ISBN 978-0-260-98575-0
PIBN 10997837

This book is a reproduction of an important historical work. Forgotten Books uses
state-of-the-art technology to digitally reconstruct the work, preserving the original format
whilst repairing imperfections present in the aged copy. In rare cases, an imperfection in
the original, such as a blemish or missing page, may be replicated in our edition. We do,
however, repair the vast majority of imperfections successfully; any imperfections that
remain are intentionally left to preserve the state of such historical works.

N. Woodard
4 Brick Court
        Temple. E.C.

THE LAW REPORTS.

DIGEST OF CASES, STATUTES, AND ORDERS
IN THE LONDON GAZETTE

FROM

1881 to 1885.

[*N.B. The Statutes and Orders of minor importance are not
here digested.*]

THE

INCORPORATED COUNCIL OF LAW REPORTING

FOR

ENGLAND AND WALES.

𝕸𝖊𝖒𝖇𝖊𝖗𝖘 𝖔𝖋 𝖙𝖍𝖊 𝕮𝖔𝖚𝖓𝖈𝖎𝖑.

Chairman—JOSEPH BROWN, Esq., Q.C.

EX-OFFICIO MEMBERS.

SIR CHARLES RUSSELL, Knt., M.P. . . . ATTORNEY-GENERAL.
SIR HORACE DAVEY, Knt. . . . . . SOLICITOR-GENERAL.

ELECTED MEMBERS.

MR. SERJEANT PULLING — Serjeants' Inn.

ARTHUR KEKEWICH, Esq., Q.C.
JOHN RIGBY, Esq., Q.C., M.P. } Lincoln's Inn.

SIR JOHN BLOSSETT MAULE, Knt., Q.C.
ARTHUR CHARLES, Esq., Q.C. } Inner Temple.

JOSEPH BROWN, Esq., Q.C.
F. A. PHILBRICK, Esq. Q.C. } Middle Temple.

JOHN A. RUSSELL, Esq., Q.C.
WILLIAM CRACROFT FOOKS, Esq., Q.C. } Gray's Inn.

WILLIAM WILLIAMS, Esq. (Firm—Messrs. Currie,
Williams, & Williams), Lincoln's Inn Fields
JOHN HOLLAMS, Esq. (Firm—Messrs. Hollams, Son,
& Coward), Mincing Lane, E.C. } Incorporated Law Society.

Secretary—JAMES THOMAS HOPWOOD, Esq., 10 Old Square, Lincoln's Inn.

THE

LAW REPORTS.
1881 TO 1885.

Under the Superintendence and Control of the
INCORPORATED COUNCIL OF LAW REPORTING FOR ENGLAND AND WALES.

Digest of Cases

DECIDED BY

THE HOUSE OF LORDS AND PRIVY COUNCIL,

AND BY

THE COURT OF APPEAL, THE SEVERAL DIVISIONS OF THE HIGH COURT OF JUSTICE,

AND THE CHIEF JUDGE IN BANKRUPTCY;

REPORTED IN THE LAW REPORTS FROM THE COMMENCEMENT OF 1881 TO THE
END OF 1885.

TOGETHER WITH A DIGEST OF THE PRINCIPAL ORDERS PUBLISHED IN THE
LONDON GAZETTE DURING THE SAME PERIOD,

AND OF

The Important Statutes.

COMPILED BY

MARTIN WARE,
OF LINCOLN'S INN,

PETER BURROWES HUTCHINS,
OF THE INNER TEMPLE,

AND

SIR G. SHERSTON BAKER, Bart.,
OF LINCOLN'S INN,
BARRISTERS-AT-LAW.

LONDON:
Printed and Published for the Council of Law Reporting,
BY WILLIAM CLOWES AND SONS, Limited,
DUKE STREET, STAMFORD STREET; AND 14, CHARING CROSS.
PUBLISHING OFFICE, 27, FLEET STREET, E.C.

1886.

LONDON:
PRINTED BY WILLIAM CLOWES AND SONS, LIMITED,
STAMFORD STREET AND CHARING CROSS.

CONTENTS.

NAMES OF EDITORS AND REPORTERS.

EDITORS.

CHANCERY DIVISION . . . G. W. HEMMING, *Queen's Counsel.*

COMMON LAW DIVISIONS . . J. R. BULWER, *Queen's Counsel.*

REPORTERS.

HOUSE OF LORDS.—ENGLISH AND IRISH APPEALS	CHARLES CLARK, J. M. MOORSOM,	*Queen's Counsel.* *Queen's Counsel.*
HOUSE OF LORDS.—SCOTCH AND DIVORCE APPEALS	GERALD J. WHEELER,	*Barrister-at-Law.*
PRIVY COUNCIL APPEALS . . .	HERBERT COWELL,	*Barrister-at-Law.*
COURT OF APPEAL	H. CADMAN JONES, MARTIN WARE, WM. LLOYD CABELL, HENRY HOLROYD, JOHN EDWARD HALL, WILLIAM PATERSON, W. WORSLEY KNOX, G. I. FOSTER COOKE, ARTHUR P. STONE, EDMUND LUMLEY, E. S. ROSCOE,	*Barristers-at-Law.*
MASTER OF THE ROLLS . . .	J. H. FORDHAM, G. I. F. COOKE, GEORGE MURRAY,	*Barristers-at-Law.*
V.-C. MALINS	T. W. GUNNING, CHARLES MARETT,	*Barristers-at-Law.*
V.-C. BACON	J. B. DAVIDSON, F. G. A. WILLIAMS, G. I. FOSTER COOKE,	*Barristers-at-Law.*

NAMES OF JUDGES,

ATTORNEYS-GENERAL AND SOLICITORS-GENERAL.

The Right Hon. The EARL OF SELBORNE,
The Right Hon. LORD HALSBURY,
} *Lord Chancellors.*

The Right Hon. LORD BLACKBURN,
The Right Hon. LORD WATSON,
The Right Hon. LORD FITZGERALD,
} *Lords of Appeal in Ordinary.*

The Right Hon. The LORD CHANCELLOR (PRE-SIDENT),
The Right Hon. The LORD CHIEF JUSTICE OF ENGLAND,
The Right Hon. The MASTER OF THE ROLLS,
The Right Hon. The PRESIDENT OF THE PROBATE, DIVORCE, AND ADMIRALTY DIVISION,
} *Ex-Officio Judges of the Court of Appeal.*

The Right Hon. SIR GEORGE JESSEL,
The Right Hon. LORD ESHER,
} *Masters of the Rolls.*

The Right Hon. SIR WILLIAM MILBOURNE JAMES,
The Right Hon. SIR RICHARD BAGGALLAY,
The Right Hon. SIR GEORGE WILLIAM WILSHERE BRAMWELL,
The Right Hon. SIR WILLIAM BALIOL BRETT,
The Right Hon. SIR HENRY COTTON,
The Right Hon. SIR ROBERT LUSH,
The Right Hon. SIR NATHANIEL LINDLEY,
The Right Hon. SIR JOHN HOLKER,
The Right Hon. SIR CHARLES SYNGE CHRISTOPHER BOWEN,
The Right Hon. SIR EDWARD FRY,
} *Lords Justices of the Court of Appeal.*

The Right Hon. The EARL OF SELBORNE, LORD CHANCELLOR (PRESIDENT),
The Right Hon. SIR GEORGE JESSEL, MASTER OF THE ROLLS,
SIR RICHARD MALINS, VICE-CHANCELLOR,
SIR JAMES BACON, VICE-CHANCELLOR,
SIR CHARLES HALL, VICE-CHANCELLOR,
SIR EDWARD FRY,
SIR E. EBENEZER KAY,
SIR JOSEPH WILLIAM CHITTY,
SIR FORD NORTH,
SIR JOHN PEARSON,
} *Judges of the Chancery Division of the High Court of Justice.*

The Right Hon. SIR ALEXANDER JAMES EDMUND
  COCKBURN, Bart., LORD CHIEF JUSTICE OF ENG-
  LAND (PRESIDENT)
The Right Hon. JOHN DUKE, LORD COLERIDGE,
  LORD CHIEF JUSTICE OF ENGLAND (PRESIDENT),
SIR WILLIAM ROBERT GROVE,
The Hon. GEORGE DENMAN,
SIR CHARLES EDWARD POLLOCK,
SIR NATHANIEL LINDLEY,
SIR WILLIAM VENTRIS FIELD,
SIR JOHN WALTER HUDDLESTON,
SIR HENRY MANISTY,
SIR HENRY HAWKINS,
SIR HENRY CHARLES LOPES,
SIR JAMES FITZJAMES STEPHEN,
SIR CHARLES SYNGE CHRISTOPHER BOWEN,
SIR CHARLES JAMES WATKIN WILLIAMS,
SIR JAMES CHARLES MATHEW,
SIR LEWIS WILLIAM CAVE,
SIR FORD NORTH,
SIR JOHN CHARLES DAY,
SIR ARCHIBALD LEVIN SMITH,
SIR ALFRED WILLS,

Judges of the Queen's Bench Division of the High Court of Justice.

The Right Hon. SIR JAMES HANNEN (PRESIDENT),
The Right Hon. SIR ROBERT PHILLIMORE,
SIR CHARLES PARKER BUTT,

Judges of the Probate, Divorce, and Admiralty Division.

The Right. Hon. LORD PENZANCE,

Dean of Arches.

SIR JAMES BACON,

Chief Judge in Bankruptcy.

SIR HENRY JAMES,
SIR RICHARD E. WEBSTER,

Attorneys-General.

SIR FARRER HERSCHELL,
SIR JOHN ELDON GORST,

Solicitors-General.

In this DIGEST OF CASES the following abbreviations are used:—

H. L.	*indicates*	HOUSE OF LORDS—ENGLISH AND IRISH APPEALS.
H. L., Sc.	,,	HOUSE OF LORDS—SCOTCH AND DIVORCE APPEALS.
P. C.	,,	PRIVY COUNCIL.
Ch.	,,	CHANCERY APPEAL CASES.
Eq.	,,	EQUITY CASES.
Q. B.	,,	QUEEN'S BENCH.
C. P.	,,	COMMON PLEAS.
Ex.	,	EXCHEQUER.
C. C.	,,	CROWN CASES RESERVED.
P. & M.	,,	PROBATE, DIVORCE, AND MATRIMONIAL CAUSES.
A. & E.	,,	ADMIRALTY AND ECCLESIASTICAL COURTS.
App. Cas.	,,	HOUSE OF LORDS (ENGLISH, IRISH, SCOTCH AND DIVORCE APPEALS), AND PRIVY COUNCIL.
Ch. D.	,,	CHANCERY DIVISION.
Q. B. D.	,,	QUEEN'S BENCH DIVISION.
C. P. D.	,,	COMMON PLEAS DIVISION.
Ex. D.	,,	EXCHEQUER DIVISION.
P. D.	,,	PROBATE, DIVORCE AND ADMIRALTY DIVISION.
L. G.	,,	LONDON GAZETTE.

(xiii)

TABLE SHEWING THE VOLUMES OF THE LAW REPORTS BELONGING
TO EACH COURT IN EACH YEAR, FROM 1881 TO 1885 INCLUSIVE.

Year.	House of Lords (English, Irish, Scotch, and Divorce Appeals) and Privy Council.	Chancery Division, Bankruptcy and Appeals therefrom.	Queen's Bench Division, Bankruptcy and Appeals therefrom and Crown Cases Reserved.	Probate Division— Probate, Divorce, Admiralty, and Ecclesiastical Courts and Appeals therefrom.
1881	6 App. Cas.	16, 17 & 18 Ch. D.	6 & 7 Q. B. D.	6 P. D.
1882	7 ,,	19, 20 & 21 ,,	8 & 9 ,,	7 ,,
1883	8 ,,	22, 23 & 24 ,,	10 & 11 ,,	8 ,,
1884	9 ,,	25, 26 & 27 ,,	12 & 13 ,,	9 ,,
1885	10 ,,	28, 29 & 30 ,,	14 & 15 ,,	10 ,,

TABLE OF CASES IN THE DIGEST.

Name of Case.	Volume and Page.	Column of Digest.
Butler, Nottingham Patent Brick and Tile Company v.	15 Q. B. D. 261	1627
Butler's Wharf Company, In re. Anderson v. Butler's Wharf Company	21 Ch. D. 131	1238
————, Anderson v. In re Butler's Wharf Company	21 Ch. D. 131	1238
Butterworth, In re. Ex parte Russell	19 Ch. D. 588	165
Button, River Lee Navigation (Conservators of) v. ..	6 App. Cas. 685	1346
Buxton, Nottage v. In re Knowles	21 Ch. D. 806	1668
Byron's Charity, In re ..	23 Ch. D. 171	1445
Bywater, In re. Bywater v. Clarke	18 Ch. D. 17	1692
———— v. Clarke. In re Bywater	18 Ch. D. 17	1692

C.

Name of Case.	Volume and Page.	Column of Digest.
" Cachapool," The	7 P. D. 217	1506
Cadogan, In re. Cadogan v. Palagi ..	25 Ch. D. 154	1693
———— v. Palagi. In re Cadogan	25 Ch. D. 154	1693
Cahill v. Cahill	8 App. Cas. 420	650
Caine, Re	10 Q. B. D. 284	650
Caithness Flagstone Quarrying Company, Sinclair v.	6 App. Cas. 340	1393
Calder, Alexander v. In re Wilson	28 Ch. D. 457	1214
Caldicott, Ex parte. In re Hart	25 Ch. D. 716	155
Caldwell v. McLaren	9 App. Cas. 392	302
Caledonian Fire and Life Insurance Co., Curtius v. ..	19 Ch. D. 534	688, 1137
Caledonian Railway Company v. North British Railway Company	6 App. Cas. 114	1398
———— v. Walker's Trustees ..	7 App. Cas. 259	1401
Calisher, Burrard v.	19 Ch. D. 644	1189
Callaghan, In re. Elliott v. Lambert ..	28 Ch. D. 186	676
Calton's Will, In re	25 Ch. D. 240	1215
Cambrian Mining Company, In re	20 Ch. D. 376	392
Camden (Marquis) v. Murray	16 Ch. D. 161	674
" Camellia " The	9 P. D. 27	1519
Cameron, In re. Nixon v. Cameron ..	26 Ch. D. 19	558
————, Nixon v. In re Cameron	26 Ch. D. 19	558
Cammell Company, Munster v.	21 Ch. D. 183	356
Camoys (Lord), Tempest v.	21 Ch. D. 571	1603
————, ———— v.	21 Ch. D. 576, n. ..	1603
Campbell, In re. Ex parte Wolverhampton Banking Company	14 Q. B. D. 32	140
————, Ex parte. In re Wallace	15 Q. B. D. 213	131
———— v. Campbell. Ex parte Campbell ..	16 Ch. D. 198	563
————, Lund v.	14 Q. B. D. 821	1220
———— v. Wardlaw	8 App. Cas. 641	1381
Campden Charities, In re	18 Ch. D. 310	288, 293
————————, (No. 2), In re	24 Ch. D. 213	294
Canada Central Railway Company v. Murray ..	8 App. Cas. 574	1128
Canada Southern Railway Company v. International Bridge Company	8 App. Cas. 723	299
Cann, In re	13 Q. B. D. 36	249
Cannell, Dyke v.	11 Q. B. D. 180	1188
Cannock and Rugeley Colliery Company, In re. Ex parte Harrison	26 Ch. D. 522 ; 28 Ch. D. 363	348
Cannon, Ex parte. In re Leicester Club and County Racecourse Company	30 Ch. D. 629	373
———— v. Smalley otherwise Cannon ..	10 P. D. 96	1113
Cape Breton Company, In re	19 Ch. D. 77	37

Name of Case.	Volume and Page.	Column of Digest.
Clarke, In re	21 Ch. D. 817	668
———, Iu re. Barker v. Perowne	18 Ch. D. 160	32
———, In re. Ex parte East and West India Dock Company	17 Ch. D. 759	173
———, Bradlaugh v.	7 Q.B. D. 38 ; 8 App. Cas. 354	996, 1052
——— v. ———	7 Q. B. D. 38	996, 1235
——— v. ———	7 Q. B. D. 151 ; 8 Q. B. D. 63	1132
———, Bywater v. In re Bywater	18 Ch. D. 17	1692
——— v. Chamberlin	16 Ch. D. 176 .. .:	1566
———, Knight v.	15 Q. B. D. 294	771
——— v. Palmer	21 Ch. D. 124	915
——— v. Skipper	21 Ch. D. 134 — ..	1187
Clarke's (J.) Estate, In re	21 Ch. D. 776	784
——— Trusts, In re	21 Ch. D. 748	644
Clarkson v. Musgrave	9 Q. B. D. 386	440, 866
Clay and Tetley, In re	16 Ch. D. 3	13, 1245
Clayton, Pountney v.	11 Q. B. D. 820	1292
———, Yorkshire Fire and Life Insurance Company v.	6 Q. B. D. 557 ; 8 Q. B. D. 421 ..	1324
Cleather v. Twisden	24 Ch. D. 731 ; 28 Ch. D. 340	1020
Cleaver v. Cleaver	9 App. Cas. 631	1112
Clemence, Ex parte. In re Carriage Co-operative Supply Association .. .. .:	23 Ch. D. 154	376
Clements v. Cheesman	27 Ch. D. 631 .. .:'	516
———, Freme v.	18 Ch. D. 499	{1082 1684
——— v. Matthews	11 Q. B. D. 808	254
Clerke v. Clerke	6 P. D. 103	1273
Clew, In re	8 Q. B. D. 511	683
Clifford v. Clifford	9 P. D. 76 .. .. .:	1118
———, Morley v.	20 Ch. D. 753	419
Clifton School Board, Scott v...	14 Q. B. D. 500	482
Clippens Oil Company v. Henderson	8 App. Cas. 873	1396
Clitheroe Estate, In re	28 Ch. D. 378	1442
Close, Ex parte. In re Hall	14 Q. B. D. 386	256.
Clover v. Adams	6 Q. B. D. 622	1539.
Clowes, Martinson v.	21 Ch. D. 857 .. .•	910
Cluff, Goodés v.	13 Q. B. D. 694	440.
Clutterbuck, Adams v.	10 Q. B. D. 403	399
Clyde Navigation Trustees, Blantyre (Lord) v. ..	6 App. Cas. 273	1402
——— v. Laird	8 App. Cas. 658	1379
Clydesdale Banking Company, M'Lean v. ...	9 App. Cas. 95	52, 1371
Coaks, Boswell v.	23 Ch. D. 302 ; 27 Ch. D. 424	582, 1537
Cobb, Powell v.	29 Ch. D. 486	1187
Cobeldick, Ex parte	12 Q. B. D. 149	1541
Cochrane, Sangster v.	28 Ch. D. 298	272
Cockburn v. Edwards	16 Ch. D, 393	1537
——— v. ———	18 Ch. D. 449	912
Cockcroft, In re. Broadbent v. Groves	24 Ch. D. 94	1679
Cockerell v. Essex (Earl of), In re Johnston	26 Ch. D. 538	{1681 1707
Cocks, Ex parte. In re Poole	21 Ch. D. 397	134
Coffin, Murphy v.	12 Q. B. D. 87	1482
Cohen, Ex parte	13 Q. B. D. 56	142
Colam v. Pagett	12 Q. B. D. 66	479
Colchester (Corporation of), Prestney v. ..	24 Ch. D. 376	1175
——— (Mayor of), Prestney v.	21 Ch. D. 111	942
Coleman v. Birmingham (Overseers of)	6 Q. B. D. 615	1061
——— v. West Middlesex Waterworks Company	14 Q. B. D. 529	1659

c

Name of Case.	Volume and Page.	Column of Digest.
Conelly v. Steer	7 Q. B. D. 520	258
Coney, In re. Coney v. Bennett	29 Ch. D. 993	1211
—— v. Bennett. In re Coney	29 Ch. D. 993	1211
——, Reg. v.	8 Q. B. D. 534	471
Connecticut Mutual Life Insurance Company of Hertford v. Moore	6 App. Cas. 644	300
Connell v. Baker. In re Baker	29 Ch. D. 711	1190
Conolan v. Leyland	27 Ch. D. 632	640
Cook, Reg. v.	13 Q. B. D. 377	610
——, Rosenberg v.	8 Q. B. D. 162	1632
——, Studd v.	8 App. Cas. 577	1383
Cooke v. Newcastle and Gateshead Water Company	10 Q. B. D. 332	1188
—— v. Wilby	25 Ch. D. 769	1191
Cookham Union, Reg. v.	9 Q. B. D. 522	1064
Cookson v. Swire	9 App. Cas. 653	243
Coomber v. Berks (Justices of)	9 Q. B. D. 17; 10 Q. B. D. 267; 9 App. Cas. 61	1326
Cooper, Ex parte. In re Morris	26 Ch. D. 693	157
——, In the Goods of	6 P. D. 34	1272
——, In re. Cooper v. Slight	27 Ch. D. 565	1089
——, In re. Cooper v. Vesey	20 Ch. D. 611	1637
——, In re. Ex parte Hall	19 Ch. D. 580	167, 190
——, Balfour v.	23 Ch. D. 472	1468
——, Bradbury v.	12 Q. B. D. 94	1154
—— v. Crabtree	19 Ch. D. 193; 20 Ch. D. 589	960
—— v. Laroche	17 Ch. D. 368	1690
——, London and Yorkshire Bank v.	15 Q. B. D. 71; 5 Q. B. D. 473	1172
—— v. Metropolitan Board of Works	25 Ch. D. 472	543, 613, 777
—— v. Prichard	11 Q. B. D. 351	144
——, Salt v.	16 Ch. D. 544	1210
—— v. Slight. In re Cooper	27 Ch. D. 565	1089
——, Titterton v.	9 Q. B. D. 473	135
—— v. Vesey. In re Cooper	20 Ch. D. 611	1637
Cooper Hall & Co., Fraser v.	21 Ch. D. 718	1138
——. Waddell v. Fraser	23 Ch. D. 685	1149
Coote v. Judd	23 Ch. D. 727	421
Cope, In re. Cope v. Cope	16 Ch. D. 49	11
Copp, In re	6 Q. B. D. 607	441
Copping Syke (Overseers of), Reg. v.	14 Q. B. D. 83	1074
Coquetdale (Justices of), White v.	7 Q. B. D. 238	681
Corbett v. Plowden	25 Ch. D. 678	904
Corfield, Wilkinson v.	6 P. D. 27	1131
Cornford v. Elliott. In re Watts	27 Ch. D. 318; 29 Ch. D. 947	290
Cornwall Minerals Railway Company, Harrison v. Fenton v. Harrison	16 Ch. D. 66; 18 Ch. D. 334; 8 App. Cas. 780	333, 1184, 1218
Corry v. Great Western Railway Company	6 Q. B. D. 237; 7 Q. B. D. 322	1290
Cory v. Burr	8 Q. B. D. 313; 9 Q. B. D. 463; 8 App. Cas. 393	694
"Cosmopolitan," The	9 P. D. 35, n.	1097
Costa Rica (Republic of) v. Strousberg	16 Ch. D. 8	1203
Cottam v. Guest	6 Q. B. D. 70	1586
Cotterell, Sbardlow v.	18 Ch. D. 280; 20 Ch. D. 90	1620
Cotton, Ex parte	11 Q. B. D. 301	257
Cotton's Trustees and School Board for London, In re	19 Ch. D. 624	1469
Cottrell v. Cottrell	28 Ch. D. 628	1444

c 2

Name of Case.	Volume and Page.	Column of Digest.
Couchman, James v.	29 Ch. D. 212	1648
Coulburn, Babbage v.	9 Q. B. D. 235	396
Couldery v. Bartrum	19 Ch. D. 394	124
Coulman, In re. Munby v. Ross	30 Ch. D. 186	1078
County Hotel Company, Strauss v.	12 Q. B. D. 27	679
Cousins, In re. Alexander v. Cross	30 Ch. D. 203	1671
Coutts & Co., Danby v.	29 Ch. D. 500	1094
Coventry, Sheppard & Co. v. Great Eastern Railway Company	11 Q. B. D. 776	537
Coverdale v. Grant	8 Q. B. D. 600; 11 Q. B. D. 543; 9 App. Cas. 470	1481
Cowburn, In re. Ex parte Firth	19 Ch. D. 419	249
Cowell, Smith v.	6 Q. B. D. 75	1210
Cowlard, Essery v.	26 Ch. D. 191	1469
Cox v. Andrews	12 Q. B. D. 126	610
—, Bristol (Mayor and Corporation of) v.	26 Ch. D. 678	1179
— v. Great Western Railway Company	9 Q. B. D. 106	867
— v. James	19 Ch. D. 55	1136
—, Johnstone v.	16 Ch. D. 571; 19 Ch. D. 17	918, 1240
—, Munster v.	10 Q. B. D. 475; 11 Q. B. D. 435; 10 App. Cas. 680	1138
— and Railton, Reg. v.	14 Q. B. D. 153	475
—, Roxburghe v.	17 Ch. D. 520	1413
Coxwell, Wilson v.	23 Ch. D. 764	566
Crabtree, Cooper v.	19 Ch. D. 193; 20 Ch. D. 589	960
——— v. Robinson	15 Q. B. D. 312	746
Craig, Scottish Widows Fund v.	20 Ch. D. 208	521
Cramer v. Matthews	7 Q. B. D. 425	444
Crawcour v. Salter	18 Ch. D. 30	161, 545
Crawford, Saunders v.	9 Q. B. D. 612	528
Crawley, In re. Acton v. Crawley	28 Ch. D. 431	1707
———, Acton v. In re Crawley	28 Ch. D. 431	1707
Credit Company, Ex parte. In re McHenry	24 Ch. D. 353	191
—————— v. Pott	6 Q. B. D. 295	248
Crédit Lyonnais, Jacobs v.	12 Q. B. D. 589	398
Credits Gerundeuse v. Van Weede	12 Q. B. D. 171	1134
Creery v. Lingwood. In re Hayward	19 Ch. D. 470	1675
Cresswell, In re. Parkin v. Cresswell	24 Ch. D. 102	1679
————, Parkin v. In re Cresswell	24 Ch. D. 102	1679
Creyke, Dawes v.	30 Ch. D. 500	1459
Crick v. Hewlett	27 Ch. D. 354	1163
Cripps v. Judge	13 Q. B. D. 583	863
Critchfield, Smith v.	14 Q. B. D. 873	1232
Croft v. London and County Banking Company	14 Q. B. D. 347	773
Crofton v. Crofton. In re Boyse	20 Ch. D. 760	1191
Croggan v. Allen	22 Ch. D. 101	553
Crombie, McEwan v.	25 Ch. D. 175	1414 1592
Crompton v. Jarratt	30 Ch. D. 298	17
Cropper v. Smith	24 Ch. D. 305	1161
——— v. ———	26 Ch. D. 700; 10 App. Cas. 249	1047
——— v. ——— (No. 2)	28 Ch. D. 148	1041
Cross, In re. Harston v. Tenison	20 Ch. D. 109	1600
———, Alexander v. In re Cousins	30 Ch. D. 203	1671
———, Saywood v.	14 Q. B. D. 53	1222
———, Percival v.	7 P. D. 234	1129
Crossfield v. Shurmur. Shurmur v. Sedgwick	24 Ch. D. 597	1648
Crossthwaite, Ex parte. In re Pearce	14 Q. B. D. 966	138

Name of Case.	Volume and Page.	Column of Digest.
Darley Main Colliery Company, Mitchell v. ..	10 Q. B. D. 457	1240
—————————————, —— v. ..	14 Q. B. D. 125	805
Darlow, Hickson v.	23 Ch. D. 690	259, 911
——, Smith v.	26 Ch. D. 605	1232
Dart & Son, Smith v. ..	14 Q. B. D. 105	1483
Dashwood, Tompson v.	11 Q. B. D. 43	499
Daubuz v. Lavington	13 Q. B. D. 347	1136
Dauvillier v. Myers	17 Ch. D. 346	1174
Davey v. London and South Western Railway Co. ..	11 Q. B. D. 213	948
—— v. ——————	12 Q. B. D. 70	948
——, Whetham v.	30 Ch. D. 574	901
David v. Howe	27 Ch. D. 533	1246
Davidson, Emley v. In re Robson	19 Ch. D. 156	289
———— v. Illidge. In re Illidge	24 Ch. D. 654; 27 Ch. D. 478	1314
———— v. Kimpton	18 Ch. D. 213	544
Davies, Ex parte. In re Sadler	19 Ch. D. 86	50
——— v. Evans	9 Q. B. D. 238	203
———, Harris v.	10 App. Cas. 279	314
——— to Jones and Evans	24 Ch. D. 190	1676
——— v. Makuna	29 Ch. D. 596 . ..	872
———, Smith v.	28 Ch. D. 650	899, 1183
———, Swansea Co-operative Building Society v. ..	12 Q. B. D. 21	1194
———, Williams v.	11 Q. B. D. 74	203
——— v. Wise ·	7 Q. B. D. 425	444
D'Avigdor, Roope v.	10 Q. B. D. 412	6
Davis v. Burton	{ 10 Q. B. D. 414; 11 Q. B. D. 537 .. .. }	246
——, Forster v. Norden v. McRae. In re McRae..	25 Ch. D. 16	1148
—— v. Harford	22 Ch. D. 128	1463
—— v. James	26 Ch. D. 778	1156
——, Lemaitre v.	19 Ch. D. 281	1557
—— v. Morris	10 Q. B. D. 436	1140
—— v. Pembrokeshire (Justices of) ..	7 Q. B. D. 513	731
—— v. Treharne	6 App. Cas. 460	887
——, Sanders v.	15 Q. B. D. 218	748
—— v. Usher	12 Q. B. D. 490	253
Davison, In re	13 Q. B. D. 50	149
———— v. Donaldson	9 Q. B. D. 623	1257
————, Fergusson v.	8 Q. B. D. 470	1226
———— v. Gillies	16 Ch. D. 347, n.	339
Dawdy, In re	15 Q. B. D. 426	37
Dawe v. Vergara	11 Q. B. D. 241	138
Dawes, Bland v.	17 Ch. D. 794	1696
——— v. Creyke	30 Ch. D. 500	1459
——— v. Tredwell	18 Ch. D. 354	1461
Dawkins v. Antrobus	17 Ch. D. 615	296
Dawson v. Beeson	22 Ch. D. 504	{ 1019 1212 }
——— v. Fox	14 Q. B. D. 377	1231
———, Howell v.	13 Q. B. D. 67	1231
Day v. Batty	21 Ch. D. 880	1226
——, Smith v.	16 Ch. D. 726	1218
——, —— v.	21 Ch. D. 421	1209
—— v. Turnell. In re Higgins	29 Ch. D. 697	1452
——, Wilkins v.	12 Q. B. D. 110	961
Deakin v. Lakin. In re Shakespear	30 Ch. D. 169	639
Dean, In re. Dean v. Wright	21 Ch. D. 581	552
—— v. Green	8 P. D. 79	1126
—— v. Wright. In re Dean	21 Ch. D. 581	552

Name of Case.	Volume and Page.	Column of Digest.
Elliott v. Smith	22 Ch. D. 236	1684
—— v. Turquand	7 App. Cas. 79	155
Ellis v. Desilva	6 Q. B. D. 521	1227
—— v. Ellis	8 P. D. 188	1108
——, Reg. v.	8 Q. B. D. 466	624
—— v. Rogers	29 Ch. D. 661	1637
——, Tenant v.	6 Q. B. D. 46	1222
Elphinstone, Clark v.	6 App. Cas. 164	308
Elsey, Gage v.	10 Q. B. D. 518	16
Elsley, Foster v.	19 Ch. D. 518	1700
Elton v. Curteis	19 Ch. D. 49	901
Eltringham, Laws v.	8 Q. B. D. 283	467
Emanuel & Co., In re	9 Q. B. D. 408	441
Emden v. Carte	17 Ch. D. 169, 768	145, 1136
—— v. ——	19 Ch. D. 311	1538
Emeny v. Sandes	14 Q. B. D. 6	1222
Emerson, Attorney-General v.	10 Q. B. D. 191	1177
Emley v. Davidson. In re Robson	19 Ch. D. 156	289
Emery v. Cichero. The "Arklow"	9 App. Cas. 136	1504
Emma Silver Mining Company v. Grant	17 Ch. D. 122	154
Emmanuel, Ex parte. In re Batey	17 Ch. D. 35	134
Emmet v. Emmet. In re Emmet's Estate	17 Ch. D. 142	1599
Emmet's Estate, In re. Emmet v. Emmet	17 Ch. D. 142	1599
"Emmy Haase," The	9 P. D. 81	1510
Empress Engineering Company, In re	16 Ch. D. 125	330
Engelhardt, Ex parte. In re Engelhardt	23 Ch. D. 706	198
English, Burton v.	10 Q. B. D. 426 ; 12 Q. B. D. 218	1485
English Channel Steamship Company v. Rolt	17 Ch. D. 715	357
Equitable Reversionary Interest Society, Burnaby v.	28 Ch. D. 416	703
Enraght, Harris v. (Perkins v. Enraght)	7 P. D. 31, 161	1123
—— v. Penzance (Lord)	7 App. Cas. 240	1122, 1123
Enraght's Case. Dale's Case	6 Q. B. D. 376	1122
Erichsen v. Last	7 Q. B. D. 12 ; 8 Q. B. D. 414	1329
Errington v. Metropolitan District Railway Company	19 Ch. D. 559	1291
——, Riddell v.	26 Ch. D. 220	1416
Escallier v. Escallier	10 App. Cas. 312	317
Esnouf v. Attorney-General for Jersey	8 App. Cas. 304	310
Essery v. Cowlard	26 Ch. D. 191	1469
Essex (Earl of), Cockerell v. In re Johnston	26 Ch. D. 538	1681, 1707
——, Reg. v.	14 Q. B. D. 753	777
—— (Justices of), Reg. v.	11 Q. B. D. 704	618
Etheridge v. Womersley. In re Womersley	29 Ch. D. 557	706
"Ettrick," The. Prehn v. Bailey	6 P. D. 127	1099
"European," The	10 P. D. 99	1505
Euston v. Smith	9 P. D. 57	1113
Evans, In re	21 Ch. D. 297	849
——, In re. Welch v. Channell	26 Ch. D. 58	669
——, Bowker v.	15 Q. B. D. 565	1146
——, Davies v.	9 Q. B. D. 238	203
——, Graff v.	8 Q. B. D. 373	684
—— v. Williamson. In re Roose	17 Ch. D. 696	1705
Evens, Nichols v.	22 Ch. D. 611	1151
Evison, Brier v. In re Brier	26 Ch. D. 238	1596
Ewing, In the Goods of	6 P. D. 19	9
—— v. Ewing	8 App. Cas. 822	1017

Name of Case	Volume and Page.	Column of Digest.
Festing, Montagu. v. In re Montagu. In re Wroughton	28 Ch. D. 82	668
Fewings, Ex parte. In re Sneyd	25 Ch. D. 338	194, 707 / 894
Field, In re.	29 Ch. D. 608	1534
——, Kay v.	8 Q. B. D. 594; 10 Q. B. D. 241	1480
——, London and Suburban Land and Building Company v.	16 Ch. D. 645	764
——, McMahon v.	7 Q. B. D. 591	485
—— v. White. In re Rownson	29 Ch. D. 358	567
Finch, In re. Abbiss v. Burney	17 Ch. D, 211	1689
——, In re. Finch v. Finch	23 Ch. D. 267	554
—— v. Finch. In re Finch	23 Ch. D. 267	554
Finchley Local Board, Charles v. ..	23 Ch. D. 767	962
Findlay, Ex parte. In re Colley.	17 Ch. D. 334	151
Finnis and Young to Forbes and Pochin (No. 1) ..	24 Ch. D. 587	286
—————————————— (No. 2) ..	24 Ch. D. 591	286
Firbank, Doughty v.	10 Q. B. D. 358	867
First Avenue Hotel Company, Parker v. ..	24 Ch. D. 282	800
Firth, Ex parte. In re Cowburn.	19 Ch. D. 419	249
Fisher, Bolckow v.	10 Q. B. D. 161	1167
——, Lees v.	22 Ch. D. 283	900
Fisherton-Angar, Clark v.	6 Q. B. D. 139	1072 / 1074
Fitzgibbon, Martin v. Pike v. Fitzgibbon ..	17 Ch. D. 454	641
——, Pike v. Martin v. —— ..	17 Ch. D. 454	641
Fitzmaurice, Edgington v.	29 Ch. D. 459	327
Flavell, In re. Murray v. Flavell ..	25 Ch. D. 89	1017
——, Murray v. In re —— ..	25 Ch. D. 89	1017
——, Reg. v.	14 Q. B. D. 364	204
Flavelle, Blackburn v.	6 App. Cas. 628	313
Fleming v. Newport Railway Company	8 App. Cas. 265	1401
—— v. Yeaman	9 App. Cas. 966	1371
Fletcher v. Bealey	28 Ch. D. 688	960
—— v. Hudson.	7 Q. B. D. 611	819
Flint, In re	15 Q. B. D. 488	38
——, Fearnside v.	22 Ch. D. 579	807
Flitcroft's Case. In re Exchange Banking Company	21 Ch. D. 519	361
Flood, Dunn v.	25 Ch. D. 629; 28 Ch. D. 586	1624
Florence Land and Public Works Company, In re. Nicol's Case. Tufnell and Ponsonby's Case ..	29 Ch. D. 421	342
Flower (C) and Metropolitan Board of Works, In re. In re Flower (M) and Same	27 Ch. D. 592	1632
—— v. Sadler	9 Q. B. D. 83; 10 Q. B. D. 572	233
Foakes, Beer v.	11 Q. B. D. 221; 9 App. Cas. 605	3
—— v. Webb	28 Ch. D. 287	1171
Foat v. Mayor of Margate	11 Q. B. D. 299	825
Fobbing (Commissioners of Sewers for) Reg. v. ..	14 Q. B. D. 561	1408
Follett v. Pettman	23 Ch. D. 337	1694
Foord, Pontifex v.	12 Q. B. D. 152	1144
Foote, Reg. v.	10 Q. B. D. 378	1235
Footitt, Drake v.	7 Q. B. D. 201	1345
Forbes v. Jackson	19 Ch. D. 615	1265
—— and Pochin, Finnis and Young to (No. 1) ..	24 Ch. D. 587	286
————————————————— (No. 2) ..	24 Ch. D. 591	286
Ford, Bacon v. In re Kensington (Lord)	29 Ch. D. 527	707

Name of Case.	Volume and Page.	Column of Digest.
Freeman, Midland Railway Company v.	12 Q. B. D. 629	405
—— v. Newman	12 Q. B. D. 373	1008
Freer, In re. Freer v. Freer	22 Ch. D. 622	1664
—— v. Freer. In re Freer	22 Ch. D. 622	1664
Freme v. Clement	18 Ch. D. 499	{1082 1684}
French, Leslie v. In re Leslie	23 Ch. D. 552 ..	688
Freston, In re	11 Q. B. D. 545	1536
"Friedeberg," The	10 P. D. 112	1103
Friedlander, In re. Ex parte Oastler	13 Q. B. D. 471	118
Friend v. Towers	10 Q. B. D. 87	1005
Fry v. Tapson	28 Ch. D. 268	1597
Fuggle v. Bland	11 Q. B. D. 711	1212
Fulham (Overseers of) Glen v.	14 Q. B. D. 328	880
Fulham (Guardians of), v. Thanet (Guardians of) ..	6 Q. B. D. 610; 7 Q. B. D. 539	1066
Fuller, Ex parte. In re Long	16 Ch. D. 617	1541
—— v. Alford	10 Q. B. D. 418	522
Furber, Ex parte. In re King	17 Ch. D. 191	115
Furness Railway Company, Dormont v.	11 Q. B. D. 496	513
Furnivall, Eager v.	17 Ch. D. 115	1696
Fussell, In re. Ex parte Allen	20 Ch. D. 341	173
—— v. Dowding	27 Ch. D. 237	1244

G.

Name of Case.	Volume and Page.	Column of Digest.
G. v. M.	10 App. Cas. 171	{1391 1405}
Gabriel v. Blankenstein	13 Q. B. D. 684	177
Gadd, In re. Eastwood v. Clark	23 Ch. D. 134	1602
"Gaetano and Maria," The	7 P. D. 1, 187	399
Gage v. Elsey	10 Q. B. D. 518	16
Gagnon, Prince v.	8 App. Cas. 103	1128
Gale, In re. Blake v. Gale	22 Ch. D. 820	806
—— Blake v. In re Gale	22 Ch. D. 820	806
Galland v. Burton. In re Fawsitt	30 Ch. D. 231	1238
Gallard v. Hawkins	27 Ch. D. 298	420
Gallaway v. Maries	8 Q. B. D. 275	611
Gandy v. Gandy	7 P. D. 77, 168	1115
—— v. ——	30 Ch. D. 57	647
Ganz, Reg. v.	9 Q. B. D. 93	571
Garbutt, Allen v.	6 Q. B. D. 165	442
Gard v. Commissioners of Sewers of the City of London	28 Ch. D. 486	837
Gardiner (H. B. S.), In the Goods of	9 P. D. 66	13
Gardner v. Jay	29 Ch. D. 50	1186
——, Knight v. In re Knight	24 Ch. D. 606; 25 Ch. D. 297	1190
—— v. Trechmann	15 Q. B. D. 154	1477
Gare's Patent, In re	26 Ch. D. 105	1041
Garnett, Orme and Hargreave's Contract, In re ..	25 Ch. D. 595	1450
——, Holroyde v.	20 Ch. D. 532	1198
Garnham v. Skipper	29 Ch. D. 566	1183
Garrard v. Lewis	10 Q. B. D. 30	231
Garrett v. Middlesex (Justices of)	12 Q. B. D. 620	682
Garrold, Dallow v. Ex parte Adams ..	{13 Q. B. D. 543; 14 Q. B. D. 543}	1539
Garrud, In re. Ex parte Newitt	16 Ch. D. 522	266
Gartside v. Silkstone and Dodworth Coal and Iron Co.	21 Ch. D. 762	496

d

Name of Case.	Volume and Page.	Column of Digest.
Great Western Railway Company, Gibbs v.	11 Q. B. D. 22 ; 12 Q. B. D. 208	867
————————, Gordon v.	8 Q. B. D. 44	1285
————————, Pigott and, In re	18 Ch. D. 146	782
———————— v. Railway Commissioners	7 Q. B. D. 182	1294
———————— and Sturge	19 Ch. D. 444	1667
———————— v. Swindon and Cheltenham Extension Railway Company	22 Ch. D. 677 ; 9 App. Cas. 787	781
———————— v. Waterford and Limerick Railway Company	17 Ch. D. 493	1294
————————, Watson v.	6 Q. B. D. 163	1228
Great Yarmouth (Justices of), Reg. v.	8 Q. B. D. 525	731
Greaves, deceased, In re. Bray v. Tofield	18 Ch. D. 551	806
————' Settlement Trusts, In re	23 Ch. D. 313	1084
Grébert-Borgnis v. Nugent	15 Q. B. D. 85	484
Green, In re. Green v. Green	26 Ch. D. 16	1540
————, Dean v.	8 P. D. 79	1126
———— v. Duckett	11 Q. B. D. 275	511
———— v. Green. In re Green	26 Ch. D. 16	1540
————, Humphreys v.	10 Q. B. D. 148	601
———— v. Humphreys	23 Ch. D. 207 ; 26 Ch. D. 474	805
———— v. Penzance (Lord). Ex parte Green	7 Q. B. D. 273 ; 6 App. Cas. 657	1125
————, M'Ilwraith v.	13 Q. B. D. 897 ; 14 Q. B. D. 766	1152
———— v. Smith. In re Smith	22 Ch. D. 586	145, 555
———— v. ———— In re ————	24 Ch. D. 672	145
Greene v. Foster	22 Ch. D. 566	899
Greenway v. Bachelor. Aldridge's Case	12 Q. B. D. 381	941
———— v. ———— Jacob's Case	12 Q. B. D. 376	1007
Greenwich County Court (Registrar of), Reg. v.	15 Q. B. D. 54	130
Greenwood, Berdan v.	20 Ch. D. 764, n.	1191
————, Wallace v.	16 Ch. D. 362	1016
Greenwood's Trusts, In re	27 Ch. D. 359	1609
Greer v. Young	24 Ch. D. 545	1539
Greetland Local Board, Dyson v.	13 Q. B. D. 946	827
Gregg, Glen v.	21 Ch. D. 513	284
Grey, D'Hormusgee v.	10 Q. B. D. 13	1181
Grey's Brewery Company, In re	25 Ch. D. 400	392
Griffin, Ex parte. Ex parte Newton. In re Bunyard	16 Ch. D. 330	149
Griffith, Ex parte. In re Wilcoxon	23 Ch. D. 69	167
———— (Edward), In the Goods of	9 P. D. 63	9
———— v. Blake	27 Ch. D. 474	1209
Griffith-Boscawen v. Scott	26 Ch. D. 358	526, 1083
Griffiths (an Infant), In re	29 Ch. D. 248	674
————, In re. Griffiths v. Lewis	26 Ch. D. 465	1223
———— v. The Earl of Dudley	9 Q. B. D. 357	864
———— v. Lewis. In re Griffiths	26 Ch. D. 465	1223
———— v. London and St. Katharine Docks Co.	12 Q. B. D. 493 ; 13 Q. B. D. 259	950
————, Morris v. In re Raw	26 Ch. D. 601	1673
Grimwade v. Mutual Society. In re Mutual Society	18 Ch. D. 530	391
Groome, Hetherington v.	13 Q. B. D. 789	245
————, London and County Banking Company v.	8 Q. B. D. 288	51
Groves, Broadbent v. In re Cockcroft	24 Ch. D. 94	1679
Grubb, Barkshire v.	18 Ch. D. 616	1661
Grundy, Stanley v.	22 Ch. D. 478	903

Name of Case.	Volume and Page.	Column of Digest.
Halliwell, In the Goods of	10 P. D. 198	9
Halsey v. Brotherhood	19 Ch. D. 386	1043
Hamilton v. Chaine	7 Q. B. D. 1, 319	248
Hamilton (Duke of) v. Dunlop	10 App. Cas. 813	1394
Hamlyn v. Betteley	6 Q. B. D. 63	1230
Hammond, In the Goods of	6 P. D. 104	10
—— v. Hocking	12 Q. B. D. 291	245
——, Jennings v.	9 Q. B. D. 225	384
Hampden v. Wallis	26 Ch. D. 746	1201
—— v. ——	27 Ch. D. 251	1151
Hampson, Imperial Hydropathic Hotel Company, Blackpool v.	23 Ch. D. 1	356
Hampstead (Vestry of) v. Hoopel	15 Q. B. D. 652	882
Hance v. Fortnum. Winyard v. Toogood	10 Q. B. D. 218	528
Hancock, Turner v.	20 Ch. D. 303	1239
Handsley, Reg. v.	7 Q. B. D. 398	1073
——, —— v.	8 Q. B. D. 383	732
Handsworth Local Board, Simcox v.	8 Q. B. D. 39	831
Hankin, Drake v.	7 Q. B. D. 201	1345
Hankinson v. Barmingham	9 P. D. 62	1129
Hannah v. Duke. In re Duke	16 Ch. D. 112	1703
Hannay v. Basham. In re Basham	23 Ch. D. 195	1592
Hansen v. Maddox	12 Q. B. D. 100	1231
Hanson, Hilliard v.	21 Ch. D. 69	1474
——, Scarlett v.	12 Q. B. D. 213	1473
Harben v. Phillips	23 Ch. D. 14	353
Harcourt, May v.	13 Q. B. D. 688	34
Hardaker v. Moorhouse	26 Ch. D. 417	1089
Hardbottle v. Terry	10 Q. B. D. 131	593
Hardiman, In re. Pragnell v. Batten	16 Ch. D. 360	1015
Harding, Glenister v. In re Turner	29 Ch. D. 985	542
—— v. Preece	9 Q. B. D. 281	175
Hardinge, Smalley v.	6 Q. B. D. 371 ; 7 Q. B. D. 524	177
Hardman v. Child	28 Ch. D. 712	1628
"Hardwick," The	9 P. D. 32	1101
Hardwick, In re	12 Q. B. D. 148	1542
Hardy, In re. Wells v. Borwick	17 Ch. D. 798	1691
—— v. Atherton	7 Q. B. D. 264	203
Hare v. Putney (Overseers of)	7 Q. B. D. 223	1069
Harford, Davis v.	22 Ch. D. 128	1463
Harland, Patman v.	17 Ch. D. 353	1640
Harle, National Provincial Bank of England v.	6 Q. B. D. 626	43
Harlock v. Ashberry	18 Ch. D. 229 ; 19 Ch. D. 539	810
—— v. ——	19 Ch. D. 84	1182
Harman and Uxbridge and Rickmansworth Railway Company, In re	24 Ch. D. 720	1641
Harmanis, Sillery v.	8 App. Cas. 99	308
Harmon v. Park	6 Q. B. D. 323	938
—— v. ——	7 Q. B. D. 369	939
Harper, Ex parte. In re Pooley	20 Ch. D. 685	188
——, Ex parte. In re Tait	21 Ch. D. 537	148
——, Lloyd's v.	16 Ch. D. 290	1262
——, Reg. v.	7 Q. B. D. 78	463
Harpham v. Shacklock	19 Ch. D. 207	1536
Harris, Ex parte. In re Richardson	16 Ch. D. 613	176
——, In re. Ex parte Graves	19 Ch. D. 1	113
—— v. Davies	10 App. Cas. 279	314
—— v. Enraght. Perkins v. Enraght	7 P. D. 31, 161	1123
—— v. Jacobs	15 Q. B. D. 247	1477

Name of Case.	Volume and Page.	Column of Digest.
Harris v. Jenkins	22 Ch. D. 481	1163
———, London Land Company v.	13 Q. B. D. 540	1206
———, Mander v. In re March	24 Ch. D. 222; 27 Ch. D. 166	1683
——— v. May	12 Q. B. D. 97	14
———, Thompson v. In re Middleton	19 Ch. D. 552	553
——— v. Truman	7 Q. B. D. 340; 9 Q. B. D. 264	163
Harris & Dixon v. Marcus, Jacobs & Co.	15 Q. B. D. 247	1477
Harris' Settled Estates, In re	28 Ch. D. 171	1416
Harrison, Ex parte. In re Betts	18 Ch. D. 127	893
———, Ex parte. In re Cannock and Rugeley Colliery Company	26 Ch. D. 522; 28 Ch. D. 363	348
———, Ex parte. In re Jordan	13 Q. B. D. 228	123
———, Ex parte. In re Peake	13 Q. B. D. 753	157
———, In re. Turner v. Hellard	30 Ch. D. 390	1686
——— v. Cornwall Minerals Railway Company. Fenton v. Harrison	16 Ch. D. 66; 18 Ch. D. 334; 8 App. Cas. 780	333 1184 1218
——— v. Harrison. In re Harrison's Trusts	28 Ch. D. 220	1567
———, Jacques v.	12 Q. B. D. 136, 165	1197
——— v. Leutner	16 Ch. D. 559	1217
——— v.	24 Ch. D. 594	1225
———, Sheffield and South Yorkshire Permanent Benefit Building Society v.	15 Q. B. D. 358	594
———, Cox, Walker, & Co., United Telephone Company v.	21 Ch. D. 720	1048
Harrison's Trusts, In re. Harrison v. Harrison	28 Ch. D. 220	1567
Harrop's Trusts, In re	24 Ch. D. 717	1448
Harston and Young's Contract, In re	29 Ch. D. 691	1624
——— v. Tenison. In re Cross	20 Ch. D. 109	1600
Hart, In re. Ex parte Caldicott	25 Ch. D. 716	155
——— v. Hart	18 Ch. D. 670	645
———, Lybbe	29 Ch. D. 8	176
———, Somerset v.	12 Q. B. D. 360	684
———, Tippett v.	10 Q. B. D. 483	1322
Hart-Davis, Hill v.	21 Ch. D. 798	1207
———, ——— v.	26 Ch. D. 470	1156
Harter v. Colman	19 Ch. D. 630	897
Hartley, Glenny & Co., In re	25 Ch. D. 611	1466
Hartmont v. Foster	8 Q. B. D. 82	1214 1230
Hartnoll, Blight v.	19 Ch. D. 294	1664 1688
———, ——— v.	23 Ch. D. 218	1685
"Harton," The	9 P. D. 44	1511
Hartopp, Drage v.	28 Ch. D. 414	1137
Harvey, Ex parte. In re Player	15 Q. B. D. 682	166
———, In re. Wright v. Woods	26 Ch. D. 179	554
———, Blake v.	29 Ch. D. 827	899 1183 1197
——— v. Croydon Union Rural Sanitary Authority	26 Ch. D. 249	1233
——— v. Farnie	6 P. D. 35; 8 App. Cas. 43	399, 628
——— v. Harvey	26 Ch. D. 644	1200
——— v. Lovekin	10 P. D. 122	1113
——— v. Municipal Permanent Investment Building Society	26 Ch. D. 273	268
Harvey's Settled Estate, In re	21 Ch. D. 123	1416
Harwood, In re	20 Ch. D. 536	1610

Name of Case.	Volume and Page.	Column of Digest.
Hood v. Newby	21 Ch. D. 605	168
Hook, Newman v. In re Bartlett	16 Ch. D. 561	1212
Hoole v. Smith	17 Ch. D. 434	910
Hoopel, Hampstead Vestry v.	15 Q. B. D. 652	882
Hooper v. Smith. In re Smith	26 Ch. D. 614	1245
"Hope," The	8 P. D. 144	1103
Hope, Edwards v.	14 Q. B. D. 922	1227
Hopkins, In re. Dowd v. Hawtin	19 Ch. D. 61	1147
———, In re. Williams v. Hopkins	18 Ch. D. 370	556
———, Williams v. In re Hopkins	18 Ch. D. 370	556
Hopkinson v. Caunt	14 Q. B. D. 592	887
——— v. Lovering	11 Q. B. D. 92	171
"Horace," The	9 P. D. 86	1103
Hornby v. Cardwell	8 Q. B. D. 329	1229
Horne and Hellard, In re	29 Ch. D. 736	335
——— v. Hughes	6 Q. B. D. 676	259
Horner, Attorney-General v.	14 Q. B. D. 245	859
Horner's Estate, In re. Pomfret v. Graham	19 Ch. D. 186	1698
Horrocks, Ex parte. In re Wood	19 Ch. D. 367	194
Horsley v. Price	11 Q. B. D. 244	1483
Horton, In re	8 Q. B. D. 434	1543
Hoskins, Wallington v.	6 Q. B. D. 206	624
Hough v. Windus	12 Q. B. D. 224	126
Houghton Estate, In re	30 Ch. D. 102	1443
——— and Hallmark's Trade-mark, In re. In re Mitchell and Co.'s Trade-mark	28 Ch. D. 666	1581
House Property and Investment Company v. H. P. Horse Nail Company	29 Ch. D. 190	1137
——— Society, Sear v.	16 Ch. D. 387	763
Household, In re. Household v. Household	27 Ch. D. 553	1465
——— v. Household. In re Household	27 Ch. D. 553	1465
Houstoun v. Sligo (Marquis of)	29 Ch. D. 448	537
Howard v. Maitland	11 Q. B. D. 695	1631
———, Scott v.	6 App. Cas. 295	1382
———, Southend Waterworks v.	13 Q. B. D. 215	828
Howarth v. Howarth	9 P. D. 218	1107
Howarth's Trusts, In re. In re Holland	16 Ch. D. 672	1610
Howe, David v.	27 Ch. D. 533	1246
——— v. Smith	27 Ch. D. 89	1633
———, Walter v.	17 Ch. D. 708	430
Howell v. Dawson	13 Q. B. D. 67	1231
——— v. Metropolitan District Railway Company	19 Ch. D. 508	1202
Howitt v. Nottingham Tramways Company	12 Q. B. D. 16	1586
Hubbuck, In re. International Marine Hydropathic Company v. Hawes	29 Ch. D. 934	565
———, Attorney-General v.	10 Q. B. D. 488 ; 13 Q. B. D. 275	1333
Huddersfield (Mayor of), Milnes v.	10 Q. B. D. 124 ; 12 Q. B. D. 443	1657
Huddlestone, Miller v.	22 Ch. D. 233	1198
Hudlestone, Gilbert v. In re Gilbert	28 Ch. D. 549	1241
Hudson, Ex parte. In re Walton	22 Ch. D. 773	196
———, In re. Hudson v. Hudson	20 Ch. D. 406	1674
———, Fletcher v.	7 Q. B. D. 611	819
——— v. Hudson. In re Hudson	20 Ch. D. 406	1674
Hudspith, Vint v.	29 Ch. D. 322	1161
———	30 Ch. D. 24	1225
Huggins, Ex parte. In re Huggins	21 Ch. D. 85	141
Hughes v. Coles	27 Ch. D. 231	809

Name of Case.	Volume and Page.	Column of Digest.
Hughes, Horne v.	6 Q. B. D. 676	259
———, Percival v. Hughes v. Percival	9 Q. B. D. 441 ; 8 App. Cas. 443	1257
———, Rigg v.	9 P. D. 68	1129
—— v. Sutherland	7 Q. B. D. 160	1496
Hughes-Hallett v. Indian Mammoth Gold Mines Co.	22 Ch. D. 561	1595
Hugo, Commissioners of French Hoek v.	10 App. Cas. 336	308
Hull, In re	9 Q. B. D. 689	431
Hull Railway and Dock Act, In re. Ex parte Rector of Kirksmeaton	20 Ch. D. 203	788
Hull Railway and Dock Company, Wilkinson v.	20 Ch. D. 323	1288
Hulme, Slade v. In re Slade	18 Ch. D. 653	1198
" Humber," The	9 P. D. 12	1098
Humphrey, Brunsden v.	11 Q. B. D. 712 ; 14 Q. B. D. 141	540, 707
Humphreys v. Green	10 Q. B. D. 148	601
———, Green v.	23 Ch. D. 207 ; 26 Ch. D. 474	805
Humphries, In re. Smith v. Millidge	24 Ch. D. 691	1666
Humphrys, Allen v.	8 P. D. 16	12
Hunnings v. Williamson	10 Q. B. D. 459	1164
—— v.	11 Q. B. D. 533	883
Hunt v. Austin	9 Q. B. D. 598	1214
—— v. Chambers. In re Martin	20 Ch. D. 365	1186
—— v. Fensham	12 Q. B. D. 162	125
—— v. Hunt	8 P. D. 161	1118
—— v. ——	28 Ch. D. 606	648
Hunter v. Edney, otherwise Hunter	10 P. D. 93	1113
—— v. Johnson	13 Q. B. D. 225	531
—— v. Myatt	28 Ch. D. 181	902
Hurd, Redgrave v.	20 Ch. D. 1	581
Hurley, Hastings v.	16 Ch. D. 734	1132
Hurst v. Hurst	21 Ch. D. 278	1668
—— v. ——	28 Ch. D. 159	553
—— v. Taylor	14 Q. B. D. 918	950
Hutcheson v. Eaton	13 Q. B. D. 861	1254
Hutchings, Reg. v.	6 Q. B. D. 300	829
Hutchinson, Palmer v.	6 App. Cas. 619	313
———'s Trusts, In re	21 Ch. D. 811	1667
Huth, Atlantic Mutual Insurance Company v.	16 Ch. D. 474	1489
Hutton, In re. Ex parte Benwell	14 Q. B. D. 301	141
—— v. Lippert	8 App. Cas. 309	307
—— v. West Cork Railway Company	23 Ch. D. 654	352
Hyatt's Trusts, In re	21 Ch. D. 846	1611
Hyde, Rolfe v.	6 Q. B. D. 673	1324
———, Stone v.	9 Q. B. D. 76	865
—— (Corporation of) v. Bank of England	21 Ch. D. 176	820
Hyett, Goodhart v.	25 Ch. D. 182	654
—— v. Mekin	25 Ch. D. 735	551
Hyman v. Helm	24 Ch. D. 531	1159
—— v. Nye	6 Q. B. D. 685	950
Hyslop, Tate v.	15 Q. B. D. 368	691

I.

Name of Case.	Volume and Page.	Column of Digest.
Ickeringill, Hinsley v. In re Ickeringill's Estate.	17 Ch. D. 151	1082
Ickeringill's Estate, In re. Hinsley v. Ickeringill	17 Ch. D. 151	1082
Iles v. West Ham Assessment Committee	8 Q. B. D. 69 ; 8 App. Cas. 386	1075

Name of Case.	Volume and Page.	Column of Digest.
Jackson v. Litchfield	8 Q. B. D. 474	{ 1140 { 1196
———, Nottage v.	11 Q. B. D. 627	{ 431 { 1218
———, Osborne v.	11 Q. B. D. 619	862
———, Rous v.	29 Ch. D. 521	1084
———, School Board for London v.	7 Q. B. D. 502	529
——— v. Talbot. In re Jackson	21 Ch. D. 786	674
———. Wallis v.	23 Ch. D. 204	1195
Jacob v. Isaac. In re Isaac	30 Ch. D. 418	1180
———, Warner v.	20 Ch. D. 220	911
Jacobs v. Crédit Lyonnias	12 Q. B. D. 589	398
———, Harris v.	15 Q. B. D. 247	1477
Jacob's Case. Greenway v. Bachelor	12 Q. B. D. 376	1007
Jacobson, Ex parte. In re Pincoffs	22 Ch. D. 312	116
Jacques (Leonard), In re	18 Ch. D. 392	1242
——— v. Harrison	12 Q. B. D. 136, 165	1197
Jagger v. Jagger	25 Ch. D. 729	5
Jakeman's Trusts, In re	23 Ch. D. 344	652
James, In re	12 Q. B. D. 332	121, 839
——— v. Couchman	29 Ch. D. 212	1648
———, Cox v.	19 Ch. D. 55	1136
———, Davis v.	26 Ch. D. 778	1156
———, Gordon v.	30 Ch. D. 249	1524
———, Neilson v.	9 Q. B. D. 546	1552
——— v. Young	27 Ch. D. 652	886
Jardine v. Jardine	6 P. D. 213	1109
———, Scarf v.	7 App. Cas. 345	1019
Jarmain v. Chatterton	20 Ch. D. 493	1233
Jarratt, Crompton v.	30 Ch. D. 298	17
Jarvis, Miles v.	24 Ch. D. 633	1673
Jay, Gardner v.	29 Ch. D. 50	1186
Jeffrey, Matthews v.	6 Q. B. D. 290	275
Jeffries, Gilbey v.	11 Q. B. D. 559	148
Jenkins, Harris v.	22 Ch. D. 481	1163
——— v. Jones	9 Q. B. D. 128	1344
———, Moyle v.	8 Q. B. D. 116	866
Jenkinson, In re. Ex parte Nottingham and Nottinghamshire Bank	15 Q. B. D. 441	164
Jenks v. Turpin	13 Q. B. D. 505	609
Jenner v. Turner	16 Ch. D. 188	1672
Jennings, Gordon v.	9 Q. B. D. 45	869
——— v. Hammond	9 Q. B. D. 225	384
——— v. Jordan	6 App. Cas. 698	897
Jermonson, Hiscooks v.	10 Q. B. D. 360	665
Jervis, Chard v.	9 Q. B. D. 178	40
——— v. Lawrence	22 Ch. D. 202	289
Jeuchner, Herman v.	15 Q. B. D. 561	411
Jewell, Rule v.	18 Ch. D. 660	381
"John McIntyre," The	6 P. D. 200	1099
	9 P. D. 135	1510
Johnson, Ex parte. In re Chapman	26 Ch. D. 338	112
———, Ex parte. In re Johnson	25 Ch. D. 112	116
———, In re. Golden v. Gillam	20 Ch. D. 389	602
———, In re. Sly v. Blake	29 Ch. D. 964	805
——— & Tustin, In re	28 Ch. D. 84	1639
———, In re	30 Ch. D. 42	1639
———, Goodier v.	18 Ch. D. 441	1689
———, Hunter v.	13 Q. B. D. 225	531

Name of Case.	Volume and Page.	Column of Digest.
Lamb v. Munster	10 Q. B. D. 110	1171
——, ——— v.	11 Q. B. D. 588	499
Lambert, Elliott v. In re Callaghan	28 Ch. D. 186	676
Lambeth Assessment Committee, Smith v. ..	9 Q. B. D. 585 ; 10 Q. B. D. 327	1068
Lamb's Trusts, In re	28 Ch. D. 77 ..	1608
Lancashire and Yorkshire Railway Co., Marsden v.	7 Q. B. D. 641	1244
——————————., Whalley v.	13 Q. B. D. 131 ..	1652
Lancashire (Justices of), Rochdale (Corporation of) v.	6 Q. B. D. 525 ; 8 Q. B. D. 12 ; 8 App. Cas. 494	622
Lancashire Telephone Company v. Manchester (Overseers of)	13 Q. B. D. 700 ; 14 Q. B. D. 267	1071
"Lancaster," The	8 P. D. 65 ; 9 P. D. 14 ..	1518
Lancaster, Ex parte. In re Marsden	25 Ch. D. 311	168
Lancaster (Justices of), Improvement Commissioners of Newton in Makerfield	15 Q. B. D. 25	623
Lancaster, Mostyn v. Taylor v. Mostyn ..	23 Ch. D. 583	1463
Lancaster (Justices of), Newton Improvement Commissioners v.	13 Q. B. D. 623	62
——————————-, Over Darwen (Mayor of) v.	13 Q. B. D. 497 ; 15 Q. B. D. 20	621
Land and Finance Corporation, Tomlinson v. ..	14 Q. B. D. 539 , ..	1180
Land and House Property Corporation, Smith v. ..	28 Ch. D. 7	1634
Land Corporation of Ireland, Guinness v. ..	22 Ch. D. 349	328
Landowners West of England and South Wales Land Drainage and Inclosure Company v. Ashford ..	16 Ch. D. 411	337
Lane v. Collins	14 Q. B. D. 193	15
—— v. Lane. In re Llewellyn	25 Ch. D. 66	1214
—— v. Rhoades. In re Rhoades	29 Ch. D. 142	1693
Langdon, Cecil v.	28 Ch. D. 1	1467
Langen v. Tate	24 Ch. D. 522	1192
Langley, Mutual Life Assurance Society v. ..	26 Ch. D. 686	902, 918
Langrish v. Archer	10 Q. B. D. 44	1618
Langriville (Overseers of), Reg. v.	14 Q. B. D. 83	1072
"Lapwing," The. The "Hochung." China Merchants Steam Navigation Company v. Bignold ..	7 App. Cas. 512	1100
Laroche, Cooper v.	17 Ch. D. 368	1690
Lascelles, Agar-Ellis v. In re Agar-Ellis ..	24 Ch. D. 317	667
———————, Genese v.	13 Q. B. D. 901	187
Last, Erichsen v.	7 Q. B. D. 12 ; 8 Q. B. D. 414	1329
—— v. London Assurance Corporation ..	12 Q. B. D. 389 ; 14 Q. B. D. 239 ; 10 App. Cas. 438 ..	338, 1329
Latham, In re. Ex parte Glegg	19 Ch. D. 7	172
Lauderdale Peerage, The	10 App. Cas. 692	515 1388 1396
Lavery, Barker v.	14 Q. B. D. 769	1160
———, Cercle Restaurant Castiglione Company v. ..	18 Ch. D 555	366
Lavington, Daubuz v.	13 Q. B. D. 347	1136
Law Society v. Skinner	9 Q. B. D. 1 ; 8 App. Cas. 407	1544
—————— v. Waterlow		
Lawes, In re. Lawes v. Lawes	20 Ch. D. 81	1470
———, Belt v.	12 Q. B. D. 356	1195
——— v. Lawes. In re Lawes	20 Ch. D. 81	1470
Lawless v. Sullivan	6 App. Cas. 373	299
Lawrence v. Accidental Insurance Company ..	7 Q. B. D. 216	689
———, Jervis v.	22 Ch. D. 202	289
——— v. Lawrence	26 Ch. D. 795	32
Lawrie v. Lees	7 App. Cas. 19	30, 1625

e

Name of Case.	Volume and Page.	Column of Digest.
Leutner, Harrison v.	16 Ch. D. 559	1217
———, ——— v.	24 Ch. D. 594	1225
Levinstein, Badische Anilin und Soda Fabrik v.	24 Ch. D. 156; 29 Ch. D. 366	1042 1045 1049
Levy, In re. Ex parte Walton	17 Ch. D. 746	176
Levy's Trusts, In re	30 Ch. D. 119	1454
Lewes and East Grinstead Railway Co., Peters v.	16 Ch. D. 703 ; 18 Ch. D. 429	783
Lewin, Holyland v.	26 Ch. D. 266	1684
Lewis, In re. Ex parte Helder	24 Ch. D. 339	139
———, In re. Foxwell v. Lewis	30 Ch. D. 654	525
———, Askew v.	10 Q. B. D. 477	259
———, Bowen v.	9 App. Cas. 890	1676
———, Foxwell v. In re Lewis	30 Ch. D. 654	525
———, Garrard v.	10 Q. B. D. 30	231
———, Griffiths v. In re Griffiths	26 Ch. D. 465	1223
———, Kaltenbach v.	24 Ch. D. 54; 10 App. Cas. 617	573
———, London and County Banking Company v.	21 Ch. D. 490	1208
———, McHenry v.	21 Ch. D. 202; 22 Ch. D. 397	1158
———, Ricketts v.	20 Ch. D. 745	13
——— v. Trask..	21 Ch. D. 862	1591
Leyland, Conolan v.	27 Ch. D. 632	640
"Libra," The	6 P. D. 139	1512
Lightbound v. Bebington Local Board	14 Q. B. D. 849	832
Lilley v. Doubleday	7 Q. B. D. 510	485
Limehouse Board of Works, Ex parte. In re Vallance	24 Ch. D. 177	1153
Limpus v. Arnold	13 Q. B. D. 246; 15 Q. B. D. 300	1695
Lindford, Otto v.	18 Ch. D. 394	1160
Lindsell v. Phillips. In re Power	30 Ch. D. 291	808
Line v. Warren	14 Q. B. D. 73, 548	941
Linger, Tucker v.	21 Ch. D. 18; 8 App. Cas. 508	743
Lingwood, Creery, v. In re Hayward	19 Ch. D. 470	1875
Linney, Moorhouse v.	15 Q. B. D. 273	939
———, Thorpe v.	15 Q. B. D. 273	939
Linton v. Linton	15 Q. B. D. 239	148
Lion Insurance Association v. Tucker	12 Q. B. D. 176	355
Lippert, Hutton v.	8 App. Cas. 309	307
Liskeard Union v. Liskeard Waterworks Company	7 Q. B. D. 505	1657
Liskeard Waterworks Company, Liskeard Union v.	7 Q. B. D. 505	1657
Lister, Ex parte. In re Halberstamm	17 Ch. D. 518	135
Lister's Petition. In re Milford Docks Company	23 Ch. D. 292	367
Litchfield, Jackson v.	8 Q. B. D. 474	1140 1196
——— v. Jones	25 Ch. D. 64	1200
Lithgow, Randall v.	12 Q. B. D. 525	1202
Little, Ingram v.	11 Q. B. D. 251	1166
——— v. Kingswood Collieries Company	20 Ch. D. 733	1535
———, Vivian v.	11 Q. B. D. 370	1176
Liverpool (Corporation of), Jones v.	14 Q. B. D. 890	861
——— (Guardians of) v. Overseers of Portsea	12 Q. B. D. 303	1063
——— (Justices of), Reg. v.	11 Q. B. D. 638	682
"Livietta," The	8 P. D. 24	1517
	8 P. D. 209	1519
Livingstone, Price v.	9 Q. B. D. 679	1478

Name of Case.	Volume and Page.	Column of Digest.
McGiffin v. Palmer's Shipbuilding Company	10 Q. B. D. 5	863
McGowan, In the Goods of	10 P. D. 197	9
——— v. Middleton	11 Q. B. D. 464	1156
M'Gregor, Gow, & Co., Mogul Steamship Company v.	15 Q. B. D. 476	401
McHenry, Ex parte. In re McHenry	24 Ch. D. 35	192
———, In re. Ex parte Credit Company	24 Ch. D. 353	191
———, In re. Ex parte Walker	22 Ch. D. 813	190
——— v. Lewis	21 Ch. D. 202; 22 Ch. D. 397	1158
Machu, In re	21 Ch. D. 838	1669
M'Ilwraith v. Green	13 Q. B. D. 897	1152
——— v. ———	14 Q. B. D. 766	1152
———, Miles v.	8 App. Cas. 120	316
"McIntyre, John," The	6 P. D. 200	1099
Mackay, Ex parte. In re Page	14 Q. B. D. 401	179
——— v. Dick	6 App. Cas. 251	{1402 {1405
Mackellar v. Bond	9 App. Cas. 715	313
M'Kenzie v. British Linen Company	6 App. Cas. 82	536, 1372
Mackenzie's Trusts, In re	23 Ch. D, 750	1445
Mackie v. Herbertson	9 App. Cas. 303	1390
Mackintosh, In re	13 Q. B. D. 235	181
Mackonochie, Martin v.	6 P. D. 87 ; 7 P. D. 94	1124
———, ——— v.	8 P. D. 191	1126
——— v. Penzance (Lord)	6 App. Cas. 424	1124
McLachlan, Angus v.	23 Ch. D. 330	680
McLaren, Ex parte. In re McColla	16 Ch. D. 534	195
———, Caldwell v.	9 App. Cas. 392	302
Maclaren v. Compagnie Francaise de Navigation à Vapeur	9 App. Cas. 640	1510
McLaren v. Home	7 Q. B. D. 477	1003
McLean, Bidder v.	20 Ch. D. 512	1153
M'Lean v. Clydesdale Banking Company	9 App. Cas. 95	52, 1371
Maclean, Sanders v.	11 Q. B. D. 327	1364
Macleod v. Jones	24 Ch. D. 289	911
Maclure, Marshall v.	10 App. Cas. 325	890
———, Yorkshire Railway Wagon Company v.	19 Ch. D. 478; 21 Ch. D. 309	1284
McMahon v. Field	7 Q. B. D. 591	485
Macmillan, Bergmann v.	17 Ch. D. 423	1041
McRae, In re. Forster v. Davis. Norden v. McRae	25 Ch. D. 16	1148
———; Norden v. Forster v. Davis. In re McRae	25 Ch. D. 16	1148
Macreight, In re. Paxton v. Macreight	30 Ch. D. 165	514
———, Paxton v. In re Macreight	30 Ch. D. 165	514
Maddever, In re. Three Towns Banking Company v. Maddever	27 Ch. D. 523	603
Maddever, Three Towns Banking Company v.	27 Ch. D. 523	603
Maddison v. Alderson	7 Q. B. D. 174; 8 App. Cas. 467	412
Maddox, Hansen v.	12 Q. B. D. 100	1231
Madge, Spiller v. In re Spiller	18 Ch. D. 614	1684
Madgwick, In re	25 Ch. D. 371	1216
Madras Irrigation and Canal Company, In re	16 Ch. D. 702	1206
———, In re. Wood v. Madras Irrigation and Canal Company	23 Ch. D. 248	1244
———, Wood v. In re Madras Irrigation and Canal Company	23 Ch. D. 248	1244
Maffet, Wakefield v.	10 App. Cas. 422	1456
Magee, In re. Ex parte Magee	15 Q. B. D. 332	190
Maggi, In re. Winehouse v. Winehouse	20 Ch. D. 545	566

Name of Case.	Volume and Page.	Column of Digest.
Montagu v. Festing. In re Montagu. In re Wroughton	28' Ch. D. 82	668
———, Hendriks v. ..	17 Ch. D. 638	387
Moody and Yates' Contract, In re	28 Ch. D. 661; 30 Ch. D. 344	1640
Moordaff, Burgoine v.	8 P. D. 205	1130
Moore, Ex parte. In re Faithfull	14 Q. B. D. 627	113
———, In re. McAlpine v. Moore	21 Ch. D. 778	1608
———, Connecticut Mutual Life Insurance Company of Hartford v.	6 App. Cas. 644	300
——— v. Kennard	10 Q. B. D. 290 ..	1003
———, McAlpine v. In re Moore	21 Ch. D. 778	1608
———, Reg. v.	7 Q. B. D. 542	680
——— v. Shelley	8 App. Cas. 285	905
Moorhouse, Allcock v.	9 Q. B. D. 366	741
———, Hardaker v.	26 Ch. D. 417	1089
——— v. Linney	15 Q. B. D. 273	939
———, Summers v.	13 Q. B. D. 388	941
Morby, Reg. v.	8 Q. B. D. 571	469
Mordaunt v. Benwell	19 Ch. D. 302	1016
Morfee v. Novis	8 Q. B. D. 200	1005
Morgan, In re	24 Ch. D. 114	1440
———, In re. Pillgrem v. Pillgrem	18 Ch. D. 93	559
——— v. London General Omnibus Company ..	12 Q. B. D. 201; 13 Q. B. D. 832	864
———, Page v.	15 Q. B. D. 228	1364
——— v. Rees	6 Q. B. D. 89, 508 ..	440
——— v. Thomas	8 Q. B. D. 575; 9 Q. B. D. 643	1676
Morgan's Case. In re Glamorganshire Banking Co.	28 Ch. D. 620	381
Morice v. Aberdeen (Commissioners of Supply of the County of)	6 App. Cas. 881	1385
Morley v. Clifford	20 Ch. D. 753	419
Morrall v. Morrall	6 P. D. 98	1115
Morrell v. Morrell	7 P. D. 68	1687
Morris, In re. Ex parte Cooper	26 Ch. D. 693	157
———, In re. Ex parte Streeter	19 Ch. D. 216	184
———, In re. Ex parte Webster	22 Ch. D. 136	244
———, Davis v.	10 Q. B. D. 436	1140
——— v. Griffiths. In re Raw	26 Ch. D. 601	1763
———, Meakin v.	12 Q. B. D. 352	665
Morrish, In re. Ex parte Dyke (Sir W. H.) ..	22 Ch. D. 410	159, 172 771
Morrison, Ex parte. In re Gillespie	14 Q. B. D. 385	187
Morse, Ward v. In re Brown	23 Ch. D. 377	1219
Mort, Liddell & Co., Parnell v.	29 Ch. D. 325	1045
Morton, Merrill v.	17 Ch. D. 382	1706
——— v. Palmer	9 Q. B. D. 89	1156
———, Peard v. In re Luddy	25 Ch. D. 394	1675
Moser, In re	13 Q. B. D. 738	178
Moss, Ex parte. In re Toward	14 Q. B. D. 310	140
Mosses, Warner v.	16 Ch. D. 100	1189
———, ——— v.	19 Ch. D. 72	1221
Most, Reg. v.	7 Q. B. D. 244	470
Mostyn v. Lancaster. Taylor v. Mostyn ..	23 Ch. D. 583	1463
———, v. Taylor v.	25 Ch. D. 48	899
——— v. Stock	9 Q. B. D. 432	138
———, Taylor v. Mostyn v. Lancaster ..	23 Ch. D. 583	1463
Mott v. Lockhart	8 App. Cas. 568	299
Mottram, Walker v.	19 Ch. D. 355	614

f

Name of Case.	Volume and Page.	Column of Digest.
Park, In re. Ex parte Koster	14 Q. B. D. 597	40
——, Harmon v.	6 Q. B. D. 323	938
——, —— v.	7 Q. B. D. 369	939
Park Gate Waggon Works Company, In re	17 Ch. D. 234	371
Parke, Blaiberg v.	10 Q. B. D. 90	244
Parker, In re	21 Ch. D. 408	995
—— (R.A.), In re	29 Ch. D. 199	1532
——, In re. Ex parte Board of Trade	15 Q. B. D. 196	129
——, In re. Ex parte Charing Cross Advance and Deposit Bank	16 Ch. D. 35	250
——, In re. Ex parte Dann	17 Ch. D. 26	111
——, In re. Ex parte Turquand	14 Q. B. D. 636	162
——, In re. Barker v. Barker	16 Ch. D. 44	1701
——, In re. Bentham v. Wilson	17 Ch. D. 262	1704
—— and Parker, In re (1). Ex parte Turquand	14 Q. B. D. 405	178
——; In re (2). Ex parte ——	14 Q. B. D. 407	129
—— v. Felgate	8 P. D. 171	1272
—— v. First Avenue Hotel Company	24 Ch. D. 282	800
——, Lea v.	13 Q. B. D. 835	445
—— v. Wells	18 Ch. D. 477	1166
——, Winder v. In re Wilson	24 Ch. D. 664	1666
Parkin v. Cresswell. In re Cresswell	24 Ch. D. 102	1679
Parkinson, Hilbers v.	25 Ch. D. 200	1457
Parkside Mining Company, Smith v.	6 Q. B. D. 67	35
Parkyns v. Priest	7 Q. B. D. 313	619
Parnell, In re. Ex parte Ball	20 Ch. D. 670	197
—— v. Mort Liddell & Company	29 Ch. D. 325	1045
Parsons v. Birmingham Dairy Company	9 Q. B. D. 172	15
——, Citizens Insurance Company of Canada v.	7 App. Cas. 96	302
——, Queen Insurance Company v.	7 App. Cas. 96	302
Partridge v. Baylis	17 Ch. D. 835	1702
Patent Lionite Company, Thomas v.	17 Ch. D. 250	367, 377
Paterson v. Poe	8 App. Cas. 678	1390
—— v. St. Andrews (Provost, &c., of)	6 App. Cas. 833	1384
Patience, In re. Patience v. Main	29 Ch. D. 967	515
—— v. Main. In re Patience	29 Ch. D. 976	515
Patman v. Harland	17 Ch. D. 353	1640
Patterson, Forster v.	17 Ch. D. 132	810
——, Washburn and Moen Manufacturing Company v.	29 Ch. D. 48	1182
Patteson, Webster v.	25 Ch. D. 626	901
Patton, Ranson v.	17 Ch. D. 767	{ 1146, 1235 }
Paul v. Paul	19 Ch. D. 47; 20 Ch. D. 742	1470
Paull, In re. In re Carthew	27 Ch. D. 485	1527
Pawley, Saunders v.	14 Q. B. D. 234	1185
Pawsey v. Armstrong	18 Ch. D. 698	1018
Pawson, Bowyear v.	6 Q. B. D. 540	1414
Paxton v. Macreight. In re Macreight	30 Ch. D. 165	514
Payne, Ex parte. In re Sinclair	15 Q. B. D. 616	139
——, In re. Randle v. Payne	23 Ch. D. 288	1159
——, Randle v. In re Payne	23 Ch. D. 288	1159
—— v. Fern	6 Q. B. D. 620	256
Peace and Waller, In re	24 Ch. D. 405	1529
Peacock, Biggs v.	20 Ch. D. 200; 22 Ch. D. 284	1015
Peake, In re. Ex parte Harrison	13 Q. B. D. 753	157
Pearce, Ex parte. In re Williams	25 Ch. D. 656	247
——, In re. Ex parte Crossthwaite	14 Q. B. D. 966	138
—— v. Foster	15 Q. B. D. 114	1178

Name of Case.	Volume and Page.	Column of Digest.
Pearce v. Scotcher	9 Q. B. D. 162	585
Peard v. Morton. In re Luddy	25 Ch. D. 394	1675
Peareth v. Marriott	22 Ch. D. 182	539–1703
Pearsall v. Brierley Hill Local Board	11 Q. B. D. 735; 9 App. Cas. 595	815
Pearson, Brown v.	21 Ch. D. 716	1196
———, Elder v. In re Bellamy	25 Ch. D. 620	653
——— v. Heys	7 Q. B. D. 260	203
——— v. Pearson	27 Ch. D. 145	614
Peat v. Jones	8 Q. B. D. 147	156
Peek v. Trower	7 P. D. 21	522
Pellew, Meager v.	14 Q. B. D. 973	643
Pelley, Ex parte. In re Anglo-French Co-operative Society	21 Ch. D. 492	359
Pembrokeshire (Justices of), Davis v.	7 Q. B. D. 513	731
Pender, Heaven v.	9 Q. B. D. 302; 11 Q. B. D. 503	949
———, Newson v.	27 Ch. D. 43	801
Peninsular and Oriental Steam Navigation Company, Ager v.	26 Ch. D. 637	421
	7 App. Cas. 795	1098
Stoomvaart Maatschappy Nederland v.	23 Ch. D. 353	1172
Penrice v. Williams	7 P. D. 19	1106
Penty v. Penty		
Penwarden v. Roberts. Heath v. Roberts. Wilson v. Roberts	9 Q. B. D. 137	243
Penzance (Lord), Enraght v.	7 App. Cas. 240	{1122 {1123
———, Green v. Ex parte Green	7 Q. B. D. 273; 6 App. Cas. 657	1125
———, Mackonochie v.	6 App. Cas. 424	1124
Penzance Union, Paris and New York Telegraph Company v.	12 Q. B. D. 552	1071
Pepperell, Mercier v.	19 Ch. D. 58	34
Percival v. Cross	7 P. D. 234	1129
——— v. Dunn	29 Ch. D. 128	43, 1154
——— v. Hughes. Hughes v. Percival	9 Q. B. D. 441; 8 App. Cas. 443	1257
Percy, In re. Percy v. Percy	24 Ch. D. 616	1663
——— v. Percy. In re Percy	24 Ch. D. 616	1663
Perkins v. Enraght. Harris v. Enraght	7 P. D. 31, 161	1123
Perowne, Barker v. In re Clarke	18 Ch. D. 160	32
Perry v. Barnett	14 Q. B. D. 467; 15 Q. B. D. 388	1259
Perth (Lord Provost of), North British Railway Company v.	10 App. Cas. 579	1398
Peruvian Guano Company v. Bookwoldt	23 Ch. D. 225	1158
———, Compagnie Financiere du Pacifique v.	11 Q. B. D. 55	1174
"Peshawur," The	8 P. D. 32	1100
Peter v. Thomas-Peter	26 Ch. D. 181	1146
Peterborough (Bishop of), Welch v.	15 Q. B. D. 432	19
——— (Corporation of) v. Overseers of Thurlby	8 Q. B. D. 586	1412
——— v. Wilsthorpe (Overseers of)	12 Q. B. D. 1	1234
Peters v. Lewes and East Grinstead Railway Co.	16 Ch. D. 703; 18 Ch. D. 429	783
Petgrave, Workman v. In re Wait	30 Ch. D. 617	1088
Pettman, Follett v.	23 Ch. D. 337	1694

Name of Case.	Volume and Page.	Column of Digest.
Plomesgate (Guardians of) v. West Ham (Guardians of)	6 Q. B. D. 576	1065
Plowden, Corbett v.	25 Ch. D. 678	904
Plumstead Board of Works v. Spackman	13 Q. B. D. 878; 10 App. Cas. 229	877
Pocock, Chandler v.	16 Ch. D. 648	1086
Pocock's Claim. In re Romford Canal Company	24 Ch. D. 85	334
Poe, Paterson v.	8 App. Cas. 678	1390
Pogose, In re. Ex parte Vanderlinden	20 Ch. D. 289	123
Pointon v. Hill	12 Q. B. D. 306	1618
Pollock, In re. Pollock v. Worrall	28 Ch. D. 552	1695
———, Noyes v.	30 Ch. D. 336	904
——— v. Rabbits	21 Ch. D. 466	1630
——— v. Worrall. In re Pollock	28 Ch. D. 552	1695
Pollok, Whyte v.	7 App. Cas. 400	1405
Pomero v. Pomero	10 P. D. 174	1110
Pomfret v. Graham. In re Horner's Estate	19 Ch. D. 186	1698
Poncia, Taylor v.	25 Ch. D. 646	1451
Ponsonby v. Ponsonby	9 P. D. 58, 122	1117
"Pontida," The	9 P. D. 102, 177	1487
Pontifex v. Foord	12 Q. B. D. 152	1144
Pookes Royle, Re	7 Q. B. D. 9	134
Poole, In re. Ex parte Cocks	21 Ch. D. 397	134
———, Walker v.	21 Ch. D. 835	1171
Pooler, Butcher v.	24 Ch. D. 273	1241
Pooley, In re. Ex parte Harper	20 Ch. D. 685	188
———, In re. Ex parte Sheard (No. 1)	16 Ch. D. 107	136
———, In re. Ex parte ——— (No. 2)	16 Ch. D. 110	184
———, Metropolitan Bank v.	10 App. Cas. 210	282
Pooley's Trustee in Bankruptcy v. Whetham	28 Ch. D. 38	1181
Poplar Union Assessment Committee, Reg. v.	11 Q. B. D. 721; 13 Q. B. D. 364	885
Popple v. Sylvester	22 Ch. D. 98	706
Poppleton, Ex parte. In re Thomas	14 Q. B. D. 379	385
Popplewell, Ex parte. In re Storey	21 Ch. D. 73	251
Port Philip Gold Mining Company, Shaw v.	13 Q. B. D. 103	536
Portal and Lamb, In re	27 Ch. D. 600; 30 Ch. D. 50	1697
Porter, Mellor v.	25 Ch. D. 158	900
Portman v. Home Hospital Association	27 Ch. D. 81, n.	764
Portsea (Overseers of), Liverpool (Guardians of) v.	12 Q. B. D. 303	1063
——— Union (Guardians of), Reg. v.	7 Q. B. D. 384	1063
Portsmouth (Corporation of) v. Smith	13 Q. B. D. 184; 10 App. Cas. 364	833
Posnanski, Salm Kyrburg v.	13 Q. B. D. 218	1200
Post v. Marsh	16 Ch. D. 395	1547
Pott v. Brassey. In re Allnutt	22 Ch. D. 275	1461
———, Credit Company v.	6 Q. B. D. 295	248
Potteries, Shrewsbury, and North Wales Railway Company, In re	25 Ch. D. 251	1282
Potteries Railway Co., Midland Waggon Co. v.	6 Q. B. D. 36	1287
Pountney v. Clayton	11 Q. B. D. 820	1292
Powell v. Apollo Candle Company	10 App. Cas. 282	314
——— v. Cobb	29 Ch. D. 486	1187
Powers, In re. Lindsell v. Phillips	30 Ch. D. 291	808
Poyser v. Minors	7 Q. B. D. 329	445
Praed, Exmouth (Viscount) v. In re Viscount Exmouth	23 Ch. D. 158	1682
Pragnell v. Batten. In re Hardiman	16 Ch. D. 360	1015
Pratt, Ex parte	12 Q. B. D. 334	127

Name of Case.	Volume and Page.	Column of Digest.
Reeves *v.* Barlow	11 Q. B. D. 610; 12 Q. B. D. 436	257
Reg. *v.* Abergavenny (Guardians of)	6 Q. B. D. 31	1066
—— *v.* Barclay	8 Q. B. D. 306, 486	828
—— *v.* Bayley	8 Q. B. D. 411	443
—— *v.* Belleau	7 App. Cas. 473	306
—— *v.* Biron	14 Q. B. D. 474	735
——, Blackwood *v.*	8 App. Cas. 82	317
—— *v.* Bridgnorth (Guardians of)	9 Q. B. D. 765; 11 Q. B. D. 314	1063
—— *v.* Brittleton	12 Q. B. D. 266	473
—— *v.* Brown	10 Q. B. D. 381	469
—— *v.* Carr	10 Q. B. D. 76	727
—— *v.* Carter	12 Q. B. D. 522	475
——, Castro *v.*	6 App. Cas. 229	476
—— *v.* Central Criminal Court (Justices of)	11 Q. B. D. 479	452
—— *v.* City of London (Judge of)	8 Q. B. D. 609	1105
—— *v.* ——————	12 Q. B. D. 115	442
—— *v.* City of London Court (Judge of)	14 Q. B. D. 818, 905	865
——, Clark *v.*	14 Q. B. D. 92	1617
—— *v.* Coney	13 Q. B. D. 963	471
—— *v.* Cook	8 Q. B. D. 534	610
—— *v.* Cookham Union	13 Q. B. D. 377	1064
—— *v.* Copping Syke (Overseers of)	9 Q. B. D. 522	1074
—— *v.* Cox and Railton	14 Q. B. D. 83	473
—— *v.* Croydon County Court (Judge of)	14 Q. B. D. 963	179
—— *v.* Cumberland (Justices of)	8 Q. B. D. 369	681
—— *v.* De Banks	13 Q. B. D. 29	464
—— *v.* Denbighshire (Justices of)	15 Q. B. D. 451	1072
—— *v.* Dibbin	14 Q. B. D. 325; 15 Q. B. D. 382	1067
—— *v.* Doutre	9 App. Cas. 745	305
—— *v.* Dudley and Stephens	14 Q. B. D. 273, 560	470
—— *v.* Duncan	7 Q. B. D. 198	476
—— *v.* Dyott	9 Q. B. D. 47	1073
—— *v.* East and West India Dock Company and Poplar Union	11 Q. B. D. 721; 13 Q. B. D. 364	885
—— *v.* Eaton	8 Q. B. D. 158	529
—— *v.* Edwards	13 Q. B. D. 586	778
—— *v.* Ellis	8 Q. B. D. 466	624
—— *v.* Essex (Justices of)	11 Q. B. D. 704	618
—— *v.* Essex	14 Q. B. D. 753	777
—— *v.* Exeter (Mayor, &c., of)	6 Q. B. D. 135	943
—— *v.* Fennell	7 Q. B. D. 147	473
—— *v.* Flavell	14 Q. B. D. 364	204
—— *v.* Fobbing (Commissioners of Sewers of)	14 Q. B. D. 561	1408
—— *v.* Foote	10 Q. B. D. 378	1235
—— *v.* Ganz	9 Q. B. D. 93	571
—— *v.* Gibbon	6 Q. B. D. 168	731
—— *v.* Great Yarmouth (Justices of)	8 Q. B. D. 525	731
—— *v.* Greenwich County Court (Registrar of)	15 Q. B. D. 54	130
—— *v.* Handsley	7 Q. B. D. 398	1073
—— *v.* ——————	8 Q. B. D. 383	732
—— *v.* Harper	7 Q. B. D. 78	463
—— *v.* Haslehurst	13 Q. B. D. 253	1067
——, Hodge *v.*	9 App. Cas. 117	301
—— *v.* Holl	7 Q. B. D. 575	997, 1235
—— *v.* Hollis	12 Q. B. D. 25	465
—— *v.* Holmes	12 Q. B. D. 23	476

Name of Case.	Volume and Page.	Column of Digest.
Reg. *v.* Hutchings	6 Q. B. D. 300	829
—— *v.* Jones	11 Q. B. D. 118	460
—— *v.* Kay	10 Q. B. D. 213	683
—— *v.* Labouchere	12 Q. B. D. 320	466
—— *v.* Langriville (Overseers of)	14 Q. B. D. 83	1072
—— *v.* Lee	9 Q. B. D. 394	823
—— *v.* Liverpool (Justices of)	11 Q. B. D. 638	682
—— *v.* Llewellyn	13 Q. B. D. 681	820
—— *v.* Local Government Board	9 Q. B. D. 600; 10 Q. B. D. 309	832
—— *v.* ————	15 Q. B. D. 70	624
—— *v.* Lovell	8 Q. B. D. 185	464
—— *v.* McDonald	15 Q. B. D. 323	464
—— *v.* Maidenhead (Corporation of)	8 Q. B. D. 339; 9 Q. B. D. 494	938
—— *v.* Mallory	13 Q. B. D. 33	474
—— *v.* Manchester (Overseers of)	8 Q. B. D. 50	1066
—— *v.* Manning	12 Q. B. D. 241	460
—— *v.* Martin	8 Q. B. D. 54	468
—— *v.* Marylebone (Guardians of)	13 Q. B. D. 15	1063
—— *v.* Maurer	10 Q. B. D. 513	572
—— *v.* Merthyr Tydvil (Justices of)	14 Q. B. D. 584	683
—— *v.* Mews	6 Q. B. D. 47; 8 App. Cas. 339	844
—— *v.* Middlesex (Justices of)	9 Q. B. D. 41	876
—— *v.* ————	11 Q. B. D. 656; 9 App. Cas. 757	1268
—— *v.* Moore	7 Q. B. D. 542	680
—— *v.* Morby	8 Q. B. D. 571	469
—— *v.* Most	7 Q. B. D. 24	470
—— *v.* Nash	10 Q. B. D. 4 4	667
—— *v.* Newman	8 Q. B. D. 70	467
—— *v.* Paget	8 Q. B. D. 15	736
—— *v.* Phillimore and Pilling	14 Q. B. D. 4 4, n.	735
—— *v.* Pirehill (Justices of)	13 Q. B. D. 6 6; 14 Q. B. D. 13	856
—— *v.* Poplar Union Assessment Committee	13 Q. B. D. 364	885
—— *v.* Portsea Union (Guardians of)	7 Q. B. D. 384	1063
—— *v.* Preston (Guardians of)	11 Q. B. D. 113	1064
—— *v.* Price	12 Q. B. D. 247	467
—— *v.* Ratcliffe	10 Q. B. D. 74	473
—— *v.* Rawlins	14 Q. B. D. 325	1067
—— *v.* ————	15 Q. B. D. 382	1067
——, Riel *v.*	10 App. Cas. 675	1128
—— *v.* Rowlands	8 Q. B. D. 530	464
——, Russell *v.*	7 App. Cas. 829	298
—— *v.* St. Albans (Bishop of)	9 Q. B. D. 454	1122
—— *v.* St. Mary Bermondsey (Overseers of)	14 Q. B. D. 351	1071
—— *v.* St. Mary, Islington (Guardians of)	15 Q. B. D. 95, 339	1062
—— *v.* Salmon	6 Q. B. D. 79	469
—— *v.* Savin	6 Q. B. D. 309	1234
—— *v.* Schneider	11 Q. B. D. 66	683
—— *v.* Sheward	9 Q. B. D. 741	778
—— *v.* Shropshire (Justices of)	6 Q. B. D. 669	746
—— *v.* Slator	8 Q. B. D. 267	474
—— *v.* Smith. In re Westfield and Metropolitan Railway Companies	12 Q. B. D. 481	786
—— *v.* Southampton County Court (Judge of)	13 Q. B. D. 142	442
—— *v.* Southend County Court (Judge of)	13 Q. B. D. 142	442

Name of Case.	Volume and Page.	Column of Digest.
Reg. v. Stephenson	13 Q. B. D. 331	467
—— v. Surrey (Judge of the County Court of)	13 Q. B. D. 963	179
—— v. —— (Justices of)	6 Q. B. D. 100	1073
—— v. Thomas	11 Q. B. D. 282	626
—— v. Thompson	12 Q. B. D. 261; 10 App. Cas. 45	204
—— v. Tonbridge (Overseers of)	11 Q. B. D. 134; 13 Q. B. D. 339	275
—— v. Weil	9 Q. B. D. 701	570
—— v. Wellard	14 Q. B. D. 63	468
—— v. West Riding of Yorkshire (Justices of)	11 Q. B. D. 417	681
——, —————— v.	8 App. Cas. 781	623
—— v. Whitchurch	7 Q. B. D. 534	1235
—— v. White	11 Q. B. D. 309; 14 Q. B. D. 358	1061
—— v. Whitfield	15 Q. B. D. 122	847
—— v. Wigan (Corporation of)	14 Q. B. D. 908	943
—— v. Williams	9 App. Cas. 418	314
—— v. Willshire	6 Q. B. D. 366	459
—— v. Wimbledon Local Board	8 Q. B. D. 459	1278
—— v. Yates	11 Q. B. D. 750; 14 Q. B. D. 648	467
Reid, Ex parte. In re Gillespie	14 Q. B. D. 963	154
—— v. Hoare	26 Ch. D. 363	1452
Reliance Permanent Building Society, West London Commercial Bank v.	27 Ch. D. 187; 29 Ch. D. 954	920
"Renpor," The	8 P. D. 115	1516
Repington v. Roberts-Gawen. In re Roberts	19 Ch. D. 520	1690
Republic of Costa Rica v. Strousberg	16 Ch. D. 8	1203
Revell, Ex parte. In re Tollemache (No. 1)	13 Q. B. D. 720	150
——————————— (No. 2)	13 Q. B. D. 727	170
Revett, Doggett v. In re Youngs	30 Ch. D. 421	1237
————, Vollum v. In re ——	30 Ch. D. 421	1237
Reynolds, Ex parte. In re Barnett	15 Q. B. D. 169	181
————, Ex parte. In re Reynolds	20 Ch. D. 294	545
————, Ex parte. In re ——	21 Ch. D. 601	189
Rhoades, In re. Lane v. Rhoades	29 Ch. D. 142	1693
————, Lane v. In re ——	29 Ch. D. 142	1693
Rhodes, In re. Ex parte Heyworth	14 Q. B. D. 49	120
——, Collins v. In re Baker	20 Ch. D. 230	1546
—— v. Rhodes	7 App. Cas. 192	1272 / 1701
—— v. Sugden. In re Wadsworth	29 Ch. D. 517	1540
—— v. Wish. In re Seaman	20 Ch. D. 230	1546
"Rhondda," The. Scicluna v. Stevenson	8 App. Cas. 549	1511
"Rhosina," The	10 P. D. 24	951
————, The	10 P. D. 131	952
Richards v. Cullerne	7 Q. B. D. 623	442
——————, Jones v.	15 Q. B. D. 439	1167
—— v. McBride	8 Q. B. D. 119	684
—— v. May	10 Q. B. D. 400	265
—— v. West Middlesex Waterworks Company	15 Q. B. D. 660	1661
Richardson, In re. Ex parte Harris	16 Ch. D. 613	176
——————, In re. Shillito v. Hobson	30 Ch. D. 396	895
——————, Robertson v.	30 Ch. D. 623	1454
—————— v. Saunders. Saunders v. Richardson	6 Q. B. D. 313; 7 Q. B. D. 388	531
Richdale, Ex parte. In re Palmer	19 Ch. D. 409	171
Richer & Co., Oriental Bank Corporation v.	9 App. Cas. 413	312

Name of Case.	Volume and Page.	Column of Digest.
Robinson, Todd v.	12 Q. B. D. 530	1052
———, —— v.	14 Q. B. D. 739	819
——— v. Trevor	12 Q. B. D. 423	913
——— v. Tucker	14 Q. B. D. 371	1230
Robson, In re. Emley v. Davidson	19 Ch. D. 156	289
Rochdale (Corporation of) v. Lancashire (Justices of)	6 Q. B. D. 525 ; 8 Q. B. D. 12 ; 8 App. Cas. 494	622
Rochfort, Sperling v. In re Van Hagan	16 Ch. D. 18	1081
Rodocanachi, Burnand v.	6 Q. B. D. 633 ; 7 App. Cas. 333	697
Roe v. Birch. In re Birch	27 Ch. D. 622	561
Rogers, Ex parte. In re Boustead	16 Ch. D. 665	181
———, Ex parte. In re Pyatt	26 Ch. D. 31	1571
———, Ex parte. In re Rogers	13 Q. B. D. 438	131
———, In re. Ex parte Challinor	16 Ch. D. 260	248
———, In re. Ex parte Rogers	13 Q. B. D. 438	131
———, Ellis v.	29 Ch. D. 661	1637
Rokeby (Lord), Elliot v.	7 App. Cas. 43	889
Rolfe v. Hyde	6 Q. B. D. 673	1324
Rolleston, Charlton v.	28 Ch. D. 237	785
Rolls v. Isaacs	19 Ch. D. 268	1049
—— v. Miller	25 Ch. D. 206 ; 27 Ch. D. 71	764
—— v. School Board for London	27 Ch. D. 639	531
Rolph, Ex parte. In re Spindler	19 Ch. D. 98	250
Rolt, English Channel Steamship Company v.	17 Ch. D. 715	357
Romford Canal Company, In re. Pocock's Claim. Trickett's Claim. Carew's Claim	24 Ch. D. 85	334
"Rona," The	7 P. D. 247	442
Rooke, Walker v.	6 Q. B. D. 631	1204
Roope v. D'Avigdor	10 Q. B. D. 412	6
Roose, In re. Evans v. Williamson	17 Ch. D. 696	1705
Roper, In re. Ex parte Bolland	21 Ch. D. 543	251
"Rory," The	7 P. D. 117	1109
Rose v. Rose	7 P. D. 225 ; 8 P. D. 98	1095
Rosenberg v. Cook	8 Q. B. D. 162	1632
Rosenthal, Ex parte. In re Dickinson	20 Ch. D. 315	186
Rosher, In re. Rosher v. Rosher	26 Ch. D. 801	1669
—— v. Rosher. In re Rosher	26 Ch. D. 801	1669
Ross v. Charity Commissioners	7 App. Cas. 463	533
———, Munby v. In re Coulman	30 Ch. D. 186	1078
—— v. Ross	7 P. D. 20	1116
Rossiter, Britain v.	11 Q. B. D. 123	600
Rotherham, Wilkins v. In re Wilkins	27 Ch. D. 703	560
Rotherham Alum and Chemical Company, In re	25 Ch. D. 103	323
Rothes (Countess of), v. Kirkcaldy and Dysart Water-works Commissioners	7 App. Cas. 694	1404
Rouch v. Hall	6 Q. B. D. 17	15
Rous v. Jackson	29 Ch. D. 521	1084
Rouse, Kinsman v.	17 Ch. D. 104	811
Rowlands, Reg. v.	8 Q. B. D. 530	464
Rownson, In re. Field v. White	29 Ch. D. 358	567
Roxburghe v. Cox	17 Ch. D. 520	1413
Royal Bank of Scotland, Chapman v.	7 Q. B. D. 136	1323
——————— v. Commercial Bank of Scotland	7 App. Cas. 366	1374
Royal Society of London and Thompson	17 Ch. D. 407	285
Royce v. Charlton	8 Q. B. D. 1	33
Royle v. Busby & Son	6 Q. B. D. 171	1473
Rudow v. Great Britain Mutual Life Assurance Society	17 Ch. D. 600	387, 1220

Name of Case.	Volume and Page.	Column of Digest.
Salm Kyrburg v. Posnanski	13 Q. B. D. 218	1200
Salmon, Reg. v.	6 Q. B. D. 79	469
Salt v. Cooper	16 Ch. D. 544	1210
—— v. Pym. In re Northen's Estate	28 Ch. D. 153	1687
Saltash (Corporation of) v. Goodman .. .. .. {	7 Q. B. D. 106 ; 7 App. Cas. 633	585
Salter, Crawcour v.	18 Ch. D. 30	161, 545
Salting, Ex parte. In re Stratton	25 Ch. D. 148	124
Sampson, Scott v.	8 Q. B. D. 491	499
Sampson and Wall, In re	25 Ch. D. 482	674
Samuelson, Heske v.	12 Q. B. D. 30	863
Sandeman v. Scottish Property and Building Society	10 App. Cas. 553	1384
Sanders, In re. Ex parte Whinney	13 Q. B. D. 476	112
—— v. Davis	15 Q. B. D. 218	748
—— v. Sanders	19 Ch. D. 373	809
—— v. Maclean	11 Q. B. D. 327	1364
——' Case. In re Albion Life Assurance Society	20 Ch. D. 403	389
Sanderson v. Berwick-upon-Tweed (Mayor of) ..	13 Q. B. D. 547	763
——, Great Northern Railway Company and, In re .. .. {	25 Ch. D. 788	1626
——, Wright v.	9 P. D. 149	1270
Sandes, Emeny v.	14 Q. B. D. 6	1222
Sandgate Local Board v. Pledge	14 Q. B. D. 730	785
—— v. Leney	25 Ch. D. 183, n.	1654
Sands to Thompson	22 Ch. D. 614	812
Sandwell, In re. Ex parte Zerfass	14 Q. B. D. 960	178
Sangster v. Cochrane	28 Ch. D. 298	272
Sastry Velaider Aronegary v. Sembecutty Vaigalie ..	6 App. Cas. 364	308
Saunders, Ex parte	11 Q. B. D. 191	820
—— v. Crawford	9 Q. B. D. 612	528
—— v. McConnell. In re McConnell ..	29 Ch. D. 76	1218
—— v. Pawley	14 Q. B. D. 234	1185
——, Richardson v. Richardson v. Saunders .. {	6 Q. B. D. 313 ; 7 Q. B. D. 388	531
——, Warder v.	1 Q. B. D. 114	1156
Savage, Bridger v.	15 Q. B. D. 363	1260
Savill, Whitecross Wire Company v. ..	8 Q. B. D. 653	1486
Savin, Reg. v.	6 Q. B. D. 809	1234
Sawtell, Hernando v. In re Hernando	27 Ch. D. 284	1087
Sawyer v. Sawyer	28 Ch. D. 595	1594
Saxby v. Gloucester Waggon Company	7 Q. B. D. 305	1048
Sayers v. Collyer	24 Ch. D. 180 ; 28 Ch. D. 103	454, 484
Saywood v. Cross	14 Q. B. D. 53	1222
Scammell, Burrow v.	19 Ch. D. 175	740
Scarf v. Jardine	7 App. Cas. 345	1019
Scarlett v. Hanson	12 Q. B. D. 213	1473
Schjott v. Schjott	19 Ch. D. 94	1142
Schmidt, Rumball v.	8 Q. B. D. 603	822
Schmitz, Ex parte	12 Q. B. D. 509	113
Schneider v. Batt	8 Q. B. D. 701	1142
——, Reg. v.	11 Q. B. D. 66	683
Scholfield v. Spooner	26 Ch. D. 94	1460
School Board for London, Cotton's Trustees and, In re	19 Ch. D. 624	1469
—————— v. Jackson	7 Q. B. D. 502	529
——————, Rolls v.	27 Ch. D. 639	532
School for Indigent Blind, Wigsell v.	8 Q. B. D. 357	483
Schuler, Young v.	11 Q. B. D. 651	542
Scicluna v. Stevenson. The "Rhondda"	8 App. Cas. 549	1511
Scotcher, Pearce v.	9 Q. B. D. 162	585

Name of Case.	Volume and Page.	Column of Digest.
Silver Valley Mines, In re	21 Ch. D. 381	390
Simcox v. Handsworth Local Board	8 Q. B. D. 39	831
Simmons, In re	15 Q. B. D. 348	1543
———— v. Mitchell	6 App. Cas. 156	500
————, Shaw v.	12 Q. B. D. 117	386
Simon v. Vernon	8 App. Cas. 542	310
Simons, In re. Ex parte Allard	16 Ch. D. 505	147
Sinclair, In re. Ex parte Chaplin	26 Ch. D. 319	110
————, In re. Ex parte Payne	15 Q. B. D. 616	139
———— v. Caithness Flagstone Quarrying Company	6 App. Cas. 340	1393
————, Daniell v.	6 App. Cas. 181	896
Singer Manufacturing Company v. Loog	18 Ch. D. 395 ; 8 App. Cas. 15	1585
Skinner v. City of London Marine Insurance Corporation	14 Q. B. D. 882	348
————, Law Society v. Law Society v. Waterlow	9 Q. B. D. 1 ; 8 App. Cas. 407	1544
Skipper, Clarke v.	21 Ch. D. 134	1187
Skipper, Garnham v.	29 Ch. D. 566	1183
Slack v. Midland Railway Company	16 Ch. D. 81	1225
Slade, In re. Slade v. Hulme	18 Ch. D. 653	1198
———— v. Hulme. In re Slade	18 Ch. D. 653	1198
Slator, Paine v.	11 Q. B. D. 120	453
————, Reg. v.	8 Q. B. D. 267	474
Sligo (Marquis of), Houstoun v.	29 Ch. D. 448	537
Slight, Cooper v. In re Cooper	27 Ch. D. 565	1089
Sly v. Blake. In re Johnson	29 Ch. D. 964	805
Small v. Smith	10 App. Cas. 119	1374
Smalley v. Hardinge	6 Q. B. D. 371 ; 7 Q. B. D. 524	177
———— otherwise Cannon, Cannon v.	10 P. D. 96	1113
Smallpage's and Brandon's Cases. In re Marseilles Extension Railway and Land Company	30 Ch. D. 598	233
Smart (W. G.), In the Goods of	9 P. D. 64	1272
————, In re. Smart v. Smart	18 Ch. D. 165	419
————, Tinnuchi v.	10 P. B. 184	39
Smethurst v. Hastings	30 Ch. D. 490	1598
Smetten, Taylor v.	11 Q. B. D. 207	610
Smith, Ex parte. In re Hepburn	14 Q. B. D. 394	153
————, In re. Green v. Smith	22 Ch. D. 586	145, 555
————, In re. ———— v. ————	24 Ch. D. 672	145
————, In re. Hooper v. Smith	26 Ch. D. 614	1245
———— v. Armitage	24 Ch. D. 727	1185
———— v. Birmingham (Corporation of)	11 Q. B. D. 195	1658
————, Booth v.	14 Q. B. D. 318	1314
———— v. Chadwick	20 Ch. D. 27 ; 9 App. Cas. 187	324
———— v. Cowell	6 Q. B. D. 75	1210
———— v. Critchfield	14 Q. B. D. 873	1232
————, Cropper v.	24 Ch. D. 305	1161
————, Cropper v.	26 Ch. D. 700 ; 10 App. Cas. 249	1047
————, Cropper v. (No. 2)	28 Ch. D. 148	1041
———— v. Dale	18 Ch. D. 516	553
———— v. Darlow	26 Ch. D. 605	1232
———— v. Dart & Son	14 Q. B. D. 105	1483
———— v. Davies	28 Ch. D. 650	899, 1183
———— v. Day	16 Ch. D. 726	1218
———— v. ————	21 Ch. D. 421	1200
————, Elliott v.	22 Ch. D. 236	1684
————, Euston v.	9 P. D. 57	1113

Name of Case.	Volume and Page.	Column of Digest.
Somerville, Ex parte. In re South Eastern Railway Company	23 Ch. D. 167	784
Sotheran v. Dening	20 Ch. D. 99	1084
Sotheron v. Scott	6 Q. B. D. 518	203
Soutar's Policy Trust, In re	26 Ch. D. 236	637
South Eastern Railway Company, In re. Ex parte Somerville	23 Ch. D. 167	748
——————————————————, Bobbett v.	9 Q. B. D. 424	1287
—————————————————— v. Railway Commissioners and Mayor, &c., of Hastings	6 Q. B. D. 586	1296
——————————————————, Thomson v.	9 Q. B. D. 320	1158
South Kensington Co-operative Stores, In re	17 Ch. D. 161	376
South Shields Union, Dinning v.	12 Q. B. D. 61; 13 Q. B. D. 25	1061
South Western Loan Company v. Robertson	8 Q. B. D 17	1205
Southall, Bollen v.	15 Q. B. D. 461	1006
Southam, In re. Ex parte Lamb	19 Ch. D. 169	186
Southampton (Corporation of), Aslatt v.	16 Ch. D. 143	942
——————, Judge of the County Court of, Reg. v.	13 Q. B. D. 142	442
—————— (Lord), Allen v. In re Southampton's (Lord) Estate. Banfather's Claim	16 Ch. D. 178	895
Southampton's (Lord) Estate. In re. Allen v. Southampton (Lord). Banfather's Claim	16 Ch. D. 178	895
Southend County Court (Judge of), Reg. v.	13 Q. B. D. 142	442
Southend Waterworks Company v. Howard	13 Q. B. D. 215	828
Southsea Railway Company, Barnes v.	27 Ch. D. 536	788
Spackman v. Foster	11 Q. B. D. 99	806
——————, Plumstead Board of Works v.	13 Q. B. D. 878; 10 App. Cas. 229	877
Spaight v. Tedcastle	6 App. Cas. 217	1515
Spain v. Mowatt. Milford Haven Railway and Estate Co. v. Mowatt. In re Lake and Taylor's Mortgage	28 Ch. D. 402	1631
Spanish Telegraph Company v. Shepherd	13 Q. B. D. 202	766
Sparrow, In re	20 Ch. D. 320	849
—————— v. Hill	7 Q. B. D. 362; 8 Q. B. D. 479.	1219
Speight, In re	13 Q. B. D. 42	187
——————, In re. Speight v. Gaunt	22 Ch. D. 727; 9 App. Cas. 1	1596
—————— v. Gaunt. In re Speight	22 Ch. D. 727; 9 App. Cas. 1	1596
Speller v. Bristol Steam Navigation Company	13 Q. B. D. 96	1145
Spence, Smith v. In re Wheatley	27 Ch. D. 606	526
Spencer, In re. Thomas v. Spencer	30 Ch. D. 183	642
—————— v. Duckworth. In re Wilkins	18 Ch. D. 634	1674
—————— (Earl), Johnstone v.	30 Ch. D. 581	419
——————, Thomas v. In re Spencer	30 Ch. D. 183	642
—————— v. Metropolitan Board of Works	22 Ch. D. 142	780
Sperling v. Rochfort. In re Van Hagan	16 Ch. D. 18	1081
Spiller, In re. Spiller v. Madge	18 Ch. D. 614	1684
—————— v. Madge. In re Spiller	18 Ch. D. 614	1684
Spindler, In re. Ex parte Rolph	19 Ch. D. 98	250
Spooner, Scholfield v.	26 Ch. D. 94	1460
Sproule v. Bouch. In re Bouch	29 Ch. D. 635	338
Spurgeon, Hill v. In re Love	29 Ch. D. 348	1593
Spurr, King v.	8 Q. B. D. 104	949
Stafford v. Stafford. In re Price	28 Ch. D. 709	639
Stait, Gray v.	11 Q. B. D. 668	747
Standing v. Bowring	27 Ch. D. 341	17
Stanford v. Roberts	26 Ch. D. 155	1532
Stanger, In re. Ex parte Geisel	22 Ch. D. 436	117, 146

Name of Case.	Volume and Page.	Column of Digest.
Stanley, In re. Ex parte Milward	16 Ch. D. 256	191
——— v. Grundy	22 Ch. D. 478	903
Stanmore, The	10 P. D. 134	1510
Stannard v. St. Giles, Camberwell (Vestry of)	20 Ch. D. 190	1208
Stedham, In the Goods of	6 P. D. 205	1687
Steed, Metropolitan Board of Works v.	8 Q. B. D. 445	881
Steel v. Dixon	17 Ch. D. 825	1262
———, Warner to. In re Warner's Settled Estates	17 Ch. D. 711	1342
——— v. Sutton Gas Company	12 Q. B. D. 68	351
Steer, Conelly v.	7 Q. B. D. 520	258
Stoere, Alloway v.	10 Q. B. D. 22	154
Stenson, In re. Ex parte Merriman	25 Ch. D. 144	148
Stenton, Webb v.	11 Q. B. D. 518	1203
Stephens, Dyke v.	30 Ch. D. 189	1173
———, Frampton, v.	21 Ch. D. 164	516
Stephenson, Ness v.	9 Q. B. D. 245	768
———, Reg. v.	13 Q. B. D. 331	467
Stevens, In re. Ex parte M'George	20 Ch. D. 697	119
——— v. Biller	25 Ch. D. 31	574
——— v. Metropolitan District Railway Company	29 Ch. D. 60	{1240 {1285
——— v. Woodward	6 Q. B. D. 318	952
Stevenson, Scicluna v. The " Rhondda "	8 App. Cas. 549	1511
Stewart, Cassels v.	6 App. Cas. 64	1396
———, Crowder v.	16 Ch. D. 368	567
———, Gullischen v.	11 Q. B. D. 186 ; 13 Q. B. D. 317	1480
——— v. Merchants Marine Insurance Company	14 Q. B. D. 555	696
———, Walker v. In re Pringle	17 Ch. D. 819	1693
——— Brothers, Gullischen v.	13 Q. B. D. 317	1480
Stigand v. Stigand	19 Ch. D. 460	1134
Stimson, Collins v.	11 Q. B. D. 142	1633
Stock v. Inglis	9 Q. B. D. 708 ; 12 Q. B. D. 546 ; 10 App. Cas. 263	691
———, Mostyn v.	9 Q. B. D. 432	138
Stocker, Bell v.	10 Q. B. D. 129	637
Stockil v. Punshon	6 P. D. 9	1682
Stoer, In re	9 P. D. 120	1107
Stöhwasser, Jones v.	16 Ch. D. 577	13
Stone v. Attorney-General. In re Sutton	28 Ch. D. 464	286
———, De Geer v.	22 Ch. D. 243	22
——— v. Hyde	9 Q. B. D. 76	865
Stoner, Durrant and, In re	18 Ch. D. 106	653
Stonor's Trusts, In re	24 Ch. D. 195	1461
Stoomvaart Maatschappy Nederland v. Peninsular and Oriental Steam Navigation Company	7 App. Cas. 795	1098
Storer, In re	26 Ch. D. 189	1528
———, Eaton v.	22 Ch. D. 91	1151
Storey, In re. Ex parte Popplewell	21 Ch. D. 73	251
Stott v. Milne	25 Ch. D. 710	1592
——— and Smith, In re	29 Ch. D. 1009, n.	794
Stovell v. New Windsor (Mayor of)	27 Ch. D. 665	821
Strains, Norman v.	6 P. D. 219	1130
Strand, In re. Ex parte Board of Trade	13 Q. B. D. 492	189
Stratton, In re. Ex parte Salting	25 Ch. D. 148	124
Strauss v. County Hotel Company	12 Q. B. D. 27	679
Strawbridge, Ex parte. In re Hickman	25 Ch. D. 266	147
Street v. Crump	25 Ch. D. 68	1161
——— v. Union Bank of Spain and England	30 Ch. D. 156	1584

Name of Case.	Volume and Page.	Column of Digest.
Streeter, Ex parte. In re Morris	19 Ch. D. 216	184
Strickland, Apap v.	7 App. Cas. 156	312
—— v. Apap	8 App. Cas. 106	312
—— v. Symons	22 Ch. D. 666; 26 Ch. D. 245	1602
—— v. Weldon	28 Ch. D. 426	288
Stringer, Ex parte	9 Q. B. D. 436	347
——, Melville v.	12 Q. B. D. 132; 13 Q. B. D. 392	247
Strong, Giblings v.	26 Ch. D. 66	1162
Strousberg, Republic of Costa Rica v.	16 Ch. D. 8	1203
Strugnell v. Strugnell	27 Ch. D. 258	1016
——, Wilson v.	7 Q. B. D. 548	410
Stuart v. Wrey. In re Wrey	30 Ch. D. 507	1701
Stubbins, Ex parte. In re Wilkinson	17 Ch. D. 58	166
Stubbs, Carter v.	6 Q. B. D. 116	1162
Studd v. Cook	8 App. Cas. 577	1383
Studds v. Watson	28 Ch. D. 305	1621
Stumore, Aste v.	13 Q. B. D. 326	1182
Sturge and Great Western Railway Company ..	19 Ch. D. 444	1667
Suffell v. Bank of England	7 Q. B. D. 270; 9 Q. B. D. 555	232
Sugden, Rhodes v. In re Wadsworth	29 Ch. D. 517	1540
Sulger, Ex parte. In re Chinn	17 Ch. D. 839	169
Sullivan, Lawless v.	6 App. Cas. 373	299
——, Trye v. In re Young	28 Ch. D. 705	641
Sully, Ex parte. In re Wallis	14 Q. B. D. 950	163
Sultan Allie, Chitty v.	8 App. Cas. 751	316
Summers v. Moorhouse	13 Q. B. D. 388	941
Sunderland Building Society, Bell v.	24 Ch. D. 618	912
—— (Guardians of) v. Sussex (Clerk of the Peace for)	8 Q. B. D. 99	1065
"Sunniside," The	8 P. D. 137	1518
Surrey County Court (Judge of), Reg. v.	13 Q. B. D. 963	179
—— (Justices of), Reg. v.	6 Q. B. D. 100	1073
—— (Treasurer of), Mullins v.	6 Q. B. D. 156; 7 App. Cas. 1	1268
Suse, In re. Ex parte Dever (No. 1) ..	13 Q. B. D. 766	235
——, In re. Ex parte Dever (No. 2)	14 Q. B. D. 611	236
Sussex (Clerk of the Peace for), Sunderland (Guardians of) v.	8 Q. B. D. 99	1065
Sutherberry, Oceanic Steam Navigation Company v.	16 Ch. D. 236	12
Sutherland, Hughes v.	7 Q. B. D. 160	1496
Sutton, In re	11 Q. B. D. 377	1525
——, In re	21 Ch. D. 855	1611
——, In re. Stone v. Attorney-General	28 Ch. D. 464	286
——, Beckett v.	19 Ch. D. 646	1610
—— v. Sutton	22 Ch. D. 511	807, 1550
Sutton Coldfield Grammer School, In re ..	7 App. Cas. 91	533
Sutton Gas Company, Steele v.	12 Q. B. D. 68	351
—— (Parish of) to Church	26 Ch. D. 173	286
Svensden v. Wallace	11 Q. B. D. 616; 13 Q. B. D. 69; 10 App. Cas. 404	1486
Swan, Grahame v.	7 App. Cas. 547	1397
Swansea Co-operative Building Society v. Davies	12 Q. B. D. 21	1194
—— (Mayor of) v. Thomas	10 Q. B. D. 48	742
Swanwick, Briggs v.	10 Q. B. D. 510	594
Sweet v. Combley	25 Ch. D. 463, n.	901
Swift v. Pannell	24 Ch. D. 210	160
Swinburn v. Ainslie. In re Ainslie	28 Ch. D. 89	1568
—— v. —— In re ——	30 Ch. D. 485	1568

Name of Case.	Volume and Page.	Column of Digest.
Swinburne, In re. Swinburne v. Pitt	27 Ch. D. 696	524, 1087
———— v. Pitt. In re Swinburne	27 Ch. D. 696	{ 524 {1087
———— v. Milburn	9 App. Cas. 844	767
Swindon and Cheltenham Extension Railway Company, Great Western Railway Company v.	22 Ch. D. 677 ; 9 App. Cas. 787	781
Swire, In re. Mellor v. Swire	21 Ch. D. 647	1148
——, In re. ———— v. ————	30 Ch. D. 239	1198
——, Cookson v.	9 App. Cas. 653	243
——, Mellor v. In re Swire	21 Ch. D. 647	1148
——, ———— v. In re ————	30 Ch. D. 239	1198
Syer v. Gladstone	30 Ch. D. 614	1676
Sykes v. Sacerdoti	15 Q. B. D. 423	1180
Sylvester, Popple v.	22 Ch. D. 98	706
Symonds v. Hallett	24 Ch. D. 346	640
Symondson, Bradford v.	7 Q. B. D. 456	696
Symons, In re. Luke v. Tonkin	21 Ch. D. 757	552
———— v. Leaker	15 Q. B. D. 629	1251
————, Strickland v.	22 Ch. D. 666 ; 26 Ch. D. 245	1602

T.

Name of Case.	Volume and Page.	Column of Digest.
Tabois, Manton v.	30 Ch. D. 92	1705
Tacquah Gold Mining Company, Macdonald v.	13 Q. B. D. 535	1202
Tadman v. D'Epineuil. In re Count D'Epineuil (No. 1)	20 Ch. D. 217	555
———— v. ————. In re ———— (No. 2)	20 Ch. D. 758	254
Tagert, Kingdon v. In re Badcook	17 Ch. D. 361	1451
Tahourdin, Great Northern Railway Company v.	13 Q. B. D. 320	1287
————, Isle of Wight Railway Company v.	25 Ch. D. 320	353
Tait, In re. Ex parte Harper	21 Ch. D. 537	148
Talbot, In re	20 Ch. D. 269	846
————, Jackson v. In re Jackson	21 Ch. D. 786	674
Tambracherry Estates Company, In re	29 Ch. D. 683	342
Tamplin, Nuth v.	8 Q. B. D. 247	1006
Tams, Bromley v. Grainger v. Aynsley	6 Q. B. D. 182	868
Tanner, Bursill v.	13 Q. B. D. 691	1136
Tanqueray-Willaume and Landau, In re	20 Ch. D. 465	{1643 {1666
Tapson, Fry v.	28 Ch. D. 268	1597
————, Raymond v.	22 Ch. D. 430	1191
Tarleton v. Bruton. In re Roberts	27 Ch. D. 346 ; 30 Ch. D. 234	1685
Tarn v. Commercial Bank of Sydney	12 Q. B. D. 294	1157
Tate, In re	20 Ch. D. 135	847, 1612
———— v. Hyslop	15 Q. B. D. 368	691
————, Langen v.	24 Ch. D. 522	1192
Tattersall v. National Steamship Company	12 Q. B. D. 297	1476
Tatton, Ex parte. In re Thorp	17 Ch. D. 512	190
Taurine Company, In re	25 Ch. D. 118	349
Taylor, Ex parte	13 Q. B. D. 128	126
————, In re. Ex parte Salaman	21 Ch. D. 394	119
————, Allen v.	16 Ch. D. 355	804
————, ———— v. In re Gyhon	29 Ch. D. 834	1183
————, Ames v. In re Ames	25 Ch. D. 72	1530
————, Hurst v.	14 Q. B. D. 918	950
———— v. Johnston	19 Ch. D. 603	665

Name of Case.	Volume and Page.	Column of Digest.
Taylor v. Mostyn	25 Ch. D. 48	899
—— v. Mostyn. Mostyn v. Lancaster	23 Ch. D. 583	1463
—— v. Pilsen Joel and General Electric Light Company	27 Ch. D. 268	341
—— v. Poncia	25 Ch. D. 646	1451
——, Ralph v. In re Ralph's Trade-mark	25 Ch. D. 194	1584
—— v. Smetten	11 Q. B. D. 207	610
—— v. Taylor	6 P. D. 29	1130
——, Wall v. Wall v. Martin	9 Q. B. D. 727; 11 Q. B. D. 102	427
Taylor's Estate, In re. Tomlin v. Underhay	22 Ch. D. 495	{1184 {1686
Teal, Barlow v.	15 Q. B. D. 403; 15 Q. B. D. 501	775
Tebbit, Barber v. In re Appleton	29 Ch. D. 893	1678
Tedcastle, Spaight v.	6 App. Cas. 217	1515
Teebay v. Manchester, Sheffield, and Lincolnshire Railway Company	24 Ch. D. 572	1620
Teevan v. Smith	20 Ch. D. 724	919
Tempest v. Camoys (Lord)	21 Ch. D. 571	1603
—— v. ——	21 Ch. D. 576, n.	1603
Templeman v. Trafford	8 Q. B. D. 397	1057
Temporalities Board, Dobie v.	7 App. Cas. 136	304
Tenant v. Ellis	6 Q. B. D. 46	1222
Tenison, Harston v. In re Cross	20 Ch. D. 109	1600
Terrell, In re	22 Ch. D. 473	1224
Terry, Graves v.	9 Q. B. D. 170	1151
——, Harbottle v.	10 Q. B. D. 131	593
——, London and County Banking Company v. In re Sherry	25 Ch. D. 692	1266
Tetley, Clay and, In re	16 Ch. D. 3	13
Teuliere v. St. Mary Abbotts, Kensington (Vestry of)	30 Ch. D. 642	881
Thames Ironworks Company, Munday v.	10 Q. B. D. 59	864
Thatcher's Trusts, In re	26 Ch. D. 426	671
Thanet (Guardians of) v. Fulham (Guardians of)	6 Q. B. D. 610; 7 Q. B. D. 539	1066
Theys, Ex parte. In re Milan Tramways Company	22 Ch. D. 122; 25 Ch. D. 587	{ 375 {1150
Thol v. Henderson	8 Q. B. D. 457	485
Thomas, In re. Ex parte Poppleton	14 Q. B. D. 379	385
——, Mayor of Swansea v.	10 Q. B. D. 48	742
——, Morgan v.	8 Q. B. D. 575; 9 Q. B. D. 643	1676 1199
—— v. Palin	21 Ch. D. 360	
—— v. Patent Lionite Company	17 Ch. D. 250	367, 377
——, Priestman v.	9 P. D. 70	537
——, —— v.	9 P. D. 210	537
——, Reg. v.	11 Q. B. D. 282	626
—— v. Sherwood	9 App. Cas. 142	318
—— v. Spencer. In re Spencer	30 Ch. D. 183	642
—— v. Williams	24 Ch. D. 558	1469
Thomas-Peter, Peter v.	26 Ch. D. 181	1146
Thompson, In re	30 Ch. D. 441	1528
——, Berkley v.	10 Q. B. D. 261; 10 App. Cas. 45	204
——, Carlisle Banking Company v.	28 Ch. D. 398	272
——, Cato v.	9 Q. B. D. 616	1633
—— and Curzon, In re	29 Ch. D. 177	638
——, Dutton v.	23 Ch. D. 278	1649

Name of Case.	Volume and Page.	Column of Digest.
Thompson v. Farrer	9 Q. B. D. 372	1495
——— v. Harris. In re Middleton	19 Ch. D. 552	553
———, Reg. v.	12 Q. B. D. 261	204
———, Royal Society of London and	17 Ch. D. 407	285
———, Sands to	22 Ch. D. 614	812
———, Waye v.	15 Q. B. D. 342	823
——— v. Wright	13 Q. B. D. 632	1231
Thomson, May v.	20 Ch. D. 705	1548
——— v. South Eastern Railway Company	9 Q. B. D. 320	1158
——— v. Weems	9 App. Cas. 671	689
Thorley, Child & Co. v.	16 Ch. D. 151	562
Thornton, Fellows v.	14 Q. B. D. 335	1203
Thorp, In re. Ex parte Tatton	17 Ch. D. 512	190
Thorpe v. Bestwick	6 Q. B. D. 311	1664
——— v. Linney	15 Q. B. D. 273	939
Three Towns Banking Company v. Maddever. In re Maddever	27 Ch. D. 523	603
Threlfall, In re. Ex parte Queen's Benefit Building Society	16 Ch. D. 274	158
——— v. Wilson	8 P. D. 18	1131
Thurlby (Overseers of), Corporation of Peterborough v.	8 Q. B. D. 586	1412
Thwaites v. Wilding	11 Q. B. D. 421 ; 12 Q. B. D. 4	769
" Thyatira," The	8 P. D. 155	1485
Tilghman's Patent Sandblast Company, Société Anonyme des Manufactures de Glaces v.	25 Ch. D. 1	1042
Tillett v. Nixon	25 Ch. D. 238	903
——— v. Ward	10 Q. B. D. 17	1687
Tilley, In re. Ex parte Solomon	20 Ch. D. 281	196
Tinnuchi v. Smart	10 P. D. 184	39
Tippett v. Hart	10 Q. B. D. 483	1322
Titterton v. Cooper	9 Q. B. D. 473	135
Tiverton and North Devon Railway Company, Loosemore v.	22 Ch. D. 25 ; 9 App. Cas. 480	781
Todd, Kirk v.	21 Ch. D. 484	551
——— v. Robinson	11 Q. B. D. 530	1052
——— v. ———	14 Q. B. D. 739	810
Todmorden Mill Company, Ormerod v.	8 Q. B. D. 664	1187
———, ——— v.	11 Q. B. D. 155	1653
Tofield, Bray v. In re Greaves, deceased	18 Ch. D. 551	806
Toke v. Andrews	8 B. B. D. 428	1150
Tollemache, In re. Ex parte Anderson	14 Q. B. D. 606	152
———, In re. Ex parte Bonham	14 Q. B. D. 604	151
———, In re. Ex parte Edwards	14 Q. B. D. 415	150
———, In re. Ex parte Revell (No. 1)	13 Q. B. D. 720	150
———, In re. Ex parte ——— (No. 2)	13 Q. B. D. 727	170
Tomlin v. Underhay. In re Taylor's Estate	22 Ch. D. 495	{1184 {1686
Tomlinson, In the Goods of	6 P. D. 209	1273
———, Ballard v.	26 Ch. D. 194 ; 29 Ch. D. 115	1653
——— v. Land and Finance Corporation	14 Q. B. D. 539	1180
Tompson v. Dashwood	11 Q. B. D. 43	499
Tonbridge (Overseers of), Reg. v.	11 Q. B. D. 184 ; 13 Q. B. D. 339	275
Tone v. Preston	24 Ch. D. 739	1557
Tonkin, Luke v. In re Symons	21 Ch. D. 757	552
Toogood, Winyard v. Hance v. Fortnum	10 Q. B. D. 218	528
Toohey, Commissioners for Railways v.	9 App. Cas. 720	314
Tottenham Local Board, United Land Company v.	13 Q. B. D. 640	625

Name of Case.	Volume and Page.	Column of Digest.
Toomer, In re. Ex parte Blaiberg	23 Ch. D. 254	259
Tootal's Trusts, In re	23 Ch. D. 532	515
Toothill, Clarbrough v.	17 Ch. D. 787	1190
Toutt's Will, In re. In re Martyn (a Lunatic)	26 Ch. D. 745	1610
Toward, In re. Ex parte Moss	14 Q. B. D. 810	140
Towers, Friend v.	10 Q. B. D. 87	1005
Townend, Adam v.	14 Q. B. D. 103	{1140 1196
Townsend v. Townsend	23 Ch. D. 100	1148
Towse v. Loveridge	25 Ch. D. 76	1144
Toye, Barnes v.	13 Q. B. D. 410	666
Tozier v. Hawkins	15 Q. B. D. 650 ; 15 Q. B. D. 680	1134
Trade-marks Registration Acts, 1875. In re J. B. Palmer's Application	22 Ch. D. 88	1161
Trafford, Templeman v.	8 Q. B. D. 397	1057
Trail, Booth v.	12 Q. B. D. 8	1204
Tramways Union Company, Société Générale de Paris v.	14 Q. B. D. 424	347
Trask, Lewis v.	21 Ch. D. 862	1501
Trechmann, Gardner v.	15 Q. B. D. 154	1477
Tredwell, Dawes v.	18 Ch. D. 354	1461
Treharne, Baillie v.	17 Ch. D. 388	703
———, Davis v.	6 App. Cas. 460	887
Treherne v. Dale	27 Ch. D. 66	1200
Trench, In re. Ex parte Brandon	25 Ch. D. 500	118
Trevor, Robinson v.	12 Q. B. D. 423	913
Trickett's Claim. In re Romford Canal Company	24 Ch. D. 85	334
Trott v. Buchanan	28 Ch. D. 446	561
Trower, Peek v.	7 P. D. 21	522
Truman, Harris v.	7 Q. B. D. 340 ; 9 Q. B. D. 264	163
——— v. London, Brighton, and South Coast Railway Company	25 Ch. D. 423 ; 29 Ch. D. 89	{959 1284
——— & Co. v. Redgrave	18 Ch. D. 547	1211
———, Hanbury & Co., Hall v.	29 Ch. D. 307	1173
Truscott v. Diamond Rock Boring Company	20 Ch. D. 251	1463
Trye v. Sullivan. In re Young	28 Ch. D. 705	641
Tuck, Seagram v.	18 Ch. D. 296	808
Tucker, Bellairs v.	13 Q. B. D. 562	326
——— v. Good. In re Bonner	19 Ch. D. 201	1704
——— v. Linger	21 Ch. D. 18; 8 App. Cas. 508	743
———, Lion Assurance Association v.	12 Q. B. D. 176	355
———, Lyons v.	6 Q. B. D. 660 ; 7 Q. B. D. 523	258
———, Robinson v.	14 Q. B. D. 371	1230
Tufnell, Shubrook v.	9 Q. B. D. 621	1233
Tufnell and Ponsonby's Case. Nicol's Case. In re Florence Land and Public Works Company	29 Ch. D. 421	342
Tugwell, In re	27 Ch. D. 309	850
Tuke, Dodds v.	25 Ch. D. 617	{1217 1592
Turnbull v. Forman	15 Q. B. D. 234	639
Turnell, Day v. In re Higgins	29 Ch. D. 697	1452
Turner, In re. Ex parte Ladbury	17 Ch. D. 532	174
———, In re. Ex parte West Riding Union Banking Company	19 Ch. D. 105	125
———, In re. Glenister v. Harding	29 Ch. D. 985	542

Name of Case.	Volume and Page.	Column of Digest.
Turner v. Bridgett	8 Q. B. D. 392	138
——— v. ———	9 Q. B. D. 55	1230
——— v. Hancock	20 Ch. D. 303	1239
——— v. Hellard. In re Harrison	30 Ch. D. 390	1686
———, Jenner v.	16 Ch. D. 188	1672
——— v. Walsh	6 App. Cas. 636	313
———, Wilson v.	22 Ch. D. 521	1465
Turner's Settled Estates, In re	28 Ch. D. 205	1081
Turpin, Jenks v.	13 Ch. D. 505	609
Turquand, Ex parte. In re Parker	14 Q. B. D. 636	129, 162
———, Ex parte. In re Parker and Parker (No. 1)	14 Q. B. D. 405	178
———, Ex parte. In re ——— (No. 2)	14 Q. B. D. 407	129
———, Elliott v.	7 App. Cas. 79	155
Tustin and Johnson, In re	28 Ch. D. 84	1639
———, In re	30 Ch. D. 42	1639
Tweddell, Lyon v.	17 Ch. D. 529	1019
Tweedie and Miles, In re	27 Ch. D. 315	1469
Tweedy, In re	28 Ch. D. 529	1609
Twisden, Cleather v.	24 Ch. D. 731 ; 28 Ch. D. 340	1020
Tyser, Mercantile Steamship Company v.	7 Q. B. D. 73	693
Tyssen, O'Brien v.	28 Ch. D. 372	290, 1153

U.

Name of Case.	Volume and Page.	Column of Digest.
Underhay, Tomlin v. In re Taylor's Estate	22 Ch. D. 495	{1184 {1686
Union Bank of London v. Ingram	20 Ch. D. 463	903
——— v.	16 Ch. D. 53	904
Union Bank of Spain and England, Street v.	30 Ch. D. 156	1584
Union Steamship Company of New Zealand v. Melbourne Harbour Trust Commissioners	9 App. Cas. 365	318
United Land Company v. Tottenham Local Board	13 Q. B. D. 640	625
"United Service," The	8 P. D. 56 ; 9 P. D. 3	1512
United Stock Exchange, Limited, In re. Ex parte Philp & Kidd	28 Ch. D. 183	365
United Telephone Company, Barney v.	28 Ch. D. 394	1043
——— v. Dale	25 Ch. D. 778	{1043 {1201
——— v. Harrison, Cox, Walker, & Co.	21 Ch. D. 720	1048
——— v. London and Globe Telephone and Maintenance Company	26 Ch. D. 776	1044
——— v. Sharples	29 Ch. D. 164	1044
———, Wandsworth Board of Works v.	13 Q. B. D. 904	879
———, Wheeler v.	13 Q. B. D. 597	1152
Universal Marine Insurance Company, Pitman v.	9 Q. B. D. 192	692
Unwin, Wilkinson & Co. v.	7 Q. B. D. 636	238
Upmann v. Forester	24 Ch. D. 231	1573
Upton v. Brown	20 Ch. D. 731	1213
——— v. ———	26 Ch. D. 588	1563
Uren, Bristol Waterworks Company v.	15 Q. B. D. 637	1660
Usher, Agnew v.	14 Q. B. D. 78	1133
———, Davis v.	12 Q. B. D. 490	253
Uxbridge and Rickmansworth Railway Company and Harman, In re	24 Ch. D. 720	1641
Uzielli v. Boston Marine Insurance Company	15 Q. B. D. 11	693

Name of Case.	Volume and Page.	Column of Digest.
V.		
Vacuum Brake Company, Lawson v...	27 Ch. D. 137	1192
Vale, Ex parte. In re Bannister	18 Ch. D. 137	169
Valiance, In re. Ex parte Limehouse Board of Works	24 Ch. D. 177	1153
———, In re. Vallance v. Blagden	26 Ch. D. 353	262
——— v. Blagden. In re Vallance	26 Ch. D. 353	262
——— v. Falle	13 Q. B. D. 109	1497
Vanderlinden, Ex parte. In re Pogose	20 Ch. D. 289	123
"Vandyck," The	7 P. D. 42	1519
Van Gheluive v. Nerinckx	21 Ch. D. 189	552
Van Hagen, In re. Sperling v. Rochfort	16 Ch. D. 18	1081
Van Werde, Credits Gerundeuse v.	12 Q. B. D. 171	1134
Vardon's Trusts, In re	28 Ch. D. 124	527
Vaughan, Ex parte. In re Riddeough	14 Q. B. D. 25	134
Vavasour (a Lunatic), In re	29 Ch. D. 306	850
"Vera Cruz," The (No. 1)	9 P. D. 88	1104
———, The (No. 2) Seward v. "Vera Cruz"	9 P. D. 96; 10 App. Cas. 59	1104
———, The (No. 2)	9 P. D. 96	1104
Vergara, Dawe v.	11 Q. B. D. 241	138
Verney, Hollins v.	11 Q. B. D. 715; 13 Q. B. D. 304	1251
Vernon v. St. James, Westminster (Vestry of)	16 Ch. D. 449	879
———, Simon v.	8 App. Cas. 542	310
Verry, Nixon v.	29 Ch. D. 196	1453
Vesey, Cooper v. In re Cooper	20 Ch. D. 611	1637
"Vesta," The	7 P. D. 240	1515
Vicary v. Great Northern Railway Company	9 Q. B. D. 168	1225
"Victor Covacevich," The	10 P. D. 40	1097
Vine v. Raleigh	24 Ch. D. 238	1416
Vint v. Hudspith	29 Ch. D. 322	1161
——— v. ———	30 Ch. D. 24	1225
Vinter v. Hind	10 Q. B. D. 63	823
Viret v. Viret	17 Ch. D. 365, n.	1452
Vivian v. Little	11 Q. B. D. 370	1176
——— v. Moat	16 Ch. D. 730	771
Voisey, Ex parte. In re Knight	21 Ch. D. 442	159
Vollum v. Revett. In re Youngs	30 Ch. D. 421	1237
Von Brockdorff v. Malcolm	30 Ch. D. 172	1088
Von Buseck (Baroness), In the Goods of	6 P. D. 211	1271
Vron Colliery Company, In re	20 Ch. D. 442	370
Vyse v. Brown	13 Q. B. D. 199	1203
W.		
Wacher, In re	22 Ch. D. 535	1611
Waddell v. Fraser. Fraser v. Cooper, Hall, & Co.	23 Ch. D. 685	1149
Wade & Thomas, In re	17 Ch. D. 348	921
——— v. Wilson	22 Ch. D. 235	903
Wadham v. North Eastern Railway Company	14 Q. B. D. 747	777
Wadsworth, In re. Rhodes v. Sugden	29 Ch. D. 517	1540
Wainwright, Ex parte. In re Wainwright	19 Ch. D. 140	192
Wait, In re. Workman v. Petgrave	30 Ch. D. 617	1088
———, Nielsen v.	14 Q. B. D. 516	1482
Waite v. Bingley	21 Ch. D. 674	543, 1015
Wake, Ex parte	11 Q. B. D. 291	824

Name of Case.	Volume and Page.	Column of Digest.
Walton v. Edge	24 Ch. D. 421; 10 App. Cas. 33	274, 379
Wandsworth Board of Works v. United Telephone Company	13 Q. B. D. 904	879
———————, Williams v.	13 Q. B. D. 211	882
Warburg, Ex parte. In re Whalley	24 Ch. D. 364	185
———, Ex parte. In re Whalley	25 Ch. D. 336	116
Warburton v. Heyworth	6 Q. B. D. 1	870
Ward, Ex parte. In re Ward	20 Ch. D. 356	115, 1552
———, Ex parte. In re Ward	22 Ch. D. 132	132
———, In re	28 Ch. D. 719	1526
———, In re. Ex parte Bennett	16 Ch. D. 541	191
——— v. Morse. In re Brown	23 Ch. D. 377	1219
——— v. National Bank of New Zealand	8 App. Cas. 755	1263
———, Ridgway v.	14 Q. B. D. 110	50
———, Tillett v.	10 Q. B. D. 17	1587
Warder v. Saunders	10 Q. B. D. 114	1156
Wardlaw, Campbell v.	8 App. Cas. 641	1381
Ward's Estates, In re	28 Ch. D. 100	787
"Warkworth," The	9 P. D. 20	1099
"	9 P. D. 145	1099
Warner v. Jacob	20 Ch. D. 220	911
——— v. Moir. In re Moir	25 Ch. D. 605	1670
——— v. Mosses	16 Ch. D. 100	1189
——— v. ———	19 Ch. D. 72	1221
——— to Steel. In re Warner's Settled Estates	17 Ch. D. 711	1342
Warner's Settled Estates, In re. Warner to Steel	17 Ch. D. 711	1342
Warren, Ex parte. In re Holland	15 Q. B. D. 48	170
———, Line v.	14 Q. B. D. 73, 548	941
Warren's Trusts, In re	26 Ch. D. 208	1455
Warrington Waterworks Company v. Longshaw	9 Q. B. D. 145	1658
Warwicker v. Bretnall	23 Ch. D. 188	687
Washburn and Moen Manufacturing Company v. Patterson	29 Ch. D. 48	1182
Waterford and Limerick Railway Company, Great Western Railway Company v.	17 Ch. D. 493	1294
Waterhouse v. Gilbert	15 Q. B. D. 569	1231
Waterlow, Law Society of the United Kingdom v. Law Society v. Skinner	9 Q. B. D. 1; 8 App. Cas. 407	1544
Watkins, Dymock v.	10 Q. B. D. 451	446
——— v. Rymill	10 Q. B. D. 178	408
Watmough, In re. Sergenson v. Beloe	24 Ch. D. 280	452
Watney, Chatterton v.	16 Ch. D. 378; 17 Ch. D. 259	1204
Watson (a person of Unsound Mind), In re	19 Ch. D. 384	1610
———, In re. Ex parte Oram	15 Q. B. D. 399	129
———, Ashbury v.	28 Ch. D. 56; 30 Ch. D. 376	328
——— v. Cave (No. 1)	17 Ch. D. 19	1236
——— v. ——— (No. 2)	17 Ch. D. 23	1238
——— v. Great Western Railway Company	6 Q. B. D. 163	1228
——— v. Holliday	20 Ch. D. 780	149
———, Jonmenjoy Coondoo v.	9 App. Cas. 561	1093
———, Kettlewell v.	21 Ch. D. 685; 26 Ch. D. 501	1635
———, Kipling & Co., In re	23 Ch. D. 500	878
———, New Zealand and Australian Land Co. v.	7 Q. B. D. 374	1256
———, Studds v.	28 Ch. D. 305	1621
——— v. Watson	7 P. D. 10	1664
——— v. Young	28 Ch. D. 436	1688

Name of Case.	Volume and Page.	Column of Digest.
West Bromwich (Overseers of), West Bromwich School Board v.	13 Q. B. D. 929	1074
West Bromwich School Board v. Overseers of West Bromwich	13 Q. B. D. 929	1074
West Cork Railway Company, Hutton v.	23 Ch. D. 654	352
West Derby (Assessment Committee of), Martin v. ..	11 Q. B. D. 145	1069
West Devon Great Consols Mine, In re	27 Ch. D. 106	381
West Ham Assessment Committee, Iles v.	8 Q. B. D. 69; 8 App. Cas. 386	1075
——— (Guardians of), Hollingbourn (Guardians of) v.	6 Q. B. D. 580	1062
———, ———, Plomesgate (Guardians of) v.	6 Q. B. D. 576	1065
West India and Panama Telegraph Company v. Home and Colonial Marine Insurance Company ..	6 Q. B. D. 51	695
West Kent Sewerage Board, Bexley Local Board v. ..	9 Q. B. D. 518	36
West London Commercial Bank v. Kitson	12 Q. B. D. 157; 13 Q. B. D. 360	358
——— ——— v. Reliance Permanent Building Society	27 Ch. D. 187; 29 Ch. D. 954	920
West Middlesex Waterworks Company, Coleman v.	14 Q. B. D. 529	1659
———, Richards v.	15 Q. B. D. 660	1661
West of England and South Wales District Bank v. Murch	23 Ch. D. 138	563 1468 1602 1642
West Riding (Justices of) Middlesborough (Overseers of) v. ..	12 Q. B. D. 239	621
——— (Justices of) Reg. v.	11 Q. B. D. 417	681
——— (Justices of) v. Reg.	8 App. Cas. 781	623
West Riding Union Banking Company, Ex parte. In re Turner	19 Ch. D. 105	125
Westbury-on-Severn Rural Sanitary Authority v. Meredith.	30 Ch. D. 387	1245
Western, Eaton v.	9 Q. B. D. 636	34
———, Leggott v.	12 Q. B. D. 287	1205
Western Counties Railway Company v. Windsor and Annapolis Railway Company	7 App. Cas. 178	298
Westhead v. Riley	25 Ch. D. 413	1211
Westlake, In re. Ex parte Willoughby	16 Ch. D. 604	1488
Weston v. Metropolitan Asylum District (Manager of)	8 Q. B. D. 387; 9 Q. B. D. 404	772
Westropp v. Elligott	9 App. Cas. 815	702
Wetley Brick and Pottery Company, General Share and Trust Company v.	20 Ch. D. 130	1197
	20 Ch. D. 260	774
Whalley, In re. Ex parte Warburg	24 Ch. D. 364	185
———, In re. Ex parte ———	25 Ch. D. 336	116
——— v. Lancashire and Yorkshire Railway Co. ..	13 Q. B. D. 131	1652
Wheater, Wood v.	22 Ch. D. 281	1205
Wheatley, In re. Smith v. Spence	27 Ch. D. 606	526
———, Lynch v.	14 Q. B. D. 504	1007
——— v. Silkstone and Haigh Moor Coal Co.	29 Ch. D. 715	835
Wheeler v. Le Marchant	17 Ch. D. 675	1179
——— v. United Telephone Company	13 Q. B. D. 597	1152
Wheelwright v. Walker	23 Ch. D. 752	1447
Whetham v. Davey	30 Ch. D. 574	901
———, Pooley's Trustee in Bankruptcy v. ..	28 Ch. D. 38	1181
Whinney, Ex parte. In re Sandars	13 Q. B. D. 476	112

h

Name of Case.	Volume and Page.	Column of Digest.
Windsor and Annapolis Railway Company, Western Counties Railway Company v.	7 App. Cas. 178	298
Windus, Hough v.	12 Q. B. D. 224	126
Winehouse v. Winehouse. In re Maggi	20 Ch. D. 545	556
Winnington, Domvile v.	26 Ch. D. 382	1453
Winslow, Weldon v.	13 Q. B. D. 784	638
Winspear v. Accident Insurance Company	6 Q. B. D 42	689
"Winston," The	8 P. D. 176; 9 P. D. 85	1514
Winter, Lumsden v.	8 Q. B. D. 650	1163
Winyard v. Toogood. Hance v. Fortnum	10 Q. B. D. 218	528
Wire, Davies v.	7 Q. B. D. 425	444
Wish, Rhodes v. In re Seaman	20 Ch. D. 280	1546
Witball v. Nixon	28 Ch. D. 413	902
Withernsea Brickworks, In re	16 Ch. D. 337	375
Withington (Local Board for), Midland Railway Co. v.	11 Q. B. D. 788	825
Wittman v. Oppenheim	27 Ch, D. 260	426
Witton, In re. Ex parte Arnal	24 Ch. D. 26	175
Wolfe v. Matthews	21 Ch. D. 194	1585
Wolverhampton and Staffordshire Banking Company v. George	24 Ch. D. 707	900
Wolverhampton Banking Company, Ex parte. In re Campbell	14 Q. B. D. 32	140
Womersley, In re. Etheridge v. Womersley	29 Ch. D. 557	706
Womersley, Etheridge v. In re Womersley	29 Ch. D. 557	706
Wood, In re. Ex parte Hall	23 Ch. D. 644	126
——, In re. Ex parte Horrocks	19 Ch. D. 367	194
——, Clack v.	9 Q. B. D. 276	396, 1164
—— and Dames, In re	27 Ch. D. 172	1629
——————, In re	29 Ch. D. 626	1629
—— v. Douglass. In re Douglass	28 Ch. D. 327	505
——, London School Board v.	15 Q. B. D. 415	530
—— v. Madras Irrigation and Canal Company. In re Madras Irrigation and Canal Company	23 Ch. D. 248	1244
—— v. Wheater	22 Ch. D. 281	1205
Woodall, Ex parte. In re Woodall	13 Q. B. D. 479	112
——, In re. Ex parte Woodall	13 Q. B. D. 479	112
Woodfin, Gill v.	25 Ch. D. 707	1162
Woodley v. Michell	11 Q. B. D. 47	1476
Woodruff v. Brecon and Merthyr Tydfil Junction Railway Company	28 Ch. D. 190	1293
Woods v. Woods	10 P. D. 172	628
——, Wright v. In re Harvey	26 Ch. D. 179	554
Woodward, Stevens v.	6 Q. B. D. 318	952
Woolley v. Colman	21 Ch. D. 169	920
Woollven, Breton v. In re Breton's Estate	17 Ch. D. 416	1647
Woolwich (Overseers of) v. Robertson	6 Q. B. D. 654	275
Worcester City and County Banking Company v. Blick. In re Pumfrey	22 Ch. D. 255	1595
Working Men's Mutual Society, In re	21 Ch. D. 831	546
Workman v. Petgrave. In re Wait	30 Ch. D. 617	1088
Worley, Holland v.	26 Ch. D. 578	801
Worrall, Pollock v. In re Pollock	28 Ch. D. 552	1695
Wormald v. Muzeen	17 Ch. D. 167	1664
Worsley, Blachford v. In re Blachford	27 Ch. D. 676	811
Worth, In re	18 Ch. D. 521	441
Worthing Local Board, Kent v.	10 Q. B. D. 118	620
Wragg's Trade-mark, In re	29 Ch. D. 551	1578
Wray v. Kemp	28 Ch. D. 169	1543

Name of Case.	Volume and Page.	Column of Digest.
Young, Greer v.	24 Ch. D. 545	1539
—— and Harston's Contract, In re	29 Ch. D. 691	1624
——, James v.	27 Ch. D. 652	886
—— v. Leamington (Corporation of) .. ..{	8 Q. B. D. 579; 8 App. Cas.} 517	817
—— v. Schuler	11 Q. B. D. 651	542
——, Watson v.	28 Ch. D. 436	1688
Youngs, In re. Doggett v. Revett .. .: ..	30 Ch. D. 421	1237
——, In re. Vollum v. Revett	30 Ch. D. 421	1237

Z.

"Zadok," The	9 P. D. 114	1508
Zerfass, Ex parte. In re Sandwell	14 Q. B. D. 960	178
Zetland (Earl of) v. Hislop	7 App. Cas. 427	1381

CASES

FOLLOWED, OVERRULED, OR SPECIALLY CONSIDERED.

Belmonte v. *Aynard* (4 C. P. D. 221, 352) distinguished　　14 Q. B. D. 539
　　See PRACTICE—SUPREME COURT—SECURITY FOR COSTS. 3.

Bengough v. *Walker* (15 Ves. 507) considered
　　　　　　　　　　[20 Ch. D. 81
　　See SETTLEMENT—SATISFACTION.

Benns v. *Mosley* (2 C. B. (N.S.) 116) followed
　　See HABEAS CORPUS.　[15 Q. B. D. 471

Berdan v. *Greenwood* (3 Ex. D. 251) followed
　　See SOLICITOR—LIEN. 1. [19 Ch. D. 311

—— v. —— (20 Ch. D. 764, n.) distinguished　-　24 Ch. D. 522
　　See PRACTICE—SUPREME COURT—EVIDENCE. 13.

Besant v. *Wood* (12 Ch. D. 605) commented on
　　　　　　　　　　[8 App. Cas. 420
　　See HUSBAND AND WIFE—WIFE'S CONVEYANCE. 3.

Besch v. *Frolich* (1 Ph. 172) followed　17 Ch. D.
　　See PARTNERSHIP—DISSOLUTION. 1. [529

Besley v. *Besley* (9 Ch. D. 103) dissented from
　　　　　　　　　　[13 Q. B. D. 351
　　See VENDOR AND PURCHASER—COMPENSATION. 2.

Best, Ex parte (18 Ch. D. 488) explained
　　　　　　　　　　[20 Ch. D. 281
　　See BANKRUPTCY—COMPOSITION. 3.

Betts v. *Burch* (4 H. & N. 506) commented on
　　See PENALTY.　　[21 Ch. D. 243

—— v. *Willmott* (Law Rep. 6 Ch. 239) distinguished　··　25 Ch. D. 1
　　See PATENT—INFRINGEMENT. 2.

Beyer v. *Adams* (26 L. J. (Ch.) 841) overruled
　　　　　　　　　　[15 Q. B. D. 363
　　See PRINCIPAL AND AGENT — PRINCIPAL'S LIABILITY. 7.

Biddle v. *Bond* (6 B. & S. 225) distinguished
　　See BAILMENT.　　[19 Ch. D. 86

Biggs v. *Head* (Sausse & Scully, 335) approved and adopted　-　20 Ch. D. 733
　　See SOLICITOR—LIABILITIES. 1.

Birmingham Canal Company v. *Cartwright* (11 Ch. D. 421) overruled　20 Ch. D. 562
　　See LANDS CLAUSES ACT—SUPERFLUOUS LANDS. 2.

Birmingham Gas Light Co., Ex parte (Law Rep. 11 Eq. 615) commented on　13 Q. B. D.
　　See BANKRUPTCY—DISTRESS. 1.　[753

Blackburn and District Benefit Building Society (24 Ch. D. 421; 10 App. Cas. 33) followed　-　28 Ch. D. 559
　　See COMPANY—DISTRIBUTION OF ASSETS. 3.

Blackett v. *Royal Exchange Assurance Co.* (2 C. & J. 244) followed　14 Q. B. D. 555
　　See INSURANCE, MARINE—POLICY. 8.

Blake v. *Izard* (16 W. R. 108) followed
　　　　　　　　　　[12 Q. B. D. 436
　　See BILL OF SALE—REGISTRATION. 4.

Bland v. *Ross* (*The Julia*) (Lush. 231; 14 Moo. P. C. 210) commented on and approved
　　See SHIP—PILOT. 7.　[6 App. Cas. 217

Blandford v. *Blandford* (8 P. D. 19) considered
　　　　　　　　　　[9 App. Cas. 205
　　See SCOTCH LAW—HUSBAND AND WIFE. 1.

Blease, Ex parte (14 Q. B. D. 123) not followed
　　　　　　　　　　[15 Q. B. D. 338
　　See BANKRUPTCY—APPEAL. 13.

Blower v. *Morrett* (2 Ves. Sen. 420) dissented from　-　-　17 Ch. D. 798
　　See WILL—PRIORITY OF LEGACIES.

Blyth and Fanshawe, In re (10 Q B. D. 207) explained　15 Q. B. D. 420
　　See SOLICITOR—BILL OF COSTS. 14.

Blyth and Young, In re (13 Ch. D. 416) considered　-　22 Ch. D. 484
　　See PRACTICE — SUPREME COURT — APPEAL. 36.

Boale v. *Dickson* (13 U. C. C. P. 337) overruled
　　　　　　　　　　[9 App. Cas. 392
　　See COLONIAL LAW—CANADA—ONTARIO. 5.

Bolckow v. *Fisher* (10 Q. B. D. 161) distinguished
　　　　　　　　　　[24 Ch. D. 110
　　See PRACTICE—SUPREME COURT—INTERROGATORIES. 6.

Bold Buccleugh, The (7 Moo. P. C. 267) considered　-　6 P. D. 106
　　See FOREIGN JUDGMENT. 2.

Borries v. *Hutchinson* (8 C. B. (N.S.) 445) distinguished　-　8 Q. B. D. 457
　　See DAMAGES—REMOTENESS. 4.

Bos v. *Helsham* (Law Rep. 2 Ex. 72) followed
　　　　　　　　　　[13 Q. B. D. 351
　　See VENDOR AND PURCHASER—COMPENSATION. 2.

Bostock v. *Floyer* (Law Rep. 1 Eq. 26) explained
　　　　　　　　　　[23 Ch. D. 727
　　See TRUSTEE—LIABILITIES. 2.

Bothamley v. *Sherson* (Law Rep. 20 Eq. 304) explained　20 Ch. D. 676
　　See WILL—SPECIFIC LEGACY.

Boughton v. *Boughton* (23 Ch. D. 169) distinguished　-　24 Ch. D. 408
　　See SOLICITOR—LIEN. 12.

Boulton, Ex parte, In re Sketchley (1 De G. & J 163) discussed　14 Q. B. D. 424
　　See COMPANY—SHARES—TRANSFER. 2.

Bower v. *Peate* (1 Q. B. D. 321) approved
　　　　　　　　　　[6 App. Cas. 740
　　See SUPPORT. 3.

—— —— —— considered
　　　　　　　　　　[8 App. Cas. 443
　　See PRINCIPAL AND AGENT—PRINCIPAL'S LIABILITY. 1.

Bowyer v. *Griffin* (Law Rep. 9 Eq. 340) considered and followed　-　21 Ch. D. 862, 865
　　See TRUSTEE—COSTS AND CHARGES. 1, 2.

Boyd's Settled Estates, In re (21 W. R. 667) overruled　-　22 Ch. D. 93
　　See PRACTICE—SUPREME COURT—PAYMENT INTO COURT. 5.

—— —— —— —— followed　-　18 Ch. D. 646
　　See LANDS CLAUSES ACT—PURCHASEMONEY. 4.

Boyes v. *Bedale* (1 H. & M. 798) disapproved
　　　　　　　　　　[17 Ch. D. 266
　　See DISTRIBUTIONS, STATUTE OF.

Carter v. *Wake* (4 Ch. D. 605) distinguished
[22 Ch. D. 549
See MORTGAGE—CONTRACT. 10.

Cassels v. *Lamb* (12 Court Sess. Cas. 4th Series, 722) affirmed - 10 App. Cas. 553
See SCOTCH LAW—HERITABLE PROPERTY. 5.

Catterina Chiazzare, The (1 P. D. 368) considered and distinguished - 21 Ch. D. 202
See PRACTICE—SUPREME COURT—STAYING PROCEEDINGS. 6.

Cawthorne v. *Cordrey* (13 C. B. (N.S.) 406; 32 L. J. (C.P) 152) distinguished
[11 Q. B. D. 123
See FRAUDS, STATUTE OF. 1.

Challinor, Ex parte (16 Ch. D. 260) explained
[19 Ch. D. 98, 419
See BILL OF SALE—FORMALITIES. 18, 21.

Chamberlain v. *West End of London Railway Company* (2 B. & S. 605) approved
[7 App. Cas. 259
See SCOTCH LAW—RAILWAY COMPANY. 4.

Chapman v. *Midland Railway* (5 Q. B. D. 167; 431) discussed - 10 Q. B. D. 71
See PRACTICE—SUPREME COURT—COSTS. 29.

———— v. *Royal Netherlands Steam Navigation Company* (4 P. D. 157) overruled
[7 App. Cas. 795
See PRACTICE—ADMIRALTY—LIMITATION OF LIABILITY. 1.

Chappell's Case (Law Rep. 6 Ch. 902) distinguished
[25 Ch. D. 118
See COMPANY—SHARES—TRANSFER. 7.

Charing Cross Advance and Deposit Bank, Ex parte (16 Ch. D. 35) distinguished
[16 Ch. D. 260
See BILL OF SALE—FORMALITIES. 17.

Charlton v. *Attorney-General* (4 App. Cas. 427) followed - - 6 Q. B. D. 548
See REVENUE—SUCCESSION DUTY. 1.

Chinery, Ex parte (12 Q. B. D. 342), explained
[14 Q. B. D. 627
See BANKRUPTCY—ACT OF BANKRUPTCY. 10.

Christopherson v. *Naylor* (1 Mer. 320) followed
[23 Ch. D. 737
See WILL—SUBSTITUTIONAL GIFT. 1.

Citizens Insurance Company of Canada v. *Parsons* (7 App. Cas. 96) approved and distinguished - - 7 App. Cas. 136
See COLONIAL LAW—CANADA—QUEBEC. 3.

Clare v. *Clare* (21 Ch. D. 865) not followed
[23 Ch. D. 195
See TRUSTEE—COSTS AND CHARGES. 3.

Clark v. *Browne* (2 Sm. & Giff. 524) not followed
See WILL—WORDS. 9. [30 Ch. D. 92

Clarke v. *Hart* (6 H. L. C. 633) distinguished
[18 Ch. D. 660
See COMPANY—COST-BOOK COMPANY. 2.

———— v. *Law* (2 K. & J. 28) approved
[21 Ch. D. 642
See PRACTICE—SUPREME COURT—EVIDENCE. 5.

Clarke's Trusts, In re (21 Ch. D. 748) questioned
[27 Ch. D. 411
See HUSBAND AND WIFE—SEPARATE ESTATE. 15.

Clayton's Case (1 Mer. 572) recognised
See BANKER—LIEN [6 App. Cas. 722

————————, distinguished
[9 App. Cas. 857
See BUILDING SOCIETY. 7.

————————, followed
[25 Ch. D. 692
See PRINCIPAL AND SURETY—LIABILITY. 2.

Clerk v. *Dumfries Commissioners of Supply* (7 Court Sess. Cas. 4th Ser. 1157) disapproved - - 9 App. Cas. 61
See REVENUE—INCOME TAX. 1.

Cobbet v. *Woodward* (Law Rep. 14 Eq. 407) overruled 21 Ch. D. 369
See COPYRIGHT—BOOKS. 1.

Cockrill v. *Sparkes* (1 H. & C. 699) distinguished
[30 Ch. D. 119
See LIMITATIONS, STATUTE OF — PERSONAL ACTIONS. 10.

Collins v. *Vestry of Paddington* (5 Q. B. D. 368) distinguished - 9 Q. B. D. 621
See PRACTICE—SUPREME COURT—APPEAL. 2.

Colvill v. *Wood* (2 C. B. 210) commented on
[9 App. Cas. 49
See WATERWORKS COMPANY — WATER RATE. 3.

Commercial Bank of India, In re (Law Rep. 6 Eq. 517) approved 27 Ch. D. 225
See COMPANY—WINDING-UP ORDER. 2.

Cooke v. *Chilcott* (3 Ch. D. 694) questioned
[8 Q. B. D. 403; 29 Ch. D. 750
See COVENANT—RUNNING WITH LAND. 2, 4.

Cork and Yougal Railway Company (Law Rep. 4 Ch. 748) followed 22 Ch. D. 61
See BUILDING SOCIETY. 7.

Corser v. *Cartwright* (Law Rep. 7 H. L. 731) followed - - 23 Ch. D. 138
See VENDOR AND PURCHASER—TITLE. 7.

Cothay v. *Sydenham* (2 Bro. C. C. 391) considered
[17 Ch. D. 437
See SOLICITOR—LIABILITIES. 2.

Cotterell v. *Stratton* (Law Rep. 8 Ch. 295) followed - 20 Ch. D. 303
See PRACTICE—SUPREME COURT—APPEAL. 25.

Cotton, In re (1 Ch. D. 232) discussed
[29 Ch. D. 331
See INFANT—MAINTENANCE. 6.

Counsel v. *Garvie* (Ir. Rep. 5 C. L. 74) considered
[13 Q. B. D. 835
See COUNTY COURT—PRACTICE. 4.

Coventry and Dixon's Case (14 Ch. D. 660) commented on - 21 Ch. D. 492, 519
See COMPANY—DIRECTOR'S LIABILITY. 3, 5.

Coverdale v. *Charlton* (4 Q. B. D. 104) followed
[13 Q. B. D. 904
See METROPOLIS—MANAGEMENT ACTS. 7.

Dillon (Lord) v. *Alvarez* (4 Ves. 357) not followed   -   -   **22 Ch. D. 397**
    See PRACTICE—SUPREME COURT—STAY-
    ING PROCEEDINGS. 6.

Dillon v. *Cunningham* (Law Rep. 8 Ex. 23) distinguished   -   -   **14 Q. B. D. 973**
    See HUSBAND AND WIFE — SEPARATE
    ESTATE. 11.

Ditton, Ex parte (3 Ch. D. 459) followed
    [**19 Ch. D. 122**
    See BANKRUPTCY—DISCLAIMER. 5.

Dixon, Ex parte (13 Q. B. D. 118) explained
    [**15 Q. B. D. 399**
    See BANKRUPTCY—RECEIVER. 8.

Dobson v. *Faithwaite* (30 Beav. 228) followed
    [**24 Ch. D. 126**
    See PRACTICE — SUPREME COURT —
    CHANGE OF PARTIES. 7.

Dodds v. *Shepherd* (1 Ex. D. 75) considered
    [**19 Ch. D. 216**
    See BANKRUPTCY—APPEAL. 1.

Doe v. *Biggs* (2 Taunt. 109) distinguished
    [**20 Ch. D. 465**
    See WILL—CHARGE OF DEBTS.

—— v. *Brindley* (12 Moo. C. P. 37) questioned
    [**16 Ch. D. 522**
    See BUILDING CONTRACT. 2.

—— v. *Harris* (5 C. & P. 592) overruled
    [**14 Q. B. D. 153**
    See CRIMINAL LAW—EVIDENCE. 5.

—— v. *Withers* (2 B. & Ad. 896) doubted **20 Ch. D.**
    See SETTLEMENT—POWERS. 3.   [**251**

Douglass v. *Howland* (24 Wendell, 35) followed
    [**17 Ch. D. 668**
    See PRINCIPAL AND SURETY—LIABILITY.
    3.

Down v. *Halling* (4 B. & C. 330) considered and
distinguished   -   -   **3 Q. B. D. 288**
    See BANKER—CHEQUE. 1.

Downes v. *Grazebrook* (3 Mer. 200) observed upon
    [**20 Ch. D. 220**
    See MORTGAGE—POWERS. 5.

Dowse, The (Law Rep. 3 A. & E. 135) followed
    [**6 Q. B. D. 165**
    See COUNTY COURT—JURISDICTION. 1.

Dronfield Silkstone Coal Company, In re (23
Ch. D. 511) not followed   **27 Ch. D. 33**
    See COMPANY—COSTS. 3.

Dundonald (Earl of) v. *Masterman* (Law Rep.
7 Eq. 504) considered   **28 Ch. D. 340**
    See PARTNERSHIP—LIABILITIES.

Durant v. *Durant* (1 Hagg. Ecc. Rep. 761) disapproved   -   -   **9 App. Cas. 205**
    See SCOTCH LAW—HUSBAND AND WIFE.
    1.

Dysart Case (6 App. Cas. 507) followed
    [**10 App. Cas. 763**
    See SCOTCH LAW—HUSBAND AND WIFE.
    4.

Eade v. *Jacobs* (3 Ex. D. 335) explained
    [**29 Ch. D. 29**
    See PRACTICE—SUPREME COURT—INTER-
    ROGATORIES. 8.

Early, Ex parte (13 Ch. D. 300) followed
    [**16 Ch. D. 655**
    See BANKRUPTCY—LIQUIDATION. 9.

East and West India Dock Company v. *Hill*
(22 Ch. D. 14) followed   **9 Q. B. D. 281**
    See BANKRUPTCY—DISCLAIMER. 12.

*East Botallack Consolidated Mining Company;
Re* (34 Beav. 82) disapproved
    [**18 Ch. D. 472**
    See COMPANY—COST-BOOK COMPANY. 1.

*Eastern Counties and London and Blackwall
Railway Companies* v. *Marriage* (9 H.
L. C. 32) distinguished **9 App. Cas.**
    See COLONIAL LAW—VICTORIA. 4.

Eccleshill Local Board, In re (13 Ch. D. 365) disapproved   -   -   **18 Ch. D. 146**
    See LANDS CLAUSES ACT—COMPULSORY
    POWERS. 5.

Edmundson, Re (17 Q. B. 67) overruled
    [**13 Q. B. D. 586**
    See LANDS CLAUSES ACT — COMPENSA-
    TION. 6.

Elbinger Actien-Gesellschaft v. *Armstrong* (Law
Rep. 9 Q. B. 473) approved
    [**15 Q. B. D. 85**
    See DAMAGES—CONTRACT. 2.

Electric Telegraph Company v. *Salford* (11 Ex.
181) followed   -   **13 Q. B. D. 700**
    See POOR-RATE—OCCUPATION. 6.

Ella A. Clark, The (Br. & L. 32) overruled
    [**10 P. D. 44**
    See SHIP—MARITIME LIEN. 1.

Ellis v. *De Silva* (6 Q. B. D. 521) followed
    [**14 Q. B. D. 841**
    See PRACTICE—SUPREME COURT—COSTS.
    42.

Ellis' Trusts, In re (Law Rep. 17 Eq. 409) followed   -   -   **21 Ch. D. 748**
    See HUSBAND AND WIFE—SEPARATE ES-
    TATE. 14.

——————————————— dis-
tinguished   -   -   **27 Ch. D. 411**
    See HUSBAND AND WIFE — SEPARATE
    ESTATE. 15.

Elworthy, Ex parte (Law Rep. 20 Eq. 742) not
followed   -   -   **18 Ch. D. 495**
    See BANKRUPTCY—COMPOSITION. 7.

Emanuel, Ex parte (17 Ch. D. 35) explained
    [**21 Ch. D. 397**
    See BANKRUPTCY—TRUSTEE. 1.

Emperor v. *Rolfe* (1 Ves. Sen. 208) followed
    [**10 App. Cas.**
    See SETTLEMENT—CONSTRUCTION. 9. [**422**

Empire Assurance Corporation, In re (17 L. T.
(N.S.) 488) discussed   **25 Ch. D. 400**
    See COMPANY—EVIDENCE. 4.

Empress Eugenie, The (Lush. 140), overruled
    [**10 P. D. 112**
    See PRACTICE—ADMIRALTY—COSTS. 7.

England v. *Marsden* (Law Rep. 1 C. P. 529)
questioned   -   **14 Q. B. D. 811**
    See INDEMNITY.

Ennor v. *Barwell* (1 D. F. & J.) 529) distinguished
    [**27 Ch. D. 356**
    See PRACTICE — SUPREME COURT — IN-
    SPECTION OF PROPERTY.

Enohin v. *Wylie* (10 H. L. C. 1), Lord Westbury's
dicta disapproved   -   **9 App. Cas. 34**
    See EXECUTOR—ACTIONS. 16.

Hobbs v. *London and South Western Railway Company* (Law Rep. 10 Q. B. 111) commented upon - - **7 Q. B. D. 591**
See DAMAGES—REMOTENESS. 3.

Hocking v. *Acraman* (12 M. & W. 170) commented on **6 Q. B. D. 84**
See BANKRUPTCY—PROTECTED TRANSACTION. 5.

Hodsoll v. *Baxter* (E. B. & E. 884) followed
[**13 Q. B. D. 302**
See PRACTICE—SUPREME COURT—WRIT SPECIALLY INDORSED. 2.

Hoffman v. *Postill* (Law Rep. 4 Ch. 673) explained
[**29 Ch. D. 29**
See PRACTICE — SUPREME COURT — INTERROGATORIES. 8.

Hogg v. *Jones* (32 Beav. 45) distinguished
See WILL—HEIRLOOM. 1. [**24 Ch. D. 102**

Hollier v. *Burne* (Law Rep. 16 Eq: 163) followed
[**18 Ch. D. 624**
See LEASEHOLD—RENEWABLE LEASE. 3.

——— v. *Laurie* (3 C. B. 334) discussed
[**14 Q. B. D. 873**
See PRACTICE—SUPREME COURT—INTERPLEADER. 12.

Holloway v. *Cheston* (19 Ch. D. 516) not followed
[**21 Ch. D. 131**
See PRACTICE — SUPREME COURT—APPEAL. 21.

Holme v. *Guy* (5 Ch. D. 901) observed upon
[**18 Ch. D. 596**
See CHARITY—COMMISSIONERS. 1.

Holmes v. *Buckley* (1 Eq. Cas. Ab. 27) discussed
[**29 Ch. D. 750**
See COVENANT—RUNNING WITH LAND. 4.

——— v. *Holmes* (1 Bro. C. C. 555) considered
[**20 Ch. D. 81**
See SETTLEMENT—SATISFACTION.

Holroyd v. *Marshall* (10 H. L. C. 191) distinguished - **20 Ch. D. 758**
See BILL OF SALE—OPERATION. 2.

——————————————— distinguished - - **12 Q. B. D. 436**
See BILL OF SALE—REGISTRATION. 2.

Home Investment Society, In re (14 Ch. D. 167), considered - - **23 Ch. D. 511**
See COMPANY—COSTS. 2.

——————————————— followed - **27 Ch. D. 33**
See COMPANY—COSTS. 3.

Hopgood v. *Parkin* (Law Rep. 11 Eq. 74) questioned **22 Ch. D. 727**
See TRUSTEE—LIABILITIES. 2.

Hopkinson v. *Rolt* (9 H. L. C. 514) followed
See BANKER—LIEN. [**6 App. Cas. 722**

——————————————— followed
[**29 Ch. D. 149**
See MORTGAGE—PRIORITY. 3.

Hopper, In re (Law Rep. 2 Q. B. 367) explained and distinguished **15 Q. B. D. 426**
See ARBITRATION—SUBMISSION. 4.

Hopton v. *Dryden* (Prec. in Ch. 179) distinguished
[**23 Ch. D. 764**
See EXECUTOR—RETAINER. 6.

Horbury Bridge Coal, Iron, and Waggon Company, In re (11 Ch. D. 109) considered
[**29 Ch. D. 159**
See COMPANY—VOLUNTARY WINDING-UP. 1.

Hornby, Re (7 W. R, 729) followed **18 Ch. D. 614**
See WILL—LAPSE. 4.

Hoskins, In re (6 Ch. D. 281) disapproved
[**20 Ch. D. 303**
See PRACTICE — SUPREME COURT—APPEAL. 25.

Houldsworth v. *City of Glasgow Bank* (5 App. Cas. 317) distinguished **18 Ch. D. 587**
See COMPANY—DEBENTURES. 2.

Howe v. *Dartmouth (Earl of)* (7 Ves. 137) distinguished - **26 Ch. D. 42**
See EXECUTOR—ADMINISTRATION. 4.

Huddersfield, Corporation of, and Jacomb, In re (10 Ch. D. 92) followed **6 Q. B. D. 67**
See ARBITRATION—AWARD. 3.

Hudson v. *Parker* (1 Robert. 14) followed
[**7 P. D. 102**
See PROBATE—EXECUTION. 1.

——— v. *Revett* (5 Bing. 368) distinguished
[**14 Q. B. D. 424**
See COMPANY—SHARES—TRANSFER. 2.

Hughes v. *Pritchard* (6 Ch. D. 24) distinguished
[**16 Ch. D. 696**
See WILL—RESIDUARY GIFT. 1.

Humble v. *Shore* (7 Hare, 247) considered
[**29 Ch. D. 142**
See WILL—RESIDUARY GIFT. 2.

Hunt v. *Hunt* (4 D. F. & J. 221; 31 L. J. (Ch.) 161) commented on **8 App. Cas. 420**
See HUSBAND AND WIFE—WIFE'S CONVEYANCE. 3.

——— v. *Wimbledon Local Board* (4 C. P. D. 48) approved - - **8 App. Cas. 517**
See LOCAL GOVERNMENT—LOCAL AUTHORITY. 3.

Hutchin v. *Mannington* (1 Ves. 366) distinguished
[**18 Ch. D. 218**
See WILL —DEATH COUPLED WITH CONTINGENCY. 2.

Hutchins v. *Hutchins* (1 Hogan, 315) approved and adopted - - **20 Ch. D. 733**
See SOLICITOR—LIABILITIES. 1.

Hutchinson v. *Copestake* (9 C. B. (N.S,) 863) considered - - **27 Ch. D. 43**
See LIGHT—TITLE. 1.

——— v. *Glover* (1 Q. B. D. 138) discussed
[**10 Q. B. D. 36**
See PRACTICE — SUPREME COURT—PRODUCTION OF DOCUMENTS. 7.

Hutchinson and Tenant, In re (8 Ch. D. 540) commented on - - **24 Ch. D. 199**
See WILL—PRECATORY TRUST. 2.

Hutchison v. *National Loan Assurance Company* (7 Court Sess. Cas. 2nd Series, 471) not approved **9 App. Cas. 671**
See INSURANCE, LIFE—POLICY. 3.

Imperial Hydropathic Hotel Company v. *Hampson* (23 Ch. D. 1) explained **27 Ch. D. 268**
See COMPANY—REDUCTION OF CAPITAL. 2.

Kensey v. *Langham* (Cas. t. Tal. 143) discussed and reconciled - - **30 Ch. D. 298**
See ADVOWSON. 1.

Khedive, The (5 App. Cas. 876) explained
See SHIP—NAVIGATION. 25. **[9 P. D. 16**

Kibble v. *Gough* (38 L. T. (N.S.) 204) followed **[15 Q. B. D. 228**
See SALE OF GOODS—CONTRACT. 3.

Kirk v. *Bell* (16 Q. B. 290) considered **[16 Ch. D. 681**
See COMPANY—DIRECTOR'S AUTHORITY. 3.

Kirkman v. *Booth* (11 Beav. 279) distinguished **[26 Ch. D. 42**
See EXECUTOR—ADMINISTRATION. 4.

Kitto v. *Luke* (28 W. R. 411) followed **[26 Ch. D. 465**
See PRACTICE—SUPREME COURT—COSTS. 27.

Knapp v. *Williams* (4 Ves. 430, n.) followed **[30 Ch. D. 544**
See CHARITY—MORTMAIN. 3.

Knight v. *Majoribanks* (2 Mac. & G. 10) approved **[7 App. Cas. 307**
See COLONIAL LAW—VICTORIA. 2.

Knowles v. *McAdam* (3 Ex. D. 23) disapproved **[6 App. Cas. 315**
See SCOTCH LAW—REVENUE.

Krehl v. *Burrell* (7 Ch. D. 551) considered **[26 Ch. D. 578**
See LIGHT—OBSTRUCTION. 2.

Labouchere v. *Dawson* (Law Rep. 13 Eq. 322) distinguished - - **19 Ch. D. 355**
See GOODWILL. 2.

————————————— over-ruled - **27 Ch. D. 145**
See GOODWILL 3.

Ladbury, Ex parte (17 Ch. D. 532), explained and distinguished - **22 Ch. D. 384**
See BANKRUPTCY—DISCLAIMER. 9.

Laing v. *Reed* (Law Rep. 5 Ch. 8) Lord Hatherley's dictum disapproved **9 App. Cas. 519**
See BUILDING SOCIETY. 9.

Lamb v. *Walker* (3 Q. B. D. 389) overruled **[14 Q. B. D. 125**
See LIMITATIONS, STATUTE OF—PERSONAL ACTIONS. 9.

Lambe v. *Eames* (Law Rep. 6 Ch. 597) commented on - - **24 Ch. D. 199**
See WILL—PRECATORY TRUST. 2.

Landore Siemens Steel Company In re (10 Ch. D. 489) not followed **16 Ch. D. 702**
See PRACTICE—SUPREME COURT—TRANSFER. 1.

Langley v. *Hammond* (Law Rep. 3 Ex. 161) not followed - - **18 Ch. D. 616**
See WAY. 1.

Large's Case (2 Leon. 82; 3 Leon. 182) explained - **26 Ch. D. 801**
See WILL—CONDITION. 2.

Latham v. *Latham* (2 Sw. & Tr. 298) overruled **[8 P. D. 188**
See PRACTICE—DIVORCE—ALIMONY. 1.

Le Marchant v. *Le Marchant* (Law Rep. 18 Eq. 414) commented on - **24 Ch. D. 199**
See WILL—PRECATORY TRUST. 2.

Lechmere & Lloyd, In re (18 Ch. D. 524) considered **[24 Ch. D. 633**
See WILL—CONTINGENT REMAINDER.

Leda, The (Swa. 40) followed - **7 P. D. 126**
See SHIP—SALVAGE. 8.

Leeming, In re (3 D. F. & J. 43) considered
See WILL—ADEMPTION. **[22 Ch. D. 622**

Leigh v. *Leigh* (15 Ves. 92) distinguished **[19 Ch. D. 520**
See WILL—PERPETUITY. 5.

Levy v. *Lovell* (14 Ch. D. 234) followed **[17 Ch. D. 74**
See BANKRUPTCY—SECURED CREDITOR. 1.

Lewis v. *Freke* (2 Ves. 507) distinguished **[23 Ch. D. 472**
See SETTLEMENT—POWERS. 14.

——— v. *Trask* (21 Ch. D. 862) followed **[23 Ch. D. 195**
See TRUSTEE—COSTS AND CHARGES. 3.

Leyland v. *Illingworth* (2 De G. F. & J. 248) distinguished - **9 Q. B. D. 616**
See VENDOR AND PURCHASER—DEPOSIT. 3.

Libra, The (6 P. D. 139) explained **8 P. D. 126**;
See SHIP—NAVIGATION 31. **[9 P. D. 47**

Life Association of Scotland v. *Foster* (11 Court Sess. Cas. 3rd. Series, 351) distinguished **[9 App. Cas. 671**
See INSURANCE, LIFE—POLICY. 3.

Lightfoot v. *Burstall* (1 H. & M. 546) considered **[29 Ch. D. 142**
See WILL—RESIDUARY GIFT. 2.

Little's Case (8 Ch. D. 806) considered and distinguished - **22 Ch. D. 484**
See PRACTICE—SUPREME COURT—APPEAL. 36.

Littledale, Ex parte, In re Pearse (6 De G. M. & G. 714) discussed - **14 Q. B. D. 424**
See COMPANY—SHARES—TRANSFER. 2.

Loane v. *Casey* (2 W. Bl. 965) followed **30 Ch. D. [15**
See EXECUTOR—RETAINER. 8.

Lloyd v. *Lloyd* (Law Rep. 2 Eq. 722) distinguished - **30 Ch. D. 623**
See SETTLEMENT—CONSTRUCTION. 6.

Loffus v. *Maw* (3 Giff. 592) disapproved **[6 App. Cas. 467**
See CONTRACT—VALIDITY. 4.

Lolley's Case (Russ. & Ry. 237) explained **[6 App. Cas. 43**
See HUSBAND AND WIFE—DIVORCE.

London and North Western Railway Company v. *Evershed* (3 App. Cas. 1029) followed **[14 Q. B. D. 209**
See RAILWAY COMPANY — RAILWAYS CLAUSES ACT. 2.

Longbottom v. *Berry* (Law Rep. 5 Q. B. 123) approved - **15 Q. B. D. 358**
See FIXTURES.

Lovat (Lord) v. *Duchess of Leeds* (2 Dr. & Sm. 62) followed - - **21 Ch. D 105**
See WILL—WORDS. 2.

Lowestoft, Yarmouth, and Southwold Tramways Company (6 Ch. D. 484) followed **[28 Ch. D. 652**
See RAILWAY COMPANY—ABANDONMENT. 3.

i 2

Lowndes v. *Davies* (6 Sim. 468) dissented from
                         [29 Ch. D. 29
    See PRACTICE—SUPREME COURT—INTER-
    ROGATORIES. 8.

Lows v. *Telford* (1 App. Cas. 414) considered
    See FORCIBLE ENTRY. 1. [17 Ch. D. 174

Lumley v. *Gye* (2 E. & B. 216; 22 L. J. (Q.B.)
    463) followed - - 6 Q. B. D. 333
    See MASTER AND SERVANT—REMEDIES.
    1.

Lynch, Ex parte (2 Ch. D. 227) overruled
                         [18 Ch. D. 109
    See BANKRUPTCY—TRADER. 3.

McAndrew v. *Barker* (7 Ch. D. 701) considered
                       [22 Ch. D. 484
    See PRACTICE—SUPREME COURT—AP-
    PEAL. 36.

McCarthy v. *Decaix* (Russ. & My. 614) dissented
    from · 8 App. Cas. 43
    See HUSBAND AND WIFE—DIVORCE.

Macdonald v. *Union Bank* (2 Court. Sess. Cas.
    3rd Series, 963) approved 9 App. Cas. 95
    See BANKER—CHEQUE. 2.

————— v. —————————— con-
    sidered - - 10 App. Cas. 692
    See SCOTCH LAW—HUSBAND AND WIFE.
    2.

McHenry v. *Lewis* (22 Ch. D. 397) approved and
    applied - - - 10 P. D. 141
    See PRACTICE—ADMIRALTY—LIS ALIBI
    PENDENS. 2.

McIntosh v. *Sinclair* (Ir. Rep. 11 C. L. 456) con-
    sidered - - 14 Q. B. D. 516
    See SHIP—CHARTERPARTY. 10.

Mackay v. *Dick* (6 App. Cas. 251) followed
                     [7 App. Cas. 49
    See SCOTCH LAW—PRACTICE. 3.

————— v. —————————— followed
                     [9 App. Cas. 95
    See SCOTCH LAW—BILL OF EXCHANGE. 1.

————— v. *Douglas* (Law Rep. 14 Eq. 106), ap-
    proved and followed 19 Ch. D. 588
    See BANKRUPTCY—VOID SETTLEMENT. 1.

Mackleay, In re (Law Rep. 20 Eq. 186), com-
    mented on - - 26 Ch. D. 801
    See WILL—CONDITION. 2.

McLeod v. *Drummond* (14 Ves. 353; 17 Ves. 152)
    distinguished - 20 Ch. D. 611
    See VENDOR AND PURCHASER—PURCHASE
    WITHOUT NOTICE. 1.

McMurray v. *Spicer* (Law Rep. 5 Eq. 527) con-
    sidered - - 27 Ch. D. 359
    See TRUSTEE ACTS—VESTING ORDERS. 3.

Macnair v. *Cathcart* (Morr. Dict. 12,832) approved
                    [7 App. Cas. 547
    See SCOTCH LAW—PUBLIC RIGHTS.

Madeline Smith (1857. 2 Irving's Justiciary Rep.
    653) considered - 10 App. Cas. 692
    See SCOTCH LAW—HUSBAND AND WIFE.
    2.

Maddy v. *Hale* (3 Ch. D. 327) followed
                    [18 Ch. D. 624
    See LEASEHOLD—RENEWABLE LEASE. 3.

Maden v. *Taylor* (45 L. J. (Ch.) 569) approved
    and followed - - 18 Ch. D. 213
    See EVIDENCE—PRESUMPTION.

Magee v. *Lavell* (Law Rep. 9 C. P. 107) com-
    mented on - - 21 Ch. D. 243
    See PENALTY.

Maghee v. *McAllister* (3 Ir. (Ch.) 604) affirmed
                    [8 App. Cas. 43
    See HUSBAND AND WIFE—DIVORCE.

Mainwaring's Settlement, In re (Law Rep. 2 Eq.
    487), observed upon 22 Ch. D. 275 ;
                      [26 Ch. D. 94
    See SETTLEMENT—FUTURE PROPERTY.
    5, 10.

Malcolm v. *Charlesworth* (1 Keen, 36) approved
    See REGISTRY ACTS. [29 Ch. D. 702

————— v. *Hodgkinson* (Law Rep. 8 Q. B. 209)
    followed - 19 Ch. D. 457
    See COMPANY—WINDING-UP ORDER. 14.

Mali Ivo, The (Law Rep. 2 A. & E. 356) con-
    sidered and distinguished 21 Ch. D. 202
    See PRACTICE—SUPREME COURT—STAY-
    ING PROCEEDINGS. 6.

Mammoth Copperopolis of Utah, In re (50 L. J.
    (Ch.) 11) distinguished - 21 Ch. D. 149
    See COMPANY—DIRECTOR'S LIABILITY. 4.

*Manchester, Union Bank of, Ex parte, In re Jack-
    son* (Law Rep. 12 Eq. 354) discussed
                    [14 Q. B. D. 424
    See COMPANY—SHARES—TRANSFER. 2.

Manson v. *Thacker* (7 Ch. D. 720) disapproved
                    [13 Q. B. D. 351
    See VENDOR AND PURCHASER—COMPEN-
    SATION. 2.

Marris v. *Ingram* (13 Ch. D. 338) distinguished
                    [20 Ch. D. 532
    See PRACTICE—SUPREME COURT—AT-
    TACHMENT. 1.

Marshall v. *Marshall* (5 P. D. 19) approved
                    [10 P. D. 188
    See PRACTICE — DIVORCE— SEPARATION
    DEED. 1.

————— v. *Smith* (Law Rep. 8 C. P. 416) distin-
    guished - - - 8 Q. B. D. 603
    See LOCAL GOVERNMENT—OFFENCES. 2.

Marson v. *Cox* (14 Ch. D. 147) discussed
                    [28 Ch. D. 296
    See BUILDING SOCIETY. 12.

Martin v. *Mackonochie* (Law Rep. 3 P. C. 409)
    approved - - 6 App. Cas. 424
    See PRACTICE—ECCLESIASTICAL—MONI-
    TION.

————— v. *Martin* (Law Rep. 2 Eq. 404) distin-
    guished - - 18 Ch. D. 218
    See WILL—DEATH COUPLED WITH CON-
    TINGENCY. 2.

————— v. *Lee* (14 Moore, P. C. 142) explained
                    [10 App. Cas. 653
    See COLONIAL LAW—CANADA—QUEBEC.
    6.

————— v. *Sedgwick* (9 Beav. 333) dissented from
                    [14 Q. B. D. 424
    See COMPANY—SHARES—TRANSFER. 2.

Mathews v. *Paul* (3 Sw. 328) observed upon
                    [26 Ch. D. 382
    See SETTLEMENT—CONSTRUCTION. 3.

National Mercantile Bank, Ex parte (15 Ch. D. 42) considered   **16 Ch. D. 35** ;
[**19 Ch. D. 98, 419**
See BILL OF SALE—FORMALITIES. 18, 20, 21.

New Callao, In re (22 Ch. D. 484) approved
[**24 Ch. D. 488**
See PRACTICE—SUPREME COURT — APPEAL. 37.

Newman, In re (4 Ch. D. 724) commented on
See PENALTY.   [**21 Ch. D. 243**

Newton v. Chorlton (10 Hare, 646) followed
[**19 Ch. D. 615**
See PRINCIPAL AND SURETY—INDEMNITY. 2.

—— *v. Harland* (1 Scott, N. R. 474) considered   **17 Ch. D. 174**
See FORCIBLE ENTRY. 1.

Niboyet v. Niboyet (4 P. D. 1) considered
[**8 App. Cas. 43**
See HUSBAND AND WIFE—DIVORCE.

Nicholls, Ex parte (22 Ch. D. 782), distinguished
[**14 Q. B. D. 310**
See BANKRUPTCY—ASSETS. 10.

Nicklin v. Williams (10 Ex. 259) discussed
[**14 Q. B. D. 125**
See LIMITATIONS, STATUTE OF — PERSONAL ACTIONS. 2

Norris v. Norris, Lawson and Mason (4 Sw. & Tr. 237 ; 30 L. J. (P. & M.) 111) distinguished   **10 P. D. 174**
See PRACTICE—DIVORCE—CONDONATION. 2.

Northam v. Hurley (1 E. & B. 665) distinguished
See WATERCOURSE. 1.   [**23 Ch. D. 566**

Northfield Iron and Steel Company, In re (14 L. T. (N.S.) 695) distinguished
[**22 Ch. D. 470**
See BANKRUPTCY—JURISDICTION. 5.

Norton v. London and North Western Railway Company (9 Ch. D. 623) considered
See LIGHT—TITLE. 3.   [**24 Ch. D. 1**

Nunn v. Fabian (Law Rep. 1 Ch. 35) considered
[**10 Q. B. D. 148**
See FRAUDS, STATUTE OF. 2.

Oliver v. Oliver (10 Ch. D. 765) considered
[**17 Ch. D. 778**
See SETTLEMENT—EQUITY TO SETTLEMENT. 1.

Omichund v. Barker (1 Atykns, 21 ; Willes, 538) followed and applied   **14 Q. B. D. 667**
See PARLIAMENT—ELECTION. 3.

Oram v. Brearey (2 Ex. D. 346) overruled
See PROHIBITION.   [**14 Q. B. D. 855**

Original Hartlepool Collieries Company v. Gibbs (5 Ch. D. 713) not followed
[**17 Ch. D. 174**
See PRACTICE—SUPREME COURT —COUNTER-CLAIM. 4.

Padstow Total Loss and Collision Insurance Association (20 Ch. D. 137) followed
[**11 Q. B. D. 563**
See COMPANY—UNREGISTERED COMPANY. 3.

Palmer v. Jones (43 L. J. (Ch.) 349) followed
[**26 Ch. D. 465**
See PRACTICE—SUPREME COURT—COSTS. 27.

—— *v. Temple* (9 Ad. & E. 508) distinguished
[**27 Ch. D. 89**
See VENDOR AND PURCHASER—DEPOSIT. 2.

Parana, The (2 P. D. 118) approved **9 P. D. 105**
See DAMAGES— REMOTENESS. 1.

Parnaby v. Lancaster Canal Company (11 Ad. & E. 223) approved   - **9 App. Cas. 418**
See COLONIAL LAW—NEW ZEALAND. 1.

Part's Case (Law Rep. 10 Eq. 622) not followed
See COMPANY—COSTS. 4. [**18 Ch. D. 530**

Paterson, Ex parte (11 Ch. D. 908) followed and approved   **22 Ch. D. 410**
See BANKRUPTCY—DISCLAIMER. 3.

—— (1 Rose, 402) followed
[**21 Ch. D. 394**
See BANKRUPTCY—TRADER. 2.

Patscheider v. Great Western Railway Company (3 Ex. D. 153) distinguished
[**14 Q. B. D. 228**
See RAILWAY COMPANY—PASSENGER'S LUGGAGE.

Paul v. Paul (15 Ch. D. 580) not followed
[**20 Ch. D. 742**
See SETTLEMENT—REVOCATION. 2.

Pawsey v. Armstrong (18 Ch. D. 698) questioned
[**27 Ch. D. 460**
See PARTNERSHIP—CONTRACT. 4.

Peacock v. Burt (4 L. J (N.S.) (Ch.) 33) not extended   - - **29 Ch. D. 954**
See MORTGAGE—REDEMPTION. 5.

Pease v. Jackson (Law Rep. 3 Ch. 576) discussed
[**28 Ch. D. 298**
See BUILDING SOCIETY. 12.

—— discussed
[**12 Q. B. D. 423**
See MORTGAGE—PRIORITY. 2.

Penysyflog Mining Company, Re (30 L. T. 861) considered   - **19 Ch. D. 118**
See COMPANY—EVIDENCE. 2.

Percival, Ex parte (Law Rep. 6 Eq. 519), considered   - - **23 Ch. D. 511**
See COMPANY—COSTS. 2.

Perry-Herrick v. Attwood (25 Beav. 205 ; 2 De G. & J. 21) explained and followed
[**21 Ch. D. 124**
See MORTGAGE—PRIORITY. 6.

Philipps v. Philipps (4 Q. B. D. 127) followed
[**26 Ch. D. 778**
See PRACTICE—SUPREME COURT—STRIKING OUT PLEADINGS. 1.

Pike v. Fitzgibbon (17 Ch. D. 454) followed
[**18 Ch. D. 531**
See SETTLEMENT—FUTURE PROPERTY. 2.

Pim v. Curell (6 M. & W. 234) discussed
See FISHERY. 1.   [**8 App. Cas. 135**

Pinnel's Case (5 Rep. 117 a) followed
[**9 App. Cas. 605**
See ACCORD AND SATISFACTION. 2.

Pinney v. *Hunt* (6 Ch. D. 98) followed
[26 Ch. D. 656
See PRACTICE—SUPREME COURT—JURIS-
DICTION. 1.

Pitt v. *Pitt* (4 Macq. 657) discussed **8 App. Cas.**
See HUSBAND AND WIFE—DIVORCE. [43

Pocock's Policy, In re (Law Rep. 6 Ch. 445) observed upon -   -   -   29 Ch. D. 535
See TRUSTEE—LIABILITIES. 10.

Pollen v. *Brewer* (7 C. B. (N.S.) 371) considered
See FORCIBLE ENTRY. 1. [17 Ch. D. 174

Pontifex v. *Foord* (12 Q. B. D. 152) followed
[26 Ch. D. 161
See PRACTICE—SUPREME COURT—THIRD
PARTY. 5.

Pool v. *Sacheverel* (1 P. Wms. 675) questioned
See CONTEMPT OF COURT. [17 Ch. D. 49

Popple v. *Sylvester* (22 Ch. D. 98) distinguished
See JUDGMENT. 3.   [25 Ch. D. 338

Portpatrick Railway Company v. *Caledonian
Railway Company* (3 Nev. & Mac. 189)
disapproved   .   -   17 Ch. D. 493
See RAILWAY COMPANY—RAILWAYS RE-
GULATION ACTS. 1.

Potter's Trusts, In re (Law Rep. 8 Eq. 52) followed   -   -   -   17 Ch. D. 788
See WILL—SUBSTITUTIONAL GIFT. 2.

Powell's Trusts, In re (39 L. J. (Ch.) 188) discussed and not followed   29 Ch. D. 521
See POWER—EXECUTION. 12.

Powell Duffryn Steam Coal Company v. *Taff Vale
Railway Company* (Law Rep. 9 Ch. 331)
distinguished   .   28 Ch. D. 190
See RAILWAY COMPANY — RAILWAY
CLAUSES ACT. 1.

Powles v. *Hargreaves* (3 D. M. & G. 453) considered   -   7 App. Cas. 366
See SCOTCH LAW—BILL OF EXCHANGE. 3.

—— v. *Hider* (6 E. & B. 207) considered
[8 Q. B. D 104
See NEGLIGENCE—LIABILITY. 1.

Preston v. *Melvill* (2 Rob. App. 107) explained
[10 App. Cas. 453
See SCOTCH LAW—JURISDICTION.

Price v. *Carver* (3 My. & Cr. 157) followed
[25 Ch. D. 158
See MORTGAGE—FORECLOSURE. 8.

—— v. *Jenkins* (5 Ch. D. 619) distinguished
[22 Ch. D. 74
See FRAUDULENT CONVEYANCE. 2.

Prince v. *Lewis* (5 B. & C. 363) considered
See MARKET. 2.   [25 Ch. D. 511

Prince of Saxe Coburg, The (3 Moo. P. C. 1), explained   -   9 P. D. 177
See SHIP—MARITIME LIEN. 2.

*Printing and Numerical Registering Company, In
re* (8 Ch. D. 535) overruled
[16 Ch. D. 337
See COMPANY—SECURED CREDITOR. 1.

Quarman v. *Burnett* (6 M. & W. 499) followed
[14 Q. B. D. 890
See MASTER AND SERVANT—MASTER'S
LIABILITY. 1.

Rabone & Co., In re (Seb. Dig. 395) followed
[28 Ch. D. 666
See TRADE-MARK—REGISTRATION. 9.

*Railway Steel and Plant Company, Ex parte, In
re Taylor* (8 Ch. D. 188) doubted
[20 Ch. D. 442
See COMPANY—INJUNCTION. 1.

Rakestraw v. *Bruyer* (Select Cas. in Ch. 55);
Mosely, 189) considered   17 Ch. D. 104
See LIMITATIONS, STATUTE OF—REALTY.
7.

Ram Sabuk Bose v. *Monomohini Dossee* (Law Rep.
2 Ind. Ap. 81) approved **7 App. Cas. 321**
See PRACTICE—PRIVY COUNCIL—LEAVE
TO APPEAL. 5.

Ramsden v. *Dyson* (Law Rep. 1 H. L. 129) approved -   -   -   9 App. Cas. 699
See COLONIAL LAW—NEW ZEALAND. 2.

Randall v. *Russell* (3 Mer. 190) considered
[29 Ch. D. 673
See LEASEHOLD—RENEWABLE LEASE. 2.

Ranelaugh (Lord) v. *Hayes* (1 Vern. 189) not followed   -   -   22 Ch. D. 561
See TRUSTEE—INDEMNITY. 3.

Ransome v. *Burgess* (Law Rep. 3 Eq. 773) disapproved -   22 Ch. D. 521
See SETTLEMENT—POWERS. 5.

Ray v. *Ray* (G. Coop. 264) distinguished
[18 Ch. D. 93
See EXECUTOR—ADMINISTRATION. 3.

Read v. *Anderson* (13 Q. B. D. 779) followed
[14 Q. B. D. 460
See PRINCIPAL AND AGENT—PRINCIPAL'S
LIABILITY. 4.

——————————————— distinguished
[14 Q. B. D. 467
See PRINCIPAL AND AGENT—PRINCIPAL'S
LIABILITY. 5.

Redondo v. *Chaytor* (4 Q. B. D. 453) followed
[28 Ch. D. 232
See PRACTICE — SUPREME COURT — SE-
CURITY FOR COSTS. 7.

Reeve v. *Whitmore* (4 De G. J. & S. 1; 33 L. J.
(Ch.) 63) distinguished   12 Q. B. D. 436
See BILL OF SALE—REGISTRATION. 2.

Reg. v. *Boyes* (1 B. & S. 311) followed   20 Ch. D.
See EVIDENCE—WITNESS. 2.   [294

—— v. *Brampton Union* (3 Q. B. D. 479) followed
[6 Q. B. D. 31
See POOR LAW—SETTLEMENT. 15.

—— v. *Dicken* (14 Cox, C. C. 8) followed
[10 Q. B. D. 74
See CRIMINAL LAW—OFFENCES AGAINST
WOMEN.

—— v. *D'Oyley* (12 Ad. & E. 139) followed
[29 Ch. D. 159
See COMPANY—VOLUNTARY WINDING-UP.
1.

—— v. *Gibbon* (6 Q. B. D. 168) disapproved
[8 Q. B. D. 383
See JUSTICES—DISQUALIFICATION. 4.

—— v. *Guardians of North Aylesford* (37 J. P.
148) explained   -   6 Q. B. D. 139
See POOR-RATE—RATEABLE VALUE. 2.

—— v. *Lewis* (9 C. & P. 523) doubted 10 Q. B. D.
[381
See CRIMINAL LAW—OFFENCES AGAINST
PERSON. 4.

Ryder v. *Wombwell* (Law Rep. 3 Ex. 90) dissented from   -   **13 Q. B. D. 410**
See INFANT—CONTRACTS. 3.

Rylands v. *Fletcher* (Law Rep. 3 H. L. 330) followed   -   **27 Ch. D. 588**
See WATER. 2.

————————————————— applied   **7 Q. B. D. 418**
See METROPOLIS—MANAGEMENT ACTS. 4.

St. Albans, Bishop of, v. *Battersby* (3 Q. B. D. 359) approved   -   **16 Ch. D. 645**
See LANDLORD AND TENANT—LEASE. 6.

St. Thomas' Dock Company, In re (2 Ch. D. 116) followed   -   **21 Ch. D. 769**
See COMPANY—WINDING-UP ORDER. 16.

Salvin v. *North Brancepeth Coal Company* (Law Rep. 9 Ch. 705) discussed **28 Ch. D. 688**
See NUISANCE—REMEDIES. 1.

Sampson v. *Hoddinott* (1 C. B. (N.S.) 590) distinguished   -   **23 Ch. D. 566**
See WATERCOURSE. 1.

Sanderson v. *Geddes* (1 Court Sess. Cas. (4th Series) 1198) approved **7 App. Cas 547**
See SCOTCH LAW—PUBLIC RIGHTS.

Sandon v. *Hooper* (6 Beav. 246; 14 L. J. (Ch.) 120) commented on   ·   **21 Ch. D. 469**
See MORTGAGE—MORTGAGEE IN POSSESSION. 8.

Sargent, Ex parte (Law Rep. 17 Eq. 273) considered   -   **26 Ch. D. 257**
See COMPANY—SHARES—TRANSFER. 1.

Saunders, Ex parte (11 Q. B. D. 191) followed
[**13 Q. B. D. 681**
See LOCAL GOVERNMENT—LOCAL AUTHORITY. 12.

Saunders v. *Crawford* (9 Q. B. D. 612) not followed   -   -   **10 Q. B. D. 218**
See ELEMENTARY EDUCATION ACTS — ATTENDANCE. 2.

———— v. *Jones* (7 Ch. D. 438) explained and discussed   -   -   **16 Ch. D. 93**
See PRACTICE—SUPREME COURT—INTERROGATORIES. 9.

———— v. *Richardson* (7 Q. B. D. 388) approved
[**12 Q. B. D. 578**
See ELEMENTARY EDUCATION ACTS — FEES. 2.

———— v. *South Eastern Railway Co.* (5 Q. B. D. 456) followed   -   -   **7 Q. B. D. 32**
See RAILWAY COMPANY—BY-LAWS.

Schomberg, Ex parte (Law Rep. 10 Ch. 172) approved and followed   -   **20 Ch. D. 697**
See BANKRUPTCY—TRADER. 1.

Schulte, Ex parte (Law Rep. 9 Ch. 409) followed
[**18 Ch. D. 137 ; 13 Q. B. D. 727**
See BANKRUPTCY—PROTECTED TRANSACTION. 4, 7.

Scott v. *Cumberland* (Law Rep. 18 Eq. 578) distinguished   ·   **28 Ch. D. 159**
See EXECUTOR—ACTIONS. 12.

Selmes v. *Judge* (Law Rep. 6 Q. B. 724) followed
[**11 Q. B. D. 788**
See LOCAL GOVERNMENT—PRACTICE. 4.

Sewell, Ex parte (13 Ch. D. 266) explained
[**22 Ch. D. 312**
See BANKRUPTCY—ACT OF BANKRUPTCY. 18.

Seymour v. *Bridge* (14 Q. B. D. 460) distinguished
[**14 Q. B. D. 467**
See PRINCIPAL AND AGENT—PRINCIPAL'S LIABILITY. 5.

Shaftoe's Charity, In re (3 App. Cas. 872) approved   -   -   **7 App. Cas. 91**
See ENDOWED SCHOOLS ACT. 3.

Shapcott v. *Chappell* (12 Q. B. D. 58) questioned
[**13 Q. B. D. 403**
See PRACTICE — SUPREME COURT — APPEAL. 7.

Sharpe v. *Birch* (8 Q. B. D. 111) followed
[**9 Q. B. D. 139**
See BILL OF SALE—FORMALITIES. 3.

Shaw, In re (49 L. J. (Ch.) 213) not followed
[**16 Ch. D. 362**
See PARTITION SUIT—SALE. 3.

Sibree v. *Tripp* (15 M. & W. 23) observed upon
[**9 Q. B. D. 37**
See ACCORD AND SATISFACTION. 1.

Silcock v. *Farmer* (46 L. T. (N.S.) 404) commented upon   -   **22 Ch. D. 410**
See BANKRUPTCY—DISCLAIMER. 3.

Simpkin v. *Justices of Birmingham* (Law Rep. 7 Q. B. 482) followed - **7 Q. B. D. 238**
See INN—LICENCE. 2.

Simpson v. *Smith* (Law Rep. 6 C. P. 87) overruled -   -   -   **10 App. Cas. 229**
See METROPOLIS—MANAGEMENT ACTS. 2.

Slade v. *Fooks* (9 Sim. 386) followed **19 Ch. D. 201**
See WILL—WORDS. 6.

Smethurst v. *Mitchell* (28 L. J. (Q.B.) 241) considered   **9 Q. B. D. 623**
See PRINCIPAL AND AGENT—PRINCIPAL'S LIABILITY. 2.

Smith, In re (6 Ch. D. 692) followed **20 Ch. D. 538**
See EXECUTOR—ACTIONS. 8.

———— v. *Butcher* (10 Ch. D. 113) distinguished
See WILL—WORDS. 10. [**25 Ch. D. 212**

———— v. *Davies* (28 Ch. D. 650) questioned
[**29 Ch. D. 827**
See PRACTICE –SUPREME COURT—JUDGMENT. 8

———— v. *Day* (21 Ch. D. 421) dictum of Jessel, M.R., dissented from - **27 Ch. D. 474**
See PRACTICE — SUPREME COURT — INJUNCTION. 9.

———— v. *Lucas* (18 Ch. D. 531) dissented from
See ELECTION. 6.   [**28 Ch. D. 124**
———————————————— followed
[**22 Ch. D. 263**
See SETTLEMENT—FUTURE PROPERTY. 3.

———— v. *Morgan* (5 C. P. D. 337) approved and followed -   -   **20 Ch. D. 545**
See EXECUTOR—ACTIONS. 20.

———— v. *Smith* (Law Rep. 20 Eq. 500) considered
[**26 Ch. D. 578**
See LIGHT—OBSTRUCTION. 2.

Society of Practical Knowledge v. *Abbott* (2 Beav. 559) distinguished   **17 Ch. D. 467**
See COMPANY—DIRECTOR'S LIABILITY. 2.

Solway Railway Company v. Jackson (1 Court Sess. Cas. 4th Series, 831) affirmed
[8 App. Cas. 265
See SCOTCH LAW—RAILWAY COMPANY. 5.

Sottomaior, In re (Law Rep. 9 Ch. 677) dissented from   -   -   -   30 Ch. D. 320
See LUNATIC—INQUISITION. 3.

Spalding v. *Ruding* (6 Beav. 376; 12 L. J. (Ch.) 503) followed -   -   7 App. Cas. 573
See SALE OF GOODS—LIEN. 1.

Sparrow v. *Farmer* (28 L. J. (Ch.) 537) distinguished   -   -   26 Ch. D 273
See BUILDING SOCIETY. 4.

Speight, In re (13 Q. B. D. 42) followed
[14 Q. B. D. 123
See BANKRUPTCY—APPEAL. 12.

————————— not followed
[15 Q. B. D. 338
See BANKRUPTCY—APPEAL. 13.

Speller v. *Bristol Steam Navigation Company* (13 Q. B. D. 96) distinguished   29 Ch D. 344
See PRACTICE—SUPREME COURT—THIRD PARTY. 7.

Staff, Ex parte (Law Rep. 20 Eq. 775) approved
[20 Ch. D. 670
See BANKRUPTCY—COMPOSITION. 6.

————————— distinguished
[16 Ch. D. 655
See BANKRUPTCY—LIQUIDATION. 9.

Stains v. *Banks* (9 Jur. (N.S.) 1049); reversed on appeal, Reg. Lib. 7 B., 1863, 1761) considered   -   -   16 Ch. D. 53
See MORTGAGE—MORTGAGEE IN POSSESSION. 3.

Stanford v. *Roberts* (26 Ch. D. 155) approved
[30 Ch. D. 28
See SOLICITOR—BILL OF COSTS. 22.

Stanhope's Trusts, Re (27 Beav. 201), followed
See WILL—CLASS. 5.   [25 Ch. D. 162

Steele v. *McKinlay* (5 App. Cas. 754) distinguished   -   -   8 App. Cas. 733
See BILL OF EXCHANGE—LIABILITY OF PARTIES.

Stelfox v. *Sugden* (1 Joh. 234) considered.
See WILL—ANNUITY. 1. [17 Ch. D. 167

Sterndale v. *Hankinson* (1 Sim. 393) observed upon   -   -   18 Ch. D. 551
See LIMITATIONS, STATUTE OF—PERSONAL ACTIONS. 4.

Stevens v. *Midland Railway Company* (10 Ex. 352) not followed   6 Q. B. D. 287
See CORPORATION. 1.

Stevenson v. *Lambard* (2 East, 575) considered
[10 Q. B. D. 48
See LANDLORD AND TENANT—ASSIGNMENT. 2.

Stewart, Ex parte, In re Shelley (4 De G. J. & S. 543) discussed -   -   14 Q. B. D. 424
See COMPANY—SHARES—TRANSFER. 2.

————— v. *Jones* (3 De G. & J. 532) followed
See WILL—LAPSE. 9.   [27 Ch. D. 346

Stockdale v. *Hansard* (9 Ad. & E. 1) commented upon and approved   12 Q. B. D. 271
See PARLIAMENT—PROCEDURE.

Stockport Waterworks Company v. *Potter* (3 H. & C. 300) approved   -   11 Q. B. D. 155
See WATERCOURSE. 2.

Stockton Iron Furnace Company, In re (10 Ch. D. 335) discussed   21 Ch. D. 442
See BANKRUPTCY—DISTRESS. 4.

Stokes Bay Railway Company v. *London and South Western Railway Company* (2 Nev. & Mac. 143) disapproved -   17 Ch. D. 493
See RAILWAY COMPANY—RAILWAYS REGULATION ACTS. 1.

Stringer's Case (Law Rep. 4 Ch. 475) distinguished   -   21 Ch. D. 149
See COMPANY—DIRECTOR'S LIABILITY. 4.

Stuart v. *Cockerell* (Law Rep. 5 Ch. 713) distinguished   -   -   28 Ch. D. 436
See WILL—PERPETUITY. 1.

Studd v. *Cook* (8 App. Cas. 577) discussed
See PROBATE—GRANT. 4. [26 Ch. D. 656

Sturgis v. *Corp* (13 Ves. 190) discussed
[23 Ch. D. 712
See HUSBAND AND WIFE — SEPARATE ESTATE. 7.

Suffell v. *Bank of England* (9 Q. B. D. 555) followed   -   11 Q. B. D. 84
See BILL OF EXCHANGE—ALTERATION. 3.

Sullivan v. *Pearson. Ex parte Morrison* (Law Rep. 4 Q. B. 153) approved   8 P. D. 144
See PRACTICE—ADMIRALTY—COSTS. 4.

Sutton v. *Sutton* (22 Ch. D. 511) followed
[22 Ch. D. 579
See LIMITATIONS, STATUTE OF — PERSONAL ACTIONS. 9.

————— v. ————— distinguished
[30 Ch. D. 291
See LIMITATIONS, STATUTE OF—PERSONAL ACTIONS. 10.

Swan v. *Swan* (8 Price, 518) commented on
[23 Ch. D. 552
See INSURANCE, LIFE—ASSIGNMENT.

Swinbanks, Ex parte (11 Ch. D. 525) distinguished
[30 Ch. D. 249
See SOLICITOR—AUTHORITY.

Swindon Waterworks Company v. *Wilts and Berks Navigation Company* (Law Rep. 7 H. L. 697) considered   -   24 Ch. D. 1
See LIGHT—TITLE. 3.

Talbot v. *Marshfield* (2 Dr. & Sm. 549) followed
[22 Ch. D. 609
See PRACTICE — SUPREME COURT—PRODUCTION OF DOCUMENTS. 27.

Tapling v. *Jones* (12 C. B. (N.S.) 826; 11 H. L. C. 290) considered   -   -   27 Ch. D. 43
See LIGHT—TITLE. 1.

Tassell v. *Smith* (2 De G. & J. 713; 27 L. J. (Ch.) 694) overruled   6 App. Cas. 698
See MORTGAGE—CONSOLIDATION. 2.

Taunton v. *Royal Insurance Company* (2 H. & M. 135) distinguished   -   23 Ch. D. 654
See COMPANY—MANAGEMENT. 2.

Taylor v. *Gillott* (Law Rep. 20 Eq. 682) commented upon   7 Q. B. D. 524
See BANKRUPTCY—DISCLAIMER. 17.

————— v. *Meltham Local Board* (47 L. J. (C.P.) 12) distinguished   11 Q. B. D. 286
See LOCAL GOVERNMENT—PRACTICE. 3

Taylor v. *Taylor* (Law Rep. 20 Eq. 155) dissented
from - - - **29 Ch. D. 250**
   See ADVANCEMENT. 1.

Templer's Trusts, In re (4 N. R. 494) considered
   [27 Ch. D. 359
   See TRUSTEE ACTS—VESTING ORDERS. 3.

Terrell, Ex parte (4 Ch. D. 293) distinguished
   [22 Ch. D. 773
   See BANKRUPTCY—COMPOSITION. 5.

Thames-Haven Dock and Railway Company v.
Rose (4 Man. & G. 552) considered
   [16 Ch. D. 681
   See COMPANY—DIRECTOR'S AUTHORITY.
   3.

Tharp, In re (2 Sim. & Giff. 578, n.), commented
on - **23 Ch. D. 552**
   See INSURANCE, LIFE—ASSIGNMENT. 1.

Thomas v. *Daw* (Law Rep. 2 Ch. 1) considered
   [28 Ch. D. 486
   See LONDON—COMMISSIONERS OF SEWERS.

Thompson v. *Waterlow* (Law Rep. 6 Eq. 36) not
followed - **18 Ch. D. 616**
   See WAY. 1.

Thracian, The (3 A. & E. 504), not followed
   [10 P. D. 1
   See PRACTICE—ADMIRALTY—COSTS. 8.

Tinker, Ex parte (Law Rep. 9 Ch. 716) distinguished
   ·· **19 Ch. D. 140**
   See BANKRUPTCY—LIQUIDATION. 5.

Todd, Ex parte (3 Q. B. D. 407) overruled
   See INN—LICÈNCE. 6. **[11 Q. B. D. 638**

Tooth v. *Hallett* (Law Rep. 4 Ch. 242) distinguished
   ·· **14 Q. B. D. 310**
   See BANKRUPTCY—ASSETS. 10.

Touche v. *Metropolitan Railway Warehousing
Company* (Law Rep. 6 Ch. 671) considered - **30 Ch. D. 57**
   See HUSBAND AND WIFE—SEPARATION
   DEED. 2.

Travis v. *Illingworth* (2 Dr. & Sm. 344) not followed
   25 Ch. D. 611
   See SETTLEMENT—POWERS. 8.

—————————— approved and followed **27 Ch. D. 333**
   See SETTLEMENT—POWERS. 9.

Treloar v. *Bigge* (Law Rep. 9 Ex. 151) followed
   [16 Ch. D. 387
   See LANDLORD AND TENANT—LEASE. 2.

Tucker v. *Morris* (1 Cr. & M. 73) distinguished
   [13 Q. B. D. 632
   See PRACTICE—SUPREME COURT—INTER-
   PLEADER. 8.

Tulk v. *Moxhay* (2 Ph. 774) considered
   [20 Ch. D. 562
   See LANDS CLAUSES ACT—SUPERFLUOUS
   LANDS. 2.

—————————— explained **8 Q. B. D.
   [403**
   See COVENANT—RUNNING WITH LAND. 2.

—————————— distinguished
   [29 Ch. D. 750
   See COVENANT—RUNNING WITH LAND. 4.

Turner, In re (12 W. R. 337) followed
   [21 Ch. D. 189
   See EXECUTOR—ACTIONS. 6.

Turner v. *Morgan* (Law Rep. 10 C. P. 587) commented on - **14 Q. B. D. 725**
   See GAME. 2.

—————— v. *Turner* (21 L. J. (Ch.) 843) distinguished - **28 Ch. D. 66**
   See WILL—WORDS. 16.

Two Ellens, The (Law Rep. 4 P. C. 161) explained - **10 P. D. 44**
   See SHIP—MARITIME LIEN. 1.

Unsworth v. *Speakman* (4 Ch. D. 620) disapproved - - **27 Ch. D. 346**
   See WILL—LAPSE. 9.

Upmann v. *Forester* (24 Ch. D. 231) followed
   [27 Ch. D. 260
   See COPYRIGHT—DESIGNS. 1.

Uruguay Central and Hyqueritas Railway Company of Monte Video (11 Ch. D. 372)
approved - **24 Ch. D. 259**
   See COMPANY—WINDING-UP ORDER. 17.

—————————————————— distinguished **27 Ch. D. 278**
   See COMPANY—WINDING-UP ORDER. 11.

Vaisey v. *Reynolds* (5 Russ. 12) disapproved of
   See WILL—WORDS. 8. **[17 Ch. D. 696**

Van Breda v. *Silberbauer* (Law Rep. 3 P. C. 84)
approved **10 App. Cas. 336**
   See COLONIAL LAW—CAPE OF GOOD
   HOPE. 4.

Vansandau v. *Rose* (2 Jac. & W. 264) discussed
and explained - **25 Ch. D. 778**
   See PRACTICE — SUPREME COURT—AT-
   TACHMENT. 9.

Vavasseur v. *Krupp* (15 Ch. D. 474) questioned
   [17 Ch. D. 174
   See PRACTICE—SUPREME COURT—COUN-
   TER-CLAIM. 4.

—————————————————— overruled
   [11 Q. B. D. 464
   See PRACTICE—SUPREME COURT—DIS-
   CONTINUANCE.

Veal v. *Veal* (27 Beav. 303) followed
   [27 Ch. D. 631
   See DONATIO MORTIS CAUSÂ.

Venables v. *Smith* (2 Q. B. D. 279) considered
   [8 Q. B. D. 104
   See NEGLIGENCE—LIABILITY. 1.

Venour's Settled Estates, In re (2 Ch. D. 522) corrected - - **22 Ch. D. 511**
   See STATUTE.

Vint v. *Padget* (2 De G. & J. 611) distinguished
   [19 Ch. D. 630
   See MORTGAGE—CONSOLIDATION. 3.

Vivian v. *Little* (11 Q. B. D. 370) distinguished
   [15 Q. B. D. 7
   See PRACTICE—SUPREME COURT—PRO-
   DUCTION OF DOCUMENTS. 3.

Vize v. *Stoney* (2 D. & Wal. 659; 1 D. & War.
337) observed upon - **30 Ch. D. 507**
   See WILL—VESTING. 2.

Wainman v. *Field* (Kay, 507) distinguished
   See WILL—LAPSE. 7. **[23 Ch. D. 218**

Walburn v. *Ingilby* (1 My. & K. 61) discussed
   [10 Q. B. D. 36
   See PRACTICE—SUPREME COURT—PRO-
   DUCTION OF DOCUMENTS. 7.

Wilkinson v. *Anglo-California Gold Mining Company* (18 Q. B. 728) distinguished
  See DEED. 2.   [10 App. Cas. 293
Williams, Ex parte (7 Ch. D. 138) discussed
    [21 Ch. D. 442
  See BANKRUPTCY—DISTRESS. 4.
———— v. *Bayley* (Law Rep. 1 H. L. 200) explained - 10 Q. B. D. 572
  See BILL OF EXCHANGE—CONSIDERATION.
———— v. *Cooke* (4 Giff. 343) distinguished
    [23 Ch. D. 181
  See HUSBAND AND WIFE—WIFE'S REAL ESTATE. 2.
———— v. *Crosling* (3 C. B. 957) followed
    [14 Q. B. D. 539
  See PRACTICE—SUPREME COURT—SECURITY FOR COSTS. 3.
———— v. *Kershaw* (5 Cl. & F. 111, n.) distinguished - 28 Ch. D. 464
  See CHARITY—GIFT TO. 1.
———— v. *Owen* (13 Sim. 597) not followed
    [19 Ch. D. 615
  See PRINCIPAL AND SURETY—INDEMNITY. 2.
Williamson v. *Williamson* (Law Rep. 9 Ch. 729) distinguished 30 Ch. D. 404
  See LANDLORD AND TENANT—LEASE. 3.
Willoughby v. *Middleton* (2 J. & H. 344) questioned - 18 Ch. D. 531
  See SETTLEMENT—FUTURE PROPERTY. 2.
Wilson, In re (28 Ch. D. 457) considered
    [29 Ch. D. 913
  See PRACTICE—SUPREME COURT—CHAMBERS. 10.
———— v. *Church* (11 Ch. D. 576) explained
    [18 Ch. D. 394
  See PRACTICE—SUPREME COURT—STAYING PROCEEDINGS. 11.
———— v. ———— (12 Ch. D. 454) considered
    [28 Ch. D. 18
  See PRACTICE—SUPREME COURT—STAYING PROCEEDINGS. 14.
———— v. *Coxwell* (23 Ch. D. 764) questioned
    [30 Ch. D. 15
  See EXECUTOR—RETAINER. 5.
———— v. *Eden* (11 Beav. 237; 5 Ex. 752; 14 Beav. 317; 18 Q. B. 474; 16 Beav. 153) discussed 28 Ch. D. 66
  See WILL—WORDS. 16.
———— v. *Hart* (Law Rep. 1 Ch. 463) considered
    [17 Ch. D. 353
  See VENDOR AND PURCHASER—TITLE. 8.
———— v. *Peake* (3 Jur. (N.S.) 155) distinguished
    [17 Ch. D. 142
  See TRUSTEE—LIABILITIES. 7.
———— v. *Strugnell* (7 Q. B. D. 548) overruled
    [15 Q. B. D. 561
  See CONTRACT—VALIDITY. 2.
Winder, Ex parte (1 Ch. D. 290, 560) considered
    [17 Ch. D. 26
  See BANKRUPTCY—ACT OF BANKRUPTCY. 2.
Wingfield v. *Wingfield* (9 Ch. D. 658) followed
  See WILL—WORDS. 10. [25 Ch. D. 212

Winter v. *Bartholomew* (11 Ex. 704) approved
    [14 Q. B. D. 873
  See PRACTICE—SUPREME COURT—INTERPLEADER. 12.
Witt v. *Corcoran* (2 Ch. D. 69) followed
    [29 Ch. D. 60
  See PRACTICE—SUPREME COURT—APPEAL. 28.
Wolley v. *Jenkins* (23 Beav. 53) discussed
    [24 Ch. D. 238
  See SETTLED ESTATES ACTS. 4.
Wolverhampton and Walsall Railway Company v. *London and North Western Railway Company* (Law Rep. 16 Eq. 433) considered - 22 Ch. D. 835
  See SPECIFIC PERFORMANCE. 3.
Womersley v. *Church* (17 L. T. (N.S.) 190) explained 26 Ch. D. 194
  See WATER. 3.
Wood, Ex parte (4 D. M. & G. 875) approved and followed - 20 Ch. D. 356
  See BANKRUPTCY—ACT OF BANKRUPTCY. 17.
Wood's Estate, In re (Law Rep. 10 Eq. 572) followed - 18 Ch. D. 624
  See LEASEHOLD—RENEWABLE LEASE. 3.
Woodgate v. *Godfrey* (5 Ex. D. 24) followed
    [7 Q. B. D. 80
  See BILL OF SALE—REGISTRATION. 4.
Woolridge v. *Woolridge* (Joh. 63) distinguished
  See ELECTION 1. [22 Ch. D. 555
Wootton's Estate, In re (Law Rep. 1 Eq. 589) followed - - 16 Ch. D. 597
  See LANDS CLAUSES ACT—PURCHASE-MONEY. 2.
———— approved 28 Ch. D. 628
  See SETTLED LAND ACT—PURCHASE-MONEY. 2.
Wright v. *Monarch Investment Building Society* (5 Ch. D. 726) approved 23 Ch. D. 103;
    [9 App. Cas. 260
  See BUILDING SOCIETY. 1, 2.
Yelverton v. *Yelverton* (1 Sw & Tr. 574) approved and followed - 13 Q. B. D. 418
  See BANKRUPTCY—BANKRUPTCY PETITION. 3.
Yewens v *Noakes* (6 Q. B. D. 530) explained
    [6 Q. B. D. 673
  See REVENUE—HOUSE DUTY. 4.
Young, Ex parte (19 Ch. D. 124) considered
    [10 Q. B. D. 436
  See PRACTICE—SUPREME COURT—PARTIES. 12.
———— v. *Brassey* (1 Ch. D. 277) not followed
    [19 Ch. D. 460
  See PRACTICE — SUPREME COURT — SERVICE. 8.
———— v. *Waterpark* (*Lord*) (13 Sim. 199) distinguished 23 Ch. D. 472
  See SETTLEMENT—POWERS. 14.
Zuns v. *South Eastern Railway Company* (Law Rep. 4 Q. B. 539) considered
    [10 Q. B. D. 178
  See CONTRACT—ACCEPTANCE. 2.

STATUTES

ABSTRACTED OR SPECIALLY REFERRED TO.

STATUTES—*continued.*

28 & 29 Vict. c. 104, ss. 31, 34, 95—*Crown Suits* - 14 Q. B. D. 667
See PARLIAMENT—ELECTION. 3.

28 & 29 Vict. c. 121, s. 3—*Fisheries*
See FISHERY ACTS. 1. [10 Q. B. D. 131

28 & 29 Vict. c. 126, ss. 4, 5, 8, 23, 44—*Prisons*
See PRISON. 3. [9 Q. B. D. 506

28 & 29 Vict. c. xxvi.—*Bristol Waterworks*
[15 Q. B. D. 637
See WATERWORKS COMPANY — WATER
RATE. 5.

1866.

29 & 30 Vict. c. 19—*Parliamentary Oath*
[7 Q. B. D. 38
See PARLIAMENT—ELECTION. 2.

——— - 8 Q. B. D. 63
See PRACTICE—SUPREME COURT—WRIT. 2.

——— - 12 Q. B. D. 271
See PARLIAMENT—PROCEDURE.

——— ss. 3, 5 - 14 Q. B. D. 667
See PARLIAMENT—ELECTION. 3.

——— s. 5 - - 11 Q. B. D. 1
See CHAMPERTY. 1.

——— . 8 App. Cas. 354
See PENAL ACTION. 2.

29 & 30 Vict. c. 32, s. 1—*Divorce* 6 P. D. 213 ;
[7 P. D. 122
See PRACTICE—DIVORCE—ALIMONY. 3, 5.

——— - - 15 Q. B. D. 239
See BANKRUPTCY—PROOF. 3.

29 & 30 Vict. c. 36, s. 8—*Income Tax*
[6 App. Cas. 315
See SCOTCH LAW—REVENUE.

——— 7 Q. B. D. 485 : 14 Q. B. D. 491
See REVENUE—INCOME TAX. 3, 4.

29 & 30 Vict. c. 52—*Prosecution Expenses.*
See JUSTICES—PRACTICE—*Statutes.*

29 & 30 Vict. c. 96, s. 5—*Bills of Sale*
[9 App. Cas. 653
See BILL OF SALE — APPARENT POSSESSION. 3.

29 & 30 Vict. c. 114, ss. 5, 7—*Libraries*
See PUBLIC LIBRARY. [8 Q. B. D. 459

29 & 30 Vict. c. 118, s. 14—*Industrial Schools*
See INDUSTRIAL SCHOOL. [10 Q. B. D. 360

29 & 30 Vict. c. cxliii.—*Middlesborough Improvement* - 12 Q. B. D. 239
See HIGHWAY—REPAIR. 1.

29 & 30 Vict. c. ccxlvii., s. 3—*Yarmouth Harbour* - - 9 P. D. 3
See SHIP—NAVIGATION. 32.

1867.

30 & 31 Vict. c. 3, ss. 65, 92—*British North America* - 10 App. Cas. 141
See COLONIAL LAW—CANADA—QUEBEC. 4.

——— ss. 91, 92 - - 7 App. Cas. 829 ;
[9 App. Cas. 157
See COLONIAL LAW — CANADA — DOMINION. 2, 3.

STATUTES—*continued.*

30 & 31 Vict. c. 3 - - 7 App. Cas. 96
See COLONIAL LAW—CANADA—ONTARIO. 3.

——— ss. 91, 92, 129 7 App. Cas. 136
See COLONIAL LAW—CANADA—QUEBEC. 3.

——— ss. 102, 109 - 8 App. Cas. 767
See COLONIAL LAW—CANADA—ONTARIO. 4.

——— s. 108 7 App. Cas. 178
See COLONIAL LAW — CANADA — DOMINION. 1.

30 & 31 Vict. c. 6—*Metropolitan Poor*
[6 App. Cas. 193
See NUISANCE—DEFINITION. 1.

30 & 31 Vict. c. 29, s. 1—*Banking Companies*
See STOCK EXCHANGE. 1. [9 Q. B. D. 546

——— 14 Q. B. D. 460; 15 Q. B. D.
[388
See PRINCIPAL AND AGENT—PRINCIPAL'S LIABILITY. 4, 5.

30 & 31 Vict. c. 48, s. 7—*Auctions*
[16 Ch. D. 561
See PRACTICE—SUPREME COURT—SALE BY COURT.

30 & 31 Vict. c. 97, s. 2, sub-s. 3—*Trusts, Scotland* 8 App. Cas. 641
See SCOTCH LAW—HERITABLE PROPERTY. 2.

30 & 31 Vict. c. 102, ss. 3, 61—*Representation of People* 10 Q. B. D. 577
See PARLIAMENT—FRANCHISE. 3.

——— s. 4 - 8 Q. B. D. 247
See PARLIAMENT—FRANCHISE. 4.

——— s. 61 8 Q. B. D. 195
See PARLIAMENT—FRANCHISE. 2.

30 & 31 Vict. c. 106, s. 27—*Poor Law Board*
[8 Q. B. D. 158
See ELEMENTARY EDUCATION ACTS—ATTENDANCE. 4.

30 & 31 Vict. c. 124, s. 9—*Merchant Shipping*
[10 P. D. 21
See PRACTICE—ADMIRALTY—LIMITATION OF LIABILITY. 3.

30 & 31 Vict. c. 127, ss. 3, 4—*Railways*
[13 Q. B. D. 320
See RAILWAY COMPANY—PROPERTY. 1.

——— s. 4 21 Ch. D. 309
See RAILWAY COMPANY—CONSTITUTION.

——— ss. 4, 23 - 6 Q. B. D. 36
See RAILWAY COMPANY—PROPERTY. 2.

——— ss. 4, 31, 35 - 18 Ch. D. 155
See RAILWAY COMPANY—ABANDONMENT. 1.

30 & 31 Vict. c. 131, s. 9—*Companies* 17 Ch. D.
[76; 29 Ch. D. 683
See COMPANY—REDUCTION OF CAPITAL. 1, 4.

——— s. 24, sub-s. 3 - 8 App. Cas. 65
See COMPANY—DIVIDENDS. 3.

——— s. 25 - - 18 Ch. D. 587
See COMPANY—DEBENTURES. 2.

——— - - 23 Ch. D. 542
See COMPANY—REDUCTION OF CAPITAL. 3.

STATUTES—*continued.*

1871.

34 & 35 Vict. c. 31, ss. 2, 3, 4—*Trade Unions*
  See TRADE UNION.   [21 Ch. D. 194

34 & 35 Vict. c. 43, ss. 12-16, 72—*Ecclesiastical Dilapidations* - · 15 Q. B. D. 222
  See ECCLESIASTICAL LAW—DILAPIDATIONS.

34 & 35 Vict. c. 44, s. 10—*Incumbents' Resignation*   17 Ch. D. 1
  See ECCLESIASTICAL LAW—CLERGY. 3.

———— -   7 Q. B. D. 626
  See PRACTICE—SUPREME COURT—COUNTER-CLAIM. 7.

34 & 35 Vict. c. 79—*Lodgers' Goods Protection.*
  See Cases under LANDLORD AND TENANT—LODGER.

34 & 35 Vict. c. 86, s. 3—*Regulation of Forces Act* - -   19 Ch. D. 17
  See MORTGAGE—PRIORITY. 12.

34 & 35 Vict. c. 87—*Sunday Observance.*
  See SUNDAY OBSERVANCE—*Statutes.*

34 & 35 Vict. c. 112, s. 19—*Prevention of Crime*   [12 Q. B. D. 522
  See CRIMINAL LAW—EVIDENCE. 6.

1872.

35 & 36 Vict. c. 33—*Ballot.*
  See PARLIAMENT—ELECTION—*Statutes.*
  MUNICIPAL CORPORATION—ELECTION—*Statutes.*

———— s. 20   - 6 Q. B. D. 323
  See MUNICIPAL CORPORATION — ELECTION. 3.

35 & 36 Vict. c. 60—*Corrupt Practices*   [10 Q. B. D. 293
  See MUNICIPAL CORPORATION — ELECTION. 2.

———— s. 13, sub-s. 6   - 6 Q. B. D. 323
  See MUNICIPAL CORPORATION — ELECTION. 3.

———— s. 14, sub-ss. 5, ss. 20, 22   [9 Q. B. D. 494
  See MUNICIPAL CORPORATION — ELECTION. 1.

35 & 36 Vict. c. 65—*Bastards.*
  See Cases under BASTARDY.

35 & 36 Vict. c. 76, s. 18—*Mines*   [14 Q. B. D. 592
  See MINE—MINES REGULATION ACTS.

35 & 36 Vict. c. 86, s. 6—*County Courts*   [11 Q. B. D. 120
  See COURT—MAYOR'S COURT. 2.

35 & 36 Vict. c. 94, s. 3—*Licensing Act*
  See INN—OFFENCES. 2. [8 Q. B. D. 373

———— ss. 3, 51   8 Q. B. D. 511
  See INN—OFFENCES. 1.

———— s. 9   - 11 Q. B. D. 417
  See INN—LICENCE. 4.

———— s. 17   · 12 Q. B. D. 360
  See INN—OFFENCES. 4.

———— s. 42 7 Q. B. D. 542 ; 14 Q. B. D. 584
  See INN—LICENCE. 1, 9.

———— s. 45   8 Q. B. D. 369
  See INN—LICENCE. 3.

STATUTES—*continued.*

1873.

36 & 37 Vict. c. 12, s. 1—*Infants Custody*
  [16 Ch. D. 115 ; 25 Ch. D. 220 ;
  [13 Q. B. D. 614
  See INFANT—CUSTODY. 1, 2, 3.

36 & 37 Vict. c. 38, s. 3—*Vagrants*
  See VAGRANT ACTS. 2. [10 Q. B. D. 44

36 & 37 Vict. c. 48—*Railways and Canals*
  See RAILWAY COMPANY—RAILWAYS REGULATION ACTS—*Statutes.*

———— - 6 Q. B. D. 586 ; 7 Q. B. D. 182
  See RAILWAY COMPANY—RAILWAYS REGULATION ACTS. 3, 5.

———— s. 8   17 Ch. D. 493
  See RAILWAY COMPANY—RAILWAYS REGULATION ACTS. 1.

———— s. 11   10 Q. B. D. 231
  See RAILWAY COMPANY — RAILWAYS REGULATION ACTS. 6.

———— ss. 15, 26 -   15 Q. B. D. 505
  See RAILWAY COMPANY—RAILWAYS REGULATION ACTS. 4.

———— s. 28   -   - 8 Q. B. D. 515
  See RAILWAY COMPANY—RAILWAYS REGULATION ACTS. 2.

36 & 37 Vict. c. 66, ss. 3, 16—*Judicature*
  [17 Ch. D. 787
  See PRACTICE—SUPREME COURT—EVIDENCE. 7.

———— s. 16 -   - 18 Ch. D. 521
  See COUNTY COURT—COSTS. 3.

————   - 28 Ch. D. 529
  See TRUSTEE ACTS—VESTING ORDERS. 2.

————   -   10 P. D. 110
  See PRACTICE—DIVORCE—APPEAL. 2.

———— ss. 16, 23   -   - 10 P. D. 122
  See PRACTICE—DIVORCE—NULLITY OF MARRIAGE. 8.

———— ss. 16, 24, 73   - 25 Ch. D. 384
  See PRACTICE—SUPREME COURT—CHAMBERS. 15.

———— ss. 16, 25, 34, 36 - 26 Ch. D. 656
  [30 Ch. D. 387
  See PRACTICE—SUPREME COURT—JURISDICTION. 1, 2.

———— s. 19   - 14 Q. B. D. 371, 377
  See PRACTICE—SUPREME COURT—INTERPLEADER. 5, 7.

————   6 Q. B. D. 323
  See MUNICIPAL CORPORATION — ELECTION. 3.

————   12 Q. B. D. 1
  See PRACTICE—SUPREME COURT—APPEAL. 3.

———— ss. 19, 45   15 Q. B. D. 76
  See PRACTICE — SUPREME COURT—APPEAL. 4.

———— ss. 19, 47   · - 10 Q. B. D. 378
  See PRACTICE—SUPREME COURT—APPEAL. 9.

———— ss. 19, 47 -   9 Q. B. D. 701
  See EXTRADITION. 1.

————   14 Q. B. D. 667
  See PARLIAMENT—ELECTION. 3.

STATUTES—*continued.*

36 & 37 Vict. c. 66, s. 22   -   **21 Ch. D. 278**
    See WILL—CONDITION. 1.

—— s. 24 -   ·   **16 Ch. D. 544**
    See PRACTICE—SUPREME COURT—RE-
    CEIVER. 1.

——   -   **12 Q. B. D. 287**
    See PRACTICE — SUPREME COURT —
    CHARGING ORDERS. 2.

—— —— sub-s. 3   -   **17 Ch. D. 174;**
    [19 Ch. D. 473; 21 Ch. D. 138
    See PRACTICE—SUPREME COURT—COUN-
    TER-CLAIM. 1, 4, 5.

—— —— s. 49   -   **8 Q. B. D. 329**
    See PRACTICE—SUPREME COURT—COSTS.
    48.

—— ——   -   **12 Q. B. D. 533**
    See PRACTICE—SUPREME COURT—THIRD
    PARTY. 3.

—— —— sub-ss. 3, 7   **8 Q. B. D. 428**
    See PRACTICE—SUPREME COURT—RE-
    PLY. 1.

—— —— sub-s. 5   **12 Q. B. D. 165**
    See PRACTICE—SUPREME COURT—JUDG-
    MENT. 5.

—— —— sub-ss. 5, 7   -   **25 Ch. D. 723**
    See PRACTICE—SUPREME COURT—RE-
    CEIVER. 7.

—— —— sub-s. 7   -   **15 Q. B. D. 549**
    See ESTOPPEL—JUDGMENT. 6.

——   -   **9 Q. B. D. 320**
    See PRACTICE—SUPREME COURT—STAY-
    ING PROCEEDINGS. 5.

—— ss. 24, 25   -   **7 App. Cas. 235**
    See LIMITATIONS, STATUTE OF—REALTY.
    4.

—— s. 24, sub-s. 7, s. 25, sub-s. 8
    [13 Q. B. D. 807
    See PRACTICE—SUPREME COURT—RE-
    CEIVER. 6.

—— —— sub-s. 8   -   **19 Ch. D. 473**
    See PRACTICE—SUPREME COURT—COUN-
    TER-CLAIM. 1.

—— s. 25, sub-s. 2   -   **18 Ch. D. 254**
    See LIMITATIONS, STATUTE OF—TRUSTS.
    2.

—— —— sub-s. 6   **22 Ch. D. 122;**
    [25 Ch. D. 587
    See COMPANY—SET-OFF. 1.

—— —— ——   -   **6 Q. B. D. 626;**
    [12 Q. B. D. 347, 511
    See ASSIGNMENT OF DEBT. 1, 2, 3.

—— ——   -   **12 Q. B. D. 518**
    See SOLICITOR—BILL OF COSTS. 5.

—— —— sub-s. 7   **11 Q. B. D. 123**
    See FRAUDS, STATUTE OF. 1.

—— —— sub-s. 8   **16 Ch. D. 660;**
    [20 Ch. D. 501
    See PRACTICE — SUPREME COURT — IN-
    JUNCTION. 3, 5.

——
    See Cases under PRACTICE — SUPREME
    COURT—RECEIVER.

—— —— ——   -   **24 Ch. D. 405**
    See SOLICITOR—BILL OF COSTS. 9.

STATUTES—*continued.*

36 & 37 Vict. c. 66, s. 25, sub-s. 8 **11 Q. B. D. 30**
    See ARBITRATION—STAYING PROCEED-
    INGS.

—— —— ——   -   **7 P. D. 15**
    See PRACTICE—DIVORCE—COSTS. 1.

—— —— —— -   **25 Ch. D. 238**
    See MORTGAGE—FORECLOSURE. 20.

——   -   **13 Q. B. D. 67**
    See PRACTICE—SUPREME COURT—IN-
    TERPLEADER. 10.

—— —— sub-s. 8, s. 34   **16 Ch. D. 143**
    See MUNICIPAL CORPORATION—QUALIFI-
    CATION.

—— —— sub-s. 9   -   **10 Q. B. D. 521**
    See SHIP—BILL OF LADING. 1.

—— —— sub-s. 10   -   **13 Q. B. D. 614**
    See INFANT—CUSTODY. 1.

—— —— sub-s. 11   **29 Ch. D. 725**
    See MORTGAGE—PRIORITY. 9.

—— —— -.   **29 Ch. D. 996**
    See HUSBAND AND WIFE—WIFE'S REAL
    ESTATE. 5.

—— ——   -   **15 Q. B. D. 280**
    See BILL OF SALE—OPERATION. 4.

—— s. 39   · -   **6 Q. B. D. 622**
    See SOLICITOR—LIEN. 3.

—— ——   -   **13 Q. B. D. 218**
    See PRACTICE—SUPREME COURT—AT-
    TACHMENT. 5.

—— s. 45 **6 Q. B. D. 309; 8 Q. B. D. 325;**
    [15 Q. B. D. 76
    See PRACTICE—SUPREME COURT—AP-
    PEAL. 4, 5, 6.

—— s. 47   -   **7 Q. B. D. 534, 575**
    See PRACTICE—SUPREME COURT—AP-
    PEAL. 8, 13.

—— ——   **12 Q. B. D. 148**
    See SOLICITOR—MISCONDUCT. 1.

—— s. 49.
    See Cases under PRACTICE—SUPREME
    COURT—APPEAL.

—— s. 49   **20 Ch. D. 611**
    See VENDOR AND PURCHASER—PURCHASE
    WITHOUT NOTICE. 1.

—— —— **8 Q. B. D. 82; 12 Q. B. D. 100**
    See PRACTICE—SUPREME COURT—INTER-
    PLEADER. 1, 9.

—— s. 50 -   -   **19 Ch. D. 326**
    See PRACTICE—SUPREME COURT—CHAM-
    BERS. 5.

—— ss. 56, 57, 58.
    See Cases under PRACTICE—SUPREME
    COURT—REFEREE.

—— s. 57   -   **25 Ch. D. 772**
    See PRACTICE—SUPREME COURT—TRIAL.
    2.

—— ss. 64, 66   -   **20 Ch. D. 538**
    See EXECUTOR—ACTIONS. 8.

—— s. 67 -   -   **27 Ch. D. 533**
    See PRACTICE—SUPREME COURT—JURIS-
    DICTION. 3.

—— s. 89 -   **7 Q. B. D. 623**
    See COUNTY COURT—JURISDICTION. 5.

TABLE

OF

TITLES, SUB-TITLES, AND CROSS-REFERENCES.

The TITLES and SUB-TITLES under which the Cases and Statutes are arranged are printed in this Table in Capitals, and the CROSS-REFERENCES in ordinary Type.

The SUB-TITLES are arranged Alphabetically (with a few trifling deviations, the object of which will be apparent) under all the TITLES except BANKRUPTCY, COMPANY, and PRACTICE.

Corrupt and Illegal Practices Prevention Act, 1883.
Cost-book Company.
Costs.
Co-Surety.
Counsel.
Counterclaim.
Counterfeit Mark.
Counterfeit Medal Act, 1883.
County.
COUNTY COURT:—
    I. APPEAL.
    II. COSTS.
    III. JURISDICTION.
    IV. PRACTICE.
County Court Rules, 1875.
County Court Rules, 1884.
County Rate.
County Stock.
County Vote.
Coupons.
COURT:—
    I. STATUTES AND GAZETTE.
    II. CENTRAL CRIMINAL COURT.
    III. LANCASTER COURT.
    IV. MAYOR'S COURT.
Cousin.
COVENANT:—
    I. BREACH.
    II. RUNNING WITH LAND.
    III. VALIDITY.
Creditor.
Creditors' Deed.
Cremation.
CRIMINAL LAW:—
    I. BIGAMY.
    II. COINING.
    III. CONSPIRACY.
    IV. EXPLOSIVES.
    V. FORGERY.
    VI. FRAUDULENT DEBTOR.
    VII. LARCENY.
    VIII. LIBEL.
    IX. MALICIOUS INJURY.
    X. MISAPPROPRIATION.
    XI. MISDEMEANOR.
    XII. NUISANCE.
    XIII. OFFENCES AGAINST PERSON.
    XIV. OFFENCES AGAINST WOMEN.
    XV. UNLAWFUL ASSEMBLY.
    XVI. EVIDENCE.
    XVII. PRACTICE.

Criminal Lunatic.
Crops.
Cross Actions.
Cross-Examination.
Cross-Notice of Appeal.
Cross-Remainders.
Crossed Cheque.
CROWN.
Crown Lands.
Cruelty.
CRUELTY TO ANIMALS.
Curtesy.
Custody of Children.
Custody of Deeds.
Custody of Goods.
Custom.
Custom House Agent.
CUSTOMS ANNUITY FUND.
Customs and Inland Revenue Acts.
Customs Regulation Act, 1879.
Customary Rent.
Customers.
Cy-près.

Damage.
DAMAGES:—
    I. CONTRACT.
    II. LORD CAIRNS' ACT.
    III. LORD CAMPBELL'S ACT.
    IV. REMOTENESS.
Danube.
De Bene Esse.
Dead Body.
Dean Forest.
Death.
Debenture.
Debenture Stock.
Debt.
Debtor.
Debtor's Summons.
Deceased Debtor.
Deceased Partner.
Deceit.
Declaration by Deceased Person.
Declaration of Future Rights.
Declaration of Legitimacy.
Declaration of Trust.
Decree Nisi.
Dedication.
DEED.

THE LAW REPORTS.

DIGEST OF CASES.

ACCOMMODATION BILLS—Proof in bankruptcy
[16 Ch. D. 330
See BANKRUPTCY—PROOF. 4.

ACCOMMODATION WORKS　20 Ch. D. 323
See RAILWAY COMPANY — RAILWAYS
CLAUSES ACT. 1.

ACCORD AND SATISFACTION.
1. —— **Cheque.**—A., being indebted to B. in
£125 7s. 9d. for goods sold and delivered, gave B.
a cheque for £100 payable on demand, which B.
accepted in satisfaction.—*Held*, a good accord and
satisfaction.—*Cumber* v. *Wane* (Stra. 426) and
Sibree v. *Tripp* (15 M. & W. 23) observed upon.
GODDARD *v.* O'BRIEN　　　　- 9 Q. B. D. 37
2. —— **Consideration** — *Contract by Creditor
to take less than Sum due.*] An agreement between
judgment debtor and creditor, that in consideration of the debtor paying down part of the judgment debt and costs, and on condition of his paying to the creditor or his nominee the residue by
instalments, the creditor will not take any proceedings on the judgment, is nudum pactum,
being without consideration, and does not prevent
the creditor after payment of the whole debt and
costs from proceeding to enforce payment of the
interest upon the judgment.—So *Held* affirming
the decision of the Court of Appeal.—*Pinnel's Case*
(5 Rep. 117 a) and *Cumber* v. *Wane* (1 Str. 426)
followed.　FOAKES *v.* BEER　　11 Q. B. D. 221;
[9 App. Cas. 605

ACCOUNT—Action for—Collegiate body
[18 Ch. D. 596
See CHARITY—COMMISSIONERS. 1.
—— Action for—Mistake of law　29 Ch. D. 902
See BUILDING SOCIETY. 8.
—— After judgment -　　　　21 Ch. D. 757
See EXECUTOR—ACTIONS. 9.
—— Auditing—Building society　28 Ch. D. 111
See BUILDING SOCIETY. 3.
—— Banker—Advances to executor　16 Ch. D.
See EXECUTOR—POWERS. 1.　　　[151
—— Bankruptcy—Duty of bankrupt to furnish
[21 Ch. D. 61
See BANKRUPTCY—EXAMINATION. 2.
—— Claim for—Particulars of demand
[28 Ch. D. 119
See PRACTICE—SUPREME COURT—PAR-
TICULARS. 1.
—— Discovery　　　　　　16 Ch. D. 93
See PRACTICE—SUPREME COURT—INTER-
ROGATORIES. 9.
—— Duty on.
See REVENUE—STAMPS—*Statutes.*
—— In Chambers—Adjournment into Court
[20 Ch. D. 731
See PRACTICE—SUPREME COURT—CHAM-
BERS. 1.
—— Mortgage—Foreclosure　29 Ch. D. 827
See MORTGAGE—FORECLOSURE. 2.
—— Mortgage—Settled account　6 App. Cas. 181
See MORTGAGE—CONTRACT. 11.
—— Mortgage—Surplus of sale by first mort-
gagee　　　　　　18 Ch. D. 254
See LIMITATIONS, STATUTE OF—TRUSTS.
2.

ACCOUNT—*continued.*
—— Mortgagee in possession　-　16 Ch. D. 53;
[22 Ch. D. 478; 30 Ch. D. 336
See MORTGAGE—MORTGAGEE IN POSSES-
SION. 1, 3, 4.
—— Order for—District Registrar 20 Ch. D. 538
See EXECUTOR—ACTIONS. 8.
—— Patent—Duty of patentee　6 App. Cas. 176
See PATENT—PROLONGATION. 2.
—— Patent—Profits　　　　17 Ch. D. 423
See PATENT—ASSIGNMENT. 1.
—— Preliminary　-　　29 Ch. D. 566, 834
See PRACTICE—SUPREME COURT — IN-
QUIRIES AND ACCOUNTS. 1, 2.
—— Settled account—Form of order 27 Ch. D. 111
See PRACTICE—SUPREME COURT—CHAM-
BERS. 2.

ACCOUNTANT—Right to appoint — Auditor—
Company　-　　　12 Q. B. D. 68
See COMPANY—MANAGEMENT. 1.

ACCUMULATIONS.
1. —— **Accumulation to pay Mortgage Debts**
—*Sale of Mortgaged Estate by Mortgagee—Right
of Tenant for Life to possession.*] A testator
devised his real estates (in the events which
happened) to the use of the Plaintiff for life;
with remainder to the use of the Plaintiff's first
and other sons successively in tail male; with
remainder over to the use of another person in
fee. The will provided that, immediately after
the death of a prior tenant for life (who died
before the testator), the trustees of the will
should receive the rents, and, after paying thereout the interest on the mortgages on the estates,
should accumulate the residue, until the amount
of the accumulations should be sufficient to discharge the principal of the mortgages. And the
testator directed that, as soon as the accumulations should be sufficient to pay off the mortgages,
the trustees should forthwith pay them off. And
he declared that the Plaintiff, or other the person
for the time being entitled for life or in tail to
the estates under the limitations of the will,
should not be entitled to receive any part of the
rents until the mortgages had been paid off.
After the testator's death the mortgagees sold
those parts of the estates which were comprised
in their mortgages. The proceeds of sale were
not enough to pay the whole of the mortgage
debts, and the balance was paid out of the accumulations of rents. A surplus of accumulations
remained :—*Held*, that the tenant for life was
entitled to be let into possession of the estates
which remained unsold, and to have the surplus
of the accumulations paid to him. NORTON *v.*
JOHNSTONE -　-　　　30 Ch. D. 649
2. —— **Thellusson Act** (39 & 40 *Geo.* 3, c. 98),
s. 1.—*Trust for Accumulation.*] The four different
periods beyond which the accumulation of income is unlawful under the 1st section of the
Thellusson Act are alternative and not cumulative; therefore when one period has been applied and exhausted, a second period cannot be
resorted to and applied, in order to extend the
time for accumulation.—In applying the Act the
Court is bound to consider not merely the events
which have happened, but also those which might
have happened.—By a post-nuptial settlement the

ACCUMULATIONS—*continued.*

husband assigned all his personal estate to trustees upon trust to apply the income to his own maintenance, and subject thereto, during the joint lives of himself and his wife, and the life of the survivor of them, to apply all or any part of the income for the maintenance of the wife and the children of the marriage, and to accumulate the surplus (if any) so that the accumulations should be added to the principal fund and follow the destination thereof, with liberty for the trustees to resort to the accumulations of any preceding years and apply the same for the maintenance of the wife and children; and after the death of the survivor of the settlor and his wife upon trust, as to both capital and income, for such of their issue as the settlor and his wife by deed jointly, or the survivor by will, should appoint, and in default for the children of the marriage as tenants in common, sons at twenty-one, and daughters at twenty-one or marriage:—
Held, that the only one of the said four periods of the Thellusson Act applicable to the case was the first, viz., the life of the settlor; and that the trust for accumulation contained in the settlement was void as from the death of the husband.
JAGGER *v.* JAGGER　　　25 Ch. D. 729

—— Allowance out of—Maintenance of infants
[17 Ch. D. 807; 19 Ch. D. 305; 22 Ch. D. 583
See INFANT—MAINTENANCE. 1, 2, 3.

—— Separate estate　　　-　30 Ch. D. 183
See HUSBAND AND WIFE — SEPARATE ESTATE. 8.

—— Trustee—Breach of trust　　17 Ch. D. 142
See TRUSTEE—LIABILITIES. 7.

ACCUMULATION FUND—Foreign life insurance
company　　-　　-　21 Ch. D. 837
See COMPANY—LIFE INSURANCE COMPANY. 1.

ACCUSED PERSON — Evidence of — Offences against women　　　　.
See CRIMINAL LAW — EVIDENCE — *Statutes.*

ACKNOWLEDGMENT—Married woman.
See HUSBAND AND WIFE—WIFE'S CONVEYANCE—*Statutes.*

—— Married woman—Fines and Recoveries Act —Varying form of certificate
[6 Q. B. D. 154
See HUSBAND AND WIFE—WIFE'S CONVEYANCE. 1.

—— Married woman — Wife's reversionary interest　　　23 Ch. D. 181, 344
See HUSBAND AND WIFE—WIFE'S REAL ESTATE. 2, 3.

—— Statute of Limitations　　26 Ch. D. 474
See LIMITATIONS, STATUTE OF — PERSONAL ACTIONS. 1.

—— Statute of Limitations　　19 Ch. D. 373 ;
[29 Ch. D. 882
See LIMITATIONS, STATUTE OF—REALTY. 1, 2.

ACQUIESCENCE—Breach of covenants—Alteration of character of property
[28 Ch. D. 103
See COVENANT—BREACH. 1.

ACQUIESCENCE—*continued.*

—— Breach of trust　-　　-　30 Ch. D. 490
See TRUSTEE—LIABILITY. 5.

—— Ultra vires act　　　　26 Ch. D. 107
See COMPANY—MEMORANDUM AND ARTICLES. 3.

ACT OF BANKRUPTCY.
See Cases under BANKRUPTCY—ACT OF BANKRUPTCY.

—— Bankruptcy Act, 1883.
See BANKRUPTCY—BANKRUPTCY ACT, 1883—*Statutes.*

—— Creditor's deed—Subsequent bankruptcy of debtor—Liability of trustee to account
[14 Q. B. D. 25
See BANKRUPTCY—TRUSTEE. 3.

—— Failure to comply with bankruptcy notice— Appeal—Stay of proceedings
[14 Q. B. D. 49
See BANKRUPTCY—BANKRUPTCY PETITION. 1.

—— Mutual dealings　　　7 App. Cas. 79
See BANKRUPTCY—MUTUAL DEALINGS. 3.

—— Notice of—Protected transaction.
See Cases under BANKRUPTCY—PROTECTED TRANSACTION.

—— Solicitor — Petitioning creditor — Payment with notice of act of bankruptcy
.　　[13 Q. B. D. 747
See BANKRUPTCY—ASSETS. 7.

—— Trader—Proof of trading　20 Ch. D. 697;
[21 Ch. D. 394
See BANKRUPTCY—TRADER. 1, 2.

ACT OF GOD—Extraordinary violence of sea
See SEA-WALL.　　[14 Q. B. D. 561

ACTING DRAMA—Copyright—Publication
[21 Ch. D. 232
See COPYRIGHT—DRAMATIC. 3.

ACTIO PERSONALIS MORITUR CUM PERSONÂ
[21 Ch. D. 484; 24 Ch. D. 439;
[9 Q. B. D. 110
See EXECUTOR—ACTIONS. 1, 2, 3.

ACTIO POPULARIS　-　　7 App. Cas. 547
See SCOTCH LAW—PUBLIC RIGHTS.

ACTION.

1. —— Alimony — *Pendente lite* — *Order of Probate and Divorce Division.*] In an action for arrears of alimony pendente lite payable under an order of the Probate and Divorce Division :—
Held, by the Divisional Court, that an order to enter final judgment under Order XIV., rule 1, could not be made:—*Held*, by the Court of Appeal, that the order for payment of alimony could only be enforced in the manner pointed out by 20 & 21 Vict. c. 85, s. 52, and therefore no action would lie to recover the arrears, and the decision must be affirmed. BAILEY *v.* BAILEY
[13 Q. B. D. 855

2. —— Cause of—*Statement of Claim shewing Felony—Demurrer.*] A statement of claim is not demurrable on the ground that it shews the cause of action to be a felony, for which the felon has not been prosecuted. ROOPE *v.* D'AVIGDOR
[10 Q. B. D. 412

ACTION—*continued.*

—— For deceit—Misrepresentation in prospectus
[17 Ch. D. 301 ; 29 Ch. D. 459 ; 9 App. Cas.
[187
See COMPANY—PROSPECTUS. 1, 3, 5.

—— Felony—Neglect to prosecute felon
See INSURANCE, FIRE. 1. [6 Q. B. D. 561

—— In personam—Dying with the person
[21 Ch. D. 484 ; 24 Ch. D. 439 ;
[9 Q. B. D. 110
See EXECUTOR—ACTIONS. 1, 2, 3.

—— In personam—Two actions on same subject
—Stay of proceedings	21 Ch. D. 202
See PRACTICE—SUPREME COURT—STAY-
ING PROCEEDINGS. 6.

—— In rem—Ship—Jurisdiction of Admiralty
Division	9 P. D. 96 ; 10 App. Cas. 59
See PRACTICE—ADMIRALTY—JURISDIC-
TION. 1.

—— Right of—Undischarged bankrupt—Per-
sonal earnings—Trustee	17 Ch. D. 768
See BANKRUPTCY—UNDISCHARGED BANK-
RUPT. 4.

AD VALOREM STAMP	17 Ch. D. 10
See REVENUE—STAMPS. 3.

ADDING PARTIES.
See Cases under PRACTICE—SUPREME
COURT—PARTIES.

—— After judgment—Foreclosure action
[25 Ch. D. 750
See PRACTICE — SUPREME COURT —
AMENDMENT. 2.

ADEMPTION—Legacy	22 Ch. D. 622
See WILL—ADEMPTION.

—— Purchase-money of estate sold - 30 Ch. D. 92
See WILL—WORDS. 9.

—— Satisfaction by advance in testator's life-
time	17 Ch. D. 701 ; 28 Ch. D. 522 ;
[15 Q. B. D. 300
See WILL—SATISFACTION. 1, 2, 3.

ADJOINING LANDOWNERS—Liability of
[9 Q. B. D. 441 ; 8 App. Cas. 443
See PRINCIPAL AND AGENT—PRINCIPAL'S
LIABILITY. 1.

ADJOINING TENEMENT—Right to easement
See EASEMENT. 1.	[22 Ch. D. 177

ADJOURNMENT TO JUDGE — Costs — Mortga-
gees' accounts	-	22 Ch. D. 5
See MORTGAGE—CONTRACT. 7.

ADJUDICATION OF BANKRUPTCY.
See Cases under BANKRUPTCY—ADJUDI-
CATION.

—— Annulment.
See Cases under BANKRUPTCY—ANNUL-
MENT.

—— Infant -	-	18 Ch. D. 109
See BANKRUPTCY—TRADER. 3.

—— Liquidating debtor	22 Ch. D. 813 ;
[24 Ch. D. 35
See BANKRUPTCY—LIQUIDATION. 1, 6.

ADJUSTMENT OF RIGHTS OF CONTRIBU-
TORIES	23 Ch. D. 297
See COMPANY—CONTRIBUTORY. 4.

ADMINISTRATION—Action for.
See Cases under EXECUTOR—ACTIONS.

ADMINISTRATION—*continued.*

—— Action for—Claim by creditor—Statute of
Limitations	-	18 Ch. D. 551
See LIMITATIONS, STATUTE OF—PER-
SONAL ACTIONS. 4.

—— Action for—Conduct of—Bankrupt execu-
tors	-	19 Ch. D. 61
See PRACTICE—SUPREME COURT—CON-
DUCT OF CAUSE. 1.

—— Action for—Costs—County Court 18 Ch. D.
See COUNTY COURT—COSTS. 3.	[521

—— Action for—Costs of defaulting trustee
[23 Ch. D. 195
See TRUSTEE—COSTS AND CHARGES. 3.

—— Action for—Costs—Remuneration of soli-
citor	-	26 Ch. D. 155
See SOLICITOR—BILL OF COSTS. 21.

—— Action for—Deceased bankrupt
[24 Ch. D. 672
See BANKRUPTCY—UNDISCHARGED BANK-
RUPT. 2.

—— Action for—Reference to chambers
[25 Ch. D. 66
See PRACTICE — SUPREME COURT —
CHAMBERS. 7.

—— Action for—Sale by Court—Leave to solicitor to bid—Fiduciary relation
[27 Ch. D. 424
See SOLICITOR—LIABILITIES. 6.

—— Amount of bond	- 10 P. D. 196, 198
See ADMINISTRATOR—GRANT. 1, 2.

—— Assets of bankrupt
See Cases under BANKRUPTCY—ASSETS.

—— Assets of deceased person
See Cases under EXECUTOR—ADMINIS-
TRATION.

—— Deceased insolvent debtor's estate—Transfer
to Bankruptcy Court.
See BANKRUPTCY — BANKRUPTCY ACT,
1883—*Statutes.*

—— Deceased insolvent debtor's estate—Transfer
to Bankruptcy Court	13 Q. B. D. 552 ;
[15 Q. B. D. 159 ; 29 Ch. D. 236
See BANKRUPTCY—DECEASED DEBTOR.
1, 2, 3.

—— Duty on	-	22 Ch. D 545
See REVENUE—SUCCESSION DUTY. 14

—— Grant of.
See Cases under ADMINISTRATOR.

—— Judgment against executor—Injunction
See JUDGMENT. 1.	[29 Ch. D. 557

—— Judgment for	29 Ch. D. 913
See PRACTICE — SUPREME COURT —
CHAMBERS. 10.

—— Retainer by executor
See Cases under EXECUTOR—RETAINER.

—— Retainer by heir-at-law	- 27 Ch. D. 478
See RETAINER.

—— Scotch law—Estate of Scotch testator
[10 App. Cas. 453
See SCOTCH LAW—JURISDICTION.

—— Severance of funds—Liability of trustees
[6 App. Cas. 855
See SCOTCH LAW—TRUSTEE.

ADMINISTRATION—*continued.*

—— Summons for—Suit of creditor **30 Ch. D. 291**
  See LIMITATIONS, STATUTE OF—PER-
  SONAL ACTIONS. 10.

ADMINISTRATION BOND—Married woman—
  Consent of husband **8 P. D. 16, 168**
  See ADMINISTRATOR—MARRIED WOMAN.
  1, 2.

ADMINISTRATION OF OATH—Commission to
  take evidence - **22 Ch. D. 341**
  See PRACTICE—SUPREME COURT—EVI-
  DENCE. 12.

ADMINISTRATOR :—   Col.
  I. GRANT - - - - 9
  II. LIMITED - - - - 10
  III. MARRIED WOMAN - - 11
  IV. NOMINEE OF CROWN - - 12
  V. POWERS - - - 12
  VI. WITH WILL ANNEXED - 13

I. ADMINISTRATOR—GRANT.

1. —— **Amount of Bond.**] An estate having
been partly administered and a further bond
become necessary, the Court allowed the administrator to take the grant for the amount then due to
the estate, and to give security only for double
that amount. IN THE GOODS OF HALLIWELL
                  [10 P. D. 198

2. —— **Amount of Bond — Sureties.**] The
Court will not by reason of the property being
large and the risk small dispense with sureties to
an administration bond or lessen the amount to
be secured. But it will allow the security to be
made up of any number of bonds. IN THE GOODS
OF EARLE - - **10 P. D. 196**
[*And see* IN THE GOODS OF McGOWAN, 10 P. D. 197.]

3. —— **Duchy of Cornwall — Evidence.**] On
motion for grant of letters of administration of
an intestate's effects to His Royal Highness the
Prince of Wales, as Duke of Cornwall, it is not
necessary, if the facts are sufficiently set forth in
the warrant, that they should be verified by affidavit. IN THE GOODS OF GRIFFITH **9 P. D. 63**

4. —— **English and Scotch Assets — Will
proved in Scotland only—Right of Legatee to insist
upon Proof in England.**] W. E. died possessed
of property of small value in England, and entitled under the will of J. O. E. to large assets
in Scotland, which were being duly administered
there. The executors of W. E. proved his will in
Scotland only. G. W. H., a legatee under W. E.'s
will, applied for a grant of administration of the
estate of W. E. in England, which application
was opposed by the executors :—*Held*, that the
Court is not bound to make such a grant, but that
its power is discretionary :—*Held*, also, that it not
having been shewn that the executors were not
doing their duty, there was no necessity for any
grant in this country. Application refused.—A
similar application was made by another legatee
upon the ground also that such a grant was necessary to substantiate proceedings in Chancery.—
Application refused, on its being proved that the
grant was not necessary for the suit in Chancery.
IN THE GOODS OF EWING - **6 P. D. 19**

5. —— **Executrix de son tort—Creditor.**] An
executrix who, without having taken probate,
had intermeddled in the estate of her testator,

I. ADMINISTRATOR—GRANT.—*continued.*

died possessed of property belonging to him :—
Held, after citation of her next of kin and their
non-appearance, that the representative of the
testator was entitled as a creditor to a general
grant of letters of administration of her estate.
IN THE GOODS OF MELLOR **8 P. D. 108**

6. —— **Insolvency of the Estate**—*Special
Circumstances*—20 & 21 *Vict. c.* 77, *s.* 73.] J. W.,
entitled to the property of his wife, E W., who
predeceased him, became indebted to the estate
of J. P. The estate of E. W. afterwards became
entitled to a share in the residuary estate of J. P.
—The executrix of J. W. refused to take out
letters of administration to E. W.'s estate, and a
grant was necessary to enable the creditors of
J. W. to obtain E. W.'s share of the residuary
estate in satisfaction of their debt :—The Court
granted (under s. 73 of 20 & 21 Vict. c. 77) administration of the estate of E. W. to a creditor
of J. W. IN THE GOODS OF WENSLEY **7 P. D. 13**

7. —— **Personal Estate, Proceeds of—Sale
under Settled Estates Acts.**] The proceeds of real
property sold under the Settled Estates Acts and
not yet converted into realty have not become
personal property in respect of which letters of
administration can be granted. IN THE GOODS
OF LLOYD - - **9 P. D. 65**

8. —— **Will not appointing Executors**—*Suppression of Will—Sale of Leaseholds by Administrator—Title of Purchaser.*] A grant of letters of
administration obtained by suppressing a will
containing no appointment of executors is not
void *ab initio*, and accordingly a sale of leaseholds by an administratrix, who had obtained a
grant of administration under such circumstances,
to a purchaser who was ignorant of the suppression of the will, was upheld by the Court, although the grant was revoked after the sale.—
Abram v. *Cunningham* (2 Lev. 182) distinguished.
BOXALL *v.* BOXALL - **27 Ch. D. 220**

II. ADMINISTRATOR—LIMITED.

1. —— **De bonis non**—38 *Geo.* 3, *c.* 87, *s.* 1 ;
21 & 22 *Vict. c.* 95, *s.* 18—*Creditor—Administrator out of the Jurisdiction.*] An assignee in bankruptcy of an administrator who is out of the
jurisdiction is a creditor within the meaning of
38 Geo. 3, c. 87, s. 1, and 21 & 22 Vict. c. 95,
s. 18, and as such may obtain administration de
bonis non of the intestate limited to the fund to
which the assignee is entitled. IN THE GOODS OF
HAMMOND - **6 P. D. 104**

2. —— **De bonis non** — *Administration with
Will annexed—Grant to Legatee—Citation—Justifying Security.*] The estate of a testatrix having
been administered, except as to one legacy, the
Court granted administration with will annexed
de bonis non to the legatee, without requiring
the representative of the executor or residuary
legatees to be cited, but ordered that the sureties
should justify. IN THE GOODS OF KING
                  [8 P. D. 162

3. —— **De bonis non**—*Attorney of Executor—
Further Grant de bonis non.*] A grant to the
attorney of an executor does not break the chain
of representation.—L., an attorney for the executor, obtained a grant of letters of administration
with the will annexed of a testatrix. The execu-

II. ADMINISTRATOR—LIMITEE—*continued.*

tor died leaving part of the property unadministered:—*Held,* that the executor's representative was entitled to deal with the property left unadministered of the testatrix, and that no further grant was necessary. IN THE GOODS OF DONNA MARIA VEA MURGUIA   **9 P. D. 236**

4. —— **Durante minore ætate**—*Power to sell.*] An administrator durante minore ætate has, for the time, all the powers of an ordinary administrator, including a power to sell the estate of the deceased for payment of debts. *In re* COPE. COPE *v.* COPE   -   **16 Ch. D. 49**

5. —— **Foreign Assets**—*Title of Administrator—Limited Administration granted to Attorney of Principal Administrator.*] E. having died in Ireland intestate, letters of administration were granted in Ireland to the Plaintiff. Part of his assets being in India, the Plaintiff sent out a power of attorney to F. & Co. in India, who procured letters of administration to be granted to them in India for the use and benefit of the Plaintiff, received the Indian assets, paid the Indian debts, and remitted the surplus to their agents in England. The Irish letters of administration were sealed in England:—*Held,* that the agents in England were bound to hand over the fund to the Plaintiff, and could not require the concurrence of the next of kin, they not having taken any legal proceedings to prevent the Plaintiff from receiving the assets.—Decision of Fry, J., affirmed. EAMES *v.* HACON
[**16 Ch. D. 407; 18 Ch. D. 347**

6. —— **Foreign Will**—*Will made abroad by a Foreigner—Property in this Country—Letters of Administration founded on a Foreign Decree—Proof of Persian Law.*] D. M. K., a Persian subject, was by a decree of a Persian Court declared entitled to certain property in this country. The decree, though founded partly upon a will, made no mention of it, and the Court which had custody of the will refused to give a copy of it.—The Court of Probate granted letters of administration limited to the property mentioned in a duly authenticated copy of the decree.—The Court allowed the law applicable to the case to be proved by a Persian ambassador. IN THE GOODS OF DOST ALY KHAN -   **6 P. D. 6**

7. —— **Pendente Lite**—*Surety — Guarantee Society.*] The "Guarantee Society" may be accepted as surety to a bond given by an administrator pending suit, even though the directors do not by the bond render themselves personally liable. CARPENTER *v.* QUEEN'S PROCTOR
[**7 P. D. 235**

III. ADMINISTRATOR—MARRIED WOMAN.

1. —— **Administration Bond**—*Consent of Husband.*] Since the Married Women's Property Act, 1882, when a married woman is administratrix it is not necessary that her husband should join in the administration bond. IN THE GOODS OF AYRES -   -   - **8 P. D. 168**

2. —— **Deed of Separation**—*Grant of Letters of Administration to Wife's Father.*] A husband agreed by deed of separation that if his wife died intestate her next of kin should be entitled to her property.—She died intestate, leaving separate property of which she had become possessed

III. ADMINISTRATOR—MARRIED WOMAN—*continued.*

by virtue of the deed, and the Court, notwithstanding that the husband objected, granted letters of administration to her father limited to that property. ALLEN *v.* HUMPHRYS   **8 P. D. 16**

IV. ADMINISTRATOR—NOMINEE OF CROWN.

The Act 47 & 48 Vict. c. 71, s. 2, enacts that where administration of the personal estate of any deceased person is granted to a nominee of the Crown, any proceeding by or against such nominee for the recovery of such personal estate shall be subject to the same rules (including Statutes of Limitation) as if the administration had been to next of kin of deceased.

Sect. 3 limits proceedings on the part of, or against, the Crown to recover personal estate, to the same time and rules as are now applicable in the case of a subject.

See also REAL ESTATE—*Statutes.*

V. ADMINISTRATOR—POWERS.

1. —— **Power to grant Underlease**—*Underlease with Option of Purchase—Breach of Trust.*] In dealing with the leaseholds of a testator or intestate, an executor or administrator may grant an underlease, if necessary for the due administration of the property, but cannot give an option of purchase at a future time.—An administrator granted an underlease of a leasehold estate of his intestate, with an option of purchase to the underlessee within seven years at a fixed price:—*Held* (affirming the decision of the Vice-Chancellor of the Lancaster Court), that the option of purchase was ultrà vires, and could not be supported against the next of kin, although it appeared from the evidence to be advantageous to the estate. OCEANIC STEAM NAVIGATION COMPANY *v.* SUTHERBERRY   **16 Ch. D. 236**

2. —— **Power to mortgage**—*Breach of Trust—Settlement of Accounts—Withdrawal of Authority—Notice.*] A., B., and C., as the only next of kin with D., the administrator, of their intestate father, signed a memorandum in 1872, authorizing D. to borrow, upon mortgage or otherwise as he might deem best, upon the security of certain house property, held by the intestate under an agreement for a lease to be granted on completion of repairs, such money as D. required for carrying out these matters, and to charge their respective shares with the interest.—A lease of the houses was soon afterwards granted to D. as the sole legal personal representative of the intestate, which, with the memorandum, was shortly afterwards deposited by D. as a security for his own debt with E.—In 1875 the administration accounts, shewing a balance due to D., were settled between A., B., C., and D., and D. then told A., B. and C. that he had not borrowed any money upon the security of their shares under the memorandum of 1872.—In 1877 D., who had previously mortgaged his share of the house property to E., executed a further mortgage to him of the entirety, reciting the authority of 1872. No notice was given by E. to A., B., and C., that he held any charge upon their shares under the memorandum: —*Held,* that, in the absence of any notice by E. to A., B., and C., of a charge to him of their shares by D. under the authority of 1872, the mortgage

V. ADMINISTRATOR—POWERS—continued.

of 1877, after that authority had been withdrawn by the settlement of accounts, did not affect their shares, and that they were entitled to an assignment from E. of their shares of the property comprised in the lease, which had been mortgaged by D. JONES v. STÖHWASSER　　　　16 Ch. D. 577

3. —— Power to mortgage—Leaseholds of Intestate—Repairs.] An administrator has no power to mortgage leaseholds of the intestate under leases not containing repairing covenants, in order to raise money for repairing the property.— And such a mortgage will be set aside as against a mortgagee who has notice of the purpose for which the money is raised. RICKETTS v. LEWIS
[20 Ch. D. 745

VI. ADMINISTRATOR — WITH WILL ANNEXED.

1. —— Charge of Debts—Renunciation by Executor—Power of Administrator with Will annexed to sell—22 & 23 Vict. c. 35, s. 16.] A testator directed that his debts should be paid by his executors thereinafter named, and in case his personal estate should be insufficient, he charged his real estate with the deficiency; and he appointed two persons his executors. Both the executors renounced probate, and an administrator with the will annexed was appointed:— Held, on summons taken out under the Vendor and Purchaser Act, 1874, that the administrator with the will annexed had no power to sell the real estate, either under the terms of the will or by virtue of the 22 & 23 Vict. c. 35, s. 16. In re CLAY AND TETLEY　　　　16 Ch. D. 3

2. —— Infant—Grant to the Guardian for use and benefit of Minor.] The next of kin of a minor, the universal legatee, were an uncle who was abroad, an aunt who was in poor circumstances, and another aunt who had renounced. The Court granted letters of administration with will annexed for the use and benefit of the minor to a guardian elected by her. IN THE GOODS OF GARDINER　　-　　-　9 P. D. 66

3. —— Interest — Sister —Legatee—Widow.] In a contest for administration with the will annexed the Court preferred the sister of the testator to the widow, as it appeared that the sister, as a legatee, had the larger interest in the property to be distributed. IN THE GOODS OF HOMAN
[9 P. D. 61

ADMINISTRATOR—Bankruptcy of—Conduct of action　　-　　-　　19 Ch. D. 61
See PRACTICE—SUPREME COURT—CONDUCT OF CAUSE. 1.

—— Deceased partner—Bankruptcy 16 Ch. D. 620
See BANKRUPTCY—PROOF. 18.

—— Default by—Attachment　-　10 P. D. 184
See ARREST—DEBTORS ACT. 1.

—— Husband—Wife's reversion - 25 Ch. D. 620
See HUSBAND AND WIFE—WIFE'S REVERSION. 1.

—— Option of purchasing freehold 24 Ch. D. 199
See LANDLORD AND TENANT—LEASE. 16.

ADMIRALTY—County Court—Jurisdiction.
See Cases under COUNTY COURT—JURISDICTION. 1—4.

ADMIRALTY—continued.

—— Discipline.
See ARMY AND NAVY—Statutes.

—— Jurisdiction—Action in rem—Lord Campbell's Act　9 P. D. 96; 10 App. Cas. 59
See PRACTICE — ADMIRALTY— JURISDICTION. 1.

—— Nautical assessors　-　　6 P. D. 84
See COUNTY COURT—PRACTICE. 2.

ADMISSION—By dead man against interest
[14 Q. B. D. 415
See BANKRUPTCY—PROOF. 8.

—— By master of ship—Evidence　10 P. D. 137
See PRACTICE—ADMIRALTY—EVIDENCE. 1.

—— By witness—Witness in bankruptcy
[19 Ch. D. 580
See BANKRUPTCY—EVIDENCE. 7.

ADMISSIONS IN PLEADINGS — Motion for judgment 21 Ch. D. 716; 23 Ch. D. 204;
[11 Q. B. D. 531
See PRACTICE—SUPREME COURT—MOTION FOR JUDGMENT. 1, 2, 3.

—— Liability of trustee—Payment into Court
[27 Ch. D. 251
See PRACTICE—SUPREME COURT—PAYMENT INTO COURT. 2.

ADULTERATION.

—— Article demanded— Sale of Food and Drugs Act, 1875 (38 & 39 Vict. c. 63), ss. 6, 25 — Written Warranty — Contract to supply Milk each Day for Six Months, whether a Warranty within the Act.] By s. 25 of the Sale of Food and Drugs Act, 1875, " if the defendant, in any prosecution under this Act, prove to the satisfaction of the justices that he had purchased the article in question as the same in nature, substance, and quality as that demanded of him by the prosecutor, and with a written warranty to that effect," he shall, under certain other specified conditions, be entitled to be discharged from the prosecution. Upon the hearing of an information against the Appellant for having, contrary to the provisions of the Act, sold, on the 12th of April, 1883, certain milk to the Respondent, which was not of the nature, substance, and quality demanded by him, as it contained a percentage of water, the Appellant proved that he had purchased the article in question under a written contract made with F. on the 24th of March, 1883, whereby F. agreed to sell to the Appellant eighty-six gallons of good and pure milk (each and every day) for six months, " the said milk to be delivered twice daily :" Held, that this contract did not constitute a written warranty within the meaning of s. 25 in respect of the specific article sold by the Appellant to the Respondent on the 12th of April; and therefore that the Appellant was not entitled to be discharged from the prosecution. HARRIS v. MAY　　-　　12 Q. B. D. 97

2. —— Article demanded—Sale of Food and Drugs Act, 1875 (38 & 39 Vict. c. 63), s. 6—Milk— Sale of Article not of the Nature, Substance, and Quality of the Article demanded—Prejudice of the Purchaser.] It was proved on an information under sect. 6 of the Sale of Food and Drugs Act, 1875, that the Appellant, who was an inspector under the Act, on asking the Respondent, a milk

ADULTERATION—*continued.*

seller, for "milk," was supplied by the Respondent with milk which had been skimmed, and which was, in consequence, as compared with normal milk as it comes from the cow, deficient in butter fat to an extent of 60 per cent:—*Held,* that on these facts it was not proved that any offence had been committed by the Respondent against the provisions of sect. 6 of the Sale of Food and Drugs Act, 1875. LANE *v.* COLLINS   14 Q. B. D.
[193

3. —— Article demanded—*Sale of Food and Drugs Act,* 1875 (38 & 39 *Vict. c.* 63), *s.* 6—*Sale of Article not of "nature, substance, and quality" demanded.*] The Sale of Food and Drugs Act, 1875, after reciting that it is desirable to amend the law regarding the sale of food and drugs in a pure and genuine condition, provides by sect. 6 that no person shall sell to the prejudice of the purchaser any article of food or any drug which is not of the nature, substance, and quality of the article demanded by such purchaser, under a penalty:—*Held,* that sect. 6 was not limited in its application to sales of adulterated articles, but that it applied also to cases in which the article sold was unadulterated but wholly different from that demanded by the purchaser. KNIGHT *v.* BOWERS -   14 Q. B. D. 845

4. —— Sample—*Sale of Food and Drugs Act,* 1875 (38 & 39 *Vict. c.* 63), *ss.* 13, 14—*Sale of Food and Drugs Act Amendment Act,* 1879 (42 & 43 *Vict. c.* 30), *s.* 3—*Sample of Milk procured for Analysis—Portion of Sample not delivered to Seller or his Agent.*] It is not necessary, where a sample of milk in course of delivery is procured for analysis under sect. 3 of the Sale of Food and Drugs Act Amendment Act, 1879, for the officer procuring such sample to notify to the seller or his agent his intention of having the sample analysed, or to deliver to the seller or his agent a portion of the sample in accordance with the provisions of sect. 14 of the Sale of Food and Drugs Act, 1875. ROUCH *v.* HALL   6 Q. B. D. 17

5. —— Sample—*Sale of Food and Drugs Act,* 1875 (38 & 39 *Vict. c.* 63), *ss.* 6, 12, 13, 14, 20, 21—*Private Purchaser—Public Officer—Penalty, Proceedings to recover—Notification to Seller of Intention to have Article analysed—Condition precedent.*] The provisions of sect. 14 of the Sale of Food and Drugs Act, 1875, apply to the purchase of an article by a private person as well as by one of the public officers named in the Act; so that it is a condition precedent to the right of a private purchaser to take proceedings for a penalty under the Act that he should have given to the seller the notification required by that section. PARSONS *v.* BIRMINGHAM DAIRY COMPANY
[9 Q. B. D. 172

6. —— Spirits—*Sale of Food and Drugs Act,* 1875 (38 & 39 *Vict. c.* 63), *ss.* 6, 8—*Sale of Food and Drugs Act Amendment Act,* 1879 (42 & 43 *Vict. c.* 30), *s.* 6—*Gin more than 35 Degrees under Proof.*] By sect. 6 of 42 & 43 Vict. c. 30, it is provided that "in determining whether an offence has been committed under 38 & 39 Vict. c. 63, s. 6, by selling to the prejudice of the purchaser spirits not adulterated otherwise than by the admixture of water, it shall be a good defence to prove that such admixture has not reduced the spirits more

ADULTERATION—*continued.*

than . . . . 35 degrees under proof for gin." The Appellant sold to the Respondent gin more than 35 degrees under proof, but, at the time of sale, brought to his knowledge a printed notice hanging up in the room to the effect that all spirits were sold "as diluted spirits, no alcoholic strength guaranteed":—*Held,* that although the Appellant had not a good defence under 42 & 43 Vict. c. 30, s. 6, he was not by that section deprived of any defence which he would have had under 38 & 39 Vict. c. 63. and that the sale not having been to the prejudice of the purchaser, no offence had been committed under 38 & 39 Vict. c. 63, s. 6. GAGE *v.* ELSEY -   -   -   10 Q. B. D. 518

ADULTERY — Condonation — Divorce — Scotch law   -   9 App. Cas. 205
    See SCOTCH LAW—HUSBAND AND WIFE. 1.

—— Conduct conducing to   -   9 P. D. 231;
[10 P. D. 177
    See PRACTICE—DIVORCE — MISCONDUCT OF PETITIONER. 1, 2.

—— Covenant against molestation—Separation deed -   -   14 Q. B. D. 792
    See HUSBAND AND WIFE—SEPARATION DEED. 3.

—— Cross-examination as to -   10 P. D. 175
    See PRACTICE—DIVORCE— NULLITY OF MARRIAGE. 5.

ADVANCE—By receiver in liquidation
[23 Ch. D. 75
    See BANKRUPTCY—RECEIVER. 3.

—— By trustee carrying on business
[26 Ch. D. 245
    See TRUSTEE—POWERS. 3.

—— By trustee—Estimated value 23 Ch. D. 483
    See TRUSTEE—LIABILITIES. 3.

—— To executor—Banker   16 Ch. D. 151
    See EXECUTOR—POWERS. 1.

ADVANCEMENT.

1. —— Portion—*Father and Child — Death of Father intestate — Statute of Distributions* 22 & 23 *Car.* 2, *c.* 10), *s.* 5.] A gift by a father to a son to enable the son to pay a debt:—*Held,* on the death of the father intestate, to be an "advancement by portion" of the son, within sect. 5 of the Statute of Distributions.—The opinion expressed by Jessel, M.R., in *Taylor* v. *Taylor* (Law Rep. 20 Eq. 155) dissented from. *In re* BLOCKLEY.   BLOCKLEY *v.* BLOCKLEY
[29 Ch. D. 250

2. —— Transfer into joint Names — *Trust — Intention to benefit—Claim to have Re-transfer.*] The Plaintiff, a widow, in the year 1880 caused a sum of £6000 Consols to be transferred into the joint names of herself and the Defendant, who was her godson, and in whose welfare she took great interest. This transfer was not made known to the Defendant. In 1882 the Plaintiff, then eighty-eight years old, married a second husband, and soon afterwards applied to the Defendant to re-transfer the stock into her name alone:—*Held,* upon the evidence, that the transfer was originally made with the deliberate intention of benefiting the Defendant, and not with a view to the creation of a trust. The Court

ADVANCEMENT—*continued.*

could not, therefore, compel the Defendant to re-transfer the stock. STANDING *v.* BOWRING

[27 Ch. D. 341
[Affirmed in the Court of Appeal, 31 Ch. D. 282.]

—— To children 17 Ch. D. 701; 15 Q. B. D. 300
See WILL—SATISFACTION. 1, 2.

ADVERSE POSSESSION—Acts of ownership
[6 App. Cas. 164
See COLONIAL LAW—CEYLON. 1.

—— Satisfied mortgagee - 22 Ch. D. 614
See LIMITATIONS, STATUTE OF—TRUSTS.
3.

ADVERTISEMENT—Contempt of Court
See CONTEMPT OF COURT. [17 Ch. D. 49

—— Petition—Reduction of capital 29 Ch. D. 683
See COMPANY—REDUCTION OF CAPITAL. 4.

—— Warning against infringement of patent
[28 Ch. D. 394
See PATENT—INFRINGEMENT. 5.

ADVOCATE—Words uttered in judicial proceed-ing—Slander · 11 Q. B. D. 588
See DEFAMATION—PRIVILEGE. 2.

ADVOWSON.

1. —— **Description**—*Freehold Hereditament "situate in the parish of D."—Parcels—General Words—Recitals.*] An advowson, although it is a hereditament, and as being the right of presen-tation to a church at a particular place, "does concern land at a certain place," is but a right collateral to land, and is not aptly described as "being situate at" a particular place.—Such a description, however, may pass an advowson under certain circumstances, e.g. when upon an examination of the whole instrument a clear in-tention is shewn that it shall pass, or upon evi-dence that there is no other property in that particular place capable of being disposed of by the instrument.—*Anon.* (3 Dyer, 323 b) and *Kensey v. Langham* (Cas. t. Tal. 143) discussed and re-conciled.—General words, although introduced for the purpose of sweeping into the assurance everything which has been omitted by mistake, apply primâ facie only to things ejusdem generis with those specifically enumerated.—G. J., tenant in tail in possession of manors, lands, and heredita-ments, devised by the will of J. J., and also of the advowson of Christ Church, Doncaster, appointed to somewhat similar uses by a separate devise in the same will, by a deed which recited only the devise of the manors, &c., disentailed and limited to the use of himself in fee, "All and singular the manors, lands, hereditaments and premises devised by the said will, and also all other the lands, hereditaments, and premises whatsoever, of which he was seised as tenant in tail in possession in anywise howsoever."—By a deed of resettle-ment executed the next day, after reciting that he was seised of "The several manors and here-ditaments comprised in the schedule subject to certain charges," and desired to settle "the same hereditaments" he assured to trustees in strict settlement, "All and singular the manors, mes-suages, farms, lands, and hereditaments comprised and described in the schedule," "and all other the freehold hereditaments of him the said G. J. situate in the parish of Doncaster." The sche-

ADVOWSON—*continued.*

dule contained a detailed description of the parcels, but neither in it nor the deed itself was there any reference to, or any provision applicable to the advowson. G. J. had property other than the advowson in the parish of D., and the advow-son was not subject to any charges. — It was admitted that some portions of the disentailed property had been intentionally omitted from the resettlement:—*Held*, by North, J., that the ad-vowson was included in the disentailing deed.—*Held*, by the Court of Appeal (affirming the decision of North, J.), that having regard to the recitals, the omission of parts of the property, and looking to the whole scope of the deed, the ad-vowson was not by force of the general words "all other hereditaments situate in the parish of D." included in the deed of resettlement. CROMP-TON *v.* JARRATT 30 Ch. D. 298

2. —— **Right of Presentation**—*Quare Im-pedit—Consolidated Benefice under 3 & 4 Vict. c. 113, and 26 & 27 Vict. c. 120.*] The vicarage of P. formerly consisted of two medieties, known re-spectively as the upper vicarage and the lower vicarage, the profits and spiritual charge being divided between two incumbents. There was only one parish church, and the right of patron-age and nomination to the upper vicarage was vested in the Lord Chancellor, and that of the lower in the Rev. H. F. Welch. In 1873, Welch presented himself to the lower vicarage. In 1875, he mortgaged the advowson thereof (with a power of sale) to Howes for 800*l.*, and in 1877 made a further charge upon it in favour of Howes of 250*l.*—In 1878, the Lord Chancellor, under 26 & 27 Vict. c. 120, conveyed to Welch the ad-vowson of the upper vicarage, subject to the then-existing incumbency. There was a proviso in the Act restricting the purchaser from selling the ad-vowson or next presentation until after the expi-ration of five years from the date of the purchase. In May, 1879, the incumbency of the lower vicar-age having become vacant, the two vicarages were under 3 & 4 Vict. c. 113 and an Order in Council consolidated, and the two medieties be-came in respect both of the profits and the spiritual charge one undivided benefice, of which Welch without any form of institution became the in-cumbent, in whom was vested the advowson or right of patronage and nomination of the whole undivided benefice. On the 1st of August, 1879, Welch mortgaged the advowson of the consoli-dated benefice to Howes, to secure the previous and further advances, with the usual power of sale.—In March, 1882, Howes died, leaving a widow, and having by his will devised and be-queathed his residuary real and personal estate to trustees, in trust for his wife for life, &c. In March, 1883, the executors of Howes contracted to sell the advowson of the undivided benefice to his widow, and she, in April, 1883, contracted to sell the same to one Ellison. In June, 1883, Welch died insolvent (the debt to Howes still remaining unpaid), having by his will devised and bequeathed all his real and personal estate to trustees in trust for his widow (the now Plain-tiff) for life, &c.—The Plaintiff and the executors of Howes each claimed the right to present to the undivided vicarage :—*Held*,—upon the authority

ADVOWSON—*continued.*
of *Hawkins* v. *Chappel* (1 Atk. 621) and *Briggs* v. *Sharp* (Law Rep. 20 Eq. 317),—that the right to nominate was in the Plaintiff, she being under her husband's will beneficial owner for life of his estate real and personal, and there being no indication of an intention that during her life the right to nominate should be exercised by any other person. WELCH v. BISHOP OF PETERBOROUGH
[15 Q. B. D. 432
—— Transfer during vacancy - 10 Q. B. D. 407
See ECCLESIASTICAL LAW—CLERGY. 2.

AFFIDAVIT—Agreement to take evidence by
[16 Ch. D. 100
. *See* PRACTICE—SUPREME COURT—EVIDENCE. 1.
—— Cross-examination on 21 Ch. D. 642 ; 25 Ch. D.
[297 ; 28 Ch. D. 669 ; 29 Ch. D. 711
See PRACTICE—SUPREME COURT—EVIDENCE. 2, 3, 4, 5.
—— Cross-examination on—Right to withdraw
[20 Ch. D. 126
See BANKRUPTCY—EVIDENCE. 1.
—— Description of deponent 24 Ch. D. 271
See TRUSTEE ACTS—NEW TRUSTEES. 1.
—— Evidence de bene esse 26 Ch. D. 1
See PRACTICE—SUPREME COURT—EVIDENCE. 18.
—— In reply—Irrelevancy 16 Ch. D. 594
See PRACTICE—SUPREME COURT—EVIDENCE. 6.
—— Of service—Non-production of—Dismissal of motion - 25 Ch. D. 84
See PRACTICE—SUPREME COURT—DEFAULT. 6.
—— Production of documents
See Cases under PRACTICE—SUPREME COURT—PRODUCTION OF DOCUMENTS.
—— Production of documents 8 App. Cas. 217
See PRACTICE—SUPREME COURT—INTERROGATORIES. 11.
—— Production of documents—Official liquidator - 22 Ch. D. 714
See COMPANY—LIQUIDATOR. 1.
—— Prolixity—Costs - 21 Ch. D. 835
See PRACTICE—SUPREME COURT—PRODUCTION OF DOCUMENTS. 1.
—— Prolixity—Taking off the file 26 Ch. D. 470
See PRACTICE—SUPREME COURT—STRIKING OUT PLEADINGS. 3.
—— Service of—Motion for attachment
[25 Ch. D. 64
See PRACTICE—SUPREME COURT—ATTACHMENT. 7.
—— Sworn abroad - 25 Ch. D. 769
See PRACTICE—SUPREME COURT—EVIDENCE. 9.
—— Sworn abroad — British Vice-Consul — Notarial certificate 15 Q. B. D. 332
See BANKRUPTCY—EVIDENCE. 6.
—— Taken on commission 9 P. D. 241
See EVIDENCE—GENERAL. 1.
—— Taxation of costs—Affidavit of increase
[16 Ch. D. 726
See PRACTICE—SUPREME COURT—COSTS. 4.

AFFIDAVIT—*continued.*
—— With bill of sale.
See Cases under BILL OF SALE—FORMALITIES.
—— With bill of sale 26 Ch. D. 338
See BANKRUPTCY—ACT OF BANKRUPTCY. 5.

AFRICA—Order in Council
See JURISDICTION—*Gazette.*

AFTER-ACQUIRED PROPERTY—Assignment of
[19 Ch. D. 342
See BANKRUPTCY—VOID SETTLEMENT. 1.
—— Bankruptcy—Discharged debtor 19 Ch. D.
See BANKRUPTCY—LIQUIDATION. 5. [140
—— Bill of sale.
See Cases under BILL OF SALE—OPERATION. 1-5.
—— Bill of sale—Statement of consideration
[13 Q. B. D. 794
See BILL OF SALE—FORMALITIES. 24.
—— Covenant to settle.
See Cases under SETTLEMENT—FUTURE PROPERTY.
—— Covenant to settle 9 Q. B. D. 337 ; 11 Q. B. D.
[27 ; 23 Ch. D. 712 ; 10 App. Cas. 1
See HUSBAND AND WIFE—SEPARATE ESTATE. 6, 7, 9.
—— Covenant to settle—Female infant
See ELECTION. 6. [28 Ch. D. 124
—— Insolvent Acts 20 Ch. D. 637
See INSOLVENCY.
—— Married woman - 28 Ch. D. 709
See HUSBAND AND WIFE — MARRIED WOMEN'S PROPERTY ACT. 10.
—— Remainder—Severance of joint tenancy
See JOINT TENANT. 2. [28 Ch. D. 416
—— Undischarged bankrupt - 24 Ch. D. 672
See BANKRUPTCY—UNDISCHARGED BANKRUPT. 2.
—— Will speaking from death 19 Ch. D. 432 ;
[30 Ch. D. 50
See WILL—SPEAKING FROM DEATH. 2, 3.

AGENCY CHARGES—Taxation - 30 Ch. D. 1
See SOLICITOR—BILL OF COSTS. 3.

AGENT.
See Cases under PRINCIPAL AND AGENT.
—— Bankruptcy of principal — Fraudulent transfer - - 24 Ch. D. 339
See BANKRUPTCY—ASSETS. 9.
—— Candidate for Parliament—Payment of expenses 21 Ch. D. 408
See PARLIAMENT—ELECTION. 1.
—— Evidence of agency — Acknowledgment under Statute of Limitations
[29 Ch. D. 882
See LIMITATIONS, STATUTE OF—REALTY. 1.
—— Factors' Act—Lien - 25 Ch. D. 31 ;
See FACTOR. 1, 2. [10 App. Cas. 617
—— Insolvency of—Liability of trustee
[26 Ch. D. 238
See TRUSTEE—LIABILITIES. 1.

AGENT—*continued.*

—— Knowledge of—Interrogatories
　　　[24 Ch. D. 110 ; 10 Q. B. D. 161
　See PRACTICE—SUPREME COURT—INTER-
　ROGATORIES. 5, 6.

—— London agent of solicitor—Refusal to pay
　lay client amount of debt recovered in
　action　　-　　-　8 Q. B. D. 262
　See SOLICITOR—LIABILITIES. 8.

—— Revocation of authority by notice of act of
　bankruptcy　　-　7 App. Cas. 79
　See BANKRUPTCY— MUTUAL DEALINGS.
　3.

—— Statement by—Admissibility of evidence
　See EVIDENCE—GENERAL. 4.[22 Ch.D.593

AGISTMENT—Distress—Exemption
　　　[15 Q. B. D. 457
　See LANDLORD AND TENANT—DISTRESS.
　1.

AGREEMENT—Application of funds of trade
　union—Injunction　21 Ch. D. 194
　See TRADE UNION.

—— By letters　-　　-　20 Ch. D. 705
　See SPECIFIC PERFORMANCE. 4.

—— Compromise—Local board -　22 Ch. D. 537
　See LOCAL GOVERNMENT—LOCAL AUTHO-
　RITY. 1.

—— Fraud—Rescission -　　26 Ch. D. 616
　See COMPANY—CONTRACTS. 3.

—— Grant of right of way—Holograph writing
　　　[6 App. Cas. 340
　See SCOTCH LAW — LANDLORD AND
　TENANT.

—— Lease.
　See Cases under LANDLORD AND TENANT
　—AGREEMENT.

—— Lease—Custom of country -　21 Ch. D. 18 ;
　　　[6 App. Cas. 508
　See LANDLORD AND TENANT—CUSTOM OF
　COUNTRY.

—— Lease—Disclaimer by trustee in bankruptcy
　　　[14 Q. B. D. 956
　See BANKRUPTCY—DISCLAIMER. 19.

—— Lease by mortgagor—Notice to pay rent to
　mortgagee　　-　　-　25 Ch. D. 678
　See MORTGAGE—MORTGAGEE IN POSSES-
　SION. 2.

—— Lease—Power in settlement　24 Ch. D. 624
　See SETTLEMENT—POWERS. 4.

—— Lease—Reservation of ground game
　　　[26 Ch. D. 559
　See LANDLORD AND TENANT—GROUND
　GAME.

—— Married woman—Release of jointure
　　　[8 App. Cas. 420
　See HUSBAND AND WIFE—WIFE'S CON-
　VEYANCE. 3.

—— Mutual mistake -　　-　10 App. Cas. 325
　See MISTAKE. 2.

—— Remuneration, between solicitor and his
　client.
　See SOLICITOR—BILL OF COSTS—*Sta-
　tutes.*

—— Remuneration of solicitor -　25 Ch. D. 279;
　　　[30 Ch. D. 114
　See SOLICITOR—BILL OF COSTS. 12, 23.

AGREEMENT—*continued.*

—— Sale of land.
　See Cases under VENDOR AND PUR-
　CHASER—AGREEMENT.

—— Several documents—Failure to prove one
　　　[16 Ch. D. 395
　See SPECIFIC PERFORMANCE. 1.

—— Tenant for life and remainderman 22 Ch. D.
　See SETTLEMENT—POWERS. 2.　　[128

—— To pay creditor in full　　18 Ch. D. 464
　See BANKRUPTCY—COMPOSITION. 11.

—— To settle　-　　17 Ch. D. 361, 365, n.
　See SETTLEMENT—ARTICLES. 1, 2.

—— To settle appointed fund—Fraud on power
　　　[28 Ch. D. 205
　See POWER—EXECUTION. 5.

AGRICULTURAL CUSTOM　　21 Ch. D. 18 ;
　　　[8 App. Cas. 508
　See LANDLORD AND TENANT—CUSTOM OF
　COUNTRY.

AGRICULTURAL HOLDINGS (ENGLAND) ACT,
　1883.
　See LANDLORD AND TENANT—FIXTURES
　　—*Statutes.*
　　LANDLORD AND TENANT—DISTRESS
　　—*Statutes.*
　　LANDLORD AND TENANT—YEARLY
　　TENANT—*Statutes.*
　　LANDLORD AND TENANT—IMPROVE-
　　MENTS—*Statutes.*

—— Half year's notice—Six months' notice
　　　[15 Q. B. D. 501
　See LANDLORD AND TENANT — YEARLY
　TENANT.

ALDERMAN—Disqualification—Insolvency
　　　[16 Ch. D. 143
　See MUNICIPAL CORPORATION—QUALIFI-
　CATION.

ALEHOUSE.
　See Cases under INN.

ALIEN.

—— Nationality—*Right to inherit Land in
　England—Descendants born Abroad of natural-
　born British Subject—Status of British Subject—
　Ambassador—Officer in Military Service of Crown
　abroad—25 Edw. 3, stat. 1—7 Anne, c. 5—4
　Geo. 2, c. 21, s. 1—13 Geo. 3, c. 21, s. 1.*] The
　status of natural-born British subjects, which, by
　the Acts 7 Anne, c. 5, 4 Geo. 2, c. 21, and 13
　Geo. 3, c. 21, is conferred on children and grand-
　children born abroad of natural-born British sub-
　jects, is a merely personal status, and is not by
　those Acts made transmissible to the descendants
　of the persons to whom that status is thereby
　given.—There is no foundation for the notion that
　by the common law of England the posterity of
　a natural-born British subject, though born
　abroad, must be treated as British subjects for
　ever.—The rule that the children born abroad of
　ambassadors in the service of the Crown of Eng-
　land abroad, are treated as natural-born British
　subjects, does not apply to the children born
　abroad of officers in the military service of the
　Crown in foreign parts. DE GEER *v.* STONE
　　　[22 Ch. D. 243

ALIEN—continued.

—— Infant　-　-　-　-　25 Ch. D. 56
　　See INFANT—WARD OF COURT. 2.

—— Will executed according to English law
　　See PROBATE—GRANT. 2.　[9 P. D. 130

ALIENATION—Forfeiture by　-　21 Ch. D. 278 ;
　　　　　　　　　　　　　　　[26 Ch. D. 801
　　See WILL—CONDITION. 1, 2.

ALIMONY.
　　See Cases under PRACTICE—DIVORCE—
　　ALIMONY.

—— Arrears—Mode of enforcing payment
　　See ACTION. 1.　　[13 Q. B. D. 855

—— Assignment of — Allowance to wife of
　　lunatic　-　27 Ch. D. 160
　　See LUNATIC—PROPERTY. 1.

—— Nullity of marriage—Decree nisi 9 P. D. 80
　　See PRACTICE — DIVORCE — NULLITY OF
　　MARRIAGE. 1.

—— Proof in bankruptcy for　15 Q. B. D. 239
　　See BANKRUPTCY—PROOF. 3.

—— Separation deed—Covenant not to sue for
　　greater allowance　7 P. D. 168
　　See PRACTICE—DIVORCE—SEPARATION
　　DEED. 2.

ALKALI WORKS REGULATION ACT, 1881
　　See LOCAL GOVERNMENT — PUBLIC
　　HEALTH—Statutes.

ALLOCATUR—Taxation of costs　20 Ch. D. 685
　　See BANKRUPTCY—COSTS. 1.

ALLOTMENT OF SHARES　-　8 Q. B. D. 685 ;
　　　　　　　　　　　　[23 Ch. D. 413 ; 29 Ch. D. 421
　　See COMPANY — SHARES — ALLOTMENT.
　　1, 2, 3.

ALLOTMENTS FOR THE POOR.
　　See POOR LAW—RELIEF—Statutes.

ALLOWANCE—Lunatic—Committee　20 Ch. D.
　　See LUNATIC—COMMITTEE. 1.　　[451

—— Lunatic—Poor relations　21 Ch. D. 297
　　See LUNATIC—PROPERTY. 2.

—— Lunatic—Tenant in tail in remainder
　　　　　　　　　　　　　　[20 Ch. D. 320
　　See LUNATIC—PROPERTY. 3.

—— Voluntary, to bankrupt　17 Ch. D. 70
　　See BANKRUPTCY—ASSETS. 14.

ALTERATION—Articles of association—Com-
　　pany—Power of general meeting
　　　　　　　　　　　　　　[23 Ch. D. 1
　　See COMPANY—DIRECTOR'S APPOINT-
　　MENT. 2.

—— Bank note　9 Q. B. D. 555 ; 11 Q. B. D. 84
　　See BILL OF EXCHANGE—ALTERATION.
　　2, 3.

—— Bill of exchange—Figures　10 Q. B. D. 30
　　See BILL OF EXCHANGE—ALTERATION. 1.

—— Character of property　-　28 Ch. D. 103
　　See COVENANT—BREACH. 1.

—— Easement—Light 27 Ch. D. 43 ; 29 Ch. D.
　　See LIGHT—TITLE. 1, 2.　　[155

—— Memorandum of association　30 Ch. D. 376
　　See COMPANY — MEMORANDUM AND
　　ARTICLES. 1.

ALTERATION—continued.

—— Order for production of documents—Place of
　　production　-　24 Ch. D. 376
　　See PRACTICE—SUPREME COURT—PRO-
　　DUCTION OF DOCUMENTS. 11.

—— Order of Court　-　29 Ch. D. 827
　　See PRACTICE—SUPREME COURT—JUDG-
　　MENT. 8.

—— Property—Will speaking from death
　　　　　　　　　　　　　　[30 Ch. D. 50
　　See WILL—SPEAKING FROM DEATH. 3.

—— Will—Position of signature　-　6 P. D. 100
　　See PROBATE—EXECUTION. 2.

ALTERNATIVE RATES　-　10 Q. B. D. 250 ;
　　　　　　　　　　　　　　[8 App. Cas. 703
　　See RAILWAY COMPANY—TRAFFIC MAN-
　　AGEMENT. 1.

ALTERNATIVE RELIEF—Specific performance
　　—Damages　28 Ch. D. 356
　　See SPECIFIC PERFORMANCE. 2.

AMBASSADOR—Certificate—Proof of foreign law
　　See PROBATE—GRANT. 7.　[9 P. D. 234

—— Children born abroad　-　22 Ch. D. 243
　　See ALIEN.

AMBIGUITY—Contract—Agreement for lease
　　　　　　　　　　　　　　[19 Ch. D. 233
　　See LANDLORD AND TENANT—AGREE-
　　MENT. 1.

—— Conveyance—Scotch law　8 App. Cas. 853
　　See SCOTCH LAW—CONVEYANCE. 1.

—— Misrepresentation—Pleading 9 App. Cas. 187
　　See COMPANY—PROSPECTUS. 1.

—— Specification of patent　-　29 Ch. D. 366
　　See PATENT—VALIDITY. 5.

—— Time policy　9 App. Cas. 345
　　See INSURANCE, MARINE—POLICY. 9.

—— Will　7 App. Cas. 400
　　See SCOTCH LAW—WILL.

AMENDMENT—Bankruptcy petition
　　　　　　　　　　　　　　[20 Ch. D. 289
　　See BANKRUPTCY—SECURED CREDITOR.

—— Bankruptcy petition　-　14 Q. B. D. 184
　　See BANKRUPTCY—BANKRUPTCY PETI-
　　TION. 6.

—— Bankruptcy petition　22 Ch. D. 529
　　See BANKRUPTCY—APPEAL. 5.

—— Judgment—Action against partners in name
　　of firm 11 Q. B. D. 435 ; 10 App. Cas. 680
　　See PRACTICE—SUPREME COURT—PAR-
　　TIES. 10.

—— Notice of motion—Court of Appeal
　　　　　　　　　　　　　　[25 Ch. D. 707
　　See PRACTICE—SUPREME COURT—DE-
　　FAULT. 4.

—— Order passed and entered　30 Ch. D. 239
　　See PRACTICE—SUPREME COURT—JUDG-
　　MENT. 9.

—— Order under Trustee Act　26 Ch. D. 432
　　See TRUSTEE ACTS—VESTING ORDERS. 1.

—— Parliamentary list　-　14 Q. B. D. 507
　　See PARLIAMENT—FRANCHISE. 9.

—— Particulars of objection—Patent　26 Ch. D.
　　　　　　　　　　　　　　[700 ; 10 App. Cas. 249
　　See PATENT—VALIDITY. 1.

AMENDMENT—*continued.*.

—— Particulars of objection—Patent   **17 Ch. D.**
     See PATENT—PRACTICE. 1.   [**137**

—— Pleadings.
     See Cases under PRACTICE — SUPREME
     COURT—AMENDMENT.

—— Pleadings   -   **26 Ch. D. 356**
     See SPECIFIC PERFORMANCE. 2.

—— Pleadings—Change of parties   **16 Ch. D. 121**
     See PRACTICE — SUPREME   COURT —
     PARTIES. 6.

—— Pleadings—Costs   ·   **11 Q. B. D. 627**
     See PRACTICE—SUPREME COURT—COSTS.
     5.

—— Pleadings—Patent suit   -   **17 Ch. D. 721;**
                    [**8 App. Cas. 5**
    ·*See* PATENT—INFRINGEMENT.   6.

—— Proof in bankruptcy   -   **19 Ch. D. 394;**
                   [**14 Q. B. D. 121**
     See BANKRUPTCY — SECURED CREDITOR.
     5, 12.

—— Special case   -   **22 Ch. D. 495**
     See PRACTICE—SUPREME COURT—SPE-
     CIAL CASE. 1.

—— Specification   **26 Ch. D. 105; 28 Ch. D. 148**
     See PATENT—AMENDMENT. 1, 2.

ANALYSIS—Adulteration of food—Sample
          [**6 Q. B. D. 17; 9 Q. B. D. 172**
     See ADULTERATION. 4, 5.

ANCIENT BUILDINGS—Right of support
        [**19 Ch. D. 281; 6 App. Cas. 740**
     See SUPPORT. ·2, 3.

ANCIENT MONUMENTS.

The Act 45 & 46 Vict. c. 73 (*the Ancient Monuments Protection Act, 1882*), *provides for the better
protection of ancient monuments*

Sect. 2. *The owner of any monument described
in the schedule to the Act may by deed under his
hand constitute the Commissioners of Her Majesty's
Works and Public Buildings the guardians of such
monument. Where the Commissioners have been
constituted guardians of a monument, they shall
thenceforth, until they shall receive notice in writing to the contrary from any succeeding owner not
bound by such deed as aforesaid, maintain such
monument, and shall, for the purpose of such
maintenance, at all reasonable times by themselves
and their workmen have access to such monument
for the purpose of inspecting it, and of bringing
such materials and doing such acts and things as
may be required for the maintenance thereof.*

*The owner of an ancient monument the
Commissioners are guardians to have, save as in
the Act expressly provided, the same estate, right,
title, and interest in and to such monument in all
respects as if the commissioners had not been constituted guardians thereof.*

*The expressions "maintain" and "maintenance,"
include the fencing, repairing, cleansing, covering
in, or doing any other act or thing which may be
required for the purpose of repairing any monument
or protecting the same from decay or injury.*

*The cost of maintenance is to be defrayed from
moneys to be provided by Parliament.*

Sect. 3. *Powers to Commissioners to purchase
ancient monuments.*

Sect. 4. *Any person may by deed or will give,*

ANCIENT MONUMENTS—*continued.*

*devise, or bequeath to the Commissioners any
ancient monument to which the Act applies.*

Sect. 5. *Commissioners to appoint inspectors of
ancient monuments.*

Sect. 6. *Penalty for injuring or defacing any
ancient monument :—*

    (1.) *Any sum not exceeding £5, and in addition
        thereto such sum as the Court may think
        just for the purpose of repairing any
        damage caused by the offender ; or,*

    (2.) *Imprisonment with or without hard labour
        for any term not exceeding one month.*

*The owner of an ancient monument not to be
punishable under the section in respect of any act
which he may do to such monument, except in cases
where the Commissioners have been constituted guardians of such monument, in which case the owner
is to be deemed to have relinquished his right of
ownership so far as relates to any injury or deface-
ment of such monument, and may be dealt with as
if he were not the owner.*

Sect. 7. *Offences and penalties under the Act to
be prosecuted and recovered in manner provided by
the Summary Jurisdiction Acts.*

*An appeal lies to a Court of general or quarter
sessions.*

Sect. 8. *The Commissioners to be a corporation
and have perpetual succession and a common seal,
and may purchase or acquire by gift, will, or otherwise, and hold without licence in mortmain, any
land or estate or interest in land for the purposes
of the Act; and any conveyance, appointment,
devise, or bequest of land, or any estate or interest
in land under the Act, to them not to be deemed a
conveyance, appointment, devise, or bequest to a
charitable use within the meaning of the Act relating to charitable uses.*

Sect. 9 *defines* "*owners*" *of ancient monuments
for the purposes of the Act to be :—*

    (1.) *Any person entitled for his own benefit, at
        law or in equity, for an estate in fee to the
        possession or receipt of the rents and
        profits of any freehold or copyhold land,
        being the site of an ancient monument,
        whether such land is or is not subject to
        incumbrances.*

    (2.) *Any person absolutely entitled in possession,
        at law or in equity, for his own benefit, to
        a beneficial lease of land, being the site of
        an ancient monument, of which not less
        than forty-five years are unexpired, whether
        such land is or is not subject to incum-
        brances ; but no lease shall be deemed to be
        a beneficial lease, within the meaning of
        the Act, if the rent reserved thereon exceeds
        one-third part of the full annual value of
        the land demised by such lease.*

    (3.) *Any person entitled under any existing or
        future settlement, at law or in equity, for
        his own benefit, and for the term of his
        own life, or for the life of any other person,
        to the possession or receipt of the rents and
        profits of land of any tenure, being the site
        of an ancient monument, whether subject
        or not to incumbrances, in which the estate
        for the time being subject to the trusts of
        the settlement is an estate for lives or years
        renewable for ever, or is an estate renewable
        for a term of not less than sixty years, or is*

ANCIENT MONUMENTS—*continued.*

an estate for a term of years of which not less than sixty are unexpired, or is a greater estate than any of the foregoing estates.

(4.) Any body corporate, any corporation sole, any trustee for charities, and any commissioners or trustees for ecclesiastical, collegiate, or other public purposes, entitled at law or in equity, and whether subject or not to incumbrances, in the case of freehold or copyhold land, being the site of an ancient monument, in fee, and in the case of leasehold land, being the site of an ancient monument, to a lease for an unexpired term of not less than sixty years.

Where any owner as aforesaid is a minor, or of unsound mind, or a married woman, the guardian, committee, or husband, as the case may be, of such owner, is the owner for the purpose of the Act ; but a married woman entitled for her separate use, and not restrained from anticipation, is to be treated as a feme sole for the purposes of the Act.

Every person deriving title to any ancient monument from, through, or under any owner who has constituted the Commissioners the guardians of such monument shall be bound by the deed executed by such owner for that purpose.

Sect. 10. List of scheduled monuments may be added to by Order in Council.

By sect. 11 the expression " ancient monument " includes the site of such monument and such portion of land adjoining the same as may be required to fence, cover in, or otherwise preserve from injury the monument standing on such site, also the means of access to such monument.

ANGLE OF 45°—Obstruction of light　24 Ch. D.
　　See LIGHT—OBSTRUCTION. 1.　　　[282

ANGLO-INDIAN DOMICIL—Legacy duty
　　See DOMICIL. 4.　　　[23 Ch. D. 532

ANIMALS—Domestic animals — Decoy birds—
Cruelty　　　　　　　　12 Q. B. D. 66
　　See CRUELTY TO ANIMALS.

—— Movement of, into proscribed districts —
Justices—Jurisdiction　12 Q. B. D 629
　　See CONTAGIOUS DISEASES (ANIMALS)
　　ACT.

ANNUAL VALUE—Water-rate　10 Q. B. D. 337 ;
　　　　　　　[14 Q. B. D. 529 ; 9 App. Cas. 49
　　See WATERWORKS COMPANY — WATER-
　　RATE. 3, 4.

—— Water rate—Definition.
　　See WATERWORKS COMPANY — WATER
　　RATE—*Statutes.*

ANNUITY—Abatement -　　-　27 Ch. D. 703
　　See EXECUTOR—ADMINISTRATION. 7.

—— Charge on capital or income　17 Ch. D. 167
　　See WILL—ANNUITY. 1.

—— Charged on land—Statute of Limitations
　　　　　　　　　　　[27 Ch. D. 231
　　See LIMITATIONS, STATUTE OF—REALTY.
　　3.

—— For life or perpetual　　-　19 Ch. D. 294
　　See WILL—ANNUITY. 2.

—— Gift of yearly sum free of all deduction—Income-tax　　-　21 Ch. D. 105 ;
　　　　　　　[22 Ch. D. 182, 269
　　See WILL—WORDS. 1, 2, 3.

ANNUITY—*continued.*

—— Payable to widow of deceased partner
　　　　　　　　　[25 Ch. D. 89
　　See PARTNERSHIP—CONTRACT. 1.

—— Perpetuity　　　　　　19 Ch. D. 294
　　See WILL—PERPETUITY. 2.

—— Widow—Voidable marriage　25 Ch. D. 685
　　See WILL--CONDITION. 11.

ANNULMENT OF BANKRUPTCY.
　　See Cases under BANKRUPTCY—ANNUL-
　　MENT.

ANTE-NUPTIAL DEBTS OF WIFE
　　　[8 Q. B. D. 380 ; 10 Q. B. D. 380
　　See HUSBAND AND WIFE—MARRIED WO-
　　MEN'S PROPERTY ACTS. 2, 3.

ANTICIPATION—Patent　　21 Ch. D. 720
　　See PATENT—VALIDITY. 2.

—— Restraint on
　　See Cases under HUSBAND AND WIFE—
　　SEPARATE ESTATE. 9—15.

—— Restraint on—Election　27 Ch. D. 606
　　See ELECTION. 5.

APPARENT POSSESSION—Bill of sale
　　See Cases under BILL OF SALE—APPA-
　　RENT POSSESSION.

APPEAL—Admiralty Court—Withdrawal—Cross-
appeal　-　　　　　10 P. D. 18
　　See PRACTICE—ADMIRALTY—APPEAL. 2.

—— Bankruptcy.
　　See Cases under BANKRUPTCY—APPEAL.

—— Bankruptcy—Costs　　14 Q. B. D. 936
　　See BANKRUPTCY- DISCHARGE. 4.

—— Bankruptcy—Costs -　　25 Ch. D. 266
　　See BANKRUPTCY—ANNULMENT. 3.

—— Bankruptcy—Evidence　22 Ch. D. 312
　　See BANKRUPTCY—ACT OF BANKRUPTCY.
　　18.

—— Bankruptcy—For costs　19 Ch. D. 140
　　See BANKRUPTCY—LIQUIDATION. 5.

—— Bankruptcy petition—Stay of proceedings
　　　　　　　　[14 Q. B. D. 49
　　See BANKRUPTCY — BANKRUPTCY PETI-
　　TION. 1.

—— Bankruptcy—Trustee　　17 Ch. D. 518
　　See BANKRUPTCY—TRUSTEE. 7.

—— Case stated by sessions　6 Q. B. D. 309
　　See PRACTICE — SUPREME COURT — AP-
　　PEAL. 5.

—— Chambers—Leave to appeal　-　9 P. D. 68
　　See PRACTICE—PROBATE—PLEADING.

—— Costs of　　-　16 Ch. D. 273 ; 19 Ch. D. 80 ;
　　　　　　　　　　　[29 Ch. D. 76
　　See PRACTICE—SUPREME COURT—COSTS.
　　1, 6, 45.

—— County Court.
　　See Cases under COUNTY COURT—AP-
　　PEAL.

—— Court of Passage—Leave to appeal
　　　　　　　　　[9 P. D. 12
　　See PRACTICE—ADMIRALTY—APPEAL. 1.

—— Criminal matter—Bail　-　10 Q. B. D. 378
　　See PRACTICE — SUPREME COURT — AP-
　　PEAL 9.

APPEAL—*continued.*

—— Criminal matter—Local Government Acts
　　　　　　　　　　[7 Q. B. D. 534
　　See PRACTICE—SUPREME COURT — AP-
　　PEAL. 8.

—— Criminal matter—Trial at bar — Notice of
　　motion　　　　14 Q. B. D. 667
　　See PARLIAMENT—ELECTION. 3.

—— Criminal matter—Mandamus 7 Q. B. D. 575
　　See PARLIAMENT — ELECTION COMMIS-
　　SIONERS.

—— Cross notice—Costs　　　18 Ch. D. 334;
　　　　　　　　　　[23 Ch. D. 98
　　See PRACTICE—SUPREME COURT—COSTS.
　　7, 8.

—— Discretion of Judge　　　20 Ch. D. 365
　　See PRACTICE—SUPREME COURT—TRIAL.
　　4.

—— Divorce Court—Application for new trial
　　　　　　　　　　[10 P. D. 110
　　See PRACTICE—DIVORCE—APPEAL. 2.

—— For costs.
　　See Cases under PRACTICE — SUPREME
　　COURT—APPEAL. 24—33.

—— For costs　　17 Ch. D. 772; 19 Ch. D. 17
　　See PRACTICE—SUPREME COURT—COSTS.
　　16, 17.

—— For costs　　　-　　- 18 Ch. D. 76
　　See COPYRIGHT—BOOKS. 5.

—— For costs　　　　　20 Ch. D. 611
　　See VENDOR AND PURCHASER—PURCHASE
　　WITHOUT NOTICE. 1.

—— For costs　　-　　-　　- 23 Ch. D. 278
　　See VOLUNTARY CONVEYANCE. 5.

—— Form of conveyance settled by Judge
　　　　　　　　　　[21 Ch. D. 466
　　See VENDOR AND PURCHASER—CONVEY-
　　ANCE. 1.

—— From summary jurisdiction
　　See JUSTICES—PRACTICE—*Statutes.*

—— High Court of Justice.
　　See Cases under PRACTICE — SUPREME
　　COURT—APPEAL.

—— Infants Custody Act　　　16 Ch. D. 115
　　See INFANT—CUSTODY. 2.

—— Interpleader—Judgment upon trial of issue
　　　　　　　　　　[14 Q. B. D. 377
　　See PRACTICE—SUPREME COURT—INTER-
　　PLEADER. 7.

—— Interpleader — Judge finally disposing of
　　whole matter　　　14 Q. B. D. 371
　　See PRACTICE—SUPREME COURT—INTER-
　　PLEADER. 5.

—— Interpleader—Summary decision at Cham-
　　bers　　　-　　- 14 Q. B. D. 569
　　See PRACTICE—SUPREME COURT—INTER-
　　PLEADER. 6.

—— Judgment by default -　　- 29 Ch. D. 322
　　See PRACTICE—SUPREME COURT — DE-
　　FAULT. 1.

—— Licence—Renewal　　-　12 Q. B. D. 620
　　See INN—LICENCE. 5.

—— Liquidator—Leave to appeal 21 Ch. D. 381
　　See COMPANY—COSTS. 1.

—— Local Government Board　12 Q. B. D. 142
　　See LOCAL GOVERNMENT—PRACTICE. 2.

APPEAL—*continued.*

—— Lower Canada—Imprisonment of debtor
　　　　　　　　　　[8 App. Cas. 530
　　See COLONIAL LAW—CANADA—QUEBEC.
　　2.

—— Municipal election—Special case
　　　　　　　　　　[14 Q. B. D. 548
　　See MUNICIPAL CORPORATION—ELECTION.
　　8. .

— — Notice of—Notice sent by post
　　　　　　　　　　[14 Q. B. D. 121
　　See BANKRUPTCY — SECURED CREDITOR.
　　12.

—— Order in Chambers · 　　- 19 Ch. D. 516
　　See PRACTICE — SUPREME COURT — AP-
　　PEAL. 20.

—— Order in Chambers — Enlarging time —
　　Powers of Judge　　- 6 Q. B. D. 116
　　See PRACTICE — SUPREME COURT—DE-
　　FAULT. 5.

—— Order of revivor　　-　　17 Ch. D. 767
　　See PRACTICE — SUPREME COURT —
　　CHANGE OF PARTIES. 5.

—— Poor law—Case stated under 12 & 13 Vict.
　　c. 45, s. 11　　-　　15 Q. B. D. 76
　　See POOR LAW—SETTLEMENT. 10.

—— Poor-rate—Case stated to Court of Appeal
　　12 & 13 Vict. c. 45, s. 11　12 Q. B. D. 1
　　See PRACTICE — SUPREME COURT — AP-
　　PEAL. 3.

—— Poor-rate—Case stated to quarter sessions
　　　　　　　　　　[15 Q. B. D. 451
　　See POOR-RATE—PROCEDURE. 3.

—— Privy Council—Leave to appeal
　　See Cases under PRACTICE — PRIVY
　　COUNCIL—LEAVE TO APPEAL.

—— Probate and Divorce Division　9 App. Cas.
　　　　　　　　　　[631
　　See PRACTICE—DIVORCE—APPEAL. 1.

—— Salvage—Amount of award　9 P. D. 14
　　See SHIP—SALVAGE. 7.

—— Scheme of Charity Commissioners
　　　　　　　　　　[18 Ch. D. 310
　　See CHARITY—MANAGEMENT. 3.

—— Scotch law　6 App. Cas. 251; 7 App. Cas. 49;
　　　　　　　　　　[10 App. Cas. 171
　　See SCOTCH LAW—PRACTICE. 1, 2, 3.

—— Security for costs.
　　See Cases under PRACTICE — SUPREME
　　COURT—SECURITY FOR COSTS. 9—12.

—— Staying proceedings.
　　See Cases under PRACTICE — SUPREME
　　COURT — STAYING PROCEEDINGS.
　　11—16.

—— Time for—Bankruptcy.
　　See Cases under BANKRUPTCY—APPEAL.
　　5—9.

—— Time for—Supreme Court.
　　See Cases under PRACTICE — SUPREME
　　COURT—APPEAL. 34—44.

—— Varying minutes—Notice　20 Ch. D. 130
　　See PRACTICE—SUPREME COURT—JUDG-
　　MENT. 6.

—— Winding-up order—Security for costs
　　See COMPANY—APPEAL. [23 Ch. D. 370

APPEAL—*continued.*

—— Withdrawal - - - **17 Ch. D. 23**
    See PRACTICE — SUPREME COURT — AP-
    PEAL. 23.

—— Witness—Winding-up **19 Ch. D. 118**
    See COMPANY—EVIDENCE. 2.

APPEAL COURT—Division of opinion—Previous
    decision. **9 P. D. 96**
    See PRACTICE—ADMIRALTY—JURISDIC-
    TION. 3.

—— Interpleader—Trial by jury—New trial
    [12 Q. B. D. 103
    See PRACTICE—SUPREME COURT—INTER-
    PLEADER. 4.

—— Order in Council as to.
    See COURT—STATUTES AND GAZETTE.

—— Summary jurisdiction—Order striking soli-
    tor off the rolls - **28 Ch. D. 614**;
    [12 Q. B. D. 148
    See SOLICITOR—MISCONDUCT. 1, 2.

APPEARANCE—Defendant to counter-claim
    [23 Ch. D. 685
    See PRACTICE — SUPREME COURT —
    COUNTER-CLAIM. 3.

—— Sequestration to compel - **16 Ch. D. 665**
    See BANKRUPTCY — STAYING PROCEED-
    INGS. 1.

APPLICATION FOR SHARES.
    See Cases under
    COMPANY—SHARES—ALLOTMENT.

APPOINTMENT—Power.
    See Cases under POWER—EXECUTION.

—— Power—Default of—Class when to be ascer-
    tained **24 Ch. D. 244**
    See SETTLEMENT—CONSTRUCTION. 8.

—— Power—Election - - **22 Ch. D. 555**
    See ELECTION. 1.

—— Power—Invalidity—Election **26 Ch. D. 208**
    See SETTLEMENT—CONSTRUCTION. 7.

—— Power—Testamentary power **23 Ch. D. 235**
    See CUSTOMS ANNUITY FUND.

—— Power—Will—Child of testator **26 Ch. D. 266**
    See WILL—LAPSE. 2.

APPOINTMENT OF MEMBER OF BOARD.
    [30 Ch. D. 350
    See LOCAL GOVERNMENT—LOCAL AU-
    THORITY. 15.

APPOINTMENT OF TRUSTEE—Power in settle-
    ment.
    See Cases under SETTLEMENT—POWERS.
    8—13.

—— Settled Land Act.
    See Cases under SETTLED LAND ACT—
    TRUSTEES. 1—4.

—— Trustee Acts.
    See Cases under TRUSTEE ACTS—NEW
    TRUSTEES.

APPORTIONMENT.

    1. —— Dividends—*Tenant for Life and Re-
mainderman—Investment.*] A testator after the
Apportionment Act, 1870, bequeathed £—— to
trustees, such sum to carry interest at 4½ per
cent. until the same should be paid or appropriated, upon trust, with the consent of his wife,
to invest the same in certain specified securities,
and to pay the annual income of the legacy and

APPORTIONMENT—*continued.*

the investments thereof, including in such income
the interest payable in respect of such legacy
to his wife for life, with remainders over.—
Interest was paid to the widow up to the day
when, pursuant to an order of the Court, the bequeathed sum was invested in stocks on some of
which five months' dividend had then accrued:—
Held, that the Apportionment Acts did not apply
and that the widow was entitled to the whole of
the dividends when received upon the purchased
stocks. *In re* CLARKE. BARKER *v.* PEROWNE
    [18 Ch. D. 160

    2. —— Parish Rates—*Company—Liquidation
—Public Health Act,* 1875, s. 211.] Parish rates
were assessed on the 20th of April for the ensuing
six months upon the premises of a company which
was wound up on the 22nd of the following
August, the business being subsequently carried
on by the liquidators as a going concern :—*Held*,
that there was no power to apportion these rates
under the Apportionment Act, and that there was
no change in the occupation under the Public
Health Act, since the liquidators were in possession under the direction of the Court; and, consequently, that the whole of the April rates
must be proved for in the liquidation. *In re*
WEARMOUTH CROWN GLASS COMPANY
    [19 Ch. D. 640

    3. —— Will before the Act—*Apportionment
Act,* 1870 (33 & 34 *Vict.* c. 35)—*Death of Tenant
for Life after the Act.*] A testator who died
before the Apportionment Act, 1870, came into
operation, gave the income of his residuary estate,
which included railway, preference, and ordinary
stock, to his wife for life, with remainder to his
nephews. The widow claimed under the old law
and received the entire dividends upon the railway stock which were declared and became receivable after the testator's death. On the death
of the widow the residuary legatees claimed the
whole of the railway dividends becoming payable
after the death of the widow:—*Held*, that the
executors of the widow were entitled, under the
new law, to an apportioned part of the dividends
up to her death. LAWRENCE *v.* LAWRENCE
    [26 Ch. D. 795

—— Annuities—Deficient estate **27 Ch. D. 703**
    See EXECUTOR—ADMINISTRATION. 7.

—— Business carried on after death of testator
    [26 Ch. D. 672
    See EXECUTOR—ADMINISTRATION. 1.

—— Capital and income—Conversion
    [24 Ch. D. 643, 649, n.
    See EXECUTOR—ADMINISTRATION. 5, 6.

—— Condition on severance of reversion
    See LANDLORD AND TENANT—LEASE—
    Statutes.

—— Contemporaneous securities **16 Ch. D. 211,**
    See MORTGAGE—CONTRACT. 4, 5. **[214, n.**

—— Costs - - **26 Ch. D. 465**
    See PRACTICE—SUPREME COURT—COSTS.
    27.

—— Costs—Administration action **19 Ch. D. 552**
    See EXECUTOR—ACTIONS. 11.

—— Costs—Appeal **18 Ch. D. 334**; **23 Ch. D. 98**
    See PRACTICE—SUPREME COURT—COSTS.
    7, 8.

APPORTIONMENT—*continued.*

—— Costs—Claim and counter-claim
　　　　　　　　　　[23 Ch. D. 377
　　See PRACTICE—SUPREME COURT—COSTS.
　　10.

—— Costs—Mortgage suit　-　27 Ch. D. 679
　　See MORTGAGE—FORECLOSURE. 5.

—— Costs—Patent suit　-　29 Ch. D. 366
　　See PATENT—PRACTICE. 3.

—— Gift to charity—Mortmain　29 Ch. D. 947
　　See CHARITY—MORTMAIN. 5.

—— Locke King's Act—Mixed fund　16 Ch. D.
　　See WILL—EXONERATION. 2.　　[322

—— Profit and loss—Settlement of business
　　See TENANT FOR LIFE.　[26 Ch. D. 588

—— Purchase-money—Leaseholds for lives
　　　　　　　　　　[18 Ch. D. 624
　　See LEASEHOLD—RENEWABLE LEASE. 3.

—— Rent—Assignment of term　10 Q. B. D. 48
　　See LANDLORD AND TENANT—ASSIGN-
　　MENT. 2.

—— Rent—Winding-up of company　17 Ch. D.
　　See COMPANY—DISTRESS. 1.　　[161

—— Rent-charge—Release of part　14 Q. B. D.
　　See RENT-CHARGE.　　　　[318

—— Salvage　-　-　-　8 P. D. 24
　　See SHIP—SALVAGE. 3.

—— Securities for bills of exchange 26 Ch. D. 755 ;
　　　　　　　　　　[29 Ch. D. 813
　　See BILL OF EXCHANGE—SECURITIES FOR.
　　4.

—— Void legacy—Mortmain　16 Ch. D. 173
　　See CHARITY—MORTMAIN. 1.

APPRENTICE.

1. —— Place of Performance — *Contract of Apprenticeship.*] A deed of apprenticeship contained the usual provision that the master should teach the apprentice, but no express provision as to the place where the contract was to be performed by the master :—*Held,* that no stipulation could be implied that it was to be performed at the place where at the time of its execution the master carried on business and the parties to the deed resided. ROYCE *v.* CHARLTON　8 Q. B. D. 1

2. —— Place of Performance — *Contract of Apprenticeship—Change of Locality of Business—Unlawful Command—Outdoor Apprentice—Division of Business.*] The Plaintiff was bound apprentice to the Defendants and their partners and successors in business in the trade of an engineer; and his father covenanted to provide him with board, lodging, and other necessaries. At the date of the indenture the business was carried on by the former Defendants in London, where also the father of the apprentice resided, but there was no stipulation in the indenture as to the place where the business should be carried on. Before the term of the apprenticeship expired the Defendants' partnership was dissolved and two firms established, one in London consisting of two of the Defendants, and the other at Derby consisting of the other two; the manufacturing part of the old business being carried on at Derby and the selling part in London. The Defendants called on the Plaintiff to attend at

APPRENTICE—*continued.*

the place of business at Derby :—*Held,* that there was an implied stipulation that the contract was to be performed at the place where the business was carried on and the parties resided at the date of the indenture ; and that the direction to the apprentice to go to Derby was an unreasonable command which he was not bound to obey.—*Held,* also, that as the business was not carried on in its entirety by either of the two new firms, neither of them was the successor of the original firm or entitled to the services of the apprentice. —*Royce* v. *Charlton* (8 Q. B. D. 1) overruled. EATON *v.* WESTERN　·　-　9 Q. B. D. 636

—— Contract not for benefit of infant — Employers and Workmen Act, 1875
　　　　　　　　　　[12 Q. B. D. 352
　　See INFANT—CONTRACTS. 1.

APPRENTICE FEES—Charity scheme
　　　　　　　　　　[18 Ch. D. 310
　　See CHARITY—MANAGEMENT. 3.

APPROPRIATION OF PAYMENTS 18 Ch. D. 449
　　See MORTGAGE—POWERS. 6.

—— Guarantee　　　25 Ch. D. 692
　　See PRINCIPAL AND SURETY—LIABILITY.
　　2.

APPROPRIATION OF SECURITIES.
　　See Cases under BILL OF EXCHANGE—
　　SECURITIES FOR.

I. ARBITRATION—AWARD.

1. —— Enlargement of Time—*Common Law Procedure Act, 1854* (17 & 18 *Vict.* c. 125), s. 15.] By a submission in writing the time within which the award was to be made was fixed at one month. The submission contained no power to enlarge the time. The award was in fact made after the expiration of the month :—*Held,* that the Court had power subsequently to the making of the award to enlarge the time under sect. 15 of the Common Law Procedure Act, 1854. MAY *v.* HARCOURT　-　13 Q. B. D. 688

2. —— Setting aside—*Objections to be specified—Common Law Procedure Act, 1852—Reg. Gen. Hil. Term, 1853, r.* 169.] A notice of motion in the Chancery Division to set aside the award of an arbitrator should specify the grounds of objection, by analogy to the practice under the Common Law Procedure Act, 1852 : Reg. Gen. Hil. Term, 1853, r. 169: an objection on "good grounds" being insufficient. MERCIER *v.* PEPPERELL　-　-　-　19 Ch. D. 58

3. —— Setting aside—*Time—Notice of Motion —9 & 10 Will.* 3, c. 15, *s.* 2.] An action having been referred to arbitration the award was published on the 14th of July. On the 24th of November (being the last day but one of the old Michaelmas Term) the Defendants moved the Court to set aside the award, but the Court refused the application on the ground that notice of motion had not been given to the Plaintiff as required by Rules of Supreme Court, 1875,

I. ARBITRATION—AWARD—*continued.*

Order LIII., rules 3 & 4. The Defendants afterwards on the same day served on the Plaintiff a notice that on the 27th of November they would move the Court to set aside the award :—*Held*, on the authority of *In re Corporation of Huddersfield and Jacomb* (Law Rep. 17 Eq. 476 ; 10 Ch. 92) that the service of notice of motion on the 24th of November was a complaint made in the Court before the last day of the next term after the publication of the award within 9 & 10 Will. 3, c. 15, s. 2, although no affidavit was filed before the last day, as had been done in that case. SMITH *v.* PARKSIDE MINING COMPANY

[6 Q. B. D. 67

II. ARBITRATION—COSTS.

"Costs of Reference " — *Award* — *Costs of Award.*] Power, in a submission to arbitration, over the " cost of the reference," includes power to award the costs of the award. *In re* AN ARBITRATION BETWEEN WALKER & SON, AND BROWN

[9 Q. B. D. 434

III. ARBITRATION—STAYING PROCEEDINGS.

Jurisdiction—*Injunction to restrain proceeding with Arbitration—Judicature Act, 1873, s. 25, sub-s. 8.*] The Judicature Act, 1873, sect. 25, sub-sect. 8, has given no power to the High Court to issue an injunction in a case in which no Court before that Act had power to give any remedy whatever.—Therefore the High Court has no jurisdiction to issue an injunction to restrain a party from proceeding with an arbitration in a matter beyond the agreement to refer, although such arbitration proceeding may be futile and vexatious :—*Semble*, per Brett, L.J., that the Judicature Act, 1873, has dealt only with procedure, and not with jurisdiction at all, and that if no Court had power to issue an injunction before that Act, the High Court has no such power now. NORTH LONDON RAILWAY COMPANY *v.* GREAT NORTHERN RAILWAY COMPANY

[11 Q. B. D. 30

IV. ARBITRATION—SUBMISSION.

1. —— Jurisdiction—*West Kent Main Sewerage Act, 38 & 39 Vict. c. clxiii.—Construction of sect. 93.*] The West Kent Sewerage Board is incorporated by a local Act of 38 & 39 Vict. c. clxiii., and by sect. 93 it is enacted that, if any difference arises between the board on the one hand and any constituted authority or person on the other hand, or between any two or more constituted authorities, or between any constituted authority and any parish or person, respecting any assessment of a main sewer rate, or any determination of the board, or any controversy or other matter under the Act, the same shall by virtue of the Act stand referred for decision to the Local Government Board, whose decision thereon and respecting the costs of the reference shall be final and binding.—A dispute having arisen between the West Kent Sewerage Board and the Bexley Local Board respecting a claim made by the local board against the sewerage board for compensation for damage done to the highways, &c., of the district, the disputants with the consent of the Local Government Board, stated a case for the opinion of this Court :—*Held*, that it was not competent to them to do so, the

IV. ARBITRATION—SUBMISSION—*continued.*

Local Government Board being by sect. 93 constituted the tribunal whose decision on the matter was to be final and binding, and this not being a submission to arbitration within sect. 5 of the Common Law Procedure Act, 1854. BEXLEY LOCAL BOARD *v.* WEST KENT SEWERAGE BOARD

[9 Q. B. D. 518

2. —— Revocation—*Appointment of Arbitrator by one Party—Common Law Procedure Act, 1854 (17 & 18 Vict. c. 125), s. 13—Revocation of Authority.*] Where there is an agreement to refer a dispute to two arbitrators, one to be appointed by each party, but no agreement to make the submission a rule of Court, and, one of the parties having failed to appoint an arbitrator, the other party, by virtue of s. 13 of the Common Law Procedure Act, 1854, appoints his arbitrator to act as sole arbitrator, the authority of such arbitrator may be revoked by either party before an award is made. FRASER *v.* EHRENSPERGER 12 Q. B. D. 310

3. —— Rule of Court—*Action—Reference to Arbitration—Enforcing Award.*] Where an action has been referred to an arbitrator by the Chancery Division it is not necessary to make the award a rule of Court before an order can be made founded on the award. JONES *v.* WEDGEWOOD

[19 Ch. D. 56

See also *In re* FORREST. BURROWES *v.* FORREST.

[19 Ch. D. 57, n.

4. —— Rule of Court—*Agreement to appoint Valuers—Landlord and Tenant—Valuation on Expiration of Tenancy—Common Law Procedure Act, 1854 (17 & 18 Vict. c. 125), s. 17.*] An agreement between landlord and tenant for the letting of a farm provided, that the tenant should be paid at the expiration of the tenancy the usual and customary valuation, as between outgoing and incoming tenant, in the same manner as he paid on entering the premises. And it was thereby mutually agreed by and between the parties thereto, that, when any valuation of the covenants should be made between the tenant and the landlord, or his incoming tenant, the persons making such valuation should take into consideration the state, condition, and usage of the farm, and, if not left in a proper and creditable state, should determine what sum of money should be paid to the landlord as compensation therefor, and should deduct such sum from the amount of the valuation. On the expiration of the tenancy, there being no incoming tenant, the landlord and tenant respectively appointed a valuer. The valuers could not agree upon the amount of the valuation, and they appointed an umpire, who held a sitting and heard witnesses, and then made and published an award in writing. The tenant, with the view of obtaining an order remitting the matters in dispute to the umpire for reconsideration, applied for an order to make the submission to arbitration contained in the agreement, together with the appointment of arbitrators and umpire, a rule of court, under s. 17 of the Common Law Procedure Act, 1854 :—*Held*, that the agreement did not contain any submission to arbitration, but that it provided only for the appointment of valuers, and that it could not, therefore, be made

IV. ARBITRATION—SUBMISSION—continued.
a rule of court.—*In re Hopper* (Law Rep. 2 Q. B. 367) explained and distinguished. *In re* DAWDY
[15 Q. B. D. 426

ARBITRATION—Building society 23 Ch. D. 103;
[9 App. Cas. 260
See BUILDING SOCIETY. 1, 2.

—— Clause of—Separation deed   18 Ch. D. 670
See HUSBAND AND WIFE—SEPARATION
DEED. 1.

—— Compensation under Public Health Act
[11 Q. B. D. 735; 9 App. Cas. 595
See LOCAL GOVERNMENT — COMPENSA-
TION. 1.

—— Costs—Event   14 Q. B. D. 321, 341
See PRACTICE—SUPREME COURT—COSTS.
13, 42.

—— Excess of jurisdiction—Sale note
[13 Q. B. 361
See PRINCIPAL AND AGENT—AGENT'S
LIABILITY. 2.

—— Lands Clauses Act -   - 30 Ch. D. 553
See LANDS CLAUSES ACT—COMPULSORY
POWERS. 6.

—— Production of documents   23 Ch. D. 353
See PRACTICE—SUPREME COURT—PRO-
DUCTION OF DOCUMENTS. 2.

—— Reconstruction of company—Inspection of
books   -   -   26 Ch. D. 620
See COMPANY—RECONSTRUCTION.

—— Railway company -   - 17 Ch. D. 493
See RAILWAY COMPANY—RAILWAYS RE-
GULATION ACTS. 1.

—— Stay of proceedings   - 9 Q. B. D. 188
See PRACTICE—SUPREME COURT—STAY-
ING PROCEEDINGS. 4.

—— Witness out of jurisdiction — " Trial " —
Evidence   -   - 12 Q. B. D. 39
See EVIDENCE—WITNESS. 1.

ARBITRATOR—Attendance of witness before
[17 Ch. D. 787
See PRACTICE—SUPREME COURT—EVI-
DENCE. 7.

—— Dwellings Improvement Act   25 Ch. D. 78
See LABOURERS' DWELLINGS ACTS. 1.

ARCHITECT—Undischarged bankrupt—Personal
earnings -   - 17 Ch. D. 768
See BANKRUPTCY—UNDISCHARGED BANK-
RUPT. 4.

ARMS—Royal Arms.
See PATENT—GAZETTE.

ARMY AND NAVY.
The Act 44 & 45 Vict. c. 57 (the Regulation of
the Forces Act, 1881), amends (in part) the Army
Discipline and Regulation Act, 1879, and other
enactments respecting the regulation of Her
Majesty's Forces.
The Act 44 & 45 Vict. c. 58 (the Army Act,
1881), as amended by 45 & 46 Vict. cc. 7 and 48
and continued by 46 & 47 Vict. c. 6, consolidate
the Army Discipline and Regulation Act, 1879,
and the subsequent Acts amending the same.
Artillery or Rifle Ranges.] By 43 & 49 Vict.

ARMY AND NAVY—continued.
c. 36, a Secretary of State may make by-laws for
Government, or Volunteer Corps, ranges.
Conveyance by Railway.] See 46 & 47 Vict.
c. 34, s. 6.
Militia.] The Act 45 & 46 Vict. c. 49 (the
Militia Act, 1882) repeals the Militia (Voluntary
Enlistment) Act, 1875, and re-enacts the same with
such modifications as are rendered necessary by
the passing of the Regulation of the Forces Act,
1881, and the Army Act, 1881.
Militia Ballot Expenses.] The Act 48 & 49
Vict. c. 59, continues the Act 28 & 29 Vict. c. 46,
until the 31st Dec. 1886.
Militia Storehouses.] The Act 45 & 46 Vict.
c. 12 (the Militia Storehouse Act, 1882) amends
the law relating to the application of moneys
arising from the sale of militia storehouses.
Navy.] The Act 47 & 48 Vict. c. 39 (Naval
Discipline Act, 1884) amends the Naval Discipline
Act, 1866.
The Act 47 & 48 Vict. c. 46 (Naval Enlistment
Act, 1884) amends the Naval Enlistment Act, 1853.
Pay and Pensions.] The Act 47 & 48 Vict. c. 55
makes further provision with regard to the pensions of soldiers, and to the pay and pensions of
the yeomanry.
Sect. 6 directs that certain penalties and sums
payable under the Yeomanry Act, 1804 (44 Geo. 3,
c. 54) may be enforced under the Summary Juris-
diction Acts.
Reserve Forces.] The Act 45 & 46 Vict. c. 48
(the Reserve Forces Act, 1882) repeals divers enactments and consolidates the Acts relating to the
Reserve Forces.
Volunteers.] Order of 14th April, 1884, amending Order of 31st July, 1880, relative to the efficiency of Volunteers under the Volunteer Act, 1863
[L. G. 1884, p. 1749
Order of 12th August, 1884, amending same
[L. G. 1885, p. 3834

—— Military Law—Habeas Corpus—Canteen-
Steward—Army Act, 1881, 44 & 45 Vict. c. 58,
s. 176, sub-s. 4.] A canteen-steward appointed by
the commanding officer of the district, acting
under a committee consisting of three officers,
and having no interest in the profits of the canteen, but receiving such pay or allowance as the
committee may think fit to award him, and being
liable to dismissal at the pleasure of the committee, though performing no military duty,
wearing no uniform, bearing no arms, and having
free ingress and egress at his pleasure to and
from the barracks,—is still a person subject to
military law within s. 176, sub-s. 4, of the Army
Act, 1881. In re FLINT   15 Q. B. D. 488

—— Domicil of British subject -   30 Ch. D. 165
See DOMICIL.

—— Officer's commission—Charge on
[19 Ch. D. 17
See MORTGAGE—PRIORITY. 12.

ARMY AGENT—Notice to—Assignment of money
payable on officer's retirement
[19 Ch. D. 17
See PRACTICE — SUPREME COURT—AP-
PEAL. 30.

—— Value of commission—Lien—Set-off
See SET-OFF. 1.   [17 Ch. D. 520

ARRANGEMENT — Bankruptcy — Approval of Court—Discretion of Registrar
[15 Q. B. D. 213
See BANKRUPTCY—SCHEME OF ARRANGEMENT. 2.

—— Dismissal of petition—"Sufficient cause"
[15 Q. B. D. 399
See BANKRUPTCY—RECEIVER. 8.

—— Preference of creditor—Fraud 15 Q. B. D. 605
See BANKRUPTCY—FRAUDULENT PREFERENCE. 2.

ARREARS — Alimony — Mode of enforcing payment - - - 13 Q. B. D. 855
See ACTION. 1.

—— Tithe rent-charge - 30 Ch. D. 84
See TITHES.

ARREST :—　　　　　　　　　Col.
  I. DEBTORS ACT　　　　　　　　39
  II. NE EXEAT REGNO　　　　　　40

I. ARREST—DEBTORS ACT.

1. —— Default by Administratrix — *Attachment—Debtors Act, 1869.*] Letters of administration had been granted to the widow of a deceased person upon the suggestion of intestacy, and she had received a sum of money, part of the deceased's property. The letters of administration were subsequently called in in an action propounding a will of the deceased, and in that action she was ordered to pay the sum of money to the administrator pending suit, which order she had not obeyed :—*Held*, that she was not protected by the Debtors Act, 1869, and therefore was liable to attachment. TINNUCHI v. SMART　　10 P. D. 184

2. —— Divorce—*Wife's Costs — Security — Debtors Act, 1869.*] Notwithstanding the provisions of the Debtors Act, 1869, a husband is liable to attachment if he does not find security for his wife's costs of suit. LYNCH v. LYNCH
[10 P. D. 183

3. —— Judgment Debt—*Commitment Order—Arrest of Debtor—Payment under Protest—Title of Trustee to Money paid—Bankruptcy Act, 1883, ss. 9, 121—County Court Rules, 1884, rr. 1-4.*] After a commitment order had been issued by the Mayor's Court in London against a judgment debtor for default in payment of an instalment of the judgment debt, a receiving order was made against him under s. 9 of the Bankruptcy Act, 1883 :—*Held*, that the commitment order was not a process for contempt of Court, but to enforce payment of a debt provable in the bankruptcy, and that after the making of the receiving order the debtor was privileged from arrest. *In re* RYLEY. *Ex parte* THE OFFICIAL RECEIVER　15 Q. B. D. 329

4. —— Means to pay—*Committal—32 & 33 Vict. c. 62, s. 5, sub-s. 2.*] The Plaintiff moved to commit the Defendant for default in payment of a judgment debt of £29 for goods supplied to him, the application being supported by an affidavit that the Defendant kept up a large establishment, and was to all appearance a man of means. The Defendant made an affidavit stating that he was an undischarged bankrupt, had no money, and was unable to pay the Plaintiff's demand, and that his wife's property was settled to her separate use   Stephen, J., made an order

I. ARREST—DEBTORS ACT—*continued.*

committing the Defendant for six weeks, or until payment, and this order was affirmed by a Divisional Court. The Defendant appealed, and filed a further affidavit shewing that he was living in a very small way, and that the expenses of the establishment were all paid by his wife out of her separate estate. The Court of Appeal being satisfied that the Defendant had no means of payment discharged the order for committal.—*Harper* v. *Scrimgeour* (5 C. P. D. 366), and the observation of James, L.J., in *Esdaile* v. *Visser* (13 Ch. D. 421) observed upon.　CHARD v. JERVIS
[9 Q. B. D. 178

5. —— Means to pay—*Judgment Summons—Order to pay Debt by Instalments—Money—arising from Gift—32 & 33 Vict. c. 62, s. 5, sub-s. 2.*] Per Cotton and Lindley, L.JJ. :—For the purpose of determining whether a judgment debtor has had "the means to pay" the judgment debt, with the view of making an order for his committal under sub-sect. 2 of sect. 5 of the Debtors Act, 1869, money derived from a gift may be taken into account. It is not necessary that the "means to pay" should have been derived from the debtor's earnings, or from a fixed income. EX PARTE KOSTER. IN RE PARK
[14 Q. B. 597

II. ARREST—NE EXEAT REGNO.

—— Service—*Debtors Act, 1869 (32 & 33 Vict. c. 62), ss. 4, 6.*] An order was made that a trustee should within seven days after service of the order pay to his cestui que trust, the Plaintiff, a sum found due to him by the Chief Clerk's certificate. The Plaintiff could not find the trustee so as to serve the order, and applied for a writ of ne exeat on the ground that the trustee was about to go out of the jurisdiction :—*Held*, that the case did not fall within the third exception in sect. 4 of the Debtors Act, 1869, the trustee not being in default, as the order only directed payment after service and had not been served, and that as the debt was not now due and payable a writ of ne exeat could not be granted. COLVERSON v. BLOOMFIELD - - - 29 Ch. D. 341

ARREST—Debtor—Bankruptcy Act, 1883.
See BANKRUPTCY—STATUTES.

—— Debtor—Bankruptcy Act, 1883
[30 Ch. D. 480
See BANKRUPTCY—RECEIVER. 10.

—— Debtors Act—Married woman
[14 Q. B. D. 973
See HUSBAND AND WIFE — SEPARATE ESTATE. 11.

—— Ship — Defendant's costs — Commission on bail - - - 10 P. D. 158
See PRACTICE—ADMIRALTY—SALVAGE. 6.

ARTICLED CLERK—Death of solicitor—Return of premium - 28 Ch. D. 409
See SOLICITOR—ARTICLED CLERK.

ARTICLES OF ASSOCIATION　25 Ch. D. 103
See COMPANY—FORMATION.

—— 22 Ch. D. 349 ; 26 Ch. D. 107 ; 30 Ch. D. 376
See COMPANY — MEMORANDUM AND ARTICLES. 1, 2, 3.

ARTICLES OF ASSOCIATION—*continued.*

—— Alteration of—Power of general meeting
[23 Ch. D. 1
See COMPANY — DIRECTOR'S APPOINT-
MENT. 2.

—— Alteration of—Reduction of capital
[27 Ch. D. 268
See COMPANY—REDUCTION OF CAPITAL.
2.

—— Payment of dividends in proportion to
shares - - 8 App. Cas. 65
See COMPANY—DIVIDENDS. 3.

ARTICLES OF PARTNERSHIP.
See Cases under PARTNERSHIP — CON-
TRACT.

ARTIFICIAL STREAM　　　27 Ch. D. 122
See WATERCOURSE. 1.

ARTILLERY RANGE
See ARMY AND NAVY—*Statutes.*

ARTIZANS' DWELLINGS ACTS
See Statutes and Cases under LABOURERS'
DWELLINGS ACTS.

ASSAULT—Judicial separation— Jurisdiction of
magistrates - - 10 P. D. 172
See HUSBAND AND WIFE — JUDICIAL
SEPARATION.

ASSEMBLY—Unlawful—Meeting for lawful pur-
pose - - 9 Q. B. D. 308
See CRIMINAL LAW—UNLAWFUL AS-
SEMBLY.

ASSESSMENT COMMITTEE—Poor-rate—Appeal
[15 Q. B. D. 451
See POOR-RATE—PROCEDURE. 3.

ASSESSORS—Nautical—Duty of—County Court
[6 P. D. 84
See COUNTY COURT—PRACTICE. 2.

ASSETS—Bankruptcy.
See Cases under BANKRUPTCY—ASSETS.

—— Executor.
See Cases under EXECUTOR—ADMINIS-
TRATION.

—— Partly in England, partly in Scotland
[10 App. Cas. 453
See SCOTCH LAW—JURISDICTION.

ASSIGNMENT—After-acquired property—Bankruptcy - 22 Ch. D. 782
See BANKRUPTCY—ASSETS. 6.

—— All debtor's property.
See Cases under BANKRUPTCY—ACT OF
BANKRUPTCY. 1—5.

—— Bill of costs　28 Ch. D. 719; 12 Q. B. D. 518
See SOLICITOR—BILL OF COSTS. 4, 5.

—— Bill of sale—Transfer - 6 Q. B. D. 676
See BILL OF SALE—REGISTRATION. 9.

—— Book debts of bankrupt - 21 Ch. D. 868
See BANKRUPTCY—ASSETS. 16.

—— Debt
See Cases under ASSIGNMENT OF DEBT.

—— Debt—Building contract—Relation back of
trustee's title - - 14 Q. B. D. 310
See BANKRUPTCY—ASSETS. 10

—— Equity of redemption—Consolidation of
mortgages - 19 Ch. D. 630
See MORTGAGE—CONSOLIDATION. 3.

ASSIGNMENT—*continued.*

—— For benefit of creditors　　22 Ch. D. 797
See BANKRUPTCY—ACT OF BANKRUPTCY.
13.

—— Future crops—Surrender of premises—Expense of cultivation - 11 Q. B. D. 808
See BILL OF SALE—OPERATION. 1.

—— Lease—Indemnity · 29 Ch. D. 254;
[9 Q. B. D. 366; 10 Q. B. D. 48
See LANDLORD AND TENANT—ASSIGN-
MENT. 1, 2, 3.

—— Mortgage—Right of mortgagor to call for
assignment - - 20 Ch. D. 724
See MORTGAGE—REDEMPTION. 2.

—— Patent - 17 Ch. D. 423; 19 Ch. D. 246
See PATENT—ASSIGNMENT. 1, 2.

—— Pendente lite—Amendment　16 Ch. D. 121
See PRACTICE — SUPREME COURT —
PARTIES. 6.

—— Property of company—Official liquidator
[17 Ch. D. 234
See COMPANY—LIQUIDATOR. 3.

—— Share of partnership　　6 App. Cas. 64
See SCOTCH LAW—PARTNERSHIP.

—— Share of testator's estate—Retainer by executor - 16 Ch. D. 202
See EXECUTOR—RETAINER. 3.

—— Voluntary—Furniture　　17 Ch. D. 416
See VOLUNTARY CONVEYANCE. 1.

—— Wife's reversion—Bankruptcy of husband
[23 Ch. D. 344
See HUSBAND AND WIFE—WIFE'S REAL
ESTATE. 3.

ASSIGNMENT OF DEBT.

1. —— Balance at Bank—*Notice of Assignment after Assignor's Death—Judicature Act,* 1873
(36 & 37 *Vict.* c. 66), s. 25, *sub-s.* 6.] By a deed
of assignment all moneys then or thereafter to be
standing to the credit of the assignor at a bank
were assigned to a trustee, on trust for the assignor
for his life, and after his death on other trusts.
At the date of the assignment the assignor's
balance at the bank was £48, at his death it was
£217. Notice of the assignment was not given
to the bank until after the assignor's death. In
an action by the trustee against the bank to recover the balance of £217:—*Held,* that the bank,
being a stranger to the assignment, could not set
up the defence that it was voluntary and therefore invalid in equity; that the balance at the
time of the assignor's death was a debt or legal
chose in action within the meaning of sect. 25,
sub-s. 6 of the Judicature Act, 1873; that notice
after the death of the assignor was sufficient; and
that the Plaintiff was entitled to recover. WALKER
v. BRADFORD OLD BANK　　12 Q. B. D. 511

2. —— Mortgage—*Charge—Judicature Act,*
1873 (36 & 37 *Vict.* c. 66), s. 25, *sub-s.* 6.] By a
mortgage deed in 1877 premises were assigned to
secure repayment of £1380 due from the mortgagor
to the mortgagee with interest, and the mortgagor
covenanted to pay debt and interest six months
thence. The mortgagee in 1878 deposited the
deed with his bankers as security for the balance
of his banking account, and by deed in 1879 assigned and transferred to them the sum of £1380
due on the mortgage deed, and all interest

ASSIGNMENT OF DEBT—*continued.*

thenceforth to become due, and all securities for principal and interest and all benefit and advantage thereof, and all his right, title, interest, and property therein to secure repayment to the bankers of £939 then due to them on his banking account, and any further sum not exceeding £1200 which might thereafter become due to them from him, with a proviso for reconveyance of the premises if the assignor should on a day named pay them back the £939 and any further sum not exceeding £1200 which might be due, with interest. The bank having given notice in writing of this assignment to the mortgagor sued him for £984 then due on the assignor's banking account:—*Held*, by Pollock, B., that the assignment to the bank by the deed of 1879 was not an "absolute assignment (not purporting to be by way of charge only)" within the Judicature Act, 1873 (36 & 37 Vict. c. 66), s. 25, sub-s. 6, and that the action could not be maintained. NATIONAL PROVINCIAL BANK OF ENGLAND *v.* HARLE　　　6 Q. B. D. 626

3. —— Mortgage — *Judicature Act,* 1873 (36 & 37 Vict. c. 66), s. 25, *sub-s.* 6.] A deed by which debts were assigned to the Plaintiff upon trust that he should receive them, and out of them pay himself a sum due to him from the assignor, and pay the surplus to the assignor:—*Held*, an "absolute assignment (not purporting to be by way of charge only)" within the Judicature Act, 1873, s. 25, sub-s. 6, and that the Plaintiff might sue in his own name for the debts. BURLINSON *v.* HALL　　　- 12 Q. B. D. 347

4. —— Order for Payment — *Equitable Assignment — Specific Fund.*] An order by a creditor to his debtor to pay a sum of money to a third person is not an equitable assignment unless it specifies the fund or debt out of which the payment is to be made. Thus, where *A.*, a builder, being a debtor to the Plaintiff, *P.*, but a creditor of the Defendant, handed to *P.* the following order signed by *A.* and addressed to the Defendant, who received due notice thereof: "Please pay *P.* the amount of his account, £42 14*s.* 6*d.* for goods supplied":—*Held*, that, the order did not operate as an equitable assignment. PERCIVAL *v.* DUNN
[29 Ch. D. 128

—— Auctioneer's charges　　-　30 Ch. D. 192
See AUCTION. 2.

ASSIGNS—Mortgage for money due from mortgagor or assigns　　-　22 Ch. D. 5
See MORTGAGE—CONTRACT. 7.

ASSIZE COURTS—Income tax　10 Q. B. D. 267;
[9 App. Cas. 61
See REVENUE—INCOME TAX. 1.

ASSOCIATION FOR GAIN.
See Cases under COMPANY—UNREGISTERED COMPANY. 1—5.

ASYLUM—Infectious diseases　6 App. Cas. 193
See NUISANCE—DEFINITION. 1.

ATTACHMENT OF DEBT — Bankruptcy — Garnishee —　-　-　17 Ch. D. 653
See BANKRUPTCY—PROTECTED TRANSACTION. 1.

—— Bankruptcy—Receiving order 30 Ch. D. 480
See BANKRUPTCY—RECEIVER. 10.

ATTACHMENT OF DEBT—*continued.*

—— Charging order
See Cases under PRACTICE — SUPREME COURT—CHARGING ORDERS.

—— Charging order—Solicitor—Lien.
See Cases under SOLICITOR—LIEN. 1—7.

—— Divorce　　-　-　7 P. D. 15
See PRACTICE—DIVORCE—COSTS. 1.; 8

—— Garnishee order
See Cases under PRACTICE — SUPREME COURT—GARNISHEE ORDERS.

—— Garnishee order absolute—"Final judgment"—Bankruptcy　　12 Q. B. D. 342
See BANKRUPTCY—ACT OF BANKRUPTCY. 9.

—— Married woman—Restraint on anticipation
[11 Q. B. D. 27
See HUSBAND AND WIFE — SEPARATE ESTATE. 9.

ATTACHMENT OF GOODS—To compel appearance　　17 Ch. D. 74
See BANKRUPTCY—SECURED CREDITOR. 1.

—— Voluntary allowance to bankrupt
[17 Ch. D. 70
See BANKRUPTCY—ASSETS. 14.

ATTACHMENT OF PERSON
See Cases under PRACTICE—SUPREME COURT—ATTACHMENT.

—— Appeal from refusal to commit 20 Ch. D. 493
See PRACTICE—SUPREME COURT—APPEAL. 1.

—— Divorce Court—Contempt — Restitution of conjugal rights　9 P. D. 52; 10 P. D. 72
See PRACTICE—DIVORCE — RESTITUTION OF CONJUGAL RIGHTS. 1, 2.

—— Non-payment of money.
See Cases under ARREST—DEBTORS ACT.

—— Notice of motion　　- 9 Q. B. D. 335
See PRACTICE—SUPREME COURT—NOTICE OF MOTION. 1.

—— Service of order on solicitor　22 Ch. D. 571
See PRACTICE—SUPREME COURT—PRODUCTION OF DOCUMENTS. 16.

—— Solicitor—Order for payment of money—Contempt 11 Q. B. D. 545; 12 Q. B. D. 545
See SOLICITOR—LIABILITIES. 4, 5. [44

—— Solicitor—Unqualified practitioner
[15 Q. B. D. 348
See SOLICITOR—UNQUALIFIED. 2.

ATTAINING TWENTY-ONE—Remoteness
[28 Ch. D. 436
See WILL—PERPETUITY 1.

ATTESTATION—Bill of sale—Affidavit.
See Cases under BILL OF SALE—FORMALITIES. 1—7.

—— Bill of sale—Statutory provisions.
See BILL OF SALE—STATUTES.

—— Will.
See Cases under PROBATE—GRANT.

ATTESTATION CLAUSE—How far part of codicil
See PROBATE—GRANT. 10. [8 P. D. 165

ATTESTING WITNESS—Will—Execution—Evidence　　[9 P. D. 149
See PROBATE—EXECUTION. 4.

ATTESTING WITNESS—*continued.*

—— Will—Marriage with devisee **6 Q. B. D. 311**
    See WILL—ATTESTING WITNESS.

ATTORNEY-GENERAL—Charity scheme
    [**22 Ch. D. 827; 28 Ch. D. 426**
    See CHARITY—MANAGEMENT. 2, 4.

—— Public injury—Illegal act— **21 Ch. D. 752**
    See PRACTICE — SUPREME COURT — IN-
JUNCTION. 1.

ATTORNEY-GENERAL OF DUCHY OF LANCAS-
TER.

—— English Information, *Right to exhibit.*]
It is not competent to the Attorney-General of
the Duchy of Lancaster to exhibit an information
in the High Court of Justice, and the Court will
order an information exhibited by him to be taken
off the file on the application of the Defendant
even after answer put in by the Defendant.
ATTORNEY-GENERAL OF DUCHY OF LANCASTER *v.*
DUKE OF DEVONSHIRE - - **14 Q. B. D. 195**

—— Right to attend proceedings in Lunacy
    [**21 Ch. D. 613**
    See LUNATIC—JURISDICTION. 4.

ATTORNMENT—Clause of—Mortgage **16 Ch. D.**
    [**226, 274; 21 Ch. D. 442**
    See BANKRUPTCY—DISTRESS. 2, 3, 4.

—— Clause of—Mortgage - **18 Ch. D. 127**
    See MORTGAGE—CONTRACT. 1.

—— Clause of—Mortgage—Bankruptcy
    [**22 Ch. D. 384**
    See BANKRUPTCY—DISCLAIMER. 9.

—— Clause of—Mortgage—Mortgagee in possession - **22 Ch. D 478**
    See MORTGAGE—MORTGAGEE IN POSSES-
SION. 1.

—— Mortgage — Tenancy — Judgment under
Order XIV. **13 Q. B. D. 347**
    See PRACTICE—SUPREME COURT—WRIT
SPECIALLY INDORSED. 5.

AUCTION.

1. —— Action against Auctioneer—*Rescission
of Contract—Return of Deposit—Staying Proceedings.*] The Plaintiff, who had bought property at an auction, and paid a deposit to the
auctioneers, brought an action against the vendors
and the auctioneers to have the contract rescinded,
the deposit repaid with interest, the costs of the
action paid, and for damages. The statement of
claim alleged that all, or nearly all, of the biddings previous to that of the Plaintiff were fictitious, and were either biddings by the vendors or
their agents, or were announced by the auctioneer
without any bidding having in fact been made.
The auctioneers applied for liberty to pay the deposit into Court, and to have the action dismissed
against them on such payment being made. The
Master of the Rolls made an order that, the vendors undertaking to pay the auctioneers their
costs of the auction without prejudice to how
they should ultimately be borne, and to pay any
interest and damages to which the Plaintiff might
be held entitled, and the auctioneers undertaking, in the event of the vendors not carrying out
their undertaking, to pay to the Plaintiff interest
on the deposit up to the time of payment into
Court, and the costs of the action up to and in-

AUCTION—*continued.*

cluding that application in the event of the Court
holding the Plaintiff entitled to such interest and
costs, the auctioneers should be at liberty to pay
the deposit into Court, and that all further proceedings against them should be stayed:—*Held,*
on appeal, that the order must be discharged, the
auctioneers not having submitted to give the
Plaintiff all the relief which he could in any event
be entitled to against them; for that if the allegations in the statement of claim were established
the Plaintiff would be entitled to have judgment
against them for the deposit with interest, and to
have an order for costs of the action against all the
Defendants. HEATLEY *v.* NEWTON **19 Ch. D. 326**

2. —— Auctioneer's Lien—*Assignment of Debt
—Marshalling—Two Funds, one subject to Lien,
the other not.*] The Defendants were auctioneers
and had sold for a customer a brewery, and part of
the proceeds of the sale was in their hands subject
to their claim for charges incurred in connection
with the sale: they had also in their hands the
balance of the price of some furniture sold by
them for the same customer. The Plaintiff was
a creditor of the Defendants' customer, and he by
letter charged the proceeds of the sale of the
brewery in favour of the Plaintiff. The Defendants wrote to the Plaintiff acknowledging the
receipt of the letter of charge. The Defendants
afterwards paid their customer the balance of the
price of the furniture, and appropriated the part
of the proceeds of the sale of the brewery in their
hands to the payment of their charges:—*Held,*
first, that the letter of charge and the Defendants'
acknowledgment thereof amounted to a good
equitable assignment in favour of the Plaintiff:—
Secondly, that the Defendants, as auctioneers,
had a lien for their charges upon the part of the
proceeds of the sale of the brewery in their
hands:—Thirdly, that the Defendants were at
liberty to appropriate the part of the proceeds of
the sale of the brewery in their hands to the payment of their charges, and were not bound to
take payment of their charges out of the price of
the furniture in order to enable the Plaintiff to
obtain payment of his charge, and that the doctrine of marshalling did not apply. WEBB *v.*
SMITH - - - **30 Ch. D. 192**

—— Charges of auctioneer **29 Ch. D. 608, 790**
    See SOLICITOR—BILL OF COSTS. 24, 25.

—— Payment of deposit by cheque **25 Ch. D. 636**
    See MORTGAGE—FORECLOSURE. 3.

—— Sale by auctioneer with notice of adverse
claim - **19 Ch. D. 86**
    See BAILMENT.

—— Statement in auction room - **25 Ch. D. 357**
    See VENDOR AND PURCHASER—CONDI-
TIONS OF SALE. 5.

—— Statute of Frauds—Identification of property - - - **20 Ch. D. 90**
    See VENDOR AND PURCHASER — AGREE-
MENT. 2.

—— Witness—Auctioneer—Expenses **21 Ch. D.**
    See EVIDENCE—WITNESS. 4. [**831**

AUDITED ACCOUNTS — Benefit society — Impeaching accounts **27 Ch. D. 111**
    See PRACTICE—SUPREME COURT—CHAM-
BERS. 2.

AUDITED ACCOUNTS—*continued.*
—— Building society　-　- 28 Ch. D. 111
　　See BUILDING SOCIETY. 3.
AUDITOR—Right to appoint accountant
　　　　　　　　　　　[12 Q. B. D. 68
　　See COMPANY—MANAGEMENT. 1.
AUSTRALIAN BANKRUPTCY - 21 Ch. D. 674
　　See PARTITION SUIT—SALE. 2.
AUSTRALIAN PROBATE　　- 21 Ch. D. 674
　　See PARTITION SUIT—SALE. 2.
AUTHORITY—Agent　-　- 24 Ch. D. 367
　　See PRINCIPAL AND AGENT—AGENT'S
　　AUTHORITY. 2.
—— To receive purchase-money—Solicitor
　　　　　　　　　　　[24 Ch. D. 387
　　See VENDOR AND PURCHASER—CONVEY-
　　ANCE. 5.
—— Withdrawal of—Administrator—Settlement
　　of accounts　　　　-　 16 Ch. D. 577
　　See ADMINISTRATOR—POWERS. 2.

AVERAGE—General.
　　See Cases under SHIP—GENERAL AVE-
　　RAGE.
—— General—Marine insurance—Warranty—
　　Adding distinct successive losses
　　together　　　-　 14 Q. B. D. 555
　　See INSURANCE, MARINE—POLICY. 8.
AVERAGE BOND — Salvage—Cargo — Duty of
　　shipowner -　-　- 10 P. D. 114
　　See SHIP—SALVAGE. 1.
AVERMENT—Pleading　　6 App. Cas. 156
　　See DEFAMATION—SLANDER. 2.
AWARD.
　　See Cases under ARBITRATION.
—— Compulsory purchase of land 27 Ch. D. 614
　　See LABOURERS' DWELLINGS ACTS. 2.
—— Law of Mauritius　　-　 8 App. Cas. 296
　　See COLONIAL LAW—MAURITIUS. 1.
—— Salvage—Apportionment　　7 P. D. 47
　　See PRACTICE —ADMIRALTY— SALVAGE.
　　3.

B.

BAIL—Action of salvage—Defendant's costs
[10 P. D. 158
See PRACTICE—ADMIRALTY—SALVAGE.
6.

—— Arrest of ship—Exorbitant amount—Costs
[9 P. D. 46
See PRACTICE—ADMIRALTY—COSTS. 1.

—— Bottomry—Private agreement 10 P. D. 141
See PRACTICE—ADMIRALTY—LIS ALIBI
PENDENS. 2.

—— Commission paid for—Damages—Salvage
action　-　-　- 9 P. D. 128
See DAMAGES—REMOTENESS. 2.

—— Money paid as indemnity—Illegality
[7 Q. B. D. 548 ; 15 Q. B. D. 561
See CONTRACT—VALIDITY. 1, 2.

BAIL-BOND—Commission on ship—Arrest
[10 P. D. 158
See PRACTICE —ADMIRALTY —SALVAGE.
6.

—— Form of -　-　-　- 10 P. D. 15
See PRACTICE—ADMIRALTY—ARREST OF
SHIP. 1.

BAILMENT.

—— Estoppel—*Jus tertii—Sale by Bailor for
Bailee after notice of adverse Claim—Right to
Proceeds of Sale—Trustee in Bankruptcy—Auctioneer—Court of Bankruptcy—Jurisdiction—
Bankruptcy Act,* 1869 (32 & 33 Vict. c. 71), s. 72.]
Although in certain cases a bailee may set up
the jus tertii, yet if he accepts the bailment with
full knowledge of an adverse claim, he cannot
afterwards set up the existence of such claim as
against his bailor.—After the filing of a liquidation petition the holder of a registered bill of sale
executed by the debtor instructed an auctioneer
to take possession of the chattels comprised in it.
The auctioneer took possession, and advertised
the goods for sale on behalf of the bill of sale
holder. The sale was stopped by injunction, and
the auctioneer remained in possession of the goods
on behalf of the receiver under the petition. On
the appointment of a trustee the auctioneer held
possession for him, and ultimately by his directions advertised the goods for sale, the advertisements and the catalogues of the goods being
headed "In liquidation. By order of the trustee."
The goods were sold, and the proceeds of sale
were received by the auctioneer. The bill of sale
holder gave him notice not to pay them to the
trustee, and he declined to pay them over. The
trustee applied to the Court of Bankruptcy for an
order for payment to him, serving notice of his
motion on the auctioneer only. On the hearing
of this motion an order was made by consent, that
the money should be paid into Court, and the
hearing adjourned, notice being meanwhile given
to the bill of sale holder. Notice was served on
him, but not a four days' notice as required by
rule 50 of the Bankruptcy Rules, 1870, and he
did not appear on the adjourned hearing. He

BAILMENT—*continued.*
had meanwhile commenced an action against the
auctioneer for the proceeds of sale :—Held (affirming the decision of Bacon, C.J.), that the Court
of Bankruptcy ought to exercise its jurisdiction
under sect. 72 of the Bankruptcy Act, 1869, and
that the money must be paid out to the trustee,
on the ground that the auctioneer had, with full
knowledge of the adverse claim, deliberately
elected to sell the goods for the trustee, and was,
therefore estopped from denying his title.—*Biddle*
v. *Bond* (6 B. & S. 225) distinguished. *Ex parte*
DAVIES. *In re* SADLER　-　　19 Ch. D. 86

—— Infant—Larceny -　- 15 Q. B. D. 323
See CRIMINAL LAW—LARCENY. 2.

—— Innkeeper—Lien -　- 23 Ch. D. 330
See INN—INNKEEPER. 2.

BAKEHOUSES.
See FACTORY ACTS—*Statutes.*

BAKER.

1. —— Weighing Bread — *Delivery by Cart
without Beam and Scales—6 & 7 Wm. 4, c. 37,
ss.* 6, 7.] The appellant, a baker, having received
through his traveller an order from a customer
for a quartern loaf, the manager of the baker's
shop selected, weighed, and appropriated to the
customer a loaf which was then carried out in a
cart and delivered to the customer, on credit, by
a servant of the baker without being provided
with any beam and scales with proper weights :
—*Held,* that the appellant was rightly convicted
under 6 & 7 Wm. 4, c. 37, s. 7, which enacts that
every baker beyond certain metropolitan limits
who shall " carry out bread for sale in and from
any cart" shall be provided with a correct beam
and scales with proper weights, in order that all
bread sold by him may be weighed in the presence of the purchaser ; and in case any such
baker shall "carry out or deliver any bread"
without being provided with such beam and scales
with proper weights, he shall be liable to a
penalty. RIDGWAY v. WARD　　14 Q. B. D. 110

2. —— Weighing Bread—*Delivery by Cart
without Beam and Scales— Delivery to oblige
Customer—6 & 7 Wm.* 4, c. 37, s. 7.] Sect. 7 of
6 & 7 Wm. 4, c. 37, provides that every baker or
seller of bread, and every servant employed by
such baker or seller of bread, who shall convey
or carry out bread for sale in and from any cart,
shall be provided with a beam and scales with
proper weights, in order that all bread sold by
any such baker or seller of bread, or his servant,
may be weighed in the presence of the purchaser
thereof ; and in case any "such baker or seller of
bread" or his servant shall carry out or deliver
any bread without being provided with such
beam and scales, every such baker or seller of
bread shall be liable to a penalty.—A customer
bought three loaves in a baker's shop. The
baker weighed the loaves in her presence, and
subsequently, at her request and to oblige her,
his servant carried them out in a cart and delivered

BAKER—*continued.*

them at her house, without being provided with any beam and scales :—*Held,* that the baker had not carried out or delivered the loaves as "such baker or seller of bread," and therefore could not be convicted of an offence under sect. 7. DANIEL *v.* WHITFIELD   -   **15 Q. B. D. 408**

BALANCE ORDER—Executor of shareholder— Retainer -   -   **29 Ch. D. 934** *See* EXECUTOR—RETAINER. 4.

—— Final judgment—Bankruptcy notice—Company   -   **13 Q. B. D. 476** *See* BANKRUPTCY—ACT OF BANKRUPTCY. 7.

BALLOT—Militia——Expenses of   - *See* ARMY AND NAVY—*Statutes.*

BANK OF ENGLAND—Duty to register stock in name of Local Board   **21 Ch. D. 176** *See* LOCAL GOVERNMENT——LOCAL AUTHORITY. 9.

—— Injunction to restrain transfer of stock [**23 Ch. D. 549** *See* PRACTICE — SUPREME COURT — INJUNCTION. 2.

BANK NOTES—Issue — Penalties—7 & 8 Vict. c. 32, ss. 11, 12   **12 Q. B. D. 605** *See* BANKER—NOTES.

BANKER :—   Col.

I. CHEQUE   -   -   - 51
II. LIEN   -   -   - 52
III. NOTES -   -   -   - 53

I. BANKER—CHEQUE.

1. —— Presentation—*Laches of Bearer.*] The rule of law as to bills of exchange and promissory notes—that an indorsee taking them after maturity takes them upon the credit of and can stand in no better position than his indorser—does not apply to cheques.—A cheque for £98, dated the 21st of August, 1880, directing the National Bank to pay that sum to A. M. or bearer, was handed by the Defendant (the drawer) to one C. under circumstances which, if C. had been suing upon it, would have been an answer to his claim. In fraud of the Defendant, C. on the 29th paid it into his account with the London and County Banking Company, who, upon the presentment and dishonour of the cheque on the same or following day, sued the drawer for the amount. There was no evidence of the absence of bona fides on the part of the Plaintiffs, or that they had notice of the alleged fraud of C. :—*Held,* by Field, J., on further consideration, that the Plaintiffs were entitled to recover.—*Down* v. *Halling* (4 B. & C. 330), and *Rothschild* v. *Corney* (9 B. & C. 388), considered and distinguished. LONDON AND COUNTY BANKING COMPANY *v.* GROOME -   - **8 Q. B. D. 288**

2. —— Negotiability—*Countermand of Drawer —Onerous Indorsee—Findings of the Court of Session on Appeal from Sheriff's Court—Judicature Act of Scotland,* 1825 (6 Geo. 4, c. 120) s. 40—*Bills of Exchange Act,* 1882 (45 & 46 Vict. c. 61, ss. 3, 73.] A banker's draft or cheque is substantially a bill of exchange, attended with many, though not all of the privileges of such ; and both in England and Scotland it is as much a negotiable instrument ; consequently, the

I. BANKER—CHEQUE—*continued.*

holder, to whom the property in it has been transferred for value, either by delivery, or by indorsation, is entitled to sue upon it if upon due presentation it is not paid.—Per Lord Blackburn : The definition given in sect. 3 of the Bills of Exchange Act, 1882, embraces in it a cheque : and that Act is declaratory of the prior law.—On a Saturday A. granted a cheque on his account with the Bank of S. for, inter alia, £250, crossed blank in favour of B. On the same day B. indorsed the cheque, and paid it into the Bank of C., of which he was a customer. The Bank of C. immediately on receipt of the cheque carried the amount to B.'s credit, and thus reduced a debit balance standing against him. On the Monday following A. stopped payment of the cheque at the Bank of S., consequently when the Bank of C. presented it, payment was refused. The Bank of C. sued A. in the Sheriff's Court for the amount. On appeal, the Court of Session found that the cheque was granted to B. to reduce the balance at his debit with the Bank of C.; that A. agreed the cheque should be so used ; and that in pursuance of that agreement the cheque was indorsed to the Bank of C. and given to them as cash, and the contents being put to B.'s credit the balance at his debit was thereby reduced :—*Held,* that in accordance with *Mackay* v. *Dick* (6 App. Cas. 251): statute 1825, s. 40, this House was limited to the findings of the Court of Session and the record : that the findings in fact were distinct, intelligible, and within the record ; that it followed from them as a matter of law that the Bank of C. were onerous holders of the cheque, and therefore the Bank of S. not having paid the cheque on demand, the Court below was right in holding that A. was liable.— *Currie* v. *Misa* (1876, Law Rep. 10 Ex. 153 ; 1 App. Cas. 554) commented on. *De la Chaumette* v. *Bank of England* (1829, 9 B. & C. 208) explained. Dicta of the Judges in *Macdonald* v. *Union Bank* (1864, 2 Court Sess. Cas. 3rd Series, 963) approved. M'LEAN *v.* CLYDESDALE BANKING COMPANY   **9 App. Cas. 95**

II. BANKER—LIEN.

—— Priority—*Deposit of Title Deeds with Bank—Loan by equitable Mortgagee after Notice of Contract of Sale—Vendor and Purchaser—Lien of Unpaid Vendor.*] The owner of land, after depositing the title deeds with a bank as security for all sums then or thereafter to become due on the general balance of his account with the bank, contracted with the knowledge of the bank to sell the land to one who had notice of the terms of the deposit. The vendor afterwards paid into his own account at the bank sums which in the whole exceeded the debt due to the bank on his balance at the time of the contract of sale, so that on the principle of *Clayton's Case* (1 Mer. 572) that debt was discharged. The bank, without giving notice to the purchaser, continued the account and made fresh advances to the vendor, so that on the general balance there was always a debt to the bank. The purchaser, who never had notice of the fresh advances, paid the purchase-money by instalments to the vendor :—*Held* (affirming the decision of the Court of Appeal), that on the principle of *Hopkinson* v. *Rolt* (9 H. L. C. 514), the bank

II. BANKER—LIEN—continued.

had no charge on the land as against the purchaser for the fresh advances.—*Held*, also, that the bank had no charge upon the purchase-money.—Per Lord Blackburn: A purchaser of land, with notice that the title deeds have been deposited with a bank as security for the general balance on the vendor's present and future account, is not bound to inquire whether the bank has after notice of the purchase made fresh advances. The burden lies on the bank advancing on the security of the unpaid vendor's lien to give the purchaser notice that it has so done or intends so to do. LONDON AND COUNTY BANKING COMPANY *v.* RATCLIFFE - - - 6 App. Cas. 722

III. BANKER—NOTES.

—— Issue — *Penalties — Bank Charter Act,* 1844 (7 & 8 *Vict. c.* 32), *ss.* 11, 12.] By sect. 11 of the Bank Charter Act, 1844, it shall not be lawful for any banker to "issue" any note payable on demand, except that any banker carrying on business as such on the 6th of May, 1844, and then lawfully issuing his own notes, may continue to issue them under specified conditions ; and, by sect. 12, if any banker, entitled after the passing of the Act to issue bank notes, "shall cease to carry on the business of a banker," it shall not be lawful for him to issue such notes at any time thereafter. In 1880 a firm of bankers, entitled to issue their own notes under the exception in sect. 11, sold their business to a limited liability company upon the following terms :—The company took over the whole of the business as a going concern, and the goodwill, except and reserving to the firm the right to issue their own notes, but including in the sale and purchase such benefit of the issue as was thereby agreed to be given to the company ; the firm were to issue their notes in the same form as theretofore, but through the company's officers only, and might nominate those officers and make the return required by statute through them: the company were to allow and pay the firm £2 per cent. interest on the amount of all notes from time to time in circulation: for the purposes of the issue only the firm might continue to use their accustomed name, but they were not to assign their rights, nor to take new partners for the purpose of continuing the issue without the consent of the company, nor to carry on the business of banking within a defined district without the like consent, except so far as related to the issue of their notes under the agreement: if the right of issue should at any time be taken away from the firm they were to pay any compensation they might receive to the company, unless the company should get an equal right of issue, in which case the firm might retain the compensation : if the company acquired a right to issue their own notes, the firm's right of issue was to cease. When the business was taken over by the company, a large number of the firm's notes being in circulation, the amount of them was deducted from the purchase-money, and the notes, when presented for payment, were cashed by the company, and reissued by them. Notes in hand when the business was taken over were treated as cash lent by the firm to the company. Daily returns were made by the company shewing the number of the firm's notes in circulation, and twice a year

III. BANKER—NOTES—continued.

the company paid £2 per cent. interest to the firm on the amount so ascertained. On an information against the firm and the company for penalties in respect of their having issued the notes contrary to the provisions of the Act :—*Held*, that the company had "issued" the notes within the meaning of sect. 11 of the Bank Charter Act, 1844 ; that the firm, in issuing the notes, were not protected by the exception in sect. 11, because after the making of the agreement they had " ceased to carry on the business of bankers" within the meaning of sect. 12 ; and therefore that all the Defendants were liable. ATTORNEY GENERAL *v.* BIRKBECK
[12 Q. B. D. 605

BANKER—Account—Over-drawing—Borrowing powers   29 Ch. D. 902 ; 9 Q. B. D. 397 ;
[9 App. Cas. 857
See BUILDING SOCIETY. 6, 7, 8.

—— Advances to executor—Separate account
[16 Ch. D. 151
See EXECUTOR—POWERS. 1.

—— Balance at—Sequestration   22 Ch. D. 233
See PRACTICE—SUPREME COURT—SEQUESTRATION. 1.

—— Bank note—Alteration   9 Q. B. D. 555 ;
[11 Q. B. D. 84
See BILL OF EXCHANGE—ALTERATION. 2, 3.

—— Bill of exchange—Specific appropriation—Accommodation acceptances
[13 Q. B. D. 740
See BILL OF EXCHANGE—SECURITIES FOR. 1.

—— Guarantee—Proof in bankruptcy 17 Ch. D.
See BANKRUPTCY—PROOF. 11.   [98

—— Lien—Army agent -   17 Ch. D. 520
See SET-OFF. 8.

—— Pledge of goods—Memorandum in bank's ledger -   14 Q. B. D. 386
See BILL OF SALE—OPERATION. 6.

BANKING COMPANY—Sale of shares—Omission to specify numbers—Broker's right to indemnity 14 Q. B. D. 460 ; 15 Q. B. D. 388
See PRINCIPAL AND AGENT—PRINCIPAL'S LIABILITY. 4, 5.

—— Sale of bank shares — Custom of Stock Exchange—Negligence of broker
See STOCK EXCHANGE. 1. [9 Q. B. D. 546

I. BANKRUPTCY—STATUTES AND GAZETTE.

BANKRUPTCY ACT, 1883.

The *Bankruptcy Act*, 1883, 46 & 47 Vict. c. 52, *repeals* (s. 169)—

  13 Edw. 1, c. 18, *in part,*
  32 & 33 Vict. c. 62, *sub-s.* (6) *of* s. 5, *and*
    ss. 21 & 22.
  32 & 33 Vict. c. 71,
  32 & 33 Vict. c. 89, s. 19,
  33 & 34 Vict. c. 76,
  34 & 35 Vict. c. 50, *ss.* 6, 7, 8.
  38 & 39 Vict. c. 77, *ss.* 9 & 32.

I. BANKRUPTCY—STATUTES AND GAZETTE—*continued.*

and amends and consolidates the Law *of* Bankruptcy.

Sect. 3. Commencement *of* Act, 31st of December, 1883.

By sect. 168, amongst other things—"*available act of bankruptcy*" means any act *of* bankruptcy available *for* a bankruptcy petition at the date *of* the presentation of the petition on which the receiving order is made.

"*Debt provable in bankruptcy*" or "*provable debt*" includes any debt or liability by the Act made provable in bankruptcy.

"*Goods*" includes chattels personal.

"*Local bank*" means any bank in or in the neighbourhood of the bankruptcy district in which the proceedings are taken.

"*Ordinary resolution*" means a resolution decided by *a* majority in value *of* the creditors present, personally or by proxy, at a meeting of creditors and voting on the resolution.

"*Person*" includes a body of persons corporate or unincorporate.

"*Property*" includes money, goods, things in action, land and every description of property, whether real or personal, and whether situate in England or elsewhere; also, obligations, easements, and every description of estate, interest, and profit, present or future, vested or contingent, arising out of or incident to property as above defined.

"*Resolution*" means ordinary resolution.

"*Secured creditor*" means a person holding a mortgage, charge, or lien on the property of the debtor, or any part thereof, as a security *for* a debt due to him.

"*Special resolution*" means a resolution decided by a majority in number and three-*f*ourths in value of the creditors present, personally or by proxy, at a meeting of creditors and voting on the resolution.

The schedules to the Act are to be construed and to take effect as part *of* the Act.

———

Part I. Proceedings *from* Act *of* Bankruptcy to Discharge.

  Part II. Disqualification of Bankrupt.
  Part III. Administration of Property.
  Part IV. Official Receivers.
  Part V. Trustees in Bankruptcy.
  Part VI. Constitution, Procedure, and Powers *of* Court.
  Part VII. Small Bankruptcies.
  Part VIII. Supplemental Provisions.

PART I. PROCEEDINGS FROM ACT OF BANKRUPTCY TO DISCHARGE.

Acts of Bankruptcy.] Sect. 4.—(1.) A debtor commits *an* act *of* bankruptcy in each *of* the following cases:—

  (*a.*) If in England or elsewhere he makes a conveyance or assignment *of* his property to a trustee or trustees *for* the benefit *of* his creditors generally :

  (*b.*) If in England or elsewhere he makes a *f*raudulent conveyance, gift, delivery, or trans*f*er *of* his property, or of any part there*of* :

I. BANKRUPTCY—STATUTES AND GAZETTE —*continued.*

(c.) *If in England or elsewhere he makes any conveyance or transfer of his property or any part thereof, or creates any charge thereon which would under this or any other Act be void as a fraudulent preference if he were adjudged bankrupt.*

(d.) *If with intent to defeat or delay his creditors he does any of the following things, namely, departs out of England, or being out of England remains out of England, or departs from his dwelling-house, or otherwise absents himself, or begins to keep house:*

(e.) *If execution issued against him has been levied by seizure and sale of his goods under process in an action in any Court, or in any civil proceeding in the High Court:*

(f.) *If he files in the Court a declaration of his inability to pay his debts or presents a bankruptcy petition against himself:*

(g.) *If a creditor has obtained a final judgment against him for any amount, and execution thereon not having been stayed, has served on him in England, or by leave of the Court, elsewhere, a bankruptcy notice under this Act, requiring him to pay the judgment debt in accordance with the terms of the judgment, or to secure or compound for it to the satisfaction of the creditor or the Court, and he does not, within seven days after service of the notice, in case the service is effected in England, and in case the service is effected elsewhere, then within the time limited in that behalf by the order giving leave to effect the service, either comply with the requirements of the notice, or satisfy the Court that he has a counter-claim, set-off or cross demand which equals or exceeds the amount of the judgment debt, and which he could not set up in the action in which the judgment was obtained:*

(h) *If the debtor gives notice to any of his creditors that he has suspended, or that he is about to suspend, payment of his debts.*

(2.) *A bankruptcy notice under this Act shall be in the prescribed form, and shall state the consequences of non-compliance therewith, and shall be served in the prescribed manner.*

Bankruptcy Petition and Receiving Order.] *Sect. 5. Subject to the conditions hereinafter specified, if a debtor commits an act of bankruptcy the Court may, on a bankruptcy petition being presented either by a creditor or by the debtor, make an order, in this Act called a receiving order, for the protection of the estate.*

Sect. 6.—(1.) *A creditor shall not be entitled to present a bankruptcy petition against a debtor unless—*

(a.) *The debt owing by the debtor to the petitioning creditor, or, if two or more creditors join in the petition, the aggregate amount of debts owing to the several petitioning creditors, amounts to fifty pounds, and*

(b.) *The debt is a liquidated sum, payable either immediately or at some certain future time, and*

I. BANKRUPTCY—STATUTES AND GAZETTE – *continued.*

(c.) *The act of bankruptcy on which the petition is grounded has occurred within three months before the presentation of the petition, and*

(d.) *The debtor is domiciled in England, or within a year before the date of the presentation of the petition, has ordinarily resided or had a dwelling-house, or place of business in England.*

(2.) *If the petitioning creditor is a secured creditor, he must, in his petition, either state that he is willing to give up his security for the benefit of the creditors in the event of the debtor being adjudged bankrupt, or give an estimate of the value of his security. In the latter case, he may be admitted as a petitioning creditor to the extent of the balance of the debt due to him, after deducting the value so estimated in the same manner as if he were an unsecured creditor.*

Sect. 7.—(1.) *A creditor's petition shall be verified by affidavit of the creditor, or of some person on his behalf having knowledge of the facts, and served in the prescribed manner.*

(2.) *At the hearing the Court shall require proof of the debt of the petitioning creditor, of the service of the petition, and of the act of bankruptcy, or, if more than one act of bankruptcy is alleged in the petition, of some of the alleged acts of bankruptcy, and if satisfied with the proof, may make a receiving order in pursuance of the petition.*

(3.) *If the Court is not satisfied with the proof of the petitioning creditor's debt, or of the act of bankruptcy, or of the service of the petition, or is satisfied by the debtor that he is able to pay his debts, or that for other sufficient cause no order ought to be made, the Court may dismiss the petition.*

(4.) *When the act of bankruptcy relied on is non-compliance with a bankruptcy notice to pay, secure, or compound for a judgment debt, the Court may, if it thinks fit, stay or dismiss the petition on the ground that an appeal is pending from the judgment.*

(5.) *Where the debtor appears on the petition, and denies that he is indebted to the petitioner, or that he is indebted to such an amount as would justify the petitioner in presenting a petition against him, the Court, on such security (if any) being given as the Court may require for payment to the petitioner of any debt which may be established against him in due course of law, and of the costs of establishing the debt, may instead of dismissing the petition stay all proceedings on the petition for such time as may be required for trial of the question relating to the debt.*

(6.) *Where proceedings are stayed, the Court may, if by reason of the delay caused by the stay of proceedings or for any other cause it thinks just, make a receiving order on the petition of some other creditor, and shall thereupon dismiss, on such terms as it thinks just, the petition in which proceedings have been stayed as aforesaid.*

(7.) *A creditor's petition shall not, after presentment, be withdrawn without the leave of the Court.*

Sect. 8.—(1.) *A debtor's petition shall allege that the debtor is unable to pay his debts, and the presentation thereof shall be deemed an act of bank-*

I. BANKRUPTCY—STATUTES AND GAZETTE
—*continued.*

ruptcy without the previous filing by the debtor of any declaration of inability to pay his debts, and the Court shall thereupon make a receiving order.

(2.) *A debtor's petition shall not, after presentment, be withdrawn without the leave of the Court.*

Sect. 9.—(1.) *On the making of a receiving order an official receiver shall be thereby constituted receiver of the property of the debtor, and thereafter, except as directed by this Act, no creditor to whom the debtor is indebted in respect of any debt provable in bankruptcy shall have any remedy against the property or person of the debtor in respect of the debt, or shall commence any action or other legal proceedings unless with the leave of the Court or on such terms as the Court may impose.*

(2.) *But this section shall not affect the power of any secured creditor to realize or otherwise deal with his security in the same manner as he would have been entitled to realize or deal with it if this section had not been passed.*

Sect. 10.—(1.) *The Court may if it is shewn to be necessary for the protection of the estate, at any time after the presentation of a bankruptcy petition, and before a receiving order is made, appoint the official receiver to be interim receiver of the property of the debtor, or of any part thereof, and direct him to take immediate possession thereof or of any part thereof.*

(2.) *The Court may at any time after the presentation of a bankruptcy petition stay any action, execution, or other legal process against the property or person of the debtor, and any Court in which proceedings are pending against a debtor may, on proof that a bankruptcy petition has been presented by or against the debtor, either stay the proceedings or allow them to continue on such terms as it may think just.*

Sect. 11. *Where the Court makes an order staying any action or proceeding, or staying proceedings generally, the order may be served by sending a copy thereof, under the seal of the Court, by prepaid post letter, to the address for service of the plaintiff or other party prosecuting such proceeding.*

Sect. 12.—(1.) *The official receiver of a debtor's estate may, on the application of any creditor or creditors, and if satisfied that the nature of the debtor's estate or business or the interests of the creditors generally require the appointment of a special manager of the estate or business other than the official receiver, appoint a manager thereof accordingly to act until a trustee is appointed, and with such powers (including any of the powers of a receiver) as may be entrusted to him by the official receiver.*

(2.) *The special manager shall give security and account in such manner as the Board of Trade may direct.*

(3.) *The special manager shall receive such remuneration as the creditors may, by resolution at an ordinary meeting, determine, or in default of any such resolution, as may be prescribed.*

Sect. 13. *Notice of every receiving order, stating the name, address, and description of the debtor, the date of the order, the Court by which the order is made, and the date of the petition, shall be gazetted and advertised in a local paper in the prescribed manner.*

Sect. 14. *If in any case where a receiving order*

has been made on a bankruptcy petition it shall appear to the Court by which such order was made, upon an application by the official receiver, or any creditor or other person interested, that a majority of the creditors in number and value are resident in Scotland or in Ireland, and that from the situation of the property of the debtor, or other causes, his estate and effects ought to be distributed among the creditors under the Bankrupt or Insolvent Laws of Scotland or Ireland, the said Court, after such inquiry as to it shall seem fit, may rescind the receiving order and stay all proceedings on, or dismiss the petition upon such terms, if any, as the Court may think fit.*

First Meeting of Creditors.] *Sect.* 15.—(1.) *As soon as may be after the making of a receiving order against a debtor a general meeting of his creditors (in this Act referred to as the first meeting of creditors) shall be held for the purpose of considering whether a proposal for a composition or scheme of arrangement shall be entertained, or whether it is expedient that the debtor shall be adjudged bankrupt, and generally as to the mode of dealing with the debtor's property.*

(2.) *With respect to the summoning of and proceedings at the first and other meetings of creditors, the rules in the first Schedule shall be observed.*

Statement of Affairs.] *Sect.* 16.—(1.) *Where a receiving order is made against a debtor, he shall make out and submit to the official receiver a statement of and in relation to his affairs in the prescribed form, verified by affidavit, and shewing the particulars of the debtor's assets, debts, and liabilities, the names, residences, and occupations of his creditors, the securities held by them respectively, the dates when the securities were respectively given, and such further or other information as may be prescribed or as the official receiver may require.*

(2.) *The statement shall be so submitted within the following times, namely:*

(i.) *If the order is made on the petition of the debtor. within three days from the date of the order.*

(ii.) *If the order is made on the petition of a creditor within seven days from the date of the order.*

But the Court may in either case, for special reasons, extend the time.

(3.) *If the debtor fails without reasonable excuse to comply with the requirements of this section, the Court may, on the application of the official receiver, or of any creditor, adjudge him bankrupt.*

(4.) *Any person stating himself in writing to be a creditor of the bankrupt may, personally or by agent, inspect this statement at all reasonable times, and take any copy thereof or extract therefrom, but any person untruthfully so stating himself to be a creditor shall be guilty of a contempt of Court, and shall be punishable accordingly on the application of the trustee or official receiver.*

Public Examination of Debtor.] *Sect.* 17.—(1.) *Where a Court makes a receiving order it shall hold a public sitting on a day to be appointed by the Court, for the examination of the debtor, and the debtor shall attend thereat, and shall be examined as to his conduct, dealings, and property.*

(2.) *The examination shall be held as soon as conveniently may be after the expiration of the*

I. BANKRUPTCY—STATUTES AND GAZETTE
—*continued.*

time for the submission of the debtor's statement of affairs.

(3.) *The Court may adjourn the examination from time to time.*

(4.) *Any creditor who has tendered a proof, or his representative authorized in writing, may question the debtor concerning his affairs and the causes of his failure.*

(5.) *The official receiver shall take part in the examination of the debtor; and for the purpose thereof, if specially authorized by the Board of Trade, may employ a solicitor with or without counsel.*

(6.) *If a trustee is appointed before the conclusion of the examination he may take part therein.*

(7.) *The Court may put such questions to the debtor as it may think expedient.*

(8.) *The debtor shall be examined upon oath, and it shall be his duty to answer all such questions as the Court may put or allow to be put to him. Such notes of the examination as the Court thinks proper shall be taken down in writing, and shall be read over to and signed by the debtor, and may thereafter be used in evidence against him; they shall also be open to the inspection of any creditor at all reasonable times.*

(9.) *When the Court is of opinion that the affairs of the debtor have been sufficiently investigated, it shall, by order, declare that his examination is concluded, but such order shall not be made until after the day appointed for the first meeting of creditors.*

Composition or Scheme of Arrangement.] Sect. 18.—(1) *The creditors may at the first meeting or any adjournment thereof, by special resolution, resolve to entertain a proposal for a composition in satisfaction of the debts due to them from the debtor, or a proposal for a scheme of arrangement of the debtor's affairs.*

(2.) *The composition or scheme shall not be binding on the creditors unless it is confirmed by a resolution passed (by a majority in number representing three-fourths in value of all the creditors who have proved) at a subsequent meeting of the creditors, and is approved by the Court.*

Any creditor who has proved his debt may assent to or dissent from such composition or scheme by a letter addressed to the official receiver in the prescribed form, and attested by a witness, so as to be received by such official receiver not later than the day preceding such subsequent meeting, and such creditor shall be taken as being present and voting at such meeting.

(3.) *The subsequent meeting shall be summoned by the official receiver by not less than seven days' notice, and shall not be held until after the public examination of the debtor is concluded. The notice shall state generally the terms of the proposal, and shall be accompanied by a report of the official receiver thereon.*

(4.) *The debtor or the official receiver may, after the composition or scheme is accepted by the creditors, apply to the Court to approve it, and notice of the time appointed for hearing the application shall be given to each creditor who has proved.*

(5.) *The Court shall, before approving a composition, or scheme, hear a report of the official receiver as to the terms of the composition or scheme and as to the conduct of the debtor, and any objec-*

I. BANKRUPTCY—STATUTES AND GAZETTE
—*continued.*

tions which may be made by or on behalf of any creditor.

(6.) *If the Court is of opinion that the terms of the composition or scheme are not reasonable, or are not calculated to benefit the general body of creditors, or in any case in which the Court is required under this Act where the debtor is adjudged bankrupt to refuse his discharge, the Court shall, or if any such facts are proved as would under this Act justify the Court in refusing, qualifying, or suspending the debtor's discharge, the Court may, in its discretion, refuse to approve the composition or scheme.*

(7.) *If the Court approve the composition or scheme, the approval may be testified by the seal of the Court being attached to the instrument containing the terms of the composition or scheme, or by the terms being embodied in an order of the Court.*

(8.) *A composition or scheme accepted and approved in pursuance of this section shall be binding on all the creditors so far as relates to any debts due to them from the debtor and provable in bankruptcy.*

(9.) *A certificate of the official receiver that a composition or scheme has been duly accepted and approved shall, in the absence of fraud, be conclusive as to its validity.*

(10.) *The provisions of a composition or scheme under this section may be enforced by the Court on application by any person interested, and any disobedience of an order of the Court made on the application shall be deemed a contempt of Court.*

(11.) *If default is made in payment of any instalment due in pursuance of the composition or scheme, or if it appears to the Court, on satisfactory evidence, that the composition or scheme cannot in consequence of legal difficulties, or for any sufficient cause, proceed without injustice or undue delay to the creditors or to the debtor, or that the approval of the Court was obtained by fraud, the Court may, if it thinks fit, on application by any creditor, adjudge the debtor bankrupt, and annul the composition or scheme, but without prejudice to the validity of any sale, disposition, or payment duly made, or thing duly done under or in pursuance of the composition or scheme. Where a debtor is adjudged bankrupt under this sub-section any debt provable in other respects, which has been contracted before the date of the adjudication, shall be provable in the bankruptcy.*

(12.) *If, under or in pursuance of a composition or scheme, a trustee is appointed to administer the debtor's property or manage his business, Part V. of this Act shall apply to the trustee as if he were a trustee in a bankruptcy, and as if the terms "bankruptcy," "bankrupt," and "order of adjudication," included respectively a composition or scheme of arrangement, a compounding or arranging debtor, and order approving the composition or scheme.*

(13.) *Part III. of this Act shall, so far as the nature of the case and the terms of the composition or scheme admit, apply thereto, the same interpretation being given to the words "trustee," "bankruptcy," "bankrupt," and "order of adjudication," as in the last preceding sub-section.*

(14.) *No composition or scheme shall be approved*

I. BANKRUPTCY—STATUTES AND GAZETTE —*continued.*

by the Court which does not provide for the payment in priority to other debts of all debts directed to be so paid in the distribution of the property of a bankrupt.

(15.) The acceptance by a creditor of a composition or scheme shall not release any person who under this Act would not be released by an order of discharge if the debtor had been adjudged bankrupt.

(19.) Notwithstanding the acceptance and approval of a composition or scheme, such composition or scheme shall not be binding on any creditor so far as regards a debt or liability from which, under the provisions of this Act, the debtor would not be discharged by an order of discharge in bankruptcy, unless the creditor assents to the composition or scheme.

Adjudication of Bankruptcy.] Sect. 20.—(1.) Where a receiving order is made against a debtor, then, if the creditors at the first meeting or any adjournment thereof by ordinary resolution resolve that the debtor be adjudged bankrupt, or pass no resolution, or if the creditors do not meet, or if a composition or scheme is not accepted or approved in pursuance of this Act within fourteen days after the conclusion of the examination of the debtor or such further time as the Court may allow, the Court shall adjudge the debtor bankrupt; and thereupon the property of the bankrupt shall become divisible among his creditors and shall vest in a trustee.

(2.) Notice of every order adjudging a debtor bankrupt, stating the name, address, and description of the bankrupt, the date of the adjudication, and the Court by which the adjudication is made, shall be gazetted and advertised in a local paper in the prescribed manner, and the date of the order shall for the purposes of this Act be the date of the adjudication.

Appointment of Trustees.] Sect. 21.—(1.) Where a debtor is adjudged bankrupt, or the creditors have resolved that he be adjudged bankrupt, the creditors may, by ordinary resolution, appoint some fit person, whether a creditor or not, to fill the office of trustee of the property of the bankrupt; or they may resolve to leave his appointment to the committee of inspection hereinafter mentioned.

(2.) The person so appointed shall give security in manner prescribed to the satisfaction of the Board of Trade, and the Board, if satisfied with the security, shall certify that his appointment has been duly made, unless they object to the appointment on the ground that it has not been made in good faith by a majority in value of the creditors voting, or that the person appointed is not fit to act as trustee, or that his connection with or relation to the bankrupt or his estate or any particular creditor makes it difficult for him to act with impartiality in the interests of the creditors generally.

(3.) Provided that where the Board make any such objection they shall, if so requested by a majority in value of the creditors, notify the objection to the High Court, and thereupon the High Court may decide on its validity.

(4.) The appointment of a trustee shall take effect as from the date of the certificate.

(5.) The official receiver shall not, save as by this Act provided, be the trustee of the bankrupt's property.

I. BANKRUPTCY—STATUTES AND GAZETTE —*continued.*

(6.) If a trustee is not appointed by the creditors within four weeks from the date of the adjudication, or, in the event of negotiations for a composition or scheme being pending at the expiration of those four weeks, then within seven days from the close of those negotiations by the refusal of the creditors to accept, or of the Court to approve, the composition or scheme, the official receiver shall report the matter to the Board of Trade, and thereupon the Board of Trade shall appoint some fit person to be trustee of the bankrupt's property and shall certify the appointment.

(7.) Provided that the creditors or the committee of inspection (if so authorized by resolution of the creditors) may, at any subsequent time, if they think fit, appoint a trustee, and on the appointment being made and certified the person appointed shall become trustee in the place of the person appointed by the Board of Trade.

(8.) When a debtor is adjudged bankrupt after the first meeting of creditors has been held, and a trustee has not been appointed prior to the adjudication, the official receiver shall forthwith summon a meeting of creditors for the purpose of appointing a trustee.

Committee of Inspection.] Sect. 22.—(1.) The creditors qualified to vote, may at their first or any subsequent meeting, by resolution, appoint from among the creditors qualified to vote, or the holders of general proxies or general powers of attorney from such creditors, a committee of inspection for the purpose of superintending the administration of the bankrupt's property by the trustee. The committee of inspection shall consist of not more than five nor less than three persons.

(2.) The committee of inspection shall meet at such times as they shall from time to time appoint, and failing such appointment, at least once a month; and the trustee or any member of the committee may also call a meeting of the committee as and when he thinks necessary.

(3.) The committee may act by a majority of their members present at a meeting, but shall not act unless a majority of the committee are present at the meeting.

(4.) Any member of the committee may resign his office by notice in writing signed by him, and delivered to the trustee.

(5.) If a member of the committee becomes bankrupt, or compounds or arranges with his creditors, or is absent from five consecutive meetings of the committee, his office shall thereupon become vacant.

(6.) Any member of the committee may be removed by an ordinary resolution at any meeting of creditors of which seven days' notice has been given, stating the object of the meeting.

(7.) On a vacancy occurring in the office of a member of the committee, the trustees shall forthwith summon a meeting of creditors for the purpose of filling the vacancy, and the meeting may, by a resolution, appoint another creditor or other person eligible as above to fill the vacancy.

(8.) The continuing members of the committee, provided there be not less than two such continuing members, may act notwithstanding any vacancy in their body; and where the number of members of the committee of inspection is for the time being less

I. BANKRUPTCY — STATUTES AND GAZETTE —*continued.*

than five, the creditors may increase that number so that it do not exceed five.

(9.) *If there be no committee of inspection, any act or thing or any direction or permission by this Act authorized or required to be done or given by the committee may be done or given by the Board of Trade on the application of the trustee.*

Composition or Scheme after Adjudication.] *Sect. 23.—*(1.) *Where a debtor is adjudged bankrupt the creditors may, if they think fit, at any time after the adjudication, by special resolution, resolve to entertain a proposal for a composition in satisfaction of the debts due to them under the bankruptcy, or for a scheme of arrangement of the bankrupt's affairs; and thereupon the same proceedings shall be taken and the same consequences shall ensue as in the case of a composition or scheme accepted before adjudication.*

(2.) *If the Court approve the composition or scheme it may make an order annulling the bankruptcy and vesting the property of the bankrupt in him or in such other person as the Court may appoint, on such terms, and subject to such conditions, if any, as the Court may declare.*

(3.) *If default is made in payment of any instalment due in pursuance of the composition or scheme, or if it appears to the Court that the composition or scheme cannot proceed without injustice or undue delay, or that the approval of the Court was obtained by fraud, the Court may, if it thinks fit, on application by any person interested, adjudge the debtor bankrupt, and annul the composition or scheme, but without prejudice to the validity of any sale, disposition, or payment duly made, or thing duly done, under or in pursuance of the composition or scheme. Where a debtor is adjudged bankrupt under this sub-section, all debts, provable in other respects, which have been contracted before the date of such adjudication, shall be provable in the bankruptcy.*

Control over Person and Property of Debtor.] *Sect. 24.—*(1.) *Every debtor against whom a receiving order is made shall, unless prevented by sickness or other sufficient cause, attend the first meeting of his creditors, and shall submit to such examination and give such information as the meeting may require.*

(2.) *He shall give such inventory of his property, such list of his creditors and debtors, and of the debts due to and from them respectively, submit to such examination in respect of his property or his creditors, attend such other meetings of his creditors, wait at such times on the official receiver, special manager, or trustee, execute such powers of attorney, conveyances, deeds, and instruments, and generally do all such acts and things in relation to his property and the distribution of the proceeds amongst his creditors, as may be reasonably required by the official receiver, special manager, or trustee, or as may be prescribed by general rules, or be directed by the Court by any special order or orders made in reference to any particular case, or made on the occasion of any special application by the official receiver, special manager, trustee, or any creditor or person interested.*

(3.) *He shall, if adjudged bankrupt, aid, to the utmost of his power, in the realization of his property and the distribution of the proceeds among his creditors.*

I. BANKRUPTCY — STATUTES AND GAZETTE —*continued.*

(4.) *If a debtor wilfully fails to perform the duties imposed on him by this section, or to deliver possession of any part of his property, which is divisible amongst his creditors under this Act, and which is for the time being in his possession or under his control, to the official receiver or to the trustee, or to any person authorized by the Court to take possession of it, he shall, in addition to any other punishment to which he may be subject, be guilty of a contempt of Court, and may be punished accordingly.*

Arrest of Debtor.] *Sect. 25.—*(1.) *The Court may, by warrant addressed to any constable or prescribed officer of the Court, cause a debtor to be arrested, and any books, papers, money, and goods in his possession to be seized, and him and them to be safely kept as prescribed until such time as the Court may order under the following circumstances :*

(a.) *If after a bankruptcy notice has been issued under this Act, or after presentation of a bankruptcy petition by or against him, it appears to the Court that there is probable reason for believing that he is about to abscond with a view of avoiding payment of the debt in respect of which the bankruptcy notice was issued, or of avoiding service of a bankruptcy petition, or of avoiding appearance to any such petition, or of avoiding examination in respect of his affairs, or of otherwise avoiding, delaying, or embarrassing proceedings in bankruptcy against him.*

(b.) *If after presentation of a bankruptcy petition by or against him, it appears to the Court that there is probable cause for believing that he is about to remove his goods with a view of preventing or delaying possession being taken of them by the official receiver or trustee, or that there is probable ground for believing that he has concealed or is about to conceal or destroy any of his goods, or any books, documents, or writings, which may be of use to his creditors in the course of his bankruptcy.*

(c.) *If, after service of a bankruptcy petition on him, or after a receiving order is made against him, he removes any goods in his possession above the value of five pounds, without the leave of the official receiver or trustee.*

(d) *If, without good cause shewn, he fails to attend any examination ordered by the Court.*

Provided that no arrest upon a bankruptcy notice shall be valid and protected unless the debtor before or at the time of his arrest shall be served with such bankruptcy notice.

(2.) *No payment or composition made or security given after arrest made under this section shall be exempt from the provisions of this Act relating to fraudulent preferences.*

Re-direction of Debtor's Letters.] *Sect. 26. Where a receiving order is made against a debtor, the Court, on the application of the official receiver or trustee, may from time to time order that for such time, not exceeding three months, as the Court thinks fit, post letters addressed to the debtor at any place, or places, mentioned in the order for*

D

I. BANKRUPTCY — STATUTES AND GAZETTE
—*continued.*

re-direction shall be re-directed, sent or delivered by the Postmaster-General, or the officers acting under him, to the official receiver or the trustee, or otherwise as the Court directs, and the same shall be done accordingly.

Discovery of Debtor's Property.] *Sect.* 27.—

(1.) *The Court may, on the application of the official receiver or trustee, at any time after a receiving order has been made against a debtor, summon before it the debtor or his wife, or any person known or suspected to have in his possession any of the estate or effects belonging to the debtor, or supposed to be indebted to the debtor, or any person whom the Court may deem capable of giving information respecting the debtor, his dealings, or property, and the Court may require any such person to produce any documents in his custody or power relating to the debtor, his dealings, or property.*

(2.) *If any person so summoned, after having been tendered a reasonable sum, refuses to come before the Court at the time appointed, or refuses to produce any such document, having no lawful impediment made known in the Court at the time of its sitting and allowed by it, the Court may, by warrant, cause him to be apprehended and brought up for examination.*

(3.) *The Court may examine on oath, either by word of mouth or by written interrogatories, any person so brought before it concerning the debtor, his dealings, or property.*

(4.) *If any person on examination before the Court admits that he is indebted to the debtor, the Court may, on the application of the official receiver or trustee, order him to pay to the receiver or trustee, at such time and in such manner as to the Court seems expedient, the amount admitted, or any part thereof, either in full discharge of the whole amount in question or not, as the Court thinks fit, without costs of the examination.*

(5.) *If any person on examination before the Court admits that he has in his possession any property belonging to the debtor, the Court may, on the application of the official receiver or trustee, order him to deliver to the official receiver or trustee such property, or any part thereof, at such time, and in such manner, and on such terms as to the Court may seem just.*

(6.) *The Court may, if it thinks fit, order that any person who if in England would be liable to be brought before it under this section shall be examined in Scotland or Ireland or in any other place out of England.*

Discharge of Bankrupt.] *Sect.* 28.—(1.) *A bankrupt may, at any time after being adjudged bankrupt, apply to the Court for an order of discharge, and the Court shall appoint a day for hearing the application, but the application shall not be heard until the public examination of the bankrupt is concluded. The application shall be heard in open Court.*

(2.) *On the hearing of the application the Court shall take into consideration a report of the official receiver as to the bankrupt's conduct and affairs, and may either grant or refuse an absolute order of discharge, or suspend the operation of the order for a specified time, or grant an order of discharge subject to any conditions with respect to*

I. BANKRUPTCY — STATUTES AND GAZETTE
—*continued.*

any earnings or income which may afterwards become due to the bankrupt, or with respect to his after-acquired property: Provided that the Court shall refuse the discharge in all cases where the bankrupt has committed any misdemeanor under this Act, or Part II. of the Debtors Act, 1869, or any amendment thereof, and shall, on proof of any of the facts hereinafter mentioned, either refuse the order, or suspend the operation of the order for a specified time, or grant an order of discharge, subject to such conditions as aforesaid.

(3.) *The facts hereinbefore referred to are—*

(a.) *That the bankrupt has omitted to keep such books of account as are usual and proper in the business carried on by him and as sufficiently disclose his business transactions and financial position within the three years immediately preceding his bankruptcy:*

(b.) *That the bankrupt has continued to trade after knowing himself to be insolvent:*

(c.) *That the bankrupt has contracted any debt provable in the bankruptcy, without having at the time of contracting it any reasonable or probable ground of expectation (proof whereof shall lie on him) of being able to pay it:*

(d.) *That the bankrupt has brought on his bankruptcy by rash and hazardous speculations or unjustifiable extravagance in living:*

(e.) *That the bankrupt has put any of his creditors to unnecessary expense by a frivolous or vexatious defence to any action properly brought against him:*

(f.) *That the bankrupt has within three months preceding the date of the receiving order, when unable to pay his debts as they became due, given an undue preference to any of his creditors:*

(g.) *That the bankrupt has on any previous occasion been adjudged bankrupt, or made a statutory composition or arrangement with his creditors:*

(h.) *That the bankrupt has been guilty of any fraud or fraudulent breach of trust.*

(4.) *For the purposes of this section the report of the official receiver shall be primâ facie evidence of the statements therein contained.*

(5.) *Notice of the appointment by the Court of the day for hearing the application for discharge shall be published in the prescribed manner and sent fourteen days at least before the day so appointed to each creditor who has proved, and the Court may hear the official receiver and the trustee, and may also hear any creditor. At the hearing the Court may put such questions to the debtor and receive such evidence as it may think fit.*

(6.) *The Court may, as one of the conditions referred to in this section, require the bankrupt to consent to judgment being entered against him by the official receiver or trustee for any balance of the debts provable under the bankruptcy which is not satisfied at the date of his discharge; but in such case execution shall not be issued on the judgment without leave of the Court, which leave may be given on proof that the bankrupt has since his discharge acquired property or income available for payment of his debts.*

I. BANKRUPTCY — STATUTES AND GAZETTE
—*continued.*

(7.) *A discharged bankrupt shall, notwithstanding his discharge, give such assistance as the trustee may require in the realization and distribution of such of his property as is vested in the trustee, and if he fails to do so he shall be guilty of a contempt of Court; and the Court may also, if it thinks fit, revoke his discharge, but without prejudice to the validity of any sale, disposition, or payment duly made or thing duly done subsequent to the discharge, but before its revocation.*

Sect. 29. *In either of the following cases; that is to say,*

(1.) *In the case of a settlement made before and in consideration of marriage where the settlor is not at the time of making the settlement able to pay all his debts without the aid of the property comprised in the settlement; or*

(2.) *In the case of any covenant or contract made in consideration of marriage for the future settlement on or for the settlor's wife or children of any money or property wherein he had not at the date of his marriage any estate or interest (not being money or property of or in right of his wife);*

If the settlor is adjudged bankrupt or compounds or arranges with his creditors, and it appears to the Court that such settlement, covenant, or contract was made in order to defeat or delay creditors, or was unjustifiable having regard to the state of the settlor's affairs at the time when it was made, the Court may refuse or suspend an order of discharge, or grant an order subject to conditions, or refuse to approve a composition or arrangement, as the case may be, in like manner as in cases where the debtor has been guilty of fraud.

Sect. 30.—(1.) *An order of discharge shall not release the bankrupt from any debt on a recognizance nor any debt with which the bankrupt may be chargeable at the suit of the Crown or of any person for any offence against a statute relating to any branch of the public revenue, or at the suit of the sheriff or other public officer on a bail bond entered into for the appearance of any person prosecuted for any such offence, and he shall not be discharged from such excepted debts unless the Treasury certify in writing their consent to his being discharged therefrom. An order of discharge shall not release the bankrupt from any debt or liability incurred by means of any fraud or fraudulent breach of trust to which he was a party, nor from any debt or liability whereof he has obtained forbearance by any fraud to which he was a party.*

(2.) *An order of discharge shall release the bankrupt from all other debts provable in bankruptcy.*

(3.) *An order of discharge shall be conclusive evidence of the bankruptcy, and of the validity of the proceedings therein, and in any proceedings that may be instituted against a bankrupt who has obtained an order of discharge in respect of any debt from which he is released by the order, the bankrupt may plead that the cause of action occurred before his discharge, and may give this Act and the special matter in evidence.*

(4.) *An order of discharge shall not release any person who at the date of the receiving order was a partner or co-trustee with the bankrupt or was jointly bound or had made any joint contract with him or any person who has been surety or in the nature of a surety for him.*

Undischarged Bankrupt obtaining Credit.] Sect. 31. *Where an undischarged bankrupt who has been adjudged bankrupt under this Act obtains credit to the extent of twenty pounds or upwards from any person without informing such person that he is an undischarged bankrupt he shall be guilty of a misdemeanor, and may be dealt with and punished as if he had been guilty of a misdemeanor under the Debtors Act, 1869, and the provisions of that Act shall apply to proceedings under this section.*

PART II. DISQUALIFICATIONS OF BANKRUPT.

Sect. 32.—(1.) *Where a debtor is adjudged bankrupt, he shall, subject to the provisions of this Act, be disqualified for—*

(a.) *Sitting or voting in the House of Lords, or on any committee thereof, or being elected as a peer for Scotland or Ireland to sit and vote in the House of Lords.*

(b.) *Being elected to, or sitting or voting in, the House of Commons, or on any committee thereof;*

(c.) *Being appointed or acting as a justice of the peace;*

(d.) *Being elected to or holding or exercising the office of mayor, alderman, or councillor;*

(e.) *Being elected to or holding or exercising the office of guardian of the poor, overseer of the poor, member of a sanitary authority, or member of a school board, highway board, burial board, or select vestry.*

(2.) *The disqualifications to which a bankrupt is subject under this section shall be removed and cease if and when,—*

(a.) *the adjudication of bankruptcy against him is annulled; or*

(b.) *he obtains from the Court his discharge with a certificate to the effect that his bankruptcy was caused by misfortune without any misconduct on his part.*

The Court may grant or withhold such certificate as it thinks fit, but any refusal of such certificate shall be subject to appeal.

(3.) *The disqualifications imposed by this section shall extend to all parts of the United Kingdom.*

Sect. 33.—(1.) *If a member of the House of Commons is adjudged bankrupt, and the disqualifications arising therefrom under this Act are not removed within six months from the date of the order, the Court shall, immediately after the expiration of that time, certify the same to the Speaker of the House of Commons, and thereupon the seat of the member shall be vacant.*

(2.) *Where the seat of a member so becomes vacant, the Speaker, during a recess of the House, whether by prorogation or by adjournment, shall forthwith, after receiving the certificate, cause notice thereof to be published in the London Gazette; and after the expiration of six days after the publication shall (unless the House has met before that day, or will meet on the day of the issue) issue his warrant to the Clerk of the Crown*

D 2

I. BANKRUPTCY — STATUTES AND GAZETTE
—*continued.*

to make out a new writ for electing another member in the room of the member whose seat has so become vacant.

(3.) *The powers of the Act of the twenty-fourth year of the reign of King George the Third, chapter twenty-six, " to repeal so much of two Acts made in the tenth and fifteenth years of the reign of His present Majesty as authorizes the Speaker of the House of Commons to issue his warrant to the Clerk of the Crown for making out writs for the election of members to serve in Parliament in the manner therein mentioned ; and for substituting other provisions for the like purposes," so far as those powers enable the Speaker to nominate and appoint other persons, being members of the House of Commons, to issue warrants for the making out of new writs during the vacancy of the office of Speaker, or during his absence out of the realm, shall extend to enable him to make the like nomination and appointment for issuing warrants, under the like circumstances and conditions, for the election of a member in the room of any member whose seat becomes vacant under this Act.*

Sect. 34. *If a person is adjudged bankrupt whilst holding the office of mayor, alderman, councillor, guardian, overseer, or member of a sanitary authority, school board, highway board, burial board, or select vestry, his office shall thereupon become vacant.*

Annulment by Adjudication.] *Sect.* 35.—(1.) *Where in the opinion of the Court a debtor ought not to have been adjudged bankrupt, or where it is proved to the satisfaction of the Court that the debts of the bankrupt are paid in full, the Court may, on the application of any person interested, by order, annul the adjudication.*

(2.) *Where an adjudication is annulled under this section, all sales and dispositions of property and payments duly made, and all acts theretofore done, by the official receiver, trustee, or other person acting under their authority, or by the Court, shall be valid, but the property of the debtor who was adjudged bankrupt shall vest in such person as the Court may appoint, or in default of any such appointment revert to the debtor for all his estate or interest therein on such terms and subject to such conditions, if any, as the Court may declare by order.*

(3.) *Notice of the order annulling an adjudication shall be forthwith gazetted and published in a local paper.*

Sect. 36. *For the purposes of this Part of this Act, any debt disputed by a debtor shall be considered as paid in full, if the debtor enters into a bond, in such sum and with such sureties as the Court approves, to pay the amount to be recovered in any proceeding for the recovery of or concerning the debt, with costs, and any debt due to a creditor who cannot be found or cannot be identified shall be considered as paid in full if paid into Court.*

PART III. ADMINISTRATION OF PROPERTY.

Proof of Debts.] *Sect.* 37.—(1.) *Demands in the nature of unliquidated damages arising otherwise than by reason of a contract, promise, or breach of trust, shall not be provable in bankruptcy.*

(2.) *A person having notice of any act of bank-*

I. BANKRUPTCY — STATUTES AND GAZETTE
—*continued.*

ruptcy available against the debtor shall not prove under the order for any debt or liability contracted by the debtor subsequently to the date of his so having notice.

(3.) *Save as aforesaid, all debts and liabilities, present or future, certain or contingent, to which the debtor is subject at the date of the receiving order, or to which he may become subject before his discharge by reason of any obligation incurred before the date of the receiving order, shall be deemed to be debts provable in bankruptcy.*

(4.) *An estimate shall be made by the trustee of the value of any debt or liability provable as aforesaid, which by reason of its being subject to any contingency or contingencies, or for any other reason, does not bear a certain value.*

(5.) *Any person aggrieved by any estimate made by the trustees as aforesaid may appeal to the Court.*

(6.) *If, in the opinion of the Court, the value of the debt or liability is incapable of being fairly estimated, the Court may make an order to that effect, and thereupon the debt or liability shall, for the purposes of this Act, be deemed to be a debt not provable in bankruptcy.*

(7.) *If, in the opinion of the Court, the value of the debt or liability is capable of being fairly estimated, the Court may direct the value to be assessed before the Court itself without the intervention of a jury, and may give all necessary directions for this purpose, and the amount of the value when assessed shall be deemed to be a debt provable in bankruptcy.*

(8.) *" Liability " shall for the purposes of this Act include any compensation for work or labour done, any obligation or possibility of an obligation to pay money or money's worth on the breach of any express or implied covenant, contract, agreement, or undertaking, whether the breach does or does not occur, or is or is not likely to occur or capable of occurring before the discharge of the debtor, and generally it shall include any express or implied engagement, agreement or undertaking to pay, or capable of resulting in the payment of money, or money's worth, whether the payment is, as respects amount, fixed and unliquidated; as respects time, present or future, certain or dependent on any one contingency or on two or more contingencies ; as to mode of valuation capable of being ascertained by fixed rules, or as matter of opinion.*

Mutual Credit and Set-off.] *Sect.* 38. *Where there have been mutual credits, mutual debts, or other mutual dealings between a debtor against whom a receiving order shall be made under this Act, and any other person proving or claiming to prove a debt under such receiving order, an account shall be taken of what is due from the one party to the other in respect of such mutual dealings, and the sum due from the one party shall be set off against any sum due from the other party, and the balance of the account, and no more, shall be claimed or paid on either side respectively ; but a person shall not be entitled under this section to claim the benefit of any set-off against the property of a debtor in any case where he had, at the time of giving credit to the debtor, notice of an act of bankruptcy committed by the debtor and available against him.*

I. BANKRUPTCY — STATUTES AND GAZETTE —*continued.*

Sect. 39. *With respect to the mode of proving debts, the right of proof by secured and other creditors, the admission and rejection of proof's, and the other matters referred to in the Second Schedule, the rules in that schedule shall be observed.*

Priority of Debts.] *Sect.* 40.—(1.) *In the distribution of the property of a bankrupt there shall be paid in priority to all other debts—*

(a.) *All parochial or other local rates due from the bankrupt at the date of the receiving order, and having become due and payable within 12 months next before such time, and all assessed taxes, land tax, property or income tax, assessed on him up to the 5th day of April next before the date of the receiving order, and not exceeding in the whole one year's assessment:*

(b.) *All wages or salary of any clerk or servant in respect of services rendered to the bankrupt during four months before the date of the receiving order, not exceeding £50: and*

(c.) *All wages of any labourer or workman, not exceeding £50, whether payable for time or piece-work, in respect of services rendered to the bankrupt during four months before the date of the receiving order.*

(2.) *The foregoing debts shall rank equally between themselves, and shall be paid in full, unless the property of the bankrupt is insufficient to meet them, in which case they shall abate in equal proportions between themselves.*

(3.) *In the case of partners, the joint estate shall be applicable in the first instance in payment of their joint debts, and the separate estate of each partner shall be applicable in the first instance in payment of his separate debts. If there is a surplus of the separate estates it shall be dealt with as part of the joint estate. If there is a surplus of the joint estate it shall be dealt with as part of the respective separate estates in proportion to the right and interest of each partner in the joint estate.*

(4.) *Subject to the provisions of this Act all debts proved in the bankruptcy shall be paid pari passu.*

(5.) *If there is any surplus after payment of the foregoing debts, it shall be applied in payment of interest from the date of the receiving order at the rate of £4 per centum per annum on all debts proved in the bankruptcy.*

(6.) *Nothing in this section shall alter the effect of sect.* 5 *of the Act* 28 & 29 *Vict. c.* 86, *"to amend the Law of Partnership," or shall prejudice the provisions of the Friendly Societies Act,* 1875.

Preferential Claims.] *Sect.* 41.—(1.) *Where at the time of the presentation of the bankruptcy petition any person is apprenticed or is an articled clerk to the bankrupt, the adjudication of bankruptcy shall, if either the bankrupt or apprentice or clerk gives notice in writing to the trustee to that effect, be a complete discharge of the indenture of apprenticeship or articles of agreement; and if any money has been paid by or on behalf of the apprentice or clerk to the bankrupt as a fee, the trustee may, on the application of the apprentice*

I. BANKRUPTCY — STATUTES AND GAZETTE —*continued.*

or clerk, or of some person on his behalf, pay such sum as the trustee, subject to an appeal to the Court, thinks reasonable, out of the bankrupt's property to or for the use of the apprentice or clerk, regard being had to the amount paid by him or on his behalf, and to the time during which he served with the bankrupt under the indenture or articles before the commencement of the bankruptcy, and to the other circumstances of the case.

(2.) *Where it appears expedient to a trustee, he may, on the application of any apprentice or articled clerk to the bankrupt, or any person acting on behalf of such apprentice or articled clerk, instead of acting under the preceding provisions of this section transfer the indenture of apprenticeship or articles of agreement to some other person.*

Sect. 42.—(1.) *The landlord or other person to whom any rent is due from the bankrupt may at any time, either before or after the commencement of the bankruptcy, distrain upon the goods or effects of the bankrupt for the rent due to him from the bankrupt, with this limitation, that if such distress for rent be levied after the commencement of the bankruptcy it shall be available only for one year's rent accrued due prior to the date of the order of adjudication, but the landlord or other person to whom the rent may be due from the bankrupt may prove under the bankruptcy for the surplus due for which the distress may not have been available.*

(2.) *For the purposes of this section the term "order of adjudication" shall be deemed to include an order for the administration of the estate of a debtor whose debts do not exceed £50, or of a deceased person who dies insolvent.*

Property available for Payment of Debts.] *Sect.* 43. *The bankruptcy of a debtor, whether the same takes place on the debtor's own petition or upon that of a creditor or creditors, shall be deemed to have relation back to, and to commence at, the time of the act of bankruptcy being committed on which a receiving order is made against him, or, if the bankrupt is proved to have committed more acts of bankruptcy than one, to have relation back to, and to commence at, the time of the first of the acts of bankruptcy proved to have been committed by the bankrupt within three months next preceding the date of the presentation of the bankruptcy petition: but no bankruptcy petition, receiving order, or adjudication shall be rendered invalid by reason of any act of bankruptcy anterior to the debt of the petitioning creditor.*

Sect. 44. *The property of the bankrupt divisible amongst his creditors, and in this Act referred to as the property of the bankrupt, shall not comprise the following particulars:—*

(1.) *Property held by the bankrupt on trust for any other person:*

(2.) *The tools (if any) of his trade and the necessary wearing apparel and bedding of himself, his wife and children, to a value, inclusive of tools and apparel and bedding, not exceeding £20 in the whole:*

But it shall comprise the following particulars:—

(i.) *All such property as may belong to or be vested in the bankrupt at the commencement of the bankruptcy, or may be acquired by or devolve on him before his discharge; and,*

(ii.) *The capacity to exercise and to take pro-*

I. BANKRUPTCY — STATUTES AND GAZETTE
—*continued.*

ceedings for exercising all such powers in or over or in respect of property as might have been exercised by the bankrupt for his own benefit at the commencement of his bankruptcy or before his discharge, except the right of nomination to a vacant ecclesiastical benefice ; and,

(iii.) *All goods being, at the commencement of the bankruptcy, in the possession, order or disposition of the bankrupt, in his trade or business, by the consent and permission of the true owner, under such circumstances that he is the reputed owner thereof ; provided that things in action other than debts due or growing due to the bankrupt in the course of his trade or business, shall not be deemed goods within the meaning of this section.*

Effect of Bankruptcy on antecedent Transactions.] *Sect.* 45.—(1.) *Where a creditor has issued execution against the goods or lands of a debtor, or has attached any debt due to him, he shall not be entitled to retain the benefit of the execution or attachment against the trustee in bankruptcy of the debtor, unless he has completed the execution or attachment before the date of the receiving order, and before notice of the presentation of any bankruptcy petition by or against the debtor, or of the commission of any available act of bankruptcy by the debtor.*

(2.) *For the purposes of this Act, an execution against goods is completed by seizure and sale ; an attachment of a debt is completed by receipt of the debt ; and an execution against land is completed by seizure, or, in the case of an equitable interest, by the appointment of a receiver.*

Sect. 46.—(1.) *Where the goods of a debtor are taken in execution, and before the sale thereof notice is served on the sheriff that a receiving order has been made against the debtor, the sheriff shall, on request, deliver the goods to the official receiver or trustee under the order, but the costs of the execution shall be a charge on the goods so delivered, and the official receiver or trustee may sell the goods or an adequate part thereof for the purpose of satisfying the charge.*

(2.) *Where the goods of a debtor are sold under an execution in respect of a judgment for a sum exceeding £20, the sheriff shall deduct the costs of the execution from the proceeds of sale, and retain the balance for fourteen days, and if within that time notice is served on him of a bankruptcy petition having been presented against or by the debtor, and the debtor is adjudged bankrupt thereon or on any other petition of which the sheriff·has notice, the sheriff shall pay the balance to the trustee in the bankruptcy, who shall be entitled to retain the same as against the execution creditor, but otherwise he shall deal with it as if no notice of the presentation of a bankruptcy petition had been served on him.*

(3.) *An execution levied by seizure and sale on the goods of a debtor is not invalid by reason only of its being an act of bankruptcy, and a person who purchases the goods in good faith under a sale by the sheriff shall in all cases acquire a good title to them against the trustee in bankruptcy.*

Voluntary Settlements.] *Sect.* 47.—(1.) *Any settlement of property not being a settlement made*

I. BANKRUPTCY — STATUTES AND GAZETTE
—*continued.*

before and in consideration of marriage, or made in favour of a purchaser or incumbrancer in good faith, and for valuable consideration, or a settlement made on or for the wife or children of the settlor of property which has accrued to the settlor after marriage in right of his wife, shall, if the settlor becomes bankrupt within two years after the date of the settlement, be void against the trustee in bankruptcy, and shall, if the settlor becomes bankrupt at any subsequent time within ten years after the date of the settlement, be void against the trustee in the bankruptcy, unless the parties claiming under the settlement can prove that the settlor was at the time of making the settlement able to pay all his debts without the aid of the property comprised in the settlement, and that the interest of the settlor in such property had passed to the trustee of such settlement on the execution thereof.

(2.) *Any covenant or contract made in consideration of marriage, for the future settlement on or for the settlor's wife or children of any money or property wherein he had not at the date of his marriage any estate or interest, whether vested or contingent, in possession or remainder, and not being money or property of or in right of his wife, shall, on his becoming bankrupt before the property or money has been actually transferred or paid pursuant to the contract or covenant, be void against the trustee in bankruptcy.*

(3.) *"Settlement" shall for the purposes of this section include any conveyance or transfer of property.*

Fraudulent Preference.] *Sect.* 48.—(1.) *Every conveyance or transfer of property, or charge thereon made, every payment made, every obligation incurred, and every judicial proceeding taken or suffered by any person unable to pay his debts as they become due from his own money in favour of any creditor, or any person in trust for any creditor with a view of giving such creditor a preference over the other creditors shall, if the person making, taking, paying, or suffering the same is adjudged bankrupt on a bankruptcy petition presented within three months after the date of making, taking, paying, or suffering the same, be deemed fraudulent and void as against the trustee in the bankruptcy.*

(2.) *This section shall not affect the rights of any person making title in good faith and for valuable consideration through or under a creditor of the bankrupt.*

Protected Transactions.] *Sect.* 49. *Subject to the foregoing provisions of this Act with respect to the effect of bankruptcy on an execution or attachment, and with respect to the avoidance of certain settlements and preferences, nothing in this Act shall invalidate, in the case of a bankruptcy—*

(a.) *Any payment by the bankrupt to any of his creditors :*

(b.) *Any payment or delivery to the bankrupt :*

(c.) *Any conveyance or assignment by the bankrupt for valuable consideration :*
Provided that both the following conditions are complied with, namely :—

(1.) *The payment, delivery, conveyance, assignment, contract, dealing or transaction, as the case may be, takes place before the date of the receiving order ; and*

(2.) *The person (other than the debtor) to, by, or*

I. BANKRUPTCY — STATUTES AND GAZETTE —*continued.*

with whom the payment, delivery, convey-ance, assignment, contract, dealing, or transaction was made, executed, or entered into, has not at the time of the payment, delivery, conveyance, assignment, contract, dealing, or transaction, notice of any available act of bankruptcy committed by the bankrupt before that time.

Realization of Property.] *Sect.* 50.—(1.) *The trustee shall, as soon as may be, take possession of the deeds, books, and documents of the bankrupt, and all other parts of his property capable of manual delivery.*

(2.) *The trustee shall, in relation to and for the purpose of acquiring or retaining possession of the property of the bankrupt, be in the same position as if he were a receiver of the property appointed by the High Court, and the Court may on his appli-cation enforce such acquisition or retention accord-ingly.*

(3.) *Where any part of the property of the bank-rupt consists of stock, shares in ships, shares, or any other property transferable in the books of any company, office, or person, the trustee may exercise the right to transfer the property to the same extent as the bankrupt might have exercised it if he had not become bankrupt.*

(4.) *Where any part of the property of the bank-rupt is of copyhold or customary tenure, or is any like property passing by surrender and admittance or in any similar manner, the trustee shall not be compellable to be admitted to the property, but may deal with it in the same manner as if it had been capable of being and had been duly surrendered or otherwise conveyed to such uses as the trustee may appoint; and any appointee of the trustee shall be admitted to or otherwise invested with the property accordingly.*

(5.) *Where any part of the property of the bank-rupt consists of things in action, such things shall be deemed to have been duly assigned to the trustee.*

(6.) *Any treasurer or other officer, or any banker, attorney, or agent of a bankrupt, shall pay and deliver to the trustee all money and securities in his possession or power, as such officer, banker, attorney, or agent, which he is not by law entitled to retain as against the bankrupt or the trustee. If he does not he shall be guilty of a contempt of Court, and may be punished accordingly on the application of the trustee.*

Seizure of Bankrupt's Property.] *Sect.* 51. *Any person acting under warrant of the Court may seize any part of the property of a bankrupt in the custody or possession of the bankrupt, or of any other person, and with a view to such seizure may break open any house, building, or room of the bankrupt where the bankrupt is supposed to be, or any building or receptacle of the bankrupt where any of his property is supposed to be; and where the Court is satisfied that there is reason to believe that property of the bankrupt is concealed in a house or place not belonging to him, the Court may, if it thinks fit, grant a search warrant to any constable or officer of the Court, who may execute it according to its tenor.*

Sequestration.] *Sect.* 52.—(1.) *Where a bank-rupt is a beneficed clergyman, the trustee may apply for a sequestration of the profits of the*

I. BANKRUPTCY — STATUTES AND GAZETTE —*continued.*

benefice, and the certificate of the appointment of the trustee shall be sufficient authority for the granting of sequestration without any writ or other proceeding, and the same shall accordingly be issued as on a writ of levari facias founded on a judgment against the bankrupt, and shall have priority over any other sequestration issued after the commencement of the bankruptcy in respect of a debt provable in the bankruptcy, except a sequestra-tion issued before the date of the receiving order by or on behalf of a person who at the time of the issue thereof had not notice of an act of bank-ruptcy committed by the bankrupt, and available for grounding a receiving order against him.

(2.) *The bishop of the diocese in which the benefice is situate may, if he thinks fit, appoint to the bankrupt such or the like stipend as he might by law have appointed to a curate duly licensed to serve the benefice in case the bankrupt had been non-resident, and the sequestrator shall pay the sum so appointed out of the profits of the benefice to the bankrupt, by quarterly instalments while he performs the duties of the benefice.*

(3.) *The sequestrator shall also pay out of the profits of the benefice the salary payable to any duly licensed curate of the church of the benefice in respect of duties performed by him as such during four months before the date of the receiving order not exceeding fifty pounds.*

(4.) *Nothing in this section shall prejudice the operation of the Ecclesiastical Dilapidations Act, 1871, or the Sequestration Act, 1871, or any mort-gage or charge duly created under any Act of Par-liament before the commencement of the bankruptcy on the profits of the benefice.*

Appropriation of Salary and Pension.] *Sect.* 53.—(1.) *Where a bankrupt is an officer of the army or navy, or an officer or clerk or otherwise employed or engaged in the civil service of the Crown, the trustee shall receive for distribution amongst the creditors so much of the bankrupt's pay or salary as the Court, on the application of the trustee, with the consent of the chief officer of the department under which the pay or salary is enjoyed, may direct. Before making any order under this sub-section the Court shall communicate with the chief officer of the department as to the amount, time, and manner of the payment to the trustee, and shall obtain the written consent of the chief officer to the terms of such payment.*

(2.) *Where the bankrupt is in the receipt of a salary or income other than as aforesaid, or is entitled to any half-pay, or pension, or to any com-pensation granted by the Treasury, the Court, on the application of the trustee, shall from time to time make such order as it thinks just for the pay-ment of the salary, income, half-pay, pension, or compensation, or of any part thereof, to the trustee to be applied by him in such manner as the Court may direct.*

(3.) *Nothing in this section shall take away or abridge any power of the chief officer of any public department to dismiss a bankrupt, or to declare the pension, half-pay, or compensation of any bankrupt to be forfeited.*

Vesting and Transfer of Property.] *Sect.* 54.— (1.) *Unless a trustee is appointed the official re-ceiver shall be the trustee for the purposes of this*

I. BANKRUPTCY — STATUTES AND GAZETTE
—continued.

Act, and immediately on a debtor being adjudged bankrupt, the property of the bankrupt shall vest in the trustee:

(2.) *On the appointment of a trustee the property shall forthwith pass to and vest in the trustee appointed.*

(3.) *The property of the bankrupt shall pass from trustee to trustee, including under that term the official receiver when he fills the office of trustee, and shall vest in the trustee for the time being during his continuance in office, without any conveyance, assignment, or transfer whatever.*

(4.) *The certificate of appointment of a trustee shall, for all purposes of any law in force in any part of the British dominions requiring registration, enrolment, or recording of conveyances or assignments of property, and may be registered, enrolled, and recorded accordingly.*

Disclaimer of Onerous Property.] *Sect.* 55.—
(1.) *Where any part of the property of the bankrupt consists of land of any tenure, burdened with onerous covenants, of shares or stock in companies, of unprofitable contracts, or of any other property that is unsaleable, or not readily saleable, by reason of its binding the possessor thereof to the performance of any onerous act, or to the payment of any sum of money, the trustee, notwithstanding that he has endeavoured to sell or has taken possession of the property, or exercised any act of ownership in relation thereto, but subject to the provisions of this section, may, by writing signed by him, at any time within three months after the first appointment of a trustee, disclaim the property : Provided that where any such property shall not have come to the knowledge of the trustee within one month after such appointment, he may disclaim such property at any time within two months after he first became aware thereof.*

(2.) *The disclaimer shall operate to determine, as from the date of disclaimer, the rights, interests, and liabilities of the bankrupt and his property in or in respect of the property disclaimed, and shall also discharge the trustee from all personal liability in respect of the property disclaimed as from the date when the property vested in him, but shall not, except so far as is necessary for the purpose of releasing the bankrupt and his property and the trustee from liability, affect the rights or liabilities of any other person.*

(3.) *A trustee shall not be entitled to disclaim a lease without the leave of the Court, except in any cases which may be prescribed by general rules, and the Court may, before or on granting such leave, require such notice to be given to persons interested, and impose such terms as a condition of granting leave, and make such orders with respect to fixtures, tenant's improvements, and other matters arising out of the tenancy as the Court thinks just.*

(4.) *The trustee shall not be entitled to disclaim any property in pursuance of this section in any case where an application in writing has been made to the trustee by any person interested in the property requiring him to decide whether he will disclaim or not, and, the trustee has for a period of twenty-eight days after the receipt of the application, or such extended period as may be allowed by the Court, declined or neglected to give notice*

I. BANKRUPTCY — STATUTES AND GAZETTE
—continued.

whether he disclaims the property or not, and in the case of a contract, if the trustee, after such application as aforesaid, does not within the said period or extended period disclaim the contract, he shall be deemed to have adopted it.

(5.) *The Court may, on the application of any person who is, as against the trustee, entitled to the benefit or subject to the burden of a contract made with the bankrupt, make an order rescinding the contract on such terms as to payment by or to either party of damages for the non-performance of the contract, or otherwise, as to the Court may seem equitable, and any damages payable under the order to any such person may be proved by him as a debt under the bankruptcy.*

(6.) *The Court may, on application by any person either claiming any interest in any disclaimed property, or under any liability not discharged by this Act in respect of any disclaimed property, and on hearing such persons as it thinks fit, make an order for the vesting of the property in or delivery thereof to any person entitled thereto, or to whom it may seem just that the same should be delivered by way of compensation for such liability as aforesaid, or a trustee for him, and on such terms as the Court thinks just ; and on any such vesting order being made, the property comprised therein shall vest accordingly in the person therein named in that behalf without any conveyance or assignment for the purpose.*

Provided always, that where the property disclaimed is of a leasehold nature, the Court shall not make a vesting order in favour of any person claiming under the bankrupt, whether as under-lessee or as mortgagee by demise except upon the terms of making such person subject to the same liabilities and obligations as the bankrupt was subject to under the lease in respect of the property at the date when the bankruptcy petition was filed, and any mortgagee or under-lessee declining to accept a vesting order upon such terms shall be excluded from all interest and security upon the property, and if there shall be no person claiming under the bankrupt who is willing to accept an order upon such terms, the Court shall have power to vest the bankrupt's estate and interest in the property in any person liable either personally or in a representative character, and either alone or jointly with the bankrupt to perform the lessee's covenants in such lease, freed and discharged from all estates, incumbrances, and interests created therein by the bankrupt.

(7.) *Any person injured by the operation of a disclaimer under this section shall be deemed to be a creditor of the bankrupt to the extent of the injury, and may accordingly prove the same as a debt under the bankruptcy.*

Powers of Trustee.] *Sect.* 56. *Subject to the provisions of this Act, the trustee may do all or any of the following things :*

(1.) *Sell all or any part of the property of the bankrupt (including the goodwill of the business, if any, and the book debts due or growing due to the bankrupt), by public auction or private contract, with power to transfer the whole thereof to any person or company, or to sell the same in parcels :*

(2.) *Give receipts for any money received by him,*

I. BANKRUPTCY — STATUTES AND GAZETTE
—*continued.*

which receipts shall effectually discharge the person paying the money from all responsibility in respect of the application thereof :

(3.) *Prove, rank, claim, and draw a dividend in respect of any debt due to the bankrupt :*

(4.) *Exercise any powers the capacity to exercise which is vested in the trustee under this Act, and execute any powers of attorney, deeds, and other instruments for the purpose of carrying into effect the provisions of this Act :*

(5.) *Deal with any property to which the bankrupt is beneficially entitled as tenant in tail in the same manner as the bankrupt might have dealt with it ; and sections fifty-six to seventy-three (both inclusive) of the Act of the session of the third and fourth years of the reign of King William the Fourth (chapter seventyfour), "for the abolition of fines and recoveries, and for the substitution of more simple modes of assurance," shall extend and apply to proceedings under this Act, as if those sections were here re-enacted and made applicable in terms to those proceedings.*

Sect. 57. *The trustee may, with the permission of the committee of inspection, do all or any of the following things :*

(1.) *Carry on the business of the bankrupt, so far as may be necessary for the beneficial winding up of the same :*

(2.) *Bring, institute, or defend any action or other legal proceeding relating to the property of the bankrupt :*

(3.) *Employ a solicitor or other agent to take any proceedings or do any business which may be sanctioned by the committee of inspection :*

(4.) *Accept as the consideration for the sale of any property of the bankrupt a sum of money payable at a future time subject to such stipulations as to security and otherwise as the committee think fit :*

(5.) *Mortgage or pledge any part of the property of the bankrupt for the purpose of raising money for the payment of his debts :*

(6.) *Refer any dispute to arbitration, compromise all debts, claims, and liabilities, whether present or future, certain or contingent, liquidated or unliquidated, subsisting or supposed to subsist between the bankrupt and any person who may have incurred any liability to the bankrupt, on the receipt of such sums, payable at such times, and generally on such terms as may be agreed on :*

(7.) *Make such compromise or other arrangement as may be thought expedient with creditors, or persons claiming to be creditors, in respect of any debts provable under the bankruptcy :*

(8.) *Make such compromise or other arrangement as may be thought expedient with respect to any claim arising out of or incidental to the property of the bankrupt, made or capable of being made on the trustee by any person, or by the trustee on any person :*

I. BANKRUPTCY — STATUTES AND GAZETTE
—*continued.*

(9.) *Divide in its existing form among the creditors, according to its estimated value, any property which from its peculiar nature or other special circumstances cannot be readily or advantageously sold.*

The permission given for the purposes of this section shall not be a general permission to do all or any of the above-mentioned things, but shall only be a permission to do the particular thing or things for which permission is sought in the specified case or cases.

Distribution of Property.] *Sect.* 58.—(1.) *Subject to the retention of such sums as may be necessary for the costs of administration, or otherwise, the trustee shall, with all convenient speed, declare and distribute dividends amongst the creditors who have proved their debts.*

(2.) *The first dividend, if any, shall be declared and distributed within four months after the conclusion of the first meeting of creditors, unless the trustee satisfies the committee of inspection that there is sufficient reason for postponing the declaration to a later date.*

(3.) *Subsequent dividends shall, in the absence of sufficient reason to the contrary, be declared and distributed at intervals of not more than six months.*

(4.) *Before declaring a dividend the trustee shall cause notice of his intention to do so to be gazetted in the prescribed manner, and shall also send reasonable notice thereof to each creditor mentioned in the bankrupt's statement who has not proved his debt.*

(5.) *When the trustee has declared a dividend he shall send to each creditor who has proved a notice shewing the amount of the dividend and when and how it is payable, and a statement in the prescribed form as to the particulars of the estate.*

Sect. 59.—(1.) *Where one partner of a firm is adjudged bankrupt, a creditor to whom the bankrupt is indebted jointly with the other partners of the firm, or any of them, shall not receive any dividend out of the separate property of the bankrupt until all the separate creditors have received the full amount of their respective debts.*

(2.) *Where joint and separate properties are being administered, dividends of the joint and separate properties shall, subject to any order to the contrary that may be made by the Court on the application of any person interested, be declared together ; and the expenses of and incident to such dividends shall be fairly apportioned by the trustee between the joint and separate properties, regard being had to the work done for and the benefit received by each property.*

Sect. 60. *In the calculation and distribution of a dividend the trustee shall make provision for debts provable in bankruptcy appearing from the bankrupt's statements or otherwise to be due to persons resident in places so distant from the place where the trustee is acting that in the ordinary course of communication they have not had sufficient time to tender their proofs, or to establish them if disputed, and also for debts provable in bankruptcy the subject of claims not yet determined. He shall also make provision for any disputed proofs or claims, and for the expenses necessary for the administration of the estate or otherwise, and, subject to the foregoing provisions, he shall distribute as dividend all money in hand.*

I. BANKRUPTCY — STATUTES AND GAZETTE
—continued.

Sect. 61. *Any creditor who has not proved his debt before the declaration of any dividend or dividends shall be entitled to be paid out of any money for the time being in the hands of the trustee any dividend or dividends he may have failed to receive before that money is applied to the payment of any future dividend or dividends, but he shall not be entitled to disturb the distribution of any dividend declared before his debt was proved by reason that he has not participated therein.*

Sect. 62. *When the trustee has realized all the property of the bankrupt, or so much thereof as can, in the joint opinion of himself and of the committee of inspection, be realized without needlessly protracting the trusteeship, he shall declare a final dividend, but before so doing he shall give notice in manner prescribed to the persons whose claims to be creditors have been notified to him, but not established to his satisfaction, that if they do not establish their claims to the satisfaction of the Court within a time limited by the notice, he will proceed to make a final dividend, without regard to their claims. After the expiration of the time so limited, or, if the Court on application by any such claimant grant him further time for establishing his claim, then on the expiration of such further time the property of the bankrupt shall be divided among the creditors who have proved their debts, without regard to the claims of any other persons.*

Sect. 63. *No action for a dividend shall lie against the trustee, but if the trustee refuses to pay any dividend the Court may, if it thinks fit, order him to pay it, and also to pay out of his own money interest thereon for the time that it is withheld, and the costs of the application.*

Sect. 64.—(1.) *The trustee, with the permission of the committee of inspection, may appoint the bankrupt himself to superintend the management of the property of the bankrupt or of any part thereof, or to carry on the trade (if any) of the bankrupt for the benefit of his creditors, and in any other respect to aid in administering the property in such manner and on such terms as the trustee may direct.*

(2.) *The trustee may from time to time, with the permission of the committee of inspection, make such allowance as he may think just to the bankrupt out of his property for the support of the bankrupt and his family, or in consideration of his services if he is engaged in winding up his estate, but any such allowance may be reduced by the Court.*

Sect. 65. *The bankrupt shall be entitled to any surplus remaining after payment in full of his creditors, with interest, as by this Act provided, and of the costs, charges, and expenses of the proceedings under the bankruptcy petition.*

PART IV. OFFICIAL RECEIVERS AND STAFF OF BOARD OF TRADE.

Sect. 66.—(1.) *The Board of Trade may, at any time after the passing of this Act, and from time to time, appoint such persons as they think fit to be official receivers of debtors' estates, and may remove any person so appointed from such office. The official receivers of debtors' estates shall act under the general authority and directions of the Board of Trade, but shall also be officers of the Courts to which they are respectively attached.*

I. BANKRUPTCY — STATUTES AND GAZETTE
—continued.

(2.) *The number of official receivers so to be appointed, and the districts to be assigned to them, shall be fixed by the Board of Trade, with the concurrence of the Treasury. One person only shall be appointed for each district unless the Board of Trade, with the concurrence of the Treasury, shall otherwise direct; but the same person may, with the like concurrence, be appointed to act for more than one district.*

(3.) *Where more than one official receiver is attached to the Court, such one of them as is for the time being appointed by the Court for any particular estate shall be the official receiver for the purposes of that estate. The Court shall distribute the receiverships of the particular estates among the official receivers in the prescribed manner.*

Sect. 67.—(1.) *The Board of Trade may, from time to time, by order direct that any of its officers mentioned in the order shall be capable of discharging the duties of any official receiver during any temporary vacancy in the office, or during the temporary absence of any official receiver through illness or otherwise.*

(2.) *The Board of Trade may, on the application of an official receiver, at any time by order nominate some fit person to be his deputy, and to act for him for such time not exceeding two months as the order may fix, and under such conditions as to remuneration and otherwise as may be prescribed.*

Sect. 68.—(1.) *The duties of the official receiver shall have relation both to the conduct of the debtor and to the administration of his estate.*

(2.) *An official receiver may, for the purpose of affidavits verifying proofs, petitions, or other proceedings under this Act, administer oaths.*

(3.) *All expressions referring to the trustee under a bankruptcy shall, unless the context otherwise requires, or the Act otherwise provides, include the official receiver when acting as trustee.*

(4.) *The trustee shall supply the official receiver with such information, and give him such access to, and facilities for inspecting the bankrupt's books and documents and generally shall give him such aid, as may be requisite for enabling the official receiver to perform his duties under this Act.*

Sect. 69. *As regards the debtor, it shall be the duty of the official receiver—*

(1.) *To investigate the conduct of the debtor and to report to the Court, stating whether there is reason to believe that the debtor has committed any act which constitutes a misdemeanor under the Debtors Act, 1869, or any amendment thereof, or under this Act, or which would justify the Court in refusing, suspending or qualifying an order for his discharge.*

(2.) *To make such other reports concerning the conduct of the debtor as the Board of Trade may direct.*

(3.) *To take such part as may be directed by the Board of Trade in the public examination of the debtor.*

(4.) *To take such part, and give such assistance, in relation to the prosecution of any fraudulent debtor as the Board of Trade may direct.*

Sect. 70.—(1.) *As regards the estate of a debtor, it shall be the duty of the official receiver—*

(a.) *Pending the appointment of a trustee, to act as interim receiver of the debtor's estate,*

I. BANKRUPTCY — STATUTES AND GAZETTE
—continued.

and, where a special manager is not appointed, as manager thereof :

(b.) To authorize the special manager to raise money or make advances for the purposes of the estate in any case where, in the interests of the creditors, it appears necessary so to do :

(c.) To summon and preside at the first meeting of creditors :

(d.) To issue forms of proxy for use at the meetings of creditors :

(e.) To report to the creditors as to any proposal which the debtor may have made with respect to the mode of liquidating· his affairs :

(f.) To advertise the receiving order, the date of the creditors' first meeting, and of the debtor's public examination, and such other matters as it may be necessary to advertise :

(g.) To act as trustee during any vacancy in the office of trustee.

(2.) For the purpose of his duties as interim receiver or manager the official receiver shall have the same powers as if he were a receiver and manager appointed by the High Court, but shall, as far as practicable, consult the wishes of the creditors with respect to the management of the debtor's property, and may for that purpose, if he thinks it advisable, summon meetings of the persons claiming to be creditors, and shall not, unless the Board of Trade otherwise order, incur any expense beyond such as is requisite for the protection of the debtor's property or the disposing of perishable goods.

Provided that when a debtor cannot himself prepare a proper statement of affairs, the official receiver may, subject to any prescribed conditions, and at the expense of the estate, employ some person or persons to assist in the preparation of the statement of affairs.

(3.) Every official receiver shall account to the Board of Trade and pay over all moneys and deal with all securities in such manner as the Board from time to time direct.

Sect. 71. The Board of Trade may, at any time after the passing of this Act, and from time to time, with the approval of the Treasury, appoint such additional officers, including official receivers, clerks and servants (if any) as may be required by the Board for the execution of this Act, and may dismiss any person so appointed.

PART V. TRUSTEES IN BANKRUPTCY.

Remuneration of Trustee.] Sect. 72.—(1.) Where the creditors appoint any person to be trustee of a debtor's estate, his remuneration (if any) shall be fixed by an ordinary resolution of the creditors or if the creditors so resolve by the committee of inspection, and shall be in the nature of a commission or percentage, of which one part shall be payable on the amount realized, after deducting any sums paid to secured creditors out of the proceeds of their securities, and the other part on the amount distributed in dividend.

(2.) If one fourth in number or value of the creditors dissent from the resolution, or the bankrupt satisfies the Board of Trade that the remune-

I. BANKRUPTCY — STATUTES AND GAZETTE
—continued.

ration is unnecessarily large, the Board of Trade shall fix the amount of the remuneration.

(3.) The resolution shall express what expenses the remuneration is to cover, and no liability shall attach to the bankrupt's estate, or to the creditors, in respect of any expenses which the remuneration is expressed to cover.

(4.) Where no remuneration has been voted to a trustee he shall be allowed out of the bankrupt's estate such proper costs and expenses incurred by him in or about the proceedings of the bankruptcy as the taxing officer may allow.

(5.) A trustee shall not, under any circumstances whatever, make any arrangement for or accept from the bankrupt, or any solicitor, auctioneer, or any other person that may be employed about a bankruptcy, any gift, remuneration, or pecuniary or other consideration or benefit whatever beyond the remuneration fixed by the creditors and payable out of the estate, nor shall he make any arrangement for giving up, or give up, any part of his remuneration, either as receiver, manager, or trustee to the bankrupt, or any solicitor or other person that may be employed about a bankruptcy.

Costs.] Sect. 73.—(1.) Where a trustee or manager receives remuneration for his services as such no payment shall be allowed in his accounts in respect of the performance by any other person of the ordinary duties which are required by statute or rules to be performed by himself.

(2.) Where the trustee is a solicitor he may contract that the remuneration for his services as trustee shall include all professional services.

(3.) All bills and charges of solicitors, managers, accountants, auctioneers, brokers, and other persons, not being trustees, shall be taxed by the prescribed officer, and no payments in respect thereof shall be allowed in the trustee's accounts without proof of such taxation having been made. The taxing-master shall satisfy himself before passing such bills and charges that the employment of such solicitors and other persons, in respect of the particular matters out of which such charges arise, has been duly sanctioned.

(4.) Every such person shall, on request by the trustee (which request the trustee shall make a sufficient time before declaring a dividend), deliver his bill of costs or charges to the proper officer for taxation, and if he fails to do so within seven days after receipt of the request, or such further time as the Court, on application, may grant, the trustee shall declare and distribute the dividend without regard to any claim by him, and thereupon any such claim shall be forfeited as well against the trustee personally as against the estate.

Receipts, Payments, Accounts, Audit.] Sect. 74.—(1.) An account, called the Bankruptcy Estates Account, shall be kept by the Board of Trade with the Bank of England, and all moneys received by the Board of Trade in respect of proceedings under this Act shall be paid to that account.

(2.) The account of the Accountant in Bankruptcy at the Bank of England shall be transferred to the Bankruptcy Estates Account.

(3.) Every trustee in bankruptcy shall, in such manner and at such times as the Board of Trade with the concurrence of the Treasury direct, pay the money received by him to the Bankruptcy Estates

I. BANKRUPTCY — STATUTES AND GAZETTE
—*continued.*

Account at the Bank of England, and the Board of Trade shall furnish him with a certificate of receipt of the money so paid.

(4.) Provided that if it appears to the committee of inspection that for the purpose of carrying on the debtor's business, or of obtaining advances, or because of the probable amount of the cash balance, or if the committee shall satisfy the Board of Trade that for any other reason it is for the advantage of the creditors that the trustee should have an account with a local bank, the Board of Trade shall, on the application of the committee of inspection, authorize the trustee to make his payments into and out of such local bank as the committee may select. Such account shall be opened and kept by the trustee in the name of the debtor's estate; and any interest receivable in respect of the account shall be part of the assets of the estate.

The trustee shall make his payments into and out of such local bank in the prescribed manner.

(5.) Subject to any general rules relating to small bankruptcies under Part VII. of this Act, where the debtor at the date of the receiving order has an account at a bank, such account shall not be withdrawn until the expiration of seven days from the day appointed for the first meeting of creditors, unless the Board of Trade, for the safety of the account, or other sufficient cause, order the withdrawal of the account.

(6.) If a trustee at any time retains for more than ten days a sum exceeding £50, or such other amount as the Board of Trade in any particular case authorize him to retain, then, unless he explains the retention to the satisfaction of the Board of Trade, he shall pay interest on the amount so retained in excess at the rate of £20 per centum per annum, and shall have no claim for remuneration, and may be removed from his office by the Board of Trade, and shall be liable to pay any expense occasioned by reason of his default.

(7.) All payments out of money standing to the credit of the Board of Trade in the Bankruptcy Estates Account shall be made by the Bank of England in the prescribed manner.

Sect. 75. No trustee in a bankruptcy or under any composition or scheme of arrangement shall pay any sums received by him as trustee into his private banking account.

Sect. 76.—(1.) Whenever the cash balance standing to the credit of the Bankruptcy Estates Account is in excess of the amount which in the opinion of the Board of Trade is required for the time being to answer demands in respect of bankrupts' estates, the Board of Trade shall notify the same to the Treasury, and shall pay over the same or any part thereof as the Treasury may require to the Treasury, to such account as the Treasury may direct, and the Treasury may invest the said sums or any part thereof in Government securities to be placed to the credit of the said account.

[By the Act 48 & 49 Vict. c. 47, the Treasury may employ so much of these sums as may be necessary, in defraying office accommodation for any officers appointed by the Board of Trade under the Bankruptcy Act, 1883.]

(2.) Whenever any part of the money so invested is, in the opinion of the Board of Trade, required to answer any demands in respect of bankrupt

I. BANKRUPTCY — STATUTES AND GAZETTE
—*continued.*

estates, the Board of Trade shall notify to the Treasury the amount so required, and the Treasury shall thereupon repay to the Board of Trade such sum as may be required to the credit of the Bankruptcy Estates Account, and for that purpose may direct the sale of such part of the said securities as may be necessary.

(3.) The dividends on the investments under this section shall be paid to such account as the Treasury may direct, and regard shall be had to the amount thus derived in fixing the fees payable in respect of bankruptcy proceedings.

Sect. 77. The Treasury may from time to time issue to the Board of Trade in aid of the votes of Parliament, out of the receipts arising from fees, fee stamps, and dividends on investments under this Act, any sums which may be necessary to meet the charges estimated by the Board of Trade in respect of salaries and expenses under this Act.

Sect. 78.—(1.) Every trustee shall, at such times as may be prescribed, but not less than twice in each year during his tenure of office, send to the Board of Trade, or as they direct, an account of his receipts and payments as such trustee.

(2.) The account shall be in a prescribed form, shall be made in duplicate, and shall be verified by a statutory declaration in the prescribed form.

(3.) The Board of Trade shall cause the accounts so sent to be audited, and for the purpose of the audit the trustee shall furnish the Board with such vouchers and information as the Board may require, and the Board may at any time require the reproduction of and inspect any books or accounts the kept by the trustee.

(4.) When any such account has been audited one copy thereof shall be filed and kept by the Board, and the other copy shall be filed with the Court, and each copy shall be open to the inspection of any creditor, or of the bankrupt, or of any person interested.

Sect. 79. The trustee shall, whenever required by any creditor so to do, and on payment by such creditor of the prescribed fee, furnish and transmit to such creditor by post a list of the creditors, shewing in such list the amount of the debt due to each of such creditors.

Sect. 80. The trustee shall keep, in manner prescribed, proper books, in which he shall from time to time cause to be made entries or minutes of proceedings at meetings, and of such other matters as may be prescribed, and any creditor of the bankrupt may, subject to the control of the Court, personally or by his agent inspect any such books.

Sect. 81.—(1.) Every trustee in a bankruptcy shall from time to time, as may be prescribed, and not less than once in every year during the continuance of the bankruptcy, transmit to the Board of Trade a statement shewing the proceedings in the bankruptcy up to the date of the statement, containing the prescribed particulars, and made out in the prescribed form.

(2.) The Board of Trade shall cause the statements so transmitted to be examined, and shall call the trustee to account for any misfeasance, neglect, or omission which may appear on the said statements or in his accounts or otherwise, and may

I. BANKRUPTCY — STATUTES AND GAZETTE
—continued.

require the trustee to make good any loss which the estate of the bankrupt may have sustained by the misfeasance, neglect, or omission.

Release of Trustee.] *Sect.* 82.—(1.) *When the trustee has realized all the property of the bankrupt, or so much thereof as can, in his opinion, be realized without needlessly protracting the trusteeship, and distributed a final dividend, if any, or has ceased to act by reason of a composition having been approved, or has resigned, or has been removed from his office, the Board of Trade shall, on his application, cause a report on his accounts to be prepared, and, on his complying with all the requirements of the Board, shall take into consideration the report, and any objection which may be urged by any creditor or person interested against the release of the trustee, and shall either grant or withhold the release accordingly, subject nevertheless to an appeal to the High Court.*

(2.) *Where the release of a trustee is withheld the Court may, on the application of any creditor or person interested, make such order as it thinks just, charging the trustee with the consequences of any act or default he may have done or made contrary to his duty.*

(3.) *An order of the Board releasing the trustee shall discharge him from all liability in respect of any act done or default made by him in the administration of the affairs of the bankrupt, or otherwise in relation to his conduct as trustee, but any such order may be revoked on proof that it was obtained by fraud or by suppression or concealment of any material fact.*

(4.) *Where the trustee has not previously resigned or been removed, his release shall operate as a removal of him from his office, and thereupon the official receiver shall be the trustee.*

Official Name.] *Sect.* 83. *The trustee may sue and may be sued by the official name of "the trustee of the property of a bankrupt," inserting the name of the bankrupt, and by that name may in any part of the British dominions or elsewhere hold property of every description, make contracts, sue, and be sued, enter into any engagements binding on himself and his successors in office, and do all other acts necessary or expedient to be done in the execution of his office.*

Appointment and Removal.] *Sect.* 84.—(1.) *The creditors may, if they think fit, appoint more persons than one to the office of trustee, and when more persons than one are appointed they shall declare whether any act required or authorized to be done by the trustee is to be done by all or any one or more of such persons, but all such persons are in this Act included under the term "trustee," and shall be joint-tenants of the property of the bankrupt.*

(2.) *The creditors may also appoint persons to act as trustees in succession in the event of one or more of the persons first named declining to accept the office of trustee, or failing to give security or not being approved of by the Board of Trade.*

Sect. 85. *If a receiving order is made against a trustee he shall thereby vacate his office of trustee.*

Sect. 86.—(1.) *The creditors may, by ordinary resolution, at a meeting especially called for that purpose, of which seven days' notice has been given, remove a trustee appointed by them, and may at the*

I. BANKRUPTCY — STATUTES AND GAZETTE
—continued.

same or any subsequent meeting appoint another person to fill the vacancy as hereinafter provided in case of a vacancy in the office of trustee.

(2.) *If the Board of Trade are of opinion that a trustee appointed by the creditors is guilty of misconduct, or fails to perform his duties under this Act, the Board may remove him from his office, but if the creditors, by ordinary resolution, disapprove of his removal, he or they may appeal against it to the High Court.*

Sect. 87.—(1.) *If a vacancy occurs in the office of a trustee the creditors in general meeting may appoint a person to fill the vacancy, and thereupon the same proceedings shall be taken as in the case of a first appointment.*

(2.) *The official receiver shall, on the requisition of any creditor, summon a meeting for the purpose of filling any such vacancy.*

(3.) *If the creditors do not within three weeks after the occurrence of a vacancy appoint a person to fill the vacancy, the official receiver shall report the matter to the Board of Trade, and the Board may appoint a trustee; but in such cases the creditors or committee of inspection shall have the same power of appointing a trustee as in the case of a first appointment.*

(4.) *During any vacancy in the office of trustee the official receiver shall act as trustee.*

Voting Powers of Trustee.] *Sect.* 88. *The vote of the trustee, or of his partner, clerk, solicitor, or solicitor's clerk, either as creditor or as proxy for a creditor, shall not be reckoned in the majority required for passing any resolution affecting the remuneration or conduct of the trustee.*

Control over Trustee.] *Sect.* 89.—(1.) *Subject to the provisions of the Act the trustee shall in the administration of the property of the bankrupt, and in the distribution thereof amongst his creditors, have regard to any directions that may be given by resolution of the creditors at any general meeting, or by the committee of inspection, and any directions so given by the creditors at any general meeting shall in case of conflict be deemed to override any directions given by the committee of inspection.*

(2.) *The trustee may from time to time summon general meetings of the creditors for the purpose of ascertaining their wishes, and it shall be his duty to summon meetings at such times as the creditors, by resolution either at the meeting appointing the trustee or otherwise may direct, or whenever requested in writing to do so by one fourth in value of the creditors.*

(3.) *The trustee may apply to the Court in manner prescribed for directions in relation to any particular matter arising under the bankruptcy.*

(4.) *Subject to the provisions of this Act the trustee shall use his own discretion in the management of the estate and its distribution among the creditors.*

Sect. 90. *If the bankrupt or any of the creditors, or any other person, is aggrieved by any act or decision of the trustee, he may apply to the Court, and the Court may confirm, reverse, or modify the act or decision complained of, and make such orders in the premises as it thinks just.*

Sect. 91.—(1.) *The Board of Trade shall take cognizance of the conduct of trustees, and in the event of any trustee not faithfully performing his duties, and duly observing all the requirements imposed on him by statute, rules or otherwise, with respect to the performance of his duties, or in the event of any complaint being made to the Board by any creditor in regard thereto, the Board shall inquire into the matter and take such action thereon as may be deemed expedient.*

(2.) The Board may at any time require any trustee to answer any inquiry made by them in relation to any bankruptcy in which the trustee is engaged, and may, if the Board think fit, apply to the Court to examine on oath the trustee or any other person concerning the bankruptcy.

(3.) The Board may also direct a local investigation to be made of the books and vouchers of the trustee.

PART VI. CONSTITUTION, PROCEDURE, AND
POWERS OF COURT.
Jurisdiction.

Sect. 92.—(1.) The Courts having jurisdiction in bankruptcy shall be the High Court and the County Courts.

(2.) But the Lord Chancellor may from time to time, by order under his hand, exclude any County Court from having jurisdiction in bankruptcy, and for the purposes of bankruptcy jurisdiction may attach its district or any part thereof to the High Court, or to any other County Court or Courts, and may from time to time revoke or vary any order so made. The Lord Chancellor may, in like manner and subject to the like conditions, detach the district of any County Court or any part thereof from the district and jurisdiction of the High Court.

(3.) The term " district," when used in this Act with reference to a County Court, means the district of the Court for the purposes of bankruptcy jurisdiction.

(4.) A County Court which, at the commencement of this Act, is excluded from having bankruptcy jurisdiction, shall continue to be so excluded until the Lord Chancellor otherwise orders.

(5.) Periodical sittings for the transaction of bankruptcy business by County Courts having jurisdiction in bankruptcy shall be holden at such times and at such intervals as the Lord Chancellor shall prescribe for each such Court.

Sect. 93.—(1.) From and after the commencement of this Act the London Bankruptcy Court shall be united and consolidated with and form part of the Supreme Court of Judicature, and the jurisdiction of the London Bankruptcy Court shall be transferred to the High Court.

(2.) For the purposes of this union, consolidation, and transfer, and of all matters incidental thereto and consequential thereon, the Supreme Court of Judicature Act, 1873, as amended by subsequent Acts, shall, subject to the provisions of this Act, have effect as if the union, consolidation, and transfer had been effected by that Act, except that all expressions referring to the time appointed for the commencement of that Act shall be construed as referring to the commencement of this Act, and, subject as aforesaid, this Act and the said abovementioned Acts shall be read and construed together.

Sect. 94.—(1.) Subject to general rules, and to

orders of transfer made under the authority of the Supreme Court of Judicature Act, 1873, and Acts amending it,—

(a.) All matters pending in the London Bankruptcy Court at the commencement of this Act; and

(b.) All matters which would have been within the exclusive jurisdiction of the London Bankruptcy Court if this Act had not passed; and

(c.) All matters in respect of which jurisdiction is given to the High Court by this Act,

shall be assigned to such Division of the High Court as the Lord Chancellor may from time to time direct.

(2.) All such matters shall, subject as aforesaid, be ordinarily transacted and disposed of by or under the direction of one of the judges of the High Court, and the Lord Chancellor shall from time to time assign a judge for that purpose.

(3.) Provided that during vacation, or during the illness of the judge so assigned, or during his absence or for any other reasonable cause such matters, or any part thereof, may be transacted and disposed of by or under the direction of any judge of the High Court named for that purpose by the Lord Chancellor.

(4.) Subject to the provisions of this Act, the officers, clerks, and subordinate persons who are, at the commencement of this Act, attached to the London Bankruptcy Court, and their successors, shall be officers of the Supreme Court of Judicature, and shall be attached to the High Court.

(5.) Subject to general rules, all bankruptcy matters shall be entitled, " In bankruptcy."

Sect. 95.—(1.) If the debtor against or by whom a bankruptcy petition is presented has resided or carried on business within the London Bankruptcy District as defined by this Act for the greater part of the six months immediately preceding the presentation of the petition, or for a longer period during those six months than in the district of any County Court, or is not resident in England, or if the petitioning creditor is unable to ascertain the residence of the debtor, the petition shall be presented to the High Court.

(2.) In any other case the petition shall be presented to the County Court for the district in which the debtor has resided or carried on business for the longest period during the six months immediately preceding the presentation of the petition.

(3.) Nothing in this section shall invalidate a proceeding by reason of its being taken in a wrong Court.

Sect. 96. The London Bankruptcy District shall, for the purposes of this Act, comprise the city of London and the liberties thereof, and all such parts of the metropolis and other places as are situated within the district of any County Court described as a metropolitan County Court in the list contained in the third schedule.

Sect. 97.—(1.) Subject to the provisions of this Act, every Court having original jurisdiction in bankruptcy shall have jurisdiction throughout England.

(2.) Any proceedings in bankruptcy may at any time, and at any stage thereof, and either with or without application from any of the parties thereto,

I. BANKRUPTCY — STATUTES AND GAZETTE
—continued.

be transferred by any prescribed authority and in the prescribed manner from one Court to another Court, or may by the like authority be retained in the Court in which the proceedings were commenced, although it may not be the Court in which the proceedings ought to have been commenced.

(3.) If any question of law arises in any bankruptcy proceeding in a County Court which all the parties to the proceeding desire, or which one of them and the judge of the County Court may desire, to have determined in the first instance in the High Court, the judge shall state the facts, in the form of a special case, for the opinion of the High Court. The special case and proceedings, or such of them as may be required, shall be transmitted to the High Court for the purposes of the determination.

Sect. 98. Subject to the provisions of this Act and to general rules the judge of the High Court exercising jurisdiction in bankruptcy may exercise in chambers the whole or any part of his jurisdiction.

Sect. 99.—(1.) The registrars in bankruptcy of the High Court, and the registrars of a County Court having jurisdiction in bankruptcy, shall have the power and jurisdiction in this section mentioned, and any order made or act done by such registrars in the exercise of the said powers and jurisdiction shall be deemed the order or act of the Court.

(2.) Subject to general rules limiting the powers conferred by this section, a registrar shall have power—

(a.) To hear bankruptcy petitions, and to make receiving orders and adjudications thereon :

(b.) To hold public examinations of debtors :

(c.) To grant orders of discharge where the application is not opposed :

(d.) To approve compositions or schemes of arrangement when they are not opposed :

(e.) To make interim orders in any case of urgency :

(f.) To make any order or exercise any jurisdiction which by any rule in that behalf is prescribed as proper to be made or exercised in chambers :

(g.) To hear and determine any unopposed or ex parte application :

(h.) To summon and examine any person known or suspected to have in his possession effects of the debtor or to be indebted to him, or capable of giving information respecting the debtor, his dealings, or property.

(3.) The registrars in bankruptcy of the High Court shall also have power to grant orders of discharge and certificates of removal of disqualifications, and to approve compositions and schemes of arrangement.

(4.) A registrar shall not have power to commit for contempt of Court.

(5.) The Lord Chancellor may from time to time by order direct that any specified registrar of a County Court shall have and exercise all the powers of a bankruptcy registrar of the High Court.

Sect. 100. A County Court shall, for the purposes of its bankruptcy jurisdiction, in addition to the ordinary powers of the Court, have all the powers and jurisdiction of the High Court, and orders of the Court may be enforced accordingly in manner prescribed.

I. BANKRUPTCY — STATUTES AND GAZETTE
—continued.

Sect. 101. Where any money or funds have been received by an official receiver, or by the Board of Trade, and the Court makes an order declaring that any person is entitled to such moneys or funds, the Board of Trade shall make an order for the payment thereof to the person so entitled as aforesaid.

Sect. 102.—(1.) Subject to the provisions of this Act, every Court having jurisdiction in bankruptcy under this Act shall have full power to decide all questions of priorities, and all other questions whatsoever, whether of law or fact, which may arise in any case of bankruptcy coming within the cognizance of the Court, or which the Court may deem it expedient or necessary to decide for the purpose of doing complete justice or making a complete distribution of property in any such case.

Provided that the jurisdiction hereby given shall not be exercised by the County Court for the purpose of adjudicating upon any claim, not arising out of the bankruptcy, which might heretofore have been enforced by action in the High Court, unless all parties to the proceeding consent thereto, or the money, money's worth, or right in dispute does not in the opinion of the judge exceed in value £200.

(2.) A Court having jurisdiction in bankruptcy under this Act shall not be subject to be restrained in the execution of its powers under this Act by the order of any other Court, nor shall any appeal lie from its decisions, except in manner directed by this Act.

(3.) If in any proceeding in bankruptcy there arises any question of fact which either of the parties desire to be tried before a jury instead of by the Court itself, or which the Court thinks ought to be tried by a jury, the Court may if it thinks fit direct the trial to be had with a jury, and the trial may be had accordingly, in the High Court in the same manner as if it were the trial of an issue of fact in an action, and in the County Court in the manner in which jury trials in ordinary cases are by law held in that Court.

(4.) Where a receiving order has been made in the High Court under this Act, the judge by whom such order was made shall have power, if he sees fit, without any further consent, to order the transfer to such judge of any action pending in any other division, brought or continued by or against the bankrupt.

(5.) Where default is made by a trustee, debtor, or other person in obeying any order or direction given by the Board of Trade or by an official receiver or any other officer of the Board of Trade under any power conferred by this Act, the Court may, on the application of the Board of Trade or an official receiver or other duly authorized person order such defaulting trustee, debtor, or person to comply with the order or direction so given; and the Court may also, if it shall think fit, upon any such application make an immediate order for the committal of such defaulting trustee, debtor, or other person ; provided that the power given by this subsection shall be deemed to be in addition to and not in substitution for any other right or remedy in respect of such default.

Judgment Debtors.] Sect. 103.—(1.) It shall be lawful for the Lord Chancellor by order to direct that the jurisdiction and powers under sect. 5 of the

I. BANKRUPTCY — STATUTES AND GAZETTE
—*continued.*

Debtors Act, 1869, *now vested in the High Court, shall be assigned to and exercised by the judge to whom bankruptcy business is assigned.*

(2.) *It shall be lawful also for the Lord Chancellor in like manner to direct that the whole or any part of the said jurisdiction and powers shall be delegated to and exercised by the bankruptcy registrars of the High Court.*

(3.) *Any order made under this section may, at any time, in like manner, be rescinded or varied.*

(4.) *Every County Court within the jurisdiction of which a judgment debtor is or resides shall have jurisdiction under sect.* 5 *of the Debtors Act,* 1869, *although the amount of the judgment debt may exceed £50.*

(5.) *Where, under sect.* 5 *of the Debtors Act,* 1869, *application is made by a judgment creditor to a Court, having bankruptcy jurisdiction, for the committal of a judgment debtor, the Court may, if it thinks fit, decline to commit, and in lieu thereof, with the consent of the judgment creditor, and on payment by him of the prescribed fee, make a receiving order against the debtor. In such case the judgment debtor shall be deemed to have committed an act of bankruptcy at the time the order is made.*

(6.) *General rules under this Act may be made for the purpose of carrying into effect the provisions of the Debtors Act,* 1869.

Appeals.] *Sect.* 104.—(1.) *Every Court having jurisdiction in bankruptcy under this Act may review, rescind, or vary any order made by it under its bankruptcy jurisdiction.*

[*By the Act* 47 *Vict. c.* 9, *sub-section* 2 *of this section is repealed; and an appeal lies at the instance of any person aggrieved from the order of a County Court to a Divisional Court of the High Court, of which the judge to whom bankruptcy business is assigned shall be a member for the time being.*

The decision of such Divisional Court is final; unless leave be given by it, or by the Court of Appeal, to appeal to the Court of Appeal, which appeal is final.]

Procedure.] *Sect.* 105.—(1.) *Subject to the provisions of this Act and to general rules, the costs of and incidental to any proceeding in Court under this Act shall be in the discretion of the Court: Provided that where any issue is tried by a jury the costs shall follow the event, unless, upon application made at the trial for good cause shewn, the judge before whom such issue is tried shall otherwise order.*

(2.) *The Court may at any time adjourn any proceedings before it upon such terms, if any, as it may think fit to impose.*

(3.) *The Court may at any time amend any written process or proceeding under this Act upon such terms, if any, as it may think fit to impose.*

(4.) *Where by this Act or by general rules, the time for doing any act or thing is limited, the Court may extend the time either before or after the expiration thereof, upon such terms, if any, as the Court may think fit to impose.*

(5.) *Subject to general rules, the Court may in any matter take the whole or any part of the evidence either vivâ voce, or by interrogatories, or upon affidavit, or by commission abroad.*

I. BANKRUPTCY — STATUTES AND GAZETTE
—*continued.*

(6.) *For the purpose of approving a composition or scheme by joint debtors, the Court may, if it thinks fit, and on the report of the official receiver that it is expedient so to do, dispense with the public examination of one of such joint debtors if he is unavoidably prevented from attending the examination by illness or absence abroad.*

Sect. 106. *Where two or more bankruptcy petitions are presented against the same debtor or against joint debtors, the Court may consolidate the proceedings, or any of them, on such terms as the Court thinks fit.*

Sect. 107. *Where the petitioner does not proceed with due diligence on his petition, the Court may substitute as petitioner any other creditor to whom the debtor may be indebted in the amount required by this Act in the case of the petitioning creditor.*

Sect. 108. *If a debtor by or against whom a bankruptcy petition has been presented dies, the proceedings in the matter shall, unless the Court otherwise orders, be continued as if he were alive.*

Sect. 109. *The Court may at any time, for sufficient reason, make an order staying the proceedings under a bankruptcy petition, either altogether or for a limited time, on such terms and subject to such conditions as the Court may think just.*

Sect. 110. *Any creditor whose debt is sufficient to entitle him to present a bankruptcy petition against all the partners of a firm may present a petition against any one or more partners of the firm without including the others.*

Sect. 111. *Where there are more respondents than one to a petition the Court may dismiss the petition as to one or more of them, without prejudice to the effect of the petition as against the other or others of them.*

Sect. 112. *Where a receiving order has been made on a bankruptcy petition against or by one member of a partnership, any other bankruptcy petition against or by a member of the same partnership shall be filed in or transferred to the Court in which the first mentioned petition is in course of prosecution, and, unless the Court otherwise directs, the same trustee or receiver shall be appointed as may have been appointed in respect of the property of the first mentioned members of the partnership, and the Court may give such directions for consolidating the proceedings under the petitions as it thinks just.*

Sect. 113. *Where a member of a partnership is adjudged bankrupt, the Court may authorize the trustee to commence and prosecute any action in the names of the trustee and of the bankrupt's partner; and any release by such partner of the debt or demand to which the action relates shall be void; but notice of the application for authority to commence the action shall be given to him, and he may shew cause against it, and on his application the Court may, if it thinks fit, direct that he shall receive his proper share of the proceeds of the action, and if he does not claim any benefit therefrom he shall be indemnified against costs in respect thereof as the Court directs.*

Sect. 114. *Where a bankrupt is a contractor in respect of any contract jointly with any person or persons, such person or persons may sue or be sued in respect of the contract without the joinder of the bankrupt.*

I. BANKRUPTCY—STATUTES AND GAZETTE
—*continued.*

Sect. 115. *Any two or more persons, being part-ners, or any person carrying on business under a partnership name, may take proceedings or be pro-ceeded against under this Act in the name of the firm, but in such case the Court may, on application by any person interested, order the names of the persons who are partners in such firm or the name of such person to be disclosed in such manner, and verified on oath, or otherwise as the Court may direct.*

Officers.] *Sect.* 116.—(1.) *No registrar or other officer attached to any Court having jurisdiction in bankruptcy shall, during his continuance in office, be capable of being elected or sitting as a member of the House of Commons.*

(2.) *No registrar or official receiver or other officer attached to any such Court shall, during his continuance in office, either directly or indirectly, by himself, his clerk, or partner, act as solicitor in any proceedings in bankruptcy or in any prosecu-tion of a debtor by order of the Court, and if he does so act he shall be liable to be dismissed from office.*

Provided that nothing in this section shall affect the right of any registrar or officer appointed before the passing of this Act to act as solicitor by himself, his clerk, or partner to the extent permitted by sect. 69 *of the Bankruptcy Act,* 1869.

Orders and Warrants of Court.] *Sect.* 117. *Any order made by a Court having jurisdiction in bank-ruptcy in England under this Act shall be enforced in Scotland and Ireland in the Courts having juris-diction in bankruptcy in those parts of the United Kingdom respectively, in the same manner in all respects as if the order had been made by the Court hereby required to enforce it; and in like manner any order made by a Court having jurisdiction in bankruptcy in Scotland shall be enforced in England and Ireland, and any order made by a Court having jurisdiction in bankruptcy in Ireland shall be enforced in England and Scotland by the Courts respectively having jurisdiction in bankruptcy in the part of the United Kingdom where the orders may require to be enforced, and in the same manner in all respects as if the order had been made by the Court required to enforce it in a case of bankruptcy within its own jurisdiction.*

Sect. 118. *The High Court, the County Courts, the Courts having jurisdiction in bankruptcy in Scotland and Ireland, and every British Court elsewhere having jurisdiction in bankruptcy or insolvency, and the officers of those Courts respec-tively, shall severally act in aid of and be auxiliary to each other in all matters of bankruptcy, and an order of the Court seeking aid, with a request to another of the said Courts, shall be deemed suffi-cient to enable the latter Court to exercise, in regard to the matters directed by the order, such jurisdiction, as either the Court which made the request, or the Court to which the request is made, could exercise in regard to similar matters within their respective jurisdictions.*

Sect. 119.—(1.) *Any warrant of a Court having jurisdiction in bankruptcy in England may be enforced in Scotland, Ireland, Isle of Man, the Channel Isles, and elsewhere in Her Majesty's dominions, in the same manner and subject to the same privileges in and subject to which a warrant*

I. BANKRUPTCY—STATUTES AND GAZETTE
—*continued.*

issued by any justice of the peace against a person for an indictable offence against the laws of England, may be executed in those parts of Her Majesty's dominions respectively in pursuance of the Acts of Parliament in that behalf.

(2.) *A search warrant issued by a Court having jurisdiction in bankruptcy for the discovery of any property of a debtor may be executed in manner prescribed, or in the same manner and subject to the same privileges in and subject to which a search warrant for property supposed to be stolen may be executed according to law.*

Sect. 120. *Where the Court commits any person to prison, the commitment may be to such convenient prison as the Court thinks expedient, and if the gaoler of any prison refuses to receive any person so committed he shall be liable for every such refusal to a fine not exceeding £100.*

PART VII. SMALL BANKRUPTCIES.

Sect. 121. *When a petition is presented by or against a debtor, if the Court is satisfied by affi-davit or otherwise, or the official receiver reports to the Court that the property of the debtor is not likely to exceed in value £300, the Court may make an order that the debtor's estate be administered in a summary manner, and thereupon the provisions of this Act shall be subject to the following modifi-cations:—*

(1.) *If the debtor is adjudged bankrupt the official receiver shall be the trustee in the bankruptcy:*

(2.) *There shall be no committee of inspection, but the official receiver may do with the permission of the Board of Trade all things which may be done by the trustee with the permission of the committee of inspection:*

(3.) *Such other modifications may be made in the provisions of this Act as may be prescribed by general rules with the view of saving expense and simplifying procedure; but nothing in this section shall permit the modification of the provisions of this Act relating to the examination or discharge of the debtor.*

Provided that the creditors may at any time, by special resolution, resolve that some person other than the official receiver be appointed trustee in the bankruptcy, and thereupon the bankruptcy shall proceed as if an order for summary administration had not been made.

Sect. 122.—(1.) *Where a judgment has been .ob-tained in a County Court and the debtor is unable to pay the amount forthwith, and alleges that his whole indebtedness amounts to a sum not exceeding £50, inclusive of the debt for which the judgment is obtained, the County Court may make an order pro-viding for the administration of his estate, and for the payment of his debts by instalments or other-wise, and either in full or to such extent as to the County Court under the circumstances of the case appears practicable, and subject to any conditions as to his future earnings or income which the Court may think just.*

(2.) *The order shall not be invalid by reason only that the total amount of the debts is found at any time to exceed £50, but in such case the County Court may, if it thinks fit, set aside the order.*

E

I. BANKRUPTCY—STATUTES AND GAZETTE
—*continued.*

(3.) *Where, in the opinion of the County Court in which the judgment is obtained, it would be inconvenient that that Court should administer the estate, it shall cause a certificate of the judgment to be forwarded to the County Court in the district of which the debtor or the majority of the creditors reside or reside, and thereupon the latter County Court shall have all the powers which it would have under this section, had the judgment been obtained in it.*

(4.) *Where it appears to the registrar of the County Court that property of the debtor exceeds in value £10, he shall, at the request of any creditor, and without fee, issue execution against the debtor's goods, but the household goods, wearing apparel, and bedding of the debtor or his family, and the tools and implements of his trade to the value in the aggregate of £20, shall to that extent be protected from seizure.*

(5.) *When the order is made no creditor shall have any remedy against the person or property of the debtor in respect of any debt which the debtor has notified to a County Court, except with the leave of that County Court, and on such terms as that Court may impose; and any County Court or inferior Court in which proceedings are pending against the debtor in respect of any such debt shall, on receiving notice of the order, stay the proceedings, but may allow costs already incurred by the creditor, and such costs may, on application, be added to the debt notified.*

(6.) *If the debtor makes default in payment of any instalment payable in pursuance of any order under this section, he shall, unless the contrary is proved, be deemed to have had since the date of the order the means to pay the sum in respect of which he has made default and to have refused or neglected to pay the same.*

(7.) *The order shall be carried into effect in such manner as may be prescribed by general rules.*

(8.) *Money paid into Court under the order shall be appropriated first in satisfaction of the costs of the plaintiff in the action, next in satisfaction of the costs of administration (which shall not exceed 2s. in the pound on the total amount of the debts), and then in liquidation of debts in accordance with the order.*

(9.) *Notice of the order shall be sent to the registrar of County Court judgments, and be posted in the office of the County Court of the district in which the debtor resides, and sent to every creditor notified by the debtor, or who has proved.*

(10.) *Any creditor of the debtor, on proof of his debt before the registrar, shall be entitled to be scheduled as a creditor of the debtor for the amount of his proof.*

(11.) *Any creditor may in the prescribed manner object to any debt scheduled, or to the manner in which payment is directed to be made by instalments.*

(12.) *Any person who after the date of the order becomes a creditor of the debtor, shall, on proof of his debt before the registrar, be scheduled as a creditor of the debtor for the amount of his proof, but shall not be entitled to any dividend under the order until those creditors who are scheduled as having been creditors before the date of the order have been paid to the extent provided by the order.*

(13.) *When the amount received under the order is sufficient to pay each creditor scheduled to the extent thereby provided, and the costs of the plaintiff, and of the administration, the order shall be superseded, and the debtor shall be discharged from his debts to the scheduled creditors.*

(14.) *In computing the salary of a registrar under the County Court Acts every creditor scheduled, not being a judgment creditor, shall count as a plaint.*

PART VIII. SUPPLEMENTAL PROVISIONS.

Application of Act.] *Sect.* 123. *A receiving order shall not be made against any corporation, or against any partnership or association, or company registered under the Companies Act, 1862.*

Sect. 124. *If a person having privilege of Parliament commits an act of bankruptcy, he may be dealt with under this Act in like manner as if he had not such privilege.*

Sect. 126. *No person not being a trader within the meaning of the Bankruptcy Act, 1861, shall be adjudged bankrupt in respect of a debt contracted before the passing of the Act.*

Administration of Deceased Insolvent Debtor's Estate.] *Sect.* 125.—(1.) *Any creditor of a deceased debtor whose debt would have been sufficient to support a bankruptcy petition against such debtor, had he been alive, may present to the Court a petition in the prescribed form praying for an order for the administration of the estate of the deceased debtor, according to the Law of Bankruptcy.*

(2.) *Upon the prescribed notice being given to the legal personal representative of the deceased debtor, the Court may in the prescribed manner, upon proof of the petitioner's debt, unless the Court is satisfied that there is a reasonable probability that the estate will be sufficient for the payment of the debts owing by the deceased, make an order for the administration in bankruptcy of the deceased debtor's estate, or may upon cause shewn dismiss such petition with or without costs.*

(3.) *An order of administration under this section shall not be made until the expiration of two months from the date of the grant of probate or letters of administration, unless with the concurrence of the legal personal representative of the deceased debtor, or unless the petitioner proves to the satisfaction of the Court that the debtor committed an act of bankruptcy within three months prior to his decease.*

(4.) *A petition for administration under this section shall not be presented to the Court after proceedings have been commenced in any Court of justice for the administration of the deceased debtor's estate, but that Court may in such case, on the application of any creditor, and on proof that the estate is insufficient to pay its debts, transfer the proceedings to the Court exercising jurisdiction in bankruptcy, and thereupon such last-mentioned Court may, in the prescribed manner, make an order for the administration of the estate of the deceased debtor, and the like consequences shall ensue as under an administration order made on the petition of a creditor.*

(5.) *Upon an order being made for the administration of a deceased debtor's estate, the property of the debtor shall vest in the official receiver of the Court, as trustee thereof, and he shall forthwith*

I. BANKRUPTCY—STATUTES AND GAZETTE —*continued.*

proceed to realize and distribute the same in accordance with the provisions of this Act.

(6.) *With the modifications hereinafter mentioned, all the provisions of Part III. of this Act, relating to the administration of the property of a bankrupt, shall, so far as the same are applicable, apply to the case of an administration order under this section in like manner as to an order of adjudication under this Act.*

(7.) *In the administration of the property of the deceased debtor under an order of administration, the official receiver shall have regard to any claim by the legal personal representative of the deceased debtor to payment of the proper funeral and testamentary expenses incurred by him in and about the debtor's estate, and such claims shall be deemed a preferential debt under the order, and be payable in full, out of the debtor's estate, in priority to all other debts.*

(8.) *If, on the administration of a deceased debtor's estate, any surplus remains in the hands of the official receiver, after payment in full of all the debts due from the debtor, together with the costs of the administration and interest as provided by this Act in case of bankruptcy, such surplus shall be paid over to the legal personal representative of the deceased debtor's estate, or dealt with in such other manner as may be prescribed.*

(9.) *Notice to the legal personal representative of a deceased debtor of the presentation by a creditor of a petition under this section shall, in the event of an order for administration being made thereon, be deemed to be equivalent to notice of an act of bankruptcy, and after such notice no payment or transfer of property made by the legal personal representative shall operate as a discharge to him as between himself and the official receiver ; save as aforesaid nothing in this section shall invalidate any payment made, or any act or thing done in good faith by the legal personal representative before the date of the order for administration.*

(10.) *Unless the context otherwise requires, "Court," in this section, means the Court within the jurisdiction of which the debtor resided or carried on business for the greater part of the six months immediately prior to his decease ; "creditor" means one or more creditors qualified to present a bankruptcy petition, as in this Act provided.*

(11.) *General rules, for carrying into effect the provisions of this section, may be made in the same manner and to the like effect and extent as in bankruptcy.*

Construction of former Acts, &c.] *Sect.* 149.—(1.) *Where in any Act of Parliament, instrument, or proceeding passed, executed, or taken before the commencement of this Act, mention is made of a commission of bankruptcy or fiat in bankruptcy, the same shall be construed, with reference to the proceedings under a bankruptcy petition, as if a commission of or fiat in bankruptcy had been actually issued at the time of the presentation of such petition.*

(2.) *Where by any act or instrument reference is made to the Bankruptcy Act, 1869, the act or instrument shall be construed and have effect as if reference were made therein to the corresponding provisions of this Act.*

Crown.] *Sect.* 150. *Save as herein provided*

I. BANKRUPTCY—STATUTES AND GAZETTE —*continued.*

the provisions of this Act relating to the remedies against the property of a debtor, the priorities of debts, the effect of a composition or scheme of arrangement and the effect of a discharge shall bind the Crown.

Audience, Right of.] *Sect.* 151. *Nothing in this Act, or in any transfer of jurisdiction effected thereby, shall take away or affect any right of audience that any person may have had at the commencement of this Act, and all solicitors and other persons who had the right of audience before the Chief Judge in Bankruptcy shall have the like right of audience in bankruptcy matters in the High Court.*

Married Women.] *Sect.* 152. *Nothing in this Act shall affect the provisions of the Married Women's Property Act, 1882.*

Evidence.] *Sect.* 132.—(1.) *A copy of the London Gazette containing any notice inserted therein in pursuance of this Act shall be evidence of the facts stated in the notice.*

(2.) *The production of a copy of the London Gazette containing any notice of a receiving order, or of an order adjudging a debtor bankrupt, shall be conclusive evidence in all legal proceedings of the order having been duly made, and of its date.*

Sect. 133.—(1.) *A minute of proceedings at a meeting of creditors under this Act, signed at the same or the next ensuing meeting, by a person describing himself as, or appearing to be, chairman of the meeting at which the minute is signed, shall be received in evidence without further proof.*

(2.) *Until the contrary is proved, every meeting of creditors in respect of the proceedings whereof a minute has been so signed shall be deemed to have been duly convened and held, and all resolutions passed or proceedings had thereat to have been duly passed or had.*

Sect. 134. *Any petition or copy of a petition in bankruptcy, any order or certificate or copy of an order or certificate made by any Court having jurisdiction in bankruptcy, any instrument or copy of an instrument, affidavit, or document made or used in the course of any bankruptcy proceedings, or other proceedings had under this Act, shall, if it appears to be sealed with the seal of any Court having jurisdiction in bankruptcy, or purports to be signed by any judge thereof, or is certified as a true copy by any registrar thereof, be receivable in evidence in all legal proceedings whatever.*

Sect. 135. *Subject to general rules, any affidavit to be used in a Bankruptcy Court may be sworn before any person authorized to administer oaths in the High Court, or in the Court of Chancery of the County Palatine of Lancaster, or before any registrar of a Bankruptcy Court, or before any officer of a Bankruptcy Court authorized in writing on that behalf by the judge of the Court, or, in case of a person residing in Scotland or in Ireland, before a judge ordinary, magistrate, or justice of the peace, or, in the case of a person who is out of the Kingdom of Great Britain and Ireland, before a magistrate or justice of the peace or other person qualified to administer oaths in the country where he resides (he being certified to be a magistrate or justice of the peace, or qualified as aforesaid by a British minister or British consul, or by a notary public).*

I. BANKRUPTCY—STATUTES AND GAZETTE
—*continued.*

Sect. 136. *In case of the death of the debtor or his wife, or of a witness whose evidence has been received by any Court in any proceeding under this Act, the deposition of the person so deceased, purporting to be sealed with the seal of the Court, or a copy thereof purporting to be so sealed, shall be admitted as evidence of the matters therein deposed to.*

Sect. 137. *Every Court having jurisdiction in bankruptcy under this Act shall have a seal describing the Court in such manner as may be directed by order of the Lord Chancellor, and judicial notice shall be taken of the seal, and of the signature of the judge or registrar of any such Court, in all legal proceedings.*

Sect. 138. *A certificate of the Board of Trade that a person has been appointed trustee under this Act, shall be conclusive evidence of his appointment.*

Sect. 139. *Where by this Act an appeal to the High Court is given against any decision of the Board of Trade, or of the official receiver, the appeal shall be brought within twenty-one days from the time when the decision appealed against is pronounced or made.*

Sect. 140.—(1.) *All documents purporting to be orders or certificates made or issued by the Board of Trade, and to be sealed with the seal of the Board, or to be signed by a secretary or assistant secretary of the Board, or any person authorized in that behalf by the President of the Board, shall be received in evidence, and deemed to be such orders or certificates without further proof unless the contrary is shewn.*

(2.) *A certificate signed by the President of the Board of Trade, that any order made, certificate issued, or act done, is the order, certificate, or act of the Board of Trade shall be conclusive evidence of the act so certified.*

Time.] *Sect.* 141.—(1.) *Where by this Act any limited time from or after any date or event is appointed or allowed for the doing of any act or the taking of any proceeding, then in the computation of that limited time the same shall be taken as exclusive of the day of that date or of the happening of that event, and as commencing at the beginning of the next following day ; and the act or proceeding shall be done or taken at latest on the last day of that limited time as is computed, unless the last day is a Sunday, Christmas Day, Good Friday, or Monday or Tuesday in Easter week, or a day appointed for public fast, humiliation, or thanksgiving, or a day on which the Court does not sit, in which case any act or proceeding shall be considered as done or taken in due time if it is done or taken on the next day afterwards, which shall not be one of the days in this section specified.*

(2.) *Where by this Act any act or proceeding is directed to be done or taken on a certain day, then if that day happens to be one of the days in this section specified, the act or proceeding shall be considered as done or taken in due time if it is done or taken on the next day afterwards, which shall not be one of the days in this section specified.*

Notices.] *Sect.* 142. *All notices and other documents for the service of which no special mode is directed may be sent by prepaid post letter to the last known address of the person to be served therewith.*

I. BANKRUPTCY—STATUTES AND GAZETTE
—*continued.*

Formal Defects.] *Sect.* 143.—(1.) *No proceeding in bankruptcy shall be invalidated by any formal defect or by any irregularity unless the Court before which an objection is made to the proceeding is of opinion that substantial injustice has been caused by the defect or irregularity and that the injustice cannot be remedied by any order of that Court.*

(2.) *No defect or irregularity in the appointment or election of a receiver, trustee, or member of a committee of inspection shall vitiate any act done by him in good faith.*

General Rules.] *Sect.* 127 *empowers the Lord Chancellor to make rules for carrying into effect the objects of the Act, which rules, when sanctioned by Parliament, are to take effect as if enacted by the Act.*

Fees.] *Sect.* 128 *empowers the Lord Chancellor to prescribe a scale of fees and percentages to be charged for in respect of proceedings under the Act.*

Sect. 129. *As to judicial salaries, &c.*

Sect. 130. *Annual accounts of receipts and expenditure in respect of bankruptcy proceedings to be laid before Parliament and to be audited.*

Sect. 131. *Bankruptcy officers to make returns of the business in their respective Courts and offices.*

Pending Proceedings.] *Sect.* 169.—(1.) *Repeal of enactments.*

(2.) *Savings.*

(3.) *Notwithstanding the repeal effected by this Act, the proceedings under any bankruptcy petition, liquidation by arrangement or composition with creditors under the Bankruptcy Act, 1869, pending at the commencement of this Act shall, except so far as any provision of this Act is expressly applied to pending proceedings, continue, and all the provisions of the Bankruptcy Act, 1869, shall, except as aforesaid, apply thereto, as if this Act had not passed.*

Sect. 170. *After the passing of this Act no composition or liquidation by arrangement under sects. 125 and 126 of the Bankruptcy Act, 1869, shall be entered into or allowed without the sanction of the Court or registrar having jurisdiction in the matter ; such sanction shall not be granted unless the composition or liquidation appears to the Court or registrar to be reasonable and calculated to benefit the general body of creditors.*

Stamp Duty.] *Sect.* 144. *Every deed, conveyance, assignment, surrender, admission, or other assurance relating solely to freehold, leasehold, copyhold, or customary property, or to any mortgage, charge, or other incumbrance on, or any estate, right, or interest in any real or personal property which is part of the estate of any bankrupt, and which, after the execution of the deed, conveyance, assignment, surrender, admission, or other assurance, either at law or in equity, is or remains the estate of the bankrupt or of the trustee under the bankruptcy, and every power of attorney, proxy paper, writ, order, certificate, affidavit, bond, or other instrument or writing relating solely to the property of any bankrupt, or to any proceeding under any bankruptcy, shall be exempt from stamp duty, except in respect of fees under this Act,*

Executions.] *Sect.* 145. *Where the sheriff sells the goods of a debtor under an execution for a sum*

I. BANKRUPTCY—STATUTES AND GAZETTE
—*continued.*

exceeding twenty pounds (including legal incidental expenses), the sale shall, unless the Court from which the process issued otherwise orders, be made by public auction, and not by bill of sale or private contract, and shall be publicly advertised by the sheriff on and during three days next preceding the day of sale.

Sect. 146.—(1.) *The sheriff shall not under a writ of elegit deliver the goods of a debtor nor shall a writ of elegit extend to goods.*

(2.) No writ of levari facias shall hereafter be issued in any civil proceeding.

Bankrupt Trustee.] *Sect.* 147. *Where a bankrupt is a trustee within the Trustee Act, 1850, sect. thirty-two of that Act shall have effect so as to authorize the appointment of a new trustee in substitution for the bankrupt (whether voluntarily resigning or not), if it appears expedient to do so, and all provisions of that Act, and of any other Act relative thereto, shall have effect accordingly.*

Corporations, &c.] *Sect.* 148. *For all or any of the purposes of this Act a corporation may act by any of its officers authorized in that behalf under the seal of the corporation, a firm may act by any of its members, and a lunatic may act by his committee or curator bonis.*

Transitory Provisions.] *Sect.* 153. *As to comptroller in bankruptcy, and other officers and their staff.*

Sect. 154 *empowers Lord Chancellor to abolish existing offices.*

Sect. 155. *As to performance of new duties by persons whose offices are abolished.*

Sect. 156. *Persons appointed to any office or employment under the Act to be selected from persons whose offices or employments have been abolished under the Act.*

Sect. 157. *As to acceptance of public employment by any person to whom a compensation annuity is granted under the Act.*

Sect. 158. *Superannuation of registrars, &c.*

Sect. 159. *In every liquidation by arrangement, under the Bankruptcy Act, 1869, pending at the commencement of this Act, if at any time after the commencement of this Act there is no trustee acting in the liquidation by reason of death, or for any other cause, such of the official receivers of bankrupts' estates as is appointed by the Board of Trade for that purpose, shall become and be the trustee in the liquidation, and the property of the liquidating debtor shall pass to and vest in him accordingly; but this provision shall not prejudice the right of the creditors in the liquidation to appoint a new trustee, in manner directed by the Bankruptcy Act, 1869, or the rules thereunder, and on such appointment the property of the liquidating debtor shall pass to and vest in the new trustee.*

The provisions of this Act with respect to the duties and responsibilities of and accounting by a trustee in a bankruptcy under this Act shall apply, as nearly as may be, to a trustee acting under the provisions of this section.

Sect. 160. *Where a bankruptcy or liquidation by arrangement under the Bankruptcy Act, 1869, has been or is hereafter closed, any property of the bankrupt or liquidating debtor which vested in the trustee and has not been realized or distributed shall vest in such person as may be appointed by*

I. BANKRUPTCY—STATUTES AND GAZETTE
—*continued.*

the Board of Trade for that purpose, and he shall thereupon proceed to get in, realize, and distribute the property in like manner, and with and subject to the like powers and obligations, as far as applicable, as if the bankruptcy or liquidation were continuing, and he were acting as trustee thereunder.

Sect. 161. *In every bankruptcy under the Bankruptcy Act, 1869, pending at the commencement of this Act, where a registrar of the London Bankruptcy Court, or of any County Court is or would hereafter but for this enactment become the trustee under the bankruptcy, such of the official receivers of bankrupts' estates as may be appointed by the Board of Trade for that purpose shall from and after the commencement of this Act be the trustee in the place of the registrar, and the property of the bankrupt shall pass to and vest in the official receiver accordingly.*

Unclaimed Funds or Dividends.] *Sect.* 162.—
(1.) *Where the trustee, under any bankruptcy, composition or scheme pursuant to this Act, shall have under his control any unclaimed dividend which has remained unclaimed for more than six months, or where, after making a final dividend, such trustee shall have in his hands or under his control any unclaimed or undistributed moneys arising from the property of the debtor, he shall forthwith pay the same to the Bankruptcy Estates Account at the Bank of England. The Board of Trade shall furnish him with a certificate of receipt of the money so paid, which shall be an effectual discharge to him in respect thereof.*

(2.) (a.) Where, after the passing of this Act, any unclaimed or undistributed funds or dividends in the hands or under the control of any trustee or other person empowered to collect, receive, or distribute any funds or dividends under any Act of Parliament mentioned in the Fourth Schedule, or any petition, resolution, deed, or other proceeding under or in pursuance of any such Act, have remained or remain unclaimed or undistributed for six months after the same became claimable or distributable, or in any other case for two years after the receipt thereof by such trustee or other person, it shall be the duty of such trustee or other person forthwith to pay the same to the Bankruptcy Estates Account at the Bank of England. The Board of Trade shall furnish such trustee or other person with a certificate of receipt of the money so paid, which shall be an effectual discharge to him in respect thereof.

(b.) The Board of Trade may at any time order any such trustee or other person to submit to them an account verified by affidavit of the sums received and paid by him under or in pursuance of any such petition, resolution, deed, or other proceeding as aforesaid, and may direct and enforce an audit of the account.

(c.) The Board of Trade, with the concurrence of the Treasury, may from time to time appoint a person to collect and get in all such unclaimed or undistributed funds or dividends, and for the purposes of this section any Court having jurisdiction in bankruptcy shall have and at the instance of the person so appointed, or of the Board of Trade, may exercise all the powers conferred by this Act with respect to the discovery and realization of the pro-

I. BANKRUPTCY—STATUTES AND GAZETTE
—*continued.*

*perty of a debtor, and the provisions of Part. I. of
this Act with respect thereto shall, with any necessary modification, apply to proceedings under this
section.*

(3.) *The provisions of this section shall not,
except as expressly declared herein, deprive any
person of any larger or other right or remedy to
which he may be entitled against such trustee or
other person.*

(4.) *Any person claiming to be entitled to any
moneys paid in to the Bankruptcy Estates Account
pursuant to this section may apply to the Board of
Trade for payment to him of the same, and the
Board of Trade, if satisfied that the person claiming is entitled, shall make an order for the payment
to such person of the sum due.*

*Any person dissatisfied with the decision of the
Board of Trade in respect of his claim may appeal
to the High Court.*

(5.) *The Board of Trade may at any time after
the passing of this Act open the account at the
Bank of England referred to in this Act as the
Bankruptcy Estates Account.*

Fraudulent Debtors, Punishment of.] Sect. 163.
—(1.) Sects. 11 and 12 of the Debtors Act, 1869,
relating to the punishment of fraudulent debtors
and imposing a penalty for absconding with property, shall have effect as if there were substituted
therein for the words " *if after the presentation of
a bankruptcy petition against him,*" the words, " *if
after the presentation of a bankruptcy petition by
or against him.*"

(2.) *The provisions of the Debtors Act, 1869, as
to offences by bankrupts shall apply to any person
whether a trader or not in respect of whose estate a
receiving order has been made as if the term
"bankrupt" in that Act included a person in
respect of whose estate a receiving order had been
made.*

Sect. 164. Sect. 16 of the Debtors Act, 1869, shall
be construed and have effect as if the term " *a
trustee in any bankruptcy*" included the official
receiver of a bankrupt's estate, and shall apply to
offences under this Act as well as to offences under
the Debtors Act, 1869.

Sect. 165.—(1.) *Where there is, in the opinion
of the Court, ground to believe that the bankrupt
or any other person has been guilty of any offence
which is by statute made a misdemeanor in case of
bankruptcy, the Court may commit the bankrupt or
such other person for trial.*

(2.) *For the purpose of committing the bankrupt
or such other person for trial the Court shall have
all the power of a stipendiary magistrate as to
taking depositions, binding over witnesses to appear,
admitting the accused to bail, or otherwise.*

*Nothing in this sub-section shall be construed as
derogating from the power or jurisdiction of the
High Court.*

Sect. 166. *Where the Court orders the prosecution
of any person for any offence under the Debtors
Act, 1869, or Acts amending it. or for any offence
arising out of or connected with any bankruptcy
proceedings, it shall be the duty of the Director of
Public Prosecutions to institute and carry on the
prosecution.*

Sect. 167. *Where a debtor has been guilty of any
criminal offence he shall not be exempt from being*

I. BANKRUPTCY—STATUTES AND GAZETTE
—*continued.*

*proceeded against therefor by reason that he has
obtained his discharge, or that a composition or
scheme of arrangement has been accepted or approved.*

THE GENERAL RULES OF 1883 MADE PURSUANT
TO SECT. 127 OF THE BANKRUPTCY ACT, 1883,
REFER TO THE FOLLOWING MATTERS:—

R. 1. *Preliminary.*
[R. 2a. *Additional*　　– 　L. G., 1884, p. 1721]
R. 4. *Forms.*

PART I. COURT PROCEDURE.

R. 5. *Court and Chambers.*
R. 8. *Proceedings.*
R. 16. *Transfer of proceedings.*
R. 19. *Motions and practice.*
R. 30. *Security in Court.*
R. 39. *Affidavits.*
R. 51. *Stamps.*
R. 53. *Witnesses and depositions.*
[R. 59 *is annulled and* r. 59a *is substituted
for it -* 　　　　　L. G., 1884, p. 536]
R. 64. *Discovery.*
R. 65. *Taking accounts of property mortgaged,
and of the sale thereof.*
R. 70. *Discovery of debtor's property.*
R. 71. *Appropriation of pay, salary, pension,
&c.*
R. 75. *Warrants, arrests, and commitments.*
R. 79. *Service and execution of process.*
R. 84. *Trial by jury.*
R. 88. *Sittings of County Court.*
R. 90. *Rules relating to the business of the High
Court.*
R. 98. *Costs.*
R. 111. *Appeals.*
[R. 114 *is annulled, and* r. 114a *is substituted
for it* 　-　　　-　　-　L. G., 1884, p. 1721]
[R. 116 *is annulled, and* r. 116a *is substituted
for it* 　-　　　-　　-　L. G., 1884, p. 1721]

PART II. PROCEEDINGS FROM ACT OF BANK-
RUPTCY TO DISCHARGE.

R. 117. *Declaration of inability to pay debts.*
R. 118. *Bankruptcy notice.*
R. 125. *Bankruptcy petition.*
R. 129. *Creditor's petition.*
R. 144. *Service of creditor's petition.*
R. 149. *Hearing of petition.*
R. 150. *Receiving order.*
R. 155. *Adjudication.*
R. 159. *Composition or scheme under sects. 18
or 23.*
R. 168. *Statement of affairs.*
R. 169. *Proof of debts.*
R. 175. *Dividends.*
R. 178. *Discharge.*
R. 183. *Proxies and voting letters.*
R. 184. *Meetings of creditors.*
R. 191. *Proceedings by company or co-partner-
ship.*
R. 192. *Proceedings by or against firm.*

PART III. SPECIAL PROCEDURES.

R. 198. *Small bankruptcies.*
R. 200. *Administration of estate of persons dying
insolvent.*

I. BANKRUPTCY—STATUTES AND GAZETTE
—*continued.*

PART IV.—OFFICERS, TRUSTEES, AUDIT, &c.

R. 203. *Gazetting.*

R. 204. *Books to be kept and returns to be made by Registrars.*

R. 207. *Accounts and audit.*

R. 218. *Trustees.*

R. 232. *Disclaimer of lease.*

R. 233. *Official receivers.*

R. 251. *Payment into and out of bank.*

R. 253. *Security by trustee or special manager.*

R. 254. *Remuneration of special manager, &c.*

R. 255. *Unclaimed funds, &c., under sect.* 162.

PART V.—MISCELLANEOUS.

R. 257. *Miscellaneous matters.*

R. 265. *Jurisdiction of High Court under sect.* 5 *of the Debtors Act,* 1869, *and sect.* 103 *of this Act.*

Department.] *Establishment of a new department to be called the Bankruptcy Department. Jan.* 1st, 1884 - L. G., **1884**, p. 8

Fees.] *Table of fees to be paid on proceedings under this Act. Dec.* 28, 1883 **L. G., 1883**, p. 6709

Amendment of above notice with regard to stamps. July 1st, 1884 **L. G., 1884**, p. 3011

Fees and percentages to be charged under the Bankruptcy Act, 1883, *after* 1st *of July,* 1885. *Order of Lord Chancellor,* 15th *of June,* 1885 [L. G., 1885, p. 2935

Notice of the appointment of one official receiver for the district of the High Court, and fixing the number of official receivers for County Courts. Jan. 1st, 1884 - - L. G., **1884**, p. 6

Receivers.] *Preliminary notice of* 25th *of August,* 1883, *of Board of Trade, under sect.* 162 *of the Bankruptcy Act of* 1883, *with regard to unclaimed dividends and other undistributed funds in the hands of persons empowered to receive the same under* 7 & 8 *Vict. c.* 70, 13 *Vict. c.* 106, 25 *Vict. c.* 134, *and* 33 *Vict. c.* 71 L. G., **1883**, p. 4229

II. BANKRUPTCY—ACT OF BANKRUPTCY.

(a.) ASSIGNMENT OF WHOLE PROPERTY.

1. —— **Secret Undertaking by Assignee to pay Debt**—*Release of existing Debt—Intent to defeat or delay Creditors*—13 *Eliz. c.* 5—*Bankruptcy Act,* 1869 (32 & 33 *Vict. c.* 71), s. 6, *sub-s.* 2.] A trader in embarrassed circumstances in July, 1882, assigned substantially the whole of his property (including his stock-in-trade, book debts, and the goodwill of his business) to a single creditor, in consideration (as expressed in the deed) of the release by that creditor of a debt of £3271 then owing to him by the debtor. In fact, at the date of the assignment, only £1370 was due by the assignor to the assignee, and the real consideration was the release by the assignee of that debt, and a secret verbal agreement between him and the assignor that he should undertake the payment of the assignor's debts (either the whole of his debts, or, at any rate, his trade debts). On the same day the assignor entered into a written agreement to manage the business as the servant of the assignee at a weekly salary. The assignee, a few days before the execution of the deed, but after the arrangement between the parties had been come to, paid out some executions for the assignor, and shortly after the execution of the

II. BANKRUPTCY—ACT OF BANKRUPTCY—
continued.

(a) ASSIGNMENT OF WHOLE PROPERTY—*contd.*

deed he paid an arrear of rent which the assignor owed to his landlord. The business was, after the execution of the deed, carried on by the assignor in his own name, just as it was before, there being nothing to shew that he was not the real, as well as the apparent, owner of it, though he was in fact acting under the directions of the assignee. None of the other creditors knew of the assignment. In March, 1883, the assignor was adjudged a bankrupt. At the date of the bankruptcy nearly all the trade debts due by the assignor at the date of the deed had been paid in the course of the carrying on of the business :—*Held,* by Cotton and Bowen, L.JJ., that the deed was void as against the trustee in the bankruptcy as an act of bankruptcy, its necessary effect being to defeat and delay the assignor's creditors in enforcing their ordinary remedies for the recovery of their debts, and there being no means by which they could compel the fulfilment by the assignee of his agreement to pay their debts :—*Held,* by Fry, L.J., that the deed was void as against the assignor's creditors under the statute 13 Eliz. c. 5. —*Held,* also, that the assignee was not entitled to payment in full out of the bankrupt's estate of the sums which he had paid under the agreement, but that he could only prove for them in the bankruptcy. *Ex parte* CHAPLIN. *In re* SINCLAIR
[26 Ch. D. 319

2. —— **Security for past Debt**—*Further Advances—Substantial Exception—Tenant Right—Contemplation of further Advances—Notice of Act of Bankruptcy.*] In order that the execution of a bill of sale of substantially the whole of the grantor's property as security for a pre-existing debt and further advances may not be an act of bankruptcy, it is necessary that there should be an agreement binding the grantee to make further advances.—It is not sufficient that further advances should have been in the contemplation of the parties, the deed being stamped so as to cover them, and further advances having been actually made after the execution of the deed.— A farmer assigned by a bill of sale, as a security for a pre-existing debt and further advances, the whole of his property, except a part of his tenant right under his agreement of tenancy. That agreement provided that the tenant should be paid on quitting the farm for all fallows made in the last year of the tenancy (not exceeding a certain proportion), for all seeds duly sown by him, for all dung made during the last year, for all hay, fodder, and straw the produce of the last year, &c., at a valuation. But it was also provided that, in case of any breach or non-performance of any of the stipulations on the part of the tenant, it should be lawful for the landlord to re-enter, and that, in case no entry should be made, the landlord should on the expiration of the tenancy be entitled to an allowance from the tenant in respect of any such breach or non-performance, to be deducted from the tenant's valuation. There was no covenant or agreement binding the grantee to make further advances, though the deed was stamped so as to cover a further advance :—*Held,* that the tenant right

II. BANKRUPTCY—ACT OF BANKRUPTCY—
continued.

(a) ASSIGNMENT OF WHOLE PROPERTY—*contd.*

did not form a substantial exception from the deed; that the execution of the deed was an act of bankruptcy by the grantor; and that it was void as against the trustee in his bankruptcy, which commenced within three months afterwards.—Some small further advances were, in fact, made by the grantee to the grantor, soon after the execution of the deed, to enable him to pay the wages of his labourers:—*Held*, that inasmuch as the grantee had made those advances with notice of the act of bankruptcy committed by the execution of the deed, he could not retain them out of the proceeds of sale of the grantor's stock which he had seized under the deed.—*Ex parte Winder* (1 Ch. D. 290, 560) considered. *Ex parte* DANN. *In re* PARKER - **17 Ch. D. 26**

3. —— **Security for past Debt**—*Further Advance—Bankruptcy Act, 1869 (32 & 33 Vict. c. 71), s. 6, sub-s. 2.*] In order that a deed, assigning the whole of a debtor's property as security for an existing debt, may not be fraudulent and an act of bankruptcy within sub-sect. 2 of sect. 6 of the Bankruptcy Act, 1869, on the ground that the assignee agreed to make further advances to the assignor, it is not necessary that the agreement should be technically binding at law or in equity; a bonâ fide promise is sufficient.—The question in all such cases is whether the arrangement was made bonâ fide with the view of enabling the debtor to continue his business, or whether it was a mere scheme to obtain payment of the existing debt.—*Ex parte Dann* (17 Ch. D. 26) commented on. *Ex parte* WILKINSON. *In re* BERRY

[22 Ch. D. 788

4. —— **Security for past Debt**—*Further Advance— Bankruptcy Act, 1869, s. 6, sub-s. 2.] Graham v. Chapman* (12 C. B. 85), so far as it decides that a bill of sale which, to secure an existing debt and a present advance, assigns the whole of the grantor's property, including that which he may purchase by means of the advance, is necessarily void as an act of bankruptcy, must be taken to have been overruled. *Ex parte* HAUXWELL. *In re* HEMINGWAY　**23 Ch. D. 626**

5. —— **Security for past Debt**—*Further Advance—Statement of Consideration—Affidavit on Registration—Jurat—Omission of Commissioner's Title—Bankruptcy Act, 1869 (32 & 33 Vict. c. 71), s. 6, sub-s. 2—Bills of Sale Act, 1878 (41 & 42 Vict. c. 31), ss. 8, 10.]* When a bill of sale of the whole of a trader's property is executed as security for an existing debt and a fresh advance, the true test whether the execution of the deed is an act of bankruptcy, is, Was the fresh advance made by the lender with the intention of enabling the borrower to continue his business, and had he reasonable grounds for believing that the advance would enable the borrower to do so? If these questions can be answered in the affirmative, the execution of the deed is not an act of bankruptcy. The Court ought not to look at the uncommunicated intention of the borrower, nor at the actual result of the loan. The consideration for a bill of sale is sufficiently stated, so as to satisfy the requirements of sect. 8 of the Bills of Sale Act, 1878, if it is stated with substantial

II. BANKRUPTCY—ACT OF BANKRUPTCY —
continued.

(a) ASSIGNMENT OF WHOLE PROPERTY—*contd.*

accuracy—if the true legal or business effect of what actually took place is stated. Strict literal accuracy of statement is not necessary. The affidavit filed on the registration of a bill of sale was sworn before a commissioner to administer oaths, but in the jurat he merely signed his name, and did not add his title as commissioner: —*Held*, that, notwithstanding this omission, the affidavit was sufficient. *Ex parte* JOHNSON. *In re* CHAPMAN　　**26 Ch. D. 338**

(b.) BANKRUPTCY NOTICE.

6. —— **Conditional Payment of Debt** *within Seven Days after Service of Notice—Promissory Note—Receiving Order—Bankruptcy Act, 1883 (46 & 47 Vict. c. 52), s. 4, sub-s. 1 (g).*] Within seven days after the service of a bankruptcy notice the debtor gave to the creditor a promissory note, payable two months after date, for the amount of the debt, which note the creditor accepted:—*Held*, that, the note being a conditional payment of the debt, the creditor could not, during the currency of the note, avail himself of the bankruptcy notice to obtain a receiving order against the debtor. *Ex parte* MATTHEW

[12 Q. B. D. 506

7. —— **Final Judgment** — *Company — Winding-up — Contributory — Balance Order — Bankruptcy Act, 1883 (46 & 47 Vict. c. 52), s. 4, sub-s. 1 (g).*] A "balance order," made in the voluntary winding-up of a company on a contributory, for the payment of calls which had been made upon him before the commencement of the winding-up, is not a "final judgment" within the meaning of sub-s. 1 (g) of sect. 4 of the Bankruptcy Act, 1883, and therefore a bankruptcy notice cannot be issued in respect of such an order. *Ex parte* WHINNEY. *In re* SANDERS　　**13 Q. B. D. 476**

8. —— **Final Judgment**—*Executor of original Judgment Creditor—Bankruptcy Act, 1883 (46 & 47 Vict. c. 52), s. 4, sub-s. 1 (g)—Rules of Supreme Court, 1883, Order XLII., r. 23.]* The executor of a creditor who has obtained a final judgment is not entitled to issue a bankruptcy notice against the judgment debtor, unless he has obtained leave from the Court, under rule 23 of Order XLII. of the Rules of the Supreme Court of 1883, to issue execution on the judgment.—Under sub-sect. 1 (g) of sect. 4 of the Bankruptcy Act, 1883, the creditor who issues a bankruptcy notice must be in a position to issue execution on the judgment. *Ex parte* WOODALL. *In re* WOODALL

[13 Q. B. D. 479

9. —— **Final Judgment** — *Garnishee Order absolute—Bankruptcy Act, 1883 (46 & 47 Vict. c. 52), s. 4, sub-s. 1 (g).*] A garnishee order absolute is not a "final judgment" against the garnishee within sub-s. 1 (g) of sect. 4 of the Bankruptcy Act, 1883, and the judgment creditor who has obtained the order cannot issue a bankruptcy notice against the garnishee in respect of it. *Ex parte* CHINERY - **12 Q. B. D. 342**

10. —— **Final Judgment**—*Judgment for Costs —Bankruptcy Act, 1883 (46 & 47 Vict. c. 52), s. 4, sub-s. 1 (g).*] At the trial of an action in the

II. BANKRUPTCY—ACT OF BANKRUPTCY—continued.

(b) BANKRUPTCY NOTICE—continued.

Chancery Division, upon motion for judgment in default of pleading, judgment was given ordering and adjudging that the Defendant should be perpetually restrained from practising as a solicitor at Liverpool or otherwise in violation of his covenant with the Plaintiff. And the Court declared that the partnership between the Plaintiff and the Defendant ought to be dissolved as from the date of the Plaintiff's notice, and ordered and decreed the same accordingly. And it was ordered that an inquiry should be made what was the amount of the damages which the Plaintiff had sustained by reason of the Defendant's breach of covenant, and that the Defendant should, within fourteen days from the date of the Chief Clerk's certificate, pay the amount of the damages, when certified, to the Plaintiff. And it was ordered that the Defendant should pay to the Plaintiff his taxed costs of the action. The costs were taxed and were partly paid by the Defendant. The inquiry as to damages was not prosecuted :— Held, that the order for the payment of costs was a "final judgment" within the meaning of sect. 4, sub-sect. 1 (g), of the Bankruptcy Act, 1883, and that the Plaintiff was entitled to serve the Defendant with a bankruptcy notice for the unpaid balance of costs.—Ex parte Chinery (12 Q. B. D. 342) explained. Ex parte MOORE. In re FAITHFULL - - 14 Q. B. D. 627

11. —— **Final Judgment**—Order for Payment of Costs—Bankruptcy Act, 1883 (46 & 47 Vict. c. 52), s. 4, sub-s. 1 (g).] The Defendants to an action for the specific performance of a contract executed the deeds necessary to carry out the contract, and an order was then made by consent that, on the Defendants paying the Plaintiff's taxed costs of the action all further proceedings in the action should be stayed. The costs were taxed, and an order was made that the Defendants should, on or before a day named, pay the taxed amount. Payment was not made within the time appointed :—Held, that the order for payment was not a "final judgment," within the meaning of sub-sect. 1 (g) of sect. 4 of the Bankruptcy Act, 1883, and that a bankruptcy notice could not be founded on it. Ex parte SCHMITZ
[12 Q. B. D. 509

(c.) DEBTOR'S SUMMONS.

12. —— **Convicted Felon**—Adjudication of Bankruptcy—33 & 34 Vict. c. 23, s. 8.] Notwithstanding the provision contained in sect. 8 of the Act 33 & 34 Vict. c. 23, that every convicted felon shall, during the time while he shall be subject to the operation of the Act, be incapable of alienating or charging any property, such a convict can pay a debt which is claimed by a debtor's summons issued and served on him after his conviction, and if he fails to pay the debt within the time limited by the summons, he will commit an act of bankruptcy, upon which an adjudication can be made against him. Ex parte GRAVES. In re HARRIS - 19 Ch. D. 1

13. —— **Dismissal**—Legal or equitable Defence to Action—Bankruptcy Act, 1869 (32 & 33 Vict. c. 71, s. 7 — Inchoate Agreement between Debtor

II. BANKRUPTCY—ACT OF BANKRUPTCY—continued.

(c.) DEBTOR'S SUMMONS—continued.

and Creditors.] In order to justify the issuing of a debtor's summons under s. 7 of the Bankruptcy Act, 1869, the alleged debt must be an exigible debt; if the debtor would have any defence, legal or equitable, to an action for the debt the summons ought to be dismissed.—Two partners in trade whose affairs were embarrassed, without filing a liquidation petition, summoned a meeting of their creditors. Nineteen out of twenty-seven creditors attended the meeting, their debts amounting to £2400 out of a total of £2628, and a resolution was passed that a deed of assignment of the debtor's estate and effects should be made to three persons named, as trustees for the benefit of the creditors, with power for them to carry on the business for such time as they should think fit, and to sell the concern as a going concern, or otherwise. One of the debtors was to have his discharge on payment of £200, or otherwise as the creditors might direct. The resolution was signed by the chairman of the meeting, but by no one else. The day after the meeting the debtors gave up possession of their assets to the persons named in the resolution as trustees, and those persons carried on the business for a few weeks, and proceeded to collect the book debts. A draft deed of assignment was prepared in accordance with the resolution, but it was never executed, the other creditors not having assented to the arrangement embodied in the resolution :— Held, that, inasmuch as all the creditors did not come in and assent to the arrangement, there was no binding agreement between the debtors and their creditors, and that, consequently, a creditor who was present at the meeting, even if he had assented to the resolution, which appeared to be doubtful, was entitled to issue a debtor's summons for his debt. Ex parte FOSTER. In re FOSTER - - - 22 Ch. D. 797

14. —— **Jurisdiction**—Residence of and carrying on of Business by Debtor—Bankruptcy Rules, 1870, r. 17.] Held, that a debtor, who was employed as a clerk in a bank, the office of which was within the district of the London Bankruptcy Court, was within the meaning of rule 17 of the Bankruptcy Rules, 1870, "carrying on business" within the district of that Court, and that consequently that Court had jurisdiction to grant a debtor's summons against him.—The debtor's private residence was in one of the suburbs, outside the district of the London Court :—Held, by James, L.J., that he was also, within the meaning of rule 17, "residing" within the district of the London Court. Ex parte BREULL. In re BOWIE
[16 Ch. D. 484

15. —— **Liquidated Demand**—Equitable Mortgage by Deposit—Interest—Bankruptcy Act, 1869, s. 6.] In April, 1879, A. deposited title deeds with B. to secure repayment of an advance of £1000, and an agreement was at the same time executed that the deeds should be held as an equitable security for payment on the 15th of July, 1879, of the £1000 and interest at $7\frac{1}{2}$ per cent. per annum, and also that A. should execute to B. a legal mortgage of the property, with power of sale and such other powers as B. might

II.·BANKRUPTCY—ACT OF BANKRUPTCY—
continued.

(c) DEBTOR'S SUMMONS—*continued.*

ɑcquire for further securing payment of the money which should then be owing on the security of the agreement, "with interest for the same after the rate aforesaid."—In January, 1881, B. took out a debtor's summons for £150, on the footing that interest continued to be paid at the rate of 7½ per cent. down to the date of demand, ɑnd not merely until the 15th of July, 1879 (in which case the debt would have been under £50) :—*Held*, that the agreement amounted to a contract that if the £1000 was not repaid in July, 1879, interest at 7½ per cent. should continue to be paid, and accordingly that there was a liquidated demand of sufficient amount within the Bankruptcy Act, 1869, sect. 6, to support the debtor's summons. *Ex parte* FURBER. *In re* KING   -   17 Ch. D. 191

16. —— Partnership—*Judgment against Firm — Debtor's Summons against Partner not served with Writ—Bankruptcy Act*, 1869, s. 7.] A partnership consisting of several members was dissolved as to one of them on the 17th of December, and the business was thenceforth continued by the others under the old firm name, and at the old place of business. On the 18th of December a creditor of the old partnership, who was ignorant of the dissolution, commenced an action ɑgainst the partners (suing them in the firm name) in respect of a debt contracted before the dissolution. On the 21st of December the writ was served personally on one of the continuing partners. The retired partner was not served in any way. No appearance was entered to the writ, and on the 29th of December the Plaintiff signed judgment by default. Execution was issued, but the sheriff found no goods of the partnership upon which to levy. No application was made under rule 8 of Order XLII. for leave to issue execution against the retired partner. In the following May, the retired partner having had no previous notice of the action, the Plaintiff served him with particulars of demand of the judgment debt, and he not having paid it, the Plaintiff served him with a debtor's summons founded on the judgment debt. He denied the debt, and applied to the Bankruptcy Court to dismiss the summons :—*Held*, by Lord Selborne, L.C., and Cotton, L.J. (dissentiente Brett, L.J.), that the judgment would not support the debtor's summons, and that the summons must be dismissed. *Ex parte* YOUNG. *In re* YOUNG
[19 Ch. D. 124

17. —— Security — *Bankruptcy Act,* 1869 (32 & 33 Vict. c. 71), s. 7.] When the proceedings on a debtor's summons are stayed, pending an action to try the validity of the alleged debt, in determining whether the alleged debtor should be required to give security regard ought to be had not only to his solvency or insolvency, but to the probability of his success in the action. If the Court can see that he has no reasonable defence he ought to be required to give security. —*Ex parte* WOOD (4 D. M. & G. 875) and *Ex parte Wier* (Law Rep. 7 Ch. 319) approved and followed. *Ex parte* WARD. *In re* WARD
[20 Ch. D. 356

II. BANKRUPTCY—ACT OF BANKRUPTCY —
continued.

(c.) DEBTOR'S SUMMONS—*continued.*

18. —— Security—*Solvent Debtor—Bonâ fide Dispute as to Debt — Bankruptcy Act,* 1869 (32 & 33 Vict. c. 71), s. 7—*Right of Respondent to insist on having his Evidence heard.*] Proceedings on a debtor's summons, pending the trial of an action for the debt, will not necessarily be stayed without security, though the alleged debtor is solvent and there is a bonâ fide dispute as to the debt. The probability of success in the action is one element to be considered.—If a Judge of first instance is prepared to decide in favour of a defendant or respondent without hearing his evidence, his counsel is entitled to insist that the evidence shall be heard before the decision is given. If, however, the counsel does not exercise that right, but accepts the decision in his favour on his opponent's evidence, the Court of Appeal has still power to allow the evidence to be taken before reversing the decision.—*Ex parte* Sewell (13 Ch. D. 266) explained. *Ex parte* JACOBSON. *In re* PINCOFFS   -   - 22 Ch. D. 312

19. —— Service—*Inaccurate Copy of Summons—Service by Clerk of Creditor—"Formal defect or irregularity"—Bankruptcy Act,* 1869 (32 & 33 Vict. c. 71), s. 82—*Bankruptcy Rules,* 1870, rr. 59, 61.] On serving a debtor with a debtor's summons the sealed copy which was delivered to him stated the amount of the debt claimed by the creditor to be £24 (instead of £74, the real amount), but these words were added, "being the sum claimed of you by him according to the particulars hereunto annexed." The particulars thus referred to were set forth on the second half of a sheet of paper, the first half of which contained the summons. The particulars stated the amount of the debt, and the circumstances under which it arose, correctly :—*Held*, that the error in the summons was a merely "formal defect" within the meaning of sect. 82, by which the debtor could not possibly have been misled, and that no substantial injustice had been caused to him by it, and, consequently, that the service of the summons was not invalidated by it, and an adjudication of bankruptcy founded on the summons could not be impeached.—The summoning creditor was a solicitor, and the service of the summons was effected by his clerk, instead of by himself or his attorney, or by an officer of the Court, as required by rule 61:—*Held*, that this irregularity also was cured by sect. 82. *Ex parte* JOHNSON. *In re* JOHNSON   25 Ch. D. 112

20. —— Service—*Time—Substituted Service —Bankruptcy Rules,* 1870, rr. 59, 61.] Rule 59 of the Bankruptcy Rules, 1870, does not apply to substituted service of a debtor's summons, but, if personal service cannot be effected, an order for substituted service may be made under rule 61 after the expiration of the time limited by rule 59 for effecting personal service, and the substituted service must be effected within such reasonable time as the Court may fix. See Bankruptcy Rules, 1883, rr. 122, 123, 144, 145. *Ex parte* WARBURG. *In re* WHALLEY
[25 Ch. D. 336

21. —— Statement of Consideration.] When a debtor's summons is founded on a judgment

II. BANKRUPTCY—ACT OF BANKRUPTCY—
continued.

(c.) DEBTOR'S SUMMONS—*continued.*

debt it is not necessary to state the consideration for the judgment in the summons, and a misstatement of the consideration will not vitiate the summons. *Ex parte* RITSO. *In re* RITSO
[**22 Ch. D. 529**

22. —— Stay of Proceedings — *Conditional Agreement for Reduction of Debt—Default in fulfilling Condition — Revivor of Original Debt—Penalty—Waiver—Bankruptcy Act,* 1869 (32 & 33 *Vict.* c. 71), s. 7.] A creditor having issued a debtor's summons in respect of a judgment debt of £344, an agreement was made that the debtor should give the creditor a cheque for £50, and three bills of exchange for £50 each, accepted by a third person, and payable respectively in three, six, and nine months, and that, upon payment of the cheque and the bills in due course, and a receipt for a debt due by the creditor to the debtor's brother being handed to the creditor, he should give a receipt in full satisfaction of the judgment debt. In default of payment of any or either of the cheque or bills, the creditor was to be at liberty to proceed for the full amount due. The cheque and the first two bills were paid in due course, but the third bill was not paid at maturity, the acceptor having forgotten to provide his bankers with funds to meet it. The creditor issued a writ against the acceptor, and he paid the dishonoured bill within a week after it became due. The creditor then issued a debtor's summons against the debtor for the unpaid balance of the original debt :—*Held,* that the provision in the agreement for the revivor of the original debt upon default being made in the performance of any of the conditions was not a penalty, but that on the dishonour of the third bill the creditor was remitted to his original right, and that he had not waived that right by suing the acceptor.—The debtor having applied to the Court of Bankruptcy to dismiss the summons :— *Held* (reversing the decision of the Registrar), that the proceedings on the summons ought not to have been stayed pending the trial of an action to determine the validity of the debt, but that the Registrar ought to have decided the question himself, and to have dismissed the application. *Ex parte* BURDEN. *In re* NEIL   **16 Ch. D. 675**

(d.) DEPARTING FROM DWELLING-HOUSE.

23. —— Onus of Proof.] A petitioning creditor, who alleges that his debtor has committed an act of bankruptcy, by departing from his dwelling-house with intent to defeat and delay his creditors, is bound to shew that the debtor is alive and in some other place. *Ex parte* GEISEL. *In re* STANGER - - -   **22 Ch. D. 436**

(e.) NOTICE OF SUSPENSION OF PAYMENT.

24. —— Verbal Notice—*Bankruptcy Act,* 1883 (46 & 47 *Vict.* c. 52), s. 4, *sub-s.* 1 (h)—*Bankruptcy Rules,* 1883, *rule* 11.] A notice by a debtor that he has suspended, or that he is about to suspend, payment of his debts need not, in order that it may constitute an act of bankruptcy, be in writing. It is sufficient if a verbal statement to that effect

II. BANKRUPTCY—ACT OF BANKRUPTCY—
continued.

(e.) NOTICE OF SUSPENSION OF PAYMENT—*contd.*

be made by the debtor to one of his creditors. *Ex parte* NICKOLL. *In re* WALKER   **13 Q. B. D. 469**

25. —— Verbal Notice of Inability—*Bankruptcy Act,* 1883 (46 & 47 *Vict.* c. 52), s. 4, *sub-ss.* 1 (f), 1 (h).] An oral statement made by a debtor to a creditor that he is unable to pay his debts in full, is not a notice he has suspended, or is about to suspend, payment of his debts, so as to constitute an act of bankruptcy within sub-s. 1 (h) of s. 4 of the Bankruptcy Act, 1883.—Such a notice may be given orally, but it must be given formally and deliberately, and with the intention of giving notice. *Ex parte* OASTLER. *In re* FRIEDLANDER
[**13 Q. B. D. 471**

(f.) REMAINING ABROAD.

26. ——Domiciled Englishman *residing Abroad* —*Bankruptcy Act,* 1869 (32 & 33 *Vict.* c. 71), s. 6, *sub-s.* 3.] A domiciled Englishman went in 1876, with his family, to reside in France, where he took a house. He was not then being pressed by any creditors in England. For a period of fourteen months in 1877 and 1878 he was in England, carrying on the business of a newspaper which he had purchased, and he then had a furnished lodging in London. During that period he retained his house in France and his wife and family lived in it. During the same period he contracted a debt for costs to a solicitor in London. At the end of the fourteen months he discontinued the business, and went back to his residence in France. In 1880 he, with his family, occupied for nine months a furnished house in England, his house in France being let furnished : at the end of the nine months he returned to that house. He then continued to reside there, paying occasional visits to England. During one of these visits he accidentally met the solicitor, who asked him why he had not paid his debt, and he answered that his newspaper speculation had left him with a number of claims, and he thought if he kept abroad he should be able to settle them more easily. The solicitor presented a bankruptcy petition against the debtor, alleging as an act of bankruptcy that he had remained out of England with intent to defeat or delay his creditors :—*Held,* that, as the debtor was remaining out of England at his own permanent residence abroad, no intent to defeat or delay his creditors could be imputed to him from that circumstance alone, and that the conversation with the petitioning creditor was not sufficient to prove such an intent. *Ex parte* BRANDON. *In re* TRENCH - - -   **25 Ch. D. 500**

—— Fraudulent transfer - **17 Ch. D. 58**
    See BANKRUPTCY—FRAUDULENT PREFERENCE. 1.

—— Notice of—Protected transaction
    See Cases under BANKRUPTCY — PROTECTED TRANSACTION.

III. BANKRUPTCY—TRADER.

1. —— Being a Trader—"*Departing from Dwelling-house or otherwise absenting himself*"— *Summary Adjudication—Bankruptcy Act,* 1869 (32 & 33 *Vict.* c. 71), s. 6, *sub-ss.* 3, 6—*Bankruptcy*

III. BANKRUPTCY—TRADER—*continued.*

Rules, 1870, r. 65.] The words " being a trader," in sub-s. 3 of sect. 6 of the Bankruptcy Act, 1869, are to be construed in the same way as the same words in sub-sect. 6 of the section, and they mean in sub-sect. 3 that the debtor must be actually carrying on a trade at the time when he is alleged to have committed any of the acts therein mentioned as acts of bankruptcy if committed by a trader. It is not sufficient that he was carrying on a trade at the time when the petitioning creditor's debt was contracted.—A summary adjudication cannot be obtained under rule 65 unless the debtor was a trader at the time when he is alleged to have "departed from his dwelling-house or otherwise absented himself."—*Ex parte Schomberg* (Law Rep. 10 Ch. 172) approved and followed. *Ex parte* M'GEORGE. *In re* STEVENS
[20 Ch. D. 697

2. —— **Being a Trader**—*Discontinuance of Trade with Intention of resuming it—Bankruptcy Act*, 1869 (32 & 33 *Vict. c.* 71), *ss.* 6, 8.] If a debtor, who has been a trader, is not actually carrying on trade at the time when it is alleged by a petitioning creditor that he has done or omitted to do that, the doing or omission of which would be an act of bankruptcy only if it was done or omitted by a trader, it is a question of intention, to be decided on the evidence, whether the debtor has permanently ceased to trade, or has only temporarily discontinued his trade with the intention of resuming it. In the latter case he is still a trader within the meaning of the Bankruptcy Act.—The law on this point is still as it was laid down in *Ex parte Paterson* (1 Rose, 402) and *Ex parte Cundy* (2 Rose, 357).—Per Jessel, M.R.. If a petitioning creditor alleges that the debtor has committed an act of bankruptcy which can be committed only by a trader, the onus is on him to prove that the debtor was, within the meaning of the Bankruptcy Act, a trader at the time when the act was committed. *Ex parte* SALAMAN. *In re* TAYLOR　　21 Ch. D. 394

3. —— *Infant—Adjudication of Bankruptcy — Trading Contract — Bankruptcy Act*, 1869 (32 & 33 *Vict. c.* 71), *ss.* 6, 125, *sub-s.* 12—*Infants' Relief Act*, 1874 (37 & 38 *Vict*, c. 62), s. 1.] An infant who has traded cannot be adjudicated a bankrupt on the petition of a person who has supplied him with goods on credit for trade purposes, but to whom he has made no express representation that he is of full age, even though he has previously filed a liquidation petition the proceedings under which have become abortive.— Nor could the Court under such circumstances make an adjudication against the infant under sub-sect. 12 of sect. 125 of the Bankruptcy Act, 1869.—Whether, if the infant had expressly represented to the petitioning creditor that he was of full age, an adjudication could be made, *quære.* The Infants' Relief Act, 1874, applies to the contracts of an infant.—Decision of Bacon, C.J., reversed.—*Ex parte Lynch* (2 Ch. D. 227) overruled. *Ex parte* JONES. *In re* JONES　-　18 Ch. D. 109

IV. BANKRUPTCY—BANKRUPTCY PETITION.

1. —— **Adjournment**—*Failure to comply with Bankruptcy Notice to pay Judgment Debt—Appeal pending from Judgment—Staying Proceedings—*

IV. BANKRUPTCY—BANKRUPTCY PETITION —*continued.*

Discretion of Registrar—Appeal—Bankruptcy Act, 1883 (46 & 47 *Vict.* c. 52), s. 7, *sub-s.* 4.] The Court of Appeal will not interfere with the exercise of discretion by the Registrar, under sub-sect. 4 of sect. 7 of the Bankruptcy Act, 1883, in adjourning the hearing of, or dismissing, a bankruptcy petition founded on non-compliance with a bankruptcy notice in respect of a judgment debt, when an appeal is pending from the judgment, unless it is clear that the Registrar could not have been right. —If the appeal appears to be a bonâ fide one, the hearing of the bankruptcy petition ought to be adjourned.—If the appeal is evidently frivolous, a receiving order ought to be made, notwithstanding its pendency. *Ex parte* HEYWORTH. *In re* RHODES　　-　　14 Q. B. D. 49

2. —— **Attorney** — *Bankruptcy Petition by Creditor — Signature — Signature by Attorney—Bankruptcy Rules*, 1883, r. 125—*Appendix, Form No.* 10.] A bankruptcy petition by a creditor may be signed on his behalf by his duly constituted attorney.—A power of attorney authorized the attorney (inter alia) " to commence and carry on, or to defend, at law or in equity, all actions, suits, or other proceedings touching anything in which I or my ships or other personal estate may be in anywise concerned " : — *Held*, that this power authorized the attorney to sign on behalf of his principal a bankruptcy petition against a debtor of the principal. *Ex parte* WALLACE. *In re* WALLACE　　-　　14 Q. B. D. 22

3. —— **Domicil of Debtor**—*Onus of Proof— Officer in British Army serving out of England —Bankruptcy Act*, 1883 (46 & 47 *Vict.* c. 52), s. 6, *sub-s.* 1 (d).] Sub-sect. 1 (d) of sect. 6 of the Bankruptcy Act, 1883, enacts that a creditor shall not be entitled to present a bankruptcy petition against a debtor unless (inter alia) " the debtor is domiciled in England " :—*Held*, that this must be taken to mean domiciled in England, as distinguished from Scotland or Ireland.—The onus is, in the first instance, on the petitioning creditor to prove the domicil, though he may adduce such primâ facie evidence as will throw the burden of disproving the domicil on the debtor. But the mere fact that the debtor bears an English name, and is an officer in the British army, does not raise any presumption that his domicil is English as distinguished from Scotch or Irish, inasmuch as his domicil of origin might have been Scotch or Irish, and in either of those cases he would not by entering into the British army have lost his domicil of origin.—*Yelverton* v. *Yelverton* (1 Sw. & Tr. 574), and *Brown* v. *Smith* (15 Beav. 444), approved and followed. The cases relating to Anglo-Indian domicil commented on and explained. *Ex parte* CUNNINGHAM. *In re* MITCHELL　-　　-　13 Q. B. D. 418

4. —— **Landlord and Tenant**—*Forfeiture on Tenant " being Bankrupt "—Bankruptcy Petition —Bankruptcy Act*, 1883 (46 & 47 *Vict.* c. 52), s. 149—*Fixtures—Notice of Breach by Landlord —Conveyancing Act*, 1881 (44 & 45 *Vict.* c. 41), s. 14.] A lease executed in 1880, of a mill and warehouse, for twenty-one years, contained a covenant by the lessors with the lessees (inter alia) (4) that certain articles mentioned in a

IV. BANKRUPTCY—BANKRUPTCY PETITION
—continued.

schedule should be the property of the lessees, and should be removable by them, they making good all damage done by such removal. The articles mentioned in the schedule were iron columns, beams, floors, brick piers and things ejusdem generis. There was a proviso (1) that in case (inter alia) the lessees should during the term be bankrupts, or file a petition in liquidation, the term should cease; (2) that the lessees might by notice determine the term at the end of seven or fourteen years; (3) that on the determination or cesser of the term all the machinery, and also all the buildings erected by the lessees (other than certain specified buildings) should be their property and should be removed by them previously to the determination or cesser of the term, unless it should be then mutually agreed that the lessors should purchase them, the lessees, in case of removal, to make good all damages which might be caused by such removal. After the Bankruptcy Act, 1883, came into operation, the lessees presented a bankruptcy petition, and a receiving order was made:—*Held*, first, that the presentation of the petition caused a forfeiture of the term; secondly, that notwithstanding the forfeiture, the official receiver was entitled to the articles mentioned in clause (4) of the covenant and clause (3) of the proviso as being property of the lessees.—*Quære*, whether the receiver was entitled to enter and remove the articles or whether he could only call on the lessors to deliver them to him.—*Held*, further, that sect. 14 of the Conveyancing Act, 1881, had no application. *Ex parte* GOULD. *In re* WALKER **13 Q. B. D. 454**

5. —— Lunatic—*Leave to Committee to file Declaration of Insolvency—Bankruptcy Act*, 1883 (46 & 47 Vict. c. 52), ss. 4, sub-s. 1 (f), 148.] Where it appears to be for the benefit of a lunatic that he should be made bankrupt, the Court will give leave to the committee in the name of the lunatic to file a declaration of insolvency, or to present a bankruptcy petition under the Bankruptcy Act, 1883, s. 4, sub-s. 1 (f). *In re* JAMES **12 Q. B. D. 332**

6. —— Petitioning Creditor—*Trustee for absolute Beneficial Owner—Joining Equitable Owner of Debt—Amendment of Petition—Bankruptcy Act*, 1883 (46 & 47 Vict. c. 52), ss. 4, sub-s. 1 (g), 5, 6, 105 (sub-s. 3).] Under the Bankruptcy Act, 1883, as under the Bankruptcy Act, 1869, a mere trustee of a debt for an absolute beneficial owner is not entitled to present a bankruptcy petition against the debtor unless the cestui que trust, if capable of dealing with the debt, joins as a co-petitioner.—*Ex parte Culley* (9 Ch. D. 307) followed.—When an act of bankruptcy has been committed by the failure of a debtor to comply with a bankruptcy summons, any creditor may avail himself of it for the purpose of presenting a bankruptcy petition against the debtor; the right to petition is not limited to the creditor who has served the bankruptcy notice.—A bankruptcy petition having been presented by a bare trustee of a debt, and dismissed on the ground that the cestui que trust ought to have been joined as a petitioner, leave was given by the Court of Appeal (though more than three months had elapsed since the presentation of the petition)

IV. BANKRUPTCY—BANKRUPTCY PETITION
—continued.

to amend it by joining the cestui que trust, with her consent, but the Appellant was ordered to pay the costs of the appeal, and the costs (if any) occasioned by the amendment. *Ex parte* DEARLE. *In re* HASTINGS **- 14 Q. B. D. 184**

V. BANKRUPTCY—SECURED CREDITOR.

(a) BANKRUPTCY ACT, 1869.

1. —— Attachment—*Tolzey Court of Bristol—Bankruptcy Act*, 1869 (32 & 33 Vict. c. 71), s. 16, sub-s. 5.] An attachment of the goods of the Defendant in an action of debt in the Tolzey Court of Bristol is only a process to compel the appearance of the Defendant, and does not make the Plaintiff a secured creditor within the meaning of sect. 16, sub-sect. 5, of the Bankruptcy Act, 1869. —The effect of an attachment in the Tolzey Court is the same as that of a foreign attachment under the custom of the Mayor's Court of London. —*Levy* v. *Lovell* (14 Ch. D. 234) followed. *Ex parte* SEAR. *In re* PRICE **- 17 Ch. D. 74**

2. —— Deposit of Goods—*Bill given for Debt indorsed away — Composition paid to Indorsee without deducting Value of Security*.] The Plaintiff gave credit to the Defendants for goods sold, and made advances to them, goods being deposited by the Defendants with the Plaintiff as security, and bills being drawn by the Plaintiff and accepted by the Defendants for the amounts of the goods sold and advances made.—The Plaintiff indorsed away such bills for value. During the currency thereof the Defendants filed a petition for liquidation by way of arrangement or composition with their creditors under the Bankruptcy Act, 1869. The creditors of the Defendants passed resolutions for the acceptance of a composition. The holders of the bills, by arrangement between themselves and the Plaintiff, claimed and were paid the composition on the total amounts of the bills, the Plaintiff paying them the balance thereof. The Plaintiff having realized his security by sale of the goods deposited claimed to hold the proceeds against the balance so paid by him upon the bills:—*Held*, that under the above circumstances the Plaintiff could not be considered to have abandoned or forfeited his right to the security, but that the Plaintiff was not entitled to stand in a better position than that which he would have occupied if he had not negotiated the bills, in which case he could only have received a composition on the balance of his debt after deducting the value of the security; and that consequently he was bound to account to the Defendants for the amount by which the composition paid on the bills exceeded that which would have been paid if the value of the security had been deducted before ascertaining the amount of the composition. BAINES *v.* WRIGHT **15 Q. B. D. 102** [Affirmed by the Court of Appeal, **16 Q. B. D. 330**]

3. —— Formal Defect—*Petition—Statement of readiness to give up Security—Valuation—Amendment—Bankruptcy Act*, 1869 (32 & 33 Vict. c. 71), ss. 6, 82—*Bankruptcy Rules*, 1870, r. 208—*Bankruptcy Forms*, 1870, No. 10.] If a petitioning creditor who holds security for his debt is willing to give an estimate of the value of his security, sect. 6

V. BANKRUPTCY — SECURED CREDITOR —
continued.

(a) BANKRUPTCY ACT, 1869—*continued.*

of the Bankruptcy Act, 1869, does not require this fact to be stated in the petition, but it is sufficient for the Petitioner to give notice of it to the Respondent, before the hearing of the petition. It is, however, proper as a matter of convenience that the Petitioner's willingness to estimate the value of his security, should, in accordance with Form No. 10, be stated in the petition. A petitioning creditor stated in his petition that he held no security for his debt. He in fact held a charge on some property of the debtor, and before the hearing of the petition his solicitors, in a letter to the debtor's solicitors, said that the security was not valued at anything, and at the hearing it was stated that the Petitioner was ready to give up his security for the benefit of the creditors. The Registrar dismissed the petition, on the ground that the Petitioner's readiness to give up his security ought in conformity with sect. 6 to have been stated in the petition:—*Held*, that the defect was a merely formal one, and that the Registrar ought to have amended the petition by adding a statement of the security and that the Petitioner was ready to give it up, and then to have made an adjudication. And the Court of Appeal made the amendment and the adjudication, but gave no costs of the appeal. *Ex parte* VANDERLINDEN. *In re* POGOSE　　-　　**20 Ch. D. 289**

4. —— **Mortgage** — *Application to Court by Equitable Mortgagee for a Sale—Insufficient Security—Conduct of Sale—Costs of Trustee—Bankruptcy Rules* 1870, *rr.* 78, 79, 80 — *Bankruptcy Rules,* 1883, *rr.* 68–70.] When an equitable mortgagee applies to the Court to realize his security, the conduct of the sale is in the discretion of the Court. As a general rule where the security is sufficient the conduct of the sale will be given to the trustee, but where the security is insufficient the conduct of the sale will be given to the mortgagee. In either case the costs, charges, and expenses of the trustee, properly incurred, will be a first charge upon the proceeds of sale. *In re* JORDAN. *Ex parte* HARRISON
[13 Q. B. D. 228

5. —— **Partnership**—*Composition—Joint Creditors—Creditors with Joint and Separate Security — Valuation of Proof for Joint Debt — Close of Composition—Action for Redemption of Security—Claim to retain Separate Security—Amendment of Proof.*] B. & Co. were creditors of a partnership for £2400, for which they held a security comprising joint property of the firm and also separate property of one of the partners. The firm being in difficulties, the joint creditors agreed to accept a composition, and B. & Co. valued their security at £800, and proved and received the composition upon the balance. Subsequently they received from their security more than £800 and interest from the date of valuation. Four years after the close of the composition the debtors brought an action to redeem their security. B. & Co. claimed to retain the security on the separate property until they had received payment in full of their claim, on the ground that they need not have deducted the separate property :—*Held*, by Jessel, M.R., that B. & Co. having received £800

V. BANKRUPTCY — SECURED CREDITOR —
continued.

(a) BANKRUPTCY ACT, 1869—*continued.*

from the security and accepted the composition on the balance, their whole debt was discharged, and they could not retain the separate security.—This decision affirmed on appeal, on the ground that although B. & Co. need not have deducted the value of the separate security, yet, inasmuch as the composition had been fixed, and the whole proceeding in the composition had been taken and completed upon the footing of the valuation of the compound security at £800, it was too late to upset the transaction :—*Held*, that leave to amend the proof could not now be given, whatever might have been the case had a proper application for that purpose been made during the pendency of the composition proceedings. COULDERY *v.* BARTRUM　　-　　**19 Ch. D. 394**

6. —— **Partnership** — *Fraudulent Pledge by Partnership Firm—Other Security held by Pledgee —Separate Guarantee of one Partner—Marshalling Securities.*] A partnership firm wrongfully pledged to their bankers, to secure a debt of the firm, the delivery warrants of some brandy which had been left in their custody in the ordinary course of business by the owner. One of the partners in the firm had no knowledge of the fraud. The debt due by the firm to the bankers was also secured by a separate guarantee of the innocent partner. The firm filed a liquidation petition, and the bankers sold the brandy, and applied the proceeds of sale in part payment of their debt. The owner of the brandy knew nothing of the pledge until the stoppage of the firm. The separate estate of the innocent partner was sufficient to pay all his separate creditors in full (including the balance remaining due to the bankers), and to leave a surplus :—*Held*, that the owner of the brandy was entitled to have the bankers' securities marshalled, and, to the extent of the value of the brandy, to have the benefit of the guarantee, and to prove against the separate estate of the innocent partner.—*Ex parte* Alston (Law Rep. 4 Ch. 168) followed. *Ex parte* SALTING. *In re* STRATTON　-　**25 Ch. D. 148**

7. —— **Proof**—*Balance of Debt above assessed Value of Security—Composition—Bankruptcy Act, 1869 (32 & 33 Vict. c. 71), s. 126—General Rules, 1870, Rule 272.*] The effect of Rule 272 of the General Rules, 1870, read together with sect. 126. of the Bankruptcy Act, 1869 (32 & 33 Vict. c. 71), is that in composition proceedings under sect. 126, a secured creditor, who proves for the balance of his debt after deducting the assessed value of his security, and afterwards realizes the security, must pay to the debtor any surplus realized above the assessed value, after allowing interest upon the assessed value from the assessment until the realization :—So *held*, affirming the decision of the Court of Appeal. SOCIÉTÉ GÉNÉRALE DE PARIS *v.* GEEN　-　-　**8 App. Cas. 606**

8. —— **Proof**—*Deduction of Value of Security —Security on Lease of Bankrupt and former Partner.*] The rule as to what securities a secured creditor of a bankrupt is bound to value and deduct on proving against the bankrupt's estate, explained.—Two partners, who were interested in

V. BANKRUPTCY — SECURED CREDITOR — *continued.*

(a) BANKRUPTCY ACT, 1869—*continued.*

equal shares in the business of the partnership, dissolved partnership. They had carried on business at some mills, of which they held a lease, granted to them, their executors, administrators, and assigns. On the dissolution, the partnership assets, other than the lease and the fixtures, were divided equally between the two partners. It was agreed that one of them should be entitled to carry on the business for seven years on his own account, and that he should pay the debts of the firm and indemnify the retiring partner against them. The retiring partner lent the other the value of his moiety of the partnership assets (other than the lease and fixtures) and granted him a lease for seven years of his moiety of the mills and fixtures. The original lease was deposited by the continuing and the retiring partners with the bankers of the former, as security for the balance which might for the time being be due from him to them, it being expressly provided that the retiring partner should be liable to the bankers only as a surety for the other. The continuing partner, before the end of the seven years, filed a liquidation petition :—*Held*, that, as to a moiety of the lease and fixtures, the bankers' security was upon separate estate of the liquidating debtor, and that, before proving in the liquidation for the balance due to them by him, they must deduct a moiety of the value of the lease and fixtures. — Decision of Bacon, C.J., affirmed. *Ex parte* WEST RIDING UNION BANKING COMPANY. *In re* TURNER　　-　19 Ch. D. 105

(b.) BANKRUPTCY ACT, 1883.

9. —— Execution—*Sale by Sheriff—Application ex parte to sell Goods by Private Contract—Discretion—Bankruptcy Act, 1883 (46 & 47 Vict. c. 52), s. 145.*] Under s. 145 of the Bankruptcy Act, 1883, the Court has a discretion to order goods taken in execution by the sheriff to be sold by private contract instead of by public auction, notwithstanding that the application for leave to sell by private contract is made by the execution creditor ex parte, and in the absence of all the other creditors of the execution debtor. HUNT *v.* FENSHAM　　-　12 Q. B. D. 162

10. —— Execution— *Seizure but not delivery of the Goods—Bankruptcy Act, 1883 (46 & 47 Vict. c. 52), ss. 146, 169.*] By the Bankruptcy Act, 1883, s. 146, "the sheriff shall not under a writ of elegit deliver the goods of a debtor, nor shall a writ of elegit extend to goods," and by s. 169, which repeals amongst other enactments so much of 13 Edw. 1, c. 18, as relates to the chattels of the debtor save only his oxen and beasts of the plough, it is enacted that "the repeal effected by this Act shall not affect anything done before the commencement of this Act under any enactment repealed by this Act, nor any right or privilege acquired or duty imposed, or liability or disqualification incurred under any enactment so repealed." Some days before the 1st of January, 1884, when the Bankruptcy Act of 1883 came into operation, the sheriff entered into possession and seized goods of the Defendant, under a writ of elegit issued under statute

V. BANKRUPTCY — SECURED CREDITOR — *continued.*

(b) BANKRUPTCY ACT, 1883—*continued.*

13 Edw. 1, c. 18, at the suit of the Plaintiff, a judgment creditor of the Defendant, but no delivery of such goods had been made to the Plaintiff before the 1st of January, 1884 :—*Held*, reversing the decision of the Queen's Bench Division, that the Bankruptcy Act, 1883, had not deprived the Plaintiff of his right to the delivery of such goods. HOUGH *v.* WINDUS　　12 Q. B. D. 224

11. —— Mortgage—*Valuation of Security—Bankruptcy Act, 1883 (46 & 47 Vict. c. 52), s. 6 (sub-s. 2) ; sched. 1, rr. 10, 12 ; sched. 2, rr. 9, 10, 11, 12, 13.*] When a secured creditor presents a bankruptcy petition against his debtor it is not necessary that the estimate given by the petitioner of the value of his security should be a true estimate ; but if an adjudication is made, the trustee in the bankruptcy will be entitled to redeem the security at the amount of the petitioner's estimate. *Ex parte* TAYLOR　13 Q. B. D. [128

12. —— Valuation of Security—*Amendment of Proof—Second Mortgagee—Notice of Appeal—Time—Notice sent by Post—Trustee—Costs—Bankruptcy Act, 1883 (46 & 47 Vict. c. 52), s. 142 ; Schedule 2, r. 13—Bankruptcy Rules, 1883, rr. 112, 114 A., 116 A. [Rules of 11th of April, 1884]—Rules of Supreme Court, 1883, Order LVIII. r. 15.*] If notice of a bankruptcy appeal is sent by post, as provided by sect. 142 of the Bankruptcy Act, 1883, *quære* whether the notice will be in time unless the letter is received by the respondent before the expiration of the twenty-one days limited for appealing.—A mortgagee who has valued his security will in a proper case be allowed, under rule 13 in schedule 2 to the Act, to amend his valuation and proof, notwithstanding the opposition of a subsequent mortgagee.—A trustee in bankruptcy who is served with notice of an appeal, and who appears and only asks for his costs, will not be allowed his costs of appearance. *Ex parte* ARDEN. *In re* ARDEN [14 Q. B. D. 121

VI. BANKRUPTCY—RECEIVER.

(a.) BANKRUPTCY ACT, 1869.

1. —— Injunction—*Undertaking as to Damages—Enforcement—Delay.*] An application to enforce an undertaking to be answerable in damages, given by a receiver in bankruptcy on the granting of an injunction to restrain proceedings in relation to property alleged to form part of the bankrupt's estate, ought to be made within a reasonable time after it is ascertained that the injunction has been improperly granted.—Unexplained and unreasonable delay in making such an application will be a sufficient ground for refusing it, even if the bankruptcy proceedings are still pending and the receiver has not obtained his discharge :—*Held*, that an unexplained delay of nearly four years in making such an application was a sufficient answer to it, though the applicant had shewn a primâ facie case. *Ex parte* HALL. *In re* WOOD—　23 Ch. D. 644

2. —— Remuneration — *Complaint against Trustee—Locus Standi—" Person aggrieved "—Bankruptcy Act, 1869 (32 & 33 Vict. c. 71), s. 20.*

VI. BANKRUPTCY—RECEIVER—*continued.*

(a) BANKRUPTCY ACT, 1869—*continued.*

—*Bankruptcy Rules*, 1871, rr. 3, 7.] A receiver in bankruptcy or liquidation has no lien upon the assets for his remuneration; he is only entitled to be paid out of the net assets.—And he is not entitled to come to the Court to complain of the conduct of the trustee in the administration of the assets.—Such a complaint can be made only by the creditors. *Ex parte* BROWNE. *In re* MALTBY　-　　　　**16 Ch. D. 497**

3. —— **Taxation**—*Receiver and Manager—Charges—Money advanced without Authority of Court—Right to Indemnity—Bankruptcy Rules, 1871, rr. 5, 6, 7.*] Under rule 5 of the Bankruptcy Rules, 1871, the charges of a receiver and manager of a business for disbursements out of pocket (e.g., travelling expenses and salaries of assistants) are liable to taxation.—A receiver and manager of a business who desires to advance money of his own for the purposes of the business may, before doing so, apply to the Court for its authority, and the Court will, as a general rule, allow him interest at 5 per cent. on the amount which it authorizes him to advance, and will give him a charge on the debtor's assets for the advance and the interest.—If the receiver and manager advances money without such a previous authority, he is entitled to an indemnity out of the assets, but he cannot obtain a personal order against the trustee for payment. *Ex parte* IZARD. *In re* BUSHELL (No. 1)
[23 Ch. D. 75

(b.) RECEIVING ORDER—BANKRUPTCY ACT, 1883.

4. —— **Act of Bankruptcy before the 1st of January, 1884**—*Pending Liquidation Proceedings—Proof of Act of Bankruptcy—Appearance of Debtor—Bankruptcy Act, 1883 (46 & 47 Vict. c. 52). ss. 4, 5, 7, 169—Bankruptcy Rules, 1883, rr. 139, 262, 263, 264.*] A receiving order can be made on a bankruptcy petition presented under the Bankruptcy Act, 1883, founded on an act of bankruptcy committed before that Act came into operation, but in respect of which no bankruptcy proceedings had been taken before that date. And the fact that liquidation proceedings under the Bankruptcy Act, 1869, were pending when the Act of 1883 came into operation, and that those proceedings afterwards came to an end by reason of the creditors failing to pass any resolution, does not affect the power of the Court to make the receiving order.—If, on the hearing of a bankruptcy petition, the act of bankruptcy alleged is not strictly proved, but the debtor appears and does not raise the objection, and a receiving order is made, he cannot on an appeal from that order raise the objection. *Ex parte* PRATT　　　　　　　　　**12 Q. B. D. 334**

5. —— **Jurisdiction**—*Petition in wrong Court—Bankruptcy Act, 1883 (46 & 47 Vict. c. 52), ss. 95, 97.*] If a bankruptcy petition is by inadvertence presented in a wrong bankruptcy court, the court to which it is presented has jurisdiction to make a receiving order.—If, however, the petition is wilfully presented in a wrong court, this is a ground for dismissing it.—The Divisional Court made a receiving order, which it held that the county court ought to have made, and to which

VI. BANKRUPTCY—RECEIVER—*continued.*

(b) RECEIVING ORDER.—BANKRUPTCY ACT, 1883 —*continued.*

the debtor had raised no other objection than want of jurisdiction, giving leave to the debtor to apply afterwards to the Divisional Court to discharge the order on any ground arising since the hearing in the county court. *Ex parte* MAY. *In re* BRIGHTMORE　　　-　　**14 Q. B. D. 37**

6. —— **Partnership**—*Notice in Name of Partners—Bankruptcy of one Partner before Hearing of Petition—Right of solvent Partner to receive Partnership Assets as against Trustee of bankrupt Partner—Bankruptcy Act, 1883 (46 & 47 Vict. c. 52), s. 4, sub-s. 1 (g).*] After the bankruptcy of a partner and the appointment of a trustee of his property his solvent partner has a right to receive, and can give a good discharge for, the partnership assets, and is entitled, for the purpose of collecting or recovering the assets, to use the name of the trustee, upon giving him an indemnity.—After one of two partners had filed a liquidation petition and a receiver had been appointed, a judgment was recovered in an action previously commenced in the names of the two partners against O., a debtor of the firm. A bankruptcy notice in the names of the two partners was then served on O.; he failed to comply with it within the seven days limited for the purpose, and a bankruptcy petition was presented against him in the names of the two partners. Before this petition came on to be heard, the creditors of the partner who had filed the liquidation petition had resolved on a liquidation by arrangement, and had appointed a trustee of his property:—*Held*, that though there was a good act of bankruptcy, a receiving order could not properly be made against O., unless the trustee in the liquidation was joined as a co-petitioner. *Ex parte* OWEN
[13 Q. B. D. 113

7. —— **Power of Court to refuse**—"*Sufficient Cause*"—*Execution of Creditors' Deed—Bankruptcy Act, 1883 (46 & 47 Vict. c. 52), s. 4. sub-s. 1 (a), s. 7, sub-s. 3, ss. 15, 16, 17, 18—Official Receiver—Appearance on Appeal—Costs.*] The fact that shortly before the presentation of a bankruptcy petition against a debtor he has, with the assent of a large majority of his creditors, executed a deed assigning the whole of his property to trustees appointed by the creditors to be administered by them as in bankruptcy, is not, within the meaning of sub-sect. 3 of sect. 7 of the Bankruptcy Act, 1883, a "sufficient cause" for refusing to make a receiving order on the petition.—As a general rule the official receiver, though served with a notice of appeal, ought not to appear on the hearing, unless there are special circumstances which he desires to bring before the Court, and in the absence of special circumstances he will not be allowed his costs of appearance. *Ex parte* DIXON -　　-　**13 Q. B. D. 118**

8. —— **Power of Court to refuse**—"*Sufficient cause*"—*Adjournment—Prior Arrangement between Debtor and Creditors—Bankruptcy Act, 1883 (46 & 47 Vict. c. 52), s. 7 (3).*] The fact that a debtor has, shortly before the presentation of a bankruptcy petition against him, entered into an arrangement with his creditors (to which the

VI. BANKRUPTCY—RECEIVER—*continued.*

(*b*) RECEIVING ORDER—BANKRUPTCY ACT, 1883 —*continued.*

petitioner has not assented) is not, however beneficial to the creditors the terms of the arrangement may be, a "sufficient cause" within the meaning of s. 7 (3) of the Bankruptcy Act, 1883, for dismissing the petition.—And, there being no jurisdiction under such circumstances to dismiss the petition, there is no jurisdiction to adjourn the hearing of it with a view to its ultimate dismissal in case the arrangement shall be found to work well.—The decision in *Ex parte Dixon* (13 Q. B. D. 118) did not depend upon the particular terms of the arrangement in that case, but on the fact that the arrangement was made at such a time and in such a manner as not to bind the dissentient creditors. *Ex parte* ORAM. *In re* WATSON - - **15 Q. B. D. 399**

9. —— **Power to rescind Order**—*Petition by Debtor*—*Payment of Creditors in full*—*Bankruptcy Act, 1883 (46 & 47 Vict. c. 52), ss. 5, 8, 104.*] A debtor presented a bankruptcy petition and a receiving order was made. The debtor's father, who was a partly secured creditor, immediately afterwards paid all the unsecured creditors in full. The only other creditor was fully secured. The debtor then applied to the Court to rescind the receiving order and to allow him to withdraw his petition. The application was assented to by the fully secured creditor and by the father. The Judge held that he had no jurisdiction to rescind the order, but he made an order staying all further proceedings under the order:—*Held*, that there was jurisdiction to grant the application. *Ex parte* WEMYSS. *In re* WEMYSS **13 Q. B. D. 244**

10. —— **Protection**—*Arrest of Debtor between Date and signing of Order*—*Bankruptcy Act, 1883, s. 9*—*Bankruptcy Rules, 1883, r. 153; Appendix, Forms 29 and 30.*] Having regard to the terms of sect. 9 of the Bankruptcy Act, 1883, as to the effect of a receiving order in protecting a debtor from arrest, the order must be deemed to have been "made" on the day it was pronounced, and therefore as protecting the debtor as from that day.—Therefore, where a debtor had been arrested under an order of the Chancery Division made after the date of a receiving order pronounced before, but not drawn up and signed by the Registrar (Bankruptcy Rules, 1883, r. 153, Appendix, Forms 29 and 30) until after the arrest, he was ordered to be discharged, notwithstanding that he had by his counsel submitted to the order of attachment.—Order of Kay, J., affirmed. *In re* MANNING - **30 Ch. D. 480**

(*c.*) OFFICIAL RECEIVER.

11. —— **Powers and Duties**—*Powers when acting as Trustee*—*Power to sell Bankrupt's Property*—*Bankruptcy Act, 1883 (46 & 47 Vict. c. 52), ss. 9, 10, 20, 21, 54, 56, 68–70, 121.*] The official receiver, when acting as trustee in a bankruptcy in the interval between the adjudication and the appointment of a trustee by the creditors, has power to sell the bankrupt's property, even though it be not of a perishable nature.—Decision of Cave, J., reversed. *Ex parte* TURQUAND. *Ex parte* BOARD OF TRADE. *In re* PARKER

[14 Q. B. D 407; 15 Q. B. D. 196

VII. BANKRUPTCY—EXAMINATION.

1. —— **Solicitor**—*Right of Audience*—*Examination of a Debtor by a Solicitor*—*Solicitor to be authorised in Writing*—*Bankruptcy Act, 1883 (46 & 47 Vict. c. 52), s. 17, sub-s. 4.*] The Bankruptcy Act, 1883, s. 17, sub-s. 4, enacts with reference to the public examination of a debtor under that Act, " that any creditor who has tendered a proof, or his representative authorized in writing, may question the debtor concerning his affairs, and the causes of his failure ":—*Held*, that a solicitor who appears at a bankruptcy court for a creditor who has tendered a proof, is the creditor's representative within the meaning of that sub-section, and is therefore not entitled so to question the debtor without being authorised in writing and producing his authority if required by the Court to do so. *Quære*, if such solicitor, when his right of audience has been so denied to him, is "a party," within the meaning of s. 43 of the County Courts Act, 1856 (19 & 20 Vict. c. 108), who is entitled to apply to the superior Court for a rule to compel the County Court Judge to give him audience. THE QUEEN *v.* REGISTRAR OF GREENWICH COUNTY COURT

[15 Q. B. D. 54

2. —— **Statement of Property**—*Duty of Bankrupt to furnish Accounts*—*Order to file Cash Account*—*Bankruptcy Act, 1869 (32 & 33 Vict. c. 71), s. 19.*] Sect. 19 of the Bankruptcy Act, 1869, gives the Court power to order a bankrupt to file a cash account of his receipts and payments for a specified period before his bankruptcy, and, if the circumstances which appear on the file of proceedings shew that such an order ought to be made, the Court can make it without any further evidence.—The Court, however, has a discretion in the matter, and such an order ought not to be made as a matter of course, but only under special circumstances.—*Ex parte Crawford* (28 L. T. (N.S.) 244) approved and followed.—A bankrupt who had been engaged in an extensive business as a promoter of public companies, had kept no accounts, and could produce no record whatever of his transactions, except his banker's pass-book, and some counterfoils of recent cheques:—*Held*, that this was a sufficient reason for ordering him to file a cash account of his receipts and payments for two years before his bankruptcy. *Ex parte* MOIR. *In re* MOIR - **21 Ch. D. 61**

VIII. BANKRUPTCY—SCHEME OF ARRANGEMENT.

1. —— **Approval of Court**—*Reasonableness*—*Discharge of Debtor left to Discretion of Committee of Inspection*—*Bankruptcy Act, 1883 (46 & 47 Vict. c. 52), s. 18.*] A scheme for the arrangement of the affairs of debtors who had presented a bankruptcy petition, duly assented to by the creditors, as provided by sect. 18 of the Bankruptcy Act, 1883, contained, inter alia, provisions for the appointment of a trustee and a committee of inspection, and also a provision that "the debtors shall be discharged when the committee of inspection shall so resolve ":—*Held*, that the latter provision was not in accordance with the intention of the Act, and was unreasonable, and that, though the debtors asked that the scheme might be approved by the Court, the approval

F

VIII. BANKRUPTCY—SCHEME OF ARRANGEMENT—continued.

ought not to be given. *Ex parte* CLARK. *In re* CLARK - **13 Q. B. D. 426**

2. —— **Approval of Court**—*Discretion of Registrar*—*Wishes of Creditors*—*Evidence of Facts justifying Court in refusing to approve*—*Report of Official Receiver*—*Bankruptcy Act, 1883 (46 & 47 Vict. c. 52), ss. 18, 28.*] The report of the official receiver is, under sect. 18 of the Bankruptcy Act, 1883 (as it is under sect. 28), primâ facie evidence of the statements contained in it.—The registrar, in deciding whether he will or will not approve a composition or scheme of arrangement accepted by the creditors of a bankrupt, is exercising a judicial discretion, and the Court of Appeal will not readily set aside his order.—It is the duty of the registrar to form his own judgment, and not to be influenced by the wishes of the creditors. *Ex parte* CAMPBELL. *In re* WALLACE
[15 Q. B. D. 213

3. —— **Approval of Court** — *Reasonableness*—*Rash and hazardous Speculation* — *Retrospective Effect of Act*—*Bankruptcy Act, 1883 (46 & 47 Vict. c. 52), ss. 18, 28, sub-s. 3 (d.).*] In determining whether a composition accepted by creditors under the provisions of sect. 18 is reasonable, the Court must exercise its own judgment, though it will take into account the fact that the creditors are mainly interested in the question.—The Court must have regard to the debtor's assets and liabilities, and if, for a large proportion of the debts set down in his statement of affairs proofs have not been tendered, or if the Court considers that the proofs which have been tendered require to be investigated by a trustee, the Court ought to decline to approve of the composition.—The Court of Appeal will not overrule the exercise of the discretion of the judge of first instance as to the approval of a composition, unless it is clearly satisfied that he was wrong.—The quasi penal provisions of sub-sects. 2 and 3 of sect. 28 are retrospective, i.e., they apply to acts done by the debtor before the Act came into operation, if the proceedings are instituted under that Act.— A trader, after he knew that one of his debtors who owed him about £32,000 was in pecuniary difficulties, allowed him, in the course of eighteen months, to increase his debt to £65,000, and to the extent of £11,000 this increase was due to accommodation bills. The trader then stopped payment, and presented a bankruptcy petition. The debt of £65,000 was apparently irrecoverable:—*Held*, that the debtor had been guilty of rash and hazardous speculations, and that on this ground (inter alia) the Court ought to refuse to approve of a composition which his creditors had, under the provisions of sect. 18, agreed to accept. *Ex parte* ROGERS. *In re* ROGERS
[13 Q. B. D. 438

IX. BANKRUPTCY—ADJUDICATION.

1. —— **Disputed Debt**—*Stay of Proceedings pending Trial of Validity of Debt*—*Discretion of Registrar*—*Waiver of Irregularity*—*Bankruptcy Rules, 1870, r. 43.*] When the proceedings on a bankruptcy petition have been stayed for the trial of the question of the validity of the petitioning creditor's debt, and the validity of the debt has

IX. BANKRUPTCY—ADJUDICATION—*contd.*

been established by the judgment of a Court of first instance, the Registrar has a judicial discretion to proceed with the hearing of the petition and to make an adjudication of bankruptcy upon it, and is not bound to wait for a final decision of a Court of Appeal on the validity of the debt.— If, however, he is satisfied that a bonâ fide appeal is pending from the judgment of the Court of first instance, he ought to adjourn the further hearing of the petition until after the appeal is disposed of.—Before fixing a day for continuing the proceedings on the petition, the Registrar is bound to require the production of the judgment establishing the debt, or an office copy of it.—But, if the day is fixed irregularly, without the production of the judgment, the irregularity will be waived by the appearance of the debtor or his solicitor on the day fixed without taking the objection, which cannot then be raised at any subsequent stage of the proceedings.—*Held*, that an appeal from an adjudication of bankruptcy ought to stand over pending the trial of an action, the result of which, it was alleged by the Appellant, would be to render a fund available to satisfy the debt claimed by the petitioning creditor. *Ex parte* YEATMAN. *In re* YEATMAN **16 Ch. D. 283**

2. —— **Petitioning Creditor's Debt**—"*Liquidated Sum*"—*Defaulter on London Stock Exchange*—*Amount of Difference fixed by Official Assignee*—*Bankruptcy Act, 1869 (32 & 33 Vict. c. 71), s. 6.*] The amount of the differences due by a defaulter on the London Stock Exchange (as fixed by the official assignee of that body under its rules) to a Stock Exchange creditor, is a "liquidated sum" within the meaning of sect. 6 of the Bankruptcy Act, 1869, and will support a bankruptcy petition by the creditor against the defaulter. *Ex parte* WARD. *In re* WARD
[22 Ch. D. 132

3. —— **Practice** — *Amendment of Petition.*] When a bankruptcy petition is amended under an order of the Court the Judge has a discretion as to requiring the amendment to be verified by affidavit, and if the alteration is an immaterial one an affidavit will not be required. *Ex parte* RITSO. *In re* RITSO - **22 Ch. D. 529**

4. —— **Prior Scotch Sequestration**—*Jurisdiction to make Adjudication*—*Discretion of Court.*] Though the Court has jurisdiction to adjudge bankrupt a debtor against whom there is existing a prior unclosed Scotch sequestration in which he has not obtained a discharge, the Court has a discretion in the matter, and it will decline to make an adjudication if it does not appear that the debtor has any assets in England, or any debts contracted since the commencement of the sequestration:—Per Jessel, M.R. : Primâ facie the existence of a Scotch sequestration is a reason for declining to make an adjudication. *Ex parte* ROBINSON. *In re* ROBINSON **22 Ch. D. 816**

5. —— **Rehearing**—*Jurisdiction*—*Act of Bankruptcy committed before Commencement of Bankruptcy Act, 1883*—*Liquidation Proceedings under Bankruptcy Act, 1869*—*Failure of Proceedings after 1st of January, 1884*—*Bankruptcy Act, 1883 (46 & 47 Vict. c. 52), ss. 4, 5, 94, 104, 169*—*Bankruptcy Act, 1869 (32 & 33 Vict. c. 71), s. 125, sub-s.*

IX. BANKRUPTCY—ADJUDICATION—contd.

12.] A debtor filed a liquidation petition in December, 1883, and a receiver of his property was appointed. On the 15th of January, 1884, the adjourned first meeting of the creditors was held, when the creditors separated without passing any resolutions, and without again adjourning the meeting. On the 21st of January one of the creditors presented a bankruptcy petition against the debtor under the Act of 1869, alleging the filing of the liquidation petition as an act of bankruptcy. On the 1st of February, the Registrar adjudicated the debtor bankrupt on the petition. The debtor was present, and raised no objection to the jurisdiction of the Court to make the order. The receiver had not been discharged. On the 14th of March (*Ex parte Pratt*, 12 Q. B. D. 334, having meanwhile been decided), the debtor applied to the Registrar for a rehearing of the petition, and a reversal of the order of adjudication, on the ground that there was no jurisdiction to make it. The Registrar refused the application:—*Held*, that the Court had no jurisdiction to make the adjudication under the Act of 1869 on the ground that an act of bankruptcy had been committed, but that it would have had jurisdiction to make it under the power given by sub-sect. 12 of sect. 125 of that Act.—*Held*, therefore, that, as the objection had not been raised before the Registrar, a rehearing ought not to be allowed.—Observations as to the exercise of the power to allow a rehearing. *Ex parte* MAY　-　12 Q. B. D. 497

—— After liquidation　-　22 Ch. D. 813
See BANKRUPTCY—LIQUIDATION. 1.

—— Annulment of adjudication.
See Cases under BANKRUPTCY—ANNULMENT.

—— Resolution for liquidation after adjudication
[16 Ch. D. 256, 541
See BANKRUPTCY—LIQUIDATION. 2, 3.

X. BANKRUPTCY—TRUSTEE.

1. —— Administration of Property — *Directions of Creditors—Application to Court for Directions—Power of Court to direct Trustee to disregard Resolution of Creditors—Bankruptcy Act, 1869 (32 & 33 Vict. c. 71), ss. 14, 20.*] Under sect. 20 of the Bankruptcy Act, 1869, a trustee in bankruptcy is entitled to apply to the Court for directions in relation to any particular matter arising under the bankruptcy, as to which the creditors have already by resolution at a general meeting, given him directions, and the Court has power for just cause shewn to direct the trustee to disregard the directions of the creditors and to act contrary to them. In such a case the Court ought not to order the resolution to be vacated or to declare it void, but simply to direct the trustee to disregard it.—Even though there be no fraud in the passing of a resolution giving the trustee directions as to the administration of the estate, yet, if the majority of the creditors have voted, not simply with the view of administering the estate in the best way for the benefit of all the creditors but with the view of favouring the debtor or persons whom he is alleged to have fraudulently preferred, the Court ought to direct the trustee to disregard the resolution.—Sect. 20 is to be construed with reference to sect. 14.—*Ex*

X. BANKRUPTCY—TRUSTEE—continued.
parte Emmanuel (17 Ch. D. 35) explained. *Ex parte* COCKS. *In re* POOLE　-　21 Ch. D. 397

2. —— Carrying on Business by Trustee—*Power of Creditors — Bankruptcy Act, 1869 (32 & 33 Vict. c. 71), ss. 14, 20, 25.*] The creditors of a bankrupt trader have no power to authorize the trustee to carry on the business of the bankrupt, except so far as may be necessary for the beneficial winding-up of the business.—If the majority of the creditors pass a resolution authorizing the trustee to carry on the business for any other purpose, such as the hope of making a profit thereby, the resolution is not binding upon the non-assenting minority, and the Court ought to interfere and to declare it invalid. *Ex parte* EMMANUEL. *In re* BATEY　-　17 Ch. D. 35

3. —— Creditors' Deed—*Act of Bankruptcy—Subsequent Bankruptcy of Debtor—Liability of Trustee under Deed to account to Trustee in Bankruptcy.*] When the trustee under a creditors' deed takes possession of the debtor's property and carries on his business under the provisions of the deed, and the debtor is subsequently adjudicated a bankrupt on the act of bankruptcy committed by the execution of the deed, the trustee in the bankruptcy must elect to treat the trustee under the deed either as a trespasser or as his agent. If he elects to treat him as a trespasser, the trustee under the deed must deliver up to him all the property of the bankrupt of which he took possession, and which remains in his possession unconverted, and must pay him the value of that property which he has converted. *Ex parte* VAUGHAN. *In re* RIDDEOUGH　-　-　-　14 Q. B. D. 25

4. —— Debt incurred by Fraud — *Action against Debtor and Trustee in Liquidation — Separate Estate of Debtor—Right of Action against Trustee.*] In an action against liquidating debtors and their trustee, to recover advances of money obtained from the Plaintiffs by the debtors through false and fraudulent representations before the liquidation, the Plaintiffs claimed, inter alia, a declaration that they were entitled to prove for the amount of the advances, and interest at 5 per cent. to the date of the liquidation, either against the joint estate of the liquidating debtors or against the separate estate, as the Plaintiffs might elect:—*Held*, on demurrer by the trustee, that, as the Plaintiffs might in this action obtain some relief against him, the claim was good. HALE *v*. BOUSTEAD　-　-　8 Q. B. D. 453

5. —— Default in rendering Accounts—*Committal for Contempt — Bankruptcy Act, 1869 (32 & 33 Vict. c. 71), s. 55—General Rules, 126 178, 179.*] The mere fact that a trustee in bankruptcy has within four days after his resignation or removal from office neglected to render the accounts prescribed by General Rule 126 of the Bankruptcy Act, 1869, is not sufficient ground for his committal to prison by the Court of Bankruptcy, as for a contempt. To warrant such committal there must be some evidence that he has after notice from the Court wilfully failed to perform the duties imposed upon him by the rule. Re POOKES ROYLE　-　-　7 Q. B. D. 9

6. —— Leasehold — *Liquidation — Election by Trustee to take Lease—Bankruptcy Act, 1869*

X. BANKRUPTCY—TRUSTEE—continued.

(32 & 33 Vict. c. 71), ss. 17, 23, 24, 83 sub-s. 6, 89, 90, 125.] The leasehold estate of a bankrupt or debtor liquidating his affairs by arrangement vests absolutely in the trustee upon his appointment, and he has no right of election to accept or decline the leases, his only remedy being by disclaimer; and if he neglects or is unable to disclaim, he becomes personally liable in respect of the covenants contained in the leases as from the date of his appointment; but he is not liable for any breach of covenant happening before his appointment.—The Plaintiff demised to M. a wharf for twenty-one years: the lease contained covenants for rent and repairs by the lessee. M. deposited the lease with S. as security for a debt. M. filed a petition for liquidation on the 8th of December, 1880, and the Defendant was appointed trustee on the 3rd of January, 1881. The Defendant never took possession of the wharf; but he negotiated with S. for the assignment of the lease to him: the negotiations proved abortive. The Plaintiff served the Defendant with a notice requiring him to disclaim; but the Defendant failed to do this. The Plaintiff then brought the present action to recover two quarters' rent, due respectively on the 25th of December, 1880, and on the 25th of March, 1881, and damages for breach of the covenant to repair:—Held, that the Plaintiff could not recover from the Defendant the quarter's rent falling due on the 25th of December, 1880, because the Defendant was not appointed trustee until the 3rd of January, 1881; but that the Defendant was personally liable for the quarter's rent due on the 25th of March, 1881, and for breach of the covenant to repair, on the grounds, first, that by virtue of his appointment as trustee all the property of the liquidating debtor vested in him without any election on his part; and, secondly, if an election on his part was necessary, he had, by his conduct, elected to accept the lease. TITTERTON v. COOPER - 9 Q. B. D. 473

7. —— Letters addressed to Bankrupt—Order for Re-direction — Appeal — Person aggrieved—Locus Standi—Bankruptcy Act, 1869 (32 & 33 Vict. c. 71), s. 85.] Under sect. 85 of the Bankruptcy Act, 1869, an application for an order for the redirection of letters addressed to a bankrupt can only be made by the trustee in the bankruptcy.—The petitioning creditor has no locus standi either to make application or to appeal from an order made on the application of the trustee if he thinks that order not sufficiently extensive.—If the trustee refuses to apply for such an order, or to appeal from an order made on his application, the petitioning creditor cannot apply to the Court himself.—Semble, that he might obtain authority to use the name of the trustee. Ex parte LISTER. In re HALBERSTAMM
[17 Ch. D. 518

8. —— Liquidation—Removal of Trustee by Court — Jurisdiction — Discretion of Registrar — "Cause shewn"—Bankruptcy Act, 1869 (32 & 33 Vict. c. 71), s. 83 (Vide Bankruptcy Act, 1883, ss. 84, 86.)] The power given to the Court by subsect. 4 of sect. 83 of the Bankruptcy Act, 1869, to "remove any trustee upon cause shewn," authorizes the removal of one of several co-trustees without the removal of all. "Cause shewn"

X. BANKRUPTCY—TRUSTEE—continued.

does not mean only conduct amounting to fraud or dishonesty on the part of the trustee; it is enough to prove conduct—such as vexatious obstruction of the realization of the estate in the interest of the debtor—which shews that it is no longer fit that the trustee should remain a trustee. Though the making of an order to remove a trustee is not a matter of pure discretion, and the Court of Appeal is bound to see that cause was shewn in order to found the jurisdiction of the registrar, yet if the facts are capable of two reasonable interpretations, the Court of Appeal will trust to the discretion of the registrar in determining which is the more reasonable interpretation of the two, and will not disturb his order for the removal of a trustee, he, from his acquaintance with the proceedings throughout, having far better means of judging than the Court of Appeal has. Ex parte NEWITT. In re MANSEL.
[14 Q. B. D. 177

9. —— Liquidation—Release and Discharge of Trustee—Power of Board of Trade to require Account—Bankruptcy Act, 1869, s. 126—Bankruptcy Act, 1883, s. 102, sub-s. 5, s. 162, sub-s. 2.] A trustee under the Bankruptcy Act, 1869, who has obtained his statutory release and discharge under that Act, after the 25th of August, 1883 (the date of the passing of the Bankruptcy Act, 1883), is not thereby relieved from rendering an account to the Board of Trade of his receipts and payments as such trustee if, on that date, he had in his hands any undistributed funds, although such funds may have been disposed of by a subsequent resolution of the creditors. In re CHUDLEY. Ex parte BOARD OF TRADE   14 Q. B. D. 402

10. —— Personal Liability—Costs.] A trustee in bankruptcy can be made personally liable for costs of a suit to which he is a party, subject to the Court of Bankruptcy allowing him to recoup himself out of the bankrupt estate, if his conduct has been bonâ fide. PITTS v. LA FONTAINE
[6 App. Cas. 482

11. —— Power of Appointment—Bankruptcy Act, 1869 & 33 Vict. c. 71), s. 15, sub-s. 4—Bankruptcy Act, 1883 (46 & 47 Vict. c. 52), s. 44 (ii.) — Property of Bankrupt — Power of Appointment.] A debtor had a general power of appointment by deed or will:—Held, that his trustee in liquidation had no power after the death of the debtor to appoint the property the subject of the power. NICHOLS TO NIXEY
[29 Ch. D. 1005

12. —— Removal of Trustee—Judicial Discretion—Bankruptcy Act, 1869 (32 & 33 Vict. c. 71), s. 83, sub-s. 4.] A trustee in bankruptcy can be removed by the Court from his office under sect. 83, sub-sect. 4, of the Bankruptcy Act. 1869, only upon good cause shewn, not at the mere discretion of the Registrar.—But, in making an order for the removal of a trustee for good cause, the Registrar is exercising a judicial discretion, and if he has exercised his discretion according to law, the Court of Appeal will not disturb his order. Ex parte SHEARD. In re POOLEY (No. 1)
[16 Ch. D. 107

—— Protection of—Costs—Annulment of bankruptcy   -   22 Ch. D. 436
See BANKRUPTCY—ANNULMENT. 1.

X. BANKRUPTCY—TRUSTEE—*continued.*

—— Relation back of title
See Cases under BANKRUPTCY—ASSETS.
6—11.

—— Removal of, before hearing of appeal
[**16 Ch. D. 110**
See BANKRUPTCY—APPEAL. 2.

—— Solicitor of—Costs - **20 Ch. D. 685**
See BANKRUPTCY—COSTS. 1.

XI. BANKRUPTCY—ASSETS.

(*a.*) EXECUTION.

1. —— "**Proceeds**" of **Sale**—*Bankruptcy Act, 1869 (32 & 33 Vict. c. 71), ss. 6, 87—Seizure and Sale—Notice to Sheriff of Petition in Bankruptcy—Sale made on two different Days.*] Sect. 87 of the Bankruptcy Act, 1869 (32 & 33 Vict. c. 71), enacts that, where the goods of any trader have been taken in execution in respect of a judgment for a sum exceeding £50, and sold, the sheriff shall retain the *proceeds of such sale* in his hands for a period of fourteen days, and, upon notice being served on him within that period of a bankruptcy petition having been presented against such trader (followed by an adjudication), shall hold the proceeds of such sale, after deducting expenses, on trust to pay the same to the trustee.—On the 29th of December, 1882, an execution was issued at the suit of the Plaintiff against the Defendants, traders, upon a judgment for £87 19s. 4d. debt and costs, and lodged with the sheriff, who on the same day seized certain goods of the Defendants and sold them on the 10th of January, 1883, realizing by that sale £41 12s. 7d. On the 12th of January other goods of the Defendants which were upon other premises occupied by them were sold under the fi. fa. and realized £74 10s. 10d. On the 24th of January, 1883, a petition in bankruptcy was presented against the Defendants, under which they were adjudicated bankrupts on the 19th of February. The sheriff had notice of the petition on the 25th of January:—*Held*, that the trustee was entitled to the whole proceeds, as the "sale" contemplated by sect. 87 of the Bankruptcy Act, 1869, was not completed until the 12th of January, within fourteen days from the receipt by the sheriff of notice of the filing of the petition. JONES v. PARCELL **11 Q. B. D. 430**

2. —— **Sum below £20**—*Sale—Notice to Sheriff of Bankruptcy Petition—Title of Trustee—Bankruptcy Act, 1883, ss. 45, 46.*] Where the sheriff sells under an execution for more than £20, and within fourteen days afterwards receives notice of a bankruptcy petition, the effect of sect. 46, sub-sect. 2, of the Bankruptcy Act, 1883, is not to render the sale absolutely void, but to deprive the execution creditor of the fruits of the sale, and to transfer them to the trustee in the bankruptcy for the benefit of the general body of the creditors.—Where, therefore, a sheriff is in possession under several writs, some for more and some for less than £20, and proceeds to sell, the writs are payable in order of priority so long as there are funds to pay; but, if he receives notice of a bankruptcy petition within fourteen days after the sale, only those writs are entitled to be paid which are for less than £20, and which

XI. BANKRUPTCY—ASSETS—*continued.*

(*a.*) EXECUTION—*continued.*

would have been paid had not bankruptcy supervened. *In re* PEARCE. *Ex parte* CROSSTHWAITE
[**14 Q. B. D. 966**

3. —— **Sum exceeding £50**—*Liquidation—Bankruptcy Act, 1869 (32 & 33 Vict. c. 71), s. 87—Abandonment of Part of Judgment Debt.*] Judgment was signed in an action against a trader for debt and costs amounting to less than £50. The judgment creditor delivered to the sheriff a writ of fi. fa. indorsed to levy the amount of the debt and costs, with the expenses of and incidental to the execution. The expenses of and incidental to the execution, added to the amount of the debt and costs, made a total exceeding £50, but upon notice of a liquidation petition against the execution debtor, the execution creditor directed the sheriff's officer not to sell for an amount exceeding £50, and accordingly goods to the amount of £49 17s. only were sold:—*Held*, that the execution creditor could, by abandoning so much of his judgment debt as might be necessary to keep the total amount for which the goods were sold under £50, avoid the operation of s. 87 of the Bankruptcy Act, 1869, and that, therefore, the execution creditor and not the trustee in liquidation was entitled to the proceeds of the execution. TURNER v. BRIDGETT - **8 Q. B. D. 392**

4. —— **Sum exceeding £50**—*Reduced by payment on Account—Payment of Balance by Trustee—Bankruptcy Act, 1869 (32 & 33 Vict. c. 71), s. 87.*] After seizure under a fi. fa. for a sum which was increased by possession money to an amount above £50, payments on account were made by the execution debtor, reducing the amount below £50. The execution creditor knew and approved of such payments, and authorized the sheriff to give the execution debtor further time to pay the balance, so that a sale might be avoided.—Proceedings in bankruptcy having been taken against the execution debtor, his trustee paid the balance to the sheriff, who gave possession of the goods to the trustee:—*Held*, that the execution creditor was entitled to the balance, as the proceeds of an execution for a sum not exceeding £50. MOSTYN v. STOCK - - **9 Q. B. D. 432**

5. —— **Sum exceeding £50**—*Partnership—Dissolution—Appointment of Receiver.*] E. and F. being in partnership as wine merchants, F. brought an action in the Chancery Division for a dissolution of the partnership, and an order was made by the Court for a dissolution, and the appointment of a receiver, under which a receiver took possession of the partnership effects and carried on the business, F. ceasing to take any part in the business, and having no other occupation than that of book-keeper to a trading company. An action having been commenced against E. and F. upon bills accepted by the firm before the receiver took possession, judgment was signed against F. and his separate property taken in execution for a sum exceeding £50:—*Held*, that F. was not at the time of the execution a "trader" within the meaning of sect. 87 of the Bankruptcy Act, 1869 (32 & 33 Vict. c. 71). DAWE v. VERGARA - - **11 Q. B. D. 241**

XI. BANKRUPTCY—ASSETS—*continued.*

(*b.*) RELATION BACK OF TRUSTEE'S TITLE.

6. —— Assignment of future Receipts — *Bankruptcy of Assignor—Relation back of Trustee's Title—Bankruptcy Act, 1869 (32 & 33 Vict. c. 71), s. 11.*] An assignment by a trader of the future receipts of his business, even if made for value, is, as regards receipts accruing after the commencement of his subsequent bankruptcy, inoperative as against the title of the trustee in the bankruptcy.—*Brice* v. *Bannister* (3 Q. B. D. 569) distinguished. *Ex parte* NICHOLS. *In re* JONES [22 Ch. D. 782

7. —— Money paid to Solicitor—*Money received by Petitioning Creditor's Solicitor during Pendency of Petition, and paid over to Petitioning Creditor—Liability of Solicitor to refund to Trustee — Principal and Agent.*] Pending the hearing of a bankruptcy petition, and with notice of the act of bankruptcy on which it was founded, the solicitor of the petitioning creditor, as his agent, received from the debtor various sums of money as consideration for successive adjournments of the hearing of the petition, and these sums he paid over, or accounted for, to his client (the petitioning creditor). Afterwards an adjudication was made on the petition :—*Held,* that, the solicitor having received the money with notice of the act of bankruptcy to which the title of the trustee related back, the payment by him was a wrongful act, and he was liable to repay the money to the trustee, and was not discharged by the payment to his own principal. *Ex parte* EDWARDS. *In re* CHAPMAN 13 Q. B. D. 747

8. —— Money paid to Solicitor—*Money paid by Debtor to his Solicitor to oppose Petition—Adjudication—Title of Trustee.*] Money bonâ fide paid by a debtor to his solicitor to defray counsel's fees and other legal expenses in opposing proceedings in bankruptcy that have been commenced against him, cannot, should adjudication follow, be recovered from the solicitor by the trustee in bankruptcy, even although the solicitor knew of the acts of bankruptcy on which the proceedings were based. *In re* SINCLAIR. *Ex parte* PAYNE - - 15 Q. B. D. 616

9. —— Payment by Agent—*Liability of Agent to Trustee in Bankruptcy of Principal—Bankruptcy Act, 1869 (32 & 33 Vict. c. 71), s. 6, sub-s. 2.*] An agent, who, in obedience to the previous direction of his principal, pays away money of the principal which is in his hands, knowing before he made the payment (though he did not know when he received the money) that the payment will when completed constitute an act of bankruptcy on the part of the principal, is not liable to the trustee in the subsequent bankruptcy of the principal for the money so paid away.—The trustee could recover the money from the agent only on the ground that he had paid away the money of the trustee, and in such a case the money would become the trustee's money only on the completion of the act of bankruptcy to which his title would relate back, i.e., not until after the money had left the agent's hands. *Ex parte* HELDER. *In re* LEWIS 24 Ch. D. 339

10. —— Ship-building Contract—*Assignment of Debt—Completion by Trustee.*] A shipbuilder agreed to build a vessel, the price to be paid in specified instalments. Part of the work having been done, but less than the value of such part having been paid to the builder, he charged in favour of a creditor the instalment due to him on the delivery of the vessel. Before the ship was completed he became bankrupt. The trustee in the bankruptcy completed the vessel, and in so doing expended less than the amount which remained to be paid by the purchaser :—*Held,* that the charge, being upon money which had been already earned by the builder, was valid as against the trustee.—*Ex parte Nicholls* (22 Ch. D. 782) and *Tooth* v. *Hallett* (Law Rep. 4 Ch. 242) distinguished. *Ex parte* MOSS. *In re* TOWARD [14 Q. B. D. 310

11. —— Withdrawal of Criminal Prosecution—*Illegal Consideration—Right of Trustee to recover from Payee.*] A banking company commenced a prosecution against a customer for having obtained credit from them under false pretences, which is, by sect. 13 of the Debtors Act, 1869, made a misdemeanour. At this time the bank had notice of an act of bankruptcy committed by the customer. On the day on which the summons was to be heard by the magistrate, H. (whose wife was an aunt of the customer's wife) signed an undertaking that, if the magistrate would allow the summons to be withdrawn, he would pay the bank the sum which the customer had obtained from them by false pretences. An application was made to the magistrate by the customer's solicitor to allow the summons to be withdrawn. The application was assented to by the bank's solicitor and was granted by the magistrate. H. then paid the money to the bank. The bank manager believed that H. was paying the money out of his own pocket. The customer was soon afterwards adjudicated a bankrupt, upon the act of bankruptcy of which the bank had notice. The trustee in the bankruptcy discovered that the money which H. had paid to the bank had been previously handed to him by the bankrupt's wife, she having, with the bankrupt's knowledge, taken it for the purpose of paying the bank out of a bag of money belonging to the bankrupt :—*Held,* that, the consideration for the payment to the bank being the stifling of a prosecution, there was no legal consideration, and that, though H., being in pari delicto, could not have recovered the money from the bank, the trustee, to whom, by virtue of the relation back of his title to the act of bankruptcy, the money really belonged, could recover it.—*Ex parte Caldecott* (4 Ch. D. 150) distinguished.—Leave to appeal to the Court of Appeal refused. *Ex parte* WOLVERHAMPTON BANKING COMPANY. *In re* CAMPBELL 14 Q. B. D. 32

(*c.*) SALARY OR INCOME.

12. —— Future Earnings of Professional Man —*Bankruptcy Act, 1869 (32 & 33 Vict. c. 71), s. 90.*] The word "income" in sect. 90 of the Bankruptcy Act, 1869, applies only to an "income" ejusdem generis with a "salary," and does not enable the Court to set aside for the benefit of the creditors of a professional man, who

XI. BANKRUPTCY—ASSETS—continued.

(c.) SALARY OR INCOME—continued.

is an undischarged bankrupt, any part of his prospective and contingent earnings in the exercise of his personal skill and knowledge. *Ex parte* BENWELL. *In re* HUTTON　　**14 Q. B. D. 301**

13. —— **Pension of Retired Judge**—*Judge of Crown Colony*—*Bankruptcy Act,* 1869 (32 & 33 *Vict. c.* 71), *ss.* 4, 15, 17, 88, 89, 90.] The effect of sects. 15 and 17 of the Bankruptcy Act, 1869, is to vest in the trustee in a bankruptcy all the " property " of the bankrupt of whatever nature, including the matters dealt with by sect. 23 and sects. 87 to 95, but subject to the exceptions and qualifications introduced by those sections.—The pension of a retired Judge of a Crown colony, granted by the Secretary of State for the Colonies, and voted annually by the Legislature of the colony, is, in case of the bankruptcy of the Judge, "property" which vests in the trustee in the bankruptcy, but it is "income" of the bankrupt within sect. 90 of the Bankruptcy Act, 1869, and is subject to the power thereby given to the Court to determine how much of it shall be set aside for the benefit of the bankrupt's creditors. *Ex parte* HUGGINS. *In re* HUGGINS　　**21 Ch. D. 85**

14. —— **Voluntary Allowance**—*Bankruptcy Act,* 1869 (32 & 33 *Vict. c.* 71), *s.* 90.] A purely voluntary allowance made to a bankrupt is not "income" within the meaning of sect. 90 of the Bankruptcy Act, 1869, and no order can be made for the payment of any part of such an allowance, when received by the bankrupt, to the trustee in the bankruptcy.—In order that sect. 90 may apply, the payment must be one to which the bankrupt has a legal or equitable claim.—Decision of Bacon, C.J., reversed. *Ex parte* WICKS. *In re* WICKS　-　　-　　-　**17 Ch. D. 70**

(d.) GENERAL.

15. —— **Assignment of Chose in Action**—*Notice of*—*Estate of Trustee in Liquidation*—*Priority*—*Stop Order*—*Bankruptcy Act,* 1849, *s.* 141—*Bankruptcy Act,* 1869, *s.* 22—*Vendor and Purchaser*—*Doubtful Title.*] A legatee of a reversionary interest under a will, which had been paid into Court in an administration suit, presented a petition for liquidation in March, 1873, and a trustee was appointed. In July he assigned his interest in the legacy to J., who obtained a stop order on the fund in Court. In November, 1876, he assigned his interest to E., without notice of the liquidation, who also obtained a stop order on the fund. Afterwards the trustee in liquidation obtained a stop order. The Plaintiffs purchased the interest of the trustee in liquidation and of J., and contracted to sell the legacy to the Defendant. The Defendant required E.'s mortgage to be abstracted as an incumbrance on the estate:—*Held,* by Jessel, M.R., that E. having obtained a stop order before the trustee in liquidation, his interest was prior to that of the trustee's, and was an incumbrance on the estate.—*In re Bright's Settlement* (13 Ch. D. 413) considered.—*Held,* by the Court of Appeal, that the question of the priority of E.'s incumbrance was too doubtful to justify the vendor in omitting it from the abstract; and the decision of

XI. BANKRUPTCY—ASSETS—continued.

(d.) GENERAL—continued.

the Master of the Rolls was accordingly affirmed. PALMER *v.* LOCKE　-　　-　　**18 Ch. D. 381**

16. —— **Books of Account** — *Assignment* — *Bankruptcy Act,* 1869 (32 & 33 *Vict. c.* 71), *s.* 22—*Bankruptcy Rules,* 1870, *r.* 110.] A bonâ fide purchaser for value of the book-debts, books, and all the interest in the partnership of his partner prior to a dissolution, will not be compelled upon the subsequent bankruptcy of such late partner to hand over to the trustee the books of account which passed by the assignment, and thereupon ceased to be property of the bankrupt within the meaning of the Bankruptcy Act, 1869, s. 22, and Bankruptcy Rules, 1870, r. 110. *In re* WEST. *Ex parte* GOOD　-　　-　　**21 Ch. D. 868**

17. —— **Gift of Chattels** — *Bankruptcy of Donor.*] In 1866 A., soon after the birth of his son T., purchased a pipe of wine for his son, and had it bottled and laid down in his cellar, and from that time it remained intact in the cellar and was known in the family and amongst their friends as T.'s wine. In 1885 A. became bankrupt:—*Held,* that there was not sufficient evidence of an intention to make an immediate present gift of the wine to T., and that it passed to the trustee in bankruptcy. *In re* RIDGWAY. *Ex parte* RIDGWAY　-　　-　　-　　**15 Q. B. D. 447**

XII. BANKRUPTCY—DISCHARGE.

1. —— **Application before close of Bankruptcy** —*Assent of Creditors*—*Meeting summoned by Trustee*—*Advertisement*—*Bankruptcy Act,* 1869 (32 & 33 *Vict. c.* 71), *ss.* 21, 48, 78—*Bankruptcy Rules,* 1870, *rr.* 89, 95, 138, 142.] When a meeting of the creditors of a bankrupt under the Bankruptcy Act, 1869, is summoned by the trustee (for the purpose, e.g. of ascertaining whether the creditors will assent to an application by the bankrupt for an order of discharge) it is only necessary that it should be summoned by means of a notice sent by the trustee to each creditor in accordance with the provisions of rule 95; it is not necessary that advertisements of the meeting should be published as provided by rule 89 in reference to the first meeting of the creditors. Sect. 78 has not the effect of incorporating the Bankruptcy Rules into the Act for the purposes of construction. But, even if the rules are to be considered as, by virtue of sect. 78, incorporated into the Act, sect. 21 does not make rule 89 applicable to meetings summoned by the trustee, a special provision for the summoning of such meetings being made by rule 95. *Ex parte* COHEN　　　**13 Q. B. D. 56**

2. —— **Certificate of Conformity**—*Effect of Suspending Order*—*Bankruptcy Act,* 1842 (5 & 6 *Vict. c.* 122), *ss.* 37, 39—*Bankrupt Law Consolidation Act,* 1849 (12 & 13 *Vict. c.* 106), *s.* 199.] In July, 1848, an order was made that the grant of a certificate of conformity to a bankrupt be suspended for three years.—During the period of suspension, the Bankruptcy Act of 1849 came into operation; which provided (s. 199) that "every certificate of conformity, allowed by any Commissioner before the time appointed for the commencement of this Act, though not confirmed according to the laws in force before that time, shall discharge the bankrupt from all debts due

XII. BANKRUPTCY—DISCHARGE—*continued.*

by him when he became bankrupt, and from all claims and demands made provable under the fiat ":—*Held*, that, as, by virtue of that section, confirmation of the order of July, 1848, was no longer required, that order became, at the expiration of the period of suspension, of itself a complete discharge to the bankrupt, and that property acquired by him after the expiration of that period belonged to him and not to the assignee in the bankruptcy. *In re* DOVE. BOUSFIELD *v.* DOVE　-　-　27 Ch. D. 687

3. —— Condition—*Contracting Debt without reasonable or probable Ground of Expectation of being able to pay it*—*Bankruptcy Act*, 1883 (46 & 47 *Vict. c.* 52), *s.* 28, *sub-s.* 3 (*c.*).] Two partners, who had no capital of their own, commenced business by means of borrowed money, assigning to the lender as security their leasehold premises, the goodwill of their business, and all their existing and after-acquired stock-in-trade, fixtures, furniture, and book-debts, giving him power to take possession at any time. They contracted debts in carrying on the business, and became bankrupts. The mortgagee took possession under his deed, and his security was insufficient. The registrar granted the bankrupts a discharge, on condition of their consenting to judgment being entered up against them by the trustee for the whole of the debts provable in the bankruptcy:—*Held*, that the bankrupts had contracted debts without having at the time of contracting them any reasonable or probable ground of expectation of being able to pay them, and that the registrar's decision was right. *Ex parte* WHITE. *In re* WHITE
[14 Q. B. D. 600

4. —— Condition—"*Rash and hazardous speculations*"—*Conduct of Bankrupt before Commencement of Act*—*Retrospective Effect of Act*—*Bankruptcy Act*, 1883 (46 & 47 *Vict. c.* 52), *s.* 28—*Costs*—*Appeal.*] Upon an application by a bankrupt under sect. 28 of the Bankruptcy Act, 1883, for an order of discharge, the Court may take into consideration conduct of the bankrupt of the nature mentioned in sub-sect. 3, though it took place before the commencement of the Act, and in that sense sect. 28 is retrospective.—*In re* White (9 L. T. (N.S.) 702) explained and distinguished. —A solicitor who had no capital of his own bought land in the city of London by means of money which he borrowed on the security of mortgages of the land, his intention being to sell at an advanced price. He afterwards borrowed more money on a further mortgage for the purpose of building on the land. The land was valued by professional valuers at considerably more than the amount borrowed. He was unable to sell or let the property, and he became a bankrupt:— *Held*, that he had been guilty of "rash and hazardous speculations," and that the registrar was right in granting him an order of discharge subject to the condition that, after setting aside out of his earnings £300 a year for the maintenance of himself and his family, he should pay over to the official receiver the balance of his earnings, until he should have paid 10*s.* in the pound on all the debts which had been, or might be, proved in the bankruptcy.—Creditors served with notice of an appeal by a bankrupt from an order grant-

XII. BANKRUPTCY—DISCHARGE—*continued.*

ing him a conditional discharge will not be allowed their costs of appearing on the hearing of the appeal when the official receiver or trustee appears. *Ex parte* SALAMAN. *In re* SALAMAN
[14 Q. B. D. 936

5. —— Effect of Order of Discharge—*Debt incurred by the Fraud or Breach of Trust of a Partner*—*Bankruptcy Act*, 1869 (32 & 33 *Vict. c.* 71), *s.* 49.] The 49th section of the Bankruptcy Act, 1869 (32 & 33 Vict. c. 71), which enacts that "an order of discharge shall not release the bankrupt from any debt or liability incurred by means of any fraud or breach of trust," is not confined to a fraud or breach of trust committed by the bankrupt personally.—Therefore, where a debt has been incurred by one of several partners for which the partnership is liable, and the partnership goes into liquidation under the Bankruptcy Act, 1869, a partner who has received his order of discharge is not thereby released from such debt if it was incurred by fraud, though he himself was innocent of such fraud. COOPER *v.* PRICHARD
[11 Q. B. D. 351

XIII. BANKRUPTCY—UNDISCHARGED BANKRUPT.

1. —— Close of Bankruptcy—*Bankrupt without Assets*—*Power of Court to reopen Proceedings*—*Rights of new Creditors*—*Bankruptcy Act*, 1869 (32 & 33 *Vict. c.* 71), *ss.* 47, 54, 71.] The Court has power under sect. 47 of the Bankruptcy Act, 1869, to make an order closing a bankruptcy in a case where it does not appear that the bankrupt has any assets.—After an order has been made closing a bankruptcy, the Court has, under sect. 71, power to reopen it.—But such an order ought not to be made without notice to the creditors of the bankrupt (if any) whose debts have been contracted after the adjudication, nor without letting them in to prove as creditors against any property of the bankrupt acquired by him after the date of the order to close the bankruptcy. *Ex parte* PITT. *In re* GOSLING
[20 Ch. D. 308

2. —— Close of Bankruptcy—*Death of Bankrupt within Three Years after Close*—*After-acquired Property*—*Rights of Old Creditors*—*Administration Action*—*Bankruptcy Act*, 1869 (32 & 33 *Vict. c.* 71), *ss.* 12, 15, 47, 48, 49, 54.] An undischarged bankrupt died intestate within three years after the close of his bankruptcy, having in the interval acquired fresh property and contracted fresh debts. Only a small dividend had been paid in the bankruptcy, and the bankrupt had not, after the close of the bankruptcy, made any further payments to the creditors who had proved. An action was brought by one of the new creditors to administer the bankrupt's estate. The estate was sufficient to pay the costs of the action, to pay the new creditors in full, and to leave a surplus. This surplus was claimed by the old creditors:—*Held*, that the administratrix was entitled to the surplus, and that the old creditors had no right to it.—The creditors of an undischarged bankrupt under the Act of 1869 have no rights against property acquired by him after the close of the bankruptcy, except such rights as are given to them by sect. 54, and those rights cannot be enforced after

XIII. BANKRUPTCY—UNDISCHARGED BANK-RUPT—*continued.*

the death of the bankrupt.—Sect. 12 applies to property acquired by an undischarged bankrupt after the close of the bankruptcy as well as to property divisible among the creditors in the bankruptcy.—*Ex parte Kelly* (7 Ch. D. 161) explained. *In re* SMITH. GREEN *v.* SMITH　　24 Ch. D. 672

3. —— **Close of Bankruptcy**—*Death of Bankrupt—Rights of Creditors—Set-off—Bankruptcy Act, 1869 (32 & 33 Vict. c. 71), ss. 12, 39, 47, 54—Judicature Act, 1875 (38 & 39 Vict. c. 77), s. 10.]* When a bankrupt has not obtained an order of discharge, a creditor who has proved in the bankruptcy, and who is being sued by the bankrupt, or by his executor, after his death, for a debt due to the bankrupt on a contract entered into after the commencement of the bankruptcy, cannot, during the period of three years from the close of the bankruptcy, set-off the unpaid balance of his proved debt against the sum claimed in the action.—The scope of the Bankruptcy Act, 1869, is that, during the period of three years after the close of the bankruptcy, none of the creditors who could prove in the bankruptcy shall be able to obtain a preference over the others, and that after the expiration of the three years, the unpaid balances of the proved debts shall be enforced against the property of the debtor only under the direction of the Court of Bankruptcy, so that any sums which may be thus recovered may be distributed among the creditors who have proved *pari passu. In re* SMITH. GREEN *v.* SMITH
[22 Ch. D. 586

4. —— **Earnings of Personal Labour**—*Architect—Bankruptcy Act, 1869 (32 & 33 Vict. c. 71), s. 17—Practice—Adding Plaintiff—Rules of Court, 1875, Order XVI., r. 13.]* The Plaintiff, who was an architect, sued for remuneration in respect of employment under a contract made in 1877, and for damages for an alleged wrongful dismissal from such 'employment in 1880. The Plaintiff was adjudicated bankrupt in 1878, and had never obtained his discharge:—*Held* (affirming the decision of Fry, J.) that the cause of action for remuneration and damages passed to the trustee, and that the proper course was to add him as co-Plaintiff in the action, and give him the conduct of the action. EMDEN *v.* CARTE
[17 Ch. D. 169, 768

XIV. BANKRUPTCY—ANNULMENT.

1. —— **Application to annul**—*Limit of Time—Protection of Trustee—Bankruptcy Act, 1869 (32 & 33 Vict. c. 71), ss. 6, 10, 71—Bankruptcy Rules, 1870, r. 143.]* In a proper case an adjudication of bankruptcy may be annulled upon an application made after the expiration of the time limited for appealing from it.—Sect. 10 of the Bankruptcy Act, 1869, has no application to an appeal from an adjudication, or to an application to annul it.—*Ex parte Brown* (Law Rep. 9 Ch. 304) explained. — *Ex parte Johnson* (12 Ch. D. 905) distinguished.—A petitioning creditor, who alleges that his debtor has committed an act of bankruptcy, by departing from his dwelling-house with intent to defeat and delay his creditors, is bound to shew that the debtor is alive and in some other place.—An order was made by the

XIV. BANKRUPTCY—ANNULMENT—*contd.*

Court of Appeal to annul an adjudication of bankruptcy, on the ground that the debtor must be presumed to have been dead when it was made. Probate had been granted of a will executed by the debtor:—*Held,* that the costs and charges of the trustee properly incurred, and the costs of all parties of the application to annul and of the appeal, must be paid out of the estate, and that the executors must confirm all acts properly done by the trustee in the bankruptcy. *Ex parte* GEISEL. *In re* STANGER -　　- 22 Ch. D. 436

2. —— **Scheme of Settlement**—*Approval of Court—Judicial Discretion—Bankruptcy Act, 1869 (32 & 33 Vict. c. 71), ss. 28, 126.]* In giving or withholding the approval of the Court to a composition with creditors, accepted by the proper majority under sect. 28 of the Bankruptcy Act, 1869, the Judge is exercising a judicial discretion, and is bound to consider the objections brought before him by a dissentient creditor and to give his decision judicially upon sufficient reasons.— The power of the Court under sect. 28 is not limited, as in the case of a composition accepted by the resolution of two meetings of creditors under sect. 126, to setting aside the resolution on the ground of fraud in the proceedings.—The propriety of the resolutions is to be judged of by the Court upon the facts as they appear at the time when its approval is sought, not as they appeared at the time when the resolutions were passed.—The exercise of the discretion by the Judge is subject to appeal, but the Court of Appeal ought not to interfere unless it is clearly shewn that the Judge has exercised his discretion wrongly—Decision of Bacon, C.J., reversed.— The fact that by composition resolutions under sect. 28 no security was given for some of the instalments, and the management of the assets was intrusted to a debtor who for several years previously had indulged in recklessly extravagant expenditure:—*Held,* to be a sufficient reason for refusing to give the approval of the Court to the resolutions. *Ex parte* MERCHANT BANKING COMPANY OF LONDON. *In re* DURHAM　16 Ch. D. 623

3. —— **Scheme of Settlement.** —*Approval of Court—Notice of Meeting of Creditors—Bankruptcy Act, 1869 (32 & 33 Vict. c. 71), s. 28—Trustee—Costs.]* Under sect. 28 of the Bankruptcy Act, 1869, the Court is not bound to approve of resolutions passed by the creditors of a bankrupt authorizing the trustee to accept a composition, or assent to a general scheme of settlement of the bankrupt's affairs, even if it sees that the majority have been acting bonâ fide in the interest of the creditors, and that better terms cannot be obtained for the creditors. It is the duty of the Court to look at all the circumstances, and to have regard to the moral aspect of the case, and not to give its approval to the proposed arrangement, although it may be for the benefit of the creditors, if it can see that the money which they are to receive under it is to be paid in order to hush up and prevent investigation into some discreditable transaction. The trustee in a bankruptcy applied to the County Court for its approval of a composition offered by the bankrupt and sanctioned by resolutions passed by the creditors under sect. 28. The Judge refused to give his approval

XIV. BANKRUPTCY—ANNULMENT—*contd.*

The trustee appealed to the Chief Judge, who held that the approval of the Court ought to be given. On the application of dissentient creditors the Court of Appeal restored the order of the County Court Judge :—*Held*, that the trustee was entitled to apply to the County Court, but that he ought not to have appealed. Consequently, though he was allowed out of the bankrupt's estate his costs of the application to the County Court, he was ordered to pay personally the costs of both appeals. *Ex parte* STRAWBRIDGE. *In re* HICKMAN　　**25 Ch. D. 266**

4. —— Scheme of Settlement — *Bankruptcy Act, 1869 (32 & 33 Vict. c. 71), s. 28 — Debtor left in Possession of Assets — Default in Payment of Composition — Rights of Trustees — Assignment of Book Debts by Debtor — Surety for Payment of Composition — Counter-Indemnity by Debtor.*] Two parties in trade filed a liquidation petition, under which a trustee of their property was appointed. Afterwards the creditors, under the provisions of sect. 28 of the Bankruptcy Act, 1869, passed resolutions authorizing the trustee to accept a composition from the debtors, and the arrangement was approved by the Court. The composition was to be paid in four instalments, part of the last of which was to be secured by a surety. One of the debtors, who was about to carry on the business alone, agreed to pay £30 to the trustee weekly, until he should have paid the amount of the composition. In case of his making default, the trustee was to be at liberty to take possession of his stock-in-trade, assets, and effects, and realise them for the benefit of the creditors of the firm. The discharge of the debtors was to be granted, the liquidation closed, and the trustee released, so soon as the trustee should certify to the Court that a sum sufficient to pay the composition had been paid to him by the debtor. The first instalment was duly paid, but the debtor afterwards made default, and the trustee took possession of his stock-in-trade and effects. It then appeared that the debtors had, shortly before the seizure, executed a deed assigning the outstanding book debts of the firm to the surety and another person, as security for moneys advanced by them, and also as a security to the surety against his liability in respect of the last instalment of the composition. The advances had been made since the passing of the resolutions, to enable the debtor to carry on the business and to pay the first instalment of the composition :—*Held*, that the resolutions of the creditors gave an implied authority to the debtor to carry on the business in the ordinary way, and to pledge the assets in order to raise money for the purposes of the business, or for the purpose of paying the composition, and that the assignees were entitled to the book debts as a security for the advances which they had made. —But *held*, that the resolutions did not authorize the pledging of the assets as an indemnity to the surety against his liability in respect of the last instalment of the composition, and that the deed could not stand as a security in that respect.—*Ex parte* Burrell (1 Ch. D. 537) distinguished. *Ex parte* ALLARD. *In re* SIMONS　　**16 Ch. D. 505**

5. —— Scheme of Settlement — *Composition under Sect. 28 of Bankruptcy Act, 1869—Locus*

XIV. BANKRUPTCY—ANNULMENT—*contd.*

Standi of Bankrupt to apply to reduce Proof of a Creditor—File of Proceedings in Bankruptcy —Estoppel.] After the creditors of a bankrupt have resolved under sect. 28 of the Bankruptcy Act, 1869, to accept a composition offered by the bankrupt, the bankrupt, though undischarged, has a locus standi to apply to the Court to reduce the amount of the proof of a creditor, and the mere fact that the proof has been upon the file of the proceedings in the bankruptcy for upwards of a year does not estop the bankrupt from making the application.—Decision of Bacon, C.J., affirmed. —The file of the proceedings in a bankruptcy is not of the nature of a record, and does not create an estoppel. *Ex parte* BACON. *In re* BOND
　　[17 Ch. D. 447

6. —— Scheme of Settlement — *Discharge of Bankrupt—Bankruptcy Act, 1869 (32 & 33 Vict. c. 71), s. 28.*] When a bankruptcy has been annulled under the Bankruptcy Act, 1869, s. 28, and a scheme of arrangement of the bankrupt's affairs has been approved of by the Court, the bankrupt is discharged from his debts, and no action is maintainable against him in respect of any debt provable under the bankruptcy. GILBEY *v.* JEFFRIES -　　-　　-　　**11 Q. B. D. 559**

XV. BANKRUPTCY—PROOF.

1. —— Admission by Trustee — *Application by Creditor to expunge — Locus Standi — Bankruptcy Act, 1869 (32 & 33 Vict. c. 71), s. 20— Bankruptcy Rules, 1870, rr. 67, 70–74.*] A creditor who has proved a debt in a bankruptcy has an interest which entitles him to apply to the Court to expunge the proof of another creditor which has been admitted by the trustee. *Ex parte* MERRIMAN. *In re* STENSON　　**25 Ch. D. 144**

2. —— Admission by Trustee—*Right to apply to expunge—Lapse of Time—Bankruptcy Rules, 1870, rr. 72, 73.*] Under rule 73 of the Bankruptcy Rules, 1870, as under the previous practice, a trustee in bankruptcy who has admitted a proof against the estate is entitled at any time afterwards to apply to the Court to expunge the proof, on the ground that it was originally wrongly admitted. Mere lapse of time is no objection to the application, but, though the proof is expunged, the creditor will be entitled to retain any dividend which he may have previously received. *Ex parte* HARPER. *In re* TAIT
　　[21 Ch. D. 537

3. —— Alimony—*"Debt or Liability"—Order of Divorce Court for Payment of monthly or weekly Alimony—29 & 30 Vict. c. 32, s. 1—Bankruptcy Act, 1883 (46 & 47 Vict. c. 52), s. 37— Debtors Act, 1869 (32 & 33 Vict. c. 62), s. 5.*] Future weekly or monthly payments of alimony, payable by a husband by virtue of an order of the Divorce Court made under sect. 1 of the Act 29 & 30 Vict. c. 32, are not capable of valuation, and are not a "debt or liability" within the meaning of sect 37 of the Bankruptcy Act, 1883. They cannot, therefore, be proved in the bankruptcy of the husband, and he is, notwithstanding his bankruptcy, liable to continue the payments.—Arrears of payments of alimony under such an order constitute a debt enforceable under sect. 5 of the Debtors Act, 1869.—Decision of Cave, J., affirmed. LINTON *v.* LINTON　　-　　**15 Q. B. D. 239**

XV. BANKRUPTCY—PROOF—_continued._

4. —— Bill of Exchange — *Accommodation Bill deposited as Security for less than its nominal Amount.*] When a bill of exchange, accepted for the accommodation of the drawer, is deposited by him as security for a debt less than the amount of the bill, the holder is entitled to prove in the bankruptcy of the acceptor for the full amount of the bill, though he cannot receive dividends in excess of the debt due to him by the drawer.— Decision of Bacon, C.J., reversed. *Ex parte* NEWTON. *Ex parte* GRIFFIN. *In re* BUNYARD
[**16 Ch. D. 330**]

5. —— Breach of Trust by Firm—*Joint and several Liability—Joint Judgment against Firm —Merger of several Liability — Bankruptcy of Firm—Right of Proof against Separate Estate.*] Where a firm is adjudicated bankrupt on a judgment debt recovered against the firm jointly, if the partners are also severally liable in respect of the same matter by reason, for instance, of its arising out of breach of trust, the several liability of the partners is not, solely by reason of the creditor having sued for and obtained a joint judgment, merged in such judgment, so as to preclude a proof by the judgment creditor against their respective separate estates. *In re* DAVISON
[**13 Q. B. D. 50**]

6. —— Covenant not to revoke Will — *Restraint of Marriage—Contingent Liability—Covenant ancillary to Mortgage — Discharge.*] An unmarried woman, having a power of appointing a sum of money by will, made a will appointing it to a mortgagee, and covenanted not to revoke the will. She afterwards became bankrupt and obtained her discharge. After her discharge she revoked her will, and made another appointing the sum of money to another person :—*Held* (affirming the decision of Kay, J.), first, that the covenant not to revoke the will was divisible, and was not wholly void, although in one alternative it was in restraint of marriage; secondly, that the contingent liability under the covenant was incapable of proof under the bankruptcy, that the covenant was not released by the bankruptcy, and that an action would lie for damages for a breach of the covenant committed after the bankruptcy. ROBINSON *v.* OMMANNEY
[**21 Ch. D. 780 ; 23 Ch. D. 285**]

7. —— Damages—*Account — Infringement of Patent—Proof for Profits—32 & 33 Vict. c. 71, s. 31—Not demurring—Costs.*] Where a patentee is entitled to recover the amount of profits made by infringing his patent, the amount of those profits is not recoverable in the nature of damages, but as money had and received to his use; and he is therefore not prevented by the 31st section of the Bankruptcy Act of 1869 from proving in the bankruptcy of the infringer for the amount of those profits.—When a bankrupt Defendant does not appear at the hearing, and his trustees appear and defend, they are liable to the costs of the action. WATSON *v.* HOLLIDAY
[**20 Ch. D. 780**]

8. —— Evidence—*Admissibility—Admission by Dead Man against Interest—Bankrupt's Statement of Affairs — Judgment Debt—Inquiry into Consideration.*] In order that an admission made by a dead man may be admissible in evidence on

XV. BANKRUPTCY—PROOF—_continued._

the ground that it was against his interest, it must have been actually against his interest at the time when it was made; it is not sufficient that it might possibly turn out afterwards to have been against his interest.—An admission made by a bankrupt in his statement of affairs that a debt is due from him, is not after his death admissible evidence as against his assignee in bankruptcy of the existence of the debt, merely because it might turn out that there was a surplus after paying the creditors. *Ex parte* EDWARDS. *In re* TOLLEMACHE - 　**14 Q. B. D. 415**

9. —— Evidence—*Admissibility—Bankrupt's Statement of Affairs—Judgment Debt—Inquiry into Consideration.*] An admission of a debt, contained in a bankrupt's statement of his affairs made after the commencement of the bankruptcy proceedings, is not evidence as against his creditors of the existence of a debt, even though the statement was verified by his oath (without cross-examination), and he has since died.—The Court of Bankruptcy is not conclusively bound by a judgment for a debt, but has power, on a claim to prove the debt in the bankruptcy of the judgment debtor, to inquire into the consideration for the debt.—But, *quære,* whether it will do so unless a *primâ facie* case of suspicion is shewn. *Ex parte* REVELL. *In re* TOLLEMACHE (No. 1)
[**13 Q. B. D. 720**]

10. —— Felony, Claim arising out of—*Compounding a Felony.*] Bankers allowed a customer to overdraw his current account on his depositing with them as security for the overdraft some bills of exchange drawn by him upon, and purporting to be accepted by, a third person. After the customer had overdrawn his account the bankers discovered that the acceptances were forgeries. They then communicated with the customer, and ultimately gave up the forged acceptances to him, receiving from him in exchange joint and several promissory notes of himself and his father. The customer was afterwards adjudicated a bankrupt. The notes were not paid at maturity :—*Held*, that though the bankers had not prosecuted the bankrupt for the felony, and whether they had or had not agreed not to prosecute him, they were entitled to prove in the bankruptcy for the balance due to them upon the bankrupt's current account. *Ex parte* LESLIE. *In re* GUERRIER 　**20 Ch. D. 131**

11. —— Guarantee to Bankers—*Payment by Surety after Proof by Creditor — Reduction of Proof—Agreement between Surety and Creditor that Receipt by Creditor of Dividends in Bankruptcy of principal Debtor shall not diminish Liability of Surety to pay in full.*] A customer gave to his bankers, as a security for the balance which might from time to time be due from him to them, the joint and several bond for £1000 of himself and a surety, the liability of the surety being expressly limited to £500. There was a proviso in the bond that any dividends received by the bankers in the bankruptcy of the customer should not, so far as concerned the surety, go in discharge of his liability; but the bankers should notwithstanding be entitled to recover on the bond against the surety to the full extent of £500, or so much thereof as should, together with the dividends, amount to 20s. in the pound on the

XV. BANKRUPTCY—PROOF—continued.

debt due by the customer to the bankers. The customer filed a liquidation petition, and the bankers proved for the debt due to them. Afterwards the surety paid the bankers £500, and he then proved in the liquidation for £500 :—Held, by Bacon, C.J., that the proof of the bankers must be reduced by £500, but that this reduction would not prejudice any right of the bankers against the surety :—Held, by the Court of Appeal, that the bankers were entitled to retain their proof for the full amount. *Ex parte* NATIONAL PROVINCIAL BANK OF ENGLAND. *In re* REES   **17 Ch. D. 98**

12. —— **Interest**—*After Adjudication—Joint and Separate Estates.*] A creditor whose proof is admitted against both the separate estates of two bankrupts who have been partners is not entitled to receive any dividend in respect of interest accrued on his debt subsequently to the date of the adjudication, until the joint creditors have been paid the principal of their debts in full. —*Warrant Finance Company's Case* (Law Rep. 5 Ch. 86), and *Warrant Finance Company's Case* (No. 2) (Law Rep. 5 Ch. 88) distinguished. *Ex parte* FINDLAY. *In re* COLLIE - **17 Ch. D. 334**

13. —— **Interest**—*Mortgage to Building Society—Principal and Interest payable by Monthly Instalments—Bankruptcy Rules,* 1870, r. 77.] A mortgage to a building society provided that the loan, with a premium and interest on the advance, should be paid in equal monthly instalments during a term of twelve years, and that each monthly instalment, when paid, should be applied (1) in payment of the interest due at the time of payment, (2) in payment of the premium till the whole should be discharged, and (3) in payment of the principal. Two years after the execution of the mortgage the mortgagor filed a liquidation petition, and the society claimed to prove in the liquidation for the total amount of the monthly instalments which remained due under the deed, less the amount at which they valued their security :—Held, that, as to so much of the sum claimed as represented interest payable subsequently to the filing of the liquidation petition, the proof must be rejected.—Decision of Bacon, C.J., reversed. *Ex parte* BATH. *In re* PHILLIPS **[22 Ch. D. 450**

14. —— **Judgment Debt**—*Evidence.*] When in support of a claim to prove a debt in a bankruptcy the only evidence of the debt is a judgment, and that judgment has been obtained after the act of bankruptcy, the judgment debt cannot be proved. *Ex parte* BONHAM. *In re* TOLLEMACHE **[14 Q. B. D. 604**

15. —— **Judgment Debt**—*Evidence — Proof of Consideration.*] When a claim is made to prove in a bankruptcy in respect of a judgment debt, though the judgment is primâ facie evidence of the debt, it is not conclusive evidence, and, if the circumstances are suspicious, the Court will call upon the claimant to prove the consideration for the judgment, and if he is unable to prove it, by reason of the loss of documents, or the lapse of time or otherwise, the proof will be rejected.—A judgment may be proved by the production of a duly certified copy of an entry in the entry book of judgments of the Court in

XV. BANKRUPTCY—PROOF—continued.

which the judgment was recovered. *Ex parte* ANDERSON. *In re* TOLLEMACHE **14 Q. B. D. 606**

16. —— **Judgment Debt**—*Power of Court to go behind Judgment.*] The Court of Bankruptcy will go behind a judgment or a compromise, and refuse to admit a proof founded upon it, if it can see that the original claim was not a bonâ fide one, but was made for purposes of extortion, the claimant knowing that he had no legal claim, but being aware of circumstances affecting the character of the Defendant which would prevent the latter from submitting to a cross-examination.— Per Brett, L.J., *Callisher* v. *Bischoffsheim* (Law Rep. 5 Q. B. 449) questioned. *Ex parte* BANNER. *In re* BLYTHE -   **17 Ch. D. 480**

17. —— **Loan from Building Society**—*Premium payable in Instalments.*] A member of a building society borrowed from the society, on the security of a mortgage, £1200, for which he was to pay £144 premium and interest at 5 per cent. per annum. The principal, premium, and interest were made payable by the borrower to the society in a fixed number of monthly instalments, each of which consisted of principal, premium, and interest. The borrower having filed a liquidation petition, and the mortgage being insufficient :—Held (affirming the decision of Bacon, C.J.), that the premium was not in the nature of interest, and that the society were entitled to prove for it in the liquidation. *Ex parte* BATH. *In re* PHILLIPS -   **27 Ch. D. 509**

18. —— **Partnership** — *Administrator of Deceased Partner—Share of Deceased Partner's Capital retained in Business without Authority.*] Three persons carried on business in partnership without any articles of partnership. The profits were divided between them in equal shares. After the death of one of them the survivors continued to carry on the business, retaining in it, without any authority, the deceased partner's share of the capital, and dividing the profits of the business between themselves equally. They afterwards filed a liquidation petition. There were still some joint debts of the partnership of the three remaining unpaid :—Held, that the administratrix of the deceased partner could not prove in the liquidation in competition with his creditors in respect of his share of the capital.—*Nanson* v. *Gordon* (1 App. Cas. 195) followed.—*Ex parte* WESTCOTT (Law Rep. 9 Ch. 626) distinguished. *Ex parte* BLYTHE. *In re* BLYTHE. **16 Ch. D. 620**

19. —— **Partnership**—*Competition with Creditors.*] The rule, that neither a partner, nor a retired partner, nor the representatives of a deceased partner, can prove in the bankruptcy of the continuing or surviving partner or partners in competition with the joint creditors of the firm of which the partner, or retired or deceased partner was a member, has no application unless there has been actually proved in the bankruptcy some debt in respect of which the bankrupt or bankrupts and the retired or deceased partner were jointly liable.—The mere possibility that such debts may be proved in the bankruptcy is not sufficient to introduce the application of the rule. *Ex parte* ANDREWS. *In re* WILCOXON **[25 Ch. D. 505**

XV. BANKRUPTCY—PROOF—*continued.*

20. —— *Partnership — Deceased Partner — Trust of Real Estate to pay Debts—No Real Estate —Debts Statute-barred—Bankruptcy of continuing Partners—Proof by Executors of Deceased Partner —Rule against proving in Competition with one's own Creditors,*] A devise of real estate upon trust to pay debts does not prevent the operation of the Statute of Limitations when the testator leaves no real estate to support the trust. A., B. and C. carried on business in co-partnership. In 1875, A. retired from the firm, his share being purchased by B. and C., the continuing partners. On his retirement, A., at the request of the continuing partners, paid certain mortgage debts of the business, and took transfers to himself of these mortgage debts with the securities for the same. He also at their request lent them money on mortgage of other portions of the partnership property. He died in 1876. B. and C. continued the business until 1883, when they became bankrupt. At this time there were cash creditors of the old firm still unpaid, who carried in proofs against the joint estate of B. and C. The executors of A. also carried in a proof against the separate estates of B. and C., for (1) the balance of the purchase-money of A.'s share ; (2) the mortgage debts paid off by A. on transfer to himself; (3) the moneys lent by A. on mortgage after his retirement. This proof was rejected by the trustee on the ground that to admit it would infringe against the rule forbidding a partner to prove in competition with his own creditors :— *Held,* that as the debts proved by the cash creditors were, as against A.'s estate, statute-barred, the rule did not apply, and that the proof must be admitted. *In re* HEPBURN. *Ex parte* SMITH - - - **14 Q. B. D. 394**

21. —— *Partnership — Partner in one Firm the secret and sole Principal in another Firm— Bankruptcy of both Firms—Right of Proof by one Firm against the other*] A. and B. traded in partnership as A. & Co. in England and abroad, A. managing the home business and B. the branch abroad. C. and D. carried on business in England as D. & Co. under an agreement by which C. was to be the sole principal of D., who was to be the manager of the business at a salary with a share of profits. Business transactions took place in England between A. & Co. and D. & Co., and on the bankruptcy of both firms a large balance was due to A. & Co. from D. & Co. C. was in fact the agent of A., who was the secret and sole principal of D., but this was unknown to B. and D. until after the bankruptcy, and D. had held himself out to A. & Co. and others as a principal. The trustee of A. & Co. tendered a proof against the estate of D. for the balance due from D. & Co. to A. & Co. :—*Held,* that the proof could not be sustained, for that, under the circumstances, there was no contract between D. and A. that D. should pay for the goods that had been supplied. *In re* WAKEHAM - - - - **13 Q. B. D. 43**

22. —— *Promoter of Company—Secret Profit —Discharge—" Unliquidated Damages "—" Contract "—" Debt incurred by means of Fraud or Breach of Trust "—Bankruptcy Act, 1869, ss. 31, 49,*] Under a secret agreement between the vendors of a mine and G., a financial agent who

XV. BANKRUPTCY—PROOF—*continued.*

was promoting and afterwards formed a company for its purchase, G. received from the vendors part of the purchase-money without the knowledge of the company. In an action by the company to make G. liable for the amount of the secret profit he had so made, a specific sum was found due from him to the company upon that footing. G. then presented a petition for liquidation, and his creditors passed a resolution for liquidation of his affairs by arrangement ; a trustee was appointed of his estate, and he obtained his certificate of discharge :—*Held,* that the company were to be at liberty to go in and prove against G.'s estate as creditors for the sum found due from him in the action, it not being a " demand in the nature of unliquidated damages arising otherwise than by reason of a contract."— *Held,* also, that the debt so due from G. was incurred by " fraud " and was also a " breach of trust " within sect. 49 of the Bankruptcy Act, 1869, and that, accordingly, G. was not released from such debt by his discharge ; and he was thereupon ordered personally to pay the debt to the company, or so much thereof as should not be received by the company under the liquidation. EMMA SILVER MINING COMPANY *v.* GRANT **17 Ch. D. 122**

—— *Secured creditor*

See Cases under BANKRUPTCY—SECURED CREDITOR.

XVI. BANKRUPTCY—MUTUAL DEALINGS.

1. —— *Set-off—Bill accepted and paid by Creditor after Notice of Debtor's Bankruptcy— Bankruptcy Act, 1883, s. 38.*] Where there are mutual dealings between a debtor and his creditors, the line as to set-off must, as a general rule, and in the absence of special circumstances, be drawn at the date of the commencement of the bankruptcy. *In re* GILLESPIE. *Ex parte* REID & SONS - - - - **14 Q. B. D. 963**

2. —— *Set-off—Landlord and Tenant— Trustee in Bankruptcy — Non-disclaimer of Tenancy, Effect of—Outgoing Tenant—Landlord's Right to set-off Rent accrued due before Bankruptcy against Trustee's Claim as outgoing Tenant for Tillages—Bankruptcy Act, 1869, s. 39.*] A debtor, who was tenant from year to year of a farm upon the terms that, at the expiration of the tenancy, he should be paid by the landlord allowances for tillages and cultivation according to the custom of the country, filed a petition for liquidation of his affairs under the Bankruptcy Act, 1869, and a trustee was appointed, who did not disclaim the tenancy, but carried on the business of the farm for the benefit of the creditors until the tenancy was determined by notice to quit. The debtor's estate was sufficient to indemnify the trustee against any personal liability in respect of the tenancy. In an action to recover the value of tillages and cultivation by the trustee during his tenancy, according to the custom :—*Held,* that the landlord was not entitled to set-off rent, accrued due from the debtor before the liquidation proceedings, against the trustee's claim. ALLOWAY *v.* STEERE **[10 Q. B. D. 22**

3. —— *Set-off—Principal and Agent—Agent's Authority not revoked till Notice of Act of Bank-*

XVI. BANKRUPTCY — MUTUAL DEALINGS — continued.

ruptcy—Bankruptcy Act, 1869, s. 39.] The object of sect. 39 of the Bankruptcy Act, 1869, is that where there are mutual accounts a secret act of bankruptcy should not stop the currency of those accounts; the existence of mutual dealings and accounts protects the credits and debts on each side from the operation of the act of bankruptcy until notice of it. The exact date at which a mutual account is to stop must depend on the circumstances of the case and the nature of the credits, but may and ought to be taken at least up to the date when the person claiming the benefit of sect. 39 has notice of an act of bankruptcy.—Where authority had been given previous to an act of bankruptcy by the bankrupts to the Defendant in the course of mutual dealings to receive the purchase-money of their estate and to place it to account, and such authority had been acted upon before notice of an act of bankruptcy:—Held, that such authority was not revoked by the act of bankruptcy; that the payment thereof to the Defendant was a rightful payment; that being so received it became a debt and an item in the account between him and the bankrupts before notice of any act of bankruptcy, and that the Defendant was entitled to set off against it, in an action brought by the trustee in bankruptcy, the debt due from the bankrupts to him. ELLIOTT v. TURQUAND - 7 App. Cas. 79

4. —— Set-off—Secured Creditor—Valuation of Security — Partnership Debt — Security on Separate Estate—Mutual Credit—Set-off—Bankruptcy Act, 1869 (32 & 33 Vict. c. 71), s. 39]. A father and son were partners in business. The father mortgaged real estate, which was his separate property, to the bankers of the firm, to secure the balance for the time being of the current account of the firm. Afterwards he contracted to sell the real estate, and the bankers joined in the conveyance to the purchaser on the terms of an agreement that the father should deposit the purchase-money with the bankers in his own name, at interest; that the deposit should be a security to the bankers for the debt of the firm, but that, subject to that security, the deposit should remain the separate property of the father; that, until payment of the debt of the firm, the father should not be entitled to withdraw any part of the deposit, but, until demand by the bankers for payment of the debt, he should be at liberty to draw out half yearly the interest on the deposit; and that, in case demand should be made by the bankers for payment, they might, at any time after the expiration of twelve months from the making of the demand, but not sooner, apply the deposit and the interest thereon from the time of making the demand, in or towards the payment of the debt of the firm. The father also entered into a covenant for payment of the debt of the firm. This arrangement was carried out:—Held, that, the arrangement being a bona fide one for the purpose of giving a security to the bankers, in substitution for their security on the real estate, the bankers could prove in the liquidation of the father and son against the joint estate for the full amount of their debt, without deducting the amount of the deposit,

XVI. BANKRUPTCY — MUTUAL DEALINGS — continued.

and that no set-off arose by virtue of sect. 39 of the Bankruptcy Act, 1869. Ex parte CALDICOTT. In re HART - 25 Ch. D. 716

5. —— Set-off — Unliquidated Damages — Action by Trustee in Liquidation — "Mutual Credits and Dealings"—Bankruptcy Act, 1869 (32 & 33 Vict. c. 71), s. 39.] The right of set-off under the Bankruptcy Act, 1869, extends to unliquidated damages.—Such set-off may be pleaded by the Defendant to an action by the trustee without recourse to a Court of Bankruptcy.—H., who had contracted to deliver iron to the Defendants by successive monthly deliveries, sued for the price, and went into liquidation. The Plaintiff, who had been appointed trustee, continued the action. The Defendants counter-claimed damages for non-delivery of part of the iron:—Held, by the Court of Appeal (Jessel, M.R., Brett, and Cotton, L.JJ.), that these unliquidated damages could be pleaded as a set-off to the Plaintiff's claim. PEAT v. JONES 8 Q. B. D. 147

6. —— Set-off — Unliquidated Damages — Fraudulent Representation on Sale of a Chattel—Bankruptcy Act, 1869, ss. 31, 39, 49.] A claim for unliquidated damages for a fraudulent representation made by a bankrupt on the sale of a chattel is within the mutual credit clause (sect. 39) of the Bankruptcy Act, 1869, and consequently may be set off in an action brought by the trustee for the unpaid price,—such fraudulent representation not being a mere personal tort, but a breach of the obligation arising out of the contract of sale. JACK v. KIPPING - - 9 Q. B. D. 113

XVII. BANKRUPTCY — PREFERENTIAL DEBTS.

—— Wages—Employer and Workman—Payment of Wages in Coin—Deductions to pay Doctor —Bankruptcy Act, 1869 (32 & 33 Vict. c. 71), s. 32—Truck Act (1 & 2 Will. 4, c. 37, ss. 1, 2, 3, 4, 23.] By an arrangement between employers and their workmen certain deductions were made from the workmen's wages (which were paid monthly) for a "doctor's fund" which was established for the purpose of paying a doctor, who attended the workmen and their families and supplied them with medicines in case of illness. The sums thus deducted were handed over by the employers to the doctor from time to time. There was no contract in writing between the employers and the workmen authorizing the employers to make the deductions, nor was there any evidence that the doctor had accepted the liability of the employers. The employers filed a liquidation petition, and at this time there stood to the credit of the "doctor's fund" in their books, a sum of £149, which had arisen from deductions thus made from the workmen's wages, and had not yet been paid over to the doctor:—Held, that there had been no valid payment (within the Truck Act) of the £149 to the workmen, and that they were entitled to be paid the £149 in full out of the employer's estate as unpaid wages.— Whether, if the £149 had been, in pursuance of the arrangement, actually paid over by the employers to the doctor, in discharge of a debt for which the workmen were liable, or if the doctor

XVII. BANKRUPTCY — PREFERENTIAL DEBTS—*continued.*

had accepted the liability of the employers, the Truck Act would, notwithstanding the absence of a contract in writing signed by the workmen, have applied,—*Quære. Ex parte* COOPER. *In re* MORRIS - - 26 Ch. D. 693

XVIII. BANKRUPTCY—DISTRESS.

1. —— Money due to Gas Company—"*Rent*"— *Bankruptcy Act*, 1869 (32 & 33 *Vict. c.* 71, s 34.] By their special Act (39 & 40 Vict. c. cxix., s. 44) the corporation of Walsall were empowered to "recover from any person any rent or charge due to them by him for gas supplied, by the like means as landlords are for the time being by law allowed to recover rent in arrear":—*Held,* that, after the filing of a liquidation petition by a customer, the corporation were entitled as against the trustee in the liquidation to levy a distress in respect of a sum due by the debtor for gas supplied to him before the filing of the petition :—*Held,* also, that the corporation were not, within the meaning of sect. 34 of the Bankruptcy Act, 1869, " other persons " to whom any rent was due by the debtor, but that, by virtue of sect. 44 of the special Act, they were entitled to the rights given to landlords by sect. 34.—The payment due to a gas company for gas supplied, though it is called " rent " in some Acts of Parliament, is not really of the nature of rent, and consequently a gas company does not come within the words " other person to whom any rent is due " in sect. 34 of the Bankruptcy Act, 1869. Those words apply only to a person who, though he is not the landlord of the bankrupt, fills a position analogous to that of a landlord, because he is entitled to receive that which is " rent " strictly so called. —Decision of Cave, J., affirmed, but on a different ground.—*Ex parte Birmingham Gas Light Co.* (Law Rep. 11 Eq. 615) and *Ex parte Hill* (6 Ch. D. 63) commented on. *Ex parte* HARRISON. *In re* PEAKE - - - 13 Q. B. D. 753

2. —— Mortgage—*Attornment Clause—Distress levied after Bankruptcy of Mortgagor—Fixtures—Bankruptcy Act,* 1869 (32 & 33 *Vict. c.* 71), *s.* 34—*Public-house—Goodwill.*] An attornment by a mortgagor to a second mortgagee is valid, notwithstanding the fact that the mortgagor has already attorned tenant to the first mortgagee of the same property. And if the amount of the rents fixed by the two attornment clauses is a fair rent of the property, so that there is no fraud on the bankrupt law, valid distresses can be levied by both mortgagees after the commencement of the bankruptcy of the mortgagor.— *Morton* v. *Woods* (Law Rep. 3 Q. B. 658; Ibid. 4 Q. B. 293) explained and followed.—A mortgage (by way of underlease) executed in 1877 of a leasehold public-house contained no express assignment of the fixtures. There was a clause by which, " for the purpose of better securing the punctual payment of the interest " on the mortgage debt, the mortgagor attorned tenant to the mortgagee of the mortgaged property at a yearly rent equal to the amount of a year's interest. And there was a proviso that the mortgagee might, at any time after the day when the first instalment of rent should become due, enter upon the property and determine the tenancy, without giving the mort-

XVIII. BANKRUPTCY—DISTRESS—*continued.*

gagor any notice to quit. Two years afterwards the mortgagor became bankrupt. The mortgagee had taken no step to determine the tenancy :— *Held,* that, as the tenancy was created only for the purpose of giving an additional security for the payment of the interest, the mortgagee did not cease to be a mortgagee because he was made a landlord, and that he was entitled as against the trustee in the bankruptcy of the mortgagor to trade fixtures which had been annexed to the public-house after the execution of the mortgage. —The goodwill of a public-house is not a personal goodwill, but on a sale of the house passes with it. *Ex parte* PUNNETT. *In re* KITCHIN
[16 Ch. D. 226

3. —— Mortgage—*Attornment Clause — Tenancy from Year to Year or at Will—Bankruptcy Act,* 1869, *s.* 34.] A mortgage deed contained an attornment clause whereby A. (the mortgagor) attorned and became tenant from year to year to B. (the mortgagee) for and in respect of the mortgaged premises, at the yearly rent of £800, to be paid by equal quarterly payments. And it was thereby agreed that it should be lawful for B., at any time after three months from the date of the mortgage, without giving previous notice of his intention so to do, to enter upon and take possession of the premises whereof A. had attorned tenant, and to determine the tenancy created by the aforesaid attornment. A. filed a liquidation petition, and on the same day a receiver was appointed, who entered into possession of A.'s estate and effects.—Notice of the petition and of the appointment of a receiver was sent to B., who two days later, by virtue of the attornment clause, distrained upon the goods and chattels on the mortgaged premises for half a year's rent then due :—*Held* (affirming the decision of Bacon, C.J.), that a tenancy from year to year and not a tenancy at will was created by the attornment clause, and that B. was entitled, under the Bankruptcy Act, 1869, s. 34, to distrain for the rent due to him from A. at the time of filing the liquidation petition.—*Morton* v. *Woods* (Law Rep. 4 Q. B. 293) explained. *In re* THRELFALL. *Ex parte* QUEEN'S BENEFIT BUILDING SOCIETY - 16 Ch. D. 274

4. —— Mortgage—*Attornment Clause—Validity — Bankruptcy of Mortgagor — Mortgage to Building Society—Advance repayable in Monthly Instalments—Monthly Tenancy—Statute of Frauds* (29 *Car.* 2, *c.* 3), *s.* 1—*Lease not in writing—" Uncertain " Rent.*] A member of a building society borrowed £7500 from the society, which was to be repaid in a series of monthly instalments of £71 17s. 6d. each, including interest at 7 per cent. The instalments were payable at the monthly meetings of the society, and, if the member neglected to pay them when due, he became liable to a fine, at the rate of 5 per cent. per month on the total amount in arrear and unpaid at each meeting. To secure the loan he executed to the trustees of the society a mortgage of real estate. The deed contained a proviso that if the member should fail for three monthly meetings to pay his subscriptions, interest, fines, or other moneys, or to observe the regulations of the society, or in the event of his becoming bankrupt, the mortgagees might enter into possession or

XVIII. BANKRUPTCY—DISTRESS—*continued.*

receipt of the rents of the mortgaged property. And "for the better securing the payments which by the rules of the society ought to be made by the mortgagor," it was agreed that, if the mortgagees should at any time become entitled to enter into possession or receipt of the rents, and the mortgagor should then or afterwards be in the occupation of the whole or part of the property, he should during such occupation be tenant thereof from month to month to the mortgagees, at a monthly rent equal in amount to the moneys which ought to be paid monthly by the mortgagor from time to time for subscriptions, interest, fines, and other moneys under the rules, and that the tenancy should commence on the day up to which he should have fully paid all and every part of such subscriptions, interest, fines, and other moneys, and the rent for the period intervening between the commencement of the tenancy and the day on which the trustees should be entitled to enter into possession or receipt of rents should be payable and paid on that day, and the monthly rent due upon and subsequently to that day should become due monthly in advance, and be payable at the monthly meetings, the first payment of rent becoming due on that day on which the mortgagees should first become entitled to enter into possession. Power was given to the mortgagees to determine the tenancy by fourteen days' notice. —The deed was not executed by the mortgagees, nor was it registered under the Bills of Sale Act. The mortgagor committed default in his payments, and was afterwards adjudicated a bankrupt:—*Held,* that the attornment clause, and distresses levied under it for rent which accrued due both before and after the commencement of the bankruptcy, were valid as against the trustee in the bankruptcy.—Decision of Bacon, C.J., affirmed.—*Held,* that it was no objection to the attornment clause that the monthly rent was fluctuating in amount.—A rent the amount of which may fluctuate according to the happening of certain events is not an uncertain rent.—*Held,* also, that the tenancy under the attornment clause was not made by sect. 1 of the Statute of Frauds, a tenancy at will.—*Ex parte Williams* (7 Ch. D. 138); *In re Stockton Iron Furnace Company* (10 Ch. D. 335) ; and *Ex parte Jackson* (14 Ch. D. 725) discussed. *Ex parte* VOISEY　*In re* KNIGHT
　　　　　　　　　　　　　　　　[21 Ch. D. 442

5. —— Rent after filing of Petition—32 & 33 *Vict. c.* 71, *s.* 34.] A landlord, between the filing of a liquidation petition by his tenant and the appointment of trustees, levied a distress for two half-year's rent accrued due before the filing of the petition. After the appointment of trustees the landlord levied a second distress for a third half-year's rent accrued due between the filing of the petition and the appointment of the trustees: —*Held,* that the second distress was void under sect. 34 of the Bankruptcy Act, 1869. *Ex parte* SIR W. HART DYKE. *In re* MORRISH
　　　　　　　　　　　　　　　　[22 Ch. D. 410

XIX. BANKRUPTCY — ORDER AND DISPOSITION.

1. —— Bills of Sale Act (41 & 42 *Vict. c.* 31), ss. 8, 20—*Bankruptcy Act,* 1869, *s.* 15, *sub-s.* 5.] During the period of seven days between the

XIX. BANKRUPTCY — ORDER AND DISPOSITION—*continued.*

making and registration of a bill of sale, the order and disposition clause (Bankruptcy Act, 1869), sect. 15, sub-sect. 5, does not apply to the goods and chattels comprised in the bill of sale, so that as against the trustee in bankruptcy, who by the receiver has before the expiration of the seven days taken possession of such goods, the bill of sale holder is entitled. *Ex parte* KAHEN. *In re* HEWER　-　21 Ch. D. 871

2. —— Bill of Sale Act—*Security—Bills of Sale Acts,* 1878 *and* 1882 (41 & 42 *Vict. c.* 31; 45 & 46 *Vict. c.* 43.] The Bills of Sale Act, 1882, repeals the 20th section of the Bills of Sale Act, 1878, in respect of bills of sale given by way of security, but not in respect of bills of sale given by way of absolute transfer, and therefore chattels comprised in a registered bill of sale given by way of absolute transfer are not in the order and disposition of the grantor within the Bankruptcy Act. SWIFT *v.* PANNELL -　-　24 Ch. D. 210

3. —— Bills of Sale Act (41 & 42 *Vict. c.* 31), *s.* 20—*Bills of Sale Act,* 1882 (45 & 46 *Vict. c.* 43), *ss.* 3, 15—*Bankruptcy Act,* 1869 (32 & 33 *Vict. c.* 71), *s.* 15, *sub-s.* 5.] Notwithstanding the repeal of sect. 20 of the Bills of Sale Act, 1878, by sect. 15 of the Bills of Sale Act, 1882, the effect of sect. 3 of the latter Act is, that the grantee of a bill of sale, registered under the Act of 1878 before the coming into operation of the Act of 1882, is, so long as the registration is subsisting, entitled to the protection afforded by sect. 20 against the "order and disposition" of the grantor, even when an act of bankruptcy is committed by the grantor after the coming into operation of the Act of 1882. *Ex parte* IZARD. *In re* CHAPPLE
　　　　　　　　　　　　　　　　[23 Ch. D. 409

4. —— Furniture—*Custom of Hiring—Bankruptcy Act,* 1869 (32 & 33 *Vict. c.* 71), *s.* 15, *sub-s.* 5.] The fact that it is the custom of furniture dealers to let out furniture on a three years' hiring and purchase agreement does not disentitle the general public to assume that an ordinary householder is the real owner of the furniture which is in his house.—The furniture in the dwelling-house of a trader having been seized under an execution, a friend of his bought it from the sheriff at a valuation, and then verbally agreed that the debtor should continue in possession of it and use it as before, paying, by way of rent, interest at 5 per cent. per annum on the purchase-money, until he should be able to repurchase it at the price given for it. This arrangement was carried out, and the debtor remained in possession of the furniture as before, until he filed a liquidation petition. He had not repurchased it. The trustee in the liquidation claimed it under the reputed ownership clause. It was admitted that there is a custom for furniture dealers to let out furniture on a three years' hiring and purchase agreement, but there was no other evidence as to the existence of any custom of hiring furniture:—*Held* (by Bacon, V.C., and by the Court of Appeal), that the trustee was entitled to the furniture. *Ex parte* BROOKS. *In re* FOWLER　-　-　23 Ch. D. 261

5. —— Furniture—*Custom of hiring—Evi-*

XIX. BANKRUPTCY — ORDER AND DISPOSITION—continued.

dence—*Custom of Trade—Professional Confidence.*] The Plaintiff lent furniture on hire to the Defendants, who were hotel-keepers, at a fixed sum to be paid by instalments, with a provision that until all the instalments were paid the property should remain in the Plaintiff, and if any instalment should not be paid when due the Plaintiff was to be at liberty to retake possession of his goods and the instalments to be forfeited, but upon all the instalments being paid the furniture to become the property of the Defendants. Upon one instalment being unpaid the Plaintiff put a man in possession of the furniture, and the Defendants executed an assignment of the lease of the hotel (which had been previously mortgaged to persons whom the Plaintiff had paid off) and of all their personal chattels and effects, including the hired furniture, to the Plaintiff, and afterwards became bankrupt :—*Held* (affirming the decision of Malins, V.C.), that the hiring agreement did not operate as a bill of sale; that the assignment of the whole property of the Defendants, which was duly registered under the Bills of Sale Act, was an act of bankruptcy, but that the Plaintiff's furniture, not having been paid for, remained the property of the Plaintiff, and was not in the order and disposition of the bankrupt, and did not pass by the assignment; that the assignment was good so far as it was a mortgage of the leasehold, but was void so far as it was an assignment of the chattels as being an act of bankruptcy ; and that the trustee in bankruptcy was entitled to all the personal effects of the bankrupt, but not to the hired furniture.—The custom of hotel-keepers holding their furniture on hire is now so well established that it ought to be taken judicial notice of. CRAWCOUR *v.* SALTER   **18 Ch. D. 30**

6. —— Furniture—*Custom of Hiring—Trade Custom — Hotel Keeper — Bankruptcy Act,* 1883 (46 & 47 *Vict.* c. 52), s. 44, *sub-s. 3—Bill of Sale — Registration — Transfer of Registered Bill of Sale—Equitable sub-Mortgage—Bills of Sale Act,* 1878 (41 & 42 *Vict.* c. 31), *ss.* 4, 10.] The custom for hotel-keepers to hire the furniture of their hotels is so notorious, and has been so often proved, that it need not now be proved, but the Court will take judicial notice of it. And the custom extends, not only to furniture in the strictest sense of the word, but to all the articles which are necessary for the furnishing of an hotel for the purpose of using it as an hotel.—The effect of the custom is absolutely to exclude the reputation of ownership by the hotel-keeper of all those articles in the hotel, at the time of his bankruptcy, which are within the scope of the custom, without regard to the question whether the particular articles are or are not in fact hired by him.—Consequently, articles which are his property subject to a mortgage by bill of sale, will be excluded from the operation of the reputed ownership clause.—A memorandum by way of equitable sub-mortgage given by the transferee of a registered bill of sale, accompanied by a deposit of the registered bill of sale and the transfer, does not require registration as a bill of sale under the Bills of Sale Act, 1878, even though, after the mortgage, the transferee

XIX. BANKRUPTCY—ORDER AND DISPOSITION—continued.

acquires by assignment the equity of redemption of the original grantor. *Ex parte* TURQUAND. *In re* PARKER - - - **14 Q. B. D. 636**

7. —— Principal and Agent—*Property, passing of, in Goods bought by Agent—Trustee—Trust Funds misapplied, following Proceeds of—Moneys held in a Fiduciary Character—Advances for particular Purpose misappropriated—False Representation—Estoppel—Trustee in Bankruptcy takes Property subject to same rights and Equities as Bankrupt—Reputed Ownership.*] The Defendants were brewers and employed F. as their " malting agent." The regular course of business between the Defendants and F. was as follows :—F. occupied the malting premises, and took out the necessary licenses. It was his duty to buy barley in his own name as principal for cash, to send in to the Defendants certain periodical accounts of the barley so bought from time to time, and the prices of the same, to submit samples to the Defendants, and if the barley was approved of by them to malt it and deliver the malt to the Defendants, receiving a commission upon the quantity of barley steeped. The quantity of malt required by large brewers being very great, the brewers, and not the malting agents, provide the capital for the purchase of the barley. In the present case the Defendants kept accounts at certain provincial banks, upon which F. was empowered to draw, and from time to time the Defendants paid in lump sums to the credit of those accounts, in accordance with current requirements, as shewn by the accounts sent in by F. of barley purchased, but these sums were not intended to, nor did they, represent any payments for any specific barley. F.'s business was to act as malting agent for the Defendants exclusively. The Defendants paid the duty as the same became payable upon the malt in F.'s premises. F. had fraudulently departed from the regular course of business. Instead of buying barley for cash and applying the balances at the provincial banks in payment for the same, he had been in the habit of sending in to the Defendants fictitious accounts of barley purchased, misapplying the sums paid in for his own purposes, and providing the malt needed for the Defendants' purposes by purchasing barley or ready-made malt upon credit. He likewise from time to time sold barley which had been brought on to the maltings to raise money for his own purposes. The Defendants believed, in consequence of the fictitious accounts and other false representations of F., that barley was from time to time purchased for cash, in accordance with the regular course of business, and on the faith thereof continued to pay sums of money into the banks for the purpose of paying for such barley, which they believed were so applied. F. subsequently absconded, leaving upon his premises barley to the value of about £22,000, and malt to the value of about £35,000, upon part of which duty had been paid by the Defendants. The value of such malt and barley was less than the amount drawn from the banks and misappropriated by F. He absconded and thereby committed an act of bankruptcy. Between the time of F.'s absconding and the time when he was adjudged a bankrupt, the Defendants seized the barley and the

G

XIX. BANKRUPTCY — ORDER AND DISPOSITION—continued.

malt left on his premises. The Plaintiff, trustee in F.'s bankruptcy, sued the Defendants for the value of the same :—*Held*, affirming the judgment of the Queen's Bench Division, that the Plaintiff could not recover, on the ground that the relation between the Defendants and F. was that of principals and agent, and that the property in the barley and the malt had vested in the Defendants, and that the barley and the malt were not in the order and disposition of F. as the reputed owner thereof, it being notorious that "malting agents" are in many instances not the owners of the barley and malt on their malting premises ; and also on the further ground that the moneys advanced by the Defendants to provide for the purchase of the barley were impressed with a trust ; that even if the barley and the malt left on the premises of F. were not bought in accordance with the authority given to him, and the legal property in the same was not vested in the Defendants but in F., nevertheless F. was a trustee for the Defendants, to the extent of the sums advanced by them. of such barley and malt, the same being either the product of the trust moneys, or in substitution for the barley in payment for which F. ought to have applied such trust moneys ; that F. could not have set up his own breach of trust or have been heard to allege that the barley was bought otherwise than according to the authority given to him by the Defendants ; and that the Plaintiff, as F.'s trustee in bankruptcy, could not in this respect stand in a better position than F. himself. HARRIS *v.* TRUMAN

[7 Q. B. D. 340; 9 Q. B. D. 264

8. —— "Trade or Business"—*Bankruptcy Act, 1869 (32 & 33 Vict c. 71), s. 15, sub-s. 5.*] When a trader is in possession at his place of business of articles not in their nature connected with his business, and the trustee in his bankruptcy claims the articles on the ground that the bankrupt was the reputed owner of them, much stronger evidence will be required to prove the reputed ownership than in the case of articles connected with the business, the inference from the nature of the articles being that they are not connected with the business. *Ex parte* LOVERING. *In re* MURRELL - 　24 Ch. D. 31

9. —— "Trade or Business"—*Home Farm—Farming and Market Gardening for Pleasure—Live and Dead Stock—Bill of Sale—Order and Disposition—Residential Estate—Bankruptcy Act, 1883, s. 44.*] A person who occupies a residential property and engages in farming and market gardening for his pleasure, and carries on the same at a profit, is not carrying on a "trade or business" within the meaning of sect. 44 of the Bankruptcy Act, 1883. even although he sells his surplus produce after supplying his household.—But if the primary intention is abandoned, and the business is carried on with a view to profit as a means of livelihood, he will come within the mischief of the section. *In re* WALLIS. *Ex parte* SULLY - 　　　- 14 Q. B. D. 950

10. —— "Trade or Business"—*Shares in Company—Bankruptcy Act, 1883 (46 & 47 Vict. c. 52), s. 44.*] J., who carried on business as a stockbroker, silversmith, and watchmaker, deposited

XIX. BANKRUPTCY—ORDER AND DISPOSITION—continued.

with his bankers the certificates of thirty shares in a joint stock company as security for the balance of his overdrawn account. There was no formal transfer of the shares. The company had notice of the deposit on the 31st of January, 1884. On the 2nd of February a petition in bankruptcy was filed against J., and a receiving order made, and he was subsequently adjudged bankrupt. The act of bankruptcy relied on was committed on the 27th of January :—*Held*, that the shares were not at the commencement of the bankruptcy "in the possession, order, or disposition of the bankrupt *in his trade or business*," within sect. 44 of the Bankruptcy Act, 1883. *In re* JENKINSON. *Ex parte* NOTTINGHAM AND NOTTINGHAMSHIRE BANK - 　　15 Q. B. D. 441

11. —— "Trade or Business"—*Shares in Incorporated Company—Chose in Action—Bankruptcy Act, 1883 (46 & 47 Vict. c. 52), s. 44, sub-s. iii.*] B. and T. were partners as stockbrokers, and their practice was from time to time to buy shares in the way of their business, and to obtain advances on them by equitable mortgage or otherwise for the purposes of their business, and for convenience the shares were generally taken in the name of B., who held them as trustee for the partnership. B. deposited the certificates together with a blank transfer of railway shares, bought with partnership moneys, and registered in his name, with a bank to secure moneys due to the bank from the firm. B. and T. became bankrupt, and no notice of the deposit was given to the railway company until after the commencement of the bankruptcy :—*Held*, that as the shares were bought with partnership moneys, and intended to be used for the purposes of the partnership business, they were at the time of the bankruptcy in the order and disposition of B. in his business, for that the business of the partnership was B.'s business, although another person was associated with him in it ; and further, that as no notice of the deposit had been given to the railway company, the shares were in the order and disposition of B., by the consent and permission of the true owner, under such circumstances that B. was the reputed owner of them :—*Held*, therefore, that the shares must pass to the trustee in bankruptcy, unless they were taken out of the reputed ownership clause, Bankruptcy Act, 1883, s. 44, sub-s. iii., by the proviso excluding choses in action from the operation of the clause.—*Held*, by Cotton and Lindley, L.JJ.. dissentiente Fry, L.J., that the shares were not choses in action within the meaning of the proviso, and that they passed to the trustee.—Order of Bacon, V.C., affirmed. COLONIAL BANK *v.* WHINNEY

[30 Ch. D. 261

12. —— Wife's Separate Property—*Property passing to Trustee—Reputed Ownership—Marriage Settlement made in Foreign Country.*] The rule that a husband is a trustee for his wife of her separate property when no other trustee has been appointed, applies to that which becomes her separate property by virtue of a marriage contract entered into in a foreign country.—When, therefore, such property is in the possession of a husband at the commencement of his bankruptcy it

XIX. BANKRUPTCY—ORDER AND DISPOSI-TION—*continued.*

does not pass to his trustee. *Ex parte* SIBETH. *In re* SIBETH　　　—　　14 Q. B. D. 417

XX. BANKRUPTCY—VOID SETTLEMENT.

1. —— Intent to delay Creditors — *Bankruptcy Act (32 & 33 Vict. c. 71), s. 91—13 Eliz. c. 5—Costs—Trustees.*] In determining whether a trader who has executed a voluntary settlement was, within the meaning of sect. 91 of the Bankruptcy Act, 1869, "at the time of making the settlement able to pay all his debts without the aid of the property comprised in such settlement," the value of the implements of his trade and of the goodwill of his business is not, if he was intending to continue his business, to be taken into account.—At any rate, if that value is to be taken into account, it can only be such a value as would be realized at a forced sale.—*Per* Lindley, L.J.: It is essential that the settlor should be able to pay his debts in the way in which he is proposing to pay them, *i.e.*, in the ordinary course of his business, if he is proposing to continue it.—A trader, who had for many years carried on the business of a baker, and had saved some money, being about to purchase a grocery business, which he intended to carry on in addition to the other, made a voluntary settlement of the bulk of his property for the benefit of his wife and children. He afterwards bought the grocery business, and carried it on for about six months, but lost money by it. He then sold it for as much money as he had given for it, and afterwards carried on the baker's business alone, until, about three years after the execution of the settlement, he filed a liquidation petition, his liabilities largely exceeding his assets. The debts which he owed at the date of the settlement had been all paid :—*Held*, that, independently of the question whether he was solvent at the date of the settlement. the settlement was void as against the trustee in the liquidation under the statute 13 Eliz. c. 5, on the ground that it was evidently executed with the view of putting the settlor's property out of the reach of his creditors in case he should fail in the speculation on which he was about to enter in carrying on a new business of which he knew nothing.—*Mackay* v. *Douglas* (Law Rep. 14 Eq. 106) approved and followed.—*Held*, also, that under the circumstances, the settlement was void against the trustee in the liquidation under sect. 91 of the Bankruptcy Act, 1869.—Decision of Bacon, C.J., reversed.—The Judge of the County Court set aside the settlement. He gave the trustee in the liquidation his costs out of the debtor's estate, but made no order as to the costs of the trustees of the settlement. The trustees of the settlement appealed to the Chief Judge, who discharged the order of the County Court. The Court of Appeal restored the order of the County Court.—*Held*, that the trustees of the settlement ought to have been satisfied with the decision of the County Court, and that they must bear their own cost of both appeals, and must pay the costs of the trustee in the liquidation of both appeals. *Ex parte* RUSSELL. *In re* BUTTERWORTH - 19 Ch. D. 588

2. —— "Settlement of Property"—*Gift of Money to Son—46 & 47 Vict. c. 52, s. 47.*] A gift of money to a son, made for the purpose of enabling him to commence carrying on business on his own account, is not a "settlement of property," within the meaning of sect. 47 of the Bankruptcy Act, 1883, which renders such settlements void in certain specified cases as against the trustee in the bankruptcy of the settlor. *In re* PLAYER. *Ex parte* HARVEY　　15 Q. B. D. 682

XXI. BANKRUPTCY—FRAUDULENT PREFERENCE.

1. —— Breach of Trust—*Application of Purchase-money of Goods to make good.Breach of Trust—Bankruptcy Act, 1869 (32 & 33 Vict. c. 71), ss. 6 (sub-s. 2), 92.*] An actual sale of goods for money, the vendor intending to use the purchase-money in making a voluntary payment and the purchaser knowing of that intention, is not a fraudulent transfer within sect. 6 (sub-sect. 2) of the Bankruptcy Act, 1869.—A voluntary preference of a creditor, though it can be set aside as a fraud on the bankrupt law, is not an act of bankruptcy.—If a debtor on the eve of bankruptcy voluntarily makes good trust money which he has misapplied, the payment cannot be set aside as a fraudulent preference of the trust estate.—Within three months before the filing of a liquidation petition the debtor, who was one of the executors of a will, sold some goods to his co-executor with the intention of applying the purchase-money in repaying to the testator's estate money which he had improperly abstracted from it. This intention was known to the co-executor, and the purchase-money was, with his knowledge, immediately after its payment by him, paid by the vendor into a bank to the credit of the executors :—*Held*, by the Court of Appeal, that the transaction was not either a fraudulent preference within sect. 92 of the Bankruptcy Act, 1869, or a fraudulent transfer of property within sect. 6 (sub-sect. 2), and that neither the co-executor nor the testator's estate could be compelled to refund the money.—Decision of Bacon, C.J., affirmed. *Ex parte* STUBBINS. *In re* WILKINSON

[17 Ch. D. 58

2. —— Composition Arrangement — *Preference of some Creditors—Fraud.*] The essence of a composition arrangement between a debtor and his creditors is equality between the creditors, and consequently a creditor who has executed a composition deed is entitled to repudiate it, if he afterwards discovers that other creditors have been induced to execute the deed by means of a secret bargain for a payment to them in excess of the composition, even if the bargain was made after his own execution of the deed.—This principle applies even if the additional payment is to be made at the expense of a third person, provided that the bargain is made with the debtor's knowledge, and it applies whether the composition arrangement is made. under the provisions of a statute or not. *Ex parte* MILNER. *In re* MILNER.

[15 Q. B. D. 605

3. —— Motive of Debtor — *Bankruptcy Act, 1869 (32 & 33 Vict. c. 71), s. 92.*] In order that a payment of money or a transfer of property made by a debtor in favour of one of his creditors should

XXI. BANKRUPTCY—FRAUDULENT PREFER-ENCE—*continued.*

be void as a fraudulent preference under sect. 92, it is sufficient that the preferring the creditor should have been the substantial, effectual, or dominant view with which the debtor made it ; it is not necessary that it should have been his sole view. *Ex parte* BIRD. *In re* BIRD.

[23 Ch. D. 695

4. —— Pressure by Creditor — *Bankruptcy Act,* 1869. s. 92.] On the 17th of February a trader told one of his creditors that he was about to stop payment. The creditor then pressed for security for his debt, and threatened to commence proceedings against the debtor at once, if he did not fulfil a verbal promise which he had on the 17th of January, when the debt was contracted, made to supply the creditor with goods, or their equivalent, as security. The creditor had on the 14th of February, before he knew that the debtor was about to stop payment. pressed the debtor for the promised security, and the debtor had then again promised to give it. On the 19th of February, the debtor delivered two bills of exchange, accepted by some other firms, to a third person, telling him to hand them to the creditor. On the 24th of February the debtor filed a liquidation petition, and on the 10th of March he was adjudicated a bankrupt :—*Held,* that the delivery of the bills of exchange amounted to a fraudulent preference of the creditor, and that it was void as against the trustee in bankruptcy under sect. 92. —*Per* Jessel, M.R. : Inasmuch as the threat to bring an action could have no influence on a man who was just about to become bankrupt, there was no real pressure exerted by the creditor on the 17th of February, and the prior pressure on the 14th of February, having been ineffectual, could not be taken into account. *Ex parte* HALL. *In re* COOPER - 19 Ch. D. 580

5. —— Statutory Definition — *Value of Old Decisions—Bankruptcy Act,* 1869 (32 & 33 *Vict.* c. 71), s. 92.] In determining whether a transaction amounts to a fraudulent preference the Court ought now to have regard simply to the statutory definition contained in sect. 92 of the Bankruptcy Act 1869.—The decisions on the subject before the Act may be useful as guides, but the standards laid down in them must not be substituted for that which is laid down in the Act. *Ex parte* GRIFFITH. *In re* WILCOXON - 23 Ch. D. 69

6. —— " Suffering Judicial Proceeding " — *Non-appearance to Writ—Bankruptcy Act,* 1869 (32 & 33 *Vict.* c. 71), s. 92.] A debtor failed to enter an appearance to a specially indorsed writ served on him by his father-in-law. Judgment was signed on the 15th of May (the earliest day possible), a writ of elegit was issued the same day, and on the 16th of May the sheriff seized the Defendant's goods. The inquisition was held on the 19th of May, and the goods were delivered to the Plaintiff in part satisfaction of his debt. On the 22nd of May the Defendant filed a liquidation petition, and his statement of affairs shewed that his debts were £6542, and his assets £607. He had committed no act of bankruptcy before the filing of the petition. He had before the writ was issued been advised by a solicitor, who acted for the father-in-law, and who issued the writ and

XXI. BANKRUPTCY—FRAUDULENT PREFER-ENCE—*continued.*

signed the judgment on his behalf. The debtor also consulted that solicitor after the issue of the elegit, and that solicitor filed the petition for him. The trustee in the liquidation claimed to set aside the judgment and the subsequent proceedings under it as a fraudulent preference :— *Held,* that though the circumstances were suspicious, yet having regard especially to the fact that, when the transactions took place, no creditor was in a position to take proceedings in bankruptcy against the debtor, he not having committed any act of bankruptcy, the trustee had failed to prove that the debtor had allowed judgment to go against him by default with the view of preferring the father-in-law. *Ex parte* LANCASTER. *In re* MARSDEN - 25 Ch. D. 311

XXII. BANKRUPTCY — PROTECTED TRANSACTION.

1. —— Attachment—*Garnishee Order—Bankruptcy Act,* 1839 (32 & 33 *Vict.* c. 71), ss. 94 (*sub-s.* 3), 95 (*sub-s.* 3).] A garnishee order, attaching a debt due to a bankrupt, is not a " dealing" with the bankrupt within sect. 94, sub-sect. 3, of the Bankruptcy Act, 1869.— Whether such an order is " an attachment against goods " of a bankrupt within sect. 95, sub-sect. 3, *quære.*—But, if it is, it is not within the protection of sect. 95, sub-sect. 3, unless the garnishor has obtained actual payment of the attached debt from the garnishee before the order of adjudication.—Decision of Bacon, C.J., reversed.—Leave to appeal to the House of Lords refused. *Ex parte* PILLERS. *In re* CURTOYS 17 Ch. D. 653

2. —— Debtor's Summons—*Notice of act of Bankruptcy available for Adjudication—Bankruptcy Act,* 1869, s. 94, *sub-s.* 3.] After the Plaintiff had commenced an action against the Defendant for dissolution of partnership, the Plaintiff took out a debtor's summons against the Defendant. The Defendant failed to comply with it, and the Plaintiff filed a petition of bankruptcy against him based on the summons.—Another creditor afterwards took out a debtor's summons against the Defendant, and on his non-compliance with it, filed a petition and obtained adjudication of bankruptcy against him. Before the adjudication and without notice of the act of bankruptcy on which it was based, the Plaintiff entered into an agreement with the Defendant for compromise of the action, which the trustee in the bankruptcy sought to impeach as void against the creditors :—*Held* (reversing the decision of Chitty, J.), that although the non-compliance with the Plaintiff's debtor's summons was not an act of bankruptcy available for adjudication on the petition of the particular creditor who obtained the adjudication against the Defendant, it was an act of bankruptcy " available for adjudication " within the meaning of the Bankruptcy Act, 1869, s. 94, and therefore the agreement for compromise between the Plaintiff and Defendant was not a protected transaction under that section.— *Ex parte* Crosbie (7 Ch. D. 123) distinguished, and the judgment of James, L.J., explained. HOOD *v.* NEWBY 21 Ch. D. 605

3. —— Execution Creditor — *Elegit against*

XXII. BANKRUPTCY — PROTECTED TRANSACTION—continued.

Goods and Chattels executed by Seizure but not by Sale after but without Notice of act of Bankruptcy—Relation back—Transaction not protected—Bankruptcy Act, 1869 (32 & 33 Vict. c. 71), ss. 11, 95 (sub-s. 3).] After an act of bankruptcy had been committed, a judgment creditor for a sum exceeding £50, without notice of the act of bankruptcy, issued an elegit against the goods of the bankrupt (there being no land); but before inquisition proceedings preparatory to sale had been commenced, a bankruptcy petition founded on the act of bankruptcy was presented, and the sheriff was restrained :—*Held,* that the transaction was not protected by sub-sect. 3 of sect. 95. *Ex parte* SULGER. *In re* CHINN　-　17 Ch. D. 839

4. —— Execution Creditor—*Notice of act of Bankruptcy—Bankruptcy Act, 1869 (32 & 33 Vict. c. 71), s. 95.]* The delivery to the execution creditor of goods seized by the sheriff under an elegit, at the value appraised by the jury on the inquisition, is a sale of the goods within the meaning of sect. 95 (sub-sect. 3) of the Bankruptcy Act, 1869, and is protected by that sub-section if the creditor had not at the time of the delivery notice of any act of bankruptcy committed by the debtor prior to the seizure, and available against him for adjudication.—Notice of an act of bankruptcy committed between the seizure and the delivery will not deprive the creditor of the protection.— *Ex parte* Schulte (Law Rep. 9 Ch. 409) followed. *Ex parte* VALE. *In re* BANNISTER 18 Ch. D. 137

5. —— Execution Creditor—*Notice of act of Bankruptcy —32 & 33 Vict. c. 71, s. 95, sub-s. 3.]* A notice to an execution creditor which states that a petition in bankruptcy against the execution debtor has been filed on a date, at a Court, and by a person, named in the notice, is sufficient notice of an act of bankruptcy to prevent the execution being a protected transaction within 32 & 33 Vict. c. 71, s. 95, sub-s. 3. since such creditor ought to know that the petition would contain a statement that the debtor has committed an act of bankruptcy :—So *held,* affirming the decision of the Common Pleas Division.—*Hocking* v. *Acraman* (12 M. & W. 170) commented on. LUCAS v. DICKER　-　-　-　6 Q. B. D. 84

6. —— Execution Creditor—*Notice to Sheriff of Bankruptcy Petition against or by Debtor—Sale under Execution—Bankruptcy Act, 1883 (46 & 47 Vict. c. 52) ss. 46 (2), 168.]* The notice of a bankruptcy petition mentioned in sub-s. 2 of sect. 46 of the Bankruptcy Act, 1883, must be served on the sheriff or his recognised agent (such as the under-sheriff), for the purpose of receiving such notices; it is not sufficient to serve it upon an ordinary bailiff or man in possession.—The effect of the provision of sect. 168 that " sheriff includes any officer charged with the execution of a writ or other process," is to bring within sect. 46 officers of inferior courts who discharge for those courts duties similar to those which the sheriff discharges for the High Court.—On F., the serjeant-at-mace of the Mayor's Court of London, proceeding to execute a warrant issued to enforce a judgment for more than £20 obtained in that court, he found H., an officer of the sheriffs of

XXII. BANKRUPTCY — PROTECTED TRANSACTION—continued.

London, in possession of the goods of the debtor under a writ issued by the Queen's Bench Division, and thereupon, in accordance with the usual practice, he delivered the warrant to H. for execution. H. sold the goods, and out of the proceeds paid the amount of the warrant to F. The next day notice was served on H. of a bankruptcy petition having been presented against the debtor on which he was afterwards adjudged bankrupt. No notice of the petition was served on F. :— *Held,* by Cave, J., that, by virtue of s. 168, H. must under the circumstances be deemed to be " the sheriff" for the purposes of s. 46, sub-s. 2 ; and that therefore the trustee in the bankruptcy was, as against the execution creditor, entitled to the money.—*Held,* by the Court of Appeal, that even if an effectual notice could ever have been served on H., a notice served on him after he had handed over the money to F., and his agency for F. had thus been determined, was ineffectual, and that consequently the execution creditor was entitled to the proceeds of sale. *Ex parte* WARREN. *In re* HOLLAND　　15 Q. B. D. 48

7. ——Onus of Proof—*Notice of Act of Bankruptcy—Judgment recovered after act of Bankruptcy.]* When a creditor claims to prove in a bankruptcy in respect of a debt which came into existence after the commission of the act of bankruptcy on which the fiat was based (the bankruptcy being under the old bankruptcy law), the onus is on him to prove that he had no notice of the act of bankruptcy before the creation of the debt.—*Ex parte Schulte* (Law Rep. 9 Ch. 409) followed. *Ex parte* REVELL. *In re* TOLLEMACHE (No. 2.)　-　-　-　13 Q. B. D. 727

8. —— Post-dated Cheque —*Bankruptcy of Payee before Date of Cheque—Duty of Drawer to stop Cheque—Holder for Value—Banker and Customer—Payment of Cheque or Bill to Customer's Credit—Bankruptcy Act, 1869 (32 & 33 Vict. c. 71), s. 94.]* The drawer of a post-dated cheque given for value is under no obligation to stop its payment before its date for the benefit of a third person.—If, for instance, before the date of payment the drawer receives notice of an adjudication of bankruptcy made against the payee since the delivery of the cheque to him upon an act of bankruptcy committed by him before the delivery he is not bound, for the benefit of the bankrupt's creditors, to give notice to his bankers not to pay the cheque and thus expose himself to the risk of an action by a bonâ fide holder of the cheque for value.—If the cheque was originally delivered by the drawer to the payee in good faith and for value, and without notice of an act of bankruptcy previously committed by the payee, on which an adjudication is subsequently made, the transaction is protected by sect. 94 (sub-s. 3) of the Bankruptcy Act, 1869, and the trustee in the bankruptcy cannot recover the amount of the cheque from the drawer.—Decision of Bacon, C.J., reversed.—When a customer pays a cheque to his bankers with the intention that the amount of it shall be at once placed to his credit, and the bankers carry the amount to his credit accordingly, they become immediately holders of the cheque for value, even though the customer's

XXII. BANKRUPTCY — PROTECTED TRANS-ACTION—*continued.*

account is not overdrawn. *Ex parte* RICHDALE. *In re* PALMER - **19 Ch. D. 409**

9. —— **Wife's Chose in Action**—*Ante-nuptial Parol Agreement to settle—Part Performance—Statute of Frauds, s. 4—Gift by Husband to Wife—Bankruptcy of Husband—Title of Trustees.*] On a marriage it was verbally agreed between the husband and the wife that a sum of money standing to the credit of the wife on deposit at a bank in her maiden name should be her separate property. Nothing further was done; but after the marriage the money, with the husband's consent, remained at the bank in the wife's maiden name; and she received the interest on it for two years after the marriage, when she drew the money out of the bank. The trustee in the subsequent liquidation of the husband having claimed payment of the money from the wife as part of her husband's property :—*Held*, by Cave, J., that there had been no such part performance by the husband of the parol contract to settle as to take the case out of the Statute of Frauds, and, therefore, that the trustee was entitled to the money subject to the wife's equity to a settlement, if any.—*Held*, by the Court of Appeal, without deciding the question on the Statute of Frauds, that there had been a gift of the money by the husband to the wife after the marriage; that he had become a trustee of it for her as her separate property; and that, consequently, it did not pass to the trustee in his liquidation. *Ex parte* WHITEHEAD. *In re* WHITE-HEAD. **14 Q. B. D. 419**

XXIII. BANKRUPTCY—DISCLAIMER.

(a) BANKRUPTCY ACT, 1869.

1. —— **Assignment by Trustee to Pauper**—*Bankruptcy of Tenant—Bankruptcy Act,* 1869 (32 & 33 Vict. c. 71), *ss.* 23, 24—*Non-disclaimer after Notice.*] Although a trustee in bankruptcy, who has taken actual possession of leasehold property of the bankrupt, receives notice from the landlord to disclaim the lease under the Bankruptcy Act, 1869 (32 & 33 Vict. c. 71), but does not disclaim, he may nevertheless relieve himself of liability to the landlord by assigning the lease, even without having previously offered to surrender it, and the mere fact that the trustee knows the assignee to be a pauper will not invalidate such assignment. HOPKINSON *v.* LOVERING **11 Q. B. D. 92**

2. —— **Fixtures**—*License by Lessor to remove after Expiration of Term—Removal by Trustee before Disclaimer—Right· of Lessor—Bankruptcy Act,* 1869 (32 & 33 Vict. c. 71), *s.* 23.] A lease contained a proviso that the lessee, his executors, administrators, and assigns, might at any time or times during the continuance of the term, or within twelve months from the expiration or other sooner determination thereof, but not afterwards, remove any buildings or machinery which he or they might have erected on the demised premises for trade purposes. The lessee filed a liquidation petition, and a trustee in the liquidation sold the trade machinery and fixtures, which were then removed by the purchaser. The trustee afterwards disclaimed the lease :—*Held*, by Bacon, C.J., that the removal of the fixtures was justified by the proviso in the lease, and that the

XXIII. BANKRUPTCY—DISCLAIMER—*contd.*

(a.) BANKRUPTCY ACT, 1869—*continued.*

trustee, notwithstanding the disclaimer, was entitled to retain the proceeds of sale.—*Held*, by the Court of Appeal, that the disclaimer having, by virtue of ·sect. 23, the operation of a surrender of the lease as from the date of the appointment of the trustee, the proviso was, by construction of the law, with all the other provisions of the lease, put an end to before the ·removal, and consequently that the removal could not be justified, and the lessor was entitled to the proceeds' of sale. *Ex parte* GLEGG. *In re* LATHAM [**19 Ch. D. 7**

3. —— **Lease determined before Disclaimer**—*Landlord and Tenant—Distress for Rent after Bankruptcy—Breach of Covenant—Forfeiture—Entry—Action to recover Possession—Proof for Damages—Set-off—Bankruptcy Act,* 1869 (32 & 33 Vict. c. 71), *ss.* 23, 34, 39.] The trustee in a bankruptcy may disclaim a lease of the bankrupt even though the lease has been determined, by effluxion of time or by forfeiture, between the appointment of the trustee and the execution of the disclaimer. And in such a case the effect of the disclaimer, when executed, is that neither the lessor nor the trustee can claim the benefit of any provisions contained in the lease which were to come into operation at the expiration or sooner determination of the term.—*Semble*, that the trustee may also disclaim a lease which has been determined before his appointment.—*Ex parte* Paterson (11 Ch. D. 908) followed and approved.—A landlord, between the filing of a liquidation petition by his tenant and the appointment of trustees, levied a distress for two half-years' rent accrued due before the filing of the petition. After the appointment of trustees the landlord levied a second distress for a third half-year's rent accrued due between the filing of the petition and the appointment of the trustees :—*Held*, that the second distress was void under sect. 34 of the Bankruptcy Act, 1869.—*Held*, also, that, in respect of breaches of covenant committed by the tenant during his occupation, the only remedy of the landlord was to prove for damages in the liquidation, and that the landlord had no right of set-off as against moneys due by him to the trustee for severed crops.—When a lease contains a proviso giving the lessor a right to re-enter in the event of breach of covenant by the lessee (but not making the lease ipso facto void in that event) :—*Quære*, whether under the present practice the mere commencement of an action by the lessor to recover possession of the property for breach of covenant, or the commencement of such action followed by appearance by the trustees, will, without actual entry, operate to determine the lease.—*Silcock* v. *Farmer* (46 L. T. (N.S.) 404) commented upon. *Ex parte* HART DYKE. *In re* MORRISH - - - **22 Ch. D. 410**

4. —— **Lease of Land and Chattels**—*Reputed Ownership—Bankruptcy Act,* 1869 (32 & 33 Vict. c. 71), *ss.* 15 (*sub-s.* 5), 23.] Sect. 15 of the Bankruptcy Act, 1869, must be read in conjunction with and as qualified by sect. 23, and the effect of a disclaimer of a lease to a bankrupt by the trustee in the bankruptcy, is to give up to the lessor the entirety of that which is

XXIII. BANKRUPTCY—DISCLAIMER—_contd._

(a.) BANKRUPTCY ACT, 1869—_continued._

comprised in the demise. Therefore, if a bankrupt be the lessee of land and personal chattels, demised to him as one subject-matter at one entire rent, a disclaimer of the lease by the trustee operates as a surrender to the lessor of the chattels, as well as the land, and the trustee cannot claim the chattels, under sect. 15 (sub-sect. 5), as having been at the commencement of the bankruptcy in the order or disposition of the bankrupt as reputed owner with the consent of the true owner. A disclaimer of a lease to a bankrupt by the trustee in the bankruptcy operates to relieve the trustee from all liability under the lease, not merely from liability as from the date of the adjudication.—_Ex parte Glegg_ (19 Ch. D. 7) explained.—Leave to appeal to the House of Lords refused. _Ex parte_ ALLEN. _In re_ FUSSELL - - - - 20 Ch. D. 341

5. —— Leave of Court—_Lease—Appeal after Execution of Disclaimer—Bankruptcy Act, 1869_ (32 & 33 Vict. c. 71), s. 23—_Bankruptcy Rules,_ 1871, r. 28.] After an unconditional leave has been given by the Court to a trustee in bankruptcy to disclaim a lease of the bankrupt and the trustee has executed a disclaimer, it is too late for the lessor to appeal from the order even for the purpose of getting conditions imposed on the trustee. The Court of Appeal has then no power to impose conditions. If the lessor desires to appeal from such an order, he ought to apply when it is made for a stay of proceedings under it.—_Ex parte Ditton_ (3 Ch. D. 459) followed. _Ex parte_ SADLER. _In re_ HAWES - 19 Ch. D. 122

6. —— Leave of Court—_Lease—Bankruptcy Act, 1869_ (32 & 33 Vict. c. 71), s. 23—_Bankruptcy Rules,_ 1871, r. 28.] In determining whether leave should be given to a trustee in bankruptcy to disclaim a leasehold interest of the bankrupt, the Court ought to have regard only to the question whether the disclaimer will be for the benefit of the persons interested in the administration of the bankrupt's estate, and ought not to have regard to any collateral consideration, such as the injury which the disclaimer might occasion to third parties.—Leave to appeal to the House of Lords refused, on the ground that the appeal would be from the discretion of the Court. _Ex parte_ EAST AND WEST INDIA DOCK COMPANY. _In re_ CLARKE - - - 17 Ch. D. 759

7. —— Leave of Court—_Lease —Conditions imposed—Bankruptcy Act, 1869_ (32 & 33 Vict. c. 71), s. 23—_Bankruptcy Rules,_ 1871, r. 28.] A lease of land and minerals was granted to two partners in trade as joint tenants. The partnership was afterwards dissolved, on the terms that the business should be carried on by one of the partners alone, and that he should purchase the interest of the other for £12,000, which was to be paid in forty equal half-yearly instalments. The retiring partner covenanted that he would stand possessed of his share and interest in the demised premises in trust for the continuing partner. The continuing partner covenanted with the retiring partner to pay the £12,000 in the manner agreed upon, and assigned to him the buildings, machinery, and fixtures on the demised premises by way of mortgage to secure the payment of the £12,000, and covenanted that the leasehold pre-

mises should stand charged therewith. A year afterwards the continuing partner filed a liquidation petition, under which a trustee of his property was appointed. The trustee occupied the demised property for some time with a view to the benefit of the debtor's estate. The rent due under the lease was paid to the landlord by the retired partner:—_Held,_ that leave to disclaim the debtor's interest in the lease ought to be given to the trustee only on condition of his paying to the retired partner the rent of the premises from the date of the trustee's appointment until the day when his beneficial occupation thereof ceased. _Ex parte_ GOOD. _In re_ SALKELD 13 Q. B. D. 731

8. —— Leave of Court—_Lease—Conditions—Bankruptcy Act, 1869_ (32 & 33 Vict. c. 71), s. 23—_Bankruptcy Rules,_ 1871, r. 28.] In giving leave to the trustee in a bankruptcy to disclaim a leasehold interest of the bankrupt, the Court has, under rule 28 of 1871, power to impose a condition (such as the payment to the lessor of the rent in full up to the date of the disclaimer) even though no third party has acquired from the bankrupt an interest in the lease. _Ex parte_ LADBURY. _In re_ TURNER 17 Ch. D. 532

9. —— Leave of Court—_Lease—Conditions—Mortgage—Attornment Clause —Mortgage to Building Society—Bankruptcy Act, 1869_ (32 & 33 Vict. c. 71), s. 23—_Bankruptcy Rules,_ 1871, r. 28.] On giving leave, under rule 28 of the Bankruptcy Rules, 1871, to the trustee in a bankruptcy to disclaim a leasehold interest of the bankrupt, the Court will not order the trustee to pay the landlord any compensation for his use and occupation of the demised property; except under special circumstances, one instance being where the trustee's occupation has been beneficial to the bankrupt's estate. Rule 28 does not mean that in every case in which leave to disclaim a lease is given, the lessor is to be placed in the same position as regards the interval before execution of the disclaimer as if there had been no disclaimer.—_Ex parte Ladbery_ (17 Ch. D. 532) explained and distinguished.—Notwithstanding the insertion of an attornment clause in a mortgage deed, the real relation between the parties is that, not of landlord and tenant, but of mortgagee and mortgagor, and this fact, as well as the nature of the rent reserved by the clause, must be taken into account in considering whether, on giving leave to the trustee in the bankruptcy of the mortgagor to disclaim the tenancy created by the attornment clause, any terms should be imposed for the benefit of the mortgagee. _Ex parte_ ISHERWOOD. _In re_ KNIGHT [22 Ch. D. 384

10. —— Leave of Court—_Lease—Compensation to Landlord—Bankruptcy Act,_ 1869 (32 & 33 Vict. c. 71), ss. 23, 24—_Bankruptcy Rules,_ 1871, r. 28.] When the trustee in a bankruptcy applies for leave to disclaim a lease of the bankrupt, the Court will not order any compensation to be paid to the landlord unless the trustee has kept him out of possession of the property, and his occupation has resulted in a benefit to the bankrupt's estate.—The principle on which the Court exer-

XXIII. BANKRUPTCY—DISCLAIMER—*contd.*

(a.) BANKRUPTCY ACT, 1869—*continued.* „

cises its discretion under rule 28 is that the trustee ought not to be allowed to increase the bankrupt's estate at the expense of the landlord.—*Ex parte Isherwood* (22 Ch. D. 384) explained. *Ex parte* IZARD. *In re* BUSHELL (No. 2) .

[**23 Ch. D. 115**

11. —— Leave of Court—*Lease—Conditions to be imposed on Trustee—Bankruptcy Act, 1869 (32 & 33 Vict. c. 71), s. 23—Bankruptcy Rules, 1871, r. 28.*] In determining whether, on giving leave to the trustee in a bankruptcy to disclaim a lease of the bankrupt, the trustee should be ordered to pay compensation to the landlord in respect of his occupation of the leasehold premises, the Court will have regard not merely to the question whether the occupation has actually produced a profit to the bankrupt's estate, but also to the question whether the possession was retained by the trustee with a view to obtaining such a profit.—The rule as laid down by Cotton, L.J., in *Ex parte Isherwood* (22 Ch. D. 384) adopted in preference to that expressed by Jessel, M.R., in *Ex parte Izard* (23 Ch. D. 115).—The imposing of conditions on the trustee is, however, a matter of judicial discretion, and the Court of Appeal will not readily interfere with the exercise of discretion by the Judge of first instance.—The Court ordered compensation to be paid by the trustee in a bankruptcy as a condition of giving him leave to disclaim the lease of the bankrupt's place of business, although during part of the time during which the trustee had been in occupation a bailiff had been in possession of the bankrupt's goods under a distress for rent, and the landlord had been allowed to place bills on the premises stating that they were to be let, and that application for that purpose was to be made to him. *Ex parte* ARNAL. *In re* WITTON　　24 Ch. D. 26

12. —— Liability of Lessee for Rent—*Lease—Liability of Bankrupt's Surety—Disclaimer of Lease by Trustee of Assignee.*] The Plaintiff being lessee of a farm for a term of years assigned the lease to P., taking the covenant of the Defendant as surety for the due payment of the rent to the lessor for the residue of the term. During the continuance of the term P. became bankrupt, and his trustee having obtained the requisite leave of the Court disclaimed all interest in the lease. Subsequently the lessor demanded from the Plaintiff the half-year's rent accruing after the bankruptcy. The Plaintiff paid the rent and brought an action to recover the amount from the Defendant under his covenant. Neither the Plaintiff nor the Defendant had entered upon or taken possession of the farm :—*Held*, by Manisty and Watkin Williams, JJ., that the Plaintiff was entitled to recover　By Manisty, J., on the ground that the disclaimer operated only as a surrender so far as was necessary to relieve the bankrupt, his estate, and the trustee, from liability without otherwise affecting third parties, and that the Plaintiff as lessee remained liable for the rent and had his remedy over against the Defendant as the bankrupt's surety.　By Watkin Williams, J., solely on the authority of *East and West India Dock Company v. Hill* (22 Ch. D. 14). HARDING *v.* PREECE -　　-　　-　　- 9 Q. B. D. 281

XXIII. BANKRUPTCY—DISCLAIMER—*contd.*

(a.) BANKRUPTCY ACT, 1869—*continued.*

13. —— Liquidation—*Lease — Covenant not to use Hay, Straw, &c.—56 Geo. 3, c. 50, s. 11—Bankruptcy Act (32 & 33 Vict. c. 71), ss. 119, 125.*] The enactment in statute 56 Geo. 3, c. 50, s. 11, that the assignee of any bankrupt shall not take or use any hay, straw, &c., on any farm of the bankrupt in any other way than the bankrupt ought to have done, is still in force, and applies to a trustee in bankruptcy or liquidation under the Bankruptcy Act, 1869.—A lessee was bound by the covenants in his lease not to sell the hay, straw, &c., grown on his farm without the consent of the landlord. The lessee became a liquidating debtor under the Bankruptcy Act, 1869, s. 125, and the trustee in the liquidation disclaimed the lease :—*Held*, that the trustee was bound by 56 Geo. 3, c. 50, s. 11, notwithstanding the disclaimer, and an injunction was granted to restrain him from selling the hay, straw, &c., grown on the farm. LYBBE *v.* HART -　　29 Ch. D. 8

14. —— Practice—*Lease—Extension of Time—Bankruptcy Act, 1869 (32 & 33 Vict. c. 71), s. 24.*] The mere fact that the lessor availed himself of the provisions contained in the debtor's lease to compel the trustee in liquidation to pay half a year's rent in advance, is not, in the absence of negotiation, or of anything to mislead the trustee, or of special circumstances to excuse the delay, a ground for enlarging the time, after the expiration of the twenty-eight days (fixed by the Bankruptcy Act, 1869, s. 24), for notice to be given by the trustee, whether he disclaims the lease or not. *In re* RICHARDSON. *Ex parte* HARRIS

[**16 Ch. D. 613**

15. —— Rights of Third Parties—*Lease—Construction of Statutes—Bankruptcy Act, 1869 (32 & 33 Vict. c. 71), s. 23—Bankruptcy Rules, 1871, r. 28.*] A disclaimer by the trustee in a bankruptcy of a lease or other onerous property of the bankrupt operates as a surrender only so far as is necessary to relieve the bankrupt and his estate and the trustee from liability, and does not otherwise affect the rights or liabilities of third parties in relation to the property disclaimed.—If, for instance, the bankrupt has granted an underlease of property demised to him, a disclaimer of the original lease by his trustee in bankruptcy does not affect the right of the lessor to distrain on the property for the rent reserved by the original lease, and to re-enter for breach of the lessee's covenants in the lease, or for non-payment of the rent reserved thereby. But, if the underlease is made at a rent less than the rent reserved by the original lease, the underlessee is, after the disclaimer, entitled to prove in the bankruptcy for the value of the difference between the two rents.—A statute may be construed contrary to its literal meaning, when a literal construction would result in an absurdity or inconsistency, and the words are susceptible of another construction which will carry out the manifest intention. *Ex parte* WALTON. *In re* LEVY -　　- 17 Ch. D. 746

16. —— Rights of Lessor against Lessee after Disclaimer—*Lease—Bankruptcy Act, 1869 (32 & 33 Vict. c. 71), s. 23.*] The assignee of a lease for a term of years became bankrupt, and his

XXIII. BANKRUPTCY—DISCLAIMER—*contd.*

(a.) BANKRUPTCY ACT, 1869—*continued.*

trustee by leave of the Court disclaimed under sect. 23 of the Bankruptcy Act, 1869 (32 & 33 Vict. c. 71), of the bankrupt's property and interest in the premises. The lessor having brought an action against the original lessee upon his covenant to pay rent for the rent accrued due since the appointment of the trustee:—*Held*, affirming the decision of the Court of Appeal, by Earl Cairns and Lords Blackburn and Watson, Lord Bramwell dissenting, that notwithstanding the disclaimer the lessee remained liable upon his covenant.　HILL *v.* EAST AND WEST INDIA DOCK COMPANY　　22 Ch. D. 14; 9 App. Cas. 448

17. —— *Sub-lease — Disclaimer by Lessee's Trustee of Lessee's Interest in Premises—8 & 9 Vict. c. 106, s. 9—Bankruptcy Act, 1869 (32 & 33 Vict. c. 71), ss. 23, 125.]* When a lessee sublets and afterwards becomes bankrupt, and his trustee, under sect. 23 of the Bankruptcy Act, 1869, and under an order of the Court of Bankruptcy, disclaims the lessee's interest in the premises, the lessor is not entitled to eject the sub-tenant.—Lessee for a term of years by deed demised part of the premises for a shorter term, and the sub-lessee entered into possession. The lessee afterwards liquidated by arrangement, under the Bankruptcy Act, 1869, and his trustee, under an order of the Court of Bankruptcy, disclaimed the lessee's interest in the premises. Notice of the application to the Court for leave to disclaim was given to the sub-lessee within a reasonable time before the order was made. The lessor having brought an action to recover possession of the part of the premises demised to the sub-lessee as from the date of the appointment of the trustee:—*Held*, reversing the judgment of Mathew, J., that the lessor was not entitled to recover possession.—*Taylor* v. *Gillott* (Law Rep 20 Eq. 682) commented upon. SMALLEY *v.* HARDINGE　6 Q. B. D. 371; 7 Q. B. D. 524

18. —— *Use and Occupation—Yearly Tenant—Bankruptcy Act, 1869, s. 23—Rule 28 of the Bankruptcy Rules, 1871.]* W., who occupied premises as a yearly tenant, was adjudicated bankrupt on the 7th of September, 1883.　The Defendant, as trustee, entered into possession of the premises and held them until the 29th of January, 1884 (when he tendered the keys to the Plaintiff, the landlord), for the purpose of winding up the bankrupt's business and realizing his assets for the benefit of the estate,—paying rent down to the 25th of December, 1883.—On the 26th of February, 1884, the trustee with the leave of the Court, and after notice to the landlord, disclaimed all interest in the term :—*Held*, that the disclaimer relating back by force of sect. 23 of the Bankruptcy Act, 1869, to the date of the adjudication, the trustee was not liable to an action in respect of his subsequent occupation of the premises (either as assignee or as a trespasser); the landlord's only remedy being by application to the Court of Bankruptcy under rule 28 of the Bankruptcy Rules, 1871.　GABRIEL *v.* BLANKENSTEIN
　　　　　　　　　　　　　　[13 Q. B. D. 684

(b.) BANKRUPTCY ACT, 1883.

19. —— *Agreement for a Lease—" Land bur-*

XXIII. BANKRUPTCY—DISCLAIMER—*contd.*

(b.) BANKRUPTCY ACT, 1883—*continued.*

dened with onerous covenants"—" Property "—Bankruptcy Act, 1883, ss. 44, 55, 168.] The right of disclaimer conferred on trustees by sect. 55 of the Bankruptcy Act, 1883, is not limited to property of the bankrupt divisible amongst his creditors as defined by sect. 44, but extends to any property as defined by sect. 168 from which no benefit can accrue to the bankrupt's estate.—A debtor held his business premises for a term of years under an agreement for a lease, and entered into a binding contract for the sale and assignment of his business and his business premises to a company, but became bankrupt before the completion of the contract :—*Held*, that the debtor's interest in the agreement for a lease was in the nature of land burdened with onerous covenants which his trustee in bankruptcy could under the circumstances disclaim.　*In re* MAUGHAN.　*Ex parte* MONKHOUSE　　　- 14 Q. B. D. 956

20. —— *Fixtures—Lease—Bankruptcy Act, 1883 (46 & 47 Vict. c. 52), s. 55.]* Where there are trade fixtures on the leasehold premises of a bankrupt, removable by the tenant, and the trustee applies for leave to disclaim the lease, the same rule will be applied as between the landlord and trustee as would obtain if the lease had been determined in an ordinary way. Therefore the landlord must either take over the fixtures at a valuation, or the trustee must have a reasonable time, before disclaiming, in which to sever and remove them.　*In re* MOSER
　　　　　　　　　　　　　　[13 Q. B. D. 738

21. —— *Landlord's Claim for Compensation—Lease — Jurisdiction — Bankruptcy Act, 1883, ss. 51, 121 — Bankruptcy Rules, 1883, r. 232.]* Where an order is made under sect. 121 of the Bankruptcy Act, 1883, for the summary administration of a bankrupt's estate, and the trustee in pursuance of the power conferred on him by rule 232 of the Bankruptcy Rules, 1883, disclaims, without any application to the Court, the leasehold premises of the bankrupt, the Court has no jurisdiction to give any compensation to the landlord out of the bankrupt's estate for the use and occupation by the trustee of the leasehold premises for the purposes of the bankruptcy, even although a benefit has thereby resulted to the estate.　*In re* SANDWELL.　*Ex parte* ZERFASS
　　　　　　　　　　　　　　[14 Q. B. D. 960

22. —— *Mortgagee—Lease—Superior Landlord — Form of Order—Bankruptcy Act, 1883, s. 55, sub-s. 6.]* On a disclaimer of leaseholds by a trustee in bankruptcy under sect. 55, sub-sect. 6, of the Bankruptcy Act, 1883, the landlord has not such an interest in the "disclaimed property" as to be entitled to a vesting order under the sub-section. The right to a vesting order is only conferred on a person claiming an interest in the property through or under the bankrupt. Where in such a case a mortgagee does not appear on the trustee's application to disclaim, the proper course is to order that the mortgagee be excluded from all interest in and security upon the property, unless he shall by a short date declare his option to take a vesting order in the terms of the sub-section.　*In re* PARKER AND PARKER (1).　*Ex parte* TURQUAND　　　- 14 Q. B. D. 405

XXIII. BANKRUPTCY—DISCLAIMER—contd.

(b.) BANKRUPTCY ACT, 1883—continued.

23.' —— Practice—Lease—Extension of Time —Bankruptcy Act, 1883, ss. 55, 105, sub-s. 4.] Although the three months given to a trustee by s. 55, sub-s. 1, within which to disclaim onerous property may have expired, the Court has power under s. 105' sub-s. 4, to grant the trustee an extension of time.—When a trustee applies for an extension of time, he should give some good reason for the indulgence he asks, and if the rights of other parties will be prejudiced by the time being extended, the Court will, as a general rule, put the trustee upon terms. In re PRICE. Ex parté FOREMAN - - 13 Q. B. D. 466

24. —— Practice—Lease—Landlord's Notice —Trustee's Neglect — Costs — Bankruptcy Act, 1883, s. 55, sub-s. 4.] When a landlord gives a trustee notice under sub-sect. 4 of the 55th section of the Bankruptcy Act, 1883, requiring him to decide whether he will disclaim or not the bankrupt's leaseholds, and the trustee declines or neglects within the twenty-eight days limited by the sub-section to give notice whether he disclaims or not, and subsequently applies to the Court for leave to disclaim, he may render himself personally liable to the payment of rent and costs. In re PAGE BROTHERS. Ex parte MACKAY - - - 14 Q. B. D. 401
—— Election to take lease - 9 Q. B. D. 473
See BANKRUPTCY—TRUSTEE. 6.

XXIV. BANKRUPTCY—JURISDICTION.

. 1. —— Conflicting Claims between Strangers —Bankruptcy Act, 1869, s. 72—Bankruptcy Act, 1883, s. 102, sub-s. 1.] The jurisdiction conferred on the Court of Bankruptcy by sub-sect. 1 of sect. 102, of the Bankruptcy Act, 1883, is identical with that conferred on that Court by sect. 72 of the Bankruptcy Act, 1869.—Where, therefore, there are conflicting claims to any part of a bankrupt's property, between parties who are strangers to the bankruptcy, and in which the trustee in bankruptcy has no interest, the Court of Bankruptcy will decline to adjudicate upon the questions at issue. In re LOWENTHAL. Ex parte BEESTY
[13 Q. B. D. 238

2. —— Contempt of Court—County Court— Committal—Prohibition—Bankruptcy Act, 1869 (32 & 33 Vict. c. 71), ss. 66, 96.] The Bankruptcy Act, 1869, s. 66, which conferred upon the Judge of a County Court sitting in bankruptcy all the powers and jurisdiction of a Judge of the Court of Chancery, thereby gave to him the power to commit for, a contempt of Court; and therefore a person who disobeyed a summons issued under sect. 96 of that statute to attend and give evidence as to the bankrupt's estate and to produce documents in his control relating thereto, might be attached for contempt; and the power of committal was not taken away by the fact that the latter section also conferred a power on the Judge of the County Court to order by warrant the person who had disobeyed the summons to be apprehended and brought up for examination, this latter remedy being only cumulative. THE QUEEN v. JUDGE OF CROYDON COUNTY COURT
[13 Q. B. D. 963

3. —— Discretion of Court—Bankruptcy Act,

XXIV. BANKRUPTCY—JURISDICTION—contd.
1869 (32 & 33 Vict. c. 71), s. 72.] Although as a general rule, cases in which the trustee in bankruptcy is asserting a claim to property by a higher title than that of the bankrupt himself ought to be tried in the Court of Bankruptcy, yet the rule is not an inflexible one, but the Court has a judicial discretion to be exercised with regard to all the circumstances of the case:—Held, that the fact that a large amount was at stake, and that questions of character were involved, were sufficient grounds for refusing to allow a case, in which the trustee in a liquidation was seeking to set aside some transactions of the debtors as fraudulent under the bankruptcy law to be tried in a County Court. Ex parte ARMITAGE. In re LEAROYD, WILTON, & Co. - 17 Ch. D. 13

4. —— Discretion of Court—Fraudulent Deed —13 Eliz. c. 5—Bankruptcy Act, 1869 (32 & 33 Vict. c. 71), s. 72.] When the trustee in a bankruptcy which is proceeding in a County Court impeaches a deed executed by the bankrupt as fraudulent under the Statute of Elizabeth if the amount at stake is beyond the ordinary jurisdiction of a County Court and serious questions of character are involved, and the person interested under the deed desires that the question should not be tried in the County Court, the Judge ought to decline to exercise the jurisdiction conferred by sect, 72, and ought to leave the matter to be tried in an action in the High Court in the ordinary way.—Ex parte Armitage (17 Ch. D. 13) approved. Ex parte PRICE. In re ROBERTS
[21 Ch. D. 553

5. —— Railway Company—Lien for Freight— Agreement for General Lien—Receiver.] A trader opened with a railway company a credit account for freight, by which it was agreed that the company should have a general lien for all moneys due by him to them on any account on all goods belonging to him in their hands. He afterwards filed a liquidation petition, under which a receiver of his property and manager of his business was appointed. In order to carry on the business the receiver bought some goods, which he paid for with his own money, and sent them to the company consigned to the trader. The company claimed the benefit of the agreement, and refused to deliver the goods until they were paid the amount which the trader owed them for freight due at the time of the filing of the petition. The receiver in order to obtain the goods paid the company £50 under protest, and then applied to the Court of Bankruptcy to order the company to repay him the £50, and an order was made accordingly:—Held, on appeal, that the Court of Bankruptcy had no jurisdiction to make the order.—But, semble, that the company would have no defence to an action by the receiver for the £50.—In re Northfield Iron and Steel Company (14 L. T. (N.S.) 695) distinguished. Ex parte GREAT WESTERN RAILWAY COMPANY. In re BUSHELL - - 22 Ch. D. 470

XXV. BANKRUPTCY — STAYING PROCEEDINGS.

(a.) BANKRUPTCY ACT, 1869.

1. —— Action against Bankrupt in Colonial Court — Sequestration to compel Appearance —

XXV. BANKRUPTCY — STAYING PROCEED-
INGS—contd.

(a.) BANKRUPTCY ACT, 1869—continued.

Bankruptcy Act, 1869 (32 & 33 Vict. c. 71), s. 13
—Bankruptcy Rules, 1870, r. 260.] Before issuing
a sequestration against real estate of a bankrupt
situate in a colony, for the purpose of compelling
his appearance in an action in the Colonial Court
to realize a mortgage given by him of other real
estate in the colony, the leave of the Court of
Bankruptcy ought to be obtained.—But where
such a sequestration had been issued without
leave, and an appearance had been entered in
the colonial action :—Held, that it was sufficient
that the Plaintiffs in the action should undertake
not to use the sequestration for any other purpose. Ex parte ROGERS. In re BOUSTEAD
[16 Ch. D. 665

(b.) BANKRUPTCY ACT, 1883.

2. —— Attachment—Pending Action in Chancery Division—Non-payment of Trust Money into
Court—Motion for Writ of Attachment—Bankruptcy of Trustee—Debt provable in Bankruptcy—
Jurisdiction of Bankruptcy Court to interfere—
Bankruptcy Act, 1883, s. 9, sub-s. 1 and s. 10,
sub-s. 2.] The Plaintiff in an action in the Chancery Division having failed to pay into Court,
when ordered, a sum of money which he had
received in a fiduciary capacity, was served with
a notice of motion for a writ of attachment against
him. He thereupon filed his petition in bankruptcy, and applied to the Court of Bankruptcy
under s. 9 of the Bankruptcy Act, 1883, to stay
further proceedings in the action on the ground
that the claim against him was a debt provable
in his bankruptcy :—Held, that his application
must be refused, for that no good reason was
shewn why the Court of Bankruptcy should interfere.—Semble, the jurisdiction conferred on the
Court of Bankruptcy by s. 9 of the Bankruptcy
Act, 1883, is discretionary, and will not, as a
general rule, be exercised in favour of a bankrupt personally, where he has by some misconduct in some other proceedings rendered himself
liable to imprisonment. In re MACKINTOSH. Ex
parte MACKINTOSH　-　　13 Q. B. D. 235

3. —— County Court—Power of County Court
to restrain Proceedings in High Court—Solicitor
—Right of Audience—Bankruptcy Act, 1883 (46
& 47 Vict. c. 52), ss. 100, 102, 151, 168.] Under
the Bankruptcy Act, 1883, a county court sitting
in bankruptcy has no power to restrain proceedings in an action in the High Court.—Decision of
Cave and Wills, JJ., reversed.—There is no
absolute rule that a question relating to the
estate of a bankrupt ought to be determined by
the Court of Bankruptcy, and not by the High
Court, whenever the trustee in the bankruptcy is,
by virtue of the bankruptcy law, claiming by a
higher title than that of the bankrupt himself.
It is a matter of judicial discretion in each case
how the question shall best be tried.—In such a
matter the Court of Appeal ought not readily to
overrule the discretion of the bankruptcy judge.
Per Cave and Wills, JJ.: A solicitor has a right
of audience on an appeal to the Divisional Court
from a county court sitting in bankruptcy. Ex
parte REYNOLDS. In re BARNETT 15 Q. B. D. 169

XXVI. BANKRUPTCY—TRANSFER.

1. —— Certificate of Judge—Discretion—Appeal—Costs—Bankruptcy Act, 1883 (46 & 47 Vict.
c. 52), ss. 97 (sub-s. 2), 104 (sub-s. 2)—Bankruptcy
Rules, 1883, rr. 16, 17, 111 (3).] The refusal of a
judge of a County Court to grant a certificate,
under rule 16 of the Bankruptcy Rules, 1883,
that in his opinion the proceedings under a bankruptcy petition would be more advantageously
conducted in another Court, is an order from
which an appeal lies, if the Judge has refused to
exercise his discretion in the matter.—In such a
case the Court of Appeal, if. it is of opinion that
the certificate ought to have been granted, will
not refer the matter back to the County Court, but
will itself grant the certificate.—Two partners in
trade presented a bankruptcy petition in a County
Court. Their statement of affairs shewed that
they had lost nearly £200,000 in five years' trading. Some of the creditors applied to the Judge
for a certificate that in his opinion the proceedings would be more advantageously conducted in
the London Court. The Judge refused the application, on the ground that it was premature. An
appeal was presented, but was afterwards withdrawn, and on this occasion some correspondence
took place between the solicitors of the applicants
and the solicitors of other creditors who opposed
the proposed transfer. The application was afterwards renewed, and there was evidence that the
debtors owed a large amount to creditors in
London, Liverpool, and other places, and that, in
order to carry out a proper investigation of their
accounts, it would be necessary to refer to the
books of various merchants in London with whom
they had traded, and also to the books of their
bankers and of the bankers' London agents. The
Judge refused the application, on the ground that
the applicants were estopped by the correspondence between the solicitors from making it :—Held,
that there was no such estoppel, and that, as the
Judge had therefore decided on a wrong ground,
he had in effect refused to exercise his discretionary power, and there was an appeal from his
decision.—Held, also, that under the circumstances the proceedings would be more advantageously conducted in the London Court, and
that the certificate asked for ought to have been
granted, and the Divisional Court itself granted
the certificate.—Per Cave, J. If an agreement
not to renew the application for a certificate had
been in fact entered into between the solicitors of
the applicants and the solicitors of the other creditors, it could not have affected the power of the
Court to make the certificate, though it might
have affected the right of the applicants to costs.
—Order made that the applicants should have
their costs out of the debtors' assets, in case the
creditors should ultimately approve of the proposed transfer. Ex parte SOANES. In re WALKER
[13 Q. B. D. 484

2. —— Judgment Summons for Committal—
County Court—Transfer to Bankruptcy Court—
Receiving Order—Notice to Judgment Debtor—
Debtors Act, 1869, s. 5—Bankruptcy Act, 1883,
s. 103, sub-ss. 4, 5—Bankruptcy Rules, 1885,
r. 268 (1) (a).] When a judgment summons for
a committal comes before the judge of a county
court, not having jurisdiction in bankruptcy, and

XXVI. BANKRUPTCY—TRANSFER—*contd.*

he, being of opinion that a receiving order should be made in lieu of a committal, makes an order transferring the matter to the Bankruptcy Court, notice of the subsequent proceedings under the order of transfer must be served on the judgment debtor.—In such a case the Court of Bankruptcy is not bound to act on the opinion of the county court judge, and to make a receiving order as of course, but must exercise its judicial discretion on hearing the case on its merits. *In re* ANDREWS. *Ex parte* ANDREWS　　-　　**15 Q. B. D. 335**

—— Deceased debtor—Administration in bankruptcy of insolvent estate—Transfer to County Court—46 & 47 Vict. c. 52, s. 125
[13 Q. B. D. 552
See BANKRUPTCY—DECEASED DEBTOR. 3.

XXVII. BANKRUPTCY—DECEASED DEBTOR.

1. —— Discovery of Debtor's Property—*Administration in Bankruptcy of Estate of Person dying Insolvent—Power to summon Person to be examined—Bankruptcy Act, 1883 (46 & 47 Vict. c. 52), ss. 27, 125—Rule 58 (Bankruptcy Rules, 1883).*] The provisions of s. 27 of the Bankruptcy Act, 1883, do not apply to an administration of the estate of a person dying insolvent under s. 125 of the Act.—There is no power in cases of such administration, either under s. 27 or under rule 58 (Bankruptcy Rules, 1883), to summon a person to be examined for the purpose of discovery of the deceased debtor's estate. *In re* HEWITT　　　　　　　**15 Q. B. D. 159**

2. —— Discretion of Court—*Administration of Insolvent Estate—Transfer to Court of Bankruptcy—Bankruptcy Act, 1883 (46 & 47 Vict. c. 52), s. 125.*] The power given by sect. 125 of the Bankruptcy Act, 1883, to transfer the proceedings in an action brought for the administration of an insolvent estate to the Court of Bankruptcy, is a discretionary one, and it will not be exercised where the estate is small, the number of creditors is small, and considerable expense has been already incurred in Chambers in the proceedings under an administration judgment.—*Semble,* that an application for transfer can only be made by a creditor who has absolutely proved his debt. *In re* WEAVER. HIGGS. *v.* WEAVER　　-　　　　**29 Ch. D. 236**

3. —— Ex parte Application—*Administration in Bankruptcy of Insolvent Estate—Transfer of Administration Proceedings from High Court to County Court—Bankruptcy Act, 1883 (46 & 47 Vict. c. 52), s. 125, sub-ss. 1, 2, 3, 4, 5—Bankruptcy Forms, 1883, Nos. 11, 31, 32.*] When proceedings for the administration of a deceased debtor's estate have been commenced in the Chancery Division of the High Court, and an order has been made, under sub-sect. 4 of sect. 125 of the Bankruptcy Act, 1883, for the transfer of the proceedings to the Court exercising jurisdiction in bankruptcy, that Court may make an administration order on an ex parte application by a creditor, but the order cannot be made until the expiration of two months from the date of the grant of probate or letters of administration, unless with the concurrence of the legal personal representative, or unless it is proved that the debtor

XXVII. BANKRUPTCY—DECEASED DEBTOR —*continued.*

committed an act of bankruptcy within three months prior to his decease. *Ex parte* MAY. *In re* MAY　　　　　　　**13 Q. B. D. 552**

XXVIII. BANKRUPTCY—APPEAL.

(a.) BANKRUPTCY ACT, 1869.

1. —— Interpleader Order—*Rehearing—1 & 2 Will. 4, c. 58, s. 6—1 & 2 Vict. c. 45, s. 2—Common Law Procedure Act, 1860 (23 & 24 Vict. c. 126), ss. 14, 17—Bankruptcy Act, 1869 (32 & 33 Vict. c. 71), ss. 65, 71—Bankruptcy Rules, 1870, r. 50—Sheriff—Interpleader—Costs.*] Any order in interpleader made by the Chief Judge in Bankruptcy can be appealed from.—The proper mode for the sheriff to apply to the Court of Bankruptcy for an interpleader order under the Act 1 & 2 Will. 4, c. 58, is by motion, of which notice is served on the claimants, and on the hearing of the motion the Court can determine their rights, without first making an order that they attend and interplead.—A person against whom an order is made on his default in appearing may appeal from the order on its merits.—*Dodds v. Shepherd* (1 Ex. D. 75) considered.—On the hearing of a motion by a sheriff in the Court of Bankruptcy for an interpleader order, one of the claimants was represented by the managing clerk of his solicitors, who was not himself a solicitor. The Registrar, supposing him to be a solicitor, allowed him to cross-examine the witnesses on the other side, but, when he discovered the mistake, he declined to hear him as an advocate, and decided against his client, and he afterwards refused an application by the client for a rehearing:—*Held,* that the Registrar ought to have adjourned the case to give the client an opportunity of being represented by counsel or a solicitor, and that the client was entitled to a rehearing.—The sheriff's costs of the appeal were ordered to be paid by the party who should ultimately be decided to be in the wrong. *Ex parte* STREETER. *In re* MORRIS　　-　　　-　　**19 Ch. D. 216**

2. —— Locus Standi—*Appeal by Trustee in Bankruptcy—Removal of Trustee before Hearing—Refusal of New Trustee to prosecute Appeal —Costs.*] The trustee in a bankruptcy presented an appeal against the admission of a proof. Before the appeal came on for hearing the Appellant had been removed from his office, and a new trustee appointed, who declined to prosecute the appeal:—*Held,* that the Appellant had no locus standi, but that the appeal must stand over for a fortnight to give the creditors an opportunity of prosecuting it. At the end of the fortnight no creditor had adopted the appeal: —*Held,* that the appeal must be dismissed, and that the Respondent was entitled to have his costs paid out of the deposit, but that no personal order for costs could be made against the Appellant. *Ex parte* SHEARD. *In re* POOLEY (No. 2)　　　　　　　**16 Ch. D. 110**

3. —— Notice—*Debtor not shewing Cause against Petition — Substituted Service — Jurisdiction — Bankruptcy Rules, 1870, rr. 36, 37.*] When a debtor gives no notice under rule 36 of his intention to shew cause against a bankruptcy petition, and the petition is consequently heard

XXVIII. BANKRUPTCY—APPEAL—*continued.*

(a.) BANKRUPTCY ACT, 1869—*continued.*

in his absence, and the Court refuses to make an adjudication, if the petitioning creditor desires to appeal against the refusal he must serve notice of the appeal on the debtor.—In a proper case the Court of Appeal has jurisdiction to make an order for substituted service of a notice of appeal, though no express provision to that effect is contained in the Rules of Court. *Ex parte* WARBURG. *In re* WHALLEY　　-　　**24 Ch. D. 364**

4. —— Notice—*Registrar—Ex parte Appeal.*] Notice of an appeal from a Registrar acting as Chief Judge ought not (even if it is *ex parte*) to be addressed to or served on the Registrar. Notice of an *ex parte* appeal was addressed to and served on the Registrar, and he appeared by counsel on the hearing :—*Held*, that the Appellant ought not to be ordered to pay the Registrar's costs. *Ex parte* IZARD. *In re* MOIR　　**20 Ch. D. 703**

5. —— Rehearing—*Limit of Time—Refusal of Adjudication—Debtor's Summons—Judgment Debt—Statement of Consideration—Amendment of Petition—Affidavit—Bankruptcy Act*, 1869 (32 & 33 Vict. c. 71), s. 71—*Bankruptcy Rules*, 1870, r. 143—*Rules of Court*, 1875, Order LVIII., r. 15.] Though as a general rule a rehearing of a bankruptcy matter ought not to be allowed after the expiration of the time limited for appealing from the order, yet, there being no time fixed by the Act or the Rules for applying for a rehearing, the Court will on special grounds allow a rehearing when it is applied for after the expiration of the time for appealing, even when the application is to rehear a bankruptcy petition which has been dismissed.—But, *semble*, that an application for a rehearing should not be made ex parte.— When a debtor's summons is founded on a judgment debt it is not necessary to state the consideration for the judgment in the summons, and a misstatement of the consideration will not vitiate the summons.—When a bankruptcy petition is amended under an order of the Court the Judge has a discretion as to requiring the amendment to be verified by affidavit, and if the alteration is an immaterial one an affidavit will not be required. *Ex parte* RITSO. *In re* RITSO　　**[22 Ch. D. 529**

6. —— Time for Appeal—*From County Court —Notice to Registrar—" Forthwith "—Bankruptcy Rules*, 1870, rr. 143, 144.] When an act is required by a statute or a rule of Court to be done " forthwith," the word "forthwith " must be construed with regard to the object of the provision and the circumstances of the case.—The London agents of the country solicitors of an appellant from an order made by a County Court in bankruptcy entered the appeal with the Registrar of Appeals in London on Friday, the 5th of August, the last possible day, but did not post a copy of the appeal notice to the country solicitors until the following day, and it was not received by them until Monday, the 8th of August, and on that day they sent a copy of the notice to the Registrar of the County Court :—*Held*, that the copy of the notice had not been sent to the Registrar of the County Court " forthwith." on entering the appeal as required by rule 144, and

XXVIII. BANKRUPTCY—APPEAL—*continued.*

(a.) BANKRUPTCY ACT, 1869—*continued.*

that consequently the appeal was out of time. *Ex parte* LAMB. *In re* SOUTHAM　　**19 Ch. D. 169**

7. —— Time for Appeal—*From County Court —Payment of Deposit "at or before" entry of Appeal — Mistake of Officer of Court — Bankruptcy Rules*, 1870, r. 145—*Bankruptcy Rules, Nov.* 1878, r. 2.] The practice laid down in *Ex parte* Rosenthal (20 Ch. D. 315) that before entering an appeal in bankruptcy the Registrar ought now to give a direction to the Bank of England to receive the deposit payable on the entry, and not to enter the appeal until he receives from the Bank a certificate that the money has been paid, applies to appeals from the Chief Judge to the Court of Appeal, as well as to appeals from a County Court to the Chief Judge. —A notice of appeal from an order made by the Chief Judge on the 24th of April was taken to the office of the Registrar of Appeals on the 28th of April. The Registrar's clerk entered the appeal, and gave a direction to the Bank to receive the deposit. The money was paid to the Bank on the 8th of May. The certificate of the Bank of the payment was then taken to the Registrar's office, but the clerk made no further entry of the appeal : —*Held*, that the clerk had made a mistake in entering the appeal before receiving the Bank's certificate of the payment of the deposit, but that as there had been no default on the part of the Appellant the appeal could be entertained. *Ex parte* LUXON. *In re* PIDSLEY　-　**20 Ch. D. 701**

8. —— Time for Appeal—*From County Court —Payment of Deposit—Formal Defect or Irregularity—Bankruptcy Act,*1869 (32 & 33 Vict. c. 71), ss. 71, 82—*Bankruptcy Rules*, 1870, r. 145—*Bankruptcy Rules, Nov.* 1878, r. 2.] Rule 2 of November, 1878, has not altered the requirement of rule 145 of 1870, that the deposit on an appeal from a County Court shall be paid " at or before the time of entering " the appeal:—*Semble*, however, that the payment would be in time if it was made at the earliest possible moment after the entry of the appeal.—An appeal was entered on the 17th of February, but the deposit was not paid till the 6th of March :—*Held*, that this was not a formal defect or an irregularity which could be cured under the power given to the Court by sect. 82, and that the appeal could not be entertained.— Having regard to rule 2 of November, 1878, the proper practice now is for the Registrar, before entering an appeal, to give a direction to the Bank of England to receive the deposit on the appeal, and, after receiving a certificate from the bank that the money has been paid, to enter the appeal. *Ex parte* ROSENTHAL. *In re* DICKINSON　　**[20 Ch. D. 315**

9. —— Time for Appeal—*From County Court —Reckoning of Time—Bankruptcy Rules*, 1870, r. 143—*Bankruptcy Rule of 26th May*, 1873—*Rules of Court*, 1875, Order LVIII., rr. 9, 15.] Notwithstanding the rules under the Judicature Acts, the time for appealing to the Chief Judge from an order made in a bankruptcy matter by a County Court is still regulated by the Bankruptcy Rules. And, in reckoning the twenty-one days allowed by rule 143 of the Bankruptcy Rules, 1870, for appealing, Sundays are, by virtue

XXVIII. BANKRUPTCY—APPEAL—*continued.*

(a.) BANKRUPTCY ACT, 1869—*continued.*

of the Rule in Bankruptcy of the 26th of May, 1873, not to be taken into account. *Ex parte* HALL. *In re* ALVEN - - **16 Ch. D. 501**

(b.) BANKRUPTCY ACT, 1883.

10. —— Committal—*Judgment Summons — Judgment under £50—Appeal from Judge of High Court—Court of Appeal—Bankruptcy Act, 1883 (46 & 47 Vict. c. 52), ss. 103, 104—Debtors Act, 1869 (32 & 33 Vict. c. 62), s. 5.*] Under the Bankruptcy Act, 1883, s. 103—which enables the jurisdiction under sect. 5 of the Debtors Act, 1869, to be delegated to and exercised by the bankruptcy registrars of the High Court, and sect. 104, by which in bankruptcy matters, an appeal lies from the order of the High Court to the Court of Appeal—an appeal from an order of the judge having jurisdiction in bankruptcy respecting the commitment of a judgment debtor must be made to the Court of Appeal and not to the Divisional Court. GENESE *v.* LASCELLES **13 Q. B. D. 901**

11. —— Preliminary Objection — *Notice — Costs.*] Where the Respondent to an appeal intends to take a preliminary objection he should give notice to the Appellant of his intention so to do. If no such notice is given and the objection prevails, the appeal will be dismissed without costs. *In re* SPEIGHT - **13 Q. B. D. 42**

12. —— Preliminary Objection — *Notice — Costs.*] A respondent to an appeal who intends to rely on a preliminary objection ought to give notice to the appellant of his intention so to do.—If he does not, and the objection is successful, the appeal will be dismissed without costs.—*In re Speight* (13 Q. B. D. 42) followed. *Ex parte* BLEASE. *In re* BLINKHORN **[14 Q. B. D. 123**

13. —— Preliminary Objection — *Notice — Costs.*] The solicitor of a respondent, if he is aware of a preliminary objection to an appeal, ought, as a matter of courtesy, to inform his opponent of it without delay, but the omission to do so is not, if the appeal is dismissed on the preliminary objection, a sufficient reason for depriving the respondent of the costs of the appeal.—*In re Speight* (13 Q. B. D. 42), and *Ex parte Blease* (14 Q. B. D. 123) not followed. *Ex parte* SHEAD. *In re* MUNDY - - **15 Q. B. D. 338**

14. —— Rejection of Proof—*Trustee—Notice of Motion—Bankruptcy Rules, 1883, rr. 19, 174.*] If a creditor desires to appeal against the rejection of his proof by the trustee he must give notice of motion in the usual way under rule 19 of the Bankruptcy Rules, 1883, and within the twenty-one days limited by the 174th rule. The old practice of applying to the Court, in the first instance, to fix a time and day for hearing such an application no longer obtains. *In re* GILLESPIE. *Ex parte* MORRISON - **14 Q. B. D. 385**

XXIX. BANKRUPTCY—COSTS.

(a.) BANKRUPTCY ACT, 1869.

1. —— Solicitor of Trustee—*Right to Costs out of Estate—Discretion of Court—Improper Conduct —Abuse of Bankruptcy Law—Taxation of Costs— Power of Court to go behind Allocatur.*] The right of the solicitor of a trustee in bankruptcy

XXIX. BANKRUPTCY—COSTS—*continued.*

(a.) BANKRUPTCY ACT, 1869—*continued.*

to be paid his costs out of the bankrupt's estate is only the right of his client, the trustee; he has no independent right. If either the trustee or the solicitor has been guilty of misconduct, the Court can refuse to allow the solicitor's costs to be paid out of the estate, and this notwithstanding that the costs have been taxed and an allocatur has been made by the Taxing Master.—It is an abuse of the bankruptcy law to purchase a debt due by a bankrupt in order so procure the appointment of a trustee favourable to the bankrupt or to a creditor or a particular class of creditors, or to purchase a debt for the purpose of making the debtor (e.g., the trustee in a bankruptcy) a bankrupt with the view, not of recovering the debt, but of putting pressure upon him for a collateral object, or of injuring him in some way.—*Ex parte Griffin* (12 Ch. D. 480) approved and followed.—The trustee in a bankruptcy and his solicitor having been engaged in transactions of this kind, the Court, after taxation of the solicitor's costs, refused to allow them to be paid out of the bankrupt's estate. *Ex parte* HARPER. *In re* POOLEY **[20 Ch. D. 685**

(b.) BANKRUPTCY ACT, 1883.

2. —— Between Solicitor and Client—*Bankruptcy Rules, 1883, r. 98.*] Rule 98 of the Bankruptcy Rules, 1883, only empowers the Court to direct that costs shall be taxed and paid as between solicitor and client at the time when the order is made awarding the costs. If such a direction is not given at that time, the Court has no power to give it subsequently. *Ex parte* SHOOLBRED. *In re* ANGELL **14 Q. B. D. 298**

3. —— Costs of Taxation—*Solicitor to Trustee in Bankruptcy—6 & 7 Vict. c. 73, ss. 37, 38, 39.*] Under an ordinary reference to tax the costs of the solicitor to a trustee in bankruptcy the taxation is regulated by the practice of the Court of Bankruptcy, and the provisions of the Act 6 & 7 Vict. c. 73, have no application.—There is no rule in the Court of Bankruptcy that, if on such a taxation the amount of the solicitor's bill is reduced by more than one-sixth, he is to pay the costs of the taxation. *Ex parte* MARSH. *In re* MARSH **[15 Q. B. D. 340**

4. —— Official Receiver—*Appeal.*] An order made by a county court, on the application of the official receiver setting aside a payment made by a debtor as a fraudulent preference, having been reversed on appeal:—*Held,* that the costs of the appellants and of the official receiver, in both courts, must be paid out of the debtor's assets, the costs of the appellants having priority. *Ex parte* LEICESTERSHIRE BANKING COMPANY. *In re* DALE - - - **14 Q. B. D. 48**

5. —— Petitioner's Costs—*Bankruptcy Petition—Costs incidental to second Meeting of Creditors—" Proceeding in Court"—Jurisdiction— Bankruptcy Act, 1883 (46 & 47 Vict. c. 52), s. 105, sub-s. 1—Bankruptcy Rules, 1883, rr. 100, 105.*] The second meeting of creditors under a bankruptcy petition (held to consider the confirmation of a scheme of arrangement of the debtor's affairs accepted at the first meeting) is not a " proceeding in court " within the meaning of sub-sect. 1 of

XXIX. BANKRUPTCY—COSTS—*continued.*

(b.) BANKRUPTCY ACT, 1883—*continued.*

sect. 105 of the Bankruptcy Act, 1883, and the Court has no power to order the costs of the petitioner incidental to that meeting to be paid out of the debtor's estate.—But the Court has power to order the petitioner's costs incidental to the public examination of the debtor to be paid out of the estate. *Ex parte* THE BOARD OF TRADE. *In re* STRAND - - - 13 Q. B. D. 492

6. —— **Sheriff's Fees**—*Poundage*—"*Costs of Execution*"—*Bankruptcy Act, 1883, s. 46, sub-ss. 1, 2.*] When the bankruptcy of a judgment debtor supervenes after seizure, but before sale, by the sheriff under a writ of fi. fa., the sheriff is not entitled to poundage under the words "costs of execution" in sub-sect. 1 of sect. 46 of the Bankruptcy Act, 1883. *In re* LUDMORE 13 Q. B. D. 415

—— Costs of trustee—Annulment of bankruptcy [22 Ch. D. 436 *See* BANKRUPTCY—ANNULMENT. 1.

XXX. BANKRUPTCY—EVIDENCE.

1. —— **Cross-examination on Affidavit**—*Right to withdraw Affidavit.*] Held (in accordance with a certificate of the Registrars of the London Court of Bankruptcy), that, according to the practice of that Court, when an affidavit has been filed by one of the parties to an application, the opposite party is not entitled to cross-examine the deponent on the affidavit, until it has been read on behalf of the party who has filed it. That party has a right, if he pleases, not to make use of the affidavit, and, if he does not use it, the deponent cannot be cross-examined on it:—*Per* Jessel. M.R.: In the High Court the deponent could be cross-examined, even if the affidavit was not used by the party who filed it. *Ex parte* CHILD. *In re* OTTAWAY - 20 Ch. D. 126

2. —— **Examination as to Bankrupt's Property**—*Jurisdiction to order Account—Bankruptcy Act, 1869 (32 & 33 Vict. c. 71), ss. 96, 97.*] Under sects. 96 and 97 of the Bankruptcy Act, 1869, the Court of Bankruptcy has no jurisdiction to order a witness to furnish an account in writing (not on oath) of money transactions between himself and the bankrupt, or property of the bankrupt received by him. *Ex parte* REYNOLDS. *In re* REYNOLDS [21 Ch. D. 601

3. —— **Examination as to Bankrupt's Property**—*Production of Documents—Discretion of Court—Bankruptcy Act, 1869 (32 & 33 Vict. c. 71), s. 96.*] In determining whether an order for the production of documents should be made under sect. 96 of the Bankruptcy Act, 1869, the Court has to exercise a discretion.—From the examination of a person summoned for examination under sect. 96, at the instance of the trustee of a bankrupt, it appeared that a policy of insurance on the life of the bankrupt's wife, which had been effected by her before her marriage with the bankrupt, and which had been after the marriage assigned by the husband and wife to trustees, on trust for the wife for her separate use, had after the bankruptcy been assigned by way of mortgage, by a deed to which the bankrupt and his wife were parties; that the mortgage had been afterwards transferred to the witness; and that the wife had subsequently executed a deed assigning the equity of redemp-

XXX. BANKRUPTCY—EVIDENCE—*continued.*

tion to him :—*Held*, that the witness must produce the mortgage deed, the deed of transfer, and the deed of assignment. *Ex parte* TATTON. *In re* THORP - - - - 17 Ch. D. 512

4. —— **Examination of Creditor**—*Composition—Jurisdiction—Bankruptcy Act, 1869 (32 & 33 Vict. c. 71), ss. 96, 125, 126—Bankruptcy Rules, 1870, rr. 166, 171.*] Sect 96 of the Bankruptcy Act, 1869, has no application to composition proceedings.—Decision of Bacon, C.J., reversed. *Ex parte* WILLEY. *In re* WRIGHT - 23 Ch. D. 118

5. —— **Examination of Creditor**—*Right to Copy of Depositions—32 & 33 Vict. c. 96—Bankruptcy Rules, 1870, rr. 9, 12.*] The Court has a discretion whether to give a copy of the short-hand notes of the deposition of a witness examined under sect. 96 of the Bankruptcy Act, 1869, but where a creditor has been so examined he was allowed a copy. *Ex parte* PRATT. *In re* HAYMAN - - - - 21 Ch. D. 439

6. —— **Notarial Certificate**—*Affidavit sworn Abroad—British Vice-consul—18 & 19 Vict. c. 42, ss. 1, 2, 3 — Bankruptcy Act, 1883, s. 135 — Schedule I., r. 14—Bankruptcy Rules, 1883, r. 50.*] When an affidavit or proof in bankruptcy is sworn abroad before a British consul, or vice-consul, a notarial certificate in verification of the signature and qualification of the consul, or vice-consul, is not required.—The notarial certificate is only required when such an affidavit or proof is sworn before a foreign functionary. *In re* MAGEE. *Ex parte* MAGEE - - 15 Q. B. D. 332

7. —— **Service of Copy of Deposition**—*Costs—Bankruptcy Rules, 1870, r. 50.*] A deposition of a witness, taken in the Court of Bankruptcy for one purpose, and filed, may be used against him as an admission in any other proceeding in the matter of the same bankruptcy.—But when a party to an application in the Court of Bankruptcy gives notice to his opponent of his intention to use as evidence on the hearing of the application a deposition which is on the file, though it was originally taken for another purpose, he ought not to serve his opponent with a copy of it, and if he does so, will not, though successful on the application, be allowed the costs of the copy thus served. *Ex parte* HALL. *In re* COOPER - 19 Ch. D. 580

XXXI. BANKRUPTCY—LIQUIDATION (ACT OF 1869).

1. —— **Adjudication**—*After Liquidation Petition—Power to adjudicate Debtor a Bankrupt—Bankruptcy Act, 1869 (32 & 33 Vict. c. 71), s. 125, sub-s. 12.*] The power given to the Court by sect. 125, sub-sect. 12 of the Bankruptcy Act, 1869, to adjudge a debtor who has filed a liquidation petition a bankrupt, may be exercised even though no liquidation or composition resolutions have been passed by the creditors. *Ex parte* WALKER. *In re* McHENRY - - - 22 Ch. D. 813

2. —— **After Adjudication**—*Subsequent Registration of Resolution for Liquidation or Composition—Bankruptcy Act, 1869, ss. 28, 80, sub-s. 10—Bankruptcy Rules, 1870, r. 266.*] The Registrar has no power to register a resolution for liquidation or composition after an adjudication of bankruptcy has been made; unless the adjudication has been

XXXI. BANKRUPTCY — LIQUIDATION (ACT OF 1869)—*continued.*

made under rule 266 of the Bankruptcy Rules, 1870, in which case the adjudication is intended to be merely ancillary to the liquidation.—*Ex parte Davis* (2 Ch. D. 231) overruled. *In re* STANLEY. *Ex parte* MILWARD   **16 Ch. D. 256**

3. —— **After Adjudication**—*Subsequent Resolutions for Liquidation by Arrangement—Vesting of Debtor's Property—Bankruptcy Act, 1869, ss. 17, 28, 83 (sub-s. 6), 125—Bankruptcy Rules, 1870, r. 266.*] After an ordinary adjudication of bankruptcy has been made (not an adjudication merely for the purpose of protecting the debtor's property pending proceedings for liquidation or composition) the creditors have no power to pass resolutions for either liquidation or composition, and such resolutions if passed will be inoperative.— *Ex parte Milward* (16 Ch. D. 256) explained and followed. *Ex parte* BENNETT. *In re* WARD
[**16 Ch. D. 541**

4. —— **Appointment of Trustee** — *Lapse of more than Six Months from filing of Petition— Bankruptcy Act, 1869 (32 & 33 Vict. c. 71), ss. 6, 125, sub-s. 7.*] A trustee can be appointed by the creditors under a liquidation petition, though more than six months have elapsed since the filing of the petition.—*Ex parte Fenning* (3 Ch. D. 455) discussed.—The last clause of sub-sect. 7 of sect. 125 relates only to the effect of the appointment of a trustee under a liquidation after he has been appointed, and does not impose on the making of the appointment any limitation similar to that which by sect. 6 is imposed on the making of an adjudication of bankruptcy, viz., that the act of bankruptcy on which the adjudication is founded must have occurred within six months before the presentation of the petition for adjudication. *Ex parte* CREDIT COMPANY. *In re* McHENRY   -   **24 Ch. D. 353**

5. —— **Close of Liquidation** — *Discharge of Debtor—Sale of Estate to Trustee—Right to after-acquired Property — Costs — Appeal for Costs— Bankruptcy Act, 1869 (32 & 33 Vict. c. 71), ss. 20, 28, 125.*] The creditors of a liquidating debtor in 1877 passed a special resolution authorizing the sale of his estate to the trustee at such a price as would pay a dividend of 5s. in the pound to the creditors, and also the costs of the liquidation. The resolution was sanctioned by the Court, and was carried out by the trustee. The debtor was not a party to the arrangement, and did not know of it for some time afterwards. The creditors did not pass any formal resolution fixing the close of the liquidation, or granting the debtor a discharge, but he commenced another business. In 1881 this came to the knowledge of the trustee, and he thereupon took possession of the debtor's stock-in-trade, claiming it on behalf of the creditors under the liquidation :—*Held*, that the resolution did not amount in substance to a close of the liquidation or a discharge of the debtor, and that consequently the trustee was entitled to the debtor's after-acquired property for the benefit of the creditors.—But, *held*, that under the circumstances, the costs might properly be the subject of appeal, and that the debtor's costs must be paid out of the estate, and (reversing the decision of Bacon, C.J.) that the trustee's costs must also

XXXI. BANKRUPTCY — LIQUIDATION (ACT OF 1869)—*continued.*

be allowed out of the estate.—*Ex parte Tinker* (Law Rep. 9 Ch. 716) distinguished. *Ex parte* WAINWRIGHT. *In re* WAINWRIGHT **19 Ch. D. 140**

6. —— **Failure to pass Resolutions**—*Delay— Power to adjudicate Debtor a Bankrupt—Pendency of Proceedings—Power to order fresh First Meeting of Creditors—Bankruptcy Act, 1869 (32 & 33 Vict. c. 71), s. 125, sub-s. 12.*] A debtor filed a liquidation petition in August, 1879. A receiver of his property was at once appointed, and injunctions were granted to restrain some of the creditors from proceeding against him for their debts. The first meeting of the creditors was held on the 20th of October, 1879, when it was resolved to adjourn to the 15th of December, 1879. Similar resolutions for adjournment were passed again and again, the meeting being ultimately, on the 15th of November, 1882, adjourned to the 28th of March, 1883. No resolutions for liquidation by arrangement or composition were passed. In January, 1883, two of the creditors applied to the Court of Bankruptcy by motion, under sub-sect. 12 of sect. 125 of the Bankruptcy Act, 1869, for an adjudication of bankruptcy against the debtor. At the adjourned meeting on the 28th of March, 1883, the creditors resolved that it was inexpedient in the interest of the creditors that any further proceedings should be taken under the petition, and that application should be made to the Court to discharge the receiver, and dismiss the petition, or stay all further proceedings under it. The Registrar, on the 3rd of May, made an adjudication. The debtor appealed, and on the hearing of the appeal an offer was made by a friend of his to pay the debts of the two creditors in full and to provide for their costs of the application, the payment to be made by the friend out of his own moneys, and an undertaking being given by him that neither directly nor indirectly should the payment be made out of the debtor's assets :—*Held*, that notwithstanding the resolution of the 28th of March, and having regard to the fact that the receiver had not been discharged the liquidation proceedings were still pending, and that if the adjudication order was discharged no other creditor would be injured, for that the Court would have jurisdiction to adjudicate the debtor a bankrupt on the application of any other creditor.—The adjudication was accordingly discharged on the terms of payment proposed, and on the undertaking of the debtor to apply to the Court of Bankruptcy for leave to summon a fresh first meeting of the creditors. —*Held*, by Baggallay and Cotton, L.JJ., and *semble* per Bowen, L.J., that the Court had jurisdiction to order a fresh first meeting of the creditors under the petition. *Ex parte* McHENRY. *In re* McHENRY -   -   **24 Ch. D. 35**

7. —— **Resolutions**—*Refusal of Registration —Power of Court to order Return of Stamp Duty paid on filing of Resolutions—Order of 1st January, 1870, as to Fees—Ex parte Appeal—Service on Registrar — Appearance by Counsel—Costs.*] When the registration of liquidation resolutions is refused, the Court has no power to order repayment of the ad valorem duty paid on the presentation of the resolutions for registration. The only mode of obtaining a return of the duty is by

XXXI. BANKRUPTCY — LIQUIDATION (ACT OF 1869)—*continued.*

a memorial to the Commissioners of Inland Revenue. Notice of an appeal from a Registrar acting as Chief Judge ought not (even if it is ex parte) to be addressed to or served on the Registrar. Notice of an ex parte appeal was addressed to and served on the Registrar, and he appeared by counsel on the hearing:—*Held*, that the Appellant ought not to be ordered to pay the Registrar's costs. *Ex parte* IZARD. *In re* MOIR
[20 Ch. D. 703

8. —— Resolutions — *Registration — Locus Standi to oppose*—"*Creditor*"—*Bankruptcy Act, 1869 (32 & 33 Vict. c. 71), s. 125 — Bankruptcy Rules, 1870, rr. 67, 70, 271, 295.*] Upon the hearing of an application to register liquidation resolutions no one has a locus standi to be heard in opposition but a creditor who has previously proved a debt in the mode prescribed by the rules. —A person who claims to be a creditor, and in that character to oppose the registration, cannot prove his debt when he comes before the Registrar to oppose. If he has not previously proved a debt he cannot be heard. *Ex parte* BAGSTER. *In re* BAGSTER　　-　　24 Ch. D. 477

9. —— Resolutions — *Registration — Small Amount of Assets—Bona fides of Creditors—Opposition by Judgment Creditor— Bankruptcy Act, 1869 (32 & 33 Vict. c. 71), s. 125—Bankruptcy Rules, 1870, r. 295.*] The statement of affairs of a debtor who had filed a liquidation petition showed that his debts were £1759 and his assets £85, the latter sum being subject to a deduction in respect to preferential debts. The creditors resolved upon a liquidation by arrangement, and gave the debtor an immediate discharge. They also voted £10 for the remuneration of the trustee. The registration of the resolutions was opposed by a creditor who had brought an action against the debtor for £182, but who had been restrained from proceeding with this action. He was in a position to sign judgment and issue execution so soon as the injunction should be dissolved :—*Held* (by Bacon, C.J., and by the Court of Appeal), that, notwithstanding the small amount of the assets, the resolutions ought to be registered, the contest being really whether the assets, such as they were, should be distributed among the creditors generally, or be swept away by the judgment creditor, and this although the judgment creditor offered in the Court of Appeal to undertake to present a bankruptcy petition against the debtor.—*Ex parte* EARLY (13 Ch. D. 300) followed.—*Ex parte Staff* (Law Rep. 20 Eq. 775) and *Ex parte Russell* (Law Rep. 10 Ch. 255) distinguished. *Ex parte* MATHEWES. *In re* SHARPE
[16 Ch. D. 655

10. —— Statement of Affairs — *Distinction between Joint and Separate Debts and Assets— Debtor formerly in Partnership—Registration of Resolutions—Bankruptcy Act, 1869 (32 & 33 Vict. c. 71), s. 125—Bankruptcy Rules, 1870, rr. 287, 295.*] A debtor, who in his liquidation petition describes himself as having been formerly in partnership, ought in his statement of affairs to distinguish between his joint and separate debts and assets, or to state expressly that no debts and no assets of the former partnership exist.—If the

---

XXXI. BANKRUPTCY—LIQUIDATION (ACT OF 1869)—*continued.*

statement of affairs fails to do this, resolutions passed by the creditors under the petition ought not to be registered.—The statement of affairs ought not to be supplemented by affidavits filed after the meeting of the creditors. *Ex parte* BUCKLEY. *In re* BUCKLEY　　16 Ch. D. 513

11. —— Statement of Affairs—*Sufficiency— Debtor in Partnership—Solvent Partner—Bankruptcy Act, 1869 (32 & 33 Vict. c. 71), ss. 125, 126.*] A debtor who carries on one business alone, and another in partnership, must when he files a liquidation petition (his partner being solvent) set forth in his statement of affairs the assets and liabilities of the partnership business in detail, as well as his own separate assets and liabilities; i.e. in each case he must give the names of the creditors, with the amount due to each and the names of the debtors, with the amount due from each. He must also state the account between himself and his partner, so as to shew the balance (if any) due to him.—If he does not give these particulars, his statement of affairs will be insufficient, and any liquidation or composition resolutions founded on it cannot be registered.—If for any reason it is impossible for the debtor to make such a statement of the affairs of the partnership, he cannot have a liquidation of his affairs by arrangement or a composition, but must submit to bankruptcy.—If without setting out the above particulars in his statement of affairs, the debtor refers (in such a way as to incorporate it with his statement) to a report made by an accountant which contains the necessary information, and which is produced to the meetings of creditors,—*Semble*, that this would be a sufficient statement. *Ex parte* AMOR. *In re* AMOR
[21 Ch. D. 594

12. —— Statement of Affairs—*Time at which Interest should be calculated— Bankruptcy Act, 1869, s. 126—Bankruptcy Rules, 1870, rr. 77, 92, 274—Bankruptcy Forms, 1870, No. 39.*] In a debtor's statement of his affairs presented to the first meeting of his creditors under a liquidation petition under the Bankruptcy Act, 1869, he is bound only to shew the state of his affairs at the date of the filing of the petition, and is not, therefore, bound to calculate interest on interest-bearing debts beyond that date. *Ex parte* FEWINGS. *In re* SNEYD　　-　　25 Ch. D. 338

13. —— Transfer to Another Court—*Meetings of Joint and Separate Creditors — Bankruptcy Rules, 1870, rr. 285, 288.*] The proceedings under a liquidation petition filed by partners cannot be transferred from the Court in which they were commenced to another Court, unless a resolution directing the transfer is passed, not only by a general meeting of the joint creditors, but also by separate general meetings of the separate creditors of each partner.—Rule 285 applies to all cases in which meetings of creditors have to be held under a liquidation petition by partners, and in all such cases separate meetings must be held of the joint creditors and of the separate creditors of each partner. *Ex parte* HORROCKS. *In re* WOOD.
[19 Ch. D. 367

—— Assets—Chose in action—Notice　18 Ch. D.
See BANKRUPTCY—ASSETS.　15.　[381.

H

XXXII. BANKRUPTCY — COMPOSITION (ACT OF 1869).

1. —— "**Extraordinary Resolution**"—*Secured Creditor—Execution levied before Registration—Bankruptcy Act*, 1869 (32 & 33 *Vict.* c. 71), *s.* 126.] A non-assenting creditor of a compounding debtor under sect. 126 of the Bankruptcy Act, 1869, against whom no equity can be raised by reason of his personal conduct, can acquire a valid security for his debt by levying an execution on the debtor's goods at any time before the registration of the extraordinary resolution accepting the composition.—The resolution does not become an "extraordinary" one until it has been confirmed at the second meeting of the creditors, and it has no validity whatever until it is registered.—The mere fact that a judgment creditor, who is entered in the debtor's statement of affairs as having no security for his debt, is present in silence at the first meeting of the creditors, not proving his debt or taking any other part in the proceedings, will not raise an equity against him so as to prevent his levying an execution on his judgment, and thus acquiring a valid security for his debt before the registration of an extraordinary resolution accepting a composition. *Ex parte* MCLAREN. *In re* MCCOLLA　-　-　- 16 Ch. D. 534

2. —— *Resolutions—Registration—Presence of Debtor at Creditors' Meetings—Bankruptcy Act*, 1869 (32 & 33 *Vict.* c. 71), *s.* 126.] The meaning of sect. 126 of the Bankruptcy Act, 1869, is that the debtor must as a rule be personally present at the meetings of his creditors to consider a proposed composition, and personally produce his statement of affairs.—It is not sufficient that he should be in a room immediately adjoining that in which the meeting is held, ready to be called in if the creditors wish to examine him, even though the creditors are informed of this.—If he is not actually present in the room, he is bound to shew that he was prevented by sickness, or that the creditors, for some other cause satisfactory to them, excused his presence. If he does not do this, any resolutions passed accepting a composition will be invalid and cannot be registered.—*Ex parte Grunelins* (Weekly Notes (1876) 244) considered. *Ex parte* BEST. *In re* BEST [18 Ch. D. 488

3. —— *Resolutions—Registration—Examination of Debtor at Creditors' Meetings—Presence of Shorthand Writer—Duty of Chairman—Statement of Affairs—Insufficiency—Irregularity of Proceedings—Order to summon fresh Meeting—Bankruptcy Act*, 1869 (32 & 33 *Vict.* c. 71), s. 126—*Bankruptcy Rules*, 1870, rr. 208, 295.] Inasmuch as the answers given by a debtor to questions put to him at the meetings of his creditors under a liquidation petition form part of his statement of affairs, it is essential that a written record of those answers should be made, and therefore a creditor who desires to examine the debtor is entitled to have a shorthand writer present at the meeting to take notes of the examination, though, if several creditors wish to employ a shorthand writer, the meeting has power to limit the number who may be present.—It is no part of the duty of the chairman of the meeting to take notes of the debtor's examination.—Per Jessel, M.R.: If for any reason a debtor who files a liquidation

XXXII. BANKRUPTCY — COMPOSITION (ACT OF 1869)—*continued.*

petition is unable to produce a proper statement of his affairs, he cannot have a liquidation by arrangement or composition, but must submit to be made a bankrupt.—A meeting of creditors under a liquidation petition refused to allow a shorthand writer to be present on behalf of one of the creditors to take notes of the debtor's examination by him, and no note of the examination was taken. The debtor's written statement of his affairs was, in the opinion of the Court, grossly insufficient. Resolutions accepting a composition were passed by the statutory majority:—*Held*, that the proceedings were irregular, and that the resolutions ought not to be registered:—But *held*, that there being no proof of *mala fides*, and as the large majority of the creditors had shewn that they desired to have a composition, a fresh meeting ought to be summoned.—And leave was given to use at the fresh meeting the proofs and proxies which were already on the file.—*Ex parte Best* (18 Ch. D. 488) explained. *Ex parte* SOLOMON. *In re* TILLEY [20 Ch. D. 281

4. —— *Resolutions — Registration — Small Amount of Assets—Abuse of Process of Court—Bankruptcy Act*, 1869, s. 126—*Bankruptcy Rules*, 1870, r. 295.] The creditors of a debtor whose debts amounted to £304 18s., and whose assets were only £8 13s., resolved to accept a composition of 3d. in the pound, the payment of which was to be secured by one of the creditors. The registration of the resolutions was opposed by a dissentient creditor:—*Held*, that, having regard to the small amount of the composition, the resolutions must have been passed solely in the interest of the debtor; that they were an abuse of the process of the Court; and that they ought not to be registered.—Decision of Bacon, C.J., reversed. *Ex parte* RUSSELL. *In re* ROBINS [22 Ch. D. 778

5. —— *Resolutions — Registration — Small Amount of Assets—Security—Bona fides—Bankruptcy Act*, 1869 (32 & 33 *Vict.* c. 71), s. 126—*Bankruptcy Rules*, 1870, r. 295.] *Held*, that resolutions accepting a composition of 1s. in the pound ought to be registered, the debtor having no assets, but the payment of the composition being secured by a third person.—The question in all such cases is whether the creditors, in accepting the composition offered, have acted bonâ fide, *i.e.*, in the interest of the creditors, and not merely with a view to benefit the debtor.—There is no hard and fast line as to the amount of composition which may be accepted, except that the sum must not be so small that no reasonable man would accept it; for in such a case the amount would in itself be evidence of want of bona fides.—There is no absolute rule that a debtor who has no assets cannot file a liquidation petition.—*Ex parte Terrell* (4 Ch. D. 293) distinguished. *Ex parte* HUDSON. *In re* WALTON [22 Ch. D. 773

6. —— *Resolutions — Registration — Small Amount of Composition—Abuse of Procedure of Court—Bankruptcy Act*, 1869 (32 & 33 *Vict.* c. 71), s. 126—*Bankruptcy Rules*, 1870, r. 295.] The statement of affairs of a debtor, who had

XXXII. BANKRUPTCY—COMPOSITION (ACT OF 1869)—*continued.*

filed a liquidation petition, shewed that his debts amounted to £1293, and that he had no assets. At the first meeting of his creditors he admitted in answer to questions put to him that he was in the receipt of a salary of £5 a week. The creditors resolved by the proper statutory majority to accept a composition of 6d. in the pound, to be paid within a month after the registration of the resolutions, and to be secured to the satisfaction of the chairman of the meeting. The resolutions were confirmed at the second meeting:—*Held,* that the proceedings were an abuse of the process of the Court, and that the resolutions ought not to be registered.—*Ex parte Staff* (Law Rep. 20 Eq. 775) approved. *Ex parte* BALL. *In re* PARNELL - - - **20 Ch. D. 670**

7. —— Resolutions—*Small Amount of Composition—Want of Bona fides — Registration—Duty of Registrar—Bankruptcy Act, 1869 (32 & 33 Vict. c. 71), s. 126—Bankruptcy Rules, 1870, r. 295.]* When the Registrar is satisfied, either from the small amount of composition offered or otherwise, that resolutions accepting a composition have been passed in the interest of the debtor, and not for the benefit of the creditors, it is his duty to refuse to register them, even though no creditor opposes the registration.—Resolutions accepting a composition of 2d. in the pound, payable in three months, and not secured in any way, were passed by the statutory majority of a debtor's creditors. His statement of affairs shewed that he had no assets:—*Held,* that the resolutions must have been passed in the interest of the debtor, not of the creditors : that they could not therefore bind the dissentient creditors; and that the Registrar was right in refusing to register them, though no creditor opposed the registration.—*Ex parte Elworthy* (Law Rep. 20 Eq. 742) not followed. *Ex parte* WILLIAMS - - - **18 Ch. D. 495**

8. —— Resolutions—*Vacating Registration—Bankruptcy Act, 1869 (32 & 33 Vict. c. 71), ss. 82, 127.]* A debtor will not be allowed, by delaying registration of the resolutions, to postpone payment of a composition which has been accepted by his creditors.—Accordingly a delay of more than three weeks, owing to non-payment by inadvertence of the fees for stamps in obtaining the registration of resolutions for a composition, is ground for vacating, on the application of a creditor, the registration. *Ex parte* WHITNALL. *In re* WHITNALL - - - **20 Ch. D. 438**

9. —— Statement of Affairs—*Creditor omitted—Application after Registration of Resolutions to admit Proof—Jurisdiction of Court—Bankruptcy Act, 1869 (32 & 33 Vict. c. 71), s. 126.]* After the registration of simple composition resolutions (by which no trustee is appointed for the receipt and distribution of the composition and no security is given for its payment) the proceedings are at an end, and the Court of Bankruptcy has no jurisdiction to entertain an application by a creditor, who was omitted from the debtor's statement of affairs, and who has taken no part in the proceedings, for the admission of a proof of his debt.—*Ex parte Carew* (Law Rep. 10 Ch. 308)

XXXII. BANKRUPTCY—COMPOSITION (ACT OF 1869)—*continued.*

explained and distinguished—*Breslauer* v, *Brown* (3 App. Cas. 672) explained.—Decision of Bacon, C.J., reversed. *Ex parte* LACEY. *In re* LACEY **[16 Ch. D. 131**

10. —— Statement of Affairs—*Misstatement of Debt—Action by Creditor—Injunction—Correction of Error—Delay—Bankruptcy Act, 1869 (32 & 33 Vict. c. 71), s. 126 — Bankruptcy Rules, 1870, r. 306.]* A liquidating debtor in his statement of affairs by mistake inserted the amount of the debt due by him to one of his creditors as £17, the amount being really £17 15s. :—*Held,* that the creditor was not bound by composition resolutions which were passed by the statutory majority, but to which he did not assent.—*Held,* also, that, after a delay of four months from the time when the debtor first became aware of the mistake, the Court would not restrain the creditor from proceeding with an action for the debt, even for the purpose of enabling the debtor to summon a general meeting of his creditors, under rule 306, in order to obtain their assent to the correction of the mistake in the statement of affairs.—*Per* Fry, L.J. : Whether, having regard to the negative words of sect. 126, an injunction could be in any case granted for such a purpose, *quære.—Burliner* v. *Royle* (5 C. P. D. 354) approved. *Ex parte* ENGELHARDT. *In re* ENGELHARDT **[23 Ch. D. 706**

11. —— Subsequent Agreement to pay one Creditor in Full—*Bankruptcy Act, 1869 (32 & 33 Vict. c. 71, s. 126.]* After composition resolutions under sect. 126 of the Bankruptcy Act, 1869, have been passed and registered, the debtor cannot, before the completion of the composition in accordance with the resolutions, enter into a valid agreement with one of the creditors who is bound by the resolutions, to pay him his debt in full even though the creditor agrees at the same time to give the debtor fresh credit.—Such an agreement would be inconsistent with good faith to the other creditors, and with the spirit of sect. 126.—The debtor does not stand in the same position as a discharged bankrupt until the composition has been fully paid.—*Jakeman* v. *Cook* (4 Ex. D. 26) distinguished, on the ground that there the debtor had obtained his discharge in a liquidation by arrangement. *Ex parte* BARROW. *In re* ANDREWS **[18 Ch. D. 464**

—— Annulment of bankruptcy.
 See Cases under BANKRUPTCY—ANNULMENT.

—— Proof under - - - **19 Ch. D. 394**
 See BANKRUPTCY—SECURED CREDITOR. 5.

BANKRUPTCY—Appellant - **10 App. Cas. 171**
 See SCOTCH LAW—PRACTICE. 1.

—— Assignee — Intestate — Administration de bonis non **6 P. D. 104**
 See ADMINISTRATOR—LIMITED. 1.

—— Australian—Real estate in England **[21 Ch. D. 674**
 See PARTITION SUIT—SALE. 2.

—— Bankrupt executor—One of two executors—Costs - - - **18 Ch. D. 516**
 See EXECUTOR—ACTIONS. 10.

BAPTISM—Register of—Date of birth
　　　　　　　　　　[29 Ch. D. 985
　　See EVIDENCE — DECLARATION BY DE-CEASED PERSON. 1.

BARE TRUSTEE—Vendor and Purchaser Act
　　　　　　　　　　[29 Ch. D. 693
　　See VENDOR AND PURCHASER—CONVEY-ANCE. 3.

BARGE-—" Ship or boat " - - 7 P. D. 126
　　See SHIP—SALVAGE. 8.

BARRATRY—Detention of ship for smuggling—Barratrous act of master—Warranty free from capture and seizure.
　　　[9 Q. B. D. 463; 8 App. Cas. 393
　　See INSURANCE, MARINE—POLICY. 3.

BARRIER—Covenant to leave—Coal mine
　　See MINE—LEASE. 2.　　[23 Ch. D. 81

BARRISTER—Law of Quebec—Remuneration
　　　　　　　　　　[9 App. Cas. 745
　　See COLONIAL LAW—CANADA—QUEBEC. 7.

BASTARDY.

1. —— Affiliation Order—*Arrears—Discretion of Justices to enforce Payment*—7 & 8 Vict. c. 101, s. 5—35 & 36 Vict. c. 65, s. 4.] By 7 & 8 Vict. c. 101, s. 5, all money payable under a bastardy order "shall be due and payable to the mother of the bastard child in respect of such time and so

BASTARDY—*continued.*

long as she lives. . . ." By 35 & 36 Vict. c. 65, s. 4, if it be made to appear to any one justice that any sum to be paid in pursuance of such order has not been paid, such justice may, by warrant, cause the putative father to be brought up before any two justices, and in case he neglect or refuse payment they may by warrant direct the sum to be recovered by distress, and may detain him until the return to the warrant of distress ; but if on the return, or by admission, it appear that no sufficient distress can be had, they may, if they see fit, cause him to be committed :—*Held,* by Grove, J., that the enforcement by the justices of the payment of sums due under such order is discretionary. By Huddleston, B., that the justices are bound to enforce it. DAVIES *v.* EVANS

[9 Q. B. D. 238

2.——**Maintenance Order**—*Marriage of Mother after making of Order—Liability of Putative Father.*] An order obtained by a single woman for the maintenance of a bastard child can be enforced against the putative father after the marriage of the mother. SOTHERON *v.* SCOTT

[6 Q. B. D. 518

3. —— **Maintenance Order**—*Marriage of Mother after making of Order—Liability of Putative Father — Ability of Husband to maintain Bastard Child.*] An order obtained by a woman for the maintenance of a bastard child can be enforced against the putative father after the marriage of the mother, although her husband is able to maintain the child. HARDY *v.* ATHERTON

[7 Q. B. D. 264

4. —— **Maintenance Order**—*Order made since 35 & 36 Vict. c. 65, for Payment until the Child attains the age of Sixteen or the Mother marries—Discretion of Justices to order Payment for less than Maximum Period.*] The justices have a discretion under 35 & 36 Vict. c. 65, to order weekly payments for the maintenance of a bastard child for a less period than the maximum period given by sect. 5 of the Act, and consequently, where the justices made an order for weekly payments until the child attained the age of sixteen or the mother married, such order was held not to be in force after the marriage of the mother. PEARSON *v.* HEYS - - 7 **Q. B. D. 260**

5. —— **Maintenance Order**—*Order for Payment until the Child attains the age of Thirteen or the Mother marries—Marriage of Mother—Power of Justices to make second Order after death of Husband.*] Upon the hearing of an affiliation summons the justices made an order under 35 & 36 Vict. c. 65, for the payment of a weekly sum until the child should attain the age of thirteen years or die, or the mother should marry. The mother married, and her husband died before the child attained the age of thirteen. The mother took out a fresh summons upon which the justices made an order for payment of a weekly allowance :—*Held* (Hawkins, J., doubting), that the matter was res judicata, and the second order was bad. WILLIAMS *v.* DAVIES - 11 **Q. B. D. 74**

6. —— **Service of Summons**—*Scotland—Jurisdiction of Justices where Putative Father resident in Scotland—Bastardy Laws Amendment Act, 1872 (35 & 36 Vict. c. 65)—Summary Jurisdiction (Process) Act, 1881 (44 & 45 Vict. c. 24), ss. 4, 6.*] The

BASTARDY—*continued.*

Summary Jurisdiction (Process) Act 1881 (44 & 45 Vict. c. 24) does not enable a bastardy summons to be issued by justices in England and served in Scotland upon the putative father domiciled and resident in Scotland ; and if a summons is so served and the putative father does not appear before the justices they have no jurisdiction to make a bastardy order against him.—So *held,* affirming the decision of the Court of Appeal. REG. *v.* THOMPSON. BERKLEY *v.* THOMPSON

[12 Q. B. D. 261 ; 10 App. Cas. 45

7. —— **Witness**—*Voluntary Attendance—Refusal to give Evidence — Power of Justices to commit—7 & 8 Vict. c. 101, s. 70—Bastardy Laws Amendment Act, 1872 (35 & 36 Vict. c. 65), s. 4.*] By 7 & 8 Vict. c. 101, s. 70, justices may, at the request of any party to bastardy proceedings before them, summon any person to appear and give evidence upon the matter of such proceedings, and if the person summoned neglect or refuse to appear the justice by warrant may require such person to be brought before him or any justices before whom such proceedings are to be had, " and if any person coming or brought before any such justice in any such proceedings refuse to give evidence thereon," the justices may commit such person to the house of correction :—*Held* (by Grove and Hawkins, JJ., Smith, J., dissenting), that the power to commit extended to any witness, and was not confined to witnesses who appeared in answer to a summons or warrant. THE QUEEN *v.* FLAVELL - 14 **Q. B. D. 364**

BASTARDY ORDERS—**Service of,** in Scotland

See JUSTICES—PRACTICE—*Statutes.*

BATH—Supply of water 25 **Ch. D. 443, 446, n.**

See WATERWORKS COMPANY—SUPPLY OF WATER. 3, 4.

BATHS AND WASH-HOUSES.

The Act 45 & 46 Vict. c. 30, amends and extends 9 & 10 Vict. c. 74, ss. 24 & 27, and gives increased facilities to local authorities for providing baths and wash-houses.

BEER—Duty—Brewer 10 **Q. B. D. 483**

See REVENUE—EXCISE.

—— Duty

See REVENUE—CUSTOMS—*Statutes.*
REVENUE—EXCISE—*Statutes.*

—— Sale of—Breach of covenant

[16 Ch. D. 645, 718

See LANDLORD AND TENANT—LEASE. 6, 7.

—— Sale of—Licence.

See Cases under INN—LICENCE.

BEER DEALERS RETAIL LICENCES AMENDMENT ACT, 1882.

See INN—LICENCE—*Statutes.*

BEERHOUSE—Covenant not to keep

[16 Ch. D. 645, 718

See LANDLORD AND TENANT—LEASE. 6, 7.

—— Covenant not to sell land for 19 **Ch. D. 258**

See COVENANT—RUNNING WITH LAND. 1.

BEGGING · - 12 **Q. B. D. 306**

See VAGRANT ACTS. 3.

BENEFICE—Mortgage—13 Eliz. c. 20

[30 Ch. D. 520

See MORTGAGE—CONTRACT. 3.

BENEFICE—*continued.*

—— Right of presentation — Consolidation —
    Quare impedit -   **15 Q. B. D. 432**
    See ADVOWSON. 2.

BETTING—Employment of agent to bet in his
    own name—Authority to pay bet.
    See GAMING. 1.   **[13 Q. B. D. 779**

—— Employment of agent to bet for principal—
    Action for the money received
        [15 Q. B. D. 363
    See PRINCIPAL AND AGENT—PRINCIPAL'S
    LIABILITY. 7.

—— Place used for betting.
    See Cases under GAMING. 4—7.

BICYCLE GROUND—Races—Betting—Liability
    of manager -   **13 Q. B. D. 377**
    See GAMING. 4.

BIGAMY—Evidence - - **11 Q. B. D. 118**
    See CRIMINAL LAW—BIGAMY. 2.

—— Presumption of duration of life
        [6 Q. B. D. 366
    See CRIMINAL LAW—BIGAMY. 1.

BILL OF COSTS.
    See Cases under SOLICITOR—BILL OF
    COSTS.

—— Charge on property recovered
    See Cases under SOLICITOR—LIEN. 1–7.

**BILL OF EXCHANGE (and PROMISSORY
NOTE):—**
               Col.
    I. STATUTES -   205
    II. ACCEPTANCE   231
    III. ALTERATION. - 231
    IV. CONSIDERATION - 232
    V. FOREIGN BILL - 233
    VI. LIABILITY OF PARTIES 233
    VII. SECURITIES FOR - 233
    VIII. TRANSFER. - 268

**I. BILL OF EXCHANGE (and PROMISSORY
NOTE)—STATUTES.**

The Act 45 & 46 Vict. c. 61 (the *Bills of Exchange Act,* 1882) repeals divers enactments (including the *Bills of Exchange Act,* 1878, and the
Crossed Cheques Act, 1876), and codifies the law
relating to bills of exchange, cheques, and promissory notes.

    1. *Bills of exchange.*
    2. *Cheques and crossed cheques.*
    3. *Dividend warrants.*
    4. *Promissory notes.*

General.] *Sect.* 2. *In the Act, unless the context otherwise requires,—*

" *Acceptance*" *means an acceptance completed
by delivery or notification.*

" *Action*" *includes counterclaim and set-off.*

" *Banker* " *includes a body of persons whether
incorporated or not who carry on the business
of banking.*

" *Bankrupt* " *includes any person whose estate is
vested in a trustee or assignee under the law
for the time being in force relating to bankruptcy.*

" *Bearer*" *means the person in possession of a
bill or note which is payable to bearer.*

" *Bill*" *means bill of exchange, and* "*note*"
means promissory note.

**I. BILL OF EXCHANGE (and PROMISSORY
NOTE)—STATUTES**—*continued.*

" *Delivery*" *means transfer of possession, actual
or constructive, from one person to another.*

" *Holder* " *means the payee or indorsee of a bill
or note who is in possession of it, or the bearer
thereof.*

" *Indorsement*" *means an indorsement completed
by delivery.*

" *Issue*" *means the first delivery of a bill or note,
complete in form to a person who takes it as
a holder.*

" *Person* " *includes a body of persons whether
incorporated or not.*

" *Value*" *means valuable consideration.*

" *Written*" *includes printed, and* "*writing*" *includes print.*

Sect. 90. *A thing is deemed to be done in good
faith, within the meaning of this Act, where it is
in fact done honestly, whether it is done negligently
or not.*

Sect. 91.—(1.) *Where, by this Act, any instrument or writing is required to be signed by any
person, it is not necessary that he should sign it
with his own hand, but it is sufficient if his signature is written thereon by some other person by or
under his authority.*

(2.) *In the case of a corporation, where, by this
Act, any instrument or writing is required to be
signed, it is sufficient if the instrument or writing
be sealed with the corporate seal.*

*But nothing in this section shall be construed as
requiring the bill or note of a corporation to be
under seal.*

Sect. 92. *Where, by this Act, the time limited for
doing any act or thing is less than three days, in
reckoning time, non-business days are excluded.*

" *Non-business days* " *for the purposes of this Act
mean—*

    (a.) *Sunday, Good Friday, Christmas Day* :
    (b.) *A bank holiday under the Bank Holidays
      Act,* 1871, *or Acts amending it* :
    (c.) *A day appointed by Royal proclamation
      as a public fast or thanksgiving day.*

Any other day is a business day.

Sect. 93. *For the purposes of this Act, where a
bill or note is required to be protested within a specified time or before some further proceeding is taken,
it is sufficient that the bill has been noted for protest
before the expiration of the specified time or the
taking of the proceeding ; and the formal protest
may be extended at any time thereafter as of the
date of the noting.*

Sect. 94. *Where a dishonoured bill or note is
authorized or required to be protested, and the services of a notary cannot be obtained at the place
where the bill is dishonoured, any householder or
substantial resident of the place may, in the presence of two witnesses, give a certificate, signed by
them, attesting the dishonour of the bill, and the
certificate shall in all respects operate as if it were
a formal protest of the bill.*

*The form given in Schedule I. of this Act may be
used with necessary modifications, and if used shall
be sufficient.*

Sect. 96 *repeals enactments mentioned in the
second schedule to this Act as from the commencement of this Act to the extent in that schedule mentioned* :

Provided that such repeal shall not affect any-

I. BILL OF EXCHANGE (and PROMISSORY NOTE)—STATUTES—*continued.*

thing done or suffered, or any right, title, or interest acquired or accrued before the commencement of the Act, or any legal proceeding or remedy in respect of any such thing, right, title, or interest.

Sect. 97.—(1.) *The rules in bankruptcy relating to bills of exchange, promissory notes, and cheques shall continue to apply thereto notwithstanding anything in this Act contained.*

(2.) *The rules of common law including the law merchant, save in so far as they are inconsistent with the express provisions of this Act, shall continue to apply to bills of exchange, promissory notes, and cheques.*

(3.) *Nothing in this Act, or in any repeal effected thereby, shall affect—*

(a.) *The provisions of the Stamp Act, 1870, or Acts amending it or any law or enactment for the time being in force relating to the revenue :*

(b.) *The provisions of the Companies Act, 1862, or Acts amending it, or any Act relating to joint stock banks or companies :*

(c.) *The provisions of any Act relating to or confirming the privileges of the Bank of England or the Bank of Ireland respectively :*

(d.) *The validity of any usage relating to dividend warrants or the indorsements thereof.*

Sect. 99. *Where any Act or document refers to any enactment repealed by this Act, the Act or document shall be construed and shall operate as if it referred to the corresponding provisions of this Act.*

1. BILLS OF EXCHANGE.

Form, Interpretation, and Acceptance.
Capacity and Authority of Parties.
Consideration.
Negotiation.
Registration.
Presentment for Acceptance and Notice of Dishonour.
Acceptance and Payment for Honour.
Liabilities of Parties.
Discharge, Alteration, and Cancellation, &c., of Bills.
Lost Bills.
Bills in a Set.
Conflict of Laws.

Form, Interpretation, and Acceptance.] *Sect.* 3. —(1.) *A bill of exchange is an unconditional order in writing, addressed by one person to another, signed by the person giving it, requiring the person to whom it is addressed to pay on demand or at a fixed or determinable future time a sum certain in money to or to the order of a specified person or to bearer.*

(2.) *An instrument which does not comply with these conditions, or which orders any act to be done in addition to the payment of money, is not a bill of exchange.*

(3.) *An order to pay out of a particular fund is not unconditional within the meaning of this section ; but an unqualified order to pay, coupled with* (a) *an indication of a particular fund out of which the drawee is to re-imburse himself or a particular account to be debited with the amount, or* (b) *a statement of the transaction which gives rise to the bill, is unconditional.*

(4.) *A bill is not invalid by reason—*

(a.) *That it is not dated :*

(b.) *That it does not specify the value given, or that any value has been given therefor :*

(c.) *That it does not specify the place where it is drawn, or the place where it is payable.*

Sect. 4.—(1.) *An inland bill is a bill which is or on the face of it purports to be* (a) *both drawn or payable within the British Islands, or* (b) *drawn within the British Islands upon some person resident therein. Any other bill is a foreign bill.*

For the purposes of the Act "British Islands" mean any part of the United Kingdom of Great Britain, the Channel Islands, and the Isle of Man.

(2.) *Unless the contrary appear on the face of the bill the holder may treat it as an inland bill.*

Sect. 5.—(1.) *A bill may be drawn payable to, or to the order of, the drawer ; or it may be drawn payable to, or to the order of, the drawee.*

(2.) *Where in a bill drawer and drawee are the same person, or where the drawee is a fictitious, person or a person not having capacity to contract, the holder may treat the instrument, at his option, either as a bill of exchange or as a promissory note.*

Sect. 6.—(1). *The drawee must be named or otherwise indicated in a bill with reasonable certainty.*

(2.) *A bill may be addressed to two or more drawees whether they are partners or not, but an order addressed to two drawees in the alternative or to two or more drawees in succession is not a bill of exchange.*

Sect. 7.—(1.) *Where a bill is not payable to bearer, the payee must be named or otherwise indicated therein with reasonable certainty.*

(2.) *A bill may be made payable to two or more payees jointly, or it may be made payable in the alternative to one of two, or one or some of several payees. A bill may also be made payable to the holder of an office for the time being.*

(3.) *Where the payee is a fictitious or non-existing person the bill may be treated as payable to bearer.*

Sect. 8.—(1.) *When a bill contains words prohibiting transfer, or indicating an intention that it should not be transferable, it is valid as between the parties thereto, but is not negotiable.*

(2.) *A negotiable bill may be payable either to order or to bearer.*

(3.) *A bill is payable to bearer which is expressed to be so payable, or on which the only or last indorsement is an indorsement in blank.*

(4.) *A bill is payable to order which is expressed to be so payable, or which is expressed to be payable to a particular person, and does not contain words prohibiting transfer or indicating an intention that it should not be transferable.*

(5.) *Where a bill, either originally or by indorsement, is expressed to be payable to the order of a specified person, and not to him or his order, it is nevertheless payable to him or his order at his option.*

Sect. 9.—(1.) *The sum payable by a bill is a sum certain within the meaning of this Act, although it is required to be paid—*

(a.) *With interest.*

(b.) *By stated instalments.*

I. BILL OF EXCHANGE (and PROMISSORY NOTE)—STATUTES—*continued.*

(c.) *By stated instalments, with a provision that upon default in payment of any instalment the whole shall become due.*

(d.) *According to an indicated rate of exchange, or according to a rate of exchange to be ascertained as directed by the bill.*

(2.) *When the sum payable is expressed in words and also in figures, and there is a discrepancy between the two, the sum denoted by the words is the amount payable.*

(3.) *Where a bill is expressed to be payable with interest, unless the instrument otherwise provides interest runs from the date of the bill, and if the bill is undated from the issue thereof.*

Sect. 10.—(1.) *A bill is payable on demand—*

(a.) *Which is expressed to be payable on demand or at sight, or on presentation, or*

(b.) *in which no time for payment is expressed.*

(2.) *When a bill is accepted or indorsed when it is overdue, it shall, as regards the acceptor who so accepts, or any indorser who so indorses it, be deemed a bill payable on demand.*

Sect. 11. *A bill is payable at a determinable future time within the meaning of this Act, which is expressed to be payable—*

(1.) *At a fixed period after date or sight.*

(2.) *On or at a fixed period after the occurrence of a specified event which is certain to happen though the time of happening may be uncertain.*

An instrument expressed to be payable on a contingency is not a bill, and the happening of the event does not cure the defect.

Sect. 12. *Where a bill expressed to be payable at a fixed period after date is issued undated, or where the acceptance of a bill payable at a fixed period after sight is undated, any holder may insert therein the true date of issue or acceptance, and the bill shall be payable accordingly.*

Provided that (1) *where the holder in good faith and by mistake inserts a wrong date, and* (2) *in every case where a wrong date is inserted, if the bill subsequently comes into the hands of a holder in due course the bill shall not be avoided thereby, but shall operate and be payable as if the date so inserted had been the true date.*

Sect. 13.—(1.) *Where a bill or an acceptance or any indorsement on a bill is dated, the date shall, unless the contrary be proved, be deemed to be the true date of the drawing, acceptance, or indorsement, as the case may be.*

(2.) *A bill is not invalid by reason only that it is ante-dated or post-dated, or that it bears date on a Sunday.*

Sect. 14. *Where a bill is not payable on demand the day on which it falls due is determined as follows :*

(1.) *Three days, called days of grace, are, in every case where the bill itself does not otherwise provide, added to the time of payment as fixed by the bill, and the bill is due and payable on the last day of grace : Provided that—*

(a.) *When the last day of grace falls on Sunday, Christmas Day, Good Friday, or a day appointed by Royal Proclamation as a public fast or thanksgiving day, the bill is, except in the case hereinafter pro-*

vided for, due and payable on the preceding business day ;

(b.) *When the last day of grace is a Bank Holiday (other than Christmas Day or Good Friday) under the Bank Holidays Act, 1871, and Acts amending or extending it, or when the last day of grace is a Sunday, and the second day of grace is a Bank Holiday, the bill is due and payable on the succeeding business day.*

(2.) *When a bill is payable at a fixed period after date, after sight, or after the happening of a specified event, the time of payment is determined by excluding the day from which the time is to begin to run, and by including the day of payment.*

(3.) *Where a bill is payable at a fixed period after sight, the time begins to run from the date of the acceptance if the bill be accepted, and from the date of noting or protest if the bill be noted or protested for non-acceptance or for non-delivery.*

(4.) *The term "month" in a bill means calendar month.*

Sect. 15. *The drawer of a bill and any indorser may insert therein the name of a person to whom the holder may resort in case of need, that is to say, in case the bill is dishonoured by non-acceptance or by non-payment. Such person is called the referee in case of need. It is in the option of the holder to resort to the referee in case of need or not, as he may think fit.*

Sect. 16. *The drawer of a bill, and any indorser, may insert therein an express stipulation—*

(1.) *Negativing or limiting his own liability to the holder :*

(2.) *Waiving as regards himself, some, or all of the holder's duties.*

Sect. 17.—(1.) *The acceptance of a bill is the signification by the drawee of his assent to the order of the drawer.*

(2.) *An acceptance is invalid unless it complies with the following conditions, namely :*

(a.) *It must be written on the bill and be signed by the drawee. The mere signature of the drawee without additional words is sufficient.*

(b.) *It must not express that the drawee will perform his promise by any other means than the payment of money.*

Sect. 18. *A bill may be accepted :*

(1.) *Before it has been signed by the drawer, or while otherwise incomplete :*

(2.) *When it is overdue, or after it has been dishonoured by a previous refusal to accept, or by non-payment :*

(3.) *When a bill payable after sight is dishonoured by non-acceptance, and the drawee subsequently accepts it, the holder, in the absence of any different agreement, is entitled to have the bill accepted as of the date of first presentment to the drawee for acceptance.*

Sect. 19.—(1.) *An acceptance is either* (a) *general or* (b) *qualified.*

(2.) *A general acceptance assents without qualification to the order of the drawer. A qualified*

I. BILL OF EXCHANGE (and PROMISSORY NOTE)—STATUTES—*continued*.

acceptance in express terms varies the effect of the bill as drawn.

In particular an acceptance is qualified which is—

    (a.) *conditional, that is to say, which makes payment by the acceptor dependent on the fulfilment of a condition therein stated :*

    (b.) *partial, that is to say, an acceptance to pay part only of the amount for which the bill is drawn :*

    (c.) *local, that is to say, an acceptance to pay only at a particular specified place :*

    An acceptance to pay at a particular place is a general acceptance, unless it expressly states that the bill is to be paid there only and not elsewhere :

    (d.) *qualified as to time :*

    (e.) *the acceptance of some one or more of the drawees, but not of all.*

Sect. 20.—(1.) *Where a simple signature or a blank stamped paper is delivered by the signer in order that it may be converted into a bill, it operates as a primâ ʃacie authority to fill it up as a complete bill for any amount the stamp will cover, using the signature for that of the drawer or the acceptor, or an indorser ; and, in like manner, when a bill is wanting in any material particular, the person in possession of it has a primâ ʃacie authority to fill up the omission in any way he thinks fit.*

(2.) *In order that any such instrument when completed may be enʃorceable against any person who became a party thereto prior to its completion, it must be filled up within a reasonable time, and strictly in accordance with the authority given. Reasonable time for this purpose is a question of fact.*

Provided that if any such instrument after completion is negotiated to a holder in due course it shall be valid and effectual for all purposes in his hands, and he may enʃorce it as if it had been filled up within a reasonable time, and strictly in accordance with the authority given.

Sect. 21.—(1.) *Every contract on a bill, whether it be the drawer's, the acceptor's, or an indorser's, is incomplete and revocable until delivery of the instrument in order to give effect thereto.*

Provided that where an acceptance is written on a bill, and the drawee gives notice to or according to the directions of the person entitled to the bill that he has accepted it, the acceptance then becomes complete and irrevocable.

(2.) *As between immediate parties, and as regards a remote party other than a holder in due course, the delivery—*

    (a.) *In order to be effectual must be made either by or under the authority of the party drawing, accepting, or indorsing, as the case may be :*

    (b.) *May be shewn to have been conditional, or for a special purpose only, and not for the purpose of transʃerring the property in the bill.*

But if the bill be in the hands of a holder in due course, a valid delivery of the bill by all parties prior to him so as to make them liable to him is conclusively presumed.

I. BILL OF EXCHANGE (and PROMISSORY NOTE)—STATUTES—*continued*.

(3.) *Where a bill is no longer in the possession of a party who has signed it as drawer, acceptor, or indorser, a valid and unconditional delivery by him is presumed until the contrary is proved.*

Capacity and Authority of Parties.] *Sect.* 22. (1.) *Capacity to incur liability as a party to a bill is co-extensive with capacity to contract.*

Provided that nothing in this section shall enable a corporation to make itself liable as drawer, acceptor, or indorser of a bill unless it is competent to it so to do under the law for the time being inʃorce relating to corporations.

(2.) *Where a bill is drawn or indorsed by an inʃant, minor, or corporation having no capacity or power to incur liability on a bill, the drawing or indorsement entitles the holder to receive payment of the bill, and to enʃorce it against any other party thereto.*

Sect. 23. *No person is liable as drawer, indorser, or acceptor of a bill who has not signed it as such :*

    Provided that

    (1) *Where a person signs a bill in a trade or assumed name, he is liable thereon as if he had signed it in his own name :*

    (2.) *The signature of the name of a firm is equivalent to the signature by the person so signing of the names of all persons liable as partners in that firm.*

Sect. 24. *Subject to the provisions of this Act, where a signature on a bill is ʃorged or placed thereon without the authority of the person whose signature it purports to be, the ʃorged or unauthorized signature is wholly inoperative, and no right to retain the bill or to give a discharge thereʃor or to enʃorce payment thereof against any party thereto can be acquired through or under that signature, unless the party against whom it is sought to retain or enʃorce payment of the bill is precluded ʃrom setting up the ʃorgery or want of authority.*

Provided that nothing in this section shall affect the ratification of an unauthorized signature not amounting to a ʃorgery.

Sect. 25. *A signature by procuration operates as notice that the agent has but a limited authority to sign, and the principal is only bound by such signature if the agent in so signing was acting within the actual limits of his authority.*

Sect. 26.—(1.) *Where a person signs a bill as drawer, indorser, or acceptor, and adds words to his signature indicating that he signs for or on behalʃ of a principal, or in a representative character, he is not personally liable thereon : but the mere addition to his signature of words describing him as an agent, or as filling a representative character, does not exempt him ʃrom personal liability.*

(2.) *In determining whether a signature on a bill is that of the principal or that of the agent by whose hand it is written, the construction most ʃavourable to the validity of the instrument shall be adopted.*

Consideration for a Bill.] *Sect.* 27.—(1.) *Valuable consideration for a bill may be constituted by—*

    (a.) *Any consideration sufficient to support a simple contract ;*

    (b.) *An antecedent debt or liability. Such a debt or liability is deemed valuable con-*

I. BILL OF EXCHANGE (and PROMISSORY NOTE)—STATUTES—*continued.*

sideration whether the bill is payable on demand or at a future time.

(2.) *Where value has at any time been given for a bill the holder is deemed to be a holder for value as regards the acceptor, and all parties to the bill who become parties prior to such time.*

(3.) *Where the holder of a bill has a lien on it arising either from contract or by implication of law, he is deemed to be a holder for value to the extent of the sum for which he has a lien.*

Sect. 28.—(1.) *An accommodation party to a bill is a person who has signed a bill as drawer, acceptor, or indorser, without receiving value therefor, and for the purpose of lending his name to some other person.*

(2.) *An accommodation party is liable on the bill to a holder for value; and it is immaterial whether, when such holder took the bill, he knew such party to be an accommodation party or not.*

Sect. 29.—(1.) *A holder in due course is a holder who has taken a bill, complete and regular on the face of it, under the following conditions; namely,*

(a.) *That he became the holder of it before it was overdue, and without notice that it had been previously dishonoured, if such was the fact:*

(b.) *That he took the bill in good faith and for value, and that at the time the bill was negotiated to him he had no notice of any defect in the title of the person who negotiated it.*

(2.) *In particular the title of a person who negotiates a bill is defective within the meaning of this Act when he obtained the bill, or the acceptance thereof, by fraud, duress, or force and fear, or other unlawful means, or for an illegal consideration, or when he negotiates it in breach of faith, or under such circumstances as amount to a fraud.*

(3.) *A holder (whether for value or not) who derives his title to a bill through a holder in due course, and who is not himself a party to any fraud or illegality affecting it, has all the rights of that holder in due course as regards the acceptor and all parties to the bill prior to that holder.*

Sect. 30.—(1.) *Every party whose signature appears on a bill is primâ facie deemed to have become a party thereto for value.*

(2.) *Every holder of a bill is primâ facie deemed to be a holder in due course; but if in an action on a bill it is admitted or proved that the acceptance, issue, or subsequent negotiation of the bill is affected with fraud, duress, or force and fear, or illegality, the burden of proof is shifted, unless and until the holder proves that, subsequent to the alleged fraud or illegality, value has in good faith been given for the bill.*

Negotiation of Bills.] *Sect.* 31.—(1.) *A bill is negotiated when it is transferred from one person to another in such a manner as to constitute the transferee the holder of the bill.*

(2.) *A bill payable to bearer is negotiated by delivery.*

(3.) *A bill payable to order is negotiated by the indorsement of the holder completed by delivery.*

(4.) *Where the holder of a bill payable to his order transfers it for value without indorsing it, the transfer gives the transferee such title as the transferor had in the bill, and the transferee in*

I. BILL OF EXCHANGE (and PROMISSORY NOTE)—STATUTES—*continued.*

addition acquires the right to have the indorsement of the transferor.

(5.) *Where any person is under obligation to indorse a bill in a representative capacity, he may indorse the bill in such terms as to negative personal liability.*

Sect. 32. *An indorsement in order to operate as a negotiation must comply with the following conditions, namely:*—

(1.) *It must be written on the bill itself and be signed by the indorser. The simple signature of the indorser on the bill, without additional words, is sufficient.*

An indorsement written on an allonge, or on a "copy" of a bill issued or negotiated in a country where "copies" are recognised, is deemed to be written on the bill itself.

(2.) *It must be an indorsement of the entire bill. A partial indorsement, that is to say, an indorsement which purports to transfer to the indorsee a part only of the amount payable, or which purports to transfer the bill to two or more indorsees severally, does not operate as a negotiation of the bill.*

(3.) *Where a bill is payable to the order of two or more payees or indorsees who are not partners all must indorse, unless the one indorsing has authority to indorse for the others.*

(4.) *Where, in a bill payable to order, the payee or indorsee is wrongly designated, or his name is mis-spelt, he may indorse the bill as therein described, adding, if he think fit, his proper signature.*

(5.) *Where there are two or more indorsements on a bill, each indorsement is deemed to have been made in the order in which it appears on the bill, until the contrary is proved.*

(6.) *An indorsement may be made in blank or special. It may also contain terms making it restrictive.*

Sect. 33. *Where a bill purports to be indorsed conditionally the condition may be disregarded by the payer, and payment to the indorsee is valid whether the condition has been fulfilled or not.*

Sect. 34.—(1.) *An indorsement in blank specifies no indorsee, and a bill so indorsed becomes payable to bearer.*

(2.) *A special indorsement specifies the person to whom, or to whose order, the bill is to be payable.*

(3.) *The provisions of this Act relating to a payee apply with the necessary modifications to an indorsee under a special indorsement.*

(4.) *When a bill has been indorsed in blank, any holder may convert the blank indorsement into a special indorsement by writing above the indorser's signature a direction to pay the bill to or to the order of himself or some other person.*

Sect. 35.—(1.) *An indorsement is restrictive which prohibits the further negotiation of the bill, or which expresses that it is a mere authority to deal with the bill as thereby directed and not a transfer of the ownership thereof, as, for example, if a bill be indorsed "Pay D. only," or "Pay D. for the account of X.," or "Pay D. or order for collection."*

(2.) *A restrictive indorsement gives the indorsee the right to receive payment of the bill and to sue*

I. BILL OF EXCHANGE (and PROMISSORY NOTE)—STATUTES—*continued.*

any party thereto that his indorser could have sued, but gives him no power to transfer his right as indorsee unless it expressly authorize him to do so.

(3.) Where a restrictive indorsement authorizes further transfer, all subsequent indorsees take the bill with the same rights and subject to the same liabilities as the first indorsee under the restrictive indorsement.

Sect. 36.—(1.) Where a bill is negotiable in its origin it continues to be negotiable until it has been (a) restrictively indorsed or (b) discharged by payment or otherwise.

(2) Where an overdue bill is negotiated, it can only be negotiated subject to any defect of title affecting it at its maturity, and thenceforward no person who takes it can acquire or give a better title than that which the person from whom he took it had.

(3.) A bill payable on demand is deemed to be overdue within the meaning and for the purposes of this section, when it appears on the face of it to have been in circulation for an unreasonable length of time. What is an unreasonable length of time for this purpose is a question of fact.

(4.) Except where an instrument bears date after the maturity of the bill, every negotiation is primâ facie deemed to have been effected before the bill was overdue.

(5.) Where a bill which is not overdue has been dishonoured, any person who takes it with notice of the dishonour, takes it subject to any defect of title attaching thereto at the time of dishonour, but nothing in this sub-section shall affect the right of a holder in due course.

Sect. 37. Where a bill is negotiated back to the drawer, or to a prior indorser or to the acceptor, such party may, subject to the provisions of this Act, reissue and further negotiate the bill, but he is not entitled to enforce payment of the bill against any intervening party to whom he was previously liable.

Sect. 38. The rights and powers of the holder of the bill are as follows :—

(1.) He may sue on the bill in his own name :

(2.) Where he is a holder in due course, he holds the bill free from any defect of title of prior parties, as well as from mere personal defences available to prior parties among themselves, and may enforce payment against all parties liable on the bill :

(3.) Where his title is defective (a) if he negotiates the bill to a holder in due course, that holder obtains a good and complete title to the bill, and (b) if he obtains payment of the bill the person who pays him in due course gets a valid discharge for the bill.

Presentment for Acceptance and Notice of Dishonour.] Sect. 39.—(1.) Where a bill is payable after sight, presentment for acceptance is necessary in order to fix the maturity of the instrument.

(2.) Where a bill expressly stipulates that it shall be presented for acceptance, or where a bill is drawn payable elsewhere than at the residence or place of business of the drawee, it must be presented for acceptance before it can be presented for payment.

I. BILL OF EXCHANGE (and PROMISSORY NOTE—STATUTES—*continued.*

(3.) In no other case is presentment for acceptance necessary in order to render liable any party to the bill.

(4.) Where the holder of a bill, drawn payable elsewhere than at the place of business or residence of the drawee, has not time, with the exercise of reasonable diligence, to present the bill for acceptance before presenting it for payment on the day that it falls due, the delay caused by presenting the bill for acceptance before presenting it for payment is excused, and does not discharge the drawer or indorsers.

Sect. 40.—(1.) Subject to the provisions of this Act, when a bill payable after sight is negotiated, the holder must either present it for acceptance or negotiate it within a reasonable time.

(2.) If he do not do so, the drawer and all indorsers prior to that holder are discharged.

(3.) In determining what is a reasonable time within the meaning of this section, regard shall be had to the nature of the bill, the usage of trade with respect to similar bills, and the facts of the particular case.

Sect. 42.—(1.) A bill is duly presented for acceptance which is presented in accordance with the following rules :

(a.) The presentment must be made by or on behalf of the holder to the drawee or to some person authorized to accept or refuse acceptance on his behalf at a reasonable hour on a business day and before the bill is overdue :

(b.) Where a bill is addressed to two or more drawees, who are not partners, presentment must be made to them all, unless one has authority to accept for all, then presentment may be made to him only :

(c.) Where the drawee is dead, presentment may be made to his personal representative :

(d.) Where the drawee is bankrupt, presentment may be made to him or his trustee :

(e.) Where authorized by agreement or usage, a presentment though the post office is sufficient.

(2.) Presentment in accordance with these rules is excused, and a bill may be treated as dishonoured by non-acceptance—

(a.) Where the drawee is dead or bankrupt, or is a fictitious person or a person not having capacity to contract by bill :

(b.) Where, after the exercise of reasonable diligence, such presentment cannot be effected :

(c.) Where although the presentment has been irregular, acceptance has been refused on some other ground :

(3.) The fact that the holder has reason to believe that the bill, on presentment, will be dishonoured does not excuse presentment.

Sect. 42.—(1.) When a bill is duly presented for acceptance and is not accepted within the customary time, the person presenting it must treat it as dishonoured by non-acceptance. If he do not, the holder shall lose his right of recourse against the drawer and indorsers.

Sect. 43.—(1.) A bill is dishonoured by non-acceptance—

(a.) when it is duly presented for acceptance, and such an acceptance as is prescribed by

I. BILL OF EXCHANGE (and PROMISSORY NOTE)—STATUTES—*continued.*

this Act is refused or cannot be obtained; or

(b.) when presentment for acceptance is excused and the bill is not accepted.

(2.) Subject to the provisions of this Act when a bill is dishonoured by non-acceptance, an immediate right of recourse against the drawer and indorsers accrues to the holder, and no presentment for payment is necessary.

Sect. 44.—(1.) The holder of a bill may refuse to take a qualified acceptance, and if he does not obtain an unqualified acceptance may treat the bill as dishonoured by non-acceptance.

(2.) Where a qualified acceptance is taken, and the drawer or an indorser has not expressly or impliedly authorized the holder to take a qualified acceptance, or does not subsequently assent thereto, such drawer or indorser is discharged from his liability on the bill.

The provisions of this sub-section do not apply to a partial acceptance, whereof due notice has been given. Where a foreign bill has been accepted as to part, it must be protested as to the balance.

(3.) When the drawer or indorser of a bill receives notice of a qualified acceptance, and does not within a reasonable time express his dissent to the holder, he shall be deemed to have assented thereto.

Sect. 45. Subject to the provisions of this Act a bill must be duly presented for payment. If it be not presented the drawer and indorsers shall be discharged.

A bill is duly presented for payment which is presented in accordance with the following rules:—

(1.) Where the bill is not payable on demand, presentment must be made on the day it falls due.

(2.) Where the bill is payable on demand, then, subject to the provisions of this Act, presentment must be made within a reasonable time after its issue in order to render the drawer liable, and within a reasonable time after its indorsement, in order to render the indorser liable.

In determining what is a reasonable time, regard shall be had to the nature of the bill, the usage of trade with regard to similar bills, and the facts of the particular case.

(3.) Presentment must be made by the holder, or by some person authorized to receive payment on his behalf, at a reasonable hour on a business day, at a proper place as hereinafter defined, either to the person designated by the bill as payer, or to some person authorized to pay, or refuse payment on his behalf, if with the exercise of reasonable diligence such person can there be found.

(4.) A bill is presented at the proper place:—

(a.) Where a place of payment is specified in the bill and the bill is there presented.

(b.) Where no place of payment is specified, but the address of the drawee or acceptor is given in the bill, and the bill is there presented.

(c.) Where no place of payment is specified and no address given, and the bill is

I. BILL OF EXCHANGE (and PROMISSORY NOTE)—STATUTES—*continued.*

presented at the drawee's or acceptor's place of business if known, and if not, at his ordinary residence if known.

(d.) In any other case if presented to the drawee or acceptor wherever he can be found, or if presented at his last known place of business or residence.

(5.) Where a bill is presented at the proper place, and after the exercise of reasonable diligence no person authorized to pay or refuse payment can be found there, no further presentment to the drawee or acceptor is required.

(6.) Where a bill is drawn upon, or accepted by two or more persons who are not partners, and no place of payment is specified, presentment must be made to them all.

(7.) Where the drawee or acceptor of a bill is dead, and no place of payment is specified, presentment must be made to a personal representative, if such there be, and with the exercise of reasonable diligence he can be found.

(8.) Where authorized by agreement or usage a presentment through the post office is sufficient.

Sect. 46.—(1.) Delay in making presentment for payment is excused when the delay is caused by circumstances beyond the control of the holder, and not imputable to his default, misconduct, or negligence. When the cause of delay ceases to operate presentment must be made with reasonable diligence.

(2.) Presentment for payment is dispensed with,—

(a.) Where, after the exercise of reasonable diligence presentment, as required by this Act, cannot be effected.

The fact that the holder has reason to believe that the bill will, on presentment, be dishonoured, does not dispense with the necessity for presentment.

(b.) Where the drawee is a fictitious person.

(c.) As regards the drawer where the drawee or acceptor is not bound, as between himself and the drawer, to accept or pay the bill, and the drawer has no reason to believe that the bill would be paid if presented.

(d.) As regards an indorser, where the bill was accepted or made for the accommodation of that indorser, and he has no reason to expect that the bill would be paid if presented.

(e.) By waiver of presentment, express or implied.

Sect. 47.—(1.) A bill is dishonoured by non-payment (a.) when it is duly presented for payment and payment is refused or cannot be obtained, or (b.) when presentment is excused and the bill is overdue and unpaid.

(2.) Subject to the provisions of this Act, when a bill is dishonoured by non-payment, an immediate right of recourse against the drawer and indorsers accrues to the holder.

Sect. 48. Subject to the provisions of this Act, when a bill has been dishonoured by non-acceptance or by non-payment, notice of dishonour must be given to the drawer and each indorser, and any drawer or indorser to whom such notice is not given is discharged; Provided that,—

I. BILL OF EXCHANGE (and PROMISSORY NOTE)—STATUTES—continued.

(1.) Where a bill is dishonoured by non-acceptance, and notice of dishonour is not given, the rights of a holder in due course subsequent to the omission, shall not be prejudiced by the omission.

(2.) Where a bill is dishonoured by non-acceptance and due notice of dishonour is given, it shall not be necessary to give notice of a subsequent dishonour by non-payment unless the bill shall in the meantime have been accepted.

Sect. 49. Notice of dishonour in order to be valid and effectual must be given in accordance with the following rules:—

(1.) The notice must be given by or on behalf of the holder, or by or on behalf of an indorser, who at the time of giving it is himself liable on the bill.

(2.) Notice of dishonour may be given by an agent, either in his own name, or in the name of any party entitled to give notice, whether that party be his principal or not.

(3.) Where the notice is given by or on behalf of the holder, it enures for the benefit of all subsequent holders and all prior indorsers who have a right of recourse against the party to whom it is given.

(4.) Where notice is given by or on behalf of an indorser entitled to give notice as hereinbefore provided, it enures for the benefit of the holder and all indorsers subsequent to the party to whom notice is given.

(5.) The notice may be given in writing or by personal communication, and may be given in any terms which sufficiently identify the bill, and intimate that the bill has been dishonoured by non-acceptance or non-payment.

(6.) The return of a dishonoured bill to the drawer or an indorser is, in point of form, deemed a sufficient notice of dishonour.

(7.) A written notice need not be signed, and an insufficient written notice may be supplemented and validated by verbal communication. A misdescription of the bill shall not vitiate the notice unless the party to whom the notice is given is in fact misled thereby.

(8.) Where notice of dishonour is required to be given to any person, it may be given either to the party himself, or to his agent in that behalf.

(9.) Where the drawer or indorser is dead, and the party giving notice knows it, the notice must be given to a personal representative if such there be, and with the exercise of reasonable diligence he can be found.

(10.) Where the drawer or indorser is bankrupt, notice may be given either to the party himself or to the trustee.

(11.) Where there are two or more drawers or indorsers who are not partners, notice must be given to each of them, unless one of them has authority to receive such notice for the others.

(12.) The notice may be given as soon as the bill is dishonoured, and must be given within a reasonable time thereafter.

I. BILL OF EXCHANGE (and PROMISSORY NOTE)—STATUTES—continued.

In the absence of special circumstances notice is not deemed to have been given within a reasonable time, unless—

(a.) where the person giving and the person to receive notice reside in the same place, the notice is given or sent off in time to reach the latter on the day after the dishonour of the bill.

(b.) where the person giving and the person to receive notice reside in different places, the notice is sent off on the day after the dishonour of the bill, if there be a post at a convenient hour on that day, and if there be no such post on that day then by the next post thereafter.

(13.) Where a bill when dishonoured is in the hands of an agent, he may either himself give notice to the parties liable on the bill, or he may give notice to his principal. If he give notice to his principal, he must do so within the same time as if he were the holder, and the principal upon receipt of such notice has himself the same time for giving notice as if the agent had been an independent holder.

(14.) Where a party to a bill receives due notice of dishonour, he has after the receipt of such notice the same period of time for giving notice to antecedent parties that the holder has after the dishonour.

(15.) Where a notice of dishonour is duly addressed and posted, the sender is deemed to have given due notice of dishonour, notwithstanding any miscarriage of the post office.

Sect. 50.—(1.) Delay in giving notice of dishonour is excused where the delay is caused by circumstances beyond the control of the party giving notice, and not imputable to his default, misconduct, or negligence. When the cause of delay ceases to operate the notice must be given with reasonable diligence.

(2.) Notice of dishonour is dispensed with :—

(a.) When, after the exercise of reasonable diligence, notice as required by this Act cannot be given to or does not reach the drawer or indorser sought to be charged.

(b.) By waiver express or implied. Notice of dishonour may be waived before the time of giving notice has arrived, or after the omission to give due notice :

(c.) As regards the drawer in the following cases, namely, (1) where drawer and drawee are the same person, (2) where the drawee is a fictitious person or a person not having capacity to contract, (3) where the drawer is the person to whom the bill is presented for payment, (4) where the drawee or acceptor is as between himself and the drawer under no obligation to accept or pay the bill, (5) where the drawer has countermanded payment :

(d.) As regards the indorser in the following cases, namely, (1) where the drawee is a fictitious person or a person not having capacity to contract and the indorser was

I. BILL OF EXCHANGE (and PROMISSORY NOTE)—STATUTES—*continued.*

aware of the fact at the time he indorsed the bill, (2) where the indorser is the person to whom the bill is presented for payment, (3) where the bill was accepted or made for his accommodation.

Sect. 51.—(1.) *Where an inland bill has been dishonoured, it may, if the holder think fit, be noted for non-acceptance or non-payment, as the case may be; but it shall not be necessary to note or protest any such bill in order to preserve the recourse against the drawer or indorser.*

(2.) *When a foreign bill, appearing on the face of it to be such, has been dishonoured by non-acceptance, it must be duly protested for non-acceptance, and where such a bill, which has not been previously dishonoured by non-acceptance, is dishonoured by non-payment, it must be duly protested for non-payment. If it be not so protested the drawer and indorsers are discharged. Where a bill does not appear on the face of it to be a foreign bill protest thereof in case of dishonour is unnecessary.*

(3.) *A bill which has been protested for non-acceptance may be subsequently protested for non-payment.*

(4.) *Subject to the provisions of this Act, when a bill is noted or protested, it must be noted on the day of its dishonour. When a bill has been duly noted, the protest may be subsequently extended as of the date of the noting.*

(5.) *Where the acceptor of a bill becomes bankrupt or insolvent or suspends payment before it matures, the holder may cause the bill to be protested for better security against the drawer and indorsers.*

(6.) *A bill must be protested at the place where it is dishonoured: Provided that—*

(a.) *When a bill is presented through the post office, and returned by post dishonoured, it may be protested at the place to which it is returned and on the day of its return if received during business hours, and if not received during business hours, then not later than the next business day:*

(b.) *When a bill drawn payable at the place of business or residence of some person other than the drawee, has been dishonoured by non-acceptance, it must be protested for non-payment at the place where it is expressed to be payable, and no further presentment for payment to, or demand on, the drawee is necessary.*

(7.) *A protest must contain a copy of the bill, and must be signed by the notary making it, and must specify—*

(a.) *The person at whose request the bill is protested:*

(b.) *The place and date of protest, the cause or reason for protesting the bill, the demand made, and the answer given, if any, or the fact that the drawee or acceptor could not be found.*

(8.) *Where a bill is lost or destroyed, or is wrongly detained from the person entitled to hold it, protest may be made on a copy or written particulars thereof.*

(9.) *Protest is dispensed with by any circumstance which would dispense with notice of dishonour. Delay in noting or protesting is excused*

I. BILL OF EXCHANGE (and PROMISSORY NOTE)—STATUTES—*continued.*

when the delay is caused by circumstances beyond the control of the holder, and not imputable to his default, misconduct, or negligence. When the cause of delay ceases to operate the bill must be noted or protested with reasonable diligence.

Sect. 52.—(1.) *When a bill is accepted generally presentment for payment is not necessary in order to render the acceptor liable.*

(2.) *When by the terms of a qualified acceptance presentment for payment is required, the acceptor, in the absence of an express stipulation to that effect, is not discharged by the omission to present the bill for payment on the day that it matures.*

(3.) *In order to render the acceptor of a bill liable it is not necessary to protest it, or that notice of dishonour should be given to him.*

(4.) *Where the holder of a bill presents it for payment, he shall exhibit the bill to the person from whom he demands payment, and when a bill is paid the holder shall forthwith deliver it up to the party paying it.*

Acceptance and Payment for Honour.] *Sect.* 65.—(1.) *Where a bill of exchange has been protested for dishonour by non-acceptance, or protested for better security, and is not overdue, any person, not being a party already liable thereon, may with the consent of the holder, intervene and accept the bill suprà protest, for the honour of any party liable thereon, or for the honour of the person for whose account the bill is drawn.*

(2.) *A bill may be accepted for honour for part only of the sum for which it is drawn.*

(3.) *An acceptance for honour suprà protest in order to be valid must—*

(a.) *be written on the bill, and indicate that it is an acceptance for honour:*

(b.) *be signed by the acceptor for honour:*

(4.) *Where an acceptance for honour does not expressly state for whose honour it is made, it is deemed to be an acceptance for the honour of the drawer.*

(5.) *Where a bill payable after sight is accepted for honour, its maturity is calculated from the date of the noting for non-acceptance, and not from the date of the acceptance for honour.*

Sect. 66.—(1.) *The acceptor for honour of a bill by accepting it engages that he will, on due presentment, pay the bill according to the tenor of his acceptance, if it is not paid by the drawee, provided it has been duly presented for payment, and protested for non-payment, and that he receives notice of these facts.*

(2.) *The acceptor for honour is liable to the holder and to all parties to the bill subsequent to the party for whose honour he has accepted.*

Sect. 67.—(1.) *Where a dishonoured bill has been accepted for honour suprà protest, or contains a reference in case of need, it must be protested for non-payment before it is presented for payment to the acceptor for honour, or referee in case of need.*

(2.) *Where the address of the acceptor for honour is in the same place where the bill is protested for non-payment, the bill must be presented to him not later than the day following its maturity: and where the address of the acceptor for honour is in the same place other than the place where it was protested for non-payment, the bill must be forwarded*

I. BILL OF EXCHANGE (and PROMISSORY NOTE)—STATUTES—*continued.*

not later than the day *following its maturity for presentment to him.*

(3.) *Delay in presentment or non-presentment is excused by any circumstance which would excuse delay in presentment for payment or non-presentment for payment.*

(4.) *When a bill of exchange is dishonoured by the acceptor for honour it must be protested for non-payment by him.*

Sect. 68.—(1.) *Where a bill has been protested for non-payment, any person may intervene and pay it suprà protest for the honour of any party liable thereon, or for the honour of the person for whose account the bill is drawn.*

(2.) *Where two or more persons offer to pay a bill for the honour of different parties, the person whose payment will discharge most parties to the bill shall have the preference.*

(3.) *Payment for honour suprà protest, in order to operate as such and not as a mere voluntary payment, must be attested by a notarial act of honour which may be appended to the protest or form an extension of it.*

(4.) *The notarial act of honour must be founded on a declaration made by the payee for honour, or his agent in that behalf, declaring his intention to pay the bill for honour, and for whose honour he pays.*

(5.) *Where a bill has been paid for honour, all parties subsequent to the party for whose honour it is paid are discharged, but the payer for honour is subrogated for, and succeeds to both the rights and duties of, the holder as regards the party for whose honour he pays, and all parties liable to that party.*

(6.) *The payer for honour on paying to the holder the amount of the bill and the notarial expenses incidental to its dishonour is entitled to receive both the bill itself and the protest. If the holder do not on demand deliver them up he shall be liable to the payer for honour in damages.*

(7.) *Where the holder of a bill refuses to receive payment suprà protest he shall lose his right of recourse against any party who would have been discharged by such payment.*

Liability of Parties.] Sect. 53.—(1.) *A bill, of itself, does not operate as an assignment of funds in the hands of the drawee available for the payment thereof, and the drawee of a bill who does not accept as required by this Act is not liable on the instrument. This sub-section shall not extend to Scotland.*

(2.) *In Scotland, where the drawee of a bill has in his hands funds available for the payment thereof, the bill operates as an assignment of the sum for which it is drawn in favour of the holder, from the time when the bill is presented to the drawee.*

Sect. 54. *The acceptor of a bill, by accepting it—*

(1.) *Engages that he will pay it according to the tenor of his acceptance :*

(2.) *Is precluded from denying to a holder in due course :*

(a.) *The existence of the drawer, the genuineness of his signature, and his capacity and authority to draw the bill :*

(b.) *In the case of a bill payable to drawer's order, the then capacity of the drawer to indorse, but not the genuineness or validity of his indorsement :*

(c.) *In the case of a bill payable to the order of a third person, the existence of the payee and his then capacity to indorse, but not the genuineness or validity of his indorsement.*

Sect. 55.—(1.) *The drawer of a bill, by drawing it—*

(a.) *Engages that on due presentment it shall be accepted and paid according to its tenor, and that if it be dishonoured he will compensate the holder or any indorser who is compelled to pay it, provided that the requisite proceedings on dishonour be duly taken.*

(b.) *Is precluded from denying to a holder in due course the existence of the payee and his then capacity to indorse.*

(2.) *The indorser of a bill, by indorsing it—*

(a.) *Engages that on due presentment it shall be accepted and paid according to its tenor, and that if it be dishonoured he will compensate the holder or a subsequent indorser who is compelled to pay it, provided that the requisite proceedings on dishonour be duly taken ;*

(b.) *Is precluded from denying to a holder in due course the genuineness and regularity in all respects of the drawer's signature and all previous indorsements ;*

(c.) *Is precluded from denying to his immediate or a subsequent indorsee that the bill was at the time of his indorsement a valid and subsisting bill, and that he had then a good title thereto.*

Sect. 56. *Where a person signs a bill otherwise than as drawer or acceptor, he thereby incurs the liabilities of an indorser to a holder in due course.*

Sect. 57. *Where a bill is dishonoured, the measure of damages, which shall be deemed to be liquidated damages, shall be as follows :*

(1.) *The holder may recover from any party liable on the bill, and the drawer who has been compelled to pay the bill may recover from the acceptor, and an indorser who has been compelled to pay the bill may recover from the acceptor or from the drawer, or from a prior indorser—*

(a.) *The amount of the bill :*

(b.) *Interest thereon from the time of presentment for payment if the bill is payable on demand, and from the maturity of the bill in any other case :*

(c.) *The expenses of noting, or when protest is necessary, and the protest has been extended, the expenses of protest.*

(2.) *In the case of a bill which has been dishonoured abroad, in lieu of the above damages, the holder may recover from the drawer or an indorser, and the drawer or an indorser who has been compelled to pay the bill may recover from any party liable to him, the amount of the re-exchange with interest thereon until the time of payment.*

(3.) *Where by this Act interest may be recovered as damages, such interest may, if justice require it, be withheld wholly or in part, and where a bill is expressed to be payable with interest at a given rate, interest as*

I. BILL OF EXCHANGE (and PROMISSORY NOTE)—STATUTES—*continued.*

damages may or may not be given at the same rate as interest proper.

Sect. 58.—(1) *Where the holder of a bill payable to bearer negotiates it by delivery without indorsing it, he is called a "transferor" by "delivery."*

(2.) *A transferor by delivery is not liable on the instrument.*

(3.) *A transferor by delivery who negotiates a bill thereby warrants to his immediate transferee being a holder for value that the bill is what it purports to be, that he has a right to transfer it, and that at the time of transfer he is not aware of any fact which renders it valueless.*

Discharge, Alteration, and Cancellation of Bill.] *Sect. 59.*—(1.) *A bill is discharged by payment in due course by or on behalf of the drawee or acceptor.*

"Payment in due course" means payment made at or after the maturity of the bill to the holder thereof in good faith and without notice that his title to the bill is defective.

(2.) *Subject to the provisions hereinafter contained, when a bill is paid by the drawer or an indorser it is not discharged; but*

(a.) *Where a bill payable to, or to the order of, a third party is paid by the drawer, the drawer may enforce payment thereof against the acceptor, but may not reissue the bill.*

(b.) *Where a bill is paid by an indorser, or where a bill payable to drawer's order is paid by the drawer, the party paying it is remitted to his former rights as regards the acceptor or antecedent parties, and he may, if he thinks fit, strike out his own and subsequent indorsements, and again negotiate the bill.*

(3.) *Where an accommodation bill is paid in due course by the party accommodated the bill is discharged.*

Sect. 60. When a bill payable to order on demand is drawn on a banker, and the banker on whom it is drawn pays the bill in good faith and in the ordinary course of business, it is not incumbent on the banker to shew that the indorsement of the payee or any subsequent indorsement was made by or under the authority of the person whose indorsement it purports to be, and the banker is deemed to have paid the bill in due course, although such indorsement has been forged and made without authority.

Sect. 61. When the acceptor of a bill is or becomes the holder of it at or after its maturity, in his own right, the bill is discharged.

Sect. 62.—(1.) *When the holder of a bill at or after its maturity absolutely and unconditionally renounces his rights against the acceptor the bill is discharged.*

The renunciation must be in writing, unless the bill is delivered up to the acceptor.

(2.) *The liabilities of any party to a bill may in like manner be renounced by the holder before, at, or after its maturity; but nothing in this section shall affect the rights of a holder in due course without renunciation.*

Sect. 63.—(1.) *Where a bill is intentionally cancelled by the holder or his agent, and the cancellation is apparent thereon, the bill is discharged.*

I. BILL OF EXCHANGE (and PROMISSORY NOTE)—STATUTES—*continued.*

(2.) *In like manner any party liable on a bill may be discharged by the intentional cancellation of his signature by the holder or his agent. In such case any indorser who would have had a right of recourse against the party whose signature is cancelled, is also discharged.*

(3.) *A cancellation made unintentionally, or under a mistake, or without the authority of the holder is inoperative; but where a bill or any signature thereon appears to have been cancelled, the burden of proof lies on the party who alleges that the cancellation was made unintentionally, or under a mistake, or without authority.*

Sect. 64.—(1.) *Where a bill or acceptance is materially altered without the assent of all parties liable on the bill, the bill is avoided except as against a party who has himself made, authorized, or assented to the alteration, and subsequent indorsers.*

Provided that

Where a bill has been materially altered, but the alteration is not apparent, and the bill is in the hands of a holder in due course, such holder may avail himself of the bill as if it had not been altered, and may enforce payment of it according to its original tenor.

(2.) *In particular the following alterations are material, namely, any alteration of the date, the sum payable, the time of payment, the place of payment, and, where a bill has been accepted generally, the addition of a place of payment without the acceptor's assent.*

Lost Bills.] *Sect. 69. Where a bill has been lost before it is overdue, the person who was the holder of it may apply to the drawer to give him another bill of the same tenor, giving security to the drawer if required to indemnify him against all persons whatever in case the bill alleged to have been lost shall be found again.*

If the drawer on request as aforesaid refuses to give such duplicate bill, he may be compelled to do so.

Sect. 70. In any action or proceeding upon a bill, the Court or a Judge may order that the loss of the instrument shall not be set up, provided an indemnity be given to the satisfaction of the Court or Judge against the claims of any other person upon the instrument in question.

Bill in a Set.] *Sect. 71.*—(1.) *Where a bill is drawn in a set, each part of the set being numbered, and containing a reference to the other parts, the whole of the parts constitute one bill.*

(2.) *Where the holder of a set indorses two or more parts to different persons, he is liable on every such part, and every indorser subsequent to him is liable on the part he has himself indorsed as if the said parts were separate bills.*

(3.) *Where two or more parts of a set are negotiated to different holders in due course, the holder whose title first accrues is as between such holders deemed the true owner of the bill; but nothing in this sub-section shall affect the rights of a person who in due course accepts or pays the part first presented to him.*

(4.) *The acceptance may be written on any part, and it must be written on one part only.*

If the drawee accepts more than one part, and such accepted parts get into the hands of different

I

I. BILL OF EXCHANGE (and PROMISSORY NOTE)—STATUTES—*continued.*

holders in due course, he is liable on every such part as if it were a separate bill.

(5.) *When the acceptor of a bill drawn in a set pays it without requiring the part bearing his acceptance to be delivered up to him, and that part at maturity is outstanding in the hands of a holder in due course, he is liable to the holder thereof.*

(6.) *Subject to the preceding rules, where any one part of a bill drawn in a set is discharged by payment or otherwise, the whole bill is discharged.*

Conflict of Laws.] *Sect. 72. Where a bill drawn in one country is negotiated, accepted, or payable in another, the rights, duties, and liabilities of the parties thereto are determined as follows :—*

(1.) *The validity of a bill as regards requisites in form is determined by the law of the place of issue, and the validity as regards requisites in form of the supervening contracts, such as acceptance, or indorsement, or acceptance suprà protest, is determined by the law of the place where such contract was made.*

Provided that—

(a.) *Where a bill is issued out of the United Kingdom it is not invalid by reason only that it is not stamped in accordance with the law of the place of issue :*

(b.) *Where a bill, issued out of the United Kingdom, conforms as regards requisites in form, to the law of the United Kingdom, it may, for the purpose of enforcing payment thereof, be treated as valid as between all persons who negotiate, hold, or become parties to it in the United Kingdom.*

(2.) *Subject to the provisions of this Act, the interpretation of the drawing, indorsement, acceptance, or acceptance suprà protest, of a bill is determined by the law of the place where such contract is made.*

Provided that where an inland bill is indorsed in a foreign country the indorsement shall, as regards the payer, be interpreted according to the law of the United Kingdom.

(3.) *The duties of the holder with respect to the presentment for acceptance or payment, and the necessity for or sufficiency of a protest or notice of dishonour, or otherwise, are determined by the law of the place where the act is done or the bill is dishonoured.*

(4.) *Where a bill is drawn out of but payable in the United Kingdom and the sum payable is not expressed in the currency of the United Kingdom, the amount shall, in the absence of some express stipulation, be calculated according to the rate of exchange for sight drafts at the place of payment on the day the bill is payable.*

(5.) *Where a bill is drawn in one country and is payable in another, the due date thereof is determined according to the law of the place where it is payable.*

2. CHEQUES AND CROSSED CHEQUES.

Sect. 73. A cheque is a bill of exchange drawn on a bank or payable on demand.

Except as otherwise provided in this part, the

I. BILL OF EXCHANGE (and PROMISSORY NOTE)—STATUTES—*continued.*

provisions of the Act applicable to a bill of exchange payable on demand apply to a cheque.

Sect. 74. Subject to the provisions of this Act—

(1.) *Where a cheque is not presented for payment within a reasonable time of its issue, and the drawer or the person on whose account it is drawn had the right at the time of such presentment as between him and the banker to have the cheque paid and suffers actual damage through the delay, he is discharged to the extent of such damage, that is to say, to the extent to which such drawer or person is a creditor of such banker to a larger amount than he would have been had such cheque been paid.*

(2.) *In determining what is a reasonable time, regard shall be had to the nature of the instrument, the usage of the trade and of bankers, and the facts of the particular case.*

(3.) *The holder of such cheque as to which such drawer or person is discharged shall be a creditor, in lieu of such drawer or person, of such banker to the extent of such discharge, and entitled to recover the amount from him.*

Sect. 75. The duty and authority of a banker to pay a cheque drawn on him by his customer are determined by—

(1.) *Countermand of payment :*

(2.) *Notice of the customer's death.*

Sect. 76.—(1.) Where a cheque bears across its face an addition of—

(a.) *The words "and company" or any abbreviation thereof between two parallel transverse lines, either with or without the words "not negotiable" ; or*

(b.) *Two parallel transverse lines simply, either with or without the words "not negotiable ;"*

that addition constitutes a crossing, and the cheque is crossed generally.

(2.) *Where a cheque bears across its face an addition of the name of a banker, either with or without the words "not negotiable," that addition constitutes a crossing, and the cheque is crossed specially and to that banker.*

Sect. 77.—(1.) A cheque may be crossed generally or specially by the drawer.

(2.) *Where a cheque is uncrossed, the holder may cross it generally or specially.*

(3.) *Where a cheque is crossed generally the holder may cross it specially.*

(4.) *Where a cheque is crossed generally or specially, the holder may add the words "not negotiable."*

(5.) *Where a cheque is crossed specially, the banker to whom it is crossed may again cross it specially to another banker for collection.*

(6.) *Where an uncrossed cheque, or a cheque crossed generally, is sent to a banker for collection, he may cross it specially to himself.*

Sect. 78. A crossing authorized by this Act is a material part of the cheque ; it shall not be lawful for any person to obliterate or, except as authorized by this Act, to add to or alter the crossing.

Sect. 79.—(1.) Where a cheque is crossed speci-

I. BILL OF EXCHANGE (and PROMISSORY NOTE)—STATUTES—*continued.*

ally to more than one banker except when crossed to an agent for collection being a banker, the banker on whom it is drawn shall refuse payment thereof.

(2.) *Where the banker on whom a cheque is drawn which is so crossed nevertheless pays the same, or pays a cheque crossed generally otherwise than to a banker, or if crossed specially otherwise than to the banker to whom it is crossed, or his agent for collection being a banker, he is liable to the true owner of the cheque for any loss he may sustain owing to the cheque having been so paid.*

Provided that where a cheque is presented for payment which does not at the time of presentment appear to be crossed, or to have had a crossing which has been obliterated, or to have been added to or altered otherwise than as authorized by this Act, the banker paying the cheque in good faith and without negligence shall not be responsible or incur any liability, nor shall the payment be questioned by reason of the cheque having been crossed, or of the crossing having been obliterated or having been added to or altered otherwise than as authorized by this Act, and of payment having been made otherwise than to a banker or to the banker to whom the cheque is or was crossed, or to his agent for collection being a banker, as the case may be.

Sect. 80. Where the banker, on whom a crossed cheque is drawn, in good faith and without negligence pays it, if crossed generally, to a banker, and if crossed specially, to the banker to whom it is crossed, or his agent for collection being a banker, the banker paying the cheque, and if the cheque has come into the hands of the payee, the drawer, shall respectively be entitled to the same rights and be placed in the same position as if payment of the cheque had been made to the true owners thereof.

Sect. 81. Where a person takes a crossed cheque which bears on it the words "not negotiable," he shall not have, and shall not be capable of giving a better title to the cheque than that which the person from whom he took it had.

Sect. 82. Where a banker in good faith and without negligence receives payment for a customer of a cheque crossed generally or specially to himself, and the customer has no title or a defective title thereto, the banker shall not incur any liability to the true owner of the cheque by reason only of having received such payment.

3. DIVIDEND WARRANTS.

By sect. 95. the provisions of the Act as to crossed cheques apply to a warrant for payment of dividend.

By sect. 97, sub-sect. 3, nothing in the Act or in any repeal effected thereby shall affect the validity of any usage relating to dividend warrants, or the indorsements thereof.

4. PROMISSORY NOTES.

Sect. 83.—(1.) *A promissory note is an unconditional promise in writing made by one person to another signed by the maker, engaging to pay, on demand or at a fixed or determinable future time, a sum certain in money, to, or to the order of, a specified person or to bearer.*

I. BILL OF EXCHANGE (and PROMISSORY NOTE)—STATUTES—*continued.*

(2.) *An instrument in the form of a note payable to maker's order is not a note within the meaning of this section unless and until it is indorsed by the maker.*

(3.) *A note is not invalid by reason only that it contains also a pledge of collateral security with authority to sell or dispose thereof.*

(4.) *A note which is, or on the face of it purports to be, both made and payable within the British Islands is an inland note. Any other note is a foreign note.*

Sect. 84. A promissory note is inchoate and incomplete until delivery thereof to the payee or bearer.

Sect. 85.—(1.) *A promissory note may be made by two or more makers, and they may be liable thereon jointly, or jointly and severally according to its tenor.*

(2.) *Where a note runs "I promise to pay" and is signed by two or more persons it is deemed to be their joint and several note.*

Sect. 86.—(1.) *Where a note payable on demand has been indorsed, it must be presented for payment within a reasonable time of the indorsement. If it be not so presented the indorser is discharged.*

(2.) *In determining what is a reasonable time, regard shall be had to the nature of the instrument, the usage of trade, and the facts of the particular case.*

(3.) *Where a note payable on demand is negotiated, it is not deemed to be overdue, for the purpose of affecting the holder with defects of title of which he had no notice, by reason that it appears that a reasonable time for presenting it for payment has elapsed since its issue.*

Sect. 87.—(1.) *Where a promissory note is in the body of it made payable at a particular place, it must be presented for payment at that place in order to render the maker liable. In any other case, presentment for payment is not necessary in order to render the maker liable.*

(2.) *Presentment for payment is necessary in order to render the indorser of a note liable.*

(3.) *Where a note is in the body of it made payable at a particular place, presentment at that place is necessary in order to render an indorser liable; but when a place of payment is indicated by way of memorandum only, presentment at that place is sufficient to render the indorser liable, but a presentment to the maker elsewhere, if sufficient in other respects, shall also suffice.*

Sect. 88. The maker of a promissory note by making it—

(1.) *Engages that he will pay it according to its tenor;*

(2.) *Is precluded from denying to a holder in due course the existence of the payee and his then capacity to indorse.*

Sect. 89.—(1.) *Subject to the provisions in this part, and, except as by this section provided, the provisions of this Act relating to bills of exchange apply, with the necessary modifications, to promissory notes.*

(2.) *In applying those provisions the maker of a note shall be deemed to correspond with the acceptor of a bill, and the first indorser of a note shall be deemed to correspond with the drawer of an accepted bill payable to drawer's order.*

I. BILL OF EXCHANGE (and PROMISSORY NOTE)—STATUTES—_continued._

(3.) *The following provisions as to bills do not apply to notes; namely, provisions relating to—*
(a.) *Presentment for acceptance;*
(b.) *Acceptance;*
(c.) *Acceptance suprà protest;*
(d.) *Bills in a set.*
(4.) *Where a foreign note is dishonoured, protest thereof is unnecessary.*
Promissory Notes.] *The Act* 48 & 49 *Vict. c.* 59, *continues the Act* 26 & 27 *Vict. c.* 105 (*Promissory Notes*) *until the* 31st *December,* 1886.

II. BILL OF EXCHANGE—ACCEPTANCE.

—— Acceptance in Blank—*Right to fill up Drawer's Name after Death of Acceptor.*] A bill of exchange accepted for valuable consideration, with the drawer's name left blank, may be completed by the drawer's name being added after the death of the acceptor. CARTER *v.* WHITE
[20 Ch. D. 225 ; 25 Ch. D. 666

III. BILL OF EXCHANGE—ALTERATION.

1. —— Acceptance in Blank — *Effect of Figures in Margin — Fraudulent Alteration of Figures—Negligence.*] The Defendant signed an acceptance, the amount in the body of which was then left in blank, but in the margin of which were the figures £14 0s. 6d., that being the sum for which the Defendant desired to accept. He then handed the acceptance to the drawer, who subsequently filled in the blank in the body of the bill for £164 0s. 6d. and fraudulently altered the figures in the margin to that sum. The bill was then indorsed by the drawer to the Plaintiffs, who took it bonâ fide for value for the larger amount :—*Held,* that the Defendant was liable on the bill for such larger amount, on the grounds that the marginal figures are not an essential part of a bill of exchange; that one who gives an acceptance in blank holds out the person he entrusts therewith as having authority to fill in the bill as he pleases within the limits of the stamp; and that no alteration (even if it be fraudulent and unauthorized) of the marginal figures can vitiate the bill as a bill for the full amount inserted in the body, when it reaches the hands of a holder for value who is unaware that the marginal figures have been improperly altered. GARRARD *v.* LEWIS - - 10 Q. B. D. 30

2. —— Bank-note—*Action on Note—Erasure of Number—Material Alteration.*] In an action against the Bank of England for the non-payment of notes payable to bearer which had been regularly issued by the bank, it appeared that the notes had been bonâ fide purchased by the Plaintiff for value, but that before the Plaintiff took them the notes had been altered by erasing the numbers upon them and substituting others, with the object of preventing the notes from being traced, as payment had been stopped and a notice issued specifying their numbers :—*Held,* reversing the decision of Lord Coleridge, C.J., that, although the alteration did not vary the contract, it was material in the sense of altering the notes in an essential part, and that therefore the notes were vitiated, so that the Plaintiff could

III. BILL OF EXCHANGE—ALTERATION—_continued._

not recover in his action on them against the bank. SUFFELL *v.* BANK OF ENGLAND
[7 Q. B. D. 270; 9 Q. B. D. 555

3. —— Bank-note—*Action on Note—Bonâ fide Transfer for Value—Rejection by Bank—*45 & 46 *Vict. c.* 61 (*Bills of Exchange Act,* 1882), *ss.* 64, 89—*Worthless Document—Action for Money paid to Transferor.*] A Bank of England note, which had been materially altered in number and date, was paid to the Plaintiff's bank for value by the Defendant, both parties believing the note to be good. The Plaintiffs paid away the note, which was afterwards presented at the Bank of England, where the alteration was perceived and payment was refused. The note was returned to the Plaintiffs as a bad one, and, after a fortnight spent in tracing the note to the Defendant, the Plaintiffs demanded payment of it from him, and on the 21st of July, 1882, sued him for the amount —On the 18th of August, 1882, the Bills of Exchange Act, 1882 (45 & 46 Vict. c. 61), received the royal assent. By sect. 64, where a bill or acceptance is materially altered, without the assent of all parties liable on the bill, the bill is avoided except as against a party who has himself made the alteration, and subsequent indorsers. Provided that where a bill has been materially altered, but the alteration is "not apparent," and the bill is in the hands of a holder in due course, such holder may avail himself of the bill as if it had not been altered, and may enforce payment of it according to its original tenor. By sect. 89 the provisions of this Act relating to bills of exchange apply, "with the necessary modifications," to promissory notes :—*Held,* that the doctrine as to notice of infirmity in bills and notes was inapplicable to a forged Bank of England note, and that the delay in giving notice of the alteration to the Defendant was no ground of defence; that before the Bills of Exchange Act, 1882, the Bank of England was not liable on the altered note; *Suffell* v. *Bank of England* (9 Q. B. D. 555); which was therefore worthless; that sect. 64 was not retrospective, and that even if it were so, the "necessary modifications" referred to in sect. 89 would exclude Bank of England notes altogether from the operation of sect. 64, and that even if the proviso of sect. 64 would otherwise have affected the altered bank note, the alteration was "apparent," as the Bank of England could at once discern and point out to the holder of the note that it had been materially altered, although the alteration was not obvious to everybody; and, consequently, that the Plaintiffs, having received from the Defendant a worthless note on which no one could be sued, were entitled to recover in the action for money had and received. LEEDS AND COUNTY BANK *v.* WALKER - 11 Q. B. D. 84

IV. BILL OF EXCHANGE—CONSIDERATION.

—— Compounding Felony — *Illegality — Liability of Acceptor—Indorsee.*] In order to render illegal the receipt of securities by a creditor from his debtor, where the debt has been contracted under circumstances which might render the debtor liable to criminal proceedings, it is not enough to shew that the creditor was thereby

IV. BILL OF EXCHANGE—CONSIDERATION—
continued.

induced to abstain from prosecuting.—*Ward* v. *Lloyd* (7 Scott, N. R. 499) followed.—*Williams* v. *Bayley* (Law Rep. 1 H. L. 200) explained.—*Semble,* per Brett and Cotton, L.JJ., in an action by an indorsee of a bill of exchange against an acceptor for valuable consideration, it is no defence that the bill was indorsed by the drawer to the Plaintiff in order to stifle a prosecution for felony. FLOWER *v.* SADLER **9 Q. B. D. 83; 10 Q. B. D. 572**

V. BILL OF EXCHANGE—FOREIGN BILL.

—— **Conflict of Law—***Foreign Indorsement—Company — Winding-up — Liquidator — Costs.*] Bills of exchange were drawn in France by a domiciled Frenchman in the French language, in English form, on an English company, who duly accepted them. The drawer indorsed the bills and sent them to an Englishman in England:—*Held,* that the acceptor could not dispute the negotiability of the bills by reason of the indorsements being invalid according to French law.—Costs of successful claims in a winding-up were not given against the liquidator personally, but out of the assets. *In re* MARSEILLES EXTENSION RAILWAY AND LAND COMPANY. SMALLPAGE'S AND BRANDON'S CASES - **30 Ch. D. 598**

VI. BILL OF EXCHANGE — LIABILITY. OF PARTIES.

—— **Promissory Notes—***Indorsement as co-Sureties—Liability of Indorsers to equal Contribution inter se.*] The liabilities inter se of successive indorsers of a bill or note must in the absence of all evidence to the contrary be determined according to the ordinary principles of the law-merchant, whereby a prior indorser must indemnify a subsequent one.—But the whole circumstances attendant upon the making, issue and transference of a bill or note may be legitimately referred to for the purpose of ascertaining the true relation to each other of the parties who put their signatures upon it either as makers or indorsers; and reasonable inferences derived from these facts and circumstances are admitted to the effect of qualifying, altering, or even inverting the relative liabilities which the law merchant would otherwise assign to them.—Where the directors of a company mutually agreed with each other to become sureties to the bank for the same debts of the company, and in pursuance of that agreement successively indorsed three promissory notes of the company:—*Held,* reversing the judgment of the Court below, that they were entitled and liable to equal contribution inter se, and were not liable to indemnify each other successively according to the priority of their indorsements.—*Reynolds* v. *Wheeler* (10 C. B. (N.S.) 561) approved; *Steele* v. *McKinlay* (5 App. Cas. 754) distinguished.—According to the Civil Code of Lower Canada (arts. 2340 and 2346) the law of England, in force on the 30th of May, 1849, is applicable to the question raised in this appeal. MACDONALD *v.* WHITFIELD - **8 App. Cas. 733**

VII. BILL OF EXCHANGE—SECURITIES FOR.

1. —— **Specific Appropriation—***Acceptances for Accommodation of Drawer—Remittances to cover Acceptances — Insolvency of Acceptor — Interest*

VII. BILL OF EXCHANGE—SECURITIES FOR—
continued.

credited by Acceptor to Drawer.] A banker in London was in the habit of accepting for the accommodation of a customer, a merchant in Sweden, bills drawn on him by the merchant, who used to remit other bills to the banker to put him in funds to meet the acceptances when they became due. The banker, with the knowledge of the customer, generally discounted the remitted bills before they fell due, and paid the proceeds to his current account with his own bankers. He rendered yearly accounts to the customer, and in those accounts he credited him with interest on the amounts of the remitted bills from their due dates, and debited him with interest on the amounts which he paid in discharge of the acceptances. The amounts of the bills remitted by the customer did not always exactly correspond with the amounts of the acceptances which they were intended to cover. In April, 1888, the banker accepted a bill for £450 drawn on him by the customer, and maturing on the 21st of July. On the 13th of July the customer sent to the banker a bill for £450 upon W., of London, payable at sight. This bill was received by the banker on the 17th of July, and the proceeds were paid to his bankers and carried to his current account. On the 20th of July the banker stopped payment. His acceptance for £450 was dishonoured the next day, and the customer had to pay it. In November, 1883, the banker filed a liquidation petition:—*Held,* that the remitted bill for £450 was not specifically appropriated to meet the banker's acceptance for £450, and that, as the amount of the bill had been received by the banker before the commencement of the liquidation, the customer was not entitled to the proceeds in specie, but could only prove for the amount as a debt in the liquidation.—*Semble,* that, if the remitted bill had remained in specie at the commencement of the liquidation, the customer would, on retiring the acceptance, have been entitled to have the bill returned to him.—*In re Gothenburg Commercial Co.* (29 W. R. 358) approved and followed. *In re* BROAD. *Ex parte* NECK
[13 Q. B. D. 740

2. —— **Specific Appropriation—***Bill of Exchange drawn against Goods—Insolvency of Acceptor—Rights of Bill-holder and Drawer—Interest credited by Acceptor to Drawer.*] Bankers in London, at the request of M., who was acting as the agent in London of S., a merchant at Shanghai, on the 16th of March, 1883, granted to S. a letter of credit for £20,000. The letter authorized S. " to draw on us four months' sight for any sums not exceeding £20,000, such draft or drafts to be accompanied by bills of lading and invoices of tea, purchased according to order of M., and shipped by steamers to London, and marine insurance policies relating thereto, and these documents to be surrendered to us against our acceptances. And we hereby agree with you, and also as a separate engagement with the bonâ fide holders respectively of the bills drawn in compliance with the terms of this credit, that the same shall be duly accepted on presentation and paid at maturity, if drawn and negotiated on or before the 31st of December, 1883." It was

VII. BILL OF EXCHANGE—SECURITIES FOR—
continued.

agreed that a commission of 1 per cent. should be paid to the bankers on all drafts drawn under the credit, and M. agreed that he would meet all the acceptances on or before their due dates, "the usual rate of 2½ per cent. being allowed on all prepayments." Bills were drawn by S. under this credit against various parcels of tea consigned by him to M. for sale. In each case the bill mentioned the parcel of tea against which it was drawn, and purported to be drawn under the letter of credit, the date of which was mentioned, and the bills of lading and other shipping documents were in each case attached to the bill. S., in each case, advised the bankers of the drawing of the bill, mentioning the tea against which it was drawn and the name of the vessel by which it was shipped. S. discounted the bills with a Chinese bank, and their agent in London presented the bills for acceptance, and in exchange for the acceptance delivered the bills of lading and other documents attached to the London bankers, in whose name the tea was then warehoused with a dock company. As M. from time to time required portions of the tea for delivery to purchasers, the bankers handed to him warrants or delivery orders, he paying them the value of the tea comprised therein. The moneys thus received were paid to the credit of the general current account of the bankers with their own bankers. In an account in their books with M., they debited him with the amounts of the acceptances and credited him with the amounts received by the sales and with 2½ per cent. according to the agreement.— The London bankers suspended payment and filed a liquidation petition before their acceptances matured :—*Held*, that, having regard to the terms of the letter of credit, the bill-holders could not claim any specific appropriation of the teas to meet the acceptances :—But, *held*, that S. was entitled to have the teas which remained in specie at the date of the suspension (but not the proceeds of the sale of the teas which were sold before the suspension) applied in payment of the acceptances. —*Frith* v. *Forbes* (4 D. F. & J. 409) distinguished. *Ex parte* DEVER. *In re* SUSE -   **13 Q. B. D. 766**

3. —— **Specific Appropriation**—*Judicial Insolvency of Drawer and Acceptor—Application of Remittances remaining in Specie — Rule in Ex parte Waring* (19 Ves. 345).] Bankers in London granted to merchants in Ceylon a letter of credit, authorizing the merchants to draw on them at three, four, or six months sight, for any sums not exceeding £10,000 at one time, the drafts to be covered within two, three, or five months (according as they had been issued at three, four, or six months), by remittances on good London houses. And the bankers thereby agreed with the merchants, and also, as a separate engagement, with the bonâ fide holders respectively of the bills, that the bills should be duly accepted on presentation, and paid at maturity. The course of dealing between the parties was this—if the remittances sent as cover for the merchants' drafts matured later than the drafts accepted, interest was debited by the bankers against the merchants from the date of the maturity of the acceptances to that of the maturity of the remittances, while, if the remit-

VII. BILL OF EXCHANGE—SECURITIES FOR —*continued.*

tances matured earlier than the acceptances, interest was credited to the merchants. In all cases the bankers dealt with the remittances as they thought expedient, and the proceeds were paid into the general banking account of their firm. Under this letter of credit a number of bills were drawn by the merchants on the bankers, and were accepted by them, and other bills were remitted by the merchants to cover the acceptances, the letters which accompanied the remittances always describing them as sent to cover particular drafts which were specified in the letters. The bankers stopped payment and filed a liquidation petition, under which a trustee was afterwards appointed. In consequence of their stoppage the merchants also stopped payment. At the date of the liquidation petition acceptances under the letter of credit to the amount of £11,535 were outstanding, to meet which the bankers had received from the merchants remittances to the amount of £3009, of which two bills remained in specie in the hands of the bankers, the others having been converted by them into cash. After the filing of the petition two other bills, which had been posted by the merchants before they knew of the stoppage of the bankers, came into the hands of the receiver appointed under the petition. The merchants' firm consisted of two partners, one of whom was insane, and resident in Germany. The sane partner procured an adjudication of insolvency against himself in Ceylon, and under this insolvency an assignee was appointed. The sane partner deposed that "under this insolvency my estate, and also the estate of my firm, so far as legally can be, is now being administered," and this evidence was not contradicted :—*Held*, that the joint estate of the merchants, as well as that of the bankers, was under a forced administration, and that consequently the rule in *Ex parte Waring* (19 Ves. 345) applied.—*Held*, therefore, that the proceeds of the four remitted bills which were in specie at the commencement of the liquidation must be applied, not in paying the whole of the acceptances rateably, nor in paying rateably all those acceptances to meet which remittances had been sent before the filing of the liquidation petition, but in paying those acceptances to meet which the four bills had been appropriated by the letters with which they were sent.—When remittances are sent under such circumstances to cover drafts of the remitter accepted by the remittee, the remittee may, so long as he is solvent, be entitled, by mercantile usage or the course of dealing between the parties, to deal with the remittances as he pleases ; but, so soon as he becomes insolvent, the remitter is entitled to insist on having the remittances applied in paying the acceptances, and that right is the foundation of the rule in *Ex parte Waring* (19 Ves. 345), but the right extends only to those remittances which remain in specie at the date of the insolvency. *Ex parte* DEVER. *In re* SUSE. (No. 2.)   -   -   **14 Q. B. D. 611**

4. —— **Specific Appropriation** — *Marginal Advice.*] A firm at Liverpool and a firm at Pernambuco employed B. as their agent at New York. According to their course of business the firm at Pernambuco received orders from persons there to

VII. BILL OF EXCHANGE—SECURITIES FOR *—continued.*

purchase goods at New York. The firm instructed the Liverpool firm, who instructed B. B. then purchased the goods in New York and shipped them to the firm at Pernambuco with the bills of lading. B. drew bills on the Liverpool firm to pay for the goods, but not for the precise amount of the shipments, and sold the bills in New York. B. advised the Liverpool firm of the bills, and with the advice forwarded a statement of his account with them. To each bill was attached a counterfoil headed "Advice of draft," and containing a memorandum of amount of the bill and the name of the drawer, with the words "Against shipments *per* (naming the vessel). Please protect the draft as advised above." The Liverpool firm on the bills being presented to them for acceptance detached the counterfoils and kept them in their own possession. The Plaintiffs were the holders for value of bills drawn on the Liverpool firm in accordance with this course of dealing, the goods having been shipped by B. to the Pernambuco firm and the bills of lading being also sent to that firm.—On the 10th of June, 1879, the Liverpool firm stopped payment.—The three bills having been dishonoured by the Liverpool firm, the Plaintiffs brought an action against the Pernambuco firm claiming to have the bills paid out of the proceeds of the goods as having been specifically appropriated to meet the bills :—*Held* (affirming the decision of Bacon, V.C.), that there was no specific appropriation of the goods either by the course of dealing or by the "advice of draft" attached to the bills.—*Frith v. Forbes* (4 D. F. & J. 409) distinguished.—*Robey & Co.'s Perseverance Ironworks v. Ollier* (Law Rep. 7 Ch. 695) approved. PHELPS, STOKES & Co. *v.* COMBER
[26 Ch. D. 755 ; 29 Ch. D. 813

5. —— Specific Appropriation—*Direction on Bill to charge it to Account of Cargo as advised —Contemporaneous Letter of Advice.*] A. purchased from B. & Co. in America a bill of exchange dated the 5th of August, 1875, payable sixty days after sight, for £2500 drawn upon K. in London, on the face of which was a direction "to charge the same on account of cheese per *Britannic* and lard per *Greece* as advised," and on the same day B. & Co, wrote to K. a letter of advice, inclosing bills of lading for the cheese and lard, and informing K. that as against these they valued on him at sixty days' sight for £2500 favour A. The bill was not accepted, K. having heard that B. & Co. had suspended payment on the 7th of August ; but, on the arrival of the consignments in England, K. took possession of them and realised them, receiving the proceeds, out of which he claimed to retain a balance due to him on the general account between him and B. & Co. —From the evidence as to the course of dealing between A. and B. and Co., it appeared that B. & Co. had for many years previously been in the habit of consigning American produce to K., and drawing bills on him in a similar form to that of the 5th of August, but that there had not been any practice of specifically appropriating the remittances to meet any particular bills.—A. brought an action against K. and the trustee in bankruptcy of B. & Co. claiming to be entitled to

a charge on the proceeds of the cheese and lard in priority to all other persons. No question was raised as between K. and the trustee in bankruptcy as to their respective rights :—*Held*, by the Court of Appeal (affirming the decision of Chitty, J.), that A. was not entitled to the charge claimed, either on (1.) on the ground that the direction on the face of the bill of exchange operated as an equitable assignment ; or (2.) that on the authority of *Frith v. Forbes* (4 D. F. & J. 409), the letter of advice created a specific appropriation of the remittances to meet the bill in favour of B. & Co., the benefit of which was transferred to A. by the direction on the bill of exchange.— The case of *Frith v. Forbes*, if and in so far as it intended to lay down that, as a general principle of law, such a letter of advice created a specific appropriation in favour of the consignors and drawers of the bills, the benefit of which was transferred by the direction on the bill to the bill-holders—is erroneous, and must not be followed. BROWN, SHIPLEY, & Co. *v.* KOUGH
[29 Ch. D. 848

VIII. BILL OF EXCHANGE—TRANSFER.

—— Reindorsement—*Indorser and Indorsee— Circuity of Action.*] The son of the Defendant bought goods of the Plaintiffs, and required credit to enable him to pay. It was agreed that the Defendant should become surety for the price of the goods. The Plaintiffs accordingly drew two bills of exchange and indorsed them to the Defendant, who reindorsed them to the Plaintiffs. The bills having been dishonoured at maturity : —*Held*, that the Plaintiffs were not precluded from suing the Defendant on the ground of circuity of action, and that they could recover the amount of the bills from the Defendant. WILKINSON & Co. *v.* UNWIN　　7 Q. B. D. 636

BILL OF EXCHANGE—Acceptor and indorser— Suretyship—Indemnity　6 App. Cas. 1
See PRINCIPAL AND SURETY—INDEMNITY. 1.

—— Bankruptcy — Composition — Payment to indorsee without deducting value of security　　　　　15 Q. B. D. 102
See BANKRUPTCY—SECURED CREDITOR. 2.

—— Cheque　　3 Q. B. D. 238 ; 9 App. Cas. 95
See BANKER—CHEQUE. 1, 2.

—— Company—No power to accept bills—Acceptance by directors " for and on behalf of company "—Personal liability
[13 Q. B. D. 360
See COMPANY—DIRECTOR'S LIABILITY. 1.

—— Forgery　 -　 -　 7 Q. B. D. 78
See CRIMINAL LAW—FORGERY.

—— Forgery—Adoption of signature 6 App. Cas.
See ESTOPPEL—CONDUCT. 1.　　　[82

—— Proof in bankruptcy—Accommodation bills
[16 Ch. D. 330
See BANKRUPTCY—PROOF. 4.

—— Scotch law　6 App. Cas. 82 ; 7 App. Cas. 366 ;
[9 App. Cas. 95
See SCOTCH LAW—BILL OF EXCHANGE. 1, 2, 3.

BILL OF EXCHANGE—*continued.*

—— Taken in payment—Loss of lien 16 Ch. D.
    See SHIP—MARITIME LIEN. 6.   [604

—— Winding-up of company—Proof 28 Ch. D.
    See COMPANY—PROOF. 3.   [634

BILL OF LADING.

    See Cases under SHIP—BILL OF LADING.

—— Exceptions—"Dangers and accidents of the
    seas" -   -   - 10 P. D. 103
    See SHIP—SALVAGE. 13.

—— Incorporation of conditions in charterparty
    [13 Q. B. D. 317 ; 15 Q. B. D. 154
    See SHIP—CHARTERPARTY. 1, 7.

—— Indorsement—Priority - 6 Q. B. D. 475 ;
    See TROVER.   [7 App. Cas. 591

—— Indorsement—Stoppage in transitu
    [7 App. Cas. 573
    See SALE OF GOODS—LIEN. 1.

—— Payment in exchange for—Tender 11 Q. B. D.
    See SALE OF GOODS—CONTRACT. 4. [327

I. BILL OF SALE—STATUTES :—

The Act 45 & 46 Vict. c. 43, *amends the Bills of Sale Act*, 1878, *and enacts :—*

Sect. 1. *Act to be cited for all purposes as the Bills of Sale Act* (1878) *Amendment Act*, 1882.

Sect. 2. *Act to come into operation on the 1st of November*, 1882.

Sect. 3. *The Act, so far as consistent with the tenor thereof, to be construed as one with the Bills of Sale Act*, 1878 (*styled* "*the principal Act*"); *but unless the context otherwise requires not to apply to any bill of sale duly registered before the commencement of the Act so long as the registration thereof is not avoided by non-renewal or otherwise.*

The expression "*bill of sale*" *and other expressions in the Act to have the same meaning as in the principal Act, except as to bills of sale or other documents mentioned in section four of the principal Act, which may be given otherwise than by way of security for the payment of money, to which last mentioned bills of sale and other documents the Act does not apply.*

Sect. 4. *Every bill of sale shall have annexed thereto or written thereon a schedule containing an inventory of the personal chattels comprised in the bill of sale ; and such bill of sale, save as hereinafter mentioned, shall have effect only in respect of the personal chattels specifically described in the said schedule ; and shall be void, except as against the grantor, in respect of any personal chattels not so specifically described.*

Sect. 5. *Save as hereinafter mentioned, a bill of sale shall be void, except as against the grantor, in respect of any personal chattels specifically described in the schedule thereto of which the grantor was not the true owner at the time of the execution of the bill of sale.*

Sect. 6. *Nothing contained in the foregoing sections of this Act shall render a bill of sale void in respect of any of the following things (that is to say) :*

    (1.) *Any growing crops separately assigned or charged where such crops were actually growing at the time when the bill of sale was executed.*

    (2.) *Any fixtures separately assigned or charged, and any plant, or trade machinery where such fixtures, plant or trade machinery are used in, attached to, or brought upon any land, farm, factory, workshop, shop, house, warehouse, or other place in substitution for any of the like fixtures, plant, or trade machinery specifically described in the schedule to such bill of sale.*

Sect. 7. *Personal chattels assigned under a bill of sale shall not be liable to be seized or taken possession of by the grantee for any other than the following causes :—*

    (1.) *If the grantor shall make default in payment of the sum or sums of money thereby secured at the time therein provided for payment, or in the performance of any covenant or agreement contained in the bill of sale and necessary for maintaining the security ;*

    (2.) *If the grantor shall become a bankrupt or suffer the said goods or any of them to be distrained for rent, rates, or taxes ;*

    (3.) *If the grantor shall fraudulently either remove or suffer the said goods or any of them to be removed from the premises ;*

    (4.) *If the grantor shall not, without reasonable excuse, upon demand in writing by the grantee, produce to him his last receipts for rent, rates, and taxes ;*

    (5.) *If execution shall have been levied against the goods of the grantor under any judgment at law ; provided that the grantor may within five days from the seizure or taking possession of any chattels on account of any of the above mentioned causes apply to the High Court or to a Judge thereof in Chambers, and such Court or Judge, if satisfied that by payment of money or otherwise the said cause of seizure no longer exists, may restrain the grantee from removing or selling the said chattels, or may make such other order as may seem just.*

Sect. 8. *Every bill of sale shall be duly attested and shall be registered under the principal Act within seven clear days after the execution thereof, or if it is executed in any place out of England then within seven clear days after the time at which it would in the ordinary course of post arrive in England if posted immediately after the execution thereof, and shall truly set forth the consideration for which it was given, otherwise such bill of sale shall be void in respect of such personal chattels comprised therein.*

Sect. 9. *A bill of sale made or given by way of security for the payment of money by the grantor thereof shall be void unless made in accordance with the form in the schedule to the Act.*

Sect. 10. *The execution of every bill of sale by the grantor shall be attested by one or more credible witness or witnesses, not being a party or parties thereto. So much of sect.* 10 *of the principal*

I. BILL OF SALE—STATUTES—*continued.*

Act as requires that the execution of· every bill of sale shall be attested by a solicitor of ·the Supreme Court, and that .the attestation shall state that before the execution of the bill of sale the effect thereof has been explained to the grantor by the attesting witness, is hereby repealed.

Sect. 11. Where the affidavit (which under sect. 10 of the principal Act is required to accompany a bill of sale when presented for registration) describes the residence of the person making or giving the same, or of the person against whom the process is issued, to be in some place outside the London bankruptcy district as defined by the Bankruptcy Act, 1869, or where the bill of sale describes the chattels enumerated therein as being in some place outside the said London Bankruptcy district, the registrar under the principal Act shall forthwith and within three clear days after registration in the principal registry and in accordance with the prescribed directions transmit an abstract in the prescribed form of the contents of such bill of sale to the County Court registrar in whose district such places are situate, and, if such places are in the district of different registrars, to each such registrar. Every abstract so transmitted shall be filed, kept, and indexed by the registrar of the County Court in the prescribed manner, and any person may search, inspect, make extracts from and obtain copies of the abstract so registered in the like manner and upon the like terms as to payment or otherwise as near as may be as in the case of bills of sale registered by the registrar under the principal Act.

Sect. 12. Every bill of sale made or given in consideration of any sum under thirty pounds shall be void.

Sect. 13. All personal chattels seized or of which possession is taken after the commencement of this Act under or by virtue of any bill of sale (whether registered before or after the commencement of this Act) shall remain on the premises where they were so seized or so taken possession of and shall not be removed or sold until after the expiration of five clear days from the day they were so seized or so taken possession of.

Sect. 14. A bill of sale· to which the Act applies to be no protection in respect of personal chattels included in such bill of sale which but for such bill of sale would have been liable to distress under a warrant for the recovery of taxes and poor and other parochial rates.

Sect. 15 repeals sects. 8 and 20 of the principal Act, and also all other enactments contained in the principal Act which are inconsistent with the Act, but the repeal is not to affect the validity of .anything done or suffered under the principal Act before the commencement of the Act.

Sect. 16 repeals so much of sect. 16 of the principal Act as enacts that any person shall be entitled at all·reasonable times to search the register, and every registered bill of sale upon·payment of one shilling for every copy of u bill of sale inspected, and enacts that from and after the commencement of the Act any person shall be entitled at all reasonable times to search the register on payment of a fee of one shilling, or such other fee as may be prescribed, and subject to such regulations as may be prescribed, and shall be entitled at all reasonable times to inspect, examine, and make extracts from

I. BILL OF SALE—STATUTES—*continued.*

any and every registered bill of sale without being required to make a written application,·or to specify any particulars in reference thereto, upon payment of one shilling for each bill of sale inspected, and such payment shall be made by a judicature stamp : Provided that the said extracts shall be limited to the dates of execution, registration, renewal of registration, and satisfaction, to the names, addresses, and occupation of the parties, to the amount of the consideration, and to any further prescribed particulars.

Sect. 17. Nothing in the Act is to apply to any debentures issued by any mortgage, loan, or other incorporated company, and secured upon the capital, stock, or goods, chattels, and effects of such company.

II. BILL OF SALE—APPARENT POSSESSION.

1. —— Man in Possession—*Bills of Sale Act.* 1878, *ss.* 4, 8.] J. having executed a bill of sale. a man was put in possession of, the goods comprised in it by the grantee. The house in which the goods were, belonged to J., and he had a key of it : he did not sleep in it, but he went in and out as he pleased :—*Held*, that the goods were in the possession or apparent possession of J. within the meaning of the Bills of Sale Act, 1878, ss. 4, 8. SEAL *v.* CLARIDGE　-　7 Q. B. D. 516

2. —— Possession of Sheriff—*Bills of Sale Act,* 1878 (41 *&* 42 *Vict.* c. 31), s. 8.] If the goods comprised in an unregistered bill of sale are, at the time of the filing of a bankruptcy petition against the grantor, in the actual visible possession of the sheriff under an execution, issued either by the grantee or by a third person, they are not, even though the grantee has himself taken no possession, in the "apparent possession" of the grantor, and the Bills of Sale Act does not apply.—*Ex parte Mutton* (Law Rep. 14 Eq. 178) not followed. *Ex parte* SAFFERY. *In re* BRENNER　　　　16 Ch. D. 668

3. —— Registration not renewed—*Bills of Sale Acts* 1854 (17 *&* 18 *Vict.* c. 36) *ss.* 1, 7—1866 (29 *&* 30 *Vict.* c. 96), *s.* 5—1878 (41 *&* 42 *Vict.* c. 31), *s.* 8—1882 (45 *&* 46 *Vict.* c. 43), s. 3.] In 1873 S. executed a bill of sale of furniture to the Respondents to secure a loan, with an absolute unconditional power to take possession and sell in case of default of payment upon demand. The bill was duly registered, but·never re-registered. In 1883 the Respondents, in order to protect the furniture from S.'s creditors, demanded payment, and on default took possession of the furniture and sold it to C., giving him a receipt for the purchase-money though no money actually passed. At the same time C., not being able to pay, executed a bill of sale of the furniture to the Respondents to secure the purchase-money. This bill was duly registered : the receipt was not registered. The transaction with C. was found by the jury to be a bonâ fide one. The furniture having been afterwards seized under a fi. fa. against S. :—*Held*, affirming the decision of the Court of Appeal, that the sale to C. being an absolute and bonâ fide transfer of the property, the bill of 1873 was spent and satisfied, and the Bills of Sale Acts of 1854, 1866, 1878, and 1882 had no application whatever to it at the time of the execution, whether the furniture was

II. BILL OF SALE—APPARENT POSSESSION—
continued.

or was not at that time in the apparent possession of S.; and that the Respondents were entitled to the furniture. COOKSON *v.* SWIRE **9 App. Cas. 653**

III. BILL OF SALE—FORMALITIES.

(a) AFFIDAVIT.

1. —— Attestation—*Solicitor—Grantee—Bills of Sale Act, 1878 (41 & 42 Vict. c. 31), ss. 4, 8, 10.*] The grantee of a bill of sale, although he may be a solicitor, cannot be the attesting witness thereof under the Bills of Sale Act, 1878, sect. 10, sub-sect. 1.   SEAL *v.* CLARIDGE　　**7 Q. B. D. 516**

2. —— Attestation — *Solicitor of Grantee— Bills of Sale Act,* 1878 (41 & 42 Vict. c. 31), *s.* 10.] The affidavit " of its due execution and attestation," filed with a registered bill of sale under 41 & 42 Vict. c. 31, s. 10, sub-s. 2, must state, inter alia, that the bill of sale was " duly attested " by the attesting solicitor, i.e. that he was present and witnessed the due execution ; an affidavit merely verifying his signature to the attestation clause, and describing his residence and occupation, is defective, and will therefore invalidate the registration.   SHARPE *v.* BIRCH　　**8 Q. B. D. 111**

3. —— Attestation—*Solicitor — Bills of Sale Act,* 1878 (41 & 42 Vict. c. 31), *ss.* 8, 10.] The affidavit which is filed on the registration of a bill of sale must shew that the solicitor whose name appears as the attesting witness to the deed did in fact attest it, i.e. was present when it was executed by the grantor.—The affidavit is not sufficient if it only verifies the signature of the solicitor to the attestation clause.—*Sharpe* v. *Birch* (8 Q. B. D. 111) followed.   FORD *v.* KETTLE　**9 Q. B. D. 139**

4. —— Attestation — *Solicitor of Grantee— Bills of Sale Act,* 1878 (41 & 42 Vict. c. 31), s. 10, *sub-s.* 1.] The execution by the grantor of a bill of sale attested and registered under the Bills of Sale Act, 1878 (41 & 42 Vict. c. 31. s. 10), may be attested by the solicitor of the grantee.   PEN-WARDEN *v.* ROBERTS.   HEATH *v.* ROBERTS.   WILSON *v.* ROBERTS　　-　　-　**9 Q. B. D. 137**

5. —— Description of Residence — *Attesting Witness—Bills of Sale Act,* 1878 (41 & 42 Vict. c. 31), s. 10, *sub-s.* 2.] The affidavit filed on registration of a bill of sale in pursuance of the Bills of Sale Act, 1878, s. 10, sub-s. 2, contained in the introductory part describing the deponent an accurate description of his residence.   The body of the affidavit contained, inter alia, the following statements :—" I (the deponent) was present and saw the said grantor of the bill of sale duly execute the said bill of sale on the 15th day of December, 1881. The name subscribed to the said bill of sale as that of the witness attesting the due execution thereof is in the proper handwriting of this deponent. I am a solicitor of the Supreme Court, and reside at —— ; " there being thus no description of the residence of the attesting witness in the body of the affidavit :—*Held,* that the affidavit was sufficient to satisfy the requirements of the Bills of Sale Act, 1878, s. 10, sub-s. 2, in respect of the description of the residence of the attesting witness.—By Manisty, J.: The body of the affidavit sufficiently incorporated by reference the description of the residence of the attesting wit-

III. BILL OF SALE—FORMALITIES—contd.

(a.) AFFIDAVIT—continued.

ness contained in the introductory part.—By North, J.: It is sufficient that the description of the occupation and residence of the attesting witness should be found in the introductory part of the affidavit.   BLAIBERG *v.* PARKE　**[10 Q. B. D. 90**

6. —— Description of Residence—*Renewal of Registration—Bills of Sale Act,* 1878 (41 & 42 Vict. c. 31), s. 11—*Shorthand Notes of Evidence—Sheriff —Interpleader—Costs.*] The affidavit made of the re-registration of a bill of sale must state the residence of the grantee as it was stated in the bill of sale, even though it was there erroneously stated.— In a bill of sale the grantee was described as of " Boldock in the county of Hereford," her residence really being at Baldock in the county of Hertford. The bill of sale was registered and was re-registered within five years. The affidavit made on the re-registration stated only the true residence of the grantee :—*Held,* that sect. 11 of the Act had not been complied with, and that the bill of sale was void as against an execution creditor of the grantor.—Costs will not be allowed of shorthand notes of evidence which are not used on the hearing of an appeal, the decision turning on a question of law.—The order on an interpleader issue between a bill of sale holder and an execution creditor gave the sheriff his costs, to be paid by the bill of sale holder. The bill of sale holder appealed, and by the notice of appeal asked that the sheriff's costs might be paid by the execution creditor. The notice was served on the sheriff, and he appeared by counsel on the hearing of the appeal. His counsel took no part in the argument of the appeal, but only asked for costs. It was not suggested that the execution creditor was not as well able to pay the sheriff's costs as the bill of sale holder ;—*Held,* that, though it was an error to serve the sheriff with a formal notice of the appeal, he ought not to have appeared on the hearing, and that he was not entitled to any costs of the appeal.   *Ex parte* WEBSTER. *In re* MORRIS -　　-　**22 Ch. D. 136**

7. —— Description of Residence—*True Copy —Clerical Error—41 & 42 Vict.* c. 31, *ss.* 8, 10.] A " true copy " of a bill of sale within the Bills of Sale Act, 1878, s. 10, sub-s. 2, must not necessarily be an exact copy, so long as any errors or omissions in the copy filed are merely clerical and of such a nature that no one could be thereby misled.—The description of the residence of the maker of a bill of sale required by the Bills of Sale Act, 1878, s. 10, sub-s. 2, to be stated in the affidavit filed therewith, is not rendered incorrect so as to avoid the bill of sale, by the fact that between the execution of the bill of sale and the date of the affidavit the maker had left his residence, as described in the affidavit, for America. —*Button* v. *O'Neill* (4 C. P. D. 354) distinguished. *In re* HEWER.   *Ex parte* KAHEN -　　**21 Ch. D. 871**

(b.) FORM IN SCHEDULE.

8. —— Agreement to pay Insurance—" *Maintenance of the Security "—Bills of Sale Act* (1878) *Amendment Act,* 1882 (45 & 46 Vict. c. 43).] An agreement in a bill of sale of chattels, that the grantor will pay all premiums necessary for in-

III. BILL OF SALE—FORMALITIES—*contd.*

(b.) FORM IN SCHEDULE—*continued.*

suring and keeping insured the chattels against loss by fire, and forthwith after every payment in respect of such insurance produce, and, if required, deliver to the grantee the receipt or voucher for the same, is not unnecessary for the maintenance of the security, and does not contravene the Bills of Sale Act (1878) Amendment Act, 1882 (45 & 46 Vict. c. 43). HAMMOND *v.* HOCKING - - - 12 Q. B. D. 291

9. —— **Agreement to pay on Demand**— *Power to seize and sell on Default in such Payment—Bills of Sale Act (1878) Amendment Act, 1882 (45 & 46 Vict. c. 43), ss. 7, 9, 13.*] A bill of sale, given by way of security for payment of money, contained an agreement by the grantor to pay the sum advanced and interest upon demand made in writing, and gave power to the grantee to seize and sell the goods on default in payment on demand in writing :—*Held,* that the agreement to pay the money on demand was not an agreement to pay it at a stipulated time in accordance with the form in the schedule to the Bills of Sale Act (1878) Amendment Act, 1882, and that therefore the bill of sale was void by sect. 9 of that Act :—*Held,* also, by Brett, M.R., and Fry, L.J. (Bowen, L.J., doubting), that the bill of sale was void on the ground that it gave power to sell on default in payment on demand without waiting for five clear days as required by sect. 13. HETHERINGTON *v.* GROOME - - 13 Q. B. D. 789

10. —— **Agreement to pay on Demand**— *Stipulated Time for Payment—Seven Days after Demand—Bills of Sale Act (1878) Amendment Act, 1882 (45 & 46 Vict. c. 43), ss. 7, 9, and Schedule.*] A bill of sale was given by way of indemnity to the grantee on his becoming security for the payment by the grantor of a sum of money, being an instalment of a composition due by him to his creditors. The grantor agreed that he would pay the said sum of money to his creditors on a given day, and the bill of sale provided that if he did not pay the money on the day named, and the grantee should be obliged to pay the same, the grantor would repay to the grantee the amount within seven days after demand in writing, with power in default to the grantee to seize and sell the goods :—*Held* (on the authority of *Hetherington* v. *Groome* (13 Q. B. D. 789)), that the bill of sale did not contain an agreement to pay the money secured at a stipulated time in accordance with the form given in the schedule to the Bills of Sale Act (1878) Amendment Act, 1882, and was therefore void. SIBLEY *v.* HIGGS, TAPLIN, CLAIMANT

[15 Q. B. D. 619

11. —— **Power to seize**—*Agreement to pay Rent, &c.—Bills of Sale Act (1878) Amendment Act, 1882 (45 & 46 Vict. c. 43), ss. 7, 9.*] The Bills of Sale Act (1878) Amendment Act, 1882, provides that a bill of sale made or given by way of security for the payment of money by the grantor thereof shall be void unless made in accordance with the form in the schedule to the Act annexed.—The Act also provides that personal chattels assigned under a bill of sale shall not be liable to be seized by the grantee for any other than the following causes, viz., among

III. BILL OF SALE—FORMALITIES—*contd.*

(b.) FORM IN SCHEDULE—*continued.*

others : 1. If the grantor shall make default in payment of the sum or sums of money thereby secured at the time therein provided for payment or in the performance of any covenant or agreement contained in the bill of sale, and necessary for maintaining the security. 2. If the grantor shall become a bankrupt, or suffer the said goods or any of them to be distrained for rent, rates, or taxes. 4. If the grantor shall. not, without reasonable excuse, upon demand in writing by the grantee, produce to him his last receipts for rent, rates, and taxes.—By a bill of sale the grantor assigned to the grantee the goods enumerated in the schedule thereto by way of security for the payment of £300 money advanced and £180 for agreed capitalised interest thereon at the rate of sixty per cent. per annum, making together the sum of £480, by instalments of a certain amount at certain specified dates. The grantor also covenanted, amongst other things, that she would deliver to the grantee the receipts for rent, rates, and taxes, in respect of the premises on which the goods assigned might be, when demanded in writing or otherwise ; and also that she would not make any assignment for the benefit of creditors, or file a petition for liquidation or composition with creditors, or do or suffer anything whereby she should render herself liable to be made or become bankrupt. It was also by the said bill of sale agreed that if the grantor should break any of the covenants, all the moneys thereby secured should immediately become due and be forthwith paid to the grantee, and it was provided that the chattels assigned should not be liable to seizure for any other cause than those specified in the Bills of Sale Act (1878) Amendment Act, 1882:—*Held,* that the bill of sale was void as not made in accordance with the form given in the schedule :—*Held,* also, that the bill of sale could not be supported, inasmuch as it enabled the grantee to seize the goods upon a failure by the grantor to produce the receipts for rent, rates, and taxes, after a verbal demand. DAVIS *v.* BURTON

[10 Q. B. D. 414; 11 Q. B. D. 537

12. —— **Power to seize**—*Bills of Sale Act (1878) Amendment Act, 1882 (45 & 46 Vict. c. 43), ss. 7, 9.*] By a bill of sale executed two days before his bankruptcy. A. (the grantor), in consideration of £30 paid to him by B., and also in consideration of £10 charged by B. by way of bonus, assigned chattels to B. by way of mortgage for payment of £40. A. thereby agreed that he would "forthwith" pay to B. the £40, together with interest and costs then due thereon, and also pay the rent, rates, and taxes, and the premiums for insurance ; and would "forthwith" after every payment produce and deliver to B. the receipts for the same. On default in payment of the sums thereby secured, " or if he should do or suffer anything whereby he should render himself liable to become a bankrupt, or remove, or suffer the chattels to be removed from the premises, or if execution should be or should have been levied against the goods of A.," or if he should make default in the performance of any of the covenants, or commit any breach thereof—

III. BILL OF SALE—FORMALITIES—*contd.*

(b.) FORM IN SCHEDULE—*continued.*

it should be lawful for B. "forthwith or when and as soon as he should think fit" to enter and take possession, and, after taking possession to relinquish and again take possession as often and whenever he should think fit. All expenses of entry and seizure (including a fee of 5 per cent. on the whole amount then due and secured by the bill of sale), and in the exercise by B. of any of the powers, rights, and remedies therein contained, were to be added thereto and to form part of the sum secured, as if such costs, charges, payments, damages, and expenses had originally constituted an integral part of the advance. It was also provided that further advances, not exceeding £100, might be made and added to the security; and it was finally provided (in the terms of the form in the schedule to the Bills of Sale Act, 1882), that the chattels thereby assigned should not be liable to seizure or to be taken possession of by B., for any cause other than those expressed in sect. 7 of the Act:—*Held*, having regard to the provision for bonus in addition to the sum actually paid by the grantee, and especially to the power to seize in events other than those mentioned in sect. 7, that this bill of sale was void as being plainly in contravention of the provisions of the Act of 1882, and the form in the schedule thereto; and that the defects were not cured by the final proviso. *In re* WILLIAMS. *Ex parte* PEARCE - - 25 Ch. D. 656

13. —— Power to seize—*Bills of Sale Act, 1882 (45 & 46 Vict. c. 43), ss. 7, 9.*] A bill of sale empowered the grantee to seize the property in case (inter alia) the grantor "shall do or suffer any matter or thing whereby he shall become a bankrupt":—*Held*, that this event was in substance equivalent to the event "if the grantor shall become a bankrupt" in which, by sect. 7 of the Bills of Sale Act, 1882, a grantee is permitted to seize under a bill of sale, and that consequently the bill of sale was not void under sect. 9. *Ex parte* ALLAM. *In re* MUNDAY
[14 Q. B. D. 43

14, —— Several Mortgagees—*Consolidation of Securities—Bills of Sale Act (1878) Amendment Act, 1882 (45 & 46 Vict. c 43), s. 9.*] A bill of sale which is in its terms so complicated as to substantially vary from the form in the schedule to the Bills of Sale Act (1878) Amendment Act, 1882, is void by sect. 9 of that Act, notwithstanding it may not contravene any of the other sections. —Therefore a bill of sale made between the grantor and four sets of mortgagees to secure different debts owing to each respectively at different times, with a declaration that in case of default in payment of any sum thereby secured or of any other default mentioned as a cause of seizure in sect. 7 of that Act, it should be lawful for the mortgagees to seize and sell the goods assigned, was held by the Court of Appeal, reversing the decision of the Queen's Bench Division, to be not in conformity with the form in the schedule, and void. —*Semble*, the sum secured should be made payable on a specified day, and a bill of sale making it payable on demand is contrary to such form. MELVILLE *v.* STRINGER　-　12 Q. B. D. 132;
[13 Q. B. D. 392

III. BILL OF SALE—FORMALITIES—*contd.*

(c.) STATEMENT OF CONSIDERATION.

15. —— Agreement to lend—*Past Debt—Bills of Sale Act, 1878 (41 & 42 Vict. c. 31), s. 8.*] A. being indebted to B., gave him a bill of sale to secure the sum of £7350, which, on stating the accounts between them, was found to be the balance due, and by such bill of sale this sum was to be paid by A. with interest on demand in writing. The bill of sale recited that B. had agreed to lend A. £7350, and the consideration for such bill of sale was stated therein to be £7350. then paid by B. to A.:—*Held*, that the bill of sale truly set forth the consideration for which it was given so as to satisfy sect. 8 of the Bills of Sale Act, 1878 (41 & 42 Vict. c. 31), although no money in fact passed from B. to A. at the time the bill of sale was given. CREDIT COMPANY *v.* POTT
[6 Q. B. D. 295

16. —— Deduction of Commission on Loan—*Bills of Sale Act, 1878 (41 & 42 Vict. c. 31), s. 8.*] At the execution of a bill of sale expressed to be "in consideration of £700 now in hand paid" a sum of £7 10s. was paid to or retained by the grantee out of the £700 for commission on the loan and expenses in connection therewith in pursuance of a previous arrangement to that effect:—*Held*, affirming the decision of the Queen's Bench Division, that the consideration was not truly stated as required by sect. 8 of the Bills of Sale Act, 1878 (41 & 42 Vict. c. 31), and that the bill of sale was void. HAMILTON *v.* CHAINE　-　-　-　7 Q. B. D. 1, 319

17. —— Deduction of Expenses—*Costs—Bills of Sale Act, 1878 (41 & 42 Vict. c. 31), s. 8.*] A bill of sale is not vitiated under sect. 8 of the Bills of Sale Act, 1878, because a part of the sum stated in it as the consideration is retained by the grantee to pay the solicitor's costs of preparing the deed and a further agreed sum for costs previously incurred, and the fee of an auctioneer for valuing the property with a view to making the loan.—Decision of Bacon, C.J., reversed.—*Ex parte Charing Cross Advance and Deposit Bank* (16 Ch. D. 35) distinguished.—The "consideration" mentioned by sect. 8 is that which the grantor receives for giving the bill of sale, not necessarily the amount secured by it.—A bill of sale was given to secure, not only a present advance, but also the amount for the time being due to the grantee upon a mortgage including future advances which had been previously given to him by the grantor. The recitals in the bill of sale in stating the amount then due on the mortgage omitted a sum which had been advanced on a bill then current:—*Held*, that this misstatement formed no objection under sect. 8 to the validity of the bill of sale. *Ex parte* CHALLINOR. *In re* ROGERS　-　-　16 Ch. D. 260

18. —— Deduction of Expenses—*Bills of Sale Act, 1878 (41 & 42 Vict. c. 31), s. 8—Appeal—Evidence—Duty of Appellant—Right to raise new Point in Court of Appeal.*] If the amount of the expenses incident to the preparation of a bill of sale, given by way of mortgage, is deducted from the sum stated in it as the consideration, and the balance only is actually paid by the lender to the borrower, the consideration is not truly stated so as to satisfy sect. 8 of the Bills of Sale Act,

III. BILL OF SALE—FORMALITIES—contd.

(c.) STATEMENT OF CONSIDERATION—continued.

1878.—*Ex parte National Mercantile Bank* (15 Ch. D. 42) and *Ex parte Challinor* (16 Ch. D. 260) must be treated as binding authorities only in so far as they decide that, if part of the sum stated in a bill of sale as the consideration is, by the grantor's direction, given at the time of the execution of the deed, applied in satisfying a then existing debt due by him, the money so applied may be properly stated in the deed to be money then paid to him.—It is the duty of an appellant to bring before the Court of Appeal the whole of the evidence, oral as well as written, on which the order appealed from was founded, and if he does not do this, his appeal ought to be dismissed.—The Court of Appeal, however, has power, by way of indulgence, in a case where a note of oral evidence has been accidentally lost, to allow that evidence to be taken over again.—An appellant will not be allowed to raise in the Court of Appeal a point which he did not raise in the Court below, even though there is some evidence in support of it, if the nature of that evidence is such that, by any possibility, the Respondent might have been able to rebut it if the point had been raised originally. *Ex parte* FIRTH. *In re* COWBURN [19 Ch. D. 419

19. —— Deduction of Expenses—Costs—Solicitor acting for both Parties—Bills of Sale Act, 1878, s. 8.] A bill of sale in its operative part was stated to be given " in consideration of the sum of £10 now paid by H. to C." In the preparation of the bill of sale D. acted as solicitor for both H. and C., and on the execution of the deed retained with C.'s consent, £9 out of the £10 in payment of his bill of costs in the matter, and only handed C. the balance of £1:—*Held*, that, under the circumstances, the consideration was truly stated in the deed so as to satisfy sect. 8 of the Bills of Sale Act, 1878, for that, on the execution of the deed, D. no longer held the money as agent for H. or had any duty to perform towards him, but held the money as C.'s agent and could with C.'s consent retain the amount of his bill of costs.—*Ex parte Firth* (19 Ch. D. 419) distinguished. *In re* CANN 13 Q. B. D. 36

20. —— Deduction of Expenses and Interest—Bills of Sale Act, 1878 (41 & 42 Vict. c. 31), s. 8.] In the operative part of a bill of sale it was expressed to be made in consideration of £120 advanced upon its execution by the grantee to the grantor. In fact, only £90 was paid to the grantor, £30 being retained by the grantee for " interest and expenses." The execution of the deed was attested by a solicitor, and the attestation clause stated that before its execution the effect of the deed was explained by him to the grantor. At the foot of the deed, immediately after the attestation clause, there was a receipt, signed by the grantor, which stated that the £90, " together with the agreed sum of £30 for interest and expenses," made the sum of £120, " the consideration money within expressed to be paid ":—*Held*, that the receipt was not part of the deed; and that the deed did not set forth the consideration for it, and was therefore made, by sect. 8 of the Bills of Sale Act, 1878, void as against the trustee in the liquidation of the

III. BILL OF SALE—FORMALITIES—contd.

(c.) STATEMENT OF CONSIDERATION—continued.

grantor.—*Ex parte National Mercantile Bank* (15 Ch. D. 42) distinguished. *Ex parte* CHARING CROSS ADVANCE AND DEPOSIT BANK. *In re* PARKER - - - - 16 Ch. D. 35

21. —— Deduction of Expenses and Rent—Bills of Sale Act, 1878 (41 & 42 Vict. c. 31), s. 8.] A bill of sale of chattels, dated the 23rd of March, was expressed to be made " in consideration of £50 by the assignee paid to the assignor at or before the execution hereof." In fact only £21 10s. was paid to the assignor on the execution of the deed, £3 10s. being retained by the assignee for the expenses of the deed, and £25 being also retained and paid by him on the 30th of March to the landlord of the assignor's house, in which the chattels comprised in the deed were, for two quarters' rent for the quarters ending respectively the 25th of March and the 24th of June. The rent of the house was payable quarterly, but there was nothing to shew that it was payable in advance. The £3 10s. and the £25 were retained upon the written request of the assignor dated the day of the execution of the deed. On the 25th of April the assignor filed a liquidation petition, and the trustee in the liquidation claimed the goods, on the ground that the consideration for the deed had not been stated in it in compliance with sect. 8 of the Bills of Sale Act, 1878 :—*Held*, by the Court of Appeal (reversing the decision of Bacon, C.J.), that the consideration was not truly stated in the deed, and that it was, therefore, void as against the trustee, 1, because the £25 was not paid to the assignor, but only agreed to be paid on his behalf; 2, because, even if the £25 were taken to have been paid to the assignor, it was not paid " at or before the execution " of the deed.—*Ex parte National Mercantile Bank* (15 Ch. D. 42) and *Ex parte Challinor* (16 Ch. D. 260) explained. *Ex parte* ROLPH. *In re* SPINDLER 19 Ch. D. 98

22. —— Defeasance or Condition—Agreement not to register—Payment of increased Bonus—Misdescription of Grantor — Bills of Sale Act, 1878 (41 & 42 Vict. c. 31), ss. 8, 10.] A bill of sale was expressed to be made in consideration of £242 advanced by the grantee to the grantors, and the grantors agreed to repay the advance, together with a sum of £100 by way of interest and bonus, in certain instalments. There was a verbal agreement by the grantee not to register the bill of sale, in consequence of which he charged a larger bonus for the advance than he would otherwise have done:—*Held*, that the agreement not to register was a mere collateral agreement, and not part of the consideration for the bill of sale, and that, therefore, it was unnecessary to state it in the deed :—*Held*, also, that the agreement was not a " defeasance or condition " to which the deed was subject within the meaning of sect. 10 of the Bills of Sale Act, 1878.—A bill of sale and the affidavit filed on its registration described the grantors (who were father and son) by their true addresses, and added that they were mantle manufacturers carrying on business together under a specified firm. They had in fact formerly carried on the business of mantle manufacturers in partnership,

III. BILL OF SALE—FORMALITIES—*contd.*

(c.) STATEMENT OF CONSIDERATION—*continued.*

but, at the time when the bill of sale was executed, the partnership had been dissolved, and the business was being carried on by the father alone, the son being in his employment as a clerk. The property comprised in the deed in fact belonged to the father alone, though both father and son joined in the assignment. The father alone filed a liquidation petition.—*Held*, that there was no misdescription of the grantors such as to affect the validity of the registration ; (1) because the son not being a bankrupt, any misdescription of him was immaterial ; (2) because as to the father, the statement that he was carrying on business with his son was mere surplusage, and was not misleading. *Ex parte* POPPLEWELL. *In re* STOREY -   **21 Ch. D. 73**

23. —— **Explanation by Attesting Solicitor** —*Bills of Sale Act*, 1878 (41 & 42 *Vict. c.* 31), *ss.* 8, 10.] A mortgage of a leasehold brewery and some chattels was stated to be made in consideration of £2000 paid by the grantee to the grantor " immediately before the execution of these presents." No money was in fact paid by the grantee to the grantor, but the £2000 was the balance due by the grantor to the grantee in respect of the purchase-money of the brewery, which had been assigned by the grantee to the grantor, in consideration of £2500, by a deed executed immediately before the mortgage. Of this sum only £500 was paid by the grantor, it being agreed that the balance of £2000 should be secured by the mortgage :—*Held*, that the consideration was truly stated in the mortgage deed, so as to satisfy sect. 8 of the Bills of Sale Act, 1878.—It is not necessary that the affidavit filed on the registration of a bill of sale should state that the solicitor who attested the execution of the deed explained the effect of it to the grantor before he executed it.—Decision of Bacon, C.J., affirmed. *Ex parte* BOLLAND. *In re* ROPER
                 [21 Ch. D. 543

24. —— **Growing Crops**—*After-acquired Property* — " *Separately assigned* " — " *By way of Security* " — " *Specifically described* " — *Bills of Sale Act*, 1878 (41 & 42 *Vict.* c. 31), *ss.* 4, 7 —*Bills of Sale Act* (1878) *Amendment Act*, 1882 (45 & 46 *Vict.* c. 43), *ss.* 4, 5, 6, *sub-s.* 1, *ss.* 8, 9, *and sch.*] A bill of sale, duly registered and dated the 30th of April, 1883, and made between one grantor and three grantees, recited that two of the grantees (R. & D.) were liable as sureties for the grantor on a bill of exchange for £60, which had been discounted at a bank : that two of the grantees (D. & E.) and one O. were liable as sureties for the grantors on a bill of exchange for £100, which had been discounted at the same bank ; that the grantor was unable to meet the said bills, and was also in urgent need for a further sum of £45, and had applied to the grantees to take up the said two bills of exchange and make him a further advance of £45, which they had agreed to do in consideration of the grantor entering into the bill of sale, " for the purpose of securing repayment to them with interest as well of the said sum of £45, as also of the said two bills of £60 and £100 respectively with all expenses due thereon." The

III. BILL OF SALE—FORMALITIES—*contd.*

(c.) STATEMENT OF CONSIDERATION—*continued.*

bill of sale then witnessed that " in consideration of the sum of £45 now paid to the said " grantor " by the said grantees (the receipt whereof the said " grantor " hereby acknowledges), and of the covenant on the part of the grantees hereinafter contained," the grantor covenanted with the grantees on demand to " pay to the grantees all and every the said several sums of £60, £100, and £45, and all costs, charges, and expenses," and meanwhile to pay interest thereon. The bill of sale also witnessed that " in further pursuance of the said agreement and in consideration of the premises," the grantor assigned unto the grantees " all the crops now growing, or which shall at any time hereafter during the continuance of this security be growing in or upon " certain farmlands in the grantor's occupation, " and also all horses, cattle, carts, carriages, implements of husbandry, farming machinery, tools, utensils, hay, straw, consumable stores, live and dead stock, furniture, and household effects, which now are, or at any time hereafter during the continuance of this security shall be, in, upon, or about the same farm, or the farmhouse, barns, stables, or other buildings or erections thereon ; and all which said crops, stock, implements, furniture, and effects are intended to be specifically described in the schedule hereunder written (but the said schedule is not to abridge the other words of description contained in these presents"). The bill of sale contained many covenants by the grantor, but none by the grantees. It did not contain the phrase " by way of security " amongst the operative words. The schedule to the bill of sale contained a list of live stock, and the words " household furniture and effects," without any list or inventory thereof, and also under the heading " crops " a list of fields with their names, acreage, and the nature of the crops growing thereon. The instruments described as " bills of exchange" were in truth, promissory notes, and had not been discounted. The goods and chattels comprised in the bill of sale were seized on behalf of execution creditors of the grantor, and an interpleader issue was directed between the grantees and the execution creditors, but no after-acquired property was seized on behalf of the execution creditors :—*Held*, that the bill of sale was valid under the Bills of Sale Act (1878) Amendment Act, 1882, except as to after-acquired property and the household furniture and effects ; for the consideration was stated with sufficient accuracy, and " was truly set forth " within the meaning of sect. 8, notwithstanding the misdescription of the promissory notes, and that the agreement to take up the bills recited in the deed was in effect a covenant to take up the promissory notes ; that the grant of the after-acquired property did not invalidate the grant of the existing property ; that the growing crops were separately assigned within the true meaning of the statute ; that the omission of the words " by way of security " was rectified by the other terms of the deed ; that in the schedule the chattels, except the " household furniture and effects," were " specifically described " within the meaning of sect. 4 ; but that the bill of sale was void as against

III. BILL OF SALE—FORMALITIES—contd.

(c.) STATEMENT OF CONSIDERATION—continued.
execution creditors of the grantor in respect of any property afterwards acquired by the grantor, and also as to the household furniture and effects because they were not specifically described within the meaning of sect. 4. ROBERTS v. ROBERTS

[13 Q. B. D. 794

25. ——— Part repayable on Demand—£30—Immediate Demand—Bills of Sale Act (1878) Amendment Act, 1882 (45 & 46 Vict. c. 43).] A bill of sale expressed to be in consideration of £30, of which £15 is repayable on demand and the rest by monthly instalments, may, in the absence of evidence that the transaction is a sham, be valid, notwithstanding the Bills of Sale Act (1878) Amendment Act, 1882, sect. 12, if £30 is bonâ fide paid to the grantor, even although, at his own request, demand for £15 is immediately made by the grantee, and it is at once returned to him. DAVIS v. USHER

[12 Q. B. D. 490

26. ——— Prior Bill of Sale—Bills of Sale Act, 1882 (45 & 46 Vict. c. 43), s. 8.] On the 12th of February a bill of sale was executed to secure an actual advance in cash of £1500. After its execution it was discovered that it contained some clauses which made it void under the Bills of Sale Acts. It was thereupon cancelled, and a new bill of sale was, on the 16th of February, executed in substitution for the first, and was registered on the 18th of February. The second deed contained nothing to shew that it was given in place of a prior bill of sale, but it purported to be given "in consideration of £1500 now paid" by the grantee to the grantor:—Held, that the consideration was truly stated, and that it was not necessary to state the whole history of the transaction. Ex parte ALLAM. In re MUNDAY 14 Q. B. D. 43

IV. BILL OF SALE—OPERATION.

1. ——— After-acquired Property—Assignment of Future Crops — Landlord and Tenant—Surrender — Rights of Bill of Sale Holder against Landlord of Grantee.] B., the tenant of a farm, by bill of sale made in September, 1880, assigned to the Plaintiff his stock-in-trade and effects on the said farm, together with all the growing and other crops "which at any time thereafter should be in or about the same or any other premises" of the said B. On the 25th of April, 1881, the Defendant, who was B.'s landlord of the said farm, distrained for rent, and afterwards agreed with B. to withdraw such distress and to forego all claim for rent on B. agreeing to give up possession and surrender the tenancy to the Defendant on the 24th of June then next. The Defendant accordingly withdrew the distress, and on the 24th of June he took possession of the farm according to the said agreement, and afterwards cultivated the crops which were growing there, and when they arrived at maturity he reaped and sold them. Between the time he withdrew the distress and the time he took possession of the farm, viz., on the 19th of May, the Defendant had notice for the first time of the Plaintiff's claim under the bill of sale to the growing crops. The amount of rent which would have been due to the Defendant had the tenancy continued, and the expenses he

IV. BILL OF SALE—OPERATION—contd.
incurred in cultivating and reaping the crops, exceeded their market value when sold:—Held, in an action by the Plaintiff against the Defendant for the value of these crops, that the description in the bill of sale of the future crops on the farm was sufficiently specific to make a valid assignment of them in equity.—Held, also, that, assuming that the Plaintiff had a right in equity to such crops as against the Defendant, yet such right was subject to the payment of the rent and of the expenses of cultivating and reaping the crops, and as such rent and expenses exceeded the value of the crops the Plaintiff had not been injured, and had no cause of action against the Defendant. CLEMENTS v. MATTHEWS

[11 Q. B. D. 808

2. ——— After-acquired Property — Charge of all Personalty.] A person by a written instrument charged "all his present and future personalty" to secure to the Plaintiff any sums he might become indebted to him, and afterwards incurred debts to the Plaintiff:—Held, that this instrument operated to charge all the personal property belonging to the debtor at the date of the instrument, but did not operate to charge after-acquired property.— Holroyd v. Marshall (10 H. L. C. 191) distinguished. In re COUNT D'EPINEUIL (2). TADMAN v. D'EPINEUIL

[20 Ch. D. 758

3. ——— After-acquired Property—Covenant to assign — Liability — Order of Discharge—Bankruptcy Act, 1869 (32 & 33 Vict. c. 71), ss. 12, 13, 49, 125, sub-s. 10.] A debtor by bill of sale assigned for value to a creditor certain specified chattels at his place of business, "and all other chattels which might be or at any time thereafter be brought thereon in addition to or in substitution thereof." The debtor became bankrupt, and after his order of discharge brought other chattels upon the premises. The creditor did not prove for his debt in the bankruptcy:—Held (reversing the decision of Hall, V.C.), that the assignment of the after-acquired chattels, although absolute in form, amounted merely to a contract to assign for the breach of which the assignor incurred a liability provable in his bankruptcy, and from which he was released by the order of discharge; that consequently the goods brought on the premises after the order of discharge could not be seized by the creditor under his bill of sale.— Whether the same rule applies to a covenant in a marriage settlement to settle future property, quære. COLLYER v. ISAACS 19 Ch. D. 342

4. ——— After-acquired Property—Prior Equitable Estate — Subsequent Legal Estate without Notice—Supreme Court of Judicature Acts, 1873, 1875 (36 & 37 Vict. c. 66; 38 & 39 Vict. c. 77.] The Supreme Court of Judicature Acts, 1873, 1875, have not abolished the distinction between legal and equitable interests, they merely enable the High Court to administer legal and equitable remedies; and therefore notwithstanding these statutes, the grant of future-acquired chattels confers only an equitable interest therein upon the grantee; and if when they come into existence, but before the grantee takes possession thereof, the legal estate and interest therein, without notice of the grantee's existing equitable interest, become

IV. BILL OF SALE—OPERATION—*continued.*

vested in another person, the latter is entitled to the future-acquired chattels comprised in the grant, and becomes the owner thereof, both at law and in equity.—By a bill of sale a jeweller, for a valuable consideration, assigned to the Plaintiff his after-acquired stock-in-trade subject to a proviso for redemption : before the Plaintiff took possession of the after-acquired stock-in-trade, the jeweller pledged a portion of it with the Defendant, who had no notice of the Plaintiff's bill of sale :—*Held*, that the Defendant was entitled to retain the stock-in-trade pledged with him as against the Plaintiff, and that no action of detinue or conversion would lie. JOSEPH *v.* LYONS
[15 Q. B. D. 280

5. —— *After-acquired Property—Subsequent Bill of Sale—Grant of Legal Interest—Seizure by Owner of Equitable Interest.*] By a bill of sale executed in 1875, R. granted to M. the after-acquired chattels which should be upon certain premises of R. The title of M. under the bill of sale ultimately vested in the Defendant. R. brought upon the premises chattels acquired by him after 1875, and before the coming into operation of the Bills of Sale Act, 1882, by a bill of sale granted to the Plaintiff, these after-acquired chattels. The Plaintiff had no notice of the bill of sale in favour of M. In January, 1884, the Defendant seized the after-acquired chattels then upon the premises of R. The Plaintiff demanded possession of them from the Defendant, who refused to give them up; and the Plaintiff thereupon brought an action to recover their value:—*Held*, that the Plaintiff was entitled to recover from the Defendant the value of the goods in question; for the grant of the after-acquired chattels to M. carried only an equitable interest, while the Plaintiff by the grant to him took the legal interest without notice of the prior equitable interest vested in M. and had a better title than the Defendant.—*Joseph v. Lyons* (15 Q. B. D. 280) followed. HALLAS *v.* ROBINSON **15 Q. B. D. 288**

6. —— Goods bought on Credit—*Banker and Customer—Pledge of Goods bought on Credit—Delivery Order—Memorandum in Bank Ledger—Bill of Sale—Possession—Bills of Sale Act, 1878* (41 & 42 Vict. c. 31), *ss.* 3, 4—*Bills of Sale Act, 1882* (45 & 46 Vict. c. 43), s. 9.] Whatever documents are included in the expression "bill of sale" as defined by the Bills of Sale Acts, they must still, by force of sect. 3 of the Bills of Sale Act, 1878, be limited to documents "whereby the holder or grantee has power to seize or take possession of any personal chattels comprised in or made subject to such " document. The Acts therefore do not include letters of hypothecation accompanying a deposit of goods or pawn tickets given by a pawnbroker, or in fact any case where the object and effect of the transaction are immediately to transfer the possession of the chattels from the grantor to the grantee.—A trader, whose banking account was largely overdrawn, and who required a further advance of £500, deposited with his bank the invoice of goods bought by him on credit and consigned to him by rail, and gave the bank a delivery order directed to the railway company requiring the company to hold the goods to the order of the bank. The invoice

IV. BILL OF SALE—OPERATION—*continued.*

shewed that the goods were bought on credit. On arrival of the goods the company sent the usual advice note to the bank stating that they held the goods to the order of the bank. The £500 was then advanced, and a minute of the transaction, stating the rate of interest on the advance, the terms on which the goods were to be redeemed, &c., was entered in the bank ledger, and was signed by the trader and stamped. Eleven months afterwards the trader became bankrupt :—*Held*, that as the effect of the transaction was immediately to transfer the possession of the goods to the bank, the delivery order and minute did not require registration as a bill of sale, and that the title of the bank was good as against the trustee in bankruptcy.—*Semble*, a pledge by a trader of stock-in-trade which he has bought on credit, and not paid for, is not a " transfer in the ordinary course of business of his trade or calling," within the exception contained in sect. 4 of the Bills of Sale Act, 1878. *In re* HALL. *Ex parte* CLOSE **14 Q. B. D. 386**

7. —— Right to Possession — *Possession by Mortgagor—Sale by Mortgagor to Third Person—Conversion.*] In consideration of a loan of money, G. [the mortgagor] by bill of sale conveyed his furniture, stock-in-trade, and other effects in and upon the farmhouse occupied by him, to the Plaintiff, and all things of the like nature which might at any time during the continuance of the security be brought on the premises. The bill of sale contained provisoes that if the mortgagor should upon demand delivered to him or his assigns pay the amount secured the security should be void, and that in case he should make default in payment of the amount, or in case he should assign the goods or permit them to be removed from the premises before such payment, it should be lawful for the Plaintiff to enter upon the premises and take possession of and sell the goods assigned. There was a further proviso that until the mortgagor or his assigns should make default, or do any act whereby the power of entry might be put in force, it should be lawful for him or his assigns to hold and possess the goods assigned. The mortgagor, while part of the consideration money remained unpaid, sold and delivered off his premises to the Defendant part of the goods assigned. The Plaintiff thereupon demanded these goods from the Defendant, and upon his refusal to give them up, brought an action for their conversion. At the trial the jury found that the sale to the Defendant was not in the ordinary course of business:—*Held*, that the Defendant was liable, for upon the true construction of the bill of sale the sale and removal of the goods gave no title to the Defendant as against the Plaintiff. PAYNE *v.* FERN **6 Q. B. D. 620**

8. —— Seizure—*"Reasonable excuse "*for Non-*production of Receipt for Rent — Relief against Seizure of Goods—Bills of Sale Act, 1878, Amendment Act, 1882* (45 & 46 Vict. c. 43), s. 7—*Bill of Sale registered before the Commencement of the Act.*] The provisions of sect. 7 of the Bills of Sale Act, 1878, Amendment Act, 1882, apply to goods seized after the date of the commencement of the Act under a bill of sale executed and registered before such date.—Where the grantor of a bill of

IV. BILL OF SALE—OPERATION—*continued.*

sale did not, upon demand in writing by the grantee, produce a receipt for rent which had only become due a few days, and of which it appeared the landlord had not yet required payment :—*Held,* that the grantor had not "without reasonable excuse" failed to produce his last receipt for rent, within the meaning of the 4th sub-section of sect. 7 of the Bills of Sale Act, 1878, Amendment, Act, 1882.—Where, after goods had been seized under a bill of sale for default in payment of instalments due thereunder, the grantor offered to pay the amount due, but the grantee refused to receive the same :—*Held,* that the Court had power, under the above-mentioned section, to make an order restraining the grantee from selling the goods on condition that the amount due was paid. *Ex parte* COTTON
[**11 Q. B. D. 301**]

V. BILL OF SALE—REGISTRATION.

1. —— Agreement to give Bill of Sale—*Bills of Sale Act,* 1878 (41 & 42 *Vict.* c. 31), *ss.* 4, 9.] A parol agreement to give a bill of sale does not require registration under the Bills of Sale Act, 1878, and a bill of sale given in pursuance of such an agreement is not void under the Act by reason of the non-registration of the agreement. —Decision of Bacon, C.J., reversed on additional evidence. *Ex parte* HAUXWELL. *In re* HEMINGWAY - - - **23 Ch. D. 626**

2. —— Building Agreement—*Clause vesting Materials in Landowner—Bills of Sale Act,* 1878 (41 & 42 *Vict.* c. 31), *s.* 4—*Amendment Act,* 1882 (45 & 46 *Vict.* c. 43).] An agreement, by a clause in an ordinary building contract, that all building and other materials brought by the builder upon the land shall become the property of the landowner, is not a bill of sale within the Bills of Sale Act, 1878 (41 & 42 Vict. c. 31).—*Brown* v. *Bateman* (Law Rep. 2 C. P. 272) and *Blake* v. *Izard* (16 W. R. 108) followed.—*Reeve* v. *Whitmore* (4 De G. J. & S. 1 ; 33 L. J. (Ch.) 63) and *Holroyd* v. *Marshall* (10 H. L. C. 191 ; 33 L. J. (Ch.) 193) distinguished. REEVES v. BARLOW **11 Q. B. D.** [**610 ; 12 Q. B. D. 436**]

3. —— Growing Crops — *Severance — Bills of Sale Act,* 1854 (17 & 18 *Vict.* c. 36), *ss.* 1, 7.] Though a bill of sale under the Bills of Sale Act, 1854, does not require registration in respect of growing crops, yet, when the crops are subsequently severed by the grantor they become personal chattels, and, if possession has not been taken of them by the grantee before the commencement of the bankruptcy of the grantor, they will pass to the trustee in the bankruptcy. *Brantom* v. *Griffits* (1 C. P. D. 349 ; 2 C. P. D. 212) distinguished. *Ex parte* NATIONAL MERCANTILE BANK. *In re* PHILLIPS **16 Ch. D. 104**

4. —— Inventory of Goods—*Receipt of Sheriff's Officer for Purchase-money of Goods sold under Execution—Bills of Sale Act,* 1878 (41 & 42 *Vict.* c. 31).] The sheriff having seized the goods of the Defendant under a writ of fi. fa. issued by C., sold them to the claimant for £65. A deposit of £40 was paid at the time of sale, and £25 on the following day ; the sheriff, thereupon, gave to the claimant an inventory of the goods, and a receipt for the price, which were never registered under

V. BILL OF SALE—REGISTRATION—*continued.*

the Bills of Sale Act, 1878. The Defendant remained in possession of the goods, which were afterwards seized by the sheriff under a writ of fi. fa. issued in the present action :—*Held,* that the inventory and receipt did not amount to a " bill of sale " within the meaning of the Bills of Sale Act, 1878 ; and that the claimant was entitled to the goods as against the Plaintiffs.— *Woodgate* v. *Godfrey* (5 Ex. D. 24) followed. MARSDEN v. MEADOWS - - **7 Q. B. D. 80**

5. —— Joint Stock Company—*Dock Warrant —Immediate Possession—Bills of Sale Act,* 1878 (41 & 42 *Vict.* c. 31)—*Bills of Sale Act,* 1882 (45 & 46 *Vict.* c. 43).] Bills of sale given by joint stock companies are within the Bills of Sale Act, 1882.—Where a security on goods with possession is given the security is valid without registration.—A wharfinger's warrant was indorsed over to a lender with an accompanying memorandum of terms of security including a power of sale :—*Held,* that there was a good security which did not require registration. *In re* CUNNINGHAM & CO., LIMITED. ATTENBOROUGH'S CASE
[**28 Ch. D. 682**]

6. —— Priority — *Bills of Sale Act,* 1878 (41 & 42 *Vict.* c. 31), *ss.* 8, 10—*Unregistered and Registered Bills of Sale.*] Chattels were assigned to the Defendant by a bill of sale which was not registered. The grantor subsequently gave another bill of sale comprising the chattels to the Plaintiff, who registered it. The Defendant afterwards took possession of the chattels under his bill of sale. In an action against him by the Plaintiff for conversion :—*Held,* reversing the judgment of the Queen's Bench Division, that the registered bill of sale took priority over the unregistered bill of sale, and that the Plaintiff was entitled to judgment. LYONS v. TUCKER
[**6 Q. B. D. 660 ; 7 Q. B. D. 523**]

7. —— Priority—*Registered Bill of Sale— Unregistered Bill of Sale—Bills of Sale Act,* 1878 (41 & 42 *Vict.* c. 31), *s.* 10.] A bill of sale attested and registered under the Bills of Sale Act, 1878, takes priority over one that is earlier but unregistered, as to any chattels which may be comprised in both. CONELLY v. STEER - **7 Q. B. D. 520**

8. —— Priority—17 & 18 *Vict.* c. 36, *s.* 1— *Execution—Unregistered Bill of Sale.*] Whether, under 17 & 18 Vict. c. 36, s. 1, the taking in execution of goods comprised in an unregistered bill of sale defeated the bill of sale wholly or only to the extent necessary to give effect to the execution, *quære.*—The position in *Richards* v. *James* (Law Rep. 2 Q. B. 285), that it has the former effect, doubted. *In re* ARTISTIC COLOUR PRINTING COMPANY. *Ex parte* FOURDRINIER
[**21 Ch. D. 510**]

9. —— Transfer—*Assignment—Bills of Sale Act,* 1878 (41 & 42 *Vict.* c. 31), *ss.* 8, 10.] A bill of sale of goods, which was duly registered, was given to secure £500 with interest, part of which was at a subsequent date paid off. A deed was afterwards made between the two parties to the bill of sale, and the Plaintiff, whereby the security was transferred and the goods assigned to him, on his paying off the amount remaining due on the

K

V. BILL OF SALE—REGISTRATION—*continued.*

bill of sale and making a further advance to the grantor, the whole amount secured by this deed being £501 15s. 9d., with interest, and the rate of interest and the times of payment being different from those of the former deed :—*Held* (by Watkin Williams and Mathew, JJ.), that this deed was a transfer and not a new bill of sale, and need not be registered under the Bills of Sale Act, 1878, to be effectual as to the whole amount secured by it, against an execution creditor.—*Held*, by the Court of Appeal (Bramwell, Baggallay, and Lush, L.JJ.), that whether or not the deed was an effectual security, without registration, for the fresh advance, it was, as to the amount which remained due on the former bill of sale, a transfer and valid to that extent without registration under the Bills of Sale Act, 1878, so as to entitle the Plaintiff to the goods. HORNE *v.* HUGHES
[6 Q. B. D. 676

10. —— **Unregistered Bill of Sale**—*Bills of Sale Act* (1878) *Amendment Act*, 1882 (45 & 46 *Vict.* c. 43), s. 8.] The Bills of Sale Act, 1882, sect. 8, which makes a bill of sale void unless it is registered within seven clear days after execution, does not avoid an unregistered bill of sale which was executed more than seven clear days before the Act came into operation. HICKSON *v.* DARLOW
[23 Ch. D. 690

11. —— **Unregistered Bill of Sale**—*Extent of Avoidance*—*Bankruptcy of Grantor*—*Bills of Sale Act*, 1878 (41 & 42 *Vict.* c. 31), s. 8.] The effect of sect. 8 of the Bills of Sale Act, 1878, in avoiding an unregistered bill of sale as against an execution creditor of the grantor is to avoid it only to the extent necessary to satisfy the execution.—*Richards v. James* (Law Rep. 2 Q. B. 285) distinguished, on the ground that the words of sect. 1 of the Bills of Sale Act, 1854, are different from those of sect. 8 of the Act of 1878.—If after the sheriff under an execution has seized the goods comprised in an unregistered bill of sale to which the Act of 1878 applies, the bill of sale holder takes a sufficient possession before the filing of a bankruptcy petition on which the grantor is afterwards adjudicated a bankrupt, and the execution is then avoided by virtue of the relation back of the title of the trustee in the bankruptcy to an act of bankruptcy committed before the levy of the execution, the execution is swept away as if it had never existed, and the bill of sale holder is entitled to the goods as against the trustee. *Ex parte* BLAIBERG. *In re* TOOMER
[23 Ch. D. 254

12. —— **Unregistered Bill of Sale**—*Rectification of Register under Bills of Sale Act*, 1878, s. 14 —*Bill of Sale void at Commencement of the Act*— *Bills of Sale Act*, 1878 (41 & 42 *Vict.* c. 31), *ss.* 14, 23.] A bill of sale, void for want of renewal of registration at the commencement of the Bills of Sale Act, 1878, cannot be renewed under sect. 14 of that Act. ASKEW *v.* LEWIS
[10 Q. B. D. 477

BILL OF SALE—Bankruptcy of grantor—Order and disposition 21 Ch. D. 871 ; 23 Ch. D. [409 ; 24 Ch. D. 210
See BANKRUPTCY—ORDER AND DISPOSITION. 1, 2, 3.

BILL OF SALE—*continued.*

—— Building contract—Power to seize materials
[16 Ch. D. 522
See BUILDING CONTRACT. 2.

—— Registration — Mortgage of machinery — Fixtures - 15 Q. B. D. 358
See FIXTURES.

—— Registration—Transfer of registered bill of sale—Equitable sub-mortgage
[14 Q. B. D. 636
See BANKRUPTCY—ORDER AND DISPOSITION. 6.

—— Statement of consideration 26 Ch. D. 338
See BANKRUPTCY—ACT OF BANKRUPTCY. 5.

—— Unregistered—Administration of estate of deceased person 20 Ch. D. 217
See EXECUTOR—ACTIONS. 17.

BIRD—Decoy bird—Cruelty - 12 Q. B. D. 66
See CRUELTY TO ANIMALS.

BIRDS PROTECTION ACT.

Wild Birds.] *The Act* 44 & 45 *Vict. c.* 51 (*the Wild Birds Protection Act*, 1881), *extends the provisions of the Wild Birds Protection Acts*, 1880 *and* 1881, *to larks.*
Sect. 1 *repeals the exception in sect.* 3 *of the Wild Birds Protection Act*, 1880, *and enacts that a person shall not be liable to be convicted under that section by exposing or offering for sale, or having the control or possession of, any wild bird recently killed, if he satisfies the Court before whom he is charged either—*
(1.) *That the killing of such wild bird, if in a place to which the said Act extends, was lawful at the time when and by the person by whom it was killed ; or*
(2.) *That the wild bird wa killed in some place to which the said Act does not extend, and the fact that the wild bird was imported from some place to which the said Act does not extend shall, until the contrary is proved, be evidence that the bird was killed in some place to which the said Act does not extend.*

BIRETTA 7 App. Cas. 240
See PRACTICE—ECCLESIASTICAL—PUBLIC WORSHIP ACT. 1.

BIRTH—Date of - - 29 Ch. D. 985
See EVIDENCE—DECLARATION OF DECEASED PERSON. 1.

BIRTHS AND DEATHS REGISTRATION ACT, 1874.
See ECCLESIASTICAL LAW—CHURCHYARDS —Statutes.

BISHOP—Colonial—Status of 7 App. Cas. 484
See COLONIAL LAW — CAPE OF GOOD HOPE. 1.

—— Power to adjudicate upon ecclesiastical offence—Promotion of suit—Interest
[9 Q. B. D. 454
See PRACTICE—ECCLESIASTICAL—CHURCH DISCIPLINE ACT. 3.

—— Refusal to institute clerk—Action by patron —Ecclesiastical law 12 Q. B. D. 404
See ECCLESIASTICAL LAW—BISHOP.

BLANKS IN WILL - - 30 Ch. D. 390
See WILL—MISTAKE. 1.

BOARD OF TRADE—Appeal—Costs 7 P. D. 207
See SHIP— MERCHANT SHIPPING ACTS.
2.

—— Discretionary power—Railway company
[10 App. Cas. 579
See SCOTCH LAW—RAILWAY COMPANY. 1.

—— Inquiry — Condition precedent — Foreign
ship—Collision - 9 P. D. 88
See PRACTICE—ADMIRALTY—JURISDIC-
TION. 2.

BOARD OF TRADE RULES, 28th August, 1872,
r. 6 . 21 Ch. D. 837
See COMPANY — LIFE INSURANCE COM-
PANY. 1.

BOARDING SHIP—Unlawfully.
See SHIP—MERCHANT SHIPPING ACTS—
Gazette.

BOAT—Canal—Children on.
See CANAL BOATS—*Statutes.*

BOAT RACE—Thames.
See RIVER—*Gazette.*

BOILER.
The Act 45 & 46 Vict. c. 22, makes better provi-
sion for inquiries with regard to boiler explosions.
Sect. 1. *Act to be cited as the Boiler Explosions*
Act, 1882.
Sect. 2 *defines " boiler " to mean any closed vessel*
used for generating steam, or for heating water, or
for heating other liquids, or into which steam is
admitted for heating, steaming, boiling, or other
similar purposes.
Sect. 3. *Act extends to the whole of the United*
Kingdom.
Sect. 4. *Act not to apply to any boiler used ex-*
clusively for domestic purposes, or to any boiler
used in the service of Her Majesty, or to any boiler
on board a steamship having a certificate from the
Board of Trade, or to any boiler explosion into
which an inquiry may be held under the provisions
of the Coal Mines Regulation Act, 1872, *and the*
Metalliferous Mines Regulation Act, 1872, *or either*
of them.
Sect. 5. *Notice of boiler explosion to be sent to*
Board of Trade within twenty-four hours of its
occurrence with certain particulars.
Penalty for not complying with requirements of
the section.
Sect. 6 *empowers Board of Trade on receipt*
of notice to direct a preliminary inquiry as to the
boiler explosion; and, if deemed ex pedient, to
direct a formal investigation before two Commis-
sioners.
Method in which formal investigation is to be
conducted.
Sect 7. *As to costs and expenses of the inquiry.*
Sect. 8. *Fines payable under the Act to be re-*
covered in manner provided by the Summary
Jurisdiction Acts.

BONA FIDES—Creditors—Resolution for liquidation 16 Ch. D. 655
See BANKRUPTCY—LIQUIDATION. 9.

—— Resolution for composition 18 Ch. D. 495;
[22 Ch. D. 773, 778
See BANKRUPTCY—COMPOSITION. 4, 5, 7.

BONA VACANTIA—Crown—Interest 17 Ch. D.
See INTEREST. 1. [771

BOND.
—— Immoral Consideration—*Continuance of*
Cohabitation—Presumption.] The testator six
months before his death gave a bond to a lady
with whom he had cohabited for more than thirty
years, conditioned for the payment to her at the
expiration of two years of a sum of money and
interest; and he continued to cohabit with her
until his death. There was nothing on the face
of the bond with reference to the cohabitation,
and there was no evidence that it was in fact
given to secure the continuance of the cohabitation.—*Held,* that the mere continuance of the
cohabitation was not enough to raise the presumption that the bond was given in consideration
of future cohabitation, and accordingly that the
bond was good.—Observations on *Gray v. Mathias*
(5 Ves. 286). *In re* VALLANCE. VALLANCE *v.*
BLAGDEN - - - 26 Ch. D. 353

—— Administration - - 10 P. D. 196, 198
See ADMINISTRATOR—GRANT. 1, 2.

—— Satisfaction of—Double portions
[20 Ch. D. 81
See SETTLEMENT—SATISFACTION.

—— Statute of Limitations—Mortgagee
[22 Ch. D. 579; 30 Ch. D. 291
See LIMITATIONS, STATUTE OF—PER-
SONAL ACTIONS. 9, 10.

—— Deposit with solicitor—Liability of partners - 28 Ch. D. 340
See PARTNERSHIP—LIABILITIES.

BOND OF CORROBORATION 10 App. Cas. 119
See SCOTCH LAW—BUILDING SOCIETY.

BONUS—Whether capital or income 29 Ch. D. 635;
[14 Q. B. D. 239; 10 App. Cas. 438
See COMPANY—DIVIDENDS.. 1, 2.

BOOK—Copyright.
See Cases under COPYRIGHT—BOOKS.

BOOTY OF WAR.
—— Royal Warrant — *Grant — Trust or*
Agency.] The Queen by Royal Warrant "granted"
booty of war to the Secretary of State for India
in Council " in trust " for the officers and men of
certain forces, to be distributed, by the Secretary
of State or by any other person he might appoint,
according to certain scales and proportions; any
doubts arising to be determined finally by the
Secretary of State or by such persons to whom he
might refer them unless the Queen should otherwise order.—An action having been brought
against the Secretary of State for India in Council
by the Appellant on behalf of himself and all
other persons entitled under the royal grant to
share in the booty, alleging a distribution of part
and possession by the Secretary of State of the
residue, and claiming an account and distribution
of the residue:—*Held,* affirming the decision of
the Court of Appeal, that the warrant did not
transfer the property, or create a trust enforceable
by the High Court of Justice : and that the
Secretary of State being merely the agent of the
Crown to distribute the fund the action could not

BOOTY OF WAR—*continued.*
be maintained. KINLOCH *v.* SECRETARY OF STATE
FOR INDIA IN COUNCIL　　-　7 App. Cas. 619

BORNEO
　See CHARTER—*Gazette.*

BOROUGH—Division of boroughs—Parliament
　See PARLIAMENT — REDISTRIBUTION OF
　　SEATS—*Statutes.*

—— Jurisdiction of mayor—No commission of
　　peace　-　　-　　7 Q. B. D. 548
　See CONTRACT—VALIDITY. 1.

—— Liability to county rate—Main roads
　　　　　　　　　　[12 Q. B. D. 239
　See HIGHWAY—REPAIR. 1.

—— Municipal—Incorporation of—School board
　　—Affected by
　See ELEMENTARY EDUCATION ACTS—
　　SCHOOL BOARD—*Statutes.*

—— New—Parliament
　See PARLIAMENT—REDISTRIBUTION OF
　　SEATS—*Statutes.*

—— Occupation franchise
　See PARLIAMENT—FRANCHISE—*Statutes.*

—— Seats in Parliament
　See PARLIAMENT — REDISTRIBUTION OF
　　SEATS—*Statutes.*

BOROUGH CONSTABLES ACT, 1883.
　See MUNICIPAL CORPORATION—*Statutes.*

BOROUGH VOTE.
　See Cases under PARLIAMENT—FRAN-
　　CHISE. 1—9.

BORROWING POWERS—Building society
　See Cases under BUILDING SOCIETY.
　　4—10.

—— Company　　-　　17 Ch. D. 715
　See COMPANY—DIRECTOR'S AUTHORITY.
　　2.

—— Company　18 Ch. D. 334 ; 8 App. Cas. 780
　See COMPANY—DEBENTURES. 1.

—— Corporation　　-　10 App. Cas. 354
　See CORPORATION. 2.

—— Railway company　　-　21 Ch. D. 309
　See RAILWAY COMPANY—CONSTITUTION.

BOTTOMRY—Foreign ship -　　-　7 P. D. 137
　See CONFLICT OF LAWS. 4.

—— Foreign ship—Necessaries　10 P. D. 44
　See SHIP—MARITIME LIEN. 1.

—— Reduction of amount—Jurisdiction of regis-
　　trar and merchants　　9 P. D. 177
　See SHIP—MARITIME LIEN. 2.

BRANCH RAILWAY—Siding—Right of user—
　　Liability of landowner　28 Ch. D. 190
　See RAILWAY COMPANY — RAILWAYS
　　CLAUSES ACT. 8.

BREACH OF TRUST—Administrator　16 Ch. D.
　　　　　　　　　　　[236, 557
　See ADMINISTRATOR—POWERS. 1, 2.

—— Attachment of trustee　20 Ch. D. 532
　See PRACTICE—SUPREME COURT — AT-
　　TACHMENT. 1.

—— Company—Directors—Shareholders
　　　　　　　　　　[21 Ch. D. 149
　See COMPANY—DIRECTOR'S LIABILITY. 4.

BREACH OF TRUST—*continued.*
—— Costs of trustee—Bankruptcy
　　　　　　　　　　[21 Ch. D. 862, 865
　See TRUSTEE—COSTS AND CHARGES. 1, 2.

—— Devastavit—Lapse of time　20 Ch. D. 230
　See SPECIALTY DEBT.

—— Liability of trustee.
　See Cases under TRUSTEE—LIABILITIES.

—— Liability of trustee—Indemnity　28 Ch. D.
　See TRUSTEE—INDEMNITY. 1.　　[595

—— Payment of purchase-money to solicitor
　　　　　　　　　　[24 Ch. D. 387
　See VENDOR AND PURCHASER—CONVEY-
　　ANCE. 5.

—— Sale of goods to make good　17 Ch. D. 58
　See BANKRUPTCY—FRAUDULENT PREFER-
　　ENCE. 1.

—— Waiver of　　-　　20 Ch. D. 109
　See TRUSTEE—LIABILITIES. 8.

BREAD—Sale of—Delivery by cart without beam
　　and scales 14 Q. B. D. 110 ; 15 Q. B. D. 408
　See BAKER. 1, 2.

BREAKING OPEN DOOR -　　-　26 Ch. D. 644
　See PRACTICE— SUPREME COURT — AT-
　　TACHMENT. 6.

BREWERS' LICENCES.
　See REVENUE—EXCISE—*Statutes.*

BRIDGE—Freedom from toll—Liability to poor-
　　rate　　　　　　　7 Q. B. D. 223
　See POOR-RATE—OCCUPATION. 2.

—— Over railway—Paving expenses
　　　[9 Q. B. D. 412 ; 8 App. Cas. 687
　See METROPOLIS — MANAGEMENT ACTS.
　　12.

—— Removal of broken bridge—Railway com-
　　pany—Scotch law -　10 App. Cas. 579
　See SCOTCH LAW—RAILWAY COMPANY. 1.

BRISTOL COURT—Tolzey Court—Attachment of
　　goods　　-　　-　17 Ch. D. 74
　See BANKRUPTCY—SECURED CREDITOR. 1.

BRITISH HONDURAS — Adverse possession
　　against the Crown　-　6 App. Cas. 143
　See COLONIAL LAW—HONDURAS.

BRITISH SUBJECT—Infant resident abroad—
　　Guardian　　　　　30 Ch. D. 324
　See INFANT—GUARDIAN. 1.

—— Military service abroad　30 Ch. D. 165
　See DOMICIL. 2.

—— Settler in colony—Privileges of English
　　law　-　　-　　10 App. Cas. 692
　See DOMICIL. 3.

—— Status of—Descendants born abroad
　See ALIEN.　　　　　　[22 Ch. D. 243

BROKER.
London.] *The Act* 47 & 48 *Vict. c.* 3, *relieves
(after the 29th September,* 1886), *brokers in the City
of London from the necessity of being admitted by
the Court of Aldermen, and from yearly payments.
It repeals* 57 *Geo.* 3, *c.* lx., *s.* 2 (*local and personal*)
and 33 & 34 *Vict. c.* 60, *s.* 6, *from the above date.*

—— Contract by　-　　-　13 Q. B. D. 635, 861
　See PRINCIPAL AND AGENT — AGENT'S
　　LIABILITY. 2, 6.

BROKER—*continued.*

—— Employment of—Loss of trust fund
[22 Ch. D. 727; 9 App. Cas. 1
See TRUSTEE—LIABILITIES. 2.

—— Right to indemnity—Usage of Stock Exchange   14 Q. B. D. 460; 15 Q. B. D. 388
See PRINCIPAL AND AGENT—PRINCIPAL'S LIABILITY. 4, 5.

BROTHEL

See CRIMINAL LAW—NUISANCE—*Statutes.*
CRIMINAL LAW—OFFENCES AGAINST WOMEN—*Statutes.*

BUILDING.—Custom of mining—Attachment to the soil 7 Q. B. D. 295; 8 App. Cas. 195
See MINE—WORKING. 1.

—— General line of   30 Ch. D. 350
See LOCAL GOVERNMENT—LOCAL AUTHORITY. 15.

—— General line of   27 Ch. D. 362; 13 Q. B. D.
[878; 10 App. Cas. 229
See METROPOLIS — MANAGEMENT ACTS. 2, 3.

—— Prohibition against—Superfluous land
[29 Ch. D. 1012
See LANDS CLAUSES ACT—SUPERFLUOUS LANDS. 4.

—— Right of support.
See Cases under SUPPORT.

BUILDING CONTRACT.

1. —— **Extras**—*Certificate of Surveyor conclusive.*] Where a contract for the erection of certain works provided that all extras or additions, payment for which the contractor should become entitled to under the said contract, should be paid for at the price fixed by the surveyor appointed by the contractor's employer :—*Held,* that this provision impliedly gave power to the surveyor to determine what were extras under the contract, and consequently that his certificate awarding a certain amount to be due for extras was conclusive. RICHARDS *v.* MAY   10 Q. B. D. 400

2. —— **Forfeiture**—*Waiver—Power for Landlord to seize Materials on Default of Builder—Seizure after act of Bankruptcy by Builder—Bill of Sale—Registration—" Licence to take Possession of Personal Chattels as Security for any Debt "—Bills of Sale Act,* 1854 (17 & 18 *Vict.* c. 36), ss. 1, 7.] A building agreement between a landowner and a builder contained a stipulation that the landowner upon the default of the builder in fulfilling his part of the agreement, might re-enter upon the land and expel the builder, and that on such re-entry all the materials then in and about the premises should be forfeited to and become the property of the landowner "as and for liquidated damages :"—*Held,* that this stipulation was not a bill of sale within the meaning of sect. 7 of the Bills of Sale Act, 1854, inasmuch as, though it was a " licence to take possession of personal chattels," the possession was not to be taken " as security for any debt."—Decision of Bacon, C.J., reversed.—*Semble,* that if the ground of forfeiture was the omission of the builder to complete the buildings on the day appointed by the agreement, and the landowner had after that day made advances of money to the builder for the purposes of the agreement, or had in any other way treated

BUILDING CONTRACT—*continued.*

the agreement as still subsisting, he would have waived the forfeiture.—The decision in *Doe* v. *Brindley* (12 Moo. C. P. 37) questioned.—Under such a stipulation, the interest of the builder in the materials being a defeasible one, the right of the landowner to seize is not defeated by the commission of an act of bankruptcy by the builder before the seizure is made. The trustee in bankruptcy of the builder takes subject to the right of the landowner under the agreement. *Ex parte* NEWITT. *In re* GARRUD   16 Ch. D. 522

—— Clause vesting materials in landowner—Bill of sale -   -   -   - 12 Q. B. D. 436
See BILL OF SALE—REGISTRATION. 2.

—— Estate in land—Tenant for life and remainderman   -   -   - 19 Ch. D. 22
See EASEMENT. 2.

BUILDING ESTATE—Alteration in estate—Restrictive covenants   28 Ch. D. 103
See COVENANT—BREACH.

—— Investment—Trustee   - 30 Ch. D. 490
See TRUSTEE—LIABILITIES. 5.

—— Mutual easements -   - 25 Ch. D. 559;
See LIGHT—TITLE. 5. [10 App. Cas. 590

BUILDING SOCIETY.

—— Arbitration.]   *The Act 47 & 48 Vict. c. 41, defines the word " disputes" in the Building Societies Acts.*

1. —— Arbitration—*Dispute between Society and Member—Mortgage*—17 & 18 *Vict.* c. 125, s. 11—37 & 38 *Vict.* c. 42, s. 34—*Summons to refer to Arbitration and to stay the Action.*] By the rules of a building society incorporated under the Building Societies Act, 1874, it was provided, pursuant to sect. 16, sub-sect. 9 of the Act, that a reference of every matter in dispute between the society and any member of the society should be referred to the arbitration of the Registrar of Friendly Societies. The Plaintiff, who was an advanced member of the society and had executed a mortgage for securing his subscriptions and fines in respect of the advance, commenced an action against the society for an account in respect of the mortgage transaction :—*Held* (affirming the decision of Pearson, J.), that the jurisdiction of the Court was ousted, and that the society was entitled to have the dispute referred to arbitration. —*Wright* v. *Monarch Investment Building Society* (5 Ch. D. 726) approved. HACK *v.* LONDON PROVIDENT BUILDING SOCIETY
[23 Ch. D. 103

2. —— Arbitration— *Jurisdiction of High Court over Dispute between Society and Member—Building Societies Act,* 1874 (37 & 38 *Vict.* c. 42), s. 16, *sub-s.* 9, s. 34.] When the rules of a benefit building society governed by 37 & 38 Vict. c. 42 provide for the settlement by arbitration of disputes between the society and any of its members, the High Court has no jurisdiction to entertain an action by the society against a member for moneys due to it under covenants in mortgage deeds executed by the member, as such, to the society :—*So held* by Lords Blackburn and Watson, the Earl of Selborne, L.C., dissenting.—*Wright* v. *Monarch Investment Building Society* (5 Ch. D.

BUILDING SOCIETY—*continued.*

726) and *Hack* v. *London Provident Building Society* (23 Ch. D. 103) approved. MUNICIPAL PERMANENT INVESTMENT BUILDING SOCIETY *v.* KENT
[9 App. Cas. 260

3. —— Audit—*Account—Order for Accounts not referring to Settled Accounts.*] Under an order directing an account, and not referring to settled accounts, the accounting party may set up settled accounts, though the order does not direct that settled accounts shall not be disturbed, and the opposite party may impeach them, though the order does not expressly give him liberty to do so.—By the rules of a benefit society it was provided that the accounts should be audited, and that, after they had been audited and signed by the auditors, the secretary and treasurer should not be answerable for any mistakes, omissions, or errors that might afterwards be proved in them. By statute 10 Geo. 4, c. 56, s. 33, it was directed that the accounts of a society of this description should be audited by two or more members of the society. In December, 1883, an order was made for an account of all moneys received by S., the late secretary. S. carried in audited accounts down to October, 1880, and claimed to have them treated as conclusive, while the Plaintiffs claimed to have them disregarded. The Court of Appeal decided (27 Ch. D. 111) that accounts audited and signed according to the rules were *primâ facie* evidence in favour of S., but that the Plaintiffs, in taking the accounts directed by the order, might impeach such audited accounts for fraud. On examination of the audited accounts, it appeared that they had throughout been audited and signed by one person only, who was not a member of the society. Bacon, V.C., made an order expressing his opinion that the accounts had been audited in accordance with the rules, and directing the account under the order of December, 1883, to commence from October, 1880, the date of the last audit :—*Held,* on appeal, that the accounts had not been duly audited in accordance with the statute and the rules, and that the order of the Vice-Chancellor must be discharged, but without prejudice to the right of the Defendant to shew that the accounts in question were to be treated as settled accounts on any other ground than that they were audited in accordance with the statute and the rules. HOLGATE *v.* SHUTT　28 Ch. D. 111

4. —— Borrowing Powers—*Loans repayable by Instalments and Premiums—Interest on Premiums—Statutory Receipt—37 & 38 Vict. c. 42, s. 42.*] Under the rules of a building society which required that loans upon a mortgage should be repaid by annual instalments and premiums spread over a certain number of years, it was held that the society was justified in adding the whole of the annual premiums to the capital, and charging interest upon the combined amount; and upon the borrower redeeming before the end of the period, he was not entitled to a rebate in respect of the premiums contracted to be paid.—Where a borrowing member of a building society has mortgaged property to the society to secure advances and all payments due from him to the society, and the society on payment off of the mortgage indorses a statutory receipt under the 42nd section of the Building Societies Act, 1874, such receipt

BUILDING SOCIETY—*continued.*

precludes them from questioning the sufficiency of the payment, and from making any further claim against the mortgagor in respect of the debt.—*Sparrow* v. *Farmer* (28 L. J. (Ch.) 537) distinguished. HARVEY *v.* MUNICIPAL PERMANENT INVESTMENT BUILDING SOCIETY　26 Ch. D. 273

5. —— Borrowing Powers—" *Monthly Subscriptions and Deposits on Loans* "—*Winding-up*—*Priority of Depositors—6 & 7 Will.* 4, *c.* 32.] One of the rules of a benefit building society, formed under the Act 6 & 7 Will. 4, c. 32, provided that the society " is established for the purpose of raising by monthly subscriptions and deposits on loans a fund to make advances to members of the value of their shares," &c. Another rule provided that the directors should meet at specified times, " for the purpose of conducting the business of the society." A third rule provided that at the end of every five years a general account of the affairs of the society should be prepared, shewing the gross receipts and expenditure and liabilities, and that " if on taking the accounts there appears to be a deficiency of income, by which the society may be prevented from meeting its anticipated expenditure and liabilities, the amount of such deficiency shall be equitably and equally apportioned by the directors between the investing and borrowing members, and be paid forthwith by such monthly or quarterly instalments as the directors shall determine " :—*Held,* that the first rule authorized the borrowing of money from persons not members of the society ; that the second rule enabled the directors to exercise the power ; and that the third rule did not enable the directors to pledge the individual credit of the members to the lenders of money to the society, but that, even if it did, and was thus ultra vires, as being inconsistent with the nature of a building society under the Act, that rule might be rejected, leaving the borrowing power unaffected.— *Held,* that the lenders of money to the society were entitled, on its being wound up, to be paid out of the assets in priority to any of the members.—Decision of Kay, J., affirmed. *In re* MUTUAL AID PERMANENT BENEFIT BUILDING SOCIETY　29 Ch. D. 182 ;
[30 Ch. D. 434

6. —— Borrowing Powers—*Overdrawn Banking Account, whether a " Loan" within the Act—Building Societies Act,* 1874 (37 & 38 Vict. c. 42), *ss.* 15, 16, 43—*Rules—Deposits or Loans in excess of Limits prescribed by the Act — Liability of Directors.*] By sect. 15 of the Building Societies Act, 1874, any society under the Act may receive deposits or loans at interest from the members or other persons within the limits provided by the section ; and in a terminating society the total amount so received on deposit or loan and not repaid may either be a sum not exceeding two-thirds of the amount for the time being secured to the society by mortgages from its members, or a sum not exceeding twelve months' subscriptions on the shares for the time being in force.—By sect. 16 the rules of every society shall set forth whether the society intends to avail itself of the borrowing powers contained in the Act, and, if so within what limits not exceeding the limits prescribed by the Act.—By sect. 43, if any society receives loans or deposits in excess of the limits prescribed by

BUILDING SOCIETY—*continued.*

the Act, the directors or committee of management of such society receiving such loans or deposits on its behalf shall be personally liable for the amount so received in excess.—Where by the rules of a terminating society the amount to be received upon deposit or loan was limited to an amount not exceeding two-thirds of the amount for the time being secured to the society by mortgages from its members :—*Held,* in an action against the directors under sect. 43, that they were personally liable in respect of sums received by the society on deposit or loan in excess of the limit prescribed by the rules, notwithstanding that the amount received on deposit or loan did not exceed the other of the alternative limits prescribed by sect. 15 :—*Held,* also, that a loan at interest to the society from its bankers, secured by deposit of title-deeds, and made by allowing the society to overdraw its account at the bank, was a "loan" within the meaning of sect. 15. LOOKER *v.* WRIGLEY. LEIGH *v.* WRIGLEY - - - 9 Q. B. D. 397

7. —— **Borrowing Powers** — *Overdrawing Banker's Account* — *Payments to withdrawing Members—Lien, equitable — Rule in Clayton's Case* (1 Mer. 572).] A benefit building society which had no power to borrow money, was allowed by its bankers to make large overdrafts. In 1876 a memorandum was signed by the officers of the society and confirmed by the directors stating that certain deeds of borrowing members which had been deposited with the bankers were deposited not only for safe custody, but as a security for the balance from time to time. In 1881 an order for winding up the society was made, and the bankers claimed to retain the deeds as security for the balance of their account. No evidence was given as to the application of the money which was drawn out by the society; but it was admitted that some part was applied in payment of members withdrawing from the society, and the remainder in payment of salaries, legal expenses, and expenses of mortgaged property.—The Court of Appeal held that the overdrafts were ultrà vires, being a borrowing not authorized by the rules, and not properly incident to the course and conduct of the society's business for its proper purposes; and that the bankers were not creditors of the society in respect of the overdrafts; but that they were entitled to hold the deeds as a security for repayment of so much only of the moneys advanced by them as was applied in payment of the debts and liabilities of the society properly payable and had not been repaid to the bankers, excluding payments to withdrawing members; that the burden of proving this lay on the bankers, and that in satisfying that burden the bankers could not have the benefit of the rule in *Clayton's Case* (1 Mer. 572).—The Court of Appeal made an order accordingly, directing inquiries; with a declaration that in making the inquiries the bankers were to be charged with all sums received by them on account of the society since it ceased to have any balance to its credit with the bankers, and that they were not to be allowed any sums advanced by them since that date which were applied in making payments to withdrawing members or otherwise than in paying such debts and liabili-

BUILDING SOCIETY—*continued.*

ties of the society as aforesaid. The society did not appeal against the order; the bankers did.—Without expressing any opinion upon the question of payments to withdrawing members, or the bankers' right to hold the securities, *held,* that the decision and order of the Court of Appeal were in other respects right. CUNLIFFE BROOKS & Co. *v.* BLACKBURN BUILDING SOCIETY
[22 Ch. D. 61 ; 9 App. Cas. 857

8. —— **Borrowing Powers** — *Overdrawing Bankers' Account*—*Action for Account—Money paid in Mistake of Law—Ratification—Payment to withdrawing Members—Priority of Securities.*] A benefit building society which had never been incorporated, and had no power to borrow money, was allowed by its bankers to make large overdrafts, and the directors of the society signed a memorandum giving the bankers a lien upon all the society's deeds, to secure all moneys which from time to time might be owing by the society to the bankers on the balance of the banking account. Annual balance-sheets, shewing the amounts due to the bankers, were sent to all the members of the society, and adopted at the annual meetings. The society was afterwards ordered to be wound up, and as the overdrafts were ultrà vires, being a borrowing unauthorized by the rules, the official liquidator brought an action against the bankers to recover all moneys which had been paid to them by the society and applied by the bankers in discharge of their loan to the society :—*Held,* that it was no answer to such action that the moneys had been so applied by the order of the directors of the society under a mistake of law as to their power to borrow, since the acts of the directors, both in borrowing and in directing the application of the moneys, were unauthorized and not binding on the society. *Held,* also, that there had been no ratification of such acts of the directors by all the members of the society, as such ratification could not be implied from merely seeing and not questioning the balance-sheet accounts which had been sent to them, and no ratification of such acts by the majority would bind the minority of the members. The bankers were, however, allowed to stand in the place of withdrawing members of the society who had been paid on notice of withdrawal out of moneys so advanced by the bankers, and to receive the amounts which would be payable to such members if they had not been paid off. The bankers were also to have the benefit of securities obtained by the society by means of overdrafts allowed by the bankers, and to have the benefit of such securities according to their order of priority without being postponed until after other securities granted to the society. BLACKBURN AND DISTRICT BENEFIT BUILDING SOCIETY *v.* CUNLIFFE BROOKS & Co. - - 29 Ch. D. 902

9. —— **Borrowing Powers**—*Unlimited Power of Borrowing — Deposit of Deeds — Preference Shares— Priorities in Winding-up—Certificate of Barrister—6 & 7 Will.* 4, c. 82.] A benefit building society, enrolled under 6 & 7 Will. 4, c. 32, by its 32nd rule authorized the directors from time to time, as occasion might require, to borrow any sums of money at interest from any persons; the borrowed money to be a first charge upon the

BUILDING SOCIETY—*continued.*

funds and property of the society.—Under this rule the directors borrowed large sums for the proper purposes of the society, and deposited with the lenders, as security, title deeds of properties which had been mortgaged to the society by advanced members:—*Held*, reversing the decision of the Court of Appeal, that the rule was valid, and that the lenders were entitled in the winding-up to payment out of the assets, after satisfaction of the outside creditors, and in priority to the claims of all shareholders or members; but that the lenders must give up their securities to the official liquidator, the claim to special equitable charges upon specific properties being inconsistent with the true meaning of the rule, which was that all the moneys borrowed under it were to have the benefit, equally and pari passu, of a first charge upon the general funds and property.— Lord Hatherley's dictum in *Laing v. Reed* (Law Rep. 5 Ch. 8) as to an unlimited power of borrowing, overruled.—The 31st rule authorized the board to issue deposit or paid-up shares for £30 each at 5 per cent. interest with the right of withdrawing the whole or part of the deposit upon notice in preference to all other shares.—This rule was struck out by the certifying barrister, but the directors printed and acted upon it by issuing shares accordingly. Some years afterwards the rule was amended, by altering £30 into £1, and the amendment was certified by the barrister; and those who had taken £30 shares had them exchanged for £1 shares, and other £1 shares were issued to new shareholders. The moneys paid by these shareholders were applied for the purposes of the society:—*Held*, affirming the decision of the Court of Appeal, that such shareholders, whether they had become so before or after the amendment was certified, and whether they had given notice of withdrawal or not, were entitled to be paid in the winding-up in preference to the unadvanced members. *In re* GUARDIAN PERMANENT BUILDING SOCIETY. MURRAY *v.* SCOTT. AGNEW *v.* MURRAY. BRINELOW *v.* MURRAY　-　　23 Ch. D. 440 ; 9 App. Cas. 519

10. —— Borrowing Powers—*Unincorporated Society—Certified Rules—Borrowing in Excess of Prescribed Limit—Agent—Authority—Holding out by Society and Directors.*] By the certified rules of an unincorporated building society the directors might borrow money not exceeding a prescribed amount. Loans were made to the society through its secretary in accordance with advertisements, issued with the authority of the directors, that such loans might be so made by bringing the money to the office of the secretary. In each case a receipt was given by the secretary for the money as a loan to the society, with a written undertaking by him " to procure the promissory note of the directors for the loan," and afterwards in pursuance of such undertaking, the receipt was exchanged for such note which always bore the date of the receipt. After an amount had been so borrowed exceeding the limit prescribed by the rules, the Plaintiffs, who had on several previous occasions lent money to the society according to the above mode, paid a sum to the secretary as a loan to the society, and received from him the usual receipt and undertaking, but no promissory note of the directors

was ever afterwards given, and the secretary absconded, appropriating that sum, with other moneys of the society, to his own use. In an action against the society and directors, the jury found that the society held out the secretary to the Plaintiffs as having authority to receive the loan on their behalf on the terms on which it was received, and that the directors did the same:— *Held*, that such finding was bad in point of law as against the society, and that, as the limit for borrowing prescribed by the rules had been exceeded when the loan was made by the Plaintiffs, the society, which had derived no benefit, was not liable for such loan:— *Held* (Bramwell, L.J., doubting), that although there was no fraud on the part of the directors they were personally liable to the Plaintiffs for the money which had been so advanced. CHAPLEO *v.* BRUNSWICK PERMANENT BUILDING SOCIETY　6 Q. B. D. 696

11. —— Incorporation—*Irregularity of Proceedings—Power of Court to declare Certificate void—Prerogative of Crown—Building Societies Act*, 1874 (37 & 38 *Vict.* c. 42), ss. 7, 9, 12, 32.] The Court has no power to declare the certificate of incorporation of a building society, given by the Registrar under the provisions of the Building Societies Act, 1874, void on the ground that it had been obtained irregularly. GLOVER *v.* GILES
[18 Ch. D. 173

12. —— Mortgages—*Mortgage Debt paid by Third Party and Deed, with Statutory Receipt indorsed thereon, handed to him—Intermediate Sale and Conveyance of Part of Mortgaged Property to Fourth Party—Effect of indorsed Receipt under s. 42 of Building Societies Act*, 1874 (37 & 38 *Vict.* c. 42).] Land and four houses thereon were vested in a building society as mortgagees, and on the society being paid off by the Plaintiff, by request of the mortgagor, the mortgage deed, with a receipt indorsed in accordance with the 42nd section of the Building Societies Act, 1874 (37 & 38 Vict. c. 42), was with other title-deeds handed to him, and the mortgagor shortly afterwards conveyed to him the property, on mortgage for a larger loan. The mortgagor had prior to the payment to the building society conveyed one house in fee to the Defendant, who was ignorant of the mortgage to the society, and he at once took possession of it, but the Plaintiff knew nothing of the sale and purchase:—*Held*, that in accordance with previous decisions, though not agreeing with them, the effect of the indorsed receipt was to vest the legal estate in the Plaintiff, and to give him, to the extent of the money paid to the society and the interest thereon, priority over Defendant's claim.—*Pease* v. *Jackson* (Law Rep. 3 Ch. 576), *Fourth City Mutual Benefit Building Society* v. *Williams, Marson* v. *Cox* (14 Ch. D. 140, 147), and *Robinson* v. *Trevor* (12 Q. B. D. 423), discussed. SANGSTER *v.* COCHRANE　28 Ch. D. 298

13. —— Mortgages—*Reconveyance—Indorsed Receipt—Priority—38 & 39 Vict. c. 60, s. 16, sub-s. 7.*] A piece of land was mortgaged to a friendly society, and by way of second mortgage to a banking company. A building society agreed to pay off the first mortgage, and to make a further advance, having no notice of the second mortgage. Accordingly by a deed indorsed on the first mortgage

BUILDING SOCIETY—_continued._

deed, the first mortgagees reconveyed to the mortgagor; and by another deed he conveyed the land to the building society to secure the repayment of the sum paid to the first mortgagees, and the further advance :—_Held_, that as the legal estate had passed by a reconveyance and not by a receipt under 38 & 39 Vict. c. 60, s. 16, sub-s. 7, it was vested in the building society, and gave them priority over the second mortgagees.—_Robinson_ v. _Trevor_ (12 Q. B. D. 423) distinguished. CARLISLE BANKING COMPANY v. THOMPSON

[26 Ch. D. 398

14. —— **Winding-up—**_Effect of Winding-up Order on Position of Members—Compulsory Withdrawal — Right of Borrowing Member to receive Credit for all Instalments, and pay up Balance of Loan, and be relieved of further Liabilities—_ 37 & 38 Vict. c. 42 (_Building Societies Act,_ 1874), _ss._ 14, 16.] A building society registered under the Building Societies Act, 1874, had for its objects : 1, to form a good investment for investors ; 2, to advance to shareholders money for building and other purposes, to a not greater extent than the amount of their shares, on their granting a bond for the same over heritable security. The rules provided that the shares were to be limited to £25 ; that a shareholder who had not received an advance was to pay up his shares by monthly instalments ; and when such instalments with profits amounted to £25 per share he was to be paid out.—As to a member who had received an advance, it was provided that he should pay up his advance by monthly instalments on his shares with interest at the rate of 5 per cent. on the loan. It was also provided that members could withdraw on giving a month's notice. On withdrawal by an unadvanced member, he was to receive the whole instalments paid on his shares with interest. On withdrawal by a borrowing member, he was to pay up the whole of his debt, interest, and penalties, after deducting the amount of the monthly instalments paid upon his shares with interest calculated thereon. A. took shares for the sole purpose of obtaining an advance. He executed a bond in common form as security ; and the society granted him a backletter, to the effect that they agreed not to enforce the bond so long as the regular payments of the instalments, interest, and other sums due upon his shares were paid. A. regularly paid his instalments with interest charged on the whole sum lent. Losses having been incurred, the society was in February, 1880, ordered to be wound up voluntarily. There were no outside creditors. In July, 1880, A. gave notice, under the rules, of withdrawal to the liquidators and claimed a discharge of his bond on his paying to them the difference between his loan and the amount in cumulo of the instalments paid by him, with interest added. The liquidators denied his right to withdraw after liquidation, unless he paid up the whole loan and left the instalments to be refunded according to the result of the liquidation :—_Held_, affirming, with a variation, the judgment of the Court below, that the advance had pro tanto been extinguished by the total amount of the instalments paid by A.; that from and after the date of the winding-up order

BUILDING SOCIETY—_continued._

A. had a right to redeem his security by paying to the liquidators the difference between his advance and his instalments with interest added thereon as against excess of interest which he had been charged ; and on payment of such difference, with interest thereon, he was entitled to be relieved of all further liability as a contributory or otherwise. BROWNLIE v. RUSSELL

[8 App. Cas. 235

15. —— **Withdrawal of Members—**_Construction of Rule " provided the funds permit"—Winding-up—Priorities in Winding-up._] The rules of a benefit building society allowed any investing member to withdraw "provided the funds permit," upon giving notice; and declared that "no further liabilities shall be incurred by the society till such member has been repaid" The society was ordered to be wound up and the assets were insufficient to pay everybody :—_Held_, affirming the decision of the Court of Appeal, that those investing members who had given notice of withdrawal and whose notices had expired before the winding-up began, were entitled to be paid out of the assets (after the outside creditors) in priority to those members who had not given notice of withdrawal, notwithstanding the fact that between the giving of the notices and the winding-up there never were any funds for payment. _In re_ BLACKBURN BENEFIT BUILDING SOCIETY. WALTON v. EDGE 24 Ch. D. 421 ; 10 App. Cas. 33

—— Mortgage to—Bankruptcy—Disclaimer
[22 Ch. D. 384
See BANKRUPTCY—DISCLAIMER. 9.

—— Mortgage to—Bankruptcy—Proof
[22 Ch. D. 450 ; 27 Ch. D. 509
See BANKRUPTCY—PROOF. 13, 17.

—— Receipt by trustees—Mortgage—Tacking
—Priorities - - 12 Q. B. D. 423
See MORTGAGE—PRIORITY. 2.

—— Scotch law - - 10 App. Cas. 119
See SCOTCH LAW—BUILDING SOCIETY.

BULLION—Liability to contribute to salvage
[6 P. D. 60
See PRACTICE—ADMIRALTY—SALVAGE. 4.

BURGESSES—Votes—Parliament
See PARLIAMENT—FRANCHISE—_Statutes._

BURGH—Common good of 7 App. Cas. 547
See SCOTCH LAW—PUBLIC RIGHTS.

BURIAL AND REGISTRATION ACTS (DOUBTS REMOVAL) ACT, 1881.
See ECCLESIASTICAL LAW—CHURCHYARDS
—_Statutes._

BURIAL BOARD.

The Act 48 & 49 Vict. c. 21, _directs that the reasonable expenses incurred in taking a poll on appointment of a burial board, or vacancy therein, shall be defrayed as if expenses of the Burial Acts._

—— Appointment of Burial Board—18 & 19 Vict. c. 128, s. 12.] The existence of a legally constituted burial board for the whole of a parish, does not prevent the vestry of an ecclesiastical district formed out of such parish under 1 & 2 Will. 4, c. 38, and which does not separately maintain its own poor, from legally

BURIAL BOARD—*continued.*

appointing a burial board for such district under 18 & 19 Vict. c. 128, s. 12. THE QUEEN *v.* OVERSEERS OF THE PARISH OF TONBRIDGE
[**11 Q. B. D. 134; 13 Q. B. D. 339**

—— Income tax—Application of surplus income in aid of poor-rate   -   13 Q. B. D. 9
See REVENUE—INCOME TAX. 2.

BURIAL GROUND.

The Act 47 & 48 Vict. c. 72 (*Disused Burial Grounds Act*), 1884), *prohibits buildings to be erected on any disused burial ground, closed by order in Council. It does not apply to any case where a faculty had been obtained before this Act, nor to such grounds sold under Act of Parliament.*

1. —— **Burial Board**—*Grave*—*Grant in Perpetuity*—*Family Rights*—*Executor*—*Purchase of Grave*—*Burial Acts* (15 & 16, Vict.. c. 85 ; 16 & 17 Vict. c. 134).] A burial board may, under the Burial Acts (15 & 16 Vict. c. 85, and 16 & 17 Vict. c. 134), grant a grave space to the grantee and his heirs, and the title to the burial rights under such grant will descend to the heirs of the grantee, and will not be vested in all members of the family of the grantee. MATTHEWS *v.* JEFFREY   -   -   -   6 Q. B. D. 290

2. —— **Dead Bodies cast on Shore** — *Tidal River*—*Liability of Parish*—48 *Geo.* 3, *c.* 75.] By 48 Geo. 3, c. 75, s. 1, the overseers of parishes throughout England in which any dead human bodies shall be found thrown in or cast on shore from the sea, by wreck or otherwise, are required to cause such bodies to be buried, and by sect. 5, the overseers are to be reimbursed such expenses by the county treasurer. A steamship was sunk by collision in the River Thames, near Woolwich, at a place below low water mark, and a number of persons were drowned. Some of the bodies were found ashore within the boundaries of Woolwich, in Kent, and were buried by the overseers. The River Thames at Woolwich and at the places where the bodies were found ashore is a navigable tidal river where great ships go :—*Held,* that the county treasurer could not be made liable for the expenses incurred by the overseers, for the bodies were not cast on shore "from the sea" within the meaning of the Act. OVERSEERS OF WOOLWICH *v.* ROBERTSON   6 Q. B. D. 654

BURNING DEAD BODY
[**12 Q. B. D. 247 ; 13 Q. B. D. 331**
See CRIMINAL LAW—MISDEMEANOR. 1, 2.

BUSINESS—Articles not connected with—Order and disposition   24 Ch. D. 31
See BANKRUPTCY—ORDER AND DISPOSITION. 8.

—— Carried on by executor   -   18 Ch. D. 93 ;
[**26 Ch. D. 19, 672**
See EXECUTOR—ADMINISTRATION. 1, 2, 3.

—— Carried on by trustee   26 Ch. D. 245
See TRUSTEE—POWERS. 3.

—— Goodwill of   19 Ch. D. 355 ; 25 Ch. D. 472 ;
See GOODWILL. 1, 2, 3. [**27 Ch. D. 145**

—— Place of carrying on   8 Q. B. D. I ;
See APPRENTICE. 1, 2. [**9 Q. B. D. 636**

—— Settlement of—Profits—Successive tenants for life   26 Ch. D. 588
See TENANT FOR LIFE.

BY-LAW—Dock company—Validity
[**10 Q. B. D. 387**
See DOCKS AND HARBOURS. 1.

—— Local government
See LOCAL GOVERNMENT — BY-LAWS — *Statutes.*

—— Local Government Acts—Validity—Swine kept near dwelling-house
[**12 Q. B. D. 617**
See LOCAL GOVERNMENT—BY-LAWS.

—— Metropolitan Board of Works—Construction
[**14 Q. B. D. 479**
See METROPOLIS—BUILDING ACTS. 8.

—— Railway company—Validity and construction of   -   -   7 Q. B. D. 32
See RAILWAY COMPANY—BY-LAWS.

—— School board—Non-payment of fees
[**15 Q. B. D. 415**
See ELEMENTARY EDUCATION ACTS — ATTENDANCE. 7.

—— Thames—Boat race.
See RIVER—*Gazette.*

—— Thames—Fishery.
See FISHERY ACTS—*Gazette.*

—— Urban authority   21 Ch. D. 621 ;
[**8 App. Cas. 798**
See LOCAL GOVERNMENT—STREETS. 4.

C.

CAB—Liability of proprietor for negligence of driver　　　-　　　8 Q. B. D. 104
　　See NEGLIGENCE—LIABILITY. 1.

CALCINING—Nuisance　　　7 App. Cas. 518
　　See SCOTCH LAW—NUISANCE.

CALL—Ultrà vires　　　-　　　16 Ch. D. 681
　　See COMPANY--DIRECTOR'S AUTHORITY. 3.

—— Unpaid—Receiver -　　　18 Ch. D. 155
　　See RAILWAY COMPANY — ABANDON-
　　MENT. 1.

CANADA, LAW OF.
　　See Cases under—
　　　COLONIAL LAW—CANADA—DOMINION.
　　　COLONIAL LAW — CANADA — NEW
　　　　BRUNSWICK.
　　　COLONIAL LAW — CANADA — NOVA
　　　　SCOTIA.
　　　COLONIAL LAW—CANADA—ONTARIO.
　　　COLONIAL LAW—CANADA—QUEBEC.

—— Practice—Appeal - 8 App. Cas. 103, 574;
　　　　　　　　　　　　　　[10 App. Cas. 675
　　See PRACTICE—PRIVY COUNCIL—LEAVE
　　TO APPEAL. 1, 2, 4.

CANAL BOATS.
　　*The Act 47 & 48 Vict. c. 75 (the Canal Boats
Act, 1884), amends the 40 & 41 Vict. c. 60 (the
Canal Boats Act, 1877).*
　　*By sect. 5, the power of the Local Government
Board to make regulations as to school certificates,
&c., includes school certificates, &c., to be used by
children in canal boats.*
　　*By sect. 10 the definition " canal boat" in sect.
14 of Act of 1877, may be extended by Local
Government Board to vessels registered under
Merchant Shipping Act, 1854.*

CANVASSERS—Election for Parliament — Expenses　　　　-　　21 Ch. D. 408
　　See PARLIAMENT—ELECTION. 1.

CAPE OF GOOD HOPE, LAW OF.
　　See Cases under COLONIAL LAW—CAPE
　　OF GOOD HOPE.

CAPITAL—Charge on annuity—Income
　　See WLL—ANNUITY. 1. [17 Ch. D. 167

—— Charge on—Land drainage　　29 Ch. D. 588
　　See SETTLED LAND ACT — PURCHASE-
　　MONEY 5.

—— Company—Application　　22 Ch. D. 349
　　See COMPANY—MEMORANDUM AND AR-
　　TICLES. 2.

—— Company—Bonus whether capital or income　　29 Ch. D. 635; 10 App. Cas. 438
　　See COMPANY—DIVIDEND. 1, 2.

—— Company—Not called up　　17 Ch. D. 715
　　See COMPANY—DIRECTOR'S AUTHORITY.
　　2.

—— Company—Payment of dividend out of
　　　　　　　　　　　　[16 Ch. D. 344
　　See COMPANY—DIVIDEND. 4.

CAPITAL—*continued.*

—— Company—Payment of dividend out of
　　　[21 Ch. D. 149, 519; 25 Ch. D. 752
　　See COMPANY — DIRECTOR'S LIABILITY.
　　4, 5, 6.

—— Company—Reduction of.
　　See Cases under COMPANY—REDUCTION
　　OF CAPITAL.

—— Income—Permanent improvements 27 Ch. D.
　　See SETTLEMENT—POWERS. 7.　[196

CAPTURE AND SEIZURE—Ship—Insurance
　　　[9 Q. B. D. 463 ; 10 Q. B. D. 432 ;
　　　　　　　　　　　[8 App. Cas. 393
　　See INSURANCE, MARINE—POLICY. 3, 4.

CARGO—Expense of re-shipping
　　　[13 Q. B. D. 69; 10 App. Cas. 404
　　See SHIP—GENERAL AVERAGE. 4.

CARRIER :—　　　　　　　　　　Col.
　　I. CARRIERS' ACT　　　-　　　278
　　II. DAMAGES　　　　　　　-　　278
　　III. GOODS -　　　　-　　　279

I. CARRIER—CARRIERS' ACT.

　　1. —— Temporary Loss of Goods—*Negligence
—Carriers' Act (11 Geo. 4 & 1 Will. 4, c. 68),
s. 1—Damages.*] A carrier is not deprived of the
protection afforded by the Carriers' Act (11 Geo. 4
& 1 Will. 4, c. 68), s. 1, merely by the fact that
the loss of the goods is temporary and not permanent, nor can the owner of goods, which ought
to have been but were not declared pursuant to
that statute, recover damages for the consequences
of the loss of them, as distinguished from the loss
itself.—The Plaintiff delivered to the Defendants,
who were carriers for hire from London to Rome,
a trunk to be sent by rail from London to Liverpool, and thence shipped by steamer for Italy,
Owing to the Defendants' negligence the trunk
was put on board a vessel bound for New York,
where it arrived, and a long time elapsed before
it was restored to the Plaintiff. The trunk contained articles within the Carriers' Act, the value
of which exceeded £10. The Plaintiff was obliged
to replace at enhanced prices the articles within
the Carriers' Act contained in the trunk :—*Held,*
that the Plaintiff could not recover from the Defendants damages either for the temporary loss of
the articles within the Carriers' Act or for being
obliged to replace them at enhanced prices, a
carrier being protected by the statute not only as
to a loss but also as to all consequences flowing
from it. MILLEN *v.* BRASCH　-　8 Q. B. D. 35 ;
　　　　　　　　　　　　[10 Q. B. D. 142

II. CARRIER—DAMAGES.

　　—— Measure of Damages — *Liability for
Delay in Transmission of Goods.*] On the 19th of
December, 1881, eighteen bales marked " Raga "
were delivered by the Plaintiffs in London to
the Defendants for conveyance to W. station in
Kent, where in the ordinary course they should

II. CARRIER—DAMAGES—*continued.*

have been delivered within twenty-four hours. By mistake they were forwarded to another place, and did not reach the W. station until the 4th of January, 1882, when, finding them to have become heated (through being packed in a damp state) and therefore unfit for the manufacture of paper, the consignees rejected them; and ultimately the rags were found useless for any purpose, and were destroyed.—There being an admitted breach of duty on the part of the Defendants, and it being conceded that the rags would have sustained no injury if they had been packed dry, the County Court Judge gave a verdict for the Plaintiffs, but for nominal damages only, on the ground that the loss was attributable to the Plaintiffs' own act in packing the rags in a damp state, without informing the Defendants that special care was necessary.—Upon a motion to enter a verdict for the Plaintiffs for the admitted value of the goods:—*Held,* that the ruling of the Judge was correct. BALDWIN & CO. *v.* LONDON, CHATHAM, AND DOVER RAILWAY COMPANY　　9 Q. B. D. 582

III. CARRIER—GOODS.

—— Freight — *Non-payment of Freight by Consignee—Liability of Consignor.*] The Defendants hired a trolly, and agreed with the owner to pay for the carriage both ways. The Defendants delivered the trolly to the Plaintiffs, to be returned to the owner under a consignment note which stated that the Defendants requested the Plaintiffs to receive and forward the trolly as per address and particulars on the note, and on the conditions stated therein. The note gave the name of the owner as consignee, and in a column headed "who pays carriage" was inserted "consignee." The Plaintiffs delivered the goods to the consignee, who declined to pay the freight on the ground that the Defendants had agreed to pay it. In an action to recover the freight from the Defendants:—*Held,* that under the circumstances the Defendants could not be treated merely as agents of the consignee to make the contract for the carriage of the trolly, but were themselves contracting parties, and liable to pay the freight. GREAT WESTERN RAILWAY COMPANY *v.* BAGGE　　-　-　-　15 Q. B. D. 625

CARRIER—Contagious Diseases (Animals) Act —Proscribed district　12 Q. B. D. 629
　　See CONTAGIOUS DISEASES (ANIMALS) ACTS.

—— Lien for freight—Bankruptcy 22 Ch. D. 470
　　See BANKRUPTCY—JURISDICTION. 5.

—— Railway company—Alternative rates
　　　　[10 Q. B. D. 250; 8 App. Cas. 703
　　See RAILWAY COMPANY—TRAFFIC MANAGEMENT. 1.

—— Railway company—Detention
　　　　[8 Q. B. D. 44
　　See RAILWAY COMPANY—LIABILITIES. 2.

—— Railway company—Passenger's luggage
　　　　[14 Q. B. D. 228
　　See RAILWAY COMPANY — PASSENGER'S LUGGAGE.

—— Railway company—Inequality of tolls— Group rates　　14 Q. B. D. 209
　　See RAILWAY COMPANY — RAILWAYS CLAUSES ACT. 2.

CASE STATED—Power to state case for opinion of Court—Reference to Local Government Board under local Act—Common Law Procedure Act, 1854　9 Q. B. D. 518
　　See ARBITRATION—SUBMISSION. 1.

—— Power of justices to state case—General district rate—Order for payment
　　　　[14 Q. B. D. 730
　　See JUSTICES—PRACTICE. 2.

—— Power of justices to state case—Railway commissioners　　15 Q. B. D. 505
　　See RAILWAY COMPANY — RAILWAYS REGULATION ACTS. 4.

CASES SPECIALLY CONSIDERED IN THIS DIGEST.
　　See TABLE OF CASES (*ante,* p. cxix).

CASH—Under control of Court　-　20 Ch. D. 203
　　See LAND CLAUSES ACT — PURCHASE-MONEY. 6.

CASUAL POOR ACT, 1882.
　　See POOR LAW—RELIEF—*Statutes.*
　　METROPOLIS—POOR ACTS—*Statutes.*

CATALOGUE—Illustrated—Copyright 21 Ch. D.
　　See COPYRIGHT—BOOKS. 1.　　[369

CATTLE—Levant and couchant—Common
　　　　[20 Ch. D. 753
　　See COPYHOLD—CUSTOM. 1.

CATTLE STATION — Nuisance—Powers of railway company　-　　29 Ch. D. 89
　　See NUISANCE—DEFINITION. 2.

CAUSE OF ACTION — Res judicata — Separate actions in respect of same wrongful act
　　See JUDGMENT. 5.　　[14 Q. B. D. 141

—— Support—Statute of Limitations—Personal actions　-　　14 Q. B. D. 125
　　See LIMITATIONS, STATUTE OF—PERSONAL ACTIONS. 2.

CENTRAL CRIMINAL COURT—Mandamus
　　　　[11 Q. B. D. 479
　　See COURT—CENTRAL CRIMINAL COURT.

CENTRAL CRIMINAL COURT (PRISONS) ACT, 1881.
　　See PRISON—*Statutes.*

CERTIFICATE — Architect — General line of buildings　-　13 Q. B. D. 878;
　　　　[10 App. Cas. 229
　　See METROPOLIS—MANAGEMENT ACTS. 2.

—— Breaches of patent　-　21 Ch. D. 720
　　See PATENT—VALIDITY. 2.

—— Competency of ship—Colonial.
　　See SHIP—MERCHANT SHIPPING ACTS— *Gazette.*

—— Conformity—Bankruptcy -　27 Ch. D. 687
　　See BANKRUPTCY—DISCHARGE. 2.

—— Engineer　　11 Q. B. D. 229
　　See CONTRACT—BREACH. 1.

—— Incorporation of building society 18 Ch. D.
　　See BUILDING SOCIETY. 11.　　[173

—— Patent suit　　29 Ch. D. 366
　　See PATENT—PRACTICE. 3.

—— Rules of building society　23 Ch. D. 440;
　　　　[9 App. Cas. 519
　　See BUILDING SOCIETY. 9.

CERTIFICATE—*continued.*
—— Survey of ship—Colonial.
　　See SHIP—MERCHANT SHIPPING ACTS—
　　Gazette.
—— Solicitor—Neglect to renew　15 Q. B. D. 467
　　See SOLICITOR—CERTIFICATE.
CERTIORARI — Discretion — Inquisition under
　　Lands Clauses Act　-　9 Q. B. D. 741
　　See LAND CLAUSES ACT — COMPENSA-
　　TION. 5.
CESTUI QUE TRUST—Improperly made party—
　　Costs　-　20 Ch. D. 611
　　See VENDOR AND PURCHASER—PURCHASE
　　WITHOUT NOTICE. 1.
—— Right of action—Breach of covenant
　　　　　　　　　　　　　　　[30 Ch. D. 57
　　See HUSBAND AND WIFE—SEPARATION
　　DEED. 2.
CEYLON—Law of.
　　See Cases under COLONIAL LAW —
　　CEYLON.
CHAIRMAN—Company—Statement by—Agent
　　　　　　　　　　　　　　　[22 Ch. D. 593
　　See EVIDENCE—GENERAL. 4.
—— Meeting of shareholders　29 Ch. D. 159
　　See COMPANY—VOLUNTARY WINDING-UP.
　　1.
CHAMBERS—Adjournment to Judge—Costs
　　　　　　　　　　　　　　　[22 Ch. D. 5
　　See MORTGAGE—CONTRACT. 7.
—— Evidence in　-　22 Ch. D. 430
　　See PRACTICE — SUPREME COURT—EVI-
　　DENCE. 8.
—— Order in—Alteration　-　29 Ch. D. 827
　　See PRACTICE—SUPREME COURT—JUDG-
　　MENT. 8.
—— Practice in.
　　See Cases under PRACTICE— SUPREME
　　COURT—CHAMBERS.
—— Practice in　-　28 Ch. D. 650
　　See MORTGAGE—FORECLOSURE. 2.
—— Practice in—Appeal from order　19 Ch. D.
　　　　　　　　　　　　　　　[516; 21 Ch. D. 131
　　See PRACTICE—SUPREME COURT — AP-
　　PEAL. 20, 21.
—— Practice in—Trustee Acts -　28 Ch. D. 529
　　See TRUSTEE ACTS—VESTING ORDERS. 2.
—— Practice in—Trustee Relief Act
　　　　　　　　　　　　　　　[22 Ch. D. 635
　　See TRUSTEE RELIEF ACT. 1.
CHAMPERTY (and MAINTENANCE).
　　1. —— Common interest, what amounts to.]
The Plaintiff having sat and voted as a member
of Parliament without having made and subscribed the oath appointed by the 5th section of
29 & 30 Vict. c. 19, the Defendant, who was also
a member of Parliament, procured C. to sue the
Plaintiff for the penalty imposed by that section
for contravention thereof.　C. was a person of
insufficient means to pay the costs in the event
of the action being unsuccessful. After the commencement of the action the Defendant gave to
C. a bond of indemnity against all costs and
expenses he might incur in consequence of the
action. It was ultimately decided in the House
of Lords that the above mentioned section does

CHAMPERTY (and MAINTENANCE)—*contd.*
not enable a common informer to sue for the
penalty, and that therefore the action would not
lie.　The Plaintiff brought an action for maintenance against the Defendant :—*Held,* that the
Defendant and C. had no common interest in the
result of the action for the penalty; that the conduct of the Defendant in respect of such action
amounted to maintenance ; and that the action
for maintenance was therefore maintainable.
BRADLAUGH *v.* NEWDEGATE　　　11 Q. B. D. 1
　　2. —— Maliciously procuring Bankruptcy—
Maintenance—Bankruptcy Act, 1869—*Order XXV.
r.* 4—*Cause of Action passing to Trustee in Bankruptcy—Company in Liquidation—Corporation.*]
A bankrupt whose adjudication in bankruptcy
has not been set aside cannot maintain an action
for maliciously procuring the bankruptcy; and
such an action may be summarily dismissed upon
summons as frivolous and vexatious.　*Whitworth*
v. *Hall* (2 B. & Ad. 695) approved.—A bankrupt
cannot maintain an action for maintenance on the
ground that the defendant incited and supported
bankruptcy proceedings in which he had no
common interest, since the cause of action (if any)
passed to the trustee in bankruptcy; and such an
action may be summarily dismissed upon summons as frivolous and vexatious:—*Held,* also by
the Earl of Selborne, L.C., that a corporation in
liquidation, as distinct from the individual liquidator, is incapable of committing such an act of
maintenance.—The inherent jurisdiction of the
Court to protect itself from abuse is recognised
and extended by Order xxv., rule 4, of the Judicature Rules of 1883.　METROPOLITAN BANK *v.*
POOLEY　-　10 App. Cas. 210
CHANCERY COURT OF YORK　7 Q. B. D. 273;
　　　　　　　　　　　　　　　[6 App. Cas. 657
　　See PRACTICE — ECCLESIASTICAL — CON-
　　TEMPT. 2.
CHANCERY DIVISION—Change of venue
　　　　　　　　　　　　　　　[26 Ch. D. 621
　　See PRACTICE—SUPREME COURT—TRIAL.
　　6.
—— Jurisdiction—Action for sum below £10
　　　　　　　　　　　　　　　[30 Ch. D. 387
　　See PRACTICE—SUPREME COURT—JURIS-
　　DICTION. 2.
—— Jurisdiction—Probate　26 Ch. D. 656
　　See PRACTICE—SUPREME COURT—JURIS-
　　DICTION. 1.
—— Probate—Revocation—Jurisdiction　9 P. D.
　　See ESTOPPEL—JUDGMENT. 1.　[210
CHANCERY FUNDS RULES, 1874, rr. 14, 19
　　　　　　　　　　　　　　　[21 Ch. D. 776
　　See LANDS CLAUSES ACT—COSTS. 5.
CHARGE—Annuity—Income or capital
　　See WILL—ANNUITY. 1. [17 Ch. D. 167
—— Debt of married woman—Separate estate—
　　Injunction -　-　16 Ch. D. 371, 660
　　See PRACTICE—SUPREME COURT—IN-
　　JUNCTION. 6.
—— Debts—Will　-　-　20 Ch. D. 465
　　See WILL—CHARGE OF DEBTS.
—— Debts—Will　-　16 Ch. D. 3
　　See ADMINISTRATOR —WITH WILL AN-
　　NEXED. 1.

CHARGE—*continued.*

—— Debts—Will—Legal estate in executors
　　See WILL—ESTATE IN REALTY. 1.
　　　　　　　　　　　　　[24 Ch. D. 190

—— Land drainage　　-　　29 Ch. D. 588
　　See SETTLED LAND ACT — PURCHASE-
　　MONEY. 5.

—— Legacies　　　　-　　26 Ch. D. 19
　　See EXECUTOR—ADMINISTRATION. 2.

—— On ecclesiastical land
　　See INCLOSURE—ECCLESIASTICAL LAND—
　　Statutes.

—— On officer's commission money 16 Ch. D. 571 ;
　　　　　　　　　　　　　[19 Ch. D. 17
　　See MORTGAGE—PRIORITY. 12.

—— On property of company—Debenture
　　　　[16 Ch. D. 411 ; 29 Ch. D. 736
　　See COMPANY—DEBENTURES. 5, 7.

—— On property recovered
　　See Cases under SOLICITOR—LIEN. 1—7.

—— On real estate—Charity
　　See Cases under CHARITY—MORTMAIN.

—— Private improvement expenses
　　　　　　　　　　　　　[17 Ch. D. 782
　　See LOCAL GOVERNMENT—STREETS. 8.

CHARGES OF TRUSTEE.
　　See Cases under TRUSTEE—COSTS AND
　　CHARGES.

CHARGING ORDER.
　　See Cases under PRACTICE — SUPREME
　　COURT—CHARGING ORDERS.

—— Solicitor's lien.
　　See Cases under SOLICITOR—LIEN. 1—7.

CHARITABLE INSTITUTION—Restrictive cove-
　　nant in lease　　　　25 Ch. D. 206 ;
　　　　　　　　　　　　　[27 Ch. D. 71
　　See LANDLORD AND TENANT—LEASE. 4.

CHARITY.　　　　　　　　　　　Col.
　　I. COMMISSIONERS　　-　　　283
　　II. GIFT TO　　　　　　　　286
　　III. MANAGEMENT　　　　　　286
　　IV. MORTMAIN　　　　　　　288

—— CHURCH BUILDING.
　　See CHURCH BUILDING ACTS.

—— ENDOWED SCHOOLS.
　　See ENDOWED SCHOOLS ACT.

I. CHARITY—COMMISSIONERS.

　　1. —— Consent — *Collegiate Body — Surplus
Revenue to be paid to Ecclesiastical Commissioners
for Administration — Action against Collegiate
Body for Accounts —Charitable Trusts Act, 1853
(16 & 17 Vict. c. 137), ss. 17, 62—Mandamus.*] By
an ancient charter a collegiate body was founded
at Manchester, and they were seised of the rectory
of the parish, and of the tithes, glebe lands, and
other property for religious and temporal purposes
in the parish. The property having considerably
increased in value, an Act of Parliament was in
1850 passed authorizing the division of the parish
into several parishes, and for the application of
the revenues. Accounts of receipts and expenditure by the collegiate body were to be rendered
yearly to the Ecclesiastical Commissioners, by
whom it was to be applied and the surplus paid,
inter alia, in payment of yearly or other sums as

I. CHARITY—COMMISSIONERS—*continued.*

to them should seem fit to each and every or any
or one or more of the incumbents of the benefices
in the parish. The accounts which were rendered
by the collegiate body to the Commissioners were
complained of by the incumbents on the ground
that many of the disbursements were illegal. A
request made to the Ecclesiastical Commissioners
to take proceedings to check the expenditure
being declined, the incumbents brought an action
against the collegiate body for the purpose of
enforcing a compliance with the statute, and the
Ecclesiastical Commissioners were made co-Defendants. A mandamus was claimed against the
collegiate body to compel them to render accounts.
Both Defendants demurred, one ground being
that the consent of the Charity Commissioners to
the action had not been obtained :—*Held,* that the
object of the action was to obtain a proper account
of the funds which ought to be transferred to the
Ecclesiastical Commissioners and which would be
administered by them as charity for the benefit of
the incumbents of the benefices, therefore the
consent of the Charity Commissioners to the action
proceeding was, under the 17th section of the
Charitable Trusts Act of 1853, necessary.—*In re
Meyrick's Charity* (1 Jur. (N.S.) 438) and *Attorney-General* v. *Sidney-Sussex College* (15 W. R.
162) followed.—*Held,* also, that, though a mandamus was the only relief sought for, the matter
would still be left within the operation of the 17th
section of the Act, because a mandamus is a proceeding for obtaining an order concerning a
charity.—*Holme* v. *Guy* (5 Ch. D. 901) observed
upon. ATTORNEY-GENERAL *v.* DEAN AND CANONS
OF MANCHESTER　　　-　　　18 Ch. D. 596

　　2. —— Consent—*College*—16 & 17 Vict. c. 137,
ss. 17, 62.] An information cannot be brought
against a college in one of the Universities without the leave of the Charity Commissioners. AT-
TORNEY-GENERAL *v.* SIDNEY-SUSSEX COLLEGE,
CAMBRIDGE　　-　　　21 Ch. D. 514, n.

　　3. —— Consent—*Place for Religious Meetings
—Registered Building*—16 & 17 Vict. c. 137, ss. 17,
62—18 & 19 Vict. c. 81, s. 9.] An action for removing the minister of a building registered as a place
of meeting for religious worship and for administering the trusts of the deed relating to such
building can be prosecuted without the certificate
of the Charity Commissioners.—*Attorney-General*
v. *Sidney-Sussex College* (21 Ch. D. 514, n.) observed
upon. GLEN *v.* GREGG　　　21 Ch. D. 513

　　4. —— Consent—*Recipient of Charity Funds
—Schoolmaster*—16 & 17 Vict. c. 137, s. 17.] The
Plaintiff had been appointed schoolmaster of a
free school by the churchwardens and overseers
of the parish, and part of his salary was paid to
him by the trustees of a charity under a scheme
of the Court of Chancery. He brought an action
against the trustees, alleging that they had refused to pay what was due to him, and claiming
an account of the income of the charity :—*Held,*
on demurrer, that the consent of the Charity
Commissioners to the action was necessary. BRIT-
TAIN *v.* OVERTON　　　25 Ch. D. 41, n.

　　5. —— Consent—*Resident Medical Officer—
Recipient of Funds of Charity—Charitable Trusts
Act,* 1853 (16 & 17 Vict. c. 137), s. 17.] The
Plaintiff had been appointed in pursuance of

I. CHARITY—COMMISSIONERS—continued.

certain rules framed by the committee of a hospital established by a trust deed of March, 1879, under the powers conferred by the deed, resident medical superintendent of the institution.for life, subject to his removal on three months' notice by the committee on proof to them of neglect of duty; and he was let into possession of a house which was annexed to the office. The funds of the hospital not being sufficient to maintain a resident medical officer, the committee gave the Plaintiff three months' notice of removal, no charge of neglect of duty being brought against him. The committee gave the notice with the intention of applying for a new scheme which would render the office unnecessary.—The Plaintiff commenced an action against the committee for a declaration that he was entitled to hold his office during good behaviour, and for an injunction to restrain them from ejecting him from his residence and from otherwise interfering with the tenure of his office:—*Held*, by Chitty, J., on motion for an injunction, that the Plaintiff before issuing his writ ought to have obtained the certificate of the Charity Commissioners as required by sect. 17 of the Charitable Trusts Act, 1853, and the motion was refused with costs.—*Held* by the Court of Appeal, that if the object of the action was anything beyond preventing the Defendants from excluding the Plaintiff, it required the sanction of the Commissioners. And the Defendants at the Bar expressing their intention not to exclude the Plaintiff unless and until a new scheme should be sanctioned, or until the trial of the action, the order of the Court below was affirmed. BENTHALL v..EARL OF KILMOREY　　-　　25 Ch. D. 39

6. —— *Consent — Royal Society — Voluntary Association — Sale of Land — Charitable Trusts Acts*, 1853, s. 62, and 1855, ss. 29, 48.] The Royal Society, a voluntary association of learned men founded in the reign of King Charles II., in 1732, purchased, out of moneys arising from the subscriptions of the members, real estate at Acton, and in 1881 sold part of it. An objection was taken by the purchaser that the consent of the Commissioners under the Charitable Trusts Acts, 1853 (16 & 17 Vict. c. 137, s. 62) and 1855 (18 & 49 Vict. c.124, s. 29), was necessary on the ground that the society was an endowed charitable institution:—*Held*, that the estate having been purchased out of the moneys arising from the voluntary contributions of members which could be by the society legally applied for such purpose, the society came within the exemptions of the 62nd section of the Charitable Trusts Act, 1853, and the 48th section of the Act of 1855, and that, notwithstanding the 29th section of the Act of 1855, the society had power to sell the estate without the consent of the Commissioners. ROYAL SOCIETY OF LONDON AND THOMPSON
[17 Ch. D. 407

7. —— *Consent—Sale of Land—16 & 17 Vict. c.* 137—18 & 19 Vict. c. 124, s. 29—5 & 6 Will. 4. c. 76—*City Ward.*] Land purchased by one of the wards of the city of London out of common moneys belonging to the ward, for the purpose, as declared by a deed of trust then executed, of providing a watch-house and suitable rooms for transacting the business and keeping the records

I. CHARITY—COMMISSIONERS—continued.

of the ward, and subsequently let out on lease, may be conveyed to a railway company (requiring to take the premises under their compulsory powers) without the consent of either the Charity Commissioners under the Charitable Trusts Acts, 1853 and 1855, or the Lords of the Treasury under the Municipal Corporations Act, 1835; nor is it necessary that the sale should be completed under the provisions of the Lands Clauses Act. FINNIS AND YOUNG TO FORBES AND POCHIN. (No. 1.)　-　-　-　24 Ch. D. 587

8. —— *Consent—Sale of Land—Charity wholly maintained by Voluntary Contributions—16 & 17 Vict. c* 137, s. 62—18 & 19 Vict. c. 124, ss. 29, 48.] Land purchased by one of the City wards and used for the purposes of the ward charity school, which had no endowment and was wholly maintained by voluntary contributions, is within the exceptions of the Charitable Trust Act, 1853, sect. 62, and sect. 48 of the Act of 1855, and may be sold without the concurrence or consent of the Charity Commissioners. FINNIS AND YOUNG TO FORBES AND POCHIN. (No. 2.)　24 Ch. D. 591

9. —— *Consent—Sale of Land — Charitable Trusts Act*, 1853 (16 & 17 Vict. c. 137), ss. 24-26 —*Charitable Trusts Amendment Act*, 1855 (18 & 19 Vict. c. 124), s. 38—*Allotments Extension Act*, 1882 (45 & 46 Vict. c. 80), ss. 4, 5, 11, 15—*Allotment Act (2 & 3 Will.* 4, c. 42).] The Allotments Extension Act, 1882, has not taken away from the Charity Commissioners the power of authorizing a sale of charity lands vested in them under the Charitable Trusts Act, 1853, and the Charitable Trusts Amendment Act, 1855. PARISH OF SUTTON TO CHURCH　　-　　-　　26 Ch. D. 173

—— Action on account of subscriptions 28 Ch. D.
See CHARITY—MANAGEMENT. 4. [426

II. CHARITY—GIFT TO.

1. —— "Charitable and deserving objects"—*Will—Construction—"Money.*"] A testatrix by her will desired "that the whole of the money over which I have a disposing power be given in charitable and deserving objects, the amount being six hundred pounds sterling":—*Held*, that this was a good charitable gift.—*Williams* v. *Kershaw* (5 Cl. & F. 111, n.) distinguished.—At the date of the will in August, 1881, the testatrix had over £600 at her bankers. In February, 1883, she invested £600 in the purchase of £586 Consols. At the date of her death in May, 1884, she had the £586 Consols, £555 at her bankers, and £8 cash in her house:—*Held*, that the word "money" in the will ought not to be extended beyond its strict meaning. *In re* SUTTON. STONE v. ATTORNEY-GENERAL　　28 Ch. D. 464

2. —— *Cy-près—Will—Charitable Legacy—Lapse.*] A legacy to an ophthalmic hospital which had ceased to exist at the date of the testator's will held to have lapsed and not to be administered cy-près. *In re* OVEY. BROADBENT v. BARROW
[29 Ch. D. 560

III. CHARITY—MANAGEMENT.

1. —— *Scheme—Alteration—Renewable Leases —Charitable Trusts Act*, 1853 (16 & 17 Vict. c. 137), s. 21.] A scheme, settled in 1856, for the administration of a charity, authorized the granting

III. CHARITY—MANAGEMENT—*continued.*

of building leases with the sanction of the Charity Commissioners for ninety-nine years absolute, or for twenty-one years with a covenant for perpetual renewal at the expiration of every twenty-one years, on payment of a fine of one half the then annual value of the demised premises. The Attorney-General applied to have this scheme amended by striking out the clause as to granting leases:—*Held,* by the Court of Appeal, affirming the decision of Chitty, J., that the clause ought to be struck out, leaving the granting of leases to be governed by the Charitable Trusts Act, 1853 (16 & 17 Vict. c. 137), s. 21. *In re* SMITH'S CHARITY (HARTLEPOOL)　　20 Ch. D. 516

2. —— Scheme—*Attorney-General—Application to Scotch Court.*] An English testator bequeathed the residue of his estate to his executors, and to trustees to be appointed by them, on trust for the benefit of the blind in Inverness-shire. The surviving executor declined to act in the trust, or even to appoint new trustees:—*Held,* that the Attorney-General, and not the surviving executor, was the person to whom liberty ought to be given to apply to the Court of Session in Scotland for the settlement of a scheme for the charity. *In re* FRASER. YEATES *v.* FRASER
[22 Ch. D. 827

3. —— Scheme — *Charity Commissioners — Cy-près—Eleemosynary Gift—Apprentice Fees—Application to Education—Discretion of Commissioners—Appeal.*] A sum of money was given by a testatrix in 1643 to be laid out in the purchase of lands of the annual value of £10, one half to be applied towards the better relief of the most poor and needy people of good life and conversation in the parish of K., to be paid to them half-yearly in the church or the porch thereof: and the other half to apprentice one poor boy or more of the parish. At that time K. was a small village, but it had now increased to a large and wealthy town, and the income of the charity estate had increased to more than £2000.—The Charity Commissioners settled a scheme by which they appropriated the income to the following objects: (*a*) The relief of poor deserving objects of the parish in case of sudden accident, sickness, or distress. (*b*) Subcriptions to dispensaries and hospitals in the parish. (*c*) Annuities for deserving and necessitous persons who had resided seven years in the parish. (*d*) The advancement of the education of children attending elementary schools. (*e*) Premiums for apprenticeship and outfits for poor boys of the parish. (*f*) Payments to encourage the continuance of scholars at public elementary schools above the age of eleven years. (*g*) Exhibitions at higher places of education. (*h*) Providing lectures and evening classes.—Some of the parishioners objected to the application of the income to educational purposes:—*Held* (reversing the decision of Hall, V.C.), that, considering the enormous increase of the income of the charity and of the population of the parish, and the change of the circumstances and habits of the people, the application of the income of the charity cy-près to educational and other charitable purposes was justifiable, and that the scheme of the Charity Commissioners ought to be confirmed.— A long continued unauthorized cy-près applica-

III. CHARITY—MANAGEMENT—*continued.*

tion of charity funds by the trustees is no ground of objection to a scheme of the Charity Commissioners directing a different cy-près application.— The Court of Appeal will not interfere with the details of a scheme of the Charity Commissioners, unless they have exceeded their authority or the scheme contains something wrong in principle or wrong in law. *In re* CAMPDEN CHARITIES
[18 Ch. D. 310

4. —— Voluntary Fund—*Action for Account — Parties — Representative Plaintiff — Attorney-General—Fund raised by Voluntary Subscriptions —Action by some Members of Committee on behalf of all against former Member—Certificate of Charity Commissioners—Charitable Trusts Act, 1853 (16 & 17 Vict. c. 137), ss. 17, 62.*] An action was brought by five of the members of a church building committee, on behalf of themselves and the other members of the committee, against a former member, claiming an account of all moneys received and paid by him in respect of the Church Building Fund during the period of his membership. The fund was raised by voluntary subscriptions ; seventeen persons having constituted themselves into a committee to receive subscriptions for the purpose of improving the church of the parish, and to apply the moneys thus collected:—*Held,* that, the members of the committee being mere agents of the subscribers, the action could not be maintained by some of the agents against others. —But *held,* also, that, even if all the subscribers were suing, the action could not be maintained in the absence of the Attorney-General.—Whether the action could be maintained without the certificate of the Charity Commissioners, *quære.* STRICKLAND *v.* WELDON　　28 Ch. D. 426

IV. CHARITY—MORTMAIN.

1. —— Apportionment—*Charge on Land — Proceeds of Sale.*] A testator gave a share of his residuary personal estate to charities. His residuary estate consisted of a legacy from another testator payable out of the proceeds of that testator's ;real and mixed estate and pure personal estate:—*Held,* that the bequests to the charities must be apportioned according to the values of the real and mixed estate and personal estate of the first testator, and that the bequests failed as to the portion attributable to the real and mixed estate, but were good as to the portion attributable to the pure personal estate. *In re* HILL'S TRUSTS
[16 Ch. D. 173

2. —— Debt payable out of Land—*Hiring Rooms.*] A settlor by deed covenanted to pay within twelve months the sum of £20,000 to trustees on trust for his wife for her life, with remainder to the settlor for his life, with remainder as his wife should by will appoint. The wife by her will appointed the £20,000 to the same trustees on trust to pay thereout legacies amounting to £2000 and certain life annuities, and to pay the residue as she should by deed appoint. By a deed-poll she appointed the residue to charitable uses. All the instruments were executed at the same time. The settlor survived his wife and died, not having paid the £20,000. Part of his estate at his death consisted of impure personalty, and the pure personalty would be insufficient for

IV. CHARITY—MORTMAIN—*continued.*

payment of the £20,000 :—*Held* (reversing the decision of Bacon, V.C.), that the £20,000 was a mere debt from the settlor's estate, and though it would be in part payable to the trustees for the charity out of the proceeds of land, the gift of the residue to charitable uses was not in any part void under the Mortmain Act.—A direction to hire rooms does not bring a gift within the Mortmain Act.—*Jeffries* v. *Alexander* (8 H. L. C. 594) considered. *In re* ROBSON. EMLEY *v.* DAVIDSON

[19 Ch. D. 156

3. —— **Harbour Commissioners' Bond**—*9 Geo. 2, c. 36—Interest in Land.*] A bond by Harbour Commissioners, in form prescribed by their Act, assigning the duties arising by virtue of·the Act (which directed the application of such duties: 1st, in payment of the costs and expenses of obtaining the Act ; 2, in payment of the interest of moneys advanced for defraying such expenses : 3, in payment of the interest of moneys borrowed under the Act ; 4, in defraying working expenses; and, 5, in payment of principal moneys borrowed under the Act), is an interest in, or affecting land within 9 Geo. 2, c. 36, and therefore cannot be given by will for charitable purposes.—*Knapp* v. *Williams* (4 Ves. 430, n.) followed ; *Attree* v. *Hawe* (9 Ch. D. 337) and *In re Harris* (15 Ch. D. 561) distinguished ; *Jervis* v. *Lawrence* (22 Ch. D. 202) not followed. *In re* CHRISTMAS. MARTIN *v.* LACON

[30 Ch. D. 544

4. —— **Improvement Bond**—*Mortgage of Rates —Pure Personalty—9 Geo. 2, c. 36.*] By an Act passed for the improvement of a suburban estate, Commissioners were empowered to make rates upon the occupiers of houses, lands, tenements, and hereditaments, within the limits of the Act, and to borrow at interest on the credit of the rates, and to assign over the rates or any part thereof as a security for repayment of·the sums borrowed. If any person rated did not pay, power was given to the Commissioners to recover the rate by action of debt, or by distress and sale of the goods and chattels of such person.—By the Metropolis Local Management Act, 1855, the powers of the Commissioners in this and other like cases were vested in the vestries of the parishes, with power to require the overseers to levy and pay over sums required for the expenses of the execution of the Act : and the overseers for the purpose of levying such rates were to proceed in the same manner and with the same powers as for levying money for the relief of the poor. In case of non-payment of any rate, any justice might on complaint by the vestry issue a warrant for levying the amount by distress and sale of the goods of the overseers ; but the vestries of certain parishes, including the parish in which this estate was situated, were themselves to levy the rates directly on the occupiers instead of on the overseers. In case of non-payment of principal or interest due on any mortgage under the Act, the mortgagee could obtain a receiver :—*Held,* that an assignment by way of mortgage of a proportion of the rates arising under the Improvement Act, to secure the repayment of a sum advanced by the assignee, did not create an interest in land within the meaning of the Mortmain Act. JERVIS *v.* LAWRENCE

[22 Ch. D. 202

IV. CHARITY—MORTMAIN—*continued.*

5. —— **Mortgage**—*Interest in Land—Mortgage of Interest of Cestui que trust in Funds invested partly on Mortgage of Real Estate—Apportionment—9 Geo. 2, c. 36, s. 3.*] A testator was entitled to £800, secured by mortgage of the life interest of a widow lady in the funds held on the trusts of her marriage settlement, and the reversionary interest of one of her children in the same funds. At the date of the mortgage and of the testator's death, part of these funds was pure personalty, and the rest was invested under a power in the settlement on mortgage of real estate. The testator bequeathed to charities such part of his residuary estate as could be so bequeathed :—*Held,* that the £800 was an interest in land within the meaning of 9 Geo. 2, c. 36, s. 3, and could not be given by will to a charity, and that there could not be any apportionment so as to make a part of the sum available for charity.—*Brook v. Badley* (Law Rep. 3 Ch. 672) approved and followed.—Observations of Jessel, M.R., in *In re Harris* (15 Ch. D. 561) explained. *In re* WATTS. CORNFORD *v.* ELLIOTT　　-　27 Ch. D. 318 ; 29 Ch. D. 947

6. —— **Secret Trust**—*Church—Mortmain Act, 9 Geo. 2, c. 36—Church Building Act, 43 Geo. 3, c. 108—Site with existing Church.*] A testator, by his will executed three months before his death, devised all his real estate, which included a piece of land of about one acre, with an unconsecrated building thereon licensed by the bishop for public worship, to his wife absolutely. The devise was in pursuance of a secret agreement between the testator and his wife, whereby the latter undertook to hold the land and building upon trust, after her husband's death, to convey the same as and for a parish or district church in perpetuity :—*Held,* that the devise was legal under the statute 43 Geo. 3, c. 108, and was not rendered illegal by any provisions of the Mortmain Act, 9 Geo. 2, c. 36. O'BRIEN *v.* TYSSEN　　28 Ch. D. 372

CHARITY—Charities of the City of London.
　　See LONDON—CHARITIES—*Statutes.*

—— Perpetuity　7 Q. B. D. 106 ; 7 App. Cas. 633
　　See FISHERY. 3.

—— Prison charity, scheme for.
　　See PRISON—*Statutes.*

—— Purchase by railway company—Interim investment　-　　-　　- 23 Ch. D. 171
　　See SETTLED LAND ACT—PURCHASE-
　　MONEY. 6.

—— Scheme--Apportionment—District parishes
　　　　　　　　　　　　[24 Ch. D. 213
　　See CHURCH BUILDING ACTS.

—— Trade or business—Covenant in lease
　　　　　　　　　　　　[27 Ch. D. 71.
　　See LANDLORD AND TENANT—LEASE. 4.

CHARTER.

Borneo.] *Charter granted, Nov. 1st., 1881, to the North British Borneo Company upon petition to the Queen in Council*　　L. G. 1881, p. 5448

—— Market—Waiver of rights　25 Ch. D. 511 ;
　　See MARKET. 2.　　　[9 App. Cas. 927

CHARTERED COMPANY.

The Act 47 & 48 Vict. c. 56, declares the law relating to the incorporation of Chartered Companies.

L

CHARTERED FREIGHT - 6 Q. B. D. 648;
[7 Q. B. D. 73 ; 7 App. Cas. 670
See INSURANCE, MARINE—POLICY. 1, 2.

CHARTERPARTY.
See Cases under SHIP—CHARTERPARTY.

—— Execution abroad—Stamping within two
months after receipt in England
See REVENUE—STAMPS 1. [9 P. D. 215

—— Option of cancelling—Marine insurance—
Concealment - - 7 Q. B. D. 73
See INSURANCE, MARINE—POLICY. 1.

—— Perils of the sea - - 6 Q. B. D. 648;
[7 App. Cas. 670
See INSURANCE, MARINE—POLICY. 1.

CHATTEL—Contract not to sell 22 Ch. D. 335
See SPECIFIC PERFORMANCE. 3.

—— Disclaimer by trustee of bankrupt 20 Ch. D.
See BANKRUPTCY—DISCLAIMER. 4. [341

CHEAP TRAINS ACT, 1883.
See RAILWAY COMPANY — PASSENGER
DUTY—Statutes.

CHECKWEIGHER—Mine—Second appointment
—Validity—35 & 36 Vict. c. 76, s. 13
[14 Q. B. D. 592
See MINE—MINES REGULATION ACTS.

CHEMICAL MANURE WORKS.
See LOCAL GOVERNMENT — PUBLIC
HEALTH ACTS—Statutes.

CHEMICAL PROCESS - - 29 Ch. D. 366
See PATENT—VALIDITY. 5.

CHEQUE—Delivery of—Accord and satisfaction
[9 Q. B. D. 37
See ACCORD AND SATISFACTION. 1.

—— Donatio mortis causâ - 27 Ch. D. 631
See DONATIO MORTIS CAUSA.

—— Laches of bearer - - 9 Q. B. D. 288
See BANKER—CHEQUE. 1.

—— Negotiability—Scotch law 9 App. Cas. 95
See SCOTCH LAW—BILL OF EXCHANGE. 1.

—— Post-dated—Bankruptcy of payee
[19 Ch. D. 409
See BANKRUPTCY—PROTECTED TRANSAC-
TION. 3.

—— Statutory enactments respecting.
See BILL OF EXCHANGE—STATUTES.

CHICORY—Substitute for.
See REVENUE—EXCISE—Statutes.

CHILD—CHILDREN Advancement by portion
Instruction - - 29 Ch. D. 260
See ADVANCEMENT. 1.

—— Class of—Gift by will.
See Cases under WILL—CLASS.

—— Custody, education, and maintenance.
See Cases under INFANT—CUSTODY.
INFANT EDUCATION.
INFANT—MAINTENANCE.

—— Custody of—Security - - 9 P. D. 161
See PRACTICE—DIVORCE—CUSTODY OF
CHILDREN.

—— Custody of - - 18 Ch. D. 670
See HUSBAND AND WIFE—SEPARATION
DEED. 1.

—— Death in lifetime of testator 19 Ch. D. 612 ;
See WILL—LAPSE. 2, 3. [28 Ch. D. 266

CHILD—CHILDREN—continued.
—— Illegitimate—Construction of will
[24 Ch. D. 691 ; 30 Ch. D. 110
See WILL—CHILDREN. 1, 2.

—— Illegitimate—Domicil - 24 Ch. D. 637
See WILL—WORDS. 13.

CHINA—Order in Council.
See JURISDICTION—Gazette.

CHINESE DOMICIL—Legacy duty
See DOMICIL. 1. [23 Ch. D. 532

CHLORINE WORKS.
See LOCAL GOVERNMENT — PUBLIC
HEALTH ACTS—Statutes.

CHOLERA—Regulations for ports.
See LOCAL GOVERNMENT — PUBLIC
HEALTH—Gazette.

—— Regulations for port of London.
See METROPOLIS—MANAGEMENT ACTS—
Gazette.

CHOSE IN ACTION—Assignment of debt—
Notice of assignment after assignor's
death - - - 12 Q. B. D. 511
See ASSIGNMENT OF DEBT. 1.

—— Assignment—Priority—Notice
[19 Ch. D. 361
See BANKRUPTCY—ASSETS. 15.

—— Married woman—Bankruptcy of husband
[23 Ch. D. 344
See HUSBAND AND WIFE—WIFE'S REAL
ESTATE. 3.

—— Sequestration - - 22 Ch. D. 233
See PRACTICE—SUPREME COURT—SE-
QUESTRATION. 1.

CHURCH—Consolidated benefice—Right of presentation—Quare impedit 15 Q. B. D. 432
See ADVOWSON. 2.

—— In South Africa—Status of 7 App. Cas. 484
See COLONIAL LAW—CAPE OF GOOD
HOPE. 1.

—— Transfer of advowson during vacancy
[10 Q. B. D. 407
See ECCLESIASTICAL LAW—CLERGY. 2.

CHURCH BUILDING ACTS.

Sites for Places of Worship.] By 45 & 46 Vict.
c. 21 (the Places of Worship Sites Amendment
Act, 1882), s. 1, the Places of Worship Sites Act,
1873, shall be construed as extending to authorize
any corporation, ecclesiastical or lay, whether sole
or aggregate, and any officers, justices of the peace,
trustees, or commissioners holding land for public,
ecclesiastical, parochial, charitable, or other purposes or objects, to grant, convey, or enfranchise for
the purposes of the Act such quantity of land as
therein mentioned, provided :

(a.) An ecclesiastical corporation sole, being
below the dignity of a bishop, shall not
make any such grant without the consent
in writing of the bishop of the diocese to
whose jurisdiction he is subject.

(b.) A municipal corporation shall not make
any such grant without the consent in
writing of the Commissioners of Her
Majesty's Treasury.

(c.) Parochial property shall not be so granted
without the consent of a majority of the
ratepayers and owners of property in the

CHURCH BUILDING ACTS—*continued.*

parish to which the property belongs, assembled at a meeting to be convened according to the mode pointed out in the Act 5 & 6 Will. 4, c. 69, and of the Local Government Board and of the guardians of the poor of the parish or of the union comprising the parish, testified by their being parties to the conveyance.

(d.) *Property held on trust for charitable purposes shall not be so granted without the consent of the Charity Commissioners for England and Wales.*

Sect. 2. *The said Act shall be construed as extending to authorize any person seised or entitled only for life or lives or to any manor or lands of freehold tenure to make such grant, conveyance, or enfranchisement as is mentioned in the said Act in cases where the person next entitled to the same for a beneficial interest in remainder in fee simple or fee tail is unborn or unascertained : provided that no such grant, conveyance, or enfranchisement made by any such person seised only for a life or lives shall be valid unless the person seised or entitled for a beneficial interest for life or lives, or for an estate in fee simple or fee tail (as the case may be) in remainder immediately expectant on the estate of such unborn or unascertained person or or to such manor or land (if any and if legally competent) shall be a party to and shall join in the same ; and if there be no such person, or if such person be not legally competent, unless the trustees or trustee, if any, of such manor or lands during the suspense or contingency of the then immediate or expectant estate in fee simple or fee tail in such manor or lands shall in like manner concur.*

The Act 47 & 48 Vict. c. 65 (the New Parishes Act and Church Buildings Acts Amendment Act, 1884), amends the New Parishes Acts and the Church Building Acts.

New Parishes.] Sect. 2. *Ecclesiastical Commissioners may with consent of the Queen in Council dissolve any district formed under New Parishes Acts, 6 & 7 Vict. c. 37, 7 & 8 Vict. c. 94, 19 & 20 Vict. c. 104, and reincorporate its area, or part thereof, in the parish or district out of which it was constituted, or add it to some other district.*

Sect. 3 *amends* sect. 1 *of* 32 & 33 Vict. c. 94.

Church Buildings.] Sect. 4. *The Commissioners may with consent of parties affected by it, revoke or alter any deed making provision for the maintenance of ministers and clerks out of pew rents under* sect. 18 *of* 1 & 2 Vict. c. 107.

Sect. 5. *Short titles for Church Building Acts.*

—— **District Parishes**—*Charity—Scheme—Apportionment—Discharge of Order—Jurisdiction—* 52 Geo. 3, c. 101—8 & 9 Vict. c. 70, s. 22.] Where under the Church Building Acts district parishes have been formed out of an original parish, and the Court has, under sect. 22 of the Church Building Act, 8 & 9 Vict. c. 70, made an order apportioning a charitable gift between these district parishes and the remainder of the original parish, such order is not to be treated as final, but the Court has jurisdiction to make fresh orders from time to time to meet the changing circumstances of such district parishes or original parish, either by discharging or varying former orders made under the section.—By an order made in 1852,

CHURCH BUILDING ACTS—*continued.*

upon a petition presented under the Church Building Act (8 & 9 Vict. c. 70), and Sir Samuel Romilly's Act (52 Geo. 3, c. 101), the Court acting under sect. 22 of the former Act, apportioned the income of certain charities established for the benefit of the poor of the parish of K., between five district parishes, which had been formed out of that parish, and the remainder of that parish, and directed the trustees of the charities to apply the income in the specified proportions. Further district parishes having been subsequently formed out of the parish of K., one of them having had assigned to it a portion of one of the original five districts, in 1879 a scheme was settled by the Charity Commissioners appropriating the income of the charities to certain objects, the scheme also providing that the trustees of the charities were, in the application of the income, to have regard to the apportionment of 1852. It being found, owing to the changes that had taken place since the order of 1852 in the populations of the various districts constituting the parish of K., impracticable to carry out the scheme of 1879 while retaining the apportionment directed by the order of 1852, the trustees presented a petition under the above Act for the discharge of that order :—*Held,* that the Court had jurisdiction to discharge the order, which was discharged accordingly. *In re* CAMPDEN CHARITIES. (No. 2.)　24 Ch. D. 213

—— Devise of land with existing church
[28 Ch. D. 372

See CHARITY—MORTMAIN. 6.

CHURCH ESTATES COMMISSIONERS.
See ECCLESIASTICAL COMMISSIONERS—
Statutes.

CHURCHWARDEN—Substitution as promoter
[7 P. D. 161
See PRACTICE—ECCLESIASTICAL—PUBLIC WORSHIP ACT. 2.

CIRCUITY OF ACTION　　7 Q. B. D. 636
See BILL OF EXCHANGE—TRANSFER.

CITY OF LONDON PAROCHIAL CHARITIES ACT, 1883.
See LONDON—CHARITIES—*Statutes.*

CIVIL CODE OF LOWER CANADA, Art. 501
[9 App. Cas. 170
See COLONIAL LAW—CANADA—QUEBEC.
8.

—— **Art. 2274**　-　8 App. Cas. 530
See COLONIAL LAW—CANADA—QUEBEC.
2.

CIVIL PROCEDURE CODE OF LOWER CANADA, Arts. 766, 1178, 1360 - 8 App. Cas. 530
See COLONIAL LAW—CANADA—QUEBEC.
2.

—— **Art. 712** -　　- 10 App. Cas. 643
See COLONIAL LAW—CANADA—QUEBEC.
1.

CIVIL PROCEDURE CODE OF MAURITIUS, Art. 174　-　-　8 App. Cas. 296
See COLONIAL LAW—MAURITIUS. 1.

CIVIL SERVICE PENSION.
See PENSION—*Statutes.*

CLAIMS AND OBJECTIONS—Registration of votes.
See PARLIAMENT — REGISTRATION —
Statutes.

CLAM AND BAIT BEDS.
 See FISHERY ACTS—*Statutes.*

CLASS—Gift to.
 See Cases under WILL—CLASS.
 —— Gift to, at twenty-one   16 Ch. D. 44
  See WILL—VESTING. 3.
 —— Gift to—Remoteness - 18 Ch. D. 441;
    [19 Ch. D. 294; 28 Ch. D. 436
  See WILL—PERPETUITY. 1, 2, 4.
 —— Original or substitutional gift 23 Ch. D. 737
  See WILL—SUBSTITUTIONAL GIFT. 1.
 —— Period of ascertaining 25 Ch. D. 458;
  See WILL—CONDITION. 4. [28 Ch. D. 523
 —— Period of ascertaining—Default of appointment - 24 Ch. D. 244
  See SETTLEMENT—CONSTRUCTION. 8.

CLAY—Exception out of conveyance to railway company - - - 20 Ch. D. 552
  See RAILWAY COMPANY — RAILWAYS CLAUSES ACT. 5.

CLAYTON'S CASE—Rule in - 22 Ch. D. 61;
    [9 App. Cas. 857
  See BUILDING SOCIETY. 7.

CLERGYMAN.
  See Cases under ECCLESIASTICAL LAW—CLERGY.

CLERICAL ERROR 21 Ch. D. 871
  See BILL OF SALE—FORMALITIES. 7.
 —— Specification of patent 26 Ch. D. 105
  See PATENT—AMENDMENT. 1.

CLOSE OF BANKRUPTCY - 20 Ch. D. 308;
    [22 Ch. D. 586; 24 Ch. D. 672
  See BANKRUPTCY—UNDISCHARGED BANKRUPT. 1, 2, 3.

CLOSE OF INSOLVENCY—After-acquired property   20 Ch. D. 637
  See INSOLVENCY.

CLOSE OF LIQUIDATION 19 Ch. D. 140
  See BANKRUPTCY—LIQUIDATION. 5.

CLUB.
 —— Power of Expulsion of Member—*Validity of Rule—Conduct injurious to Character and Interests of Club—Bona fides—Irregularity—Interference of Court.*] The Court will not interfere against the decision of the members of a club professing to act under their rules, unless it can be shewn either that the rules are contrary to natural justice, or that what has been done is contrary to the rules, or that there has been mala fides or malice in arriving at the decision.—One of the rules of a club provided that a general meeting might alter any of the standing rules affecting the general interests of the club, provided this was done with certain formalities and by a certain majority :—*Held*, that a rule providing for the expulsion of members who should be guilty of conduct injurious to the interest of the club was within the regulation, and could be validly passed by a general meeting.—One of the rules of a club provided that in case the conduct of any member should, in the opinion of the committee, be injurious to the character and interests of the club, the committee should be empowered to recommend such member to resign, and if he should not comply, the committee should then call a general meeting, and if a majority of two-thirds of the meeting agreed by ballot to the

CLUB—*continued.*
expulsion of such member, he should be expelled. —The Plaintiff, a member of the club, sent a pamphlet which reflected on the conduct of S., a gentleman in a high official position, also a member of the club, to S., at his official address, enclosed in an envelope on the outside of which was printed " Dishonourable Conduct of S." The committee being of opinion that this action was injurious to the character and interests of the club, called upon the Plaintiff for an explanation, which he refused to give. They then called on him to resign, and as he did not comply with their recommendation, they duly summoned a general meeting, at which a resolution was passed by the requisite majority expelling the Plaintiff from the club :—*Held* (affirming the decision of Jessel, M.R.), that the Court would not interfere to restrain the committee from excluding the Plaintiff from the club.—The fact that a decision is unreasonable may be strong evidence of malice, but it is not conclusive, and may be rebutted by evidence of bona fides. DAWKINS *v.* ANTROBUS
    [17 Ch. D. 615

 —— Gaming — Baccarat — Liability of proprietor and players 13 Q. B. D. 505
  See GAMING. 2.
 —— Licensing Acts—Sale by retail
  See INN—OFFENCES. 2. [8 Q. B. D. 373

CLYDE NAVIGATION 6 App. Cas. 273
  See SCOTCH LAW—RIVER.
 —— Harbour dues 8 App. Cas. 658
  See SCOTCH LAW—HARBOUR. 2.

COAL MINE.
  See Cases under MINE.
 —— Income tax 6 App. Cas. 315
  See SCOTCH LAW—REVENUE.
 —— Scotch law - 8 App. Cas. 641
  See SCOTCH LAW—HERITABLE PROPERTY. 2.
 —— Scotch law—Liberty of working
    [10 App. Cas. 813
  See SCOTCH LAW—MINE. 1.
 —— Settlement of 23 Ch. D. 583
  See SETTLEMENT—POWERS. 1.

COCKLES.
  See FISHERY ACTS—*Statutes.*

CODE OF TELEGRAPHY—Copyright
  See COPYRIGHT—BOOKS. 4. [26 Ch. D. 637

CO-DEFENDANTS—Costs - 17 Ch. D. 600;
    [18 Ch. D. 236
  See PRACTICE—SUPREME COURT—COSTS. 14, 15.

CODICIL—Confirmation of will 23 Ch. D. 337
  See WILL—REVOCATION. 2.
 —— Incorporation in subsequent codicil 6 P. D. 9
  See WILL—INCORPORATED DOCUMENTS. 1.
 —— Unattested—Made abroad } 25 Ch. D. 373
  See POWER—EXECUTION. 4.
 —— Revocation - ‣ 8 P. D. 169 ; 23 Ch. D. 337
  See WILL—REVOCATION. 1, 2.

COFFEE, SUBSTITUTE FOR.
  See REVENUE—EXCISE—*Statute.*

COHABITATION — Consideration of bond—Immorality - 26 Ch. D. 353
  See BOND.

COHABITATION—*continued.*

—— Scotch marriage　　-　　**6 App. Cas. 489**
　　See SCOTCH LAW—HUSBAND AND WIFE.
　　3.

COLLATERAL SECURITY　16 Ch. D. 211, 214, n.
　　See MORTGAGE—CONTRACT.　4, 5.

COLLEGE BOOKS—Entry in　-　17 Ch. D. 429
　　See EVIDENCE—ENTRY BY DECEASED
　　PERSON.

COLLEGIATE BODY — Ecclesiastical Commissioners　18 Ch. D. 596; 21 Ch. D. 514, n.
　　See CHARITY—COMMISSIONERS.　1, 2.

COLLISION.
　　See Cases under SHIP—NAVIGATION.

—— Damages—Loss of market—Remoteness
　　　　　　　　　　　　　[9 P. D. 105
　　See DAMAGES—REMOTENESS.　1.

—— Inspection of lights—Trinity Masters
　　　　　　　　　　　　　[10 P. D. 40
　　See PRACTICE—ADMIRALTY—INSPECTION
　　OF PROPERTY.

—— Negligence—"Perils of the sea"
　　　　　　[10 Q. B. D. 521; 11 Q. B. D. 47
　　See SHIP—BILL OF LADING.　1, 3.

—— Sailing rules.
　　See Cases and Gazettes under SHIP—
　　NAVIGATION.

—— Thames Rules.
　　See Cases under SHIP—NAVIGATION.　28–
　　31.

COLLUSION—Judgment obtained by 30 Ch. D. 421
　　See PRACTICE — SUPREME COURT — AP-
　　PEAL.　18.

COLONIAL CERTIFICATES.
　　See SHIP—MERCHANT SHIPPING ACTS—
　　Gazette.

COLONIAL COURT—Sequestration—Bankruptcy
　　　　　　　　　　　　[16 Ch. D. 665
　　See BANKRUPTCY—STAYING PROCEED-
　　INGS.　1.

COLONIAL COURTS OF INQUIRY.
　　See SHIP—MERCHANT SHIPPING ACTS—
　　Statutes.

COLONIAL LAW:—　　　　　　　Col.

COLONIAL LAW—*continued.*

I. COLONIAL LAW—CANADA—DOMINION.

1. —— Legislative Power—*British North
America Act,* 1867, *s.* 108—*Power of Canadian
Legislature—Construction of Dominion Act,* 37
Vict. c. 16.] Under the British North America
Act, 1867, s. 108, read in connection with the 3rd
schedule thereto, all railways belonging to the province of Nova Scotia, including the railway in suit,
passed to and became vested on the 1st of July
1867, in the Dominion of Canada; but not for
any larger interest therein than at that date
belonged to the province.—The railway in suit
being at the date of the statutory transfer subject
to an obligation on the part of the provincial
Government, confirmed by provincial Act, 30 Vict.
c. 36, to enter into a traffic arrangement with the
respondent company, the Dominion Government,
in pursuance of that obligation entered into a
further agreement relating thereto of the 22nd of
September, 1871 :—*Quære,* whether it was ultrà
vires the Dominion Parliament by an enactment
to that effect to extinguish the rights of the respondent company under the said agreement.—
But *held,* that Dominion Act, 37 Vict. c. 16, did
not, upon its true construction, purport so to do.
And although it authorized a transfer of the
railway to the Appellant, it did not enact such
transfer in derogation of the Respondent's rights
under the agreement of the 22nd of September,
1871, or otherwise. WESTERN COUNTIES RAILWAY
COMPANY *v.* WINDSOR AND ANNAPOLIS RAILWAY
COMPANY　　　　　　-　　**7 App. Cas. 178**

2. —— Legislative Powers—*Dominion Parliament—British North America Act,* 1867, *ss.* 91,
92, *sub.-ss.* 9, 13, 16—*Validity of Canada Temperance Act,* 1878.] *Held,* that the Canada Temperance Act, 1878, which in effect, wherever
throughout the Dominion it is put in force, uniformly prohibits the sale of intoxicating liquors
except in wholesale quantities, or for certain
specified purposes, regulates the traffic in the
excepted cases, makes sales of liquors in violation
of the prohibitions and regulations contained in
the Act criminal offences, punishable by fine and
for the third or subsequent offence by imprisonment, is within the legislative competence of the
Dominion Parliament.—The objects and scope of
the Act are general, viz., to promote temperance
by means of a uniform law throughout the
Dominion.　They relate to the peace, order, and
good government of Canada, and not to the class
of subjects "property and civil rights."　Provision for the special application of the Act to
particular places does not alter its character as
general legislation. RUSSELL *v.* THE QUEEN
　　　　　　　　　　　　[**7 App. Cas. 829**

3. —— Legislative Powers—*Dominion Parliament—British North America Act,* 1867, *ss.* 91, 92
—*Canadian Act,* 37 *Vict. c.* 103.] *Held,* that
Canadian Act, 37 Vict. c. 103, which created a
corporation with power to carry on certain definite
kinds of business within the Dominion was within
the legislative competence of the Dominion Parlia-

I. COLONIAL LAW — CANADA—DOMINION— *continued.*

ment. The fact that the corporation chose to confine the exercise of its powers to one province and to local and provincial objects did not affect its status as a corporation, or operate to render its original incorporation illegal as ultrà vires of the said Parliament.— *Held,* further, that the corporation could not be prohibited generally from acting as such within the province; nor could it be restrained from doing specified acts in violation of the provincial law upon a petition not directed and adapted to that purpose. COLONIAL BUILDING AND INVESTMENT ASSOCIATION *v.* ATTORNEY-GENERAL OF QUEBEC　　**9 App. Cas. 157**

4. —— **Railway** — *Canadian Act, 20 Vict. c. 227, s. 16—22 Vict. c. 124—Power to levy Tolls —Reasonableness of Charges.*] *Held,* that the International Bridge Company was under Canadian Act, 20 Vict. c. 227, s. 16, entrusted with a general and unqualified power of making byelaws and regulations as to the use of its bridge and the terms on which it should be used in point of payment; and that there is nothing in sect. 2 of the amending Act (22 Vict. c. 124), when read and construed together with the principal Act, which cuts down that power as to the regulation of the use of the bridge and as to the terms on which it may be used by railway trains.—As to the reasonableness of charges, the principle is not what profit it may be reasonable for a company to make, but what it is reasonable to charge to the person who is charged. CANADA SOUTHERN RAILWAY COMPANY *v.* INTERNATIONAL BRIDGE COMPANY
　　[8 App. Cas. 723

II. COLONIAL LAW—CANADA—NEW BRUNSWICK.

—— **Income Tax**—*31 Vict. c. 36, s. 4—Balance of Gain over Loss.*] The tax imposed by sect. 4 of New Brunswick Act, 31 Vict c. 36, upon "income" is leviable in respect of the balance of gain over loss made in the fiscal year, and where no such balance of gain has been made there is no income or fund which is capable of being assessed. There is nothing in the said section or in the context which should induce a construction of the word "income," when applied to the income of a commercial business for a year, otherwise than its natural and commonly - accepted sense, as the balance of gain over loss. LAWLESS *v.* SULLIVAN　　**6 App. Cas. 373**

III. COLONIAL LAW—CANADA—NOVA SCOTIA.

—— **Lease**—*Nova Scotia Revised Statutes, 4th Series, c. 9—Right to lease—Priority of Application.*] Nova Scotia Revised Statutes, 4th Series, c. 9, contemplates the grant of both licenses and leases in all districts whether proclaimed or unproclaimed. The first applicant, whether for a license or a lease, is entitled. Applications must be made in writing to the Commissioner or Deputy-Commissioner. A licensee is entitled to a lease under sect. 42. "Occupying and staking off" is not a condition precedent to all leases in an unproclaimed district. MOTT *v.* LOCKHART
　　[8 App. Cas. 568

IV. COLONIAL LAW—CANADA—ONTARIO.

1. —— *Jurisdiction—Court of Queen's Bench and Supreme Court—Law Reform Act (Ontario)—*

IV. COLONIAL LAW—CANADA—ONTARIO— *continued.*

38 Vict. c. 11 (Canada), s. 22.—Rule to set aside Verdict—Misdirection—New Trial.] Upon a rule nisi calling upon the Plaintiff in an action upon a policy of life insurance to shew cause why a verdict obtained by her should not be set aside and a nonsuit or verdict entered for the Defendant pursuant to the Law Reform Act, or a new trial had between the parties, said verdict being contrary to law and evidence, and the finding virtually for the Defendant; and for misdirection in that the jury had not been directed on the evidence to find for the Defendant, the Court of Queen's Bench for Ontario ordered the verdict for the Plaintiff to be set aside and the same to be entered for the Defendant, while the Supreme Court eventually reversed this order and restored the verdict for the Plaintiff, being of opinion that they had no power to direct a new trial on the ground of the verdict being against the weight of evidence :— *Held,* that although the Court of Queen's Bench would have had power to enter the verdict in accordance with what they deemed to be the true construction of the findings coupled with other facts admitted or beyond controversy, they had no power to set aside the verdict for the Plaintiff and direct a verdict to be entered for the Defendant in direct opposition to the finding of the jury on a material issue.—Under 38 Vict. c. 11 (Canada), the Supreme Court has power to make any order or to give any judgment which the Court below might or ought to have given, and amongst other things to order a new trial on the ground either of misdirection or the verdict being against the weight of evidence ; and that power is not taken away by sect. 22 in this case, in which the Court below did not exercise any discretion as to the question of a new trial, and where the appeal from their judgment did not relate to that subject.—Although the Privy Council have the right, if they think fit, to order a new trial on any ground, that power will not be exercised merely where the verdict is not altogether satisfactory, but only where the evidence so strongly preponderates against it as to lead to the conclusion that the jury have either wilfully disregarded the evidence or failed to understand or appreciate it. CONNECTICUT MUTUAL LIFE INSURANCE COMPANY OF HERTFORD *v.* MOORE　　**6 App. Cas. 644**

2. —— **Legislative Power** — *British North America Act, 1867, ss. 91, 92—Liquor License Act of 1877, c. 181, Revised Statutes of Ontario—Powers of Local Legislature—Regulations of Local Board —Imprisonment with Hard Labour.*] Subjects which in one aspect and for one purpose fall within sect. 92 of the British North America Act, 1867, may in another aspect and for another purpose fall within sect. 91.—*Russell* v. *The Queen* (7 App. Cas. 829) explained and approved.—*Held,* that "The Liquor License Act of 1877, c. 181, Revised Statutes of Ontario," which in respect of sects. 4 and 5, makes regulations in the nature of police or municipal regulations of a merely local character for the good government of taverns, &c., does not in respect of those sections interfere with "the general regulation of trade or commerce," but comes within Nos. 8, 15, and 16, of sect. 92 of the Act of 1867, and is within the

IV. COLONIAL LAW — CANADA—ONTARIO—
continued.

powers of the provincial legislature.—*Held,* further, that the local legislature had power by the said Act of 1867 to entrust to a Board of Commissioners authority to enact regulations of the above character, and thereby to create offences and annex penalties thereto. "Imprisonment" in No. 15 of sect. 92 of the Act of 1867 means imprisonment with or without hard labour. HODGE *v.* THE QUEEN - - - 9 App. Cas. 117

3. —— Legislative Power — *British North America Act, 1867, ss. 91, 92*—"*Property and civil rights* —"*Regulation of trade and commerce*" —*Validity of Ontario Act, 39 Vict. c. 24*—*Construction—Statutory Condition of Policies of Insurance—Interim Notes.*] Sects. 91 and 92 of the British North America Act, 1867, must in regard to the classes of subjects generally described in sect. 91, be read together, and the language of one interpreted and, where necessary, modified by that of the other, so as to reconcile the respective powers they contain and give effect to all of them. Each question should be decided as best it can, without entering more largely than is necessary upon an interpretation of the statute. —*Held,* that;—In No. 13 of sect. 92, the words "property and civil rights in the province" include rights arising from contract (which are not in express terms included under sect. 91) and are not limited to such rights only as flow from the law, e.g., the status of persons.—In No. 2 of sect. 91, the words "regulation of trade and commerce" include political arrangements in regard to trade requiring the sanction of parliament, regulation of trade in matters of inter-provincial concern, and, it may be, general regulation of trade affecting the whole dominion; but do not include the regulation of the contracts of a particular business or trade such as the business of fire insurance in a single province, and therefore do not conflict with the power of property and civil rights conferred by sect. 92, No. 13.—Consequently :— (Ontario) Act, 39 Vict. c. 24, which deals with policies of insurance entered into or in force in the Province of Ontario for insuring property situate therein against fire, and prescribes certain conditions which are to form part of such contracts, is a valid Act, applicable to the contracts of all such insurers in Ontario, including corporations and companies, whatever may be their origin, whether incorporated by British authority or by foreign or colonial authority.—*Held,* further, that the said Ontario Act is not inconsistent with Dominion Act, 38 Vict. c. 20, which requires all insurance companies whether incorporated by foreign dominion or provincial authority to obtain a license, to be granted upon compliance with the conditions prescribed by the Act.—*Held,* further, that according to the true construction of the Ontario Act, whatever may be the conditions sought to be imposed by insurance companies, no such conditions shall avail against the statutory conditions, and the latter shall alone be deemed to be part of the policy and resorted to by the insurers, notwithstanding any conditions of their own, unless the latter are indicated as variations in the manner prescribed by the Act. The penalty for not observing that manner is that the policy

IV. COLONIAL LAW — CANADA—ONTARIO—
continued.

becomes subject to the statutory conditions, whether printed or not. Where a company has printed its own conditions and failed to print the statutory ones it is not the case that the policy must be deemed to be without any conditions at all.—An interim note being merely an agreement for interim insurance preliminary to the grant of a policy is not a policy within the meaning of that term in the Ontario Act. "Subject to all the usual terms and conditions of this company" in such note means that such conditions ought to be read into the interim contract to the extent to which they may lawfully be made a part of the policy when issued by following the directions of the statute, subject always to the statutable condition that they should be held to be just and reasonable by the Court or judge. CITIZENS INSURANCE CO. OF CANADA *v.* PARSONS. QUEEN INSURANCE CO. *v.* PARSONS　7 App. Cas. 96

4. —— Escheats—*Rights of the Province—British North America Act, ss. 102, 109.*] *Held,* that lands in Canada escheated to the Crown for defect of heirs belong to the province in which they are situated, and not to the Dominion.—At the date of passing the British North America Act, 1867, the revenue arising from all escheats to the Crown within the then province of Canada was subject to the disposal and appropriation of the Canadian Legislature, and not of the Crown. Although sect. 102 of the Act imposed upon the Dominion the charge of the general public revenue as then existing of the provinces; yet by sect. 109 the casual revenue arising from lands escheated to the Crown after the Union was reserved to the provinces—the words "lands, mines, minerals, and royalties," therein including, according to their true construction, royalties in respect of lands, such as escheats. ATTORNEY-GENERAL OF ONTARIO *v.* MERCER 8 App. Cas. 767

5. —— Timber—*Right to float Timber down the Streams—Right to use Improvements without Compensation—Canadian Act, 12 Vict. c. 87, s. 5.*] *Held,* that the right conferred to float timber and logs down streams by Canadian Statute, 12 Vict. c. 87, s. 5, is not limited to such streams as in their natural state, without improvements, during freshets, permit said logs, timber, &c., to be floated down them, but extends to the user without compensation of all improvements upon such streams, even when such streams have been rendered floatable thereby.—*Boale v. Dickson* (13 U. C. C. P. 337) overruled.—Such right is only conferred by the statute during freshets; *quære* as to the rights at other seasons of the year of the parties, that is, of the lumberers on the one side, and the owners of the improvements and the bed of the stream whereon they have been effected, on the other. CALDWELL *v.* MCLAREN
[9 App. Cas. 392

V. COLONIAL LAW—CANADA—QUEBEC.

1. —— Execution—*Sheriff's Sale of an Immeuble—Duty of Vendor to give Possession—Rights of Purchaser.*] A sheriff's sale of a sugar factory with the fixed machinery therein, as of an immeuble, having taken place on the distinct footing

V. COLONIAL LAW — CANADA — QUEBEC — *continued.*

that the property was sold free of all charges, the customs authorities on the next day, acting under a *bref d'assistance,* seized the whole machinery and refused to give or allow delivery until the whole duties chargeable in respect of the machinery were paid:—*Held,* that whether the claim of the Crown was well founded or not, the seizing and detaining the machinery was in virtue of a warrant *ex facie* regular, and effectually prevented the seller from giving possession, and consequently relieved the purchaser from his obligation to pay the price.—There is nothing either in the Civil or Procedure Code of Lower Canada which casts upon such a purchaser the obligation to pay the price and thereafter get possession from a third party as he may. Sect. 712 of the C. P. L. C. relates to dispossessing the judgment debtor only. PRÉVOST *v.* LA COMPAGNIE DE FIVES-LILLE **- 10 App. Cas. 643**

2. —— **Imprisonment for Debt**—*Civil Code of Lower Canada, art.* 2274 — *Consolidated Statutes of Lower Canada, c.* 87, *s.* 12—*Code of Civil Procedure of Lower Canada, arts.* 766, 1178, *and* 1360—*Right of Appeal—Special Leave of Appeal.*] The general intention of the Canadian Legislature seems to have been that the Civil Code and the Code of Civil Procedure, which latter Code came into force ten months after the former, should stand together and be construed together; *quære,* therefore whether sect. 1360 of the latter Code repealed not only all laws in force before the passing of either Code, but also all parts of the former Code which touched procedure.—*Held,* that Art. 2274 C. C. should be read as meaning that any debtor imprisoned or held to bail in a cause wherein judgment for a sum of $80 or upwards is rendered, is obliged to make a statement under oath, and a declaration of abandonment of all his property according to the rules and subject to the penalty of imprisonment in certain cases provided in c. 87 of the Consolidated Statutes *until the Code of Civil Procedure comes into force* and *then* in the manner and form specified in the Code of Civil Procedure; the italicized words being interpolated so as to fulfil (see art. 12 of C. C.) the intention of the Legislature and to attain the object for which the article was passed.—Consequently the penalty of a year's imprisonment cannot be imposed on a person refusing to perform the duty prescribed by sect. 766 of the C. C. P., inasmuch as the same is not authorized by any of the provisions of the said Code. As to how he is compellable to perform such duty,—*quære.*—*Held,* that under Art. 1178 C. C. P., no appeal lies as of right from a judgment of the Court of Queen's Bench for Lower Canada in the matter of a penalty of imprisonment. Special leave of appeal granted on the ground of the importance of the question at issue. CARTER *v.* MOLSON **[8 App. Cas. 530**

3. —— **Legislative Power** — *Corporation*—*British North America Act,* 1867, *ss.* 91, 92, 129—*Canada Act,* 22 *Vict. c.* 66—*Invalidity of Quebec Act,* 38 *Vict. c.* 64—*Right to sue—Powers of Synod.*] The powers conferred by the British North America Act, 1867, s. 129, upon the provincial Legislatures of Ontario and Quebec, to repeal

V. COLONIAL LAW — CANADA — QUEBEC — *continued.*

and alter the statutes of the old Parliament of Canada, are precisely co-extensive with the powers of direct legislation with which those bodies are invested by the other clauses of the Act of 1867. —*Held,* that 22 Vict. *c.* 66 (of the Parliament of Canada), which created a corporation, having its corporate existence and rights in the provinces of Ontario and Quebec, could not be repealed or modified by the Legislature of either province or by the conjoint operation of both, but only by the Parliament of the Dominion. — *Held,* further, that the Quebec Act, 38 Vict. c. 64, which assumed to repeal and amend the said 22 Vict. c. 66 and (1) to destroy a corporation created by the Canadian Parliament and substitute a new one; (2) to alter materially the class of persons interested in the corporate funds, and not merely to impose conditions upon the transaction of business by the corporation within the province, was invalid.—*Citizens Insurance Company of Canada v. Parsons* (Law Rep. 7 App. Cas. 96), approved and distinguished—In a suit for a declaration of the invalidity of the Quebec Act and relief: *held,* that the Plaintiff as a contributor to the fund affected by 22 Vict. c. 66, was entitled to sue, and that his suit was not barred by reason of the Quebec Act having been passed in conformity with the resolution of a synod of the Church to which he belonged. DOBIE *v.* BOARD FOR THE MANAGEMENT OF THE TEMPORALITIES FUND OF THE PRESBYTERIAN CHURCH OF CANADA **7 App. Cas. 136**

4. —— **Legislative Power** — *British North America Act,* 1867, *ss.* 65, 92, *sub-ss.* 2, 14—*Quebec Act,* 43 & 44 *Vict. c.* 9—*Duty upon Exhibits.*] *Held,* that Quebec Act (43 & 44 Vict. c. 9) which imposed a duty of 10 cents. upon every exhibit filed in Court in any action depending therein is ultrà vires of the provincial legislature. ATTORNEY-GENERAL FOR QUEBEC *v.* REED. **[10 App. Cas. 141**

5. —— **Mortgage**—*Notice—Right of Intervention—Sect.* 154 *of Civil Procedure Code.*] Where a registered deed referred to and by reference incorporated certain other transfers and agreements whereby it appeared that the deed, though professedly one of sale, was in substance and reality the transfer to the ostensible purchaser of an estate which had been specifically allotted to him as part of his share of the residue under his father's will; *held* that a mortgagee from the said purchaser must be treated as having full knowledge that the property was by the will grèvé de substitutions in favour of the mortgagor's wife and family, his usufruct being not arrestable for his debts, especially as the mortgagee's agent was personally cognizant of the transfers and agreements of which the deed gave notice.—Certain rents and dividends of the said mortgagor having been attached, *held* that under sect. 154 of the Civil Procedure Code those who were only entitled under the will to the corpus of the property and the shares had no right to intervene in a proceeding between the mortgagor and mortgagee to declare such rents and dividends insaisissables during the mortgagor's life. CARTER *v.* MOLSON. HOLMES *v.* CARTER **10 App. Cas. 664**

V. COLONIAL LAW — CANADA — QUEBEC —
continued.

6. —— Power—*Power to apportion amongst a Class includes Power of Exclusion—Illusory Appointments—Will—Construction.*] Where a testator domiciled in Lower Canada bequeathed a portion of his residuary estate to his executors upon trust to " pay upon the death of his son, the capital thereof to such son's children in such proportion as my said son shall decide by his last will and testament, but in default of such decision then share and share alike as their absolute property for ever":—*Held*, that the son had not only the right to apportion the capital between all his children, as well those of his then existing marriage as those of any future marriage, but also the right to dispose of the property in favour of one or more of his children to the exclusion of the others.—The English doctrine as to illusory and unsubstantial appointments under a power is not and never was any part of the old French law or of the law of Lower Canada.—An English will by a testator domiciled in Lower Canada must be interpreted with regard to the law of Lower Canada, and not that of England.—*Martin* v. *Lee* (14 Moore, P. C. 142) explained. McGIBBON v. ABBOTT　　　　　　**10 App. Cas. 653**

7. —— Rights of Barristers—*Quantum meruit —Canada Petition of Right Act, 1876, sect. 19, sub-s. 3.*] According to the law of Quebec, a member of the Bar is entitled, in the absence of special stipulation, to sue for and recover on a quantum meruit in respect of professional services rendered by him, and may lawfully contract for any rate of remuneration which is not contra bonos mores, or in violation of the rules of the Bar.— Where a member of the Bar of Lower Canada (Quebec) was retained by the Government as one of their counsel before the Fisheries Commission sitting in Nova Scotia, *held*, that in the absence of stipulation to the contrary, express or implied, he must be deemed to have been employed upon the usual terms according to which such services are rendered, and that his status in respect both of right and remedy was not affected either by the lex loci contractûs or the lex loci solutionis.— *Held*, further, that the Petition of Right, Canada, Act, 1876, sect' 19, sub-sect. 3, does not in such case bar the remedy against the Crown by petition.—*Kennedy* v. *Brown* (13 C. B. (N.S.) 677) commented upon. THE QUEEN v. DOUTRE
　　　　　　　　　　　　　[9 App. Cas. 745

8. —— Riparian Proprietors — *Servitudes— Accumulation of Flow of Water—Civil Code of Lower Canada, sect. 501.*] By sect. 501 of the Civil Code of Lower Canada the proprietor of the higher land can do nothing to aggravate the servitude of the lower land. Where the Plaintiffs, being entitled to a flow of water from their land, executed certain works which had the effect of accumulating the volume of water, and probably of increasing the depth of its channel:—*Held*, that to the extent of such accumulation and consequent increase of flow, they had aggravated the servitude of the lower land, and to that extent had no right to demand a free course for the water sent down by them. Having insisted on their right to the existing flow, and refused to allege and prove a case for relief pro tanto, their suit was

V. COLONIAL LAW —CANADA — QUEBEC—
continued.

dismissed with costs. FRECHETTE v. LA COMPAGNIE MANUFACTURIÈRE DE ST. HYACINTHE
　　　　　　　　　　　　　[9 App. Cas. 170

9. —— Timber Limits—*Consolidated Statutes of Canada, c. 23—Priority of Licenses—Warranty on Sale.*] On a sale of "timber limits" held under licenses in pursuance of the Consolidated Statutes of Canada, c. 23, a clause of simple warranty (garantie de tous troubles généralement quelconques) does not operate to protect the purchaser against eviction by a person claiming to be entitled under a prior license to a portion of the limits sold. DUCONDU v. DUPUY
　　　　　　　　　　　　　[9 App. Cas. 150

10. —— Turnpike Roads — *Canadian Act (16 Vict. c. 235)—Debentures issued by Trustees of the Quebec Turnpike Roads—Liability of Province.*] *Held*, that the debentures in suit which had been issued under the authority of the Canadian Act (16 Vict. c. 235) by the trustees of the Quebec turnpike roads, appointed under Ordinance 4 Vict. c 17, and empowered thereby to borrow moneys "on the credit and security of the tolls thereby authorized to be imposed, and of other moneys which might come into the possession and be at the disposal of the said trustees, under and by virtue of the Ordinance, and not to be paid out of or chargeable against the general revenue of this province," did not create a liability on the part of the province in respect of either the principal or the interest thereof:—*Held*, further, that the province of Canada had not by its conduct and legislation recognised its liability to pay the same. The 7th section of the Act 16 Vict. expressly took away the power which had been conferred by the 27th section of the Ordinance to make advances out of provincial funds for the payment of interest, and by its proviso distinguished these debentures from those which had a provincial guarantee. THE QUEEN v. BELLEAU
　　　　　　　　　　　　　[7 App. Cas. 473

VI. COLONIAL LAW—CAPE OF GOOD HOPE.

1. —— Church of South Africa—*Endowments of the Church of England in South Africa—Construction of Articles of Constitution—Effect of Proviso repudiating Privy Council Decisions.*] The Church of the Province of South Africa is not a Church in connection with the Church of England as by law established.—Although there are in the articles of the constitution of the Church of the Province of South Africa general expressions affirming in the strongest way the connection of the Church of the Province with the Church of England, and its adherence to the faith and doctrine of the Church of England, yet by the proviso in the said articles to the effect that in the interpretation of such faith and doctrine it is not bound by the decisions of the tribunals of the Church of England, it is practically declared that the connection is not maintained.—In a suit by the Bishop of Graham's Town (one of the dioceses of the Church of the Province) against the officiating minister in possession of the church of St. George in Graham's Town to enforce sentences of the Diocesan Court of Graham's Town, whereby the Defendant, a member of the Church of the

VI. COLONIAL LAW—CAPE OF GOOD HOPE—
continued.

Province, subject to its constitution and canons, and to the episcopal jurisdiction of the Plaintiff, had been found guilty of contumacious disobedience, suspended from his ministerial functions until he should engage not to repeat the offence of preventing the bishop from preaching or ministering in the church of St. George, and finally excommunicated: it appeared that the church of St. George had been duly dedicated to ecclesiastical purposes in connection with the Church of England as by law established, and for no other purposes, and was held by trustees for those purposes:—*Held,* that the Plaintiff had no right in the said church of St. George, and that his suit must be dismissed. MERRIMAN *v.* WILLIAMS - - - - 7 App. Cas. 484

2. —— **Equitable Jurisdiction** — *Removal of Trustees.*] There is a jurisdiction in Courts of Equity to remove old trustees and substitute new ones in cases requiring such a remedy.—The main principle on which such jurisdiction should be exercised is the welfare of the beneficiaries and of the trust estate.—Case in which their Lordships, overruling the decree of the Court below, held that the trustees (the Board of Executors of Cape Town, a body incorporated by an ordinance of the Cape of Good Hope) should, in the special circumstances of the case, be removed without costs of appeal, the Appellant having persisted in charges of fraud which the evidence did not sustain. LETTERSTEDT *v.* BROERS 9 App. Cas. 371

3. —— **Principal and Agent**—*Cape of Good Hope Act* 11 *of* 1863, s. 2—*Construction of Contract.*] Where a contract between the Defendant and E. in terms purported to be one of guarantee or agency, the Defendant guaranteeing the sale of E.'s property in whole or by lots at a fixed price, E. giving the Defendant a power of attorney to deal with the property as he thinks fit, and agreeing that he should receive any surplus over and above the fixed price as his commission on and recompense for the said guarantee; but the real effect of the transaction was to give E. every right which a vendor could legally claim, and to confer on the Defendant every right which a purchaser could legally demand:—*Held,* that the defendant was liable to pay duty on his purchase-money under Act 11 of 1863, sect. 2. HUTTON *v.* LIPPERT - - 8 App. Cas. 309

4. —— **Watercourse** — *Prescription* — *Roman-Dutch Law*—*Rights of the Owner of Springs—Rights of Riparian Proprietors.*] The Respondent's predecessor in title in 1820 constructed a watercourse on Crown lands, by means of which he diverted the water of two springs which rose thereon, so that they mingled with the waters of a private stream admittedly belonging to the farm, of which the Respondent owned a portion. He did so with the license of those who acted as agents for the Government, in order to have the permanent use of the water for his farm, and continued his user for the period of prescription, after which the Respondent applied for and obtained from the Colonial Government a renewal of the license originally granted to his predecessor:—*Held,* that the user of the diverted water by the

VI. COLONIAL LAW—CAPE OF GOOD HOPE—
continued.

Respondent's predecessor was not precarious, and that the act of the Respondent had not deprived him of the prescriptive right acquired by the predecessor so as to enable the Crown to give to the Plaintiffs in 1881 a title to the said water.—It is very doubtful whether, by Dutch-Roman law, the owner of the sources of streams has exclusive dominion over their waters. They are at least subject to rights of user acquired by prescription, and probably also to the rights which English law recognises in riparian proprietors to water flowing in a known or definite channel.—*Miner v. Gilmour* (12 Moore's Ind. Ap. Ca. 131) and *Van Breda* v. *Silberbauer* (Law Rep. 3 P. C. 84) approved.—When a prescriptive right is once acquired, it cannot be lost by any subsequent act not amounting to a surrender, even though such act would have, previous to the acquisition of such right, rendered the user precarious. COMMISSIONERS OF FRENCH HOEK *v.* HUGO [10 App. Cas. 336

VII. COLONIAL LAW—CEYLON.

1. —— **Adverse Possession** — *Ceylon Ordinances, No.* 8 *of* 1834, *No.* 22 *of* 1871—*Acts of Ownership.*] Ceylon Ordinances No. 8 of 1834, and No. 22 of 1871, require that a Defendant should have had ten years' undisturbed and uninterrupted possession, meaning actual and not ideal possession, of land in dispute in order to be entitled to the benefit of such Ordinances. Although acts done upon parts of a district of land may be evidence of possession of the whole, yet as regards lands within a disputed boundary acts of ownership by either party outside the boundary are no evidence of title to the lands within it. CLARK *v.* ELPHINSTONE - 6 App. Cas. 164

2. —— **Judgment Debtor**—*Execution—Ceylon Ordinance, No.* 4, 1867, *ss.* 53, 54—*Application to set aside Sale for Irregularity—Rule as to Thirty Days imperative.*] By Ceylon Ordinance No. 4, 1867, sects. 53, 54, any application by a judgment debtor to set aside a sale in execution of immovable property must be made within thirty days, and the absence of the judgment debtor from Ceylon is no excuse for non-compliance with the positive terms of the Ordinance. SILLERY *v.* HARMANIS [8 App. Cas. 99

3. —— **Presumption of Marriage**—*Onus Probandi.*] According to the Roman-Dutch law there is a presumption in favour of marriage rather than of concubinage. According to the law of Ceylon, as in England, where a man and woman are proved to have lived together as man and wife, the law will presume, unless the contrary be clearly proved, that they were living together in consequence of a valid marriage, and not in a state of concubinage. Where it is proved that they have gone through a form of marriage, and thereby shewn an intention to be married, *held,* that those who claim by virtue of the marriage are not bound to prove that all necessary ceremonies have been performed. SASTRY VELAIDER ARONEGARY *v.* SEMBECUTTY VAIGALIE [6 App. Cas. 364

4. —— **Right to sue the Crown**—*Roman-Dutch Law of Holland—Right of Set-off between the*

VII. COLONIAL LAW—CEYLON—_continued._

Crown and the Subject.] There is no authority for saying that the Roman-Dutch law of Holland, which was in force in Ceylon at the date of its conquest by the British, and has not since been abrogated, empowered the subject to sue the Government.—But since the conquest a very extensive practice of suing the Crown has sprung up and·has been recognised by the Legislature: see the 117th section of Ordinance No. 11 of 1868, which re-enacted an Ordinance of 1856:— _Held,_ therefore, that such suits are now incorporated into the law of the land.—_Held,_ further, that where the Crown is Plaintiff and the Defendants sue in reconvention, the Court is not bound to give separate judgments, but may set off the amount awarded to the Defendants against ·that awarded to the Crown, and give judgment for the balance. HETTIHEWAGE APPU _v._ THE QUEEN'S ADVOCATE　　　9 App. Cas. 571

VIII. COLONIAL LAW—GRIQUALAND.

—— Grant of Land—_Griqualand West—Indefeasible British Title — Conditions of Grant._] _Held,_ that the Plaintiff, who had obtained a judgment from the Land Court of Griqualand West in respect of certain lands, was entitled to the grant of an indefeasible British title thereto under the seal of the province in confirmation·of the Presidential grant of the 3rd of December, ·1862; and that he was not compellable to accept a title containing conditions not expressed in that grant, and not shewn to be incidents implied therein, nor to be duties or ·regulations since established concerning lands granted upon the like conditions.—_Held,_ further, that he might reasonably object to the clause "that the issue of this title without the express reservation to Government of its rights to all precious stones gold, or silver found on or under the surface of the said land shall in no degree prejudice the position of the Government in regard to the same."—_Quære,_ whether the Civil Commissioner of the district was the proper officer to be sued in respect of title to lands·in his district; but, _held,_ that he as Respondent could not by such objection defend the judgment which he had obtained or defeat an appeal therefrom. WEBB _v._ WRIGHT

[8 App. Cas. 318

IX. COLONIAL LAW—HONDURAS.

—— Territorial Sovereignty—_Adverse Possession against the Crown._] _Held,_ in an information of intrusion relating to land in British Honduras, that the Defendants having shewn sixty years' ·adverse possession there from before 1817, by ·themselves and their predecessors in title, without disturbance or effectual claim by the Crown, such information must be dismissed. Although British Honduras was formerly declared to be a ·British Colony, and formally annexed to British dominions·by a proclamation of Her Majesty, dated the 12th of May, 1862, yet grants of land ·having been made therein by the Crown as early as ·1817; ·_held,_ overruling the opinion of the ·Supreme Court, that the territorial sovereignty of the Crown must be deemed to have been acquired in or before that year. ATTORNEY-GENERAL FOR BRITISH HONDURAS _v._ BRISTOWE

[6 App. Cas. 143

X. COLONIAL LAW—JERSEY.

1. —— Criminal Cases — _Practice — Special Leave to appeal—Order in Council of 13th of May,_ 1572.] An order of Court directing a Defendant to plead to an information (or other analogous proceeding), for libel, and directing that having pleaded he should be tried·without a jury, is· not a specific sentence within the meaning of·the Order of Council of 13th·of May, 1572. Special leave to appeal therefrom refused.— _Quære,_ as to granting· special leave to appeal in criminal cases in Jersey, or where there has been no definitive sentence. ESNOUF _v._ ATTORNEY-GENERAL FOR·JERSEY -　　- 8 App. Cas. 304.

2. —— Public Register — _Registration by Order of Court—Hypothec._] The legal effect of the registration in the public register of Jersey pursuant to an order of the Royal Court of a marriage contract, is to confer a right of hypothec in respect of its provisions from the date of the said order. SIMON _v._ VERNON　　8 App. Cas. 542·

3. —— Set-off—_Liquid Demand._] According to the law of Jersey a claim by way of compensation or set-off is admissible, when it is for a liquid demand.—Such claims having been dismissed by the Court below the case was remanded to ascertain whether·they were in whole or in part liquid debts or debts "incontestées ou du moins incontestables" as alleged by the Appellants. DYSON _v._ GODFRAY　　-　　9 App. Cas. 726·

XI. COLONIAL LAW—MALTA.

1. —— Primogenitura·—_Construction of Deed._] B. by deed (1673) gave· all his property to his nephew, reserving the right quoad the "bona stabilia" to establish a primogenitura. After the death of his nephew he executed a deed (1686) which recited the gift and the death of the donee without ·establishing the primogenitura, and directed that at the death of the donor, the donee's eldest son Martinus Antonius should ·succeed. The deed then contained the following clauses, under the first of which N. succeeded as· a primogenitus· mas and died in 1875.—·1. "Scilicet quod deinde censeantur bona predicta vinculata et fideicommisso perpetuo supposita pro omnibus primogenitis maribus legittimis et naturalibus, et· ex legittimo matrimonio nascituris, per directam lineam ex dicto Martino Antonio de primogenito in primogenitum in infinitum,·cunctisque futuris· temporibus, et sine ulla temporis perfinitione."— 3. "Et in defectu primogeniti maris ex dicto Domino Martino Antonio, dicta bona pervenire· debeant ac perveniant et pervenire debeant ad filios ejusdem Domini Martini Antonj, legittimos et naturales, et ex legittimo· matrimonio nascituros quousque in secundo gradu nepotum dioti Domini Martini Antonij nasceretur masculus ex aliqua de filiabus dicti D. Martini Antonij legittimis et naturalibus et ex legittimo matrimonio, cui nepoti nato statim dicta bona devolvant cum onere ut supra transeundi de primogenito nepote dioti Martini Antonj in primogenitum nepotem legittimum et de legittimo matrimonio nasciturum."—On the death without· issue in 1875 of N.'s daughter's son who had succeeded under clause 3, the succession· opened. —In a suit by G. the daughter's son (born 1861) of a younger sister of the deceased, claiming as·

XI. COLONIAL LAW- MALTA—*continued.*

the male descendant in the nearest collateral line, the Defendant, the son (born 1834) of the youngest sister of the deceased, contended that he was entitled by priority of birth under the 3rd clause, and denied that G. was a primogenitus mas within the meaning of the deed :—*Held,* that G. was entitled to the estate by virtue of the ordinary rules of law applicable to the primogenitura established by clause 1. Although the primogenitura as created by clause 1 is so far qualified in favour of males as in the events which happened to devolve on G. in preference to his mother, it is not an agnatial primogenitura so as to prevent females from constituting lines of descent ; line is to be considered in preference to degree, sex, or age ; and therefore G. succeeds, being in a nearer collateral line, viz., that of the elder sister, than the Appellant, who though born first is in the line of the younger sister.—A deviation from the ordinary mode in which a primogenitura descends is not to be construed as interfering with that mode of descent more than is necessary to give effect to such deviation ; and therefore assuming that in the event contemplated by clause 3 females are to take collectively, it by no means follows that all or any of them are prevented from forming lines of descent. The clause applies only to the case therein stated, viz., when upon the opening of the succession there is no " primogenitus mas," in which case the estate devolves on females who are to be displaced by the first male born from any of them. G. being a primogenitus mas in existence at the death of the deceased, clause 3 had no operation. APAP *v.* STRICKLAND

[7 App. Cas. 156

2. —— Primogenitura—*Construction of Deed.*]
The general rule governing the succession to a primogenitura is that line is to be considered in the first place, degree in the second, sex in the third, and age in the fourth. A prescribed deviation therefrom must not be construed as interfering therewith more than is necessary to give effect to the deviation.—The deed of foundation of a primogenitura prescribed that sex should be preferred to line and degree, and gave certain powers of nomination. Under clause 3, which directed that in the events which happened the succession should go "ad unum e masculis descendentibus a feminis de eadem linea masculina ;" N. succeeded. The clause further provided that in subsequent successions the order of line should be the direct before the collateral, the nearer collateral before the more remote.—The deed contained also the following clause :—5. " Quod quilibet possessor pro tempore præsentis primogenituræ, si fuerit masculus, possit nominare et eligere suum immediatum successorem aliquem vel aliquam ex vocatis in præsenti instrumento ad sui libitum, etiam si sit sibi magis remotus vel remota, vel minor natu, dummodo non pervertat ordinem vocationis et prælationis superius præscriptum ; et non facta hujusmodi nominatione et electione censeatur semper nominatus magis proximus ultimo possessori pro tempore in gradu naturæ, et in paritate gradus major ætate."—On the death in 1875 of N. without issue, the succession opened.—In a suit by the Respondent, the son (born 1834) of N.'s youngest sister claiming as nearest in degree of

XI. COLONIAL LAW—MALTA—*continued.*

nature; the Appellant, the grandson (born 1861) of an elder sister of N. contended that he was entitled by priority of line :—*Held,* that the Appellant was entitled.—The devolution of the primogenitura in the absence of nomination must be ascertained by construing clause 5 relatively to the power of nomination given thereby, which merely enables the possessor to regulate the order of succession within the prescribed order of lines. Priority of line is always to be regarded, and in the absence of nomination priority in degree, and then in age must also be attended to. STRICKLAND *v.* APAP

[8 App. Cas. 106

XII. COLONIAL LAW—MAURITIUS.

1. —— Arbitration —*Tierce Opposition— Judgment Creditors claiming under their Debtor are bound by his acts — Civil Procedure Code, Art.* 474.] Where accounts between a firm and one of its debtors had been settled by a reference and an award made thereunder, *held,* that the judgment creditors of the firm could not without alleging fraud or collusion in the proceedings on the reference be admitted to impeach the award by way of tierce opposition or otherwise. Although they were not parties to the reference and were hostile to the firm down to judgment, yet by virtue of the judgment they derived rights under a party to the reference within the meaning of Art. 474 of the Code de Procédure Civile. MARTIN *v.* BOULANGER   8 App. Cas. 296

2. —— Bankrupt —*Mauritius Ordinance of* 1853, *No.* 33, *ss.* 40, 43, 50—*Validity of Adjudication.*] The Court of Bankruptcy of the Mauritius has jurisdiction to order adjudication against a firm on the petition of the sole member of that firm. Such order is valid against the petitioner personally.—Under sects. 40, 43, and 50 of Ordinance No. 33 of 1853, a creditor cannot challenge the validity of such order on the ground that the bankrupt has not made it appear to the satisfaction of the Court that his estate is sufficient to pay his creditors at least five shillings in the pound clear of all bankruptcy charges. Such qualified solvency is not a fact to be put in issue and proved, but provisionally to appear to the satisfaction of the Court, the propriety of whose conclusion cannot by any process be contested. ORIENTAL BANK CORPORATION *v.* RICHER & Co.

[9 App. Cas. 413

XIII. COLONIAL LAW—NATAL.

1. —— Public Officer —*Jurisdiction — Suit against Public Officer in his Official Capacity— Liability of Servants of the Crown—Petition of Right.*] In a suit against Her Majesty's Deputy Commissary-General for Natal, and as such representing Her Majesty's Commissariat Department, to recover certain moneys as the price or hire of certain waggons and oxen, for the carriage of certain goods, for damages for illegal acts of Defendant or his employés, and for general damage :— *Held,* on exceptions by the Defendant to the jurisdiction of the Court and to the declaration that the Defendant could not be sued, either personally, or in his official capacity, upon a contract entered into by him on behalf of the Commissariat Department; and that there was no cause of action against him.—The Government revenue

XIII. COLONIAL LAW—NATAL—_continued._

cannot be reached by a suit against a public officer in his official capacity.—_Quære_, whether the Court would have had jurisdiction if a petition of right had been presented and the Crown had ordered that right should be done.　PALMER _v._ HUTCHINSON　　　**6 App. Cas. 619**

2. —— **Surety Bond by a Woman**—_Effect of Non-Renunciation of Legal Privileges._] By the law which prevails in Natal a woman cannot be effectually bound as a surety, unless she specially renounces the privileges secured to her by the Senatûs Consultum Villeianum and other rules of law.—Where a husband under a general power of attorney from his wife professed to bind her personally as surety under a mortgage bond duly executed, _held_, that, there being no authority to renounce as aforesaid, express or implied, given by the power of attorney, such deed was void. MACKELLAR _v._ BOND　　　**9 App. Cas. 715**

XIV. COLONIAL LAW—NEW SOUTH WALES.

1. —— **Crown Lands**—_Dedication of Land to Public Purposes by the Crown—Presumption from User—Crown Lands Alienation Act, 1861, ss. 3, 5 —5 & 6 Vict. c. 36._] From long-continued user of a way by the public, whether land belongs to to the Crown or to a private owner, dedication from the Crown or private owner, as the case may be, in the absence of anything to rebut the presumption may and ought to be presumed.—The same presumption from user should be made in the case of Crown lands in the colony of New South Wales, apart from the Crown Lands Alienation Act, 1861, though the nature of the user and the weight to be given to it vary in each particular case.—Assuming that the effect of the 3rd and 5th sections of the Act is that any dedication by the Crown must since 1861 be in manner prescribed by the statute :—_Held_, that from a continuous user of twenty-one years before the statute continued since 1861 down to the time of the action without any interruption or interference on the part of the Crown, a dedication prior to the statute, and at a time when the Crown had power to dedicate, might be presumed; and that that presumption was strengthened by the subsequent user.—5 & 6 Vict. c. 36, of the Imperial Parliament leaves the power of the Crown with regard to public roads as it existed by the common law, and does not interfere with its right to dedicate lands for that purpose.　TURNER _v._ WALSH　　　**6 App. Cas. 636**

2. —— **Crown Lands**—_Lands forfeited to the Crown cannot be conditionally sold—Crown Lands Alienation Act, 1861, s. 13._] Lands taken under a conditional sale and afterwards forfeited to the Crown are not open to a conditional purchase under sect. 13 of the Crown Lands Alienation Act, 1861. The Crown has, under the 18th section, the option either to sell them by public auction or to retain them in its own hands. BLACKBURN _v._ FLAVELLE　　　**6 App. Cas. 628**

3. —— **Legislative Powers**—11 _Vict. No._ 13, _s._ 1—_Costs of Action of Slander._] _Held_, that the Legislature of New South Wales had power to repeal the Statute of James (21 Jac. 1, c. 16), s. 6, and had impliedly done so by 11 Vict. No. 13, s. 1, which, according to its true construction,

XIV. COLONIAL LAW—NEW SOUTH WALES —_continued._

placed an action for words spoken upon the same footing as regards costs and other matters as an action for written slander.　HARRIS _v._ DAVIES 　　　**[10 App. Cas. 279**

4. —— **Legislative Powers**—_Customs Regulation Act of 1879, s._ 133—_Duties levied under an Order in Council._] A Colonial Legislature is not a delegate of the Imperial Legislature. It is restricted in the area of its powers, but within that area it is unrestricted.—_Held_, that the Customs Regulation Act of 1879, s. 133, was within the plenary powers of legislation conferred upon the New South Wales Legislature by the Constitution Act (scheduled to 18 & 19 Vict. c. 54), ss. 1 and 45.—_Held_, further, that duties levied by an Order in Council issued under sect. 133, are really levied by authority of the Legislature and not of the Executive. Also that under sect. 133 "the opinion of the collector," whether right or wrong, authorizes the action of the Governor. POWELL _v._ APOLLO CANDLE COMPANY　**10 App. Cas. 282**

5. —— **Tramways**—_New South Wales Act, 43 Vict. No._ 25, _ss._ 3, 5—_Right to run Steam Motors on Tramways._] _Held_, that the Commissioner for Railways in New South Wales has, according to the true construction of Act 43 Vict. No. 25, sect. 3, a legal right to run steam motors upon the tramway lines mentioned in the 2nd schedule thereto.—_Semble_, sect. 5 is sufficient to legalise the use of steam motors upon the other tramways governed by the said Act. COMMISSIONER FOR RAILWAYS _v._ TOOHEY　9 App. Cas. 720

XV. COLONIAL LAW—NEW ZEALAND.

1. —— **Harbour**—_New Zealand Crown Suits Act, 1881 (45 Vict. No._ 8), _sect._ 37—_Executive Government—Liability for Negligence — Reasonable Care—Damage to Vessels using the Defendant's Staiths._] Where the Executive Government possessed the control and management of a tidal harbour with authority to remove obstructions in it, and the public had a right to navigate therein, subject to the harbour regulations and without payment of harbour dues; the staiths and wharves belonging to the Executive Government which received wharfage and tonnage dues in respect of vessels using them :—_Held_, that there was a duty imposed by law upon the Executive Government to take reasonable care that vessels using the staiths in the ordinary manner might do so without damage to the vessel. Reasonable care is not shewn when after notice of danger at a particular spot, no inquiry is made as to its existence and extent, and no warning is given.—The principle of liability for negligence established by _Parnaby_ v. _Lancaster Canal Company_ (11 Ad. & E. 223) and _Mersey Docks Trustees_ v. _Gibbs_ (Law Rep. 1 H. L. 93) approved of and applied to the Executive Government in the above circumstances, which were distinguishable in respect of non-receipt of harbour dues; notwithstanding the Crown Suits Act, 1881, sect. 37. THE QUEEN _v._ WILLIAMS　-　-　**9 App. Cas. 418**

2. —— **Public Works**—_Compensation—Wellington Harbour Board and Corporation Act, 1880 —The Public Works Act, 1882, s._ 4—" _Estate or interest in land._"] Land having become vested in

XV. COLONIAL LAW—NEW ZEALAND—contd.

the Respondents under the Wellington Harbour Board and Corporation Land Act, 1880 (44 Vict. No. 21), the Appellants claimed compensation under the Public Works Act, 1882 (46 Vict. No. 37), on the ground of their having some estate or interest therein within the meaning of the latter Act.—It appeared that the Appellants' lessor (or his predecessor in title) had in 1848 erected a wharf on the said land, with the permission of the Government, and in 1855 a jetty; that in 1856, at the request and for the benefit of the Government, he incurred large expenditure for the extension of his jetty and for the erection of a warehouse; that in subsequent years the Government used, paid for, and, with the consent of the said lessor, improved the said land and works:—Held, that the lessor must be deemed to have occupied the ground from 1848 under a revocable license to use it for the purposes of a wharfinger; that by virtue of the transactions of 1856 such license ceased to be revocable at the will of the Government, whereby the lessor acquired an indefinite, that is, practically, a perpetual right to the jetty for the purposes aforesaid. The equitable right so acquired is an "estate or interest in, to or out of land" within the wide meaning of the Act of 1882, which directs that in ascertaining title to compensation the Court should not be bound to regard strict legal rights only but should do what is reasonable and just.—Ramsden v. Dyson (Law Rep. 1 H. L. 129) approved. PLIMMER v. MAYOR, &c., OF WELLINGTON
[9 App. Cas. 699

XVI. COLONIAL LAW—QUEENSLAND.

—— Principal and Agent—Queensland Constitution Act of 1867, ss. 6, 7—Estoppel.] In an action to recover penalties against the Defendant for having contrary to the Queensland Constitution Act of 1867 sat in the Legislative Assembly as a member thereof and voted therein; it appeared that M., M., & Co. had in 1878 "for and on behalf of the owners of the ship S. H.," but contrary to the express direction of the Defendant (one of such owners), concluded a charterparty with the local Government; that such charterparty was made in pursuance of an agreement between M., M., & Co. and the Government to supply ships of a particular description to carry emigrants, which agreement did not provide for any privity of contract between the owners of such ships and the Government; that M., M., & Co. were the general agents of the Defendant to charter ships in which he held shares, and that one of the firm was registered as managing owner of S. H.; and that it was neither alleged nor proved that the Government ever knew that M., M., & Co., or any member of that firm had general authority to bind the Defendant, and had acted upon the belief that such general authority continued unrestricted:—Held, that under such circumstances the Government could not have held the Defendant bound to them, and consequently that he was not disqualified under the Act.—Freeman v. Cooke (2 Ex. 654) approved.—Quære, whether in the absence of any notice to the Government of such special restriction, the general authority of the agent if known to the Government would have sufficed to bind the De-

XVI. COLONIAL LAW—QUEENSLAND—contd.

fendant so as to disqualify him under the Act.—Quære, also, as to the meaning of "presume to sit and vote" in sect. 7 of the Act, and as to what knowledge by a member of his disqualification is implied thereby. MILES v. McILWRAITH
[8 App. Cas. 120

XVII. COLONIAL LAW—SOUTH AUSTRALIA.

—— Unregistered Deed—South Australian Act 22 of 1861, s. 39—Equitable Right.] Although an unregistered deed is not effectual to pass any interest in land under sect. 39 of Act 22 of 1861, yet it is effectual to pass an equitable right to set aside a certificate of title relating thereto which has been obtained by fraud. McELLISTER v. BIGGS
[8 App. Cas. 314

XVIII. COLONIAL LAW—STRAITS SETTLEMENTS.

1. —— Evidence—Penang—Ordinance 8 of 1873, s. 12, sub-s. 2 and s. 26—Insufficient Cancellation—Additional Stamp—Admissibility in Evidence.] Sect. 26 of Ordinance 8 of 1873, applies to all cases where a document has not been duly stamped, and for which a special provision in the ordinance has not been previously made, as in the case of bills of exchange and other documents.—Where an agreement, liable to stamp duty under Schedule A. had not been cancelled in manner provided by sect. 12, sub-sect. 2 (the date of cancellation only, and not the initials appearing thereon):—Held, that it could be and was rendered admissible in evidence by means of an additional stamp under sect. 26. ALLEN v. MEERA PULLAY
[7 App. Cas. 172

2. —— Treaty—Construction—Grant to A. his Heirs and Successors.] Case where the grant by a treaty between two sovereigns of a monthly pension to A., his heirs and successors, was held, according to its true construction, not to confer such an interest therein upon A. as to enable him to assign it beyond the period of his own life. RAVENA MANA CHENA ALLAGAPPA CHITTY v. TUNKU ALLUM BIN SULTAN ALLIE ISKANDER SHAH
[8 App. Cas. 751

XIX. COLONIAL LAW—TRINIDAD.

—— Legitimacy—Status of Children born before Marriage—Law of Inheritance—Ordinance No. 24 of 1845, s. 5, and No. 7 of 1858, s. 7.] According to the Spanish laws originally in force in Trinidad, children born before marriage (contracted before the 12th of March, 1846), have the same rights of inheritance from their father and mother as children born after marriage.—Sect. 12 of Ordinance No. 24 of 1845, while preventing marriage after that date from legitimating the ante nati children, does not take away the status of legitimacy previously acquired.—Where a mother married before that date, died intestate in 1862, leaving seven children, three of whom were ante nati and four post nati, held, that each by inheritance took one seventh of the estate which she had acquired by purchase under sect. 5 of No. 24 of 1845:—Held, with regard to the shares of two ante nati who had died thereafter intestate without issue, that under sect. 5 above cited and sect. 7 of No. 7 of 1858, they were divisible equally amongst the four surviving children, whether

XIX. COLONIAL LAW—TRINIDAD—*continued.*
ante nati or post nati, and the issue of a deceased daughter. FISCALLIER *v.* ESCALLIER
[10 App. Cas. 312

XX. COLONIAL LAW—VICTORIA.

1. —— *Insolvency—Real Estate in England.*] Real estate in England does not vest in an assignee under a Victorian insolvency. WAITE *v.* BINGLEY 　　-　　21 Ch. D. 674

2. —— *Insolvency—Suit to set aside Release of Equity of Redemption — Misrepresentation—Onus Probandi.*] In a suit by the Respondent (lately an insolvent) to set aside on the ground of misrepresentation or mutual mistake a release by the official assignee of the Respondent's equity of redemption of a certain mortgage, for accounts against the Appellants, the mortgagees, and in effect to have the benefit of a subsequent resale by the releasee's purchaser, it appeared that the official assignee had in the release admitted the truth of the representations made to him, and that the Respondent had thereafter taken a conveyance from him of all the estate vested in him under the insolvency:—*Held,* that the onus was upon the Respondent, who was primâ facie bound by the admissions under the seal of his vendor, to prove the falsehood of the representations, and not upon the Appellants to establish their truth. —*Held,* further, that where a mortgagor in consideration of the mortgage debt releases the equity of redemption to the mortgagee, the parties should be regarded, until the contrary is shewn by the party impeaching the deed, as on the ordinary footing of vendor and purchaser.—*Knight* v. *Marjoribanks* (2 Mac. & G. 10) approved.—If such release is voidable an equity to set it aside is an equitable interest in the property to which it relates, and therefore in this case was part of the estate vested in the official assignee. The Respondent, under his conveyance from the official assignee, obtained a locus standi to maintain this suit. MELBOURNE BANKING CORPORATION *v.* BROUGHAM 　　　7 App. Cas. 307

3. —— *Lex Domicilii—Lex Loci as applied to the Personal Assets of a Testator—Victorian Act No. 388 of 1870, s. 2, sub-s. 7—Probate Duty.*] Although the law of a testator's domicil governs the foreign personal assets of his estate for the purpose of succession and enjoyment, yet those assets are, for the purpose of legal representation, of collection and of administration, as distinguished from distribution among the successors, governed by the law of their own locality and not by that of the testator's domicil.—*Held,* that, according to the true construction and intention of Victorian Act No. 388 of 1870, "The Duties on the Estates of Deceased Persons Statute, 1870," a legal personal representative in Victoria should, as regards the "personal estate" of the deceased mentioned in sect. 2, sub-sect. 7, take accounts only of so much thereof as comes under his control by virtue of his Victorian probate. BLACKWOOD *v.* THE QUEEN 　　-　　8 App. Cas. 82

4. —— *Notice of Action—Melbourne Harbour Trust Act, sect. 46—Interpretation—Acts divided into Headings.*] *Held,* that an action against the Melbourne Harbour Trust Commissioners was an action brought against a "person" within the

XX. COLONIAL LAW—VICTORIA—*continued,*
meaning of sect. 46 of the Melbourne Harbour Trust Act; and that notice in writing thereof complying in form or in substance with the requirements of the section was necessary.— Remarks as to the effect upon interpretation of dividing an Act into parts with appropriate headings.—*Eastern Counties and London and Blackwall Railway Companies* v. *Marriage* (9 H. L. C. 32), distinguished. UNION STEAMSHIP COMPANY OF NEW ZEALAND *v.* MELBOURNE HARBOUR TRUST COMMISSIONERS 9 App. Cas. 365

5. —— *Solicitor—Victorian Common Law Procedure Act, s. 369—Power of Court to order delivery of Attorney's Bill.*] Under sect. 396 of the Victorian Common Law Procedure Act, the Court has power to order delivery of his bill by an attorney, whether or not it has been paid, and whether or not it is one which it would have jurisdiction to refer to taxation. DUFFETT *v.* McEVOY 　　-　　10 App. Cas. 300

XXI. COLONIAL LAW—WEST AUSTRALIA.

1. —— *Foreign Country—Conflict of Laws— Liability of Foreign Corporation—Lex Loci Contractûs.*] *Held,* that the Western Australian Joint Stock Companies Ordinance Act, 1858, does not apply to foreign corporations or to companies incorporated out of Western Australia and properly and lawfully carrying on business as such. Consequently a limited company incorporated elsewhere, not having complied with its provisions, can nevertheless carry on business and make contracts in Western Australia by its agent without its members being liable individually for its debts and engagements.—*Held,* further, that a company duly registered and incorporated in Victoria could not be again registered as a company in Western Australia.—*Bulkeley* v. *Schutz* (Law Rep. 3 P. C. 764) approved. BATEMAN *v.* SERVICE
[6 App. Cas. 386

2. —— *Railway—Western Australian Railways Act of 1878 (42 Vict. No. 31), ss. 14 and 16 —Notice—Right of Resumption—Compensation.*] *Held,* in a case where the Crown had a power of resumption under the terms of its grant, and had given lawful notice in exercise of such power, such notice must not be deemed to be under sect. 12 of the Railways Act of 1878 (entitling the parties affected to compensation under sect. 14); *secus* where notice could not have been lawfully given except under this Act. THOMAS *v.* SHERWOOD 　　-　　9 App. Cas. 142

COLONIAL LAW—Anglo-Indian domicil
　　See DOMICIL. 4.　　[23 Ch. D. 532

—— Canada—Bill of exchange 8 App. Cas. 733
　　See BILL OF EXCHANGE—LIABILITY OF PARTIES.

—— Jamaica 　　-　　7 App. Cas. 79
　　See BANKRUPTCY—MUTUAL DEALINGS. 3.

—— Practice—Leave to appeal to Privy Council.
　　See Cases under PRACTICE—PRIVY COUNCIL—LEAVE TO APPEAL.

COLONIAL REGISTERS.
　　See COMPANY — SHARES — REGISTER — Statutes.

COLONIAL STATUTES SPECIALLY REFERRED TO IN THIS DIGEST.
　See TABLE OF STATUTES, COLONIAL (*ante*, p. clxxvii).

COLONY—English settlers—Privileges of English law　-　　10 App. Cas. 692
　See SCOTCH LAW—HUSBAND AND WIFE. 2.

—— Evidence in.
　See EVIDENCE—GENERAL—*Statutes.*

—— User of invention in　-　19 Ch. D. 268
　See PATENT—VALIDITY. 4.

COMITY OF NATIONS—Infant resident abroad
　See INFANT—GUARDIAN. 1. [30 Ch. D. 324

COMMENCEMENT OF TITLE　　28 Ch. D. 586
　See VENDOR AND PURCHASER — CONDITIONS OF SALE. 1.

COMMENCING BUSINESS—Company
　　　　　　　　　　　[21 Ch. D. 209
　See COMPANY—WINDING-UP ORDER. 1.

COMMISSION—Bail bond—Arrest of ship—Damages　　　　　10 P. D. 158
　See PRACTICE—ADMIRALTY—SALVAGE. 6.

—— Mortgage payable by instalments 22 Ch. D.
　See MORTGAGE—CONTRACT. 10.　　[549

COMMISSION IN ARMY—Army agent's lien—Set-off　　　-　17 Ch. D. 520
　See SET-OFF. 1.

—— Value of, on retirement—Charge on
　　　　　[16 Ch. D. 571; 19 Ch. D. 17
　See MORTGAGE—PRIORITY. 12.

COMMISSION TO EXAMINE WITNESS.
　See Cases under PRACTICE — SUPREME COURT—EVIDENCE. 10—16.

—— Evidence by.
　See EVIDENCE—GENERAL—*Statutes.*

COMMISSIONERS—Charity.
　See Cases under CHARITY—COMMISSIONERS.

—— Ecclesiastical　　-　　20 Ch. D. 208
　See ECCLESIASTICAL COMMISSIONERS.

—— Endowed Schools Act　　10 App. Cas. 304
　See ENDOWED SCHOOLS ACT. 1.

—— Land.
　See SETTLED LAND ACT—*Statutes.*

—— National debt.
　See NATIONAL DEBT COMMISSIONERS—*Statutes.*

—— Parliamentary elections.
　See Statutes and Cases under PARLIAMENT—ELECTION COMMISSIONERS.

—— Sewers　　　　　28 Ch. D. 486
　See LONDON—COMMISSIONERS OF SEWERS.

—— Sewers — Disqualification by reason of interest　　　　14 Q. B. D. 561
　See SEA WALL.

COMMITTAL — Appeal from Judge of High Court—Court of Appeal 13 Q. B. D. 901
　See BANKRUPTCY—APPEAL. 10.

—— Contempt—Appeal　-　20 Ch. D. 493
　See PRACTICE — SUPREME COURT—APPEAL. 1.

—— Contempt of Court　-　17 Ch. D. 49
　See CONTEMPT OF COURT.

—— County Court—Power to enforce interlocutory order　　-　7 Q. B. D. 623
　See COUNTY COURT—JURISDICTION. 5.

COMMITTAL—*continued.*

—— Order for — Judgment debtor — Privilege from arrest　-　・15 Q. B. D. 329
　See ARREST—DEBTORS' ACT. 3.

—— Order to pay debt by instalments—" Means to pay "　9 Q. B. D. 178; 14 Q. B. D. 597
　See ARREST—DEBTORS ACT. 4, 5.

COMMITTEE—Church building—Voluntary subscriptions　-　-　28 Ch. D. 426
　See CHARITY—MANAGEMENT. 4.

—— Directors of company　　25 Ch. D. 118
　See COMPANY—SHARES—TRANSFER. 7.

—— Stock Exchange　-　20 Ch. D. 356
　See STOCK EXCHANGE. 2.

COMMITTEE OF LUNATIC.
　See Cases under LUNATIC—COMMITTEE.

—— Suit by committee for dissolution of lunatic's marriage　-　　-　6 P. D. 12
　See PRACTICE—DIVORCE—PARTIES. 3.

COMMON.

—— ' Common of Pasturage and Herbage'—*Jus secandi vel falcandi*—*Common of Estovers*—*Prescription*—*Profit à prendre in alieno solo*—2 & 3 *Will.* 4, c. 71, s. 1.] Previous to the disafforestation and grant of A. Forest in 1677, the Crown was absolute owner of the soil of the forest and possessed of all the rights belonging to such ownership including vert and venison. The tenants of the adjoining manors had customary rights of common of pasture, herbage, and pannage, but the Court Rolls and other documents contained no evidence of any customary right in the commoners to cut and carry away from the forest brakes, fern, and litter, except by permission of the forest officers, and afforded negative evidence that no such right was ever claimed or lawfully exercised.—In a suit instituted in 1691, for the purpose of determining how much of the forest might properly be inclosed having regard to the rights of common, the commoners by their answers claimed rights of pasturage, and pannage for swine, and, as to such of them as had houses, certain quantities of fuel wood for their houses, but made no claim in respect of any other estovers. By the decree made in 1693, after allotting to the owners for inclosure and improvement portions of the forest within which the commoners were to be excluded and debarred from any common of pasture, herbage, or pannage, the residue of the forest (containing 6400 acres) was allotted to remain open and uninclosed, " and the said defendants, their heirs, tenants, and assigns, and all other persons having right of common in the said forest according to their respective interests therein, shall from time to time have and take the sole common pasturage and herbage of all and every the lands allotted and left for common as aforesaid "—the owners, their heirs and assigns, tenants and farmers, being for ever excluded " from having or claiming any common of pasture or herbage upon or in the said lands so left for common as aforesaid." In an action brought by the owner of the inheritance in 1878 to restrain one of the commoners from cutting and carrying away brakes, fern, and litter from the 6400 acres, for use upon the copyhold tenement in respect of which he had his right of common, the Defendant

COMMON—*continued.*

claimed this right as one of the commoners entitled to the benefit of the decree in 1693, and also alternatively by prescription in respect of his particular tenement:—*Held*, by Bacon, V.C., and by the Court of Appeal, 1. That upon the construction of the decree of 1693, by which the respective rights of the lord and the commoners were defined and determined, the right of the commoners over the 6400 acres was limited to common of pasturage and herbage, and did not include the right to cut and carry away the brakes, fern, heather, and litter growing therein. —2. That the existence at the date of that decree of any special custom authorizing the commoners to cut and carry away brakes, &c., and litter in that which had been a royal forest, had not been established, and was negatived by the absence of any claim to such a custom by the commoners in the suit in which that decree was made.—3. That evidence of usage subsequent to the date of the decree of 1693 could not affect the construction of that decree, which in its terms was clear and unambiguous.—*Held*, by Bacon, V.C., that the alternative claim to the alleged right by prescription in respect of the particular tenement being a claim of a profit à prendre in alieno solo could not be sustained.—*Held*, on appeal, that as the Defendant and his predecessors in title were shewn to have claimed to take, and to have actually taken, as of right and without any permission from the lord, litter from 6400 acres for the use of the tenement for upwards of sixty years immediately before the action, they had, under the Prescription Act (2 & 3 Will. 4, c. 71), acquired a right to do so, although they had claimed to do the acts complained of under the mistaken supposition that all the commoners were entitled to do them.—In order to establish a right under the Prescription Act, it is only necessary to shew that the benefit claimed has been actually enjoyed by the claimant for the requisite period as of right and not by permission, and that the right claimed is one which could have a legal origin by custom, prescription, or grant, and it is immaterial on what ground the claimant rested his alleged right to enjoy it. EARL DE LA WARR *v.* MILES - - 17 Ch. D. 535

—— Appurtenant—Copyholder - **20 Ch. D. 753**
See COPYHOLD—CUSTOM. 1.

—— Extinguishment of right—Inclosure
See INCLOSURE. 2, 3. [8 Q. B. D. 437;
[20 Ch. D. 380

—— Land for recreation - **6 App. Cas. 833**
See SCOTCH LAW—HIGHWAY. 1.

COMMON INFORMER—Recovery of penalty—
Offence against Crown 7 Q. B. D. 38;
See PENAL ACTION. 2. [8 App. Cas 354

COMMON LAW PROCEDURE ACT—Victoria
[10 App. Cas. 300
See COLONIAL LAW—VICTORIA. 5.

COMMONABLE RIGHTS COMPENSATION ACT,
1882.
See INCLOSURE—*Statutes.*
METROPOLIS—COMMONS ACTS—*Statutes.*

COMMUTATION OF PENSIONS.
See PENSION—*Statutes.*

COMPANIES ACT, 1883.
See COMPANY—PREFERENTIAL DEBTS—
Statutes.

COMPANIES (COLONIAL REGISTERS) ACT,
1883.
See COMPANY — SHARES — REGISTER —
Statutes.

COMPANY.

—— BUILDING SOCIETY.
See BUILDING SOCIETY.

—— CHARTERED COMPANY.
See CHARTERED COMPANY.

—— RAILWAY COMPANY.
See RAILWAY COMPANY.

I. COMPANY—FORMATION.

—— Costs of Formation—*Claim by Solicitor of Promoter against the Company.*] M. employed P. as solicitor in the formation of a limited company for the purpose of taking over M.'s business. The company was formed, and the articles provided that all expenses incurred about the formation of the company should be paid by the company. After the company was formed P. acted

M

I. COMPANY—FORMATION—*continued*.

as its solicitor, and M. was one of the directors. At a meeting of the directors, at which M. was present. P. asked for payment of his costs incurred about the formation of the company, and a conversation took place tending to shew that the company would undertake to pay them, but nothing appeared on the minutes. At a subsequent meeting a resolution was passed on the proposal of M. that a cheque for £39 should be given to P. in discharge of a certain part of these costs. The company having been ordered to be wound up, P. carried in a claim for his bill of costs, which was referred to the Taxing Master. The Taxing Master disallowed all items incurred before the formation of the company, and Bacon, V.C., refused to disturb his decision. P. appealed:—*Held*, that P. could not maintain his claim on the ground that the company having had the benefit of his services was bound to pay for them, as his services had been rendered on the retainer of M.—*In re Hereford and South Wales Waggon and Engineering Company* (2 Ch. D. 621) considered.—*Held*, further, that P. could not maintain his claim on the ground of novation, the conversation at the first meeting not being supported by anything in the minutes, and the subsequent giving of the cheque being capable of being referred to the obligation of the company to indemnify M. against the costs incurred in its formation, and so not being sufficient evidence of an agreement by the company with P. to pay him. *In re* ROTHERHAM ALUM AND CHEMICAL COMPANY　　-　25 Ch. D. 103

II. COMPANY—PROSPECTUS.

1. —— Misrepresentation—*Ambiguous statement—Action of Deceit — Burden of Proof on Plaintiff.*] The prospectus of a company which was being formed to take over ironworks, contained a statement that "the present value of the turnover or output of the entire works is over £1,000,000 sterling per annum." If that statement meant that the works had actually in one year turned out produce worth at present prices more than a million, or at that rate per year, it was untrue. If it meant only that the works were capable of turning out that amount of produce it was true. In an action of deceit for fraudulent misrepresentation whereby the Plaintiff was induced to take shares he swore in answer to interrogatories that he "understood the meaning" of the statement "to be that which the words obviously conveyed," and at the trial was not asked either in examination or cross-examination 'what interpretation he had put upon the words:—*Held*, by the Earl of Selborne, L.C. and Lords Blackburn and Watson, affirming the decision of the Court of Appeal, that the statement taken in connection with the context was ambiguous and capable of the two meanings; that it lay on the Plaintiff to prove that he had interpreted the words in the sense in which they were false and had in fact been deceived by them into taking the shares, and that as he had as a matter of fact failed to prove this the action could not be maintained.—*Held*, by Lord Bramwell, that the statement was capable only of the meaning in which it was untrue, and that the Plaintiff had proved that he had understood it in that sense;

II. COMPANY—PROSPECTUS—*continued*.

but that there was not sufficient evidence that the statement was fraudulent on the part of the Defendants, and that the decision of the Court of Appeal should be affirmed on that ground. SMITH *v.* CHADWICK　　-　20 Ch. D. 27; 9 App. Cas. 187

2. —— Misrepresentation—*Change of Directors—Shareholder's Name removed.*] An applicant for shares in a company received a letter of allotment, and at the same time a letter informing him that two of the four directors named in the prospectus had retired. The applicant on the same day wrote to the company stating that he had applied for shares entirely in consequence of these two directors being directors, and asking to have the allotment cancelled:—*Held*, that under the circumstances the applicant was entitled to have his name removed from the register of shareholders.—*Hallows* v. *Fernie* (Law Rep. 3 Ch. 467) distinguished. *In re* SCOTTISH PETROLEUM COMPANY. ANDERSON'S CASE 17 Ch. D. 373

3. —— Misrepresentation — *Concealment of Contract—Companies Act, 1867, s. 38 —Action of Deceit—Measure of Damages.*] The prospectus of a company formed for taking over a business, after mentioning the price to be paid by the company for the business, stated that the remuneration of the directors would be fixed by the shareholders, and that it was proposed that they should be paid only by a commission on the profits made, and that no promotion money would be paid to them by the company. The vendors of the business, who became directors, received part payment in 3000 fully paid-up shares of the company, and an agreement for such part payment was disclosed in the prospectus. Shortly after the formation of the company the vendors transferred 800 of these shares (being of the nominal amount of £4000), as to 350 to the solicitors who had acted in the formation of the company, and as to the remaining 450 to the directors other than the vendors. The Plaintiff took shares on the faith of the prospectus and paid them up in full. Some time afterwards the shareholders discovered the transfer of the 800 shares and removed the directors. A claim was made on behalf of the company against the directors who had received the 450 shares, and they by way of compromise surrendered those shares to the company. The Plaintiff retained his shares, and nearly two years after the transfer to the directors had been discovered he commenced an action against the old directors and the solicitors, alleging that the Defendants other than the vendors had agreed to become promoters on the terms of receiving as remuneration £4000 in fully paid-up shares or money, out of the shares or money to be received by the vendors; that the nominal purchase-money included this promotion money of £4000 as well as the real purchase-money; that the value of the property was not so much as the nominal purchase-money, less £4000; and that the statements in the prospectus were false; and he claimed as damages the whole nominal amount of his shares, on the ground that they had become utterly worthless. It appeared in evidence that at the time when the prospectus was issued, or at least before the Plaintiff took his shares, there was an understanding between the vendors and the other directors

II. COMPANY—PROSPECTUS—*continued.*

that the other directors should receive from the vendors some remuneration, and that on the day when the Plaintiff's application was accepted the transfer of the 450 shares to the other directors was agreed to; but there was no evidence of there having been any understanding for remuneration at the time of the contract for sale to the company, and it appeared that the price agreed to be given by the company was a fair one :—*Held,* by Fry, J., that although the understanding that the directors should receive remuneration was not such a contract as is required to be specified in the prospectus by sect. 38 of the Companies Act, 1867, the concealment of the arrangement was a material misrepresentation, and made the prospectus fraudulent irrespectively of the statute ; and that the Plaintiff was entitled to recover by way of damages the excess of the money paid for his shares over the real value of them at the time when he took them.—*Held,* on appeal, that the case was to be decided, not according to the principles applicable to an action to rescind the agreement by the Plaintiff to take shares, but according to the principles applicable to a common law action for deceit ; that, there being no arrangement for the directors to receive any promotion money from the company, the prospectus did not contain any misstatement on which an action for deceit could be grounded ; and that the action must be dismissed. ARKWRIGHT *v.* NEWBOLD - - - 17 Ch. D. 301

4. —— Misrepresentation—*False and Fraudulent Statements.*] The Plaintiff was a dealer in stocks and shares, and had formerly been a member of the Stock Exchange. The Defendants were largely interested as shareholders in the Date-Coffee Company, a company whose objects were declared to be (amongst others) the acquisition of licenses to use an invention for manufacturing from dates a substitute for coffee, for which a patent had been granted to Henley (one of the Defendants), and to sell, &c., the patent-rights when acquired by the company. Of this company Haymen (another of the Defendants) was chairman, the Defendant Tucker was the solicitor, and Henley consulting engineer.— Henley was also possessed of a patent for the manufacture and sale of date-coffee in France ; and a company was formed for that purpose, called The French Date-Coffee Company, with a capital of £100,000 in 100,000 shares of £1 each (under substantially the same management as that of the English company), by whom Henley's patent for France was purchased for £50,000, which sum it was agreed should be divided as a bonus amongst the shareholders in the English company. Early in February, 1881, the Defendants prepared and issued a prospectus of the French company, containing the following passage,—" From the success attending the company formed for the working of Henley's English patent, when a duty of 2*d.* per lb. is payable, and the coffee sold at 1*s.* per lb., the directors feel justified in stating they confidently believe the profits of this company will be more than sufficient to pay dividends of at least 50 per cent. on the nominal capital, and will exceed those of the company working the English patent, which,

II. COMPANY—PROSPECTUS—*continued.*

having only been formed a little over twelve months, has entered into a contract which will yield the return by way of annual dividends of a sum equal to the whole paid-up capital of the company of £34,000."—At the time at which this prospectus was issued the period had not arrived at which "profits" in a commercial sense could have been acquired by the English company ; but the article had been sold in the English market and received with some favour, and an agreement had been entered into by the company with a merchant or broker in London to take all they could make.—The Plaintiff, influenced, as he said, partly by the above statement in the prospectus, partly from information derived from another source, and partly by the favourable opinion he had formed of the article to be manufactured, purchased 100 shares in the French company, and paid the deposit. He had no connection with the English company. Owing, as it was said, to the duty imposed upon the date-coffee in England, and to other circumstances, the hopes held out in the prospectus were not realized, and the French Date-Coffee Company was ultimately wound up ; and, after the lapse of nearly two years, when the Plaintiff was called upon as a contributory, he sought to recover from the Defendants the sum he had paid as deposit money and the amount of calls for which he had become and would become liable, as damages for the alleged false and deceitful representations contained in the above statements in the prospectus :—*Held,* that the statements complained of, though expressing the strongest confidence that the company referred to would be successful and would make large profits by the sale of the article to be manufactured, could not fairly be read as alleging that profits in a commercial sense had actually been made, and consequently that there was no evidence which could be properly left to a jury in support of the charge of wilful and fraudulent misrepresentation. BELLAIRS *v.* TUCKER

[13 Q. B. D. 562

5. —— Misrepresentation—*Issue of Debentures—Misstatement of Object of Loan—Contributory Mistake of Plaintiff.*] A misstatement of the intention of the Defendant in doing a particular act may be a misstatement of fact, and if the Plaintiff was misled by it, an action of deceit may be founded on it.—Where a Plaintiff has been induced both by his own mistake and by a material misstatement by the Defendant to do an act by which he receives injury, the Defendant may be made liable in an action for deceit.—The directors of a company issued a prospectus inviting subscriptions for debentures, and stating that the objects of the issue of debentures were to complete alterations in the building of the company, to purchase horses and vans, and to develop the trade of the company. The real object of the loan was to enable the directors to pay off pressing liabilities. The Plaintiff advanced money on some of the debentures under the erroneous belief that the prospectus offered a charge upon the property of the company, and stated in his evidence that he would not have advanced his money but for such belief, but that he also relied upon the statements contained in

M

II. COMPANY—PROSPECTUS—*continued.*

the prospectus. The company became insolvent:—*Held* (affirming the decree of Denman, J.), that the misstatement of the objects for which the debentures were issued was a material misstatement of fact, influencing the conduct of the Plaintiff, and rendered the directors liable to an action for deceit, although the Plaintiff was also influenced by his own mistake. EGDINGTON *v.* FITZMAURICE　　　　　　　　　**29 Ch. D. 459**

6. —— Misrepresentation—*Notice — Delay— Companies Act,* 1862 (25 & 26 *Vict. c.* 89), *s.* 35; *Table A, Articles* 95, 97.] The provisions of articles 95, 97, of Table A to the Companies Act, 1862, for the service of notices by a company on its members, apply only to notices relating to the ordinary business of a company, and service in the way there pointed out is not sufficient for the purpose of fixing a shareholder with knowledge of a misrepresentation which would entitle him to repudiate his shares, unless he had been guilty of laches after notice of the misrepresentation. *In re* LONDON AND STAFFORDSHIRE FIRE INSURANCE COMPANY　　　　　**24 Ch. D. 149**

III. COMPANY—MEMORANDUM AND ARTICLES.

1. —— Alteration of Articles—*Preference and Ordinary Shares—Subsequent Special Resolutions acted upon for ten years, altering the Appropriation of Revenue, invalid—Rights of Shareholders under original Contract—25 & 26 Vict. c.* 89, *s.* 12.] The memorandum of association of a company incorporated under the Companies Act, 1862 (25 & 26 Vict. c. 89), stated that a portion of the shares were to have a right of receiving a dividend by preference to the other shares, and that the preference shares should have a right to a dividend of 7 per cent. per annum in priority over the ordinary shares, and to one-fifth of the remainder of the net revenue after a deduction of a sum sufficient for paying 7 per cent. per annum on the ordinary shares; and also that those shares should have a right to the rest of the dividend, whatever it might be, up to 7 per cent. after paying 7 per cent. to the preference shares and to four-fifths of the remainder of the net revenue, after deduction of a sum sufficient to pay the dividends to the preference and ordinary shares.—The directors applied the profits of the company in substantial accordance with the provisions in the articles of association till November, 1872, when the company passed special resolutions which altered the priorities and payments of the net revenue as between the preference and ordinary shareholders, and which provided for the redemption of shares out of the surplus profits, and they were acted upon without any objection being raised to them by any of the members of the company till July, 1883, when the company passed a special resolution by which the original appropriation of the revenue as provided by the memorandum of association was restored;—*Held* (affirming the decision of Kay, J.), that the resolutions of 1872 were not valid, as they altered a condition in the memorandum of association in contravention of sect. 12 of the Companies Act, 1862:—*Held,* also, that even if the resolutions of 1872 would be valid if ratified by every member of the company, there was no evidence on which the Court, acting as a jury, ought to infer that every member of the

III. COMPANY—MEMORANDUM AND ARTICLES—*continued.*

company had ratified such resolutions with full knowledge of what had been done. ASHBURY *v.* WATSON　　-　　**23 Ch. D. 56; 30 Ch. D. 376**

2. —— Articles inconsistent with Memorandum—*Application of Capital.*] By the memorandum of association of a company limited by shares it was stated that the objects of the company were, the cultivation of lands in Ireland, and other similar purposes there specified, and to do all such other things as the company might deem incidental or conducive to the attainment of any of these objects, and that the capital of the company was £1,050,000, divided into 140,000 A shares of £5 each, and 3500 B shares of £100 each. By the 8th of the contemporaneous articles of association it was provided that the capital produced by the issue of B shares should be invested, and that the income, and so far as necessary the capital, should be applied so as to make good to the holders of A shares a preferential dividend of £5 per cent. on the amounts paid up on the A shares. Subject to this, the B fund was to belong to the owners of B shares. The profits of the company, after paying the £5 per cent. dividend to the A shareholders were to be applied in payment of a non-cumulative dividend of £5 per cent. to the B shareholders, and the surplus was to be divided rateably between the A shareholders and B shareholders according to the amounts paid up on their respective shares:— *Held,* by Chitty, J., and by the Court of Appeal, that article 8 was invalid, as it purported to make the B capital applicable to purposes not within the objects of the company as defined by the memorandum of association, and in a way not incidental or conducive to the attainment of those objects, and that the directors must be restrained from acting upon it.—The articles of association of a company cannot, except in the cases provided for by sect. 12 of the Companies Act, 1862, modify the memorandum of association in any of the particulars required by the Act to be stated in the memorandum. GUINNESS *v.* LAND CORPORATION OF IRELAND　　　**22 Ch. D. 349**

3. —— Ultrā Vires—*Liability of Directors— Acquiescence—Ratification.*] The objects of a company were stated by the memorandum of association to be " the carrying on for profit or gain the trades or businesses of discounters, lenders of, and dealers in money" . . . " the advancing and lending of money on real, personal, or mixed securities . . on stocks and shares of railway, canal, dock, and other joint stock companies, corporations, associations, and other undertakings of whatever nature or description . . . on ships, goods, merchandize, materials, produce, works, plant, chattels, debts, choses in action, articles and effects, or on any other property of whatever kind and description . . . in the making of purchases, investments, sales, or any other dealings of or in any of the above-named articles or securities . . . and the entering into and carrying on of any monetary and financial arrangements or operations, and the doing of all matters and things which may appear to the company to be incident or conducive to the objects aforesaid, or any of them " :—*Held,* that the entering into an

III. COMPANY—MEMORANDUM AND ARTICLES—*continued.*

agreement to purchase "on joint account" with two other parties, for £310,000, an estate, on which one of the other parties (K. & L.) undertook to finish a building (the Alexandra Palace), grounds, racecourse and stand, lodges, roads, terraces, and drainage, for a sum not exceeding £200,000, the company undertaking to float another (the Alexandra Palace) company for the purpose of acquiring materials and building the palace, was a transaction within the powers of the company :—*Held*, further, that such an agreement did not constitute a partnership between the three parties to it.—Observations on the effect of acquiescence by shareholders in the contracts and acts of their directors. LONDON FINANCIAL ASSOCIATION *v.* KELK - - - **26 Ch. D. 107**

—— Alteration—Power of general meeting—Dismissal of directors · **23 Ch. D. 1**
See COMPANY—DIRECTOR'S APPOINTMENT. 2.

—— Alteration—Power to reduce capital [**27 Ch. D. 268**]
See COMPANY—REDUCTION OF CAPITAL. 2.

—— Application of rules to winding-up—Withdrawing and continuing members—Charge on particular fund **24 Ch. D.** [425, n ; 26 Ch. D. 559 ; 10 App. Cas. 33
See COMPANY—DISTRIBUTION OF ASSETS. 1, 2, 3.

—— General meeting—Resolution for winding-up - **29 Ch. D. 159**
See COMPANY—VOLUNTARY WINDING-UP. 1.

IV. COMPANY—CONTRACTS.

1. —— **Contract by Directors — Loan to Company—Whether Directors personally liable.**] By agreement between the T. Company and the Plaintiff, the Defendants, describing themselves as "we the undersigned, three of the directors," agreed to repay £500 advanced by the Plaintiff "to the company," and assigned to the Plaintiff as security for the advance certain "machines and tools," which were the property of the company :—*Held*, after hearing parol evidence to explain the ambiguity of the agreement, that the Defendants were personally liable to repay the £500. MCCOLLIN *v.* GILPIN **6 Q. B. D. 516**

2. —— **Contract by Promoters—Ratification by Company—Contract to pay Money to Third Party.**] A. and B. agreed with C. on behalf of a company intended to be formed, that A. and B. should sell and the company buy a certain business, and it was a term of the agreement that sixty guineas should be paid to J. & P. solicitors, for their expenses and charges in registering the company. The memorandum of association adopted this agreement, and the directors subsequently ratified it. An order having been made for winding-up the company, J. & P. claimed to prove for the sixty guineas :—*Held* (affirming the decision of the Vice-Chancellor of the County Palatine), that the claim must be disallowed, for that the contract between A. and B. and C. having been entered into before the company was in existence, could not by mere ratification be made binding on the company, and that a

IV. COMPANY—CONTRACTS—*continued.*

contract between A. and B. and the company, to which J. & P. were in no way parties, that the company should pay money to J. & P., would not entitle J. & P. to proceed against the company.—*Gregory* v. *Williams* (3 Mer. 582) explained. *In re* EMPRESS ENGINEERING COMPANY **16 Ch. D. 125**

3. —— **Fraudulent Agreement—Rescinding Fraudulent Agreement—Winding-up.**] B., for the purpose of enabling a company to have a fictitious credit in case of inquiries at their bankers, placed money to their credit which they were to hold in trust for him. Some of the money having been drawn out with B.'s consent, and the company having been ordered to be wound up while a balance remained :—*Held* (affirming the decision of Bacon, V.C.), that B. could not claim to have the balance paid to him. *In re* GREAT BERLIN STEAMBOAT COMPANY **26 Ch. D. 616**

4. —— **Winding-up — Running Contract — Charge on Moneys payable under the Contract—Winding-up of contracting Company—Set-off—Salvage Money—Moneys payable under concurrent Contracts—Notice—Mutual Credit—Bankruptcy Act, 1869 (32 & 33 Vict. c. 71), s. 39.**] By the terms of a contract between the Commissioners of Sewers and a wood paving company, the company were to pave a particular street called Victoria Street, and the Commissioners were to pay 60 per cent. of the moneys due a month after the engineer certified the works to be complete ; 30 per cent. within three months afterwards ; and 10 per cent. at the expiration of two years. During the two years the company were to keep the wood surface of the roadway in repair, and if, before the expiration of the two years, the Commissioners should give them notice, the company were also to keep the roadway in repair for fifteen years upon being paid for the same at the annual rate of 6d. per square yard. The Commissioners were to be at liberty to retain from time to time "out of any money payable by them to the contractors," an amount equal to the above annual charge, by way of security ; and in the event of failure by the company to perform the contract, the moneys retained were to be forfeited, and to be held by the Commissioners as liquidated damages for the default ; and it was provided that whenever "according to the terms of this contract," any money should be due from the company to the Commissioners for damages or otherwise, the Commissioners might either sue for such money or deduct or set off the same against any money due from them to the company.—The contract being dated on the 22nd of September, 1882, the company on the 15th of November, 1882, gave to L. and C., timber merchants, a charge on all their interest in the contract to secure a debt for goods sold and delivered ; and on the 9th of December, 1882, notice of this charge was given to the Commissioners.—On the same 9th of December, 1882, but after the notice, the company presented a petition for a winding-up order, and on the 12th and 16th of December the provisional official liquidator was empowered and ordered to complete the contract and to obtain the necessary timber on security of the moneys to be received subject to L. and C.'s charge. On the 13th of January, 1883, the winding-up order was made : on the 29th of January

IV. COMPANY—CONTRACTS—*continued.*

the liquidator, having completed the work, sent in a claim to the Commissioners, and on the 8th of March, 1883, the engineer certified the work to be complete. On the 19th of March, 1883, the Commissioners sent to the liquidator a claim of set-off for anticipated loss by breach of the contract to repair for fifteen years, the amount of such claim being estimated by the difference between 1s. a square yard, which the Commissioners considered they would have to pay for the repairs, and the 6d. a square yard provided for by the agreement. They also claimed to set off damages accrued and anticipated under other contracts for paving other streets. Except as to a trifling sum, it was not alleged that any cause of action for breach of any of these contracts accrued before the 27th of January, 1883. On the 25th of May, 1883, the Commissioners served the company (in liquidation) with formal notice to repair for fifteen years from the 8th of March, 1885 :—*Held,* that the liquidator was not entitled to a first charge on the moneys payable under the contract for the cost of completing the work incurred by him since the winding-up.—Decision of Bacon, V.C., reversed.—*Held,* further, that the chargees, L. and C., were entitled to a charge on 90 per cent. of the moneys payable under the contract (subject as above) undiminished by any retainer or set-off by the Commissioners either under the Victoria Street contract or otherwise.—Decision of Bacon, V.C., affirmed.—*Held,* further, that the Commissioners might prove for their cross-claim under the contract of the 22nd of September, 1882.—Decision of Bacon, V.C., affirmed.—*Held,* further, that the Commissioners were not entitled to retain any moneys due under the contract of the 22nd of September, 1882, in respect of moneys due under any of the concurrent contracts. — Decision of Bacon, V.C., affirmed. *In re* ASPHALTIC WOOD PAVEMENT COMPANY. LEE & CHAPMAN'S CASE　[26 Ch. D. 624 ; 30 Ch. D. 216

V. COMPANY—ACTIONS (by and against).

—— Leave to sue in Name of Company—*Winding-up.*] An order was made on the application of R., in a winding-up, directing that he should receive his costs of the application out of the assets. H. & Co. were his solicitors in this application, but had no other connection with the company or its affairs. The costs were not paid, and R. became bankrupt. Subsequently Malins, V.C., made an order, on the application of H. & Co., that they should be at liberty, on giving such indemnity as the Judge should direct, to institute such proceedings as they might be advised against the former directors and promoters, to recover certain sums from them, the applicants undertaking to pay into the bank to the credit of the liquidators whatever was recovered, and also to abide by any order the Court or Judge might make as to the costs of such proceedings. H. & Co. thereupon commenced this action in the name of the company, against the former directors and promoters without having taken any steps to have the indemnity fixed by the Judge. The Defendants moved that all further proceedings might be stayed, or the suit and all proceedings under it set aside, on the ground that the action had been commenced

V. COMPANY — ACTIONS (by and against)— *continued.*

without proper authority. This application was refused by Malins, V.C., who expressed his opinion that the undertaking of H. & Co., contained in the order, was a sufficient indemnity :—*Held,* on appeal, that as H. & Co. were strangers to the company, being neither creditors nor contributories, and having no charge on the assets, there was no jurisdiction to give them leave to sue in the name of the company :—*Held,* also, that if there had been jurisdiction to make such an order, the action would still have been commenced without authority, the condition precedent of H. & Co. giving indemnity not having been complied with :—*Held,* therefore, that the action must be dismissed, as having been instituted without authority, and that H. & Co. must pay the costs of all parties, including the official liquidators ; the costs of the company being taxed as between solicitor and client, and the other costs as between party and party. CAPE BRETON COMPANY *v.* FENN -　-　-　- 17 Ch. D. 198

VI. COMPANY — DEBENTURES (and MORT-GAGES).

1. —— Borrowing Powers—*Debenture Stock—Mortgages—Companies Clauses Act, 1863 (26 & 27 Vict. c. 118), Part III.—Priority—Debenture Stock "at any time created by the Company"—Practice—Rules of Court, 1875, Order LVIII., r. 6—Costs—Cross Notice of Appeal.*] By the Cornwall Minerals Railway Act, 1873, the Cornwall Minerals Railway Company was empowered to borrow on mortgage to the extent of £250,000, and to issue debenture stock subject to the provisions of the Companies Clauses Act, 1863, Part III., but notwithstanding anything therein contained, the interest of all debenture stock, at any time created by the company was to rank pari passu with the interest of all mortgages "at any time granted by the company" and should have priority over all principal money secured by such mortgages.—By a later Act of 1875, the company were empowered to raise additional capital ; and after providing that the principal secured by all mortgages granted by the company before the passing of the Act, should have priority over the principal secured by all mortgages granted by virtue of that Act, the company was empowered to issue debenture stock subject to the provisions of the Companies Clauses Act, 1863, but the interest of all debenture stock created and issued at any time after the passing of that Act was to rank pari passu with the interest of all mortgages granted after the passing of that Act, and should have priority over all principal moneys secured by such mortgages.—By another Act of 1877 power to raise a further sum by the issue of debenture stock under provisions similar to those in the Act of 1875 was given to the company.—The company granted mortgages and issued debenture stock under the powers of the Act of 1873 before the passing of the Act of 1875.—They also issued further debenture stock under the powers of the Act of 1873 after the passing of the Act of 1875, but before the passing of the Act of 1877. They also issued further debenture stock under the powers of the Act of 1873 after the passing of the Act of 1877 ; and also issued

VI. COMPANY — DEBENTURES (and MORT-GAGES—*continued.*

debenture stock under the powers of the Acts of 1875 and 1877 after the passing of the Act of 1877.—The company being unable to pay the interest on all these mortgages and debenture stock in full, a receiver of the undertaking was appointed by the Court, and a special case settled for ascertaining the priorities :—*Held*, first, that notwithstanding the words "at any time" in the Act of 1873 the enactment therein contained applied only to the mortgage debt and debenture stock for which provision was made by that Act. —Secondly, that upon the true construction of the several Acts of 1873, 1875, and 1877, the order of priority of the interest on the mortgages and debenture stocks was as follows :—(1.) The interest on the mortgages and debenture stocks granted and issued under the powers of the Act of 1873 previously to the passing of the Act of 1875.—(2.) The interest on the debenture stock issued under the Act of 1873 after the passing of the Act of 1875, but before the Act of 1877.— (3.) The interest on the debenture stock created under any of the Acts, after the passing of the Act of 1877. — Thirdly, that the principal of mortgages for the time being due had priority of payment next after the interest of the debenture stock issued before the passing of the Act of 1875.—The decision of Hall, V.C., substantially affirmed. HARRISON *v.* CORNWALL MINERALS RAILWAY COMPANY. FENTON *v.* HARRISON

[16 Ch. D. 66 ; 18 Ch. D. 334 ; 8 App. Cas. 780

2. —— Cancellation—*Debentures given up to be cancelled—Contract by Company to issue fully paid-up Shares—Consideration—Contributory—Proof for Damages in the Liquidation—Companies Act, 1867, s. 25.*] A., a director, and the solicitor of the Great Australian Gold Mining Company, obtained by assignments from K., one of the vendors of a mine, situate in South Australia, to the company two debentures of and which were given by the company for £500 each in part payment of the purchase-money ; and in consideration of A. giving them up to be cancelled the company contracted to issue to him 500 £2 fully paid-up shares. No contract was ever registered under the provisions of the 25th section of the Companies Act, 1867. A. had been by order of the Court placed on the list of contributories for the 500 shares.—On summons taken out by A. :— *Held*, that there was no duty cast upon him to register the contract ; and that the breach of the contract by the company having been established, A. was entitled to prove in the liquidation for damages for calls made or which might be made on the shares.—*Mudford's Claim* (14 Ch. D. 634) followed.—*Houldsworth v. City of Glasgow Bank* (5 App. Cas. 317) distinguished. GREAT AUSTRALIAN GOLD MINING COMPANY. *Ex parte* APPLEYARD - - - 18 Ch. D. 587

3. —— Irregularity in Issue — *Companies Clauses Consolidation Act, 1845—Transferee for Value without Notice—Estoppel.*] Where a company has power to issue legally transferable securities an irregularity in the issue cannot be set up against even the original holder if he has a right to presume omnia rite acta. If such securities

VI. COMPANY — DEBENTURES (and MORT-GAGES—*continued.*

be legally transferable such an irregularity and a fortiori any equity against the original holder, cannot be asserted by the company against a bonâ fide transferee for value without notice. Nor can such an equity be set up against an equitable transferee, whether the securities were transferable at law or not, if by the original conduct of the company in issuing the securities or by their subsequent dealing with the transferee he has a superior equity. If the original conduct of the company in issuing debentures was such that the public were justified in treating it as a representation that they were legally transferable, there would be an equity on the part of any person who had agreed for value to take a transfer of these debentures to restrain the company from pleading their invalidity, although that might be a defence at law to an action by the transferor.— A company having, subject to the conditions in the Companies Clauses Consolidation Act, 1845 (8 & 9 Vict. c. 16), the power of borrowing, issued, after resolutions passed at a meeting at which an insufficient number of shareholders were present, debentures to the contractor J. B. P., who was present at the meeting and knew of the irregularities of the company.—J. B. P. transferred some of the debentures to Y., a sub-contractor, for a nominal consideration, and some to C. for value. —Y. had a bill against J. B. P., and P. discounted it and took as security a deposit of some of the debentures which had been registered in the name of J. B. P. These debentures were not transferred to P. and the transfer to Y. was not registered.—T. took a transfer of other debentures from Y. for a nominal consideration which had not been registered in the name of J. B. P., but the transfer to Y. had been registered and T. alleged that he gave value to Y. Registration of the transfer to T. was refused. He brought an action against the company for payment and for registration, but it was stopped by the winding-up. C. had a transfer for full value and registered :—*Held*, that C. had a valid claim to be paid his debentures, and that the company were estopped from setting up the irregularity in the issue of them :—*Held*, also, that P. and T. must be treated as equitable transferees only, but without reason to suspect any irregularity in the issue, and that they could be allowed to recover only such a sum as each of them might be able to prove he bonâ fide advanced upon the securities which he received. *In re* ROMFORD CANAL COMPANY. POCOCK'S CLAIM. TRICKETT'S CLAIM. CAREW'S CLAIM

[24 Ch. D. 85

4. —— Power of Company to deal with Property—*Charge on General Undertaking—Mortgage—Priority.*] The directors of a company with power to borrow or create mortgages or issue debentures, issued debentures purporting to charge the undertaking and the hereditaments and effects of the company with the payment of the sums mentioned in the debentures respectively, to the intent that the debentures might rank equally as a first charge on the undertaking, hereditaments and effects of the company. They

VI. COMPANY — DEBENTURES (and MORT-GAGES)—continued.

afterwards, in consideration of £4000 advanced and applied to the purposes of the company, deposited with the Plaintiff the title-deeds of the colliery the property of the company, and by a written agreement charged the property comprised in the deeds with the payment to the Plaintiff of £4000 and interest:—*Held*, that the mortgage to the Plaintiff had priority over the debentures. WHEATLEY *v.* SILKSTONE AND HAIGH MOOR COAL COMPANY - - 29 Ch. D. 715

5. —— Power of Company to deal with Property—*Charge on all Property present and future—Floating Security.*] A company which carried on the business of ironmasters and manufacturers, issued debentures for a total sum of £500,000, by which they charged their undertaking, works, stock-in-trade, plant, moneys, and other real and personal property, both present and future, with the payment of the sums secured by the debentures "to the intent that the same charge shall, until default in the payment of the principal or interest or become payable in respect of the said sum of £500,000, or some part thereof, be a floating security upon the undertaking, works, and property of the company, not hindering sales or leases of, or other dealings with, any of the property or assets of the company in the course of its business as a going concern." The company afterwards contracted to sell some of their land:—*Held*, that the purchaser was entitled to reasonable evidence that there had been no default in the payment of the principal or interest of the debentures.—*In re Florence Land and Public Works Company* (10 Ch. D. 530) and *In re Colonial Trusts Corporation* (15 Ch. D. 465) distinguished. *In re* HORNE AND HELLARD

[29 Ch. D. 736

6. —— Priority—*Costs of Realization—Action by Debenture-holders—Receiver and Manager—Trustees—Practice — Set-off — Rules of Supreme Court*, 1883, *Order LXV., r.* 27, *sub-s.* 21.] In a suit instituted by a debenture-holder of a company, on behalf of himself and the other debenture-holders, against the company and the trustees of a deed, by which leasehold collieries and plant of the company were assigned to trustees to secure the payment of the debentures, to enforce the security, a receiver and manager was appointed. He worked the collieries for some years at a loss. Ultimately the property was sold, the Plaintiff having the conduct of the sale, and the purchase-money was paid into Court. The fund was insufficient. The original Plaintiff became bankrupt in the course of the proceedings, and another debenture-holder was substituted for him as Plaintiff. On the further consideration of the suit:—*Held*, that the costs and other expenses must be paid out of the fund in the following order:—(1.) The Plaintiff's costs of the realization of the property, including the costs of an abortive attempt to sell. (2.) The balance due to the receiver and manager (including his remuneration) and his costs of the suit. (3.) The costs, charges, and expenses of the trustees of the deed. (4.) The two Plaintiffs' costs of the suit, *pari passu.*—When the second Plaintiff was

VI. COMPANY — DEBENTURES and MORT-GAGES—continued.

substituted for the first, an order was made that the solicitors of the first Plaintiff should, without prejudice to their lien (if any) deliver up to the solicitor of the second Plaintiff all documents in their possession relating to the conduct and prosecution of the suit:—*Held*, that the solicitors of the first Plaintiff had no lien on the documents which could entitle them to priority in respect of their costs.—Two summonses taken out by the Plaintiff were heard with the further consideration of the suit, and were dismissed with costs.—*Held*, that these costs must be set off against the costs which the Plaintiff was entitled to receive out of the fund. BATTEN *v.* WEDGWOOD COAL AND IRON COMPANY - - 28 Ch. D. 317

7. —— Priority—*Salvage—Statutory Charge —Condition Precedent—" Owner of a Limited Interest in Land " — Special Act — Borrowing Powers—Directory Clauses—Companies Clauses Consolidation Act*, 1845 (8 & 9 *Vict.* c. 16), *ss.* 41, 42.] The special Act (11 & 12 Vict. c. 142) incorporating a company for the purpose (inter alia) of draining and reclaiming land, empowered the "owner of a limited interest in land" to contract with the company for the execution of drainage and reclamation works, and for that purpose to charge on the land (in the manner provided by the Act), the cost of executing the works. The Act defined the term "owner of a limited interest in land," as including "any person entitled to any land subject to any mortgage or charge thereon, provided such person shall be in possession of the land mortgaged or charged":—*Held*, that this definition included a purchaser in possession of land upon which the vendor had a lien for unpaid purchase-money.—The Act provided (by sect. 34) that "from and after the due execution of the works mentioned in any contract" (between the company and an owner of land) "or any part of any such works, such execution, together with the amount due in respect of the same, being duly certified by three directors of the company under the seal of the company, the company shall be entitled to, and shall have a lien and charge upon the lands so drained, &c., for the moneys or money mentioned in such certificate as aforesaid. . . . and such lien or charge shall have priority over every other charge or incumbrance affecting the same land," except ground rents and tithe commutation rent-charge:—*Held*, that the certificate of the directors was not conclusive, but only primâ facie evidence of the due execution of the works mentioned in it, and that if, notwithstanding the certificate, it was shewn that the works had not been duly executed according to the contract, the company would not be entitled to the statutory charge on the land as against a prior incumbrancer, or even as against the equitable owner. A second mortgagee who is in possession of the mortgaged property and expends money in permanently improving or preserving it, is not entitled as against the first mortgagee to any charge on the property for the money so expended.—The 41st and 42nd sections of the Companies Clauses Act, 1845, requiring mortgages to be duly stamped and the

VI. COMPANY — DEBENTURES (and MORT-GAGES)—*continued.*

consideration to be duly stated, do not make void an instrument the consideration for which is apparent, though it is not in terms stated.— A provision in a company's special Act that moneys were to be borrowed by order of a general meeting:—*Held,* to be directory only, and not to postpone money borrowed without such order to other mortgages of the company, ranking in other respects pari passu.—The borrowing powers of companies and the priorities of mortgagees under the 42nd section of the Companies Clauses Act considered. LANDOWNERS WEST OF ENGLAND AND SOUTH WALES LAND DRAINAGE AND INCLOSURE COMPANY *v.* ASHFORD

[16 Ch. D. 411

—— Misrepresentation as to object of loan

[29 Ch. D. 459

See COMPANY—PROSPECTUS. 5.

VII. COMPANY—DIVIDENDS.

1. —— **Bonus**—*Capital or Income—Tenant for Life and Remainderman.*] A testator died in 1876 having bequeathed his residuary personal estate to his executor T. B. in trust for the testator's wife for life, and after her death to T. B. Part of the residuary estate consisted of 600 shares in a company whose directors had power, before recommending a dividend, to set apart out of the profits such sum as they thought proper as a reserved fund, for meeting contingencies, equalizing dividends, or repairing or maintaining the works. The shares were £10 shares on which £7 10s. per share had been paid up. In 1880 the reserved fund was £100,000, which had been made up in the testator's lifetime, and there was also an " undivided profit " fund of £36,070, more than half of which arose from profits earned in his lifetime. In September, 1880, the directors proposed to add to the " undivided profit " fund £7246, and recommended that the £100,000, and £38,000 out of the undivided profit fund, should be distributed as a " bonus dividend " of £2 10s. per share, and that there should be created new £10 shares amounting in number to one-third of the original shares, so that one new share might be allotted to each shareholder for every three original shares which he held, £7 10s. per share to be paid on allotment, which £7 10s. the bonus would enable him to pay. At a general meeting these recommendations were adopted, and special resolutions were passed, authorizing the directors, with the sanction of a general meeting, to declare a bonus out of the reserved and undivided profit fund, and providing for the issue and allotment of new shares. These resolutions were confirmed at a subsequent meeting, at which an ordinary resolution was passed for paying the bonus of £2 10s. per share. The warrant for the bonus had at its foot a memorandum to be signed by the shareholder directing the registrar of the company to apply the bonus in payment of the call. T. B. accepted the 200 new shares allotted to him, and signed the memorandum, and the new shares were registered in his name. After the death of the testator's wife in 1883, the question was raised whether the bonus of 1880 and the new shares belonged to the widow as tenant for life, or to T. B. as entitled to the capital of

VII. COMPANY—DIVIDENDS—*continued.*

the testator's estate at her death:—*Held,* by Kay, J., that they were capital and belonged to T. B.—*Held,* on appeal, that there is no rule that where a sum, whether called bonus or dividend, is distributed by a company among its shareholders, it must, if it is paid out of the accumulated profits of past years, be treated between tenant for life and remainderman as capital. In most, if not all, cases, the inquiry when the profits out of which it is paid were earned is immaterial, the question being whether the company, having the power of distributing its profits as dividend, or of converting them into capital, has taken the former or the latter course.—*Held,* that in the present case the company had not, by setting aside profits to a reserved fund applicable for purposes several of which were not such as ought to be satisfied out of capital, or to an undivided profits fund, made them capital;—that the distribution of the bonus was not conditional on the shareholders accepting the new shares, and that it was not converted into capital by the offer of the new shares, the shareholders not being bound to apply it in taking them, that it must therefore be treated as income belonging to the tenant for life, and that the new shares acquired by means of it belonged to her estate. *In re* BOUCH. SPROULE *v.* BOUCH　　29 Ch. D. 635

2. —— **Bonus**—*Income Tax—Insurance Company—" Annual Profits or Gains "—Sums paid as Bonuses to participating Policy-holders — 5 & 6 Vict. c. 35, s. 54.*] A life insurance company issued "participating policies," at an increased premium, according to the terms of which at the end of each quinquennial period " the gross profits " of such policies were thus dealt with : two-thirds were returned by way of bonus or abatement of premiums to the holders of such policies then in force : the remaining third went to the company who bore the whole expenses of the business, the portion remaining after payment of expenses constituting the only profit available for division among the shareholders :—*Held* reversing the decision of the Court of Appeal, by Lords Blackburn and FitzGerald, Lord Bramwell dissenting, that the two-thirds returned to the policy-holders were " annual profits or gains," and assessable to income tax. LAST *v.* LONDON ASSURANCE CORPORATION　-　12 Q. B. D. 389;

[14 Q. B. D. 239; 10 App. Cas. 438

3. —— **Payment in " proportion to Shares "**—*Shares fully and partly paid up—Participation equally in Dividend—Construction of Articles of Association—Companies Act,* 1862 (25 & 26 Vict. c. 89), *1st Sched., Table A., Reg.* 72 ; *and Companies Amendment Act,* 1867 (30 & 31 Vict. c. 131), *s.* 24, *sub-s.* 3.] The capital of a company, incorporated under the Acts of 1862 and 1867, consisted of 60,000 shares of £1 ; 40,000 were fully paid-up, and 20,000 to the extent of only 5s. per share. By the 71st article of association the directors may " declare a dividend to be paid to the members in proportion to their shares." By the definition clauses the word " capital " was declared to mean the capital for the time being of the company, and the word " shares " the shares into which the capital is divided. In a question whether the directors could competently recom-

VII. COMPANY—DIVIDENDS—continued.

mend a dividend payable to each shareholder in proportion to the amount paid up upon the shares held by him :—Held, affirming the decision of the Court below, that such a declaration of dividend was incompetent, because upon the true construction of the articles of association, read with the Acts of 1862 and 1867, all the shares were entitled to participate equally in dividend, without regard to the amount paid up upon each.—See opinions of the Lords at pp. 74, 77, 99, as to the effect of sub-sect. 3, sect. 24, of the Companies Amendment Act, 1867. OAKBANK OIL COMPANY v. CRUM

[8 App. Cas. 65

4. —— Payment out of Capital — *Tramway Company—Maintenance of Works—Depreciation of Capital—Reinstating Capital—Reserve Fund — Ordinary Shareholders — Preference Shareholders—"Net Profits"—Profits of particular Year.*] The articles of association of a limited tramway company provided that no dividend should be declared except "out of profits"; that the directors should, with the sanction of the company, declare annual dividends "out of profits": and that the directors should, before recommending a dividend, set aside "out of profits," subject to the sanction of the company, "a reserve fund for maintenance, repairs, depreciation, and renewals." The company had for several years carried on their business, paying a dividend half-yearly on their ordinary shares; but they failed to set apart a reserve fund adequate for the maintenance of their tramway, which eventually became worn out. The company having again declared a half-yearly dividend on their ordinary shares, and the total sum appropriated for the dividend being, as it appeared, much less than the sum required to reinstate the tramway :—Held, that the company could only declare a dividend out of the net profits, and that the net profits could not be ascertained without first restoring the tramway to an efficient condition, or making due provision for the purpose out of the company's assets. An injunction was accordingly granted restraining the company from paying the half-yearly dividend they had declared, but leave was given them to move to dissolve the injunction, in the event of their being able to satisfy the Court that there were profits available for the dividend :—Held, however that the holders of preference shares, the dividend on which was "dependent on the profits of the particular year only," were entitled to a dividend out of the profits of any year after setting aside a proportionate amount sufficient for the maintenance of the tramway for that year only; and were not to be deprived of that dividend in order to make good the sums which in previous years should have been set aside by the company for maintenance, but which had been improperly applied by them in paying dividends. DENT v. LONDON TRAMWAYS COMPANY - 16 Ch. D. 344

See also DAVISON v. GILLIES - 16 Ch. D. 347, n.

—— Liability of directors—Payment of dividends out of capital - 21 Ch. D. 149, 519;

[25 Ch. D. 752

See COMPANY — DIRECTOR'S LIABILITY. 4, 5, 6.

VIII. COMPANY—REDUCTION OF CAPITAL.

1. —— Purchase by Company of its own Shares —*Companies Act, 1862, ss. 12, 23—Companies Act, 1867, s. 9.*] The memorandum of association of a limited colliery company gave the company power to do all things which it should consider conducive to the attainments of its objects, but did not in terms give any power to purchase its own shares. The 10th clause of the articles empowered the directors to purchase for the company any shares in the company, and directed that the shares so purchased should be dealt with as if they had never been issued, and that any profit arising on the re-issuing or subsequent sale of such shares should be deemed profits of the year in which they were re-issued or sold. In 1872, disputes having arisen as to the conduct of the business, the directors agreed with W., the largest shareholder, who was also one of the directors, to purchase for the company his shares and also his interest as landlord of the mines worked by the company. This arrangement was confirmed by an extraordinary general meeting of the company, and was carried into effect by an assignment of his interest in the mines to the company for a specific sum, and by a transfer to the company of his shares for another specific sum. The company was entered in the share register as holder of these shares, and in all the subsequent returns to the Registrar of Joint Stock Companies the company was entered as such holder. The company for some time was prosperous, but afterwards fell into difficulties, and in 1879 an order was made for winding it up :—Held, by Jessel, M.R., that the power to the company to purchase its own shares was illegal, and that W. must be placed on the list of contributories.—Held, on appeal, that although the articles could not effectually authorize a general trafficking in shares, as that would be extending the business of the company in a way not authorized by the memorandum, there was nothing illegal in a clause authorizing a purchase of shares, not for profit, but for carrying into effect an arrangement considered to be for the benefit of the company; that such a purchase did not reduce the capital of the company in any sense in which such reduction is prohibited by the Companies Acts; and that W. had effectually surrendered his shares to the company and ceased to be a shareholder from the date of the surrender, and was not a contributory :—Held, further, that if the transaction, supposing it to have been carried into effect without the sanction of the extraordinary general meeting, would have been questionable, the company having confirmed it, and taken the benefit of it, could not now have impeached it, and that the liquidator had no better right. *In re* DRONFIELD SILKSTONE COAL COMPANY 17 Ch. D. 76

2. —— Purchase by Company of its own Shares—*Power to alter Articles of Association—Resolution effecting two Objects.*] A company having formed a scheme for reducing their capital by the purchase of fully paid shares, and this being in violation of their articles of association, passed a resolution at a general meeting : "That notwithstanding anything contained in the articles, the directors be authorized to carry out

VIII. COMPANY—REDUCTION OF CAPITAL—
continued.

the following compromise or modification of the agreement with the vendors," which was in effect to cancel 12,000 fully paid vendors' £5 shares upon payment of £1 3s. 4d. per share:—*Held*, that this resolution was valid, notwithstanding that'the effect of it was to carry out two distinct objects, viz., to set aside for the purpose of this transaction the article forbidding the purchase of shares, and to authorize the directors to carry out the proposed scheme. — *Imperial Hydropathic Hotel Company* v. *Hampson* (23 Ch. D. 1) discussed and explained.—*Campbell's Case* (Law Rep. 9 Ch. 1) followed. TAYLOR *v.* PILSEN JOEL AND GENERAL ELECTRIC LIGHT COMPANY

[27 Ch. D. 268

3. —— Sanction of Court—*Notice to Creditors —Advertisement of Petition—Companies Act,* 1862, *Sched.* 1, *Table A.,* arts. 26 *and* 27—*Companies Act,* 1877—*Gen. Ord. Nov.,* 1862, *r.* 53—*Gen. Ord. March,* 1868, *rr.* 4, 5.] A company was empowered by its articles of association to increase its capital by the issue of new shares and to issue such shares at a discount; also to reduce its capital. Of the company's original capital, which was made up of £10 shares, some of the shares taken were fully paid up, and others were issued and taken at the price of £2 per share, £8 per share being credited as paid in pursuance of a contract duly registered under sect. 25 of the Companies Act, 1867. Part of their capital having been lost the company passed a resolution for the reduction of its nominal amount by writing off £7 from each fully paid £10 share and from each £10 share on which £8 had been credited as paid, and by reducing all shares remaining unissued from £10 to £3 per share.—A petition was then presented under the Companies Acts, 1867 and 1877, to obtain the sanction of the Court to this resolution, the petition being supported by evidence that all the creditors of the company had been paid up to a recent date, except one, who appeared and consented to the petition. The Court made the order as prayed, and dispensed with the usual notices to creditors and advertisement of the petition. *In re* PLASKYNASTON TUBE COMPANY

[23 Ch. D. 542

5. —— Sanction of Court—*Notice to Creditors —Advertisement of Petition—Companies Act,* 1867 —*Companies Act,* 1877—*Gen. Ord. March,* 1868, *r.* 5.] A limited company whose shares were all fully paid up, having lost part of its capital, presented a petition to reduce the nominal capital by the amount of the loss, reducing the nominal amount of each share from £1 to 12s. 6d. Bacon, V.-C., refused to hear the petition until its presentation had been advertised as prescribed by the 5th rule of the General Order of 1868, made under the Companies Act, 1867 : — *Held,* on appeal, that a petition for reduction of capital authorized by the Companies Act, 1877, ought primâ facie to be advertised as directed by the General Order of 1868, though the Judge has a discretion to dispense with advertisements if he is satisfied that the interests of creditors cannot be affected by what is proposed, and that as in the present case the Judge in his discretion thought that the petition ought to be advertised,

VIII. COMPANY—REDUCTION OF CAPITAL—
continued.

the Court of Appeal would not interfere. *In re* TAMBRACHERRY ESTATES COMPANY 29 Ch. D. 683

4. —— Special Resolution—*Computation of Time—Companies Act,* 1862 (25 & 26 *Vict.* c. 89), s. 51.] The interval of not less than fourteen days which under sect. 51 of the Companies Act, 1862, is to elapse between the meetings passing and confirming a special resolution of a company is an interval of fourteen clear days, exclusive of the respective days of meeting, and therefore a special resolution for reduction of capital passed at a meeting held on the 25th of February, 1885, and confirmed at a meeting held on the 11th of March, 1885, was held to be bad. *In re* RAILWAY SLEEPERS SUPPLY COMPANY 29 Ch. D. 204

IX. COMPANY—SHARES—ALLOTMENT.

1. —— Contract—*Rescission—Cancellation of Shares—Companies Act,* 1862, *s.* 23.] W. T. and P. applied for shares in a limited company established for the purpose of purchasing and working a concession from a foreign Government. T. & P. were directors of the company. The directors sent letters of allotment to the applicants, in which they called on them to pay the allotment money by a certain day. But their names were never entered on the register, nor was any allotment money paid nor certificates of shares issued. Three years afterwards the directors made a fresh arrangement with the owners of the concession under which they purported to cancel the old allotments and to allot all the shares, except a few reserved for the directors and other persons, to the vendor of the concession and his nominees. The shares were accordingly entered in the register in their names. Soon afterwards the company was ordered to be wound up, and the liquidator applied to the Court to rectify the register by placing on it the names of W. T. & P. for the number of shares allotted to them, and to diminish the number of shares for which the vendor of the concession was entered on the register to a like amount :—*Held* (affirming the decision of Chitty, J.), that whether the effect of the application and allotment was that W. T. & P. became actual members of the company in respect of the shares allotted to them or only agreed to become such members, it was now too late, under the circumstances which had occurred, for the company to insist on placing their names on the register.—But, *semble,* according to the true construction of the 23rd section of the Companies Act, 1862, they did not become members in respect of the allotted shares, the entry on the register being a condition precedent to such membership.—*Held* also, that the fact that T. & P. were directors whose duty it was to place the allottees on the register did not affect the question. *In re* FLORENCE LAND AND PUBLIC WORKS COMPANY. NICOL'S CASE. TUFNELL & PONSONBY'S CASE   -   -   29 Ch. D. 421

2. —— Director — *Calls — Estoppel.*] The Plaintiff company was constituted by seven persons signing the memorandum of association. Afterwards they all were summoned to attend a meeting, but only four attended and they elected three directors. These three elected three other

IX. COMPANY — SHARES — ALLOTMENT — continued.

directors. The three original directors resigned, and afterwards one of the remaining directors sent in his resignation. The Defendant then applied for fifty shares. The two remaining directors resolved that fifty shares should be allotted to the Defendant, that he should be appointed a director, and that the resignation of the retiring director should be accepted. The Defendant afterwards attended a meeting of the directors, confirmed the allotment to himself, and joined in passing a resolution, that the shares allotted to himself should be paid up in full forthwith. The Defendant subsequently withdrew his application and refused to pay the amount of the shares allotted to him. By the articles of association the number of the directors was to be not less than three, and any casual vacancy occurring in the board might be filled up by the board, and the continuing board might act notwithstanding any vacancy in their body :—*Held*, that the Defendant was liable to pay the amount of the shares.

YORK TRAMWAYS COMPANY *v.* WILLOWS
[8 Q. B. D. 685

3. —— **Repudiation of voidable Contract to take Shares**—*Change of Directors—Quorum of Directors.*] By the articles of association of a limited company it was provided that the number of directors should not be less than four or more than seven, and G., R., S., and Y., were named the first directors. It was provided that two directors should form a quorum, and that the continuing directors might act notwithstanding any vacancy in the Board. The directors were empowered to fill up casual vacancies. A prospectus was issued giving the names of the directors and mentioning G. as chairman. W., who was acquainted with G., after communicating with him, applied for shares on the faith of G. and R. being directors. At the first meeting of directors on the 12th of November, 1880, S. and Y. only were present, G. and R. having sent in their resignation on that day; S. and Y. elected a third diretor who was not present, and proceeded to allot shares. A letter of allotment in the common form was received by W. about the 15th of November, accompanied with a letter stating that G. and R. had resigned. W. on the 27th wrote to withdraw his offer to take shares on the ground of G. and R. not being directors. The company refused to withdraw his name. On the 3rd of February, 1881, Anderson, another shareholder, obtained an order to remove his name from the register on the ground of the change in the board, but no agreement was shewn that the proceedings in his case should govern the cases of other repudiating allottees :—*Held*, that although there was not a board of four directors, a quorum of two was competent to allot shares.—*Held*, also, that the letter accompanying the letter of allotment, and stating the fact of the retirement of G. and R. did not qualify the letter of allotment, so as to prevent it from being an unconditional acceptance of W.'s offer to take shares.—*Held*, therefore, that the allotment was not void.—*Held*, by Kay, J., that W. never had any right to repudiate his shares, but held by the Court of Appeal, approving *Anderson's Case* (17 Ch. D. 373), that

as the application to take shares was made on the faith of G. and R. being directors, and they had ceased to be so before allotment, the allotment was voidable.—Whether a repudiation by W. so late as the 27th of November would in the case of a going concern have entitled him to be relieved from the shares *quære.*—But, *held*, by Kay, J., and by the Court of Appeal that assuming W. to have had a right to rescind, still as he had not before the winding-up taken any proceedings to have his name removed from the register, and no agreement was shewn that the cases of other repudiating allottees should be governed by the result of the proceedings in *Anderson's Case*, W. must be on the list of contributories.—*Fox's Case* (Law Rep. 5 Eq. 118) observed upon. *In re* SCOTTISH PETROLEUM COMPANY　23 Ch. D. 413

X. COMPANY—SHARES—ISSUE.

1. —— **Issue at a Discount**—*Registered Contract—Ultrà Vires—Companies Act, 1867, s. 25.*] A limited company may, where so authorized by its articles of association, issue shares at a discount under a contract duly registered pursuant to sect. 25 of the Companies Act, 1867. *In re* INCE HALL ROLLING MILLS COMPANY 23 Ch. D. 545, n. [*See also In re* PLASKYNASTON TUBE COMPANY 23 Ch. D. 542]

2. —— **Numbers of Shares**—*Paid-up Shares—Companies Act, 1867 (30 & 31 Vict. c. 131), s. 25.*] A contract to issue fully paid-up shares for a consideration other than money, registered under the Companies Act, 1867, sect. 25, need not specify the numbers of the shares. *In re* DELTA SYNDICATE, LIMITED. *Ex parte* FORDE　30 Ch. D. 153

XI. COMPANY—SHARES—TRANSFER.

1. —— **Blank Transfer**—*Pledge of Shares.*] F., the registered holder of shares in a company, deposited the certificates with C. as security for £150, and gave him a transfer signed by F., with the consideration, the date, and the name of the transferee left in blank. C. deposited the certificates and the blank transfer with Q. as security for £250. C. died insolvent, after which Q. filled in his own name as transferee, and sent in the transfer for registration. The shares were accordingly registered in Q.'s name, but whether this was done before notice given by F. to the company and to Q. that F. denied the validity of the transfer, was doubtful on the evidence:—*Held*, affirming the decision of Fry, J , that Q. had no title against F. except to the extent of what was due from F. to C.—A person who without inquiry takes from another an instrument signed in blank by a third party, and fills up the blanks, cannot, even in the case of a negotiable instrument, claim the benefit of being a purchaser for value without notice, so as to acquire a greater right than the person from whom he himself received the instrument.—If a debtor delivers to his creditor a blank transfer by way of security, that does not enable the creditor to delegate to another person authority to fill it up for purposes foreign to the original contract.—*Ex parte* Sargent. (Law Rep. 17 Eq. 273) observed upon. FRANCE *v.* CLARK　22 Ch. D. 830; 26 Ch. D. 257

XI. COMPANY — SHARES — TRANSFER — *continued.*

2. —— **Blank Transfer**—*Transfer of Shares by Deed—Delivery of Transfer by Transferor as his Deed—Equitable Mortgage of Shares — Notice — Priority—Maxim, " Qui prior est tempore, potior est jure "—Companies Act, 1862 (25 & 26 Vict. c. 89), s. 30—Mode of giving Notice to Company—Notice to Secretary as an Individual.*] Where the shares of a company registered under the Companies Act, 1862, are pursuant to the articles of association thereof to be transferred by deed, a transfer at the time when the transferor parts with the possession and control thereof, must contain the name of the transferee and must identify the shares; and a transfer in blank, that is, a transfer, which at the time above mentioned neither contains the name of the transferee nor identifies the shares, is void, even although the name of the transferee and the number and the numbers of the shares afterwards, but not in the presence nor by the direction of the transferor, are filled in, and he then adopts and acknowledges the transfer; for the mere adoption and acknowledgment by the transferor of the transfer after it has been filled in, it not being either in his possession or under his control at the time of the adoption and acknowledgment, do not amount to a delivery of the transfer by him as his deed.—*Hudson* v. *Revett* (5 Bing. 368) distinguished.—The principle established in *Dearle* v. *Hall* (3 Russ. 1), as to the effect of notice in determining the priorities of equitable rights, does not extend to the shares of companies registered under the Companies Act, 1862, or to companies governed by regulations having a provision similar to sect. 30 of that Act.—The Companies Act, 1862, s. 30, forbids the entry of any trust on the register of companies, and where the shares of a company either registered under that statute, or containing a regulation to the like effect with sect. 30 thereof, are either assigned or mortgaged more than once, the priority of the assignees or mortgagees will be determined by the priority of the assignments or mortgages, and not by the priority of the notices thereof given to the company :—So *held* by Brett, M.R., on the ground that a notice of an equitable assignment or mortgage, in order to be effectual, must turn the person to whom it is addressed into a trustee, and the Companies Act, 1862, s. 30, and any regulation of a company of a like nature, not only forbid the entry of any trust on the register, but also exempt the company from any liability for acting in contravention of a notice of the equitable assignment or mortgage:—By Cotton, L.J., on the ground that although the directors may be personally liable for permitting a transfer to be registered in contravention of equitable rights of which they have actual notice, nevertheless the company itself is not bound to recognise trusts, and cannot be made liable for accepting a transfer by any notice not to allow it:—By Lindley, L.J., on the ground that although the directors may be personally liable if they allow a transfer to be registered which they know to be fraudulent, nevertheless the only right of an equitable assignee or mortgagee against the company is to apply to the High Court under 5 Vict. c. 5, s. 4, and Rules of the Supreme Court, 1883, Order XLVI., for an order restraining the company from allowing a

XI. COMPANY — SHARES — TRANSFER — *continued.*

transfer to be made in contravention of his rights, and the company itself is not bound to take notice of equitable interests in shares not followed up in a reasonable time by proceedings to restrain a transfer.—*Semble*, by Brett, M.R., that the directors and secretary of the company will not be personally liable for disregarding a notice of a trust as to shares and for allowing them to be transferred in contravention thereof.—*Martin* v. *Sedgwick* (9 Beav. 333) dissented from.—*Ex parte Littledale, In re Pearse* (6 De G. M. & G. 714); *Ex parte Stewart, In re Shelley* (4 De G. J. & S. 543); *Ex parte Boulton, In re Sketchley* (1 De G. & J. 163); *Ex parte Union Bank of Manchester, In re Jackson* (Law Rep. 12 Eq. 354); and *Ex parte Agra Bank, In re Worcester* (Law Rep. 3 Ch. 555) discussed. —In order that a notice to a company may be effectual, either it must be given to the company itself through its proper officers, or it must be received by the company in the course of the transaction of its business : casual knowledge, acquired by the secretary as an individual and not whilst he is engaged in transacting the business of the company, cannot be deemed notice to the company. —In March, 1881, M. deposited with S. the certificates and a blank transfer of 100 shares in a company as security for money advanced. In February, 1882, S. died, and the secretary of the company, who was a relative of S., attended his funeral, and during a discussion of the deceased's affairs became acquainted with the existence of the charge on the shares. In December, 1882, M. was heavily in debt to the Plaintiffs, and as they pressed him for payment, he fraudulently delivered to them another blank transfer of the same shares. Some days afterwards, the transfer to the Plaintiffs was in the absence of M. filled up with the name of the Plaintiff C. as transferee and with the numbers of the shares. The company refused to register the transfer to the Plaintiffs on the ground that the certificates were not produced, and thereupon M. offered to indemnify the company against any other claim, but shortly after the executors of S. gave notice to the company of the existence of the charge in favour of their testator. The company was registered under the Companies Act, 1862, and one of the articles of association provided that the shares should be transferred by deed, and another provided that the company should not be bound by or recognise any equitable interest. In an action by the Plaintiffs against the executors of S. to obtain a declaration of their title to the 100 shares :—*Held*, first, that the knowledge acquired by the secretary of the company at the funeral of S. of the existence of the charge in his favour could not be deemed notice of its existence to the company itself:—*Held*, secondly, that the offer of M. to indemnify the company could not be deemed to be a delivery of the transfer as his deed, after it had been filled in with the name of C. as transferee and with the numbers of the 100 shares, and that the shares had not been legally transferred to the Plaintiffs who had only an equitable mortgage :—*Held*, thirdly, that the notice by the Plaintiffs to the company of the charge existing in their favour was notice of a trust, and therefore was invalid, and that the charge in favour of S. being prior in point of time, his execu-

XI. COMPANY — SHARES — TRANSFER — continued.

tors had the better title in equity to the shares. Société Générale de Paris v. Tramways Union Company - - - 14 Q. B. D. 424 [Affirmed in the House of Lords, 11 App. Cas. 20.]

3. —— Lien of Company—*Priority—Deposit of Certificates of Shares—Lien of Company on Shares for Moneys due from Shareholder—Notice.*] The articles of association of a company provided that the company should have a first and permanent lien and charge, available at law and in equity, on every share, for all debts due from the shareholder to the company. A shareholder deposited the certificates of his shares with his bankers as security for the balance then due from him to them on his current account, and notice of the deposit was given to the company.—*Held*, that *Hopkinson* v. *Rolt* (9 H. L. C. 514) applied, and that the company could not claim priority over the bankers in respect of moneys which became due from the shareholder to the company after notice of the bankers' advance, but that the bankers were entitled to priority. Bradford Banking Company v. Briggs & Co.
[29 Ch. D. 149
[Reversed by the Court of Appeal, 31 Ch. D. 19.]

4. —— Refusal to register Transfer — *Company's Lien on Shares — Companies Act, 1862 (25 & 26 Vict. c. 89), s. 35, Sched. 1, Table A., clause 10.*] Table A in the 1st schedule to the Companies Act, 1862, contains regulations which may be adopted for the management of a company limited by shares. The 10th clause of the Table provides that "the company may decline to register any transfer of shares made by a member who is indebted to them":—*Held*, that this provision is not limited to cases where the member is indebted for calls or otherwise in respect of the particular share proposed to be transferred, but enables the company to decline to register the transfer if the member is indebted to them on any account whatever. *Ex parte* Stringer - - - 9 Q. B. D. 436

5. —— Refusal to register Transfer—*Shareholder indebted to Company—Liquidation of Shareholder—Trustee.*] By the articles of association of a company it was provided that the directors might refuse to register a transfer of shares while the shareholder making the same was indebted to the company, or if they should consider the transferee an irresponsible person. It was also provided that persons becoming entitled to shares in consequence of the death, insolvency, or bankruptcy of a shareholder might be registered on the production of such evidence as might from time to time be required by the directors, and that any transfer or pretended transfer of shares not being approved by the directors should be absolutely void.—A holder of shares in the company executed transfers of such shares to the nominees of a bank as a security for advances. The company refused to register these transfers, on the ground that the transferor was indebted to the company. Subsequently, the transferor having filed a liquidation petition, a trustee in liquidation was duly appointed. Such trustee, with the consent of the bank and their nominees, applied to the directors of the company to be registered as

the owner of the shares, but they refused the application. The bank, though consenting to the trustee's registration, had never waived their security :—*Held* (by the Earl of Selborne, L.C., Brett, M.R., and Cotton, L.J.), that the declining to register the transfers by the directors was not a disapproval of them so as to render them void within the meaning of the articles, that the trustee was not entitled to the shares within the meaning of the articles so long as the transfers remained in force, and that the trustee was not entitled to be registered, notwithstanding the consent of the transferees. *Ex parte* Harrison. *In re* Cannock and Rugeley Colliery Company - - 26 Ch. D. 522; 28 Ch. D. 363

6. —— Refusal to register Transfer—*Measure of Damages — Companies Act, 1867 (30 & 31 Vict. c. 131), s. 26.*] The Plaintiff transferred shares of his in a registered company to A. B. on an agreement between them that if A. B. was accepted as shareholder by the company the shares should be taken by him at their market value in reduction of a debt due to him from the Plaintiff. The consideration was stated in the transfer to be only the sum of 5s., and the transfer was brought to the company for registration without any notice of the said agreement between the Plaintiff and A. B. The company refused to register, on the ground that the plaintiff was indebted to them, and on its being established after an interval of eighteen months that the Plaintiff was not so indebted, the company registered the transfer. In an action against the company for wrongfully refusing to register, the Plaintiff sought to recover as damages the loss in the market value of the shares between the time when the transfer was brought to the company to be registered and the time when it was in fact registered :—*Held*, that the Plaintiff was entitled to recover only nominal damages, as the contract between the Plaintiff and A. B. was a special one, of which the company had had no notice, and the ordinary contract on the sale of registered shares was only that the seller should give to the purchaser a valid transfer and do all required to enable the purchaser to be registered as member in respect of such shares, the duty of the purchaser, which has not been altered by sect. 26 of the Companies Act, 1867, being to get himself registered as such member. Skinner v. City of London Marine Insurance Corporation
[14 Q. B. D. 882

7. —— Winding-up—*Transfer of Shares pending Proceedings for Voluntary Liquidation — Voluntary Winding-up followed by Compulsory Winding-up — Commencement of Winding-up — Committee of Directors*] The articles of a company enabled the board of directors to appoint committees of their own number, and to delegate to any such committee all or any of the powers of the board. Transfers of shares were to be effected only by instruments executed both by the transferor and transferee, and were not to be made without the approval of the board, which had an absolute discretion as to accepting a transfer. On the 2nd of November, 1874, the board appointed H. B. a committee with all the powers of

XI. COMPANY — SHARES — TRANSFER —
continued.

the board. On the 24th of December, 1874, a board meeting was held, at which only H. B. and the secretary were present. At this meeting transfers, which had on the previous day been executed by X. and Y. to various persons of 1519 shares standing in the joint names of X. and Y., were approved, and the transferees placed on the register. H. B. deposed that all formalities had been waived, and there was no evidence whether the transfers had been executed by the transferees. On the same day a general meeting of shareholders was held, at which resolutions were passed for a voluntary winding-up of the company, and the transfer of its business to a new company, each shareholder in the old company taking the same number of shares in the new, and this was confirmed by a meeting of the 15th of January, 1875. At neither of these meetings did the transferors vote in respect of the shares transferred, but several of the transferees did, and the transferees were registered as shareholders in the new company. It did not appear that the old company was insolvent, but it was considered desirable to reconstitute it. In March, 1877, a petition was presented by some of the transferees for the compulsory winding-up of the old company, upon which an order was made on the 17th of the same month. The transferees were placed on the list of contributories. In 1881 some creditors, pursuant to leave given, applied in the name of the official liquidator to put X. and Y. on a supplemental list of contributories of the old company for the 1519 shares, and if not then on a B list as past members. The application was refused by Bacon, V.C.:—*Held,* that the fact that the transferors knew that the company was on on the eve of being wound up voluntarily did not take away their power of transferring their shares, and that the transfers of the 1519 shares were not invalid on that ground.—*Chappell's Case* (Law Rep. 6 Ch. 902) distinguished.—*Held,* also, that a committee of the board of directors need not consist of more than one person, and that H. B. had authority to approve the transfers: —*Held,* also, that it was not to be inferred in the absence of express evidence that the transfers had not been executed by the transferees.—*Held,* that, if they had not been so executed they were not a nullity but only irregular, and that after they had been acted upon and treated as valid for so long a period they could not be impeached: *Held,* therefore, that X. and Y. could not be placed on the list of contributories as present members :—*Held,* by Lindley and Fry, L.JJ., that X. and Y. could not be placed on the B list as past members, for that the winding-up was to be treated as having commenced at the presentation of the petition, which was more than twelve months after they transferred their shares; dissentiente, Cotton, L.J., who was of opinion that it commenced from the date of the resolution for voluntary winding-up, at which time X. and Y. had not ceased for twelve months to be shareholders. *In re* TAURINE COMPANY **25 Ch. D. 118**

XII. COMPANY—SHARES—REGISTER.

Form of Register.] *Alteration by the Board of Trade on 14th April, 1885, of Form E., in the second*

XII. COMPANY—SHARES—REGISTER—*contd.*

schedule of 25 & 26 Vict. c. 89 (the Companies Act, 1862), by virtue of s. 71 of that Act

[L. G. 1885, p. 1672

Colonial Register.] *The Act* 46 & 47 *Vict. c. 30 (the Companies Colonial Registers Act, 1883), which is to be construed as one with the Companies Acts, 1862 to 1880, enacts—*

Sect. 3.—(1.) *Any company whose objects comprise the transaction of business in a colony may, if authorized so to do by its regulations, as originally framed or as altered by special resolution, cause to be kept in any colony in which it transacts business a branch register or registers of members resident in such colony.*

(2.) *The company shall give to the registrar of joint stock companies notice of the situation of the office where any such branch register (in this Act called a colonial register) is kept, and of any change therein, and of the discontinuance of any such office in the event of the same being discontinued.*

(3.) *A colonial register shall, as regards the particulars entered therein, be deemed to be a part of the company's register of members, and shall be primâ facie evidence of all particulars entered therein. Any such register shall be kept in the manner provided by the Companies Acts, 1862 to 1880, with this qualification, that the advertisement entered in sect. 33 of the Companies Act, 1862, shall be inserted in some newspaper circulating in the district wherein the register to be closed is kept, and that any competent Court in the colony where such register is kept shall be entitled to exercise the same jurisdiction of rectifying the same as is by sect. 35 of the Companies Act, 1862, vested, as respects a register, in England and Ireland, in Her Majesty's superior Courts of Law or Equity, and that all offences under sect. 32 of the Companies Act, 1862, may as regards a colonial register, be prosecuted summarily before any tribunal in the colony where such register is kept having summary criminal jurisdiction.*

(4.) *The company shall transmit to its registered office a copy of every entry in its colonial register or registers as soon as may be after such entry is made, and the company shall cause to be kept at its registered office, duly entered up from time to time, a duplicate or duplicates of its colonial register or registers. The provisions of sect. 32 of the Companies Act, 1862, shall apply to every such duplicate, and every such duplicate shall, for all the purposes of the Companies Acts, 1862 to 1880, be deemed to be part of the register of members of the company.*

(5.) *Subject to the provisions of this Act, with respect to the duplicate register, the shares registered in a colonial register shall be distinguished from the shares registered in the principal register, and no transaction with respect to any shares registered in a colonial register shall, during the continuance of the registration of such shares in such colonial register, be registered in any other register.*

(6.) *The company may discontinue to keep any colonial register, and thereupon all entries in that register shall be transferred to some other colonial register kept by the company in the same colony, or to the register of members kept at the registered office of the company.*

XII. COMPANY—SHARES—REGISTER—contd.

(7.) *In relation to stamp duties the following provisions shall have effect :—*

(a.) *An instrument of transfer of a share registered in a colonial register under this Act shall be deemed to be a transfer of property situated out of the United Kingdom, and unless executed in any part of the United Kingdom shall be exempt from British stamp duty.*

(b.) *Upon the death of a member registered in a colonial register under this Act, the share or other interest of the deceased member shall for the purposes of this Act so far as relates to British duties be deemed to be part of his estates and effects situated in the United Kingdom for or in respect of which probate or letters of administration is or are to be granted, or whereof an inventory is to be exhibited and recorded in like manner as if he were registered in the register of members kept at the registered office of the company.*

(8.) *Subject to the provisions of this Act any company may, by its regulations as originally framed, or as altered by special resolution, make such provisions as it may think fit respecting the keeping of colonial registers.*

XIII. COMPANY—MANAGEMENT.

1. —— Auditor — *Right of, to appoint Accountant—Companies Clauses Act, 1845 (8 & 9 Vict. c. 16), s. 108.]* An auditor appointed under the Companies Clauses Act, 1845, is entitled to appoint an accountant under sect. 108 of that Act, without the consent of his co-auditor. STEELE *v.* SUTTON GAS COMPANY　　**12 Q. B. D. 68**

2. —— General Meeting—*Gratuities to Servants—Remuneration to Directors for past Services—Companies Clauses Act, 1845 (8 & 9 Vict. c. 16), ss. 67, 90, 91,]* A company carrying on business has power, by the vote of a general meeting, to expend a portion of its funds in gratuities to servants or directors, provided such grants are made for the purpose of advancing the interests of the company. But this does not apply to a case where the company has transferred its undertaking to another company and is being wound up.—A railway company which had no provision in its articles for paying remuneration to directors, and had never paid any, sold its undertaking to another company at a price to be determined by an arbitrator. By the Act authorizing the transfer it was provided that on the completion of the transfer the company should be dissolved except for the purpose of regulating their internal affairs and winding up the same and of dividing the purchase-money. The purchase-money was to be applied in paying the costs of the arbitration and in paying off any revenue debts or charges of the company, and the residue was to be divided among the debenture holders and shareholders. After the completion of the transfer a general meeting of the company was held at which a resolution was passed to apply £1050 of the purchase-money in compensating the paid officials of the company for their loss of employment although they had no legal claim for any compensation, and £1500 in remuneration to the directors for their past services ;—*Held,* by the

XIII. COMPANY—MANAGEMENT—*continued.*

Court of Appeal (dissentiente Baggallay, L.J.), that the resolution was invalid, as the company was no longer a going concern, and only existed for the purpose of winding-up.—*Hampson* v. *Price's Patent Candle Company* (24 W. R. 754) and *Taunton* v. *Royal Insurance Company* (2 H. & M. 135) distinguished.—*Per* Baggallay, L.J.: The vote was within the powers of the company as it still retained the power of regulating its internal affairs. — *Per* Fry, L.J.: Remuneration for past services of directors cannot be voted at an ordinary general meeting unless special notice be given of the intention to propose such a resolution. HUTTON *v.* WEST CORK RAILWAY COMPANY　　　　　　　　**23 Ch. D. 654**

3. —— General Meeting—*Poll—Mode of taking Poll—Chairman, Direction of—Companies Act, 1862, Table A, Art. 43.]* The articles of association of a company provided (in the terms of art. 43 of Table A to the Companies Act, 1862) that if at any general meeting of the company a poll should be demanded it should be taken "in such manner as the chairman shall direct."—A poll having been demanded at a meeting summoned to consider a resolution for a voluntary winding-up, the chairman directed the poll be taken then and there. It was so taken, and the resolution was carried :—*Held,* that the poll had been rightly taken. *In re* CHILLINGTON IRON COMPANY
　　　　　　　　　　　　　　　[29 Ch. D. 159

4. —— General Meeting—*Proxies.]* By the 65th of the articles of association of a steamship company, it was provided that votes might be given personally or by proxy. Article 66 provided that the instrument appointing a proxy should be in writing under the hand of the appointor, and should be attested by one or more witness or witnesses, and that no person should be appointed a proxy who was not a member of the company. Article 68 gave a form of proxy containing an attestation clause. By a special resolution, article 68 was repealed, and a new form given without an attestation clause, but the resolution did not purport to repeal art. 66 : — *Held,* by Chitty, J., and by the Court of Appeal, that as the special resolution did not purport to affect art. 66, the provision requiring the signature to be attested remained in force, and that it was not merely directory, but that attestation was essential to the validity of a proxy, and that unattested proxies must be rejected.—Disputes arose as to the number of directors to be appointed, as to the change of the port of the company, and as to the amount of dividend to be declared. There having been seven directors, five of whom remained in office, a poll was taken to determine whether M. and T. should be elected, and the number of directors continued at seven, or whether the five Plaintiffs should be elected, and the number of directors increased to ten. A poll was also taken on the question whether the dividend proposed by the old directors should be paid or a larger dividend which had been proposed by persons who sided with the Plaintiffs. A poll was also taken on the question whether the port should be changed or should remain where it was. In each case the result of the poll was in favour of the first alternative if unattested proxies were

XIII. COMPANY—MANAGEMENT—*continued.*

admitted, but for the second, if they were excluded. The chairman in each case held the proxies admissible. The five old directors and M. and T. accordingly claimed to be the board of directors, and excluded the Plaintiffs. The Plaintiffs thereupon commenced their action on behalf of themselves and all other the shareholders except the Defendants, making the company a co-Plaintiff, against the seven to restrain them from paying any dividend except the increased dividend, and from excluding the Plaintiffs, and from doing anything contrary to the resolution against changing the port, and to restrain M. and T. from acting as directors. After the action was commenced a requisition was handed in to the board to call an extraordinary general meeting for the purpose of considering certain proposed resolutions, the effect of which would be to confirm the resolutions in favour of which the unattested proxies had been given, and to rescind the resolutions on which the Plaintiffs relied. The Defendants summoned the meeting. The Plaintiffs then amended their writ, and asked for an injunction against the holding the meeting. Chitty. J., granted an injunction to restrain M. and T. from acting as directors, to restrain the Defendants from excluding the Plaintiffs, to restrain them changing the port, and to restrain them from holding the meeting :—The Court of Appeal considered that the matters in dispute were matters to be determined by the shareholders, and upon undertakings being given by both parties to keep matters in statu quo, discharged the order of Chitty, J., for an injunction, and directed the appeal to stand over until the sense of the shareholders had been taken at a general meeting to be convened for that purpose. Such meeting was held, and a resolution was passed by a large majority rescinding the election of the Plaintiffs as directors.—The Court of Appeal, though holding that the resolution not having been passed as a special resolution was not an effectual exercise of the power given by the articles to remove directors, refused to grant an interlocutory injunction to prevent the exclusion of the Plaintiffs, but exacted an undertaking that M. and T. should not act. HABBEN *v.* PHILLIPS **23 Ch. D. 14**

5. —— General Meeting—*Requisition to call a Meeting—Power to remove Directors— Companies Clauses Consolidation Act,* 1845 (8 & 9 *Vict.* c. 16), *ss.* 70, 88, 89, 91.] A sufficient number of shareholders required the directors of a railway company to call a meeting of the company for the following objects : 1. To appoint a committee to inquire into the working and general management of the company, and the means of reducing the working expenses, to empower such committee to consolidate offices, to remove any of the officers and appoint others, and to authorize and require the directors to carry out the recommendations of the committee ; 2. To remove, if deemed necessary or expedient, any of the present directors, and to elect directors to fill any vacancy in the board. The directors issued a notice for a meeting " for the purpose of considering and determining upon a demand of the requisitionists for the appointment of a committee to inquire into the working and general manage-

XIII. COMPANY—MANAGEMENT—*continued.*

ment of the company and the means of reducing the working expenses." The requisitionists gave notice that they should not attend the meeting, as the notice did not provide for all their objects, they did not attend, and they then themselves issued a notice under sect. 70 of the Companies Clauses Act, calling a meeting for the purposes mentioned in their requisition. The directors brought an action in the name of the company to restrain the requisitionists from holding the meeting :—*Held,* by Kay, J., that everything in the first part of the requisition beyond the appointment of a committee was illegal, for that it proposed to transfer the powers of the directors to a committee, and that the directors were therefore justified in not entertaining the latter part of the first head of the requisition :—*Held,* also, by Kay, J., that the second head of the requisition was too vague and did not " fully express the object of the meeting," and that the directors had no power to call a meeting for that purpose, whether a general meeting had power to remove directors or not :—*Held,* therefore, by Kay, J., that the directors had not failed to call a meeting within the meaning of the Companies Clauses Act, 1845, s. 70, that the power of the shareholders to call it had therefore not arisen, and that an injunction must be granted.—*Held,* on appeal, that all the objects of the first part of the requisition were objects that could be carried out in a legal way, that the Court will not restrain the holding of a meeting because the notice calling it is so expressed that consistently with its terms resolutions might be passed which would be ultrà vires, and that the directors were not justified in excluding from their notice the objects in the first part of the requisition other than the appointment of a committee :—*Held,* also, that under sect. 91 of the Companies Clauses Act a general meeting has power to remove directors, that a notice of a proposal to remove "any of the directors" was sufficiently distinct, that the general meeting could at all events fill up vacancies in the board if all the directors were removed or if the directors declined to exercise the power given by sect. 89, and that the directors were therefore bound to include in their notice the objects mentioned in the second part of the requisition :—*Held,* therefore, that the requisitionists were entitled to call a meeting, and that the injunction must be discharged. ISLE OF WIGHT RAILWAY COMPANY *v.* TAHOURDIN **25 Ch. D. 320**

XIV. COMPANY—MEMBER'S LIABILITY.

1. —— Charge—*Contribution—Locke King's Act* (17 & 18 *Vict.* c. 113).] A testator held shares in a banking company by whose deed of settlement it was provided that if any shareholder did not on demand pay all moneys due from him to the company, the directors might declare his shares forfeited, and that nevertheless he should still be liable to pay the debt, and it was also provided that a shareholder must have paid all moneys due from him to the company before he could transfer his shares. The testator borrowed money from the company, and deposited the deeds of certain real estate with them as security. By his will he gave the above estate to his son A., and his residuary property to his

N

XIV. COMPANY — MEMBER'S LIABILITY — continued.

other sons. A. claimed that the testator's shares in the bank should contribute rateably to payment of the debt:—*Held*, by Chitty, J., and by the Court of Appeal, that the provisions of the deed of settlement did not create a charge or lien on the shares for a debt due from the holder, and that no case for contribution arose:—*Held*, also that if the deed of settlement had charged the shares with all debts due from the shareholder to the company, a debt for which real estate had been specifically mortgaged would still have been payable out of the mortgaged estate before resorting to the shares which were only subject to a general lien. *In re* DUNLOP. DUNLOP *v.* DUNLOP　　　21 Ch. D. 583

2. —— Mutual Marine Insurance Association —*Company limited by Guarantee—Memorandum and Articles of Association—Limitation of Liability in the Event of winding up the Association—Companies Act,* 1862 (25 & 26 *Vict.* c. 89), *ss.* 9, 38.] The Defendant was the owner of a ship insured and entered in a certain class of a mutual insurance association, which was limited by guarantee and incorporated under the Companies Act, 1862. The object of the association was the mutual insurance of ships of members, or in which they were interested. According to its rules a person by entering his ship to be insured, as the Defendant had done, became a member of the association, and whilst his ship was insured by the other members of his own class he was an assurer of the vessels of such other members entered in the same class as that in which his own had been so entered. By the memorandum of association the declaration of the undertaking required, by sect. 9 of the Companies Act, 1862, on the part of a member of an association limited by guarantee was as follows : " Every member of the association undertakes to contribute to the assets of the association in the event of the same being wound up during the time that he is a member, or within one year afterwards, for payment of the debts and liabilities of the association contracted before the time at which he ceases to be a member, and the costs, charges, and expenses of winding up the same, and for the adjustment of the rights of the contributories amongst themselves, such amount as may be required, not exceeding £5." Whilst the Defendant's ship continued to be so insured and the Defendant was such member the association resolved to be wound up voluntarily:—*Held*, that the Defendant was liable to pay his proportion of losses in respect of vessels entered and insured in the same class as his own, and that his liability was not limited to £5, since the debts and liabilities mentioned in the declaration of undertaking were those of the association as against its members, and in respect of which the 9th section of the statute required such declaration to be contained in the memorandum of association, and were not the debts and liabilities to which the members by the rules of the association were to contribute as insurers or as assured. LION MUTUAL MARINE INSURANCE ASSOCIATION *v.* TUCKER　　-　　12 Q. B. D. 176

3. —— *Trustee of Shares—Lien on Shares for Debt of Trustee—Equitable Title to Shares—Pri-*

XIV. COMPANY — MEMBER'S LIABILITY — continued.

ority.] The trustees of a marriage settlement which authorized them to invest in the shares of any trading company, invested part of their trust funds in the purchase of shares in a limited banking company, which were transferred into their joint names. By the articles it was provided that the company should have a first and paramount charge on the shares of any shareholder for all moneys owing to the company from him alone or jointly with any other person, and that when a share was held by more persons than one the company should have a like lien and charge thereon in respect of all moneys so owing to them from all or any of the holders thereof alone or jointly with any other person. One of the trustees was a partner in a firm which afterwards went into liquidation, at which time it owed the company a debt which had arisen long after the registration of the shares in the names of the trustees:—*Held*, by Bacon, V.C., and by the Court of Appeal, that the bank had a lien on the shares for this debt which must prevail over the title of the cestuis que trust.—Whether as between themselves and the cestuis que trust the trustees were authorized to make such an investment, *quære.* NEW LONDON AND BRAZILIAN BANK *v.* BROCKLEBANK　　　21 Ch. D. 302

XV. COMPANY—DIRECTOR'S APPOINTMENT

1. —— Casual Vacancy — *General Meeting.*] The articles of association of a company provided that the directors might fill up any casual vacancy on the board.—A casual vacancy occurred, and before it was filled up by the board a general meeting of the company was held.—The vacancy was not filled up by the general meeting :—*Held*, that the power of the board to fill up the vacancy remained.—*Semble*, the general meeting could have filled up the vacancy. MUNSTER *v.* CAMMELL COMPANY　-　　　-　　　21 Ch. D. 183

2. —— Dismissal of Directors — *Power of General Meeting — Alteration of Articles—Costs out of Company's Funds.*] A joint stock company whose directors are appointed for a definite period has no inherent power to remove them before the expiration of that period.—If the articles of association of a company contain no power to remove directors before the expiration of their period of office, but authorize the shareholders by special resolution to alter any of the articles, there must be a separate special resolution altering the articles so as to give power to remove directors before a resolution can be passed to remove any of them. — Certain shareholders who were appointed directors by a general meeting in the place of the existing directors, brought an action in the name of the company against the existing directors to restrain them from acting. The Court held that the new directors were not duly appointed, and refused the relief prayed with costs ; but inasmuch as the Plaintiffs substantially represented the wishes of the majority of the shareholders, although technically they had no right to use the name of the company, the Court allowed the costs to be paid out of the company's assets. IMPERIAL HYDROPATHIC HOTEL COMPANY, BLACKPOOL *v.* HAMPSON　　-　　　-　　　23 Ch. D. 1

XV. COMPANY—DIRECTOR'S APPOINTMENT
continued.

—— Dismissal of directors—Power of general
meeting - - - **25 Ch. D. 320**
See COMPANY—MANAGEMENT. 5.

XVI. COMPANY—DIRECTOR'S AUTHORITY.

1. —— Application of Funds—*Directors—Ultrà
Vires—Winding-up Petition.*] A proviso in the
articles of association of a company that the directors may "at any time direct any action or other
legal proceedings to be commenced and prosecuted
on behalf of the company in the name of the company or of such officer or other person as the
directors may be advised; and may defend any
action, &c., and may release, discontinue, or compromise any such action or other proceeding as
they shall deem expedient; and they shall be
indemnified out of the funds of the company
against all costs, damages, and expenses by reason
of such action, suit, or proceedings," does not
authorize the application by the directors of the
assets of the company in paying the costs of a
petition for winding up the company presented
by themselves, but opposed by a number of the
shareholders and a minority of the directors, and
the costs of an appeal from the dismissal of such
petition; and such intended application will be
restrained as an act illegal and ultrà vires. SMITH
v. DUKE OF MANCHESTER - - **24 Ch. D. 611**

2. —— Mortgage—*Ultrà Vires—Limit—Capital not called up—Shares not issued.*] Among
the objects of a company was to purchase ships;
and the directors were empowered to do all need-
ful acts in furtherance of the objects of the company; they were also expressly authorized to
borrow, on the security of the property of the company, any sum of money not exceeding two-thirds
of the capital of the company not called up.—
The directors mortgaged a ship, the only property
of the company, to secure the payment of a sum
of money advanced to the company, and of unpaid
purchase-money of the ship; the amount so secured much exceeding two-thirds of the amount
not called up of the shares actually issued, but
being within two-thirds of the whole nominal
capital not called up:—*Held,* that the mortgage
was within the powers of the directors, and was
valid; and that the term "capital not called up"
included shares which had not been issued. ENG-
LISH CHANNEL STEAMSHIP COMPANY *v.* ROLT
[17 Ch. D. 715

3. —— Quorum of Directors—*Articles of Association—Business to be conducted by not less than
a certain Number — Call — Forfeiture — Ultrà
Vires.*] Where the articles of association of a
company provide that "the business of the company shall be conducted by not less than" a specified number of directors, the words are imperative,
not merely directory: consequently a call made
or a forfeiture of shares declared by less than the
specified number of directors is invalid. — The
articles of association of a limited company provided (Art. 35) that "the business of the company should be conducted by not less than five
nor more than seven directors;" also that the
office of director should be vacated on bankruptcy
or insolvency; and that "the directors might determine the quorum necessary for the transaction

XVI. COMPANY—DIRECTOR'S AUTHORITY—
continued.

of business."—The articles named six persons
only as directors, of whom B. was one. These
directors fixed three of their number as a quorum.
—In October, 1877, the number of directors being
then reduced by death to five, B. became insolvent, and therefore disqualified as a director.—In
November the company passed, at an ordinary
meeting, a resolution altering article 35 by substituting "three" directors for "five." This resolution was admitted to be invalid as not having
been passed in accordance with the articles.—In
December the four remaining directors made a
call. B. having made default in payment of this
call, as well as a former call made prior to his insolvency, the same directors passed a resolution
declaring his shares forfeited.—The company
afterwards passed a resolution for a voluntary
winding-up, in the course of which it turned out
that there were surplus assets available for division among the shareholders:—*Held,* that the
second call and the forfeiture, having been made
and declared by four directors only, were invalid:
and, therefore, that B. was entitled, on payment
of his calls to the liquidator, to be treated as a
shareholder, and to participate in the surplus
assets accordingly.—*Thames - Haven Dock and
Railway Company v. Rose* (4 Man. & G. 552), and
Kirk v. Bell (16 Q. B. 290) considered. *In re*
ALMA SPINNING COMPANY. BOTTOMLEY'S CASE
[16 Ch. D. 631

XVII. COMPANY—DIRECTOR'S LIABILITY.

1. —— Acceptance of Bills *"for and on behalf
of Company"— Personal Liability.*] A bill of
exchange payable to order and addressed to the
B. & I. Company, which was incorporated under
local Acts and had no power to accept bills,
was accepted by the Defendants, who were two
of the directors of the company, and also by the
secretary, as follows:—"Accepted for and on
behalf of the B. & I. Company, G. K., F. S. P.
directors; B. W. secretary." The bill was so
accepted and given by the Defendants to the
drawer, the engineer of the company, on account
of the company's debt to him for professional
services, and although he was told by the Defendants that they gave him the bill on the understanding that he should not negotiate it, but
merely as a recognition of the company's debt
to him, as the company had no power to accept
bills, yet the Defendants knew that he would get
it discounted, and they meant that he should have
the power of doing so. The bill was indorsed by
the drawer to the Plaintiffs for value, and without
notice of the understanding between him and the
Defendants:—*Held,* affirming the decision of the
Queen's Bench Division, that the Defendants were
personally liable, as by their acceptance they represented that they had authority to accept on
behalf of the company, which being a false representation of a matter of fact and not of law, gave
a cause of action to the Plaintiffs, who had acted
upon it. WEST LONDON COMMERCIAL BANK *v.*
KITSON - - **12 Q. B. D. 157; 13 Q. B. D. 360**

2. —— Fiduciary Relation—*Company intended
to be worked as a Private Partnership—Shareholders subsequently admitted.*] A company was
formed and registered consisting of eight persons,

XVII. COMPANY—DIRECTOR'S LIABILITY—
continued.

seven of whom were directors and the eighth the solicitor, for the purchase and working of a patent belonging to some of the members. The directors allotted shares without consideration to some of their number. It was proved to the satisfaction of the Court that it was intended at that time to work the company as a private partnership, and to admit no other members. All the members consented to what was done, and it was sanctioned at a general meeting of the company. No prospectus was issued. Rather more than a year afterwards, the company being in need of more capital, some fresh shareholders were admitted, who alleged that they were not informed of the manner in which the original shares had been allotted. The company was ordered to be wound up:—*Held* (affirming the decision of Jessel, M.R.), that no fraud had been committed on the company, and that the official liquidator, as representing the company, could not call upon the directors under the 165th section of the Companies Act, 1862, to account for the value of the shares so allotted to them.—*Society of Practical Knowledge* v. *Abbott* (2 Beav. 559) distinguished. *In re* BRITISH SEAMLESS PAPER BOX COMPANY
[**17 Ch. D.** 467

3. —— **Misappropriation of Funds**—*Repayment by Directors—Investment by Money misappropriated in Debentures of the Company—Set-off by Director—Companies Act, 1862 (25 & 26 Vict. c. 89), ss. 101, 165.*] The directors of a company passed a resolution to pay £3000 to P., who was one of the promoters, for services rendered, upon an understanding, which was not reduced into writing, that he should expend £400 in advertisements and advance the residue to the company on the security of debentures. The directors accordingly paid P. the money, and he spent £400 as arranged, and advanced the remaining £2600 to the company on debentures, which he divided between himself and certain of the directors. The company was afterwards wound up:—*Held*, (affirming the decision of Hall, V.C.), that the directors were jointly and severally liable to repay the £2600 to the company; that the advance of the money to the company on debentures was not a repayment to the company; and that it made no difference whether the arrangement to invest the money in debentures under which it was originally paid to P., was binding or not.—At the time of the winding-up the company was indebted to one of the directors who were thus held liable, for money advanced for expenses:—*Held*, that he could not set off the debt against his liability for the misappropriation of the company's money.—*Coventry and Dixon's Case* (14 Ch. D. 660) commented on. *In re* ANGLO-FRENCH CO-OPERATIVE SOCIETY. *Ex parte* PELLY - - - 21 Ch. D. 492

4. —— **Payment of Dividend out of Capital**—*Money borrowed to pay Dividend—Measure of Damages—Shareholders and Creditors Parties to Breach of Trust—Indemnity—Delay—Stale Demand.—Companies Act, 1862 (25 & 26 Vict. c. 89), s. 165.*] The articles of association of a company provided that all dividends on shares should be made only out of the clear profits of the company, and that all moneys borrowed by the company and

all moneys received under insurances of the company's property against destruction or damage by fire should be deemed capital.—A building of the company having been destroyed by fire, the company resolved to increase the capital by £150,000 for the purpose of reconstructing the building and to issue for this purpose 15,000 preference shares. These shares were issued, and during the reconstruction of the building, no profits having been earned by the company, the directors paid four dividends on the shares. The first dividend was paid out of moneys received from an insurance company in respect of the loss occasioned by the fire. The other three dividends were paid by means of moneys borrowed expressly for the purpose from the contractors of the company and a financial company, both of whom had notice of the purpose for which the money was borrowed, and both of whom held a large number of the preference shares:—*Held*, that the directors were, under sect. 165 of the Companies Act, 1862, jointly and severally liable to pay to the liquidator the amount of the first dividend.—But with respect to the other three dividends, *held* that the result of the transactions, as a whole, had been only to increase the amount of the proofs against the company by the amount of the loans, and that, consequently the directors were jointly and severally liable to pay to the liquidator only such a sum as would enable him to pay on all the debts of the company a dividend equal to that which would have been paid on all the debts (other than the loans), in case no proof had been made in respect of the loans.—But, *held*, that the order must be made without prejudice to the right of the directors to be indemnified by any shareholders or creditors of the company who were parties or privies to the payment of the dividends out of capital, and that three months from the date of the Chief Clerk's certificate of the amount payable by the directors must be given to them to make the payment.—The dividends in question were paid in January and July, 1874, and in January and July, 1875. The order to wind up the company was made in November, 1876. A liquidator was appointed in December. 1876; he afterwards retired, and his successor was appointed in December, 1878. The summons against the directors was issued in February, 1880:—*Held*, that there had been no such delay. as to disentitle the liquidator to make the application.—*Stringer's Case* (Law Rep. 4 Ch. 475) and *In re Mammoth Copperopolis of Utah* (50 L. J. (Ch.) 11) distinguished. *In re* ALEXANDRA PALACE COMPANY 21 Ch. D. 149

5. —— **Payment of Dividend out of Capital**—*Set-off—Statute of Limitations.*] The directors of a limited company for several years presented to the general meetings of shareholders reports and balance-sheets in which various debts known by the directors to be bad were entered as assets, so that an apparent profit was shewn though in fact there was none. The shareholders, relying on these documents, passed resolutions declaring dividends, which the directors accordingly paid. An order having been made to wind up the company the liquidator applied, under sect. 165 of the

XVII. COMPANY—DIRECTOR'S LIABILITY—
continued.

Companies Act, 1862, for an order on the directors to replace the amount of dividends thus paid out of capital :—*Held,* by Bacon, V.C., and by the Court of Appeal, that as regards each half-yearly dividend the persons who were directors when it was paid were liable for the whole amount paid for the dividends of that half-year, and that *In re National Funds Assurance Company* (10 Ch. D. 118) is in no way affected by *Coventry and Dixon's Case* (14 Ch. D. 660). The order of Bacon, V.C., declared them to be jointly liable, but this was varied on appeal by declaring them jointly and severally liable :—*Held,* that even if the shareholders had known the true facts, so that their ratification of the payment of dividends would have bound themselves individually, they could not bind the company, for that the payment of dividends out of corpus was ultrà vires the company, and incapable of ratification by the shareholders :—*Held,* further, that the fact that the capital thus improperly applied was distributed pro ratâ among the whole body of shareholders did not protect the directors, for that the shareholders were not the corporation, and that payment to them would not prevent the corporation before winding-up, or the liquidator after winding-up, from compelling the directors to replace the money that it might be applied to proper purposes :—*Held,* further, that the directors could not set off any money due from the company to them against the amounts which they were ordered to replace : *Held,* also, that the claim was for a breach of trust, and that the Statute of Limitations could not be set up. *In re* EXCHANGE BANK-ING COMPANY. FLITCROFT'S CASE 21 Ch. D. 519

6. —— Payment of Dividend out of Capital— *—Negligence — Misfeasance—Breach of Trust— Innocent Director—Companies Act, 1862 (25 & 26 Vict. 89),* s. 165.] An innocent director of a company is not liable for the fraud of his co-directors in issuing to the shareholders false and fraudulent reports and balance sheets if the books and accounts of the company have been kept and audited by duly appointed and responsible officers, and he has no ground for suspecting fraud. Consequently, if such a director has received, together with the other shareholders, dividends declared and paid in pursuance of such reports and balance sheets, such dividends having been, in fact, payments out of capital, he cannot be called upon, under sect. 165 of the Companies Act, 1862, to repay the dividends so paid, nor even the dividends received by himself. A director is not bound to examine entries in any of the company's books; nor is the doctrine of constructive notice to be so extended as to impute to him a knowledge of the contents of the books. —The articles of association of a company vested in D., the vendor to the company and its chairman, the "supreme control" of its management and business; also power "to the exclusion of general meetings and the board" to determine the amount of dividend, and, generally, power to exercise any of the authorities thereby conferred on the general meetings and boards of directors, and in doing so to "supersede the authority of general meetings and boards." The articles then,

XVII. COMPANY—DIRECTOR'S LIABILITY—
continued.

"subject and without prejudice to the authorities thereby given to" D., vested the general conduct and management of the business of the company in the board of directors, and required them to keep and render proper accounts, reports, and balance sheets. The articles also prohibited the payment of dividends except out of profits. The company had a regular book-keeper and duly appointed auditors. During a period of four years printed annual reports, with balance sheets annexed, were issued to the shareholders purporting to shew profits each year available for a 15 per cent. dividend, which was declared and paid accordingly. Each report was headed with the names of the four directors of the company including D., the chairman, and ended with the words, "By order of the directors—D., chairman"; the balance sheets being signed as approved by the auditors. C. was one of the directors named at the head of the reports, but he never attended any of the board meetings or took any actual part in the preparation or issue of the reports and balance sheets, and during the four years he only occasionally attended the company's general meetings, at one of which, at D.'s request, he formally moved the resolution declaring the 15 per cent. dividend for that year.—On the company having subsequently been ordered to be wound up, it was found that the dividends for the four years had been paid out of capital and not out of profits, and that in order to shew profits available for the 15 per cent. dividend the accounts had been fraudulently manipulated by D. and the book-keeper, though without the knowledge of C., who had no grounds for suspecting misconduct on the part of any of the officers of the company. A summons having been taken out under sect. 165 of the Companies Act, 1862, by certain creditors of the company to compel C. to repay the amount of dividends so paid out of capital :—*Held,* that C. was not personally responsible for the fraudulent reports and balance sheets and the dividends paid under them, the words, "By order of the directors" at the foot of the reports not being alone sufficient to fix him with individual liability; and that—having regard to the powers by the articles vested in D., and to the fact that the books had been kept and audited by duly authorised officers, and that C. had had no reason to suspect any misconduct—C. had not been guilty of such negligence or abnegation of duty as to render himself liable to repay the whole amount of capital paid away as dividends to himself and the other shareholders, nor even the amount received by himself alone as a shareholder, nor the single dividend for which he had formally moved the resolution. *In re* DENHAM & Co. 25 Ch. D. 752

XVIII. COMPANY—DIRECTOR'S QUALIFICA-TION.

1. —— Contract to obtain Qualification—*Subscriber of Memorandum—Reasonable Time for Performance — Abortive Company—Companies Act, 1862,* s. 23.] A company was registered in June, 1879. B. and H. signed the memorandum of association as subscribers for one share each. By the articles B. and H. were named as original directors, and it was provided that the qualifica-

XVIII. COMPANY—DIRECTOR'S QUALIFICA-TION—continued.

tion of a director should be fifty shares. B. and H. attended meetings of the directors, but no shares were allotted to them, nor did their names appear on the register for any shares except those for which they had signed the memorandum. In September B. resigned his office, but H. continued a director. No business was ever done by the company, and in November a resolution was passed to wind up the company. The liquidator placed B. and H. on the list of contributories for fifty shares each :—*Held* (affirming the decision of Kay, J.), that assuming that the contract entered into by B. and H. to obtain a qualification amounted to an agreement to take fifty shares within the 23rd section of the Companies Act, 1862, they were entitled to a reasonable time for performing the agreement, and that under the circumstances such reasonable time had not elapsed at the commencement of the winding-up of the company. Consequently they could not be held liable as contributories in respect of the fifty shares.—Whether the contract amounted to an agreement to take the fifty shares within the 23rd section, *quære. In re* COLOMBIA CHEMICAL FACTORY MANURE AND PHOSPHATE WORKS. HEWITT'S CASE. BRETT'S CASE　-　　- 25 Ch. D. 283

2. —— Provided by Promoter—*Joint and several Liability.*] The first five directors of a company being bound by the articles of association to hold twenty shares each as a qualification, accepted, with the knowledge and approval of each other, twenty fully paid shares each from the promoter who had received them as cash from the company :—*Held,* upon summons by the official liquidator in the winding-up, that all the directors were jointly and severally liable to pay the full value of the shares.—One only of the five directors, upon finding that he was not justified in receiving the shares without payment, offered to pay the full sum due from him, and gave a cheque for the amount, which, however, was accepted as an advance to the company, and was added to previous advances made by him for preliminary expenses :—*Held,* that this director was not at liberty to set off the value of his shares against the amount paid in respect of advances, though he would have a claim against the company for those advances. *In re* CARRIAGE CO-OPERATIVE SUPPLY ASSOCIATION　- 27 Ch. D. 322

XIX. COMPANY—WINDING-UP ORDER.

1. —— Commencing Business—*Business of the Company at Home and Abroad—Companies Act,* 1862 (25 & 26 Vict. c. 89), s. 79, *sub-s.* 2.] When a company is incorporated to carry on business in the United Kingdom and in other parts of the world, and it has commenced to carry on its business in a foreign country, and there appears a bonâ fide intention to commence business in the country, the mere fact that it has not actually commenced in this country the objects for which it was incorporated within a year from its incorporation is not a sufficient ground for ordering the company to be wound up under the Companies Act, 1862, s. 79, sub-s. 2.—*Princess of Reuss* v. *Bos* (Law Rep. 5 H. L. 176) discussed and distinguished. *In re* CAPITAL FIRE INSURANCE ASSOCIATION　-　　-　　- 21 Ch. D. 209

XIX. COMPANY — WINDING-UP ORDER — continued.

2. —— Foreign Company—*Branch Office in England—Jurisdiction to wind up — Pending Foreign Liquidation — Companies Act,* 1862, s. 199.] The Court has jurisdiction under sect. 199 of the Companies Act, 1862, to wind up an unregistered joint stock company, formed, and having its principal place of business in New Zealand, but having a branch office, agent, assets, and liabilities in England.—The pendency of a foreign liquidation does not affect the jurisdiction of the Court to make a winding-up order, in respect of the company under such liquidation, although the Court will as a matter of international comity have regard to the order of the foreign Court.—It being alleged that proceedings to wind up the company were pending in New Zealand, the Court, in order to secure the English assets until proceedings should be taken by the New Zealand liquidators to make them available for the English creditors pari passu with those in New Zealand, sanctioned the acceptance of an undertaking by the solicitor for the English agent of the company, that the English assets should remain in statu quo until the further order of the Court.—*In re Commercial Bank of India* (Law Rep. 6 Eq. 517) approved. *In re* MATHESON BROTHERS, LIMITED -　　- 27 Ch. D. 225

3. —— Foreign Company—*Jurisdiction—Companies Act, 1862* (25 & 26 Vict. c. 89), *s.* 199.] There is no jurisdiction under the Companies Act, 1862, to wind up a foreign company which has carried on business in England by means of agents, but which has no branch office of its own there. *In re* LLOYD GENERALE ITALIANO
[29 Ch. D. 219

4. —— Impossibility of carrying on Business —*Failure of Object of Company — " Just and Equitable Cause "] or Winding-up—Companies Act,* 1862, s. 79, *sub-s.* 5—*General Words in Memorandum of Association.*] The memorandum of association of a company stated that it was formed for working a German patent which had been or would be granted for manufacturing coffee from dates, and also for obtaining other patents for improvements and extensions of the said inventions or any modifications thereof or incident thereto ; and to acquire or purchase any other inventions for similar purposes, and to import and export all descriptions of produce for the purpose of food, and to acquire or lease buildings either in connection with the above-mentioned purposes or otherwise, for the purposes of the company.—The intended German patent was never granted, but the company purchased a Swedish patent, and also established works at Hamburg, where they made and sold coffee made from dates without a patent. Many of the shareholders withdrew from the company on ascertaining that the German patent could not be obtained; but the large majority of those who remained desired to continue the company, which was in solvent circumstances.—A petition having been presented by two shareholders :—*Held,* (affirming the decision of Kay, J.), that the substratum of the company had failed, and it was impossible to carry out the objects for which it was formed ; and therefore it was just and equitable that the company should be wound up,

XIX. COMPANY — WINDING-UP ORDER — *continued.*

although the petition was presented within a year from its incorporation.—The effect of general words describing the objects of a company in the memorandum of association considered. *In re* GERMAN DATE COFFEE COMPANY　20 Ch. D. 169

5. —— **Impossibility of carrying on Business** —*"Just and Equitable Cause" for Winding-up—Majority of Shareholders desirous of going on—Fraud — Companies Act, 1862, s. 79, sub-s. 5.*] Where the Court is satisfied that the subject-matter of the business for which a company was formed has substantially ceased to exist, it will make an order for winding-up the company, although the large majority of the shareholders desire to continue to carry on the company,—Therefore, where a company was established for working a gold mine in New Zealand and it turned out that the company had no title to the mine, and had no prospect of obtaining possession of it, except as to a small portion for a few months, a winding-up order was made, although there were general words in the memorandum of association enabling the company to purchase and work other mines in New Zealand, and the large majority of the shareholders wished to continue the company.—But, *semble*, the mere fact of there having been fraud in the formation of the company, or fraudulent misrepresentation in the prospectus, would not in itself be sufficient to induce the Court to make a winding-up order, because the majority of the shareholders would have power at a general meeting to waive the fraud and confirm the transactions affected by it.—The decision of Bacon, V.C., reversed. *In re* HAVEN GOLD MINING COMPANY　-　20 Ch. D. 151

6. —— **Petition —** *Costs—Withdrawal — Advertisements — Contributories — Companies Act, 1862. (25 & 26 Vict. c. 89), s. 82 — Rules of November, 1862, r. 2.*] A winding-up petition had appeared in the Court paper from time to time which had never been advertised:—*Held,* that the petition could be withdrawn without payment of the costs of a shareholder appearing to oppose. *In re* UNITED STOCK EXCHANGE, LIMITED. *Ex parte* PHILP & KIDD 28 Ch. D. 183

7. —— **Petition —** *Costs—Dismissal of Petition on Application of Petitioner—Shareholders and Creditors appearing to consent.*] Where a winding-up petition is dismissed on the application of the petitioner, shareholders and creditors appearing either to oppose or support the petition are entitled to their costs.—*In re Jablochkoff Electric Light and Power Company* (Weekly Notes, 1883, p. 189) distinguished. *In re* NACUPAI GOLD MINING COMPANY -　-　28 Ch. D. 65

8. —— **Petition—**Costs—*Rival Petitions.*] A creditor who presents a petition for winding-up in ignorance of a prior petition, is entitled to his costs up to the time when he has notice of the prior petition, but if he then proceeds, he will not be allowed his further costs ; unless he has good reason to suppose that the other petition is not bonâ fide, in which case he is justified in proceeding and may be allowed his costs. *In re* GENERAL FINANCIAL BANK　20 Ch. D. 276

9. —— **Petition—**Creditor whose Debt is dis-

XIX. COMPANY — WINDING-UP ORDER — *continued.*

puted—*Jurisdiction—Solvent Company—Injunction.*] The Court has jurisdiction to restrain by injunction a person claiming to be a creditor of a company, from presenting a petition to wind up the company, where the debt is bonâ fide disputed, and the company is solvent. CERCLE RESTAURANT CASTIGLIONE COMPANY v. LAVERY　18 Ch. D. 555 NIGER MERCHANTS COMPANY v. CAPPER 18 Ch. D. [557, n.

10. —— **Petition—**Creditor whose Debt is disputed — Evidence of Insolvency — Dismissal of Petition on Motion.] B., a dismissed servant of a company, claimed £15 for arrears of salary, and £95 damages for alleged wrongful dismissal. The company disputed both claims. B. filed a petition to wind up the company, alleging it to be insolvent, but there was no evidence of insolvency except the common statutory affidavit of the Petitioner. The company at once moved to stay proceedings on the petition, and in support of the motion filed an affidavit by their secretary shewing that the claims of the Petitioner were bonâ fide disputed, and that the company was solvent. Bacon V.C., ordered that on payment by the company of £110 into Court all proceedings should be stayed until an action to be brought by the Petitioner had been tried. The company paid the £110 into Court and appealed : —*Held,* by the Court of Appeal, that where a petition to wind up is improperly filed the Court has jurisdiction on motion to stay all proceedings under it, or to dismiss it; that the present petition was an abuse of the process of the Court, being brought to compel payment of a small debt which was bonâ fide disputed, and being unsupported by any evidence that the company was insolvent; that the petition therefore must be dismissed with costs, and the £110 returned to the company. *In re* GOLD HILL MINES 23 Ch. D. 210

11. —— **Petition—**Creditor—Debenture-holder —Trust Deed—Debenture payable to Bearer—Debenture held as Security—Inquiry as to existence of Assets—Appointment of Provisional Liquidator with Powers of Official Liquidator—Companies Act, 1862 (25 & 26 Vict. c. 89), ss. 86, 92.] A company issued debentures payable to bearer, the payment of which was secured by a deed by which the company purported to assign all their present and future property to trustees, on trust for the benefit of the debenture-holders, and covenanted with the trustees for payment of the principal and interest of the debentures. By the debentures the company agreed to pay the amount thereby secured to the bearer:—*Held,* that the holder of some of the debentures the interest on which was overdue (the debentures having been deposited with him by the original holder as security for a debt) was entitled to petition for the winding-up of the company.—*In re Uruguay Central and Hygueritas Railway Company of Monte Video* (11 Ch. D. 372) distinguished. —There being some evidence that the company had no assets beyond the property comprised in the trust deed, the Court directed an inquiry in Chambers whether the company had any and what assets not included in the deed and available for the general creditors, and referred it to

XIX. COMPANY — WINDING-UP ORDER — *continued.*

Chambers to appoint a provisional liquidator, with all the powers of an official liquidator, but the liquidator was to take no steps without the direction of the Judge in Chambers, beyond taking possession of the company's property within the jurisdiction, including their books and papers. *In re* OLATHE SILVER MINING COMPANY - 27 Ch. D. 278

12. —— Petition—*Creditor's Debt—Companies Act, 1862, ss. 80, 82—Lands Clauses Act, 1845.*] A claim against a limited company by a landowner for the amount of purchase and compensation money in respect of land taken, which has been assessed by arbitration under the provisions of the Lands Clauses Act, 1845, does not, until the title has been investigated and accepted by the company, constitute a debt in respect of which the landowner is entitled as an unpaid creditor within the Companies Act, 1862, s. 82, to apply for a winding-up order. *In re* MILFORD DOCKS COMPANY. LISTER'S PETITION 23 Ch. D. 292

13. —— Petition — *Insolvent Contributory — Trustee—Companies Act, 1867 (30 & 31 Vict. c. 131), s. 40—Period of Six Months—"Held"—Companies Act, 1862 (25 & 26 Vict. c. 89)—Bankruptcy Act, 1869 (32 & 33 Vict. c. 71), ss. 11, 15, 94, 95, 115.*] A contributory of a company may present a petition to wind up the company where his name appears on the register as the holder of shares, though a trustee may have been appointed under a liquidation petition filed by such contributory, during the period of six months mentioned in sect. 40 of the Companies Act, 1867.— The word "*held*" in such section has no technical meaning, the true meaning of the word being that the name of the contributory has been on the register as the holder of shares for the period in question. *In re* WALA WYNAAD INDIAN GOLD MINING COMPANY - 21 Ch. D. 849

14. —— Petition—*Security for Costs—Subsequent Petition by same Petitioner for Liquidation of his own Affairs.*] After the presentation and before the hearing of a winding-up petition, the petitioner filed a petition for the liquidation of his own affairs under the 125th and 126th sections of the Bankruptcy Act, 1869 (32 & 33 Vict. c. 71):—*Held*, that he must give security for costs in the winding-up petition.—*Malcolm* v. *Hodgkinson* (Law Rep. 8 Q. B. 209) and *Brocklebank* v. *King's Lynn Steamship Company* (3 C. P. D. 365) followed. *In re* CARTA PARA MINING COMPANY [19 Ch. D. 457

15. —— Previous Voluntary Winding-up.] A compulsory order for winding-up does not avoid ab initio all the proceedings under a previous resolution for voluntary winding-up. THOMAS *v.* PATENT LIGNITE COMPANY - 17 Ch. D. 250

16. —— Wishes of Creditors—*Companies Act, 1862 (25 & 26 Vict. c. 89), s. 91.*] In determining whether regard should be paid to the wishes of creditors who oppose the making of a winding-up order, the Court ought to consider not only the number of the creditors and the amount of their debts, but also the reasons which they assign for their conclusion.—The primâ facie right of an unpaid creditor of a company to a winding-

XIX. COMPANY — WINDING-UP ORDER — *continued.*

up order is rebutted when it is shewn that a large mass of other creditors oppose the making of such an order.—A creditor's winding-up petition ordered to stand over for six months upon terms similar to those imposed in *In re St. Thomas' Dock Company* (2 Ch. D. 116). *In re* GREAT WESTERN (FOREST OF DEAN) COAL CONSUMERS' COMPANY. [21 Ch. D. 769

17. —— Wishes of Creditors—*Right to a Winding-up Order ex debito justitiæ—Companies Act, 1862, s. 91.*] Although as a general rule an unpaid creditor of a company which cannot pay its debts is entitled to a winding-up order, that order will not be made when it is shewn that the petitioning creditor cannot gain anything by a winding-up order, and, à fortiori, it will not be made under those circumstances if the other creditors oppose it.—*In re Uruguay Central and Hygueritas Railway Company of Monte Video* (11 Ch. D. 372) approved.—The 91st section of the Companies Act, 1862, is not confined to cases where a winding-up order has been made, but applies also where a petition for winding-up is before the Court.—The colliery belonging to a colliery company was subject to a large mortgage payable by instalments, and all its assets had been assigned to trustees upon trust for its debenture holders, who had no present right of action against the company for the principal of their debts, which was not payable till 1885, but only for the arrears of interest, which were considerable. The colliery was not worth so much as the mortgage money, but it was worked at a profit, and the instalments of the mortgage debt were being paid, but nothing was left to pay interest to the debenture holders. There appeared, however, to be reason to think that if the business were continued, and the coal trade improved, there would be something for the debenture holders. The colliery was leasehold and liable to forfeiture if the company was wound up. A holder of debentures to a small amount presented a petition to wind up the company, the debt on the footing of which he petitioned being the arrears of interest on his debentures. A vast majority of the other debenture holders opposed the petition, and none of them supported it. Kay, J., thought the case not a proper one for making a winding-up order, but directed the petition to stand over for six months :—*Held*, on appeal, that the petition ought to be dismissed at once. *In re* CHAPEL HOUSE COLLIERY COMPANY - 24 Ch. D. 259

XX. COMPANY—VOLUNTARY WINDING-UP

1. —— General Meeting — *Poll — Mode of taking Poll — Chairman, Direction of—Companies Act, 1862, Table A, Art. 43.*] The articles of association of a company provided (in the terms of art. 43 of Table A to the Companies Act, 1862) that if at any general meeting of the company a poll should be demanded it should be taken "in such manner as the chairman shall direct."—A poll having been demanded at a meeting summoned to consider a resolution for a voluntary winding-up, the chairman directed the poll be taken then and there. It was so taken, and the resolution was carried :—*Held*, that the poll had been rightly taken.—*Reg.* v. *D'Oyly* (12 Ad. & E.

XX. COMPANY—VOLUNTARY WINDING-UP
—continued.

139) followed.—Observations on the *dicta* of Jessel, M.R., and Brett, L.J., in *In re Horbury Bridge, Coal, Iron, and Waggon Company* (11 Ch. D. 109, 114). *In re* CHILLINGTON IRON COMPANY - - - 29 Ch. D. 159

2. —— Special Resolution *requiring Confirmation—Resolution appointing Liquidator—Notice of proposed Resolution—Necessity for—Companies Act,* 1862 (25 & 26 *Vict.* c. 89), *ss.* 67, 133, *sub-s.* 2, 141.] A resolution appointing a liquidator is operative only when there is an effective resolution to wind up. — Where therefore a special resolution to wind up voluntarily which requires confirmation, has been passed at the first meeting, although it is unobjectionable to pass at the same meeting a resolution appointing a liquidator, the latter resolution by itself can have no effect; and if at the subsequent meeting the latter is rejected it is immaterial that the principal resolution, i.e. to wind up, has been confirmed—nor is it possible to fall back upon the resolution appointing a liquidator which was passed at the first meeting and treat it as binding.—The chairman of a general meeting has *primâ facie* authority to decide all incidental questions which arise at such meeting, and necessarily require decision at the time, and the entry by him in the minute book of the result of a poll, or of his decision of all such questions, although not conclusive, is *primâ facie* evidence of that result, or of the correctness of that decision, and the onus of displacing that evidence is thrown on those who impeach the entry.—Where the chairman at a confirmation meeting disallowed certain votes which had been given against the confirmation of a resolution passed at the first meeting appointing a liquidator, the effect of such disallowance being to confirm such resolution, and he made an entry in the minute book that such resolution had been confirmed, the Court in the absence of evidence that the votes were improperly disallowed, declined to question the decision of the chairman. But, having regard to the unsatisfactory state of the evidence, the Court of Appeal in the interest of all parties by its own order confirmed the appointment of the liquidator. *In re* INDIAN ZOEDONE COMPANY 26 Ch. D. 70

XXI. COMPANY — INJUNCTION (and LEAVE TO PROCEED).

1. —— Execution — *Companies Act,* 1862 (25 & 26 *Vict.* c. 89, *ss.* 85, 163)—*Forbearance by Creditor.*] A creditor of a mining company made repeated applications for payment through the year 1881, and on the 21st of December obtained a payment on account, and being unable to obtain more, he, on the 28th of December, issued a writ. On the 4th of January, 1882, a paid-up shareholder in the company who was under considerable liability as a surety for the company, presented a petition to wind it up, setting out a balance sheet which shewed that the assets greatly exceeded the liabilities, but not alleging as a fact that they did so, stating that the company was unable to pay its debts, and that it was just and equitable that it should be wound up. On the 6th of January the creditor recovered final judgment without notice of the winding-up petition, and on the following day issued execu-

XXI. COMPANY — INJUNCTION (and LEAVE TO PROCEED)—*continued.*

tion. On the 14th of January the petition came on to be heard and was supported by creditors, and a winding-up order was made. The creditor then applied for leave to go on with the execution :—*Held,* by Bacon, V.C., that leave ought to be granted :—*Held,* by the Court of Appeal, that the petition could not be treated as a petition collusively presented on behalf of a solvent company for the purpose of defeating the execution, for that the balance sheet could not be treated as proving the company to be solvent, and the Petitioner, though not legally a creditor, was virtually such, and by amending the petition by joining one of the supporting creditors it might have been made a creditor's petition; and consequently that leave to proceed with the execution ought not to be given :—*Held,* also, that leave ought not to be given on the ground that the creditor had given indulgence to the company, as he had never given time to the company in the sense of binding himself not to sue, but had merely abstained from suing :—Whether the having given indulgence to a company is a sufficient reason for allowing a creditor to continue his proceedings notwithstanding a winding-up, *quære.*—*Ex parte Railway Steel and Plant Company, In re Taylor* (8 Ch. D. 183) and *In re Richards & Co.* (11 Ch. D. 676) doubted. *In re* VRON COLLIERY COMPANY 20 Ch. D. 442

2. —— Execution—*Companies Act,* 1862 (25 & 26 *Vict.* c. 89), *s.* 163.] Where an execution against the goods of a company which is being wound up is avoided by the Companies Act, 1862, s. 163, it is avoided altogether, and the creditor retains no interest under it. *In re* ARTISTIC COLOUR PRINTING COMPANY. *Ex parte* FOURDRINIER - - - 21 Ch. D. 510

—— Injunction against winding-up petition [18 Ch. D. 555
See COMPANY—WINDING-UP ORDER, 9.

—— Staying proceedings—Delay 17 Ch. D. 600
See COMPANY — UNREGISTERED COMPANY. 7.

XXII. COMPANY—LIQUIDATOR.

1. —— Official—*Affidavit embracing distinct Cases against different Parties—Affidavit of Documents by Official Liquidator—Companies Act,* 1862, s. 165.] The official liquidator of a company applied under sect. 165 of the Companies Act, 1862, to make a number of gentlemen, some of whom were and others had been directors, responsible for acts of misfeasance. The alleged acts were 107 in number. E. had been a director only during the period in which the first eleven of these acts were done, and it was not sought to make him liable in respect of any others. The liquidator filed an affidavit of 1150 folios, including all the cases. E., who appeared alone, applied for an order that the liquidator might state what paragraphs he intended to read against E. It appeared that E.'s solicitor had borrowed the affidavit and was, on his own shewing, able to make out what parts of the affidavit affected E. :—*Held,* affirming the decision of Chitty, J., that E.'s application must be refused, for that although the Court would interfere if the cases against different parties were mixed up together

XXII. COMPANY—LIQUIDATOR—continued.

in a way which was oppressive, a Defendant must, as a general rule, ascertain for himself what part of the Plaintiff's evidence affects him, and that there were no circumstances in the present case to take it out of the general rule.— E. applied that the official liquidator might be ordered to make the usual affidavit as to documents in his possession :—*Held*, affirming the decision of Chitty. J., that such an order ought not to be made, for that the official liquidator, being an officer of the Court, is not, even in proceedings under sect. 165, in the position of an ordinary litigant, and will not in the absence of special circumstances, be required to make an affidavit as to documents in his possession, though he is bound to produce to the adverse litigant the documents which the latter requires to see. *In re* MUTUAL SOCIETY - - **22 Ch. D. 714**

2. —— Official—*Appointment.*] An official liquidator ought not to be appointed on the hearing of a winding-up petition, it being now the settled practice to direct a reference to Chambers for that purpose. *In re* GENERAL FINANCIAL BANK - **20 Ch. D. 276**

3. —— Official—*Assignment by Official Liquidator of all the Property of a Company—Claims against Directors for Misfeasance—Companies Act, 1862, s. 95, sub-s. 3.*] A company being in course of winding-up, an arrangement was entered into with the sanction of the Court, in pursuance of which the official liquidators assigned to W., in the most general terms, all the estate, property and effects of the company which the liquidators had power to dispose of, in consideration of certain payments to be made by W., and which were duly made. W. entered into the arrangement on behalf of E., an officer of the company. After this the liquidators brought forward claims against E. and some of the directors, alleging that they had improvidently sold property of the company at an undervalue, and seeking to make them liable for the loss, and also alleging that E. and some of the directors had purchased for the company certain property, and concealed the fact that it had shortly before been bought by E. for little more than half the amount, and seeking to make them liable for the difference. The existence of these claims was not known at the time when the above arrangement was entered into. E. took out a summons to restrain the liquidators from prosecuting these claims without his consent, which application was refused by Hall, V.C.:— *Held*, on appeal, that claims of this nature were "things in action" of the company within the meaning of the Companies Act, 1862, s. 95, sub-s. 3, and could be assigned by the official liquidator, that they were assigned by the deed, and that E. was entitled to the order which he asked, but that the order ought to be made without prejudice to any application which the liquidators might make to the Vice-Chancellor to enforce the claims, in case they should be successful in the proceedings to set aside the arrangement. *In re* PARK GATE WAGGON WORKS COMPANY - - - **17 Ch. D. 234**

4. —— Official—*Remuneration—Internal Litigation.*] Where the assets of a company in compulsory liquidation are insufficient for payment

XXII. COMPANY—LIQUIDATOR—continued.

of the costs of the winding-up, the official liquidator is not entitled to any remuneration. *In re* DRONFIELD SILKSTONE COAL COMPANY (No. 2) [**23 Ch. D. 511**

—— Costs of official liquidator **21 Ch. D. 381** *See* COMPANY—COSTS.˜ 1.

—— Payment of rates—Beneficial occupation [**23 Ch. D. 500; 28 Ch. D. 470, 474** *See* COMPANY—RATES. 1, 2, 3.

XXIII. COMPANY—CONTRIBUTORY.

1. —— Husband in his Wife's Name.] S. (a Parsee merchant) applied for 300 shares in the London, Bombay, and Mediterranean Bank, 100 in his own name and 200 in the name of his wife, M., paying the deposit on the whole 300 out of his own moneys. The company allotted the shares accordingly, and S. subscribed the memorandum and articles of association on M.'s behalf as well as his own, and paid all calls upon all the shares. S. afterwards sold and transferred 140 of the shares allotted to M., executing the transfers for her, or in her name. All these transactions took place without M.'s knowledge.—In 1866 the company was ordered to be wound up, and at that date the name of "M. the wife of S." was on the register as a past holder of 140 shares, and the then holder of sixty shares—S. died shortly afterwards, and the name of M. was placed upon the A list of contributories in respect of sixty shares, and upon the B list in respect of 140 shares.— M. had no separate estate.—Upon an application by the liquidator to have the B list rectified by placing thereon the names of S.'s executors instead of the name of M. :—*Held*, that the company having accepted the wife as a shareholder without any misrepresentation or concealment on the part of the husband, his estate was not liable, and the company were not entitled to any rectification of the list. *In re* LONDON, BOMBAY, AND MEDITERRANEAN BANK **18 Ch. D. 581**

2. —— Insolvent — *Jurisdiction — Application by Stranger—Companies Act, 1862 (25 & 26 Vict. c. 89), s. 77.*] R., a contributory, became bankrupt. After this he took out a summons asking that the official liquidator might be directed to take proceedings against a director to recover sums of money alleged to have been improperly received by him. Fry, J., made an order that on R.'s depositing £100 the liquidator should take the opinion of counsel on the case alleged against the director, and on obtaining his opinion should apply to the Judge for directions. Two contributories and creditors who had liberty to attend proceedings appealed from this order :—*Held*, by the Court of Appeal, that R., having become bankrupt, was a stranger to the company—that there was no jurisdiction to make any order on his application, and that the order must therefore be discharged without any regard to the question whether it was right or wrong on the merits. *In re* CAPE BRETON COMPANY - **19 Ch. D. 77**

3. —— Insolvent—*Winding-up of Company after and pending the Liquidation—Order of Discharge—Subsequent Call—Contributory—Provable Debt or Liability—Companies Act, 1862 (25 & 26 Vict. c. 89), ss. 75, 77—Bankruptcy Act, 1869 (32 & 33 Vict. c. 71), s. 31.*] The liability in respect

XXIII. COMPANY—CONTRIBUTORY—*contd.*

of calls of a liquidating member of a company where the liquidation proceedings commence prior to the winding-up of the company, and are pending at the time of the winding-up, is a debt or liability which is not "incapable of being fairly estimated," and which is therefore provable in the liquidation. When, therefore, under those circumstances, a company winding up has failed to carry in a proof in the liquidation proceedings of a member of the company for calls, and the liquidating member obtains his discharge, he cannot afterwards be placed on the list of contributories. —*Furdoonjee's Case* (3 Ch. D. 264) discussed and not followed. *In re* MERCANTILE MUTUAL MARINE INSURANCE ASSOCIATION　　-　**25 Ch. D. 415**

4.　—— **Jurisdiction**—*Adjustment of Rights of Contributories*—*Companies Act*, 1862 (*25 & 26 Vict. c. 89*), s. 109.] Under sect. 109 of the Companies Act, 1862, the Court has jurisdiction to adjust the rights *inter se* of contributories; it cannot enforce equities which persons who, as tortfeasors (being also contributories), have been ordered to pay money under sect. 165, may have against other persons, who happen also to be contributories, to compel them to make good the money so ordered to be paid. *In re* ALEXANDRA PALACE COMPANY
　　　　　　　　　　　　[23 Ch. D. 297

XXIV. COMPANY—PROOF.

1.　—— **Directors' Fees**—*Companies Act*, 1862 (*25 & 26 Vict. c. 89*), s. 38, sub-s. 7—*Priorities of Debts.*] In a company where directors were obliged to be members:—*Held*, that a director's unpaid fees were debts due to him in his character of member, and to be postponed to outside creditors. *In re* LEICESTER CLUB AND COUNTY RACECOURSE COMPANY. *Ex parte* CANNON　-　**30 Ch. D. 629**

2.　—— **Fire Insurance**—*Fires before and after Winding-up Order*—*Right of Proof*—*Companies Act*, 1862, s. 158—*Gen. Ord. November*, 1862, r. 25— *Bankruptcy Act*, 1869, s. 31—*Bankruptcy Rules*, 1870, r. 27—*Judicature Act*, 1875, s. 10.] The holder of a fire policy issued by a fire insurance company is entitled, upon the company being ordered to be wound up, to prove in the winding-up for the full amount of loss covered by the policy and sustained by him through a fire which has occurred in the course of the winding-up although after the date of the winding-up order, and whether the time limited for sending in claims in the winding-up has expired or not.—*A fortiori*, a claim on account of a fire which has occurred after the presentation of the petition but before the order to wind up, is entitled to proof. *In re* NORTHERN COUNTIES OF ENGLAND FIRE INSURANCE COMPANY. MACFARLANE'S CLAIM　　　**17 Ch. D. 337**

3.　—— **Payments without Notice of Winding-up**—*Companies Act*, 1862 (*25 & 26 Vict. c. 89*), ss. 84, 153.] In consideration of moneys paid in at a distant foreign branch of a banking company whose head office was in London, drafts on the head office were given after presentation of a petition to wind up the company, and appointment of a provisional liquidator in England, but before (from want of direct telegraphic communication) any notice of the stoppage of the bank in London had been received at the foreign branch, and before the date of the winding-up order:—*Held*, that the

XXIV. COMPANY—PROOF—*continued.*

contract which was entered into by the officers of the foreign branch on behalf of the company without any notice of the winding-up proceedings, and therefore before revocation of their authority, was not invalidated by the Companies Act, 1862, s. 153; and accordingly that the creditors in respect of such transaction were not entitled to have their money refunded as on the footing of a void transaction, but merely to prove for the amount under the winding-up *pari passu* with the other creditors.—As between the holders for value of the drafts and the persons by whom the consideration was paid, the holders were held entitled to prove. *In re* ORIENTAL BANK CORPORATION. *Ex parte* GUILLEMIN　**28 Ch. D. 634**
—— Servants' wages　-　-　**16 Ch. D. 373**
　　　See COMPANY—PREFERENTIAL DEBTS.

XXV. COMPANY—PREFERENTIAL DEBTS.

The Act 46 & 47 *Vict. c.* 28 (*Companies Act*, 1883), *which came into operation on the 1st of September*, 1883, *enacts*:

Sect. 4. *In the distribution of the assets of any company being wound up under the Companies Acts*, 1862 *and* 1867, *there shall be paid in priority to other debts*,—

(a.) *All wages or salary of any clerk or servant in respect of service rendered to the company during four months before the commencement of the winding-up not exceeding £50; and*

(b.) *All wages of any labourer or workman in respect of services rendered to the company during two months before the commencement of the winding-up.*

Sect. 5. *The foregoing debts shall rank equally among themselves, and shall be paid in full, unless the assets of the company are insufficient to meet them, in which case they shall abate in equal proportions between themselves.*

Sect. 6. *Subject to the retention of such sums as may be necessary for the cost of administration or otherwise, the liquidator or liquidators or official liquidator shall discharge the foregoing debts forthwith, so far as the assets of the company are and will be sufficient to meet them, as and when such assets come into the hands of such liquidator or liquidators or official liquidator.*

—— **Wages**—*Rule in Bankruptcy*—32 & 33 *Vict. c.* 71, s. 32.] The rule in bankruptcy that servants' wages shall be paid in priority to all other debts, is, by sect. 10 of the Judicature Act, 1875, extended to windings-up.— *In re* Albion *Steel and Wire Company* (7 Ch. D. 547) followed. *In re* ASSOCIATION OF LAND FINANCIERS
　　　　　　　　　　　　[16 Ch. D. 373

XXVI. COMPANY—SET-OFF.

1.　—— **Assignment of Claim**—*Claim against Company assigned to Debtor to Company and again assigned by him*—*Judicature Act*, 1875, s. 10— *Rules of Court*, 1875, *Order XIX.*, r. 3.] A company in 1877 was ordered to be wound up. In 1879 H. took assignments for value of the debts proved by and certified to be due to several creditors. On the 23rd of January, 1880, the liquidator took out a summons under sect. 165 of the Companies Act, 1862, that H., who had been a director, might be ordered to pay £2000, the

XXVI. COMPANY—SET-OFF—*continued.*.

nominal value of certain shares in the company received by him from the promoter, or to make compensation on the ground of misfeasance. On the 25th of February, 1880, H. assigned the above debts to T. for value, T. knowing nothing of the claims against H., and notice of the assignment was at once given to the liquidator. In July, 1880, an order was made on the summons for H. to pay £2000 to the liquidator. On the 4th of August, 1881, an order was made giving the liquidator liberty to declare a dividend of 11s. in the pound on the debts of the company. T. applied for payment of this dividend on the debts assigned to him, but the liquidator claimed to retain the dividend by way of set-off against the £2000:—*Held* (affirming the decision of Kay, J.), that the liquidator had no such right of set-off, and that T. was entitled to receive the dividend. *In re* MILAN TRAMWAYS COMPANY. *Ex parte* THEYS　　　22 Ch. D. 122; 25 Ch. D. 587

2. —— **Contract before Winding-up**—*Goods delivered after Commencement of Winding-up—Companies Act,* 1862 (25 & 26 Vict. c. 89).] In an action by a limited company in the course of compulsory winding-up by the Court for the price of goods supplied to the Defendants by the company after, but in pursuance of a contract entered into before, the commencement of the winding-up, i.e., the presentation of the petition for winding-up, such contract not being a sale of specific goods:—*Held,* that the Defendants could not set off a debt from the Plaintiffs to themselves incurred prior to the commencement of the winding-up. INCE HALL ROLLING MILLS COMPANY *v.* DOUGLAS FORGE COMPANY　-　-　8 Q. B. D. 179

XXVII. COMPANY—SECURED CREDITOR.

1. —— **Execution Creditor**—*Judicature Act,* 1875, s. 10—*Bankruptcy Act,* 1869, s. 87—*Companies Act,* 1862, ss. 85, 87.] A creditor having recovered judgment against a company, the sheriff, on the 10th of July, 1880, seized the goods of the company under a fi. fa. for £89. On the 14th of July a winding-up petition was presented, and on the 15th of July an order was made restraining all further proceedings in the action until the petition was disposed of or withdrawn. The sheriff thereupon withdrew from possession. On the 30th of July a winding-up order was made. On the 31st of July the creditor applied for leave to enforce his judgment, and the value of the goods seized being much greater than the amount of the debt, an order was made by Malins, V.C., that the liquidator should pay the amount of the debt:—*Held,* on appeal, that this order was right.—Sect. 87 of the Bankruptcy Act, 1869, which deprives execution creditors of the fruits of the execution where the sheriff has notice of a bankruptcy within fourteen days after sale, is not made applicable to the winding-up of companies by the Judicature Act, 1875, s. 10.—*In re Richards & Co.* (11 Ch. D. 676) approved.—*In re Printing and Numerical Registering Company* (8 Ch. D. 535) overruled. *In re* WITHERNSEA BRICKWORKS　　16 Ch. D. 337

2. —— **Failure of Security**—*Creditors' Right to prove*— *Companies Act,* 1862 (25 & 26 Vict. c. 89), s. 107—*Judicature Act,* 1875 (38 & 39 Vict. c. 77), s. 10—*Bankruptcy Rules,* 1870, rr. 99–102.]

XXVII. COMPANY — SECURED CREDITOR — *continued.*

A creditor of a company, believing himself to be fully secured by the hypothecation under the hand of the managing director of a call on the company's shares, made no claim for his debt in the winding-up. The security turning out defective, by reason of the call moneys having been paid away partly before and partly since the letter of hypothecation:—*Held,* that the creditor, never having assessed the value of his security, was not prevented by the operation of sect. 10 of the Judicature Act. 1875, and rule 101 of the Bankruptcy Rules, 1870, from coming in and proving for the unsecured balance of his debt, on the terms of his disturbing no past dividend. *In re* KIT HILL TUNNEL. *Ex parte* WILLIAMS　　16 Ch. D. 590

XXVIII. COMPANY—DISTRESS.

1. —— **Apportionment of Rent**—*Apportionment Act,* 1870 (33 & 34 Vict. c. 35).] Where a company in liquidation continued in the possession of leasehold premises for the purpose of carrying on their business:—*Held,* that the rent of the premises must be apportioned under the Act 33 & 34 Vict. c. 35, the landlord of the premises being entitled to prove jointly with the other creditors for so much rent as became due up to the date of the presentation of the petition for winding up, when a provisional liquidator was appointed, and being entitled to distrain for the full rent due after that day.—*Quære,* whether there would be any such apportionment in a case where the landlord sought to proceed by re-entry instead of by distress. *In re* SOUTH KENSINGTON CO-OPERATIVE SOCIETY -　-　17 Ch. D. 161

2. —— **Collateral Security**—*Companies Act,* 1862 (25 & 26 Vict. c. 89), ss. 85, 163.] The rule that a landlord will not be allowed to realize a distress for rent levied on the goods of a company between the presentation of a winding-up petition and the making of a winding-up order, if he is a creditor entitled to prove in the winding-up for the rent distrained for:—*Held,* not to apply to a case in which the company were not tenants of the landlord (but undertenants of his lessee), and the landlord had accepted as collateral security for the overdue rent a promissory note of the company upon which he was entitled to prove in the winding-up:—*Held,* that in such a case the landlord ought to be allowed to realize his distress. *In re* CARRIAGE CO-OPERATIVE SUPPLY ASSOCIATION. *Ex parte* CLEMENCE 23 Ch. D. 154

3. —— **Commencement of Winding-up** — *Voluntary Winding-up—Compulsory Winding-up—Appointment of Liquidator—*25 & 26 Vict. c. 89, ss. 87, 163—*Judicature Act,* 1875 (38 & 39 Vict. c. 77), s. 10.] After an extraordinary resolution for the voluntary winding-up of a company had been passed, but before a liquidator had been appointed, a landlord distrained for rent due from the company before the resolution was passed. Immediately afterwards an action was commenced on behalf of the debenture holders of the company, in whose favour the company had made a mortgage of its assets, and the company moved for and obtained in this action an order to restrain the landlords from proceeding with their distress. A receiver appointed in the action thereupon

XXVIII. COMPANY—DISTRESS—continued.

took possession of the chattels distrained, and by arrangement a sum of money was set apart to meet the claim of the landlords if the Court should hold them entitled to the benefit of their distress. Subsequently an order for the compulsory winding-up of the company was made which did not refer to the proceedings in the voluntary winding-up:—Held, by Malins, V.C., that the distress was good; first, because at the time when it was made there was no liquidator to interfere; and secondly, because the voluntary winding-up was superseded by the compulsory winding-up, and ordered the rent to be paid to the landlords out of the proceeds of the chattels.—Held, on appeal, that the distress was avoided by sect. 163 of the Companies Act, 1862, unless sufficient grounds could be shewn for inducing the Court to exercise the discretionary power given by sect. 87, and that the circumstances of the case did not furnish any such ground, the case not being one where the landlords could not prove for rent.— The making a compulsory order for winding up a company does not avoid ab initio all the proceedings under a previous resolution for voluntary winding-up.—The 10th section of the Judicature Act, 1875, does not import into winding-up the 34th section of the Bankruptcy Act, 1869, which gives a landlord priority for a year's rent. THOMAS v. PATENT LIONITE COMPANY

[17 Ch. D. 250

4. —— Mine.] E. demised a colliery to a limited company for twenty-five years from January, 1858. The company mortgaged it by underlease. In 1878 an agreement was come to between E. and the company for a new lease of the colliery and of the mines under 163 acres of adjoining land, these latter mines to be worked by outstroke. The company then brought plant and machinery on the 163 acres, sunk trial pits, and found coal, but no new lease was granted. On the 28th of January, 1880, the mortgagees took possession of the colliery, but did not interfere with the 163 acres. On the 31st of January, 1880, a petition was presented to wind up the company, on which an order was made. The liquidator did not take possession either of the colliery or of the 163 acres, or the minerals under them, nor did he take any steps to give the demised property up to E. The plant and machinery brought on the 163 acres remained there. In May, 1880, the liquidator had the whole plant and machinery, both on the colliery and on the 163 acres, valued, with a view to a sale of these chattels to the mortgagees, that they might sell the property as a going concern, but this purchase by the mortgagees was not carried into effect. In May, 1881, the liquidator advertised the whole plant and machinery for sale. On the 30th of May, 1881, E. took out a summons for leave to distrain on the plant and machinery on the 163 acres, or to have the proceeds paid to him. In June, 1881, the plant and machinery were sold. In January, 1882, Kay, J., made an order on the summons that the liquidator should pay to E. all the rent accrued since the commencement of the winding-up:—Held, on appeal, that no case has gone the length of deciding that a landlord is entitled to distrain for or be paid in full rent accrued since the commencement

XXVIII. COMPANY—DISTRESS—continued.

of the winding-up, where the liquidator has done nothing except abstain from trying to get rid of the property of which the company is lessee, and that the facts that the liquidator left the company's plant and machinery where he found them, that he had them valued for sale in May, 1880, and that he took no steps to surrender the company's interest in the colliery and the 163 acres, did not entitle the landlord to distrain or to be paid in full, and that the summons ought to have been dismissed. In re OAK PITS COLLIERY COMPANY   -   -   - 21 Ch. D. 322

5. —— Mine—Power to distrain and stop working—Payment of full Rent.] The owner of a coal mine leased to a company, having power to distrain for rent in arrear and to stop the working of the mine, gave notice to the liquidator requiring payment of a half-year's rent which became due after the winding-up of the company, or that the working should be stopped. The liquidator neither paid the rent nor stopped the working:— Held, upon summons by the lessor for leave to distrain, that the liquidator having elected to continue the working for the advantage of the company, must pay the full rent out of the first assets. In re SILKSTONE AND DODWORTH COAL AND IRON COMPANY   -   17 Ch. D. 158

6. —— Mortgage—Stay of Action—Interest on Mortgage Debt.] Mortgagees having a right of distress to enforce payment of interest will be allowed to distrain after a winding-up for interest accrued while the liquidators were in possession, but not for arrears accrued before the winding-up. In re BROWN, BAYLEY, & DIXON. Ex parte ROBERTS AND WRIGHT   -   18 Ch. D. 649

XXIX. COMPANY—RATES.

1. —— Beneficial Occupation — Voluntary Winding-up—Poor's and Local Board of Health Rates—Summons for Payment in full dismissed.] Where the occupation by the liquidator of the property of a company in liquidation had not been beneficial, an application for payment in full of poor's rates and Local Board of Health rates made after the liquidation commenced was refused. In re WATSON, KIPLING, & Co.   -   23 Ch. D. 500

2. —— Beneficial Occupation—Winding-up— Business carried on by the Liquidator.] An hotel company was wound up under an order of the Court, and the liquidator was directed to sell the hotel, but with liberty to carry on the business till the sale, so as to sell it as a going concern. The liquidator accordingly carried on the business in the hotel, but made no profit by it. Shortly after the commencement of the winding-up a poor-rate was made, and the overseers claimed payment of the rate from the liquidator in respect of his occupation of the hotel:—Held (affirming the decree of the Vice-Chancellor of the county palatine of Lancaster) that the rate must be paid in full.—In re West Hartlepool Iron Company (34 L. T. (N.S.) 568), and In re Watson, Kipling, & Co. (23 Ch. D. 500), distinguished. In re INTERNATIONAL MARINE HYDROPATHIC COMPANY   -   -   - 28 Ch. D. 470

3. —— Beneficial Occupation—Winding-up— Business Premises, Occupation of, by Liquidator.] A company was being wound up under

XXIX. COMPANY—RATES—*continued.*

supervision, the liquidation commencing in 1882. The liquidator did not keep the concern in full work, but remained in occupation of the business premises for the purpose of carrying out some pending contracts, finishing a quantity of unfinished articles, and storing and keeping in order a quantity of completed articles with a view to selling them. In March, 1883, a rating authority made a rate for 1883 on all the property within the district. The liquidator allowed the time for appealing against the assessment to go by. The rating authority applied to the Court for payment of the rate in full:—*Held*, that as the liquidator had from the commencement of the winding-up occupied the property for the purposes of the company, and with a view to acquiring gain or avoiding loss to the company, the rate ought to be paid in full.—Whether, in order to entitle the rating authority to be paid in full, it is necessary for the liquidator to have any more beneficial occupation of the property than is required under the ordinary law as to rating, *quære.* The test in *In re West Hartlepool Iron Company* (34 L. T. (N.S.) 568) doubted.—Where the liquidator, being in possession, does not appeal against the assessment, the Court will not refuse to order payment of the rate in full on the ground of its being too high, except perhaps in extreme cases. *In re* NATIONAL ARMS AND AMMUNITION COMPANY

[**28 Ch. D. 474**

XXX. COMPANY—DISTRIBUTION OF ASSETS.

1. —— **Withdrawal of Members—***Winding-up —Payment out of " existing Moneys"—Applicability of Rules to Winding-up.*] One of the rules of a mutual loan society permitted that members who wished to withdraw should be entitled to have their money repaid, but such payments were to be made solely out of moneys existing at the time in a special fund, and they were to be repaid in rotation according to the date of their notices of withdrawal. The company being wound up :—*Held*, that the rule as to withdrawing members was only applicable to the company as a going concern, and that the members who had given notice before the winding-up had no priority of those who had given no notice. *In re* MUTUAL SOCIETY

[**24 Ch. D. 425, n.**

2. —— **Withdrawal of Members—***Winding-up —Construction of Rule "provided the funds permit"—Priorities in Winding-up.*] The rules of a benefit building society allowed any investing member to withdraw " provided the funds permit," upon giving notice; and declared that " no further liabilities shall be incurred by the society till such member has been repaid." The society was ordered to be wound up and the assets were insufficient to pay everybody :—*Held*, affirming the decision of the Court of Appeal, that those investing members who had given notice of withdrawal and whose notices had expired before the winding-up began, were entitled to be paid out of the assets (after the outside creditors) in priority to those members who had not given notice of withdrawal, notwithstanding the fact that between the giving of the notices and the winding-up there never were any funds for payment. *In re* BLACKBURN BENEFIT BUILDING SOCIETY. WALTON v. EDGE **24 Ch. D. 421 ; 10 App. Cas. 33**

XXX. COMPANY—DISTRIBUTION OF ASSETS —*continued.*

3. —— Withdrawal of **Members**—*Winding-up —Mutual Loan Society—Payment out of Special Fund — Applicability of Rules to Winding-up.*] The rules of an unlimited mutual loan society provided that a separate fund should be formed by the subscriptions of members joining in each year, which subscriptions might, with the consent of the directors, be paid in advance. The accounts of each fund were to be kept distinct, and the members were to receive advances called " appropriations," out of the accumulations of the particular fund to which they subscribed. The appropriations were to be repaid by instalments extending over twenty years. Members might withdraw on giving notice, and were in that case entitled to a return of their subscriptions, together with payment of the bonuses declared in respect of their shares, such payments to be made in the order of the dates of their notices, and only out of moneys received after the date of their notices in repayment of appropriations.—When appropriations had been made to all members of a fund, or before that under certain circumstances, the fund was to be declared closed and the accumulations were to be divided among the continuing members of the fund.—The company was wound up voluntarily, and the liquidator applied for the direction of the Court as to the distribution of the assets among the members, there being no outside creditors.—There were four classes of members whose interests were in dispute :—1. Members who had given notice of withdrawal before the closing of their funds, and before the commencement of the winding-up.—2. Members who had given notice of withdrawal after the closing of their funds, but before the commencement of the winding-up.—3. Continuing members who had paid subscriptions in advance. — 4. Continuing members who had not paid any subscriptions in advance.—*Held*, by Kay, J., that the provision for the repayment of withdrawing members out of the particular fund ceased to apply on the winding-up of the company, and that those members who had given notice of withdrawal before the commencement of the winding-up had no priority over the continuing members :—*Held*, also, that the continuing members who had paid their subscriptions in advance had no priority over the other members :—But, *held*, by the Court of Appeal, that, according to the true construction of the articles, members who had given notice of withdrawal before the closing of their fund and before the commencement of the winding-up had a charge on the repayments of appropriations belonging to their particular funds; that such charge did not cease on the closing of the fund or on the winding-up, and that they were therefore entitled to be paid in full out of such repayments in priority to all other members.—*In re Blackburn and District Benefit Building Society* (24 Ch. D. 421; 10 App. Cas. 33) followed.—*In re Mutual Society* (24 Ch. D. 425, n.) distinguished. *In re* ALLIANCE SOCIETY　-　-　**28 Ch. D. 559**

XXXI. COMPANY—RECONSTRUCTION.

—— Dissentient Member — *Winding-up — Right of dissentient Member to inspect before going into Arbitration—Companies Act, 1862, ss. 161,*

XXXI. COMPANY—RECONSTRUCTION—*contd.*

162.] A banking company being in the course of voluntary winding-up for the purpose of reconstruction, one of the members having been, with the others, offered 5s. in the pound for her holding in the old company, gave notice to arbitrate under the 161st section, as a dissentient. She then claimed the right to examine the books of the company in order to see whether it would be better for her to accept the offer of 5s. or go on with the arbitration.—Application refused, with costs of adjournment into Court. *In re* GLAMORGANSHIRE BANKING COMPANY. MORGAN'S CASE
　　　　　　　　　　　　　[28 Ch. D. 620

XXXII. COMPANY—COST-BOOK COMPANY.

1. —— Business never commenced—*Mine— Jurisdiction of High Court—Stannaries Court— Companies Act,* 1862, *ss.* 81, 116.] The words " engaged in working" mines in the 81st section of the Companies Act, 1862, mean, " is or has been engaged in working," or " now or formerly engaged in working" mines in Cornwall, and do not apply to a case where the company, although they have purchased a mine in Cornwall, have not begun to work it.—Where, therefore, a company was formed to purchase mines in " Cornwall or elsewhere in England," and contracted to purchase a right to have a lease of a mine in Cornwall, but never acquired the lease or began to work the mine :—*Held,* that the High Court of Justice had jurisdiction to make a winding-up order.—*Re East Botallack Consolidated Mining Company* (34 Beav. '82) disapproved of. *In re* SILVER VALLEY MINES -　　- 18 Ch. D. 472

2. —— Delay— *Mine — Partner — Claim — Lying-by.*] At a meeting of the partners in a cost-book mine held in 1874, it was stated that the mine was £2003 in debt, and a call of £25 was made upon each of the six shares in the mine. Two of the partners did not pay this call, and were in arrear for other calls. At subsequent meetings in June, 1874, the shares of these partners were declared [to be forfeited. These two partners took no steps as to the mine until July, 1879, when they made a claim, and in September, 1880, they brought an action, alleging that the shares had not been regularly forfeited, and claiming to be still partners. It appeared that the mine was in debt in 1878 :—*Held,* that even assuming the shares not to have been regularly forfeited, the Plaintiffs, under the circumstances, could not, after lying-by for more than six years, successfully assert their claim to be partners.— *Clarke* v. *Hart* (6 H. L. C. 633) distinguished. RULE v. JEWELL -　　-　　18 Ch. D. 660

3. —— Inspection of Documents—*Winding-up Petition—Stannaries Court—*18 & 19 *Vict. c.* 32, *s.* 22.] The practice of the Stannaries Court is the same as that of the High Court of Justice, that the mere fact of a winding-up petition is not enough to justify an order for inspection of books. But if grounds are shewn, the petition may properly be ordered to stand over to allow the petitioner to enforce his right as a shareholder to inspection.— The right of inspection under the 22nd section of the Stannaries Act, 1855, is personal to the shareholder, and does not extend to his solicitors or agents. *In re* WEST DEVON GREAT CONSOLS MINE
　　　　　　　　　　　　　[27 Ch. D. 106

XXXII. COMPANY—COST-BOOK COMPANY— *continued.*

4. —— Retiring Shareholder — *Mine —Contribution.*] In a company formed on the cost-book system the practice had been for a shareholder to be at liberty to retire on the terms that if the company was solvent he received from the company a sum of money equally to his rateable proportion of the excess of the assets above the liabilities, but if the company was insolvent he paid to the company his rateable proportion of the excess of the liabilities above the assets... In every case in which a shareholder had retired when the liabilities were in excess of the assets the purser in calculating the value of the assets had entered all the arrears of calls as good debts, and the shareholder retired on paying only his proportionate part of the excess of the liabilities over the assets according to the number of shares, without regard to the solvency or insolvency of the other shareholders.—C. gave notice to retire in November, 1879, but no account was made out shewing what he was to pay. In March, 1880, an order was made to wind up the company. The liquidator, in 1882, made out an account shewing what C. was to pay, and in estimating the assets omitted all arrears of calls owing by insolvent shareholders, and then calculated C.'s contribution by dividing the excess of liabilities over assets rateably among C. and the other solvent shareholders. The Vice-Warden of the Stannaries held that this was correct, and ordered payment by C. of the amount with which he was thus charged :—*Held,* on appeal, that this decision was correct in principle, and that the fact that on all previous occasions the assets had been reckoned without any allowance for the insolvency of persons owing arrears of calls, and the contribution of the retiring shareholder ascertained without reference to the insolvency of any of the continuing shareholders, was not sufficient evidence of an agreement among the shareholders that the contribution of a retiring shareholder should be calculated on that footing.—The course of practice followed by an officer of a company is not so strong evidence of an agreement sanctioning that practice as a course of practice in an ordinary partnership of few members.—But, *held,* that C. was entitled to have the assets of the company valued on the footing of its being a going concern, which it was when he gave notice of retirement, and that the solvency of the persons who owed calls, and of the continuing shareholders, must be taken as matters stood at the date of the notice of retirement, and not at the time when the account was made out. *In re* FRANK MILLS MINING COMPANY　　23 Ch. D. 52

XXXIII. COMPANY — UNREGISTERED COMPANY.

1. —— Association of more than Twenty Members—*Illegality—Companies Act,* 1862, *s.* 4 *—Gain by Individual Members—Company, the formation of which is prohibited.*] By the rules of a mutual marine insurance association, which was not registered under the Companies Act, it was provided that all persons who effected an insurance with the association should be members. No ship was to be insured for more than three-fourths of its value, the person insuring paid a

XXXIII. COMPANY—UNREGISTERED COMPANY—continued.

deposit of 25s. per cent. on the amount of the insurance, and in case of the total loss of a vessel, the members were to pay the loser the amount for which he had insured it rateably, according to the amounts assured to them respectively. The association consisted of more than twenty members. A vessel insured by R. was lost, and the amount of the loss was referred to arbitration. R. assigned his claim to his bankers, who obtained judgment in R.'s name on the award, and, not obtaining payment, presented a petition to wind up the association, the petition stating that the association consisted of more than seven members, but not stating that it consisted of more than twenty. The petition was served at the abandoned office of the association which had ceased to carry on business, and the proper advertisements were issued. On the 28th of May, 1880, a winding-up order was made, no one appearing to oppose. In November, 1881, another member of the association heard, for the first time, of the winding-up order, and within a week applied for leave to appeal against it:—Held, that the order having been made by a superior Court having jurisdiction in winding-up, and having authority to decide as to its own competency, must, if the association was one which ought not to be wound up, be treated merely as an erroneous order, and not as an order void for want of jurisdiction, and that the proper manner of getting rid of it was to appeal:—Held, that as the Appellant was not a party to the order, and applied for leave to appeal as soon as he knew of it, he ought to have leave to appeal notwithstanding the lapse of time:—Held, that although the business of the association had not for its object the acquisition of gain by the association, it had for its object the acquisition of gain by the individual members; that as it consisted of more than twenty members and was not registered, its formation was forbidden by the Companies Act, 1862, s. 4; that the Court, therefore, could not recognise it as having any legal existence, and that the order for winding it up must be discharged. *In re* PADSTOW TOTAL LOSS AND COLLISION ASSURANCE ASSOCIATION
[20 Ch. D. 137

2. —— Association of more than Twenty Members—*Loan Society—Illegality—Companies Act,* 1862 (25 & 26 *Vict.* c. 89), s. 4—*Association having for its Object the Acquisition of Gain.*] Persons to a number exceeding twenty had formed themselves into a society called the " Ipswich Mechanics Mutual Benefit Society." From the rules of the society it appeared that there were four hundred shares in the society of £10 each, and that no member could hold more than twenty shares. The object of the society was to raise by monthly subscriptions and payments payable by the members in respect of their shares a fund for the purpose of making advances to members. From time to time as soon as the fund in hand amounted to a certain sum it was put up for sale by auction amongst the members, the highest bidder receiving the amount on loan from the society at interest. No member could receive on loan more than the nominal amount of the share or shares held by him, but ultimately every

member, who did not withdraw his share under the rule providing for such withdrawal, was to have advanced or allotted to him out of the funds accruing to the society the sum of £10 for every share held by him. The society was not registered under the Companies Act, 1862 :—*Held,* that the society was illegal by reason of the provisions of the Companies Act, 1862, s. 4, which prohibits the formation of any company, association, or partnership consisting of more than twenty persons for the purpose of carrying on any business (other than banking) that has for its object the acquisition of gain by the company, association, or partnership, or by the individual members thereof, unless registered as a company under the Act :—*Held* also, that a promissory note given by a member to the trustee of the society to secure a sum of money advanced to such member under the rules of the society was invalid, and no action could be maintained thereon. JENNINGS *v.* HAMMOND　　9 Q. B. D. 225

3. —— Association of more than Twenty Members—*Loan Society—Illegality—Association having for its Object the Acquisition of Gain—Gain by Individual Members—Companies Act,* 1862 (25 & 26 *Vict.* c. 89), s. 4.] T. was the president of a loan society. The objects of the society were to form a fund from which money might be advanced to enable shareholders to build or purchase a dwelling-house or other buildings, or to lend money to each other on approved personal security; five per cent. interest was to be charged on all moneys advanced by the society. The society consisted of more than twenty members, and was not registered under any statute. The society advanced a sum of money to the Defendants, who signed promissory notes by way of security for the loan; and when T. went out of office, he indorsed the promissory notes to the Plaintiff, who succeeded him. The Plaintiff having sued upon the notes for the benefit of the society :—*Held,* that the society not having been registered, was rendered illegal by the Companies Act, 1862 (25 & 26 Vict. c. 89), s. 4, it being an association having " for its object the acquisition of gain," within the meaning of that enactment; that the Plaintiff could not be in a better position than the society, and therefore could not recover upon the promissory notes.—*In re Padstow Total Loss and Collision Assurance Association* (20 Ch. D. 137) followed. *Jennings Hammond* (9 Q. B. D. 225) approved. SHAW *v.* BENSON　　11 Q. B. D. 563

4. —— Association of more than Twenty Persons—*Freehold Land Society—Illegality—Business for the Acquisition of Gain—Companies Act,* 1862 (25 & 26 *Vict.* c. 89), s. 4.] In 1873 an association of more than twenty persons was formed for the object, as stated in its deed of settlement, of purchasing a freehold estate and reselling it in allotments to the members of the association. The deed was executed by all the members, the name of each, the number of his allotment, the total amount he was to pay, and the amount of his monthly payment to be made in respect of it, being specified in a schedule to the deed. The property was vested in trustees, and its manage-

XXXIII. COMPANY — UNREGISTERED COMPANY—*continued.*

ment was vested in a president, vice-president, treasurer, secretary, and a committee. The deed contained provisions for the conveyance to the members of their allotments when they had paid up the whole amount payable in respect of them, and for forfeiture and sale of the allotments of defaulting members. Powers were given to the committee to make roads, drains, &c., on the land, and powers were given to the trustees of borrowing money on mortgage with the consent of a general meeting. When all mortgages had been paid off and all the allotments had been conveyed the society was to come to an end. The society was not registered under the Companies Act, 1862:—*Held*, that the society was not an association formed for the purpose of carrying on any business that had for its object the acquisition of gain, and was not made illegal by the Companies Act, 1862, s. 4.—*Crowther v. Thorley* (32 W. R. 330) followed.—*Wigfield v. Potter* (45 L. T. (N. S.) 612) approved. *In re* SIDDALL
[**29 Ch. D. 1**]

5. —— **Association of more than twenty Members**—*Loan Society—Illegality— Subsequent Increase of Members—Borrowing Member—Acquiescence—Bankruptcy of Borrowing Member—Proof for Loan—Companies Act, 1862 (25 & 26 Vict. c. 89), s. 4.*] An unregistered money club, which in its inception comprises less than twenty members, becomes an illegal association within sect. 4 of the Companies Act, 1862, so soon as it comprises upwards of twenty members. Such a society is none the less within the mischief of the Act because its business is carried on and managed by a committee of seven members as the agents of the society, although they may have full powers as to management and may make by-laws.—*Crowther v. Thorley* (32 W. R. 330) distinguished.—In 1881 seven persons formed a loan society, and when business was commenced their members had increased to twenty. In June, 1883, the society was registered under the Companies Act, 1862, with the knowledge and consent of all the members. In 1881 the society advanced 100*l.* to a borrowing member, repayable by monthly instalments, and he duly paid the instalments as they fell due until December, 1883, when he became bankrupt:—*Held*, that under the circumstances the inference was, that all the members had, either expressly or by acquiescence, mutually agreed that all the transactions of the society previous to its registration should continue to be binding on the registered society; and, consequently, that the registered society could prove for the balance of the loan. *In re* THOMAS. *Ex parte* POPPLETON
[**14 Q. B. D. 379**]

6. —— **Formation before the Companies Act, 1862**—*Change of Members—Companies Act, 1862 (25 & 26 Vict. c. 89), s. 4.*] An association, consisting of more than twenty persons, was formed before the commencement of the Companies Act, 1862, to receive contributions from the members, and sell the money in hand, from time to time, in shares varying from £20 to £100, to the highest bidder among them. The premiums paid by the purchasers were divided as profits among all the members. When the amount of the contributions

XXXIII. COMPANY — UNREGISTERED COMPANY—*continued.*

and profits of a member who had purchased a share equalled the amount of such share, or, in the case of a member who did not borrow, when the amount of his contributions and profits equalled the amount of the share in respect of which he had joined, and he was paid off, membership ceased in respect of such share. New members, however, were continually joining, and the existence of the society was continuous:—*Held*, that the association was not "formed" within the meaning of sect. 4 of the Act, on each occasion of a change of membership, and did not require to be registered under the Act. SHAW *v.* SIMMONS   -   -   -   **12 Q. B. D. 117**

7. —— **Petition to wind up**—*Part IV. of Companies Act, 1862 — Application to Unregistered Companies—Companies Act, 1862, ss. 85, 199, 201, 204—Judgment against Company after Petition to wind up.*] W. being entitled to the money payable on a policy of insurance on the life of his wife, who had lately died, assigned it to R. R. brought an action against the insurance company, which was an unregistered company, and W., to recover the money. The company paid it into Court. The Plaintiff applied by summons to have it paid out to her, and to have her costs taxed and paid by the company; and W. took out a summons for payment of his costs. On the 6th of August, 1880, an order was made for payment of the money to the Plaintiff, and for payment of her costs by the company; and all proceedings were stayed, except on W.'s summons, which was adjourned. The Plaintiff's costs were taxed and paid. In October, 1880, two petitions were presented for winding-up the company. On the 3rd of December, 1880, W.'s summons was heard, and the Vice-Chancellor ordered the Plaintiff to pay W.'s costs, and ordered the company to repay the Plaintiff what he should so pay, no objection being taken by the company on the ground of the pendency of the winding-up petitions, although the claim was resisted on other grounds. The Plaintiff paid W.'s costs, and applied to the company for repayment, which was refused: and the company applied in the action to restrain the Plaintiff from issuing execution for these costs. The winding-up petitions were still pending, and no order for winding up had been made:—*Held*, by Bacon, V.C., that the company being unregistered, and no winding-up order having been made, sect. 85 of the Companies Act, 1862, did not apply; and that there was no jurisdiction to make the order.—*Held*, by the Court of Appeal, that where proceedings are pending for winding-up an unregistered company, all the provisions of Part IV. of the Companies Act, 1862, other than those expressly excepted, are applicable; and that under sect. 85 the Court had jurisdiction to make the order asked for; the direction in sect. 204, that "an unregistered company shall not, except in the event of its being wound up, be deemed to be a company under this Act," not being intended to confine the application of the Act to a company which has been actually ordered to be wound up:—But *held*, that as the company had allowed the order of the 3rd of December, 1880, to be made without raising

O

XXXIII. COMPANY — UNREGISTERED COMPANY—*continued.*

the objection that the pendency of the winding-up proceedings made such an order improper, and had lain by till that order could not be appealed from, the Court ought not now to exercise in their favour the discretionary power to stay proceedings which is given by sect. 85. RUDOW *v.* GREAT BRITAIN MUTUAL LIFE ASSURANCE SOCIETY
[17 Ch. D. 600

8. —— **Similarity of Name**—*Intended Registration of New Company—Companies Act, 1862, s. 20—Injunction quia timet.*] A company not registered under the Companies Act, 1862, can restrain the registration under that Act of a projected new company, which is intended to carry on the same business as the unregistered company and to bear a name so similar to that of the unregistered company as to be calculated to deceive the public. HENDRIKS *v.* MONTAGU
[17 Ch. D. 638

9. —— **Tramway Company** — *Winding-up — Unregistered Company—"Railway Company"—Companies Act, 1862 (25 & 26 Vict. c. 89), s. 199.*] An unregistered tramway company incorporated by a special Act does not fall within the exception of "railway companies incorporated by Act of Parliament" in sect. 199 of the Companies Act, 1862, and it may therefore be wound up under that section. *In re* BRENTFORD AND ISLEWORTH TRAMWAYS COMPANY　26 Ch. D. 527

XXXIV. COMPANY—LIFE INSURANCE COMPANY.

1. —— **Foreign Company**—*Return of Deposit —Accumulation Fund in Foreign Country—Life Assurance Companies Acts, 1870 to 1872—Life Assurance Companies Act, 1870, s. 3—Board of Trade Rules, 28th August, 1872, r. 6.*] On a petition by depositors under the Life Assurance Companies Acts, 1870 to 1872, and the Board of Trade Rules thereunder, for payment out to them of the £20,000 required to be deposited in Court by a foreign life assurance company before commencing business in this country, the Court will, having regard to rule 6 of the Board of Trade Rules, make the order notwithstanding that the Life Assurance Companies Act, 1870, sect. 3, enacts that the deposit shall be returned " to the company."—The life assurance fund required by that section to have been accumulated prior to the return of the deposit may consist of accumulations already existing abroad and arising from the original business of the company. *In re* COLONIAL MUTUAL LIFE ASSURANCE SOCIETY　21 Ch. D. 837

2. —— **Jurisdiction** — *Winding-up Order — Mutual Insurance Society — Contributory — Liability of Members—Disputed Claim—Evidence—Reduction of Contracts — Companies Act, 1862 (25 & 26 Vict. c. 89), s. 91 — Life Assurance Companies Act, 1870 (33 & 34 Vict. c. 61), ss. 21, 22.*] The Court has, by virtue of sect. 2 of the Life Assurance Companies Act, 1870, jurisdiction to wind up an unregistered mutual life assurance society under the Companies Act, 1862.—But, *semble,* that the holders of policies in such a society are not liable to contribute to the payment of any debts; and that all that can be

XXXIV. COMPANY—LIFE INSURANCE COMPANY—*continued.*

done in the winding-up is after payment of the costs to distribute the funds of the society among the policy-holders in proportion to the amounts of their respective claims.—When a company, Respondents to a winding-up petition, dispute the validity of the Petitioner's debt they must adduce on the hearing such evidence as will shew the Court that there is a question to be tried. If they fail to do this, a winding-up order ought to be made. Two petitions having been presented by policy-holders for the winding-up of a mutual life assurance society, the society admitted their insolvency, and a winding-up order was made on the second petition, on the ground that the validity of the first Petitioner's debt was disputed. But liberty was given to the first Petitioner to apply for the costs of her petition, if her claim should be ultimately established. She appealed, and before the appeal came on for hearing a committee of policy-holders was formed, who desired that the Court should exercise the power given to it by sect. 22 of the Life Assurance Companies Act, 1870, of reducing the amount of the contracts of the society instead of making a winding-up order:—*Held,* that this power could not be exercised so long as the winding-up order remained, and that the order ought to be discharged, and a meeting of the policy-holders summoned in order to ascertain their wishes. And the further hearing of the appeal was adjourned until after the meeting should have been held. *In re* GREAT BRITAIN MUTUAL LIFE ASSURANCE SOCIETY
[16 Ch. D. 246

3. —— **Participating Policy**—*Winding-up—Mutual Insurance Society — Contributory — Liability of Shareholders and participating Policy-holders inter se — Partnership—Participation in Profit and Loss.*] The articles of association of an unlimited mutual insurance society provided that the company should at first consist of two classes of members, namely, shareholders, so long as there should be any, and assurance members, who were policy-holders with participation in the profits and registered as members; and that when the shareholders should be paid off under the scheme provided for, then the company should consist of assurance members only. The shareholders were to have £6 per cent. on their paid-up calls, and every three years the profits were to be calculated, and one fourth paid to the shareholders, and the other three-fourths carried to the assurance fund and appropriated by way of bonus to the policies of the participating policy-holders who have paid five years' premiums. The company was wound up ,before the shareholders had been paid off, and the participating policy-holders were declared by the Court to be contributories:—*Held* (affirming the decision of Malins, V.C.), that although the participating policy-holders were members and contributories under the special terms of the articles, they could not be called upon to contribute until the shareholders had been exhausted.—The presumption of law that the absence of express stipulation partners must share losses in the same proportion as they share profits, *held* not to apply to such a case, the assured members having no direct

XXXIV. COMPANY—LIFE INSURANCE COM-
PANY—*continued.*

participation in profits. *In re* ALBION LIFE
ASSURANCE SOCIETY　　　　16 Ch. D. 83

4. —— Participating Policy—*Winding-up—*
Mutual Insurance Society—Contributory—Assign-
ment of Policy.] It having been held in *In re*
Albion Life Assurance Society (16 Ch. D. 83) that
assurance members, being participating policy-
holders of the Albion Society, were contributories
in the winding-up of the company :—*Held,* that
a policy-holder who had assigned his policy
ceased to be liable as a contributory, although
no other person had been made liable to contribute in respect of his policy in his stead. *In re*
ALBION LIFE ASSURANCE SOCIETY. BROWN'S CASE
[18 Ch. D. 639

5. —— Participating Policy—*Winding-up—*
Mutual Insurance Society—Contributory—Assign-
ment — Evidence of Transfer — Rectification of
Register.] Under the articles of association of
an assurance society "members" included "the
holders of participating policies duly registered,"
and payment of premium was to be deemed an
agreement to become a member.—The directors
of the company had power to require evidence
of the assignment of policies before registering the
assignees as members.—A participating policy
had been assigned, and the assignee had paid a
premium on it five months before the winding-
up of the company, but no evidence of the assignment had been offered to or required by the
directors ; and the name of the assignee was not
entered upon the register of members :—*Held,*
that the assignee was not a contributory. *In re*
ALBION LIFE ASSURANCE SOCIETY. SANDERS' CASE
[20 Ch. D. 403

6. —— Reduction of Contracts—*Winding-up*
—*Life Assurance Companies Act, 1870 (33 & 34*
Vict. c. 71), s. 22—Date at which Contracts to be
ascertained.] A petition having been presented
for the winding-up of a life assurance company, an
order was made under the Life Assurance Companies Act, 1870, sect. 22, directing a scheme to
be prepared for the reduction of the contracts of
the company :—*Held* (affirming the decision of
Hall, V.C.), that in the absence of special circumstances the contracts to be included in a scheme
for reduction are to be ascertained, not at the
time of settling the scheme, nor at the date of
the order directing a scheme, but at the date of
the presentation of the winding-up petition, so
that no persons whose contracts have not matured
into debts until after the presentation of the
petition are entitled to be paid in full. *In re*
GREAT BRITAIN MUTUAL LIFE ASSURANCE SOCIETY
[19 Ch. D. 39; 20 Ch. D. 351

XXXV. COMPANY—APPEAL.

—— Security for Costs—*Winding-up Order—*
Appeal by Company.] Where a limited company
alone appeals from a winding-up order without
joining any one personally responsible for costs,
it will generally be ordered to give security for
costs. *In re* PHOTOGRAPHIC ARTISTS' COOPERA-
TIVE SUPPLY ASSOCIATION　　- 23 Ch.D. 370

XXXVI. COMPANY—COSTS.

1. —— Liquidator—*Winding-up—Application*
for Leave to appeal—Rules of Court, 1875, Order

XXXVI. COMPANY—COSTS—*continued.*

LV.] On the 29th of July, 1881, a petition was
presented to wind up a company. On the same
day an order was made by Bacon, V.C., on an
application by A. that his name should be taken
off the register of shareholders and his money
returned to him. This order was made in ignorance that a winding-up petition had been presented, and was drawn up as of the 24th of
August, 1881. On the 26th of August a winding-
up order was made by Hall, V.C. A. claimed as
a creditor for the moneys ordered to be refunded
to him, and his claim was allowed. The liquidator was advised he ought to obtain a decision
on the question whether V.C. Bacon's order was
right, he thereupon took out a summons to have
the claim of A. to rank as a creditor disallowed.
Kay, J., on the 24th of June, 1882, dismissed the
summons as misconceived, since he had no jurisdiction to disturb V.C. Bacon's order, and refused
to give the liquidator his costs out of the estate.
The liquidator on the 29th of June took out a summons for leave to appeal against V.C. Bacon's order
of the 24th of August, 1881, and Mr. Justice Kay's
order of the 24th of June, 1882. Kay, J., dismissed
the summons with costs, refusing the liquidator
his costs out of the estate. The liquidator applied
to vary this order :—*Held,* that an official liquidator is a person who as a general rule is entitled
to his costs out of the estate, and that under
Order LV. an appeal would lie.—But, *held,* that
as the application of the 24th of June was a
manifest mistake it was competent to the Judge
below to refuse the liquidator his costs of it, and
the Court of Appeal would not interfere with his
decision.—A liquidator, though in some sense a
trustee, is a paid agent bound to discharge his
duties with reasonable care and skill, and may be
deprived of costs for a mistake which would not
be sufficient to disentitle an ordinary gratuitous
trustee to costs.—*Held,* that a liquidator who
applies for leave to appeal from an order is as a
general rule entitled to the costs of the application, but they will be refused if the appeal would
be frivolous.—*Held,* that if the application of the
29th of June had only been for leave to appeal
against the order of the 24th of June, 1882, the
Court of Appeal would not have interfered as to
the costs, but that an application for leave to
appeal against the order of the 24th of August,
1881, was reasonable, and that as the including
in the application liberty to appeal against the
other order did not increase the costs, the liquidator must be allowed his costs of that application
out of the estate.—Leave to appeal against the
order of the 24th of August, 1881, so as to entitle
the liquidator to costs in any event was however
refused on the ground of lapse of time. — The
principles upon which applications by official
liquidators for leave to appeal are to be dealt
with, considered. *In re* SILVER VALLEY MINES
[21 Ch. D. 381

2. —— Liquidator—*Winding-up—Remunera-*
tion— Cost of Realization—General Costs—Insuf-
ficiency of Assets—Priority—Internal Litigation.]
Where the assets of a company in compulsory
liquidation are insufficient for payment of the
costs of the winding-up, the official liquidator is
not entitled to any remuneration.—Where in the

XXXVI. COMPANY—COSTS—*continued.*

compulsory winding-up of a company the assets are insufficient for the payment in full of costs, the costs of realization are payable out of the assets in priority to costs incurred in internal litigation, and these latter costs, including those of the liquidator, are payable, rateably, without regard to priority in the dates of the orders under which such costs have been directed to be paid.— *Ex parte Percival* (Law Rep. 6 Eq. 519), *Cape Breton Company* v. *Fenn* (17 Ch. D. 198), and *In re Home Investment Society* (14 Ch. D. 167) considered. *In re* DRONFIELD SILKSTONE COAL COMPANY (No. 2) - .. - 23 Ch. D. 511

3. —— Priority—*Winding-up—Costs of Successful Litigant—General Costs of Liquidation.*] In the winding-up of a company the liquidator changed his solicitor. The first solicitor claimed to be paid his costs. The liquidator set up in defence that he had, in pursuance of an order of the Court, paid away part of the assets in discharging the costs of an unsuccessful attempt to settle an alleged shareholder on the list of contributories, and that the only remaining assets amounted to £9, which was quite insufficient to pay the applicant, and which he claimed to retain for costs out of pocket :—*Held* (affirming the decision of Pearson, J.), that the successful litigant whose costs were ordered to be paid by the liquidator, was entitled to immediate payment of those costs in priority to the general costs of liquidation including costs of realization ; and that the remaining assets, amounting to £9, must be apportioned equally between the liquidator and the applicant. —*In re Home Investment Society* (14 Ch. D. 167) followed ; *In re Dronfield Silkstone Coal Company* (23 Ch. D. 511) not followed.—The order giving the costs to the successful litigant directed that they should be paid by the official liquidator, and that he should be at liberty to retain them out of the assets of the company :—*Held*, that this form of order gave the official liquidator the right to repay himself the costs out of the assets in priority to all other creditors. *In re* DOMINION OF CANADA PLUMBAGO COMPANY 27 Ch. D. 33

4. —— Representative Case—*Costs—Winding-up.*] In a representative case for the opinion of the Court in the winding-up of a company, the costs of the parties will be allowed out of the estate as between party and party only, and not as between solicitor and client.—*Part's Case* (Law Rep. 10 Eq. 622) not followed on this point. *In re* MUTUAL SOCIETY. GRIMWADE *v.* MUTUAL SOCIETY [18 Ch. D. 530

XXXVII. COMPANY—EVIDENCE.

1. —— Interrogatories—*Winding-up—Practice—Action—Corporation—Rules of Court, 1875, Order XXXI, rr.* 1, 4.] The liquidator of a company is entitled to deliver interrogatories to a person claiming to prove who has made an affidavit of documents. *In re* ALEXANDRA PALACE COMPANY - - - - 16 Ch. D. 58

2. —— Witness — *Winding-up* — *Companies Act*, 1862, *s.* 115—*Examination by Liquidator—by Contributories—Locus Standi of, to appeal.*] The only ground on which a witness summoned to attend for examination can contest the validity of the summons is a want of jurisdiction to issue

XXXVII. COMPANY—EVIDENCE—*continued.*

the summons or make the order. If the jurisdiction exists, a witness has no locus standi to appeal against the order.—The examination under the 115th section of the Companies Act, 1862, is as a general rule entrusted to the liquidator, but it is discretionary with the Judge whether he will entrust either the whole or any part of the examination to creditors or contributories, and whether he will or will not confine that examination within certain limits.—*Re Penysyflog Mining Company* (30 L. T. (N.S.) 861) considered. *In re* SILKSTONE AND DODWORTH COAL AND IRON COMPANY. WHITWORTH'S CASE - 19 Ch. D. 118

3. —— Witness—*Winding-up—Examination of Witness under Companies Act, 1862 (25 & 26 Vict.* c. 89), s. 115—*Presence of Counsel and Solicitor on behalf of Person summoned for Examination —Right to take and carry away Notes—Re-examination.*] A person summoned for the purpose of being examined under the Companies Act, 1868, s. 115, is entitled to have counsel and solicitor on his behalf present during his examination, and to be re-examined for the purpose of explaining his examination-in-chief, but the re-examination must be limited to that purpose ; and his counsel and solicitor are entitled to take and carry away notes of the examination, but only to use such notes for the purpose of the re-examination. *In re* CAMBRIAN MINING COMPANY 20 Ch. D. 376

4. —— Witness—*Winding-up—Examination before an Examiner—Creditors' Right of attending —Companies Act, 1862 (25 & 26 Vict* c. 89), s. 115 —*Bankrupt Law Consolidation Act, 1849 (12 & 13 Vict.* c. 106), s. 120—*General Order of the 11th of November,* 1862, *Rule LX—Bankruptcy Act,* 1869 (32 & 33 *Vict.* c. 71), s. 96.] Admitted creditors of a company in course of winding-up have not a general right under rule LX. of the General Order to regulate the proceedings under the Companies Act, 1862, of the 11th of November, 1862, to attend an examination of witnesses before an examiner summoned under sect. 115 of the Companies Act, 1862. But the Court in its discretion may allow the attendance.—The word " proceedings " in that rule cannot be held to include an examination before an examiner which is strictly of a private character.—*In re Empire Assurance Corporation* (17 L. T. (N.S.) 488) and *In re Merchants' Company* (Law Rep. 4 Eq. 454) discussed. *In re* GREY'S BREWERY COMPANY 25 Ch. D. 400

5. —— Witness—*Winding-up—Examination of former Officer under Companies Act, 1862 (25 & 26 Vict.* c. 89), s. 115—*General Order of the 11th of November,* 1862, *Rule LX.—Leave to Creditor to attend " the Proceedings"—Right of Creditor to be present.*] A person who had brought in a large claim as creditor of a company which was being wound up, obtained an order giving him liberty " to attend the proceedings in this matter at his own expense." The liquidator afterwards took out a summons under sect. 115 for the examination of a former officer of the company with a view to obtaining information as to the circumstances under which the claim of the alleged creditor arose, the alleged creditor claimed a right to be present at the examination :—*Held* (affirming the decision of Bacon, V.C.), that he ought

XXXVII. COMPANY—EVIDENCE—*continued.*
not to be allowed to be present at the examination.
In re NORWICH EQUITABLE FIRE ASSURANCE
COMPANY　-　　-　　-　　- 27 Ch. D. 515

COMPANY—Bill of sale by　　- 28 Ch. D. 682
　See BILL OF SALE—REGISTRATION.

—— Charging orders—Sale of shares
　　　　　　　　　　[12 Q. B. D. 287
　See PRACTICE—SUPREME COURT—CHARG-
　ING ORDERS. 2.

—— Costs — Liquidator — Successful claims
　against　-　　-　　- 30 Ch. D. 598
　See BILL OF EXCHANGE—FOREIGN BILL.

—— Certificates of shares—Reputed ownership—
　Bankruptcy　-　　- 15 Q. B. D. 441
　See BANKRUPTCY—ORDER AND DISPOSI-
　TION. 10.

—— Chartered company.
　See CHARTERED COMPANY—*Statutes.*

—— Detention of shares—Second action for same
　cause of action　- 15 Q. B. D. 549
　See ESTOPPEL—JUDGMENT. 6.

—— Director—Misfeasance　- 29 Ch. D. 795
　See PRINCIPAL AND AGENT—AGENT'S
　LIABILITY.

—— Forged certificate -　　- 13 Q. B. D. 103
　See ESTOPPEL—CONDUCT. 2.

—— Foreign corporation　- 6 App. Cas. 386
　See COLONIAL LAW—WEST AUSTRALIA.
　1.

—— Lease to—Clause of re-entry—Distress
　　　　　　　　　　[20 Ch. D. 260
　See LANDLORD AND TENANT—RE-ENTRY.
　8.

—— Malicious prosecution—Petition to wind up
　—Reasonable and probable cause
　　　　　　　　　　[11 Q. B. D. 674
　See MALICIOUS PROSECUTION. 1.

—— Plaintiff in action—Security for costs
　　　　　　　　　　[23 Ch. D. 358
　See PRACTICE—SUPREME COURT—SECU-
　RITY FOR COSTS. 1.

—— Purchase of lands—Lands Clauses Act.
　See Cases under LANDS CLAUSES ACT.

—— Purchase-money—Reinvestment—Land tax
　—Costs　-　　-　　- 17 Ch. D. 378
　See PRACTICE—SUPREME COURT—COSTS.
　39.

—— Railway company.
　See Cases under RAILWAY COMPANY.

—— Set-off in winding-up　- 9 Q. B. D. 648 ;
　　　　　　　　　　[9 App. Cas. 434
　See SALE OF GOODS—RESCISSION. 2.

—— Voluntary winding-up — Liquidator—Pro-
　duction of documents　15 Q. B. D. 473
　See PRACTICE—SUPREME COURT—PRO-
　DUCTION OF DOCUMENTS. 3.

—— Winding-up—Apportionment of rates
　See APPORTIONMENT. 2. [19 Ch. D. 640

—— Winding-up—Balance order — Retainer by
　executor　-　　-　　- 29 Ch. D. 934
　See EXECUTOR—RETAINER. 4.

—— Winding-up—Crown debts　28 Ch. D. 643
　See CROWN.

COMPANY—*continued.*
—— Winding-up order—Solicitor's lien on docu-
　ments　-　　-　　- 24 Ch. D. 406
　See SOLICITOR—LIEN. 12.

COMPENSATION—Agricultural improvements.
　See LANDLORD AND TENANT—IMPROVE-
　MENTS—*Statutes.*

—— Conditions of sale—Error discovered after
　execution of conveyance 13 Q. B. D. 351
　See VENDOR AND PURCHASER—COMPEN-
　SATION. 2.

—— Damage to surface　- 10 Q. B. D. 547 ;
　See INCLOSURE. 1.　[9 App. Cas. 286

—— Damage—Support of surface 6 App. Cas. 833
　See SCOTCH LAW—MINE. 2.

—— Death by accident—Lord Campbell's Act
　　　　[25 Ch. D. 409 ; 9 Q. B. D. 160
　See DAMAGES—LORD CAMPBELL'S ACT.
　1, 2.

—— Improvement in streams - 9 App. Cas. 392
　See COLONIAL LAW—CANADA—ONTARIO.
　5.

—— Incumbent of benefice—Mortgage
　　　　　　　　　　[30 Ch. D. 520
　See MORTGAGE—CONTRACT. 3.

—— Labourers' Dwellings Act - 27 Ch. D. 614
　See LABOURERS' DWELLINGS ACT. 2.

—— Lands Clauses Act.
　See Cases under LANDS CLAUSES ACT—
　COMPENSATION.

—— Public Health Act.
　See Cases under LOCAL GOVERNMENT—
　COMPENSATION.

—— Public Works Act—New Zealand
　　　　　　　　　　[9 App. Cas. 699
　See COLONIAL LAW—NEW ZEALAND. 2.

—— Railway—Scotch law　- 7 App. Cas. 259 ;
　　　　　　　　　　[8 App. Cas. 265
　See SCOTCH LAW—RAILWAY COMPANY.
　4, 5.

—— Railway company—Resumption of grant by
　Crown -　　-　　- 9 App. Cas. 142
　See COLONIAL LAW—WEST AUSTRALIA. 2.

—— Sale of land—Misrepresentation 28 Ch. D. 309
　See VENDOR AND PURCHASER—CONDI-
　TIONS OF SALE. 7.

COMPETENCY—Colonial certificate of.
　See SHIP—MERCHANT SHIPPING ACT—
　Gazette.

COMPOSITION — Tithe rent-charge—Statute of
　Limitations　-　　- 10 App. Cas. 14
　See LIMITATIONS, STATUTE OF—REALTY.
　8.

COMPOSITION WITH CREDITORS.
　See Cases under
　　　BANKRUPTCY—COMPOSITION.
　　　BANKRUPTCY — SCHEME OF AR-
　　　RANGEMENT.

—— After bankruptcy.
　See Cases under BANKRUPTCY—ANNUL-
　MENT. 2-6.

—— Disqualification of alderman　16 Ch. D. 143
　See MUNICIPAL CORPORATION—QUALIFI-
　CATION.

COMPOSITION WITH CREDITORS—*continued.*

—— Forfeiture on insolvency—Settlement
[29 Ch. D. 196
See SETTLEMENT—CONSTRUCTION. 4.

—— Preference of creditor - 15 Q. B. D. 605
See BANKRUPTCY — FRAUDULENT PRE-
FERENCE. 2.

—— Proof—Secured creditor - 19 Ch. D. 394;
[15 Q. B. D. 102; 8 App. Cas. 606
See BANKRUPTCY — SECURED CREDITOR.
2, 5, 7.

—— Right of retainer by executor of creditor
[16 Ch. D. 202
See EXECUTOR—RETAINER. 3.

—— Witness - 23 Ch. D. 118
See BANKRUPTCY—EVIDENCE. 4.

COMPOUND INTEREST - 6 App. Cas. 181
See MORTGAGE—CONTRACT. 11.

—— Proof in bankruptcy 20 Ch. D. 131
See BANKRUPTCY—PROOF. 10.

—— Trustee—Breach of trust 17 Ch. D. 142
See TRUSTEE—LIABILITIES. 7.

COMPOUNDING FELONY—Liability of acceptor
—Indorsee 10 Q. B. D. 572
See BILL OF EXCHANGE—CONSIDERATION.

COMPROMISE — Administration suit — Locke
King's Act - 24 Ch. D. 94
See WILL—EXONERATION. 3.

—— Divorce suit - - - 18 Ch. D. 670
See HUSBAND AND WIFE—SEPARATION
DEED. 1.

—— Infant - - - 16 Ch. D. 41
See INFANT—CONTRACTS. 2.

—— Local board - - 22 Ch. D. 537
See LOCAL GOVERNMENT—LOCAL AUTHO-
RITY. 1.

COMPTROLLER OF TRADE-MARKS
[27 Ch. D. 681
See TRADE-MARK—REGISTRATION. 5.

COMPULSORY PILOTAGE.
See Cases under SHIP—PILOT.

COMPULSORY POWERS — Commissioners of
Sewers 28 Ch. D. 486
See LONDON—COMMISSIONERS OF SEWERS.

—— Labourers' Dwellings Act 27 Ch. D. 614
See LABOURERS' DWELLINGS ACTS. 2.

—— Lands Clauses Act.
See Cases under LANDS CLAUSES ACT—
COMPULSORY POWERS.

—— Minerals—Railway company 19 Ch. D. 559
See RAILWAY COMPANY — RAILWAYS
CLAUSES ACT. 4.

—— Scotch Law—Harbour trustees
[8 App. Cas. 623
See SCOTCH LAW—HARBOUR. 1.

—— School Board—Elementary Education Act
[27 Ch. D. 639
See ELEMENTARY EDUCATION ACTS —
SCHOOL BOARD.

COMPUTATION OF TIME—Notice of meeting of
company - - - 29 Ch. D. 204
See COMPANY—REDUCTION OF CAPITAL.
5.

CONCEALMENT—Material fact—Marine insurance - 6 Q. B. D. 222; 15 Q. B. D. 368
See INSURANCE, MARINE—CONCEALMENT.
1, 2.

CONCURRENT SUITS—Conduct of proceedings.
See Cases under PRACTICE — SUPREME
COURT—CONDUCT OF CAUSE.

—— Staying proceedings.
See Cases under PRACTICE — SUPREME
COURT—STAYING PROCEEDINGS.

CONDITION.

1. —— Condition Precedent—*Furnished House
—Agreement to deliver up House and Furniture
and pay Sum for Damage to be ascertained by
Valuers.*] Where by a written agreement a tenant
of a furnished house agrees at the expiration of the
tenancy to deliver up possession of the house and
the furniture in good order, and in the event of
loss, damage, or breakage, to make good or pay
for the same, the amount of such payment if disputed to be settled by two valuers, the settlement
of the amount of the payment by the valuers is a
condition precedent to the right of the landlord
to bring an action in respect of the dilapidations.
BABBAGE *v.* COULBURN - - 9 Q. B. D. 235

2. —— Condition rendered impossible by Defendant—"*Title to be approved by my Solicitor.*"]
The Plaintiff's claim was for commission on the
sale of a piece of land by A. to the Defendant, one
term of the Plaintiff's contract being that A.'s
title should be approved by the Defendant's solicitor. The Defendant broke off the sale of his own
accord, so that A.'s title was never submitted to
the Defendant's solicitor:—*Held,* that the Plaintiff
could not succeed without proving that the Defendant's solicitor had approved A.'s title, or else that
such a title was submitted to him as it was unreasonable for him to disapprove. CLACK *v.* WOOD
[9 Q. B. D. 276

—— Bill of costs—Conditional payment
[30 Ch. D. 441
See SOLICITOR—BILL OF COSTS. 7.

—— Conditional acknowledgment — Statute of
Limitations 23 Ch. D. 207; 26 Ch. D. 474
See LIMITATIONS, STATUTE OF—PERSONAL
ACTIONS. 1.

—— Conditional application—Shares
[17 Ch. D. 373
See COMPANY—PROSPECTUS. 2.

—— Conditional debt—Garnishee order
[19 Ch. D. 508
See PRACTICE—SUPREME COURT—GAR-
NISHEE ORDER. 5.

—— Disclaimer by trustee in bankruptcy—Con-
ditions imposed by Court.
See Cases under BANKRUPTCY—DIS-
CLAIMER. 5—11.

—— Feu charter—Right of co-feuar to enforce
[6 App. Cas. 560
See SCOTCH LAW—CONVEYANCE. 2.

—— Life estate—Settled Land Act 30 Ch. D. 161
See SETTLED LAND ACT—DEFINITIONS. 2.

—— Option of purchase - - 30 Ch. D. 203
See WILL—CONDITION. 7.

CONDITION—*continued.*

—— Precedent—Agreement for lease—Nominee
of lessee   -   -   - 22 Ch. D. 441
See LANDLORD AND TENANT—AGREE-
MENT. 2.

—— Precedent—Charterparty—Efficiency of ship
[6 Q. B. D. 648; 7 App. Cas. 670
See INSURANCE, MARINE—POLICY. 2.

—— Precedent—Compulsory purchase
[22 Ch. D. 142
See LANDS CLAUSES ACT—COMPULSORY
POWERS. 1.

—— Precedent—Covenant to renew lease—Notice
of option -   -   - 22 Ch. D. 640
See LANDLORD AND TENANT—LEASE. 13.

—— Precedent—Performance of covenants
[18 Ch. D. 238
See LANDLORD AND TENANT—LEASE. 12.

—— Reduction of debt—Non-performance
[16 Ch. D. 675
See BANKRUPTCY—ACT OF BANKRUPTCY.
22.

—— Subsequent—Heirlooms - 23 Ch. D. 158
See WILL—HEIRLOOM. 4.

—— Will.
See Cases under WILL—CONDITION.

CONDITIONS OF SALE.
See Cases and Statutes under VENDOR
AND PURCHASER—CONDITIONS OF SALE

—— Lands forfeited to Crown 6 App. Cas. 628
See COLONIAL LAW—NEW SOUTH WALES.
2.

—— Misdescription—Error discovered after execution of conveyance—Compensation -
[13 Q. B. D. 351
See VENDOR AND PURCHASER—COMPEN-
SATION. 2.

CONDONATION—Adultery.
See Cases under PRACTICE—DIVORCE—
CONDONATION.

—— Adultery—Scotch law - 9 App. Cas. 205
See SCOTCH LAW—HUSBAND AND WIFE. 1.

CONDUCT OF CAUSE.
See Cases under PRACTICE—SUPREME
COURT—CONDUCT OF CAUSE.

CONDUIT—Interference with - 25 Ch. D. 182
See WATERCOURSE. 3.

**CONFERENCES OF LOCAL GOVERNMENT
AUTHORITIES.**
See LOCAL GOVERNMENT — RATES —
Statutes.

CONFESSION—Admissibility of—Evidence
[7 Q. B. D. 147
See CRIMINAL LAW—EVIDENCE. 1.

CONFIRMATION—Settlement—Infant
[22 Ch. D. 263
See SETTLEMENT—FUTURE PROPERTY. 3.

—— Will—Reference in will - 23 Ch. D. 337
See WILL—REVOCATION. 2.

CONFLICT OF LAWS.
1. —— Contract — *Construction and enforcement of a Contract made in England between Merchants residing there, for the delivery in London
of Goods shipped at a foreign Port by a foreign
Company — Vis Major.*] The Defendants, a

CONFLICT OF LAWS—*continued.*
London firm, contracted in London to sell to the
Plaintiffs, merchants in London, 20,000 tons of
Algerian esparto, to be shipped by a French
company at an Algerian port, at certain prices,
according to specified qualities, on board vessels
to be provided by the Plaintiffs in London, and
to be paid for by the Plaintiffs in London by
cash on or before arrival of the ship or ships at
her or their port of destination, less interest at
5 per cent. per annum for the unexpired portion
of three months from date of bill of lading, for
the full amount of the invoice based on shipping
weight.—The Defendants caused to be delivered
and were paid for 9000 tons of esparto, but failed
to deliver the remaining 11,000 tons.— In an
action for this breach of contract:—*Held,* affirming the judgment of the Queen's Bench Division,
that the contract was an English contract, and to
be construed and dealt with according to the law
of this country; and, consequently, that it was
no answer to say that by the French law (which
prevailed at the port of shipment) the Defendants
were excused from performing their contract if
prevented from so doing by "force majeure," viz.,
the prohibition by the constituted authorities of
the export of esparto from Algeria, by reason of
an insurrection and consequent hostilities in that
country. JACOBS v. CRÉDIT LYONNAIS
[12 Q. B. D. 589

2. —— Foreign Divorce—*Marriage in England between Scotchman domiciled in Scotland and
Englishwoman—Decree of Divorce by Scotch Court,
by reason of Husband's Adultery only—Validity
of Divorce in England*] The English Courts
will recognise as valid the decision of a competent
foreign Christian tribunal dissolving the marriage
between a domiciled native in the country where
such tribunal has jurisdiction, and an English
woman, when the decree of divorce is not impeached by any species of collusion or fraud.
And this, although the marriage may have been
solemnized in England, and may have been dissolved for a cause which would not have been
sufficient to obtain a divorce in England.—When
an English woman marries a domiciled foreigner,
the marriage is constituted according to the lex
loci contractus; but she takes his domicil and is
subject to his law.—A domiciled Scotchman married, in England, an English woman. Immediately after the ceremony the married couple
went to Scotland and resided there as their matrimonial home. Two years after the wife obtained in Scotland a divorce à vinculo matrimonii,
on the ground of her husband's adultery only.
The husband came to England, and married there
another English woman, the first wife being still
alive. In a suit for a declaration of the nullity of
the second marriage at the instance of the second
wife:—*Held,* affirming the decision of the Court
below, that the divorce in Scotland was a sentence of a Court of competent jurisdiction, not
only effectual within that jurisdiction but entitled to recognition in the Courts of this country
also.—*Lolley's Case* (Russ. & Ry. 237) explained;
Warrender v. *Warrender* (2 Cl. & F. 488); *Geils*
v. *Geils* (1 Macq. 255) undistinguishable; *Maghee*
v. *M'Alister* (3 Ir. (Ch.) 604) also undistinguishable and affirmed; *M'Carthy* v. *Decaix* (2 Russ.

CONFLICT OF LAWS—*continued.*

& My. 614) dissented from.—*Quære*, Whether a bonâ fide change of domicil which was English at the date of the contract would affect the question of dissolution; and whether *Pitt* v. *Pitt* (4 Macq. 627) would govern cases like *Niboyet* v. *Niboyet* (4 P. D. 1) if they arose in Scotland. HARVEY *v.* FARNIE   6 P. D. 35; 8 App. Cas. 43

3. —— Incorporeal Hereditament — *Lease made in England by Englishmen of Sporting Right over Land in Scotland—Absence of Seal—Action in England—Enjoyment of Right.*] By Scotch law an instrument under seal is not necessary for the conveyance of a sporting right, and therefore the stipulations of an unsealed lease made between Englishmen in England of a sporting right over land in Scotland may be enforced by action in the English Courts, as the provision of the law of England that an instrument under seal is necessary for the conveyance of a right to an incorporeal hereditament, is not part of the lex fori.—Even if such lease were invalid for want of a seal, the lessee, after having had an enjoyment of the right, could not set up the invalidity as a defence to an action for breach of a stipulation in the lease to leave a good breeding stock of game on the ground at the termination of the lease. ADAMS *v.* CLUTTERBUCK   10 Q. B. D. 403

4. —— Ship—*Bottomry—Foreign Ship—Law of the Flag.*] The owner of cargo who ships it on board a foreign vessel, ships it to be dealt with by the master according to the law of the flag, that is the law of the country to which the vessel belongs, unless that authority be limited by express stipulation at the time of the shipment. Therefore a bond made by the master of a foreign ship hypothecating cargo laden on board such ship if valid according to the law of the flag of the ship, will be enforced by the English Admiralty Court, on the arrest of the ship and cargo at the Port of London (the port of discharge within the meaning of the bond), although the conditions imposed by English law as essential to the validity of such bond have not been complied with. THE "GAETANO AND MARIA"   [7 P. D. 1, 137

5. —— Ship—*Law applicable in Case of Collision between British and Foreign Vessel.*] In an action in personam, brought by the owners of a British vessel against the owners of a Spanish vessel to recover damages caused to the British vessel by collision with the Spanish vessel on the high seas, the Defendants pleaded that they were Spanish subjects, and that if there was any negligence on the part of those in charge of the Spanish vessel it was negligence for which the master and crew alone, and not the Defendants, were liable according to the law of Spain:—*Held*, bad on demurrer. THE "LEON" -   6 P. D. 148

—— Foreign bill of exchange -   30 Ch. D. 598
   See BILL OF EXCHANGE—FOREIGN BILL.
—— Foreign corporation -   6 App. Cas. 386
   See COLONIAL LAW—WEST AUSTRALIA. 1.
—— Foreign decree—Property in this country
     [6 P. D. 6
   See ADMINISTRATOR—LIMITED. 6.

CONFLICT OF LAWS—*continued.*

—— Legitimacy—Bequest to children
   See WILL—WORDS. 13. [24 Ch. D. 637
CONJUGAL RIGHTS—Restitution—Decree.
   See PRACTICE—DIVORCE—RESTITUTION OF CONJUGAL RIGHTS—*Statutes.*
—— Restitution—Contempt—Attachment
     [9 P. D. 52; 10 P. D. 72
   See PRACTICE—DIVORCE—RESTITUTION OF CONJUGAL RIGHTS. 1, 2.
CONSANGUINITY—Nephew—Will   17 Ch. 382
   See WILL—WORDS. 12.
CONSENT—Action—Strangers to action
     [6 App. Cas. 560
   See SCOTCH LAW—CONVEYANCE. 2.
—— Assignment of lease—Unreasonable refusal
     [16 Ch. D. 387
   See LANDLORD AND TENANT—LEASE. 2.
—— Charity Commissioners.
   See Cases under CHARITY — COMMISSIONERS.
—— Marriage with consent of guardians
   See WILL—CONDITION. 9. [18 Ch. D. 61
—— Order by consent -   - 26 Ch. D. 249
   See PRACTICE—SUPREME COURT—CONSENT.
—— Power of advancement—Tenant for life—Bankruptcy -   27 Ch. D. 565
   See POWER—EXTINCTION. 2.
—— Sale of land—Settled Land Act
     [24 Ch. D. 144
   See SETTLED LAND ACT—TRUSTEES. 8.
—— Scotch marriage—Evidence 6 App. Cas. 489
   See SCOTCH LAW—HUSBAND AND WIFE. 3.
—— Tenant for life—Assignment 23 Ch. D. 583
   See SETTLEMENT—POWERS. 1.
CONSIDERATION—Accord and satisfaction
   [9 Q. B. D. 37; 11 Q. B. D. 221; 9 App. Cas. 605
   See ACCORD AND SATISFACTION. 1, 2.
—— Assignment of all debtor's property.
   See Cases under BANKRUPTCY—ACT OF BANKRUPTCY. 1—5.
—— Bill of exchange—Illegality 10 Q. B. D. 572
   See BILL OF EXCHANGE—CONSIDERATION.
—— Bond—Immorality -   - 26 Ch. D. 353
   See BOND.
—— Statement of—Bill of sale.
   See Cases under BILL OF SALE—FORMALITIES. 15—26.
—— Statement of—Judgment debt 22 Ch. D. 529
   See BANKRUPTCY—ACT OF BANKRUPTCY. 21.
CONSIGNMENTS—Appropriation to meet bills.
   See Cases under BILL OF EXCHANGE—SECURITIES FOR.
CONSOLIDATED ORDERS XXII., r. 10
     [21 Ch. D. 360
   See PRACTICE—SUPREME COURT—ATTACHMENT. 3.
—— XXXIII. r. 7 -   16 Ch. D. 594
   See PRACTICE—SUPREME COURT—EVIDENCE. 6.
—— XXXV., r. 1 -   22 Ch. D. 635
   See TRUSTEE RELIEF ACT. 1.

CONSOLIDATED ORDERS—*continued.*
—— XXXV., r. 1   -   - 28 Ch. D. 529
  See TRUSTEE ACTS—VESTING ORDERS. 2.
CONSOLIDATED STATUTES OF LOWER
    CANADA, c. 87, s. 12   8 App. Cas. 530
  See COLONIAL LAW—CANADA—QUEBEC.
    2.
CONSOLIDATION OF MORTGAGES.
    See Cases under MORTGAGE—CONSOLI-
    DATION.
—— Restriction of.
    See MORTGAGE—CONSOLIDATION—*Sta-
    tutes.*
CONSPIRACY.
—— Combination for unlawful Object — *Interim or Interlocutory Injunction — Irreparable
Damage.*] A confederation or conspiracy by an
associated body of shipowners which is calculated
to have and has the effect of driving the ships of
other merchants or owners, and those of the Plaintiffs in particular, out of a certain line of trade,—
even though the immediate and avowed object be,
not to injure the Plaintiffs, but to secure to the
conspirators themselves a monopoly of the carrying trade between certain foreign ports and this
country,—is, or may be, an indictable offence, and
therefore actionable if private and particular
damage can be shewn.—To warrant the Court,
however, in granting an interim or interlocutory
injunction to restrain the parties from continuing
to pursue the objectionable course, those who com·
plain must at least shew that they have sustained
or will sustain "irreparable damage,"—that is,
damage for which they cannot obtain adequate
compensation without the special interference
of the Court. MOGUL STEAMSHIP COMPANY *v.*
M'GREGOR, GOW, & CO. -   15 Q. B. D. 476
—— Criminal law   -   - 12 Q. B. D. 241
    See CRIMINAL LAW—CONSPIRACY.
CONSTABLE—Notice of Action—*Trial in County,
where Fact committed*—1 & 2 *Will.* 4, c. 41, ss. 5,
19—2 & 3 *Vict.* c. 93, s. 8—*Contagious Diseases
(Animals) Act,* 1878 (41 & 42 *Vict.* c. 74), s. 50.]
An officer of police, appointed under 2 & 3 Vict.
c. 93, s. 8, who is sued for anything done in intended pursuance of the duties imposed and powers
conferred upon him by the Contagious Diseases
(Animals) Act, 1878, s. 50, is not entitled by
virtue of 1 & 2 Will. 4, c. 41, ss. 5, 19, to notice
of action and to have the action tried in the
county where the alleged grievance has been
committed ; for, although 2 & 3 Vict. c. 93, s. 8,
incorporates 1 & 2 Will. 4, c. 41, nevertheless the
protection afforded by sect. 19 of the last-named
statute extends by force of sect. 5 only to those
cases where a constable appointed under it is
intending to act with the power and authority
given to a constable by the common law or by
some statute existing when 1 & 2 Will. 4, c. 41,
was passed. BRYSON *v.* RUSSELL   14 Q. B. D. 720
—— Borough constable.
    See MUNICIPAL CORPORATION—CONSTI-
    TUTION—*Statutes.*
—— Costs as Defendant in action—Liability of
    borough fund   -   - 6 Q. B. D. 135
    See MUNICIPAL CORPORATION—RATES.

CONSTITUENCY—Parliament.
    See PARLIAMENT—REDISTRIBUTION OF
    SEATS—*Statutes.*
CONSTRUCTION—Settlement.
    See Cases under SETTLEMENT.
—— Statute   -   -   - 6 App. Cas. 114
    See SCOTCH LAW—RAILWAY COMPANY. 2.
—— Will.
    See Cases under WILL.
CONSTRUCTIVE NOTICE—Vendor's lien
                [26 Ch. D. 501
    See VENDOR AND PURCHASER—LIEN. 2.
CONTAGIOUS DISEASES (ANIMALS) ACTS.
    The Act 47 & 48 *Vict.* c. 13 (*the Contagious
Diseases Animals Act,* 1884), *extends the power of
the Privy Council to prohibit the landing or export
of animals: and amends* 41 & 42 *Vict. c.* 74 (*the
Contagious Diseases Animals Act,* 1878).
    The Act 47 & 48 *Vict.* c. 47 (*the Contagious
Diseases Animals Transfer of Parts of Districts
Act,* 1884), *enables local authorities to transfer the
whole or certain parts of their districts for the
purposes of the Contagious Diseases Animals Act,*
1878, *to the districts of neighbouring local authorities.*

ORDERS IN COUNCIL UNDER THE CONTAGIOUS
    DISEASES ANIMALS ACT, 1878.

    Order in Council of 5th February, 1884, *revok-
ing certain earlier Orders* - L. G., 1884, p. 643
    Order in Council of 5th February, 1884 (*the
Animals Order of* 1884) *provides for the management of diseased animals, their disinfection,
transit and otherwise.*

        Analysis of this Order.

        PART I. PRELIMINARY.

        PART II. DISEASE.

    1. *Cattle plague.*
    2. *Pleuro-pneumonia.*
    3. *Foot-and-mouth disease.*
    4. *Sheep-pox.*
    5. *Sheep-scab.*
    6. *Glanders and farcy.*
    7. *Swine fever.*
    8. *Agreements of local authorities respecting
movement.*
    9. *General regulations as to movement licences.*
    10. *Offences.*
    11. *Pleuro-pneumonia, or foot-and-mouth dis-
ease, or swine fever found in a market, railway
station, grazing park, or other like place, or during
transit.*
    12. *Exposure or movement of diseased animals,
horses, asses, and mules.*
    13. *Removal of dung or other things.*
    14. *Carcases.*
    15. *Slaughter houses.*
    16. *Regulation by local authorities of markets,
fairs, and other places.*

        PART III. DISINFECTION.

    17. *Water traffic.*
    18. *Railway traffic.*
    19. *Road traffic.*
    20. *Landing places.*
    21. *Miscellaneous.*

CONTAGIOUS DISEASES (ANIMALS) ACTS—
continued.

22. *Offences.*
23. *Markets, fairs, sale-yards, places of exhibition, lairs, and other places.*

Part IV. Transit.

24. *Transit by water.*
25. *Shipping and unshipping places.*
26. *Transit by railway.*
27. *Offences.*
28. *Water supply on railways.*

Part V. General.

29. *Inspectors and Forms.*
30. *Miscellaneous.*

Schedules.

[L. G., 1884, p. 645

Order in Council of 5th of February, 1884, declaring the foot-and-mouth disease. Temporary Order of 1884 - **L. G., 1884, p. 738**
Order in Council of 11th of November, 1884, revokes so much of last as applies specially to the Metropolis - **L. G., 1884, p. 4889**
Order in Council of 4th of April, 1884, revokes art. 105 of the Animals Order of 1884 and enables local authorities to make regulations for cleansing and disinfection of animals - L. G., 1884, p. 1603
Order in Council of 12th of May, 1884, provides for foreign animals landed at an Admiralty wharf
[L. G., 1884, p. 2125
Order in Council of 16th of May, 1884, revokes art. 62 of the Animals Order of 1884, and provides for swine affected with swine fever
[L. G., 1884, p. 2176
Order in Council of 29th of July, 1884, provides for the formation of swine fever infected circles
[L. G., 1884, p. 3482
Order in Council of 13th of November, 1884, adds rules to the rules contained in the 4th Schedule of 41 & 42 Vict. c. 74, with regard to foot-and-mouth disease infected places L. G., 1884, p. 4890
Order in Council of 13th of February, 1885 (the Foot and Mouth Disease Slaughter Order of 1885), declares concerning slaughter in cases of foot-and-mouth disease - **L. G., 1885, p. 627**
Order in Council of 15th of June, 1885 (the Foreign Animals Order of 1885), declares concerning foreign animals landed in England, Wales and Scotland.

Analysis of this Order.

4. *Interpretation.*
5. *Prohibited countries.*
6. *Ports having foreign animals wharves.*
7. *Conditions of landing.*
8. *Exception in favour of Admiralty wharves.*
9. *Regulations applying to landing stage.*
10. *Charge of animals on landing.*
11. *Disposal of animals on landing.*
12. *Regulations applying to reception lair.*
13. *Regulations applying to all parts of foreign animals wharf (other than reception lair) on detection of disease.*
14. *Feeding and watering.*
15. *Time for slaughter.*
16. *Movement of carcases, manure, &c.*
17. *Disinfection of foreign animals wharf.*
18. *Restriction on use of foreign animals wharf.*

CONTAGIOUS DISEASES (ANIMALS) ACTS—
continued.

19. *Ports having quarantine stations.*
20. *Animals intended for reshipment to a foreign country.*
21. *Animals intended for purposes of exhibition, or for other exceptional purposes (other than reshipment.)*
22. *Movement of carcases.*
23. *Disinfection of dung and manure.*
24. *Disinfection of quarantine station.*
25. *Restriction on use of quarantine station.*
26. *Free countries.*
27. *Landing place.*
28. *Conditions of landing.*
29. *Twelve hours detention.*
30. *Examination and consequences.*
31. *Continuance of one cargo.*
32. *Detention of suspected animals.*
33. *Movement of animals, carcases, manure, &c.*
34. *Disinfection of landing place.*
35. *Restriction on use of landing place.*
36. *Landing of other foreign animals.*
37. *Channel Islands.*
38. *Isle of Man.*
39. *Ship's cows and goats.*
40. *Landing and disposal of dung, fodder, litter, utensils, and other things.*
42. *Removal from wharf or station or landing place.*
43. *Vessels.*
44. *Moveable gangways and other apparatus.*
45. *Substitution in existing orders.*
46. *Fittings of vessels.*
47. *Shorn sheep.*
48. *Gangways for sheep pens.*
49. *Detention.*
50. *Water.*
51. *Food.*
52. *Disinfection of persons and clothes.*
53. *Foreign animals injured on voyage.*
54. *Carcases of animals dying on voyage.*
55. *General power of detention.*
56. *Duties of local authorities and police.*
57. *Offences.*
List of prohibited countries.
List of free countries.
Rules for foreign animals wharf.

[L. G., 1885, p. 2741

Order in Council of 15th June, 1885 (the Dairies, Cowsheds, and Milkshops Order of 1885), provides concerning registration of dairymen, construction of new dairies, contamination of milk, disease in cow-sheds, &c. - L. G., 1885, p. 2751

Order in Council of 4th December, 1885, approves of a landing place in the port of London (Thames Haven) for foreign animals L. G., 1885, p. 5933

—— Justices — Jurisdiction—41 & 42 Vict. c. 74—Offences against Act — Carriers—Persons "causing or permitting" Movement of Animals into Proscribed Districts.] By an Order of Council made under the Contagious Diseases (Animals) Act, 1878, if an animal is moved in contravention of the regulations of any local authority, the person "causing, directing, or permitting" the movement shall be deemed guilty of an offence against the Act. The local authority of the county of Dorset having by regulations

CONTAGIOUS DISEASES (ANIMALS) ACTS—
continued.

prohibited the movement of animals into their district except under specified conditions, animals were consigned to a place within the district, with through bills from Cork viâ Bristol and a specified route. The Appellants were no parties to the contract with the consignor, but in furtherance of the scheme of carriage carried the animals on their railway over a portion of the route to a point outside the county of Dorset whence they were subsequently carried into that county by another company :—*Held*, that the Appellants were liable to be convicted of an offence against the Act as persons "causing, directing, or permitting" the movement of the animals within the meaning of the Order of Council; and that the justices of the county of Dorset had jurisdiction to convict. MIDLAND RAILWAY COMPANY *v.* FREEMAN　-　-　-　**12 Q. B. D. 629**

—— Notice of action—Trial in county where fact committed　-　-　**14 Q. B. D. 720**
　See CONSTABLE.

CONTEMPORANEOUS CONVEYANCES—Easements　-　-　**16 Ch. D. 355**
　See LIGHT—TITLE. 6.

—— Priority　-　-　-　**21 Ch. D. 762**
　See DEED. 1.

CONTEMPORANEOUS EXPLANATION — Statutes　-　-　-　**8 App. Cas. 658**
　See SCOTCH LAW—HARBOUR. 2.

CONTEMPORANEOUS SECURITIES—Freehold and leasehold　**16 Ch. D. 211, 214, n.**
　See MORTGAGE—CONTRACT. 4, 5.

CONTEMPT—Admiralty Court—Notice of warrant—Removal of ship　**10 P. D. 120**
　See PRACTICE—ADMIRALTY—ARREST OF SHIP. 2.

—— Attachment.
　See Cases under PRACTICE — SUPREME COURT—ATTACHMENT.

—— Attachment—Divorce Court—Payment of costs　-　**9 P. D. 52; 10 P. D. 72**
　See PRACTICE—DIVORCE—RESTITUTION OF CONJUGAL RIGHTS. 1, 2.

—— Attachment—Solicitor—Order for payment of money **11 Q. B. D. 545; 12 Q. B. D. 44**
　See SOLICITOR—LIABILITIES. 4, 5.

—— Attachment—Solicitor—Unqualified person
　　[8 Q. B. D. 187; 15 Q. B. D. 348
　See SOLICITOR—UNQUALIFIED. 1, 2.

—— Bankruptcy—Trustee—Default in rendering accounts　-　-　**7 Q. B. D. 9**
　See BANKRUPTCY—TRUSTEE. 5.

—— County Court　-　-　**13 Q. B. D. 963**
　See BANKRUPTCY—JURISDICTION. 2.

—— Ecclesiastical Court 7 P. D. 94; 7 Q. B. D. 273;
　　　　　　　　　[6 App. Cas. 657
　See PRACTICE — ECCLESIASTICAL—CONTEMPT. 1, 2.

—— Refusal to commit—Right to appeal
　　　　　　　　　[20 Ch. D. 493
　See PRACTICE—SUPREME COURT—APPEAL. 1.

—— Ward of Court　-　-　**25 Ch. D. 482**
　See INFANT—SETTLEMENT. 1.

CONTEMPT OF COURT.

—— Advertisement for *Subscription to defend a Suit—Advertisement of Reward for Evidence.*] An injunction having been granted to restrain the Defendants from infringing a patent for nickel-plating, they gave notice of appeal and published in a newspaper an advertisement inviting the trade to subscribe towards the expenses of the appeal, and also an advertisement offering a reward of £100 to any one who could produce documentary evidence that nickel-plating was done before 1869. The Plaintiffs moved to commit the publishers of the newspaper for contempt of Court in publishing these advertisements, as being an interference with the course of justice, stating at the same time that they did not press for a committal, but would be satisfied with an expression of regret and an undertaking not to repeat the advertisements :—*Held*, that as all persons engaged in the trade of plating had a common interest in resisting the claims of the Plaintiffs, an advertisement asking them to contribute to the expenses of defending the proceedings was open to no objection :—*Held*, also, that the advertisement offering a reward for documentary evidence was free from objection.—*Pool v. Sacheverel* (1 P. Wms. 675) questioned.—The Court will discourage motions to commit where no real case for committal is made, and only an apology and costs are asked for. PLATING COMPANY *v.* FARQUHARSON　-　**17 Ch. D. 49**

CONTEXT—Reference to—Misdescription
　See WILL—MISTAKE. 3. [28 Ch. D. 153

CONTINGENT INTEREST　-　**16 Ch. D. 691;**
　　　　　　　　　[30 Ch. D. 186
　See POWER—EXECUTION. 1, 14.

—— Heirlooms—Vesting　-　**24 Ch. D. 102**
　See WILL—HEIRLOOM. 1.

—— Tenant for life—Settled Land Act
　　　　　　　　　[24 Ch. D. 114
　See SETTLED LAND ACT—DEFINITIONS. 1.

CONTINGENT LEGACY -　-　**18 Ch. D. 614**
　See WILL—LAPSE. 4.

—— Interim income 23 Ch. D. 360; 25 Ch. D. 743
　See WILL—INTERIM INCOME. 2, 3.

—— Intermediate income.
　See Cases under INFANT—MAINTENANCE. 4—7.

—— Proof in administration　-　**17 Ch. D. 342**
　See EXECUTOR—ACTIONS. 19.

CONTINGENT LIABILITY—Covenant not to revoke will 21 Ch. D. 780; 23 Ch. D. 285
　See BANKRUPTCY—PROOF. 6.

CONTINGENT REMAINDER—Will　**18 Ch. D.**
　　　　　　[524; 24 Ch. D. 633
　See WILL — CONTINGENT REMAINDER. 1, 2.

—— Will　-　-　-　**17 Ch. D. 211**
　See WILL—PERPETUITY. 3.

CONTINUANCE OF ACTION—Trustee in bankruptcy—Adoption of previous proceedings　-　-　-　**28 Ch. D. 53**
　See PRACTICE — SUPREME COURT — CHANGE OF PARTIES. 2.

CONTINUANCE OF ACTION—*continued.*

—— Trustee in bankruptcy—Suing in official name　-　**26 Ch. D. 38**
See PRACTICE—SUPREME COURT—SECU-·RITY FOR COSTS. 8.

CONTINUING BREACH—Covenant—Lease
[7 App. Cas. 19
See VENDOR AND PURCHASER—CONDI-TIONS OF SALE. 3

CONTRACT.　　　　　　　　　Col.
　　I. ACCEPTANCE　-　-　-　- 407
　　II. BREACH　　-　-　-　— 408
　　III. VALIDITY　-　-　-　— 410

—— SALE OF GOODS :
　　See SALE OF GOODS.

—— SALE OF LAND :
　　See VENDOR AND PURCHASER.

I. CONTRACT—ACCEPTANCE.

1. —— *Correspondence—Consensus ad idem —Misunderstanding of Parties as to Subject-matter of Negotiation.*] A negotiation took place as to the sale by L. to P. of a British patent and certain foreign patents for the same inventions, and ultimately an offer was made for sale at £500 and accepted by letter, but it was not quite clear whether the offer and acceptance related to all the patents, or to the British patent only. P. brought his action for specific performance, treating the contract as including all the patents, and moved for an injunction to restrain L. from parting with them. At the hearing of the motion he asked for leave to amend his writ, and for an injunction as to the British patent only :—*Held*, by Kay, J., that as L. had understood that he was negotiating about the British patent only, and P. that he was negotiating as to all the patents, there never was the consensus ad idem which is necessary to make a contract; that there was, therefore, no contract which P. could enforce; and that an injunction must be refused.—*Held*, on appeal, that an injunction should be granted, for that where a written agreement has been signed, though it is in some cases a defence to an action for specific performance according to its terms that the defendant did not understand it according to what the Court holds to be its true construction, the fact that the plaintiff has put an erroneous construction upon it, and insisted that it included what it did not include, does not prevent there being a contract, nor preclude the plaintiff from waiving the question of construction and obtaining specific performance according to what the defendant admits to be its true construction. PRESTON *v.* LUCK　-　- **27 Ch. D. 497**

2. —— *Incorporation of Conditions—Repository for Sale of Horses and Carriages—Receipt delivered to Customer—Incorporation of Conditions exhibited upon Premises—Presumption of Assent.*] The Defendant was keeper of a repository for the sale on commission of horses and carriages. The Plaintiff delivered to him a waggonette to be sold, and took from him a printed form which contained a receipt for the waggonette, followed by the words, "Subject to the conditions as exhibited upon the premises." By one of the conditions exhibited upon the premises the De-

I. CONTRACT—ACCEPTANCE—*continued.*

fendant had power to sell any property sent to the repository which remained over one month unless all expenses were previously paid. The Plaintiff did not read this receipt, but put it into his pocket without noticing it. The Defendant having sold the waggonette in the exercise of the power of sale in the conditions, the Plaintiff brought an action to recover its value, and at the trial the jury, having been directed that the question was whether the Defendant had or had not given the Plaintiff reasonable notice of the conditions, found a verdict for the Plaintiff :—*Held*, that the jury had been misdirected, for the condition was not unreasonable, and, having regard to the circumstances, there was nothing to take the case out of the general rule that if a document in a common form is delivered by one of two contracting parties to and accepted without objection by the other, it is binding upon him, whether he informs himself of its contents or not, and that judgment ought to be entered for the Defendant without a new trial, for there was no evidence upon which the jury could have properly found for the Plaintiff.—*Zunz* v. *South Eastern Railway Company* (Law Rep. 4 Q. B. 539); *Henderson* v. *Stevenson* (Law Rep. 2 H. L., Sc. 470); *Burke* v. *South Eastern Railway Company* (5 C. P. D. I) considered. WATKINS *v.* RYMILL. **10 Q. B. D. 178**

II. CONTRACT—BREACH.

1. —— *Certificate of Engineer—Local Government Acts—Public Health Act, 1875 (38 & 39 Vict. c. 55), s. 174—Wallasey Improvement Acts, 1858 (21 & 22 Vict. c. lxiii.) and 1861 (24 & 25 Vict. c. iv.)*] The Wallasey Local Board, a local board of health under the Public Health Act, 1848 (11 & 12 Vict. c. 63), and an urban sanitary authority under the Public Health Act, 1875 (38 & 39 Vict. c. 55), were authorized by the Wallasey Improvement Acts, 1858 and 1861, to acquire and work certain ferries between Liverpool and the Cheshire side of the Mersey, amongst others Seacombe Ferry. In May, 1878, they entered into a contract under their seal with the Plaintiff for the removal by dredging of a large quantity of soil from the bed of the river at Seacombe Ferry for £5000, the work to be executed under the direction and to the satisfaction of the engineer of the board by a given day, subject to an extension of time (as the engineer might think reasonable) in case the staging on the site to be dredged (which belonged to another contractor) should not be removed in time to enable the Plaintiff to complete the work by the day named.—The general superintendence of the works connected with their ferries was intrusted by the board to the engineer, subject to the control of a "ferry-works committee" appointed under sect. 200 of the Public Health Act, 1875, and acting under the powers conferred by that Act. The contract between the board and the Plaintiff contained a clause that, "if any difference shall arise between the local board and the contractor concerning the work hereby contracted for, or any part thereof, *or concerning anything in connection with this contract*, such difference shall be referred to the engineer, and his decision thereon shall be final and binding on the local board and the contractor."—In answer to a complaint by the Plaintiff on the 15th of January,

II. CONTRACT—BREACH—_continued._

1879, that his progress was obstructed by the non-removal of the staging, the engineer wrote, " I note that you are put to extra expense consequent on this delay, and I am prepared to compensate you for it on settlement." This was reported by the engineer to the ferry works committee, with an intimation that, " inasmuch as the Plaintiff was not able to complete his contract until the piles had been removed, the board would be liable for the rent of the dredgers until the Plaintiff could recommence." The committee thereupon by a minute which was subsequently confirmed by the board, ordered the engineer to use all speed in the removal of the piles. The staging referred to was not in fact removed until September, 1879, and the Plaintiff was put to considerable expense in consequence of this delay, by the detention of his plant and for the hire of dredgers and machinery, &c. The works were completed on the 11th of November.—After some correspondence between the Plaintiff and the engineer as to the amount due to the former on account of the contract and for delay, the latter gave the Plaintiff the following certificate :—" I certify that Mr. George Lawson has completed to my satisfaction the work which he contracted to execute at Seacombe Ferry for the Wallasey Local Board, and that he is therefore entitled to the sum of £500, being the balance of the sum of £5000 mentioned in his contract after deducting £4500 already paid him on account; and I further certify that Mr. George Lawson is entitled to the further sum of £565 19s. 2d. for extra work executed by him at Seacombe Ferry in connection with the said contract, being the balance of £1324 10s., after deducting £758 10s. 10d. paid by the Wallasey Local Board at his request for the hire of dredger, tug, hoppers, and insurance ; and that such several balances of £500 and £565 19s. 2d. are to be received by Mr. George Lawson in full satisfaction of all his claims on the Wallasey Local Board for work executed by him at Seacombe pursuant to the contract and _in connection with it._"—The Plaintiff declined to accept those sums in satisfaction, but claimed a balance of £2489 3s. 11d.—It was admitted that none of the forms prescribed by the Public Health Act, 1875, sect. 174, were complied with, that there was no consideration for any contract entered into or action taken by the Defendant board except as appeared in the case, and that no document other than the original contract was under the seal of the board :—_Held_, first, that, looking at the terms of the contract, which provided for a definite amount of dredging to be done by a certain time, with power to the engineer to extend that time as he should think reasonable in case of the non-removal of staging, there was an implied contract on the part of the board that the removal of the staging should not be unreasonably delayed ; and that for this breach, if proved, the Plaintiff would be entitled to recover damages from the Defendants,—the proper measure of such damages being the loss which the Plaintiff had unavoidably sustained in consequence of such unreasonable delay ; secondly, that this was not a difference " concerning a matter in connection with the contract," as to which the decision of the engineer was to be conclusive. LAWSON _v._ WALLASEY LOCAL BOARD - - 11 Q. B. D. 229

II. CONTRACT—BREACH—_continued._

2. —— Condition of Article—_Implied Undertaking—State of Repair and fitness for Use._] The Plaintiff, a master mariner, contracted with the Defendants, for a lump sum to be paid him by the Defendants, to take a certain specified steam-tug of the Defendants, towing six sailing barges, from Hull to the Brazils, the Plaintiff paying the crew and providing provisions for all on board for seventy days. The engines of the steam-tug were damaged and out of repair at the time of the contract, but neither the Plaintiff nor Defendants were then aware of this. The consequence however of the engines being so defective was that the time occupied in the voyage was increased, and the Plaintiff's gain in performing his contract was much less than it would otherwise have been :—_Held_, by Brett and Cotton, L.JJ., that as the contract related to a specified vessel, there was no implied undertaking by the Defendants that it should be reasonably efficient for the purposes of the voyage, and that therefore the defective state of the engines gave the Plaintiff no cause of action, it not appearing that the engines were in a worse state when the Plaintiff took possession of the vessel than they were at the time of the contract.—_Held_, contra, by Bramwell, L.J., that the defective state of the engines gave the Plaintiff a cause of action, as there was an implied undertaking by the Defendants that the engines were not so defective. ROBERTSON _v._ AMAZON TUG AND LIGHTERAGE COMPANY 7 Q. B. D. 598

III. CONTRACT—VALIDITY.

1. —— Bail in Criminal Case—_Indemnity of Surety—Contract against Public Policy—Municipal Corporations Act (5 & 6 Will. 4, c. 76), s. 57—Borough without Commission of Peace—Mayor a Justice of the Peace for Borough._] The mayor of a borough, without a commission of the peace, before whom a person was brought charged with embezzlement, remanded the accused to the next meeting of the justices of the peace for the county in which the borough was situated, and admitted him to bail, taking the recognizance of the Defendant in £100 for the appearance of the accused. The accused paid to the Defendant £100 to indemnify him against liability under the recognizances. The accused did not appear before the county justices, who, not recognizing the authority of the mayor to remand prisoners for appearance before the County bench, took no steps on the information preferred before him, but proceeded on a fresh information, and issued a warrant against the accused which was not executed. It did not appear that the Defendant's recognizance had been either forfeited or discharged or that he had paid anything under it. The accused having been adjudicated bankrupt, the Plaintiff, as trustee, sued to recover the £100 from the Defendant :—_Held_ (by Stephen, J.), that, by sect. 57 of the Municipal Corporations Act, the mayor was a justice of the peace for the borough, and the recognizance was valid ; that the £100 was paid to the Defendant in pursuance of a contract which was contrary to public policy, but that the contract had not been executed, and therefore the Plaintiff was entitled to recover. WILSON _v._ STRUGNELL [7 Q. B. D. 548

2. —— Bail in Criminal Case—_Indemnity of_

III. CONTRACT—VALIDITY—continued.

Surety—Deposit of Money with Surety—Action to recover Money deposited.] A contract is illegal, whereby a Defendant in a criminal case, who has been ordered to find bail for his good behaviour during a specified period, deposits money with his surety upon the terms that the money is to be retained by the surety during the specified period for his own protection against the Defendant's default, and at the expiration of that period is to be returned; and no action by the Defendant in the criminal case will lie to recover back the money deposited with the surety either before or after the expiration of the specified period, although the defendant in the criminal case has not committed any default, and although the surety has not been compelled to pay the amount for which he has become bound.— *Wilson v. Strugnell* (7 Q. B. D. 548) as to this point overruled. HERMAN *v.* JEUCHNER　　15 Q. B. D. 561

3. —— **Fraud on Bankrupt Law**—*Shipbuilding Contract—Power for Buyer in the event of Bankruptcy of Builder to use Materials belonging to Builder in completion of Ship.*] A contract for the building of a ship provided that, if at any time the builder should cease working on the ship for fourteen days, or should allow the time for completion and delivery of the ship to expire for one month without the same having been completed and ready for delivery, or in the event of the bankruptcy or insolvency of the builder, it should be lawful then and thenceforth for the buyer to cause the ship to be completed by any person he might see fit to employ, or to contract with some other person for the completion of the work agreed to be done by the builder, and to employ such materials belonging to the builder as should be then on his premises, and which should either have been intended to be, or be considered fit and applicable for the purpose:— *Held,* that, so far as this clause applied to the bankruptcy of the builder, it was void as against the trustee in his bankruptcy as being an attempt to control the user after bankruptcy of property vested in the bankrupt at the date of the bankruptcy, and as depriving the trustee of the right to elect whether he would complete the ship or not as might seem most advantageous for the creditors under the bankruptcy, and transferring that right of election to the buyer:—*Held,* also, that, this clause having been put in force by the buyer on the filing of a liquidation petition by the builder, the user of the builder's goods in the completion of the ship could not be justified on the ground of a subsequent cesser of work on the ship. *Ex parte* BARTER. *Ex parte* BLACK. *In re* WALKER　-　　26 Ch. D. 510

4. —— **Representation influencing Conduct**—*Parol Contract relating to Interest in Land—Part Performance—Statute of Frauds, s. 4.*] An intestate induced a woman to serve him as his housekeeper without wages for many years and to give up other prospects of establishment in life by a verbal promise to make a will leaving her a life estate in land, and afterwards signed a will, not duly attested, by which he left her the life estate:—*Held,* that there was no contract, and that even if there had been and although the woman had wholly performed her part by serving till the in-

testate's death without wages, yet her service was not unequivocally and in its own nature referable to any contract, and was not such a part performance as to take the case out of the operation of the Statute of Frauds, s. 4; and that she could not maintain an action against the heir for a declaration that she was entitled to a life estate in the land.—*Loffus v. Maw* (3 Giff. 592) disapproved.　MADDISON *v.* ALDERSON　7 Q. B. D. 174; [8 App. Cas. 467

CONTRACT—Breach of—Damages [8 Q. B. D. 357; 15 Q. B. D. 85 *See* DAMAGES—CONTRACT. 1, 2.

—— Breach of contract—Summary jurisdiction [6 Q. B. D. 182; 13 Q. B. D. 618 *See* MASTER AND SERVANT—REMEDIES. 2, 3.

—— Building contract—Extras—Certificate of surveyor　-　　10 Q. B. D. 400 *See* BUILDING CONTRACT. 1.

—— Company. *See* Cases under COMPANY—CONTRACTS.

—— Company—Prospectus　17 Ch. D. 301 *See* COMPANY—PROSPECTUS. 3.

—— Company—To obtain qualification [25 Ch. D. 283 *See* COMPANY — DIRECTOR'S QUALIFICATION. 1.

—— Company—To take shares　23 Ch. D. 413; [29 Ch. D. 421 *See* COMPANY — SHARES — ALLOTMENT. 1, 3.

—— Company—To take shares—Agent's authority　-　-　24 Ch. D. 367 *See* PRINCIPAL AND AGENT — AGENT'S AUTHORITY. 2.

—— Consideration—Contract by creditor to take less than due, whether valid 9 Q. B. D. 37; [11 Q. B. D. 221; 9 App. Cas. 605 *See* ACCORD AND SATISFACTION. 1, 2.

—— Corporation — Appointment of officer not under seal　-　-　14 Q. B. D. 500 *See* CORPORATION. 3.

—— Damages—Loss of profit on contract to resell　-　-　8 Q. B. D. 457 *See* DAMAGES—REMOTENESS. 4.

—— For benefit of third party　-　16 Ch. D. 290 *See* PRINCIPAL AND SURETY—CONTRACT.

—— Forfeiture—Liquidated damages *See* PENALTY.　[21 Ch. D. 243

—— Husband and wife　-　8 App. Cas. 420 *See* HUSBAND AND WIFE—WIFE'S CONVEYANCE. 3.

—— Interest of officials in. *See* LOCAL GOVERNMENT—LOCAL AUTHORITY—*Statutes.*

—— Local Board. *See* Cases under LOCAL GOVERNMENT—LOCAL AUTHORITY. 1—8.

—— Married woman　-　30 Ch. D. 169 *See* HUSBAND AND WIFE—MARRIED WOMEN'S PROPERTY ACT. 12.

—— Partnership articles. *See* Cases under PARTNERSHIP — CONTRACT.

CONTRACT—*continued.*

—— Privity of - - - 19 Ch. D. 246
    See PATENT—ASSIGNMENT. 2.

—— Privity of 24 Ch. D. 54; 10 App. Cas. 617
    See FACTOR. 1.

—— Procuring breach of—Master and servant
    [6 Q. B. D. 333
    See MASTER AND SERVANT—REMEDIES.

—— Promoters of company—Formation
    [25 Ch. D. 103
    See COMPANY—FORMATION.

—— Rescission—Contract for delivery by instalments 9 Q. B. D. 648; 9 App. Cas. 434
    See SALE OF GOODS—RESCISSION. 2.

—— Rescission—Misrepresentation 20 Ch. D. 1
    See FALSE REPRESENTATION. 1.

—— Sale of goods.
    See Cases under SALE OF GOODS.

—— Sale of goods—Scotch law 6 App. Cas.
    [251, 588
    See SCOTCH LAW—SALE OF GOODS. 1, 2.

—— Sale of land.
    See Cases under VENDOR AND PURCHASER.

—— Sale of land—Confirmation 26 Ch. D. 220
    See SETTLED ESTATES ACT. 2.

—— Sale of land—Implied conditions.
    See VENDOR AND PURCHASER—CONDITIONS OF SALE—*Statutes.*

—— Service—Wages—Forfeiture 6 Q. B. D. 1
    See MASTER AND SERVANT—WAGES. 2.

—— Validity—Lunatic - 21 Ch. D. 615
    See LUNATIC—MAINTENANCE. 1.

—— Wife with husband—Agreement to assign real estate—Heir-at-law 9 Q. B. D. 576
    See HUSBAND AND WIFE—WIFE'S REAL ESTATE. 6.

CONTRACTOR—Liability - 19 Ch. D. 281;
    See SUPPORT. 2, 3. [6 App. Cas. 740

—— Liability of principal - 8 App. Cas. 443
    See PRINCIPAL AND AGENT—PRINCIPAL'S LIABILITY. 1.

CONTRARY INTENTION—Will speaking from death - - 30 Ch. D. 50
    See WILL—SPEAKING FROM DEATH. 3.

CONTRIBUTION—Costs—Co-Defendants
    [18 Ch. D. 236
    See PRACTICE—SUPREME COURT—COSTS. 14.

—— Co-surety 17 Ch. D. 44, 825; 24 Ch. D. 709
    See PRINCIPAL AND SURETY—CONTRIBUTION. 1, 2, 3.

—— Tenants in common - 15 Q. B. D. 60
    See TENANT IN COMMON.

—— Mortgage of land and charge on shares
    [21 Ch. D. 583
    See COMPANY—MEMBER'S LIABILITY. 1.

—— Shareholders of cost-book mine 23 Ch. D. 52
    See COMPANY—COST-BOOK COMPANY. 4.

—— Ship—General average loss.
    See Cases under SHIP—GENERAL AVERAGE.

—— Third party - - 26 Ch. D. 161
    See PRACTICE—SUPREME COURT—THIRD PARTY. 5.

CONTRIBUTORY — Company — Winding-up — Costs—Winding-up petition
    [28 Ch. D. 183
    See COMPANY—WINDING-UP ORDER. 6.

—— Director—Qualification - 27 Ch. D. 322
    See COMPANY—DIRECTOR'S QUALIFICATION. 2.

—— Executor of shareholder—Retainer
    [29 Ch. D. 934
    See EXECUTOR—RETAINER. 4.

—— Life insurance company — Participating policy-holder.
    See Cases under COMPANY—LIFE INSURANCE COMPANY.

CONTRIBUTORY MISTAKE - 29 Ch. D. 459
    See COMPANY—PROSPECTUS. 5.

CONTRIBUTORY NEGLIGENCE—Collision
    [6 P. D. 76; 9 App. Cas. 136, 640, 873
    See SHIP—NAVIGATION. 2, 21, 28, 31.

—— Damage to ship - - 6 App. Cas. 217
    See SHIP—PILOT. 7.

CONTUMACY—Ecclesiastical law 7 P. D. 94;
    [7 Q. B. D. 273; 6 App. Cas. 657
    See PRACTICE — ECCLESIASTICAL—CONTEMPT. 1, 2.

CONVENIENCE—Accommodation works — Discretion of railway company 20 Ch. D. 323
    See RAILWAY COMPANY — RAILWAYS CLAUSES ACT. 1.

—— Balance of—Injunction - 27 Ch. D. 43
    See LIGHT—TITLE. 1.

—— Balance of—Injunction—Trade circular
    [25 Ch. D. 1
    See PATENT—INFRINGEMENT. 2.

CONVERSION OF GOODS—Demand and refusal—Limitations - 11 Q. B. D. 99
    See LIMITATIONS, STATUTE OF—PERSONAL ACTIONS. 3.

—— Warehouseman - - 6 Q. B. D. 475;
    See TROVER. [7 App. Cas. 591

CONVERSION OF REAL AND PERSONAL ESTATE — Accumulations of personal estate—Investment in realty
    [14 Q. B. D. 895
    See REVENUE—PROBATE DUTY. 1.

—— Bequest to separate use—Power of anticipation - - 21 Ch. D. 748
    See HUSBAND AND WIFE — SEPARATE ESTATE. 14.

—— Direction in will - 26 Ch. D. 601
    See WILL—CONVERSION.

—— Election to take personalty as realty
    See ELECTION. 3. [30 Ch. D. 654

—— Lunatic's estate—Partition suit 17 Ch. D.
    [241; 27 Ch. D. 309
    See LUNATIC—PROPERTY. 8, 9.

—— Order for sale - 25 Ch. D. 735
    See EXECUTOR—ACTIONS. 4.

—— Power of sale of land—Reinvestment in Government funds - 16 Ch. D. 648
    See POWER—EXECUTION. 15.

—— Realty forming partnership assets—Probate duty - - 13 Q. B. D. 275
    See REVENUE—PROBATE DUTY. 2.

CONVERSION OF REAL AND PERSONAL ESTATE—*continued.*

—— Sale under Partition Act—Married woman
[16 Ch. D. 362; 18 Ch. D. 612; 19 Ch. D. 302
See PARTITION SUIT—SALE. 3, 4, 6.

—— Trust for—Apportionment   24 Ch. D. 643,
[649, n.
See EXECUTOR—ADMINISTRATION. 5, 6.

CONVEYANCE.
See Cases and Statutes under VENDOR
AND PURCHASER—CONVEYANCE.

—— By married woman.
See Cases under HUSBAND AND WIFE—
WIFE'S CONVEYANCE.

—— By married woman—Wife's reversion
[18 Ch. D. 106
See HUSBAND AND WIFE—WIFE'S RE-
VERSION. 2.

—— Costs of—Lands Clauses Act 23 Ch. D. 167
See LANDS CLAUSES ACT—COSTS. 1.

—— Execution of.
See VENDOR AND PURCHASER — CON-
VEYANCE—*Statutes.*

—— Fraudulent—13 Eliz. c. 5.
See Cases under FRAUDULENT CONVEY-
ANCE.

—— Objection to—Right to rescind 28 Ch. D. 712
See VENDOR AND PURCHASER—CONDI-
TIONS OF SALE. 9.

—— Payment of purchase-money 27 Ch. D. 592
See VENDOR AND PURCHASER—CONVEY-
ANCE. 6.

—— To oneself.
See DEED—*Statutes.*

—— Voluntary—27 Eliz. c. 4.
See Cases under VOLUNTARY CONVEY-
ANCE.

CONVEYANCE OF TROOPS.
See ARMY AND NAVY—*Statutes.*

CONVEYANCE OF VOTERS.
See PARLIAMENT—ELECTION—*Statutes.*

CONVEYANCING ACT, 1881.
*The Act 44 & 45 Vict. c. 41, simplifies and im-
proves the practice of conveyancing ; vests in
trustees, mortgagees, and others, various powers
commonly conferred by provisions inserted in settlements, mortgages, wills, and other instruments ;
and amends in various particulars the law of property.*
Adoption of Act.] *Sect.* 66.—(1.) *It is hereby
declared that the powers given by this Act to any
person, and the covenants, provisions, stipulations,
and words which under this Act are to be deemed
included or implied in any instrument, or are by
this Act made applicable to any contract for sale or
other transaction, are and shall be deemed in law
proper powers, covenants, provisions, stipulations,
and words, to be given by or to be contained in any
such instrument, or to be adopted in connection with
or applied to, any such contract or transaction ;
and a solicitor shall not be deemed guilty of neglect
or breach of duty, or become in any way liable, by
reason of his omitting in good faith, in any such
instrument, or in connection with any such contract
or transaction, to negative the giving, inclusion,
implication, or application of any of those powers,*

CONVEYANCING ACT, 1881—*continued.*
*covenants, provisions, stipulations, or words, or to
insert or apply any others in place thereof, in any
case where the provisions of this Act would allow
of his doing so.*
(2.) *But nothing in this Act shall be taken to
imply that the insertion in any such instrument, or
the adoption in connection with, or the application
to, any contract or transaction, of any further or
other powers, covenants, provisions, stipulations or
words is improper.*
(3.) *Where the solicitor is acting for trustees,
executors, or other persons in a fiduciary position,
those persons shall also be protected in like manner.*
(4.) *Where such persons are acting without a
solicitor they shall be protected in like manner.*
Commencement of Act.] *By sect.* 1 *the Act
came into operation on the 31st of December,* 1881.
Conditions of Sale.] *See* VENDOR AND PUR-
CHASER—CONDITIONS OF SALE—*Statutes.*
Discharge of Incumbrances.] *See* VENDOR AND
PURCHASER—CONVEYANCE—*Statutes.*
Deeds—Construction.] *See* DEEDS—*Statutes.*
Execution of Purchase Deed.] *See* VENDOR
AND PURCHASER—CONVEYANCE—*Statutes.*
Infants.] *See* INFANT—PROPERTY—*Statutes.*
Leases.] *See* LANDLORD AND TENANT—LEASE
—*Statutes.*
Long Terms.] *See* LEASEHOLD—LONG TERMS
—*Statutes.*
Married Women.] *See* HUSBAND AND WIFE—
WIFE'S CONVEYANCE—*Statutes.*
Mortgages.]
See MORTGAGE—POWERS—*Statutes.*
MORTGAGE—CONSOLIDATION—*Statutes.*
MORTGAGE—REDEMPTION—*Statutes.*
MORTGAGE—FORECLOSURE—*Statutes.*
Power of Attorney.] *See* POWER OF ATTORNEY
—*Statutes.*
Rent-charges.] *See* RENT-CHARGE—*Statutes.*
Trust estates.] *See* WILL—TRUST ESTATES—
Statutes.
Trustees.] *See* TRUSTEE—*Statutes.*
Procedure.] *Sect.* 67.—(1.) *Any notice required
or authorized by this Act to be served shall be in
writing.*
(2.) *Any notice required or authorized by this
Act to be served on a lessee or mortgagor shall be
sufficient, although only addressed to the lessee or
mortgagor by that designation, without his name,
or generally to the persons interested, without any
name, and notwithstanding that any person to be
affected by the notice is absent, under disability,
unborn, or unascertained.*
(3.) *Any notice required or authorized by this
Act to be served shall be sufficiently served if it is
left at the last-known place of abode or business in
the United Kingdom of the lessee, lessor, mortgagee,
mortgagor, or other person to be served, or in case
of a notice required or authorized to be served on a
lessee or mortgagor, is affixed or left for him on the
land or any house or building comprised in the
lease or mortgage, or, in case of a mining lease, is
left for the lessee at the office or counting-house of
the mine.*
(4.) *Any notice required or authorized by this
Act to be served shall also be sufficiently served, if
it is sent by post in a registered letter addressed to
the lessee, lessor, mortgagee, mortgagor, or other
person to be served, by name, at the aforesaid place:*

CONVEYANCING ACT, 1881—*continued.*

of abode or business, office, or counting-house, and if that letter is not returned though the post-office undelivered; and that service shall be deemed to be made at the time at which the registered letter would in the ordinary course be delivered.

(5.) This section does not apply to notices served in proceedings in this Court.

Sect. 68. The Act 5 & 6 Will. 4, c. 62, shall, by virtue of this Act, have the short title of the Statutory Declarations Act, 1835, and may be cited by that short title in any declaration made for any purpose under or by virtue of that Act, or in any other document, or in any Act of Parliament.

Sect. 69.—(1.) All matters within the jurisdiction of the Court under this Act shall, subject to the Acts regulating the Court, be assigned to the Chancery Division of the Court.

(2.) Payment of money into Court shall effectually exonerate therefrom the person making the payment.

(3.) Every application to the Court shall, except where it is otherwise expressed, be by summons at Chambers.

(4.) On an application by a purchaser notice shall be served in the first instance on the vendor.

(5.) On an application by a vendor notice shall be served in the first instance on the purchaser.

(6.) On any application notice shall be served on such persons, if any, as the Court thinks fit.

(7.) The Court shall have full power and discretion to make such order as it thinks fit respecting the costs, charges, or expenses of all or any of the parties to any application.

(8.) General Rules for purposes of this Act shall be deemed Rules of Court within sect. 17 of the Appellate Jurisdiction Act, 1876, and may be made accordingly.

(9.) The powers of the Court may, as regards land in the County Palatine of Lancaster, be exercised also by the Court of Chancery of the County Palatine; and rules for regulating proceedings in that Court shall be from time to time made by the Chancellor of the Duchy of Lancaster, with the advice and consent of a Judge of the High Court acting in the Chancery Division, and of the Vice-Chancellor of the County Palatine.

(10.) General Rules, and Rules of the Court of Chancery of the County Palatine, under this Act may be made at any time after the passing of this Act, to take effect on or after the commencement of this Act.

Sect. 70.—(1.) An order of the Court under any statutory or other jurisdiction shall not as against a purchaser, be invalidated on the ground of want of jurisdiction, or of want of any concurrence, consent, notice, or service, whether the purchaser has notice of any such want or not.

(2.) This section shall have effect with respect to any lease, sale, or other act under the authority of the Court, and purporting to be in pursuance of the Settled Estates Act, 1877, notwithstanding the exception in sect. 40 of that Act, or to be in pursuance of any former Act repealed by that Act, notwithstanding any exception in such former Act.

(3.) This section applies to all orders made before or after the commencement of this Act, except any order which has before the commencement of this Act been set aside or determined to be invalid on

CONVEYANCING ACT, 1881—*continued.*

any ground, and except any order as regards which an action or proceeding is at the commencement of this Act pending for having it set aside or determined to be invalid.

Repeals.] *Sect. 71 repeals 8 & 9 Vict. c. 119; 23 & 24 Vict. c. 145, ss. 11–30.*

—— sect. 25　—　-　21 Ch. D. 169
　　See MORTGAGE—REDEMPTION. 4.

—— sect. 70　　-　　21 Ch. D. 41
　　See SETTLED ESTATES ACT. 1.

CONVEYANCING ACT, 1882 (45 & 46 Vict. c. 39).
　　See EXECUTORY LIMITATION—*Statutes.*
　　HUSBAND AND WIFE — WIFE'S CONVEYANCE—*Statutes.*
　　LEASEHOLD—LONG TERM—*Statutes.*
　　MORTGAGE—REDEMPTION—*Statutes.*
　　POWER—EXTINCTION—*Statutes.*
　　POWER OF ATTORNEY—*Statutes.*
　　TRUSTEE—APPOINTMENT—*Statutes.*
　　VENDOR AND PURCHASER — CONDITIONS OF SALE—*Statutes.*
　　VENDOR AND PURCHASER—PURCHASE WITHOUT NOTICE—*Statutes.*
　　VENDOR AND PURCHASER—TITLE—*Statutes.*

CONVEYANCING BUSINESS—Remuneration of solicitor　25 Ch. D. 301; 26 Ch. D. 155;
　　　　　　　　　　　　　[29 Ch. D. 199
　　See SOLICITOR—BILL OF COSTS. 19, 20, 21.

CO-OWNERSHIP—Action of restraint—Form of bail bond　-　　-　　10 P. D. 15
　　See PRACTICE—ADMIRALTY—ARREST OF SHIP. 1.

—— Charter—Managing owner—Commission
　　　　　　　　　　　　　[10 P. D. 69
　　See SHIP—CHARTERPARTY. 15.

—— Order of sale—Admiralty　-　10 P. D. 4
　　See SHIP—OWNERS. 1.

COPARCENERS—Trustee Act—Vesting order
　　　　　　　　　　　　　[27 Ch. D. 359
　　See TRUSTEE ACTS—VESTING ORDERS. 3.

COPY—Bill of sale—Registration　21 Ch. D. 871
　　See BILL OF SALE—FORMALITIES. 7.

—— Depositions in bankruptcy—Service
　　　　　　　　　　　　　[19 Ch. D. 580
　　See BANKRUPTCY—EVIDENCE. 7.

—— Pleadings—Costs　　-　19 Ch. D. 72
　　See PRACTICE—SUPREME COURT—COSTS. 16.

—— Summons—Inaccurate copy　25 Ch. D. 112
　　See BANKRUPTCY—ACT OF BANKRUPTCY. 19.

COPYHOLD :—　　　　　　　　Col.
　　I. CUSTOM　　　-　　-　　418
　　II. SURRENDER AND ADMITTANCE　-　419

Fees.] *List of fees ordered by Copyhold Commissioners to be taken in respect of enfranchisements and other transactions under the Copyhold and other Acts in accordance with 31 & 32 Vict. c. 89, s. 6*　-　　L. G., 1882, p. 2477

I. COPYHOLD—CUSTOM.

1. —— Common—*Appurtenant—Prescription Act (2 & 3 Will. 4, c. 71), s. 1—Cattle levant and couchant.*] A copyholder cannot lawfully claim

I. COPYHOLD—CUSTOM—continued.

common appurtenant without stint in respect of
his copyhold tenement, but such common must
be limited to the cattle levant and couchant on
the tenement to which it is annexed, or the number must be ascertained by the Court rolls or in
some other manner. MORLEY v. CLIFFORD
[20 Ch. D. 753

2. —— Descent—*Jus Representationis.*] The
custom of a manor was stated to be that all copyholds descended to the youngest son or daughter,
brother or sister, uncle or aunt.—A tenant died
intestate seised of customary lands of the manor,
leaving neither son, daughter, brother, sister,
uncle, nor aunt; but leaving sons of deceased
uncles:—Held, that the youngest son of the
youngest uncle was not entitled, and that the
heir-at-law was entitled to the lands. *In re*
SMART. SMART v. SMART　　18 Ch. D. 165

**II. COPYHOLD — SURRENDER AND ADMIT-
TANCE.**

1. —— Arbitrary Fine—*Omission to demand
fixed Sum—Three Years' improved Annual Value.*]
A lord, who is entitled by the custom of the
manor to a reasonable fine upon admission to a
copyhold tenement, may demand and recover such
fine by the description of three years' improved
annual value of the tenement to which the admittance relates, and without stating in money
the precise amount of the fine. FRASER v. MASON
[10 Q. B. D. 398; 11 Q. B. D. 574

2. —— Right to split Admittance—*Purchase
of several distinct Tenements under one Disposition—Fines—Special Custom—Evidence.*] There
is no general copyhold law that, in manors in
which a fine is only payable on the first admittance of a tenant, a purchaser of several distinct
copyhold tenements under one disposition —
whether a will, or surrender, or otherwise—is
entitled as of right to split his admittances, i.e.,
is entitled to compel the lord of the manor to
admit him to any one or more of such several
tenements, and to take admittance to the others
at any subsequent time, as and when he pleases.
—A special custom in a manor, that a purchaser
of several distinct copyhold tenements under one
disposition, must take admittance to all at one
and the same time, and pay one general fine in
respect of all, is good.—Such a special custom may
be evidenced by a uniform course of practice or
usage in the manor for a number of years, although
it does not otherwise appear either on the Court
rolls, or in any custumal or other record, of the
manor. JOHNSTONE v. EARL SPENCER
[30 Ch. D. 581

3. —— Trustees — *Customary Heiress of Devisee of Surviving Trustee—Right of Escheat—
Mandamus.*] A testatrix who died in 1851 devised her copyhold property to a trustee in trust
to pay the rents and profits to J. King for life,
and after her death to certain charitable purposes
which were void under the Mortmain Acts. The
testatrix died without heirs. The trustee named
in the will refused the trust, and two trustees
were appointed by order of the Court in 1853, who
were admitted upon the court rolls to hold upon
the trusts of the will. One trustee died in 1873,
and the surviving trustee, who died in 1877,

**II. COPYHOLD — SURRENDER AND ADMIT-
TANCE—**continued.

devised his trust estates to two trustees, neither of
whom was admitted to the copyholds. The
survivor of these trustees made no devise of his
trust estates and died leaving his youngest
daughter, Janet Hawkins, his customary heiress
according to the custom of this manor. The
tenant for life under the will died in 1883:—
Held, that Janet Hawkins, who claimed by
escheat and under a resulting trust, was entitled
to be admitted as tenant to the copyhold property
for her own benefit as against the lord of the
manor. GALLARD v. HAWKINS　27 Ch. D. 298

COPYHOLD — Enfranchisement — Acknowledgment of right to production of deeds
[25 Ch. D. 600
See VENDOR AND PURCHASER — TITLE
DEEDS.

—— Enfranchisement—Lunatic　20 Ch. D. 514
See LUNATIC—PROPERTY. 4.

—— Trustee dying without heir—Vesting order
[23 Ch. D. 205
See TRUSTEE ACT—VESTING ORDERS. 4.

COPYRIGHT:—　　　　　　　　　　　Col.

I. COPYRIGHT—BOOKS.

1. —— Illustrated Catalogue—*Book of Engravings—Copyright Act (5 & 6 Vict. c. 45).*]
The Plaintiffs, who were upholsterers, published
an illustrated catalogue of articles of furniture
which was duly registered under the Copyright
Acts as a book. The illustrations were engraved
from original drawings made by artists employed
by the Plaintiffs, but the book contained no letterpress of such a description as to be the subject of
copyright, and it was not published for sale, but
was used by the Plaintiffs as an advertisement.
The Defendants published an illustrated catalogue,
many of the illustrations in which were copied
from those in the Plaintiff's book:—Held, by the
Court of Appeal (affirming the decision of Vice-
Chancellor Hall), that the Plaintiffs were entitled
to an injunction restraining the Defendants from
publishing any catalogue containing illustrations
copied from the Plaintiffs' book.—A collection of
prints published together in a volume is a book
within the meaning of the Copyright Acts and
the proper subject of copyright, though it contains no such letterpress as could be the subject
of copyright, and it makes no difference that the
book is not published for sale but only used as
an advertisement.—Cobbett v. Woodward (Law
Rep. 14 Eq. 407) overruled. MAPLE & Co. v.
JUNIOR ARMY AND NAVY STORES　21 Ch. D. 369

2. —— Lecture in Manuscript—*Delivered from
Memory—Audience admitted by Tickets — Notes
taken by Shorthand Writer—Publication of Lecture in "Phonographic Lecturer"—Implied Contract—Injunction.*] N., an author and a lecturer
upon various scientific subjects, delivered from
memory, though it was in manuscript, a lecture

I. COPYRIGHT—BOOKS—*continued.*

at the Working Men's College upon "The Dog as the Friend of Man." The audience were admitted to the room by tickets issued gratuitously by the committee of the college. P., the author of a system of shorthand writing, and the publisher of works intended for instruction in the art of shorthand writing, attended the lecture, and took notes, nearly verbatim, in shorthand of it, and afterwards published the lecture in his monthly periodical "The Phonographic Lecturer."—On motion for an injunction to restrain the publication :—*Held*, that where a lecture of this kind is delivered to an audience, limited and admitted by tickets, the understanding between the lecturer and the audience is that, whether the lecture has been committed to writing beforehand or not, the audience are quite at liberty to take the fullest notes for their own personal purposes, but they are not at liberty to use them afterwards for the purpose of publishing the lecture for profit; and the publication of the lecture in shorthand characters is not regarded as being different in any material sense from any other; and injunction accordingly.—*Abernethy* v. *Hutchinson* (3 L. J. (Ch.) (O.S.) 209 ; 1 H. & T. 28) discussed. NICOLS v. PITMAN -　-　- 26 Ch. D. 374

3. —— **Registration**—*Pleading*—*Objections*—*Copyright Act, 1842* (5 & 6 *Vict.* c. 45), *ss.* 13, 16, 24.] Registration of a copyright is bad, if the name entered as that of "the publisher " is not that of the first publisher.—*Weldon* v. *Dicks* (10 Ch. D. 247) followed.—In an action for infringement of copyright, where objections to the registration are not delivered within the prescribed time, the action may nevertheless be dismissed if a defect in the registration is brought out from the Plaintiff's evidence. COOTE v. JUDD
[23 Ch. D. 727

4. —— **Telegraphy**—*Telegraphic Code compiled from the Words for use of Agents*—*Infringement of Copyright*—*Injunction.*] The Plaintiff published "The Standard Telegram Code," a book of words selected from eight languages, for use in telegraphic transmissions of messages, and it was accompanied by figure cyphers for reference or private interpretation. The book was registered under the Copyright Act, 5 & 6 Vict. c. 45. The Defendant bought a copy of the book, and compiled for their own use with its aid a new and independent work, as alleged, which was their own private telegraph code, and they distributed copies of their book amongst their agents at home and abroad, but they had not printed their book for sale or exportation :—*Held*, that the Defendants had infringed the copyright of the Plaintiff, and that a perpetual injunction must be granted. AGER v. PENINSULAR AND ORIENTAL STEAM NAVIGATION COMPANY　26 Ch. D. 637

5. —— **Title of Book**—*Registration of Part of a Book*—*Practice*—*Appeal for Costs.*] The Plaintiff published in numbers, in a weekly periodical called "Every Week," a tale intituled "Splendid Misery ; or, East End and West End," by C. A. Hazlewood. The Defendant subsequently commenced issuing in weekly parts, in a newpaper published by him, a tale by Miss Braddon intituled "Splendid Misery." Plaintiff was registered as the proprietor of "Every Week" before the publi-

I. COPYRIGHT—BOOKS—*continued.*

cation of it began, and after the tale had been completed he had himself registered as tho proprietor of "Splendid Misery ; or, East End and West End," giving the date of publication of the number of "Every Week" which contained the first number of the tale as the date of the publication of the tale. He then commenced an action to restrain the Defendant from continuing his publication of Miss Braddon's tale under the title of "Splendid Misery," and moved for an injunction. Before the motion was made, the Defendant had altered the title of Miss Braddon's tale, and the motion was ordered to stand over till the trial, the Defendant undertaking not to alter the new title in the meantime. The tale was finished under the new title before the trial. It was proved that a novel which once had a large circulation had been published in 1801 under the title of "Splendid Misery," and that second-hand copies could still be met with. At the trial Bacon, V.C., *held* that the Defendant had infringed the Plaintiff's copyright, and made an order containing no declaration of right, but simply ordering the Defendant to pay the whole costs of the action. The Defendant appealed, contending that the Plaintiff had no title, and that the action ought to have been dismissed :— *Held*, that it is not within the discretion of the Court to make a Defendant pay the whole costs of an action if the Plaintiff has no right to sue, that there was therefore implied in the order a declaration that the Plaintiff had a good cause of action, and that an appeal would lie.—*Held*, that though the registration of "Every Week" being made before any part of that periodical was published was not a good registration, the subsequent registration of the first number of the tale was a good registration to enable him to sue in respect of infringement of copyright in the title of the tale, supposing such copyright to exist :—But *held*, that the Plaintiff had no copyright in the title "Splendid Misery," for that copyright can only exist in something original, and the mere adopting as a title a hackneyed phrase, which moreover had been used as the title of a novel many years before, and which for anything that appeared might have been copied from that novel, could not give any copyright in that title :—*Held*, therefore that the Plaintiff had no title to sue for infringement of copyright, and that as it was clear that the public could not be misled into purchasing the Defendant's tale under the belief that it was the same as that of the Plaintiff, so that there was no ground for the interference of the Court on the principles applicable to trade-marks, the action ought to be dismissed with costs.—*Semble*, that as a general rule, there cannot be any copyright in the title of a book.—*Weldon* v. *Dicks* (10 Ch. D. 247) considered. DICKS v. YATES
[18 Ch. D. 76

II. COPYRIGHT—DESIGNS.

The Act 46 & 47 *Vict.* c. 57, s. 113 (*Patents, Designs and Trade Marks Act*, 1883), *repeals* (*inter alia*)

5 & 6 *Vict.* c. 100,
6 & 7 *Vict.* c. 65,
13 & 14 *Vict.* c. 104,
21 & 22 *Vict.* c. 70,

P 2

II. COPYRIGHT—DESIGNS—*continued.*

24 & 25 Vict. c. 73,
28 & 29 Vict. c. 3,
33 & 34 Vict. c. 27,
33 & 34 Vict. c. 97, s. 65,
38 & 39 Vict. c. 93,

and consolidates and amends the law relating to Copyright in Designs.

Sect. 3. Act to commence on the 31st of December, 1883.

Definitions.] *Sect.* 60. In and for the purposes of this Act

"Design" means any design applicable to any article of manufacture, or to any substance artificial or natural, or partly artificial and partly natural, whether the design is applicable for the pattern, or for the shape or configuration, or for the ornament thereof, or for any two or more of such purposes, and by whatever means it is applicable, whether by printing, painting, embroidery, weaving, sewing, modelling, casting, embossing, engraving, staining, or any other means whatever, manual, mechanical, or chemical, separate or combined, not being a design for a sculpture, or other thing within the protection of the Sculpture Copyright Act of the year 1814 (54 Geo. 3, c. 56).

"Copyright" means the exclusive right to apply a design to any article of manufacture or to any such substance as aforesaid in the class or classes in which the design is registered.

Sect. 61. The author of any new and original design shall be considered the proprietor thereof, unless he executed the work on behalf of another person for a good or valuable consideration, in which case such person shall be considered the proprietor, and every person acquiring for a good or valuable consideration a new and original design, or the right to apply the same to any such article or substance as aforesaid, either exclusively of any other person or otherwise, and also every person on whom the property in such design or such right to the application thereof shall devolve, shall be considered the proprietor of the design in respect to which the same may have been so acquired, and to that extent, but not otherwise.

Duration of Copyright.] *Sect.* 50.—(1.) When a design is registered, the registered proprietor of the design shall, subject to the provisions of this Act, have copyright in the design during five years from the date of registration.

(2.) Before delivery on sale of any articles to which a registered design has been applied, the proprietor must (if exact representations or specimens were not furnished on the application for registration), furnish to the Comptroller the prescribed number of exact representations or specimens of the design; and if he fails to do so, the Comptroller may erase his name from the register, and thereupon his copyright in the design shall cease.

Sect. 51. Before delivery on sale of any articles to which a registered design has been applied, the proprietor of the design shall cause each such article to be marked with the prescribed mark, or with the prescribed word or words or figures, denoting that the design is registered; and if he fails to do so the copyright in the design shall cease, unless the proprietor shews that he took all proper steps to ensure the making of the article.

Sect. 52.—(1.) During the existence of copyright

II. COPYRIGHT—DESIGNS—*continued.*

in a design, the design shall not be open to inspection except by the proprietor, or a person authorised in writing by the proprietor, or a person authorized by the Comptroller or by the Court, and furnishing such information as may enable the Comptroller to identify the design, nor except in the presence of the Comptroller, or of an officer acting under him, nor except on payment of the prescribed fee; and the person making the inspection shall not be entitled to take any copy of the design, or of any part thereof.

(2.) When the copyright in a design has ceased, the design shall be open to inspection, and copies thereof may be taken by any person on payment of the prescribed fee.

Sect. 53. On the request of any person producing a particular design, together with its mark of registration, or producing only its mark of registration, or furnishing such information as may enable the Comptroller to identify the design, and on payment of the prescribed fee, it shall be the duty of the Comptroller to inform such person whether the registration still exists in respect of such design, and if so, in respect of what class or classes of goods, and stating also the date of registration, and the name and address of the registered proprietor.

Sect. 54. If a registered design is used in manufacture in any foreign country and is not used in this country within six months of its registration in this country, the copyright in the design shall cease.

Exhibition at Industrial and International Exhibitions.] *Sect.* 57. The exhibition at an industrial or international exhibition, certified as such by the Board of Trade, or the exhibition elsewhere during the period of the holding of the exhibition, without the privity or consent of the proprietor, of a design, or of any article to which a design is applied, or the publication, during the holding of any such exhibition, of a description of a design, shall not prevent the design from being registered, or invalidate the registration thereof, provided that both the following conditions are complied with; namely,—

(a.) The exhibitor must, before exhibiting the design or article, or publishing a description of the design, give the Comptroller the prescribed notice of his intention to do so; and

(b.) The application for registration must be made before or within six months from the date of the opening of the exhibition.

Fees.] *Sect.* 56. There shall be paid in respect of applications and registration and other matters under this part of this Act such fees as may be from time to time, with the sanction of the Treasury, prescribed by the Board of Trade; and such fees shall be levied and paid to the account of Her Majesty's Exchequer in such manner as the Treasury shall from time to time direct.

Legal Proceedings.] *Sect.* 58. During the existence of copyright in any design—

(a.) It shall not be lawful for any person without the license or written consent of the registered proprietor to apply such design or any fraudulent or obvious imitation thereof, in the class or classes of goods in which such design is registered, for purposes of sale to any article of manufacture or to

II. COPYRIGHT—DESIGNS—*continued.*

any substance artificial or natural or partly artificial and partly natural; and

(b.) It shall not be lawful for any person to publish or expose for sale any article of manufacture or any substance to which such design or any fraudulent or obvious imitation thereof shall have been so applied, knowing that the same has been so applied without the consent of the registered proprietor.

Any person who acts in contravention of this section shall be liable for every offence to forfeit a sum not exceeding £50 to the registered proprietor of the design, who may recover such sum as a simple contract debt by action in any Court of competent jurisdiction.

Sect. 59. Notwithstanding the remedy given by this Act for the recovery of such penalty as aforesaid, the registered proprietor of any design may (if he elects to do so) bring an action for the recovery of any damages arising from the application of any such design, or of any fraudulent or obvious imitation thereof for the purpose of sale, to any article of manufacture or substance, or from the publication, sale, or exposure for sale by any person of any article or substance to which such design or any fraudulent or obvious imitation thereof shall have been so applied, such person knowing that the proprietor had not given his consent to such application.

Register of Designs.] Sect. 55.—(1.) There shall be kept at the Patent Office a book called the Register of Designs wherein shall be entered the names and addresses of proprietors of registered designs, notifications of assignments and of transmissions of registered designs, and such other matters as may from time to time be prescribed.

(2.) The register of designs shall be primâ facie evidence of any matters by this Act directed or authorized to be entered therein.

Registration of Designs.] Sect. 47. The Comptroller may, on application by or on behalf of any person claiming to be the proprietor of any new or original design not previously published in ·the United Kingdom, register the design under this part of this Act.

(2.) The application must be made in the form set forth in the 1st Schedule to this Act, or in such other form as may be from time to time prescribed, and must be left at, or sent by post to, the Patent Office in the prescribed manner.

(3.) The application must contain a statement of the nature of the design, and the class or classes of goods in which the applicant desires that the design be registered.

(4.) The design may be registered in more than one class.

(5.) In case of doubt as to the class in which a design ought to be registered, the Comptroller may decide the question.

(6.) The Comptroller may, if he thinks fit, refuse to register any design presented to him for registration, but any person aggrieved by any such refusal may appeal therefrom to the Board of Trade.

(7.) The Board of Trade shall, if required, hear the applicant and the Comptroller, and may make an order determining whether, and subject to what conditions, if any, registration is to be permitted.

Sect. 48.—(1.) On application for registration of

II. COPYRIGHT—DESIGNS—*continued.*

a design the applicant shall furnish to the Comptroller the prescribed number of copies of drawings, photographs, or tracings of the design sufficient, in the opinion of the Comptroller, for enabling him to identify the design; or the applicant may, instead of such copies, furnish exact representations or specimens of the design.

(2.) The Comptroller may, if he thinks fit, refuse any drawing, photograph, tracing, representation, or specimen which is not, in his opinion, suitable for the official records.

Sect. 49.—(1.) The Comptroller shall grant a certificate of registration to the proprietor of the design when registered.

(2.) The Comptroller may, in case of loss of the original certificate, or in any other case in which he deems it expedient, grant a copy or copies of the certificate.

General.] Sects. 82–102 provide for the constitution of the Patent Office and the proceedings thereat, including the rectification and alteration of the register.

Sects. 103, 104 relate to International and Colonial arrangements.

Sects. 105, 106, as to offences against the Act,

And see PATENT—STATUTES.

1. —— Article erroneously marked—*Patents, Designs, and Trade-marks Act,* 1883 (46 & 47 Vict. c. 57), ss. 51, 113—*Designs Rules,* 1883, r. 32—*Costs—Innocent Infringer—Notice before Action.*] Sect. 51 of the Patents, Designs, and Trade-marks Act, 1883, applies to the delivery on sale of articles to which a design registered under the Act 5 & 6 Vict. c. 100, has been applied, and the marking of such goods since the Act of 1883 came into operation is regulated by that Act. Consequently, the proprietor of a design registered under the Act 5 & 6 Vict. c. 100, is in a proper case entitled to the benefit of the proviso contained in sect. 51, which relieves him from the forfeiture of his copyright resulting from the omission to mark the articles with the prescribed mark, if he shews that he "took all proper steps to ensure the marking."—The proprietor of a registered design instructed the manufacturer, who made for him the articles to which the design was applied, to stamp the proper mark upon them, and furnished him with a die for the purpose. By inadvertence the manufacturer marked some of the articles with a mark which belonged to another design registered by the same proprietor, the copyright of which had expired, using for the purpose by mistake an old die which remained in his possession, and the proprietor, after the Act of 1883 came into operation, sold some of the articles thus wrongly marked without observing the error. The letters Rd. formed part of both the marks :— Held, that the proprietor had not forfeited his copyright, but that he was protected by the proviso in sect. 51.—Held, that an innocent infringer of a registered design must pay the costs of a motion for an injunction to restrain him from infringing, though the Plaintiff had given him no notice of the infringement before serving him with the writ in the action.—*Upmann v. Forester* (24 Ch. D. 231) followed. WITTMAN v. OPPENHEIM ·   **27 Ch. D. 260**

2. —— New or Original Design — *Patents,*

II. COPYRIGHT—DESIGNS—continued.

Designs, and Trade-marks Act, 1883 (46 & 47 *Vict. c.* 57), *s.* 47.] A design is not a proper subject of registration under the Patents, Designs, and Trade-marks Act, 1883, unless there is a clearly marked and defined difference involving substantial novelty between it and any design previously in use.—A design for a shirt collar was registered, the advantages claimed for which were —the height of the collar above the stud which fastened it in front, the cutting away of the corners in a segment of a circle, and the absence of a band. A collar was shewn to have been previously in use which had no band, and in which the corners were cut away in arcs of circles; but the cutting away was not so wide, and the height above the stud was not so great, as in the registered design :—*Held,* that the registered design was not new or original within the meaning of the Act, and must be removed from the register. LE MAY *v.* WELCH. *In re* LE MAY'S REGISTERED DESIGN

[28 Ch. D. 24

III. COPYRIGHT—DRAMATIC.

1. —— **Place of Entertainment**—3 & 4 *Wm.* 4, *c.* 15, *ss.* 1, 2—5 & 6 *Vict. c.* 45, *ss.* 20, 21.] The 3 & 4 Wm. 4, c. 15, s. 1, gives the author of a dramatic piece not printed or published the sole liberty of representing it at any place of dramatic entertainment, and sect. 2 enacts that if any person shall, during the continuance of such sole liberty, without the consent of the author, represent such piece at any place of dramatic entertainment, " every such offender ". shall be liable for each and every such representation to the payment of not less than 40s. or to the full amount of the benefit arising from such representation or the loss sustained therefrom, whichever shall be the greater damages.—The 5 & 6 Vict. c. 45, by sect. 20, enacts that the 3 & 4 Wm. 4, c. 15, shall apply to musical compositions, and that the sole liberty of representing any dramatic piece or musical composition shall be the property of the author and his assigns for the term mentioned, and by sect. 21 enacts that the person who shall have such sole liberty of representing such dramatic piece or musical composition, " shall have and enjoy the remedies given and provided by 3 & 4 Wm. 4, c. 15, as if the same were re-enacted" in that Act :—*Held,* affirming the judgment of the Queen's Bench Division (Cotton, L.J., dissenting), that the person whose right under sect. 20 of 5 & 6 Vict. c. 45, to such sole liberty of representing a musical composition, has been infringed, is entitled to recover the penalty of 40s. given by sect. 2 of 3 & 4 Wm. 4, c. 15, although such musical composition has not been represented at a place of dramatic entertainment. WALL *v.* TAYLOR. WALL *v.* MARTIN 9 Q. B. D. 727;

[11 Q. B. D. 102

2. —— **Place of Entertainment**—*Performance in Private Room*—*Admission without Payment*— 3 & 4 *Wm.* 4, *c.* 15, *ss.* 1, 2.] The Defendant and others joined in representing a dramatic piece in a room of an hospital, without the consent of the proprietor of the copyright in the drama. The performance was merely for the entertainment of the nurses, attendants, and others connected with the hospital, who were admitted free of charge :— *Held,* by Brett, M.R., and Bowen, L.J. (Fry, L.J.,

III. COPYRIGHT—DRAMATIC—continued.

dissenting), that the room where the drama was represented was not a place of public entertainment, and consequently that the Defendant was not liable to damages or penalties under 3 & 4 Wm. 4, c. 15, ss. 1, 2.—Judgment of the Queen's Bench Division affirmed. DUCK *v.* BATES

[12 Q. B. D. 79; 13 Q. B. D. 843

3. —— **Printing and Publishing** -- *Musical Composition*—*Acting or Performing*—3 & 4 *Wm.* 4, *c.* 15, *s.* 1—5 & 6 *Vict. c.* 45, *ss.* 2, 20, 22.] The publication in this country of a dramatic piece, or musical composition, as a book before it has been publicly represented or performed does not deprive the author of such dramatic piece or musical composition, or his assignee, of the exclusive right of representing or performing it. CHAPPELL *v.* BOOSEY - - 21 Ch. D. 232

IV. COPYRIGHT—MUSIC.

By 45 & 46 *Vict. c.* 40 (*Copyright Musical Compositions Act,* 1882), *s.* 1, on and after the passing of the Act (10th of August, 1882) the proprietor of the copyright in any musical composition first published after the passing of the Act, or his assignee, who shall be entitled to and be desirous of retaining in his own hands exclusively the right of public representation or performance of the same, shall print or cause to be printed on the titlepage of every published copy of such musical composition a notice to the effect that the right of public representation or performance is reserved.

Sect. 2. *In case, after the passing of the Act, the right of public representation or performance of, and the copyright in, any musical composition shall be or become vested before publication of any copy thereof in different owners then, if the owner of the right of public representation or performance shall desire to retain the same, he shall, before any such publication of any copy of such musical composition, give to the owner of the copyright therein notice in writing requiring him to print upon every copy of such musical composition a notice to the effect that the right of public representation or performance is reserved ; but in case the right of public representation or performance of, and the copyright in, any musical composition shall, after publication of any copy thereof subsequently to the passing of the Act, first become vested in different owners, and such notice as aforesaid shall have been duly printed on all copies published after the passing of the Act previously to such vesting, then, if the owner of the right of performance and representation shall desire to retain the same, he shall, before the publication of any further copies of such musical composition, give notice in writing to the person in whom the copyright shall be then vested, requiring him to print such notice as aforesaid on every copy of such musical composition to be thereafter published.*

Sect. 3. *If the owner for the time being of the copyright in any musical composition shall, after due notice being given to him or his predecessor in title at the time, and generally in accordance with the last preceding section, neglect or fail to print legibly and conspicuously upon every copy of such composition published by him or by his authority, or by any person lawfully entitled to publish the same, and claiming through or under him, a note or memorandum stating that the right of public*

IV. COPYRIGHT—MUSIC—continued.

representation or performance is reserved, then and in such case the owner of the copyright at the time of the happening of such neglect or default, shall forfeit and pay to the owner of the right of public representation or performance of such composition the sum of £20 to be recovered in any Court of competent jurisdiction.

Sect. 4. *Notwithstanding the provisions of 3 & 4 Will.* 4, *c.* 15, *or any other Act in which those provisions are incorporated, the costs of any action or proceeding for penalties or damages in respect of the unauthorized representation or performance of any musical composition published before the 10th of August,* 1882, *shall in cases in which the plaintiff shall not recover more than* 40s. *as penalty or damages, be in the discretion of the Court or judge before whom such action or proceeding shall be tried.*

V. COPYRIGHT—NEWSPAPERS.

Registration.] *By the Newspaper Libel and Registration Act,* 1881 (44 & 45 Vict. c. 60), *s.* 8, *a register of newspaper proprietors as defined by the Act is to be established under the superintendence of a Registrar.*

Sect. 1 *defines* (inter alia) *the word* " *newspaper* " *to mean any paper containing public news, intelligence, or occurrences, or any remarks or observations therein, printed for sale and published in England or Ireland periodically, or in parts or numbers, at intervals not exceeding twenty-six days between the publication of any two such papers, parts, or numbers.*

Also any paper printed in order to be dispersed and made public weekly or oftener, or at intervals not exceeding twenty-six days, containing only or principally advertisements.

The word " *proprietor* " *to mean and include as well the sole proprietor of any newspaper, as also, in the case of a divided proprietorship, the persons who, as partners or otherwise, represent and are responsible for any share or interest in the newspaper as between themselves and the persons in like manner representing or responsible for the other shares or interests therein, and no other person.*

Sect. 7. *Where in the opinion of the Board of Trade inconvenience would arise or be caused in any case from the registry of the names of all the proprietors of the newspaper (either owing to minority, coverture, absence from the United Kingdom, minute subdivision of shares, or other special circumstances) it shall be lawful for the Board of Trade to authorize the registration of such newspaper in the name or names of some one or more responsible* " *representative proprietors.*"

Sect. 9. *Printers and publishers of newspapers to make annual returns on or before the* 31st *of July in every year, according to scheduled form, of :—*

 (a.) *The title of a newspaper.*
 (b.) *The names of all the proprietors of such newspapers, together with their respective occupations, places of business (if any), and places of residence.*

Sect. 10. *Penalty for omitting to make annual return within one month of the specified time.*

Sect. 11. *Power to any party to a transfer or transmission of or dealing with any share of or interest in any newspaper, whereby any person*

V. COPYRIGHT—NEWSPAPERS—continued.

ceases to be a proprietor, or any new proprietor is introduced, at any time to make a return according to a prescribed form.

Sect. 12. *Penalty for knowingly and wilfully making a misleading return.*

Sect. 13. *Register to be kept by registrar and to be open to public inspection, &c., during business hours.*

Sect. 14. *Fees to be paid in making returns and for inspecting, &c., register.*

Sect. 15. *Copies of entries in and extracts from register to be evidence.*

Sect. 16. *Penalties to be recovered before a Court of summary jurisdiction in manner provided by the Summary Jurisdiction Acts ; and summary orders to be enforced in manner provided by sect.* 34 *of the Summary Jurisdiction Act,* 1879, *which section is made applicable to Ireland.*

Sect. 17 *defines a* " *court of summary jurisdiction* " *and the expression* " *Summary Jurisdiction Acts.*"

Sect. 18 *provisions of the Act as to registration of newspaper proprietors not to apply to any newspaper which belongs to a joint stock company incorporated under the Companies Acts,* 1862 *to* 1879.

—— Registration — *Newspaper Article* — *Author*—*Injunction*—*Copyright Act* (5 & 6 Vict. c. 45).] A newspaper is within the Copyright Act (5 & 6 Vict. c. 45), and requires registration under that Act in order to give the proprietor the copyright in its contents and so enable him to sue in respect of a piracy :—*Cox* v. *Land and Water Journal Company* (Law Rep. 9 Eq. 324) not followed.—Also to enable the proprietor of a newspaper to sue in respect of a piracy of any article therein, he must shew, not merely that the author of the article has been paid for his services, but that it has been composed on the terms that the copyright therein shall belong to such proprietor. WALTER v. HOWE - 17 Ch. D. 708

VI. COPYRIGHT—PICTURES.

—— Photograph—"*Author*"—*Joint Authors* —*Copyright Act,* 1862 (25 & 26 Vict. c. 68), *ss.* 1, 4—*Amendment of Pleadings*—*Costs.*] A. and B. carried on business in copartnership as photographers under the firm of the L. Company. They did not take photographs themselves, but employed managers and a large staff of photographic artists and assistants. One of their managers, thinking that the photograph of the Australian Cricketers would sell well, arranged for the photographs to be taken without any payment being made for taking them, and sent one of the artists in the employ of the firm to take the negative. From this negative the photograph was in the usual way produced and sold by the firm in the ordinary course of business ; and A. and B. registered themselves under the Copyright Act, 1862, in their individual names as the proprietors and authors of the photograph. In an action by the firm to restrain the pirating of their copyright in the photograph :—*Held*, that A. and B. were not the authors of the photograph.—*Semble*, that the person who took the negative was the author.— Two or more persons may be registered under the Act as the "authors" of a painting, or a drawing, or a photograph ; but in such a case quære,

VI. COPYRIGHT—PICTURES—*continued.*

whether the copyright would subsist for the joint lives of the authors, and seven years afterwards, or for the lives and life of the survivors and survivor and seven years afterwards. NOTTAGE *v.* JACKSON - - 11 Q. B. D. 627

CORN RETURNS.

The Act 45 & 46 Vict. c. 37 (the Corn Returns Act, 1882), *repeals* 5 & 6 *Vict. c.* 14, 27 & 28 *Vict. c.* 87, *and s.* 56 *of* 6 & 7 *Wm.* 4, *c.* 71, *and amends the law respecting the obtaining of weekly returns of purchases of British corn so as to ascertain the average price of British corn.*

CORNER HOUSE 27 Ch. D. 362
    See METROPOLIS—MANAGEMENT ACTS. 3.

CORNWALL—Company for working mine in.
    See Cases under COMPANY— COST-BOOK COMPANY.

—— Duchy — Intestacy — Administration—Evidence - - 9 P. D. 63
    See ADMINISTRATOR—GRANT. 3.

CORONER.

—— **Misbehaviour in Office** — *Unnecessary Delay—Neglect or refusal to hold Inquest—Sudden Death without Information as to Cause—Discretion of Coroner as to holding Inquest.*] A coroner is not justified in delaying the inquest upon a dead body in a state of decomposition for so long a period as five days in order that the body may be identified, and buried and registered under the right name, and the mere fact that it has been placed in a mortuary can make no difference.—A coroner received from the proper police authorities a report with a view to an inquest, that a man within his district, aged sixty-one, had been found dead in his bed. It did not appear on the one hand that there had been any previous disease or illness, or on the other hand that there was any suspicion of violence, suicide, or crime. A medical man, moreover, refused to give a certificate of the cause of death, and the friends and relatives of the deceased made no objection to an inquest:—*Held,* that the coroner had, in the absence of further information as to the cause of death, no discretion to refuse to hold an inquest upon the ground that it was unnecessary. *In re* HULL
                    [9 Q. B. D. 689

—— Justice of the peace—Disqualification
                    [7 Q. B. D. 513
    See JUSTICES—DISQUALIFICATION. 1.

—— Prevention of inquest—Burning dead body
      [12 Q. B. D. 247 ; 13 Q. B. D. 331
    See CRIMINAL LAW—MISDEMEANOR. 1, 2.

CORPORATE AND INCORPORATE BODIES—
    Duty on.
    See REVENUE—STAMPS—*Statutes.*

CORPORATION.

1. —— Action for Malicious Prosecution.] An action for a malicious prosecution will lie against an incorporated company.—*Stevens* v. *Midland Railway Company* (10 Ex. 352) not followed.— The employment of a policeman by a company to protect their property is an act within the scope of the incorporation of the company. EDWARDS *v.* MIDLAND RAILWAY COMPANY 6 Q. B. D. 287

CORPORATION—*continued.*

2. —— **Borrowing Powers** — *Ultrà vires.*] The Respondents were constituted a company by an Act of Geo. 2, for the purpose of recovering and preserving the navigation of the River Dee. This Act was amended by subsequent Acts, but none of them expressly authorized or forbade the company to borrow, till the Act 14 & 15 Vict. c. lxxxvii., which, by sect. 24, empowered the company to borrow at interest for the purposes of their Acts upon bond or mortgage of the lands recovered and inclosed by them, or partly upon bond and partly upon such mortgage, a sum not exceeding £25,000, and also a further sum, not exceeding £25,000, upon mortgage of their tolls, rates and duties :—*Held,* affirming the decision of the Court of Appeal, that whether the earlier Acts gave an implied power to borrow or not, the company was prohibited by the 14 & 15 Vict. c. lxxxvii. from borrowing except in accordance with the provisions of that Act.—By Lord Blackburn :—The law laid down by the House of Lords in *Ashbury Company* v. *Riche* (Law Rep. 7 H. L. 653) applies to all companies created by any statute for a particular purpose, and not only to companies created under the Companies Act, 1862 (25 & 26 Vict. c. 89). BARONESS WENLOCK *v.* RIVER DEE COMPANY - 10 App. Cas. 354

3. —— Contract not under Seal—*School Board —Appointment of Architect—Orders to—Minutes of Board duly signed—Validity—*33 & 34 *Vict. c.* 75, *s.* 30, *sub-ss.* 1, 4, 6—*Sect.* 35—*Third Schedule,* 7.] By 33 & 34 Vict. c. 75 (the Elementary Education Act, 1870), s. 30, sub-s. (1), " The school board shall be a body corporate . . . . having a perpetual succession and a common seal . . . ," sub-sect. (4) "any minute made of proceedings at meetings of the school board, if signed by . . . . the chairman . . . . shall be receivable in evidence in all legal proceedings without further proof . . . ." sub-sect. (6) "the rules contained in the third schedule . . . shall be observed."—By sect. 35 "a school board may appoint a clerk and a treasurer and other necessary officers . . . ."—By the Third Schedule, 7, "the appointment of any officer of the board may be made by a minute of the board, signed by the chairman of the board, and countersigned by the clerk (if any) of the board, and any appointment so made shall be as valid as if it were made under the seal of the board."—By a minute signed by the chairman of a school board and countersigned by the clerk, the plaintiff was appointed architect of the board, and under orders given by subsequent minutes so signed and countersigned and communicated to him, he prepared plans for the board :—*Held,* that by virtue of the provisions of the Act he was entitled to recover payment for his services although the appointment and orders were not under seal. SCOTT *v.* CLIFTON SCHOOL BOARD - 14 Q. B. D. 500

—— Contract with.
    See Cases under LOCAL GOVERNMENT— LOCAL AUTHORITY. 1—8.

—— Municipal corporation—Resignation of office —Power to withdraw resignation
                    [14 Q. B. D. 908
    See MUNICIPAL CORPORATION—RESIGNATION.

CORPORATION—*continued.*

—— Discovery—Winding-up - **16 Ch. D. 58**
  See COMPANY—EVIDENCE. 1.

—— Income tax - - **8 App. Cas. 891**
  See REVENUE—INCOME TAX. 6.

—— Law of Canada - - **7 App. Cas. 136**
  See COLONIAL LAW—CANADA—QUEBEC.
  3.

—— Maintenance—Maliciously procuring bankruptcy - **10 App. Cas. 210**
  See CHAMPERTY. 2.

CORRESPONDENCE—Ante litem motam
  [22 Ch. D. 609
  See PRACTICE—SUPREME COURT — PRO-
  DUCTION OF DOCUMENTS. 27.

CORROBORATION—Claim against estate of deceased person - **23 Ch. D. 267**
  See EXECUTOR—ACTIONS. 15.

—— Claim for separate estate - **21 Ch. D. 657**
  See HUSBAND AND WIFE — SEPARATE
  ESTATE. 3.

**CORRUPT AND ILLEGAL PRACTICES PRE-
VENTION ACT,** 1883 — Municipal
  election.
  See MUNICIPAL CORPORATION—ELECTION
  —*Statutes.*

—— Parliamentary election.
  See PARLIAMENT—ELECTION—*Statutes.*

—— Parliamentary election—Repeal of dis-
  qualification of certain persons
  See PARLIAMENT—REDISTRIBUTION OF
  SEATS—*Statutes.*

COST-BOOK COMPANY.
  See Cases under COMPANY — COST-BOOK
  COMPANY.

COSTS.
  See Cases under PRACTICE — SUPREME
  COURT—COSTS.

—— Action by debenture-holder **28 Ch. D. 317**
  See COMPANY—DEBENTURE. 6.

—— Action in name of company **23 Ch. D. 1**
  See COMPANY — DIRECTOR'S APPOINT-
  MENT. 2.

—— Action of salvage—Commission on bail
  [10 P. D. 158
  See PRACTICE—ADMIRALTY — SALVAGE.
  6.

—— Administration action.
  See Cases under EXECUTOR—ACTIONS.
  10—14.

—— Administration proceedings **29 Ch. D. 913**
  See PRACTICE—SUPREME COURT—CHAM-
  BERS. 10.

—— Administration action—BankruptDefendant
  [21 Ch. D. 862, 865
  See TRUSTEE—COSTS AND CHARGES. 1, 2.

—— Administration action — Solicitors' Remuneration Act - **26 Ch. D. 155**
  See SOLICITOR—BILL OF COSTS. 21.

—— Admiralty.
  See Cases under PRACTICE—ADMIRALTY
  —COSTS.

—— Affidavit—Prolixity - **21 Ch. D. 835**
  See PRACTICE—SUPREME COURT — PRO-
  DUCTION OF DOCUMENTS. 1.

COSTS—*continued.*

—— Appeal—Bankruptcy **16 Ch. D. 110**
  See BANKRUPTCY—APPEAL. 2.

—— Appeal—Cross notice **19 Ch. D. 17**
  See PRACTICE — SUPREME COURT —
  APPEAL. 30.

—— Appeal—Scotch law - **6 App. Cas. 833**
  See SCOTCH LAW—HIGHWAY. 1.

—— Appeal for.
  See Cases under PRACTICE — SUPREME
  COURT—APPEAL. 24—33.

—— Appeal for - **19 Ch. D. 140**
  See BANKRUPTCY—LIQUIDATION. 5.

—— Appeal for - - **18 Ch. D. 76**
  See COPYRIGHT—BOOKS. 5.

—— Arbitration—Lands Clauses Act
  [11 Q. B. D. 345
  See LANDS CLAUSES ACT—COSTS. 1.

—— Assignment of bill of costs **12 Q. B. D. 518;**
  [26 Ch. D. 719
  See SOLICITOR—BILL OF COSTS. 4, 5.

—— Bankruptcy
  See Cases under BANKRUPTCY—COSTS.

—— Bankruptcy—Appeal - **25 Ch. D. 266**
  See BANKRUPTCY—ANNULMENT. 3.

—— Bankruptcy — Appeal — Preliminary objection **13 Q. B. D. 42 ; 14 Q. B. D. 123 ;**
  [15 Q. B. D. 338
  See BANKRUPTCY—APPEAL. 11, 12, 13.

—— Bankruptcy — Appeal — Creditors served
  with notice - **14 Q. B. D. 936**
  See BANKRUPTCY—DISCHARGE. 4.

—— Bankruptcy—Mortgagor and mortgagee—
  Application by equitable mortgagee for
  sale — Insufficient security — Costs of
  trustee - **13 Q. B. D. 228**
  See BANKRUPTCY—SECURED CREDITOR. 4.

—— Bankruptcy—Official receiver—Appearance
  on appeal **13 Q. B. D. 118**
  See BANKRUPTCY—RECEIVER. 7.

—— Bankruptcy—Trustee served with notice of
  appeal - - **14 Q. B. D. 121**
  See BANKRUPTCY—SECURED CREDITOR.
  12.

—— Between solicitor and client **16 Ch. D. 393**
  See SOLICITOR—LIABILITIES. 7.

—— Board of Trade — Shipping casualty —
  Appeal - - - **7 P. D. 207**
  See SHIP—MERCHANT SHIPPING ACTS. 2.

—— Breach of sailing rules—Collision—Inevitable accident - **6 P. D. 152**
  See SHIP—NAVIGATION. 11.

—— Case stated by justices—Jurisdiction
  [13 Q. B. D. 680
  See JUSTICES—PRACTICE. 1.

—— Case stated by sessions—Practice
  [6 Q. B. D. 139
  See POOR-RATE—PROCEDURE. 4.

—— Copies of deed—Transfer of mortgage
  [17 Ch. D. 348
  See MORTGAGE—REDEMPTION. 6.

—— Counsel—Allowance of three counsel
  [9 P. D. 126
  See PRACTICE—ADMIRALTY—COSTS. 6.

COSTS—*continued.*

—— County Court.
　See Cases under COUNTY COURT—COSTS.

—— County Court—Statute respecting.
　See COUNTY COURT—COSTS—*Statutes.*

—— Country solicitor—Taxation　**26 Ch. D. 189**
　See SOLICITOR—BILL OF COSTS. 8.

—— Discretion of Court -　　-　**22 Ch. D. 611**
　See PRACTICE—SUPREME COURT—PAY-
　MENT INTO COURT. 1.

—— District registry—Administration action
　　　　　　　　　[**27 Ch. D. 242**
　See PRACTICE—SUPREME COURT—DIS-
　TRICT REGISTRY.

—— Divorce—Attachment—Contempt
　　　　　　　　　[**10 P. D. 72**
　See PRACTICE—DIVORCE—RESTITUTION
　OF CONJUGAL RIGHTS. 2.

—— Divorce—Failure of husband to give security
　for wife's costs—Debtors Act, 1869　.
　　　　　　　　　[**10 P. D. 183**
　See ARREST—DEBTORS ACT. 2.

—— Divorce—Variation of settlements
　[**7 P. D. 228 ; 9 P. D. 122 ; 10 P. D. 179**
　See PRACTICE—DIVORCE—SETTLEMENTS.
　3, 5, 6.

—— Former action — Staying proceedings in
　second action　**23 Ch. D. 288 ; 25 Ch. D.**
　　　　　　　　　[**12**
　See PRACTICE—SUPREME COURT—STAY-
　ING PROCEEDINGS. 9, 10.

—— Infringement of copyright — Innocent in-
　fringer　　-　　**27 Ch. D. 260**
　See COPYRIGHT—DESIGNS. 1.

—— Injunction against sheriff -　**21 Ch. D. 69**
　See SHERIFF. 4.

—— Interpleader—Appeal　-　**8 Q. B. D. 82**
　See PRACTICE—SUPREME COURT—INTER-
　PLEADER. 1.

—— Interpleader — Power of Master to order
　Plaintiff to pay Defendant's costs
　　　　　　　　　[**12 Q. B. D. 100**
　See PRACTICE—SUPREME COURT—INTER-
　PLEADER. 9.

—— Lands Clauses Act.
　See Cases under LANDS CLAUSES ACT—
　COSTS.

—— Lands Clauses Act—Petition　**24 Ch. D. 119**
　See REVENUE—STAMPS. 5.

—— Lien for—Solicitor and client.
　See Cases under SOLICITOR—LIEN.

—— Married woman　-　　-　**30 Ch. D. 159**
　See HUSBAND AND WIFE — SEPARATE
　ESTATE. 10.

—— Member of vestry　-　　**23 Ch. D. 60**
　See METROPOLIS—MANAGEMENT ACTS.
　15.

—— Mortgage—Adjournment to Judge
　　　　　　　　　[**22 Ch. D. 5**
　See MORTGAGE—CONTRACT. 7.

—— Mortgage suit **22 Ch. D. 566 ; 25 Ch. D. 795 ;**
　　　　　　　　　[**27 Ch. D. 679**
　See MORTGAGE—FORECLOSURE. 4, 5, 6.

COSTS—*continued.*

—— Offences against women
　See CRIMINAL LAW—OFFENCES AGAINST
　WOMEN—*Statutes.*

—— Official liquidator -　　-　**21 Ch. D. 381**
　See COMPANY—COSTS. 1.

—— Official receiver—Bankruptcy — Personal
　liability—Unsuccessful appeal
　　　　　　　　　[**14 Q. B. D. 48**
　See BANKRUPTCY—COSTS. 4.

—— Official solicitor　-　　-　**21 Ch. D. 776**
　See LANDS CLAUSES ACT—COSTS. 5.

—— Order for payment—"Final judgment"—
　Bankruptcy **12 Q. B. D. 509 ; 14 Q. B. D.**
　　　　　　　　　[**627**
　See BANKRUPTCY—ACT OF BANKRUPTCY.
　10, 11.

—— Order for payment by solicitor—Appeal
　　　　　　　　　[**15 Q. B. D. 635**
　See PRACTICE—SUPREME COURT—AP-
　PEAL. 32.

—— Order in Chambers—Discretion—Appeal
　　　　　　　　　[**10 Q. B. D. 457**
　See PRACTICE—SUPREME COURT—AP-
　PEAL. 29.

—— Overseers of parish—Opposition to bill in
　Parliament　-　　-　**14 Q. B. D. 858**
　See POOR LAW—MANAGEMENT.

—— Patent action　-　　-　**29 Ch. D. 325, 366**
　See PATENT—PRACTICE. 2, 3.

—— Payment into Court—Denial of liability—
　Action for several breaches of contract—
　Acceptance in satisfaction of all demands
　　　　　　　　　[**14 Q. B. D. 766**
　See PRACTICE—SUPREME COURT—PAY-
　MENT INTO COURT. 8.

—— Payment by solicitor personally **19 Ch. D. 94**
　See PRACTICE—SUPREME COURT—NEXT
　FRIEND. 2.

—— Petition to vary settlements -　**9 P. D. 122**
　See PRACTICE—DIVORCE—SETTLEMENTS.
　7.

—— Practice in Chambers　　**20 Ch. D. 731**
　See PRACTICE—SUPREME COURT—CHAM-
　BERS. 3.

—— Previous application　-　**25 Ch. D. 182**
　See WATERCOURSE. 3.

—— Probate suit—Set-off against legacies
　　　　　　　　　[**18 Ch. D. 300**
　See EXECUTOR—RETAINER. 5.

—— Railway Commissioners—Successful Defend-
　ant not liable to pay costs **8 Q. B. D. 515**
　See RAILWAY COMPANY—RAILWAYS RE-
　GULATION ACTS. 2.

—— Reference—Award -　　-　**9 Q. B. D. 434**
　See ARBITRATION—COSTS.

—— Reference—Discretion of Court **10 P. D. 112**
　See PRACTICE—ADMIRALTY—COSTS. 7.

—— Respondent to appeal　　**22 Ch. D. 484**
　See PRACTICE—SUPREME COURT—AP-
　PEAL. 36.

—— Salvage—Abandonment　-　**9 P. D. 27**
　See SHIP—SALVAGE. 9.

COSTS—*continued.*

—— Salvage—Amount of tender　　7 P. D. 199
　　See PRACTICE — ADMIRALTY — SALVAGE.
　　9.

—— Salvage—Tender after action　　10 P. D. 1
　　See PRACTICE—ADMIRALTY—COSTS. 8.

—— Security for.
　　See Cases under PRACTICE—SUPREME
　　COURT—SECURITY FOR COSTS.

—— Security for—Action remitted to County
　　Court—Practice　-　13 Q. B. D. 835
　　See COUNTY COURT—PRACTICE. 4.

—— Security for — Administration — Married
　　woman　　-　8 P. D. 18
　　See PRACTICE—PROBATE—COSTS. 4.

—— Security for—Appeal from winding-up order
　　See COMPANY—APPEAL　[23 Ch. D. 370

—— Security for—Next friend of married woman
　　　　　　　　　[19 Ch. D. 94
　　See PRACTICE—SUPREME COURT—NEXT
　　FRIEND. 2.

—— Sequestration for　-　17 Ch. D. 433
　　See PRACTICE—SUPREME COURT—SE-
　　QUESTRATION. 3.

—— Settled Land Act　-　-　25 Ch. D. 651
　　See SETTLED LAND ACT — PURCHASE-
　　MONEY. 3.

—— Sheriff　　-　　22 Ch. D. 136
　　See BILL OF SALE—FORMALITIES. 6.

—— Shorthand notes　　-　22 Ch. D. 136
　　See BILL OF SALE—FORMALITIES. 6.

—— Solicitor—Defendant in person
　　　　　　　　　[13 Q. B. D. 872
　　See PRACTICE—SUPREME COURT—COSTS.
　　47.

—— Solicitor—Order to pay costs personally
　　　　　　　　　[15 Q. B. D. 635
　　See PRACTICE — SUPREME COURT—AP-
　　PEAL. 32.

—— Solicitor and client—County Court 18 Ch. D.
　　[521; 6 Q. B. D. 607; 9 Q. B. D. 408
　　See COUNTY COURT—COSTS. 1, 2, 3.

—— Solicitor and client — Taxation— Bill of
　　costs.
　　See Cases under SOLICITOR—BILL OF
　　COSTS.

—— Special directions as to—Appeal　26 Ch. D.
　　　　　　　　　[614
　　See PRACTICE—SUPREME COURT—AP-
　　PEAL. 44.

—— Staying proceedings pending appeal
　　　　　　　　　[20 Ch. D. 669
　　See PRACTICE—SUPREME COURT—STAY-
　　ING PROCEEDINGS. 13.

—— Supreme Court—Practice.
　　See Cases under PRACTICE—SUPREME
　　COURT—COSTS.

—— Taxation of bill of costs　·　-　27 Ch. D. 485
　　See SOLICITOR—BILL OF COSTS. 6.

—— Tenant for life—Protection of estate
　　　　　　　　　[16 Ch. D. 587, 588, n.
　　See TRUSTEE RELIEF ACT. 4, 5.

—— Third party　　-'　-　21 Ch. D. 198
　　See PRACTICE—SUPREME COURT—THIRD
　　PARTY. 2.

COSTS—*continued.*

—— Trade-mark—Innocent consignee
　　　　　　　　　[24 Ch. D. 231
　　See TRADE-MARK—INFRINGEMENT. 2.

—— Trustee.
　　See Cases under TRUSTEE—COSTS AND
　　CHARGES.

—— Trustee—Administration action　29 Ch. D.
　　　　　　　　　[495
　　See PRACTICE—SUPREME COURT—AP-
　　PEAL. 26.

—— Trustee—Appeal　-　19 Ch. D. 588
　　See BANKRUPTCY—VOID SETTLEMENT. 1.

—— Trustee in bankruptcy　6 App. Cas 482
　　See PRACTICE—PRIVY COUNCIL—JURIS-
　　DICTION.

—— Trustee of void settlement　23 Ch. D. 278
　　See VOLUNTARY CONVEYANCE. 5.

—— Vendor and purchaser—Making out title
　　　　　　　[28 Ch. D. 84; 30 Ch. D. 42
　　See VENDOR AND PURCHASER—TITLE. 1.

—— Victoria, Law of—Slander 10 App. Cas. 300
　　See COLONIAL LAW—VICTORIA. 5.

—— When payable—Arbitration—Lands Clauses
　　Act　-　-　-　11 Q. B. D. 345
　　See LANDS CLAUSES ACT—COSTS. 1.

—— Wife's costs payable by husband—Limita-
　　tion of amount　.　·　6 P. D. 119
　　See PRACTICE—DIVORCE—COSTS. 4.

—— Will—Residuary legatee under prior will
　　　　　　　　　[7 P. D. 239
　　See PRACTICE—PROBATE—COSTS. 3.

—— Winding-up of company.
　　See Cases under COMPANY—COSTS.

—— Winding-up—Liquidation -　30 Ch. D. 598
　　See BILL OF EXCHANGE—FOREIGN BILL.

—— Winding-up petition　　20 Ch. D. 276;
　　　　　　　　　[28 Ch. D. 65, 183
　　See COMPANY — WINDING-UP ORDER.
　　6, 7, 8.

—— Witness　　-　　21 Ch. D. 831
　　See EVIDENCE—WITNESS. 4.

—— Wreck Commissioner — Appeal— Shipping
　　casualty　-　-　-　6 P. D. 182
　　See SHIP—MERCHANT SHIPPING ACTS. 8.

CO-SURETY—Indorsers of promissory note
　　　　　　　　　[8 App. Cas. 733
　　See BILL OF EXCHANGE—LIABILITY OF
　　PARTIES.

—— Release of one　　-　8 App. Cas. 755
　　See PRINCIPAL AND SURETY—DISCHARGE.
　　. . 1. .

—— Right to contribution　17 Ch. D. 44, 825 ;
　　　　　　　　　[24 Ch. D. 709
　　See PRINCIPAL AND SURETY—CONTRIBU-
　　TION. 1, 2, 3.

COUNSEL—Fees　　-　　-　16 Ch. D. 517
　　See PRACTICE—SUPREME COURT—COSTS.
　　38.

—— Fees -　　-　30 Ch. D. 1; 15 Q. B. D. 420
　　See SOLICITOR—BILL OF COSTS. 3, 14.

—— For witness—Winding-up of company
　　　　　　　　　[20 Ch. D. 376
　　See COMPANY—EVIDENCE.　8.

COUNSEL—*continued.*

—— Request for sale by—Married woman
[16 Ch. D. 362
See PARTITION SUIT—SALE. 1.

COUNTER-CLAIM.

See Cases under PRACTICE—SUPREME
COURT—COUNTER-CLAIM.

—— Collision—Security for damages—Foreign
government   10 P. D. 33
See PRACTICE—ADMIRALTY—COUNTER-
CLAIM.

—— Costs—Claim and counter-claim 6 Q. B. D.
[691 ; 10 Q. B. D. 286 ; 14 Q. B. D. 821 ;
[23 Ch. D. 377
See PRACTICE—SUPREME COURT—COSTS.
10—13.

—— Default in pleading -   25 Ch. D. 68
See PRACTICE—SUPREME COURT—DE-
FAULT. 2.

—— Discontinuance of action 11 Q. B. D. 464
See PRACTICE—SUPREME COURT—DIS-
CONTINUANCE.

—— Salvage—Misconduct of salvors 8 P. D. 147
See SHIP—SALVAGE. 10.

—— Security for costs—Defendant out of juris-
diction -   - 15 Q. B. D. 423
See PRACTICE — SUPREME COURT — SE-
CURITY FOR COSTS. 2.

—— Set-off—Winding-up of company
[9 Q. B. D. 648 ; 9 App. Cas. 434
See SALE OF GOODS—RESCISSION 2.

—— Specific performance—Transfer to Chancery
Division -   - 13 Q. B. D. 540
See PRACTICE—SUPREME COURT—TRANS-
FER. 2.

COUNTERFEIT MARK — Silver wares — Party
grieved -   7 Q. B. D. 465
See PENAL ACTION. 1.

COUNTERFEIT MEDAL ACT, 1883.

See CRIMINAL LAW—COINING—*Statutes.*

COUNTY—Dead bodies cast on shore by sea—
Expenses of burial - 6 Q. B. D. 654
See BURIAL GROUND. 2.

—— Highway—Disturnpiked road.
See Cases under HIGHWAY—REPAIR. 2–6.

—— Main roads—Expense of removing snow
[10 Q. B. D. 480
See HIGHWAY—REPAIR. 3.

—— Number of members—Parliament
See PARLIAMENT—REDISTRIBUTION OF
SEATS—*Statutes.*

I. COUNTY COURT—APPEAL.

1. —— Leave of Judge—*Discretion of Judge
under 30 & 31 Vict. c. 142, s. 13.*] A County Court
judge having given a Defendant leave to appeal,
but subject to a condition that he should pay the
Plaintiff's costs of the appeal in any event, and
should also, in case the appeal were unsuccessful,
pay the costs of the trial upon the higher scale,

I. COUNTY COURT—APPEAL—*continued.*

the Divisional Court held that it had no power to
interfere with the discretion vested in him by
30 & 31 Vict. c. 142, s. 13. GOODES *v.* CLUFF
[13 Q. B. D. 694

2. —— Point not raised at Trial—*Condition
Precedent—County Courts Act, 1875 (88 & 39 Vict.
c. 50), s. 6.*] It is a condition precedent to the
right to appeal under sect. 6 of the County Courts
Act, 1875, that the question of law upon which
it is desired to appeal should have been raised
before the County Court Judge at the trial. CLARK-
SON *v.* MUSGRAVE -   9 Q. B. D. 386

3. —— Request to Judge to take Note—*Application to compel Judge to sign Note or to hear Case
—Adjournment of Trial in County Court—38 & 39
Vict. c. 50, s. 6—Order XXXVII., rule 26 of County
Court Rules, 1875—Appeal—19 & 20 Vict. c. 108,
s. 44.*] Rule 26 of Order XXXVII. of the County
Court Rules, 1875, which enables parties to a
County Court action, "at any time before the
action is called on, by consent and without payment of any trial fee, to postpone the trial to
such subsequent Court as the Judge shall direct,"
does not enable such parties to adjourn the trial
without the consent of the Judge ; and therefore
where, after a cause has been adjourned by the
Judge, the parties by agreement amongst themselves further adjourn the trial without the sanction of the Judge, he has jurisdiction to hear and
dispose of the cause as if there had been no such
further adjournment.—A request to a County
Court Judge, at the commencement of the trial,
and before any specific question of law has been
raised, that he should take a note of the evidence,
as it was an important case and might go to the
superior Court, is not a sufficient request within
the meaning of sect. 6 of the County Courts Act,
1875 (38 & 39 Vict. c. 50) ; and therefore a note
which the Judge afterwards took, and which he
stated was an incomplete one, and not such as
he would have taken if he had been requested to
take a note of any specific question of law and of
the evidence in relation thereto, is not a note taken
under that section which the Court will order him
to sign.—The right to appeal from an order of a
Divisional Court, discharging a rule for an order
on a County Court judge to hear an action, is not
taken away because sect. 44 of 19 & 20 Vict. c. 108,
which substitutes such rule for a mandamus to
the County Court judge, enacts that, where any
superior Court shall have refused such rule, no
other superior Court shall grant it. MORGAN *v.*
REES -   - 6 Q. B. D. 89, 508

—— Prohibition   8 Q. B. D. 9
See COUNTY COURT—PRACTICE. 5.

II. COUNTY COURTS—COSTS.

The Act 45 & 46 Vict. c. 57, sect. 2, *repeals so
much of sect. 91 of the County Courts Act, 1846, as
was then still in force ; and in lieu thereof enacts
that no person other than a solicitor of the Supreme
Court shall be entitled to have or recover any fee or
reward for appearing or acting on behalf of any
other party in any proceeding in a County Court :
provided that nothing in the Act contained shall
affect the right of any barrister-at-law to appear or
act in any County Court, or of any solicitor of the
Supreme Court to recover costs in respect of his*

II. COUNTY COURT—COSTS—continued.

employment of a barrister-at-law to appear or act as aforesaid.

By sect. 4 the 5th section of 30 & Vict. c. 142 shall be read and construed as if the words " less than" were substituted for the words "not exceeding."

Sect. 5. Notwithstanding any Act of Parliament or any rule to the contrary, it shall be in the power of the judge of a County Court to award costs on the higher scale to the Plaintiff on any amount recovered, however small, or to the Defendant who successfully defends an action brought for any amount, however small, provided the said Judge certify that the action involved some novel or difficult point of law, or that the question litigated was of importance to some class or body of persons, or of general or public interest.

1. —— Action under £20—Work done before and after Action—County Courts Act, 1875 (38 & 39 Vict. c. 50), s. 8 ; 19 & 20 Vict. c. 108, s. 36.] The scale of costs and charges in actions in the County Court under £20 framed in pursuance of 38 & 39 Vict. c. 50, s. 8, does not prevent a solicitor from recovering charges other than those specified in the scale for work done out of Court before and after the commencement of an action, although there has been no agreement in writing for further costs under 19 & 20 Vict. c. 108, s. 36. Re EMANUEL & Co.　　9 Q. B. D. 408

2 —— Between Solicitor and Client—Limit where not more than £20 claimed—County Courts Act, 1856 (19 & 20 Vict. c. 108), s. 36.] The 38th section of the County Courts Act, 1856, which fixes a limit to costs, as between solicitor and client, in actions where not more than £20 is claimed, applies to County Court actions only. In re COPP -　　-　　-　　6 Q. B. D. 607

3. —— Between Solicitor and Client—Taxation—Jurisdiction of High Court—Attorneys and Solicitors Act, 1843 (6 & 7 Vict. c. 73), s. 37— County Courts Act, 1856 (19 & 20 Vict. c. 108), ss. 35, 36—Judicature Act, 1873 (36 & 37 Vict. c. 66), s. 16—County Courts Act, 1875 (38 & 39 Vict. c. 50), s. 8—County Courts Rules, 1875, Order XXXVI., r. 1.] By the combined operation of the Attorneys and Solicitors Act, 1843 (6 & 7 Vict. c. 73), s. 37, and the Judicature Act, 1873, s. 16, as modified by the County Courts Act, 1856, s. 36, the costs as between solicitor and client in a County Court action in which the claim exceeds £20 may be taxed in the High Court of Justice ; consequently, the costs as between solicitor and client in a County Court administration action may be taxed in the Chancery Division. In re WORTH　　[18 Ch. D. 521

III. COUNTY COURT—JURISDICTION.

Districts.] Order in Council of 23rd of August, 1883, respecting limits of certain districts of County Courts　　-　　L. G. 1883, p. 4210

Judges.] Rank and precedence of County Court Judges. August 7th, 1884 - L. G. 1884, p. 3569

1. —— Admiralty—Action for Necessaries— British Ship—Owners domiciled in Great Britain —County Courts Admiralty Jurisdiction Act, 1868 (31 & 32 Vict. c. 71), s. 2—County Courts Admiralty Jurisdiction Amendment Act, 1869 (32 & 33 Vict. c. 51), ss. 2, 3.] A County Court having

III. COUNTY COURT—JURISDICTION—contd.

Admiralty jurisdiction has no greater jurisdiction in respect of a claim for necessaries than that possessed by the Admiralty Division of the High Court, and consequently cannot entertain an action for necessaries supplied to a British ship, the owners of which are domiciled in Great Britain. —The Dowse (Law Rep. 3 A. & E. 135) followed. —The Alina (5 Ex. D. 227) distinguished. ALLEN v. GARBUTT　　-　　-　　6 Q. B. D. 165

2. —— Admiralty—Claim in relation to the carriage of Goods in any Ship—County Courts Admiralty Jurisdiction Act, 1868 (31 & 32 Vict. c. 71), s. 3—County Courts Admiralty Jurisdiction Act Amendment Act, 1869 (32 & 33 Vict. c. 51), s. 2.] A Court having County Court Admiralty jurisdiction under the County Courts Admiralty Acts, 1868 and 1869, has jurisdiction to try and determine an action at the suit of the holder of a bill of lading against a British ship to recover for a breach of the contract of carriage in the bill of lading, notwithstanding that it is shewn to the Court that at the time of the institution of the suit the owner of the ship proceeded against was domiciled in England or Wales.—The Cargo ex Argos (Law Rep. 5 P. C. 134) and The Alina (5 Ex. D. 227) followed. THE " RONA "　　-　　-　　7 P. D. 247

3. —— Admiralty—Claim in relation to the carriage of Goods in any Ship—City of London Court—Passengers' Luggage—County Courts Admiralty Jurisdiction Amendment Act, 1869 (32 & 33 Vict. c. 51), s. 2.] Passengers' luggage carried on board a ship is not " goods " within the meaning of the County Courts Admiralty Jurisdiction Amendment Act, 1869, and consequently the Act does not confer jurisdiction to try a claim arising out of the loss of such luggage on a County Court having Admiralty jurisdiction. THE QUEEN v. JUDGE OF CITY OF LONDON COURT 12 Q. B. D. 115

4. —— Admiralty — Claims under Charterparties—Maritime Causes—Actions under £50— County Courts Admiralty Jurisdiction Act, 1868 (31 & 32 Vict. c. 71), ss. 3, 5—County Courts Admiralty Jurisdiction Amendment Act, 1869 (32 & 33 Vict. c. 51), s. 2.] The statutes 31 & 32 Vict. c. 71, and 32 & 33 Vict. c. 51, do not deprive County Courts not having Admiralty jurisdiction of their jurisdiction to try actions to recover freight under charterparties where the amount claimed is less than £50. THE QUEEN v. JUDGE OF THE SOUTHEND COUNTY COURT　　-　　13 Q. B. D. 142

5. —— Contempt — Interlocutory Order enforced by Committal — Judicature Act, 1873 (36 & 37 Vict. c. 66), s. 89, Order XLII., r. 5.] The power of a County Court under the Judicature Act, 1873, s. 89, in actions within the jurisdiction to enforce obedience to its orders by committal extends to interlocutory as well as to final orders. RICHARDS v. CULLERNE　　-　　7 Q. B. D. 623

6. —— Mandamus—Brighton Intercepting and Outfall Sewers Act, 1870 (33 & 34 Vict. c. c.)— Mandamus to the Judge of the Sussex County Court to hear and determine a Dispute between the Sewers Board and the Hove Commissioners, under s. 93 of the Act.] By sect. 93 of 33 & 34 Vict. c. c., an Act the main object of which was the diverting of the sewage of Brighton from the existing storm-

III. COUNTY COURT—JURISDICTION—*contd.*

outfalls and carrying it to a distance from the town,—it was enacted that "any dispute which might from time to time arise between the sewers board and any local authority with respect to carrying into effect the provisions of the Act or incidental thereto might, at the instance of either party, be referred to the Judge for the time being of the Sussex County Court, who should hear and determine such dispute, and whose decision should be final and conclusive."—A dispute having arisen between the sewers board and the Hove Commissioners (one of the local authorities) with respect to the mode of carrying out the provisions of the Act, and the sewers board requiring it to be referred to the County Court Judge :—*Held*, that the County Court Judge was bound to hear and determine the matter, and that mandamus was the proper course to compel him to do so, and not a rule or order under 19 & 20 Vict. c. 108, s. 43,—this not being a matter within his ordinary jurisdiction, but a special duty imposed upon him by statute. *Re* BRIGHTON SEWERS ACT 9 Q. B. D. 723

7. —— Transfer to County Court—*Action sent from the High Court—Power to stay Proceedings —30 & 31 Vict. c. 142 s. 10.*] Where an action, commenced in the High Court, has been transferred to a County Court under 30 & 31 Vict. c. 142, s. 10, the County Court Judge has power to make an order staying the proceedings until the Plaintiff has paid the costs of a previous action brought by him in the High Court against the same Defendant. THE QUEEN *v.* BAYLEY
[8 Q. B. D. 411

8. —— Transfer to County Court—*Action sent for Trial from the High Court—Action for Unliquidated Damages—Indorsement of Amount of Claim upon Writ—19 & 20 Vict. c. 108, s. 26.*] There is no power under 19 & 20 Vict. c. 108, s. 26, of the Judicature Act, 1875, to order an action for unliquidated damages to be tried in a County Court, even where the writ is indorsed with a claim for a specified sum. KNIGHT *v.* ABBOTT
[10 Q. B. D. 11

IV. COUNTY COURT—PRACTICE.

THE COUNTY COURT RULES OF 1886, *made the 7th December, 1885, under 19 & 20 Vict. c. 108, s. 32,* REFER TO THE FOLLOWING MATTERS :—

O. 1. *Court and offices.*
O. 2. *Officers.*
O. 3. *Parties.*
O. 4. *Joinder of causes of action.*
O. 5. *Commencement of action.*
O. 6. *Particulars and statement of claim.*
O. 7. *Plaint note and summons.*
O. 8. *Consolidation of actions or stay of proceedings.*
O. 9. *Discontinuance, confession, admission, and payment into or out of Court.*
O. 10. *Special defences.*
O. 11. *Claim for contribution, indemnity, &c.*
O. 12. *Interlocutory and interim orders and proceedings.*
O. 13. *Receiver.*
O. 14. *Amendment.*
O. 15. *Application for directions.*
O. 16. *Discovery and inspection.*
O. 17. *Change of parties.*

IV. COUNTY COURT—PRACTICE—*continued.*

O. 18. *Evidence.*
O. 19. *Affidavits.*
O. 20. *Arbitration.*
O. 21. *Assessors (County Courts Act, 1875).*
O. 22. *Trial.*
23. *Judgments and orders.*
24. *Accounts and inquiries.*
25. *Enforcement of judgments and orders.*
O. 26. *Attachment of debts.*
O. 27. *Interpleader.*
O. 28. *Transmission of proceeds of warrants from foreign districts.*
O. 29. *Security.*
O. 30. *Proceedings by and against executors and administrators.*
O. 31. *New trial.*
O. 32. *Appeals.*
O. 33. *Actions or matters remitted from or transferred to the High Court of Justice.*
O. 34. *Replevin.*
O. 35. *Bills of Exchange Act, 1855.*
O. 36. *Registry of judgments.*
O. 37. *Funds (County Courts Act, 1865).*
O. 38. *Trustee Relief Acts, the Settled Land Act, 1882, the County Courts Act, 1867, s. 24.*
O. 39. *Admiralty actions.*
O. 40. *Agricultural Holdings (England) Acts, 1875 and 1883.*
O. 41. *The Friendly Societies Act, 1875, &c.*
O. 42. *Winding-up of companies and societies.*
O. 43. *The Local Loans Act, 1875.*
O. 44. *The Employers Liability Act, 1880.*
O. 45. *Inferior Courts Judgments Extension Act, 1882.*
O. 46. *Married Women's Property Act, 1882.*
O. 47. *Acknowledgments by married women.*
O. 48. *Charitable Trusts.*
O. 49. *Probate or Letters of administration.*
O. 50. *Costs.*
O. 51. *General provisions.*
O. 52. *Interpretation of terms.*

1. —— Interpleader—*Deposit—Request—Sale by High Bailiff—19 & 20 Vict. c. 108, s. 72—30 & 31 Vict. c. 142, s. 31—County Court Order XXI., r. 1.*] Under Order XXI., rule 1, of the County Courts Orders and Rules, 1875, it is not necessary for the high bailiff, before selling goods seized in execution and claimed, to request the claimant to deposit the amount of the value of the goods or possession money, and, if no such deposit be made, the high bailiff is entitled under 19 & 20 Vict. c. 108 (the County Courts Act, 1856), s. 72, to sell the goods without first applying for an interpleader summons under 30 & 31 Vict. c. 142 (the County Courts Act, 1867), s. 31. DAVIES *v.* WISE ; CRAMER & CO., Claimants ; CRAMER *v* MATTHEWS 7 Q. B. D. 425

2. —— Nautical Assessors—*Admiralty Jurisdiction Act, 1868 (31 & 32 Vict. c 71), ss. 3, 11.*] Nautical assessors summoned under the County Courts Admiralty Jurisdiction Act, 1868, to attend at the hearing of an Admiralty action tried by a County Court Judge, are present merely to advise the Judge, and the Judge ought to decide the case in accordance with his own opinion as to the law and merits of the case. THE "AID"
[6 P. D. 84

3. —— Nonsuit—*Order XVI., rule 17 of County*

IV. COUNTY COURT—PRACTICE—continued.

Court Orders, 1875—Authority to make such Rule —County Courts Act, 1856 (19 & 20 Vict. c. 108), s. 32.] By Order XVI., rule 17, of County Court Orders, 1875, "any judgment of nonsuit, unless the Judge otherwise directs, shall have the same effect as a judgment upon the merits for the Defendant." Such rule is a copy of Order XLI., rule 6, of the Judicature Orders, and was made by a committee of County Court Judges with the approval of the Lord Chancellor under the authority of sect. 32 of the County Courts Act, 1856 (19 & 20 Vict. c. 108), which authorizes such County Court Judges with such approval to frame rules and orders for "regulating the practice of the Courts and forms of proceedings therein:"— *Held,* that unless rule 17 of the County Court Orders was ultrà vires a judgment of nonsuit in a County Court not appealed against nor set aside, was a bar to an action by the Plaintiff for the same debt in the superior Court. *Held,* also (Bramwell, L.J., dissenting), that rule 17 was not ultrà vires but was covered by the authority given to the committee of County Court Judges by the County Courts Act, 1856, s. 32. POYSER v. MINORS
[7 Q. B. D. 329

4. —— Security for Costs—Remission of Action to County Court—"Visible Means" of Plaintiff— *County Courts Act, 1867 (30 & 31 Vict. c. 142), s. 10.]* By the term "visible means" as used in sect. 10 of the County Courts Act, 1867, is intended such means as could be fairly ascertained by a reasonable person in the position of the Defendant.—On the filing of the affidavit the jurisdiction of the Judge arises, and he is to satisfy himself not merely whether the Plaintiff has any "visible means," but whether he has any means at all of paying the costs, and the Judge has a judicial discretion whether he will make the order.—On an application under sect. 10 of the County Courts Act, 1867, it appeared from the affidavit that the Defendant was in possession of certain property of the Plaintiff under a claim for rent for £5929, that the Plaintiff had no property upon which an execution under a judgment for £2404 could be levied, that his furniture had been sold under an execution, and that he had assigned his property for the benefit of his creditors. It also appeared that the Plaintiff was being employed as a colliery manager at a weekly wage of £4, the employment being determinable on three months' notice, or on payment of three months' salary in lieu of notice, or without notice in the event of wilful misconduct:—*Held,* that, whether or not the salary could be attached, the Plaintiff had no substantial means of paying the costs of the action in the event of the verdict being for the Defendant, and that an order was rightly made under s. 10.—*Counsel v. Garvie* (Ir. R. 5 C. L. 74) considered. LEA v. PARKER　　-　　**13 Q. B. D. 835**

5. —— Time—Action to recover Lands—De- *livery of Summons to Bailiff—County Court Rules, 1875, Order VIII., r. 7—Jurisdiction—Appeal—Prohibition.]* By Order VIII., rule 7, of the County Court Rules, 1875, "the summons in an action brought to recover lands shall be delivered to the Bailiff forty clear days at least before the return day, and shall be served thirty-five clear days before the return day thereof." The

IV. COUNTY COURT—PRACTICE—continued.

Plaintiff in an action in the County Court to recover lands delivered the summons to the bailiff thirty-nine clear days and the bailiff served it upon the Defendant thirty-eight clear days, before the return day. At the hearing the County Court Judge ruled that the service was good, and tried the case, giving judgment for the Plaintiff:— *Held,* that the provision in rule 7 with respect to the time of delivering the summons to the bailiff was obligatory, and not merely directory, and therefore that the Judge ought not to have tried the case. *Held,* also, that the Defendant's proper remedy was to appeal from the Judge's ruling, and not to apply for a prohibition against the issue of execution on the judgment. BARKER v. PALMER　　　-　　　**8 Q. B. D. 9**

6. —— Trial—Right of Defendant to sum up *Evidence—17 & 18 Vict. c. 125, s. 18.]* An action remitted from the Queen's Bench Division to a County Court was tried before the County Court Judge with a jury. After the Defendant's evidence had closed his counsel claimed to address the jury, but the Judge refused to allow it. The jury having given a verdict for the Plaintiff the Defendant applied for a rule nisi for a new trial on the ground that his counsel ought to have been allowed to sum up the evidence:—*Held,* affirming the decision of a Divisional Court, that as the right claimed did not exist at common law, and the 18th section of the Common Law Procedure Act, 1854, which gave such a right in the superior Courts, did not apply to County Courts, there was no ground for interfering with the practice of any County Court in which the Defendant was not allowed to sum up the evidence. DYMOCK v. WATKINS -　　　-　　　**10 Q. B. D. 451**

COUNTY COURT—Action remitted for trial—Costs —Order LXV., IT. 1, 4　-　**14 Q. B. D. 6**
　　See PRACTICE—SUPREME COURT—COSTS. 20.

——Action remitted—New trial
　　　　　　　　[14 Q. B. D. 55
　　See PRACTICE—SUPREME COURT — NEW TRIAL. 2.

—— Action remitted for trial—Trial before judge without jury　-　-　**12 Q. B. D. 21**
　　See PRACTICE—SUPREME COURT—NEW TRIAL. 1.

—— Admiralty jurisdiction—Costs—Certificate
　　　　　　　　[6 Q. B. D. 46
　　See PRACTICE—SUPREME COURT—COSTS. 21.

—— Admiralty jurisdiction—Dock
　　　　　　　　[8 Q. B. D. 609
　　See PRACTICE—ADMIRALTY — JURISDICTION. 6.

—— Admiralty—Appeal　-　-　**9 P. D. 12**
　　See PRACTICE—ADMIRALTY—APPEAL. 1.

—— Appeal—Notice of motion　**13 Q. B. D. 403**
　　See PRACTICE — SUPREME COURT—APPEAL. 7.

—— Bankruptcy—Appeal　　**16 Ch. D. 501；**
　　　　　　[19 Ch. D. 169; 20 Ch. D. 315, 701
　　See BANKRUPTCY—APPEAL. 6—9.

COUNTY COURT—*continued.*

—— Bankruptcy—Contempt　　13 **Q. B. D.** 963
　　See BANKRUPTCY—JURISDICTION. 2.

—— Bankruptcy—Power to restrain proceedings
　　in High Court　-　15 **Q. B. D.** 169
　　See BANKRUPTCY— STAYING PROCEED-
　　INGS. 3.

—— Bankruptcy — Transfer of proceedings —
　　Certificate of judge—Discretion—Appeal
　　—Costs　　-　　13 **Q. B. D.** 484
　　See BANKRUPTCY—TRANSFER. 1.

—— Costs—Breach of promise to marry—Verdict
　　in High Court for £20　14 **Q. B. D.** 53
　　See PRACTICE—SUPREME COURT—COSTS.
　　19.

—— Employers' Liability Act—Action of tort—
　　Stay of proceedings　　14 **Q. B. D.** 905
　　See MASTER AND SERVANT — MASTER'S
　　LIABILITY. 11.

—— Employers' Liability Act — Certiorari to
　　remove action -　　- 10 **Q. B. D.** 59
　　See MASTER AND SERVANT — MASTER'S
　　LIABILITY. 10.

—— Motion for new trial—Improper rejection of
　　evidence　-　　- 12 **Q. B. D.** 58
　　See PRACTICE—SUPREME COURT—NEW
　　TRIAL. 3.

—— Transfer of action -　　27 **Ch. D.** 533
　　See PRACTICE—SUPREME COURT—JURIS-
　　DICTION. 3.

—— Transfer of action—Appeal to Court of Ap-
　　peal　　-　　8 **Q. B. D.** 325
　　See PRACTICE— SUPREME COURT — AP-
　　PEAL. 6.

COUNTY COURT RULES, 1875—Order VIII. r. 7
　　[8 **Q. B. D.** 9
　　See COUNTY COURT—PRACTICE. 5.

—— Order XVI., r. 17　　-　7 **Q. B. D.** 329
　　See COUNTY COURT—PRACTICE. 3.

—— Order XX., r. 1　-　　- 27 **Ch. D.** 533
　　See PRACTICE—SUPREME COURT—JURIS-
　　DICTION. 3.

—— Order XXI., r. 1　　7 **Q. B. D.** 425
　　See COUNTY COURT—PRACTICE. 1.

—— Order XXXVII., r. 26　　- 6 **Q. B. D.** 508
　　See COUNTY COURT—APPEAL. 3.

COUNTY COURT RULES, 1884—Rules 1–4
　　[15 **Q. B. D.** 329
　　See ARREST—DEBTORS ACT. 3.

COUNTY RATE—Criminal lunatic—Maintenance
　　of　-　6 **Q. B. D.** 47; 8 **App. Cas.** 339
　　See LUNATIC—CRIMINAL.

—— Expenses of conveyance of prisoners
　　[6 **Q. B. D.** 156; 7 **App. Cas.** 1
　　See PRISON. 2.

—— Expenses of maintaining highway—Contri-
　　bution.
　　See Cases under HIGHWAY— REPAIR.
　　1–6.

COUNTY STOCK—Duty on.
　　See REVENUE—STAMPS—*Statutes.*

COUNTY VOTE—Occupation franchise.
　　See PARLIAMENT—FRANCHISE—*Statutes.*

COUNTY VOTE—*continued.*

—— Rent-charge—Actual possession—2 & 3 Wm.
　　4, c. 45, s. 26　　　12 **Q. B. D.** 369
　　See PARLIAMENT—FRANCHISE. 11.

—— Rent-charge for life or lives below £5
　　[12 **Q. B. D.** 365
　　See PARLIAMENT—FRANCHISE. 12.

COUPONS—Foreign—Income tax on.
　　See REVENUE—INCOME TAX—*Statutes.*

COURT :—　　　　　　　　　　　Col.
　　I. STATUTES AND GAZETTES　-　- 448
　　II. CENTRAL CRIMINAL COURT -　- 452
　　III. LANCASTER COURT　-　- 452
　　IV. MAYOR'S COURT　　-　- 452

—— ADMIRALTY COURT.
　　See PRACTICE—ADMIRALTY.

—— COUNTY COURT.
　　See COUNTY COURT.

—— COURT OF REVISION.
　　See PARLIAMENT—FRANCHISE.

—— DIVORCE COURT.
　　See PRACTICE—DIVORCE.

—— ECCLESIASTICAL COURT.
　　See PRACTICE— ECCLESIASTICAL.

—— PRIVY COUNCIL.
　　See PRACTICE—PRIVY COUNCIL.

—— STANNARIES COURT.
　　See COMPANY—COST-BOOK COMPANY.

—— SUPREME COURT.
　　See PRACTICE—SUPREME COURT.

I. COURT—STATUTES AND GAZETTE.

　　The Act 44 & 45 Vict. c. 68 (*the Supreme Court
of Judicature Act,* 1881), *amends the constitution
of Her Majesty's Court of Appeal, and makes
further provision concerning the Supreme Court
of Judicature and the officers thereof, and other
matters.*

　　Sect. 2. *Master of the Rolls to be a Judge of
Appeal only.*

　　Sect. 3. *Existing vacancy in Court of Appeal
not to be filled up.*

　　Sect. 4. *President of Probate, &c., Division to be
an ex-officio Judge of the Court of Appeal.*

　　Sect. 5. *A new Judge of High Court to be appointed instead of Master of the Rolls.*

　　Sect. 6. *Judges of Chancery Division to be not
less than five in number.*

　　Sect. 7. *Rolls Court Chambers and clerks, &c., to
be attached to a Judge of the Chancery Division.*

　　Sect. 8 *amends sect.* 4 *of the Supreme Court of
Judicature Act,* 1877.

　　Sect. 9. *As to appeals under Divorce Acts.*

　　Sect. 10. *As to appeal against decree nisi for
dissolution or nullity of marriage.*

　　Sect. 11. *Qualification of Judges of divisional
Courts to sit on appeals.*

　　Sect. 12. *In cases of urgency, illness, &c., one
Judge may officiate for another.*

　　Sect. 13. *Judges for trial of election petitions to
be selected from Queen's Bench Division.*

　　Sect. 14. *As to jurisdiction of High Court on
appeals on questions of law in municipal and
parliamentary, borough registration, and election
cases.*

　　Sect. 15. *Five or more of the Judges of the High*

I. COURT—STATUTES AND GAZETTE—*contd.*

Court may exercise the jurisdiction and authority in relation to questions of law arising in criminal trials which under sect. 47 of the Supreme Court of Judicature Act, 1873, is vested in such Judges.

Sect. 16. *Proceedings with regard to nomination of sheriffs.*

Sect. 17. *Presentation and swearing in of Lord Mayor of London.*

Sect. 18. *As to fixing sessions of Central Criminal Court.*

Sect. 19. *Power to make rules under 39 & 40 Vict. c. 59.*

Sect. 20 *extends sect. 14 of 32 & 33 Vict. c. 91, to all officers of the Supreme Court, and all officers in Lunacy.*

Sect. 21. *As to notice of vacancies in offices of the Supreme Court.*

Sect. 22. *Solicitors may be appointed district registrars.*

Sect. 23. *Appointments to keep order, &c., in Royal Courts of Justice.*

Sect. 24. *Powers as to solicitors.*

Sect. 25. *Chief Justice of England to have powers of Chief Justice of Common Pleas and Chief Baron of the Exchequer.*

Sect. 26. *Certain appointments of commissioners for acknowledgments by married woman declared valid.*

Sect. 27. *Powers to make rules for County Courts.*

Act of 1884.] *The Act 47 & 48 Vict. c. 61 (the Supreme Court of Judicature Act, 1884), amends the Supreme Court of Judicature Acts 1873 to 1879 and 1881.*

Sect. 3. *The rank of President of Probate, &c., Division in Court of Appeal fixed.*

Sect. 4 *amends 39 & 40 Vict. c. 39, s. 17.*

Sect. 5. *Any Judge of any Division of the High Court may act for another absent from illness, &c., or as an additional Judge of any Division.*

Sect 7. *13 & 14 Vict. c. 25, extended to Judges of County Courts.*

Sect. 8 *extends sect. 45 of 36 & 37 Vict. c. 66, to all appeals from compulsory reference to arbitration in any cause in the Queen's Bench Division.*

Sect. 10. *In all cases where matter may be referred to Master, &c., under sects. 3, 6, or 12 of Common Law Procedure Act, 1854, such matter may now be referred to official referee.*

Sect. 11. *Parties under agreement of reference may refer to official referee.*

Sect. 12. *Saving as to district registrars.*

Sect. 13. *Sect. 16 of 18 & 19 Vict. c. 134, extends to all applications under any existing or future Act, by virtue of which a Court or Judge may make orders upon petition or motion in a summary way.*

Sect. 14. *Execution of instruments by order of the Court.*

Sect. 15. *Proceedings in quo warranto are deemed civil proceedings.*

Sect. 16 *amends 17 & 18 Vict. c. 34, s. 1, as to process.*

Sect. 17. *Power to transfer interpleader proceedings not exceeding £500 in value to County Court.*

Sect. 18. *Jurisdiction of Inferior Courts in counter-claims under 36 & 37 Vict. c. 66, ss. 89 and 90.*

I. COURT—STATUTES AND GAZETTE—*contd.*

Sect. 19. *Patronage under 42 & 43 Vict. c. 78.*

Sect. 20. *Civil Service certificates for officers of Supreme Court under 42 & 43 Vict. c. 78.*

Sect. 21. *Appointment of circuit officers.*

Sect. 22. *Abolishes the offices of sworn clerks to examiners in Chancery.*

Sect. 23. *The power to make rules under 38 & 39 Vict. c. 77, includes power to make rules concerning appeals from inferior Courts.*

Sect. 24. *The power of making rules for the procedure of an inferior Court of civil jurisdiction is to be subject to the concurrence of the authority empowered to make rules for the Supreme Court.*

Inferior Courts.] *By 46 & 47 Vict. c. 49, s. 8, it shall be lawful for the Queen from time to time by Order in Council to extend to any inferior Court of civil jurisdiction any of the provisions of the Supreme Court of Judicature Act, 1873, and Acts amending it, or of the Rules of Court made thereunder, with any such modifications as may be necessary or desirable, in the same manner as and to the like extent that the provisions of the Common Law Procedure Acts, 1852, 1854, and 1860, and of the general rules made thereunder, might, under the powers given by those Acts, have been extended to any such Court.*

Pay Office.] *The Act 46 & 47 Vict. c. 29, consolidates the accounting departments of the Supreme Court of Judicature.*

Sect. 1 *establishes one accounting department for the Supreme Court of Judicature.*

Sect. 2. *As to funds in Chancery Division.*

Sect. 3. *As to funds paid into Court in any other division of the High Court.*

Sect. 4 *empowers Lord Chancellor to make rules to give effect to sect. 3.*

Sect. 5. *All acts to be done by Paymaster-General pursuant to rules to be valid.*

Sect. 6. *Crossed cheques or other documents remitted by post to any person pursuant to the rules to be equivalent to delivery of such cheques or documents to such person.*

Sect. 7 *amends 35 & 36 Vict. c. 44, s. 10.*

Sect. 8. *Act to be cited as Supreme Court of Judicature (Funds, &c.) Act, 1883.*

Bristol.] *Order that certain sections of 1 & 2 Will. 4, c. 58, shall apply to the Tolzey Court and Pie Poudre Court of the City and County of Bristol - - - L. G., 1883, p. 3707*

Clerks.] *Courts of Justice (Salaries and Funds) Act, 1868. Pay, constitution, &c., of clerks in Central Office. Treasury Order of 30th June, 1882*
[L. G., 1882, p. 3644

Ditto, clerks in the Admiralty Division. Treasury Order of 10th July, 1882 L. G., 1882, p. 3647
Ditto, clerks in the Probate and Divorce Division. Treasury Order of 14th July, 1882
[L. G., 1882, p. 3644

Court of Appeal.] *Order in Council as to sittings of the Court of Appeal. Dec. 12th, 1883*
[L. G., 1883, p. 6567

Fees.] *Supreme Court of Judicature, amending Order of July 12th, 1881 - L. G., 1881, p. 3452*
Schedule of fees of Clerk of the Crown in Chancery Office. August 8th, 1881 L. G., 1881, p. 4188

Guildhall.] *Order in Council, under 28 & 29 Vict. c. 48, of May 22nd, 1883, directing that in future all issues in cases at Nisi Prius hitherto*

Q

I. COURT—STATUTES AND GAZETTE—*contd.*

tried and executed in the City of London be now tried at the Royal Courts of Justice

[L. G., 1883, p. 2733

Vacation.] *Order that the Trinity sittings of the Court of Appeal, and in London and Middlesex of the High Court of Justice, shall extend till 12th August inclusive, that the Long Vacation shall commence 13th August, that the Michaelmas Sittings of the same Courts shall commence on 24th October, and that the Long Vacation shall terminate on 23rd October -　　-　　* **L. G., 1883, p. 6567**

Crown Offices Rules, 1886.] *These rules were made the 18th of December, 1885, and come into force 28th April, 1886.*

R. 1. *All existing rules or practice on the Crown side, inconsistent with these rules, are hereby repealed, and the following rules shall henceforth be in force.*

R. 2. *No order or rule annulled by any former order shall be revived by any of these rules, unless expressly so declared, and where no other provision is made by these rules, the present procedure and practice remain in force.*

R. 3.　*Custody of records.*
R. 4.　*Date of proceedings.*
R. 5.　*Affidavits.*
R. 28.　*Certiorari.*
R. 43.　*Indictments and informations.*
R. 51.　*Quo warranto.*
R. 60.　*Mandamus.*
R. 80.　*Orders in the nature of mandamus.*
R. 81.　*Prohibition.*
R. 83.　*Appearance to indictment, information, and inquisition.*
R. 99.　*Outlawry.*
R. 113.　*Reversal of outlawry.*
R. 122.　*Bail.*
R. 123.　*Recognizances.*
R. 127.　*Scire facias.*
R. 128.　*Pleadings.*
R. 138.　*Copies of proceedings and service.*
R. 140.　*Special cases and demurrers.*
R. 143.　*Paper books.*
R. 148.　*Notice of trial.*
R. 155.　*Continuances.*
R. 156.　*Entering record for trial.*
R. 158.　*Jury.*
R. 159.　*View.*
R. 160.　*Trial at bar.*
R. 166.　*New trial.*
R. 170.　*Judgment by default.*
R. 171.　*Judgment.*
R. 183.　*Error.*
R. 207.　*Error upon judgments in the Queen's Bench Division.*
R. 216.　*Appeals.*
R. 217.　*Execution.*
R. 229.　*Writs.*
R. 235.　*Habeas corpus.*
R. 250.　*Motions.*
R. 261.　*Attachment for contempt.*
R. 277.　*De contumace capiendo—de excommunicato capiendo.*
R. 280.　*Articles of the peace.*
R. 293.　*Time.*
R. 299.　*Amendment.*
R. 300.　*Costs.*
R. 302.　*Notices.*
R. 303.　*Non-compliance.*

I. COURT—STATUTES AND GAZETTE—*contd.*

R. 304.　*Applications at chambers.*
R. 306.　*Interpretation clause.*
R. 307.　*Repeal.*
R. 308.　*Forms.*

II. COURT—CENTRAL CRIMINAL COURT.

——— Mandamus — 4 & 5 *Will.* 4, c. 36.] Mandamus will not lie to the judges and justices of the Central Criminal Court.—The Recorder of London, upon the trial and conviction of a prisoner charged with larceny, having refused to order (under 24 & 25 Vict. c. 96, s. 100) the person with whom the stolen property was pledged to restore it to the prosecutor,—the Queen's Bench refused to grant a mandamus directed to "the judges and justices of the Central Criminal Court," to compel the Recorder to make such order. THE QUEEN *v.* JUSTICES OF CENTRAL CRIMINAL COURT

[11 Q. B. D. 479

III. COURT—LANCASTER COURT.

——— Service out of Jurisdiction — *Chancery Court of County Palatine—*17 & 18 *Vict.* c. 82, s. 8.] Where the sole Defendant to an action commenced in the Chancery Court of the County Palatine of Lancaster is resident out of the jurisdiction of that Court leave to serve the writ of summons upon him out of the jurisdiction, if it will be granted to all (as to which *quære*), will only be granted under very special circumstances. *In re* WATMOUGH. SERGENSON *v.* BELOE

[24 Ch. D. 280

IV. COURT—MAYOR'S COURT.

1. ——— Foreign Attachment—*Garnishee.*] The process against a garnishee, to enforce obedience to the jurisdiction of the Lord Mayor's Court in foreign attachment, is personal, and cannot be applied to a corporation aggregate. — Where, therefore, a corporation aggregate was cited, as garnishee, to appear in the Lord Mayor's Court, it was held entitled to maintain prohibition.—The suit of foreign attachment is founded upon ancient custom, and in itself is perfectly valid. The process by which it is sought to be enforced must be strictly pursued according to the custom. Fictitious summonses and returns will render the suit invalid.—No payment, but a payment made by compulsion of law, can discharge a garnishee from his original liability to his creditor. CORPORATION OF LONDON *v.* LONDON JOINT STOCK BANK

[6 App. Cas. 393

2. ——— Judgment—*Execution issued from High Court upon Judgment of Mayor's Court—Mayor's Court of London Procedure Act, 1857* (20 & 21 *Vict.* c. clvii.), s. 48—*Borough and Local Courts of Record Act,* 1872 (35 & 36 *Vict.* c.86), s. 6—*Statute, Construction of—Repeal by Implication—Permissive Words.*] By the Mayor's Court of London Procedure Act, 1857, sect. 48, execution might be issued in a superior Court upon a judgment obtained in the Mayor's Court. By the Borough and Local Courts of Record Act, 1872, sect. 6, where final judgment has been obtained in any local Court for a sum not exceeding £20, "such Court shall be at liberty to send a writ or precept for the recovery of the same to the registrar of any County Court within the jurisdiction of

IV. COURT—MAYOR'S COURT—*continued.*

which the Defendant may possess any goods or chattels . . . . and thereupon the high bailiff of such County Court shall execute the same in the same manner as if such writ or precept had been issued out of such County Court" :—*Held*, that the two statutes were not inconsistent, and that the Mayor's Court of London Procedure Act. 1857, sect. 48, had not been repealed by the Borough and Local Courts of Record Act, 1872, sect. 6; and that notwithstanding the latter statute execution might be issued in the High Court of Justice upon a judgment for a sum not exceeding £20 obtained in the Mayor's Court. PAINE *v.* SLATER　　11 Q. B. D. 120

3. —— **Jurisdiction**—*Power to give Judgment under Order* XL., *Rule* 10—*Judicature Act,* 1873, s. 89.] The Judge of the Mayor's Court, London, has no power, on a motion before that Court for a new trial, to direct judgment to be entered for either of the parties in the action, as a Judge of the High Court can do under Order XL., rule 10, no rules having been made for applying the rules of the Judicature Acts to that Court, and no such power being given to an inferior Court by sect. 89 of the Judicature Act, 1873.—Where, notwithstanding such want of power, the Judge of the Mayor's Court has acted as if he had such power, an appeal will lie to the Court of Appeal in respect of his having so erroneously acted. PRYOR *v.* CITY OFFICES COMPANY　　-　10 Q. B. D. 504

4. —— **Jurisdiction** — *Prohibition* — *Mayor's Court Procedure Act* (20 & 21 *Vict. c. clvii.*), s. 12 —*Cause of Action arising wholly or in part within the City of London or Liberties thereof.*] The terms of a sale of the lease, goodwill and fixtures of a business carried on in Surrey having been agreed upon, two counterpart documents were drawn up, embodying such terms. One of these was signed by the purchaser at Bow in the county of Middlesex. The other was subsequently signed by the vendor in the city of London. The two documents were then exchanged between the parties, and the deposit was paid at the office of the purchaser's solicitor in the city of London. The sum of £50, part of the purchase-money, being unpaid, the vendor sued for the same in the Mayor's Court :—*Held*, that the cause of action did not in part arise within the jurisdiction of the Mayor's Court, and that therefore a writ of prohibition must issue. ALDERTON *v.* ARCHER
　　　　　　　　　　　　　　[14 Q. B. D. 1

5. —— **New Trial**—*Mayor's Court Procedure Act,* 1857 (20 & 21 *Vict. c. clvii.*), *ss.* 10, 22.] Where a rule has been obtained to enter a nonsuit or for a new trial in the Mayor's Court, London, under sect. 22 of 20 & 21 Vict. c. clvii., it is not competent to the unsuccessful party afterwards, even with the leave of the Judge, to move the Divisional Court under sect. 10. MEARS *v.* CHITTICK　　　　　　-　9 Q. B. D. 35

COURT—Appeal Court—Jurisdiction— Previous decision　　　　　　　9 P. D. 96
　　See PRACTICE—ADMIRALTY— JURISDIC-
　　　　TION. 3.

—— Appeal Court—Jurisdiction of—Misconduct of solicitor　　-　28 Ch. D. 614
　　See SOLICITOR—MISCONDUCT. 2.

COURT—*continued.*

—— Lancaster Court—Concurrent suits
　　　　　[21 Ch. D. 647; 23 Ch. D. 100
　　See PRACTICE—SUPREME COURT—CON-
　　DUCT OF CAUSE. 2, 3.

—— Lancaster Court—Rehearing—Jurisdiction
　　　　　　　　　　　　[24 Ch. D. 488
　　See PRACTICE—SUPREME COURT—AP-
　　PEAL. 37.

—— Of record—Municipal election—Amendment of orders　　-　9 Q. B. D. 494
　　See MUNICIPAL CORPORATION — ELEC-
　　TION. 1.

—— Of session—Equitable jurisdiction
　　　　　　　　　　[7 App. Cas. 547
　　See SCOTCH LAW—PUBLIC RIGHTS.

COUSIN—Will—Construction—First and second cousins - 17 Ch. D. 262; 19 Ch. D. 201;
　　　　　　　　　　　[30 Ch. D. 512
　　See WILL—WORDS. 4, 5, 6.

COVENANT :—　　　　　　　　Col.
　　I. BREACH　　-　　-　　-　-　454
　　II. RUNNING WITH LAND　　　　455
　　III. VALIDITY　　　　　　.　-　456

—— IN CONVEYANCE.
　　See VENDOR AND PURCHASER—CONVEY-
　　ANCE.

—— IN LEASE.
　　See LANDLORD AND TENANT—LEASE.

I. COVENANT—BREACH.

1. —— **Alteration of Character of Estate**— *Mutual Restrictive Covenants*—*Building Estate*— *Acquiescence.*] A building estate was laid out in lots, which were sold by the owners of the estate to different purchasers, each of whom covenanted with the vendors and with the purchasers of the other lots entitled to the benefit of the covenant not to build a shop on his land, or to use his house as a shop or to carry on any trade therein. The purchaser of one of the lots, who occupied his house as a private residence, brought an action against the purchaser of another lot, who was using his house as a beershop with an "off" licence, to restrain him from breaking his covenant and for damages. The Plaintiff had known for three years before the action was commenced that the Defendant was using his house as a beer-shop, and had himself bought beer at the shop. There was evidence that some of the houses built on other lots had been for some time used as shops notwithstanding the covenant, and that some of the houses near the Plaintiff's house were occupied, not each by a single tenant, but by two families at weekly rents :—*Held*, that the change in the character of the neighbourhood was not in itself a ground for refusing relief to the Plaintiff, as the change was not caused by his conduct ; but that the Plaintiff had lost the right to enforce his covenant either by injunction or damages, through his acquiescence in the proceedings of the Defendant.—*Duke of Bedford v. Trustees of the British Museum* (2 My. & K. 552) explained. SAYERS *v.* COLLYER 24 Ch. D. 180; 28 Ch. D. 103
　　　　　　　　　　　　　　　　　　Q 2

II. COVENANT — RUNNING WITH LAND.

1. —— Beershop—*Off Licence—Notice—Damages.*] Upon the sale in 1863, to A., for the purposes of a public-house, of part of an estate intended to be laid out for building, the trustees of the estate covenanted with A., his heirs and assigns, that they, their heirs and assigns, would not thereafter sell any portions of the estate without requiring the purchaser to enter into a covenant "not to erect thereon or use or permit to be used any building to be erected thereon as a tavern, public-house, or beershop." —— Further portions of the estate were sold in 1870 by the then trustees to G., who covenanted with the vendors not to use or permit to be used any buildings erected on the land and premises intended to be thereby assured as a tavern, public-house, or beershop. The rest of the estate was sold to other persons. In 1879 H. purchased from G. part of the land comprised in G.'s purchase of 1870, and entered into a covenant with G., in terms similar to those of the covenant in the deed of 1870.—I., a yearly tenant under H. of one of the houses, having obtained an "off licence." sold under it beer which was not drunk upon the premises :—*Held,* that the property was bound by the restrictive covenant entered into by the vendors in 1863, and that B., an assign of A., was entitled to an injunction and damages against H. and I., in respect of the breach of covenant in selling beer under an " off licence." NICOLL *v.* FENNING　　19 Ch. D. 258

2. —— Land subject to Rent-charge—*Covenant by Grantee to build and repair Buildings—Assignment of Land and Rent-charge—Whether Assignee of Land liable on Covenant to Repair—Notice.*] Where land has been granted in fee in consideration of a rent-charge and a covenant to build and repair buildings, the assignee of the grantee of the land is not liable, either at law or in equity, on the ground of notice, to the assignee of the grantee of the rent-charge on the covenant to repair.—*Tulk* v. *Moxhay* (2 Ph. 774) explained. —*Cooke* v. *Chilcott* (3 Ch. D. 694) questioned. HAYWOOD *v.* BRUNSWICK PERMANENT BENEFIT BUILDING SOCIETY　　　8 Q. B. D. 403

3. —— Land subject to Rent-charge —*Restrictive Covenant—Assignee.*] Land was granted in fee in consideration of a rent-charge, and the deed of grant contained a covenant to build houses on the land the rent of which should be double the value of the rent reserved by the deed, without limiting any time within which such building was to be required.—*Held,* that such covenant was unusually restrictive.—*Semble,* that although the assignee of the grantee of the land was not liable affirmatively on such covenant, he might be called on to allow the house to be built in accordance with the covenant. ANDREW *v.* AITKIN
[22 Ch. D. 218

4. —— To repair—*Assigns—Personal Covenant—Notice, Equitable Doctrine of.*] The doctrine in *Tulk* v. *Moxhay* (2 Ph. 774) is limited to restrictive stipulations, and will not be extended so as to bind in equity a purchaser taking with notice of a covenant to expend money on repairs or otherwise which does not run with the land at law.—*Semble,* that the burden of a covenant (not involving a grant) never runs with the land at

II. COVENANT — RUNNING WITH LAND —
continued.

law, except as between landlord and tenant.— *Cooke* v. *Chilcott* (3 Ch. D. 694) overruled on this point.—*Morland* v. *Cook* (Law Rep. 6 Eq. 252) explained.—*Holmes* v. *Buckley* (1 Eq. C. Ab. 27) discussed. Consideration of the circumstances under which a covenant will be held to touch or concern the land of the covenantee so that the benefit may run with the land.—A., by deed, conveyed for value to trustees in fee a piece of land as part of the site of a road intended to be made and maintained by the trustees under the provisions of a contemporaneous trust deed (being a deed of settlement for the benefit of a joint stock company established to raise the necessary capital for making the road) ; and in the conveyance the trustees covenanted with A., his heirs and assigns, that they, the trustees, their heirs and assigns, would make the road and at all times keep it in repair, and allow the use of it by the public subject to tolls. The piece of land so conveyed was bounded on both sides by other lands belonging to A. The trustees duly made the road, which afforded the necessary access to A.'s adjoining lands. A. afterwards sold his adjoining lands to the Plaintiff, and the trustees sold the road to the Defendants, both parties taking with notice of the covenant to repair :—*Held* (affirming the decision of the Vice-Chancellor of the Duchy of Lancaster), that the Plaintiff could not enforce the covenant against the Defendants. AUSTERBERRY *v.* CORPORATION OF OLDHAM　　-　　- 29 Ch. D. 750

III. COVENANT—VALIDITY.

—— Not to revoke Will.] A covenant not to revoke a will is not necessarily against public policy as being in restraint of marriage. ROBINSON *v.* OMMANNEY 21 Ch. D. 780 ; 23 Ch. D. 285

COVENANT—Binding on representatives.
　　　See DEED—*Statutes.*

—— Breach—Continuing breach　7 App. Cas 19
　　　See VENDOR AND PURCHASER—CONDITIONS OF SALE. 3.

—— Breach—Proof in bankruptcy 22 Ch. D. 410
　　　See BANKRUPTCY—DISTRESS. 5.

—— Debt under—Retainer by executor
[30 Ch. D. 15
　　　See EXECUTOR—RETAINER. 8.

—— For title implied.
　　　See DEED—*Statutes.*

—— Interest—Judgment—Merger 25 Ch. D. 338
　　　See JUDGMENT. 3.

—— Lapse of time—Laches　-　20 Ch. D. 230
　　　See SPECIALTY DEBT.

—— Lease—Disclaimer by trustee　29 Ch. D. 8
　　　See BANKRUPTCY—DISCLAIMER. 13.

—— Leaseholds—Indemnity of trustees
[16 Ch. D. 723
　　　See TRUSTEE—LIABILITIES. 9.

—— Mining lease　-　-　-　23 Ch. D. 81
　　　See MINE—LEASE. 1.

—— Mortgagor—Judgment in foreclosure action
[28 Ch. D. 181
　　　See MORTGAGE—FORECLOSURE. 18.

COVENANT—*continued.*

—— Not to revoke will—Proof in bankruptcy
[23 Ch D. 285
See BANKRUPTCY—PROOF. 6.

—— Notice of - 17 Ch. D. 353
See VENDOR AND PURCHASER—TITLE. 3.

—— Offensive trade 9 Q. B. D. 404
See LANDLORD AND TENANT—RE-ENTRY.
4.

—— Partnership articles—Annuity of widow of
deceased partner - 25 Ch. D. 89
See PARTNERSHIP—CONTRACT. 1.

—— Proof in administration 17 Ch. D. 342
See EXECUTOR—ACTIONS. 19.

—— Quiet enjoyment—Breach—General system
of drainage - 13 Q. B. D. 547
See LANDLORD AND TENANT—LEASE. 1.

—— Renewable lease - 9 App. Cas. 844
See LANDLORD AND TENANT—LEASE. 14.

—— Restrictive—Conveyance settled by Judge
[21 Ch. D. 466
See VENDOR AND PURCHASER—CONVEY-
ANCE. 1.

—— Restrictive—Non-disclosure to purchaser—
Right to rescind - 15 Q. B. D. 261
See VENDOR AND PURCHASER—CONDI-
TIONS OF SALE. 8.

—— Restrictive—Objection to title 21 Ch. D. 95
See VENDOR AND PURCHASER—TITLE. 6.

—— Running with property — Assignment of
patent - 19 Ch. D. 246
See PATENT—ASSIGNMENT. 2.

—— Running with reversion.
See LANDLORD AND TENANT—LEASE—
Statutes.

—— Separation deed.
See Cases under HUSBAND AND WIFE—
SEPARATION DEED.

—— Stamp duty on.
See REVENUE—STAMPS—Statutes.

—— Statute of Limitations—Mortgage
[22 Ch. D. 511
See LIMITATIONS, STATUTE OF —PER-
SONAL ACTIONS. 8.

—— To pay annuity—Power to reduce amount
[8 P. D. 159
See PRACTICE—DIVORCE—SETTLEMENTS.
2.

—— To pay money free from all deductions
[29 Ch. D. 697
See SETTLEMENT—CONSTRUCTION. 1.

—— To pay premiums on policy—Surety
[19 Ch. D. 615
See PRINCIPAL AND SURETY—INDEMNITY.
2.

—— To pay rates—Metropolis Management Acts
[9 Q. B. D. 632 ; 13 Q. B. D. 1
See LANDLORD AND TENANT — LEASE.
9, 10.

—— To pay rates—Water supplied by waterworks company - 13 Q. B. D. 202
See LANDLORD AND TENANT—LEASE. 11.

—— To pay rent, how far divisible 10 Q. B. D. 48
See LANDLORD AND TENANT—ASSIGN-
MENT. 2.

COVENANT—*continued.*

—— To re-convey—Railway company — Super-
fluous lands 20 Ch. D. 562
See LANDS CLAUSES ACT—SUPERFLUOUS
LANDS. 2.

—— To renew lease 18 Ch. D. 238 ; 22 Ch. D.
[640 ; 9 App. Cas. 844
See LANDLORD AND TENANT—LEASE. 12,
13, 14.

—— To repair road - 29 Ch. D. 750
See HIGHWAY—DEDICATION.

—— To settle 19 Ch. D. 342
See BANKRUPTCY—VOID SETTLEMENT. 1.

—— To settle after-acquired property.
See Cases under SETTLEMENT—FUTURE
PROPERTY.

—— To settle future property 9 Q. B. D. 337 ;
[10 App. Cas. 1
See HUSBAND AND WIFE — SEPARATE
ESTATE. 6.

—— To settle—Severance of joint tenancy
See JOINT TENANT. 2. [17 Ch. D. 388

—— To settle—Female infant 28 Ch. D. 124
See ELECTION. 6.

—— Underlease - 30 Ch. D. 404
See LANDLORD AND TENANT—LEASE. 3.

CRABS.
See FISHERY ACTS—Statutes.

CREDITOR — Claim in administration suit —
Statute of Limitations - 18 Ch. D. 551
See LIMITATIONS, STATUTE OF—PER-
SONAL ACTIONS. 4.

—— Examination of—Bankruptcy—Composition
[23 Ch. D. 118
See BANKRUPTCY—EVIDENCE. 4.

—— Execution against company 20 Ch. D. 442
See COMPANY—INJUNCTION. 1.

—— Grant of administration to— Special circumstances - 7 P. D. 13
See ADMINISTRATOR—GRANT. 6.

—— Opposition to registration of liquidation
resolutions - 24 Ch. D. 477
See BANKRUPTCY—LIQUIDATION. 8.

—— Partnership— Action against estate of de-
ceased partner - 23 Ch. D. 16
See PRACTICE—SUPREME COURT—CON-
DUCT OF CAUSE. 4.

—— Power of, to authorize trustee to carry on
business 17 Ch. D. 35
See BANKRUPTCY—TRUSTEE. 2.

—— Resolution of creditors—Direction to trustees - 21 Ch. D. 397
See BANKRUPTCY—TRUSTEE. 1.

—— Rights of—Lunatic—Insolvent estate
[23 Ch. D. 577
See LUNATIC—MAINTENANCE. 2.

—— Secured—Administration action— Rules of
bankruptcy - 20 Ch. D. 545
See EXECUTOR—ACTIONS. 20.

—— Secured—Bankruptcy.
See Cases under BANKRUPTCY—SECURED
CREDITOR.

—— Winding up of company — Attendance at
examination of witnesses 25 Ch. D. 283 ;
[27 Ch. D. 515
See COMPANY—EVIDENCE. 4, 5.

CREDITOR—*continued.*

—— Winding-up petition by.
　See Cases under COMPANY—WINDING-UP
　ORDER.　8—12.

CREDITORS' DEED.

—— Time for executing.] Incumbrancers
who had claimed priority over a creditors' deed
and failed in their contention were not allowed
afterwards to execute and take the benefit of the
deed. *In re* MEREDITH. MEREDITH *v.* FACEY
　　　　　　　　　　　[29 Ch. D. 745

—— Costs of trustees　-　25 Ch. D. 617
　See TRUSTEE—COSTS AND CHARGES.　6.

CREMATION—Dead body　20 Ch. D. 659
　See EXECUTOR—POWERS.　3.

—— Dead body—Misdemeanor　12 Q. B. D. 247
　See CRIMINAL LAW—MISDEMEANOR.　1.

—— Dead body—Prevention of inquest—Obstruction of coroner　-　13 Q. B. D. 331
　See CRIMINAL LAW—MISDEMEANOR.　2.

CRIME—Prevention of.
　See CRIMINAL LAW—PRACTICE—*Statutes.*

CRIMINAL LAW:—　　　　　　　Col.
　I. BIGAMY　-　-　-　459
　II. COINING　-　-　-　460
　III. CONSPIRACY　-　-　460
　IV. EXPLOSIVES　-　-　460
　V. FORGERY　-　-　463
　VI. FRAUDULENT DEBTOR　-　463
　VII. LARCENY　-　-　464
　VIII. LIBEL　-　-　465
　IX. MALICIOUS INJURY　-　467
　X. MISAPPROPRIATION　467
　XI. MISDEMEANOR　-　467
　XII. NUISANCE　467
　XIII. OFFENCES AGAINST PERSON　468
　XIV. OFFENCES AGAINST WOMEN　-　471
　XV. UNLAWFUL ASSEMBLY　-　473
　XVI. EVIDENCE　-　473
　XVII. PRACTICE　-　-　-　475

I. CRIMINAL LAW—BIGAMY.

1. —— Evidence—*Duration of Life, Presumption of—Conflicting Presumptions.*] In 1864, W.
married A. In 1868 he was charged with bigamy
in marrying B. in 1868, his wife A. being then
alive, and was on such charge convicted. In
1879 he married C., and in 1880, C. being then
alive, he married D. Afterwards, upon a charge
of bigamy in marrying D., C. being then alive,
W. was convicted, it being held by the presiding
Judge that there was no evidence that A. was
alive when W. married C., or that the marriage
with C. was invalid by reason of A. being then
alive :—*Held,* by the Court (Lord Coleridge, C.J.,
Lindley, Hawkins, Lopes, and Bowen, JJ.), that
the conviction could not be sustained, as the
question should have been left to the jury whether
upon the above facts A. was alive or not when W.
married C. THE QUEEN *v.* WILLSHIRE
　　　　　　　　　　　[6 Q. B. D. 366

2. —— Evidence—*Presumption of continuance
of Cohabitation*—24 & 25 Vict. c. 100, s. 57.] The
prisoner was convicted of bigamy. It was proved

I. CRIMINAL LAW—BIGAMY—*continued.*
that he had married W. in 1865, and lived with
her after the marriage, but for how long was not
known; that in 1882, W. being still alive, he had
gone through the form of marriage with another
woman, but there was no evidence as to the prisoner and W. having ever separated or as to
when, if separated, they last saw each other—:
Held, by the Court (Lord Coleridge, C.J., Pollock, B., Manisty, Lopes, and Stephen, JJ.), that
the prisoner was rightly convicted. THE QUEEN
v. JONES　-　-　-　-　11 Q. B. D. 118

II. CRIMINAL LAW—COINING.

By the Counterfeit Medal Act, 1883 (46 & 47 Vict.
c. 45), s. 2, *any person who, without due authority
or excuse (the proof whereof lies on the person
accused), makes or has in his possession for sale, or
offers for sale, or sells, any medal, cast, coin, or
other like thing made wholly or partially of metal
or any metallic combination, and resembling in
size, figure, and colour any of the Queen's current
gold or silver coin, or having thereon a device
resembling any device on any of the Queen's current
gold or silver coin, or being so formed that it can
by gilding, silvering, colouring, washing, or other
like process, be so dealt with as to resemble any of
the Queen's current gold or silver coin, shall be
guilty of a misdemeanor, and on being convicted
shall be liable to be imprisoned for any term not
exceeding one year, with or without hard labour.*

*Sect. 3. "The Queen's current gold and silver
coin" includes any gold or silver coin coined in or
for any of Her Majesty's mints, or lawfully current
by virtue of any proclamation or otherwise in any
part of Her Majesty's dominions, whether within the
United Kingdom or otherwise.*

III. CRIMINAL LAW—CONSPIRACY.

—— *Indictment against Two for conspiring
together—Acquittal or Conviction of both.*] Where
two persons are indicted for conspiring together
and they are tried together, both must be acquitted
or both convicted. THE QUEEN *v.* MANNING
　　　　　　　　　　　[12 Q. B. D. 241

IV. CRIMINAL LAW—EXPLOSIVES.

The Act 46 & 47 Vict. c. 3 (*Explosive Substances
Act,* 1883) *amends the law relating to explosive
substances.*

*Sect. 2. Any person who unlawfully and mali-
ciously causes by any explosive substance an explosion of a nature likely to endanger life or to
cause serious injury to property shall, whether any
injury to person or property has been actually caused
or not, be guilty of felony, and on conviction shall
be liable to penal servitude for life, or for any less
term (not less than the minimum term allowed by
law), or to imprisonment with or without hard
labour for a term not exceeding two years.*

*Sect. 3. Any person who within or (being a sub-
ject of Her Majesty) without Her Majesty's dominions unlawfully and maliciously—*

(a.) *Does any act with intent to cause by an explosive substance, or conspires to cause by
an explosive substance an explosion in the
United Kingdom of a nature likely to endanger life or to cause serious injury to
property; or*

(b.) *Makes or has in his possession or under his*

IV. CRIMINAL LAW—EXPLOSIVES—contd.

control any explosive substance with intent by means thereof to endanger life, or cause serious injury to property in the United Kingdom, or to enable any other person by means thereof to endanger life or cause serious injury to property in the United Kingdom, shall, whether any explosion does or not take place, and whether any injury to person or property has been actually caused or not, be guilty of felony, and on conviction shall be liable to penal servitude for a term not exceeding twenty years, or to imprisonment with or without hard labour for a term not exceeding two years, and the explosive substance shall be forfeited.

Sect. 4.—(1.) Any person who makes or knowingly has in his possession or under his control any explosive substance, under such circumstances as to give rise to a reasonable suspicion that he is not making it or does not have it in his possession or under his control for a lawful object, shall, unless he can shew that he made it or had it in his possession or under his control for a lawful object, be guilty of felony, and on conviction, shall be liable to penal servitude for a term not exceeding fourteen years, or to imprisonment for a term not exceeding two years with or without hard labour, and the explosive substance shall be forfeited.

(2.) In any proceeding against any person for a crime under this section, such person and his wife, or husband, as the case may be, may, if such person thinks fit, be called, sworn, examined, and cross-examined as an ordinary witness in the case.

Sect. 5. Any person who within or (being a subject of Her Majesty) without Her Majesty's dominions by the supply of or solicitation for money, the providing of premises, the supply of materials, or in any manner whatsoever procures, counsels, aids, abets, or is accessory to, the commission of any crime under this Act, shall be guilty of felony, and shall be liable to be tried and punished for that crime, as if he had been guilty as a principal.

Sect. 6.—(1.) Where the Attorney-General has reasonable ground to believe that any crime under this Act has been committed, he may order an inquiry under this section, and thereupon any justice for the county, borough, or place in which the crime was committed, or is suspected to have been committed, who is authorized in that behalf by the Attorney-General, may, although no person may be charged before him with the commission of such crime, sit at a police court, or petty sessional or occasional court house, or police station in the said county, borough, or place, and examine on oath concerning such crime any witness appearing before him, and may take the deposition of such witness, and, if he see cause, may bind such witness by recognizance to appear and give evidence at the next petty sessions, or when called upon within three months from the date of such recognizance; and the law relating to the compelling of the attendance of a witness, before a justice and required to give evidence concerning the matter of an information or complaint, shall apply to compelling the attendance of a witness for examination and to a witness attending under this section.

(2.) A witness examined under this section shall not be excused from answering any question on the

ground that the answer thereto may criminate or tend to criminate himself; but any statement made by any person in answer to any question put to him on any examination under this section shall not, except in the case of an indictment or other criminal proceeding for perjury, be admissible in evidence against him in any proceeding, civil or criminal.

(3.) A justice who conducts the examination under this section of a person concerning any crime shall not take part in the committal for trial of such person for such crime.

(4.) Whenever any person is bound by recognizance to give evidence before justices, or any criminal Court, in respect of any crime under this Act, any justice, if he sees fit, upon information being made in writing, and on oath, that such person is about to abscond, or has absconded, may issue his warrant for the arrest of such person, and if such person is arrested any justice, upon being satisfied that the ends of justice would otherwise be defeated, may commit such person to prison until the time at which he is bound by such recognizance to give evidence, unless in the meantime he produces sufficient sureties: Provided that any person so arrested shall be entitled on demand to receive a copy of the information upon which the warrant for his arrest was issued.

Sect. 7.—(1.) If any person is charged before a justice with any crime under this Act, no further proceeding shall be taken against such person without the consent of the Attorney-General, except such as the justice may think necessary by remand, or otherwise, to secure the safe custody of such person.

(2.) In framing an indictment the same criminal act may be charged in different counts as constituting different crimes under this Act, and upon the trial of any such indictment the prosecutor shall not be put to his election as to the count on which he must proceed.

(3.) For all purposes of and incidental to arrest, trial, and punishment, a crime for which a person is liable to be punished under this Act, when committed out of the United Kingdom, shall be deemed to have been committed in the place in which such person is apprehended or is in custody.

(4.) This Act shall not exempt any person from any indictment or proceeding for a crime or offence which is punishable at common law, or by any Act of Parliament other than this Act, but no person shall be punished twice for the same criminal act.

Sect. 8.—(1.) Sects. 73, 74, 75, 89, and 96 of the Explosives Act, 1875 (which sections relate to the search for, seizure, and detention of explosive substances, and the forfeiture thereof, and the disposal of explosive substances, seized or forfeited), shall apply in like manner as if a crime or forfeiture under this Act were an offence or forfeiture under the Explosives Act, 1875.

(2.) Where the master or owner of any vessel has reasonable cause to suspect that any dangerous goods or goods of a dangerous nature which, if found, he would be entitled to throw overboard in pursuance of the Merchant Shipping Act, 1873, are concealed on board his vessel, he may search any part of such vessel for such goods, and for the purpose of such search may, if necessary, break open any box, package, or parcel, or receptacle on board the vessel, and such master or owner, if he finds any such dangerous goods, or goods of a dangerous

IV. CRIMINAL LAW—EXPLOSIVES—contd.

nature, shall be entitled to deal with the same in manner provided by the said Act, and if he do not find the same, he shall not be subject to any liability, civil or criminal, if it appears to the tribunal, before which the question of his liability is raised, that he had reasonable cause to suspect that such goods were so concealed as aforesaid.

By sect. 9. The expression " explosive substance," shall be deemed to include any materials for making any explosive substance; also any apparatus, machine, implement, or materials used, or intended to be used, or adapted for causing, or aiding in causing, any explosion in or with any explosive substance; also any part of any such apparatus, machine, or implement.

Explosives Act. 1875.] Notice as to fees for licences. Dated March 31, 1882
　　　　　　　　　　[L. G., 1882, p. 1472

Keeping Explosives—Certificates.] Orders in Council under Explosives Act, 1875, all dated 20th April, 1883　L. G., 1883, pp. 2099, 2101, 2102

Fees.] Notice as to fees for amending licences for toy fireworks factories. Dated Feb. 26, 1884
　　　　　　　　　　[L. G., 1884, p. 971

Fireworks.] Order of Sept. 1, 1884, placing explosives of the 7th (Firework) class under the Explosives Act, 1875, s. 40, sub-s. 9
　　　　　　　　　　[L. G., 1884, p. 2994

Premises registered for keeping Explosives.] Order of 12th July, 1885, revoking part of order of Nov. 27, 1875, and prescribing in lieu thereof
　　　　　　　　　　[L. G., 1885, p. 3779

V. CRIMINAL LAW—FORGERY.

—— Bill of Exchange — Inchoate Negotiable Instrument.] H. purchased goods upon the terms that he should give to the vendors his acceptance for the price, indorsed by a solvent third party. The vendors sent to him for such acceptance and indorsement a document in the form of a bill of exchange, for the price, but without any drawer's name thereon. H. returned this document accepted by himself, and with what purported to be an indorsement by a solvent third party. This indorsement was fictitious and had been forged by H. No drawer's name was ever placed upon the document:—Held, by the Court (Lord Coleridge, C J., Grove, Hawkins, Lopes, and Stephen, JJ.), that the document was not a bill of exchange, as it bore no drawer's name, and that H. could not be convicted of feloniously forging or feloniously uttering an indorsement on a bill of exchange.—Semble, that he might have been convicted of a common law forgery. THE QUEEN v. HARPER　　-　　- 7 Q. B. D. 78

VI. CRIMINAL LAW—FRAUDULENT DEBTOR.

—— Removing Property—Debtors Act, 1869 (32 & 33 Vict. c. 62), s. 13 (3) — Execution, removing Property to defeat — Evidence — Indictment—Execution Creditor.] A., B., and C., were convicted, under sect. 13, sub-sect. 3, of 32 & 33 Vict. c. 62, of having, with intent to defraud the creditors of A., removed the property of A. since the date of an unsatisfied judgment against A.— The evidence was, that on the next night after a judgment, which was still unsatisfied, had been obtained against A., the property of A. was removed from his house by A., B. and C., in order

VI. CRIMINAL LAW—FRAUDULENT DEBTOR —continued.

to defeat the creditor who had obtained the judgment, and to prevent him from levying thereon to satisfy the judgment. There was no evidence that A. had any other creditors, or that there was any intention to defeat the claims of any creditors of A. other than this particular creditor.— No petition in bankruptcy had been presented against A., nor had any proceedings been taken to have his affairs liquidated by arrangement:— Held, by Lord Coleridge, C.J., Denman, Stephen, Mathew, and Cave, JJ., that the absence of proceedings in bankruptcy or for liquidation was not material; that the provisions in question of the above statute applied to all persons; but that the conviction must nevertheless be quashed, inasmuch as an intent to defraud creditors was charged but was not proved. THE QUEEN v. ROWLANDS　　-　　8 Q. B. D. 530

VII. CRIMINAL LAW—LARCENY.

1. —— Bailment of Money — Larceny by Bailee.] A prisoner was convicted of larceny under the following circumstances:—The prosecutor gave a mare of his into the care of the prisoner, telling him that it was to be sold on the next Wednesday. On the next Wednesday the prosecutor did not go himself to sell his mare, but sent his wife, who went to where the prisoner was and saw him riding the mare about a horse fair, and sell her to a third party, and receive on such sale some money. The prosecutor's wife after such sale asked the prisoner to give her the money, saying she would pay his expenses: this the prisoner declined to do, and eventually he absconded with the money and without accounting:—Held, by the Court (Lord Coleridge, C.J., Grove, Field, and Smith, JJ., Stephen, J., dissenting) that there was evidence that the prisoner was a bailee of the money thus paid to him, and that the conviction could be supported. THE QUEEN v. DE BANKS　　-　　13 Q. B. D. 29

2. —— Bailment to Infant—24 & 25 Vict. c. 96, s. 3.] An infant over fourteen years of age fraudulently converted to his own use goods which had been delivered to him by the owner under an agreement for the hire of the same:—Held, that he was rightly convicted of larceny as a bailee of the goods under 24 & 25 Vict. c. 96, s. 3. THE QUEEN v. McDONALD　　15 Q. B. D. 323

3. —— Money demanded with Menaces.] The prosecutrix gave L., a travelling grinder, six knives to grind for her, the ordinary charge for grinding which would be 1s. 3d. L. ground the knives, and then demanded with threats 5s. 6d. as his charge from the prosecutrix. The prosecutrix, being thus frightened, in consequence of her fears paid L. the sum demanded:—The jury found that the money was obtained by menaces, and convicted L. of larceny:—Held, by the Court (Lord Coleridge, C.J., Lindley, Hawkins, Lopes, and Bowen, JJ.), that the conviction was right.— Reg. v. M'Grath (L. R. 1 C. C. R. 205) followed. THE QUEEN v. LOVELL　　-　　8 Q. B. D. 185

4. —— Ringing the Changes — Larceny by Trick.] The two prisoners by a series of tricks fraudulently induced a barmaid to pay over money of her master to them, without having received

VII. CRIMINAL LAW—LARCENY—continued.

from them in return the proper change; the barmaid had no authority to pay over money without receiving the proper change, and had no intention of or knowledge that she was so doing:—*Held*, by the Court (Lord Coleridge, C.J., Denman, Hawkins, Williams, and Mathew, JJ.), that the prisoners were properly convicted of larceny. THE QUEEN *v.* HOLLIS - - 12 Q. B. D. 25

5. —— **Water stored in Pipes,** *whether the subject of Larceny at Common Law.*] Water supplied by a water company to a consumer, and standing in his pipes, may be the subject of a larceny at common law. FERENS *v.* O'BRIEN
[11 Q. B. D. 21

VIII. CRIMINAL LAW—LIBEL.

The Act 44 & 45 Vict. c. 60 (*Newspaper Libel and Registration Act,* 1881) *amends the law affecting civil actions and criminal prosecutions for newspaper libel.*

Sect. 1 *defines* (inter alia) *the word "newspaper" to mean any paper containing public news, intelligence, or occurrences, or any remarks or observations thereon, printed for sale and published in England or Ireland periodically, or in parts or numbers, at intervals not exceeding twenty-six days between the publication of any two such papers, parts or numbers.*

Also any paper printed in order to be dispersed and made public weekly or oftener, or at intervals not exceeding twenty-six days, containing only or principally advertisements.

The word "proprietor" to mean and include as well the sole proprietor of any newspaper, as also, in the case of a divided proprietorship, the persons who as partners or otherwise represent and are responsible for any share or interest in the newspaper as between themselves and the persons in like manner representing or responsible for the other shares or interests therein, and no other person.

Sect. 2. *Any report published in any newspaper of the proceedings of a public meeting shall be privileged, if such meeting was lawfully convened for a lawful purpose and open to the public, and if such report was fair and accurate, and published without malice, and if the publication of the matter complained of was for the public benefit; provided always, that the protection intended to be afforded by this section shall not be available as a defence in any proceeding if the Plaintiff or prosecutor can shew that the Defendant has refused to insert in the newspaper in which the report containing the matter complained of appeared a reasonable letter or statement of explanation or contradiction by or on behalf of such Plaintiff or prosecutor.*

Sect. 3. *No criminal prosecution shall be commenced against any proprietor, publisher, editor, or any person responsible for the publication of a newspaper, for any libel published therein without the written fiat or allowance of the Director of Public Prosecutions in England or Her Majesty's Attorney-General in Ireland being first had and obtained.*

◊| Sect. 4. *A Court of summary jurisdiction upon the hearing of a charge against a proprietor, publisher, or editor, or any person responsible for the publication of a newspaper, for a libel published therein, may receive evidence as to the publication*

VIII. CRIMINAL LAW—LIBEL—continued. :

being for the public benefit, and as to the matters charged in the libel being true, and as to the report being fair and accurate, and published without malice, and as to any matter which under this or any other Act, or otherwise, might be given in evidence by way of defence by the person charged on his trial on indictment, and the Court, if of opinion after hearing such evidence, that there is a strong or probable presumption that the jury on the trial would acquit the person charged, may dismiss the case.

Sect. 5. *If a Court of summary jurisdiction upon the hearing of a charge against a proprietor, publisher, editor, or any person responsible for the publication of a newspaper, for a libel published therein, is of opinion that though the person charged is shewn to have been guilty the libel was of a trivial character, and that the offence may be adequately punished by virtue of the powers of this section, the Court shall cause the charge to be reduced into writing and read to the person charged and then address a question to him to the following effect: "Do you desire to be tried by a jury or do you consent to the case being dealt with summarily?" and if such person assents to the case being dealt with summarily, the Court may summarily convict him and adjudge him to pay a fine not exceeding fifty pounds.*

Sect. 27 *of the Summary Jurisdiction Act,* 1879, *shall so far as is consistent with the tenor thereof apply to every such proceeding as if it were herein enacted and extended to Ireland, and as if the Summary Jurisdiction Acts were therein referred to instead of the Summary Jurisdiction Act,* 1848.

Sect. 6. *Every libel, or alleged libel, and every offence under this Act shall be deemed to be an offence within and subject to the provisions of the Act* 22 *&* 23 *Vict. c.* 17, *intituled "An Act to prevent vexatious indictments for certain misdemeanors."*

1. —— **Discretion of Court—***Leave to file Information—Libel upon Deceased Foreign Nobleman—Applicant resident Abroad.*] Upon application for leave to file a criminal information in respect of a libel upon a deceased foreign nobleman made by his representative who was not resident in this country:—*Held*, that the Court, in the exercise of its discretion, must reject the application, for the rule to be collected from the modern decisions is that a criminal information for libel can only be granted at the suit of persons who are in some public office or position, and not at the suit of private persons:—*Held*, also, that the fact that the applicant does not reside in this country is a strong reason for rejecting such an application.—*Semble*, that an application for a criminal information for a libel upon a deceased person made by his representative will not be granted. THE QUEEN *v.* LABOUCHERE - - 12 Q. B. D. 320

2. —— **Newspaper** — *Criminal Information for Libel—Newspaper Libel and Registration Act,* 1881 (44 & 45 Vict. v. 60), s. 3—*Information filed without Fiat of Director of Public Prosecutions.*] The 3rd section of the Newspaper Libel and Registration Act, 1881, which enacts that no criminal prosecution shall be commenced against any proprietor, publisher, or editor, or any person

VIII. CRIMINAL LAW—LIBEL—*continued.*

responsible for the publication of a newspaper, for any libel published therein, without the written fiat or allowance of the Director of Public Prosecutions in England, or her Majesty's Attorney General in Ireland, being first had and obtained, does not apply to a criminal information for libel filed by order of the Court. YATES *v.* THE QUEEN

[11 Q. B. D. 750; 14 Q. B. D. 648

IX. CRIMINAL LAW — MALICIOUS INJURY TO PROPERTY.

—— **Herbage Right** — *Malicious Injuries to Property Act (24 & 25 Vict. c. 97), s. 52—"Real or Personal Property" — Incorporeal Hereditament.*] The soil of a town moor was vested in the corporation of the town in fee, but freemen and widows of deceased freemen of the town were under statute entitled to the "full right and benefit to the herbage" of the town moor for two milch cows:—*Held,* that this right to the herbage was not "any real or personal property whatsoever" within the meaning of the Malicious Injuries to Property Act (24 & 25 Vict. c. 97), s. 52, which applies only to tangible property and not to a mere incorporeal right. LAWS *v.* ELTRINGHAM   8 Q. B. D. 283

X. CRIMINAL LAW—MISAPPROPRIATION.

—— **Property intrusted for safe Custody**—*Larceny Act (24 & 25 Vict. c. 96), ss. 75, 76.*] N., a solicitor, was intrusted by a client with money to invest on mortgage on the client's behalf: he, instead of so doing, fraudulently appropriated the money to his own use: *Held,* by Lord Coleridge, C.J., Denman, Stephen, Mathew, and Cave, JJ., that N. was not intrusted with such money for "safe custody" within sect. 76 of 24 & 25 Vict. c. 96 (the Larceny Act). THE QUEEN *v.* NEWMAN

[8 Q. B. D. 706

XI. CRIMINAL LAW—MISDEMEANOR.

1. —— **Burning Dead Body**—*Nuisance—Inquest—Preventing Inquest being held.*] To burn a dead body, instead of burying it, is not a misdemeanor, unless it is so done as to amount to a public nuisance.—If an inquest ought to be held upon a dead body, it is a misdemeanor so to dispose of the body as to prevent the coroner from holding the inquest. THE QUEEN *v.* PRICE

[12 Q. B. D. 247

2. —— **Obstructing Coroner**—*Inquest, Destruction of Body to prevent—Misdemeanor, obstructing Justice—Burning Dead Body.*] It is a misdemeanor to burn or otherwise dispose of a dead body, with intent thereby to prevent the holding upon such body of an intended coroner's inquest, and so to obstruct a coroner in the execution of his duty, in a case where the inquest is one which the coroner has jurisdiction to hold. A coroner has jurisdiction to hold, and is justified in holding, an inquest if he honestly believes information which has been given to him to be true, which, if true, would make it his duty to hold such inquest. THE QUEEN *v.* STEPHENSON

[13 Q. B. D. 331

XII. CRIMINAL LAW—NUISANCE.

Brothel.] *The Act 48 & 49 Vict. c. 69, s. 13, enables summary proceedings to be taken against*

XII. CRIMINAL LAW—NUISANCE—*contd.*

a brothel keeper, &c., under the Summary Jurisdiction Act, 1879 (42 & 43 *Vict. c.* 49). *The enactments contained in* 25 *Geo.* 2, *c.* 36, *ss.* 5, 6, *and* 7, *and* 58 *Geo.* 3, *c.* 70, *to apply to these summary proceedings.*

—— **Indecent Exposure**—*Public Place—Public Nuisance* — 14 & 15 *Vict. c.* 100, *s.* 29.] The prisoner was convicted of indecently exposing his person to divers subjects of the Queen in a certain public place, upon evidence shewing that the place in question was out of sight of the public footpath, but was a place to which the prisoner had gone with several little girls, though without any legal right to go there, and was a place to which persons were in the habit of going without having any strict legal right so to do, and that persons so going were never in any way hindered or interfered with:—*Held,* by the Court (Lord Coleridge, C.J., Grove, J., Huddleston, B., Manisty, and Mathew, JJ.), that the conviction was correct, and that the jury were justified in finding that the place was public.—*Semble,* that the offence may be indictable if committed before divers subjects of the realm, even if the place be not public. THE QUEEN *v.* WELLARD

[14 Q. B. D. 63

XIII. CRIMINAL LAW—OFFENCES AGAINST PERSON.

Indecent Act with Male Person.] *The Act* 48 & 49 *Vict. c.* 69, *s.* 11, *punishes as a misdemeanor any commission, or attempted commission, by a male person of any act of gross indecency with another male person, in public or private.*

1. —— **Grievous Bodily Harm** — *Malice* — 24 & 25 *Vict. c.* 100, *s.* 20.] Shortly before the conclusion of a performance at a theatre, M., with the intention and with the result of causing terror in the minds of persons leaving the theatre, put out the gaslights on a staircase which a large number of such persons had to descend in order to leave the theatre, and he also, with the intention and with the result of obstructing the exit, placed an iron bar across a doorway through which they had in leaving to pass.—Upon the lights being thus extinguished a panic seized a large portion of the audience, and they rushed in fright down the staircase forcing those in front against the iron bar. By reason of the pressure and struggling of the crowd thus created on the staircase, several of the audience were thrown down or otherwise severely injured, and amongst them A. and B.—On proof of these facts the jury convicted M. of unlawfully and maliciously inflicting grievous bodily harm upon A. and B. :—*Held,* by the Court (Lord Coleridge, C.J., Field, Hawkins, Stephen, and Cave, JJ.), that M. was rightly convicted. THE QUEEN *v.* MARTIN

[8 Q. B. D. 54

2. —— **Manslaughter**—*Death caused by dangerous Act performed without proper Precautions—Fire-arms, negligent use of—Joint Wrongdoers.*] A., B., and C. went into a field in proximity to certain roads and houses, taking with them a rifle which would be deadly at a mile, for the purpose of practising firing with it. B. placed a board, which was handed to him by A., in the presence of C., in a tree in the field as a target.

XIII. CRIMINAL LAW—OFFENCES AGAINST PERSON—*continued.*

All three fired shots directed at the board *so* placed, from a distance of about 100 yards.—-No precautions of any kind were taken to prevent danger from such firing.—One of the shots thus fired by one, though it was not proved by which one, of them, killed a boy in a tree in a garden near the field, at a spot distant 393 yards from the firing point. A., B., and C., were all found guilty by a jury of manslaughter:—*Held,* by the Court (Lord Coleridge, C.J., Field, Lopes, Stephen, and Williams, JJ.), that A., B., and C., had been guilty of a breach of duty in firing at the spot in question, without taking proper precautions to prevent injury to others, and were rightly convicted of manslaughter. THE QUEEN v. SALMON, HANCOCK, AND SALMON　-　6 Q. B. D. 79

3. —— Manslaughter—*Neglect of Parent to provide Medical Aid for Child—Evidence—*31 & 32 *Vict. c.* 122, *s.* 37.] M. was convicted of the manslaughter of his son, a child of tender years. The child died of confluent small-pox, and the prisoner, though able to do so, did not, owing to certain religious views he held, employ any medical practitioner, nor afford to the child during its illness any medical aid or attendance. It was proved that proper medical aid and attendance might have saved or prolonged the child's life, and would have increased its chance of recovery, but that it might have been of no avail; and there was no positive evidence that the death was caused or accelerated by the neglect to provide medical aid or attendance:—*Held,* by Lord Coleridge, C.J., Grove, Stephen, Mathew, and Cave, JJ., that under the above circumstances the conviction could not be sustained. THE QUEEN v. MORBY　　　8 Q. B. D. 571

4. —— Murder—*Attempt to commit—*24 & 25 *Vict. c.* 100, *ss.* 14, 15.] B. drew a loaded pistol from his pocket for the purpose of murdering S., but before he had time to do anything further in pursuance of his purpose the pistol was snatched out of his hand, and he was at once arrested:—*Held,* by the Court (Lord Coleridge, C.J., Pollock, B., Huddleston, B., Manisty and Stephen, JJ.), that the offence was not within sect. 15 of 24 & 25 Vict. c. 100, under which section the prisoner had been tried and convicted.—*Semble,* that the offence was within sect. 14 of 24 & 25 Vict. c. 100.—*Reg.* v. *St. George* (9 C. & P. 483), and *Reg.* v. *Lewis* (9 C. & P. 523), doubted. THE QUEEN v. BROWN　　-　10 Q. B. D. 381

5. —— Murder—*Inciting to—Foreign Sovereign, Newspaper Article inciting to Murder of—*24 & 25 *Vict. c.* 100, *s.* 4.] M. was indicted under 24 & 25 Vict. c. 100, s. 4. The encouragement and endeavour to persuade to murder, proved at the trial, was the publication and circulation by him of an article, written in German in a newspaper published in that language in London, exulting in the recent murder of the Emperor of Russia, and commending it as an example to revolutionists throughout the world. The jury were directed that if they thought that by the publication of the article M. did intend to, and did, encourage or endeavour to persuade any person to murder any other person, whether a subject of Her Majesty or not, and whether within the Queen's dominions or not, and that such encouragement and endeavouring to persuade was the natural and reasonable effect of the article, they should find him guilty:—*Held,* by the Court (Lord Coleridge, C.J., Grove, and Denman, JJ., Huddleston, B., and Watkin Williams, J.), that such direction was correct, and that the publication and circulation of a newspaper article might be an encouragement, or endeavour to persuade to murder, within sect. 4 of 24 & 25 Vict. c. 100, although not addressed to any person in particular. THE QUEEN v. MOST　　7 Q. B. D. 244

6. —— Murder—*Killing and eating Flesh of Human Being under Pressure of Hunger—" Necessity"—Special Verdict—Certiorari—Offence on High Seas—Jurisdiction of High Court.*] A man who, in order to escape death from hunger, kills another for the purpose of eating his flesh, is guilty of murder; although at the time of the act he is in such circumstances that he believes and has reasonable ground for believing that it affords the only chance of preserving his life. At the trial of an indictment for murder it appeared, upon a special verdict, that the prisoners D. and S., seamen, and the deceased, a boy between seventeen and eighteen, were cast away in a storm on the high seas, and compelled to put into an open boat: that the boat was drifting on the ocean, and was probably more than 1000 miles from land; that on the eighteenth day, when they had been seven days without food and five without water, D. proposed to S. that lots should be cast who should be put to death to save the rest, and that they afterwards thought it would be better to kill the boy that their lives should be saved; that on the twentieth day D., with the assent of S., killed the boy, and both D. and S. fed on his flesh for four days; that at the time of the act there was no sail in sight nor any reasonable prospect of relief; that under these circumstances there appeared to the prisoners every probability that unless they then or very soon fed upon the boy, or one of themselves, they would die of starvation:—*Held,* that upon these facts, there was no proof of any such necessity as could justify the prisoners in killing the boy, and that they were guilty of murder. THE QUEEN v. DUDLEY AND STEPHENS
[14 Q. B. D. 273

7. —— Prize-fight — *Aiding and Abetting.*] Two men fought with each other in a ring, formed by ropes supported by posts, in the presence of a large crowd. Amongst that crowd were the prisoners. It did not appear that the prisoners took any active part in the management of the fight, or that they said or did anything. They were tried and convicted of assault, as being principals in the second degree.—The jury were directed that prize-fights are illegal, and that all persons who go to a prize-fight to see the combatants strike each other, and who are present when they do so, are guilty in law of an assault, and that if the persons charged were not casually passing by, but stayed at the place, they encouraged the fight by their presence, although they did not do or say anything. Upon this direction the jury found the prisoners guilty; but added, that they did so in consequence of

XIII. CRIMINAL LAW—OFFENCES AGAINST PERSON—continued.

such direction of law, as they found that the prisoners did not aid or abet:—*Held*, by Denman, J., Huddleston, B , Manisty, Hawkins, Lopes, Stephen, Cave, and North, JJ. (Lord Coleridge, C.J., Pollock, B., and Mathew, J., dissenting), that the above direction was not correct, that mere voluntary presence at a fight does not as a matter of law necessarily render persons so present guilty of an assault as aiding and abetting in such fight, and that the conviction could not be sustained:—*Held*, by Lord Coleridge, C.J., Pollock, B., and Mathew, J., that the conviction could be sustained, that the legal inference to be drawn from mere presence, as a voluntary spectator, at a prize-fight is, in the absence of other evidence to rebut such inference, that the person so present is encouraging, aiding and abetting such fight, and consequently guilty of assault:—*Held*, by the whole Court, that a prize-fight is illegal, and that all persons aiding and abetting therein are guilty of assault, and that the consent of the persons actually engaged in fighting to the interchange of blows does not afford any answer to the criminal charge of assault:—*Semble*, that mere presence of a person, unexplained, at a prize-fight affords some evidence for the consideration of a jury of an aiding or abetting in such fight. THE QUEEN *v.* CONEY - 8 Q. B. D. 534

—— Rape—Girl between twelve and thirteen
[10 Q. B. D. 74

See CRIMINAL LAW—OFFENCES AGAINST WOMEN.

XIV. CRIMINAL LAW—OFFENCES AGAINST WOMEN.

The Act 48 & 49 *Vict.* c. 69 (*the Criminal Law Amendment Act*, 1885), *makes further provision for the protection of women.*

Repeal.] *Sect.* 19 *repeals* 24 & 25 *Vict.* c. 100, s. 49, *and of sect.* 52 *the words* " *or any attempt to have carnal knowledge of any girl under* 12 *years of age,*" *and the whole of* 38 & 39 *Vict.* c. 94 (*Offences against the Person Act*, 1875).

Procuration.] *Sect.* 2 (1), *procuration of females not of known immoral character, and under twenty-one years, for immorality within or without the Queen's dominions ; or,*

(2, 3, 4), *procuration of females of any age for common prostitution or for brothels within or without the Queen's dominions,*

is a misdemeanor. *One witness will not suffice for a conviction, unless corroborated in some material particular.*

Defilement] *Sect.* 3. *The procuring of defilement of any female by threats or fraud within or without the Queen's dominions or by drugs within the Queen's dominions, is a misdemeanor.*

One witness will not suffice for a conviction unless corroborated in some material particular.

Girls under 13.] *Sect.* 4. *Defilement of a girl under thirteen years is felony. Attempt to defile the same is a misdemeanor.*

An offender whose age does not exceed sixteen years may be whipped instead, under 25 & 26 *Vict.* c. 18, *and in addition may be sent to a reformatory.*

The girl or any other child of tender years may give evidence although not on oath. This evidence

XIV. CRIMINAL LAW—OFFENCES AGAINST WOMEN—continued.

will not suffice for a conviction unless corroborated in some material particular.

Girls under 16.] *Sect.* 5 (1). *Defilement or attempted defilement of a girl above thirteen years and under sixteen years ;* or (2), *of any female idiot, is a misdemeanor.*

Reasonable belief that the girl was over sixteen years is a defence to sub-sect. 1. *No prosecution to be commenced under this sub-section after three months from the offence.*

Rape.] *Sect.* 4. *Connection with a married woman by personating her husband, is rape.*

Householder permitting Defilement on his Premises.] *Sect.* 6. *Any person occupying or managing premises inducing or suffering a girl to be on his premises for defilement—*

(1) *is guilty of felony if the girl is under thirteen years ;*

(2) *is guilty of misdemeanor if the girl be under sixteen years.*

Reasonable belief that the girl was over sixteen years is a defence to sub-sect. 1.

Abduction.] *Sect.* 7. *Abduction from parents, or person in charge, of unmarried girl under eighteen for defilement is a misdemeanor.*

Reasonable belief that the girl was over eighteen years is a defence.

Detention.] *Sect.* 8. *Detention of a female against her will*

(1) *on any premises with intent to defile her ;* or

(2) *in any brothel,*

is a misdemeanor.

Detention of apparel or goods of a female, or threat to take legal proceedings against her for taking away apparel lent her, is, under certain circumstances, a detention under this section.

Indictment.] *Sect.* 9. *Power on indictment for rape or offences under sect.* 4 *of this Act to convict of certain misdemeanors.*

Sect. 17. *Every misdemeanor to be within Vexatious Indictments Act* (22 & 23 *Vict.* c. 17).

No indictment to be tried at Quarter Sessions.

Search.] *Sect.* 10. *A justice may on information that a female is unlawfully detained for immoral purposes issue a warrant for superior officer of police to search for and detain the same in a place of safety, and may by warrant cause any person unlawfully detaining the female to be apprehended. A female may not be detained for immoral purposes if (a) she be under sixteen years,* or (b) *if over sixteen and under eighteen years she be detained against her own will or that of her parent or guardian,* or (c) *if over eighteen years, she be detained against her will,*

Custody of Girls under 16.] *Sect.* 12. *Power to take girl under sixteen from parents, guardians, &c., where her prostitution is favoured by them, and place her in charge of guardians until she be twenty-one years of age.*

Other Proceedings.] *Sect.* 16. *This Act is not derogatory to other proceedings, provided that no one be punished twice for same offence.*

Costs.] *Sect.* 18. *Costs of prosecution under this Act of misdemeanors allowed as in felonies.*

Evidence.] *See* CRIMINAL LAW—EVIDENCE—*Statutes.*

—— Rape—*Girl between Twelve and Thirteen*

XIV. CRIMINAL LAW—OFFENCES AGAINST WOMEN—*continued.*

—*Statutes* 24 & 25 *Vict.* c. 100, *ss.* 48, 51 ; 38 & 39 *Vict.* c. 94, s. 4.] The statute 38 & 39 Vict. c. 94, s. 4, which enacted that " whosoever shall unlawfully and carnally know and abuse any girl being above the age of twelve years and under the age of thirteen years, whether with or without her consent, shall be guilty of a misdemeanor," &c., did not operate to prevent a conviction for felony, under 24 & 25 Vict. c. 100, s. 48, of a person committing a rape upon a girl between those ages.— *Reg.* v. *Dicken* (14 Cox, C. C. 8) followed. THE QUEEN *v.* RATCLIFFE - 10 Q. B. D. 74

XV. CRIMINAL LAW — UNLAWFUL ASSEMBLY.

—— Meeting for lawful Purpose—*Knowledge that others will commit a Breach of the Peace.*] The Appellants assembled with others for a lawful purpose, and with no intention of carrying it out unlawfully, but with the knowledge that their assembly would be opposed, and with good reason to suppose that a breach of the peace would be committed by those who opposed it :—*Held*, by Field and Cave, JJ., that they could not be rightly convicted of an unlawful assembly. BEATTY *v.* GILLBANKS 9 Q. B. D. 308

XVI. CRIMINAL LAW—EVIDENCE.

By 48 & 49 *Vict.* c. 69, *s.* 20, *every person charged under this Act, or under* 24 & 25 *Vict.* c. 100, *ss.* 48, *and* 52 *to* 55 *inclusive, may give evidence. The same as to husband or wife of party charged.*

1. —— Confession—*Admissibility of.*] On a trial for larceny, evidence was received of a confession made by the prisoner to the prosecutor in the presence of a police inspector, immediately after the prosecutor had said to the prisoner, " The inspector tells me you are making housebreaking implements ; if that is so, you had better tell the truth, it may be better for you " :—*Held*, by the Court (Lord Coleridge, C.J., Grove, Hawkins, Lopes, and Stephen, JJ.), that the confession was not admissible in evidence. THE QUEEN *v.* FENNELL - - - 7 Q. B. D. 147

2. —— Husband and Wife—*Larceny by Wife —Witness, Competency of—Married Women's Property Act,* 1882 (45 & 46 *Vict.* c. 75), *ss.* 12, 16.] Upon the trial of a married woman jointly with another person for larceny of the property of her husband, the husband was called as a witness against his wife :—*Held*, by the Court (Lord Coleridge, C.J., Hawkins, Lopes, and Mathew, JJ. ; Stephen, J., doubting), that the evidence of the husband was improperly received, and that the conviction which had taken place founded upon it was bad as against both the prisoners. THE QUEEN *v.* BRITTLETON - 12 Q. B. D. 266 [But see 47 & 48 Vict. c. 14.]

3. —— Husband and Wife—*Statement of Wife in presence of Husband—Admission.*] Upon the trial of a prisoner for feloniously receiving stolen property, a list of the stolen articles which the prisoner, who was a marine store dealer, had bought, was received in evidence in order to shew that he had bought at an under value. The circumstances under which the list was written were

XVI. CRIMINAL LAW—EVIDENCE—contd.

as follows : A police constable asked the prisoner to consider when he had bought the stolen property, to which the prisoner replied that his wife should make out a list of it, and on the next day the prisoner's wife in her husband's presence handed to another constable the list tendered in evidence, saying in her husband's hearing " this is a list of what we bought, and what we gave for them." The question reserved was whether such list was properly admitted in evidence :—*Held*, by the Court (Lord Coleridge, C.J., Grove, Field, Stephen and Smith, JJ.), that the list was clearly admissible in evidence. THE QUEEN *v.* MALLORY [13 Q. B. D. 33

4. —— Perjury—*Indictment — Information— Corrupt Practices Prevention Act,* 1863 (26 & 27 *Vict.* c. 29), s. 7.] By sect. 7 of the Corrupt Practices Prevention Act, 1863, no person summoned as a witness before any commissioners appointed under the Corrupt Practices Acts shall be excused from answering any question relating to corrupt practices forming the subject of inquiry on the ground that the answer would tend to criminate himself, " provided that no statement made by any person in answer to any question put by or before such commissioners shall, except in cases of indictments for perjury, be admissible in evidence in any proceeding civil or criminal :"— *Held*, that the exception in the proviso did not apply to an ex officio information by the Attorney-General for perjury. THE QUEEN *v.* SLATER [8 Q. B. D. 267

5. —— Privileged Communication—*Solicitor and Client, Communications between—Communication in Furtherance of Criminal Purpose.*] All communications between a solicitor and his client are not privileged from disclosure, but only those passing between them in professional confidence and in the legitimate course of professional employment of the solicitor. Communications made to a solicitor by his client before the commission of a crime for the purpose of being guided or helped in the commission of it, are not privileged from disclosure.—C. and R. were partners under a deed of partnership. M. brought an action against R. & Co., and obtained judgment therein, and issued execution against the goods of R. The goods seized in execution were then claimed by C. as his absolute property under a bill of sale executed in his favour by R. at a date subsequent to the above-mentioned judgment. An interpleader issue was ordered to determine the validity of the bill of sale, and upon the trial of this issue, the partnership deed was produced on C.'s behalf, bearing an indorsement purporting to be a memorandum of dissolution of the said partnership, prior to the commencement of the action by M. Subsequently C. and R. were tried and convicted upon a charge of conspiring to defraud M., and upon that trial the case for the prosecution was, that the bill of sale was fraudulent, that the partnership between R. and C. was in truth subsisting when it was given, and that the memorandum of dissolution indorsed on the deed was put there after M. had obtained judgment, and fraudulently ante-dated, the whole transaction being, it was alleged, a fraud intended to cheat M. of the fruits of his

XVI. CRIMINAL LAW—EVIDENCE—contd.

execution. Upon the trial a solicitor was called on behalf of the prosecution to prove that after M. had obtained the judgment C. and R. together consulted him as to how they could defeat M.'s judgment, and as to whether a bill of sale could legally be executed by R. in favour of C. so as to defeat such judgment, and that no suggestion was then made of any dissolution of partnership having taken place. The reception of this evidence being objected to, on the ground that the communication was one between solicitor and client, and privileged, the evidence was received, but the question of whether it was properly received was reserved for this Court:—Held, by the Court (Grove, J., Pollock and Huddleston, BB., Hawkins, Lopes, Stephen, Watkin Williams, Mathew, Day, and Smith, JJ.), that the evidence was properly received.—Cromack v. Heathcote (2 B. & B. 4); Rex v. Smith (1 Phil. & Arn. on Evidence, 118); and Doe v. Harris (5 C. & P. 592) overruled.—Follett v. Jefferyes (1 Sim. (N.S.) 1); Russell v. Jackson (9 Hare, 387); and Gartside v. Outram (26 L. J. (Ch.) 113) approved. THE QUEEN v. COX AND RAILTON 14 Q. B. D. 153

6. —— Receiving Stolen Goods—Guilty Knowledge—Prevention of Crimes Act, 1871 (34 & 35 Vict. c. 112), s. 19.] Upon the trial of a prisoner for receiving stolen property with a guilty knowledge, evidence was admitted that shortly before the stealing of the property in question he had been in possession of other stolen property of a similar character, though he had parted with the possession of such other property before the date of the stealing of the property charged in the indictment:—Held, by the Court (Lord Coleridge, C.J., Hawkins, Stephen, Williams, and Mathew, JJ.), that such evidence was inadmissible, and did not fall within the words of sect. 19 of the Prevention of Crimes Act, 1871. THE QUEEN v. CARTER　　12 Q. B. D. 522

XVII. CRIMINAL LAW—PRACTICE.

Public Prosecutor.] The Act 47 & 48 Vict. c. 58 (the Prosecution of Offences Act, 1884), revokes all appointments made in pursuance of 42 & 43 Vict. c. 22 (the Prosecution of Offences Act, 1879), and appoints the Solicitor of the Treasury to be director of public prosecutions.
Sect. 5 repeals the first paragraph of sect. 2, and sects. 3 & 4 of 42 & 43 Vict. c. 22.
Prevention of Crime.] The 48 & 49 Vict. c. 75, amends the Prevention of Crimes Act, 1871 (34 & 35 Vict. c. 112), s. 12.

1. —— Lunatic—India—Inquiry as to Sanity of Accused—Removal to England—Detention in Asylum—14 & 15 Vict. c. 81, s. 1.] By 14 & 15 Vict. c. 81, s. 1, if any person shall be indicted for or charged with any crime or offence in any Court in India, and shall be acquitted of or not be tried for such crime or offence on the ground of his being found to be of unsound mind, he may be removed to England in the manner prescribed by the Act.—A European British subject in India having been arrested for homicide, a district magistrate was informed of it, and went with witnesses to a private house in the presidency, where the accused was detained. On seeing him and receiving medical testimony on oath as to his

XVII. CRIMINAL LAW—PRACTICE—contd.

state of mind, the magistrate deemed him insane and unfit to be tried, and so reported to the Government of the Presidency. The Government made an order under 14 & 15 Vict. c. 81, s. 1, for the removal of the prisoner to England. By virtue of the order he was brought in custody to England, and on his arrival a Royal warrant was issued, under sect. 2, for his reception into a lunatic asylum, where he was accordingly kept:—Held, that the prisoner was charged with a crime in a "Court," and "not tried" on the ground of being "found" to be of unsound mind within the meaning of sect. 1, and that his detention was lawful. In re MALTBY　　7 Q. B. D. 18

2. —— Misdemeanor — Indictment — Two Counts—General Verdict—Second Term of Punishment beginning at the end of the First.] An indictment for perjury contained two counts, charging perjury to have been committed by the Defendant on two different occasions, one in the progress of a trial, the other in an affidavit in Chancery. Both acts of perjury had the same object in view:—Held, 1. That they were distinct offences, and a punishment might be inflicted in respect of each.—2. That though the offences were in this way distinct, they might both be included in the same indictment, and that a general finding of guilty on the charges contained in both counts was good.—3. That the full punishment of seven years' penal servitude might be inflicted for each offence, and that the second term of penal servitude was properly made to begin at the termination of the first term,—4. The 2 Geo. 2, c. 25, s. 2, authorizes the Judge before whom a person shall be convicted of perjury, to order such person to be sent to a house of correction for seven years, there to be kept to hard labour; "and thereupon judgment shall be given that the person convicted shall be committed accordingly, over and beside such punishment as shall be adjudged to be inflicted upon such person, agreeable to the laws now in being":—Held, that this statute did not impose on the Court the necessity of awarding any punishment previous to that of penal servitude so as to give the sentence of penal servitude the form of an additional punishment.—The conclusion to a count "contra formam statuti" is now, by 14 & 15 Vict. c. 100, s. 24, no longer necessary. CASTRO v. THE QUEEN 6 App. Cas. 229

3. —— Obstruction of Highway—Acquittal—New Trial.] Upon the trial of an indictment for obstructing a highway the Defendant was acquitted:—Held, that a new trial on the ground of misreception of evidence, misdirection, and that the verdict was against evidence, could not be granted. THE QUEEN v. DUNCAN 7 Q. B. D. 198

4. —— Venue — False Pretences—Place of Trial.] H. wrote and posted at N. in England a letter, addressed to G. at a place out of England, containing a false pretence by means of which he fraudulently induced G. to transmit to N. a draft for £150 which he there cashed:—Held, by the Court (Lord Coleridge, C.J., Denman, Hawkins, Williams, and Mathew, JJ.), that there was jurisdiction to try H. at N., that the pretence was made at N., where also the money obtained by means of it was received. THE QUEEN v. HOLMES [12 Q. B. D. 23

CRIMINAL LAW—Bail—Indemnity to surety—
Action to recover deposit **15 Q. B. D. 561**
See CONTRACT—VALIDITY. 2.

—— Colony—Appeal to Privy Council
[**10 App. Cas. 675**
See PRACTICE—PRIVY COUNCIL—LEAVE
TO APPEAL. 1.

—— Fugitive offenders.
See JURISDICTION—*Statutes.*

—— Extradition—Jurisdiction of magistrate —
Decision of magistrate conclusive —
Weight of evidence **10 Q. B. D. 513**
See EXTRADITION. 3.

—— Jersey - - - **8 App. Cas. 304**
See COLONIAL LAW—JERSEY. 1.

—— Larceny from British ship at foreign port—
Felonious receiving - **10 Q. B. D. 76**
See JURISDICTION. 2.

—— Riot—Felonious demolition—Action against
hundred - **7 Q. B. D. 201**
See RIOT.

CRIMINAL LUNATIC.
See LUNATIC—CRIMINAL—*Statutes.*

—— Maintenance **6 Q. B. D. 47; 8 App. Cas. 339**
See LUNATIC—CRIMINAL.

CROPS—Assignment—Bill of sale—Distress—
Landlord and tenant - **11 Q. B. D. 808**
See BILL OF SALE—OPERATION. 1.

—— Bill of sale—Separate assignment
[**13 Q. B. D. 794**
See BILL OF SALE—FORMALITIES. 24.

—— Valuation of - - **22 Ch. D. 769**
See LANDLORD AND TENANT—LEASE. 13.

CROSS ACTIONS—Res judicata - **29 Ch. D. 448**
See ESTOPPEL—JUDGMENT. 2.

CROSS-EXAMINATION—Affidavit **20 Ch. D. 126**
See BANKRUPTCY—EVIDENCE. 1.

—— Affidavit—Costs of deponent **24 Ch. D. 606**;
[**25 Ch. D. 297**
See PRACTICE—SUPREME COURT—COSTS.
22.

—— Affidavit—Withdrawal - **21 Ch. D. 642**
See PRACTICE—SUPREME COURT—EVI-
DENCE. 5.

—— As to adultery - - **10 P. D. 175**
See PRACTICE—DIVORCE — NULLITY OF
MARRIAGE. 5.

—— Expenses of witnesses **25 Ch. D. 297**;
[**29 Ch. D. 711**
See. PRACTICE—SUPREME COURT—EVI-
DENCE. 3, 4.

CROSS NOTICE OF APPEAL - **18 Ch. D. 334**;
[**23 Ch. D. 98**
See PRACTICE—SUPREME COURT—COSTS.
7, 8.

—— - - - - **19 Ch. D. 17**
See PRACTICE — SUPREME COURT—AP-
PEAL. 30.

CROSS REMAINDERS - **20 Ch. D. 406**
See WILL—CROSS REMAINDERS.

CROSSED CHEQUE—Statutory enactments re-
specting.
See BILLS OF EXCHANGE ACT, 1882—
Statutes.

CROWN.

—— Prerogative—*Companies Act*, 1862 (25 &
26 *Vict.* c. 89)—*Judicature Act*, 1875, s. 10—*Bankruptcy Act*, 1883 (46 & 47 *Vict.* c. 52), *ss.* 30, 40, 150.]
The provisions of the Bankruptcy Act, 1883, which
take away the priority of the Crown over other
creditors in the distribution of assets in bankruptcy, have not, by virtue of the assimilating
provisions contained in the Judicature Act, 1875,
s. 10, been incorporated into the Companies Act,
1862, so as to bar the prerogative right of the
Crown to issue process and thus to obtain payment in full, in priority over other creditors, in
respect of a debt due from a company in course
of liquidation under the Companies Act. *In re*
ORIENTAL BANK CORPORATION. *Ex parte* THE
CROWN - **28 Ch. D. 643**

—— Administration by nominee of—Proceedings.
See ADMINISTRATOR — NOMINEE OF
CROWN—*Statutes.*

—— Adverse possession against **6 App. Cas. 143**
See COLONIAL LAW—HONDURAS.

—— Booty of war - - **7 App. Cas. 619**
See BOOTY OF WAR.

—— Forfeiture of gale—Election **27 Ch. D. 652**
See MINE—FREE MINERS.

—— Lands Clauses Act—Claim for purchase-
money - **24 Ch. D. 253**
See LANDS CLAUSES ACT — PURCHASE-
MONEY. 1.

—— Mandamus—Commissioners of Inland Revenue **12 Q. B. D. 461**
See MANDAMUS. 2.

—— Payment of interest by—Bona vacantia
See INTEREST. 1. [**17 Ch. D. 771**

—— Prerogative — Incorporation of building
society—Irregularity **18 Ch. D. 173**
See BUILDING SOCIETY. 11.

—— Prerogative—Recovery of penalty
. [**7 Q. B. D. 36; 8 App. Cas. 354**
See PENAL ACTION. 2.

—— Reservation of rights of—Prolongation of
patent -- - **6 App. Cas. 174**
See PATENT—PROLONGATION. 4.

—— Right of subject to sue Crown—Set-off
[**9 App. Cas. 571**
See COLONIAL LAW—CEYLON. 4

—— Servants of—Liability - **6 App. Cas. 619**
See COLONIAL LAW—NATAL. 1.

—— Service of—Domicil - **30 Ch. D. 165**
See DOMICIL. 2.

CROWN LANDS.

The Act 48 & 49 *Vict.* c. 79 (*the Crown Lands
Act*, 1885), amends the law relating to the manage-
ment of the woods, forests, and land revenues of the
Crown, and amends 10 Geo. 4, c. 50, and 14 & 15
Vict. c. 42.

CROWN LANDS—continued.
—— Griqualand　-　　- 8 App. Cas. 318
　　See COLONIAL LAW—GRIQUALAND.

—— New South Wales　6 App. Cas. 628, 636
　　See COLONIAL LAW—NEW SOUTH WALES.
　　1, 2.

—— Sale of.
　　See REAL ESTATE—Statutes.

CROWN OFFICE RULES.
　　See COURT—STATUTES AND GAZETTE.

CRUELTY—Condonation　　　- 8 P. D. 98
　　See PRACTICE—DIVORCE—CONDONATION.
　　1.

CRUELTY TO ANIMALS.
　　" Domestic Animals " — 12 & 13 Vict.
　　c. 92, ss. 2, 29—17 & 18 Vict. c. 60, s. 3—
　　Birds trained and kept as Decoy Birds.] Birds
　　kept in a state of captivity and trained as decoy
　　birds for the purpose of bird-catching are "do-
　　mestic animals" within the meaning of 12 & 13
　　Vict. c. 92, the Act for the more effectual Preven-
　　tion of Cruelty to Animals. COLAM v. PAGETT
　　　　　　　　　　　　　　[12 Q. B. D. 66

CURTESY—Devise to married daughter—Death
　　before testator　-　　　17 Ch. D. 115
　　See WILL—SPEAKING FROM DEATH. 1.

CUSTODY OF CHILDREN.
　　See Cases under INFANT—CUSTODY.

—— Covenant respecting　　·　18 Ch. D. 670
　　See HUSBAND AND WIFE—SEPARATION
　　DEEDS. 1.

—— Girls under sixteen.
　　See CRIMINAL LAW—OFFENCES AGAINST
　　WOMEN—Statutes.

CUSTODY OF DEEDS—Acknowledgment on con-
　　veyance.
　　See TITLE DEEDS—Statutes.

—— Trustee in bankruptcy　- 26 Ch. D. 31
　　See TITLE DEEDS.

CUSTODY OF GOODS—Innkeeper 23 Ch. D. 330
　　See INN—INNKEEPER. 2.

CUSTOM—Borough—Individual benefit of free-
　　men　-　　　-　21 Ch. D. 111
　　See MUNICIPAL CORPORATION—PROPERTY.

—— Country—Right to sell flints 21 Ch. D. 18；
　　　　　　　　　　　　　　[8 App. Cas. 508
　　See LANDLORD AND TENANT—CUSTOM
　　OF COUNTRY.

—— Manor　　18 Ch. D. 165; 20 Ch. D. 753
　　See COPYHOLD—CUSTOM. 1, 2.

—— Manor—Admittance　　- 30 Ch. D. 581
　　See COPYHOLD—SURRENDER AND ADMIT-
　　TANCE. 2.

—— Mine—Right of miner to remove buildings
　　　　　　[7 Q. B. D. 295; 8 App. Cas. 195
　　See MINE—WORKING. 1.

—— Stock Exchange—Sale of bank shares
　　　　　[14 Q. B. D. 460; 15 Q. B. D. 388
　　See PRINCIPAL AND AGENT—PRINCIPAL'S
　　LIABILITY. 4, 5.

CUSTOM—continued.
—— Stock Exchange—Sale of shares—Illegality
　　See STOCK EXCHANGE. 1. [9 Q. B. D. 546

—— Trade—Hiring furniture　- 18 Ch. D. 30；
　　　　　　　　　　　　　　　[23 Ch. D. 261
　　See BANKRUPTCY—ORDER AND DISPOSI-
　　TION. 4, 5.

—— Trade—Implied contract between manufac-
　　turer of iron plates and customer
　　　　　　　　　　　　　　[7 Q. B. D. 438
　　See SALE OF GOODS—CONTRACT. 1.

—— Trade—Port of discharge—Evidence
　　　　　　　　　　　　　　　[6 P. D. 68
　　See SHIP—CHARTERPARTY. 16.

CUSTOM HOUSE AGENT—Infringement of patent
　　—Transshipment　　- 17 Ch. D. 721；
　　　　　　　　　　　　　　[8 App. Cas. 5
　　See PATENT—INFRINGEMENT. 6.

CUSTOMARY RENT　　　16 Ch. D. 730
　　See LANDLORD AND TENANT—RE-ENTRY.
　　2.

CUSTOMERS—Solicitation of　·· 27 Ch. D. 145
　　See GOODWILL. 3.

—— Solicitation of　　　22 Ch. D. 504
　　See PARTNERSHIP—DISSOLUTION. 3.

CUSTOMS ANNUITY FUND.
　　—— Power of Subscriber to bequeath Sum
　　assured.] The Customs Annuity and Benevolent
　　Fund was established for the benefit of the
　　widows, children, or other relatives of officers of
　　the Customs, by Act of Parliament, which gave
　　power to frame rules for its management. By
　　the rules it was provided that the fund should
　　be raised by subscriptions on the principle of life
　　insurance, and should form a fund for the bene-
　　fit of widows, children, relatives, and nominees
　　of the subscribers. It was provided that the ad-
　　mission of a nominee by the directors should
　　take place during the life of the subscriber; that
　　the capital money forthcoming at a subscriber's
　　death under his insurance should, subject to the
　　regulations thereinafter contained, be appropriated
　　according to the directions contained in his will
　　or in any instrument deposited with the directors
　　as therein mentioned; that the widow's share
　　should not be less than one-third, nor a life in-
　　terest in two-thirds, and that the remainder should
　　be applied according to the directions of the sub-
　　scriber for the benefit of his widow, children,
　　blood relations, or any of them, or his nominee or
　　nominees who had been duly admitted by the di-
　　rectors; that if the widow was otherwise provided
　　for as therein mentioned the whole money should
　　be subject to the directions of the subscriber " in
　　favour of his widow, children, blood relations, or
　　nominees, or any of them as aforesaid；" that if
　　the widow received the income of two-thirds the
　　capital of the two-thirds should be held, subject
　　to the directions of the subscriber, to take effect
　　at the death of the widow, and the remaining
　　capital, subject to the directions of the subscriber,
　　to take effect at his own death; that if the widow
　　was provided for as thereinbefore mentioned, or if
　　there was no widow, then the whole capital should
　　be " subject to the directions of the subscriber as
　　aforesaid；" that if a subscriber died leaving issue

CUSTOMS ANNUITY FUND—*continued.*

without having by will or such other instrument as aforesaid directed the application of the capital placed at his disposal, it should go to his children and the issue of deceased children as therein mentioned, and if none, to his next of kin. A subscriber died a widower leaving children. No nominee had been accepted by the directors in his lifetime. By his will he bequeathed the fund coming from his insurance to a stranger in blood:—*Held*, by Bacon, V.C., that the legatee was entitled:—*Held*, by the Court of Appeal, that the subscriber had no property in the fund, but only a limited power of appointment over it, and that this power could only be exercised in favour of his widow, children, blood relations, and nominees admitted by the directors in his lifetime; that he had therefore no power to bequeath the fund to a stranger in blood, who had not in his lifetime been accepted by the directors as a nominee, and

CUSTOMS ANNUITY FUND—*continued.*

that the fund therefore belonged to the children. *In re* WILLIAM PHILLIPS' INSURANCE
[23 Ch. D. 235

CUSTOMS AND INLAND REVENUE ACTS.
See REVENUE—CUSTOMS—*Statutes.*
REVENUE—EXCISE—*Statutes.*
REVENUE—INCOME TAX—*Statutes.*
REVENUE—LEGACY DUTY—*Statutes.*
REVENUE—PROBATE DUTY—*Statutes.*
REVENUE—STAMPS—*Statutes.*

CUSTOMS REGULATION ACT, 1879—New South Wales - - 10 App. Cas. 282
See COLONIAL LAW—NEW SOUTH WALES. 4.

CY-PRÈS—Charity—Scheme - 18 Ch. D. 310
See CHARITY—MANAGEMENT. 3.
—— Charity which has ceased to exist
See CHARITY, GIFT TO. 2. [29 Ch. D. 560

R

D.

DAMAGE—Amendment—Mistake in preliminary
act - - **7 P. D. 185**
See PRACTICE—ADMIRALTY—PRELIMI-
NARY ACT.

—— Harbour master—Harbour Commissioners—
Liability - **10 P. D. 24, 131**
See NEGLIGENCE—LIABILITY. 9, 10.

—— Limitation of liability—Tonnage of ship
[6 P. D. 200
See PRACTICE — ADMIRALTY — LIMITA-
TION OF LIABILITY. 4.

DAMAGES :— Col.
    I. CONTRACT - - - 483
    II. LORD CAIRNS' ACT - 484
    III. LORD CAMPBELL'S ACT - - 484
    IV. REMOTENESS - - 485

I. DAMAGES—CONTRACT.

1. ' —— Measure of Damages—Cost *of Performance not the Measure.*] The grantees of certain land
had covenanted with the grantor, since deceased,
that the land, except as to the entrance to be
made by them towards an intended new road,
should be and be kept enclosed on all the sides abutting on the land of the grantor with a brick wall
seven feet high. The grantees not having erected
a wall in pursuance of the covenant, an action was
brought against them by the executors and devisees of the grantor for damages for the breach of
covenant. It appeared that, in the events that
had happened, the value of the adjoining land of
the Plaintiffs was not decreased by the non-erec-
tion of the wall to anything like the amount which
it would have cost to build the wall :—*Held,* that,
the true measure of damages being the pecuniary
amount of the difference between the position of
the Plaintiffs upon the breach of contract and what
it would have been if the contract had been performed, under the circumstances of the case the
amount that it would cost to build the wall was
not the correct measure of the damages. WIGSELL
v. SCHOOL FOR THE INDIGENT BLIND **8 Q. B. D. 357**

2. —— Measure of Damages—*Sale of Goods to
fulfil a Contract by Vendee.*] The Defendants contracted with the Plaintiff to deliver goods to him of
a particular shape and description at certain prices
and by instalments at different times. When the
contract was made the Defendants knew that,
except as to price, it corresponded with and was
substantially the same as a contract which the
Plaintiff had entered into with a French customer
of his, and that it was made in order to enable
the Plaintiff to fulfil such last-mentioned contract.
The Defendants broke their contract, and there
being no market for goods of the description contracted for, the Plaintiff's customer recovered
damages against him in the French Court to the
amount of £28 :—*Held,* in an action against the
Defendants for their breach of contract, that the
Plaintiff was not only entitled to recover as
damages the amount of profit he would have

I. DAMAGES—CONTRACT—*continued.*

made had he been able to fulfil his contract with
his customer, but also damages in respect of his
liability to such customer, and that in estimating
such last-mentioned damages the £28 which the
French Court had given might be treated as not an
unreasonable sum at which such damages might be
assessed.—The case of *Elbinger Actien-Gesellschaft* v. *Armstrong* (Law Rep. 9 Q. B. 473) approved of. GRÉBERT-BORGNIS *v.* NUGENT
[15 Q. B. D. 85

II. DAMAGES—LORD CAIRNS' ACT.

—— Nominal Damages—*Repeal of Act.*] Lord
Cairns' Act (21 & 22 Vict. c. 27) is applicable to
cases where the damage sustained by the Plaintiff is only nominal, as well as to cases where he
is entitled to substantial damages.—The repeal
of Lord Cairns' Act by 46 & 47 Vict. c. 49 has
not affected the jurisdiction of the Court.—*Per*
Fry, L.J.: An amount of acquiescence on the
part of the Plaintiff which would not be sufficient
to bar his action, may be sufficient to induce the
Court to give damages instead of an injunction.
SAYERS *v.* COLLYER - **28 Ch. D. 103**

III. DAMAGES—LORD CAMPBELL'S ACT.

1. —— Distribution of the Fund—*Railway Accident — Compensation—Compromise—No action
brought—*Lord Campbell's Act (9 & 10 Vict. c. 93)
—*Amendment Act (27 & 28 Vict. c. 95).*] A sum
of money was received from a railway company by
way of compensation by the executors of a person
whose death had resulted from injuries received in
an accident on the railway, no action having been
brought under Lord Campbell's Act (9 & 10 Vict.
c. 93).—The executors brought an action in the
Chancery Division, to which all the relatives of
the deceased referred to in sect. 2 of 9 & 10 Vict.
c. 23, were parties, asking for a declaration as to
the persons entitled to the money :—*Held,* that
the Court could distribute the fund amongst such
of the relatives of the deceased as suffered damage
by reason of the death, in the same manner as a
jury could have done in an action under the Act.
BULMER *v.* BULMER **25 Ch. D. 409**

2. —— Evidence of Pecuniary Loss—*Action
for causing Death through Negligence—*9 & 10 *Vict.*
c. 93), s. 2—*Pecuniary Loss to surviving Relative.*] In an action brought, under 9 & 10 Vict.
c. 93, for the benefit of the father of the deceased,
evidence was given that the father, who was fifty-
nine years of age, was nearly blind and injured in
his leg and hands, and was not so able to work as
he had been, but worked when he could; that
the son used to contribute to his support; that
five or six years previously, the father being out of
work for six months, the son had assisted him
pecuniarily out of his earnings, but had not done so
since :—*Held,* that there was evidence for the jury
of pecuniary injury to the father from the son's
death. HETHERINGTON *v.* NORTH EASTERN RAIL-
WAY COMPANY - **9 Q. B. D. 160**

IV. DAMAGES—REMOTENESS.

1. —— *Collision—Loss of Market.*] A ship having been damaged by a collision with another ship, the owners of cargo on the former claimed damages from the owners of the latter ship. The cargo-owners claimed, inter alia, for damages in respect of the loss of market in consequence of a portion of the cargo having been delayed in its arrival at the port of destination:—*Held,* affirming the judgment of Sir James Hannen, that loss of market was too remote a consequence to be considered as an element of damage, and that there was no difference in the principles which regulate the measure of damages in an action of collision, and an action for a breach of duty under a shipping contract.—*The Parana* (2 P. D. 118) approved. THE "NOTTING HILL" 9 P. D. 105

2. —— **Commission for Bail**—*Salvage Action.*] Commission paid for bail in a salvage action will not be allowed as part of the damages recoverable by the salved vessel in an action of damage. THE "BRITISH COMMERCE" - 9 P. D. 128

3. —— **Innkeeper.**] The Defendant, an innkeeper, contracted with the Plaintiff, a horse-dealer, to provide him with stabling for a number of horses during a fair at which they were to be sold, but in consequence of the Defendant, in breach of such contract, having let his stables to another person, the Plaintiff's horses, after they had been put into the Defendant's stables on their arrival there, from a railway journey, were turned out by that person, assisted by the Defendant's servant, without their clothing, and they remained in the Defendant's yard exposed to the weather for some time until the Plaintiff could find suitable stables for them elsewhere. Owing to this exposure several of them caught cold, which depreciated their value in the market:—*Held,* that the damage in respect of such cold was recoverable, as it was the probable consequence of the Defendant's breach of contract, and was not therefore too remote.—*Hobbs* v. *London and South Western Railway Company* (Law Rep. 10 Q. B. 111) commented on. McMAHON v. FIELD 7 Q. B. D. 591

4. —— **Loss of Profit** *on Contract to resell.*] In an action for breach of contract to deliver goods it was shewn that the goods were not procurable in the market, that the Plaintiff had entered into a contract of subsale, which in consequence of the non-delivery he could not perform, that such contract was not known to the Defendant at the time of sale, but that he knew that the goods had been purchased by the Plaintiff for resale:—*Held,* by Grove, J., that the Plaintiff was not entitled to recover damages for loss of profit on the resale.—*Borries* v. *Hutchinson* (8 C. B. (N.S.) 445) distinguished. THOL v. HENDERSON 8 Q. B. D. 457

5. —— **Warehouseman**—*Breach of Contract—Negligence.*] The Defendant contracted to warehouse certain goods for the Plaintiff at a particular place, but he warehoused a part of them at another place where, without any negligence on his part, they were destroyed. In an action to recover as damages the value of the goods:—*Held* (by Grove, Lindley, and Stephen, JJ.), that the damage was not too remote, and that the Defendant, by his breach of contract, had rendered himself liable for the loss of the goods. LILLEY v. DOUBLEDAY - - 7 Q. B. D. 510

DAMAGES—Abandonment of railway — Landowner [25 Ch. D. 251
See RAILWAY COMPANY—ABANDONMENT. 2.

—— Agreement for lease—Lessor only entitled to moiety - 19 Ch. D. 175
See LANDLORD AND TENANT—AGREEMENT. 3.

—— Application for new trial—Power of Court to reduce damages - 12 Q. B. D. 356
See PRACTICE—SUPREME COURT—NEW TRIAL. 4.

—— Breach of covenant—Proof in bankruptcy [22 Ch. D. 410
See BANKRUPTCY—DISTRESS. 5.

—— Cargo—Reshipment—Use of damaged cargo *See* SHIP—NAVIGATION. 3. [10 P. D. 167

—— Carrier—Negligence — Temporary loss of goods - 10 Q. B. D. 142
See CARRIER—CARRIERS' ACT.

—— Collision—Apportionment 7 App. Cas. 512
See PRACTICE — ADMIRALTY — APPORTIONMENT OF DAMAGE.

—— Company—Neglect to register transfer of shares - 14 Q. B. D. 882
See COMPANY—SHARES—TRANSFER. 6.

—— Covenant for quiet enjoyment 9 Q. B. D. 128
See RIGHT OF ENTRY. 2.

—— Damage to estate of intestate arising out of injury to his person 9 Q. B. D. 110
See EXECUTOR—ACTIONS. 1.

—— Defamation - 11 Q. B. D. 407
See DEFAMATION—SLANDER. 4.

—— Divorce—Condonation 10 P. D. 174
See PRACTICE—DIVORCE—CONDONATION. 2.

—— False representation - 20 Ch. D. 1
See FALSE REPRESENTATION. 1.

—— Forcible entry - 17 Ch. D. 174
See FORCIBLE ENTRY. 1.

—— Infringement of patent—Proof in bankruptcy - 20 Ch. D. 780
See BANKRUPTCY—PROOF. 7.

—— Inquiry as to - 16 Ch. D. 81
See PRACTICE—SUPREME COURT—COSTS. 33.

—— Liquidated—Penalty - 21 Ch. D. 243
See PENALTY.

—— Lord Cairns' Act—Light — Discretion of Court 26 Ch. D. 578
See LIGHT—OBSTRUCTION. 2.

—— Lord Campbell's Act—Widow of workman how far bound by his contract not to claim compensation - 9 Q. B. D. 357
See MASTER AND SERVANT—MASTER'S LIABILITY. 8.

—— Malicious arrest of ship—Salvage [10 P. D. 158
See PRACTICE—ADMIRALTY—SALVAGE. 6.

—— Measure of—Action of deceit 17 Ch. D. 301
See COMPANY—PROSPECTUS. 3.

—— Measure of—Collision - 8 P. D. 109
See SHIP—NAVIGATION. 1.

DAMAGES—*continued.*

—— Measure of—Collision—Compulsory pilotage -   -   - **8 P. D. 218**
    See SHIP—PILOT. 4.

—— Measure of—Delay in transmission of goods
    [9 Q. B. D. 582
    See CARRIER—DAMAGES.

—— Measure of—Guarantee   **16 Ch. D. 290**
    See PRINCIPAL AND SURETY—CONTRACT.

—— Measure of—Improper sale by solicitor
    [16 Ch. D. 393
    See SOLICITOR—LIABILITIES. 7.

—— Measure of—Principal and agent—Consignment of goods not of description ordered
    [11 Q. B. D. 797
    See PRINCIPAL AND AGENT—AGENT'S LIABILITY. 3.

—— Measure of—Warranty of authority
    [24 Ch. D. 367
    See PRINCIPAL AND AGENT—AGENT'S AUTHORITY. 2.

—— Recovered in previous action—Res judicata
    See JUDGMENT. 5.   **[14 Q. B. D. 141**

—— Set-off—Misconduct of director   **22 Ch. D.**
    [122 ; 25 Ch. D. 587
    See COMPANY—SET-OFF. 1.

—— Slander of title   **19 Ch. D. 386**
    See PATENT—INFRINGEMENT. 4.

—— Specific performance—Alternative relief
    [28 Ch. D. 356
    See SPECIFIC PERFORMANCE. 2.

—— Undertaking as to   **21 Ch. D. 421 ;**
    [27 Ch. D. 474
    See PRACTICE — SUPREME COURT — INJUNCTION. 8, 9.

—— Undertaking as to—Receiver in bankruptcy
    [23 Ch. D. 644
    See BANKRUPTCY—RECEIVER. 1.

—— Undischarged bankrupt—Right of action
    [17 Ch. D. 768
    See BANKRUPTCY—UNDISCHARGED BANKRUPT. 4.

DANUBE—Navigation of—Collision
    [10 App. Cas. 276
    See SHIP—NAVIGATION. 4.

DE BENE ESSE—Evidence   **16 Ch. D. 100 ;**
    [19 Ch. D. 224 ; 26 Ch. D. 1
    See PRACTICE—SUPREME COURT—EVIDENCE. 1, 17, 18.

DEAD BODY—Cast on shore—Burial—Liability of county   -   **6 Q. B. D. 654**
    See BURIAL GROUND. 2.

—— Cremation of **12 Q. B. D. 247 ; 13 Q. B. D. 331**
    See CRIMINAL LAW—MISDEMEANOR. 1, 2.

—— Right of property—Executor **20 Ch. D. 659**
    See EXECUTOR—POWERS. 3.

DEAN FOREST   **27 Ch. D. 652**
    See MINE—FREE MINERS.

DEATH—Acceptor of bill drawn in blank—Subsequent completion of bill   **20 Ch. D.**
    [225 ; 25 Ch. D. 663
    See BILL OF EXCHANGE—ACCEPTANCE.

—— Before completion of contract.
    See VENDOR AND PURCHASER—CONVEYANCE—*Statutes.*

DEATH—*continued.*

—— Before date of will—Class—Substitutional gift   **17 Ch. D. 788 ; 23 Ch. D. 737**
    See WILL—SUBSTITUTIONAL GIFT. 1, 2.

—— Before payment   **30 Ch. D. 512**
    See WILL—WORDS. 4.

—— Before testator.
    See Cases under WILL—LAPSE.

—— Before testator   **22 Ch. D. 111**
    See WILL—CLASS. 3.

—— Before testator   **16 Ch. D. 18**
    See POWER—EXECUTION. 6.

—— Coupled with some contingency—Construction of will
    See Cases under WILL—DEATH COUPLED WITH CONTINGENCY.

—— Party to reference before award—Right of executor   **15 Q. B. D. 565**
    See PRACTICE — SUPREME COURT — CHANGE OF PARTIES. 4.

—— Protector of settlement—Estate tail
    See TENANT IN TAIL. 2. **[16 Ch. D. 176**

DEBENTURE.
    See Cases under COMPANY — DEBENTURES.

—— Contemporaneous deeds—Priority of operation   -   **21 Ch. D. 762**
    See DEED. 1.

—— Holder of—Petition to wind up company
    [27 Ch. D. 278
    See COMPANY—WINDING-UP ORDER. 12.

—— Investment of money—Misappropriated by directors -   **21 Ch. D. 492**
    See COMPANY—DIRECTOR'S LIABILITY. 3.

—— Misstatement of object of loan—Action of deceit   -   **29 Ch. D. 459**
    See COMPANY—PROSPECTUS. 5.

—— Mortgage of chattels—Exception from Act.
    See BILL OF SALE—STATUTES.

—— Property of lunatic -   **17 Ch. D. 515**
    See LUNATIC—PROPERTY. 5.

—— Right to rolling stock   **21 Ch. D. 309**
    See RAILWAY COMPANY—CONSTITUTION.

—— Stamp duty   -   -   **7 Q. B. D. 165**
    See REVENUE—STAMPS. 2.

—— Stamp duty—Statute respecting.
    See REVENUE—STAMPS—*Statutes.*

—— Turnpike roads—Law of Canada
    [7 App. Cas. 473
    See COLONIAL LAW—CANADA—QUEBEC. 10.

DEBENTURE STOCK—Investment **23 Ch. D. 750**
    See SETTLED LAND ACT—PURCHASE-MONEY. 7.

—— Priority—Borrowing powers **18 Ch. D. 334 ;**
    [8 App. Cas. 780
    See COMPANY—DEBENTURES. 1.

DEBT—Accord and satisfaction.
    See Cases under ACCORD AND SATISFACTION.

—— Assignment.
    See Cases under ASSIGNMENT OF DEBT.

—— Attachment of.
    See Cases under PRACTICE — SUPREME COURT—GARNISHEE ORDERS.

DEBT—*continued.*

—— Bequest of " estate and effects "　22 Ch. D.
　　See WILL—WORDS. 7.　　　[573

—— Charge of debts　-　　- 20 Ch. D. 465
　　See WILL—CHARGE OF DEBTS.

—— Direction to pay debts—Estate of trustees
　　See WILL—TRUSTEES. 1. [21 Ch. D. 790

—— Disputed—Debtor's summons
　　　　　　　　　[22 Ch. D. 312
　　See BANKRUPTCY—ACT OF BANKRUPTCY.
　　18.

—— Disputed—Petition for adjudication
　　　　　　　　　[16 Ch. D. 283
　　See BANKRUPTCY—ADJUDICATION. 1.

—— Disputed—Petition for winding up.
　　[18 Ch. D. 555, 557, n. ; 23 Ch. D. 210
　　See COMPANY—WINDING-UP ORDER. 9,
　　10.

—— Incurred by fraud—Proof in bankruptcy
　　　　　　　　　[17 Ch. D. 122
　　See BANKRUPTCY—PROOF. 22.

—— Inquiry as to debts　- 20 Ch. D. 465
　　See WILL—CHARGE OF DEBTS.

—— Married woman—Separate estate
　　　　　　　　　[20 Ch. D. 749
　　See HUSBAND AND WIFE — SEPARATE
　　ESTATE. 12.

—— Mortgage—How far " absolute assignment "
　　within 36 & 37 Vict. c. 66, s. 25
　　　　　　　　　[12 Q. B. D. 347
　　See ASSIGNMENT OF DEBT. 3.

—— Of record—Balance due from receiver
　　　　　　　　　[18 Ch. D. 296
　　See LIMITATIONS, STATUTE OF — PER-
　　SONAL ACTIONS. 11.

—— Payable out of real estate　19 Ch. D. 156
　　See CHARITY—MORTMAIN. 2.

—— Payment of, by felon　· 19 Ch. D. 1
　　See BANKRUPTCY—ACT OF BANKRUPTCY.
　　12.

—— Relinquishment of—Condition 21 Ch. D. 431
　　See WILL—CONDITION. 8.

—— Specialty　-　- 20 Ch. D. 230
　　See SPECIALTY DEBT.

DEBTOR—Arrest of.
　　See Cases under ARREST—DEBTOR'S ACT.

—— Arrest of—Bankruptcy Act, 1883.
　　See BANKRUPTCY—STATUTES.

—— Imprisonment of—Appeal—Law of Lower
　　Canada　-　- 8 App. Cas. 530
　　See COLONIAL LAW—CANADA—QUEBEC.
　　2.

DEBTORS ACT—Order for payment of damages
　　into registry—Default　10 P. D. 185
　　See PRACTICE—DIVORCE—DAMAGES.

DEBTOR'S SUMMONS.
　　See Cases under BANKRUPTCY—ACT OF
　　BANKRUPTCY. 12—22.

—— Act of bankruptcy—Discontinuance of trade
　　　　　　　　　[21 Ch. D. 394
　　See BANKRUPTCY—TRADER. 2.

DEBTOR'S SUMMONS—*continued.*

—— Act of bankruptcy available for adjudication
　　　　　　　　　[21 Ch. D. 605
　　See BANKRUPTCY—PROTECTED TRANSAC-
　　TION. 2.

—— Judgment debt　- 22 Ch. D. 529
　　See BANKRUPTCY—APPEAL. 5.

—— Partner, on judgment against firm
　　　　　　　　　[19 Ch. D. 124
　　See PRACTICE—SUPREME COURT—PAR-
　　TIES. 11.

DECEASED DEBTOR—Administration of estate
　　in bankruptcy.
　　See BANKRUPTCY—STATUTES.
　　　Cases under BANKRUPTCY — DE-
　　CEASED DEBTOR.

—— Claim against—Corroboration 23 Ch. D. 267
　　See EXECUTOR—ACTIONS. 15.

DECEASED PARTNER—Administration action—
　　Joint creditors -　25 Ch. D. 16
　　See PRACTICE—SUPREME COURT—CON-
　　DUCT OF CAUSE. 4.

—— Share of　-　8 App. Cas. 822
　　See PARTNERSHIP—CONTRACT. 2.

DECEIT—Action for 17 Ch. D. 301 ; 20 Ch. D. 27 ;
　　　　　　　　　[9 App. Cas. 187
　　See COMPANY—PROSPECTUS. 1, 3.

DECLARATION OF DECEASED PERSON
　　　　　　　[29 Ch. D. 985 ; 13 Q. B. D. 818
　　See EVIDENCE—DECLARATION BY DE-
　　CEASED PERSON. 1, 2.

—— Scotch law　-　6 App. Cas. 489
　　See SCOTCH LAW—HUSBAND AND WIFE.
　　3.

DECLARATION OF FUTURE RIGHTS—Appeal
　　　　　　　　　[21 Ch. D. 1
　　See PRACTICE—SUPREME COURT — AP-
　　PEAL. 34.

DECLARATION OF LEGITIMACY—Appeal from
　　grant or refusal of.
　　See PRACTICE — DIVORCE — APPEAL —
　　Statutes.

DECLARATION OF TRUST　17 Ch. D. 416
　　See VOLUNTARY CONVEYANCE. 1.

DECREE NISI—Re-marriage before decree abso-
　　lute -　　- 6 P. D. 11
　　See PRACTICE—DIVORCE—DECREE. 3.

DEDICATION—Highway　16 Ch. D. 449
　　See METROPOLIS—MANAGEMENT ACTS. 6.

—— Highway　-　29 Ch. D. 750
　　See HIGHWAY—DEDICATION.

—— Land to public purposes - 6 App. Cas. 636
　　See COLONIAL LAW—NEW SOUTH WALES.
　　1,

DEED.

_ Construction and Effect.] *The Act* 44 & 45 *Vict.*
　c. 41 (*Conveyancing Act*, 1881), *enacts, sect.* 2 :—
　In this Act—
　(i.) *Property, unless a contrary intention ap-
　pears, includes real and personal property, and
　any estate or interest in any property, real or
　personal, and any debt, and anything in action,
　and any other right or interest :*
　(ii.) *Land, unless a contrary intention appears,
　includes land of any tenure, and tenements and*

DEED—*continued.*

hereditaments, corporeal or incorporeal, and houses and other buildings, also an undivided share in land :

(v.) *Conveyance, unless a contrary intention appears, includes assignment, appointment, lease, settlement, and other assurance, and covenant to surrender, made by deed, on a sale, mortgage, demise, or settlement of any property, or on any other dealing with or for any property ; and convey, unless a contrary intention appears, has a meaning corresponding with that of conveyance.*

Conveyance to oneself.] *Sect.* 6.—(1.) *Freehold land or a thing in action may be conveyed by a person to himself jointly with another person by the like means by which it might be conveyed by him to another person ; and may, in like manner, be conveyed by a husband to his wife.*

(2.) *This section applies only to conveyances made after the commencement of this Act*—31st *of December,* 1881.

Covenants binding Representatives.] *Sect.* 58.—
(1.) *A covenant relating to land of inheritance, or devolving on the heir as special occupant, shall be deemed to be made with the covenantee his heirs and assigns, and shall have effect as if heirs and assigns were expressed.*

(2.) *A covenant, relating to land not of inheritance, or not devolving on the heir as special occupant, shall be deemed to be made with the covenantee, his executors, administrators, and assigns, and shall have effect as if executors, administrators, and assigns were expressed.*

(3.) *This section applies only to covenants made after the commencement of this Act.*

Sect. 59.—(1.) *A covenant, and a contract under seal, and a bond or obligation under seal, though not expressed to bind the heirs, shall operate in law to bind the heirs and real estate, as well as the executors and administrators and personal estate, of the person making the same, as if heirs were expressed.*

(2.) *This section extends to a covenant implied by virtue of this Act.*

(3.) *This section applies only if and as far as a contrary intention is not expressed in the covenant, contract, bond, or obligation, and shall have effect subject to the terms of the covenant, contract, bond, or obligation, and to the provisions therein contained.*

(4.) *This section applies only to a covenant, contract, bond, or obligation made or implied after the commencement of this Act.*

Sect. 60.—(1.) *A covenant, and a contract under seal, and a bond or obligation under seal, made with two or more jointly, to pay money or to make a conveyance, or to do any other act, to them or for their benefit, shall be deemed to include, and shall, by virtue of this Act, imply, an obligation to do the act to, or for the benefit of, the survivor or survivors of them, and to, or for the benefit of, any other person to whom the right to sue on the covenant, contract, bond, or obligation devolves.*

(2.) *This section extends to a covenant implied by virtue of this Act.*

(3.) *This section applies only if and as far as a contrary intention is not expressed in the covenant, contract, bond, or obligation, and shall have effect subject to the covenant, contract, bond, or obligation, and to the provisions therein contained.*

DEED—*continued.*

(4.) *This section applies only to a covenant, contract, bond, or obligation made or implied after the commencement of this Act.*

Sect. 64. *In the construction of a covenant or proviso, or other provision, implied in a deed by virtue of this Act, words importing the singular or plural number, or the masculine gender, shall be read as also importing the plural or singular number, or as extending to females, as the case may require.*

Covenants for Title, when implied.] *Sect.* 7.—
(1.) *In a conveyance there shall in the several cases in this section mentioned, be deemed to be included, and there shall in those several cases, by virtue of this Act, be implied, a covenant to the effect of this section stated, by the person or by each person who conveys, as far as regards the subject-matter or share of subject-matter expressed to be conveyed by him, with the person, if one, to whom the conveyance is made, or with the persons jointly, if more than one, to whom the conveyance is made as joint tenants, or with each of the persons, if more than one, to whom the conveyance is made as tenants in common, that is to say :* —

(A.) *In a conveyance for valuable consideration, other than a mortgage, the following covenants by a person who conveys and is expressed to convey as beneficial owner* (namely):

　Right to convey.
　Quiet enjoyment.
　Freedom from incumbrances.
　Further assurance.

(in which covenant a purchase for value shall not be deemed to include a conveyance in consideration of marriage).

(B.) *In a conveyance of leasehold property for valuable consideration, other than a mortgage, the following further covenant by a person who conveys and is expressed to convey as beneficial owner* (namely):

　Validity of lease,

(in which covenant a purchase for value shall not be deemed to include a conveyance in consideration of marriage).

(C.) *In a conveyance by way of mortgage, the following covenants by a person who conveys and is expressed to convey as beneficial owner* (namely):

　Right to convey.
　Quiet enjoyment.
　Freedom from incumbrances.
　Further assurance.

(D.) *In a conveyance by way of mortgage of leasehold property, the further following covenants by a person who conveys and is expressed to convey as beneficial owner* (namely):

　Validity of lease.
　Payment of rent and performance of covenants.
　To indemnify against breach of covenants.

(E.) *In a conveyance by way of settlement, the following covenants by a person who conveys and is expressed to convey as settlor* (namely):

　For further assurance limited.

(F.) *In any conveyance the following covenant by every person who conveys and is expressed to convey as trustee or mortgagee, or as personal representative of a deceased person, or as committee of a lunatic so found by inquisition, or under an order of the Court, which covenant shall be deemed*

DEED—*continued.*

to extend, to every such person's own acts only (namely):

　　Against incumbrances.

(2.) *Where in a conveyance it is expressed that by direction of a person expressed to direct as beneficial owner another person conveys, then, within this section, the person giving the direction, whether he conveys and is expressed to convey as beneficial owner or not, shall be deemed to convey and to be expressed to convey as beneficial owner the subject-matter so conveyed by his direction; and a covenant on his part shall be implied accordingly.*

(3.) *Where a wife conveys and is expressed to convey as beneficial owner, and the husband also conveys and is expressed to convey as beneficial owner, then, within this section, the wife shall be deemed to convey and to be expressed to convey by direction of the husband, as beneficial owner; and, in addition to the covenant implied on the part of the wife, there shall also be implied, first, a covenant on the part of the husband as the person giving that direction, and secondly, a covenant on the part of the husband in the same terms as the covenant implied on the part of the wife.*

(4.) *Where in a conveyance a person conveying is not expressed to convey as beneficial owner, or as settlor, or as trustee, or as mortgagee, or as personal representative of a deceased person, or as committee of a lunatic so found by inquisition, or under an order of the Court, or by direction of a person as beneficial owner, no covenant on the part of the person conveying shall be, by virtue of this section, implied in the conveyance.*

(5.) *In this section a conveyance includes a deed conferring the right to admittance to copyhold or customary land, but does not include a demise by way of lease at a rent, or any customary assurance, other than a deed, conferring the right to admittance to copyhold or customary land.*

(6.) *The benefit of a covenant implied as aforesaid shall be annexed and incident to, and shall go with, the estate or interest of the implied covenantee, and shall be capable of being enforced by every person in whom that estate or interest is, or for the whole or any part thereof, from time to time vested.*

(7.) *A covenant implied as aforesaid may be varied or extended by deed, and, as so varied or extended, shall, as far as may be, operate in the like manner, and with all the like incidents, effects, and consequences, as if such variations or extensions were directed in this section to be implied.*

(8.) *This section applies only to conveyances made after the commencement of this Act.*

Easement.]　*Sect.* 62.—(1.) *A conveyance of freehold land to the use that any person may have, for an estate or interest not exceeding in duration, the estate conveyed in the land, any easement, right, liberty, or privilege in, or over, or with respect to that land, or any part thereof, shall operate to vest in possession in that person that easement, right, liberty, or privilege, for the estate or interest expressed to be limited to him; and he, and the persons deriving title under him, shall have, use, and enjoy the same accordingly.*

(2.) *This section applies only to conveyances made after the commencement of this Act.*

Estate Clause.]　*Sect.* 63.—(1.) *Every convey-*

DEED—*continued.*

ance shall, by virtue of this Act, be effectual to pass all the estate, right, title, interest, claim, and demand which the conveying parties respectively have, in, to, or on the property conveyed, or expressed or intended so to be, or which they respectively have powers to convey in, to, or on the same.

(2.) *This section applies only if and so far as a contrary intention is not expressed in the conveyance, and shall have effect subject to the terms of the conveyance and to the provisions therein contained.*

(3.) *This section applies only to conveyances made after the commencement of this Act.*

Forms.]　*Deeds in the form of and using the expressions in the forms given in the fourth schedule to this Act, or in the like form or using expressions to the like effect, shall, as regards form and expression in relation to the provisions of this Act be sufficient.*

General Words.]　*Sect.* 6.—(1.) *A conveyance of land shall be deemed to include, and shall, by virtue of the Act, operate to convey with the land all buildings, erections, fixtures, commons, hedges, ditches, fences, ways, waters, watercourses, liberties, privileges, easements, rights, and advantages, whatsoever, appertaining or reputed to appertain to the land, or any part thereof, or at the time of conveyance demised, occupied, or enjoyed with, or reputed or known as part or parcel of or appurtenant to the land or any part thereof.*

(2.) *A conveyance of land, having houses or other buildings thereon, shall be deemed to include and shall by virtue of the Act operate to convey, with the land, houses, or other buildings, all outhouses, erections, fixtures, cellars, areas, courts, courtyards, cisterns, sewers, gutters, drains, ways, passages, lights, watercourses, liberties, privileges, easements, rights and advantages, whatsoever, appertaining or reputed to appertain to the land, houses, and other buildings conveyed, or any of them, or any part thereof, or at the time of conveyance demised, occupied, or enjoyed with, or reputed or known as part or parcel of or appurtenant to the land, houses, or other buildings conveyed, or any of them or any part thereof.*

(3.) *A conveyance of a manor shall be deemed to include and shall by virtue of the Act operate to convey, with the manor, all pastures, feedings, wastes, warrens, commons, mines, minerals, quarries, furzes, trees, woods, underwoods, coppices, and the ground and soil thereof, fishings, fisheries, fowlings, courts leet, courts baron, and other courts, view of frankpledge and all that to view of frankpledge doth belong, mills, mulctures, customs, tolls, duties, reliefs, heriots, fines, sums of money, amerciaments, waifs, estrays, chief-rents, quit-rents, rentscharge, rents seck, rents of assize, fee farm rents, services, royalties, jurisdictions, franchises, liberties, privileges, easements, profits, advantages, rights, emoluments, and hereditaments whatsoever, to the manor appertaining or reputed to appertain, or at the time of conveyance demised, occupied, or enjoyed with the same, or reputed or known as part, parcel, or member thereof.*

(4.) *This section applies only if and as far as a contrary intention is not expressed in the conveyance, and shall have effect subject to the terms of the conveyance and to the provisions therein contained.*

DEED—*continued.*

(5.) *This section shall not be construed as giving to any person a better title to any property, right, or thing in this section mentioned than the title which the conveyance gives to him to the land or manor expressed to be conveyed, or as conveying to him any property, right, or thing in this section mentioned, further or otherwise than as the same could have been conveyed to him by the conveying parties.*

(6.) *This section applies only to conveyances made after the commencement of this Act.*

Joint Account Clause.] *Sect.* 61.—(1.) *Where in a mortgage, or an obligation for payment of money, or a transfer of a mortgage or of such an obligation, the sum, or any part of the sum, advanced or owing is expressed to be advanced by or owing to more persons than one out of money, or as money, belonging to them on a joint account, or a mortgage, or such an obligation, or such a transfer is made to more persons than one, jointly, and not in shares, the mortgage money, or other money, or money's worth for the time being due to those persons on the mortgage or obligation, shall be deemed to be and remain money or money's worth belonging to those persons on a joint account, as between them and the mortgagor or obligor; and the receipt in writing of the survivors or last survivor of them, or of the personal representatives of the last survivor, shall be a complete discharge for all money or money's worth for the time being due, notwithstanding any notice to the payer of a severance of the joint account.*

(2.) *This section applies only if and as far as a contrary intention is not expressed in the mortgage, or obligation, or transfer, and shall have effect subject to the terms of the mortgage, or obligation, or transfer, and to the provisions therein contained.*

(3.) *This section applies only to a mortgage, or obligation, or transfer made after the commencement of this Act.*

Receipts.] *Sect.* 54.—(1.) *A receipt for consideration money or securities in the body of a deed shall be a sufficient discharge for the same to the person paying or delivering the same, without any further receipt for the same being indorsed on the deed.*

(2.) *This section applies only to deeds executed after the commencement of this Act.*

Sect. 55.—(1.) *A receipt for consideration money or other consideration in the body of a deed or indorsed thereon shall, in favour of a subsequent purchaser, not having notice that the money or other consideration thereby acknowledged to be received was not in fact paid or given, wholly or in part, be sufficient evidence of the payment or giving of the whole amount thereof.*

(2.) *This section applies only to deeds executed after the commencement of this Act.*

Sect. 56.—(1.) *Where a solicitor produces a deed, having in the body thereof or indorsed thereon a receipt for consideration money or other consideration, the deed being executed, or the indorsed receipt being signed, by the person entitled to give a receipt for that consideration, the deed shall be sufficient authority to the person liable to pay or give the same for his paying or giving the same to the solicitor, and without the solicitor producing any separate or other direction or authority in that*

behalf *from the person who executed or signed the deed or receipt.*

(2.) *This section applies only in cases where consideration is to be paid or given after the commencement of this Act.*

Supplemental Deed.] *Sect.* 53.—(1.) *A deed expressed to be supplemental to a previous deed, or directed to be read as an annex thereto shall, as far as may be, be read and have effect as if the deed so expressed or directed were made by way of indorsement on the previous deed or contained a full recital thereof.*

(2.) *This section applies to deeds executed either before or after the commencement of this Act.*

Word "Grant" unnecessary.] *Sect.* 49.—(1.) *It is hereby declared that the use of the word grant is not necessary in order to convey tenements or hereditaments, corporeal or incorporeal.*

(2.) *This section applies to conveyances made before or after the commencement of this Act.*

Words of Limitation.] *Sect.* 51.—(1.) *In a deed it shall be sufficient, in the limitation of an estate in fee simple, to use the words in fee simple, without the word heirs; and in the limitation of an estate in tail, to use the words in tail without the words heirs of the body; and in the limitation of an estate in tail male or in tail female, to use the words in tail male, or in tail female, as the case requires, without the words heirs male of the body or heirs female of the body.*

(2.) *This section applies only to deeds executed after the commencement of this Act.*

1. —— Deeds executed on same day—*Priority of Operation—Debentures of Company.*] When two deeds relating to the same subject-matter are executed on the same day, the Court will inquire which of them was executed first.—But if there is anything in the deeds themselves to shew an intention either that they shall take effect pari passu, or that one should take effect in priority to the other, the Court will presume that they were executed in such an order as to give effect to the manifest intention.—One hundred and fifty debentures of a company, each for £100, were all sealed with the company's seal on the same day. They bore the numbers 501 to 650. Each of the first hundred (Nos. 501 to 600) contained a provision that it " and all other debentures of the company to the amount of £10,000 (the amount intended to be now borrowed by the company), or such of them as shall be for the time being due and unpaid, shall be all taken and considered, as between the company and the several holders thereof, as one debenture, and shall not be entitled to any preference or priority by reason of priority of date or otherwise, but shall be paid pari passu out of the funds of the company." Each of the other fifty debentures contained a similar provision, substituting the sum of £5000 for £10,000. There was evidence that the company's seal was affixed to the debentures in the order of their numbers, beginning with the earliest. The company being in liquidation : — *Held*, that the holders of the debentures for £10,000 were entitled to priority over the holders of the debentures for £5000. GARTSIDE *v.* SILKSTONE AND DODWORTH COAL AND IRON COMPANY

[21 Ch. D. 762

DEED—*continued.*

2. —— Execution of Deed of Assignment— *Effect of Note appended to Signature.*] Not every attempt by a form of execution to restrain the full operation of a deed can be treated as a non-execution of it.—Where a deed of assignment by debtors to a trustee for the benefit of all creditors who should execute the deed was executed by the Plaintiffs, who appended a note that they executed only in respect of certain claims scheduled to the deed and amounting to £73,531, and it appeared that subsequently thereto they received a sum of money from the trustee by virtue of their execution of the deed :—*Held,* that the Plaintiffs were bound. The note did not amount to a refusal to execute ; and the Plaintiffs having received payment under the deed could not be heard to repudiate it, and deny their execution.— *Wilkinson* v. *Anglo-Californian Gold Mining Company* (18 Q. B. 728) held to be inapplicable. EXCHANGE BANK OF YARMOUTH *v.* BLETHEN

[**10 App. Cas. 293**]

—— Delivery of—Foreclosure　　　**22 Ch. D. 566** *See* MORTGAGE—FORECLOSURE. 4.

—— Deposit of—Banker　-　**6 App. Cas. 722** *See* BANKER—LIEN.

—— Deposit of—Bonds—Solicitor—Liability of partner　　　　　　　**28 Ch. D. 340** *See* PARTNERSHIP—LIABILITIES.

—— Deposit of—Building society **30 Ch. D. 434**; [**9 App. Cas. 519** *See* BUILDING SOCIETY. 5, 9.

—— Deposit of—Equitable mortgage—Priority [**18 Ch. D. 560** *See* MORTGAGE—PRIORITY. 4.

—— Execution of—Knowledge of contents [**20 Ch. D. 611** *See* VENDOR AND PURCHASER—PURCHASE WITHOUT NOTICE. 1.

—— Not in vendor's possession—Expense of production　　　-　　　**30 Ch. D. 42** *See* VENDOR AND PURCHASER—TITLE. 1.

DEFAMATION :—　　　　　　　　Col.
　I. LIBEL　　-　　-　　-　497
　II. PRIVILEGE　　　　　-　499
　III. SLANDER　-　　-　　-　500

I. DEFAMATION—LIBEL.

Newspaper.] *The Act* 44 & 45 *Vict.* c. 60 (*the Newspaper Libel and Registration Act,* 1881), *amends the law affecting civil actions and criminal prosecutions for newspaper libel.*

Sect. 1 *defines* (*inter alia*) *the word "newspaper" to mean any paper containing public news, intelligence,* or *occurrences,* or *any remarks* or *observations thereon, printed for sale and published in England* or *Ireland periodically,* or *in parts* or *numbers, at intervals not exceeding twenty-six days between the publication of any two such papers, parts* or *numbers.*

Also any paper printed in order to be dispersed and made public weekly or oftener, or at intervals not exceeding twenty-six days, containing only or *principally advertisements.*

The word "proprietor" to mean and include as well the sole proprietor of any newspaper, as also, in the case of a divided proprietorship, the per-

I. DEFAMATION—LIBEL.—*continued.*

sons who as partners or otherwise represent and are responsible for any share or interest in the newspaper as between themselves and the persons in like manner representing or responsible for the other shares or interests therein, and no other person.

Sect. 2. *Any report published in any newspaper of the proceedings of a public meeting shall be privileged, if such meeting was lawfully convened for a lawful purpose and open to the public, and if such report was fair and accurate, and published without malice, and if the publication of the matter complained of was for the public benefit ; provided always, that the protection intended to be afforded by this section shall not be available as a defence in any proceeding if the Plaintiff or prosecutor can shew that the Defendant has refused to insert in the newspaper in which the report containing the matter complained of appeared a reasonable letter or statement of explanation or contradiction by or on behalf of such Plaintiff or prosecutor.*

1. —— Innuendo—*Evidence of Defamatory Meaning.*] H. & Sons were in the habit of receiving, in payment from their customers, cheques on various branches of a bank, which the bank cashed for the convenience of H. & Sons at a particular branch. Having had a squabble with the manager of that branch H. & Sons sent a printed circular to a large number of their customers (who knew nothing of the squabble)—" H. & Sons hereby give notice that they will not receive in payment cheques drawn on any of the branches of the " bank. The circular became known to other persons ; there was a run on the bank and loss inflicted. The bank having brought an action against H. & Sons for libel, with an innuendo that the circular imputed insolvency :—*Held,* affirming the decision of the Court of Appeal (Lord Penzance dissenting) that in their natural meaning the words were not libellous : that the inference suggested by the innuendo was not the inference which reasonable persons would draw : that the onus lay on the bank to shew that the circular had a libellous tendency ; that the evidence consisting of the circumstances attending the publication, failed to shew it ; that there was no case to go to the jury ; and that the Defendants were entitled to judgment. CAPITAL AND COUNTIES BANK *v.* HENTY -　-　**7 App. Cas. 741**

2. —— Justification—*Evidence of Plaintiff's general bad Character — Rumours of Plaintiff having committed Offences charged in Libel— Mitigation of Damages—Facts not stated in Pleadings—Order XIX., r. 4.*] Action for a libel alleging that the Plaintiff, a theatrical critic, had endeavoured to extort money by threatening to publish defamatory matter concerning a deceased actress. Defence—that the allegation was true in substance and fact :—*Held,* by Mathew, and Cave, JJ., that evidence of rumours before the publication of the libel that the Plaintiff had committed the offences charged in it, and evidence of particular facts and circumstances tending to shew the misconduct of the Plaintiff as a theatrical critic could not be admitted in reduction of damages :—*Held,* further, that assuming such evidence to be material it was rightly rejected, for the particular facts

I. DEFAMATION—LIBEL—continued.

and circumstances were not stated or referred to in the pleadings as required by Order XIX., r. 4. SCOTT v. SAMPSON　　-　　**8 Q. B. D. 491**

II. DEFAMATION—PRIVILEGE.

1. —— **Charity Organisation Society.**] A. interested herself in obtaining subscriptions for the relief of the Plaintiff, a lady in distressed circumstances. B., who was interested in the case, applied to the Defendant, the Secretary of the Charity Organisation Society, for information as to the Plaintiff's character, and received an unfavourable report which, by leave of the secretary, she communicated to A. The subscriptions were thereupon withdrawn. The Plaintiff then sued the secretary for libel. The society was formed for the purpose (inter alia) of investigating the cases of applicants for charitable relief :—*Held*, that the report was a privileged communication, and that, in the absence of proof of malice, the action could not be maintained. WALLER v. LOCH.
[**7 Q. B. D. 619**

2. —— **Judicial Proceeding—**Advocate—Relevancy—Malice.] No action will lie against an advocate for defamatory words spoken with reference to, and in the course of, an inquiry before a judicial tribunal, although they are uttered by the advocate maliciously and not with the object of supporting the case of his client, and are uttered without any justification or even excuse, and from personal ill-will or anger towards the person defamed arising out of a previously existing cause, and are irrelevant to every issue of fact which is contested before the tribunal.—H. was charged before a Court of petty sessions with administering drugs to the inmates of M.'s house in order to facilitate the commission of a burglary at it. M. was the prosecutor, and L., who was a solicitor, appeared for the defence of H. There was some evidence, although of a very slight character, that a narcotic drug had been administered to the inmates of M.'s house upon the evening before the burglary, and H. had been at M.'s house on that evening. During the proceedings before the Court of petty sessions, L., acting as advocate for H., suggested that M. might be keeping drugs at his house for immoral or criminal purposes. There was no evidence that M. kept any drugs for those purposes :—*Held*, that no action by M. for defamation would lie against L.—*Kendillon* v. *Maltby* (Car. & M. 402 ; 2 M. & R. 438) dissented from. MUNSTER v. LAMB　　-　　**11 Q. B. D. 588**

3. —— **Publication by Mistake—**Negligence.] The Defendant wrote defamatory statements of the Plaintiff in a letter to W. under circumstances which made the publication of the letter to W. privileged, but by mistake the Defendant placed it in an envelope directed to another person who received and read the letter. In an action for libel :—*Held*, that the letter having been written to W. under circumstances which caused the legal implication of malice to be rebutted, the publication to the other person, though made through the negligence of the Defendant, was privileged in the absence of malice in fact on his part. TOMPSON v. DASHWOOD　-　　-　　**11 Q. B. D. 43**

4. —— **Witness—** Parliament — Select Committee of House of Commons.] To an action of

II. DEFAMATION—PRIVILEGE—continued.

slander Defendant pleaded that the statements complained of were part of the evidence given by him in the character of a witness before a Select Committee of the House of Commons :—*Held*, that the statements so made were privileged, and that the action would not lie. GOFFIN v. DONNELLY　-　　-　　-　　**6 Q. B. D. 307**

III. DEFAMATION—SLANDER.

1. —— **Innuendo—**Criminal Offence—Indictable Offence—Words actionable per se.] Words imputing that the Plaintiff has been guilty of a criminal offence will support an action for slander, without special damage ; and it is not necessary to allege in the statement of claim that they impute an indictable offence. WEBB v. BEAVAN
[**11 Q. B. D. 609**

2. —— **Innuendo —** Prefatory Averment.] Words merely conveying suspicion will not sustain an action for slander. Where such words admit fairly, and in their natural sense, of two meanings, the one being an imputation of suspicion only, the other of guilt, the sense in which they were uttered should be left to the jury.— The innuendoes not declaring that the words were spoken with the intention of imputing to the Plaintiff a felony, and not importing to enlarge the meaning of those words :—*Held*, that the prefatory averments which only professed to give the motives of the Defendant could not be substituted for those innuendoes whereby the Plaintiff undertook to give the meaning of the words spoken. SIMMONS v. MITCHELL　**6 App. Cas. 156**

3. —— **Letters** addressed to Agent at the Principal's Office—Mandatory Injunction.] B. was employed to manage one of L.'s branch offices for the sale of machines, and resided on the premises. He was dismissed by L., and on leaving gave the postmaster directions to forward to his private residence all letters addressed to him at L.'s branch office. He admitted that among the letters so forwarded to him were two which related to L.'s business, and that he did not hand them to L., but returned them to the senders. After his dismissal he went about among the customers, making oral statements reflecting on the solvency of L., and advised some of them not to pay L. for machines which had been supplied through himself. L. brought an action to restrain B. from making statements to the customers or any other person or persons that L. was about to stop payment, or was in difficulties or insolvent, and from in any manner slandering L. or injuring his reputation or business, and from giving notice to the post-office to forward to B.'s residence letters addressed to him at L.'s office, and also asking that he might be ordered to withdraw the notice already given to the post-office :—*Held*, by Pearson, J., and the Court of Appeal, that the Court has jurisdiction to restrain a person from making slanderous statements calculated to injure the business of another person, and that this jurisdiction extends to oral as well as written statements, though it requires to be exercised with great caution as regards oral statements ; and that in the present case an injunction ought to be granted :—*Held*, also, by Pearson, J., and by the Court of Appeal,

III. DEFAMATION—SLANDER—*continued.*

that the Defendant had no right to give a notice to the post-office the effect of which would be to hand over to him letters of which it was probable that the greater part related only to L.'s business; and that the case was one in which a mandatory injunction compelling the Defendant to withdraw his notice could properly be made, the Plaintiff being put under an undertaking only to open the letters at certain specified times, with liberty for the Defendant to be present at the opening. HERMANN LOOG *v.* BEAN　26 Ch. D. 306

4. —— Remoteness of Damage—*Damage not natural and probable Consequence of Words spoken.*] Claim, that the Plaintiff was a candidate for membership of the R. Club, but upon a ballot of the members was not elected; that a meeting of the members was called to consider an alteration of the rules regarding the election of members; that the Defendant falsely and maliciously spoke and published of the Plaintiff as follows : " The conduct of the " Plaintiff " was so bad at a club in M. that a round robin was signed urging the committee to expel " him ; " as however " he was " there only for a short time, the committee did not proceed further ;" whereby the Defendant induced a majority of the members of the club to retain the regulations under which the Plaintiff had been rejected, and thereby prevented the Plaintiff from again seeking to be elected to the club :—*Held,*upon demurrer, that the claim disclosed no cause of action; for the words complained of, not being · actionable in themselves, must be supported by special damage in order to enable the Plaintiff to sue; and the damage alleged was not pecuniary or capable of being estimated in money, and was not the natural and probable consequence of the Defendant's words. CHAMBERLAIN *v.* BOYD - 　- 　11 Q. B. D. 407

DEFAMATION — Criminal information—Newspaper libel—Fiat of director of public prosecutions - 　- 　14 Q. B. D. 648
　　See CRIMINAL LAW—LIBEL. 2.

—— Criminal prosecution—Newspaper.
　　See CRIMINAL LAW—LIBEL—*Statutes.*

—— Injunction to restrain 　- 　20 Ch. D. 501 ;
　　　　　　　　　　　　[21 Ch. D. 798
　　See PRACTICE— SUPREME COURT — INJUNCTION. 4, 5.

—— Interrogatories—Libel—Handwriting
　　　　　　　　　　　　[15 Q. B. D. 439
　　See PRACTICE—SUPREME COURT—INTERROGATORIES. 7.

—— Leave to file information—Libel upon deceased foreign nobleman — Applicant resident abroad 　- 　12 Q. B. D. 320
　　See CRIMINAL LAW—LIBEL. 1.

—— Particulars of persons to whom slander uttered - 　- 　- 　12 Q. B. D. 94
　　See PRACTICE—SUPREME COURT—PARTICULARS. 2.

—— Publication—Interrogatories 10 Q. B. D. 110
　　See PRACTICE—SUPREME COURT—INTERROGATORIES. 15.

—— Slander uttered abroad—Service out of jurisdiction - 　- 　7 Q. B. D. 434
　　See PRACTICE—SUPREME COURT—SERVICE. 11.

DEFAULT—Pleading—Practice.
　　See Cases under PRACTICE — SUPREME COURT—DEFAULT.

DEFAULTER—Stock Exchange 　20 Ch. D. 356
　　See STOCK EXCHANGE. 2.

DEFEASANCE—Bill of sale 　- 　21 Ch. D. 73
　　See BILL OF SALE—FORMALITIES. 22.

DEFEATING AND DELAYING CREDITORS
　　　　　　　[25 Ch. D. 500; 26 Ch. D. 319
　　See BANKRUPTCY—ACT OF BANKRUPTCY. 1, 23, 26.

—— - 　- 　20 Ch. D. 389; 22 Ch. D. 74, 436
　　See FRAUDULENT CONVEYANCE. 1, 2, 3.

—— Bankruptcy—Trader 　- 　20 Ch. D. 697
　　See BANKRUPTCY—TRADER. 1.

—— Bankruptcy—Voluntary settlement
　　　　　　　　　　　　[19 Ch. D. 588
　　See BANKRUPTCY—VOID SETTLEMENT. 1.

DEFECT IN TITLE—Removable or irremovable
　　　　　　　　　　　　[23 Ch. D. 320
　　See VENDOR AND PURCHASER—TITLE. 9.

DEFENCE—Delivered after proper time
　　　　　　　[25 Ch. D. 707; 26 Ch. D. 66
　　See PRACTICE—SUPREME COURT—DEFAULT. 3, 4.

—— Omitting to deny Plaintiff's title
　　　　　　[6 Q. B. D. 645 ; 8 App. Cas. 456
　　See PRACTICE—SUPREME COURT—DEFENCE.

—— Putting in new defence—Fraud of solicitors
　　　　　　　　　　　　[20 Ch. D. 672
　　See PRACTICE—SUPREME COURT—AMENDMENT. 3.

—— Withdrawal of—Costs 　- 　18 Ch. D. 362
　　See PRACTICE—SUPREME COURT—COSTS. 23.

DEFENDANT—Adding - 　- 　28 Ch. D. 414
　　See PRACTICE—SUPREME COURT—PARTIES. 5.

—— Bankruptcy of 7 Q. B. D. 413; 28 Ch. D. 53
　　See PRACTICE — SUPREME COURT — CHANGE OF PARTIES. 1, 2.

—— Cross-examination of 　29 Ch. D. 711
　　See PRACTICE—SUPREME COURT—EVIDENCE. 4.

DEFILEMENT—Of women.
　　See CRIMINAL LAW—OFFENCES AGAINST WOMEN—*Statutes.*

—— On premises.
　　See CRIMINAL LAW—NUISANCE—*Statutes.*

DELAY—Agreement to settle 　- 　17 Ch. D. 361
　　See SETTLEMENT—ARTICLES. 1.

—— Devastavit by executor 　27 Ch. D. 622
　　See EXECUTOR—LIABILITIES. 1.

—— Expunging proof - 　- 　21 Ch. D. 537
　　See BANKRUPTCY—PROOF. 2.

—— Forfeiture of shares—Cost-book mine
　　　　　　　　　　　　[18 Ch. D. 660
　　See COMPANY—COST-BOOK COMPANY. 9.

—— Loading of ship—Frost 　10 Q. B. D. 241 ;
　　　　　　[11 Q. B. D. 543 ; 9 App. Cas. 470
　　See SHIP—CHARTERPARTY. 8, 9.

—— Misconduct of directors 　21 Ch. D. 149
　　See COMPANY—DIRECTOR'S LIABILITY. 4.

DELAY—*continued.*

—— Mistake in statement of debts—Delay in correcting mistake   23 Ch. D. 706
See BANKRUPTCY—COMPOSITION. 10.

—— Motion for security for costs   22 Ch. D. 83
See PRACTICE—SUPREME COURT—SECURITY FOR COSTS. 9.

—— Nullity of marriage—Impotence 10 P. D. 75
See PRACTICE—DIVORCE—NULLITY OF MARRIAGE. 3.

—— Petition for divorce—Poverty - 8 P. D. 21
See PRACTICE—DIVORCE—DELAY.

—— Presentment of cheque   8 Q. B. D. 288
See BANKER—CHEQUE. 1.

—— Principal—Discharge of surety
[25 Ch. D. 666
See PRINCIPAL AND SURETY—DISCHARGE. 3.

—— Rectification of register   24 Ch. D. 149
See COMPANY—PROSPECTUS. 6.

—— Revivor of suit   -   20 Ch. D. 398
See PRACTICE — SUPREME COURT — CHANGE OF PARTIES. 6.

—— Setting aside fraudulent conveyance
[27 Ch. D. 523
See FRAUDULENT CONVEYANCE. 3.

—— Specialty debt   -   20 Ch. D. 230
See SPECIALTY DEBT.

—— Undertaking as to damages   23 Ch. D. 644
See BANKRUPTCY—RECEIVER. 1.

DELIVERY—Bill of costs—Taxation   30 Ch. D.
See SOLICITOR—BILL OF COSTS. 7. [441

—— Goods—Before bankruptcy—Scotch law
[6 App. Cas. 588
See SCOTCH LAW—SALE OF GOODS. 2.

—— Goods—Instalments   -   9 Q. B. D. 648 ;
[9 App. Cas. 434
See SALE OF GOODS—RESCISSION. 2.

DEMURRAGE.
See Cases under SHIP—CHARTERPARTY. 2, 5—13.

DEMURRER.
See Cases under PRACTICE — SUPREME COURT—DEMURRER.

——   .   -   -   26 Ch. D. 35
See PRACTICE—SUPREME COURT—PARTIES. 16.

—— Parties   -   -   -   20 Ch. D. 208
See ECCLESIASTICAL COMMISSIONERS.

—— Proceedings in lieu of   28 Ch. D. 372
See PRACTICE — SUPREME COURT—DEMURRER. 3.

DENIAL OF PLAINTIFF'S TITLE 18 Ch. D. 477
See PRACTICE — SUPREME COURT — INTERROGATORIES. 3.

—— Omission of 6 Q. B. D. 645 ; 8 App. Cas. 456
See PRACTICE — SUPREME COURT — DEFENCE.

DEPARTING FROM DWELLING-HOUSE
[20 Ch. D. 697
See BANKRUPTCY—TRADER. 1.

——   -   22 Ch. D. 436
See BANKRUPTCY—ACT OF BANKRUPTCY. 23.

DEPOSIT—Appeal   -   -   20 Ch. D. 701
See BANKRUPTCY—APPEAL. 7.

—— Foreign life insurance company
[21 Ch. D. 837
See COMPANY — LIFE INSURANCE COMPANY. 1.

—— Forfeiture of   .   27 Ch. D. 89
See VENDOR AND PURCHASER—DEPOSIT. 2.

—— Forfeiture of   21 Ch. D. 243
See PENALTY.

—— Loan to building society   -   30 Ch. D. 434
See BUILDING SOCIETY. 5.

—— Parliamentary—Railway company
[18 Ch. D. 155 ; 25 Ch. D. 251 ;
[28 Ch. D. 652
See RAILWAY COMPANY — ABANDONMENT. 1, 2, 3.

DEPOSIT OF DEEDS—Banker   6 App. Cas. 722
See BANKER—LIEN.

—— Bonds—Solicitor—Liability of partner
[28 Ch. D. 340
See PARTNERSHIP—LIABILITIES.

—— Building society   23 Ch. D. 440 ;
[9 App. Cas. 519
See BUILDING SOCIETY. 9.

—— Mortgage—Priority   18 Ch. D. 560 ;
[29 Ch. D. 725
See MORTGAGE—PRIORITY. 4, 9.

—— Mortgage—Transfer   -   30 Ch. D. 396
See MORTGAGE—CONTRACT. 8.

DEPOSITION — Bankruptcy — Admission — Service of copy   19 Ch. D. 580
See BANKRUPTCY—EVIDENCE. 7.

—— Bankruptcy—Right of witness to copy
[21 Ch. D. 439
See BANKRUPTCY—EVIDENCE. 5.

DEPRIVATION—Contumacy   6 P. D. 157
See PRACTICE—ECCLESIASTICAL—CHURCH DISCIPLINE ACT. 1.

—— Sentence of—Jurisdiction   22 Ch. D. 316
See PRACTICE—ECCLESIASTICAL—JURISDICTION. 2.

DERELICT—Abandonment by salvors—Distribution of salvage reward   6 P. D. 193
See PRACTICE—ADMIRALTY — SALVAGE. 7.

—— Right to freight after abandonment of ship
See SHIP—FREIGHT. 2.   [7 P. D. 5

DERIVATIVE SETTLEMENT—Settled Land Act
[27 Ch. D. 707
See SETTLED LAND ACT—DEFINITIONS. 7.

DESCENT.

—— **Ex parte Paternâ** or **Ex parte Maternâ**
—*Inheritance Act* (3 & 4 *Will.* 4, c. 106), s. 2.]
A testator who died in 1853 devised as his own an estate which had devolved on his late wife in fee as heiress-at-law of her mother. The devise was to trustees in fee, on trust to pay the rents to the testator's only son and to his two daughters in equal shares, and to the survivors or survivor of them, with remainder on trust for the children of the son and the daughters respectively in fee, with an ultimate remainder unto and to the use of the testator's own right heirs.

DESCENT—*continued.*
The son and both the daughters survived the testator, but they all died without issue. The son survived the daughters, and died intestate. He was the heir-at-law of his father, and also of his mother. The testator had also devised real estate of his own to the son, who elected to confirm the will :—*Held*, that the equitable estate, which the son took under the will and by virtue of his election, merged in the legal estate which descended to him from his mother, and that the descent was regulated by the legal estate, and that, consequently, on his death intestate and without issue, the property descended to the heir of his maternal grandmother, who was the last purchaser of the legal estate, and not to his own heir. *In re* DOUGLAS. WOOD *v.* DOUGLAS　-　28 Ch. D. 327

—— Custom of manor—Youngest son
　　　　　　　　　　　　[18 Ch. D. 165
　　See COPYHOLD—CUSTOM. 2.

—— Law of Malta　-　-　7 App. Cas. 156
　　See COLONIAL LAW—MALTA. 1.

DESCRIPTION OF RESIDENCE　21 Ch. D. 371 ;
　　　　　　[22 Ch. D. 136; 10 Q. B. D. 90
　　See BILL OF SALE—FORMALITIES. 5, 6. 7.

DESERTION.
　　See Cases under PRACTICE—DIVORCE—
　　　　DESERTION.

—— Condonation — Subsequent adultery — Revival　-　-　-　8 P. D. 19
　　See PRACTICE—DIVORCE—CONDONATION. 3.

—— Wife by husband—Settlement by residence
　　　　　　　　　　　　[9 Q. B. D. 522
　　See POOR-LAW—SETTLEMENT. 8.

DESIGNS—Copyright in.
　　See COPYRIGHT—DESIGNS—*Statutes.*

—— Copyright in　27 Ch. D. 260; 28 Ch. D. 24
　　See COPYRIGHT—DESIGNS. 1, 2.

DESTRUCTION OF MACHINE　26 Ch. D. 766
　　See PATENT — SUPREME COURT — INFRINGEMENT. 8.

DETENTION—Scholar -　-　13 Q. B. D. 225
　　See ELEMENTARY EDUCATION ACTS—
　　　　HOME LESSONS.

—— Woman, for immoral purposes.
　　See CRIMINAL LAW—OFFENCES AGAINST
　　　　WOMEN—*Statutes.*

DEVASTAVIT　-　27 Ch. D. 622
　　See EXECUTOR—LIABILITIES. 1.

—— Claim against executor—Statute of Limitations　22 Ch. D. 820; 26 Ch. D. 783
　　See LIMITATIONS, STATUTE OF—PERSONAL
　　　　ACTIONS. 5, 6.

—— Debt barred by Statute of Frauds
　　　　　　　　　　　　[29 Ch. D. 358
　　See EXECUTOR—RETAINER. 10.

—— Lapse of time　-　20 Ch. D. 230
　　See SPECIALTY DEBT.

DEVISE.
　　See Cases under WILL.

—— Foreclosure - Infant heir of mortgagor
　　　　　　　　　　　　[25 Ch. D. 158
　　See MORTGAGE—FORECLOSURE. 8.

DICTATION—Written agreement—Scotch law
　　　　　　　　　　　　[6 App. Cas. 340
　　See SCOTCH LAW — LANDLORD AND
　　　　TENANT.

DIFFERENCES—Stock Exchange　22 Ch. D. 132
　　See BANKRUPTCY—ADJUDICATION. 2.

DIGGING UP SOIL—Inspection of property
　　　　　　　　　　　　[27 Ch. D. 356
　　See PRACTICE—SUPREME COURT—INSPECTION OF PROPERTY.

DILAPIDATIONS (ECCLESIASTICAL)—Repairs done by sequestrator — Objection to accounts　-　-　15 Q. B. D. 222
　　See ECCLESIASTICAL LAW — DILAPIDATIONS.

DIRECTOR—Appointment and dismissal
　　　　　　[21 Ch. D. 183; 23 Ch D. 1
　　See COMPANY — DIRECTOR'S APPOINTMENT. 1, 2.

—— Authority of　16 Ch. D. 681; 17 Ch. D. 715;
　　　　　　　　　　　　[24 Ch. D. 611
　　See COMPANY—DIRECTOR'S AUTHORITY. 1, 2, 3.

—— Charge of　-　23 Ch. D. 413
　　See COMPANY—SHARES—ALLOTMENT. 3.

—— Committee of directors　25 Ch. D. 118
　　See COMPANY—SHARES—TRANSFER. 7.

—— Fees—Proof—Winding-up　30 Ch. D. 629
　　See COMPANY—PROOF. 1.

—— Liability of　-　26 Ch. D. 107
　　See COMPANY—MEMORANDUM AND ARTICLES. 3.

—— Liability of　-　-　29 Ch. D. 795
　　See PRINCIPAL AND AGENT — AGENT'S
　　　　LIABILITY. 1.

—— Liability for calls -　8 Q. B. D. 685
　　See COMPANY—SHARES—ALLOTMENT. 2.

—— Liability for misconduct.
　　See Cases under COMPANY—DIRECTOR'S
　　　　LIABILITY.

—— Liability for misconduct—Right of action
　　　　　　　　　　　　[17 Ch. D. 234
　　See COMPANY—LIQUIDATOR. 3.

—— Liability on contract　6 Q. B. D. 516
　　See COMPANY—CONTRACTS. 1.

—— Qualification　25 Ch. D. 283; 27 Ch. D. 322
　　See COMPANY—DIRECTOR'S QUALIFICATION. 1, 2.

—— Quorum of—Forfeiture of shares
　　　　　　　　　　　　[16 Ch. D. 681
　　See COMPANY—DIRECTOR'S AUTHORITY. 3.

—— Quorum of—Power to allot shares
　　　　　　　　　　　　[23 Ch. D. 413
　　See COMPANY—SHARES—ALLOTMENT. 3.

—— Remuneration—Gratuity—Power of general meeting　-　23 Ch. D. 654
　　See COMPANY—MANAGEMENT. 2.

—— Retirement of—Application for shares
　　　　　　　　　　　　[17 Ch. D. 373
　　See COMPANY—PROSPECTUS. 2.

—— Statement by—Agent　22 Ch. D. 593
　　See EVIDENCE—GENERAL. 4.

DISABILITY—Statute of Limitations
[17 Ch. D. 104, 132
See LIMITATIONS, STATUTE OF—REALTY.
6, 7.

DISBURSEMENTS — Master of ship—Maritime
lien   -   -   -   8 P. D. 48
See SHIP—MARITIME LIEN. 4.

DISCHARGE—Bankruptcy.
See Cases under BANKRUPTCY — DIS-
CHARGE.

—— Bankruptcy—After-acquired chattels
[19 Ch. D. 342
See BILL OF SALE—OPERATION. 3.

—— Bankruptcy—Bankruptcy Act, 1883.
See BANKRUPTCY — BANKRUPTCY ACT,
1883—*Statutes*.

—— Bankruptcy—Subsequent breach of covenant   -   -   23 Ch. D. 285
See BANKRUPTCY—PROOF. 6.

—— Liquidation -   -   19 Ch. D. 140
See BANKRUPTCY—LIQUIDATION. 5.

—— Liquidation—Member of company
[25 Ch. D. 415
See COMPANY—CONTRIBUTORY. 3.

—— Prisoner in custody for contempt
[21 Ch. D. 230
See PRACTICE — SUPREME COURT—AT-
TACHMENT. 2.

—— Surety   -   25 Ch. D. 666
See PRINCIPAL AND SURETY—DISCHARGE.
5.

DISCHARGE OF INCUMBRANCES.
See VENDOR AND PURCHASER—CONVEY-
ANCE—*Statutes*.

DISCLAIMER—Lessor's title—Ejectment
[16 Ch. D. 730
See LANDLORD AND TENANT—RE-ENTRY.
2.

—— Onerous legacy   22 Ch. D. 573; 30 Ch. D.
See WILL—DISCLAIMER. 1, 2.   [614

—— Second mortgagee—Costs -   22 Ch. D. 566
See MORTGAGE—FORECLOSURE. 4.

—— Trustee in bankruptcy.
See Cases under BANKRUPTCY — DIS-
CLAIMER.

—— Trustee in liquidation   -   29 Ch. D. 8
See BANKRUPTCY—DISCLAIMER. 13.

—— Trustee in liquidation—Election to take
lease   -   -   -   9 Q. B. D. 473
See BANKRUPTCY—TRUSTEE. 6.

—— Specification -   -   28 Ch. D. 148
See PATENT—AMENDMENT. 3.

DISCONTINUANCE OF ACTION—Costs
[16 Ch. D. 559
See PRACTICE—SUPREME COURT—COSTS.
2.

—— Counter-claim   -   11 Q. B. D. 464
See PRACTICE—SUPREME COURT — DIS-
CONTINUANCE.

DISCOUNT—Issue of shares at   23 Ch. D. 545, n.
See COMPANY—SHARES—ISSUE. 1, 2.

DISCOVERY—Books of account of bankrupt
[21 Ch. D. 868
See BANKRUPTCY—ASSETS. 16.

DISCOVERY—*continued*.
—— Depositions before Receiver of Wreck
[9 P. D. 6
See PRACTICE — ADMIRALTY — PRODUC-
TION OF DOCUMENTS.

—— Disobedience to order   -   25 Ch. D. 64
See PRACTICE — SUPREME COURT—AT-
TACHMENT. 7.

—— Inspection of books of company—Arbitration   -   28 Ch. D. 620
See COMPANY—RECONSTRUCTION.

—— Interrogatories.
See Cases under PRACTICE — SUPREME
COURT—INTERROGATORIES.

—— Interrogatories—Winding-up   16 Ch. D. 58
See COMPANY—EVIDENCE. 1.

—— Production of documents.
See Cases under PRACTICE — SUPREME
COURT—PRODUCTION OF DOCUMENTS.

—— Property of deceased debtor 15 Q. B. D. 159
See BANKRUPTCY—DECEASED DEBTOR. 1.

—— Solicitor and client—Injunction   20 Ch. D.
See SOLICITOR—LIABILITIES. 1.   [733

DISCRETION—Charity Commissioners—Appeal
[18 Ch. D. 310
See CHARITY—MANAGEMENT. 3.

—— Court—Appeal   -   9 P. D. 122
See PRACTICE—DIVORCE—SETTLEMENTS.
7.

—— Court—Bankruptcy -   -   17 Ch. D. 13;
[21 Ch. D. 553
See BANKRUPTCY—JURISDICTION. 3, 4.

—— Court—Bankruptcy   -   16 Ch. D. 623
See BANKRUPTCY—ANNULMENT. 2.

—— Court—Bankruptcy—Costs   20 Ch. D. 685
See BANKRUPTCY—COSTS. 1.

—— Court—Bankruptcy—Disclaimer by trustee
[23 Ch. D. 115
See BANKRUPTCY—DISCLAIMER. 10.

—— Court—Bankruptcy—Removal of trustee
[16 Ch. D. 107
See BANKRUPTCY—TRUSTEE. 12.

—— Court—Bankruptcy—Scotch sequestration
[22 Ch. D. 816
See BANKRUPTCY—ADJUDICATION. 4.

—— Court—Costs   -   22 Ch. D. 611
See PRACTICE—SUPREME COURT—PAY-
MENT INTO COURT. 4.

—— Court— Costs—Compulsory purchase
[24 Ch. D. 669
See PRACTICE—SUPREME COURT—COSTS.
24.

—— Court—Injunction or damages 26 Ch. D. 578
See LIGHT—OBSTRUCTION. 2.

—— Court—Notice to third party   16 Ch. D. 489
See PRACTICE—SUPREME COURT—THIRD
PARTY. 4.

—— Court—Refusal to commit—Appeal
[20 Ch. D. 493
See PRACTICE—SUPREME COURT—AP-
PEAL. 1.

—— Court—Revivor   -   20 Ch. D. 398
See PRACTICE — SUPREME COURT —
CHANGE OF PARTIES. 6.

DISTRESS DAMAGE FEASANT.

—— *Impounding on Premises — Tender of Damages — Excessive Demand — Payment under Protest—Action for Money had and received—Extortion.*] Where an animal distrained as damage feasant is impounded on private premises, and not in a common pound, a subsequent tender of sufficient compensation for the damage actually done is good ; and if the distrainor, by demanding an

DISTRESS DAMAGE FEASANT—*continued.*
excessive sum for damages as the condition of his release of the animal, obtains payment of such sum from the owner, such payment is not voluntary, and the sum paid may be recovered in an action for money had and received. GREEN *v.* DUCKETT - - - **11 Q. B. D. 275**

DISTRESS WARRANT—Justices—Power to delay execution · **7 Q. B. D. 398**
　　See POOR-RATE—PROCEDURE. 6.

DISTRIBUTIONS, STATUTE OF.
—— Next of Kin—*Brother's Child—Intestate domiciled in England—Child legitimated by subsequent Marriage—22 & 23 Car. 2, c. 10, ss. 6, 7—Foreign Law.*] The Statute of Distributions being a statute not for Englishmen only but for all persons, English or not, dying intestate and domiciled in England, and applying universally to persons of all countries, races, and religions whatsoever, the proper law for determining the "kindred" under that statute is the international law adopted by the comity of states.—Therefore a child born before wedlock, of parents who were at her birth domiciled in Holland, but legitimated according to the law of Holland by the subsequent marriage of her parents:—*Held* (by James and Cotton, L.JJ., dissentiente Lush, L.J.), entitled to a share in the personal estate of an intestate dying domiciled in England as one of her next of kin, under the Statute of Distributions.—*Boyes* v. *Bedale* (1 H. & M. 798) disapproved.—The decision of Jessel, M.R., reversed. *In re* GOODMAN'S TRUSTS **17 Ch. D. 266**
—— Advancement ·· **29 Ch. D. 250**
　　See ADVANCEMENT. 1.

DISTRICT BOARD—Liability for acts of predecessors - **17 Ch. D. 685**
　　See LOCAL GOVERNMENT—LOCAL AUTHORITY. 13.

DISTRICT PARISHES—Apportionment of charities - **24 Ch. D. 213**
　　See CHURCH BUILDING ACTS.

DISTRICT REGISTRY—Administration action—Order for account **20 Ch. D. 538**
　　See EXECUTOR—ACTIONS. 8.
—— Taxation of costs - **27 Ch. D. 242**
　　See PRACTICE—SUPREME COURT — DISTRICT REGISTRY.

DISTRINGAS—Notice in lieu of **23 Ch. D. 549**
　　See PRACTICE— SUPREME COURT — INJUNCTION. 2.

DISUSED BURIAL-GROUND.
　　See BURIAL-GROUND—*Statutes.*

DIVERSION OF FOOTPATH—Duty to fence
[14 Q. B. D. 918
　　See NEGLIGENCE—LIABILITY. 5.

DIVIDEND—Bonus, whether capital or income
**[29 Ch. D. 635; 14 Q. B. D. 239; 10 App.
[Cas. 438
　　See COMPANY—DIVIDENDS. 1, 2.
—— Legacy—Apportionment **18 Ch. D. 160**
　　See APPORTIONMENT. 1.
—— Payment in proportion to shares
[8 App. Cas. 65
　　See COMPANY—DIVIDENDS. 3.

DIVIDEND—*continued.*
—— Payment out of capital **21 Ch. D. 149, 519;**
[25 Ch. D. 752
　　See COMPANY—DIRECTOR'S LIABILITY. 4, 5, 6.
—— Payment out of capital **16 Ch. D. 344**
　　See COMPANY—DIVIDENDS. 4.

DIVIDEND WARRANT—Statutory enactments respecting.
　　See BILL OF EXCHANGE—*Statutes.*

DIVISIBLE GIFT—Remoteness **28 Ch. D. 436**
　　See WILL—PERPETUITY. 1.

DIVISIONS OF METROPOLIS — School board affected by.
　　See ELEMENTARY EDUCATION ACTS— SCHOOL BOARD—*Statutes.*

DIVORCE.
　　See Cases under PRACTICE—DIVORCE.
—— Alimony—Lunatic – **27 Ch. D. 160**
　　See LUNATIC—PROPERTY. 1.
—— Alimony — Order for payment of—Bankruptcy—Proof - **15 Q. B. D. 239**
　　See BANKRUPTCY—PROOF. 3.
—— Dower **21 Ch. D. 164**
　　See DOWER. 1.
—— Scotch divorce—English wife **6 P. D. 35;**
[8 App. Cas. 43
　　See HUSBAND AND WIFE—DIVORCE.
—— Scotch law - **9 App. Cas. 205; 10 App.
[Cas. 171
　　See SCOTCH LAW—HUSBAND AND WIFE. 1, 7.

DIVORCE COURT—Practice in.
　　See Cases under PRACTICE—DIVORCE.

DIVORCE SUIT—Appeal from decree.
　　See PRACTICE—DIVORCE—APPEAL—*Statutes.*
—— Compromise of - **18 Ch. D. 670**
　　See HUSBAND AND WIFE—SEPARATION DEED. 1.
—— Sequestration in - **18 Ch. D. 653**
　　See PRACTICE — SUPREME COURT — SEQUESTRATION. 2.

DIVORCED HUSBAND—Legacy to husband
　　See WILL—WORDS. 11. [**22 Ch. D. 619**

DIVORCED WIFE—Annuity during widowhood
[22 Ch. D. 597; 25 Ch. D. 685
　　See WILL—CONDITION. 11.

DOCK—Admiralty jurisdiction **8 Q. B. D. 609**
　　See PRACTICE—ADMIRALTY—JURISDICTION. 6.
—— Entering—Arrival at port **11 Q. B. D. 782;**
[6 App. Cas. 38
　　See SHIP—CHARTERPARTY. 5, 6.

DOCK COMPANY—Railway ancillary to docks— Taking railway plant in execution
[13 Q. B. D. 320
　　See RAILWAY COMPANY—PROPERTY. 1.

DOCK WARRANT—Indorsement **28 Ch. D. 682**
　　See BILL OF SALE—REGISTRATION. 5.

DOCKS AND HARBOURS.
　　1. —— **By-laws** - *Validity of — Harbours, Docks, and Piers Clauses Act, 1847 (10 & 11 Vict. c. 27), s. 83—Dock Company—Ship—Dis-*

DOCKS AND HARBOURS—*continued.*

charge of Cargo—Employment of Lumpers.] By 10 & 11 Vict. c. 27, s. 83, the undertakers authorized by any special Act to construct a dock may from time to time make such by-laws as they shall think fit for (amongst other purposes) regulating the shipping, unshipping, and removing of all goods within the limits of the dock, and for regulating the duties and conduct of all persons, as well the servants of the undertakers as others, employed in the dock. A dock company, who were the undertakers under a special Act, made by-laws that no lumpers should be allowed to work on board any vessel in the dock, but such as were authorized by the company, unless permission in writing had been previously obtained from the superintendent of the dock, and that servants of the company only should be allowed to work within the dock premises, whether on ship, lighter, or shore:—*Held*, that the by-laws were in excess of the power conferred upon the dock company by sect. 83, and were therefore invalid. DICK *v.* BADART FRÈRES - - - 10 Q. B. D. 387

2. —— **Removal of Wreck**—*Harbour Authority, Liability of—Acts, Local and General, Construction of.*] By Act of Parliament 26 & 27 Vict. c. lxxxix. the Harbour of B. was vested in the Defendants, the limits were defined, and the Defendants had jurisdiction over the harbour of P. and the channel of P. beyond those limits for the purpose of, inter alia, buoying "the said harbour and channel," but they were not to levy dues or rates beyond the harbour of B. By 42 & 43 Vict. c. cxlvi. a moiety of the residue of light duties to which ships entering or leaving the harbour of P. contributed, were to be paid to the Defendants and to be applied by them in, inter alia, buoying and lighting the harbour and channel of P. A vessel was wrecked in the channel of P., which under the Wrecks Removal Act, 1877 (40 & 41 Vict. c. 16), s. 4, the Defendants had power to, and did partially, remove. The wreck not removed was not buoyed, and the Plaintiff's vessel was in consequence wrecked:—*Held*, that the statutes imposed upon the Defendants· an obligation to remove the wreck from the channel or to mark its position by buoys, and that not having done so they were liable in damages to the Plaintiff. DORMONT *v.* FURNESS RAILWAY CO. 11 Q. B. D. 496

DOCUMENTARY EVIDENCE ACT, 1882.
See EVIDENCE—DOCUMENTS—*Statutes.*

DOCUMENTS—Contemporaneous   20 Ch. D. 27;
[9 App. Cas. 187
See COMPANY—PROSPECTUS. 1.

—— Evidence - 17 Ch. D. 833; 21 Ch. D. 674;
[25 Ch. D. 472
See EVIDENCE—DOCUMENTS. 1, 2, 3.

—— Evidence—Entry in college books
[17 Ch. D. 429
See EVIDENCE — ENTRY BY DECEASED PERSON.

—— Evidence—Public documents.
See· EVIDENCE — PUBLIC DOCUMENTS — *Statutes.*

—— Inspection of—Deceased'lunatic
[16 Ch. D. 673
See LUNATIC—DECEASED LUNATIC.

DOCUMENTS—*continued.*

—— Inspection of—Stannaries Court
[27 Ch. D. 106
See COMPANY—COST-BOOK COMPANY. 3.

—— Lien on—Solicitor.
See Cases under SOLICITOR—LIEN. 8—12.

—— Production of.
See Cases under PRACTICE—SUPREME COURT—PRODUCTION OF DOCUMENTS.

—— Production of—Bankruptcy   17 Ch. D. 512
See BANKRUPTCY—EVIDENCE. 3.

—— Production of—Books on account of bankrupt   -   -   21 Ch. D. 868
See BANKRUPTCY—ASSETS. 16.

—— Production of—Costs   16 Ch. D. 517
See PRACTICE—SUPREME COURT—COSTS. 38.

—— Valueless
See RECORD OFFICE—STATUTES AND GAZETTE.

DOMICIL.

—— **Abandonment**—*Acquired Domicil—Probate—Construction of Will expressed in Terms of Foreign Law.*] A Scotchman came to live in England and acquired an English domicil. He afterwards went for two years to France and returned to England, where he soon after died. He left an unsigned will of personal estate, made in 1827, which was drawn by a Scotch lawyer, and contained several technical words of Scotch law. The will was admitted to probate by the English Court. It was held by Pearson, J.:—(1), that the grant of the probate was not conclusive that the testator was domiciled in England: (2), that the Scotch domicil of the testator had revived, and that he died a domiciled Scotchman; (3), that the will must be construed according to Scotch law; and (4), that upon the true construction of the will the Plaintiff was entitled to the estate:—*Held*, by the Court of Appeal, that whether the testator was domiciled in Scotland or England, and whether the will was to be construed according to English or Scotch law, on the true construction of the will the Plaintiff was entitled to the estate; and therefore the question of domicil was immaterial.—But, *semble*, the testator died domiciled in England, his residence in France not being sufficient evidence of his intention to abandon his English domicil.—*Semble*, also, the use of some technical Scotch terms in his will did not furnish sufficient indication of the intention of the testator to induce the Court to construe it according to Scotch law. BRADFORD *v.* YOUNG
[29 Ch. D. 617

2. —— **Abandonment** — *Acquired Domicil— British Subject in Military Service of Crown.*] The rule that a British subject does not, by entering into and remaining in the military service of the Crown, abandon the domicil which he had when he entered into the service, applies to an acquired domicil as well as to a domicil of origin. —An infant, whose father was then living in Jersey, where he had acquired a domicil in place 'of his English domicil of origin, obtained a commission in the British army in 1854 and joined his regiment in England. He served with the

S

DOMICIL—*continued.*

regiment in different parts of the world, and ultimately, in 1863, he died in Canada, where he then was with the regiment. He had in the meantime paid occasional visits to Jersey while on leave :—*Held*, that he retained his Jersey domicil at the time of his death. *In re* MACREIGHT. PAXTON *v.* MACREIGHT   30 Ch. D. 165

3. —— Abandonment—*Evidence—Settlers in Colony.*] A change of domicil must be a residence *sine animo revertendi.* A temporary residence for the purposes of health, travel or business does not change the domicil. Also (1) every presumption is to be made in favour, of the original domicil; (2) no change can occur without an actual residence in a new place; and (3) no new domicil can be obtained without a clear intention of abandoning the old.—*Per* Lord Blackburn: When English settlers go out to a colony and settle there they carry with them, so far as may be applicable to their purpose, all the immunities and privileges of the law of England as the law of England was at that time. THE LAUDERDALE PEERAGE   10 App. Cas. 692

4. —— Chinese Domicil — *Petition—Legacy Duty—Anglo-Indian Domicil.*] Notwithstanding the constitution of the Supreme Court of China and Japan, and the jurisdiction conferred on that Court over British subjects having a fixed place of residence in China, a British subject cannot acquire by residence in China a new domicil so as to exempt his personal estate on death from the operation of the Legacy Duty Acts.—British subjects resident in Chinese territory cannot acquire in China a domicil similar to that existing in India, and commonly known as Anglo-Indian. *In re* TOOTAL'S TRUSTS   23 Ch. D. 532

5. —— Unsettled Residence—*Territorial Limits of England—Domicil of Origin.*] P. was born in Scotland, in 1792, of Scotch parents. In 1810 he obtained a commission in the army, and immediately proceeded with his regiment on foreign service, and served abroad till 1860, when he retired from the army. From 1860 till his death he resided in lodgings, hotels, and boarding-houses in various places in England, dying in 1882, intestate and a bachelor, in a private hotel in London, leaving no real estate in England, and no property whatsoever in Scotland. From the year 1810 till his death he never revisited Scotland, and for the last twenty-two years of his life never left the territorial limits of England —*Held*, that the domicil of the intestate at his death was Scotch. *In re* PATIENCE. PATIENCE *v.* MAIN   [29 Ch. D. 976

—— Alien—Execution of will   9 P. D. 130
    See PROBATE—GRANT. 2.

—— Bankruptcy—Officer in British army serving out of England -   13 Q. B. D. 418
    See BANKRUPTCY—BANKRUPTCY PETITION. 3.

—— Foreign—Administration   16 Ch. D. 407;
    [18 Ch. D. 347
    See ADMINISTRATOR—LIMITED. 5.

—— Foreign—Administration—English assets—Foreign creditors   28 Ch. D. 175
    See EXECUTOR—ADMINISTRATION. 8.

DOMICIL—*continued.*

—— Foreign husband—English settlement   [27 Ch. D. 284
    See POWER—EXECUTION. 16.

—— Foreign—Succession duty—Fund in Court   [21 Ch. D. 100
    See REVENUE—SUCCESSION DUTY. 2.

—— Illegitimate children   17 Ch. D. 266
    See DISTRIBUTIONS, STATUTE OF.

—— Law of—Representatives   8 App. Cas. 82
    See COLONIAL LAW—VICTORIA. 3.

—— Legitimacy—Will -   24 Ch. D. 637
    See WILL—WORDS. 13.

—— Probate of will—Estoppel -   29 Ch. D. 268
    See ESTOPPEL—JUDGMENT. 4.

—— Proof of—Probate of will -   26 Ch. D. 656
    See PROBATE—GRANT. 4.

—— Residence in Scotland or Ireland—Service of writ   20 Ch. D. 240; 12 Q. B. D. 50;
    [14 Q. B. D. 78
    See PRACTICE—SUPREME COURT—SERVICE.2, 3, 10.

—— Scotch—Action for administration in England   22 Ch. D. 456; 9 App. Cas. 34
    See EXECUTOR—ACTIONS. 16.

—— Scotch divorce—Validity in England   [6 P. D. 35; 8 App. Cas. 43
    See HUSBAND AND WIFE—DIVORCE.

DOMINION OF CANADA.
    See Cases under COLONIAL LAW — CANADA—DOMINION.

DONATIO MORTIS CAUSÂ.

—— Cheque *payable to', Donor or Order.*] A cheque payable to the donor or order and, without having been indorsed by him, given by the donor during his last illness to his son, stands on the same footing as a promissory note or bill of exchange payable to the donor or order, and, following *Veal* v. *Veal* (27 Beav. 303), will pass to the son by way of *donatio mortis causâ.* CLEMENT *v.* CHEESMAN -   27 Ch. D. 631

—— Duty on.
    See REVENUE—STAMPS—*Statutes.*

DOUBLE INSOLVENCY—Bill of exchange —Doctrine of *Ex parte Waring*   [7 App. Cas. 366
    See SCOTCH LAW—BILL OF EXCHANGE 3.

—— -   14 Q. B. D. 611
    See BILL OF EXCHANGE—SECURITIES FOR. 3.

DOUBLE PORTIONS -   20 Ch. D. 81
    See SETTLEMENT—SATISFACTION.

DOUBTFUL TITLE—Specific performance—Vendor and purchaser   18 Ch. D. 381
    See BANKRUPTCY—ASSETS. 15.

DOWER.

1. —— Divorce—20 & 21 *Vict.* c. 85.] A wife having obtained a decree for dissolution of marriage in the Court for Divorce and Matrimonial Causes on the ground of her husband's misconduct :—*Held*, by so doing to have lost her right to dower. FRAMPTON *v.* STEPHENS   21 Ch. D. 164

DOWER—*continued.*

2. —— **Release of** *by Widow to Mortgagee—Reconveyance.*] The owner in fee of certain lands died intestate, leaving a widow entitled to dower thereout. The heir-at-law executed a mortgage of the lands to secure a sum of money advanced to him by a building society. The widow was a party to the mortgage deed, by which, "for the purpose of extinguishing her right to dower," she granted and released the lands to the mortgagees, the trustees of the building society. It was provided by the deed that, upon repayment of the moneys secured thereby, a receipt should be indorsed thereon in the form given by 6 & 7 Will. 4, c. 32, to the intent that the deed should be vacated and the property comprised therein be revested in the person or persons for the time being interested in the equity of redemption therein. The moneys secured by the deed having been repaid, and the statutory receipt indorsed thereon:—*Held,* that the widow was, notwithstanding the release of her dower contained in the mortgage deed, entitled to have dower assigned to her out of the premises comprised in the deed.—*Dawson* v. *Bank of Whitehaven* (6 Ch. D. 218) distinguished. MEEK v. CHAMBERLAIN   -   -   8 Q. B. D. 31

DRAINAGE   - ˙   27 Ch. D. 665
  See LOCAL GOVERNMENT—LOCAL AUTHORITY. 14.

—— Cost of—Ordinary outgoings 28 Ch. D. 431
  See WILL—WORDS. 14.

—— Nuisance by Local Board   22 Ch. D. 221
  See NUISANCE—REMEDIES. 4.

—— Right to use -   -   - 17 Ch. D. 246
  See METROPOLIS—MANAGEMENT ACTS. 9.

DRAMA—Copyright in˙   -   13 Q. B. D. 843;
                  [21 Ch. D. 232
  See COPYRIGHT—DRAMATIC. 2, 3.

DRAWER—Bill of exchange—Name in blank
                  [25 Ch. D. 666
  See BILL OF EXCHANGE—ACCEPTANCE.

—— Cheque—Bankruptcy of payee — Duty to stop cheque   -   - 19 Ch. D. 409
  See BANKRUPTCY — PROTECTED TRANSACTION. 8.

DUCHY OF LANCASTER—Attorney-General of—Right to file information in High Court
                  [14 Q. B. D. 195
  See ATTORNEY-GENERAL OF DUCHY OF LANCASTER.

—— Attorney-General of—Right to attend proceedings in lunacy   - 21 Ch. D. 613
  See LUNATIC—JURISDICTION. 4.

DUES—Harbour—Scotch law   8 App. Cas. 658
  See SCOTCH LAW—HARBOUR. 2.

DURANTE MINORE ÆTATE   - 16 Ch. D. 49
  See ADMINISTRATOR—LIMITED. 4.

DUTY—Public revenue.
  See Statutes and Cases under REVENUE.

DWELLING-HOUSE—Occupation of part of
                  [12 Q. B. D. 381
  · *See* MUNICIPAL CORPORATION — FRANCHISE.

—— Occupation of part of   -   8 Q. B. D. 195;
                  [10 Q. B. D. 577
  See PARLIAMENT—FRANCHISE. 2, 3.

—— Separate estate   -   - 24 Ch D. 346
  See HUSBAND AND WIFE — SEPARATE ESTATE. 2.

DYING WITHOUT ISSUE   - 9 App. Cas. 890
  See WILL—ESTATE IN REALTY. 2.

E.

EARNINGS—Personal labour of bankrupt
　　　　　　　　　　　　　[17 Ch. D. 768
　　See BANKRUPTCY—UNDISCHARGED BANK-
　　　RUPT. 4.

EASEMENT.

—— LIGHT.
　　See LIGHT.
—— SUPPORT.
　　See SUPPORT.
—— WATERCOURSE.
　　See WATERCOURSE.
—— WAY.
　　See WAY.

1. —— *Fascia—Adjoining Tenement—Common Landlord.*] The Plaintiff was lessee of a house numbered 152 in A. Street, but which lay behind Nos. 151 and 153 in that street, and at the bottom of a court approached by a passage from A. Street, half of which passage was under the first floor of No. 151, and the other half under the first floor of No. 153. The passage was closed by a gate in the plane of the front of 151 and 153, which was hung on the wall of 153, but was admitted to be part of the Plaintiff's premises. All three houses belonged to the same landlord. Above the gate was a fascia of cement eight feet long, half of which was on the wall of 151, and the other half on that of 153. The fascia had existed from about 1845, and the number of the Plaintiff's house and the name and business of the occupier for the time being had always been painted on it. No. 153 was demised to the Defendant in 1874 without any express reservation of the fascia, and the Plaintiff became lessee of No. 152 in 1876 :—*Held* (affirming the decision of Kay, J.), that the fascia must be held to be a parcel of the property demised to the Plaintiff, and that he was entitled to prevent the Defendant from interfering with it. FRANCIS *v.* HAY-
WARD　　-　　20 Ch. D. 773; 22 Ch. D. 177

2. —— *Foreshore—Prescription Act (2 & 3 Will. 4, c. 71), s. 8—" Person entitled to any reversion"—Building Agreement by Tenant for Life—Amendment of Pleadings—Practice.*] In an action to restrain the removal of shingle from, and the placing of bathing-machines upon, a part of the foreshore of the sea at M., the Plaintiff claimed to be tenant in possession of the locus in quo under a building agreement granted him by the lord of the manor of M., who was tenant for life of the property under a settlement. By his statement of defence the Defendant set up a forty years' uninterrupted user and enjoyment of the locus in quo by himself and his predecessors in title for the purposes complained of, and denied that the Plaintiff was or ever had been in possession of the locus in quo "save subject to the right of the Defendant." At the trial, Fry, J., refused the Defendant leave to amend his statement of defence by striking out the qualifying words, so as to make his denial of the Plaintiff's possession an unqualified one :—*Held*, on appeal, that the

EASEMENT—*continued.*
amendment ought to have been allowed.—*Golding* v. *Wharton Saltworks Company* (1 Q. B. D. 374) explained.—*Held*, also, per Fry, J., that the words " person entitled to any reversion" in the 8th section of the Prescription Act (2 & 3 Will. 4, c. 71) included a person entitled as a remainderman; that the Plaintiff being in possession of the locus in quo under the agreement at least as tenant at will to the reversioner, was also a person "entitled to any reversion" within the section, and could therefore maintain the action.—But, *held*, by the Court of Appeal, 1. That on the true construction of the building agreement the Plaintiff had no estate whatever in the locus in quo, but only a right of entry thereon for the purposes of that agreement, and therefore could not maintain the action; 2. That it was, therefore, unnecessary to decide the question raised on the 8th section of the Prescription Act; but their Lordships intimated that it must not be concluded that they agreed with the decision of the Court below on that point. LAIRD *v.* BRIGGS
　　　　　　　　　　[16 Ch. D. 440; 19 Ch. D. 22.

—— Grant of.
　　See DEED—*Statutes.*

—— Railway—Right to cross lands of another company 22 Ch. D. 677; 9 App. Cas. 787
　　See LANDS CLAUSES ACT—COMPULSORY
　　　POWERS. 3.

—— Railway—Right to make tunnel
　　　　　　　　　　　　　　[21 Ch. D. 143
　　See LANDS CLAUSES ACT—COMPULSORY
　　　POWERS. 2.

—— Right of way — Forty years' enjoyment — Remainderman —Reversion expectant on term of life or years -　15 Q. B. D. 629.
　　See PRESCRIPTION. 2.

EAST INDIA STOCK—Investment of money in Court　　　　　　　　　　22 Ch. D. 93.
　　See PRACTICE—SUPREME COURT—PAY-
　　　MENT INTO COURT. 5.

ECCLESIASTICAL COMMISSIONERS.

Church Estates Commissioners.] *The Act* 14 *& 15 Vict. c. 104, so far as it is not repealed, and the several Acts amending the same are continued until the 31st of December,* 1886, *by the Act* 48 & 49 *Vict. c.* 59.

The Act 48 & 49 *Vict. c.* 55, *explains sect.* 34 *of the Ecclesiastical Commissioners Act,* 1840.

Tatenhill Rectory.] *By the Act* 48 & 49 *Vict. c.* 31, *the Act* 3 & 4 *Vict. c.* 113, *and Acts amending the same, apply to rectory of Tatenhill.*

—— Glebe Lands—*Drainage and Improvement Company—Rent-charge—Inclosure Commissioners, Order by—Arrears—Sale of Lands—Demurrer.*] A rent-charge for a certain period of time, in arrear, charged by an order made by the Inclosure Commissioners upon the inheritance of the glebe lands of a rectory, under the provisions of the General Land Drainage and Improvement Com-

ECCLESIASTICAL COMMISSIONERS—*contd.*

pany's Act of 1849 (12 & 13 Vict. c. xci.), was, under the provisions of the same Act, ordered to be raised by a sale of the glebe lands.—In an action by the owners of a rent-charge in arrear, charged on glebe lands, for a declaration that they were entitled under the order made by the Inclosure Commissioners to a charge on the lands for the sums due and to become due of the rent-charge, and asking for a sale of the lands, the Ecclesiastical Commissioners were made Defendants :— *Held*, on demurrer, that they were not necessary parties. SCOTTISH WIDOWS' FUND *v.* CRAIG

[20 Ch. D. 208

—— Action against collegiate body 18 Ch. D. 596
See CHARITY—COMMISSIONERS. 1.

—— Inclosure of commons.
See INCLOSURE—*Statutes.*

—— Land of—Easement - 19 Ch. D. 281
See SUPPORT. 2.

ECCLESIASTICAL JURISDICTION.

See ECCLESIASTICAL LAW — BISHOP—*Statutes.*

ECCLESIASTICAL LAW :—　　　　　　Col.

I. BISHOP	-	-	-	- 521
II. CHURCH	-	-	-	- 521
III. CHURCHYARD	-	-	-	522
IV. CLERGY			-	522
V. DILAPIDATIONS	-			523

—— PRACTICE.
See PRACTICE—ECCLESIASTICAL.

I. ECCLESIASTICAL LAW—BISHOP.

Jurisdiction.] *Such of the provisions of the Act 10 & 11 Vict. c. 98 as are continued by 21 & 22 Vict. c. 50, are continued by 48 & 49 Vict. c. 59, until the 31st of December, 1886.*

—— Quare Impedit—*Benefice — Refusal of Bishop to institute Clerk—Grounds of Refusal—Fitness of Clerk—Offences against Ecclesiastical Law.*] A bishop refused to institute a clerk in holy orders to a benefice on the grounds that he had, whilst acting as curate to a former holder of the benefice, habitually committed offences against ecclesiastical law and failed to observe the Book of Common Prayer, by wearing unlawful vestments and doing unlawful acts in respect of matters of ritual when officiating in the communion service; and that he declined to undertake not to repeat the offences in the future. In an action against the bishop in which the patron claimed a declaration that he was entitled to have the clerk instituted :—*Held*, that the Defendant had acted within his discretion in refusing to institute the clerk upon the grounds stated, and was therefore entitled to judgment. HEYWOOD *v.* BISHOP OF MANCHESTER - 12 Q. B. D. 404

II. ECCLESIASTICAL LAW—CHURCH.

—— Faculty—*Judicial Discretion—Opinion of Parishioners—Matters of Taste and Fancy.*] Where the incumbent and churchwardens with the approval of the vestry apply for a faculty for alterations in their parish church, and the grant or refusal of the faculty is merely a matter for the discretion of the ordinary, the faculty ought not to be granted unless it is proved to the satisfaction

II. ECCLESIASTICAL LAW—CHURCH—*contd.*

of the ordinary that if the proposed alterations are carried out, the church will be thereby rendered more convenient, more fit for the accommodation of the parishioners who worship there, more suitable, more appropriate or more adequate to its purposes, or that there exists either on the part of the parishioners generally, or of the parishioners actually attending the church, a general desire in favour of the faculty being granted. PEEK *v.* TROWER - - 7 P. D. 21

III. ECCLESIASTICAL LAW—CHURCHYARD.

The Act 44 & 45 Vict. c. 2 (the Burial and Registration Act Doubts Removal Act, 1881), sect. 1 enacts: Nothing in the 11th section of the Burial Laws Amendment Act, 1880, shall have, or be deemed in law to have had, the effect of repealing, or in any manner altering, any of the provisions contained in the 17th section of the Births and Deaths Registration Act, 1874, in any case whatever, save and except only the case of a burial under the Burial Laws Amendment Act, 1880.

IV. ECCLESIASTICAL LAW—CLERGY.

The Act 48 & 49 Vict. c. 54, amends the law relating to Pluralities.

1. —— District — *New Parish — Marriages, Right to solemnize—Marriage Fees, Right to—New Parish Act, 1843 (6 & 7 Vict. c. 37), ss. 11, 15—New Parish Act, 1856 (19 & 20 Vict. c. 104), ss. 14, 15.*] The publication of the banns of marriage and the solemnization of marriage are "ecclesiastical purposes" within the meaning of 19 & 20 Vict. c. 104, s. 14, and, where a district becomes within this section a separate and distinct parish for ecclesiastical purposes, the incumbent of such parish has the exclusive right of performing the office of marriage in the case of persons resident in his parish, and of receiving the fees for such marriages, and consequently the incumbent of the mother parish has no right to solemnize such marriages in the church of the mother parish or to receive the fees for the same. FULLER *v.* ALFORD

[10 Q. B. D. 418

2. —— Donative—*Transfer of Advowson by Patron during Vacancy—Trust to appoint Nominee—Nomination of Self—Right to Benefice.*] The patron of a donative benefice, being a qualified clergyman and officiating curate of the church, by deed-poll, executed during a vacancy of the benefice, granted the advowson to a trustee in trust to present whomsoever the patron should nominate; the patron then by word of mouth nominated himself, and the trustee by deed-poll granted the office of rector to him :—*Held*, that the transaction was valid, and that he thereupon became rector and entitled to the profits of the benefice. LOWE *v.* BISHOP OF CHESTER

[10 Q. B. D. 407

3. —— Incumbents' Resignation Act, 1871 (34 & 35 Vict. c. 44), s. 10—*Retired Clerk—Pension—Debt due by retired Clerk to Incumbent—Set-off.*] By the 10th section of the Incumbents' Resignation Act, 1871, the pension allowed to a retiring clerk is made a charge upon the revenues of the benefice, "and shall be recoverable as a debt at law or in equity from the incumbent of the said benefice by the retired clerk, his execu-

IV. ECCLESIASTICAL LAW—CLERGY—contd.

tors, administrators, and assigns, ... but shall not be transferable at law or in equity."—In an action by a retired clerk against the incumbent of the benefice for payment of the arrears of the pension that had been allowed him under the Act :—Held, that the incumbent could not set off against such arrears a judgment debt previously due to him from the retired clerk. GATHERCOLE v. SMITH
[17 Ch. D. 1

V. ECCLESIASTICAL LAW—DILAPIDATIONS.

—— Sequestration of Benefice—Dilapidations of Glebe Buildings—Repairs done by Sequestrator—Ecclesiastical Dilapidations Act, 1871 (34 & 35 Vict. c. 43), ss. 12–16, 72—Accounts of Sequestrator, Objection to.] A benefice having been sequestrated under a writ of sequestration in an action, an inspection of the glebe buildings by the diocesan surveyor was directed by the bishop, and a report made by such surveyor under the Ecclesiastical Dilapidations Act, 1871. The report estimated the cost of the necessary repairs to the buildings at £140, and no objections were taken to such report under s. 16 of the Act. The sequestrator, being subsequently of opinion that the repairs provided for by the surveyor's report were inadequate, expended on the repairs of the buildings a much larger sum than £140. No inspection or report, except as before mentioned, was ordered by the bishop or made by the surveyor :—Held, that the sequestrator had no authority to expend on repairs out of the proceeds of the benefice a larger sum than that estimated as necessary by the surveyor's report under the Ecclesiastical Dilapidations Act, 1871, and that such expenditure must be disallowed. KIMBER v. PARAVICINI
[15 Q. B. D. 222

ECCLESIASTICAL LAW — Church of South Africa - - 7 App. Cas. 484
See COLONIAL LAW—CAPE OF GOOD HOPE. 1.

—— Advowson—Consolidated benefice — Right of presentation—Quare impedit
See ADVOWSON. 2. [15 Q. B. D. 432

EDUCATION—Application of charitable gift to [18 Ch. D. 310
See CHARITY—MANAGEMENT. 3.

—— Appropriation of charitable gift to [7 App. Cas. 463
See ENDOWED SCHOOLS ACT. 2.

—— Infant—Right to control - 21 Ch. D. 817 ; [24 Ch. D. 317 ; 28 Ch. D. 82
See INFANT—EDUCATION. 1, 2, 3.

EJECTMENT—Disclaimer of lessor's title [16 Ch. D. 730
See LANDLORD AND TENANT—RE-ENTRY. 2.

—— Discovery 20 Ch. D. 484 ; 8 App. Cas. 217
See PRACTICE—SUPREME COURT—INTERROGATORIES. 11.

—— Relief against forfeiture—Non-payment of rent—Disallowance of costs to Plaintiff [14 Q. B. D. 347
See LANDLORD AND TENANT—RE-ENTRY. 7.

EJECTMENT—continued.

—— Statute of Limitations—Mortgage [6 Q. B. D. 345 ; 7 App. Cas. 235
See LIMITATIONS, STATUTE OF—REALTY. 4.

—— Tenant holding over—Expiration of landlord's title—Writ of possession [15 Q. B. D. 294
See LANDLORD AND TENANT—RE-ENTRY. 3.

EJUSDEM GENERIS—Bequest in will
See WILL—WORDS. 9. [30 Ch. D. 92

ELDEST SON 26 Ch. D. 363, 382
See SETTLEMENT—CONSTRUCTION. 2, 3.

ELECTION.

1. —— Appointment.] A testator, having power under a settlement to appoint the settled hereditaments to children of his first marriage only, appointed the settled hereditaments (describing them as his own property) in favour of a son of the first marriage subject to a charge in favour of his other children, including the children of his second marriage, and he devised property of his own to the same son subject to the same charges in favour of his other children " so as to equalise the shares of all his children in all his property ":—Held, that a case of election arose in favour of the children of the second marriage.—Woolridge v. Woolridge (Joh. 63) distinguished. WHITE v. WHITE - 22 Ch. D. 555

2. —— Appointment—Special Power — Appointment to Persons not Objects of Power—Direction to pay Debts of Appointor.] A testatrix had, under the will of a brother who had predeceased her, a power to appoint his property by will among his nephews and nieces and the children or child of deceased nephews and nieces. She, by her will, gave all the real and personal estate of which she might be seised or possessed at the time of her death, or over which she might have any testamentary power of disposition, to trustees, upon trust for sale and conversion, and to stand possessed of the proceeds (which she described as " my said trust funds ") upon trust to pay costs and expenses, and to pay her debts and funeral expenses and certain pecuniary legacies, and then upon trust as to two one-fourth parts of her trust funds respectively for persons who were objects of the power ; and upon trust as to the other two one-fourth parts respectively for persons who were not objects of the power. And she declared that, in case of the failure of the trusts thereinbefore declared of any of the one-fourth parts of her trust funds, the one-fourth part, or so much thereof of which the trusts should fail, should be held upon the trusts thereinbefore declared of the others or other of the fourth parts of which the trusts should not fail :—Held, that the testatrix had manifested an intention to exercise the power, and that as to one moiety of the brother's property the power was well exercised :—Held, also, that, as to the other moiety of the brother's property, the appointment was invalid, but that, by virtue of the gift " in case of the failure of any of the trusts thereinbefore declared," that moiety went to the persons to whom the first moiety was

ELECTION—*continued.*

well appointed, and that, consequently, no case of election arose. *In re* SWINBURNE. SWINBURNE *v.* PITT - - 27 Ch. D. 696

3. —— *Conversion—Real and Personal Estate —Election to take Personalty as Realty—Real Estate in Lease with Option to Tenant to purchase Reversion.*] A testator by his will gave his real estate and the residue of his personal estate to trustees, on trust to sell his real estate, and to convert and get in his residuary personal estate, and to stand possessed of the moneys arising from both, on trust to invest the same, and to pay the income to his wife during her life or widowhood, and, after her death or second marriage, upon trust to divide the trust funds equally between such of his children as should be living at his death, and the issue of such of them as might be then dead. The testator died in 1869. The wife and two infant children survived him. There were no issue of any deceased child. Both the children died before the wife unmarried and intestate, the one who died last dying in 1876. The wife did not marry again, and she died in 1885 intestate. The only real estate of the testator was a house, of which he had in 1869 agreed to grant a lease for twenty years, with an option to the tenant to purchase the reversion at any time during the term. At the death of the widow this option had not been exercised, and the house had not been sold by the trustees. After the deaths of the children the widow continued in receipt of the rent of the house :—*Held*, that by reason of the tenant's option to purchase the house, the widow's continued receipt of the rent was no evidence of an election by her to take the property as real estate, and that on her death it descended as personalty to her next of kin.—*In re Gordon* (6 Ch. D. 531) distinguished. *In re* LEWIS. FOXWELL *v.* LEWIS - - - 30 Ch. D. 654

4. —— *Married Woman — Appointment— Donee unaware of Power—Exercise of Power— Approbation and Reprobation.*] A married woman being (although unaware of it) the donee of a general power of appointment by deed or will over policy moneys payable upon her own death, concurred with her husband in settling certain family estates by an indenture which treated the policy moneys as the husband's own property, and settled them also. Her concurrence in the settlement was for a purpose entirely unconnected with the policy moneys, and under it she took a life interest in remainder after her husband's death in the estates, but no interest in the policy moneys. She survived her husband, received in respect of her life interest in the estates sums exceeding the amount of the policy moneys, and died, having by her will given all property over which she had any disposing power to certain beneficiaries :—*Held*, that by her will she had exercised her general power so as to make the policy moneys her own assets, and *Held* also, that having taken under the settlement, benefits exceeding the value of the policy moneys, she could not by the exercise of the power take the policy moneys out of the settlement, without making good to the settlement beneficiaries an equal amount from her own estate; and accordingly that the policy moneys must be paid to the settlement trustees.

ELECTION—*continued.*

—*Semble,* The concurrence of the donee of the power in the deed of settlement, for purposes unconnected with the policy moneys subject to the power, and in ignorance of the existence of the power, could not operate as an exercise of the power although the deed purported to pass the policy moneys. GRIFFITH-BOSCAWEN *v.* SCOTT [26 Ch. D. 358

5. —— *Married Woman — Restraint on Anticipation.*] In the case of a married woman to whom an interest with a restraint on anticipation attached thereto is given by the same instrument as that which gives rise to a question of election, the doctrine of election does not apply, as the value of her interest in the property to be relinquished by way of compensation has, by the terms of the instrument, been made inalienable. *In re* WHEATLEY. SMITH *v.* SPENCE - 27 Ch. D. 606

6. —— *Married Woman—Settlement on Marriage of Female Infant—Life Interest for Separate Use—Restraint on Anticipation—Covenant by her to settle after-acquired Property—Bequest to her after Twenty-one during Coverture for her Separate Use—Voidable Covenant—Approbation and Reprobation—Sequestration of Life Interest.*] The doctrine of election is founded upon the rule that a person cannot take under and against the same instrument, and the equity is not that the person electing to take against the instrument shall be required to assign, but that he shall not be permitted to take, the benefit given to him thereunder.—Accordingly the Court is not prevented from enforcing this rule by the incapacity of the person so electing to alienate the interest taken under the settlement. And upon this principle the Court can, notwithstanding a restraint on anticipation attaching thereto, sequester the life interest of a married woman electing to take against a settlement until compensation has been made thereout to the persons disappointed under the settlement by such election.—Upon the marriage of a female infant in 1860 personalty was settled by her father upon trusts under which she took the first life interest for her separate use without power of anticipation, and the settlement contained a covenant by her to settle all her after-acquired property upon trusts under which the husband took the first life interest. In 1883 and during the coverture personal property was bequeathed to her for her separate use, and she chose to avoid her covenant and to take this property instead of bringing it into the settlement. She also contended that she was entitled to keep the life interest under the settlement which she was restrained from anticipating without making compensation thereout to the persons disappointed under the settlement, upon the ground that as she was restrained from alienating such life interest the Court could not impound it :—*Held*, that as the married woman had elected to defeat one of the provisions of the settlement, she was not competent to take a life interest under another of them, and that, notwithstanding the restraint on anticipation, the income which would have been payable to her if she had not so elected, ought to be applied in making compensation to the persons disappointed by her election for the benefits of which they had been thereby deprived, and that

ELECTION—*continued.*

the trustees of the settlement must retain and apply the same accordingly.— *Smith* v. *Lucas* (18 Ch. D. 531) and *In re Wheatley* (27 Ch. D. 606) dissented from. *In re* VARDON'S TRUSTS

[28 Ch. D. 124

[Reversed by the Court of Appeal, 31 Ch. D. 275.]

—— Invalid appointment   -   26 Ch. D. 208
See SETTLEMENT—CONSTRUCTION. 7.

—— Lunatic — Confirmation of settlement by married woman—Election by Court

[22 Ch. D. 263

See SETTLEMENT—FUTURE PROPERTY. 3.

—— Married woman—Separate estate—Restraint on anticipation -   -   18 Ch. D. 531
See SETTLEMENT—FUTURE PROPERTY. 2.

—— Of remedy—Concurrent actions   22 Ch. D.

[397 ; 23 Ch. D. 225

See PRACTICE—SUPREME COURT—STAYING PROCEEDINGS. 6, 7.

—— Sale under partition action—Married woman

[16 Ch. D. 362

See PARTITION SUIT—SALE. 3.

—— To charge old or new firm   7 App. Cas. 345
See PARTNERSHIP—DISSOLUTION. 4.

ELECTION AGENT.
See PARLIAMENT—ELECTION—*Statutes.*

ELECTION COMMISSIONERS—Expenses of
See PARLIAMENT — ELECTION COMMISSIONERS—*Statutes.*

ELECTION FOR PARLIAMENT.
See Cases and Statutes under
    PARLIAMENT—ELECTION.
    PARLIAMENT—FRANCHISE.

ELECTION FOR SCHOOL BOARD.
See ELEMENTARY EDUCATION ACTS—SCHOOL BOARD—*Statutes.*

ELECTION, MUNICIPAL.
See Cases and Statutes under
    MUNICIPAL CORPORATION—ELECTION.
    MUNICIPAL CORPORATION—FRANCHISE.

ELECTION PETITION.
See Cases and Statutes under
    PARLIAMENT—ELECTION PETITION.
    MUNICIPAL CORPORATION — ELECTION.

ELECTRIC LIGHT.
The Act 45 & 46 *Vict. c.* 56 (*the Electric Lighting Act,* 1882), *facilitates and regulates the supply of electricity for lighting and other purposes in the United Kingdom.*

ELEGIT—Application for receiver   6 Q. B. D. 75
See PRACTICE — SUPREME COURT — RECEIVER. 2.

—— Bankruptcy—Seizure but not delivery of possession -   12 Q. B. D. 224
See BANKRUPTCY—SECURED CREDITOR. 10.

—— Bankruptcy—Protected transaction

[18 Ch. D. 137

See BANKRUPTCY—PROTECTED TRANSACTION. 4.

I. ELEMENTARY EDUCATION ACTS — ATTENDANCE.

1. —— Employment of Child—39 & 40 *Vict. c.* 79, *ss.* 8, 11, *sub-s,* 1 ; 41 & 42 *Vict. c.* 16, *Sched.*— "*Full Time Employment.*"] By 39 & 40 Vict. c. 79, s. 11, sub-s. 1, if the parent of any child above the age of five years "who is under this Act prohibited from being taken into full time employment," habitually and without reasonable excuse neglects to provide efficient elementary instruction for his child, a court of summary jurisdiction may order that the child do attend school :—*Held,* that sub-sect. 1 refers to sect. 8, which applies certain sections of the Factory Acts to the employment and education of children, and that, as those sections have been repealed by 41 & 42 Vict. c. 16, Sched., there can be no child within the terms of 39 & 40 Vict. c. 79, s. 11, sub-s. 1, "who is under this Act prohibited from being taken into full time employment," and therefore sub-sect. 1 has ceased to operate. SAUNDERS *v.* CRAWFORD   9 Q. B. D. 612

2. —— Employment of Child—"*Full Time Employment*"—39 & 40 *Vict. c.* 79, *ss.* 4, 5, 8, 11.] By sect. 5 of the Elementary Education Act, 1876, a person shall not take into his employment any child (1) who is under the age of ten years, or (2) who, being of the age of ten years or upwards, has not obtained the certificate of proficiency, or of due attendance at school, prescribed by the Act, unless such child, being of the age of ten years and upwards, is employed and attending school under the Factory Acts, or any by-law made under the Elementary Education Act, 1870. —By sect. 11, if the parent of any child above the age of five years, "who is under this Act prohibited from being taken into full time employment," habitually, and without reasonable excuse, "neglects to provide efficient elementary instruction for such child, an order that the child attend one of the prescribed schools may be obtained by the local authority of the district before a Court of summary jurisdiction.—By sect. 48 "a child in this Act means a child between the ages of five and fourteen years."— An attendance order was applied for, under sect. 11, in respect of two children aged nine and thirteen years respectively. Neither of the children were in any employment, nor attending any school, nor had either of them obtained any certificate under sect. 5 :—*Held,* that the words of sect. 11 "any child who is under this Act prohibited from being taken into full time employment" applied to any child prohibited from being taken into employment by sect. 5, and therefore that an attendance order could be made in respect of each child.—*Saunders* v. *Crawford* (9 Q. B. D. 612) not followed. WINYARD *v.* TOOGOOD. HANCE *v.* FORTNUM   -   10 Q. B. D. 218

3. —— Employment of Child—33 & 34 *Vict. c.* 75, *s.* 74, *and* 39 & 40 *Vict. c.* 79—*By-laws* —*Reasonable Excuse.*] A school board made a by-law under sect. 74 of the Elementary Educa-

I. ELEMENTARY EDUCATION ACTS—ATTEN-
DANCE—*continued.*

tion Act, 1870, providing that "the parent of every child of not less than five nor more than thirteen years of age shall cause such child to attend school, unless there be a reasonable excuse for non-attendance," and that "any of the following reasons shall be a reasonable excuse, namely, that the child is under efficient instruction in some other manner; that the child has been prevented from attending school by sickness or any unavoidable cause; that there is no public elementary school open, which the child could attend, within two miles from the residence of such child." Where it was shewn that non-attendance was caused by the child, a girl aged twelve, with fair elementary instruction, having been in respectable employment, earning wages, which she gave to her parents, who were poor, industrious, and respectable people, and applied them to the support of their other children, whom otherwise, from no fault of the parents, they would have been unable sufficiently to support: *Held*, that these facts constituted a "reasonable excuse" for non-attendance. LONDON SCHOOL BOARD *v.* DUGGAN　　-　　- 13 Q. B. D. 176

4. —— Justices—*Jurisdiction in Cases under the Elementary Education Acts—Union extending into several Counties—Elementary Education Act, 1876 (39 & 40 Vict. c. 79), ss. 12, 34; Poor Law Amendment Act, 1867 (30 & 31 Vict. c. 106, s. 27.]* The effect of sect. 34 of the Elementary Education Act, 1876 (39 & 40 Vict. c. 79)—which incorporates for certain purposes all enactments relating to guardians and their officers—is to enable proceedings before justices for non-compliance with attendance orders and for breach of by-laws under the Elementary Education Acts, in cases where the parents proceeded against reside in a union extending into different counties, to be taken before the justices of either county. THE QUEEN *v.* EATON　　-　　- 8 Q. B. D. 158

5. —— Liability of Parent—*33 & 34 Vict. c. 75, s. 3—Neglect to educate a Child—Liability where Child in the Actual Custody of some other Person.]* The Respondent was summoned for non-compliance with an order under sect. 11 of the Elementary Education Act, 1876, to educate a child of which she was the parent. The child was not residing with the Respondent, but with a relative, and the magistrate on that ground refused to convict:—*Held* (by Lord Coleridge, C.J., Pollock, B., and Manisty, J.), that sect. 3 of 33 & 34 Vict. c. 75, which declares that the term parent shall include "guardian and every person who is liable to maintain, or has the actual custody of any child," does not affect the primary liability of the parent, if there be one, and that the Respondent ought to have been convicted. SCHOOL BOARD FOR LONDON *v.* JACKSON
[7 Q. B. D. 502

6. —— Liability of Parent—*33 & 34 Vict. c. 75; 39 & 40 Vict. c. 79; 43 & 44 Vict. c. 23— "Reasonable Excuse"—By-laws.]* A by-law made under the Elementary Education Acts provided that, "The parent of every child of not less than five nor more than thirteen years of age, shall cause such child to attend school, unless there be a reasonable excuse for non-attendance.

I. ELEMENTARY EDUCATION ACTS—ATTEN-
DANCE—*continued.*

Reasonable excuses.—Any of the following reasons shall be a reasonable excuse, namely: (*a.*) That the child is under efficient instruction in some other manner; (*b.*) That the child has been prevented from attending school by sickness or an unavoidable cause; (*c.*) That there is no public elementary school open which the child can attend within two miles. . . ."—From the 18th of May to the 23rd of September, the Respondent, an engine-driver, caused his child to be sent daily from home in time to arrive at school when it opened. He did not receive any notice that the child had not duly attended, except on two occasions. On both occasions the Respondent's wife corrected the child. Nevertheless it often failed to attend school. At the hearing of an information, which charged that the Respondent on and ever since the 18th of May had neglected the by-law in not causing his child to attend school, the justices found that he had done all that could reasonably be expected of him to secure the attendance of the child at school, and had reasonable grounds for believing, and did believe, the child was duly attending school, and had, therefore, a "reasonable excuse" for not causing the child to attend school:—*Held*, that there may be other "reasonable excuses" within the meaning of the by-law besides the three reasons therein specified, and that the justices were right. BELPER SCHOOL ATTENDANCE COMMITTEE *v.* BAILEY
[9 Q. B. D. 259

7. —— Non-payment of Fees—*Causing Child to attend School, what is—By-law—Penalty—Elementary Education Act, 1870 (33 & 34 Vict. c. 75), s. 74.]* The London School Board made by-laws, under s. 74 of the Elementary Education Act, 1870, providing that the parent of every child, if not less than five nor more than thirteen years of age, should cause such child to attend school unless there was a reasonable cause for non-attendance, and that every parent who should not observe or neglect any by-law should be liable upon conviction to a penalty.—The Respondent sent his child, aged ten, to one of the Board's schools, but did not pay, though he was able to pay, the weekly fees for tuition prescribed by the School Board with the consent of the Education Department. The child was admitted to the school, and received instruction therein:—*Held*, that the Respondent had not caused his child to attend school within the meaning of the by-laws, and therefore was liable to the penalty. LONDON SCHOOL BOARD *v.* WOOD　　15 Q. B. D. 415

II. ELEMENTARY EDUCATION ACTS—FEES.

1. —— Liability of Parent—*Child attending Board School without Fees—33 & 34 Vict. c. 75, s. 17; 39 & 40 Vict. c. 79, ss. 10, 11, 12; 43 & 44 Vict. c. 23, s. 4.]* A parent who, under an order by a court of summary jurisdiction that his child shall attend a board school, and that he do see that the order is complied with, causes the child to attend school, but without the school fees, and without having applied to the guardians under 33 & 34 Vict. c. 75, for payment of such fees, or to the school board under sect. 17 for a remission of them, is liable to be convicted under the Elementary Education Act, 1876 (39 &

II. ELEMENTARY EDUCATION ACTS—FEES—
continued.

40 Vict. c. 79), s. 10, for non-compliance with the
order.—*In re Murphy* (2 Q. B. D. 397) discussed.
RICHARDSON *v.* SAUNDERS. SAUNDERS *v.* RICHARD-
SON　　　　6 Q. B. D. 313; 7 Q. B. D. 388

2. —— Liability of Parent—*Action to recover
Fees for Tuition—Implied Promise to pay Fees—
Action of Debt upon Statutes—By-laws—33 & 34
Vict. c. 75—36 & 37 Vict. c. 86—39 & 40 Vict.
c. 79—43 & 44 Vict. c. 23.*] No action to recover
arrears of fees for tuition can be maintained
by a school board against the parent of a child
attending a public elementary school; for, it
being compulsory upon the parent to cause his
child to attend a school, his act in sending the
child to school is not voluntary, and no promise
to pay the fees can be implied; and the Elementary Education Acts, 1870 to 1880, contemplate that the remedy to enforce payment of fees
shall be by an attendance order and by summary
proceedings before justices and not by action.—
Saunders v. *Richardson* (7 Q. B. D. 388) approved.
SCHOOL BOARD FOR LONDON *v.* WRIGHT
[12 Q. B. D. 578

**III. ELEMENTARY EDUCATION ACTS—HOME
LESSONS.**

—— Detention of Scholar—*Assault—33 & 34
Vict. c. 75—39 & 40 Vict. c. 79.*] The Elementary Education Acts, 1870 and 1876, do not
authorize the setting of lessons to be prepared at
home by children attending a board school. The
detention at school after school hours of a child
for not doing home lessons is therefore unlawful,
and renders the master who detains the child
liable to be convicted for an assault. HUNTER *v.*
JOHNSON -　　-　　-　　13 Q. B. D. 225

**IV. ELEMENTARY EDUCATION ACTS—SCHOOL
BOARD.**

*The Act 47 & 48 Vict. c. 70, s. 38, repeals
section 33 of 33 & 34 Vict. c. 75 (the Elementary
Education Act, 1870).*

*The Act 48 & 49 Vict. c. 38 (the School Boards
Act, 1885) amends the law relating to school boards
so far as affected by the incorporation of a municipal borough and as respects the divisions of the
metropolis.*

Election.] *Order modifying the General Orders
regulating the triennial election of school boards in
boroughs and parishes.* 4th Oct., 1882.
[L. G., 1882, p. 4563

—— Compulsory Purchase of Lands—*Elementary Education Act, 1870 (33 & 34 Vict. c. 75),
ss. 19, 20, 22—Agreement for Exchange with Third
Party prior to Notice to Treat.*] A School Board
served on R. the customary notice to treat for
land belonging to him, all the requisite prelimi-
naries required by the Elementary Education
Act, 1870, having previously been complied with.
—Prior, however, to the service of such notice to
treat and to the passing of the Confirmation Act
as required by the above Act, the Board had
entertained and adopted, subject to the sanction
of the Education Department, a proposal from one
B., a neighbouring landowner, for exchanging a
portion of the land to be acquired by the Board
from R. for a piece of B.'s land, he undertaking

**IV. ELEMENTARY EDUCATION ACTS—SCHOOL
BOARD—***continued.*

to form the land so to be conveyed to him by the
Board into a public road. There was evidence to
shew that. such road, when made, would be advantageous to the school intended to be erected :—
Held, on motion by R. for an injunction to restrain
the Board from putting in force their statutory
powers with respect to so much of the land comprised in the notice to treat as they proposed to
convey to B., that the Board were justified in the
course they had taken, and could, if they obtained
the sanction of the Education Department, carry
out the proposal. ROLLS *v.* SCHOOL BOARD FOR
LONDON -　　-　　-　　27 Ch. D. 639

—— School Board—Poor-rate—Rateability
[13 Q. B. D. 929
See POOR-RATE—RATEABLE VALUE. 3.

EMBARRASSING PLEADINGS -　26 Ch. D. 778
See PRACTICE—SUPREME COURT—STRIK-
ING OUT PLEADINGS. 2.

——　　-　　-　　-　　22 Ch. D. 481
See PRACTICE — SUPREME COURT —
AMENDMENT. 1.

——　.　　-　　-　　-　　29 Ch. D. 344
See PRACTICE—SUPREME COURT—THIRD
PARTY. 7.

EMPLOYER AND WORKMAN—Apprenticeship
deed—Contract not for the benefit of
infant—38 & 39 Vict. c. 90, ss. 5, 6
[12 Q. B. D. 352
See INFANT—CONTRACTS.

—— Liability of master.
See Cases under MASTER AND SERVANT—
MASTER'S LIABILITY.

—— Summary proceeding before justices—Neglect of seamen to join ship
See SHIP—SEAMEN. [11 Q. B. D. 225

ENDOWED SCHOOLS ACT.

*The Act 48 & 49 Vict. c. 59, continues as to cer-
tain powers the Endowed Schools Act, 1869 (32 &
33 Vict. c. 56), and the several Acts amending the
same, until the 31st of December, 1886.*

1. —— Powers of Commissioners—*32 & 33
Vict. c. 56, ss. 9, 19, sub-s. 2—36 & 37 Vict. c. 87,
s. 7—Denominational School—Original Subscribers
—Effect of Regulations.*] Where the Commissioners
by their scheme provided that certain endowments
which had theretofore been applied in carrying on
the schools of a particular parish, should thenceforth be applied in exhibitions for the benefit of a
larger area of schools ; *Held,* that this was within
their powers under sect. 9 of the Act of 1869, and
that being so the way in which those powers had
been exercised was not the proper subject of appeal.—*Held,* that a charity which has no instrument of foundation, or statutes, or duly authorized
regulations impressing upon it a denominational
character, does not fall within the 19th clause of
the Act of 1869, or the 7th clause of the Act of
1873. Its trustees cannot impress upon it that
character, nor is any practice for the time being
as to the application of its funds sufficient evidence of there ever having been regulations in
existence which prescribed it.—Where a charity

ENDOWED SCHOOLS ACT—*continued.*
is established by subscriptions, the original subscribers alone are the founders, the later benefactions are on the footing of the original foundation. If its regulations are relied upon as impressing upon it a denominational character, they must be shewn to have been authorized by all the founders, and to have been issued before fifty years from their deaths. *In re* ST. LEONARD, SHOREDITCH, PAROCHIAL SCHOOLS　　　-　10 App. Cas. 304

2. —— Vested Interests—32 & 33 *Vict.* c. 56, ss. 5, 11, 14, sub-s. 1 ; s. 19, sub-s. 2—*Appropriation of Charitable Endowments to Educational Purposes by Order of Court—Due Regard to Educational Interests.*] Endowments originally given for charitable uses but made applicable to the purposes of education by a scheme and an order of the Court of Chancery are educational endowments within the meaning of the Endowed Schools Act, 1869, s. 5.—Where such endowments were actually given more than fifty years before the passing of the Act, *Held* that such subsequent appropriation of them as aforesaid cannot be deemed to be an original gift thereof within the meaning of sect. 14, sub-sect. 1, or of sect. 19, sub-sect. 2, so as to require the assent of their governing body to any scheme or provision made by the Charity Commissioners relating thereto.—Where the scheme of the Charity Commissioners increased the amount of tuition fees previously payable by a certain class of boys and added the condition that the trustees shall be satisfied that aid is needed by their parents, *Held* that such provision does not fail in due regard to their educational interests within the meaning of sect. 11 of the Act of 1869, and sect. 5 of the Amendment Act of 1873. ROSS *v.* CHARITY COMMISSIONERS
[7 App. Cas. 463

3. —— Vested Interests—32 & 33 *Vict.* c. 56, s. 39—*Petition by Inhabitants of Locality.*] In an appeal under sect. 39 of the Endowed Schools Act, 1869, by the corporation of Sutton Coldfield against two schemes of the Charity Commissioners, by which it was proposed to withdraw from that part of the funds of the corporation which was applicable for educational purposes a sum equal to £15,000, to be applied as part of the foundation of Sutton Coldfield Grammar School :—*Held,* that the scheme could not be regarded as wanting in the finality required by the Act, because it was expressed to be without prejudice to a future scheme to be framed in accordance with the Acts of Parliament, words to that effect being surplusage.—*Held* further, that sect. 11 of the Act of 1869 protects vested interests only, that is the privileges or educational advantages to which the class of persons thereby or by later Acts designated have a legal title, and cannot be invoked to protect benefits which have been enjoyed by the permission or bounty of another.—In a similar appeal by the inhabitants of the locality, *Held,* that such inhabitants had no locus standi to present it.—*In re Shaftoe's Charity* (3 App. Cas. 872) approved. *In re* SUTTON COLDFIELD GRAMMAR SCHOOL　　　-　　　-　7 App. Cas. 91

ENDOWMENT—Church of England in South Africa -　　　7 App. Cas. 484
　See COLONIAL LAW—CAPE OF GOOD HOPE. 1.

ENFRANCHISEMENT — Acknowledgment of right to production of deeds
[25 Ch. D. 600
　See VENDOR AND PURCHASER—TITLE DEEDS.

—— Copyhold—Lunatic's estate　20 Ch. D. 514
　See LUNATIC—PROPERTY. 4.

ENGINEER—Certificate　　-　11 Q. B. D. 229
　See CONTRACT—BREACH. 1.

—— Lien on ship　　　16 Ch. D. 604
　See SHIP—MARITIME LIEN. 6.

ENGLISH WILL—Scotch lands　8 App. Cas. 577
　See SCOTCH LAW—HERITABLE PROPERTY. 4.

ENGRAVINGS—Book of—Copyright.　21 Ch. D.
　See COPYRIGHT—BOOKS. 1.　　　[369

ENTAIL—Scotch law　　-　7 App. Cas. 713
　See SCOTCH LAW—ENTAIL.

—— Scotch law—English will　8 App. Cas, 577
　See SCOTCH LAW—HERITABLE PROPERTY. 4.

ENTRY IN BOOKS—College—Evidence
[17 Ch. D. 429
　See EVIDENCE — ENTRY BY DECEASED PERSON.

ENTRY INTO HOUSE—Forcible　17 Ch. D. 174;
　See FORCIBLE ENTRY. 1, 2. [18 Ch. D. 189

ENTRY OF APPEAL—Payment of deposit
[20 Ch. D. 701
　See BANKRUPTCY—APPEAL. 7.

ENTRY ON LAND—Railway company
[22 Ch. D. 25 ; 9 App. Cas. 480
　See LANDS CLAUSES ACT—COMPULSORY POWERS. 4.

ENTRY, RIGHT OF—Pretenced title—Purchase —Forfeiture　-　　-　9 Q. B. D. 128 ;
[15 Q. B. D. 491
　See RIGHT OF ENTRY. 1, 2.

EPIDEMIC AND OTHER DISEASES PREVENTION ACT, 1883.
　See LOCAL GOVERNMENT — PUBLIC HEALTH ACTS— *Statutes.*

EQUITABLE ASSETS　　-　18 Ch. D. 182
　See EXECUTOR—RETAINER. 7.

EQUITABLE EXECUTION　　-　16 Ch. D. 544;
[25 Ch. D. 413 ; 29 Ch. D. 993
　See PRACTICE—SUPREME COURT—RECEIVER. 1, 3, 4.

EQUITABLE MORTGAGE — Foreclosure—Form of order　22 Ch. D. 283 ; 25 Ch. D. 158
　See MORTGAGE—FORECLOSURE. 7, 8.

EQUITY OF REDEMPTION—Assignment of— Consolidation of mortgages　19 Ch. D.
　See MORTGAGE—CONSOLIDATION. 3. [630

—— Release of—Bill to set aside　7 App. Cas.
　See COLONIAL LAW—VICTORIA. 2. [307

—— Seizure in execution—Duty of sheriff
　See SHERIFF. 1.　　　[12 Q. B. D. 213

EQUITY TO SETTLEMENT　　16 Ch. D. 376 ;
[17 Ch. D. 778 ; 27 Ch. D. 220
　See SETTLEMENT—EQUITY TO SETTLEMENT. 1, 2, 3.

EQUIVALENT—Chemical process　24 Ch. D. 156
　See PATENT—INFRINGEMENT. 1.

EQUIVALENT—continued.

—— Use of - - 21 Ch. D. 720
　　See PATENT—VALIDITY. 2.

ESCHEAT.
　　See REAL ESTATE—Statutes.

—— Admission to copyholds 27 Ch. D. 298
　　See COPYHOLD—SURRENDER AND AD-
　　MITTANCE. 3.

—— Dominion of Canada - 8 App. Cas. 767
　　See COLONIAL LAW—CANADA—ONTARIO.
　　4.

ESTATE CLAUSE—When implied.
　　See DEED—Statutes.

ESTATE TAIL.
　　See Cases under TENANT IN TAIL.

——After-acquired property of wife 25 Ch. D. 200
　　See SETTLEMENT—FUTURE PROPERTY. 1.

—— Rule in Shelley's Case 9 App. Cas. 890
　　See WILL—ESTATE IN REALTY. 2.

—— Title of dignity—Settled Land Act
　　　　　　　　　　　[30 Ch. D. 136
　　See SETTLED LAND ACT—RESTRICTIONS.
　　2.

ESTOPPEL:— Col.
　　I. CONDUCT - - - - 535
　　II. JUDGMENT - - - - 537

I. ESTOPPEL—CONDUCT.

1. —— Forgery—Bill of Exchange—Silence—Adoption of Signature.] A person who knows that a bank is relying upon his forged signature to a bill, cannot lie by and not divulge the fact until he sees that the position of the bank is altered for the worse. But there is no principle on which his mere silence for a fortnight from the time when he first knew of the forgery, during which the position of the bank was in no way altered or prejudiced, can be held to be an admission or adoption of liability, or an estoppel. The names of A. and B. appeared on a bill as drawers and indorsers to the B. L. Co. The B. L. Co.'s Inverness bank discounted it for C., who signed it as acceptor. They had no previous dealings with A. or B. Being dishonoured when due, notice to that effect was sent to A. and B., and received late on a Saturday, but they did not communicate with the bank. On the following Monday, being the 14th of April, C. brought to the B. L. Co. a blank bill with A. and B.'s names as drawers and indorsers, apparently in the same handwriting as the previous bill. It was agreed to accept it as a renewal of the previous bill but for a less amount, the difference being paid in cash by C. Three days before it was due, notice was sent to A. and B., and again when it was dishonoured, and then through the B. L. Co.'s law agent. A fortnight after the first notice the B. L. Co. were informed for the first time that A. and B.'s signatures were forgeries, and that they declined to pay the amount in the bill. A. alleged that he called on C. on the 14th of April about the first bill, that C. admitted that he had forged his name, handed him the bill, and solemnly assured him that it had been taken up by cash; and so assured he did not think it necessary to communicate with the bank. He admitted that on that day he drank with C. and borrowed £4

I. ESTOPPEL—CONDUCT—continued.

of him. He denied positively any knowledge of the second bill until he received the bank notices. C. was convicted of the forgery. The B. L. Co. charged A. with payment of the bill on the ground that he had either authorized the use of his name, or had subsequently adopted, and accredited the bill, and therefore was estopped from denying his liability :—Held, reversing the decision of the Court below, that on the facts proved A. had neither authorized nor assented to the use of his name: nor did the circumstances of the case raise any estoppel against him.—Dictum of Parke, B., as to estoppel in Freeman v. Cooke (2 Ex. 654), approved of. M'KENZIE v. BRITISH LINEN COMPANY - - 6 App. Cas. 82

2. —— Forgery—Share Certificate issued by Secretary—Principal and Agent—Scope of Employment.] It was the duty of a secretary of a company to procure the execution of certificates of shares in the company with all requisite and prescribed formalities, and to issue them to the persons entitled to receive the same. By a resolution of the directors of the company it was provided that certificates of shares should be signed by one director, the secretary, and the accountant. The secretary of the company having executed a deed purporting to transfer certain shares in the company to one G., a purchaser of such shares, issued to G. a certificate stating that he had been registered as the owner of the shares. Such certificate was in the usual and authorized form, and sealed with the company's seal, but the signature of the director appended thereto was a forgery, and the seal of the company was, in fact, affixed thereto without the authority of the directors.—G. deposited the certificate with the Plaintiff as a security for advances, and subsequently executed a transfer of the shares to the Plaintiff. Neither G. nor the Plaintiff had any knowledge or reason to suspect that the certificate was otherwise than a genuine document, or that the matters stated therein were untrue.—The company refused to register the Plaintiff as owner of the shares, stating that there were no such shares standing in G.'s name in their books:—Held, that the company were estopped by the certificate issued by their secretary from disputing the Plaintiff's title to the shares. SHAW v. PORT PHILIP GOLD MINING COMPANY - 13 Q. B. D. 103

3. —— Negligence—Proximate Cause—Railway Company — Delivery Order.] The Defendants received a consignment of wheat and issued a delivery order for it, which came into the hands of B. Upon this delivery order B. obtained advances from the Plaintiffs. Shortly afterwards the Defendants issued a second delivery order in respect of the same consignment of wheat. The two delivery orders were different, and such as might be reasonably supposed to relate to distinct consignments of wheat. Upon this second delivery order B. obtained further advances from the Plaintiffs, who were under the belief that the delivery orders related to distinct consignments of wheat. B. having afterwards become insolvent :—Held, that the Defendants were estopped by their negligence from shewing that the two delivery orders related only to one consignment

I. ESTOPPEL—CONDUCT—*continued.*

of wheat, and that they were liable to compensate the Plaintiffs for the loss sustained by them through the advances to B. COVENTRY *v.* GREAT EASTERN RAILWAY COMPANY   **11 Q. B. D. 776**

II. ESTOPPEL—JUDGMENT.

1. —— **Chancery and Probate Divisions—***Revocation of Probate — Forgery—Jurisdiction of Chancery Division.*] In an action in the Probate Division T. and G. propounded an earlier and P. a later will. The action was compromised, and by consent verdict and judgment were taken for establishing the earlier will. Subsequently P. discovered that the earlier will was a forgery, and in an action in the Chancery Division, to which T. and G. were parties, obtained the verdict of a jury to that effect, and judgment that the compromise should be set aside. In another action in the Probate Division for revocation of the probate of the earlier will:—*Held,* affirming the decision of the President of the Probate Division, that T. and G. were estopped from denying the forgery.—*Semble,* a Court of the Chancery Division has no jurisdiction to revoke the probate of a will. PRIESTMAN *v.* THOMAS   **9 P. D. 70, 210**

2. —— **English and Irish Courts—***Res Judicata—Pleading—Evidence of Proceedings in Irish Action—Report of Judge.*] Held, by Pearson, J., that in order to raise the defence of res judicata it is not necessary to set forth in detail in the defence the pleadings in the other action the judgment in which is said to operate as res judicata, but, in order to judge whether the same questions were at issue in the first action as in the second, the Court will look at the pleadings in the first action, though they were not set forth in the defence in the second action. Whether a judgment obtained in one action before the trial of another can operate by way of estoppel as res judicata, unless the judgment was obtained before the issue of the writ in the second action, *quære,*—On appeal by the Defendant an order was taken by arrangement:—*Held,* by the Court of Appeal, that a report made by an Irish Judge to a Divisional Court in Ireland to be used on an application to set aside the verdict, was evidence in an English action between the same parties of what took place at the trial and what the Judge decided.—An affidavit verifying the shorthand note of the judgment in the action pleaded as res judicata was also admitted. HOUSTOUN *v.* MARQUIS OF SLIGO   **29 Ch. D. 448**

3. —— **Judgment by Consent—***Limitation of Liability — Right of Claim.*] In an action for damages by collision between the owners of the *A.* and the *B.,* the Court, by consent of the parties, made a decree dismissing the action. Subsequently another action was brought by the owners of the cargo on the *A.* against the *B.* in respect of the same collision, and the Court found both vessels to blame. The owners of the *B.* then commenced an action against the owners of cargo on the *A.* for the purpose of limiting their liability in respect of all claims arising out of this collision, and paid the amount of their statutory liability into Court. Subsequently, again by consent of the owners of the *A.* and the *B.,* the assistant registrar rescinded the decree by consent

II. ESTOPPEL—JUDGMENT—*continued.*

in the first action, and the owners of the *A.* then brought in a claim in the limitation action against the fund in Court. The registrar held such claim to be inadmissible. On motion to confirm the report:—*Held,* that the report should be confirmed, as the owners of the *A.* and *B.* could not by consent rescind the decree of the Court, and that the decree by consent was a bar to a claim against the fund in Court, as it estopped the owners of the *A.* from bringing any further action against the *B.* THE "BELLCAIRN"   **10 P. D. 161**

4. —— **Judgment in rem—***Res Judicata — Finding on Issues on which Judgment in rem is founded.*] A native of Chili made his will in London, in November, 1859, and died in February, 1860. A caveat having been entered on behalf of the testator's daughter, the will was propounded by the executors in solemn form, the executors alleging that the testator was domiciled in England. The daughter alleged that the testator was domiciled in Chili, and that his will was not executed according to Chilian law. In July, 1860, the Judge of the Probate Court made a decree by which he pronounced for the validity of the will, found that the testator was domiciled in England, and decreed probate to the executors. In September, 1860, the executors filed a bill against the residuary legatee and a pecuniary legatee for administration of the estate, in which a decree was made in November, 1860. In 1862, the daughter filed a bill against the executors, alleging that the testator was a domiciled Chilian, that his will being executed in England, according to English law, was good by the law of Chili, but so far only as the testator could by the law of Chili dispose of his property by will : that according to that law he could only dispose by will of one-fourth of his personal estate, and that the other three-fourths belonged to the Plaintiff. The executors by answer set up the decree of the Probate Court as a bar, and no further steps were taken in the suit. In 1877, an order was made staying proceedings in the latter suit, and in another suit, but giving liberty to any of the parties to apply to add to the decree in the former cause all accounts and inquiries necessary to determine all questions in the suits so stayed. Pursuant to this leave, the daughter and her husband applied to add to the decree inquiries as to the legitimacy of the daughter and the domicil of the testator, and as to what part of his personal estate he could according to Chilian law dispose of by will, and an order was made in 1878 directing inquiries as to the legitimacy the rest of the application to stand over. In 1881 and 1882 orders were made transfering the conduct of the cause from the Plaintiff, the surviving executor, to the residuary legatee, dispensing with services of any notices or proceedings on the Plaintiff, and appointing the residuary legatee to represent the estate of the testator in the cause. In 1884 the application for an inquiry as to domicil was renewed against the residuary legatee, but without notice to the executor, and Bacon, V.C., made an order directing the inquiry as asked. The residuary legatee appealed:—*Held,* that the decree of the Probate Court was not conclusive in rem as to the domicil, for that it

II. ESTOPPEL—JUDGMENT—*continued.*

did not appear that the decree was necessarily based on the finding as to domicil. And, *quære,* whether the findings on which a judgment in rem is based are in all cases conclusive against the world.—*Held,* further, that the finding by the Probate Court as to domicil was not binding inter partes as between the daughter and the residuary legatee, for that it was a finding between the daughter and the executors, that the executors could not by litigating in that suit a question of domicil, which it was not necessary to decide for the purposes of the suit, conclude the residuary legatee as to the extent of the testator's power of disposing of his property, and did not represent him for that purpose, and that as the residuary legatee was not bound, the daughter could not be bound, since estoppel must be mutual.—*Held,* therefore, that the inquiry was properly directed, and this notwithstanding that the application had not been served on the executor.—An application by counsel for the executor for leave to be heard on the appeal was refused. DE MORA *v.* CONCHA - 29 Ch. D. 268

5. —— **Order not declaring Rights** — *Res Judicata* — *" Until Further Order " — Leave to appeal.*] Testator directed trustees to stand possessed of residuary real and personal estate upon trust to pay thereout to his wife, during her life, such an annual sum as, together with the income of a settled fund of £10,000, should produce to her " a clear annual income of £1500." He gave several legacies and annuities, and towards the end of his will declared that " no deduction shall be made from any of the legacies given by this my will, or to be given by any codicil thereto, for the legacy tax or any other matter, cause, or thing whatever."—An administration suit having been brought, an order was made in 1861 that the trustees of the will should repay to the widow certain sums which had been deducted from her annuity by mistake for succession duty, and that they should pay her until further order an annuity of £1500 free of all deductions except income tax, but no express declaration of her rights was made. This order was acted upon until 1882, when a petition was presented by the widow asking that the income tax which had been deducted might be paid to her, and that in future her annuity might be paid free of income tax:—*Held,* by the Court of Appeal, that the order of 1861 amounted to a declaration of the right of the widow to receive the annuity free of all deductions except income tax, notwithstanding the words "until further order," and that the matter was res judicata and could not now be reconsidered:—*Held,* also, that considering the lapse of time leave ought not to be given to appeal from the order. PEARETH *v.* MARRIOTT - - - 22 Ch. D. 182

6. —— **Second Action for same Cause of Action**—*Injunction — Res Judicata — Prayer for "further or other Relief"—Chancery Amendment Act,* 1858 (21 & 22 Vict. c. 27), *s. 2—Judicature Act,* 1873, *s.* 24, *sub-s.* 7.] In March, 1881, the Plaintiff handed to one Bird, a broker, shares in a mining company, with a transfer signed (a blank being left for the name of the transferee), for the purpose of sale. Bird died; and it was

II. ESTOPPEL—JUDGMENT—*continued.*

then discovered that he had, without the knowledge or authority of the Plaintiff, lodged the shares with the Defendant's firm as security for an advance. Having received notice from the company that they were about to register the shares in the name of the Defendant, the Plaintiff commenced an action in the Chancery Division of the High Court to restrain the Defendant's firm and the company from parting with the shares or registering the Defendant as transferee,—concluding with the usual prayer for " such further or other relief as the nature of the case might require."—On the 23rd of February, 1882, the Defendants in that action consented to an order for the delivery up of the shares to the Plaintiff forthwith. The order directed that, " upon delivery of the deed or form of transfer and the securities representing the same, and upon payment of costs to the Plaintiff and the mining company, all proceedings in the said Chancery action should be stayed."—The shares were not delivered up to the Plaintiff until the 28th of April, 1882, when they were sold at a considerable loss.—In an action against the Defendant in the Queen's Bench Division to recover damages for this detention, the jury found that the Plaintiff did not authorize Bird to pledge the shares for his own debt, or lend them to him for that purpose :—*Held,* that the Plaintiff was estopped by the consent order made in the Chancery action on the 23rd of February, 1882, from recovering in this action damages for such detention, and that the Defendant was not responsible for the detention of the shares by the mining company after the order had been made in the suit in the Chancery Division. SERRAO *v.* NOEL
[15 Q. B. D. 549

7. —— **Separate Actions in respect of same wrongful Act**—*Damage to Property and Injury to Person—Damages recoverable in previous Action —Maxim, " Nemo debet bis vexari pro unâ et eâdem causâ"—Maxim, " Interest reipublicæ ut sit finis litium."*] Damage to goods and injury to the person, although they have been occasioned by one and the same wrongful act, are infringements of different rights, and give rise to distinct causes of action ; and therefore the recovery in an action of compensation for the damage to the goods is no bar to an action subsequently commenced for the injury to the person.—So *held* by Brett, M.R., and Bowen, L.J., Lord Coleridge, C.J., dissenting.—The Plaintiff brought an action in a County Court for damage to his cab occasioned by the negligence of the Defendant's servant, and, having recovered the amount claimed, afterwards brought an action in the High Court of Justice against the Defendant, claiming damages for personal injury sustained by the Plaintiff through the same negligence :—*Held,* by Brett, M.R., and Bowen, L.J., Lord Coleridge, C.J., dissenting, that the action in the High Court was maintainable, and was not barred by the previous proceedings in the County Court. — Judgment of the Queen's Bench Division reversed. BRUNSDEN *v.* HUMPHREY - 11 Q. B. D. 712; 14 Q. B. D. 141

ESTOPPEL—Bailee—Sale with notice of adverse claims - - - 19 Ch. D. 86
See BAILMENT.

ESTOPPEL—*continued.*

—— Director—Calls - - 8 Q. B. D. 685
   See COMPANY—SHARES—ALLOTMENT. 2.

—— Justices—Res judicata · 6 Q. B. D. 300
   See LOCAL GOVERNMENT—STREETS. 1.

—— Petition—Discovery of fresh evidence
                [28 Ch. D. 516
   See NATIONAL DEBT COMMISSIONERS.

—— Probate of will—Whether conclusive as to
   domicil - - - 26 Ch. D. 656
   See PROBATE—GRANT. 3.

—— Patentee—Denying validity of patent
      [26 Ch. D. 700 ; 10 App. Cas. 249
   See PATENT—VALIDITY. 1.

—— Proceedings in bankruptcy — Amount of
   debt - - 17 Ch. D. 447
   See BANKRUPTCY—ANNULMENT. 5.

—— Representations by agent 18 Ch. D. 560
   See MORTGAGE—PRIORITY. 4.

—— Trustee - 9 Q. B. D. 264
   See BANKRUPTCY—ORDER AND DISPOSI-
   TION. 7.

ESTOVERS - - - 17 Ch. D. 535
   See COMMON.

EVIDENCE :— Col.
   I. GENERAL - - - 541
   II. DECLARATION BY DECEASED PERSON 542
   III. DOCUMENTS - - 543
   IV. ENTRY BY DECEASED PERSON - 543
   V. PRESUMPTION - - - 543
   VI. PUBLIC DOCUMENTS - - 544
   VII. WITNESS - - - 544

I. EVIDENCE—GENERAL.

Evidence by Commission.] *The Act* 48 & 49
Vict. c. 74, *amends the law for taking evidence by
commission in the colonies and elsewhere, and
amends the Act* 22 *Vict.* c. 20.

1. —— Affidavit sworn Abroad—*Consul refusing to administer Oath.*] · Where by German
law a British consul is not allowed to administer
an oath, the affidavit may be sworn before a
German Judge. IN THE GOODS OF FAWOUS
                  [9 P. D. 241

2. —— Illegitimacy—*Bequest to Children of
C. equally—Non-access of Husband and Wife—
Presumption of Legitimacy rebutted.*] Testator
bequeathed Government annuities upon trust for
his daughter C. for life, and after her decease for
her children equally. C. married H. G., and by
him had two children at the time when H. G.
deserted her and his family. C. went to live
with a man named J. H., and while living with
him had five children, the eldest of whom was
M., who was, according to the evidence, born
during the lifetime of H. G. M. claimed a share
of the fund in Court :—*Held*, that, considering
all the circumstances from which non-access between the husband and wife might be inferred,
the presumption of the legitimacy of M. was
rebutted, and that she was not entitled to any
share of the fund. HAWES *v.* DRAEGER
                [23 Ch. D. 173

3. —— Signature by Agent *both for Principal and in his own Right—Guarantee—Parol*

I. EVIDENCE—GENERAL—*continued.*

Evidence.] By articles of agreement under seal
between J. A. & Co. and Y. & Co., Y. & Co.
agreed to do certain work for which J. A. & Co.
were to make certain payments, and the agreement contained this clause, " It· is further understood between the parties to this contract that
J. O. Schuler guarantees payment to Y. & Co. of
all moneys due to them under this contract."
The attestation clause was "signed and delivered
by the said J. A. & Co. in the presence of C. T.,"
and Schuler, acting under a power of attorney,
signed as follows: "P.P.A—J. A &. Co., J. O.
Schuler." Y. & Co. sued Schuler as guarantor,
and evidence was given at the trial of statements
by Schuler at the time of execution that he intended to sign on his own behalf as well as on
that of A. & Co. A verdict was found for the
Plaintiffs. Schuler moved for a new trial on the
ground that he had not signed the guarantee :—
Held, affirming the decision of the Queen's Bench
Division, that evidence that Schuler intended to
sign in his own right as well as on behalf of
A. & Co. did not contradict the document, and
was admissible, and that Schuler must be taken
to have signed as a contracting party. YOUNG *v*
SCHULER - - 11 Q. B. D. 651

4. —— Statement by Agent—*Admissibility—
Company — Director —Rectification of Register.*]
A shareholder in a company applied to have his
name removed from the register of members on
the ground that he had been induced to become
a shareholder by a material misrepresentation in
a prospectus issued by the company. The only
evidence of the untruth of the representation was
a statement made by the chairman of the company in a speech addressed by him to a meeting
of the shareholders :—*Held*, that this statement
was not admissible evidence against the company,
inasmuch as the chairman in making it was not
acting as the agent of the company in a transaction between them and a third party, but was
making a confidential report to his own principal.
—*Meux's Executors' Case* (2 D. M. & G. 522) distinguished. *In re* DEVALA PROVIDENT GOLD
MINING COMPANY - - - 22 Ch. D. 593

II. EVIDENCE—DECLARATION BY DECEASED
PERSON.

1. —— Legitimacy — *Baptismal Register —
Entry of Date of Birth—Declarations of deceased
Father.*] Although an entry in a baptismal
register by the officiating clergyman of the day
when the baptized child was born furnishes uo
proof per se that the child was born on the day
stated, the entry will not be rejected altogether
as an item of evidence upon an inquiry as to the
legitimacy, from its birth before or after the marriage of its reputed parents, of the child in question.—Declarations by a reputed father contained
in business letters written by one of his daughters
in his name and under his dictation admitted as
evidence after his death of the date of their birth
upon the question of their legitimacy. *In re*
TURNER. GLENISTER *v.* HARDING 29 Ch. D. 985

2. —— Pedigree—*Hearsay—Proof of Birth—
Declaration of Deceased Parent.*] · The rule which
admits hearsay evidence in pedigree cases is confined to the proof of pedigree, and does not apply

II. EVIDENCE—DECLARATION BY DECEASED PERSON—*continued.*

to proof of the facts which constitute a pedigree, such as birth, death, and marriage, when they have to be proved for other purposes.—Therefore in an action for goods sold, to which the defence was infancy, an affidavit stating the date of the Defendant's birth, which had been made by his deceased father in an action to which the plaintiff was not a party, was held inadmissible as evidence of the age of the Defendant in support of his defence. HAINES *v.* GUTHRIE **13 Q. B. D. 818**

III. EVIDENCE—DOCUMENTS.

1. —— **Notary Public**—*Chancery Procedure Act, 1852 (15 & 16 Vict. c. 86), s. 22.*] The execution of a release was attested by a notary in a colony. There was no evidence that the attestation was for the purpose of using the deed in Court :—*Held*, nevertheless, that it was a document to be used in Court within 15 & 16 Vict. c. 86, s. 22, and that the Court would take judicial notice of the notary's seal and signature. BROOKE *v.* BROOKE　　　　-　　　　**17 Ch. D. 833**

2. —— **Report of Surveyor**—*Resolution of Public Body.*] A public body passed a resolution directing their solicitor to write a letter to the Plaintiff, the resolution being based upon the report of their own surveyor. The Plaintiff wished to put the report in evidence to shew the grounds for passing the resolution, and to explain the letter :—*Held*, that the report was not admissible. COOPER *v.* METROPOLITAN BOARD OF WORKS　　　　-　　　　**25 Ch. D. 472**

3. —— **Will of Real Estate** *made in Colony.*] For the purposes of the usual preliminary judgment in a partition action letters testimonial of the Supreme Court of the Colony of Victoria, Probate Jurisdiction, setting out the will verbatim, were accepted as sufficient proof of a will made in Victoria of real estate in England. WAITE *v.* BINGLEY　　　　-　　　　**21 Ch. D. 674**

IV. EVIDENCE—ENTRY BY DECEASED PERSON.

—— **Entry in College Books**—*Admissibility.*] It was the practice that the proceedings of the Provost and Fellows of King's College Cambridge, should be entered in a book, and that the entries should be signed by the Registrar of the College, who was a notary public, and who signed the entries in that character. One or two of the entries were not so signed :—*Held*, that an unsigned entry was not admissible in evidence, notwithstanding that it was proved to be in the handwriting of the person who usually made the entries at the time when it was made. FOX *v.* BEARBLOCK　　　　-　　　　**17 Ch. D. 429**

V. EVIDENCE—PRESUMPTION.

—— **Woman past Child bearing**—*Will—Construction—"Survivor."*] A testator bequeathed the dividends of a sum of £10,000 Consols unto and equally between his four daughters, and from and immediately after their several and respective deceases he bequeathed the £10,000 to their children respectively—viz., one fourth part thereof unto and equally between the children of each daughter. And, in case any one or more of the daughters should die without leaving issue her or

V. EVIDENCE—PRESUMPTION—*continued.*

them surviving, he bequeathed the share or shares of the stock so bequeathed to and intended for the issue (had there been such) "unto the survivors or survivor" of the four daughters, equally if more than one, and if but one, to that one absolutely. Three of the daughters married, and died leaving children. The fourth was the longest liver, and was a spinster of the age of fifty-four :—*Held*, that on her death without leaving issue she would be entitled to her own one-fourth share of the £10,000 absolutely; that it might be assumed that she would never have any children; and that the share might be transferred to her at once.—*Maden v. Taylor* (45 L. J. (Ch.) 569) approved and followed. DAVIDSON *v.* KIMPTON　　**18 Ch. D. 213**

VI. EVIDENCE—PUBLIC DOCUMENTS.

The Act 45 & 46 Vict. c. 9 (Documentary Evidence Act, 1882) amends the Documentary Evidence Act, 1868, and other enactments relating to the evidence of documents by means of copies printed by the Government Printers.

Sect. 2. Where any enactment, whether passed before or after the passing of this Act, provides that a copy of any Act of Parliament, proclamation, order, regulation, rule, warrant, circular, list, gazette, or document shall be conclusive evidence, or evidence, or have any other effect, when purporting to be printed by the Government Printer, or a printer authorized by Her Majesty, or otherwise under Her Majesty's authority, whatever may be the precise expression used, such copy shall also be conclusive evidence, or evidence, or have the said effect (as the case may be) if it purports to be printed under the superintendence or authority of Her Majesty's Stationery Office.

Sect. 3. If any person prints any copy of any Act, proclamation, order, regulation, &c., which falsely purports to have been printed under the superintendence or authority of Her Majesty's Stationery office, or tenders in evidence any copy which falsely purports to have been printed as aforesaid, knowing that the same was not so printed, he shall be guilty of felony, and shall, on conviction, be liable to penal servitude for a term not exceeding seven years, or to be imprisoned for a term not exceeding two years, with or without hard labour.

VII. EVIDENCE—WITNESS.

1. —— **Out of Jurisdiction**—*Arbitration—Reference of Action and "All Matters in Difference"—"Trial"—17 & 18 Vict. c. 34, s. 1.*] When an action and "all matters in difference" between the parties have been referred by consent to an arbitrator, no writ of subpœna will be granted under 17 & 18 Vict. c. 34, s. 1, in order to compel the attendance at the hearing before the arbitrator of witnesses residing within the United Kingdom but out of the jurisdiction of the Queen's Bench Division ; for the hearing before the arbitrator is not a "trial" within the meaning of that enactment. HALL *v.* BRAND　　**12 Q. B. D. 39**

2. —— **Privilege**—*Answer tending to criminate—Refusal to answer—Power of Judge—Bankruptcy Act, 1869 (32 & 33 Vict. c. 71), s. 96.*] Where a witness refuses to answer a question put to him on the ground that his answer might tend to criminate himself, his mere statement of his belief that his answer will have that effect is

VII. EVIDENCE—WITNESS—*continued.*

not enough to excuse him from answering, but the Court must be satisfied from the circumstances of the case, and the nature of the evidence which the witness is called upon to give, that there is reasonable ground to apprehend danger to him from his being compelled to answer.—But, if it is once made to appear that the witness is in danger, great latitude should be allowed to him in judging for himself of the effect of any particular question.—Subject, however, to that reservation, the Judge is bound to insist on the witness answering, unless he is satisfied that the answer will tend to place him in peril.—Decision of the Court of Queen's Bench in *Reg.* v. *Boyes* (1 B. & S. 311) approved and followed. *Ex parte* REYNOLDS. *In re* REYNOLDS　　　20 Ch. D. 294

3. —— **Privilege** — *Professional Correspondence—Solicitor—Execution of Deed.*] A solicitor employed to obtain the execution of a deed, and who is one of the witnesses, is not precluded, on the ground of a breach of professional confidence, from giving evidence as to what passed at the time of execution, by which the deed may be proved invalid. CRAWCOUR v. SALTER
　　　　　　　　[18 Ch. D. 30

4. —— **Professional Witness** — *Auctioneer—Expenses—Loss of Time.*] An auctioneer summoned to give evidence before a special examiner appointed under proceedings in the Chancery Division is, as a professional witness, entitled to be paid a guinea a day by way of compensation for his loss of time, together with the amount of his travelling expenses, if any, including therein his railway fare, first class, from his residence to the place of his examination and back again. And, although sworn, he may refuse to answer any questions until a sum sufficient to cover these amounts has been paid him. *In re* WORKING MEN'S MUTUAL SOCIETY　　-　21 Ch. D. 831

EVIDENCE.
　　　See Cases under PRACTICE — SUPREME
　　　COURT—EVIDENCE.

—— Admiralty Court—Appeal—Leave to adduce fresh evidence　　-　9 P. D. 12
　　　See PRACTICE—ADMIRALTY—APPEAL. 1.

—— Admission by master of ship　10 P. D. 137
　　　See PRACTICE—ADMIRALTY—EVIDENCE. 1.

—— Admission of debt—Bankrupt's admission—How far binding on trustee　13 Q. B. D.
　　　See BANKRUPTCY—PROOF. 9.　　　[720

—— Admission of deceased person against interest—Bankruptcy　14 Q. B. D. 415
　　　See BANKRUPTCY—PROOF. 8.

—— Agreement in several documents　16 Ch. D.
　　　See SPECIFIC PERFORMANCE. 1.　　[395

—— Appeal　　　　　19 Ch. D. 419
　　　See BILL OF SALE—FORMALITIES. 18.

—— Attesting witness—Execution　9 P. D. 149
　　　See PROBATE—EXECUTION. 4.

—— Bankruptcy.
　　　See Cases under BANKRUPTCY—EVIDENCE.

—— Bankruptcy — Administration of estate of person dying insolvent—Power to summon persons to be examined 15 Q. B. D. 159
　　　See BANKRUPTCY—DECEASED DEBTOR. 1.

EVIDENCE—*continued.*

—— Bought and sold notes—Liability of brokers
　　　　　　　　　[13 Q. B. D. 635
　　　See PRINCIPAL AND AGENT — AGENT'S LIABILITY. 6.

—— Claim against estate of deceased person—Corroboration　-　　23 Ch. D. 267
　　　See EXECUTOR—ACTIONS. 15.

—— Connection of papers constituting will
　　　　　　　　　　[6 P. D. 1
　　　See PRACTICE—PROBATE—EVIDENCE. 2.

—— Contemporaneous documents　20 Ch. D. 27;
　　　　　　　　　　[9 App. Cas. 187
　　　See COMPANY—PROSPECTUS. 1.

—— Criminal law.
　　　See Cases under CRIMINAL LAW—EVIDENCE.

—— Custom of manor　-　　30 Ch. D. 581
　　　See COPYHOLD—SURRENDER AND ADMITTANCE. 2.

—— Custom—Port of discharge　-　6 P. D. 68
　　　See SHIP—CHARTERPARTY. 16.

—— Damage to salving ship 8 P. D. 137; 9 P. D.
　　　See SHIP—SALVAGE. 5, 6.　　　[182

—— Declaration of deceased person—Scotch law
　　　　　　　　　[6 App. Cas. 489
　　　See SCOTCH LAW—HUSBAND AND WIFE. 3.

—— Desertion　-　　-　　-　9 P. D. 245
　　　See PRACTICE—DIVORCE—DESERTION. 1.

—— Discovery of fresh　25 Ch. D. 231; 28 Ch. D.
　　　　　　　　　　　[516
　　　See NATIONAL DEBT COMMISSIONERS.

—— Divorce Court — Commission to examine witnesses　-　　　9 P. D. 8
　　　See PRACTICE—DIVORCE—EVIDENCE. 1.

—— Divorce Court—Perpetuation of testimony
　　　　　　　　　[9 P. D. 120
　　　See PRACTICE—DIVORCE—EVIDENCE. 2.

—— Engineer's log—Action of damage 10 P. D. 31
　　　See PRACTICE—ADMIRALTY—EVIDENCE. 2.

—— Entry against interest　29 Ch. D. 882
　　　See LIMITATIONS, STATUTE OF—REALTY. 1.

—— Family repute—Hearsay evidence
　　　　　　　　　[10 App. Cas. 763
　　　See SCOTCH LAW—HUSBAND AND WIFE. 4.

—— Gift of husband to separate use of wife—Corroboration　-　21 Ch. D. 657
　　　See HUSBAND AND WIFE — SEPARATE ESTATE. 3.

—— Husband and wife—Criminal law 12 Q. B. D.
　　　　　　　　　[266; 13 Q. B. D. 33
　　　See CRIMINAL LAW—EVIDENCE. 2, 3.

—— Infant—Necessaries　　13 Q. B. D. 410
　　　See INFANT—CONTRACTS. 3.

—— Insolvency—Winding-up petition
　　　　　　　　　[23 Ch. D. 210
　　　See COMPANY—WINDING-UP ORDER. 10.

—— Interruption of easement　-　19 Ch. D. 462
　　　See LIGHT—TITLE. 4.

T

EVIDENCE—*continued.*

—— Irish inquisition—Transcript of record
　　　　　　　　　　　[20 Ch. D. 269
　　See LUNATIC—JURISDICTION. 1.
—— Judgment debt—Proof 14 Q. B. D. 604, 606
　　See BANKRUPTCY—PROOF. 14, 15.
—— Libel　-　8 Q. B. D. 491; 7 App. Cas. 741
　　See DEFAMATION—LIBEL. 1, 2.
—— Licensing Act.
　　See INN—OFFENCES—*Statutes.*
—— Malicious prosecution—Burden of proof
　　　　　　　　　　　[11 Q. B. D. 440
　　See MALICIOUS PROSECUTION. 3.
—— Marriage—Ceylon　　6 App. Cas. 364
　　See COLONIAL LAW—CEYLON. 3.
—— Marriage—Scotch marriage 6 App. Cas. 489;
　　　　　　　　　　[10 App. Cas. 692, 763
　　See SCOTCH LAW—HUSBAND AND WIFE.
　　2, 3, 4.
—— Misrepresentation—Impeaching deed
　　　　　　　　　　　[7 App. Cas. 307
　　See COLONIAL LAW—VICTORIA. 2.
—— Negligence—Carriage and driver
　　　　　　　　　　　[6 Q. B. D. 145
　　See NEGLIGENCE—EVIDENCE. 2.
—— Offences against women.
　　See CRIMINAL LAW—EVIDENCE—*Statutes.*
—— Poor-rate—Diminution of income—Alteration of valuation list　13 Q. B. D. 364
　　See METROPOLIS—VALUATION ACTS.
—— Possession—Judgment in former action
　　See FISHERY. 1.　　[8 App. Cas. 135
—— Precognitions　-　-　6 App. Cas. 489
　　See SCOTCH LAW—HUSBAND AND WIFE.
　　3.
—— Presumption—Evidence to rebut　29 Ch. D.
　　See WILL—EXECUTORS.　　　　[893
—— Presumption of continuance of cohabitation between husband and wife
　　　　　　　　　　　[11 Q. B. D. 118
　　See CRIMINAL LAW—BIGAMY. 2.
—— Presumption of duration of life 6 Q. B. D. 366
　　See CRIMINAL LAW—BIGAMY. 1.
—— Proceedings in Irish action — Shorthand notes　-　-　29 Ch. D. 448
　　See ESTOPPEL—JUDGMENT. 2.
—— Proof of foreign law　　　6 P. D. 6
　　See ADMINISTRATOR—LIMITED. 6.
—— Proof of foreign law—Certificate of ambassador　-　-　9 P. D. 234
　　See PROBATE—GRANT. 7.
—— Register in church—Memorandum by rector
　　　　　　　　　　[10 App. Cas. 692
　　See SCOTCH LAW—HUSBAND AND WIFE.
　　2.
—— Right to sum up　　-　10 Q. B. D. 451
　　See COUNTY COURT—PRACTICE. 6.
—— Sale of land—Intention of parties to conveyance　-　9 Q. B. D. 506
　　See PRISON. 3.
—— Service of writ out of jurisdiction
　　　　　　　　　　　[20 Ch. D. 240
　　See PRACTICE—SUPREME COURT—SERVICE. 3.

EVIDENCE—*continued.*

—— Stamps　-　　　7 App. Cas. 172
　　See COLONIAL LAW—STRAITS SETTLEMENTS. 1.
—— Statement of deceased person
　　　　　　　　　　　[6 App. Cas. 489
　　See SCOTCH LAW—HUSBAND AND WIFE.
　　3.
—— Statement of third person—Hearsay
　　　　　　　　　　　[7 P. D. 151
　　See NEGLIGENCE—LIABILITY. 8.
—— Statements post litem motam　10 App. Cas.
　　　　　　　　　　　　　　　　[763
　　See SCOTCH LAW—HUSBAND AND WIFE.
　　4.
—— Surveyor's certificate　　28 Ch. D. 661;
　　　　　　　　　　　[30 Ch. D. 644
　　See VENDOR AND PURCHASER—TITLE. 2.
—— Technical meaning of " beerhouse "
　　　　　　　　　　　[16 Ch. D. 718
　　See LANDLORD AND TENANT—LEASE.
　　7.
—— Will proved in Victoria　-　21 Ch. D. 674
　　See PARTITION SUIT—SALE. 2.
—— Winding-up petition　　16 Ch. D. 246
　　See COMPANY — LIFE INSURANCE COMPANY. 2.
—— Witness—Voluntary attendance—Refusal to give evidence　-　14 Q. B. D. 364
　　See BASTARDY. 7.

EX PARTE APPEAL—Bankruptcy 20 Ch. D. 703
　　See BANKRUPTCY—LIQUIDATION. 7.

EX PARTE APPLICATION—Injunction—Parting with legal estate　21 Ch. D. 490
　　See PRACTICE — SUPREME COURT — INJUNCTION. 7.

—— Leave to serve third party　16 Ch. D. 489
　　See PRACTICE—SUPREME COURT—THIRD PARTY. 4.

—— Registration of trade-mark　26 Ch. D. 187
　　See TRADE-MARK—REGISTRATION. 8.

EX PARTE ORDER—Taxation　25 Ch. D. 279
　　See SOLICITOR—BILL OF COSTS. 23.

EX PARTE PATERNÂ—*Ex parte maternâ*
　　See DESCENT.　　　　[28 Ch. D. 327

EXAMINATION—Alleged lunatic—Justices
　　　　　　　　　　　[15 Q. B. D. 122
　　See LUNATIC—JURISDICTION. 2.

—— Bankrupt.
　　See BANKRUPTCY—STATUTES.
—— Bankrupt　15 Q. B. D. 54; 21 Ch. D. 61
　　See BANKRUPTCY—EXAMINATION. 1, 2.
—— Bankrupt—De bene esse　16 Ch. D. 100
　　See PRACTICE — SUPREME COURT—EVIDENCE. 1.
—— Compounding debtor　-　20 Ch. D. 281
　　See BANKRUPTCY—COMPOSITION. 3.
—— Judgment debtor　-　16 Ch. D. 8
　　See PRACTICE—SUPREME COURT—GARNISHEE ORDERS. 6.
—— Married woman—Settled Estates Act.
　　　　　　　[26 Ch. D. 220; 28 Ch. D. 171
　　See SETTLED ESTATES ACT. 2, 3.

EXAMINATION—*continued.*

—— Witness abroad.
See Cases under PRACTICE — SUPREME COURT—EVIDENCE. 9—16.

—— Witness in bankruptcy.
See Cases under BANKRUPTCY — EVIDENCE.

—— Witness in winding-up.
See Cases under COMPANY—EVIDENCE.

EXCHANGE—Agreement for—Before notice to treat -   - 27 Ch. D. 639
See ELEMENTARY EDUCATION ACT — SCHOOL BOARD.

EXCEPTION—Residuary gift—Intestacy
See WILL—LAPSE. 7.   [23 Ch. D. 218

—— Substantial—Assignment of all debtor's property   17 Ch. D. 26
See BANKRUPTCY—ACT OF BANKRUPTCY. 2.

EXECUTION—Abandonment of part of judgment debt   - 8 Q. B. D. 392
See BANKRUPTCY—ASSETS. 3.

—— Action against partner in name of firm
[11 Q. B. D. 435; 10 App. Cas. 680
See PRACTICE — SUPREME COURT — PARTIES. 10.

—— Bankruptcy—Application to sell by private contract   - 12 Q. B. D. 162
See BANKRUPTCY—SECURED CREDITOR. 9.

—— Before composition   16 Ch. D. 534
See BANKRUPTCY—COMPOSITION. 1.

—— Equitable—Receiver of debts 16 Ch. D. 544;
[25 Ch. D. 413; 29 Ch. D. 993
See PRACTICE—SUPREME COURT—RECEIVER. 1, 3, 4.

—— Equity of redemption—Duty as sheriff
See SHERIFF. 1.   [12 Q. B. D. 213

—— Leave to proceed after winding-up of company   - 20 Ch. D. 442; 21 Ch. D. 510
See COMPANY—INJUNCTION. 1, 2.

—— Levy for a sum with possession money above £50   .   9 Q. B. D. 432
See BANKRUPTCY—ASSETS. 4.

—— Rule to set aside—Ceylon law
[8 App. Cas. 99
See COLONIAL LAW—CEYLON. 2.

—— Sale by sheriff—Notice of bankruptcy petition   - 15 Q. B. D. 48
See BANKRUPTCY — PROTECTED TRANSACTION. 6.

—— Seizure without sale—Notice of act of bankruptcy   -   17 Ch. D. 839
See BANKRUPTCY—PROTECTED TRANSACTION. 3.

—— Unregistered bill of sale - 23 Ch. D. 254
See BILL OF SALE—REGISTRATION. 11.

—— Unregistered bill of sale—Apparent possession   -   - 16 Ch. D. 668
See BILL OF SALE—APPARENT POSSESSION. 2.

—— Winding-up order -   16 Ch. D. 337
See COMPANY—SECURED CREDITOR. 1.

—— Wrongful seizure 21 Ch. D. 69; 9 Q. B. D.
See SHERIFF. 3, 4.   [340

EXECUTION OF DEED—Creditor's deed 29 Ch. D.
See CREDITOR'S DEED.   [745

—— Evidence of—Professional confidence
[18 Ch. D. 30
See EVIDENCE—WITNESS. 3.

—— Qualified execution   - 10 App. Cas. 293
See DEED. 2.

—— Statutory effect.
See VENDOR AND PURCHASER—CONVEYANCE—*Statutes.*

EXECUTION OF WILL.
See Cases under PROBATE—EXECUTION.

EXECUTIVE GOVERNMENT—Liability of
[9 App. Cas. 418
See COLONIAL LAW—NEW ZEALAND. 1.

EXECUTOR.   Col.

I. ACTIONS (BY AND AGAINST)   -   550
  (a) ACTION FOR TRESPASS.
  (b) ADMINISTRATION ACTION.
  (c) COSTS.
  (d) EVIDENCE.
  (e) FOREIGN ASSETS.
  (f) INSOLVENT ESTATES.

II. ADMINISTRATION   -   556
  (a) CARRYING ON BUSINESS.
  (b) CONVERSION.
  (c) PAYMENT OF DEBTS AND LEGACIES.

III. LIABILITIES (AND DUTIES)   -   561
IV. POWERS   -   -   -   562
V. RETAINER   -   -   -   564

I. EXECUTOR—ACTIONS (by and against).

(a) ACTION FOR TRESPASS.

1. —— Actio personalis moritur cum personâ—*Action for Damage to Estate of Intestate arising out of Injury to his Person—Medical Expenses—Loss of Wages.*] The Plaintiff sued as the administratrix of her late husband, who, whilst crossing the Defendants' railway at a level crossing, was, through the negligence of the Defendants, run over by an engine and sustained personal injuries which prevented him from following his occupation and earning wages, and caused him to incur expenses for medical attendance and nursing, whereby his personal estate was diminished in value:—*Held*, that the Plaintiff could not sue in respect of damage to the intestate's estate arising, as above mentioned, from the tortious injury to the intestate's person, and that the action was therefore not maintainable. PULLING *v.* GREAT EASTERN RAILWAY COMPANY
[9 Q. B. D. 110

2. —— Actio personalis moritur cum personâ—*Continuance of Action against Executors—3 & 4 Wm. 4, c. 42, s. 2—Death of sole Defendant trading under Name of Firm—Executors carrying on Trade under same Firm—Rules of Court, 1875, Order XII., r. 12a.; Order L.*] The Plaintiff brought his action for damages and an injunction against the firm of T. & Co. for torts committed by the firm. The firm consisted of T. alone, who died more than six months after the commencement of action, and the action was continued against his executors:—*Held* (affirming the decision of Hall V.-C.), that T. having died more than six months after the

T 2

I. EXECUTOR—ACTIONS (by and against)—
continued.

(a) ACTION FOR TRESPASS—*continued.*

commission of the acts complained of, no action either for damages or injunction could be maintained against his executors; although the action had been commenced in the lifetime of the testator, and although the executors continued the business in the name of the firm. KIRK *v.* TODD
[21 Ch. D. 484

3. —— Actio personalis moritur cum personâ —*Benefit received by Trespasser.*] By the decree in 1870 it was declared that H. & F. and the estate of their deceased partner were liable to the Plaintiffs for minerals taken by them under the Plaintiff's farm, and that H. & F. were liable to compensate the Plaintiffs for user of all roads and passages under the farm, and inquiries were directed—1. As to the quantity of minerals taken and the value. 2. What quantities of minerals had been carried by the Defendants through the roads or passages under the farm. 3. What upon the result of the second inquiry ought to be paid by the Defendants as wayleave for the user of the roads and passages. 4. Whether the farm, and the mineral property of the Plaintiffs under it, had sustained any and what damage by reason of the way in which the Defendants had worked under the farm. Pending these inquiries F. died, and his executrix moved to stay proceedings under the second, third, and fourth inquiries :—*Held*, by Pearson, J., that the fourth inquiry must be stayed, but that as the estate of F. had derived profit from the trespasses to which the second and third inquiries related, it was liable after his death and that those inquiries must be prosecuted :— *Held*, on appeal by Cotton and Bowen, L.JJ., dissentiente Baggallay, L.J., that proceedings under the second and third inquiries must also be stayed, for that, apart from cases of breach of contract, a remedy for a wrongful act done by a deceased person cannot be pursued against his estate, unless property or the proceeds or value of property belonging to another person have been appropriated by the deceased person and added to his estate. PHILIPS *v.* HOMFRAY　　24 Ch. D. 439

(b) ADMINISTRATION ACTION.

4. —— Order for Sale—*Power of Sale in Trustees—Conversion.*] An absolute order for sale made within the jurisdiction of the Court in an administration suit operates as a conversion from the date of the order and before any sale has taken place. HYETT *v.* MEKIN　　25 Ch. D. 735

5. —— Payment into Court—*Legacy for Life — Residuary Legatee — Administration by the Court.*] The rule that if personal property consisting of money or stock is limited to A. for life, and after his death to B. absolutely, it will be ordered into Court for administration in an action by B. for the purpose, is not absolute, and will only be enforced as against A. where there is reasonable ground, such as danger to the fund, for the application. *In re* BRAITHWAITE. BRAITHWAITE *v.* WALLIS　-　21 Ch. D. 121

6. —— Protection of Executor—*Judgment— Registration—Priority—Order of Administration —4 & 5 Wm. & M. c. 20, s. 3—23 & 24 Vict. c. 38, s. 3.*] The meaning of sect. 3 of the Act 23 & 24

I. EXECUTOR—ACTIONS (by and against)—
continued.

(b.) ADMINISTRATION ACTION—*continued.*

Vict. c. 38, like that of sect. 3 of the Act 4 & 5 Wm. & M. c. 20, is not merely that protection is given to an executor or administrator against an action for a devastavit by a judgment creditor of the testator or intestate whose judgment has not been registered, but that such a judgment debt is not entitled in the administration of the estate to any priority over the simple contract debts of the testator or intestate.—*In re Turner* (12 W. R. 337) followed. VAN GHELUIVE *v.* NERINCKX
[21 Ch. D. 189

7. —— Revocation of Probate—*Dismissal of Action.*] A decree was made at the suit of residuary legatees for the administration of the real and personal estate of a testator. After this a subsequent will was discovered by which the estate was disposed of in a different way. Probate of the old will was recalled, and letters of administration with the later will annexed were granted to one of the beneficiaries.—Under these circumstances the Court of Appeal made an order dismissing the action. *In re* DEAN. DEAN *v.* WRIGHT　-　　21 Ch. D. 581

8. —— Wilful Default—"*Ordinary Account*" —*District Registrar—Jurisdiction—Form of Report—Judicature Act*, 1873 (36 & 37 Vict. c. 66), *ss. 64, 66—Rules of Court*, 1875, *Order III., r. 8— Order XV., r. 1—Order XXXV., rr. 1a, 4.*] A claim against an executor for an account on the footing of wilful default is not a "case of ordinary account " within the meaning of rule 8 of Order III., and consequently a summary order for such an account cannot be made under rule 1 of Order XV. —By virtue of rules 1a and 4 of Order XXXV., a District Registrar has power to make an order for an account under rule 1 of Order XV., and if the order so directs (but not otherwise) he can then proceed to take the account himself.—*In re Smith* (6 Ch. D. 692) followed.—In making a report to the Court under sect. 66 of the Judicature Act, 1873, of the result of an account in an administration action, the District Registrar ought to adopt the form of a Chief Clerk's certificate, and to state in the report the persons who were present before him, and the materials upon which he proceeded. *In re* BOWEN. BENNETT *v.* BOWEN
[20 Ch. D. 538

9. —— Wilful Default—*Adding Accounts and Inquiries after Judgment—Rules of Court*, 1875, *Order XXXIII.*] When the statement of claim in an administration action against an executor alleges that he has committed wilful default, but the judgment at the trial gives no relief on that footing (the claim to such relief not being, however, dismissed), the Court can at any subsequent stage of the proceedings, if evidence of wilful default is adduced, direct further accounts and inquiries to be taken and made on that footing.— *Job* v. *Job* (6 Ch. D. 562) as explained by *Mayer* v. *Murray* (8 Ch. D. 424) followed. *In re* SYMONS. LUKE *v.* TONKIN　-　-　-　21 Ch. D. 757

(c) COSTS.

10. —— Executors appearing by same Solicitor—*Defaulting Executor—Bankruptcy.*] Two executors, Defendants in an administration ac-

I. EXECUTOR — ACTIONS (by and against)—
continued.

(c.) COSTS—*continued.*

tion, were represented by the same solicitor, to whom they had given a joint retainer. One of them was a debtor to the estate, and became bankrupt :—*Held,* that the costs incurred by them prior to the bankruptcy should be distinguished, and that the solvent executor should be allowed only his own proportion out of the fund, the defaulter's proportion being set off against the debt due from him : but that the costs incurred by both subsequently to the bankruptcy should be allowed in full.—*Watson* v. *Row* (Law Rep. 18 Eq. 680) dissented from. SMITH *v.* DALE
　　　　　　　　　　　　　[18 Ch. D. 516

11. —— Real and Personal Estate—*Inquiries as to Real Estate—Apportionment of Costs.*] It is the now settled practice of the Chancery Division that the costs of an administration action so far as they have been increased by the administration of the real estate are to be borne by that real estate. —An action was brought by the heir-at-law of a testatrix who had given by will certain legacies, but had died intestate as to her real estate and residuary personalty, for the administration of her real and personal estate:—*Held,* by Fry, J., that the entire costs of the action were payable primarily out of the residuary personal estate :— *Held,* by the Court of Appeal, varying the order of Fry, J., that the costs of the action, so far as they had been increased by the administration of the real estate, must be borne by the real estate.— *Per* Jessel, M.R. : When an estate is insufficient the Plaintiff does not necessarily get his costs in priority to the Defendants. *In re* MIDDLETON. THOMPSON *v.* HARRIS　　-　　19 Ch. D. 552

12. —— Real Estate—*Descended Real Estate —Interest accruing to Heir by Reason of Forfeiture under Provisions of Will.*] Real estate which had descended to a testator's heir-at-law, not because it was not originally disposed of by the will, but by reason of a subsequent forfeiture by the devisee under the provisions of the will, *held* not liable to pay the costs of an action to administer the testator's estate in priority to specifically devised and bequeathed freehold and leasehold estate.—*Scott v. Cumberland* (Law Rep. 18 Eq. 578), *Gowan* v. *Broughton* (Law Rep. 19 Eq. 77), and *Row* v. *Row* (Law Rep. 7 Eq. 414) distinguished. HURST *v.* HURST　　-　　-　　28 Ch. D. 159

13. —— Residuary Estate—*Accounts.*] In an administration action no costs ought to be given out of the estate, except for those proceedings that are in their origin directed with some shew of reason and a proper foundation for the benefit of the estate, or which have in their result conduced to the benefit thereof.—A tenant for life under a will who had duly received the income of the estate, and whose solicitors had expressed themselves satisfied with the accounts rendered by the executors, instituted an action for the administration of the estate. The accounts taken shewed that the Plaintiff had been slightly overpaid:—*Held,* that the Plaintiff must have no costs of the action, and must pay the costs of the rendering of the income account. CROGGAN *v.* ALLEN　-　　-　　-　　- 22 Ch. D. 101

I. EXECUTOR—ACTIONS (by and against)—
continued.

(c.) COSTS—*continued.*

14. —— Solicitor and Client—*Residuary Legatee Plaintiff—Insufficient Estate.*] A residuary legatee Plaintiff in an administration action is entitled to his costs as between solicitor and client where the estate is insufficient for payment of legacies, provided it is sufficient for payment of debts, but not otherwise. *In re* HARVEY. WRIGHT *v.* WOODS　-　-　-　　26 Ch. D. 179

(d.) EVIDENCE.

15. —— Evidence of Claimant—*Corroboration.*] The rule that a claim upon the estate of a deceased person cannot be maintained upon the unsupported testimony of the claimant applies to cases of alleged debt as well as to cases of alleged gift. —*Per* Jessel, M.R. : The rule is a rule of prudence rather than of law; and in an action tried by a jury it is the duty of the Judge to recommend the jury to disregard the unsupported evidence of the claimant; but if they should decline to do so, and should find for the claimant, *quære* if their verdict could be interfered with. An English widow lady residing in Paris in a house which belonged to her for her separate use, married an English gentleman, and by the marriage settlement certain plate which formerly belonged to her first husband was settled to her separate use. After the marriage, her husband having family plate of his own, sent it to his wife's house in Paris, and she then sent her own plate to her son by her first marriage. Upon the death of the husband his family plate, and also a marble bust of himself, was in his wife's house at Paris. In a suit for the administration of his estate his wife claimed the plate as having been given her in exchange for her own plate, and the bust as having been presented to her by her husband :—*Held* (reversing the decision of Kay, J.), that the surrounding circumstances did not furnish corroborative evidence in support of the claim by the wife to the plate and bust, and that as the claim rested on her unsupported testimony it could not be allowed. *In re* FINCH. FINCH *v.* FINCH　　23 Ch. D. 267

(e.) FOREIGN ASSETS.

16. —— Jurisdiction of English Court over Scotch Assets of Testator domiciled in Scotland— Scotch Assets.] A testator domiciled in Scotland, and possessed of a large personal and some heritable property in Scotland and of a comparatively small personal property in England, by will made in Scotch form appointed several persons to be executors and trustees, some of whom resided in England and some in Scotland. The trustees obtained a confirmation of the will in Scotland, and the confirmation was sealed by the English Court of Probate under 21 & 22 Vict. c. 56. An infant legatee resident in England brought by his next friend an action here to administer the estate, and the writ was served upon some of the trustees in England, and (under an order) upon the Scotch trustees in Scotland. The trustees appeared without protest and took no steps to discharge the order, but obtained an order of reference to inquire whether the further prosecution of the action would be for the benefit of the infant plaintiff; upon which an order (not

I. EXECUTOR — ACTIONS (by and against)— *continued.*

(e.) FOREIGN ASSETS—*continued.*

appealed from) was made for the further prosecution of the action. The trustees removed all the English personalty into Scotland before the action came on for trial :—*Held,* affirming the decision of the Court of Appeal, that the English Court had jurisdiction to administer the trusts of the will as to the whole estate, both Scotch and English ; and that as no proceedings were pending in a Scotch Court (if such were possible) by which the interests of the infant plaintiff could have been equally protected, the jurisdiction was not discretionary, but that the decree was a matter of course.—The dicta of Lord Westbury in *Enohin* v. *Wylie* (10 H. L. C. 1) disapproved. EWING *v.* ORR EWING　　-　　22 Ch. D. 456 ;

[9 App. Cas. 34

[As to jurisdiction of Scotch Courts, see S. C. 10 Ch. D. 453.]

(f.) INSOLVENT ESTATE.

17. —— Bankruptcy Rules—*Judicature Act, 1875, s. 10—Bill of Sale.*] The 10th section of the Judicature Act, 1875, is not intended to enlarge the assets of an insolvent estate, but only to vary the rights of the persons entitled to the assets.— And therefore that section does not apply the rules of bankruptcy so as to make an unregistered bill of sale void as against the unsecured creditors of an insolvent estate. *In re* COUNT D'EPIN-BUIL (1). TADMAN *v.* EFINEUIL　　20 Ch. D. 217

18. —— Bankruptcy Rules—*Mutual Credits—Judicature Act, 1875 (38 & 39 Vict. c. 77), s. 10.*] The mutual credit clause (sect. 39) of the Bankruptcy Act, 1869, will not be applied in the administration of the estate of a deceased person until it is shewn that the estate is insolvent, but the Court may direct that a debt claimed on behalf of the estate from a creditor shall be paid into Court to a separate account, with liberty to the creditor to apply, in case the estate shall prove to be insolvent. *In re* SMITH. GREEN *v.* SMITH

[22 Ch. D. 586

19. —— Bankruptcy Rules, 1870, r. 77—*Proof—Judicature Act, 1875, s. 10—Bankruptcy Act, 1869, s. 31—Covenant to pay on certain Event—Annuity—Valuation—Contingent Liabilities—Contingency happening during Administration—Proof of Debts—Rebate of Interest.*] A testator covenanted by deed for payment to his daughter of a sum of £5000, with interest at 4 per cent. per annum, within one month after the death of his wife ; also for payment to his daughter of an annuity of £100 during the joint lives of himself and his wife and the life of the survivor, if his daughter should so long live.—The testator died in 1879, insolvent, leaving his widow and daughter surviving, and a judgment was made, in a creditor's action for administration of his estate.—The daughter having sent in claims in respect of the principal sum and the annuity, they were both allowed on a valuation as at the date of the judgment, but subsequently the widow died. No certificate had yet been made in the action :—*Held,* applying the rules in bankruptcy as to contingent liabilities (Judicature Act, 1875, s. 10), that the daughter was entitled to prove for the full amount of the £5000,

I. EXECUTOR—ACTIONS (by and against)— *continued.*

(f.) INSOLVENT ESTATE—*continued.*

less a rebate of interest at 4 per cent. per annum for the period between the date of the judgment and the death of the widow, and that her proof in respect of the annuity must be treated on the same principle. *In re* BRIDGES. HILL *v.* BRIDGES

[17 Ch. D. 342

20. —— Bankruptcy Rules—*Secured and unsecured Creditors—Priority—Judgment recovered against Executors before Administration Judgment—Judicature Act, 1875 (38 & 39 Vict. c. 77), s. 10—Bankruptcy Act, 1869 (32 & 33 Vict. c. 71), s. 32.*] Sect. 10 of the Judicature Act, 1875, does not introduce into the administration of insolvent estates of deceased persons the provision of sect. 32 of the Bankruptcy Act, 1869, that all debts (with certain exceptions) are to be paid pari passu.— Sect. 10 affects only the rights of the class of secured creditors as conflicting with those of the class of unsecured creditors ; it does not affect the rights inter se of the members of those classes.— Therefore if a creditor of an insolvent testator recovers judgment for his debt against the executor before the date of a judgment in an administration action, he is, notwithstanding sect. 10, entitled to be paid out of the assets in priority to the other creditors of equal degree. — *Smith* v. *Morgan* (5 C. P. D. 337) approved and followed. *In re* MAGGI. WINEHOUSE *v.* WINEHOUSE 20 Ch. D. 545

21. —— Bankruptcy Rules, 1870, rr. 99, 100, 101—*Secured Creditor — Judicature Act, 1875, s. 10.*] An equitable mortgagee obtained a common decree for administration of his deceased debtor's estate, and sent in a claim for the whole amount of his debt. When the certificate of debts came to be settled the mistake was pointed out, and the Chief Clerk required the Plaintiff to put a value on his security. He did so, and was admitted as a creditor for the balance, £28. The estate was then believed to be insolvent, but the fact had not been formally established. After the certificate had become binding the Plaintiff took out a summons asking that the property might be sold, and that he might be allowed to prove for the deficiency. A sale was ordered, and the summons directed to stand over. The property sold for much less than the value set upon it, and the summons was then brought on again :—*Held,* by Fry, J., and by the Court of Appeal, that by sect. 10 of the Judicature Act, 1875, rule 101 of the Bankruptcy Rules of 1870 was made applicable to the case, and that the Plaintiff could only stand as a creditor for £28. *In re* HOPKINS. WILLIAMS *v.* HOPKINS　　-　　18 Ch. D. 370

—— Retainer — Right of, after administration judgment　16 Ch. D. 198 ; 22 Ch. D. 604

See EXECUTOR—RETAINER. 1, 2.

II. EXECUTOR—ADMINISTRATION.

(a.) CARRYING ON BUSINESS.

1. —— Apportionment of Loss—*Tenant for Life and Remainderman—Settlement by Will of Share of Business.*] A trader devised and bequeathed to trustees all his real and personal estate, including his share in the business in which he was a partner, on trust as to one moiety thereof to pay the annual proceeds (including the

II. EXECUTOR—ADMINISTRATION—contd.

(a) CARRYING ON BUSINESS—continued.

net profits of the business) to his daughter for her life, for her separate use without power of anticipation, and after her death the moiety was to be held in trust for her children or remoter issue. He directed his trustees to carry on the business after his death until the expiration of the partnership term, and authorized them to use, not only such capital as he should have in the business at the time of his death, but also such other part of the trust premises as they should think fit. The partnership deed authorized the partners to dispose of their shares by will; it did not provide how any loss in carrying on the business should be borne. The will contained no provision as to the mode in which any such loss should be borne as between the persons interested in the testator's estate. It had been the practice of the firm in prosperous years to divide the whole profit among the partners, and in years in which there was a loss to write off each partner's proportion of the loss from his share of the capital. The testator died in 1879. After his death the business was carried on by his trustees in partnership with the other partners. Up to the end of 1880 it was carried on at a profit, and half the testator's share of that profit was paid by the trustees to the daughter. For the year 1881 there was a loss, and the testator's share of the loss was written off from his share of the capital in the books of the firm. For the year 1882 there was a profit:—*Held*, that the daughter was entitled to receive half that share of the profits which the testator, according to the practice of the firm, would have received if he had been alive, and that, consequently, she was entitled to receive half his share of the profits for the year 1882, without any deduction for the purpose of making good the corpus of the settled share in the interest of the remaindermen. GOW v. FORSTER

[26 Ch. D. 672

2. —— Occupation of Business Premises— *Direction to Executors to pay Legacies "out of my Estate"—Direction to carry on Testator's Business.*] A testator, after giving legacies and annuities, proceeded to say: "My executors may realize such part of my estate as they think right and in their judgment to pay the aforenamed legacies." He then directed his business to be carried on till his son attained the age of thirty, but did not dispose of the profits, nor did his will contain any further disposition of his real or personal estate, except a gift of a particular house. The testator carried on his business in a freehold mill which was his own property. *Held*, by the Vice-Chancellor of the Court of the County Palatine of Lancaster, that the testator died intestate as to his real estate except the house, that his business was to be carried on till the son attained thirty or further order, and that the profits after providing for the legacies and annuities went to the next of kin. That the testator died intestate as to his residuary personal estate, and that an occupation rent should be paid to the heir-at-law from the testator's death in respect of the real estate and the fixtures forming part thereof which were used in the business. *Held*, on appeal (affirming the decision of the Vice-

II. EXECUTOR—ADMINISTRATION—contd.

(a.) CARRYING ON BUSINESS—continued.

Chancellor), that the legacies were not charged on the real estate, for that the direction to the executors to realize such parts of his estate as they thought right to pay the legacies was satisfied by holding it to apply to property which they took as executors. *Held* (reversing the decision of the Vice-Chancellor), that so long as the testator's business was continued for the purposes and under the directions of the will, the executors were entitled to the free use and occupation of the business premises, and of the fixed plant and machinery therein without paying any rent for the same. But *held* (varying the decision of the Vice-Chancellor), that the descended real estate could not be affected by the direction to carry on the testator's business any further or otherwise than such carrying on might be necessary for payment of the legacies and annuities given by the will, and that, so soon as they were provided for, the direction to carry on the business became inoperative, and ceased to be binding either on the heir-at-law or the next of kin, and that any surplus profits which had arisen since the testator's decease, after providing for the legacies and annuities, must be apportioned between the heir-at-law and the next of kin according to the values of the real and personal estate employed in the business. *In re* CAMERON. NIXON v. CAMERON - 26 Ch. D. 19

3. —— Pledging Testator's Assets— *Testator's Goods seized under Fi. Fa. against Executor— Lapse of Time—Acquiescence—Renewal of Testator's Lease in Executor's own Name—Deposit to secure Executor's own Debt—Equities—Priority— Purchaser for Value without Notice—Possession of Title Deeds—Order to give up Deed to facilitate Sale.*] If an executor, in pursuance of the directions contained in the testator's will, carries on the testator's business, and in so doing contracts debts, the fact that he has carried on the business in his own name and that the testator's assets employed in it are ostensibly the executor's own property, will not entitle a judgment creditor of the executor to take in execution the testator's assets.— Lapse of time and an enjoyment of the assets in a manner inconsistent with the trusts of the will, coupled with the consent of the beneficiaries, may, however, raise an inference of a gift of the assets by them to the executor, and entitle his judgment creditor to take them in execution. But, when the possession and the time which has elapsed are in accordance with the trusts of the will, no such inference can arise.—*Ray* v. *Ray* (G. Coop. 264) distinguished.—An executor, six years after the death of the testator, surrendered a lease belonging to the testator, and took a renewed lease, including additional property, and at an increased rent, in his own name. He afterwards deposited the lease as security for money advanced to him, which he applied to his own purposes. The renewed lease contained no mention of the surrender, and the mortgagee did not know that the borrower was an executor, or that he was not the beneficial owner of the lease. He did not, however, make any inquiry into the title. An action was afterwards brought to administer the testator's estate, and a consent order was made for the

II. EXECUTOR—ADMINISTRATION—*contd.*

(a) CARRYING ON BUSINESS—*continued.*

sale of the leasehold property, without prejudice to any right, the mortgagee giving up the lease to facilitate the sale. He claimed to be paid the amount due to him by the executor out of the proceeds of sale.—*Held* (affirming the decision of Fry, J.), that the lease was in equity part of the testator's estate, and that the equity of the estate being prior to the equity of the mortgagee, must prevail against it :—*Held*, also, that the equitable mortgagee was not injured by the order to give up the indenture of lease, and did not thereby acquire any claim upon the proceeds of the sale. *In re* MORGAN. PILLGREM *v.* PILLGREM
[18 Ch. D. 93

4. —— Profits until Sale—*Trust for Sale—Direction as to interim Profits—Capital or Income.*] A testator devised and bequeathed his real and personal estate upon usual trusts for sale and conversion, the proceeds to be invested and to be held upon trust for his wife for life, and, after her death, for his children. The will contained the usual power to postpone the sale and conversion of the real and personal estate, and the usual direction that until sale and conversion the rents, profits, and income thereof should be paid and applied to the same persons and in the same manner as the income of the trust estate. The will contained no reference whatever to the business of the testator, which comprised the bulk of his estate. The executors carried on the business for nearly two years with a view to its sale as a going concern, and the question arose whether the profits of the business during that period were to be treated as capital or income :—*Held*, that the executors had power to carry on the business for a reasonable period with a view to its sale as a going concern ; and that, as the testator had expressly directed that the profits of his personal estate until conversion were to be treated as income, the general rule laid down in *Howe* v. *Earl of Dartmouth* (7 Ves. 137) did not apply, and therefore the widow was entitled to the profits of the business.—*Brown* v. *Gellatly* (Law Rep. 2 Ch. 751) and *Kirkman* v. *Booth* (11 Beav. 279) distinguished. *In re* CHANCELLOR. CHANCELLOR *v.* BROWN
[26 Ch. D. 42

(b.) CONVERSION.

5. —— Power to postpone—*Residue—Tenant for Life and Remainderman—Apportionment between Capital and Income—Compound Interest.*] A testator died entitled to an annuity secured on the grantor's estate in land expectant on the death of his father, and also to a mortgage debt on the same estate. The testator devised his residuary estate to trustees upon trust to convert at their uncontrolled discretion, and to pay the income to his wife for life, and after her death to his children. The mortgaged estate did not fall into possession till several years after testator's death, and the arrears of the annuity and the mortgage debt were then paid :—*Held*, that the amount ought to be apportioned between capital and income, on the principle of ascertaining the amount which if put out at interest on the death of the testator at compound interest would with the accumulations have amounted on the day of payment to the sum actually paid, and the sum so ascertained should

II. EXECUTOR—ADMINISTRATION—*contd.*

(b.) CONVERSION—*continued.*

be treated as capital, and the difference between that sum and the sum actually paid should be treated as income, and paid to the tenants for life. BEAVAN *v.* BEAVAN　-　-　24 Ch. D. 649, n.

6. —— Power to postpone—*Will—Residuary Gift—Tenant for Life and Remainderman—Expectancy—Property falling in after Testator's Death—Apportionment between Capital and Income, how made—Compound Interest—Yearly Rests.*] Where a testator has bequeathed his residuary personal estate to trustees upon trust for conversion, with power to postpone such conversion at their discretion, and to hold the proceeds upon trust for a person for life with remainders over, and such residue includes outstanding personal estate, the conversion of which the trustees, in the exercise of their discretion, postpone for the benefit of the estate, and which eventually falls in some years after the testator's death—as for instance a mortgage debt with arrears of interest, or arrears of an annuity with interest, or moneys payable upon a life policy—such outstanding personal estate should, on falling in, be apportioned as between capital and income by ascertaining the sum which, put out at interest at 4 per cent. per annum on the day of the testator's death, and accumulating at compound interest calculated at that rate with yearly rests and deducting income tax, would, with the accumulations of interest, have produced, at the day of receipt, the amount actually received ; and the sum so ascertained should be treated as capital, and the residue as income.—*Beavan* v. *Beavan* (24 Ch. D. 649, n.) followed. *In re* EARL OF CHESTERFIELD'S TRUSTS　　　24 Ch. D. 643

(c.) PAYMENT OF DEBTS AND LEGACIES.

7. —— Deficient Estate—*Abatement of Annuities—Apportionment—Direction to pay Annuity free of Legacy Duty—Costs of Plaintiff in Legatee's Administration Action.*] When a testator's estate is insufficient (after payment of his debts) to pay in full annuities given by his will, the fund must (after payment of costs) be apportioned between the annuitants in the proportion which the sums composed of the arrears of the annuity in each case plus the present value of the future payments bear to each other, and this rule applies in a case in which the annuitants are all living at the time of distribution.—*Heath* v. *Nugent* (29 Beav. 226) followed.—A testator gave an annuity of £150 to his widow, an annuity of £100 to a stranger in blood, and he directed that the second annuity should be paid free of legacy duty, which should be paid out of his estate. After payment of his debts, the estate was insufficient to pay the annuities in full :—*Held*, that (after payment of costs) the fund must be apportioned as above between the two annuitants ; that the legacy duty payable on the sum apportioned to the second annuitant must be deducted from the whole fund, and the balance then divided in the same proportion between the two annuitants. —It is the settled rule that the plaintiff in a legatee's administration action is, when the estate is insufficient to pay the legacies in full, entitled to receive his costs out of the fund as between

II. EXECUTOR—ADMINISTRATION—contd.

(c) PAYMENT OF DEBTS AND LEGACIES—contd.

solicitor and client, and this rule applies even when there is a contest between him and another legatee as to the proper mode of dividing the fund. *In re* WILKINS. WILKINS *v.* ROTHERHAM
[27 Ch. D. 703

8. —— Domicil—Priorities.] In the administration of the English estate of a deceased domiciled abroad, foreign creditors are entitled to dividends *pari passu* with English creditors. *In re* KLŒBE. KANNREUTHER *v.* GEISELBRECHT
[28 Ch. D. 175

9. —— Exoneration of General Personal Estate —Trust for Payment of Debts.] The rule that a charge of debts on real estate does not of itself exonerate the personal estate applies to a case where a charge for payment of debts after the grantor's death is created by deed. But no such rule applies to specific personal estate given on similar trusts; in such a case the specific personal estate will be the primary fund for the payment of the debts.—A testator by a deed executed in his lifetime conveyed and assigned real and personal estate to trustees, in trust for himself during his life, and after his death to sell and convert the property, and to stand possessed of the proceeds on trust, after payment of costs, to pay all the debts which should be due from him, and his funeral expenses, and, after such payment as aforesaid, upon trusts for his sons and their children. By his will the testator, after reciting the deed, devised and bequeathed all and every the residue of his real and personal estate not comprised in and subject to the trusts of the deed, to his wife for her life, with remainders over, and he appointed his wife and one of the trustees of the deed executors of his will, which was proved by the widow and one of the trustees:—Held, that, as regarded the real estate comprised in the deed, the testator's general personal estate was not exonerated from its primary liability to pay his debts.—But *held*, that the personal estate comprised in the deed was the primary fund for the payment of the debts.—*French* v. *Chichester* (2 Vern. 568; 3 Bro. P. C. 2nd Ed. p. 16) discussed and explained. TROTT *v.* BUCHANAN　　　28 Ch. D. 446

III. EXECUTOR—LIABILITIES (and DUTIES).

1. —— Laches — Devastavit.] Mere laches in abstaining from calling upon the executors to realise for the purpose of paying his debt will not deprive a creditor of his right to sue the executors for devastavit, unless there has been such a course of conduct, or express authority, on his part that the executors have been thereby misled into parting with the assets, available to answer his claim. *In re* BIRCH. ROE *v.* BIRCH　　27 Ch. D. 622

2. —— Purchase by Executor who has not proved—Suit to set aside Sale.] Held, that a sale is not to be avoided merely because when entered upon the purchaser has the power to become trustee of the property purchased, as for instance by proving the will which relates thereto, though in point of fact he never does become such. Such a purchaser is under no disability, and in order to avoid such sale it must be shewn

III. EXECUTOR—LIABILITIES (and DUTIES) —continued.

that he in fact used his power in such a way as to render it inequitable that the sale should be upheld. CLARK *v.* CLARK　-　9 App. Cas. 733

IV. EXECUTOR—POWERS.

By 44 & 45 Vict. c. 41, s. 37.—(1.) *An executor may pay or allow any debt or claim on any evidence that he thinks sufficient.*

(2.) *An executor may, if and as he thinks fit, accept any composition or any security, real or personal, for any debt, or for any property, real or personal, claimed, and may allow any time for payment of any debt, and may compromise, compound, abandon, submit to arbitration, or otherwise settle any debt, account, claim, or thing whatever relating to the testator's estate, and for any of those purposes may enter into, give, execute, and do such agreements, instruments of composition or arrangement, releases, and other things as to him seems expedient, without being responsible for any loss occasioned by any act or thing so done by him in good faith.*

The section applies to executorships constituted or created either before or after the commencement of the Act.

By sect. 38.—(1.) *Where a power is given to two or more executors jointly, then unless the contrary is expressed in the instrument, if any, creating the power, the same may be exercised or performed by the survivor or survivors of them for the time being.*

(2.) *The section applies only to executorships constituted after or created by instruments coming into operation after the commencement of the Act—31st of December, 1881.*

1. —— Advances to an Executor—Bankers—Executorial Purposes—Separate Account of Executor.] One of two executors, who was himself a residuary legatee, entered an account with a banker in his own name for executorial purposes, and the banker, without notice of the dispositions under the will, made advances to the executor for payments connected with the executorship, and securities were deposited for repayment of the advances. The co-executor assented to the first advance, but upon a second advance being made to the acting executor upon other securities, he withdrew his assent, and objected to the banker being repaid out of the trust property, on the ground that the money had been placed to the separate account of the acting executor. The advances were duly applied to the purposes of the administration. Upon an action being brought by the banker for a lien upon the second securities for repayment of his advances:—Held, that the banker was justified in advancing money to the acting executor for executorial purposes, and that the assent of the co-executor in the first instance was a further justification for placing confidence in the acting executor and in making further advances to him. The repayment was therefore decreed with mortgagee's costs. CHILD & Co. *v.* THORLEY -　-　16 Ch. D. 151

2. —— Charge of Debts—Partnership Property—Power of Executor to sell—23 & 24 Vict. c. 145, s. 30.] A testator, who carried on business in partnership with his brother, by his will, dated

IV. EXECUTOR—POWERS—*continued.*

the 23rd of November, 1861, directed payment of his debts, and, after bequeathing specific and pecuniary legacies, he devised and bequeathed all his real and leasehold and personal estate to trustees, upon trust for sale and conversion into money, and to hold the proceeds of sale on certain trusts. In 1872 the brother and the testator's widow, who was then the sole trustee and executrix of the will, joined in selling and conveying real estate, of which the brother and the testator had been tenants in common, and which was in fact partnership property, to a limited company who purchased the business. The purchase-money was to be paid partly in cash and partly in fully paid-up shares and debentures of the company. At the same time an arrangement was made for the handing over of the whole purchase-money to the bankers of the partnership, to whom the partnership was largely indebted, and whose debt was secured by mortgages of the partnership property, in satisfaction of the debt due to the bankers, the bankers undertaking to pay the other creditors of the partnership, and handing back to the executrix a sum of cash and some of the debentures, and providing certain other benefits for the brother. The conveyance of the real estate to the company contained a recital that the brother and the widow were entitled to the property in equal undivided moieties, and the widow purported to convey as trustee of her husband's will, but it was not stated in the deed that she was his executrix or that the property was partnership property.—On a subsequent sale of the property by the company, the purchaser objected that the sale by the widow was not authorized by the trust for sale, the consideration not being entirely paid in money:—*Held,* that the arrangement as to the disposition of the purchase-money amounted to a compromise by the widow with the creditors and with the surviving partner into which it was competent to her as executrix to enter under sect. 30 of the Act 23 & 24 Vict. c. 145:—And *held,* on the authority of *Corser v. Cartwright* (Law Rep. 7 H. L. 731), that this being so, and the real estate being partnership property which the widow, as executrix, was entitled to sell, and inasmuch as she, as trustee, had the legal estate, and as executrix was the proper person to receive the purchase-money, the sale to the company was a valid one and their title good. WEST OF ENGLAND AND SOUTH WALES DISTRICT BANK *v.* MURCH   23 Ch. D. 138

3. —— **Dead Body**—*Property—Possession—Direction by Will—Cremation—Claim founded on Fraud.*] A testator directed W. to burn his body, and directed his executors to repay W. the expense of so doing. The body was buried in unconsecrated ground with the assent of the executors. Afterwards W. representing to the Under-Secretary of State that she intended to bury it in consecrated ground, obtained his license to remove it. She caused it to be burnt in Italy, and then brought an action against the executors for the expenses. The action was dismissed:—*Held,* that there is no property in a dead body, but the executors have a right to the possession

IV. EXECUTOR—POWERS—*continued.*

of the body, and their duty is to bury it.—*Held,* that a direction by will as to the disposition of the testator's body cannot be enforced.—Whether it is lawful to burn a dead body, *quære.* WILLIAMS *v.* WILLIAMS   20 Ch. D. 659

V. EXECUTOR—RETAINER.

1. —— **Administration Action** — *Executor suing on behalf of himself and all other Creditors.*] In the administration of a testator's estate, the right of an executor to retain for his debt is not affected by the circumstances that he is himself the Plaintiff, suing on behalf of himself and all other creditors, and that he has submitted to account in the ordinary form of an administration decree. *Ex parte* CAMPBELL CAMPBELL *v.* CAMPBELL - - - - 16 Ch. D. 198

2. —— **Administration Action**—*Solicitor—Conflict of Interest and Duty—Appointment of Receiver.*] In a creditor's administration action, brought against the administrator of an intestate (the Defendant being a solicitor, and a member of the firm of solicitors who were acting for the Plaintiff) after judgment for administration had been pronounced, an order was made on the application of the Plaintiff by his solicitors for the appointment of a specified person, "upon his giving security," to receive the rents of the intestate's real estate, and to collect and get in his outstanding personal estate. On the application for this order the Defendant made an affidavit stating his approval of the person proposed. Before the receiver had perfected his security some money arising from the sale of furniture belonging to the intestate was received by the Defendant's firm, and appropriated by him, and he claimed to retain out of it a debt due to him by the intestate:—*Held,* that, by reason of the relation in which the Defendant stood to the Plaintiff as a member of the firm of solicitors who were acting for him, the Defendant stood in no better position than he would have stood after the receiver had perfected his security, and that the Defendant could not under the circumstances exercise his right of retainer.—*Wickens v. Townshend* (1 Russ. & My. 661) applied. *In re* BIRT. BIRT *v.* BIRT   -   22 Ch. D. 604

3. —— **Bequest to Bankrupt Debtor**—*Composition—Assignment by Debtor of Share of Estate.*] D., who was indebted to his father L., on a bill of sale, and a promissory note, was adjudicated bankrupt. At a meeting of the creditors of D., a composition of 2s. 6d. in the pound was accepted in satisfaction of the debts due to them, and the bankruptcy was annulled. L., who did not prove his debt, and was not paid the composition, died, having bequeathed to D. a share of his estate. The executors who proved the will (D. being an executor who did not prove) did not prove the debt under the composition. D. assigned his share of the estate to B., who brought an action for the administration of L.'s estate. The executors claimed a right of retainer against B. for the debt:—*Held,* that the amount of composition was substituted for the provable debts, whether such debts were proved by the creditors or not; and

V. EXECUTOR—RETAINER—continued.

that the executors were not entitled to the right of retainer against the bequest of the share of the estate for the whole debt, but only for the composition on the debt and interest ; six years' arrears of interest on the promissory note, and the whole arrears on the bill of sale. In re ORPEN. BES-WICK v. ORPEN - 16 Ch. D. 202

4. —— Contributory to Company — Liquidator—Balance Order—Joint Creditor—Companies Act, 1882, ss. 75, 76, 103, 105, 106—Gen. Ord. Nov. 1862, r. 35; Sched. III., Form 39.] Where under sects. 76 and 103 of the Companies Act, 1862, and Rule 35 of Gen. Ord. Nov. 1862, a balance order has been obtained by the official liquidator of a company against the legal personal representative of a deceased contributory for payment of a call made after the death, the order being in accordance with Form 39 in Sched. III. to the Gen. Ord., and directing the legal personal representative to pay the call "out of the assets of the deceased in his hands as such legal personal representative to be administered in due course of administration," such an order is not in the nature of a judgment so as to constitute the liquidator a judgment creditor; it is to be treated simply as analogous to a common administration judgment, or as a step to the administration judgment which may be obtained by the liquidator under sect. 105 of the Companies Act, 1862, and which is his proper remedy in case the legal personal representative has failed to comply with the order; and therefore the order, whether followed by an administration judgment or not, leaves untouched all priorities and rights usually existing in the due course of the administration of the estate of a deceased person, including an executor's right of retainer. Thus, the order, if obtained against executors, does not give the liquidator priority over a debt due to one of them from the testator, and therefore retained by that executor out of the assets, even though the order be prior in date to notice of the retainer.—One of several executors is entitled to a right of retainer in respect of a mortgage debt due from the testator to a body of trustees of whom that executor is one.—Decision of Bacon, V.C., reversed. In re HUBBACK. INTERNATIONAL MARINE HYDROPATHIC COMPANY v. HAWES - - - - 29 Ch. D. 934

5. —— Costs incurred in Probate Suit against Legacy.] Legatees who were also next of kin of the testator, brought an action against the executor, seeking a revocation of the probate, but failed, and were ordered to pay the executor's costs of the action. While the action was pending, some of the Plaintiffs assigned and others mortgaged their shares whether under the will or on an intestacy. Afterwards the legatees commenced an action against the executor in the Chancery Division for the administration of the estate :—Held (affirming the decision of Hall, V.C.), that the executor was entitled to set off the costs in the probate suit against the legacies, notwithstanding the assignments and incumbrances. In re KNAPMAN. KNAPMAN v. WREFORD - 18 Ch. D. 300

6. —— Creditor in higher Degree—Executor of Executor of original Testator—Hinde Palmer's Act (32 & 33 Vict. c. 46), s. 1.] The right of retainer by an executor has not been abolished by Hinde Palmer's Act, nor has it been enlarged so as to enable the executor to retain his debt as against a creditor of higher degree than himself. —Notwithstanding the Act, an executor who is only a simple contract creditor of his testator cannot retain his debt as against a specialty creditor.—If an executor dies after having claimed a right of retainer, but without having actually exercised it, leaving another executor of the original testator surviving, the executors of the deceased executor have the right of retainer for the benefit of his estate.—Hopton v. Dryden (Prec. in Ch. 179) distinguished.—A right of retainer being claimed on behalf of the estate of an executor who was a simple contract creditor of the testator, and there being a specialty creditor :—Held, that the assets must (after payment of costs) be apportioned on the footing of giving an equal dividend to all the creditors (specialty and simple contract) ; that the dividend must be paid in full to the specialty creditor ; that the executor must then retain his debt out of the residue ; and that the surplus (if any) must be divided equally among the simple contract creditors. WILSON v. COXWELL -. - - 23 Ch. D. 764

7. —— Equitable Assets—Real Estate—3 & 4 Will. 4, c. 104.] Real estate is, by the statute 3 & 4 Will. 4, c. 104, made assets for the payment of debts only in equity, and an executor has no right of retainer against it. Personal estate being the primary fund for the payment of specialty debts, the circumstance that the specialty debts of a testator, whose personal estate is insufficient to pay those debts in full, have been actually paid in the first instance partly out of the proceeds of the sale of real estate, will not give the executor a right to retain his own simple contract debt out of personal estate subsequently realized, which he would not have had if the whole personal estate had been applied in the first instance in payment of the specialty debts. WALTERS v. WALTERS - 18 Ch. D. 182

8. —— Executor of Executor—Assets received or paid into Court after Death of Executor — Debt under Covenant—Arbitrary Damages.] An executor's right of retainer is limited to so much of the assets of his testator as comes into the possession or under the control of the executor, or is paid into Court during his lifetime.—If an executor asserts in his lifetime a right of retainer, but dies without having exercised it, his representatives may exercise that right for the benefit of his estate only as to anything which came into the actual possession or under the actual control of their testator, or which was paid into Court during his lifetime.—Wilson v. Coxwell (23 Ch. D. 764), unless restricted in this way, must be treated as overruled.—Claims by an executor for breach of a covenant to assign a policy, and to replace furniture, if sold, by other furniture of like value, are claims for damages for breach of pecuniary contracts for which there is a certain standard or measure, and may therefore, on the authority of Loane v. Casey (2 W. Bl. 965), be retained. In re COMPTON. NORTON v. COMPTON 30 Ch. D. 15

V. EXECUTOR—RETAINER—*continued.*

9. —— **Joint Creditors**—*One Executor*—32 & 33 *Vict.* c. 46.] One of three executors who is also one of two joint creditors has a right of retainer in respect of his joint debt. The right of retainer is not affected by the Act abolishing the distinction between specialty and simple contract debts. CROWDER *v.* STEWART **16 Ch. D. 368**

10. —— **Statute of Frauds, Debt barred by—**Devastavit.] An executor or administrator would commit a devastavit who paid a debt to a creditor who is prevented from enforcing it by the Statute of Frauds. And for the same reason an executor or administrator cannot retain such debt if due to himself.—A father in consideration of the marriage of his daughter made a verbal promise to pay his daughter and her husband £500. He died intestate without performing his promise, and the daughter took out administration to his estate:—*Held* (affirming the decision of Kay, J.), that the administratrix could not retain the debt out of the assets. *In re* ROWNSON. FIELD *v.* WHITE **29 Ch. D. 358**

EXECUTOR—According to tenor - **8 P. D. 215**
See PROBATE—GRANT. 6.

—— Action commenced before probate—Staying proceedings **12 Q. B. D. 294**
See PRACTICE—SUPREME COURT—STAYING PROCEEDINGS. 3.

—— Adopting Conveyancing Act—Protection of.
See CONVEYANCING ACT, 1881—*Statutes.*

—— Bankruptcy of—Conduct of cause
[**19 Ch. D. 61**
See PRACTICE—SUPREME COURT—CONDUCT OF CAUSE. 1.

—— Charge of debts—Legal title **24 Ch. D. 190**
See WILL—ESTATE IN REALTY. 1.

—— Charge of debts—Power to sell
[**20 Ch. D. 465**
See WILL—CHARGE OF DEBTS.

—— Debtor to estate—Set-off - **25 Ch. D. 175**
See SET-OFF. 3.

—— Devastavit—Statute of Limitations
[**22 Ch. D. 320; 26 Ch. D. 783**
See LIMITATIONS, STATUTE OF—PERSONAL ACTIONS. 5, 6.

—— Indefinite trust **26 Ch. D. 531**
See WILL—TRUSTEES.

—— Judgment creditor—Bankruptcy
[**13 Q. B. D. 479**
See BANKRUPTCY—ACT OF BANKRUPTCY. 8.

—— Legacy to - - - **29 Ch. D. 893**
See WILL—EXECUTORS.

—— Liability of—Insolvency of agent
[**26 Ch. D. 238**
See TRUSTEE—LIABILITIES. 1.

—— Married woman—Power of appointment—Separate estate - **7 P. D. 61**
See PROBATE—MARRIED WOMAN. 5.

—— One suing alone—Application to add the other - - **28 Ch. D. 414**
See PRACTICE — SUPREME COURT — PARTIES. 5.

EXECUTOR—*continued.*

—— Order of reference—Death of party before making of award **15 Q. B. D. 565**
See PRACTICE — SUPREME COURT — CHANGE OF PARTIES. 4.

—— Renunciation - - - **16 Ch. D. 3**
See ADMINISTRATOR—WITH WILL ANNEXED. 1.

—— Solicitor—Professional charges
[**27 Ch. D. 584**
See SOLICITOR—BILL OF COSTS. 15.

EXECUTORY DEVISE - - **18 Ch. D. 524;**
[**24 Ch. D. 633**
See WILL—CONTINGENT REMAINDER. 1, 2.

—— Remoteness - **17 Ch. D. 211**
See WILL—PERPETUITY. 3.

—— Leaseholds for lives **18 Ch. D. 624**
See LEASEHOLD—RENEWABLE LEASE. 3.

EXECUTORY LIMITATION.

By 45 & 46 *Vict.* c. 39 (*Conveyancing Act,* 1882), *Sect.* 10.—(1.) *Where there is a person entitled to land for an estate in fee, or for a term of years absolute or determinable on life, or for term of life, with an executory limitation over on default or failure of all or any of his issue, whether within or at any specified period of time or not, that executory limitation shall be or become void and incapable of taking effect, if (and as soon as) there is living any issue who has attained the age of twenty-one years, of the class on default or failure whereof the limitation over was to take effect.*
(2.) *This section applies only where the executory limitation is contained in an instrument coming into operation after the commencement of this Act—31st December,* 1882.

—— Implication - - **20 Ch. D. 406**
See WILL—CROSS-REMAINDERS.

—— Perpetuity **20 Ch. D. 562**
See LANDS CLAUSES ACT—SUPERFLUOUS LAND. 2.

—— Tenant for life—Settled Land Act
[**24 Ch. D. 114**
See SETTLED LAND ACT—DEFINITIONS. 1.

EXECUTRIX— Married woman — Husband objecting to probate - **6 P. D. 103**
See PROBATE—MARRIED WOMAN. 2.

EXHIBITS—Costs of perusal - **24 Ch. D. 684**
See PRACTICE—SUPREME COURT—COSTS. 37.

—— Duty on—Canadian law **10 App. Cas. 141**
See COLONIAL LAW—CANADA—QUEBEC. 4.

EXONERATION—Lapsed bequest **29 Ch. D. 145**
See WILL—EXONERATION. 1.

—— Mortgaged estate - **16 Ch. D. 322**
See WILL—EXONERATION. 2.

—— Personal estate—Trust for payment of debts
[**28 Ch. D. 446**
See EXECUTOR—ADMINISTRATION. 9.

—— Purchased estate—Vendor's lien **24 Ch. D.**
See WILL—EXONERATION. 3. [**94**

EXPENSES—Election for Parliament   **21 Ch. D.**
    See PARLIAMENT—ELECTION.   1.   [**408**

—— Prisoner—Conveying to prison **6 Q. B. D. 156**;
    See PRISON.   2.   [**7 App. Cas. 1**

—— Winning coal—Reimbursement **7 App. Cas.**
    See MINE—WORKING.   2.   [**43**

—— Witness - -   **21 Ch. D. 831**
    See EVIDENCE—WITNESS.   4.

EXPERIMENT—User for—Infringement of patent   **29 Ch. D. 164**
    See PATENT—INFRINGEMENT.   7.

EXPERT—Advice to Court -   **24 Ch. D. 156**
    See PATENT—VALIDITY.   5.

EXPLOSIONS—Causing—Criminal law.
    See CRIMINAL LAW—EXPLOSIVES—*Sta-
tutes.*

EXPLOSIVES—Having in possession.
    See CRIMINAL LAW—EXPLOSIVES—*Sta-
tutes.*

—— Patent for protecting -   **17 Ch. D. 721**;
                 [**8 App. Cas. 5**
    See PATENT—INFRINGEMENT.   6.

EXPRESS TRUST—Statute of Limitations
    [**18 Ch. D. 254; 22 Ch. D. 614; 27 Ch. D.**
                 [**676**
    See LIMITATIONS, STATUTE OF—TRUSTS.
    1, 2, 3.

EXPULSION—Member of club -   **17 Ch. D. 615**
    See CLUB.

—— Partner—Soliciting customers **22 Ch. D. 504**
    See PARTNERSHIP—DISSOLUTION.   3.

EXTENSION OF TIME—Appeal.
    See Cases under PRACTICE — SUPREME
        COURT—APPEAL.   35—38.

——-Disclaimer—Trustee in bankruptcy **16 Ch D.**
    See BANKRUPTCY—DISCLAIMER.   14. [**613**

—— Indorsement on writ -   **16 Ch. D. 734**
    See PRACTICE—SUPREME COURT—WRIT.
    1.

EXTINCTION OF POWER— Alienation of interest   **26 Ch. D. 417; 27 Ch. D. 565**
    See POWER—EXTINCTION.   1, 2.

EXTRADITION.
    *Treaties under the Extradition Acts, 1870 to
1873, entered into since 1st Jan. 1881, by Great
Britain with the*
     Netherlands. Order in Council, March 2nd,
       1881 - -   **L. G., 1881, p. 983**
     Salvador. Order in Council, Dec. 16th, 1882
                 [**L. G., 1883, p. 1**
     Switzerland. Order in Council, May 18th,
       1881 - -   **L. G., 1881, p. 2609**
     Tonga. Order in Council, Nov. 30th, 1882.
                [**L. G., 1882, p. 6136**
     Uruguay. Order in Council, March 5th, 1885.
                [**L. G., 1885, p. 1028**
      And see JURISDICTION—*Statutes.*
    Canada.] *Suspension of Act of* 1870 *in Canada
so far as relates to foreign states. Order in Council,
Dec. 28th,* 1882 - -   **L. G., 1883, p. 81**
    Cyprus.] *Order in Council, of July 15th,* 1881,
*for the surrender under Foreign Jurisdiction Acts,
1843 to 1878 (and any enactment amending the*

EXTRADITION—*continued.*
*same), by Cyprus of fugitives from any foreign
country or from any part of the Ottoman dominions*
                [**L. G, 1881, p. 3652.**
    *Straits Settlements.] Order in Council, Nov.
29th, 1884, rescinding an earlier Order in Council
rendering it obligatory on the governor. of the
Straits Settlements to surrender fugitive criminals to
foreign states under the statute 29 & 30 Vict. c. 115.*
                . [**L. G., 1884, p. 5657**

    1. —— " **Apprehension** "—*Person already in
Custody—Arrest without a Warrant—Extradition
Act, 1870 (33 & 34 Vict. c. 52), s. 8—Court of Appeal— Jurisdiction — Criminal Matter — Habeas
Corpus — Judicature Act, 1873 (36 & 37 Vict.
c. 66), ss. 19, 47.]* Under sect. 8 of the Extradition Act, 1870, a fugitive criminal who is already
in custody may be detained for an offence coming
within the Act, even though he was originally
arrested without any warrant. The word "apprehension " in sect. 8 includes " detention."—*Semble,*
per Brett, L.J., that a constable would be justified
in arresting without a warrant a fugitive from a
foreign country on reasonable grounds of suspicion that he has committed a crime which would
be a felony if committed in the United Kingdom.
Whether the Court of Appeal has any jurisdiction
to entertain an appeal from the refusal of a Divisional Court to issue a writ of habeas corpus, on
the application of a person who has been arrested
for an alleged extradition crime, *quære.* THE
QUEEN *v.* WEIL - -   **9 Q. B. D. 701**

    2. —— **Foreign Warrant of Arrest**—*Authen-
tication of—Extradition of Subject of State not
party to Extradition Treaty— Extradition Act,.
1870 (33 & 34 Vict. c. 52), ss. 10, 15, 26.]* An
extradition treaty between the United Kingdom
and the Netherlands provided that the Governments, parties to the treaty, should reciprocally
deliver up to each other any persons who, being
accused of any of certain specified crimes committed within the jurisdiction of the party
requiring the extradition, should be found in the
territories of the other party. The treaty further
provided that neither of the contracting governments should be bound to deliver up its own
subjects, and that a person arrested under the
treaty in either country should be discharged, if
within fourteen days a requisition should not have
been made for his surrender by the diplomatic
agent of " his " country :—*Held,* that the provisions for the extradition of criminals under the
treaty were not confined to persons who were
subjects of the state requiring the extradition,
but applied to all persons who had committed any
of the specified crimes within the jurisdiction
of such state of whatever nationality they might
be, except subjects of the state from which extradition was required. A document produced
before a magistrate as the "foreign warrant" of
arrest under sect. 10 of the Extradition Act, 1870,.
was sealed with the seal of the department of
justice at the Hague, and purported to be a copy
of the record or minutes of a certain order or
decree of the Criminal Court of Justice there,
setting forth the charges against the criminal
whose extradition was sought, and authorizing
proceedings against him and his arrest :—*Held,*

EXTRADITION—*continued.*

that the production of such a document before the magistrate was a sufficient compliance with the provisions of sect. 10 of the Extradition Act, 1870, which provides that the magistrate may commit the criminal to prison, if, inter alia, the foreign warrant authorizing his arrest is duly authenticated.—*Semble,* such document must be regarded as in the nature of an original for this purpose. THE QUEEN *v.* GANZ　'-　-　**9 Q. B. D. 93**

3. —— Jurisdiction of Magistrate—*Decision of Magistrate conclusive—Weight of Evidence— 33 & 34 Vict. c. 52, ss. 9, 10.*] Upon an application for a habeas corpus in the case of a fugitive criminal committed by a police magistrate under the Extradition Act, the Court has no power to review the decision of the magistrate on the

EXTRADITION—*continued.*

ground that it was against the weight of evidence laid before him, there being sufficient evidence before him to give him jurisdiction in the matter. THE QUEEN *v.* MAURER -　　**10 Q. B. D. 513**

—— Jurisdiction.
　　See JURISDICTION—*Statutes.*

EXTRAORDINARY FLOOD—Damage from
　　　　　　　　　[7 App. Cas. 694
　　See SCOTCH LAW—STATUTORY DUTY.

EXTRAORDINARY RESOLUTION 16 Ch. D. 534
　　See BANKRUPTCY—COMPOSITION. 1.

EXTRAS—Certificate of surveyor—How far conclusive -　　-　　- **10 Q. B. D. 400**
　　See BUILDING CONTRACT. 1.

F.

FACT, MATTER OF—Matter of opinion
[9 App. Cas. 671
See INSURANCE, LIFE—POLICY. 3.

FACTOR.

1. —— *Lien—Advances by Brokers to Agents for Sale—Antecedent Debt—Privity of Contract—Money had and received—Factors Act,* 5 & 6 Vict. c. 39, *ss.* 3, 7.] The Appellants, merchants at Singapore, employed M. in London as agent to sell, without authority to pledge, cargoes which they from time to time consigned to him. M. employed the Respondents, London brokers, to sell the Appellants' consignments, and also in speculative purchases on his own account. The Respondents purchased shellac for M. without disclosing that they were buying as agents, and therefore were personally liable to the vendors on the contracts. Subsequently they made advances to M. to enable him to pay deposits on the shellac, and took as security bills of lading of some of the Appellants' cargoes. They had no notice that M. was acting improperly in pledging the cargoes. On obtaining the advances M. gave the Respondents cheques for the amount of the deposits, which were then paid by the Respondents :—*Held*, affirming in this respect the decision of the Court of Appeal, that the obligation under which M. lay to the Respondents to pay the deposits and thus prevent their being called upon to pay them, did not constitute an antecedent debt within the meaning of the Factors Act (5 & 6 Vict. c. 39), s. 3, and that the pledges were made in respect of bonâ fide advances and not of antecedent debts, and were valid against the Appellants.—M. also pledged with the Respondents pepper consigned to him for sale by the Appellants, to secure an advance protected by the Factors Acts. The goods had been sold for M. by the Respondents, but not delivered to the purchasers, nor paid for, when M. died insolvent and heavily indebted to the Respondents on a general account. After the sale, but before receiving the proceeds, the Respondents had notice that the Appellants claimed the pepper and the proceeds :—*Held*, reversing in this respect the decision of the Court of Appeal, that after repayment of the Respondents' advance the surplus proceeds of sale belonged to the Appellants ; that the Appellants could sue the Respondents for such surplus, whether on the ground of privity of contract, or on the ground of property, or under the Factors Act (5 & 6 Vict. c. 39), s. 7.— *New Zealand and Australian Land Company* v. *Watson* (7 Q. B. D. 374) distinguished and explained. KALTENBACH v. LEWIS   -   **24 Ch. D. 54; 10 App. Cas. 617**

2. —— *Lien—Restrictions placed by Principal on Powers of Factor.*] An agent who is entrusted with the possession of goods for the purpose of sale does not lose his character of factor, or the

FACTOR—*continued.*
right of lien attached to it, by reason of his acting under special instructions from his principal to sell the goods at a particular price and to sell in the principal's name. STEVENS v. BILLER
[25 Ch. D. 31

3. —— *Lien—Undisclosed Principal—Foreign Merchants—Privity of Contract between Principal and Consignee—Money had and received—Notice or Knowledge—Set-off—Factors Act* (6 Geo. 4, c. 94), s. 1.] Merchants in London, upon the instruction of shipping agents at Havannah with respect to a cargo of tobacco to be consigned to the London merchants and after receiving the shipping documents, effected policies of marine insurance in the ordinary form on behalf and for the benefit of all parties whom it might concern. The Havannah agents shipped and consigned the tobacco in their own names, but were in fact acting as commission agents for Havannah merchants to whom the tobacco belonged; and the London merchants before effecting the policies had notice that the Havannah agents had an unnamed principal. A total loss having occurred, the London merchants received the policy moneys, but before receipt had notice that the moneys were claimed by the Havannah principals :—*Held*, affirming the decision of the Court of Appeal, that an action lay by the Havannah principals against the London merchants for the policy moneys ; that the London merchants were not entitled to a lien upon the moneys for the balance of their general account with the Havannah agents, and could not in that action set off their claim to that balance, or set off anything except the premiums, stamps and commission in respect of the insurance.— *Held* also by Lord Blackburn, that the case fell within the Factors Act (6 Geo. 4, c. 94), s. 1.— Sed *quære* by Lord FitzGerald. MILDRED v. MASPONS   ·   **9 Q. B. D. 530; 8 App. Cas. 874**

FACTORY ACTS.

The Act 46 & 47 *Vict.* c. 53, *amends the law relating to certain Factories and Bakehouses.*

Sect. 1. *Act to be cited as the Factory and Workshop Act,* 1883.

WHITE LEAD FACTORIES.

Sect. 2. *It is unlawful to carry on a white lead factory unless such factory is certified by an inspector to be in conformity with the Act.*

Sect. 3. *Certificate of conformity not to be granted unless scheduled conditions have been complied with.*

Sect. 4. *How certificate is to be obtained.*

Sect. 5. *Certificate may be withdrawn if default is made in complying with the conditions.*

Sect. 6. *Penalty on carrying on factory without certificate.*

FACTORY ACTS—*continued.*

Sect. 7. *Special rules to be established for every white lead factory,*

Sect. 8. *As to framing and approval of special rules.*

Sect. 9. *Special rules how to be amended.*

Sect. 10. *Penalty for making false statement with respect to special rules, and for not transmitting special rules for approval.*

Sect. 11. *Publication of special rules.*

Sect. 12. *Penalty for defacing, &c., special rules.*

Sect. 13 *explains s.* 53 *of the Factory and Workshop Act,* 1878, *as to the employment of young persons and women.*

Sect. 14 *amends ss.* 12 *and* 14 *of the Factory and Workshop Act,* 1878, *as to the period of employment of children in certain cases.*

BAKEHOUSES.

Sect. 15. *Regulations for new bakehouses.*

Sect. 16. *Penalty for any bakehouse being unfit on sanitary grounds for use as a bakehouse.*

Sect. 17. *Enforcement of law as to retail bakehouses by local authorities.*

Sect. 18. *Act to be construed as one with the Factory, &c., Act,* 1878.

Definitions.

Schedule of conditions for certificate.

ORDERS BY THE HOME SECRETARY WITH REFERENCE TO THE STATUTE 41 VICT. C. 16 (FACTORY AND WORKSHOP ACT, 1878).

Lime-washing.] *Order of December* 20th, 1882 . *Regulations under sect.* 33 *of the Act not to apply to factories and workshops in Schedule A, nor, under certain provisions, to Schedule B.*

Schedule A.

The whole of the following non-textile factories and workshops :—

Blast furnaces.
Copper mills.
Iron mills.
Foundries.
Distilleries.
Breweries.
Sugar factories.
Cement works.
Manure works.
Stone and marble works.
Paint, colour, and varnish works.
Chemical works.
Works in which alkali is used.
Glass factories.
Flax scutch mills in which neither children nor young persons are employed, and which are worked intermittently for not more than six months in the year.
Works in which there are no glazed windows.

Schedule B.

Parts of non-textile factories and workshops as hereinafter mentioned :—

1. *Such warerooms or other rooms in any non-textile factory or workshop as are used for the storage of articles (whether on shelves or otherwise), and not for the constant carrying on therein of any manufacturing process or handicraft.*

2. *Such parts of any non-textile factory or workshop as are subject to the influence of steam involved in the processes of manufacture.*

3. *Such parts of any non-textile factory or workshop as are places in which pitch, tar, or like material is used.*

4. *Such parts of any non-textile factory or workshop as are places in which unpainted or unvarnished wood is manufactured.*

5. *Such parts of any non-textile factory as are places in which metal is moulded, cast, or founded.*

6. *Such walls of a workshop in a dwelling-house as are prepared.*

7. *Such ceilings or tops of rooms in any non-textile factory or workshop as are of slate or iron, or are at least twenty feet from the floor.*

8. *All ceilings or tops of rooms in any non-textile factory or workshop in which any of the following occupations are carried on :—*

Print works.
Bleach works.
Dye works.
Engineering and machine shops.
Agricultural implement making.
Coachmaking.
Fellmongers, curriers, tanners.
Making of aërated water.
Making of preserved fruits, sweetmeats, bonbons.
Engraving.
Manufacture of soap, starch, candles.
Corn flour mills.
Manufacture of watch movements, shaving, boring, turning, and fitting of brass.

[L. G., 1882, p. 6524

Meals, Places forbidden for.] *Order of December* 20th, 1882. *Prohibition under sect.* 39 *of the Act to extend to the following :—*

Every part of a factory or workshop in which part wool or hair is sorted or dusted, or in which rags are sorted, dusted, or ground.

Every part of a textile factory in which part gassing is carried on.

Every part of a printwork, bleachwork, or dyework, in which part singeing is carried on.

Every part of a factory or workshop in which part any of the following processes are carried on :—

Grinding, glazing, or polishing on a wheel.
Brass casting, type founding.
Dipping metal in aquafortis or other acid solution.
Metal bronzing.
Majolica painting on earthenware.
Cat-gut cleaning and repairing.
Cutting, turning, polishing, bone, ivory, pearl-shell, snail-shell.

Every factory or workshop in which chemicals or artificial manures are manufactured, except any room used solely for meals.

Every factory or workshop in which white lead is manufactured, except any room thereof used solely for meals.

Every part of a factory or workshop in which part dry powder or dust is used in any of the following processes :—Lithographic printing. Playing-card making. Fancy box making. Paper staining. Almanac making. Artificial flower making. Paper colouring and enamelling. Colour making   -   -   - **L. G., 1882, p. 6525**

FACTORY ACTS—*continued.*

Period of Employment : 8 A.M. to 8 P.M.] *Order of December 20th, 1882. Exception under sect. 42 of the Act to extend to the following:—*
Paper-staining works.
Lace warehouses.
Hosiery warehouses.
The manufacture of :—
Silver plate.
Electro-plate.
Britannia metal.
Cutlery.
Scissors.
Files.
Saws.
Jewellery.
Enamelling.
Ornaments and appliances for personal use.
Die sinking.
Tobacco.
Non-textile factories and workshops in which card-making and straw-board lining are carried on.
Ribbon warehouses being workshops. Turning and cutting wood, bone, and ivory. Cabinet and furniture making - - L. G., 1882, p. 6525
Period of Employment : 9 A.M. to 9 P.M.] *Order of December 20th, 1882. Exception under sect. 43 of the Act to apply to workshops in which the curing of fish is carried out* L. G., 1882, p. 6520
Substitution of another Day for Saturday.] *Substitution allowed under sect. 46 of the Act in following places :—*
(a.) *Non-textile factories in which is carried on the printing of newspapers, or of periodicals, or of railway time tables, or of law or parliamentary proceedings.*
(b.) *Non-textile factories or workshops in which any manufacturing process or handicraft is carried on in connection with a retail shop on the same premises.*
(c.) *Non-textile factories and workshops in which is carried on the making of any article of wearing apparel or of food.*
(d.) *Non-textile factories and workshops in places in which the market day is Saturday, or in which a special day has been set apart for weekly half-holiday.*
The following non-textile factories and workshops, viz. :—Dressing floors, tin streams, china clay-pits, and quarries, in the county of Cornwall
[L. G., 1882, p. 6526
Five Hours' Spell.] *Order of December 20th, 1882. Exception under sect. 48 of this Act extended to hosiery factories, woollen factories in the counties of Oxford, Wilts, Worcester, Gloucester, and Somerset, factories in which the only processes carried on are those of winding and throwing raw silk, or either of such processes*
[L. G., 1882, p. 6526
Different Holidays to different Sets.] *Order of December 20th, 1882; exception granted under sect. 49 of the Act to the following :—*
(a.) *Non-textile factories in which is carried on the printing of newspapers, or of periodicals, or of railway time tables, or of law or parliamentary proceedings.*
(b.) *Non-textile factories and workshops in which any manufacturing process or handicraft is carried*

FACTORY ACTS—*continued.*

on in connection with a retail shop on the same premises.
(c.) *Non-textile factories and workshops in which is carried on the making of any article of wearing apparel or of food.*
(d.) *Non-textile factories in which is carried on the manufacture of plate glass* L. G., 1882, p. 6527
Meal Hours, different.] *Order of December 20th, 1882; exception under sect. 52 of the Act in favour of the following:—*
(a.) *Textile factories wherein female young persons or women, employed in a distinct department in which there is no machinery, commence work at a later hour than the men and other young persons, subject to condition that all in the same department shall have their meals at the same time.*
(b.) *Non-textile factories and workshops wherein is carried on the making of wearing apparel.*
(c.) *Non-textile factories and workshops wherein there are two or more departments or sets of young persons, subject to condition that all in the same department or set shall have their meals at the same time.*
(d.) *The following non-textile factories and workshops, viz. :—Dressing floors, tin streams, china clay-pits, and quarries, in the county of Cornwall*
[L. G., 1882, p. 6527
Meal Hours, Employment, &c., during.] *Order of December 20th, 1882; exception under sect. 52 of the Act in favour of the factories and workshops in the last schedule mentioned* L. G., 1882, p. 6527
Additional two Hours.] *Order of 20th December, 1882. Exception under sect. 53 of the Act in favour of the following:—*
The occupation of die-sinking, card-board making, paper colouring, and enamelling, rolling of tea-lead.
The occupation of the making of gas-holders, boilers, and other apparatus, partly manufactured in the open air.
The following non-textile factories and workshops, viz. :—Dressing floors, tin streams, china clay-pits, and quarries, in the county of Cornwall.
Non-textile factories in which the only processes carried on are the processes of calendering, finishing, hooking, lapping, or making up and packing up of any yarn or cloth, or any of such processes.
Workshops wherein the manufacture of fireworks is carried on - - *- L. G., 1882, p. 6528*
Watermills—Lost Time.] *Order of 20th December, 1882. Exception permitting employment from 6 A.M. to 7 P.M. under sect. 57 of the Act, for factories in which water power alone is used to move the machinery -* - *L. G., 1882, p. 6528*
Nightwork.—Male Young Persons above Sixteen.] *Order of 20th December, 1882. Exception in favour of work, under sect. 58 of the Act, in the following places :—*
Oil and seed crushing mills (factories).
Copper and yellow metal rolling mills.
Iron and metal tube works, in which the furnaces used are Siemens' gas furnaces.
The knocking-out and cutting departments of non-textile factories engaged in the refining of loaf sugar.
Such parts of mineral dressing-floors in Cornwall (whether non-textile factories or workshops) as

U

FACTORY ACTS—*continued.*

are appropriated to the processes of calcining and stamping - - - L. G., 1882, p. 6529

Overtime 30 Minutes.—Incomplete Process.] *Order of 20th December*, 1882. *Exception in favour of working overtime, under sect.* 54 *of the Act, in the following places* —.

Non-textile factories and workshops, or parts thereof, in which is carried on the process of baking of bread or biscuits.

The following non-textile factories and workshops, viz.:—Dressing-floors, tin streams, china clay-pits, and quarries, in the county of Cornwall [L. G., 1882, p. 6529

Overtime —Condition under which the additional two Hours may be worked.] *Order of 20th December*, 1882, *directing, under sect.* 63 *of the Act, it to be a condition of the employment in any factory or workshop under Part* 3, *Schedule* 3, *of the Act, of any young person or woman in pursuance of exceptions under sect.* 53 *of the Act, that there be a cubic space of at least* 400 *feet for every young person and woman so employed* [L. G., 1882, p. 6529

Overtime, additional two Hours.] *Order of 22nd November*, 1883. *Exception under sect.* 53 *of the Act in favour of factories and workshops for the making of pork pies* - - L. G., 1883, p. 5861

Period of Employment: 9 A.M. to 9 P.M.] *Order of 12th January*, 1884. *Exception under sect.* 43, *in favour of factories in the Metropolis, in which bookbinding is carried on* - - L. G., 1884, p. 292

Overtime, additional two Hours.] *Order of 12th March*, 1884. *Exception under sect.* 53 *of the Act in favour of factories and workshops for the processes of warping, winding, or filling, or either of them, as incidental to the weaving of ribbons in workshops* - - - L. G., 1884, p. 1263

Period of Employment : 9 A.M. to 9 P.M.] *Order of 15th April*, 1884. *Exception under sect.* 43 *of the Act to workrooms in connection with drapers' retail establishments, within the boroughs of Manchester and Salford* - - L. G., 1884, p. 1769

Overtime, additional two Hours.] *Order of 27th August*, 1884. *Exception under sect.* 53 *in favour of the processes carried on in non-textile factories of calendering, finishing, hooking, lapping, or making up and packing of any yarn or cloth, or any of such processes, and none other* [L. G., 1884, p. 3958

Period of Employment : 8 A.M. to 8 P.M.] *Order of August* 30th, 1884, *extending exception under sect.* 42, *in favour of print works, bleach works, and dyeworks* - - L. G., 1884, p. 3958

FAILURE OF PARTICULAR ESTATE   21 Ch. D.
See WILL—TRUSTEES. 1.   [790

FALSE PRETENCES—Place of trial
[12 Q. B. D. 23
See CRIMINAL LAW—PRACTICE. 4.

FALSE REPRESENTATION.

1. **Opportunity of discovering Truth**—*Specific Performance—Rescinding Contract — Reasonable Diligence—Damages.*] The Plaintiff, a solicitor, published in the *Law Times* an advertisement headed "Law Partnership," stating that the advertiser, an elderly solicitor of moderate practice, with extensive connections, shortly retiring, and

FALSE REPRESENTATION—*continued.*

having no successor, would first take as partner an efficient lawyer who would not object to purchase the advertiser's suburban residence, value £1600. The Defendant answered the advertisement, and had an interview with the Plaintiff, at which the latter stated that his business brought in about £800 a year. The Defendant wrote saying that he should like to have some idea of the amount of business done for the last three years, and asking an interview for the purpose. At this interview the Plaintiff produced three summaries shewing a business of not quite £200 a year. The Defendant asked how the difference was made up, and the Plaintiff shewed him a number of papers which he said related to other business not included in the summaries. These papers, which the Defendant did not examine, shewed only a most trifling amount of business, and the gross returns of the business were in fact only about £200 a year. The Defendant shortly afterwards signed an agreement to purchase the house for £1600, and paid a deposit, the Plaintiff refusing to have any reference to the business inserted in the agreement. The Defendant took possession, but finding, as he alleged, that the business was worthless, refused to complete. The Plaintiff brought his action for specific performance. The Defendant put in a defence, in which he disputed the right to specific performance on the ground of misrepresentations as to the business, and by counter-claim claimed on the same ground to have the contract rescinded, and to have damages on the ground of the expenses he had been put to and the loss incurred by giving up his own practice. He did not in his counter-claim specifically state what representations had been made, nor allege that they were false to the Plaintiff's knowledge:—*Held*, by FRY, J., that the Defendant having had opportunity afforded him of ascertaining the truth of the representations made to him as to the amount of the business, and having to some extent, though carelessly and inefficiently, inquired into it, must be taken not to have relied on the representations, and that the Plaintiff was entitled to specific performance:—*Held*, on appeal, that where one person induces another to enter into an agreement with him by a material representation which is untrue, it is no defence to an action to rescind the contract that the person to whom the representation was made had the means of discovering, and might with reasonable diligence have discovered, that it was untrue:—*Held*, further, that it is no defence in such an action that the Defendant made a cursory and incomplete inquiry into the facts, for that if a material representation is made to him he must be taken to have entered into the contract on the faith of it; and in order to take away his right to have the contract rescinded if it is untrue, it must be shewn either that he had knowledge of facts which shewed it to be untrue, or that he stated in terms, or shewed clearly by his conduct, that he did not rely on the representation :—*Held*, therefore, that the Defendant was entitled to have the contract rescinded and the deposit returned, but that as he had not pleaded knowledge on the part of the Plaintiff that the statements us to the business were untrue, and had not specifically alleged the state-

FALSE REPRESENTATION—*continued.*

ments in his counter-claim, he could not recover damages.—*Atwood v. Small* (6 Cl. & F. 232) considered and explained. REDGRAVE *v.* HURD
[20 Ch. D. 1

2. —— **Vendor and Purchaser**—*Sale under the Direction of the Court—Misrepresentation by Purchaser—Suppression of Facts by Purchaser.*] The life interest of H. in a fund of about £300,000 was put up for sale in a suit for the administration of the estate of a testator who had purchased it. An attempted sale by auction having proved abortive, C., a solicitor, and B., an actuary, stated to L. & Co., the solicitors who conducted the sale, that they could produce evidence as to the life of H. which would induce the Court to accept a less sum than the supposed value, and that they were prepared to make an offer on behalf of themselves and four others, including H. The negotiation proceeded, and pending the settlement of a draft contract, B. prepared and sent to L. & Co., to be laid before the Judge, a "skeleton case," which stated that H. had been examined by three specified medical men on behalf of the three insurance offices of which they were the respective medical examiners, and set out their joint opinion that the insurance of the life of H. was very hazardous, and should not be accepted at a less addition than fifteen years to his age, and that the whole premiums should be paid within ten years. It further stated that one of the three medical men had informed B. that he should advise his office to decline the proposal—which was thereupon withdrawn; that another of the offices refused to insure; and that the third consented to insure for £5000 at a £12 per cent. premium. It set out separate opinions of later date by two of the three medical men which were at least as unfavourable as the joint opinion, and concluded with the statement that H. had not since been examined on behalf of any life office. The Judge upon these materials took the opinions of actuaries, and when their reports were brought before him B. urged upon him that the income was liable to be reduced to £9000 by investment in Consols, and he sanctioned an agreement for purchase at £40,000, which was about the value of the life interest if the income was taken at £9000 and the life as only insurable at a £12 per cent. premium. The sale was completed, and nine years afterwards an action was brought on behalf of the creditors of the testator to impeach it. It appeared that, at the time when the skeleton case was made out, C. and B. had in their hands a later opinion by one of the above-mentioned medical officers to the effect that a £10 per cent. premium would be the fair one, and before the contract was approved by the Judge several Scotch offices had agreed to grant, at premiums of £10 11s. payable for ten years, insurances for sums sufficient in the whole to cover the purchase-money, and an English office had expressed its willingness to grant an insurance for £4000 on still more favourable terms. None of these facts were mentioned in the skeleton case or disclosed to the Judge :—*Held* (reversing the judgment of Fry, J.), that the sale must be set aside, for that C. and B. knew that the materials which they laid before the Judge to enable him to form his

FALSE REPRESENTATION—*continued.*

opinion whether the sale should be sanctioned were incomplete, and calculated to produce the false impression that the life could only be insured at £12 per cent., and that the sanction of the Judge must therefore be regarded as obtained by fraud.—A person desirous of buying property which is being sold under the direction of the Court must either abstain from laying any information before the Court in order to obtain its approval, or he must lay before it all the information he possesses which is material to enable the Court to form a correct opinion, and he will not be held excused from so doing because the Court does not ask for further information :—*Held*, that if the Scotch insurances were known to L. & Co., the solicitors conducting the sale (a fact which the Court considered not proved), the Defendants could not successfully contend that they were not responsible for the failure of L. & Co. to mention them to the Judge, for that it was the duty of B., who took an active personal part in obtaining the sanction of the Judge, and who had reason to believe that the Judge did not know of them, to see that he was informed of them. BOSWELL *v.* COAKS - - 23 Ch. D. 302 ; 27 Ch. D. 424
[Reversed by the House of Lords.]

—— Misrepresentation in prospectus of company.
See Cases under COMPANY—PROSPECTUS.

—— Life insurance - 9 App. Cas. 671
See INSURANCE, LIFE—POLICY. 3.

—— Sale of land—Action for damages
[11 Q. B. D. 255
See VENDOR AND PURCHASER—COMPENSATION. 1.

FANCY NAME—Trade-mark - 27 Ch. D. 681 ;
[29 Ch. D. 877
See TRADE-MARK—REGISTRATION. 5, 6.

FARMING STOCK—Bequest of 17 Ch. D. 696
See WILL—WORDS. 8.

FASCIA—Right to use 20 Ch. D. 773 ; 22 Ch. D.
See EASEMENT. 1. [177

FATHER—Advancement to child—Distribution
See ADVANCEMENT. 1. [29 Ch. D. 250

—— Right to custody of child 25 Ch. D. 220
See INFANT—CUSTODY. 3.

—— Right to receive income for maintenance of child - 22 Ch. D. 521
See SETTLEMENT—POWERS. 5.

—— Undue influence 18 Ch. D. 188
See UNDUE INFLUENCE.

—— Wishes of—Religious education 21 Ch. D.
See INFANT—EDUCATION. 2. [817

FEES—Counsel's - 16 Ch. D. 517
See PRACTICE—SUPREME COURT—COSTS. 38.

—— Counsel's - - - 30 Ch. D. 1
See SOLICITOR—BILL OF COSTS. 3.

—— Court.
See COURT—GAZETTE.

—— Directors of company—Proof in winding-up
See COMPANY—PROOF. 1. [30 Ch. D. 629
U 2

FEES—*continued.*

—— School board 7 **Q. B. D.** 388; 12 **Q. B. D.** 578
　See ELEMENTARY EDUCATION ACTS—
　FEES. 1, 2.

FELO DE SE.

The Act 45 & 46 Vict. c. 19, repeals 4 Geo. 4, c. 52 (which provided that the remains of persons against whom a verdict of felo de se should be found should be privately buried by night in the parish churchyard), and enacts that the remains of such persons felo de se shall be interred in the churchyard or other burial-ground of the parish or place where the remains of such person might by laws or custom of England be interred if the verdict of felo de se had not been found.

By sect. 3 the interment of any such felo de se may be made in any of the ways prescribed or authorized by the Burial Laws Amendment Act, 1880.

By sect. 4 the rites of Christian burial are not to be performed on interment.

FELON—Bankruptcy of　-　- 19 **Ch. D.** 1
　See BANKRUPTCY—ACT OF BANKRUPTCY. 12.

FELONIOUS DEMOLITION — Action against
hundred -　　-　　7 **Q. B. D.** 201
　See RIOT.

FELONY—Claim arising out of—Proof in bankruptcy　　-　　20 **Ch. D.** 131
　See BANKRUPTCY—PROOF. 10.

—— Compounding—Bill of exchange
　　　　　　　　[10 **Q. B. D.** 572
　See BILL OF EXCHANGE — CONSIDERA-
　TION.

—— Prosecution before action　10 **Q. B. D.** 412
　See ACTION. 2.

—— Prosecution before action　- 6 **Q. B. D.** 561
　See INSURANCE, FIRE. 1.

—— Sale of goods in market overt 8 **Q. B. D.** 109
　See SALE OF GOODS—CONTRACT. 2.

FEU CHARTER　　-　　6 **App. Cas.** 560
　See SCOTCH LAW—CONVEYANCE. 2.

—— Restrictions in　　-　　7 **App. Cas.** 427
　See SCOTCH LAW—HERITABLE PROPERTY. 1.

FEU CONTRACT　8 **App. Cas.** 265; 10 **App. Cas.**
　　　　　　　　[147
　See SCOTCH LAW—RAILWAY COMPANY. 3, 5.

FEU DUTY—Failure to pay　10 **App. Cas.** 553
　See SCOTCH LAW—HERITABLE PROPERTY. 5.

FIAR—Scotch law—Coal mine　8 **App. Cas.** 641
　See SCOTCH LAW—HERITABLE PROPERTY. 2.

FICTITIOUS SALE—Railway company
　　　　　　　　[21 **Ch. D.** 309
　See RAILWAY COMPANY—CONSTITUTION. 1.

FIDUCIARY RELATION—Director 17 **Ch. D.** 467
　See COMPANY—DIRECTOR'S LIABILITY. 2.

—— Executor who has not proved
　　　　　　　　[9 **App. Cas.** 733
　See VENDOR AND PURCHASER—FRAUD. 1.

FIDUCIARY RELATION—*continued.*

—— Mortgagees—Power of sale　21 **Ch. D.** 857;
　　　　　　　　[24 **Ch. D.** 289
　See MORTGAGE—POWERS. 2, 4.

—— Physician　　-　　- 8 **Q. B. D.** 587
　See GIFT.

—— Solicitor—Improper sale　- 16 **Ch. D.** 393
　See SOLICITOR—LIABILITIES. 7.

FIERI FACIAS—Assets of testator—Debt incurred by executor　　18 **Ch. D.** 93
　See EXECUTOR—ADMINISTRATION. 3.

—— Wrongful seizure　　21 **Ch. D.** 69
　See SHERIFF. 4.

FIFTY POUNDS RENTAL VOTER.
　See PARLIAMENT — REGISTRATION —
　Statutes.

FINE—Copyhold　-　- 30 **Ch. D.** 581
　See COPYHOLD—SURRENDER AND ADMIT-
　TANCE. 2.

FIRE INSURANCE.
　See Cases under INSURANCE—FIRE.

—— Law of Canada　　- 7 **App. Cas.** 96
　See COLONIAL LAW—CANADA—ONTARIO. 3.

FIRST MEETING—Fresh first meeting—Compounding debtor　　20 **Ch. D.** 281
　See BANKRUPTCY—COMPOSITION. 3.

—— Fresh first meeting—Liquidation
　　　　　　　　[24 **Ch. D.** 35
　See BANKRUPTCY—LIQUIDATION. 6.

FISHERY.

1. —— **Navigable Tidal River**—*Prescription —Evidence—Judgment in Possessory Suit—Judgment by Default.*] In an action for trespass to a several fishery in a navigable tidal river in Ireland the Defendants justified on the ground that the public had the right of fishing. The Plaintiff's paper title (if the possession and enjoyment were consistent with it) afforded irresistible ground for a presumption that the fishery was put in defence before Magna Charta. As evidence of possession and user the Plaintiff tendered (inter alia) the proceedings and decree in 1687 in a "possessory suit" brought in the Court of Chancery in Ireland by C. (the Plaintiff's predecessor in title) against strangers to the present action; by which decree an injunction was awarded to quiet C. and his undertenants in such possession of their fishing as they had at the time of exhibiting the bill and three years before, to continue until evicted by due course of law, both parties being at liberty to take proceedings at law against each other for ascertaining their titles :—*Held*, that as the decree was a solemn and final adjudication, not collusive, and as it could not have been made except upon proof of unbroken user and enjoyment for at least three years before the bill, inconsistent with any actual exercise at that time of a public right of fishing, the proceedings and decree were admissible; and that the effect of this evidence (not being met by any counter evidence applicable to the same period) was extremely strong to establish possession and enjoyment of the fishery in the latter

FISHERY—*continued.*

part of the 17th century, consistent with the paper title and exclusive of the public.—*Pim v. Curell* (6 M. & W. 234) discussed.—*Held,* also, that a judgment obtained by the Plaintiff in 1826 in an action against a stranger for trespass by fishing in the locus in quo, in which action the Defendant appeared but allowed judgment to go by default of pleading, was evidence in the present action of possession in. 1826. . The Defendants proved that cot-fishing had been carried on in the locus in quo with the knowledge of the Plaintiff or his agents and without interruption by them as far back as living memory extended : —*Held,* that if the Plaintiff's right to a several fishery were once proved the exercise of cot-fishing could not ·take it away or confer any right on the public ; for the public cannot in law prescribe for a profit à prendre in alieno solo, nor acquire any right adversely to the owner under any statute of limitation ; and an incorporeal hereditament such as a several fishery, which can only pass by deed, cannot be "abandoned." NEILL *v.* DUKE OF DEVONSHIRE　8 App. Cas. 135

2. —— **Non-tidal River**—*River in part Navigable.*] There can be no public right of fishing in non-tidal waters, even where they are to some extent "navigable rivers." PEARCE *v.* SCOTCHER
[9 Q. B. D. 162

3. —— **Oysters** — *Prescription* — *Profit à prendre in alieno solo* — *Presumption of lawful Origin* — *User* — *Charitable Trust* — *Perpetuity.*] A prescriptive right to a several oyster fishery in a navigable tidal river was proved to have been exercised from time immemorial by a borough corporation and its lessees, without any qualification except that the free inhabitants of ancient tenements in the borough had from time immemorial without interruption, and claiming as of right, exercised the privilege of dredging for oysters in the locus in quo from the 2nd of February to Easter Eve in each year, and of catching and carrying away the same without stint for sale and otherwise. This usage of the inhabitants tended to the destruction of the fishery, and if continued would destroy it :—*Held* (Lord Blackburn dissenting), that the claim of the inhabitants was not to a profit à prendre in alieno solo : that a lawful origin for the usage ought to be presumed if reasonably possible : and that the presumption which ought to be drawn, as reasonable in law and probable in fact, was that the original grant to the corporation was subject to a trust or condition in favour of the free inhabitants of ancient tenements in the borough in accordance with the usage. GOODMAN *v.* MAYOR OF SALTASH　-　　　7 Q. B. D. 106 ;
[7 App. Cas. 633
—— Tidal navigable river　-　8 Q. B. D. 626
See JUSTICES—JURISDICTION.

FISHERY ACTS.

Fresh Water Fish.] *The Act* 47 & 48 Vict. c. 11 (*Fresh Water Fisheries Act,* 1884) *extends the powers of Boards of Conservators for the further protection of fish other than salmon in fresh waters. It·· is to be construed with 41 & 42 Vict. c.. 39 (Fresh Water Fisheries Act,* 1878).

FISHERY ACTS—*continued.*

Oyster, Crab, and Lobster.] *The Act* 47 & 48 Vict. c. 26 (*Fisheries Oyster, Crab, and Lobsters Act,* 1877, *Amendment Act,* 1884) *enables the Board of Trade to direct that the proviso in the last paragraph of sect.* 8 *of* 40 & 41 Vict. c. 42, *shall not apply within any certain area.*

Registry of Fishing Boats of Barrow-in-Furness.] *Regulations of May* 3rd, 1882, *for lettering, numbering, and registering of sea fishing boats of Barrow-in-Furness under the Sea Fisheries Act,* 1868 (31 & 32 Vict. c. 45), s. 23　L. G., 1882, p. 2127

Sea Fisheries.] *The Sea Fisheries* (*Clam and Bait Beds*) *Act,* 1881 (44 & 45 Vict. c. 11), *further amends the law relating to Sea Fisheries by providing for the protection of clam and other bait beds.*

The Act 46 & 47 Vict. c. 22. (*Sea Fisheries Act,* 1883), *carries into effect an International Convention concerning the fisheries in the North Sea, and amends the laws relating to British Sea Fisheries.*

The Act 47 & 48 Vict. c. 27 (*Sea Fisheries Act,* 1884) *extends the powers conferred by Part III. of the Sea Fisheries Act,* 1868, *upon the Board of Trade, and enables it to make orders with regard to cockles.*

Salmon.] *Sect.* 31 *of the Act* 24 & 25 Vict. c. 109, *as to the appointment of inspectors, is continued until the* 31*st of December,* 1886, *by the* 48 & 49 Vict. c. 59.

Thames Fishery By-laws, 1883.] *Order in Council of July* 19, 1883, *allows the following by-laws for the protection, preservation, and regulation of the fisheries in the River Thames, made by the Conservators of the River Thames, in exercise of the power and authority vested in them by the Thames Conservancy Acts,* 1857 *and* 1864, *the Thames Navigation Act,* 1866, *the Thames Conservancy Act,* 1867, *the Thames Navigation Act,* 1870, *and the Thames Conservancy Act,* 1878, *and otherwise.*

4. *These by-laws extend and apply to the rivers Thames and Isis hereinafter called the River Thames, from Cricklade in the county of Wilts, to Yantlet Creek in the county of Kent, save and except where the application thereof is hereby expressly limited to any particular part of the said river, or to any particular and specified class of fish and to that extent only.*

5. *In these by-laws, unless there is something inconsistent in the context, the words and expressions hereinafter mentioned shall have respectively the meanings hereby assigned to them, that is to say :—*

"*Person*" *shall include any body of persons, corporate or incorporate.*

"*Court*" *shall mean two or more justices assembled in petty sessions or a stipendiary magistrate.*

"*Fishery*" *shall include oyster and shell fisheries.*

"*Fish*" *shall include oysters and shell fish, and also the spawn, brood or fry of fish, oysters and shell fish.* .

"*Vessel*" *shall mean any ship, lighter, keel, barge, boat, punt, wherry, raft, or craft, or any other kind of vessel whatever, whether navigated by steam or otherwise.*

6. *Subject to the reservation of rights in these*

FISHERY ACTS—*continued.*

by-laws contained, every net or engine, or apparatus for taking or attempting to take fish, which is not expressly authorized by these by-laws, shall be deemed to be a prohibited net or engine, or apparatus within the same, and the following nets or engines shall be deemed to be nets or engines authorized to be used within the limits under-mentioned :—

(1.) For pike, jack, perch, roach, dace, chub, and barbel . *A flew or stream net of a mesh not less than three inches throughout when wet, and not more than sixteen fathoms long. To be used only in the river below Richmond Bridge.*

(2.) For flounders and soles . *A net of a mesh not less than two and a half inches throughout when wet, and not more than sixteen fathoms long. To be used only in the river below Richmond Bridge.*

(3.) For roach and dace . . *A single blay net, of a mesh not less than two inches and a quarter when wet, and not more than thirteen fathoms long ; to fleet with the stream with a boat and buoy attached to it. To be used only in the river below Richmond Bridge.*

(4.) For eels . *Grig weels to be used for eels only in the river below the City Stone at Staines.*

(5.) For smelts . *A net of not less than one inch and a quarter in the mesh when wet, and not more than sixteen fathoms long, except in the middle of the net where a space of six fathoms long shall be one inch in the mesh when wet ; to be worked by fleeting with the stream, with a boat and buoy attached to it. To be used only in the river below Richmond Bridge.*

(6.) For shrimps . *A trawl net of a mesh not less than one inch when wet, except near the cod end, wherever that may be, but not smaller than half an inch mesh when wet, to be used only in the river between Greenhithe and Yantlet Creek ; or a trim-tram net, with a mesh of not less than half an inch when wet, and a weighted beam of twenty-one feet in length. To be used only in the river below Richmond Bridge.*

(7.) For sprats . *A stow-boat net not less than one inch in the mesh when wet. To be used only in the river below Richmond Bridge.*

(8.) For whitebait . *A stow-boat net not less than half an inch in the mesh when wet. To be used only in the river below Richmond Bridge.*

(9.) For minnows . *A round drop minnow net not exceeding three feet in diameter, which may be used in all parts of the river.*

(10.) . . . *A small landing net for securing fish taken in angling, which may be used in all parts of the river.*

(11.) . . . *A hand or well net, to be used for removing fish from the well of a boat, or for carrying or preserving fish after capture, which may be used in all parts of the river.*

For General use . *A casting or bait net, not exceeding thirty feet in circumference, to be used only by assistant river keepers or registered fishermen in obtaining bait to be employed in angling, the sack or purse thereof not being more than six inches in depth when extended to the utmost, which may be used in all parts of the river.*

(12.) . . .

7. *No fish of the species hereinafter mentioned, shall be taken in or out of the River Thames, or having been taken, shall be had in possession, or exposed for sale on the River Thames, or on the shore thereof, or any lands adjoining or near to the river, of less than the respective sizes and dimensions following :—(This section is not intended to apply to any person who takes such fish accidentally, and forthwith returns the same to the water with the least possible injury.)*

Pike or jack .	. Extreme length, 18 inches.
Perch . . .	,, ,, 8 ,,
Chub . . .	,, ,, 10 ,,
Roach . . .	,, ,, 7 ,,
Dace . . .	,, ,, 6 ,,
Barbel . . .	,, ,, 13 ,,
Trout . . .	,, ,, 16 ,,
Grayling . .	,, ,, 9 ,,
Bream . . .	,, ,, 10 ,,
Carp . . .	,, ,, 10 ,,
Tench . . .	,, ,, 8 ,,
Rudd . . .	,, ,, 6 ,,
Gudgeon . . .	,, ,, 4 ,,
Flounders . .	,, ,, 7 ,,
Smelts . . .	,, ,, 5½ ,,
Shrimps . . .	to be sifted through a sieve of ⅜-in. between the wires, and those only taken which will not pass through such a sieve.
Soles or slips .	Extreme length, 7 inches.
Whiting . .	,, ,, 7 ,,
Plaice or dab .	,, ,, 8 ,,

FENCE SEASON.

8. *The times and seasons for fishing in the River Thames, and for taking the following fish therein,*

FISHERY ACTS—*continued.*

and the close, or fence seasons, when such fish shall not be fished for or taken therein, are as follows :—

—	Times when fishing is permitted.	Fence Season, when fishing is not permitted.
Salmon, salmon trout, trout and char . .	From the 1st of April to the 10th September inclusive.	From the 11th September in each year, to the 31st March in the following year, both days inclusive.
Eels . . .	May be taken all the year, but not by rod and line from the 15th of March to the 15th of June.	Not by rod and line from the 15th March to the 15th June, both days inclusive.
Pike or jack Perch Roach Dace Chub Rudd Barbel Carp Tench Bream Grayling Gudgeon Pope Crayfish Bleak Minnow, and every other kind of fish known as fresh-water fish, except as aforesaid	From the 16th of June to the 14th of March following, both days inclusive.	From the 15th March in each year to the 15th June following, both days inclusive.
Flounders, plaice, soles, and dabs Whitings Shrimps	May be taken all the year.	
Smelts . . .	From the 26th of July to the 24th of March following, inclusive.	From the 25th March to the 25th July following, both days inclusive.
Lamperns . .	From the 24th August to the 31st March following.	From the 1st April to the 23rd August following, both days inclusive.

Nothing in this section shall apply to any person who shall during the period between the 1st day of April and the 10th day of September, both days inclusive, take, or attempt to take, bleak, minnows or gudgeon for or use as bait for trout.

9. The places hereinafter mentioned are the preserves staked and marked by the conservators for the preservation of the fishery, and no person shall take up or remove any stake, burr, boat, punt, or any other thing placed for the purpose of impeding fishing, or wilfully disturb the said preserves or spawning beds in any way, and no person shall fish or attempt to take fish in any of the said places, except by angling with rod and line and grig weels for eels only, by fishermen therein.

Richmond. . From Richmond Bridge to the Duke of Buccleuch's grounds—a distance of 700 yards in length, or thereabouts.

FISHERY ACTS—*continued.*

Twickenham . From the upper end of the lawn at Pope's Villa to the island, being 400 yards in length.

Kingston . . From Mr. Park's lawn at Teddington through the backwater (the Crowlock) up to the Lower Malthouse at Hampton Wick, being 1960 yards in length.

Thames Ditton From Lord Henry Fitzgerald's—eastward, 512 yards in length.

Hampton . . From Moulsey Lock to Garrick's Lawn, Hampton, being 1514 yards in length, or thereabouts.

Sunbury . . From Sunbury Weir—683 yards in length, to the eastward.

Walton . Walton Sale—250 yards in length.

Shepperton . Upper Deep—240 yards eastward of Creek Rails. Lower Deep—200 yards eastward of the public drain.

Weybridge . From Shepperton Lock round the course of the river to the weir—830 yards in length.

Chertsey . From the weir to 80 yards below the bridge, being 445 yards in length.

Penton Hook. From the weir round the island and up to the lock at Penton Hook, being 1150 yards in length.

Staines . . From the City Stone to a point 210 yards below the road bridge at Staines.

10, No person shall do, aid, or assist in doing the following things, or any of them, that is to say :—

(a.) Fish with, use, trawl, lay or set a prohibited net or engine, or apparatus.

(b.) Have in his possession while on the river, or on the shore thereof, or on any lands adjoining or near to the river, a prohibited net or engine, unless he shews to the satisfaction of the justices before whom he is charged, that he had not the same in his possession with intent at the time of such possession to fish with, use, trawl, lay or set the same in the river.

(c.) Fish for or take, or attempt to take, any fish by using baited or unbaited hooks, or wire or snare, or any other engine for the purpose of foul hooking commonly called snatching or snaring.

(d.) Fish from any vessel, boat, or punt, for or take, or attempt to take, above Richmond Bridge any fish except in the daytime, that is to say, between the beginning of the last hour before sunrise, and the end of the first hour after sunset.

(e.) Fish for or take, or attempt to take, any fish within the fence season for the same.

(f.) Buy, sell, or expose for sale or have in his possession any fish that has been caught or taken within the fence season for the same, in the River Thames.

(g.) Take, or attempt to take, or disturb any fish when spawning.

(h.) Take, destroy, or spoil any spawn, fry or brood of fish, or spat of oysters.

FISHERY ACTS—*continued.*

(i.) *Use more than two rods at any one and the same time for angling.*

(j.) *Use eel spears commonly so called for the purpose of taking fish.*

(k.) *Attach any net, engine or other device to any anchor, or fix the same in any manner so as to cross any part of the River Thames.*

(l.) *Lay night hooks or night lines of any description whatever, or any fixed hooks or lines by night or day above Kew Bridge.*

(m.) *Use double walled net or nets with false or double bottoms with cod or pouse.*

11. *On and after the 1st day of January, 1883, every person following the business of a fisherman on the River Thames, or who shall keep to be let for hire for fishing in the River Thames any boat, punt, or vessel, shall cause his name and place of abode to be duly registered in a book to be kept for that purpose by the secretary to the Conservators of the River Thames, at their office in London, which is now situate at 41, Trinity Square, Tower Hill, and every such person shall pay one shilling for every registry of each boat, punt, or vessel, and on every registry the secretary to the said Conservators shall deliver a number for each boat, punt, or vessel, to such person, and such person shall cause to be painted and kept in legible characters of not less than two inches long and broad in proportion on the stern, and on each bow of each boat, punt, or vessel, such number together with his name and place of abode, so as to be plainly seen in the day-time ; and if such person shall neglect to cause such boat, punt, or vessel to be duly registered, or such number together with his name and place of abode to be painted and preserved in legible characters as aforesaid, or shall wilfully suffer the same to be altered or defaced, and if not renewed he shall be liable to a penalty for a breach of these by-laws, and it shall not be lawful for any person following the business of a fisherman on the River Thames, and having a boat, punt, or vessel for that purpose, or who shall keep a boat or boats, punts or vessels, to be let for hire for fishing, to use or let for hire for fishing any boat, punt, or vessel without having the same registered, and his name and place of abode, together with the registered number, legibly painted thereon as hereinbefore mentioned.*

12. *No person shall put down in the River Thames, at the mouth of any creek, river, or back-water communicating with the River Thames, or running into the said river, or at any mill or sluice, any net or device whatever to stop, catch, or hinder the fish, or spawn or fry of fish, from coming into the said River Thames.*

When a prohibited net or engine or other apparatus is seized under the provisions of the Acts or any or either of them in such case made, or these by-laws, the same may be burnt, or otherwise destroyed, by order of the justices before whom the same is brought, without prejudice to the infliction of a penalty on or other remedy against the person offending, in respect of such net, engine or apparatus.

13. *Nothing in these by-laws shall prevent any person, provided he has the previous consent of the Conservators in writing under their common seal, from obtaining fish for the purposes of artificial propagation or scientific purposes, or from having*

in his possession salmon roe or trout roe for any of those purposes, or for taking or attempting to take salmon or trout when spawning, or near the spawning beds.

14. *Nothing in these by-laws except the provisions relative to the fence season, shall take away, or abridge the right, if any, of the owner or occupier of a private fishery, if any, or any person having authority in writing from any such owner or occupier, to do any of the following things within the limits of such private fishery only ; that is, to fish for, or to take or attempt to take fish and eels by means of nets commonly called cast nets and cray-fish nets, or by grig or ground weels for eels, or by night lines, or by means of eel bucks or stages, so far only as the same or any of them can be legally used irrespective of these by-laws. Provided that on a special license being obtained from the Conservators in writing, under their common seal, and not otherwise, such owners or occupiers, or persons having authority as aforesaid, may in such private fishery only take fish by means of a net commonly called a hoop net, having a mesh of not less than two inches from knot to knot when wet, or eight inches all round, and not being more than six yards long, or by means of a net commonly called a drag net, and having a mesh of not less than two inches from knot to knot when wet, or eight inches all round.*

15. *Any person committing any breach of or in any way infringing any of these by-laws other than and except catching or attempting to catch or kill any fresh-water fish during the fence season, shall be liable to a penalty of, and shall forfeit a sum not exceeding £5, and for catching or attempting to catch or kill any fresh-water fish during such fence season shall be liable on a first conviction to a penalty of and shall forfeit a sum not exceeding 40s., and on a second or any subsequent conviction to a penalty of and shall forfeit a sum not exceeding £5, which said penalties respectively shall be recovered, enforced, and applied according to the provisions of " The Thames Acts, 1857 to 1878," and of the statutes in such case made and provided.*

Repeal of earlier By-laws, Rules, &c.] The rules and ordinances made in pursuance of the Act of 30 Geo. 2, by the mayor and aldermen of the city of London, on the 4th day of October, 1785, and duly approved and confirmed on the 22nd and 24th days of the same month, and by the Conservators of the River Thames, in pursuance of the same Act, on the 23rd day of January, 1860, and duly approved and confirmed on the 28th day of the same month ; and

The rules and by-laws made by the Conservators of the River Thames on the 14th day of June, 1869, and duly allowed by Her Majesty in Council, on the 11th day of November, following; and

The rules and by-laws made by the said Conservators on the 7th day of July, 1873, and duly allowed by Her Majesty in Council, on the 30th day of September, following ; and

The rules and by-laws made by the said Conservators and duly allowed by Her Majesty in Council, on the 28th day of October, 1878, and all other (if any) the rules, ordinances, and by-laws heretofore made by the Conservators of the River Thames, and heretofore in force for protecting, preserving,

FISHERY ACTS—*continued.*

*or regulating the fisheries of the River Thames,
are all hereby repealed*　　　L. G., 1883, p. 3635
　　　　And see RIVER—*Statutes.*

1. —— **Salmon Fishery** (28 & 29 Vict. c.
121), s. 3—*Fishery Districts—Definition of Limits
by Secretary of State's Certificate—River—"Tributary," what is—Reservoirs.*] By 28 & 29 Vict.
c. 121, the limits of a river shall be defined, and
a fishery district shall be formed, for the purpose
of the Salmon Fishery Acts, by a Secretary of
State's certificate describing the limits of the
river and district, and, by sect. 3 "river" shall
include "such portion of any stream with its
tributaries" as may be declared in the certificate.
Prior to 1845 the Whittle Burn in the county of
Northumberland was a tributary of the Tyne.
In 1845 a water company, under powers given by
local Acts, constructed works for the supply of
water to a neighbouring town, by placing a dam
across the stream of the Whittle Burn, and
forming a series of reservoirs; the water being
taken by underground pipes from the stream
into the highest reservoir, and from thence to the
others. All water not required for the reservoirs
was allowed to pass down a watercourse running
outside the reservoirs into the ancient watercourse of the burn, down which it flowed into
the Tyne. Sometimes all the water coming down
the Whittle Burn was taken into, and impounded
in, the reservoirs, and none flowed into the Tyne.
At other times all the water flowed into the Tyne
without having entered the reservoirs. There
were outlets with sluices from the reservoirs by
which surplus water flowed into the Tyne down
watercourses also running into the ancient watercourse of the burn. In 1866, the Fishery District of the River Tyne was formed, and the
Secretary of State's certificate defined the limits
as "so much of the River Tyne with its tributaries" as was situate (inter alia) in the county
of Northumberland :—*Held,* that the reservoirs
were not tributaries of the Tyne within the meaning of the certificate. HARBOTTLE *v.* TERRY
　　　　　　　　　　　　　[10 Q. B. D. 131

2. —— **Salmon Fishery**—*Placing a Device to
catch Fish—Permanent Structure erected before
the passing of the Act.*] The 15th section of
the Salmon Fishery Act, 1873 (36 & 37 Vict.
c. 71), enacts that no person between the 1st day
of January and the 24th day of June shall place
in any inland water any device whatsoever to
catch or obstruct any fish descending the stream.
—A permanent structure for the purpose of
catching eels had been erected at a weir upon a
river before the passing of the above-mentioned
Act. The nature of such structure was as follows :—There were floodgates or shuttles in the
weir, and a grating of iron bars, through which
the eels could not pass, was fixed below such
floodgates. When the floodgates were raised the
rush of water through them carried the eels on to
and over the end of the grating into a trough,
which communicated with a well from which
they could not escape. The Appellant, on a day
between the 1st of January and the 24th of June,
1882, raised the floodgates and so brought the
trap into action, with the result that eels were
caught in the trap :—*Held,* that by so doing the

FISHERY ACTS—*continued.*

Appellant had been guilty of an offence within
the above-mentioned section. BRIGGS *v.* SWAN-
WICK　　-　　-　　-　　10 Q. B. D. 510

FISHING BOATS.
　　　　See SHIP—MERCHANT SHIPPING ACTS—
　　　　Statutes.

FIXTURES—*Mortgagor and Mortgagee—Driving-
belts—Bills of Sale Act,* 1854 (17 & 18 Vict.
c. 36).] A wheel-factory, including the machinery
and gear, was mortgaged to the Plaintiffs. The
deed of mortgage was not registered as a bill of
sale. Leathern driving-belts were used in working the machinery at the factory; they were fastened to certain wheels or drums, but could be
removed at pleasure when the machinery was
thrown out of gear. They were necessary parts of
the machinery. The mortgagor having liquidated
his affairs under the Bankruptcy Act, 1869, the
Defendant, his trustee, sold the belts :—*Held,* that
the belts passed to the Plaintiffs under the mortgage, and that they were entitled to maintain an
action of conversion against the defendant.—
Longbottom v. *Berry* (Law Rep. 5 Q. B. 123) approved. SHEFFIELD AND SOUTH YORKSHIRE PER-
MANENT BUILDING SOCIETY *v.* HARRISON
　　　　　　　　　　　　　[15 Q. B. D. 358

—— Agricultural Holdings Act.
　　　　See LANDLORD AND TENANT—FIXTURES
　　　　—*Statutes.*

—— Bankruptcy — Disclaimer of leasehold in-
　　　terest　　-　　-　　13 Q. B. D. 738
　　　　See BANKRUPTCY—DISCLAIMER. 20.

—— Buildings for working mine　7 Q. B. D. 295
　　　　　　　　　　　　　[8 App. Cas. 195.
　　　　See MINE—WORKING. 1.

—— Landlord and tenant—Forfeiture on tenant
　　　"being bankrupt"—Right of removal
　　　　　　　　　　　　　[13 Q. B. D. 454
　　　　See BANKRUPTCY — BANKRUPTCY PETI-
　　　　TION. 4.

—— Law of Lower Canada — Sale of fixed
　　　machinery　　　　10 App. Cas. 643
　　　　See COLONIAL LAW—CANADA—QUEBEC.
　　　　1.

—— Mortgage of—Distress　　16 Ch. D. 226
　　　　See BANKRUPTCY—DISTRESS. 2.

—— Mortgage of—Lease by mortgagor after
　　　mortgage—Rights of tenant
　　　　　　　　　　　　　[15 Q. B. D. 218
　　　　See LANDLORD AND TENANT—FIXTURES.

—— Removal of　-　-　-　19 Ch. D. 7
　　　　See BANKRUPTCY—DISCLAIMER. 2.

FLANGEWHEEL—User upon tramway
　　　　　　　　　　　　　[6 Q. B. D. 70
　　　　See TRAMWAY COMPANY. 1.

FLINTS—Right to sell　-　· 21 Ch. D. 18 ;
　　　　　　　　　　　　　[8 App. Cas. 508
　　　　See LANDLORD AND TENANT — CUSTOM
　　　　OF COUNTRY.

FLOOD—Damage from　　　7 App. Cas. 694
　　　　See SCOTCH LAW—STATUTORY DUTY.

FOG—Collision—Sailing rules—Articles 13, 18.
　　　　See Cases under SHIP — NAVIGATION.
　　　　14—18, 23.

FORCIBLE ENTRY.

1. —— Damages — Independent Wrong — Injury to Furniture — 5 Rich. 2, stat. 1, c. 8.] Damages cannot be recovered against the rightful owner for a forcible entry on land, for the statute 5 Rich. 2, stat. 1, c. 8, only makes a forcible entry an indictable offence, and does not create any civil remedy for it. But for any independent wrong (such as an assault or an injury to furniture) committed in the course of the forcible entry, damages can be recovered, even by a person whose possession was wrongful, for the statute makes a possession obtained by force unlawful, even when it is so obtained by the rightful owner. — *Newton v. Harland* (1 Scott, N. R. 474), *Pollen v. Brewer* (7 C. B. (N.S.) 371), and *Lows v. Telford* (1 App. Cas. 414) considered. BEDDALL *v.* MAITLAND　-　-　**17 Ch. D. 174**

2. —— License to eject—Landlord and Tenant —5 Rich. 2, stat. 1, c. 8.] A license by a tenant to his landlord to eject him on a specified day without any process of law is void, as authorizing the commission of an act which is made illegal by the Act 5 Rich. 2, stat. 1, c. 8.—If a person who has a legal right of entry upon land which is in the possession of a wrongdoer is allowed to enter peaceably through the outer door, it is still illegal for him to turn out the wrongdoer with violence. EDWICK *v.* HAWKES　　**18 Ch. D. 199**

—— Attachment　-　**26 Ch. D. 644**
　　See PRACTICE — SUPREME COURT—ATTACHMENT. 6.

FORECLOSURE—Action for.
　　See Cases under MORTGAGE—FORECLOSURE.

—— Action for—Statute of Limitations
　　　　　　　　[19 Ch. D. 539; 6 Q. B. D. 345;
　　　　　　　　[7 App. Cas. 235
　　See LIMITATIONS, STATUTE OF—REALTY. 4, 5.

—— Action for—Writ of possession
　　　　　　　　　　[22 Ch. D. 281
　　See PRACTICE—SUPREME COURT—WRIT OF POSSESSION.

—— Order in Chambers—Alteration **29 Ch. D. 827**
　　See PRACTICE—SUPREME COURT—JUDGMENT. 8.

—— Payment by instalments　　**22 Ch. D. 549**
　　See MORTGAGE—CONTRACT. 10.

FOREIGN ACTION—Election　22 Ch. D. 397;
　　　　　　　　[23 Ch. D. 225; 24 Ch. D. 531
　　See PRACTICE—SUPREME COURT—STAYING PROCEEDINGS. 6, 7, 8.

FOREIGN ASSETS—Title of administrator
　　　　　　　　　　[18 Ch. D. 347
　　See ADMINISTRATOR—LIMITED. 5.

FOREIGN ATTACHMENT　-　6 App. Cas. 393
　　See COURT—MAYOR'S COURT. 1.

FOREIGN BILL OF EXCHANGE—Estoppel
　　　　　　　　　　[6 App. Cas. 82
　　See ESTOPPEL—CONDUCT. 1.

—— Indorsement—Conflict of laws **30 Ch. D. 598**
　　See BILL OF EXCHANGE—FOREIGN BILL.

FOREIGN COMPANY—Jurisdiction to wind up
　　　　　　　　[27 Ch. D. 225; 29 Ch. D. 219
　　See COMPANY—WINDING-UP ORDER. 2, 3.

FOREIGN CORPORATION　-　6 App. Cas. 386
　　See COLONIAL LAW—WEST AUSTRALIA. 1.

FOREIGN CREDITORS — Administration—English assets　-　**28 Ch. D. 175**
　　See EXECUTOR—ADMINISTRATION. 8.

FOREIGN DIVORCE—English marriage—Scotch divorce　6 P. D. 35; 8 App. Cas. 43
　　See CONFLICT OF LAWS. 2.

FOREIGN DOMICIL—Testator—English assets
　　　　　　　　　　[28 Ch. D. 175
　　See EXECUTOR—ADMINISTRATION. 8.

FOREIGN GOVERNMENT—Collision—Counterclaim—Security for damages 10 P. D. 33
　　See PRACTICE—ADMIRALTY —COUNTERCLAIM.

FOREIGN JUDGMENT.

1. —— Fraud—Action in English Court.] A foreign judgment obtained by the fraud of a party to the suit in the foreign Court cannot be afterwards enforced by him in an action brought in an English Court, even although the question whether the fraud had been perpetrated was investigated in the foreign Court, and it was there decided that the fraud had not been committed. —To an action claiming the value of certain goods and brought upon a foreign judgment, whereby the Defendants were ordered to return to the Plaintiff the goods or to pay to her their value, the defence alleged that the Plaintiff obtained the foreign judgment by fraudulently representing to the foreign Court that the goods were not then in her possession, and by fraudulently concealing from the foreign Court that the goods then were in her possession and were concealed by her:—*Held*, upon demurrer, that the defence was good. ABOULOFF *v.* OPPENHEIMER
　　　　　　　　　　[10 Q. B. D. 295

2. —— Ship—Maritime Lien—Jurisdiction—Action in rem to enforce Judgment of Foreign Tribunal of Commerce.] The Plaintiffs brought an action and obtained judgment in the Tribunal of Commerce at Lisbon against the captain and owners of a British ship for damages for injury caused by a collision with the Plaintiffs' ship. The Portuguese Courts recognise no distinction between actions in personam and actions in rem. The Defendants' ship having come into a British Court, the Plaintiffs commenced an action in rem against the ship, claiming to enforce the judgment of the Portuguese Court against it, and arrested the ship:—*Held*, reversing the decision of Sir R. Phillimore, that the action in the Portuguese Court was a personal action, and that the writ in the present action and all proceedings under it must be set aside, the Court having no jurisdiction to enforce a judgment in a personal action by proceedings in rem. — All civilised nations recognise the validity of maritime lien, and will enforce it when it has been declared by a foreign Court; but it is essential that it should appear from the proceedings of the foreign Court that the object of the suit was the sale of the ship, and not a personal remedy against the captain or owners.—*The Bold Buccleugh* (7 Moo. P. C. 267) considered. THE "CITY OF MECCA" **6 P. D. 106**

FOREIGN JUDGMENT—continued.
—— Writ specially indorsed — Power to sign judgment under Order XIV.
[13 Q. B. D. 302
See PRACTICE—SUPREME COURT—WRIT SPECIALLY INDORSED. 2.

FOREIGN LAW—Conflict of laws.
See Cases under CONFLICT OF LAWS.
—— Construction of will   - 29 Ch. D. 617
See DOMICIL. 1.
—— Domicil—Alien   -   - 9 P. D. 130
See PROBATE—GRANT. 2.
—— English and Spanish wills—Probate of English will only   - 9 P. D. 64
See PROBATE—GRANT. 9.
—— Evidence—Consul refusing to administer oath—Affidavit   9 P. D. 241
See EVIDENCE—GENERAL. 1.
—— Foreign decree—Property in this country—Absence of will   -   6 P. D. 6
See ADMINISTRATOR—LIMITED. 6.
—— Illegitimate children   17 Ch. D. 266
See DISTRIBUTIONS, STATUTE OF.
—— Lex loci — Contract in England between residents for delivery of cargo to be shipped at foreign port by foreign company   -   12 Q. B. D. 589
See CONFLICT OF LAWS. 1.
—— Probate of will abroad   - 8 P. D. 167
See PROBATE—GRANT. 8.
—— Royal family of Russia—Proof of Russian law -   -   - 9 P. D. 234
See PROBATE—GRANT. 7.
—— Will—Construction   6 P. D. 211;
[26 Ch. D. 656
See PROBATE—GRANT. 1, 4.

FOREIGN LIFE INSURANCE COMPANY —
Deposit -   -   - 21 Ch. D. 837
See COMPANY—LIFE INSURANCE COMPANY. 1.

FOREIGN MANUFACTURE—User in England
[17 Ch. D. 721; 8 App. Cas. 5
See PATENT—INFRINGEMENT. 6.

FOREIGN PATENT—Accounts of profits
[6 App. Cas. 176; 9 App. Cas. 592
See PATENT—PROLONGATION. 1, 2.
—— Licence—Right to sell articles in England
[25 Ch. D. 1
See PATENT—INFRINGEMENT. 2.

FOREIGN PROBATE—Payment out of Court
[24 Ch. D. 177
See PRACTICE—SUPREME COURT—PAYMENT OUT OF COURT.

FOREIGN SECURITY—Stamp duty on.
See REVENUE—STAMPS—Statutes.

FOREIGN SHIP—Action for wages   8 P. D. 121
See JURISDICTION. 3.
—— Action in rem—Board of Trade inquiry—Condition precedent   - 9 P. D. 88
See PRACTICE — ADMIRALTY — JURISDICTION. 2.
—— Action in rem—Jurisdiction—Lord Campbell's Act   9 P. D. 96; 10 App. Cas. 59
See PRACTICE — ADMIRALTY — JURISDICTION. 1.

FOREIGN SHIP—continued.
—— Application of measurement of tonnage to.
See SHIP—MERCHANT SHIPPING ACTS—Gazette.
—— Application of Wages and Rating Act to.
See SHIP—MERCHANT SHIPPING ACTS—Gazette.
—— Compulsory pilotage -   - 7 P. D. 240
See SHIP—PILOT. 5.
—— Crew space—Limitation of liability
[10 P. D. 21
See PRACTICE—ADMIRALTY—LIMITATION OF LIABILITY. 3.
—— English port—Necessaries—Lien 10 P. D. 44
See SHIP—MARITIME LIEN. 1.

FOREIGN SOVEREIGN—Incitement to murder
[7 Q. B. D. 244
See CRIMINAL LAW—OFFENCES AGAINST PERSON. 5.

FOREIGN TRADE-MARK   - 27 Ch. D. 570
See TRADE-MARK—REGISTRATION. 7.

FOREIGN WILL — Unattested — Power of appointment   25 Ch. D. 373
See POWER—EXECUTION. 4.

FOREIGNER—Marriage of—English settlement
[27 Ch. D. 284
See POWER—EXECUTION. 16.

FORESHORE   -   -   - 19 Ch. D. 22
See EASEMENT. 2.

FORFEITURE—Bankruptcy—Composition
[29 Ch. D. 196; 30 Ch. D. 119, 623
See SETTLEMENT—CONSTRUCTION. 4, 5, 6.
—— Bankruptcy—Estate of tenant for life
[30 Ch. D. 605
See SETTLED LAND ACT—DEFINITIONS. 6.
—— Building contract   16 Ch. D. 522
See BUILDING CONTRACT. 2.
—— Condition in will.
See Cases under WILL—CONDITION. 1—6.
—— Condition in will—Costs of administration action   -   28 Ch. D. 159
See EXECUTOR—ACTIONS. 12.
—— Cost-book mine   -   18 Ch. D. 660
See COMPANY—COST-BOOK COMPANY. 2.
—— Defaulting vassal—Scotch law
[10 App. Cas. 553
See SCOTCH LAW—HERITABLE PROPERTY. 5.
—— Deposit   21 Ch. D. 243
See PENALTY.
—— Deposit—Purchase of land   27 Ch. D. 89
See VENDOR AND PURCHASER—DEPOSIT. 2.
—— Sale   -   -   27 Ch. D. 652
See MINE—FREE MINERS.
—— Land   -   - 6 App. Cas. 628
See COLONIAL LAW—NEW SOUTH WALES. 2.
—— Lease—Relief against.
See LANDLORD AND TENANT—RE-ENTRY—Statutes.

FORFEITURE—*continued.*

—— Lease — Relief against — Disallowance of
costs to Plaintiff   -   14 Q. B. D. 347
See LANDLORD AND TENANT—RE-ENTRY.
7.

—— Recovery of land—Setting aside judgment
—Equitable mortgagees 12 Q. B. D. 165
See PRACTICE—SUPREME COURT—JUDG-
MENT. 5.

—— Sale of right of entry—Fictitious title
[9 Q. B. D. 128; 15 Q. B. D. 491
See RIGHT OF ENTRY. 1, 2.

—— Shares—Ultra vires   16 Ch. D. 681
See COMPANY—DIRECTOR'S AUTHORITY.
3.

FORGERY — Action in Chancery Division —
Estoppel   -   9 P. D. 210
See ESTOPPEL—JUDGMENT. 1.

—— Bill of exchange—Inchoate instrument
[7 Q. B. D. 78
See CRIMINAL LAW—FORGERY.

—— Company—Share certificate issued by secretary—Principal and agent
[13 Q. B. D. 103
See ESTOPPEL—CONDUCT. 2.

—— Deed   -   -   20 Ch. D. 611
See VENDOR AND PURCHASER—PURCHASE
WITHOUT NOTICE. 1.

FRANCHISE—Fishery.
See Cases under FISHERY.

—— Market.
See Cases under MARKET.

FRAUD — Action in English Court — Foreign
judgment   -   -   10 Q. B. D. 295
See FOREIGN JUDGMENT. 1.

—— Allegations of   -   26 Ch. D. 717
See PRACTICE—SUPREME COURT—PRO-
DUCTION OF DOCUMENTS. 10,

—— Appointment under power   21 Ch. D. 332;
[28 Ch. D. 205
See POWER—EXECUTION. 3, 4.

—— Charge of—Trial of action   24 Ch. D. 727
See PRACTICE—SUPREME COURT—TRIAL.
1.

—— Company—Cause for winding-up
[20 Ch. D. 151
See COMPANY—WINDING-UP ORDER. 5.

—— Company—Fictitious balance at banker
[26 Ch. D. 616
See COMPANY—CONTRACTS. 3.

—— Complicity in—Notice of prior fraud
[29 Ch. D. 500
See POWER OF ATTORNEY. 2.

—— Composition with creditors — Undue pre-
ference -   -   15 Q. B. D. 605
See BANKRUPTCY — FRAUDULENT PRE-
FERENCE. 2.

—— Concealment—Statute of Limitations
[9 Q. B. D. 59
See LIMITATIONS, STATUTE OF — PER-
SONAL ACTIONS. 7.

—— Debt incurred by—Action against debtor
and trustee in liquidation 8 Q. B. D. 453
See BANKRUPTCY—TRUSTEE. 4.

FRAUD—*continued.*

—— Debt incurred by—Proof in bankruptcy
[17 Ch. D. 122
See BANKRUPTCY—PROOF. 22.

—— False representation   -   20 Ch. D. 1;
[27 Ch. D. 424
See FALSE REPRESENTATION. 1, 2.

—— False representation—Prospectus of company. ..
See Cases under COMPANY—PROSPECTUS.

—— False representation—Sale of land
[28 Ch. D. 7
See VENDOR AND PURCHASER—FRAUD. 2.

—— Forged deed   -   20 Ch. D. 611
See VENDOR AND PURCHASER—PURCHASE
WITHOUT NOTICE. 1.

—— On bankruptcy laws   26 Ch. D. 510
See CONTRACT—VALIDITY. 3.

—— On company   ..   17 Ch. D. 467
See COMPANY—DIRECTOR'S LIABILITY. 2.

—— Solicitor—Conduct of action—Rehearing
[20 Ch. D. 672
See PRACTICE — SUPREME COURT —
AMENDMENT. 3.

—— Title of literary work—Fraud on public
[16 Ch. D. 395
See SPECIFIC PERFORMANCE. 1.

—— User of trade-mark   -   27 Ch. D. 570
See TRADE-MARK—REGISTRATION. 7.

FRAUDS, STATUTE OF.

1. —— Contract not to be performed within.
a Year.—*Sect.* 4—*Implied Contract—Part Performance — Supreme Court of Judicature Act,
1873* (36 & 37 Vict. c. 66), s. 25, sub-s. 7.] A
contract to serve for one year, the service to
commence on the second day after that on which
the contract is made, is a contract not to be performed within a year within the meaning of the
Statute of Frauds, s. 4.—*Cawthorne* v. *Cordrey*
(13 C. B. (N.S.) 406; 32 L. J. (C.P.) 152) distinguished.—A contract, which is not enforceable
by reason of the provisions of the Statute of
Frauds, s. 4, nevertheless is an existing contract
and is not void altogether, and a fresh contract
cannot be implied from acts done in pursuance of
it.—The doctrine as to part performance, whereby a contract not enforceable by an action at law,
owing to the provisions of the Statute of Frauds,
s. 4, was rendered enforceable in equity, was confined to suits as to the sale of interests in land,
and its operation has not been extended by the
provisions of the Supreme Court of Judicature
Act, 1873. BRITAIN v. ROSSITER 11 Q. B. D. 123

2. —— Interest in Land—29 Car. 2, c. 3, s. 4
—*Verbal Promise to devise such Interest by Will
—Part Performance.*] The general principle as
to the circumstances under which a part performance of a parol contract relating to land will be
regarded as sufficient to take it out of the operation of the Statute of Frauds is accurately stated
in the judgment in *Alderson* v. *Maddison* (7
Q. B. D. at p. 178):—*Held*, also, by. Baggallay, L.J., that the illustration which is there
given of such general principle that "payment of.
part or even of the whole of the purchase-money
is not sufficient to exclude the operation of the
statute" is rightly qualified by the following

FRAUDS, STATUTE OF—*continued.*

words which are there stated, " unless it is shewn that the payment was made in respect of the particular land, and the particular interest in the land, which is the subject of the parol agreement," those qualifying words being used to cover such a case as *Nunn* v. *Fabain* (Law Rep. 1 Ch. 35).—*Semble,* per Brett, L.J., that *Nunn* v. *Fabian* (Law Rep. 1 Ch. 35) is not an authority for those qualifying words, and that mere payment of part, or even of the whole, of the purchase-money will not be sufficient under any circumstances to exclude the operation of the statute. HUMPHREYS v. GREEN   **10 Q. B. D. 148**

3. —— Interest in Land—*Sect. 4—Right of Shooting—Right to take away Game shot.*] A grant of a right to shoot over land and to take away a part of the game killed is a grant of an interest in land and within the Statute of Frauds. WEBBER v. LEE   -   -   - **9 Q. B. D. 315**

4. —— Memorandum in Writing—*Sect. 4— Reference to Document containing Terms of Agreement.*] The Plaintiff had signed a memorandum setting forth the terms of a contract by which the Plaintiff agreed to let a carriage to the Defendant for the period of a year. The Defendant in a subsequent letter to the Plaintiff signed by him referred to " our arrangement for the hire of your carriage."—There was no other arrangement for the hire of a carriage than that the terms of which were contained in the memorandum signed by the Plaintiff:—*Held,* that the Defendant's letter sufficiently referred to the document containing the terms of the contract, to constitute a good memorandum of the contract within the Statute of Frauds, sect. 4.   CAVE v. HASTINGS

[7 Q. B. D. 125

—— Acceptance—*Sect.* 17—*Act recognising the contract   -   -   - 15 Q. B. D. 228 See* SALE OF GOODS—CONTRACT. 3.

—— Agreement for lease
[19 Ch. D. 233; 22 Ch. D. 441 *See* LANDLORD AND TENANT—AGREEMENT. 1, 2.

—— Contract for sale of land. *See* Cases under VENDOR AND PURCHASER —AGREEMENT.

—— Debt barred by—Retainer by executor
[29 Ch. D. 358 *See* EXECUTOR—RETAINER. 10.

—— Husband and wife—Agreement for settlement—Part performance—Bankruptcy
[14 Q. B. D. 419 *See* BANKRUPTCY — PROTECTED TRANSACTION. 9.

—— Lease not in writing   **21 Ch. D. 442** *See* BANKRUPTCY—DISTRESS. 4.

—— Representation influencing conduct—Promise to make will
[7 Q. B. D. 174; 8 App. Cas. 467 *See* CONTRACT—VALIDITY. 4.

—— Specific performance—Reference to formal contract -   -   - **20 Ch. D. 705** *See* SPECIFIC PERFORMANCE. 4.

FRAUDULENT APPOINTMENT   21 Ch. D. 232;
[25 Ch. D. 373 *See* POWER—EXECUTION. 3, 4.

FRAUDULENT CONVEYANCE.

1. —— Defeating and delaying Creditors— 13 *Eliz.* c. 5.] By a deed of gift J. granted farming property in trust for her daughters, in consideration of which they covenanted to pay the debts " incurred by J. up to the date of the deed in connection with the working arrangement of the farm," and to maintain J.—J. had no other property than that comprised in the deed, and the Plaintiff's debt not having been incurred by J. in connection with the farm, was defeated by the deed.—The Court found that the deed was an honestly intended family arrangement, and was not executed with the object of defeating creditors :—*Held,* that the deed was valid under stat. 13 Eliz. c. 5. *In re* JOHNSON. GOLDEN v. GILLAM   -   -   -   - **20 Ch. D. 389**

2. —— Defeating and delaying Creditors — 13 *Eliz.* c. 5.] In 1872 R. R. gave to the W. Bank a guarantee to secure the balance due from his son R. H. R. on his banking account to the extent of £1000. On the 25th of May, 1877, R. H. R.'s account was overdrawn by £1515. On that day R. R. made a voluntary settlement of a leasehold property worth £200 a-year, which he held at a rent of £3 10s. His only other property was furniture worth less than £200, and a debt of £1500 due to him from R. H. R. In 1880 R. H. R., whose account was then overdrawn by £1313, went into liquidation and paid a dividend of 3s. in the pound. There was some general evidence that R. H. R. was solvent at the date of the settlement. R. R. having died, the Bank took proceedings to set aside the settlement and to have the leasehold treated as assets of R. R. in a suit for administration of his estate in which the Bank had been admitted creditors for £1000 on the guarantee :—*Held,* by Bacon, V.-C., that the settlement was valid against creditors, as there was no evidence that it was made with intent to defeat or delay creditors.—*Held,* by the Court of Appeal, that the settlement was not a settlement for value within the meaning of 13 Eliz.' c. 5, the doctrine of *Price* v. *Jenkins* (5 Ch. D. 619) not being applicable to cases under that statute.—But *held,* reversing the decision below, that the settlement was invalid as against creditors, for that under the circumstances the liability under the guarantee ought to have been regarded as a substantial one; that R. R. had no right to treat the £1500 due from R. H. R. as a good debt; that the settlement must therefore be looked' upon as a settlement of all his property, leaving to him nothing out of which he could meet his liability under the guarantee, and that an intention to defeat or delay creditors must be inferred. *In re* RIDLER. RIDLER v. RIDLER   -   -   -   - **22 Ch. D. 74**

3. —— Laches—13 *Eliz.* c. 5.] A specialty creditor brought an action to set aside a conveyance as fraudulent under 13 Eliz. c. 5, nearly ten years after the death of the grantor. The Plaintiff had been aware of the facts during the whole of that period, and gave no satisfactory reason for his delay :—*Held* (affirming the decision of North, J.), that as the Plaintiff was coming to enforce a legal right his mere delay to take proceedings was no defence, as it had not continued long enough to bar his legal right, the case

FRAUDULENT CONVEYANCE—*continued.*
standing on a different footing from a suit to set aside on equitable grounds a deed which was valid at law. *In re* MADDEVER. THREE TOWNS BANKING COMPANY *v.* MADDEVER   27 Ch. D. 523

—— Impeached by trustee in bankruptcy
[21 Ch. D. 553
See BANKRUPTCY—JURISDICTION. 4.

—— Void under bankruptcy law   19 Ch. D. 588
See BANKRUPTCY—VOID SETTLEMENT. 1.

FRAUDULENT DEBTOR—Punishment of.
See BANKRUPT—BANKRUPTCY ACT, 1883
—*Statutes.*

FRAUDULENT PLEDGE—Marshalling securities
[25 Ch. D. 148
See BANKRUPTCY—SECURED CREDITOR. 6.

FRAUDULENT PREFERENCE.
See Cases under BANKRUPTCY—FRAUDULENT PREFERENCE.

FREE MINERS   27 Ch. D. 652
See MINE—FREE MINERS.

FREEMAN—Honorary.
See MUNICIPAL CORPORATION—CONSTITUTION—*Statutes.*

—— Municipal corporation—Custom of borough
[21 Ch. D. 111
See MUNICIPAL CORPORATION — PROPERTY.

—— Registration of.
See PARLIAMENT — REDISTRIBUTION OF SEATS—*Statute.*

FREIGHT—Carrier—Liability of consignor
See CARRIER—GOODS.   [15 Q. B. D. 625

—— Insurance   6 Q. B. D. 648 ; 7 Q. B. D. 73 ;
[7 App. Cas. 670
See INSURANCE, MARINE—POLICY. 1, 2.

—— Insurance — Sum of money in nature of freight—Advance for necessaries.
See SHIP—FREIGHT. 1.   [8 P. D. 155

—— Liability of indorsee of bill of lading
[13 Q. B. D. 159 ; 10 App. Cas. 74
See SHIP—BILL OF LADING. 4.

—— Lien for   -   15 Q. B. D. 154
See SHIP—CHARTERPARTY. 1.

—— Right to freight after abandonment of ship
See SHIP—FREIGHT. 2.   [7 P. D. 5

—— Right to freight—Final sailing from last port   9 Q. B. D. 679 ; 15 Q. B. D. 580
See SHIP—CHARTERPARTY. 3, 4.

FRESHWATER FISH.
See FISHERY ACTS—*Gazette.*

FRIENDLY SOCIETY.
The Act 45 & 46 Vict. c. 35, s. 2, repeals so much of sect. 14 of the Friendly Societies Act, 1875 (38 & 39 Vict. c. 60), and of the second schedule to that Act, as relates to sending to the registrar every five years a return to be called a quinquennial return of the sickness and mortality experienced by Friendly Societies, or as relates to such return.
The Act 46 & 47 Vict. c. 47, extends the power

FRIENDLY SOCIETY—*continued.*
of nomination in Friendly and Industrial, &c., Societies, and makes further provision for cases of intestacy in respect of personal property of small amount.
    Sect. 1. Act to be cited as the Provident Nomination and Small Intestacies Act, 1883.
    Sect. 2. Interpretation of terms.
    Sect. 3 extends sub-sections 3 and 4 of sect. 15 of the Friendly Societies Act, 1875, sub-sections 5 and 6 of sect. 11 of the Industrial and Provident Societies Act, 1876, sect. 10 of the Trade Union Act Amendment Act, 1876, sects. 41, 42, and 43 of the Trustee Savings Bank Act, 1863, sect. 10 of the Act 7 & 8 Vict. c. 83, and sub-head (e) of sect. 6 of the Government Annuities Act, 1882, to sums not exceeding £100.
    Sect. 4. How a nomination may be made.
    Sect. 5. Nominations by savings bank depositors.
    Sect. 6 extends sub-section 3 of sect. 15 of the Friendly Societies Act, 1875, to deposits made under sect. 18 of the same Act, and moneys accumulated under sect. 19 of the same Act, and sub-sections 5 and 6 of sect. 11 of the Industrial and Provident Societies Act, 1876, to loans and deposits made under sub-section (2) of sect. 10 of that Act.
    Sect. 7. Provisions in case of intestacy and no nomination.
    Sect. 8. Provision for illegitimacy.
    Sect. 9. Payments made by directors under the powers given above to be valid.
    Sect. 10. Conditions to be observed where fund exceeds £80. Nomination or payment under the Act not to affect liability to probate duty.
    Sect. 11. As to Channel Islands and Isle of Man.
    The Act 48 & 49 Vict. c. 27, declares the true meaning of sect. 22 of 38 & 39 Vict. c. 60 (the Friendly Societies Act, 1875).

—— Powers of Investment — Illegal Loan—38 & 39 Vict. c. 60.] The trustees of a friendly society lent out of the surplus funds of the society a sum of £300 to A. on the security of a joint and several promissory note made by A., and by B. and C. as his sureties. None of the makers was a member of the society. C. having died, the trustees claimed to prove against his estate on the note:—*Held*, by Fry, J., that the loan on personal security to a person not a member of the society was forbidden by the Friendly Societies Act, that the transaction therefore was illegal, and that as C. had not received any money of the society, and the society had no claim against his estate except under the contract, the proof must be rejected.—*Held*, on appeal, that as it was not alleged that the money was borrowed for an illegal purpose, the contract was not illegal, but merely unauthorized ; that it was not competent to the makers of the note to allege by way of defence that the payee had no authority to lend the money, and that the proof, therefore, must be admitted. *In re* COLTMAN. COLTMAN *v.* COLTMAN   19 Ch. D. 64

—— Libel—Injunction   21 Ch. D. 798
See PRACTICE — SUPREME COURT—INJUNCTION. 4.

FRIVOLOUS ACTION   -   -   26 Ch. D. 35
See PRACTICE—SUPREME COURT—PARTIES. 16.

FROST—Preventing loading of ship   10 Q. B. D.
    [241; 11 Q. B. D. 543; 9 App. Cas. 470
    See SHIP—CHARTERPARTY. 8, 9.

FRUIT PICKERS.
    See LOCAL GOVERNMENT — PUBLIC
    HEALTH ACTS—*Statutes.*

FUGITIVE OFFENDERS.
    See JURISDICTION—*Statutes.*

FUND IN COURT—Proceeds of real estate—Suc-
    cession duty—Illegitimate children
                  [21 Ch. D. 100
    See REVENUE—SUCCESSION DUTY. 2.

—— Stop order—Notice   29 Ch. D. 786
    See MORTGAGE—PRIORITY. 10.

—— Stop order—Priority   -   23 Ch. D. 497
    See PRACTICE — SUPREME COURT —
    CHARGING ORDERS. 3.

FURNITURE—Custom of hiring—Bankruptcy
            [18 Ch. D. 30; 23 Ch. D. 261
    See BANKRUPTCY—ORDER AND DISPOSI-
    TION. 4, 5.

—— Gift of—Things ejusdem generis 30 Ch. D. 92
    See WILL—WORDS. 9.

FURTHER CONSIDERATION—Report of official
    referee   -   19 Ch. D. 644
    See PRACTICE—SUPREME COURT—RE-
    FEREE. 6.

FUTURE RIGHTS—Declaration of—Appeal
                   [21 Ch. D. 1
    See PRACTICE—SUPREME COURT—AP-
    PEAL. 34.

FUTURITY—Words of   -   6 App. Cas. 471
    See WILL—ESTATE IN REALTY. 4.

G.

GALE—Forfeiture of　　··　-　27 Ch. D. 652
　　　See MINE—FREE MINERS.

GAME.

1. —— Injury to Crops—*Reservation of Right of Shooting — Overstocking Land with Game— Right of Action.*] Where land is let to a tenant reserving the right of shooting over the land, the tenant may maintain an action against the persons entitled to the right of shooting for overstocking the land with game so as to cause damage to the tenant's crops. FARRER *v.* NELSON 15 Q. B. D. 258

2. —— Poaching — *Search by Constable in Highway—Seizure—25 & 26 Vict.* c. 114, s. 2.] A police constable saw the Appellant in a highway with some rabbits slung over his back. The Appellant left the highway and ran across a meadow followed by the police constable, and on being overtaken, at a distance from the highway, he threw the rabbits on the ground, and they were then and there taken possession of by the police constable. On appeal against a conviction under 25 & 26 Vict. c. 114, s. 2:—*Held,* that the conviction was right—*Turner* v. *Morgan* (Law Rep. 10 C. P. 587) commented on. LLOYD *v.* LLOYD -　　　-　-　14 Q. B. D. 725

—— Ground Game Act　　-　- 26 Ch. D. 559
　　　See LANDLORD AND TENANT — GROUND GAME.

GAMING.

1. —— Betting—*Employment of Agent to bet in his own Name—Implied Authority to pay Bet— When Authority is irrevocable—8 & 9 Vict.* c. 109, *s.* 18.] The employment of an agent to make a bet in his own name on behalf of his principal may imply an authority to pay the bet if lost, and on the making of the bet that authority may become irrevocable.—So *held,* by Bowen and Fry, L.JJ., Brett, M.R., dissenting. READ *v.* ANDERSON　　10 Q. B. D. 100; 13 Q. B. D. 779

2. —— Common Gaming House—*Unlawful Gaming within 17 & 18 Vict.* c. 38, *s.* 4—"*Baccarat.*"] The 4th section of 17 & 18 Vict. c. 38, enacts that "any person, being the owner or occupier or having the use of any house, room, or place, who shall use the same for the purpose of unlawful gaming being carried on therein; and any person who, being the owner or occupier of any house or room, shall knowingly and wilfully permit the same to be opened, kept, or used by any other person for the purpose aforesaid; and every person having the care or management of or in any manner assisting in conducting the business of any house, room, or place opened, kept, or used for the purpose aforesaid; and any person who shall advance or furnish money for the purpose of gaming with persons frequenting such house, room, or place, may, on summary conviction thereof before any two justices of the peace, &c.," forfeit and pay a penalty not exceeding £500.—A. was the proprietor of the Park Club, and was also occupier of the premises used by the

GAMING—continued.
club, and received the profits. B., C., D., and E. were members of the committee of management, whose duty it was to regulate the internal management of the club, and (amongst other things) to make by-laws and regulations for the carrying it on and for the government of its members, who were elected by them. F., G., and H. were members of the club.—By the rules and regulations of the club, hazard was not to be played, dice were excluded, and the points at whist were limited to £1; all games were to be played for ready money: and under no pretence were strangers to be admitted in the card-room.—An entrance fee of 10 guineas and an annual subscription of 6 guineas was paid by each member of the club. The kitchen was conducted at a loss, and wines and cigars supplied at a slight excess over cost price. The profits accruing to the proprietor arose from the entrance-fees and subscriptions and what was called "card money." Members' cheques were cashed by the proprietor to the amount of £200, for which he charged 1 per cent.—The game of baccarat was played nightly, as follows:—About twelve persons at a time played at it. A special table was provided, with arrangements for the banker and players. Three packs of cards shuffled together were used. One card was dealt to each person, the banker included. The object of the game was to get 9 in pips or as near thereto as possible. After each had a card dealt to him and had seen it, it was at his option whether he would stand upon it or take another; and in the exercise of this option consisted the only semblance of skill in the game. If the banker had 9, and none of the others had, he swept the board: if he had not 9 but a less number, he won from all who were further from 9, and paid to all who were nearer to 9 than he was. The banker had a slight advantage, inasmuch as he had an extra "draw," and consequently with luck would win more quickly than an ordinary player.—Play commenced at 4.30 P.M., and continued till 7.30; commencing again at 10.30 P.M., and continuing till 3 and sometimes till 8 A.M. There was a fresh bank about every twenty minutes. A "regulation bank" was one held by any member who chose to take it by putting his name on a slate: it must not be less than £50. Every third bank before 2 A.M. was a regulation bank. The other banks (which originally ranged from £25 to £300, but sometimes extended to £1000 and even more) were offered at auction. Each banker paid 1 per cent., and the punters (players) 5s. each, which was called "card money," up to 2 A.M.; after that hour 5s. an hour was charged until 5 A.M., when £1 an hour was charged. The banker had to put down ready money to the amount of £300.—Upon an information charging the eight persons above named with having committed offences against sect. 4 of 17 & 18 Vict. c. 38, A., the proprietor, was adjudged to have been guilty of "keeping and using the Park Club for the purpose of unlawful

GAMING—*continued.*

gaming," and fined £500. The four committee-men were adjudged to have been guilty, as persons "having the care or management of and assisting in conducting the business " of the house so kept and used for the purpose of unlawful gaming, and each fined £500. The three players were also adjudged to have been guilty of the offence, as persons who "assisted by playing in conducting the business of the house so kept and used for the purpose of unlawful gaming," and were each fined £100:—*Held*, that the proprietor of the club and the four members of the committee were properly convicted : but that the players—though possibly liable to be indicted for unlawful gaming in a common gaming-house—were not liable to be summarily convicted under this statute.—Per Hawkins, J.: If the house in question had been opened and used for a double purpose, viz. as an honest social club for those who did not desire to play, as well as for the purposes of gaming for those who did, it would not the less be a house opened and kept "for the purpose of gaming."—To constitute "unlawful gaming," it is not necessary that the games played shall be *unlawful* games : it is enough that the play is carried on in a "common gaming-house." The expression "*unlawful* games" was intended by the Legislature to cover and include some games which, being lawful in themselves, were only made unlawful when played in particular places or by particular persons.—It makes no difference that the use of the house and the gaming therein is limited to the subscribers or members of the club, and that it is not open to *all* persons who might be desirous of using it. It is not a *public*, but a *common* gaming-house, that is prohibited.—" Baccarat " is a game of chance, and unlawful within 17 & 18 Vict. c. 38, s. 4.—Excessive gaming, per se, is not any longer a legal offence : it was not an offence at common law ; and there now exists no statute against it. But the fact that it is habitually carried on in a house kept for the purpose of gaming is cogent evidence for a jury or other tribunal called upon to determine whether the house in which it is carried on is a common gaming-house, so as to make the keeper of it liable to be indicted for a nuisance at common law.—Per Smith, J.: A " common gaming-house" is a house kept or used for playing therein at any game of chance, or any mixed game of chance and skill, in which (1) a bank is kept by one or more of the players exclusively of the others, or (2) in which any game is played the chances of which are not alike favourable to all the players, including among the players the banker or other person by whom the game is managed or against whom the other players stake, play, or bet.—It is immaterial whether the bank is kept by the owner or occupier or keeper of the house or by one of the players. JENKS *v.* TURPIN　　13 Q. B. D. 505

3. —— Lottery—*Sale of Packets of Tea containing Coupons for Prizes*—42 *Geo.* 3, c. 119, s. 2.] By 42 Geo. 3, c. 119, s. 2, it is made an offence to keep any office or place to exercise any lottery not authorized by Parliament.—The Appellant erected a tent, in which he sold packets, each containing a pound of tea, at 2s. 6d. a packet. In each packet was a coupon entitling the purchaser to a

GAMING—*continued.*

prize, and this was publicly stated by the Appellant before the sale, but the purchasers did not know until after the sale what prizes they were entitled to, and the prizes varied in character and value. The tea was good and worth the money paid for it :—*Held*, that what the Appellant did constituted a lottery within the meaning of the statute. TAYLOR *v.* SMETTEN -　11 Q. B. D. 207

4. —— Place used for Betting — *Bicycle Grounds—Manager of—Betting there—Liability of Manager* (16 & 17 *Vict.* c. 119, ss. 1, 3).] The Appellant was manager of bicycle grounds. Bicycle races, at which 20,000 spectators were present, took place there. Placards with the words " No betting allowed," were posted in the grounds, and twelve police constables were employed there by the manager, but some betting took place about twenty yards from the winning-post where he stood, acting as judge of the races. He was aware that betting would and did take place, but could not have wholly prevented it under the circumstances, although he might have repressed it to a certain extent with the aid of the constables :—*Held*, that as the business of the grounds was not that of illegal betting within 16 & 17 Vict. c. 119, s. 1, he was not liable to conviction under sect. 3, as a " person having the care or management of or in any manner assisting in conducting the business of any . . . . place opened, kept, or used for the purposes aforesaid." THE QUEEN *v.* COOK -　　- 13 Q. B. D. 377

5. —— Place used for Betting—*Information or Advice with respect to Bet or Wager—Advertisement—Betting Acts*, 1853 *and* 1874 (16 & 17 *Vict.* c. 119 *and* 37 & 38 *Vict.* c. 15).] The Betting Act, 1874, is confined to such bets as are mentioned in the Betting Act, 1853—that is, to bets made in any house, office, or place kept for betting—and the Act does not apply to advertisements offering information for the purpose of bets not to be made in any house, office, or place kept for that purpose. COX *v.* ANDREWS　12 Q. B. D. [126

6. —— Place used for Betting—*Payment for Admission*—16 & 17 *Vict.* c. 119, ss. 1, 3.] Dog-races were held in an inclosed field hired for the purpose by a committee, the public being admitted to a reserved portion of the field on payment of a small sum. The Appellant attended the races, and moved about the reserved portion, making bets with various persons there :—*Held*, that the Appellant did not use a place for the purpose of betting with persons resorting thereto, within the meaning of sects. 1 and 3 of 16 & 17 Vict. c. 119, and therefore was not liable to be convicted for an offence under those sections. SNOW *v.* HILL -　　-　　-　14 Q. B. D. 588

7. —— Place used for Betting—*Station of Betting Man at a moveable Box within Ring at Races*—16 & 17 *Vict.* c. 119, s. 3.] By 16 & 17 Vict. c. 119, s. 3, "any person who, being the owner or occupier of any house, office, room, or other place, or a person using the same, shall open, keep, or use the same for the purposes" of betting with persons resorting thereto, is liable to a penalty. The Respondent and a companion, having paid for admission, were in a railed inclo-

X

GAMING—*continued.*

sure of the grand stand at a race meeting. The companion stood on a small wooden box not attached to the ground, and he and the Respondent called out offering to make and making bets with other persons. The companion received the money for bets made, and the Respondent booked the same. They stood together in one place within the inclosure during the races :—*Held,* that the fixed and ascertained spot defined in the inclosure by the box at which the Respondent orally advertised his willingness to bet was a "place" used by him for the purpose of betting with persons resorting thereto, and he was liable to a penalty under 16 & 17 Vict. c. 119, s. 3.
GALLAWAY *v.* MARIES　　-　8 Q. B. D. 275

—— Licensed premises — Knowledge of servant
—Licensing Acts　　.　12 Q. B. D. 360
See INN—OFFENCES. 4.

—— Railway carriage　　-　10 Q. B. D. 44
See VAGRANT ACTS. 2.

GARNISHEE ORDER — " Final judgment "—
Bankruptcy notice　　12 Q. B. D. 342
See BANKRUPTCY—ACT OF BANKRUPTCY.
9.

—— Foreign attachment　　6 App. Cas. 393
See COURT—MAYOR'S COURT. 1.

—— Practice—Supreme Court.
See Cases under PRACTICE — SUPREME
COURT—GARNISHEE ORDER.

—— Salary of secretary -　-　9 Q. B. D. 45
See MASTER AND SERVANT—WAGES. 1.

—— Solicitor's lien—Priority　-　14 Q. B. D. 543
See SOLICITOR—LIEN. 4.

GAS COMPANY.

—— Injury to Pipes—*Highway—Repair of Streets—Use of Steam Rollers—Statutable Rights.*]
The Plaintiffs, a gas company, laid down pipes under the surface of certain streets, as they were bound by statute to do, for the purpose of supplying gas to light the streets and houses in the streets. The streets were vested in the Defendants, the vestry of the parish, by certain statutes which gave them the authority of the surveyor of highways, and with the duty to repair, but without prescribing any particular mode of repair. The Defendants used steam-rollers for the repair of the streets, as being a mode of repair most advantageous to both the ratepayers and the public, but the rollers they used were so heavy as to frequently injure the Plaintiffs' pipes, though the pipes were sufficiently below the surface not to have been injured by the ordinary mode of repair if such rollers had not been used :—*Held,* that the Plaintiffs were entitled not only to recover damages for the injury which had been done, but also to have an injunction to restrain the Defendants from using steam rollers in such a way as to injure the pipes of the Plaintiffs. GAS LIGHT AND COKE COMPANY *v.* VESTRY OF ST. MARY ABBOTT'S, KENSINGTON　　15 Q. B. D. 1

—— Bankruptcy of consumer — Distress for amount due—Preferential debt
[13 Q. B. D. 753
See BANKRUPTCY—DISTRESS. 1.

GAS LIQUOR WORKS.
See LOCAL GOVERNMENT — PUBLIC
HEALTH ACTS—*Statutes.*

GENERAL AVERAGE.
See Cases under SHIP—GENERAL AVERAGE.

GENERAL LINE OF BUILDINGS 27 Ch. D. 362 ;
[9 Q. B. D. 41 ; 13 Q. B. D. 878 ;
[10 App. Cas. 229
See METROPOLIS — MANAGEMENT ACTS.
1, 2, 3.

—— -　-　30 Ch. D. 350
See LOCAL GOVERNMENT—STREETS. 3.

GENERAL MEETING—Company 23 Ch. D. 654 ;
[25 Ch. D. 320 ; 29 Ch. D. 159
See COMPANY—MANAGEMENT. 3, 4, 5.

GENERAL ORDER, AUG., 1882—Solicitors' Remuneration Act.
See Cases under SOLICITOR — BILL OF
COSTS. 18—25.

—— r. 35, Sched. III., Form 39　-　29 Ch. D. 984
See EXECUTOR—RETAINER. 4.

GENERAL ORDERS IN CHANCERY, 1st FEB.
1861　　18 Ch. D. 646 ; 22 Ch. D. 93
See LANDS CLAUSES ACT — PURCHASEMONEY. 4, 5.

GENERAL ORDERS UNDER COMPANIES ACT,
NOV. 1862.
—— r. 25　-　-　17 Ch. D. 337
See COMPANY—PROOF. 2.

—— r. 53　　-　-　23 Ch. D. 542
See COMPANY—REDUCTION OF CAPITAL.
3.

—— r. 60 -　　25 Ch. D. 400 ; 27 Ch. D. 515
See COMPANY—EVIDENCE. 4, 5.

GENERAL ORDERS UNDER COMPANIES ACT,
MARCH, 1868, rr. 4, 5　　23 Ch. D. 542 ;
[29 Ch. D. 683
See COMPANY—REDUCTION OF CAPITAL.
3, 4.

GENERAL RULES, Hil. Term, 1853, r. 169
[19 Ch. D. 58
See ARBITRATION—AWARD. 2.

GENERAL WORDS—Conveyance　18 Ch. D. 616
See WAY. 1.

—— Ejusdem generis　-　-　30 Ch. D. 298
See ADVOWSON. 1.

—— Memorandum of association—Object of company　　-　20 Ch. D. 169
See COMPANY—WINDING-UP ORDER. 4.

—— Policy of insurance -　　6 Q. B. D. 51
See INSURANCE, MARINE—POLICY. 6.

—— Statutory effect.
See DEED—*Statutes.*

GIBRALTAR—Orders in Council.
See JURISDICTION—*Gazette.*

GIFT.

—— Fiduciary Relation—*Physician and Patient—Independent Advice.*] Although a gift made to a person standing in a confidential relation to the donor, as by a patient to a physician, may be voidable, yet, if after the confidential relation has ceased to exist, the donor intentionally

GIFT—*continued.*

elects to abide by the gift, and does in fact abide by it, it cannot be impeached after his death, even if it is not proved that the donor was aware that the gift was voidable at his election. The Plaintiffs were executors of G., to whom the Defendant had acted as medical adviser. G. made a gift of £800 to the Defendant. At the time of the gift no independent advice was given to G., and the relation of physician and patient then existed; but the Defendant had not been guilty of any undue influence, and after the relation of physician and patient had ceased, G. elected to abide by the gift, and did in fact abide by it during the rest of her life. It was not proved that G. was aware that the gift was voidable :—*Held,* that the gift made by G. to the Defendant could not be impeached after her death.—*Rhodes* v. *Bate* (Law Rep. 1 Ch. 252) commented on. MITCHELL *v.* HOMFRAY - - - **8 Q. B. D. 587**

—— By infant - - **19 Ch. D. 603**
   See INFANT—ACTS.

—— By will.
   See Cases under WILL.

—— Chattels—Parent and child—Assets
               [15 Q. B. D. 447
   See BANKRUPTCY—ASSETS. 17.

—— Furniture - - - **17 Ch. D. 416**
   See VOLUNTARY CONVEYANCE. 1.

—— Money — Father to son—Voluntary settlement—Bankruptcy—Void settlement
               [15 Q. B. D. 682
   See BANKRUPTCY—VOID SETTLEMENT. 2.

GIN—Adulteration - **10 Q. B. D. 518**
   See ADULTERATION. 6.

GIRLS—Under thirteen.
   See CRIMINAL LAW—OFFENCES AGAINST WOMEN—*Statutes.*

—— Under sixteen.
   See CRIMINAL LAW—OFFENCES AGAINST WOMEN—*Statutes.*

GLEBE LANDS — Purchase-money — Lands Clauses Act - **20 Ch. D. 203**
   See LANDS CLAUSES ACT — PURCHASE-MONEY. 6.

—— Sale of—Rent-charge—Land drainage company - - **20 Ch. D. 208**
   See ECCLESIASTICAL COMMISSIONERS.

GOODWILL.

1. —— Mortgage — *Trade Premises.*] Although in some cases the goodwill of trade premises passes to a mortgagee, that does not apply to a case where the goodwill depends on the personal skill of the owner. COOPER *v.* METROPOLITAN BOARD OF WORKS **25 Ch. D. 472**

2. —— Sale of—*Rights of Purchaser—From Vendor personally—From Trustees in Bankruptcy—Solicitation of Old Customers.*] The rule of *Labouchere* v. *Dawson* (Law Rep. 13 Eq. 322), by which in the case of a voluntary sale the vendor of the goodwill of a business is precluded from afterwards soliciting the former customers of that business, cannot be extended to the case of a compulsory alienation. The obligation enforced by the rule is purely personal, and not a mere incident to the transfer of property. Therefore the purchaser of the goodwill of a business from a

GOODWILL—*continued.*

trustee in bankruptcy or liquidation has no right to restrain the bankrupt or liquidating debtor from setting up bonâ fide a fresh business and soliciting the customers of his former business, and it is immaterial whether the bankrupt has or has not joined in the conveyance of the goodwill to the purchaser.—Per Lindley and Lush, L.JJ.: The case of *Labouchere* v. *Dawson* is still applicable to the case of voluntary sales.—The decision in that case questioned by Baggallay, L.J.—*Cruttwell* v. *Lye* (17 Ves. 335) followed. WALKER *v.* MOTTRAM - - **19 Ch. D. 355**

3. —— Sale—*Vendor setting up new Business—Right to solicit old Customers.*] T. P., as trustee of a will, carried on a business which had been carried on by the testator under the name of James P. By an agreement made to compromise a suit, James P., a son of the testator and a beneficiary under his will, agreed to sell to T. P. all his interest in the business, and in the property on which it was carried on. And it was provided that nothing in the agreement should prevent James P. from carrying on the like business where he should think fit, and under the name of James P. T. P. brought this action to enforce this agreement, and to restrain James P. from soliciting the customers of the old firm. An injunction was accordingly granted by Kay, J., on the authority of *Labouchere* v. *Dawson* (Law Rep. 13 Eq. 322) and the cases in which it had been followed :—*Held,* by Baggallay and Cotton, L.JJ., dissentiente Lindley, L.J., that *Labouchere* v. *Dawson* was wrongly decided, and ought to be overruled, and that even apart from the proviso in the agreement, the Plaintiff was not entitled to the injunction which he had obtained.—*Held,* by the whole Court, that the proviso in the agreement authorized the Defendant to carry on business in the same way as any stranger might lawfully do, and took the case out of the authority of *Labouchere* v. *Dawson,* supposing that case to have been well decided. PEARSON *v.* PEARSON **27 Ch. D. 145**

—— Compensation—Mortgage · **25 Ch. D. 472**
   See LANDS CLAUSES ACT—COMPENSATION. 1.

—— Sale of—Bankruptcy - **16 Ch. D. 226**
   See BANKRUPTCY—DISTRESS. 2.

—— Sale of—Dissolution of partnership
               [18 Ch. D. 698
   See PARTNERSHIP—CONTRACT. 3.

GOVERNMENT ANNUITIES.
   See NATIONAL DEBT COMMISSIONERS—*Statutes.*
   FRIENDLY SOCIETY—*Statutes.*

GOVERNMENT STOCK—Local board—Vesting—Duty of Bank of England
               [21 Ch. D. 176
   See LOCAL GOVERNMENT—LOCAL AUTHORITY. 9.

GOVERNOR OF PRISON—Superannuation allowance **11 Q. B. D. 656; 9 App. Cas. 757**
   See PRISON. 1.

GRAMMAR SCHOOL - - **7 App. Cas. 91**
   See ENDOWED SCHOOLS ACT. 3.

GRANT—Crown—Booty of war **7 App. Cas. 619**
   See BOOTY OF WAR.

                       K 2.

GRANT—*continued.*

—— Crown lands—Resumption of grants
　　　　　　　　　　　[9 **App. Cas.** 142
　　　See COLONIAL LAW—WEST AUSTRALIA. 2.

—— Implied—Right to support　　21 **Ch. D.** 559
　　　See SUPPORT. 1.

—— Monthly pensions—"Heirs and successors"
　　　　　　　　　　　[8 **App. Cas.** 751
　　　See COLONIAL LAW—STRAITS SETTLE-
　　　MENTS. 2.

GRATUITY—Servants and directors of company
　　—Power of general meeting　　23 **Ch. D.**
　　　See COMPANY—MANAGEMENT. 2. [654

GRAVE—Grant in perpetuity -　6 **Q. B. D.** 290
　　　See BURIAL-GROUND. 1.

GRAZING—Right of—Poor-rate—Occupation
　　　　　　　　　　　[6 **Q. B. D.** 10
　　　See POOR-RATE—OCCUPATION. 4.

GREEK MARRIAGES.

　　*The Act 47 & 48 Vict. c. 20, renders valid cer-
tain marriages celebrated in the Greek Church in
London between 1836 and 1857.*

GROUND GAME—Reservation of　26 **Ch. D.** 559
　　　See LANDLORD AND TENANT — GROUND
　　　GAME.

GROWING CROPS—Bill of sale—Registration
　　　　　　　　　　　[16 **Ch. D.** 104
　　　See BILL OF SALE—REGISTRATION. 3.

GUARANTEE—Construction -　16 **Ch. D.** 290
　　　See PRINCIPAL AND SURETY—CONTRACT.

—— Death of surety—Appropriation of pay-
　　ments　　　　　- 25 **Ch. D.** 692
　　　See PRINCIPAL AND SURETY—DISCHARGE.
　　　3.

—— Directors of railway company 19 **Ch. D.** 478
　　　See RAILWAY COMPANY —CONSTITUTION.

—— Discharge　9 **Q. B. D.** 783 ; 8 **App. Cas.** 755
　　　See PRINCIPAL AND SURETY—DISCHARGE.
　　　1, 2.

GUARANTEE—*continued.*

—— One of several partners　　25 **Ch. D.** 148
　　　See BANKRUPTCY—SECURED CREDITOR. 6.

—— Proof in bankruptcy -　-　17 **Ch. D.** 98
　　　See BANKRUPTCY—PROOF. 11.

GUARANTEE SOCIETY -　-　7 **P. D.** 235
　　　See ADMINISTRATOR—LIMITED. 7.

GUARDIAN—Administration—Grant for benefit
　　of minor　　　　　9 **P. D.** 66
　　　See ADMINISTRATOR—WITH WILL AN-
　　　NEXED. 2.

—— Consent to marriage -　-　18 **Ch. D.** 61
　　　See WILL—CONDITION. 9.

—— Infant resident abroad　-　30 **Ch. D.** 324
　　　See INFANT.—GUARDIAN. 1.

—— Religious education　　21 **Ch. D.** 317
　　　See INFANT—EDUCATION. 2.

—— Vouchers of expenditure　-　26 **Ch. D.** 58
　　　See INFANT—GUARDIAN. 2.

GUARDIAN AD LITEM—Infant　19 **Ch. D.** 460
　　　See PRACTICE—SUPREME COURT—SER-
　　　VICE. 8.

—— Interrogatories—Answer -　11 **Q. B. D.** 251
　　　See PRACTICE—SUPREME COURT—INTER-
　　　ROGATORIES. 4.

—— Probate action　　-　-　7 **P. D.** 234
　　　See PRACTICE—PROBATE—GUARDIAN.

GUARDIANS OF POOR.
　　　See POOR LAW—MANAGEMENT—*Statutes.*

—— Disqualification—Clerk of highway or school
　　board　　　-　　15 **Q. B. D.** 382
　　　See POOR-RATE—GUARDIANS.

—— Maintenance of lunatic　-　27 **Ch. D.** 710
　　　See LUNATIC—MAINTENANCE. 3.

GUILDHALL.
　　　See COURT—*Gazette.*

GUNPOWDER—Used in mines.
　　　See MINE—MINES REGULATION ACT—
　　　Statutes.

H.

HABEAS CORPUS—*Prisoner—Party to Motion.*]
The Court cannot grant a habeas corpus to a
party to a suit, in custody, to enable him to appear in Court merely for the purpose of arguing
his case in person.—*Benns* v. *Mosley* (2 C. B.
(N.S.) 116) followed. WELDON *v.* NEAL
　　　　　　　　　　　　[15 Q. B. D. 471

—— Custody of infant—Discretion 13 Q. B. D. 614
　　See INFANT—CUSTODY. 1.

—— Military law—Canteen steward
　　See ARMY AND NAVY. [15 Q. B. D. 488

HABIT AND REPUTE—Scotch marriage
　　　　　　　　　　　[6 App. Cas. 489
　　See SCOTCH LAW—HUSBAND AND WIFE.
　　3.

HANDWRITING—Comparison — Interrogatories
　　—Libel　　-　-　15 Q. B. D. 439
　　See PRACTICE—SUPREME COURT—INTER-
　　ROGATORIES. 7.

HARBOUR—Dues leviable　-　8 App. Cas. 658
　　See SCOTCH LAW—HARBOUR. 2.

—— Duties—Assignment—Mortmain
　　　　　　　　　　　[30 Ch. D. 544
　　See CHARITY—MORTMAIN. 3.

—— Infringement of regulations　-　9 P. D. 3
　　See SHIP—NAVIGATION. 32.

—— Removal of wreck -　　11 Q. B. D. 496
　　See DOCKS AND HARBOURS. 2.

—— Trustees of—Lands Clauses Act—Scotch
　　law　-　　-　8 App. Cas. 623
　　See SCOTCH LAW—HARBOUR. 1.

HARBOUR MASTER—Damage to ship—Mooring
and beaching of vessels—Harbour Commissioners—Liability　10 P. D. 24, 131
　　See NEGLIGENCE—LIABILITY. 9, 10.

HAWKER OF PETROLEUM.
　　See PETROLEUM—*Statutes.*

HEARSAY EVIDENCE—Family repute
　　　　　　　　　　　[10 App. Cas. 763
　　See SCOTCH LAW—HUSBAND AND WIFE.
　　4.

HEDGES—In west of England.
　　See HIGHWAY—REPAIR—*Statutes.*

HEIR-AT-LAW—Customary heir—Jus represen-
　　tationis　　-　　18 Ch. D. 165
　　See COPYHOLD—CUSTOM. 2.

—— Retainer for debts　-　-　27 Ch. D. 478
　　See RETAINER.

HEIRLOOM.
　　See Cases under WILL—HEIRLOOM.

—— Sale of—Settled Land Act　27 Ch. D. 179;
　　　　　　　　　　　[30 Ch. D. 136
　　See SETTLED LAND ACT.—RESTRICTIONS.
　　1, 2.

—— Sale of—Settled Land Act 30 Ch. D. 102, 127
　　See SETTLED LAND ACT — PURCHASE-
　　MONEY. 1, 4.

—— Tenant for life's power of sale over.
　　See SETTLED LAND ACT—STATUTES.

HERBAGE—Common of -　　-　17 Ch. D. 535
　　See COMMON.

—— Malicious injury—"Real or personal pro-
　　perty "　-　　-　　-　8 Q. B. D. 283
　　See CRIMINAL LAW—MALICIOUS INJURY
　　TO PROPERTY.

HERITABLE PROPERTY.
　　See Cases under SCOTCH LAW — HERI-
　　TABLE PROPERTY.

HERITAGE—Conveyance of -　8 App. Cas. 853
　　See SCOTCH LAW—CONVEYANCE. 1.

HIGH BAILIFF—City of London Court—War-
　　rant of arrest—Service—Clerk
　　　　　　　　　　　[10 P. D. 36
　　See PRACTICE—ADMIRALTY—SERVICE. 1.

HIGH PEAK MINE—Custom—Erection of build-
　　ings　7 Q. B. D. 295; 8 App. Cas. 195
　　See MINE—WORKING. 1.

HIGHER OR LOWER SCALE—Costs.
　　See Cases under PRACTICE—SUPREME
　　COURT—COSTS.

HIGHWAY.　　　　　　　　　Col.
　　I. BOARD　-　　-　　-　-　618
　　II. DEDICATION　　　　　　　618
　　III. LOCOMOTIVE　　-　　-　619
　　IV. NUISANCE　　　　　-　619
　　V. OBSTRUCTION　　-　　　620
　　VI. RATE　　　　　-　　620
　　VII. REPAIR　-　　-　　-　620
　　　　(*a.*) COUNTY RATE.
　　　　(*b.*) DISTURNPIKED ROADS.
　　　　(*c.*) EXTRAORDINARY EXPENSES.
　　　　(*d.*) MATERIALS.
　　VIII. STOPPING-UP　-　　-　-　625
　　IX. WAYWARDEN　-　　-　626

I. HIGHWAY—BOARD.
　　The Act 44 & 45 Vict. c. 72, amends sect. 13 of
the Highways and Locomotives (Amendment) Act,
1878.

—— Dissolution of Highway District—*Highway Board existing after such Dissolution—Highway Act, 1862 (25 & 26 Vict. c. 61), ss. 9 and
39.*] By the dissolution of a highway district, in
respect of which a highway board had been constituted under the Highway Act, 1862, the highway board, though it ceases to have any control
over the highways in its district, does not cease to
exist as a corporate body for the performance of
its other duties, such as those of suing or being
sued, and of acting generally for the purpose of
winding up its affairs. THE QUEEN *v.* JUSTICES OF
ESSEX　　-　　　　-　-　11 Q. B. D. 704

II. HIGHWAY—DEDICATION.
　　—— Reservation of Tolls-—*Private Owners—
Tolls—" Highway repairable by Inhabitants at
large "—38 & 39 Vict. c. 55, ss. 4, 150.*] The

II. HIGHWAY—DEDICATION—continued.

promoters of an intended road by deed declared that the road should not only be enjoyed by them for their individual purposes, but "should be open to the use of the public at large for all manner of purposes in all respects as a common turnpike road," but subject to the payment of tolls by the persons using it:—*Held*, that this was not a dedication of the road to the public, and that the road was not a highway repairable by the inhabitants at large under sect. 150 of the Public Health Act, 1875.—*Semble*, an individual cannot, without legislative authority, dedicate a road to the public if he reserves the right to charge tolls for the user; and the mere fact that a number of persons form themselves into a company for making and maintaining a road, and erect gates and bars and charge tolls, does not make the road a "turnpike road" in the sense of a turnpike road made such by Act of Parliament, and so dedicated to the public. AUSTERBURY *v.* CORPORATION OF OLDHAM - - - **29 Ch. D. 750**

III. HIGHWAY—LOCOMOTIVE.

The Act 48 & 49 Vict. c. 59, continues the Locomotives Act, 1865 (28 & 29 Vict. c. 83), and the Acts amending the same until the 31st of December, 1886.

—— **Tricycle**—*Locomotives Act, 1861 (24 & 25 Vict. c. 70), ss. 8, 12—Locomotives Act, 1865 (28 & 29 Vict. c. 83), ss. 3, 4, 7—Highways and Locomotives (Amendment) Act, 1878 (41 & 42 Vict. c. 77), ss. 28, 29, 38.*] A tricycle was capable of being propelled by the feet of the rider, or by steam as an auxiliary, or by steam alone. There was no smoke, nor escape of steam into the air, nor anything to indicate that it was being worked by steam, nor anything which could frighten horses, or cause danger to the public using the highway beyond any ordinary tricycle. The weight was about two hundred weight, and the tires of the wheels about one and a half inches in width. The tires being of india-rubber, no injury would be done to the surface of the road by working the machine on it:—*Held*, by Lord Coleridge, C.J., Pollock, B., and Manisty, J., that the tricycle was a "locomotive" within the definition in sect. 38 of the Highways and Locomotives (Amendment) Act, 1878 (41 & 42 Vict. c. 77), and was therefore subject to the rules and regulations for the use of locomotives on highways prescribed by sects. 28 and 29 of that Act, by the Locomotives Act, 1861 (24 & 25 Vict. c. 70), s. 12, and the Locomotives Act, 1865 (28 & 29 Vict. c. 83), ss. 3, 4, 7. PARRYNS *v.* PREIST - - - **7 Q. B. D. 313**

IV. HIGHWAY—NUISANCE.

—— **Cover of Water Valve**—*Projection of—Wearing away of Road—Local Board—Water and Highway Authority, Liability of—38 & 39 Vict. c. 55 (Public Health Act, 1875), s. 149.*] The iron cover of a valve connected with a water main was properly fixed in a highway by the Defendants, but in consequence of the ordinary wearing away of the highway the valve cover projected an inch above it. The Plaintiff's horse using the highway stumbled over the valve cover and was hurt. In an action against the Defendants, who were both the water authority and the highway autho-

IV. HIGHWAY—NUISANCE—continued.

rity, for the injury to the horse :—*Held*, that it was the duty of the Defendants to make such arrangements that works under their care should not become a nuisance to the highway, and that the Plaintiff was entitled to recover. KENT *v.* WORTHING LOCAL BOARD OF HEALTH
[10 Q. B. D. 118

[*And see* METROPOLIS—MANAGEMENT ACTS. 5.]

V. HIGHWAY—OBSTRUCTION.

—— **Omission to remove Obstruction**—*Highway Act, 1835 (5 & 6 Will. 4 c. 50), s. 72.*] In order to constitute wilful obstruction of a highway within 5 & 6 Will. 4, c. 50, s. 72, it is not necessary that there should be any act of commission, but the offence may be complete by an omission on the part of the person whose duty it is to remove an obstruction to do so after notice. GULLY *v.* SMITH
[12 Q. B. D. 121

VI. HIGHWAY—RATE.

The Act 45 & 46 Vict. c. 27, extends certain provisions of the Poor Rate Assessment and Collection Act, 1869, to the Highway Rate.

Sect. 1. Act to be cited as the Highway Rate Assessment and Expenditure Act, 1882.

Sect. 2. Extent of Act.

Sect. 3. Sect. 3 and 4 of the Poor Rate Assessment and Collection Act, 1869 to extend to and include the highway rate.

Power to rate and compound with owners of small tenements.

Repeal of 5 & 6 Will. 4, c. 50, s. 30.

Sect. 4. Valuation lists to be conclusive for highway rate.

Sect. 5. Provision for balances of outgoing surveyor.

Sect. 6. Power to maintain milestones and to fence.

Sect. 7. Extends and applies 41 & 42 Vict. c. 77, and 42 & 43 Vict. c. 6, as to waywarden's rate accounts.

Sect. 8. As to recovery and payment of certified balances.

Sect. 9. Provision as to excluded parts of parishes.

Sect. 10. Interpretation of terms.

VII. HIGHWAY—REPAIR.

The Act 48 & 49 Vict. c. 13, enables highway authorities in the counties of Wilts, Dorset, Somerset, Devon, and Cornwall to cut hedges, lop trees, &c., to avert shade.

(a.) COUNTY RATE.

1. —— **Borough**—*Liability to County Rate—Middlesborough Extension and Improvement Act, 1874 (37 & 38 Vict. c. cviii.)—Highways and Locomotives Amendment Act, 1878 (41 & 42 Vict. c. 77), s. 13*]. By a local Act passed in 1874 the limits of the borough of Middlesborough were extended. By sect. 20 of that Act it was enacted that the extended area "shall be exempt from all county rates save only in respect of the purposes for which any county rates are now leviable within the existing borough." At the time of the passing of that Act general county rates were leviable within the existing borough for all purposes for which general county rates could be levied in any

VII. HIGHWAY—REPAIR—*continued.* ·

(a.) COUNTY RATE—*continued.*

part of the riding. By sect. 13 of the Highways and Locomotives Amendment Act, 1878, any road which has ceased to be a turnpike road in manner described by the Act shall be deemed to be a main road, and one-half of the expenses incurred by the highway authority in the maintenance of such road shall be contributed out of the county rate:—*Held*, that as within the borough existing at the time of the passing of the local Act general county rates were leviable for all purposes, the saving of such liability rendered the exemption in sect. 20 inoperative; and therefore the inhabitants of the extended area of the borough were not exempt from liability to pay county rates for the maintenance of a road under sect. 13 of the Highways and Locomotives Amendment Act, 1878.—The decision of the Queen's Bench Division affirmed. OVERSEERS OF MIDDLESBOROUGH *v.* JUSTICES OF NORTH RIDING OF YORKSHIRE　　11 Q. B. D. 490; [12 Q. B. D. 239

2. —— Borough—*Expenses of Maintenance—Contribution from County Authority—Highway Act,* 1862 (25 & 26 *Vict. c.* 61), *s.* 2—*Highways and Locomotives (Amendment) Act,* 1878 (41 & 42 *Vict. c.* 77), *ss.* 13, 38.] By the Highway Act, 1862 (25 & 26 Vict. c. 61), s. 2, defining the word " county," " for the purposes of this Act all liberties and franchises except boroughs . . . . shall be considered as forming part of that county by which they are surrounded."—By the Highways and Locomotives (Amendment) Act, 1878 (41 & 42 Vict. c. 77), s. 38, " in this Act 'county' has the same meaning as it has in the Highway Acts, 1862 and 1864," and by sect. 13 any road which has between the 31st of December, 1870, and the date of the Act ceased to be a turnpike road . . . . shall be deemed to be a main road, and one-half of the expenses incurred in the maintenance shall, as to every part thereof which is within the limits of any highway area, be paid to the highway authority of such area " by the county authority of the county in which such road is situate " out of the county rate.—A road in the borough and highway area of Over Darwen, in Lancashire, ceased to be a turnpike road in 1877 :—*Held*, that, although for the purposes of the Highway Act, 1862, boroughs are not to be considered as forming parts of counties, yet as the road was within the geographical limits of Lancashire, the county of Lancaster was the " county in which such road is situate " within 41 & 42 Vict. c. 77, s. 13, and the county authority was liable to pay half the expenses incurred in the maintenance of such road. —Judgment of the Queen's Bench Division affirmed. MAYOR, &C., OF OVER DARWEN *v.* JUSTICES OF LANCASTER　　13 Q. B. D. 497 ; 15 Q. B. D. 20

3. —— Expense of removing Snow—*Liability of County Authority—Highways and Locomotives (Amendment) Act,* 1878 (41 & 42 *Vict. c.* 77), *s.* 13.] The main roads within the district of a highway authority became impassable from snow, which the highway authority removed, and they claimed one-half of the expense of doing so from the county authority under the Highways and Locomotives (Amendment) Act, 1878, s. 13:—*Held*, that this was an " expense incurred in the maintenance " of such roads within that sec-

VII. HIGHWAY—REPAIR—*continued.*

(a.) COUNTY RATE—*continued.*

tion, and that the county authority were liable. GUARDIANS OF AMESBURY *v.* JUSTICES OF WILTS [10 Q. B. D. 480

(b.) DISTURNPIKED ROADS.

4. ——. Ceasing to be Turnpike Road—*Main Road—Highways and Locomotives (Amendment) Act,* 1878 (41 & 42 *Vict. c.* 77), *s.* 13.] The Highways and Locomotives (Amendment) Act, 1878 (41 & 42 Vict. c. 77), by sect. 13, enacts that any road which has " between the 31st of December, 1870, and the date of this Act ceased to be a turnpike road " . . . . " shall be deemed to be a main road, and one-half of the expenses incurred from and after the 29th of September, 1878, by the highway authority in the maintenance of such road, shall, as to every part thereof which is within the limits of any highway area, be paid to the highway authority of such area by the county authority of the county in which such road is situate, out of the county rate."—The corporation of the town and borough of R. was the highway authority of the R. highway area. Under sects. 47–50 of the Towns Improvement Clauses Act, 1847 (10 & 11 Vict. c. 34), such portions of the turnpike roads entering it, as came within the area of the town were taken out of the turnpike trusts, and the obligation to repair the same was imposed upon the corporation. By a local Act in 1872, the boundaries of the borough were enlarged and all the provisions of the Acts relating to the " town " were made applicable to the enlarged area of the borough. The effect was that the further portions of the turnpike roads, thus for the first time brought within the area of the borough, were taken out of the turnpike trusts by the operation of the Towns Improvement Clauses Act, 1847, and ceased to be turnpike roads :—*Held*, reversing the decision of the Court of Appeal, that these further portions, being only parts of turnpike roads, had not " ceased to be turnpike roads," and were not to be deemed to be " main roads " within sect. 13 of the Highways and Locomotives (Amendment) Act, 1878 : and that the county authority were not liable to pay half the expenses of their maintenance. CORPORATION OF ROCHDALE *v.* JUSTICES OF LANCASHIRE [6 Q. B. D. 525 ; 8 Q. B. D. 12 ; 8 App. Cas. 494

5. —— Continuing to be Turnpike Road—*Highways and Locomotives (Amendment) Act,* 1878 (41 & 42 *Vict. c.* 77), *s.* 13.] The Highways and Locomotives (Amendment) Act, 1878, s. 13, provides for the maintenance of roads which have since the 31st of December, 1870, ceased to be turnpike roads. A provision in turnpike Acts coming into operation before the 31st of December, 1870, that turnpike trustees shall not spend money or levy toll upon certain portions of turnpike roads does not prevent such portions of the roads from being still turnpike roads on the 31st of December, 1870, within the meaning of sect. 13 of the Highways and Locomotives (Amendment) Act, 1878. So as to an agreement under the Local Government Act, 1858 (21 & 22 Vict. c. 98), s. 41, made before the 31st of December, 1870, between turnpike trustees and a corporation, under which the turnpikes upon certain portions of turnpike

VII. HIGHWAY—REPAIR—*continued.*

(*b.*) DISTURNPIKED ROADS—*continued.*

roads were removed and the repair of such portions was undertaken by the corporation:—So *held*, affirming the decision of the Court of Appeal. JUSTICES OF WEST RIDING OF YORK *v.* THE QUEEN **[8 App. Cas. 781**

6. —— Main Road—*Contribution from County for Repair—Highways and Locomotives (Amendment) Act, 1878 (41 & 42 Vict. c. 77), s. 13—18 & 19 Vict. c. c.—Towns Improvement Clauses Act, 1847 (10 & 11 Vict. c. 34), ss. 47, 49, 50, 51—Expiration of Turnpike Trusts in 1877—Cesser of Turnpike Road.*] By a local Act (18 & 19 Vict. c. c.) passed in 1855, and incorporating the Towns Improvement Clauses Act, 1847 (10 & 11 Vict. c. 34), the maintenance of all highways within a district, including a turnpike road, became vested in commissioners. The trustees of the turnpike road thereupon ceased to repair it within the limits of the district. The turnpike trust expired in 1877. The commissioners were the "highway authority" for the district, which was a "highway area" within the Highways and Locomotives (Amendment) Act, 1878 (41 & 42 Vict. c. 77), s. 13:—*Held*, that, notwithstanding the special legislation in 1855 providing for the maintenance of part of the road by the commissioners, it only "ceased to be a turnpike road" within the meaning of sect. 13 of the Highways and Locomotives (Amendment) Act, 1878, on the expiration of the turnpike trust between 1870 and the date of passing that Act, and therefore should be "deemed to be a main road," and one-half of the expenses of the maintenance of the part within the highway area should be paid to the highway authority by the county authority under sect. 13.—Judgment of the Queen's Bench Division affirmed. IMPROVEMENT COMMISSIONERS OF NEWTON IN MAKERFIELD *v.* JUSTICES OF LANCASTER - **13 Q. B. D. 623; 15 Q. B. D. 25**

7. —— Main Road — *Provisional Order to declare Ordinary Highway—Highways and Locomotives Amendment Act, 1878 (41 & 42 Vict. c. 77), s. 16 — Road disturnpiked between the 31st of December, 1870, and the passing of the Act.*] The 16th section of the Highways and Locomotives Amendment Act, 1878, provides as follows: "If it appears to a county authority that any road within their county which, within the period between the 31st of December, 1870, and the date of the passing of this Act, ceased to be a turnpike road, ought not to become a main road in pursuance of this Act, such authority shall, before the 1st of February, 1879, make an application to the Local Government Board for a provisional order declaring that such road ought not to become a main road." The section further provides that, "Subject as aforesaid, where it appears to a county authority that any road within their county, which has become a main road in pursuance of this Act, ought to cease to be a main road and become an ordinary highway, such authority may apply to the Local Government Board for a provisional order declaring that such road has ceased to be a main road and become an ordinary highway:—*Held*, that a road which had ceased to be a turnpike road within the period specified by the first of the above-

VII. HIGHWAY—REPAIR—*continued.*

(*b.*) DISTURNPIKED ROADS—*continued.*

mentioned provisions, and had become a main road, there being no application for a provisional order before the 1st of February, 1879, was not excluded from the operation of the second of the above-mentioned provisions, and that the Local Government Board had, therefore, jurisdiction to make a provisional order declaring such road an ordinary highway upon an application made subsequently to the 1st of February, 1879. THE QUEEN *v.* LOCAL GOVERNMENT BOARD **15 Q. B. D. [70**

(*c.*) EXTRAORDINARY EXPENSES.

8. —— Excessive Weight—*Branch Road—Conveyance of Manure to Farm—Traction Engines—Highways and Locomotives Amendment Act, 1878 (41 & 42 Vict. c. 77), s. 23.*] Justices having made an order charging the expenses of repairing a highway upon the Appellants as being extraordinary expenses within 41 & 42 Vict. c. 77, s. 23, it appeared that the highway communicated at either end with main roads, and was principally used by farmers and occupiers of land adjoining it for ordinary farm traffic. The Appellants having been employed to convey a quantity of manure to a farm adjoining the road, carried it there by means of a traction engine and trucks, the engine weighing eight and the truck five tons. The road, which had not been prepared for, and was not adapted to, the weight of traction engines, was, in consequence of such traffic, rendered unfit for use. The carriage of farm materials and produce by traction engines was usual in the neighbourhood, though not upon this particular road:—*Held*, that the order was right, the passage of traction engines and trucks being "extraordinary traffic" upon the particular road. THE QUEEN *v.* ELLIS - **8 Q. B. D. 466**

9. —— Excessive Weight—*Traffic from recognised [Business in Neighbourhood—Highways and Locomotives Amendment Act, 1878 (41 & 42 Vict. c. 77), s. 23.*] Upon the hearing of a complaint made by a highway board under the Highways and Locomotives Amendment Act, 1878 (41 & 42 Vict. c. 77), s. 23, for the purpose of recovering from the Appellant extraordinary expenses incurred by the board by reason of traffic conducted by him, it appeared that he was owner or occupier of stone quarries in the district, and that the stone was conveyed in heavy loads over the highways, so as to make the cost of repairing them much larger than if they had been subject to ordinary agricultural traffic; but that the stone traffic was a recognised business in the neighbourhood, and the waggon loads of the usual weight in such traffic. The justices having upon these facts found, first, that the traffic was not extraordinary, secondly, that the weights were excessive, and thirdly, that the expenses were extraordinary :—*Held*, that the first finding, which was warranted by the evidence, shewed that the expenses were not "extraordinary" within the meaning of the section, and that they could not be recovered from the Appellant. WALLINGTON *v.* HOSKINS - **6 Q. B. D. 206**

10. —— Excessive Weight—*Traffic caused in building a House—Highways and Locomotives*

VII. HIGHWAY—REPAIR—continued.

(c.) EXTRAORDINARY EXPENSES—continued.

Amendment Act, 1878 (41 & 42 Vict. c. 77), s. 23.] Materials for building a house were carried by the Respondent over a highway, and he was summoned under sect. 23 of the Highways and Locomotives Amendment Act, 1878, by the Appellants to recover the amount of expenses incurred by them by reason of the damage to the highway. The justices dismissed the summons, subject to a special case in which they found that the traffic conducted by the Respondent was in aggregate weight and in quantity excessive and extraordinary as compared with the ordinary traffic along the highway, which was light agricultural traffic, that the highway had been damaged thereby, that the amount expended on the highway by reason thereof was in excess of the average expense of repairing highways in the neighbourhood, and was an extraordinary expense incurred by reason of such damage, but that the traffic did not materially differ in character from that to be expected on the highway :—Held (by Grove and Lopes, JJ.), that the Respondent was not liable for the damage to the highway. PICKERING LYTHE EAST HIGHWAY BOARD v. BARRY　-　-　8 Q. B. D. 59

(d.) MATERIALS.

11. —— Gathering Stones—Inclosed Land—Right to Compensation—5 & 6 Will. 4, c. 50, s. 51.] Under the Highway Act, 5 & 6 Will. 4, c. 50, s. 51, justices are entitled to grant the surveyor of highways a licence to gather stones upon inclosed land within the parish for the repair of its highways, without making any compensation to the owner for the value of such stones. ALRESFORD RURAL SANITARY AUTHORITY v. SCOTT　7 Q. B. D. 210

12. —— Licence to get Materials—5 & 6 Will. 4, c. 50, s. 54—"Search for, dig, and get in or through"—Avenue to a House.] A licence may be granted to get materials for the repair of the highways under 5 & 6 Will. 4, c. 50, s. 54, although the materials when got must be carried away by an "avenue to a house," the exception of such an avenue (inter alia) in the section referring only to the digging or getting of the materials, not to the carrying of them away when got. RAMSDEN v. YEATES　-　6 Q. B. D. 583

VIII. HIGHWAY—STOPPING-UP.

—— Expenses—Right of Board to employ a Solicitor at the Cost of the Party—Highway Act, 1835 (5 & 6 Wm. 4, c. 50), ss. 84, 85, 101—Public Health Act, 1875 (38 & 39 Vict. c. 55), ss. 144, 189.] The charges of a solicitor employed by an urban authority to conduct proceedings at the instance of an individual for the stopping-up or diverting a highway under sects. 84, 85 of the Highway Act, 5 & 6 Wm. 4, c. 50, are not "expenses" within sect. 84 of the Act, so as to be recoverable in the manner pointed out by sect. 101.—Semble, that all the steps required by sect. 85 to be taken for the purpose of obtaining the order of sessions, are ministerial acts which ought to be done by the surveyor of the local authority. UNITED LAND COMPANY v. TOTTENHAM LOCAL BOARD　-　-　13 Q. B. D. 640

IX. HIGHWAY—WAYWARDEN.

—— Election—Waywardens—Several Elections—Demand of Poll—Time for—Mandamus.] At a vestry meeting held to elect waywardens for eleven townships, different candidates were successively and separately nominated, proposed, and seconded, and, after show of hands, declared by the chairman to be duly elected waywardens for each township. After waywardens had been thus elected for all the townships, an elector demanded a poll in respect of the sixth and seventh townships in order of election. The chairman ruled that the demand was too late, and refused a poll.—On a rule for a mandamus to the Defendants to reassemble the meeting, and proceed to an election of waywardens for the two townships :—Held, that the proceeding in respect of each township was a separate election, and that the demand for a poll was too late, as it should, in each case, have been made upon the declaration of the show of hands. THE QUEEN v. THOMAS　11 Q. B. D. 282

HIGHWAY — Clerk of highway board — Disqualification as guardian of parish or union　15 Q. B. D. 382
　See POOR-RATE—GUARDIANS.

—— Dedication　16 Ch. D. 449
　See METROPOLIS—MANAGEMENT ACTS. 6.

—— Houses abutting upon—Subsidence of land
　[6 Q. B. D. 264
　See LOCAL GOVERNMENT — COMPENSATION. 3.

—— Indictment for obstruction of—New trial
　[7 Q. B. D. 196
　See CRIMINAL LAW—PRACTICE. 3.

—— Injury to pipes—Repair of street—Use of steam rollers　-　15 Q. B. D. 1
　See GAS COMPANY.

—— Nuisance — Flap covering water-meter in street—Liability of vestry 9 Q. B. D. 451
　See METROPOLIS—MANAGEMENT ACTS. 5.

—— Obstruction　12 Q. B. D. 110
　See NUISANCE—REMEDIES. 3.

—— Rates　13 Q. B. D. 946
　See LOCAL GOVERNMENT—RATES. 1.

—— Scotch law　-　6 App. Cas. 833, 881;
　[10 App. Cas. 378
　See SCOTCH LAW—HIGHWAY. 1, 2, 3.

—— Surveyor—Local Government Acts—Period of limitation　-　11 Q. B. D. 286
　See LOCAL GOVERNMENT—PRACTICE. 3.

HIRING FURNITURE—Custom of trade
　[18 Ch. D. 30; 23 Ch. D. 261
　See BANKRUPTCY—ORDER AND DISPOSITION. 4, 5.

HIRING ROOMS—Mortmain　19 Ch. D. 156
　See CHARITY—MORTMAIN. 2.

HOLOGRAPH AGREEMENT—Scotch law
　[6 App. Cas. 340
　See SCOTCH LAW—LANDLORD AND TENANT.

HOLOGRAPH WILL—Scotch law 7 App. Cas. 400
　See SCOTCH LAW—WILL.

HOME FOR WORKING GIRLS—Covenant not to carry on business ;　-　27 Ch. D. 71
　See LANDLORD AND TENANT—LEASE. 4.

HOSPITAL—Covenant not to carry on business
[27 Ch. D. 81, n.
See LANDLORD AND TENANT—LEASE. 5.

—— Nuisance   **6 App. Cas. 193**
See NUISANCE—DEFINITION. 1.

HOTCHPOT—Advancement—Interest payable—
Presumption of intention **15 Q. B. D. 300**
See WILL—SATISFACTION. 1.

—— Advances to children   **17 Ch. D. 701**
See WILL—SATISFACTION. 2.

HOURS OF POLL—Parliament.
See PARLIAMENT—ELECTION—*Statutes.*

HOUSE—Direction to block up   **21 Ch. D. 667**
See WILL—LAPSE. 6.

—— Notice to treat   -   - **27 Ch. D. 536**
See LANDS CLAUSES ACT—COMPULSORY
POWERS. 7.

—— Occupation—Qualification—Municipal elec-
tion   -   -   - **12 Q. B. D. 381**
See MUNICIPAL CORPORATION — FRAN-
CHISE.

HOUSE DUTY.
See Cases under REVENUE—HOUSE DUTY.

HOUSE OF COMMONS—Procedure—Jurisdiction
of Courts   -   - **12 Q. B. D. 271**
See PARLIAMENT—PROCEDURE.

HOUSEHOLD FRANCHISE.
See PARLIAMENT—FRANCHISE—*Statutes.*

HUMBER RULES — Stern light — Compulsory
pilotage—Collision   - **10 P. D. 65**
See SHIP—NAVIGATION. 8.

HUNDRED—Action against—Damage to houses
See RIOT.   [7 Q. B. D. 201

HUSBAND AND WIFE.   Col.
  I. DIVORCE   -   -   627
  II. JUDICIAL SEPARATION   628
  III. LIABILITY OF HUSBAND   628
  IV. MARRIED WOMEN'S PROPERTY ACTS   629
  V. SEPARATE ESTATE -   640
  VI. SEPARATION DEED   645
  VII. WIFE'S CONVEYANCE   -   -   649
  VIII. WIFE'S REAL ESTATE   -   650
  IX. WIFE'S REVERSION   -   -   653

—— PRACTICE OF DIVORCE COURT.
See Cases under PRACTICE—DIVORCE.

I. HUSBAND AND WIFE—DIVORCE.

—— **English Marriage—Scotch Divorce—**
*Marriage in England between Scotchman domiciled
in Scotland and Englishwoman—Decree of Divorce
by Scotch Court, by reason of Husband's Adultery
only—Validity of Divorce in England.*] The English Courts will recognise as valid the decision of
a competent foreign Christian tribunal dissolving
the marriage between a domiciled native in the
country where such tribunal has jurisdiction, and
an English woman, when the decree of divorce is
not impeached by any species of collusion or
fraud. And this, although the marriage may
have been solemnized in England, and may have
been dissolved for a cause which would not have
been sufficient to obtain a divorce in England.—
When an English woman marries a domiciled
foreigner, the marriage is constituted according to

I. HUSBAND AND WIFE—DIVORCE—*contd.*
the lex loci contractûs; but she takes his domicil
and is subject to his law.—A domiciled Scotchman married, in England, an English woman.
Immediately after the ceremony the married
couple went to Scotland and resided there as their
matrimonial home. Two years after the wife
obtained in Scotland a divorce à vinculo matrimonii, on the ground of her husband's adultery
only. The husband came to England, and married
there another English woman, the first wife being
still alive. In a suit for a declaration of the
nullity of the second marriage at the instance of the
second wife :—*Held*, affirming the decision of the
Court below, that the divorce in Scotland was a
sentence of a Court of competent jurisdiction, not
only effectual within that jurisdiction, but entitled to recognition in the Courts of this country
also.—*Lolley's Case* (Russ & Ry. 237) explained;
Warrender v. Warrender (2 Cl. & F..488) ; *Geils
v. Geils* (1 Macq. 255) undistinguishable; *Maghee
v. M'Allister* (3 Ir. (Ch.) 604) also undistinguishable and affirmed ; *M'Carthy v. Decaix* (2 Russ. &
My. 614) dissented from.—*Quære*, Whether a bonâ
fide change of domicil which was English at the
date of the contract would affect the question of
dissolution ; and whether *Pitt v. Pitt* (4 Macq.
627) would govern cases like *Niboyet v. Niboyet*
(4 P. D. 1) if they arose in Scotland. HARVEY *v.*
FARNIE   **6 P. D. 35 ; 8 App. Cas. 43**

**II. HUSBAND AND WIFE—JUDICIAL SEPARA-
TION.**

—— Jurisdiction of Magistrates—*Aggravated
Assault—Matrimonial Causes Act, 1878—24 &
25 Vict. c. 100, s. 43.*] If a husband has been
convicted of an aggravated assault the magistrates
may grant a judicial separation, even though
they do not fine or imprison him. WOODS *v.*
WOODS   -   -   - **10 P. D. 172**

**III. HUSBAND AND WIFE — LIABILITY OF
HUSBAND.**

—— Necessaries — *Agency — Notice not to
trust.*] Where the husband neither does, nor
assents to, any act to shew that he has held out
his wife as his agent, to pledge his credit for
goods supplied on her order, the question whether
she bears that character must be examined upon
the circumstances of the case. That question is
one of fact. The management of the husband's
house would raise a presumption of agency as to
matters necessarily connected with that management, which might not be got rid of by a mere
private arrangement between husband and wife.
Otherwise where such management did not exist.
A. was the manager of a limited company's
hotel at Bradford—where his wife acted as
manageress—they cohabited—he made his wife an
allowance for clothes, but forbade her to pledge his
credit for them. She purchased clothes in London,
the bills for which were at first made out in her
name and were paid by her. She afterwards incurred, with the same tradesmen, a debt for clothes,
payment for which was demanded from the husband, with whom, previously, they had had no
communication :—*Held* (affirming the judgment of
the Court below), that the husband was not liable
—that under the circumstances here the mere
fact of cohabitation did not raise a presumption

III. HUSBAND AND WIFE — LIABILITY OF
HUSBAND—*continued.*

of agency, nor require a proof of notice not to
trust his wife. DEBENHAM *v.* MELLON

[6 App. Cas. 24

IV. HUSBAND AND WIFE — MARRIED WO-
MEN'S PROPERTY ACTS.

*The Act 45 & 46 Vict. c. 75, consolidates and
amends the Married Women's Property Acts.*

*Sect. 27. The Act is to be cited as the Married
Women's Property Act, 1882.*

*Sect. 25. The date of the commencement of the
Act is the 1st of January, 1883.*

*Sect. 22 repeals the Married Women's Property
Act, 1870, and the Married Women's Property Act,
1870, Amendment Act, 1874: provided that such
repeal shall not affect any act done or right acquired
while either of those Acts was in force, or any
right or liability of any husband or wife, married
before the 1st of January, 1883, to sue or be sued
under the provisions of those Acts or either of
them for or in respect of any debt, contract, wrong,
or other matter or thing whatsoever, for or in
respect of which any such right or liability shall
have accrued to or against such husband or wife
before the 1st of January, 1883.*

*Sect. 19. Nothing in this Act contained shall
interfere with or affect any settlement or agreement
for a settlement made or to be made, whether before
or after marriage, respecting the property of any
married woman, or shall interfere with or render
inoperative any restriction against anticipation at
present attached or to be hereafter attached to the
enjoyment of any property or income by a woman
under any settlement, agreement for a settlement,
will, or other instrument; but no restriction against
anticipation contained in any settlement or agreement for a settlement of a woman's own property
to be made, or entered into by herself shall have any
validity against debts contracted by her before
marriage, and no settlement or agreement for a
settlement shall have any greater force or validity
against creditors of such woman than a like settlement or agreement for a settlement made or entered
into by a man would have against his creditors.*

*Sect. 24. The word "contract" in the Act in-
cludes the acceptance of any trust, or of the office
of executrix or administratrix, and the provisions
of the Act as to liabilities of married women extends to all liabilities by reason of any breach of
trust or devastavit committed by any married
woman being a trustee or executrix or administratrix either before or after her marriage, and her
husband shall not be subject to such liabilities
unless he has acted or intermeddled in the trust or
administration. The word "property" in the Act
includes a thing in action.*

Ante-nuptial Debts and Liabilities of Wife.]
*Sect. 13. A woman after her marriage shall con-
tinue to be liable in respect and to the extent of her
separate property for all debts contracted, and all
contracts entered into or wrongs committed by her
before her marriage, including any sums, or which
she may be liable as a contributory, either before or
after she has been placed on the list of contributories, under or by virtue of the Acts relating to
joint stock companies; and she may be sued for
any such debt and for any liability in damages or
otherwise under any such contract, or in respect of*

IV. HUSBAND AND WIFE — MARRIED WO-
MEN'S PROPERTY ACTS—*continued.*

*any such wrong; and all sums recovered against
her in respect thereof, or for any costs relating
thereto, shall be payable out of her separate property; and, as between her and her husband,
unless there be any contract between them to the
contrary, her separate property shall be deemed to
be primarily liable for all such debts, contracts, or
wrongs, and for all damages or costs recovered in
respect thereof: provided always, that nothing in
this Act shall operate to increase or diminish the
liability of any woman married before the commencement of this Act for any such debt, contract,
or wrong as aforesaid except as to any separate
property to which she may become entitled by
virtue of this Act, and to which she would not have
been entitled for her separate use under the Acts
hereby repealed or otherwise, if this Act had not
passed.*

*Sect. 14. A husband shall be liable for the debts
of his wife contracted, and for all contracts entered
into and wrongs committed, before marriage, including any liabilities to which she may be so
subject under the Acts relating to joint stock companies as aforesaid, to the extent of all property
whatsoever belonging to his wife which he shall
have acquired or become entitled to from or through
his wife, after deducting therefrom any payments
made by him, and any sums for which judgment
may have been bonâ fide recovered against him in
any proceeding at law in respect of any such debts,
contracts, or wrongs for or in respect of which his
wife was liable before her marriage as aforesaid;
but he shall not be liable for the same any further
or otherwise; and any Court in which a husband
shall be sued for any such debt shall have power to
direct any inquiry or proceedings which it may
think proper for the purpose of ascertaining the
nature, amount, or value of such property: provided always, that nothing in this Act contained
shall operate to increase or diminish the liability
of any husband married before the commencement
of this Act for or in respect of any such debt or
other liability of his wife as aforesaid.*

*Sect. 15. A husband and wife may be jointly
sued in respect of any such debt or other liability
(whether by contract or for any wrong) contracted
or incurred by the wife before marriage as aforesaid, if the Plaintiff in the action shall seek to
establish his claim, either wholly or in part, against
both of them; and if in any such action, or in any
action brought in respect of any such debt or liability against the husband alone, it is not found
that the husband is liable in respect of any property of the wife so acquired by him or to which
he shall have become so entitled as aforesaid, he
shall have judgment for his costs of defence, whatever may be the result of the action against the
wife if jointly sued with him; and in any such
action against husband and wife jointly, if it
appears that the husband is liable for the debt or
damages recovered, or any part thereof, the judgment to the extent of the amount for which the
husband is liable shall be a joint judgment against
the husband personally and against the wife as to
her separate property; and as to the residue, if
any, of such debt and damages, the judgment shall
be a separate judgment against the wife as to her
separate property only.*

IV. HUSBAND AND WIFE—MARRIED WO-MEN'S PROPERTY ACTS—*continued.*

Criminal Acts by Wife.] *Sect.* 16. *A wife doing any act with respect to any property of her husband, which, if done by the husband with respect to the property of the wife, would make the husband liable to criminal proceedings by the wife under this Act, shall in like manner be liable to criminal proceedings by her husband.*

Life Insurance.] *Sect.* 11. *A married woman may by virtue of the power of making contracts hereinbefore contained effect a policy upon her own life or the life of her husband for her separate use ; and the same and all benefit thereof shall enure accordingly.*

A policy of assurance effected by any man on his own life, and expressed to be for the benefit of his wife, or of his children, or of his wife and children, or any of them, or by any woman on her own life, and expressed to be for the benefit of her husband, or of her children, or of her husband and children, or any of them, shall create a trust in favour of the objects therein named ; and the moneys payable under any such policy shall not, so long as any object of the trust remains unperformed, form part of the estate of the insured, or be subject to his or her debts : Provided, that if it shall be proved that the policy was effected and the premiums paid with intent to defraud the creditors of the insured, they shall be entitled to receive, out of the moneys payable under the policy, a sum equal to the premiums so paid. The insured may by the policy, or by any memorandum under his or her hand, appoint a trustee or trustees of the moneys payable under the policy, and from time to time appoint a new trustee or new trustees thereof, and may make provision for the appointment of a new trustee or new trustees thereof, and for the investment of the moneys payable under any such policy. In default of any such appointment of a trustee, such policy, immediately on its being effected, shall vest in the insured and his or her legal personal representatives, in trust for the purposes aforesaid. If, at the time of the death of the insured, or at any time afterwards, there shall be no trustee, or it shall be expedient to appoint a new trustee or new trustees, a trustee or trustees or a new trustee or new trustees may be appointed by any Court having jurisdiction under the provisions of the Trustee Act, 1850, or the Acts amending and extending the same. The receipt of a trustee or trustees duly appointed, or, in default of any such appointment or in default of notice to the insurance office, the receipt of the legal personal representative of the insured, shall be a discharge to the office for the sum secured by the policy, or for the value thereof, in whole or in part.

Loans by Wife to Husband.] *Sect.* 3. *Any money or other estate of the wife lent or entrusted by her to her husband for the purpose of any trade or business carried on by him, or otherwise, shall be treated as assets of her husband's estate in case of his bankruptcy, under reservation of the wife's claim to a dividend as a creditor for the amount or value of such money or other estate after, but not before, all claims of the other creditors of the husband for valuable consideration in money or money's worth have been satisfied.*

Maintenance of Children and Husband.] *Sect.* 20. *Where in England the husband of any woman*

having separate property becomes chargeable to any union or parish, the justices having jurisdiction in such union or parish may, in petty sessions assembled, upon application of the guardians of the poor, issue a summons against the wife, and make and enforce such order against her for the maintenance of her husband out of such separate property as by the 33rd section of the Poor Law Amendment Act, 1868, they may now make and enforce against a husband for the maintenance of his wife if she becomes chargeable to any union or parish. Where in Ireland relief is given under the provisions of the Acts relating to the relief of the destitute poor to the husband of any woman having separate property, the cost price of such relief is hereby declared to be a loan from the guardians of the union in which the same shall be given, and shall be recoverable from such woman as if she were a feme sole by the same actions and proceedings as money lent.

Sect. 21. *A married woman having separate property shall be subject to all such liability for the maintenance of her children and grandchildren as the husband is now by law subject to for the maintenance of her children and grandchildren : provided always, that nothing in this Act shall relieve her husband from any liability imposed upon him by law to maintain her children or grandchildren.*

Question of Title to Property.] *Sect.* 17. *In any question between husband and wife as to the title to or possession of property, either party, or any such bank, corporation, company, public body, or society as aforesaid in whose books any stocks, funds, or shares of either party are standing, may apply by summons or otherwise in a summary way to any Judge of the High Court of Justice in England or in Ireland, according as such property is in England or Ireland, or (at the option of the applicant irrespectively of the value of the property in dispute) in England to the Judge of the County Court of the district, or in Ireland to the chairman of the Civil Bill Court of the division in which either party resides, and the Judge of the High Court of Justice or of the County Court, or the chairman of the Civil Bill Court (as the case may be) may make such order with respect to the property in dispute, and as to the costs of and consequent on the application, as he thinks fit, or may direct such application to stand over from time to time, and any inquiry touching the matters in question to be made in such manner as he shall think fit : Provided always, that any order of a Judge of the High Court of Justice to be made under the provisions of this section shall be subject to appeal in the same way as an order made by the same Judge in a suit pending or on an equitable plaint in the said Court would be ; and any order of a County or Civil Bill Court under the provisions of this section shall be subject to appeal in the same way as any other order made by the same Court would be, and all proceedings in a County Court or Civil Bill Court under this section in which, by reason of the value of the property in dispute, such Court would not have had jurisdiction if this Act or the Married Women's Property Act, 1870, had not passed, may, at the option of the Defendant or Respondent to such proceedings, be removed as of right into the High Court of Justice*

IV. HUSBAND AND WIFE—MARRIED WO-
MEN'S PROPERTY ACTS—*continued.*

*in England or Ireland (as the case may be), by
writ of certiorari or otherwise as may be prescribed by any rule of such High Court; but any
order made or act done in the course of such proceedings prior to such removal shall be valid,
unless order shall be made to the contrary by such
High Court: Provided also, that the Judge of the
High Court of Justice or of the County Court, or
the chairman of the Civil Bill Court, if either party
so require, may hear any such application in his
private room: Provided also, that any such bank,
corporation, company, public body, or society as
aforesaid, shall, in the matter of any such application for the purposes of costs or otherwise, be
treated as a stakeholder only.*

Separate Estate.]　*Sect.* 6. *All deposits in any
post office or other savings bank, or in any other
bank, all annuities granted by the Commissioners
for the Reduction of the National Debt, or by any
other person, and all sums forming part of the
public stocks, or funds, or of any other stocks or
funds transferable in the books of the Governor
and Company of the Bank of England, or of any
other bank, which at the commencement of this Act
are standing in the sole name of a married woman,
and all shares, stock, debentures, debenture stock,
or other interests of or in any corporation, company, or public body, municipal, commercial, or
otherwise, or of or in any industrial, provident,
friendly, benefit, building, or loan society, which at
the commencement of this Act are standing in her
name, shall be deemed, unless and until the contrary be shewn, to be the separate property of such
married woman; and the fact that any such deposit, annuity, sum forming part of the public
stocks or funds, or of any other stocks or funds
transferable in the books of the Governor and Company of the Bank of England, or of any other bank,
share, stock, debenture, debenture stock, or other
interest as aforesaid, is standing in the sole name
of a married woman, shall be sufficient primâ facie
evidence that she is beneficially entitled thereto for
her separate use, so as to authorize and empower
her to receive or transfer the same, and to receive
the dividends, interest, and profits thereof, without
the concurrence of her husband, and to indemnify
the Postmaster-General, the Commissioners for the
Reduction of the National Debt, the Governor and
Company of the Bank of England, the Governor
and Company of the Bank of Ireland, and all
directors, managers, and trustees of every such
bank, corporation, company, public body, or society
as aforesaid, in respect thereof.*

Sect. 7. *All sums forming part of the public
stock or funds, or of any other stocks or funds
transferable in the books of the Bank of England
or of any other bank, and all such deposits and
annuities respectively as are mentioned in the last
preceding section, and all shares, stock, debentures,
debenture stock, and other interests of or in any
such corporation, company, public body, or society
as aforesaid, which after the commencement of this
Act shall be allotted to or placed, registered, or
transferred in or into or made to stand in the sole
name of any married woman, shall be deemed,
unless and until the contrary be shewn, to be her
separate property, in respect of which so far as
any liability may be incident thereto her separate*

*estate shall alone be liable, whether the same shall
be so expressed in the document whereby her title
to the same is created or certified, or in the books
or register wherein her title is entered or recorded,
or not.*

*Provided always, that nothing in this Act shall
require or authorize any corporation or joint stock
company to admit any married woman to be a
holder of any shares or stock therein to which any
liability may be incident, contrary to the provisions
of any Act of Parliament, charter, by-law, articles
of association, or deed of settlement regulating such
corporation or company.*

Sect. 8. *All the provisions hereinbefore contained
as to deposits in any post-office or other savings
bank, or in any other bank, annuities granted by
the Commissioners for the Reduction of the National
Debt, or by any other person, sums forming part of
the public stocks or funds, or of any other stocks or
funds transferable in the books of the Bank of
England, or of any other bank, shares, stocks, debentures, debenture stock, or other interests of or in
any such corporation, company, public body, or
society as aforesaid respectively, which at the commencement of this Act shall be standing in the sole
name of a married woman, or which after that
time shall be allotted to or placed, registered, or
transferred to or into, or made to stand in; the sole
name of a married woman, shall respectively extend
and apply, so far as relates to the estate, right, title
or interest of the married woman, to any of the
particulars aforesaid which, at the commencement
of this Act, or at any time afterwards, shall be
standing in, or shall be allotted to, placed, registered or transferred to or into, or made to stand in,
the name of any married woman jointly with any
persons or person other than her husband.*

Sect. 9. *It shall not be necessary for the husband
of any married woman, in respect of her interest,
to join in the transfer of any such annuity or deposit as aforesaid, or any sum forming part of the
public stocks, or funds, or of any other stocks or
funds transferable, as aforesaid, or any share,
stock, debenture, debenture stock, or other benefit,
right, claim, or other interest of or in any such
corporation, company, public body, or society as
aforesaid, which is now or shall at any time hereafter be standing in the sole name of any married
woman, or in the joint names of such married
woman, and any other person or persons not being
her husband.*

Sect. 10. *If any investment in any such deposit
or annuity as aforesaid, or in any of the public
stocks, or funds, or in any other stocks or funds
transferable as aforesaid, or in any share, stock,
debenture, or debenture stock, of any corporation,
company, or public body, municipal, commercial,
or otherwise, or in any share, debenture, benefit,
right, or claim whatsoever in, to, or upon the funds
of any industrial, provident, friendly, benefit,
building, or loan society, shall have been made by a
married woman by means of moneys of her husband, without his consent, the Court may, upon an
application under sect.* 17 *of this Act, order such
investment, and the dividends thereof, or any part
thereof, to be transferred and paid respectively to
the husband; and nothing in this Act contained
shall give validity as against creditors of the*

**IV. HUSBAND AND WIFE—MARRIED WO-
MEN'S PROPERTY ACTS**—*continued.*

*husband to any gift by a husband to his wife of any
property which, after such gift, shall continue to be
in the order and disposition or reputed ownership
of the husband, or to any deposit or other investment of moneys of the husband made by or in the
name of his wife in fraud of his creditors; but
any moneys so deposited or invested may be followed as if this Act had not been passed.*

[*See also sects. 1, 2, 4 and 5, infra.*]

Status of Married Woman.] *Sect.* 1.—(1.) *A
married woman shall, in accordance with the provisions of this Act, be capable of acquiring, holding,
and disposing by will or otherwise, of any real or
personal property as her separate property, in the
same manner as if she were a feme sole, without
the intervention of any trustee.*

(2.) *A married woman shall be capable of entering into and rendering herself liable in respect of
and to the extent of her separate property on any
contract, and of suing and being sued, either in
contract or in tort, or otherwise, in all respects as
if she were a feme sole, and her husband need not
be joined with her as plaintiff or defendant, or be
made a party to any action or other legal proceeding brought by or taken against her; and any
damages or costs recovered by her in any such action
or proceeding shall be her separate property; and
any damages or costs recovered against her in any
such action or proceeding shall be payable out of
her separate property, and not otherwise.*

(3.) *Every contract entered into by a married
woman shall be deemed to be a contract entered into
by her with respect to and to bind her separate property, unless the contrary be shewn.*

(4.) *Every contract entered into by a married
woman with respect to and to bind her separate
property shall bind not only the separate property
which she is possessed of or entitled to at the date
of the contract, but also all separate property which
she may thereafter acquire.*

(5.) *Every married woman carrying on a trade
separately from her husband shall, in respect of her
separate property, be subject to the bankruptcy laws
in the same way as if she were a feme sole.*

Sect. 2. *Every woman who marries after the
commencement of this Act shall be entitled to have
and to hold as her separate property and to dispose
of in manner aforesaid all real and personal property which shall belong to her at the time of marriage, or shall be acquired by or devolve upon her
after marriage, including any wages, earnings,
money, and property gained or acquired by her in
any employment, trade, or occupation, in which she
is engaged, or which she carries on separately from
her husband, or by the exercise of any literary,
artistic, or scientific skill.*

Sect. 4. *The execution of a general power by will
by a married woman shall have the effect of making
the property appointed liable for her debts and other
liabilities in the same manner as her separate estate
is made liable under this Act.*

Sect. 5. *Every woman married before the commencement of this Act shall be entitled to have and
to hold and to dispose of in manner aforesaid as
her separate property all real and personal property, her title to which, whether vested or contingent, and whether in possession, reversion, or remainder, shall accrue after the commencement of*

**IV. HUSBAND AND WIFE—MARRIED WO-
MEN'S PROPERTY ACTS**—*continued.*

*this Act, including any wages, earnings, money,
and property so gained or acquired by her as
aforesaid.*

Sect. 12. *Every woman, whether married before
or after this Act, shall have in her own name against
all persons whomsoever, including her husband, the
same civil remedies, and also (subject as regards
her husband, to the proviso hereinafter contained)
the same remedies and redress by way of criminal
proceedings, for the protection and security of her
own separate property, as if such property belonged
to her as a feme sole, but, except as aforesaid, no
husband or wife shall be entitled to sue the other
for a tort. In any indictment or other proceeding
under this section it shall be sufficient to allege such
property to be her property; and in any proceeding
under this section a husband or wife shall be competent to give evidence against each other, any
statute or rule of law to the contrary notwithstanding; provided always, that no criminal proceeding
shall be taken by any wife against her husband by
virtue of this Act while they are living together, as
to or concerning any property claimed by her, nor
while they are living apart, as to or concerning any
act done by the husband while they were living
together, concerning property claimed by the wife,
unless such property shall have been wrongfully
taken by the husband when leaving or deserting, or
about to leave or desert, his wife.*

Sect. 18. *A married woman who is an executrix
or administratrix alone or jointly with any other
person or persons of the estate of any deceased
person, or a trustee alone or jointly as aforesaid of
property subject to any trust, may sue or be sued,
and may transfer or join in transferring any such
annuity or deposit as aforesaid, or any sum forming part of the public stocks or funds, or of any
other stocks or funds transferable as aforesaid, or
any share, stock, debenture, debenture stock, or
other benefit, right, claim, or other interest of or in
any such corporation, company, public body, or
society in that character, without her husband, as
if she were a feme sole.*

Sect. 23. *For the purposes of this Act the legal
personal representative of any married woman
shall in respect of her separate estate have the
same rights and liabilities, and be subject to the
same jurisdiction as she would be if she were
living.*

Evidence.] *The Act 47 & 48 Vict. c. 14, enacts
that in any criminal proceeding under the Married
Women's Property Act, 1882, against a husband
or a wife (whether under sect. 12 or any other
section) the same shall be competent witnesses, and
except when defendant compellable to give evidence.*

And see PRACTICE—DIVORCE—RESTITU-
TION OF CONJUGAL RIGHTS—*Statutes.*

1. —— **Action for Assault** — *Limitations.
Statute of* (21 Jac. 1, c. 16), ss. 3, 7—*Married
Woman—"Discovert"* — *Married Women's Property Act, 1882* (45 & 46 Vict. c. 75).]—A
married woman can maintain in her own name an
action for an assault and false imprisonment committed before the coming into operation of the
Married Women's Property Act, 1882, even although the cause of action accrued more than four
years before suit, provided the action be brought

IV. HUSBAND AND WIFE—MARRIED WO-
MEN'S PROPERTY ACTS—*continued.*

within four years after the coming into operation
of that statute, for she thereby has become "discovert" within the meaning of 21 Jac. 1, c. 16,
s. 7. LOWE v. FOX　　15 Q. B. D. 667

2. —— Debts before Marriage—*Liability of
Husband after Wife's Death—Married Women's
Property Act* (1870) *Amendment Act,* 1874
(37 & 38 *Vict. c.* 50), *ss.* 1, 2.] A husband is not
liable under the Married Women's Property Act
(1870) Amendment Act, 1874 (37 & 38 Vict.
c. 50), after his wife's death, for her debts contracted before the marriage. BELL v. STOCKER
[10 Q. B. D. 129

3. —— Debts before Marriage—"*Subsequent
Action*"—*Married Women's Property Act* (1870)
Amendment Act, 1874 (37 & 38 *Vict. c.* 50), *s.* 5.]
The Married Women's Property Act, 1874, sect. 5,
enacts that when a husband after marriage has a
judgment bonâ fide recovered against him in any
action brought under the Act to recover a debt of
the wife contracted before marriage, "then to the
extent of such judgment the husband shall not in
any subsequent action be liable":—*Held,* that
the words "any subsequent action" mean any
action commenced subsequently to the time of
bringing the action in which judgment has been
recovered, and not merely any action commenced
subsequently to the recovery of the judgment.
FEAR v. CASTLE　　-　　8 Q. B. D. 380

4. —— Policy of Assurance—*Trust for Wife
and Children of Assured—Petition for Appointment of Trustees—Title of Petition—Married
Women's Property Act,* 1870 (33 & 34 *Vict. c.* 93),
s. 10 —*Married Women's Property Act,* 1882
(45 & 46 *Vict. c.* 75), *ss.* 11, 22.] A petition (presented since the coming into operation of the
Married Women's Property Act, 1882) for the
appointment of trustees of the proceeds of a life
policy effected by a husband, under the provisions
of the Married Women's Property Act, 1870, for
the benefit of his wife and children, ought to be
entitled in the matter of the Act of 1882. *In re*
SOUTAR'S POLICY TRUST　-　　- 26 Ch. D. 236

5. —— Policy of Assurance—*Trust for Wife
and Children—"Separate use"—Married Women's Property Act,* 1870, *s.* 10—*Married Women's
Property Act,* 1882, *s.* 11—*Form of Order.*] A husband effected a policy for the benefit of his wife and
children under the Married Women's Property
Act, 1870, and died insolvent. His wife and one
child of the marriage predeceased him. Upon a
petition by his surviving children, under the 10th
section of the Act, for the appointment of a
trustee of the policy-money and for a declaration
as to the rights of the petitioners:—*Held,* that
the Court had, under that section, no jurisdiction
to do more than make the order appointing a
trustee; but since under the policy there was a
trust either for the wife for life with remainder to
the children, or, in the alternative, for the wife
and children as joint tenants, the order was directed to be prefaced with an expression of opinion
that the wife took no interest, and that the surviving children took as joint tenants.—*In re
Mellor's Policy Trusts* (6 Ch. D. 127; 7 Ch. D.
200) not followed.—*Semble,* a policy effected by a
husband under sect. 10 of the Married Women's

IV. HUSBAND AND WIFE—MARRIED WO-
MEN'S PROPERTY ACTS—*continued.*

Property Act, 1870, "for the benefit of his wife
and children," should be read in conjunction with
that section, and should, by virtue of the words
"separate use" in the section, be considered as
giving the wife a life interest only, with remainder
to the children. *In re* ADAM'S POLICY TRUSTS
[23 Ch. D. 525

6. —— Power to sue—*Married Woman, Right
of, to sue alone*—45 & 46 *Vict. c.* 75, *s.* 1, *sub-s.* 2—
Cause of Action before Act.] A married woman
may, by virtue of the Married Women's Property
Act, 1882, sue alone for a tort committed before
that Act came into operation. WELDON v. WIN-
SLOW　　-　　- 13 Q. B. D. 784

7. —— Reversionary Interest—45 & 46 *Vict.
c.* 75, *s.* 5—*Accruer of Title in Possession after
Commencement of Act.*] Property to which a
married woman was, at the commencement of the
Married Women's Property Act, 1882, entitled
in reversion or remainder, and which since the
Act has fallen into possession, is within sect. 5,
and may be transferred and paid to her upon her
separate receipt. BAYNTON v. COLLINS
[27 Ch. D. 604

8. —— Reversionary Interest—*Devise of Real
Estate for Life and in Remainder—Marriage of
Female Reversioner in 1878—Married Women's
Property Act,* 1882 (45 & 46 *Vict. c.* 75), *s.* 5—
—*Death of Tenant for Life in 1884—Separate
Estate.*] Testator, who died in 1875, devised his
real estate to his wife for life, with remainder to
his children. One daughter married in 1878, and
the tenant for life died in 1884:—*Held,* following
the decision in *Baynton* v. *Collins* (27 Ch. D. 604),
that under the operation of sect. 5 of the Married
Women's Property Act, 1882 (45 & 46 Vict. c. 75),
the married woman's share in the estate was her
separate property, and could be disposed of by her
without the concurrence of her husband. *In re*
THOMPSON AND CURZON　-　　29 Ch. D. 177

9. —— Separate Property—*Action by Husband against Wife—Money paid by Husband for
Wife before and after Marriage*—45 & 46 *Vict.
c.* 75, *s.* 1, *sub-ss.* 2, 3, 4; *ss.* 3, 12, 13.] A
husband is entitled to maintain an action against
his wife, and to charge her separate property for
money lent by him to her after their marriage,
and for money paid by him for her after their
marriage at her request made before or after their
marriage, but he is not entitled, even since the
Married Women's Property Act, 1882 (45 & 46
Vict. c. 75), to maintain any action against her
for money lent to her or money paid for her before their marriage at her request. BUTLER v.
BUTLER　-　　-　　-　　- 14 Q. B. D. 831
[Affirmed by Court of Appeal, 16 Q. B. D. 374.]

10. —— Separate Property — *After-acquired
Property*—1882 (45 & 46 *Vict. c.* 75), *ss.* 1, 23—
Will—Wills Act (1 *Vict. c.* 26), *s.* 24.] Sect. 1,
sub-sect. 1, of the Married Women's Property
Act, 1882, gives a married woman power to dis-
pose by will only of property of which she is
seised or possessed while she is under coverture.
—Consequently, notwithstanding sect. 24 of the
Wills Act, her will made during coverture is not,
unless it is re-executed after she has become

IV. HUSBAND AND WIFE—MARRIED WO-MEN'S PROPERTY ACTS—continued.

discovert, effectual to dispose of property which she acquires after the coverture has come to an end. *In re* PRICE. STAFFORD v. STAFFORD **28 Ch. D. 709**

11. —— Separate Property—*Contract made by Married Woman before the Act not binding on after-acquired Separate Property—Married Women's Property Act, 1882 (45 & 46 Vict. c. 75), s. 1, sub-s. 4—Construction not retrospective.*] Sub-s. 4 of s. 1 of the Married Women's Property Act, 1882, is not retrospective ; and, therefore, in an action on a contract made by a married woman before the passing of that Act, judgment cannot be ordered in such terms as to be available against separate property to which the Defendant became entitled after the date of the contract. TURNBULL v. FORMAN **15 Q. B. D. 234**

12. —— Separate Property — *Contract — Married Women's Property Act, 1882 (45 & 46 Vict. c. 75), s. 1, sub-s. 4.*] The contract entered into by a married woman "to bind her separate property," referred to in sect. 1, sub-sect. 4, of the Married Women's Property Act, 1882, is a contract entered into at a time when she has existing separate property. — If the married woman commits a breach of such a contract, and a judgment is recovered against her for the breach, the judgment can be enforced against any separate property which she then has. — But sect. 1, sub-sect. 4, does not enable a married woman who has no existing separate property to bind by a contract any separate property which she may possibly thereafter acquire. *In re* SHAKESPEAR. DEAKIN v. LAKIN **30 Ch. D. 169**

13. —— Separate Property—*House in sole occupation of Wife—33 & 34 Vict. c 93, and 45 & 46 Vict. c. 75—Trespass for entering—Right of Wife to sue.*] A married woman in the sole occupation of a house, bought by her out of her own earnings, since the Married Women's Property Act, 1870, can now, after the Married Women's Property Act, 1882, sue alone, without her husband, in an action for trespass, a person who has entered such house against her will, though he did no injury to the house and entered it with the authority of her husband, but for a purpose unconnected with the husband's desire to live with his wife.—*Quære,* if the husband has himself a right to enter such house. WELDON v. DE BATHE **[14 Q. B. D. 339**

14. —— Separate Property—*45 & 46 Vict. c. 75, s. 1 (3) and (4)—Order of Reference by Consent.*] Sect. 1 (3) and (4) of the Married Women's Property Act, 1882, have not a retrospective operation so as to include contracts entered into by a married woman before the date of the commencement of the Act.—But an order made after the commencement of the Act by consent in an action by a creditor against a married woman in respect of her contract before the Act, by which order all questions under the contract were referred to an arbitrator, and the parties bound themselves to abide by, obey, perform, and keep the award, is an agreement by the married woman after the commencement of the Act, within sect. 1 (3), and therefore by sect. 1 (4) any separate estate which she had at or after the date

IV. HUSBAND AND WIFE—MARRIED WO-MEN'S PROPERTY ACTS—continued.

of such agreement is liable to pay the amount found by the award to be due from her under the contract. CONOLAN v. LEYLAND **27 Ch. D. 632**

V. HUSBAND AND WIFE—SEPARATE ES-TATE.

Restraint on Anticipation.] *By 44 & 45 Vict. c. 41 (Conveyancing Act, 1881), s. 39.—(1.) Notwithstanding that a married woman is restrained from anticipation, the Court may, if it thinks fit, where it appears to the Court to be for her benefit, by judgment or order, with her consent, bind her interest in any property.*

(2.) This section applies only to judgments or orders made after the commencement of the Act, 31st December, 1881.

1. —— *Agreement not signed by Wife—Fee Simple of Wife—Renunciation of Marital Rights by Husband—Will of Wife—Statute of Frauds (29 Car. 2, c. 3), s. 7.*] In order that the fee simple of an intended wife may be affected with a trust for her separate use by an agreement made between the intended husband and wife before marriage, the agreement must be in writing and signed by the wife as well as by the husband : if it is signed by the husband alone, it is, owing to the Statute of Frauds, sect. 7, invalid as a declaration of trust for separate use as to the fee simple, a husband having in his wife's land only an estate for the joint lives of himself and his wife with a possible estate by the curtesy ; and upon the death of the wife without issue during her husband's lifetime, her heir-at-law, and not her devisee, will be entitled to the land of which she is seised in fee simple.—Mere renunciation by an intended husband of his marital rights in his wife's real property is not sufficient to clothe her with a testamentary power, or to constitute a valid declaration of trust of the fee.—*Rippon* v. *Dawding* (Ambl. 565) commented on. DYE v. DYE **[13 Q. B. D. 147**

2. —— House — *Proceedings for Judicial Separation—Husband claiming proprietary Right to House—Interim Injunction.*] On a marriage a leasehold house was settled upon the usual trusts for the wife for life, for her separate use, and the husband and wife continued to reside in the house. Differences arose between them, they ceased to cohabit, and the wife instituted proceedings for divorce or judicial separation. The husband claimed the right to go to and to use the house when and as he thought fit, not for the purpose of consorting with his wife, but for his own purposes. In an action by the wife against the trustees and her husband claiming administration of the trusts of the settlement and an injunction to restrain the husband from entering the house ;—*Held,* that, under the circumstances, the wife was entitled to an interim injunction. SYMONDS v. HALLETT - - **24 Ch. D. 346**

3. —— Intention of Husband — *Evidence — Absence of Corroboration.*] In the absence of proof of an unequivocal, complete, and final intention on the part of a husband to constitute himself a trustee for his wife, the Court will not after his death, upon her uncorroborated statement that he expressly authorized her to carry on the business,

V. HUSBAND AND WIFE—SEPARATE ES-
TATE—*continued.*

on her own account, of a farm which she had
rented before marriage, and to treat the proceeds
as her separate property, admit her claim as
against his estate to the proceeds of the farm
which were invested by him during his lifetime.
In re WHITTAKER. WHITTAKER *v.* WHITTAKER
                                    [21 Ch. D. 657

4. —— Joint Investments — Survivorship.]
Banking accounts were kept in the joint names
of husband and wife, and investments in railway
stock were made in their joint names. The wife
survived her husband five days, having executed
a will during coverture :—*Held,* that the balances
of the joint accounts and the joint investments
survived to the wife, but did not pass under her
will. *In re* YOUNG. TRYE *v.* SULLIVAN
                                    [28 Ch. D. 705

5. —— Liability — General Engagements of
Married Woman—Judgment—Existing Property
—Restraint on Anticipation.] Held, by Malins,
V.C., that the general engagements of a married
woman entitled to separate estate will be enforced
by a Court of Equity against such separate estate
as she has at the time when judgment is given,
including (if her husband be then dead) estate
limited to her separate use, without power of
anticipation.—*Held,* on appeal, that they can be
enforced only against so much of the separate
estate to which she was entitled, free from any
restraint on anticipation, at the time when the
engagements were entered into, as remains at the
time when judgment is given, and not against
separate estate to which she became entitled after
the time of the engagements, nor against separate
estate to which she was entitled at the time of the
engagements subject to a restraint on anticipation.
PIKE *v.* FITZGIBBON. MARTIN *v.* FITZGIBBON
                                    [17 Ch. D. 454

6. —— Liability — Debts contracted before
Marriage—33 & 34 Vict. c. 93, s. 12—Practice—In-
terpleader—Power of Court of Appeal—Rules of
Court, 1875, Orders I., r. 2, XL., r. 10.] A married
woman was sued without her husband for debts
contracted before her marriage. By her ante-
nuptial settlement it was agreed that all property
coming to her or to her husband in her right
during the coverture should be vested in two trustees, except jewels, which were to be for her separate use. The creditors obtained judgment and
issued execution against her separate estate. The
sheriff seized jewels which belonged to her before
her marriage, and an interpleader issue was ordered
between her husband and the execution creditor.
The jury found that the jewels belonged to the
husband :—*Held,* by the Court of Appeal, on an
application for a new trial, that the jewels belonged to the wife for her separate use, and that
the execution creditor was entitled to seize them :
—That the creditor was right in suing the wife
without making her husband a party :—That the
Court of Appeal had power under Order XL.,
rule 10, to order judgment in the interpleader
issue to be entered for the execution creditor
without directing a new trial. And this judgment
was affirmed by the House of Lords. WILLIAMS *v.*
MERCIER   9 Q. B. D. 337; 10 App. Cas. 1

V. HUSBAND AND WIFE—SEPARATE ES-
TATE—*continued.*

7. —— Liability—Wife's Contract — Charge
on Separate Estate—Trust for Separate Use not
arising till after Contract—Policies on Life of
Husband.] By a post-nuptial settlement made in
pursuance of ante-nuptial articles, certain policies
of insurance on the life of the husband were
assigned to trustees upon trust to receive the
money and pay the income to the wife during her
life for her separate use, independently of any
future husband whom she might marry. There
was no restraint on anticipation. During the life
of her first husband the wife made promissory
notes in favour of the Plaintiff, and the Plaintiff,
the first husband being still alive, brought an
action claiming a charge on the policies :—*Held*
(reversing the decision of Kay, J.), that the trust
for separate use did not arise till after the death
of the husband, and that as the contracts of a
married woman can only be enforced against property which formed part of her separate estate at
the date of the contract, the action could not be
maintained.—*In re Gaffee* (1 Mac. & G. 541), *In*
re Molyneux' Estate (L. R. 6 Eq. 411), and *Sturgis*
v. Corp. (13 Ves. 190), discussed. KING *v.* LUCAS
                                    [23 Ch. D. 712

8. —— Restraint on Anticipation—Accumu-
lations.] A testator directed surplus income of
real and personal estate, after providing an
annuity, to be accumulated during the life of his
wife, and after her death he gave the capital to
his children : he directed that the shares of his
daughters should be for their separate use, without power of alienation or anticipation during the
wife's life :—*Held,* that his married daughters
during the life of their mother were entitled to
receive only the income of invested income. *In*
re SPENCER. THOMAS *v.* SPENCER   30 Ch. D. 183

9. —— Restraint on Anticipation — Attach-
ment of Debts—Order XLV., r. 1.] Judgment
having been signed in an action against the Defendants, a man and his wife, it was sought to
attach in execution moneys in the hands of
trustees, forming part of the income of trust funds
payable to the wife to her separate use, which
had accrued since the judgment. The will by
which the trust was created contained a clause
restraining anticipation by the wife. It appeared
that the action was for the amount of a promissory
note made by the husband and wife jointly during
the coverture :—*Held,* that the moneys in question
could not be attached in execution. CHAPMAN *v.*
BIGGS   -   -   -   -   11 Q. B. D. 27

10. —— Restraint on Anticipation—Costs—
Proceedings improperly instituted.] A married
woman who, under a will, was entitled to income
for her separate use, with a restraint on anticipation, instituted (without a next friend) against
the trustees proceedings in the course of which
she took out a summons which was refused :—
Held, that the restraint on anticipation did not
prevent the Court from giving the trustees liberty
to retain their costs of the proceedings out of the
married woman's income. *In re* ANDREWS.
EDWARDS *v.* DEWAR   -   -   30 Ch. D. 159

11. —— Restraint on Anticipation—Judgment
                                                Y

V. HUSBAND AND WIFE—SEPARATE ES-TATE—*continued.*

Summons—Order for Payment—Debtors Act, 1869 (32 & 33 Vict. c. 62), *s.* 5.] Upon a judgment summons issued under sect. 5 of the Debtors Act, 1869, against a married woman who has only separate estate which she is restrained from anticipating, an order for payment cannot be made unless it is shewn that, since the date of the judgment, she has received some of her separate income.—If in the judgment execution is limited to separate estate which she is not restrained from anticipating, *quære,* whether sect. 5 of the Debtors Act, 1869, applies at all.—*Dillon v. Cunningham* (Law Rep. 8 Ex. 23) distinguished. MEAGER *v.* PELLEW -　　14 Q. B. D. 973

12. —— Restraint on Anticipation—*Removal by Court—Payment of Debts—Consent—Conveyancing and Law of Property Act,* 1881 (44 & 45 Vict. c. 41), *s.* 39.] A married woman was entitled to the income of a fund in Court for her life, for her separate use without power of anticipation, with remainder in trust for her children, and in default of issue, in trust for such persons as she should, whether covert or sole, by will appoint, and, in default of appointment, to herself absolutely. She having had no children, and being past the age of childbearing, and having contracted a number of debts, for payment of which the creditors were pressing her and causing her great annoyance, she with her husband applied to the Court to exercise its power under sect. 39 of the Conveyancing Act, 1881, to remove the restraint on anticipation, and to order part of the fund to be paid out to her to enable her to pay her debts :—*Held,* that, whether she did or did not exercise her power of appointment, the fund would at her death be subject to the payment of her debts, and that under the circumstances the restraint on anticipation ought to be removed and a portion of the fund paid out to the applicant.—*In re Harvey's Estate* (13 Ch. D. 216) followed.—The order was made upon the evidence of the married woman's consent afforded by an affidavit made by her in support of the application, and a letter written by her to her solicitors, strongly urging them to obtain the money for her.—But, *quære,* whether such an order ought in general to be made without ascertaining the consent of the married woman by a separate examination in the ordinary way. HODGES *v.* HODGES 20 Ch. D. 749

13. —— Restraint on Anticipation—*Right to receive Capital—Income producing Fund.*] Gift by a testatrix of real and personal estate to trustees upon trust to convert and invest, and to stand possessed of the stocks, funds, and securities representing the same in trust for her children who, being male, attained twenty-one, or being female, attained that age or married under that age; with a declaration that the shares of daughters should be for their sole and separate use without power of anticipation. Power was given to the trustees, upon the marriage of any of the daughters, to revoke the trusts so far as related to the share of any daughter so marrying, and to settle the same for the benefit of the daughter and her issue as to the trustees should seem fit.—The residuary estate was represented by a sum of cash and certain leasehold houses.—

Held, that the gift being of an income-producing fund with a restraint upon anticipation, the trustees could not pay to the daughters during coverture their shares upon their separate receipt. *In re* BENTON. SMITH *v.* SMITH　19 Ch. D. 277

14. —— Restraint on Anticipation—*Right to receive Capital—Payment on Separate Receipt—Income-bearing Fund—Personal Estate—Conversion.*] A testator bequeathed an annuity to his wife. And he directed his trustees and executors to provide for the same, either by setting apart a sufficient portion of the produce of his residuary personal estate, or by purchasing an annuity. And, after bequeathing some pecuniary legacies, he devised and bequeathed all his real estate, and the residue of his personal estate, to his two daughters, their heirs, &c., as tenants in common, so that the same might be enjoyed by them, during any and every coverture, as separate property free from marital control, and without power of anticipation. The executors paid the testator's debts, funeral and testamentary expenses, and legacies, and purchased an annuity for the widow. The residue of the estate then consisted of two sums of stock and a sum of cash. One of the daughters was married :—*Held,* that the will did not require the conversion of the residue into money, except so far as might be necessary to provide for the annuity :—*Held,* also, that the married daughter's share of the stocks, they being income-bearing funds, could not be transferred to her, but that only the income arising from them could be paid to her :—But *held,* that her share of the cash might be paid to her on her separate receipt.—*In re Ellis' Trusts* (Law Rep. 17 Eq. 409) followed.—*In re Croughton's Trusts* (8 Ch. D. 460) distinguished. *In re* CLARKE'S TRUSTS
　　　　　　　　　　　　　　　　　[21 Ch. D. 748

15. —— Restraint on Anticipation—*Right to receive Capital—Income-producing Fund.*] Where a testator makes a bequest to a married woman for her separate use absolutely, and follows it by a clause restraining her from anticipation, the question whether the restraint on anticipation is effectual does not depend on the question whether it is a gift of an income-bearing fund or of a sum of cash, but whether the testator has or has not shewn an intention that the trustees should keep the investment and pay the income to the married woman.— A testatrix directed her trustees to raise and invest a sum of £4500, and to pay the income to B. during her life, and after her death to hold two shares in trust for two of her nieces for life, and then for their children, and as to one other share to pay it to the daughters of a deceased niece, and as to the remaining share to pay it to H.,ʻa married woman, for her separate use without power to anticipate the same, and her receipt alone to be a sufficient discharge.—*Held* (reversing the decision of Kay, J.), on the construction of the will, that on the death of B., H. was entitled to receive the capital of her share, notwithstanding the restraint on anticipation.—*In re Ellis' Trusts* (Law Rep. 17 Eq. 409) distinguished. *In re Clark's Trusts* (21 Ch. D. 748) questioned. *In re Croughton's Trusts* (8 Ch. D. 460) followed. *In re* BOWN. O'HALLORAN *v.* KING　27 Ch. D. 411

VI. HUSBAND AND WIFE — SEPARATION DEED.

.. 1. —— **Compromise of Divorce Suit**—*Specific Performance of Separation Deed—Jurisdiction of Court—Custody of Children by Wife—Agreement not too vague—" Usual Covenants "—Dum Casta Clause—Reference to Arbitration — Evidence — Mistake.*] The Plaintiff, Mrs. H., who was the wife of the Defendant, claimed specific performance of an agreement for a separation entered into upon the compromise of a suit in the Divorce Court which was instituted by the husband against the wife for a divorce on the ground of adultery. The agreement was signed by both husband and wife after the husband's evidence in support of his case had been heard and before the wife's defence had been commenced, and was in these terms :—" Petition and answer dismissed. Deed of separation with usual covenants ; costs of preparing deed to be borne by Mr. H. Mr. H. to pay Mrs. H. for herself and child or children £150 a year quarterly. Mrs. H. to maintain the child or children. Mr. H. to pay wife's costs. In case of difference in working out these terms matter to be referred to Mr. W. and Dr. D." (the leading counsel on each side) :—*Held*, that this Court had power to enforce specific performance of an agreement for a separation deed and for the compromise of a suit in the Divorce Court without infringing the Judicature Act prohibiting interference with proceedings pending in another branch of the Court :—That the Court would not refuse specific performance of an agreement for a separation deed on the ground that it provided for the wife having the custody of the children :— That husband and wife were competent to make a binding agreement for compromise of a divorce suit, and that this agreement was not too vague to be enforced by the Court :—That a dum casta clause did not come within the term " usual covenants " in a separation deed agreed to as part of the terms of compromise of a divorce suit :—That the Court would construe the term " usual covenants " in reference to surrounding circumstances, but the adultery of the wife not having been proved could not form an element for the consideration of the Court :—That the agreement on the face of it being complete, the arbitration clause could only come into force in case of difference between the parties, and did not oust the jurisdiction of the Court to settle the deed itself. —Decree for specific performance; the deed of separation to be settled in Chambers if the parties differed, and no dum casta clause to be inserted :— It is no answer to a suit for specific performance for Defendant to say that though he understood what the words of the agreement were, he was under a mistake as to their legal effect. HART v. HART - 18 Ch. D. 670

2. —— **Covenant to maintain Children**—*Right of Child to sue—Cestui que trust—Stranger suing on Covenant—Practice —Action —Parties —Mistake—Amendment—Rules of Supreme Court, 1883, Order XVI., r. 2.*] To entitle a third person, not named as a party to a contract, to sue either of the contracting parties, the third person must possess an actual beneficial right which places him in the position of cestui que trust under the contract.— By a deed of separation between husband and

VI. HUSBAND AND WIFE — SEPARATION DEED—*continued.*

wife, the husband covenanted with the trustees to pay to them an annuity for the use of the wife and two eldest daughters, and also to pay to the trustees all the expenses of the maintenance and education of the two youngest daughters, provided that the trustees permitted them to go to such school as the husband should direct, and provided also that the covenants by the trustees were duly observed and performed : provided, also, that the two youngest daughters should live at such place (being reasonable and proper for the purpose) as the husband should direct, and should be maintained and educated at his expense, the husband and wife to have all reasonable access to them. And the trustees covenanted with the husband that they would, during the continuance of the separation, keep him indemnified against all liability for the maintenance of the wife and the two eldest daughters, and against all molestation by them, and that the wife would not take any proceedings against the husband for alimony, except as aforesaid ; and that they, the trustees, would, on the husband defraying all the expenses connected therewith, carry out his desires as to the school at which the two youngest daughters should be educated, and the place at which they should live, and would permit them, if they so desired, and without any interference on the part of the wife, to accept any invitation of the husband to reside with him.—On one of the two youngest daughters subsequently attaining sixteen, the husband refused any longer to maintain her, whereupon she brought an action, by her next friend, against the husband and the trustees of the separation deed to enforce the husband's covenant, the trustees having refused to allow their names to be used as plaintiffs, and Bacon, V.C., gave a judgment for enforcing the covenant :— *Held*, on appeal, that upon the construction of the deed, the Plaintiff was not in the position of cestui que trust under the covenant so as to entitle her to maintain the action, but liberty was given to her, under the Rules of the Supreme Court, 1883, Order XVI., r. 2, to amend the writ, by adding the trustees, the wife, and the other daughters, or any of them, as Plaintiffs.—*Touche* v. *Metropolitan Railway Warehousing Company* (Law Rep. 6 Ch. 671) considered.—The trustees refusing to be joined as co-Plaintiffs, the statement of claim was amended by making the wife a co-Plaintiff : —*Held*, that she had such an interest as entitled her to sue, the deed being an arrangement between the husband and wife, and the trustees being introduced on her behalf in order to get over the difficulty that the husband and wife could not at law sue each other, so that the trustees were to be considered trustees for the wife, and if they refused to sue she could sue in equity.—After the separation deed the husband committed adultery, and a decree was made for judicial separation, giving the custody of the two youngest daughters to the wife. After this the wife applied for increased alimony, which was granted by the President, but his decision was reversed on appeal (7 P. D. 168), both the arguments and the judgment of the Court of Appeal proceeding on the footing (though the Court did not expressly decide the point) that the husband remained liable under

Y 2

VI. HUSBAND AND WIFE — SEPARATION DEED—*continued.*

the deed to pay for the maintenance and education of the two youngest daughters. He now contended that his covenant was put an end to by the custody of the youngest daughters being given to his wife:—*Held*, that he was not at liberty to retain the benefit of a decision given on the footing that his liability under the covenant continued, and at the same time to insist that his liability under it had determined, and the appeal was ordered to stand over, with liberty to the wife to apply to the Divorce Court for increased alimony, if she should be so advised. GANDY *v.* GANDY　　　　　　　　- 　30 Ch. D. 57

3. —— Covenant to pay Annuity—*Adultery by Wife—Condition Precedent—Independent Covenants—Covenant against Molestation—Molestation, what amounts to.*] In a separation deed a covenant, by which the husband undertakes to pay his wife an annuity without restricting his liability to such time as she shall be chaste, is good and is not against public policy, and the covenant remains in force and the annuity continues payable, although the wife afterwards commits adultery.— But, *semble*, per Cotton, L.J., on the authority of *Evans* v. *Carrington* (2 De G. F. & J. 481), that if the covenant had been inserted in the separation deed with the intent that the wife might be at liberty to commit adultery, the deed would have been void.—Covenants in a separation deed, by which respectively the husband has covenanted to pay an annuity to a trustee for the wife, and the trustee has covenanted that the wife shall not molest the husband, must be construed as independent covenants in the absence of any express terms making them dependent; and therefore a breach of the covenant, that a wife shall not molest the husband, is not an answer to an action for the annuity.—Neither adultery alone by the wife, nor adultery by her followed by the birth of a spurious child, is a breach of a covenant in a separation deed against molestation by the wife.—But, *semble*, adultery by the wife followed by the birth of a spurious child whom she puts forward as the child of her husband, especially if this is done with intent to claim a title or property to which the legitimate offspring of her husband would be entitled, is evidence of a breach of a covenant against molestation by her.—By Brett, M.R., in order to constitute a breach of a covenant in a separation deed against molestation by a wife, some act must be done by her or by her authority with intent to annoy her husband and which is in fact an annoyance to him, or at least some act must be done by her or by her authority with a knowledge that it must of itself without more annoy her husband or annoy a husband with reasonable and proper feeling. FEARON *v.* EARL OF AYLESFORD　12 Q. B. D. 539 ; 14 Q. B. D. 792

4. —— Separation Deed—*Reconciliation.*] A husband and wife when before the Divorce Court agreed that if judicial separation was decreed the wife should be permitted to enjoy during her life certain furniture. Judicial separation was decreed, and the wife took possession of the furniture. The husband and wife afterwards resumed cohabitation:—*Held*, in an action by the wife to recover

VI. HUSBAND AND WIFE — SEPARATION DEED—*continued.*

the furniture, that the agreement came to an end when cohabitation was resumed:—*Held*, that, as the wife was entitled to the furniture during separation only, she took nothing under 20 & 21 Vict. c. 85, s. 25, which relates to property acquired by a wife during separation. NICOL *v.* NICOL　　　　　　-　　30 Ch. D. 143

[**Affirmed by the Court of Appeal.**]

5. —— Ward of Court—*Custody of Children—Access.*] By a deed of separation made in 1880 between H., a medical officer in the army, and his wife, provision was made as to the custody of their four children (of whom the eldest was eleven and the youngest three years of age) during the approaching absence of the husband in India, after which he was to resume the entire custody of them, but he covenanted that full and free liberty of access to them should be always accorded to the wife, to the extent at least of her having the opportunity of spending one day in every fortnight with them. In 1884 he was ordered to Egypt and proposed to take the first and third of the children with him. Mrs. H. applied for an injunction to restrain him from doing so:—*Held*, by Pearson, J., that H. was bound by the covenant to keep the children in such a place that Mrs. H. could have free access to them, and that an injunction ought to be granted:—*Held*, by the Court of Appeal, that the covenant did not bind H. to keep the children in a place where Mrs. H. could conveniently have access to them, and did not preclude him from taking them with him to any place where he might be ordered in the course of his duties, and that the injunction must be dissolved, there being no case made that he was removing them for the purpose of preventing Mrs. H. from having access to them. HUNT *v.* HUNT

　　　　　　　　　　　　[28 Ch. D. 606

VII. HUSBAND AND WIFE — WIFE'S CONVEYANCE.

Acknowledgment of Deeds by Married Women.] *By* 45 & 46 *Vict. c.* 39 (*Conveyancing Act,* 1882), *s.* 7.—(1.) *In sect.* 79 *of the Fines and Recoveries Act, and sect.* 70 *of the Fines and Recoveries* (*Ireland*) *Act, there shall, by virtue of this Act, be substituted for the words* "*two of the perpetual commissioners, or two special commissioners,*" *the words* "*one of the perpetual commissioners, or one special commissioner ;*" *and in sect.* 83 *of the Fines and Recoveries Act, and sect.* 74 *of the Fines and Recoveries* (*Ireland*) *Act, there shall, by virtue of this Act, be substituted for the word* "*persons*" *the word* "*person,*" *and for the word* "*commissioners*" *the words* "*a commissioner ;*" *and for the word* "*commissioner,*" *and all other provisions of those Acts, and all other enactments having reference in any manner to the sections aforesaid, shall be read and have effect accordingly.*

(2.) *Where the memorandum of acknowledgment by a married woman of a deed purports to be signed by a person authorized to take the acknowledgment, the deed shall, as regards the execution thereof by the married woman, take effect at the time of acknowledgment, and shall be conclusively taken to have been duly acknowledged.*

(3.) *A deed acknowledged before or after the commencement of this Act by a married woman,*

VII. HUSBAND AND WIFE — WIFE'S CON-VEYANCE—continued.

before a judge of the High Court of Justice in England or Ireland, or before a judge of a county court in England, or before a chairman in Ireland, or before a perpetual commissioner or a special commissioner, shall not be impeached or impeachable by reason only that such judge, chairman, or commissioner was interested or concerned either as a party, or as solicitor, or clerk to the solicitor for one of the parties, or otherwise, in the transaction giving occasion for the acknowledgment; and General Rules shall be made for preventing any person interested or concerned as aforesaid from taking an acknowledgment; but no such Rules shall make invalid any acknowledgment; and those Rules shall, as regards England, be deemed Rules of Court within sect. 17 of the Appellate Jurisdiction Act, 1876, as altered by sect. 19 of the Supreme Court of Judicature Act, 1881, and shall, as regards Ireland, be deemed Rules of Court within the Supreme Court of Judicature Act (Ireland), 1877, and may be made accordingly, for England and Ireland respectively, at any time after the passing of this Act, to take effect on or after the commencement of this Act.

(4.) repeals 3 & 4 Will. 4, c. 74, ss. 85–88 ; 4 & 5 Will. 4, c. 92, ss. 75 (in part) and 76–79 ; 17 & 18 Vict. c. 75 ; and 41 & 42 Vict. c. 23.

(5.) The foregoing provisions of this section, including the repeal therein, apply only to the execution of deeds by married women after the commencement of this Act.

(6.) Notwithstanding the repeal or any other thing in this section, the certificate, if not lodged before the commencement of this Act, of the taking of an acknowledgment by a married woman of a deed executed before the commencement of this Act, with any affidavit relating thereto, shall be lodged, examined, and filed in the like manner, and with the like effects and consequences as if this section had not been enacted.

(7.) There shall continue to be kept in the proper office of the Supreme Court of Judicature an index to all certificates of acknowledgments of deeds by married women lodged therein, before or after the commencement of this Act, containing the names of the married women and their husbands, alphabetically arranged, and the dates of the certificates and of the deeds to which they respectively relate, and other particulars found convenient; and every such certificate lodged after the commencement of this Act shall be entered in the index as soon as may be after the certificate is filed.

(8.) An office copy of any such certificate filed before or after the commencement of this Act shall be delivered to any person applying for the same; and every such office copy shall be received as evidence of the acknowledgment of the deed to which the certificate refers.

1. ——Acknowledgment of Deed under 3 & 4 Will. 4, c. 74, s. 84—Varying the Certificate by omitting the Words "of full Age."] By order of a Vice-Chancellor indentures of settlement were directed to be executed by a married woman who was an infant. The Court allowed the certificate of acknowledgment under 3 & 4 Will. 4, c. 74, s. 84, to be varied by omitting the words "of full age." In re LACEY - - 6 Q. B. D. 154

VII. HUSBAND AND WIFE — WIFE'S CON-VEYANCE—continued.

2. —— Husband's Concurrence—Conveyance of Wife's Property under 3 & 4 Will. 4, c. 74, s. 91.] Where a husband and wife were living apart and, the wife being devisee under a will of real property on trust for sale, the husband refused to concur in a conveyance of such property upon a sale under the trusts of the will, unless he received a sum of money for doing so, the Court granted an order dispensing with the concurrence of the husband under 3 & 4 Will. 4, c. 74, s. 91, although it was admitted by the affidavit that the husband had, since he had left his wife, to a slight extent contributed to her support. In re CAINE

[10 Q. B. D. 284

3. —— Specific Performance—Fines and Recoveries, Act for abolition of (Ireland) (4 & 5 Will. 4, c. 92), ss. 68, 71.] A married woman was entitled by an ante-nuptial settlement to a jointure rent-charge after her husband's death secured upon his real estates in Ireland. The wife having left him, the husband commenced a suit for restitution of conjugal rights; with a view to a compromise by an agreement for separation a document was drawn up and signed by the husband, which stipulated that the wife should release part of her jointure. The wife signed this document with a qualification, that no further steps were taken in the matrimonial suit, but it was not stayed or dismissed. A deed was prepared to carry out the terms of the compromise and was executed by the husband, but the wife refused to execute it or to return to her husband, and the husband afterwards died :—Held, reversing the decision of the Court of Appeal in Ireland, that the wife was not, when she signed the document, in all respects in the same position as a feme sole, and that even if any final agreement had been come to she would not have been bound by it, there having been no acknowledgment as required by 4 & 5 Will. 4, c. 92, ss. 68, 71 ; and that specific performance of the agreement to release her jointure could not be decreed against her.—Hunt v. Hunt (4 D. F. & J. 221 ; 31 L. J. (Ch.) 161) and Besant v. Wood (12 Ch. D. 605) commented on by the Earl of Selborne, L.C. CAHILL v. CAHILL

[8 App. Cas. 420

VIII. HUSBAND AND WIFE—WIFE'S REAL ESTATE.

1. —— Articles of Settlement—Infant—Married Woman suing alone — Trust Property — Order XVI., r. 8—Jus tertii.] The Plaintiff's husband, who married her when he was an infant of about seventeen, agreed in writing shortly before the marriage, and in consideration of the same, to assign all her property to a trustee for her sole and separate use. At the time of the marriage the Plaintiff was possessed of some leasehold property in her own right, and of other leasehold property in trust for her son by a former marriage, and the Defendant was her agent appointed by her to receive the rents of the said leasehold property, and as such agent he received the rents both before and after the last marriage. Immediately after the last marriage the Plaintiff was deserted by her husband, and she obtained a protection order from a police magistrate, under 20 & 21 Vict. c. 85, s. 21, protecting all her

VIII. HUSBAND AND WIFE—WIFE'S REAL ESTATE—*continued.*

earnings and property acquired since the desertion. The action was brought by the Plaintiff alone without her husband (who was still an infant) for the rents received by the Defendant after the marriage. The husband made no claim to any of the rents, but the Defendant having had notice of the marriage, refused to pay them to the Plaintiff; and he applied to stay the action until the Plaintiff added a next friend or gave security for costs. This application was refused at Chambers, and on appeal by a Divisional Court :—*Held*, that the agreement to assign was void as against the infant husband :—*Held*, also, that the protection order did not apply, but that the effect of the Court to stay the action on the Defendant's application was to give leave to the Plaintiff to sue alone without her husband, in exercise of the authority given to a Court or Judge by Order xvi., rule 8, and which might be so exercised after action brought, and that therefore the Plaintiff was entitled to sue alone and to recover the money received from the property of which she was trustee :—*Held*, however, by Lord Selborne, L.C., and Baggallay, L.J., that the agreement to assign being void against her husband she could not recover the money received from the property which belonged to her absolutely before her last marriage :—*Held*, by Brett, L.J., that she could, since the husband had made no claim, and therefore the Defendant, who was not defending by his authority, could not set up the husband's right as an answer to the action. KINGSMAN *v.* KINGSMAN   **6 Q. B. D. 122**

2. —— **Interest in Land**—*Mortgage Debt—Acknowledged Deed—Fines and Recoveries Act (3 & 4 Will. 4, c. 74), ss. 1, 77.*] Under the will of a testator who died in 1843, his three children, T., W., & S., a married woman, were each entitled to one-third of his residuary estate, subject to the life interest therein of his widow.—In 1844 T. died a bachelor and intestate.—By a deed executed in 1854 (before Sir R. Malins' Act), to which the tenant for life, the trustees of the will, W., and S. and her husband, were parties, and which was acknowledged by S. under the Fines and Recoveries Act (3 & 4 Will. 4, c. 74), two mortgage debts, secured to the trustees on real estate and forming part of the testator's residuary estate, were assigned by the tenant for life and W. and by S. and her husband, with the privity of the trustees, by way of mortgage.—The deed was executed under the erroneous assumption that, according to the terms of a gift over in the will, T. took no share in the testator's estate, and consequently his administrator was not made a party.—*Held*, that the deed was not effectual to pass S.'s share of the two mortgage debts.—*Williams v. Cooke* (4 Giff. 343) distinguished.   *In re* NEWTON'S TRUSTS
 [23 Ch. D. 181

3. —— **Interest in Land**—*Devise in Trust for Sale—Proceeds of Sale—Husband—Bankruptcy—Creditors' Deed—Concurrence in Wife's Assignment—Acknowledged Deed—Fines and Recoveries Act (3 & 4 Will. 4, c. 74), s. 77—Bankruptcy Act, 1849, s. 141—Bankruptcy Act, 1861.*] Under the will of a testator, who died in March, 1862, M., a married woman, was entitled in reversion expect-

VIII. HUSBAND AND WIFE—WIFE'S REAL ESTATE—*continued.*

ant on the death of a tenant for life to a share of the proceeds of real estate devised to trustees in trust for sale on that event. In August, 1862, in the lifetime of the tenant for life, M.'s husband executed a general assignment, under the Bankruptcy Act, 1861, of all his property to a trustee for the benefit of his creditors. In August, 1866, he was adjudged bankrupt, and in December following he obtained his discharge. The tenant for life died in January, 1869. By a deed executed in February following, and duly acknowledged by M. under sect. 77 of the Fines and Recoveries Act (3 & 4 Will. 4, c. 74), M. and her husband assigned all moneys which should become due to them or either of them under the testator's will to S. by way of mortgage. Shortly afterwards the trustees of the will sold the real estate, and ultimately paid M.'s share of the proceeds into Court under the Trustee Relief Act :—*Held*, that the husband was not precluded by the creditors' deed of 1862 or by his bankruptcy in 1866 from concurring with his wife in the mortgage of 1869, and accordingly that the mortgage was valid against the trustee of the creditors' deed and the assignee in bankruptcy.   *In re* JAKEMAN'S TRUSTS
 [23 Ch. D. 344

4. —— **Nature of Settlement**—*Duty of Mortgagee to inquire as to Settlement.*] When a married woman executes a mortgage there is no obligation on the mortgagee to inquire whether a settlement was made on her marriage. LLOYD'S BANKING COMPANY *v.* JONES -   -   - **29 Ch. D. 221**

5. —— **Non-concurrence of Husband**—*Fines and Recoveries Act, 1833 (3 & 4 Will. 4, c. 74), s. 91—Husband's Interest in Rents and Profits—Judicature Act, 1873, s. 25, sub-s. 11—Wife's Equity to a Settlement.*] An order in the usual form obtained under s. 91 of the Fines and Recoveries Act, 1833, by a married woman, empowering her to dispose of her real estate without the concurrence of her husband, does not deprive him of the common law rights which he acquired in the property by reason of the coverture.—Where, therefore, under such an order, a married woman sold and conveyed all her estate and interest in real estate, her husband refusing to join :— *Held*, that the husband's common law right to the rents during the coverture remained unaffected by the wife's alienation, but that (she asserting her equity to a settlement) he was bound, whether his estate was legal or equitable, to provide for her out of the rents; and, under the circumstances, the whole of the rents were settled upon her. FOWKE *v.* DRAYCOTT   **29 Ch. D. 996**

6. —— **Post-nuptial Contract**—*Contract by the Wife with the Husband in respect of her Real Estate—3 & 4 Will. 4, c. 74, ss. 77, 79.*] A married woman immediately after the marriage, and in consideration thereof and of her husband undertaking the management of lands and tenements of which she was seised in fee, and of his paying off incumbrances and defraying the expense of managing and keeping the premises in repair, verbally agreed to convey the lands and tenements to him, and to settle them upon him absolutely, and to do all such acts as might be

VIII. HUSBAND AND WIFE—WIFE'S REAL ESTATE—*continued.*

legally necessary for effectuating such conveyance and settlement. The husband performed his part of the agreement, but the wife died without having executed or acknowledged a deed:—*Held*, that this contract could not be set up as an equitable defence to a claim by her heir-at-law to recover the land. WILLIAMS *v.* WALKER

[9 Q. B. D. 576

IX. HUSBAND AND WIFE—WIFE'S REVERSION.

1. —— *Chattels Real not vested in Possession during Coverture—Reversionary Interest of Wife after Life Interest in Leaseholds for Years—Wife predeceasing Tenant for Life—Title of Husband surviving.*] A wife entitled to a term subject to a life estate therein predeceased her husband during the subsistence of the life estate :—*Held*, that it was not necessary for the husband to take out letters of administration to her in order to complete his title to the leaseholds. *In re* BELLAMY. ELDER *v.* PEARSON - 25 Ch. D. 620

2. —— *Interest in Land—Money invested in Land—Fines and Recoveries Act* (3 & 4 Will. 4, c. 74), *s.* 77.] A fund of personalty was settled in 1842 upon trust during the joint lives of a husband and wife for the wife for her separate use without power of anticipation, then for the survivor during his or her life, and after the death of the survivor for such of their children as being sons should attain twenty-one, or being daughters attain that age or marry, in equal shares. There was no power to invest in purchase of land. The trustees bought a freehold house with part of the fund. The only children were two daughters, who attained twenty-one and married. After this the trustee, the husband and wife, and the daughters and their husbands, by deed duly acknowledged by the daughters, conveyed the estate to such uses as the father and mother should jointly appoint, and in default as the survivor should by deed or will appoint. After the death of the mother the father contracted to sell the estate. The purchaser objected to the title on the ground that, as the purchase of real estate was unauthorized, the interest of the daughters was still to be treated as a reversionary interest in personalty of which they could not dispose :—*Held* (reversing the decision of Hall, V.C.), that the father could make a good title. *In re* DURRANT AND STONER

[18 Ch. D. 106

—— Agreement not signed by wife—Fee simple of wife - - - 13 Q. B. D. 147
See HUSBAND AND WIFE — SEPARATE ESTATE. 1.

HUSBAND AND WIFE—Action by executrix and her husband—Costs 30 Ch. D. 24
See PRACTICE—SUPREME COURT—COSTS. 35.

—— Appointment by wife—Will 22 Ch. D. 238
See POWER—EXECUTION. 11.

—— Bankruptcy — Ante-nuptial agreement for settlement—Part performance—Statute of Frauds - 14 Q. B. D. 419
See BANKRUPTCY — PROTECTED TRANSACTION. 9.

HUSBAND AND WIFE—*continued.*

—— Bankruptcy — Wife's separate property in possession of husband—Reputed ownership - - 14 Q. B. 417
See BANKRUPTCY—ORDER AND DISPOSITION. 12.

—— Bequest by will to—Unity of person—Married Women's Property Act
[27 Ch. D. 166
See WILL—JOINT TENANCY.

—— Consent of wife—Examination 26 Ch. D. 220
See SETTLED ESTATES ACT. 2.

—— Conveyance—Bare trustee 29 Ch. D. 693
See VENDOR AND PURCHASER — CONVEYANCE. 3.

—— Covenant to settle after-acquired property.
See Cases under SETTLEMENT—FUTURE PROPERTY.

—— Criminal law — Husband witness against wife—Married Women's Property Act, 1882 - - 12 Q. B. D. 266
See CRIMINAL LAW—EVIDENCE. 2.

—— " Desertion " - 9 Q. B. D. 522
See POOR LAW—SETTLEMENT. 8.

—— Divorce—Assignment of alimony 27 Ch. D.
See LUNATIC—PROPERTY. 1. [160

—— Divorced husband—Legacy 22 Ch. D. 619
See WILL—WORDS. 11.

—— Dower - 21 Ch. D. 164; 8 Q. B. D. 31
See DOWER. 1, 2.

—— Election by wife - - 26 Ch. D. 358;
[27 Ch. D. 606; 28 Ch. D. 124
See ELECTION. 4, 5, 6.

—— Equity to settlement - 16 Ch. D. 376;
[17 Ch. D. 778; 27 Ch. D. 220
See SETTLEMENT—EQUITY TO SETTLEMENT. 1, 2, 3.

—— Evidence of marriage—Ceylon 6 App. Cas.
See COLONIAL LAW—CEYLON. 3. [364

—— Evidence of marriage—Scotch law
[6 App. Cas. 489; 10 App. Cas. 692
See SCOTCH LAW—HUSBAND AND WIFE. 2, 3.

—— Evidence of non-access - 23 Ch. D. 173
See EVIDENCE—GENERAL. 2.

—— Evidence of, on behalf of the other—Offences against women.
See CRIMINAL LAW—OFFENCES AGAINST WOMEN—*Statutes.*

—— Judgment against married woman
[8 Q. B. D. 177; 13 Q. B. D. 691
See PRACTICE—SUPREME COURT—WRIT SPECIALLY INDORSED. 3, 4.

—— Legacy to wife - 17 Ch. D. 798
See WILL—PRIORITY OF LEGACIES.

—— Married woman executrix — Husband objecting to probate - - 6 P. D. 103
See PROBATE—MARRIED WOMAN. 2.

—— Married woman—Third party—Summons for directions - 12 Q. B. D. 533
See PRACTICE—SUPREME COURT—THIRD PARTY. 3.

HUSBAND AND WIFE—*continued.*

—— Married woman suing separately—Security for costs   -   **9 Q. B. D. 52**
See PRACTICE—SUPREME COURT—SECURITY FOR COSTS. 4.

—— Married Women's Property Act—Wife suing as feme sole—Security for costs
[30 Ch. D. 418
See PRACTICE—SUPREME COURT—SECURITY FOR COSTS. 5.

—— Natal—Law of –Surety bond by wife
[9 App. Cas. 715
See COLONIAL LAW—NATAL. 2.

—— Nullity of marriage—Impotence—Scotch law   -   -   **10 App. Cas. 171**
See SCOTCH LAW—HUSBAND AND WIFE. 7.

—— Order upon husband for maintenance of wife—Amount of relief granted by guardians   -   **13 Q. B. D. 25**
See POOR LAW—MAINTENANCE. 2.

—— Policy of insurance—Felonious act of wife of assured   -   -   **6 Q. B. D. 561**
See INSURANCE, FIRE. 1.

—— Poor law—Adultery of wife   **7 Q. B. D. 89**
See POOR LAW—MAINTENANCE. 1.

—— Post-nuptial settlement — Wife's separate estate   -   **24 Ch. D. 597**
See VOLUNTARY CONVEYANCE. 3.

—— Production of documents   **29 Ch. D. 899**
See PRACTICE — SUPREME COURT—PRODUCTION OF DOCUMENTS. 4.

—— Protection order—Setting aside—Death of wife   -   **6 P. D. 54**
See PROBATE—MARRIED WOMAN. 3.

—— Request for sale in partition suit   **18 Ch. D.**
See PARTITION SUIT—SALE. 4.   **[612**

HUSBAND AND WIFE—*continued.*

—— Restitution of conjugal rights.
See Cases and Statutes under PRACTICE — DIVORCE — RESTITUTION OF CONJUGAL RIGHTS.

—— Scotch law.
See Cases under SCOTCH LAW—HUSBAND AND WIFE.

—— Separate estate—Bill of costs   **24 Ch. D. 405**
See SOLICITOR—BILL OF COSTS. 9.

—— Separate estate—Injunction against married woman   -   **16 Ch. D. 660**
See PRACTICE — SUPREME COURT — INJUNCTION. 5.

—— Separate estate—Sale under Lands Clauses Act   -   **18 Ch. D. 429**
See LANDS CLAUSES ACT—COMPULSORY POWERS. 8.

—— Separate examination of wife   **28 Ch. D. 171**
See SETTLED ESTATES ACT. 3.

—— Separate use—Will.
See Cases under WILL—SEPARATE USE.

—— Settlement on marriage.
See Cases under SETTLEMENT.

—— Settlement—After-acquired property
[24 Ch. D. 114
See SETTLED LAND ACT—DEFINITIONS. 1.

—— Shares taken in wife's name   **18 Ch. D. 581**
See COMPANY—CONTRIBUTORY. 1.

—— Subsequent marriage—Child illegitimate
[17 Ch. D. 266
See DISTRIBUTIONS, STATUTE OF.

—— Voidable marriage—Annuity to widow
See WILL—CONDITION. 11. **[25 Ch. D. 685**

—— Wife tenant for life—Custody of deeds—Bankruptcy of husband   **26 Ch. D. 31**
See TITLE DEEDS.

HYPOTHEC—Law of Jersey   -   **8 App. Cas. 542**
See COLONIAL LAW—JERSEY. 2.

I.

IDENTIFICATION OF PROPERTY—Statute of Frauds   20 Ch. D. 90
See VENDOR AND PURCHASER—AGREEMENT. 2.

ILLEGALITY—Contract to indemnify bail
      [7 Q. B. D. 548; 15 Q. B. D. 561
See CONTRACT—VALIDITY. 1, 2.

—— Contract—Public body - 8 App. Cas. 623
See SCOTCH LAW—HARBOUR. 1.

—— Contract — Local authority— Officer concerned in contract.
See Cases under LOCAL GOVERNMENT—LOCAL AUTHORITY. 4—7.

—— Loan—Friendly society—Investment
See FRIENDLY SOCIETY.   [19 Ch. D. 64

—— Payment of bankrupt's money to procure withdrawal of criminal prosecution—Relation back of trustee's title
      [14 Q. B. D. 32
See BANKRUPTCY—ASSETS. 11.

—— Practices at municipal election.
See MUNICIPAL CORPORATION—ELECTION—*Statutes.*

—— Practices at parliamentary elections.
See PARLIAMENT—ELECTION—*Statutes.*

—— Right of Attorney-General to sue
      [21 Ch. D. 752
See PRACTICE—SUPREME COURT—INJUNCTION. 1.

—— Seizure of goods—Mortgagor in possession
      [8 App. Cas. 285
See MORTGAGE—MORTGAGOR IN POSSESSION.

—— Unregistered company of more than twenty members.
See Cases under COMPANY — UNREGISTERED COMPANY.

ILLEGITIMACY—Suit to perpetuate testimony
      [9 P. D. 120
See PRACTICE—DIVORCE—EVIDENCE. 2.

—— Trinidad, Law of   ·   10 App. Cas. 312
See COLONIAL LAW—TRINIDAD.

ILLEGITIMATE CHILD—Construction of will
      [24 Ch. D. 691; 30 Ch. D. 110
See WILL—CHILDREN. 1, 2.

—— Domicil   -   -   24 Ch. D. 637
See WILL—WORDS. 13.

—— Evidence of non-access   -   23 Ch. D. 173
See EVIDENCE—GENERAL. 2.

—— Lunatic—Duchy of Lancaster 21 Ch. D. 613
See LUNATIC—JURISDICTION. 4.

—— Right to custody -   10 Q. B. D. 454
See INFANT—CUSTODY. 4.

—— Subsequent marriage   -   17 Ch. D. 266
See DISTRIBUTIONS, STATUTE OF.

ILLEGITIMATE CHILD—*continued.*
—— Succession duty—Fund in Court
      [21 Ch. D. 100
See REVENUE—SUCCESSION DUTY. 2.

ILLUSORY APPOINTMENT — Law of Lower Canada   -   10 App. Cas. 653
See COLONIAL LAW—CANADA—QUEBEC. 6.

IMITATION—Trade-mark   -   7 App. Cas. 219
See TRADE-MARK—INFRINGEMENT. 1.

IMMORAL CONSIDERATION—Bond
See BOND.   [26 Ch. D. 353

IMPLICATION—Contract with lunatic
      [21 Ch. D. 615
See LUNATIC—MAINTENANCE. 1.

—— Cross remainders   -   20 Ch. D. 406
See WILL—CROSS REMAINDERS.

—— Grant—Easement—Light   25 Ch. D. 559;
See LIGHT—TITLE. 5. [10 App. Cas. 590

—— Right of support—Grant - 21 Ch. D. 559
See SUPPORT. 1.

—— Obligation—Covenant to buy beer of landlord   -   -   18 Ch. D. 199
See LANDLORD AND TENANT—LEASE. 8.

—— Revocation of will -   23 Ch. D. 337
See WILL—REVOCATION. 2.

IMPORTATION—Patented article 17 Ch. D. 721;
      [8 App. Cas. 5
See PATENT—INFRINGEMENT. 6.

IMPOSSIBILITY OF CARRYING ON BUSINESS—Winding-up   20 Ch. D. 151, 169
See COMPANY—WINDING-UP ORDER. 4, 5.

IMPOTENCE—Nullity of marriage—Practice
      [6 P. D. 13; 7 P. D. 16; 10 P. D. 75
See PRACTICE—DIVORCE—NULLITY OF MARRIAGE. 2, 3, 4.

—— Nullity of marriage—Scotch law
      [10 App. Cas. 171
See SCOTCH LAW—HUSBAND AND WIFE. 7.

IMPRISONMENT — Debtor — Law of Lower Canada   -   -   8 App. Cas. 530
See COLONIAL LAW—CANADA—QUEBEC. 2.

—— Law of Ontario -   -   9 App. Cas. 117
See COLONIAL LAW—CANADA—ONTARIO. 2.

IMPROVEMENTS—Compensation for.
See LANDLORD AND TENANT—IMPROVEMENTS—*Statutes.*

—— Lunatic's estate—Charge   29 Ch. D. 306
See LUNATIC—PROPERTY. 6.

—— Settled Land Act -   -   30 Ch. D. 102
See SETTLED LAND ACT — PURCHASE-MONEY. 1.

IMPROVEMENTS—continued.
—— Settled Land Act.
　　See SETTLED LAND ACT—STATUTES.

IMPROVEMENT BOND—Mortmain 22 Ch. D. 202
　　See CHARITY—MORTMAIN. 4.

INCLOSURE.

Commons.] *By 45 & 46 Vict. c. 15 (Commonable Rights Compensation Act, 1882), s. 1, moneys
paid, under the provisions of the Lands Clauses
Consolidation Act, 1845, and of railway and other
special Acts of Parliament, by way of compensation for the compulsory acquisition of Common
Lands and the extinguishment of Rights of Common may be applied in one or more of the following ways :*

　(a.) *In the improvement of the remainder of the
　　common land in respect of a portion of
　　which such money has been paid :*
　(b.) *In defraying the expense of any proceedings
　　under the Metropolitan Commons Acts or
　　under the Inclosure Acts, 1845 to 1878,
　　with reference to a scheme for the local
　　management, or a provisional order for
　　the regulation, of such common land, or
　　of any application to Parliament for a
　　private bill or otherwise for the preserva-
　　tion and management of such common land
　　as an open space ;*
　(c.) *In defraying the expense of any legal pro-
　　ceedings for the protection of such common
　　land, or the commoners' rights over the
　　same ;*
　(d.) *In the purchase of additional land to be
　　used as common land ;*
　(e.) *In the purchase of land to be used as a re-
　　creation ground for the neighbourhood.*

*Any land so purchased as aforesaid for use as
common land to be conveyed to and vest in trustees
to be appointed by the Inclosure Commissioners.*

*Any land so purchased as aforesaid for use as
recreation ground to be conveyed to and vest in the
local authority.*

*Sect. 3. As to application of compensation money
paid for recreation grounds and field gardens.*

*Sect. 4. Provision for cases where money paid
by way of compensation has already been applied
in manner authorized by the Act.*

Ecclesiastical Land.] *The Act 47 & 48 Vict.
c. 67, enacts that the Inclosure Commissioners shall
not sanction ecclesiastical land to be charged for
improvement under 27 & 28 Vict. c. 114, without
the consent of patron and bishop.*

1. —— Construction of Act—Mines—Manorial
Rights—Support—Damage to Surface—Compensation.] An Inclosure Act enacted that allotments should be made to the persons having a
right of common upon the waste of the manor,
that is, to the owners of every separate ancient
dwelling-house within the manor; that all right
of common should be extinguished; and that the
allotments should be held and enjoyed by the
allottees by the same tenure and estates as the
respective dwelling-houses: provided that nothing
should prejudice, lessen, or defeat the title and
interest of the lords of the manor to and in the
royalties, but that the lords and their successors as
owners of the royalties should for ever hold and
enjoy all "rents, courts, perquisites, profits, mines,

INCLOSURE—continued.
power of using or granting wayleave, waifs, estrays,
and all other royalties and jurisdictions whatsoever " to the owners of the manor appertaining
"in as full, ample, and beneficial manner to all
intents and purposes as they could or might have
held and enjoyed the same in case this Act had not
been made." Provided further, that in case the
lords or any persons claiming under them should
work any mines lying under any allotment, or
should lay, make, or use any way or ways over any
allotment, such persons so working the mines, or
laying. making, or using such way or ways, should
make "satisfaction for the damages and spoil of
ground occasioned thereby to the person or persons
who shall be in possession of such ground at the
time or times of such damage or spoil;" such
satisfaction to be settled by arbitration and "not
to exceed the sum of £5 yearly during the time
of working such mines or continuing or using
such way or ways for every acre of ground so
damaged or spoiled."—At the time of passing the
Act there were no customs which enlarged or cut
down the common law rights of the lords to work
the minerals under the wastes of the manor.
Under the Act an allotment was made in 1772 to
a commoner in respect of an ancient freehold
dwelling-house. At that time no house had been
built upon the allotment. More than twenty
years after a house had been built upon it, the
minerals underlying it were worked by lessees of
the lords of the manor so as to cause the surface
of the land to subside, whereby the house was
damaged to an amount exceeding the sum recoverable under the proviso. The land would have
subsided if there had been no house. An action
for damages having been brought against the
lessees by the allottee's successor in title and by
his tenant in possession:—Held, affirming the
decision of the Court of Appeal, that upon the
true construction of the Act, the proviso for satisfaction did not apply to damage from subsidence ;
that there was nothing in the Act giving the
lords the right to let down the surface ; that the
Plaintiffs were entitled to have the house and land
supported by the minerals, and to recover damages
for the subsidence. LOVE v. BELL 10 Q. B. D.
　　　　　　　　　　　　[547 ; 9 App. Cas. 286

2. —— Extinguishment of Right of Common
—Allotment—Lease of Land, to which Right of
Common was formerly attached—8 & 9 Vict.
c. 118.] When upon the inclosure of waste lands
under 8 & 9 Vict. c. 118, rights of common over
them have been extinguished, the allotments
awarded in lieu of rights of common are not to
be deemed parts of the lands to which the rights
of common were annexed, but are to be deemed
to have been granted to the owner of those lands;
and a lease of land, to which rights of common
were formerly attached, will not, after they have
been extinguished by an inclosure of the waste
lands, pass by general words the right to the possession of the allotment.—Rights of common over
H. were attached to a farm. In 1857 a provisional
order was made for inclosing H., and the rights of
common over it were extinguished as from May,
1859. Allotments were made to the owner of the
farm in lieu of the rights of common. In 1866 a
lease for sixty years of the farm was granted at a

INCLOSURE—*continued.*.

fixed rent : the lease contained the usual general words:—*Held*, that the right to the possession of the allotments did not pass with the lease. WILLIAMS *v.* PHILLIPS　　8 Q. B. D. 437

3. —— **Property in Underwood**—*Waste Lands of Manor*—29 Geo. 2, c. 36—*Agreement between Lord and Tenants under*—*Right of Common of Pasture*—*Freehold Tenants with right of Property in Underwood.*] In the year 1769 the lord of a manor, the freehold tenants of which were not only entitled to common of pasture, but were also collectively the owners of the bushes and underwoods growing on the wastes of the manor, entered into an agreement, under 29 Geo. 2, c. 36, with the major part of such tenants for the periodical inclosure of parts of the wastes of the manor for the growth and preservation of timber and underwood; and this agreement appeared to have been from time to time acted upon from the year 1773 until, in the year 1880, two of the freehold tenants of the manor brought an action on behalf of themselves and all other the freehold tenants against the lord of the manor to restrain him from further infringement of their rights:—*Held*, in a special case stated in that action, that the Act of 29 Geo. 2, c. 36, applied only to agreements by persons entitled to common of pasture, and not to agreements by persons who were the owners of the bushes and underwood; that the agreement of 1769 was inoperative against such owners; and that the lord had no right to inclose as against them. NICHOLLS *v.* MITFORD　　20 Ch. D. 380

INCLOSURE COMMISSIONERS.

　See INCLOSURE—*Statutes.*

—— Rent-charge—Land drainage company
　　　　　　　　　　　　　[20 Ch. D. 208
　See ECCLESIASTICAL COMMISSIONERS.

INCOME — Application of — Purchase-moneys under Lands Clauses Act 16 Ch. D. 597
　See LANDS CLAUSES ACT — PURCHASE-MONEY. 2.

—— Bankrupt—Voluntary allowance
　　　　　　　　　　　　　[17 Ch. D. 70
　See BANKRUPTCY—ASSETS. 14.

—— Charge on—Annuity　　-　17 Ch. D. 167
　See WILL—ANNUITY. 1.

—— Interim　　　-　　16 Ch. D. 691
　See POWER—EXECUTION. 14.

—— Interim—Legacy　.　-　22 Ch. D. 573 ;
　　　　　　　[23 Ch. D. 360; 25 Ch. D. 743
　See WILL—INTERIM INCOME. 1, 2, 3.

—— Maintenance of infant.
　See Cases under INFANT—MAINTENANCE.

—— Property of lunatic—Jurisdiction 26 Ch. D.
　See LUNATIC—PROPERTY. 7.　　[496

—— Purchase-money—Settled Land Act
　　　　　　　　　　　　　[28 Ch. D. 628
　See SETTLED LAND ACT — PURCHASE-MONEY. 2.

—— Trust estate—Expenses of action
　　　　　　　　　　　　　[25 Ch. D. 710
　See TRUSTEE—COSTS AND CHANGES. 5.

INCOME-PRODUCING FUND -　19 Ch. D. 277;
　　　　[21 Ch. D. 743; 27 Ch. D. 411
　See HUSBAND AND WIFE—SEPARATE ESTATE. 13, 14, 15.

INCOME-TAX.

　See Cases under REVENUE — INCOME TAX.

—— Bequest of annuity free from all deductions
　　　　[21 Ch. D. 105; 22 Ch. D. 182, 269
　See WILL—WORDS. 1, 2, 3.

—— New Brunswick　　-　6 App. Cas. 373
　See COLONIAL LAW — CANADA — NEW BRUNSWICK.

—— Scotch law　　-　　-　6 App. Cas. 315
　See SCOTCH LAW—REVENUE.

INCOMING TENANT　-　　-　22 Ch. D. 769
　See LANDLORD AND TENANT—LEASE. 15.

INCONGRUITY—Mistake in description
　　　　　　　　　　　[28 Ch. D. 153
　See WILL—MISTAKE. 3.

INCONSISTENT CLAUSES—Will　18 Ch. D. 17
　See WILL—REPUGNANCY.

INCORPORATION OF DISTRICT—Local board
　　　　　　　　　　　　[21 Ch. D. 176
　See LOCAL GOVERNMENT — LOCAL AUTHORITY. 1.

INCORPORATION OF DOCUMENTS—Testamentary instrument　　-　6 P. D. 9, 30 ;
　　　　　　　　　　　　　[8 P. D. 14
　See WILL—INCORPORATED DOCUMENTS. 1, 2, 3.

INCUMBENT OF CHURCH——Compensation on retirement—Mortgage　　30 Ch. D. 520
　See MORTGAGE—CONTRACT. 3.

—— Resignation　　-　　-　17 Ch. D. 1
　See ECCLESIASTICAL LAW—CLERGY. 3.

INCUMBRANCES—Discharge of.
　See VENDOR AND PURCHASER — CONVEYANCE—*Statutes.*

—— Discharge of — Conveyancing Act, 1881
　　　　　　　　　　　　[25 Ch. D. 788
　See VENDOR AND PURCHASER — CONDITIONS OF SALE. 6.

—— Discharge of—Settled Land Act
　　　　　[29 Ch. D. 588 ; 30 Ch. D. 127
　See SETTLED LAND ACT — PURCHASE-MONEY. 4, 5.

INDECENCY—Exposure of person—Public place
　　　　　　　　　　　　[14 Q. B. D. 63
　See CRIMINAL LAW—NUISANCE.

—— Male persons.
　See CRIMINAL LAW—OFFENCES AGAINST THE PERSON—*Statutes.*

INDEFEASIBLE TITLE—Land in Griqualand
　　　　　　　　　　　　[8 App. Cas. 318
　See COLONIAL LAW—GRIQUALAND.

INDEFINITE TRUST—Gift by will
　See WILL—TRUSTEES. 2. [26 Ch. D. 531

INDEMNITY.

　—— *Goods lawfully seized for another's Debt.*] As a general rule, where one person's goods are lawfully seized for another's debt, the owner of the goods is entitled to redeem them, and to be reimbursed by the debtor against the money paid to redeem them, and in the event of the goods being sold to satisfy the debt the owner is entitled to recover the value of them from the debtor ; and the right to indemnity exists although there may be no agreement to indemnify, and although there

INDEMNITY—*continued.*

may be in that sense no privity between the owner of the goods and the debtor.—*England* v. *Marsden* (Law Rep. 1 C. P. 529) questioned.—The Defendant bought the business of an ironmonger in his own name for his two sons; he paid the greater part of the purchase-money. The banking account of the business was kept by him, and he drew the cheques on that account. A society having obtained judgment in an action against the Defendant, certain goods of his sons were seized by the sheriff: the sons claimed the goods; but upon an interpleader summons taken out by the sheriff, the claim of the sons was barred, and the goods were sold. They realised £1300, and this sum was paid into Court in the action by the society against the Defendant as a security for what might be found due to the society from the Defendant upon taking certain accounts. The Defendant's sons were afterwards adjudicated bankrupts, and the Plaintiff was appointed their trustee. The Defendant agreed with the Plaintiff that in consideration of his sons' goods having been seized and sold on behalf of the society in respect of an alleged claim against him, he would pay £300 per annum to the Plaintiff until he should have paid a sufficient sum to pay the trade creditors of his sons in full. The Plaintiff having brought the present action to recover £1200 due by virtue of the above-mentioned agreement, or in the alternative £1300, the value of the goods seized:—*Held*, that even if the Defendant's express promise to pay £1200 was not legally binding upon him, nevertheless the action was maintainable; for although the decision upon the interpleader summons did not estop the Defendant from shewing that the seizure by the sheriff was unlawful, nevertheless he had by his conduct led to the seizure, and the goods of his sons had been legally taken for his debt; the Defendant, therefore, was bound to indemnify his sons, and the Plaintiff, as their trustee in bankruptcy, was entitled to have judgment entered for him for the sum of £1200, which he was willing to accept instead of £1300, the value of the goods seized. EDMUNDS *v.* WALLINGFORD   -   -   14 Q. B. D. 811

——— Assignment of lease   -   29 Ch. D. 254
 See LANDLORD AND TENANT—ASSIGNMENT. 3.

——— Claim for—Third party.
 See Cases under PRACTICE—SUPREME COURT—THIRD PARTY. 5—9.

——— Landlord and tenant—Contract of subtenant to perform covenants of lease
        [8 Q. B. D. 329
 See PRACTICE—SUPREME COURT—COSTS. 48.

——— Misconduct of director—Shareholders and creditors   -   -   21 Ch. D. 149
 See COMPANY—DIRECTOR'S LIABILITY. 4.

——— Receiver in liquidation   23 Ch. D. 75
 See BANKRUPTCY—RECEIVER. 3.

——— Surety—Composition   16 Ch. D. 505
 See BANKRUPTCY—ANNULMENT. 4.

——— Trustee   -   -   22 Ch. D. 255, 561, 666;
        [28 Ch. D. 595
 See TRUSTEE—INDEMNITY. 1, 2, 3.

INDEMNITY—*continued.*

——— Trustee—Leaseholds—Covenants
        [16 Ch. D. 723
 See TRUSTEE—LIABILITIES. 9.

——— Trustee—Severance of trust funds
        [6 App. Cas. 855
 See SCOTCH LAW—TRUSTEE.

INDIA—Criminal law—Inquiry as to sanity of accused—Removal to England
        [7 Q. B. D. 18
 See CRIMINAL LAW—PRACTICE. 1.

INDIA STOCK—Investment of money in Court
        [22 Ch. D. 93
 See PRACTICE—SUPREME COURT—PAYMENT INTO COURT. 5.

INDICTMENT — Conspiracy — Two persons indicted together—Acquittal or conviction of both   -   -   -   12 Q. B. D. 241
 See CRIMINAL LAW—CONSPIRACY.

——— Obstruction of highway—New trial
        [7 Q. B. D. 198
 See CRIMINAL LAW—PRACTICE. 3.

——— Offences against women.
 See CRIMINAL LAW—OFFENCES AGAINST WOMEN—*Statutes.*

——— Two counts—Sentence   -   6 App. Cas. 229
 See CRIMINAL LAW—PRACTICE. 2.

INDORSEMENT — Bill of lading — Passing of property   13 Q. B. 159; 10 App. Cas. 74
 See SHIP—BILL OF LADING. 4.

——— Bill of exchange—Right of indorsee to be indemnified by acceptor   6 App. Cas. 1
 See PRINCIPAL AND SURETY — INDEMNITY. 1.

——— Foreign bill of exchange   -   30 Ch. D. 598
 See BILL OF EXCHANGE—FOREIGN BILL.

——— Dock warrant   28 Ch. D. 682
 See BILL OF SALE—REGISTRATION. 5.

——— Order of attachment   21 Ch. D. 360;
        [27 Ch. D. 66
 See PRACTICE—SUPREME COURT—ATTACHMENT. 3, 4.

——— Order for discovery of documents
        [26 Ch. D. 746
 See PRACTICE—SUPREME COURT—ATTACHMENT. 8.

——— Promissory note—Co-sureties
        [8 App. Cas. 733
 See BILL OF EXCHANGE—LIABILITY OF PARTIES.

——— Receipt—Mortgage to building society
        [28 Ch. D. 398
 See BUILDING SOCIETY. 13.

——— Writ—Extension of time   -   16 Ch. D. 734
 See PRACTICE—SUPREME COURT—WRIT. 1.

——— Writ—Motion on admission   23 Ch. D. 204
 See PRACTICE — SUPREME COURT—MOTION FOR JUDGMENT. 1.

INDUSTRIAL SCHOOL.

Order in Council.] *Directing that certain provisions of the Industrial Schools Act, 1866, and the Acts amending the same, shall apply to certified day industrial schools. October 25th, 1881*
        [L. G., 1881, p. 5294

INDUSTRIAL SCHOOL—*continued.*

—— **Living in Disorderly House**—*House resided in by Prostitutes*—*Industrial Schools Act, 1866 (29 & 30 Vict. c. 118), s. 14*—*Industrial Schools Act Amendment Act, 1880 (43 & 44 Vict. c. 15), s. 1.*] A child under fourteen who lives with and under the guardianship of her mother in "a house resided in by prostitutes" may be ordered to be sent to an industrial school under 29 & 30 Vict. c. 118, s. 4, although there is no evidence of any act of prostitution on the part of the mother. HISCOCKS *v.* JERMONSON
[10 Q. B. D. 360

INDUSTRIAL SOCIETY.
See FRIENDLY SOCIETY—*Statutes.*

INFANT:—

		Col.
I.	ACTS	665
II.	CONTRACTS	665
III.	CUSTODY	666
IV.	EDUCATION	667
V.	GUARDIAN	668
VI.	MAINTENANCE	669
VII.	PROPERTY	671
VIII.	SETTLEMENT	674
IX.	WARD OF COURT	675

I. INFANT—ACTS.

—— **Undue Influence**—*Gift of Personal Estate.*] In the absence of proof of the exercise of control or influence on the part of the donee, or of the existence of the relation of guardian and ward between the donee and the donor, a gift of her property within a month before her death by an infant aged twenty, of business habits, firm will, and fully capable of managing her own affairs, to a relative with whom she had been residing from her father's death, for a period of five months until her own death, is not invalid. TAYLOR *v.* JOHNSTON - - 19 Ch. D. 603

II. INFANT—CONTRACTS.

1. —— **Apprenticeship Deed**—*Contract not for Benefit of Infant—Employers and Workmen Act, 1875 (38 & 39 Vict. c. 90), ss. 5, 6.*] An infant was apprenticed by a deed containing a provision that the master should not be liable to pay wages to the apprentice so long as his business should be interrupted or impeded by or in consequence of any turn-out, and that the apprentice might during any such turn-out employ himself in any other manner or with any other person for his own benefit:—*Held*, that, this provision not being for the benefit of the infant, the apprenticeship deed could not be enforced against the infant under the Employers and Workmen Act, 1875, ss. 5, 6. MEAKIN *v.* MORRIS - 12 Q. B. D. 352

2. —— **Compromise.**] An order having been made approving, on behalf of infant Defendants, a compromise which was objected to by their guardian and opposed by their counsel:—*Held*, that the Court had no jurisdiction to enforce a compromise against infants against the opinion of their advisers, and that the order must be discharged. *In re* BIRCHALL. WILSON *v.* BIRCHALL
[16 Ch. D. 41

3. —— **Necessaries**—*Evidence.*] Where an

II. INFANT—CONTRACTS—*continued.*

infant is sued for the price of goods supplied to him on credit, he may, for the purpose of shewing that they were not necessaries, give evidence that, when the order was given, he was already sufficiently supplied with goods of a similar description, and it is immaterial whether the Plaintiff did or did not know of the existing supply.—*Ryder* v. *Wombwell* (Law Rep. 3 Ex. 90) dissented from. BARNES *v.* TOYE 13 Q. B. D. 410

III. INFANT—CUSTODY.

1. —— **Infants Custody Act**—*Habeas Corpus*—*36 & 37 Vict. c. 12, s. 1*—*Judicature Act, 1873 (36 & 37 Vict. c. 66), s. 25, sub-s. 10.*] In the exercise of its discretion under 36 & 37 Vict. c. 12, s. 1, and sect. 25, sub-sect. 10 of the Judicature Act, 1873 (36 & 37 Vict. c. 66), the Court will look at all the surrounding circumstances before they will accede to the application of the father of a female child of tender years to remove her from the custody of the mother and other relations whose conduct with regard to the child is unimpeached, and place her under his control.—A mariner who had no fixed home, and who had already married a woman who left him and went to America more than seven years before and (as he said) died there, went through the ceremony of marriage with another woman at a registry-office at Portsmouth. Shortly after her marriage, the second wife, being informed by a stranger that she had received a letter from the first wife after the ceremony at the registry-office, quitted her supposed husband, and went to reside with her parents at Southampton, where she gave birth to a female child. She afterwards took proceedings against her husband for bigamy; but, for want of proof that the first wife was living at the time of the second marriage, these became abortive.—The child having reached the age of nine, the father (without shewing any efforts to ascertain whether his first wife was living or not) applied to a Judge at Chambers for a habeas corpus to obtain its custody. The Judge refused the application. The father appealed.—The Court,—not being satisfied that the second was a valid marriage, or that the father was in a position properly to maintain and educate the child:—*Held*, that the Judge had wisely exercised his discretion, and dismissed the appeal, and also that the failure of the prosecution for bigamy was not entitled to any weight upon a motion of this kind. *In re* ETHEL BROWN
[13 Q. B. D. 614

2. —— **Infants Custody Act** (36 & 37 Vict. c. 12), s. 1—*Order "till further order"—Subsequent Application to vary—Appeal.*] When an order is made under sect. 1 of the Infants Custody Act, 1873, on the petition of a mother, giving the custody of an infant child to her "until further order," an application to vary the order by reason of something subsequent to its date should be made, not by way of appeal, but by motion before the Judge of first instance. Such a motion can be made by the Respondent to the original petition. The provision of sect. 1 of the Act, that the application shall be made by the mother by her next friend, applies only to the original petition. *In re* HOLT - - 16 Ch. D. 115

3. —— **Infants Custody Act** (36 & 37 Vict.

III. INFANT—CUSTODY—*continued.*

c. 12), *s.* 1—*Right of Mother—Breach of Marital Duty by Father.*] In determining whether the custody of an infant child ought to be given to or retained by the mother, the Court will take into consideration three matters—the paternal right, the marital duty, and the interest of the child.— For this purpose the marital duty includes, not only the duty which the husband and wife owe to each other, but the responsibility of each of them towards their children so to live that the children shall have the benefit of the joint care and affection of both father and mother. In a case where a father had committed a breach of the marital duty as thus defined :—*Held*, for this among other reasons, that the mother, in whose custody two children of the marriage of tender years were, ought to retain the custody until further order. *In re* ELDERTON   -   25 Ch. D. 220

4. —— **Mother of Illegitimate Child.**] A woman placed her illegitimate female child soon after its birth with N. and wife, who were labouring people, intending to pay them for it. She fell into ill health and was unable to continue her payments, but N. and wife continued to maintain the child till it was nearly seven years old. The mother then applied to have the child delivered to her, which N. and wife refused. She therefore applied for a habeas corpus, which was refused by North, J., but granted by a Divisional Court. N. and wife appealed. The mother, who was a kept mistress, did not propose that the child should live with her, but with a respectable married sister, whose husband was in a station superior to that of N. :—*Held*, that the appeal must be dismissed, for that the mother of an illegitimate infant has a natural right to its custody, which will be regarded by the Court. THE QUEEN *v.* NASH   -   10 Q. B. D. 454

IV. INFANT—EDUCATION.

1. —— **Father's Authority—***Infant above Sixteen—Free Access to and by Mother restricted—Jurisdiction of Court—*12 *Car.* 2, *c.* 24.] A father has a legal right to control and direct the education and bringing up of his children until they attain the age of twenty-one years, even although they are wards of Court, and the Court will not interfere with him in the exercise of his paternal authority, except (1) where by his gross moral turpitude he forfeits his rights, or (2) where he has by his conduct abdicated his paternal authority, or (3) where he seeks to remove his children, being wards of Court, out of the jurisdiction without the consent of the Court.—A father put restrictions on the intercourse between his daughter in her seventeenth year, who was a ward of Court, and her mother, on the plea that he believed the mother would alienate the daughter's affections from him. The Court refused to interfere. *In re* AGAR-ELLIS. AGAR-ELLIS *v.* LASCELLES   [24 Ch. D. 317

2. —— **Religious Education —** *Guardian — Wishes of deceased Father — Abandonment of Father's Right.*] An Englishman, who was a Protestant, in October, 1869, married in Germany a German lady who was a Roman Catholic. Previously to the marriage a written agreement was signed by them both, which provided that the

IV. INFANT—EDUCATION—*continued.*

children (if any) of the marriage should be educated in the Roman Catholic faith. After the marriage the husband and wife lived together in Germany. He never attended a Protestant place of worship, but often went to mass with his wife. There were three children of the marriage—a daughter born in 1871, a son born in 1873, and another daughter born, just after the death of the father, in April, 1876. The first two children were, with the father's knowledge, baptized as Roman Catholics, and, in the case of the son, a Roman Catholic priest in England, whom the father knew, acted as godfather at the request of the father himself. The father allowed the mother to bring up the two children as Roman Catholics. He died intestate, and had not appointed any guardian to his children. His only property was some real estate in Lancashire, worth more than £2000 a year, which passed to his infant son as his heir-at-law, subject to the life estate of the paternal grandfather, who died in 1881. The mother had no fortune of her own. She, as next friend of the infant son, in 1882 took out a summons for the appointment of a guardian and the settlement of a scheme for his maintenance and education. She desired that he should be educated in the Roman Catholic faith. The paternal relations, on the contrary, wished that the infant should be brought up as a Protestant :—*Held*, that the father by his conduct had abandoned his right to have the child brought up in his own faith, and had indicated a wish that he should be brought up as a Roman Catholic :—*Held*, also, that under the circumstances it would be most for the benefit of the infant that he should be educated in the Roman Catholic faith.—*Hawksworth* v. *Hawksworth* (Law Rep. 6 Ch. 539), *Andrews* v. *Salt* (Law Rep. 8 Ch. 622), and *Hill* v. *Hill* (10 W. R. 400) considered. *In re* CLARKE   21 Ch. D. 817

3. —— **Religious Education —** *Jurisdiction.*] Infants interested in real estate in England, whose father was dead, were living in charge of their mother, who was resident out of the jurisdiction, and was one of their testamentary guardians. At the instance of their other two guardians an order was made declaring in what faith they ought to be educated. *In re* MONTAGU. *In re* WROUGHTON. MONTAGU *v.* FESTING 28 Ch. D. 82

V. INFANT—GUARDIAN.

1. —— **Jurisdiction—***Grandchild born Abroad of natural-born British Subject—Status of British Subject—*7 *Anne, c.* 5—4 *Geo.* 2, *c.* 21, *s.* 1—13 *Geo.* 3, *c.* 21, *s.* 1—*International Comity.*] If an infant be born abroad whose paternal grandfather was a natural-born British subject, the Court has jurisdiction to appoint a guardian of such infant, although the infant is resident abroad and has no property in this country.—A Frenchwoman, who was the mother of such an infant, and entitled by the law of France to the status of natural guardian of the infant, was not a person who would have been appointed guardian if she and the infant had been domiciled in England, and she had brought proceedings in the French Courts for the appointment of guardians, which proceedings had been directed to stand over until it should be ascertained what course the English Courts would adopt :—

V. INFANT—GUARDIAN—*continued.*

Held, by Kay, J., that this was a case in which the English Court should exercise its jurisdiction; and a guardian of the infant appointed accordingly; and *held* by the Court of Appeal, that under the circumstances the decision of the Court below was right. *In re* WILLOUGHBY - 30 Ch. D. 324

2. —— **Voucher of Items of Expenditure.**] H. and C. were trustees and executors of a will, and guardians of the testator's daughters. The daughters during their infancy were maintained by C., and H. allowed him to receive the income for that purpose. After they attained majority judgment was given for administration of the testator's estate, in which the usual accounts of the personal estate were directed, and an inquiry how and by whom each of the daughters was maintained during infancy, and what was proper to be allowed and to whom out of the income of her share for her maintenance and education. A dispute having arisen in taking the accounts and inquiry, H. applied for a declaration that the receipts by C. of the income of the shares of the daughters for maintenance were a good discharge to H., and that H. was not to be called upon to produce vouchers in respect of the particular manner in which the income was applied. Kay, J., made an order expressing the opinion of the Court that the accounts of the trustees should be taken as directed by the judgment as between guardian and ward, and ordering H. to pay the costs of the application :—*Held,* on appeal, that H., as trustee, was not discharged by the evidence of payment of the income to C., as a guardian, but that under the inquiry H. was not bound to vouch the items of expenditure; and if it was shewn that C. had properly maintained and educated the children, the sum proper for that purpose would be allowed against the balance found due on the account, without vouching the details of the application. *In re* EVANS. WELCH *v.* CHANNELL 26 Ch. D. 58

VI. INFANT—MAINTENANCE.

1. —— **Accumulations** *for Twenty-one Years* —*Tenant for Life*—*Infants in Remainder*—*Allowance for Benefit of Infants.*] A testator left property to the value of £10,000 a year to be accumulated for twenty-one years, and directed the accumulations to be laid out in the purchase of land, to be then held in trust for Sir H. Havelock for life, and afterwards for his eldest son for life and his first and other sons in tail, with a similar trust for Sir H. Havelock's second son and his issue, with subsequent limitations over :—*Held,* that as Sir H. Havelock was possessed of a moderate income only, which was insufficient for the maintenance and education of his sons, to fit them for their prospective positions in life, a sum of £2700 per annum should be allowed him for the benefit of the infants. HAVELOCK *v.* HAVELOCK. *In re* ALLAN 17 Ch. D. 807

2. —— **Accumulations** — *Defeasible Estate*— *Lord Cranworth's Act* (23 & 24 *Vict. c.* 145), *s.* 26.] Property was bequeathed to trustees in trust for an infant, with a gift over in case of his death under twenty-one.—The trustees accumulated the income of the property not required for his maintenance, in pursuance of the powers given by sect. 26 of Lord Cranworth's Act.—The infant

VI. INFANT—MAINTENANCE—*continued.*

died under twenty-one.—*Held,* that the accumulations of income to the time of the death of the infant, belonged to the infant, and were not to be held for the benefit of the remainderman who ultimately became entitled to the property from which the accumulations arose. *In re* BUCKLEY'S TRUSTS - 22 Ch. D. 583

3. —— **Allowance beyond Provision in Will**— *Trust for Accumulation of Surplus Income*— *Jurisdiction on Summons.*] A testator gave the residue of his estate to trustees, upon trust out of the income to pay an annuity of £220 to his widow, and then to pay to his daughter two yearly sums of £100 for the maintenance and education of her infant son and daughter respectively (by a former marriage), as regarded the son so long as he should be under twenty-five, and as regarded the daughter so long as she should be under twenty-one or unmarried. The residue of the income was to be accumulated during the life of the widow, and on her death the testator, after certain provisions for his son and daughter, directed his trustees to pay £10,000 to his daughter's son on his attaining twenty-five; and to pay to her daughter £10,000 on her attaining twenty-one, or marrying under that age, and in the event of her dying before she should have attained twenty-one or married, the £10,000 was to fall into the residue. And the testator gave the residue of the trust estate equally between his daughter and her two children.—Upon a summons taken out after the testator's death in the matter of and on behalf of the infants, with the consent of the testator's widow (who was seventy-seven years of age), and of their mother and her second husband (so far as they were able to consent), an order was made increasing the allowances for the maintenance and education of the infant son and daughter by £150 and £120 per annum respectively, to be paid out of the income of the estate and the accumulations thereof.—But it was ordered that the trustees should hold the interests of the infants respectively under the testator's will as a security for the purpose of recouping to any person entitled thereto such sums of money as would be equivalent to the sums which would have arisen from such part of the income as should be applied in payment of the increased allowances, in case the same, instead of having been so applied, had been accumulated as directed by the will. *In re* COLGAN - 19 Ch. D. 305

4. —— **Contingent Legacy** — *Directions for Accumulation of Income until happening of Contingency*—"*Contrary Intention*" — *Conveyancing and Law of Property Act,* 1881 (44 & 45 *Vict. c.* 41), *s.* 43.] A testator gave a fund to trustees, on trust for all the children of A. equally, who being sons should attain twenty-one, or being daughters should attain twenty-one, or marry, with benefit of survivorship amongst them, and he directed his trustees to accumulate the income of the shares of the children, and to pay the same to them as and when their presumptive shares should become payable under the previous trust :—*Held,* that the will did not express a "contrary intention" within the meaning of sect. 43 of the Conveyancing Act, 1881, and.

VI. INFANT—MAINTENANCE—*continued.*

that, the children being infants and unmarried, the trustees might at their discretion apply the income of the trust fund in or towards the maintenance and education of the infants. *In re* THATCHER'S TRUSTS -   **26 Ch. D. 426**

5. —— Contingent Legacy—*Interim Income —Conveyancing Act,* 1881, *s.* 43.] Trustees cannot, under sect. 43 of the Conveyancing Act, 1881, apply the income of an infant's contingent legacy for the benefit of the infant, unless the income will go along with the capital of the legacy if and when such capital vests. *In re* JUDKIN'S TRUSTS   **25 Ch. D. 743**

6. —— Contingent Legacy—*Interim Income —Conveyancing and Law of Property Act,* 1881 (44 & 45 *Vict. c.* 41), *s.* 43.] Sect. 43 of the Conveyancing and Law of Property Act, 1881, empowering trustees to apply towards the maintenance of an infant the income of property held in trust for him contingently on his attaining the age of twenty-one years, does not authorize the allowance of maintenance where, apart from the Act, the infant on attaining twenty-one would only be entitled to the legacy without interest.—*In re* Cotton (1 Ch. D. 232) and *In re* George (5 Ch. D. 837) discussed. *In re* DICKSON. HILL *v.* GRANT   **28 Ch. D. 291; 29 Ch. D. 331**

7. —— Contingent Legacy — *Jurisdiction* — *Discretion of Trustees.*] A female infant was entitled contingently on her attaining twenty-one, or marrying, to a fund of which her deceased mother had been tenant for life. The trustees had power "to apply all or any part" of the income (about £598 a year) for her maintenance and education. On a summons in the matter of the infant, Bacon, V.C., held that he had jurisdiction to control the discretion of the trustees as to the quantum to be allowed, and made an order on them to pay £400 a year to the father for her maintenance and education. The trustees appealed, and in answer to an inquiry by the Court stated their intention to allow £250 to the father for her maintenance and education:—*Held,* that the order of the Vice-Chancellor was irregular, and must be discharged, the Court having no jurisdiction on a summons in the matter of an infant to make any order for payment by trustees or other persons.—Whether the Court could control the discretion of the trustees as to the amount to be allowed for maintenance and education, so long as such discretion was honestly exercised, *quære. In re* LOFTHOUSE   **29 Ch. D. 921**

VII. INFANT—PROPERTY.

Management.] *By* 44 & 45 *Vict. c.* 41 (*Conveyancing Act,* 1881).

Sect. 41. *Where a person in his own right seised of or entitled to land for an estate in fee simple, or for any leasehold interest at a rent, is an infant, the land shall be deemed to be a settled estate within the Settled Estates Act,* 1877.

Sect. 42—(1.) *If and as long as any person who would but for this section be beneficially entitled to the possession of any land is an infant, and being a woman is also unmarried, the trustees appointed for this purpose by the settlement, if any, or if there are none so appointed, then the persons, if any, who*

VII. INFANT—PROPERTY— *continued.*

are for the time being under the settlement trustees with power of sale of the settled land, or of part thereof, or with power of consent to or approval of the exercise of such a power of sale, or if there are none, then any persons appointed as trustees for this purpose by the Court, on the application of a guardian or next friend of the infant, may enter into and continue in possession of the land; and in every such case the subsequent provisions of this section shall apply.

(2.) *The trustees shall manage or superintend the management of the land, with full power to fell timber or cut underwood from time to time in the usual course for sale, or for repairs or otherwise, and to erect, pull down, rebuild, and repair houses, and other buildings and erections, and to continue the working of mines, minerals, and quarries which have usually been worked, and to drain or otherwise improve the land or any part thereof, and to insure against loss by fire, and to make allowances to and arrangements with tenants and others, and to determine tenancies, and to accept surrenders of leases and tenancies, and generally to deal with the land in a proper and due course of management; but so that, where the infant is impeachable for waste, the trustees shall not commit waste, and shall cut timber on the same terms only, and subject to the same restrictions, on and subject to which the infant could, if of full age, cut the same.*

(3.) *The trustees may from time to time, out of the income of the land, including the produce of the sale of timber and underwood, pay the expenses incurred in the management, or in the exercise of any power conferred by this section, or otherwise in relation to the land, and all outgoings not-payable by any tenant or other person, and shall keep down any annual sum, and the interest of any principal sum, charged on the land.*

(4.) *The trustees may apply at discretion any income which, in the exercise of such discretion, they deem proper, according to the infant's age, for his or her maintenance, education, or benefit, or pay thereout any money to the infant's parent or guardian, to be applied for the same purposes.*

(5.) *The trustees shall lay out the residue of the income of the land in investment on securities on which they are by the settlement, if any, or by law, authorized to invest trust money, with power to vary investments; and shall accumulate the income of the investments so made in the way of compound interest, by from time to time similarly investing such income and the resulting income of investments: and shall stand possessed of the accumulated fund arising from income of the land and from investments of income on the trusts following* (namely):

  (i.) *If the infant attains the age of twenty-one years, then in trust for the infant;*

  (ii.) *If the infant is a woman and marries while an infant, then in trust for her separate use, independently of her husband, and so that her receipt after she marries, and though still an infant, shall be a good discharge; but*

  (iii.) *If the infant dies while an infant, and being a woman without having been married, then, where the infant was, under a settlement, tenant for life, or by*

VII. **INFANT—PROPERTY**——*continued.*

purchase tenant in tail or tail male or tail female, on the trusts, if any, declared of the accumulated fund by that settlement; but where no such trusts are declared, or the infant has taken the land from which the accumulated fund is derived by descent, and not by purchase, or the infant is tenant for an estate in fee simple, absolute or determinable, then in trust for the infant's personal representatives as part of the infant's personal estate;

but the accumulations, or any part thereof, may at any time be applied as if the same were income arising in the then current year.

(6.) *Where the infant's estate or interest is in an undivided share of land, the powers of this section relative to the land may be exercised jointly with persons entitled to possession of, or having power to act in relation to the other undivided share or shares.*

(7.) *This section applies only if and as far as a contrary intention is not expressed in the instrument under which the interest of the infant arises, and shall have effect subject to the terms of that instrument and to the provisions therein contained.*

(8.) *This section applies only where that instrument comes into operation after the commencement of this Act.*

Sect. 43.—(1.) *Where any property is held by trustees in trust for an infant, either for life, or for any greater interest, and whether absolutely, or contingently on his attaining the age of twenty-one years, or on the occurrence of any event before his attaining that age, the trustees may, at their sole discretion, pay the infant's parent or guardian, if any, or otherwise apply for or towards the infant's maintenance, education, or benefit, the income of that property, or any part thereof, whether there is any other fund applicable to the same purpose, or any person bound by law to provide for the infant's maintenance or education, or not.*

(2.) *The trustees shall accumulate all the residue of that income in the way of compound interest, by investing the same and the resulting income thereof from time to time on securities on which they are by the settlement, if any, or by the Court, authorized to invest trust money, and shall hold those accumulations for the benefit of the person who ultimately becomes entitled to the property from which the same arise; but so that the trustees may at any time, if they think fit, apply those accumulations, or any part thereof, as if the same were income arising in the then current year.*

(3.) *This section applies only and if as far as a contrary intention is not expressed in the instrument under which the interest of the infant arises, and shall have effect subject to the terms of that instrument and to the provisions therein contained.*

(4.) *This same applies whether that instrument comes into operation before or after the commencement of this Act.*

1. —— **Real Estate**—*Power of Court to mortgage for Repairs.*] When an infant was absolutely entitled subject to certain trusts to the beneficial interest in real estate, the legal estate

VII. **INFANT—PROPERTY**—*continued.*

being in trustees:— *Held,* that the Court had jurisdiction to direct the raising of money by means of a mortgage of the estate for the purpose of paying the cost of repairs certified by the Chief Clerk to be absolutely necessary. *In re* JACKSON. JACKSON *v.* TALBOT   **21 Ch. D. 786**

2. —— **Real Estate**—*Sale of Infant's Property—Discretion of Trustees—Large Increase of Income—Refusal of Court to order a Sale.*] Two trustees having power to sell the freehold property of an infant at the request of the guardians, and one trustee having declined upon such request to exercise the power of sale, the Court refused to control the discretion of the trustees by ordering them to sell the estate—there being no absolute necessity for raising money and the existing income being sufficient to keep down the charges upon the estate—notwithstanding that the effect of the sale would be to increase very considerably the income of the property. MARQUIS CAMDEN *v.* MURRAY - **16 Ch. D. 161**

3. —— **Surrender of Lease** — 11 *Geo.* 4 & 1 *Will.* 4, c. 65, ss. 12, 14.] The provisions of the Act 11 Geo. 4 & 1 Will. 4, c. 65, for the surrender of a lease to which an infant is entitled, apply to a lease to which an infant is only beneficially entitled, the legal estate being vested in a trustee for him. *In re* GRIFFITHS **29 Ch. D. 248**

VIII. **INFANT—SETTLEMENT.**

—— **Ward of Court** — *Form of Settlement — Infants Settlements Act (18 & 19 Vict. c. 43)— Settlement "upon" Marriage—Contempt—Power to enforce Settlement against Ward.*] A gentleman having, in wilful defiance of an order of the Court, married an infant ward of Court, the usual directions were given for a settlement of her property, and a settlement was prepared which provided that the power of testamentary appointment given to her in default of issue should not be exercised in favour of the husband. The wife objected to this exclusion of the husband, and to the proposed trustees, with whom she was not on friendly terms, and she refused to execute the settlement unless it was altered in these particulars. There was no objection to the trustees except her personal dislike to them. On an application in the matter of the infant and under the Infants Settlements Act (18 & 19 Vict. c. 43), Kay, J., made an order for the husband and wife to execute the settlement as it stood.—The wife appealed. — *Held,* by Earl Selborne, L.C., and Fry, L.J. (dubitante Cotton, L.J.), that under the Act 18 & 19 Vict. c. 43, a settlement of an infant's property may be made on the occasion of his or her marriage after the marriage has taken place. —*Held,* by Cotton and Fry, L.JJ. (absente Earl of Selborne, L.C.), that the wife ought not to be prevented from exercising in favour of her husband the power of testamentary appointment in default of issue, and that it was desirable not to appoint trustees with whom she was on unpleasant terms, and that the settlement ought to be modified in these respects; and the wife being willing to execute the settlement so modified, the Court declined to decide whether she could be compelled to execute it. *In re* SAMPSON AND WALL, INFANTS -   -   **25 Ch. D. 482**

Z

IX. INFANT—WARD OF COURT.

1. —— Administration Action—*Payment into Court—Summons for Appointment of Guardian.*] In an administration action to which an infant was not a party, moneys were paid in to her separate account:—*Held*, that this was sufficient to constitute the infant a ward of Court.—A summons for the appointment of a guardian to the infant was taken out before the action, and upon the hearing of the summons no order was made, but, upon the suggestion of the Judge, an arrangement was made as to access to the infant.—*Semble*, this was of itself sufficient to constitute the infant a ward of Court. DE PEREDA *v*. DE MANCHA　-　-　19 Ch. D. 451

2. —— Alien—*Infant Member of Class mentioned in Title to Account.*] A fund was carried over in an administration action to a separate account, intituled "The account of A. B., and of X. Y., and his issue," to answer a settled legacy under the will of the testator, wherein A. B. and X. Y. had life interests.—X. Y. was a domiciled Frenchman, and he died leaving issue three daughters only, who were all French and married to Frenchmen, two of them having married under age, and one being still an infant. A. B. having also died, these three daughters and their husbands petitioned for payment out to them of their respective shares :—*Held*, that the Court would not in the exercise of its discretion treat the two daughters who had married under age as wards of Court.—*Semble*, the carrying of a fund to separate account of an infant in an action to which the infant is not a party will not constitute such infant a ward of Court, and even if such carrying over would have constituted a natural born British subject a ward of Court, it would not have that effect in the case of an alien not resident in this country.—Observations on *De Pereda* v. *De Mancha* (19 Ch. D. 451). BROWN *v*. COLLINS
[25 Ch. D. 56

3. —— Out of Jurisdiction—*Leave to take Ward of Court out of the Jurisdiction.*] A resident in Jamaica died leaving two children, who were born there, and resided there with their mother till 1875, when the elder, a daughter, was sent to England to be educated. The mother came to England in 1876 to place her son at school, and returned to Jamaica in 1878. In 1880 she came to England to see her children and had remained there, the daughter, upon leaving school, living with her. With the above exceptions the mother had always lived in Jamaica, and regarded it as her home. She now wished to return thither permanently, and to take with her the daughter aged twenty years and three months, the son, who was apprenticed to an engineer, remaining in England. The children were wards of Court, and the mother had been appointed by the Court sole guardian :—*Held*, by Kay, J., that the Court would not allow a ward of Court to be taken out of the jurisdiction except under very special circumstances, and that there were not in the present case any such special circumstances, as would justify giving the permission :—*Held*, on appeal, that leave may be given to take a ward out of the jurisdiction without a case of necessity being shewn, the Court having only to be satisfied that the step is for the benefit of the ward, and

IX. INFANT—WARD OF COURT—*continued.*
that there is sufficient security that future orders will be obeyed. Leave was accordingly given upon a relative resident in England being appointed guardian along with the mother. *In re* CALLAGHAN. ELLIOTT *v*. LAMBERT 28 Ch. D. 186

INFANT—Adjudication of bankruptcy
[18 Ch. D. 109
　See BANKRUPTCY—TRADER. 3.

—— Bailment to—Larceny　-　15 Q. B. D. 323
　See CRIMINAL LAW—LARCENY. 2.

—— Compromise—How far binding　6 P. D. 219
　See PRACTICE—PROBATE—COMPROMISE.

—— Custody—Covenant in separation deed
[18 Ch. D. 670 ; 28 Ch. D. 606
　See HUSBAND AND WIFE—SEPARATION DEED. 1, 5.

—— Joint tenant—Severance　-　28 Ch. D. 416
　See JOINT TENANT. 1.

—— Maintenance—Legacy　16 Ch. D. 44, 47
　See WILL—VESTING. 3, 5.

—— Maintenance—Right of father to income
[22 Ch. D. 521
　See SETTLEMENT—POWERS. 5.

—— Marriage settlement—Minority of husband
—Wife suing alone　-　6 Q. B. D. 122
　See HUSBAND AND WIFE—WIFE'S REAL ESTATE. 1.

—— Married female—Election　-　28 Ch. D. 124
　See ELECTION. 6.

—— Married female—Waiver of equity to settlement　-　16 Ch. D. 376
　See SETTLEMENT—EQUITY TO SETTLEMENT. 2.

—— Mortgagor—Foreclosure　-　24 Ch. D. 707 ;
[25 Ch. D. 158
　See MORTGAGE—FORECLOSURE. 8, 9.

—— Next friend　-　25 Ch. D. 243
　See PRACTICE—SUPREME COURT—NEXT FRIEND. 1.

—— Next friend—Production of accounts
[30 Ch. D. 189
　See PRACTICE — SUPREME COURT—PRODUCTION OF DOCUMENTS. 5.

—— Order for administration　28 Ch. D. 457 ;
[29 Ch. D. 913
　See PRACTICE—SUPREME COURT—CHAMBERS. 9, 10.

—— Property of—Solicitor's lien　24 Ch. D. 545
　See SOLICITOR—LIEN. 2.

—— Settled Land Act—Powers as tenant for life.
　See SETTLED LAND ACT—STATUTES.

—— Settled Land Act—Sale　24 Ch. D. 114, 129
　See SETTLED LAND ACT—DEFINITIONS. 1.

—— Settled Land Act—Sale　27 Ch. D. 552
　See SETTLED LAND ACT—DISABILITIES. 1.

—— Settlement by—Confirmation—Lunatic
[22 Ch. D. 263
　See SETTLEMENT—FUTURE PROPERTY. 3.

—— Supplemental action—Inquiry if for his benefit　-　-　26 Ch. D. 181
　See PRACTICE—SUPREME COURT—CHANGE OF PARTIES. 3.

INFANT—*continued.*

—— Trustee of stock—Vesting order
[20 Ch. D. 536
See TRUSTEE ACTS—VESTING ORDERS. 5.

INFECTIOUS DISEASES.
See METROPOLIS—MANAGEMENT ACTS—
Statutes.

INFERIOR COURTS—Jurisdiction.
See COURT—STATUTES.

—— Jurisdiction　-　-　10 Q. B. D. 504
See COURT—MAYOR'S COURT. 3.

INFERIOR COURTS JUDGMENTS EXTENSION
ACT, 1882.
See JUDGMENT—*Statutes.*

INFORMATION — English' information — At-
torney-General　-　14 Q. B. D. 195
See ATTORNEY-GENERAL OF DUCHY OF
LANCASTER.

—— Libel　-　12 Q. B. D. 320; 14 Q. B. D. 648
See CRIMINAL LAW—LIBEL. 1. 2.

INFORMER — Recovery of penalty — Offence
against Crown　7 Q. B. D. 38 ; 8 App.
See PENAL ACTION. 2.　　[Cas. 354

INFRINGEMENT—Copyright.
See Cases under COPYRIGHT.

—— Patent.
See Cases under PATENT — INFRINGE-
MENT.

—— Patent—Scotch law　8 App. Cas. 873
See SCOTCH LAW—PATENT.

—— Trade-mark.
See Cases under TRADE-MARK.

—— Trade-name.
See Cases under TRADE-NAME.

INHABITED HOUSE DUTY—Exemption—"Servant *or other person*"　6 Q. B. D. 530,
[673; 14 Q. B. D. 838
See REVENUE—HOUSE DUTY. 3, 4, 5.

INHERITANCE—Descent ex parte paterná or ex
parte materná　-　28 Ch. D. 327
See DESCENT.

—— Law of Trinidad　·　10 App. Cas. 312
See COLONIAL LAW—TRINIDAD.

INHIBITION　-　-　7 App. Cas. 240
See PRACTICE—ECCLESIASTICAL—PUBLIC
WORSHIP ACT. 1.

INJUNCTION.
See Cases under PRACTICE — SUPREME
COURT—INJUNCTION.

—— Abstraction of water　27 Ch. D. 122
·*See* WATERCOURSE. 1.

—— Action by creditor after composition—Error
in settlement of debts　23 Ch. D. 706
See BANKRUPTCY—COMPOSITION. 10.

—— Advertisement warning against infringement of patent　-　28 Ch. D. 394
See PATENT—INFRINGEMENT. 5.

—— Application of funds of trade union
See TRADE UNION.　[21 Ch. D. 194

—— Bankruptcy　-　16 Ch. D. 665
See BANKRUPTCY — STAYING PROCEED-
INGS. 1.

INJUNCTION—*continued.*

—— Committal for breach of　-　25 Ch. D. 778
See PRACTICE — SUPREME COURT—AT-
TACHMENT. 9.

—— Contract for exclusive personal service—
Procuring breach of contract
[6 Q. B. D. 333
See MASTER AND SERVANT— REMEDIES.
1.

—— Contract not to sell -　-　22 Ch. D. 835
See SPECIFIC PERFORMANCE. 3.

—— Copyright—Infringement of.
See Cases under COPYRIGHT.

—— Disqualification of alderman—Election of
successor -　-　16 Ch. D. 143
See MUNICIPAL CORPORATION—QUALIFI-
CATION.

—— Husband and wife—Separate estate—Dwell-
ing-house　-　-　24 Ch. D. 346
See HUSBAND AND WIFE — SEPARATE
ESTATE. 2.

—— Judgment creditor—Administration action
See JUDGMENT. 1.　[29 Ch. D. 557

—— Licence to use metropolitan stage carriage
[12 Q. B. D. 105
See METROPOLIS — PUBLIC CARRIAGES
ACTS.

—— Light—Obstruction of.
See Cases under LIGHT.

—— Metropolitan main drainage　17 Ch. D. 246
See METROPOLIS—MANAGEMENT ACTS.
9.

—— Mortgagor—Interference with possession
[18 Ch. D. 547
See PRACTICE—SUPREME COURT—RE-
CEIVER. 5.

—— Nuisance.
See Cases under NUISANCE.

—— Nuisance—District board　17 Ch. D. 685
See LOCAL GOVERNMENT — LOCAL AU-
THORITY. 13.

—— Patent—Infringement of.
See Cases under PATENT.

—— Receiver in another action　25 Ch. D. 723
See PRACTICE — SUPREME COURT—RE-
CEIVER. 7.

—— Registration of company　-　17 Ch. D. 638
See COMPANY—UNREGISTERED COMPANY.
8.

—— Restraining party from proceeding with
arbitration　-　-　11 Q. B. D. 30
See ARBITRATION—STAYING PROCEED-
INGS.

—— Restrictive covenants—Alteration of property　-　24 Ch. D. 180 ; 28 Ch. D. 103
See COVENANT—BREACH.

—— Sale by mortgagee　-　20 Ch. D, 220 ;
[23 Ch. D. 690 ; 24 Ch. D. 289
See MORTGAGE—POWERS. 3, 4, 5.

—— Slanderous statement about business
[26 Ch. D. 306
See DEFAMATION—SLANDER. 3.

Z 2

INJUNCTION—*continued.*

—— Soliciting customers—Expelled partner
[22 Ch. D. 504
See PARTNERSHIP—DISSOLUTION. 3.

—— Soliciting customers—Sale of goodwill
[19 Ch. D. 355; 27 Ch. D. 145
See GOODWILL. 2, 3.

—— Solicitor acting against former client'
[20 Ch. D. 733
See SOLICITOR—LIABILITIES. 1.

—— Trade circular—Infringement of patent
[25 Ch. D. 1
See PATENT—INFRINGEMENT. 2.

—— Trade-mark—Infringement.
See Cases under TRADE-MARK.

—— Trade-name—Telegraphic address
See TRADE-NAME. 1.   [30 Ch. D. 156

—— Undertaking as to damages 23 Ch. D. 644
See BANKRUPTCY—RECEIVER. 1.

—— Undertaking as to damages 27 Ch. D. 474
See PRACTICE — SUPREME COURT — IN-
JUNCTION. 10.

—— Waterworks company   28 Ch. D. 138
See WATERWORKS COMPANY—SUPPLY OF
WATER. 1.

—— Winding-up petition—Solvent company
[18 Ch. D. 555
See COMPANY—WINDING-UP ORDER. 9.

INJURIOUSLY AFFECTING LANDS — Scotch
railway   8 App. Cas. 265
See SCOTCH LAW—RAILWAY COMPANY. 5

INLAND REVENUE BUILDINGS ACT, 1881.
See REVENUE—MANAGEMENT—*Statutes.*

INN :—   Col.
  I. INNKEEPER - - - 679
  II. LICENCE. - - 680
  III. OFFENCES. - - - 683

I. INN—INNKEEPER.

1. —— **Liability**—*Property of Guest—Temporary Refreshment.*] The Plaintiff arrived at
Carlisle with the intention of spending the night
at the Defendants' hotel, which adjoined the
railway station. He delivered his luggage to
one of the porters of the hotel, but, after reading
a telegram which was waiting for him, decided
not to spend the night at Carlisle, and went into
the coffee-room to order some refreshments. He
was not able to obtain in the coffee-room exactly
what he required, and went into the station
refreshment-room, which was under the same
management as the hotel, and connected with it
by a covered passage. Shortly afterwards he went
out, telling the porter to lock up his luggage, and
it was locked up in a room near the refreshment-
room. On his return he found that part of it was
missing:—*Held*, that at the time of the loss of
the Plaintiff's goods there was no evidence of the
relation of landlord and guest between him and
the Defendants, so as to make them responsible.
STRAUSS *v.* COUNTY HOTEL AND WINE COMPANY
[12 Q. B. D. 27

2. —— **Lien**—*Effect of taking Security—Bailee
—Custody of Goods.*] An innkeeper who accepts

I. INN—INNKEEPER—*continued.*

security from his guest for the payment of hotel
charges does not waive his lien at common law
upon the goods of the guest for the amount of
such charges unless there is something in the
nature of the security, *or* in the circumstances
under which it was taken, which is inconsistent
with the existence *or* continuance of the lien
and therefore destructive of it.—An innkeeper
retaining the goods of his guest by virtue of
such lien is not bound to use greater care as to
their custody than he uses as to his own goods of
a similar description.—Observations on *Cowell* v.
Simpson (16 Ves. 275). ANGUS *v.* MCLACHLAN
[23 Ch. D. 330

II. INN—LICENCE.

The Act 45 & 46 Vict. c. 34, *amends the Beer
Dealers' Retail Licences Act, 1880, and enacts
(sect. 1) that notwithstanding anything in sect. 8
of the Wine and Beerhouse Act, 1869, or in any
other Act now in force, the licensing justices shall
be at liberty, in their free and unqualified discretion, either to refuse a certificate for any licence
for sale of beer by retail to be consumed off the
premises on any grounds appearing to them sufficient, or to grant the same to such persons as they
in the execution of their statutory powers and in
the exercise of their discretion deem fit and proper.
Sect. 2. Such certificates to be granted at annual
licensing meetings only.
Sect. 3. Act to be cited as the Beer Dealers'
Retail Licences (Amendment) Act, 1882.*

1. —— **Continuance by Owner**—*Authority to
Owner of Premises to continue the Business, where
the Occupier's Licence has been forfeited under s. 15
of the Licensing Act, 1874 (37 & 38 Vict. c. 49)—
Discretion of Justices.*] Where the occupier of a
beerhouse has forfeited his licence by being guilty
of an offence under sect. 15 of the Licensing Act,
1874 (37 & 38 Vict. c. 49), the grant by the petty
sessions of an authority to the owner to carry on
the business until the next special sessions for
licensing purposes, is in the discretion of the
justices, under sects. 1, 4, and 14 of the Licensing
Act, 1828 (9 Geo. 4, c. 61); and the person applying for such authority is not entitled to notice
under sect. 42 of the Act of 1872 (35 & 36 Vict.
c. 94) of the objections intended to be urged
against his application. THE QUEEN *v.* MOORE
[7 Q. B. D. 542

2. —— **Death of Licence-holder**—*Licence for
Sale of Exciseable Liquors—Death of Licence-holder
before Expiration of Licence—Expiration of Licence
—Application to Special Sessions—9 Geo. 4, c. 61,
ss. 4, 13, 14.*] K., licensed to sell intoxicating
liquors under 9 Geo. 4, c. 61, died on the 27th of
September. At the general annual licensing meeting on the 2nd of October application was made
by the lessees of the house for a fresh licence,
without giving the requisite notices under 35 & 36
Vict. c. 94, as there was no time to give them.
This application was rejected on the ground that
they were not in occupation of or about to occupy
the premises. K.'s licence expired on the 10th of
October. On the 13th of November W., as assignee
of the heir of K., gave notice that he would apply
at the special sessions on the 4th of December for
a new licence in respect of the house under 9 Geo. 4,
c. 61, s. 14 :—*Held*, following *Simpkin* v. *Justices*

II. INN—LICENCE—continued.

of Birmingham (Law Rep. 7 Q. B. 482), that the justices had no jurisdiction to entertain the application, as it was made after the expiration of the period for which the previous licence remained in force. WHITE v. JUSTICES OF COQUETDALE

[7 Q. B. D. 238

[But see INN—LICENCE. 6.]

3. —— "Off" Licence — Application for Licence—Value of House—3 & 4 Vict. c. 61, s. 1—Licensing Act, 1872 (35 & 36 Vict. c. 94), s. 45—Notice to Applicant of Grounds of Refusal—Wine and Beerhouse Act, 1869 (32 & 33 Vict. c. 27), s. 8.] An application for a licence to sell beer by retail not to be consumed on the premises was refused by justices, on the ground that the house was not duly qualified by law, not being of sufficient value under 3 & 4 Vict. c. 61, s. 1. The Wine and Beerhouse Act, 1869, s. 8, requires the justices, where such an application is refused on the ground that the house is not duly qualified as by law required, to specify in writing to the applicant the grounds of their decision. A minute of the decision with the grounds of it was made and read out by the chairman in Court, in the presence of the applicant, but no copy was delivered to him. On a rule for a mandamus to the justices to hear and determine the application:—Held (by Field and Cave, JJ.), that the provisions as to rating qualification for houses for the sale of beer and cider for consumption off the premises under 3 & 4 Vict. c. 61, s. 1, had not been affected by the Licensing Act, 1872, s. 45, which must be construed as applying only to premises licensed before the Act, or to be licensed under it, for the sale of intoxicating liquor thereupon.—Held, also, that, in the absence of any request by the applicant for a writing shewing the reasons for the decision of the justices, the notice was sufficient. THE QUEEN v. JUSTICES OF CUMBERLAND

[8 Q. B. D. 369

4. —— Renewal—Conviction—Forfeiture of Licence — Application by Owner of Premises to Special Sessions for Licence, Refusal of—Right of Appeal to Quarter Sessions—9 Geo. 4, c. 61, ss. 4, 14; 35 & 36 Vict. c. 94, s. 9; 37 & 38 Vict. c. 49, s. 15.] The appeal clauses of 9 Geo. 4, c. 61 (the Intoxicating Liquors Licensing Act, 1828), are incorporated in 37 & 38 Vict. c. 49 (the Licensing Act, 1874), sect. 15, and therefore when the licence of a public-house keeper is forfeited by conviction under 35 & 36 Vict. c. 94, s. 9, and the owner of the premises duly applies under 37 & 38 Vict. c. 49, s. 15, to special sessions for a licence and it is refused, he has a right of appeal to quarter sessions. THE QUEEN v. JUSTICES OF WEST RIDING

[11 Q. B. D. 417

5. —— Renewal—Mortgagor and Mortgagee—Appeal—Quarter Sessions—9 Geo. 4, c. 61, s. 27 —32 & 33 Vict. c. 27, s. 19.] The tenant and occupier of a house, licensed for the sale of beer on the premises, in 1876 assigned all his interest in the premises for the residue of his term of years, and the benefit of the licence, to the Appellants by way of first mortgage to secure the repayment of moneys advanced by them; and by the mortgage deed irrevocably constituted the Appellants his attorneys, in his name, and as his act and deed, to do all acts necessary to procure a transfer of the

II. INN—LICENCE—continued.

licence. In 1883, the moneys secured by the mortgage being still unpaid, the occupier sent a written application for a renewal of his licence to the justices at their annual licensing meeting, and they adjourned the hearing of the application. At the adjourned hearing the Appellants applied, as mortgagees and under their power of attorney, for a renewal of the licence to the occupier, who appeared, but stated that he did not wish for a renewal. No objection was made to the renewal on any of the grounds specified in 32 & 33 Vict. c. 27, which Act applied to the occupier's licence. The justices refused the application, and the Appellants appealed to quarter sessions in their own names as mortgagees, and also as attorneys of the occupier, and in his name, and for and on his behalf. At the hearing the occupier again appeared, and stated that he did not wish the licence to be renewed, and the quarter sessions thereupon affirmed the order of the licensing justices:—Held, first, that the Appellants were persons aggrieved, within 9 Geo. 4, c. 61, s. 27, by the refusal of the licensing justices to renew the occupier's licence; and were therefore entitled to appeal to quarter sessions; secondly, that upon the facts stated the licensing justices and the court of quarter sessions were bound to grant the application of the Appellants for a renewal of the licence to the occupier. GARRETT v. JUSTICES OF MIDDLESEX

[12 Q. B. D. 620

6. —— Renewal—Neglect of Occupier about to remove to apply for Renewal—Expiration of Licence—Application to Special Sessions—9 Geo. 4, c. 61, s. 14.] S., tenant of a house and licensed to sell excisable liquors therein, made over the house in June, 1881, to W., who forthwith sub-let it to B. B. applied at a special sessions for a transfer of the licence, which was opposed by S., and refused. At the time of the general licensing meeting B. was in occupation, but was about to leave owing to illness in her family, and did not apply for a renewal of the licence. She left shortly afterwards and the house was shut up, and no excisable liquors had been sold there since June. In September, after the close of the licensing meeting, the landlord learnt that the house was vacant and took possession. The licence expired on the 10th of October. The landlord afterwards let to D., who, in January, 1882, applied to a special sessions for a renewal of the licence:—Held, that B. as occupier, though not holding a licence, was a person entitled to apply at the general sessions for a renewal of the licence, and that the event mentioned in 9 Geo. 4, c. 61. s. 14, of the occupier of a house being about to quit the same neglecting to apply at the general meeting for a licence to continue to sell excisable liquors therein, had occurred, so that an application under that section could be made:—Held, also, overruling Ex parte Todd (3 Q. B. D. 407), and White v. Justices of Coquetdale (7 Q. B. D. 238), that it was not necessary that the application should be made before the expiration of the period for which the old licence was in force, and that the justices in special sessions had jurisdiction to grant the application. THE QUEEN v. JUSTICES OF LIVERPOOL　　-　　-　　- 11 Q. B. D. 638

II. INN—LICENCE—continued.

7. —— Renewal—" Off " Licences—Appeal—Beer Dealers' Retail Licences Act, 1882 (45 & 46 Vict. c. 34), s. 1.] The right of appeal to quarter sessions, from a refusal of licensing justices to renew a certificate for a licence to sell beer not to be consumed on the premises, has not been taken away by the Beer Dealers' Retail Licences Act, 1882 (45 & 46 Vict. c. 34), s. 1. THE QUEEN v. SCHNEIDER　　　-　　　11 Q. B. D. 66

8. —— Renewal—" Off " Licences—Discretion to refuse—Beer Dealers' Retail Licences Act, 1882 (45 & 46 Vict. c. 34), s. 1.] The unqualified discretion which the licensing justices have under the Beer Dealers' Retail Licences Act, 1882 (45 & 46 Vict. c. 34), s. 1, to refuse a certificate for any licence for sale of beer by retail to be consumed off the premises may be exercised, not only on an application for such certificate in respect of premises not theretofore similarly licensed, but also on an application for such certificate by way of renewal. - THE QUEEN v. KAY　10 Q. B. D. 213

9. —— Renewal—Proceedings where no Notice of Opposition—Objection not made in open Court—Licensing Act, 1872 (35 & 36 Vict. c. 94), s. 42.] By sect. 42 of the Licensing Act, 1872, justices at the general annual licensing meeting shall not entertain any objection to the renewal of a licence, or take any evidence with respect to the renewal thereof, unless written notice of an intention to oppose the renewal has been served upon the holder of the licence in the prescribed manner: " Provided that the justices may, notwithstanding that no notice has been given, on an objection being made, adjourn the granting of any licence to a future day, and require the attendance of the holder of the licence on such day, when the case will be heard and the objection considered, as if the notice hereinbefore prescribed had been given:"—Held, that an objection to the renewal of a licence made privately to justices before they came into court at the general annual licensing meeting was not a good " objection made " within the meaning of the proviso to sect. 42, and that, therefore, the justices had no power to adjourn the case. THE QUEEN v. JUSTICES OF MERTHYR TYDVIL - - -　　　14 Q. B. D. 584

III. INN—OFFENCES.

The Act 47 & 48 Vict. c. 29 (Licensing Evidence Act, 1884), extends sect. 41 of 35 & 36 Vict. c. 94, with respect to licences wilfully withheld by holders.

1. —— Conviction—Fine or Imprisonment—No Order of Distress—35 & 36 Vict. c. 94, ss. 3, 51—Summary Jurisdiction Act, 1879 (42 & 43 Vict. c. 49), s. 21, sub-s. 3.] The Summary Jurisdiction Act, 1879 (42 & 43 Vict. c. 49), s. 21, sub-s. 3, does not apply to the Licensing Act, 1872 (35 & 36 Vict. c. 94), sect. 3, sub-sect. 1, and sect. 51, sub-sect. 2, so as to give justices jurisdiction to order imprisonment for non-payment of a penalty exceeding £5, under sect. 3, without first ordering a distress.—By the Licensing Act, 1872, sect. 2, an unlicensed person selling intoxicating liquors is liable to a penalty or to imprisonment:—Held, that a conviction imposing a penalty exceeding £5, and, in default of payment, imprisonment, was bad. In re CLEW　-　- 8 Q. B. D. 511

III. INN—OFFENCES—continued.

2. —— " Sale by Retail "—Club—Intoxicating Liquors—Licensing Act, 1872 (35 & 36 Vict. c. 94), s. 3.] The Appellant was manager of an institution carried on bonâ fide as a club, under rules by which members paid an entrance fee and subscription; trustees were appointed in whom all the club property was vested, and there was a committee of management (for whom the Appellant acted) to conduct the general business. The club was not licensed for the sale of intoxicating liquors, but these were supplied; at fixed prices, to members for consumption on and off the premises, 33 per cent. above the cost price being charged for liquors to be consumed off the premises, and the money produced thereby going to the general funds of the club. The Appellant having, in the course of his employment as manager, supplied intoxicating liquors to a member (who paid for them) for consumption off the premises:—Held, that the Appellant did not " sell by retail " intoxicating liquors within the meaning of sect. 3 of the Licensing Act, 1872, and therefore was not liable to conviction for an offence under the section. GRAFF v. EVANS
[8 Q. B. D. 373

3. —— Sale to Drunken Person—Knowledge of Condition of Customer—Licensing Act, 1872 (35 & 36 Vict. c. 94), s. 13.] The Licensing Act, 1872, sect. 13, makes it an offence for any licensed person to sell any intoxicating liquor to any drunken person. A publican sold intoxicating liquor to a drunken person who had given no indication of intoxication, and without being aware that the person so served was drunk :—Held, that the prohibition was absolute, and that knowledge of the condition of the person served with liquor was not necessary to constitute the offence. CUNDY v. LE COCQ - - - 13 Q. B. D. 207

4. —— Suffering Gaming — Licensing Act, 1872 (35 & 36 Vict. c. 94)—Knowledge of Servant—Mens rea.] Where gaming had taken place upon licensed premises to the knowledge of a servant of the licensed person employed on the premises, but there was no evidence to shew any connivance or wilful blindness on the part of the licensed person, and it did not appear that the servant was in charge of the premises :—Held, that the justices were right in refusing to convict the licensed person of suffering gaming on the premises under the Licensing Act, 1872, s. 17.—Mullins v. Collins (Law Rep. 9 Q. B. 292) discussed. SOMERSET v. HART　12 Q. B. D. 360

5. —— Sunday Closing (Wales) Act, 1881 (44 & 45 Vict. c. 61), s. 3—Commencement of Act.] By sect. 3 of the Sunday Closing (Wales) Act, 1881 (44 & 45 Vict. c. 61), passed on the 27th of August, 1881, " This Act shall commence and come into operation with respect to each division or place in Wales on the day next appointed for the holding of the general annual licensing meeting for that division or place" :—Held, that " the day next appointed " is the day which shall, after the passing of the Act, be next appointed for the holding of the meeting. RICHARDS v. MCBRIDE
[8 Q. B. D. 119

6. —— Sunday Closing (Wales) Act, 1881 (44 & 45 Vict. c. 61)—" Christmas Day and Good Friday "] By sect. 3 of the Licensing Act, 1874

III. INN- OFFENCES—*cont.'nued.*

(37 & 38 Vict. c. 49), " all premises in which intoxicating liquors are sold by retail, wherever situate, shall be closed on Christmas Day and Good Friday, as if Christmas Day and Good Friday were respectively Sunday."—By sect. 1 of the Sunday Closing (Wales) Act, 1881 (44 & 45 Vict. c. 61), all such premises are to be closed "during the whole of Sunday":—*Held,* that the word "Sunday" in the Welsh Act only has its ordinary meaning, and that a conviction under that Act for unlawfully keeping open premises for the sale of intoxicating liquors on Christmas Day was bad. FORSDIKE *v.* COLQUHOUN

[11 Q. B. D. 71

INNUENDO—Libel   -   **7 App. Cas. 741**
See DEFAMATION—LIBEL. 1.

—— Slander   -   -   **6 App. Cas. 156**
See DEFAMATION—SLANDER. 2.

INQUEST—Obstruction—Burning dead body
[12 Q. B. D. 247; 13 Q. B. D. 331
See CRIMINAL LAW—MISDEMEANOR. 1, 2.

—— Refusal to hold   -   - **9 Q. B. D. 689**
See CORONER.

INQUISITION—Lunatic   -   **18 Ch. D. 26;**
[27 Ch. D. 116; 30 Ch. D. 320
See LUNATIC—INQUISITION. 1, 2.

INSANITY.
See Cases under LUNATIC.

—— Nullity of marriage   -   - **10 P. D. 80**
See PRACTICE—DIVORCE—NULLITY OF MARRIAGE. 6.

INSOLVENCY.

—— Close of Insolvency—*After-acquired Property—Subsequent Insolvency and Bankruptcy—32 & 33 Vict. c. 83, s. 15—"Pending Matter."*] In June, 1836, C. took the benefit of the Insolvent Act (7 Geo. 4. c. 57) and obtained his discharge having executed a warrant of attorney upon which judgment was entered up. Two creditors' assignees were then appointed, one being W., a creditor. C. subsequently became three times insolvent, and in July, 1854, he became bankrupt under the Act of 1849, and obtained his certificate. He died in January, 1880. C. had married the only daughter of a man who died possessed of very considerable property a few months after his first insolvency, whereupon he became entitled, in right of his wife, to that money, which came into his possession on her death in 1877. W., the survivor of the two creditors' assignees 'under the first insolvency, and himself a creditor, now applied for leave to prove his debt in an action to administer C.'s estate:—*Held* (affirming the decision of Kay, J.), that, under the Act to provide for the winding-up of the business of the Insolvency Courts (32 & 33 Vict. c. 83), the close of the insolvency provided for by sect. 15 was intended to be an absolute close, and that if no steps were taken to postpone the closing within twelve months from the commencement of the Act, then at the expiration of twelve months from the commencement of the Act, or at the expiration of twenty years from the filing of the petition, it became the duty of the Court to refuse leave to issue execution; and by analogy it was the duty of this Court to refuse leave to prove the debts in

INSOLVENCY—*continued.*

insolvency in the administration action.—Per Jessel, M.R.: A "pending matter" in any Court of Justice means one in which some proceeding may still be taken. *In re* CLAGETT'S ESTATE. FORDHAM *v.* CLAGETT -   **20 Ch. D. 637**

—— Disqualification of alderman—Election of successor   **16 Ch. D. 143**
See MUNICIPAL CORPORATION—QUALIFICATION.

—— Evidence of—Winding-up petition
[23 Ch. D. 210
See COMPANY—WINDING-UP ORDER. 10.

—— New South Wales—Forfeiture **30 Ch. D. 119**
See SETTLEMENT—CONSTRUCTION. 5.

—— Security for costs—Trustee in bankruptcy
[28 Ch. D. 38
See PRACTICE—SUPREME COURT—SECURITY FOR COSTS. 8.

INSPECTION OF DOCUMENTS.
See Cases under PRACTICE — SUPREME COURT—PRODUCTION OF DOCUMENTS.

—— Books of company—Arbitration
[28 Ch. D. 620
See COMPANY—RECONSTRUCTION.

—— Deceased lunatic   -   **16 Ch. D. 673**
See LUNATIC—DECEASED LUNATIC.

INSPECTION OF PROPERTY   **27 Ch. D. 356**
See PRACTICE — SUPREME COURT—INSPECTION OF PROPERTY.

INSPECTION OF SHIP'S LIGHTS — Trinity masters   -   -   - **10 P. D. 40**
See PRACTICE—ADMIRALTY—INSPECTION OF PROPERTY.

INSTALMENTS—Mortgage to building society—Proof in bankruptcy   **22 Ch. D. 450**
See BANKRUPTCY—PROOF. 13.

INSURABLE INTEREST—Marine insurance
[12 Q. B. D. 564; 10 App. Cas. 263
See INSURANCE, MARINE — INSURABLE INTEREST.

INSURANCE COMPANY.
See Cases under COMPANY—LIFE INSURANCE COMPANY.

—— Income tax—" Annual profits or gains"
[14 Q. B. D. 239; 10 App. Cas. 438
See REVENUE—INCOME TAX. 9.

INSURANCE, FIRE.

1. —— Felonious Act—*Loss occasioned by the Felonious Act of the Wife of the Assured—Rights of the Insurer—Risks covered by Policy—Action maintainable without shewing that Felon has been prosecuted.*] An insurance company granted a fire policy to S., and during the currency of the policy S.'s wife feloniously burnt the property insured. The company, not admitting any claim on the policy, brought an action against S. and his wife for the damage done by the act of the wife:—*Held,* first, that the action could not be maintained, as the insurer has no rights other than those of his assured, and can enforce those only in his name and after admitting the claim on the policy. Secondly, that the action for the felony if it were maintainable was maintainable without shewing

INSURANCE, FIRE—*continued.*

that the felon had been prosecuted.—*Semble*, that a felonious burning by the wife of the assured, without his privity, is covered by the ordinary fire policy. MIDLAND INSURANCE COMPANY *v.* SMITH AND WIFE - - **6 Q. B. D. 561**

2. —— Settled Estate—*Tenant in Tail—Payment of Premiums out of Rents—Policy Moneys, who entitled to.*] During the infancy of a tenant in tail of freehold estates devised in strict settlement, part of which consisted of a corn-mill let on lease, the rents were received by his mother on his behalf, and she thereout paid the premiums necessary for keeping up a policy which had been effected in her name for insuring the mill against fire. The will contained no provision for fire insurance.—The mill having been burnt down, and it not being considered for the benefit of any person interested in the settled estates that it should be rebuilt:—*Held*, that the insurance moneys belonged to the infant tenant in tail as his personal estate, and were not to be treated as real estate for the benefit of all persons interested in the settled estates. WARWICKER *v.* BRETNALL **[23 Ch. D. 188**

3. —— Vendor and Purchaser—*Fire after Contract but before Completion—Right to Insurance Money.*] A vendor contracted with a purchaser for the sale of a house which had been insured by the vendor against fire. The contract contained no reference to the insurance. After the date of the contract but before the time fixed for completion the house was damaged by fire, and the vendor received a sum of money from the office:—*Held*, by Brett, and Cotton, L.JJ. (affirming the decision of Jessel, M.R.), James, L.J., dissentiente, that the purchaser, who had completed his contract, was not entitled as against the vendor to the benefit of the insurance. RAYNER *v.* PRESTON **[16 Ch. D. 1**

4. —— Vendor and Purchaser—*Insurance by Vendor—Fire after Contract but before Completion—Right to Insurance Moneys—Subrogation.*] According to the doctrine of subrogation, as between the insurer and the assured, the insurer is entitled to the advantage of every right of the assured, whether such right consists in contract, fulfilled or unfulfilled, or in remedy for tort capable of being insisted on or already insisted on, or in any other right, whether by way of condition or otherwise, legal or equitable, which can be, or has been, exercised or has accrued, and whether such right could or could not be enforced by the insurer in the name of the assured, by the exercise or acquiring of which right or condition the loss against which the assured is insured, can be or has been diminished.—A vendor contracted with a purchaser for the sale, at a specified sum, of a house, which had been insured by the vendor with an insurance company against fire. The contract contained no reference to the insurance. After the date of the contract, but before the date fixed for completion, the house was damaged by fire, and the vendor received the insurance money from the company. The purchase was afterwards completed, and the purchase-money agreed upon, without any abatement on account of the damage by fire, was paid to the vendor:—*Held*, in an action by the company against the vendor, that

INSURANCE, FIRE—*continued.*

the company were entitled to recover a sum equal to the insurance-money from the vendor for their own benefit. CASTELLAIN *v.* PRESTON **8 Q. B. D. [613; 11 Q. B. D. 380**

—— By mortgagee.
    See MORTGAGE—POWERS—*Statutes.*

—— Law of Canada - **7 App. Cas. 96**
    See COLONIAL LAW—CANADA—ONTARIO. 3.

—— Proof in winding-up - **17 Ch. D. 337**
    See COMPANY—PROOF. 2.

INSURANCE, LIFE:—   Col.
    I. ASSIGNMENT   688
    II. POLICY   -   -   688

—— Insurance Company.
    See COMPANY—LIFE INSURANCE COMPANY.

I. INSURANCE, LIFE—ASSIGNMENT.

1. —— Lien—*Payment of Premiums by Stranger or Part Owner—Salvage.*] When a person, not the sole beneficial owner, pays the premiums to keep up a policy of life insurance, he is entitled to a lien on the policy or its proceeds in the following cases: (1.) By contract with the beneficial owner; (2.) By reason of the right of trustees to an indemnity out of their trust property for money expended by them in its preservation; (3.) By subrogation to their right of some person who, at the request of trustees, had advanced money for the preservation of the property; (4.) By reason of the right of a mortgagee to add to his charge any money paid by him to preserve the property.—In no other cases can a lien on a policy for premiums paid be acquired either by a stranger or by a part owner of the policy.—*In re Tharp* (2 Sm. & Giff. 578, n.); *Swan* v. *Swan* (8 Price, 518); and *Hamilton* v. *Denny* (1 B. & B. 199) commented on. *In re* LESLIE. LESLIE *v.* FRENCH **[23 Ch. D. 552**

2. —— Parties—*Absence of Personal Representative of Person insured—15 & 16 Vict. c. 86, s. 44.*] In an action by an equitable mortgagee of a policy of insurance against the insurance company for payment of the policy money the Court has jurisdiction under the 44th section of the 15 & 16 Vict. c. 86, to dispense with a legal personal representative of the assured where none exists. CURTIUS *v.* CALEDONIAN FIRE AND LIFE INSURANCE COMPANY - - **19 Ch. D. 534**

II. INSURANCE, LIFE—POLICY.

1. —— Construction—*Injury by Accident—Drowning — Epileptic Fit.*] W. effected an insurance with the Defendants against accidental injury, and by the terms of the policy the Defendants agreed to pay the amount insured to W.'s legal representatives, should he sustain "any personal injury caused by accidental, external, and visible means," and the direct effect of such injury should occasion his death. The policy also contained a proviso that the insurance should not extend "to any injury caused by or arising from natural disease or weakness or exhaustion consequent upon disease." During the time the policy

II. INSURANCE, LIFE—POLICY—continued.

was in force, and whilst he was crossing and fording a stream, W. was seized with an epileptic fit and fell into the stream, and was there drowned whilst suffering from the fit, but he did not sustain any personal injury to occasion death other than drowning:—*Held,* that W.'s death was occasioned by an injury within the risk covered by the policy, and to which the proviso did not apply. WINSPEAR *v.* ACCIDENT INSURANCE COMPANY
[6 Q. B. D. 42

2. —— Construction—*Insurance against Accident—"Sole Cause of Death"—Sudden Fit—Fall from Platform upon Railway.*] A policy of insurance against death from accidental injury contained the following condition : "This policy insures payment only in case of injuries accidentally occurring from material and external causes operating upon the person of the insured, where such accidental injury is the direct and sole cause of death to the insured, but it does not insure in case of death arising from fits . . . . or any disease whatsoever arising before or at the time or following such accidental injury, whether consequent upon such accidental injury or not, and whether causing such death directly or jointly with such accidental injury."—The insured, while at a railway station, was seized with a fit and fell forwards off the platform across the railway, when an engine and carriages which were passing went over his body and killed him :—*Held,* that the death of the insured was caused by an accident within the meaning of the policy, and that the insurers were liable. LAWRENCE *v.* ACCIDENTAL INSURANCE COMPANY - - - 7 Q. B. D. 216

3. —— Validity—*Truth of Answers to Queries of Life Insurance Company—Express Warranty—"Strictly Temperate"—Matter of Fact and Matter of Opinion.*] A. applied to an insurance office to effect a policy on his life. He received a printed form of proposal containing questions. Among these was the following : "Question 7 (a) Are you temperate in your habits ? (b) and have you always been strictly so ? A. answered (a) "Temperate;" (b) "Yes." Subjoined to the printed questions was a declaration, which A. signed, to the effect that the foregoing statements were true, and that the assured agreed that this declaration should be the basis of the contract, and that if any untrue averment, &c., was made the policy was to be absolutely void and all moneys received as premium forfeited. The policy recited the above declaration as the basis of the contract. After A.'s decease the insurance company refused payment of the policy on the ground that the above-mentioned answer was false in fact. In an action on the policy :—*Held,* reversing the decision of the Court below, that the declaration of A., taken in connection with the policy, constituted an express warranty that the answer to Question 7 was true in fact; and as the evidence clearly proved that A.'s averment as to his temperance was untrue, the policy was absolutely null and void.—*Life Association of Scotland* v. *Foster* (11 Court Sess. Cas. 3rd Series, 351) distinguished.—*Hutchison* v. *National Loan Assurance Company* (7 Court Sess. Cas. 2nd Series, 467) not approved of. THOMSON *v.* WEEMS
[9 App. Cas. 671

INSURANCE, LIFE—Customs Annuity Fund
[23 Ch. D. 235
See CUSTOMS ANNUITY FUND.

—— Government, contracts of insurance by.
See NATIONAL DEBT COMMISSIONERS—Statutes.

—— Husband or wife, by.
See HUSBAND AND WIFE — MARRIED WOMEN'S PROPERTY ACTS—*Statutes.*

—— Husband, by, for benefit of wife
[23 Ch. D. 525 ; 26 Ch. D. 236
See HUSBAND AND WIFE — MARRIED WOMEN'S PROPERTY ACTS. 4, 5.

—— Insurance company.
See Cases under COMPANY — LIFE INSURANCE COMPANY.

INSURANCE, MARINE :—　　　Col.
I. CONCEALMENT　　690
II. INSURABLE INTEREST　　691
III. LOSS, PARTIAL　　691
IV. LOSS, TOTAL　　692
V. POLICY　　693
VI. RISK -　　696
VII. SALVAGE　　696

I. INSURANCE, MARINE—CONCEALMENT.

1. —— Material Fact—*Open Policies—Declaration of Shipments at less than real Value—Policies set aside.*] The concealment by the assured at the time of effecting a marine policy of insurance of a fact which is material to enable a rational underwriter, governing himself by the principles on which underwriters in practice act, to judge whether he shall accept the risk at all, or at what rate, will vitiate the policy, although the fact may not be material with regard to the risk incurred.—The Defendants effected with the Plaintiff, a Lloyd's underwriter, a series of open policies for certain specified sums to cover shipments to be declared and valued as interest might appear. The policies were effected at different dates, and were to succeed each other in the order of date. The value of the shipments was declared at considerably less than their real value, so that when the later policies were effected the earlier policies were in fact more exhausted than they would appear to be from the declarations. The undervaluation of the shipments was systematically and fraudulently made by the Defendants, and the fact that they had been so undervalued was concealed from the Plaintiff when he underwrote the later policies :—*Held,* that, under these circumstances, a jury would be justified in finding that the concealment was of a fact of which it was material that the Plaintiff should have been informed, in order to guide him in deciding whether he would underwrite these later policies or not, or at what rate ; and that on the jury so finding the Plaintiff was entitled to have such later policies set aside and cancelled. RIVAZ *v.* GERUSSI - - - 6 Q. B. D. 222

2. —— Material Fact—*Arrangement by Assured to employ a particular Lighterman—Risk on Craft.*] On policies of marine insurance on goods, which included risks on crafts and lighters, underwriters to the knowledge of the Plaintiffs

I. INSURANCE, MARINE—CONCEALMENT—
continued.

charged a higher rate of premium where the insurance was with no recourse against lightermen (which meant where the lighterage was done on the terms that the liability of the lightermen was to be less than that of common carriers, namely, for negligence only), than they charged where there was such recourse and the liability of the lightermen was to be that of common carriers. The Plaintiffs effected with the Defendant, a Lloyd's underwriter, a policy of marine insurance on goods which included risk on craft and lighters, and was not with no recourse against lightermen. At the time of effecting such policy the Plaintiffs had an arrangement with one H., by which he was to do all the Plaintiffs' lighterage on the terms that he was only to be liable for negligence:—*Held,* that if the Plaintiffs intended that the goods so insured should be landed under such arrangement with H., it was a fact which a prudent and experienced underwriter would take into consideration in estimating the premium, and that therefore a jury would be justified in finding that the non-communication of it to the Defendant was the concealment of a material fact which vitiated the policy.—A mere disclosure of the existence of such arrangement to the Defendant's solicitor is not notice of it to the Defendant. TATE *v.* HYSLOP -　-　-　15 Q. B. D. 368

II. INSURANCE, MARINE—INSURABLE INTEREST.

——— Goods at Purchasers' Risk—*Sale of Goods "f.o.b."*] D. sold to B. 200 tons of German sugar "f.o.b. Hamburg; payment by cash in London in exchange for bill of lading;", the price to be variable according to the percentage of saccharine matter, which was not to exceed or fall short of certain limits. B. resold to the Respondent the same quantity at an increased price, but otherwise upon similar terms. D. also sold to the Respondent 200 tons upon similar terms. To fulfil these contracts 390 tons (being ten tons short) were shipped in bags on one vessel at Hamburg for Bristol, no bags being set apart for one contract more than the other. Each bag was marked with its percentage of saccharine matter, and bills of lading with marks corresponding to the bags were sent to D. to be retained till payment in accordance with the contracts. The Respondent was insured in floating policies upon "any kind of goods and merchandises" between Hamburg and Bristol, and duly declared in respect of this cargo. The ship sailed from Hamburg for Bristol and was lost. After receiving news of the loss D. allocated 2000 bags or 200 tons to B.'s contract, and 1900 bags or 190 tons to the other contract. In an action upon the policies:—*Held,* affirming the decision of the Court of Appeal, that the sales being "f. o. b. Hamburg" the sugar was at the Respondent's risk after shipment; that he had an insurable interest in it; and that the underwriters were liable. INGLIS *v.* STOCK　-　9 Q. B. D. 708 ;
[12 Q. B. D. 564; 10 App. Cas. 263

III. INSURANCE, MARINE—LOSS, PARTIAL.

——— Perils insured against—*Owner selling instead of repairing —Mode of estimating Liability*

III. INSURANCE, MARINE—LOSS, PARTIAL
—*continued.*

of Underwriters.] Where a ship that is insured is injured by perils insured against, and the owner instead of repairing, sells her during the continuance of the risk, the loss to be made good by the underwriters depends on the depreciation in the value of the ship and not on the amount that it would have cost to repair her with an allowance in respect of new materials for old.—The estimated cost of repairs, though rejected as a direct measure of loss, might be the measure of the difference between the ship's sound and damaged values, if no other means can be found for arriving at the loss really sustained.—The depreciation in value is to be ascertained by taking the value of the ship, if sound, at the port of distress, and her value there in her damaged condition. To ascertain the liability of the insurers, the proportion so arrived at should be applied to the real value of the ship at the commencement of the risk, if the policy be open, or to the agreed value if the policy be valued:—So *held,* by Lindley, J., affirmed (except as to the mode of ascertaining the depreciation in value) on appeal by the majority of the Court; Jessel, M.R., and Cotton, L.J.; Brett, L.J., dissenting.—*Held,* by B.ett, L.J., that the matter against which the owner was indemnified was the cost of repairs and not any diminution in the saleable value of the ship, and that therefore loss or gain by the sale of the ship was outside the contract of insurance and was not a matter to be considered between the assured and the underwriter in adjusting either a total or a partial loss on ship. PITMAN *v.* UNIVERSAL MARINE INSURANCE COMPANY　-　-　9 Q. B. D. 192

IV. INSURANCE, MARINE—LOSS, TOTAL.

——— Re-insurance—*Constructive Total Loss—Notice of Abandonment— Suing and Labouring Clause.*] Upon a constructive total loss happening to the ship insured, notice of abandonment need not be given to the underwriters of a policy of re-insurance. The owners of a ship insured her for twelve months in an ordinary Lloyd's policy, which contained a suing and labouring clause. The underwriters of the Lloyd's policy re-insured themselves with a French company which re-insured itself with the Defendants. The policy underwritten for the French company by the Defendants was for £1000, bound them to pay as might be paid on the original policy, was to cover the risk of total loss only, and contained a suing and labouring clause. Whilst the policy was in force, the ship went ashore and was much damaged. Her owners gave notice of abandonment to the underwriters of the Lloyd's policy, but notice of abandonment was not given to the Defendants: the underwriters of the ship ultimately settled with her owners at 88 per cent. They expended more than £5000 in floating the ship, and sold her to a builder, who repaired her at a cost of £9000, and resold her for £11,200. The cost of floating the ship (after deducting the price paid by the shipbuilders) being added to the 88 per cent. represented a loss of 112 per cent. In an action by the French company as re-insurers against the Defendants:—*Held,* that a constructive total loss had occurred, and that as the Defendants had bound themselves to pay as might

IV. INSURANCE, MARINE — LOSS, TOTAL — *continued.*

be paid on the original policy, they were liable to the extent of £1000 ; but that they could not be held liable for more, as the underwriters of the Lloyd's policy were not the " factors, servants, or assigns " of the Plaintiffs within the meaning of the suing and labouring clause, and that the Defendants were not liable, at least by virtue of that clause, for any part of the expenses incurred in floating the ship. UZIELLI *v.* BOSTON MARINE INSURANCE COMPANY - **15 Q. B. D. 11**

V. INSURANCE, MARINE—POLICY.

1. —— Chartered Freight — *Interest — Commencement of—Risks "incident to Steam Navigation" — Option of cancelling Charterparty — Concealment.*] The Plaintiffs, on the 29th of July, 1875, chartered their ship G. for a voyage from New York to Odessa. The freight was agreed " during the voyage aforesaid " at £5500 in cash at Hull, England, on the discharge of the cargo in Odessa. " If the vessel has not arrived at the port of New York on or before the 1st of September, 1875, charterers have option of cancelling this charterparty." The Plaintiffs, on the 7th of August, 1875, effected an insurance with the Defendant "at and from London to New York while there, and thence to Odessa, viâ Constantinople," on their chartered freight, including, besides the ordinary ones, all risks "incident to steam navigation." The clause in the charterparty giving the option to cancel was not mentioned to the Defendant.—The ship started from England on the 7th of August, but owing to the failure of her machinery in the British Channel was obliged to put back for repairs, which occupied so much time that she did not reach New York until after the 1st of September, whereupon the charterers cancelled the charter and the freight was lost :—*Held* (by Lord Coleridge, C.J.), that the interest in the chartered freight had commenced at the time when the charter was cancelled, but that the Defendant was not liable, for the freight was not lost by any of the perils insured against, but by the exercise of the option to cancel in the charterparty ; and, further, that the withholding from the Defendant information as to the power to cancel vitiated the policy. MERCANTILE STEAMSHIP COMPANY *v.* TYSER **7 Q. B. D. 73**

2. —— Chartered Freight—*Loss—Perils of the Seas — Causa proxima—Charterparty — Condition precedent.*] A ship was chartered for time on monthly hire : the charterers agreeing to pay the freight during employment and efficient performance of the service, and the owner covenanting that the ship should be seaworthy during the continuance of the charter ; provided that if at any time it should appear to the charterers that the ship became inefficient it should be lawful for them to put her out of pay, or to make such abatement by way of mulct out of the hire or freight as they should adjudge fit. The owner effected a time policy of insurance "on freight outstanding." During the time the ship became inefficient through perils of the seas and the charterers refused to pay freight after that date. The owner having brought an action on the policy :—*Held*, affirming the decision of the Court of Appeal, that

V. INSURANCE, MARINE—POLICY—*contd.*

on the true construction of the charterparty the efficiency of the ship was not a condition precedent to the earning of the freight ; that the pecuniary loss was caused by the charterers availing themselves of the abatement clause, and not by the perils of the seas ; and that the underwriters were not liable. INMAN STEAMSHIP COMPANY *v.* BISCHOFF - 6 Q. B. D. 648 ; 7 App. Cas. 670

3. —— Construction — *Barratry — Perils insured—Warranty "free from Capture and Seizure" —Whether Barratry causing Capture within Warranty.*] In a time policy of marine insurance the ordinary perils insured against (including " barratry of the master ") were enumerated, and the subject-matter of the insurance was warranted "free from capture and seizure." During the continuance of the policy, in consequence of the barratrous act of the master, the ship was seized and detained for smuggling. In an action on the policy to recover expenses incurred by the owner in obtaining the release of the ship :—*Held*, affirming the decision of the Court of Appeal, that the loss must be imputed to ' capture and seizure " and not to the barratry of the master, and that the underwriter was not liable. CORY *v.* BURR **[8 Q. B. D. 313 ; 9 Q. B. D. 463 ; 8 App. Cas. 393**

4. —— Construction—" *Capture and Seizure" —Intention to keep the Ship, whether necessary to constitute " Seizure."*] In an action on a policy of insurance upon a ship, in which the subject-matter was warranted " free from capture and seizure, and the consequence of any attempt thereat," it was proved that during the continuance of the risk some natives took forcible possession of the ship in the Brass River, plundered the cargo, and damaged her so that she became a constructive total loss, and that their intention in so taking possession was only to plunder the cargo, and not to keep the ship :—*Held*, that the acts of the natives constituted a " seizure" within the meaning of the warranty, and therefore that the underwriters were not liable. JOHNSTON *v.* HOGG - - **10 Q. B. D. 432**

5. —— Construction—*Constructive total Loss —By-laws — Insurance confined to " Absolute Damage caused by the Perils insured against."*] A policy of marine insurance effected by the Plaintiff with the Defendants, a mutual insurance company, incorporated certain by-laws of the company indorsed thereon. The policy (inter alia) expressed it to be thereby declared that the acts of the assurer or assured in recovering, saving, or preserving the property insured should not be considered a waiver or acceptance of abandonment. One of the by-laws provided that in the event of any ship being stranded or damaged, and not taken into a place of safety, it should be lawful for the directors of the company to use every possible means in their power to procure the safety of the ship, the owner bearing his proportion of the expense incurred ; and that no acts of the company or its agents under or in pursuance of the power thereby reserved to the company should be deemed, or taken to be, an acceptance or recognition of any abandonment, of which the assured might have given notice to such company, and the company under any circumstances should only pay for the absolute damage caused by the

V. INSURANCE, MARINE—POLICY—*contd.*

perils insured against, which was in no case to exceed the sum insured. The Plaintiff's vessel was, while the policy was in force, damaged by perils of the sea to such an extent that the cost of repairing would have amounted to more than the ship would have been worth when repaired. The Plaintiff within a reasonable time gave notice of abandonment :—*Held*, that a constructive total loss was covered by the policy and by the by-laws, and that the Plaintiff could maintain an action. FORWOOD *v.* NORTH WALES INSURANCE COMPANY - - - 9 Q. B. D. 732

6. —— Construction— *General Words — Explosion of Boiler of Steamer, whether a Peril insured against—Contributory Cause of Loss, and proximate Cause*] The explosion of the boiler of a steamer is a peril insured against by a marine policy in the ordinary form.—A steamer insured by a time policy became a wreck, by reason of the explosion of her boiler in ordinary weather under ordinary pressure of steam. The *causa sine quâ non* of the explosion was that the boiler had become from external and internal corrosion by bilge water and "scale," too thin to resist the steam. The corrosion might have been discovered, and in some measure prevented, by ordinary care :—*Held*, affirming the judgment of Baggallay, L.J., that though unseaworthiness was a *causa sine quâ non* of the loss, the explosion was a proximate cause, and a peril insured against. WEST INDIA AND PANAMA TELEGRAPH COMPANY *v.* HOME AND COLONIAL MARINE INSURANCE COMPANY
[6 Q. B. D. 51

7. —— Constructive total Loss—*Collision—Recovery of Damages from Owner of Ship in default—Claim by Underwriter on Ship after Payment of Sum insured to Compensation received for Loss of Freight—Subrogation.*] Freight to be earned under a charterparty is not an incident to the ownership of the vessel ; and therefore although an underwriter of a policy of insurance upon the vessel herself becomes, by abandonment to him upon a constructive total loss happening through the fault of another vessel, entitled after payment of the sum secured by the policy to every benefit accruing from the ownership of the insured vessel, he cannot claim any part of the damages recovered from the owners of the wrongdoing vessel on account of loss of freight intended to be earned by the insured vessel.—The Defendants being owners of a ship chartered her upon a voyage, and insured her with the Plaintiffs, and they insured the freight intended to be earned with other underwriters. The Defendant's ship became a constructive total loss through a collision with the C. occasioned by negligence in navigating the latter vessel. The Plaintiffs settled with the Defendants for a total loss of the insured ship. No freight was earned under the charterparty. Afterwards the Defendants recovered from the owners of the C. damages for the loss of their ship and of her freight :—*Held*, that the Plaintiffs were not entitled to any part of the damages recovered from the owners of the C. on account of the loss of the freight intended to be earned by the Defendants' ship. SEA INSURANCE COMPANY *v.* HADDEN
[13 Q. B. D. 706

8. —— Time Policy— *Memorandum against*

V. INSURANCE, MARINE—POLICY—*contd.*

Average under 3 per cent.—Adding distinct successive Losses together.] In a time policy of marine insurance the ship was warranted free from average under 3 per cent. unless general, or the ship be stranded, sunk, or burnt :—*Held*, following *Blackett* v. *Royal Exchange Assurance Co.* (2 C. & J. 244), that distinct successive losses on the ship during the period insured, each less than 3 per cent., but in the aggregate amounting to more than 3 per cent., were not within the exception and were to be borne by the underwriters. STEWART *v.* MERCHANTS MARINE INSURANCE COMPANY
[14 Q. B. D. 555
[Reversed by the Court of Appeal, 16 Q. B. D. 619.]

9. —— Time Policy—*Negative Words—Where no General Custom of Merchants what Facts to be considered—Maxim "contra proferentem."*] A time policy of marine insurance on A.'s ship, from the 29th of May, 1878, to the 28th of May, 1879, contained the words "warranted no St. Lawrence between the 1st of October and the 1st of April." The vessel was lost on the voyage home. The underwriters refused A.'s claim for a total loss on the ground of breach of warranty, inasmuch as the vessel had navigated in the Gulf of St. Lawrence during the prescribed period. A. contended that the above words referred exclusively to the River St. Lawrence. Admittedly no general custom of merchants could be proved : but the facts established that the great river which discharges the waters of the North American lakes, and the gulf into which it flows, both bear the name of "St. Lawrence"; that the navigation of both, though of the gulf in a less degree than of the river, was within the prohibited period dangerous :—*Held*, reversing the decision of the Court below, that the evidence disclosed no ambiguity or uncertainty sufficient to prevent the application of the ordinary rules of construction ; and according to those rules the whole St. Lawrence navigation, both gulf and river, was within the fair and natural meaning of these negative words, and therefore prohibited during the months in question. BIRRELL *v.* DRYER
[9 App. Cas. 345

VI. INSURANCE, MARINE—RISK.

—— Re-insurance — *Policy attaching — Voyage ended when Policy effected—Action for Premium.*] The Defendant, who had insured a cargo by a certain vessel lost or not lost for a certain voyage, believing such vessel to be overdue, effected a policy of re-insurance with the Plaintiff on the same cargo and risk.—Before effecting the policy of re-insurance, the vessel and cargo had in fact arrived safely at the port of destination ; but this was not known to either the Plaintiff or Defendant at the time the policy was effected :—*Held*, that the policy had attached, and that therefore the Plaintiff was entitled to the premium at which it had been effected. BRADFORD *v.* SYMONDSON - - 7 Q. B. D. 456

VII. INSURANCE, MARINE—SALVAGE.

—— Valued Policy—*Loss—Indemnity.*] The Respondents effected with underwriters valued policies of insurance (including war risks) on a cargo, which was afterwards destroyed by the *Alabama*, a Confederate cruiser, and the under-

VII. INSURANCE, MARINE—SALVAGE—*contd.*

writers paid to the Respondents as on an actual total loss the valued amounts, which were less than the real value. The United States, out of a compensation fund created after the loss and distributed under an Act of Congress passed subsequently to the loss, paid to the Respondents the difference between their real total loss and the sum received from the underwriters. Under the Act of Congress no claim was allowed for any loss for which the party injured should have received compensation from any insurer, but if such compensation should not have been equal to the loss actually suffered, allowance might be made for the difference; and no claim was allowed by or on behalf of any insurer either in his own right or in that of the party insured :—*Held*, affirming the decision of the Court of Appeal, that the underwriters were not entitled to recover. the compensation from the Respondents. BURNAND *v.* RODOCANACHI **6 Q. B. D. 633; 7 App. Cas. 333**

INSURANCE, MARINE—Mutual association— Limitation of liability **12 Q. B. D. 176**
   See COMPANY—MEMBER'S LIABILITY. 2.

—— Payment of premiums — How far necessaries - - - **10 P. D. 44**
   See SHIP—MARITIME LIEN. 1.

—— Subrogation—Advanced freight **8 P. D. 155**
   See SHIP—FREIGHT. 1.

—— Total loss—Sale of ship - **16 Ch. D. 474**
   See SHIP—MASTER. 1.

—— Undisclosed principal — Right to policy moneys—Set-off - **9 Q. B. D. 530;**
                  [8 App. Cas. 874
   See PRINCIPAL AND AGENT—PRINCIPAL'S LIABILITY. 6.

INTENT TO DELAY CREDITORS—Bankruptcy —Trader.
   See Cases under BANKRUPTCY—TRADER.

—— Fraudulent conveyance - **20 Ch. D. 389;**
                 [22 Ch. D. 74
   See FRAUDULENT CONVEYANCE. 1, 2.

—— Settlement - **19 Ch. D. 588**
   See BANKRUPTCY—VOID SETTLEMENT. 1.

INTENTION—Exercise of power **30 Ch. D. 617**
   See POWER—EXECUTION. 19.

INTERDICT—Costs - **7 App. Cas. 547**
   See SCOTCH LAW—PUBLIC RIGHTS.

—— Nuisance - - - **7 App. Cas. 518**
   See SCOTCH LAW—NUISANCE.

—— Patent - - **8 App. Cas. 873**
   See SCOTCH LAW—PATENT.

—— Restraining action—Compensation
                 [8 App. Cas. 265
   See SCOTCH LAW—RAILWAY COMPANY. 5.

INTEREST.

1. —— **Bona Vacantia** — *Administration by Executors—Assignment to the Crown—Claim by Next of Kin—Interest payable by the Crown.*] The trustees and executors of a will administered the estate, and upon its being decided in a suit instituted for the purpose that there was an intestacy, and no heir or next of kin being discovered, the trustees assigned the leasehold property to the Solicitor for the Treasury, to be held for the benefit of the Crown. The claimants, six years

INTEREST—*continued.*

afterwards, established their claim as next of kin of the testator, and the Court declared them entitled :—*Held* (reversing the decision of Malins, V.C.), that the Crown was not chargeable with interest on the rents and profits received from the property while in its possession. *In re* GOSMAN
                 [17 Ch. D. 771

2. —— **Legacy.**] Under a bequest of £1000 upon trust to invest the same upon mortgage of the B. borough fund, and pay the interest as the same should arise to his widow during her life and widowhood, and after her death or second marriage in favour of testator's children by a former marriage, interest does not become payable to the widow except from the end of a year from the testator's death. *In re* WHITTAKER. WHITTAKER *v.* WHITTAKER - **21 Ch. D. 657**

—— Advances to children—Hotchpot
                 [17 Ch. D. 701
   See WILL—SATISFACTION. 2.

—— Breach of trust—Accumulations—Unauthorized investment - **17 Ch. D. 142**
   See TRUSTEE—LIABILITIES. 7.

—— Compound—Administration of estate—Conversion - - **24 Ch. D. 643, 649, n.**
   See EXECUTOR—ADMINISTRATION. 5, 6.

—— Covenant in mortgage deed — Merger in judgment - - **25 Ch. D. 338**
   See JUDGMENT. 3.

—— Debtor's summons - - **17 Ch. D. 191**
   See BANKRUPTCY—ACT OF BANKRUPTCY. 15.

—— Legacy - - **24 Ch. D. 616**
   See WILL—ABSOLUTE GIFT. 1.

—— Legacy—Statute of Limitations
                 [27 Ch. D. 676
   See LIMITATIONS, STATUTE OF—TRUSTS. 1.

—— Money in Court—Staying proceedings pending appeal - - **20 Ch. D. 669**
   See PRACTICE—SUPREME COURT—STAYING PROCEEDINGS. 13.

—— Mortgage - - **6 App. Cas. 181**
   See MORTGAGE—CONTRACT. 11.

—— Mortgage—Arrears - **18 Ch. D. 449**
   See MORTGAGE—POWERS. 6.

—— Mortgage — Distress for — Winding-up of company - - **18 Ch. D. 649**
   See COMPANY—DISTRESS. 6.

—— Mortgage—Foreclosure - **19 Ch. D. 49**
   See MORTGAGE—FORECLOSURE. 10.

—— Mortgage—Proviso for reduction of
                 [16 Ch. D. 53
   See MORTGAGE—MORTGAGEE IN POSSESSION. 3.

—— Mortgage—Tenant for life **30 Ch. D. 614**
   See WILL—DISCLAIMER. 2.

—— Payment of—Statute of Limitations
                 [29 Ch. D. 882
   See LIMITATIONS, STATUTE OF—REALTY. 1.

—— Premiums—Loan by building society
   See BUILDING SOCIETY. 4. **[26 Ch. D. 273**

—— Proof in administration - **17 Ch. D. 342**
   See EXECUTOR—ACTIONS. 19.

INTESTACY—*continued*.

—— Right of Crown waived.
　See REAL ESTATE—*Statutes*.

—— Statute of Distributions—Illegitimate children　-　　-　　-　**17 Ch. D. 266**
　See DISTRIBUTIONS, STATUTE OF.

—— Trust not disclosed to executor
　See WILL—TRUSTEES. 2. [**26 Ch. D. 531**

INVALIDITY—Covenant—Restraint of marriage
　　　　　　　　　　[**23 Ch. D. 285**
　See COVENANT—VALIDITY.

—— Patent.
　See Cases under PATENT—VALIDITY.

INVESTMENT—Capital money.
　See SETTLED LAND ACT—*Statutes*.

—— Friendly society—Illegal loan　**19 Ch. D. 64**
　See FRIENDLY SOCIETY.

—— Interim—Money to be laid out in land—
　Settled Land Act　　**23 Ch. D. 171, 750**
　See SETTLED LAND ACT — PURCHASE-
　MONEY. 6, 7.

—— Investment in joint names—Husband and
　wife　-　　-　　**28 Ch. D. 705**
　See HUSBAND AND WIFE—SEPARATE ES-
　TATE. 4.

—— Liability of trustee.
　See Cases under TRUSTEE—LIABILITY.
　3–7.

—— Liability of trustees—Shares of company
　　　　　　　　　　[**21 Ch. D. 302**
　See COMPANY—MEMBER'S LIABILITY. 3.

—— Money in Court—Lands Clauses Act.
　See Cases under LANDS CLAUSES ACT—
　PURCHASE-MONEY.

—— Personal estate in cultivation of real
　　　　　　　　　　[**27 Ch. D. 553**
　See SETTLEMENT—POWERS. 6.

—— Purchase-money of leaseholds for lives
　　　　　　　　　　[**18 Ch. D. 624**
　See LEASEHOLD—RENEWABLE LEASE. 3.

—— Sanctioned by Court—Lands Clauses Act
　　　　　　　　　　[**22 Ch. D. 93**
　See PRACTICE—SUPREME COURT—PAY-
　MENT INTO COURT. 5.

—— Severance of trust funds　**6 App. Cas. 855**
　See SCOTCH LAW—TRUSTEE.

IRELAND — Residence in Ireland—Service of
　writ　-　　-　　**12 Q. B. D. 50**
　See PRACTICE—SUPREME COURT—SER-
　VICE. 10.

IRISH ESTATE—Charge on—Rate of interest
　　　　　　　　　　[**23 Ch. D. 472**
　See SETTLEMENT—POWERS.. 14.

IRISH INQUISITION—Transcript of record
　　　　　　　　　　[**20 Ch. D. 269**
　See LUNATIC—JURISDICTION. 1.

IRISH LAND LAW ACT.

—— Pasture—*Land Law (Ireland) Act*, 1881
(44 & 45 *Vict. c.* 49), *s.* 58 *sub-s.* 3 — *Landlord and Tenant—Land let to be used wholly or
mainly for Pasture.*] By a lease in 1861 lands

IRISH LAND LAW ACT—*continued*.
in Ireland of more than 100 acres were demised
for twenty-one years, the tenant covenanting that
he would not without the landlord's consent break
up or have in tillage in any one year any greater
quantity than ten acres, out of a certain specified
portion, and that he would manage the land in
a good and husbandlike manner and in due and
regular course so that the same might not be in
any way injured :—At the time of the demise
there were only fifteen acres in tillage, and the
rest was used as pasture, but was not ancient
pasture, the whole farm having been put in tillage (in different portions at different times)
between 1852 and 1861. The tenant used the farm
as a dairy farm : frequently meadowing different
portions (about twenty acres each year), and sometimes selling hay off the land :—*Held*, affirming
the decision of the Court of Appeal (Ireland),
that the farm was not a "holding let to be used
wholly or mainly for the purpose of pasture "
within the Land Law (Ireland) Act, 1881 (44 & 45
Vict. c. 49), s. 58, sub-s. (3). WESTROPP *v.* ELLIGOTT
　　　　　　　　　　[**9 App. Cas. 815**

IRISH TITHE RENT-CHARGE—Statute of Limi-
　tations -　　-　　-　**10 App. Cas. 14**
　See LIMITATIONS, STATUTE OF—REALTY.
　8.

IRONWORKS—Nuisance　-　**7 App. Cas. 518**
　See SCOTCH LAW—NUISANCE.

IRREGULARITY—Ceylon law　**8 App. Cas. 99**
　See COLONIAL LAW—CEYLON. 2.

—— Dismissal of motion — Non-production of
　affidavit of service　-　**25 Ch. D. 84**
　See PRACTICE — SUPREME COURT—DE-
　FAULT. 6.

—— Incorporation of building society
　See BUILDING SOCIETY. 11. [**18 Ch. D. 173**

—— Issue of debentures—Estoppel　**24 Ch. D.**
　See COMPANY—DEBENTURES. 3.

—— Order under Settled Estates Act　**21 Ch. D.**
　See SETTLED ESTATES ACT. 1.　　[**41**

—— Service of inaccurate copy -　**25 Ch. D. 112**
　See BANKRUPTCY—ACT OF BANKRUPTCY.
　19.

IRRELEVANCY — Affidavits on interlocutory
　motion　-　　-　　**16 Ch. D. 594**
　See PRACTICE—SUPREME COURT—EVI-
　DENCE. 6.

IRRITANT CLAUSE　-　**10 App. Cas. 553**
　See SCOTCH LAW—HERITABLE PROPERTY.
　5.

ISOMERIC SUBSTANCES　-　**29 Ch. D. 366**
　See PATENT—VALIDITY. 5.

ISSUE—Read "Children"　-　**26 Ch. D. 208**
　See SETTLEMENT—CONSTRUCTION. 7.

ISSUES—Fact or law　-　　**7 App. Cas. 49**
　See SCOTCH LAW—PRACTICE. 3.

—— Of fact—Staying proceedings on
　　　　　　　　　　[**22 Ch. D. 88**
　See PRACTICE—SUPREME COURT—STAY-
　ING PROCEEDINGS. 16.

J.

JAMAICA—Law of—Bankruptcy 7 App. Cas. 79
    See BANKRUPTCY—MUTUAL DEALINGS. 3.
JAPAN—Order in Council.
    See JURISDICTION—*Gazette.*
JERSEY—Law of.
    See Cases under COLONIAL LAW—JERSEY.
JEWELS—Gift of—Heirlooms - 26 Ch. D. 538
    See WILL—HEIRLOOM. 3.
—— Separate use   10 App. Cas. 1
    See SETTLEMENT—FUTURE PROPERTY. 6.
JOINDER OF ACTIONS—Claim for recovery of
    land—Counter-claim - 21 Ch. D. 138
    See PRACTICE—SUPREME COURT—COUN-
    TER-CLAIM. 5.
JOINT ACCOUNT CLAUSE—Effect of.
    See DEED—CONSTRUCTION—*Statutes.*
JOINT AND SEPARATE DEBTS—Joint judg-
    ment against firm—Proof against sepa-
    rate estate - 13 Q. B. D. 50
    See BANKRUPTCY—PROOF. 5.
—— Liquidation 16 Ch. D. 513 ; 19 Ch. D. 367
    See BANKRUPTCY—LIQUIDATION. 10, 13.
JOINT AND SEPARATE ESTATES—Bankruptcy
    —Interest on debts - 17 Ch. D. 334
    See BANKRUPTCY—PROOF. 12.
JOINT CREDITORS—Joint and separate security
    —Composition 19 Ch. D. 394
    See BANKRUPTCY—SECURED CREDITOR. 5.
—— Retainer by executor 16 Ch. D. 368 ;
    [29 Ch. D. 934
    See EXECUTOR—RETAINER. 4, 9.
JOINT TENANT.
    1. —— **Severance**—*Infant.*] A marriage set-
tlement contained a proviso for the settlement of
the present and after-acquired property of the
intended wife, who was an infant. She was then
entitled in remainder jointly with two others to a
share in Bank annuities standing in the names of
trustees : — *Held,* that the joint tenancy was
severed. BURNABY *v.* EQUITABLE REVERSIONARY
INTEREST SOCIETY - - 28 Ch. D. 416
    2. —— **Severance** — *Marriage* — *Covenant to
settle.*] By their marriage settlement the intended
husband and wife each covenanted to assign and
settle any personal estate which should, during
the coverture, vest in the wife or in the husband
in her right. At that time the wife was entitled,
as one of two joint tenants, to personal estate in
expectancy on the death of a person who died
during the coverture :—*Held,* that the marriage
and the covenant to settle each operated to sever
the joint tenancy. BAILLIE *v.* TREHARNE
    [17 Ch. D. 388
——Bequest to husband and wife—Unity of
    person. - - 27 Ch. D. 166
    See WILL—JOINT TENANCY.
—— Tenant in common 19 Ch. D. 492 ;
    [21 Ch. D. 352
    See POWER—EXECUTION. 3.

JOINTURE—Release of ·· 8 App. Cas. 420
    See HUSBAND AND WIFE—WIFE'S CON-
    VEYANCE. 3.
JOURNEYS—Solicitor's costs - 26 Ch. D. 189
    See SOLICITOR—BILL OF COSTS. 8.
JUDGE—Colonial—Salary of—Bankruptcy
    [21 Ch. D. 85
    See BANKRUPTCY—ASSETS. 13.
JUDGMENT.
    *The Act 45 & 46 Vict. c. 31, renders judgments
obtained in certain inferior Courts in England,
Scotland, and Ireland respectively, effectual in any
other part of the United Kingdom.*
    *Sect. 1. Act to be cited for all purposes as the
Inferior Courts Judgments Extension Act, 1882.*
    *Sect. 2. Interpretation of terms (inter alia):—
"judgment" includes decreet, civil bill decree, dismiss, or order. "Inferior Court" includes County
Courts, Civil Bill Courts, and all Courts in England and Ireland having jurisdiction to hear and
determine civil causes, other than the High Court
of Justice; and in Ireland, Courts of Petty Sessions and the Court of Bankruptcy; and in Scotland, the Sheriffs' Courts and the Courts held under
the Small Debts and Debts Recovery Acts.*
    *Sect. 3. Where judgment shall hereafter be ob-
tained or entered up in any of the inferior Courts
of England, Scotland, or Ireland respectively, for
any debt, damages, or costs, the registrar of such
inferior Court or other proper officer shall after the
time for appealing against such judgment shall
have elapsed, and in the event of such judgment
not being reversed on appeal or of execution thereunder not being stayed, upon the application of
the party who has recovered such judgment, and
upon proof that the same has not been satisfied, and
upon payment of the prescribed fee, grant a certificate in the prescribed form.*
    *Sect. 4. On production to the registrar or other
proper officer of an inferior Court in England,
Scotland, or Ireland of a certificate under the Act
purporting to be signed by the registrar or other
proper officer of the inferior Court where such
judgment was obtained, such certificate shall, on
payment of the prescribed fee, be registered in the
prescribed form by such registrar or other proper
officer to whom the same shall be produced for that
purpose; and all reasonable costs and charges
attendant upon the obtaining and registering such
certificate shall be added to and recovered in like
manner as if the same were part of the original
judgment.*
    *No certificate of any such judgment shall be
registered as aforesaid in any inferior Court in
the United Kingdom more than twelve months after
the date of such judgment.*
    *Sect. 5. Where a certificate of a judgment of any
of the inferior Courts aforesaid has been registered
under this Act, process of execution may issue
thereon out of the Court in which the same shall
have been so registered against any goods or chattels
of the person against whom such judgments shall*

JUDGMENT—*continued.*

have been obtained which are within the jurisdiction of such last-mentioned Court in the same or the like manner as if the judgment to be executed had been obtained in the Court in which such certificate shall be so registered as aforesaid.

Sect. 6. *The Courts of Great Britain and Ireland to which this Act applies shall, in so far as relates to execution under this Act, have and exercise the same control and jurisdiction over and with respect to the execution of any judgment, a certificate of which shall be registered under this Act, as they now have and exercise over and with respect to the execution of any judgment in their own Courts.*

Sect. 7. *On proof of the setting aside or satisfaction of any judgment of which a certificate shall have been registered under this Act, the Court in which such certificate is so registered may order the registration thereof to be cancelled.*

Sect. 8. *In any action brought in any of the inferior Courts aforesaid for the purpose of enforcing any judgment which might be registered under this Act in the country in which such action is brought, the party bringing such action shall not recover or be entitled to any costs or expenses unless the Court in which such action shall be brought shall otherwise order.*

Sect. 9. *Nothing contained in this Act shall authorize the registration in an inferior Court of the certificate of any judgment for a greater amount than might have been recovered if the action or proceeding had been originally commenced in such inferior Court.*

Provided that, where a judgment obtained in an inferior Court in Scotland cannot be registered in an inferior Court in England or Ireland by reason of its being for a greater amount than might have been recovered if the action or proceeding had been originally commenced in such inferior Court, it shall be competent to register a certificate of such judgment in the register directed to be kept in the Court of Common Pleas at Westminster and Dublin respectively, to be called " The Register of Scotch Judgments," by sect. 3 *of the Judgments Extension Act,* 1868, *in the same manner, to the same effect, and subject to the same provisions as if the said certificate had been a certificate of an extracted decreet of the Court of Session registered in the said register under the said Act.*

Sect. 10. *This Act shall not apply to any judgment pronounced by any inferior Court in England against any person domiciled in Scotland or Ireland at the time of the commencement of any action unless the whole cause of action shall have arisen or the obligation to which the judgment relates ought to have been fulfilled within the district of such inferior Court and the summons was served upon the Defendant personally within the said district, nor to any judgment pronounced by any inferior Court in Scotland against any person domiciled in England or Ireland at the time of the commencement of any action unless the whole cause of action shall have arisen or the obligation to which the judgment relates ought to have been fulfilled within the district of such inferior Court and the summons was served upon the Defendant personally within the said district, nor to any judgment pronounced by any inferior Court in Ireland against any person domiciled in England or Scotland at the time of the commencement of any action unless the whole cause of action shall*

JUDGMENT—*continued.*

have arisen or the obligation to which the judgment relates ought to have been fulfilled within the district of such inferior Court and the summons was served upon the Defendant personally within the said district.

Provided that it shall be competent to any person against whom any judgment to which this Act does not apply as aforesaid is sought to be enforced by registration in the register of an inferior Court in England and Ireland to apply for or obtain from one of the superior Courts of England or Ireland a prohibition or injunction against the enforcement of such judgment and of any execution thereupon, and that it shall be competent to any person against whom any judgment to which this Act does not apply as aforesaid is sought to be enforced by registration in the register of an inferior Court in Scotland to apply for and obtain from the Bill Chamber or Court of Session in Scotland suspension or suspension and interdict of or against the enforcement of such judgment and any diligence thereon and in any such proceeding as aforesaid the unsuccessful party may be found liable in costs.

Sect. 11. *Rules to be made from time to time for the purposes of the Act.*

1. —— Administration Action — *Judgment Creditor* — *County Court*— *Injunction.*] Previously to the administration order in a creditor's action another creditor had obtained judgment in a County Court against the Defendant, a sole executrix. The Court refused to restrain the creditor from pursuing his remedy in the County Court against the executrix personally, but ordered payment to the creditor by the receiver of the estate, without prejudice to the question whether the executrix should be allowed the payment. *In re* WOMERSLEY. ETHERIDGE *v.* WOMERSLEY.

[29 Ch. D. 557

2. —— Merger — *Covenant — Mortgage.*] By a mortgage deed the mortgagor covenanted to pay the debt on a day named, and by a separate covenant) to pay interest at £7 per cent., so long as the £3000 or any part thereof should remain due.—The mortgagee obtained a judgment for the principal and interest due at the date of the judgment with interest at £4 per cent. on the sum made up by such principal and interest:—*Held,* that the security of the mortgage was not merged in the judgment, but that the mortgagee was entitled to sue for the difference between interest at £7 per cent. on the mortgage debt and the interest at £4 per cent. paid under the judgment. POPPLE *v.* SYLVESTER - 22 Ch. D. 98

3. —— Merger — *Covenant — Mortgagor and Mortgagee—Costs—Liquidation Petition—Composition.*] A mortgage deed contained a covenant by the mortgagor for payment of the principal sum on the expiration of six months next after a specified day, together with interest thereon at 5 per cent. per annum for the six months. And there was a further covenant by the mortgagor that if the principal sum, or any part thereof, should remain unpaid after the expiration of the six months, the mortgagor would, so long as the same sum or any part thereof should remain unpaid, pay to the mortgagee interest for the principal sum, or for so much thereof as should for the time being remain unpaid at 5 per cent. per annum. After the

2 A

JUDGMENT—*continued.*

expiration of the six months, the mortgagee recovered judgment against the mortgagor on the covenant for the principal sum and interest in arrear.—*Held*, that, the covenant being merged in the judgment, the mortgagee was, as from the date of the judgment, entitled only to interest on the judgment debt at the rate of 4 per cent., and was not entitled under the covenant to interest at the rate of 5 per cent. on the principal sum.—Decision of Bacon, C.J., reversed.—*Popple* v. *Sylvester* (22 Ch. D. 98) dsitinguished. *Ex parte* FEWINGS. *In re* SNEYD -　　25 Ch. D. 338

4. —— Registration—*Omission to re-register within Five Years—Priorities*—1 & 2 *Vict. c.* 110, *s.* 19—2 & 3 *Vict. c.* 11, *s.* 4—3 & 4 *Vict. c.* 82, *s.* 2.] A., B., and C. were judgment creditors of D. A. registered his judgment on the 12th of March, 1840, but never re-registered; B. registered his judgment in April, 1842, and re-registered in March, 1848; C. registered his judgment on the 18th of March, 1845, and re-registered on the 16th of March, 1850. Questions having arisen as to the priorities of the several judgment creditors, the fund in Court being insufficient for payment in full :—*Held*, that on the construction of the statutes 1 & 2 Vict. c. 110, s. 19, 2 & 3 Vict. c. 11, s. 4, and 3 & 4 Vict. c. 82, s. 2, and upon the principle laid down in *Beavan* v. *Earl of Oxford* (6 D. M. & G. 492), C. was first entitled to take out of the fund the sum found due on A.'s judgment, and then that B. was entitled to be paid the full amount of his judgment before C. took anything more in respect of his judgment. *In re* LORD KENSINGTON. BACON v. FORD　　29 Ch. D. 527

5. —— Res Judicata — *Cause of Action — Separate Actions in respect of same wrongful Act —Damage to Property and Injury to Person— Damages recoverable in previous Action—Maxim, " Nemo debet bis vexari pro unâ et eâdem causâ " —Maxim, " Interest reipublicæ ut sit finis litium."*] Damage to goods and injury to the person, although they have been occasioned by one and the same wrongful act, are infringements of different rights, and gave rise to distinct causes of action ; and therefore the recovery in an action of compensation for the damage to the goods is no bar to an action subsequently commenced for the injury to the person. So *held* by Brett, M.R., and Bowen, L.J., Lord Coleridge, C.J., dissenting.—The Plaintiff brought an action in a County Court for damage to his cab occasioned by the negligence of the Defendant's servant, and having recovered the amount claimed, afterwards brought an action in the High Court of Justice against the Defendant, claiming damages for personal injury sustained by the Plaintiff through the same negligence :—*Held*, by Brett, M.R., and Bowen, L.J., Lord Coleridge, C.J., dissenting, that the action in the High Court was maintainable, and was not barred by the previous proceedings in the County Court.—Judgment of the Queen's Bench Division reversed. BRUNSDEN v. HUMPHREY -　11 Q. B. D. 712; 14 Q. B. D. 141

—— Action against partner in name of firm
[19 Ch. D. 124; 11 Q. B. D. 435;
[10 App. Cas. 680
See PRACTICE—SUPREME COURT—PARTIES. 10, 11, 12.

JUDGMENT—*continued.*

—— Against company after winding-up ·
[17 Ch. D. 600,
See COMPANY—UNREGISTERED COMPANY. 7.

—— Against firm—Proceeding against partners
[8 Q. B. D. 474 ; 9 Q. B. D. 355; 14 Q. B. D. 103,
See PRACTICE—SUPREME COURT—JUDGMENT. 1, 2, 3.

—— Against married woman—Separate estate
[17 Ch. D. 454
See HUSBAND AND WIFE — SEPARATE ESTATE. 5.

—— Against principal -　- 17 Ch. D. 668
See PRINCIPAL AND SURETY—LIABILITY. 3.

—— Bankruptcy — How far judgment against bankrupt binding on trustee
[13 Q. B. D. 720
See BANKRUPTCY—PROOF. 9.

—— Bankruptcy—Power to go behind judgment
[17 Ch. D. 480; 14 Q. B. D. 415,
See BANKRUPTCY—PROOF. 8, 16.

—— By default　　25 Ch. D. 707 ; 29 Ch. D. 322,
See PRACTICE — SUPREME COURT—DEFAULT. 1, 4.

—— By default—Admiralty -　- 9 P. D. 84,
See PRACTICE—ADMIRALTY—DEFAULT.

—— By default—Evidence in subsequent actions
See FISHERY. 1.　[8 App. Cas 135

—— Estoppel by previous judgment.
· *See* Cases under ESTOPPEL—JUDGMENT.

—— Executor of judgment creditor—Bankruptcy notice -　　13 Q. B. D. 479,
See BANKRUPTCY—ACT OF BANKRUPTCY. 8.

—— Foreclosure action—Amendment
[25 Ch. D. 750,
See PRACTICE — SUPREME COURT — AMENDMENT. 2.

—— Form of—Obstruction of light 24 Ch. D. 282,
See LIGHT—OBSTRUCTION. 1.

—— Note of—Costs of appeal -　29 Ch. D. 76,
See PRACTICE—SUPREME COURT—COSTS. 6.

—— Obtained by collusion—Appeal 30 Ch. D. 421,
See PRACTICE — SUPREME COURT—APPEAL. 18.

—— Order to sign — Alimony pendente lite — Practice—　　- 13 Q. B. D. 855,
See ACTION. 1.

—— Practice—Supreme Court.
See Cases under PRACTICE — SUPREME COURT—JUDGMENT.

—— Reference—Law of Mauritius　8 App. Cas.,
See COLONIAL LAW—MAURITIUS. 1. [296,

—— Rescission by consent—Third parties
[10 P. D. 161
See ESTOPPEL—JUDGMENT. 3.

—— Set-off—Pension due to retired clergyman
[17 Ch. D. 1
See ECCLESIASTICAL LAW—CLERGY. 3.

—— Unregistered—Priority over simple contract debts -　　21 Ch. D. 189,
See EXECUTOR—ACTIONS. 6.

JUDGMENT CREDITOR—Garnishee order.
　　See Cases under PRACTICE —SUPREME
　　　COURT—GARNISHEE ORDERS.
—— Opposition to resolution for liquidation
　　　　　　　　　　　　[16 Ch. D. 655
　　See BANKRUPTCY—LIQUIDATION. 9.
JUDGMENT DEBTOR—Ceylon law　8 App. Cas.
　　See COLONIAL LAW—CEYLON. 2.　[99
JUDGMENT SUMMONS.
　　See BANKRUPTCY — BANKRUPTCY ACT,
　　　1883—*Statutes.*
—— Appeal from Judge of High Court—Court
　　of Appeal　-　-　13 Q. B D. 901
　　See BANKRUPTCY—APPEAL. 10.
—— Committal — County Court — Transfer to
　　Bankruptcy Court　-　15 Q. B. D. 335
　　See BANKRUPTCY—TRANSFER.. 2.
—— Married woman—Separate estate
　　　　　　　　　　　　[14 Q. B. D. 973
　　See HUSBAND AND WIFE—SEPARATE
　　　ESTATE. 11.
—— Order for committal—" Means to pay "
　　　[9 Q. B. D. 178; 14 Q. B. D. 597
　　See ARREST—DEBTORS' ACT. 4, 5.
JUDICIAL COMMITTEE.
　　See PRIVY COUNCIL—*Statutes.*
—— Effect of order　-　-　6 App. Cas. 482
　　See PRACTICE—PRIVY COUNCIL—JURIS-
　　　DICTION.
JUDICIAL SEPARATION—After-acquired pro-
　　perty　-　-　30 Ch. D. 500
　　See SETTLEMENT.—FUTURE PROPERTY. 4.
—— Jurisdiction of magistrates　10 P. D. 172
　　See HUSBAND AND WIFE — JUDICIAL
　　　SEPARATION.
—— Separate estate—Dwelling-house
　　　　　　　　　　　　[24 Ch. D. 346
　　See HUSBAND AND WIFE—SEPARATE ES-
　　　TATE. 2.
JUNCTION—Siding on railway—Rights of land-
　　owner　-　-　-　28 Ch. D. 190
　　See RAILWAY COMPANY — RAILWAYS
　　　CLAUSES ACTS. 8.
JURAT—Bill of sale　-　-　26 Ch. D. 338
　　See BANKRUPTCY—ACT OF BANKRUPTCY.
　　5.

JURISDICTION.
　　Fugitive Offenders.] *The Act* 44 & 45 *Vict.
c.* 69, *repeals* 6 & 7 *Vict. c.* 34 *(the Fugitive
Offenders Act,* 1843*), and amends the law with
respect to* fugitive offenders *in Her Majesty's dominions, and for other purposes connected with the
apprehension and trial of offenders.*
　　Sect. 1. *Act to be cited as the Fugitive Offenders
Act,* 1881.

PART I. RETURN OF FUGITIVES.

　　Sect. 2. *Liability of* fugitive *to be apprehended
and returned to that part of. Her Majesty's
dominions* from *which he is a* fugitive.
　　Sect. 3. *Warrant issued in one part of Her
Majesty's dominions may be indorsed in another
part of same dominions for apprehension of
fugitive.*
　　Sect. 4. *As to issue of provisional warrant in*

JURISDICTION—*continued.*
*any part of Her Majesty's dominions for appre-
hension of a* fugitive.
　　Sect. 5. *As to dealing with* fugitive *when apprehended.*
　　Sect. 6. *As to return of* fugitive *by warrant to
that part of Her Majesty's dominions* from *which
he* is *a* fugitive.
　　Sect. 7. *As to discharge of person apprehended
if not returned as a* foresaid *within one month.*
　　Sect. 8. *Person apprehended and returned may,
if not prosecuted within six months or acquitted,
be sent back* free *of cost, to where he was apprehended.*
　　Sect. 9. *Part I. of the Act applies to treason
and piracy, and to every offence, whether called
felony, misdemeanor, crime, or by any other
name, which is for the time being punishable in
the part of Her Majesty's dominions in which it
was committed, either on indictment or* infor-
*tion, by imprisonment with hard labour for a term
of twelve months or more, or by any greater punishment; and for the purposes of the section rigorous
imprisonment and any confinement in a prison
combined with labour, by whatever name it is
called, is to be deemed imprisonment with hard
labour.*
　　*Part I. of the Act to apply to an offence not-
withstanding that by the law of the part of Her
Majesty's dominions in or on his way to which the*
fugitive *is or is suspected of being it is not an
offence, or not an offence to which Part I. applies.*
　　Sect. 10. *Where it is made to appear to a
superior Court that by reason of the trivial nature
of the case, or by reason of the application for the
return of a* fugitive *not being made in good* faith
*in the interests of justice or otherwise, it would,
having regard to the distance, to the* facilities *for
communication, and to all the circumstances of the
case, be unjust or oppressive or too severe a punishment to return a* fugitive *either at all or until the
expiration of a certain period, such Court may
discharge the* fugitive, *either absolutely or on bail,
or order that he shall not be returned until after
the expiration of the period named in the order,
or make such other order in the premises as to the
Court seems just.*
　　Sect. 11. *As to the persons in Ireland by whom
the powers conferred by Part I. are to be exercised.*

PART II. INTER-COLONIAL BACKING OF WARRANTS
AND OFFENCES.

　　Sect. 12. *Part II. of the Act to apply only to
those groups of British possessions to which, by
reason of their contiguity or otherwise, Her Majesty
may by order in Council apply the same.*
　　Sect. 13. *As to backing in one British possession
of warrant issued in another of same group.*
　　Sect. 14. *As to return of prisoner apprehended
under a backed warrant.*
　　Sect. 15. *As to backing in one British possession
of summons, &c., for attendance of witnesses issued
in another possession of the same group.*
　　Sect. 16. *As to issue of provisional warrant in
group of British possessions.*
　　Sect. 17. *As to discharge of person apprehended
under backed warrant if not returned within one
month to British possession of same group.*
　　Sect. 18. *As to sending back of prisoner returned
under backed warrant, if not prosecuted within*

JURISDICTION—*continued.*

six months or acquitted, to British possession of same group.

Sect. 19. As to discharge of prisoner sought to be returned where offence is too trivial, &c.

PART III. TRIAL &C., OF OFFENCES.

Sect. 20. Where two British possessions adjoin, a person accused of an offence committed on or within the distance of 500 yards from the common boundary of such possessions may be apprehended, tried, and punished in either of such possessions.

Sect. 21. As to trial of offences committed on journey between two British possessions.

Sect. 22. A person accused of the offence (under whatever name it is known) of swearing or making any false deposition, or of giving or fabricating any false evidence, for the purposes of the Act, may be tried either in the part of Her Majesty's dominions in which such deposition or evidence is used, or in the part in which the same was sworn, made, given, or fabricated, as the justice of the case may require.

Sect. 23. Supplemental provision as to trial of person in any place.

Sect. 24. As to issue of search warrants.

Sect. 25. As to removal of prisoner by sea from one place to another in a British possession.

PART IV. SUPPLEMENTAL.

Sect. 26. As to indorsement of warrants under the Act.

Sect. 27. As to conveyance of fugitives and witnesses from any part of Her Majesty's dominions to another part.

Sect. 28. As to escape, recapture, and trial of escaped prisoners.

Sect. 29. Depositions, &c., to be receivable in evidence when duly authenticated.

Sect. 30. The jurisdiction under Part I. of the Act to hear a case, and commit a fugitive to prison to await his return shall be exercised in England by a chief magistrate of the metropolitan police courts, or one of the other magistrates of the metropolitan police court at Bow Street.

If a fugitive is apprehended and brought before a magistrate who has no power to exercise the jurisdiction under the Act in respect of that fugitive, that magistrate shall order the fugitive to be brought before some magistrate having that jurisdiction, and such order shall be obeyed.

Sect. 31. Power to make and revoke Orders in Council.

Sect. 32. Power to Legislature of British possessions to pass laws for carrying into effect the Act.

Sect. 33. Where an offence is triable in more than one part of Her Majesty's dominions, a warrant for the apprehension of the offender may be issued in any part of Her Majesty's dominions in which he can, if he happens to be there, be tried.

Sect. 34 applies the Act to convicts unlawfully at large before the expiration of their sentence.

Sect. 35. Where a person accused of an offence is in custody in some part of Her Majesty's dominions, and the offence is triable in some other part of Her Majesty's dominions, such offender may be removed to some other part of Her Majesty's dominions in which he can be tried.

Sect. 36. Power to apply Act by Order in Council to any place out of Her Majesty's dominions in which Her Majesty has jurisdiction.

JURISDICTION—*continued.*

Sect. 37 extends Act to Channel Islands and the Isle of Man.

Sect. 38. Applies Act to offences committed before the commencement of the Act.

Sect. 39. Definitions.

THE FOLLOWING ORDERS IN COUNCIL ARE MADE UNDER THE FOREIGN JURISDICTION ACTS, 1843 TO 1878 :—

China and Japan.] *The China and Japan Order in Council of 25th Oct. 1881, for the exercise of British jurisdiction in China and Japan, repeals part of the China and Japan Order in Council of 1865 and confirms the rest.*

2. This Order shall, except as otherwise expressed, commence and take effect from and immediately after the 31st day of December, 1881, which time is in this Order referred to as the commencement of this Order.

3. In this Order—

"China" means the dominions of the Emperor of China:

"Japan" means the dominions of the Mikado of Japan:

"Minister" means superior diplomatic representative, whether ambassador, envoy, minister plenipotentiary, or chargé d'affaires:

"Consular officer" includes every officer in Her Majesty's consular service, whether consul-general, consul, vice-consul, or consular agent, or person authorized to act in any such capacity in China or in Japan:

"British subject" means a subject of Her Majesty whether by birth or by naturalization:

"Foreigner" means a subject of the Emperor of China or of the Mikado of Japan, or a subject or citizen of any other state in amity with Her Majesty:

"Treaty" includes convention, and any agreement, regulations, rules, articles, tariff, or other instrument annexed to a treaty, or agreed on in pursuance of any stipulation thereof:

"Month" means calendar month:

Words importing the plural or the singular may be construed as referring to one person or thing, or more than one person or thing, and words importing the masculine as referring to females (as the case may require).

Repeal.

4. Subject to the provisions of this Order, articles 85 to 91 inclusive, of the China and Japan Order in Council, 1865, authorizing the making o regulations for the purposes and by the authority therein mentioned, and the regulations made thereunder, dated respectively July 11, 1866, and November 16, 1866, relating to mortgages, bills of sale, and proceedings against partnerships or partners or agents thereof, and rule 252 of the Rules of the Supreme Court and other Courts in China and Japan of May 4, 1865, relating to proceedings by or against partnerships, and articles 117 and 118 of the China and Japan Order in Council, 1865, relating to foreigners and foreign tribunals, are hereby repealed, as from the commencement of this Order; but this repeal does not affect any right, title, obligation or liability acquired or accrued before the commencement of this Order.

Confirmation of Regulations not repealed.

5. Such regulations as are described in the

JURISDICTION—*continued.*

schedule to this Order, being *regulations made or expressed or intended to be made under or in execution of the powers conferred by articles* 85 *to* 91 *of the China and Japan Order in Council,* 1865, *and all other regulations made or expressed or intended to be so made and having been approved, or, in case of urgency, not disapproved, under that Order, before the commencement of this Order, except the regulations expressed to be repealed by this Order, are hereby confirmed, as from the passing of this Order, and the same, as far as they are now in force, shall be in force, and shall be deemed to have always been of the like validity and effect as if they had been originally made by Order in Council.*

Authority for further Regulations.

6. *Her Majesty's minister in China may from time to time, subject and according to the provisions of this Order, make such regulations as to him seem fit for the peace, order, and good government of British subjects, resident in or resorting to China.*

7. *The power aforesaid extends to the making of regulations for securing observance of the stipulations of treaties between Her Majesty, her heirs and successors, and the Emperor of China, and for maintaining friendly relations between British subjects and Chinese subjects and authorities.*

8. *Her Majesty's minister in China may, as he thinks fit, make any regulation under this Order extend either throughout China, or to some one or more only of the consular districts in China.*

9. *Her Majesty's minister in China, in the exercise of the powers aforesaid, may, if he thinks fit, join with the ministers of any foreign powers in amity with Her Majesty in making or adopting regulations with like objects as the regulations described in the schedule to this order, commonly called the Shanghai Land Regulations, or any other regulations for the municipal government of any foreign concession or settlement in China; and, as regards British subjects, joint regulations so made shall be as valid and binding as if they related to British subjects only.*

10. *Her Majesty's minister in China may, by any regulation made under this Order, repeal or alter any regulation made under the China and Japan Order in Council,* 1865, *or under any prior like authority.*

11.—(a.) *Regulations made under this Order shall not have effect unless and until they are approved by Her Majesty the Queen, that approval being signified through one of Her Majesty's Principal Secretaries of State,—save that, in case of urgency declared in any such regulations, the same shall take effect before that approval, and shall continue to have effect unless and until they are disapproved by Her Majesty the Queen, that disapproval being signified through one of Her Majesty's Principal Secretaries of State, and until notification of that disapproval has been received and published by Her Majesty's minister in China.*

(b) *That approval, where given, shall be conclusive, and the validity or regularity of any regulations so approved shall not be called in question in any legal proceeding whatever.*

12. *Any regulations made under this Order may, if Her Majesty's minister in China thinks fit, impose penalties for offences against the same.*

JURISDICTION—*continued.*

13. *Penalties so imposed shall not exceed the following, namely,—for any offence imprisonment for three months, with or without hard labour, and with or without a fine of* $500, *or a fine of* $500, *without imprisonment,—with or without a further fine, for a continuing offence, of* $25 *for each day during which the offence continues after the original fine is incurred.*

14. *Regulations imposing penalties shall be so framed as to allow in every case of part only of the highest penalty being inflicted.*

15. *All regulations made under this Order, whether imposing penalties or not, shall be printed, and a printed copy thereof shall be affixed, and be at all times kept exhibited conspicuously in the public office of each consulate in China.*

16. *Printed copies of the regulations shall be kept on sale at such reasonable price as Her Majesty's minister in China from time to time directs.*

17. *Where a regulation imposes a penalty, the same shall not be enforceable in any consular district until a printed copy of the regulation has been affixed in the public office of the consulate for that district, and has been kept exhibited conspicuously there during one month.*

18. *A charge of an offence against a regulation made under this Order, imposing a penalty, shall be inquired of, heard, and determined as an ordinary criminal charge under the China and Japan Order in Council,* 1865, *except that (notwithstanding anything in that Order) where the regulation is one for securing observance of the stipulations of a treaty, the charge shall be heard and determined in a summary way, and (where the proceeding is before a Provincial Court) without assessors.*

19. *A printed copy of a regulation, purporting to be made under this Order and to be certified under the hand of Her Majesty's minister in China, or under the hand and consular seal of one of Her Majesty's Consular officers in China, shall be conclusive evidence of the due making of the regulation, and of its contents.*

20. *The foregoing provisions authorizing regulations for China are hereby extended to Japan, with the substitution of Japan for China, and of the Mikado of Japan for the Emperor of China, and of Her Majesty's minister in Japan for Her Majesty's minister in China, and of Her Majesty's consular officers in Japan for Her Majesty's consular officers in China.*

Prison Regulations.

21. *The respective powers aforesaid extend to the making of regulations for the governance, visitation, care, and superintendence of prisons in China or in Japan, and for the infliction of corporeal or other punishment on prisoners committing offences against the rules or discipline of a prison; but the provisions of this Order respecting penalties, and respecting the printing, affixing, exhibiting, and sale of regulations, and the mode of trial of charges of offences against regulations, do not apply to regulations respecting prisons and offences of prisoners.*

Mortgages.

22. *A deed or other instrument of mortgage, legal or equitable, of lands or houses in China or in Japan, executed by a British subject, may be*

JURISDICTION—*continued.*

registered at any time after its execution at the consulate of the consular district wherein the property mortgaged is situate.

23. *Registration is made as follows:* The original and a copy of the deed or other instrument of mortgage, and an affidavit verifying the execution and place of execution thereof, and verifying the copy, are brought into the consulate; and the copy and affidavit are left there.

24. If a deed or other instrument of mortgage is not registered at the consulate aforesaid within the respective time following (namely):

(i.) Within fourteen days after its execution, where it is executed in the consular district wherein the property mortgaged is situate:

(ii.) Within two months after its execution, where it is executed in China or Japan, elsewhere than in that consular district, or in Hong Kong:

(iii.) Within six months after its execution, where it is executed elsewhere than in China, Japan, or Hong Kong:

then, and in every such case, the mortgage debt secured by, the deed or other instrument and the interest thereon shall not have priority over judgment or simple contract debts contracted before the registration of that deed or other instrument.

25. Registered deeds or other instruments of mortgage, legal, or equitable, of the same lands or houses have, as among themselves, priority in order of registration.

26.—(a.) The provisions of this Order do not apply to a deed or other instrument of mortgage executed before the commencement of this Order.

(b.) As regards a deed or other instrument of mortgage executed before the commencement of this Order, the regulations repealed by this Order shall, notwithstanding that repeal, be in force, and shall be deemed to have always been of the like validity and effect as if they had originally been made by Order in Council.

27. The power conferred on the Chief Justice of the Supreme Court for China and Japan by Article 127 of the China and Japan Order in Council, 1865, of framing rules from time to time, is hereby extended to the framing of rules for prescribing and regulating the making and keeping of indexes, and of a general index, to the register of mortgages, and searches in those indexes, and other particulars connected with the making, keeping, and using of those registers and indexes, and for authorizing and regulating the unregistering of any deed or other instrument of mortgage, or the registering of any release or satisfaction in respect thereof.

Bills of Sale.

28. The provisions of this Order relating to bills of sale—

(i.) Apply only to such bills of sale executed by British subjects as are intended to affect chattels in China or in Japan:

(ii.) Do not apply to bills of sale given by sheriffs or others under or in execution of process authorizing seizure of chattels.

29.—(a.) Every bill of sale must conform with the following rules (namely):

(1.) It must state truly the name, description, and address of the grantor.

JURISDICTION—*continued.*

(2.) It must state truly the consideration for which it is granted.

(3.) It must have annexed thereto or written thereunder an inventory of the chattels intended to be comprised therein.

(4.) Any defeasance, condition, or declaration of trust affecting the bill not contained in the body of the bill must be written on the same paper as the bill.

(5.) The execution of the bill must be attested by a credible witness, with his address and description.

(b.) Otherwise, the bill is void in China and in Japan to the extent following, but not further (that is to say):

(i.) In the case of failure to conform with the rule respecting an inventory, as far as regards chattels omitted from the inventory; and

(ii.) In any other case, wholly.

(c.) The inventory, and any defeasance, condition, or declaration as aforesaid, respectively, is for all purposes deemed part of the bill.

30. A bill of sale conforming, or appearing to conform, with the foregoing rules, may be registered, if it is intended to affect chattels in China, at the Supreme Court; and if it is intended to affect chattels in Japan, at the Court for Japan; or in either case at the Consulate of the Consular district wherein the chattels are; within the respective time following and not afterwards (namely):

(i.) Within fourteen days after its execution, where it is executed in the consular district wherein the chattels are:

(ii.) Within two months after its execution, where it is executed in China or in Japan, elsewhere than in that consular district, or in Hong Kong:

(iii.) Within six months after its execution, where it is executed elsewhere than in China, Japan, or Hong Kong.

31. Registration is made as follows: The original and a copy of the bill of sale, and an affidavit verifying the execution, and the time and place of execution, and the attestation thereof, and verifying the copy, are brought into the proper office of the Court or the Consulate; and the copy and affidavit are left there.

32. If a bill of sale is not registered at a place and within the time by this Order appointed and allowed for registration thereof, it is, from and after the expiration of that time, void in China or in Japan, according as that place is in China or in Japan, to the extent following, but not further (that is to say):

(i.) As against trustees or assignees of the estate of the grantor, in or under bankruptcy, liquidation, or assignment for benefit of creditors; and

(ii.) As against all sheriffs and others seizing chattels under process of any Court, and any person on whose behalf the seizure is made; but only

(iii.) As regards the property in, or right to, the possession of such chattels comprised in the bill as, at or after the filing of the petition for bankruptcy or liquidation, or the execution of the assignment, or the seizure, are in the grantor's possession, or apparent possession.

JURISDICTION—*continued.*

33. *Registered bills of sale affecting the same chattels have as among themselves priority in order of registration.*

34. *Chattels comprised in a registered bill of sale are not in the possession, order, or disposition of the grantor within the law of bankruptcy.*

35. *If in any case there is an unregistered bill of sale, and within or on the expiration of the time by this Order allowed for registration thereof, a subsequent bill of sale is granted affecting the same or some of the same chattels, for the same or part of the same debt, then the subsequent bill is, to the extent to which it comprises the same chattels and is for the same debt, absolutely void, unless the Supreme Court for China and Japan, or the Court for Japan, as the case may require, is satisfied that the subsequent bill is granted in good faith for the purpose of correcting some material error in the prior bill, and not for the purpose of unlawfully evading the operation of this Order.*

36. *The registration of a bill of sale must be renewed once at least every five years.*

37. *Renewal of registration is made as follows: An affidavit stating the date of and parties to the bill of sale, and the date of the original registration, and of the last renewal, and that the bill is still a subsisting security, is brought in to the proper office of the Court or the Consulate of original registration, and is left there.*

38. *If the registration of a bill of sale is not so renewed in any period of five years, then on and from the expiration of that period the bill is deemed to be unregistered.*

39. *The provisions of this Order relating to renewal apply to bills of sale registered under the regulations repealed by this Order.*

40. *A transfer or assignment of a registered bill of sale need not be registered; and renewal of registration is not necessary by reason only of such a transfer or assignment.*

41. *Where the time for registration or renewal of registration of a bill of sale expires on a Sunday, or other day on which the office for registration is closed, the registration or renewal is valid if made on the first subsequent day on which the office is open.*

42. *If in any case the Supreme Court for China and Japan, or the Court for Japan, as the case may require, is satisfied that failure to register or to renew the registration of a bill of sale in due time, or any omission or misstatement connected with registration or renewal, was accidental or inadvertent, the Court may, if it thinks fit, order the failure, omission, or misstatement to be rectified in such manner and on such terms, if any, respecting security, notice by advertisement or otherwise, or any other matter, as the Court thinks fit.*

43. (a.) *The provisions of this Order, except as regards renewal of registration, do not apply to a bill of sale executed before the commencement of this Order.*

(b.) *As regards a bill of sale executed before the commencement of this Order, the regulations repealed by this Order shall, notwithstanding that repeal, be in force, and shall be deemed to have always been of the like validity and effect as if they had originally been made by Order in Council.*

44. *The power conferred on the Chief Justice*

JURISDICTION—*continued.*

of the Supreme Court for China and Japan by Article 127 of the China and Japan Order in Council, 1865, of framing rules from time to time, is hereby extended to the framing of rules for prescribing and regulating the making and keeping of indexes, and of a general index, to the registers of bills of sale, and searches in those indexes, and other particulars connected with the making, keeping, and using of those registers and indexes, and for authorizing and regulating the unregistering of any bill of sale, or the registering of any release or satisfaction in respect thereof.

Suits by or against Partners.

45. (a.) *The following are Rules of Procedure of Her Majesty's Courts in China and in Japan, under the China and Japan Order in Council, 1865:*

(1.) *Persons claiming or being liable as partners may sue or be sued in the firm name, if any.*

(2.) *Where partners sue in the firm name, they must, on demand in writing on behalf of any defendant, forthwith declare the names and addresses of the partners.*

(3.) *Otherwise, all proceedings in the suit may, on application, be stayed on such terms as the Court thinks fit.*

(4.) *When the names of the partners are so declared, the suit proceeds in the same manner, and the same consequences in all respects follow, as if they had been named as the plaintiffs in the petition.*

(5.) *All subsequent proceedings nevertheless continue in the firm name.*

(6.) *Where partners are sued in the firm name, the petition must be served either on one or more of the partners within the jurisdiction, or at the principal place of the partnership business within the jurisdiction on some person having then and there control or management of the partnership business.*

(7.) *Where one person, carrying on business in the name of a firm apparently representing more persons than one, is sued in the firm name, the petition may be served at the principal place of the business within the jurisdiction on some person having then and there control or management of the business.*

(8.) *Where partners are sued in the firm name, they must appear individually in their own names.*

(9.) *All subsequent proceedings nevertheless continue in the firm name.*

(10.) *Where a person, carrying on business in the name of a firm apparently representing more persons than one, is sued in the firm name he must appear in his own name.*

(11.) *All subsequent proceedings nevertheless continue in the firm name.*

(12.) *In any case not hereinbefore provided for, where persons claiming or being liable as partners sue or are sued in the firm name, any party to the suit may, on application to the Court, obtain a statement of the names of the persons who are partners in the firm, to be furnished and verified on oath or otherwise, as the Court thinks fit.*

(13.) *Where a judgment is against partners in the firm name, execution may issue—*

(1.) *Against any property of the partners a such; and*

JURISDICTION—*continued.*

(ii.) *Against any person who has admitted in the suit that he is a partner, or who has been adjudged to be a partner ; and*

(iii.) *Against any person who has been served in the suit as a partner, and has failed to appear.*

(14.) *If the party who has obtained judgment claims to be entitled to issue execution against any other person, as being a partner, he may apply to the Court for leave so to do ; and the Court, if the liability is not disputed, may give such leave, or if it is disputed may order that the question of the liability be tried and determined as a question in the suit, in such manner as the Court thinks fit.*

(b.) *The foregoing rules may be from time to time varied by Rules of Procedure made under the China and Japan Order in Council, 1865.*

(c.) *Printed copies of the foregoing rules must be exhibited conspicuously in each Court and Consulate in China and Japan, with the other Rules of Procedure for the time being in force under the China and Japan Order in Council, 1865, and be sold at such reasonable price as the Chief Justice of the Supreme Court from time to time directs.*

(d.) *A printed copy of the foregoing rules purporting to be certified under the hand of the Chief Justice of the Supreme Court and the seal of that Court is for all purposes conclusive evidence thereof.*

46.—(a.) *The provisions of this Order do not apply to proceedings instituted by or against partnerships or partners or agents thereof, before the commencement of this Order.*

(b.) *As regards proceedings instituted by or against partnerships or partners or agents thereof before the commencement of this Order, the regulations repealed by this Order shall, notwithstanding that repeal, be in force, and shall be deemed to have always been of the like validity and effect as if they had been Rules of Procedure made under the China and Japan Order in Council, 1865 ; and, as regards the same proceedings, the Rule of Procedure (252) repealed by this Order shall continue to have effect, notwithstanding that repeal, subject always to the operation of the regulations repealed by this Order.*

Suits by or against Foreigners.

47.—(a.) *Where a foreigner desires to institute or take a suit or proceeding of a civil nature against a British subject, or a British subject desires to institute or take a suit or proceeding of a civil nature against a foreigner, the Supreme Court for China and Japan, and the Court for Japan, and a Provincial Court, according to the respective jurisdiction of the Court, may entertain the suit or proceeding, and hear and determine it ; and, if all parties desire, or the Court directs, a trial with a jury or assessors, then, with a jury or assessors, at a place where such a trial might be had if all parties were British subjects, but in all other respects according to the ordinary course of the Court :*

(b.) *Provided, that the foreigner first obtains and files in the Court the consent in writing of the competent authority of his own nation to his submitting, and that he does submit, to the jurisdiction of the Court, and, if required by the Court, gives security to the satisfaction of the Court, and*

JURISDICTION—*continued.*

to such reasonable amount as the Court directs, by deposit or otherwise, to pay fees, damages, costs, and expenses, and abide by and perform the decision to be given either by the Court or on appeal.

(c.) *A counter-claim or cross-suit cannot be brought or instituted in the Court against a plaintiff, being a foreigner, who has submitted to the jurisdiction, by a defendant, except by leave of the Court first obtained.*

(d.) *The Court, before giving leave, requires proof from the defendant that his claim arises out of the matter in dispute, and that there is reasonable ground for it, and that it is not made for vexation or delay.*

(e.) *Nothing in this provision prevents the defendant from instituting or taking in the Court against the foreigner, after the termination of the suit or proceeding in which the foreigner is plaintiff, any suit or proceeding that the defendant might have instituted or taken in the Court against the foreigner if no provision restraining counter-claims or cross-suits had been inserted in this Order.*

(f.) *Where a foreigner obtains in the Court an Order against a defendant being a British subject, and in another suit that defendant is plaintiff and the foreigner is defendant, the Court may, if it thinks fit, on the application of the British subject, stay the enforcement of the order pending that other suit, and may set off any amount ordered to be paid by one party in one suit against any amount ordered to be paid by the other party in the other suit.*

(g.) *Where a plaintiff, being a foreigner, obtains in the Court an order against two or more defendants, being British subjects, jointly, and in another suit one of them is plaintiff, and the foreigner is defendant, the Court may, if it thinks fit, on the application of the British subject, stay the enforcement of the order pending that other suit, and may set off any amount ordered to be paid by one party in one suit against any amount ordered to be paid by the other party in the other suit, without prejudice to the right of the British subject to require contribution from his co-defendants under the joint liability.*

(h.) *Where a foreigner is co-plaintiff in a suit with a British subject who is within the particular jurisdiction, it is not necessary for the foreigner to make deposit or give security for costs, unless the Court so directs ; but the co-plaintiff British subject is responsible for all fees and costs.*

Chinese, Japanese, or Foreign Tribunals.

48.—(a.) *Where it is shewn to the Supreme or other Court that the attendance of a British subject to give evidence, or for any other purpose connected with the administration of justice, is required in a Chinese or Japanese Court, or before a Chinese or Japanese judicial officer or in a Court or before a judicial officer of any state in amity with Her Majesty, the Supreme or other Court may, if it thinks fit, in a case and in circumstances in which it would require his attendance before itself, order that he do attend as so required.*

(b.) *A Provincial Court, however, cannot so order attendance at any place beyond its particular jurisdiction.*

JURISDICTION—*continued.*

(c.) *If the person ordered to attend, having reasonable notice of the time and place at which he is required to attend, fails to attend accordingly, and does not excuse his failure to the satisfaction of the Supreme or other Court, he is, independently of any other liability, guilty of an offence against this Order, and for every such offence, on conviction thereof, by summary trial, is liable to a fine not exceeding $500, or to imprisonment for not exceeding one month, in the discretion of the Court.*

And the Foreign Office is to give the necessary directions herein.

Schedule.

I.—*Regulations made by Sir Rutherford Alcock while Her Majesty's Minister in China, intituled or designated as Land Regulations, Regulations, and By-Laws annexed to the Land Regulations, for the Foreign quarter of Shanghai north of the Yang - King - Pang, and commonly called the Shanghai Land Regulations.*

II.—*Port, Consular, Customs, and Harbour Regulations applicable to all the Treaty ports in China, dated 31st of May, 1869.*　　**L. G., 1881, p. 5289**

China, Japan, and Corea.] *The China, Japan, and Corea Order of 26th June, 1884, provides for the exercise of British jurisdiction in Corea in accordance with the provisions of the China and Japan Orders in Council* -　**L. G., 1884, p. 2991**

The China, Japan, and Corea Order of 9th of September, 1884 (Supplemental) makes further provision for the exercise of British jurisdiction in Corea -　-　-　**L. G., 1884, p. 4115**

The Order in Council of 26th of March, 1885, establishes new tables of Consular fees in China, Japan, and Corea -　-　**L. G., 1885, p. 1527**

Cyprus.] *Neutrality Order in Council of May 18th, 1881, makes provision for the regulation of the conduct of the inhabitants of Cyprus, and other persons residing therein during the existence of hostilities between States with which Her Majesty is at peace* -　**L. G., 1881, p. 2795**

Order in Council of 15th of July, 1881, making provision for appeals from the decisions of the High Court of Justice for Cyprus, and from the Ottoman Court there, called the Temyiz Court
　　　　　　　　　　[L. G., 1881, p. 3589

Ottoman Dominions.] *The Ottoman Order in Council of May 3rd, 1882.*

1.—(a.) *This Order may be cited as the Ottoman Order in Council, 1882.*

(b.) *The Order in Council made at Windsor, the 12th day of December, 1873, for the regulation of consular jurisdiction in the Ottoman dominions, may be cited as the Ottoman Order in Council, 1873.*

(c.) *That Order and this Order may be cited together as the Ottoman Orders in Council, 1873 and 1882.*

Commencement.

2. *This Order shall commence and have effect from and immediately after the 31st day of May, 1882.*

Interpretation.

3. *In this Order—*
"*Her Majesty's Ambassador*" *includes Her*

JURISDICTION—*continued.*

Majesty's Chargé d'Affaires, or other chief diplomatic representative in the Ottoman dominions for the time being.

"*Administration*" *means letters of administration, including the same with will annexed, or granted for special or limited purposes.*

"*Ship*" *includes any vessel used in navigation, howsoever propelled, with her tackle, furniture, and apparel, and any boat or other craft.*

"*Ottoman waters*" *means the territorial waters of the Ottoman dominions.*

Other words have the same meaning as in the Ottoman Order in Council, 1873.

Repeal.

4. *The following parts of the Ottoman Order in Council, 1873, are hereby repealed:*

(a.) *Art. 11.—The last two paragraphs.*
(b.) *Art. 12.—The last paragraph.*
(c.) *Art. 13.—The words " and for that purpose shall have the like jurisdiction and authority as the assistant judge."*
(d.) *Art. 93.*
(e.) *Art. 266.—In the first paragraph the words " the judge of ;" and the last paragraph.*

Assistant Judge of Supreme Court.

5.—(a.) *The Assistant Judge of the Supreme Court shall be, at the time of his appointment, a member of the Bar of England, Scotland, or Ireland, of seven years' standing.*

(b.) *The assistant judge shall hear and determine such causes and matters, civil and criminal, and transact such other part of the business of the Supreme Court as the Judge of the Supreme Court, from time to time, by general order or otherwise, directs.*

(c.) *For that purpose the assistant judge shall have all the like jurisdiction, power, and authority as the judge.*

(d.) *Any party to a civil suit or proceeding, wherein any matter or question is heard and determined by the assistant judge, and any party to a criminal proceeding, other than a proceeding by summary trial, wherein any question of law is heard and determined by the assistant judge, shall be entitled, as of course, to a re-hearing of the matter or question aforesaid before the judge, sitting with the assistant judge, or, in the unavoidable absence of the assistant judge, alone; provided that an application for the re-hearing be made within three days after the day of the decision of the assistant judge.*

(e.) *If, on any such re-hearing, there is a difference of opinion between the judge and the assistant judge, the opinion of the judge shall prevail.*

Acting Judge or Acting Assistant Judge of Supreme Court.

6. *In case of the death or illness, or the absence or intended absence from the district of the Consulate-General of Constantinople, of the Judge or Assistant Judge of the Supreme Court, Her Majesty's Ambassador may appoint a fit person to be the acting judge, or to be the acting assistant judge, as the case may require; but, unless in any case the Secretary of State otherwise directs, the assistant judge, if present, and able to act, shall always be appointed to be the acting judge.*

JURISDICTION—*continued.*

Offences on Board Ship.

7. Sect. 11 of the Merchant Shipping Act, 1867, is hereby extended to the Ottoman dominions, with such adaptations and modifications that the same will, as regards those dominions, read as follows (namely):

If in the Mediterranean Sea, or the Sea of Azof, or if in the Adriatic, Ægean, or Black Sea, out of Ottoman waters, a British subject commits an offence on board a British ship, or on board a foreign ship to which he does not belong, the Supreme Court, sitting within the district of the Consulate-General of Constantinople, shall have jurisdiction to hear and determine the case as if the offence had been committed on board a British ship in Ottoman waters; and the Supreme Court may exercise that jurisdiction accordingly if in any case the Court, in its discretion, having regard to all the circumstances, thinks it fit and expedient so to do.

Detention of Ship.

8. Where the Supreme Court issues a summons or warrant against any person on a charge of an offence committed on board of or in relation to a British ship, then, if it appears to the Court that the interests of public justice so require, the Supreme Court may issue a warrant or order for the detention of the ship, being within the district of the Consulate-General of Constantinople, and may cause the ship to be detained accordingly, until the charge is heard and determined and the order of the Court thereon is fully executed, or for such shorter time as the Court thinks fit; and the Supreme Court shall have power to make, from time to time, all such orders as appear to it necessary or proper for carrying this provision into effect.

Offences partly out of Jurisdiction.

9. The Admiralty Offences Colonial Act, 1860, is hereby extended to the Ottoman dominions, with such adaptations and modifications that the same will, as regards those dominions and the jurisdiction of the Court, read as follows (namely):

Where a person, being feloniously stricken, poisoned, or otherwise hurt, in the Ottoman dominions, dies of such stroke, poisoning, or hurt, on the sea, or out of the Ottoman dominions, then every offence committed in respect of any such case, whether amounting to murder or to manslaughter, or to the being accessory before the fact to murder, or after the fact to murder or to manslaughter, may be dealt with, inquired of, tried, determined, and punished in the Ottoman dominions in all respects as if such offence had been wholly committed in the Ottoman dominions.

Fugitive Offenders.

10. The Fugitive Offenders Act, 1881, except Part II. thereof, or so much thereof, except that part, as is for the time being in force, and any enactment for the time being in force amending or substituted for the same, are hereby extended to the Ottoman dominions, with the adaptations following (namely):

(i.) Her Majesty's ambassador is hereby substituted for the governor of a British possession:

JURISDICTION—*continued.*

(ii.) The Supreme Court, or the Court for Egypt, or the Court for Tunis (as the case requires), is hereby substituted for a Superior Court in a British possession:

(iii.) Each Court under the Ottoman Order in Council, 1873, according to its jurisdiction, is substituted for a magistrate of any part of Her Majesty's dominions.

Coroner's Inquests.

11.—(a.) The Supreme Court shall, for and within the district of the Consulate-General of Constantinople, and the Court for Egypt shall, for and in Egypt, and the Court for Tunis shall, for and in Tunis, have and discharge all the powers, rights, and duties appertaining to the office of coroner in England, in relation not only to deaths of British subjects happening in that respective district or country, but also to deaths of any persons having happened at sea on board British ships arriving in that respective district or country, and to deaths of British subjects having happened at sea on board foreign ships so arriving.

(b.) Every inquest shall be held with a jury of not less than three persons comprised in the jury list of the Court summoned for that purpose.

(c.) If any person fails to attend according to such summons, he shall be liable to the like fine, to be levied in the like manner, as is in the Ottoman Order in Council, 1873, provided with respect to juries in civil and criminal proceedings.

Jurisdiction as regards Embassy.

12. The Court shall not exercise any jurisdiction in any proceeding whatsoever over Her Majesty's ambassador, or his official or other residences, or his official or other property; nor shall the Court, except with the consent of Her Majesty's ambassador, signified in writing to the Court, exercise any jurisdiction in a civil action or proceeding over any person attached to or being a member of Her Majesty's embassy, or being a domestic servant of Her Majesty's ambassador.

Evidence.

13. If in any case it is made to appear to the Court that the attendance of Her Majesty's ambassador, or of any person attached to or being a member of Her Majesty's embassy, or being a domestic servant of Her Majesty's ambassador, to give evidence before the Court, is requisite in the interest of justice, the Court shall address to Her Majesty's ambassador a request in writing for such attendance.

14. A person attending to give evidence before the Court shall not be compellable to give any evidence or to produce any document if, in the opinion of Her Majesty's ambassador, signified by him personally or in writing to the Court, the giving or production thereof would be injurious to Her Majesty's service.

15. Sections 7 and 11 of the Evidence Act, 1851, are hereby extended to the Ottoman dominions.

16. The following Acts (namely):

The Foreign Tribunals Evidence Act, 1856.

The Evidence by Commission Act, 1859,— or so much thereof as is for the time being in force, and any enactment for the time being in force

JURISDICTION—continued.

amending or substituted for the same, are hereby extended to the Ottoman dominions, with the adaptations following (namely):

The Supreme Court, or the Court for Egypt, or the Court for Tunis (as the case requires), is hereby substituted for a Supreme Court in a colony.

Ascertainment of Law.

17. The following Acts (namely):
The British Law Ascertainment Act, 1859,
The Foreign Law Ascertainment Act, 1861,—
or so much thereof as is for the time being in force, and any enactment for the time being in force amending or substituted for the same, are hereby extended to the Ottoman dominions, with the adaptations following (namely):

The Supreme Court, or the Court for Egypt, or the Court for Tunis (as the case requires), is hereby substituted for a Superior Court in a colony.

Probate.

18.—(a.) Where probate, administration, or confirmation is granted in England, Ireland, or Scotland, and therein, or by a memorandum thereon signed by an officer of the Court granting the same, the testator or intestate is stated to have died domiciled in England, Ireland, or Scotland (as the case may be), and the probate, administration, or confirmation is produced to, and a copy thereof is deposited with, the Supreme Court, the Court shall write thereon a certificate of that production and deposit; and thereupon, notwithstanding anything in the Ottoman Order in Council, 1873, the probate, administration, or confirmation shall, with respect to the personal property in the Ottoman dominions of the testator or intestate, have the like effect as if he had been resident in those dominions at his death, and probate or administration to his personal property there had been granted by the Supreme Court.

(b.) Any person who, in reliance on an instrument purporting to be a probate, administration, or confirmation granted in England, Ireland, or Scotland, and to bear such a certificate of the Supreme Court as in this article prescribed, makes or permits any payment or transfer, in good faith, shall be, by virtue of this Order, indemnified and protected in respect thereof, in the Ottoman dominions, notwithstanding anything affecting the validity of the probate, administration, or confirmation.

(c.) The following shall be the terms of the certificate of the Supreme Court in this article prescribed (namely):

This probate has [or these letters of administration have or this confirmation has] been produced to this Court, and a copy thereof has been deposited with this Court.

19. Section 51 of the Conveyancing (Scotland) Act, 1874, and any enactment for the time being in force amending or substituted for the same, are hereby extended to the Ottoman dominions, with the adaptation following (namely):

The Supreme Court is hereby substituted for a Court of Probate in a Colony.

Recovery against Ships.

20. Where money ordered by the Court to be

JURISDICTION—continued.

paid is due for seamen's wages, or is other money recoverable under the Merchant Shipping Acts or other law relating to ships, and the person ordered to pay is master or owner of a ship, and the money is not paid as ordered, the Court, in addition to other powers for compelling payment, shall have power to direct that the amount unpaid be levied by seizure and sale of that ship.

Judicial Notice.

21. Judicial notice shall be taken of the Ottoman Order in Council, 1873, and of the several Orders in Council amending the same, passed or to be passed, and of this Order, and of the appointment of all judges, officers, and persons acting thereunder, and of their signatures, and of all seals used thereunder; and no proof thereof shall be necessary.

And the Foreign Office, the Treasury, and the Admiralty are to give the necessary directions herein as to them may respectively appertain.

[L. G., 1882, p. 2209

Ottoman Dominions—Tunis.] Order in Council of 18th May, 1881, making further regulation for the exercise of British jurisdiction in the Regency of Tunis -　-　L. G., 1881, p. 2617
Order in Council abandoning British Consular jurisdiction in Tunis, 31st Dec., 1884
[L. G., 1884, p. 71

Siam.] The Siam Order in Council of 26th June, 1884, provides for the exercise of British jurisdiction in the dominions of the Kings of Siam
[L. G., 1884, p. 3049
Ditto, Supplemental Order of 9th September, 1884 -　-　-　-　L. G., 1884, p. 4115

South Africa.] Order in Council of 27th January, 1885, to exercise British jurisdiction in parts of South Africa situate west of the boundary of the South African Republic, as defined by Convention of 27th February, 1884. L. G., 1885, p. 417

West Africa.] Order in Council of 26th March, 1885, to exercise British jurisdiction in parts of West Africa situate west of the 25th meridian of east longitude, south of the 30th parallel of north latitude, and north of 25th parallel of south latitude -　-　-　-　L. G., 1885, p. 1617

Zanzibar.] The Zanzibar Order in Council of 29th November, 1884, makes provision for the exercise of British jurisdiction in the dominions of the Sultan of Zanzibar　　L. G., 1884, p. 5649

The following Orders have been also made as to foreign jurisdiction:—

Fees.] Order in Council of 26th March, 1885 (not under the Foreign Jurisdiction Acts) establishing the Consular Fees to be taken in all foreign countries other than China, Japan, and Corea, in pursuance of the Acts 6 Geo. 4, c. 87, and 12 & 13 Vict. c. 68 -　-　-　L. G., 1885, p. 1523
Gibraltar.] The law of England as it existed on 31st December, 1883, to be, subject to some exceptions, hereafter in force in the city, garrison, and territory of Gibraltar. Jurisdiction of the Supreme Court of Gibraltar from the 2nd February, 1884
[L. G., 1884, p. 579

1. —— Land in Foreign Country—Parties resident in England.] The title to immoveable pro-

JURISDICTION—*continued.*

perty in Saxony was in dispute between A. and B. A. sold the property in Saxony, received part of the purchase-money, and took a mortgage for the balance. Both A. and B. being in England. an action by B. to make A. account for the purchase-money was dismissed for want of jurisdiction. *In re* HAWTHORNE. GRAHAM *v.* MASSEY
[23 Ch. D. 743

2. —— **Larceny from British Ship at Foreign Port**—*Feloniously receiving Property stolen from British Ship at Foreign Port—Admiralty, Jurisdiction of—Criminal Jurisdiction over British Ship afloat Abroad—High Seas, Criminal Jurisdiction on.*] Certain bonds or valuable securities were stolen from a British ocean-going merchant ship whilst she was lying afloat, in the ordinary course of her trading, in the river at Rotterdam, in Holland, moored to the quay, and were afterwards wrongfully received in England by the prisoners with a knowledge that they had been thus stolen. The place where the ship lay at the time of the theft was in the open river, sixteen or eighteen miles from the sea, but within the ebb and flow of the tide. There were no bridges between the ship and the sea, and the place where she lay was one where large vessels usually lay. It did not appear who the thief was, or under what circumstances he was on board the ship:—*Held* (by Lord Coleridge, C.J., Pollock B., Lopes, Stephen, and Watkin Williams, JJ.), that the prisoners could be properly tried and convicted at the Central Criminal Court in this country, as the larceny took place within the jurisdiction of the Admiralty of England. THE QUEEN *v.* CARR 10 Q. B. D. 76

3. —— **Wages** — **Foreign Ship** — *Protest by Foreign Consul — Discretion of Court.* In an action for wages and damages for wrongful dismissal by British seamen who had served on a Spanish ship under Spanish articles, the Spanish consul at Liverpool protested against the exercise of the jurisdiction of the Court, and the Court accordingly dismissed the action:—*Held,* on appeal, that to enable the Court of Appeal to overrule the discretion of the Court below as to entertaining the action, the Judge must be shewn to have exercised it on wrong principles or wrongly or unfairly.—*Held,* further, that though no express provision of the Spanish code was referred to in the articles, and though it did not appear in evidence that the Spanish code compelled the seamen to abide by the decision of a Spanish tribunal, yet, under the circumstances, it must be inferred that they had agreed to do so. THE "LEON XIII." - - 8 P. D. 121

—— Admiralty Court.
See Cases under PRACTICE—ADMIRALTY —JURISDICTION.

—— Allowance for maintenance of infant — Summons 19 Ch. D. 305
See INFANT—MAINTENANCE. 3.

—— Appellant out of 22 Ch. D. 83
See PRACTICE—SUPREME COURT—SECURITY FOR COSTS. 9.

—— Appointment of guardian to infant abroad
[30 Ch. D. 324
See INFANT—GUARDIAN. 1.

JURISDICTION—*continued.*

—— Arbitration—Public Health Act, 1875
[11 Q. B. D. 735 ; 9 App. Cas. 595.
See LOCAL GOVERNMENT—COMPENSATION. 1.

—— Bankruptcy Court.
See Cases under BANKRUPTCY—JURISDICTION.

—— Bankruptcy Court 16 Ch. D. 131
See BANKRUPTCY—COMPOSITION. 1.

—— Bankruptcy Court 19 Ch. D. 86
See BAILMENT.

—— Bankruptcy Court—Bankruptcy Act, 1883.
See BANKRUPTCY—STATUTES.

—— Bankruptcy Court—Debtor's summons
[16 Ch. D. 484
See BANKRUPTCY—ACT OF BANKRUPTCY. 14.

—— Bankruptcy—Disclaimer of lease—Landlord's claim for compensation "
[14 Q. B. D. 960
See BANKRUPTCY—DISCLAIMER. 21.

—— Bankruptcy—Petition presented in wrong court—Receiving order 14 Q. B. D. 37
See BANKRUPTCY—RECEIVER. 5.

—— Bankruptcy Court—Scotch sequestration
[22 Ch. D. 816
See BANKRUPTCY—ADJUDICATION. 4.

—— Bankruptcy Court—Substituted service of appeal - 24 Ch. D. 364
See BANKRUPTCY—APPEAL. 3.

—— Chancery Division—Probate of will
[26 Ch. D. 656
See PRACTICE—SUPREME COURT—JURISDICTION. 1.

—— Church Building Acts 24 Ch. D. 213
See CHURCH BUILDING ACTS.

—— Committee out of—Appointment 17 Ch. D.
See LUNATIC—COMMITTEE. 2. [775

—— Compromise by infant - 16 Ch. D. 41
See INFANT—CONTRACTS. 8.

—— Costs under Trustee Act 26 Ch. D. 82
See TRUSTEE—COSTS AND CHARGES. 8.

—— County Court—Admiralty.
See Cases under COUNTY COURT—JURISDICTION.

—— Court of Appeal—Solicitor 28 Ch. D. 614
See SOLICITOR—MISCONDUCT. 2.

—— Court of Queen's Bench—Supreme Court of Canada - 6 App. Cas. 644
See COLONIAL LAW—CANADA— ONTARIO. 1.

—— Ecclesiastical Court - 7 App. Cas. 240
See PRACTICE—ECCLESIASTICAL—PUBLIC WORSHIP ACT. 1.

—— Ecclesiastical Court 22 Ch. D. 316 ; 8 P. D. 191
See PRACTICE—ECCLESIASTICAL—JURISDICTION. 1, 2.

—— Ecclesiastical Court
See ECCLESIASTICAL LAW — BISHOP — *Statutes.*

—— Equitable—Removal of trustees 9 App. Cas.
[371
See COLONIAL LAW — CAPE OF GOOD HOPE. 2.

JURISDICTION—*continued.*

—— Foreign decree—Absence of will　6 P. D. 6
　　See ADMINISTRATOR—LIMITED. 6.

—— Foreign ship—Board of Trade—17 & 18
　　Vict. c. 104, s. 512　　-　9 P. D. 88
　　See PRACTICE—ADMIRALTY—JURISDIC-
　　TION. 2.

—— High Court of Justice　-　9 Q. B. D. 518
　　See ARBITRATION—SUBMISSION. 1.

—— High Court of Justice—Action for sum
　　below £10　　-　　-　30 Ch. D. 387
　　See PRACTICE—SUPREME COURT—JURIS-
　　DICTION. 2.

—— High Court of Justice—Dispute in building
　　society -　　　-　　9 App. Cas. 260
　　See BUILDING SOCIETY. 2.

—— High Court of Justice—Winding-up of
　　mining company—Stannaries Court
　　　　　　　　　　[18 Ch. D. 472
　　See COMPANY—COST-BOOK COMPANY. 1.

—— Infant's real estate -　　-　21 Ch. D. 786
　　See INFANT—PROPERTY. 1.

—— Inferior Court—Prohibition 14 Q. B. D. 855
　　See PROHIBITION.

—— Injunction to restrain election of alderman
　　　　　　　　　　[16 Ch. D. 143
　　See MUNICIPAL CORPORATION—QUALIFI-
　　CATION.

—— Injunction to restrain proceedings before
　　justices -　　　-　　20 Ch. D. 190
　　See PRACTICE — SUPREME COURT—IN-
　　JUNCTION. 7.

—— Injunction to restrain winding-up petition
　　　　　　　　　　[18 Ch. D. 555
　　See COMPANY—WINDING-UP ORDER. 9.

—— Judge under Public Worship Regulation
　　Act　　-　　-　6 Q. B. D. 376
　　See PRACTICE—ECCLESIASTICAL--CHURCH
　　DISCIPLINE ACT. 2.

—— Justices—Contagious Diseases (Animals)
　　Act—Movement of animals into pro-
　　scribed districts　-　12 Q. B. D. 629
　　See CONTAGIOUS DISEASES (ANIMALS)
　　ACTS.

—— Justices—Public Health Act, 1875
　　　　　　　　　　[12 Q. B. D. 142
　　See LOCAL GOVERNMENT—PRACTICE. 2.

—— Justices—Right of fishing—Tidal navigable
　　river　　-　　　-　8 Q. B. D. 626
　　See JUSTICES—JURISDICTION.

—— Lancaster Palatine Court—Service
　　　　　　　　　　[24 Ch. D. 280
　　See COURT—LANCASTER COURT.

—— Lunacy.
　　See Cases and Statutes under LUNATIC
　　—JURISDICTION.

—— Lunacy—Property of small amount
　　　　　　　　　　[26 Ch. D. 496
　　See LUNATIC—PROPERTY. 7.

—— Maritime lien—Foreign judgment　6 P. D.
　　See FOREIGN JUDGMENT. 2.　　[106

—— Master of the Rolls—Patent　26 Ch. D. 105
　　See PATENT—AMENDMENT. 1.

—— Mother of infant resident out of 28 Ch. D. 82
　　See INFANT—EDUCATION. 3.

JURISDICTION—*continued.*

—— Murder on high seas　-　14 Q. B. D. 273
　　See CRIMINAL LAW—OFFENCES AGAINST
　　PERSON. 6.

—— Partition suit　22 Ch. D. 284; 24 Ch. D. 622
　　See PARTITION SUIT—JURISDICTION. 1, 2.

—— Plaintiff out of—Security for costs 28 Ch. D.
　　　　　　　　　　[232
　　See PRACTICE—SUPREME COURT—SECU-
　　RITY FOR COSTS. 7.

—— Probate Division—Married woman—Will of
　　realty　　-　　　-　6 P. D. 209
　　See PROBATE—MARRIED WOMAN. 4.

—— Registrar and merchants—Bottomry—Re-
　　duction of amount　　-　9 P. D. 177
　　See SHIP—MARITIME LIEN. 2.

—— Scotch assets — Administration action in
　　England 22 Ch. D. 456; 9 App. Cas. 34
　　See EXECUTOR—ACTIONS. 16.

—— Scotch Courts — Assets in England and
　　Scotland　-　　-　10 App. Cas. 453
　　See SCOTCH LAW—JURISDICTION.

—— Sequestration—Payment of money in Court
　　to sequestrator -　　　18 Ch. D. 653
　　See PRACTICE—SUPREME COURT—SE-
　　QUESTRATION. 2.

—— Service out of.
　　See Cases under PRACTICE — SUPREME
　　COURT—SERVICE. 2—10.

—— Specific performance of separation deed
　　　　　　　　　　[18 Ch. D. 670
　　See HUSBAND AND WIFE—SEPARATION
　　DEED. 1.

—— Suit against public officer　6 App. Cas. 619
　　See COLONIAL LAW—NATAL. 1.

—— Transfer of action　-　-　16 Ch. D. 702
　　See PRACTICE—SUPREME COURT—TRANS-
　　FER. 1.

—— Transfer of action　　-　27 Ch. D. 533
　　See PRACTICE—SUPREME COURT—JURIS-
　　DICTION. 3.

—— Vice-Admiralty Court　　8 App. Cas. 329
　　See PRACTICE—ADMIRALTY—JURISDIC-
　　TION. 5.

—— Vice-Admiralty Court　-　9 App. Cas. 356
　　See SHIP—MARITIME LIEN. 7.

—— Ward of Court　　-　28 Ch. D. 186
　　See INFANT—WARD OF COURT. 3.

—— Waterworks company—Settlement of dis-
　　putes　　　-　　28 Ch. D. 138
　　See WATERWORKS COMPANY—SUPPLY OF
　　WATER. 1.

—— Winding-up Acts　19 Ch. D. 77; 23 Ch. D.
　　　　　See COMPANY—CONTRIBUTORY. 2, 4. [297

—— Winding-up of foreign company　27 Ch. D.
　　　　　　　　　[225; 29 Ch. D. 219
　　See COMPANY—WINDING-UP ORDER. 2, 3.

JURY—Trial by　20 Ch. D. 365; 21 Ch. D. 134;
　　　　　　　　　[25 Ch. D. 772; 29 Ch. D. 50
　　See PRACTICE—SUPREME COURT—TRIAL.
　　2—5.

—— Trial by—Probate　　-　8 P. D. 205
　　See PRACTICE—PROBATE—TRIAL.

JUS REPRESENTATIONIS　-　18 Ch. D. 165
　　See COPYHOLD—CUSTOM. 2.

JUS SECANDI VEL FALCANDI　17 Ch. D. 535
　See COMMON.

JUS TERTII—Bailment—Estoppel　19 Ch. D. 86
　See BAILMENT.

JUSTICES (OF THE PEACE):—　　　Col.
　I. DISQUALIFICATION　-　-　731
　II. JURISDICTION　　　-　732
　III. PRACTICE　-　　-　732

I. JUSTICES—DISQUALIFICATION.

1. —— Coroner.] A justice of the peace does not become disqualified from acting as such, by reason of his being elected coroner for the county or division for which he so acts as justice. DAVIS *v.* JUSTICES OF PEMBROKESHIRE　**7 Q. B. D. 513**

2. —— Interest—Bias—Litigant in similar Cases—Waiver of Objection.] At a special sessions for appeals against a poor-rate, the chairman of the magistrates, who was himself Appellant in one of the cases for hearing, took part in the decision of all the cases except his own. When his own case was called on, he left the bench and went to the body of the Court and conducted the case himself. On a rule for a certiorari to bring up all the orders for the purpose of quashing them :—*Held*, by Field and Bowen, JJ., that the chairman, being a litigant in a matter similar to the other matters before the Court, was disqualified from acting as a justice, and that the orders were bad.—Before the sessions were held the Appellants gave notice to the clerk of the justices that objection would be made " if any justices who were rated in Yarmouth heard the appeals." At the hearing this objection, and no other, was made, and it was overruled by the justices :—*Held*, that the Appellants were not precluded by the form of their notice from contending, in support of the rule for a certiorari, that the chairman, even if not disqualified by reason of his being rated, was disqualified by reason of his being himself a litigant; although this latter objection was not specifically mentioned in the notice, or made before the justices. THE QUEEN *v.* JUSTICES OF GREAT YARMOUTH　**8 Q. B. D. 525**

3. —— Interest—Urban Sanitary Authority—Municipal Corporation—Summons issued by Member of Corporation.] By a local Act for the improvement of a borough the corporation was made the authority for the execution of the Act, with power to direct prosecutions for this purpose. An information for an offence under the Act having been preferred by an officer on behalf of the corporation, a summons was issued upon it by a justice, who was also an alderman and member of the corporation, but came on for hearing before justices, none of whom were connected with the corporation :—*Held*, notwithstanding, that such justices could not proceed with the hearing of the summons, for it had been issued by one who was virtually prosecutor. THE QUEEN *v.* GIBBON
　　　　　　　[6 Q. B. D. 168

4. —— Interest — Public Health Act, 1875 (38 & 39 Vict. c. 55), s. 258—Town Council—Enforcing Borough Rate.] Where by statute a member of the town council of a borough may act as a justice of the peace in matters arising under the Act, in order to disqualify him from so acting it is not sufficient to show that, as a member

I. JUSTICES—DISQUALIFICATION—continued.

of the town council, he has a pecuniary interest in the result of the information or complaint, or that the corporation of which he is a member are the prosecutors, but it must be established that he has such a substantial interest in the result of the hearing as to make it likely that he has a real bias in the matter.—*Reg.* v. *Gibbon* (6 Q. B. D. 168) disapproved.—An officer of a corporation appointed to collect the borough rate obtained a summons against a ratepayer in arrear. In so doing he acted in the discharge of his duty, but on his own responsibility and without consulting the town council. At the hearing the justices dismissed the summons, on the ground that one of the sitting magistrates being a town councillor was thereby disqualified from adjudicating upon the summons. On motion for a mandamus to the justices to hear and adjudicate on the summons :—*Held* (by Field and Cave, JJ.), that there was no ground for supposing either substantial interest or likelihood of bias, and consequently no disqualification. THE QUEEN *v.* HANDSLEY
　　　　　　　[8 Q. B. D. 383

II. JUSTICES—JURISDICTION.

—— Reasonable Claim of Right — Fishing; Public Right of—Tidal navigable River—Tide, what constitutes — Damming back of Water by exceptionally High Tides.] An information was laid against the Appellant for unlawfully fishing in a river wherein the Respondents had a private right of fishery. It was proved that the river was navigable, and that at the place where the Appellant fished the water was not salt, and that in ordinary tides it was unaffected by any tidal influence, but that upon the occasion of very high tides the rising of the salt water in the lower part of the river dammed back the fresh water and caused it upon those occasions to rise and fall with the flow and ebb of the tide. The Appellant contended that, the river being navigable and tidal at the place in question, there was a presumption that the public had a right to fish there, and that the jurisdiction of the justices was therefore ousted by a reasonable claim of right :—*Held*, that the river at the place in question could not be considered as tidal within the meaning of the rule of law which gives the public a right to fish in navigable tidal rivers, and therefore there was no claim of title set up sufficient to oust the justices' jurisdiction. REECE *v.* MILLER
　　　　　　　[8 Q. B. D. 626

III. JUSTICES—PRACTICE.

The Act 44 & 45 Vict. c. 24 (the Summary Jurisdiction Process Act, 1881), amends the law respecting the Service of Process of Courts of Summary Jurisdiction in England and Scotland.

Bastardy Orders.]　Sect. 6. *A Court of summary jurisdiction in England and a Sheriff Court in Scotland shall respectively have jurisdiction by order or decree to adjudge a person within the jurisdiction of the Court to pay for the maintenance and education of a bastard child of which he is the putative father, and for the expenses incidental to the birth of such child, and for the funeral expenses of such child, notwithstanding that such person ordinarily resides, or the child has been born, or the mother of it ordinarily*

III. JUSTICES—PRACTICE—*continued*.

resides, where the Court is English in Scotland, or where the Court is Scotch, in England, in like manner as the Court has jurisdiction in any other case. Any process issued in England or Scotland to enforce obedience to such order or decree must be indorsed and executed in Scotland and England respectively in manner provided by this Act with respect to process of a Court of summary jurisdiction.

Any bastardy order of a Court of summary jurisdiction in England may be registered in the books of a Sheriff Court in Scotland, and thereupon a warrant of arrestment may be issued in like manner as if such order were a decree of the said Sheriff Court.

Service of Process.] *Subject to the provisions of this Act any process issued under the Summary Jurisdiction Acts may if issued by a Court of summary jurisdiction in England and indorsed by a Court of summary jurisdiction in Scotland, or issued by a Court of summary jurisdiction in Scotland and indorsed by a Court of summary jurisdiction in England, be served and executed within the jurisdiction of the indorsing Court in like manner as it may be served and executed within the jurisdiction of the issuing Court, and that by an officer either of the issuing or of the indorsing Court.*

For the purposes of this Act:

(1.) *Any process may be issued and indorsed under the hand of any such person as is declared by this Act to be a Court of summary jurisdiction, and may be indorsed upon proof alone of the handwriting of the person issuing it, and such proof may be either on oath or by such solemn declaration as is mentioned in sect. 41 of the Summary Jurisdiction Act of 1879, or by any like declaration taken in Scotland before a sheriff, justice of the peace, or other magistrate having the authority of a justice of the peace. Such indorsement may be in the form contained in the schedule to this Act annexed or in a form to the like effect.*

(2.) *Where any process requiring the appearance of a person to answer any information or complaint has been served in pursuance of this section, the Court before issuing a warrant for the apprehension of such person for failure so to appear shall be satisfied on oath that there is sufficient primâ facie evidence in support of such information or complaint.*

(3.) *If the process is to procure the attendance of a witness, the Court issuing the process shall be satisfied on oath of the probability that the evidence of such witness will be material, and that the witness will not appear voluntarily without such process, and the witness shall not be subject to any liability for not obeying the process unless a reasonable amount for his expenses has been paid or tendered to him.*

(4.) *This Act shall not apply to any process requiring the appearance of a person to answer a complaint issued by an English Court of summary jurisdiction for the recovery of a sum of money which is a civil debt within the meaning of the Summary*

III. JUSTICES—PRACTICE—*continued*.

Jurisdiction Act, 1879, or if issued by a Scotch Court in a case which falls within the definition of "civil jurisdiction" contained in the Summary Procedure Act, 1864.

Sect. 5. Where a person is apprehended under any process executed in pursuance of this Act such person shall be forthwith taken to some place within the jurisdiction of the Court issuing the process, and be there dealt with as if he had been there apprehended.

Warrant of Distress.] *Sect. 5. A warrant of distress issued in England when indorsed in pursuance of this Act, shall be executed in Scotland as if it were a Scotch warrant of poinding and sale, and a Scotch warrant of poinding and sale, when indorsed in pursuance of this Act, shall be executed in England as if it were an English warrant of distress, and the enactments relating to the said warrants respectively shall apply accordingly, except that any account of the costs and charges in connection with the execution, or of the money levied thereby or otherwise relating to the execution, shall be made, and any money raised by the execution shall be dealt with in like manner as if the warrant had been executed within the jurisdiction of the Court issuing the warrant.*

Prosecution Expenses.] *The Act 48 & 49 Vict. c. 59, continues the Act 29 & 30 Vict. c. 52, until the 31st of December, 1886.*

Act of 1884.] *The Act 47 & 48 Vict. c. 43 (the Summary Jurisdiction Act, 1884) repeals divers enactments rendered unnecessary by the Summary Jurisdiction Acts, and provides for uniformity of proceedings in Courts of summary jurisdiction.*

Appeal.] *Sect. 6. Where a person is authorized by any Act passed before the commencement of the Summary Jurisdiction Act, 1879, to appeal from the conviction or order of a Court of summary jurisdiction made in pursuance of the Summary Jurisdiction Acts, or from the refusal to make any conviction or order in pursuance of those Acts to a Court of General or Quarter Sessions, he shall after the passing of this Act appeal to such Court subject to the conditions and regulations contained in the Summary Jurisdiction Act, 1879, with respect to an appeal to a Court of General or Quarter Sessions.*

Doubts.] *Sect. 7 removes certain doubts as to 42 & 43 Vict. c. 49, s. 50.*

Sect. 8 removes certain doubts as to 42 & 43 Vict. c. 49, s. 30, and declares that a petty sessional court-house may be outside the limits of such division.

Sect. 9 removes certain doubts as to 42 & 43 Vict. c. 49, s. 38.

Enactments repealed.] *Sect. 4 repeals parts of certain Acts as to England.*

Sect. 5. The jurisdiction of justices to act summarily in any matter referred to in any enactments by this Act repealed, is not taken away.

Forms.] *Sect. 12. A form authorized by any rules for the time being in force in pursuance of s. 29 of the Summary Jurisdiction Act, 1879, shall be of the same effect as if it were contained in the Summary Jurisdiction Act, 1848 (11 & 12 Vict. c. 43), or in any other Act to which the form is made applicable.*

Obsolete Punishment.] *Sect. 3 repeals so much*

III. JUSTICES—PRACTICE—*continued.*

of any Act as enacts that a person, on non-payment of a sum of money adjudged to be paid by the conviction or order of a Court of summary jurisdiction in England, shall be liable to whipping, or to any other punishment than imprisonment with or without hard labour.

Rates.] Sect. 10. This Act does not alter the procedure for the recovery of poor or other rates, the payment of which is not adjudged by the conviction or order of a Court of Summary Jurisdiction.

Sect. 11. Payments certified by district auditors may be enforced as if poor rates.

1. —— **Case stated**—*Case stated under 20 & 21 Vict. c. 43, and remitted for amendment, but not returned—Jurisdiction over Costs.]* A case having been stated by justices under 20 & 21 Vict. c. 43, and remitted to them for an amended statement, but not returned within the proper time, and therefore abandoned :—*Held,* that the Court still had jurisdiction to order the Appellant to pay the Respondent's costs. CROWTHER *v.* BOULT
[13 Q. B. D. 680

2. —— **Case stated**—*Power of Justices to state —Summary Jurisdiction Act (42 & 43 Vict. c. 49), s. 33—Order, Determination, or other Proceeding of a Court of Summary Jurisdiction—General District Rate, Order for Payment of—Public Health Act, 1875 (38 & 39 Vict. c. 55), s. 256—Functions of Justices in enforcing General District Rate.]* A special case may be stated by justices under the 33rd section of the Summary Jurisdiction Act, 1879, upon an application to enforce payment of a general district rate under the 256th section of the Public Health Act, 1875.—On an application under the last-mentioned section to enforce a general district rate good on the face of it, the justices may not refuse to make an order for payment of the rate on the ground that there is a concurrent rate made for the same purpose. SAND-GATE LOCAL BOARD *v.* PLEDGE   14 Q. B. D. 730

3. —— **Rule against Justices** — *Refusal to do Act relating to Duties of Office—Rule under 11 & 12 Vict. c. 44, s. 5 — Mandamus.]* The application of the 5th section of 11 & 12 Vict. c. 44, is not confined to cases where the justice requires protection in respect of the act he is called upon to do.—*Reg.* v. *Percy* (Law Rep. 9 Q. B. 64) not followed. THE QUEEN *v.* BIRON   14 Q. B. D.
[474

[*See also* REG. *v.* PHILLIMORE, 14 Q. B. D. 474, n.]

4. —— **Sum "claimed to be due"**—*Summary Jurisdiction Act, 1879 (42 & 43 Vict. c. 49), ss. 6, 21, 35—Railways Clauses Consolidation Act (8 & 9 Vict. c. 20), ss. 103, 145—Penalty for Travelling with intent to avoid Payment of Fare—Distress Warrant—Procedure.]* The penalty imposed by sect. 103 of the Railways Clauses Consolidation Act (8 & 9 Vict. c. 20), for travelling in a railway carriage without having paid the fare and with intent to avoid the payment of it, is not "a sum of money claimed to be due and recoverable on complaint to a Court of summary jurisdiction"

III. JUSTICES—PRACTICE—*continued.*

within the meaning of sect. 6 of the Summary Jurisdiction Act, 1879 (42 & 43 Vict. c. 49), and is not subject to the procedure for the recovery of civil debts in a Court of summary jurisdiction prescribed by sect. 35 of the same Act. The QUEEN *v.* PAGET -   -   8 Q. B. D. 151

JUSTICES (OF THE PEACE)—Assize Court—Income tax 10 Q. B. D. 267 ; 9 App. Cas. 61
    See REVENUE—INCOME TAX. 1.

—— Compensation under Lands Clauses Act—Order—Limitation of time
[13 Q. B. D. 586
    See LANDS CLAUSES ACT — COMPENSATION. 6.

—— Expenses of sewering street—Jurisdiction
[12 Q. B. D. 142
    See LOCAL GOVERNMENT—PRACTICE. 2.

—— Injunction to restrain proceedings before
[20 Ch. D. 190
    See PRACTICE — SUPREME COURT—INJUNCTION. 7.

—— Jurisdiction — Bastardy—Service of summons in Scotland - 12 Q. B. D. 261 ;
    See BASTARDY. 6.   [10 App. Cas. 45

—— Jurisdiction to grant judicial separation—Aggravated assault - 10 P. D. 172
    See HUSBAND AND WIFE — JUDICIAL SEPARATION.

—— Jurisdiction—Union extending into different counties -   -   8 Q. B. D. 158
    See ELEMENTARY EDUCATION ACTS — ATTENDANCE. 4.

—— Landlord and tenant—Fraudulent removal —Notice of appeal - 6 Q. B. D. 669
    See LANDLORD AND TENANT—DISTRESS. 3.

—— Lunatic—Custody—Personal examination
[15 Q. B. D. 122
    See LUNATIC—JURISDICTION. 2.

—— Member of sanitary committee—Disqualification—Local Government Acts
[9 Q. B. D. 394
    See LOCAL GOVERNMENT—PRACTICE. 1.

—— Quarter sessions—Case stated 8 Q. B. D. 586
    See SESSIONS.

—— Res judicata—Estoppel   6 Q. B. D. 300
    See LOCAL GOVERNMENT—STREETS. 1.

—— Salvage—Jurisdiction—Appeal 7 P. D. 126
    See SHIP—SALVAGE. 8.

—— Summary proceeding — Exclusion of civil remedy -   -   11 Q. B. D. 225
    See SHIP—SEAMEN.

K

KNOWLEDGE OF SERVANT—Interrogatories—Sufficiency of answer 10 Q. B. D. 161 ;
        [24 Ch. D. 110
    See PRACTICE—SUPREME COURT—INTERROGATORIES. 5, 6.

L.

LABOURERS' DWELLINGS ACTS.

The Act 45 & 46 Vict. c. 54, amends the Artizans' and Labourers' Dwellings Improvement Acts, 1875 and 1879, and the Artizans' and Labourers' Dwellings Acts, 1868 and 1879, and makes further provision for the accommodation of the working classes, and for the purchase and pulling down of buildings unfit for human habitation, and for the opening of alleys.

The Act 48 & 49 Vict. c. 72, amends the law relating to dwellings of the working classes generally.

Sect. 4 amends 31 & 32 Vict. c. 130 (Artizans' and Labourers' Dwellings Act, 1868).

Sects. 7 and 8 amend the sanitary law generally, and the Act 38 & 39 Vict. c. 55, s. 90 (Public Health Act, 1875).

Sect. 9 amends 29 & 30 Vict. c. 90, s. 19 (Sanitary Act, 1866).

Sect. 11 amends 45 & 46 Vict. c. 38 (Settled Land Act, 1882).

It repeals part of 14 & 15 Vict. c. 34; part of sects. 4, 6, and 7 of 29 & 30 Vict. c. 28; sects. 5 and 6 of 42 & 43 Vict. c. 64; part of sect. 2 of 38 & 39 Vict. c. 36; sect. 11 of 45 & 46 Vict. c. 54.

1. —— **Compensation**—38 & 39 Vict. c. 36, s. 19, Sched., s. 6—*Publication—Notice to treat —Arbitrator—Lands Clauses Act, 1845, ss. 18, 121.*] Sect. 121 of the Lands Clauses Act as to compensation for interests less than a year is incorporated in the Artizans' and Labourers' Dwellings Improvement Act, 1875.—The publication of the requisition under sect. 6 of the schedule to the Dwellings Improvement Act is analogous to the notice to treat under the Lands Clauses Act, and a landowner affected by it cannot afterwards alter his position.—An arbitrator under the Dwellings Improvement Act may, when a claim for compensation is brought before him, assess the amount of compensation without deciding as to the right of the claimant. WILKINS *v.* MAYOR OF BIRMINGHAM　　　-　　　**25 Ch. D. 78**

2. —— **Payment into Court**—38 & 39 Vict. c. 36 —*Compulsory taking of Land—Arbitration Award —Appeal—Verdict of Jury for larger Sum—Payment of Difference into Court—Time of taking Possession—Interest on Difference.*] Where, under the provisions of the Artizans' and Labourers' Dwellings Improvement Act, 1875, a sum of money has been paid into Court by a local authority under the award of an arbitrator for lands taken compulsorily by them, and on appeal a verdict for a larger sum is given by a jury, the difference between the two sums being subsequently paid into Court, interest at £4 per cent. per annum from the date of the first payment to the date of the second payment in is payable on such difference. *In re* SHAW AND THE CORPORATION OF BIRMINGHAM　　-　　**27 Ch. D. 614**

LACHES.

See DELAY AND NEGLIGENCE.

LANCASTER, DUCHY OF—Attorney-General— Right to exhibit information
　　　　　　　[14 Q. B. D. 195
See ATTORNEY-GENERAL OF DUCHY OF LANCASTER.

—— Attorney-General—Right to attend proceedings in lunacy　-　　**21 Ch. D. 613**
See LUNATIC—JURISDICTION.　4.

LANCASTER PALATINE COURT　24 Ch. D. 280
See COURT—LANCASTER COURT.

—— Contempt　7 Q. B. D. 273; 6 App. Cas. 657
See PRACTICE — ECCLESIASTICAL—CONTEMPT.　2.

—— Concurrent suits　21 Ch. D. 647; 23 Ch. D.
　　　　　　　　　　　　　　　[100
See PRACTICE—SUPREME COURT—CONDUCT OF CAUSE.　2, 3.

—— Rehearing—Jurisdiction　-　**24 Ch. D. 488**
See PRACTICE — SUPREME COURT—APPEAL.　37.

LAND—Belonging to the Crown.
See CROWN LANDS—*Statutes.*

—— Injuriously affected—Railway—Scotch law
　　　　　　　　[7 App. Cas. 259
See SCOTCH LAW—RAILWAY COMPANY.　4.

—— In foreign country—Parties to contest in England -　　　-　　**23 Ch. D. 743**
See JURISDICTION.　1.

—— Power to take　　　　**28 Ch. D. 486**
See LONDON—COMMISSIONERS OF SEWERS.

—— Property of lunatic—Sale　**28 Ch. D. 514**
See LUNATIC—PROPERTY.　10.

—— Taken by railway company.
See Cases under LANDS CLAUSES ACT— COMPULSORY POWERS.

LAND COMMISSIONERS.

The Act 48 & 49 Vict. c. 59, continues until the 31st of December, 1886, so much of the Act 4 & 5 Vict. c. 35, and Acts amending the same, as relates to the appointment of and the period for holding office by Copyhold, Inclosure, and Tithe Commissioners (now Land Commissioners).

—— Constitution of—Settled Land Act.
See SETTLED LAND ACT—STATUTES.

LAND COMPANY—Illegality—Unregistered company　-　　-　　-　**29 Ch. D. 1**
See COMPANY—UNREGISTERED COMPANY.　4.

LAND DRAINAGE—Charge on capital
　　　　　　　　[29 Ch. D. 588
See SETTLED LAND ACT — PURCHASE MONEY.　5.

—— Rent-charge　　　-　**20 Ch. D. 203**
See LANDS CLAUSES ACT—PURCHASE MONEY.　6.

LAND LAW (IRELAND) ACT　9 App. Cas. 815
See IRISH LAND LAW ACT.

2 B

LAND TAX COMMISSIONERS.
See REVENUE—MANAGEMENT—*Statutes.*

—— LONG TERMS.
See LEASEHOLD—LONG TERMS.
—— RENEWABLE LEASE.
See LEASEHOLD—RENEWABLE LEASE.

I. LANDLORD AND TENANT—AGREEMENT.

1. —— **Ambiguous Contract**—*Specific Performance — Statute of Frauds.*] An executory agreement for a lease does not satisfy the Statute of Frauds, unless it can be collected from it on what day the term is to begin, and there is no inference that the term is to commence from the date of the agreement in the absence of language pointing to that conclusion.—*Jacques* v. *Millar* (6 Ch. D. 153) overruled.—The Plaintiff offered to take a lease of furnaces from the Defendant, conditionally upon his being able to make arrangements with other persons as to ore. A loosely-drawn memorandum was shortly afterwards signed by the parties, substituting certain other rents for the rents mentioned in the letter, which in other respects was to form the basis of the agreement. The Defendant, understanding that the lease was to begin immediately, offered possession to the Plaintiff at once, but the Plaintiff refused to take it, as he had not yet made arrangements for ores, and continued to treat the agreement as conditional on his making those arrangements. Ultimately the parties differed as to the covenants to be inserted in the lease, and the Plaintiff commenced his action for specific performance:—*Held*, although where an agreement is clear the Court must act upon its own view of the construction without regard to the view entertained by the parties, yet where a party has throughout insisted on one construction of an obscure agreement, he cannot get specific performance on the footing of the opposite construction. MARSHALL *v.* BERRIDGE　-　**19 Ch. D. 233**

2. —— **Condition Precedent** — *Specific Performance—Agreement to grant Lease to Nominee of Plaintiff—No Nominee appointed—Agreement by Letter—Statute of Frauds.*] A lessee wrote to his lessor offering to surrender his lease and to take a fresh lease for twenty-one years to a nominee, or to a company which he intended to form, at an increased rent, but otherwise on the same terms as the existing lease; and by a subse-

I. LANDLORD AND TENANT—AGREEMENT—*continued.*

quent letter offered to instruct his solicitor to prepare a draft lease. The lessor telegraphed to him in reply to get the lease prepared. Afterwards correspondence took place between the solicitors as to the form of the lease, and the lessee's solicitor prepared a formal agreement. Differences having arisen, the lessor refused to grant the lease, and the lessee brought an action for specific performance of the agreement to grant a lease and for damages. No company had been formed and no nominee appointed by the Plaintiff before the trial of the action:—*Held* (reversing the decision of Kay, J.), that assuming that there was a binding agreement for a lease, the formation of a company or appointment of a nominee was a condition precedent, and that the Plaintiff could not maintain an action for specific performance of the contract, as he had not performed the condition. —But, *held*, also, on the construction of the correspondence, that there was no binding agreement between the parties, and therefore the action entirely failed. WILLIAMS *v.* BRISCO
[22 Ch. D. 441

3. —— **Partial Interest of Lessor**—*Contract to sell the Entirety—Remedy of Purchaser.*] By a memorandum in writing, Defendant agreed to let, the Plaintiffs agreed to take, business premises for one year, with an option for Plaintiffs at the end of the year to have a lease for seven, fourteen, or twenty-one years. Plaintiffs, having gone into possession under the agreement, and having laid out money in alterations, at the end of the year gave notice of their intention to exercise the option; but when the Defendant's title came to be investigated it was found that she was possessed of only a moiety of the premises, the other moiety being vested in her son, a minor. The Defendant was decreed to perform specifically so much of the contract as she was able to perform, with an abatement of one moiety of the rent. An inquiry as to damages was refused, there being no evidence that the Plaintiffs had sustained any damage. BURROW *v.* SCAMMELL
[19 Ch. D. 175

4. —— **Right of Distress**—*Executory Agreement—Minimum Rent—Rent payable in Advance.*] The Defendant on the 29th of May, 1879, agreed to grant and the Plaintiff to accept a lease of a mill for seven years at the rent of 30s. a year for each loom run, the Plaintiff not to run less than 540 looms. The lease to contain such stipulations as were inserted in a certain lease of the 1st of May, which was a lease at a fixed rent made payable in advance, and contained a stipulation that there should at all times be payable in advance on demand one whole year's rent in addition to the proportion, if any, of the yearly rent due and unpaid for the period previous to such demand. The Plaintiff was let into possession and paid rent quarterly, not in advance, down to the 1st of January, 1882, inclusive, having run in 1881 560 looms. In March, 1882, the Defendant demanded payment of £1005 14s. (£840 as one whole year's rent for 560 looms at 30s., and £165 14s. as the proportionate part of the rent from the 1st of January last), and put in a distress. The Plaintiff thereupon commenced his action for damages for illegal distress,

I. LANDLORD AND TENANT—AGREEMENT—
continued.

for an injunction, and for specific performance,
and moved for an injunction. Fry, J., granted
the injunction on the terms of the Plaintiff
paying the £1005 14s. into Court. The Plaintiff
appealed.—*Held,* that since the Judicature Acts
the rule no longer holds that a person occupying
under an executory agreement for a lease is only
made tenant from year to year at law by the payment of rent, but that he is to be treated in every
Court as holding on the terms of the agreement:
—*Held,* therefore, that the Plaintiff holding under
the agreement was subject to the same right of
distress as if a lease had been granted, and that
if under the terms of the lease a year's rent would
have been payable in advance on demand a distress for that was lawful.—*Semble,* that such lease
ought to reserve a minimum rent of £810 (30s. a
piece on 540 looms), and that the stipulation in
the lease of the 1st of May as to payment in
advance would be applicable to such minimum
rent though not to the whole rent. And the
Defendant being willing to submit to the injunction on having £810 paid into Court, order varied
accordingly, the Court being inclined to the view
that there was a right of distress for that amount
though the time had not arrived for finally determining the question. WALSH *v.* LONSDALE

[21 Ch. D. 9

II. LANDLORD AND TENANT—ASSIGNMENT.

1. —— Assignment of Reversion—*Action by
Assignee against original Tenant—Yearly Tenancy
—Privity—4 Anne, c. 16, s. 9—8 & 9 Vict. c. 106,
s. 6.*] S. made a parol demise of a tenement to
M. from year to year at a rent. M. by deed assigned all his estate, interest, and term in the
tenement to a third party, but S. refused to accept
the third party as his tenant. Afterwards S.
assigned his reversion to the Plaintiffs, who never
accepted the third party as their tenant, and
brought an action against M. for rent in arrear:—
Held, affirming the judgment of the Queen's
Bench Division, that as no estate remained in M.
after his assignment of his yearly tenancy, the
Statute 4 Anne, c. 16, s. 9, did not apply; that
there was no privity of estate or of contract between the Plaintiffs and M., and therefore the
action could not be maintained. ALLCOCK *v.*
MOORHOUSE　　　-　　9 Q. B. D. 366

2. —— Assignment of Reversion—*Part of Demised Premises—Privity of Contract—Covenant to
pay Rent, whether divisible—Apportionment—32
Hen. 8, c. 34.*] The Defendant, being tenant of
land under a lease for years granted by the Plaintiffs and containing the usual lessee's covenant to
pay rent, assigned all her interest in the term.
Subsequently the Plaintiffs granted their reversion in part of the demised premises. No rent
having been paid by the assignees of the Defendant, the Plaintiff sued her for arrears of rent
accrued due since the grant of their reversion in
part of the premises, the sum claimed being a fair
apportionment of the rent in respect of the other
part, the reversion of which remained in the
Plaintiffs :—*Held,* that the covenant to pay rent
was divisible; that the rent could be apportioned, although the action was founded on a

II. LANDLORD AND TENANT—ASSIGNMENT
—*continued.*

privity of contract only; and therefore that the
Plaintiffs were entitled to recover.—*Stevenson* v.
Lambard (2 East, 575) considered. CORPORATION
OF SWANSEA *v.* THOMAS　　-　　10 Q. B. D. 48

3. —— Indemnity—*Right of Assignor to Indemnity—Dilapidations—Mercantile Law Amendment Act,* 1856 (19 & 20 *Vict. c.* 97), *s.* 5.] On
the dissolution of a partnership between H. and
R., H. assigned to R. all his interest in two houses
belonging to the partnership held under sub-leases
from C. and D., and R. covenanted to pay the
rents and observe the covenants and keep H. indemnified against them. R.'s executors sold the
houses to B., and B. to a company which went
into liquidation. The landlords C. and D. thereupon sued H. for the rent, and he paid it for the
whole of the year 1882. D. also made a large
demand against H. for breaches of covenants to
repair, but H. made no payment. On the 15th of
March, 1883, D. assigned his reversion to H., and
in May H. acquired C.'s reversion. In June,
1883, H. bought the leasehold interest in both
houses from the liquidators of the company, and
covenanted thenceforth to pay the rent and observe
the covenants. H. sought to prove against the
estate of R. for the sums paid for rent, for the
rent payable at Lady Day, 1883, on D.'s house,
and for the amount of the dilapidations in that
house :—*Held,* that the right of H., under R.'s
covenant of indemnity, to prove for the rents
which he had paid, was not taken away by his
covenant in the assignment by the liquidators,
which could not be extended to rents already due
and paid :—*Held,* also, that this right was not
defeated on the ground that the right of R.'s representatives, if they paid rent, to recover it from
the owner of the lease for the time being, was interfered with by the assignment from the liquidators to H., for that this assignment could not take
away any right of action which R.'s executors
might have against the persons entitled to the
houses at the end of 1882, and that an assignor
who pays rent has no lien on the term, and so
cannot be prejudiced by its subsequent assignment :—*Held,* further, that the right was not
defeated on the ground that H. on paying the
rent became entitled to a right of distress from
the reversioners, which he had destroyed by taking
an assignment of the leases, and had therefore
discharged the estate of R. by releasing a remedy
to the benefit of which R. as a surety was entitled,
for that a right of distress is not a security or
remedy to the benefit of which a surety paying
rent is entitled under the Mercantile Law Amendment Act (19 & 20 *Vict. c.* 97), *s.* 5:—*Held,*
therefore, that H. was entitled to prove against
R.'s estate for the rent paid in 1882, on both
houses :—*Held,* also, that he was entitled to prove
for the Lady Day rent on D.'s house :—But *held,*
that H. was not entitled to prove for the amount
of dilapidations, for that he had sustained no
damage by reason of them, inasmuch as he bought
the leases from the liquidators at a less price in
consequence of the breaches of the covenant to
repair; nor for the Lady Day rent of C.'s house.
In re RUSSELL. RUSSELL *v.* SHOOLBRED

[29 Ch. D. 254

2 B 2

III. LANDLORD AND TENANT—CUSTOM OF COUNTRY.

1. —— "**Mines and Minerals**"—*Whether reservation of, includes Flints.*] A farm was let under a written agreement reserving to the landlord "all mines and minerals, sand, quarries of stone, brick earth and gravel pits." A local custom (which, it was suggested, had grown up within the last 30 or 40 years) allowed tenants of such farms, let with a similar reservation, to take away the flints that were turned up in the ordinary course of good husbandry and to sell them for their own benefit. If the flints were not turned up and removed such farms could not be properly cultivated:—*Held*, affirming the decision of the Court of Appeal, that the custom was reasonable and valid; and when read into the written agreement was not inconsistent with the reservation, even assuming (but without deciding) that the reservation of "mines and minerals" included such flints. TUCKER *v.* LINGER   **21 Ch. D. 18 ; 8 App. Cas. 508**

IV. LANDLORD AND TENANT—DISTRESS.

The Act 46 & 47 Vict. c. 61 (Agricultural Holdings Act, 1883), enacts, sect. 44, after the commencement of this Act (1st January, 1884), it shall not be lawful for any landlord entitled to the rent of any holding to which this Act applies, to distrain for rent, which, becoming due in respect of such holding, more than one year before the making of such distress, except in the case of arrears of rent in respect of a holding to which this Act applies, existing at the time of the passing of this Act, which arrears shall be recoverable by distress up to the first day of January, 1885, to the same extent as if this Act had not passed. Provided that where it appears that, according to the ordinary course of dealing between the landlord and tenant of a holding, the payment of the rent of such holding has been allowed to be deferred until the expiration of a quarter of a year or half a year after the date at which such rent legally became due, then, for the purpose of this section, the rent of such holding shall be deemed to have become due at the expiration of such quarter or half year as aforesaid, as the case may be, and not at the date at which it legally became due.

Sect. 45. Where live stock belonging to another person has been taken in by the tenant of a holding to which this Act applies, to be fed at a fair price agreed to be paid for such feeding by the owner of such stock to the tenant, such stock shall not be distrained by the landlord for rent where there is other sufficient distress to be found, and if so distrained, by reason of other sufficient distress not being found, there shall not be recovered by such distress a sum exceeding the amount of the price so agreed to be paid for the feeding, or if any part of such price has been paid exceeding the amount remaining unpaid, and it shall be lawful for the owner of such stock, at any time before it is sold, to redeem such stock by paying to the distrainer a sum equal to such price as aforesaid, and any payment so made to the distrainer shall be in full discharge as against the tenant of any sum of the like amount which would be otherwise due from the owner of the stock to the tenant in respect of the price of feeding : Provided always, that so long as any portion of such live stock shall remain on the said holding the right to distrain such portion

shall continue to the full extent of the price originally agreed to be paid for the feeding of the whole of such live stock, or if part of such price has been bonâ fide paid to the tenant under the agreement, then to the full extent of the price then remaining unpaid.

Agricultural or other machinery which is the bonâ fide property of a person other than the tenant, and is on the premises of the tenant under a bonâ fide agreement with him for the hire or use thereof in the conduct of his business, and live stock of all kinds which is the bonâ fide property of a person other than the tenant, and is on the premises of the tenant solely for breeding purposes, shall not be distrained for rent in arrear.

Sect. 46. Where any dispute arises—

(a.) *in respect of any distress having been levied contrary to the provisions of this Act ; or*

(b.) *as to the ownership of any live stock distrained, or as to the price to be paid for the feeding of such stock ; or*

(c.) *as to any other matter or thing relating to a distress on a holding to which this Act applies :*

such dispute may be heard and determined by the County Court or by a Court of summary jurisdiction, and any such County Court or Court of summary jurisdiction may make an order for restoration of any live stock or things unlawfully distrained, or may declare the price agreed to be paid in the case where the price of the feeding is required to be ascertained, or may make any other order which justice requires; any such dispute as mentioned in this section shall be deemed to be a matter in which a Court of summary jurisdiction has authority by law to make an order on complaint in pursuance of the Summary Jurisdiction Acts ; but any person aggrieved by any decision of such Court of summary jurisdiction under this section may, on giving such security to the other party as the Court may think just, appeal to a Court of general or quarter sessions.

Sect. 47. Where the compensation due under this Act, or under any custom or contract, to a tenant has been ascertained before the landlord distrains for rent due, the amount of such compensation may be set off against the rent due, and the landlord shall not be entitled to distrain for more than the balance.

Sect. 48. An order of the County Court or of a Court of summary jurisdiction under this Act shall not be quashed for want of form, or be removed by certiorari or otherwise into any superior Court.

Sect. 49. No person whatsoever making any distress for rent on a holding to which this Act applies when the sum demanded and due shall exceed the sum of £20 for or in respect of such rent shall be entitled to any other or more costs and charges for and in respect of such distress or any matter or thing done therein than such as are fixed and set forth in the Second Schedule hereto.

Sect. 50. So much of an Act passed in the second year of the reign of their Majesties King William the Third and Mary, chapter five, as requires appraisement before sale of goods distrained is hereby repealed as respects any holding to which this Act applies, and the landlord or other person levying a distress on such holding may sell the goods and

IV. LANDLORD AND TENANT—DISTRESS—
continued.

chattels distrained without causing them to be previously appraised; and for the purposes of sale the goods and chattels distrained shall, at the request in writing of the tenant or owner of such goods and chattels, be removed to a public auction room or to some other fit and proper place specified in such request, and be there sold. The costs and expenses attending any such removal, and any damage to the goods and chattels arising therefrom, shall be borne and paid by the party requesting the removal.

Sect. 51. The period of five days provided in the said Act of William and Mary, chapter five, within which the tenant or owner of goods and chattels distrained may replevy the same shall, in the case of any distress on a holding to which this Act applies, be extended to a period of not more than fifteen days, if the tenant or such owner make a request in writing in that behalf to the landlord or other person levying the distress, and also give security for any additional costs that may be occasioned by such extension of time. Provided that the landlord or person levying the distress may, at the written request or with the written consent of the tenant, or such owner as aforesaid, sell the goods and chattels distrained or part of them at any time before the expiration of such extended period as aforesaid.

Sect. 52. From and after the commencement of this Act no person shall act as a bailiff to levy any distress on any holding to which this Act applies unless he shall be authorized to act as a bailiff by a certificate in writing under the hand of the judge of a County Court; and every County Court judge shall, on or before the 31st day of December, 1883, and afterwards from time to time as occasion shall require, appoint a competent number of fit and proper persons to act as such bailiffs as aforesaid. If any person so appointed shall be proved to the satisfaction of the said judge to have been guilty of any extortion or other misconduct in the execution of his duty as a bailiff, he shall be liable to have his appointment summarily cancelled by the said judge.

Sect. 35 applies the Act to Crown lands.

Sect. 36 applies the Act to lands of the Duchy of Lancaster.

Sect. 37 applies the Act to lands of the Duchy of Cornwall.

Sects. 38–40 designate the persons who are to exercise the powers conferred by the Act in the case of ecclesiastical and charity lands.

By sect. 54 nothing in the Act applies to a holding that is not either wholly agricultural or wholly pastoral, or in part agricultural and as to the residue pastoral, or in whole or in part cultivated as a market-garden, or to any holding let to the tenant during his continuance in any office, appointment, or employment held under the landlord.

Sect. 60. General saving of rights exercisable by landlord, tenant, or other person under any other Act or law, or under any custom of the country, or otherwise.

Sect. 62 repeals the Agricultural Holdings (England) Act. 1875 and 1876, saving existing rights and obligations thereunder.

SECOND SCHEDULE.

Levying distress. Three per centum on any sum exceeding £20 and not exceeding £50. Two and a half per centum on any sum exceeding £50.

To bailiff for levy, £1 1s.

To man in possession, if boarded, 3s. 6d. per day; if not boarded, 5s. per day.

For advertisements the sum actually paid.

To auctioneer. For sale five pounds per centum on the sum realised not exceeding £100, and four per centum on any additional sum realised not exceeding £100, and on any sum exceeding £200 three per centum. A fraction of £1 to be in all cases considered £1.

Reasonable costs and charges where distress is withdrawn or where no sale takes place, and for negotiations between landlord and tenant respecting the distress; such costs and charges in case the parties differ to be taxed by the registrar of the County Court of the district in which the distress is made.

I. —— Agistment of Cattle for "fair price" —Payment in kind—Protection from Distress— 46 & 47 Vict. c. 61, s. 45.] Live stock agisted for a fair equivalent is within 46 & 47 Vict. c. 61, s. 45 (the Agricultural Holdings Act, 1883), as taken in to be fed at a "fair price," and may, therefore, be exempt from distress, even although such equivalent be not money.—Cows were agisted on the terms "milk for meat," i.e., that the agister should take their milk in exchange for their pasturage:—Held, that the agistment was within the Act. LONDON AND YORKSHIRE BANK v. BELTON

[15 Q. B. D. 457

2. —— Entry—Raising Window partly open.] Entry into a house for the purpose of distraining may lawfully be made by further opening a window which is partly open. CRABTREE v. ROBINSON

[15 Q. B. D. 312

3. —— Fraudulent Removal of Goods—11 Geo. 2, c. 19, ss. 4, 5; 12 & 13 Vict. c. 45, s. 1; 42 & 43 Vict. c. 49, s. 31, sub-s. 2, s. 32.] An appeal from an order of justices under 11 Geo. 2, c. 19, ss. 4, 5, by a person adjudged guilty of fraudulently removing goods to prevent a distress, is subject to the conditions and regulations prescribed in the Summary Jurisdiction Act, 1879 (42 & 43 Vict. c. 49), s. 31, sub-s. 2, and s. 32, and therefore notice of appeal must be given within seven days after the decision appealed against. REG. v. JUSTICES OF SHROPSHIRE　　-　-　6 Q. B. D. 669

4. —— Fraudulent Removal of Goods—Termination of Tenancy—Possession of Tenant— 8 Anne, c. 14, ss. 6, 7—11 Geo. 2, c. 19, s. 1.] A landlord cannot follow and distrain his tenant's goods which have been fraudulently removed to prevent a distress for rent due, if at the time of the distress the tenant's interest in the demised premises has come to an end and he is no longer in possession.—The Plaintiff was tenant to the Defendant of a house. The Defendant having terminated the tenancy, the Plaintiff removed his goods on the day of its termination, and on the same day gave up possession of the house to the Defendant. One quarter's rent was due on the day when the tenancy terminated, and as that remained unpaid, within thirty days of the removal the Defendant followed the Plaintiff's goods

IV. LANDLORD AND TENANT—DISTRESS—
continued.

to the place of removal, and there distrained them. An action having been brought for wrongful distress, the jury found that the goods had been fraudulently removed in order to prevent a distress:—*Held,* that, notwithstanding the finding of the jury, the Plaintiff was entitled to judgment.
GRAY *v.* STAIT - **11 Q. B. D. 668**

—— Protection of lodger.
    See Cases under LANDLORD AND TENANT
    —LODGER.

V. LANDLORD AND TENANT—FIXTURES.

By 46 & 47 Vict. c. 61, s. 34, where after the commencement of the Act (1st of January, 1884) a tenant affixes to his holding any engine, machinery, fencing, or other fixtures, or erects any building for which he is not under this Act or otherwise entitled to compensation, and which is not so affixed or erected in pursuance of some obligation in that behalf or instead of some fixture or building belonging to the landlord, then such fixture or building shall be the property of and be removable by the tenant before or within a reasonable time after the termination of the tenancy.
  Provided as follows:—

1. *Before the removal of any fixture or building the tenant shall pay all rent owing by him, and shall perform or satisfy all other his obligations to the landlord in respect to the holding:*

2. *In the removal of any fixture or building the tenant shall not do any avoidable damage to any other building or other part of the holding:*

3. *Immediately after the removal of any fixture or building the tenant shall make good all damage occasioned to any other building or other part of the holding by the removal:*

4. *The tenant shall not remove any fixture or building without giving one month's previous notice in writing to the landlord of the intention of the tenant to remove it:*

5. *At any time before the expiration of the notice of removal the landlord, by notice in writing given by him to the tenant, may elect to purchase any fixture or building comprised in the notice of removal, and any fixture or building thus elected to be purchased shall be left by the tenant, and shall become the property of the landlord, who shall pay the tenant the fair value thereof to an incoming tenant of the holding; and any difference as to the value shall be settled by a reference under this Act, as in case of compensation (but without appeal).*

Sect. 35 applies the Act to Crown lands.

Sect. 36 applies the Act to lands of the Duchy of Lancaster.

Sect. 37 applies the Act to lands of the Duchy of Cornwall.

Sects. 38–40 designate the persons who are to exercise the powers conferred by the Act with respect to ecclesiastical and charity lands.

By sect. 54, nothing in the Act applies to a holding that is not either wholly agricultural or wholly pastoral, or in part agricultural and as to the residue pastoral, or in whole or in part cultivated as a market-garden, or to any holding let to the

V. LANDLORD AND TENANT—FIXTURES—
continued.

tenant during his continuance in any office, appointment, or employment, held under the landlord.

Sect. 60. General saving of rights exercisable by the landlord, tenant, or other person under any other Act or law, or under any custom of the country, or otherwise.

Sect. 62 repeals the Agricultural Holdings (England) Act, 1875 and 1876, saving existing rights and obligations thereunder.

—— **Mortgage** — *Lease by Mortgagor after Mortgage—Rights of Tenant.*] A mortgagor in possession of premises let them to a tenant who brought on to them certain trade fixtures. The mortgagee subsequently entered and sold the premises under the power of sale contained in the mortgage:—*Held,* that the fixtures did not pass under the mortgage, but remained the property of the tenant. SANDERS *v.* DAVIS **15 Q. B. D. 218.**

VI. LANDLORD AND TENANT — GROUND GAME.

1. —— **Agreement for Lease**—*Ground Game Act, 1880 (43 & 44 Vict. c. 47.*] When at the date of the passing of the Ground Game Act, 1880, land is in the occupation of a tenant with a legal interest, as tenant from year to year, expiring after the commencement of the Act, but also with an equitable interest under an agreement prior to the Act for a lease for fourteen years to commence from the expiration of the legal interest, and reserving to the landlord the right to the ground game on the land, such right in the landlord as against the tenant is preserved by the provisions of the saving clause of the Act (sect. 5): the phrase "is vested" not being confined to an actual legal vesting under a lease in possession, but including an equitable vesting of the right under an agreement for a lease, contract, of tenancy, or other contract bonâ fide made for valuable consideration. ALLHUSEN *v.* BROOKING
    [26 Ch. D. 559.

VII. LANDLORD AND TENANT —IMPROVEMENTS.

The Act 46 & 47 Vict. c. 61 (*the Agricultural Holdings (England) Act, 1883), enacts, sect. 1: Subject as in this Act mentioned, where a tenant has made on his holding any improvement comprised in the first Schedule hereto, he shall, on and after the commencement of this Act, be entitled on quitting his holding at the determination of a tenancy to obtain from the landlord as compensation under this Act for such improvement such sum as fairly represents the value of the improvement to an incoming tenant: Provided always, that in estimating the value of any improvement in the first Schedule hereto, there shall not be taken into account as part of the improvement made by the tenant what is justly due to the inherent capabilities of the soil.*

As to Improvements before the Act.] *Sect. 2. Compensation under this Act shall not be payable in respect of improvements executed before the commencement of this Act, with the exceptions following, that—*

  (1.) *Where a tenant has within ten years before the commencement of this Act made an*

VII. LANDLORD AND TENANT — IMPROVE-MENTS—*continued.*

improvement mentioned in the third part of the first Schedule hereto, and he is not entitled under any contract, or custom, or under the Agricultural Holdings (England) Act, 1875, to compensation in respect of such improvement ; or

(2.) *Where a tenant has executed an improvement mentioned in the first or second part of the said first Schedule within ten years previous to the commencement of this Act, and he is not entitled under any contract, or custom, or under the Agricultural Holdings (England) Act, 1875, to compensation in respect of such improvement, and the landlord within one year after the commencement of this Act declares in writing his consent to the making of such improvement, then such tenant on quitting his holding at the determination of a tenancy after the commencement of this Act may claim compensation under this Act in respect of such improvement in the same manner as if this Act had been in force at the time of the execution of such improvement.*

As to Improvements after the Act.] *Sect.* 3. *Compensation under this Act shall not be payable in respect of any improvement mentioned in the first part of the First Schedule hereto, and executed after the commencement of this Act, unless the landlord, or his agent duly authorized in that behalf, has, previously to the execution of the improvement and after the passing of this Act, consented in writing to the making of such improvement, and any such consent may be given by the landlord unconditionally, or upon such terms as to compensation, or otherwise, as may be agreed upon between the landlord and the tenant, and in the event of any agreement being made between the landlord and the tenant, any compensation payable thereunder shall be deemed to be substituted for compensation under this Act.*

Sect. 4. *Compensation under this Act shall not be payable in respect of any improvement mentioned in the second part of the First Schedule hereto, and executed after the commencement of this Act, unless the tenant has, not more than three months and not less than two months before beginning to execute such improvement, given to the landlord, or his agent duly authorized in that behalf, notice in writing of his intention so to do, and of the manner in which he proposes to do the intended work, and upon such notice being given, the landlord and tenant may agree on the terms as to compensation or otherwise on which the improvement is to be executed, and in the event of any such agreement being made, any compensation payable thereunder shall be deemed to be substituted for compensation under this Act, or the landlord may, unless the notice of the tenant is previously withdrawn, undertake to execute the improvement himself, and may execute the same in any reasonable and proper manner which he thinks fit, and charge the tenant with a sum not exceeding £5 per centum per annum on the outlay incurred in executing the improvement, or not exceeding such annual sum payable for a period of twenty-five years as will repay such outlay in the said period, with interest at the rate of three per centum per annum, such*

VII. LANDLORD AND TENANT — IMPROVE-MENTS—*continued.*

annual sum to be recoverable as rent. In default of any such agreement or undertaking, and also in the event of the landlord failing to comply with his undertaking within a reasonable time, the tenant may execute the improvement himself, and shall in respect thereof be entitled to compensation under this Act.

The landlord and tenant may, if they think fit, dispense with any notice under this section, and come to an agreement in a lease or otherwise between themselves in the same manner and of the same validity as if such notice had been given.

Sect. 5. *Where, in the case of a tenancy under a contract of tenancy current at the commencement of this Act, any agreement in writing or custom, or the Agricultural Holdings (England) Act, 1875, provides specific compensation for any improvement comprised in the First Schedule hereto, compensation in respect of such improvement, although executed after the commencement of this Act, shall be payable in pursuance of such agreement, custom, or Act of Parliament, and shall be deemed to be substituted for compensation under this Act.*

Where in the case of a tenancy under a contract of tenancy beginning after the commencement of this Act, any particular agreement in writing secures to the tenant for any improvement mentioned in the third part of the First Schedule hereto, and executed after the commencement of this Act, fair and reasonable compensation, having regard to the circumstances existing at the time of making such agreement, then in such case the compensation in respect of such improvement shall be payable in pursuance of the particular agreement, and shall be deemed to be substituted for compensation under this Act.

The last preceding provision of this section relating to a particular agreement shall apply in the case of a tenancy under a contract of tenancy current at the commencement of this Act in respect of an improvement mentioned in the third part of the first Schedule hereto, specific compensation for which is not provided by any agreement in writing, or custom, or the Agricultural Holdings Act, 1875.

Regulations as to Compensation for Improvements.] *Sect.* 6. *In the ascertainment of the amount of the compensation under this Act payable to the tenant in respect of any improvement there shall be taken into account in reduction thereof :*

(a.) *Any benefit which the landlord has given or allowed to the tenant in consideration of the tenant executing the improvement ; and*

(b.) *In the case of compensation for manures, the value of the manure that would have been produced by the consumption on the holding of any hay, straw, roots, or green crops sold off or removed from the holding within the last two years of tenancy, or other less time for which the tenancy has endured, except as far as a proper return of manure to the holding has been made in respect of such produce so sold off or removed therefrom ; and*

(c.) *Any sums due to the landlord in respect of rent, or in respect of any waste committed or permitted by the tenant, or in respect of any breach of covenant or other agreement*

VII. LANDLORD AND TENANT — IMPROVE-
MENTS—*continued.*

connected with the contract *of* tenancy committed by the tenant, also any taxes, rates,
and like rent-charges due or becoming due
in respect *of* the holding to which the tenant
is liable as between him and the landlord,
There shall be taken into account in augmentation
of the tenant's compensation :—

(d.) Any sum due to the tenant for compensation
in respect *of* a breach *of* covenant or other
agreement connected with a contract *of*
tenancy and committed by the landlord.

Nothing in this section shall enable a landlord
to obtain under this Act compensation in respect *of*
waste by the tenant, or *of* breach by the tenant, committed or permitted in relation to a matter *of*
husbandry more than *f*our years be*f*ore the determination *of* the tenancy.

Procedure.] *Sect.* 7. A tenant claiming compensation under this Act shall, two months at least
be*f*ore the determination *of* the tenancy, give notice
in writing to the landlord *of* his intention to make
such claim.

Where a tenant gives such notice, the landlord
may, be*f*ore the determination *of* the tenancy, or
within *f*ourteen days therea*f*ter, give a counter-
notice in writing to the tenant of his intention to
make a claim in respect *of* any waste or any breach
of covenant or other agreement.

Every such notice and counter-notice shall state,
as far as reasonably may be, the particulars and
amount *of* the intended claim.

Sect. 8. The landlord and the tenant may agree
on the amount and mode and time *of* payment *of*
compensation to be paid under this Act.

If in any case they do not so agree the difference
shall be settled by a re*f*erence.

Sect. 9. Where there is a reference under this
Act, a re*f*eree, or two re*f*erees and an umpire, shall
be appointed as *f*ollows :—

(I.) If the parties concur, there may be a single
re*f*eree appointed by them jointly :

(2.) If be*f*ore award the single re*f*eree dies or
becomes incapable *of* acting, or *f*or seven
days a*f*ter notice *f*rom the parties, or either
of them, requiring him to act, *f*ails to act,
the proceedings shall begin a*f*resh, as if no
re*f*eree had been appointed :

(3.) If the parties do not concur in the appointment *of* a single re*f*eree, each *of* them shall
appoint a re*f*eree :

(4.) If be*f*ore award one *of* two re*f*erees dies or
becomes incapable of acting, or *f*or seven
days a*f*ter notice *f*rom either party requiring him to act, *f*ails to act, the party
appointing him shall appoint another
re*f*eree :

(5.) Notice *of* every appointment *of* a re*f*eree by
either party shall be given to the other
party ;

(6.) If *f*or *f*ourteen days a*f*ter notice by one party
to the other to appoint a referee, or another
re*f*eree, the other party *f*ails to do so, then,
on the application *of* the party giving notice,
the County Court shall within *f*ourteen
days appoint a competent and impartial
person to be a re*f*eree :

(7.) Where two re*f*erees are appointed, then
(subject to the provisions *of* this Act) they

VII. LANDLORD AND TENANT—IMPROVE-
MENTS—*continued.*

shall, be*f*ore they enter on the re*f*erence,
appoint an umpire :

(8.) If be*f*ore award an umpire dies or becomes
incapable *of* acting, the re*f*eree shall appoint another umpire :

(9.) If *f*or seven days a*f*ter request *f*rom either
party the re*f*erees *f*ail to appoint an
umpire, or another umpire, then, on the
application *of* either party, the County
Court shall within *f*ourteen days appoint
a competent and impartial person to be
the umpire :

(10.) Every appointment, notice, and request
under this section shall be in writing.

Sect. 10. Provided that, where two re*f*erees are
appointed, an umpire may be appointed as follows :—

(1.) If either party, on appointing a re*f*eree,
requires, by notice in writing to the other,
that the umpire shall be appointed by the
Land Commissioners *f*or England, then the
umpire, and any successor to him, shall be
appointed, on the application *of* either
party, by those Commissioners.

(2.) In every other case, if either party on appointing a re*f*eree requires, by notice in
writing to the other, that the umpire shall
be appointed by the County Court, then,
unless the other party dissents by notice in
writing there*f*rom, the umpire, and any
successor to him, shall on the application
of either party be so appointed, and in case
of such dissent the umpire, and any successor to him, shall be appointed, on the
application *of* either party, by the Land
Commissioners *f*or England.

Sect. 11. The powers *of* the County Court under
this Act relative to the appointment *of* a referee or
umpire shall be exercisable by the judge *of* the
Court having jurisdiction whether he is without or
within his district, and may, by consent *of* the
parties, be exercised by the registrar *of* the Court.

Sect. 12. The delivery to a re*f*eree *of* his appointment shall be deemed a submission to a reference by
the party delivering it ; and neither party shall
have power to revoke a submission, or the appointment *of* a re*f*eree, without the consent *of* the other.

Sect. 13. The re*f*eree or re*f*erees or umpire may
call *f*or the production *of* any sample, or voucher,
or other document, or other evidence which is in the
possession or power *of* either party, or which either
party can produce, and which to the re*f*eree or
re*f*erees or umpire seems necessary *f*or determination *of* the matters re*f*erred, and may take the
examination *of* the parties and witnesses on oath,
and may administer oaths and take affirmations ;
and if any person so sworn or affirming wilfully
and corruptly gives *f*alse evidence he shall be guilty
of perjury.

Sect. 14. The re*f*eree or re*f*erees or umpire may
proceed in the absence *of* either party where the
same appears to him or them expedient, a*f*ter notice
given to the parties.

Sect. 15. The award shall be in writing, signed
by the referee or re*f*erees or umpire.

Sect. 16. A single re*f*eree shall make his award
ready *f*or delivery within twenty-eight days a*f*ter
his appointment.

VII. LANDLORD AND TENANT—IMPROVE-MENTS—continued.

Two referees shall make their award ready for delivery within twenty-eight days after the appointment of the last appointed of them, or within such extended time (if any) as they from time to time jointly fix by writing under their hands, so that they make their award ready for delivery within a time not exceeding in the whole forty-nine days after the appointment of the last appointed of them.

Sect. 17. In any case provided for by sects. 3, 4, or 5, if compensation is claimed under this Act, such compensation as under any of those sections is to be deemed to be substituted for compensation under this Act, if and so far as the same can, consistently with the terms of the agreement, if any, be ascertained by the referees or the umpire, shall be awarded in respect of any improvements thereby provided for, and the award shall, when necessary, distinguish such improvements and the amount awarded in respect thereof ; and an award given under this section shall be subject to the appeal provided by this Act.

Sect. 18. Where two referees are appointed and act, if they fail to make their award ready for delivery within the time aforesaid, then, on the expiration of that time, their authority shall cease, and thereupon the matters referred to them shall stand referred to the umpire.

The umpire shall make his award ready for delivery within twenty-eight days after notice in writing given to him by either party or referee of the reference to him, or within such extended time (if any) as the registrar of the County Court from time to time appoints, on the application of the umpire or of either party, made before the expiration of the time appointed by or extended under this section.

Sect. 19. The award shall not award a sum generally for compensation, but shall, so far as possible, specify—

  (a.) *The several improvements, acts, and things in respect whereof compensation is awarded, and the several matters and things taken into account under the provisions of this Act in reduction or augmentation of such compensation ;*

  (b.) *The time at which each improvement, act, or thing was executed, done, committed, or permitted ;*

  (c.) *The sum awarded in respect of each improvement, act, matter, and thing ; and*

  (d.) *Where the landlord desires to charge his estate with the amount of compensation found due to the tenant, the time at which, for the purposes of such charge, each improvement, act, or thing, in respect of which compensation is awarded is to be deemed to be exhausted.*

Sect. 20. The costs of and attending the reference, including the remuneration of the referee or referees, and umpire, where the umpire has been required to act, and including other proper expenses, shall be borne and paid by the parties in such proportion as to the referee or referees or umpire appears just, regard being had to the reasonableness or unreasonableness of the claim of either party in respect of amount, or otherwise, and to all the circumstances of the case.

The award may direct the payment of the whole

VII. LANDLORD AND TENANT—IMPROVE-MENTS—continued.

or any part of the costs aforesaid by the one party to the other.

The costs aforesaid shall be subject to taxation by the registrar of the County Court, on the application of either party, but that taxation shall be subject to review by the judge of the County Court.

Sect. 21. The award shall fix a day, not sooner than one month after the delivery of the award, for the payment of money awarded for compensation, costs, or otherwise.

Sect. 22. A submission or award shall not be made a rule of any Court, or be removable by any process into any Court, and an award shall not be questioned otherwise than as provided by this Act.

Sect. 23. Where the sum claimed for compensation exceeds £10, either party may, within seven days after delivery of the award, appeal against it to the judge of the County Court on all or any of the following grounds :—

1. *That the award is invalid ;*
2. *That the award proceeds wholly or in part upon an improper application of or upon the omission properly to apply the special provisions of sects. 3, 4, or 5, of this Act ;*
3. *That compensation has been awarded for improvements, acts, or things, breaches of covenants or agreements, or for committing or permitting waste, in respect of which the party claiming was not entitled to compensation ;*
4. *That compensation has not been awarded for improvements, acts, or things, breaches of covenants or agreements, or for committing or permitting waste, in respect of which the party claiming was entitled to compensation ;*

and the judge shall hear and determine the appeal, and may, in his discretion, remit the case to be re-heard as to the whole or any part thereof by the referee or referees or umpire, with such directions as he may think fit.

If no appeal is so brought, the award shall be final.

The decision of the judge of the County Court on appeal shall be final, save that the judge shall, at the request of either party, state a special case on a question of law for the judgment of the High Court of Justice, and the decision of the High Court on the case, and respecting costs and any other matter connected therewith, shall be final, and the judge of the County Court shall act thereon.

Sect. 24. Where any money agreed or awarded or ordered on appeal to be paid for compensation, costs, or otherwise, is not paid within fourteen days after the time when it is agreed or awarded or ordered to be paid, it shall be recoverable, upon order made by the judge of the County Court, as money ordered by a County Court under its ordinary jurisdiction to be paid is recoverable.

Sect. 25. Where a landlord or tenant is an infant without a guardian, or is of unsound mind, not so found by inquisition, the County Court, on the application of any person interested, may appoint a guardian of the infant or person of unsound mind for the purposes of this Act, and may change the guardian if and as occasion requires.

Sect. 26. Where the appointment of a person to act as the next friend of a married woman is

VII. LANDLORD AND TENANT — IMPROVEMENTS—continued.

required for the purposes of this Act, the County Court may make such appointment, and may remove or change that next friend if and as occasion requires.

A woman married before the commencement of the Married Women's Property Act, 1882, entitled for her separate use to land, her title to which accrued before such commencement as aforesaid, and not restrained from anticipation, shall, for the purposes of this Act, be in respect of land as if she was unmarried.

Where any other woman married before the commencement of the Married Women's Property Act, 1882, is desirous of doing any act under this Act in respect of land, her title to which accrued before such commencement as aforesaid, her husband's concurrence shall be requisite, and she shall be examined apart from him by the County Court, or by the judge of the County Court for the place where she for the time being is, touching her knowledge of the nature and effect of the intended act, and it shall be ascertained that she is acting freely and voluntarily.

Sect. 27. The costs of proceedings in the County Court under this Act shall be in the discretion of the Court.

The Lord Chancellor may from time to time prescribe a scale of costs for those proceedings, and of costs to be taxed by the registrar of the Court.

Sect. 28. Any notice, request, demand, or other instrument under this Act may be served on the person to whom it is to be given, either personally or by leaving it for him at his last known place of abode in England, or by sending it through the post in a registered letter addressed to him there ; and if so sent by post it shall be deemed to have been served at the time when the letter containing it would be delivered in ordinary course ; and in order to prove service by letter it shall be sufficient to prove that the letter was properly addressed and posted, and that it contained the notice, request, demand, or other instrument to be served.

Charge of Tenant's Compensation.] *Sect. 29. A landlord, on paying to the tenant the amount due to him in respect of compensation under this Act, or in respect of compensation authorized by this Act to be substituted for compensation under this Act, or on expending such amount as may be necessary to execute an improvement under the second part of the First Schedule hereto, after notice given by the tenant of his intention to execute such improvement in accordance with this Act, shall be entitled to obtain from the County Court a charge on the holding, or any part thereof, to the amount of the sum so paid or expended.*

The Court shall, on proof of the payment or expenditure, and on being satisfied of the observance in good faith by the parties of the conditions imposed by this Act, make an order charging the holding, or any part thereof, with repayment of the amount paid or expended, with such interest, and by such instalments, and with such directions for giving effect to the charge, as the Court thinks fit.

But, where the landlord obtaining the charge is not absolute owner of the holding for his own benefit, no instalment or interest shall be made payable after the time when the improvement in respect whereof compensation is paid will, where an award has

VII. LANDLORD AND TENANT—IMPROVEMENTS—continued.

been made, be taken to have been exhausted according to the declaration of the award, and in any other case after the time when any such improvement will in the opinion of·the Court, after hearing such evidence (if any) as it thinks expedient, have become exhausted.

The instalments and interest shall be charged in favour of the landlord, his executors, administrators, and assigns.

The estate or interest of any landlord holding for an estate or interest determinable or liable to forfeiture by reason of his creating or suffering any charge thereon shall not be determined or forfeited by reason of his obtaining a charge under this Act, anything in any deed, will, or other instrument to the contrary thereof notwithstanding.

Capital money arising under the Settled Land Act, 1882, may be applied in payment of any moneys expended and costs incurred by a landlord under or in pursuance·of this Act in or about the execution of any improvement mentioned in the first or second parts of the schedule hereto, as for an improvement authorized by the said Settled Land Act ; and such money may also be applied in discharge of any charge created on a holding under or in pursuance of this Act in respect of any such improvement as aforesaid, as in discharge of an incumbrance authorized by the said Settled Land Act to be discharged out of such capital money.

Sect. 30. The sum charged by the order of a County Court under this Act shall be a charge on the holding, or the part thereof charged, for the landlord's interest therein, and for all interests therein subsequent to that of the landlord ; but so that the charge shall not extend beyond the interest of the landlord, his executors, administrators, and assigns, in the tenancy where the landlord is himself a tenant of the holding.

Sect. 31. Where the landlord is a person entitled to receive the rents and profits of any holding as trustee, or in any character otherwise than for his own benefit, the amount due from such landlord in respect of compensation under this Act, or in respect of compensation authorized by this Act to be substituted for compensation under this Act, shall be charged and recovered as follows and not otherwise ; (that is to say,)

(1.) *The amount so due shall not be recoverable personally against such landlord, nor shall he be under any liability to pay such amount, but the same shall be a charge on and recoverable against the holding only.*

(2.) *Such landlord shall, either before or after having paid to the tenant the amount due to him, be entitled to obtain from the County Court a charge on the holding to the amount of the sum required to be paid or which has been paid, as the case may be, to the tenant.*

(3.) *If such landlord neglect or fail within one month after the tenant has quitted his holding to pay to the tenant the amount due to him, then after the expiration of such one month the tenant shall be entitled to obtain from the County Court in favour of himself, his executors, administrators, and assigns, a charge on the holding to the amount of the sum due to him, and of all costs pro-*

VII. LANDLORD AND TENANT — IMPROVE-MENTS—*continued.*

perly incurred by him in obtaining the charge or in raising the amount due thereunder.

(4.) *The Court shall on proof of the tenant's title to have a charge made in his favour, make an order charging the holding with payment of the amount of the charge, including costs, in like manner and form as in case of a charge which a landlord is entitled to obtain.*

Sect. 32. *Any company now or hereafter incorporated by Parliament, and having power to advance money for the improvement of land, may take an assignment of any charge made by a County Court under the provisions of this Act, upon such terms and conditions as may be agreed upon between such company and the person entitled to such charge, and such company may assign any charge so acquired by them to any person or persons whomsoever.*

Ecclesiastical and Charity Lands.] *Sect.* 38. *Where lands are assigned or secured as the endowment of a see, the powers by this Act conferred on a landlord shall not be exercised by the archbishop or bishop, in respect of those lands, except with the previous approval in writing of the Estates Committee of the Ecclesiastical Commissioners for England.*

Sect. 39. *Where a landlord is incumbent of an ecclesiastical benefice, the powers by this Act conferred on a landlord shall not be exercised by him in respect of the glebe land or other land belonging to the benefice, except with the previous approval in writing of the patron of the benefice, that is, the person, officer, or authority, who, in case the benefice were vacant, would be entitled to present thereto, or of the Governors of Queen Anne's Bounty (that is, the Governors of the Bounty of Queen Anne for the Augmentation of the Maintenance of the Poor Clergy).*

In every such case the Governors of Queen Anne's Bounty may, if they think fit, on behalf of the incumbent, out of any money in their hands, pay to the tenant the amount of compensation due to him under this Act; and thereupon they may, instead of the incumbent, obtain from the County Court a charge on the holding, in respect thereof, in favour of themselves.

Every such charge shall be effectual notwithstanding any change of the incumbent.

Sect. 40. *The powers by this Act conferred on a landlord in respect of charging the land shall not be exercised by trustees for ecclesiastical or charitable purposes, except with the previous approval in writing of the Charity Commissioners for England and Wales.*

Resumption for Improvements and Miscellaneous.] *Sect.* 41. *Where on a tenancy from year to year a notice to quit is given by the landlord with a view to the use of land for any of the following purposes:—*

The erection of farm labourers' cottages or other houses, with or without gardens;

The providing of gardens for existing farm labourers' cottages or other houses;

The allotment for labourers of land for gardens or other purposes;

The planting of trees;

VII. LANDLORD AND TENANT—IMPROVE-MENTS—*continued.*

The opening or working of any coal, ironstone, limestone, or other mineral, or of a stone-quarry, clay, sand, or gravel pit, or the construction of any works or buildings to be used in connection therewith;

The obtaining of brick earth, gravel, or sand;

The making of a watercourse or reservoir;

The making of any road, railway, tramroad, siding, canal, or basin, or any wharf, pier, or other work connected therewith:

and the notice to quit so states, then it shall, by virtue of this Act, be no objection to the notice that it relates to part only of the holding.

In every such case the provisions of this Act respecting compensation shall apply as on determination of a tenancy in respect of an entire holding.

The tenant shall also be entitled to a proportionate reduction of rent in respect of the land comprised in the notice to quit, and in respect of any depreciation of the value to him of the residue of the holding, caused by the withdrawal of that land from the holding or by the use to be made thereof, and the amount of that reduction shall be ascertained by agreement or settled by a reference under this Act, as in case of compensation (but without appeal).

The tenant shall further be entitled, at any time within twenty-eight days after service of the notice to quit, to serve on the landlord a notice in writing to the effect that he (the tenant) accepts the same as a notice to quit the entire holding, to take effect at the expiration of the then current year of tenancy; and the notice to quit shall have effect accordingly.

Sect. 42. *Subject to the provisions of this Act in relation to Crown, duchy, ecclesiastical, and charity lands, a landlord, whatever may be his estate or interest in his holding, may give any consent, make any agreement, or do or have done to him any act in relation to improvements in respect of which compensation is payable under this Act which he might give or make or do or have done to him if he were in the case of an estate of inheritance owner thereof in fee, and in the case of a leasehold possessed of the whole estate in the leasehold.*

Sect. 43. *When, by any Act of Parliament, deed, or other instrument, a lease of a holding is authorized to be made, provided that the best rent or reservation in the nature of rent, is by such lease reserved, then, whenever any lease of a holding is, under such authority, made to the tenant of the same, it shall not be necessary, in estimating such rent or reservation, to take into account against the tenant the increase (if any) in the value of such holding arising from any improvements made or paid for by him on such holding.*

General Provisions.] *Sect.* 53. *The Act comes into force on the 1st day of January,* 1884.

Sect. 54. *Nothing in this Act shall apply to a holding that is not either wholly agricultural or wholly pastoral, or in part agricultural, and as to the residue pastoral, or in whole or in part cultivated as a market-garden, or to any holding let to the tenant during his continuance in any office, appointment, or employment held under the landlord.*

Sect. 55. *Any contract, agreement, or covenant made by a tenant, by virtue of which he is deprived*

VII. LANDLORD AND TENANT — IMPROVE-MENTS—*continued.*

of his right to claim compensation under this Act in respect of any improvement mentioned in the first Schedule hereto (except an agreement providing such compensation as is by this Act permitted to be substituted for compensation under this Act) shall, so far as it deprives him of such right, be void, both at law and in equity.

Sect. 56. *Where an incoming tenant has, with the consent in writing of his landlord, paid to an outgoing tenant any compensation payable under or in pursuance of this Act in respect of the whole or part of any improvement, such incoming tenant shall be entitled in quitting the holding to claim compensation in respect of such improvement or part in like manner, if at all, as the outgoing tenant would have been entitled if he had remained tenant of the holding, and quitted the holding at the time at which the incoming tenant quits the same.*

Sect. 57. *A tenant shall not be entitled to claim compensation by custom or otherwise than in manner authorized by this Act in respect of any improvement for which he is entitled to compensation under or in pursuance of this Act, but where he is not entitled to compensation under or in pursuance of this Act he may recover compensation under any other Act of Parliament, or any agreement or custom, in the same manner as if this Act had not passed.*

Sect. 58. *A tenant who has remained in his holding during a change or changes of tenancy shall not thereafter on quitting his holding at the determination of a tenancy be deprived of his right to claim compensation in respect of improvements by reason only that such improvements were made during a former tenancy or tenancies, and not during the tenancy at the determination of which he is quitting.*

Sect. 59. *Subject as in the section mentioned, a tenant shall not be entitled to compensation in respect of any improvements, other than manures as defined by this Act, begun by him, if he holds from year to year, within one year before he quits his holding, or at any time after he has given or received final notice to quit, and, if he holds as a lessee, within one year before the expiration of his lease.*

A final notice to quit means a notice to quit which has not been waived or withdrawn, but has resulted in the tenant quitting his holding.

The foregoing provisions of this section shall not apply in the case of any such improvement as aforesaid—

(1.) *Where a tenant from year to year has begun such improvement during the last year of his tenancy, and in pursuance of a notice to quit thereafter given by the landlord, has quitted his holding at the expiration of that year; and*

(2.) *Where a tenant, whether a tenant from year to year or a lessee, previously to beginning any such improvement, has served notice on his landlord of his intention to begin the same, and the landlord has either assented or has failed for a month after the receipt of the notice to object to the making of the improvement.*

Sect. 60. *Except as in this Act expressed, nothing in this Act shall take away, abridge or prejudicially affect any power, right, or remedy of a landlord, tenant or other person vested in or exercisable by him by virtue of any other Act or law, or under any custom of the country, or otherwise, in respect of a contract of tenancy or other contract, or of any improvements, waste, emblements, tillages, away-going crops, fixtures, tax rate, tithe, rent-charge, rent or other thing.*

Sect. 61. *Definitions; amongst others—*

" Contract of tenancy " means a letting of or agreement for the letting land for a term of years, or for lives, or for lives and years, or from year to year;

A tenancy from year to year under a contract of tenancy current at the commencement of the Act shall for the purposes of this Act be deemed to continue to be a tenancy under a contract of tenancy current at the commencement of this Act until the first day on which either the landlord or tenant of such tenancy could, the one by giving notice to the other immediately after the commencement of this Act, cause such tenancy to determine, and on and after such day as aforesaid shall be deemed to be a tenancy under a contract of tenancy beginning after the commencement of this Act;

" Landlord " in relation to a holding means any person for the time being entitled to receive the rents and profits of any holding;

" Tenant " includes the executors, administrators, assigns, legatee, devisee, or next of kin, husband, guardian, committee of the estate or trustees in bankruptcy of a tenant, or any person deriving title from a tenant; and the right to receive compensation in respect of any improvement made by a tenant shall enure to the benefit of such executors, administrators, assigns, and other persons as aforesaid;

" Person " includes a body of persons and a corporation aggregate or sole;

" Manures " mean any of the improvements numbered 22 and 23 in the third part of the First Schedule hereto;

The designations of landlord and tenant shall continue to apply to the parties until the conclusion of any proceedings taken under or in pursuance of this Act in respect of compensation for improvements or under any agreement made in pursuance of this Act.

Sects. 62 *repeals the Agricultural Holdings (England) Act, 1875, and the Agricultural Holdings (England) Act, 1875, Amendment Act, 1876, saving—*

(a.) *Any thing duly done or suffered, or any proceedings pending under or in pursuance of any enactment hereby repealed; or*

(b.) *Any right to compensation in respect of improvements to which the Agricultural Holdings (England) Act, 1875, applies, and which were executed before the commencement of this Act; or*

(c.) *Any right to compensation in respect of any improvement to which the Agricultural Holdings (England) Act, 1875, applies, although executed by a tenant after the commencement of this Act if made under a contract of tenancy current at the commencement of this Act; or*

VII. LANDLORD AND TENANT — IMPROVE-MENTS—*continued.*

(d.) *Any right in respect of fixtures affixed to a holding before the commencement of this Act;*

and any right reserved by this section may be enforced after the commencement of this Act in the same manner in all respects as if no such repeal had taken place.

Sect. 63. *The Act is to be cited for all purposes as the Agricultural Holdings (England) Act,* 1883.

FIRST SCHEDULE.

PART I. IMPROVEMENTS TO WHICH CONSENT OF LANDLORD IS REQUIRED.

(1.) *Erection or enlargement of buildings.*
(2.) *Formation of silos.*
(3.) *Laying down of permanent pasture.*
(4.) *Making and planting of osier beds.*
(5.) *Making of water meadows or works of irrigation.*
(6.) *Making of gardens.*
(7.) *Making or improving of roads or bridges.*
(8.) *Making or improving of watercourses, ponds, wells, or reservoirs, or of works for the application of water power or for supply of water for agricultural or domestic purposes.*
(9.) *Making of fences.*
(10.) *Planting of hops.*
(11.) *Planting of orchards or fruit bushes.*
(12.) *Reclaiming of waste land.*
(13.) *Warping of land.*
(14.) *Embankment and sluices against floods.*

PART II. IMPROVEMENT IN RESPECT OF WHICH NOTICE TO LANDLORD IS REQUIRED.

(15.) *Drainage.*

PART III. IMPROVEMENTS TO WHICH CONSENT OF LANDLORD IS NOT REQUIRED.

(16.) *Boning of land with undissolved bones.*
(17.) *Chalking of land.*
(18.) *Clay-burning.*
(19.) *Claying of land.*
(20.) *Liming of land.*
(21.) *Marling of land.*
(22.) *Application to land of purchased artificial or other purchased manure.*
(23.) *Consumption on the holding by cattle, sheep, or pigs of cake or other feeding stuff not produced on the holding.*

VIII. LANDLORD AND TENANT—LEASE.

Apportionment of Conditions on Severance of Reversion.] *The Act* 44 & 45 *Vict.* c. 41 (*Conveyancing Act,* 1881), enacts:—

Sect. 12.—(1.) *Notwithstanding the severance by conveyance, surrender, or otherwise, of the reversionary estate in any land comprised in a lease, and notwithstanding the avoidance or cesser in any other manner of the term granted by a lease as to part only of the land comprised therein, every condition or right of re-entry, and every other condition, contained in the lease, shall be apportioned. and shall remain annexed to the severed parts of the reversionary estate as severed, and shall be in force with respect to the term whereon each severed part is reversionary, or the term in any land which has*

VIII. LANDLORD AND TENANT—LEASE—continued.

not been surrendered, or as to which the term has not been avoided or has not otherwise ceased, in like manner as if the land comprised in each severed part, or the land as to which the term remains subsisting, as the case may be, had alone originally been comprised in the lease.

(2.) *This section applies only to leases made after the commencement of the Act—31st December,* 1881.

Covenants to run with Reversion.] Sect. 10.—
(1.) *Rent reserved by a lease, and the benefit of every covenant or provision therein contained, having reference to the subject-matter thereof, and on the lessee's part to be observed or performed, and every condition of re-entry and other condition therein contained, shall be annexed and incident to and shall go with the reversionary estate in the land, or in any part thereof, immediately expectant on the term granted by the lease, notwithstanding severance of that reversionary estate, and shall be capable of being recovered, received, enforced, and taken advantage of by the person from time to time entitled, subject to the term, to the income of the whole or any part, as the case may require, of the land leased.*

(2.) *This section applies only to leases made after the commencement of the Act.*

Sect 11.—(1.) *The obligation of a covenant entered into by a lessor with reference to the subject-matter of the lease shall, if and as far as the lessor has power to bind the reversionary estate immediately expectant on the term granted by the lease, be annexed and incident to and shall go with that reversionary estate, or the several parts thereof, notwithstanding severance of that reversionary estate, and may be taken advantage of and enforced by the person in whom the term is from time to time vested by conveyance, devolution in law, or otherwise: and, if and as far as the lessor has power to bind the person from time to time entitled to that reversionary estate, the obligation aforesaid may be taken advantage of and enforced against any person so entitled.*

(2.) *This section applies only to leases made after the commencement of the Act.*

(a.) COVENANTS.

1. —— For quiet Enjoyment.] In order to constitute a breach of covenant for quiet enjoyment in a lease of land, it is sufficient that the lessee's ordinary and lawful enjoyment of the demised land be substantially interfered with by the acts of the lessor or those lawfully claiming under him, although neither the title to the land nor the possession of the land be otherwise affected.—By a general system of drainage made by the Defendants in a particular district, various farms in that district were drained by several underground drains, by which the water was carried through all such farms. The Defendants let one of these farms to the Plaintiff with the usual covenant for quiet enjoyment against the acts of the lessors or any person lawfully claiming through or under them. The Defendants had previously let another of such farms adjoining, but lying above the Plaintiff's farm, to one C., with a right to use the drains through the Plaintiff's land, so far as they were adequate to carry

VIII. LANDLORD AND TENANT — LEASE —
continued.

(a.) COVENANTS—*continued.*

the water from C.'s farm. C. during the Plaintiff's tenancy, first, by an excessive user of the drainage system, which was properly constructed for the purpose of drainage, caused the water passing down the drains in his farm to escape and overflow into the Plaintiff's farm and damage his crops; secondly, by a proper user by C. of the drains passing through the Plaintiff's farm, damage was also done to a field in Plaintiff's farm by the escape of water, but this arose from one of the drains there having been imperfectly and improperly constructed:—*Held,* that the Defendants were liable to the Plaintiff for a breach of their covenant for quiet enjoyment in respect of this last damage, as there had been within the meaning of such covenant a substantial interruption by a person who lawfully claimed through the Defendants. But that the Defendants were not liable for the damage done by the excessive user by C. of the drainage system, which was properly constructed, either under their covenant for quiet enjoyment or under the law of trespass or nuisance. SANDERSON *v.* MAYOR OF BERWICK-UPON-TWEED　　　　**13 Q. B. D. 547**

2. —— Not to assign without Consent —
Unreasonable Refusal—Qualification of Covenant.]
A lessee, in a lease of a house and premises to him for twenty-one years, covenanted with the lessor, his executors, &c., that he would not carry or suffer to be carried on any other business upon the premises than that of a grocer and tea-dealer without the previous consent in writing of the lessor, his executors, &c., and that he, his executors and permitted assigns, should not assign or underlease the premises without the like previous consent in writing, "but such consent not to be unreasonably withheld," and on the granting of such consent the lessee should pay a certain fee for the preparation of it, and give notice of any assignment to the lessor.—The premises were afterwards conveyed by the lessor, subject to the lease. The lessee applied for the necessary consent to enable him to mortgage the premises by way of underlease, and it was refused. —On demurrer to an action for an injunction, and for specific performance of the covenant, or for damages:—*Held,* that the words "but such consent not to be unreasonably withheld" did not amount to a contract on the part of the lessor, but were a qualification of the covenant by the lessee.—*Treloar* v. *Bigge* (Law Rep. 9 Ex. 151) followed. SEAR v. HOUSE PROPERTY AND INVESTMENT SOCIETY　　　　**16 Ch. D. 387**

3. —— Not to assign without Consent —
Underlease — Agreement that Underlease shall contain the same Covenants as original Lease.]
The Plaintiff, who was lessee of part of the property of a hospital, agreed with the Defendant to grant him an underlease " to contain all usual covenants (including a covenant not to assign or underlet without the consent of the Plaintiff, such consent not to be withheld if the proposed assignee or tenant be respectable and responsible), together with such other covenants, clauses, and provisoes as are contained in the lease under which the premises are held." The original

(a.) COVENANTS—*continued.*

lease contained (1) a covenant that if any dispute relating to the demised premises should arise between the lessee and any other tenant of the hospital, it should be referred to the arbitration of the hospital; (2) that the lessee, his executors, administrators, or assigns would not assign or sublet without the licence of the hospital; (3) that all demises and assignments of the demised premises should be prepared by the solicitors of the hospital:—*Held,* by Pearson, J., and by the Court of Appeal, that the covenants in the original lease were not to be taken as models and inserted into the underlease with the names of the underlessor and underlessee substituted for the names of the original lessors and lessee respectively, but that the Plaintiff was entitled to have them inserted without modification, so as to bind the underlessee to refer disputes with tenants of the hospital to the arbitration of the hospital, not to assign or underlet without the consent of the hospital, and to have his demises and assignments prepared by the solicitors of the hospital.— *Williamson* v. *Williamson* (Law Rep. 9 Ch. 729) distinguished. HAYWOOD v. SILBER **30 Ch. D. 404**

4. —— Restriction against Trade—*Business —Charitable Institution where no Payment received—Home for Working Girls.*] The lease of a house contained a covenant that the lessee should not use, exercise, or carry on upon the premises any trade or business of any description whatsoever:—*Held* (affirming the decision of Pearson, J.), that a charitable institution called a "Home for Working Girls," where the inmates were provided with board and lodging, whether any payment was taken or not, was a business, and came within the restrictions of the covenant. —It is not essential that there should be payment in order to constitute a business; nor does payment necessarily make that a business which without payment would not be a business. ROLLS v. MILLER － **25 Ch. D. 206; 27 Ch. D. 71**

5. —— Restriction against Trade—*Business, Occupation, or Calling—Hospital.*] The covenants of a lease restrained the tenant from using the house in the exercise of any trade, business, occupation, or calling whatsoever. The Defendants were an incorporated association for providing patients willing to pay with medical attendance, nursing, &c.;—*Held,* that this was a violation of the covenant. PORTMAN v. HOME HOSPITAL ASSOCIATION　　　-　　　**27 Ch. D. 81, n.**

6. —— Restriction against Trade — ***Not to use Premises as a Public-house, Tavern, or Beershop—Sale of Beer to be consumed off the Premises.*] A deed contained a covenant by the grantee of a piece of land that no building to be erected on the land should be used as a public-house, tavern, or beershop.—A lessee of the grantee obtained an off license authorizing him to sell at his shop, on the land, beer not to be drunk on the premises, and sold beer there accordingly:—*Held* (affirming the decision of the Master of the Rolls), that this was a breach of the covenant.—*Bishop of St. Alban's* v. *Battersby* (3 Q. B. D. 359) approved. LONDON AND SUBURBAN LAND AND BUILDING COMPANY v. FIELD　　-　　-　　**16 Ch. D. 645

VIII. LANDLORD AND TENANT — LEASE — *continued*

(a.) COVENANTS—*continued*.

7. —— Restriction against Trade— *Not to use Premises as a Public-house, &c.—" Beerhouse" —Construction—Technical Meaning — Evidence.*] A person who had entered into a covenant not to use a house as a public-house, tavern, or beer-house, opened a grocer's shop there, at which he carried on the sale of beer to be drunk off the premises as an ancillary business to his grocer's business :—*Held*, that this was no infringement of the covenant.—Evidence to shew that the word "beerhouse" was understood in the trade in a technical sense rejected. HOLT & CO. *v.* COLLYER
[16 Ch. D. 718

8. —— Restriction against Trade — *To buy Beer of Landlord—Implied Obligation on Cove-nantee.*] A covenant by the tenant of a public-house to purchase of his landlord all beer to be sold or consumed in or upon the premises, is not broken by the tenant buying through an agent, without the knowledge of the landlord, beer made by the landlord.—*Semble*, that where such a covenant is entered into by a tenant, there is, in the absence of express stipulation, an im-plied obligation on the part of the landlord to supply the tenant with such kinds of beer as he requires, and if this obligation is not fulfilled the tenant is at liberty to buy the beer which he re-quires elsewhere. EDWICK *v.* HAWKES
[18 Ch. D. 199

9. —— To pay Rates—*Paving Rate—"Rates charged upon the Premises or on the Occupier in respect thereof"—Metropolis Management Acts—18 & 19 Vict. c. 120, s. 105—25 & 26 Vict. c. 102, s. 96.*] The lessee of a house in a new street within the metropolitan district for seven, four-teen, or twenty-one years, covenanted with his lessor to pay all rates and assessments taxed, rated, charged, assessed, or imposed upon the demised premises, or upon or payable by, the occupier or tenant in respect thereof;—*Held*, that the propor-tion of the expense of paving the new street assessed upon the demised house under 25 & 26 Vict. c. 102, s. 96, was not a rate payable by the tenant under this covenant. ALLUM *v.* DICKINSON
[9 Q. B. D. 632

10. —— To pay Rates—*"Rates, taxes, and assessments"—Metropolis Local Management Acts, 1855 and 1862 (18 & 19 Vict. c. 120, s. 105, and 25 & 26 Vict. c. 102, s. 96).*] By an agreement of lease the tenant agreed to pay "all rates, taxes, and assessments payable in respect of the premises during the term" :—*Held*, that a sum assessed upon the owners as their proportion of the ex-pense of paving the street upon which the pre-mises abutted, was not a rate, tax, or assessment within the meaning of the covenant, but a charge imposed upon the owner for the permanent im-provement of his property. WILKINSON *v.* COLLYER
[13 Q. B. D. 1

11. —— To pay Rates—*"Rates chargeable in respect of the demised premises"—Water supplied to Tenant by Water Company—Water-rate.*] In a lease of a shop and basement and of three rooms on the third floor of the same house, the lessor covenanted to pay "all rates and taxes chargeable in respect of the demised premises." Water was separately supplied by a water company to the shop and basement, and paid for by the tenant. In an action to recover from the lessor the amount so paid :—*Held*, that such charge was a "rate" within the meaning of the covenant. DIRECT SPANISH TELEGRAPH CO. *v.* SHEPHERD
[13 Q. B. D. 202

12. —— To renew Lease—*Condition Prece-dent—Performance of Covenants*] The lease of a house contained a covenant by the lessee to pay the rent and keep the premises in repair, and to paint the outside and inside at certain fixed periods ; and the lessor covenanted that the lessee should be entitled, on giving six months' notice before the end of the term, to have a further lease for twenty-one years "upon paying the rent and performing and observing the covenants" in his lease. The lessee applied for a renewal of his lease, but the lessor refused to grant such renewal, on the ground that the covenants had not been fulfilled either at the date of the six months' notice or at its expiration :—*Held*, that the per-formance of the covenants was a condition pre-cedent to the lessee's privilege of having a re-newed lease, and, the requisite painting and repairs not having been completed either when the six months' notice was given or when it ex-pired, the lessee was not entitled to a renewal of his lease. BASTIN *v.* BIDWELL　　18 Ch. D. 238

13. —— To renew Lease—*Condition Prece-dent—Notice of Option to renew—Payment of Fine—Notice by Secretary to Company—Notice to one of Three Trustees.*] A lease of household property was granted in the year 1818 to the trustees of an insurance company for twenty-one years at a rent of £100, with a covenant that the lessor, his heirs or assigns, would from time to time, at any time before the expiration of the term, and also before the expiration of every succeeding term to be granted by every future or renewed lease, whenever required by the lessees or the person interested in the term, or any suc-ceeding term, and upon payment of a fine or premium of £1000, grant a renewed lease for twenty-one years, and in every such new lease there should be a similar covenant for renewal at or before the end of every twenty-one years, it being the intention of the parties that this lease should be renewable for ever at the option of the lessees, their executors, administrators, or assigns ; and there was a covenant by the lessees that in case the option to renew was not exercised they would before the expiration of the term rebuild or reinstate the buildings and premises as a dwelling-house.—There were two renewals of the lease, one in 1839 and one in 1860, which last lease expired on the 24th of June, 1881. The persons then entitled under the original lessor were G. S., who was tenant for life of a moiety of the property, and three trustees, of whom G. S. was one, of the entirety subject to the life inte-rest.—Under arrangements made by the insurance company this lease with other property was vested in five trustees upon trust to indemnify a certain class of stockholders and subject thereto for the

VIII. LANDLORD AND TENANT — LEASE — *continued.*

(a.) COVENANTS—*continued.*

company. One H. was secretary to these trustees and also to the company, and it was his duty to attend to the renewal of the lease.—On the 23rd of June, 1881, G. S. gave notice to H. that the lease would expire on the following day. H. answered that the directors of the company "would of course renew the lease." Subsequently renewal was refused:—*Held*, in an action for specific performance, that it was not necessary for the lessees to pay the fine of £1000, or execute a new lease before the expiration of the term, but that it was necessary that notice of an intention to renew should be given before the end of the term; and that the informal notice by H. to G. S. was sufficient. Specific performance decreed, with payment of the premium and interest at £5 per cent. from the end of the prior lease. NICHOLSON v. SMITH　-　**22 Ch. D. 640**

14. —— To renew Lease—*Lease for Lives— Covenant for renewal on dropping of one or more Lives—Construction.*] A lessor demised hereditaments to the lessee, his heirs and assigns, for the natural lives of the lessee and two other persons and the longest liver of them, with a covenant that the lessor, his heirs and assigns (upon the lessee, his heirs or assigns " surrendering this present demise as hereinafter mentioned "), should at any time thereafter at the request of the lessee, his heirs or assigns, "as often as one or two life or lives of and in the said hereditaments " should drop and be determined, renew and grant a further term "for any other life or two lives of any other person or persons to be nominated by the lessee, his heirs or assigns, in the stead of the persons life or lives so dropping or determining;" the lessee, his heirs or assigns, paying to the lessor, his heirs or assigns, " for every such renewal for every life or lives of such person or persons so to be renewed as aforesaid the sum of 40s. only, and at the same time surrendering this present demise to be cancelled ":—*Held*, reversing the decision of the Court of Appeal, that upon the true construction of the covenant the right of renewal was neither perpetual, nor limited to one renewal for not more than two new lives, but was a right of renewal as often as any of the three original lives should drop, so that any such renewal might take place either on the dropping of any one of the said three lives, or after the dropping of any two of them, as the lessee might from time to time request. SWINBURNE v. MILBURN　　　**9 App. Cas. 844**

(b.) INCOMING AND OUTGOING TENANTS.

15. —— Valuation of Crops.] An owner in fee demised a farm for seven years, and agreed at the expiration of the term to pay for the tenant's property in and upon the farm at a valuation. He devised the land to trustees for a term of 1000 years, upon trust to raise money in aid of his personal estate for payment of debts, funeral and testamentary expenses, and legacies, and subject thereto to the Plaintiff for life, with divers remainders over. On the testator's death the Plaintiff took possession On the expiration of the term a new tenant could not be found. The Plaintiff paid the outgoing

VIII. LANDLORD AND TENANT—LEASE— *continued.*

(b.) INCOMING AND OUTGOING TENANTS—*contd.*

tenant for his property in the farm, and claimed to be repaid the amount out of the testator's estate :— *Held*, that the liability to pay the outgoing tenant was a liability attaching to the land, and that the landlord for the time being was the person primarily liable; that the Plaintiff being in receipt of the rents and profits, was the landlord, and not the trustees of the term, that he therefore was the person primarily liable, and had no claim to be repaid wholly or in part either out of the testator's estate or by persons entitled in remainder. MANSELL v. NORTON **22 Ch. D. 769**

(c.) OPTION TO PURCHASE FREEHOLD.

16. —— Real and Personal Representatives— *Nature of Interest conferred on Lessee.*] A lease of land contained a covenant by the lessor with the lessee, his executors, administrators, and assigns, that if the lessee, his executors, administrators, or assigns, should at any time thereafter be desirous of purchasing the fee simple of the demised land, and should give notice in writing to the lessor, his heirs or assigns, then the lessor, his heirs or assigns, would accept £1200 for the purchase of the fee simple, and on the receipt thereof would convey the fee simple to the lessee, his heirs or assigns, or as he or they should direct. The lessee died intestate, and nearly twenty years after his death, but before the expiration of the term, his heir, who was also administrator of his personal estate, called on the devisee of the lessor to convey the fee simple to him in accordance with the covenant, and a conveyance was executed accordingly. The heir afterwards contracted to sell part of the property thus conveyed to him :— *Held* (affirming the decision of Pearson, J.), that on the true construction of the covenant the option to purchase was attached to the lease and passed with it ; that it consequently passed as part of the lessee's personal estate to the administrator, and that the administrator could not make a good title to the purchaser unless the next of kin of the lessee concurred in the sale.—*Green* v. *Low* (22 Beav. 625) distinguished. *In re* ADAMS AND THE KENSINGTON VESTRY　　　**24 Ch. D. 199;** **[27 Ch. D. 394**

IX. LANDLORD AND TENANT—LODGER.

1. —— Protection from Distress –"*Lodger*" —*Lodgers' Goods Protection Act,* 1871 (34 & 35 *Vict. c.* 79).] If the landlord, reserving a room in a house, lets the rest of it to a person, but retains such control and dominion over it as is usually retained by masters of houses let in lodgings, the relation of landlord and "lodger" may exist between the parties within the meaning of the Lodgers' Goods Protection Act, 1871 (34 & 35 Vict. c. 79), although the lodger has the right of exclusively occupying the greater part of the premises, and has separate and uncontrolled power of ingress and egress, and neither the landlord nor his agent sleeps or resides in the house, and the lodger acts as caretaker of the part reserved.—The existence of the relationship of landlord and lodger is a question of fact. NESS v. STEPHENSON　-　　-　　- **9 Q. B. D. 245**

2. —— Protection from Distress—34 & 35

IX. LANDLORD AND TENANT — LODGER — *continued.*

Vict. c. 79, *s.* 1—*Declaration by Lodger inoperative against subsequent Distress—Illegal Distress —Voluntary Abandonment.*] A declaration under the Lodgers' Goods Protection Act, s. 1, will not protect a lodger's goods against seizure and sale by a superior landlord for rent due from his immediate tenant, unless it has been made after the distress has been levied or authorized, or threatened; a declaration is inoperative against a distress subsequently levied, which has not been authorized or threatened before the declaration is made.—The Plaintiff was a lodger in one of three rooms let to T., who was the immediate tenant of the Defendant. Rent to the amount of £8 being due from T. to the Defendant, the Defendant distrained the goods in the rooms including the Plaintiff's. She thereupon made a declaration under the Lodgers' Goods Protection Act, s. 1, which was correct in all respects. T. and the Defendant came to an arrangement whereby £1 was to be paid down, and the remaining £7 by instalments; and the distress was thereupon withdrawn by the Defendant. None of the agreed instalments having been paid by T., and a further sum of £1 having accrued due for rent, the Defendant afterwards levied a second distress for the sum of £8, under which the Plaintiff's goods were again seized and sold. She made no further declaration under the Lodgers' Goods Protection Act, but she owed no rent to T.:—*Held*, that no action of trespass would lie against the Defendant for distraining the Plaintiff's goods; for the declaration made at the time of levying the first distress was ineffectual against the second, and the first distress had not been voluntarily abandoned.　THWAITES *v.* WILDING　11 Q. B. D. 421;
　　　　　　　　　　　　　　　　[12 Q. B. D. 4

3. —— Protection from Distress — 34 & 35 *Vict. c.* 79, *ss.* 1, 2—"*Lodger,*" *who is—Sleeping and Residence on Premises—Occupation for Business Purposes.*] The Appellant occupied the first floor and basement of premises at a yearly rent, carrying on the business of a publisher there, but sleeping and residing elsewhere. He had no key of the outer door, which was under the control of his immediate landlord, who admitted him every morning:—*Held*, that the Appellant was not a "lodger" within the meaning of s. 1 of the Lodgers' Goods Protection Act, 1871. HEAWOOD *v.* BONE　-　-　-　-　13 Q. B. D. 179

4. —— Protection from Distress—*Sale of Distress before Expiration of Five Days*—2 *Wm.* & *M.* sess. 1, *c.* 5, *s.* 2—*Lodgers' Goods Protection Act,* 1871 (34 & 35 *Vict. c.* 79), *ss.* 1, 2.] A landlord having on the 17th of October distrained for rent goods of his tenant's lodger upon the demised premises, sold the same on the 22nd, *i.e.*, before the expiration of five clear days from the distress, contrary to the provisions of 2 Wm. & M., sess. 1, c. 5, s. 2 :—*Held*, that an action is maintainable by the lodger against the landlord for so selling his goods.　SHARP *v.* FOWLE　12 Q. B. D. 385

X. LANDLORD AND TENANT—RE-ENTRY.

The Act 44 & 45 Vict. c. 41 (*Conveyancing Act,* 1881) enacts, sect. 14.—(1.) *A right of re-entry or forfeiture under any proviso or stipulation in a*

X. LANDLORD AND TENANT—RE-ENTRY— *continued.*

lease, shall not be enforceable, by action or otherwise, unless and until the lessor serves on the lessee a notice specifying the particular breach complained of, and, if the breach is capable of remedy, requiring the lessee to remedy the breach, and, in any case, requiring the lessee to make compensation in money for the breach, and the lessee fails, within a reasonable time thereafter, to remedy the breach, if it is capable of remedy, and to make reasonable compensation in money, to the satisfaction of the lessor, for the breach.

(2.) Where a lessor is proceeding, by action or otherwise, to enforce such a right of re-entry or forfeiture, the lessee may, in the lessor's action, if any, or in any action brought by himself, apply to the Court for relief; and the Court may grant or refuse relief, as the Court, having regard to the proceeding and conduct of the parties under the foregoing provisions of this section, and to all the other circumstances, thinks fit; and in case of relief may grant it on such terms, if any, as to costs, expenses, damages, compensation, penalty, or otherwise including the granting of an injunction to restrain any like breach in the future, as the Court, in the circumstances of each case, thinks fit.

(3.) For the purposes of this section a lease includes an original or derivative underlease, also a grant at a fee farm rent, or securing a rent by condition; and a lessee includes an original or derivative under-lessee, and the heirs, executors, administrators, and assigns of a lessee, also a grantee under such a grant as aforesaid, his heirs and assigns; and a lessor includes an original or derivative under-lessor and the heirs, executors, administrators, and assigns of a lessor, also a grantor as aforesaid, and his heirs and assigns.

(4.) This section applies although the proviso or stipulation under which the right of re-entry, or forfeiture accrues is inserted in the lease in pursuance of the directions of any Act of Parliament.

(5.) For the purposes of this section a lease limited to continue as long only as the lessee abstains from committing a breach of covenant shall be and take effect as a lease to continue for any longer term for which it could subsist, but determinable by a proviso for re-entry on such a breach.

(6.) This section does not extend,

  (i.) *To a covenant or condition against the assigning, underletting, parting with the possession, or disposing of the land leased; or to a condition for forfeiture on the bankruptcy of the lessee, or on the taking in execution of the lessee's interest; or*

  (ii.) *In case of a mining lease, to a covenant or condition for allowing the lessor to have access to or inspect books, accounts, records, weighing machines or other things, or to enter or inspect the mine or the workings thereof.*

(7.) Repeals 22 & 23 *Vict. c.* 35, *ss.* 4–9, *and* 23 & 24 *Vict. c.* 126, *s.* 2.

(8.) This section shall not affect the law relating to re-entry or forfeiture or relief in case of non-payment of rent.

(9.) This section applies to leases made either before or after the commencement of this Act, and shall have effect notwithstanding any stipulation to the contrary.

2 C

X. LANDLORD AND TENANT—RE-ENTRY—
continued.

1. —— Commencement of Action—*No actual Re-entry—No Proviso to make Lease void.*] When a lease contains a proviso giving the lessor a right to re-enter in the event of breach of covenant by the lessee (but not making the lease ipso facto void in that event):—*Quære,* whether under the present practice the mere commencement of an action by the lessor to recover possession of the property for breach of covenant, or the commencement of such action followed by appearance by the trustees, will, without actual entry, operate to determine the lease.—*Silcock v. Farmer* (46 L. T. (N.S.) 404) commented upon. *Ex parte* Sir W. Hart Dyke. *In re* Morrish

[**22 Ch. D. 410**

2. —— Disclaimer of Plaintiff's Title—*Ejectment—Notice to Quit—"Customary Rent."*] In an action of ejectment it was proved that the Plaintiffs, who claimed to be landlords of certain tenements, had given notice to the Defendants, as their tenants, that the rent of the tenements would be raised, and that the Defendants had thereupon written a letter stating that they "disputed the Plaintiffs' alleged right to raise the rent and were willing and offered to pay what was due in respect of the customary rent of 11s. a year, being all that they were liable to pay in respect of the property":—*Held,* that this letter was a repudiation of the relation of landlord and tenant and an assertion of a right to hold the tenements upon payment of a customary rent in the sense of a quit rent, and that the Plaintiffs were entitled to eject, upon proving their title, without proving a valid notice to quit. Vivian v. Moat - - - **16 Ch. D. 730**

3. —— Ejectment—*Holding over after Expiration of Term—Writ of Possession when Plaintiff's Title has expired.*] Where a landlord has recovered judgment in an action against his tenant for the possession of premises which had been held over after the expiration of the tenancy, he will be allowed to issue the writ of possession notwithstanding that his estate in the premises terminated after the commencement of the action and before the trial, unless it be unjust and futile to issue such writ, and it is for the Defendant to shew affirmatively that this will be the result of issuing such writ. Knight v. Clarke

[**15 Q. B. D. 294**

4. —— Forfeiture — *Carrying on Offensive Trade—Extra Rent reserved in case of Breach of such Covenant.*] The Defendants were assignees of the lease of certain premises which had been demised by the Plaintiffs for a term of years, the reddendum being as follows: "yielding and paying a yearly rent of £30 by equal quarterly payments" on the usual quarter days, "and a like yearly rent of £25 by like equal payments in case any of the trades, occupations, or things hereinafter covenanted not to be carried on or done upon the said premises shall be carried on or done."—The lessees, among other usual covenants, covenanted not to carry on upon the premises certain specified trades or businesses, nor any offensive, noisome, or noisy trade or business whatsoever, nor do nor suffer to be done anything which might be or grow to the damage or annoy-

X. LANDLORD AND TENANT—RE-ENTRY—
continued.

ance of the lessors. The lease contained a condition of re-entry if the said yearly rent of £30 or the said further rent of £25, in case the same should become payable, were in arrear, or if and whenever there should be a breach of any of the covenants thereinbefore contained on the part of the lessees.—The Defendants having carried on upon the demised premises a business within the terms of the above-mentioned covenant, the Plaintiffs sued to recover the premises upon a forfeiture of the lease:—*Held,* affirming the decision of the Queen's Bench Division, that the lease could not be construed as meaning that the Defendants were entitled to carry on the business in question upon payment of the additional rent mentioned in the reddendum, and that the Plaintiffs were entitled to re-enter under the condition for re-entry should they choose to exercise their option, instead of requiring the payment of the additional rent. Weston v. Managers of the Metropolitan Asylum District

[**8 Q. B. D. 387; 9 Q. B. D. 404**

5. —— Forfeiture — *Tenant "being Bankrupt"—Bankruptcy Petition under Bankruptcy Act, 1883—Bankruptcy Act, 1883 (46 & 47 Vict. c. 52), s. 149—Fixtures—Notice of Breach by Landlord—Conveyancing Act, 1881 (44 & 45 Vict. c. 41), s. 14.*] A lease (executed in 1880) of a mill and warehouse, for twenty-one years, contained a covenant by the lessors with the lessees (inter alia): (4) that certain articles mentioned in a schedule should be the property of the lessees, and should be removable by them, they making good all damage done by such removal. The articles mentioned in the schedule were iron columns, beams, floors, brick piers, and things ejusdem generis. There was a proviso (1) that in case (inter alia) the lessees should during the term be bankrupts, or file a petition in liquidation, the term should cease; (2) that the lessees might by notice determine the term at the end of seven or fourteen years; (3) that on the determination or cesser of the term all the machinery, and also all the buildings erected by the lessees (other than certain specified buildings) should be their property and should be removed by them previously to the determination or cesser of the term, unless it should be then mutually agreed that the lessors should purchase them, the lessees, in case of removal, to make good all damages which might be caused by such removal. After the Bankruptcy Act, 1883, came into operation, the lessees presented a bankruptcy petition, and a receiving order was made:—*Held,* first, that the presentation of the petition caused a forfeiture of the term; secondly, that notwithstanding the forfeiture, the official receiver was entitled to the articles mentioned in clause (4) of the covenant and clause (3) of the proviso as being property of the lessees.—*Quære,* whether the receiver was entitled to enter and remove the articles or whether he could only call on the lessors to deliver them to him.—*Held,* further, that sect. 14 of the Conveyancing Act, 1881, had no application. *Ex parte* Gould. *In re* Walker

[**13 Q. B. D. 454**

6. —— Forfeiture — *Relief — Conveyancing*

X. LANDLORD AND TENANT—RE-ENTRY—
continued.

and Law of Property Act, 1881 (44 & 45 Vict. c. 41), s. 14—Pending Proceedings—Order LVIII., r. 5—Power of Court of Appeal.] A landlord brought an action to recover the demised property under a proviso of re-entry for breach of a covenant to insure. The Defendant claimed relief under statute 22 & 23 Vict. c. 35, s. 4. The Plaintiff obtained judgment on the 4th of July, 1881. On the 4th of August the Defendant appealed. A stay of proceedings was granted and continued so that the Plaintiff never obtained possession. On the 1st of January, 1882, the Conveyancing and Law of Property Act (44 & 45 Vict. c. 41), came into operation, after which the appeal came on to be heard :—*Held*, that the Conveyancing and Law of Property Act, 1881, s. 14, sub-s. 2, is not confined to breaches taking place after the Act came into operation, but extends also to breaches committed before the Act, and to proceedings pending when the Act came into operation, and that as the landlord had not obtained possession, but the action was still pending, there was jurisdiction to grant relief to the tenant under that sub-section :—*Held*, also, that assuming the judgment of the Court below to have been correct according to the law as it then stood, the Court of Appeal could grant to the tenant the relief to which he was entitled according to the law as it stood at the hearing of the appeal, since the general orders provide that appeals shall be by way of re-hearing, and give power to the Court of Appeal not merely to make any order which ought to have been made by the Court below, but to make such further or other order as the case may require. QUILTER *v.* MAPLESON　　-　　9 Q. B. D. 672

7. —— Forfeiture—*Relief—Non-payment of Rent—Relief after Trial—Disallowance of Costs to Plaintiff—Common Law Procedure Act, 1852 (15 & 16 Vict. c. 76), s. 210; Common Law Procedure Act, 1860 (23 & 24 Vict. c. 126), s. 1.*] Where in an action of ejectment upon a forfeiture by non-payment of rent the Plaintiff obtains judgment, but without costs, the Defendant may obtain relief from the forfeiture under the Common Law Procedure Act, 1860 (23 & 24 Vict. c. 126), s. 1, without being required to pay the Plaintiff any costs other than those of the summons for relief. CROFT *v.* LONDON AND COUNTY BANKING CO.
[14 Q. B. D. 347

8. —— Forfeiture—*Winding-up of Company—Distress by Landlord of Company—Clause of Re-entry.*] Mines were demised to a company by a lease which contained a power of re-entry if the rents or royalties, or any part thereof, should be in arrear for thirty days, or if the company " should be wound up voluntarily or by compulsion or otherwise under the provisions of any Act or Acts of Parliament." An action was brought against the company by the debenture holders, and a receiver was appointed. Rent being in arrear, the landlord took out a summons for leave to distrain or re-enter. After the summons had been returnable, but before it was heard, an order was made for winding up the company. The summons was then amended by intituling it in the winding-up as well as in the

X. LANDLORD AND TENANT—RE-ENTRY—
continued.

action :—*Held*, by Hall, V.C., that as the landlord was a creditor of the company, leave could not be given him to distrain, and that the claim to re-enter ought to be left to be tried in an action : — *Held*, by the Court of Appeal, that according to the true construction of the proviso for re-entry, a right to re-enter accrued on the making of a winding-up order, and that, the title of the landlord to re-enter being clear, the Court ought to order possession to be given to him, and ought not to put him to the useless expense of bringing an action to which there was no defence. GENERAL SHARE AND TRUST COMPANY *v.* WETLEY BRICK AND POTTERY COMPANY
[20 Ch. D. 260

9. —— Notice—*Power to determine Tenancy by delivering Notice to Tenant—Tenant not to be found—Delivery of Notice at demised Premises.*] A lease of premises for twenty-one years contained a proviso that it should be lawful for the landlord or his assigns to put an end to the demise at the end of the first fourteen years by delivering to the tenant or his assigns six calendar months' previous notice in writing of his intention to do so. In an action by the assignee of the reversion to recover possession of the premises on the ground that the demise had been duly determined by notice under the proviso, it appeared that the lessee had disappeared some years previously, after having mortgaged the premises by way of underlease, that his address could not be found, and that written notice to determine the tenancy directed to him had been sent to his last known address, and had also been delivered to the mortgagee and to the occupier of the premises :—*Held*, that the action could not be maintained, as there had been no service of the notice on the lessee, and as he had not assigned the premises no other service would satisfy the terms of the proviso. HOGG *v.* BROOKS　　-　　14 Q. B. D. 475 ; 15 Q. B. D. 256

XI. LANDLORD AND TENANT — YEARLY TENANT.

Notice to quit.] *By 46 & 47 Vict. c. 61, s. 33, where a half year's notice expiring with a year of tenancy is by law necessary and sufficient for determination of a tenancy from year to year, in the case of any such tenancy under a contract of tenancy made either before or after the commencement of the Act (1st of January, 1884), a year's notice so expiring shall by virtue of the Act be necessary and sufficient for the same, unless the landlord and tenant of the holding, by writing under their hands, agree that this section shall not apply, in which case a half-year's notice shall continue to be sufficient ; but nothing in this section shall extend to a case where the tenant is adjudged bankrupt, or has filed a petition for composition or arrangement with his creditors.*

Sect. 35 applies the Act to Crown lands.

Sect. 36 applies the Act to lands of the Duchy of Lancaster.

Sect. 37 applies the Act to lands of the Duchy of Cornwall.

Sects. 38–40 designate the persons who are to exercise the powers conferred by the Act in the case of ecclesiastical and charity lands.

By sect. 54, nothing in the Act applies to a hold-

2 C 2

XI. LANDLORD AND TENANT — YEARLY TENANT— *continued.*

ing that is not either wholly agricultural or wholly pastoral, or in part agricultural and as to the residue pastoral, or in whole or in part cultivated as a market-garden, or to any holding let to the tenant during his continuance in any office, appointment, or employment held under the landlord. Sect. 62 repeals the Agricultural Holdings (England) Acts, 1875 and 1876, saving existing rights and liabilities thereunder.

—— **Notice** — *Half-year's Notice and Six Months' Notice, Distinction between—Agricultural Holdings Act, 1883 (46 & 47 Vict. c. 61), s. 33.]* A tenancy under a written agreement from year to year " until six months' notice shall have been given . . . in the usual way to determine the tenancy," is not one " where a half-year's notice . . . is by law necessary" within the Agricultural Holdings Act, 1883 (46 & 47 Vict. c. 61), s. 33, which, therefore, does not apply so as to render a year's notice necessary for the determination of the tenancy.—Judgment of the Queen's Bench Division affirmed. BARLOW v. TEAL
[15 Q. B. D. 403, 501

LANDLORD AND TENANT — Agreement for lease by mortgagor   25 Ch. D. 678
See MORTGAGE—MORTGAGEE IN POSSESSION. 2.

—— Agreement—Scotch law   6 App. Cas. 340
See SCOTCH LAW—LANDLORD AND TENANT.

—— Bankruptcy—Disclaimer by trustee.
See Cases under BANKRUPTCY — DISCLAIMER.

—— Bankruptcy—Forfeiture on tenant "being bankrupt "—Removal of fixtures—Official receiver   -   13 Q. B. D. 454
See BANKRUPTCY — BANKRUPTCY PETITION. 4.

—— Bankruptcy—Period of vesting in trustee
[9 Q. B. D. 473
See BANKRUPTCY—TRUSTEE. 6.

—— Bankruptcy—Trustee—Outgoing tenant—Set-off—Tillages   -   10 Q. B. D. 22
See BANKRUPTCY—MUTUAL DEALINGS. 2.

—— Contract by sub-tenant to perform covenants of lease — Whether contract of indemnity   -   -   8 Q. B. D. 329
See PRACTICE—SUPREME COURT—COSTS. 48.

—— Distress after bankruptcy.
See Cases under BANKRUPTCY—DISTRESS.

—— Distress after winding-up.
See Cases under COMPANY—DISTRESS.

—— Distress—Crops—Bill of sale—Surrender—Expenses of cultivation   11 Q. B. D. 808
See BILL OF SALE—OPERATION. 1.

—— Forcible entry   -   18 Ch. D. 199
See FORCIBLE ENTRY. 2.

—— Incorporeal hereditament—Conflict of laws
[10 Q. B. D. 403
See CONFLICT OF LAWS. 3.

—— Irish Land Law Act   9 App. Cas. 815
See IRISH LAND LAW ACT.

LANDLORD AND TENANT—*continued.*

—— Licensee—Obligation to fence 9 Q. B. D. 80
See NEGLIGENCE—LIABILITY. 6.

—— Right of shooting—Overstocking land with game—Injury to crops   15 Q. B. D. 258
See GAME. 1.

—— Tenancy in common — Ordinary repairs—Contribution   -   15 Q. B. D. 60
See TENANT IN COMMON.

—— Tenancy under mortgage deed — Action to recover land — Judgment under Order XIV.   -   13 Q. B. D. 347
See PRACTICE—SUPREME COURT—WRIT SPECIALLY INDORSED. 5.

—— Valuation on expiration of tenancy—Agreement to appoint valuers—Rule of Court
[15 Q. B. D. 426
See ARBITRATION—SUBMISSION. 4.

LANDOWNER—Compensation—Abandonment of railway   -   25 Ch. D. 251
See RAILWAY COMPANY — ABANDONMENT. 2.

—— Right to use of siding on railway—Renewing junction   -   28 Ch. D. 190
See RAILWAY COMPANY — RAILWAYS CLAUSES ACT. 8.

LANDS CLAUSES ACT :—   Col.
I. COMPENSATION   -   776
II. COMPULSORY POWERS   -   779
III. COSTS   -   784
IV. PURCHASE-MONEY   -   -   786
V. SUPERFLUOUS LANDS   -   788

I. LANDS CLAUSES ACT—COMPENSATION.

Appointment of Umpire.] *The Act 46 & 47 Vict. c. 15, extends the powers of the Board of Trade under sect. 28 of the Lands Clauses Consolidation Act, 1845, in relation to the appointment of any umpire under the provisions of that section, and enacts that after the passing of the Act that section shall be read and have effect as follows :—* " If in either of the cases aforesaid the said arbitrators shall refuse or shall for seven days after request of either party to such arbitration neglect to appoint an umpire, the Board of Trade shall, on the application of either party to such arbitration, appoint an umpire, and the decision of such umpire on the matter on which the arbitrators shall differ, or which shall be referred to him under this or the special Act, shall be final."

1. —— **Goodwill of Business**—*Special Agreement—Occupier of House—Title — Metropolitan Streets Improvement Act, 1877—Mortgage.]* A public body acting under the powers of their Act and of the Lands Clauses Consolidation Act gave notice to the Plaintiff, who was a tailor, as to his house, which was leasehold. After some negotiation they offered him £400, of which £150 was to be apportioned to his leasehold interest and £250 to his trade damage and personal expenses, to which the Plaintiff agreed. The Plaintiff had mortgaged his leasehold interest and could not make a good title. The Plaintiff then brought an action for specific performance of the agreement, and the Defendants afterwards paid the £400 into Court under the 76th section of the

I. LANDS CLAUSES ACT — COMPENSATION—
continued.

Lands Clauses Act, executed a deed-poll, and took possession :—*Held* (affirming the decree of Bacon, V.C.), that the Plaintiff was entitled to judgment in the action, and to have the £250 paid at once to him, with interest from the time when the Defendants took possession.—Although in some cases the goodwill of trade premises passes to a mortgagee, that does not apply to a case where the goodwill depends on the personal skill of the owner. COOPER *v.* METROPOLITAN BOARD OF WORKS　　　-　25 Ch. D. 472

2. —— **Land injuriously affected—**8 & 9 *Vict. c.* 18—*House—Special Value as a Public-house—Compensation for.*] Under statutory powers conferred by an Act incorporating the Lands Clauses Act, 1845 (8 & 9 Vict. c. 18), a railway company stopped up a street in which were a house and premises used as an hotel, whereby the value thereof for using, selling, or letting as an hotel and public-house was diminished :—*Held,* that the owner was entitled to compensation under the Lands Clauses Act, 1845, for the depreciation in the special value of the premises as an hotel and public-house. WADHAM *v.* NORTH EASTERN RAILWAY COMPANY　-　-　14 Q. B. D. 747 [Affirmed by the Court of Appeal, 16 Q. B. D. 227]

3. —— **Land injuriously affected—**8 & 9 *Vict. c.* 18, *s.* 63—*Part of Building Estate taken for Sewage Farm—Value of other Parts thereby depreciated—Compensation for "injuriously affecting" same.*] Part of land laid out as a building estate was taken by a local board under an Act incorporating the Lands Clauses Act, 1845 (8 & 9 Vict. c. 18), for the purposes of a sewage farm, whereby the value of other parts of the land near to the part so taken was depreciated, even in the absence of any nuisance arising from the sewage farm when made :—*Held,* that the owner of the estate was entitled to compensation under the Lands Clauses Act, 1845 (8 & 9 Vict. c. 18), s. 63, not only in respect of the land taken, but also for damage sustained by reason of the "injuriously affecting" the other lands by the exercise of the statutory powers. THE QUEEN *v.* ESSEX　14 Q. B. D. 753 [Reversed by the Court of Appeal.]

4. —— **Land injuriously affected —** *Sewer— Right of Access to—Injuriously affecting such Right —Compensation — Lands Clauses Consolidation Act,* 1845, *s.* 68—*Railways Clauses Consolidation Act,* 1845, *s.* 6.] The Plaintiffs, in 1843, under the authority of a local Act, constructed a sewer on land part of which had been bought by the Defendants, a railway company, but had not then been used for their works. Part of the remainder was bought by the Defendants after the construction of the sewer, but no part of the land was the Plaintiffs', or had ever been granted to them. The local Act not only authorized the Plaintiffs to make the sewer, but vested it in them, with the duty to repair it, without, however, giving them any express right of access thereto. In 1863 the Defendants, in exercise of the powers conferred on them by their special Act, with which was incorporated the Railways Clauses Consolidation Act, 1845, constructed an embankment over the sewer which, though it made it less easy, did not prevent the Plaintiffs getting access to the sewer in

order to repair it. The Plaintiffs being obliged afterwards to repair, and having incurred extra expense in doing so in consequence of the embankment, claimed compensation from the Defendants under s. 68 of the Lands Clauses Consolidation Act, 1845, and s. 6 of the Railways Clauses Consolidation Act, 1845, for injuriously affecting the Plaintiffs' interest in the sewer :—*Held,* by the Queen's Bench Division, that the Plaintiffs had no interest in land within the meaning of the Lands Clauses Consolidation Act, 1845, s. 68, and therefore could not maintain the claim to compensation :—*Held,* by the Court of Appeal, that as a right of access to the sewer had not been expressly given by the local Act but had to be implied, the right of access which ought to be implied was not any particular mode of access, but such only as was reasonably necessary for enabling the repair of the sewer to be done, and as that had not been prevented by the Defendants' embankment, but only rendered less easy and convenient, the Plaintiffs had no right to compensation. MAYOR OF BIRKENHEAD *v.* LONDON AND NORTH WESTERN RAILWAY COMPANY [15 Q. B. D. 572

5. —— **Matter not the subject of Compensation** *—Application to quash Inquisition—Certiorari. Writ of—Discretion—Lands Clauses Act,* 1845 (8 & 9 *Vict. c.* 18).] Application having been made to the High Court of Justice for a writ of certiorari, to bring up and quash the proceedings upon an inquisition before the sheriff as to the amount of compensation to be awarded to a claimant under the Lands Clauses Consolidation Act, 1845, on the ground that the jury in assessing the compensation had taken into consideration matters which were not legally the subject of compensation ; it was proved that the applicants for the writ had allowed five months to expire without taking any objection to the proceedings :—*Held,* that as the time allowed for setting aside an award made under the provisions of the above-mentioned Act had expired before the application was made, the writ of certiorari ought not to be granted. THE QUEEN *v.* SHEWARD [9 Q. B. D. 741

6. —— **Settlement by Justices—***Lands Clauses Act,* 1845 (8 & 9 *Vict. c.* 18), *s.* 24—*Railways Clauses Act,* 1845 (8 & 9 *Vict. c.* 20), *ss.* 6, 140— *Settlement by Justices of the Amount—Limitation of Time—*11 & 12 *Vict. c.* 43, *s.* 11.] The determination by justices under sect. 24 of the Lands Clauses Act, 1845, of the compensation to be paid by a railway company to a landowner for having in the construction of the railway injuriously affected his land, is not an order of the justices for the payment of money within sect. 11 of 11 & 12 Vict. c. 43 (which limits the time for making a complaint to six months from the time when the matter of such complaint arose), and therefore the justices have jurisdiction under sect. 24 of the Lands Clauses Act, 1845, to hear and determine the question of such disputed compensation, although the application be made more than six months after the land has been so injuriously affected.—*Re Edmundson* (17 Q. B. 67) overruled. THE QUEEN *v.* EDWARDS　-　13 Q. B. D. 586

II. LANDS CLAUSES ACT — COMPULSORY POWERS.

1. —— Conditions Precedent — *Metropolitan Street Improvements Act, 1877 (40 & 41 Vict. c. ccxxxv.)—Lands Clauses Consolidation Act, 1845 (8 & 9 Vict. c. 18), s. 18—Meaning of Word "take."*] By an Act of 1877, with which the Lands Clauses Act was incorporated, the Metropolitan Board of Works were authorized to effect certain street improvements, and by sect. 5 were authorized to " enter upon, take, use, and hold " any of the lands in the deposited plans and books of reference, with the exception of certain specified lands. By sect. 33, after reciting that it was expedient to make provision for the accommodation of such of the labouring classes as would be displaced by the improvements, the Board were directed to acquire or appropriate lands and sell them or let them on building lease for the purpose of the erection of suitable houses for the labouring classes. And it was provided that before the Board should, without the consent of one of the Secretaries of State, " take for the purposes of this Act" fifteen houses or more occupied at the passing of the Act wholly or partially by persons of the labouring classes, they should prove to the satisfaction of such Secretary of State that suitable accommodation had been provided elsewhere for the same number of persons as had been accommodated in the houses to be taken. The Board served on the Plaintiff notice to treat for the purchase of more than fifteen houses belonging to him, which were occupied at the passing of the Act by the labouring classes. The Plaintiff sent in his claim without prejudice to any question as to the right of the Board to exercise their powers before complying with the proviso of sect. 33. The Board then served notice of their intention to summon a jury. It was admitted that the conditions of the proviso had not yet been complied with. The Plaintiff brought his action to restrain the Board from proceeding on their notices till they had complied with the conditions :—*Held*, by Chitty, J., that the word "take" in the proviso was not confined to taking possession, but included purchasing, and that the Board ought to be restrained from taking any steps to acquire a title to the land till they had complied with the conditions precedent. An injunction was therefore granted.—On appeal, *held*, by Jessel, M.R., and Bowen, L.J., dissentiente Cotton, L.J., that as the conditions precedent to taking the Plaintiff's land were conditions which the Board were able and compellable to comply with, the land in question was land which the Board were " authorized to purchase or take " within the meaning of the Lands Clauses Consolidation Act, 1845, s. 18, and that they were entitled to serve a notice to treat and summon a jury.—*Held*, by Jessel, M.R., and Bowen, L.J., that the prohibition against "taking" the land till the conditions had been complied with did not prohibit the Board from taking before such compliance any proceeding prior to the conveyance, Jessel, M.R., giving no opinion whether they were prohibited from taking a conveyance or only from taking possession, and Bowen, L.J. (with whom on this point Cotton, L.J., concurred) holding that the getting a conveyance from the landlord without entering into possession came

II. LANDS CLAUSES ACT — COMPULSORY POWERS—*continued.*

within the meaning of the word " take."—*Held*, therefore, by Jessel, M.R., and Bowen, L.J. (dissentiente Cotton, L.J.), that the injunction must be dissolved. SPENCER *v.* METROPOLITAN BOARD OF WORKS -   **22 Ch. D. 142**

2. —— Easement — *Railway — Compulsory Powers—Lands Clauses Consolidation Act, 1845 (8 & 9 Vict. c. 18), s. 85.*] A railway company was entitled by a special Act to acquire compulsorily an easement of tunnelling under land, unless a jury should determine that such easement could not be acquired by the company without material detriment to the remainder of such land :—*Held*, that the company might enter upon the land for the purpose of making the tunnel under sect. 85 of the Lands Clauses Consolidation Act upon depositing the value of the easement, and could not be compelled to deposit the value of the whole land. HILL *v.* MIDLAND RAILWAY COMPANY   **[21 Ch. D. 143**

3. —— Easement—*Railway Company—Hereditaments—" Land," whether includes Incorporeal Hereditaments—Lands Clauses Consolidation Act, 1845 (8 & 9 Vict. c. 18),ss. 3, 16, 84, 85.*] By a special Act the S. Co. were authorized to make a railway and to carry it across the railway of the G. W. Co., at one point by a bridge over and at another by an archway under that railway, the archway to remain the property of the G. W. Co. The Act by sect. 8, which was inserted at the instance of the G. W. Co. for their protection, provided that the S. Co. should not purchase and take any land of the G. W. Co. which the S. Co. were authorized to use, enter upon or interfere with, but that the S. Co. might purchase and take, and the G. W. Co. should sell and grant accordingly, an easement or right of using the same in perpetuity for the purposes of the Act; and by sect. 9 that if any dispute should arise respecting the matters aforesaid it should be settled by an arbitrator to be appointed under the Act. The Lands Clauses Act, 1845 (except where expressly varied by the Act), was incorporated therewith, and it was enacted that the words and expressions to which meanings were assigned by the Lands Clauses Act should have the same respective meanings unless there was something in the subject or context repugnant to such construction.—The S. Co. gave the G. W. Co. a notice to treat for the purchase of an easement or right in or over lands of the G. W. Co. for the purposes of the crossings, and shortly afterwards a notice of their desire to enter upon and use the lands for those purposes, and of their intention to apply to the Board of Trade to appoint a surveyor to determine the value of such easement or right. The valuation was made, and the S. Co. deposited the amount and entered into a bond under sect. 85 of the Lands Clauses Act.—The G. W. Co. having brought an action for an injunction to restrain the S. Co. from entering or continuing upon the lands mentioned in the notice to treat, or from putting in force any of the powers of the special Act or of the Lands Clauses Act in relation to the compulsory purchase of land, on the ground that the capital of the S. Co. had not been duly subscribed as required by sect. 16 of the Lands Clauses

II. LANDS CLAUSES ACT — COMPULSORY POWERS—*continued.*

Act:—*Held*, by Lords Bramwell and FitzGerald, affirming the decision of the Court of Appeal, Lord Watson dissenting, that the S. Co. could not be restrained on that ground :—By Lord FitzGerald, That (1) the assertion of the rights conferred by sect. 8 of the special Act was not a "putting in force of the powers of the Lands Clauses Act or of the special Act in relation to the compulsory taking of land" : and (2) that even if the perpetual easements created by sect. 8 of the special Act would constitute "land" within sect. 16 of the Lands Clauses Act, yet the case had been taken out of the compulsory powers of the Lands Clauses Act by sect. 8 of the special Act. GREAT WESTERN RAILWAY COMPANY *v.* SWINDON AND CHELTENHAM RAILWAY COMPANY 22 Ch. D. 677 ; 9 App. Cas. 787

4. —— **Expiration of Period**—*Railway Company—Entry under s. 85 of the Lands Clauses Act, 1845, shortly before Expiration of Period allowed for Completion of Railway—Right of Company to take Possession without Sheriff—Lands Clauses Consolidation Act, 1845 (8 & 9 Vict. c. 18), ss. 68, 84, 85, 91.*] The special Act of a railway company enacted that "the powers of the company for the compulsory purchase of lands for the purposes of this Act shall not be exercised after the expiration of three years from the passing of this Act ;" and that "if the railways are not completed within five years from the passing of this Act, then on the expiration of that period the powers by this Act granted to the company for making and completing the railways or otherwise in relation thereto, shall cease to be exercised except as to so much thereof as is then completed." A few days before the expiration of the three years the company served on a landowner a notice to treat for part of his land. A correspondence ensued, no agreement was come to, and the compensation was not assessed. Thirteen days before the expiration of the five years the company, having complied with the requirements of sect. 85 of the Lands Clauses Act, 1845, entered and proceeded to make the railway, the landowner objecting and resisting. The land was *bonâ fide* required for the railway :—*Held*, reversing the judgment of the Court of Appeal and restoring the judgment of Fry, J., that whether the railway could or could not have been completed within the thirteen days, the entry under sect. 85 was lawful ; that the company could not be restrained by injunction, but were entitled to remain and complete the railway after the expiration of the five years. TIVERTON AND NORTH DEVON RAILWAY COMPANY *v.* LOOSEMORE 22 Ch. D. 25 ; 9 App. Cas. 480

5. —— **Interest on Purchase-money**—*Interest, from what time payable — Conveyance — Settled Lands—Trustees with Power of Sale— Tenant for Life, Sale by—Lands Clauses Consolidation Act, 1845, ss. 75, 85.*] A complete contract being established between a railway company and a landowner by the notice to treat, and an award under the Lands Clauses Consolidation Act, 1845, fixing the amount of the purchase-money, the ordinary rules as between vendor and purchaser apply to such a contract, including the liability of the purchasing company, in a proper case, to pay interest on their unpaid purchase-money.—Thus,

II. LANDS CLAUSES ACT — COMPULSORY POWERS—*continued.*

where the title has not been accepted before the award, and the company, not being in possession, delay paying or depositing the purchase-money, they are liable to pay interest at 4 per cent. per annum, not from the date of the award, but from the time they might prudently have taken possession ; that is, when a good title was shewn.— *In re Eccleshill Local Board* (13 Ch. D. 365) disapproved of.—Where a railway company has given notices to treat to a legal tenant for life under a settlement and to the trustees of the settlement who have a bare power of sale with his consent, and the purchase-money for the life estate is fixed as between the company and the tenant for life by award under a reference to arbitration under the Lands Clauses Act in the usual way, the trustees taking no part in the reference, the company cannot require the sale to be completed as a sale by the trustees, but it must be completed as a sale by the tenant for life under the Act. *In re* PIGOTT AND THE GREAT WESTERN RAILWAY COMPANY 18 Ch. D. 146

6. —— **Notice to Treat**—*Sects. 18, 19, 23, 25, 27, 28, 30—Service on Occupier of Part of Premises — Notice adopted by Owner — Validity of Service— Reference to Arbitration — Arbitrator neglecting or refusing to act—Power of other Arbitrator to proceed ex parte.*] Where arbitrators have been appointed under sect. 25 of the Lands Clauses Act, 1845, and one arbitrator refuses or neglects for seven days to concur in the appointment of an umpire, the other arbitrator has power, under sect. 30 of the Act, to proceed ex parte to make an award, and the previous appointment of an umpire is not in such a case a condition precedent to the ex parte proceedings.—A corporation, three days before the expiration of their compulsory powers, without making any attempt to discover and serve the owner of the property, served a notice to treat on an occupier of part of the premises comprised in the notice to treat, who was the agent of the owner for the management of his property. The occupier took it the same day to the solicitor of the owner, and also wrote to the owner ; but it did not appear that, as a matter of fact, the notice came to the hands of the owner before the three days had expired. The owner, however, after the expiration of the three days gave a counter notice under sect. 92 requiring the corporation to take the whole of his property. This notice he subsequently withdrew, and required the corporation to proceed with the purchase of the land specified in their notice to treat, which they declined to do :—*Held*, that the service of the notice to treat was irregular and invalid, and that the owner could not, by his subsequent adoption of the notice, cure the irregularity and compel the corporation to proceed with it.—The conditions necessary for service of a notice to treat discussed. SHEPHERD *v.* CORPORATION OF NORWICH　-　30 Ch. D. 553

7. —— **Part of House**—*Railway Company— Notice to treat—Company taking part of a House to take the whole—Close—Private Road—Lands Clauses Consolidation Act, 1845 (8 & 9 Vict. c. 18), s. 92.*] A house and garden were surrounded by a wall. A gateway in the wall opened into a

II. LANDS CLAUSES ACT — COMPULSORY POWERS—continued.

paddock surrounded by a high hedge of an ornamental kind. From the gateway the back road to the house passed through the paddock to a public road which ran along the far side of the paddock fence :—Held, that the paddock was part of the house within sect. 92 of the Lands Clauses Consolidation Act, 1845. BARNES v. SOUTHSEA RAILWAY COMPANY   -   27 Ch. D. 536

8. —— Sale by Trustees—Persons absolutely entitled—Lands Clauses Act, 1845, ss. 7, 9—Married Women entitled for Separate Use—Trustee acting as Surveyor under the 9th section —Power of Sale, Determination of.] A testator devised his residuary real estate (which comprised land in respect of which notice to treat had been given by a railway company) to trustees in trust for his wife for life, and after her death to assure the same to his two married daughters, in equal shares, for their separate use as tenants in common, with a gift over in favour of their issue in events which did not happen ; and "for the purpose of division" he empowered his trustees to sell his residuary estate : and declared that his trustees might receive payment for all business done by them in relation to the estate.—The testator's wife, his two daughters and their husbands survived the testator : and after the death of the widow the trustees sold and conveyed the lands to a railway company for a price which had been determined by the valuation of two surveyors, as provided by the 9th section of the Lands Clauses Act, 1845, the trustees having first, for the purposes of such valuation, appointed one of themselves as the surveyor on their behalf. One of the testator's daughters disputed the validity of the sale, and brought an action to restrain the company from taking or using the land :—Held, first, that whether the power of sale under the will was still in existence or not, the trustees did not exercise it, but professed to convey the land under the provisions of the Lands Clauses Act, and therefore the validity of the sale must be determined without reference to the power.—Secondly, that the trustees, being trustees of the land for femes covertes who were absolutely entitled for their separate use, were not persons competent to contract with a railway company for the sale of the land under the 7th section of the Lands Clauses Act, 1845, and that the sale was for that reason invalid.—Thirdly, that the sale was also invalid by reason of the appointment by the trustees of one of themselves as surveyor to value the land under the 9th section of the Lands Clauses Act, 1845.—Per Jessel, M.R. : The mere fact of trustees having the price fixed by two surveyors, and then agreeing to sell for that price, instead of first agreeing to sell for a certain price and then testing the price by the valuation of two surveyors, would not in itself invalidate a sale under the 9th section of the Lands Clauses Act.—Per Jessel, M.R.: The power of sale given to the trustees by the will did not determine on the death of the tenant for life, but might have been exercised within a reasonable time afterwards for the purpose of dividing the property. PETERS v. LEWES AND EAST GRINSTEAD RAILWAY COMPANY 16 Ch. D. 703 ; 18 Ch. D. 429

III. LANDS CLAUSES ACT—COSTS.

1. —— Arbitration—Lands Clauses Acts, 1845, 1869 (8 & 9 Vict. c. 18, ss. 23, 34 ; 32 & 33 Vict. c. 18)—Settlement of Purchase-money by Arbitration —Payment due before Conveyance.] Where the amount of compensation payable to the owner of lands taken under the Lands Clauses Acts, 1845 and 1869, is settled by arbitration, and the amount and the costs of the arbitration are awarded to the owner, the taxed costs of the arbitration become payable to him within a reasonable time, and the execution of the conveyance by him of the lands taken is not a condition precedent to payment of such costs. CAPELL v. GREAT WESTERN RAILWAY COMPANY   9 Q. B. D.
[459 ; 11 Q. B. D. 345

2. —— Conveyance—Taxation—8 & 9 Vict. c. 18, s. 83.] A railway company cannot under the 83rd section of the Lands Clauses Consolidation Act, tax the costs of conveyance after payment by them of the costs. In re SOUTH EASTERN RAILWAY COMPANY. Ex parte SOMERVILLE   -   -   23 Ch. D. 167

3. —— Incumbrancers—8 & 9 Vict. c. 18, s. 80 —Payment out of Court.] After payment into Court by a company of the purchase-money of land belonging to a tenant for life and remaindermen, some of the latter mortgaged their reversionary interests in the fund.—Upon the death of the tenant for life, the owners of the fund and their incumbrancers presented a petition for payment of the fund out of Court :—Held, that the company were not liable to pay the costs incurred by the mortgagees in proving their incumbrances. Ex parte GREAT WESTERN RAILWAY COMPANY. In re GOUGH'S TRUSTS   -   24 Ch. D. 569

4. —— Litigation between adverse Claimants —8 & 9 Vict. c. 18, s. 80.] Property which was in the possession of a mortgagee was taken by the London School Board, and the purchase-money paid into Court pursuant to the Lands Clauses Act, 1845. The mortgagor's trustee in liquidation presented a petition asking for an inquiry what was due on the mortgage, for payment to the mortgagee of what should be so found due, and for payment of the residue of the purchase-money to himself :—Held (reversing the decision of Fry, J), that the Board must pay the costs of the inquiry. In re BAREHAM   -   17 Ch. D. 329

5. —— Official Solicitor—Chancery Funds Rules, 1874, r. 91—Chancery Funds Amended Orders, 1874, r. 14—Railway Company—Payment out of Court—Fund exceeding £500 not dealt with for Fifteen Years.] Where a fund in Court exceeding £500 in value and representing the purchase-moneys of settled lands taken by a railway company, with accumulated interest, had not been dealt with for upwards of fifteen years, and it had become necessary under the Chancery Funds Rules, 1874, r. 91, and the Chancery Funds Amended Orders, 1874, Order 14, to serve the official solicitor with the petition for the payment out of the fund :—Held, first, that his costs were not payable by the railway company ; secondly, that such costs having been occasioned by the default of the tenant for life, were properly payable out of the portion of the fund which came to his estate. In re J. CLARKE'S ESTATE   -   21 Ch. D. 776

III. LANDS CLAUSES ACT—COSTS—*continued.*

6. —— "**Taking Land**"—8 & 9 *Vict. c.* 18, *ss.* 80, 85—*Entry on Land—Abandonment of Railway.*] A railway company gave notice to treat for a piece of land, and no agreement having been come to with the owners, they entered on the land under the powers of the 85th section of the Lands Clauses Act, and paid the deposit into Court. Afterwards the company obtained an Act by which they were empowered to abandon that part of their undertaking, but it was enacted that the abandonment should not prejudice any landowner's rights to compensation for damage done by entry and occupation, and that the compensation should be determined in the manner provided by the Lands Clauses Act. The owners of the land then entered into an agreement with the company fixing the amount of compensation at £1350, but providing that this should not include costs, charges and expenses which the owners might be entitled to recover under the company's Acts, but that such costs, charges, and expenses should be recoverable from the company in addition to the compensation as if the agreement had not been entered into. The company objected to pay the costs of ascertaining the amount of the compensation on the ground that the land had not been taken within the meaning of the 80th section of the Lands Clauses Act. They also objected to pay the costs of the preparation of the agreement:—*Held* (affirming the decision of Kay, J.), that the land had been "taken" within the meaning of the 80th section, and that the company must pay the costs of ascertaining the amount of compensation and of the preparation of the agreement. CHARLTON *v.* ROLLESTON - - - **28 Ch. D. 237**

7. —— Verdict of Jury—*Lands Clauses Consolidation Act,* 1845 (8 & 9 *Vict. c.* 18), *ss.* 38, 51 —"*Sum previously offered.*"] By sect. 38 of the Lands Clauses Consolidation Act, 1845, the promoters of an undertaking, before issuing their warrant for causing a jury to be summoned in cases of disputed compensation, shall give not less than ten days' notice of their intention to summon a jury to the other party, and in such notice shall state what sum of money they are willing to give for the interest in the lands sought to be purchased from him, and for the damage to be sustained by him by the execution of the works; and by sect. 51, on every such inquiry before a jury where the verdict of the jury shall be given for a greater sum "than the sum previously offered" by the promoters, all the costs of the inquiry shall be borne by the promoters, but if the verdict be given for a less sum the costs shall be borne equally between the parties in the manner specified in that section.—In a proceeding to take and purchase the claimant's lands under the Lands Clauses Consolidation Act, 1845, the promoters, on the 9th of March, gave him the notice required by sect. 38, and stated that they were willing to give him £600 as and for purchase-money and compensation. On the 19th of March, the promoters served a second notice upon the claimant that they were willing, and thereby offered, to pay £900 as purchase-money and compensation. This notice did not refer to the previous one. Neither offer was accepted by the claimant, and on the 29th of March

III. LANDS CLAUSES ACT—COSTS—*continued.*

the promoters issued their warrant for causing a jury to be summoned, who assessed the sum to which the claimant was entitled at £750.—*Held,* first, that in cases to which sect. 38 was applicable the words "the sum previously offered" in sect. 51 applied only to an offer made under sect. 38; secondly, that the promoters were not entitled to rely upon their second offer of £900 as an offer made under sect. 38, and that the costs of the inquiry must, therefore, be borne by them. THE QUEEN *v.* SMITH - - **12 Q. B. D. 481**

IV. LANDS CLAUSES ACT—PURCHASE-MONEY.

1. —— Adverse Claimants—*Claim of the Crown* —8 & 9 *Vict. c.* 18, *s.* 76.] A railway company under the powers of its Act gave notice to a lord of the manor to take a piece of land on the sea-shore, which he claimed as part of the waste of his manor. The purchase-money was assessed by arbitration, but an adverse claim having been made by the Crown, the company paid the purchase-money into Court under the 76th section of the Lands Clauses Act. The Crown filed an information against the lord of the manor claiming the land together with other land as part of the foreshore. The lord of the manor having filed a petition for payment of the purchase-money to him:—*Held* (affirming the decree of Kay, J.), that as the Crown could not be brought before the Court under the Lands Clauses Act to contest the claim of the Petitioner, the petition ought to stand over till the information had been heard.— *Quære* as to the course which ought to have been pursued if the rival claimant had been a subject. *In re* MANOR OF LOWESTOFT AND GREAT EASTERN RAILWAY COMPANY. *Ex parte* REEVE **24 Ch. D. [253**

2. —— Application of Income—8 & 9 *Vict. c.* 18, *s.* 74—*Lands subject to beneficial Leases taken by Railway Company—Tenant for Life and Remainderman—Form of Order.*] A railway company took freeholds settled by a will, and subject to eight leases, one granted by the testator and the other seven granted under powers in the will, either by the trustees or the tenant for life, and containing covenants by the lessee to repair or rebuild. The company purchased the leasehold interests from the tenants themselves, and paid the purchase-moneys of the fee, subject to the lessee's interests, into Court under the Lands Clauses Consolidation Act, 1845. The income of the purchase-moneys when invested would be greater than the aggregate rents payable under the leases:—*Held,* upon petition by the tenant for life for investment and payment to him of the dividends, that, having regard to the 74th section of the Lands Clauses Consolidation Act, 1845, he was entitled, during the continuance of the leases, to so much only of the dividends as equalled the amount of the rents he would have received in case the property had not been taken by the railway company; that the rest of the rents must be accumulated; and that, upon the date of falling in of each lease, the tenant for life would be entitled to an additional annual sum representing the income of so much of the capital of the purchase-moneys as was attributable to the property comprised in the lease which had fallen in, and of the accumulations thereof, less the rent under

IV. LANDS CLAUSES ACT—PURCHASE-MONEY
—continued.

such lease.—*In re Wootton's Estate* (Law Rep. 1 Eq. 589) followed.—Form of order. *In re* WILKES' ESTATE   **16 Ch. D. 597**

3. —— Payment out of Court—*Person "becoming absolutely entitled"—Trustees with Power of Sale—Lands Clauses Consolidation Act, 1845 (8 & 9 Vict. c. 18), s. 69].* A share of stock in Court, which represented money paid into Court by a railway company for the purchase of land taken under their statutory powers, had been assigned by the beneficial owner to trustees, on trust for sale and conversion, at the request in writing of herself during her life and afterwards at the discretion of the trustees, and to hold the proceeds on certain trusts:—*Held,* that the settlor joining in the petition, and the company not objecting, the share might be transferred to the trustees as persons "becoming absolutely entitled" within the meaning of sect. 69 of the Lands Clauses Consolidation Act, 1845. *In re* WARD'S ESTATES
[**28 Ch. D. 100**

4. —— Reinvestment—*Cash under Control of Court—23 & 24 Vict. c. 38, s. 10—General Order of Court of Chancery, 1st February, 1861, r. 1—Lands Clauses Consolidation Act, 1845 (8 & 9 Vict. c. 18), s. 70.]* Money paid into Court under the Lands Clauses Act, 1845, or under any other Act which directs money so paid in to be invested in specified securities, is not "cash under the control of the Court," within the meaning of the Act 23 & 24 Vict. c. 38, s. 10, and the General Order of the 1st of February, 1861, r. 1, and the Court cannot order such money to be invested in any securities but those which are specified in the Act under which it is paid in.—*In re Boyd's Settled Estate* (21 W. R. 667) followed. *Ex parte* VICAR OF ST. MARY, WIGTON   **18 Ch. D. 646**

5. —— Reinvestment—*Cash under Control of the Court—Money paid in under Lands Clauses Act, 1845 (8 & 9 Vict. c. 18)—Law of Property Act, 1860 (23 & 24 Vict. c. 38), s. 10—General Order, Feb. 1, 1861.]* Money paid into Court under the Lands Clauses Act is "cash under the control of the Court" within the meaning of the Act 23 & 24 Vict. c. 38, s. 10, and the General Order of the 1st of February, 1861, and may be invested in any of the securities sanctioned by the Court.—The expression "cash under the control of the Court" means cash standing in Court in any cause or matter.—*In re Boyd's Settled Estates* (21 W. R. 667) overruled.—Cash under the control of the Court may be invested in East India 3½ per cent. Stock created since the date of the General Order. *Ex parte* ST. JOHN BAPTIST COLLEGE, OXFORD. *In re* METROPOLITAN AND DISTRICT RAILWAYS ACT   **22 Ch. D. 93**

6. —— Reinvestment—*Glebe Lands taken by Railway Company — Incumbrance — Rent-charge —8 & 9 Vict. c. 18, s. 69—Cash under Control of Court.]* A railway company took part of glebe lands which were subject to a yearly rent-charge created under the General Land Drainage and Improvement Company's Act, 1849, to repay money borrowed by a former rector for outlay on the glebe. The company paid the purchase-moneys into Court under the Lands Clauses Consolidation Act, 1845, and the in-

IV. LANDS CLAUSES ACT—PURCHASE-MONEY
—continued.

cumbrancer being willing to take a lump sum in lieu of the remaining payments of the rent-charge (eleven in number), the rector petitioned to have this sum paid off out of the fund in Court, and to have the residue of the fund invested as if it were cash under the control of the Court:—*Held,* first, that even supposing that the rector could himself have charged the inheritance of the glebe to provide for or to repay similar outlay, the Court ought not to disturb the existing state of things and allow the fund in Court to be applied in anticipating the future payments of the rent-charge.—Secondly, that money paid into Court under the Lands Clauses Consolidation Act, 1845, is not to be invested as cash under the control of the Court, but only in the manner specified in the Act.—*In re Fryer's Settlement* (Law Rep. 20 Eq. 468) not followed. *Ex parte* RECTOR OF KIRKSMEATON. *In re* HULL RAILWAY AND DOCK ACT   -   **20 Ch. D. 203**

7. —— Reinvestment—*8 & 9 Vict. c. 18, s. 69—Tenant for Life—Remainderman—Trust Estate—Permanent Repairs—Recouping Trustee.]* Under a will A. was tenant for life of a copyhold house and two leasehold houses. The latter having been taken under the Lands Clauses Consolidation Act, the purchase-money was paid into Court under the 69th section. The trustee of the will having entered into a contract for putting the copyhold house into permanent repair, and there being no trust funds in hand out of which the expense could be defrayed, the Court, upon a petition for re-investment presented by the tenant for life and the trustee, and without requiring service on the remaindermen, ordered the contract price of the repairs to be paid to the trustee out of the fund in Court, and the remainder to be invested in consols, and the dividends paid to the trustee. *In re* ALDRED'S ESTATE   **21 Ch. D. 228**

V. LANDS CLAUSES ACT — SUPERFLUOUS LANDS.

1. —— Sale by Company—*Railway Company —Landowner — Pre-emption—Conveyance—Ultra Vires—Lands Clauses Consolidation Act (8 & 9 Vict. c. 18), 1845, s. 128.]* The mere fact of a railway company purporting to convey away lands acquired by them for the purposes of their undertaking is not conclusive to shew that the lands so conveyed are superfluous lands within the meaning of sect. 128 of the Lands Clauses Consolidation Act, 1845.—The M. Railway Company having, under their special Act passed in 1872, acquired for the purposes of their undertaking certain lands forming part of a farm belonging to H., purported, acting in excess of their parliamentary powers, to sell and convey the lands to the S. Railway Company under a bonâ fide arrangement by which they were to be held and used for the purposes of the undertakings of both companies.—Upon an action brought by H. against both companies to establish his right of pre-emption under sect. 128 of the Lands Clauses Consolidation Act, 1845, in the lands conveyed, the ten years from the time fixed by the M. Company's Act for the completion of their works not having yet expired:—*Held,* that the mere fact of the conveyance was not sufficient to shew that the lands were super-

V. LANDS CLAUSES ACT — SUPERFLUOUS LANDS—*continued.*

fluous within the meaning of that section ; and that, inasmuch as it appeared from the evidence that, had the lands remained in the hands of the M. Company, they would not have been superfluous for the purposes of that company within that section, the Plaintiff's right of pre-emption had not yet arisen ; but that the conveyance from the M. Company to the S. Company must be set aside as ultrà vires. HOBBS *v.* MIDLAND RAILWAY COMPANY - - 20 Ch. D. 418

2. —— **Sale by Company**—*Railway Company—Lands Clauses Consolidation Act, 1845 (8 & 9 Vict. c. 18), s. 127—Covenant to reconvey—Ultrà Vires—Perpetuity—Land required or Purposes of Railway.*] By a deed dated in August, 1865, which recited that the Plaintiff company were seised in fee simple of certain land which was no longer required for the purposes of their railway, the company conveyed the land to G. P. in fee for £100, and G. P. covenanted with the company that he, his heirs or assigns, would at any time thereafter whenever the land might be required for the railway or works of the company, and whenever thereunto requested by the company on a six calendar months' notice, and upon receiving £100, reconvey the land to the company. In 1879 the Defendant purchased the land from G. P.'s heir, with notice of the above covenant. In 1880 the company gave the Defendant notice to reconvey the land, and upon his refusal to do so this action was brought for specific performance of the covenant. The company had power in 1865 by their special Act to purchase land by agreement, though not compulsorily, and that power was extended to the present time by subsequent Acts :—*Held,* by Kay, J., that the transaction of 1865 was not ultrà vires the company, that as there was at that time a strong probability that the land would be required for the purposes of the company, it was within their power to enter into a prospective contract to purchase it, and that the sale was not a conditional sale, but an absolute sale with a personal contract by the purchaser to resell :—*Held,* also, by Kay, J., that an executory interest in property to arise on a future event which may not happen within the limits of the rule against perpetuities is void, though it be limited to an ascertained person who can release it at any time.—The dictum in *Gilbertson* v. *Richards* (4 H. & N. 277, 297) and the decision in *Birmingham Canal Company* v. *Cartwright* (11 Ch. D. 421) dissented from.—But, *Held,* by Kay, J., that in the present case the covenant did not create any estate or interest in land, and therefore was not obnoxious to the rule against perpetuities, and that specific performance must be decreed, the covenant being binding on an alienee with notice on the principle of *Tulk* v. *Moxhay* (2 Ph. 774).—*Held,* by the Court of Appeal, that the covenant in the deed of 1865 reserved to the company an interest in the land, and that the sale was ultrà vires and void, for that under the Lands Clauses Consolidation Act, 1845, s. 127, land sold by a company as superfluous land must be sold absolutely without reserving any interest to the company :—*Held,* also, that as the covenant gave to the company an exe

V. LANDS CLAUSES ACT — SUPERFLUOUS LANDS—*continued.*

cutory interest in land to arise on an event which might occur after the period allowed by the rules as to remoteness, it was invalid on the ground of remoteness. — *Birmingham Canal Company* v. *Cartwright* (11 Ch. D. 421) overruled.—The doctrine of *Tulk* v. *Moxhay* (2 Ph. 774) only applies to restrictive covenants and not to covenants to do acts relating to the land. LONDON AND SOUTH WESTERN RAILWAY COMPANY *v.* GOMM
[20 Ch. D. 562

3. —— **Sale by Company**—*Railway Company—8 & 9 Vict. c. 18, ss. 127, 128—Restrictive Covenant.*] A railway company selling its superfluous land is at liberty to impose such restrictive conditions upon the user and enjoyment of the land as may most conduce to their advantage as vendors, and there is nothing in the Lands Clauses Consolidation Act, 1845, to deprive them in this respect of the rights of ordinary vendors. *In re* HIGGINS AND HITCHMAN'S CONTRACT　　　21 Ch. D. 95

4. —— **Sale by Company**—*Railway Company—Restrictions—Land subject to statutory Prohibition against building.*] An Inclosure Act passed in 1806 provided that no buildings should at any time thereafter be erected on a certain strip of land. In 1865 a railway company under their statutory powers acquired a portion of the strip of land for the purposes of their undertaking. A part of the land thus acquired became superfluous land, and the company in 1868 sold and conveyed the superfluous part to a purchaser who demised it to the Defendant. The Defendant in 1885 commenced building on the land :—*Held,* that the land acquired by the company was freed from the prohibition of building only for the purposes of the company's undertaking, and that, when part of it was sold as superfluous land, the prohibition of building revived in respect of that part.—An injunction to restrain the Defendant from building on the land in contravention of the provisions of the Inclosure Act was granted at the suit of an owner of adjoining land. BIRD *v.* EGGLETON
[29 Ch. D. 1012

LANDS CLAUSES ACT—Compensation — Dwellings Improvement Act　　25 Ch. D. 78
　See LABOURERS' DWELLINGS ACTS. 1.

—— Compulsory purchase—Unstamped deed
　See REVENUE—STAMPS. 5. [24 Ch. D. 119

—— Costs—Solicitor's charges　-　30 Ch. D. 28
　See SOLICITOR—BILL OF COSTS. 22.

—— Lunatic's land—Conversion　27 Ch. D. 309
　See LUNATIC—PROPERTY. 8.

—— Payment out of Court — Re-investment—
　Summons in Chambers.
　See Cases under PRACTICE — SUPREME
　　COURT—CHAMBERS. 11—16.

—— Scotland　　　　-　8 App. Cas. 623
　See SCOTCH LAW—HARBOUR. 1.

LAPSE—Appointed share　-　17 Ch. D. 151
　See POWER—EXECUTION. 7.

—— Direction that share shall fall into residue
[29 Ch. D. 142
　See WILL—RESIDUARY GIFT. 2.

—— Devise on condition　-　21 Ch. D. 431
　See WILL—CONDITION. 8.

LAPSE—*continued.*

—— Devise to daughter—Curtesy   **17 Ch. D. 115**
See WILL—SPEAKING FROM DEATH. 1.

—— Legacy.
See Cases under WILL—LAPSE.

—— Mortmain—Exoneration from debts
[**29 Ch. D. 145**
See WILL—EXONERATION. 1.

LAPSE OF TIME.
See DELAY.

LARCENY.
See Cases under CRIMINAL LAW—LAR-
CENY.

—— By wife—Evidence of husband
[**12 Q. B. D. 266**
See CRIMINAL LAW—EVIDENCE. 2.

—— Misappropriation of property intrusted for
safe custody   -   -   **8 Q. B. D. 706**
See CRIMINAL LAW—MISAPPROPRIATION.

—— Ship—Foreign port—Jurisdiction
See JURISDICTION. 2.   [**10 Q. B. D. 76**

LARCH TREES—Windfalls ▾ **28 Ch. D. 89, 220;**
See TIMBER. 1, 2.   [**30 Ch. D. 485**

LARKS.
See WILD BIRDS PROTECTION ACT, 1881
—*Statutes.*

LAUNCH—Reasonable precautions—Mersey
[**7 P. D. 217; 8 P. D. 119**
See SHIP—NAVIGATION. 6, 7.

LEASE.
See Cases under LANDLORD AND TENANT
—LEASE.

—— Agreement for.
See Cases under LANDLORD AND TENANT
—AGREEMENT.

—— Agreement for—Custom of country
[**21 Ch. D. 18; 8 App. Cas. 508**
See LANDLORD AND TENANT —CUSTOM
OF COUNTRY.

—— Apportionment of conditions on severance
of reversion.
See LANDLORD AND TENANT—LEASE—
Statutes.

—— Covenants in.
See Cases under LANDLORD AND TENANT
—LEASE. 1—14.

—— Covenants—Continuing breach—Conditions
of sale   --   **7 App. Cas. 19**
See VENDOR AND PURCHASER— CONDI-
TIONS OF SALE. 3.

—— Covenants running with the reversion.
See LANDLORD AND TENANT—LEASE—
Statutes.

—— Disclaimer by trustee in bankruptcy.
See Cases under BANKRUPTCY — DIS-
CLAIMER.

—— Distress—Bankruptcy.
See Cases under BANKRUPTCY—DISTRESS.

—— Distress—Winding-up of company.
See Cases under COMPANY—DISTRESS.

—— Forfeiture, relief against.
See Cases under LANDLORD AND TENANT
—RE-ENTRY.

LEASE—*continued.*

—— Forfeiture, relief against—Statute respect-
ing.
See LANDLORD AND TENANT—RE-ENTRY
—*Statutes.*

—— Land subject to—Purchase-money –Appli-
cation of income   -   **16 Ch. D. 597**
See LANDS CLAUSES ACT— PURCHASE-
MONEY. 2.

—— Licence to assign   -   -   **29 Ch. D. 661**
See VENDOR AND PURCHASER — RESCIS-
SION. 1.

—— Mine   **23 Ch. D. 81; 6 App. Cas. 460**
See MINE—LEASE. 1, 2.

—— Mines—Nova Scotia   **8 App. Cas. 568**
See COLONIAL LAW — CANADA — NOVA
SCOTIA.

—— Mistake—Rectification   -   **28 Ch. D. 255**
See MISTAKE. 1.

—— Mortgagor's power to grant.
See MORTGAGE—POWERS—*Statutes.*

—— Power of leasing.
See Cases under SETTLEMENT—POWERS.
1—4.

—— Renewable.
See Cases under LEASEHOLD—RENEW-
ABLE LEASE.

—— Renewal of, by executor   **18 Ch. D. 93**
See EXECUTOR—ADMINISTRATION. 3.

—— Surrender of—Infant   -   **29 Ch. D. 248**
See INFANT—PROPERTY. 3.

LEASEHOLD.   Col.
  I. LONG TERMS   792
 II. RENEWABLE LEASE   -   794

I. LEASEHOLD—LONG TERMS.

*By 44 & 45 Vict. c. 41 (Conveyancing Act, 1881),
sect. 65 (1), where a residue unexpired of not less
than 200 years of a term, which, as originally
created, was for not less than 300 years, is subsisting in land, whether being the whole land originally
comprised in the term, or part only thereof, without
any trust or right of redemption affecting the term
in favour of the freeholder, or other person entitled
in reversion expectant on the term, and without any
rent, or with merely a peppercorn rent or other rent
having no money value, incident to the reversion, or
having had a rent, not being merely a peppercorn
rent or other rent having no money value, originally
so incident, which subsequently has been released
or has become barred by lapse of time, or has in
any other way ceased to be payable, then the term
may be enlarged into a fee simple in the manner,
and subject to the restrictions, in this section provided.*

(2.) Each of the following persons (namely):
*(i.) Any person beneficially entitled in right of
the term, whether subject to any incumbrance or not, to possession of any land
comprised in the term; but, in case of a
married woman, with the concurrence of
her husband, unless she is entitled for her
separate use, whether with restraint on
anticipation or not, and then without his
concurrence;*
*(ii.) Any person being in receipt of income as
trustee, in right of the term, or having the*

I. LEASEHOLD—LONG TERMS—*continued.*

term vested in him in trust, or sale, whether subject to any incumbrance or not :

(iii.) *Any person in whom, as personal representative of any deceased person, the term is vested, whether subject to any incumbrance or not ;*

shall, as far as regards the land to which he is entitled, or in which he is interested, in right of the term, in any such character as aforesaid, have power by deed to declare to the effect that, from and after the execution of the deed, the term shall be enlarged into a fee simple.

(3.) *Thereupon, by virtue of the deed and of this Act, the term shall become and be enlarged accordingly, and the person in whom the term was previously vested shall acquire and have in the land a fee simple instead of the term.*

(4.) *The estate in fee simple so acquired by enlargement shall be subject to all the same trusts, powers, executory limitations over, rights, and equities, and to all the same covenants and provisions relating to user and enjoyment, and to all the same obligations of every kind, as the term would have been subject to if it had not been so enlarged.*

(5.) *But where any land so held for the residue of a term has been settled in trust by reference to other land, being freehold land, so as to go along with that other land as far as the law permits, and, at the time of enlargement, the ultimate beneficial interest in the term, whether subject to any subsisting particular estate or not, has not become absolutely and indefeasibly vested in any person, then the estate in fee simple acquired as aforesaid shall, without prejudice to any conveyance or value previously made by a person having a contingent or defeasible interest in the term, be liable to be, and shall be, conveyed and settled in like manner as the other land, being freehold land, aforesaid, and until so conveyed and settled shall devolve beneficially, as if it had been so conveyed and settled.*

(6.) *The estate in fee simple so acquired shall, whether the term was originally created without impeachment of waste or not, include the fee simple in all mines and minerals which at the time of enlargement have not been severed in right, or in fact, or have not been severed or reversed by an Inclosure Act or award.*

(7.) *This section applies to every such term as aforesaid subsisting at or after the commencement of this Act.*

By 45 & 46 Vict. c. 39 (*Conveyancing Act,* 1882), sect. 11. *Sect.* 65 *of the Conveyancing Act of* 1881 *shall apply to and include, and shall be deemed to have always applied to and included, every such term as in that section mentioned, whether having as the immediate reversion thereon the freehold or not ; but not—*

(i.) *Any term liable to be determined by re-entry for condition broken ; or*

(ii.) *Any term created by sub-demise out of a superior term, itself incapable of being enlarged into a fee simple.*

1. —— **Enlargement into Fee**—"*Rent having no money value*" — *Conveyancing and Law of Property Act,* 1881 (44 & 45 Vict. c. 41), s. 65.] Land was demised for a term of 500 years from Michaelmas, 1646, at the yearly rent of "one

I. LEASEHOLD—LONG TERMS—*continued.*

silver penny, if lawfully demanded" :—*Held,* that this rent was a "rent having no money value," within the meaning of sect. 65 of the Conveyancing Act, 1881, and that the owner of the term in 1884 had power under that section to enlarge the term into a fee. *In re* CHAPMAN AND HOBBS
[29 Ch. D. 1007

2. —— **Enlargement into Fee**—"*Rent having a money value*"—44 & 45 Vict. c. 41, s. 65.] Land was demised for 1000 years from 1607 at a yearly rent of 3s. In 1882 the land was sold as freehold :—*Held,* that the rent of 3s. had a money value, and that the owner had no power to enlarge the term into a freehold under the 65th section of the Conveyancing Act, 1881. *In re* SMITH AND STOTT　-　- 29 Ch. D. 1009, n.

II. LEASEHOLD—RENEWABLE LEASE.

1. —— **Leasehold for Lives**—*Settlement on Trust for Tenant for Life and Remaindermen—Overriding Trust for Renewal—Renewal become impossible—Purchase of Reversion by Assignee of first Tenancy for Life and ultimate Remainder—Rights of other Cestuis que Trustent.*] A leasehold for lives was devised by a testator who died in 1820 to trustees, on trust for a tenant for life and other persons in remainder, the ultimate remainder in fee being given to the tenant for life. The first trust was to renew the lease from time to time, paying the necessary fines and expenses out of the rents, or raising them by mortgage. In 1825 the trustees obtained a renewed lease for three lives, one of which was that of the tenant for life. In 1855 and 1859 respectively the other two lives dropped. In October, 1876, the tenant for life contracted to sell all his interest in the property to B., and a conveyance was executed in March, 1879. In December, 1876, the Ecclesiastical Commissioners, in whom the reversion subject to the lease was then vested, and who would not renew the lease, contracted to sell the reversion to B., and in August, 1879, they executed a conveyance to him, the conveyance being expressly made subject to "such trusts, equities, estates, and interests" as then affected the leasehold interest. In June, 1878, the School Board for London, under their statutory powers, took part of the property, and in January, 1880, they paid the purchase-money and compensation money into Court. The legal estate in the lease was outstanding in the representatives of the last surviving trustee of the will :—*Held,* that irrespectively of the form of the conveyance of the reversion to B., it was, according to the ordinary doctrine of a Court of Equity, impossible for him to purchase the reversion otherwise than as a trustee for the persons interested in the lease under the trusts of the will, and that, subject to his right to be recouped the purchase-money, he was only entitled to an order for payment on the interest on the fund in Court during the life of the tenant for life under the will. — *Hardman* v. *Johnson* (3 Mer. 347) distinguished. *In re* LORD RANELAGH'S WILL　-　- 26 Ch. D. 590

2. —— **Leasehold for Lives** — *Renewals by Tenant for Life—Purchase by Tenant for Life of Reversion — Ownership of the Fee — Customary Right of Renewal—Devise of Leaseholds for Life, with Remainder over.*] The doctrine that a re-

II. LEASEHOLD—RENEWABLE LEASE—*contd.*

newal of leaseholds by a tenant for life enures for the benefit of the remaindermen applies equally to a purchase of the reversion.—*Randall* v. *Russell* (3 Mer. 190) considered.—Testatrix devised leaseholds, renewable by custom, to J. P. for the residue of the term, and after the death of J. P., during the residue of the term, to the children of J. P. in equal shares. J. P. renewed the leaseholds more than once, and finally purchased the reversion:—*Held*, that the fee simple in the property passed by the devise in the will to the children of J. P., and became subject to the trusts of the will. PHILLIPS *v.* PHILLIPS　　-　　29 **Ch. D. 673**

3. —— Leasehold for Lives—*Successive Limitations—Executory Devise—Power of Alienation —Tenant for Life and Remainderman — Overriding Trust for Renewal—Refusal of Reversioner to renew—Sale under Settled Estates Act—Application of Purchase-money.*] When an estate pur autre vie is made the subject of successive limitations, the power of alienation of the successive takers is to be regulated, as far as possible, by analogy to the rules which govern similar limitations of an estate in fee simple.—Therefore an executory devise of an estate pur autre vie cannot be defeated by the prior taker of a quasi estate in fee simple.—Leaseholds for lives were devised on trust for J. in fee, but, if he should die without leaving issue living at his death, then on trust for W. in fee, and there was an overriding trust for renewal of the lease out of the rents. After the death of the testator the reversioner refused to renew the lease or to sell the reversion, and the lease was sold under the provisions of the Settled Estates Act:—*Held*, that the purchase-money must be invested in ordinary securities, and the income only paid to J. for his life.—*In re Wood's Estate* (Law Rep. 10 Eq. 572), *Hollier* v. *Burne* (Law Rep. 16 Eq. 163), and *Maddy* v. *Hale* (3 Ch. D. 327) followed. *In re* BARBER'S SETTLED ESTATES　　-　　-　　**18 Ch. D. 624**

4. —— Mortgage—*Purchase of Reversion by Mortgagor—Mortgage of Reversion — Rights of Mortgagees—14 & 15 Vict. c. 104, s. 3—23 & 24 Vict. c, 124, s. 35.*] An ecclesiastical lease of a house for a term of years, which was renewable by custom, though it contained no covenant by the lessors for renewal, was mortgaged, and the equity of redemption was afterwards assigned for value. The Ecclesiastical Commissioners, in whom the reversion had become vested, would not renew the lease, but before its expiration they agreed to sell the reversion to the assignee of the equity of redemption. The conveyance was not executed till after the expiration of the lease. While the negotiation for the purchase of the reversion was in progress the assignee borrowed £300, giving the lender a memorandum in writing, which stated that the money was to be secured by a mortgage from him of the house "so soon as he had completed the enfranchisement of the property from the Commissioners." The lender had no notice of the mortgage of the lease :—*Held*, that the mortgagor could only hold the fee simple of the property subject to the mortgage of the lease, and that he (and consequently the lender of the £300) was not entitled to any prior lien on the property for the purchase-money of the reversion, notwith-

II. LEASEHOLD—RENEWABLE LEASE—*contd.*

standing the fact that the mortgagor was under no obligation to the mortgagees of the lease to obtain a renewal of it, or to purchase the reversion. LEIGH *v.* BURNETT　　-　　29 **Ch. D. 231**

LEASEHOLD—Bequest of, to go with peerage
　　See WILL—HEIRLOOM. 3. [**26 Ch. D. 538**

—— Devise of real estate　　-　　28 **Ch. D. 66**
　　See WILL—WORDS. 16.

—— Power of administrator to mortgage
　　　　　　　　　　[**20 Ch. D. 745**
　　See ADMINISTRATOR—POWERS. 3.

—— Renewable—Charity scheme　20 **Ch. D. 516**
　　See CHARITY—MANAGEMENT. 1.

—— Title to—Peppercorn rent　30 **Ch. D. 344**
　　See VENDOR AND PURCHASER. 2.

—— Wife's reversionary interest　25 **Ch. D. 620**
　　See HUSBAND AND WIFE—WIFE'S REVERSION. 1.

LEAVE OF COURT—Disclaimer by trustee in bankruptcy.
　　See Cases under BANKRUPTCY—DISCLAIMER. 5—11.

—— Settled Land Act　-　-　30 **Ch. D. 102**
　　See SETTLED LAND ACT — PURCHASE-MONEY. 1.

—— Third party procedure　　25 **Ch. D. 76**
　　See PRACTICE—SUPREME COURT—THIRD PARTY. 8.

—— To amend—Application at trial—Appeal
　　　　　　　　　　[**16 Ch. D. 663**
　　See PRACTICE — SUPREME COURT—APPEAL. 41.

—— To appeal—Person not a party　16 **Ch. D. 1**
　　See PRACTICE — SUPREME COURT—APPEAL. 16.

—— To appeal—Privy Council.
　　See Cases under PRACTICE — PRIVY COUNCIL—LEAVE TO APPEAL.

—— To appeal—Privy Council—Criminal law
　　　　　　　　　　[**8 App. Cas. 304**
　　See COLONIAL LAW—JERSEY. 1.

—— To serve writ out of jurisdiction
　　　　　　　　　　[**19 Ch. D. 460**
　　See PRACTICE—SUPREME COURT—SERVICE. 8.

—— To use name of company　17 **Ch. D. 198**
　　See COMPANY—ACTIONS.

LECTURE—Oral delivery—Copyright
　　　　　　　　　　[**26 Ch. D. 374**
　　See COPYRIGHT—BOOKS. 2.

LEE NAVIGATION　　　6 **App. Cas. 685**
　　See RIVER.

LEGACY.
　　See Cases under WILL.

—— Charged on real estate　-　26 **Ch. D. 19**
　　See EXECUTOR—ADMINISTRATION. 2.

—— Income of—Infant—Maintenance.
　　See Cases under INFANT—MAINTENANCE.

—— Interest on　-　-　-　21 **Ch. D. 657**
　　See HUSBAND AND WIFE—SEPARATE ESTATE. 3.

LEGACY—*continued.*

—— Interest on—Statute of Limitations
　　　　　　　　　[27 Ch. D. 676
　　See LIMITATIONS, STATUTE OF—LEGACY.

—— Life interest—Action by remainderman—
　　Payment into Court　　21 Ch. D. 121
　　See EXECUTOR—ACTIONS. 5.

—— Set-off—Costs in probate suit 18 Ch. D. 300
　　See EXECUTOR—RETAINER. 5.

LEGACY DUTY.
　　See REVENUE—LEGACY DUTY—*Statutes.*

—— Direction to pay annuity free of duty
　　　　　　　　　[27 Ch. D. 703
　　See EXECUTOR—ADMINISTRATION. 7.

—— Foreign domicil　-　23 Ch. D. 532
　　See DOMICIL. 4.

—— Legacies to be paid free of duty
　　See WILL—HEIRLOOM. 3. [26 Ch. D. 538

—— Valuation of property by executor
　　　　　　　　　[11 Q. B. D. 16
　　See REVENUE—LEGACY DUTY.

LEGAL ESTATE—Charge of debts—Executors
　　　　　　　　　[24 Ch. D. 190
　　See WILL—ESTATE IN REALTY. 1.

—— Injunction against parting with
　　　　　　　　　[21 Ch. D. 490
　　See PRACTICE—SUPREME COURT—IN-
　　JUNCTION. 7.

—— Mortgage—Priority　-　19 Ch. D. 207
　　See SOLICITOR—LIABILITIES. 3.

LEGISLATIVE ASSEMBLY—Queensland—Dis-
　　qualification -　- 8 App. Cas. 120
　　See COLONIAL LAW—QUEENSLAND.

LEGISLATURE OF CANADA—Power of
　　　　　　　　　[7 App. Cas. 178, 829
　　See COLONIAL LAW — CANADA — DO-
　　MINION. 1, 2.

—— ——　　　-　　7 App. Cas. 96
　　See COLONIAL LAW—CANADA—ONTARIO.
　　3.

—— ——　　　-　　7 App. Cas. 136
　　See COLONIAL LAW—CANADA—QUEBEC.
　　3.

LEGITIMACY—Domicil—Will -　24 Ch. D. 637
　　See WILL—WORDS. 13.

—— Evidence of non-access　-　23 Ch. D. 173
　　See EVIDENCE—GENERAL. 2.

—— Scotch law—Subsequent marriage
　　　　　　　　　[10 App. Cas. 692
　　See SCOTCH LAW—HUSBAND AND WIFE.
　　2.

LESSOR—Title of—Notice　-　17 Ch. D. 353
　　See VENDOR AND PURCHASER—TITLE. 3.

LETTERS—Addressed to bankrupt—Redirection
　　　　　　　　　[17 Ch. D. 518
　　See BANKRUPTCY—TRUSTEE. 7.

—— Addressed to agent -　-　26 Ch. D. 306
　　See DEFAMATION—SLANDER. 3.

—— Agreement by　　　-　22 Ch. D. 441
　　See LANDLORD AND TENANT—AGREE-
　　MENT. 2.

—— Agreement by　　-　-　27 Ch. D. 497
　　See CONTRACT—ACCEPTANCE. 1.

LETTERS—*continued.*

—— Letter of advice—Bill of exchange—Con-
　　signment of goods　-　29 Ch. D. 848
　　See BILL OF EXCHANGE—SECURITIES FOR.
　　5.

—— Promise by—Marriage articles
　　　　　　　　　[17 Ch. D. 361; 17 Ch. D. 365, n.
　　See SETTLEMENT—ARTICLES. 1, 2.

—— Protection of.
　　See POST OFFICE—*Statutes.*

LETTERS OF ADMINISTRATION—Duty on.
　　See REVENUE—PROBATE DUTY—*Statutes.*

LEX DOMICILII—Personal assets of testator
　　　　　　　　　[8 App. Cas. 82
　　See COLONIAL LAW—VICTORIA. 3.

LEX LOCI—Foreign corporation 6 App. Cas. 386
　　See COLONIAL LAW—WEST AUSTRALIA. 1.

—— Personal assets of testator -　8 App. Cas. 82
　　See COLONIAL LAW—VICTORIA. 3.

LIABILITY—Agent.
　　See Cases under PRINCIPAL AND AGENT
　　—AGENT'S LIABILITY.

—— Director of company.
　　See Cases under COMPANY—DIRECTOR'S
　　LIABILITY.

—— Director of company　26 Ch. D. 107
　　See COMPANY—MEMORANDUM AND AR-
　　TICLES. 3.

—— Member of company　21 Ch. D. 302, 583
　　See COMPANY—MEMBER'S LIABILITY. 1.

—— Member of vestry　　23 Ch. D. 60
　　See METROPOLIS — MANAGEMENT ACTS.
　　15.

—— Partner—Misappropriation by co-partner
　　　　　　　　　[28 Ch. D. 340
　　See PARTNERSHIP—LIABILITIES.

—— Principal for act of agent
　　See Cases under PRINCIPAL AND AGENT
　　—PRINCIPAL'S LIABILITY.

—— Retiring partner　　-　7 App. Cas. 345
　　See PARTNERSHIP—DISSOLUTION. 4.

—— Surety.
　　See Cases under PRINCIPAL AND SURETY
　　—LIABILITY.

—— Surety—Proof in bankruptcy　17 Ch. D. 98
　　See BANKRUPTCY—PROOF. 11.

—— To repair turnpike-road.
　　See TURNPIKE ACTS—GENERAL—*Sta-
　　tutes.*

—— Trustee.
　　See Cases under TRUSTEE—LIABILITIES.

LIBEL.
　　See Cases and Statutes under
　　DEFAMATION—LIBEL.
　　DEFAMATION—PRIVILEGE.

—— Criminal information—Discretion of Court
　　　　　　　　　[12 Q. B. D. 320
　　See CRIMINAL LAW—LIBEL. 1.

—— Criminal information—Fiat of Director of
　　Public Prosecutions -　14 Q. B. D. 648
　　See CRIMINAL LAW—LIBEL. 2.

—— Injunction -　20 Ch. D. 501; 21 Ch. D. 798
　　See PRACTICE—SUPREME COURT — IN-
　　JUNCTION. 3, 4.

LIBEL—*continued.*

—— Interrogatories—Handwriting **15 Q. B. D. 439**
　　See PRACTICE—SUPREME COURT—INTER-
　　ROGATORIES. 7.

—— Publication—Interrogatories **10 Q. B. D. 110**
　　See PRACTICE—SUPREME COURT—INTER-
　　ROGATORIES. 15.

LIBERTY TO APPLY—Omission of **23 Ch. D. 353**
　　See PRACTICE—SUPREME COURT—PRO-
　　DUCTION OF DOCUMENTS. 2.

LIBERTY TO ATTEND—Costs　　**21 Ch. D. 830**
　　See PRACTICE—SUPREME COURT—COSTS.
　　36.

LIBRARY.
　　See PUBLIC LIBRARY—*Statutes.*

LICENCE—Patent　　　　··　　**19 Ch. D. 268**
　　See PATENT—VALIDITY. 4.

—— Patent　　　　　　**17 Ch. D. 423**
　　See PATENT—ASSIGNMENT. , 1.

—— Patent in two countries　　**25 Ch. D. 1**
　　See PATENT—INFRINGEMENT. 2.

—— Public-house.
　　See Cases and Statutes under INN—
　　LICENCE.

—— Public-house—Off-licence　**19 Ch. D. 258**
　　See COVENANT—RUNNING WITH LAND. 1.

—— Timber limits　　-　　· **9 App. Cas. 150**
　　See COLONIAL LAW—CANADA—QUEBEC.
　　9.

—— Trade-mark　　　　**25 Ch. D. 194**
　　See TRADE-MARK—REGISTRATION. 15.

LICENSING ACTS.
　　See Statutes and Cases under INN—
　　LICENCE.

—— Ontario　　-　　- **9 App. Cas. 117**
　　See COLONIAL LAW—CANADA—ONTARIO.
　　2.

LIEN—Auctioneer　　-　　**30 Ch. D. 192**
　　See AUCTION. 2.

—— Carrier—Bankruptcy—Receiver
　　　　　　　　[**22 Ch. D. 470**
　　See BANKRUPTCY—JURISDICTION. 5.

—— Company—Debt of shareholders
　　　　　　　　[**29 Ch. D. 149**
　　See COMPANY—SHARES—TRANSFER. 3.

—— Company—Shares - **21 Ch. D. 302, 583**
　　See COMPANY — MEMBER'S LIABILITY.
　　1, 3.

—— Factors Act **25 Ch. D. 31; 10 App. Cas. 617**
　　See FACTOR. 1, 2.

—— Freight—Bill of lading—Incorporation of
　　conditions in charterparty
　　　　　　　　[**15 Q. B. D. 154**
　　See SHIP—CHARTERPARTY. 1.

—— Innkeeper　-　　　- **23 Ch. D. 330**
　　See INN—INNKEEPER. 2.

—— Maritime.
　　See Cases under SHIP—MARITIME LIEN.

—— Maritime—Foreign judgment　**6 P. D. 106**
　　See FOREIGN JUDGMENT. 2.

LIEN—*continued.*

—— Policy of insurance—Payment of premiums
　　　　　　　　[**23 Ch. D. 552**
　　See INSURANCE, LIFE—ASSIGNMENT. 1.

—— Purchase-money advanced by trustee
　　　　　　　　[**22 Ch. D. 255**
　　See TRUSTEE—INDEMNITY. 2.

—— Receiver—Bankruptcy　　**16 Ch. D. 497**
　　See BANKRUPTCY—RECEIVER. 2.

—— Shares — Company — Refusal to register
　　transfer -　　　-　**9 Q. B. D. 436**
　　See COMPANY—SHARES—TRANSFER. 4.

—— Solicitor—Costs.
　　See Cases under SOLICITOR—LIEN.

—— Unpaid vendor—Sale of goods—Stoppage in
　　transitu.
　　See Cases under SALE OF GOODS—LIEN.

—— Unpaid vendor—Sale of land **21 Ch. D. 243,**
　　　　　　　[**685 ; 26 Ch. D. 501**
　　See VENDOR AND PURCHASER—LIEN. 1, 2.

—— Unpaid vendor — Deposit of deeds with
　　banker -　　　-　　**6 App. Cas. 722**
　　See BANKER—LIEN.

—— Unpaid vendor — Devise of estate—Locke
　　King's Act　　-　　　**24 Ch. D. 94**
　　See WILL—EXONERATION. 3.

LIFE ESTATE—Determination of, on bankruptcy
　　—Children born afterwards
　　See WILL—CONDITION. 4. [**28 Ch. D. 523**

LIFE INSURANCE.
　　See Cases under INSURANCE, LIFE.

—— Married woman—Petition - **26 Ch. D. 236**
　　See HUSBAND AND WIFE — MARRIED
　　WOMEN'S PROPERTY ACTS. 4.

LIFE INSURANCE COMPANY.
　　See Cases under COMPANY—LIFE INSUR-
　　ANCE COMPANY.

LIFE RENTER—Scotch law—Coal mine
　　　　　　　　[**8 App. Cas. 641**
　　See SCOTCH LAW—HERITABLE PROPERTY.
　　2.

LIGHT :—　　　　　　　　　Col.
　　I. OBSTRUCTION　　　　　　800
　　II. TITLE　-　　　　　　　801

I. LIGHT—OBSTRUCTION.

　　1. —— Angle of 45°—*Injunction—Form of
Judgment.*] There is no conclusion of law that a
building will not obstruct the light coming to a
window if it permits the light to fall on the
window at an angle of not less than 45° from the
vertical. The question of the amount of obstruction is always a question of fact which depends
on the evidence in each case. Therefore a Plaintiff whose ancient light is obstructed is entitled
to a judgment in general terms, without referring
to the angle of incidence of the light, unless there
is some special evidence justifying the insertion
of such a clause.—*Hackett* v. *Baiss* (Law Rep.
20 Eq. 494) considered. PARKER v. FIRST AVENUE
HOTEL COMPANY　　　　**24 Ch. D. 282**

　　2. —— Injunction or Damages—*Discretion of*

I. LIGHT—OBSTRUCTION—*continued.*

Court—Lord Cairns' Act (21 & 22 Vict. c. 27), s. 2.] In exercising the discretion given by sect. 2 of Lord Cairns' Act, to award damages in substitution for an injunction, in the case of a substantial interference with the Plaintiff's ancient lights, the Court will not, when the result of the Defendant's buildings would be, if they were allowed to continue, to render the Plaintiff's property absolutely useless to him, compel the Plaintiff to sell his property out and out to the Defendant. But, if the injury to the Plaintiff will be less serious, and his property will remain substantially useful to him, if the Defendant's buildings are permitted to continue, the Court may exercise its discretion by awarding the Plaintiff damages in lieu of an injunction, and for the purpose of exercising that discretion the Court will take into consideration the nature and situation of the property, e.g., the circumstance that it is situate in the centre of a large city, such as London.—*Aynsley* v. *Glover* (Law Rep. 18 Eq. 544), *Krehl* v. *Burrell* (7 Ch. D. 551), and *Smith* v. *Smith* (Law Rep. 20 Eq. 500), considered. HOLLAND *v.* WORLEY　　-　　**26 Ch. D. 578**

II. LIGHT—TITLE.

1. —— Alteration of Windows—*Interim Injunction—Balance of Convenience.*] The Plaintiffs being the owners of an ancient building which had numerous windows pulled it down and rebuilt it. A few of the windows in the new house included the space occupied by ancient windows but were of larger dimensions; several others included some portion of the space occupied by ancient windows; and in some cases the spaces occupied by ancient windows were entirely built up in the new house. The Defendants commenced to build a house on the opposite side of the street, which if completed according to the plans, would materially interfere with the light coming to the Plaintiffs' windows.—On a motion for an interim injunction the Court, holding that the Plaintiffs had shewn an intention to preserve, and not to abandon, their ancient lights, and that there was a fair question of right to be tried at the hearing, and considering that the balance of convenience was in favour of granting an injunction rather than of allowing the Defendants to complete their building with an undertaking to pull it down if required to do so, granted an injunction till the hearing.—The order of Bacon, V.C., affirmed.—*Hutchinson* v. *Copestake* (9 C. B. (N.S.) 863) and *Tapling* v. *Jones* (12 C. B. (N.S.) 826; 11 H. L. C. 290) considered. NEWSON *v.* PENDER　**27 Ch. D. [43**

2. —— Alteration of Windows—*Rebuilding—Preservation of Ancient Light.*] In rebuilding a house, which had an ancient light in its ground floor front room, the front wall, which originally stood out beyond the general building line four feet at one end and seven feet at the other, was set back into the general building line; and in the new front wall was placed a window the position of which corresponded to a great extent with the position of the ancient light in the old front wall. The new room was about the same frontage breadth as the old, but included little more than half the site of it, viz., a depth of nine feet at one end, and less than four feet at the

II. LIGHT—TITLE—*continued.*

other :—*Held*, that the right to the ancient light had not been lost. BULLERS *v.* DICKINSON　　　**[29 Ch. D. 155**

3. —— Easement over Railway—*Adjoining Landowner—Interlocutory Injunction.*] The Plaintiff was owner of a house some of the windows of which overlooked a piece of land belonging to a railway company and used as a goods yard of a station. When the house had been built sixteen years the company put up a screen opposite the Plaintiff's windows to prevent his acquiring an easement of light and air. The Plaintiff brought an action for an injunction to restrain the company from interfering with his light and air; and moved for an interlocutory injunction till the hearing :—*Held* (reversing the decision of Bacon, V.C.), that the Plaintiff had no equity to restrain the company from taking measures to prevent prescriptive rights from being acquired for windows looking upon their land. The injunction was therefore refused.—*Norton* v. *London and North Western Railway Company* (9 Ch. D. 623) and *Swindon Waterworks Company* v. *Wilts and Berks Canal Navigation Company* (Law Rep. 7 H. L. 697) considered. BONNER *v.* GREAT WESTERN RAILWAY COMPANY　　**24 Ch. D. 1**

4. —— Evidence—*Enjoyment—Interruption—Notice—Prescription Act (2 & 3 Will. 4, c. 71), s. 4—Onus probandi.*] *Semble*, that the person who asserts that an alleged twenty years' enjoyment of light has been interrupted during that period is bound, under sect. 4 of the Prescription Act, to prove that some notice (other than that which arises from the mere existence of a physical obstruction) was given to the person interrupted by the person by whose authority the interruption was made.—A Plaintiff who alleges a twenty years' enjoyment of light must prove affirmatively a prim âfacie case of enjoyment. But, when he has done this, the Defendant may displace the primâ facie case, either by proving the existence of an obstruction at the commencement of the twenty years, or a statutory interruption of the enjoyment at some time during the twenty years, or by shewing by other evidence that the Plaintiff's evidence of enjoyment cannot be relied upon. In either way the Defendant will discharge the onus which is cast on him. SEDDON *v.* BANK OF BOLTON　　　**[19 Ch. D. 462**

5. —— Implied Reservation—*Notice—Building Scheme—Merger of Lease—Surrender.*] By seven simultaneous leases seven plots of land marked respectively A, B, C, D, E, F, and G, and forming together one square block, were demised by the owner to J. with a ground plan on each lease, and with covenants for the erection and maintenance of buildings upon each plot according to certain plans. The leases were granted with a view to the erection upon the whole block of one large edifice, of which the several parts and the internal arrangements were to be connected together for a common use and occupation; so however as to be separable (if desired) into seven separate buildings. J. being in the occupation of the whole, while the buildings were being erected mortgaged C, F, and G, by a sub-lease which recited the building scheme and the original leases of C, F, and G, and contained

2 D

II. LIGHT—TITLE—*continued.*

stipulations for the completion of the buildings on C, F, and G. After the buildings had been substantially completed J. mortgaged E by a deed which recited the lease of E and assigned the buildings thereon, subject to the covenants in the lease, to one who had notice of the general plan of the buildings. J. then mortgaged B. On J.'s bankruptcy the several mortgagees obtained foreclosure decrees in respect of B, C, and E. respectively :— *Held*, reversing the decision of the Court of Appeal and restoring the decision of Bacon, V.C., Lord Blackburn dissenting, that though there was no express reservation of the right to light, yet looking at the plans, the covenants in the original leases, and the mortgage deeds, the mortgagees of C and E respectively were by reasonable implication precluded from interfering with the light to the windows in B which looked out upon C and E respectively, and might be restrained accordingly in an action by the mortgagee of B :—*Held*, also, that the mortgagee of B could maintain such an action, although he had surrendered the lease of B and taken a fresh lease from the original lessor ; for—without deciding what effect the merger of the original lease might have—whenever the lease of B came to an end either by surrender, forfeiture, or otherwise, the original lessor would have the same rights to light as the mortgage would have had if the original lease had subsisted.—*Semble*, by the Earl of Selborne, that if on a sale and conveyance of land adjoining a house to be built by the vendor, it is mutually agreed that one of the outer walls of that house may stand wholly or partly within the verge of the land sold and shall have in it particular windows opening upon and overlooking the land sold, and if the house is erected accordingly, the purchaser cannot afterwards build upon the land sold so as to prevent or obstruct the access of light to those windows. RUSSELL *v.* WATTS　　25 Ch. D. 559; [10 App. Cas. 590

6. —— **Purchase by different Persons from same Vendor**—*Contemporaneous Conveyances— Injunction.*] Where the owner of a dwelling-house and adjoining land sells the house to one person and the land to another under contemporaneous conveyances, either purchaser being aware of the conveyance to the other, the purchaser of the land is not entitled to build thereon so as to obstruct the lights of the house.—A testator being owner in fee of a piece of land with two dwelling-houses thereon, and of another piece of land immediately adjoining, with a warehouse at the further end thereof, devised his real estate to his two sons and another person in trust for sale, giving his two sons, or either of them, an option of purchasing any part of his real estate. By two separate but contemporaneous conveyances, executed by the trustees of the will, the one piece of land and the two dwelling-houses thereon were conveyed for value, " together with all lights thereunto belonging," and all the estate, &c., to the one son in fee, and the other adjoining piece of land and the warehouse were conveyed for value, together with all lights, &c., and all the estate, &c., to the other son in fee :—An injunction was granted restraining the successor in title to the purchaser of the last-mentioned piece of

II. LIGHT—TITLE—*continued.*

land and warehouse from building on his land in such a way as to obstruct his neighbour's lights. —*Wheeldon v. Burrows* (12 Ch. D. 31) considered. ALLEN *v.* TAYLOR -　　16 Ch. D. 355

—— Trespass—Nuisance—Injury to reversion [20 Ch. D. 589 *See* NUISANCE—REMEDIES.　2.

LIGHTERMAN—Marine insurance—Contract as to lighterage—Concealment from underwriter -　　　15 Q. B. D. 368 *See* INSURANCE, MARINE—CONCEALMENT. 2.

LIGHTS—Regulation as to　-　7 App. Cas. 512 *See* PRACTICE—ADMIRALTY—APPORTIONMENT OF DAMAGE. *And see* SHIP—NAVIGATION—*Gazette.*

LIGHTHOUSE — Poor-rate — Rateable value— Telegraph station and premises [14 Q. B. D. 770 *See* POOR-RATE—RATEABLE VALUE.　1. *And see* SHIP — MERCHANT SHIPPING ACTS.—*Gazette.*

LIMITATION OF ACTION—Surveyor of highways —Urban authority　　11 Q. B. D. 286 *See* LOCAL GOVERNMENT—PRACTICE.　3.

LIMITATION OF LIABILITY—Admiralty *See* Cases under PRACTICE—ADMIRALTY —LIMITATION OF LIABILITY.

—— Rescission of judgment by consent [10 P. D. 161 *See* ESTOPPEL—JUDGMENT.　3.

LIMITATION OF USER—Trade-mark *See* Cases under TRADE-MARK—REGISTRATION.　8—11.

I. LIMITATIONS, STATUTE OF—LEGACY.

—— Administration—*Statutory Bar—23 & 24 Vict. c. 38, s. 13—" Dying Intestate "—" Present right to receive"—Part Payment.*] The operation of 23 & 24 Vict. c. 38, s. 13, is retrospective, so that the limitation of twenty years " next after a present right to receive the same shall have accrued" thereby imposed (in analogy to 3 & 4 Will. 4, c. 27, s. 40) upon claims to recover personal estate of " any person dying intestate, possessed by the legal personal representative of such intestate," is not confined to the case of persons dying intestate after the 31st of December, 1860, the time fixed by the section for commencement of the operation of the enactment. —Accordingly a claim by next of kin for general administration of the estate of an intestate who died in 1848 was barred at the end of twenty-one years from that date; and leave to revive an administration suit relating to the same estate in which no proceeding had been taken since the decree in 1855 was refused.—But with respect to assets of the intestate not received by the administrator until 1870 (more than twenty years after the death, and within twenty years before the

I. LIMITATIONS STATUTE OF—LEGACY—
continued.

issue of the writ) the claim of the next of kin to administration, limited to such assets, was not barred ; there being no "present right to receive" on the part of the next of kin until the assets had been actually recovered by the administrator.— Part payment by the administrator out of a particular asset which has so fallen in will not revive the right to sue for general administration which was at the time of payment barred by statute. *In re* JOHNSON. SLY *v.* BLAKE　　29 Ch. D. 964

II. LIMITATIONS, STATUTE OF—PERSONAL ACTIONS.

1. —— **Acknowledgment**—21 *Jac.* 1, *c.* 16, *s.* 3.] J. H. was a trustee of a settlement by which the T. B. estate was settled on the wife of the Defendant for life to her separate use without power of anticipation. J. H. lent money to the Defendant, and for some time, with the wife's consent, the rents of the T. B. estate were applied towards payment of the debt, the wife giving receipts for them. In October, 1879, the Defendant wrote to J. H., "I thank you for your very kind intention to give up the rent of T. B. next Christmas, but I am happy to say at that time both principal and interest will have been paid in full."—*Held*, that this was an acknowledgment which would take the debt out of the Statute of Limitations.—Decision of Pollock. B., reversed. GREEN *v.* HUMPHREYS
[23 Ch. D. 207 ; 26 Ch. D. 474

2. —— **Cause of Action**—21 *Jac.* 1, *c.* 16— *Recovery of Damages for Injury after Satisfaction for Previous Injury arising from same Act —Support—Action for Subsidence after Compensation for previous Subsidence.*] The Plaintiff was the owner of certain land, and in 1867 and 1868, but not afterwards, the Defendants worked a seam of coal lying under and near to the Plaintiff's land, which subsided in consequence of the Defendants' excavations. Some cottages of the plaintiff standing on his land were damaged by the subsidence and were repaired by the Defendants. In 1882 a second subsidence of the Plaintiff's land occurred owing to the Defendants' workings in 1867 and 1868, and the Plaintiff's cottages were again damaged :—*Held*, that the Plaintiff was entitled to maintain an action for the damage done to his cottages in 1882, and that his right to sue was not barred by the Statute of Limitations.—*Nicklin* v. *Williams* (10 Ex. 259), *Backhouse* v. *Bonomi* (E. B. & E. 622 ; 9 H. L. C. 503), *Whitehouse* v. *Fellowes* (10 C. B. (N.S.) 765) discussed.—*Lamb* v. *Walker* (3 'Q. B. D. 389) overruled. MITCHELL *v.* DARLEY MAIN COLLIERY CO.
[14 Q. B. D. 125
[Affirmed in the House of Lords.]

3. —— **Conversion**—*Demand and Refusal— Title Deeds.*] Title deeds of the Plaintiffs were fraudulently taken from them and deposited by a third person, without their knowledge, with the Defendant in 1859, who held them without knowledge of the fraud to secure the repayment of a loan. The Plaintiffs on discovering the loss of the deeds in 1882, demanded them of the Defendant and upon his refusal to give them up brought an action to recover them, to which the Defendant

II. LIMITATIONS, STATUTE OF—PERSONAL ACTIONS—*continued.*

pleaded the Statute of Limitations :—*Held*, that until demand and refusal to give up the deeds to the real owners they had no right of action against which the statute would run. SPACKMAN *v.* FOSTER -　　-　　-　　-　　11 Q. B. D. 99

4. —— **Decree for Administration**—*Creditors* —21 *Jac.* 1, *c.* 16.] In an administration action commenced in December, 1878, by one executor of a testator, who was also a creditor of his testator, against his co-executor, the usual judgment in a creditor's action was pronounced in December, 1879, and some time afterwards a claim was brought in by a creditor against the estate upon a promissory note of the testator dated in November, 1873 :—*Held*, that the claim was barred by the statute.—*Sterndale* v. *Hankinson* (1 Sim. 393) observed upon. *In re* GREAVES, DECEASED. BRAY *v.* TOFIELD　　18 Ch. D. 551

5. —— **Devastavit**—*Executor—Mortgagor and Mortgagee.*] Testator mortgaged an estate to Plaintiffs, and devised it to three executors upon trusts in favour of his daughters, and after the death of all his children for sale.—The executors distributed the whole personal estate without providing for the mortgage debt. After this one of the executors died. The daughters occupied the farm for twenty years after the distribution of the personal estate, paying rent to the executors, and until 1880 paying the interest on the mortgage. The mortgagees then brought an action for foreclosure or sale, and claimed to have any deficiency made good by the two surviving executors and the executors of the deceased executor :—*Held*, that any claim founded on the devastavit in distributing the personal estate was barred after six years, but that the Plaintiffs were entitled to foreclosure and to an order for administration of the mortgagor's estate. *In re* GALE. BLAKE *v.* GALE　　22 Ch. D. 820

6. —— **Devastavit**—*Executor of Mortgagor.*] A testator mortgaged leaseholds and died. His executors took possession of his estate, recovered the rents of the leaseholds, paid the interest on the mortgage debt, made certain payments to the beneficiaries under the will. In the course of proceedings by the mortgagee for the realization of his security and by the legatee for administration, the executor carried in an account in which he claimed credit for all payments made to the beneficiaries on the ground that under the circumstances the mortgagee must be taken to have acquiesced in such payments, and further, that as to such of the said payments as were made upwards of six years before the action any claim on a devastavit was barred after six years by the Statute of Limitations :—*Held*, that there was no sufficient proof of acquiescence, and that the executors having acknowledged the mortgage debt by payment of interest, and being bound in equity by a trust properly to deal with the assets, could not set up their own wrong by way of devastavit as a defence in order to claim the benefit of the Statute of Limitations.—*In re Gale* (22 Ch. D. 820) considered. *In re* MARSDEN. BOWDEN *v.* LAYLAND. GIBBS *v.* LAYLAND
[26 Ch. D. 783
2 D 2

II. LIMITATIONS, STATUTE OF—PERSONAL ACTIONS—*continued.*

7. —— **Fraud**—*Absence of reasonable Means of Discovery.*] In an action to recover by way of damages money lost by the fraudulent representations of the Defendant, a reply to a defence of the Statute of Limitations that the Plaintiff did not discover and had not reasonable means of discovering the fraud within six years before action, and that the existence of such fraud was fraudulently concealed by the Defendant until within such six years, was *held* good by the Court of Appeal (Lord Coleridge, C.J., and Brett, L.J., Holker, L.J., dissenting), affirming the judgment of Field, J.　GIBBS *v.* GUILD　- 8 Q. B. D. 296 ;
[9 Q. B. D. 59

8. —— **Mortgage Debt**—*Covenant in Mortgage Deed*—37 & 38 *Vict. c.* 57, *s.* 8.] The limitation of twelve years imposed by the Real Property Limitation Act, 1874, s. 8, to action and suits for the recovery of money charged on land applies to the personal remedy on the covenant in a mortgage deed as well as to the remedy against the land.　SUTTON *v.* SUTTON
[22 Ch. D. 511

9. —— **Mortgage Debt**—*Collateral Bond—Real Property Limitation Act,* 1874 (37 & 38 *Vict. c.* 57), *s.* 8.] When a mortgage debt is secured by a collateral bond the remedy on the bond is, under sect. 8 of the Real Property Limitation Act, 1874, barred by the lapse of twelve years since the last payment of interest or acknowledgment of the debt, equally with the remedy against the land comprised in the mortgage.—*Sutton* v. *Sutton* (22 Ch. D. 511) followed. FEARNSIDE *v.* FLINT　-　22 Ch. D. 579

10. —— **Mortgage Debt**—*Bond by Sureties for Payment of Mortgage Debt—Real Property Limitation Act,* 1874 (37 & 38 *Vict. c.* 57), *s.* 8—*Rules of Supreme Court,* 1883, *Order* LV., *r.* 10—*Order for Administration at Suit of Creditor.*] In 1867 T. P. mortgaged an estate to L. & A. for £1000, and at the same time E. P. and C. P. gave to L. & A. a joint and several bond in the penal sum of £400 reciting that the £1000 had been advanced at the request of E. P. and C. P., and that they had agreed to give as a better security for part thereof a bond conditioned for payment of £200 and interest. The bond was conditioned to be void if the mortgagor paid the mortgage money and interest according to his covenant. T. P. paid the interest till December, 1877, after which it fell into arrear, and in 1880 the mortgagees entered into possession. E. P. died in 1883 without having made any payment or given any acknowledgment. L. & A., as creditors under the bond, took out a summons for administration of his estate. E. P.'s representatives disputed the claim on the ground that this was a proceeding to recover money secured on land, and was barred by the lapse of twelve years under the Real Property Limitation Act, 1874. Bacon, V.C., without giving any opinion on this question, dismissed the summons under the discretion given by Order LV., rule 10, on the ground that a disputed debt ought not to be tried on summons :—*Held*, by the Court of Appeal, that as there were no facts in dispute the Vice-Chancellor ought to have decided the question of law on the

II. LIMITATIONS, STATUTE OF—PERSONAL ACTIONS—*continued.*

summons :—*Held*, further, that this was not a proceeding to recover money secured on land, but to recover damages because another person failed to pay money secured on land, and that it did not come within the scope of the Real Property Limitation Act, 1874, sect. 8 :—*Held*, further, that if remedy on the bond had been barrable by the lapse of twelve years under that section, the payments of interest by the mortgagor would have prevented the bar :—*Held*, therefore, that L. & A. were entitled to rank as creditors against the estate of E. P., and that if his representatives did not admit assets, an administration order must be made.—*Sutton* v. *Sutton* (22 Ch. D. 511), *Fearnside* v. *Flint* (22 Ch. D. 579), and *Cockrill* v. *Sparkes* (1 H. & C. 699), distinguished. *In re* POWERS.　LINDSELL *v.* PHILLIPS　30 Ch. D. 291

11. —— **Receiver**—*Debt of Record—Trustee.*] Money not accounted for and due from a receiver under the Court is, by his recognizance, made a debt of record, although the balance due has not been ascertained.—The receiver is a trustee of such money for the persons entitled thereto, and cannot, as against them, avail himself of the Statute of Limitations, although his final accounts have been passed and the recognizances vacated. SEAGRAM *v.* TUCK　-　18 Ch. D. 296

III. LIMITATIONS, STATUTE OF—REALTY—

1. —— **Acknowledgment**—*Entry against Interest—Payment of Interest—Agency.*　The representative of a deceased mortgagee brought in 1884 a foreclosure action against the mortgagor, who pleaded the Statutes of Limitations. There was no evidence that any interest had been paid since 1866, except an entry in the books of the mortgagee of £50 as paid in 1878 by the mortgagor for rent and interest :—*Held*, that though as an acknowledgment of money received it was against the interest of the person who made the entry, yet as it would prove the revival of a simple contract debt then barred, it was for his interest, and therefore could not be received as evidence on behalf of his representatives.—The solicitor of a mortgagor paid the interest to the mortgagee, and it was taken into account between them up to 1866. From that time the solicitor continued to pay the interest, but there was no proof that he acted as agent for the mortgagor or that the mortgagor furnished the money :—*Held*, in a foreclosure action brought in 1884, that there had been no sufficient payment of interest to take the case out of the Statute of Limitations, and that the action was barred.　NEWBOULD *v.* SMITH
[29 Ch. D. 882

2. —— **Acknowledgment**—*Tenant in Common—Expiration of Twenty Years*—3 & 4 *Will.* 4, v. 27, *s.* 34.]　T. and J. became entitled in possession to a freehold as tenants in common in 1833. In 1879, persons claiming under J. brought an action for sale or partition. The Defendant, who claimed under T., alleged that T. was in receipt of the rents of the entirety from 1833 to 1864, without accounting, and claimed the benefit of the Statute of Limitations. The parties entered into admissions, which stated that T. received the rents of the entirety from 1833 till his death

III. LIMITATIONS, STATUTE OF—REALTY—
continued.

in 1877, and that T. paid to the solicitors of J.'s mortgagees a moiety of the rents due in November, 1864, and continued to pay to them a moiety of the rents till his death. The admissions did not state, nor was there any evidence, whether T. did or did not account for a moiety of the rents before 1864:—*Held,* by Malins, V.C., that the acknowledgment by T. of J.'s title, though after twenty years' adverse possession, excluded the operation of the Statute of Limitations, and that the Plaintiffs were entitled to judgment.—*Held,* by the Court of Appeal, that where a tenant in common has gained by the statute an adverse title to another share of the property, no payment of rent or acknowledgment by him can restore the title which has been extinguished by the statute:—But, *held,* that the payment of a moiety of the rents to persons claiming under J. from 1864 to 1877, raised a presumption that a similar payment was made previously, and that as the admissions did not negative this inference, the defence on the Statute of Limitations could not be supported:—*Held,* also, that the Defendant ought not to be allowed to bring forward fresh evidence on the appeal to shew that T. had not accounted for a moiety of the rents prior to 1864. SANDERS *v.* SANDERS　-　19 Ch. D. 373

3. —— Annuity charged on Land *and the Rents thereof—Right first accrued in* 1851—*Claim first made in* 1884—*Statute of Limitations* (3 & 4 *Will.* 4, c. 27), *s.* 1—*Real Property Limitation Act,* 1874 (37 & 38 *Vict.* c. 57), *ss.* 1, 9, 10.] By an indenture executed in 1833, real estate was conveyed to trustees and their heirs, upon trust as to one moiety that immediately after the death of M. C. they should out of the moiety and the rents and profits thereof pay unto J. M., and to his heirs and assigns, or permit him or them to receive it, an annuity of £8 half-yearly. M. C. died in 1857. No payment was ever made in respect of the annuity, and the annuitant first made a claim in 1884. The Chief Clerk had certified that he was entitled to a perpetual annuity. On summons to vary the certificate:—*Held,* that, by sect. 1 of the Act 37 & 38 Vict. c. 57, no proceeding to recover any "rent," which, inasmuch as by sect. 9 the Act must be construed with the 3 & 4 Will. 4, c. 27, meant by the interpretation clause of that Act, any annuity charged upon land, could be taken after twelve years from the time when the right first accrued, therefore if there had not been any trust, those twelve years having elapsed, none of the past instalments of the annuity could be recovered, and that the effect of sect. 10 of the 37 & 38 Vict. c. 57, was that no payment of the annuity which became due before the application was made was recoverable, the remedy being only the same as if there had not been any trust. HUGHES *v.* COLES　　27 Ch. D. 231

4. —— Mortgage—*Foreclosure—Ejectment—* 3 & 4 *Will.* 4, c. 27, *ss.* 2, 3, 24, 34; 7 *Will.* 4 & 1 *Vict.* c. 28 — *Judicature Act,* 1873, *ss.* 24, 25.] A legal mortgage of freehold land in 1856; no possession by the mortgagee, and no payment of principal or interest to him, nor any acknowledgment of his title. In 1870 a

III. LIMITATIONS, STATUTE OF—REALTY—
continued.

bill by the mortgagee for redemption or foreclosure; in 1874 a decree nisi for redemption or foreclosure; and in 1877 an order absolute for foreclosure. In 1878 an action by the mortgagees to recover possession of the land:—*Held,* affirming the judgment of the Court of Appeal, that although brought more than twenty-years after the date of the mortgage deed the action was not barred by the Statutes of Limitations (3 & 4 Will. 4, c. 27, and 7 Will. 4 & 1 Vict. c. 28).—*Semble,* per Earl Cairns, that the action, being brought by one who had become absolute owner of the land under the foreclosure decree, was an action as to which the right to bring it must be taken to have accrued within sect. 2 of 3 & 4 Will. 4, c. 27, at the date of that decree; and that sect. of that Act in defining when the right shall be deemed to have accrued is not necessarily exhaustive, or otherwise inconsistent with this view. PUGH *v.* HEATH　6 Q. B. D. 345; 7 App.
[Cas. 235

5. —— Mortgage—*Foreclosure Action — Recovery of Land—Payment of Principal or Interest by Mortgagor or his Agent—*3 & 4 *Will.* 4, c. 27, *ss.* 2, 24, 40—7 *Will.* 4 & 1 *Vict.* c. 28.] A foreclosure action is an action for the recovery of land, and is therefore not within sect. 40 of 3 & 4 Will. 4, c. 27, but is within sects. 2 and 24, and consequently within the supplementary enactment of 7 Will. 4 & 1 Vict. c. 28.—A payment to come within the 7 Will. 4 & 1 Vict. c. 28, must be a payment of principal or interest, and must be made by the mortgagor or some person bound to pay principal or interest on his behalf.—So the word "paid" in 3 & 4 Will. 4, c. 27, s. 40, involves by implication the addition of "by the person liable to pay."—A payment of rent made by a tenant of the mortgaged property to the mortgagee in consequence of a notice by the mortgagee requiring the rent to be paid to him is not such a payment.—The principle underlying all the Statutes of Limitations is that a payment to prevent the barring by statute must be an acknowledgment by the person making the payment of his liability, and an admission of the title of the person to whom the payment is made.—Judgment of Fry, J., reversed. HARLOCK *v.* ASHBERRY　-　-　18 Ch. D. 229; 19 Ch. D. 539

6. —— Mortgage—*Mortgagee in Possession—Redemption Action — Limitation—Disabilities—Statute of Limitations* (37 & 38 *Vict.* c. 57), *s.* 7.] Under the Real Property Limitation Act, 1874, the twelve years' bar to a redemption suit from the time when the mortgagee took possession, or from the last written acknowledgment, is absolute, and not to be extended by reason of any disability of the mortgagor. FORSTER *v.* PATTERSON　-　-　-　17 Ch. D. 132

7. —— Mortgage—*Mortgagor in possession of Part of Mortgaged Property—Mortgagee in Possession of Remainder—Right to redeem—Persons under Disability—Absence of Mortgagor beyond Seas—Statute of Limitations* (3 & 4 *Will.* 4, c. 27), *ss.* 16, 28.] The rule that prevailed prior to the Statute of Limitations (3 & 4 Will. 4, c. 27), that

III. LIMITATIONS, STATUTE OF—REALTY—
continued.

no lapse of time barred the right of a mortgagor of lands to redeem the whole provided he held possession of part (*Rakestraw v. Bruyer*, Select Cas. in Ch. 55; Mosely, 189) has been abolished by sect. 28 of the statute.—Accordingly, where a mortgagee had been in undisturbed possession of part of the land comprised in the mortgage for upwards of twenty years, the right of the mortgagor to redeem was held to be barred by that section, although he held possession of the remainder of the land.—Sect. 16 of the Statute of Limitations (3 & 4 Will. 4, c. 27), saving the rights of persons under disability, such as absence beyond seas, does not apply as between a mortgagor and mortgagee. KINSMAN *v.* ROUSE
[17 Ch. D. 104

8. —— **Tithe Rent-charge** — *Ireland* — *Non-payment for more than Twenty Years—Statute of Limitations* (3 & 4 Will. 4, c. 27), ss. 1, 2, 29— 1 & 2 Vict. c. 109.] The right to the tithe rent-charge in Ireland was vested in a spiritual corporation sole until 1871, when it was transferred by statute to a lay corporation. In 1877 the lay corporation brought an action against the persons liable to pay tithe rent-charge to recover six years' arrears. For more than twenty years next before action there had been no payment and no acknowledgment in writing:—*Held*, affirming the decision of the Irish Court of Appeal, that tithe rent-charge was "rent" within sect. 1 of the Statute of Limitations (3 & 4 Will. 4, c. 27), and not a "composition" within the exception to sect. 1, compositions in Ireland having been abolished by 1 & 2 Vict. c. 109; that sect. 2 of 3 & 4 Will. 4, c. 27, applied as between the owner and the persons liable to tithe rent-charge : that the lay corporation could not avail themselves of the provisions of sect. 29 in favour of spiritual corporations sole ; and that the action was barred by the lapse of twenty years. COMMISSIONERS OF IRISH CHURCH TEMPORALITIES *v.* GRANT - 10 App. Cas. 14

—— Mortgage—Satisfaction—Legal estate in the mortgagee - 22 Ch. D. 614
See LIMITATIONS, STATUTE OF—TRUSTS. 3.

IV. LIMITATIONS, STATUTE OF—TRUSTS.

1. —— **Interest**—*Delay in realization of Estate* —37 & 38 Vict. c. 57, s. 10.] The property of a testatrix who died in 1869 consisted mainly of a reversionary interest. This interest was not sold by the executors, and it did not fall into possession until 1881. In the opinion of the Court the executors had acted for the benefit of the estate in not selling the reversion:—*Held*, that legatees under the will who had waited for the payment of their legacies until after the falling in of the reversion were entitled, not merely to six years' arrears of interest, but to interest on their legacies from the expiration of one year after the death of the testatrix. *In re* BLACHFORD, BLACHFORD *v.* WORSLEY
[27 Ch. D. 676

2. —— **Mortgage of Ship**—*Express Trust— Sale by First Mortgagee— Claim for an Account by Second Mortgagee — Express and Constructive*

IV. LIMITATIONS, STATUTE OF—TRUSTS— *continued.*

Trust.] The second mortgagee of a ship claimed an account against the first mortgagee, who had sold the vessel upon the mortgagor becoming bankrupt. Defendant offered to pay a specific amount. The action having been commenced more than six years after the sale, the Defendant pleaded the Statute of Limitations. The Plaintiff set up an express trust as a bar to the statute:—*Held*, that there was no express trust ; that in case of an ascertained surplus the first mortgagee might be constructively a trustee of the surplus, but after six years, evidence could not be adduced to prove a surplus :—But *held*, that although the statute was not avoided on the ground of express trust, it was in this case avoided by an acknowledgment within six years of an unsettled account pending, which by itself would have sufficed, and also by a promise to pay what should be found due. The Plaintiff was therefore entitled to an account.—Where the mortgagee of his own mere motion realized the mortgaged property, he was held not to be entitled to interest in lieu of notice.—An express trust bars the statute equally as to personalty and realty by force of the Judicature Act, 1873, sect. 25, sub-sect. 2. BANNER *v.* BERRIDGE 18 Ch. D. 254

3. —— **Mortgage** — *Satisfaction — Express Trust—Legal Estate—Tenancy at Will—3 & 4 Will.* 4, c. 27, ss. 7, 25, 34—37 & 38 Vict. c. 57, s. 1.] When the money due upon a mortgage has been paid to the mortgagee, but no reconveyance has been executed, the mortgagor becomes from the date of such payment a tenant at will to the mortgagee, and the legal estate of the mortgagee is extinguished by thirteen years' adverse possession of the mortgagor.—The 25th section of the Statute of Limitations (3 & 4 Will. 4, c. 27) relates to express trusts only, and does not apply to the relation between a mortgagee whose mortgage has been satisfied and the mortgagor. SANDS to THOMPSON - 22 Ch. D. 614

LIMITATIONS, STATUTE OF—Action for penalty —Selling silver with counterfeit mark
See PENAL ACTION. 1. [7 Q. B. D. 465

—— Adverse possession - . 9 Q. B. D. 424
See RAILWAY COMPANY—PROPERTY. 3.

—— Ceylon - - - 6 App. Cas. 164
See COLONIAL LAW—CEYLON. 1.

—— Devise upon trust to pay debts—No real estate - - . 14 Q. B. D. 394
See BANKRUPTCY—PROOF. 20.

—— Married woman—Discoverture 15 Q. B. D. [667
See HUSBAND AND WIFE — MARRIED WOMEN'S PROPERTY ACTS. 1.

—— Misappropriation of money by directors
[21 Ch. D. 519
See COMPANY—DIRECTOR'S LIABILITY. 5.

—— Sale of right of entry — Fictitious title— Knowledge of buyer - 15 Q. B. D. 491
See RIGHT OF ENTRY. 1.

—— Supply of necessaries to lunatic
[21 Ch. D. 615
See LUNATIC—MAINTENANCE. 1.

LIMITED ADMINISTRATION.
  See Cases under ADMINISTRATOR —
  LIMITED.

LIMITED OWNER—Settled Land Act.
  See SETTLED LAND ACT—STATUTES.
  Cases under SETTLED LAND ACT—
  DEFINITIONS.

LIQUID DEMAND—Law of Jersey
                [9 App. Cas. 726
  See COLONIAL LAW—JERSEY. 3.

LIQUIDATED DAMAGES   -   21 Ch. D. 243
  See PENALTY.

LIQUIDATED SUM—Debtor's summons
                [17 Ch. D. 191
  See BANKRUPTCY—ACT OF BANKRUPTCY.
  15.

—— Petitioning creditor's debt   22 Ch. D. 132
  See BANKRUPTCY—ADJUDICATION. 2.

LIQUIDATION BY ARRANGEMENT.
  See Cases under BANKRUPTCY—LIQUI-
  DATION.

—— Member of company   -   25 Ch. D. 415
  See COMPANY—CONTRIBUTORY. 3.

—— Receiver   16 Ch. D. 497 ; 12 Q. B. D. 334
  See BANKRUPTCY—RECEIVER. 2, 4.

—— Release and discharge of trustee—Power of
  Board of Trade to require account
                [14 Q. B. D. 402
  See BANKRUPTCY—TRUSTEE. 9.

—— Removal of trustee by Court
                [14 Q. B. D. 177
  See BANKRUPTCY—TRUSTEE. 8.

LIQUIDATOR.
  See Cases under COMPANY—LIQUIDATOR.

—— Carrying on business—Rates
        [23 Ch. D. 500 ; 28 Ch. D. 470, 474
  See COMPANY—RATES. 1, 2, 3.

—— Carrying on mine—Distress   17 Ch. D. 158
  See COMPANY—DISTRESS. 5.

—— Costs of -   - 21 Ch. D. 381 ; 23 Ch. D.
                [511 ; 27 Ch. D. 33
  See COMPANY—COSTS. 1, 2, 3.

—— Costs of   -   -   30 Ch. D. 598
  See BILL OF EXCHANGE—FOREIGN BILL.

—— Official—Appointment of   20 Ch. D. 276 ;
                [27 Ch. D. 278
  See COMPANY — WINDING-UP ORDER.
  8, 11.

—— Voluntary winding-up—Appointment
                [26 Ch. D. 70
  See COMPANY—VOLUNTARY WINDING-
  UP. 2.

LIS ALIBI PENDENS   -   22 Ch. D. 397
  See PRACTICE—SUPREME COURT—STAY-
  ING PROCEEDINGS. 6.

LIS PENDENS—Divorce—Variation of marriage
  settlement—Charge   -   7 P. D. 228
  See PRACTICE—DIVORCE—SETTLEMENTS.
  3.

—— Protection of property   21 Ch. D. 490
  See PRACTICE — SUPREME COURT — IN-
  JUNCTION. 7.

LIST OF VOTERS—Parliament.
  See PARLIAMENT—FRANCHISE—Statutes.

LITERARY WORK — Title-page — Fraud on
  public   -   16 Ch. D. 395
  See SPECIFIC PERFORMANCE. 1.

LOADING—Delay of—Frost - 10 Q. B. D. 241 ;
          [11 Q. B. D. 543 ; 9 App. Cas. 470
  See SHIP—CHARTERPARTY. 8, 9.

LOAN (LOCAL) ACT, 1875.
  See LOCAL GOVERNMENT — POWERS —
  Statutes.

LOAN SOCIETY—Illegality - 9 Q. B. D. 225 ;
        [11 Q. B. D. 563 ; 14 Q. B. D. 379
  See COMPANY—UNREGISTERED COMPANY.
  2, 3, 5.

LOBSTER.
  See FISHERY ACTS—Statutes.

LOCAL BOARD.
  See Statutes and Cases under LOCAL
  GOVERNMENT—LOCAL AUTHORITY.

—— Nuisance by—Sewage   -   20 Ch. D. 595 ;
                [22 Ch. D. 221 ; 23 Ch. D. 767
  See NUISANCE—REMEDIES. 4, 5, 6.

—— Ontario   -   - 9 App. Cas. 117
  See COLONIAL LAW—CANADA—ONTARIO.
  2.

LOCAL GOVERNMENT :—   Col.
  I. BY-LAWS   -   -   - 814
  II. COMPENSATION   -   - 814
  III. LOCAL AUTHORITY   816
    (a) CONTRACTS
    (b) POWERS.
  IV. OFFENCES   822
  V. PRACTICE -   - 823
  VI. PUBLIC HEALTH ACTS   - 825
  VII. RATES   -   827
  VIII. SEWERS   828
  IX. STREETS   - 828

—— LONDON (CITY OF).
  See LONDON.

—— METROPOLITAN DISTRICT.
  See METROPOLIS.

I. LOCAL GOVERNMENT—BY-LAWS.

  Confirmation of By-laws.] *The Act 47 & 48
Vict. c. 12, relates to the confirmation of by-laws
made under the Public Health Act, 1875, or under
certain Acts incorporated therewith.*
  Lodging-houses.] *The Act 48 & 49 Vict. c. 72,
s. 8 extends the powers of the Public Health Act,
1875 (38 & 39 Vict. c. 55), s. 90, with regard to
by-laws for lodging-houses.*
  —— Validity—*Public Health Act, 1875 (38 &
39 Vict. c. 55), ss. 44, 276—Nuisance—Swine kept
near Dwelling-house.*] A rural sanitary authority,
purporting to act under the powers of ss. 44 and
276 of the Public Health Act, 1875, made a by-
law prohibiting the keeping of swine within the
distance of fifty feet from any dwelling-house
within their district :—*Held,* that the by-law was
unreasonable, and therefore bad. HEAP *v.* BURN-
LEY UNION   -   - 12 Q. B. D. 617

II. LOCAL GOVERNMENT—COMPENSATION.

  1. —— Arbitration—*Public Health Act, 1875
(38 & 39 Vict. c. 55), ss. 179, 180, 308—Jurisdiction
of Arbitrator when Liability under the Act is bonâ*

II. LOCAL GOVERNMENT—COMPENSATION—
continued.

fide disputed.] When a claim for compensation is made against a local authority for damage caused by the exercise of the powers conferred upon them by the Public Health Act, 1875, the arbitrator has jurisdiction to hold the arbitration and make his award as to the fact of damage and the amount of compensation under sects. 179, 180, and 308, although the local authority bonâ fide dispute their liability to make compensation at all under the Act. Their proper course is to raise the question of liability, in their defence to an action upon the award.—So *held*, affirming the decision of the Court of Appeal. BRIERLEY HILL LOCAL BOARD *v.* PEARSALL **11 Q. B. D. 735 ;**
[9 App. Cas. 595

2. —— Nuisance — *Urinal* — *Public Health Act,* 1875 (38 & 39 Vict. c. 55), *ss.* 39, 149, 264, 308 — *Compensation* — *Mandatory Injunction* — *Public Highway.*] A local board, assuming to act under the authority of sect. 39 of the Public Health Act, 1875 (38 & 39 Vict. c. 55), erected a public urinal partly upon a highway and partly upon a strip of land belonging to the Plaintiff, and so near to other adjoining land of the Plaintiff as to be a nuisance to her and her tenants and to depreciate the value of her property :—*Held*, that the Plaintiff was entitled to a mandatory injunction to restrain the board from continuing the urinal upon her land or so near thereto as to cause injury or annoyance to her or her tenants :— *Held* also, that it was not a matter in respect of which the Plaintiff's remedy was by compensation under sect. 308 of the Act.—In such a case notice of action under sect. 264 is not required.— Abutting upon the highway the Plaintiff had land upon which an inn and some stabling were erected. These stood back from the highway, and in front of them was an open space (forming part of the same land) which had been left open to and on a level with the highway until the Defendants in exercise of their powers under s. 149 of the Act, and for the convenience of the public, placed kerb-stones and a raised foot-path at the side of the highway, leaving openings so that carriages could still pass at convenient places to and from the Plaintiff's land and premises :— *Held*, that the Plaintiff was not entitled to a mandatory injunction directing the Defendants to remove the kerb-stones, and that in the absence of any unreasonable conduct the remedy for any injury caused by the kerb-stones would be by compensation under sect. 308 of the Act. SELLORS *v.* MATLOCK BATH LOCAL BOARD **14 Q. B. D. 928**

3. —— Subsidence of Land—*Highway—Houses abutting — Raising of Road by Local Board— Raising of Houses by Owners—Compensation for Cost of—Liability of Local Board—*38 & 39 Vict. c. 55 *(Public Health Act,* 1875), ss. 144, 149, 179, 308.] The Plaintiffs were owners of houses abutting on a highway which was vested in the Defendants, a local board acting under 38 & 39 Vict. c. 55 (Public Health Act, 1875), and having the powers and liabilities of surveyor of highways. The abstraction of salt from a bed beneath them caused from time to time a subsidence of the ground upon which the houses and highway were situate. The houses were rebuilt in 1870 on

II. LOCAL GOVERNMENT—COMPENSATION—
continued.

timber, so that they might be raised by screwjacks. In 1876 the surface of the highway in front of the houses had subsided considerably, and the houses had subsided with it. The surface of the roadway remained continuous, so that traffic could pass along it as before; but the roadway was in a curved hollow, and at the level to which it had subsided was liable to be flooded, and in fact was flooded at times, so as to render traffic impossible. The Defendants put materials on the roadway so as to make the surface immediately above the point of the lowest subsidence about 4 ft. 3 in. higher than it was at the commencement of the work. The Plaintiffs having had notice from the Defendants, raised their houses simultaneously with the works to the roadway, and then claimed under sect. 308 of the Act, and were awarded compensation for the cost of raising the houses.—Having regard to the obstruction to traffic caused by floods, the raising of the road was reasonably necessary to put it in a proper state for traffic ; but, excluding the consideration of floods, the raising of the road to the extent described, though a reasonable and prudent act, was not necessary to put the road into a proper state for traffic :—*Held*, that as the highway was vested in the Defendants, no action of trespass could have been maintained by the Plaintiffs, even if more materials had been placed on the road than a surveyor of highways could justify, and that the Plaintiffs had no right to have the road maintained at the level to which it accidentally and recently sank; and that the works of the Defendants were not done " in exercise of any of the powers" of the Act within the terms of sect. 308—which mean powers created by the Act, and not simply powers transferred by sect. 144 from the surveyor to the local board —but were done, if not strictly in pursuance of their duty as surveyors of highways, at all events in exercise of such powers as surveyors of highways have, and, consequently, that the Plaintiffs were not entitled to compensation. BURGESS *v.* NORTHWICH LOCAL BOARD **6 Q. B. D. 264**

III. LOCAL GOVERNMENT—LOCAL AUTHORITY.

Interest.] *The Act* 48 & 49 Vict. c. 53 *(Public Health Members and Officers Act,* 1885) *amends sect.* 193 *of* 38 & 39 Vict. c. 55 *(Public Health Act,* 1875) *and permits officers of a local authority under certain conditions to be interested in certain contracts with the local authority.*

Sect. 3. *Restriction on recovery of penalties under rule* 70 *of Schedule II. of Public Health Act,* 1875.

Sect. 4. *Removal of disqualification from any member of a local authority having an interest in a newspaper in which such local authority advertises.*

Loans.] *The Act* 48 & 49 Vict. c. 30, *amends* 38 & 39 Vict. c. 83 *(the Local Loans Act,* 1875), *as regards the provision of sinking funds for the discharge of local loans.*

(*a*) CONTRACTS.

1. —— Contract not under Seal—*Agreement to compromise—Public Health Act,* 1875 (38 & 39

III. LOCAL GOVERNMENT—LOCAL AUTHO-
RITY—*continued.*

(a.) CONTRACTS—*continued.*

Vict. c. 55), *ss.* 173, 174.] An agreement between a local board and a person against whom an action to restrain his interference with a public highway had been commenced by the local board, that the action should be settled by his paying the costs of the board (which exceeded £50), and undertaking not to build on the unbuilt land, the board agreeing not to proceed further as to pulling down the obstruction, is not a contract within the Public Health Act, 1875, necessary for carrying the Act into execution (sect. 173) so as to require to be sealed with the common seal of the local board under sect. 174; and therefore such agreement, though not under seal, is capable of being enforced by the board. ATTORNEY-GENERAL *v.* GASKILL　　　- 22 Ch. D. 537

2. —— Contract not under Seal—*Contract exceeding £50 in Value or Amount—Corporation—Public Health Act, 1875 (38 & 39 Vict. c. 55), ss. 174, 200—Urban Authority.*] Sect. 174 of the Public Health Act, 1875, which directs a contract made by an urban authority to be under their common seal, if " the value or amount exceeds £50," applies only to a contract to which the parties at the time of entering into it contemplate that it shall exceed that sum. Scarlet fever having broken out, an urban sanitary authority appointed a committee under sect. 200 of the Public Health Act, 1875, and the committee provided hospital tents. A medical man agreed verbally with the committee on behalf of the urban sanitary authority, to attend the patients at the rate of 5s. 3d. per tent per day, and attended until the amount due was nearly £100:—*Held,* affirming the judgment of Stephen, J., that the committee men were not liable to pay the medical man; but—*Held,* reversing the judgment of Stephen, J., that although more than £50 became due, it was not a contract " whereof the value or amount exceeds £50 " within the meaning of the Public Health Act, 1875, s. 174, because at the time of entering into it, the parties had not ascertained that it would exceed £50, and that the urban sanitary authority were liable to the medical man. EATON *v.* BASKER
　　　[6 Q. B. D. 201; 7 Q. B. D. 529

3. —— Contract not under Seal but executed—*Urban Authority—Public Health Act, 1875 (38 & 39 Vict. c. 55), ss. 173, 174.*] Sub-sect. 1 of sect. 174 of the Public Health Act, 1875 (38 & 39 Vict. c. 55) enacts that " every contract made by an urban authority whereof the value or amount exceeds £50 shall be in writing and sealed with the common seal of such authority," is obligatory and not merely directory, and applies to an executed contract of which the urban authority have had the full benefit and enjoyment, and which has been effected by their agent duly appointed under their common seal.—*Hunt* v. *Wimbledon Local Board* (4 C. P. D. 48) approved. YOUNG *v.* MAYOR, &c. OF LEAMINGTON SPA
　　　[8 Q. B. D. 579; 8 App. Cas. 517

4. —— Contract with Board—*Contract not under Seal—Affixing Seal where Contract partly performed, Effect of—Urban Authority—Illegality—Officer concerned in Contract, whether Contract*

III. LOCAL GOVERNMENT—LOCAL AUTHO-
RITY—*continued.*

(a.) CONTRACTS—*continued.*

void—Public Health Act, 1875 (38 & 39 Vict. c. 55), ss. 174, 193.] By sect. 174 of the Public Health Act, 1875, every contract made by an urban authority whereof the value or amount exceeds £50 shall be in writing and sealed with the common seal of such authority.—The Defendants, an urban authority, by contract not under seal employed the Plaintiffs as engineers to perform certain work. The Plaintiffs performed part of the work exceeding in value £50, and then required the Defendants to affix their seal to the contract. This the Defendants did, believing that it was for the benefit of the ratepayers of the district that the contract should be completed :—*Held,* that as part of the work was unperformed when the seal was affixed, and there was consideration for affixing it in the Plaintiffs' promise to complete the work, it was competent for the Defendants to constitute the contract a good contract under seal, within sect. 174, in respect of the work already done, and therefore that the Plaintiffs were entitled to maintain their action for the value of that work.—By sect. 193, officers or servants employed under this Act by the local authority shall not in anywise be concerned or interested in any bargain or contract made with such authority for any of the purposes of this Act; and if any such officer or servant is so concerned or interested he shall be incapable of afterwards holding or continuing in any office or employment under this Act, and shall forfeit and pay the sum of £50, to be recovered by any person in the prescribed manner :—*Held,* that this section intended to limit the penal consequences of a breach of its provisions to the specified penalties; and therefore that the enactment did not render a contract made by an officer with the local authority void, so as to disentitle him to sue upon it. MELLISS *v.* SHIRLEY LOCAL BOARD　　　-　　　-　14 Q. B. D. 911
　　[Reversed on the second point by Court of
　　　　Appeal, 16 Q. B. D. 446.]

5. —— Contract with Board—*Officer—"Concerned or interested in any bargain or contract" with Board—Demise of Rooms to Local Board —"Allowance" in addition to Salary—Public Health Act, 1875 (38 & 39 Vict. c. 55), ss. 174, 175, 189, 193, 265.*] A demise of rooms is a " bargain or contract" within the meaning of sect. 193 of the Public Health Act, 1875, and if an officer, employed by a local board constituted under that statute, lets rooms to the board at a rent payable by it to him although the rooms are used by it in the transaction of its business, he becomes liable to the penalty imposed by that section ; for the rent payable by the local board cannot be considered as an " allowance " to the officer in addition to his salary within the meaning of sects. 189, 193, it being unconnected with the performance of any services in the course of his employment under the board. BURGESS *v.* CLARK　　　-　　14 Q. B. D. 735

6. —— Contract with Board—*Officer—Shareholder in Company—"Interested in any bargain or contract" with Local Board—Public Health Act, 1875 (38 & 39 Vict. c. 55), s. 193.*] An

III. LOCAL GOVERNMENT — LOCAL AUTHO-
RITY—*continued.*

(*a.*) CONTRACTS—*continued.*

officer of a local board, who is a shareholder in a company having a contract with the board, is, so long as the contract exists, "interested in a bargain or contract" with the board within the meaning of the Public Health Act, 1875, sect. 193, and if the contract is capable of producing any profit to the shareholders of the company, he is liable to the penalty imposed by that enactment.　TODD *v.* ROBINSON　　**14 Q. B. D. 739**

7. —— **Contract with Board**—*Public Health Act, 1875—Local Board, Member of—Liability to Penalty for acting as Member when disabled.*] By rule 64 of schedule 2 to the Public Health Act, 1875 (38 & 39 Vict. c. 55), it is declared that any member of a local board who "in any manner is concerned in any bargain or contract entered into by such board" shall "cease to be such member, and his office as such shall thereupon become vacant;" and rule 70 imposes a penalty of £50 on "any person who, not being duly qualified to act as member of the local board," "or being disabled from acting by any provisions of this Act, acts as such member":—*Held,* by Brett and Cotton, L.JJ. (Bramwell, L.J., dissenting), that a member of such board, who having been concerned in a contract by the board has thereupon ceased to be such member by force of rule 64, is a person disabled from acting as a member by a provision of the Act within the meaning of rule 70, and consequently that if afterwards he does so act he is liable to the penalty of £50.　FLETCHER *v.* HUDSON　-　　-　　-　　**7 Q. B. D. 611**

8. —— **Contract with Board**—*Public Health Act, 1875 (38 & 39 Vict. c. 55), ss. 150, 174, 257— Sewering and paving—Liability for Proportion of Expenses—Contract not under Seal.*] In an action by a local authority to recover from the Defendant his proportion of the cost of sewering, paving, &c., a street under the powers of the Public Health Act, 1875, s. 150, it appeared that part of the work, to an amount exceeding £50, had been done by contractors employed by the local authority, but that no written contract under the common seal of the authority had been made with them (as provided by sect. 174):—*Held,* by Hawkins, J., and Smith, J., that the Defendant was nevertheless liable.— By Smith, J., that the objection, if valid, would have been an objection to the apportionment, which could only be raised in the time and manner provided by sect. 257.　BOURNEMOUTH COMMISSIONERS *v.* WATTS　　**14 Q. B. D. 87**

(*b*) POWERS.

9. —— **Incorporation of District**—*Vesting of Property—Government Stock—Bank of England— Public Health Act, 1875 (38 & 39 Vict. c. 55), s. 310 —National Debt Act, 1870 (33 & 34 Vict. c. 71), s. 22.*] The words "council of such borough" in sect. 310 of the Public Health Act, 1875, mean the mayor, aldermen, and burgesses acting by the council.—The effect of the section, therefore, is that, when the district of a local board is incorporated as a borough all the property of the board (including property acquired by them by purchase after the passing of the Act) vests at once in the corporation, without the necessity of

III. LOCAL GOVERNMENT — LOCAL AUTHO-
RITY—*continued.*

(*b.*) POWERS—*continued.*

any conveyance or transfer.—In such a case the Bank of England are bound, on the request of the corporation, to register in their corporate name Government stock previously standing in the books of the bank in the name of the local board, without requiring any transfer to be executed. CORPORATION OF HYDE *v.* BANK OF ENGLAND
[21 Ch. D. 176

10. —— **Notice to abate Nuisance** — *Public Health Act, 1875 (38 & 39 Vict. c. 55), ss. 94, 96— Order of Justices—Works necessary for the Purpose.*] A nuisance existed consisting of a privy and ashpit in such a state as to be a nuisance, and the local sanitary authority gave notice to the owner under the Public Health Act, 1875, s. 94, to abate the same, and for that purpose to fill up the ashpit, abandon the privy, and build a pail closet. The owner failed to do so, and the justices thereupon, under sect. 96, ordered the owner to fill up the ashpit, to abandon the privy, and to construct a proper and sufficient pail closet in lieu thereof. On a rule for a certiorari to quash the order of justices:—*Held,* by Pollock, B., and Stephen, J., that the order was bad, as the justices had no power under sect. 96 to order the erection of the pail closet.　*Ex parte* WHITCHURCH
[6 Q. B. D. 545

11. —— **Notice to abate Nuisance**—*Power of Justices to order Specific Works—Public Health Act, 1875 (38 & 39 Vict. c. 55), ss. 94-96.*] A water-closet in the centre of a house being a nuisance, the sanitary authority gave notice to the owner of the house under the 94th section of the Public Health Act, 1875, to abate the nuisance, and for that purpose to remove the said closet from the centre of the house and place the same near an outer wall where there might be efficient ventilation, and to fix the soil-pipe outside the walls. The owner making default in so doing, justices thereupon, under sect. 96, ordered him to do the things above specified:—*Held,* that they had jurisdiction under the 96th section to make the order.—*Ex parte Whitchurch* (6 Q. B. D. 545) distinguished.　*Ex parte* SAUNDERS
[11 Q. B. D. 191

12. —— **Notice to abate Nuisance**—*Power of Justices to order specific Works—Public Health Act, 1875 (38 & 39 Vict. c. 55), ss. 94-96.*] A privy openly discharged nightsoil and offensive matter on the bank of a river, the sanitary authority served the owner of the premises with a notice to abate the nuisance, and for that purpose " to remove the present pipes and pan, level the floor under the seat of the privy, and provide a galvanized double-handle pail under the seat, the cover of which said seat to be moveable, so that the premises should no longer be a nuisance or injurious to health." And the justices at sessions made an order in the terms of the notice :—*Held,* that they had jurisdiction to make the order.— *Ex parte Saunders* (11 Q. B. D. 191) followed ; and *Ex parte Whitchurch* (6 Q. B. D. 545) distinguished or dissented from.　THE QUEEN *v.* LLEWELLYN
[13 Q. B. D. 681

13. —— **Power to bind Successors**—*Action in*

III. LOCAL GOVERNMENT—LOCAL AUTHO-RITY—*continued.*

(b.) Powers—*continued.*

Nature of Supplemental Suit—Nuisance—Injunction—District Board—38 & 39 Vict., c. 55, s. 275.] A decree was made in 1875 against the corporation of B., as the sanitary authority of B., granting a perpetual injunction to restrain them from allowing sewage to flow into a river so as to be injurious to health or a nuisance to the Plaintiffs; but the injunction was suspended for five years, to give the corporation an opportunity to execute certain works. After the expiration of that period the Plaintiffs desired to enforce the injunction, but in the meantime the B., T., and R. District Board had been constituted under the Public Health Act, 1875 (38 & 39 Vict. c. 55), as the sanitary authority of the district, in the place of the corporation of B.—The Plaintiffs brought an action against the B., T., and R. Board, claiming a declaration that they were entitled to the same benefit of the decree as against the Defendants in the present action as if they had been Defendants in the former suit. The Defendants demurred:—*Held* (reversing the decision of Bacon, V.C.), that the B., T., and R. Board were not made by the Public Health Act subject to any liabilities of their predecessors except those attaching under the Act, and were, therefore, not bound by the decree against them; and that, there being no allegation of any nuisance committed by the B., T., and R. Board, the Plaintiffs had no cause of action, and the demurrer must be allowed. ATTORNEY-GENERAL *v.* BIRMINGHAM, TAME, AND REA DRAINAGE BOARD   -   - 17 Ch. D. 685

14. —— Power to bind Successors—*Public Health Act, 1848* (11 & 12 *Vict. c.* 63), *s.* 48—*—Trustees—Improvident Bargain—Ultrà vires—Change of Circumstances.*] Under the Public Health Act, 1848, sect. 48, the owner of land adjoining a district by deed agreed with the local board to do certain works and pay £10 a year, and the board gave him leave to drain through their drain all sewage from the property and houses then belonging to the landowner and from any houses hereafter to be erected on the property. Many more houses were afterwards erected, and the urban sanitary authority (which had succeeded the local board) were under a new Act of Parliament prevented from passing as before the sewage through the drain into the Thames:—*Held,* that the deed was not *ultrà vires,* and that the board could bind their successors as to the sewage of houses not then in existence.—*Held,* that though the board were trustees for the ratepayers they had exercised their discretion, and the agreement did not appear at the time improvident, and its turning out badly for them did not affect it.—*Held,* that the law being altered so as to prevent the discharge of sewage into the Thames was no ground for setting aside the deed. MAYOR OF NEW WINDSOR *v.* STOVELL   -   - 27 Ch. D. 665

15. —— Quorum—*Public Health Act,* 1875 (38 & 39 *Vict. c.* 55), *ss.* 155, 158; *Sched. I.,* rr. 2, 9; *Sched. II., Part I.,* r. 65; *Part II.,* r. 2—*Casual Vacancy—Lapse of Board—Informality.*] Several members of a local board constituted under the Public Health Act, 1875, and consisting of nine

III. LOCAL GOVERNMENT—LOCAL AUTHO-RITY—*continued.*

(b.) Powers—*continued.*

members, resigned, so that the quorum of three required by Sched. I., r. 2, was not left. The two remaining members proceeded to fill up the vacancies. The board as thus constituted prescribed a building line under sect. 155 of the Act :—*Held,* by Pearson, J., that, as the resignations reduced the number of members to less than a quorum, the board had lapsed, that the two remaining members could not fill up the vacancies, that there was therefore no board, that the building line was therefore not well prescribed, and that Sched. I., rule 9, to the Act did not cure the defect.—*Held,* by the Court of Appeal, that the filling up of vacancies was "business" within the meaning of Sched. I., rule 2, that the two members were not competent to transact it, and that the new members therefore were not duly elected, but that by Sched. I., rule 9, the objection to the building line, founded on the fact that some of the members of the board were not duly elected, was removed. NEWHAVEN LOCAL BOARD *v.* NEWHAVEN SCHOOL BOARD   -   - 30 Ch. D. 350

IV. LOCAL GOVERNMENT—OFFENCES.

1. —— Accumulation or Deposit—"*Nuisance or Injurious to Health*"—*Absence of Injury to Health—Public Health Act,* 1875 (38 & 39 *Vict. c.* 55), *sub-s.* 4.] By sect. 91 of the Public Health Act, 1875, "any accumulation or deposit which is a nuisance or injurious to health" shall be deemed to be a nuisance liable to be dealt with summarily under the Act:—*Held,* that an offence within the section was committed where the accumulation emitted offensive smells which interfered with the personal comfort of persons living in the neighbourhood; but did not cause injury to health.—*Great Western Railway Company v. Bishop* (Law Rep. 7 Q. B. 550) distinguished. BISHOP AUCKLAND LOCAL BOARD *v.* BISHOP AUCKLAND IRON COMPANY 10 Q. B. D. 138

2. —— Continuing Offence — *Information—Time—Public Health Act,* 1875 (38 & 39 *Vict. c.* 55), *ss.* 156, 252.]. By sect. 156 of the Public Health Act, 1875, it is an offence to bring forward or build any addition to a house in a street beyond the front of the house or building on either side without the consent of the urban authority; and "any person offending against this enactment shall be liable to a penalty not exceeding 40s. for every day during which the offence is continued after written notice in this behalf from the urban authority :"—*Held,* that an offence to which the penalty was applicable continued so long as the addition to the house was maintained after written notice from the urban authority, notwithstanding that the addition was completed before the notice was given.—*Marshall v. Smith* (Law Rep. 8 C. P. 416) distinguished. RUMBALL *v.* SCHMIDT
          [8 Q. B. D. 603.

3. —— Keeping Swine—*Absence of Injury to Health—Public Health Act,* 1875 (38 & 39 *Vict. c.* 55), *s.* 47.] It is an offence under the Public Health Act, 1875, s. 47, to keep swine so as to be a "nuisance" in the common law meaning of the term. It is not necessary to such offence that

IV. LOCAL GOVERNMENT—OFFENCES—*contd.*

there should be any injury to health. BANBURY URBAN SANITARY AUTHORITY *v.* PAGE
[8 Q. B. D. 97

4. —— Unwholesome Meat—*Evidence of State of Meat—Public Health Act,* 1875 (38 & 39 *Vict. c.* 55), *s.* 117—*Condemnation by Justice—Proceedings for Penalty.*] When unwholesome meat has been condemned by a justice, and proceedings are afterwards taken before a Court of summary jurisdiction, under 38 & 39 Vict. c. 55 (Public Health Act, 1875), s. 117, against the owner of the meat, evidence may be given by him as to the state of the meat at the time of condemnation. WAYE *v.* THOMPSON   -   15 Q. B. D. 342

5. —— Unwholesome Meat—*Exposure for Sale—Purchase by Customer — Seizure —Condemnation—Liability of Seller to Penalty—Public Health Act,* 1875 (38 & 39 *Vict. v.* 55), *ss.* 116, 117.] The Respondent, a butcher, exposed for sale part of a cow which had died of disease, and sold the meat to a customer, who took it home for food, and some days afterwards at the request of the Appellant, an inspector of nuisances, handed it over to him, and it was condemned by a justice as unfit for the food of man:—*Held,* that the meat was not "so seized" and condemned as is prescribed by sects. 116, 117, of the Public Health Act, 1875, and therefore the Respondent was not liable, as the person to whom the same "did belong at the time of the exposure for sale," to a penalty under sect. 117. VINTER *v.* HIND
[10 Q. B. D. 63

V. LOCAL GOVERNMENT—PRACTICE.

1. —— Justices of the Peace—*Bias—Disqualification—Town Council—Urban Sanitary Authority—Public Health Act,* 1875 (38 & 39 *Vict. c.* 55), *s.* 258.] By sect. 258 of the Public Health Act, 1875, " no justice of the peace shall be deemed incapable of acting in cases arising under this Act by reason of his being a member of any local authority."—In the borough of Wakefield the sanitary committee of the town council, who were the local authority under the Public Health Act, 1875, passed a resolution directing the town clerk to prosecute S. for exposing for sale meat unfit for human food, contrary to the provisions of the Act, and at the hearing of an information laid in pursuance of this resolution S. was convicted before four justices of the borough, who imposed a penalty upon him. One of the justices was a member of the sanitary committee, and had been present at the meeting at which the resolution was passed:—*Held,* that sect. 258 did not remove the disqualification which attached to the justice by reason of his having acted as a member of the sanitary committee in directing the prosecution, and that a rule for a certiorari to bring up and quash the conviction must be made absolute. THE QUEEN *v.* LEE   -   9 Q. B. D. 394

2. —— Justices of the Peace—*Jurisdiction —Summary Proceedings—Expenses of sewering Street — Appeal to Local Government Board — Public Health Act,* 1875 (38 & 39 *Vict. v.* 55), *ss.* 150, 268.] Upon the hearing of a complaint preferred before a police magistrate by the urban authority of the district acting under sect. 150 of the Public Health Act, 1875, to recover the

V. LOCAL GOVERNMENT—PRACTICE—*contd.*

amount apportioned upon a frontager in respect of expenses incurred by the urban authority in sewering, &c., a street, the frontager objected that the plans referred to in the notice requiring him to execute the work, shewed that part of the work in respect of which upon his failure to comply with the notice the expenses were incurred, was executed upon land belonging to private owners : *Held,*—that, as part of the work was executed on a street, the urban authority had power to fix the sum to be apportioned, and the magistrate had jurisdiction to entertain the complaint, and could only make an order for payment of the apportioned sum, and if the frontager was aggrieved by what the urban authority had done his only remedy was to appeal to the Local Government Board under sect. 268 of the Public Health Act, 1875.—*Ex parte* WAKE ; WAKE *v.* MAYOR, &c., of SHEFFIELD   11 Q. B. D. 291 ; 12 Q. B. D. 142

3. —— Limitation of Action — *Highway— Urban Authority — Surveyors of Highways constituted by Local Act—5 & 6 Will.* 4, *c.* 50, *s.* 109 —5 & 6 *Vict. c.* 97, *s.* 5—*Public Health Act,* 1875 (38 & 39 *Vict. c.* 55), *ss.* 144, 264, 341.] By a local Act passed in 1862, the corporation of Salford were constituted surveyors of highways within the borough, having and being subject to all such powers and liabilities as any surveyors of highways had or were subject to by virtue of the law for the time being in force. Sect. 109 of 5 & 6 Will. 4, c. 50 (the Highway Act of 1835), limits the period within which any action may be brought for anything done under the authority of that Act to three months after the act committed for which the action is brought. Sect. 5 of 5 & 6 Vict. c. 97, limits the period within which any action may be brought for anything done under the authority of the local Acts to two years after the cause of action. By the Public Health Act, 1875, s. 144, urban authorities (including by sect. 6 corporations of boroughs) are constituted surveyors of highways within their district, having and being subject to all the powers, duties, and liabilities (so far as the same are not inconsistent with the provisions of that Act) of surveyors of highways under the law for the time being in force. Sect. 264 limits the period within which actions may be brought for anything done under that Act to six months after the cause of action accrued ; and by sect. 341, all powers given by that Act shall be deemed to be in addition to and not in derogation of any other powers conferred by statute, and such other powers may be exercised in the same manner as if that Act had not passed. In an action against the corporation for negligence, as surveyors of highways, commenced more than three but less than six months after the cause of action accrued :—*Held,* that the Defendants were entitled to rely on the limitation of three months provided by 5 & 6 Will. 4, c. 50, and therefore that the action could not be maintained.—*Taylor v. Meltham Local Board* (47 L. J. (C.P.) 12) distinguished. BURTON *v.* CORPORATION OF SALFORD -   -   11 Q. B. D. 286

4. —— Limitation of Action — *Money paid under Mistake of Fact—Money received for Plaintiff's use—Public Health Act,* 1875 (38 & 39 *Vict. c.* 55), *s.* 264.] The Defendants, under the

V. LOCAL GOVERNMENT—PRACTICE—*contd.*

Public Health Act, 1875, s. 150, gave notice to the Plaintiffs, as adjoining owners, to pave a part of a road situate within the Defendants' district. It was then believed by both the Plaintiffs and the Defendants that the road was not repairable by the inhabitants at large.　The Plaintiffs not having done the work, the Defendants did it and charged the cost to the Plaintiffs, who paid it. It was afterwards discovered that the road was repairable by the inhabitants at large, and therefore that the Plaintiffs were not liable, as adjoining owners. to pave the road.　The Plaintiffs thereupon demanded back from the Defendants the money paid by them as the cost of paving the part of the road ; but the Defendants refused to return it.　The Plaintiffs, thereupon, sued to recover it as money paid under a mistake of fact and as money received to their use : but the Plaintiffs did not give the Defendants notice of action, and the action was commenced more than six months after the cost of paving the part of the road had been paid to the Defendants :—*Held*, that notice of action was necessary, and that the action was brought too late, and that the provisions of the Public Health Act, 1875, s. 264, applied.—*Waterhouse* v. *Keen* (4 B. & C. 200), and *Selmes* v. *Judge* (Law Rep. 6 Q. B. 724), followed.　MIDLAND RAILWAY COMPANY *v.* WITHINGTON LOCAL BOARD　　**11 Q. B. D. 788**

5. —— **Limitation of Action** — *Recovery of Land—Public Health Act, 1875* (38 & 39 *Vict.* c. 55), s. 264.] Sect. 264 of the Public Health Act, 1875 (38 & 39 Vict. c. 55),—which enacts that no writ or process shall be sued out against any local authority for anything done or intended to be done under the provisions of the Act until one month after written notice of action, &c., and that any person to whom any such notice of action is given, may tender amends to the Plaintiff within one month under the service of such notice—does not apply to an action for the recovery of land.　FOAT *v.* MAYOR, &c., OF MARGATE　-　　-　　-　　**11 Q. B. D. 299**

VI. LOCAL GOVERNMENT—PUBLIC HEALTH ACTS.

Alkali, &c., Works.] *The Alkali, &c., Works Regulations Act*, 1881 (44 & 45 Vict. c. 37), *repeals the Alkali Act*, 1863 (26 & 27 Vict. c. 124), *the Act* (31 & 32 Vict. c. 36), *which made perpetual the Alkali Act*, 1863, *the Alkali Act*, 1874 (37 & 38 Vict. c. 43) ; *directs* (sects. 3–10) *the manner in which alkali works, sulphuric acid works, and certain other scheduled works shall be carried on ; provides* (sects. 11–20) *for the registration and inspection of all such works ; and* (sects. 21–28) *prescribes the procedure to be adopted in recovering fines for offences against the Act.*

Fines are to be recovered by action in the County Court, and an appeal lies in the form of a special case to the High Court of Justice.

By sect. 25 the owner of a work is not to be liable in certain cases for an offence against the Act, if he proves that the offence was committed without his knowledge, consent, or connivance, by some agent, servant, or workman, whom he shall charge by name as the actual offender.

By sect. 28 where a nuisance, arising from any

VI. LOCAL GOVERNMENT—PUBLIC HEALTH ACTS—*continued.*

noxious or offensive gas or gases, is wholly or partially caused by the acts or defaults of several persons, any person injured by such nuisance may proceed against any one or more of such persons and may recover damages from each person made a defendant in proportion to the extent of the contribution of such defendant to the nuisance, notwithstanding that the act or default of such defendant would not separately have caused a nuisance.

The section is not to apply to any defendant who can produce a certificate from the chief inspector that in the works of such defendant the requirements of the Act have been complied with, and were complied with when the nuisance arose.

Scheduled Works.
Sulphuric Acid Works,
Chemical Manure Works,
Gas Liquor Works,
Nitric Acid Works,
Sulphate of Ammonia Works,
Chlorine Works,
and works of a similar character.

Epidemic Diseases.] *The Epidemic and other Diseases Prevention Act* (46 & 47 Vict. c. 59), 1883, *makes better provision for the prevention of outbreaks of formidable epidemic, endemic, or infectious diseases, and amends the Public Health Act,* 1875.

Fruit-pickers.] *The Act* 45 & 46 Vict. c. 23, *extends sect.* 214 *of the Public Health Act,* 1875, *and empowers any local authority to make by-laws for securing the decent lodging and accommodation of persons engaged in the picking of fruit and vegetables.*

Penalties.] *The Act* 47 & 48 Vict. c. 74, *prohibits proceedings for any penalty under the Public Health Act,* 1875, s. 193, *to be taken without the consent of the Attorney-General.*

Sewers.] *The Act* 46 & 47 Vict. c. 37, *amends the Public Health Act, 1875, and makes provision with respect to the support of public sewers and sewage works in mining districts.*

Sect. 1. *Act to be cited as Public Health Act,* 1875 (*Support of Sewers*) *Amendment Act,* 1883, *and to be construed as one with Public Health Act,* 1875.

Sect. 2. *Interpretation of terms, "sanitary works" and "support."*

Sect. 3. *Application of provisions of the Waterworks Clauses Act,* 1847 (10 & 11 Vict. c. 17), *with respect to mines, to any sanitary work of a local authority.*

Sect. 4. *Limitation of right to support for sanitary works over mines.*

Sect. 5. *Savings.*

Amendment.] *The Act* 48 & 49 Vict. c. 72, *amends sect.* 90 *of the Public Health Act,* 1875.

Port Sanitary Authority.] *The Act* 48 & 49 Vict. c. 35, *by sect.* 2 *amends sect.* 110 *of* 38 & 39 Vict. c. 55 (*the Public Health Act,* 1875), *and by sect.* 3 *enables the Local Government Board to permanently constitute a port sanitary authority by order.*

Cholera.] *General Regulations* (12th July, 1883) *of Local Government Board under Public Health Act,* 1875, s. 130, *for all port sanitary authorities*

VI. LOCAL GOVERNMENT—PUBLIC HEALTH ACTS—*continued.*

(*except the port of London*), *customs ports not within a port sanitary authority, and others*
[**L. G., 1883, p. 3535**

Order (*21st April, 1884*) *of Local Government Board, amending above cholera regulations with respect to approval of the Queen's Harbour Master in certain ports* - - **L. G., 1884, p. 1813**

Medical Officer.] *Order of Local Government Board under Public Health Act, 1875, s. 287, with respect to every medical officer of health appointed or reappointed on or after the 1st of August, 1883, where any portion of the salary of such officer is paid by Parliament* - **L. G., 1883,**
[**p. 3653**

Ditto, where no portion of such salary is paid by Parliament - - **L. G., 1883, p. 3655**

Inspector of Nuisances.] *Order of Local Government Board under Public Health Act, 1875, s. 287, with respect to every inspector of nuisances appointed or reappointed on or after the 1st August, 1883, where any portion of the salary of such officer is paid by Parliament* - **L. G., 1883, p. 3657**

VII. LOCAL GOVERNMENT—RATES.

Conference.] *The Act 48 & 49 Vict. c. 22, provides for the expenses incurred in relation to conferences of the public health and local government authorities.*

1. —— Highway Rate—*Local Board—Urban Authority—Surveyors of Highways—Limit upon Amount of Highway Rate—Highway Act, 1835* (5 & 6 Will. 4, c. 50), ss. 5, 29—*Public Health Act, 1875* (38 & 39 Vict. c. 55), ss. 144, 216, 217.] The Respondents were the local board for the district of G. Part of their district, called the outer district, was not rated for works of paving, water supply, and sewerage. The Respondents under the Public Health Act, 1875, ss. 216, 217, made a highway rate of 3s. 4d. in the pound upon the inhabitants of the outer district, whose consent to the rate had not been obtained : — *Held,* that, although the local board were surveyors of highways within the outer district, pursuant to the Public Health Act, 1875, s. 144, yet the limit imposed upon rates made by surveyors of highways under the Highway Act, 1835, s. 29 (10d. in the pound for one rate and 2s. 6d. in the pound for one year) unless the consent of the parishioners had been obtained, did not apply to the highway rates made by a local board pursuant to the Public Health Act, 1875, ss. 216, 217, and that the rate of 3s. 4d. in the pound made by the Respondents was valid. DYSON v. GREETLAND LOCAL BOARD - - - **13 Q. B. D. 946**

2. —— Owner rated instead of Occupier—*Rate in respect of Tenements whether occupied or unoccupied—Reduced Estimate—Proportion of annual Value—Public Health Act, 1875* (38 & 39 Vict. c. 55), s. 211.] By the Public Health Act, 1875 (38 & 39 Vict. c. 55), s. 211, the owner instead of the occupier may, at the option of the urban authority, be rated to general district rates, provided that in cases where the owner is rated instead of the occupier he shall be assessed on such reduced estimate as the urban authority deem reasonable of the nett annual value, not being less than two-thirds nor more than four-

VII. LOCAL GOVERNMENT—RATES—*contd.*

fifths of the nett annual value ; and where such reduced estimate is in respect of tenements whether occupied or unoccupied, then such assessment may be made on one half of the amount at which such tenements would be liable to be rated if the same were occupied, and the rate were levied on the occupiers :—*Held,* affirming the decision of the Queen's Bench Division, that a discretionary power is given to the urban authority by that enactment to rate the owner in respect of premises whether occupied or unoccupied, but where the owner is so rated the assessment must only be upon one-half of the rateable value. THE QUEEN v. BARCLAY - - **8 Q. B. D. 306, 486**

3. —— Water—Supply to House—*Notice to Owner to obtain Proper Supply—Non-compliance with Notice — Power to charge Rates — Public Health Act, 1875* (38 & 39 Vict. c. 55), s. 62.] A local authority caused a supply of water to be brought in main water-pipes along the street in which a house was situate, and gave notice to the owner of the house, under sect. 62 of the Public Health Act, 1875, to obtain a proper supply and do all such works as might be necessary for that purpose. That notice was not complied with, and the local authority did not exercise the power given to them by that section of executing the works necessary to connect the house with the main. In an action by the water company for water-rates:—*Held,* that the Defendant was liable, and that it was not a condition precedent to such liability that the works necessary to bring the water into the house should have been executed. SOUTHEND WATERWORKS COMPANY v. HOWARD
[**13 Q. B. D. 215**

VIII. LOCAL GOVERNMENT—SEWERS.

1. —— Obligation of Landowner— *Subjacent Support—Compensation for Deprivation of Power to work Mines—Public Health Act, 1875* (38 & 39 Vict. c. 55), ss. 15, 16, 175, 308.] The Public Health Act, 1875, imposes on landowners, through whose land a sewer is run under that Act, an obligation to preserve to such sewer subjacent support, and gives them a right to immediate compensation for being deprived of free power to work subjacent mines, but not for the risk of percolation of sewage into the subjacent mines. *In re* CORPORATION OF DUDLEY **8 Q. B. D. 86**

2. —— Vesting in Local Authority—*Public Health Act, 1875* (38 & 39 Vict. c. 55), s. 13—*Obstruction by Owner of Soil—Injunction*]. A sewer made by the owner of some only of the houses in a street not yet a highway, though made for the purpose of draining his own amongst other houses, is not a sewer made by a person " for his own profit " within the meaning of the exception in sect. 13 of the Public Health Act, 1875.—The word " sewer " in that Act should receive the largest possible interpretation, and a drain is a " sewer " within the meaning of sect. 13 when more than one house has been connected with it. ACTON LOCAL BOARD v. BATTEN **28 Ch. D. 283**

IX. LOCAL GOVERNMENT—STREETS.

1. —— Finding by Justices—*Estoppel — Res judicata—Justices, Summary Proceedings before—Adjudication that Street is a Highway—Public Health Act, 1875* (38 & 39 Vict. c. 55), s. 150.] An

IX. LOCAL GOVERNMENT—STREETS—*contd.*

application to justices by a local board under the Public Health Act, 1875, for a recovery of a proportion of the expenses of sewering a street from the owner of premises abutting thereon, was dismissed by the justices on the ground ,that the street was a highway repairable by the inhabitants at large. The local board some years afterwards made an application against the same person for the recovery of a proportion of paving expenses subsequently incurred in respect of the same street, and a stipendiary magistrate made an order for the payment of such expenses:—*Held*, that the adjudication of the justices that the street was a highway repairable by the inhabitants at large on the first application was beyond the jurisdiction of such justices, which was only to make or refuse the order for the expenses claimed, and that, therefore, such adjudication on the first application did not estop the local board from claiming the expenses they claimed on the second application, and consequently that the magistrate might make the order which he made for their payment. THE QUEEN *v.* HUTCHINGS

[6 Q. B. D. 300

2. —— **Finding by Justices**—"*Street,*" *Definition of*—*Public Health Act,* 1875 (38 & 39 *Vict.* c. 55), *ss.* 4, 150.] By sect. 4 of the Public Health Act, 1875, "in this Act, if not inconsistent with the context, the following words and expressions have the meaning hereinafter respectively assigned to them," and (amongst other definitions) "street includes any road," &c. By sect. 150 where any street within any urban district (not being a highway repairable by the inhabitants at large) is not sewered, paved, and channelled to the satisfaction of the urban authority they may give notice to the owners of the adjoining premises to sewer, &c., the street, and on failure to comply with the notice the urban authority may execute the works themselves, and recover the expense of so doing from the adjoining owners in a summary manner. Summary proceedings having been taken by an urban authority to recover, under sect. 150, the expense of sewering, &c., a road within the district which was not a highway repairable by the inhabitants at large:—*Held*, that it was a question of fact for the justices to determine whether or not the road was a street within sect. 150, and that they were not bound to find as matter of, law that it was a street by the terms of the definition in sect. 4. MAUDE *v.* BAILDON LOCAL BOARD 10 Q. B. D. 394

3. —— **General Line of Buildings**—*Informality* —*Acquiescence*—*Public Health Act,* 1875, *ss.* 155, 158.] The Defendants being about to pull down a school and erect a new one, submitted plans to the local board. The local board objected to the plans, giving as a reason that they violated a by-law, which obliged a person laying out a new street to leave it of a certain width. This by-law was not applicable, as South Lane, on which the school fronted, was not a new street. The Defendants disregarded the objection, commenced their works on the 5th of January, 1885, laid the foundations of the main wall towards South Lane on the 12th, and proceeded rapidly with the erection of it. On the 22nd of January, the local board prescribed a building line which

IX. LOCAL GOVERNMENT—STREETS—*contd.*

did not interfere with the main wall, but would prevent the erection of certain annexes not then commenced, lying between South Lane and the main walls, which annexes were shewn on the plans laid before the board. The Defendants had ground enough to allow of the annexes being erected elsewhere. The Defendants proceeded with the annexes, and the board brought their action to restrain them from building beyond the line, and to compel them to pull down what they had built beyond it:—*Held*, that where a building is taken down to be rebuilt, a building line may be prescribed under sect. 155, for any portion of it which has not been commenced, although other portions have been commenced, unless what has been commenced necessarily involves as a matter of construction a projection beyond the line afterwards prescribed, and that here no such necessity existed, as the annexes could be erected elsewhere. That the commencement of the main building therefore did not preclude the board from laying down a line which would prevent the erection of the annexes which had not then been commenced.—*Held*, also, that as the notice given by the board, though ineffectual for the purpose of empowering them to pull down the erection under sect. 155, gave the Defendants to understand that the board objected on the ground that buildings according to the plan would make the street too narrow, the board had not done anything to induce the Defendants to believe that they would not prescribe a building line, and that there was no equity to prevent the board from exercising their powers under sect. 155 on the ground that they had misled the Defendants. NEWHAVEN LOCAL BOARD *v.* NEWHAVEN SCHOOL BOARD   -   -   - 30 Ch. D. 350

4. —— "**New Street**" — *Bringing forward Buildings*—*Public Health Act,* 1848 (11 & 12 *Vict.* c. 63), *s.* 2—*Local Government Act,* 1858 (21 & 22 *Vict.* c. 98), *s.* 34 — *Public Health Act,* 1875 (38 & 39 *Vict.* c. 55), *ss.* 4, 156, 157.] The Public Health Act, 1875 (38 & 39 Vict. c. 55), s. 157, enables an urban authority to make by-laws with respect (inter alia) to the level, width, and construction of new streets:—*Held*, affirming the decision of the Court of Appeal, that the words " new streets" in that section are not confined to streets constructed for the first time, but apply also to an old highway, formerly a country lane, which has long been a "street" within the interpretation clause (sect. 4) of that Act, and which by the building of houses on each side of it has recently become a street in the popular sense of the term.—A by-law made by an urban authority under that section provided that every new street should be laid out and formed of such width and at such level as the urban authority should in each case·determine :—*Held*, reversing the decision of the Court of Appeal, that "width" in sect. 157 of the Public Health Act, 1875, and in the above by-law meant width of roadway, and not width between houses on each side of the street; and that the urban authority were not entitled under the above by-law (or any other of their existing by-laws) to disapprove of and pull down houses in the course of erection in a new street on the ground that the building line was too

IX. LOCAL GOVERNMENT—STREETS—*contd.*
near the roadway. ROBINSON *v.* LOCAL BOARD
OF BARTON-ECCLES 21 Ch. D. 621 ; 8 App. Cas. 798

5. —— Notice to several Owners—*Default by
one only—Right to execute Works without giving
fresh Notice — Apportionment, when conclusive—
Summary Proceedings—Delay between Complaint
and Summons—Paving Expenses—38 & 39 Vict.
c. 55, ss. 150, 257.*] The Appellant and five
others were the owners of premises within the
district of the Respondents, an urban authority
under the Public Health Act, 1875. These premises abutted upon a street (not being a highway), which street was not sewered, levelled,
paved, flagged, and channelled to the satisfaction
of the Respondents. The Respondents gave a
separate notice to each of such owners requiring
them to sewer, level, pave, flag, and channel the
parts of the street in front of their premises,
within a specified time. Five of the owners
executed the works in front of their premises,
but the Appellant made default. The Respondents thereupon executed the works required to
be done in front of her premises, and their surveyor having made his apportionment, gave her
a notice stating that the expenses had been
apportioned by their surveyor, who had settled
that £213 13s. 6d. was payable by her according
to the frontage of her premises, and that they
required payment of that sum : — *Held*, first,
that the Respondents were not bound before executing such works to give the Appellant a fresh
notice specifying the particular works which
remained to be done by her ; secondly, that the
Respondent not having given notice to dispute
the apportionment, it became binding on her
within the three months limited by sect. 257, and
that summary proceedings might be taken under
that section for the recovery of the amount due
from her; thirdly, that in such summary proceedings it was no objection to the validity of a
summons that it was issued more than a year
after the complaint upon which it was founded;
fourthly, that the notice of apportionment, which
concluded with a demand of payment of the
amount apportioned, was not a "notice of demand"
within sect. 257, and that the six months within
which, under sect. 252, summary proceedings
must be taken, were not to be reckoned from
it but from a subsequent notice of demand.
SIMCOX *v.* LOCAL BOARD FOR HANDSWORTH,
STAFFORD -   -   **8 Q. B. D. 39**

6. —— Paving Expenses—*Apportionment—
Premises "adjoining or abutting on" a newly-
made Street—Public Health Act, 1875 (38 & 39
Vict. c. 55), s. 150.*] A. was the owner of three
houses fronting a street called York Place,
and adjoining or abutting at the rear upon a
footpath at the end of a street called St. Julian
Street, which formed a cul-de-sac. The ground
at the back of these houses was five feet above
the level of St. Julian Street, and the wall,
which was the property of A., was about twelve
feet high on the outside. There was no access
from A.'s premises to St. Julian Street :—*Held*,
that his premises "adjoined or abutted on"
St. Julian Street within the Act, and consequently that he was chargeable with his proportion of the expenses of paving, &c., that street,

IX. LOCAL GOVERNMENT—STREETS—*contd.*
under the Public Health Act, 1875 (38 & 39
Vict. c. 55), s. 150. NEWPORT URBAN SANITARY
AUTHORITY *v.* GRAHAM -   -   **9 Q. B. D. 183**

7. —— Paving Expenses—*Apportionment—
Premises "fronting, adjoining, or abutting"—
Public Health Act, 1875 (38 & 39 Vict. c. 55),
s. 150.*] The Appellant owned premises separated from a street by a wall five feet high,
belonging, together with the land on which it
stood, to another person. The Appellant had no
direct access from his premises to the street, but in
order to reach it had to pass for a short distance
down a public footpath, or over other intervening
land :—*Held*, that the Appellant was not the
owner of premises "fronting, adjoining, or abutting" on the street within the meaning of sect. 150
of the Public Health Act, 1875, and therefore
was not liable to contribute to the expenses of
sewering and paving the street under that section.
LIGHTBOUND *v.* HIGHER BEBINGTON LOCAL BOARD
[14 Q. B. D. 849
[Affirmed by the Court of Appeal, 16 Q. B. D. 577]

8. —— Paving Expenses—*Private Improvement Expenses — Charge upon "Premises"—
Leasehold Interest—Charge on Total Ownership
—Public Health Act, 1875 (38 & 39 Vict. c. 55),
ss. 4, 257.*] The charge created by sect. 257 of
the Public Health Act, 1875, for expenses incurred by a local authority for sewering and
other works, and for the payment whereof the
owner of the premises in respect of which the
same are incurred is liable under that Act, is a
charge upon the "premises" as defined by sect. 4 ;
accordingly, it is a charge, not on the interest of
any particular owner of the premises, but on the
total ownership, that is to say, on the respective
interest of every owner for the time being in proportion to the value of his interest. CORPORATION
OF BIRMINGHAM *v.* BAKER -   -   **17 Ch. D. 782**

9. —— Paving Expenses, *Recovery of—Public
Health Act, 1875 (38 & 39 Vict. c. 55), ss. 150,
257, 268—Appeal to Local Government Board—
Prohibition.*] Under 38 & 39 Vict. c. 55, s. 150,
notice was given by an urban authority to the
owner of premises fronting a street to pave part
of it, and on his default the authority executed
the work, and their surveyor gave him notice of
apportionment of the expenses for which the
owner was liable, and demand was made upon
him for the amount.—Under sect. 268, he, deem-
ing himself aggrieved by the "decision" of the
authority, addressed a memorial by way of appeal
to the Local Government Board, stating the
grounds of his complaint.—On a rule for a prohibition to the Local Government Board :—*Held*,
that an appeal lay by the memorial to the Local
Government Board, and that no prohibition
ought to be granted. THE QUEEN *v.* LOCAL
GOVERNMENT BOARD   **9 Q. B. D. 600 ;**
[10 Q. B. D. 309

10. —— Paving Expenses—*Road made good
and afterwards paved and flagged—Liability of
adjoining Owners—Towns Improvement Clauses
Act 1847 (10 & 11 Vict c. 34), s. 53.*] In
1857 a local Act was passed which incorporated
sect. 53 of the Towns Improvement Clauses
Act, 1847 (10 & 11 Vict. c. 34). In 1874 the
Appellants, in their capacity as the corporation

IX. LOCAL GOVERNMENT—STREETS—*contd.*
of P., bought some land of the Respondents abutting upon a country high road within the district to which the local Act applied, and, in pursuance of an agreement then made with the Respondents, at their own expense widened and improved the road and laid out a footpath along the side, and gravelled, channelled, and kerbed the footpath. In 1879 the Appellants, in their capacity as the urban authority, paved and flagged the footpath and sought to recover the expense of so doing from the Respondents as adjoining owners under the powers of sect. 53. The jury found that before the paving and flagging in 1879 the road was not a street in the popular sense of the term, and that the footpath had been "made good" within sect. 53:—*Held*, affirming the decision of the Court of Appeal, that the Respondents were not liable, upon the ground that the footpath had been "theretofore made good" within the meaning of sect. 53, but without deciding whether the road was a "street" within the meaning of that section.—The word "theretofore" in sect. 53 refers to the period before the work is done by the commissioners, not to the period before the passing of the special Act. MAYOR, &c. OF PORTS-MOUTH *v.* SMITH **13 Q. B. D. 184; 10 App. Cas. 364**

LOCAL GOVERNMENT—Appeal to Court of Appeal—Criminal cause or matter
　　　　　　　　　　　　　　　[7 Q. B. D. 534
　　　See PRACTICE — SUPREME COURT — APPEAL. 8.

—— Highway—Costs of proceedings for stopping up　　　　　　　　**13 Q. B. D. 640**
　　　See HIGHWAY—STOPPING UP.

—— Municipal corporation—Local authority—Justice member of corporation—Disqualification　　　-　　**6 Q. B. D. 168**
　　　See JUSTICES—DISQUALIFICATION. 3.

—— Penalty — Officer interested in contract—Rescission by Crown　　**12 Q. B. D. 530**
　　　See PENAL ACTION. 3.

—— Reference to Local Government Board under local Act—Power to state case for opinion of Court—Common Law Procedure Act, 1854　　　-　　**9 Q. B. D. 518**
　　　See ARBITRATION—SUBMISSION. 1.

—— Scotland—Power to make road
　　　　　　　　　　　　　　　[6 App. Cas. 833
　　　See SCOTCH LAW—HIGHWAY. 1.

LOCKS ON THE THAMES.
　　　See RIVER—*Gazette.*

LOCKE KING'S ACT 16 Ch. D. 322; 24 Ch. D. 94
　　　See WILL—EXONERATION. 2, 3.

—— Mortgage of land and charge on shares
　　　　　　　　　　　　　　　[21 Ch. D. 583
　　　See COMPANY—MEMBER'S LIABILITY. 1.

LOCOMOTIVES—On road.
　　　See HIGHWAY—LOCOMOTIVE—*Statutes.*

—— On road　-　-　**7 Q. B. D. 313**
　　　See HIGHWAY—LOCOMOTIVE.

LOCUS STANDI—Appeal in bankruptcy
　　　　　　　　　　　　　　　[16 Ch. D. 110
　　　See BANKRUPTCY—APPEAL. 2.

—— Appeal—Witness in winding-up
　　　　　　　　　　　　　　　[19 Ch. D. 118
　　　See COMPANY—EVIDENCE. 2.

LODGER—Franchise　　　**8 Q. B. D. 195, 247;**
　　　　　　　　　　　　　　[10 Q. B. D. 577
　　　See PARLIAMENT—FRANCHISE. 2, 3, 4.

—— Franchise.
　　　See PARLIAMENT—FRANCHISE—*Statutes.*

—— Distress—Lodgers' Goods Protection Act.
　　　See Cases under LANDLORD AND TENANT —LODGER.

LODGING-HOUSE—By-laws.
　　　See LOCAL GOVERNMENT—BY-LAWS— *Statutes.*

LOG BOOK — Engineer — Evidence — Action of damage　　-　　-　　**10 P. D. 31**
　　　See PRACTICE—ADMIRALTY—EVIDENCE. 2.

LONDON (CITY OF):—　　　　　　Col.
　　I. CHARITIES　　　　-　　-　**834**
　　II. COMMISSIONERS OF SEWERS　-　**837**

—— METROPOLITAN DISTRICT.
　　　See METROPOLIS.

I. LONDON—CHARITIES.
Charities.] *The Act 46 & 47 Vict. c. 36, provides for the better application and management of the Parochial Charities of the City of London.*
Sect. 1. *Act to be cited as the City of London Parochial Charities Act,* 1883.

I. *Appointment and Powers of Commissioners.*
Sect. 2. *Charity Commissioners for England and Wales to be Commissioners under the Act, and*
(1.) *To exercise any of the powers vested in them by the Charitable Trusts Act,* 1853.
(2.) *To exercise the like jurisdiction, &c., as might be exercised by the High Court of Justice if the matters and questions referred to them had come before that Court;*
(3.) *To determine whether any property is or is not charity property subject to the powers of the Act.*
Sect. 3 *provides for the appointment of two additional Charity Commissioners.*
Sect. 4. *Powers of Commissioners to continue until end of year* 1887, *and may be extended to end of* 1889, *but not further.*

II. *Inquiry and Statement.*
Sect. 5. *Commissioners to inquire into the charity property of the City of London, and to classify same in two schedules, one of ecclesiastical and the other of general charity property.*
Sect. 6. *Where property is mixed, Commissioners to determine how much is ecclesiastical and how much general.*
Sect. 7. *As to vested interests and equitable claims.*
Sect. 8. *Commissioners to publish statement embodying results of inquiry.*
Sect. 9. *Commissioners to send copy of statement to governing bodies, &c.*
Sect. 10. *Any person claiming any vested interest affecting any endowment mentioned in any such statement, and alleging that the Commissioners have not duly recognised such vested interest, or any person or persons alleging that any property, which the Commissioners have determined to be charity property within the meaning of the Act, is not charity property, but that he or they is or are entitled to the same free from any charitable trust*

2 E

I. LONDON—CHARITIES—*continued*.

affecting the same, may within two months from the date of the publication of such statement apply to the High Court of Justice, by petition or summons at Chambers, asking for a declaration that he has a vested interest affecting such endowment, or that such property is not charity property (as the case may be). The Commissioners may appear upon any such proceedings, and the decision of the Judge before whom such petition or summons is heard shall be final (unless special leave to appeal shall be by him given). The Judge shall make a declaration in conformity with the justice of the case, and shall have power to order that the costs of the application shall be paid out of the endowment or property in question, or by any party to the application as he may think right.

III. *Schemes for better Application of Charity Funds.*

Sect. 11. *After publication of statement, Commissioners to frame scheme for charity property.*

Sect. 12. *Every such scheme shall provide—*

(a.) *For the vesting of all real estate in the official trustee of charity lands appointed under the Charitable Trusts Acts, 1853 to 1869, and of all personal estate in the official trustee of charitable funds appointed under the same Acts, subject to all equities, &c.;*

(b.) *For the expenses of Commissioners in carrying out the Act;*

(c.) *For saving or making due compensation for vested interests.*

Sect. 13. *Special provisions to be inserted in schemes relating to parishes in first Schedule.*

Sect. 14. *Special provisions to be inserted in schemes relating to parishes in second Schedule.*

Sect. 15. *Schemes relating to parishes in the first Schedule may provide for union of governing bodies.*

Sect. 16. *Scheme relating to parishes in second schedule may provide for payment of moneys to trustees of existing institutions.*

Sect. 17. *In schemes relating to property, belonging to parishes in second schedule, Commissioners may create new bodies of trustees.*

Sect. 18. *In schemes relating to property belonging to parishes in second Schedule, Commissioners may retain or modify existing bodies of trustees.*

Sect. 19. *More schemes than one may be made, and other objects may be provided for.*

Sect. 20. *Scheme need not specify precise application of general charity property.*

Sect. 21. *No scheme to affect any endowment originally given to charitable uses less than fifty years before the commencement of the Act.*

Sect. 22. *Educational interests of girls as well as boys to be regarded.*

Sect. 23. *Schemes need not be prepared for endowments which are educational endowments within 32 & 33 Vict. c. 56, s. 5.*

IV. *Procedure for Approving Schemes.*

Sect. 24. *Schemes to be printed and sent to governing bodies, and otherwise circulated.*

Sect. 25. *Commissioners to receive and consider suggestions respecting schemes.*

Sect. 26. *Scheme may be revised, reprinted, and circulated anew.*

I. LONDON—CHARITIES—*continued.*

Sect. 27. *Scheme to be submitted to and approved by Committee of Council on Education, and when approved to be published and circulated with notice stating unless within two months after publication of scheme, when approved, a petition is presented to the Committee of Council on Education, such scheme may be approved by Her Majesty without being laid before Parliament.*

Scheme may be laid before Parliament on a petition within said two months to Committee of Council on Education by the governing body or not less than twenty inhabitant ratepayers.

Sect. 28. *Any person aggrieved by any provision of a scheme, on the ground of its not making due compensation for any vested interest to which he has been declared entitled as aforesaid, may petition against the scheme to Her Majesty in Council, and counsel may be heard in support of and against the petition.*

Sect. 29. *Where a scheme is remitted, the Commissioners may amend the scheme or prepare another scheme, subject to the like right of petition to Her Majesty in Council as before directed.*

Sect. 30. *As to laying of schemes before Parliament where a petition has been presented.*

Sect. 31. *Where scheme relates to an endowment producing less than £100 per annum no petition lies to Her Majesty in Council.*

Sect. 32. *On non-approval of scheme by Her Majesty, a new scheme to be prepared.*

Sect. 33. *Schemes may be framed for amending schemes approved under the Act.*

V. *Supplemental Provisions.*

Sect. 34. *No scheme to take effect unless approved by Order in Council.*

Sect. 35. *Effect and operation of scheme when approved.*

Sect. 36. *Order in Council approving scheme to be conclusive evidence of validity of scheme.*

Sect. 37. *Scheme to be approved by three Commissioners before being submitted to Committee of Council on Education.*

Sect. 38 *extends sect. 11 of the Charitable Trusts Act, 1853, and sects. 6, 7, 8, and 9 of Charitable Trusts Act, 1855, to Commissioners appointed under the Act.*

Sect. 39. *Commissioners to have power to direct sale of charity property and invest proceeds.*

Sect. 40. *During the continuance of the power of making schemes under the Act, no Court or Judge shall, with respect to any charity property or endowment which can be dealt with by a scheme under the Act, make any scheme or appoint any new trustee without the consent of the Commissioners.*

Sect. 41. *Persons acquiring rights after the passing of the Act to be subject to schemes. Temporary restrictions on powers of governing bodies.*

Sect. 42. *As to service of notices and documents on governing bodies.*

Sect. 43. *Notices and documents may be sent by post.*

Sect. 44 *provides for the payment of salaries paid and expenses incurred in carrying the Act into effect.*

Sect. 45. *Requisitions, &c., of Commissioners to be made under their seal.*

Sect. 46. *All orders of Commissioners to be subject to provisions of the Charitable Trusts Acts.*

I. LONDON—CHARITIES—continued.

Sect. 47. *Commissioners to make annual report to be laid before Parliament.*

VI. New Governing Body.

Sect. 48. *New governing body to be established, to be called " The Trustees of the London Parochial Charities," and to be a body corporate.*

Sect. 49. *Commissioners to make a scheme for regulating nomination of members of new governing body, &c.*

Sect. 50. *Schemes affecting general charity property to contain no preference for any religious denomination.*

Sect. 51. *Commissioners to determine costs of parliamentary proceedings.*

Sect. 52. *Saving for endowments at Christ's Hospital.*

Sect. 53. *Interpretation of terms.*

Sect. 54. *Act to be construed together with Charitable Trusts Acts, Schedules.*

II. LONDON—COMMISSIONERS OF SEWERS.

—— Power to take Land—57 Geo. 3, c. xxix. —Right of Pre-emption—14 & 15 Vict. c. xci. s. 54.] Two houses adjoining Wood Street, in the city of London, having been destroyed by fire, the outer walls only being left standing, the Commissioners of Sewers adjudicated that it was desirable to widen Wood Street, and that the two houses, and the land on which they stood, projected into and prevented them from widening the street, and that the possession and purchase of those houses was necessary for that purpose, and they directed their solicitor to treat for the purchase. Notice to treat was accordingly given for the whole of the houses. The owners brought their action for an injunction to restrain the Commissioners from proceeding on this notice. It was admitted by the Commissioners that they only meant to use a strip of 5½ feet in breadth for widening the street, and intended to sell the rest without giving the Plaintiffs any option of pre-emption :—*Held*, by Kay, J., and by the Court of Appeal, that the Plaintiffs were entitled to an injunction, for that the adjudication was ultrà vires, the Commissioners having no power to adjudicate that the possession of the whole of a piece of land is necessary for the purpose of improvements when they only intend to use a small part of it for that purpose, though if they made such an adjudication in the belief that they should require the whole for the improvements, the correctness of the adjudication could not be questioned.—If part of a piece of land prevents an improvement, the Commissioners have power to take part compulsorily, their power of proceeding compulsorily not being limited to taking the whole.—Whether the Commissioners, if they only want a part of the site of an existing house for the purpose of an improvement, can adjudicate that the possession and purchase of the whole house are necessary *quære.—Thomas* v. *Daw* (Law Rep. 2 Ch. 1), considered.—By Kay, J., *semble*, that the right of pre-emption given by 57 Geo. 3, c. xxix., s. 96, is not taken away by the City of London Sewers Act, 1851 (14 & 15 Vict. c. xci.), s. 54. GARD *v.* COMMISSIONERS OF SEWERS OF THE CITY OF LONDON - - - 28 Ch. D. 486

LONDON—City of London Court—Warrant of arrest—Service · 10 P. D. 36
See PRACTICE—ADMIRALTY—SERVICE. 1.

LONG TERM—Enlargement into fee
[29 Ch. D. 1007, 1009, n.
See LEASEHOLD—LONG TERM, 1, 2.

LONG VACATION.
See COURT—GAZETTE.

LORD CAIRNS' ACT—Repeal of 28 Ch. D. 103
See DAMAGES—LORD CAIRNS' ACT.

LORD CAMPBELL'S ACT - 25 Ch. D. 409;
[9 Q. B. D. 160
See DAMAGES—LORD CAMPBELL'S ACT. 1, 2.

—— Ship—Jurisdiction of Admiralty Division
[9 P. D. 96; 10 App. Cas. 59
See PRACTICE — ADMIRALTY—JURISDIC-TION. 1.

LOWER CANADA—Law of.
See Cases under COLONIAL LAW—CAN-ADA—QUEBEC.

LUGGAGE—Delivery to passenger—Termination of railway company's risk 14 Q. B. D. 228
See RAILWAY COMPANY — PASSENGER'S LUGGAGE.

LUNACY ORDERS, Nov. 1862, rr. 7, 8 26 Ch. D.
See LUNATIC—PROPERTY. 7. [496

—— 1883, Orders 35, 36, 45 - 23 Ch. D. 577
See LUNATIC—MAINTENANCE. 2.

—— 1883, rr. 61, 62 - 26 Ch. D. 496
See LUNATIC—PROPERTY. 7.

I. LUNATIC—COMMITTEE.

1. —— **Allowance without Account**—*Power to mortgage or deal with Allowance.*] An order was made that the brother of a lunatic, who was committee of his estate, should be allowed to retain the family mansion and grounds and the heirlooms therein for his own occupation and use, and that of his unmarried sisters, and that £4000 a year should be allowed him for his expenses in reference thereto. The committee with his sisters occupied the mansion accordingly, and incurred heavy and, as it was alleged, unreasonable expenses about the establishment. The income being insufficient to pay the allowance, it fell into arrear, and the committee mortgaged the arrears. He subsequently was removed from being committee and became bankrupt, and a large amount of bills incurred in keeping up the establishment remained unpaid. A surplus having arisen applicable to payment of the arrears, the new committee presented a petition for direction as to its application :—*Held*, that although the allowance was made to the former committee without any obligation to account, and with an intention indirectly to confer a benefit on him and his

2 E 2

I. LUNATIC—COMMITTEE—continued.

sisters, still it was an allowance made to a person in a fiduciary position for a particular purpose, and which he had no right to mortgage, and that the mortgagee could stand in no better position than the committee himself :—Held, also, that the person to whom an allowance of this kind is made has no such right to arrears as will prevent the Court from dealing with them in such way as it may consider just, and, if the Court finds that the expenses incurred for the purposes for which the allowance was granted remain unpaid, it will stop the arrears, and make provision for payment of such expenses.—An inquiry was therefore directed as to which of the debts of the committee were properly incurred in keeping up the establishment at the mansion. *In re* WELD **20 Ch. D. 451**

2. —— **Appointment out of Jurisdiction.**] It being proposed to appoint as committee a person resident out of the jurisdiction, the Master in Lunacy reported that as the proposed committee was resident out of the jurisdiction he could not approve of him. The Court, though satisfied of the expediency of appointing him, declined to do so until the Master had certified that the proposed committee was a person whom, if resident within the jurisdiction, he should have approved. *In re* BRUÈRE - **17 Ch. D. 775**

3. —— **Bankruptcy**—*Adjudication in Bankruptcy.*] Leave given to the committee of the estate of a lunatic trader to consent to an adjudication in bankruptcy against the lunatic. *In re* LEE - ·· **23 Ch. D. 216**

4. —— **Bankruptcy**—*Leave to Committee to file Declaration of Insolvency—Bankruptcy Act, 1883 (46 & 47 Vict. c. 52), ss. 4, sub-s. 1 (f), 148.*] Where it appears to be for the benefit of a lunatic that he should be made bankrupt, the Court will give leave to the committee in the name of the lunatic to file a declaration of insolvency, or to present a bankruptcy petition under the Bankruptcy Act, 1883, s. 4, sub-s. 1 (f). *In re* JAMES **[12 Q. B. D. 332**

5. —— **Execution of Lease.**] By a lease expressed to be made between a lunatic by A. B. and C. D., his two committees, and other parties, the lunatic acting by his committees demised. The testimonium clause was " In witness whereof the said parties to these presents have hereunto set their hands and seals." A. B. signed his name against one seal and C. D. his against another; and the attestation clause was "signed, sealed, and delivered by A. B. and C. D. in the presence of &c." :—Held (affirming the decision of the Court of Appeal) that the lease was well executed on behalf of the lunatic. LAWRIE *v.* LEES **[7 App. Cas. 19**

II. LUNATIC—CRIMINAL.

The Act 46 & 47 Vict. c. 38 (*the Trial of Lunatics Act, 1883*), amends the law respecting the trial and custody of insane persons charged with offences.

Sect. 2.—(1.) *Where in any indictment or information any act or omission is charged against any person as an offence, and it is given in evidence on the trial of such person for that offence that he was insane, so as not to be responsible, according to law, for his actions at the time when the act was done or omission made, then, if it appears to the*

II. LUNATIC—CRIMINAL—continued.

jury before whom such person is tried that he did the act or made the omission charged, but was insane as aforesaid at the time when he did or made the same, the jury shall return a special verdict to the effect that the accused was guilty of the act or omission charged against him, but was insane as aforesaid at the time when he did the act or made the omission.

(2.) *Where such special verdict is found, the Court shall order the accused to be kept in custody as a criminal lunatic, in such place and in such manner as the Court shall direct till Her Majesty's pleasure shall be known ; and it shall be lawful for Her Majesty thereupon, and from time to time, to give such order for the safe custody of the said person during pleasure, and in such place and in such manner as to Her Majesty may seem fit.*

(3.) *Repealed by the Act 47 & 48 Vict. c. 64.*

(4.) *All provisions in any existing Act or in any rules or orders made in pursuance of any existing Act, having reference to a person or persons acquitted on the ground of insanity, shall apply to a person or persons in respect of whom a special verdict is found under this Act.*

Sect. 4 repeals 39 & 40 Geo. 3, c. 94, s. 1 ; 1 & 2 Geo. 4, c. 33, s. 16 ; and 3 & 4 Vict. c. 54, s. 3 ; but any unrepealed enactment referring to any enactment thereby repealed, shall be construed to apply to the corresponding provisions of the Act.

Act of 1884.] *The Act 47 & 48 Vict. c. 64* (*Criminal Lunatics Act, 1884*), consolidates and amends the law relating to criminal lunatics.

Sect. 2. *Where it appears to any two members of the visiting committee of a prison that a prisoner is insane, they shall with two medical practitioners examine such prisoner, and may certify in writing that he is insane. The Secretary of State may by warrant direct such prisoner to be removed to an asylum, and, subject to the provisions of this Act relating to discharge, the prisoner shall be detained in such asylum. Provision for prisoner under sentence of death.*

Sect. 3. *A criminal lunatic found to be sane shall be remitted to prison.*

Sect. 16. " *Prison*" *means any prison or place of confinement to which a person may be committed whether on remand or for trial, safe custody, or punishment, or otherwise, under any other than civil process ; and "prisoner" means any person so committed. "Asylum," means an asylum within 16 & 17 Vict. c. 97, and an asylum for criminal lunatics within 23 & 24 Vict. c. 75, and includes a hospital registered for the reception of lunatics, but does not include a licensed house. Such hospital as above is not obliged to receive a criminal lunatic.*

Sect. 4. *A periodical report of criminal lunatics shall be made to the Secretary of State.*

Sect. 5. *A Secretary of State may transfer or discharge (absolutely or conditionally) a criminal lunatic, or by warrant cause him to be again taken into custody. See 23 & 24 Vict. c. 75, s. 9, 27 & 28 Vict. c. 29, s. 2, and 30 Vict. c. 12, ss. 4, 5.*

Sect. 6. *On expiration of sentence the superintendent of the asylum shall, unless satisfied that the person is sane, place him in care of friends or in a lunatic asylum.*

Sect. 7 —(1.) *Where a person being a criminal lunatic is detained in an asylum or other place,*

II. LUNATIC—CRIMINAL—*continued.*

or being a prisoner in a prison is certified in manner provided in this Act to be insane, but has not been directed by the Secretary of State to be removed to an asylum, and it is made to appear to any justice of the peace having jurisdiction where such asylum or place or prison is situate, or being a member of the visiting committee of such prison, by notice in writing signed by the superintendent of such asylum or place, or by the governor of such prison, either—

　(a.) that such person is about to be absolutely discharged ; or

　(b.) that any term of penal servitude or imprisonment to which such person is subject is about to determine,

and that in the opinion of such superintendent or governor such person is insane and unfit to be at large, the said justice shall examine such person and make any inquiry and take any medical or other evidence which he may deem necessary respecting him.

　(2.) The said justice, if satisfied on such examination and inquiry that such person is insane and a proper person to be detained under care and treatment, shall make an order for his detention as a lunatic in the asylum or place of confinement for lunatics named in the order ; and if within one month after the date of the said notice such criminal lunatic is absolutely discharged, or such term of penal servitude or imprisonment determines, the said order shall thereupon take effect, and he shall be deemed to be a pauper lunatic.

　(3.) An order under this section shall be in such form as may be prescribed by a Secretary of State, and there shall be inserted in every such order, wherever it be possible, the name and address of one or more of the relations of the lunatic.

　(4.) At any time before a person for whose detention an order is made under this section is detained in an asylum or place of confinement for lunatics in pursuance thereof, such order may be amended or cancelled and a new order made by the justice who made the original order, or, if such justice is unable to act, by any other justice having jurisdiction in the same place.

　Sect. 8.—(1.) Where by virtue of an order made by a justice under this Act a person becomes a pauper lunatic, such person shall for the purposes of this Act be deemed to be prima facie chargeable to the union or parish in the United Kingdom in which it appears to the justice making the order that the ordinary residence of such person was situate at the time when the offence in respect of which he became a criminal lunatic was alleged to have been committed, and, if such residence is not shewn to the satisfaction of the said justice, then to such union or parish in the United Kingdom as follows, namely,—

　(a.) To that in which it appears to the said justice that the said offence was alleged to have been committed ; or

　(b.) If it appears that the offence was alleged to have been committed out of the United Kingdom, to that in which it appears to the said justice, that such person was first apprehended for such offence ; or

　(c.) If such person appears to have been so apprehended out of the United Kingdom, to that in which it appears to the said justice

II. LUNATIC—CRIMINAL—*continued.*

　that such person first landed in the United Kingdom :

　Provided that, if such person appears to the justice making the order to have been a man in the naval or military service of Her Majesty, or to have been the wife or infant child of a man in such naval or military service, at the time when the offence was alleged to have been committed, such person shall for the purposes of this Act be deemed to be prima facie chargeable to the union or parish in the United Kingdom to which the man in such naval or military service appears to the said justice from the statements in the declaration made on his entry in the naval service of Her Majesty, or in his attestation paper on enlistment, or from other available information, to be by law chargeable for the purposes of the Acts relating to the relief of the poor.

　(2.) Subject as hereinafter mentioned, an order made by a justice under this Act for the detention of a person as a lunatic shall, on such person becoming a pauper lunatic, have the same effect as an order of a justice, and medical certificate, made in pursuance of section sixty-eight of 16 & 17 Vict. c. 97 (the Lunatic Asylums Act, 1853), in the case of a lunatic found wandering at large in the union or parish to which such person is prima facie chargeable, and all the provisions of 8 & 9 Vict. c. 100 (the Lunacy Act, 1845), and of 16 & 17 Vict. c. 97 (the Lunatic Asylums Act, 1853), and of any Acts amending those Acts, or either of them, shall apply accordingly in like manner as if such person had been sent from that union or parish :

　And such person on becoming a pauper lunatic, if detained in an asylum or place of confinement to which lunatics may be sent in pursuance of the said Lunatic Asylums Act, 1853, shall be deemed to have been received therein in pursuance of the said order of detention, and if detained elsewhere shall be removed by a person named in the order. or any constable, to the asylum or place of confinement for lunatics named in the order, being one to which a justice can send a lunatic found wandering at large in the aforesaid union or parish :

　Provided that if such pauper lunatic is certified by a legally qualified medical practitioner to be unfit for removal to such last-mentioned asylum or place of confinement, he may either be removed to and detained in any nearer asylum or place of confinement for lunatics willing to receive him, or may be detained in any asylum or place in which a criminal lunatic may be detained, but in either case he shall be deemed to have been sent to the asylum or place of confinement in which he is so detained, in pursuance of section sixty-eight of the Lunatic Asylums Act, 1853, and the expenses incurred in relation to such lunatic shall be defrayed, and the lunatic, when fit to be removed, may be removed accordingly, and where the lunatic is detained in any asylum or place to which lunatics cannot be sent, in pursuance of the Lunatic Asylums Act, 1853, the provisions of the above-mentioned Acts shall apply as if such asylum or place were an asylum within the meaning of the Lunatic Asylums Act, 1853, and the council of supervision or other persons having control thereof were visitors.

　Sub-sects. (3), (4), and (5), refer to cases where the union chargeable is in Scotland or Ireland.

　Sect. 9 regulates the transfer by warrant of a

II. LUNATIC—CRIMINAL—continued.

Secretary of State, and the removal by order of a justice under this Act, of a person from a criminal lunatic asylum under 23 & 24 Vict. c. 75, to an asylum under 16 & 17 Vict. c. 97.

Sect. 10—(1.) Subject as in this section mentioned, all expenses incurred under this Act in relation to a criminal lunatic while detained in an asylum, and all expenses of removing a person on his becoming under this Act a pauper lunatic to an asylum or place of confinement for lunatics in any part of the United Kingdom, shall be defrayed out of moneys provided by Parliament, and the costs of maintenance of a criminal lunatic in any asylum within the meaning of the Lunatic Asylums Act, 1853, shall be at the same rate as if he was a lunatic sent from a union or parish situate elsewhere than in the county or borough to which the asylum belongs.

(2.) Where a person, being a criminal lunatic, is absolutely discharged before the expiration of any term of penal servitude or imprisonment to which he is subject, or is conditionally discharged in pursuance of this Act, the Commissioners of Her Majesty's Treasury may from time to time contribute, out of moneys provided by Parliament, such sum or sums, on the recommendation of a Secretary of State, as they from time to time think fit towards the costs of the maintenance of such person, until the expiration of the said sentence, or so long as he continues to be subject to any conditions of discharge (as the case may be).

(3.) Sect. 104 of the Lunatic Asylums Act, 1853, with respect to the application of the property of a lunatic for his maintenance and for the other charges in the said section mentioned, and the other sections of the Lunatic Asylums Act, 1853, which are ancillary to the said sect. 104, shall extend to a criminal lunatic wherever he may be detained, and to his property, in like manner as if the said sections were herein re-enacted, and in terms made applicable thereto, and any power exercisable by justices under the said section may, for the purposes of this section, be exercised by two justices of the county or place where such lunatic is detained.

The Lord Chancellor, or other authority having power to make orders with respect to the property of a lunatic, under sects. 12, 13, and 14 of the Lunacy Regulation Act, 1862, shall, if satisfied by affidavit or otherwise that a person is or has been a criminal lunatic, and continues to be insane and to be in confinement, have power to make any such order with respect to the property of such person, and the application thereof for the maintenance or benefit of him or his family, or for carrying on his trade or business, as may be made in pursuance of the said sections of the Lunacy Regulation Act, 1862.

(4.) When the criminal lunatic was a person removed from India in pursuance of the Lunatics Removal (India) Act, 1851, all expenses attending the removal of any such person from India, and his safe custody and maintenance, shall continue to be defrayed in the same manner as if this Act had not been passed.

Sect. 11. Sects. 11 and 12 of 23 & 24 Vict. c. 75 (the Criminal Lunatic Asylums Act, 1860), referring to recapture of escaped lunatics, &c., apply to every asylum for criminal lunatics.

Sect. 12 refers to regulations for persons in

II. LUNATIC—CRIMINAL—continued.

prisons (not necessarily lunatics) suffering from imbecility of mind.

Sect. 13. Saving of authority of Crown to make orders with respect to safe custody of persons.

Sect. 14. Provisions as to existing criminal lunatics.

Sect. 15. The warrant under this Act to be under the hand of a Secretary of State or of an Under-Secretary of State, and to be executed by the person to whom addressed, or by a constable.

Repeal.] By sect. 17 the following Acts or portions of Acts are repealed:—3 & 4 Vict. c. 54; 6 & 7 Vict. c. 26, s. 21; 16 & 17 Vict. c. 96, part of s. 38; 23 & 24 Vict. c. 75, part of s. 2, and ss. 7, 9, and 10; 25 & 26 Vict. c. 86, s. 15; 27 & 28 Vict. c. 29; 29 & 30 Vict. c. 109, part of s. 80; 30 & 31 Vict. c. 22; 32 & 33 Vict. c. 78; 44 & 45 Vict. c. 58, part of s. 130; 46 & 47 Vict. c. 38, s. 2, sub-s. 3.

—— County Rate—Maintenance—Upon what Funds chargeable—3 & 4 Vict. c. 54, s. 2—27 & 28 Vict. c. 29, s. 2—Prison Act, 1877 (40 & 41 Vict. c. 21), ss. 4, 57.] When a pauper prisoner without a settlement becomes insane during confinement in a prison to which the Prison Act, 1877 (40 & 41 Vict. c. 21) applies, the expenses of inquiring into his insanity and of removing him to a county lunatic asylum and of his maintenance in such asylum during the currency of his sentence are, by sects. 4 and 57 of that Act, to be defrayed out of moneys provided by Parliament; and the effect of those sections is to repeal the provisions of 3 & 4 Vict. c. 54, s. 2, which made the county liable.—So held, reversing the decision of the Court of Appeal. THE QUEEN v. MEWS   6 Q. B. D. 47; [8 App. Cas. 339

III. LUNATIC—CUSTODY—Order for Detention —Order for Discharge—8 & 9 Vict. c. 100, ss. 72, 99—16 & 17 Vict. c. 96, s. 4, sched. A, No. 1.] The Plaintiff was detained in a private asylum for lunatics, of which the Defendant was superintendent, under an order signed by her husband. In the statement annexed to the order the question " Whether first attack," was answered thus : " For the last twenty years has been subject to what is termed hysteria;" and the question, " When and where previously under care and treatment," was answered, "During this period of twenty years has been constantly under treatment ":—Held, that the order, together with the statement, was sufficient under 16 & 17 Vict. c. 96, s. 4, sched. A (No. 1), and afforded a defence under 8 & 9 Vict. c. 100, s. 99, to an action for assault and false imprisonment.—The Plaintiff's husband, having received a letter from the Commissioners in Lunacy intimating that she ought to be discharged, wrote to the Defendant as follows : " After the Commissioners' letter I suppose that I must consent to Mrs. Lowe's discharge, and beg you will carry out their suggestion as soon as you may think it advisable ":—Held, that the letter of the Plaintiff's husband was not an order of discharge within 8 & 9 Vict. c. 100, s. 72. LOWE v. FOX - - - - 15 Q. B. D. 667

IV. LUNATIC—DECEASED LUNATIC.

—— Inspection of Documents — Practice — Order to inspect Documents by a Person claiming

IV. LUNATIC—DECEASED LUNATIC—contd.

under a Deceased Lunatic.] A lunatic having died intestate, and an action having been commenced for recovery of his real estate :—*Held,* that the Defendant, who produced primâ facie evidence of his being heir-at-law of the lunatic, was entitled to an order to inspect the documents relating to the estate which were in the custody of the Registrars in Lunacy, although it was sworn on the other side, and not contradicted, that the lands had descended to the lunatic from his mother, and that the Defendant was no relation to the mother. *In re* SMYTH - 16 Ch. D. 673

V. LUNATIC—INQUISITION.

——— *Access to alleged Lunatic—Order for Visitors in Lunacy to see the alleged Lunatic—Inquiry in London as to State of Mind of Person in the Country.*] A petition for an inquiry into the state of mind of an alleged lunatic having been presented, and disputes having arisen as to the terms under which access of medical witnesses should be allowed, the Court made an order that two of the visitors in lunacy should see the alleged lunatic and report to the Court.—The rule is not inflexible that an inquiry by a jury as to the state of mind of an alleged lunatic must take place near his place of residence, and there being reason to believe that a strong local feeling as to the proceedings existed in the neighbourhood where the alleged lunatic resided, the inquiry was directed to be held in London.— When the medical witnesses for the alleged lunatic had seen her alone it was held that they were not entitled to be present when the medical witnesses for the Petitioner saw her. *In re* ANON., AN ALLEGED LUNATIC - 18 Ch. D. 26

2. ——— **Inquiry before Judge of High Court**—*Lunacy Regulation Act,* 1862 (25 & 26 *Vict.* c. 86), *s.* 4—8 & 9 *Vict.* c. 109, s. 19.] When an issue is directed by an order in Lunacy to try the question of the insanity of an alleged lunatic before a Judge of the High Court of Justice under the Lunacy Regulation Act, 1862, sect. 4, it is not necessary to commence the proceedings by a writ of summons, the order for the issue being sufficient to give jurisdiction to the Judge. *In re* SCOTT - - - 27 Ch. D. 116

3. ——— **Inquiry when Lunacy commenced**—*Lunacy Regulation Act,* 1862 (25 & 26 *Vict.* c. 86), *s.* 3.] The Lunacy Regulation Act, 1862, s. 3, takes away the power existing under the Lunacy Regulation Act, 1853, s. 47, of directing an inquiry from what time an alleged lunatic has been of unsound mind.—Opinion expressed by James, L.J., in *In re Sottomaior* (Law Rep. 9 Ch. 677) dissented from. *In re* DANBY - 30 Ch. D. 320

VI. LUNATIC—JURISDICTION.

The Act 45 & 46 *Vict.* c. 82 (*the Lunacy Regulation Amendment Act,* 1882), amends the Lunacy Regulation Acts.

Sect. 2. The Act to be construed as one with the 16 & 17 *Vict.* c. 70, *and* 25 & 26 *Vict.* c. 86 (*the Lunacy Regulation Acts,* 1853 and 1862).

By sect. 3 the 12th section of the Lunacy Regulation Act, 1862, *is to have effect as though the words "two thousand pounds in value" had been inserted therein instead of "one thousand in*

VI. LUNATIC—JURISDICTION—continued.

value," and the words "one hundred pounds per annum" instead of "fifty pounds per annum."

By sect. 4 the 20th section of the Lunacy Regulation Act, 1862, *is to be construed as if the word "twice" had been inserted therein instead of "four times," and as if the words "eight months" had been inserted therein instead of the words "four months," and as if instead of the proviso therein there had been inserted the following words : provided always, that every lunatic resident in a private house shall, during the two years next following inquisition, be so visited at least four times in every year.*

Pauper Lunatic.] *The Act* 48 & 49 *Vict.* c. 52, enacts :—

Sect. 2. Where a pauper lunatic or other person liable to be apprehended under 16 & 17 *Vict.* c. 97, *by order of a justice or otherwise, requires immediate control, the relieving officer may remove him to the workhouse and carry out the requirements of the statute afterwards.*

Sect. 3 (1). Lunatics liable under 16 & 17 *Vict.* c. 97, *ss. 67 and 68 to be removed to any asylum, may by order of a justice be removed to the workhouse instead.*

(2.) *Limits of such detention.*

Sect. 4. Construction of Act.

1. ——— **Irish Inquisition**—*Transcript of Record —Jurisdiction of English Court over Proceedings in Ireland—Lunacy Regulation Act,* 1853 (16 & 17 *Vict.* c. 70, *ss.* 41, 52).] Where an order in lunacy has been made in Ireland by the Court having jurisdiction for that purpose, and a transcript of the record has, under the provisions of sect. 52 of the Lunacy Regulation Act, 1853, been transmitted to this country, the English Court must treat the order as a binding order, and has no jurisdiction to entertain an application either for the purpose of setting aside the proceedings in Ireland, or for a supersedeas. Any such application must be made to the Court which originally made the order.—The right of an alleged lunatic to demand a jury is confined to the original inquiry. *In re* TALBOT - 20 Ch. D. 269

2. ——— **Justices**—*Lunatic Asylums Act,* 1853 (16 & 17 *Vict.* c. 97), *s.* 68—*Personal Examination by Justices of alleged Lunatic.*] In order to give two justices jurisdiction to make an order under sect. 68 of the Lunatic Asylums Act, 1853, for the reception of a person into a lunatic asylum as a lunatic who is not a pauper, and not wandering at large, but who is not under proper care and control, it is not necessary that they should examine such person in the presence of the medical man whom they have called to their assistance, nor that the examination should be made with the knowledge of the alleged lunatic, so that he should have the opportunity of explaining, if he could, what might otherwise be signs of insanity. Though his examination must not be a sham, yet if it be made by the justices bonâ fide for the purpose of satisfying themselves of the sanity or insanity of the person examined, it is sufficient, and their order is not without jurisdiction because the examination lasted only four or five minutes and was made at the door of the carriage in which the alleged lunatic was seated with his attendants preparatory to his being taken to the

VI. LUNATIC—JURISDICTION—continued.

asylum:—So held by Sir James Hannen and Lindley, L.J. (Lord Coleridge, C.J., dissenting):—Held, by Lord Coleridge, C.J., that where the person deemed to be a lunatic is examined by two justices at his place of abode or elsewhere, the 68th section requires that one of such two justices must already have had, as a condition precedent to the vesting of the jurisdiction of the justices, either an information upon oath or private or personal knowledge of his own as to the insanity of such person. THE QUEEN v. WHITFIELD

[15 Q. B. D. 122

3. —— Married Woman—Power of Election—Person of Unsound Mind.] If a married woman who is entitled to exercise an election is of unsound mind the Court will make an election on her behalf, it having jurisdiction to bind the equitable interests of lunatics, not so found by inquisition, when it appears to be for their benefit. Jones v. Lloyd (Law Rep. 18 Eq. 265) followed. WILDER v. PIGOTT　-　-　22 Ch. D. 263

4. —— Parties entitled to attend Proceedings —Illegitimate Person—Attorney-General—Attorney-General of Duchy of Lancaster.] A lunatic, who was illegitimate and unmarried, was resident in Lancashire, and part of her property consisted of copyholds held of the Duchy of Lancaster:—Held, that the Attorney-General of the Duchy of Lancaster was not entitled to attend the proceedings in the lunacy; the Queen's rights being sufficiently represented by the Queen's Attorney-General, who had leave to attend. In re KERSHAW　-　21 Ch. D. 613

5. —— Trustee Relief Act.] Where a person who has been found lunatic is entitled to a fund which has been paid into Court under the Trustee Relief Act, a petition may be presented in Chancery under the Trustee Relief Act and in Lunacy, and the Court has jurisdiction to make an immediate order for the transfer of the fund to the account of the lunatic. In re TATE

[20 Ch. D. 135

VII. LUNATIC—MAINTENANCE.

1. —— Allowance for past Maintenance — Out of what Fund—Statute of Limitations—Supply of Necessaries to Lunatic.] Where a lunatic has property to which he is entitled for life under a settlement as well as property to which he is absolutely entitled, the Court will apply the life interest in the first place towards his maintenance ; unless the trustees of the settled property have an absolute discretion whether to employ the whole or any part of the income for the lunatic's benefit.—Therefore where property was held upon trust to pay the income in such way, at such time, and in such manner as the trustees should think fit towards the maintenance of a lunatic during her life, with power to invest any surplus not required for the purpose as capital, it was held that the trustees had no such discretion as would oust the jurisdiction of the Court to apply the whole of the income in the lunatic's maintenance in exoneration of her absolute property.—Gisborne v. Gisborne (2 App. Cas. 300) distinguished.—The brother of a lunatic lady not so found by inquisition advanced money for the maintenance of his sister for several years under circumstances which

VII. LUNATIC—MAINTENANCE—continued.

left it doubtful whether he intended it for a gift or expected to be repaid. He died, and his sister was then found to be lunatic by inquisition. His executors having brought in a claim against the lunatic's estate for repayment of the advances, the Court made an allowance to the testator's estate for past maintenance, but limited it to advances made within six years before the testator's death. —Whether a person who supplies a lunatic with necessaries, knowing him to be lunatic, can maintain an action against him on the ground of an implied contract quære. In re WEAVER

[21 Ch. D. 615

2. —— Creditors, Rights of—Maintenance, past and Future—Insolvent Estate—16 & 17 Vict. c. 70, s. 116— 25 & 26 Vict. c. 86, s. 16—Lunacy Orders, 1883, Orders 35, 36, 45.] In managing the estates of lunatics the Court will have regard to the maintenance and comfort of the lunatic in preference to the claims of his creditors, although the estate be insolvent. The Master in Lunacy made a certificate finding that the property of a lunatic produced an income of £163, and that his debts amounted to £7000, including £250 for his past maintenance in an asylum, and £374 for the past maintenance of his wife and children expended by the committee :—Held, on a summons taken out under Order 45 of the Lunacy Orders, 1883, on which some of the ordinary creditors appeared and claimed payment of their debts, that the expenses of past maintenance of the lunatic, his wife and children, must be paid in full, that capital producing £110 a year should be set aside for the lunatic's future maintenance, and that the residue should be divided among the ordinary creditors pro ratâ, who were to have a charge on the reserved capital, with liberty to apply on the lunatic's death. In re PINK

[23 Ch. D. 577

3. —— Pauper—Expenses of Maintenance—Right of Poor Law Guardians to recover against Estate of Lunatic after his Death—Lunatic Asylums Act, 1853 (16 & 17 Vict. c. 97), ss. 94, 104.] A pauper lunatic having died seised of a small amount of real estate :—Held, that the amount of sums paid by guardians of the union to which the pauper was chargeable (though not the union in which he died), in respect of his maintenance at a lunatic asylum, was a debt recoverable in a creditor's action against his personal and real representatives, though no steps to recover payment of expenses incurred in respect of such maintenance were taken by the guardians in the pauper's lifetime. In re WEBSTER. GUARDIANS OF DERBY UNION v. SHARRATT　27 Ch. D. 710

VIII. LUNATIC—PROPERTY.

1. —— Allowance—Divorced Wife—Permanent Alimony—Assignment—20 & 21 Vict. c. 85, s. 25.] On a decree for judicial separation an order was made for payment of £60 a year to the wife as permanent alimony. The husband was afterwards found lunatic by inquisition, and by an order in Lunacy and Chancery the dividends of a sum of stock to which he was entitled in a Chancery suit were ordered to be carried to his account in the lunacy and £60 a year to be paid out of them to his wife in respect of her alimony

VIII. LUNATIC—PROPERTY—*continued.*

till further order. The wife assigned the annuity to a purchaser, who presented a petition in Lunacy and in the suit to have the annuity paid to her :—*Held*, that the petition must be refused, on the ground that whether the annuity was considered as alimony *or* as an allowance made to the wife by the Court in Lunacy, it was not assignable. *In re* ROBINSON - -· **27 Ch. D. 160**

2. —— **Allowance** — *Poor Relations.*] The income of a lunatic being much more than was required for his maintenance, a respectable aged clergyman, a first cousin, and one of the next of kin of the lunatic, who had been reduced to indigence by unavoidable misfortune, applied for an allowance out of the surplus income. It was not shewn that the lunatic had ever known of the existence of the applicant, and it was not suggested that any evidence could be obtained that the lunatic, when sane, had ever done anything for him *or* expressed any intention in his favour :—*Held*, that the application must be refused.—The practice of granting allowances out of a lunatic's property to relations for whom he is under no legal obligation to provide, is rather to be narrowed than to be extended. *In re* EVANS
[**21 Ch. D. 297**

3. —— **Allowance** — *Tenant in Tail in remainder—Next of Kin not consenting—Allowance sanctioned upon Terms—Charge on Inheritance—Protector of Settlement.*] A lunatic, aged sixty-four, was tenant for life of certain real estates, of which his nephew, aged twenty-eight, was tenant in tail in remainder, producing a considerable yearly income. The nephew had been found heir-at-law and one of the next of kin of the lunatic.—The Court upon the nephew's petition, directed an allowance of £500 per annum to be made to him out of the surplus income of the lunatic after providing for a yearly sum for the lunatic's maintenance, in spite of the opposition of some of the next of kin, upon the terms of the Petitioner charging the estate with the repayment of the sums received in respect of such allowance, the Lords Justices consenting as protector of the settlement to the Petitioner barring his estate tail, but only so far as to let in the charge. *In re* SPARROW - - **20 Ch. D. 320**

4. —— **Copyhold**—*Enfranchisement—Devolution of Enfranchised Estate.*] The Court on sanctioning proceedings for carrying into effect the enfranchisement of a copyhold estate belonging to a lunatic, the rules of descent as to which were different from those as to the descent of freeholds, made a declaration that in the event of his dying intestate as to the enfranchised property his heir-at-law would stand seised thereof in trust for the person who would have been entitled thereto as his heir according to the custom of the manor if it had not been enfranchised. *In re* H. D. RYDER
[**20 Ch. D. 514**

5. —— **Debenture**—*Lunacy Regulation Act,* 1853 (16 & 17 *Vict. c.* 70), *s.* 141.] A debenture bond of a limited company, according to the constitution of which debentures were transferred by deed, and the deeds of transfer upon presentation to the company were registered in the company's book of mortgages, ordered to be transferred under

VIII. LUNATIC—PROPERTY—*continued.*

sect. 141 of the Lunacy Regulation Act, 1853.. *In re* MITCHELL - - - **17 Ch. D. 515**

6. —— **Expenses of Improvements**—*Lunacy Regulation Act,* 1853 (16 & 17 *Vict. c.* 70), *s.* 118.] A lunatic was tenant for life of the H. estate, and tenant in tail in possession of the D. estate. Expenses were incurred by the committee in improvements on both estates, but chiefly on the former :—*Held*, that there was no jurisdiction to charge the D. estate with the expenses incurred on the H. estate. *In re* VAVASOUR **29 Ch. D. 306**

7. —— **Property of Small Amount**—*Petition for Application of Income—Opposition by alleged Lunatic—Jurisdiction—Lunacy Regulation Act,* 1862 (25 & 26 *Vict. c* 86), *s.* 12—*General Orders in Lunacy, Nov.* 1862, *rr.* 7, 8—*Lunacy Orders,* 1883, *rr.* 61, 62.] The power given to the Lord Chancellor, by sect. 12 of the Lunacy Regulation Act, 1862 (extended by sect. 3 of the Lunacy Regulation Amendment Act, 1882), to make an order for the application of the property of a person of unsound mind for his maintenance or benefit, when the property is below a specified amount, without directing any inquiry under a commission of lunacy, ought not, even if the jurisdiction extends in cases in which the alleged lunatic appears and denies unsoundness of mind, to be exercised in such cases. *In re* LEES - **26 Ch. D. 496**

8. —— **Sale under Lands Clauses Act** (8 & 9 *Vict. c.* 18), *s.* 7—*Purchase of Land of Lunatic not so found—Conversion—Real and Personal Representatives.*] Sect. 7 of the Lands Clauses Consolidation Act, 1845, does not authorize a person of unsound mind to sell land to a company or public body who have statutory power to take it ; the section only authorizes the committee of a lunatic to sell.—A public body having given notice under their statutory powers to take land belonging to a lady of unsound mind not so found, the value of the land was ascertained by two surveyors, one appointed by an uncle of the lady, who purported to act on her behalf, and the other by the public body ; the sum thus ascertained was paid into Court, and the public body took possession of the land. The lady afterwards died intestate, being still of unsound mind, and her heir-at-law petitioned for payment of the money to him :—*Held*, that the land had never been converted into personalty, and that the heir was entitled to the money.—*Ex parte* Flamank (1 Sim. (N.S.) 260) dissented from. *In re* TUGWELL **27 Ch. D. 309**

9. —— **Sale under Partition Act**—*Conversion —Real and Personal Representatives—Partition Act,* 1868 (31 & 32 *Vict. c.* 40), *s.* 8—*Settled Estates Act* (19 & 20 *Vict. c.* 120), *s.* 23.] By an order made in a partition suit a share of real estate belonging to a lunatic was sold, and the proceeds paid into Court to the credit of the matter of the lunacy, but they were not carried to a real estate account.—The lunatic died intestate, and his administrator claimed the money as part of the lunatic's personal estate :—*Held*, that the money retained the character of real estate, and passed to the lunatic's heir-at-law.—The words of the 23rd section of the Settled Estates Act when imported into the 8th section of the Partition Act are not to be restricted to a sale

VIII. LUNATIC—PROPERTY—*continued.*

of estates in settlement, but apply to all sales effected under the Partition Act.—The payment of the money into Court to the credit of the lunacy was not a payment "to a person becoming absolutely entitled" within the meaning of the 23rd section of the Settled Estates Act. *In re* BARKER
[17 Ch. D. 241

10. —— **Sale of Share in Real Estate**—*Lunacy Regulation Act,* 1853 (16 & 17 *Vict.* c. 70), *ss.* 116, 124.] The 124th section of the Lunacy Regulation Act, 1853, does not give jurisdiction to authorize the committee of a lunatic to sell the lunatic's undivided share of land to the owner of the other shares. *In re* WELD - -   28 Ch. D. 514

—— Powers of committee.
See Cases under LUNATIC—COMMITTEE.

LUNATIC—Business carried on in name of firm —Service on manager   10 Q. B. D. 471
See PRACTICE—SUPREME COURT—SERVICE. 1.

—— Government annuity—Payment.
See NATIONAL DEBT COMMISSIONERS— *Statutes.*

—— Illegitimacy—Suit to perpetuate testimony
[9 P. D. 120
See PRACTICE—DIVORCE—EVIDENCE. 2.

—— India -   -   -   - 7 Q. B. D. 18
See CRIMINAL LAW—PRACTICE. 1.

LUNATIC—*continued.*

—— Married woman—Power of Court to elect for
[22 Ch. D. 263
See SETTLEMENT—FUTURE PROPERTY. 3.

—— New trustee—Deceased lunatic
[23 Ch. D. 217; 24 Ch. D. 271
See TRUSTEE ACTS—NEW TRUSTEES. 1, 4.

—— Removal—Separation of husband and wife
[11 Q. B. D. 113
See POOR LAW—SETTLEMENT. 9.

—— Sale of stock—Ademption of legacy
See WILL—ADEMPTION. [22 Ch. D. 622

—— Tenant for life—Powers of.
See SETTLED LAND ACT—STATUTES.

—— Tenant for life—Settled Land Act
[25 Ch. D. 464
See SETTLED LAND ACT—DISABILITIES. 2.

—— Title deeds—Inspection—Custody of Court
[11 Q. B. D. 370
See PRACTICE—SUPREME COURT—PRODUCTION OF DOCUMENTS. 17.

—— Trustee—Vesting order.
See Cases under TRUSTEE ACTS—VESTING ORDERS. 6—9.

LUNATIC REMOVAL (INDIA) ACT, 1851.
See LUNATIC—CRIMINAL—*Statutes.*

M.

MAIN ROAD — Expenses of maintenance and repair.
> See Cases under HIGHWAY — REPAIR. 1—7.

MAINTENANCE.
—— Children.
> See Cases under INFANT—MAINTENANCE.
—— Children—By married woman.
> See HUSBAND AND WIFE — MARRIED WOMEN'S PROPERTY ACTS—Statutes.
—— Children—Clause in settlement 22 Ch. D. 521
> See SETTLEMENT—POWERS. 5.
—— Children—Divorce—Security by Respondent
> [8 P. D. 161
> See PRACTICE—DIVORCE—CUSTODY OF CHILDREN.
—— Children—Legacy—Vesting 16 Ch. D. 44, 47
> See WILL—VESTING. 3, 5.
—— Lunatic - 21 Ch. D. 615; 23 Ch. D. 577;
> [27 Ch. D. 710
> See LUNATIC—MAINTENANCE. 1, 2, 3.
—— Lunatic—Criminal - 6 Q. B. D. 47;
> [8 App. Cas. 339
> See LUNATIC—CRIMINAL.
—— Pauper husband.
> See HUSBAND AND WIFE — MARRIED WOMEN'S PROPERTY ACTS—Statutes.
—— Prisoner - 6 Q. B. D. 156; 7 App. Cas. 1
> See PRISON. 2.
—— Wife—Divorce.
> See Cases under PRACTICE—DIVORCE—ALIMONY.
—— Wife—Separation deed—Subsequent divorce
> 6 P. D. 98
> See PRACTICE — DIVORCE — SEPARATION DEED. 3.

MAINTENANCE OF SUIT - 11 Q. B. D. 1;
> See CHAMPERTY. 1, 2. [10 App. Cas. 210

MAJORITY OF CREDITORS—Winding-up of company 21 Ch. D. 769; 24 Ch. D. 255
> See COMPANY—WINDING-UP ORDER. 16, 17.

MAJORITY OF SHAREHOLDERS 20 Ch. D. 151
> See COMPANY—WINDING-UP ORDER. 5.

MALICIOUS PROSECUTION.

1. —— **Reasonable and Probable Cause—Malicious Presentation of Petition to wind up Trading Company.**] An action will lie for falsely and maliciously and without reasonable or probable cause presenting a petition under the Companies Acts, 1862, 1867, to wind up a trading company, even although no pecuniary loss or special damage to the company can be proved, for the presentation of the petition is, from its very nature, calculated to injure the credit of the company.—The Defendant, who had been a shareholder in the Plaintiff company, instructed certain brokers to sell his shares, and signed a transfer. The brokers informed him that they could not sell

MALICIOUS PROSECUTION—continued.
the shares, but the transfer was not returned to him. After waiting ten or eleven days he presented a petition to wind up the company on the ground of fraud in its formation, and of the impossibility that it could carry on business at a profit. At the time of presenting the petition the company, which was a trading company, had property of a large amount, and its debts were trifling. The Defendant was not then in fact a shareholder: his shares had been sold, and the transfer had been registered. Upon discovering that his shares had been sold, he gave notice that the petition would be withdrawn, and it was ultimately dismissed without costs. The company having brought an action for falsely and maliciously and without reasonable or probable cause presenting the petition, at the trial no proof of damage to the company was given beyond the liability to pay its own costs of defending itself against the petition; and upon this ground the company was nonsuited at the close of its case :—*Held*, that although the liability to pay "extra costs" was not a ground of legal damage, nevertheless the nonsuit was wrong, and a new trial must be had, because an action would lie for falsely and maliciously and without reasonable or probable cause presenting the petition to wind up, which was necessarily injurious to the credit of the company :—*Held*, further, that as at the time of presenting the petition the company was an existing and going concern, and had valuable property and was solvent, unless other facts could be shewn, there was a want of reasonable and probable cause for presenting the petition, and the opinion of the jury ought to have been taken whether the Defendant had been actuated by malice :—*Held*, further, that if the Defendant as a matter of business ought, in the opinion of the jury, to have inferred from the failure of the brokers to return the transfer, that the shares had been sold, the Defendant would have had no reasonable or probable cause to suppose that he was still a shareholder.—*Johnson* v. *Emerson* (Law Rep. 6 Ex. 329) commented upon. QUARTZ HILL GOLD MINING COMPANY v. EYRE 11 Q. B. D. 674

2. —— **Reasonable and Probable Cause—Onus of Proof—Direction to Jury.**] At the hearing of a plaint in a County Court to recover rent the tenant's son was called as a witness, and swore that he had given up the key of the premises to the landlord before the rent accrued due. The landlord denied this, and subsequently proscouted the witness for perjury. He was acquitted, and brought an action against the landlord for malicious prosecution. At the trial the Plaintiff and Defendant repeated their evidence as to the key, and the Judge directed the jury alternatively that if they could not arrive at a conclusion as to which of the parties was speaking the truth, the Plaintiff had not made out his case, and the Defendant was entitled to a verdict; and that if they thought the Plaintiff did give up

MALICIOUS PROSECUTION—*continued.*

the key, but the Defendant owing to a defective memory had forgotten the occurrence and went on with the prosecution honestly believing that the Plaintiff had sworn falsely and corruptly, then the jury would not be justified in saying that the Defendant maliciously and without reasonable and probable cause prosecuted the Plaintiff, and the Defendant would be entitled to their verdict :—*Held*, that the direction was right. HICKS *v.* FAULKNER - **8 Q. B. D. 167**

3. —— **Reasonable and Probable Cause**— *Burden of Proof—Direction to Jury.*] In an action for malicious prosecution the burden of proof as to all the issues arising therein lies upon the Plaintiff; and although the Plaintiff proves that he was innocent of the charge laid against him, and although the Judge in order to enable himself to determine the issue of reasonable and probable cause, leaves subsidiary questions of fact to the jury, nevertheless the onus of proving the existence of such facts as tend to establish the want of reasonable and probable cause on the part of the Defendant, rests upon the Plaintiff. The Plaintiff, a surgeon, had attended one M. for bodily injuries alleged to have been sustained in a collision upon the Defendants' railway. M. brought an action against the Defendants, which was compromised by the Defendants paying a large sum for damages and costs. Subsequently the directors of the Defendant company, having received certain information, caused the statements of certain persons to be taken by a solicitor; these statements tended to shew that the injuries of which M. complained were not caused at the collision, but were produced wilfully by the Plaintiff, with the consent of M., for the purpose of defrauding the Defendants. These statements were laid before counsel, who advised that there was good ground for prosecuting the Plaintiff and M. for conspiracy. The Defendants accordingly prosecuted the Plaintiff, but he was acquitted. In an action for malicious prosecution, the Judge directed the jury to find whether the Defendants had taken reasonable care to inform themselves of the true state of the case, and whether they honestly believed the case which they laid before the magistrates; the jury having answered these questions in the affirmative, the Judge entered the judgment for the Defendants:— *Held*, by the Court of Appeal, reversing the decision of the Queen's Bench Division, that the direction to the jury was correct, that upon the facts and the findings of the jury, the Defendants had reasonable and probable cause for prosecuting the Plaintiff, and that the Judge had rightly entered the judgment for the Defendants. ABRATH *v.* NORTH EASTERN RAILWAY COMPANY

[11 Q. B. D. 79, 440

[Affirmed by the House of Lords.]

—— Action against corporation 6 Q. B. D. 287 *See* CORPORATION. 1.

MANAGEMENT OF COMPANY.
See Cases under COMPANY—MANAGEMENT.

MANDAMUS.
—— **Pleading to Return**—*Return of unconditional Compliance—Rules of Supreme Court,*

MANDAMUS—*continued.*

1883, Order LIII., r. 9; Order LXVIII., r. 1; Order LXXII., r. 2—9 Anne, c. 20 [*Revised Ed. Statutes, 9 Anne, c. 25*]—1 Wm. 4, c. 21—46 & 47 Vict. c. 49.] A return of unconditional compliance to a writ of mandamus, which is not a peremptory writ, may be pleaded to, notwithstanding Order LIII., rule 9, since the procedure of pleading to the return to such writ as regulated by the repealed statute 9 Anne, c. 20 [Revised Ed. Statutes, 9 Anne, c. 25], and 1 Wm. 4, c. 21, is preserved by Order LXVIII., rule 1, and Order LXXII., rule 2. THE QUEEN *v.* JUSTICES OF PIREHILL NORTH

[13 Q. B. D. 696; 14 Q. B. D. 13

2. —— **Servants of the Crown**—*Commissioners of Inland Revenue—Return of Probate Duty— 5 & 6 Vict. c. 79, s. 23.*] Sect. 23 of 5 & 6 Vict. c. 79, provides for the return by the Commissioners of Stamps and Taxes of probate duty on proof by oath and proper vouchers to their satisfaction of the payment of debts of the deceased, whereby the amount of probate duty payable on the estate is reduced below the amount which has been paid. By a subsequent Act the Commissioners of Inland Revenue are substituted for the Commissioners of Stamps and Taxes. On an application by an administrator for a mandamus to the commissioners to pay to the applicant the amount of duty overpaid by him, on the ground that he had supplied evidence of overpayment and had no other legal remedy :—*Held*, that the mandamus ought not to issue, for the statute created no duty between the commissioners and the applicant, whose remedy, if the decision of the commissioners could be reviewed, was by petition of right.—*Rex* v. *Lords Commissioners of the Treasury* (4 A. & E. 286) disapproved of. *In re* NATHAN - **12 Q. B. D. 461**

—— Central Criminal Court - **11 Q. B. D. 479** *See* COURT—CENTRAL CRIMINAL COURT.

—— Charity - **18 Ch. D. 596** *See* CHARITY—COMMISSIONERS. 1.

—— Corrupt Practices Act—Criminal matter— Appeal - **7 Q. B. D. 575** *See* PARLIAMENT — ELECTION COMMISSIONERS.

—— Judge of County Court - **9 Q. B. D. 723** *See* COUNTY COURT—JURISDICTION. 6.

—— Justices—Prison Act, 1877 **11 Q. B. D. 656**; *See* PRISON. 1. [9 App. Cas. 757

—— Refusal of justice to do act relating to the duties of his office **14 Q. B. D. 474** *See* JUSTICES—PRACTICE. 3.

MANOR—Copyhold.
See Cases under COPYHOLD.

—— Waste lands—Common - **20 Ch. D. 380** *See* INCLOSURE. 3.

MANSION-HOUSE—Sale of—Settled Land Act

[27 Ch. D. 179

See SETTLED LAND ACT—RESTRICTIONS. 1.

MANSLAUGHTER—Neglect of parent to provide medical aid - - **8 Q. B. D. 571** *See* CRIMINAL LAW—OFFENCES AGAINST PERSON. 3.

MANSLAUGHTER—*continued.*

—— Negligent use of firearms   -   6 Q. B. D. 79
    See CRIMINAL LAW—OFFENCES AGAINST
    PERSON. 2.

MANUFACTURED ARTICLE —Name of
    [18 Ch. D. 395; 8 App. Cas. 315
    See TRADE NAME. 3.

MARGINAL ADVICE—Bill of exchange—Con-
    signment of goods   -   29 Ch. D. 813
    See BILL OF EXCHANGE—SECURITIES FOR.
    4.

MARGINAL NOTE—Act of Parliament
    See STATUTE.   [22 Ch. D. 511

MARINE INSURANCE.
    See Cases under INSURANCE, MARINE.

MARITIME LIEN.
    See Cases under SHIP—MARITIME LIEN.

—— Jurisdiction   -   -   6 P. D. 106
    See FOREIGN JUDGMENT. 2.

MARKET.

1. —— Disturbance—*Statutory Market—Extinguishment of Old Franchise by Statute.*] Under
the powers of an Act of 1844, the corporation of
Manchester purchased the manorial rights of the
manor of Manchester, which was co-extensive
with one of the six townships included in the
borough.—Among these rights was an ancient
franchise to hold a market, which appeared to
have been a Saturday market. After this, by the
Manchester Market Act, 1846, the corporation
were empowered to hold markets on such days as
they should think fit at any places within the
borough which they should appropriate as market places, and to charge any tolls not exceeding
those mentioned in the schedule to the Act (which
were higher than the old accustomed tolls), and
to make certain charges for weighing which could
not have been made under the old franchise :—
Held (affirming the decision of the Vice-Chancellor of the county palatine of Lancaster), that
there being under the Act a change of time, a
change of place, an alteration of the old charges,
an imposition of new charges, and an extension of
the market from the township to the borough, the
effect of the Act was to give the corporation new
rights of holding markets in substitution for the
old franchise, and that the old franchise was
extinguished.—The corporation brought an action
to restrain the Defendants from selling eggs and
dried fish on market days in their shop. The
shop was situated in a street which adjoined one
side of one of the Plaintiffs' markets, and was on
the opposite side of the street from, but not opposite to, the entrance from that street to the market.
The Defendants only sold their own goods in
their shop in the ordinary course of business.:—
Held (affirming the decision of the Vice-Chancellor), that this was no disturbance of the statutory right of market.   CORPORATION OF MAN-
CHESTER v. LYONS -   -   -   22 Ch. D. 287
    [*See also* CORPORATION OF MANCHESTER v.
    PEVERLEY, 22 Ch. D. 294, n.]

2. —— Disturbance — *Charter, Force of —
Waiver of Statutory Rights—Accommodation provided by Lord of Market.*] A charter of 1st Edward III. made by the King " with the assent of
the prelates, earls, barons, and all the commons

MARKET—*continued.*

of our realm assembled in our present Parliament," granted to the citizens of the city of
London certain privileges, and among them "that
no market within seven miles round about the city
shall be granted by us or our heirs to any one."
By letters patent in the 34th Charles II., reciting
an inquisition founded on a writ of ad quod
damnum, the King granted to the Respondents'
predecessor in title the right of holding markets
on Thursday and Saturday in every week in
Spittal Square within the seven miles.—User of
the market was proved since 1723. The Appellant company set up a depôt or row of stalls at
their terminus within 300 yards of Spittal Square
and let them to dealers for the purpose of selling
fruit and vegetables brought up by their railway
and justified their depôt on the ground that the
Respondents' market was very crowded, that it
was difficult for dealers to get stalls there, and
that if any persons other than the Respondents'
tenants wished to sell in the Respondents' market
there would be no room for them; and that the
respondents' market infringed the provisions of
certain Paving Acts :—*Held,* affirming the decision of the Court of Appeal, that the charter of
Edward III. had, at the most, the force of a private or personal statute, and concerned the corporation of London only and not the general
public; that the consent of the corporation was
to be presumed to the letters patent of Charles II.;
that the letters patent of Charles II. conferred a
valid right of market; that the company's depôt
was in fact a rival market, and a disturbance of
the Respondents' right of market, and entitled the
Respondents to an injunction to restrain the company from using their depôt in the above manner
or so as to interfere with the Respondents' rights;
and that even if the company had proved that
there was not sufficient accommodation in the
Respondents' market, or that the Paving Acts had
been infringed, those circumstances would have
afforded no answer to the action for an injunction.
GREAT EASTERN RAILWAY COMPANY v. GOLDSMID
    [25 Ch. D. 511; 9 App. Cas. 927

3. —— Market not limited by Metes and
Bounds—*Extension of Market—Streets subject to
Market Rights — Street Acts of Parliament not
affecting Market — Usage — Presumption of lost
Grant.*] By letters patent in 34 Charles II. the
King granted to the predecessor in title of those
under whom the Defendant claimed as lessee the
right to hold two markets—one on Thursday and
the other on Saturday—in every week, " in or
next to Spital Square." The market-place and
four inner streets connected therewith were made
by the grantee on the square piece of land which
had formerly been Spital Square, and which land
he had acquired when the charter was granted to
him, but he never acquired the adjoining land
which surrounded such square piece, and on which,
subsequently to the charter, were made certain
outer streets, into which the four inner streets
ran. By letters patent in 4 James II., made void
by 2 Wm. & M. sess. 1, c. 8, a third market was
given, viz., on Monday in every week, and a
market on Wednesday substituted for that on
Thursday.—In proceedings taken at the instance
of the local authority to restrain the Defendan

MARKET—*continued.*

from licensing the sale of goods in either the outer or the inner streets adjoining the market, the local authority relied on certain Paving Acts of Geo. 3, which empowered such authority to remove the obstruction caused by selling articles in those specific streets, and the Defendant proved a usage from the time of living memory to sell vegetables and fruit in any of those streets, and to pay toll to the market-owner for so doing, when by reason of the market being so crowded it was impossible to get nearer to the inside market, and he also proved such usage to hold the market on other days of the week besides on Thursday and Saturday :—*Held*, that the market was a market without metes and bounds, and might extend, therefore, from time to time, as the crowded state of the market might require, over any of these surrounding streets, all of which were to be presumed to have been dedicated to the public subject to the exercise of the market franchise, notwithstanding the Paving Acts, as such Acts were not to be construed as interfering with the market rights : —*Held*, also, that the right to hold the market was confined to the two days mentioned in the charter of Charles II., and that under the particular circumstances of the case a lost grant for the other days of the week was not to be inferred. ATTORNEY-GENERAL *v.* HORNER **14 Q. B. D. 245** [Affirmed by the House of Lords, 11 App. Cas. 66.]

MARRIAGE—Breach of promise — Pleading— Matter of aggravation　**6 Q. B. D. 190** *See* PRACTICE—SUPREME COURT—STRIK- ING OUT PLEADINGS.　1.

—— Consent of guardians　-　**18 Ch. D. 61** *See* WILL—CONDITION.　9.

—— In Greek Church. *See* GREEK MARRIAGES—*Statutes.*

—— Non-solemnization of—Revocation of settle- ment　-　**26 Ch. D. 191** *See* SETTLEMENT—REVOCATION.　1.

—— Presumption of—Law of Ceylon [**6 App. Cas. 364** *See* COLONIAL LAW—CEYLON.　3.

—— Restraint of -　-　**23 Ch. D. 285** *See* COVENANT—VALIDITY.

—— Right to solemnize—Fees　**10 Q. B. D. 418** *See* ECCLESIASTICAL LAW—CLERGY.　1.

—— Scotch—Habit and repute　**6 App. Cas. 489** *See* SCOTCH LAW—HUSBAND AND WIFE. 3.

—— Severance of joint tenancy　**17 Ch. D. 368** *See* JOINT TENANT.　2.

MARRIAGE CONTRACT — Settlement — Scotch law　-　- **9 App. Cas. 303** *See* SCOTCH LAW—HUSBAND AND WIFE. 5.

MARRIAGE SETTLEMENT. *See* Cases under SETTLEMENT.

MARRIED WOMAN. *See* Cases and Statutes under HUSBAND AND WIFE.

—— Action by—Costs of former action not paid [**23 Ch. D. 288** *See* PRACTICE—SUPREME COURT—STAY- ING PROCEEDINGS.　7.

MARRIED WOMAN—*continued.*

—— Action by—Security for costs　**30 Ch. D. 418** ; [**9 Q. B. D. 52** *See* PRACTICE—SUPREME COURT—SECU- RITY FOR COSTS.　4, 5.

—— Administratrix　-　- **8 P. D. 16, 168** *See* ADMINISTRATOR—MARRIED WOMAN. 1, 2.

—— Breach of trust—Indemnity of trustees [**28 Ch. D. 595** *See* TRUSTEE—INDEMNITY.　1.

—— Compromise—How far binding　**6 P. D. 219** *See* PRACTICE—PROBATE—COMPROMISE.

—— Consent—Settled Estates Act　**26 Ch. D. 220** *See* SETTLED ESTATES ACT.　2.

—— Conveyance—Vendor and Purchaser Act [**29 Ch. D. 693** *See* VENDOR AND PURCHASER—CONVEY- ANCE.　3.

—— Election—Female infant　-　**28 Ch. D. 124** *See* ELECTION.　6.

—— Equity to settlement　-　**16 Ch. D. 376** ; [**17 Ch. D. 778 ; 27 Ch. D. 220** *See* SETTLEMENT—EQUITY TO SETTLE- MENT.　1, 2, 3.

—— Executrix. *See* Cases under PROBATE—MARRIED WOMAN.

—— Injunction against parting with separate estate　-　-　-　**16 Ch. D. 660** *See* PRACTICE — SUPREME COURT — IN- JUNCTION.　6.

—— Law of Natal—Surety bond　**9 App. Cas. 715** *See* COLONIAL LAW—NATAL.　2.

—— Maintenance of children and husband. *See* HUSBAND AND WIFE — MARRIED WOMEN'S PROPERTY ACTS—*Statutes.*

—— Next friend -　-　**19 Ch. D. 94** *See* PRACTICE—SUPREME COURT—NEXT FRIEND.　2.

—— Power of attorney. *See* POWER OF ATTORNEY—*Statutes.*

—— Sale in partition action—Request for sale [**16 Ch. D. 362** *See* PARTITION SUIT—SALE.　3.

—— Scotch law. *See* Cases under SCOTCH LAW—HUSBAND AND WIFE.

—— Separate examination　-　**28 Ch. D. 171** *See* SETTLED ESTATES ACT.　3.

—— Tenant for life—Powers of. *See* SETTLED LAND ACT—STATUTES.

—— Testamentary appointment　**22 Ch. D. 238** *See* POWER—EXECUTION.　11.

MARRIED WOMEN'S PROPERTY ACTS. *See* Cases and Statutes under HUSBAND AND WIFE—MARRIED WOMEN'S PRO- PERTY ACTS.

MARRIED WOMEN'S PROPERTY ACT (SCOT- LAND)　-　**8 App. Cas. 678** *See* SCOTCH LAW—HUSBAND AND WIFE. 6.

MARSHALLING—Securities—Bankruptcy [**25 Ch. D. 148** *See* BANKRUPTCY—SECURED CREDITOR. 6.

MASTER AND SERVANT :—　　　Col.
  I. MASTER'S LIABILITY　-　-　861
    (a.) GENERAL.
    (b.) COMMON EMPLOYMENT.
    (c.) DEFECTIVE MACHINERY, &c.
    (d.) PERSON ENTITLED TO COM-
        PENSATION.
    (e.) PRACTICE.
    (f.) RAILWAYS.
  II. REMEDIES　-　　-　-　867
  III. WAGES　-　　-　-　868

**I. MASTER AND SERVANT—MASTER'S LIA-
BILITY.**

(a.) GENERAL.

1. —— **Servant hired to drive Cart**—*Liability
of Hirer for.*] D. contracted with the Defendants,
an urban authority, to supply by the day a driver
and horse to drive and draw a watering-cart belonging to the Defendants. The driver was employed and paid by D., and was not under the
Defendants' direction or control otherwise than
that their inspector directed him what streets to
water. In an action to recover damages for injuries caused by the negligent conduct of the
driver whilst in charge of the cart :—*Held*, that
the Defendants were not liable.—*Quarman v. Burnett* (6 M. & W. 499) followed ; *Rourke v. White
Moss Colliery Co.* (2 C. P. D. 205) distinguished.
JONES *v.* CORPORATION OF LIVERPOOL　14 Q. B. D.
[890

(b.) COMMON EMPLOYMENT.

2. —— **Orders of Fellow Workman**—*Employers'
Liability Act,* 1880 (43 & 44 Vict. c. 42), s. 1, *sub-s.* 3
—*Injury resulting to Workman from having conformed to Orders or Directions of Fellow Workman.*] The 1st section of the Employers' Liability
Act, 1880, provides that, where personal injury
is caused to a workman (3) by reason of the
negligence of any person in the service of the
employer to whose orders or directions the workman at the time of the injury was bound to
conform, and did conform, where such injury
resulted from his having so conformed, the workman or, in case the injury resulted in death, his
legal personal representatives, shall have the
same right of compensation against the employer
as if the workman had not been a workman of nor
in the service of the employer nor engaged in his
work.—The Plaintiff, a boy employed by the Defendants, a railway company, was assisting a carman of the Defendants, under whose directions he
was, in unloading from a van three large iron window frames. The frames were standing upright in
the van, secured at each end to the hooks of the van
by a string. The carman untied the string at one
end of the frames, and the Plaintiff untied the
string at the other end. The carman did not expressly order the Plaintiff to untie the string but
the Plaintiff stated that he did so without orders
because he had done so on previous occasions and
that the carman saw him untie the string and
made no objection. The carman then removed
one of the frames without retying the two remaining frames, leaving them standing unsecured.
They directly afterwards fell on the Plaintiff,
causing him injuries in respect of which he sued

(b.) COMMON EMPLOYMENT—*continued.*

the Defendants for compensation under the Employers' Liability Act, 1880 :—*Held*, that there
was on the above facts evidence of an injury to
the Plaintiff by reason of the negligence of a
fellow workman to whose orders he was bound to
conform, and did conform, and which resulted
from his having so conformed. MILLWARD *v.*
MIDLAND RAILWAY COMPANY　　14 Q. B. D. 68

3. —— **Superintendent**—"*Person having superintendence entrusted to him*"—*Employers' Liability Act,* 1880 (43 & 44 Vict. c. 42), s. 1 (*sub-s.* 2),
s. 8.] The Plaintiff and one J. were employed
with others by the Defendants in loading sacks
of corn into the hold of a ship. J.'s duty was to
guide the beam of the crane by means of a guy-
rope, and to give directions when to lower and
hoist the chain. He neglected to use the guy-
rope, and the sacks in consequence fell down the
hatchway, and hurt the Plaintiff, who was working in the hold :—*Held*, that J. was "engaged in
manual labour," and was not "a person having
superintendence entrusted to him," within the
meaning of the Employers' Liability Act, 1880
(43 & 44 Vict. c. 42), s. 1, sub-s. 2, as defined by
sect. 8. SHAFFERS *v.* GENERAL STEAM NAVIGA-
TION COMPANY　-　-　-　10 Q. B. D. 356

4. —— **Superintendent**—*Superintendent assisting in Manual Labour*—*Employers' Liability Act,*
1880 (43 & 44 Vict. c. 42), s. 1.] An employer
may be liable under the Employers' Liability Act,
1880 (43 & 44 Vict. c. 42), s. 1, where personal injury is caused to a workman (sub-s. 2), "by reason of the negligence of any person in the service
of the employer who has any superintendence
entrusted to him whilst in the exercise of such
superintendence," although the superintendent,
when negligent, is voluntarily assisting in manual
labour. OSBORNE *v.* JACKSON -　　11 Q. B. D. 619

(c.) DEFECTIVE MACHINERY, &c.

5. —— **Machinery**—*Employers' Liability Act,*
1880 (43 & 44 Vict. c. 42), s. 1, *sub-s.* 1—"*Defect
in condition of machinery*"—*Machine unsuited
for Purpose to which it was applied.*] The Employers' Liability Act, 1880 (43 & 44 Vict. c. 42)
—which gives a workman a right of action against
his employer for personal injury by reason of any
defect in the condition of the machinery used in
the business of the employer—applies to a case
where the machine, though not defective in its
construction, was, under the circumstances in
which it was used, calculated to cause injury to
those using it. The deceased, a workman in the
employment of the Defendants, was killed by a
piece of coke falling from a lift used at a blast
furnace belonging to them. The lift consisted
of two platforms which ascended and descended
alternately, and at the time when the deceased
was injured he was removing empty barrows from
the platform which was at rest at the bottom of
the lift. There was evidence that the accident
arose either from the sides of the lift not being
fenced so as to prevent coke from falling over, or
from the lower platform not being roofed so as to
protect those working on it from falling coke :—
Held, that under the circumstances there was a

I. MASTER AND SERVANT—MASTER'S LIA-BILITY—*continued.*

(c.) DEFECTIVE MACHINERY, &c.—*continued.*

" defect in the condition " of the lift for which the Defendants were liable. HESKE *v.* SAMUELSON & Co. - - - 12 Q. B. D. 30

6. —— Plant—*Employers' Liability Act*, 1880 (43 & 44 *Vict.* c. 42), s. 1 (1), s. 2 (1)—*Plant unfit for Purpose !'or which it was used—Negligence of Employer.*] The Employers' Liability Act, 1880, which gives a workman a right of action against his employer for personal injury by reason of any defect in the condition of the plant used in the business of the employer, applies to a case where the plant is unfit for the purpose for which it is used, though no part of it is shewn to be unsound. —Plaintiff, a workman in Defendants' employment, was injured by reason of the breaking of a ladder, which was being used to support a scaffold. The ladder was insufficient for the purpose for which it was being used, and the scaffold and ladder had been placed and were being used under the directions of one of the Defendants :—*Held* that, under the above circumstances, there was evidence that the Plaintiff had been injured by reason of a defect in the condition of the plant, owing to the negligence of his employer, within the meaning of the Employers' Liability Act, 1880.—*Heske* v. *Samuelson* (12 Q. B. D. 30) approved and followed. CRIPPS *v.* JUDGE
[13 Q. B. D. 583

7. —— Roadway—*Obstruction — Employers' Liability Act,* 1880 (43 & 44 *Vict.* c. 42), *s.* 1, *sub-s.* 1.] A workman was employed in the Defendants' ironworks, and part of his duty was to take iron in balls, by means of a two-wheeled car, along a roadway of iron plates. While he was so engaged the car struck against a piece of a substance used for lining the furnaces, which had been negligently placed projecting into the roadway, and a ball fell on him, causing personal injuries from which he died. In an action against the employers :—*Held* (by Field and Stephen, JJ.), that the obstruction caused by the substance projecting into the roadway was not a defect in the condition of the way within the meaning of the Employers' Liability Act, 1880, s. 1, sub-s. 1, and that the Defendants were not liable. MCGIFFIN *v.* PALMER'S SHIPBUILDING AND IRON COMPANY
[10 Q. B. D. 5

(d.) PERSON ENTITLED TO COMPENSATION.

8. —— Contract not to claim — *Employers' Liability Act,* 1880 (43 & 44 *Vict.* c. 42), s. 1— *Contract against Public Policy—Injury resulting in Death—Lord Campbell's Act (9 & 10 Vict.* c. 93)—*Widow of Workman, whether bound by his Contract not to claim Compensation.*] It is competent to a workman to contract with his employer not to claim compensation for personal injuries under the Employers' Liability Act, 1880.—By sect. 1 of the Employers' Liability Act, 1880, where personal injury is caused to a workman in certain specified cases, the workman, or, in case the injury results in death, his legal personal representatives and any person entitled in case of death " shall have the same right of compensation and remedies against the employer as if the workman had not been a workman of, nor in the service of, the

I. MASTER AND SERVANT—MASTER'S LIA-BILITY—*continued.*

(d.) PERSON ENTITLED TO COMPENSATION — *continued.*

employer, nor engaged in his work."—A workman having contracted with his employer for himself and his representatives, and any person entitled in case of death, not to claim any compensation under the Act for personal injury whether resulting in death or not :—*Held,* that sect. 1 only affected the contract of service so far as to negative the implication of an agreement by the workman to bear the risks of the employment, and therefore did not render the workman's express contract not to claim compensation invalid.—*Held,* also, that the contract was not against public policy, and that the workman's widow, suing for damages under Lord Campbell's Act, was bound by it. GRIFFITHS *v.* EARL OF DUDLEY - - - 9 Q. B. D. 357

9. —— Omnibus Conductor—*Employers' Liability Act,* 1880 (43 & 44 *Vict.* c. 42), s. 8—*Employers and Workmen Act,* 1875 (38 & 39 *Vict.* c. 90), *s.* 10—" *Journeyman*" — "*Labourer*"— "*Otherwise engaged in Manual Labour.*"] An omnibus conductor engaged at daily wages, paid daily, is not a "person to whom the Employers and Workmen Act, 1875, applies," and therefore is not entitled to the benefit of the Employers' Liability Act, 1880.—Judgment of the Queen's Bench Division affirmed. MORGAN *v.* LONDON GENERAL OMNIBUS CO. 12 Q. B. D. 201 ;
[13 Q. B. D. 832

(e.) PRACTICE.

10. —— Action in County Court—*Removal of —Employers' Liability Act* (43 & 44 *Vict.* c. 42), s. 6.] By the Employers' Liability Act, 1880 (43 & 44 Vict. c. 42), s. 6, " Every action for recovery of compensation under this Act shall be brought in a County Court. but may, upon the application of either Plaintiff or defendant, be removed into a superior Court in like manner and upon the same conditions as an action commenced in a County Court may by law be removed."—A Plaintiff having brought in the County Court an action against his employers, to recover compensation under the Act for an injury through the breaking of a chain, applied for a certiorari to remove the action into the superior Court on the grounds that his notice given under the Act was defective ; that he desired to consolidate the action with one brought by him in the superior Court to recover damages for the same injury from the Defendants on their common law liability, and that the questions arising were of considerable complexity and legal difficulty :— *Held,* that the power of removal ought only to be exercised in exceptional cases, and that no such special grounds had been shewn as to induce the Court in its discretion to grant the application. MUNDAY *v.* THAMES IRONWORKS AND SHIPBUILDING COMPANY 10 Q. B. D. 59

11. —— Action in County Court—*Stay of Proceedings — Employers' Liability Act,* 1880 (43 & 44 *Vict.* c. 42), s. 6—*Action of Tort—* 19 & 20 *Vict.* c. 108, *s.* 39.] Sect. 39 of the County Courts Act, 1856, entitles the Defendant " in any action of tort " where the claim exceeds

I. MASTER AND SERVANT—MASTER'S LIA-
BILITY—*continued.*

(e.) PRACTICE—*continued.*

£5 to a stay of proceedings, upon certain conditions as to giving security for the amount claimed
and the costs of trial in one of the superior Courts
of common law :—*Held,* affirming that the decision of
the Queen's Bench Division, that this section was
intended to apply only to actions which could be
brought either in one of the superior Courts or in
a County Court, and therefore did not apply to
an action under the Employers' Liability Act,
1880, which by sect. 6 of that Act must be
brought in a County Court. THE QUEEN *v.*
JUDGE OF CITY OF LONDON COURT
[14 Q. B. D. 818, 905

12. —— Notice of Injury—*Defect or Inaccuracy in Notice—Omission of Date of Injury—
Employers' Liability Act, 1880 (43 & 44 Vict. c. 42),
s. 7.]* Sect. 4 of the Employers' Liability Act,
1880, provides that an action to recover compensation under the Act shall not be maintainable
unless notice of injury is given as provided by the
Act. By sect. 7, the notice shall state (inter alia)
the date of the injury ; and " a notice under this
section shall not be deemed invalid by reason of
any defect or inaccuracy therein" unless the
Judge who tries the action shall be of opinion
that the Defendant is prejudiced in his defence by
such defect or inaccuracy, and that it was for the
purpose of misleading. A notice of injury given
under sect. 4 omitted to state the date of the
injury, and the Judge at the trial found that the
Defendant was not prejudiced in his defence by
the omission, and that it was not for the purpose
of misleading :—*Held,* that the omission of the
date was a "defect or inaccuracy" in the notice
within the meaning of sect. 7, and therefore did
not render the notice invalid. CARTER *v.* DRYS-
DALE　　-　　- 12 Q. B. D. 91

13. —— Notice of Injury—*Inaccuracy—Employers' Liability Act, 1880 (43 & 44 Vict. c. 42),
s. 7.]* The notice of injury under sect. 7 of the
Employers' Liability Act, 1880 (43 & 44 Vict. c. 42),
need not be expressed in strictly technical language : it is enough if it substantially conveys to
the mind of the person to whom it is given, the
name and address of the person injured and the
cause and date of the injury.—A letter from the
Plaintiff's solicitor gave only the date of the injury, and stated that the Plaintiff was and had for
some time past been under treatment at a hospital
"for injury to his leg:"—*Held,* that having regard
to the proviso at the end of sect. 7 the defect in
the notice did not render it invalid. STONE *v.*
HYDE　　-　　-　　9 Q. B. D. 76

14. —— Notice of Injury—*Statement of Cause
of Injury—Employers' Liability Act, 1880 (43 & 44
Vict. c. 42), s. 7.]* In an action to recover compensation for injuries under the Employers' Liability
Act, 1880, the Plaintiff's notice of injury stated
that she was injured in consequence of the Defendants' negligence in leaving a certain hoist in
their warehouse unprotected whereby her foot
was caught in the casement of the hoist and
crushed. At the trial, the jury found that the
accident occurred through the negligence of a
superintendent in the warehouse, in allowing the
Plaintiff, a young girl, to go in the hoist alone ;—

I. MASTER AND SERVANT—MASTER'S LIA-
BILITY—*continued.*

(e.) PRACTICE—*continued.*

Held, that the notice of injury sufficiently stated
the "cause of the injury" within sect. 7 of the
Employers' Liability Act, 1880. CLARKSON *v.*
MUSGRAVE -　　-　　　9 Q. B. D. 386

15. —— Notice of Injury— *Written Notice
necessary—Employers' Liability Act, 1880 (43 & 44
Vict. c. 42), ss. 4, 7.]* By the Employers' Liability
Act, 1880 (43 & 44 Vict. c. 42), s. 4, an action for
the recovery under this Act of compensation for
an injury shall not be maintainable, unless " notice that injury has been sustained " is given
within six weeks. By sect. 7 notice in respect of
an injury under this Act shall give the name and
address of the person injured, and shall state in
ordinary language the cause of the injury and
the date, and shall be served on the employer,
and may be served by delivery or by post :—*Held,*
that notice under the Act must be in writing.
MOYLE *v.* JENKINS　　-　　- 8 Q. B. D. 116

16. —— Notice of Injury— *Written Notice
necessary—Sufficiency of Notice—Employers' Liability Act, 1880 (43 & 44 Vict. c. 42), ss. 4, 7.]*
The notice of injury sustained by a workman
which is to be given to an employer under the
Employers' Liability Act, 1880 (43 & 44 Vict.
c. 42), must contain in writing all the particulars
required by sect. 7 in order to fulfil the condition
precedent to bringing an action enacted by sect. 4.
—*Quære,* if such notice can be made by one writing
referring to another writing.—Where a workman,
on the day he had been injured, made a verbal
report of such injury to his employer's inspector,
who took the details down in writing and sent
them to the employer's superintendent, and afterwards the workman's solicitor wrote a letter to
the employer, stating that he was instructed by
such workman to apply for compensation for injuries received on the employer's premises, "particulars of which have already been communicated
to your superintendent" :—*Held,* that such letter
did not refer to any other writing, and was not a
notice in compliance with the Act. KEEN *v.*
MILLWALL DOCK COMPANY　　- 8 Q. B. D. 482

(f.) RAILWAYS.

17. —— Person in Charge—*Employers' Liability Act, 1880 (43 & 44 Vict. c. 42), s. 1, sub-s. 5
—Railway Company—Person having " Charge or
Control " of Points.]* In an action for compensation under the Employers' Liability Act, 1880,
the evidence shewed that it was the duty of F., a
workman employed in the signal department of
the Defendants' railway, to clean, oil, and adjust
the points and wires of the locking apparatus at
various places along a portion of the line, and to
do slight repairs, that for these purposes he was,
with several other men, subject to the orders of
an inspector in the same department, who was responsible for the points and locking gear, which
were moved and worked by men in the signal
boxes, being kept in proper condition, and that F.
having taken the cover off some points and locking gear in order to oil them, negligently left it
projecting over the metals of the line, whereby
injury was caused to a fellow workman :—*Held,*
affirming the decision of the Queen's Bench Divi-

2 F

**I. MASTER AND SERVANT—MASTER'S LIA-
BILITY**—continued.

(f.) RAILWAYS—continued.

sion, that there was no evidence for the jury that
F. had "charge or control" of the points within
the meaning of sect. 1, sub-sect. 5, of the Employers' Liability Act, 1880, so as to make the
Defendants liable for his negligence. GIBBS v.
GREAT WESTERN RAILWAY COMPANY
[11 Q. B. D. 22; 12 Q. B. D. 208

18. —— **Person in Charge**—Negligence of a
Person "in Charge of a Train upon a Railway"
—Employers' Liability Act, 1880 (43 & 44 Vict.
c. 42), s. 1, sub-s. 5.] H., who was in the employ
of a railway company as a "capstan man," without giving the usual warning, propelled a series
of trucks along a line of rails in a goods station,
and injured the Plaintiff, who was engaged in
similar work at the other end of the line about
100 yards off. The capstan was set in motion by
hydraulic power communicated to it by H. from
a stationary engine at a distance:—Held, that
there was evidence to warrant the jury in finding
that H. was a person who had the charge or control of "a train upon a railway" under sect. 1,
sub-sect. 5, of the Employers' Liability Act, 1880
(43 & 44 Vict. c. 42). COX v. GREAT WESTERN
RAILWAY COMPANY   -   - 9 Q. B. D. 106

19. —— **"Railway," Meaning of**—Employers'
Liability Act, 1880 (43 & 44 Vict. c. 42), s. 1,
sub-s. 5.] The meaning of the term "railway"
as used in the 5th sub-section of the 1st section
of the Employers' Liability Act, 1880, is not confined to railways belonging to railway companies
such as are subject to the provisions of the Railway Regulation Acts; but the sub-section applies
also to a temporary railway laid down by a contractor for the purposes of the construction of
works. DOUGHTY v. FIRBANK   10 Q. B. D. 358

II. MASTER AND SERVANT—REMEDIES.

1. —— **Exclusive Personal Service**—Action for
procuring a Breach of such Contract—Damages
where Injunction only claimed—21 & 22 Vict. c. 27,
s. 2.] An action lies against a third person who
maliciously induces another to break his contract
of exclusive personal service with an employer,
which thereby would naturally cause, and did in
fact cause, an injury to such employer, although
the relation of master and servant may not strictly
exist between the employer and employed.—So
held by Lord Selborne, L.C., and Brett, L.J.,
affirming the decision of the majority of the
Judges in Lumley v. Gye (2 E. & B. 216; 22 L. J.
(Q.B.) 463), Lord Coleridge, C.J., dissentient.—
Where in such an action the employed was also
a Defendant, but as against him the Plaintiff
claimed only an injunction and not damages, it
was held that damages might, in the discretion
of the Court, be given under Lord Cairns' Act
(21 & 22 Vict. c. 27), and that the jury, therefore,
should be directed by the Judge, in the event of
a verdict for the Plaintiff, to find such damages
as should be awarded; first, if the Court should
think it a proper case both for injunction and
damages; and secondly, if the Court should think
it a proper case for damages only, and not also for
an injunction. BOWEN v. HALL   6 Q. B. D. 333

2. —— **"Workman"**—Inventor—Employers

II. MASTER AND SERVANT—REMEDIES—
continued.

and Workmen Act, 1875 (38 & 39 Vict. c. 90).] By
an agreement in writing between H. & Co., manufacturers, and J.,—reciting that J. having a knowledge of mechanics, and H. & Co. requiring the
services of a person having such knowledge "to-
assist the firm as a practical working mechanic
in developing ideas they the firm might wish to-
carry out, and to himself originate and carry out
ideas and inventions suitable to the business of
such firm if such inventions were approved by
them,"—it was mutually agreed that J. should
be employed by the firm "for the purpose above
specified":—Held, that J. was not "a mechanic
or workman" within the Employers and Workmen Act, 1875. JACKSON v. HILL
[13 Q. B. D. 618

3. —— **"Workman"**—Potter's Printer—
Breach of his Contract through Strike of Assistants
employed by him—38 & 39 Vict. c. 90, ss. 4, 10.]
By the Employers and Workmen Act, 1875 (38 & 39
Vict. c. 90), s. 4, "a dispute under this Act between an employer and a workman may be heard
and determined by a Court of summary jurisdiction, and such Court, for the purposes of this Act,
shall be deemed to be a Court of civil jurisdiction" limited to £10. By sect. 10 "In this Act
the expression 'workman' . . . means any person
who, being a labourer, servant in husbandry,
journeyman, artificer, handicraftsman, miner, or
otherwise engaged in manual labour, . . . has
entered into, or works under a contract with an
employer, whether the contract be . . . a contract
of service or a contract personally to execute any
work or labour."—The expression "court of summary jurisdiction" means (inter alia) a stipendiary magistrate:—Held, that a potter's printer,
under a contract with his employers to do work
in which he was assisted by "transferrers" whom
he himself engaged and paid, was a "workman"
within the Act, and liable in proceedings before a
magistrate to pay damages for a breach of his
contract with his employers, caused by his transferrers' refusal to do the work, although he was
ready and willing to do it. GRAINGER v. AYNES-
LEY. BROMLEY v. TAMS   - 6 Q. B. D. 182

III. MASTER AND SERVANT—WAGES.

Payment in Public-houses prohibited.] By
46 & 47 Vict. c. 31 (Payment of Wages in Public-
houses Prohibition Act, 1883), s. 3, no wages are to
be paid to any workman at or within any public-
house, beer-shop, or place for the sale of any spirits,
wine, cyder, or other spirituous or fermented liquor,
or any office, garden, or place belonging thereto or
occupied therewith, save and except such wages as
are paid by the resident owner or occupiers of such
public-house, beer-shop, or place to any workmen
bonâ fide employed by him.

Every person who contravenes or fails to comply
with or permits any person to contravene or fail to
comply with the Act is guilty of an offence against
the Act.

And in the event of any wages being paid by any
person in contravention of the provisions of the Act
for or on behalf of any employer, such employer
shall himself be guilty of an offence against the Act,
unless he proves that he had taken all reasonable

III. MASTER AND SERVANT—WAGES—*contd.*

means in his power for enforcing the provisions of the Act and to prevent such contravention.

By sect. 4 *every person who is guilty of an offence against the Act is liable to a penalty not exceeding £10 for each offence; and all offences against the Act may be prosecuted and all penalties under the Act may be recovered by any person summarily in manner provided by the Summary Jurisdiction Acts.*

Sect. 2 *defines "workman" to mean any person who is a labourer, servant in husbandry, journeyman, artificer, handicraftsman, or is otherwise engaged in manual labour, whether under the age of twenty-one years or above that age; but does not include a domestic or menial servant, nor any person employed in or about any mine to which the Coal Mines Regulation Act,* 1872, *or the Metalliferous Mines Regulation Act,* 1872, *applies.*

1. —— Attachment of Debts—*Garnishee Order —Wages Attachment Abolition Act,* 1870 (33 & 34 *Vict. c.* 30), *s.* 1—*Salary of Secretary attachable.*] The salary of a secretary to a company amounting to £200 a year is not "wages" of a "servant" within the Wages Attachment Abolition Act (33 & 34 Vict. c. 30), and is therefore not exempted from attachment by that Act. GORDON *v.* JENNINGS - - 9 Q. B. D. 45

2. —— Forfeiture of Wages—*Employer and Workmen—Employers and Workmen Act,* 1875 (38 & 39 *Vict. c.* 90), *s.* 11—*Wages due but not payable—Piece Work—Women.*] A weaver, a woman subject to the provisions of the Factory Acts, was employed at a mill in which amongst the rules were rule 15, that no person shall leave his or her work without giving fourteen days' previous notice, such notice to be given on a Saturday, and rule 16, that any person leaving without giving such notice "shall forfeit all wages then due, or earned, or unpaid." She was paid by the piece and all work done was booked up at three o'clock on the Wednesday afternoon in each week, and paid for on the following Saturday, all work booked after three o'clock on the Wednesday afternoon being carried forward to the following week. She left the mill before three o'clock on a Wednesday afternoon without giving the required notice, having previously carried in and had booked certain work which she had completed. On the following Saturday she applied for the wages due at the time she left and when she had completed her work, but payment was refused on the ground that the same was forfeited by rules 15 and 16. No claim was, however, made for damage sustained by the employer.— The 11th section of the Employers and Workmen Act, 1875, enacts that "in the case of a child, young person, or woman, subject to the provisions of the Factory Acts, any forfeiture on the ground of absence or leaving work shall not be deducted from or set off against a claim for wages or other sum due for work done before such absence or leaving work, except to the amount of the damage, if any, which the employer may have sustained by reason of such absence or leaving work":— *Held,* that the above facts did not shew a weekly hiring at weekly wages, but shewed that the price for the work done and booked when the weaver left on the Wednesday was then earned and due,

III. MASTER AND SERVANT—WAGES—*contd.*

though not then payable, and that the same would have been forfeited by rules 15 and 16, but that as there was no damage and the weaver was a woman subject to the Factory Acts she was protected by the said 11th section, and could not be deprived of what she had so earned. WARBURTON *v.* HEYWORTH - - 6 Q. B. D. 1

MASTER AND SERVANT—Apprentice
[8 Q. B. D. 1; 9 Q. B. D. 636
See APPRENTICE. 1, 2.

—— Negligence — Unsafe premises — Ignorance of servant 13 Q. B. D. 259
See NEGLIGENCE—LIABILITY. 7.

MASTER OF SHIP—Disbursements 8 P. D. 48
See SHIP—MARITIME LIEN. 4.

—— Sale by - 10 P. D. 13; 16 Ch. D. 574
See SHIP—MASTER. 1, 2.

MASTER OF THE ROLLS—Jurisdiction
[26 Ch. D. 105
See PATENT—AMENDMENT. 1.

MATERIAL MEN—Wages—Lien—Priority
See SHIP—MARITIME LIEN. 5. [9 P. D. 37

MATRIMONIAL CAUSES ACT, 1884
See PRACTICE — DIVORCE—RESTITUTION OF CONJUGAL RIGHTS—*Statutes.*

MAURITIUS—Law of - 8 App. Cas. 296;
[9 App. Cas. 413
See COLONIAL LAW—MAURITIUS. 1, 2.

MAXIMS OF LAW—"Actio personalis moritur cum personâ" - 15 Q. B. D. 565
See PRACTICE — SUPREME COURT — CHANGE OF PARTIES. 4.

—— "Actio personalis moritur cum personâ"
[21 Ch. D. 484; 24 Ch. D. 439;
[9 Q. B. D. 110
See EXECUTOR—ACTIONS. 1, 2, 3.

—— "Interest reipublicæ ut sit finis litium"
[14 Q. B. D. 141
See ESTOPPEL—JUDGMENT. 7.

—— "Nemo debet bis vexari pro unâ et eâdem causâ" - - 14 Q. B. D. 141
See ESTOPPEL—JUDGMENT. 7.

—— "Omnia præsumuntur rite acta"
[10 App. Cas. 692
See SCOTCH LAW—HUSBAND AND WIFE 2..

—— "Qui prior est tempore potior est jure"
[14 Q. B. D. 424
See COMPANY—SHARES—TRANSFER. 2.

—— "Quicquid plantatur solo solo cedit"
[7 Q. B. D. 295; 8 App. Cas. 195
See MINE—WORKING. 1.

MAYOR—Borough without commission of peace —Jurisdiction - 7 Q. B. D. 548
See CONTRACT—VALIDITY. 1.

MAYOR'S COURT—London.
See Cases under COURT — MAYOR'S COURT.

MEASURE
See WEIGHTS AND MEASURES—*Statutes.*

MEASURE OF DAMAGES — Abandonment of railway—Landowner 25 Ch. D. 251
See RAILWAY COMPANY—ABANDONMENT. 2.

MEASURE OF DAMAGES—*continued*.

—— Carrier—Liability for delay in transmission
　of goods—　-　-　9 Q. B. D. 582
　See CARRIER—DAMAGES.

—— Collision　-　8 P. D. 109; 10 P. D. 167
　See SHIP—NAVIGATION. 1, 3.

—— Collision—Compulsory pilotage　8 P. D. 218
　See SHIP—PILOT. 4.

—— Guarantee　-　16 Ch. D. 290
　See PRINCIPAL AND SURETY—CONTRACT.

—— Improper sale by solicitor　-　16 Ch. D. 393
　See SOLICITOR—LIABILITIES. 7.

—— Misrepresentation in prospectus of company
　[17 Ch. D. 301
　See COMPANY—PROSPECTUS. 3.

—— Principal and agent—Consignment of goods
　not of description ordered
　[11 Q. B. D. 797
　See PRINCIPAL AND AGENT—AGENT'S
　LIABILITY. 3.

—— Warranty of authority　-　24 Ch. D. 367
　See PRINCIPAL AND AGENT—AGENT'S
　AUTHORITY. 2.

MEDICAL OFFICER — Action by—Consent of
Charity Commissioners　-　25 Ch. D. 39
See CHARITY—COMMISSIONERS. 5.

MEDICAL PRACTICE—Sale of　-　20 Ch. D. 705
See SPECIFIC PERFORMANCE. 4.

MEDICAL PRACTITIONER—*Unqualified Person
—Right to sue—Apothecaries Act* (55 Geo. 3, c. 194),
s. 14—*Medical Act,* 1858 (21 & 22 Vict. c. 90),
ss. 32, 40.] The Act 55 Geo. 3, c. 194, prohibiting medical practice by unqualified persons is not
repealed by implication by the Medical Act,
1858.—The Defendant, a duly qualified medical
practitioner, agreed with the Plaintiff, a medical
practitioner not duly qualified, but who was described in the agreement as "medical practitioner," to serve the Plaintiff as assistant in
his profession as a medical practitioner, and not
to practise at R. within five years after the close
of the engagement. The Plaintiff applied for an
injunction to prevent the Defendant from practising at R. in breach of this agreement:—*Held,*
by Pearson, J., that the Medical Act of 1858 does
not prohibit unqualified persons from practising
medicine, its object being only to enable the public
to distinguish between qualified and unqualified
practitioners—that the use by an unqualified person in a private agreement with another medical
man, of any of the titles for the wilful use of
which by an unqualified person, for the purpose
of deceiving the public, penalties are imposed by
sect. 40 of the Act, is not an offence within that
section—that the agreement therefore was not
illegal, and that the Plaintiff could enforce its
terms, and was entitled to an injunction.—The
Defendant appealed, and on appeal shewed that
the Plaintiff had given various certificates of
cause of death, which shewed that the Plaintiff
had attended the deceased persons during their
last illness, and from which it was to be inferred
that he attended patients in the way in which a
medical practitioner ordinarily attends, and in
fact personally acted as an apothecary:—*Held,*
that his doing so was made illegal by the Act
55 Geo. 3, c. 194, s. 14, that the agreement there-

MEDICAL PRACTITIONER—*continued*.

fore was to assist the Plaintiff in carrying on a
business which he could not lawfully carry on,
and that the agreement was illegal and could not
be enforced:—*Semble,* if the Plaintiff had carried
on his business by means of duly qualified assistants, without personally acting as a physician,
surgeon, or apothecary, the agreement might
have been legal. DAVIES *v.* MAKUNA
[29 Ch. D. 596

MEDICAL RELIEF—Municipal election.
See MUNICIPAL CORPORATION—ELECTION
　—*Statutes.*

—— Parliament—Vote.
See PARLIAMENT—FRANCHISE—*Statutes.*

MEDICAL WITNESS　-　18 Ch. D. 26
See LUNATIC—INQUISITION. 1.

MEETING OF CREDITORS — Bankruptcy —
Scheme of arrangement　25 Ch. D. 266
See BANKRUPTCY—ANNULMENT. 3.

—— Composition　18 Ch. D. 488; 20 Ch. D. 281
See BANKRUPTCY—COMPOSITION. 2, 3.

—— Liquidation -　19 Ch. D. 367; 24 Ch. D. 35
See BANKRUPTCY—LIQUIDATION. 6, 13.

MEETING OF SHAREHOLDERS — Fourteen
days' notice—Computation of time
[29 Ch. D. 204
See COMPANY—REDUCTION OF CAPITAL.
5.

—— Poll　-　29 Ch. D. 159
See COMPANY—MANAGEMENT. 3.

—— Power of　21 Ch. D. 183; 23 Ch. D. 1
See COMPANY — DIRECTOR'S APPOINT-
MENT. 1, 2.

—— Power of—Gratuities to directors and servants　-　23 Ch. D. 654
See COMPANY—MANAGEMENT. 2.

—— Proxies　-　23 Ch. D. 14
See COMPANY—MANAGEMENT. 4.

MELBOURNE HARBOUR TRUST -　9 App. Cas.
See COLONIAL LAW—VICTORIA. 4. [365

MEMBER OF CLUB—Expulsion　17 Ch. D. 615
See CLUB.

MEMORANDUM OF ASSOCIATION.
See Cases under COMPANY—MEMORAN-
DUM AND ARTICLES.

—— Subscriber of -　-　25 Ch. D. 283
See COMPANY—DIRECTOR'S QUALIFICA-
TION. 1.

**MERCHANT SEAMEN PAYMENT OF WAGES
AND RATING ACT,** 1880, *s.* 5, applied
to foreign ships.
See SHIP—MERCHANT SHIPPING ACTS—
Gazette.

MERCHANT SHIPPING ACTS.
See Cases, Statutes and Gazette under
SHIP—MERCHANT SHIPPING ACTS.

MERGER—Lease—Easement -　25 Ch. D. 559;
[10 App. Cas. 590
See LIGHT—TITLE. 5.

—— Mortgage debt—Judgment -　22 Ch. D. 98
See JUDGMENT. 2.

MERSEY—Launch—Reasonable precautions
　　　　　　　　　[7 P. D. 217 ; 8 P. D. 119
　　　See SHIP—NAVIGATION. 6, 7.

METER—Waterworks company - **25 Ch. D. 443**
　　　See WATERWORKS COMPANY. 3.

METROPOLIS :—　　　　　　　　　Col.

I. METROPOLIS—BUILDING ACTS.

The Act 45 & 46 Vict. c. 14, amends the Metropolitan Building Act, 1855, and the Acts amending the same, and confers further powers on the Metropolitan Board of Works with respect to the removal of temporary buildings and structures, and with respect to dilapidated, neglected, and dangerous structures.

1. —— Party-Wall—*Dangerous Structure—Complaint against one Owner—Expenses incurred by Board of Works—Reasonableness of Charges—Metropolitan Building Act,* 1855 (18 & 19 *Vict. c.* 122), *Part II., ss.* 73, 97.] A structure within the metropolis having been surveyed by the Board of Works under 18 & 19 Vict. c. 122, ss. 69, 73, an order was made by a magistrate for the owner to take down or otherwise secure the party-walls. Upon his default the board themselves executed the works and took out a summons against the owner for the expenses incurred :—*Held*, first, that upon the hearing of such summons the owner could not object to his being made liable for expenses actually incurred, by merely shewing that they included items which were in excess of the market price of labour and materials at the date of the execution of the works. Secondly, that he could not require that the other owners of the party-walls should be summoned in order that the expenses might be distributed among them. DEBENHAM *v.* METROPOLITAN BOARD OF WORKS
　　　　　　　　　　　[6 Q. B. D. 112

2. —— Party-wall—*United Buildings — Appeal — Conviction — Metropolitan Building Act,* 1855 (18 & 19 *Vict. v.* 122), *ss.* 27, 28, 106).] By sect. 9 of the Metropolitan Building Act, 1855, an addition to an old building is subject to the regulations of the Act ; by sect. 27, rule 4, certain buildings containing more than 216,000 cubic feet are to be divided by party walls ; and by sect. 28, rule 2, no buildings shall be united, if when so united they will be in contravention of the Act. A new building was added to an old building, the united building containing more than 216,000 cubic feet :—*Held*, that the united building was

I. METROPOLIS—BUILDING ACTS—*continued.*
not within the words of the Act, and need not be divided by a party-wall.—An appeal from the decision of a magistrate will lie under sect. 106 of the Act, although there has not been a conviction. SCOTT *v.* LEGG　-　　-　　-　**10 Q. B. D. 236**

3. —— Site of Building—*Removal of fæcal, animal, or vegetable Matter from Site— By-laws of Metropolitan Board of Works, Construction of—Metropolis Management and Building Acts Amendment Act,* 1878 (41 & 42 *Vict. c.* 32), *ss.* 14, 16.] By the Metropolis Management and Building Acts Amendment Act, 1878, sect. 16, the Metropolitan Board of Works were empowered to make by-laws with respect to " the foundations of houses, buildings, and other erections, and the sites of houses, buildings, and other erections to be constructed after the passing of this Act, and the mode in which and the materials with which such foundations and sites shall be made, formed, excavated, filled up, prepared, and completed for securing stability, the prevention of fires, and for purposes of health." By sect. 14 the term " site " is defined to mean " the whole space to be occupied by such house, building, or other erection between the level of the bottom of the foundations and the level of the base of the walls." The Metropolitan Board of Works made the following by-law : " No house, building, or other erection shall be erected upon any site or portion of any site which shall have been filled up or covered with any material impregnated or mixed with any fæcal, animal, or vegetable matter, or which shall have been filled up or covered with dust, or slop, or other refuse, or in or upon which any such matter or refuse shall have been deposited, unless and until such matter or refuse shall have been properly removed by excavations or otherwise from such site " :—*Held*, that the meaning of the word " site " in the by-law was governed by the interpretation of that word in the Act, so that the by-law did not authorize the Metropolitan Board of Works to direct the removal of fæcal, animal, or vegetable matter in the soil below the level of the bottom of the foundations. BLASHILL *v.* CHAMBERS　　-　　　　**14 Q. B. D. 479**

II. METROPOLIS—COMMONS ACT.

The Act 45 & 46 Vict. c. 15 (Commonable Rights Compensation Act, 1882), *provides for the better application of moneys paid by way of compensation, under the provisions of the Lands Clauses Consolidation Act,* 1845, *and of railway and other special Acts of Parliament, for the extinction of commonable rights, or for lands, being common lands or in the nature thereof, the right to the soil of which belongs to the commoners.*
　　　　　　　　[*See also* INCLOSURE.]

III. METROPOLIS—MANAGEMENT ACTS.

Board of Works.] *The Act 48 & 49 Vict. v. 33, further amends 18 & 19 Vict. c. 120, and confers additional members on the Metropolitan Board of Works.*

Infectious Diseases.] *The Act 46 & 47 Vict. c. 35, makes better provision as regards the Metropolis for the isolation and treatment of persons suffering from cholera and other infectious diseases. Sect.* 1. *Act to be cited as the Diseases Prevention (Metropolis) Act,* 1883.

III. METROPOLIS — MANAGEMENT ACTS —
continued.

Sect. 2. *Managers of the Metropolitan Asylum District to be a local authority for certain purposes of the Diseases Prevention Act,* 1855.

Sect. 3 *empowers the managers to contract with hospital authorities for the reception of cholera patients.*

Sect. 4 *provides for expenses of managers and other local authority.*

Sect. 5 *empowers vestries and district boards to borrow for hospitals.*

Sect. 6. *Managers to provide places for embarkation, &c., of patients.*

Sect. 7. *Admission into hospital of person suffering infectious disease to be no disqualification of or for any right or privilege.*

Sect. 8 *empowers Local Government Board to assign to port sanitary authority of Port of London the duties, &c., of an urban sanitary authority under the Public Health Act,* 1875.

Sect. 9. *Saving for duties, &c., of local authorities.*

Sect. 10 *empowers Local Government Board to make regulations.*

Sect. 11 *extends Diseases Prevention Act,* 1885, *to hamlet of Nottingham.*

Sect. 12. *Definitions.*

Sect. 13. *Act not to continue in force after the 1st of September,* 1884, *except so far as regards any property acquired, act done, liability incurred under it prior to that date, and except as regards the Port Sanitary Authority of London.*

The Act 48 & 49 Vict. c. 59, *continues this Act to the 31st of December,* 1886.

Cholera.] *Regulations of* 12th July, 1883, *for the Port of London made by the Local Government Board under the Sanitary Act,* 1866, s. 52, *and Public Health Act,* 1875, s. 130 **L. G.** 1883, **p.** 3533

The Act 47 & 48 Vict. c. 60, *provides that works carried out under s. 6 of* 46 & 47 Vict. c. 35, *shall be deemed to have been and to be purposes for which money may be borrowed in pursuance of the Metropolitan Poor Act,* 1867, *and other Acts.*

The Act 48 & 49 Vict. c. 72, s. 9, *amends* 29 & 30 Vict. c. 90, s. 19 (*Sanitary Act,* 1866).

Loans by the Metropolitan Board of Works.] *The Act* 44 & 45 Vict. c. 48 (*Metropolitan Board of Works Money Act,* 1881), *as amended by* 45 & 46 Vict. c. 33, *and the Acts* 46 & 47 Vict. c. 27 (*Metropolitan Board of Works Money Act,* 1883), *and* 47 & 48 Vict. c. 50 (*Metropolitan Board of Works Money Act,* 1884), *amend the Acts relating to the raising of money by the Metropolitan Board of Works.*

The Act 48 & 49 Vict. c. 50 (*Metropolitan Board of Works Money Act,* 1885), *amends the earlier Acts relating to the raising of money by the Metropolitan Board of Works.*

Open Spaces.] *The Act* 44 & 45 Vict. c. 34 (*the Metropolitan Open Spaces Act,* 1880), *amends the Metropolitan Open Spaces Act,* 1877.

Sect. 1. *Interpretation clause.*

Sect. 2. *Power to trustees to transfer certain open spaces to local authority.*

Sect. 3. *Power to any owner to transfer open spaces to local authority.*

Sect. 4. *Power to transfer disused burial grounds to local authority.*

Sect. 5. *Powers and duties of local authority.*

III. METROPOLIS — MANAGEMENT ACTS —
continued.

Sect. 6. *By-laws.*

Sect. 7. *Metropolitan Board and vestry or district board may carry out Act jointly.*

Sect. 8. *Provision for extra-parochial places.*

Sect. 9. *Provision for compensation.*

Sect. 10. *Expenses.*

Sect. 11. *Extent of Act.*

Sect. 12. *Application in City of London.*

Sect. 13. *Short title.*

Offensive Business.] *The Order of Metropolitan Board of Works, under* 37 & 38 Vict. c. 67, s. 3, *declaring the business of a gut scraper to be an offensive business, confirmed by Local Government Board,* 4th January, 1881 - **L. G.** 1881, **p.** 130

Streets.] *The Act* 45 & 46 Vict. c. 14, *amends the* 18 & 19 Vict. c. 120 (*an Act for the better Local Management of the Metropolis*), *and the Acts amending the same, and confers further powers upon the Metropolitan Board of Works with respect to the management of existing streets and the formation of new streets for carriage traffic or foot traffic only.*

(a.) GENERAL LINE OF BUILDINGS.

1. —— Appeal—*Justice of the Peace—Quarter Sessions—Whether Appeal lies to Quarter Sessions from Order of Justice for Demolition of Building —Metropolis Management Act,* 1855 (18 & 19 Vict. c. 120), s. 231 — *Metropolis Management Amendment Act,* 1862 (25 & 26 Vict. c. 102), s. 75.] An appeal to quarter sessions will not lie against the order of a justice directing the demolition of buildings under sect. 75 of the Metropolis Management Amendment Act, 1862.—By sect. 231 of the Metropolis Management Act, 1855, any person aggrieved by any adjudication of a justice " with respect to any penalty or forfeiture under the provisions of the Act" may appeal to quarter sessions.—By sect. 75 of the Metropolis Management Amendment Act, 1862 (which, by sect. 110, is to be construed as one Act with the Act of 1855), where a building is erected beyond the general line of buildings in a street without the consent of the Metropolitan Board of Works, a justice of the peace is empowered, upon complaint made and after inquiry held as the Act directs, to order the owner or occupier to demolish the building, and in default of compliance with the order the vestry of the parish or Board of Works for the district shall demolish the building, and may remove and sell the materials, and recover the expenses of so doing from the owner or occupier:—*Held,* that the order of a justice directing the demolition of a building under sect. 75 of the Act of 1872, was not an adjudication "with respect to a penalty or forfeiture " within sect. 231 of the Act of 1855, and therefore that no appeal to quarter sessions would lie against the order. THE QUEEN *v.* JUSTICES OF MIDDLESEX. *Re* ELSDON - **9 Q. B D.** 41

2. —— Certificate of Architect — *Metropolis Management Act,* 1862 (25 & 26 Vict. c. 102), s. 75.] The certificate of the superintending architect of the Metropolitan Board of Works made under the Metropolis Management Amendment Act, 1862 (25 & 26 Vict. c. 102), s. 75, and fixing the "general line of buildings " in a road is conclusive as to a building erected before the certificate is made;

III. METROPOLIS — MANAGEMENT ACTS — *continued.*

(a.) GENERAL LINE OF BUILDINGS—*continued.*

and on the hearing of a summons (issued after the making of the certificate) for an offence under s. 75 alleged to have been committed in respect of such building, the justice has no jurisdiction to review the architect's decision or decide for himself whether the line fixed by the certificate is the true general line.—So *held*, affirming the decision of the Court of Appeal.—*Simpson* v. *Smith* (Law Rep. 6 C. P. 87) overruled. SPACK-MAN *v.* PLUMSTEAD BOARD OF WORKS
[13 Q. B. D. 878 ; 10 App. Cas. 229

3. —— **House on Vacant Land** — *Metropolis Management Amendment Act,* 1862 (25 & 26 *Vict. c.* 102), *ss.* 74, 75 — *House at Corner of Two Streets* — *Order of Magistrate* — *Reduction into Writing—Time of Service.*] The Plaintiff purchased a large piece of land abutting on a highway called the K. Road, on which were standing a public-house and several other houses fronting the highway. He pulled down the house, and made a new street through the piece of land, running into the K. Road at right angles with it, which he called D. Gardens, and sold portions of the land on each side of the new street to a builder. The builder erected a row of houses in D. Gardens, and the superintending architect of the Metropolitan Board certified the general line of buildings in D. Gardens. The Plaintiff built a row of houses fronting the K. Road, one of which was at the corner of the K. Road and D. Gardens. The side of the corner house abutting on D. Gardens projected beyond the general line of buildings in D. Gardens. The house was not built on the site of any one of the old houses in the K. Road, but on the site of part of the garden of the public-house. A magistrate's order having been obtained by the vestry for the removal of the projecting part of the corner house, the Plaintiff brought an action to restrain the vestry from interfering with his house :—*Held*, reversing the decision of Bacon, V.C., (1.) that the general line of buildings in D. Gardens extended to the K. Road ; (2.) that the projecting part of the corner house was a new building and came within sect. 75 of the Metropolis Management Amendment Act, 1862, and not within sect. 74, which applies to existing buildings ; and (3.) that although the corner house formed part of a row in K. Road it was also in D. Gardens, and the owner was bound to keep it within the general line of buildings of D. Gardens. The action was therefore dismissed. —*Lord Auckland* v. *Westminster District Board of Works* (Law Rep. 7 Ch. 597) distinguished.—An order was made by a magistrate under sect. 75 of the Metropolis Management Amendment Act, 1862, for pulling down the projecting part of a building within eight weeks. The order was made in the presence of the owner who was summoned, but was not reduced into writing and served on him till the day on which the eight weeks expired :—*Held*, that the order was binding : the Act being silent as to service of the order on the owner, although it requires to be in writing. BARLOW *v.* KENSINGTON VESTRY
[27 Ch. D. 362
[Reversed by the House of Lords.]

III. METROPOLIS — MANAGEMENT ACTS — *continued.*

(b.) NUISANCE.

4. —— **Accumulation of Water from a Sewer**— *Liability of Metropolitan Board of Works* — *Metropolis Local Management Act,* 1855 (18 & 19 *Vict. c.* 120), *ss.* 135, 136—*Act of God.*] The Defendants, under the powers conferred upon them by the Metropolis Local Management Act, 1855 (18 & 19 Vict. c. 120), ss. 135, 136, constructed, and properly constructed, a sewer having its outfall at Deptford Creek, a little above the Plaintiff's coal wharf, with water-gates which it was the duty of the person in charge of them to open when the water within them became eight feet deep,—a depth which was reached only in heavy rainfalls. On the 29th of August, 1879, there was an exceptionally heavy rainfall, and it became necessary to open the water-gates to prevent a large district from being flooded. This having been done, and the rain increasing in violence, the rush of water from the sewer carried away a portion of the Plaintiff's wharf, with a barge moored thereto, and a quantity of coals deposited therein and thereon : —*Held*, that the injury complained of was occasioned by the opening of the water-gates, and not by the act of God, and therefore the Defendants were *primâ facie* liable for the damage done, within the principle of *Fletcher* v. *Rylands* (Law Rep. 3 H. L. 330) ; but that, as they were a public body acting in the discharge of a public duty, and as that which happened was only the inevitable result of what Parliament had authorized them to do, they were not liable. DIXON *v.* METROPOLITAN BOARD OF WORKS - .. 7 Q. B. D. 418

5. —— **Flap of Water-Meter**—*Highway—Improper State of Flap—Liability of Vestry*—18 & 19 *Vict. c.* 120, *ss.* 96, 116.] A water-meter, which was the property of a water company and used for measuring the water supplied ·by the company to the Defendants, the vestry of a parish, for watering the streets, was placed by the Defendants in a box of theirs sunk in the footway of one of the streets and covered with an iron flap. The Defendants as such vestry were by sect. 96 of the Metropolis Management Act, 1855 (18 & 19 Vict. c. 120), the surveyors of highways, and by sect. 116 authorized to cause the streets in their parish to be watered. The Plaintiff whilst walking along the street stepped on the iron flap, and by reason of its having been worn smooth and become slippery and dangerous, he fell and was injured. In an action by him against the Defendants for damages for such injury :—*Held*, that though the Defendants might not be liable as surveyors of the highway for negligence in not keeping the iron flap in a proper state, they were in their capacity as the authority for watering the street, in which capacity they had placed the iron flap there.— *White* v. *Hindley Local Board* (Law Rep. 10 Q. B. 219) affirmed. BLACKMORE *v.* VESTRY OF MILE END OLD TOWN - - - 9 Q. B. D. 451
[*And see* HIGHWAY—NUISANCE.]

6. —— **Urinal**—*Dedication of Court to Public* —*No Thoroughfare*—*Metropolis Management Act,* 1855 (18 & 19 *Vict. c.* 120), *s.* 88.] A court which was not a thoroughfare had for seventy or eighty years been at all hours open to the

III. METROPOLIS — MANAGEMENT ACTS — *continued.*

(b.) NUISANCE—*continued.*

public, and had been paved, lighted, and cleansed by the parish vestry, and the owners of the soil were not shewn to have during that time exercised any rights of ownership over the soil of the court :—*Held*, by Malins, V.C., that the court had been dedicated to the public so as to bring it under the vestry according to the Metropolis Local Management Act.—Under the Metropolis Local Management Act (18 & 19 Vict. c. 120), s. 88, the vestry has power to provide and maintain urinals in situations where they deem such accommodation to be required :—*Held*, by Malins, V.C., that any question whether one place or another was more fit for the erection of an urinal must be left to the decision of the vestry; but that the vestry would be controlled by the Court if they acted in an unreasonable manner and occasioned a nuisance to the owners of adjoining property :—*Held*, by the Court of Appeal, that as the erection of an urinal was not necessarily a nuisance, the provision of the Act authorizing the vestry to erect urinals did not empower them to erect one where it would be a nuisance to the owners of adjoining property, there being no words in the Act which expressly or by necessary implication authorized them to create a nuisance. VERNON *v.* VESTRY OF ST. JAMES, WESTMINSTER **[16 Ch. D 449**

7. —— Wire across Street—*Telephone Company*—*Metropolis Management Act,* 1855 (18 & 19 *Vict. c.* 120), *s.* 96 — *" Street "* — *Property of Vestry or District Board in " Street "*—*Telegraph Act,* 1863 (26 & 27 *Vict. c.* 112), *ss.* 2, 3, 12—*Telegraph Act,* 1868 (31 & 32 *Vict. c.* 110), *s.* 2—*Telegraph Act,* 1869 (32 & 33 *Vict. c.* 73), *ss.* 2, 3 —*" The Company "*—*" Telegraph Company "*—*Consent of Local Authority*—*Trespass*—*Injunction.*] The Metropolis Management Act, 1855, does not by sect. 96 confer upon a vestry or a board of works (constituted under that statute) such a property in the streets situate within their district, as to entitle them to maintain an action for an injunction against the erection of a telephone wire across a street, the telephone wire being erected at a great height and causing no appreciable danger to the public or to the traffic in the street.—*Coverdale v. Charlton* (4 Q. B. D. 104) followed.—Notwithstanding the Telegraph Act, 1869, sect. 3, a telephone company registered under the Companies Act, 1862, and not incorporated under any special Act, does not fall within the phrase " the company " used in the Telegraph Act, 1863, and therefore is not forbidden by sect. 12 of the last-named Act to erect its wires across a street, unless the consent of the body having the control of the street is obtained. BOARD OF WORKS FOR WANDSWORTH DISTRICT *v.* UNITED TELEPHONE COMPANY **13 Q. B. D. 904**

(c.) RATES.

8. —— Sealing Order—*Order of Board to Overseers to levy Rate*—*Issue of Order*—18 & 19 *Vict. c.* 120, *ss.* 158-161.] By the Metropolis Management Act, 1855 (18 & 19 Vict. c. 120), sect. 158, every vestry and district board shall from time to time " by order under their seal require " the

III. METROPOLIS — MANAGEMENT ACTS— *continued.*

(c.) RATES—*continued.*

overseers of their parish to levy the sums which such vestry or board may require for defraying the expenses of the execution of the Act.—By sect. 161 the overseers " to whom any such order as aforesaid is issued shall levy the amount mentioned therein according to the exigency thereof " :—*Held* (per Stephen and Mathew, JJ., Day, J., dissenting), that such an order became effective when sealed, and service of it on the overseers was not necessary to authorize them to levy rates, but that rates made by overseers in pursuance of such order, after notice of it having been sealed, were valid. GLEN *v.* OVERSEERS OF FULHAM - - **14 Q. B. D. 328**

(d.) SEWERS.

9. —— Metropolitan Main Drainage—*Metropolitan Area, Persons outside*—*Right to use Drainage* — *Injunction* — *Metropolis Management Act,* 1855 (18 & 19 *Vict. c.* 120), *s.* 135—*Metropolis Management Amendment Act,* 1862 (25 & 26 *Vict. c.* 102), *s.* 61.] The Metropolis Management Act, 1855, vested in the Plaintiffs an open sewer, called the Stamford Brook.—The Metropolis Management Amendment Act, 1862, s. 61, enacted that no person should make or branch any sewer or drain, or make any opening into any sewer vested in the Plaintiffs, without their previous consent in writing; provided that any person might, with such consent, at his own expense, make or branch any drain into any such sewer in such manner as the Plaintiff should direct. After the passing of the Act of 1855, the Plaintiffs allowed four old cottages belonging to the Defendants, on land just outside the Metropolitan area and bounded by the Stamford Brook, to continue to drain through an eighteen-inch brick drain into Stamford Brook. They subsequently, at the request of the Defendants, who paid half the cost, covered in the brook and converted it into a main sewer. When they did this, they made a drain-eye in the newly covered-in sewer as a communication for the eighteen-inch drain.—The Defendants afterwards built other cottages on the same land, and claimed the right to use the eighteen-inch drain for the purpose of draining the new cottages through the communication into the sewer :—*Held*, 1. That as the Defendants had not proved any prescriptive right to use the eighteen-inch drain for the sewage of the new cottages, nor obtained the written consent of the Plaintiffs for that purpose under sect. 61 of the Act of 1862, they were not entitled to use the eighteen-inch drain for any other purposes than those for which they used it when the brook was covered in. 2. That, therefore, the Plaintiffs were entitled to an injunction to restrain the Defendants from permitting their additional cottages, or any buildings other than the four old cottages, to drain into the Stamford Brook.—*Semble*, that if the Plaintiffs had given their written consent and fixed the size of the communication under the 61st section of the Act of 1862, the Defendants could then have used the eighteen-inch drain to the full extent of its capacity for all purposes. METROPOLITAN BOARD OF WORKS *v.* LONDON AND NORTH WESTERN RAILWAY COMPANY **[17 Ch. D. 246**

III. METROPOLIS — MANAGEMENT ACTS — *continued.*

(e.) STREETS.

10. —— Compulsory Purchase — 57 *Geo.* 3, *c. xxix.*, *ss.* 80, 82—*Severance—Vestry.*] A metropolitan vestry required, for the purpose of widening a street, a part of the buildings and site of an orphanage that would leave a substantial portion of the premises:—*Held*, that (the owners wishing to sell the part required only) the vestry could not take the whole. TEULIERE *v.* VESTRY OF ST. MARY ABBOTTS, KENSINGTON - 30 Ch. D. 642

11. —— Formation of Streets—"*Open at both ends*"—*Metropolis Management Act,* 1862 (25 & 26 *Vict. c.* 102), *s.* 98.] By the Metropolis Management Act, 1862 (25 & 26 Vict. c. 102), s. 98, no road being of less width than forty feet shall hereafter be formed or laid out for building as a street for the purposes of carriage traffic unless such road be widened to the full width of forty feet, or for the purposes of foot traffic only unless such road be widened to the full width of twenty feet, "or" unless such streets respectively shall be open at both ends:—*Held*, that such street must be of the width prescribed and be also open at both ends. METROPOLITAN BOARD OF WORKS *v.* STEED
[8 Q. B. D. 445

12. —— Paving New Street—*Owner of Land bounding or abutting on new Street—Railway in Cutting—Bridge carrying new Street over Railway* — *Metropolis Management Acts,* 1855 *and* 1862, 18 & 19 *Vict. c.* 120, *ss.* 96, 105, 250, *and* 25 & 26 *Vict. c.* 102, *s.* 77.] A railway line ran in a deep cutting much below the level of a highway, which was carried over the railway (nearly at right angles) by a bridge built by the railway company under statutory powers and in pursuance of sects. 46–51 of the Railways Clauses Consolidation Act, 1845 (8 & 9 Vict. c. 20). The parapets of the bridge consisted of two walls resting upon arches which had their foundations (outside the lines of the roadway) in the railway company's land. The walls were not used by the company otherwise than as fences for the bridge. The district board of works having paved the highway, which was admitted to be a new street within sect. 105 of the Metropolis Management Act, 1855 (18 & 19 Vict. c. 120):—*Held* by Lords Blackburn, Watson, and FitzGerald, reversing the decision of the Court of Appeal, that assuming the fence walls to be the railway company's land, the company were not "owners of land bounding or abutting on" the highway within sect. 77 of the Metropolis Management Act, 1862 (25 & 26 Vict. c. 102), and were not liable as owners of the fence walls to contribute to the expenses of paving.—*Held*, also, by Lords Blackburn and Watson, that the railway line and slopes being much below the level of the highway, the company were not in respect of such line and slopes "owners of land bounding or abutting on" the highway within the above section, and were not liable as owners of the line and slopes to contribute to the expenses of paving. HACKNEY DISTRICT BOARD OF WORKS *v.* GREAT EASTERN RAILWAY COMPANY
[9 Q. B. D. 412; 8 App. Cas. 687

13. —— Paving New Streets — "*Owner*" *of Land—Land subject to Covenants — Expenses of*

III. METROPOLIS — MANAGEMENT ACTS— *continued.*

(e.) STREETS—*continued.*

paving New Street—Metropolis Management Act, 1855 (18 & 19 *Vict. v.* 120), *s.* 250—*Metropolis Management Amendment Act,* 1862 (25 & 26 *Vict. c.* 102), *s.* 77.] By the Metropolis Management Act, 1855, s. 250, the word "owner" shall mean the person for the time being receiving the rack-rent of the lands or premises in connection with which the word is used, or who would so receive the same if such lands or premises were let at a rack-rent; and by the Metropolis Management Amendment Act, 1862, s. 77 (which is to be read as one with the Act of 1855) "owners" of land abutting on any new street are made liable to contribute towards the expenses of paving the same. The Appellant having a strip of land about 4 inches wide and 265 feet in length, abutting upon the north side of a new street, had erected a boundary fence upon the land along its whole extent, under a covenant to erect and for ever after maintain a fence thereon made with his vendor, who was owner of the land adjoining the strip on the north side:—*Held*, that the Appellant was the "owner" of the strip of land within the meaning of sect. 250 of the Metropolis Management Act, 1855, and therefore liable to contribute towards the expense of paving the new street. WILLIAMS *v.* WANDSWORTH BOARD OF WORKS 13 Q. B. D. 211

14. —— Paving New Street—*Power to make Branch Drains to Sewer—Metropolis Management Act,* 1855 (18 & 19 *Vict. c.* 120), *ss.* 78, 250—*Metropolis Management Amendment Act,* 1862 (25 & 26 *Vict. c.* 102), *s.* 112.] A builder made drains from certain houses in a road to the boundary of the forecourts of the houses. The road was what is known as a builder's road, made and coated with gravel and ballasted. The footpaths were made with gravel and kerbed with granite. The houses on either side of the road were not completed and inhabited, but the road was open for carriages and foot-passengers. It was lighted by the parish but had not been taken to as a public road. The vestry made branches from the drains into a sewer which belonged to them and ran along the centre of the road, and for that purpose they opened the road and footway. The builder declined to repay to the vestry the expenses incurred thereby:—*Held*, (1), that the road was not the less a street within the definitions in sect. 250 of the Metropolis Management Act, 1855, and sect. 112 of the Metropolis Management Amendment Act, 1862, because it came within the definition of a new street in the last-mentioned section;—(2.) That sect. 78 of the Metropolis Management Act, 1855, which authorizes the opening of the pavement of any street for the purpose of branching private drains into a sewer, applies equally to streets and to new streets;—(3.) That, looking to the definition of the word "pave" in sect. 112 of the Metropolis Management Amendment Act, 1862, the road was paved:—That, consequently, the vestry had opened a part of the pavement of a street and were entitled under sect. 78 of the Metropolis Management Act, 1855, to recover the expenses incurred by them. HAMPSTEAD VESTRY *v.* HOOPEL
[15 Q. B. D. 652

III. METROPOLIS — MANAGEMENT ACTS —
continued.

(f.) VESTRY.

15. —— Improper Expenditure of Rates—*Injunction—Vestrymen made Parties for Purpose of Costs—Metropolis Management Act, 1855 (18 & 19 Vict. c. 120).*] A metropolitan vestry incorporated under the Act 18 & 19 Vict. c. 120, has no power to apply the rates in paying the expenses of a dinner or a ball, or other ceremonies in connection with the opening of a new vestry hall.—A vestry having passed resolutions authorizing such an expenditure, an action was brought by the Attorney-General, at the relation of a ratepayer, and by the ratepayer as Plaintiff, against the vestry and six of the vestrymen, who had proposed, or seconded, or voted for the resolutions, to restrain the proposed application of the rates. The statement of claim did not allege that any of the parish funds had been applied in the proposed way, but it alleged an intention on the part of the vestry so to apply the funds. No such intention was alleged on the part of the other Defendants, and under the Act they had no control over the funds. The statement of claim asked that the individual Defendants might pay the costs of the action, but costs were not asked against the vestry. On a motion for an interim injunction against the vestry only, an order for a perpetual injunction was consented to, but without costs. The other Defendants delivered no defences, and the Plaintiff moved for judgment against them in default of pleading :—*Held*, that the individual Defendants were not properly made parties for the purpose of obtaining costs from them, and that the action must be dismissed as against them.—*Attorney-General v. Compton* (1 Y. & C. (Ch.) 417) distinguished.—Whether, if the vestry had been made liable for costs, they could have recovered them from the members who had induced them to act illegally, *quære.* ATTORNEY-GENERAL *v.* VESTRY OF BERMONDSEY 23 Ch. D. 60

16. —— Member interested in Contract—*Acting as Member—Penalty—Evidence—Minute-book—18 & 19 Vict. c. 120, ss. 54, 60.*] The brother of the Defendant entered into a contract with a vestry constituted under the Metropolis Management Act, 1855, and in order to enable him to carry it out, borrowed money from the Defendant, who by way of security took an assignment of the contract. Afterwards the Defendant was elected a member of the vestry. An action for penalties having been brought against the Defendant for acting as member of the vestry, an attendance-book of the members signed by the Defendant and the minute-book of the vestry containing his name as a member in attendance were put in as evidence at the trial:—*Held*, that sect. 54 of the Metropolis Management Act, 1855, applied to contracts made as well before as after the election of a member, and that the Defendant was "interested" in the contract in question within the meaning of that section; that there was evidence under sect. 60 that the Defendant had acted as member of the vestry; and that he was liable to penalties for having acted after he had "ceased" to be a member. HUNNINGS *v.* WILLIAMSON

[11 Q. B. D. 533

17. —— Qualification of Vestryman—*Metro-*

III. METROPOLIS — MANAGEMENT ACTS —
continued.

(f.) VESTRY—*continued.*

polis Management Act, 1855 (18 & 19 Vict. c. 120), s. 6 — Rating — Occupation.] By 18 & 19 Vict. c. 120 (Metropolis Management Act, 1855), s. 6, "the vestry elected under this Act in any parish shall consist of persons rated or assessed to the relief of the poor upon a rental of not less than £40 per annum; and no person shall be capable of acting or being elected as one of such vestry for any parish, unless he be the occupier of a house, lands, tenements, or hereditaments in such parish, and be rated or assessed as aforesaid upon such rental as aforesaid within such parish":—*Held*, that to be qualified as a vestryman under the Act a person must be the occupier of real property in the parish and be himself rated or assessed in respect of such occupation to the required amount. MOGG *v.* CLARK

[15 Q. B. D. 82
[Affirmed by the Court of Appeal, 16 Q. B. D. 79.]

IV. METROPOLIS—POLICE ACTS.

Streets.] *The Act 48 & 49 Vict. c. 18, extends limits of the Metropolitan Streets Act, 1867 (30 & 31 Vict. c. 134), to six miles.*

Superannuation.] *The 48 & 49 Vict. c. 68, amends the Metropolitan Police Staff Superannuation Act, 1875.*

V. METROPOLIS—POOR ACTS.

The Act 45 & 46 Vict. c. 36 (the Casual Poor Act, 1882), amends the Pauper Inmate Discharge and Regulation Act, 1871, prescribes the time when a casual pauper may discharge himself from a casual ward, and directs that persons obtaining poor relief by false statements shall be dealt with under sect. 3 of 5 Geo. 4, c. 83.

VI. METROPOLIS—PUBLIC CARRIAGES ACTS.

—— Stage Carriage—*Licence to use—Manager—Injunction—2 & 3 Wm. 4, c. 120—32 & 33 Vict. c. 115, and Rules thereunder.*] The Plaintiff as manager of an omnibus company became, under the provisions of the statutes and rules for the regulation of metropolitan stage-carriages, the licensee of their vehicles. Having ceased to be such manager :—*Held*, that he was entitled to an injunction to restrain the company from continuing to use his name upon the number plates affixed to their carriages. HODGES *v.* LONDON TRAMS OMNIBUS CO. -   12 Q. B. D. 105

VII. METROPOLIS—VALUATION ACTS.

The Act 47 & 48 Vict. c. 5 (Valuation (Metropolis) Amendment Act, 1884), amends the Valuation (Metropolis) Act, 1869, and enables owners and lessees to appeal against valuation lists.

—— Supplemental Valuation List—*Valuation (Metropolis) Act, 1869 (32 & 33 Vict. c. 67), ss. 36, 46, 47) — Alteration during preceding twelve Months—Diminution of Income—Evidence—How rateable Value in Supplemental List to be ascertained.*] On an appeal from the assessment committee as to a supplemental valuation list under the Valuation (Metropolis) Act, 1869 (32 & 33 Vict. c. 67), evidence of a falling off in receipts of tonnage rates on vessels coming to certain docks during the twelve months preceding the making

VII. METROPOLIS—VALUATION ACTS—*contd.*
of the supplemental list when the rates were the same, and which, as compared with former years, shews a continuous and not accidental falling off, is sufficient if not explained or rebutted to shew an alteration in the rateable value of the docks during that period within the meaning of sect. 46. —When such alteration has been established, and it has therefore to be entered in a supplemental list, the rateable value of the docks is to be ascertained, not by opening up the previous quinquennial or supplemental list, but by assuming the value in the list then in force to be the correct value at the commencement of the twelve months preceding, and by deducting from it the diminution in value from the alteration during that period.—(Fry, L.J., dissenting). THE QUEEN *v.* EAST AND WEST INDIA DOCK COMPANY. THE QUEEN *v.* POPLAR UNION　-　11 Q. B. D. 721;
　　　　　　　　　　　　　　[13 Q. B. D. 364

METROPOLIS MANAGEMENT ACTS.
　See Cases and Statutes under METRO-POLIS—MANAGEMENT ACTS.
—— Covenant to pay "rates, taxes and assessments"　　9 Q. B. D. 632; 13 Q. B. D. 1
　See LANDLORD AND TENANT—LEASE. 9, 10.

METROPOLIS MANAGEMENT AND BUILDING ACTS (AMENDMENT) ACT, 1882.
　See METROPOLIS — MANAGEMENT ACTS —*Statutes.*
　　METROPOLIS—BUILDING ACTS—*Statutes.*

METROPOLIS VALUATION LIST—Discretion of overseers　　-　　14 Q. B. D. 351
　See POOR-RATE—PROCEDURE. 1.

METROPOLITAN BOARD OF WORKS (MONEY) ACTS, 1881 AND 1883.
　See METROPOLIS—MANAGEMENT ACTS—*Statutes.*

METROPOLITAN BUILDING ACT, 1855 (18 & 19 Vict. c. 122), part II., ss. 73, 97
　　　　　　　　　　　　[6 Q. B. D. 112
　See METROPOLIS—BUILDING ACTS. 1.

METROPOLITAN OPEN SPACES ACT, 1881.
　See METROPOLIS—MANAGEMENT ACTS—*Statutes.*

METROPOLITAN POOR ACT—Nuisance
　　　　　　　　　　　　[6 App. Cas. 193
　See NUISANCE—DEFINITION. 1.

METROPOLITAN PUBLIC CARRIAGES ACT.
　　　　　　　　　　　　[12 Q. B. D. 105
　See METROPOLIS — PUBLIC CARRIAGES ACTS.

METROPOLITAN STREET IMPROVEMENT ACT —Compensation　　-　25 Ch. D. 472
　See LANDS CLAUSES ACT—COMPENSATION. 1.

MIDDLESEX REGISTRY ACTS　29 Ch. D. 702
　See REGISTRY ACTS.

——　　-　　-　　20 Ch. D. 611
　See VENDOR AND PURCHASER—PURCHASE WITHOUT NOTICE. 1.

MILITARY LAW — Canteen steward—Habeas corpus　　-　　-　15 Q. B. D. 488
　See ARMY AND NAVY.

MILITIA—Ballot expenses.
　See ARMY AND NAVY—*Statutes.*

MILITIA ACT, 1882.
　See ARMY AND NAVY—*Statutes.*

MILITIA STOREHOUSES ACT, 1882.
　See ARMY AND NAVY—*Statutes.*

MILK—Adulteration—Sample　-　6 Q. B. D. 17;
　[9 Q. B. D. 172; 12 Q. B. D. 97; 14 Q. B. D. 193
　See ADULTERATION. 1, 2, 4, 5.

MINE (and MINERALS):—　　　　　　Col.
　　I. FREE MINERS　　-　　-　　- 886
　　II. LEASE　　　-　　-　　-　　- 886
　　III. MINES REGULATION ACTS　　- 887
　　IV. WORKING -　　-　　-　　- 888

I. MINE—FREE MINERS.
　—— Forfeiture of Gale—*Forest of Dean — Election—Time of Application — Empty Gale.*] According to the Acts and rules regulating the working of mines in the Forest of Dean, a gale or lease is not forfeited by not being worked, unless and until the Crown claims the forfeiture. The Crown is under no obligation to claim the forfeiture. An application for a gale will not be valid, unless the gale is at the time empty. A gale is forfeited and becomes empty when notice that the Crown claims the forfeiture has been given to the galee, and an officer has been ordered to take possession, though possession is not immediately taken. The free miner who applies first after that notice has been given is entitled to the gale. JAMES *v.* YOUNG -　　-　　- 27 Ch. D. 652

II. MINE—LEASE.
　　1. —— Covenant to leave Barriers—*Support for underlying Strata.*] The owner of land under which there were several strata of coal, demised one of the upper strata to the Plaintiff, reserving to himself and his lessees the right of working any coal not included in that demise, and the same powers and privileges with respect to such last-mentioned coal as if that demise had not been made : provided always, that in exercising such powers and privileges the working of the coal then demised should not be prevented or unnecessarily interfered with, and that compensation should be made to the Plaintiff for any necessary interference with the workings.—The landowner afterwards demised some of the strata of coal underlying the coal demised to the Plaintiff, to the M. company. The Plaintiff brought an action for an injunction against the landowner and the company :—*Held,* by Kay, J., on the construction of the lease, that working under a barrier between the demised coal and an adjoining worked-out mine, in such a way as might probably endanger the barrier, and thereby let in a sufficiently large quantity of water to delay and impede the working of the upper strata, was an "unnecessary interference" within the meaning of the proviso in the lease.— *Held,* by the Court of Appeal, that the proviso in the lease was unintelligible and could not determine the rights of the parties : that if a lessor wished to reserve rights in derogation of his grant, he must do so in plain. terms : and that on that ground the Plaintiff was entitled to an injunction if he could prove that the works threatened by the Defendants would in all probability affect the

II. MINE—LEASE—*continued.*

security of his mine. Further evidence was directed on this point; and the Court ultimately granted the injunction. MUNDY *v.* DUKE OF RUTLAND　　-　　-　　**23 Ch. D. 81**

2. —— Injury to the Surface.] A clause in a mining lease that the lessee may work the mines "in the usual and most approved way in which the same is performed in other works of the like kind in the county," refers simply to the mode of carrying on the underground works for mining purposes; but does not suppose a custom to work the mines so as to injure or interfere with the rights of other people. Nor did the words that the mining lessee should have liberty to enter upon the land and carry away the minerals, and to erect buildings, and "do and execute all such other acts, works, and things upon, in, or under, or above, the said premises, as shall be necessary or convenient for working and carrying away the same," making compensation, &c., enlarge the power so to deal with the mines as to let down the surface.—*Per* Lord Blackburn : In common right the person who owns the surface has a right to have it properly supported below by minerals. A Court of Law has to look at the documents to see whether the parties have agreed upon something different from the common right. DAVIS *v.* TREHARNE　　-　　-　　**6 App. Cas. 460**

III. MINE—MINES REGULATION ACTS.

Stratified Ironstone.] *The Act* 44 *&* 45 *Vict.* c. 26, *amends the law relating to the use of gunpowder in certain Stratified Ironstone Mines.*

Slate Mines.] *The Act* 45 *&* 46 *Vict.* c. 3 (*Slate Mines Gunpowder Act,* 1883) *empowers the Secretary of State to exempt slate mines from the regulations contained in sect.* 23 (*sub-sect.* 2) *of the Metalliferous Mines Regulations Act,* 1872, *with respect to the use of gunpowder or other explosive substances.*

—— Check-weigher—*Coal Mines Regulation Act,* 1872 (35 *&* 36 *Vict. c.* 76), s. 18—*Qualification — Person "Employed in the Mine."*] By the Coal Mines Regulation Act, 1872, sect. 18, the persons employed in a mine, and paid according to the weight of the mineral gotten by them, may, at their own cost, station a check-weigher at the place appointed for the weighing of such mineral, in order to take an account of the weight thereof on behalf of the persons by whom he is so stationed : and "the check-weigher shall be one of the persons employed either in the mine at which he is so stationed, or in another mine belonging to the owner of that mine."—The Plaintiff, a check-weigher, duly appointed under sect. 18, received a fortnight's notice to quit his employment from the men employed in the mine. Before the notice expired, the men held a fresh election, at which the Plaintiff (with others) presented himself as a candidate, and was again appointed :—*Held,* that the true construction of sect. 18 was to limit the class of persons from whom the men might appoint a check-weigher to persons employed in the mine by the mine-owner ; that the Plaintiff ceased to have any employment under the mine-owner when he was first appointed check-weigher by the men ; and therefore that his second appointment was invalid. HOPKINSON *v.* CAUNT　　-　　-　　-　　**14 Q. B. D. 592**

IV. MINE—WORKING.

1. —— Fixtures—*High Peak Mining Customs and Mineral Courts Act,* 1851 (14 *&* 15 *Vict. c. xciv.*)—*Right of Miner to remove Buildings erected for Mining Purposes—Maxim "quicquid plantatur solo solo cedit."*] Miners working under customs established by the High Peak Mining Customs and Minerals Courts Act, 1851 (14 & 15 Vict. c. xciv.) lawfully erected machinery and buildings accessory thereto on surface land, of which the miners were entitled to the exclusive use for mining purposes, but the freehold of which belonged to others. The buildings were attached so as to be part of the soil, and so that they could not be removed without some disturbance, which would not amount to a destruction, of the soil. The buildings were from the first intended to be accessory to the mining, and there was nothing to shew that the property in them was intended to be irrevocably annexed to the soil :—*Held,* that the maxim "quicquid plantatur solo solo cedit," was not applicable, and that the miners were entitled to pull down and remove the buildings while their interest in the mine continued, and were not liable to the surface owners for so doing. WAKE *v.* HALL　　**7 Q. B. D. 295 ;** [**8 App. Cas. 195**

2. —— Winning Coal.] By a deed of grant and licence the licensee was empowered to win and work all and every or any of the coal mines, seam and seams of coal under certain lands, and to reimburse himself all expenses incurred in the winning out of the profits from the sale of the coal ; and it was provided that after payment to the licensee of all expenses in winning the said colliery, coal mines, or coal mine seam or seams of coal, he should pay the grantor such royalty for the coals yearly wrought out of the said coal mines, seam or seams as should from time to time be awarded by two arbitrators once in every five years whilst the said coal mines, seam, or seams of coal should continue to be wrought.—More than one seam of coal lay under the lands. The licensee after winning one seam went on to win another :—*Held* (reversing the decision of the Court of Appeal upon this point), that the whole colliery was not won when the first seam was won, but that the deed was to be read separatim as to the winning of each seam, and that the licensee was entitled to reimburse himself the expenses of winning the second seam before any royalty was payable as to that seam. ELLIOT *v.* LORD ROKEBY [**7 App. Cas. 43**

MINE—Conveyance to railway company—Open working　　**20 Ch. D. 552** *See* RAILWAY COMPANY — RAILWAYS CLAUSES ACT. 5.

—— Cost-book mine. *See* Cases under COMPANY—COST-BOOK COMPANY.

—— Custom of country—Selling flints **21 Ch. D.** [**18 ; 8 App. Cas. 508** *See* LANDLORD AND TENANT—CUSTOM OF COUNTRY.

—— Inclosure Act—Manorial rights [**10 Q. B. D. 547 ; 9 App. Cas. 286** *See* INCLOSURE. 1.

MINE—*continued.*

—— Income tax   -   -   6 App. Cas. 315
   See SCOTCH LAW—REVENUE.

—— Land taken by railway company
       [22 Ch. D. 25 ; 9 App. Cas. 480
   See LANDS CLAUSES ACT—COMPULSORY
   POWERS. 4.

—— Lease—Distress—Winding-up of company
       [17 Ch. D. 158
   See COMPANY—DISTRESS. 5.

—— Lease—Settled Land Act -   24 Ch. D. 129
   See SETTLED LAND ACT—TRUSTEES. 6.

—— Nova Scotia—Lease of gold mine
       [8 App. Cas. 568
   See COLONIAL LAW—CANADA—NOVA
   SCOTIA.

—— Power of leasing   -   23 Ch. D. 583
   See SETTLEMENT—POWERS. 1.

—— Railway company—Purchase by   19 Ch. D.
      [559 ; 20 Ch. D. 552 ; 30 Ch. D. 634
   See RAILWAY COMPANY — RAILWAYS
   CLAUSES ACT. 4. 5, 6.

—— Railway company—Right of support
       [11 Q. B. D. 820
   See RAILWAY COMPANY — RAILWAYS
   CLAUSES ACT. 7.

—— Reservation of minerals—Support—Inclosure   10 Q. B. D. 547 ; 9 App. Cas. 286
   See INCLOSURE. 1.

—— Scotch law—Reservation of liberty of working coal   -   -   10 App. Cas. 813
   See SCOTCH LAW—MINE. 1.

—— Scotch law—Reservation of minerals—Support   -   -   8 App. Cas. 833
   See SCOTCH LAW—MINE. 2.

—— Scotch law—Right to profits   8 App. Cas.
       [641
   See SCOTCH LAW—HERITABLE PROPERTY.
   2.

MINISTER—Removal of—Leave of Charity Commissioners   -   21 Ch. D. 513
   See CHARITY—COMMISSIONERS. 3.

MINUTES—Motion to vary   20 Ch. D. 130;
       [21 Ch. D. 621
   See PRACTICE—SUPREME COURT—JUDG-
   MENT. 6, 7.

MISCONDUCT—Directors.
   See Cases under COMPANY—DIRECTOR'S
   LIABILITY.

—— Solicitor   28 Ch. D. 614 ; 12 Q. B. D. 148
   See SOLICITOR—MISCONDUCT. 1, 2.

MISDEMEANOR—Sentence—Two counts
       [6 App. Cas. 229
   See CRIMINAL LAW—PRACTICE. 2.

MISDIRECTION—Canada Court 6 App. Cas. 644
   See COLONIAL LAW—CANADA—ONTARIO.
   1.

MISJOINDER—Solicitor—Discovery and costs
       [26 Ch. D. 35
   See PRACTICE—SUPREME COURT—PAR-
   TIES. 16.

MISLEADING CONDITIONS OF SALE
       [24 Ch. D. 11 ; 25 Ch. D. 357
   See VENDOR AND PURCHASER—CONDI-
   TIONS OF SALE. 4, 5.

MISREPRESENTATION   ··   -   20 Ch. D. 1;
       [27 Ch. D. 424
   See FALSE REPRESENTATION. 1, 2.

—— Agent—Sale of land   -   22 Ch. D. 194
   See PRINCIPAL AND AGENT—AUTHORITY.
   1.

—— Answers to queries of life insurance com-
   .pany   .   .   9 App. Cas. 671
   See INSURANCE, LIFE—POLICY. 3.

—— Prospectus of company.
   See Cases under COMPANY—PROSPECTUS.

—— Release of equity of redemption 7 App. Cas.
   See COLONIAL LAW—VICTORIA. 2.   [307

—— Sale of land -   -   -   28 Ch. D. 309
   See VENDOR AND PURCHASER—FRAUD. 2.

MISTAKE.

1. —— Lease—*Rectification*]. Where there
is mutual mistake in a deed or contract the remedy is to rectify by substituting the terms
really agreed to. Where the mistake is unilateral
the remedy is not rectification but rescission, but
the Court may give to a defendant the option of
taking what the plaintiff meant to give in lieu of
rescission.—Plaintiff wrote a letter offering to the
Defendant to make a lease to him of a portion of
a block of three houses, consisting of the first,
second, third, and fourth floors of all three houses,
at a rent of £500 a year.   Defendant wrote in
answer, accepting the offer; and a lease was
executed whereby all the upper floors of the block
were demised by the Plaintiff to the Defendant
at the rent of £500.—Plaintiff alleged that the
first floor of one of the houses was included in the
offer, and in the lease, by mistake, and that he
always intended to reserve such first floor for his
own use.   Defendant denied that he accepted the
offer, or executed the lease, under any mistake.—
The Court having found upon the evidence that
a common mistake was not sufficiently proved,
but that mistake on the part of the Plaintiff was,
gave judgment for rescission with an option to
the Defendant to accept rectification instead.
PAGET *v.* MARSHALL   -   28 Ch. D. 255

2. —— Memorandum of Agreement—"*His
share*" *equivalent to Share of Firm*.] Case in
which it was held, that according to the true construction, having regard to all the circumstances
of the case, of a memorandum of mutual agreement between M., the Plaintiffs, and three other
firms, whereby M. agreed to surrender to the
Plaintiffs "his share" in a certain mortgage held
by him as trustee, the share of M.'s firm therein
passed, and not merely his own individual share
as between himself and his partner.   MARSHALL
v. MACLURE   -   -   10 App. Cas. 325

3. —— Money paid—*Delay in reclaiming—
Alteration of Position of Payee.*]   The Plaintiff,
by mistake, paid to the Defendants, who were
owners of the tithes of a parish, tithe rent-charge
in respect of lands not in his occupation.   The
Plaintiff did not discover the mistake until the
two years limited by 6 & 7 Will. 4, c. 71, for
the recovery of a tithe rent-charge had expired
and the Defendants had lost their remedy for the
arrears against the lands actually chargeable :—
Held, that there was no duty cast on the Plaintiff
in relation to the Defendants which made his

MISTAKE—*continued.*

delay in discovering the mistake laches on his part; and that he was entitled to recover back the amount paid as money paid under a mistake of fact. DURRANT *v.* ECCLESIASTICAL COMMISSIONERS FOR ENGLAND AND WALES 6 Q. B. D. 234

—— Charging compound interest 6 App. Cas. 181
    See MORTGAGE—CONTRACT. 11.

—— Contributory - - - 29 Ch. D. 459
    See COMPANY—PROSPECTUS. 5.

—— Disentailing deed—Rectification 29 Ch. D.
    See TENANT IN TAIL. 1.   [133

—— Execution of will—Incomplete will
                [6 P. D. 204
    See PROBATE—EXECUTION. 3.

—— Fact—Money had and received—Notice of
    action - 11 Q. B. D. 788
    See LOCAL GOVERNMENT—PRACTICE. 4.

—— Law — Ultrà vires act — Overdrawing
    banker's account - 29 Ch. D. 902
    See BUILDING SOCIETY. 8.

—— Misdescription of grantor—Bill of sale
                [21 Ch. D. 73
    See BILL OF SALE—FORMALITIES. 22.

—— Misdescription—Particulars of sale—Compensation - 13 Q. B. D. 351
    See VENDOR AND PURCHASER—COMPENSATION. 2.

—— Misunderstanding as to contract
                [27 Ch. D. 497
    See CONTRACT—ACCEPTANCE. 1.

—— Order of Court—Amendment 30 Ch. D. 239
    See PRACTICE—SUPREME COURT—JUDGMENT. 9.

—— Payment by—Interest on purchase-money
                [29 Ch. D. 691
    See VENDOR AND PURCHASER—CONDITIONS OF SALE. 2.

—— Separation deed—Specific performance
                [18 Ch. D. 670
    See HUSBAND AND WIFE—SEPARATION DEED. 1.

—— Statement in attestation clause 8 P. D. 165
    See PROBATE—GRANT. 10.

—— Statement of debts by compounding debtor
                [23 Ch. D. 706
    See BANKRUPTCY—COMPOSITION. 10.

—— Time for appeal - - 22 Ch. D. 484
    See PRACTICE — SUPREME COURT — APPEAL. 36.

—— Voluntary settlement—Rectification
                [29 Ch. D. 212
    See VOLUNTARY CONVEYANCE. 4.

—— Will.
    See Cases under WILL—MISTAKE.

MITTIMUS - 7 Q. B. D. 273; 6 App. Cas. 657
    See PRACTICE — ECCLESIASTICAL—CONTEMPT. 2.

MIXED FUND—Exoneration - 16 Ch. D. 322
    See WILL—EXONERATION. 2.

MOLESTATION—Separation deed—Covenant
         [12 Q. B. D. 539; 14 Q. B. D. 792
    See HUSBAND AND WIFE—SEPARATION DEED. 3.

MONEY—Bequest of "money"—Consols.
    See CHARITY—GIFT TO. 1. [28 Ch. D. 464

—— Bequest of "the money of which I am possessed" - - - 25 Ch. D. 154
    See WILL—RESIDUARY GIFT. 4.

—— In Court—Investment—Lands Clauses Act.
    See Cases under LANDS CLAUSES ACT—PURCHASE-MONEY.

—— In Court—Investments sanctioned by the
    Court - - 22 Ch. D. 93
    See PRACTICE—SUPREME COURT—PAYMENT INTO COURT. 5.

—— In Court — Staying proceedings pending
    appeal - - - 20 Ch. D. 669
    See PRACTICE—SUPREME COURT—STAYING PROCEEDINGS. 13.

—— To be invested in land—Appointment
                [23 Ch. D. 313
    See POWER—EXECUTION. 10.

MONEY HAD AND RECEIVED—Extortion—Payment under protest 11 Q. B. D. 275
    See DISTRESS DAMAGE FEASANT.

—— Local Government Acts—Notice of action
                [11 Q. B. D. 788
    See LOCAL GOVERNMENT—PRACTICE. 4.

—— Worthless bank note - 11 Q. B. D. 84
    See BILL OF EXCHANGE—ALTERATION. 3.

MONEY ORDERS.
    See POST OFFICE—*Statutes.*

MONEY PAID — Indemnity — Goods lawfully seized for another's debt 14 Q. B. D. 811
    See INDEMNITY.

MONITION - 7 App. Cas. 240
    See PRACTICE—ECCLESIASTICAL— PUBLIC WORSHIP ACT. 1.

—— - - - - 6 App. Cas. 424
    See PRACTICE—ECCLESIASTICAL—MONITION.

MONTHLY TENANCY—Uncertain rent—Distress
                [21 Ch. D. 442
    See BANKRUPTCY—DISTRESS. 4.

MONUMENT.
    See ANCIENT MONUMENTS—*Statutes.*

MORTGAGE :—			Col.
I. CONTRACT -	-	-	892
II. CONSOLIDATION		-	896
III. FORECLOSURE			897
IV. MORTGAGEE IN POSSESSION			903
V. MORTGAGOR IN POSSESSION			905
VI. POWERS -	-	-	905
VII. PRIORITY -	-	-	912
VIII. REDEMPTION	-	-	918
IX. STATUTORY FORM -		-	921

I. MORTGAGE—CONTRACT.

1. —— Attornment Clause—*Distress—Application of Proceeds.*] The proceeds of a distress for rent levied under an attornment clause in a mortgage deed are, in the absence of any provision to the contrary in the deed, applicable to the payment of principal as well as interest.—The fact that the yearly rent reserved by the attornment clause is equal in amount to the yearly interest of the mortgage debt as provided

I. MORTGAGE—CONTRACT—*continued.*

by the deed, and is made payable on the same days, is not of itself sufficient to displace the primâ facie right of the mortgagee to apply the proceeds of the distress in satisfaction of principal as well as interest.—*Hampson* v. *Fellows* (Law Rep. 6 Eq. 575) not followed. *Ex parte* HARRISON. *In re* BETTS　　**18 Ch. D. 127**

2. —— Attornment Clause—*Distress—Seizure of Goods of Stranger.*] If a mortgage is created by way of demise for a term of years, and the mortgagor attorns and becomes tenant to the mortgagee at a certain rent, the relation of landlord and tenant is created, and upon failure to pay the rent the mortgagee is entitled to distrain the goods even of a stranger. J., being lessee for a term of years, demised to P., by way of mortgage, all his interest in the term save one day, and J. attorned and became tenant to P. at a certain rent. J., being mortgagor, let the mortgaged premises to K., who assigned his goods thereon to R. The rent due from J. to P. being unpaid, P. distrained the goods assigned by K. to R. No rent was then due from K.—R. having brought an action against P. for the seizure of the goods:—*Held,* that by the attornment J. had become tenant to P., and that the distress was lawful. KEARSLEY v. PHILIPS
　　　　　　　　　　　　　[11 Q. B. D. 621

3. —— Benefice with Cure—*Validity*—13 *Eliz.* c. 20—*Union of Benefices Act,* 1860 (23 & 24 *Vict. c.* 142)—*Compensation payable to retiring Incumbent.*] In pursuance of an Order in Council under the Union of Benefices Act, 1860, uniting two City benefices, certain annuities were granted to the retiring incumbent and his assigns out of the annual income of the united benefice, and made a first charge thereon during the joint lives of himself and the incumbent of the united benefice, so long as he should perform in person, or by substitute to be approved of by the bishop, the duties of curate of the united benefice under the style of vicar in charge, with a provision for the retiring incumbent after the death of the incumbent of the united benefice:—*Held,* that such annuities were not a benefice with cure within 13 Eliz. c. 20, and accordingly could be validly mortgaged by the retired incumbent. McBEAN v. DEANE　　-　　**30 Ch. D. 520**

4. —— Contemporaneous Mortgages—*Incidence of Mortgage Debt—Apportionment—Collateral Security.*] A mortgagor deposited title deeds with an insurance company for securing the repayment of an advance of £1200. About the same time he executed an assignment of policies of insurance to secure the repayment of a similar sum. Only one sum of £1200 was really advanced:—*Held,* that the security on the land and on the policies must bear the mortgage debt rateably. EARLY v. EARLY. WILLIAMS v. EARLY
　　　　　　　　　　　　[16 Ch. D. 214, n.

5. —— Contemporaneous Mortgages — *Mortgage of Freeholds—Contemporaneous Security of Leaseholds for Mortgage Debt — " Collateral " Security—Incidence of Mortgage Debt.*] A mortgagor conveyed freeholds by way of mortgage by an indenture which recited an agreement by the mortgagees to advance him the principal moneys upon having the repayment thereof with interest secured " as hereinafter mentioned and by a

I. MORTGAGE—CONTRACT—*continued.*

collateral security or indenture intended to bear even date with" those presents.—On the same day the mortgagor demised leaseholds by way of mortgage to the same mortgagees to secure the same advance by an indenture which recited the mortgage of the freeholds, and that on the treaty for the advance " it was agreed that the same principal and interest should be further secured by these presents."—Each of the two indentures contained a covenant for the payment of the mortgage debt and interest.—In an action to administer the estate of the mortgagor:—*Held* (affirming the decision of Hall, V.C.), both on the frame of the deeds themselves, and upon the evidence as to the circumstances attending the advance, that the leasehold security was not " collateral " in the sense of " secondary " ; and accordingly that, as between the real and personal representatives of the mortgagor, the mortgage debt was payable rateably out of the freeholds and leaseholds comprised in the two securities, and not primarily out of the freeholds.—Observations upon *Marquis of Bute* v. *Cunynghame* (2 Russ. 275) and upon the meaning of the words " collateral security." *In re* ATHILL. ATHILL v. ATHILL　　-　　-　　**- 16 Ch. D. 211**

6. —— Costs and Expenses—*Right of Action against Mortgagor.*] Costs and expenses properly incurred by a mortgagee in relation to the mortgaged property, and which the mortgagor will be compelled to pay as a condition of being allowed to redeem the property; do not constitute a debt in respect of which an action can be maintained by the mortgagee against the mortgagor. *Ex parte* FEWINGS. *In re* SNEYD
　　　　　　　　　　　　　[25 Ch. D. 338

7. —— Costs of Mortgagee—*Costs of Adjournment to Judge—Mortgage to secure Moneys due from Mortgagor " his Executors, Administrators, or Assigns "—Advance to Assign.*] W., the owner and occupier of a public-house, gave to H. & Co., brewers, a mortgage to secure £1300, and also all sums which should at any time be owing to them from W., " his executors, administrators, or assigns " on any account whatsoever. W. died giving, by will, all his property to his wife for life, without any directions as to carrying on his business. Letters of administration, with the will annexed, were granted to the widow. The widow carried on the business, and was supplied with beer by H. & Co., to whom she from time to time made payments which discharged the moneys due to them from W. at his decease other than the £1300, but a balance of £138 was due from her to them at her decease for beer supplied. H. & Co. sold the property under a power of sale, and claimed to retain not only the £1300 but the £138. The question was raised on summons in an action for the administration of W.'s estate. The Chief Clerk was prepared to make an order without costs against H. & Co. to pay into Court the balance of purchase-money in their hands without deducting the £138; but H. & Co. insisted on having the case heard by the Judge. Kay, J., held that they must pay in the balance without deducting the £138, and ordered them to pay the costs of the adjournment to him as being in the nature of an unsuccessful appeal :—*Held,*

I. MORTGAGE—CONTRACT—continued.

on appeal, that as the widow was assign of the public-house, the £138 was covered by the security, and H. & Co. were entitled to retain it :— *Held*, also, that the adjournment to the Judge was not in the nature of an appeal, it being the right of H. & Co. to have the point heard by the Judge personally, and that even if they had been wrong on the merits they ought not to have been ordered to pay costs, for that a mortgagee cannot be deprived of costs merely because he claims bonâ fide something more than the Court holds him entitled to. *In re* WATTS. SMITH *v.* WATTS.

[22 Ch. D. 5

8. —— **Equitable Mortgage—***Deposit of Deed —Invalid Transfer of Charge—Right to Deed.*] Equitable mortgagee by a deposit of a deed cannot pass his interest in the property by a parol voluntary gift accompanied by delivery of the deed ; and as his interest in the deed is only incidental to his interest in the mortgage, the donee of the deed has no right to retain it. *In re* RICHARDSON. SHILLITO *v.* HOBSON 30 Ch. D. 396

9. —— **Equitable Mortgage —***Transferee— Confidential Solicitor—Constructive Notice.*] A deposited deeds with his confidential solicitor with a memorandum of deposit by way of equitable mortgage to secure the repayment of £3000. The solicitor handed the deeds and memorandum to B. as security for £2000, together with a memorandum signed by himself that the £2000, part of the annexed £3000 security, then belonged to B., with interest at 5 per cent. The solicitor afterwards obtained a return of the deeds from B. upon an assurance that in lieu thereof others of equal value should be deposited. Other deeds were subsequently deposited, which proved to be worthless. The mortgage of £3000 was paid off by A.'s representatives, and the genuine deeds were given up to them by the solicitor without the memorandum of deposit. No notice of B.'s security had been given to A. B. then claimed payment of the £2000 against the estate of A., upon the ground of constructive notice to A. through his confidential solicitor :—*Held*, that B., by neglecting to give notice to A. of the transfer of the mortgage, and by giving up the documents originally deposited with him, had lost any right he might have had against A.'s estate. *In re* LORD SOUTHAMPTON'S ESTATE. ALLEN *v.* LORD SOUTHAMPTON. BANFATHER'S CLAIM - - - 16 Ch. D. 178

10. —— **Instalments—***Advance to be repaid by Instalments—Stipulation for Payment of " Commission " on Instalments not duly repaid—Sale— Foreclosure—One Time for Redemption.*] A mortgagee agreed to advance to a mortgagor a sum to be repaid at specified dates by instalments, with interest at £6 per cent. per annum, and if the bank rate should exceed £4 per cent. additional interest equal to the excess. If default was made in payment of any instalment at due date there was also to be paid a " commission " of £1 per cent. for every month or part of a month from the due date to the date of payment of such instalment :—*Held*, that this " commission " was not in the nature of a penalty, and that the mortgagee was entitled to charge for it in taking the account.—Foreclosure ordered with one term of redemption for all the puisne mortgagees, as in

I. MORTGAGE—CONTRACT—continued.

Bartlett v. Rees (Law Rep. 12 Eq. 395).—On a security upon railway shares with power of sale, under which the shares were transferred to the lenders :—*Held*, that the lender was entitled to foreclosure, and that *Carter v. Wake* (4 Ch. D. 605) did not apply. GENERAL CREDIT AND DISCOUNT COMPANY *v.* GLEGG - 22 Ch. D. 549

11. —— **Settled Account** *re-opened, Compound Interest charged by Mistake—Mutual Mistake of Law.*] In the absence of special agreement simple interest only can be charged in a mortgage account. —Where such mortgage account had been settled on the footing of compound interest with half-yearly rests, both parties wrongly understanding the mortgage deed to require the same :—*Held*, that such settled account might be re-opened.— Although under certain circumstances the giving credit in account may be treated as so far equivalent to payment under mistake of law as to prevent sums wrongly credited being recoverable at law ; yet in equity the line between mistakes in law and mistakes in fact has not been so clearly and sharply drawn. DANIELL *v.* SINCLAIR

[6 App. Cas. 181

II. MORTGAGE—CONSOLIDATION.

Restriction on Consolidation.] *The Act 44 & 45 Vict. c. 41 (Conveyancing Act, 1881), enacts, Sect. 17.—(1.) A mortgagor seeking to redeem any one mortgage, shall, by virtue of this Act, be entitled to do so, without paying any money due under any separate mortgage made by him, or by any person through whom he claims, on property other than that comprised in the mortgage which he seeks to redeem.*

(2.) This section applies only if and as far as a contrary intention is not expressed in the mortgage deeds or one of them.

(3.) This section applies only where the mortgages or one of them are or is made after the commencement of this Act—31st Dec. 1881.

1. —— **One Mortgage ceasing to exist—***Mortgage in the Name of Trustees.*] Two persons partners in a mercantile firm. who held a leasehold house, made an equitable mortgage of it to W. Afterwards the firm took in another partner who acquired a share in the equity of redemption. The firm then mortgaged their interest in another house, which they held as joint tenants, to W. for a further debt. The firm having become bankrupt, the lease on the first-mentioned house was determined by the bankruptcy, and the lessor re-entered. W. claimed to consolidate both debts, so that the second-mentioned house should not be redeemed without paying both debts :—*Held*, that one mortgaged property having ceased to exist, there could be no consolidation of the two debts.—Whether a mortgage by three persons can be consolidated with a mortgage by two in trust for the three, *quære. In re* RAGGETT. *Ex parte* WILLIAMS

[16 Ch. D. 117

2. —— **Redemption Suit —***Parties—Trustees —Rules of Court, 1875, Order XVI., r. 7.*] The mortgagor of one property assigned the equity of redemption, and afterwards mortgaged another property to the mortgagee of the first. The assignee of the equity of redemption having

II. MORTGAGE—CONSOLIDATION—*continued.*

brought an action to redeem the first property, the mortgagee claimed to consolidate the mortgages :—*Held* (affirming the decision of the Court of Appeal), that the right of the purchaser of an equity of redemption cannot be affected by a mortgage created after the purchase, and that the assignee was entitled to redeem the first mortgage without redeeming the second.—Also that under Order XVI., rule 7, trustees of an equity of redemption sufficiently represent their cestui que trust in a redemption suit, no direction to the contrary having been made by the Court.—*Tassel v. Smith* (2 De G. & J. 713; 27 L. J. (Ch.) 604) overruled.—*Beevor v. Luck* (Law Rep. 4 Eq. 537) commented on.—*White v. Hillacre* (3 Y. & C. (Ex.) 597) approved. JENNINGS v. JORDAN

[**6 App. Cas. 698**]

3. —— Union of Mortgages on different Estates *after Assignment of Equity of Redemption of one of them.*] When two mortgages, made by the same mortgagor to different mortgagees on different estates, become united for the first time in one person after the mortgagor has assigned (by way either of sale or mortgage) the equity of redemption of one of them, the owner of the two mortgages cannot consolidate them as against the assignee of the equity of redemption, even though both the mortgages were created before the assignment.—The assignee of an equity of redemption takes it subject to all equities which affect the assignor in respect of it at the date of the assignment, but the possibility that the mortgage may, by virtue of its subsequent union in the same person with a mortgage of another estate made, previously to the assignment, by the same mortgagor to a different mortgagee, become liable to consolidation, is not such an equity.—*White v. Hillacre* (3 Y. & C. Ex. 597) approved and followed.—*Beevor v. Luck* (Law Rep. 4 Eq. 537) disapproved and not followed, on the ground that its authority has been much impaired by the observations made upon it by Lord Chancellor Selborne and Lord Blackburn in *Jennings v. Jordan* (6 App. Cas. 698).—*Vint v. Padget* (2 De G. & J. 611) distinguished. HARTER v. COLMAN

[**19 Ch. D. 630**]

4. —— Voluntary Settlement by Mortgagor— *Subsequent Mortgages by same Mortgagor of the settled and also of other Property.*] A. B. having executed a voluntary settlement of the W. estate mortgaged it in fee to X. Y. He afterwards mortgaged the Q. estate, and that mortgage became vested in X. Y. :—*Held,* that X. Y. was not entitled to consolidate as against the persons claiming under the voluntary settlement the mortgages on the W. and Q. estates. *In re* WAL-HAMPTON ESTATE — — — 26 Ch. D. 391

III. MORTGAGE—FORECLOSURE.

The Act 44 & 45 *Vict.* c. 41 (*Conveyancing Act,* 1881), *enacts*—

Sect. 25.—(1.) *Any person entitled to redeem mortgaged property may have a judgment or order for sale instead of for redemption in an action brought by him either for redemption alone, or for sale alone, or for sale or redemption, in the alternative.*

(2.) *In any action, whether for foreclosure, or for*

III. MORTGAGE—FORECLOSURE—*continued.*

redemption, or for sale, or for the raising and payment in any manner of mortgage money, the Court, on the request of the mortgagee, or of any person interested either in the mortgage money or in the right of redemption, and, notwithstanding the dissent of any other person, and notwithstanding that the mortgagee or any person so interested does not appear in the action, and without allowing any time for redemption or for payment of any mortgage money, may, if it thinks fit, direct a sale of the mortgaged property, on such terms as it thinks fit, including, if it thinks fit, the deposit in Court of a reasonable sum fixed by the Court, to meet the expenses of sale and to secure performance of the terms.

(3.) *But, in an action brought by a person interested in the right of redemption and seeking a sale, the Court may, on the application of any Defendant, direct the Plaintiff to give such security for costs as the Court thinks fit, and may give the conduct of the sale to any Defendant, and may give such directions as it thinks fit respecting the costs of the Defendants or any of them.*

(4.) *In any case within this section the Court may, if it thinks fit, direct a sale without previously determining the priorities of incumbrances.*

(5.) *This section applies to actions brought either before or after the commencement of this Act—31st December, 1881.*

(6.) *Repeals 15 & 16 Vict. c. 86, s. 48.*

1. —— Accounts — *Decree—Right of Defendant to insist on Plaintiff bringing in Accounts — Practice—Amendment of Form of Summons.*] Mortgagees for the term of a colliery brought an action for foreclosure, seeking declarations that the original mortgage deed was a good exercise of a power of leasing, and that the sums secured by a later deed were also charged on the term created by the first deed. They obtained a decree giving them the declarations asked, and directing the usual accounts in the case of mortgagees in possession, with directions for foreclosure in default of payment. A summons was taken out by the Defendant to proceed with the judgment, and the Chief Clerk directed the Plaintiffs to bring in their accounts by a certain day, but no order to that effect was drawn up. The Plaintiffs afterwards having refused to bring in their accounts on the ground that, as they alleged, the moneys remaining due to them were many times more than the value of the mortgaged property, and that taking the accounts would therefore be useless, the Defendants applied on summons for an order that the Plaintiffs might bring them in in four days, not asking any alternative relief. Pearson, J., refused the application on the ground that the Defendants were not entitled to a four-day order. The Defendants appealed :—*Held,* that the summons must be treated as if it had been asked that the Plaintiffs might bring in their accounts in four days, or in such other time as the Court might think fit, the summons if necessary, being amended :—*Held,* that as the Plaintiffs had taken a foreclosure decree, the Defendants were entitled to have the accounts brought in, but that the order should be prefaced with a statement that they required them to be brought in.—Whether this statement would give

2 G

III. MORTGAGE—FORECLOSURE—*continued.*

the Court jurisdiction as to the costs if it turned out that the accounts had been asked for vexatiously and unreasonably, *quære.*—Whether the Court would not on a substantive application by the Plaintiffs stay the taking the accounts if it was satisfactorily shewn that taking them would be useless, *quære.* TAYLOR *v.* MOSTYN 25 Ch. D. 48

2. —— Accounts and Inquiries—*Rules of Supreme Court, 1883, Order* XV., *rr.* 1, 2]. In foreclosure actions where there is no preliminary question to be tried, the Plaintiff may obtain, under Rules of Supreme Court, 1883, Order XV., an order for an account with all necessary inquiries, and the usual directions as in a common foreclosure judgment *nisi.* Such order should be applied for by summons in Chambers and not by motion in Court, and only the costs of a summons in Chambers attended by counsel will be allowed. SMITH *v.* DAVIES　-　28 Ch. D. 650

[*But see* BLAKE *v.* HARVEY, 29 Ch. D. 827.]

3. —— Costs—*Abortive Sale — Cheque for Deposit dishonoured—Practice of Auctioneers—Personal Order for Payment—Form of Order.*] The custom of auctioneers to accept, on sales of large properties, a cheque in lieu of cash for the deposit, is reasonable, and a mortgagee-vendor was held to be justified in acting on it, and not to be guilty of negligence in the conduct of the sale, though the cheque was dishonoured.—In such a case a mortgagee, who has endeavoured to sell under his powers, is entitled to add the costs of the abortive sale to his security.—The proper order in a foreclosure action, when an account and an order for personal payment of what may be found due is asked for against the mortgagor, is to direct payment of principal and interest within one month after the date of the Chief Clerk's certificate on the taking of the accounts.—*Semble,* if a mortgagee wants an immediate order for personal payment, he must ask for it by his pleadings and prove the amount due for principal and interest at the trial. FARRER *v.* LACY, HARTLAND & Co. -　　25 Ch. D. 636

[Affirmed by the Court of Appeal, 31 Ch. D. 42.]

4. —— Costs — *Delivery up of Deeds—Disclaimer.*] When a judgment for foreclosure is given against a puisne mortgagee, the Plaintiff is not entitled to delivery up of deeds of subsequent date to his own mortgage, dealing only with the title to the equity of redemption.— A Defendant to a foreclosure action, who was originally properly made a party, is entitled to his costs incurred subsequently to his making a proper offer to disclaim.—After the commencement of a foreclosure action the solicitors of the Defendants (who were second mortgagees) wrote to the Plaintiff's solicitors, offering to consent to the dismissal of the action without costs, and to hand over a release at Plaintiff's expense. The Plaintiff brought the action to a trial, insisting that he was entitled to delivery up by the Defendants of some deeds which affected only the title to the equity of redemption:—*Held,* that the letter contained a proper offer to disclaim; that the Defendants were entitled to their costs subsequent to its date; and that the Plaintiff was not entitled to the deeds which he claimed. GREENE *v.* FOSTER　-　22 Ch. D. 566

III. MORTGAGE—FORECLOSURE—*continued.*

5. —— Costs—*Mortgages of two Estates—Redemption — Apportionment of Costs of Action — Conveyancing and Law of Property Act, 1881 (44 & 45 Vict. c. 41), s. 17.*] An action was brought by a mortgagee for the foreclosure of two mortgages of two distinct estates, executed by the same mortgagor to secure two different advances. Both mortgages were executed since the Conveyancing Act, 1881, came into operation:—*Held,* that the whole of the costs of the action ought to be included in the account relating to each estate, and that the mortgagor could not redeem either estate separately without paying the whole of the costs of the action. CLAPHAM *v.* ANDREWS
[27 Ch. D. 679

6. —— Costs—*Special.*] The plaintiff in a foreclosure action is as a general rule entitled to an account of only principal and interest due to him on his mortgage, and of the costs of the action. To entitle him to an account of any other costs he must make out a special case.— But, where the Plaintiff was the transferee of a mortgage, on which interest was overdue at the date of the transfer, and the mortgagor was a bankrupt :—*Held,* that the Plaintiff was entitled to an account of costs generally. BOLINGBROKE *v.* HINDE　-　25 Ch. D. 795

7. —— Equitable Mortgage—*Form of Order —Practice.*] A decree for foreclosure in the case of an equitable mortgage ought not to omit the word "foreclose," but ought to contain directions that upon default the mortgagor will be foreclosed, that the hereditaments will be discharged from all equity of redemption, and that a conveyance must be executed. LEES *v.* FISHER
[22 Ch. D. 283

8. —— Infant — *Equitable Mortgage—Mortgagor's Estate in infant Heir-at-Law—Day to shew Cause—Form of Decree.*] In an action by an equitable mortgagee, without any memorandum of deposit of title deeds, against the widow and infant heir-at-law of the mortgagor for foreclosure :—*Held,* on motion for judgment, the Defendants not having appeared, that the infant heir must be ordered to shew cause at the time when he attained the age of twenty-one years, and that he must have a day to shew cause in the usual way.—*Price v. Carver* (3 My. & Cr. 157) followed. MELLOR *v.* PORTER　　25 Ch. D. 158

9. —— Infant—*Immediate Foreclosure Judgment Absolute against Infant.*] Judgment for an immediate foreclosure absolute against an infant granted, the Plaintiffs offering to pay the Defendant's costs of the action as between solicitor and client, and the Defendant's counsel not asking for liberty to redeem, or that an account should be taken of what was due to the Plaintiffs, upon the Court being satisfied by evidence that the value of the property was not sufficient to pay the amount of the principal sum due on the mortgage, together with interest and the costs of the action, and that it would be for the benefit of the infant to give judgment in that form. WOLVERHAMPTON AND STAFFORDSHIRE BANKING COMPANY *v.* GEORGE　　24 Ch. D. 707

10. —— Interest subsequent to Certificate.] When a judgment for foreclosure, obtained by a

III. MORTGAGE—FORECLOSURE—*continued:*

first mortgagee against subsequent mortgagees and the mortgagor, directs successive redemptions, and forecloses in default of redemption, and a puisne mortgagee fails to pay the amount found due from him to the prior mortgagee for principal, interest, and costs, and is accordingly foreclosed, in taking the account against the person next entitled to redeem, subsequent interest ought to be computed on the whole sum found due from the person who has failed to redeem, i.e., upon the interest found due from him, as well as upon the principal and costs. ELTON *v.* CURTEIS
[19 Ch. D. 49

11. —— **Opening** Foreclosure—*Receipt of Rents by Mortgagee before Final Judgment—Further Account.*] In an action by executors of a mortgagee against the mortgagor and a puisne mortgagee an order nisi for foreclosure was made, giving successive periods of redemption. After the time fixed for redemption and before final judgment was obtained against the puisne mortgagee, and before the expiration of the time allowed to the mortgagor, the Plaintiffs received a sum of money for rent. A further account had been taken against the mortgagor, and a further day fixed for redemption by him;—*Held,* that it was irregular to fix a further time for the mortgagor to redeem until the puisne mortgagee had been finally foreclosed ; and that the receipt of moneys for rent after the time fixed for the puisne mortgagee to redeem and before final judgment obtained against him did not open the foreclosure against him.—The order was to foreclose the puisne mortgagee absolutely, and to take a further account against the mortgagor. WEBSTER *v.* PATTESON - - - 25 Ch. D. 626

12. —— **Partnership, Share of**—*Date at which Account of mortgaged Share is to be taken —Form of Order.*]・ When a partner mortgages his share in the partnership, and the mortgagee brings an action to realise his mortgage, the proper order is to direct an account of what the mortgagor's interest in the partnership was at the date when the mortgagee proceeded to take possession under his mortgage, i.e., at the date of the writ; but if a dissolution of the partnership has previously taken place, the date of the dissolution is the date at which the account is to be taken. WHETHAM *v.* DAVEY　30 Ch. D. 574

13. —— **Period of Redemption**—*Several Defendants.*] In an action for foreclosure by first mortgagees against a second mortgagee and the mortgagor :—*Held,* that successive periods for redemption ought to be allowed to the Defendants. SWEET *v.* COMBLEY　25 Ch. D. 463, n.

14. —— **Period of Redemption**—*Several Defendants.*] Where there were two Defendants to a foreclosure action—the mortgagor and second mortgagee who had joined in the Plaintiff's security to postpone his previously prior right, and as surety for the Plaintiff :—*Held,* that only one period of six months should be allowed for redemption by both Defendants. — *Bartlett v. Rees* (Law Rep. 12 Eq. 395) and *General Credit and Discount Company* v. *Glegg* (22 Ch. D. 549) followed. SMITH *v.* OLDING　- 25 Ch. D. 462

15. —— **Period of Redemption**—*Several De-*

III. MORTGAGE—FORECLOSURE—*continued.*

fendants.] As a general but not invariable rule, when there are several defendants to a foreclosure action, one period for redemption should be allowed to all the defendants. MUTUAL LIFE ASSURANCE SOCIETY *v.* LANGLEY　26 Ch. D. 686

16. —— **Period of Redemption** — *Subsequent Incumbrancers.*] A first mortgagee is *primâ facie* entitled to a judgment in a foreclosure action limiting only one period for redemption, both as against subsequent incumbrancers and the mortgagor, and where there are conflicting claims as to priority between co-Defendants the practice, as settled by *Bartlett* v. *Rees* (Law Rep. 12 Eq. 395), is to grant only one period for redemption. Where, however, the Defendants have put in a defence or appeared at the bar and have proved or offered to prove their incumbrances, and there is no question of priority between them, the Court will at the request of the puisne incumbrancers, but not at the request of the mortgagor, limit successive periods for redemption. A mortgagor has no right in himself to more than one period of six months to redeem. In a foreclosure action by the transferee of the first mortgagee, the statement of claim alleged that the Defendants other than the mortgagor claimed to have some charge upon the mortgaged premises subsequent to the Plaintiff's charge. None of the Defendants, including the mortgagor, put in a defence or appeared at the bar :—*Held,* that the Plaintiff was entitled to a foreclosure judgment on the pleadings, allowing one period for redemption as against all the Defendants. PLATT *v.* MENDEL　27 Ch. D. 246

17. —— **Period of Redemption**—*Subsequent Incumbrances.*] In a foreclosure judgment against the mortgagor and subsequent incumbrancers, only one period for redemption will be fixed where none of the defendants appear on the motion for judgment; whether it is alleged by the statement of claim that the subsequent incumbrancers are " entitled " or only that they " claim to be entitled " to charges upon the mortgaged premises. DOBLE *v.* MANLEY　- 28 Ch. D. 664

18. —— **Personal Judgment against Mortgagor**—*Form of Judgment.*] Form of judgment in a foreclosure action, when a personal judgment is taken against the mortgagor on his covenant for payment of principal and interest.—The form in *Grundy v. Grice* (Seton on Decrees, 4th Ed. vol. ii. p. 1036 (Form No. 2)), modified. HUNTER *v.* MYATT - - - 28 Ch. D. 181

19. —— **Possession** — *Form of Judgment.*] Where an order *nisi* for foreclosure and possession had been made the order absolute also provided for possession and was made *ex parte.* WITHALL *v.* NIXON - - - 28 Ch. D. 413

20. —— **Receiver** — *Judicature Act,* 1873 (36 & 37 Vict. c. 66), s. 25, *sub-s.* 8 — *Conveyancing Act* 1881 (44 & 45 Vict. c. 41), s. 19, *sub-s.* 3.] A legal mortgagee being in possession of the mortgaged property, applied to the Court for the appointment of a receiver :—*Held,* that although the mortgagee might, under the Conveyancing Act, 1881, appoint a receiver without coming to the Court, it was more desirable, where an action was pending, that the appoint.

III. MORTGAGE—FORECLOSURE—*continued.*

ment should be made by the Court under the Judicature Act, 1873. TILLETT *v.* NIXON

[25 Ch. D. 238

21. —— Sale — *Conveyancing and Law of Property Act, 1881 (44 & 45 Vict. c. 41), s. 25.*] A decree for successive redemption and foreclosures having been obtained in an action by a second mortgagee against the first mortgagee and several successive incumbrancers, the second mortgagee redeemed the first, and then applied for a sale of the mortgaged property:—*Held,* that under the Conveyancing and Law of Property Act, 1881, sect. 25, the Court has jurisdiction to order a sale of mortgaged property in a foreclosure or redemption action at any time before the suit is concluded by foreclosure absolute, and a sale was ordered. UNION BANK OF LONDON *v.* INGRAM

[20 Ch. D. 463

22. —— Sale — *Conveyancing and Law of Property Act, 1881 (44 & 45 Vict. c. 41), s. 25.*] When at the trial of a foreclosure action the Plaintiff asks for a sale of the property, and the mortgagor does not appear, the Court will order an account of what is due to the Plaintiff to be first taken, and then that so much of the property be sold as will be sufficient to satisfy what is found due to the Plaintiff. WADE *v.* WILSON

[22 Ch. D. 235

IV. MORTGAGE—MORTGAGEE IN POSSESSION.

1. —— Account — *Attornment Clause.*] In taking the account in a foreclosure action between first mortgagee and second mortgagee and mortgagor, an attornment clause in his mortgage deed will not render the first mortgagee liable to account on the footing of mortgagee in possession in respect of the rent reserved by the attornment clause. STANLEY *v.* GRUNDY - 22 Ch. D. 478

2. —— Lease subsequent to Mortgage— *Notice by Mortgagee to Tenant to pay Rent to him.*] C., the owner of a leasehold estate which was subject to a mortgage, entered without the privity of the mortgagees into an agreement with P. to grant him a lease for twenty-one years, and in 1875 P. took possession under this agreement. On the 25th of March, 1881, the mortgagees' solicitors wrote to P. stating that they, on behalf of the mortgagees, had withdrawn C.'s authority to receive the rents and asking him to pay the rent due that day and all future rent to them. P. wrote to ask C. whether he ought to pay according to the notice, and C. replied that he would be correct in doing so. P. consulted his solicitors, who inspected the mortgage deed, and advised him that the mortgagees could claim rent from him. P. therefore paid the mortgagees the rent due on the 25th of March, and on the 22nd of June gave them notice to determine his tenancy at Christmas. At the end of the year the mortgagees refused to accept possession, and in June, 1882, they and C. commenced this action to compel P. to take a lease according to the agreement:—*Held,* affirming the decision of Pollock, B., that the notice by the mortgagees to the tenant to pay rent to them and the payment accordingly did away with the agreement between C. and P. and made P. tenant from year to year to the mort-

IV. MORTGAGE—MORTGAGEE IN POSSESSION —*continued.*

gagees, and that specific performance of the agreement could not be decreed. CORBETT *v.* PLOWDEN

[25 Ch. D. 678

3. —— Proviso for Reduction of Interest—*Accounts—Right to Higher Rate of Interest.*] Under a proviso in a mortgage deed for reduction of interest on punctual payment, a mortgagee in possession through the default of the mortgagor is entitled, on the accounts being taken, to charge the mortgagor with the higher rate of interest ; and, also, in a proper case, with the commission paid to a receiver for collecting the rents.— *Stains* v. *Banks* (9 Jur. (N.S.) 1049; reversed on appeal, Reg. Lib. 7 B. 1863, 1761) considered. UNION BANK OF LONDON *v.* INGRAM 16 Ch. D. 53

4. —— Rents and Profits—*Account—Liberty to surcharge.*] The Defendants had by the judgment in the action been held to be mortgagees in possession of certain mortgaged estates, and the usual accounts and inquiries as against mortgagees in possession were directed. The Defendants brought in an account purporting to shew their receipts in respect of the rents and profits of the mortgaged estates, but which in fact only shewed certain lump sums received by them from one J. H. Blood, then deceased, their agent.—On motion by the Plaintiff for a further and better account :— *Held,* by Pearson, J., that the account was sufficient and that the Plaintiff's proper course was to surcharge the Defendants :—*Held,* by the Court of Appeal (reversing the decision of Pearson, J.), that the Defendants were bound to render the further account, for that the receipts of Blood were as between the Plaintiff and the Defendants the receipts of the Defendants; the Defendants were bound to deliver an account shewing not only what they had received from Blood but what he had received from the tenants, and that it was a question not of technicality but of substance, for without the knowledge derived from such an account the Plaintiff would be unable to proceed on the inquiry as to wilful default, which was a matter of surcharge, and that the death of the Defendants' agent could not excuse the Defendants from this liability. NOYES *v.* POLLOCK

[30 Ch. D. 336

5. —— Sale by Mortgagee—*Use and Occupation—Permanent Improvements.*] If a mortgagee in possession, or a mortgagee selling under his power of sale, has reasonably expended money in permanent works on the property, he is entitled on primâ facie evidence to that effect to an inquiry whether the outlay has increased the value of the property, and if it has done so, he is entitled to be repaid his expenditure so far as it has increased such value. And in such case it is immaterial whether the mortgagor had notice of the expenditure.—Notice to the mortgagor is only material when the expenditure is unreasonable, for the purpose of shewing that he acquiesced in it.—*Sandon* v. *Hooper* (6 Beav. 246; 14 L. J. (Ch.) 120) commented on.—A mortgagee in possession sold the property under his power of sale, a day being fixed for the completion of the sale and for letting the purchaser into possession. At the request of the purchaser the mortgagee let him into possession four months before the

IV. MORTGAGE—MORTGAGEE IN POSSESSION
—*continued.*

appointed day, but did not require him to pay any rent :—*Held*, in an action by the mortgagor for ascertaining the amount of the balance due to him, that the mortgagee could not be charged with an occupation rent for the interval during which the purchaser had been in possession before the appointed day.—Whether in such a case the mortgagee might be charged with wilful default in not requiring a rent from the purchaser, *quære.*—The decision of Kay, J., reversed. SHEPARD *v.* JONES - 21 Ch. D. 469

—— Power of sale - - 18 Ch. D. 449
See MORTGAGE—POWERS. 6.

V. MORTGAGE—MORTGAGOR IN POSSESSION.

—— *Trespass—Default in Payment on Demand—Damages for Illegal Seizure.*] Where by the terms of a mortgage deed the Plaintiffs were to remain in possession on their own account, and manage the mortgaged property until they should make default in payment of the mortgage money upon demand in writing in manner specified, and such demand was made on the wife of one of the Plaintiffs during the Plaintiffs' absence by a person who represented himself as the Defendant's agent, and upon non-payment the Defendant forthwith entered upon possession and seized the mortgaged property :—*Held*, in an action of trespass against the mortgagee, that such non-payment before the Plaintiffs had had any opportunity to inquire into the truth of the alleged agency did not constitute default, and that the Defendant was liable to the mortgagors in substantial damages. MOORE *v.* SHELLEY 8 App. Cas. 285

VI. MORTGAGE—POWERS.

Power of leasing.] *The Act 44 & 45 Vict. c. 41 (Conveyancing Act, 1881) enacts—*

Sect. 18—(1.) *A mortgagor of land while in possession shall, as against every incumbrancer, have, by virtue of this Act, power to make from time to time any such lease of the mortgaged land, or any part thereof, as is in this section described and authorized.*

(2.) *A mortgagee of land while in possession shall, as against all prior incumbrancers, if any, and as against the mortgagor, have, by virtue of this Act, power to make from time to time any such lease as aforesaid.*

(3.) *The leases which this section authorizes are—*
(i.) *An agricultural or occupation lease for any term not exceeding twenty-one years ; and*
(ii.) *A building lease for any term not exceeding ninety-nine years.*

(4.) *Every person making a lease under this section may execute and do all assurances and things necessary or proper in that behalf.*

(5.) *Every such lease shall be made to take effect in possession not later than twelve months after its date.*

(6.) *Every such lease shall reserve the best rent that can reasonably be obtained, regard being had to the circumstances of the case, but without any fine being taken.*

(7.) *Every such lease shall contain a covenant by the lessee for payment of the rent, and a condition of re-entry on the rent not being paid within a time therein specified not exceeding thirty days.*

VI. MORTGAGE—POWERS—*continued.*

(8.) *A counterpart of every such lease shall be executed by the lessee and delivered to the lessor, of which execution and delivery the execution of the lease by the lessor shall, in favour of the lessee and all persons deriving title under him, be sufficient evidence.*

(9.) *Every such building lease shall be made in consideration of the lessee, or some person by whose direction the lease is granted, having erected, or agreeing to erect within not more than five years from the date of the lease, buildings, new or additional, or having improved or repaired buildings, or agreeing to improve or repair buildings within that time, or having executed, or agreeing to execute, within that time, on the land leased, an improvement for or in connection with building purposes.*

(10.) *In any such building lease a peppercorn rent, or a nominal or other rent less than the rent ultimately payable, may be made payable for the first five years, or any less part of the term.*

(11.) *In case of a lease by the mortgagor, he shall, within one month after making the lease, deliver to the mortgagee, or, where there are more than one, to the mortgagee first in priority, a counterpart of the lease duly executed by the lessee ; but the lessee shall not be concerned to see that this provision is complied with.*

(12.) *A contract to make or accept a lease under this section may be enforced by or against every person on whom the lease if granted would be binding.*

(13.) *This section applies only if and as far as a contrary intention is not expressed by the mortgagor and mortgagee in the mortgage deed, or otherwise in writing, and shall have effect subject to the terms of the mortgage deed or of any such writing and to the provisions therein contained.*

(14.) *Nothing in this Act shall prevent the mortgage deed from reserving to or conferring on the mortgagor or the mortgagee, or both, any further or other powers of leasing or having reference to leasing ; and any further or other powers so reserved or conferred shall be exerciseable, as far as may be, as if they were conferred by this Act, and with all the like incidents, effects, and consequences, unless a contrary intention is expressed in the mortgage deed.*

(15.) *Nothing in this Act shall be construed to enable a mortgagor or mortgagee to make a lease for any longer term or on any other conditions than such as could have been granted or imposed by the mortgagor, with the concurrence of all the incumbrancers, if this Act had not been passed.*

(16.) *This section applies only in case of a mortgage made after the commencement of this Act ; but the provisions thereof, or any of them, may, by agreement in writing made after the commencement of this Act, between mortgagor and mortgagee, be applied to a mortgage made before the commencement of this Act, so, nevertheless, that any such agreement shall not prejudicially affect any right or interest of any mortgagee not joining in or adopting the agreement.*

(17.) *The provisions of this section referring to a lease shall be construed to extend and apply, as far as circumstances admit, to any letting, and to an agreement, whether in writing or not, for leasing or letting.*

VI. MORTGAGE—POWERS—*continued.*

Power of Sale, &c.] *The Act* 44 & 45 *Vict. c.* 41 (*Conveyancing Act,* 1881) *enacts, sect.* 19—

(1.) *A mortgagee, where the mortgage is made by deed, shall, by virtue of this Act, have the following powers, to the like extent as if they had been in terms conferred by the mortgage deed, but not further (namely):—*

(i.) *A power, when the mortgage-money has become due, to sell, or to concur with any other person in selling, the mortgaged property, or any part thereof, either subject to prior charges, or not, and either together or in lots, by public auction or by private contract, subject to such conditions respecting title, or evidence of title, or other matter, as he (the mortgagee) thinks fit, with power to vary any contract for sale, and to re-sell, without being answerable for any loss occasioned thereby ; and*

(ii.) *A power at any time after the date of the mortgage deed, to insure and keep insured against loss or damage by fire any building, or any effects or property of an insurable nature, whether affixed to the freehold or not, being or forming part of the mortgaged property, and the premiums paid for any such insurance shall be a charge on the mortgaged property, in addition to the mortgage-money and with the same priority ; and with interest at the same rate, as the mortgage-money ; and*

(iii.) *A power, when the mortgage-money has become due, to appoint a receiver of the income of the mortgaged property, or of any part thereof ; and*

(iv.) *A power, while the mortgagee is in possession, to cut and sell timber and other trees ripe for cutting, and not planted or left standing for shelter or ornament, or to contract for any such cutting and sale, to be completed within any time not exceeding twelve months from the making of the contract.*

(2.) *The provisions of this Act relating to the foregoing powers, comprised either in this section, or in any subsequent section regulating the exercise of those powers, may be varied or extended by the mortgage deed, and, as so varied or extended, shall, as far as may be, operate in the like manner and with all the like incidents, effects, and consequences, as if such variations or extensions were contained in this Act.*

(3.) *This section applies only if and as far as a contrary intention is not expressed in the mortgage deed, and shall have effect subject to the terms of the mortgage deed and, to the provisions therein contained.*

(4.) *This section applies only where the mortgage deed is executed after the commencement of this Act.*

Sect. 20. *A mortgagee shall not exercise the power of sale conferred by this Act unless and until—*

(i.) *Notice requiring payment of the mortgage-money has been served on the mortgagor or one of several mortgagors, and default has been made in payment of the mortgage-money, or of part thereof, for three months after such service ; or*

VI. MORTGAGE—POWERS—*continued.*

(ii.) *Some interest under the mortgage is in arrear and unpaid for two months after becoming due ; or*

(iii.) *There has been a breach of some provision contained in the mortgage deed or in this Act, and on the part of the mortgagor, or of some person concurring in making the mortgage, to be observed or performed, other than and besides a covenant for payment of the mortgage-money or interest thereon.*

Sect. 21.—(1.) *A mortgagee exercising the power of sale conferred by this Act shall have power, by deed, to convey the property sold, for such estate and interest therein as is the subject of the mortgage, freed from all estates, interests, and rights to which the mortgage has priority, but subject to all estates, interests, and rights which have priority to the mortgage ; except that, in the case of copyhold or customary land, the legal right to admittance shall not pass by a deed under this section, unless the deed is sufficient otherwise by law, or is sufficient by custom, in that behalf.*

(2.) *Where a conveyance is made in professed exercise of the power of sale conferred by this Act, the title of the purchaser shall not be impeachable on the ground that no case had arisen to authorize the sale, or that due notice was not given, or that the power was otherwise improperly or irregularly exercised, but any person damnified by an unauthorised, or improper, or irregular exercise of the power, shall have his remedy in damages against the person exercising the power.*

(3.) *The money which is received by the mortgagee, arising from the sale, after discharge of prior incumbrances to which the sale is not made subject, if any, or after payment into Court under this Act of a sum to meet any prior incumbrance, shall be held by him in trust to be applied by him, first, in payment of all costs, charges, and expenses, properly incurred by him, as incident to the sale or any attempted sale, or otherwise ; and secondly, in discharge of the mortgage-money, interest, and costs, and other money, if any, due under the mortgage, and the residue of the money so received shall be paid to the person entitled to the mortgaged property, or authorized to give receipts for the proceeds of the sale thereof.*

(4.) *The power of sale conferred by this Act may be exercised by any person for the time being entitled to receive and give a discharge for the mortgage-money.*

(5.) *The power of sale conferred by this Act shall not affect the right of foreclosure.*

(6.) *The mortgagee, his executors, administrators, or assigns, shall not be answerable for any involuntary loss happening in or about the exercise or execution of the power of sale conferred by this Act, or of any trust connected therewith.*

(7.) *At any time after the power of sale conferred by this Act has become exerciseable, the person entitled to exercise the same may demand and recover from any person, other than a person having in the mortgaged property an estate, interest, or right in priority to the mortgage, all the deeds and documents relating to the property, or to the title thereto, which a purchaser under the power of sale would be entitled to demand and recover from him.*

VI. MORTGAGE—POWERS—*continued.*

Sect. 22.—(1.) *The receipt in writing of a mortgagee shall be a sufficient discharge for any money arising under the power of sale conferred by this Act, or for any money or securities comprised in his mortgage, or arising thereunder; and a person passing or transferring the same to the mortgagee shall not be concerned to inquire whether any money remains due under the mortgage.*

(2.) *Money received by a mortgagee under his mortgage or from the proceeds of securities comprised in his mortgage shall be applied in like manner as in this Act directed respecting money received by him arising from a sale under the power of sale conferred by this Act; but with this variation, that the costs, charges, and expenses payable shall include the costs, charges, and expenses properly incurred of recovering and receiving the money or securities, and of conversion of securities into money, instead of those incident to sale.*

Sect. 23.—(1.) *The amount of an insurance effected by a mortgagee against loss or damage by fire under the power in that behalf conferred by this Act shall not exceed the amount specified in the mortgage deed, or, if no amount is therein specified, then shall not exceed two-third parts of the amount that would be required, in case of total destruction, to restore the property insured.*

(2.) *An insurance shall not, under the power conferred by this Act, be effected by a mortgagee in any of the following cases (namely):*

(1.) *Where there is a declaration in the mortgage deed that no insurance is required:*

(ii.) *Where an insurance is kept up by or on behalf of the mortgagor in accordance with the mortgage deed:*

(iii.) *Where the mortgage deed contains no stipulation respecting insurance, and an insurance is kept up by or on behalf of the mortgagor, to the amount in which he has by this Act authorized to insure.*

(3.) *All money received on an insurance effected under the mortgage deed or under this Act shall, if the mortgagee so requires, be applied by the mortgagor in making good the loss or damage in respect of which the money is received.*

(4.) *Without prejudice to any obligation to the contrary imposed by law, or by special contract, a mortgagee may require that all money received on an insurance be applied in or towards discharge of the money due under his mortgage.*

Sect. 24.—(1.) *A mortgagee entitled to appoint a receiver under the power in that behalf conferred by this Act shall not appoint a receiver until he has become entitled to exercise the power of sale conferred by this Act, but may then, by writing under his hand, appoint such person as he thinks fit to be receiver.*

(2.) *The receiver shall be deemed to be the agent of the mortgagor; and the mortgagor shall be solely responsible for the receiver's acts or defaults unless the mortgage deed otherwise provides.*

(3.) *The receiver shall have power to demand and recover all the income of the property of which he is appointed receiver, by action, distress, or otherwise, in the name either of the mortgagor or of the mortgagee, to the full extent of the estate or interest which the mortgagor could dispose of, and to give effectual receipts, accordingly, for the same.*

VI. MORTGAGE—POWERS—*continued.*

(4.) *A person paying money to the receiver shall not be concerned to inquire whether any case has happened to authorize the receiver to act.*

(5.) *The receiver may be removed, and a new receiver may be appointed, from time to time, by the mortgagee in writing under his hand.*

(6.) *The receiver shall be entitled to retain out of any money received by him, for his remuneration, and in satisfaction of all costs, charges, and expenses incurred by him as receiver, a commission at such rate, not exceeding 5 per centum on the gross amount of all money received, as is specified in his appointment, and if no rate is so specified, then at the rate of 5 per centum on that gross amount, or at such higher rate as the Court thinks fit to allow on application made by him for that purpose.*

(7.) *The receiver shall, if so directed in writing by the mortgagee, insure and keep insured against loss or damage by fire, out of the money received by him, any building, effects, or property comprised in the mortgage, whether affixed to the freehold or not, being of an insurable nature.*

(8.) *The receiver shall apply all money received by him as follows (namely):—*

(i.) *In discharge of all rents, taxes, rates, and outgoings whatever affecting the mortgaged property; and*

(ii.) *In keeping down all annual sums or other payments, and the interest on all principal sums, having priority to the mortgage in right whereof he is receiver; and*

(iii.) *In payment of his commission, and of the premiums on fire, life, or other insurances, if any, properly payable under the mortgage deed or under this Act, and the cost of executing necessary or proper repairs directed in writing by the mortgagee; and*

(iv.) *In payment of the interest accruing due in respect of any principal money due under the mortgage:*

and shall pay the residue of the money received by him to the person who, but for the possession of the receiver, would have been entitled to receive the income of the mortgaged property, or who is otherwise entitled to that property.

1. —— Power of Sale—*Notice to Mortgagor or his Assigns.*] A mortgage contained a power of sale with a proviso that the mortgagee was not to execute the power without giving notice to the mortgagor or his assigns. The mortgagor assigned his equity of redemption by way of mortgage to a second mortgagee :—*Held*, that such second mortgagee was entitled to receive notice of the first mortgagee's intention to exercise his power of sale, and was entitled to damage from him for default in giving such notice. HOOLE *v.* SMITH

[17 Ch. D. 434]

2. —— Power of Sale—*Purchase by Secretary of Mortgagees.*] At a sale by auction under the direction of a building society as mortgagees, the secretary of the society openly bid for and became the purchaser of two lots on his own account. There was no proof of undervalue. — *Held*, that under the circumstances the sale to the secretary could not be maintained as against the mortgagor. —*Robertson v. Norris* (1 Giff. 421) disapproved of. MARTINSON *v.* CLOWES   - 21 Ch. D. 857

VI. MORTGAGE—POWERS—*continued.*

3. —— Power of Sale—*Restraining Sale—Payment into Court.*] The general rule is that a sale by a mortgagee will be restrained only on payment into Court by the mortgagor of the amount which the mortgagee swears to be due to him, but this does not apply where the Court can see on the terms of the deed that this amount cannot be due on the security.—*Hill* v. *Kirkwood* (28 W. R. 358) considered. HICKSON *v.* DARLOW

[**23 Ch. D. 690**

4. —— Power of Sale—*Restraining Sale—Payment of Money into Court—Mortgagee in fiduciary Position—Solicitor and Client.*] The ordinary rule that the Court will not grant an interlocutory injunction restraining a mortgagee from exercising his power of sale except on the terms of the mortgagor paying into Court the sum sworn by the mortgagee to be due for principal, interest, and costs, does not apply to a case where the mortgagee at the time of taking the mortgage was the solicitor of the mortgagor. In such a case the Court will look to all the circumstances of the case, and will make such order as will save the mortgagor from oppression without injuring the security of the mortgagee.—The Plaintiff was a lady who was entitled to a life interest in leasehold property which she had mortgaged to various persons. The Defendant acted as her solicitor, and with her sanction in order to release her from embarrassment bought up several of the incumbrances with his own money and took a transfer of them to himself; having previously taken a mortgage of the life interest to secure his past costs and the costs which he might incur in paying off the incumbrances. Afterwards the Plaintiff discharged the Defendant, and employed another solicitor, who applied to the Defendant for information respecting the securities transferred. The Defendant refused to give this information unless the payment of what was due to him was guaranteed, and threatened to proceed to a sale of the property. The Plaintiff then brought an action to impeach the securities and to restrain the sale of the property, and moved for an injunction till the hearing:—*Held*, that considering all the circumstances, an injunction ought to be granted, on the Plaintiff paying into Court such a sum as the Court considered would cover the amount actually advanced by the Defendant, and amending the writ so as to make it a simple action for redemption and injunction. MACLEOD *v.* JONES -   **24 Ch. D. 289**

5. —— Power of Sale—*Restraining Sale—Undervalue—Trustee.*] If a mortgagee exercises his power of sale bonâ fide for the purpose of realizing his debt and without collusion with the purchaser, the Court will not interfere even though the sale be very disadvantageous unless the price is so low as in itself to be evidence of fraud. A mortgagee in exercising his power of sale is not (except as to the balance of the purchase-money after a sale) a trustee for the mortgagor even if the mortgage is in the form of a trust for sale.—*Downes* v. *Grazebrook* (3 Mer. 200) and *Robertson* v. *Norris* (1 Giff. 421) observed upon. WARNER *v.* JACOB -   -   - **20 Ch. D. 220**

6. —— Power of Sale—*Solicitor and Client—Mortgage by Client to Solicitor—Appropriation of*

VI. MORTGAGE—POWERS—*continued.*

rents by Mortgagee in Possession.] A solicitor advanced money to his client on a second mortgage, in which was inserted a power of sale exerciseable at any time without the usual proviso requiring that notice should be given, or some interest should be three months in arrear ; and it was not shewn that he explained to the client that the power was not in the usual form. The solicitor afterwards took possession, and for several years received the rents, which, together with some payments made by the mortgagor, exceeded the interest on both mortgages. He then sold the property without notice.—*Held* (affirming the decision of Fry, J.), in an action by the mortgagor against the solicitor, that the omission from the power of sale of the usual qualifying clause was a breach of duty, and that the mortgagee was liable in damages as for an improper sale, unless it could be shewn that some interest was three months in arrear : and whether the absence of explanation did not make it improper even if there was interest in arrear, *quære.*—*Held*, that the fact that the mortgagee had received rents to an amount more than sufficient to pay the interest would not by itself prove that there was no interest in arrear if no appropriation was shewn to have been made.—The dictum in *Brocklehurst* v. *Jessop* (7 Sim. 442) overruled.—But *held*, that, as in an account sent by the mortgagee to the mortgagor the interest was treated as satisfied up to a certain day out of the rents, there was evidence of an arrangement that the rents should be applied in discharge of interest, and that, as the final account shewed that if the rents were thus appropriated there would be no interest in arrear at the time of sale, the sale was improper.—Whether a mortgagee in possession having a balance of rents in hand more than sufficient for payment of the interest and all expenses he has incurred can be heard to say that interest is in arrear so as to justify a sale because no account has been rendered and no appropriation made, *quære.*—*Held* (reversing the decision of Fry, J.), that the difference between party and party costs and solicitor and client costs of the present action could not be given to the Plaintiff by way of damages. COCKBURN *v.* EDWARDS -   -   **18 Ch. D. 449**

—— Sale by mortgagee in possession—Permanent improvements -   **21 Ch. D. 469** *See* MORTGAGE—MORTGAGEE IN POSSESSION. 5.

VII. MORTGAGE—PRIORITY.

1. —— Bankruptcy of Mortgagor—*Purchase by Trustee in Bankruptcy of Mortgaged Estate—Right of Second Mortgagee.*] A trustee in bankruptcy does not by purchasing from the first mortgagee of the bankrupt extinguish the first mortgage, and make the second mortgagee the first incumbrancer on the estate.—But such a purchase does not extinguish the right of the second mortgagee to redeem. BELL *v.* SUNDERLAND BUILDING SOCIETY -   **24 Ch. D. 618**

2. —— Building Society—*Tacking—Receipt by Trustees of Building Society—6 & 7 Wm. 4, c. 32, s. 5—Vendor and Purchaser Act, 1874 (37 & 38 Vict. c. 78), s. 7—Land Transfer Act, 1875 (38 & 39 Vict. c. 87), s. 129.*] The lessee of a term, in November, 1865, mortgaged it to the

VII. MORTGAGE—PRIORITY—*continued.*

trustees of a building society of which he was a member, to secure the payment by him of all moneys which might become due from him pursuant to the rules of the society. In September, 1868, the lessee of the term again mortgaged it to the Plaintiff to secure the sum of £70 then due from him to the Plaintiff, and such further sums as should thereafter be advanced by the Plaintiff. Notice of the mortgage to the Plaintiff was not given to the building society.—Previously to June, 1875, the lessee of the term applied to the Defendants to advance to him the sum of £150 on the security thereof. He informed them that the property was subject to the mortgage to the building society, but was not subject to any other incumbrance. In July, 1875, the Defendants paid to the trustees of the building society the sum of £57 18s. 11d., being the full amount due from the lessee of the term, and thereupon the trustees, under 6 & 7 Wm. 4, c. 32, s. 5, signed a receipt indorsed on the deed of mortgage to the society, acknowledging that all moneys intended to be secured by the mortgage to the building society had been paid. In the same month the Defendants paid to the lessee of the term the sum of £92 1s. 1d., being the balance of the sum of £150 agreed to be advanced, and thereupon he executed a mortgage of the term to the Defendants to secure payment of the sum of £150. The lessee of the term afterwards became insolvent. The present action for foreclosure having been brought in a County Court, the Judge, by his decree, declared that the hereditaments were subject, first, to a charge of what might be due to the Defendants in respect of the £57 18s. 11d. paid by them to the building society; secondly, to a charge of what might be due to the Plaintiff by virtue of the mortgage to him; thirdly, to a charge of what might be due to the Defendants on the security of their mortgage, so far as the same might not be included in the first charge:—*Held*, affirming the decision of the Queen's Bench Division, that the priorities were correctly ascertained, and that the decree of the County Court was right.—Per Brett, M.R., and Bowen, L.J., that the present case fell within the principles laid down in *Pease* v. *Jackson* (Law Rep. 3 Ch. 576).—Per Baggallay, L.J., first, on the authority of *Pease* v. *Jackson* (Law Rep. 3 Ch. 576), that the Defendants had the better equity, and consequently the better right to call for the legal estate, and that the legal estate in the property comprised in the mortgage to the building society had vested in the Defendants by virtue of the indorsed receipt; nevertheless that the security acquired by the Defendants by reason of the legal estate becoming vested in them, did not extend beyond the amount advanced by them to pay off the building society; and that, as regarded the further advance, they were incumbrancers puisne to the Plaintiff; secondly, that notwithstanding the Land Transfer Act, 1875, s. 129, the Defendants, owing to the Vendor and Purchaser Act, 1874, were precluded from treating the property vested in them as security for the further sum advanced by them to the lessee of the term. —*Fourth City Mutual Benefit Building Society* v. *Williams* (14 Ch. D. 140) commented on. ROBINSON v. TREVOR　-　　-　　12 Q. B. D. 423

VII. MORTGAGE—PRIORITY—*continued.*

3. —— **Company** —*Deposit*— *Certificates of Shares*—*Lien of Company on Shares for Moneys due from Shareholder*—*Notice.*] The articles of association of a company provided that the company should have a first and permanent lien and charge, available at law and in equity, on every share, for all debts due from the shareholder to the company. A shareholder deposited the certificates of his shares with his bankers as security for the balance then due from him to them on his current account, and notice of the deposit was given to the company :—*Held*, that *Hopkinson* v. *Rolt* (9 H. L. C. 514) applied, and that the company could not claim priority over the bankers in respect of moneys which became due from the shareholder to the company after notice of the bankers' advance, but that the bankers were entitled to priority. BRADFORD BANKING COMPANY v. BRIGGS & Co. 29 Ch. D. 149 [Reversed by Court of Appeal, 31 Ch. D. 19.]

4. —— **Deposit** — *Equitable Priorities* — *Incumbrancers without Notice*—*Fraud*—*Possession of Title Deeds*—*Estoppel.*] In 1873, D., in order to carry out a fraudulent scheme, obtained a transfer to himself of mortgages of freehold property, and after various dealings with it the legal estate was, in September, 1875, conveyed by a mortgagee to H. in trust for M., and in March, 1876, by H. to M. M. was alleged to have been an accomplice of and trustee for D.—In August, 1874, in pursuance of this scheme, T., claiming to be entitled to this property under a fictitious lease for ninety-eight years, purporting to have been granted to him in March, 1870, by a merely fictitious freeholder (an agent and accomplice of D.), demised the property by way of mortgage to A.— In November, 1874, M., claiming to be entitled to the same property under a fictitious lease for ninety-nine years, also dated March, 1870, and purporting to be granted to him by T., demised the property by way of mortgage to B., the mortgage deed being executed by M. only.— In January, 1877, M. (to whom the legal estate had been conveyed in March, 1876) deposited the genuine title deeds of the property with C. upon a memorandum charging his estate and interest in the lands comprised in the deeds and a statutory declaration of title; and further advances were made to M. and D., who came forward and stated that M. was merely a trustee for him of the property.—In 1878, D., M., and T. were convicted and sentenced to penal servitude for forgery and fraud in connection with this property, and C., as equitable mortgagee, entered into possession.—In an action by A. to settle the priorities of himself, B., and C., as incumbrancers on the property :— *Held* : 1. That, assuming T. to have been the agent of D., so that his representations to A. of having a good title were binding on D., such representations followed by the acquisition of the property beneficially by D. did not bind the estate so as to give A. a prior equitable charge as against subsequent purchasers for value without notice.— 2. That the like representations of M. to B., followed by the acquisition, first, of the equitable, and afterwards of the legal estate by M., did not put B. in any better position, and that the doctrine of estoppel did not apply so as to convert the ficti-

VII. MORTGAGE—PRIORITY—continued.

tious title acquired by B. from N. in November, 1874, into a valid legal title ab initio upon the conveyance of the legal estate to M. in March, 1876.—3. That as purchaser for value without notice by deposit of the genuine title deeds, C., though subsequent in date, was entitled in priority over A. and B.　KEATE v. PHILLIPS

[18 Ch. D. 560

5. —— Deposit—*Loan by equitable Mortgagee after Notice of Contract of Sale—Vendor and Purchaser—Lien of Unpaid Vendor.*] The owner of land, after depositing the title deeds with a bank as security for all sums then or thereafter to become due on the general balance of his account with the bank, contracted with the knowledge of the bank to sell the land to one who had notice of the terms of the deposit. The vendor afterwards paid into his own account at the bank sums which in the whole exceeded the debt due to the bank on his balance at the time of the contract of sale, so that on the principle of *Clayton's Case* (1 Mer. 585) that debt was discharged. The bank, without giving notice to the purchaser, continued the account and made fresh advances to the vendor, so that on the general balance there was always a debt to the bank. The purchaser, who never had notice of the fresh advances, paid the purchase-money by instalments to the vendor: —*Held* (affirming the decision of the Court of Appeal), that on the principle of *Hopkinson* v. *Rolt* (9 H. L. C. 514), the bank had no charge on the land as against the purchaser for the fresh advances. — *Held*, also, that the bank had no charge upon the purchase-money. — Per Lord Blackburn: A purchaser of land, with notice that the title deeds have been deposited with a bank as security for the general balance on the vendor's present and future account, is not bound to inquire whether the bank has after notice of the purchase made fresh advances. The burden lies on the bank advancing on the security of the unpaid vendor's lien to give the purchaser notice that it has so done or intends so to do.　LONDON AND COUNTY BANKING COMPANY v. RATCLIFFE

[6 App. Cas. 722

6. —— Negligence of First Mortgagee—*Possession of Deeds.*] P. mortgaged estates to M., and was allowed to retain possession of the title deeds. He subsequently mortgaged one of the estates to A. B., who obtained possession of the deeds, and all the estates to C., who advanced his moneys after ascertaining the position of the deeds, and upon the faith that A. B. was the only prior mortgagee:—*Held*, that M., by not obtaining possession of the deeds, enabled P. to deal with his estates as an unincumbered owner; that A. B. having been diligent in obtaining the deeds acquired priority, and that C. also having been diligent in ascertaining that A. B. had the deeds, apparently as first mortgagee, the same principle extended to him, and he also had priority over M. —The case of *Perry-Herrick* v. *Attwood* (25 Beav. 205; 2 De G. & J. 21) explained and followed. CLARKE v. PALMER　-　21 Ch. D. 124

7. —— Negligence of First Mortgagee — *Possession of Deeds.*] C., the manager of a joint stock company, executed a legal mortgage to the company of his own freehold estate, and handed

VII. MORTGAGE—PRIORITY—continued.

over the title deeds to them. The deeds were placed in a safe of the company, which had only one lock having duplicate keys, one of which was intrusted to C., as manager. Some time afterwards, C. took out of the safe the deeds except the mortgage, and handed them to W., to whom at the same time he executed a mortgage for money advanced to him by her, without notice of the company's security :—*Held*, reversing the decision of the Vice-Chancellor of the Court of the County Palatine of Lancaster, that the mortgage of the company had priority over the mortgage to W.—The Court will postpone a legal mortgage to a subsequent equitable security: (1) where the legal mortgagee has assisted in or connived at the fraud which led to the creation of the subsequent equitable estate, of which assistance or connivance the omission to use ordinary care in inquiring after or keeping the title deeds may be sufficient evidence where such conduct cannot otherwise be explained; or (2), where the legal mortgagee has made the mortgagor his agent with authority to raise money, and the security given for raising such money has by misconduct of the agent been represented as the first estate.—But the Court will not postpone a legal mortgage to a subsequent equitable mortgagee on the ground of any mere carelessness or want of prudence on the part of the legal mortgagee.　NORTHERN COUNTIES OF ENGLAND FIRE INSURANCE COMPANY v. WHIPP 26 Ch. D. 482

8. —— Negligence of First Mortgagee—*Possession of Deeds—Postponement of Holder of Legal Estate—Trustee of Marriage Settlement—Notice of Marriage of Mortgagor—Duty of Mortgagee to inquire as to Settlement.*] In November, 1875, a husband deposited with his bankers the title deeds of some leasehold houses, together with a memorandum of deposit, as a continuing security to the bankers for any overdraft of his wife's current account with them. In November, 1876, he died, having bequeathed all his property to his wife, and appointed her his executrix. After his death the deeds remained with the bankers, and the widow was allowed on the security of them to overdraw her account. In May, 1877, she married again. Prior to the marriage the houses were assigned by her to a trustee on trust for herself for life, and after her death on trust for an infant son of her first marriage absolutely. Power was given to the trustee to sell the houses during the life of the wife, at her request, and after her death at the discretion of the trustee. The trustee made no inquiry about the title deeds, and no notice of the settlement was given to the bankers. In June, 1877, the husband and wife gave notice to the bankers of their marriage, and at their request a balance, which then stood to the credit of the wife's current account, was transferred to a new current account opened by the bankers with the husband. The deeds remained with the bankers, but no notice of the settlement was given to them. In November, 1877, at the request of the bankers, the probate of the first husband's will was sent to them, and at their request a new memorandum of deposit was in January, 1878, signed by the husband and wife, making the deeds a continuing security to the bankers for any overdraft of the

VII. MORTGAGE—PRIORITY—*continued.*

husband's current account. In April, 1878, the wife died. The deeds were still with the bankers, and at that time the husband's current account was in credit. In 1883 the trustee made some inquiries, and then discovered that the deeds, which he had believed to be in the custody of the solicitor who had prepared the settlement, were with the bankers. He then gave the bankers notice of the settlement, and claimed the deeds. This was the first notice that the bankers had had of the settlement:—*Held*, that the omission of the trustee to inquire for the title deeds was negligence of such a character as prevented him from availing himself of the legal estate to give him priority over the equitable charge of the bankers, and that the cestui que trust stood in no better position.—*Held*, that the bankers were entitled to priority in respect of the amount due to them on their security at the time when they received notice of the settlement. — When a married woman executes a mortgage there is no obligation on the mortgagee to inquire whether a settlement was made on her marriage. LLOYD'S BANKING COMPANY *v.* JONES   -   29 Ch. D. 221

9. —— **Negligence of First Mortgagee**—*Postponement of Legal Mortgage—Deposit of Deeds—Priority—Recovery of Deeds—Purchase for Value without Notice — Judicature Act, 1873, s. 25, sub-s. 11.*] A legal mortgagee had asked for the deeds which the mortgagor, who was his solicitor, made excuses for not giving to him. The mortgagor afterwards deposited the deeds with another mortgagee as security for money advanced without notice of the legal mortgage :—*Held*, in an action by the legal mortgagee for foreclosure, that he had not been guilty of fraud or negligence amounting to fraud, and that he could not be postponed to the mortgagee by deposit by reason of any negligence short of that :—*Held*, that the legal mortgagee was entitled to recover the deeds from the mortgagee by deposit, notwithstanding he was a purchaser for value without notice; and that sect. 25, sub-sect. 11, of the Judicature Act, 1873, did not alter the rule of law on the subject. MANNERS *v.* MEW   -   -   29 Ch. D. 725

10. —— **Notice**—*Fund in Court—Notice of Prior Incumbrance to Second Incumbrancer—Stop Order.*] A second incumbrancer of a fund in Court, who at the time of taking his security had notice of the existence of the first incumbrance, cannot by obtaining a stop order gain priority over the first incumbrancer, even although the latter never obtains a stop order. *In re* HOLMES
[29 Ch. D. 786

11. —— **Notice**—*Fund partly in Court and partly in Hands of Trustees—Notice—Stop Order.*] When an assignment is made of an interest in a trust fund part of which is in Court and part in the hands of the trustees, the assignee in order to complete his title must, as regards the fund in Court, obtain a stop order, and, as regards the fund in the hands of the trustees, give notice to the trustees. Notice to the trustees will be ineffectual as regards the fund in Court, and as to that fund the priorities of different assignees will be determined by the dates at which they have obtained stop orders. An assignee who has obtained a stop order is entitled (as regards the

VII. MORTGAGE—PRIORITY—*continued.*

fund in Court) to priority over a prior assignee (of whose assignment he had no notice), who had given notice to the trustees before the date of the stop order, but who had not himself obtained any stop order. MUTUAL LIFE INSURANCE SOCIETY *v.* LANGLEY   -   -   -   -   26 Ch. D. 686
[Affirmed by the Court of Appeal.]

12. —— **Notice**—*Officer's Commission—Regulation of the Forces Act, 1871 (34 & 35 Vict. c. 86), s. 3.*] When an officer retires from 'Her Majesty's service, the amount in respect of his commission to which he is entitled under 34 & 35 Vict. c. 86, s. 3, "upon his retirement," though it has been previously lodged by the Army Purchase Commissioners with the army agents, and by them entered in their books under the officer's name, is not the money of the officer so as to be capable of being affected by notice from an incumbrancer to the army agents until the retirement is gazetted.—A first incumbrancer gave notice after the money was transferred by the Army Purchase Commissioners to the agents and again gave notice five days after the *Gazette.* Second and third incumbrancers gave simultaneous notices on the day after the *Gazette* :—*Held*, that the order of priorities was : 1. Second incumbrancer ; 2. Third incumbrancer ; 3. First incumbrancer. JOHNSTONE *v.* COX
[16 Ch. D. 571 ; 19 Ch. D. 17

13. —— **Notice**—*Policy—Incumbrance—Legal Estate—Trustee.*] A trustee who has the legal estate and takes from his cestui que trust an assignment of the equitable interest by way of security for money advanced to the cestui que trust, can avail himself of the legal estate as a pro ection against a prior incumbrance of which he t had no notice. — The note in Sugden's Vendors and Purchasers (14th Ed. p. 879) on *Browne* v. *Savage* (4 Drew. 635) corrected. The Act 30 & 31 Vict. c. 144, is intended to apply only as between the insurance office and the persons interested in the policy, and does not affect the rights of those persons *inter se.* Accordingly where a first incumbrancer on a policy had not given such notice as prescribed by the Act, and a second incumbrancer with notice of the prior charge had given the statutory notice :—*Held*, that the second incumbrancer did not thereby obtain priority. NEWMAN *v.* NEWMAN   -   -   -   28 Ch. D. 674

VIII. MORTGAGE—REDEMPTION.

The Act 44 & 45 Vict. c. 41 (*Conveyancing Act, 1881*), enacts, Sect. 15.—(1.) *Where a mortgagor is entitled to redeem, he shall, by virtue of this Act, have power to require the mortgagee, instead of reconveying, and on the terms on which he would be bound to re-convey, to assign the mortgage debt and convey the mortgaged property to any third person, as the mortgagor directs ; and the mortgagee shall, by virtue of this Act, be bound to assign and convey accordingly.*

(2.) *This section does not apply in the case of a mortgagee being or having been in possession.*

(3.) *This section applies to mortgages made either before or after the commencement of this Act (31st Dec. 1881), and shall have effect notwithstanding any stipulation to the contrary.*

VIII. MORTGAGE—REDEMPTION—*continued.*

By 45 & 46 Vict. c. 39 (*Conveyancing Act*, 1882), s. 12, *the right of the mortgagor, under sect.* 15 *of the Conveyancing Act*, 1881, *to require a mortgagee, instead of re-conveying, to assign the mortgage debt and convey the mortgaged property to a third person, shall belong to and be capable of being enforced by each incumbrancer, or by the mortgagor, notwithstanding any intermediate incumbrance; but a requisition of an incumbrancer shall prevail over a requisition of the mortgagor, and, as between incumbrancers, a requisition of a prior incumbrancer shall prevail over a requisition of a subsequent incumbrancer.*

Inspection of Title-deeds.] *By the 44 & 45 Vict. c. 41, s. 16.*—(1.) *A mortgagor, as long as his right to redeem subsists, shall, by virtue of this Act, be entitled from time to time, at reasonable times, on his request, and at his own cost, and on payment of the mortgagee's costs and expenses in this behalf, to inspect and make copies or abstracts of or extracts from the documents of title relating to the mortgaged property in the custody or power of the mortgagee.*

(2.) *This section applies only to mortgages made after the commencement of this Act, and shall have effect notwithstanding any stipulation to the contrary.*

1. —— Action to enforce Security—*Notice to pay off Mortgage Debt.*] A son who was residuary legatee under his father's will, mortgaged his interest under that will to H. The son died having made P. his executor and A. his residuary legatee. A., as residuary legatee, and H., on behalf of himself and the other creditors, brought an action against the executors of the son for administration of the son's estate, and H. brought an action against the executors of the father for administration of the father's estate. Shortly after this P. gave notice to H. that he should pay off the mortgage in six calendar months, and this notice was accepted by H.:—*Held*, that notwithstanding the giving and acceptance of the notice, H. having taken proceedings to recover his mortgage money was bound to accept in satisfaction of his claims his principal money and costs with interest up to the time of payment, though such payment was made before the expiration of the notice. *In re* ALCOCK. PRESCOTT *v.* PHIPPS

[23 Ch. D. 372

2. —— Right of Mortgagor to call for Assignment—*Rights of Puisne Mortgagee—Conveyancing and Law of Property Act*, 1881 (44 & 45 Vict. c. 41), s. 15.] If there are first and subsequent mortgages of the same estate, the mortgagor cannot require the first mortgagee to assign the debt and property to a nominee of his own, under the 15th section of the Conveyancing Act, 1881, without the consent of the puisne mortgagee. The "mortgagor entitled to redeem" in that section means a mortgagor, or person claiming under the mortgagor, who has a right to require a reconveyance from the mortgagee; and no other person can take advantage of that section.—The decision of Fry, J., affirmed. TEEVAN *v.* SMITH

[20 Ch. D. 724

3. —— Right of Mortgagor to call for Assignment *to any Third Person*—"*On the terms*"—*Tenant for Life—Conveyancing and Law of Pro-*

VIII. MORTGAGE—REDEMPTION—*continued.*

perty Act, 1881 (44 & 45 Vict. c. 41), s. 15.] A tenant for life of mortgaged premises who has failed to keep down the interest and who has obtained the usual order permitting him to redeem the mortgage, is not of right entitled under sect. 15 of the Conveyancing and Law of Property Act, 1881, to require the mortgagee to transfer the mortgage debt and premises to a third person. ALDERSON *v.* ELGEY - 26 Ch. D. 567

4. —— Sale—*Conduct of Sale—Conveyancing and Law of Property Act*, 1881 (44 & 45 Vict. c. 41), s. 25.] Under sect. 25 of the Conveyancing and Law of Property Act, 1881, the Court has power in a redemption action to order a sale of the mortgaged property on an interlocutory application made before the trial of the action by a person interested in the equity of redemption.—In an action by the owner of the equity of redemption of property subject to several mortgages for the redemption of the mortgages, the Plaintiff, soon after the issue of the writ, applied by summons for an order giving him liberty to sell the mortgaged property, and asking that he might have the conduct of the sale. The first and second mortgagees opposed the application, the others supported it:—*Held*, that an order for sale ought to be made, but that a reserve price must be fixed large enough to cover what was due on the first and second mortgages, and that the Plaintiff must give security for the costs of the sale. The conduct of the sale was given to the Plaintiff on the ground that he was more interested than the first or second mortgagees in obtaining as large a price as possible for the property.—And it was ordered that the sale should take place out of Court, and that the proceeds of sale should be paid into Court. WOOLLEY *v.* COLMAN - 21 Ch. D. 169

5. —— Sale—*Mortgagor and First Mortgagee —Notice of Second Mortgage—Proceeds of Sale, how to be applied.*] A mortgagor of a leasehold house, with the concurrence of the first mortgagees, who had a notice of a second equitable mortgage, sold the property. Upon completion, the balance of the purchase-money, after payment of the first mortgagees, was handed to the mortgagor. In an action by the second mortgagees against the mortgagor (who did not appear) and the first mortgagees:—*Held* (affirming Bacon, V.C., that the first mortgagees were liable to make good to the Plaintiffs the amount of their security to the extent of the balance of the purchase-money.—The doctrine in Peacock v. Burt (4 L. J. (N.S.) (Ch.) 33) will not be extended.—Dictum of Wood, V.C., in Bates v. Johnson (Joh. 304, 313, 314), as to the right of a first mortgagee to transfer to a third mortgagee in preference to the second, questioned. WEST LONDON COMMERCIAL BANK *v.* RELIANCE PERMANENT BUILDING SOCIETY 27 Ch. D. 187;

[29 Ch. D. 954

6. —— Transferee—*Taxation—Mortgagee—Draft Mortgage or Transfer—Copies.*] A firm of solicitors acting for a number of sets of persons (five in all) interested in moneys secured upon mortgage, on the mortgage being paid off, in their bill of costs charged the executors of the mortgagor with the cost of five copies of the draft deed of transfer, and the Taxing Master having disallowed the charge for four such copies :—

VIII. MORTGAGE—REDEMPTION—*continued.*

Held, that the Taxing Master was right in allowing the costs of only one copy.—A mortgagee or transferee of a mortgage, though entitled to keep a fair copy of the draft deed for his own protection until the transaction is completed, has no right to keep copies of the mortgage deed or deed of transfer after he is paid off, but whatever copies he has are as a general rule copies paid for by the mortgagor, and to be delivered up to him when he pays off the mortgage. *In re* WADE & THOMAS　-　-　-　-　**17 Ch. D. 348**

—— Consolidation of mortgages.

See Statutes and Cases under MORTGAGE —CONSOLIDATION.

IX. MORTGAGE—STATUTORY FORM.

The Act 44 & 45 *Vict. c.* 41 *(Conveyancing Act, 1881), enacts—Sect.* 26.—(1.) *A mortgage of freehold or leasehold land may be made by a deed expressed to be made by way of statutory mortgage, being in the form given in Part I. of the Third Schedule to the Act, with such variations and additions, if any, as circumstances may require, and the following provisions shall apply thereto.*

(2.) *There shall be deemed to be included, and there shall by virtue of the Act be implied, in the mortgage deed :—*

First, a covenant with the mortgagee by the person expressed therein to convey as mortgagor to the effect following (namely):

That the mortgagor will, on the stated day, pay to the mortgagee the stated mortgage money, with interest thereon in the meantime, at the stated rate, and will thereafter, if and as long as the mortgage money, or any part thereof, remains unpaid, pay to the mortgagee interest thereon, or on the unpaid part thereof, at the stated rate, by equal half-yearly payments, the first thereof to be made at the end of six calendar months from the day stated for payment of the mortgage money.

Secondly, a proviso to the effect following (namely):

That if the mortgagor, on the stated day, pays to the mortgagee the stated mortgage money, with interest thereon in the meantime, at the stated rate, the mortgagee at any time thereafter, at the request and cost of the mortgagor, shall reconvey the mortgaged property to the mortgagor, or as he shall direct.

Sect. 27.—(1.) *A transfer of a statutory mortgage may be made by a deed expressed to be made by way of statutory transfer of mortgage, being in such one of the three forms* (A) *and* (B) *and* (C) *given in Part II. of the Third Schedule to the Act as may be appropriate to the case, with such variations and additions, if any, as circumstances may require, and the following provisions shall apply thereto.*

(2.) *In whichever of those three forms the deed of transfer is made, it shall have effect as follows (namely):—*

(i.) *There shall become vested in the person to whom the benefit of the mortgage is expressed to be transferred, who, with his executors, administrators, and assigns, is hereafter in this section designated the transferee, the right to demand, sue for, recover, and give receipts for the mortgage money, or the unpaid part thereof, and the*

IX. MORTGAGE—STATUTORY FORM—*contd.*

interest then due, if any, and thenceforth to become due thereon, and the benefit of all securities for the same, and the benefit of and the right to sue on all covenants with the mortgagee, and the right to exercise all powers of the mortgagee ;

(ii.) *All the estate and interest, subject to redemption, of the mortgagee in the mortgaged land shall vest in the transferee, subject to redemption.*

(3.) *If the deed of transfer is made in the form* (B) *there shall also be deemed to be included, and there shall by virtue of the Act be implied therein, a covenant with the transferee by the person expressed to join therein as covenantor to the effect following (namely),*

That the covenantor will, on the next of the days by the mortgage deed fixed for payment of interest, pay to the transferee the stated mortgage money, or so much thereof as then remains unpaid, with interest thereon, or on the unpaid part thereof, in the meantime, at the rate stated in the mortgage deed ; and will thereafter, as long as the mortgage money, or any part thereof, remains unpaid, pay to the transferee interest on that sum, or the unpaid part thereof, at the same rate, on the successive days by the mortgage deed fixed for payment of interest.

(4.) *If the deed of transfer is made in the form* (C), *it shall, by virtue of the Act, operate not only as a statutory transfer of mortgage, but also as a statutory mortgage, and the provisions of this section shall have effect in relation thereto accordingly ; but it shall not be liable to any increased stamp duty by reason only of it being designated a mortgage.*

Sect. 28. *In a deed of statutory mortgage, or of statutory transfer of mortgage, where more persons than one are expressed to convey as mortgagors, or to join as covenantors, the implied covenant on their part shall be deemed to be a joint and several covenant by them ; and where there are more mortgagees or more transferees than one, the implied covenant with them shall be deemed to be a covenant with them jointly, unless the amount secured is expressed to be secured to them in shares or distinct sums, in which latter case the implied covenant with them shall be deemed to be a covenant with each severally in respect of the share or distinct sum secured to him.*

Sect. 29. *A re-conveyance of a statutory mortgage may be made by a deed expressed to be made by way of statutory re-conveyance of mortgage, being in the form given in Part III. of the third Schedule to the Act with such variations and additions, if any, as circumstances may require.*

MORTGAGE—Action for recovery of land—Application by equitable mortgagee to set aside judgment　-　**12 Q. B. D. 165**
See PRACTICE—SUPREME COURT—JUDGMENT. 5.

—— Assignment of debt　-　**6 Q. B. D. 626 ;**
[12 Q. B. D. 347
See ASSIGNMENT OF DEBT. 2, 3.

—— Attornment clause—Disclaimer **22 Ch. D. 384**
See BANKRUPTCY—DISCLAIMER. 9.

MORTGAGE—*continued.*

—— Attornment clause—Distress 16 Ch. D. 226,
[274; 21 Ch. D. 442
See BANKRUPTCY—DISTRESS. 1, 2, 3.

—— Attornment clause—Distress—Winding-up
of company - - 18 Ch. D. 649
See COMPANY—DISTRESS. 6.

—— Attornment clause — Tenancy — Judgment
under Order XIV. 13 Q. B. D. 347
See PRACTICE—SUPREME COURT—WRIT
SPECIALLY INDORSED. 5.

—— Bankruptcy—Application by mortgagee for
sale of security—Costs of trustee
[13 Q. B. D. 228
See BANKRUPTCY—SECURED CREDITOR. 4.

—— Building society.
See Cases under BUILDING SOCIETY.

—— Building society—Bankruptcy—Proof
[22 Ch. D. 450
See BANKRUPTCY—PROOF. 13.

—— By administrator—Leaseholds 20 Ch. D. 745
See ADMINISTRATOR—POWERS. 3.

—— Charity—Gift to—Mortmain 29 Ch. D. 947
See CHARITY—MORTMAIN. 5.

—— Committee of lunatic—Mortgage by
[20 Ch. D. 451
See LUNATIC—COMMITTEE. 1.

—— Company.
See Cases under COMPANY—DEBENTURES.

—— Covenant by surety to pay premiums on
policy . 19 Ch. D. 615
See PRINCIPAL AND SURETY—INDEMNITY.
2.

—— Devise of mortgaged estate—Keeping down
interest - 30 Ch. D. 614
See WILL.—DISCLAIMER. 2.

—— Executor—Mortgage of lease of testator
[18 Ch. D. 93
See EXECUTOR—ADMINISTRATION. 3.

—— Fixtures—Driving belts—Bills of Sale Act,
1854 - - - 15 Q. B. D. 358
See FIXTURES.

—— Fixtures—Lease by mortgagor after mortgage—Rights of tenant 15 Q. B. D. 218
See LANDLORD AND TENANT—FIXTURES.

—— Foreclosure—Amendment after judgment
[25 Ch. D. 750
See PRACTICE—SUPREME COURT—AMEND-
MENT. 2.

—— Foreclosure—Ejectment ¦ 6 Q. B. D. 345;
[7 App. Cas. 235
See LIMITATIONS, STATUTE OF—REALTY.
4.

—— Foreclosure—Writ of possession
[22 Ch. D. 281
See PRACTICE—SUPREME COURT—WRIT
OF POSSESSION.

—— Forged deed - - - 20 Ch. D. 611
See VENDOR AND PURCHASER—PURCHASE
WITHOUT NOTICE. 1.

—— Goodwill — Right of mortgagee to trade
name - - - 22 Ch. D. 660
See TRADE-NAME. 2.

—— Insufficient security—Valuation 23 Ch. D.
[483; 28 Ch. D. 268
See TRUSTEE—LIABILITIES. 3, 4.

MORTGAGE—*continued.*

—— Insurance by mortgagee.
See MORTGAGE—POWERS—*Statutes.*

—— Lease by mortgagor after mortgage—Right
to trade fixtures - 15 Q. B. D. 218
See LANDLORD AND TENANT—FIXTURES.

—— Lease of partnership premises 19 Ch. D. 105
See BANKRUPTCY—SECURED CREDITOR. 8.

—— Lower Canada - - 10 App. Cas. 664
See COLONIAL LAW—CANADA—QUEBEC.
5.

—— Merger in judgment debt—Interest
See JUDGMENT. 2. [22 Ch. D. 98

—— Partition suit by mortgagee 21 Ch. D. 674
See PARTITION SUIT—SALE. 2.

—— Payment off—Authority of solicitor to receive
money - - - 30 Ch. D. 249
See SOLICITOR—AUTHORITY.

—— Power of sale—Garnishee order—Proceeds
of sale - - 17 Ch. D. 259
See PRACTICE—SUPREME COURT—GAR-
NISHEE ORDER. 8.

—— Priority—Creditors' deed - 29 Ch. D. 745
See CREDITORS' DEED.

—— Priority—Middlesex Registry Act
See REGISTRY ACTS. [29 Ch. D. 702

—— Rates—Mortmain - 22 Ch. D. 202
See CHARITY—MORTMAIN. 4.

—— Receiver—Injunction - 18 Ch. D. 547
See PRACTICE—SUPREME COURT—RE-
CEIVER. 5.

—— Release of equity of redemption—Bill to set
aside - - - 7 App. Cas. 307
See COLONIAL LAW—VICTORIA. 2.

—— Renewable lease - - 29 Ch. D. 231
See LEASEHOLD—RENEWABLE LEASE. 4.

—— Salvage—Money expended by second mortgagee - - 16 Ch. D. 411
See COMPANY—DEBENTURES. 7.

—— Several mortgagees—Consolidation of securities—Bill of sale - 13 Q. B. D. 392
See BILL OF SALE—FORMALITIES. 2.

—— Ship—Action by master for wages—Misconduct—Liability of mortgagee
See SHIP—MASTER. 2. [10 P. D. 13

—— Solicitor and client - 19 Ch. D. 207
See SOLICITOR—LIABILITIES. 3.

—— Solicitor a mortgagee—Profit costs
[27 Ch. D. 544
See SOLICITOR—BILL OF COSTS. 10.

—— Stamps - - - 17 Ch. D. 10
See REVENUE—STAMPS. 3.

—— Statute of Limitations.
See Cases under LIMITATIONS, STATUTE
OF—REALTY. 2, 4—7.

—— Statute of Limitations.
See Cases under LIMITATIONS, STATUTE
OF—PERSONAL ACTIONS. 5, 6, 8, 9, 10.

—— Statute of Limitations—Express trust
[18 Ch. D. 254; 22 Ch. D. 614
See LIMITATIONS, STATUTE OF—TRUSTS.
2, 3.

—— Stop order—Priority—Notice 23 Ch. D. 497
See PRACTICE—SUPREME COURT—CHARG-
ING ORDERS. 3.

MORTGAGE—*continued.*

—— Tenant for life with power of leasing
[23 Ch. D. 583
See SETTLEMENT—POWERS. 1.

—— Title deeds—Solicitor's lien on 16 Ch. D. 617
See SOLICITOR—LIEN. 10.

—— To be paid off out of accumulations of rents
See ACCUMULATIONS. 1. [30 Ch. D. 649

—— Wife's reversionary interest 23 Ch. D. 181
See HUSBAND AND WIFE—WIFE'S REAL
ESTATE. 2.

MORTMAIN.

See Cases under CHARITY—MORTMAIN.

—— Lapsed bequest—Exoneration from debts
[29 Ch. D. 145
See WILL—EXONERATION. 1.

MOTHER—Right to custody of child 16 Ch. D.
[115; 25 Ch. D. 220; 13 Q. B. D. 614
See INFANT—CUSTODY. 1, 2, 3.

MOTION—Dismissal of—Affidavit of service
[25 Ch. D. 84
See PRACTICE—SUPREME COURT—DE-
FAULT. 6.

—— For attachment—Notice 9 Q. B. D. 335
See PRACTICE—SUPREME COURT—NOTICE
OF MOTION. 1.

—— For attachment—Notice - 27 Ch. D. 66
See PRACTICE — SUPREME COURT—AT-
TACHMENT. 4.

—— For judgment—Admissions 21 Ch. D. 716;
[23 Ch. D. 204; 11 Q. B. D. 531
See PRACTICE — SUPREME COURT—MO-
TION FOR JUDGMENT. 1, 2, 3.

—— For judgment—Counter-claim 25 Ch. D. 68
See PRACTICE — SUPREME COURT—DE-
FAULT. 2.

—— For judgment—Report of referee
[32 Ch. D. 722
See PRACTICE—SUPREME COURT — RE-
FEREE. 3.

—— Short notice of - - 22 Ch. D. 504
See PRACTICE—SUPREME COURT—NOTICE
OF MOTION. 3.

—— To discharge order in Chambers
[19 Ch. D. 326
See PRACTICE—SUPREME COURT—CHAM-
BERS. 5.

—— To discharge order in Chambers
[21 Ch. D. 131
See PRACTICE—SUPREME COURT—AP-
PEAL. 21.

—— To dismiss winding up petition
[23 Ch. D. 210
See COMPANY—WINDING-UP ORDER. 10.

—— To vary minutes 20 Ch. D. 130; 21 Ch. D. 621
See PRACTICE—SUPREME COURT—JUDG-
MENT. 6, 7.

MUNICIPAL CORPORATION:—

**I. MUNICIPAL CORPORATION — CONSTITU-
TION.**

. *The Act 45 & 46 Vict. c. 50, repeals the Municipal Corporations Act, 1835, and divers other enactments relating to municipal corporations (see the
1st schedule to the Act), and re-enacts and consolidates the same with amendments.*

*Sect. 1. The Act to be cited as the Municipal Cor-
porations Act, 1882.*

Sect. 2. Division into Parts.
Part I.—Preliminary
*Part II.—Constitution and government of
borough.*
*Part III.—Preparations for and procedure at
elections.*
*Part IV.—Corrupt practices and election peti-
tions.*
Part V.—Corporate property and liabilities.
*Part VI.—Charitable and other trusts and
powers.*
*Part VII.— Borough fund, borough rate,
county rate.*
Part VIII.—Administration of justice.
Part IX.—Police.
Part X.—Freemen.
Part XI.—Grant of charters.
Part XII.—Legal proceedings.
Part XIII.—General.

Sect. 3. Extent of Act.
*Sect. 4. Act to commence the 31st of December,
1882.*

PART I. PRELIMINARY.

Sect. 5 repeals enactments in first schedule.
Sect. 6. Application of Act.
Sect. 7. Interpretation and construction of terms.

PART II. CONSTITUTION AND GOVERNMENT OF
BOROUGH.

Sect. 8. As to name of municipal corporation.
Sect. 9. As to qualification of burgess.
Sect. 10. Constitution of council of the borough.
Sect. 11. Qualification for office of councillor.
Sect. 12. Disqualification for being councillor.
*Sect. 13. Term of office and rotation of coun-
cillors.*
*Sect. 14. As to number, term of office, and rota-
tion of aldermen.*
*Sect. 15. Qualification, term of office, salary, pre-
cedence, and powers of mayor.*
*Sect. 16. Power of mayor to appoint deputy,
powers of deputy.*
*Sect. 17. As to appointment, term of office, and
duties of town clerk, and his deputy.*
Sect. 18. As to appointment, &c., of treasurer.
Sect. 19. As to other borough officers.
*Sect. 20. As to security to be given by and re-
muneration of officers.*
Sect. 21. Every officer to account to council.
*Sect. 22. Rules in second schedule of the Act to
be observed. Quarterly and other meetings of
council and power to appoint committees. Minutes
to be kept, &c.*
Sect. 23. Power to council to make by-laws.
*Sect. 24. Production of written copy of by-law,
under corporate seal, to be sufficient evidence of
by-law.*
*Sect. 25. As to number, qualification, term of
office, and duties of borough auditors.*
*Sect. 26. Treasurer to make up half-yearly
accounts.*

I. **MUNICIPAL CORPORATION — CONSTITU-TUTION**—*continued.*

Sect. 27. As to audit and publication of treasurer's accounts.

Sect. 28. Town clerk to make annual returns of municipal receipts and expenditure to the Local Government Board.

Penalty for not making return.

Sect. 29. As to qualification, number, and term of office of revising assessors in non-parliamentary boroughs.

Sect. 30. Procedure for division of borough into wards or alteration of wards.

Sect. 31. Sole and exclusive use of part of a house, shop, &c., to be deemed a separate occupation for the purpose of describing a qualification.

Sect. 32. Occupier's name to be placed on the rate book when he claims to be rated to and pays the poor-rate.

Sect. 33. Rules as to qualification of burgess in succession, &c., to property.

Sect. 34. A qualified person when elected to a corporate office to accept the office or pay a fine.

Sect. 35. As to declaration on acceptance of office.

Sect. 36. A person elected to a corporate office may at any time resign on payment of a fine.

Sect. 37. Re-eligibility of office holders.

Sect. 38. Mayor and aldermen to continue members of council.

Sect. 39. Avoidance of office of mayor, alderman, or councillor, by bankruptcy or absence from borough.

Sect. 40. As to filling of casual vacancies in a corporate office.

Sect. 41. Penalty on unqualified person acting in office.

Sect. 42. Validity of acts done whilst in possession of corporate office notwithstanding disqualification, &c.

Sect. 43. As to person by whom duties of town clerk, deputy town clerk, or treasurer are to be performed during vacancy or incapacity.

PART III. PREPARATIONS FOR AND PROCEDURE AT ELECTIONS.

Sect. 44. As to preparation and revision of parish burgess lists.

Sect. 45. As to burgess roll and ward rolls.

Sect. 46. As to arrangement of lists and rolls.

Sect. 47. As to correction of burgess roll.

Sect. 48. As to printing and sale of burgess roll and other documents.

Sect. 49. Separate lists to be made of persons qualified to be councillors but not to be burgesses.

Sects. 50–59. As to election of councillors and procedure thereon.

Sect. 60. Time and mode of election of aldermen.

Sect. 61. Time and mode of election of mayor.

Sect. 62. Time and mode of election of auditors and assessors.

Sect. 63. Right of women to vote.

Sect. 64. As to polling districts.

Sect. 65. Notices of elections, how to be given.

Sect. 66. Time for filling casual vacancies.

Sect. 67. Person by whom duties of mayor or returning officer are to be performed in case of illness, absence, &c., of mayor or returning officer.

Sect. 68. Person elected councillor for more than one ward to be put to his election.

Sect. 69. Elections not to be held in any church, &c.

I. **MUNICIPAL CORPORATION — CONSTITU-TION**—*continued.*

Sect. 70. When an election is not held on the appointed day or becomes void, the High Court to appoint a day for the election.

Sect. 71. Burgess roll to be in operation until revision of new burgess roll.

Sect. 72. Elections not necessarily invalid because of non-compliance with rules.

Sect. 73. Every election to be valid unless questioned within twelve months.

Sect. 74. Penalty for offences in relation to nomination papers.

Sect. 75. Penalty for offences in relation to lists and election.

Sect. 76. Revival of former law if Ballot Act, 1872, ceases to be in force.

PART IV. (*Partly repealed by 47 & 48 Vict. c. 70*). CORRUPT PRACTICES AND ELECTION PETITIONS.

Sect. 77 (repealed in part). Defines "bribery," "treating," "undue influence," "personation," "corrupt practices," &c.

Sect. 78 (repealed).

Sects. 79, 80 (repealed).

Sect. 81. Avoidance of election for general corruption.

Sects. 82, 83, 84 (repealed).

Sect. 85. As to striking off votes.

Sect. 86. As to personation.

Sect. 87. Election to be questioned by petition.

Sect. 88. Petition to be presented within twenty-one days of election by four or more voters or by candidate.

Sect. 89. Security for the costs of the petition to be given within three days.

Sect. 90. As to when petition is at issue.

Sect. 91. List of election petitions to be made and kept.

Sect. 92 (repealed in part). Constitution of Election Court.

Sect. 93 prescribes manner in which election petitions are to be tried.

Sect. 94 (repealed in part). As to summoning, &c., of witnesses.

Sect. 95. As to withdrawal of petitions.

Sect. 96. Petition to abate by death of petitioner, but another person may be substituted as petitioner.

Sect. 97. As to withdrawal and substitution of respondents before trial of petition.

Sect. 98 (repealed in part). As to costs of election petitions.

Sect. 99. Reception and attendance on Election Court.

Sect. 100. Rules to be made to regulate the practice, procedure, and costs of petition. Jurisdiction of High Court over election petitions.

Sect. 101. As to remuneration and expenses of election Court.

Sect. 102. Acts done by an elected candidate pending a petition not to be invalidated.

Sect. 103. Provisions as to elections in the room of persons unseated on petition.

Sect. 104. No person to be required to state for whom he has voted.

PART V. CORPORATE PROPERTY AND LIABILITIES.

Sect. 105. Corporation may purchase land for town hall, &c.

2 H

I. MUNICIPAL CORPORATION — CONSTITU-TION—*continued.*

Sect. 174. *County coroner to act in borough not having a separate Court of quarter sessions.*

Sect. 175. *Judge of borough Civil Court where there is a recorder.*

Sect. 176. *Judge of borough Civil Court where there is no recorder.*

Sect. 177. *Tenure of Judge of borough Civil Court.*

Sect. 178. *As to registrar and other officers and fees.*

Sect. 179. *Registrar of borough Civil Court not to practise as a solicitor in the Court.*

Sect. 180. *Borough Civil Court to be held four times a year.*

Sect. 181. *Procedure.*

Sect. 182. *Power for Judge to make rules of procedure.*

Sect. 183. *Borough Civil Court to have jurisdiction in personal actions where sum claimed does not exceed £20, and in ejectment actions where the annual rent does not exceed £20.*

Sect. 184. *Nothing in the Act to restrict existing jurisdiction, &c., of a borough Civil Court, or to affect the Borough and Local Courts of Record Act, 1872.*

Sect. 185. *Jurisdiction of borough Civil Court may be extended over adjacent district.*

Sect. 186. *Provisions as to juries in borough having separate Court of quarter sessions.*

Sect. 187. *Grants to boroughs of separate Court of quarter sessions, &c., not to be affected by subsequent grants to counties.*

Sect. 188. *As to trial of offences committed in borough being a county of a city or county of a town.*

Sect. 189. *As to jurisdiction in places which cease to be part of a borough.*

PART IX. POLICE.

Sects. 190–196 *provide for the appointment of a watch committee; the appointment, duties and powers of borough constables, and special constables.*

Sects. 197–200 *provide for the making and levying of a watch rate.*

PART X. FREEMEN.

Sect. 201. *Definition of freemen.*

Sect. 202. *No person to be admitted a freeman by gift or by Purchase.*

Sect. 203. *Freeman's roll to be kept.*

Sect. 204. *As to admission to freedom.*

Sect. 205. *Reservation of rights of property to freemen and others.*

Sect. 206. *Limit of value and saving under preceding section.*

Sect. 207. *Saving for power to question right or title of any freeman.*

Sect. 208. *Reservation of beneficial exemptions to freemen and others.*

Sect. 209. *Reservation of parliamentary franchise, &c., to freemen.*

And see 48 & 49 Vict. c. 29, *infra.*

PART XI. GRANT OF CHARTERS.

Sect. 210. *Power to Crown in granting charter to borough to extend to it the provisions of the Municipal Corporations Acts.*

Sect. 211. *Every petition for charter to be referred to Committee of Privy Council.*

I. MUNICIPAL CORPORATION — CONSTITU-TION—*continued.*

Sect. 212. *Power by charter to settle wards, and by fixing dates and otherwise to adapt the Municipal Corporations Acts to first constitution of new borough.*

Sect. 213. *Scheme for continuance or abolition of and adjustment of rights of existing local authority and officers.*

[*This is modified by* 45 & 46 Vict. c. 50.]

Sect. 214. *Supplemental provisions as to scheme and charter.*

Sect. 215. *Provision as to police force in new borough.*

Sect. 216. *Validity of charters granted under the Act.*

Sect. 217. *Power to Privy Council to settle scheme in cases where charter granted within seven years before the 14th of August, 1877.*

Sect. 218. *Power to Privy Council to amend scheme.*

And see ELEMENTARY EDUCATION ACTS — SCHOOL BOARD.—*Statutes.*

PART XII. LEGAL PROCEEDINGS.

Sect. 219. *Summary proceedings for offences and fines under the Act to be commenced within six months after commission of the offence.*

An appeal lies to a Court of quarter sessions.

Sect. 220. *Convictions, &c., not to be quashed for want of form, and not to be removed by certiorari or otherwise into the High Court.*

Sect. 221. *As to application of fines, penalties, &c., in quarter sessions borough.*

Sect. 222. *Duties of clerk of the peace as to fines and forfeitures.*

Sect. 223. *As to service of summons or warrants.*

Sect. 224. *Penal actions against corporate officers to be brought only by a burgess of the borough within three months after cause of action arisen. Procedure thereon.*

Sect. 225. *As to proceedings on quo warranto and mandamus.*

Sect. 226. *Provision for protection of persons acting under the Act.*

Sect. 227. *Power for borough constables to take bail.*

PART XIII. GENERAL.

Sect. 228. *As to boundaries of boroughs and transfer of parts to counties.*

Sect. 229. *As to adjustment of rates between boroughs and counties on change of boundaries.*

Sect. 230. *As to computation of time.*

Sect. 231. *As to measurement of distances.*

Sect. 232. *Notices, where to be posted.*

Sect. 233. *As to inspection and taking copies of documents.*

Sect. 234. *Tables of fees to be posted.*

Sect. 235. *Penalty for forgery of seals and signatures.*

Sect. 236. *Notice of intended applications to and correspondence with Treasury to be posted on town hall.*

Sect. 237. *Acts of any deputy under the Act not to be invalidated by any defect in his appointment.*

Sect. 238. *As to notices to and acts done by overseers.*

Sect. 239. *Power to administer oaths, &c.*

Sect. 240. *Form in Schedule to be used.*

I. MUNICIPAL CORPORATION — CONSTITU-TION—continued.

　Sect. 241. *Misnomer or inaccurate description not to hinder operation of the Act.*

　Sect. 242. *The Act to be substituted for 5 & 6 Will. 4, c. 76, in reference to the latter in unrepealed enactments.*

　Sect. 243. *As to short titles of Acts partly repealed.*

　Sect. 244. *Mayor of certain boroughs to be returning officer in parliamentary elections.*

　Sect. 245. *As to electors in disfranchised boroughs.*

　Sect. 246. *Explanation of term "town corporate," &c., in Licensing Acts.*

　Sect. 247. *Right of free trading in boroughs.*

　Sect. 248. *Special provisions as to certain of the Cinque Ports.*

　Sect. 249. *Vice-Chancellor of Cambridge may be a justice for the borough of Cambridge.*

　Sect. 250. *Saving of charters, privileges, &c., granted to existing corporations before commencement of the Act.*

　Sect. 251. *Nothing in Act to affect any local Act of Parliament.*

　Sects. 252–260. *Various special savings.*

　The Act 46 & 47 Vict. c. 18 (*Municipal Corporations Act,* 1883), makes provision respecting certain municipal corporations and other local authorities not subject to the *Municipal Corporations Act,* 1882.

　Borough Constable.] By the *Borough Constable Act* (46 & 47 Vict. c. 44), 1883, s. 2, nothing in sect. 195 of the *Municipal Corporations Act,* 1882, shall be taken to have repealed sect. 20 of the *Town Police Clauses Act,* 1847, or sect. 12 of the *Prevention of Crimes Act,* 1871.

　Freeman.] The Act 48 & 49 Vict. c. 29, enables municipal corporations to confer the honorary freedom of boroughs upon persons of distinction.

II. MUNICIPAL CORPORATION—ELECTION.

　By 44 & 45 Vict. c. 68 (the *Supreme Court of Judicature Act,* 1881), s. 14, the jurisdiction of the High Court of Justice to decide questions of law upon appeal or otherwise under the Act 6 & 7 Vict. c. 18, the *Corrupt Practices* (*Municipal Elections*) *Act,* 1872, the *Parliamentary and Municipal Registration Act,* 1878, or any of the said Acts, or any Act amending the same respectively, shall be final and conclusive, unless in any case it shall seem fit to the said High Court to give special leave to appeal therefrom to Her Majesty's Court of Appeal, whose decision in such case shall be final and conclusive.

　The Act 48 & 49 Vict. c. 59, continues 35 & 36 Vict. c. 33 (the *Ballot Act,* 1872), so far as it is not repealed, and the 45 & 46 Vict. c. 50 (*Municipal Elections Act,* 1882), until the 31st of December, 1886.

　Poll.] The Act 48 & 49 Vict. c. 10 (*Elections Hours of Poll Act,* 1885), directs that at every election of a councillor, or other person named in the Act, in any municipal borough being subject to the *Municipal Corporations Act,* 1882 (45 & 46 Vict. c. 50), the poll shall be open from 8 a.m. to 8 p.m.

　Act of 1884.] The Act 47 & 48 Vict. 70 (the *Municipal Elections Corrupt and Illegal Practices Act,* 1884), enacts as follows :—

　Corrupt Practices.] Sect. 2 defines the expression "corrupt practices" at a municipal election and its punishment.

II. MUNICIPAL CORPORATION—ELECTION—continued.

　Sect. 3 enacts the incapacity of any candidate who is reported by an election Court under 45 & 46 Vict. c. 50 for corrupt practice.

　Illegal Practices.] Sect. 4. Certain expenditure to be deemed illegal practice.

　Sect. 5. Subject to the exceptions in this Act no expense shall be incurred by or on behalf of a candidate.

　Sect. 6. Voting by a prohibited person, or the publication of false statements of the withdrawal of a candidate to be an illegal practice.

　Sect. 7. The punishment of a person guilty of an illegal practice.

　Sect. 8. An illegal practice to be deemed to be an offence against Part 4 of 45 & 46 Vict. c. 50. Any candidate guilty of such offence to be incapable of being elected to or of holding any corporate office during a certain period, and to be subject to other penalties.

　Illegal Payment, Employment, and Hiring.]— Sect. 9. Where a person knowingly provides money for any payment contrary to the provisions of this Act, or for any expenses in excess of the maximum allowed by this Act, or for replacing any money expended in any such payment, except where allowed by this Act he shall be guilty of illegal payment.

　Sect. 10.—(1.) A person shall not let, lend, or employ for the purpose of the conveyance of electors to or from the poll, any public stage or hackney carriage, or any horse or other animal kept or used for drawing the same, or any carriage, horse, or other animal which he keeps or uses for the purpose of letting out for hire, and if he does so knowing that it is for the above purpose he shall be guilty of illegal hiring.

　(2.) A person shall not use for the purpose of the conveyance of electors to or from the poll any carriage, horse, or other animal which he knows the owner thereof is prohibited by this section to employ for that purpose, and if he does so he shall be guilty of illegal hiring.

　(3.) This Act does not prevent a carriage, &c., being used by an elector, or several electors at their joint cost, for the purpose of conveyance to or from the poll.

　(4.) No person is liable to pay any duty or take out a license for any carriage by reason only of such carriage being used without payment for the conveyance of electors to or from the poll.

　Sect. 11. Any person corruptly withdrawing, or inducing another to withdraw, from an election is guilty as of an illegal payment.

　Sect. 12.—(1.) No payment for the purpose of promoting the election of a candidate shall be made on account of bands of music, torches, flags, banners, cockades, ribbons, or other marks of distinction.

　(2.) Subject to such exception as may be allowed in pursuance of this Act, any payment made in contravention of this section, either before, during, or after an election, is an illegal payment, and any person being a party to such contract shall be guilty of illegal payment if he knew that the same was made contrary to law.

　Sect. 13.—(1.) No person shall, for the purpose of promoting the election of a candidate be engaged for payment for any purpose except as follows :—

　(a.) A number of persons may be employed as

II. MUNICIPAL CORPORATION—ELECTION—
continued.

clerks or messengers, not exceeding two
for a borough or ward, and if the number
of electors in such borough or ward exceeds
two thousand, one additional person may
be employed for every thousand electors
and incomplete part of a thousand electors
over and above the said two thousand ;
and,

(b.) *One polling agent may be employed in each
polling station :*

This section does not apply to any engagement
bonâ fide made with any person in the ordinary
course of business.

(2.) Subject to any exception allowed in pursuance of this Act, if any person is employed in contravention of this section, either before, during, or
after an election, the person employing him shall
be guilty of illegal employment, and the person so
employed shall also be guilty of illegal employment
if he knew that he was engaged in contravention of
this Act.

(3.) A person legally employed for payment
under this section may or may not be an elector, but
may not vote.

Sect. 14. Every bill or placard referring to an
election is to bear the name of the printer and
publisher. Any person printing, etc., any bill
without such name is (if a candidate) guilty of
illegal practice, and if not a candidate is liable to
a fine.

Sect. 15. The rights of creditors, ignorant of any
contravention of this Act, are preserved in respect
of prohibited contracts or expenses.

Sect. 16. The use of certain premises for com-
mittee-rooms or election meetings to be deemed an
illegal hiring.

Sect. 17. Punishment of illegal payment, employment, or hiring.

Sect. 18. Consequences where illegal practices,
&c. have affected the result of the election.

Excuse and Exception for Practices forbidden
by this Act.] *Sect. 19.* The election Court may
report exonerating a candidate in certain cases of
corrupt and illegal practice by his agents.

Sect. 20. Power of High Court and election
Court to except an innocent act from being an
illegal practice.

Sect. 21—(1.) Claims to be sent in within 14
days, and to be paid within 21 days after election.

(2.) Agent to make return in writing to candidate
of all expenses within 23 days after election.

(3.) Candidate elected as councillor to send return to town clerk accompanied by a declaration
within 28 days of all expenses.

(4.) Candidate if elected not to sit in council
until he has made the above return and declaration.

(5.) Candidate failing to make return, &c., or
making same falsely.

(6.) Claims sent in after time limited by this
section, when allowed.

(7.) Candidate when excused for failing to
make return, &c., or for making false statement.

(8) and (9.) *Ditto.*

(10) and (11.) The return and declaration to be
kept for 12 months, and to be open to inspection.

Sect. 22. Votes of persons guilty of corrupt
practices and other offences against this Act are
void.

II. MUNICIPAL CORPORATION—ELECTION—
continued

Sect. 23. Portions of sections 37 & 38 of 46 & 47
Vict. c. 51 (Corrupt and Illegal Practices Prevention Act, 1883), to be part of this Act.

Disqualification of Electors.] *Sect. 24.* Town
clerk to make out list of persons who become after
commencement of this Act incapable of voting on
account of corrupt or illegal practices, and to
send this list not less than 14 days before the
publication of the parish burgess lists in the borough
to the overseers.

Any person in such list may object, and the
revising authority shall determine the claim.

The revising authority may, after notice, insert
in such list the name of any incapacitated person,
which is not already therein.

Any town clerk or overseer failing to carry out
this section is liable to a fine under 45 & 46 Vict.
c. 50, s. 75.

Proceedings on Election Petitions.] *Sect. 25*—
(1.) A municipal election petition complaining of
the election on the ground of an illegal practice
may be presented at any time before the expiration
of fourteen days after the day on which the town
clerk receives the return and declaration respecting
election expenses by the candidate to whose election
the petition relates, or where there is an authorized
excuse for failing to make the return and declaration then within the like time after the date of the
allowance of the excuse.

(2.) A municipal election petition, complaining
of the election on the ground of an illegal practice,
and specifically alleging a payment of money or
other act made or done since the election by the
candidate elected at such election, or by an agent
of the candidate, or with the privity of the candidate, in pursuance or in furtherance of such illegal
practice, may be presented at any time within
twenty-eight days after the date of such payment
or act, whether or not any other petition against
that person has been previously presented or tried.

(3.) Any election petition presented within the
time limited by the Municipal Corporations Act,
1882, may, for the purpose of complaining of the
election upon an allegation of an illegal practice,
be amended with the leave of the High Court within the time within which a petition complaining of
the election on the ground of that illegal practice
can. under this section, be presented.

(4.) This section shall apply notwithstanding
the illegal practice is also a corrupt practice.

Sect. 26. Withdrawal of election petition.

Sect. 27. Continuation of election petition.

Sect. 28—(1.) Duty of the Director of Public
Prosecutions to attend on the trial of an election
petition.

(3.) Duty of the same to prosecute where necessary.

(4.) An election Court may punish a person
guilty of corrupt practice by imprisonment with
or without hard labour for a term not exceeding
six months, or by a fine not exceeding £200, and
may punish a person guilty of an illegal practice
by a fine.

A person charged with corrupt practice may
claim a jury.

(5.) The election Court may, if expedient, order a
person to be tried before some other Court than
itself.

II. MUNICIPAL CORPORATION—ELECTION—
continued.

(7.) *Such order cannot be discharged or varied under 45 & 46 Vict. c. 50, s. 92, sub-s. 6.*

(9.) *Costs of prosecution in the first instance to be paid by the Treasury.*

Sect. 29. *Costs where a corrupt practice is not proved. Rules of Supreme Court to apply so far as practicable to taxation.*

Miscellaneous.] Sect. 30. *General provisions as to prosecution of offences, and certificates of indemnity.*

Sect. 31. *A person incapacitated by conviction or report of election Court to vacate his seat or office.*

Sect. 32. *Recovery of costs.*

Sect. 33. *Services of notices or summons by registered letter and otherwise.*

Sect. 34. *Definitions.*

Sect. 35. *This Act and Part IV. of 45 & 46 Vict. c. 50 (Municipal Corporations Act, 1882) apply, subject to certain exceptions, to municipal elections in the City of London; and*

Sect. 36. *To elections for the offices mentioned in the 1st Schedule of this Act. Commissioners to be appointed for the trial of election petitions under Part IV. of 45 & 46 Vict. c. 50.*

Sect. 37. *The elections for the offices mentioned in the said 1st Schedule are exempt from provisions of this Act as to maximum expenses.*

Sect. 38. *Repeal of Acts 33 & 34 Vict. c. 75, s. 33, and part of 45 & 46 Vict. c. 50.*

Sect. 41. *Act to be in force to end of year 1886.*

Medical Relief.] *The Act 48 & 49 Vict. c. 46, declares that medical relief at the expense of the poor-rate shall not deprive a person of right to be registered or to vote as a voter at any municipal election, or as a burgess, or as a voter at any election to an office under the provisions of any statute.*

1. —— Certificate of Commissioners of Treasury—*Expenses of Election Court—Amendment of Order—Court of Record — Rate — Mandamus — Corrupt Practices (Municipal Elections) Act, 1872 (35 & 36 Vict. c. 60), s. 14, sub-s. 5, ss. 20, 22.*] Upon the trial of a petition against the return of a borough councillor under the Corrupt Practices (Municipal Elections) Act, 1872, the barrister in delivering judgment said that he found the councillor guilty of personal bribery, and that all the costs of the inquiry were to be borne by him, and made an order in writing for the payment by the councillor of certain costs under sect. 19 of the Act. The written order made no provision for the remuneration and allowances to the barrister and other persons under sect. 22. The Lords Commissioners of the Treasury paid the amount of such remuneration and allowances and certified the payment to the borough treasurer, and required him to repay them the amount out of the borough fund or rates as provided by sect. 22. A rate was accordingly made and levied. The commissioners, afterwards, on receiving from the barrister a letter that he had always intended to visit all the costs upon the councillor, and had said so in giving judgment, cancelled their certificate, and the borough corporation abandoned their rate and returned the sums levied to the ratepayers. Afterwards the commissioners, finding that the barrister had made no written order

for the payment of the remuneration and allowances under sect. 22, issued a fresh certificate requiring the borough treasurer to repay them out of the borough fund or rates the amount of such remuneration and allowances. These facts being raised upon the return to a mandamus commanding the treasurer to repay the commissioners out of the borough fund or rate, and the corporation to cause such repayment:—*Held*, that no valid order was made by the barrister for the payment o such allowances and remuneration under sect. 22; that the election court for the trial of petitions under the Act was by virtue of sect. 14, sub-sect. 5, a Court of record, and that neither the Queen's Bench Division nor the Court of Appeal on the return to the mandamus could amend the barrister's order so as to make it include the payment of such remuneration and allowances; that the act of the commissioners in certifying was not a judicial act, and that they had the power to make the second certificate, and were entitled to a peremptory mandamus compelling the treasurer to repay to them the amount of such remuneration and allowances out of the borough fund or rate, and compelling the corporation to order such amount to be levied by a borough rate. THE QUEEN *v.* CORPORATION OF MAIDENHEAD

[8 Q. B. D. 339; 9 Q. B. D. 494]

2. —— Corrupt Practices—*Time for delivery of Particulars — Corrupt Practices (Municipal Elections) Act, 1872 (35 & 36 Vict. c. 60).*] In a municipal election petition the Respondent applied for an order for delivery of particulars of the alleged corrupt practices :—*Held*, that, in the absence of exceptional circumstances, the Petitioners should not be ordered to deliver particulars more than seven clear days before the hearing of the petition. LENHAM *v.* BARBER

[10 Q. B. D. 293]

3. —— Mayor—*Complaint of Conduct of—Returning Officer—Corrupt Practices (Municipal Elections) Act, 1872 (35 & 36 Vict. c. 60), s. 13, sub-s. 6—Ballot Act (35 & 36 Vict. c. 33), s. 20—Municipal Corporations Act (5 & 6 Will. 4, c. 76), s. 43—Municipal Election Petition Rules, 1872, rule 44—Judicature Act, 1873, s. 19.*] Where a mayor had bonâ fide given a decision under 38 & 39 Vict. c. 40, s. 1, sub-s. 3, on the validity of an objection made to a nomination paper, a complaint of such decision as erroneous is not a "complaint of the conduct" of such mayor within the meaning of 35 & 36 Vict. c. 60, s. 13, sub-s. 6. —At the election of a councillor for a ward in a borough the mayor is not the returning officer within the meaning of sect. 20 of the Ballot Act, unless he also happens to be alderman of such ward, or unless the office of alderman in such ward be vacant.—From an order of a Divisional Court upon an interlocutory matter arising in an election petition, an appeal lies to the Court of Appeal. HARMON *v.* PARK - 6 Q. B. D. 323

4. —— Nomination Paper—*Municipal Elections Act, 1875 (38 & 39 Vict. c. 40), s. 1, sub-s. 2 —Christian Name of Candidate—Abbreviation of "William."*] A nomination paper at the election of a town councillor pursuant to the Municipal Elections Act, 1875, sufficiently states the chris-

II. MUNICIPAL CORPORATION—ELECTION—
continued.

tian name "William," of the person nominated by the abbreviation "Wm." HENRY *v.* ARMITAGE

[12 Q. B. D. 257

5. —— **Nomination Paper** — *Subscription of Nomination Papers—Assenting Burgesses—Municipal Elections Act,* 1875 (38 & 39 *Vict. c.* 40), *s.* 1, *sub-s.* 2.] Sect. 1, sub-sect. 2 of the Municipal Elections Act. 1875, provides that every candidate at a municipal election shall be nominated in writing subscribed by ' two burgesses as proposer and seconder, and by eight others as assenting to the nomination, and that "each candidate shall be nominated by a separate nomination paper, but the same burgesses, or any of them, may subscribe as many nomination papers as there are vacancies to be filled, but no more." —At a municipal election where there were four vacancies to be filled a burgess subscribed four nomination papers, which were delivered within due time, and subsequently he subscribed a fifth nomination paper, which was also delivered in due time. In each case he subscribed as one 'of the eight assenting burgesses required by the Act :—*Held*, that the first four nomination papers were valid, and that the fifth was invalid. BURGOYNE *v.* COLLINS - 　 - 　 **8 Q. B. D. 450**

6. —— **Nomination Paper** — *Subscription of assenting Burgess — Defect in Entry on Burgess Roll — Variance — Municipal Corporations Act,* 1882 (45 & 46 *Vict. c.* 50), *s.* 241.] A nomination paper at an election of town councillors was subscribed with the full and correct name of " Charles Arthur Burman" as an assenting burgess; but his name was erroneously entered upon the burgess roll as " Charles Burman " only :— *Held*, that the defect was not such as was remedied by 45 & 46 Vict. c. 50, s. 241, enacting that " no misnomer or inaccurate description of any person . . . . named in any roll . . . . required by this Act shall hinder the full operation of this Act with respect to that person . . . . provided the description of that person . . . . be such as to be commonly understood." — The words " commonly understood " in this proviso mean " commonly understood by any person comparing the nomination paper and the burgess roll." MOORHOUSE *v.* LINNEY. THORPE *v.* LINNEY 　 **15 Q. B. D. 273**

7. —— **Nomination Paper** — *Substitution of different Proposer without privity of assenting Burgesses—Municipal Elections Act,* 1875 (38 & 39 *Vict. c.* 40), *s.* 1, *sub-s.* 2.] By the Municipal Elections Act, 1875 (38 & 39 Vict. c. 40), s. 1, sub-s. 2, at any municipal election (of councillors) every candidate shall be nominated in writing; the writing shall be subscribed by two enrolled burgesses of such borough or ward as proposer and seconder, and by eight other enrolled burgesses of such borough or ward as assenting to the nomination.—At an election of a ward councillor a burgess was nominated in a paper signed by B. and H. as proposer and seconder, and by eight other burgesses as assenting to the nomination. After the nomination paper had been delivered to the town clerk it was altered in the absence of the seconder and assenting burgesses by striking out the name of B. as proposer and substituting that of G., another duly enrolled

II. MUNICIPAL CORPORATION—ELECTION—
continued.

burgess :—*Held*, that the nomination was invalid. HARMON *v.* PARK - 　 - 　 - 　 **7 Q. B. D. 369**

8. —— **Petition against some only—***Validity of the Election as a whole—Municipal Corporations Act,* 1882 (45 & 46 *Vict. c.* 50), *ss.* 87, 88, 91, 93, 242, *Sch.* 3, *Part II., rr.* 3 *and* 10—*Appeal—Municipal Election Petition—Special Case—Supreme Court of Judicature Act,* 1881 (44 & 45 *Vict. c.* 68), *s.* 14.] An election petition may be presented under the Municipal Corporations Act, 1882, s. 87, against some only of the persons returned at a municipal election, although the ground of the petition is one affecting the validity of the election as a whole; and the Court can on such petition declare the persons so petitioned against not to have been duly elected.—The three Respondents and six other persons were nominated as candidates to fill four vacancies in the town council of a borough under the Municipal Corporations Act, 1882. An objection having been made to the nomination papers of H., and three other candidates (not the Respondents), on the ground that they were invalid under Sch. 3, Part II., rule 10, because the persons subscribing the paper in each case had subscribed nomination papers of other candidates, the mayor erroneously held the objection to be good, being of opinion that rule 10 applied to a case where there were several vacancies. The objection to H. was withdrawn; but the three other candidates objected to were prevented from going to the poll, and at the election which was afterwards held, H., and the three Respondents were declared duly elected. Upon a petition against the return of the Respondents, to which H. was not a party, it was admitted that an election of town councillors where there are several vacancies, is governed by the Municipal Corporations Act, 1882, Sch. 3, Part II., rule 3, which provides that the same burgesses may subscribe as many nomination papers as there are vacancies, and that rule 10 does not apply to a case of several vacancies; and it was further admitted that as the objection would have been valid against all the candidates returned, the whole election might have been declared void if H. had been a party to the petition ; but it was contended that as he was not before the Court, and therefore as his election could not be questioned, the return of the Respondents must stand good :—*Held*, that although the erroneous decision of the mayor affected the validity of the whole election, nevertheless the Court had power to deal with those candidates returned who were petitioned against, and; that the return of the Respondents must be declared void, notwithstanding that the return of H. could not be questioned, he not being a party to the petition.—Judgment of the Queen's Bench Division affirmed.—Notwithstanding sect. 93, sub-sect. 7, of the Municipal Corporations Act, 1882, which enacts that the decision of the High Court upon a petition questioning a. municipal election shall be final, nevertheless an appeal, if leave be given, lies from a judgment of the Queen's Bench Division upon a petition of that nature to the Court of Appeal, owing to sect. 242 of the statute above-mentioned, which in effect incorporates.the Supreme Court of Judicature Act, 1881, s. 14,.

II. MUNICIPAL CORPORATION—ELECTION—
continued.

whereby in certain cases an appeal is allowed from the High Court of Justice to the Court of Appeal, if special leave be given. LINE *v.* WARREN
[14 Q. B. D. 73, 548

9. —— Voting Paper—*Election of Aldermen—Insertion of Wrong Name—Signature—Ambiguity —Parol Evidence—Municipal Corporations Act,* 1882 (45 & 46 *Vict.* c. 50), *s.* 60, *sub-s.* 4.] By the Municipal Corporations Act, 1882, s. 60, sub-s. 4, any person entitled to vote at an election of aldermen may vote " by signing and personally delivering at the meeting to the chairman, a voting paper containing the surnames and other names and places of abode and descriptions of the persons for whom he votes." A voting paper was delivered commencing, "I, the undersigned A. B.," and ending with the signature " C. D." ; and upon a petition against the return of the persons elected, the commissioner received evidence shewing that the town clerk had inserted A. B.'s name in order that the voting paper might be used by him, but by inadvertence it was handed to C. D., who signed and personally delivered it to the chairman without discovering the mistake :—*Held,* that the vote was valid, and that the commissioner was right, in receiving evidence of the circumstances under which it was given. SUMMERS *v.* MOORHOUSE 13 Q. B. D. 388

III. MUNICIPAL CORPORATION—FRANCHISE.

—— Qualification—*Inhabitant Householder—Dwelling-house, Occupation of. Part of—Parliamentary and Municipal Registration Act,* 1878 (41 & 42 *Vict.* c. 26), *s.* 5—*Municipal Corporations Act,* 1882 (45 & 46 *Vict.* c. 50), *ss.* 9, 31.] Occupation of part of a dwelling-house, for the purposes of a private dwelling only, constitutes occupation of a " house " within sects. 9 and 31 of the Municipal Corporations Act, 1882, so as to confer the municipal franchise upon the occupier. GREENWAY *v.* BACHELOR. ALDRIDGE'S CASE
[12 Q. B. D. 381

IV. MUNICIPAL CORPORATION—PROPERTY.

—— Action by Freemen—*Property of Borough applied for individual Benefit of Freemen—Custom of Borough — Municipal Corporations Act,* 1835 (5 & 6 *Will.* 4, c. 76), *s.* 2—*Pleading.*] In an action by some (on behalf of all) of the freemen of a borough to establish the right of all individual freemen to share for their private benefit the net proceeds of certain properties vested in the corporation :—*Held,* on demurrer, that the effect of the saving of rights in sect. 2 of the Municipal Corporations Act of 1835 was to legalise the beneficial interests therein mentioned, without reference to the legality of their origin, and, in particular, to obviate any objection which might otherwise arise in respect of the tendency towards a perpetuity of any such beneficial interest.—An action to establish such rights as aforesaid may be brought by parties claiming to be entitled, without an information by the Attorney-General.—In such an action it was held on demurrer that in order to enable the Plaintiffs to avail themselves of such saving of rights as aforesaid, it was sufficient for them, after stating the title of the corporation by charter or otherwise to the property in

IV. MUNICIPAL CORPORATION — PROPERTY *—continued.*

question, to aver that at the time of the passing of the Act the rents, tolls, and profits claimed by them were not, nor ever had been, nor ought to have been, held and applied to public purposes, but then were, and always had been, held and applied for the particular benefit of the freemen, and without pleading that such rents, tolls, and profits had been enjoyed or acquired by virtue of any specific statute, charter, by-law or custom, or expressly to aver that any custom to such effect as aforesaid existed. PRESTNEY *v.* CORPORATION OF COLCHESTER AND THE ATTORNEY-GENERAL
[21 Ch. D. 111

V. MUNICIPAL CORPORATION—QUALIFICATION.

The Act 48 & 49 *Vict.* c. 9, *removes disqualification for voting at a municipal election in a borough, in respect of occupation, where during a part of the qualifying period, not exceeding four months, a man has permitted his house to be occupied as a furnished dwelling-house by some other person, and has not then resided within seven miles of the borough.*

—— Alderman—*Disqualification—Insolvency —Composition with Creditors—Avoiding Office—Municipal Corporation Act,* 1835 (5 & 6 *Will.* 4, c. 76), *s.* 52—*Debtors Act,* 1869, *s.* 21—*Jurisdiction—Injunction—Assigned Business—Judicature Act,* 1873, *s.* 25, *sub-s.* 8 ; *s.* 34.] The Plaintiff, an alderman of a borough, made a composition with his creditors, but executed no composition deed ; nor were any composition proceedings taken under the Debtors Act, 1869. He had, however, executed a bill of sale, duly registered, to a person not a creditor, to secure a sum of money advanced by him to meet the amount of the composition. A meeting of the corporation of the borough having been summoned by notice for the purpose of declaring the office held by the Plaintiff void under the Municipal Corporation Act, 1835 (5 & 6 Will. 4, c. 76), s. 52, and the Debtors Act, 1869, s. 21, and electing a successor :—An injunction was granted, at the instance of the Plaintiff, restraining the corporation from proceeding under their notice on the ground, (1) that, having regard to the express words of the above sections, the Plaintiff had not become disqualified from holding office ; (2) that under sect. 25, sub-s. 8, of the Judicature Act, 1873, the Court had jurisdiction to grant the injunction ; and (3) that, having regard to sect. 34 of the same Act, the action which claimed the injunction only, had been properly brought in the Chancery Division.—The jurisdiction of the Chancery Division to interfere by injunction under Judicature Act, 1873, s. 25, sub-s. 8 considered. ASLATT *v.* CORPORATION OF SOUTHAMPTON 16 Ch. D. 143

VI. MUNICIPAL CORPORATION—RATES.

—— Constable—*Costs of Action for Malicious Prosecution against—Borough Fund and Rates, Illegal Charge upon—Municipal Corporation Act* (5 & 6 *Will.* 4, c. 76), *s.* 82.] The chief constable of a borough having, by direction of borough magistrates, laid an information against a person for conspiracy, an action for malicious prosecution was brought by such person against him and a

VI. MUNICIPAL CORPORATION — RATES — *continued.*

verdict recovered for £200 :—*Held*, that it was not competent to the town council to order payment of the chief constable's costs out of the borough fund or rate under 5 & 6 Will. 4, c. 76, s. 82. THE QUEEN *v.* CORPORATION OF EXETER

[6 Q. B. D. 135

VII. MUNICIPAL CORPORATION — RESIGNATION.

—— **Withdrawal** — *Resignation of Corporate Office* — *Delivery of Resignation to Town Clerk* — *Power to withdraw Resignation* — *Municipal Corporations Act,* 1882 (45 & 46 *Vict.* c. 50), *s.* 36.] Under the Municipal Corporations Act, 1882 (45 & 46 Vict. c. 50), s. 36,—which enacts that a person elected to a corporate office may at any time, by writing signed by him and delivered to the town clerk, resign the office, on payment of the fine provided for non-acceptance thereof,— the resignation is completed by the delivery of the writing to the town clerk and the payment of the fine, and cannot afterwards, even with the assent of the corporation, be withdrawn. THE QUEEN *v.* CORPORATION OF WIGAN 14 Q. B. D. 908

MUNICIPAL CORPORATION—Borough without commission of peace—Mayor, a justice of the peace for borough 7 Q. B. D. 548
See CONTRACT—VALIDITY. 1.

—— Information for penalties—Justice member of corporation—Interest 6 Q. B. D. 168
See JUSTICES—DISQUALIFICATION. 3.

MUNICIPAL ELECTIONS CORRUPT AND IL-LEGAL PRACTICES ACT, 1884.
See MUNICIPAL CORPORATION—ELECTION —*Statutes.*

MURDER—Attempt to—Criminal law
[10 Q. B. D. 381
See CRIMINAL LAW—OFFENCES AGAINST PERSON. 4.

—— Inciting to - - 7 Q. B. D. 244
See CRIMINAL LAW—OFFENCES AGAINST PERSON. 5.

—— Killing and eating flesh of human being under pressure of hunger 14 Q. B. D. 273
See CRIMINAL LAW—OFFENCES AGAINST PERSON. 6.

MUSEUM.
See PUBLIC LIBRARY—*Statutes.*

MUSICAL COMPOSITION—Copyright
[21 Ch. D. 232; 11 Q. B. D. 102
See COPYRIGHT—DRAMATIC. 1, 3.

—— Right of public performance of.
See COPYRIGHT—MUSIC—*Statutes.*

MUTUAL CREDIT—Administration action
[22 Ch. D. 586
See EXECUTOR—ACTIONS. 18.

—— - - - 30 Ch. D. 216
See COMPANY—CONTRACTS. 4.

MUTUAL DEALINGS—Bankruptcy.
See Cases under BANKRUPTCY—MUTUAL DEALINGS.

MUTUAL LIFE INSURANCE COMPANY—Wind-ing-up.
See Cases under COMPANY — LIFE IN-SURANCE COMPANY.

MUTUAL LOAN SOCIETY - 28 Ch. D. 559
See COMPANY—DISTRIBUTION OF ASSETS. 3.

N.

NAME—Company—Leave to use 17 Ch. D. 198
 See COMPANY—ACTIONS.

—— Firm—Trade-mark - - 27 Ch. D. 681
 See TRADE-MARK—REGISTRATION. 5.

—— Gift to persons bearing particular name
       [19 Ch. D. 520
 See WILL—PERPETUITY. 5.

—— Use of, in trade 22 Ch. D. 660; 30 Ch. D. 156;
      [8 App. Cas. 315
 See TRADE NAME. 1, 2, 3.

NAME AND ARMS CLAUSE 17 Ch. D. 211
 See WILL—PERPETUITY. 3.

—— - - - 26 Ch. D. 792
 See WILL—CONDITION. 5.

NATAL—Law of 6 App. Cas. 619; 9 App. Cas. 715
 See COLONIAL LAW—NATAL. 1, 2.

NATIONAL DEBT COMMISSIONERS.

Government Annuities and Contracts of Insurance.] *The Act* 45 & 46 *Vict.* c. 51 (*Government Annuities Act*, 1882, amends and extends the Acts relating to the purchase of small Government annuities and to assuring payments of money on death or at a specified age.

By sect. 2 an annuity (in the Act referred to as a *Savings Bank Annuity*) may be granted of any amount not exceeding £100 to any person not under five years of age.

By sect. 3 the National Debt Commissioners may contract with any person for a payment to be made on the attainment by him of a specified age or sooner in case of his death (such contract in the Act referred to as a savings bank insurance).

Sect. 4. A savings bank insurance may be granted for any amount not exceeding £100 to a person not over the age of sixty-five years and not under fourteen years of age, or if the amount does not exceed £5, not under the age of eight years.

Sect. 5. Tables to be constructed for saving banks annuities and insurances.

Sect. 6. Regulations to be observed in granting such annuities and insurances.

Sect. 7. Applies the Savings Banks Acts for the purposes of this Act.

Sect. 8. Trusts not to be noticed, except such trusts as are from time to time recognised by law in relation to deposits in savings banks, and except such trusts as are provided for by sect. 10 of the Married Women's Property Act, 1870, or any enactment now or hereafter to be passed relating to the property of married women.

A savings bank annuity or insurance depending on the life of one person may be granted to two or more persons, and may be the subject of transfer.

Sect. 9. Where any person, entitled to a savings bank annuity or insurance, is insane or otherwise incapacitated to act, then the payment of such annuity or insurance may be made at such times, in such sums, and to such persons as may seem proper.

Sect. 10 amends 27 & 28 Vict. c. 43, ss. 8, 11, as

NATIONAL DEBT COMMISSIONERS—continued. to surrender of policy or assignment of policy after payment of five years' premiums.

Sect. 11. As to forfeiture of annuity or insurance exceeding the maximum or where holder makes any false declaration with respect thereto.

Sect. 12. Penalty for receiving annuity or insurance in fraud of the Commissioners.

Sect. 13. As to application and investment of sums paid for annuities and insurances.

Sect. 14. Definitions.

Sect. 15 repeals in part the Government Annuities Acts, 1853 and 1864.

National Debt.] *The Act* 46 & 47 *Vict.* c. 54 (*National Debt Act*, 1883) makes further provision respecting the National Debt, and the investment of moneys in the hands of the National Debt Commissioners on account of Savings Banks, and otherwise.

The Act 45 & 46 *Vict.* c. 72, ss. 18–26, provides for the application of the accumulations of fractions of a penny on dividends of the National Debt, for payment of the annual deficiency in the value of the securities held by the National Debt Commissioners for Friendly Societies, and for other purposes.

The Act 47 & 48 *Vict.* c. 2 (*National Debt Act*, 1884) makes further provision respecting the conversion into 2½ per cent. annuities of 3 per cent. annuities held by the National Debt Commissioners on account of Savings Banks; and for the redemption of the Indian Loan Annuity, 1881.

Conversion of 3 per cent. Stock into Stock of lower Denomination.] *The Act* 47 & 48 *Vict.* c. 23 (*National Debt Conversion of Stock Act*, 1884) provides for the creation of new 2¾ per cent. stock, or additional 2½ per cent. stock, and for the exchange of 3 per cent. stock into 2¾ per cent. or 2½ per cent. stock.

By sect. 5 the regulations made in pursuance of the Savings Bank Act, 1880, with respect to investments through the Post Office, are adapted to the new stock and to the 2½ per cent. stock.

By sect. 6, 3 per cent. stock held in trust may be exchanged for the new stock or for 2½ per cent. stock.

—— Res Judicata—Petition for re-transfer of Stock—Dismissal of former Petition by same Petitioner—Discovery of Fresh Evidence—National Debt Act, 1870 (33 & 34 Vict. c. 71), ss. 51, 54, 55.] The jurisdiction given to the Court by sect. 55 of the National Debt Act, 1870, to decide upon petition as to the validity of a claim for the re-transfer of stock, which has been transferred to the National Debt Commissioners under the provisions of sect. 51, is to be exercised in the mode in which the ordinary jurisdiction of the Court is exercised. Therefore, if a petition for the re-transfer of stock is heard on its merits, and is dismissed on the ground that the Petitioner has failed to make out his title, he cannot, on the subsequent discovery of fresh evidence in support

NATIONAL DEBT COMMISSIONERS—*continued.*
of his title, present a fresh petition for the same object, without leave of the Court previously obtained.—Decision of Pearson, J., affirmed. *In re* MAY　-　　- 25 Ch. D. 231 ; 28 Ch. D. 516

NATIONALITY—Descendants of British subject born abroad　-　　- 22 Ch. D. 243
See ALIEN.

NAUTICAL ASSESSORS　-　　6 P. D. 84
See COUNTY COURT—PRACTICE. 2.

NAVIGABLE RIVER　-　　- 9 Q. B. D. 162 ;
See FISHERY. 1. 2.　[8 App. Cas. 135

—— Scotland -　-　　- 6 App. Cas. 273
See SCOTCH LAW—RIVER.

NAVIGATION—Collision.
See Cases under SHIP—NAVIGATION.

NAVY.
See ARMY AND NAVY—*Statutes.*

NE EXEAT REGNO　-　　29 Ch. D. 341
See ARREST—NE EXEAT REGNO.

NECESSARIES—For infant　　13 Q. B. D. 410
See INFANT—CONTRACTS. 3.

—— For lunatic—Supplied to lunatic
[21 Ch. D. 615
See LUNATIC—MAINTENANCE. 1.

—— For ship　'-　10 P. D. 44 ; 16 Ch. D. 604 ;
[9 App. Cas. 356
See SHIP—MARITIME LIEN. 1, 6, 7.

—— For ship—Action for—Admiralty—County Court　-　　- 6 Q. B. D. 165
See COUNTY COURT—JURISDICTION. 1.

—— For ship—Managing owner—Authority to bind other owners　6 Q. B. D. 93
See SHIP—OWNERS. 2.

—— For wife—Liability of husband
[6 App. Cas. 24
See HUSBAND AND WIFE—LIABILITY OF HUSBAND.

NEGLIGENCE :—　　　　　Col.
　I. EVIDENCE -　-　-　- 947
　II. LIABILITY -　-　-　- 948

I. NEGLIGENCE—EVIDENCE.

1. —— Contributory Negligence — *Licensee.*] The deceased was employed by a builder to watch and protect certain unfinished buildings. Workmen were employed by the Defendant, a contractor, on the land near to where the deceased was on duty, to excavate the earth for the foundations of other buildings. In the performance of this operation they employed a steam-crane and winch to which were attached a chain and iron bucket by means of which the earth was raised from the excavation and thence to the carts which were to carry it away. The deceased had nothing to do with the excavations, but was standing where he need not have been, watching the Defendant's men at work, and allowing the bucket to pass some three feet over his head, when the chain broke and the bucket and its contents falling upon him so injured him that he subsequently died :—*Held,* that there was no evidence of negligence in the Defendant's workmen ; that the deceased was at the most a bare licensee ; and that he

I. NEGLIGENCE—EVIDENCE—*continued.*
stood where he did subject to all the risks incident to the position in which he had placed himself. BATCHELOR *v.* FORTESCUE　-　11 Q. B. D. 474

2. —— Driving Carriage—*Public Thoroughfare.*] A horse drawing a brougham under the care of the Defendant's coachman in a public street, suddenly and without any explainable cause bolted, and, notwithstanding the utmost efforts of the driver to control him, swerved on to the footway and injured the Plaintiff :—*Held,* no evidence of negligence to go to a jury.—And *held,* that the fact that the horse had cast a shoe shortly after he bolted, and that the driver did not under the circumstances in which he was placed call out or give any warning did not alter the case.—*Hammack* v. *White* (11 C. B. (N.S.) 588 ; 31 L. J. (C.P.) 129), upheld. MANZONI *v.* DOUGLAS
[6 Q. B. D. 145

3. —— Level Crossing—*Contributory Negligence.*] The Defendant's railway crossed a public footway on the level. About half-past four o'clock in the afternoon of the 29th of March, the Plaintiff, a foot-passenger, while crossing from the down side to the up side of the railway, was knocked down and injured at the crossing by a train of the Defendants on the up line. Owing to the position of certain buildings which stood by the line it was impossible for any one crossing from the down side to see a train coming until he got within a step or two from the down line, but a person standing on the down line or the six-foot had a clear and uninterrupted view up and down the line for several hundred yards. The Plaintiff, who lived near and was well acquainted with the crossing, stated that before crossing he looked to the right along the down line, but he admitted that he did not look to the left along the up line, and that if he had looked he must have seen the train coming. The engine-driver did not whistle. There was a servant of the Defendants employed as a gatekeeper at the crossing, whose duty it was to open the carriage gates there when carriages could safely be admitted, and to close them at other times. He was standing at the time on the opposite side of the crossing talking to two boys, with a furled flag in his hand ; but he gave no warning to the Plaintiff that a train was coming. The Plaintiff having brought an action against the Defendants to recover compensation for his injuries, was nonsuited on the above facts being proved at the trial :—*Held,* by Brett, M.R., and Bowen, L.J. (Baggallay, L.J., dissenting), that the nonsuit was right as, although there was evidence of negligence on the part of the Defendants, yet according to the undisputed facts of the case the Plaintiff had shewn that the accident was solely caused by his omission to use the care which any reasonable man would have used.—Decision of the Queen's Bench Division affirmed. DAVEY *v.* LONDON AND SOUTH WESTERN RAILWAY COMPANY
[11 Q. B. D. 213 ; 12 Q. B. D. 70

II. NEGLIGENCE—LIABILITY.

1. —— Cab Proprietor—*Liability for Negligence of Driver—Horse provided by Driver—Metropolitan Hackney Carriages Acts* (1 & 2 Will. 4, c. 22), ss. 6, 20, 23 ; (6 & 7 Vict. c. 86), ss. 10, 21, 24, 28, 35.] The Plaintiff's cart and pony were

II. NEGLIGENCE—LIABILITY—*continued.*

injured by a cab plying in the streets of London, owing to the negligence of the cab-driver. The Defendant was proprietor of the cab and licensed to ply it for hire. He had let the cab to the driver for a weekly payment, the horse, harness, and whip being provided by the driver with whom the Defendant had nothing to do beyond receiving money from him :—*Held,* that under the circumstances there was nothing in the Metropolitan Hackney Carriages Acts (1 & 2 Wm. 4, c. 22, and 6 & 7 Vict. c. 86), to make the Defendant liable for the negligence of the driver.—*Powles* v. *Hider* (6 E. & B. 207), and *Venables* v. *Smith* (2 Q. B. D. 279) considered. KING v. SPURR
[8 Q. B. D. 104

2. —— **Defective Article**—*Supply of—Injury to Stranger—Liability of Person supplying a defective Article causing Injury to Stranger.*] The Defendant supplied and erected a staging round a ship under a contract with the shipowner. The Plaintiff was a workman in the employ of a ship painter who had contracted with the shipowner to paint the outside of the ship, and in order to do the painting the Plaintiff went on and used the staging, when one of the ropes by which it was slung, being unfit for use when supplied by the Defendant, broke, and by reason thereof the Plaintiff fell into the dock and was injured :—*Held,* reversing the decision of the Queen's Bench Division, that the Plaintiff, being engaged on work on the vessel in the performance of which the Defendant, as dock owner, was interested, the Defendant was under an obligation to him to take reasonable care that at the time he supplied the staging and ropes they were in a fit state to be used, and that for the neglect of such duty the Defendant was liable to the Plaintiff for the injury he had sustained :—*Held,* also, by Brett, M.R., that whenever one person is by circumstances placed in such a position with regard to another, that every one of ordinary sense who did think would at once recognise that if he did not use ordinary care and skill in his own conduct with regard to those circumstances he would cause danger of injury to the person or property of the other, a duty arises to use ordinary care and skill to avoid such danger. HEAVEN v. PENDER
[9 Q. B. D. 302 ; 11 Q. B. D. 503

3. —— **Defect in Carriage**—*Jobmaster—Warranty of Fitness.*] The Plaintiff hired from the Defendant, a jobmaster, for a specified journey, a carriage, a pair of horses, and a driver. During the journey a bolt in the under part of the carriage broke, the splinter bar became displaced, the horses started off, the carriage was upset, and the Plaintiff injured. In an action against the Defendant for negligence, the jury were directed that, if in their opinion the Defendant took all reasonable care to provide a fit and proper carriage, their verdict ought to be for him. The jury found a verdict for the Defendant, and in particular that the carriage was reasonably fit for the purpose for which it was hired, and that the defect in the bolt could not have been discovered by the Defendant by ordinary care and attention :—*Held,* that the direction was wrong, and that it was the duty of the Defendant to supply a carriage as fit for the purpose for which it was hired as care and skill

II. NEGLIGENCE—LIABILITY—*continued.*

could render it, and the evidence was not such as to shew that the breakage of the bolt was, in the proper sense of the word, an accident not preventible by any care or skill, or to warrant the finding of the jury that the carriage was reasonably fit for the purpose for which it was hired. HYMAN v. NYE - - - **6 Q. B. D. 685**

4. —— **Defect in Carriage**—*Articles sold consigned in Defective Truck to Vendee—Injury to Servant of Vendee.*] The Defendant, a colliery owner, consigned coals sold by him to the buyers by rail in a truck rented by him from a waggon company for the purposes of the colliery. Through the negligence of the Defendant's servants the truck was allowed to leave the colliery in a defective state. In consequence of the defect in the truck injury was occasioned to the Plaintiff, one of the buyers' servants, who was employed in unloading the coals, and had got into the truck for that purpose :—*Held,* that there was a duty on the part of the Defendant towards the Plaintiff to exercise reasonable care with regard to the condition of the truck, and the Defendant was therefore liable to the Plaintiff in respect of the injuries sustained by him. ELLIOTT v. HALL
[15 Q. B. D. 315

5. —— **Diversion of Highway**—*Owner of Land—Duty to fence.*] A duty is cast upon those who, in the exercise of statutory powers, divert a public footpath, to protect, by fencing or otherwise, reasonably careful persons using the footpath from injury through going astray at the point of diversion. HURST v. TAYLOR
[14 Q. B. D. 918

6. —— **Landlord of House**—*Licensee—Obligation to fence—Private Way.*] The Defendant was the landlord of a house which was let out in apartments to several tenants, each of whom had the privilege of using the roof (which was flat and covered with lead, having an iron rail on its outer edge), for the purpose of drying their linen ; the access to the roof being by means of a low door at the stair-head about two feet from the rail. The Plaintiff, the occupier of one of the rooms, went upon the roof for the purpose of removing some linen, when, his foot slipping, and the rail being out of repair (and known by the landlord to be so), he fell through to the court-yard below, and was injured :—*Held,* that the mere licence to the lodgers to use the roof as a drying-ground imposed no duty upon the Defendant to fence it or to keep the fence in repair. IVAY v. HEDGES - - - - **9 Q. B. D. 80**

7. —— **Master and Servant**—*Unsafe Premises —Knowledge of Master—Ignorance of Servant.*] In an action for negligence brought by a servant against his master for personal injury resulting from the unsafe state of the premises upon which the servant was employed, the statement of claim must allege not only that the master knew, but that the servant was ignorant of, the danger.—Judgment of the Queen's Bench Division affirmed. GRIFFITHS v. LONDON AND ST. KATHARINE DOCKS COMPANY - - 12 Q. B. D. 493 ; 13 Q. B. D. 259

8. —— **Ship** — *Harbour : Master — Collision caused by Vessel approaching the Spot where Navigation of River rendered Dangerous by Sunken*

II. NEGLIGENCE—LIABILITY—continued.

Vessel—Vessel sunk by Collision for which her Owner alone to blame—Removal of Wrecks Act, 1877 (40 & 41 Vict. c. 16), s. 4—Act done in course of Duty—Warning to Harbour-master—Hearsay Evidence—Wrongful Rejection of Evidence.] The *D.* in consequence of the sole default of her master and crew had sunk in the Thames, and had become a wreck obstructing the navigation of the river. Her mate sent a message to the harbour-master at G. to inform him of the accident, who said that he would cause the wreck to be lighted. A few hours afterwards, the wreck not having been lighted, a vessel without any fault on the part of those on board her came into collision with the wreck and sustained damage. An action of damage having been instituted on behalf of the owner of the damaged vessel against the owners of the *D.*, the Judge at the trial refused to admit the evidence shewing that the mate of the *D.* had sent a message to the harbour-master, and that the latter had promised to light the wreck :—*Held*, that the evidence was wrongly rejected, that the collision had not been caused by the negligence of the owners of the wreck, and that they were not liable for the damage done. THE " DOUGLAS "　　　7 P. D. 151

9. ——— Ship—*Harbour Master—Harbour Commissioners—Harbours, Docks, and Piers Clauses Act, 1847 (10 & 11 Vict. c. 27), ss. 51, 52, 53—Falmouth Harbour By-laws.*] The *R.*, which was anchored in F. outer harbour, having to be beached in the inner harbour, S., the harbour master, directed the master of the *R.* where to beach her. Before the *R.* left the outer harbour, S. came on board, although a Trinity House pilot was in the vessel, and when she had arrived near the place where she was to be beached gave directions as to the lowering of her anchor. The *R.* overran her anchor and grounded on it, sustaining damage. In an action against the harbour commissioners and S., the Court found as a fact that there was negligence on the part of S., and that the place where the *R.* grounded was outside the jurisdiction of the harbour commissioners :—*Held*, that the duties of the harbour master comprised directions as to the mooring and beaching of vessels ; that by giving directions when he went on board, S. had resumed his functions as harbour master, and that he and the commissioners were therefore liable for the damage done to the *R.*—*Held* further, that S. was personally liable as a volunteer. THE "RHOSINA"　　- 10 P. D. 24

10. ——— Ship—*Harbour Master—Harbour Commissioners—Harbours, Docks, and Piers Clauses Act, 1847 (10 & 11 Vict. c. 27), s. 52.*] The *R.*, which was anchored in F. outer harbour, having to be beached in the inner harbour, S., the harbour master, directed the master of the *R.* where she was to be beached. Before the *R.* left the outer harbour S. came on board, and when she arrived near the place where she was to be beached, S. gave orders as to the lowering of her anchor. The *R.* overran her anchor and grounded on it, sustaining damage. The *R.* grounded, and the order was given outside the jurisdiction of the harbour commissioners, but the spot where the *R.* was to be beached was within their jurisdiction. The Court below found that S. had been negligent in

fact :—*Held* by the Court of Appeal, affirming the decision of Sir James Hannen (10 P. D. 24), that the commissioners were liable, for under the circumstances the order given by S. was within the scope of his authority as harbour master. THE " RHOSINA "　-　　-　-　10 P. D. 131

11. ——— Solicitor and Clerk—*Scope of Authority.*] The Plaintiffs occupied premises beneath the offices of the Defendants who were solicitors. One of the Defendants had a room of the offices, and in it was a lavatory for his own use exclusively, and his orders to his clerks were that no clerk should come into his room after he had left. A clerk went into the room to wash his hands at the lavatory after his employer had left, turned the water tap, and negligently left it so that water flowed from it into the Plaintiff's premises and damaged them.—In an action for negligence :—*Held*, that the act of the clerk was not within the scope of his authority, or incident to the ordinary duties of his employment, and that there was no evidence of negligence for which the Defendants were liable. STEVENS *v.* WOODWARD
[6 Q. B. D. 318

NEGLIGENCE — Common employment — Master and servant
See Cases under MASTER AND SERVANT—MASTER'S LIABILITY

——— Condition exempting from liability 9 P. D. 3
See SHIP—NAVIGATION. 32.

——— Contributory—Navigation.
See Cases under SHIP—NAVIGATION.

——— Death through negligence 25 Ch. D. 409 ;
[9 Q. B. D. 160
See DAMAGES—LORD CAMPBELL'S ACT. 1, 2.

——— Death through negligence—Widow of workman how far bound by his contract not to claim compensation - 9 Q. B. D. 357
See MASTER AND SERVANT—MASTER'S LIABILITY. 8.

——— Delivery order—Estoppel 11 Q. B. D. 776
See ESTOPPEL—CONDUCT. 3.

——— Director　　-　　25 Ch. D. 752
See COMPANY—DIRECTOR'S LIABILITY. 6.

——— Driver of cart—Liability of hirer
[14 Q. B. D. 890
See MASTER AND SERVANT—MASTER'S LIABILITY. 1.

——— Employers' Liability Act, 1880—Superintendent 10 Q. B. D. 356 ; 11 Q. B. D. 619
See MASTER AND SERVANT—MASTER'S LIABILITY. 3, 4.

——— Executive Government—Liability
[9 App. Cas. 418
See COLONIAL LAW—NEW ZEALAND. 1.

——— Infringement of sailing rules—Contributory negligence—Action in rem 9 P. D. 96 ;
[10 App. Cas. 59
See PRACTICE—ADMIRALTY — JURISDICTION. 1.

——— Master of tug　　　9 P. D. 3
See SHIP—NAVIGATION. 32.

——— Mortgage—Priority　-　21 Ch. D. 124 ;
[26 Ch. D. 482 ; 29 Ch. D. 221, 725
See MORTGAGE—PRIORITY.　6—9

NEGLIGENCE—*continued.*

—— Railway company—"Charge or control" of points　-　**12 Q. B. D. 208**
　　See MASTER AND SERVANT—MASTER'S
　　LIABILITY. 17.

—— Railway company—Liability to fence against adjoining lands—Injury to cattle
　　　　　　　　　　　　[**7 Q. B. D. 322**
　　See RAILWAY COMPANY — RAILWAYS
　　CLAUSES ACT. 3.

—— Railway company—Person in charge of train　-　　　**9 Q. B. D. 106**
　　See MASTER AND SERVANT—MASTER'S
　　LIABILITY. 18.

—— Servant.
　　See Cases under MASTER AND SERVANT
　　—MASTER'S LIABILITY.

—— Sewer—Accumulation of water—Liability of Metropolitan Board of Works
　　　　　　　　　　　　[**7 Q. B. D. 418**
　　See METROPOLIS—MANAGEMENT ACTS. 4.

—— Ship—Collision.
　　See Cases under SHIP—NAVIGATION.

—— Solicitor　-　-　**17 Ch. D. 437**
　　See SOLICITOR—LIABILITIES. 2.

—— Solicitor's bill of costs—Taxation
　　　　　　　　　　　　[**26 Ch. D. 459**
　　See SOLICITOR—BILL OF COSTS. 11.

—— Tramway—Road authority　**12 Q. B. D. 16**
　　See TRAMWAY COMPANY. 2.

—— Trustee　**22 Ch. D. 727; 28 Ch. D. 268;**
　　　　　　　　　　　　[**9 App. Cas. 1**
　　See TRUSTEE—LIABILITIES. 2, 4.

—— Unavoidable accident—Steam-steering gear
　　See SHIP—NAVIGATION. 5. [**10 P. D. 99**

—— Warehouseman—Damages　**7 Q. B. D. 510**
　　See DAMAGES—REMOTENESS. 5.

NEPHEWS AND NIECES—Will—Construction
　　See WILL—WORDS. 12. [**17 Ch. D. 382**

NET PROFITS—Payment of dividend of company　-　　**16 Ch. D. 344**
　　See COMPANY—DIVIDENDS. 4.

NEW PARISH.
　　See CHURCH BUILDING ACTS—*Statutes.*

NEW SOUTH WALES—Law of.
　　See Cases under COLONIAL LAW—NEW
　　SOUTH WALES.

NEW STREET.
　　See Cases under
　　　LOCAL GOVERNMENT—STREETS.
　　　METROPOLIS—MANAGEMENT ACTS.
　　　10—14.

NEW TRIAL.
　　See Cases under PRACTICE—SUPREME
　　COURT—NEW TRIAL.

—— Canadian Court　-　-　**6 App. Cas. 644**
　　See COLONIAL LAW—CANADA—ONTARIO.
　　1.

—— Divorce Court—Application for—Time for appealing　-　　-　**10 P. D. 110**
　　See PRACTICE—DIVORCE—APPEAL. 2.

—— Indictment for obstruction of highway
　　　　　　　　　　　　[**7 Q. B. D. 198**
　　See CRIMINAL LAW—PRACTICE. 3.

NEW TRUSTEES — Appointment of — Conveyancing Act, 1881　　**23 Ch. D. 13;**
　　　　　　　　　　　　[**24 Ch. D. 698**
　　See SETTLEMENT—POWERS. 12, 13.

—— Appointment of—Petition　　**26 Ch. D. 236**
　　See HUSBAND AND WIFE — MARRIED
　　WOMEN'S PROPERTY ACT. 4.

—— Appointment of—Settled Land Act.
　　See Cases under SETTLED LAND ACT—
　　　TRUSTEES,
　　　and SETTLED LAND ACT—STATUTES.

—— Power to appoint　-　-　**25 Ch. D. 611;**
　　　　　　　　[**27 Ch. D. 333; 28 Ch. D. 1**
　　See SETTLEMENT—POWERS. 8, 9, 10.

—— Refusal of executor of trustee to appoint
　　　　　　　　　　　　[**26 Ch. D. 82**
　　See TRUSTEE—COSTS AND CHARGES. 8.

—— Trustee Acts.
　　See Cases under TRUSTEE ACTS—NEW
　　TRUSTEES.

NEW ZEALAND—Law of　**9 App. Cas. 418, 699**
　　See COLONIAL LAW—NEW ZEALAND. 1, 2.

—— Probate in—Payment out of Court
　　　　　　　　　　　　[**24 Ch. D. 177**
　　See PRACTICE—SUPREME COURT—PAYMENT OUT OF COURT.

NEWSPAPER—Copyright　　**17 Ch. D. 708**
　　See COPYRIGHT—NEWSPAPERS.

—— Libel in.
　　See CRIMINAL LAW—LIBEL—*Statutes.*
　　DEFAMATION—LIBEL—*Statutes.*

—— Libel in — Criminal information—Fiat of Director of Public Prosecutions
　　　　　　　　　　　　[**14 Q. B. D. 648**
　　See CRIMINAL LAW—LIBEL. 2.

—— Post Office.
　　See POST OFFICE—*Statutes.*

—— Registration.
　　See COPYRIGHT—NEWSPAPERS—*Statutes.*

NEXT FRIEND　　**19 Ch. D. 94; 25 Ch. D. 243**
　　See PRACTICE—SUPREME COURT—NEXT
　　FRIEND. 1, 2.

—— Married woman—Costs of former action not paid　-　-　**23 Ch. D. 288**
　　See PRACTICE—SUPREME COURT—STAYING PROCEEDINGS. 10.

—— Married woman—Security for costs
　　　　　　　　　　　　[**30 Ch. D. 418**
　　See PRACTICE — SUPREME COURT —
　　SECURITY FOR COSTS. 5.

—— Production of documents　**30 Ch. D. 189**
　　See PRACTICE—SUPREME COURT—PRODUCTION OF DOCUMENTS. 5.

NEXT OF KIN—Appointment to　**30 Ch. D. 186**
　　See POWER—EXECUTION. 1.

—— Bequest to—Time of ascertaining class
　　See WILL—CLASS. 4. [**19 Ch. D. 444**

—— Claim of interest from the Crown
　　See INTEREST. 1. [**17 Ch. D. 771**

NITRIC ACID WORKS.
　　See LOCAL GOVERNMENT — PUBLIC
　　HEALTH ACTS—*Statutes.*

NOTICE—continued.

—— Motion for attachment　　9 Q. B. D. 335
　　　See PRACTICE—SUPREME COURT—NOTICE
　　　OF MOTION. 1.

—— Motion—Short—Irregularity　22 Ch. D. 504
　　　See PRACTICE—SUPREME COURT—NOTICE
　　　OF MOTION. 2.

—— Motion to set aside award -　6 Q. B. D. 67;
　　　　　　　　　　　[19 Ch D. 58
　　　See ARBITRATION—AWARD. 2, 3.

—— Motion to vary minutes　-　20 Ch. D. 130
　　　See PRACTICE—SUPREME COURT—JUDG-
　　　MENT. 6.

—— Not to trust wife　-　- 6 App. Cas. 24
　　　See HUSBAND AND WIFE—LIABILITY OF
　　　HUSBAND.

—— Objection—Borough franchise—Mistake—
　　　Power of amendment -　8 Q. B. D. 259;
　　　　　　　　　　[15 Q. B. D. 461
　　　See PARLIAMENT—FRANCHISE. 5, 6.

—— Objection — List of county voters—Omis-
　　　sion of date　-　-　12 Q. B. D. 373
　　　See PARLIAMENT—FRANCHISE. 10.

—— Option to renew lease　-　22 Ch. D. 640
　　　See LANDLORD AND TENANT—LEASE. 13.

—— Power to determine tenancy—Delivery to
　　　tenant—Absence of tenant　-
　　　　　　　　　　[15 Q. B. D. 256
　　　See LANDLORD AND TENANT—RE-ENTRY.
　　　9.

—— Publication of poor-rate -　9 Q. B. D. 47
　　　See POOR-RATE—PROCEDURE. 7.

—— Repair of road—Winding-up of company
　　　　　　　　　　[30 Ch. D. 216
　　　See COMPANY—CONTRACTS. 4.

—— Sale of land—Trustee—Settled Land Act
　　　　　　　　　　[23 Ch. D. 752
　　　See SETTLED LAND ACT—TENANT FOR
　　　LIFE. 4.

—— Second mortgagee—Proceeds of sale
　　　　　　　　　　[29 Ch. D. 954
　　　See MORTGAGE—REDEMPTION. 5.

—— Service on shareholders — Misrepresenta-
　　　tion　-　-　24 Ch. D. 149
　　　See COMPANY—PROSPECTUS. 6.

—— Third party procedure
　　　See Cases under PRACTICE—SUPREME
　　　COURT—THIRD PARTY.

—— To quit—Disclaimer of lessor's title
　　　　　　　　　　[16 Ch. D. 730
　　　See LANDLORD AND TENANT—RE-ENTRY.
　　　2.

—— To quit—Half-year's notice—Six months'
　　　notice　-　-　- 15 Q. B. D. 501
　　　See LANDLORD AND TENANT—YEARLY
　　　TENANT.

—— To quit—Statute.
　　　See LANDLORD AND TENANT—YEARLY
　　　TENANT—Statutes.

—— To treat—Dwellings Improvement Act
　　　　　　　　　　[25 Ch. D. 78
　　　See LABOURERS' DWELLINGS ACTS. 1.

—— To treat—Lands Clauses Act 30 Ch. D. 553
　　　See LANDS CLAUSES ACT—COMPULSORY
　　　POWERS. 6.

NOTICE—continued.

—— To trustees—Settled Land Act
　　　　　　　　　　[25 Ch. D. 464
　　　See SETTLED LAND ACT—TRUSTEES. 5.

—— Transfer of shares—Equitable mortgage—
　　　Priority　-　- 14 Q. B. D. 424
　　　See COMPANY—SHARES—TRANSFER. 2.

—— Trial—Right of Defendant to give
　　　　　　　　　　[14 Q. B. D. 234
　　　See PRACTICE—SUPREME COURT—NOTICE
　　　OF TRIAL.

—— Trial—Want of prosecution　27 Ch. D. 354
　　　See PRACTICE—SUPREME COURT—DE-
　　　FAULT. 7.

—— Trust—Recitals in deed　- 24 Ch. D. 720
　　　See VENDOR AND PURCHASER—TITLE. 4.

—— Trustee—Charge on fund -　26 Ch. D. 686
　　　See MORTGAGE—PRIORITY. 11.

—— Undisclosed principal　9 Q. B. D. 530;
　　　　　　　　　　[8 App. Cas. 874
　　　See PRINCIPAL AND AGENT—PRINCIPAL'S
　　　LIABILITY. 6.

—— Vendor's lien—Register county
　　　　　　　　　　[26 Ch. D. 501
　　　See VENDOR AND PURCHASER—LIEN. 2.

—— Winding-up—Proof　-　28 Ch. D. 634
　　　See COMPANY—PROOF. 3.

—— Withdrawal of members—Building society
　　　　　　　[24 Ch. D. 421; 10 App. Cas. 33
　　　See BUILDING SOCIETY. 15.

—— Withdrawal of members — Mutual loan
　　　society　-　-　- 24 Ch. D. 425, n.
　　　See COMPANY—DISTRIBUTION OF ASSETS.
　　　1.

NOTOUR BANKRUPTCY—Scotch law
　　　　　　　　　　[9 App. Cas. 966
　　　See SCOTCH LAW—BANKRUPTCY.

NOVA SCOTIA—Law of　-　8 App. Cas. 568
　　　See COLONIAL LAW — CANADA — NOVA
　　　SCOTIA.

NOVATION—Company—Promoter .25 Ch. D. 103
　　　See COMPANY—FORMATION.

NOVELTY—Patent　-　- 7 Q. B. D. 305;
　　　　　　　[19 Ch. D. 268; 21 Ch. D. 720
　　　See PATENT—VALIDITY. 2, 3, 4.

NUISANCE:—　　　　　　　　Col.
　　I. DEFINITION　-　-　-　- 958
　　II. REMEDIES　-　-　-　- 959

I. NUISANCE—DEFINITION.

1. —— Hospitals—Metropolitan Poor Act.]
The Metropolitan Poor Act, 1867 (30 & 31 Vict.
c. 6), authorizes the formation of districts and district asylums for the care and cure of sick and in-
firm poor, creates corporations for that purpose,
gives authority to the Poor Law Board (now the
Local Government Board) to issue directions to
these corporations, enables them to purchase lands
and erect buildings for the purposes of the Act, and
makes the rates of parishes and unions liable for
the outlay thus incurred: But it does not, by
direct and imperative provisions, order these
things to be done, so that if, in doing them, a
nuisance is created to the injury of the health or
property of persons resident in the neighbourhood
of the place where the land is purchased or the

I. NUISANCE—DEFINITION—*continued.*

buildings erected, it does not afford to these acts a statutory protection. And therefore, where such nuisance was found as a fact :—*Held*, that the District Board could not set up the statute, nor the orders of the Poor Law Board under it, as an answer to an action, or to prevent an injunction issuing to restrain the Board from continuing the nuisance.—Per Lord Blackburn: On those who seek to establish that the Legislature intended to take away the private rights of individuals, lies the burden of shewing that such an intention appears by express words or necessary implication.—Per Lord Watson : Where the terms of a statute are not imperative, but permissive, the fair inference is that the Legislature intended that the discretion, as to the use of the general powers thereby conferred, should be exercised in strict conformity with private rights. METROPOLITAN ASYLUM DISTRICT *v.* HILL

[**6 App. Cas. 193**

2. —— Railway Company—*Cattle Station—Parliamentary Powers.*] A railway company were by their Act authorized, among other things, to carry cattle, and were also authorized to purchase by agreement (in addition to the lands which they were empowered to purchase compulsorily) any lands not exceeding in the whole fifty acres, in such places as should be deemed eligible, for the purpose of providing additional station yards, &c., for receiving, loading, or keeping any cattle or any goods, &c., conveyed or intended to be conveyed by the railway, and for making convenient ways thereto, or for any other purposes connected with the undertaking which the company should judge requisite; and they were empowered to sell the additional lands, and to purchase in lieu thereof other lands which they should deem more eligible for their additional purposes, and afterwards to sell the same as aforesaid, and so from time to time. The company bought under this power a piece of land adjoining one of their stations and used it as a cattle dock. The noise of the cattle and drovers was a nuisance to the occupiers of certain houses near the station, and they brought an action to restrain the company from continuing the nuisance :—*Held* (affirming the decision of North, J.), that the Plaintiffs were entitled to an injunction, for that there was nothing in the Act which by necessary implication authorized the creation of a nuisance on the additional lands. TRUMAN *v.* LONDON, BRIGHTON, AND SOUTH COAST RAILWAY COMPANY 25 Ch. D. 423 ; 29 Ch. D. 89 [Reversed by the House of Lords, 11 App. Cas. 45.]

II. NUISANCE—REMEDIES.

1. —— Injunction—*Fouling Stream—Quia Timet Action.*] In order to maintain a *quia timet* action to restrain an apprehended injury the Plaintiff must prove imminent danger of a substantial kind, or that the apprehended injury, if it does come, will be irreparable.—*Earl of Ripon v. Hobart* (3 My. & K. 169), *Attorney-General v. Corporation of Kingston* (13 W. R. 888), and *Salvin v. North Brancepeth Coal Company* (Law Rep. 9 Ch. 705) discussed.—The Plaintiff was a manufacturer of paper, his mills being situate on the bank of a river, the water of which he used to a large extent in his process of manufacture,

II. NUISANCE—REMEDIES—*continued.*

for which it was essential that the water should be very pure. The Defendants, who were alkali manufacturers, were depositing on a piece of land close to the river, and about one mile and a half higher up than the Plaintiff's mills, a large heap of refuse from their works. It was proved that in the course of a few years a liquid of a very noxious character would flow from the heap, and would continue flowing for forty years or more, and that if this liquid should find its way into the river to any appreciable extent the water would be rendered unfit for the Plaintiff's manufacture, and his trade would be ruined. The Plaintiff did not allege that he had as yet sustained any actual injury. The Defendants said that they intended to use all proper precautions to prevent the noxious liquid from getting into the river :—*Held*, that, it being quite possible by the use of due care to prevent the liquid from flowing into the river, and it being also possible that, before it began to flow from the heap, some method of rendering it innocuous might have been discovered, the action could not be maintained, and must be dismissed with costs.—But the dismissal was expressly declared to be without prejudice to the right of the Plaintiff to bring another action hereafter, in case of actual injury or imminent danger. FLETCHER *v.* BEALEY

[**28 Ch. D. 688**

2. —— Obstruction of Light—*Injunction—Cause of Action—Reversioner.*] The Plaintiff was the owner in fee of a cottage, the Defendant owned some land immediately adjoining. The Plaintiff alleged that the Defendant had erected on the Plaintiff's land a hoarding on poles in order to block out the access of light to a window in the cottage, and had in so doing committed a trespass. The Plaintiff also alleged that the poles and hoarding produced a rattling and creaking noise which was an intolerable nuisance to the Plaintiff and his tenants. The Plaintiff claimed an injunction to restrain the trespass and the nuisance. At the trial it was proved that the cottage was in the occupation of a weekly tenant of the Plaintiff, who was not a party to the action. There was no evidence that the acts of the Defendant had caused any diminution of value of, or other injury to, the reversion :—*Held* (affirming the decision of Fry, J.), that the poles and hoarding not being of such a permanent character as to injure the reversion the Plaintiff could not maintain an action for trespass; and that the erection of the poles on the Plaintiff's land was too trifling an injury to entitle the Plaintiff to an injunction.—*Rochdale Canal Company v. King* (2 Sim. (N.S.) 78) distinguished. COOPER *v.* CRABTREE　-　　19 Ch. D. 193;

[**20 Ch. D. 589**

3. —— Obstruction on Highway.] The Defendant farmed land on either side of a highway. His servants removed a roller from one of his fields across the highway to the gate of the opposite field, and taking away the horses, left the roller on the green-sward at the roadside with its shafts turned up (but projecting a few inches over the metalled part of the road), intending it to remain there until it should suit their convenience to draw it away. The Plain-

II. NUISANCE—REMEDIES—*continued.*

tiff's wife drove past the spot, and her pony shied at the roller, overturned the carriage, and caused her death.—In an action under Lord Campbell's Act (9 & 10 Vict. c. 93), the jury found that the accident was caused by an unreasonable user by the Defendant of the highway: —*Held,* that the verdict was warranted by the evidence, and that the Plaintiff was entitled to judgment. WILKINS *v.* DAY **12 Q. B. D. 110**

4. —— Sewage—*Local Board—Right to send Sewage into Sewers of adjoining District—Injunction—Trivial Damage—Claim of Right—Mandatory Injunction—Stopping up existing Drains—Suspension of Injunction—Metropolis Local Management Act,* 1855 (18 & 19 Vict. c. 120), *ss.* 135, 220—*Public Health Act,* 1875 (38 & 39 Vict. c. 55), *ss.* 15, 23.] Notwithstanding the obligation imposed on a local board by the Public Health Act, 1875, to drain their district, their right to send the sewage of their district, directly or indirectly, into the sewers belonging to the sanitary authority of an adjoining district is, in the absence of express enactment or agreement, no higher than the right of a landowner to send sewage from his land on to the land or into the drains of a neighbouring landowner. — If, therefore, a prescriptive right has been acquired to send some sewage from one district into the sewers of another, the burden cannot be increased without the consent of the sanitary authority of the latter district. The ratio decidendi of *Metropolitan Board of Works* v. *London and North Western Railway Company* (17 Ch. D. 246) applies to a local board just as it does to an ordinary landowner.—Injunction granted in the absence of proof of substantial damage, on the ground that the Defendants by their pleading claimed a right to continue doing that which the Court held they were not entitled to do.—In an action by a sanitary authority to restrain the sanitary authority of a neighbouring district from authorizing or directing sewage from their district to flow into the sewers of the Plaintiffs, the Court granted an injunction as to the future, but refused to grant a mandatory injunction to compel the stopping up of existing drains (1), Because to do so would cause serious inconvenience to the district, and (2), Because it is doubtful whether a local board have power to stop up drains which they have once authorized to be connected with their sewers. And, inasmuch as the injunction granted applied only to the future, the Court refused to suspend its operation. ATTORNEY-GENERAL *v.* ACTON LOCAL BOARD **22 Ch. D. 221**

5. —— Sewage—*Pollution of Stream—Local Board—Neglect of Public Duty—Mandamus—Injunction—Vesting of Sewers in Local Authority—Public Health Act,* 1875 (38 & 39 Vict. c. 55), s. 17 — *Rivers Pollution Act,* 1876 (39 & 40 Vict. c. 75), *ss.* 2, 3, 8.] A sanitary authority in whom the sewers are vested have only a limited ownership in them; they are not in the same position as to responsibility for fouling a stream as a private individual, because they cannot stop the sewers on account of the damage to the inhabitants of the neighbourhood. And although, perhaps, the sanitary authority might obtain an injunction to restrain persons from using the sewers who had

II. NUISANCE—REMEDIES—*continued.*

no right to do so, a landowner complaining of the nuisance cannot bring an action against them for not doing so; because an action cannot be maintained either at Law or in Equity to compel a person to bring an action for the purpose of restraining a nuisance which he cannot himself prevent. Where a sanitary authority have not themselves constructed sewers which are a nuisance, but only permitted them to be used as formerly by the inhabitants, they are not doing an act which can be restrained under the Public Health Acts, or the Rivers Pollution Act, 1876. But if they are neglecting their duty in providing a sufficient sanitary scheme for the neighbourhood the remedy of an aggrieved landowner is by mandamus.—Per Jessel, M.R.: The Court will not make an order against a public body or against individuals to do an act unless it is satisfied that it is within their power to do it.—Per Jessel, M.R.: In dealing with the question of restraining a public body from continuing a state of things which existed before the commencement of their powers, the Court must take into consideration the balance of convenience.—*Glossop* v. *Heston and Isleworth Local Board* (12 Ch. D. 102) approved and followed.—The order of Hall, V.C., affirmed. ATTORNEY-GENERAL *v.* GUARDIANS OF POOR OF UNION OF DORKING **20 Ch. D. 595**

6. —— Sewage—*Right to compel an Action against Third Party—Power of Local Board to stop Nuisance—Public Health Act,* 1875, *s.* 21.] On a motion for an injunction to restrain a local board from allowing sewage to flow into a brook opposite the Plaintiff's house, whereby a nuisance was occasioned, it appeared that the nuisance was in fact caused by C. P., not a party to the action, who had passed the sewage of his house into the brook through a pipe, which, by agreement with the Defendants, he was only entitled to use for surface or rain water:—*Held,* that although the Local Board could not be compelled to construct an improved system of drainage except by mandamus; nor to bring an action for an injunction against a third party, particularly in cases where the legal right was doubtful; still where the third party was acting in violation of an agreement entered into with the Local Board to pass surface water only through the pipe, and where no special inconvenience would be caused to other neighbours, the Plaintiff was entitled to an injunction against the Defendants on the ground that they could themselves prevent any nuisance being caused, by stopping up the pipe which was being used in contravention of the agreement, under the powers given them by the Public Health Act, and this, notwithstanding that they would be preventing the third party from exercising his right of passing surface water only through the pipe.—*Attorney-General* v. *Guardians of Poor of Union of Dorking* (20 Ch. D. 595) distinguished. CHARLES *v.* FINCHLEY LOCAL BOARD **[23 Ch. D. 767**

NUISANCE—Abatement—Public Health Act—Power of justices to order specific works **[6 Q. B. D. 545; 11 Q. B. D. 191; [13 Q. B. D. 681**

See LOCAL GOVERNMENT—LOCAL AUTHORITY. 10, 11, 12.

2 I

NUISANCE—*continued.*

—— Action against district board—Liability of successors in title   -   **17 Ch. D. 685**
    See LOCAL GOVERNMENT—LOCAL AUTHORITY. **13.**

—— Alkali works.
    See LOCAL GOVERNMENT — PUBLIC HEALTH ACTS—*Statutes.*

—— Burning dead body   -   **12 Q. B. D. 247**
    See CRIMINAL LAW—MISDEMEANOR. **1.**

—— Flap covering water meter in street—Liability of vestry -   -   **9 Q. B. D. 451**
    See METROPOLIS—MANAGEMENT ACTS. **5.**

—— Highway—Local board -   **10 Q. B. D. 138**
    See LOCAL GOVERNMENT—OFFENCES. **1.**

—— Indecent exposure -   -   **14 Q. B. D. 63**
    See CRIMINAL LAW—NUISANCE.

—— Ironworks -   -   **7 App. Cas. 518**
    See SCOTCH LAW—NUISANCE.

—— Offensive business.
    See METROPOLIS—MANAGEMENT ACTS—*Statutes.*

—— Percolation of water   -   **27 Ch. D. 588**
    See WATER. **2.**

NUISANCE—*continued.*

—— Swine kept near dwelling-house
                  [12 Q. B. D. 617
    See LOCAL GOVERNMENT—BY-LAWS.

—— Swine kept near dwelling-house
                  [8 Q. B. D. 97
    See LOCAL GOVERNMENT—OFFENCES. **3.**

—— Urinal   -   **16 Ch. D. 449**
    See METROPOLIS—MANAGEMENT ACTS. **6.**

—— Urinal—Public Health Act **14 Q. B. D. 928**
    See LOCAL GOVERNMENT — COMPENSATION. **2.**

NULLITY OF MARRIAGE.
    See Cases under PRACTICE—DIVORCE—NULLITY OF MARRIAGE.

—— After divorce in Scotland   **8 App. Cas. 43**
    See HUSBAND AND WIFE—DIVORCE.

—— Appeal from decree.
    See PRACTICE — DIVORCE — APPEAL — *Statutes.*

—— Scotch law   -   **10 App. Cas. 171**
    See SCOTCH LAW—HUSBAND AND WIFE. **7.**

O.

OATH—Administration of—Commission to take
evidence abroad - 22 Ch. D. 841
  See PRACTICE—SUPREME COURT—EVI-
  DENCE. 12.
—— Parliament—Claim to affirm 7 Q. B. D. 38
  See PARLIAMENT—ELECTION. 2.
—— Parliament—Disbelief in Supreme Being—
  Penalty - 14 Q. B. D. 667
  See PARLIAMENT—ELECTION. 3.
—— Parliament — Proceedings of House of
  Commons - 12 Q. B. D. 271
  See PARLIAMENT—PROCEDURE.

OBJECTION—For want of parties 16 Ch. D. 59
  See PRACTICE—SUPREME COURT—PAR-
  TIES. 7.
—— Registration of copyright 23 Ch. D. 727
  See COPYRIGHT—BOOKS. 3.
—— To qualification of voter 8 Q. B. D. 259;
  [12 Q. B. D. 376; 15 Q. B. D. 461
  See PARLIAMENT—FRANCHISE. 5, 6, 7.
—— To title.
  See Cases under VENDOR AND PURCHASER
  —TITLE.

OBSOLETE PUNISHMENT.
  See JUSTICES—PRACTICE—Statutes.

OBSTRUCTION—Highway - 12 Q. B. D. 121
  See HIGHWAY—OBSTRUCTION.
—— Light.
  See Cases under LIGHT.

OCCUPATION—Parliamentary franchise.
  See Cases and Statutes under
  PARLIAMENT—FRANCHISE.
  PARLIAMENT—REGISTRATION.
—— Rates.
  See Cases under POOR-RATE—OCCUPATION.
—— Rates—Company in liquidation
  [23 Ch. D. 500; 28 Ch. D. 470, 474
  See COMPANY—RATES. 1, 2, 3.

OCCUPIER—Lands Clauses Acts—Compensation
  [25 Ch. D. 472
  See LANDS CLAUSES ACTS—COMPENSA-
  TION. 1.

OFFICIAL ASSIGNEE—Stock Exchange
  See STOCK EXCHANGE. 2. [20 Ch. D. 356

OFFICIAL LIQUIDATOR.
  See Cases under COMPANY—LIQUIDATOR.
—— Appointment of - 20 Ch. D. 276
  See COMPANY—WINDING-UP ORDER. 8.
—— Costs—Appeal - 21 Ch. D. 381
  See COMPANY—COSTS. 1.

OFFICIAL RECEIVER.
  See BANKRUPTCY — BANKRUPTCY ACT,
  1883—Statutes.
—— Bankruptcy 13 Q. B. D. 118; 15 Q. B. D. 169
  See BANKRUPTCY—RECEIVER. 7, 11.
—— Bankruptcy—Costs—Appeal 14 Q. B. D. 48
  See BANKRUPTCY—COSTS. 5.

OFFICIAL RECEIVER—continued.
—— Report as to composition of scheme of
  arrangement—How far prima facie evi-
  dence - 15 Q. B. D. 213
  See BANKRUPTCY—SCHEME OF ARRANGE-
  MENT. 2.

OFFICIAL REFEREE.
  See Cases under PRACTICE — SUPREME
  COURT—REFEREE.

OFFICER—In army—Bankruptcy—Domicil
  [13 Q. B. D. 418
  See BANKRUPTCY — BANKRUPTCY PETI-
  TION. 3.
—— In army—Children born abroad
  See ALIEN. [22 Ch. D. 243
—— In army—Money payable on retirement—
  Priority of assignment 19 Ch. D. 17
  See MORTGAGE—PRIORITY. 12.
—— Public—Suit against - 6 App. Cas. 619
  See COLONIAL LAW—NATAL. 1.

OMISSION OF WORDS—Will—Probate
  [7 App. Cas. 192
  See PROBATE—GRANT. 11.

OMNIBUS—Conductor — Employers and Work-
  men Act - 13 Q. B. D. 832
  See MASTER AND SERVANT—MASTER'S
  LIABILITY. 9.
—— Manager — Injunction to restrain use of
  name - - 12 Q. B. D. 105
  See METROPOLIS — PUBLIC CARRIAGES
  ACTS.

ONEROUS HOLDER—Cheque - 9 App. Cas. 95
  See SCOTCH LAW—BILL OF EXCHANGE.
  1.

ONEROUS LEGACY—Disclaimer 22 Ch. D. 573;
  [30 Ch. D. 614
  See WILL—DISCLAIMER. 1, 2.

ONTARIO—Law of.
  See Cases under COLONIAL LAW —
  CANADA—ONTARIO.

ONUS PROBANDI—Easement - 19 Ch. D. 462
  See LIGHT—TITLE. 4.
—— Evidence of marriage - 6 App. Cas. 364
  See COLONIAL LAW—CEYLON. 3.
—— Impeaching voluntary settlement 18 Ch. D.
  See VOLUNTARY CONVEYANCE. 6. [668
—— Misrepresentation—Impeaching deed
  [7 App. Cas. 307
  See COLONIAL LAW—VICTORIA. 2.
—— Purchase by conservators of river
  See RIVER. [6 App. Cas. 685
—— Undue influence - 18 Ch. D. 188
  See UNDUE INFLUENCE.

OPEN SPACES.
  See METROPOLIS—MANAGEMENT ACTS—
  Statutes.

OPENING BIDDINGS—Sale by Court 16 Ch. D. 561
  See PRACTICE—SUPREME COURT—SALE
  BY COURT.

P.

I. PARLIAMENT—ELECTION.

The Act 48 & 49 Vict. c. 59, continues 35 & 36 Vict. c. 33, the Ballot Act, 1872, so far as it is not repealed, until the 31st of December, 1886.

Conveyance of Voters.] *The Act 48 & 49 Vict. c. 59, continues the Act 43 Vict. c. 18, until the 31st of December, 1886.*

Returning Officers.] *The Act 46 & 47 Vict. c. 51, s. 32, amends the Act 38 & 39 Vict. c. 84; the Act 48 & 49 Vict. c. 59, continues the latter until the 31st of December, 1886.*

The Act 48 & 49 Vict. c. 62, amends the law relating to the charges of returning officers at parliamentary elections.

I. PARLIAMENT—ELECTION—*continued.*

Corrupt Practices.] *The Act 46 & 47 Vict. c. 51 (Corrupt and Illegal Practices Prevention Act, 1883), repeals (sect. 66 and Schedule 5) divers enactments relating to parliamentary elections and to corrupt and . illegal practices at such elections, and provides for the better prevention of corrupt and illegal practices at such elections.*

By sect. 65 the Act and the Corrupt Practices Prevention Acts may be cited together as the Corrupt Practices Prevention Acts, 1854 to 1883.

By sect. 66 the Act came into operation on the 15th of October, 1886.

By sect. 64 the expression " committee room " shall not include any house or room occupied by a candidate at an election as a dwelling, by reason only of the candidate there transacting business with his agents in relation to such election; nor shall any room or dwelling be deemed to be a committee room for the purposes of the Act by reason only of the candidate or any agent of the candidate addressing therein electors, committee-men or others.

" Election " means the election of a member or members to serve in Parliament.

" Election court " means two Judges presiding at the trial of an election petition, or, if the matter comes before the High Court of Justice, that Court.

" Election petition " means a petition presented in pursuance of the Parliamentary Elections Act, 1868, as amended by this Act.

" Elector " means any person whose name is for the time being on the register roll or book containing the names of the persons entitled to vote at the election with reference to which the word is used.

" Payment " includes any pecuniary or other reward; and " pecuniary reward " and " money " include any office, place, or employment, and any valuable security or other equivalent for money, and any valuable consideration, and expressions referring to money shall be construed.

" Person " includes an association or body of persons, corporate or incorporate, and where any act is done by any such association or body, the members of such association or body who have taken part in the commission of such act shall be liable to any fine or punishment imposed for the same by this Act.

" Personal expenses " as used with respect to the expenditure of any candidate in relation to any election includes the reasonable travelling expenses of his living at hotels or elsewhere for the purposes of and in relation to such election.

" Polling agent " means an agent of the candidate appointed to attend at a polling station in pursuance of the Ballot Act, 1872, or of the Acts therein referred to or amending the same.

" Public office " means any office under the Crown or under the charter of a city or municipal borough or under the Acts relating to Municipal Corporations or to the Poor Law, or under the Elementary Education Act, 1870, or under the Public Health Act, 1875, or under any Acts amending the above-

I. PARLIAMENT—ELECTION—*continued.*

mentioned *Acts, or under any other Acts for the time being in force (whether passed before or after the commencement of this Act), relating to local government, whether the office is that of mayor, chairman, alderman, councillor, guardian, member of a board, commission, or other local authority in any county, city, borough, union, sanitary district, or other area, or is the office of clerk of the peace, town clerk, clerk or other officer under a council, board, commission, or other authority, or is any other office, to which a person is elected or appointed under any such charter or Act as above-mentioned, and includes any other municipal or parochial office.*

Candidate.] *Sect. 63.*—(1.) *In the Corrupt Practices Prevention Acts, as amended by this Act, the expression " candidate at an election" and the expression "candidate" respectively mean, unless the context otherwise requires, any person elected to serve in Parliament at such election, and any person who is nominated as a candidate at such election, or is declared by himself or by others to be a candidate, on or after the day of the issue of the writ for such election, or after the dissolution or vacancy in consequence of which such writ has been issued;*

(2.) *Provided that where a person has been nominated as a candidate or declared to be a candidate by others, then—*

(a.) *If he was so nominated or declared without his consent, nothing in this Act shall be construed to impose any liability on such person, unless he has afterwards given his assent to such nomination or declaration or has been elected; and*

(b.) *If he was so nominated or declared, either without his consent or in his absence, and takes no part in the election, he may, if he thinks fit, make the declaration respecting election expenses contained in the second part of the Second Schedule to this Act, and the election agent shall, so far as circumstances admit, comply with the provisions of this Act with respect to expenses incurred on account of or in respect of the conduct or management of the election in like manner as if the candidate had been nominated or declared with his consent.*

Corrupt and Illegal Practices.] *Sect.* 1. *Whereas under sect. 4 of the Corrupt Practice Prevention Act, 1854, persons other than candidates at parliamentary elections are not liable to any punishment for treating, and it is expedient to make such persons liable; be it therefore enacted in substitution for the said sect. 4 as follows:*—

(1.) *Any person who corruptly by himself or by any other person, either before, during, or after an election directly or indirectly gives or provides, or pays wholly or in part the expense of giving or providing any meat, drink, entertainment, or provision to or for any person, for the purpose of corruptly influencing that person or any other person to give or refrain from giving his vote at the election, or on account of such person or any other person having voted or refrained from voting, or being about to vote or refrain from voting at such election, shall be guilty of treating.*

I. PARLIAMENT—ELECTION—*continued.*

(2.) *And every elector who corruptly accepts or takes any such meat, drink, entertainment, or provision shall also be guilty of treating.*

Sect. 2. *Every person who shall directly or indirectly, by himself or by any other person on his behalf, make use of or threaten to make use of any force, violence, or restraint, or inflict or threaten to inflict, by himself or by any other person, any temporal or spiritual injury, damage, harm, or loss upon or against any person in order to induce or compel such person to vote or refrain from voting, or on account of such person having voted or refrained from voting at any election, or who shall by abduction, duress, or any fraudulent device or contrivance impede or prevent the free exercise of the franchise of any elector, or shall thereby compel, induce, or prevail upon any elector either to give or to refrain from giving his vote at any election, shall be guilty of undue influence.*

Sect. 3. *The expression " corrupt practice" as used in this Act means any of the following offences; namely, treating and undue influence, as defined by this Act, and bribery, and personation, as defined by 17 & 18 Vict. c. 102, ss. 2 & 3; 30 & 31 Vict. c. 102, s. 49; and 35 & 36 Vict. c. 33, s. 24; and aiding, abetting, counselling, and procuring the commission of the offence of personation, and every offence which is a corrupt practice within the meaning of this Act shall be a corrupt practice within the meaning of the Parliamentary Elections Act, 1868.*

Sect. 4. *Where upon the trial of an election petition respecting an election for a county or borough, the Election Court, by the report made to the Speaker in pursuance of sect. 11 of the Parliamentary Elections Act, 1868, reports that any corrupt practice other than treating or undue influence has been proved to have been committed in reference to such election by or with the knowledge and consent of any candidate at such election, or that the offence of treating or undue influence has been proved to have been committed in reference to such election by any candidate at such election, that candidate shall not be capable of ever being elected to or sitting in the House of Commons for the said county or borough, and if he has been elected, his election shall be void; and he shall further be subject to the same incapacities as if at the date of the said report he had been convicted on an indictment of a corrupt practice.*

Sect. 5. *Upon the trial of an election petition respecting an election for a county or borough, in which a charge is made of any corrupt practice having been committed in reference to such election, the Election Court shall report in writing to the Speaker whether any of the candidates at such election has been guilty by his agents of any corrupt practice in reference to such election; and if the report is that any candidate at such election has been guilty by his agents of any corrupt practice in reference to such election, that candidate shall not be capable of being elected to or sitting in the House of Commons for such county or borough for seven years after the date of the report, and if he has been elected his election shall be void.*

Sect. 6—(1.) *A person who commits any corrupt practice other than personation, or aiding, abetting, counselling, or procuring the commission of the offence of personation, shall be guilty of a mis-*

I. PARLIAMENT—ELECTION—*continued.*

demeanor, and on conviction on indictment shall be liable to be imprisoned, with or without hard labour, for a term not exceeding one year, or to be fined any sum not exceeding two hundred pounds.

(2.) A person who commits the offence of personation, or of aiding, abetting, counselling, or procuring the commission of that offence, shall be guilty of felony, and any person convicted thereof on indictment shall be punished by imprisonment for a term not exceeding two years, together with hard labour.

(3.) A person who is convicted on indictment of any corrupt practice shall (in addition to any punishment as above provided) be not capable during a period of seven years from the date of his conviction ;

　(a.) *of being registered as an elector or voting at any election in the United Kingdom, whether it be a parliamentary election or an election for any public office within the meaning of this Act ; or,*

　(b.) *of holding any public or judicial office within the meaning of this Act, and if he holds any such office the office shall be vacated.*

(4.) Any person so convicted of a corrupt practice in reference to any election shall also be incapable of being elected to and of sitting in the House of Commons during the seven years next after the date of his conviction, and if at that date he has been elected to the House of Commons his election shall be vacated from the time of such conviction.

Sect. 7.—(1.) No payment or contract for payment shall, for the purpose of promoting or procuring the election of a candidate at any election be made—

　(a.) *on account of the conveyance of electors to or from the poll, whether for the hiring of horses or carriages, or for railway fares, or otherwise ; or*

　(b.) *to an elector on account of the use of any house, land, building, or premises for the exhibition of any address, bill, or notice, or on account of the exhibition of any address, bill, or notice ; or*

　(c.) *on account of any committee room in excess of the number allowed by the first Schedule to this Act.*

(2.) Subject to such exception as may be allowed in pursuance of this Act, if any payment or contract for payment is knowingly made in contravention of this section either before, during, or after an election, the person making such payment or contract shall be guilty of an illegal practice, and any person receiving such payment or being a party to any such contract, knowing the same to be in contravention of this Act, shall also be guilty of an illegal practice.

(3.) Provided that where it is the ordinary business of an elector as an advertising agent to exhibit for payment bills and advertisements, a payment to or contract with such elector, if made in the ordinary course of business, shall not be deemed to be an illegal practice within the meaning of this section.

Sect. 8.—(1.) Subject to such exception as may be allowed in pursuance of this Act, no sum shall be paid and no expense shall be incurred by a candidate at an election or his election agent,

I. PARLIAMENT—ELECTION—*continued.*

whether before, during, or after an election, on account of or in respect of the conduct or management of such election, in excess of any maximum amount in that behalf specified in the first Schedule of this Act.

(2.) Any candidate or election agent who knowingly acts in contravention of this section shall be guilty of an illegal practice.

Sect. 9.—(1.) If any person votes or induces or procures any person to vote at any election, knowing that he or such person is prohibited, whether by this or any other Act from voting at such election, he shall be guilty of an illegal practice.

(2.) Any person who before or during an election knowingly publishes a false statement of a withdrawal of a candidate at such election for the purpose of promoting or procuring the election of another candidate shall be guilty of an illegal practice.

(3.) Provided that a candidate shall not be liable, nor shall his election be avoided, for any illegal practice under this section committed by his agent other than his election agent.

Sect. 10. A person guilty of an illegal practice whether under the foregoing sections or under the provisions hereinafter contained in this Act, shall on summary conviction be liable to a fine not exceeding £100, and be incapable during a period of five years from the date of his conviction as being registered as an elector or voting at any election (whether it be a parliamentary election or an election for a public office within the meaning of this Act) held for or within the county or borough in which the illegal practice has been committed.

Sect. 11. Whereas by sub-sect. 14 of sect. 11 of the Parliamentary Elections Act, 1868, it is provided that, where a charge is made in an election petition of any corrupt practice having been committed at the election to which the petition refers, the Judge shall report in writing to the Speaker as follows :—

　(a.) *" Whether any corrupt practice has or has not been proved to have been committed by or with the knowledge and consent of any candidate at such election, and the nature of such corrupt practice ;"*

　(b.) *The names of all persons, if any, who have been proved at the trial to have been guilty of any corrupt practice ;*

　(c.) *" Whether corrupt practices have, or whether there is reason to believe corrupt practices have, extensively prevailed at the election to which the petition relates :"*

And whereas it is expedient to extend the said subsection to illegal practices :

Be it therefore enacted as follows.—

Sub-sect. 14 of sect. 11 of the Parliamentary Elections Act, 1868, shall apply as if that subsection were herein re-enacted with the substitution of illegal practice within the meaning of this Act for corrupt practice ; and upon the trial of an election petition respecting an election for a county or borough, the Election Court shall report in writing to the Speaker the particulars required by the said sub-section as herein re-enacted, and shall also report whether any candidate at such election has been guilty by his agents of any illegal practice within the meaning of this Act in reference to such election, and the following consequences shall ensue

I. PARLIAMENT—ELECTION—*continued.*

upon the report by the Election Court to the Speaker (that is to say),

(a.) *If the report is that any illegal practice has been proved to have been committed in reference to such election by or with the knowledge and consent of any candidate at such election, that candidate shall not be capable of being elected to or sitting in the House of Commons for the said county or borough for seven years next after the date of the report, and if he has been elected his election shall be void: and he shall further be subject to the same incapacities as if at the date of the report he had been convicted of such illegal practice; and*

(b.) *If the report is that a candidate at such election has been guilty by his agents of any illegal practice in reference to such election, that candidate shall not be capable of being elected to or sitting in the House of Commons for the said county or borough during the Parliament for which the election was held, and if he has been elected, his election shall be void.*

Sect. 12. *Whereas by the Election Commissioners Act,* 1852, *as amended by the Parliamentary Elections Act,* 1868, *it is enacted that where a joint address of both Houses of Parliament represents to Her Majesty that an Election Court has reported to the Speaker that corrupt practices have, or that there is reason to believe that corrupt practices have, extensively prevailed at an election in any county or borough, and prays Her Majesty to cause inquiry under that Act to be made by persons named in such address (being qualified as therein mentioned), it shall be lawful for Her Majesty to appoint the said persons to be Election Commissioners for the purpose of making inquiry into the existence of such corrupt practices:*

And whereas it is expedient to extend the said enactment to the case of illegal practices:

Be it therefore enacted as follows:—

When Election Commissioners have been appointed in pursuance of the Election Commissioners Act, 1852, *and the enactments amending the same, they may make inquiries and act and report as if "corrupt practices" in the said Act and the enactments amending the same included illegal practices; and the Election Commissioners Act,* 1852, *shall be construed with such modifications as are necessary for giving effect to this section, and the expression "corrupt practice" in that Act shall have the same meaning as in this Act.*

Sect. 13. *Where a person knowingly provides money for any payment which is contrary to the provisions of this Act, or for any expenses incurred in excess of any maximum amount allowed by this Act, or for replacing any money expended in any such payment or expenses, except where the same may have been previously allowed in pursuance of this Act to be an exception, such person shall be guilty of illegal payment.*

Sect. 14.—(1.) *A person shall not let, lend, or employ for the purpose of the conveyance of electors to or from the poll, any public stage or hackney carriage, or any horse or other animal kept or used for drawing the same, or any carriage, horse, or other animal which he keeps or uses for the purpose of letting out for hire, and if he lets, lends, or*

I. PARLIAMENT—ELECTION—*continued.*

employs such carriage, horse, or other animal, knowing that it is intended to be used for the purpose of the conveyance of electors to or from the poll, he shall be guilty of an illegal hiring.

(2.) *A person shall not hire, borrow, or use for the purpose of the conveyance of electors to or from the poll any carriage, horse, or other animal which he knows the owner thereof is prohibited by this section to let, lend, or employ for that purpose, and if he does so he shall be guilty of an illegal hiring.*

(3.) *Nothing in this Act shall prevent a carriage, horse, or other animal being let to or hired, employed, or used by an elector, or several electors at their joint cost, for the purpose of being conveyed to or from the poll.*

(4.) *No person shall be liable to pay any duty or to take out a licence for any carriage by reason only of such carriage being used without payment or promise of payment for the conveyance of electors to or from the poll at an election.*

Sect. 15. *Any person who corruptly induces or procures any other person to withdraw from being a candidate at an election, in consideration of any payment or promise of payment, shall be guilty of illegal payment, and any person withdrawing, in pursuance of such inducement or procurement, shall also be guilty of illegal payment.*

Sect. 16.—(1.) *No payment or contract for payment shall, for the purpose of promoting or procuring the election of a candidate at any election, be made on account of bands of music, torches, flags, banners, cockades, ribbons, or other marks of distinction.*

(2.) *Subject to such exception as may be allowed in pursuance of this Act, if any payment or contract for payment is made in contravention of this section, either before, during, or after an election, the person making such payment shall be guilty of illegal payment, and any person being a party to any such contract or receiving such payment shall also be guilty of illegal payment if he knew that the same was made contrary to law.*

Sect. 17.—(1.) *No person shall, for the purpose of promoting or procuring the election of a candidate at any election, be engaged or employed for payment or promise of payment for any purpose or in any capacity whatever, except for any purposes or capacities mentioned in the first or second parts of the First Schedule to this Act, or except so far as payment is authorized by the first or second parts of the First Schedule to this Act.*

(2.) *Subject to such exception as may be allowed in pursuance of this Act, if any person is engaged or employed in contravention of this section, either before, during, or after an election, the person engaging or employing him shall be guilty of illegal employment, and the person so engaged or employed shall also be guilty of illegal employment if he knew that he was engaged or employed contrary to law.*

Sect. 18. *Every bill, placard, or poster having reference to an election shall bear upon the face thereof the name and address of the printer and publisher thereof; and any person printing, publishing, or posting, or causing to be printed, published, or posted any such bill, placard, or poster as aforesaid, which fails to bear upon the face thereof the name and address of the printer and publisher, shall, if he is the candidate or the election*

I. PARLIAMENT—ELECTION—*continued.*

agent of the candidate, be guilty of an illegal practice, and if he is not the candidate, or the election agent of a candidate, shall be liable on summary conviction to a fine not exceeding £100.

Sect. 19. *The provisions of this Act prohibiting certain payments and contracts for payments, and the payment of any sum, and the incurring of any expense in excess of a certain maximum, shall not affect the right of any creditor, who, when the contract was made or the expense was incurred was ignorant of the same being in contravention of this Act.*

Sect. 20.—(a.) *Any premises on which the sale by wholesale or retail of any intoxicating liquor is authorized by a licence (whether the licence be for consumption on or off the premises), or*

(b.) *Any premises where any intoxicating liquor is sold, or is supplied to members of a club, society, or association other than a permanent political club, or*

(c.) *Any premises whereon refreshment of any kind, whether food or drink, is ordinarily sold for consumption on the premises, or*

(d.) *The premises of any public elementary school or in receipt of an annual parliamentary grant, or any part of any such premises, shall not be used as a committee room for the purpose of promoting or procuring the election of a candidate at an election, and if any person hires or uses any such premises or any part thereof for a committee room he shall be guilty of illegal hiring, and the person letting such premises or part, if he knew it was intended to use the same for a committee room, shall also be guilty of illegal hiring :*

Provided that nothing in this section shall apply to any part of such premises which is ordinarily let for the purpose of chambers or offices or the holding of public meetings or of arbitrations, if such part has a separate entrance and no direct communication with any part of the premises on which any intoxicating liquor or refreshment is sold or supplied as aforesaid.

Sect. 21.—(1.) *A person guilty of an offence of illegal payment, employment or hiring shall, on summary conviction, be liable to a fine not exceeding £100.*

(2.) *A candidate or an election agent of a candidate who is personally guilty of an offence of illegal payment, employment, or hiring shall be guilty of an illegal practice.*

Sect. 22. *Where, upon the trial of an election petition respecting an election for a county or borough, the Election Court report that a candidate at such election has been guilty by his agents of the offence of treating and undue influence, and illegal practice, or of any such offences in reference to such election, and the Election Court further report that the candidate has proved to the Court—*

(a.) *That no corrupt or illegal practice was committed at such election by the candidate or his election agent, and the offences mentioned in the said report were committed contrary to the orders and without the sanction or connivance of such candidate or his election agent ; and*

(b.) *That such candidate and his election agent took all reasonable means for preventing the commission of corrupt and illegal practices at such election ; and*

I. PARLIAMENT—ELECTION—*continued.*

(c.) *That the offences mentioned in the said report were of a trivial, unimportant, and limited character ; and*

(d.) *That in all other respects the election was free from any corrupt or illegal practice on the part of such candidate and of his agents.*

Then the election of such candidate shall not by reason of the offences mentioned in such report, be void, nor shall the candidate be subject to any incapacity under this Act.

Sect. 23. *Where, on application made, it is shewn to the High Court or to an Election Court by such evidence as seems to the Court sufficient—*

(a.) *that any act or omission of a candidate at any election, or of his election agent or of any other agent or person, would by reason of being a payment, engagement, employment, or contract in contravention of this Act, or being the payment of a sum or the incurring of expense in excess of any maximum amount allowed by this Act, or of otherwise being in contravention of any of the provisions of this Act, be but for this section an illegal practice, payment, employment, or hiring ; and*

(b.) *that such act or omission arose from inadvertence or from accidental miscalculation or from some other reasonable cause of a like nature, and in any case did not arise from any want of good faith ; and*

(c.) *that such notice of the application has been given in the county or borough for which the election was held as to the Court seems fit ;*

and under the circumstances it seems to the Court to be just that the candidate and the said election and other agent and person, or any of them, should not be subject to any of the consequences under this Act of the said act or omission, the Court may make an order allowing such act or omission to be an exception from the provisions of this Act which would otherwise make the same an illegal practice, payment, employment, or hiring, and thereupon such candidate, agent, or person shall not be subject to any of the consequences under this Act of the said act or omission.

Corrupt Practices Prevention Acts.] *By sect.* 65 *the enactments referred to in the Act as the Corrupt Practices Prevention Acts are* 17 & 18 Vict. c. 102, 26 & 27 Vict. c. 29, 30 & 31 Vict. c. 102, 31 & 32 Vict. c. 125, 35 & 36 Vict. c. 32 (*Part III.*), *and* 42 & 43 Vict. c. 75.

Disqualification of Electors.] Sect. 36. *Every person guilty of a corrupt or illegal practice or of illegal employment, payment, or hiring at an election is prohibited from voting at such election. and if any such person votes his vote shall be void.*

Sect. 37. *Every person who, in consequence of conviction or of the report of any Election Court or Election Commissioners under this Act, or under the Corrupt Practices (Municipal Elections) Act,* 1872, *or under Part IV. of the Municipal Corporations Act,* 1882, *or under any other Act for the time being in force relating to corrupt practices at an election for any public office, has become incapable of voting at any election, whether a parliamentary election or an election to any public office, is pro-*

I. PARLIAMENT—ELECTION—*continued.*

hibited *from* voting at any such election, and his vote shall be void.

Sect. 38—(1.) *Before a person, not being a party to an election petition nor a candidate on behalf of whom the seat is claimed by an election petition, is reported by an Election Court, and before any person is reported by Election Commissioners, to have been guilty, at an election, of any corrupt or illegal practice, the Court or Commissioners, as the case may be, shall cause notice to be given to such person, and if he appears in pursuance of the notice, shall give him an opportunity of being heard by himself and of calling evidence in his defence to shew why he should not be so reported.*

(2.) *Every person reported by Election Commissioners to have been guilty at any election of any corrupt or illegal practice may appeal against such report to the next Court of oyer and terminer or goal delivery held in and for the county or place in which the offence is alleged to have been committed, and such Court may hear and determine the appeal; and subject to rules of Court such appeal may be brought, heard, and determined in like manner as if the Court were a Court of Quarter Sessions and the said Commissioners were a Court of summary jurisdiction, and the person so reported had been convicted by a Court of summary jurisdiction for an offence under this Act, and notice of every such appeal shall be given to the Director of Public Prosecutions in the manner and within the time directed by rules of Court, and subject to such rules then within three days after the appeal is brought.*

(3.) *Where it appears to the Lord Chancellor that appeals under this section are interfering or are likely to interfere with the ordinary business transacted before any Courts of oyer and terminer or goal delivery, he may direct that the said appeals, or any of them, shall be heard by the judges for the time being on the rota for election petitions, and in such case one of such judges shall proceed to the county or place in which the offences are alleged to have been committed, and shall there hear and determine the appeals in like manner as if such judge were a Court of oyer and terminer.*

(4.) *The provisions of the Parliamentary Elections Act, 1868, with respect to the reception and powers of and attendance on an Election Court, and to the expenses of an Election Court, and of receiving and accommodating an Election Court shall apply as if such Judge were an Election Court.*

(5.) *Every person who after the commencement of this Act is reported by any Election Court or Election Commissioners to have been guilty of any corrupt or illegal practice at an election, shall, whether he obtained a certificate of indemnity or not, be subject to the same incapacity as he would be subject to if he had at the date of such election been convicted of the offence of which he is reported to have been guilty ; Provided that a report of any Election Commissioners inquiring into an election for a county or borough shall not avoid the election of any candidate who has been declared by an Election Court on the trial of a petition respecting such election to have been duly elected at such election, or render him incapable of sitting in the House of Commons for the said county or borough during the Parliament for which he was elected.*

(6.) *Where a person who is a justice of the peace is reported by any Election Court or Election*

I. PARLIAMENT—ELECTION—*continued.*

Commissioners to have been guilty of any corrupt practice in reference to an election, whether he has obtained a certificate of indemnity or not, it shall be the duty of the Director of Public Prosecutions to report the case to the Lord High Chancellor of Great Britain with such evidence as may have been given as to such corrupt practice, and where any such person acts as a justice of the peace by virtue of his being, or having been, mayor to a borough, the Lord High Chancellor shall have the same power to remove such person from being a justice of the peace as if he was named in a commission of the peace.

(7.) *Where a person who is a barrister, or a solicitor, or who belongs to any profession the admission to which is regulated by law, is reported by any Election Court or Election Commissioners to have been guilty of any corrupt practice in reference to an election, whether such person has obtained a certificate of indemnity or not, it shall be the duty of the Director of Public Prosecutions to bring the matter before the Inn of Court, High Court, or tribunal having power to take cognizance of any misconduct of such person in his profession, and such Inn of Court, High Court, or tribunal may deal with such person in like manner as if such corrupt practice were misconduct by such person in his profession.*

(8.) *With respect to a person holding a licence or certificate under the Licensing Acts (in this section referred to as a licensed person) the following provisions shall have effect:—*

(a.) *If it appears to the Court by which any licensed person is convicted of the offence of bribery or treating, that such offence was committed on his licensed premises, the Court shall direct such conviction to be entered in the proper register of licences.*

(b.) *If it appears to an Election Court or Election Commissioners that a licensed person has knowingly suffered any bribery or treating in reference to any election to take place upon his licensed premises, such Court or Commissioners (subject to the provisions of this Act as to a person having an opportunity of being heard by himself and producing evidence before being reported) shall report the same; and whether such person obtained a certificate of indemnity or not it shall be the duty of the Director of Public Prosecutions to bring such report before the licensing justices from whom or on whose certificate the licensed person obtained his licence, and such licensing justices shall cause such report to be entered in the proper register of licences :*

(c.) *Where an entry is made in the register of licences of any such conviction of or report respecting any licensed person as above in this section mentioned, it shall be taken into consideration by the licensing justices in determining whether they will or will not grant to such person the renewal of his licence or certificate, and may be a ground, if the justices think fit, for refusing such renewal.*

(9.) *Where the evidence shewing any corrupt practice to have been committed by a justice of the peace, barrister, solicitor, or other professional*

I. PARLIAMENT—ELECTION—*continued.*

person, or any licensed person, was given before Election Commissioners, those Commissioners shall report the case to the Director of Public Prosecutions, with such information as is necessary or proper for enabling him to act under this section.

(10.) *This section shall apply to an Election Court under this Act, or under Part IV. of the Municipal Corporations Act, 1882, and the expression election shall be construed accordingly.*

Sect. 39.—(1.) *The registration officer in every county or borough shall annually make out a list containing the names and descriptions of all persons who, though otherwise qualified to vote at a parliamentary election for such county or borough respectively, are not capable of voting by reason of having after the commencement of this Act been found guilty of a corrupt or illegal practice on conviction or by the report of any Election Court or Election Commissioners whether under this Act, or under Part IV. of the Municipal Corporations Act, 1882, or under any other Act for the time being in force relating to a parliamentary election or an election to any public office ; and such officer shall state in the list (in this Act referred to as the corrupt and illegal practices list), the offence of which each person has been found guilty.*

(2.) *For the purpose of making out such list he shall examine the report of any Election Court or Election Commissioners who have respectively tried an election petition or inquired into an election where the election (whether a parliamentary election or an election to any public office) was held in any of the following places ; that is to say,*

　(a.) *if he is the registration officer of a county, in that county, or in any borough in that county ; and*

　(b.) *if he is the registration officer of a borough, in the county in which such borough is situate, or in any borough in that county.*

(3.) *The registration officer shall send the list to the overseers of every parish within his county or borough, together with his precept, and the overseers shall publish the list together with the list of voters and shall also, in the case of every person in the corrupt and illegal practices list, omit his name from the list of persons entitled to vote, or, as circumstances require, add "objected" before his name in the list of claimants or copy of the register published by them, in like manner as is required by law in any other cases of disqualification.*

(4.) *Any person named in the corrupt and illegal practices list may claim to have his name omitted therefrom, and any person entitled to object to any list of voters for the county or borough may object to the omission of the name of any person from such list. Such claims and objections shall be sent in within the same time and be dealt with in like manner, and any such objection shall be served on the person referred to therein in like manner, as nearly as circumstances admit, as other claims and objections under the enactments relating to the registration of parliamentary electors.*

(5.) *The revising barrister shall determine such claims and objections and shall revise such list in like manner, as nearly as circumstances admit, as in the case of other claims and objections, and of any list of voters.*

(6.) *Where it appears to the revising barrister that a person not named in the corrupt and illegal*

I. PARLIAMENT—ELECTION—*continued.*

practices list is subject to have his name inserted in such list, he shall (whether an objection to the omission of such name from the list has or has not been made, but) after giving such person an opportunity of making a statement to shew cause to the contrary, insert his name in such list and expunge his name from any list of voters.

(7.) *A revising barrister in acting under this section shall determine only whether a person is incapacitated by conviction or by the report of any Election Court or Election Commissioners, and shall not determine whether a person has or has not been guilty of any corrupt or illegal practice.*

(8.) *The corrupt and illegal practices list shall be appended to the register of electors, and shall be printed and published therewith wherever the same is printed or published.*

Election Agent and Expenses.] *Sect.* 24.—(1.) *On or before the day of nomination at an election, a person shall be named by or on behalf of each candidate as his agent for such election (in this Act referred to as the election agent).*

(2.) *A candidate may name himself as election agent, and thereupon shall, so far as circumstances admit, be subject to the provisions of this Act both as a candidate and as an election agent ; and any reference in this Act to an election agent shall be construed to refer to the candidate acting in his capacity of election agent.*

(3.) *On or before the day of nomination the name and address of the election agent of each candidate shall be declared in writing by the candidate or some other person on his behalf to the returning officer, and the returning officer shall forthwith give public notice of the name and address of every election agent so declared.*

(4.) *One election agent only shall be appointed for each candidate, but the appointment, whether the election agent appointed be the candidate himself or not, may be revoked, and in the event of such revocation or his death, whether such event is before, during, or after the election, then forthwith another election agent shall be appointed, and his name and address declared in writing to the returning officer, who shall forthwith give public notice of the same.*

Sect. 25.—(1.) *In the case of the elections specified in that behalf in the First Schedule to this Act an election agent of a candidate may appoint the number of deputies therein mentioned (which deputies are in this Act referred to as sub-agents), to act within different polling districts.*

(2.) *As regards matters in a polling district the election agent may act by the sub-agent for that district, and anything done for the purposes of this Act by or to the sub-agent in his district shall be deemed to be done by or to the election agent, and any act or default of a sub-agent which, if he were the election agent, would be an illegal practice or other offence against this Act, shall be an illegal practice and offence against this Act committed by the sub-agent, and the sub-agent shall be liable to punishment accordingly ; and the candidate shall suffer the like incapacity as if the said act or default had been the act or default of the election agent.*

(3.) *One clear day before the polling the election agent shall declare in writing the name and address of every sub-agent to the returning officer, and the*

I. PARLIAMENT—ELECTION—*continued.*

returning officer shall forthwith give public notice of the name and address of every sub-agent so declared.

(4.) *The appointment of a sub-agent shall not be vacated by the election agent who appointed him ceasing to be election agent, but may be revoked by the election agent for the time being of the candidate, and in the event of such revocation or of the death of a sub-agent another sub-agent may be appointed, and his name and address shall be forthwith declared in writing to the returning officer, who shall forthwith give public notice of the same.*

Sect. 26.—(1.) *An election agent at an election for a county or borough shall have within the county or borough, or within any county of a city or town adjoining thereto, and a sub-agent shall have within his district, or within any county of a city or town adjoining thereto, an office or place to which all claims, notices, writs, summonses, and documents may be sent, and the address of such office or place shall be declared at the same time as the appointment of the said agent to the returning officer, and shall be stated in the public notice of the name of the agent.*

(2.) *Any claim, notice, writ, summons, or document delivered at such office or place and addressed to the election agent or sub-agent as the case may be, shall be deemed to have been served on him, and every such agent may in respect of any matter connected with the election in which he is acting be sued in any Court having jurisdiction in the county or borough in which the said office or place is situate.*

Sect. 27.—(1.) *The election agent of a candidate by himself or by his sub-agent shall appoint every polling agent, clerk, and messenger employed for payment on behalf of the candidate at an election, and hire every committee room hired on behalf of the candidate.*

(2.) *A contract whereby any expenses are incurred on account of or in respect of the conduct or management of an election shall not be enforceable against a candidate at such election unless made by the candidate himself or by his election agent, either by himself or by his sub-agent; provided that the inability under this section to enforce such contract against the candidate shall not relieve the candidate from the consequences of any corrupt or illegal practice having been committed by his agent.*

Sect. 28.—(1.) *Except as permitted by or in pursuance of this Act, no payment and advance or deposit shall be made by a candidate at an election or by any agent on behalf of the candidate or by any other person at any time, whether before, during, or after such election, in respect of any expenses incurred on account of or in respect of the conduct or management of such election, otherwise than by or through the election agent of the candidate, whether acting in person or by a sub-agent; and all money provided by any person other than the candidate for any expenses incurred on account of or in respect of the conduct or management of the election, whether as gift, loan, or advance, or deposit, shall be paid to the candidate or his election agent and not otherwise: Provided that this section shall not be deemed to apply to a tender of security to or any payment by the returning officer or to any sum disbursed by any person out of his own money for any small expense legally incurred by himself, if such sum is not repaid to him.*

I. PARLIAMENT—ELECTION—*continued.*

(2.) *A person who makes any payment, advance, or deposit in contravention of this section, or pays in contravention of this section any money so provided as aforesaid, shall be guilty of an illegal practice.*

Sect. 29.—(1.) *Every payment made by an election agent, whether by himself or a sub-agent, in respect of any expenses incurred on account of or in respect of the conduct or management of an election, shall except where less than forty shillings be vouched for by a bill stating the particulars and by a receipt.*

(2.) *Every claim against a candidate at an election, or his election agent in respect of any expenses incurred on account of or in respect of the conduct or management of such election which is not sent in to the election agent within the time limited by this Act shall be barred and shall not be paid; and subject to such exception as may be allowed in pursuance of this Act, an election agent who pays a claim in contravention of this enactment shall be guilty of an illegal practice.*

(3.) *Except as by this Act permitted, the time limited by this Act for sending in claims shall be fourteen days after the day on which the candidates returned are declared elected.*

(4.) *All expenses incurred by or on behalf of a candidate at an election, which are incurred on account of or in respect of the conduct or management of such election, shall be paid within the time limited by this Act and not otherwise, and subject to such exception as may be allowed in pursuance of this Act, an election agent who makes a payment in contravention of this provision shall be guilty of an illegal practice.*

(5.) *Except as by this Act permitted, the time limited by this Act for the payment of such expenses as aforesaid shall be twenty-eight days after the day on which the candidates returned are declared elected.*

(6.) *Where the Election Court reports that it has been proved to such Court by a candidate that any payment made by an election agent in contravention of this section was made without the sanction or connivance of such candidate, the election of such candidate shall not be void, nor shall he be subject to any incapacity under this Act by reason only of such payment having been made in contravention of this section.*

(7.) *If the election agent in the case of any claim sent in to him within the time limited by this Act disputes it, or refuses or fails to pay it within the said period of twenty-eight days, such claim shall be deemed to be a disputed claim.*

(8.) *The claimant may, if he thinks fit, bring an action for a disputed claim in any competent Court; and any sum paid by the candidate or his agent in pursuance of the judgment or order of such Court shall be deemed to be paid within the time limited by this Act, and to be an exception from the provisions of this Act requiring claims to be paid by the election agent.*

(9.) *On cause shewn to the satisfaction of the High Court, such Court on application by the claimant or by the candidate or his election agent may by order give leave for the payment by a candidate or his election agent of a disputed claim, or of a claim for any such expenses as aforesaid, although sent in after the time in this section*

I. PARLIAMENT—ELECTION—*continued.*

mentioned for sending in claims, or although the same was sent in to the candidate and not to the election agent.

(10.) *Any sum specified in the order of leave may be paid by the candidate or his election agent, and when paid in pursuance of such leave shall be deemed to be paid within the time limited by this Act.*

Sect. 30. *If any action is brought in any competent Court to recover a disputed claim against a candidate at an election, or his election agent, in respect of any expenses incurred on account or in respect of the conduct or management of such election, and the defendant admits his liability, but disputes the amount of the claim, the said amount shall, unless the Court, on the application of the plaintiff in the action, otherwise directs, be forthwith referred for taxation to the master, official referee, registrar, or other proper officer of the Court, and the amount found due on such taxation shall be the amount to be recovered in such action in respect of such claim.*

Sect. 31.—(1.) *The candidate at an election may pay any personal expenses incurred by him on account of or in connexion with or incidental to such election to an amount not exceeding one hundred pounds, but any further personal expenses so incurred by him shall be paid by his election agent.*

(2.) *The candidate shall send to the election agent within the time limited by this Act for sending in claims a written statement of the amount of personal expenses paid as aforesaid by such candidate.*

(3.) *Any person may, if so authorized in writing by the election agent of the candidate, pay any necessary expenses for stationery, postage, telegrams, and other petty expenses, to a total amount not exceeding that named in the authority, but any excess above the total amount so named shall be paid by the election agent.*

(4.) *A statement of the particulars of payments made by any person so authorized shall be sent to the election agent within the time limited by this Act for the sending in of claims, and shall be vouched for by a bill containing the receipt of that person.*

Sect. 32.—(1.) *So far as circumstances admit, this Act shall apply to a claim for his remuneration by an election agent and to the payment thereof in like manner as if he were any other creditor, and if any difference arises respecting the amount of such claim the claim shall be a disputed claim within the meaning of this Act, and be dealt with accordingly.*

(2.) *The account of the charges claimed by the returning officer in the case of a candidate and transmitted in pursuance of sect.* 4 *of the Parliamentary Elections (Returning Officers) Act,* 1875, *shall be transmitted within the time specified in the said section to the election agent of the candidate. and need not be transmitted to the candidate.*

Sect. 33.—(1.) *Within thirty-five days after the day on which the candidates returned at an election are declared elected, the election agent of every candidate at that election shall transmit to the returning officer a true return (in this Act referred to as a return respecting election expenses), in the form set forth in the Second Schedule to this Act or*

I. PARLIAMENT—ELECTION—*continued.*

to the like effect, containing, as respects that candidate,—

(a.) *A statement of all payments made by the election agent, together with all the bills and receipts (which bills and receipts are in this Act included in the expression " return respecting election expenses");*

(b.) *A statement of the amount of personal expenses, if any, paid by the candidate :*

(c.) *A statement of the sums paid to the returning officer for his charges, or, if the amount is in dispute, of the sum claimed and the amount disputed ;*

(d.) *A statement of all other disputed claims of which the election agent is aware ;*

(e.) *A statement of all the unpaid claims, if any, of which the election agent is aware, in respect of which application has been or is about to be made to the High Court :*

(f.) *A statement of all money, securities, and equivalent of money received by the election agent from the candidate or any other person for the purpose of expenses incurred or to be incurred on account of or in respect of the conduct or management of the election, with a statement of the name of every person from whom the same may have been received.*

(2.) *The return so transmitted to the returning officer shall be accompanied by a declaration made by the election agent before a justice of the peace in the form in the Second Schedule to this Act (which declaration is in this Act referred to as a declaration respecting election expenses).*

(3.) *Where the candidate has named himself as his election agent, a statement of all money, securities, and equivalent of money paid by the candidate shall be substituted in the return required by this section to be transmitted by the election agent for the like statement of money, securities, and equivalent of money received by the election agent from the candidate ; and the declaration by an election agent respecting election expenses shall be modified as specified in the Second Schedule to this Act.*

(4.) *At the same time that the agent transmits the said return, or within seven days afterwards, the candidate shall transmit or cause to be transmitted to the returning officer a declaration made by him before a justice of the peace, in the form in the first part of the Second Schedule to this Act (which declaration is in this Act referred to as a declaration respecting election expenses).*

(5.) *If in the case of an election for any county or borough the said return and declarations are not transmitted before the expiration of the time limited for the purpose, the candidate shall not after the expiration of such time sit or vote in the House of Commons as member for that county or borough until either such return and declarations have been transmitted, or until the date of the allowance of such an authorized excuse for the failure to transmit the same, as in this Act mentioned, and if he sits and votes in contravention of this enactment he shall forfeit £100 for every day on which he so sits or votes to any person who sues for the same.*

(6.) *If without such authorized excuse as in this Act mentioned, a candidate or an election agent*

I. PARLIAMENT—ELECTION—continued.

fails to comply with the requirements of this section, he shall be guilty of an illegal practice.

(7.) *If any candidate or election agent knowingly makes the· declaration required by this section falsely, he shall be guilty of an offence, and on conviction thereof on indictment shall be liable to the punishment for wilful and·corrupt perjury; such offence shall also be deemed to be a corrupt practice within the meaning of this Act.*

(8.) *Where the candidate is out of· the·United Kingdom at· the time when·the return is so transmitted to the returning ·officer, the declaration required by this section may be made by him within fourteen days after his return to the United Kingdom, and in that case shall be forthwith transmitted to the returning officer, but the delay hereby authorized in making such declaration shall not. exonerate the election agent from complying with the provisions of this Act as to the return and declaration respecting election expenses.*

(9.) *Where, after the date at which the return respecting election expenses is transmitted, leave is given by the High Court for any claims to be paid, the candidate or his election agent shall, within seven days after the payment thereof, transmit to the returning officer a return of the sums paid in pursuance of such·leave accompanied by·a copy of the order of the Court giving the leave, and in default he shall be deemed to have failed to comply with the requirements of this section without such authorized excuse as in this Act mentioned.*

Sect. 34.—(1.) *Where the return and declarations respecting election expenses of a candidate at an election for a county or borough have not been transmitted as required by this .Act, or being transmitted contain some error or false statement, then—*

(a.) *If the candidate applies to the High Court or an Election Court and shews that the failure to transmit such return and declarations, or any of them, or any part thereof, or any error or false statement therein, has arisen by reason of his illness, or of. the absence, death, illness, or misconduct of his election agent or sub-agent, or of any clerk or officer of such agent, or by reason of inadvertence or of any reasonable cause of a like nature, and not by reason of any want of good faith on the part of the applicant, or*

(b.) *If the election agent of the candidate applies to the High Court or an Election Court and shews that the failure to transmit the return and declarations which he was required to transmit, or any part thereof, or any error or false statement therein, arose by reason of. his illness or of the death or illness of any prior election agent of the candidate, or of the absence, death, illness, or misconduct of any sub-agent, clerk, or officer of an election agent of the candidate, or by reason of inadvertence or of any reasonable cause of a like nature, and not by reason of any want of good faith on the part of the applicant,*

the Court may, after such notice of the application in the said county or borough, and on production of such evidence of the grounds stated in the application, and of the good faith of the applica-

I. PARLIAMENT—ELECTION—continued.· ···

tion, and otherwise, as to the Court seems fit, make such order for allowing an authorized excuse for the failure to transmit such return and declaration, or for an error or ·false statement in such return and declaration, as to the Court seems just. ·

(2.) *Where it appears to the Court that any person being or having been ·election agent or sub-agent has refused or failed to make such return or to supply such particulars as will enable the candidate and his election agent respectively to comply with the provisions of this Act as to the return and declaration respecting election expenses, the Court before making an order allowing the excuse as in this section mentioned shall order such person to attend before the Court, and on his attendance shall, unless he shews cause to the contrary, order him to make the return and declaration, or to deliver a statement of the particulars required to be contained in the return, as to the Court seems just, and to make or deliver the same within such time and to such person and in such manner as the Court may direct, or may order him to be examined with respect to such particulars, and may in default of compliance with any such order order him to pay a fine not exceeding £500.*

(3.) *The order may make the allowance conditional upon the making of the return and declaration in a modified form or·within an extended time, and upon the compliance with such other terms as to the Court seem best calculated for carrying into effect the objects of this Act; and an order allowing an authorized excuse shall relieve the applicant for the order from any liability or consequences under this Act in respect of the matter excused by the order; and where it is proved by the candidate to the Court that any act or omission of the election agent in relation to the return and declaration respecting election expenses was without the sanction or connivance of the candidate, and that the candidate took all reasonable means for preventing such act or omission, the Court shall relieve the candidate from the consequences of such act or omission on the part of his election agent.*

(4.) *The date of the order, or if conditions and terms are to be complied with, the date at which the applicant fully complied with them, is referred to in this Act as the date of the allowance of the excuse.*

Sect. 35.—(1.) *The returning officer at an election within ten days after he receives from the election agent of a candidate a return respecting election expenses shall publish a summary of the return in not less than two newspapers circulating in the county or borough for which the election was held. accompanied by a notice of the time and place at which the return and declarations (including the accompanying documents) can be inspected, and may charge the candidate in respect of such publication, and the amount of such charge shall be the sum allowed by the Parliamentary Elections (Returning Officers) Act, 1875.*

(2.) *The return and declarations (including the accompanying documents) sent to the returning officer by an election agent shall be kept at the office of the returning officer, or some convenient place appointed by him, and shall at all reasonable times during two years next after they are received by the returning officer be open to inspection by any person on payment of a fee of one shilling, and the return-*

I. PARLIAMENT—ELECTION—continued.

ing officer, shall on demand furnish copies thereof or any part thereof at the price of twopence for every seventy-two words. After the expiration of the said two years the returning officer may cause the said return and declarations (including the accompanying documents) to be destroyed, or, if the candidate or his election agent so require, shall return the same to the candidate.

Polling Places.] Sect. 47.—(1.) Every county shall be divided into polling districts, and a polling place shall be assigned to each district in such manner that, so far as is reasonably practicable, every elector resident in the county shall have his polling place within a distance not exceeding three miles from his residence, so nevertheless that a polling district need not in any case be constituted containing less than one hundred electors.

(2.) In every county the local authority who have power to divide that county into polling districts shall from time to time divide the county into polling districts, and assign polling places to those districts, and alter those districts and polling places in such manner as may be necessary for the purpose of carrying into effect this section.

(3.) The power of dividing a borough into polling districts vested in a local authority by the Representation of the People Act, 1867, and the enactments amending the same, may be exercised by such local authority from time to time, and as often as the authority think fit, and the said power shall be deemed to include the power of altering any polling district, and the said local authority shall from time to time, where necessary for the purpose of carrying this section into effect, divide the borough into polling districts in such manner that—

(a.) Every elector resident in the borough, if other than one hereinafter mentioned, shall be enabled to poll within a distance not exceeding one mile from his residence, so nevertheless that a polling district need not be constituted containing less than 300 electors; and

(b.) Every elector resident in the boroughs of East Retford, Shoreham, Cricklade, Much Wenlock, and Aylesbury, shall be enabled to poll within a distance not exceeding three miles from his residence, so nevertheless that a polling district need not be constituted containing less than 100 electors.

(4.) So much of sect. 5 of the Ballot Act, 1872, and the enactments amending the same as is in force and is not repealed by this Act, shall apply as if the same were incorporated in this section.

(5.) The expenses incurred by the local authority of a county or borough under this or any other Act in dividing their county or borough into polling districts, and, in the case of a county, assigning polling places to such districts, and in altering any such districts or polling places, shall be defrayed in like manner as if they were expenses incurred by the registration officer in the execution of the enactments respecting the registration of electors in such county or borough, and those enactments, so far as is consistent with the tenor thereof, shall apply accordingly.

Sect. 48. Where the nature of a county is such that any electors residing therein are unable at an election for such county to reach their polling place

I. PARLIAMENT—ELECTION—continued.

without crossing the sea, or a branch or arm thereof, this Act shall not prevent the provision of means for conveying such electors by sea to their polling place, and the amount of payment for such means of conveyance may be in addition to the maximum amount of expenses allowed by this Act.

Sect. 49. Notwithstanding the provisions of the Act 15 & 16 Vict. c. 57, or any amendment thereof, in any case where, after the passing of this Act, any Commissioners have been appointed, on a joint address of both Houses of Parliament, for the purpose of making inquiry into the existence of corrupt practices in any election, the said Commissioners shall not make any inquiries concerning any election that shall have taken place prior to the passing of this Act, and no witness called before such Commissioners, or at any election petition after the passing of this Act, shall be liable to be asked or bound to answer any question for the purpose of proving the commission of any corrupt practice at or in relation to any election prior to the passing of this Act: Provided that nothing herein contained shall affect any proceedings that shall be pending at the time of such passing.

Procedure, &c.] Sect. 45. Where information is given to the Director of Public Prosecutions that any corrupt or illegal practices have prevailed in reference to any election, it shall be his duty, subject to the regulations under the Prosecution of Offences Act, 1879, to make such inquiries and institute such prosecutions as the circumstances of the case appear to him to require.

Sect. 46. Where a person has, either before or after the commencement of this Act, become subject to any incapacity under the Corrupt Practices Prevention Acts or this Act by reason of a conviction or of a report of any Election Court or Election Commissioners, and any witness who gave evidence against such incapacitated person upon the proceeding for such conviction or report is convicted of perjury in respect of that evidence, the incapacitated person may apply to the High Court, and the Court, if satisfied that the conviction or report so far as respects such person was based upon perjury, may order that such incapacity shall thenceforth cease, and the same shall cease accordingly.

Sect. 50. Where an indictment as defined by this Act for any offence under the Corrupt Practices Prevention Acts or this Act is instituted in the High Court or is removed into the High Court by a writ of certiorari issued at the instance of the Attorney-General, and the Attorney-General suggests on the part of the Crown that it is expedient for the purposes of justice that the indictment should be tried in the Central Criminal Court, or if a special jury is ordered, that it should be tried before a Judge and jury at the Royal Courts of Justice, the High Court may, if it thinks fit, order that such indictment shall be so tried upon such terms as the Court may think just, and the High Court may make such orders as appear to the Court necessary or proper for carrying into effect the order for such trial.

Sect. 51.—(1.) A proceeding against a person in respect of the offence of a corrupt or illegal practice or any other offence under the Corrupt Practices Prevention Acts or this Act shall be commenced within one year after the offence was committed, or if it was committed in reference to an election with

I. PARLIAMENT—ELECTION—*continued.*

respect to which an inquiry is held by Election Commissioners shall be commenced within one year after the offence was committed, or within three months after the report of such commissioners is made, whichever period last expires, so that it be commenced within two years after the offence was committed, and the time so limited by this section shall, in the case of any proceeding under the Summary Jurisdiction Acts for any such offence, whether before an Election Court or otherwise, be substituted for any limitation of time contained in the last-mentioned Acts.

(2.) For the purposes of this section the issue of a summons, warrant, writ, or other process shall be deemed to be a commencement of a proceeding, where the service or execution of the same on or against the alleged offender is prevented by the absconding or concealment or act of the alleged offender, but save as aforesaid the service or execution of the same on or against the alleged offender, and not the issue thereof, shall be deemed to be the commencement of the proceeding.

Sect. 52. *Any person charged with a corrupt practice may, if the circumstances warrant such finding, be found guilty of an illegal practice (which offence shall for that purpose be an indictable offence), and any person charged with an illegal practice may be found guilty of that offence, notwithstanding that the act constituting the offence amounted to a corrupt practice, and a person charged with illegal payment, employment, or hiring, may be found guilty of that offence, notwithstanding that the act constituting the offence amounted to a corrupt or illegal practice.*

Sect. 53.—(1.) *Sects.* 10, 12, *and* 13 *of the Corrupt Practices Prevention Act,* 1854, *and sect.* 6 *of the Corrupt Practices Prevention Act,* 1863 *(which relate to prosecutions for bribery and other offences under those Acts), shall extend to any prosecution on indictment for the offence of any corrupt practice within the meaning of this Act, and to any action for any pecuniary forfeiture for an offence under this Act, in like manner as if such offence were bribery, within the meaning of those Acts, and such indictment or action were the indictment or action in those sections mentioned, and an order under the said sect.* 10 *may be made on the defendant; but the Director of Public Prosecutions or any person instituting any prosecution in his behalf or by direction of an Election Court shall not be deemed to be a private prosecutor, nor required under the said sections to give any security.*

(2.) On any prosecution under this Act, whether on indictment or summarily, and whether before an Election Court or otherwise, and in any action for a pecuniary forfeiture under this Act, the person prosecuted or sued, and the husband or wife of such person, may, if he or she think fit, be examined as an ordinary witness in the case.

(3.) On any such prosecution or action as aforesaid it shall be sufficient to allege that the person charged was guilty of an illegal practice, payment, employment, or hiring within the meaning of this Act, as the case may be, and the certificate of the returning officer at an election that the election mentioned in the certificate was duly held, and that the person named in the certificate was a candidate at such election, shall be sufficient evidence of the facts therein stated.

I. PARLIAMENT—ELECTION—*continued.*

Sect. 54.—(1.) *All offences under this Act punishable on summary conviction may be prosecuted in manner provided by the Summary Jurisdiction Acts.*

(2.) A person aggrieved by a conviction by a Court of summary jurisdiction for an offence under this Act may appeal in general or quarter sessions against such conviction.

Sect. 55.—(1.) *Except that nothing in this Act shall authorize any appeal against a summary conviction by an Election Court, the Summary Jurisdiction Acts shall, so far as is consistent with the tenor thereof, apply to the prosecution of an offence summarily before an Election Court, in like manner as if it were an offence punishable only on summary conviction, and accordingly the attendance of any person may be enforced, the case heard and determined and any summary conviction by such Court be carried into effect and enforced, and the costs thereof paid, and the record thereof dealt with under those Acts in like manner as if the Court were a petty sessional Court for the county or place in which such conviction took place.*

(2.) The enactments relating to charges before justices against persons for indictable offences shall, so far as is consistent with the tenor thereof, apply to every case where an Election Court orders a person to be prosecuted on indictment in like manner as if the Court were a justice of the peace.

Sect. 56.—(1.) *Subject to any Rules of Court, any jurisdiction vested by this Act in the High Court may, so far as it relates to indictments or other criminal proceedings, be exercised by any Judge of the Queen's Bench Division, and in other respects may either be exercised by one of the Judges for the time being on the rota for the trial of the election petitions sitting either in Court or at chambers, or may be exercised by a Master of the Supreme Court of Judicature in manner directed by and subject to an appeal to the said Judges;*

Provided that a Master shall not exercise jurisdiction in the case either of an order declaring any act or omission to be an exemption from the provisions of this Act with respect to illegal practices, payments, employments, or hirings, or of an order allowing an excuse in relation to a return or declaration respecting election expenses.

(2.) Rules of Court may from time to time be made, revoked, and altered for the purposes of this Act, and of the Parliamentary Elections Act, 1868, *and the Acts amending the same, by the same authority by whom Rules of Court for procedure and practice in the Supreme Court of Judicature can for the time being be made.*

Sect. 57.—(1.) *The Director of Public Prosecutions in performing any duty under this Act shall act in accordance with the regulations under the Prosecutions of Offences Act,* 1879, *and subject thereto in accordance with the directions (if any) given to him by the Attorney-General; and any assistant or representative of the Director of Public Prosecutions in performing any duty under this Act shall act in accordance with the said regulations and directions, if any, and with the directions given to him by the Director of Public Prosecutions.*

(2.) Subject to the provisions of this Act, the costs of any prosecution or indictment for an offence punishable under this Act, whether by the

I. PARLIAMENT—ELECTION—*continued.*

Director of Public Prosecutions or his representative or by any other person, shall, so far as they are not paid by the defendant, be paid in like manner as costs in the case of a prosecution for felony are paid.

Sect. 58.—(1.) *Where any costs or other sums (not being costs of a prosecution or indictment) are, under an order of an Election Court, or otherwise under this Act, to be paid by a county or borough, the Commissioners of Her Majesty's Treasury shall pay those costs or sums, and obtain repayment of the amount so paid, in like manner as if such costs and sums were expenses of Election Commissioners paid by them, and the Election Commissioners Expenses Acts, 1869 and 1871, shall apply accordingly as if they were herein re-enacted and in terms made applicable to the above mentioned costs and sums.*

(2.) *Where any costs or other sums are, under the order of an Election Court or otherwise under this Act, to be paid by any person, those costs shall be a simple contract debt due from such person to the person or persons to whom they are to be paid, and if payable to the Commissioners of Her Majesty's Treasury shall be a debt to Her Majesty, and in either case may be recovered accordingly.*

Sect. 59.—(1.) *A person who is called as a witness respecting an election before any Election Court shall not be excused from answering any question relating to any offence at or connected with such election on the ground that the answer thereto may criminate or tend to criminate himself or on the ground of privilege.*

Provided that:—

    (a.) *A witness who answers truly all questions which he is required by the Election Court to answer shall be entitled to receive a certificate of indemnity under the hand of a member of the Court stating that such witness has so answered; and*

    (b.) *An answer by a person to a question put by or before any Election Court shall not, except in the case of any criminal proceeding for perjury in respect of such evidence, be in any proceeding, civil or criminal, admissible in evidence against him.*

(2.) *Where a person has received such a certificate of indemnity in relation to, an election, and any legal proceeding is at any time instituted against him for any offence under the Corrupt Practices Prevention Acts or this Act committed by him previously to the date of the certificate at or in relation to the said election, the Court having cognizance of the case shall on proof of the certificate stay the proceeding, and may in their discretion award to the said person such costs as he may have been put to in the proceeding.*

(3.) *Nothing in this section shall be taken to relieve a person receiving a certificate of indemnity from any incapacity under this Act or from any proceeding to enforce such incapacity (other than a criminal prosecution).*

(4.) *This section shall apply in the case of a witness before any Election Commissioners, in like manner as if the expression "Election Court" in this section included Election Commissioners.*

(5.) *Where a solicitor or person lawfully acting as agent for any party to an election petition respecting any election for a county or borough has not taken any part or been concerned in such*

I. PARLIAMENT—ELECTION—*continued.*

election, the Election Commissioners inquiring into such election shall not be entitled to examine such solicitor or agent respecting matters which came to his knowledge by reason only of his being concerned as solicitor or agent for a party to such petition.

Sect. 60. *An Election Court or Election Commissioners, when reporting that certain persons have been guilty of any corrupt or illegal practice, shall report whether those persons have or have not been furnished with certificates of indemnity; and such report shall be laid before the Attorney-General (accompanied in the case of the Commissioners with the evidence on which such report was based) with a view to his instituting or directing a prosecution against such persons as have not received certificates of indemnity, if the evidence should, in his opinion, be sufficient to support a prosecution.*

Sect. 61.—(1.) *Sect.* 11 *of the Ballot Act,* 1872, *shall apply to a returning officer or presiding officer or clerk who is guilty of any wilful misfeasance or wilful act or omission in contravention of this Act in like manner as if the same were in contravention of the Ballot Act,* 1872.

(2.) *Sect.* 97 *of the Parliamentary Registration Act,* 1843, *shall apply to every registration officer who is guilty of any wilful misfeasance or wilful act of commission or omission contrary to this Act in like manner as if the same were contrary to the Parliamentary Registration Act,* 1843.

Sect. 62.—(1.) *Any public notice required to be given by the returning officer under this Act shall be given in the manner in which he is directed by the Ballot Act,* 1872, *to give a public notice.*

(2.) *Where any summons, notice, or document is required to be served on any person with reference to any proceeding respecting an election for a county or borough, whether for the purpose of causing him to appear before the High Court or any Election Court, or Election Commissioners, or otherwise, or for the purpose of giving him an opportunity of making a statement, or shewing cause, or being heard by himself, before any Court or Commissioners, for any purpose of this Act, such summons, notice, or document may be served either by delivering the same to such person, or by leaving the same at, or sending the same by post by a registered letter to, his last known place of abode in the said county or borough, or if the proceeding is before any Court or Commissioners, in such other manner as the Court or Commissioners may direct, and in proving such service by post it shall be sufficient to prove that the letter was prepaid, properly addressed, and registered with the post office.*

(3.) *In the form of notice of a parliamentary election set forth in the Second Schedule to the Ballot Act,* 1872, *the words "or any illegal practice" shall be inserted after the words "or other corrupt practices," and the words the "Corrupt and Illegal Practices Prevention Act,* 1883," *shall be inserted after the words "Corrupt Practices Prevention Act,* 1854."

Continuance.] *The Act* 48 & 49 *Vict. c.* 59, *continues the* 46 & 47 *Vict. c.* 51, *until the* 31st *of December,* 1886.

Repeal.] *The Acts* 41 & 42 *Vict. c.* 4 *(Parliamentary Elections Metropolis Act,* 1878), *and* 47 & 48 *Vict. v.* 34 *(Elections Hours of Poll Act,* 1884), *were repealed on the* 18th *of November,* 1885, *by virtue of the* 48 & 49 *Vict. c.* 10.

I. PARLIAMENT—ELECTION—*continued.*

Hours of Poll.] *The Act* 48 & 49 *Vict ʼc.* 10 (*the Elections Hours of Poll Act*, 1885) *directs that at every parliamentary or municipal election the poll shall commence at* 8 *a.m., and be kept open till* 8 *p.m. of the same day and no longer. It does not apply to any university.*

Leave of Absence.] *The Act* 48 & 49 *Vict. c.* 56, *declares the conditions on which an employer may give leave of absence to employés to record their votes at a parliamentary election.*

1. —— Expenses—*Payment of Canvassers by Sub-Agent—*26 & 27 *Vict. c.* 29, *s.* 2.] It is unlawful for any election agent or sub-agent, except the expense agent, to make payments on behalf of the candidate even for current disbursements, and such payments cannot be recovered from the candidate.—An election sub-agent, who was a solicitor, employed canvassers for the work of the election, and paid them out of his own moneys. The expense agent having disallowed these payments the sub-agent brought an action against the candidate in the district registry for the money expended. The candidate obtained the common order to tax the Plaintiff's account as a solicitor's bill of costs, and then obtained an order to stay further proceedings in the action pending the taxation. On the taxation the candidate objected to the payments as illegal under the 2nd section of the Corrupt Practices Act, 1863 (26 & 27 Vict. c. 29):—*Held* (affirming the decision of Chitty, J.), that the payments were illegal; that although the sub-agent had an implied authority to employ canvassers, he had no implied authority to pay them, and therefore he could not recover the amount expended from the candidate: *Held*, also, that the candidate could take the objection of illegality on the taxation of the bill of costs.—Whether the order to stay proceedings in the action pending the taxation was regular, *quære. In re* PARKER -   **21 Ch. D. 408**

2. —— Oath of Allegiance—*Claim to affirm— Parliamentary Oaths Act*, 1866 (29 & 30 *Vict. c.* 19)—*Promissory Oaths Act*, 1868 (31 & 32 *Vict. c.* 72)—*Evidence Further Amendment Act*, 1869 (32 & 33 *Vict. c.* 68)—*Evidence Amendment Act*, 1870 (33 & 34 *Vict. c.* 49).] The Defendant was sued under the Parliamentary Oaths Act, 1866, for a penalty for sitting and voting in the House of Commons without having made and subscribed the oath appointed by that Act, as amended by the Promissory Oaths Act, 1868, to be taken by members. Sect. 4 of the Act of 1866 provides that "Quakers and every other person for the time being by law permitted to make a solemn affirmation or declaration instead of taking an oath" may, instead of taking and subscribing the oath, make an affirmation in the form given by the Act. The Defendant pleaded that he was a person who by reason of the Evidence Further Amendment Act, 1869, and the Evidence Amendment Act, 1870, was by law permitted to make a solemn affirmation, instead of taking an oath, because an oath would have no binding effect on his conscience, and that he came within the exemption of the Parliamentary Oaths Act, 1866, and that he had duly made an affirmation in conformity with that Act before sitting and voting. On demurrer:—*Held* (by the Court of Appeal, Bram-

I. PARLIAMENT—ELECTION—*continued.*

well, Baggallay, and Lush, L.JJ., affirming the judgment of Mathew, J.), that sect. 4 of the Parliamentary Oaths Act, 1866, exempted only persons having a general right to affirm on all occasions on which otherwise they would take an oath, and that the defence was therefore bad, as the Evidence Further Amendment Act, 1869, and the Evidence Amendment Act, 1870, applied only to persons called to give evidence as witnesses. The Plaintiff replied that the Defendant was a person who, by want of religious belief, was not entitled by the Parliamentary Oaths Act, 1866, or the Promissory Oaths Act, 1868, to make and subscribe a solemn affirmation. On demurrer: —*Held* (by Mathew, J.), that the reply was bad, as the statute contains contains no proviso that none but persons of religious belief were or could be entitled to the benefit of the exemption in sect. 4 from taking the oath. CLARKE *v.* BRADLAUGH   -   -   **7 Q. B. D. 38** [Reversed on another point -   **8 App. Cas. 354**] *See* PENAL ACTION. 2,

3. —— Oath of Allegiance—*Disbelief in a Supreme Being — Oath not binding upon the Person taking it as an Oath, but only as a Solemn Promise — Penalty — Parliamentary Oaths Act*, 1866 (29 & 30 *Vict. c.* 19), *ss.* 3, 5—"*Solemnly and publicly made and subscribed*"—*Promissory Oaths Act*, 1868 (31 & 32 *Vict. c.* 72)—*Evidence— Journals of House of Commons—Practice of House of Commons—Practice—Appeal—Information by Attorney General to recover Penalty—*"*Criminal Cause or Matter*"—*Trial at Bar—Motion for New Trial on Ground of Misdirection and Misreception of Evidence—Notice of Motion—Supreme Court of Judicature Act*, 1873 (36 & 37 *Vict. c.* 66), *ss.* 19, 47.] A member of parliament, who does not believe in the existence of a Supreme Being, and upon whom an oath has no binding effect as an oath but .only as a solemn promise, is, owing to his want of religious belief, incapable by law of "making and subscribing" the oath of allegiance appointed by the Parliamentary Oaths Act, 1866, ss. 1, 3, as amended by the Promissory Oaths Act, 1868; and if he takes his seat and votes as a member, although he has gone through the form of making and subscribing the oath appointed by those statutes, he will be liable upon an information at the suit of the Attorney General to the penalty imposed by the Parliamentary Oaths Act, 1866, s. 5.—*Omichund* v. *Barker* (1 Atkyns, 21 ; Willes, 538) followed and applied.—In order that the oath of allegiance imposed upon members of the House of Commons upon taking their seats by the Parliamentary Oaths Act, 1866, as amended by the Promissory Oaths Act, 1868, may be "solemnly and publicly made and subscribed" within the meaning of sect. 3 of the former statute. it must be taken by a member with the assent of the House according to the requirements of the Standing Orders, and after he has been called upon by the Speaker to be sworn.—Upon the trial of an information at the suit of the Attorney General against a member of the House of Commons for voting without having taken the oath of allegiance within the meaning of the Parliamentary Oaths Act, 1866, as amended by the Promissory Oaths Act, 1868, evidence of the practice

I. PARLIAMENT—ELECTION—continued.

observed in the House of Commons as to taking the oath of allegiance is admissible for the purpose of explaining the construction of those statutes, and the journals of the House of Commons are admissible as evidence for the purpose of shewing, from the member's conduct as therein recorded, that owing to his want of religious belief he is by law incapable of taking an oath.—By Brett, M.R., and Lindley, L.J., Cotton, L.J., doubting, an information at the suit of the Attorney General to recover penalties under sect. 5 of the Parliamentary Oaths Act, 1866, from a member of Parliament for voting without having taken the oath of allegiance required by that statute, as amended by the Promissory Oaths Act, 1868, is not a "criminal cause or matter" within the meaning of the Supreme Court of Judicature Act, s. 47, and an appeal may be brought from any order or judgment therein of the High Court to the Court of Appeal:—By Brett, M.R., on the ground that the information is in its nature a civil proceeding, and, therefore, that an appeal lies under the Supreme Court of Judicature Act, 1873, s. 19:—By Lindley, L.J., on the ground that even although the information may be to some extent of a criminal nature, nevertheless before the passing of the Supreme Court of Judicature Acts, 1873, 1875, an appeal would have lain under the Crown Suits Act, 1865 (28 & 29 Vict. c. 104), ss. 31, 34, 35, from a decision of the Court of Exchequer to the Court of Exchequer Chamber, and that the Supreme Court of Judicature Acts, 1873, 1875, do not take away any right of appeal existing before the passing of those statutes.—Semble, by Brett, M.R., that even if the information could be regarded as a criminal proceeding, nevertheless an appeal would lie, for by the Supreme Court of Judicature Act, 1873, s. 47, the right of appeal is taken away only in the case of indictments, of criminal informations for indictable misdemeanors filed in the Queen's Bench Division, and of criminal proceedings before justices. An appeal lies to the Court of Appeal from any order or judgment made or given by the Queen's Bench Division either during, or afterwards with respect to, a trial at bar of a civil proceeding, and whether or not the appeal is brought from a decision upon a motion for a new trial on the ground of misdirection or wrongful reception of evidence; but the appeal must be brought on by notice of motion, an ex parte application for a rule nisi to the Court of Appeal being irregular. THE ATTORNEY GENERAL v. BRADLAUGH - 14 Q. B. D. 667

II. PARLIAMENT — ELECTION COMMISSIONERS.

The Act 48 & 49 Vict. c. 59, continues 32 & 33 Vict. c. 21, the Corrupt Practices Commission Expenses Act, 1869, as amended by 34 & 35 Vict. c. 61, until the 31st of December, 1886.

1. —— Certificate to Witness—Mandamus—Jurisdiction to hear Appeal—Supreme Court of Judicature Act, 1873, s. 47—Criminal Matter—Corrupt Practices Prevention Act (26 & 27 Vict. c. 29), s. 7.] Where the Commissioners appointed to inquire into corrupt practices at a parliamentary election have, with reference to a witness before them on such inquiry, exercised their judgment as to the right of such witness to receive

II. PARLIAMENT — ELECTION COMMISSIONERS—continued.

their certificate under sect. 7 of the Corrupt Practices Prevention Act (26 & 27 Vict. c. 29), their decision refusing such certificate is conclusive, and cannot be reviewed by mandamus.—Reg. v. Price (Law Rep. 6 Q. B. 411) dissented from. —The decision of a Divisional Court discharging a rule for a mandamus to such Commissioners to grant such certificate, which certificate if given would be a protection to the witness against criminal proceedings for bribery, does not relate to a criminal cause or matter, within the meaning of the Supreme Court of Judicature Act, 1873, s. 47, and the Court of Appeal is not therefore deprived of jurisdiction to hear an appeal against such decision. THE QUEEN v. HOLL
[7 Q. B. D. 575

III. PARLIAMENT—ELECTION PETITION.

The Act 46 & 47 Vict. c. 51 (Corrupt and Illegal Practices Prevention Act, 1883), which continues in force by virtue of the 48 & 49 Vict. c. 59, until the 31st of December, 1886), enacts:

Sect. 40.—(1.) Where an election petition questions the return or the election upon an allegation of an illegal practice, then notwithstanding anything in the Parliamentary Elections Act, 1868, such petition, so far as respects such illegal practice, may be presented within the time following; (that is to say,)

  (a.) At any time before the expiration of fourteen days after the day on which the returning officer receives the return and declarations respecting election expenses by the member to whose election the petition relates or his election agent.

  (b.) If the election petition specifically alleges a payment of money, or some other act to have been made or done since the said day by the member, or an agent of the member, or with the privity of the member or his election agent in pursuance or in further-ance of the illegal practice alleged in the petition, the petition may be presented at any time within twenty-eight days after the date of such payment or other act.

(2.) Any election petition presented within the time limited by the Parliamentary Elections Act, 1868, may for the purpose of questioning the return or the election upon an allegation of an illegal practice be amended with the leave of the High Court within the time within which a petition questioning the return upon the allegation of that illegal practice can under this section be presented.

(3.) This section shall apply in the case of an offence relating to the return, and declarations respecting election expenses, in like manner as if it were an illegal practice, and also shall apply notwithstanding that the act constituting the alleged illegal practice amounted to a corrupt practice.

(4.) For the purposes of this section—

  (a.) Where the return and declarations are received on different days, the day on which the last of them is received, and

  (b.) Where there is an authorised excuse for failing to make and transmit the return and declarations respecting election expenses, the date of the allowance of the excuse, or if there was a failure as regards

2 K 2

III. PARLIAMENT — ELECTION PETITION — *continued.*

two or more of them, and the excuse was allowed at different times, the date of the allowance of the last excuse shall be substituted for the day on which the return and declarations are received by the returning officer.

(5.) For the purposes of this section, time shall be reckoned in like manner as it is reckoned for the purposes of the Parliamentary Elections Act, 1868.

Sect. 41.—(1.) Before leave for the withdrawal of an election petition is granted, there shall be produced affidavits by all the parties to the petition, and their solicitors, and by the election agents of all of the said parties who were candidates at the election, but the High Court may on cause shewn dispense with the affidavit of any particular person if it seems to the Court on special grounds to be just so to do.

(2.) Each affidavit shall state that, to the best of the deponent's knowledge and belief, no agreement or terms of any kind whatsoever has or have been made, and no undertaking has been entered into, in relation to the withdrawal of the petition; but if any lawful agreement has been made with respect to the withdrawal of the petition, the affidavit shall set forth that agreement, and shall make the foregoing statement subject to what appears from the affidavit.

(3.) The affidavits of the applicant and his solicitor shall further state the ground on which the petition is sought to be withdrawn.

(4.) If any person makes any agreement or terms, or enters into any undertaking, in relation to the withdrawal of an election petition, and such agreement, terms, or undertaking, is or are for the withdrawal of the election petition in consideration of any payment, or in consideration that the seat shall at any time be vacated, or in consideration of the withdrawal of any other election petition, or is or are (whether lawful or unlawful) not mentioned in the aforesaid affidavits, he shall be guilty of a misdemeanor, and shall be liable on conviction on indictment to imprisonment for a term not exceeding twelve months, and to a fine not exceeding £200.

(5.) Copies of the said affidavit shall be delivered to the Director of Public Prosecutions a reasonable time before the application for the withdrawal is heard, and the Court may hear the Director of Public Prosecutions, or his assistant or other representative (appointed with the approval of the Attorney-General), in opposition to the allowance of the withdrawal of the petition, and shall have power to receive the evidence on oath of any person or persons whose evidence the Director of Public Prosecutions, or his assistant or other representative, may consider material.

(6.) Where in the opinion of the Court the proposed withdrawal of a petition was the result of any agreement, terms, or undertaking prohibited by this section, the Court shall have the same power with respect to the security as under sect. 35 of the Parliamentary Elections Act, 1868, where the withdrawal is induced by a corrupt consideration.

(7.) In every case of the withdrawal of an election petition the Court shall report to the Speaker whether, in the opinion of such Court, the withdrawal of such petition was the result of any agree-

ment, terms, and undertaking, or was in consideration of any payment, or in consideration that the seat should at any time be vacated, or in consideration of the withdrawal of any other election petition, or for any other consideration, and if so, shall state the circumstances attending the withdrawal.

(8.) Where more than one solicitor is concerned for the petitioner or respondent, whether as agent for another solicitor or otherwise, the affidavit shall be made by all such solicitors.

(9.) Where a person not a solicitor is lawfully acting as agent in the case of an election petition, that agent shall be deemed to be a solicitor for the purpose of making an affidavit in pursuance of this section.

Sect. 42. The trial of every election petition so far as is practicable, consistently with the interests of justice in respect of such trial, shall be continued de die in diem on every lawful day until its conclusion, and in case the rota of Judges for the year shall expire before the conclusion of the trial, or of all the proceedings in relation or incidental to the petition, the authority of the said Judges shall continue for the purpose of the said trial and proceedings.

Sect. 43.—(1.) On every trial of an election petition the Director of Public Prosecutions shall by himself or by his assistant, or by such representative as hereinafter mentioned, attend at the trial, and it shall be the duty of such director to obey any directions given to him by the Election Court with respect to the summoning and examination of any witness to give evidence on such trial, and with respect to the prosecution by him of offenders, and with respect to any person to whom notice is given to attend with a view to report him as guilty of any corrupt or illegal practice.

(2.) It shall also be the duty of such Director, without any direction from the Election Court, if it appears to him that any person is able to give material evidence as to the subject of the trial, to cause such person to attend the trial, and with the leave of the Court to examine such person as a witness.

(3.) It shall also be the duty of the said Director, without any direction from the Election Court, if it appears to him that any person who has not received a certificate of indemnity has been guilty of a corrupt or illegal practice, to prosecute such person for the offence before the said Court, or if he thinks it expedient in the interests of justice before any other competent Court.

(4.) Where a person is prosecuted before an Election Court for any corrupt or illegal practice and such person appears before the Court, the Court shall proceed to try him summarily for the said offence, and such person, if convicted thereof upon such trial, shall be subject to the same incapacities as he is rendered subject to under this Act upon conviction, whether on indictment or in any other proceeding for the said offence; and further, may be adjudged by the Court, if the offence is a corrupt practice, to be imprisoned, with or without hard labour, for a term not exceeding six months, or to pay a fine not exceeding £200, and if the offence is an illegal practice, to pay such fine as is fixed by this Act for the offence;

III. PARLIAMENT—ELECTION PETITION—
continued.

Provided that, in the case of a corrupt practice, the Court, before proceeding to try summarily any person, shall give such person the option of being tried by a jury.

(5.) *Where a person is so prosecuted for any such offence, and either he elects to be tried by a jury or he does not appear before the Court, or the Court thinks it in the interests of justice expedient that he should be tried before some other Court, the Court, if of opinion that the evidence is sufficient to put the said person upon his trial for the offence, shall order such person to be prosecuted on indictment or before a Court of summary jurisdiction, as the case may require, for the said offence; and, in either case may order him to be prosecuted before such Court as may be named in the order; and for all purposes preliminary and of and incidental to such prosecution the offence shall be deemed to have been committed within the jurisdiction of the Court so named.*

(6.) *Upon such order being made,*

(a.) *If the accused person is present before the Court, and the offence is an indictable offence, the Court shall commit him to take his trial, or cause him to give bail to appear and take his trial for the said offence; and*

(b.) *If the accused person is present before the Court, and the offence is not an indictable offence, the Court shall order him to be brought before the Court of summary jurisdiction before whom he is to be prosecuted, or cause him to give bail to appear before that Court; and*

(c.) *If the accused person is not present before the Court, the Court shall as circumstances require issue a summons for his attendance, or a warrant to apprehend him and bring him before a Court of summary jurisdiction, and that Court, if the offence is an indictable offence, shall, on proof only of the summons or warrant and the identity of the accused, commit him to take his trial, or cause him to give bail to appear and take his trial for the said offence, or if the offence is punishable on summary conviction, shall proceed to hear the case, or if such Court be not the Court before whom he is directed to be prosecuted, shall order him to be brought before that Court.*

(7.) *The Director of Public Prosecutions may nominate, with the approval of the Attorney-General, a barrister or solicitor of not less than ten years' standing to be his representative for the purpose of this section, and that representative shall receive such remuneration as the Commissioners of Her Majesty's Treasury may approve; there shall be allowed to the Director and his assistant, or representative, for the purposes of this section, such allowance for expenses as the Commissioners of Her Majesty's Treasury may approve.*

(8.) *The costs incurred in defraying the expenses of the Director of Public Prosecutions under this section (including the remuneration of his representative) shall, in the first instance, be paid by the Commissioners of Her Majesty's Treasury, and so far as they are not in the case of any prosecution paid by the defendant shall be deemed to be expenses*

III. PARLIAMENT—ELECTION PETITION—
continued.

of the Election Court; but if for any reasonable cause it seems just to the Court so to do, the Court shall order all or part of the said costs to be repaid to the Commissioners of Her Majesty's Treasury by the parties to the petition, or such of them as the Court may direct.

Sect. 44.—(1.) *Where upon the trial of an election petition respecting an election for a county or borough, it appears to the Election Court that a corrupt practice has not been proved to have been committed in reference to such election by or with the knowledge and consent of the respondent to the petition, and that such respondent took all reasonable means to prevent corrupt practices being committed on his behalf, the Court may make one or more orders with respect to the payment either of the whole or such part of the costs of the petition as the Court may think right as follows :—*

(a.) *If it appears to the Court that corrupt practices extensively prevailed in reference to the said election, the Court may order the whole or part of the costs to be paid by the county and borough; and*

(b.) *If it appears to the Court that any person or persons is or are proved, whether by providing money or otherwise, to have been extensively engaged in corrupt practices, or to have encouraged or promoted extensive corrupt practices in reference to such election, the Court may, after giving such person or persons an opportunity of being heard by counsel or solicitor, and examining and cross-examining witnesses to shew cause why the order should not be made, order the whole or part of the costs to be paid by that person, or those persons, or any of them, and may order that if the costs cannot be recovered from one or more of such persons, they shall be paid by some other of such persons, or by either of the parties to the petition.*

(2.) *Where any person appears to the Court to have been guilty of the offence of a corrupt or illegal practice, the Court may, after giving such person an opportunity of making a statement to shew why the order should not be made, order the whole or any part of the costs of or incidental to any proceeding before the Court in relation to the said offence or to the said person to be paid by the said person.*

(3.) *The rules and regulations of the Supreme Court of Judicature with respect to costs to be allowed in actions, causes, and matters in the High Court, shall, in principle, and so far as is practicable, apply to the costs of petitions and other proceedings under the Parliamentary Elections Act, 1868, and under this Act, and the taxing officer shall not allow any costs, charges, or expenses on a higher scale than would be allowed in any action, cause, or matter, in the High Court on the higher scale, as between solicitor and client.*

[*And see Sects. 45, 46, and 50–62 under* PARLIAMENT—ELECTION.]

1. —— **Inspection and Discovery** — *Parliamentary Elections Act*, 1868 (31 & 32 Vict. c. 125), ss. 2, 26—*Rules of Michaelmas Term*, 1868, r. 44.]
In a parliamentary election petition the Court or

III. PARLIAMENT — ELECTION PETITION — *continued.*

a Judge at Chambers has no jurisdiction to make orders against the sitting member for inspection and discovery of documents. MOORE *v.* KENNARD

[10 Q. B. D. 290

2. —— Witness—*Expenses— Certificate of Registrar—Taxation by Master—31 & 32 Vict. c. 125, ss. 34, 41, and Rules.*] Although the amount of the reasonable expenses to be paid to any witness in an election petition may, under 31 & 32 Vict. c. 125 (the Parliamentary Elections Act, 1868), s. 34, and rule 5, of its Additional General Rules, January, 1875, be ascertained and certified by the registrar, his certificate is not conclusive of the amount as between the Petitioner and Respondent, but it is, as part of the general costs of the petition, subject under sect. 41 to taxation by a master, who must exercise his discretion on the expenses certified. MCLAREN *v.* HOME

[7 Q. B. D. 477

IV. PARLIAMENT—FRANCHISE.

The Act 48 & 49 Vict. c. 3 (the Representation of the People Act, 1884), amends [*the law relating to the representation of the people of the United Kingdom.*

Household and Lodger Franchise.]—*Sect.* 2 *establishes a uniform household franchise, and a uniform lodger franchise in all counties and boroughs throughout the United Kingdom. Every man possessed of either of the above qualifications in a county in England may be registered as a voter for that county.*

Sect. 3. Where a man inhabits a dwelling-house by virtue of any office or employment, and it is not inhabited by any person under whom he serves, he is deemed as a tenant.

Prohibition of Multiplication of Votes.] *Sect. 4 prohibits :—*

(1.) *A man to vote in respect of a rent-charge, except the owner* '*of the whole of the tithe rent-charge of a benefice to which an apportionment of rent-charge shall have been made in respect of a portion of tithes.*

(2.) *More than one of joint tenant or tenants in common to vote for same estate in land. Exceptions for traders, descent, marriage, and some other cases.*

Assimilation of Occupation Qualification.] *Sect. 5. Every man occupying land in a county or borough of a clear yearly value of not less than £10, may vote at elections for such county or borough in respect of such occupation.*

Supplemental Provisions.] *Sect. 6. A voter not to vote for county in respect of occupation of property in a borough.*

Sect. 7. With respect to England :—

(1.) "*Household qualification" means the qualification enacted by sect. 3 of 30 & 31 Vict. c. 102 (Representation of the People Act, 1867.)*

(3.) "*Lodger qualification," means the qualification enacted by sect. 4 of 30 & 31 Vict. c. 102.*

(6.) "*County occupation franchise" means the franchise enacted by sect. 6 of 30 & 31 Vict. c. 102.*

(7.) "*Borough occupation franchise," means the franchise enacted by sect. 27 of 2 & 3 Will. 4, c. 45.*

Sect. 8. Enactments in Registration Acts shall with necessary variations extend to counties.

Sect. 9.—(2.) *Duty of overseers to ascertain*

IV. PARLIAMENT—FRANCHISE—*continued.*

whether any man other than the owner or person rated, is entitled to be registered as a voter in respect of his being an inhabitant occupier.

(8.) *Where a man inhabits a dwelling-house by virtue of office or employment and is deemed to be an inhabitant occupier of such dwelling-house as a tenant, and another person is rated, the rating of the other person shall be deemed to be that of the inhabitant occupier. So much of the 32 & 33 Vict. c. 41 and 41 & 42 Vict. c. 26, and 42 & 43 Vict. c. 10 as is mentioned in the first Schedule to this Act shall apply to such inhabitant occupier, and in construing such enactments the word " owner " shall include a person rated as aforesaid.*

(9.) *A man who inhabits a dwelling-house for which through exemption no one is rated, shall not thereby be disentitled to vote.*

Sect. 10. A person who at the date of this Act is registered in respect of a county or borough may be registered in respect of his qualification as if this Act had not passed. But if he is also qualified under this Act he shall be registered under this Act only.

This Act shall not confer vote on anyone subject to a legal incapacity.

Sect. 11. This Act shall be construed as far as consistent with other Acts being Representation of the People Acts.

Sect. 12. The franchises conferred by this Act are in substitution for the franchises conferred by the enactments mentioned in the 1st and 2nd parts of the Second Schedule, and those enactments are repealed to the extent in the said Schedule mentioned.

Sect. 13. The Act came into operation on 1st January, 1885.

Modification of the 30 & 31 Vict. c. 102 (Representation of the People Act, 1867.)] *In this Act, the 31st December, shall be substituted for 5th January, the 1st May for 1st June, and 20th May for 20th June. Sect. 6 of 30 & 31 Vict. c. 102, is repealed.*

Medical Relief.] *The Act 48 & 49 Vict. c. 46, declares that medical relief at the expense of the poor-rate shall not deprive a person of right to be registered or to vote as a parliamentary voter.*

(a.) BOROUGH VOTE.

1. —— Dwelling-house—*Amendment of Description of Qualification under Parliamentary and Municipal Registration Act, 1878 (41 & 42 Vict. c. 26), s. 28, sub-ss. 12, 13.*] The Respondent had a sufficient qualification for the borough franchise as the occupier of a dwelling-house under the Representation of the People Act, 1867, s. 3, but not under the Reform Act, 1832, s. 27, the yearly value of the house being under £10.—The Respondent's qualification was described in the list as " house." The Respondent being objected to, the revising barrister was of opinion that such description was sufficient, but he amended it by adding the word " dwelling " to the word " house," and retained the Respondent's name on the list :—*Held* (without determining whether the description as it originally stood was sufficient), that the case came within the provisions of the Parliamentary and Municipal Registration Act, 1878, s. 28, sub-s. 12, and the revising barrister had power to make the amend-

IV. PARLIAMENT—FRANCHISE—*continued.*

(a.) BOROUGH VOTE—*continued.*

ment, and his decision was therefore correct. FRIEND *v.* TOWERS　-　- 10 Q. B. D. 87

2. —— Dwelling-house—*Part of a House— Occupation as Lodger*—30 & 31 *Vict. c.* 102, *s.* 61— 41 & 42 *Vict. c.* 26, *s.* 5.] Although by the Parliamentary and Municipal Registration Act, 1878 (41 & 42 Vict. c. 26), s. 5, the term "dwellinghouse" in the Representation of the People Act, 1867 (30 & 31 Vict. c. 102), is to mean part of a house separately occupied, yet in order to be entitled to the borough franchise as the occupier of a dwelling-house, the person must have an occupation in respect of which he can be rated to the relief of the poor, and therefore he is not entitled to such dwelling-house franchise by reason of the occupation of a part of a house if he occupies such part as a lodger.—The tenant of two rooms which he took unfurnished at a weekly rent, had the exclusive use of such rooms, and a key of the outer door of the house. His landlord had also a key of the outer door, and resided in all the rest of the house, but supplied no attendance or service to such tenant :—*Held*, that such tenant occupied the rooms as a lodger, and consequently that in respect of such occupation he could not acquire the dwelling-house franchise under the Representation of the People Act, 1867. —The tenant of two rooms which he took unfurnished at a weekly rent, had in common with the other tenants of the house, which was wholly let out on similar tenancies, the use of the passages, staircase, street-door, and usual conveniences of the house. The landlord and not the tenant was rated, and the landlord did all repairs inside and out, but he did not reside in the house, nor did he, save as aforesaid, retain the control and dominion over the house, or render any services to any of the tenants :—*Held*, that such tenant did not occupy the rooms as a lodger, but as an occupying tenant under the Representation of the People Act, 1867, and that he could therefore acquire the dwelling-house franchise in respect of such occupation. BRADLEY *v.* BAYLIS ; MORFEE *v.* NOVIS ; KIRBY *v.* BIFFEN　-　8 Q. B. D. 195

3. —— Dwelling-house—*Part of a House— Vacant Room— Occupation as Householder or Lodger*—30 & 31 *Vict. c.* 102, *ss.* 3, 61—41 & 42 *Vict. c.* 26, *s.* 5.] The claimant of a borough vote had during the qualifying period occupied as sole tenant at a weekly rent a room in a house, which he furnished himself, as his residence. At the commencement of the qualifying period all the rooms in the house were similarly let off to tenants as their residences, each tenant having a key to his room and a key of the front door. During the qualifying period the tenant of one of the other rooms relinquished his tenancy, and gave up the key of his room and his front door key to the landlord, who thereupon took the usual steps to obtain a new tenant of the vacant room. The landlord did not during any part of the qualifying period reside in the house or any part of it, either personally or by any servant, nor did he exercise any control over it, except such control, if any, as might by law be conferred on him by reason of the vacating of the room and the delivery of the keys to him by the outgoing

IV. PARLIAMENT—FRANCHISE—*continued.*

(a.) BOROUGH VOTE—*continued.*

tenant as aforesaid :—*Held*, affirming the judgment of the Queen's Bench Division, that the claimant was entitled to the franchise as an inhabitant occupier of a dwelling-house. ANCKETILL *v.* BAYLIS -　-　10 Q. B. D. 577

4. —— Lodger—*Declaration— Primâ facie Evidence—Representation of the People Act, 1867* (30 & 31 *Vict. c.* 102), *s.* 4—*Parliamentary and Municipal Registration Act, 1878* (41 & 42 *Vict. c.* 26,) *ss.* 22, 23.] Sect. 23 of the Parliamentary and Municipal Registration Act, 1878, which enacts that in the case of a person claiming to vote as a lodger the declaration annexed to his notice of claim shall, for the purposes of revision, be primâ facie evidence of his qualification, is general, and applies to lodgers claiming for the first time under sect. 4 of the Representation of the People Act, 1867, as well as to claims under sect. 22 of the Parliamentary and Municipal Registration Act, 1878, by lodgers retaining the same lodgings in successive years. NUTH *v.* TAMPLIN　-　-　8 Q. B. D. 247

5. —— Practice—*Notice of Objection—Description of List, where more than One—Parliamentary and Municipal Registration Act, 1878* (41 & 42 *Vict. c.* 26), *s.* 28, *sub-s.* 2, *and Sched.* Form I. 1, 2.] A notice of objection given to overseers was as follows : "I hereby give you notice that I object to the name of W. B. being retained in the Blockhouse list of persons, Division 1, entitled to vote at the election of members to serve in parliament for the parliamentary borough of W." There were three lists of parliamentary voters for the Blockhouse, viz. 1,—householders and occupiers. 2. freemen,—3. lodgers. The first of these only had divisions. The name of W. B. was on the parliamentary list 1, Division 1, for the Blockhouse :—*Quære*, whether this notice was a sufficient compliance with Form I. No. 1, in the schedule to the Parliamentary and Municipal Registration Act, 1878 (41 & 42 Vict. c. 26):— *Held*, that, if not, the inaccurate description of the list was a "mistake" which the revising barrister had power to correct, under s. 28, sub-s. 2, of the Act. BOLLEN *v.* SOUTHALL 15 Q. B. D. 461

6. —— Practice—*Notice of Objection—Omission of Place of Abode of Objector—Mistake— Power of Amendment*—41 & 42 *Vict. c.* 26, *s.* 28, *sub-s.* 2.] An objector described himself in the notice of objection as "on the list of parliamentary voters for the parish of H," but omitted to insert his place of abode. He was a solicitor practising at H., was a clerk to the magistrates and coroner, and had resided at H. all his life. It was admitted that the insertion of the words "of H." would have sufficiently described the objector's place of abode, and the revising barrister found as a fact that no one had been misled or deceived by the omission :—*Held*, that under the circumstances the omission was a "mistake" within the meaning of 41 & 42 Vict. c. 26, s. 28, sub-s. 2, which the revising barrister had power to amend. ADAMS *v.* BOSTOCK　-　-　8 Q. B. D. 259

7. —— Practice—*Registration of Voters—Lists —Divisions of List—Parliamentary and Municipal Registration Act, 1878* (41 & 42 *Vict. c.* 26),

IV. PARLIAMENT—FRANCHISE—*continued.*

(a.) BOROUGH VOTE—*continued.*

s. 15, *sub-s.* 2 ; *s.* 28, *sub-s.* 15—*Transfer of Names —Objection to Qualification for one Franchise.*] Sect. 15 of the Parliamentary and Municipal Registration Act, 1878, enacts that where the whole or part of the area of a municipal borough is co-extensive with or included in the area of a parliamentary borough, the lists of parliamentary voters shall, so far as practicable, be made out and revised together; and specifies the mode in which overseers of parishes shall make out the lists. By sub-sect. 2, where the parish is situate wholly or partly both in the parliamentary borough and the municipal borough, the lists shall be made out in three divisions : Division I. shall comprise the names of the persons entitled both to be registered as parliamentary voters and to be enrolled as burgesses : Division II. shall comprise the names of the persons entitled to be registered as parliamentary voters, but not to be enrolled as burgesses : Division III. shall comprise the names of the persons entitled to be enrolled as burgesses, but not to be registered as parliamentary voters. By sect. 28, sub-sect. 15, where a list is made out in divisions, the revising barrister shall place the name of any person in the division in which it should appear according to the result of the revision, regard being had to the title of the person to be on the list both as a parliamentary voter and a burgess, or only in one of those capacities, and shall expunge the name from the other division (if any) in which it appears.—An objection in respect only of a voter's qualification for the parliamentary franchise having been taken to the retention of his name in Division I., the revising barrister struck the name off Division I.; and was thereupon asked to place it in Division III., but refused so to do unless proof was given of a qualification entitling the voter to be on the burgess roll:—*Held,* that the decision of the revising barrister was right, and that he was not bound, under sect. 28, sub.-sect. 15, to place the name in Division III. GREENWAY *v.* BACHELOR. JACOB'S CASE - **12 Q. B. D. 376**

8. —— Practice—*Registration—Qualification in List—Mistake in Statement of—Correction— 41 & 42 Vict. c. 26, s. 28, sub-s. 12.*] The qualification of a voter was stated in the third column of the list to be "offices, successive occupation," and in the fourth column "High Street and Charles Street," whereas it was proved that during the whole of the qualifying period he had occupied one office only, namely, in High Street, and would have had by reason of such occupation a good and sufficient qualification. The misdescription was an error of the overseers :—*Held,* that the revising barrister had power under 41 & 42 Vict. c. 26, s. 28, to correct the mistake, and should have amended the list by striking out the words " successive occupation " and " Charles Street." LYNCH *v.* WHEATLEY　　　　　14 Q. B. D. 504

9. —— Practice — *Registration—Revision of List—Description of qualifying Property—Houses in Succession—Omission of one—Mistake—Amendment—41 & 42 Vict. c. 26, s. 28.*] The nature of the qualification of a voter was described on the parliamentary list as " Dwelling houses in succession," and the name and situation of the

IV. PARLIAMENT—FRANCHISE—*continued.*

(a.) BOROUGH VOTE—*continued.*

qualifying property were described in the fourth column of the list as " 44, Oxford Street and 34, Prospect Place, Cowick Street." He had, in fact, occupied three houses in succession during the qualifying period, but the overseer by mistake omitted to specify the third house, viz. 31, Prospect Place, and the occupation of the two only as they appeared on the list was insufficient to give the vote. These facts were proved before the revising barrister, and he was asked to amend the fourth column, and did so by striking out the figures " 44 " and " 34 ":—*Held,* by Stephen and Cave, JJ. (Lord Coleridge, C.J , dissenting), that under 41 & 42 Vict. c. 26, s. 28, the revising barrister had power to correct the mistake, although it should not have been corrected by striking out the numbers, and that the list should be amended by inserting " and 31 " after the words " Oxford Street " in the fourth column of the list. FORD *r.* HOAR - - - - **14 Q. B. D. 507**

(b.) COUNTY VOTE.

10. —— Practice—*Notice of Objection—Omission of Date—Parliamentary Registration Act, 1843 (6 & 7 Vict. c. 18), s. 7.*] Where a notice of objection to a person on the list of voters for any county is delivered to overseers and is defective under the Parliamentary Registration Act, 1843, s. 7, the defect is not cured by the publication by the overseers, under sect. 8 of the name of the person objected to.—The omission of part of the date from such a notice is a defect which invalidates it, and cannot be amended. FREEMAN *r.* NEWMAN *r.* - - **12 Q. B. D. 373**

11. —— Rent - charge — *Actual Possession under 2 & 3 Wm. 4, c. 45, s. 26—Statute of Uses, 27 Hen 8, c. 10.*] A. being possessed of a rent-charge issuing out of freehold lands, granted it unto B., C., and D., and their heirs, to hold the same unto B., C., and D., and their heirs, to the use of A., B., C., and D., their heirs and assigns for ever, in equal one-fourth shares as tenants in common :—*Held,* that all the grantees took under the Statute of Uses, and that by force of the statute and on the authority of *Heelis v. Blain* (18 C. B. (N.S.) 90 ; 34 L. J. (C.P.) 88), they were from the date of the deed in actual possession of their shares of the rent-charge within sect. 26 of 2 & 3 Wm. 4, c. 45. LOWCOCK *v.* OVERSEERS OF BROUGHTON - - **12 Q. B. D. 369**

12. —— Rent-charge—*For Life or Lives below value of £5 — Occupation — Reform Act, 1832 (2 & 3 Wm. 4, c. 45), ss. 18, 26.*] By sect. 18 of the Reform Act, 1832, no person shall be entitled to a county vote in respect of any freehold lands or tenements of which he may be seised for a life or lives, except he shall be " in the actual and bonâ fide occupation of such lands or tenements," or except the same shall be of the clear yearly value of not less than £10 (reduced to £5 by a subsequent Act) :—*Held,* that a rent-charge for life below the yearly value of £5, being incapable of occupation, was not within the exception in sect. 18, and therefore did not confer a county vote. DRUITT *v.* OVERSEERS OF CHRISTCHURCH **[12 Q. B. D. 365**

V. PARLIAMENT—PROCEDURE.

By 44 & 55 *Vict. c.* 68 (*the Supreme Court of Judicature Act,* 1881), *s.* 14, *the jurisdiction of the High Court of Justice to decide questions of law, upon appeal or otherwise, under the Act* 6 & 7 *Vict. c.* 18, *the County Voters Registration Act,* 1865, *the Parliamentary Elections Act,* 1868, *the Parliamentary and Municipal Registration Act,* 1878, *or any of the said Acts, or any Act amending the same respectively, shall be final and conclusive, unless in any case it shall seem fit to the said High Court to give special leave to appeal therefrom to Her Majesty's Court of Appeal, whose decision in such case shall be final and conclusive.*

1. —— **Privilege of House of Commons—*Internal Regulation of its own Procedure—Parliamentary Oaths Act,* 1866 (29 & 30 *Vict. c.* 19).]** The House of Commons is not subject to the control of her Majesty's Courts in its administration of that part of the statute law which has relation to its internal procedure only. What is said or done within its walls cannot be inquired into in a Court of law.—A resolution of the House of Commons cannot change the law of the land. But a Court of law has no right to inquire into the propriety of a resolution of the House restraining a member from doing within the walls of the House itself something which by the general law of the land he had a right to do, viz., take the oath prescribed by the Parliamentary Oaths Act, 1866 (29 & 30 Vict. c. 19).—An action will not lie against the Serjeant-at-Arms of the House of Commons for excluding a member from the House in obedience to a resolution of the House directing him to do so; nor will the Court grant an injunction to restrain that officer from using necessary force to carry out the order of the House.—The Plaintiff, having been returned as member for the borough of N., required the Speaker of the House of Commons to call him to the table for the purpose of taking the oath required by 29 & 30 Vict. c. 19. In consequence of something which had transpired on a former occasion the Speaker declined to do so : and the House, upon motion, resolved "that the Serjeant-at-Arms do exclude Mr. B. (the Plaintiff) from the House until he shall engage not further to disturb the proceedings of the House."—In an action against the Serjeant-at-Arms praying for an injunction to restrain him from carrying out this resolution :—*Held*, that this being a matter relating to the internal management of the procedure of the House of Commons, the Court of Queen's Bench had no power to interfere. — *Burdett* v. *Abbot* (14 East, 1), and *Stockdale* v. *Hansard* (9 Ad. & E. 1) commented upon and approved. BRADLAUGH r. GOSSETT

[12 Q. B. D. 271

VI. PARLIAMENT—REGISTRATION.

The Act 48 & 49 *Vict. c.* 15 (*the Registration Act,* 1885), *assimilates the registration law of occupation voters in counties and boroughs.*

Sect. 1.—(1.) *Subject to this Act the registration of occupation voters in parliamentary counties is to be conducted the same as that of occupation voters in parliamentary boroughs. The Parliamentary Registration Acts (i.e.,* 6 & 7 *Vict. c.* 18, *and* 41 & 42 *Vict. c.* 26, *and Acts amending them), shall apply to parliamentary counties as well as to parliamentary boroughs.*

VI. PARLIAMENT—REGISTRATION—*contd.*

(2.) *Subject to this Act sects.* 9, 27, 28, *and* 29 *of the Parliamentary and Municipal Registration Act,* 1878, 41 & 42 *Vict. c.* 26, *shall apply to the registration of ownership voters in parliamentary counties the same as that of occupation voters.*

(3.) *The modifications necessary to apply the above Acts to the above purposes.*

Sect. 2. *Adaptation of above Acts as regards lists of parliamentary county voters.*

Sect. 3.—(1.) *In parliamentary counties and boroughs notices of claims and objections to be given on or before* 20th *August. In Parliamentary Registration Acts,* 20th *to be substituted for* 25th *August.*

(2.) *Overseers in parliamentary counties and boroughs to publish lists before* 25th *August, and to deliver to town clerk and clerk of peace the papers mentioned in sects.* 9 *and* 19 *of* 6 & 7 *Vict. c.* 18. *The* 25th *August to be substituted in Parliamentary Registration Acts for* 29th *August and* 1st *September. The first fourteen days after* 25th *August to be substituted for first fourteen days of September.*

Sect. 4.—(1.) *Court for revision of lists of voters in parliamentary county may be held in same period as for parliamentary borough. Seven days notice of holding of court sufficient.*

(2.) *Declarations made under sect.* 10 *of* 28 & 29 *Vict. c.* 36, *County Voters Registration Act,* 1865, *to be transmitted to clerk of peace before* 12th *September.*

(3.) *Evening sitting of revision Court in an urban sanitary district of more than* 10,000 *inhabitants.*

(4.) *The local authority for assigning polling places may cause revision Court to be held in a town outside the county near the polling district of the parliamentary county.*

(5.) (6.) (7.) (8.) *directions for list of voters.*

(9.) *Substitution of new provisions for parliamentary counties in lieu of sub-sect.* 14 *of sect.* 28 *of* 41 & 42 *Vict. c.* 26.

Sect. 5. *Provision as to double entries in parliamentary borough lists.*

Municipal Boroughs.] *Sect.* 6. *Saving as to registration of burgesses and voters in parishes in municipal boroughs.*

Sect. 7.—(1.) *Clerks of the peace and town clerks to send their precepts to overseers within seven days before the* 15th *April (except in* 1885.)

(2.) *and* (3.) *Provisions where a parliamentary county is co-extensive with a county quarter sessional area.*

Sect. 8. *Application of* 30 & 31 *Vict. c.* 102, *s.* 31, *to remuneration of clerk of the peace.*

Sect. 9. *Divided parishes.*

Sect. 10. *Special provisions as to voters under sect.* 3 *of the Representation of the People Act,* 1884.

Sect. 11. *A voter in respect of* £50 *rental to be registered as an "occupation voter," and not as an ownership voter.*

Sect. 12. *The period of qualification for any voter in a parliamentary county to be computed to* 15th *July instead of the last day of July.*

Sect. 13. *Constitution of polling districts by Court of Quarter Sessions.*

Sect. 14. *Expenses incurred by quarter sessions in constituting polling districts.*

VI. PARLIAMENT—REGISTRATION—*contd.*

Sect. 16. *Information as to persons disqualified by receipt of parochial relief to be furnished to any parliamentary voter by clerk of guardians on payment of fees allowed by* 41 & 42 *Vict. c.* 26.

Sect. 18. *The forms and instructions in 2nd and 3rd Schedules of this Act to be used.*

Sect. 19. "Ownership voter" *means a person entitled to vote in respect of the ownership of property whether freehold, leasehold, or copyhold.*

"Fifty pounds rental voter" *means a person who on 6th December, 1884, was registered as a voter for a county under* 2 & 3 *Will.* 4, *c.* 35, *s.* 20 (*Reform Act, 1832*), *in respect of any tenement for which he was liable to a yearly rent of not less than £50, and who continues under* 48 & 49 *Vict. c.* 3 (*Representation of the People Act, 1884*), *s.* 10, *to be registered for such occupation.*

"Occupation voter" *means* (1) *as regards a parliamentary county, a person entitled to vote in respect of any qualification conferred by* 48 & 49 *Vict. c.* 3, *and* (2) *as regards a parliamentary borough, a person entitled to vote in respect of any qualification conferred by* 48 & 49 *Vict. c.* 3, *s.* 5, *or of a household or a lodger qualification as defined by that Act.*

"Parliamentary county" *means a county, or division of a county, returning members of parliament.*

"Court of county quarter sessions" *means the justices in general or quarter sessions for a county, or for part of a county having a separate quarter sessions, and includes the Isle of Ely.*

Repeal.] *Sect.* 15. *Repeal of* 2 & 3 *Will.* 4, *c.* 45, *s.* 78.

Sect. 17. *Repeal of* 6 *Vict. c.* 18, *s.* 40, *and Schedule A.;* 28 & 29 *Vict. c.* 36, *ss.* 4, 5, 12, *and Schedule A.;* 30 & 31 *Vict. c.* 102, *so much of sect.* 30 *as relates to persons entitled to vote for a county in respect of the occupation of premises other than lodgings;* 31 & 32 *Vict. c.* 58, *ss.* 17 *and* 19.

VII. PARLIAMENT — REDISTRIBUTION OF SEATS.

The Act 48 & 49 *Vict. c.* 23 (*the Redistribution of Seats Act,* 1885); *redistributes seats at parliamentary elections.*

PART I.

Boroughs.] *Sect.* 2. *Certain parliamentary boroughs cease, as boroughs, to return members. Certain counties of cities and towns are included in counties at large.*

Sect. 3. *The parliamentary boroughs reported for corrupt practices in* 1880, *cease to return members.*

Sect. 4. *City of London to return only two members. Certain parliamentary boroughs to return only one member.*

Sect. 5. *Certain parliamentary boroughs to have additional members.*

Sect. 6. *New boroughs.*

Sect. 7. *Alteration of boundaries of some boroughs.*

Sect. 8. *Division of some parliamentary boroughs into certain divisions.*

Counties.] *Sect.* 9 (1.) *Certain counties shall return so many members, and for that purpose shall be divided into the same number of divisions as the number of members.*

VII. PARLIAMENT — REDISTRIBUTION OF SEATS—*continued.*

(2.) *The names, contents, and boundaries of these divisions specified.*

(3.) *Each division to be a separate constituency.*

PART II. SUPPLEMENTAL PROVISIONS.

Sect. 10. *Qualification by occupation (otherwise than as lodger) of premises in immediate succession in a divided borough.*

Sect. 11. *Provisions as to Warwick and Pembroke.*

Sect. 12. *Returning officers in new boroughs.*

Sect. 13. *Returning officers in boroughs divided into divisions.*

Sect. 14. *Registration of freemen in divided boroughs, and where to vote.*

Voting of Election Agent and Others.] *Sect.* 15. *For the purposes of the schedule to* 46 & 47 *Vict. c.* 51 (*Corrupt and Illegal Practices Prevention Act, 1883*), *a parliamentary borough divided into divisions shall be deemed one borough.*

Place of Election.] *Sect.* 16 (1.) *In the case of a division of a county at large, the election to be in such town in the said county, or in such county of a city adjourning the said county, as the local authority, or in default thereof, as the returning officer, may determine.*

(2.) *In the case of a parliamentary borough, or division thereof, the election to be in such room as the returning officer may determine.*

Sect. 17. *Saving of rights of voters on change of parliamentary area, if otherwise qualified,*

Alteration of Parishes.] *Sect.* 18. *Any constitution of new parishes or alteration of boundaries thereof, for poor law purposes, effected prior to* 26th *of March,* 1885, *and any incidental alteration of the boundary of a county to have effect also in parliamentary elections.*

Sect. 18. *Transitory provisions as to registers of voters.*

Sect. 19. *Boundaries of parliamentary boroughs and divisions of same to be marked.*

Sect. 21. *Writs and other documents relating to election or registration to be adapted to this Act,* and to 48 & 49 *Vict. c.* 3 (*Representation of the People Act,* 1884).

Sect. 22. *Existing election law to remain in force subject to this Act.*

Sect. 23. *Definition of expressions in the Schedules to this Act.*

Sect. 24. *Definition of expressions in this Act.*

PART III. DISQUALIFICATION OF VOTERS FOR CORRUPT PRACTICES.

Sect. 27 *repeals the following statute laws (whereby certain persons were declared not to have certain rights of voting), viz.:*—30 & 31 *Vict. c.* 102, *ss.* 13, 14, 15, 16; 33 & 34 *Vict. c.* 21, *ss.* 2, 3, 4, 5; 33 & 34 *Vict. c.* 25; 33 & 34 *Vict. c.* 38, *ss.* 2, 3, 4; 33 & 34 *Vict. c.* 54; 34 & 35 *Vict. c.* 77.

Sect. 28. *Enactments concerning persons reported for corrupt practices in certain boroughs by the Commissioners in* 1880.

PART IV. ACCELERATION OF REGISTRATION IN 1885.

Sects. 29 *to* 34. *Temporary provisions for* 1885.

VII. PARLIAMENT — REDISTRIBUTION OF SEATS—*continued.*

Revising Barristers.] *Order under* 36 & 37 *Vict. c.* 70 (*the Revising Barrister Act,* 1873), *s.* 3, *varying number of revising barristers. Dated 9th July.* 1885 - - - - L. G., 1885, 3173

PARLIAMENT — Committee — Privilege of witness - - - 6 Q. B. D. 307
See DEFAMATION—PRIVILEGE. 4.

—— Perjury—Indictment—Information
[8 Q. B. D. 267
See CRIMINAL LAW—EVIDENCE. 4.

—— Special Act—Power to charge interest upon poor-rate—Opposition to bill by overseers—Costs - - 14 Q. B. D. 358
See POOR LAW—MANAGEMENT.

PARLIAMENT OF DOMINION OF CANADA
[7 App. Cas. 178, 829; 9 App. Cas. 157
See COLONIAL LAW — CANADA — DOMINION. 1, 2, 3.

PARLIAMENTARY DEPOSIT - 16 Ch. D. 155
See RAILWAY COMPANY—ABANDONMENT. 1.

PAROL CONTRACT—Not to be performed within a year 7 Q. B. D. 125; 11 Q. B. D. 123
See FRAUDS, STATUTE OF. 1, 4.

—— Relating to land 7 Q. B. D. 174; 8 App. Cas.
See CONTRACT—VALIDITY. 4. [467

—— —— - 9 Q. B. D. 315; 10 Q. B. D. 148
See FRAUDS, STATUTE OF. 2, 3.

PART OF HOUSE—Notice to treat 27 Ch. D. 536
See LANDS CLAUSES ACT—COMPULSORY POWERS. 7,

PART PERFORMANCE—Parol contract relating to land 7 Q. B. D. 174; 8 App. Cas. 467
See CONTRACT—VALIDITY. 4.

—— Parol contract relating to land
[10 Q. B. D. 148
See FRAUDS, STATUTE OF. 2.

—— Parol contract not to be performed within a year - - - 11 Q. B. D. 123
See FRAUDS, STATUTE OF. 1.

PARTIAL INTEREST—Contract to lease entirety
[19 Ch. D. 175
See LANDLORD AND TENANT — AGREEMENT. 3.

PARTICIPATING POLICY-HOLDER.
See Cases under COMPANY—LIFE INSURANCE COMPANY. 2—5.

PARTICIPATION IN PROFITS 18 Ch. D. 693;
[37 Ch. D. 460
See PARTNERSHIP—CONTRACT. 3, 4.

PARTICULARS—Admiralty—Damage to cargo
[7 P. D. 117
See PRACTICE—ADMIRALTY—PLEADING. 1.

—— Ecclesiastical law—Criminal suit 10 P. D. 20
See PRACTICE — ECCLESIASTICAL—PARTICULARS.

—— Of breaches—Patent—Costs 29 Ch. D. 366
See PATENT—PRACTICE. 3.

—— Of demand 16 Ch. D. 13; 28 Ch. D. 119
See PRACTICE—SUPREME COURT—PARTICULARS. 1, 3.

PARTICULARS—*continued.*

—— Of objections—Patent action 17 Ch. D. 137;
[22 Ch. D. 629; 29 Ch. D. 325
See PATENT—PRACTICE. 1, 2, 4.

—— Of objections—Patent action
[26 Ch. D. 700; 10 App. Cas. 249
See PATENT—VALIDITY. 1.

—— Of persons to whom slander was uttered
[12 Q. B. D. 94
See PRACTICE—SUPREME COURT—PARTICULARS. 2.

—— Probate - - 9 P. D. 23, 62
See PRACTICE—PROBATE—PARTICULARS. 1, 2.

PARTIES.
See Cases under PRACTICE — SUPREME COURT—PARTIES.

—— Action against firm - 21 Ch. D. 484
See EXECUTOR—ACTIONS. 2.

—— Action by some members of committee against others - - 28 Ch. D. 426
See CHARITY—MANAGEMENT. 4.

—— Change of parties—Adding parties.
See Cases under PRACTICE — SUPREME COURT—CHANGE OF PARTIES.

—— Demurrer for want of - 19 Ch. D. 246
See PRACTICE—SUPREME COURT—DEMURRER. 1.

—— Divorce Court - 6 P. D. 12; 7 P. D. 19;
[8 P. D. 217
See PRACTICE—DIVORCE—PARTIES. 1, 2, 3.

—— Ecclesiastical Commissioners 20 Ch. D. 208
See ECCLESIASTICAL COMMISSIONERS.

—— Liberty to attend—Costs - 21 Ch. D. 830
See PRACTICE—SUPREME COURT—COSTS. 36.

—— Partition suit—Sale - 16 Ch. D. 360
See PARTITION SUIT—SALE. 1.

—— Partition suit—Sale—Vesting order
[19 Ch. D. 646
See TRUSTEE ACTS—VESTING ORDERS. 10.

—— Redemption suit—Trustees 6 App. Cas. 698
See MORTGAGE—CONSOLIDATION. 2.

—— Third party.
See Cases under PRACTICE — SUPREME COURT—THIRD PARTY.

—— Trustees and cestui que trust 20 Ch. D. 611
See VENDOR AND PURCHASER—PURCHASE WITHOUT NOTICE. 1.

I. PARTITION SUIT—JURISDICTION.

1. —— **Power of Sale**—A decree for the partition of property can be granted notwithstanding the existence of a power given to trustees to sell the property for the purpose of a division. BOYD *v.* ALLEN - - - 24 Ch. D. 622

2. —— Trust for **Sale**—*Partition Act,* 1868

I. PARTITION SUIT—JURISDICTION—contd.

(31 & 32 Vict. c. 40), s. 4—*All Cestuis que trust sui juris.*] A testator directed the trustees of his will at such times and in such manner as they should think fit to sell his copyhold estate, and to hold the proceeds in trust for his widow for life, and after her death for his children. He left six children, all of whom attained a vested interest and were sui juris.—The widow and three children brought an action for partition of the estate; the other children who were Defendants, demurred :—*Held* (affirming the decision ·of Bacon, V.C.), that the trustees had a. trust for sale, not a mere power; and that it was not put an end to by all the reversioners attaining a vested interest; and therefore the Court had no jurisdiction to decree a partition under the Partition Act. BIGGS v. PEACOCK
[20 Ch. D. 200; 22 Ch. D. 284

II. PARTITION SUIT—SALE.

1. —— **Absent Parties**—*Order for Sale—Dispensing with Service of Judgment—Partition Act, 1876 (39 & 40 Vict. c. 17), s. 3—Form of Judgment.*] In a partition action, the Court, in ordering a sale at the request of the parties to the action, will not in the absence of the other parties interested, preface the judgment order for sale with an expression of its opinion that a sale is more beneficial than a partition.—Form of judgment order for sale in a partition action providing that service of the judgment may be dispensed with under sect. 3 of the Partition Act, 1876. *In re* HARDIMAN. PRAGNELL v. BATTEN
[16 Ch. D. 360

2. —— **Disputed Title**—*Co-tenant in Common, Mortgagee of Entirety—Australian Bankruptcy — Real Estate in England — Will of Realty —Evidence.*] Where a tenant in common of a freehold messuage subject to a mortgage in fee, had procured the transfer of the mortgage to himself and was in possession thereunder, his co-tenant in common was held entitled in a partition action to a sale of the property subject to the mortgage.—Real estate in England does not vest in an assignee under a Victorian insolvency.—For the purposes of the usual preliminary judgment in a partition action letters testimonial of the Supreme Court of the colony of Victoria, Probate Jurisdiction, setting out the will verbatim, were accepted as sufficient proof of a will made in Victoria of real estate in England. WAITE v. BINGLEY
[21 Ch. D. 674

3. —— **Married Woman**—*Request for Sale—Authority to act on her behalf—Request by Counsel — Purchase-money — Conversion — Fund under £200—Election—Separate Examination — Partition Act, 1876 (39 & 40 Vict. c. 17), s. 6.*] In a partition action, an order for sale of a married woman's share of real estate when made with her consent or at her request under sect. 6 of the Partition Act, 1876, operates as a conversion of such share into personal estate.—In a partition action a request for sale on the part of a married woman, under sect. 6 of the Partition Act, 1876, should be made by a person specially authorized to act on her behalf in the action: a request by her counsel is not sufficient.—*Crookes v. Whitworth* (10 Ch. D. 289) not followed.—Where, in a partition action, the share of a married woman in

II. PARTITION SUIT—SALE—continued.

the proceeds of sale of real estate is under £200, the Court will order the same to be paid out to her upon her separate receipt and upon an affidavit of no settlement, and will dispense with her separate examination as to her election to take the money as personal estate.—*In re Shaw* (49 L. J. (Ch.) 213) not followed. WALLACE v. GREENWOOD　-　-　16 Ch. D. 362

4. —— **Married Woman** — *Request for Sale —Partition Act 1876 (39 & 40 Vict. c. 17), s. 6.*] The request for sale in a partition action, when made on behalf of a married woman, should be a writing signed by her authorizing and requesting her solicitor to instruct counsel to ask for a sale. GRANGE v. WHITE　　-　18 Ch. D. 612

5. —— **Parties not sui juris**—*Sale out of Court—Partition Act, 1868 (31 & 32 Vict. c. 68), s. 8.*] Where some of the parties beneficially interested are not *sui juris*, and the trustees have no power of sale under their trust deed, there is no jurisdiction under the Partition Act, 1868, s. 8, to order a sale out of Court. STRUGNELL v. STRUGNELL　-　-　27 Ch. D. 258

6. —— **Real Estate**—*Proceeds of Sale—Real and Personal Representatives—Conversion—Partition Act, 1868 (31 & 32 Vict. c. 40), s. 8—Leases and Sales of Settled Estates Act, 1856 (19 & 20 Vict. c. 120), ss. 23-25—Settled Estates Act, 1877 (40 & 41 Vict. c. 18), ss. 34-36.*] A decree for the sale of real estate having been made in a partition suit, the property was sold and the proceeds of sale were paid into Court. Three of the persons entitled to shares in the property died intestate before the money was distributed, leaving their father their heir-at-law and sole next of kin. He took out administration to each of them and then died intestate :—*Held*, that the father took his children's shares of the money as their heir-at-law, but that he took them as money, and that on his death they passed to his personal representative, and not to his heir-at-law. MORDAUNT v. BENWELL　　　19 Ch. D. 302

PARTITION SUIT—Vesting order—Persons not under disability　-　19 Ch. D. 646
See TRUSTEE ACTS—VESTING ORDERS. 10.

I. PARTNERSHIP—CONTRACT.

1. —— **Benefit of Third Party**—*Right to enforce—Trust—Covenant to pay Annuity for Benefit of Widow of deceased Partner.*] Articles of partnership between two solicitors provided that the partnership should be for the term of ten years from the 1st of May, 1875, if both the partners should so long live. The partnership was also made determinable by notice. There was a further provision that from the determination of the partnership the retiring partner, his executors or administrators, or the executors or administrators, of the deceased partner, should be entitled to receive out of the net profits of the partnership business, during so much (if any) of the term of five years from the 1st of May, 1880, as should

I. PARTNERSHIP—CONTRACT—*continued.*

remain after the determination of the partnership, the yearly sum of £350, and during so much (if any) of the term of five years from the 1st of May, 1885, as either the retiring partner, or a widow of the retiring or deceased partner, should be living, the yearly sum of £250, any sum which might under this provision for the time being become payable to the executors or administrators of a deceased partner to be applied in such manner as such partner should by deed or will direct for the benefit of his widow and children, and in default of such direction to be paid to such widow, if living, for her own benefit. It was further provided that the annuity should, so far as legally might be, be constituted a charge on the net profits of the business. One of the partners died in 1883, leaving a widow, but without having given any direction as to the application of the annuity. By his will he appointed his widow his universal legatee and sole executrix. He died insolvent, and an action was brought by the creditor to administer his estate;—*Held*, by North, J., and by the Court of Appeal, that the annuity did not form part of the testator's estate, but that by the articles a trust of it was created in favour of the widow, and that she was entitled to it free from the claims of the testator's creditors. *In re* FLAVELL. MURRAY *v.* FLAVELL   **25 Ch. D. 89**

2. —— *Deceased Partner's Share — Interest thereon how paid—Construction of Articles.*] A deed of partnership provided that in the event of the death of any of the partners, and in the event of the surviving partners electing to continue the business, the amount at the credit of the deceased partner as at the last balance "shall be paid out to his representative by instalments of equal amount at six, twelve, &c., up to sixty months' date," "from the date of the surviving partners declaring their election," "with interest thereon from the date of the balance."—The chief partner, whose interest was about £394,340 in the concern, died. The surviving partners having elected to continue the business, sought to pay his representative by ten equal instalments, with interest on the amount of each instalment from substantially the date of the death to the date of payment. In a claim by a deceased partner's representative that interest should be added to each instalment on the balance of the capital sum remaining unpaid at the date of the payment of each such instalment; thus reaping an advantage of about £2365 from the earlier payment of the larger sums of interest:—*Held* (Lord Watson dissenting), affirming the decision of the Court below, that the interest to be paid with each instalment was interest calculated upon the balance of the capital sum unpaid at that date, and not interest upon the amount of each instalment. ORR EWING & Co. *v.* ORR EWING   -   - **8 App. Cas. 822**

3. —— *Participation in Profit and Loss—Legal Effects of Contract—Dissolution—Sale of Assets and Goodwill.*] The Plaintiff, having been a clerk in the Defendant's firm, entered into a verbal agreement with him for a share of profit and loss in the proportion of one-fifth to the Plaintiff and four-fifths to the Defendant, it being stipulated that the building in which the business was carried on should remain the property of the

I. PARTNERSHIP—CONTRACT—*continued.*

Defendant. The Plaintiff alleged that the agreement was for a partnership, and claimed a dissolution and an account of assets. The Defendant denied the partnership, and alleged that the Plaintiff was only manager:—*Held*, that the agreement for sharing profit and loss in certain proportions conferred all the rights of partnership inter se, subject to the stipulation as to the buildings remaining the property of one partner; that the Defendant could not maintain that the legal effects of partnership should not follow such a contract, and that the Plaintiff had a right to a dissolution and sale of the assets of the partnership, including the goodwill:- such sale to be conducted by an independent firm of solicitors, with power to either partner to bid. PAWSEY *v.* ARMSTRONG   -   -   - **18 Ch. D. 698**

4. —— *Participation in Profit and Loss — Receiver—Injunction*] Although an agreement for participation in profit and loss is *primâ facie* evidence of a 'partnership between the contracting parties as between themselves, yet the question of partnership must in all cases depend upon the intention of the parties as it appears on the contract.—By an agreement between the Plaintiff and the firm of H. & Co., the members of which were the two Defendants, it was agreed that for the part taken by the Plaintiff in the business, he should receive a fixed salary of £180, and in addition should receive one-eighth share of the net profits, and bear one-eighth share of the losses, as shewn by the books when balanced; and the Plaintiff agreed to advance £1500 to the business. The agreement was to be determined on four months' notice on either side. The Plaintiff had been previously a clerk of the Defendants, and he continued to perform similar duties after the execution of the agreement, and was not introduced to the customers as a member of the firm, and did not sign the name of the firm to bills. The Defendants being dissatisfied with the Plaintiff gave him notice to determine the agreement, and excluded him from the place of business. The Plaintiff brought an action for winding up the partnership, and moved for an injunction and receiver. Pearson, J., refused the motion, on the terms of the Defendants paying £1500 into Court:—*Held*, by the Court of Appeal (affirming the order of Pearson, J.), that on the true construction of this agreement the Plaintiff was in the position of a servant, and that there was no such partnership between the Plaintiff and the Defendants as to entitle the Plaintiff to an injunction or receiver.— *Pawsey v. Armstrong* (18 Ch. D. 698) questioned. WALKER *v.* HIRSCH   -   - **27 Ch. D. 460**

II. PARTNERSHIP—DISSOLUTION.

1. —— *Dissolution by Court — Date from which Dissolution is ordered—Terms of Dissolution.*] In an action for dissolution of partnership on the ground of disputes between the partners, where there is no distinct breach of the partnership articles, the dissolution will not be made retrospective, but will be ordered from the date of the judgment.—*Besch v. Frolich* (1 Ph. 172) followed. —The terms of dissolution in such a case as to return of premium and other matters are within the discretion of the Judge, and his conclusions

II. PARTNERSHIP—DISSOLUTION—*continued.*

will not be interfered with by the Court of Appeal except on very sufficient grounds. LYON *v.* TWEDDELL - - - - 17 Ch. D. 529

2. —— **Dissolution by Court**—*Premium— Order for Accounts being prosecuted—Summons for Direction for a Return of Part of Premium.*] Where a Plaintiff, who entered into a partnership for a long term of years and paid a premium, of which in certain events, that did not happen, he was to have a proportion returned to him, obtained judgment for a dissolution and an order for accounts and inquiries, and after the accounts had been prosecuted, asked, by summons, for a direction that he was entitled to be credited with a sum as for return of premium, the Court *held*, that though it had the power to make an addition to the judgment, yet as the Plaintiff knew all the facts at the time when it was pronounced, had present to his mind the question whether he was or not entitled to any such return, and came to the conclusion that he was not, this was not a case in which the relief asked for should be granted, and dismissed the summons with costs. —In partnership cases relief is given by directing a return of premium as for partial failure of the consideration, but such relief ought not to be granted without the leave of the Court, after decree made declaring the partnership dissolved, and directing the usual accounts to be taken ; and leave ought not to be given unless the circumstances are such as would have authorized the Court to give leave leave to bring a supplemental action. EDMONDS *v.* ROBINSON 29 Ch. D. 170

3. —— **Expulsion of Partner**—*Injunction to restrain expelled Partner from soliciting Customers of old Firm.*] A partner who had been expelled under a provision in the articles of partnership, and has been repaid his share of the capital, will not be restrained from carrying on the business on his own account, and soliciting the old customers of the firm. — *Walker* v. *Mottram* (19 Ch. D. 355) followed. DAWSON *v.* BEESON [22 Ch. D. 504

4. —— **Liability of retiring Partner**—*Election to charge old or new Firm.*] A firm of two partners dissolved ; one retired and the other carried on the business with a new partner under the same style. A customer of the old firm sold and delivered goods to the new firm after the change but without notice of it. After receiving notice he sued the new firm for the price of the goods, and upon their bankruptcy proved against their estate ; and afterwards brought an action for the price against the late partner :—*Held*, reversing the decision of the Court of Appeal, that the liability of the late partner was a liability by estoppel only, and not jointly with the members of the new firm ; that the customer might at his option have sued the late partner or the members of the new firm, but could not sue all three together ; and that having elected to sue the new firm he could not afterwards sue the late partner. SCARF *v.* JARDINE [7 App. Cas. 345

—— Rights of partners under articles 18 Ch. D. *See* PARTNERSHIP—CONTRACT. 3. [698

III. PARTNERSHIP—LIABILITIES.

—— Scope of Business—*Firm of Solicitors—*

III. PARTNERSHIP—LIABILITIES—*continued.* *Deposit of Bonds with one Partner — Liability of Firm.*] Trustees under a will deposited certain bonds payable to bearer with P., a member of the firm of solicitors who were acting for the estate. His partners had no knowledge of this, but letters referring to the bonds were copied in the letter-book of the firm and were charged for in the bill of costs of the firm, and the bonds were included in a statement of account which the firm made out for the trustees. P. paid some of the interest of the bonds by cheques of the firm, but on each occasion recouped the firm by a cheque for the same amount on his private account. P. misappropriated the bonds :—*Held* (reversing the judgment of Denman, J.), that the cheques, letters, and entries were too ambiguous to affect the other partners with acquiescence in P. having the custody of the bonds as part of the partnership business, and that they could not be held liable for their misappropriation.—*Harman* v. *Johnson* (2 E. & B. 61) and *Earl of Dundonald* v. *Masterman* (Law Rep. 7 Eq. 504) considered. CLEATHER *v.* TWISDEN [24 Ch. D. 731 ; 28 Ch. D. 340

PARTNERSHIP—Action against firm—Executors carrying on same business 21 Ch. D. 484 *See* EXECUTOR—ACTIONS. 2.

—— Action against firm—Judgment 9 Q. B. D. [355 ; 14 Q. B. D. 103 *See* PRACTICE—SUPREME COURT—PARTIES. 14, 15.

—— Action against partner in name of firm *See* Cases under PRACTICE — SUPREME COURT—PARTIES. 10—13.

—— Administration action against estate of deceased partner - 25 Ch. D. 16 *See* PRACTICE—SUPREME COURT—CONDUCT OF CAUSE. 4.

—— Bankruptcy—Proof by executor of deceased partner - - 14 Q. B. D. 394 *See* BANKRUPTCY—PROOF. 20.

—— Bankruptcy—Proof by partner 16 Ch. D. 620 ; [25 Ch. D. 505 ; 13 Q. B. D. 43 *See* BANKRUPTCY—PROOF. 18, 19, 21.

—— Bankruptcy— Right of solvent partner to receive partnership assets [13 Q. B. D. 113 *See* BANKRUPTCY—RECEIVER. 6.

—— Bequest of share of business 19 Ch. D. 432 *See* WILL—SPEAKING FROM DEATH. 2.

—— Breach of trust by partner—Bankruptcy— Liability of co-partner 11 Q. B. D. 351 *See* BANKRUPTCY—DISCHARGE. 5.

—— Business carried on by trustees of deceased partner—Apportionment of loss [26 Ch. D. 672 *See* EXECUTOR—ADMINISTRATION. 1.

—— Composition with creditors—Joint and separate security - - 19 Ch. D. 409 *See* BANKRUPTCY—PROTECTED TRANSACTION. 8.

—— Dissolution —Scotch law - 6 App. Cas. 64 *See* SCOTCH LAW—PARTNERSHIP.

PARTNERSHIP—*continued.*

—— Executor of deceased partner—Costs—Appeal   -   24 Ch. D. 273
See PRACTICE—SUPREME COURT—APPEAL. 31.

—— Fraudulent pledge — Liability of innocent partner -   25 Ch. D. 148
See BANKRUPTCY—SECURED CREDITOR. 6.

—— Lease of premises— Mortgage — Proof in bankruptcy   -   -   19 Ch. D. 105
See BANKRUPTCY—SECURED CREDITOR. 8.

—— Liquidation of one partner—Statement of debts and assets -   -   21 Ch. D. 594
See BANKRUPTCY—LIQUIDATION. 11.

—— Mortgage of share -   -   30 Ch. D. 574
See MORTGAGE—FORECLOSURE. 12.

—— Participation in profits—Policy holders.
See Cases under COMPANY—LIFE INSURANCE COMPANY. 2—5.

—— Patent—Denying validity of patent — Estoppel 26 Ch. D. 700; 10 App. Cas. 249
See PATENT—VALIDITY. 1.

—— Production of documents — Sealing up entries   -   -   25 Ch. D. 247
See PRACTICE—SUPREME COURT—PRODUCTION OF DOCUMENTS. 15.

—— Property—Power of executor to sell
[23 Ch. D. 138
See VENDOR AND PURCHASER—TITLE. 7.

—— Realty forming part of partnership assets—Probate duty—Conversion
[13 Q. B. D. 275
See REVENUE—PROBATE DUTY. 2.

—— Satisfaction of bond -   -   20 Ch. D. 81
See SETTLEMENT—SATISFACTION.

PARTY WALL — Cut through by contractor—Liability of employer   9 Q. B. D. 441;
[8 App. Cas. 443
See PRINCIPAL AND AGENT—PRINCIPAL'S LIABILITY. 1.

—— Metropolitan Building Act
[6 Q. B. D. 112; 10 Q. B. D. 236
See METROPOLIS—BUILDING ACTS. 1, 2.

PASSAGE, COURT OF—Leave to appeal 9 P. D. 12
See PRACTICE—ADMIRALTY—APPEAL. 1.

PASSENGER ACT, 1855.
See SHIP—MERCHANT SHIPPING ACTS—Gazette.

PASSENGER DUTY—Railway—Sleeping accommodation   -   -   6 Q. B. D. 216
See RAILWAY COMPANY — PASSENGER DUTY.

—— Statute respecting.
See RAILWAY COMPANY — PASSENGER DUTY—*Statutes.*

PASSENGER SHIPS.
See SHIP—MERCHANT SHIPPING ACT—Gazette.

PASTURE—Common of -   -   17 Ch. D. 535
See COMMON.

—— Common of—Inclosure   -   20 Ch. D. 380
See INCLOSURE. 3.

PATENT :—   Col.
I. STATUTES AND GAZETTE   -   1022
II. AMENDMENT   -   1040
III. ASSIGNMENT   -   1041
IV. INFRINGEMENT   -   1042
V. PRACTICE   -   -   1044
VI. PROLONGATION   -   -   1045
VII. VALIDITY -   -   -   1046

I. PATENT—STATUTES AND GAZETTE.

The Act 46 & 47 *Vict. c.* 57, *s.* 113, *repeals (inter alia),*
21 *James* 1, *c.* 3,
5 & 6 *Will.* 4, *c.* 62, *s.* 11
5 & 6 *Will.* 4, *c.* 83,
2 & 3 *Vict. c.* 67,
15 & 16 *Vict. c.* 83,
16 & 17 *Vict. c.* 5,
16 & 17 *Vict. c.* 115,
22 *Vict. c.* 13,
28 & 29 *Vict. c.* 3,
43 & 44 *Vict. c.* 10, *s.* 5,
45 & 46 *Vict. c.* 72, *s.* 16,
and consolidates and amends the law touching letters patent for inventions.

Sect. 3. *Act commenced on the 31st of December,* 1883.

Sect. 46. "*Patentee*" *means the person for the time being entitled to the benefit of a patent.*

"*Invention*" *means any manner of new manufacture the subject of letters patent and grant of privilege within sect.* 6 *of* 21 *James* 1, *c.* 3 (*the Statute of Monopolies*), *and includes an alleged invention.*

Existing Patents.] *Sect.* 45.—(1.) *The provisions of this Act relating to applications for patents and proceedings thereon shall have effect in respect only of applications made after the commencement of this Act.*

(2.) *Every patent granted before the commencement of this Act, or on an application then pending, shall remain unaffected by the provisions of this Act relating to patents binding the Crown, and to compulsory licenses.*

(3.) *In all other respects (including the amount and time of payment of fees) this Act shall extend to all patents granted before the commencement of this Act, or on application then pending, in substitution for such enactments as would have applied thereto if this Act had not been passed.*

(4.) *All instruments relating to patents granted before the commencement of this Act required to be left or filed in the Great Seal Patent Office shall be deemed to be so left or filed if left or filed before or after the commencement of this Act in the Patent Office.*

PATENTS.

Application for and Grant of Patent.] *Sect.* 4.—(1.) *Any person, whether a British subject or not, may make an application for a patent.*

(2.) *Two or more persons may make a joint application for a patent, and a patent may be granted to them jointly.*

[*Confirmed by* 48 & 49 *Vict. c.* 63, *s.* 5.]

Sect. 5.—(1.) *An application for a patent must be made in the form set forth in the First Schedule to this Act, or in such other form as may be from time to time prescribed; and must be left at, or sent*

I. PATENT—STATUTES AND GAZETTE—*contd.*

by post to, the Patent Office in the prescribed manner.

(2.) *An application must contain a declaration to the effect that the applicant is in possession of an invention, whereof he, or in the case of a joint application, one or more of the applicants, claims or claim to be the true and first inventor or inventors, and for which he or they desires or desire to obtain a patent; and must be accompanied by either a provisional or complete specification.*

[*The Act 48 & 49 Vict. c. 63, declares that this declaration may either be a statutory declaration or as otherwise prescribed.*]

(3.) *A provisional specification must describe the nature of the invention, and be accompanied by drawings, if required.*

(4.) *A complete specification, whether left on application or subsequently, must particularly describe and ascertain the nature of the invention, and in what manner it is to be performed, and must be accompanied by drawings, if required.*

(5.) *A specification, whether provisional or complete, must commence with the title, and in the case of a complete specification must end with a distinct statement of the invention claimed.*

Sect. 6. *The Comptroller shall refer every application to an examiner, who shall ascertain and report to the Comptroller whether the nature of the invention has been fairly described, and the application, specification, and drawings (if any) have been prepared in the prescribed manner, and the title sufficiently indicates the subject matter of the invention.*

Sect. 7.—(1.) *If the examiner reports that the nature of the invention is not fairly described, or that the application specification or drawings has not or have not been prepared in the prescribed manner, or that the title does not sufficiently indicate the subject matter of the invention, the Comptroller may require that the application specification or drawings be amended before he proceeds with the application.*

(2.) *Where the Comptroller requires an amendment, the applicant may appeal from his decision to the law officer.*

(3.) *The law officer shall, if required, hear the applicant and the Comptroller, and may make an order determining whether and subject to what conditions, if any, the application shall be accepted.*

(4.) *The Comptroller shall, when an application has been accepted, give notice thereof to the applicant.*

(5.) *If after an application has been made, but before a patent has been sealed, an application is made, accompanied by a specification bearing the same or a similar title, it shall be the duty of the examiner to report to the Comptroller whether the specification appears to him to comprise the same invention, and if he reports in the affirmative, the Comptroller shall give notice to the applicants that he has so reported.*

(6.) *Where the examiner reports in the affirmative, the Comptroller may determine, subject to an appeal to the law officer, whether the invention comprised in both applications is the same, and if so he may refuse to seal a patent on the application of the second applicant.*

Sect. 8.—(1.) *If the applicant does not leave a complete specification with his application, he may*

I. PATENT—STATUTES AND GAZETTE—*contd.*

leave it at any subsequent time within nine months from the date of application.

(2.) *Unless a complete specification is left within that time the application shall be deemed to be abandoned.*

[*Amended by* 48 & 49 *Vict. c.* 63.]

Sect. 9.—(1.) *Where a complete specification is left after a provisional specification, the Comptroller shall refer both specifications to an examiner for the purpose of ascertaining whether the complete specification has been prepared in the prescribed manner, and whether the invention particularly described in the complete specification is substantially the same as that which is described in the provisional specification.*

(2.) *If the examiner reports that the conditions hereinbefore contained have not been complied with, the Comptroller may refuse to accept the complete specification unless and until the same shall have been amended to his satisfaction; but any such refusal shall be subject to appeal to the law officer.*

(3.) *The law officer shall, if required, hear the applicant and the Comptroller, and may make an order determining whether and subject to what conditions, if any, the complete specification shall be accepted.*

(4.) *Unless a complete specification is accepted within twelve months from the date of application, then (save in the case of an appeal having been lodged against the refusal to accept) the application shall, at the expiration of those twelve months, become void.*

(5.) *Reports of examiners shall not in any case be published or be open to public inspection, and shall not be liable to production or inspection in any legal proceeding, other than an appeal to the law officer under this Act, unless the Court or officer having power to order discovery in such legal proceeding shall certify that such production or inspection is desirable in the interests of justice, and ought to be allowed.*

[*Amended by* 48 & 49 *Vict. c.* 63.]

Sect. 10. *On the acceptance of the complete specification the Comptroller shall advertise the acceptance; and the application and specification or specifications with the drawings (if any) shall be open to public inspection.*

Sect. 11.—(1.) *Any person may at any time within two months from the date of the advertisement of the acceptance of a complete specification give notice at the Patent Office of opposition to the grant of the patent on the ground of the applicant having obtained the invention from him, or from a person of whom he is the legal representative, or on the ground that the invention has been patented in this country on an application of prior date, or on the ground of an examiner having reported to the Comptroller that the specification appears to him to comprise the same invention as is comprised in a specification bearing the same or a similar title and accompanying a previous application, but on no other ground.*

(2.) *Where such notice is given the Comptroller shall give notice of the opposition to the applicant, and shall, on the expiration of those two months, after hearing the applicant and the person so giving notice, if desirous of being heard, decide on the case, but subject to appeal to the law officer.*

(3.) *The law officer shall, if required, hear the*

I. **PATENT—STATUTES AND GAZETTE**—*contd.*

applicant and any person so giving notice and being, in the opinion of the law officer, entitled to be heard in opposition to the grant, and shall determine whether the grant ought or ought not to be made.

(4.) The law officer may, if he thinks fit, obtain the assistance of an expert, who shall be paid such remuneration as the law officer, with the consent of the Treasury, shall appoint.

Sect. 12.—(1.) If there is no opposition, or, in case of opposition, if the determination is in favour of the grant of a patent, the Comptroller shall cause a patent to be sealed with the seal of the Patent Office.

(2.) A patent so sealed shall have the same effect as if it were sealed with the Great Seal of the United Kingdom.

(3.) A patent shall be sealed as soon as may be, and not after the expiration of fifteen months from the date of application except in the cases hereinafter mentioned, that is to say—

(a.) Where the sealing is delayed by an appeal to the law officer, or by opposition to the grant of the patent, the patent may be sealed at such time as the law officer may direct.

(b.) If the person making the application dies before the expiration of the fifteen months aforesaid, the patent may be granted to his legal representative and sealed at any time within twelve months after the death of the applicant.

[Amended by 48 & 49 Vict. c. 63.]

Sect. 13. Every patent shall be dated and sealed as of the day of the application : Provided that no proceedings shall be taken in respect of an infringement committed before the publication of the complete specification : Provided also, that in case of more than one application for a patent for the same invention, the sealing of a patent on one of those applications shall not prevent the sealing of a patent on an earlier application.

Provisional Protection.] Sect. 14. Where an application for a patent in respect of an invention has been accepted, the invention may during the period between the date of the application and the date of sealing such patent be used and published without prejudice to the patent to be granted for the same ; and such protection from the consequences of use and publication is in this Act referred to as provisional protection.

Protection by Complete Specification.] Sect. 15. After the acceptance of a complete specification and until the date of sealing a patent in respect thereof, or the expiration of the time for sealing, the applicant shall have the like privileges and rights as if a patent for the invention had been sealed on the date of the acceptance of the complete specification ; Provided that an applicant shall not be entitled to institute any proceeding for infringement unless and until a patent for the invention has been granted to him.

Duration of Patent.] Sect. 16. Every patent when sealed shall have effect throughout the United Kingdom and the Isle of Man.

Sect. 17. The term limited in every patent for the duration thereof shall be fourteen years from its date.

(2.) But every patent shall, notwithstanding any-

I. **PATENT—STATUTES AND GAZETTE**—*contd.*

thing therein or in this Act, cease if the patentee fails to make the prescribed payments within the prescribed times.

(3.) If, nevertheless, in any case, by accident mistake or inadvertence, a patentee fails to make any prescribed payment within the prescribed time, he may apply to the Comptroller for an enlargement of the time for making that payment.

(4.) Thereupon the Comptroller shall, if satisfied that the failure has arisen from any of the above-mentioned causes, on receipt of the prescribed fee for enlargement, not exceeding ten pounds, enlarge the time accordingly, subject to the following conditions :

(a.) The time for making any payment shall not in any case be enlarged for more than three months.

(b.) If any proceeding shall be taken in respect of an infringement of the patent committed after a failure to make any payment within the prescribed time, and before the enlargement thereof, the Court before which the proceeding is proposed to be taken may, if it shall think fit, refuse to award or give any damages in respect of such infringement.

Amendment of Specification.] Sect. 18.—(1.) An applicant or a patentee may, from time to time, by request in writing left at the Patent Office, seek leave to amend his specification, including drawings forming part thereof, by way of disclaimer, correction, or explanation, stating the nature of such amendment and his reasons for the same.

(2.) The request and the nature of such proposed amendment shall be advertised in the prescribed manner, and at any time within one month from its first advertisement any person may give notice at the patent office of opposition to the amendment.

(3.) Where such notice is given the Comptroller shall give notice of the opposition to the person making the request, and shall hear and decide the case subject to an appeal to the law officer.

(4.) The law officer shall, if required, hear the person making the request and the person so giving notice, and being in the opinion of the law officer entitled to be heard in opposition to the request, and shall determine whether and subject to what conditions, if any, the amendment ought to be allowed.

(5.) Where no notice of opposition is given, or the person so giving notice does not appear, the Comptroller shall determine whether and subject to what conditions, if any, the amendment ought to be allowed.

(6.) When leave to amend is refused by the Comptroller, the person making the request may appeal from his decision to the law officer.

(7.) The law officer shall, if required, hear the person making the request and the Comptroller, and may make an order determining whether, and subject to what conditions, if any, the amendment ought to be allowed.

(8.) No amendment shall be allowed that would make the specification, as amended, claim an invention substantially larger than or substantially different from the invention claimed by the specification as it stood before amendment.

(9.) Leave to amend shall be conclusive as to the right of the party to make the amendment allowed, except in case of fraud ; and the amendment shall

2 L

1. PATENT—STATUTES AND GAZETTE—*contd.*

in all Courts and for all purposes be deemed to form part of the specification.

(10.) The foregoing provisions of this section do not apply when and so long as any action for infringement or other legal proceeding in relation to a patent is pending.

Sect. 19.—(1.) In an action for infringement of a patent, and in a proceeding for revocation of a patent, the Court or a Judge may at any time order that the patentee shall, subject to such terms as to costs and otherwise as the Court or a Judge may impose, be at liberty to apply at the Patent Office for leave to amend his specification by way of disclaimer, and may direct that in the meantime the trial or hearing of the action shall be postponed.

Sect. 20. Where an amendment by way of disclaimer, correction, or explanation has been allowed under this Act, no damages shall be given in any action in respect of the use of the invention before the disclaimer, correction or explanation, unless the patentee establishes to the satisfaction of the Court that his original claim was framed in good faith and with reasonable skill and knowledge.

Sect. 21. Every amendment of a specification shall be advertised in the prescribed manner.

Compulsory Licenses.] *Sect.* 22. If on the petition of any person interested it is proved to the Board of Trade that by reason of the default of a patentee to grant licenses on reasonable terms :

(a.) The patent is not being worked in the United Kingdom; or

(b.) The reasonable requirements of the public with respect to the invention cannot be supplied; or

(c.) Any person is prevented from working or using to the best advantage an invention of which he is possessed;

the Board may order the patentee to grant licenses on such terms as to the amount of royalties, security for payment, or otherwise, as the Board, having regard to the nature of the invention and the circumstances of the case, may deem just, and any such order may be enforced by mandamus.

Register of Patents.] *Sect.* 23.—(1.) There shall be kept at the Patent Office a book called the Register of Patents, wherein shall be entered the names and addresses of grantees of patents, notifications of assignments and of transmissions of patents, of licenses under patents, and of amendments, extensions, and revocations of patents, and such other matters affecting the validity or proprietorship of patents as may from time to time be prescribed.

(2.) The register of patents shall be *primâ facie* evidence of any matters by this Act directed or authorized to be inserted therein.

(3.) Copies of deeds, licenses, and any other documents affecting the proprietorship in any letters patent or in any license thereunder, must be supplied to the Comptroller in the prescribed manner for filing in the Patent Office.

Fees.] *Sect.* 24.—(1.) There shall be paid in respect of the several instruments described in the Second Schedule to this Act, the fees in that schedule mentioned, and there shall likewise be paid, in respect of other matters under this part of the Act, such fees as may be from time to time, with the sanction of the Treasury, prescribed by

I. PATENT—STATUTES AND GAZETTE—*contd.*

the Board of Trade; and such fees shall be levied and paid to the account of Her Majesty's Exchequer in such manner as the Treasury may from time to time direct.

(2.) The Board of Trade may from time to time, if they think fit, with the consent of the Treasury, reduce any of those fees.

Extension of Term of Patent.] *Sect.* 25.—(1.) A patentee may, after advertising in manner directed by any rules made under this section his intention to do so, present a petition to Her Majesty in Council, praying that his patent may be extended for a further term ; but such petition must be presented at least six months before the time limited for the expiration of the patent.

(2.) Any person may enter a caveat, addressed to the Registrar of the Council at the Council Office, against the extension.

(3.) If Her Majesty shall be pleased to refer any such petition to the Judicial Committee of the Privy Council, the said Committee shall proceed to consider the same, and the petitioner and any person who has entered a caveat shall be entitled to be heard by himself or by counsel on the petition.

(4.) The Judicial Committee shall, in considering their decision, have regard to the nature and merits of the invention in relation to the public, to the profits made by the patentee as such, and to all the circumstances of the case.

(5.) If the Judicial Committee report that the patentee has been inadequately remunerated by his patent, it shall be lawful for Her Majesty in Council to extend the term of the patent for a further term not exceeding seven, or in exceptional cases fourteen years ; or to order the grant of a new patent for the term therein mentioned, and containing any restrictions, conditions, and provisions that the Judicial Committee may think fit.

(6.) It shall be lawful for Her Majesty in Council to make, from time to time, rules of procedure and practice for regulating proceedings on such petitions, and subject thereto such proceedings shall be regulated according to the existing proceedings and practice in patent matters of the Judicial Committee.

(7.) The costs of all parties of and incident to such proceedings shall be in the discretion of the Judicial Committee ; and the orders of the Committee respecting costs shall be enforceable as if they were orders of a division of the High Court of Justice.

Revocation.] *Sect.* 26.—(1.) The proceeding by scire facias to repeal a patent is hereby abolished.

(2.) Revocation of a patent may be obtained on petition to the Court.

(3.) Every ground on which a patent might, at the commencement of this Act, be repealed by scire facias shall be available by way of defence to an action of infringement and shall also be a ground of revocation.

(4.) A petition for revocation of a patent may be presented by—

(a.) The Attorney-General in England or Ireland, or the Lord Advocate of Scotland.

(b.) Any person authorized by the Attorney-General in England or Ireland or the Lord Advocate in Scotland.

(c.) Any person alleging that the patent was obtained in fraud of his rights, or of the

I. PATENT—STATUTES AND GAZETTE—contd.

rights of any person under or through whom he claims.

(d.) Any person alleging that he, or any person under or through whom he claims, was the true inventor of any invention included in the claim of the patentee.

(e.) Any person alleging that he, or any person under or through whom he claims an interest in any trade, business, or manufacture, had publicly manufactured, used, or sold, within this realm, before the date of the patent, anything claimed by the patentee as his invention.

(5.) The plaintiff must deliver with his petition particulars of the objections on which he means to rely, and no evidence shall, except by leave of the Court or a Judge, be admitted in proof of any objection of which the particulars are not so delivered.

(6.) Particulars delivered may be from time to time amended by leave of the Court or a Judge.

(7.) The defendant shall be entitled to begin, and give evidence in support of the patent, and if the plaintiff gives evidence impeaching the validity of the patent the defendant shall be entitled to reply.

(8.) Where a patent has been revoked on the ground of fraud, the Comptroller may, on the application of the true inventor made in accordance with the provisions of this Act, grant to him a patent in lieu of and bearing the same date as the date of revocation of the patent so revoked, but the patent so granted shall cease on the expiration of the term for which the revoked patent was granted.

Crown.] Sect. 27.—(1.) A patent shall have to all intents the like effect as against Her Majesty the Queen, her heirs and successors, as it has against a subject.

(2.) But the officers or authorities administering any department of the service of the Crown may, by themselves, their agents, contractors, or others, at any time after the application, use the invention for the service of the Crown on terms to be before or after the use thereof agreed on, with the approval of the Treasury, between those officers or authorities and the patentee, or, in default of such agreement, on such terms as may be settled by the Treasury after hearing all parties interested.

Legal Proceedings.] Sect. 28.—(1.) In an action or proceeding for infringement or revocation of a patent, the Court may, if it thinks fit, and shall, on the request of either of the parties to the proceeding, call in the aid of an assessor specially qualified, and try and hear the case wholly or partially with his assistance; the action shall be tried without a jury unless the Court shall otherwise direct.

(2.) The Court of Appeal or the Judicial Committee of the Privy Council may, if they see fit, in any proceeding before them respectively, call in the aid of an assessor as aforesaid.

(3.) The remuneration, if any, to be paid to an assessor under this section shall be determined by the Court or the Court of Appeal or Judicial Committee, as the case may be, and be paid in the same manner as the other expenses of the execution of this Act.

Sect. 29.—(1.) In an action for infringement of a patent the plaintiff must deliver with his statement of claim, or by order of the Court or the

I. PATENT—STATUTES AND GAZETTE—contd.

Judge, at any subsequent time, particulars of the breaches complained of.

(2.) The defendant must deliver with his statement of defence, or, by order of the Court or a Judge, at any subsequent time, particulars of any objections on which he relies in support thereof.

(3.) If the defendant disputes the validity of the patent, the particulars delivered by him must state on what grounds he disputes it, and if one of those grounds is want of novelty must state the time and place of the previous publication or user alleged by him.

(4.) At the hearing no evidence shall, except by leave of the Court or a judge, be admitted in proof of any alleged infringement or objection of which particulars are not so delivered.

(5.) Particulars delivered may be from time to time amended, by leave of the Court or a Judge.

(6.) On taxation of costs regard shall be had to the particulars delivered by the plaintiff and by the defendant; and they respectively shall not be allowed any costs in respect of any particular delivered by them unless the same is certified by the Court or a Judge to have been proven or to have been reasonable and proper, without regard to the general costs of the case.

Sect. 30. In an action for infringement of a patent, the Court or a Judge may, on the application of either party, make such order for an injunction, inspection or account, and impose such terms and give such directions respecting the same and the proceedings thereon as the Court or a Judge may see fit.

Sect. 31. In an action for infringement of a patent, the Court or a Judge may certify that the validity of the patent came in question; and if the Court or a Judge so certifies, then in any subsequent action for infringement, the plaintiff in that action on obtaining a final order or judgment in his favour shall have his full costs, charges, and expenses as between solicitor and client, unless the Court or Judge trying the action certifies that he ought not to have the same.

Sect. 32. Where any person claiming to be the patentee of an invention by circulars, advertisements, or otherwise threatens any other person with any legal proceeding or liability in respect of any alleged manufacture, use, sale, or purchase of the invention any persons or person aggrieved thereby may bring an action against him, and may obtain an injunction against the continuance of such threats, and may recover such damage (if any) as may have been sustained thereby, if the alleged manufacture, use, sale, or purchase to which the threats related was not in fact an infringement of any legal rights of the person making such threats: Provided that this section shall not apply if the person making such threats with due diligence commences and prosecutes an action for infringement of his patent.

Miscellaneous.] Sect. 33. Every patent may be in the form in the First Schedule to this Act, and shall be granted for one invention only, but may contain more than one claim; but it shall not be competent for any person in an action or other proceeding to take any objection to a patent on the ground that it comprises more than one invention.

Sect. 34.—(1.) If a person possessed of an invention dies without making application for a

I. PATENT—STATUTES AND GAZETTE—*contd.*

patent for the invention, application may be made by, and a patent for the invention granted to, his legal representative.

(2.) *Every such application must be made within six months of the decease of such person, and must contain a declaration by the legal representative that he believes such person to be the true and first inventor of the invention.*

Sect. 35. *A patent granted to the true and first inventor shall not be invalidated by an application in fraud of him, or by provisional protection obtained thereon, or by any use or publication of the invention subsequent to that fraudulent application during the period of provisional protection.*

Sect. 36. *A patentee may assign his patent for any place in or part of the United Kingdom, or Isle of Man, as effectually as if the patent were originally granted to extend to that place or part only.*

Sect. 37. *If a patent is lost or destroyed, or its non-production is accounted for to the satisfaction of the Comptroller, the Comptroller may at any time cause a duplicate thereof to be sealed.*

Sect. 38. *The law officers may examine witnesses on oath and administer oaths for that purpose under this part of this Act, and may from time to time make, alter, and rescind rules regulating references and appeals to the law officers and the practice and procedure before them under this part of this Act; and in any proceeding before either of the law officers under this part of this Act, the law officer may order costs to be paid by either party, and any such order may be made a rule of the Court.*

Sect. 39. *The exhibition of an invention at an industrial or international exhibition, certified as such by the Board of Trade, or the publication of any description of the invention during the period of the holding of the exhibition, or the use of the invention for the purpose of the exhibition in the place where the exhibition is held, or the use of the invention during the period of the holding of the exhibition by any person elsewhere, without the privity or consent of the inventor, shall not prejudice the right of the inventor or his legal personal representative to apply for and obtain provisional protection and a patent in respect of the invention or the validity of any patent granted on the application, provided that both the following conditions are complied with, namely—*

(a.) *The exhibitor must, before exhibiting the invention, give the Comptroller the prescribed notice of his intention to do so; and*

(b.) *The application for the patent must be made before or within six months from the date of the opening of the exhibition.*

Sect. 40.—(1.) *The Comptroller shall cause to be issued periodically an illustrated journal of patented inventions, as well as reports of patent cases decided by Courts of law, and any other information that the Comptroller may deem generally useful or important.*

(2.) *Provision shall be made by the Comptroller for keeping on sale copies of such journal, and also of all complete specifications of patents for the time being in force, with their accompanying drawings, if any.*

(3.) *The Comptroller shall continue, in such form*

I. PATENT—STATUTES AND GAZETTE—*contd.*

as he may deem expedient, the indexes and abridgments of specifications hitherto published, and shall from time to time prepare and publish such other indexes, abridgments of specifications, catalogues, and other works relating to inventions, as he may see fit.

Sect. 41 *transfers and vests the control and management of the existing Patent Museum and contents to the Department of Science and Art.*

Sect. 42 *empowers the Department of Science and Art to require a patentee to furnish them with a model of his invention on payment to the patentee of the cost of the manufacture of the model: the amount to be settled, in case of dispute, by the Board of Trade.*

Sect. 43.—(1.) *A patent shall not prevent the use of an invention for the purposes of the navigation of a foreign ship within the jurisdiction of any of Her Majesty's Courts in the United Kingdom or Isle of Man, or the use of an invention in a foreign vessel within that jurisdiction, provided it is not used therein for or in connection with the manufacture or preparation of anything intended to be sold in or exported from the United Kingdom or Isle of Man.*

(2.) *But this section shall not extend to vessels of any foreign state of which the laws authorize subjects of such foreign state, having patents or like privileges for the exclusive use or exercise of inventions within its territories, to prevent or interfere with the use of such inventions in British vessels while in the ports of such foreign state, or in the waters within the jurisdiction of its Courts, where such inventions are not so used for the manufacture or preparation of anything intended to be sold in or exported from the territories of such foreign state.*

Sect. 44.—(1.) *The inventor of any improvement in instruments or munitions of war, his executors, administrators, or assigns (who are in this section comprised in the expression the inventor) may (either for or without valuable consideration) assign to Her Majesty's Principal Secretary of State for the War Department (hereinafter referred to as the Secretary of State), on behalf of Her Majesty, all the benefit of the invention and of any patent obtained or to be obtained for the same; and the Secretary of State may be a party to the assignment.*

(2.) *The assignment shall effectually vest the benefit of the invention and patent in the Secretary of State for the time being on behalf of Her Majesty, and all covenants and agreements therein contained for keeping the invention secret and otherwise shall be valid and effectual (notwithstanding any want of valuable consideration), and may be enforced accordingly by the Secretary of State for the time being.*

(3.) *Where any such assignment has been made to the Secretary of State, he may at any time before the application for a patent for the invention, or before publication of the specification or specifications, certify to the Comptroller his opinion that, in the interest of the public service, the particulars of the invention and of the manner in which it is to be performed should be kept secret.*

(4.) *If the Secretary of State so certifies, the application and specification or specifications with the drawings (if any), and any amendment of the specification or specifications, and any copies of*

I. PATENT—STATUTES AND GAZETTE—contd.

such documents and drawings, shall, instead of being left in the ordinary manner at the patent office, be delivered to the Comptroller in a packet sealed by authority of the Secretary of State.

(5.) Such packet shall until the expiration of the term or extended term during which a patent for the invention may be in force, be kept sealed by the Comptroller, and shall not be opened save under the authority of an order of the Secretary of State, or of the law officers.

(6.) Such sealed packet shall be delivered at any time during the continuance of the patent to any person authorized by writing under the hand of the Secretary of State to receive the same, and shall if returned to the Comptroller be again kept sealed by him.

(7.) On the expiration of the term or extended term of the patent, such sealed packet shall be delivered to any person authorized by writing under the hand of the Secretary of State to receive it.

(8.) Where the Secretary of State certifies as aforesaid, after an application for a patent has been left at the Patent Office, but before the publication of the specification or specifications, the application specification or specifications, with the drawings (if any), shall be forthwith placed in a packet sealed by authority of the Comptroller, and such packet shall be subject to the foregoing provisions respecting a packet sealed by authority of the Secretary of State.

(9.) No proceeding by petition or otherwise shall lie for revocation of a patent granted for an invention in relation to which the Secretary of State has certified as aforesaid.

(10.) No copy of any specification or other document or drawing, by this section required to be placed in a sealed packet, shall in any manner whatever be published or open to the inspection of the public, but save as in this section. otherwise directed, the provisions of this part of this Act shall apply in respect of any such invention and patent as aforesaid.

(11.) The Secretary of State may, at any time by writing under his hand, waive the benefit of this section with respect to any particular invention and the specifications documents and drawings shall be thenceforth kept and dealt with in the ordinary way.

(12.) The communication of any invention for any improvement in instruments or munitions of war to the Secretary of State, or to any person or persons authorized by him to investigate the same or the merits thereof, shall not, nor shall anything done for the purposes of the investigation, be deemed use or publication of such invention so as to prejudice the grant or validity of any patent for the same.

PATENT OFFICE AND PROCEEDINGS THEREAT.

Sect. 82.—(1.) The Treasury may provide for the purposes of this Act an office with all requisite buildings and conveniences, which shall be called, and is in this Act referred to as, the Patent Office.

(2.) Until a new Patent Office is provided, the offices of the Commissioners of Patents for inventions and for the registration of designs and trade-marks existing at the commencement of this Act shall be the Patent Office within the meaning of this Act.

I. PATENT—STATUTES AND GAZETTE—contd.

(3.) The Patent Office shall be under the immediate control of an officer called the Comptroller General of Patents, Designs, and Trade-marks, who shall act under the superintendence and direction of the Board of Trade.

(4.) Any act or thing directed to be done by or to the Comptroller may, in his absence, be done by or to any officer for the time being in that behalf authorized by the Board of Trade.

Sect. 83.—(1.) The Board of Trade may at any time after the passing of this Act, and from time to time, subject to the approval of the Treasury, appoint the Comptroller-General of Patents, Designs, and Trade-marks, and so many examiners and other officers and clerks, with such designations and duties as the Board of Trade think fit, and may from time to time remove any of those officers and clerks.

(2.) The salaries of those officers and clerks shall be appointed by the Board of Trade, with the concurrence of the Treasury, and the same and the other expenses of the execution of this Act shall be paid out of money provided by Parliament.

Sect. 84. There shall be a seal for the Patent Office, and impressions thereof shall be judicially noticed and admitted in evidence.

Sect. 85. There shall not be entered in any register kept under this Act, or be receivable by the Comptroller, any notice of any trust expressed implied or constructive.

Sect. 86. The Comptroller may refuse to grant a patent for an invention, or to register a design or trade-mark, of which the use would, in his opinion, be contrary to law or morality.

Sect. 87. Where a person becomes entitled by assignment, transmission, or other operation of law to a patent, or to the copyright in a registered design, or to a registered trade-mark, the Comptroller shall on request, and on proof of title to his satisfaction, cause the name of such person to be entered as proprietor of the patent, copyright in the design, or trade-mark, in the register of patents, designs, or trade-marks, as the case may be. The person for the time being entered in the register of patents, designs, or trade-marks. as proprietor of a patent, copyright in a design, or trade-mark, as the case may be, shall, subject to any rights appearing from such register to be vested in any other person, have power absolutely to assign, grant licenses as to, or otherwise deal with the same, and to give effectual receipts for any consideration for such assignment, license, or dealing. Provided that any equities in respect of such patent, design, or trade-mark may be enforced in like manner as in respect of any other personal property.

Sect. 88. Every register kept under this Act shall at all convenient times be open to the inspection of the public, subject to such regulations as may be prescribed; and certified copies, sealed with the seal of the Patent Office, of any entry in any such register shall be given to any person requiring the same on payment of the prescribed fee.

Sect. 89. Printed or written copies or extracts purporting to be certified by the Comptroller and sealed with the seal of the Patent Office of or from patents, specifications, disclaimers, and other documents in the Patent Office, and of or from registers and other books kept there, shall be admitted in evidence in all Courts in Her Majesty's dominions

I. PATENT—STATUTES AND GAZETTE—contd.

and in all proceedings without further proof or production of the originals.

Sect. 90.—(1.) The Court may on the application of any person aggrieved by the omission without sufficient cause of the name of any person from any register kept under this Act, or by any entry made without sufficient cause in any such register, make such order for making, expunging, or varying the entry, as the Court thinks fit ; or the Court may refuse the application ; and in either case may make such order with respect to the costs of the proceedings as the Court thinks fit.

(2.) The Court may in any proceeding under this section decide any question that it may be necessary or expedient to decide for the rectification of a register, and may direct an issue to be tried for the decision of any question of fact, and may award damages to the party aggrieved.

(3.) Any order of the Court rectifying a register shall direct that due notice of the rectification be given to the Comptroller.

Sect. 91. The Comptroller may, on request in writing accompanied by the prescribed fee,—

(a.) Correct any clerical error in or in connexion with an application for a patent, or for registration of a design or trade-mark ; or

(b.) Correct any clerical error in the name, style or address of the registered proprietor of a patent, design, or trade-mark.

(c.) Cancel the entry or part of the entry of a trade-mark on the register : Provided that the applicant accompanies his request by a statutory declaration made by himself, stating his name, address, and calling, and that he is the person whose name appears on the register as the proprietor of the said trade-mark.

Sect. 92.—(1.) The registered proprietor of any registered trade-mark may apply to the Court for leave to add to or alter such mark in any particular, not being an essential particular within the meaning of this Act, and the Court may refuse or grant leave on such terms as it may think fit.

(2.) Notice of any intended application to the Court under this section shall be given to the Comptroller by the applicant ; and the Comptroller shall be entitled to be heard on the application.

(3.) If the Court grants leave, the Comptroller shall, on proof thereof and on payment of the prescribed fee, cause the register to be altered in conformity with the order of leave.

Sect. 93. If any person makes or causes to be made a false entry in any register kept under this Act, or a writing falsely purporting to be a copy of an entry in any such register, or produces or tenders or causes to be produced or tendered in evidence any such writing, knowing the entry or writing to be false, he shall be guilty of a misdemeanor.

Sect. 94. Where any discretionary power is by this Act given to the Comptroller, he shall not exercise that power adversely to the applicant for a patent, or for amendment of a specification, or for registration of a trade-mark or design, without (if so required within the prescribed time by the applicant) giving the applicant an opportunity of being heard personally or by his agent.

Sect. 95. The Comptroller may, in any case of doubt or difficulty arising in the administration of

I. PATENT—STATUTES AND GAZETTE—contd.

any of the provisions of this Act, apply to either of the law officers for directions in the matter.

Sect. 96. A certificate purporting to be under the hand of the Comptroller as to any entry, matter, or thing which he is authorized by this Act, or any general rules made thereunder, to make or do, shall be primâ facie evidence of the entry having been made, and of the contents thereof, and of the matter or thing having been done or left undone.

Sect. 97.—(1) Any application, notice, or other document authorized or required to be left, made, or given at the Patent Office or to the Comptroller, or to any other person under this Act, may be sent by a prepaid letter through the post ; and if so sent, shall be deemed to have been left, made, or given, respectively at the time when the letter containing the same would be delivered in the ordinary course of post.

(2.) In proving such service or sending, it shall be sufficient to prove that the letter was properly addressed and put into the post.

Sect. 98. Whenever the last day fixed by this Act, or by any rule for the time being in force, for leaving any document or paying any fee at the Patent Office shall fall on Christmas Day, Good Friday, or on a Saturday or Sunday, or any day observed as a holiday at the Bank of England, or any day observed as a day of public fast or thanksgiving, herein referred to as excluded days, it shall be lawful to leave such document or to pay such fee on the day next following such excluded day or days if two or more of them occur consecutively.

Sect. 99. If any person is by reason of infancy, lunacy, or other inability, incapable of making any declaration or doing anything required or permitted by this Act or by any rules made under the authority of this Act, then the guardian or committee (if any) of such incapable person, or if there be none, any person appointed by any Court or Judge possessing jurisdiction in respect of the property of incapable persons, upon the petition of any person on behalf of such incapable person or of any other person interested in the making such declaration or doing such thing, may make such declaration or a declaration as nearly corresponding thereto as circumstances permit, and do such thing in the name and on behalf of such incapable person, and all acts done by such substitute shall for the purposes of this Act be as effectual as if done by the person for whom he is substituted.

Sect. 100. Copies of all specifications, drawings, and amendments left at the Patent Office after the commencement of this Act, printed for and sealed with the seal of the Patent Office, shall be transmitted to the Edinburgh Museum of Science and Art, and to the Enrolments Office of the Chancery Division in Ireland, and to the Rolls Office in the Isle of Man, within twenty-one days after the same shall respectively have been accepted or allowed at the Patent Office ; and certified copies of or extracts from any such documents shall be given to any person requiring the same on payment of the prescribed fee ; and any such copy or extract shall be admitted in evidence in all Courts in Scotland and Ireland and in the Isle of Man without further proof or production of the originals.

Sect. 101.—(1.) The Board of Trade may from time to time make such general rules and do such

I. PATENT—STATUTES AND GAZETTE—*contd.*

things as they think expedient, subject to the provisions of this Act—

(a.) For regulating the practice of registration under this Act:

(b.) For classifying goods for the purposes of designs and trade-marks:

(c.) For making or requiring duplicates of specifications, amendments, drawings, and other documents:

(d.) For securing and regulating the publishing and selling of copies, at such prices and in such manner as the Board of Trade think fit, of specifications, drawings, amendments, and other documents:

(e.) For securing and regulating the making, printing, publishing, and selling of indexes to, and abridgments of, specifications and other documents in the Patent Office; and providing for the inspection of indexes and abridgments and other documents:

(f.) For regulating (with the approval of the Treasury) the presentation of copies of Patent Office publications to patentees and to public authorities, bodies, and institutions at home and abroad.

(g.) Generally for regulating the business of the Patent Office, and all things by this Act placed under the direction or control of the Comptroller, or of the Board of Trade,

(2.) Any of the forms in the First Schedule to this Act may be altered or amended by rules made by the Board as aforesaid.

(3.) General rules may be made under this section at any time after the passing of this Act, but not so as to take effect before the commencement of this Act, and shall (subject as hereinafter mentioned) be of the same effect as if they were contained in this Act, and shall be judicially noticed.

(4.) Any rules made in pursuance of this section shall be laid before both Houses of Parliament, if Parliament be in session at the time of making thereof, or, if not, then as soon as practicable after the beginning of the then next session of Parliament, and they shall also be advertised twice in the official journal to be issued by the Comptroller.

(5.) If either House of Parliament, within the next forty days after any rules have been so laid before such House, resolve that such rules or any of them ought to be annulled, the same shall after the date of such resolution be of no effect, without prejudice to the validity of anything done in the meantime under such rules or rule or to the making of any new rules or rule.

Sect. 102. The Comptroller shall, before the 1st day of June in every year, cause a report respecting the execution by or under him of this Act to be laid before both Houses of Parliament, and therein shall include for the year to which such report relates, all general rules made in that year under or for the purposes of this Act, and an account of all fees, salaries, and allowances, and other money received and paid under this Act.

INTERNATIONAL AND COLONIAL ARRANGEMENTS.

Sect. 103.—(1.) If Her Majesty is pleased to make any arrangement with the Government or Governments of any foreign state or states for

I. PATENT—STATUTES AND GAZETTE—*contd.*

mutual protection of inventions, designs, and trademarks, or any of them, then any person who has applied for protection for any invention, design, or trade-mark in any such state shall be entitled to a patent for his invention or to registration of his design or trade-mark (as the case may be) under this Act, in priority to other applicants; and such patent or registration shall have the same date as the [date of the application (see 48 & 49 Vict. c. 63)] in such foreign state.

Provided that his application is made, in the case of a patent within seven months, and in the case of a design or trade-mark within four months, from his applying for protection in the foreign state with which the arrangement is in force.

Provided that nothing in this section contained shall entitle the patentee or proprietor of the design or trade-mark to recover damages for infringements happening prior to the date of the actual acceptance of his complete specification, or the actual registration of his design or trade-mark in this country, as the case may be.

(2.) The publication in the United Kingdom or the Isle of Man during the respective periods aforesaid of any description of the invention, or the use therein during such periods of the invention, or the publication therein during such periods of a description or representation of the design, or the use therein during such periods of the trade-mark, shall not invalidate the patent which may be granted for the invention, or the registration of the design or trade-mark.

(3.) The application for the grant of a patent, or the registration of a design, or the registration of a trade-mark under this section must be made in the same manner as an ordinary application under this Act: Provided that, in the case of trade-marks, any trade-mark the registration of which has been duly applied for in the country of origin may be registered under this Act:

(4.) The provisions of this section shall apply only in the case of those foreign states with respect to which Her Majesty shall from time to time by Order in Council declare them to be applicable, and so long only in the case of each state as the Order in Council shall continue in force with respect to that state.

Sect. 104.—(1.) Where it is made to appear to Her Majesty that the legislature of any British possession has made satisfactory provision for the protection of inventions, designs, and trade-marks, patented or registered in this country, it shall be lawful for Her Majesty from time to time, by Order in Council, to apply the provisions of the last preceding section, with such variations or additions, if any, as to Her Majesty in Council may seem fit, to such British possession.

(2.) An Order in Council under this Act shall, from a date to be mentioned for the purpose in the Order, take effect as if its provisions had been contained in this Act; but it shall be lawful for Her Majesty in Council to revoke any Order in Council made under this Act.

OFFENCES AGAINST THE ACT.

Sect. 105.—(1.) Any person who represents that any article sold by him is a patented article, when no patent has been granted for the same, or describes any design or trade-mark applied to any

I. PATENT—STATUTES AND GAZETTE—*contd.*

article sold by him as registered which is not so, shall be liable for every offence on summary conviction to a fine not exceeding five pounds.

(2.) *A person shall be deemed, for the purposes of this enactment, to represent that an article is patented or a design or a trade-mark is registered, if he sells the article with the word "patent," "patented," "registered," or any word or words expressing or implying that a patent or registration has been obtained for the article stamped, engraved, or impressed on, or otherwise applied to, the article.*

Sect. 106. *Any person who, without the authority of Her Majesty, or any of the Royal Family, or of any government department, assumes or uses in connection with any trade, business, calling, or profession, the Royal arms, or arms so nearly resembling the same as to be calculated to deceive, in such a manner as to be calculated to lead other persons to believe that he is carrying on his trade, business, calling, or profession by or under such authority as aforesaid, shall be liable on summary conviction to a fine not exceeding twenty pounds.*

GENERAL.

Sects. 107–111 *apply the Act to Scotland and Ireland.*

Sect. 112 *extends the Act to the Isle of Man.*

Sect. 113 *repeals and savings for past operation of repealed enactments, &c.*

Sect. 114. *Former registers to be deemed continued.*

Sect. 115. *Saving for existing rules.*

Sect. 116. *Saving for Royal Prerogative.*

Sect. 117. *General definitions.*

THE FIRST SCHEDULE.

THE SECOND SCHEDULE.

Fees on Instruments for obtaining Patents, and Renewal.

(a.) *Up to sealing.*

	£ s. d.	£ s. d.
On application for provisional protection	1 0 0	
On filing complete specification	3 0 0	
		4 0 0

or

On filing complete specification with first application	4 0 0

(b.) *Further before end of four years from date of patent.*

On certificate of renewal	50 0 0

(c.) *Further before end of seven years, or in the case of patents granted after the commencement of this Act, before the end of eight years from date of patent.*

On certificate of renewal	100 0 0

Or in lieu of the fees of £50 and £100 the following annual fees :—

I. PATENT—STATUTES AND GAZETTE—*contd.*

Before the expiration of the—			£ s. d.
Fourth year from the date of the patent			10 0 0
Fifth	"	"	10 0 0
Sixth	"	"	10 0 0
Seventh	"	"	10 0 0
Eighth	"	"	15 0 0
Ninth	"	"	15 0 0
Tenth	"	"	20 0 0
Eleventh	"	"	20 0 0
Twelfth	"	"	20 0 0
Thirteenth	"	"	20 0 0

Foreign States.] *By Order in Council dated 26th June, 1884, the provisions of sect. 103 of Patents, Designs, and Trade-marks Act, 1883, apply to :—*

Belgium.	Portugal.
Brazil.	Salvador.
Ecuador	Servia.
France.	Spain.
Guatemala.	Switzerland.
Italy.	Tunis.
Netherlands.	[L. G., 1884 p. 2993

San Domingo.] *By Order in Council, of 27th January, 1885, the Patents, Designs, and Trade-marks Act, 1883, applies to San Domingo.*
　　　　　　　　　　　　[L. G., 1885, p. 418

Queensland.] *Ditto to Colony of Queensland. Order in Council, 17th Sept., 1885*
　　　　　　　　　　　　[L. G., 1885, p. 4429

Royal Arms.] *Notice of Board of Green Cloth that there is a penalty under 46 & 47 Vict. c. 57, for improperly using the Royal Arms. Dated Feb. 19, 1884.* -　　L. G., 1884, p. 887

II. PATENT—AMENDMENT.

1. —— Clerical Error—*Specification—Amendment—Jurisdiction of the Master of the Rolls—Patents, Designs, and Trade-marks Act, 1883 (46 & 47 Vict. c. 57), s. 18.]* The 18th section of the Patents, Designs, and Trade-marks Act, 1883, does not affect the jurisdiction of the Master of the Rolls to allow an amendment in a patent specification which has been filed under sects. 27 and 28 of the Patent Law Amendment Act, of 1852, or has otherwise become a record. So long as it is in the Patent Office, any one applying for amendment must proceed under sect. 18 of the Act of 1883. *In re* GARE'S PATENT　　26 Ch. D. 105

2. —— Disclaimer — *Patents, Designs, and Trade-marks Act, 1883 (46 & 47 Vict. c. 57), ss. 18, 19—Application for Leave to amend Specification by way of Disclaimer—Appeal to the House of Lords in Action relating to the Patent, after Application for Leave to amend—"Action for Infringement"—Pending Action—"Other Legal Proceeding"—Revocation of Patent.]* In an action for infringement of their patent, the Plaintiffs obtained a judgment against the Defendants S. & H., but on appeal, that judgment was reversed as against S., but maintained as against H. (26 Ch. D. 700). The Plaintiffs afterwards applied under the Patents, Designs, and Trade-marks Act, 1883 (46 & 47 Vict. c. 57), s. 18, for leave to amend their specification by way of disclaimer, which application was opposed by the Defendants. Subsequently, H.

II. PATENT—AMENDMENT—*continued.*

lodged an appeal in the House of Lords against the decision of the Court of Appeal.⧸ The Comptroller-General then declined to proceed with the Plaintiffs' application until the opinion of the Court had been taken under sect. 19 of the Act, as he doubted whether or not the appeal to the House of Lords was a pending litigation within sect. 18, sub-sect. 10 of the Act, and the Plaintiffs thereupon took out a summons that they might be at liberty to disclaim :—*Held*, that the words "other legal proceeding in relation to a patent," in sect. 18, sub-sect. 10, refer to a proceeding for the revocation of a patent, and that an "action for infringement . . . . pending'" means an action before judgment, and that being so there was no action for infringement or other legal proceeding pending, and the summons was dismissed. CROPPER *v.* SMITH (No. 2) 28 Ch. D. 148

III. PATENT—ASSIGNMENT.

1. —— Principal and Agent—*Account—Assignment by Principal of Part of Interest to Third Party—License to work Patent—Assignment of Part of Royalty.*] When an assignment is made of a share of profits (arising, e.g., from the working of a patent by licensees), the assignee is entitled to an account from the licensee, but the account must be taken once for all in the presence of all the parties interested. The licensee is not bound to account to the assignor and to each assignee of a share separately.—And the assignee who asks for an account must place himself in the position of the assignor by offering to pay to the accounting party anything which may be due to him by the assignor.—An account of profits will not be directed if it is clear that no profits have been made. BERGMANN *v.* MACMILLAN 17 Ch. D. 423

2. —— Privity of Contract—*Covenant running with Property.*] A patentee assigned letters patent to A. and B., who covenanted with him that they, their executors, administrators, and assigns would use their best endeavours to introduce the invention by granting licenses or working the patent or selling it, and that the patentee should be entitled to receive £5 per cent. of all net profits, whether arising from royalties, sale, or otherwise, which should be received by A. and B. or the survivor of them, or the executors or administrators of the survivor, their or his assigns, and that an account of profits should be rendered yearly to the patentee, and his share of profits paid to him by A. and B. and the survivor of them, and the executors or administrators of such survivor, their or his assigns, with a proviso that after a sale had been made of the patent the interest of the patentee in the profits should cease, and a final account be come to. A. and B. had taken the assignment with a view to forming a company to work the patent. The company was formed and the patent made over to them. The patentee sued the company for an account of profits. The company demurred, on the ground that there was no privity between them and the Plaintiff, and that the Plaintiff's right, if any, was against A. and B. only :—*Held*, by Bacon, V.C., and by the Court of Appeal, that the Plaintiff could sue the company for an account of profits, for that the stipulations of the assignment to A. and B. amounted to a contract that the owners for

III. PATENT—ASSIGNMENT—*continued.*

the time being of the patent should [account for and pay to the Plaintiff a share of profits unless a sale within the meaning of the deed was effected, and that no person taking the patent with notice of this contract could refuse to give effect to it. WERDERMAN *v.* SOCIÉTÉ GÉNÉRALE D'ÉLECTRICITÉ
[19 Ch. D. 246

IV. PATENT—INFRINGEMENT.

1. —— Chemical Process—*Known Chemical Equivalents—Production of similar Results.*] In an action for infringement of a patent for producing colouring matter for dyes the Defendant alleged that in the manufacture of his dyes he used a secret process entirely different from that of the Plaintiffs, and he was allowed to decline answering any questions in cross-examination which would disclose his secret process.—In the course of the arguments the Court being of opinion that the patent was valid, gave the Defendant leave to state his secret process in camerâ. The short-hand writer's notes, which would disclose the secret process, were ordered to be impounded in Court, with liberty to apply :—*Held*, that where a patent is for a process arriving at a known result any person may use another process without its being an infringement ; but where the patent is for a new result, coupled with an effectual process, the patentee is protected from the use of any other process for the same result. The Defendant had not invented new materials but had used the same materials and arrived at a similar result, though by a process different from that of the Plaintiffs and not known at the date of the patent, and this was an infringement. BADISCHE ANILIN UND SODA FABRIK *v.* LEVINSTEIN   24 Ch. D. 156

2. —— Sale in England—*Foreign Manufacture — Slander of Title — Circular warning against Infringement of Patent— Balance of Convenience.*] The Defendants, who were the owners of patents in Belgium and England for an invention for making glass lamp globes, by a deed executed in Belgium granted a licence to the Plaintiffs to manufacture articles under their invention in Belgium, but not elsewhere. The deed contained a clause for submitting disputes to arbitration. The Plaintiffs under this licence manufactured articles in Belgium and sold them in England. The Defendants issued a circular warning persons engaged in the trade that the importation and sale of articles made in foreign countries under their invention, except by themselves, would be a violation of their patent. The Plaintiffs brought an action to restrain the issue of this circular until the matters in dispute had been determined by arbitration.—*Held* (affirming the decision of Pearson, J.), that the grant of the licence to use the patent in Belgium did not imply permission to sell the manufactured article in England in violation of the Defendants' English patent.—*Betts* v. *Willmott* (Law Rep. 6 Ch. 239) distinguished.—Where a trade circular is issued bonâ fide, an interim injunction will not be granted to restrain it unless it is in violation of some contract between the Plaintiff and Defendant, however much the balance of convenience may be in favour of granting. SOCIÉTÉ ANONYME DES MANUFACTURES DE GLACES *v.* TILGHMAN'S PATENT SAND BLAST COMPANY   -   25 Ch. D. 1

IV. PATENT—INFRINGEMENT—continued.

3. —— Sale of component Parts.] Semble, that an injunction granted to restrain the sale of a complete machine, the subject of a patent, will be violated by a sale of the component parts of the machine in such a way that they can easily be put together by any one. UNITED TELEPHONE COMPANY v. DALE   25 Ch. D. 778

4. —— Slander of Title—Damages—Injunction.] The holder of a patent, the validity of which is not impeached, who issues notices against purchasing certain articles alleging that they are infringements of his patent and threatening legal proceedings against those who purchase them, is not liable to an action for damages by the vendor of those articles for the injury done to the vendor's trade by his issuing them, provided they are issued bonâ fide in the belief that the articles complained of are infringements of his patent. Nor is he liable to be restrained by injunction from continuing to issue them until it is proved that they are untrue, so that this further issuing them would not be bonâ fide. — Decision of Jessel, M.R., affirmed. HALSEY v. BROTHERHOOD 19 Ch. D. 386

5. —— Slander of Title—Threat of Legal Proceedings — Injunction — Patents, Designs, and Trade-marks Act, 1883 (46 & 47 Vict. c. 57), s. 32.] On motion under the Patents, Designs, and Trademarks Act, 1883, s. 32, to restrain the publication of advertisements warning the public that the invention claimed by the applicant is an infringement of patent rights claimed by the advertisers, and that all necessary proceedings will be taken to protect such rights should any attempt be made to manufacture or supply the invention claimed by the applicant, the applicant, as a condition precedent to obtaining an injunction, must shew that there has been no infringement on his part. And if in opposition to the motion a case of alleged infringement is raised by the respondents' affidavits, an injunction will not be granted, although the respondents decline to take legal proceedings in respect of such alleged infringement against the applicant. BARNEY v. UNITED TELEPHONE COMPANY   -   28 Ch. D. 394

6. —— User—Importation and transshipment of patented Article — Custom House Agents — Foreign Manufacture.] A patent was granted in England for an invention rendering nitro-glycerine less dangerous. Foreigners imported into England an article compounded of nitro-glycerine and other substances which they had manufactured abroad according to the patent process. The Respondents, acting as Custom House agents for the importers, passed the article through the Custom House, and obtained permission (as required by the Explosives Act, 1875) for landing it and storing it in magazines belonging to the importers :—Held, affirming the decision of the Court of Appeal, that the Respondents being only Custom House agents for the importers, and not themselves the importers, and having neither possession of nor control over the goods, their acts did not amount to an exercise or user of the patent, and that no action could be maintained against them for an infringement of the patent. NOBEL'S EXPLOSIVES COMPANY v. JONES, SCOTT, & CO.   -   -   17 Ch. D. 721 ; 8 App. Cas. 5

7. —— User—Importation and User of Ap-

IV. PATENT—INFRINGEMENT—continued.

paratus made Abroad according to the Specification of an English Patent—Infringement—User for Experiment and Instruction.] User of a pirated article for the purpose of experiment and instruction is user for advantage, and an infringement of the patent.—The Defendant, an English electrician, purchased and imported from foreign manufacturers apparatus which if made here would have infringed the Plaintiffs' patent. The Defendant maintained that he had only purchased the apparatus for examination and experiment by himself and his pupils, as certain royalty-paid instruments in his possession were too expensive to be taken to pieces ; and he insisted that he had never sold, and had never otherwise used the apparatus :—Held, that such user of the pirated apparatus by the Defendant was a user for advantage and an infringement of the patent. UNITED TELEPHONE COMPANY v. SHARPLES 29 Ch. D. 164

8. —— User—Non-destruction of infringing Machines.] Defendants, a telephone company, contracted with an American agent for the purchase of a number of telephones. These machines, known as Blake's transmitters, having been accordingly made in America, were sent to this country, and came into the possession of the Defendants, who kept them unused in a warehouse. The Blake transmitters were protected by English and American patents. The Plaintiffs, another telephone company, having in the meantime obtained an assignment of Blake's English patent, brought an action for infringement, claiming an injunction and delivery up of the machines. Defendants dismantled the machines by taking out the Blake elements, and kept the separate parts stored in a warehouse :—Held, that the possession of the machines by the Defendants was an infringement of the Plaintiffs' patent rights ; and injunction granted.—The Court refused to order the destruction or the delivery up of the infringing machines. UNITED TELEPHONE COMPANY v. LONDON AND GLOBE TELEPHONE AND MAINTENANCE COMPANY   -   26 Ch. D. 766

V. PATENT—PRACTICE.

1. —— Amended Particulars of Objection — 15 & 16 Vict. c. 83, s. 41—Costs—Form of Order.] In granting the Defendant in a patent action after issue joined, and a day has been fixed for the hearing, leave to amend his particulars of objection, the Court will place the Plaintiff in the same position as to discontinuing the action, or disclaiming a portion of his invention, as he would have been if the original particulars of objection had contained the new instances of prior publication proposed to be introduced by amendment ; and accordingly all costs incurred by the Plaintiff subsequently to the delivery of the original particulars of objection will be ordered to be paid to him by the Defendant in case he elects, within a time fixed by the order, to discontinue his action. —Form of order. EDISON TELEPHONE COMPANY v. INDIA RUBBER COMPANY.   -   17 Ch. D. 137

2. —— Costs — Discretion — Patent Law Amendment Act, 1852 (15 & 16 Vict. c. 83), s. 43 —Lord Cairns' Act (21 & 22 Vict. c. 27)— Sir J. Rolt's Act (25 & 26 Vict. c. 42).] In an action in the Court of the County Palatine to restrain

V. PATENT—PRACTICE—*continued.*

infringement of a patent the Defendants delivered particulars of objection. At the trial the Judge held the patent invalid for an objection appearing on the face of it, and dismissed the action with costs, stating his opinion that the Defendants ought to have the costs of the witnesses brought up to support their particulars of objection, though they had not been called, as the Plaintiffs virtually had been non-suited. On taxation the Registrar disallowed these costs, but the Vice-Chancellor held that they must be allowed. The Plaintiffs appealed.—*Held*, that neither Lord Cairns' Act (21 & 22 Vict. c. 27) nor Sir J. Rolt's Act (25 & 26 Vict. c. 42) made it obligatory on a Court of Equity to follow the rule as to costs of particulars of objections laid down by the Patent Law Amendment Act, 1852 (15 & 16 Vict. c. 83), s. 43, and that the rule which applied to Courts having no discretion as to costs ought not to be followed by analogy by a Court which has discretion as to costs; that the Vice-Chancellor had therefore power to give these costs, and that they must be allowed. PARNELL *v.* MORT, LIDDELL, & COMPANY - - - 29 Ch. D. 325

3. —— *Costs—Plaintiff successful on some Issues and not on others—Certificate as to Validity —15 & 16 Vict. c. 83, s. 43.*] A patentee failed in establishing the validity of his patent, but succeeded on the issue of infringement :—*Held*, that the Plaintiff must pay the general costs of the action, but that the Defendant must pay the costs occasioned by the issue of infringement, the one set of costs to be set off against the other.—A certificate under 15 & 16 Vict. c. 83, s. 43, that the validity of a patent came in question in the action cannot be obtained by the Defendant in an action for infringement. BADISCHE ANILIN UND SODA FABRIK *v.* LEVINSTEIN - 24 Ch. D. 156;
[29 Ch. D. 366

4. —— *Interrogatories—Further Particulars —Patent Law Amendment Act, 1852 (15 & 16 Vict. c. 83), s. 41—Common Law Procedure Act, 1854 (17 & 18 Vict. c. 125.]* In a patent action where the Plaintiff or Defendant, as the case may be, makes out a proper case the Court has jurisdiction to order interrogatories to be answered notwithstanding the provision in the Patent Law Amendment Act, 1852, for the delivery of particulars.—The Plaintiff is also entitled under the 41st section of the same Act to the names and addresses of the persons by whom prior user is alleged to have been made as well as the places where the prior user has taken place. BIRCH *v.* MATHER - - - 22 Ch. D. 629

5. —— *Scientific Expert—Chemical Process.*] In an action to restrain the infringement of a patent, if there is contradictory evidence on a scientific question, the Court is at liberty to employ independent expert evidence to give advice upon which the Court may form its judgment. BADISCHE ANILIN UND SODA FABRIK *v.* LEVINSTEIN
[24 Ch. D. 156

VI. PATENT—PROLONGATION.

1. —— *Accounts of Foreign Profits—46 & 47 Vict. c. 57, s. 25, cl. 4.*] *Held*, that 46 & 47 Vict. c. 57, s. 25, cl. 4, does not alter the rules adopted by the Judicial Committee. It is the

VI. PATENT—PROLONGATION—*continued.*

duty of a patentee applying for a prolongation to produce accounts of all the profits received under foreign patents in respect of his invention. *In re* NEWTON'S PATENTS - - 9 App. Cas. 592

2. —— *English and Foreign Patents—Foreign Patents should be stated in Petition—Renewal of English Patent although Foreign Patent expired —Duty of Patentee as to Accounts.*] Where a patentee, whether English or foreign, has obtained foreign patents they should be stated to their Lordships and the fullest information afforded as to the profits thereof.—An English patent may be renewed though a foreign one has been taken out and allowed to expire. A patentee should preserve the clearest evidence of everything which has been paid and received on account of the patent. Whether or not his remuneration has been adequate, his furnishing a satisfactory account is a condition precedent to his obtaining an extension of his term. *In re* ADAIR'S PATENT
[6 App. Cas. 176

3. —— *Patents, Designs, and Trade-marks Act, 1883 (ss. 25, 113)—Practice—Petition.*] *Held*, that the enactments of 46 & 47 Vict. c. 57, do not affect any patent granted before the commencement of the Act, nor any right or privilege which had accrued to the patentee before or at the commencement of the said Act, including the privilege of applying for a renewal. *In re* BRANDON'S PATENT. *Ex parte* DOTY
[9 App. Cas. 589

4. —— *Rights of the Crown—New Patent limited in its Application.*] When a patent is prolonged, if the invention is likely to be used by the Government, it is usual to insert a condition reserving the rights of the Crown. *In re* NAPIER'S PATENT - - - - 6 App. Cas. 174

VII. PATENT—VALIDITY.

1. —— *Estoppel—Particulars of Objection delivered by one of two Partners in Action against both—15 & 16 Vict. c. 83, s. 41.*] If a patentee becomes bankrupt, and his trustee in bankruptcy assigns the patent the patentee is not estopped from afterwards denying the validity of the patent, as against the assignee.—So *held*, affirming the decision of the Court of Appeal.—A patentee having gone into liquidation his trustee in liquidation assigned the patent. The patentee afterwards went into a trade partnership with S. The assignees of the patent brought an action against the patentee and S. for an injunction and damages for infringements of the patent alleged to have been committed in partnership. The defence alleged the invalidity of the patent, and the Defendants delivered particulars of objections, viz., that the Defendants would deny the infringement; and that the Defendant S. would rely on their objections to the validity of the letters patent on the ground of want of novelty and insufficiency of the specification :—*Held*, reversing the decision of the Court of Appeal, that under 15 & 16 Vict. c. 83, s. 41, it was not necessary for every one of two or more defendants defending in the same interest to deliver particulars of objections, and that the patentee was not precluded from setting up at the trial the invalidity of the patent on the ground of want of novelty and

VII. PATENT—VALIDITY—*continued.*

insufficiency of the specification. SMITH *v.* CROPPER　-　　- 26 Ch. D. 700; 10 App. Cas. 249

2. —— **Novelty**—*Anticipation—Prior Publication—Book in Foreign Language—Validity—Variation between Provisional and Complete Specification—Insufficiency of Provisional Specification—Infringement— Use of Equivalent — Discovery after Date of Patent—Practice— Certificate of Proof of Breaches—Patent Law Amendment Act, 1852 (15 & 16 Vict. c. 83), ss. 6, 43.*] An instrument which was alleged to be an anticipation of an invention, patented in 1876, for improvements in electric telephony and telephonic apparatus, was described in a paper written in German in a scientific journal, called the "*Zeitschrift*" of the Germo-Austrian Telegraph Union, which was published in Berlin, in 1862. The description was illustrated by figures. A copy of the "*Zeitschrift*," was in the library of the Patent Office in London, and another copy was in the library of the institute of Civil Engineers in London, where it was accessible to all the members, more than 3000 in number, and to friends introduced by them. It was, however, entered in the catalogue only under the head of "Journals," not under the head of "Telephones," or "Telegraphs." A telegraphic engineer gave evidence that, before the date of the patent, he had seen the description in the "*Zeitschrift*," and that, though he could not read German, yet, from his knowledge of the technical words used, he was able, with the assistance of the plates, to understand the substance of the invention:—*Held,* that there had been a sufficient publication in England of the prior invention before the date of the patent.—But *held,* upon the facts, that the prior invention was not an anticipation of the patented invention. —A patent held void on the ground that the nature of part of the invention described in and claimed by the complete specification, had not been sufficiently described in the provisional specification.—In a patent for "improvements in instruments for controlling by sound the transmission of electric currents, and the reproduction of corresponding sounds at a distance," the patentee claimed (1) "In an instrument for transmitting electric impulses by sound a diaphragm or tympan of mica, substantially as set forth; (2) In an instrument for transmitting electric impulses by sound, the combination with a diaphragm or tympan of electric tension regulators substantially as hereinbefore described for varying the resistance in a closed circuit substantially as set forth." The Plaintiffs, the owners of the patent, in the instruments which they manufactured and sold, used a diaphragm or tympan of mica to receive the air vibrations produced by the voice; below this diaphragm and in its centre, but of smaller size than it, was a cork, below the cork was a piece of platina foil of the same size as the cork, and in a cavity or box below the platina was placed the substance which was used as a tension regulator. The platina foil formed one electrode and the bottom of the box the other, the current of electricity passing from one to the other through the tension regulator. The Plaintiffs used for this purpose lampblack, artificially compressed into a button. The Defendants made and sold similar instruments, but they dispensed with the mica diaphragm and the cork, the air vibrations being in their instruments received directly on the platina foil, below which was placed the substance used as a tension regulator. The Defendants employed loose particles of coke for this purpose. At the date of the Plaintiff's patent it was not known that the instrument would work without the independent mica diaphragm; this was a subsequent discovery. The Defendants adduced evidence to shew that their instrument would work equally well if the platina foil above the tension regulator was removed and the air vibrations were received directly on the particles of coke:—*Held,* that in the Defendants' instrument the platina foil acted as a diaphragm or tympan, and that the Defendants had infringed the Plaintiffs' patent. When, at the trial of an action for the infringement of a patent, the Court is of opinion that there has been an infringement by the Defendant, but holds on a legal ground that the patent is void, it will not give the Plaintiff a certificate, under sect. 43 of the Patent Law Amendment Act, 1852, that breaches of the patent by the Defendant have been proved. UNITED TELEPHONE COMPANY *v.* HARRISON, COXWALKER, & Co.　-　　- 21 Ch. D. 720

3. —— **Novelty**—*Combination of existing Inventions.*] The Plaintiff obtained in 1874 a patent for certain improvements in interlocking apparatus for railway points and signals. Patents had been previously obtained in 1870 and 1871 for inventions of apparatus for similar purposes. In an action for infringement of the Plaintiff's patent of 1874 by the Defendants it was admitted by the Plaintiff's witnesses that, taking the two inventions of 1870 and 1871 together, and discarding all superfluous parts, every element of the patent of 1874 was to be found in one or other of those inventions; and that no new result was obtained by their combination in the patent of 1874 different from that which had been obtained by the previous inventions, but it was contended for the Plaintiff that the combination of the two inventions of 1870 and 1871, effected by the Plaintiff's invention of 1874, required such an exercise of skill and ingenuity as to constitute the subject of a valid patent. There was, however, evidence, with which the Court was satisfied, to shew that any person of ordinary skill and knowledge of the subject, placing the two inventions of 1870 and 1871 side by side, could effect the combination of the two in a manner similar to that of the Plaintiff's invention without making any further experiments or obtaining any further information:— *Held,* that the Plaintiff's invention was not of sufficient novelty to constitute the subject of a valid patent. SAXBY *v.* GLOUCESTER WAGGON COMPANY　-　　- 7 Q. B. D. 305

4. —— **Novelty**—*Prior User in British Colony —License to use Invention in the United Kingdom.*] The district of Natal is a British colony with a separate Government, under a Governor appointed by the Crown; and a law has been passed by the Legislative Council of Natal, providing for the granting, in the colony, of patents for inventions: —*Held,* that the validity of letters patent under the Great Seal for license to use an invention in

VII. PATENT—VALIDITY—*continued.*
the United Kingdom of Great Britain and Ireland,
the Channel Islands, and the Isle of Man, would
not be impeached by the fact, if proved, of prior
use of the invention in Natal. ROLLS *v.* ISAACS
[19 Ch. D. 268

5. —— **Sufficiency of Specification**—*Utility—
Ambiguity — Chemical Process — Isomeric Substances*] Two isomeric forms of a chemical product N., called A. N. and B. N., were known to
exist at the date of Plaintiffs' patent, but one only
was known in commerce, the other being only
mentioned in scientific books. B. N. had only
been known for a few years, before which time,
and to some extent afterwards, A. N. had been
known as N. The Plaintiff's specification, which
was from its nature addressed to advanced students
of organic chemistry, mentioned N. as an important factor in his process, without stating whether
it was A. N. or B. N.—*Held,* by the Court of
Appeal (dissentiente Baggallay, L.J.), that the specification was insufficient for ambiguity.—When
the specification of a patent for a chemical process
applies equally to several isomeric substances, but
one only would produce a useful result, and it can
only be ascertained by experiment which that is,
the patent is invalid.—Observations on the necessity of proof by the Plaintiff that the invention
has been worked, when the utility of the invention and the sufficiency of the specification are in
issue. BADISCHE ANILIN UND SODA FABRIK *v.*
LEVINSTEIN   24 Ch. D. 156 ; 29 Ch. D. 366

PATENT—Co-owners—Action by one
[16 Ch. D. 59
See PRACTICE—SUPREME COURT—PAR-
TIES. 9.

—— Infringement—Injunction -   25 Ch. D. 778
See PRACTICE—SUPREME COURT—AT-
TACHMENT. 9.

—— Infringement—Proof for profits in bankruptcy   -   -   20 Ch. D. 780
See BANKRUPTCY—PROOF. 7.

—— Infringement—Scotch law   8 App. Cas. 873
See SCOTCH LAW—PATENT.

—— Statutory declaration for
See REVENUE—STAMPS—*Statutes.*

PATRIOTIC FUND.
The Act 44 & 45 Vict. c. 46 *(the Patriotic Fund
Act,* 1881) *amends the Patriotic Fund Act,* 1867.

PAUPER—Discharge from casual ward.
See POOR LAW—RELIEF—*Statutes.*
METROPOLIS—POOR ACTS—*Statutes.*

—— Husband, maintenance of, by wife.
See HUSBAND AND WIFE—MARRIED WO-
MEN'S PROPERTY ACT—*Statutes.*

—— Lunatic.
See LUNATIC—JURISDICTION—*Statutes.*

—— Lunatic—Maintenance   27 Ch. D. 710
See LUNATIC—MAINTENANCE. 3.

—— Settlement—Removal.
See Cases under POOR LAW—SETTLE-
MENT.

PAVING EXPENSES.
See Cases under LOCAL GOVERNMENT—
STREETS.
METROPOLIS—MANAGEMENT ACTS.

PAY AND PENSIONS.
See ARMY AND NAVY—*Statutes.*

PAY OFFICE OF SUPREME COURT.
See COURT—STATUTES.

"PAYABLE"—Vesting -   -   17 Ch. D. 835
See WILL—VESTING. 6.

PAYMENT — After bankruptcy notice—Promissory note   -   12 Q. B. D. 506
See BANKRUPTCY—ACT OF BANKRUPTCY:
6.

—— Appropriation—Guarantee   25 Ch. D. 692
See PRINCIPAL AND SURETY—DISCHARGE.
3.

—— Commencement of—Construction of statute
[6 App. Cas. 114
See SCOTCH LAW—RAILWAY COMPANY.
2.

—— Direction as to—Will—Inconsistency
See WILL—REPUGNANCY. [18 Ch. D. 17

—— Illegal, at municipal election.
See MUNICIPAL CORPORATION—ELECTION
—*Statutes.*

—— In exchange for bills of lading—Tender of
one bill only   -   11 Q. B. D. 327
See SALE OF GOODS—CONTRACT. 4.

—— Interest on mortgage—Statute of Limitations   ·   -   19 Ch. D. 539
See LIMITATIONS, STATUTE OF—REALTY.
5.

—— Mortgage debt—Notice to pay
[23 Ch. D. 372
See MORTGAGE—REDEMPTION. 1.

—— On demand—Mortgagor in possession
[8 App. Cas. 285
See MORTGAGE—MORTGAGOR IN POSSES-
SION.

—— Wages in public-houses—Prohibition Act,
1883.
See MASTER AND SERVANT—WAGES —
Statutes.

PAYMENT INTO COURT.
See Cases under PRACTICE—SUPREME
COURT—PAYMENT INTO COURT.

—— Action by remainderman   - 21 Ch. D. 121
See EXECUTOR—ACTIONS. 5.

—— Lands Clauses Act—Investment.
See Cases under LANDS CLAUSES ACT—
PURCHASE-MONEY.

—— Redemption of mortgage—Bankruptcy of
mortgagor '   -   -   28 Ch. D. 402
See VENDOR AND PURCHASER—CONVEY-
ANCE. 4.

—— Restraining sale by mortgagee
[23 Ch. D. 690
See MORTGAGE—POWERS. 3.

PAYMENT OUT OF COURT—Costs—Compulsory
purchase   -   24 Ch. D. 669
See PRACTICE—SUPREME COURT—COSTS
24.

—— Costs—Lands Clauses Act   21 Ch. D. 776
See LANDS CLAUSES ACT—COSTS. 5.

—— Fund of infant married woman
[16 Ch. D. 376
See SETTLEMENT—EQUITY TO SETTLE-
MENT. 2.

PAYMENT OUT OF COURT—*continued.*
—— Lands Clauses Act.
   See Cases under LANDS CLAUSES ACT—
     PURCHASE-MONEY.
—— Lands Clauses Act—Practice in Chambers
         [30 Ch. D. 541
   See Cases under PRACTICE—SUPREME
    COURT—CHAMBERS. 11—16.
—— New Zealand—Probate in - 24 Ch. D. 177
   See PRACTICE—SUPREME COURT—PAY-
    MENT OUT OF COURT.
—— Settled Land Act   24 Ch. D. 662, 717
   See SETTLED LAND ACT — TRUSTEES.
    1, 2.
—— Staying proceedings pending appeal
         [28 Ch. D. 18
   See PRACTICE—SUPREME COURT—STAY-
    ING PROCEEDINGS. 14.
—— Trustee Relief Act   22 Ch. D. 635
   See TRUSTEE RELIEF ACT. 1.

PEDIGREE—Declaration by deceased parent—
   Proof of birth - - 13 Q. B. D. 318
   See EVIDENCE — DECLARATION BY DE-
    CEASED PERSON. 2.

PEDLAR.
   *The Act 44 & 45 Vict. c. 45 (the Pedlars Act,
1881) amends the Pedlars Act, 1871, and enacts
(sect. 2) that a pedlar's certificate granted under
the Pedlars Act, 1871, shall during the time for
which it continues in force authorize the person to
whom it is granted to act as a pedlar within any
part of the United Kingdom.*
—— Selling petroleum.
   See PETROLEUM—*Statutes.*
PEERAGE—Scotch law - 6 App. Cas. 489 ;
         [10 App. Cas. 692, 763
   See SCOTCH LAW—PEERAGE. 1, 2, 3.

PENAL ACTION.
   1. —— Limitation of Time — *Common Informer—Selling Silver Wares with Counterfeit
Mark*—" *Party grieved* "—7 & 8 Vict. c. 22, s. 3—
3 & 4 Will. 4, c. 42, s. 3—31 Eliz. c. 5.] An action
by an officer of one of the Companies of Goldsmiths
mentioned in 7 & 8 Vict. c. 22, for penalties under
sect. 3 of that Act, is not an action by a common
informer within 31 Eliz. c. 5, nor is it an action
by a " party grieved " within 3 & 4 Will. 4, c. 42,
s. 3, and consequently can be brought more than
two years after the cause of action accrued :—So
held, reversing the judgment of the Queen's Bench
Division. ROBINSON v. CURREY 6 Q. B. D. 21 ;
         [7 Q. B. D. 465
   2. —— Oath of Allegiance—*Claim to affirm
—Common Informer — Prerogative of Crown—
Parliamentary Oaths Act, 1866 (29 & 30 Vict.
c. 19), s. 5.*] Where a penalty is created by
statute and nothing is said as to who may recover
it, and it is not created for the benefit of a party
grieved, and the offence is not against an individual, it belongs to the Crown, and the Crown
alone can maintain a suit for it.—To enable a
common informer to maintain an action for a
penalty created by statute, an interest in the
penalty must be given to him by express words
or by sufficient implication.—The penalty of £500,
" to be recovered by action in one of Her Ma-

PENAL ACTION—*continued.*
jesty's Superior Courts at Westminster," which is
imposed by the Parliamentary Oaths Act, 1866
(29 & 30 Vict. c. 19), s. 5, upon any Member of
the House of Commons voting as such in the
House or sitting during any debate after the
Speaker has been chosen without having taken
and subscribed the oath thereby appointed, cannot be recovered in an action by a common informer, and can be sued for only by the Crown :—
So held, reversing the decision of the Court of Appeal (Lord Blackburn dissenting). BRADLAUGH
v. CLARKE - 7 Q. B. D. 38 ; 8 App. Cas. 354
   3. —— Remission—*22 Vict. c. 32—Local Government Acts—Officer interested in Contract with
Local Authority—Public Health Act, 1875 (38 &
39 Vict. c. 55), s. 193.*] Under 22 Vict. c. 32—
which enables the Crown to remit penalties imposed by statute on convicted offenders—there
is no power to remit the penalty to which the
officers of local authorities are liable under sect. 193
of the Public Health Act, 1875, for being interested in any contract made with such local
authorities. TODD v. ROBINSON 12 Q. B. D. 530

PENALTY.
   —— Liquidated Damages—*Breach of Contract
to pay a Sum certain—Breach of several Stipulations of various importance—Forfeiture of Deposit
—Lien for Money expended by Party who breaks
the Contract.*] The Plaintiff entered into a contract with the Defendant, who was a builder, to
sell him an estate for £70,000, which was to be
expended by the Defendant in building on the
estate. The contract contained numerous provisions, and amongst other things that a deposit of
£5000 should be paid by the Defendant into the
bankers to the joint account of the Plaintiff and
Defendant, of which £500 was to be paid on the
execution of the contract and the remainder
within seven months. If the Plaintiff could not
make a good title the deposit of the £500 was to
be returned, and the Plaintiff was to pay the
Defendant £5000 as liquidated damages. And if
the Defendant should commit a substantial breach
of the contract, either in not proceeding with due
diligence to carry out the works, or in failing to
perform any of the provisions of the contract,
then and in either of such events the deposit of
£5000 should be forfeited, and if it had not been
paid the Defendant should forfeit and pay to the
Plaintiff £5000 by way of liquidated damages, and
the agreement should be void and of no effect,
and the Plaintiff should regain possession of the
estate ; but credit was to be given to the Defendant for all moneys actually expended ; and it
was provided that such breach should not be the
consequence of a misconstruction of the meaning
of any of the provisions of the contract.—The Defendant did not pay the £500 deposit, and altogether failed in carrying out the contract, and the
Plaintiff brought an action to recover £5000 as
liquidated damages :—Held (affirming the decision
of Fry, J.), that the condition of forfeiture was
not intended to apply to the payment of the deposit of £500 which was to be paid on the execution of the contract, but to a substantial breach of
any of the subsequent stipulations, and therefore
the £5000 was not be regarded as a penalty but
as liquidated damages, the payment of which

PENALTY—*continued.*

could be enforced against the Defendant. Where a contract contains a condition for payment of a sum of money as liquidated damages for the breach of stipulations of varied importance, none of which is for payment of an ascertained sum of money, the general rule is that the sum named is not to be treated as a penalty, but as liquidated damages. —But whether it would not be treated as a penalty if one of the stipulations was of very trivial importance :—*Quære.*—Where there is a condition for the forfeiture of a deposit for the breach of various stipulations, even though some of them may be very trivial, or for payment of a fixed sum of money, the forfeiture will be enforced and not treated as a penalty.—*Astley* v. *Weldon* (2 B, & P. 346); *Kemble* v. *Farren* (6 Bing. 141); *Atkyns* v. *Kinnier* (4 Ex. 776); *Magee* v. *Lavell* (Law Rep. 9 C.P. 107); *In re Newman* (4 Ch. D. 724); and *Betts* v. *Burch* (4 H. & N. 506), commented on.—*Per* Fry, J.: A man who enters into a contract to expend a certain sum of money on land, and after spending part of it declines to perform the contract, has no lien on the land for the money which he has expended. WALLIS *v.* SMITH   -   -   21 Ch. D. 243

—— Action for—Criminal law 7 Q. B. D. 38, 465 ;
          [12 Q. B. D. 530; 8 App. Cas. 354
   See PENAL ACTION. 1, 2, 3.

—— Action for—Interrogatories 10 Q. B. D. 459
   See PRACTICE—SUPREME COURT—INTER-
   ROGATORIES. 1.

—— Adulteration of food.
   See Cases under ADULTERATION.

—— Continuing offence -   -   8 Q. B. D. 603
   See LOCAL GOVERNMENT—OFFENCES. 2.

—— Default of performance of condition
          [16 Ch. D. 675
   See BANKRUPTCY—ACT OF BANKRUPTCY.
   22.

—— Parliamentary Oaths Act -   7 Q. B. D. 38;
          [14 Q. B. D. 667
   See PARLIAMENT—ELECTION. 2, 3.

—— Public Health Act.
   See LOCAL GOVERNMENT — PUBLIC
   HEALTH ACTS—PENALTIES—*Statutes.*

—— Unqualified person acting as solicitor
          [9 Q. B. D. 1; 8 App. Cas. 407
   See SOLICITOR—UNQUALIFIED. 4.

—— Vestry—Member interested in contract
          [11 Q. B. D. 533
   See METROPOLIS—MANAGEMENT ACTS.
   16.

PENANG—Law of   -   7 App. Cas. 172
   See COLONIAL LAW—STRAITS SETTLE-
   MENTS. 1.

PENDENTE LITE—Assignment of cause of action
          [16 Ch. D. 121
   See PRACTICE — SUPREME COURT —
   PARTIES. 6.

PENDING BUSINESS—Remuneration of solicitor
          [29 Ch. D. 608
   See SOLICITOR—BILL OF COSTS. 24.

PENDING PROCEEDINGS—Administration action—Appointment of new trustees
          [24 Ch. D. 553
   See SETTLEMENT—POWERS. 17.

—— Administration action—New practice—Re-
   ference to Chambers   -   25 Ch. D. 66
   See PRACTICE—SUPREME COURT—CHAM-
   BERS. 7.

—— Administration action—Sale under Settled
   Land Act   -   -   30 Ch. D. 531
   See SETTLED LAND ACT—TENANT FOR
   LIFE. 1.

—— Costs of trustee—New and Old Rules of
   Court   -   -   29 Ch. D. 495
   See PRACTICE — SUPREME COURT—AP-
   PEAL. 6.

—— Default in pleading—New practice
          [25 Ch. D. 68
   See PRACTICE—SUPREME COURT—DE-
   FAULT. 2.

—— Final determination of controversy
          [18 Ch. D. 544
   See PRACTICE—SUPREME COURT—RE-
   CEIVER. 1.

—— Legal demand   -   -   21 Ch. D. 278
   See WILL—CONDITION. 1.

—— Liquidation—Adjudication of bankruptcy
          [24 Ch. D. 35
   See BANKRUPTCY—LIQUIDATION. 6.

—— Stay of action -   -   -   10 P. D. 141
   See PRACTICE—ADMIRALTY—LIS ALIBI
   PENDENS. 2.

—— Patent—Action—Amendment of specification of   -   -   -   28 Ch. D. 148
   See PATENT—AMENDMENT. 2.

—— Transfer to Supreme Court—Insolvency
   See INSOLVENCY.   [20 Ch. D. 637

—— Voluntary winding-up—Transfer of shares
          [25 Ch. D. 118
   See COMPANY—SHARES—TRANSFER. 7.

PENSION.

Civil Service Pension.] *The Act 44 & 45 Vict. c. 44 (the Superannuation Act, 1881) extends the Superannuation Act Amendment Act, 1873, to certain persons admitted into subordinate situations in the departments of the Postmaster General and the Commissioners of Her Majesty's Works and Public Buildings. The Act 47 & 48 Vict. c. 57, further extends the Superannuation Act Amendment Act, 1873.*

Commutation of Pensions.] *The Act 45 & 46 Vict. c. 44, amends the Pensions Commutation Act, 1871, and empowers the Treasury to commute a portion of a pension.*

—— Indian officer—Sequestration   8 P. D. 163
   See PRACTICE — DIVORCE — SEQUESTRA-
   TION.

—— Judge of colony—Bankruptcy 21 Ch. D. 85
   See BANKRUPTCY—ASSETS. 13.

—— Retired incumbent -   -   17 Ch. D. 1
   See ECCLESIASTICAL LAW—CLERGY. 3.

PEPPERCORN RENT—Receipt for 28 Ch. D. 661 ;
          [30 Ch. D. 344
   See VENDOR AND PURCHASER—TITLE. 2

PER STIRPES—"According to the stocks"
  See WILL—CLASS. 1.   [24 Ch. D. 664

PERCENTAGE—Remuneration of solicitor
                [25 Ch. D. 301
  See SOLICITOR—BILL OF COSTS. 19.

PERILS OF THE SEAS   6 Q. B. D. 648; 7 App.
                              [Cas. 670
  See INSURANCE, MARINE—POLICY. 2.

PERIOD OF DISTRIBUTION — Erroneous reference to   -   16 Ch. D. 212
  See WILL—VESTING. 7.

PERJURY—Commissioners to inquire into corrupt practices — Indictment—Information   -   -   8 Q. B. D. 267
  See CRIMINAL LAW—EVIDENCE. 4.

—— Sentence—Two counts - 6 App. Cas. 229
  See CRIMINAL LAW—PRACTICE. 2.

PERMANENT IMPROVEMENTS—Capital or income   -   27 Ch. D. 196
  See SETTLEMENT—POWERS. 7.

—— Mortgagee in possession   21 Ch. D. 469
  See MORTGAGE—MORTGAGEE IN POSSES-
  SION. 5.

PERPETUITY—Covenant to reconvey
                [20 Ch. D. 562
  See LANDS CLAUSES ACT—SUPERFLUOUS
  LANDS. 2.

—— Power of appointment   29 Ch. D. 521;
                [30 Ch. D. 172
  See POWER—EXECUTION. 12, 18.

—— Power of re-entry -   25 Ch. D. 629
  See VENDOR AND PURCHASER—CONDI-
  TIONS OF SALE. 1.

—— Power of sale—Settlement - 19 Ch. D. 624
  See SETTLEMENT—POWERS. 15.

—— Will—Construction.
  See Cases under WILL—PERPETUITY.

PERSIAN LAW—Proof of -   6 P. D. 6
  See ADMINISTRATOR—LIMITED. 6.

"PERSON"—Meaning of—Notice of action
                [9 App. Cas. 365
  See COLONIAL LAW—VICTORIA. 4.

PERSON AGGRIEVED—Appeal in bankruptcy
                [17 Ch. D. 518
  See BANKRUPTCY—TRUSTEE. 7.

—— Bankruptcy—Complaint against trustee
                [16 Ch. D. 497
  See BANKRUPTCY—RECEIVER. 2.

—— Recovery of penalty   - 7 Q. B. D. 465
  See PENAL ACTION. 1.

—— Registration of trade-mark 25 Ch. D. 194;
                [26 Ch. D. 48
  See TRADE-MARK—REGISTRATION. 14, 15.

PERSONÆ DESIGNATÆ -   25 Ch. D. 162
  See WILL—CLASS. 5.

PERSONAL ACTION—Dying with the person
  [21 Ch. D. 464; 24 Ch. D. 439; 9 Q. B. D.
  See EXECUTOR—ACTIONS. 1, 2, 3. [110

PERSONAL OBLIGATION—Conveyance of heritable property   6 App. Cas. 295
  See SCOTCH LAW—HERITABLE PROPERTY.
  3.

PERSONAL REPRESENTATIVE—Power to dis-
  pense with   -   19 Ch. D. 534
  See PRACTICE—SUPREME COURT—PAR-
  TIES. 1.

PETITION—Adjudication of bankruptcy—Petitioning creditor's debt   16 Ch. D. 283;
                [22 Ch. D. 132
  See BANKRUPTCY—ADJUDICATION. 1, 5.

—— Adjudication of bankruptcy—Offer to give
  up security   -   20 Ch. D. 289
  See BANKRUPTCY—SECURED CREDITOR. 3.

—— Adjudication of bankruptcy—Surety
                [17 Ch. D. 44
  See PRINCIPAL AND SURETY—CONTRIBU-
  TION. 1.

—— Adjudication of bankruptcy—Trader
                [21 Ch. D. 394
  See BANKRUPTCY—TRADER. 2.

—— Company—Reduction of capital—Sanction
  of Court   23 Ch. D. 542; 29 Ch. D. 683
  See COMPANY—REDUCTION OF CAPITAL.
  3. 4.

—— Liquidation   24 Ch. D. 35
  See BANKRUPTCY—LIQUIDATION. 6.

—— Re-transfer of stock—National Debt Commissioners   -   25 Ch. D. 231
  See NATIONAL DEBT COMMISSIONERS.

—— Settled Estates Act—Persons to present
                [24 Ch. D. 238
  See SETTLED ESTATES ACT. 4.

—— Winding-up.
  See Cases under COMPANY—WINDING-UP
  ORDER.

—— Winding-up—Inspection of documents
                [27 Ch. D. 106
  See COMPANY—COST-BOOK COMPANY. 3.

—— Winding-up—Policy-holders 16 Ch. D. 246
  See COMPANY — LIFE INSURANCE COM-
  PANY. 2.

—— Withdrawal of—Filing of second petition
                [6 P. D. 10
  See PRACTICE—DIVORCE—PLEADING. 2.

PETITION OF RIGHT—Canada 9 App. Cas. 745
  See COLONIAL LAW—CANADA—QUEBEC.
  7.

—— Natal—Jurisdiction   - 6 App. Cas. 619
  See COLONIAL LAW—NATAL. 1.

PETROLEUM.

  *The Act 44 & 45 Vict. c. 67 (Petroleum Hawkers
  Act, 1881), s. 1, empowers any person who is
  licensed in pursuance of the Petroleum Act, 1871,
  to keep petroleum to which that Act applies, subject to the enactments for the time being in force
  with respect to hawkers and pedlars, to hawk such
  petroleum by himself or his servants.*
  *Sect. 2 prescribes the regulations to be observed
  in the hawking of petroleum. The Act to apply to
  any petroleum other than that to which the Petroleum Act, 1871, applies while in any carriage used
  for the hawking of petroleum to which the Petroleum
  Act, 1871, applies.*
  *Penalty for any contravention of the prescribed
  regulation.*
  *Sect. 3 modifies the conditions annexed to licenses
  granted under the Petroleum Act, 1881.*

PETROLEUM—*continued.*

Sect. 4 empowers a constable to seize and detain petroleum where he has reasonable cause to believe a contravention of the Act is being committed.

Sect. 5 saves rights of municipal boroughs.

Sect. 6 defines the expressions "carriage" and "hawker of petroleum."

PHARMACY ACTS.

Nux vomica.] *Order in Council under the Pharmacy Act,* 1868, 31 & 32 Vict. c. 121, s. 2, *declaring nux vomica and its preparations to be poison. 28th of July,* 1882   L. G. 1882, p. 3514

—— *Poison, Sale of—Label—Name and Address of "Seller"—Pharmacy Act,* 1868 (31 & 32 Vict. c. 121), *s.* 17.] The Pharmacy Act, 1868 (31 & 32 Vict. c. 121), sect. 17, enacts that it shall be unlawful to sell any poison unless the box, bottle, vessel, wrapper, or cover in which such poison is contained be distinctly labelled with the name of the article and the word poison, and with the name and address of the seller of the poison, and any person selling poison otherwise shall upon summary conviction be liable to a penalty, and for the purposes of this section the person on whose behalf any sale is made by any apprentice or servant shall be deemed to be the seller.—The Respondent sold at his shop in Friar Street, Oxford, a packet of poison labelled only, "W. Paterson, chemist and druggist, 3, Cowley Road, Oxford"—the name and address of a registered chemist who had supplied the poison to the Respondent, and paid him a commission on the sale:—*Held,* that the Respondent was the "seller," with whose name and address the packet should have been labelled, and he was liable to a penalty under sect. 17, which applies to the person keeping the shop or conducting the business in which the sale is made. TEMPLEMAN *v.* TRAFFORD
[8 Q. B. D. 397

PHOTOGRAPH—"Author"—Copyright
[11 Q. B. D. 627
See COPYRIGHT—PICTURES.

PHYSICIAN—Gift to—Fiduciary relation
See GIFT.   [8 Q. B. D. 587

PILOT—PILOTAGE.
See Cases under SHIP—PILOT.

PLAINTIFF—Adding Plaintiff   17 Ch. D. 169;
[19 Ch. D. 55; 29 Ch. D. 190, 584
See PRACTICE—SUPREME COURT—PARTIES. 1—4.

—— Death of—Revivor -   - 24 Ch. D. 126
See PRACTICE — SUPREME COURT — CHANGE OF PARTIES. 7.

PLACE OF ELECTION—Parliament
See PARLIAMENT—REDISTRIBUTION OF SEATS—*Statutes.*

PLACES OF WORKSHOP SITES AMENDMENT ACT, 1882.
See CHURCH BUILDING ACTS—*Statutes.*

PLATE—Duty on.
See REVENUE—CUSTOMS—*Statutes.*

PLEADING—Action by freemen of borough—Custom of borough - 21 Ch. D. 111
See MUNICIPAL CORPORATION — PROPERTY.

PLEADING—*continued.*

—— Action on guarantee   - 8 App. Cas. 755
See PRINCIPAL AND SURETY—DISCHARGE. 1.

—— Admiralty Court.
See Cases under PRACTICE—ADMIRALTY —PLEADING.

—— Amendment of—Supreme Court
See Cases under PRACTICE — SUPREME COURT—AMENDMENT.

—— Amendment of 16 Ch. D. 440; 19 Ch. D. 22
See EASEMENT. 2.

—— Copyright action -   23 Ch. D. 727
See COPYRIGHT—BOOKS. 3.

—— Divorce Court.
See Cases under PRACTICE—DIVORCE.

—— Ecclesiastical Courts.
See Cases under PRACTICE—ECCLESIASTICAL.

—— Facts not stated—Libel—Justification
[8 Q. B. D. 491
See DEFAMATION—LIBEL. 2.

—— Probate Court—Embarrassing matter—Appeal from chambers -   9 P. D. 68
See PRACTICE—PROBATE—PLEADING.

—— Slander   11 Q. B. D. 609; 6 App. Cas, 156
See DEFAMATION—SLANDER. 1, 2.

—— Striking out   26 Ch. D. 470, 778;
[6 Q. B. D, 190
See PRACTICE—SUPREME COURT—STRIKING OUT PLEADINGS. 1, 2, 3.

—— Supplemental action against successors in title -   - 17 Ch. D. 685
See LOCAL GOVERNMENT—LOCAL AUTHORITY. 13.

—— Supreme Court.
See Cases under PRACTICE—SUPREME COURT.

PLEDGE—Bill of lading—Indorsement
[13 Q. B. D. 159; 10 App. Cas. 74
See SHIP—BILL OF LADING. 4.

—— Shares in company -   - 26 Ch. D. 257
See COMPANY—SHARES—TRANSFER. 1.

PLURALITIES.
See ECCLESIASTICAL LAW — CLERGY — *Statutes.*

POACHING—Search by constable in highway
See GAME. 2.   [14 Q. B. D. 725

POISON—Sale—Pharmacy Act   8 Q. B. D. 397
See PHARMACY ACTS.

—— Sale—Nux vomica.
See PHARMACY ACTS—Gazette.

POLICE—Constable—Notice of action
See CONSTABLE.   [14 Q. B. D. 720

—— Constable—In boroughs
See MUNICIPAL CORPORATION—CONSTITUTION—*Statute* 45 & 46 VICT. c. 50, PARTS IX. and X.

—— Constable—Allowance—Attachment of debt
[12 Q. B. D. 8
See PRACTICE—SUPREME COURT—GARNISHEE ORDERS. 10.

2 M

POLICE ACTS.
　See METROPOLIS—POLICE ACTS—*Statutes.*

POLICE STATION—Income tax　**10 Q. B. D. 267;**
　　　　　　　　　　　　　[9 App. Cas. 61
　See REVENUE—INCOME TAX.　1.

POLICY OF INSURANCE—Fire.
　See Cases under INSURANCE, FIRE.

—— Fire—Law of Canada　-　**7 App. Cas. 96**
　See COLONIAL LAW—CANADA—ONTARIO.
　3.

—— Life.
　See Cases under INSURANCE, LIFE.

—— Life—Assignment—Payment in absence of
　representatives of persons insured
　　　　　　　　　　　　　[19 Ch. D. 534
　See PRACTICE—SUPREME COURT—PAR-
　TIES.　7.

—— Life—Covenant by surety to pay premiums
　—Right to securities　**19 Ch. D. 615**
　See PRINCIPAL AND SURETY—INDEMNITY.
　2.

—— Life—Husband—Settled to separate use—
　Contract by wife　-　**23 Ch. D. 712**
　See HUSBAND AND WIFE — SEPARATE
　ESTATE.　7.

—— Life—Married Women's Property Act—
　Separate use　-　-　**23 Ch. D. 525;**
　　　　　　　　　　　　　[26 Ch. D. 236
　See HUSBAND AND WIFE—MARRIED WO-
　MEN'S PROPERTY ACTS.　4, 5.

—— Life—Notice of charge—Priority
　　　　　　　　　　　　　[28 Ch. D. 674
　See MORTGAGE—PRIORITY.　13.

—— Life—Sureties　　**24 Ch. D. 709**
　See PRINCIPAL AND SURETY—CONTRIBU-
　TION.　2.

—— Marine.
　See Cases under INSURANCE, MARINE.

POLICY-HOLDER—Participating—Contributory.
　See Cases under COMPANY—LIFE IN-
　SURANCE COMPANY.

POLL—Meeting of shareholders.　**29 Ch. D. 159**
　See COMPANY—MANAGEMENT.　3.

—— Municipal election
　See MUNICIPAL CORPORATION—ELECTION
　—*Statutes.*

—— Parliament—Hours of
　See PARLIAMENT—ELECTION—*Statutes.*

—— Parliament—Leave of absence to employés
　See PARLIAMENT—ELECTION—*Statutes.*

—— Right to demand　-　-　**8 Q. B. D. 459**
　See PUBLIC LIBRARY.

—— Time for demanding　**11 Q. B. D. 282**
　See HIGHWAY—WAYWARDEN.

POLLING DISTRICTS
　See PARLIAMENT — REGISTRATION —
　Statutes.

POLLUTION—Stream　-　-　**20 Ch. D. 595;**
　　　　　　　　　　　　　[28 Ch. D. 688
　See NUISANCE—REMEDIES.　1, 5.

—— Underground water　-　**29 Ch. D. 115**
　See WATER.　3.

POOR-LAW:—　　　　　　　　　　Col.
　I. MANAGEMENT　-　-　-　1060
　II. MAINTENANCE　-　-　-　1061
　III. RELIEF　-　-　-　1061
　IV. SETTLEMENT (and REMOVAL)　1062
　　(*a.*) DERIVATIVE SETTLEMENT.
　　(*b.*) HUSBAND AND WIFE.
　　(*c.*) RESIDENCE.

I. POOR LAW—MANAGEMENT.
　The Act 45 & 46 *Vict. c.* 58 (*the Divided Parishes
　and Poor Law Amendment Act,* 1882), *amends the
　Divided Parishes and Poor Law Act,* 1876.

　　(*a.*) *Divided Parishes.*
　Sect. 2. *Detached parts of parishes to form part
　of the parishes surrounding them.*
　Sect. 3. *Provision for parishes not separately
　maintaining highway.*
　Sect. 4. *Detached parts with a population ex-
　ceeding* 300 *may be made separate parishes.*
　Sect. 5. *Provision as to school districts.*
　Sect. 6 *extends* 39 & 40 *Vict. c.* 61, *s.* 5, *to any
　parish in a highway district.*
　Sect. 7. *Interpretation of county.*

　　(*b.*) *Poor Law Amendment.*
　Sect. 8. *Power to Local Government Board to alter
　wards for the election of guardians in certain cases.*
　Sect. 9. *Adjustment of liabilities in asylum dis-
　tricts.*
　Sect. 10. *Provision for separate rate.*
　Sect. 11. *Adjustment of liabilities not to be re-
　quired in certain cases.*
　Sect. 12. *Mode of consent by guardians and
　manager.*
　Sect. 13. *As to maintenance and education of
　pauper children by guardians of union.*
　Sect. 14. *Repeal of enactments.*
　Register of Securities to be kept.

　Register.] *General Order of Local Government
　Board of December* 8*th,* 1882, *under* 45 & 46 *Vict.
　c.* 58, *s.* 14, *prescribing register of securities to be
　kept by guardians*　-　**L. G. 1882, p. 6252**
　Expenses of Guardians.] *The Act* 46 & 47 *Vict.
　c.* 11 (*Poor Law Conferences Act,* 1883), *provides
　for the expenses incurred by guardians of the poor
　in relation to Poor Law Conferences.*
　Order of September. 13, 1883, *of Local Govern-
　ment Board empowering guardians of the poor
　under the Poor Law Conferences Act,* 1883, *s.* 2, *to
　pay the reasonable expenses incurred in attending
　any conference under that section*
　　　　　　　　　　　　　[L. G. 1883, p. 4585
　Election of Guardians.] *General Order of*
　29*th of October,* 1881, *of the Local Government
　Board altering the General Order of* 1877
　　　　　　　　　　　　　[L. G. 1881, p. 5356

—— Overseers of Parish—*Bill in Parliament
　affecting Parish—Opposition by Overseers—Costs
　of Opposition.*] A private bill before Parliament
　provided for the punctual payment of interest on
　the share capital of the undertaking for which
　authority was sought by declaring that the over-
　seers of the parish in which the undertaking was
　situated should, when required to do so, raise as
　part of the poor-rate money for the payment of
　such interest. The overseers, with the authority
　of the vestry, successfully opposed the bill, and in

I. POOR-LAW—MANAGEMENT—*continued.*

so doing incurred certain expenses which were not immoderate and were allowed by the auditor:—*Held*, reversing the decision of the Queen's Bench Division, that the overseers were entitled to charge the expenses so incurred upon the poor-rate. THE QUEEN *v.* WHITE　　**11 Q. B. D. 309;**
[14 Q. B. D. 358

II. POOR-LAW—MAINTENANCE.

1. —— Married Woman—*Husband and Wife—Non-liability of Husband to maintain Adulterous Wife*—31 & 32 *Vict.* c. 122, s. 33.] A husband is not liable to be ordered, under 31 & 32 Vict. c. 122, s. 33, to maintain a wife with whom he has ceased to cohabit in consequence of her adultery. CULLEY *v.* CHARMAN　　**7 Q. B. D. 89**

2. —— Married Woman— *Order upon Husband towards Cost of Relief*—31 & 32 *Vict.* c. 122, s. 33.] It is not a condition precedent to the power of justices under 31 & 32 Vict. c. 122, s. 33, to order the husband to pay for the maintenance of his pauper wife, that the guardians should have fixed the sum for her relief. Therefore, although the guardians have not fixed any sum for her future relief, but have given her a small weekly sum, the justices may, under the 33rd section, order the husband to pay for her maintenance such weekly sum as, considering the condition of the husband and all the circumstances, may be proper, although it may exceed the amount of the relief previously given to her by the guardians.—Decision of the Queen's Bench Division reversed. DINNING *v.* SOUTH SHIELDS UNION **12 Q. B. D. 61;**
[13 Q. B. D. 25

3. —— Married Woman—*Maintenance by Relations — Grandmother — Married Woman with Separate Estate*—43 *Eliz.* c. 2, s. 7—*Married Women's Property Act*, 1870 (33 & 34 *Vict.* c. 93), s. 14.] A woman whose husband is alive is not liable under the Poor Law Acts to contribute to the support of her grandchildren, even though she has separate estate and is able, independently of her husband, to support them. COLEMAN *v.* OVERSEERS OF BIRMINGHAM **6 Q. B. D. 615**

III. POOR LAW—RELIEF.

Allotments for the Poor.] *The Act* 45 & 46 *Vict.* c. 80 (*the Allotments Extension Act*, 1882) *extends the benefits of the Act* 2 *Will.* 4, c. 42, *to all the irremoveable poor, and to all lands, whether cultivated or uncultivated, held for the benefit of the poor as thereinafter described, and provides a summary remedy for the recovery of arrears of rent and of possession where tenant refuses to quit.*

Discharge of Pauper.] *The Act* 45 & 46 *Vict.* c. 36 (*the Casual Poor Act*, 1882), *repeals* sect. 5 *of the Pauper Inmates Discharge and Regulation Act,*1871, *and enacts* (sect. 4) *that a casual pauper shall not be entitled to discharge himself from a casual ward before 9 o'clock in the morning of the second day following his admission, nor before he has performed the work prescribed for him.*

Provision for case where a casual pauper has been admitted on more than one occasion into any casual ward of the same union.

Sect. 5. Person obtaining poor relief by false statement to be dealt with as a disorderly person under sect. 3 of 5 Geo. 4, c. 83.

Local Government Board.] *Regulations of 18th*

III. POOR-LAW—RELIEF—*continued.*

December, 1882, *with respect to casual paupers under "Pauper Inmates Discharge and Regulation Act,* 1871," *and* "*Casual Poor Act,* 1882"
[L. G. 1882, p. 6461

Casual Paupers.] *General Order of Local Government Board. Regulations of December 21,* 1882, *with respect to casual paupers*
[L. G. 1882, p. 6520

IV. POOR-LAW—SETTLEMENT(and REMOVAL)

(a.) DERIVATIVE SETTLEMENT.

1. —— Children—*Divided Parishes and Poor Law Amendment Act*, 1876 (39 & 40 *Vict.* c. 61), s. 35.] Where the settlement of a widowed mother, as well as the settlement of her legitimate children, who are unemancipated and under the age of sixteen, has to be inquired into, the children take the settlement of their widowed mother under the first clause of sect. 35 of the Divided Parishes and Poor Law Amendment Act 1876 (39 & 40 Vict. c. 61) and are not to be deemed to be settled in the parish where they were born under the last clause of that section, although it cannot be shewn what settlement the children derived from their widowed mother without inquiring into her derivative settlement.—So *held* by Lindley and Mathew, JJ. GUARDIANS OF HOLLINGBOURN UNION *v.* GUARDIANS OF WEST HAM UNION **6 Q. B. D. 580**

2. —— Children—*Divided Parishes Act*, 1876 (39 & 40 *Vict.* c. 61), s. 35—*Pauper above Sixteen.*] Since 39 & 40 Vict. c. 61 (Divided Parishes Act, 1876), s. 35, enacting that "no person shall be deemed to have derived a settlement from any other person, . . . except . . . in the case of a child under the age of sixteen, which child shall take the settlement of its father . . . up to that age and shall retain the settlement so taken until it shall acquire another," paupers who are above the age of sixteen at the time of the inquiry as to their settlement cannot take the settlement of their father. THE QUEEN *v.* GUARDIANS OF ST. MARY, ISLINGTON -　　**15 Q. B. D. 95, 339**

3. —— Children—*Divided Parishes Act*, 1876 (39 & 40 *Vict.* c. 61), s. 35.] Where neither the father nor mother of a pauper child has acquired a settlement in his or her own right, and after the father has died the widowed mother has deserted such child, who is under the age of sixteen, and has not acquired a settlement for itself, such child is by 39 & 40 Vict c. 61, s. 35, to be deemed to be settled in the parish in which it was born, and an order for its removal to a parish in which it was not born but in which its father was born was quashed, because, in that case, it could not be shewn what settlement such child derived from its father or mother without inquiring into the derivative settlement of such parent, which was prohibited by that section. GUARDIANS OF HEADINGTON UNION *v.* GUARDIANS OF ST. OLAVE'S UNION
[13 Q. B. D. 293

4. —— Children—*Divided Parishes Act* (39 & 40 *Vict.* c. 61), s.35—*Widow and Children—Birth Settlement of Father.*] Upon appeal against an order for the removal of a widow and her children, it appeared that the widow had acquired no settlement since her husband's death. Her husband, the father of her children, was born in the appellant parish, but never acquired a settlement

2 M 2

IV. POOR LAW — SETTLEMENT (and RE-MOVAL)—*continued.*

(a.) Derivative Settlement—continued.

for himself and there was no evidence as to the settlement of his parents:—*Held, that* under 39 & 40 Vict. c. 61, s. 35, the children took a settlement from their father in the appellant parish, and that the order for their removal was right. Guardians of Liverpool *v.* Overseers of Portsea - 12 Q. B. D. 303

5. —— Illegitimate Child—*Divided Parishes Act,* 1876 (39 & 40 Vict. c. 61), s. 35.] Under the Divided Parishes Act, 1876 (39 & 40 Vict. c. 61), an illegitimate child under sixteen does not take the settlement of its mother, where such settlement has been derived from the mother's father, but such child is remitted to its birth settlement. The Queen *v.* Guardians of Marylebone - 13 Q. B. D. 15

6. —— Illegitimate Child *under Sixteen*—39 & 40 Vict. c. 61, s. 35.] Under 39 & 40 Vict. c. 61, s. 35, illegitimate children under sixteen do not take the settlement of their mother where such settlement has been derived from her marriage, although the birth of the children and the marriage of the mother were before the passing of the Act. The Queen *v.* Guardians of Portsea [7 Q. B. D. 384

7. —— Wife and Children—*Divided Parishes Act,* 1876 (39 & 40 Vict. c. 61), s. 35.] An order for the removal of a pauper wife and her three children, aged respectively five years, three years, and one year, on the ground that the settlement of her husband was the birth settlement of his father within the union to which the removal was made, having been made and appealed against, the birth settlement of the husband's father in such union was proved, but no other settlement either of the husband or of his father being set up, the order was quashed by an order of the Court of quarter sessions and the Queen's Bench Division confirmed such order of the sessions:—*Held,* affirming the decision of the Queen's Bench Division, that evidence of the settlement of the husband's father was inadmissible, and could not be acted upon in making the order of removal, as it went to prove the derivative settlement of the parent of the children contrary to sect. 35 of the Divided Parishes Act, 1876 (39 & 40 Vict. c. 61), and that consequently the order of removal was rightly quashed. The Queen *v.* Guardians of Bridgnorth [9 Q. B. D. 765; 11 Q. B. D. 314

(b.) Husband and Wife.

8.—— "Desertion" *of Wife by her Husband—Misconduct of Wife—*24 & 25 Vict. c. 55, s. 3.] By 24 & 25 Vict. c. 55, s. 3, "where a married woman shall have been or shall be deserted by her husband, and shall after his desertion reside for three years in such a manner as would if she were a widow render her exempt from removal, she shall not be liable to be removed from the parish where she shall be resident unless her husband return to cohabit with her."—One night in June, 1873, the pauper, a married woman, who had been drinking at a public-house with a man named Wyatt, with whom her husband reasonably suspected her of too much intimacy, came home

IV. POOR LAW — SETTLEMENT (and RE-MOVAL—*continued.*

(b.) Husband and Wife—continued.

the worse for drink and found the door of her husband's house locked. She forced her way in; and in the morning, after some words, her husband threatened to lock her in. He then went out to his work, and when he came back he found his wife absent, and that part of his furniture and clothes had been carried away. The pauper took a room elsewhere, and shortly afterwards went away with Wyatt, with whom she lived in adultery until his death in 1879. After Wyatt's death, the pauper wrote to her husband asking him to receive her back. He took no notice of her letter, and if she had gone back to him he would not have received her.—In August, 1881, she became chargeable to the parish of Liverpool as a pauper lunatic, and an order of justices was made for her removal to her husband's parish, which order was confirmed by the quarter sessions. Upon appeal against the last-mentioned order.—*Held,* that the above facts disclosed no reasonable evidence of desertion of the wife by the husband, within the statute.—*Reg. v. Maidstone Union* (5 Q. B. D. 31) distinguished. The Queen *v.* Cookham Union [9 Q. B. D. 522

9. —— Lunatic Wife—*Removal of—Consent of Husband—*25 & 26 Vict. c. 111, s. 20—*Separation of Husband and Wife.*] A wife having become insane and chargeable to the union in which her husband dwelt, was taken from his house to the workhouse of the union, and the medical officer thereof certified, under 25 & 26 Vict. c. 111, s. 20, that the lunatic was a proper person to be kept in a workhouse. An order was then made by justices for her removal alone to another union containing her husband's last place of settlement. The husband consented to the removal order: the wife was mentally incapable of consent:—*Held,* that the order of removal made under these circumstances did not contravene the policy of the law with regard to the separation of husband and wife, and was good. The Queen *v.* Guardians of Preston 11 Q. B. D. 113

(c.) Residence.

10. —— Children—*Under Sixteen—Evidence.*] Upon appeal to the quarter sessions from an order of the justices adjudging that two pauper children under sixteen years of age were settled in a parish within the Holborn Union, in which their father had a settlement at the time of his death, it appeared that seven years before the order the children, then under seven years old, were on the death of their mother placed by their father in the care of K. and his wife, who resided at Chertsey within the Chertsey Union, and lived with them from that time continuously until they became chargeable. After they went to Chertsey the children were visited by their father on three occasions only, and then only for a few hours at a time, but he made a weekly payment for their maintenance which was continued to his death:—*Held,* reversing the decision of the Divisional Court, that there was evidence on which the justices might find, as they must be taken to have done, that the father had never

IV. POOR LAW — SETTLEMENT (and RE-MOVAL)—*continued.*

(c.) RESIDENCE—*continued.*

given up the intention that his children should return to him when he was in a position to receive them, and that therefore there was no ground for quashing the order of the justices. GUAR-DIANS OF HOLBORN *v.* GUARDIANS OF CHERTSEY
[14 Q. B. D. 289; 15 Q. B. D. 76

11. —— Illegitimate Child above Sixteen — *Idiot—Residence as part of Family—24 & 25 Vict. c. 55, s. 10 : 28 & 29 Vict. c. 79, s. 8 ; 39 & 40 Vict. c. 61, s. 34.*] The pauper, an illegitimate child, and an idiot from her birth, resided after the age of sixteen for more than three years continuously in P. with her mother and her mother's husband, living as part of their family :—*Held,* that, notwithstanding the circumstances of her residence, she had under the Divided Parishes Act (39 & 40 Vict. c. 61), s. 34, acquired a settlement in P. GUARDIANS OF SALFORD *v.* OVERSEERS OF MANCHESTER - - - 10 Q. B. D. 172

12. —— Parish—Union—*39 & 40 Vict. c. 61, s. 34.*] A person resided in parish A. for a term of three years which expired before the passing of 39 & 40 Vict. c. 61, in such manner and under such circumstances in each of such years as would render him irremoveable. He then left parish A. and went to reside in parish B. in the same union, from which he continued irremoveable down to a date subsequent to the passing of the said Act :—*Held,* that he had not acquired a settlement in parish A. under 39 & 40 Vict. c. 61, s. 34. GUAR-DIANS OF SUNDERLAND UNION *v.* CLERK OF THE PEACE FOR SUSSEX - - 8 Q. B. D. 99

13. —— Parish—Union—*Divided Parishes and Poor Law Amendment Act, 1876 (39 & 40 Vict. c. 61), ss. 34, 44.*] "Parish" in sect. 34 of the Divided Parishes and Poor Law Amendment Act, 1876 (39 & 40 Vict. c. 61), does not include "union." A pauper resided for more than three years in a union, residing continuously for more than two and less than three years of the period in one parish of the union and for more than one and less than two years of the period in another parish of the same union, in such manner and under such circumstances, as would, in accordance with the several statutes in that behalf, render her irremoveable :—*Held,* by Lindley and Mathew, JJ., that such a residence did not constitute a settlement within sect. 34 of 39 & 40 Vict. c. 61. GUARDIANS OF PLOMESGATE UNION *v.* GUARDIANS OF WEST HAM UNION - 6 Q. B. D. 576

14. —— Penitentiary—*"Bonâ fide Charitable Gift"—54 Geo. 3, c. 170, s. 6—9 & 10 Vict. c. 66, s. 1—39 & 40 Vict. c. 61, s. 34.*] A pauper had resided for upwards of three years in a building in the parish of F., occupied as a home or reformatory for women. This home was supported by money collected at church offertories without the parish, and by annual subscriptions and donations from persons resident in all parts of the kingdom the money being applied in providing for the supervision, instruction, maintenance, and clothing of the inmates. The pauper during the whole term paid no money for her maintenance and clothing :—*Held,* affirming the judgment of the

IV. POOR LAW — SETTLEMENT (and RE-MOVAL)—*continued.*

(c.) RESIDENCE—*continued.*

Queen's Bench Division, that the money collected for her maintenance in the home was a "bonâ fide charitable gift," and that she had not been maintained by a rate or subscription raised in a parish in which she did not reside, within the meaning of the proviso to 9 & 10 Vict. c. 66, s. 1, and that she was irremoveable from and settled within the parish of F., under 39 & 40 Vict. c. 61, s. 34. GUARDIANS OF FULHAM *v.* GUARDIANS OF THANET - 6 Q. B. D. 610 ; 7 Q. B. D. 539

15. —— Removal, *Order of, made without Corroboration—Corroboration before Sessions on Appeal —39 & 40 Vict. c. 61, s. 34.*] An order of removal was made by justices in respect of an alleged settlement under 39 & 40 Vict. c. 61, s. 34, which provides that an order of removal in respect of a settlement acquired under that section shall not be made upon the evidence of the person to be removed without such corroboration as the justices or Court think sufficient. There was no corroborative evidence before the justices who made the order. Upon appeal to the quarter sessions against the order, the grounds of appeal were, first, that the pauper had not acquired a settlement under 39 & 40 Vict. c. 61, s. 34 ; and, secondly, that there was no corroborative evidence before the justices who made the order of removal. Corroborative evidence was tendered on behalf of the Respondents at the sessions, and received by the Court, who considered the same sufficient, but quashed the order of removal on the ground that, as a matter of law upon the facts proved, the pauper had not acquired a settlement under 39 & 40 Vict. c. 61, s. 34 :—*Held,* that the sessions were right in receiving the corroborative evidence, but that (the case being governed by *Reg.* v. *Brampton Union* (3 Q. B. D. 479)), they were wrong in holding that the settlement was not acquired, and that consequently the order of removal must stand good. THE QUEEN *v.* GUAR-DIANS OF ABERGAVENNY - 6 Q. B. D. 31

16. —— Status of Irremoveability—*Effect of Break of Residence of Husband on Status of Wife —9 & 10 Vict. c. 66, s. 1—11 & 12 Vict, c. 111, s. 1.*] A husband who had acquired a status of irremoveability in the P. union went to America in January, 1880, intending to reside there, leaving his wife and children resident in that union ; there was no evidence of desertion. In March, 1880, he died in America : in May of the same year the wife and children became chargeable to the union. In April, 1881, an order was made by justices removing the wife and children to Manchester, the husband's last place of settlement :—*Held,* that the break of residence by the husband was, in law, a break in the wife's residence, and that the order of removal was good. THE QUEEN *v.* OVERSEERS OF MANCHESTER - 8 Q. B. D. 50

POOR LAW—Bond to guardians for collection of rates —Negligence of overseers
[9 Q. B. D. 683
See PRINCIPAL AND SURETY—LIABILITY. 1.

—— Maintenance of lunatic　　27 Ch. D. 710
See LUNATIC—MAINTENANCE. 3.

POOR LAW—*continued.*

—— Settlement by residence—Constructive residence of children — Appeal — Case stated under 12 & 13 Vict. c. 45, s. 11
[15 Q. B. D. 76

See PRACTICE—SUPREME COURT—APPEAL. 4.

POOR LAW CONFERENCES ACT, 1883.

See POOR LAW—MANAGEMENT—*Statutes.*

I. POOR RATE—APPLICATION.

—— Roman Catholic Clergyman—*Ministrations in Workhouse—Auditor—Disallowance.*] By a general order of the Poor Law Board, dated the 19th of August, 1867, it was provided that the guardians might employ such persons as they should deem requisite in or about the workhouse, or workhouse premises, or on the land occupied for the employment of the pauper inmates of the workhouse, or otherwise in or about the relief of the indoor poor, upon such terms and conditions as should appear to them to be suitable :—*Held,* that, under this order it was competent to the guardians to appoint and pay a Roman Catholic clergyman to minister to the religious wants of the Roman Catholic inmates of the workhouse. THE QUEEN *v.* HASLEHURST - - - 13 Q. B. D. 253

II. POOR-RATE—EXEMPTIONS.

Stock-in-trade.] *The Act 3 & 4 Vict. c. 89, which exempts stock-in-trade from poor-rates is continued by the 48 & 49 Vict. c. 59, until the 31st of December, 1886.*

III. POOR-RATE—GUARDIANS.

—— Salary—*Disqualification of Guardian—5 & 6 Vict. c. 57, s. 14—Clerk of Highway Board—Clerk of School Board—Payment out of Funds raised in a Poor-rate—27 & 28 Vict. c. 101, s. 32 ; 33 & 34 Vict. c. 75.*] The Act 5 & 6 Vict. c. 57, s. 14, which enacts that "no person receiving any fixed salary . . . from the poor-rates in any parish or union shall be capable of serving as a guardian in such parish or union" does not apply to the clerk of a highway board or of a school board whose salary is paid out of the highway or school board fund which is a fund supplied from moneys contributed by parishes in pursuance of precepts issued under the Highway Act, 1864, 27 & 28 Vict. c. 101, or the Elementary Education Act, 1870, 33 & 34 Vict. c. 75, respectively. THE QUEEN *v.* RAWLINS. THE QUEEN *v.* DIBBIN
[14 Q. B. D. 325; 15 Q. B. D. 382

IV. POOR-RATE—OCCUPATION.

The Act 45 & 46 Vict. c. 20, amends sect. 16 of the Poor Rate Assessment and Collection Act, 1869, and directs (sect. 3) that the payment of rates by an outgoing occupier shall be proportionate to the time of his occupation, notwithstanding he may not

IV. POOR-RATE—OCCUPATION—*continued. be succeeded in his occupation by an incoming tenant.*

Sect. 4. As to the publication of poor-rate where there is no parish church.

1. —— Bookstalls on a Railway Platform—*Exclusive Occupation—Valuation (Metropolis) Act, 1869 (32 & 33 Vict. c. 67)—Licence or Demise.*] By indenture the South Western Railway Company granted to S. & S. (therein called "the tenants") for seven years "the sole and exclusive licence and privilege to vend, sell, lend, and exhibit for sale and loan, newspapers, books, periodicals, stationery, &c., and such other like articles required for the convenience of passengers by railway as should be approved by the secretary of the company, at all their stations," &c. ; and also full liberty for the tenants, subject to the approval of the engineer of the company, to erect and place bookstands, &c., on the platforms for exhibiting and keeping their books, &c., and to post and exhibit advertisements and placards on the station walls; and also full and free ingress and egress at all reasonable times for the "tenants," their servants and agents, to and from the several stations for the purposes of the grant. The persons employed by S. & S. were to be under the control of the station-master and liable to immediate removal from the station in case of insobriety or misconduct. S. & S. were to pay the company certain fixed monthly rents, and also a percentage (quarterly) on the gross amounts received by S. & S. for the posting of the advertisements, &c.,—with a proviso that, in case the rent or the quarterly payments should be in arrear for fourteen days after notice, the same should be recoverable by the company, in addition to any other remedies, "by distress as in the case of rent in arrear." And it was provided that the "tenants" should not vend or offer for sale, or exhibit or publish, any books or advertisements or placards of an indecent, immoral, or seditious character, or which should be forbidden by the company ; and should abide by and observe the regulations from time to time made by the company, touching the placing on the platforms any of the necessary bookstands ; and the company warranted to the "tenants" "the quiet and peaceable enjoyment and benefit thereby granted for the period and upon the terms and stipulations and in manner aforesaid."—S. & S. erected bookstands upon the platforms at W. station, and had the exclusive use of them; and these bookstands were closed at night with shutters, and were locked up, the keys being kept by their servants. No rights of ingress or egress to and from the station, or of access to the bookstands, were exercised by S. & S., or their agents or servants, except under the provisions and for the purposes of the indenture. The company were assessed to the poor-rate for the station generally ;—*Held,* that S. & S. had no "exclusive occupation" of any portion of the platforms, so as to render them liable to be rated in respect of these bookstands.—Judgment of the Queen's Bench Division affirmed. SMITH *v.* LAMBETH ASSESSMENT COMMITTEE
[9 Q. B. D. 585; 10 Q. B. D. 327

2. —— Occupier ceasing to occupy—*Liability to pay Rate—Beneficial Occupation—Bridge free*

IV. POOR-RATE—OCCUPATION—continued.

of Toll—32 & 33 Vict. c. 41, s. 16.] An occupier assessed in a poor-rate, but who ceases to occupy before the rate has been wholly discharged, is not relieved by 32 & 33 Vict. c. 41, s. 16, from liability to pay the whole rate, unless some one succeeds or comes into the occupation who is liable to pay a proportionate part of such rate, and, semble, that such occupier remains liable to the whole rate until the name of some one liable to be assessed is substituted for his in the rate book.—The Metropolitan Board of Works purchased Putney Bridge of the Fulham Bridge Company, who transferred the bridge to the board under the provisions of an Act of Parliament which required the tolls in respect of the bridge to cease, and enacted that the bridge should be open free to the public and should be maintained by the board, the justices of Surrey paying an annual sum to the board in discharge of the liability of that county to maintain the bridge. Before the transfer the Fulham Bridge Company received tolls for the passage over the bridge, and were duly assessed in the poor-rate in the parish of Putney in respect of the bridge, and at the time of the transfer there remained undischarged a rate for which the bridge company had been so assessed, and which had been made by the parish for a period extending beyond the transfer:—Held, that the board had no beneficial occupation of the bridge in respect of which they were capable of being rated, and that therefore as there was no succeeding occupier liable to be rated the bridge company remained liable for the whole rate. Hare v. Churchwardens and Overseers of Putney - 7 Q. B. D. 223

3. —— Residence of Police Officer—Residence when not part of the Police Station—Rateability —Building for Public Purposes.] A superintendent of the police for a county police division had as his quarters a house, which was rented for him by the county authorities, and which he furnished; his rent was paid out of the police rates, and the amount deducted from his salary as superintendent. The house was liable to be examined and its fitness reported by one of Her Majesty's inspectors, and to be used for purposes connected with the police force as the chief constable might direct, but no room in it was specially set apart for any other purpose than for the use of the superintendent and his family. The house was a quarter of a mile from the police station, within a convenient distance of which it was necessary that the superintendent should reside for the performance of his duties; and he was compelled to live in it as long as it was rented for him by the county authorities, but he was liable to be removed from it at any time, and from one police division to another:—Held, that such superintendent was rateable to the poor rate in respect of such house as his occupation was a beneficial one, and the house, being no part of the police station, did not come within the recognised heads of property which is treated as Crown property.—The case of Gambier v. Overseers of Lydford (3 E. & B. 346; 23 L. J. (M.C.) 69) approved. Martin v. West Derby Assessment Committee 11 Q. B. D. 145

4. —— Sale of Grass on Land—Right of Grazing.] The Appellant was the owner of

IV. POOR-RATE—OCCUPATION—continued.

certain land, and such land being unlet, he sold the grass upon it by auction. The conditions of sale described the sale as a sale of grass for a certain time, and set forth certain conditions under which the purchasers were to be entitled to turn cattle in to eat the grass. The conditions also provided that the purchasers should dress the dung, cut the thistles, and leave the fences in good repair. It was a term of the sale that the vendor should pay the rates and taxes. The Appellant was rated to the poor-rate in respect of the land in question for a period coincident with part of the period for which the grass was sold. An application having been made to the justices to enforce the rate against him :—Held, that there was evidence that the Appellant was the occupier of the land; that the effect of the sale of the grass was not to put the purchasers in occupation of the land, but merely to license them to graze their cattle thereon; and that, consequently, the Appellant was liable to be rated. Mogg v. Overseers of Yatton - - - 6 Q. B. D. 10

5. —— Telegraph Wires—Exclusive Occupation—Rateable Subject under 43 Eliz. c. 2—Licence of Exclusive Use.] By agreement between a telegraph company and the Postmaster-General, the latter covenanted with the company that he would provide, and thenceforth during the continuance of the agreement keep appropriated and maintain for the exclusive use of the company certain telegraph wires, called in the agreement "special wires," between the landing-place of a foreign telegraphic cable near the Land's End and an office of the company at Penzance, and thence to their office in London, with the necessary translators for working them, and a pneumatic tube; such wires, &c., to remain the property of the Postmaster-General,—the Postmaster-General to repair all accidental defects or interruptions to the working of the wires, &c., but to be paid for making good any damage to the wires occasioned by the neglect or default of the company or their servants; the company not to use the wires for the transmission of any except certain specified messages. And, in consideration of the appropriation and maintenance by the Postmaster-General of the wires, translators, batteries, and pneumatic tube, the company covenanted to pay him certain rents; and they also covenanted not to part with the possession of the special wires or any of them, or underlet or assign the benefit of the agreement, without the consent of the Postmaster-General; and that, in the event of their doing so, the Postmaster-General was to be at liberty to determine the contract by notice: and it was further provided that, upon the expiration or determination of the agreement, it should be lawful for the Postmaster-General to resume the possession of the special wires, &c. The telegraph posts remained the property of the Postmaster-General, and carried between Penzance and London several wires beyond those appropriated to the use of the company :—Held, —Lord Coleridge, C.J., doubting,—that this agreement did not give the company such an exclusive occupation of the special wires as to make them rateable to the relief of the poor in respect thereof, even in the parish where the special wires were

IV. POOR-RATE—OCCUPATION—continued.

the only wires affixed to the posts. COMPAGNIE FRANÇAISE DU TÉLÉGRAPHIE DE PARIS À NEW YORK v. PENZANCE UNION　-　12 Q. B. D. 552

6. —— Telephone Company —Rateable Occupation — "Wayleaves" — Overhead Wires and Apparatus attached to Roofs and Chimneys of Houses.] A telephone company were possessed of an exchange by means of which subscribers could communicate by telephone with each other, and also of wires and telephone apparatus unconnected with the exchange for the use of persons renting them. For the purpose of this business they laid wires from their office to the business premises of their subscribers, and also erected wires for the use of those who rented them. All these wires were overhead wires and were carried from the office of the company to the different premises, being supported and steadied either by poles fixed in the ground, or by being attached to the roofs, chimneys, or walls of some of the buildings over which they passed. The attachments were made in the case of a single wire by an iron spike driven into the building, or by a bolt screwed into the ridge, or by an iron bracket nailed to the corner of the chimney to which the wire was attached, or in the case of a number of wires by means of standards or ridge-saddles attached to the roofs of the buildings and fastened by iron bolts or stays. The consent of the owners or occupiers of the lands or buildings was given by agreements in which the company undertook to pay an annual rent and to remove the wires and attachments, upon a certain notice. The company had no key of the outside doors, and could only obtain access to the roofs by the permission of the occupiers:—Held, affirming the decision of the Queen's Bench Division, that upon these facts there was proof of an occupation of land by the wires of the company, and that they were rateable. LANCASHIRE TELEPHONE COMPANY v. OVERSEERS OF MANCHESTER

[13 Q. B. D. 700 ; 14 Q. B. D. 267

V. POOR-RATE—PROCEDURE.

1. —— Alteration of Value—Valuation (Metropolis) Act, 1869 (32 & 33 Vict. c. 67), s. 47—Alteration of Value of Hereditament during Year—Provisional List—Default by Overseers in sending Provisional List—Discretion of Overseers.] Where a requisition is made to the overseers of a parish to make and send to the assessment committee a provisional list under sect. 47 of the Valuation (Metropolis) Act, 1869, containing the gross and rateable value of an hereditament, on the ground that the value has been increased or diminished during the year, the overseers are not bound to comply with the requisition if they are of opinion that no such alteration in value has taken place, and a mandamus will not be granted to compel them to do so. THE QUEEN v. ST. MARY MAGDALENE, BERMONDSEY　-　14 Q. B. D. 351

2. —— Amendment of Valuation List—Union Assessment Committee Acts (25 & 26 Vict. c. 103), s. 19 : (27 & 28 Vict. c. 39), s. 1—"Notice of objection in manner provided by 25 & 26 Vict. c. 103, with respect to objections"—Omission to give Notice of Meeting of Committee to Overseers.] Under the "Union Assessment Committee

V. POOR-RATE—PROCEDURE—continued.

Amendment Act, 1864," 27 & 28 Vict. c. 39, s. 1, —which enables the assessment committee to hear objections against a valuation list approved by the committee, and to amend such list, "after notice given at any time in the manner prescribed by 25 & 26 Vict. c. 103, with respect to objections,"—an amendment of the list is valid, although no notice of the meeting of the committee was given to the overseers of the parish to which the list relates as required by 25 & 26 Vict. c. 103, s. 19. THE QUEEN v. OVERSEERS OF LANGRIVILLE. THE QUEEN v. OVERSEERS OF COPPING SYKE　-　-　-　14 Q. B. D. 83

3. —— Appeal —Assessment Committee — Failure to obtain Relief on Objection to Valuation List—Appeal against second Rate—27 & 28 Vict. c. 39, s. 1.] A person who has once given to the assessment committee notice of objection against a valuation list and failed to obtain such relief as he deems just, may appeal to quarter sessions against any subsequent poor-rate made in conformity with the list, and 27 & 28 Vict. c. 39, s. 1, does not make it a condition precedent of such appeal that previously thereto he should repeat his application to the committee for relief. THE QUEEN v. JUSTICES OF DENBIGHSHIRE　15 Q. B. D.

[451

4. —— Appeal—Case stated by Sessions—Costs —Civil Proceeding—Rules of 1880, Order LXII., r. 2.] Where a case is stated by sessions upon appeal against a poor-rate, the proceeding is a civil proceeding on the Crown side of the Queen's Bench Division, within the rules of 1880, Order LXII., rule 2, and the costs are in the discretion of the Court under Order LV. CLARK v. FISHERTON-ANGAB　　6 Q. B. D. 139

5. —— Appeal—Reasonable Time for giving Notice of Appeal—Entry of Appeal—Next Sessions —17 Geo. 2, c. 38, s. 4.] A poor-rate for the parish of L. was made and allowed on Saturday, the 20th of March, and published on the following day. S. & Son, who are the occupiers of bookstalls at certain railway stations in the parish, were included in the rate. The quarter sessions next after the publication of the rate were held on the 6th of April. A party desirous of appealing against the rate would therefore, if bound by law to bring his appeal to such April sessions, have had to give notice of appeal upon the 22nd of March, the day immediately succeeding that of the publication of the rate, in accordance with the provisions of 12 & 13 Vict. c. 45, s. 1, which requires fourteen clear days' notice to be given to the overseers. S. & Son gave notice of appeal against the rate on the 7th of June for the then next sessions, which were held on the 5th of July. The Court of quarter sessions refused to hear the appeal on the ground that it ought to have been brought to the April sessions :—Held, that an Appellant against a poor-rate is entitled to a reasonable time, before giving notice of appeal, to allow of his considering whether he shall appeal, and the grounds on which his appeal shall be based, and that one day is not a reasonable time for that purpose ; and that consequently S. & Son were not bound to give notice of appeal for the April sessions.—Held, further, that under

V. POOR-RATE—PROCEDURE—*continued.*

the circumstances they were not even bound to enter and respite their appeal at the April sessions. THE QUEEN v. JUSTICES OF SURREY
[**6 Q. B. D. 100**

6. —— **Distress Warrant**—*Power of Justices to delay Execution.*] Justices in issuing a distress warrant for the recovery of poor-rates have no power to order that there shall be any delay in the execution of the warrant. THE QUEEN v. HANDSLEY - - - **7 Q. B. D. 398**

7. —— **Notice**—*Publication—Extra-parochial Places—Publication of Poor-rate in Parishes where no Church or Chapel—17 Geo. 2, c. 3, s. 1—7 Will. 4 & 1 Vict. c. 45, s. 2—20 Vict. c. 19, s. 1.*] By 17 Geo. 2, c. 3, s. 1, public notice of every rate for the relief of the poor shall be given in the parish church the next Sunday after the allowance of the rate by the justices, "and no rate shall be esteemed or reputed valid and sufficient so as to collect or raise the same unless such notice shall have been given ;" and by 7 Will. 4 & 1 Vict. c. 45, a written notice, to be affixed on the doors of all the churches or chapels in the parish, is substituted for any notice theretofore by any law or statute given in churches or chapels. By 20 Vict. c. 19, s. 1, every extra-parochial place wherein no rate is levied for the relief of the poor shall for all purposes of assessment to the poor-rate and the relief of the poor "be deemed a parish."—The overseer of a parish which, before the passing of 20 Vict. c. 19, was an extra-parochial place, made a rate for the relief of the poor, but did not publish any notice of the rate within the parish, in which there was no church or chapel :—*Held*, that the rate could not be collected. THE QUEEN v. DYOTT - - - **9 Q. B. D. 47**

VI. POOR-RATE—RATEABLE VALUE.

1. —— **Lighthouse**—*Mersey Docks and Harbour Board—Rateability of Lighthouse vested in and under the Management of the Board—Telegraph Station and Premises—Rateable Value enhanced by reason of Neighbourhood — Merchant Shipping Act, 1854 (17 & 18 Vict. c. 104), s. 430.*] The Mersey Docks and Harbour Board were possessed of a tower used as a lighthouse and also as a telegraph station, in respect of which they received tolls from vessels using their docks or entering the port of Liverpool, which tolls were directed by the statutes under which the board derived their authority to be so fixed, that, with the other receipts of the board applicable to conservancy purposes, they should not be higher than was necessary to meet the conservancy expenditure : —*Held*, that, inasmuch as the tower was incapable of profitable occupation, it was not rateable to the relief of the poor.—Two dwelling-houses adjoining the tower were used by the light-keepers, and if not so used in connection with the lighthouse might be let to tenants at a rent, and the rent would be enhanced by the fact that they had been built in the neighbourhood of the tower :—*Held*, that the rateable value of the dwelling-houses must be ascertained with reference to the fact, that they had been built in the neighbourhood of the tower.—By Lord Coleridge, C.J., and Mathew, J., sitting as judges of the Queen's Bench Division, the lighthouses which are exempted from

VI. POOR-RATE—RATEABLE VALUE—*contd.*

rating by sect. 430 of the Merchant Shipping Act, 1854 (17 & 18 Vict. c. 104), are those only the superintendence and management of which is by sect. 389 vested in the Trinity House, the Commissioners of Northern Lighthouses, and the Port of Dublin Corporation, and not lighthouses under the control and management of local authorities, such as the Mersey Docks and Harbour Board. MERSEY DOCKS AND HARBOUR BOARD v. OVERSEERS OF LLANEILIAN - - - **14 Q. B. D. 770**

2. —— **Refreshment Rooms**—*Railway Station —Rent reserved—Evidence of Actual Profits.*] The refreshment rooms upon a railway station having been let to a contractor for a term of years at a fixed annual rent, he appealed against a poor-rate made upon him as occupier of the premises, and at the hearing of the appeal sought to prove by his own testimony and by his account books, shewing the receipts and expenditure during the past year in respect of the refreshment rooms, that the business was carried on at a loss, and that the rent reserved did not represent the true annual value of the premises :—*Held*, that such evidence ought to have been received as an element in ascertaining the rateable value.—*Reg.* v. *Guardians of North Aylesford* (37 J. P. 148) explained. CLARK v. FISHERTON-ANGAR - **6 Q. B. D. 139**

3. —— **School**—*Public Elementary School— Elementary Education Act, 1870 (33 & 34 Vict. c. 75).*] A school board are rateable to the relief of the poor in respect of a public elementary school, whether they are owners or lessees of the site thereof. WEST BROMWICH SCHOOL BOARD v. OVERSEERS OF WEST BROMWICH **13 Q. B. D. 929**

4. —— **Sporting Rights** — *Woodland — Game —Rating Act, 1874 (37 & 38 Vict. c. 54), s. 4, sub-s. (a).*] The Appellant was the owner and occupier of certain woodlands in respect of which he was rated to the poor-rate. He used the lands in question as plantations and woods and exercised the right of sporting over them. In the case of each piece of land a certain amount per acre was added to the rateable value of the land in respect of such right of sporting :—*Held*, that the right of sporting was properly taken into account in estimating the rateable value of the land in its natural and unimproved state. EYTON v. OVERSEERS OF MOLD - - **6 Q. B. D. 13**

5. —— **Statutory Restrictions**—*Railway Company—Running Powers—Rent fixed by Special Act —Private Act—Construction.*] A private Act of Parliament will be construed more strictly than a public one as regards provisions made by it for the benefit of the persons who obtained it, but, when once the true construction is ascertained, the effect of a private Act is the same as that of a public Act.—The special Act which authorized the making of a railway by the C. company, provided that the L. company should have the right to run their traffic over a part of the line, on payment of a fixed annual rent to the C. company. The rent was much less than the actual value of the traffic passed over that part of the line by the L. Co. :— *Held*, that the C. Company could not be rated for poor-rate in respect of that traffic at a higher sum than the fixed rent. ALTRINCHAM UNION v. CHESHIRE LINES COMMITTEE - **15 Q. B. D. 597**

VII. POOR-RATE—RATING OF OWNERS.

—— Rent above £20—"*Sturges Bourne's Act*," 59 *Geo.* 3, c. 12, s. 19—*Whether Owners rateable, where Weekly Rent amounting to more than £20 by the Year.*] The owner of a house let " on any agreement by which the rent is reserved or made payable at any shorter period than three months," cannot be assessed to the poor-rates instead of the actual occupier under Sturges Bourne's Act (59 Geo. 3, c. 12), s. 19, if the rent is at a rate which amounts to more than £20 by the year :— So *held*, affirming the decision of the Court of Appeal. ASSESSMENT COMMITTEE OF WEST HAM UNION *v.* ILES   **8 Q. B. D. 69; 8 App. Cas. 386**

POOR-RATE—Appeal—Case stated—12 & 13 Vict. c. 45, c. 11 -   **12 Q. B. D. 1** *See* PRACTICE—SUPREME COURT—APPEAL. 3.

—— Company in liquidation — Occupation by liquidator **23 Ch. D. 500; 28 Ch. D. 470,** *See* COMPANY—RATES. 1, 2, 3.   [474

POOR-RATE ASSESSMENT AND COLLECTION ACT AMENDMENT ACT, 1882. *See* POOR-RATE — OCCUPATION — Statutes.

—— Metropolis—Valuation Act **13 Q. B. D. 364** *See* METROPOLIS—VALUATION ACTS.

PORT.
See LOCAL GOVERNMENT — PUBLIC HEALTH—*Gazette.*
METROPOLIS—MANAGEMENT ACTS—*Gazette.*
SHIP—MERCHANT SHIPPING ACTS—*Gazette.*

PORT SANITARY AUTHORITY.
See LOCAL GOVERNMENT — PUBLIC HEALTH ACTS—*Statutes.*

PORTIONS -   -   -   **26 Ch. D. 363** *See* SETTLEMENT—CONSTRUCTION. 2.

—— Appointment before required—Fraud **[21 Ch. D. 332** *See* POWER—EXECUTION. 3.

—— Interest on—Irish estates—Rate allowed by Court   **23 Ch. D. 472** *See* SETTLEMENT—POWERS. 14.

—— Satisfaction—Double portions **20 Ch. D. 81** *See* SETTLEMENT—SATISFACTION.

—— Vesting -   **21 Ch. D. 806** *See* WILL—CLASS. 6.

POSSESSION—Bill of sale—Apparent possession **[16 Ch. D. 668 ; 7 Q. B. D. 516 ; [9 App. Cas. 653** *See* BILL OF SALE—APPARENT POSSESSION. 1, 2, 3.

—— Bill of sale—Unregistered **28 Ch. D. 682** *See* BILL OF SALE—REGISTRATION. 5.

—— Engineer—Ship -   **16 Ch. D. 604** *See* SHIP—MARITIME LIEN. 6.

—— Order for—Foreclosure **28 Ch. D. 413** *See* MORTGAGE—FORECLOSURE. 19.

—— Right to take—Railway company **[22 Ch. D. 25; 9 App. Cas. 480** *See* LANDS CLAUSES ACT—COMPULSORY POWERS. 4.

POSSESSION—*continued.*

—— Taken by purchaser—Waiver of objections to title -   -   **23 Ch. D. 320** *See* VENDOR AND PURCHASER—TITLE. 9.

—— Writ of -   -   -   **22 Ch. D. 281** *See* PRACTICE—SUPREME COURT—WRIT OF POSSESSION.

POSSESSION MONEY -   **26 Ch. D. 605** *See* PRACTICE—SUPREME COURT—INTERPLEADER. 11.

—— Levy for a sum above £50   **9 Q. B. D. 432** *See* BANKRUPTCY—ASSETS. 4.

POST OFFICE.

Congo.] *Treasury Warrant of 5th Nov., 1885, relative to transmission of letters, postcards, and newspapers between the United Kingdom and Congo Free State* -   -' **L. G. 1885, p. 5134**

Land.] *The Act 44 & 45 Vict. c. 20, amends the law with respect to the acquisition of land and the execution of instruments for the purposes of the Post Office.*

Money Orders.] *The Post Office Money Orders Act (46 & 47 Vict. c. 58), 1883, amends the Post Office Money Orders Acts, 1848 and 1880, and extends the same to Her Majesty's Dominions out of the United Kingdom.*

Post Office regulations, 28th Jan., 1884, under the Post Office Money Orders Acts, 1848 to 1883, extending money orders to Gibraltar **[L. G., 1884, p. 847**

Ditto (17th Dec., 1885), varying above regulations, and arranging for the issue and payment in Gibraltar, and in the United Kingdom and Constantinople respectively, of postal money orders **[L. G., 1885, p. 6249**

Regulations under 46 & 47 Vict. c. 58, extending money orders to British India (5th July, 1884), Hong Kong (17th July, 1884), and amending as to Malta (12th Dec., 1884)   **L. G., 1884, pp. 3325, [3486, 6013**

Ditto to the Straits Settlements (1st April, 1885) **[L. G., 1885, p. 1746**

Newspapers.] *The Act 44 & 45 Vict. c. 19 repeals, in part, sect. 6 of the Post Office Act, 1870, and further regulates the transmission of newspapers.*

Parcels Post.] *The Act 45 & 46 Vict. c. 74 (the Post Office Parcels Act, 1882), amends the Post Office Acts with respect to and provides for the conveyance of parcels by post not exceeding seven pounds in weight.*

Treasury warrant of 29th June, 1883, establishes the parcel post in the United Kingdom **[L. G., 1883, p. 3379**

Ditto of 14th April, 1885, extends the same to British India, Aden, and British Burmah **[L. G., 1885, p. 1856**

Ditto of 14th April, 1885, requires a declaration for the Customs in the case of parcels sent under last mentioned warrant. **L. G., 1885, p. 1856**

Ditto of Nov. 5th, 1885, establishing a Parcels Post between the United Kingdom and Ceylon and Labuan; and between Ceylon and Labuan and Malta and Gibraltar -   - **L. G., 1885, p. 5131**

Ditto of Nov. 18th, 1885, Parcels Post between the United Kingdom and Cape of Good Hope **[L. G., 1885, p. 5305**

POST OFFICE—continued.

Ditto of 1st Dec., 1885, Parcels Post between the United Kingdom and Leeward Islands .
　　　　　　　　　　　　[L. G., 1885, p. 5872
Ditto of 2nd Dec., 1885, Parcels Post between the United Kingdom and British Post Office, Constantinople　-　-　-　L. G., 1885, p. 5986
Ditto of 10th Dec., 1885, Parcels Post between the United Kingdom and British Guiana and Cyprus　-　-　-　L. G., 1885, p. 6070
Ditto of 18th Dec., 1885, Parcels Post between the United Kingdom and Germany
　　　　　　　　　　　　[L. G., 1885, p. 6194
Ditto of 19th Dec., 1885, Parcels Post between the United Kingdom and Belgium
　　　　　　　　　　　　[L. G., 1885, p. 6197
Reply Post Cards.] The Act 45 & 46 Vict. c. 2, authorizes the use of Reply Post Cards.

Act of 1884.] The Act 47 & 48 Vict. c. 76 (Post Office Protection Act, 1884), amends the law with respect to the protection of the Post Office. This Act is a Post Office Act within 7 Will. 4 & 1 Vict. c. 36 (Post Office Offences Act, 1837).

Officers.] Sect. 9 prohibits the obstruction of any officer of the Post Office.

Sect. 10 directs the surrender of clothing by an officer of the Post Office on ceasing to be such officer. A justice of the peace may issue a warrant to enforce such surrender.

Telegrams.] Sect. 11 punishes any person who forges or transmits a fictitious telegram, or who improperly divulges the purport of a telegram.

Prosecution.] Sect. 12 directs prosecution of summary offences under this Act, or under the Post Office Acts, to be under 42 & 43 Vict. c. 49 (Summary Jurisdiction Act, 1879). Indictable offences under this Act to be deemed to be indictable offences within first schedule of the above Act of 1879.

Sect. 13 gives power to mitigate punishments.

Sect. 14. Sums recovered to be paid into Exchequer.

Supplemental.] Sect. 15 declares that any instrument may be executed for the Postmaster-General by a secretary.

By sect. 16 no person shall be exempt by this Act from being proceeded against otherwise, but shall not be punished twice for the same offence.

Sect. 19 defines meaning of expressions in this Act and in 7 Will. 4 & 1 Vict. c. 36 (Post Office Offences Acts, 1837).

Sect. 20 defines meaning of expressions in this Act.

Protection.] Sect. 3 prohibits the placing of injurious substances, or nuisance, in or against post office letter boxes.

Sect. 4 prohibits the sending by post of inflammable or deleterious substances, noxious animals, or indecent prints, words, &c. See 3 & 4 Vict. c. 96, s. 62.

Sect. 5 prohibits the affixing of placards, notices, &c., on post offices or letter boxes. It also modifies power under sect. 9 of 41 & 42 Vict. c. 26 (Parliamentary and Municipal Registration Act, 1878) of fixing notices on a post office.

Sect. 6 prohibits the imitation of stamps, envelopes, forms, and marks of the Post Office, or of any foreign or colonial post office.

Sect. 7 prohibits fictitious stamps of English colonial or foreign government.

POST OFFICE—continued.

Sect. 8 prohibits false notices as to reception of letters or telegrams.

Repeal.] Sect. 17 substitutes 32 & 33 Vict. c. 18, s. 1, in 41 & 42 Vict. c. 76, for 31 & 32 Vict. c. 119, s. 33.

Sect. 21 repeals part of 7 Will. 4 & 1 Vict. c. 36, of 3 & 4 Vict. c. 96, of 38 & 39 Vict. c. 22, of 42 & 43 Vict. c. 49, of 44 & 45 Vict. c. 20, and of 44 & 45 Vict. c. 33.

Letter Carriers.] New regulations of Postmaster-General relative to employment of letter carriers, 10th Feb., 1885　-　L. G., 1885, p. 633.
And see TELEGRAPH—Statutes.

—— Government annuities.
　　See REVENUE—COLLECTION—Statutes.
—— Telegrams.
　　See TELEGRAPH—Statutes.

POST OFFICE PROTECTION ACT, 1884.
　　See POST OFFICE—Statutes.

POST OFFICE SAVINGS BANK—Investments in stocks.
　　See NATIONAL DEBT COMMISSIONERS—Statutes.

POST-NUPTIAL SETTLEMENT -　24 Ch. D. 597
　　See VOLUNTARY CONVEYANCE. 3.

POUND—Tender of damages—Action for money had and received　　　　11 Q. B. D. 275
　　See DISTRESS DAMAGE FEASANT.

POUNDAGE—Sheriff's fees—"Costs of execution"—Bankruptcy　-　13 Q. B. D. 415
　　See BANKRUPTCY—COSTS. 6.

POWER :—　　　　　　　　　　　　　Col.
I. EXECUTION　-　-　-　-　-　1078
　　(a.) EXCESSIVE APPOINTMENT.
　　(b.) FRAUDULENT APPOINTMENT.
　　(c.) TESTAMENTARY APPOINTMENT.
II. EXTINCTION　-　-　-　1088

I. POWER—EXECUTION.

(a.) EXCESSIVE APPOINTMENT.

1. —— Appointment to Next of Kin—Contingent Exercise.] An appointment to an object of a power for life with remainder to his next of kin will take effect if at the death of the tenant for life his next of kin are objects of the power. In re COULMAN. MUNBY v. ROSS　　　30 Ch. D. 186

2. —— Appointment to Second Set of Trustees—Wilful Default.] Property was assigned to trustees on trust for S. for life, and after her death to such of her issue as she should by will appoint; the settlor and S. during their joint lives, and the survivor, had a power of appointment of new trustees and discretion as to the investments, and the settlor had a power of revocation, which however he did not exercise. S. by her will appointed to B. and N. the property as trustees for her son. After her death the settlor appointed L. and N. trustees of the settlement, and the property was transferred to them. The son of S. died, and B. died. L. had allowed the property to remain in the hands of N., who had made away with it.—The persons beneficially entitled under the will of the son recovered judgment for the property made away with against

I. POWER—EXECUTION—*continued.*

(a.) EXCESSIVE APPOINTMENT—*continued.*

the executor of the son on the ground of wilful default. The executor brought an action against L. for the property as having been lost by his wilful default in allowing it to remain in the hands of N. :—*Held*, that S. had power to appoint the property to trustees for her son ; that as he took the whole beneficial interest the trustees of the settlement had no duties to perform except to hand the property over to the surviving trustee of the will; that therefore N. was rightfully in possession of the property, and L. was not liable for having allowed it to remain in the hands of N.—*In re Pocock's Policy* (Law Rep. 6 Ch. 445), *Ferrier* v. *Jay* (Law Rep. 10 Eq. 550), and *Busk* v. *Aldam* (Law Rep. 19 Eq. 16), observed upon. SCOTNEY v. LOMER ・ - 29 Ch. D. 535 [Affirmed by the Court of Appeal, 31 Ch. D. 380.]

(b.) FRAUDULENT APPOINTMENT.

3. —— Appointment before required—*Fraud on Power.*] B. P. W. having a power of charging portions for younger children on real estate under a settlement which gave him in the clearest terms power to fix the ages and times at which the portions should vest, and contained no provision for raising portions in default of appointment, and having three daughters aged nine, seven, and one, appointed by deed in 1828 £10,000 (being the full amount he was entitled to charge) for the portions of the daughters, to be a vested interest in the three daughters respectively immediately on the execution of the deed, the portions to be paid to them at such times and in such proportions as he should by deed or will appoint, and in default of - appointment to be paid to them share and share alike, at twenty-one or marriage, if the same age or time should happen after his decease, but if in his lifetime, then the payment to be postponed till after his death, unless he should -signify his consent in writing to their being raised and paid in his lifetime ; maintenance at £4 per cent. to be raised from his death, and the deed contained a power of revocation. In 1832 he made by a deed a similar appointment by way of confirmation of the former, the portions to be vested immediately on the execution of the deed. One daughter married and attained twenty-one, and in 1851 B. P. W. appointed £5000, part of the £10,000, to her. The other two died infants and spinsters, one in 1836, the other in 1845. B. P. W. assigned to the Plaintiff for value in 1875 the £5000 appointed to the two deceased daughters, and after his death the Plaintiff brought this action to have it raised :—*Held* (reversing the decision of Kay, J., who had dismissed the action as against the owners of the settled estate), that where a donee of a power of charging portions on real estate has, under the terms of the power, clear authority to fix the times at which portions shall vest, and appoints a portion to vest immediately, there is no rule of law which prohibits its being raised in the event of the child dying under twenty-one and unmarried, and that that the decision could not be supported on the ground that the appointment, so far as it made the portions vest immediately, was not within the power.— *Lord Hinchinbroke* v. *Seymour* (1 Bro. C. C. 395),

I. POWER—EXECUTION—*continued.*

(b.) FRAUDULENT APPOINTMENT—*continued.*

considered and examined.—*Held*, also, that the decision could not be supported on the ground that the appointment, so far as it made the portions vest immediately, was a fraud on the power as being made with a view to secure a benefit to the appointor; for that having regard to the fact that if the father had died without making any appointment, the children would have been unprovided for, it was manifestly for the benefit of the children that the father should make an appointment, and that as there was nothing to lead to the conclusion that when the appointments were made the children were likely to die young, and as in the event of the early death of the appointor the children might have derived a benefit from the absolute vesting of their portions, there was no ground for attributing to him an intention to benefit himself by making the portions vest immediately.—*Held*, therefore, that the Plaintiff was entitled to have the £5000 raised. HENTY v. WREY ‐ - 19 Ch. D. 492; 21 Ch. D. 332

4. —— Bargain by Appointor with Appointee —*Valid Exercise by Will—Subsequent Fraud on Power—Unattested Codicil—Wills Act* (1 Vict. c. 26), *ss.* 9, 10—*24 & 25 Vict. c.* 114.] The donee of a power of appointment amongst his children, exercisable by deed or will, having one son and one daughter, by will in 1862 made a valid appointment to the daughter of the whole fund subject to the power. By a French settlement, not under seal, made in 1866, upon the marriage of his daughter, he purported to appoint the whole fund to her, reserving to himself the power of disposing of a life interest in a portion of the fund in favour of his second wife ; and by a holograph codicil, dated in 1871, made in France, and unattested, after reciting an arrangement made when his daughter was married between himself, his daughter, and her intended husband, that such second wife should have such provision, he in effect appointed that if his daughter and her husband should carry out this arrangement they should have the whole of the fund. This codicil was admitted to probate under 24 & 25 Vict. c. 114.—*Held*, that though admitted to probate the codicil was invalid as a testamentary exercise of the power (sects. 9 and 10 of the Wills Act not being repealed by 24 & 25 Vict. c. 114) and did not revoke the appointment by will.—*Held*, also, that the codicil could not be treated as a defective attempt to exercise the power by deed which the Court would aid.—*Held*, also, that the appointments by the settlement and codicil were frauds upon the power.—*Held*, also, that the arrangements made by the settlement and codicil involved a threat to revoke the will if they were not carried into effect, and that consequently the will, being an ambulatory instrument, was vitiated and became a fraud upon the power, although at the date of its execution it was not open to objection.—Observations on *Kennard* v. *Kennard* (Law Rep. 8 Ch. 227). *In re* KIRWAN'S TRUSTS [25 Ch. D. 373

5. —— Bargain to settle appointed Property.] Real estate was vested in trustees under a will, upon trust as to one moiety to pay the rents to

I. POWER—EXECUTION—*continued.*

(b.) FRAUDULENT APPOINTMENT—*continued.*

A. for life, and after his death to convey it to and among his children who should attain twenty-one, and if he had no such child then on the trusts of the other moiety, and as to the other moiety on similar trusts for B. and his children. The will empowered the trustees if they should think fit to convey the shares of A. and B., or either of them, to them in fee. In 1882 A. and B., the younger of whom was of the age of sixty-two, and neither of whom had any child, having incumbered their interests, and being pressed by their mortgagees, applied to the trustees to exercise the power of giving them their shares of the estate in fee. An arrangement was made between A. and B. and the trustees that the trustees should, in exercise of their power, convey the estate to A. and B., as tenants in common in fee, and that, subject to such mortgages as should be approved by the trustees for raising money to pay off the existing mortgages, a part of the property should be settled upon trusts which gave A. and B. respectively powers of appointment in favour of their respective children and remoter issue, and powers of jointuring their wives. The trustees accordingly conveyed to A. and B., as tenants in common in fee, and the re-settlement, which vested the equity of redemption in new trustees, with a power of sale, upon the trusts which had been arranged, was made by a deed which recited that the trustees had exercised the power on condition that the settlement should be made :—*Held*, on appeal, that looking at all the circumstances of the case, it was not shewn that the bargain for the re-settlement induced the appointment, or that if the bargain had not been entered into the appointment would not have been made, and that the appointment and settlement were therefore valid, and that the trustees of the settlement could make a good title. *In re* TURNER'S SETTLED ESTATES　　　　　**28 Ch. D. 205**

(c.) TESTAMENTARY APPOINTMENT.

6. —— **General Power**—*Death of Appointee before Testatrix—Real Estate.*] A testator gave to his mother a general testamentary power of appointment over real estate, provided that, should his mother die without any will, then the estate was to go to E. C. The mother by will gave all her real estate, including that over which she had any power of appointment, to trustees in trust for G. G., who died in her lifetime :— *Held*, by Malins, V.C., that, the property being real estate, the case was not governed by authorities having reference solely to personal property ; that the mere circumstance of the testatrix making an appointment which failed did not shew an intention to make the appointed estate part of her general property, and that the estate went as in default of appointment.—*Held*, on appeal, that for this purpose there was no distinction between real and personal estate, and that the property belonged to the trustees of the mother's will, subject to a resulting trust for her heir-at-law (if any). *In re* VAN HAGAN. SPERLING *v.* ROCHFORT
　　　　　　　　　　　　　　[16 Ch. D. 18

7. —— **General Power**—*Death of Appointee*

I. POWER—EXECUTION—*continued.*

(c.) TESTAMENTARY APPOINTMENT—*continued.*

before Appointor—Next of Kin of Appointor entitled—Bequest of Legacy for Life—Residuary Gift.] Testator by his will gave a sum of money to his son M. upon trust to invest and to pay the income unto his daughter A. for her separate use for life, and after her death upon trust to pay the principal sum and interest unto such persons as A. should by deed or will appoint, and in default of appointment upon trust for M.'s own benefit. The testator bequeathed to M. his residuary estate, and appointed him sole executor. The money was invested by M. upon mortgages, and the income paid to A. till her death. A., who was not seised or possessed of any other property, by her will gave all her money and securities for money, furniture, and all other her personal estate and effects, and property, and all her real estate, if any, unto her two sisters H. and C. in proportion, i.e., one-third part of all her real estate and personal property and effects to H., and two-thirds of all her real and personal property and effects to C. absolutely, and she appointed C. sole executrix, and charged her property and effects with the payment of her debts and funeral and testamentary expenses. C. died in 1868, and A. in 1880, and H. was appointed administratrix of the will :—*Held*, that the two thirds of the moneys, subject to the payment thereout of a proportion of the debts, and funeral and testamentary expenses, belonged to the next of kin of A., and not to M., the residuary legatee. *In re* ICKERINGILL'S ESTATE. HINSLEY *v.* ICKERINGILL -　**17 Ch. D. 151**

8. —— **General or Special Power**—*"Devise"—Wills Act* (1 *Vict. c.* 26)—*Power created before but exercised after Act—Void Appointment falling into residuary Appointment.*] An instrument exercising a special or general power of appointment over property must be executed and construed according to the rules for the time being applicable to instruments of that kind, although the power may have been created before, but exercised after, an alteration in the law as to the construction and mode of execution of such instruments.—The word "devise" in the Wills Act includes in general a devise by way of appointment under a special or general power : consequently, where a testator makes a will operating as an exercise of a special or general power, a devise of real estate by way of appointment which fails or is void, falls, under sect. 25, into the residuary devise (if any) by way of appointment, unless a contrary intention appears by the will. FREME *v.* CLEMENT -　　　　　**18 Ch. D. 499**

9. —— **General Power** — *Donee unaware of Power—Exercise of Power — Election—Approbation and Reprobation.*] A married woman being (although unaware of it) the donee of a general power of appointment by deed or will over policy moneys payable upon her own death, concurred with her husband in settling certain family estates by an indenture which treated the policy moneys as the husband's own property, and settled them also. Her concurrence in the settlement was for a purpose entirely unconnected with the policy moneys, and under it she took a life interest in remainder after her husband's death in the estates, but no interest in the policy moneys.

I. POWER—EXECUTION—*continued.*

(c.) TESTAMENTARY APPOINTMENT—*continued.*

She survived her husband, received in respect of her life interest in the estates sums exceeding the amount of the policy moneys, and died, having by her will given all property over which she had any disposing power to certain beneficiaries:— *Held*, that by her will she had exercised her general power so as to make the policy moneys her own assets, and *Held*, also, that having taken under the settlements, benefits exceeding the value of the policy moneys, she could not by the exercise of her power take the policy moneys out of the settlement, without making good to the settlement beneficiaries an equal amount from her own estate; and accordingly that the policy moneys must be paid to the settlement trustees. —*Semble*, The concurrence of the donee of the power in the deed of settlement, for purposes unconnected with the policy moneys subject to the power, and in ignorance of the existence of the power, could not operate as an exercise of the power although the deed purported to pass the policy moneys. GRIFFITH-BOSCAWEN *v.* SCOTT

[26 Ch. D. 358

10. —— General Power—*General Devise or Bequest—Money liable to be invested in Land— Wills Act (1 Vict. c. 26), s. 27.*] By a marriage settlement executed in March, 1823, real estate was conveyed to trustees in fee, to their use during the life of the wife, on trust to pay the rents to her for her life, and after her death to such uses as the husband should by deed or writing, to be by him executed and delivered in the presence of and attested by two witnesses, appoint, and, in default of appointment and subject thereto, to the common dower uses in favour of the husband. There was a power for the trustees to sell the property with the consent of the husband and wife during their joint lives, and the money to arise from any sale was to be laid out in the purchase of other land, to be settled to the same uses, and until the re-investment should be made the money was to be invested in (inter alia) the public funds, and the income was to be payable to the persons to whom the rents of the land to be purchased would go. During the joint lives of the husband and wife, and before the date of the husband's will, the land was sold, and the proceeds of the sale were invested in New 3 per Cents. in the names of the trustees. No purchase of land was ever made, but the income of the stock was paid to the wife during her life. In October, 1844, the husband made his will (which was signed by him and sealed, and attested by two witnesses). The will contained the following bequest : "I also give and bequeath all the money and moneys that I die possessed of, whether in the public funds or in the care of W., or elsewhere, after my funeral expenses are paid, unto the sole use and behoof of my children hereinbefore named, share and share alike." W. was one of the trustees of the will, and at the time of the testator's death he had in his hands some money belonging to the testator. The testator had no money of his own in the funds, nor had he any power of appointment other than that contained in the settlement. The testator died on the 28th of December, 1851. His

I. POWER—EXECUTION—*continued.*

(c.) TESTAMENTARY APPOINTMENT—*continued.*

wife died on the 24th of October, 1881. After her death the question arose whether the testator had by his will exercised the power of appointment contained in the settlement, or whether the sum of stock passed as unappointed to his heir-at-law:—*Held*, that inasmuch as the wife had a right to call for the reinvestment of the stock in land, it must be considered as having been land at the time of the testator's death, and that the will did not operate as an exercise of the power of appointment:—*Held*, consequently, that the stock passed to the testator's heir-at-law. *In re* GREAVES' SETTLEMENT TRUSTS - 23 Ch. D. 313

11. —— General Power—*Married Woman— Will.*] A testatrix devising property by will by virtue of a power of appointment :—*Held*, upon the construction of the will, to have made the property her own, so that on the death of the devisee in her lifetime the gift over in default of appointment did not take effect.—*Hoare* v. *Osborne* (12 W. R. 661 ; 33 L. J. (Ch.) 586) disapproved. WILLOUGHBY OSBORNE *v.* HOLYOAKE

[22 Ch. D. 238

12. —— General Power—*Married Woman— Execution of Power—Ownership—Remoteness— Testamentary Power.*] A married woman exercised a general testamentary power :—*Held*, that time under the rule against perpetuities ran from her death, and not from the date of the instrument creating the power.—*In re Powell's Trusts* (39 L. J. (Ch.) 188) discussed and not followed. ROUS *v.* JACKSON - - 29 Ch. D. 521

13. —— General Power—*Revocation by General Clause in Subsequent Will.*] A general clause in a will revoking all former wills revokes- a prior testamentary appointment. — *In the Goods of Merritt* (1 Sw. & Tr. 112) and *In the Goods of Joys* (4 Sw. & Tr. 214) considered.—A married woman having a general power of appointment by will over real estate executed a will appointing the estate. After the death of her husband, she made another will revoking all former wills and containing a general devise and bequest of all her real and personal estate. She afterwards made a third will, also revoking all former wills and bequeathing her personal estate, but not devising or appointing her real estate. She had no real estate except that subject to her power of appointment: —*Held* (affirming the decision of the Master of the Rolls), that the testamentary appointment under the first will was revoked by the second will, and the second will by the third, and that the real estate went as in default of appointment. SOTHERAN *v.* DENING - - 20 Ch. D. 99

14. —— General Power—*Settlement—Will— Partial Invalidity—Appointment of Share of Trust Fund—Contingent Interest—Postponed Enjoyment of Capital—Intermediate Income.*] Where a testator, having a power of appointment over personalty, appoints a share of the fund to an object of the power upon the happening of a certain event, the appointment carries with it all the intermediate accretions to that share, whether in the shape of income or otherwise.—Under a settlement made on the second marriage of M., a widow, a trust fund belonging to her was vested in a

I. POWER—EXECUTION—*continued.*

(*c.*) TESTAMENTARY APPOINTMENT—*continued.*

trustee upon trust for her three children, nominatim, in such shares as she should by deed or will appoint, and in default of appointment for such three children equally.—By her will M. appointed that the trustee of the settlement should stand possessed of the trust fund, as to one-third part thereof, upon trust to pay the income thereof to her son C. (an object of the power) during his life, or until anticipation; and from and after his death or the determination of his estate, upon trust to pay the said one-third part to her grandson (not an object of the power) when he should attain twenty-one; and in case he should die before he should attain twenty-one, upon trust to pay the said one-third part to her daughter S. (an object of the power).—C. survived the testatrix and died, the grandson being then an infant:—*Held,* that although the appointment to the grandson was void, the appointment over to S. was good, and that the income from C.'s death of the one-third so appointed would pass with the capital to S., if the grandson died under twenty-one; but that, if that event did not happen, both income and capital would pass under the settlement as in default of appointment. LONG *v.* OVENDEN - - - 16 Ch. D. 691

15. —— General Power—*Settlement—Real Estate — Power of Sale — Direction to lay out Money in Purchase of Land — Conversion—Reinvestment in Government Funds—Will—General Bequest of Personal Estate—Exercise of Power of Appointment—Wills Act,* 1837 (1 *Vict. c.* 26), *ss.* 1, 27.] By A.'s marriage settlement, dated in 1832, her father settled certain real estate to the use of A. for life, and after her death, and in default of issue of the marriage, to the use of such persons as she should by will appoint, and in default of appointment to the use of the person under whom the Plaintiff claimed. The settlement contained a power for the trustee to sell the real estate, with a direction to lay out the proceeds, with A.'s consent, in the purchase of other hereditaments to be settled to the like uses, with a power of interim investment, with the like consent, in Government securities. By his will dated in 1831, and confirmed, subject to the settlement, by a codicil executed shortly after the settlement, A.'s father devised the property, subject to the settlement, and all other his real estate, to the use of A. for life, and in default of her having any issue, to such uses as she should by will appoint. —Some years afterwards, A.'s father and husband both having died, and there having been no issue of the marriage, the trustees of the settlement, at A.'s request, sold all the settled real estate for a sum of £24,226 2s. 0d. consols, which they transferred to her.—A. died a widow in 1879, having by her will, made shortly after the transfer to her of the consols, after appointing executors and bequeathing pecuniary legacies amounting to upwards of £30,000 bequeathed "all the residue of my personal estate and effects whatsoever" to two persons absolutely. The personal estate to which A. was entitled at the date of her will and of her death, independently of the consols, did not amount to more than £6000 :—*Held* (affirming the decision of Jessel, M.R.), that the general

I. POWER—EXECUTION—*continued.*

(*c.*) TESTAMENTARY APPOINTMENT—*continued.*

bequest of personal estate contained in A.'s will operated as an execution of the powers of appointment over the real estate given to her by her marriage settlement and by her father's will, and passed the consols. CHANDLER *v.* POCOCK [16 Ch. D. 648

16. —— General Power—*Settlement—Marriage of Englishwoman with Foreigner—Domicil—Settlement in English Form—Separate Use—Power of testamentary Disposition—Power of Appointment by " writing at any time hereafter"—Exercise by Will previously executed—Wills Act* (1 *Vict. c.* 26), *ss.* 24, 27.] On the 20th of December, 1881, prior to the marriage (solemnized in England) of a domiciled Englishwoman (a widow) with a domiciled Spaniard, real estate in England of the intended wife was vested by her in a trustee in fee, to such uses as the intended wife should by deed or will appoint, and, subject thereto, to the use of the intended wife, for her separate use. The settlement was made with the approbation of the intended husband, and the deed contained a statement that this approbation was given in consideration of a renunciation the same day executed by the intended wife of any rights which she would otherwise have acquired by her marriage in respect of the property of the intended husband according to the law of Spain. The deed also contained a declaration that it was to take effect and be construed according to the law of England. The marriage was solemnized on the next day. On the 23rd of February, 1882, the wife (being then domiciled in Spain) executed a deed-poll, in accordance with the provisions of the settlement, whereby she, in exercise of the power given to her by the settlement, appointed the real estate to the use of herself in fee for her separate use. By another deed executed the same day, to which the husband was a party, she, with the consent of the husband, appointed and conveyed, and the husband conveyed, the real estate to the use of a trustee in fee, upon trust for sale, and out of the proceeds of sale to pay certain specified debts, and, subject thereto, in trust for such person or persons as the wife " shall at any time or times hereafter by any writing or writings from any to time appoint," and, in default of any appointment and subject thereto, in trust for the wife absolutely for her separate use. Under this deed the trustee sold the property, and out of the proceeds of sale paid the specified debts, and there then remained a surplus in his hands. The wife died in June, 1882, having by a will, executed immediately after her marriage, and which purported to be made in exercise of the powers reserved to her by her marriage settlement, and of all other powers enabling her, directed, appointed, and declared that the real and personal estate over which she had any disposing power at the time of her death should be held and applied in the payment of certain legacies and annuities, and, subject thereto, she gave four-fifths of her real and personal estate, in case she should leave no children, to her husband absolutely. And she gave the remaining one-fifth of her property, charged with the before-mentioned annuities and legacies, to her brother and sisters, or to the

I. POWER—EXECUTION—*continued.*

(c.) TESTAMENTARY APPOINTMENT—*continued.*

children per stirpes of such of them as should die before her leaving children. The testatrix died without issue. The husband survived her. According to the law of Spain under such circumstances two-thirds of her property belonged to her father and mother, notwithstanding that she had left a will:—*Held*, that, whether the will was or was not a good exercise of the power reserved by the deed of February, 1882, it was a valid testamentary disposition by virtue of the limitation in default of appointment to the separate use of the testatrix ; that it took effect according to English law, and that the legatees named in it (including the husband) were entitled to the benefits given to them by it.—*Semble*, that, on the authority of *Boyes* v. *Cook* (14 Ch. D. 53) the will was a valid exercise of the power of appointment given by the deed of February, 1882. *In re* HERNANDO. HERNANDO *v.* SAWTELL - - 27 Ch. D. 284

17. —— Special Power—*Appointment to Persons not Objects of Power—Direction to pay Debts of Appointor—Election.*] A testatrix had, under the will of a brother who had predeceased her, a power to appoint his property by will among his nephews and nieces and the children or child of deceased nephews and nieces. She, by her will, gave all the real and personal estate of which she might be seised or possessed at the time of her death, or over which she might have any testamentary power of disposition, to trustees, upon trust for sale and conversion, and to stand possessed of the proceeds (which she described as "my said trust funds") upon trust to pay costs and expenses and to pay her debts and funeral expenses and certain pecuniary legacies, and then upon trust as to two one-fourth parts of her trust funds respectively for persons who were objects of the power ; and upon trust as to the other two one-fourth parts respectively for persons who were not objects of the power. And she declared that, in case of the failure of the trusts thereinbefore declared of any of the one-fourth parts of her trust funds, the one-fourth part, or so much thereof of which the trusts should fail, should be held upon the trusts thereinbefore declared of the others or other of the fourth parts of which the trusts should not fail :—*Held*, that the testatrix had manifested an intention to exercise the power, and that as to one moiety of the brother's property the power was well exercised :— *Held*, also, that as to the other moiety of the brother's property, the appointment was invalid, but that, by virtue of the gift "in case of the failure of any of the trusts thereinbefore declared." that moiety went to the persons to whom the first moiety was well appointed, and that, consequently, no case of election arose. *In re* SWINBURNE. SWINBURNE *v.* PITT - 27 Ch. D. 696

18. —— Special Power—*Exercise by Will— Bequest of all Property over which Testator at the Time of his Death should have "any beneficial disposing power by will"—Remoteness—Intervention of Trustees.*] A testator, who had under a settlement a power of appointment over leasehold and other personal estate among his children or grandchildren or other issue, by his will, which contained no reference to the power, gave "all the

I. POWER—EXECUTION—*continued.*

(c.) TESTAMENTARY APPOINTMENT—*continued.*

real and personal estate and effects whatsoever, and wheresoever, whether in possession, reversion, remainder, or expectancy, over which at the time of my decease, I shall have any beneficial disposing power by this my will" to trustees, upon trusts partly for persons who were objects of the power, and partly in excess of the power :—*Held*, that the use of the word "beneficial" did not conclusively shew that the testator could not have intended to exercise a power which he could not exercise for his own benefit or the benefit of his estate.—*Ames* v. *Cadogan* (12 Ch. D. 868) discussed.—There being, in the opinion of the Court, upon the will taken as a whole, a sufficient indication of an intention to exercise the power :— *Held*, that the power was exercised by the will, the trusts, so far as they were in excess of the power, being inoperative.—The testator gave a moiety of the property on trust for his daughters who should survive him, and attain twenty-four, in equal shares. The testator's youngest daughter was more than three years old at the time of his death :—*Held*, that the appointment was not void for remoteness.—*Held*, also, that the appointed fund ought to be retained by the trustees of the settlement on the trusts of the will, so far as they were valid. VON BROCKDORFF *v.* MALCOLM
[30 Ch. D. 172

19. —— Special Power—*Exercise by Will — Intention.*] If a testator manifests an intention to exercise by his will a special power of appointment, by reason of his making some gifts of property which he describes as "my" property, but the words of which gifts cannot be satisfied unless they pass property subject to the power, the Court will assume that he intended also to exercise the power in the case of other gifts in the will which are capable of passing other property subject to the power, although the words of gift can be satisfied by means of property belonging to the testator himself.—A testator had under a settlement a special power to appoint by will two estates at B. and at S. respectively, and also some shares in the B. Colliery. By his will he made gifts of "my estate at B." and of "my estate at S.," and he made another gift of "all my share and interest in the B., H., and W. Colliery Companies." He had no property of his own at either B. or S., but he had some shares of his own in the B. Colliery :—*Held*, that the will operated as an exercise of the power, not only as regarded the estates at B. and S., but also as regarded the settled shares in the B. Colliery. *In re* WAIT. WORKMAN *v.* PETGRAVE 30 Ch. D. 617

II. POWER—EXTINCTION.

By 44 & 45 Vict. c. 41 (*Conveyancing Act*, 1881), *sect.* 52.— (1.) *A person to whom any power, whether coupled with an interest or not, is given, may by deed release, or contract not to exercise the power.*

(2.) *The section applies to powers created by instruments coming into operation before or after the commencement of this Act.*

Disclaimer by Trustee.] *By* 45 & 46 Vict. c. 39 (*Conveyancing Act*, 1882), *sect.* 6.—(1.) *A person to whom any power, whether coupled with an*

II. **POWER—EXTINCTION**—*continued.*

interest or not, is given, may, by deed, disclaim the power; and, after disclaimer, shall not be capable of exercising or joining in the exercise of the power.

(2.) *On such disclaimer, the power may be exercised by the other or others, or the survivors or survivor of the others, of the persons to whom the power is given, unless the contrary is expressed in the instrument creating the power.*

(3.) *This section applies to powers created by instruments coming into operation either before or after the commencement of this Act.*

1. —— **Alienation of Interest**—*Settlement— Power to appoint New Trustees—Subsequent Exercise of Power—Consent of Alienees.*] A power to appoint new trustees may be exercised by a tenant for life, after aliening his interest. By a settlement, property partly real and partly personal, was conveyed to trustees upon trust to provide an annuity for A., a widow, for life, and subject thereto for B., her son, absolutely. The settlement provided that B., during his life, and after his death the trustees or trustee for the time being, or the executors or administrators of the last acting trustee, should have power to appoint new trustees, if necessary. B. mortgaged his whole interest under the settlement, and the real estate (subject to A.'s annuity) was sold by the mortgagees to C. The personal estate was not sold by the mortgagees:—*Held*, that B., could still exercise the power to appoint new trustees, without the consent of C. HARDAKER *v.* MOORHOUSE - - - - **26 Ch. D. 417**

2. —— **Alienation of Interest**—*Will—Power of Advancement — Consent of Life Tenant — Bankruptcy of Life Tenant—Effect of.*] A testatrix who died in 1884 gave a moiety of a trust fund to trustees upon trust to pay the income to J. C. during his life, and after his death in trust for W. J. (an infant), empowering the trustees to raise any part not exceeding one half of W. J.'s share for his advancement, subject to the consent in writing of J. C. during his life.—The trustees were desirous of exercising the power, but J. C. had become a bankrupt, and was still undischarged:—*Held*, that J. C.'s power of consenting to the advancement was not extinguished by his bankruptcy, but could not be exercised without the sanction of his trustee in bankruptcy acting under the direction of the Court of Bankruptcy. *In re* COOPER. COOPER *v.* SLIGHT **27 Ch. D. 565**

POWER—Appointment—Election **22 Ch. D. 555**
  See ELECTION. 1.

—— Appointment—Exercise by trustee in liquidation - - **29 Ch. D. 1005**
  See BANKRUPTCY—TRUSTEE. 11.

—— Appointment—Invalidity—Election
  [26 Ch. D. 208
  See SETTLEMENT—CONSTRUCTION. 7.

—— Appointment—Will—Children of testator
  See WILL—LAPSE. 2. **[26 Ch. D. 266**

—— Default of appointment - **24 Ch. D. 244**
  See SETTLEMENT—CONSTRUCTION. 8.

—— Discretion of trustees—Interference of Court
  [21 Ch. D. 571, 576, n.; 29 Ch. D. 913
  See TRUSTEE—POWERS. 4, 5, 6.

POWER—*continued.*

—— Executor.
  See EXECUTOR—POWERS—*Statutes.*

—— Illusory—Law of Lower Canada
  [10 App. Cas. 653
  See COLONIAL LAW—CANADA—QUEBEC. 6.

—— Maintenance clause—Settlement
  [22 Ch. D. 521
  See SETTLEMENT—POWERS. 5.

—— Of appointing new trustees.
  See Cases under SETTLEMENT—POWERS. 8—13.

—— Of appointing new trustees **23 Ch. D. 134, 138**
  See TRUSTEE—POWERS. 1, 2.

—— Of bequeathing by will - **23 Ch. D. 235**
  See CUSTOMS ANNUITY FUND.

—— Of borrowing—Corporation **10 App. Cas. 354**
  See CORPORATION. 2.

—— Of charging portions—Rate of interest
  [23 Ch. D. 472
  See SETTLEMENT—POWERS. 14.

—— Of investment - - **19 Ch. D. 64**
  See FRIENDLY SOCIETY.

—— Of leasing.
  See Cases under SETTLEMENT—POWERS. 1—4.

—— Of leasing by mortgagor.
  See MORTGAGE—POWERS—*Statutes.*

—— Of managing - - **27 Ch. D. 196, 553**
  See SETTLEMENT—POWERS. 6, 7.

—— Of mortgaging—Administrator
  [16 Ch. D. 577; 20 Ch. D. 745
  See ADMINISTRATOR—POWERS. 2, 3.

—— Of pledging—Power of attorney
  [9 App. Cas. 561
  See POWER OF ATTORNEY 1.

—— Of purchasing land—Settlement
  [22 Ch. D. 255
  See TRUSTEE—INDEMNITY. 2.

—— Of revocation **18 Ch. D. 668; 29 Ch. D. 212**
  See VOLUNTARY CONVEYANCE. 4, 6.

—— Of revocation—Settlement **19 Ch. D. 47;**
  [20 Ch. D. 742
  See SETTLEMENT—REVOCATION. 2.

—— Of sale—Administration with will annexed
  [16 Ch. D. 3
  See ADMINISTRATOR—WITH WILL ANNEXED. 1.

—— Of sale—Administrator - **16 Ch. 49**
  See ADMINISTRATOR—LIMITED. 4.

—— Of sale—Charity Commissioners
  [26 Ch. D. 173
  See CHARITY—COMMISSIONERS. 9.

—— Of sale—Determination of—Separate estate
  [18 Ch. D. 429
  See LANDS CLAUSES ACT—COMPULSORY POWERS. 8.

—— Of sale—Executor - - **23 Ch. D. 138**
  See VENDOR AND PURCHASER—TITLE. 7.

—— Of sale—Mortgage.
  See Cases and Statutes under MORTGAGE —POWERS.

2 N

POWER—*continued.*

—— Of sale—Mortgage—Abortive sale
[**25 Ch. D. 636**]
    See MORTGAGE—FORECLOSURE. 3.

—— Of sale — Mortgage — Garnishee order—
    Proceeds of sale   **17 Ch. D. 259**
    See PRACTICE—SUPREME COURT—GAR-
    NISHEE ORDERS. 8.

—— Of sale—Pledge—Shares in company
[**26 Ch. D. 257**]
    See COMPANY—SHARES—TRANSFER. 1.

—— Of sale—Settled Land Act.
    See Cases under SETTLED LAND ACT.

—— Of sale—Settlement.
    See Cases under SETTLEMENT—POWERS.
    15—18.

—— Of sale—Trustee—Conveyancing Act, 1881.
    See TRUSTEE—POWERS—*Statutes.*

—— Of sale—Will—Conversion   **26 Ch. D. 601**
    See WILL—CONVERSION.

POWER OF ATTORNEY.

By 44 & 45 *Vict. c.* 41 (*Conveyancing Act,*1881),
sect. 46.—(1.) *The donee of a power of attorney
may, if he thinks fit, execute or do any assurance,
instrument, or thing, in and with his own name
and signature and his own seal, where sealing is
required, by the authority of the donor of the power ;
and every assurance, instrument, and thing so
executed and done shall be as effectual in law, to
all intents, as if it had been executed or done by
the donee of the power in the name and with the
signature and seal of the donor thereof.*

(2.) *This section applies to powers of attorney
created by instruments executed either before or
after the commencement of this Act.*

Sect. 47.—(1.) *Any person making or doing any
payment or act, in good faith, in pursuance of a
power of attorney, shall not be liable in respect of
the payment or act by reason that before the payment or act the donor of the power had died or
become lunatic, of unsound mind, or bankrupt, or
had revoked the power, if the fact of death, lunacy,
unsoundness of mind, bankruptcy, or revocation
was not at the time of the payment or act known
to the person making or doing the same.*

(2.) *But this section shall not affect any right
against the payee of any person interested in any
money so paid ; and that person shall have the like
remedy against the payee as he would have had
against the payer if the payment had not been made
by him.*

(3.) *This section applies only to payments and
acts made and done after the commencement of this
Act—*31st *of December,* 1881.

Sect. 48.—(1.) *An instrument creating a power
of attorney, its execution being verified by affidavit,
statutory declaration, or other sufficient evidence,
may, with the affidavit or declaration, if any, be
deposited in the Central Office of the Supreme Court
of Judicature.*

(2.) *A separate file of instruments so deposited
shall be kept, and any person may search that file,
and inspect every instrument so deposited, and an
office copy thereof shall be delivered out to him on
request.*

(3.) *A copy of an instrument so deposited may
be presented at the office, and may be stamped or*

POWER OF ATTORNEY—*continued.*

*marked as an office copy, and when so stamped or
marked shall become and be an office copy.*

(4.) *An office copy of an instrument so deposited
shall without further proof be sufficient evidence of
the contents of the instrument and of the deposit
thereof in the Central Office.*

(5.) *General Rules may be made for purposes of
this section, regulating the practice of the Central
Office, and prescribing, with the concurrence of the
Commissioners of Her Majesty's Treasury, the fees
to be taken therein.*

(6) *This section applies to instruments creating
powers of attorney executed either before or after
the commencement of this Act.*

Act of 1882.] *By* 45 & 46 *Vict. c.* 39 (*Conveyancing Act,* 1882), *Sect.* 8.—(1.) *If a power of
attorney given for valuable consideration is in the
instrument creating the power expressed to be irrevocable, then, in favour of a purchaser—*

    (i.) *The power shall not be revoked at any time,
either by anything done by the donee of the
power without the concurrence of the donee
of the power, or by death, marriage, lunacy,
unsoundness of mind, or bankruptcy of the
donor of the power ; and*

    (ii.) *Any act done at any time by the donee of
the power, in pursuance of the power, shall
be as valid as if anything done by the donor
of the power without the concurrence of the
donee of the power, or the death, marriage,
lunacy, unsoundness of mind, or bankruptcy
of the donor of the power, had not been
done or happened ; and*

    (iii.) *Neither the donee of the power nor the pur-
chaser shall at any time be prejudicially
affected by notice of anything done by the
donor of the power, without the concurrence
of the donee of the power, or of the death,
marriage, lunacy, unsoundness of mind, or
bankruptcy of the donor of the power.*

(2.) *This section applies only to powers of
attorney created by instruments executed after the
commencement of this Act—*31st *of December,*
1882.

Sect. 9.—(1.) *If a power of attorney, whether
given for valuable consideration or not, is in the
instrument creating the power expressed to be irrevocable for a fixed time therein specified, not exceeding one year from the date of the instrument, then,
in favour of a purchaser,—*

    (i.) *The power shall not be revoked, for and
during that fixed time, either by anything
done by the donor of the power without the
concurrence of the donee of the power, or
by the death, marriage, lunacy, unsoundness of mind, or bankruptcy of the donor of
the power ; and*

    (ii.) *Any act done within that fixed time, by the
donee of the power, in pursuance of the
power, shall be as valid as if anything done
by the donor of the power without the concurrence of the donee of the power, or the
death, marriage, lunacy, unsoundness of
mind, or bankruptcy of the donor of the
power, had not been done or happened ;
and*

    (iii.) *Neither the donee of the power, nor the pur-
chaser, shall at any time be prejudicially
affected by notice either during or after*

POWER OF ATTORNEY—*continued.*

that fixed time of anything done by the donor of the power during that fixed time, without the concurrence of the donee of the power, or of the death, marriage, lunacy, unsoundness of mind, or bankruptcy of the donor of the power within that fixed time.

(2.) This section applies only to powers of attorney created by instruments executed after the commencement of this Act.

Married Woman.] *By* 44 & 45 *Vict. c.* 41 (*Conveyancing Act*, 1881), *sect.* 40.—(1.) *A married woman, whether an infant or not, shall by virtue of this Act have power, as if she were unmarried and of full age, by deed, to appoint an attorney on her behalf for the purpose of executing any deed or doing any other act which she might herself execute or do; and the provisions of this Act relating to instruments creating powers of attorney shall apply thereto.*

(2.) This section applies only to deeds executed after the commencement of this Act.

1. —— *Power to pledge—Power to sell or purchase does not include Power to pledge.*] A power of attorney gave to the holders authority "for the purposes aforesaid to sign for me and in my name and on my behalf any and every contract or agreement, acceptance, or other document," the purposes aforesaid being "from time to time to negotiate, make sale, dispose of, assign, and transfer" Government promissory notes, and "to contract for, purchase, and accept the transfer" of the same:—*Held*, that upon the true construction of this power the holders were authorized to sell or purchase such notes, but not to pledge them.—*Bank of Bengal v. Macleod* (5 Moore, Ind. Ap. 1; 7 Moore, P. C. 35) distinguished. JONMENJOY COONDOO *v.* WATSON

[9 App. Cas. 561

2. —— *Recital—Control of operative Part—Complicity in Fraud — Notice.*] The operative part of a power of attorney appointed X. and Y. to be the attorneys of the Plaintiff without in terms limiting the duration of their powers, but it was preceded by a recital that the Plaintiff was going abroad, and was desirous of appointing attorneys to act for him during his absence:—*Held*, that the recital controlled the generality of the operative part of the instrument, and limited the exercise of the powers of the attorneys to the period of the Plaintiff's absence from this country. —During the Plaintiff's absence from England, and again after his return, X. and Y., without his knowledge and purporting to act under the power, which empowered them to borrow money on mortgage, borrowed moneys from a bank upon the security of charges on the Plaintiff's property, which moneys they afterwards misappropriated. Upon the occasion of the first advance the power was produced to the bankers and registered by their clerk, but it was not examined by them, nor were they aware that the Plaintiff was in England when they made the second advance:—*Held*, that the charge given during the Plaintiff's absence was valid, and that the charge given after his return was invalid.—The Plaintiff went abroad a second time, and before going gave a fresh power to X. and Y., by which, after referring to the former power, and reciting that he had been in

POWER OF ATTORNEY—*continued.*

England for a short time, and was returning abroad, he appointed X. and Y. his attorneys, giving them power to borrow money for him with or without giving security. During his second absence, and without his knowledge, X. and Y., who themselves had an overdrawn account with the bankers, borrowed from them further moneys, alleging that it was to enable them to make payments for the Plaintiff; and under the second power of attorney they charged the Plaintiff's property as a security for the loan, applying the borrowed moneys in reduction of their own debt to the bank. Upon this occasion the second power was produced to the solicitor of the bank, but he was unacquainted with the former transactions, and neither the bankers nor any of their clerks were aware that the Plaintiff had been in England:—*Held*, that in order to make out that the bank were so put upon inquiry as to invalidate the transaction, the Plaintiffs must shew that the recitals in the second power were seen by some agent of theirs who knew of the previous transactions, and would by these recitals have been rendered suspicious of the good faith of X. and Y.; and consequently that there having been no such notice or knowledge on the part of the bank, wilful blindness could not be imputed to them, and the last-mentioned charge was valid. DANBY *v.* COUTTS & CO. -　**29 Ch. D. 500**

I. PRACTICE—ADMIRALTY—PRELIMINARY ACT.

—— *Amendment—Refusal to amend Preliminary Act.*] The Court will refuse to allow a mistake in a preliminary act to be amended, even though the application for an amendment is made before the hearing of the suit and be supported by affidavit. THE "MIRANDA"

[7 P. D. 185

II. PRACTICE—ADMIRALTY—SERVICE.

1. —— *Warrant of Arrest—City of London Court—London (City) Small Debts Extension Act,* 1852 (15 & 16 *Vict. c. lxxvii.*), *s.* 18 — *County Courts Admiralty Jurisdiction Act,* 1868 (31 & 32

2 N 2

II. PRACTICE — ADMIRALTY — SERVICE— *continued.*

Vict. c. 71, s. 23.)] A warrant of arrest in an action in rem was issued from the City of London Court directed to the high bailiff, and others, the bailiffs thereof, but was, without authority from the Court, served by a clerk in the high bailiff's office :—*Held,* affirming the decision of the judge of the City of London Court, that this was not a proper service of the warrant.—*Per* Sir James Hannen : "Any officer" mentioned in 31 & 32 Vict. c. 71, s. 23, means any officer duly authorized by the Court.—*Per* Butt, J.: That it means any officer whose ordinary duty it is to serve processes, or one duly authorized so to do. THE "PALOMARES" - - 10 P. D. 36

2. —— Writ in Personam—*Incorrect Address of Defendant — Refusal of Consolidation Order before service of Writ.*] The Court will refuse to consolidate cross actions of damage in personam where there has been no service of the writ in the principal action. — A shipowner, residing and carrying on business in Scotland, having been described on the face of a writ of summons for service within the jurisdiction sued out against him in an action of damage in personam as "of the city of London" applied before service of the writ and after a cross action of damage in respect of the same collision had been instituted on his behalf that the writ should be set aside. The Court refused the motion. THE "HELENSLEA." THE "CATALONIA" 7 P. D. 57

3. —— Writ in Rem—*Action by default—Rules of the Supreme Court, 1883, Order IX., rr. 11, 12; Order XIII., rr. 12, 13, Order LVII., r. 14.*] In an action in rem the writ of summons was served in the manner provided by Order IX., rule 12, no appearance was entered, and the action came on for judgment by default under Order XIII., rules 12, 13. The affidavit of service of the writ was made by the solicitor's clerk who had served such writ :—*Held,* that service of a writ in rem by a solicitor or his clerk, and not by the marshal or his substitute was a valid service, and that the affidavit was sufficient. THE "SOLIS" [10 P. D. 62

III. PRACTICE—ADMIRALTY—PLEADING.

1. —— Damage to Cargo—*Particulars.*] The rule as to giving the opposite party particulars of any general allegation in pleadings ought to be the same in the Admiralty as in the Queen's Bench Division. Where, therefore, in an action in the Admiralty Division by cargo owners against shipowners for delivery of cargo in a damaged condition, the statement of claim alleged that the damage was not occasioned by any of the excepted perils mentioned in the bill of lading under which the cargo has been shipped, but was occasioned by the defective condition of the vessel or by the negligence or breach of duty of the Defendants or their servants, it was *held* by the Court of Appeal (Lord Coleridge, C.J., and Brett and Holker, L.JJ.), reversing the decision of Sir Robert Phillimore, that the Defendants were entitled to particulars of the defects rendering the vessel not fit to carry the cargo. THE "RORY" [7 P. D. 117

2. —— Salvage—*Statement of Claim—Rules*

III. PRACTICE—ADMIRALTY—PLEADING— *continued.*

of Supreme Court, 1883. Order XLX., rr. 5, 7— Appendix C., Form No. 6.] A statement of claim in a salvage action was drawn in the Form No. 6 of Appendix C. to the Rules of the Supreme Court,. 1883; on motion by the Defendants under Order XIX., rule 7, for a further and better statement of claim or particulars :—*Held,* that the Plaintiffs must deliver a fuller statement of claim, and that in salvage actions a fuller form than that given in Appendix C, No. 6, should generally be followed. THE "ISIS" - - - - 8 P. D. 227

IV. PRACTICE—ADMIRALTY—DEFAULT.

—— Time—*Order XIII., rr. 12, 13.*] In order to obtain judgment by default of appearance in an action in rem under Order XIII., r. 12, the ten days stated in Order XXI., r. 6, must elapse, and a notice of trial under Order XXXVI., r. 11, must be filed in the registry. THE "AVENIR" [9 P. D. 84

V. PRACTICE — ADMIRALTY — COUNTER - CLAIM.

—— Security for Damages—*Foreign Government—24 & 25 Vict.* c. 10, s. 34.] The Court has jurisdiction by 24 & 25 Vict. c. 10, s. 34, to order a Plaintiff in an action for damage by collision to give security for damages to a Defendant who brings a counter-claim. The Court can exercise this power when such Plaintiff is a foreign sovereign whose ship cannot be arrested. THE. "NEWBATTLE" - - 10 P. D. 33.

VI. PRACTICE—ADMIRALTY—THIRD PARTY.

—— Embarrassing Pleading—*Tow and Tug—Rules of Supreme Court, 1875, Order XVI., rr. 18, 21.*] In an action for damage by collision brought by a vessel at anchor against a vessel in tow of a. tug, the owners of the tug were made third parties. under Order XVI. rule 18, as the Defendants claimed to be indemnified by the owners of the. tug against the Plaintiff's claim on the ground that the improper navigation, if any, was that: of the tug. An application for directions under Order XVI. rule 21 was subsequently made, and. the Plaintiffs thereupon asked that the third parties should be dismissed from the action on the ground that the Plaintiffs would be embarrassed by the proceedings between the Defendants and the third parties :—*Held,* that the third parties must be dismissed, as under the circumstances questions would probably arise between them and the Defendants by which the Plaintiffs might be embarrassed, as they were different from those upon which the action between the Plaintiffs and Defendants would turn. THE. "BIANCA" - - - - 8 P. D. 91

VII. PRACTICE — ADMIRALTY — ARREST OF SHIP.

1. —— Restraint—*Bail Bond — Form.*] In an action of restraint the bail bond should not be given to pay what may be adjudged against the Defendant in an action, but simply for the appraised or agreed value of the Plaintiff's shares,. in case the ship does not return to the particular port named in the bond. THE "ROBERT DICKINSON" - - - 10 P. D. 15.

2. —— Warrant—*Notice—Telegram.*] When.

VII. PRACTICE—ADMIRALTY—ARREST OF SHIP—*continued.*

the marshal sends by telegram to his substitute at an outport notice of the issue of a warrant, and such substitute communicates it to the master of the ship against which it is issued, it is a contempt of Court to move the ship from the place where it is lying. THE "SERAGLIO" 10 P. D. 120

VIII. PRACTICE—ADMIRALTY—CONCURRENT ACTIONS.

—— Transfer of Action from Inferior Court —*Cross Action in High Court—Plaintiffs.*] When an action is transferred from an inferior Court and consolidated with a cross-action begun in the High Court, the plaintiffs in the action in the inferior Court will be placed in the position of plaintiffs in the consolidated actions, if they began the action in the inferior Court before the cross-action in the High Court. THE "NEVER DESPAIR"
[9 P. D. 34

[*See also* THE "COSMOPOLITAN," 9 P. D. 35, n; *and* THE "BJORN," Ibid. 36, n.]

IX. PRACTICE—ADMIRALTY—EVIDENCE.

1. —— Admission by Master of Ship—*Letter.*] A letter from the master of a ship to her owners is admissible as evidence against them in regard to the facts therein stated; but the opinion of the master in such a letter is not evidence. THE "SOLWAY" - 10 P. D. 137

2. —— Engineer's Log.] In an action of damage the engineer's log is admissible as evidence against the shipowner by whom the engineer is employed. THE "EARL OF DUMFRIES "
[10 P. D. 31

X. PRACTICE — ADMIRALTY — PRODUCTION OF DOCUMENTS.

—— Depositions before Receiver of Wreck—*Discovery.*] Depositions of the master and crew of a British ship, the *R.*, in regard to a collision had been taken by the Receiver of Wreck, and the Board of Trade refused to give copies of such depositions to the owners of the *P.* in an action arising out of the collision between these vessels. Copies had however been obtained for the purpose of the action by the solicitors to the owners of the *R.*, whose master and crew had made the depositions. On motion by the owners of the *P.* for leave to inspect and take copies of the copies of the depositions in the possession of the solicitors of the owners of the *R.* :—*Held*, that these copies were privileged. THE "PALERMO"
[9 P. D. 6

XI. PRACTICE — ADMIRALTY — INSPECTION OF PROPERTY.

—— Trinity Masters — 24 & 25 Vict. c. 10, *s.* 18.] Before the hearing of an action an application was made under 24 & 25 Vict. c. 10, s. 18, by the Plaintiffs, that two Trinity masters should inspect the lights of the Defendants' ship :—*Held*, that the application was premature and ought to be refused. THE "VICTOR COVACEVICH"
[10 P. D. 40

XII. PRACTICE—ADMIRALTY—TRIAL.

—— Consequential Damage — *Tribunal to decide Question.*] Although it is the usual practice of the Court in collision cases to refer all questions

XII. PRACTICE — ADMIRALTY — TRIAL — *continued.*

involving the amount of damages to the Registrar assisted by merchants, yet when consequential damages are claimed, it is in the discretion of the Court to deal at the hearing of the action, with the question whether such damages are recoverable. THE "MAID OF KENT" 6 P. D. 178

XIII. PRACTICE—ADMIRALTY—APPEAL.

1. —— Court of Passage—*Leave to appeal—County Courts Admiralty Jurisdiction Act, 1868* (31 & 32 Vict. c. 71), ss. 26, 27—*County Courts Act, 1875* (38 & 39 Vict. c. 50). *s. 6—Application for Leave to adduce fresh Evidence.*] Appeals from County Courts may still be brought under the County Courts Admiralty Jurisdiction Act, 1868, ss. 26, 27, as well as under the County Courts Act, 1875, s. 6. Leave to appeal was granted after the expiration of ten days from the trial when it was shewn that no injustice would be done to the other side—Application to adduce fresh evidence on the appeal refused. THE "HUMBER" - - - - 9 P. D. 12

2. —— Withdrawal of Appeal—*Order LVIII., r. 6.*—When a Respondent under Order LVIII., rule 6, has given notice that he will on the hearing of an appeal contend that the decision of the Court below should be varied, and the Appellant subsequently withdraws his appeal, such notice entitles the Respondent to elect whether to continue or withdraw his cross-appeal. If he continues his cross-appeal the Appellant has the right to give a cross notice that he will bring forward his original contention on the hearing of the Respondent's appeal. THE "BEESWING"
[10 P. D. 18

XIV. PRACTICE—ADMIRALTY—LIMITATION OF LIABILITY.

1. —— Collision — *Merchant Shipping Act, 1862* (25 & 26 Vict. c. 63), s. 54.] Two ships V. and K. having come into collision, the owners of the V. brought an action in rem in the Admiralty Division against the owners of the K., who counter-claimed, and both ships were held to blame. The owners of the K. brought an action in the Admiralty Division to limit their liability under the Merchant Shipping Amendment Act, 1862 (25 & 26 Vict. c. 63), s. 54, and paid the amount of their liability into Court. The damage to the V. was greater than that to the K., and the fund in Court was not sufficient to satisfy all the claims for which the owners of the K. were answerable in damages :—*Held* (Lord Bramwell doubting) that the owners of the V. were entitled to prove against the fund for a moiety of their damage, less a moiety of the damage sustained by the K., and to be paid in respect of the balance due to them after such deduction, pari passu with the other claimants out of such fund.—*Chapman* v. *Royal Netherlands Steam Navigation Company* (4 P. D. 157) overruled. STOOMVAART MAATSCHAPPY NEDERLAND *v.* PENINSULAR AND ORIENTAL STEAM NAVIGATION COMPANY - - 7 App. Cas. 795

2. —— Collision—*Improper Navigation—25 & 26 Vict. c. 63; s. 54, sub-s. 4.*] The words "improper navigation" in 25 & 26 Vict. c. 63, s. 54, sub-s. 4, are not to be restricted to the negligent

XIV. PRACTICE—ADMIRALTY—LIMITATION OF LIABILITY—*continued.*

navigation of a vessel by her master and crew, for the statute includes all damage wrongfully done by a ship to another whilst it is being navigated, where the wrongful action is due to the negligence of a person for whom the owner is responsible. Therefore when a vessel, owing to the negligence of a person on shore in overlooking the machinery, steered so badly that she came into collision with another vessel, and Butt, J., in an action for limitation of liability gave a decree in her favour:—*Held*, by the Court of Appeal, that such judgment was right, and that the statute applied to such a case. THE "WARKWORTH" **9 P. D. 20, 145**

3. —— Deductions — *Foreign Ship — Crew Space—Merchant Shipping Act*, 1854 (17 & 18 *Vict. c.* 104), *s.* 21—*Merchant Shipping Act*, 1867 (30 & 31 *Vict. c.* 124), *s.* 9.] The owners of a foreign ship with a closed-in space on the upper deck solely appropriated to the berthing of the crew, are entitled, in limiting their liability, to deduct such space under the Merchant Shipping Act, 1854, s. 21, sub-s. 4, though the provisions of the Merchant Shipping Act, 1867, s. 9, have not been complied with.—*The Franconia* (3 P. D. 164) explained. THE "PALERMO" **10 P. D. 21**

4. —— Deductions—*Tonnage of Ship at Time of Collision—Merchant Shipping Act*, 1862 (25 & 26 *Vict. c.* 63), *s.* 54.] In a suit of limitation of liability in respect of damage arising from a collision, the shipowners claimed deductions on account of screw space which appeared on the register of their vessel at the time of their application for a decree:—*Held*, that they were not entitled to the benefit of any deductions not appearing on the register in force at the time of the collision. THE "JOHN MCINTYRE"
[6 P. D. 200

5. —— Payment into Court—*Wrongdoer—Salvage— Cargo—Thames Conservancy— Powers under Two Acts of Parliament.*] The payment into Court of £8 a ton under 25 & 26 Vict. c. 63, s. 54, does not place the shipowner in the position of a person who has not done wrong.—The owner of a ship sunk by a collision in the Thames admitted it to be his fault, and paid into Court £8 a ton in a suit to limit his liability. The Thames Conservators, having powers under the Removal of Wrecks Act, 1877, and the Thames Conservancy Acts, raised the ship and delivered the ship and cargo to the owner, he undertaking to pay the expenses of raising. Part of the cargo was some wool, which was damaged by being sunk:—*Held*, that the shipowner was bound to deliver the wool to the owner of the wool without claiming from him, by way of contribution to salvage, any part of the expenses of raising the ship and cargo. —Where a public body has powers under two Acts, it must be taken to have proceeded under that which gave it the most advantages. PREHN *v.* BAILEY. THE "ETTRICK" **6 P. D. 127**

XV. PRACTICE — ADMIRALTY —APPORTIONMENT OF DAMAGE.

—— Collision—*Infringement of the Rule with respect to Lights—Merchant Shipping Act*, 1873 (36 & 37 *Vict. c.* 85), *s.* 17.] Where two ships incurred damage in a collision and it was found

XV. PRACTICE — ADMIRALTY—APPORTIONMENT OF DAMAGE—*continued.*

that one of them was to blame for improper navigation, and that the other had infringed the regulations with respect to lights:—*Held*, that in the absence of proof that such infringement could not possibly have contributed to the collision, the damage must be divided according to the ordinary rule of the Court of Admiralty.—*The Fanny M. Carvill* (Aspinall's Maritime Cases (N.S.) vol. 2, p. 569) approved. CHINA MERCHANTS' STEAM NAVIGATION COMPANY *v.* BIGNOLD. THE "HOCHUNG." THE "LAPWING" - **7 App. Cas. 512**

XVI. PRACTICE — ADMIRALTY — LIS ALIBI PENDENS.

1. —— Stay of Proceedings.] In an action of damage in personam by the owners of the ship G. against the owners of the ship P. it appeared that a cause of damage in rem relating to the same collision had, prior to the proceedings in this Court, been instituted by the owners of the P. against the G. in a Vice-Admiralty Court abroad, and was then pending. The Court, on the application of the owners of the ship P., stayed the proceedings in this Court until after the hearing of the cause in the Vice-Admiralty Court abroad. THE "PESHAWUR" - **8 P. D. 32**

2. —— Stay of Proceedings—*Action in rem—Bail.*] The Plaintiffs, the owners of the German vessel J., commenced an action in rem against the Danish vessel C. in an Admiralty Court in Holland, in respect of a collision on the high seas, and the C. was arrested in this action. The Plaintiff's agent in Holland and the Dutch Court allowed the C. to be released on the underwriters of the C. guaranteeing to the parties interested to the amount of 175,000 gulden, for the compensation which the C. might eventually have to pay by legal decision in Holland. While these proceedings were pending in Holland, the Plaintiffs began an action in rem in England in respect of the same collision, and the C. was arrested in the English action. On a motion by the Defendants for the release of the C.—the Plaintiffs on such motion expressing their willingness to cease proceedings in Holland and pay the costs—Sir James Hannen held that the C. ought to be released, as it was *primâ facie* oppressive to institute an action in another Court in respect of the same subject-matter when there was no evidence that the Court, in which the action was first brought, would not do full justice to the Plaintiffs:—*Held*, on appeal, by Baggallay and Fry, L.JJ., that the decision of Sir James Hannen was right, for bail being the equivalent of the ship, and it having been given in Holland, an action in England against the ship should not be allowed to proceed at the same time as the Dutch action:—*Held*, also, that if the guarantee given in Holland was not equivalent to bail, but was a private agreement, the arrest of the ship in England was against good faith:—*Held*, by Lord Esher, M.R., that the decision of Sir James Hannen was wrong, because though it was not *primâ facie* oppressive to institute an action in a foreign and in an English Court in respect of the same collision, it would be oppressive if bail were given in both Courts, but in this case the guarantee not being equivalent to bail, the Plaintiffs had

XVI. PRACTICE — ADMIRALTY — LIS ALIBI PENDENS—*continued.*

not so good a remedy in Holland as in England, and were therefore entitled to bring an action in the English Admiralty Court.—*McHenry* v. *Lewis* (22 Ch. D. 397) approved and applied. THE "CHRISTIANSBORG" - - - 10 P. D. 141

XVII. PRACTICE — ADMIRALTY — SALVAGE.

1. —— **Admissions**—*Evidence—Order XXXII.,* r. 1.] When the Defendant admits all the facts pleaded in the statement of claim in a salvage action, the Plaintiff will not be allowed to call evidence except by permission of the Court, and on special grounds. THE "HARDWICK" 9 P. D. 32

2. —— **Agreement**—*Action by Seamen.*] An agreement was made between the masters of the *W.* and the *N.*, which was in need of assistance, that the *W.* should tow the *N.* to Queenstown for the sum of £200. There was no evidence at the trial to shew that the master of the *W.* consulted the officers and crew as to the terms of the agreement. The service was duly performed, and subsequently thirteen of the officers and crew of the *W.* brought an action of salvage against the *N.* The Defendants pleaded, inter alia, that they had tendered £200 to the owners of the *W.*, but this sum was not paid into Court :—*Held*, first, that a plea of tender without a payment into Court was bad ; secondly, that the agreement must be upheld, and the £200 apportioned amongst the owners and crew of the *W.* ; thirdly, that when a fair salvage agreement has been made in a bonâ fide manner by the masters of the salving and the salved vessels the officers and seamen of the salving ship ought not to bring an action of salvage, and that the Plaintiffs must therefore pay the costs of the action. THE "NASMYTH" 10 P. D. 41

3. —— **Award**—*Apportionment.*] In a suit instituted to recover salvage reward in respect of services rendered in towing a disabled vessel into safety, the Court awarded a total sum of £4000, of which £3000 was apportioned to the owners. THE "KENMURE CASTLE" 7 P. D. 47

4. —— **Bullion**—*Liability to contribute in the same Proportion as other Property.*] Where steam tugs rendered salvage services by towing a sinking vessel with passengers, cargo, and bullion on board into safety, it was held that the bullion was liable to contribute to the salvage reward in proportion to its value rateably with the other property salved. THE "LONGFORD" 6 P. D. 60

5. —— **Damages**—*Commission for Bail—Salvage Action.*] Commission paid for bail in a salvage action will not be allowed as part of the damages recoverable by the salved vessel in an action of damage. THE "BRITISH COMMERCE" [9 P. D. 128

6. —— **Damages**—*Ship—Arrest—Commission on Bail Bond.*] Commission on bail is not part of the Defendant's costs in an action of salvage or damage, but it may be recovered as damages from the Plaintiff where the arrest of the vessel is made maliciously, or with gross negligence. THE "COLLINGROVE." THE "NUMIDA" - 10 P. D. 158

7. —— **Derelict**—*Abandonment of Derelict by Salvors—Waiver of Salvage—Remuneration—*

XVII. PRACTICE—ADMIRALTY—SALVAGE—*continued.*

Amount of Award.] The barque N. fell in with the K. a derelict barque, in the Atlantic, and put five hands on board of her who navigated her for three days. The K. then fell in with the barque B., and the five hands on board of the K., were, at their own request, taken on board the B. The B. then sent some of her own crew on board the K., and took her in tow, and towed her until the tow-rope broke, when the vessels parted company, and the hands on board the K., with the assistance of the L., a steamship which they afterwards fell in with, brought the K. into Falmouth. In suits instituted on behalf of the masters, owners, and crews of the N., the B. and the L., the Court held, that the master, owners, and crew of the N. were not entitled to salvage reward, but awarded salvage to the remaining Plaintiffs. THE "KILLEENA" 6 P. D. 193

8. —— **Misconduct of Salvors**—*Diminishing amount of Reward.*] Violent and overbearing conduct on the part of salvors, although it may not amount to such wilful misconduct as to cause an entire forfeiture of salvage reward, will yet operate to induce the Court to diminish the amount of the reward. THE "MARIE" 7 P. D. 203

9. —— **Tender**—*Adequate, but illiberal Tender —Costs.*] In a case of salvage, in which the Defendants pleaded a tender and payment into Court of £300, the Court pronounced for the tender and condemned the Defendants in costs up to the time of payment into Court, but made no order as to the costs incurred after that time. THE "LOTUS" 7 P. D. 199

—— **Contribution**—Salvage—Shipowner paying money into Court - - 6 P. D. 127 *See* PRACTICE—ADMIRALTY—LIMITATION OF LIABILITY. 5.

—— **Pleading**—Statement of claim 8 P. D. 227 *See* PRACTICE—ADMIRALTY—PLEADING. 2.

XVIII. PRACTICE—ADMIRALTY—COSTS.

1. —— **Arrest**—*Bail.*] A ship was arrested, and bail required for an exorbitant sum :—*Held*, that the Plaintiffs must pay the costs and expenses incurred by the Defendants in giving this bail. THE "GEORGE GORDON" 9 P. D. 46

2. —— **Collision**—*Both Ships to blame.*] Where a collision has occurred between two vessels, through the bad navigation of each of them, the owners of the ships are not entitled to the costs of any litigation arising out of the collision. THE "HECTOR" - 8 P. D. 218

3. —— **Collision**—*Both Ships to blame—Costs of Reference.*] Where in an action of damage the Defendant sets up a counter-claim relating to the collision in respect of which the action is brought, and both ships are held to blame, and a reference is ordered to ascertain the amount of damage sustained by each ship, each party is, as a general rule, entitled to the costs of establishing his claim before the Registrar, provided that not more than one-fourth of his claim has been disallowed. THE "MARY" - - 7 P. D. 201

4. —— **Compromise**—*Solicitors' Costs.*] In an Admiralty action for wages the Plaintiffs and

XVIII. PRACTICE — ADMIRALTY — COSTS — continued.

Defendants compromised the action by payment to each of the Plaintiffs of a certain sum in discharge of the claim and costs. The Plaintiffs left the country without paying their solicitors' costs:— *Held*, by the Court of Appeal, reversing the judgment of Sir R. J. Phillimore, that as there was no evidence that the parties had made the settlement with the intention of depriving the Plaintiffs' solicitors of their lien for their costs, the Defendants ought not to be ordered to pay the Plaintiffs' taxed costs.—*Brunsdon v. Allard* (2 E. & E. 19), *In re Sullivan v. Pearson, Ex parte Morrison* (L. R. 4 Q. B. 153) approved. THE "HOPE"
[8 P. D. 144

5. —— **Higher and Lower Scale** — *Rules of the Supreme Court, 1883, Order* LXV., *r.* 9, *App. N.*] Costs on the higher scale will only be granted when special grounds of urgency or importance are shewn, as it was intended that the lower scale should be the ordinary scale.—An award of £2400 having been made in a salvage action, an application under Order LXV., rule 9, for costs on the higher scale was made to the Court :—*Held*, that this was not a special ground so as to take the case out of the ordinary rule. THE "HORACE" - 9 P. D. 86

6. —— Printing—*Order* LXVI., *r.* 7 — *Third Counsel.*] The parties to an action between the owners of the *B.* and the *C.* agreed that the evidence taken in an action between the owners of the *A.* and the *C.*, and printed for the purpose of an appeal, should be used in the action between the *B.* and the *C.* The Plaintiffs paid the solicitors of the *A.* for such prints, and charged the sums so paid in addition to the regular charge of 3*d.* per folio, as though the printing had been done in this action, under Order LXVI., rule 7:—*Held*, on objection to the taxation, that the charge of 3*d.* per folio was not improper.—In an action arising out of a collision where damage had been done to the amount of £2000 :—*Held*, that the charges of a third counsel should not be disallowed. THE "MAMMOTH" - - 9 P. D. 126

7. —— Reference.] As by Order LXV., rule 1, of the Rules of the Supreme Court, 1883, the costs of all proceedings are in the discretion of the Court, the general rule of practice in the Admiralty Court as to the costs of reference, namely, that when more than a fourth is struck off a claim, each party pays his own costs, and when more than a third the claimant pays the other party's costs, is wrong, and the Court must exercise its discretion according to the circumstances of each particular case.—*The Empress Eugénie* (Lush. 140) overruled. THE "FRIEDEBERG" - 10 P. D. 112

8. —— Tender—*Rules of Court, 1883, Order* LXV., *rule* 1.] The Defendant in an action for salvage, after action brought, tendered and paid into Court £200 in respect of the claim. The Court upheld the tender. On an application by the Defendants to be allowed the whole costs of the action :—*Held*, that the discretion vested in the Court by Order LXV., rule 1, ought to be exercised in this case and in similar cases by giving Plaintiffs the costs up to the date of payment into Court, and Defendants those subsequent to that event. But that this general rule

would be departed from when salvors unreasonably refuse an offer made before suit :—*Held*, further, that an offer of a sum in respect of salvage services should not include any sum in respect of the Plaintiff's costs.—*The Thracian* (3 A. & E. 504) not followed. THE "WILLIAM SYMINGTON"
[10 P. D. 1

XIX. PRACTICE — ADMIRALTY — JURISDICTION.

1. —— Action in rem—*Action under Lord Campbell's Act* (9 & 10 *Vict. c.* 93)—*Admiralty Court Act, 1861* (24 & 25 *Vict. c.* 10), *ss.* 7, 35.] The Admiralty Court Act, 1861 (24 & 25 Vict. c. 10) which by sect. 7 gave the Court of Admiralty "jurisdiction over any claim for damage done by any ship," did not give jurisdiction over claims for damages for loss of life under Lord Campbell's Act (9 & 10 Vict. c. 93): and the Admiralty Division cannot entertain an action in rem for damages for loss of life under Lord Campbell's Act :—So held affirming the decision of the Court of Appeal.—*The Franconia* (2 P. D. 163) overruled. SEWARD *v.* "VERA CRUZ." THE "VERA CRUZ" - 9 P. D. 96 ; 10 App. Cas. 59

2. —— Action in rem—*Foreign Ship—Board of Trade—17 & 18 Vict. c.* 104, *s.* 512.] A refusal by the Board of Trade to institute an inquiry under 17 & 18 Vict. c. 104, s. 512, is not a condition precedent to an action in rem against a foreign ship. THE "VERA CRUZ" (No. 1)
[9 P. D. 88

3. —— Previous Decision—*Court of Appeal.*] When the Court of Appeal is equally divided so that the decision appealed against stands unreversed, the result of the case in the Court of Appeal affects the actual parties to the litigation only, and the Court, when a similar case is brought before it, is not bound by the result of the previous case. THE "VERA CRUZ" (No. 2)
[9 P. D. 96

4. —— Transfer of Action *after Judgment recovered—Pending Actions in High Court—Discretion—County Courts Admiralty Jurisdiction Act, 1868* (31 & 32 *Vict. c.* 71), *s.* 6.] A foreign vessel was under arrest in three actions of necessaries, one in the City of London Court and the other two in this Court, and after judgment pronounced in the City of London Court was about to be sold by the bailiff of that Court. In these circumstances the Plaintiff in one of the actions in this Court applied for an order to transfer the action in the City of London Court to this Court, alleging that a sale by the marshal would be to the benefit of all parties.—The Court made the order, but directed that it should be without prejudice to any priorities claimed by the Plaintiff in the action ordered to be transferred. THE "IMMACOLATA CONCEZIONE" - - 8 P. D. 34

5. —— Vice-Admiralty Jurisdiction—*Suit by six Seamen for Wages and Compensation—Orders in Council* (2 & 3 *Will.* 4, *c.* 51), *s.* 15—*Merchant Shipping Act, 1854, s.* 189.] By an Order in Council, sect. 15, passed in pursuance of 2 & 3 Will. 4, c. 51, the Vice-Admiralty Court has jurisdiction to entertain a suit brought by any number of seamen not exceeding six, to recover their wages.

XIX. PRACTICE—ADMIRALTY—JURISDIC-
TION—*continued.*

The Merchant Shipping Act, 1854, sect. 189,
does not take away such right of suit so long as
the total aggregate amount claimed by such
seamen exceeds £50.—Where in a suit brought
by six seamen in the Vice-Admiralty Court, the
Judge found that a total amount of £203 19s. 8d.
was due to them, partly for wages and partly for
wrongful dismissal, but that the amount due to
each was less than £50 :—*Held*, that under the
above rule and section the Judge was wrong in
dismissing the suit for want of jurisdiction, and
that a decree for £203 19s. 8d. should be made.
PHILLIPS *v.* HIGHLAND RAILWAY COMPANY. THE
"FERRET"　-　-　-　8 App. Cas. 329

6. —— Waters not part of High Seas—*Docks
—County Court—3 & 4 Vict. c. 65, s. 6—Admiralty Courts Act,* 1861 (24 & 25 Vict. c. 10), s. 7.]
A collision occurred in a dock connected with the
River Thames by channels provided with gates
and locks. An action was brought in a County
Court having Admiralty jurisdiction in respect
of damages arising out of the collision. On an
application for a prohibition :—*Held*, that the
claim was within the Admiralty Courts Act, 1861,
s. 7, and that the County Court had jurisdiction.
THE QUEEN *v.* THE JUDGE OF THE CITY OF LON-
DON COURT　-　-　-　8 Q. B. D. 609

PRACTICE—BANKRUPTCY.
See Cases under BANKRUPTCY.

PRACTICE—CENTRAL CRIMINAL COURT
[11 Q. B. D. 479
See COURT—CENTRAL CRIMINAL COURT.

PRACTICE—COUNTY COURT.
See Cases under COUNTY COURT.

I. PRACTICE—DIVORCE—SERVICE.

—— Out of Jurisdiction — *Restitution of
Conjugal Rights—Service of Petition—Jurisdiction.*] The Court has no power to allow service
abroad of a petition for restitution of conjugal
rights. CHICHESTER *v.* CHICHESTER 10 P. D. 186

II. PRACTICE—DIVORCE—PARTIES.

1. —— Alleged Adulteress.] In a suit by a
wife for dissolution of marriage, the Court, upon
application on behalf of the person with whom it
was alleged that the husband had committed
adultery, directed that she be made a Respondent.
BELL *v.* BELL　-　-　8 P. D. 217

2. —— Co-Respondents.] If a petition alleges
adultery with persons unknown the order of the
Court must be obtained dispensing with making
them co-Respondents, notwithstanding that there
are already other co-Respondents who have been
served with process. PENTY *v.* PENTY 7 P. D. 19

3. —— Lunatic Petitioner—*Dissolution of Marriage—Committee.*] The lunacy of a husband
or wife is not a bar to a suit by the committee for
the dissolution of the lunatic's marriage.—Such a
suit may be instituted by the committee of the
lunatic. BAKER *v.* BAKER　-　6 P. D. 12

III. PRACTICE—DIVORCE—PLEADING.

1. —— Affidavit verifying Petition.] A
petitioner in a divorce suit being on military
service, and unable to make the usual affidavit
verifying the petition, the Court allowed the petition to be filed if verified by the affidavit of his
solicitor, but ordered that the Petitioner's affidavit
should also be filed as soon as possible. *Ex parte*
BRUCE　-　-　6 P. D. 16

2. —— Desertion—*Petition filed after Desertion for a few Months—Second Petition after
Desertion for Two Years.*] A wife's petition for
dissolution of marriage by reason of cruelty and
adultery was, by leave of the Court, withdrawn,
and petition afterwards filed for dissolution of
marriage by reason of the same adultery and also
by reason of desertion for two years, which had
not accrued at the date of the first petition.
KNAPP *v.* KNAPP　-　6 P. D. 10

IV. PRACTICE—DIVORCE—EVIDENCE.

1. —— Commission to examine Witnesses—
*Commission addressed to a Court which has ceased
to exist.*] In a divorce suit a commission to examine witnesses in India was issued addressed to
" The Judges of the Supreme Court at Calcutta,
or such person or persons as they or one of them
may depute." The Supreme Court at Calcutta
had been abolished in 1861, and all its powers
transferred to a new Court called "The High
Court of Judicature at Fort William in Bengal."
The witnesses were examined by a person de-
puted by a Judge of the High Court at Fort
William :—*Held*, affirming the decision of the
President, that the evidence was receivable, for
that the commission must be taken to be addressed to the Judges of the highest Court for the
time being at Calcutta. WILSON *v.* WILSON
[9 P. D. 8

2. —— Lunatic—*Suit to perpetuate Testimony—
Illegitimacy—Rules of Court,* 1883, *Order XXXVII.,
r.* 35.] A lunatic who had several children was
divorced from his wife on the ground of the wife's
adultery. One of the wife's children born before
the divorce was alleged to be illegitimate, and
the committee presented a petition that proceedings might be taken to perpetuate the testimony
of the illegitimacy :—*Held*, that the proper course
to pursue was for the Court to make a settlement

IV. PRACTICE—DIVORCE—EVIDENCE—contd.
of some of the lunatic's property on his children, and for the legitimate children to raise the question of the right of the alleged illegitimate child to participate, and then to bring an action to perpetuate the testimony. IN RE STOER **9 P. D. 120**

V. PRACTICE—DIVORCE—INTERVENTION.
—— "Material Facts *not brought before the Court*"—23 & 24 *Vict. c.* 144, *s.* 7.] A wife sued for dissolution of marriage on the ground of adultery and cruelty. The husband alleged that the wife had been guilty of adultery. At the trial a decree nisi for dissolution was made. The husband applied for a new trial on the ground that fresh evidence had been discovered to shew the wife's adultery before the decree nisi, and filed affidavits alleging facts not known at the trial which went to prove adultery. He obtained a rule nisi, but the rule was discharged on argument. The husband appealed. Immediately afterwards an uncle of the husband entered an appearance as intervener, and filed affidavits which were substantially the same as those used on the application for a new trial. There was nothing to shew that he was acting on behalf of or in collusion with the Respondent. The wife moved to make the decree for dissolution absolute. This was refused, but leave was given her to move the Court to reject the intervention. The husband abandoned his appeal from the refusal of a new trial. After this the motion of the wife to reject the intervention of the uncle was heard by the President and refused. The wife appealed:—*Held*, by the Court of Appeal, that the Act 23 & 24 Vict. c. 144, *s.* 7, authorizes intervention by any person where material facts have not been brought before the Court, whether by intention or through accident.—Whether where the petitioner, after the decree nisi, is guilty of conduct disentitling him or her to have the decree made absolute, the right to intervene is confined to the Queen's Proctor, *quære:—Held*, that the words "not brought before the Court," mean, not brought before the Court at a time when the Court can act upon them for the purpose of seeing whether a decree nisi ought to be made, and that the bringing them before the Court on an application for a new trial is not bringing them before the Court within the meaning of this clause, so as to prevent an intervention.—Whether the rules as to granting a new trial on the ground of fresh evidence discovered shewing misconduct in the petitioner are the same as in a case between ordinary litigants, *quære.—*Where a respondent is not entitled to a new trial, intervention on the ground of fresh evidence as to acts prior to the decree nisi will not be allowed if the intervener is merely acting on behalf of and in collusion with the Respondent; but the fact that he is a near relative of the Respondent is no ground for rejecting the intervention:—*Held*, therefore, that in the present case, the facts alleged being undoubtedly material, and the affidavits making a case which shewed that there was ground for investigating them, the intervention had rightly been allowed. HOWARTH *v.* HOWARTH - - - **9 P. D. 218**

VI. PRACTICE—DIVORCE—ALIMONY.
—— Pendente lite—*Decree Nisi*—20 & 21 *Vict.*

VI. PRACTICE—DIVORCE—ALIMONY—contd..
c. 85, *s.* 32—23 & 24 *Vict. c.* 144, *s.* 7.] The Court has power to order alimony pendente lite notwithstanding a decree nisi has been made for dissolution of marriage.—*Latham* v. *Latham* (2 Sw. & Tr. 298) overruled. ELLIS *v.* ELLIS **8 P. D. 188**

2. —— Permanent Maintenance —*Dissolution of Marriage*—20 & 21 *Vict. c.* 85, *s.* 32.] A decree nisi for dissolution of marriage was made against a wife on the 3rd of August, 1880, and was made absolute in due course. The wife appealed, and her appeal was dismissed on the 19th of July, 1881. On the 30th of July she took out a summons to have permanent maintenance allowed her. Owing to her absence abroad the summons was not heard till December, 1882, when the President dismissed it. The wife appealed : *Held*, on appeal, that as the application to the President was out of time, and he had exercised a discretion under the special circumstances of the case, the Court would not interfere with his decision.—Whether special circumstances are required to induce the Court to give permanent alimony to a wife against whom a decree for dissolution is made, and who has no means of support, *quære*. ROBERTSON *v.* ROBERTSON **8 P. D. 94**

3. —— Permanent Maintenance — 20 & 21 *Vict. c.* 85, *s.* 32—29 & 30 *Vict.* c. 32,) *s.* 1—*Husband's Property Abroad.*] The provisions of 20 & 21 Vict. c. 85, s. 32, respecting permanent maintenance empower the Court to order a gross or annual sum to be secured for the benefit of the wife, but not to make a direct order on the husband to pay a gross or annual or other periodical sum to the wife.—The qualification that the maintenance is to be for the wife "dum sola et casta vixerit" is not usually inserted in the order but in the deed of security.—The provisions of 29 & 30 Vict. c. 32, respecting the payment of monthly or weekly sums to the wife do not apply to the case of a husband who has property abroad sufficient and available for a security :—Per Jessel, M.R., an order for maintenance cannot be made in the alternative for securing a gross or annual sum of money, or else for the payment of monthly or weekly sums by the husband. MEDLEY *v.* MEDLEY - **7 P. D. 122**

4. —— Permanent Maintenance — *Lunatic's Estate, Allowance out of—Assignment*—20 & 21 *Vict.* c. 85, *s.* 23.] On a decree for judicial separation an order was made for payment of £60 a year to the wife as permanent alimony. The husband was afterwards found lunatic by inquisition, and by an order in Lunacy and Chancery the dividends of a sum of stock to which he was entitled in a Chancery suit were ordered to be carried to his account in the Lunacy and £60 a year to be paid out of them to his wife in respect of her alimony till further order. The wife assigned the annuity to a purchaser, who presented a petition in Lunacy and in the suit to have the annuity paid to her — *Held*, that the petition must be refused, on the ground that whether the annuity was considered as alimony, or as an allowance made to the wife by the Court in Lunacy, it was not assignable. *In re* ROBINSON **27 Ch. D. 160**

5. —— Permanent Maintenance—*Weekly or Monthly Payments — Variation — 29 & 30 Vict.*

VI. PRACTICE—DIVORCE—ALIMONY—contd.

c. 32.] The provisions of 29 & 30 Vict. c. 32, do not apply exclusively to the case of a poor man, and the Court may order sums of considerable amount to be paid weekly or monthly as permanent maintenance, and may from time to time modify the order. JARDINE v. JARDINE
[6 P. D. 213

—— Nullity of marriage - - 9 P. D. 80
See PRACTICE—DIVORCE—NULLITY OF MARRIAGE. 1.

VII. PRACTICE—DIVORCE—DESERTION.

1. —— Adultery.] A husband in 1880 ceased to reside with his wife on the pretence that his business compelled him to be absent, but he supplied her with necessaries and corresponded with her and visited her occasionally, and a child was born in February, 1884. In January, 1884, the wife discovered that he had for years been living with another woman:—Held, that his conduct did not amount to desertion for two years.—Semble, that desertion commenced from the time when his wife discovered the adultery, and that after a lapse of two years from that time she would be entitled to a dissolution of her marriage FARMER v. FARMER - 9 P. D. 245

2. —— Desertion by Petitioner — Agreement to live separate.] A husband, without reasonable excuse, obtained from his wife an agreement that they should live apart from each other, which they accordingly did, and she subsequently committed adultery:—Held, that under the circumstances he had deserted her, and that a petition by him for dissolution of the marriage must be dismissed. DAGG v. DAGG - 7 P. D. 17

3. —— Desertion by Wife—Judicial Separation.] Judicial separation decreed by reason of the wife's desertion of her husband for two years and upwards without reasonable cause. MILLAR v. MILLAR - 8 P. D. 187

VIII. PRACTICE—DIVORCE—CONDONATION.

1. —— Cruelty—Condonation by Deed—Revival by subsequent Adultery.] A husband had been guilty of cruelty. He and his wife separated under the provisions of a deed by which it was agreed that no proceedings should be taken by either party against the other in respect of any cause of complaint which had arisen before the date of the deed, and that every offence, if any, committed by either party against the other should be considered as condoned, and that in any proceedings by either party against the other in respect of any cause of complaint which might thereafter arise, no offence committed by either party before the deed should be pleaded or be admissible in evidence:—Held, affirming the decision of the President, that subsequent adultery by the husband did not revive the wife's right to complain of the cruelty committed before the deed, so as to enable her to obtain a decree for dissolution of the marriage.—Whether adultery by a husband which has been condoned is a bar to his obtaining a dissolution on the ground of subsequent adultery of the wife, quære. ROSE v ROSE 7 P. D. 225 ; 8 P. D. 98

2. —— Damages.] Condonation of the wife's adultery is no answer to the husband's claim for

VIII. PRACTICE— DIVORCE — CONDONATION—continued.

damages against the co-Respondent.—Norris v. Norris, Lawson and Mason (4 Sw. & Tr. 237 ; 30 L. J. (P. & M.) 111) distinguished. POMERO v. POMERO 10 P. D. 174

3. —— Desertion — Revival.] A husband having been guilty of desertion and adultery the wife forgave him and they returned to cohabitation. He subsequently committed adultery :—Held, that the subsequent adultery revived the desertion, and that the wife was entitled to a dissolution of the marriage. BLANDFORD v. BLANDFORD - - - 8 P. D. 19

IX. PRACTICE—DIVORCE—MISCONDUCT OF PETITIONER.

1. —— Adultery — Wife's Petition — Decree Nisi—Discretion.] A husband obtained a decree nisi by reason of his wife's adultery, but the decree was rescinded, and his petition dismissed by reason of his cruelty and adultery. The parties lived together again, and he committed other acts of cruelty, and was also guilty of rape, when the wife filed a petition for dissolution of the marriage. The Court under the circumstances granted the wife a decree nisi. COLLINS v. COLLINS
[9 P. D. 231.

2. —— Conduct conducing to Adultery.] A Petitioner and Respondent separated by mutual consent shortly after the marriage, and only met once afterwards. The Petitioner allowed her a small sum for her support, and sixteen years after the marriage discovered that she had committed adultery:—Held, under the circumstances, that the Petitioner had conduced to the adultery. Petition dismissed. HAWKINS v. HAWKINS
[10 P. D. 177

3. —— Wilful Neglect — Imprisonment for Criminal Offence.] Semble, that the conviction of a wife for an offence against the criminal law is no justification for refusing further cohabitation with her, and that, if such refusal conduces to her adultery, the Court will not grant her husband a dissolution of his marriage. WILLIAMSON v. WILLIAMSON - - - 7 P. D. 76

X. PRACTICE—DIVORCE—DELAY.

—— Poverty of Petitioner—Previous Decree for Judicial Separation.] A husband in 1878 obtained a judicial separation, and £50 damages against the co-Respondent, but he took no steps to recover the damages. The wife continued to cohabit with the co-Respondent, and in 1882 the husband petitioned for a dissolution of his marriage. The reason which he gave for the delay and for not enforcing the claim for damages was that he had no money, being only in receipt of weekly wages, and that he hoped his wife would come back and live with him :—Held, reversing the decision of the President, that the delay was not unreasonable, and that the Petitioner was entitled to a decree. MASON v. MASON
[7 P. D. 233 ; 8 P. D. 21

XI. PRACTICE—DIVORCE—DECREE.

1. ——Bigamy of Petitioner.] A husband believing that his wife was dead married again, and subsequently discovered that his wife was alive and had committed adultery :—Held, that,

XI. PRACTICE—DIVORCE—DECREE—contd.

notwithstanding the bigamy, he was entitled to a dissolution of his marriage. FREEGARD v. FREE-GARD, COWPER & LUCAS　-　　8 P. D. 186

2. —— **Maintenance**—*Dum Casta Clause.*] A deed had been executed securing a maintenance for the wife after the decree absolute. The deed did not contain a dum casta clause :—*Held*, that the Court had no power to set aside the deed by reason that the wife was no longer chaste. BRADLEY v. BRADLEY　　　　　7 P. D. 237

3. —— **Re-marriage before Decree absolute.**] A. R. W. obtained in 1868 a decree nisi for dissolution of her marriage, and in 1871, believing that the decree had been made absolute, she married again.—The Court, the Queen's Proctor not opposing, made the decree absolute. WICKHAM v. WICKHAM　　-　　-　　6 P. D. 11

XII. PRACTICE—DIVORCE—DAMAGES.

—— **Payment into Court**—*Proceedings under the Debtors Act.*] The Court having ordered damages to be paid into the registry, and proceedings in default being impracticable, as there was no one to institute them, the Court ordered the damages to be paid to the Petitioner, he undertaking to pay them into Court. GYTE v. GYTE
[10 P. D. 185

XIII. PRACTICE—DIVORCE—APPEAL.

By 44 & 45 Vict. c. 68 (*the Supreme Court of Judicature Act*, 1881), s. 9, *all appeals which, under sect.* 55 *of* 20 & 21 *Vict. c.* 85, *or under any other Act, might be brought to the full Court established by the said first-mentioned Act, are to be brought to Her Majesty's Court of Appeal, and not to the said full Court.*

The decision of the Court of Appeal on any question arising under the Acts relating to divorce and matrimonial causes, or to the declaration of legitimacy, is final, except where the decision either is upon the grant or refusal of a decree on a petition for dissolution or nullity of marriage, or for a declaration of legitimacy, or is upon a question of law on which the said Court of Appeal give leave to appeal; and, save as aforesaid, no appeal lies to the House of Lords under the said Acts.

Subject to any order made by the House of Lords in accordance with the Appellate Jurisdiction Act, 1876, every appeal to the House of Lords against any such decision is to be brought within one month after the decision appealed against is pronounced by the Court of Appeal if the House of Lords is then sitting, or, if not, within fourteen days after the House of Lords next sits.

The section, so far as is consistent with the tenor thereof, is to be construed as one with the said Acts.

Sect. 10. No appeal lies from an order absolute for dissolution or nullity of marriage in favour of any party who, having had time and opportunity to appeal from the decree nisi on which such order is founded, has not appealed therefrom.

And see PRACTICE—DIVORCE—RESTITUTION OF CONJUGAL RIGHTS—*Statutes.*

1. —— **Time for appealing**—*Appeal from Decision of Court of Appeal in Cases from Probate and Divorce Division—Divorce and Matrimonial Act, 1868—Appellate Jurisdiction Act, 1876—Judicature Act, 1881.*] Since the Judicature Act of

XIII. PRACTICE—DIVORCE—APPEAL—contd.

1881, an appeal to the House of Lords in a matrimonial cause (where an appeal lies) can only be from a decision of the Court of Appeal ; and such an appeal must be brought within one month after the decision appealed against is pronounced by the Court of Appeal, if the House of Lords is then sitting, or if not, within fourteen days after the House of Lords next sits CLEAVER v. CLEAVER　　-　　-　　9 App. Cas. 631

2. —— **Time for appealing**—*Application for New Trial*—23 & 24 Vict. c. 144, s. 2; 36 & 37 Vict. c. 66, s. 16 ; 38 & 39 Vict. c. 77, s. 18 ; 44 & 45 Vict. c. 68, s. 9.] An appeal from a decision of a judge of the Probate Division granting or refusing a new trial in the Divorce Court must be made within fourteen days in accordance with the Divorce Court Act, 1860 (23 & 24 Vict. c. 144), s. 2. AHIER v. AHIER　-　　10 P. D. 110

XIV. PRACTICE — DIVORCE — NULLITY OF MARRIAGE.

1. —— **Alimony**—*Decree Nisi.*] In a suit for nullity alimony continues payable after the decree nisi until the decree is made absolute. S. FALSELY CALLED B. v. B.　-　　-　9 P. D. 80

2. —— **Application by Respondent** *to make Decree absolute.*] The Court will not upon the application of the Respondent make a decree nisi absolute for nullity of marriage by reason of the impotence of the Respondent. HALFEN v. BODDINGTON　　-　　-　　6 P. D. 13

3. —— **Impotence** — *Delay — Sincerity.*] At the end of seven years' cohabitation a marriage had not been consummated through the impotence of the alleged husband. The alleged wife subsequently cohabited with another man, and upon the alleged husband discovering her misconduct she instituted a suit for nullity of marriage against him and he a suit for dissolution of marriage against her :—*Held*, that the proof of impotence being clear her conduct did not shew such a want of sincerity as to deprive her of her right to have the marriage annulled.—When the impotence is undoubted mere delay is not sufficient to disentitle the injured party to relief. M. OTHERWISE D. v. D. -　　-　　10 P. D. 75

4. —— **Impotence**—*Possible Cure.*] After a partial cohabitation of two years and eight months it appeared that the woman was impotent, but that she might probably be cured if she would submit to an operation involving no great risk of life. This she refused to do. The Court made a decree nisi of nullity of marriage. L. v. L. FALSELY CALLED W. -　　-　7 P. D. 16

5. —— **Impotence**—*Suits for Nullity of Marriage and Dissolution of Marriage—Cross-examination as to Adultery.*] A suit had been instituted for nullity of marriage by reason of impotence, and a cross-suit for dissolution of marriage by reason of adultery :—*Held*, that, in the first suit, the petitioner in that suit might be cross-examined as to her improper intimacy with the co-Respondent in the cross-suit. M. v. D.
[10 P. D. 175

6. —— **Insanity.**] The burden of shewing that the Respondent was insane at the time of the marriage lies upon the party asserting it, and the Court has to determine whether the Respondent

XIV. PRACTICE — DIVORCE — NULLITY OF MARRIAGE—*continued.*

was capable of understanding the nature of the contract, and the duties and responsibilities which it creates, and was free from the influence of morbid delusions upon the subject. DURHAM *v.* DURHAM. HUNTER *v.* EDNEY, OTHERWISE HUNTER. CANNON *v.* SMALLEY, OTHERWISE CANNON

[10 P. D. 80

7. —— **Interrogatories.**] In a suit for nullity of marriage the Court has power to order interrogatories. EUSTON *v.* SMITH (FALSELY CALLED EUSTON) ‘　　　　-　　9 P. D. 57

8. —— **Interrogatories**—*Jurisdiction of Divorce Division—Supreme Court of Judicature Act, 1873 (36 & 37 Vict. c. 66), ss. 16, 23—Interrogatories necessarily criminating—Felony.*] In a suit for nullity of marriage, the Court has power to give leave to administer interrogatories between the parties to the suit; for suits of that kind were formerly within the jurisdiction of the Ecclesiastical Courts, which had power to allow interrogatories to be administered between the parties, and now all the jurisdiction of the Ecclesiastical Courts as to suits for nullity of marriage (including matters of practice and procedure)' is vested in the Probate, Divorce, and Admiralty Division. And, further, even if the power to allow interrogatories to be administered between the parties did not otherwise exist, it would be conferred upon the Probate, Divorce, and Admiralty Division by the Supreme Court of Judicature Act, 1873 ; for at the time of passing that statute the Superior Courts of Common Law and the Court of Chancery had power to allow interrogatories to be administered between the parties to a suit; and by s. 16, all the jurisdiction of those Courts, including the ministerial powers and authorities incident thereto, was transferred to and vested in the High Court of Justice, and by s. 23 the jurisdiction transferred to the High Court may (so far as regards procedure and practice) be exercised in the same manner, as it might have been exercised by any of the Courts whose jurisdiction has been transferred.—Leave to administer interrogatories ought not to be refused on the ground, that it is plain from the nature of the case that they must necessarily criminate the party interrogated, who cannot answer them without admitting that he has' been guilty of felony : he may, however, decline to answer them.—*Semble,* that inasmuch as proceedings for divorce and for other matrimonial causes are excluded from the operation of the Rules of the Supreme Court, 1883, by Order LXVIII., rule 1 (*d*), an application for leave to administer interrogatories between the parties to a suit ought not to be made to a registrar of the Divorce Division ; but it ought to be made in the first instance to one of the judges of the Court. HARVEY *v.* LOVEKIN　　　-　　10 P. D. 122

9. —— **Variation of Settlements.**] A marriage having been annulled, the Court ordered all the property of the alleged wife to be reconveyed to her freed from the trusts of the settlement upon the alleged marriage. A. *v.* M. -　10 P. D. 178

XV. PRACTICE — DIVORCE — RESTITUTION OF CONJUGAL RIGHTS.

The Act 47 & 48 Vict. c. 68 (*the Matrimonial

XV. PRACTICE—DIVORCE—RESTITUTION OF CONJUGAL RIGHTS—*continued.*

Causes Act, 1884), *declares that a decree for restitution of conjugal rights shall not be enforced by attachment. Where the application is made by the wife the Court may order that in the event of the decree not being complied with the respondent shall make payments as for alimony. This may be secured by a proper deed settled by one of the Conveyancing Counsel of the Court.*

Sect. 3. Where the application is made by the husband the Court may order the property of the wife to be paid or settled for the benefit of the petitioner and children of the marriage.

Sect. 4. The Court may vary any order for payment.

Sect. 5. Non-compliance with the decree shall be deemed desertion, and a suit for judicial separation may be instituted. When any husband has also been guilty of adultery, the wife may petition for dissolution of marriage.

Sect. 6. The Court may before final decree for restitution of conjugal rights, or after final decree if not complied with, make orders with respect to custody and education of children.

1. —— **Attachment**—*Sufficient Obedience.*] The duty of the Court to issue an attachment for non-obedience of a decree for restitution of conjugal rights was the same since the Divorce Acts as it was before.—It was not a sufficient compliance by a husband with a decree for restitution of conjugal rights that he had provided his wife with a suitable establishment and sufficient income. WELDON *v.* WELDON　　　-　　9 P. D. 52

2. —— **Contempt**—*Attachment—Payment of Costs.*] A Respondent being in contempt for non-obedience of an order for restitution of conjugal rights, the petitioner applied for a writ of attachment against him :—*Held,* that since the passing of the Matrimonial Causes Act, 1884, the writ could not be issued notwithstanding that the contempt existed prior to that Act :—*Held,* also, that the writ could not issue for non-payment of costs. Application refused. WELDON *v.* WELDON

[10 P. D. 72

—— Service—Out of jurisdiction - 10 P. D. 186
See PRACTICE—DIVORCE—SERVICE.

XVI. PRACTICE — DIVORCE — SEPARATION DEED.

1. —— **Agreement not to sue**—*Covenant by Wife not to sue for Restitution of Conjugal Rights.*], By a deed of separation between the husband, the wife, and a trustee, containing a recital that the husband and wife had agreed to live separate, the husband covenanted with the trustee to pay the wife £25 a year till their only child should attain twenty-one, or die under that age or become chargeable to the husband, and to allow her to enjoy all her present and future property for her separate use, and the trustee covenanted with the husband to indemnify him against the debts of the wife, and that the wife should not take any proceedings to compel him to live with her. The annuity was paid until the child died, a minor. The wife after this presented her petition for the restitution of conjugal rights, and the husband pleaded the separation deed. Butt, J., dismissed the petition.—

Held, that an agreement entered into by a wife-

XVI. PRACTICE — DIVORCE — SEPARATION DEED—*continued.*

for valuable consideration, and without fraud or duress, that she will not take proceedings to compel her husband to return to cohabitation, is a bar to such proceedings :—*Held*, also, that the recital of the agreement to live separate, being contained in a deed to which the wife was a party, was evidence of a contract by her to allow her husband to live separate from her. and that after accepting benefits under the deed, she could not be heard to say that she had not contracted, because the covenant not to sue was entered into only by the trustee and not by her.—*Marshall* v. *Marshall* (5 P. D. 19) approved. CLARK *v.* CLARK
[10 P. D. 188

2. —— **Maintenance**—*Covenant not to sue for greater Allowance—Subsequent Adultery—Permanent Alimony.*] A husband having committed adultery, disputes arose between him and his wife which led to his committing acts of legal cruelty. A separation deed was then executed, by which he agreed to allow her £250 a year, and to maintain the two youngest children, who were not to be in her custody ; and she covenanted not to take any proceedings to compel the husband to allow her a larger amount of alimony. Subsequently the husband committed adultery, and the wife obtained a decree for judicial separation and an order that she should have the custody of the two youngest children. The husband had since the date of the separation deed become wealthy, and the wife applied for an inquiry as to his means with a view to obtaining increased alimony :—*Held*, by the Court of Appeal, that increased alimony could not be ordered, for that as the Court had not, as it would have had in the case of a decree for dissolution, power to alter the separation deed, the covenant by the wife not to sue for increased alimony was binding on her, and must have effect given to it, the husband not having, in the opinion of the Court, been guilty of such misconduct as under the circumstances of the case would disentitle him to claim the benefit of the deed. GANDY *v.* GANDY -   7 P. D. 77, 168

3. —— Maintenance—*Subsequent Adultery—Further Maintenance.*] A wife, by a deed of separation, agreed to accept certain sums as a provision for her support, and not to sue her husband for any further maintenance. Subsequently having discovered that he had been guilty of incestuous adultery, she obtained a decree for dissolution of the marriage :—*Held*, that notwithstanding the deed, she was entitled to the usual order for permanent maintenance. MORRALL *r.* MORRALL
[6 P. D. 98

XVII. PRACTICE—DIVORCE—SETTLEMENTS.

1. —— Variation—*Conduct of Parties—Discretion of Court*—22 '& 23 Vict. c. 61, s. 5—41 & 42 Vict. c. 19, s. 3.] The fortune of a wife was settled as to a part producing £950 a year on the husband for life, then on the wife for life ; as to the residue producing £1200 a year on the wife for life, then on the husband for life ; and after the decease of the survivor, in default of children of the marriage, then as to the whole property on such trusts as the wife should by will appoint, and in default of appointment to

XVII. PRACTICE—DIVORCE—SETTLEMENTS —*continued.*

the husband absolutely. There was no child of the marriage. The wife obtained a decree for dissolution of the marriage on the ground of adultery and cruelty. The husband had mortgaged his life interest for debts incurred in keeping up the joint establishment, and alleged that he had incurred other debts for the same purpose. The President of the Divorce Court, upon the wife's petition, made an order that the trustees of the settlement should stand possessed of all the funds upon the trusts which would be applicable thereto if the husband were dead, and had died in the lifetime of the wife, and free from the ultimate trust in default of appointment, but subject to the wife undertaking to pay the charges made by the husband on the trust funds :—*Held*, on appeal, that the order must be affirmed, with this variation, that an account should be taken of all debts due from the husband incurred for the purpose of the joint establishment, and that the wife must undertake to pay them.—Though the power given to the Court of varying settlements is not given for the purpose of punishing the guilty party, but of making due provision for the parties, their conduct is to be taken into consideration in determining what provisions ought to be made for them respectively.—The Judge has an absolute judicial discretion as to the provisions to be made for the parties respectively out of settled property, and the Court of Appeal will not interfere with that discretion, unless there has been a clear miscarriage in its exercise. WIGNEY *v.* WIGNEY
[7 P. D. 177

2. —— Variation—*Covenant to pay Annuity.*] The Court has power to vary a post-nuptial settlement contained in a deed of separation by reducing the amount of an annuity which the husband had covenanted to pay. JUMP *v.* JUMP
[6 P. D. 159

3. —— Variation — *Lis pendens — Rights of Third Parties — Charge for Solicitor's Costs.*] Upon a petition for variation of settlements the Court has power to make an order in favour of the interest of third parties created before the filing of that petition.—Until a decree has been made for dissolution of a marriage, there is no lis pendens with reference to the property included in the marriage settlements.—Before a decree nisi was made for dissolution of the marriage, the Respondent had charged his interest under the marriage settlement with payment of his solicitor's costs of suit :—*Held*, that, under the circumstances, the charge was valid and that the Respondent's interests could not be extinguished without providing for this charge. WIGNEY *r.* WIGNEY   -   7 P. D. 228

4. —— Variation — *Petition — Signature.*] A petition for variation of settlements must usually be signed by the petitioner, but the Court will, under special circumstances, allow his solicitor to sign it on his behalf. ROSS *r.* ROSS
[7 P. D. 20

5. —— Variation—*Power of Appointment—Costs of Suit.*] A marriage had been dissolved at the suit of the husband. By the marriage settlements the wife had certain interests in her

XVII. PRACTICE — DIVORCE — SETTLEMENTS
—*continued.*

husband's property, and had also power to appoint a portion of her own property for the benefit of any husband she might marry after the death of her late husband, and for the children of that marriage.—She and her husband had at present about £400 a year each, but she was entitled to reversionary property of great value, and was liable to pay the costs of the suit.—The Court gave half of the wife's present and reversionary income to the husband for himself and the two children of the marriage, and—*Held*, that her interest in her husband's property must be extinguished, and that her powers of appointment in favour of a future husband and children must not take effect until after the death of her late husband:—*Held*, also, that in varying the settlements the Court must not take into consideration in her favour that she has to pay the costs of the suit. NOEL *v.* NOEL　-　-　**10 P. D. 179**

6. —— Variation — *Power to deal with Capital* — 22 & 23 Vict. c. 61, *s.* 5—*Appeal—Discretion of Judge—Costs.*] On a petition for variation of a settlement the Judge refused to give the wife, the petitioner, any part of the capital of the fund, which had been all settled by the husband, although there were no children of the marriage, or to order payment of the petitioner's costs out of the funds. And he gave a portion only of the income to the wife.—The Court of Appeal affirmed the decision, holding that although the Court had undoubted jurisdiction to deal with the capital it was not for the benefit of the wife to give her any portion of it; and the Court refused to interfere with the discretion of the Judge as to the amount of income awarded to her. PONSONBY *v.* PONSONBY
[9 P. D. 58, 122

7. —— Variation — *Power to appoint New Trustee.*] In the variation of settlements the Court has jurisdiction to extinguish a joint power of appointment of new trustees. OPPENHEIM *v.* OPPENHEIM AND RICOTTI　　**9 P. D. 60**

8. —— Variation—*Separation Deed—Power to vary Settlements after Dissolution of Marriage—* 22 & 23 Vict. c. 61, *s.* 5.] In June, 1881, a deed of separation was executed by which the husband agreed to pay for the benefit of the wife £52 a year. Shortly after the separation she committed adultery, and in November, 1882, a decree for dissolution of the marriage was made absolute. In April, 1883, the husband obtained leave to present a petition to vary the deed, on payment of all arrears up to that time. There were three children of the marriage who were living with the husband. A petition having been presented, the matter was referred to the registrar, who reported that the wife had no means of support, and that the husband's income was about £270 a year. Butt, J., treated the case as one of alimony depending mainly on the husband's means, and refused to vary the deed:—*Held*, on appeal, that the case was not to be treated as one of alimony, but was one in which the Court had a discretion as to the amount of allowance which ought to be made to the wife under all the circumstances; and that, having regard to the circumstances, and the conduct of the wife in the suit, the hus-

XVII. PRACTICE — DIVORCE — SETTLEMENTS
continued.

band ought to be allowed to retain one-half of the allowance provided by the deed. CLIFFORD *v.* CLIFFORD　-　**9 P. D. 76**

—— Nullity of marriage—Reconveyance of property　-　-　**10 P. D. 178**
See PRACTICE—DIVORCE — NULLITY OF MARRIAGE. 9.

XVIII. PRACTICE — DIVORCE — CUSTODY OF CHILDREN.

—— **Maintenance**—*Security.*] Upon a decree for judicial separation when the Court has ordered a provision to be made for the children it has no power to order also that the Respondent shall secure the payment. HUNT *v.* HUNT **8 P. D. 161**

XIX. PRACTICE — DIVORCE — SEQUESTRATION.

1. —— Indian Officer's Pension.] The pension of an officer in the Indian army is not liable to sequestration for payment of costs and permanent maintenance. BIRCH *v.* BIRCH **8 P. D. 163**

2. —— Previous Writ of Attachment—*Personal Service.*] The Respondent in a suit for restitution of conjugal rights was evading service of the decree, and an order as to custody of children. The Court, though she was not abroad, ordered a writ of sequestration to issue, without a previous writ of attachment or personal service of the decree or order. ALLEN *v.* ALLEN　-　**10 P. D. 187**

XX. PRACTICE—DIVORCE—COSTS.

1. —— Attachment of Debt—*Judicature Act,* 1873, *s.* 25, *sub-s.* 8.] Under sub-sect. 8 of sect. 25 of the Judicature Act, 1873, the Court of Divorce has power to attach a debt due to a Respondent in order to compel obedience to an order of that Court for payment of costs. WHITTAKER *v.* WHITTAKER　-　-　**7 P. D. 15**

2. —— Respondent's Costs—*Full Costs.*] In a divorce suit the usual order had been obtained for securing the wife's costs of the hearing, and there had been no appeal from that order and no further costs were asked for at the hearing. Subsequently the case of *Robertson* v. *Robertson* (6 P. D. 119) was decided in the Court of Appeal, and the Divorce Court was thereupon asked to order payment of the wife's full costs. Application refused.—In future, if in a divorce suit in which a wife is found guilty the Court is asked to order payment of her full costs, the Court will postpone its decision until after her bill of costs has been taxed.—The case of *Robertson* v. *Robertson* (6 P. D. 119) referred to. SMITH *v.* SMITH
[7 P. D. 84

3. —— Security for Costs — *Bankruptcy of Petitioner.*] In a petition for dissolution of marriage, the husband, who was an uncertificated bankrupt, claimed damages. Upon application by the co-Respondent:—*Held*, that unless the claim for damages was withdrawn the petitioner must give security for the costs of the action. SMITH *v.* SMITH　　**7 P. D. 227**

4. —— Wife's Costs—*Limit.*] In a divorce suit, the costs of the wife payable by the husband are not limited to the amount paid into Court or

XX. PRACTICE—DIVORCE—COSTS—*continued.*
secured by the husband for that purpose.—Order
of the Divorce Court varied. ROBERTSON *v.*
ROBERTSON　　　　　　　　　　　**6 P. D. 119**

—— Security—Attachment　-　**10 P. D. 183**
　See ARREST—DEBTORS' ACT. 1.

**I. PRACTICE — ECCLESIASTICAL — PARTICU-
LARS.**

—— **Criminal Suit.**] In a criminal· suit containing charges of misconduct against a clerk in
holy orders, an order was made after the close of
the pleadings that the promoter should give particulars of the charges.—Such particulars should
as a rule be applied for on the admission of articles.
BISHOP OF SALISBURY *v.* OTTLEY　　**10 P. D. 20**

**II. PRACTICE — ECCLESIASTICAL — CHURCH
DISCIPLINE ACT.**

　1. —— **Contumacy** — *Continuous Offences
against Ritual—Deprivation ab officio et a beneficio—3 & 4 Vict. c. 86.*] The Official Principal
of the Court of Arches has jurisdiction to deprive
ab officio et beneficio a clergyman in holy orders
holding a benefice in the province of Canterbury
who has been articled against in a criminal suit
in the Court of Arches by virtue of letters of request under the Church Discipline Act, and is in
such suit proved to have been guilty within two
years of the institution of the suit of contumacy,
of incorrigible disobedience to the Ordinary and
to the Canons of the Church, and of having failed
to observe the Book of Common Prayer. COMBE
v. DE LA BERE　　-　　　　　　**6 P. D. 157**

　2. —— **Contumacy**—*Significavit, Power to
issue — Requisition, Monition, and Inhibition,
Form of—Absence of Statements shewing Jurisdiction—37 & 38 Vict. c. 85, ss. 7, 9, 13, 16, 19—
Forms given by Rules and Orders of 1875, 1879,
of Statutory Authority—" Rules regulating Procedure " includes Forms of Proceedings—127th
Canon not binding on Official Principal appointed
by Public Worship Regulation Act, 1874—Style
of Judge under Public Worship Regulation Act,
1874—Requirement as to Place of hearing Cause
—Writ de Contumace Capiendo issued in Vacation and not brought into Court—Petty Bag Act,
12 & 13 Vict. c. 109, s. 26.*] A representation
under the Public Worship Regulation Act, 1874,
was made in July, 1878, by the churchwardens
of a parish to the bishop of the diocese, complaining of the incumbent for certain illegal
practices in the conduct of Divine worship. The
bishop and archbishop being alternate patrons of
the benefice, the bishop of the diocese of E. was
appointed to act in the place of such bishop and
archbishop in the matter of the representation
under the 16th section of the above-mentioned
Act. The bishop of E. having considered the
representation sent a requisition to the Judge
under the Public Worship Regulation Act, 1874,

**II. PRACTICE — ECCLESIASTICAL — CHURCH
DISCIPLINE ACT**—*continued.*
requiring him to hear the case in London or
Westminster, or within the diocese. The requisition followed as nearly as possible the form
given by the Rules and Orders of 1875, issued
under the Public Worship Regulation Act, 1874.
It did not state that a copy of the representation·
had been sent to the party complained of, or that
the parties had been required to state whether
they would submit to the directions of the bishop·
touching the matter of the representation, as
provided· for by sect. 9 of the Public Worship
Regulation Act, 1874. It stated, however, that
the parties had not stated within the prescribed
time that they were willing to submit to the·
directions of the bishop :—*Held*, by the Queen's-
Bench Division, that the requisition under the
9th section of the Public Worship Regulation
Act must name the limits within which, under
the section, the hearing is to take place, but need·
not name the particular place within such limits—
that the requisition made by the bishop of E.
was valid, and that the form of it was sufficient
on the following grounds, first, that it sufficiently
shewed by necessary implication that the parties·
had been required to state whether they were
willing to submit to the directions of the bishop ;
secondly, that it was not competent to the party·
complained of to object to the form of the requisition to the Judge if all the facts essential to the·
jurisdiction in truth existed ; and thirdly, that the·
requisition was in substantial accordance with
the form given by the Rules and Orders. This
decision was not questioned on appeal.—The
Judge under the Public Worship Regulation Act
proceeded to hear the matter of the above-mentioned representation, and issued a monition commanding the incumbent complained of to abstain
from certain practices which he pronounced unlawful. The incumbent disregarded such monition, and continued the said practices, whereupon
the Judge issued an inhibition inhibiting the incumbent from the performance of Divine service
and the exercise of the cure of souls within the·
diocese for three months, and thereafter until the
inhibition should be relaxed. The monition issued
while the Rules and Orders of 1875 (1 P. D. 1)·
were in force, but the inhibition issued after the
amended Rules of 1879 (4 P. D. 250) had come
into force. In the monition the Judge was styled·
the official principal of the Arches Court of Canterbury (he having become such official principal under the 7th section of the Act upon the·
resignation of the previous official principal), but
except in this respect the monition exactly followed the form given by the Rules and Orders of
1875. The inhibition exactly followed the form
given by the Rules and Orders of 1879 :—*Held*,
by the Queen's Bench Division, that, assuming
an official principal of the Arches Court of Canterbury to be within the 127th of the Canons·
of 1603, 1604, the Judge under the Public Worship Regulation Act, 1874, was constituted by
the 7th section of that Act upon the happening
of a vacancy ex officio official principal of the·
Arches Court of Canterbury, without any obligation to take the oaths and subscribe the articles
as required by that canon. This decision was not
questioned on appeal :—*Held*, also, by the Queen's·

II. PRACTICE — ECCLESIASTICAL — CHURCH DISCIPLINE ACT—*continued.*

Bench Division, that the Judge was rightly described in the monition as official principal of the Arches Court of Canterbury without setting forth how he became such official principal. This was not questioned on appeal :—*Held*, by the Queen's Bench Division and by the Court of Appeal, that the power given by the Public Worship Regulation Act, 1874, s. 19, to make rules and orders regulating the procedure under the Act, includes the power to make forms, and that consequently the forms given by the Rules and Orders of 1875 and 1879 are of statutory authority, and the monition and inhibition, whether they would have otherwise sufficiently shewn jurisdiction or not, were valid as being in accordance with the forms so given.—The incumbent disregarded the inhibition, and continued to exercise the cure of souls. The Judge then issued a significavit against him for contempt. A writ de contumace capiendo was thereupon issued from the Petty Bag Office on the 29th of October, and recorded in the Queen's Bench on the following day (the Court not being then sitting), and delivered to the sheriff. Under this writ the incumbent was arrested and lodged in prison :—*Held*, by the Queen's Bench Division and by the Court of Appeal, that the Judge under the Public Worship Regulation Act, 1874, is not the Judge of a new Court constituted by the Act, but is the official principal of the old Court of Arches, and has all the old powers of that Court, including the power of signifying for contempt if his orders are disobeyed, and that as the Act does not contain any special power of enforcing an inhibition issued under it, such inhibition can be enforced by significavit under 53 Geo. 3, c. 127 :—*Held*, by the Queen's Bench Division, that the provisions of 5 Eliz. c. 23, s. 2, incorporated by 53 Geo. 3, c. 127, s. 1, that the writ de contumace capiendo, when brought into the Court of Queen's Bench, should there, in the presence of the justices, be opened and delivered of record to the sheriff, were impliedly repealed by the 26th section of the Petty Bag Act, 12 & 13 Vict. c. 109, and were not revived by the repeal of that section by 38 & 39 Vict. c. 66, and 42 & 43 Vict. c. 59 ; that the writ was effectual, and that the incumbent was lawfully arrested under it :—*Held*, on appeal, that though the Petty Bag Act authorized the issuing of the writ in vacation, it did not repeal the enactment that the writ should be opened in the Queen's Bench in the presence of the justices, and that as it had only been brought into the Crown Office at a time when the Judges were not sitting, the requisitions of 53 Geo. 3, c. 127, had not been complied with, and the incumbent was entitled to be discharged from custody.—A monition commanded an incumbent, inter alia, to abstain from wearing in the administration of the Holy Communion the vestments known as an alb, a chasuble, and a biretta, and from all practices acts, matters, and things of the same or a like nature to those thereinbefore particularly set forth, or any of them, or from unlawfully permitting the same, or any of them. The inhibition stated that the incumbent had failed to obey the monition in regard to the matters therein mentioned, and proceeded to specify various acts,

II. PRACTICE — ECCLESIASTICAL — CHURCH DISCIPLINE ACT—*continued.*

most of which were expressly forbidden by the monition, and also that the incumbent had permitted his curate to wear at the Communion Service certain unlawful ecclesiastical vestments, to wit, a biretta and a stole, and it inhibited him from officiating for three months, and thereafter until the inhibition should be relaxed :—*Held*, that it was within the jurisdiction of the Judge to decide whether the wearing a stole was not an unlawful act of the same or a like nature to those mentioned in the monition ; that if he had decided wrongly the case was one for appeal, and that even if the Act gave no appeal in such a case, there was no ground for saying that the Judge had exceeded his jurisdiction. A prohibition to restrain proceedings on the inhibition was therefore refused.—Whether the including among the grounds of the inhibition an act not prohibited by the monition along with acts which were so prohibited would make the inhibition invalid—*quære.* DALE'S CASE. ENRAGHT'S CASE **6 Q. B. D. 376** [*And see* ENRAGHT *v.* LORD PENZANCE (7 App. Cas. 240).

PRACTICE — ECCLESIASTICAL — PUBLIC WORSHIP ACT. 1.]

3. —— Prohibition—3 & 4 Vict. c. 86, ss. 3, 5, 7, 11, 13, 24—*Proceedings against Clerk in Orders—Bishop Promoter of Suit—Power to adjudicate thereon — Interest—Costs.*] Under the Church Discipline Act, 1840 (3 & 4 Vict. c. 86), which empowers a bishop to hear and determine a charge against a clerk in orders of having committed an ecclesiastical offence, if the bishop be not patron of any preferment held by the party accused, the mere fact that the bishop is, by his secretary, promoter of the suit does not, in the absence of any personal interest or bias, disqualify him from adjudicating upon the case. THE QUEEN *v.* BISHOP OF ST. ALBANS **9 Q. B. D. 454**

III. PRACTICE — ECCLESIASTICAL — PUBLIC WORSHIP ACT.

1. —— Monition—*Vestments—Biretta—Stole —Inhibition—Jurisdiction—Prohibition*—37 & 38 Vict. c. 85.] A monition, precisely following a judgment pronounced by the Judge under the Public Worship Regulation Act, 1874, admonished a clerk to abstain for the future when officiating in his church from doing each of certain specified acts, and (amongst them) from wearing the vestments known as an alb, a chasuble, and a biretta ; and from causing to be formed a procession at the commencement of Morning Service ; and also "from all practices, acts, matters and things of the same or a like nature to those hereinbefore particularly set forth or any of them, or from unlawfully permitting the same or any of them."—A subsequent inhibition, after reciting the monition and the disobedience of the clerk thereto in regard to several other matters, recited his disobedience in permitting his curate to wear a vestment known as a biretta and a vestment known as a stole, and also in permitting his curate to form a procession between Morning Prayer and the Communion Service, and for such his disobedience inhibited the clerk from performing services for three months and until relaxation. The clerk having applied for

2 O

III. PRACTICE — ECCLESIASTICAL — PUBLIC WORSHIP ACT—*continued.*

a writ of prohibition :—*Held* (affirming the decision of the Court of Appeal) that the Judge had jurisdiction (subject to correction on appeal) to insert the alia similia clause in the monition.—And that under sect. 13 of the Public Worship Regulation Act, 1874, the Judge had jurisdiction to determine whether the wearing of a stole, and the forming a procession between Morning Prayer and the Communion Services were practices, acts, matters and things of the same or a like nature to those particularly set forth in the monition ; and that if he had determined that question wrongly it might be the subject of appeal—if an appeal lies—but could not afford any ground for prohibition.—And that even if the wearing of a stole and the forming a procession between Morning Prayer and the Communion Service were not breaches of the monition, yet as it appeared on the face of the inhibition that the clerk had committed several other acts of disobedience any one of which would have justified an inhibition for the full period, there was no excess of jurisdiction and no ground for prohibition. ENRAGHT *v.* LORD PENZANCE　-　　　**7 App. Cas. 240**

2. —— Promoter — *Substitution of succeeding Churchwarden as Promoter of a Suit.*] There is no power given by the Public Worship Regulation Act, 1874, to substitute succeeding churchwardens for a churchwarden who has instituted a suit for acts committed during the time he was churchwarden.—*Quære,* as to the effect upon a suit of the churchwarden who instituted it ceasing to be a churchwarden or a parishioner. PERKINS *v.* ENRAGHT. HARRIS *v.* ENRAGHT　**7 P. D. 31, 161**

IV. PRACTICE — ECCLESIASTICAL — MONITION.

—— **Prohibition**—*Definitive Sentence—Subsequent Enforcement of the Monition.*] In 1874 a suit was instituted by letters of request in the Arches Court, according to the provisions of the 3 & 4 Vict. c. 86 (the Church Discipline Act) against a clerk for unlawful practices in the performance of divine service. A sentence of suspension ab officio for six weeks was pronounced against him, and he was "monished" not to repeat the practices. He did repeat them, and was again admonished. He continued to repeat them, was twice summoned before the Court to answer, but did not appear ; and in June, 1878, the Dean of the Arches "pronounced, decreed, and declared" that the acts alleged to have been done by the clerk had been fully proved, " and that in so doing he had repeated the offences alleged against him in the articles exhibited against him in this suit," and had thereby disobeyed and contravened the monitions served upon him. "For which disobedience the Judge did pronounce him to have been guilty of contumacy. And for the conduct aforesaid the Judge did further decree and declare," that he should be suspended ab officio et beneficio for three years :—*Held,* that this was a matter of ecclesiastical procedure alone, and was not, therefore, the subject of a proceeding in prohibition. The suspension was only a step in the proceedings which had been regularly instituted in 1874, and was in itself perfectly regular.—*Per* Lord Blackburn : The temporal Court, proceeding in prohibi-

IV. PRACTICE — ECCLESIASTICAL — MONITION—*continued.*

tion, is not bound by a decision of even the highest Court of Appeal in ecclesiastical matters.—*Martin* v. *Mackonochie* (Law Rep. 3 P. C. 409) and *Hebbert* v. *Purchas* (Law Rep. 4 P. C. 301) approved. MACKONOCHIE *v.* LORD PENZANCE
　　　　　　　[6 App. Cas. 424

V. PRACTICE — ECCLESIASTICAL — CONTEMPT.

1. —— **Appropriate Sentence obligatory** — *Court of Final Appeal will not decide in the first instance—Contumacy—New Suit for fresh Offences whilst Sentence in a former Suit is not enforced.*] A Judge has no discretion, while finding a Defendant guilty of ecclesiastical offences, to absolve him from all ecclesiastical censure or punishment for those offences, but should pronounce that which he considers to be an appropriate sentence.—Case remitted to the Court below for that purpose as, except under peculiar circumstances, a Court of final appeal ought not to decide any cause in the first instance.—Although it may not be proper to institute a new suit for the mere purpose of punishing contumacy or disobedience to orders passed in a former suit, yet a new suit may be brought for new substantial offences, and the former disobedience be relied upon as a matter of aggravation. An order having the force of a definitive sentence may inflict canonical punishment (such as deprivation, degradation, and excommunication) which cannot lawfully be inflicted for mere contumacy or contempt. MARTIN *v.* MACKONOCHIE　　·　**6 P. D. 87 ; 7 P. D. 94**

2. —— **Chancery Court of York**—*Contumacy—Writ de contumace capiendo—Mittimus—County Palatine of Lancaster—Public Worship Regulation Act,* 1874 (37 & 38 Vict. c. 85), *ss.* 7, 9, 13—5 *Eliz. c.* 23, *ss.* 2, 11—53 *Geo.* 3, *c.* 127, *s.* 1—2 & 3 *Will.* 4, *c.* 93, *s.* 1—*Rules of Supreme Court, Order II., rule* 8.] A representation having been made against a clerk, rector of a parish within the county palatine of Lancaster, in the province of York, under the Public Worship Act, 1874, for offences against sect. 8 of that Act committed in the parish church, the bishop of the diocese sent the matter to the Archbishop of York, who sent a requisition to Lord Penzance—the Judge appointed under the Act, who had since the passing of the Act become official principal of the Chancery Court of York—requiring him to hear and determine the matter of the representation at any place in London or Westminster, or within the province of York or diocese of Manchester, as he might deem fit. The Judge heard it at Westminster, and there pronounced judgment, and issued a monition ordering the clerk to abstain from the practices complained of. The clerk having disobeyed the monition to the Judge, sitting at Westminster, issued an inhibition inhibiting the clerk for three months and thereafter until relaxation from performing any service of the church within the diocese, and on his persisting in his disobedience, pronounced him contumacious and issued a significavit under 53 Geo. 3, c. 127, s. 1. The tenor of the significavit was sent by mittimus from the Petty Bag Office to the Chancellor of the county palatine of Lancaster. In accordance with an order made by the Vice-Chancellor of the

V. PRACTICE — ECCLESIASTICAL — CONTEMPT—*continued.*

county palatine sitting at Lincoln's Inn a writ de contumace capiendo was issued, under which the clerk was arrested by the sheriff of Lancashire and lodged in Lancaster Goal. On a motion for a habeas corpus :—*Held* (affirming the decision of the Court of Appeal), that the matter so heard before the Judge, as official principal of the Chancery Court of York, was a cause cognizable in an Ecclesiastical Court within the meaning of 53 Geo. 3, c. 127, s. 1, and that the Judge had power to pronounce the contumacy and issue the significavit under that Act :—That the county palatine being one of the exempt jurisdictions mentioned in 5 Eliz. c. 23, s. 11, the procedure required by that section as to the mittimus and the issue of the writ de contumace capiendo was applicable and was duly followed :—That the mittimus was not one of the writs referred to in Order II., rule 8, of the Rules of the Supreme Court, and was properly tested as in the name of the Queen by the Master of the Rolls :—That under the Public Worship Regulation Act, 1874 (37 & 38 Vict. c. 85), s. 9, the Judge had power not merely to "hear" but also to hear and determine the matter, and to do all the acts which he did at Westminster :— That all the proceedings were regular and there was no ground for a habeas corpus. GREEN *v.* LORD PENZANCE **7 Q. B. D. 273 ; 6 App. Cas. 657**

3. —— **Discharge**—*Application by Bishop of Diocese for Discharge of Clerk in Custody for Contempt—Deprivation under Provisions of Statute Law — Satisfaction of Contempt by involuntary Obedience—Public Worship Regulation Act, 1874 (37 & 38 Vict. c. 85), s. 13—53 Geo. 3, c. 127.*] At the hearing of the matter of a representation made under the Public Worship Regulation Act against the rector of a parish church in the diocese of Manchester and province of York, the Official Principal of the Chancery Court of York pronounced that the Defendant when officiating in the parish church had committed certain offences against ecclesiastical law, and on the 27th of June, 1879, issued a monition admonishing him to refrain from such offences for the future. The Defendant failed to obey the monition, and the Official Principal, in August, 1879, by an inhibition under the Public Worship Regulation Act, inhibited him for three months, and, until the inhibition had been relaxed, from performing the services of the church or exercising the cure of souls within the diocese of Manchester. Whilst the inhibition was still in force the Defendant disobeyed it by officiating in the parish church on several occasions, and thereupon his contempt was signified to the Queen in Chancery, and he was in March, 1881, taken into custody under a writ de contumace capiendo. In August, 1882, the Defendant still remained in custody under the writ, but, by the operation of the Public Worship Regulation Act, ceased to be rector of the parish. The Bishop of Manchester then applied to the Official Principal for the discharge of the Defendant. The application was neither supported by the Defendant nor opposed by the complainants :— *Held*, that the application was rightly made by the bishop of Manchester :—*Held*, also, that the Defendant had "satisfied his contempt" within

V. PRACTICE — ECCLESIASTICAL — CONTEMPT—*continued.*

the meaning of 53 Geo. 3, c. 127, and that a writ of deliverance in the form prescribed by that statute ought to issue for his discharge. DEAN *v.* GREEN **[8 P. D. 79**

VI. PRACTICE—ECCLESIASTICAL—JURISDICTION.

1. —— **Deprivation**—*Church Discipline Act (3 & 4 Vict. c. 86)—Offences against Ritual—Resignation of Benefice pending a Suit—Operation of Sentence of Deprivation.*] The ordinary sentence of deprivation in use in the Ecclesiastical Courts is not limited to the particular preferment or benefice stated in the articles to be held by the Respondent, but extends to all ecclesiastical promotions within the jurisdiction held by the Respondent at the time that sentence is pronounced.—It is contrary to the practice of the Court of Arches to pronounce a sentence of perpetual suspension from the performance of divine service against a Respondent who holds a benefice of which the Court has jurisdiction to deprive him.—The articles in a criminal suit by letters of request under the Church Discipline Act contained allegations charging that the Respondent was perpetual curate of the parish of A., in the diocese of London, and that he had within two years of the institution of the suit committed repeated and aggravated offences against the laws ecclesiastical in matters of ritual whilst officiating in the performance of divine service in the parish church of A. At the hearing of the suit the above-mentioned allegations were held to be proved, and the Official Principal, in his discretion, condemned the Respondent in costs, but refused to pronounce any sentence of deprivation or canonical punishment. The promoter appealed, and the appeal having been allowed the Queen in Council remitted the cause, with an intimation that the Respondent ought to be canonically punished. After the cause had been so remitted, but before the terms of the remission had been complied with, the Respondent resigned the perpetual curacy of A. and was instituted to the incumbency of P. in the diocese of London.—On the cause subsequently coming on for sentence, the Official Principal of the Court of Arches pronounced sentence depriving the Respondent of all ecclesiastical promotions within the province of Canterbury of which he was possessed when the sentence was pronounced and of all the ecclesiastical emoluments thereto belonging. MARTIN *v.* MACKONOCHIE (THIRD SUIT) - - - **8 P. D. 191**

2. —— **Deprivation** — *Prohibition—House of Lords—Palace of Westminster—Royal Peculiar—Royal Palace—Royal Residence—Church Discipline Act, 1840 (3 & 4 Vict. c. 86).*] A suit having been brought against a clerk in the Court of Arches, under the Church Discipline Act, a sentence of suspension for six months was pronounced against him on the 9th of March, 1878, but was made conditional on an affidavit being filed. Afterwards the affidavit was filed, and an unconditional sentence was pronounced on the 23rd of March and served on the Defendant.—A fresh suit was instituted in 1880 for fresh offences, and also for contumacious disobedience to the sentence of the 23rd of March, 1878. These offences

2 O 2

VI. PRACTICE — ECCLESIASTICAL — JURIS-DICTION—*continued.*

being proved, the Defendant was sentenced to be deprived of his benefice. This sentence was pronounced by the Dean of Arches in Committee Room E of the House of Lords.—A motion for a prohibition having been brought to restrain the Court of Arches from enforcing the sentence :—*Held*, first, that the sentence of the 9th of March was an interlocutory order which did not end the suit, and therefore the Court was not functus officio when it pronounced the unconditional sentence of suspension :—Secondly. That even if the unconditional sentence had been void, the Court would not have exceeded its jurisdiction in passing the sentence of deprivation, as there were other offences proved which would have supported it :—Thirdly. That the site of the old Palace of Westminster is no longer a peculiar, but is within the diocese of London and the jurisdiction of the Court of Arches :—Fourthly. That the new Palace of Westminster is not exempt from the jurisdiction of the ordinary Civil and Ecclesiastical Courts on the ground of privilege, inasmuch as it had ceased to be a royal residence :—Whether Committee Room E of the House of Lords is within the precincts of the old Palace of Westminster, *quære.* COMBE *v.* DE LA BERE
[22 Ch. D. 316

—— County Palatine of Lancaster—Official Principal of Chancery Court of York—Judge appointed under Public Worship Regulation Act—Contempt 7 Q. B. D. 273 ;
[6 App. Cas. 657
See PRACTICE — ECCLESIASTICAL—CONTEMPT. 2.

PRACTICE—LANCASTER COURT 24 Ch. D. 280
See COURT—LANCASTER COURT.

PRACTICE—MAYOR'S COURT.
See Cases under COURT—MAYOR'S COURT.

PRACTICE—PRIVY COUNCIL :—   Col.
  I. JURISDICTION - 1127
  II. LEAVE TO APPEAL 1127

I. PRACTICE—PRIVY COUNCIL—JURISDICTION.

—— Effect of Order of the Queen in Council—*Trustee's Liability for Costs.*] When a decision of the Judicial Committee has been reported to Her Majesty and has been sanctioned it becomes the decree or order of the final Court of Appeal : and it is the duty of every subordinate tribunal to whom the order is addressed to carry it into execution.—A trustee in bankruptcy can be made personally liable for costs of a suit to which he is a party, subject to the Court of Bankruptcy allowing him to recoup himself out of the bankrupt estate, if his conduct has been bonâ fide. PITTS *v.* LA FONTAINE - - 6 App. Cas. 482

II. PRACTICE—PRIVY COUNCIL—LEAVE TO APPEAL.

1. —— Criminal Case—*Validity of 43 Vict. c. 25 (Canada).*] The rule of the Judicial Committee is not to grant leave to appeal in criminal cases except where some clear departure from the requirements of justice is alleged to have taken place.—*Held*, that 34 & 35 Vict. c. 28, which

II. PRACTICE—PRIVY COUNCIL—LEAVE TO APPEAL—*continued.*

authorizes the Parliament of Canada to provide for " the administration, peace, order, and good government of any territory not for the time being included in any province" vests in that Parliament the utmost discretion of enactment for the attainment of those objects. Accordingly Canadian Act 43 Vict. c. 25, is intrà vires the legislature.—Sect. 76, sub-sect. 7, which prescribes that full notes of evidence be taken is literally complied with when those notes are taken in shorthand. RIEL *v.* THE QUEEN
[10 App. Cas. 675

2. —— Importance of Case.] Their Lordships will not advise Her Majesty to admit an appeal from the Supreme Court of the Dominion of Canada save where the case is of gravity, involving matter of public interest or some important question of law, or affecting property of considerable amount, or where the case is otherwise of some public importance or of a very substantial character.—Petition for special leave to appeal refused, the case depending on a disputed matter of fact whether there had been a gift or sale of certain goods of the value of £1000. PRINCE *v.* GAGNON
[8 App. Cas. 103

3. —— Imprisonment—*Importance of Case*] No appeal lies as of right from a judgment of the Court of Queen's Bench of Lower Canada in the matter of a penalty of imprisonment. Special leave was granted on the ground of the importance of the question at issue. CARTER *v.* MOLSON
[8 App. Cas. 530

4. —— Issue of Fact.] Petition for special leave to appeal in a case involving only an issue of fact refused.—Such petition must state fully but succinctly the grounds upon which it is based ; the record not being before their Lordships until forwarded by the proper authorities.
CANADA CENTRAL RAILWAY COMPANY *v.* MURRAY
[8 App. Cas. 574

5. —— Misstatements.] The petition of special leave to appeal in this case stated correctly two valid grounds for granting the same ; but contained misstatements of fact which affected the third ground relied upon by the Petitioner :—*Held*, that any such petition is liable at any time to be rescinded with costs if it contains any misstatement or any concealment of facts which ought to be disclosed. It appearing however that there was in this case no intention to mislead, the appeal was heard and allowed, but without costs.—*Ram Sabuk Bose v. Monomohini Dossee* (Law Rep. 2 Ind. Ap. 81) approved. MUSSOORIE BANK *v.* RAYNOR - - 7 App. Cas. 321

—— Leave to appeal - 8 App. Cas. 304
See COLONIAL LAW—JERSEY. 1.

PRACTICE—PROBATE :—   Col.
  I. CITATION 1129
  II. GUARDIAN - - - 1129
  III. PLEADING - - 1129
  IV. PARTICULARS - - 1129
  V. EVIDENCE - 1129
  VI. TRIAL - 1130
  VII. COMPROMISE 1130
  VIII. COSTS 1130

I. PRACTICE—PROBATE—CITATION.

—— Realty—*Assignee—Leave to cite*—20 & 21 Vict. c. 77, s. 61.] In an action as to the validity of a will the Court will not order the assignee of the heir-at-law of the testatrix to be cited as a person having or pretending interest in the real estate affected by the will.　JONES v. JONES
[7 P. D. 66

II. PRACTICE—PROBATE—GUARDIAN.

—— Infant—*Guardian ad litem*.] When a will is disputed by a guardian ad litem on behalf of infants, the Court of Probate has power to inquire whether the suit is for their benefit PERCIVAL v. CROSS · - - 7 P. D. 234

III. PRACTICE—PROBATE—PLEADING.

—— *Appeal direct from Chambers—Embarrassing Matter in Pleading—Rules of Supreme Court*, 1883, *Order XIX., r.* 27.] Appeals from orders made in Chambers are to be subject to the same rules in the Probate Division as in the Chancery Division, and will not be entertained unless the Judge gives leave to appeal direct, or certifies that he does not require to hear further argument. —The Plaintiff propounded for probate a will of September, 1880. A Defendant counter-claimed to prove a will of May, 1881. The Plaintiff replied (inter alia) that the testatrix was not of sound mind when she executed the will of May, 1881, and (5), that if she did duly execute it when of sound mind she duly revoked it by a will of June, 1881, executed when she was in a similar state of mind:—*Held*, by the President and by the Court of Appeal, that clause 5 of the reply, ought not to be struck out as embarrassing. *In re* SMITH. RIGG v. HUGHES　　9 F. D. 68

IV. PRACTICE—PROBATE—PARTICULARS.

1. —— Incapacity.] In an action for probate the Court will not order particulars to be given of incapacity. HANKINSON v. BARNINGHAM 9 P. D. 62

2. —— Undue Influence.] The Defendant in a probate action alleged that the will had been procured by the undue influence of the Plaintiff "and others." The Plaintiff applied for particulars of the names of the persons charged with undue influence and particulars of the acts of undue influence alleged, and the times when and places where each of the acts was alleged to have taken place. The President ordered the Defendant to give the names of the persons charged with undue influence, but refused to order him to give particulars of the acts. The Plaintiff appealed:—*Held*, by the Court of Appeal, that as it was admitted to have been the long settled practice of the Probate Court, and subsequently of the Probate Division, not to require a party alleging undue influence to give particulars of the acts of undue influence, such practice ought not now to be disturbed; and—*Semble* (per Lindley and Fry, L.JJ.), that this rule of practice was founded on good reason. LORD SALISBURY v. NUGENT · - 9 P. D. 23

V. PRACTICE—PROBATE—EVIDENCE.

1. —— Commission to examine Witness.] Under sect. 26 of 20 & 21 Vict. c. 77, the Court has power to order a commission to issue to

V. PRACTICE — PROBATE — EVIDENCE — *continued.*

examine a person as to her knowledge of a testamentary paper. BANFIELD v. PICKARD 6 P. D. 33

2. —— Parol Evidence of Intention.] Statements of a testatrix, whether made before or after the execution of the will, are admissible to shew what papers constitute the will. GOULD v. LAKES
[6 P. D. 1

VI. PRACTICE—PROBATE—TRIAL.

—— Right to Trial by Jury—*Probate Act*, 1857 (20 & 21 Vict. c. 77), s. 35—*General Orders XXXVI., rr.* 3, 26.] In an action by an executor to establish a will, the heir-at-law was cited. The Plaintiff gave notice of trial by jury. The action was twice tried by a special jury, before Sir J. Hannen, and in each case the jury disagreed and were discharged. The Plaintiff having set the action down for trial again before a special jury, the Defendants applied for special directions as to the further trial. Sir J. Hannen, the heir-at-law appearing and not opposing, made an order that the action should be tried by a Judge without a jury. The Plaintiff appealed:—*Held*, that the case was one where, under 20 & 21 Vict. c. 77, s. 35, as the heir-at-law did not ask for a jury, the Judge could, before the Judicature Act, without any consent, have ordered the action to be tried without a jury; that a choice of the mode of trial under Order XXXVI., rule 3, did not exclude the application of rule 26, and that the Judge therefore had jurisdiction to make the order appealed from :—*Held*, further, that though the order was subject to appeal, the Court of Appeal would not interfere with the discretion of the Judge except in a strong case, and that there was no ground for holding that his discretion had been wrongly exercised. BURGOINE v. MOORDAFF　8 P. D. 205

VII. PRACTICE—PROBATE—COMPROMISE.

—— Married Women or Infants.] *Semble*, in an action as to the validity of a will when terms of compromise are agreed to by the parties who are sui juris, the Court of Probate will not make an order binding married women or infants to the terms of a compromise. NORMAN v. STRAINS
[6 P. D. 219

VIII. PRACTICE—PROBATE—COSTS.

1. —— Administrator pending Suit—*Receiver pending Suit—Termination*.] The duties of an administrator and receiver pending suit commence from the date of the order of appointment, and if the decree in the action is appealed from do not cease until the appeal has been disposed of. Costs of the administrator and receiver pending suit and of his solicitor allowed from the date of the appointment until the dismissal of the appeal. TAYLOR v. TAYLOR - - 6 P. D. 29

2. —— Codicil propounded by Legatee—*Costs as of Executor proving.*] A legatee who has propounded a codicil and succeeded is entitled to the same costs as an executor under similar circumstances. The Defendant, the executor of the will of R. C., had proved the will only. The Plaintiffs propounded a codicil. The Court having pronounced for the codicil, condemned the Defendant in costs, and gave the Plaintiffs also out of the estate such sum nomine expensarum as would

VIII. PRACTICE—PROBATE—COSTS—*contd.*
cover the additional expenses. WILKINSON *v.*
CORFIELD - - - **6 P. D. 27**

3. —— Proof in solemn Form—*Rules of 20th
July*, 1862,' *Rule 41—Residuary Legatee under
prior Will.*] The rule and practice by which a
party may compel proof of a will in solemn form,
without liability for costs, do not extend to a
residuary legatee under a prior will. HOCKLEY *v.*
WYATT - - **7 P. D. 239**

4. —— Security for Costs—*Married Women.*]
Married women suing as plaintiffs without their
husbands being joined :—*Held*, since the Married
Women's Property Act, 1882 (45 & 46 Vict. c. 75),
not liable to give security for costs. THRELFALL
v. WILSON - - **8 P. D. 18**

I. PRACTICE—SUPREME COURT—WRIT.

1. —— Extension of Time—*Indorsement on
Writ of Date of Service—Rules of Court*, 1875,
Order IX., *r.* 13 ; *Order LVII.*, *r.* 6.] Under rule 6
of Order LVII. of Rules of Court, 1875, the Court
has power to extend the time fixed by rule 13 of
Order IX. for the making an indorsement on a
writ of the date of service. HASTINGS *v.* HURLEY
         [16 Ch. D. 734

2. —— Time from which Writ takes effect—
*Day, Fractions of—Writ of Summons issued on
the same day as Cause of Action accrued—Fiction
of Law—Distinction between original and judicial
Writ—Effect of Statute Law Revision Act*, 1875,
on Parliamentary Oaths Act, 1866 (29 & 30 Vict.
c. 19), *and Promissory Oaths Act*, 1868 (31 & 32
Vict. c. 72).] To issue a writ of summons is not a
judicial act, and the Court may inquire at what
period of the day it was issued. It appeared from
the statement of claim that the writ of summons
in the action was issued on the 2nd of July, and
that the cause of action arose on the same day,
but before the issue of the writ. The statement
of claim was demurred to on the ground that the
issuing of the writ was a judicial act, and must,
therefore, be presumed to have taken place at the
earliest moment of the day, before the cause of
action accrued :—*Held*, affirming the judgment
of the Queen's Bench Division, that the Court
could inquire whether or not the writ was in fact
issued after the cause of action accrued.—The
penal clauses of the Parliamentary Oaths Act,
1866, are not repealed by the Statute Law Revision Act, 1875. CLARKE *v.* BRADLAUGH
       [7 Q. B. D. 151 ; 8 Q. B. D. 63

II. PRACTICE—SUPREME COURT—SERVICE.

1. —— Lunatic Defendant—*Business carried on in Name of Firm—Service on Manager—Rules of Court.* 1875, *Order* IX., rr. 5, 6, 6a—*Order* XIII., r. 1.] The Defendant, who carried on business in the name of a firm apparently consisting of more than one person, was sued in her firm name; the writ was served at her place of business upon the manager according to Order IX., r. 6a ; and judgment signed in default of appearance. At the time of the service of the writ she was of unsound mind and confined in an asylum, but this was unknown to the Plaintiff :—*Held,* that the judgment must be set aside, as the writ ought to have and had not been served under Order XIII., r. 1. FORE STREET WAREHOUSE CO. *v.* DURRANT

[10 Q. B. D. 471

2. —— Out of Jurisdiction—*Action for Rent of Land in England—Defendants domiciled or ordinarily resident in Scotland—Rules of Court,* 1883, *Order* XI., r. 1 (b), (e).] Order XI., r. 1, does not enable the Court or a judge to allow service out of the jurisdiction of a writ in an action for non-payment of rent due under a lease of land in England against Defendants who are domiciled or ordinarily resident in Scotland. AGNEW *v.* USHER - - - 14 Q. B. D. 78

3. —— Out of Jurisdiction—*Admissibility of Evidence—Rules of Court,* 1875, *Order* XI., rr. 1, 1a, 3.] Where a Plaintiff has obtained leave under Order XI. to serve a writ out of the jurisdiction, and the Defendant moves to discharge the order, affidavits are admissible to contest the question whether the cause of action arose within the jurisdiction. — *Great Australian Gold Mining Company* v. *Martin* (5 Ch. D. 1) overruled on this point.—The sufficiency of the Plaintiff's affidavit under Order XI., r. 3, considered.—In cases where the Defendant is resident in Scotland or Ireland, the omission of the statement that he is a British subject is not material.—Rule 1a, of Order XI., giving a discretion to the Judge when the Defendant resides in Scotland or Ireland, only relates to actions on contracts and will not be applied to other actions. FOWLER *v.* BARSTOW

[20 Ch. D. 240

4. —— Out of Jurisdiction—*Discretion of Court—Rules of Court,* 1883, *Order* XI., r. 1.] The Court will exercise discretion in allowing or disallowing service out of the jurisdiction, and in so doing will consider evidence as to the merits. SOCIÉTÉ GÉNÉRALE DE PARIS *v.* DREYFUS BROTHERS 29 Ch. D. 239

5. —— Out of Jurisdiction—*Foreigner—Service of Notice of Appointment of Receiver.*] The Plaintiff having obtained judgment against the Defendant, a foreigner resident out of the jurisdiction, a summons was issued by leave of a Judge at chambers calling on the Defendant to shew cause why a receiver should not be appointed. On an application for leave to serve this summons on the Defendant out of the jurisdiction :—*Held,* that there was no jurisdiction to grant such leave. WELDON *v.* GOUNOD - 15 Q. B. D. 622

6. —— Out of Jurisdiction — *Libel—Injunction—Jurisdiction of Court—Rules of Court,* 1883, *Order* XI., r. 1 (f).] A writ of summons claiming an injunction to restrain the Defendant

II. PRACTICE—SUPREME COURT—SERVICE— *continued.*

(resident out of the jurisdiction) from sending libels to the Plaintiff (residing within the jurisdiction) and publishing the same within the jurisdiction, and claiming also damages, may, by leave of the Court, be issued and served upon the Defendant, at least if it does not appear that the Defendant never comes within the jurisdiction.—Judgment of the Queen's Bench Division affirmed. TOZIER *v.* HAWKINS 15 Q. B. D. 650, 680

7. —— Out of Jurisdiction—*Interpleader—Rules of Court,* 1883, *Order* LVII.] Where the Plaintiffs sued for goods in the possession of the Defendant, and it appeared that a foreigner residing out of the jurisdiction claimed the right to the same goods and would probably sue the Defendant in respect of them, the Court gave the Defendant leave to serve an interpleader summons out of the jurisdiction upon the foreigner.—The effect of service out of the jurisdiction in such a case is to give the foreigner notice of the proceedings within the jurisdiction, so that he may appear and prosecute his claim, or, if he does not appear, so that any future claim, prosecuted by him against the Defendant in respect of the subject-matter of the section within the jurisdiction may be barred. CREDITS GERUNDEUSE *v.* VAN WEEDE 12 Q. B. D.

[171

8. —— Out of Jurisdiction—*Leave to issue—Leave to serve—Rules of Court,* 1875, *Orders* II., r. 4, *and* XI., rr. 1 and 3.] Applications for leave to issue a writ for service out of the jurisdiction, and for leave to serve out of the jurisdiction the writ when issued, should be made in Chambers; and such applications may be made either simultaneously or separately.—Evidence is only requisite upon the application for leave to serve. If the applications are simultaneous, the affidavit in support of the application for leave to serve should be intituled in the matter of the intended action, if separate in the action.—Statement of the practice.—*Young* v. *Brassey* (1 Ch. D. 277) not followed. STIGAND *v.* STIGAND 19 Ch. D. 460

9. —— Out of Jurisdiction—*Old and New Practice—Rules of Court,* 1875, *Order* XI., r. 1.] The old practice as to service out of the jurisdiction is no longer in force. No leave to serve a Defendant out of the jurisdiction can be given except in the cases specified in Order XI., r. 1. *In re* EAGER. EAGER *v.* JOHNSTONE 22 Ch. D. 86

· . 10. —— Out of Jurisdiction—*Scotland and Ireland—Action for Breach of Contract—Rules of Court,* 1883, *Order* XI., rr. 1 (e) and 2—*Defendant domiciled or ordinarily resident in Scotland or Ireland.*] There is no power to allow service of a writ out of the jurisdiction in actions for breach of contract under Order XI., rule 1 (e), where the Defendant is domiciled or ordinarily resident in Scotland or Ireland. LENDERS *v.* ANDERSON

[12 Q. B. D. 50

11. —— Out of Jurisdiction—*Slander uttered Abroad—Special Damage within Jurisdiction—"Act done"—Rules of Court,* 1875, *Order* II., rule 4 —*Order* XI., *rule* 1.] On an application for leave to issue a writ of summons for service out of the jurisdiction, it appeared that the cause of action was an alleged slander uttered abroad and fol-

II. PRACTICE—SUPREME COURT—SERVICE
—continued.

lowed by special damage in England:—*Held*, by Denman and Watkin Williams, JJ., that the special damage in England was not an act done within the jurisdiction, so as to give the Court power to allow service of the writ out of the jurisdiction under Order XI., rule 1; *Held*, by the Court of Appeal (Bramwell, Brett, and Cotton, L.JJ.), that the writ ought not to issue, for as it was not shewn that the slander was intended to be transmitted to England the special damage, if it was the cause of action, was not the act of the person who uttered the slander, or an act for which he was responsible, so that there was no act done by him within the jurisdiction within Order XI., rule 1.
BREE *v.* MARESCAUX   -   -   **7 Q. B. D. 434**

—— Partner   -   -   **19 Ch. D. 124**
    See PRACTICE—SUPREME COURT—PARTIES. 11.

—— Substituted—Solicitor   -   **26 Ch. D. 746**
    See PRACTICE — SUPREME COURT—ATTACHMENT. 8.

—— Substituted—Solicitor   **9 Q. B. D. 598**
    See PRACTICE—SUPREME COURT—CHAMBERS. 6.

—— Third party notice -   **13 Q. B. D. 96**
    See PRACTICE—SUPREME COURT—THIRD PARTY. ·10.

III. PRACTICE — SUPREME COURT — WRIT SPECIALLY INDORSED.

1. —— **Demurrer** — *Rules of Court*, 1875, *Order XXI., r.* 4—*Objection on Ground of Insufficiency.*] A writ was specially indorsed, "The Plaintiff's claim is against the Defendant as the acceptor of a bill of exchange. The following are particulars:—Bill of exchange for £180, dated 27th of March, 1882, drawn by C. upon and accepted by Defendant, payable three months after date."—The Plaintiff having delivered a notice under Order XXI., r. 4, that his claim was that which appeared by the indorsement on the writ, the Defendant demurred on the ground that the statement was insufficient and disclosed no cause of action:—*Held*, that there was no ground of demurrer, and that the Defendant's remedy, if any, was to apply for a further statement under the rule.—*Robertson v. Howard* (3 C. P. D. 280) disapproved. FAWCUS *v.* CHARLTON
[**10 Q. B. D. 516**

2. —— **Foreign Judgment**—*Rules of Court*, 1883, *Order III., r.* 6—*Order XIV.*] In an action upon a foreign judgment in which the writ of summons has been specially indorsed under Order XIV., the Plaintiff may obtain an order empowering him to sign final judgment.—*Hodsoll v. Baxter* (E. B. & E. 884) followed. GRANT *v.* EASTON   -   -   **13 Q. B. D. 302**

3. —— **Married Woman**—*Judgment against—Rules of Court*, 1875, *Order XIV., r.* 1—*Form of Order.*] An order having been obtained under Order XIV., r. 1, for leave to sign final judgment against a married woman in an action for the price of goods supplied to her during coverture:—*Held*, that the order was wrongly made, inasmuch as there can be no judgment against a married woman personally in respect of such a claim. DURRANT *v.* RICKETTS AND WIFE   **8 Q. B. D. 177**

III. PRACTICE — SUPREME COURT — WRIT SPECIALLY INDORSED—*continued.*

4. —— **Married Woman**—*Judgment against —Form of—Separate Estate—Restraint on Anticipation—45 & 46 Vict. c.* 75, *ss.* 1, 19—*Rules of Court*, 1883, *Order XIV.*] An order giving leave to enter final judgment against a married woman in respect of her separate estate by virtue of the Married Women's Property Act, 1882 (45 & 46 Vict. c. 75), ss. 1, 19, should state that execution is to be limited to such separate estate as the Defendant is not restrained from anticipating unless such restraint exists under any settlement or agreement for a settlement of her own property made or entered into by herself. BURSILL *v.* TANNER
[**13 Q. B. D. 691**

5. —— **Mortgage**—*Action against Mortgagor for possession of Land—Tenancy created by Deed of Mortgage — Special Indorsement of Writ — Rules of Court*, 1883, *Order III., r.* 6 (*f*) — *Order XIV.*] The relationship of landlord and tenant may be created by a mortgage deed, and therefore, in an action for recovery of land by mortgagees from a mortgagor in possession under a mortgage deed creating a tenancy between them, the writ may be specially indorsed under Order III., rule 6 (*f*), so that Order XIV. will apply, and final judgment may be ordered. DAUBUZ *v.* LAVINGTON.
[**13 Q. B. D. 347**

IV. PRACTICE—SUPREME COURT—PARTIES.

1. —— **Adding Plaintiff**—*Change of Plaintiff —Rules of Court*, 1875, *Order XVI., r.* 13.] The Court cannot substitute one Plaintiff for another under Rules of Court, 1875, Order XVI., r. 13, except by the first Plaintiff's consent, and where he admits that he has commenced his action improperly; but in a proper case the Court will add a Plaintiff and give him the conduct of the action. EMDEN *v.* CARTE   **17 Ch. D. 169**

2. —— **Adding Plaintiff**—*Consent—Rules of Court*, 1875, *Order XVI., r.* 13.] The consent which Order XVI., r. 13 (Rules of Court, 1875), requires to be given by a person whom it is proposed to add as Plaintiff need not be in writing; it is sufficient if the solicitor for the existing Plaintiff states that he consents on behalf of the proposed new Plaintiff, the solicitor taking the ordinary responsibility of using the Plaintiff's name. COX *v.* JAMES
[**19 Ch. D. 55**

3. —— **Adding Plaintiff**—*Rules of Court*, 1883, *Order XVI., r.* 11.] In an action by a company, lessees for a long term of eleven houses, of which ten were unlet and in their possession when the writ was issued, and by their tenant of the remaining house as co-Plaintiff, for an injunction and damages in respect of an alleged nuisance from noise; the tenant, after delivery of the statement of claim and notice of trial, refused to go on with the action as co-Plaintiff. The other ten houses having in the meantime been let, the Plaintiff company applied at the trial for leave to amend by adding as co-Plaintiffs two of the new tenants, who consented to be added.—Application granted as being within the discretion given by Rules of the Supreme Court, 1883, Order XVI., rule 11, of allowing the names of any parties, whether plaintiffs or defendants — "whose presence before the Court may be necessary in order

IV. PRACTICE—SUPREME COURT—PARTIES
—*continued.*

to enable the Court effectually and completely to adjudicate upon and settle all the questions involved in the cause or matter"—to be added. HOUSE PROPERTY AND INVESTMENT COMPANY *v.* H. P. HORSE NAIL COMPANY　　29 Ch. D. 190

4. —— Adding Plaintiff—*Rules of Court*, 1883, *Order* XVI., *r.* 11.] The tenant for life of a trust fund brought an action against the trustees to make them liable for an improper investment. The trustees by their defence alleged that they had made the investment in question at the request of the Plaintiff. The Plaintiff thereupon applied for leave to amend by adding as co-Plaintiff his son, who had a reversionary interest in the fund, and Bacon, V.C., made an order giving him leave :—*Held*, on appeal, that the order must be discharged, for that Order XVI., rule 11 does not authorize the allowing a Plaintiff who has no right to sue, to amend by joining as co-Plaintiff a person who has such right. WALCOTT *v.* LYONS
[29 Ch. D. 584

5. —— Adding Defendant—*Executor—Rules of Court*, 1883, *Order* XVI., *r.* 11.] One of two executors having absconded, the other executor sued a mortgagor. The Court refused on the application of the Defendant to add the absconding executor as Defendant. DRAGE *v.* HARTOPP
[28 Ch. D. 414

6. —— Assignment of Cause of Action— *Change of Plaintiff—Amendment of Title of Action and of Pleadings—Rules of Court*, 1875, *Order* XVI., *r.* 13.] A trustee in bankruptcy commenced an action to obtain a declaration that a deed, which purported to be an absolute conveyance of real estate by the bankrupt, was in fact a mortgage, and to redeem such mortgage: and subsequently sold and assigned his interest in the subject-matter of the action to C., who claimed to carry on the action in the name of the original Plaintiff :—*Held*, on the application of the Defendant, that C. was bound to amend the title of the action so as to shew that he was the real Plaintiff, and to introduce such averments in the statement of claim as would disclose his title. SERAB *v.* LAWSON　-　-　-　16 Ch. D. 121

7. —— Assignment of Policy of Insurance— *Absence of Personal Representative of Person insured*—15 & 16 *Vict. c.* 86, *s.* 44.] In an action by an equitable mortgagee of a policy of insurance against the insurance company for payment of the policy money the Court has jurisdiction under the 44th section of the 15 & 16 Vict. c. 86, to dispense with a legal personal representative of the assured where none exists.—In a case where the mortgage debt was larger than the policy money, and the estate of the assured was insolvent :—*Held* (affirming the decision of the Master of the Rolls), that the jurisdiction to dispense with the personal representative was rightly exercised.—The dicta of James and Cotton, L.JJ., in *Webster* v. *British Empire Mutual Life Insurance Company* (15 Ch. D. 169) commented on. CURTIUS *v.* CALEDONIAN FIRE AND LIFE INSURANCE COMPANY　-　-　-　19 Ch. D. 534

8. —— Bondholder of Railway Company— *Rules of Court*, 1875, *Order* XVI., *r.* 9.] The

IV. PRACTICE—SUPREME COURT—PARTIES
—*continued.*

Plaintiff, a bondholder of a railway company, sued " on behalf of himself and all the bondholders of the company other than the Defendant B.," but did not obtain an order under Order XVI., rule 9, that B. should be sued as representing all bondholders who dissented from the Plaintiff's claim.—One of the bondholders took out a summons whereby he stated that neither the Plaintiff nor the Defendant B. properly represented the interests of himself and certain other bondholders, and applied to be made a defendant : —*Held*, that the applicant was entitled to be made a defendant, to represent the bondholders being dissentient from the Plaintiff's view. FRASER *v.* COOPER, HALL & Co.　-　-　21 Ch. D. 718

9. —— Co-owners of a Patent—*Right of one Co-owner to sue—Rules of Court*, 1875, *Order* XVI., *rr.* 13, 14, 17.] One of several co-owners of a patent has a right to sue alone for the recovery of profits due for the use of the patent.—An objection by a Defendant that other persons should have been joined as Plaintiffs should be made promptly, under Rules of Court, 1875, Order XVI., rules 13 and 14, and may not be postponed till the hearing where no impediment exists to raising the objection at once. SHEEHAN *v.* GREAT EASTERN RAILWAY COMPANY　-　-　16 Ch. D. 59

10. —— Partners—*Action against Partners in Name of Firm—Appearance by one Partner only— Judgment entered against Partner appearing instead of against Firm—Application to issue Execution against other Partner—Amendment of Judgment— Rules of Court*, 1875, *Order* XII., *r.* 12 ; *Order* XLII., *r.* 8.] To a writ issued against R. & Co., and claiming damages for libel, an appearance was entered for " R. trading as R. & Co. the Defendant in this action." The statement of claim was delivered against " R. sued as R. & Co." and the proceedings continued in that form down to judgment. At the trial by consent a verdict was found for the Plaintiff for 40*s* and judgment entered accordingly. After issuing execution against R. the Plaintiff, under the Rules in force before 1883, took out a summons for liberty to amend the judgment (and the pleadings if necessary) by striking the words " R. sued as " from the title of the action ; to enter judgment against R. & Co. so as to correspond with the writ, and to issue execution against C., on the ground that C. had been since discovered to be a partner in the firm :—*Held*, affirming the decision of the Court of Appeal, that the proceedings having been conducted against R. only, and judgment having been signed by consent against him alone, the judgment could not be converted into a judgment against the firm. MUNSTER *v.* RAILTON. MUNSTER *v.* COX 10 Q. B. D. 475 ; 11 Q. B. D. 435 ;
[10 App. Cas. 680

11. —— Partners—*Action against Partners in name of Firm—Firm dissolved before Writ issued—Service on one Member of Firm—Judgment by Default — Debtor's Summons against Member not served with Writ—Bankruptcy Act*, 1869 (32 & 33 *Vict. c.* 71), *s.* 7—*Rules of Court*, 1875, *Order* IX., *r.* 6 ; *Order* XII., *r.* 12 ; *Order* XVI., *r.* 10 ; *Order* XLII., *r.* 8.] Per Lord Selborne, L.C.: Whether the provisions of Order XVI., rule 10, that partners may be sued in

IV. PRACTICE—SUPREME COURT—PARTIES
—continued

the name of their firm, applies, not only to a partnership existing at the time when the writ is issued, but also to a partnership dissolved before the issue of the writ in respect of a cause of action which arose during its existence, *quære*.—But, if it does, still judgment in the action is not *per se* binding on any member of the dissolved firm who has not been served with the writ as a partner, or has not admitted on the pleadings that he is or has been adjudged to be a partner. Leave ought not to be given to issue execution on the judgment against such a person, if he disputes his liability, without the previous determination of the question of his liability ; nor can a debtor's summons be properly issued against him on the judgment per se.—*Per* Cotton, L.J. : Order XVI., rule 10, applies only to a partnership existing at the time when the writ is issued. It does not apply to a partnership dissolved before the issue of the writ.—*Per* Brett, L.J. : Order XVI., rule 10, authorizes the suing in the name of their firm the members of a partnership dissolved before the issue of the writ, in respect of a cause of action which arose during the existence of the firm, and service of the writ on one of the former partners is, under rule 6 of Order IX., a good service on the others ; and a judgment obtained after such a service only is binding on a former partner who has not admitted that he is nor has been adjudged to be a partner, so that a debtor's summons can properly issue on the judgment, though execution cannot issue without the leave of the Court.—A partnership consisting of several members was dissolved as to one of them on the 17th of December, and the business was thenceforth continued by the others under the old firm name, and at the old place of business. On the 18th of December a creditor of the old partnership, who was ignorant of the dissolution, commenced an action against the partners (suing them in the firm name) in respect of the debt contracted before the dissolution. On the 21st of December the writ was served personally on one of the continuing partners. The retired partner was not served in any way. No appearance was entered to the writ, and on the 29th of December the Plaintiff signed judgment by default. Execution was issued, but the sheriff found no goods of the partnership upon which to levy. No application was made under rule 8 of Order XLII. for leave to issue execution against the retired partner. In the following May, the retired partner having had no previous notice of the action, the Plaintiff served him with particulars of demand of the judgment debt, and, he not having paid it, the Plaintiff served him with a debtor's summons founded on the judgment debt. He denied the debt, and applied to the Bankruptcy Court to dismiss the summons :—*Held*, by Lord Selborne, L.C., and Cotton, L.J. (dissentiente Brett, L.J.), that the judgment would not support the debtor's summons, and that the summons must be dismissed. *Ex parte* YOUNG. *In re* YOUNG
                        [19 Ch. D. 124

12. ——— **Partners**—*Action against Partners in Name of Firm—Right to proceed against existing Partners together with former Partner—Presump-*

IV. PRACTICE—SUPREME COURT—PARTIES
—continued.

tion as to Partners intended to be sued as Defendants under Name of Firm—Judgment by Default — Rules of Court, 1875, Order XVI., r. 10 ; Order XLII., r. 8.] The Plaintiffs having brought an action and obtained judgment against the firm of " H. & D.," applied to a Judge under Order XLII., rule 8, for leave to issue execution against M. as being a member of the firm. It appeared that the action was upon a bill of exchange drawn by D. at a time when M. H. & D. were partners in the firm of H. & D., but that M. had retired from the partnership prior to the issuing of the writ, and that the firm of H. & D. then continued, but consisted of H. & D. only. The bill was drawn without the knowledge or consent of M., and for a purpose unconnected with the partnership.—*Held*, by Watkin Williams, J., first, that under Order XVI., rule 10 — which enables two or more persons being liable as co-partners to be sued in the name of their firm —the right to sue partners in the name of a firm is not limited to the case of partners carrying on business at the date of the writ ; secondly, that it was a question of fact, having regard to the circumstances and the proceedings subsequent to the writ, whether the Plaintiff intended to sue under the firm name those partners only who were members of the firm at the commencement of the action, or the same persons together with any former partner. — *Ex parte Young* (19 Ch. D. 124) considered. DAVIS *v.* MORRIS   **10 Q. B. D. 436**

13. ——— **Partners**—*Action against Name of Firm—Rules of Court, 1875, Order IX., r. 6, and Order XLII. r. 8.*] Where the writ in an action is issued against a partnership firm in the name of the firm the judgment must be against the firm, and it cannot be separately entered against an individual member of the firm who has made default in appearing to the action. JACKSON *v.* LITCHFIELD   **[8 Q. B. D. 474**

14. ——— **Partners**—*Action against Firm — Service of Writ on one Member of a Trading Partnership—Appearance by him only "as a partner of the firm"—Rules of Court, 1883, Order XII., r. 15.*] A writ was issued against a trading partnership (unincorporated), and served upon a member of the firm, who entered an appearance, " W. N., a partner of the firm of W. T. & Co." There was no service upon or appearance by the other members of the firm :—*Held*, that leave to sign judgment against the firm for default of appearance could not be granted. — *Jackson v. Litchfield* (8 Q. B. D. 474) followed. ADAM *v.* TOWNEND   **14 Q. B. D. 103**

15. ——— **Partners**—*Judgment against Firm— Action on Judgment—Execution—Rules of Court, 1875, Order XLII., r. 8.*] Where judgment has been recovered against a partnership firm in the name of the firm, the Plaintiff may bring an action on the judgment against the individual members of the firm, and is not confined to the remedy given by Order XLII., rule 8, with respect to the issue of execution. CLARK *v.* CULLEN   **9 Q. B. D. 355**

16. ——— **Solicitors, for Purposes of Discovery or Costs**—*Demurrer—Frivolous Action—Misjoinder —Dismissal of Action — Rules of Court, 1883,*

IV. PRACTICE—SUPREME COURT—PARTIES —*continued.*

Order xxv., rr. 1, 3, 4; *Order xviii., r.* 1.] Order xxv. of the Rules of 1883, although in form abolishing demurrers, has merely substituted other modes of procedure by which the objects of a demurrer, so far as it served a beneficial purpose in obtaining a speedy decision of the point at issue, can now be attained. Where the cause of action against one Defendant is totally disconnected with that against the other Defendant, except so far as it arises out of an incident in the same transaction, there is a misjoinder, and it is not the case contemplated by Order xviii., rule 1. Solicitors who were made parties with other Defendants to an action, the statement of claim in which shewed no reasonable cause of action as against them :—*Held,* entitled under Order xxv., rule 4, to an order dismissing the action as against them with costs and striking their names out of the proceedings. To make solicitors or others parties to an action without seeking any relief against them, except payment of costs or discovery, is vexatious. BURSTALL *v.* BEYFUS　-　　　**26 Ch. D. 35**

V. PRACTICE — SUPREME COURT — NEXT FRIEND.

1. —— **Infant.**] Doubts having arisen as to the proper custody of an infant, a suit was commenced in her name for the administration of her father's estate. A next friend was appointed who was a friend of the Defendants, the executors and trustees of the will, and guardians of the infant, and accepted the office at their request, and on an indemnity from their father. The solicitors on the record for the Plaintiff were the solicitors of the executors. On an application in the name of the infant by M., the husband of her paternal aunt, as next friend pro hâc vice, to remove the next friend and substitute M. :—*Held,* reversing the decision of Bacon, V.C., that although nothing was alleged against the character, circumstances, or conduct of the next friend, his connection with the executors made him an improper person to act as next friend, and that he ought to be removed and M. substituted. *In re* BURGESS. BURGESS *v.* BOTTOMLEY　-　**25 Ch. D. 243**

2. —— **Married Woman**—*Authority—Security or Costs.*] An action was commenced in the name of a married woman by her next friend against her husband and the trustee of a separation deed to enforce payment of an annuity under the deed. The Defendants moved that the action might be dismissed, or that the next friend might be ordered to give security for costs. This was supported by an affidavit of the husband that he believed that his wife had given no authority to commence the action. The husband's solicitors joined in the affidavit, and deposed to the facts that the next friend was not a householder, and had no visible means of paying the costs. The next friend replied by affidavit that he had sufficient means to pay any costs that he might be ordered to pay, but said nothing as to his having authority from the married woman to commence the action, and did not produce any authority :—*Held,* by Bacon, V.C., that the next friend of a married woman will not be called upon to prove his authority on the

V. PRACTICE — SUPREME COURT — NEXT FRIEND—*continued.*

mere allegation of a Defendant that he has no authority :—*Held,* also, that the next friend could not be ordered to give security for costs on the ground that he was not a householder when he deposed that he had sufficient means to pay costs. —*Held,* by the Court of Appeal, that the action must be dismissed with costs, to be paid by the solicitors of the next friend, as he, when challenged to shew his authority to commence the action, did not shew any. SCHJOTT *v.* SCHJOTT

[19 Ch. D. 94

VI. PRACTICE — SUPREME COURT—THIRD PARTY.

1. —— **Directions** *as to Mode of having Questions in Action determined—Refusal of Court to order one Trial—Dismissal of Third Party from Action—Rules of Court,* 1875, *Order xvi., rr.* 18, 21.] The Plaintiff having sued for breach of contract in respect of goods, the Defendants, under the Rules of the Supreme Court, 1875, Order xvi., r. 18, brought in as a third party P. from whom they themselves had bought the goods. The Defendants afterwards, under Order xvi., rule 21, applied for directions as to the mode of having the questions in the action determined ; but the Court refused to give any directions. The Defendants delivered a claim to the third party, who in turn delivered to them a defence. The action, having been tried between the Plaintiff and the Defendants, the latter delivered a reply to the third party, and gave notice of trial :—*Held,* that the reply and notice of trial must be set aside, for it must be taken that the action came to an end as regarded the third party, when the Court refused to give directions. SCHNEIDER *v.* BATT

[8 Q. B. D. 701

2. —— **Directions** *as to Questions between Defendant and Third Party—Costs to be paid by Third Party—Rules of Court,* 1875, *Order xvi., rr.* 17, 18, 19, 20, 21.] No questions can be determined between a Defendant and a third party brought into the action by the Defendant unless an order be obtained under Order xvi., rule 17, giving directions that such question shall be determined.—The Court has power under Order xvi., rule 21, to order the third party so brought into the action to pay to the Plaintiff the costs occasioned by his defence. PILLER *v.* ROBERTS

[21 Ch. D. 198

3. —— **Directions**—*Summons for—Appearance—Judgment on—Judicature Act,* 1873, *s.* 24, *sub-s.* 3—*Judicature Act,* 1875, *s.* 24—*Rules of Court,* 1875, *Order xvi., r.* 52—*Married Women's Property Act,* 1882, 45 & 46 *Vict. c.* 75, *s.* 1.] Under Order xvi., rule 52, judgment against a third party who has appeared pursuant to a third party notice, but, at the hearing of an application by the Defendant for directions, declines to state any defence, may be ordered, if the Judge is not satisfied that there is any question proper to be tried as to the liability of the third party. The rule is consistent with the Judicature Act, 1873, s. 24, sub-s. 3, and the Judicature Act, 1875, s. 24, and is not ultrâ vires. Such judgment under the rule may, since the Married Women's Property Act, 1882, be ordered against a married woman, third

VI. PRACTICE — SUPREME COURT — THIRD PARTY—*continued.*

party, as a feme sole, declaring her separate estate chargeable even in respect of a liability created before that Act. GLOUCESTERSHIRE BANKING COMPANY *v.* PHILLIPS   -   - 12 Q. B. D. 533

4. —— **Discretion of Court**—*Ex parte Application—Rules of Court*, 1875, *Order* XVI., rr. 18, 20, 21.] An application by the Defendant in an action for leave to serve a third-party notice under Order XVI., rule 18, ought to be made on notice to the Plaintiff, and not ex parte.—In an action by a company against its directors and others, seeking to make the Defendants personally liable in respect of certain dividends alleged to have been improperly paid out of capital, the Defendants applied under Order XVI., rule 18, for leave to serve third party notices on all the shareholders of the company, 450 in number, on the ground that if they, the Defendants, were held liable, they would have a right over against the shareholders to recover from them the sums received by them by way of dividend:—*Held* (affirming the decision of Hall, V.C.), that the granting of the leave asked for would materially embarrass the Plaintiffs in the conduct of their action, and that, therefore, the Court in the exercise of its discretion ought to refuse the application. WYE VALLEY RAILWAY COMPANY *v.* HAWES
[16 Ch. D. 489

5. —— **Indemnity**—*Claim for Indemnity from co-Defendant—Rules of Court*, 1883, *Order* XVI., r. 55.] An action by a vendor against the purchaser of a house and premises, and the auctioneer who advertised and sold them, for specific performance of the contract or damages. The purchaser stated that he was induced to purchase the property in consequence of the advertisement in the newspapers inserted by the auctioneer, representing that the purchase-moneys would be allowed to remain on mortgage. The representation was alleged to have been unauthorized, and the purchaser applied by summons under Rules of Supreme Court, 1883, Order XVI., rule 55, for leave to serve his co-Defendant—the auctioneer—with a notice claiming indemnity from him against the claim of the vendor.—*Held,* that this was not a case for indemnity within rule 55, and that the summons must be dismissed.—*Pontifex v. Foord* (12 Q. B. D. 152) followed. CATTON *v.* BENNETT
[26 Ch. D. 161

6. —— **Indemnity** — *Contribution — Rules of Court*, 1883, *Order* XVI., rr. 48, 52.] The Plaintiff sued the Defendant for breach of a covenant to repair contained in a lease of a dwelling-house for a term of twenty-one years from Michaelmas, 1861. The Defendant obtained leave to serve and served a third party notice claiming contribution or indemnity from a sub-lessee to whom he had let the premises from Midsummer, 1869, for the remainder of the original term less ten days. The underlease contained a covenant to repair, which was in terms precisely similar to those of the covenant in the original lease, and for breach of which the Defendant claimed relief against the sub-lessee:—*Held,* that, inasmuch as the terms of the covenant to repair must in each case be construed with reference to the age and character of the premises at the time of the

demise, the covenant in the underlease could not be construed as a covenant to indemnify the Defendant against or to perform the covenant in the original lease; that the Defendant's claim was not one for contribution or indemnity from the third party within Order XVI., rule 25, and that therefore, no directions as to trial could be given under that rule. PONTIFEX *v.* FOORD
[12 Q. B. D. 152

7. —— **Indemnity** — *Embarrassing Pleading—Rules of Court*, 1883, *Order* XVI., r. 48.] In giving leave to a Defendant to serve notice of claim for contribution or indemnity on a third party, the Court will not consider whether the claim is a valid one, but only whether the claim is bonâ fide, and whether if established it will result in contribution or indemnity.—The Plaintiff, who was the owner of stock in a public company registered in her name, ascertained that it had been transferred to F. by virtue, as she alleged, of a forged transfer. She brought an action against the company to have her name reinstated in the books of the company. The company obtained leave to serve F. with a claim for indemnity:—*Held,* by the Court of Appeal, without deciding that the claim for indemnity was valid, that leave to serve F. was rightly given.—*Speller v. Bristol Steam Navigation Company* (13 Q. B. D. 96) distinguished. CARSHORE *v.* NORTH EASTERN RAILWAY COMPANY   -   - 29 Ch. D. 344

8. —— **Indemnity**—*Leave of Court or a Judge — Rules of Supreme Court*, 1883, *Order* XVI., rr. 48, 55.] Under rule 55 of Order XVI., a Defendant need not obtain the leave of the Court or a Judge before issuing to a co-Defendant a notice claiming contribution or indemnity from him. But it will be open to the co-Defendant, after he has been served with the notice, to move to set aside the service. TOWSE *v.* LOVERIDGE
[25 Ch. D. 76

9. —— **Indemnity**—*Non-admission of Liability — Application by Defendant for Directions — Liberty to appear at Trial—Rules of Court*, 1883, *Order* XVI., r. 48.] Where in an action for damages in respect of alleged injury to the Plaintiffs' premises, the Defendant, claiming to be entitled to indemnity over against a person not a party to the action, had served such person with a third-party notice under Order XVI., rule 48, and he had appeared thereto, the Court, upon a summons for directions taken out by the Defendant, gave the third party, who did not admit his liability, liberty to appear at the trial of the action and take such part as the Judge should direct, and be bound by the result, and ordered the question of his liability to indemnify the Defendant to be tried at the trial of the action but subsequent thereto.—In case a third party served with notice appears and admits his liability to indemnify, the Court will give him leave to defend the action.—Form of the order made. COLES *v.* CIVIL SERVICE. SUPPLY ASSOCIATION   -   - 26 Ch. D. 529

10. —— **Indemnity**—*Service out of Jurisdiction—Rules of Court*, 1883, *Order* XVI, r. 48; *Order* XI., r. 1 (g).] Where a Defendant is not entitled to claim contribution against a person not a party

VI. PRACTICE—SUPREME COURT—THIRD PARTY—*continued.*

to the action, he can only be entitled under Order XVI., rule 48, to issue a third-party notice to such person, where under a contract express or implied he is entitled to indemnity over against him.—Therefore, where the Defendants were sued for damages to the Plaintiffs' goods while on board a vessel of the Defendants on a certain voyage, by reason of the vessel being not seaworthy for the voyage, it was held by the Court of Appeal, that the Defendants were not entitled to a third-party notice under Order XVI., rule 48, to the persons of whom the Defendants had hired the vessel with a warranty that she was tight, staunch, strong, and fitted for the service.—By Order XI., rule 1, service out of the jurisdiction of a ... notice of a writ of summons may be allowed by the Court or a Judge whenever ... (*g*) any person out of the jurisdiction is a necessary or proper party to an action properly brought against some other person duly served within the jurisdiction:—*Held* (by the Queen's Bench Division), that Order XI., rule 1 (*g*), does not apply to service out of the jurisdiction of a third-party notice on a third party domiciled or ordinarily resident in Scotland. SPELLER & Co. *v.* BRISTOL STEAM NAVIGATION COMPANY

[13 Q. B. D. 96

—— Counter-claim by third party 28 Ch. D. 333
See PRACTICE — SUPREME COURT — COUNTER-CLAIM. 9.

VII. PRACTICE—SUPREME COURT—CHANGE OF PARTIES.

1. —— Bankruptcy of Defendant — *Making Trustee a Party to the Action—Rules of Court, 1875, Order L., r. 2.*] After issue joined in an action by the indorsees against the acceptor of a bill of exchange, in which the defence was that the Plaintiffs took the bill without value, and after notice that the Defendant had been defrauded of it, the Defendant who was a sole Defendant, filed a petition in liquidation, and a trustee was appointed. The Bankruptcy Court refused to restrain the action, but restrained the Plaintiffs from enforcing any 'judgment' they might obtain in the action either against the property or person of the debtor, and the trustee declined to admit the Plaintiff's claim:—*Held*, that the Bankruptcy Court was the proper Court in which Plaintiffs ought to prove their debt, and that there was no ground for making an order under Order L., rule 2, that the trustee be made a party to the action or be served with notice thereof. BARTER *v.* DUBEUX　　7 Q. B. D. 413

2. —— Bankruptcy of Defendant — *Trustee adopting Bankrupt's Defence — Costs.*] An interlocutory order for an injunction and receiver having been made against the Defendants in an action, they gave notice of appeal, and shortly afterwards became bankrupt. An order was made for carrying on the proceedings against their trustee. The trustee gave notice to the Plaintiff that he should not proceed with the appeal. Shortly after this the trustee entered an appearance and called for a statement of claim. He declined to undertake to pay the costs of the appeal incurred by the Plaintiff before the notice

VII. PRACTICE—SUPREME COURT—CHANGE OF PARTIES—*continued.*

that the appeal would not be proceeded with, and the appeal came on that the question as to the costs might be decided:—*Held*, that the appeal must be dismissed with costs to be paid by the trustee, for that having adopted the defence of the bankrupts he had placed himself in their position as to the whole of the action, and could not reject part of the proceedings in it. BORNEMAN *v.* WILSON　　　28 Ch. D. 53

3. —— Birth of Infant—*Rules of Court, 1883, Order XVII., rr. 4, 5—Carrying on Proceedings—Supplemental Action—Form of Order.*] Where proceedings have been taken in an action after it has become defective by the birth of an infant who is a necessary party thereto, the infant should be made a party by the common order under Rules of Supreme Court, 1883, Order XVII., rule 4, to carry on proceedings between the continuing parties and such infant; and the order (as in Seton (page 1527, Form 3)) should go on to direct an inquiry whether any proceedings affecting the interest of the infant have been taken in the action since his birth, and if so, whether it will be fit and proper and for the benefit of the infant that he should be bound thereby; and if so certified the infant to be bound accordingly.—If such inquiry be answered in the negative, the Plaintiff or person having the conduct can still proceed by supplemental action. PETER *v.* THOMAS-PETER 26 Ch. D. 181

4. —— Death of Party—*Order of Reference—Action for Tort—Death of Party before making of Award—Maxim, "Actio personalis moritur cum personâ."*] The parties to an action for a tort agreed before trial to refer the matter in dispute to an arbitrator. The order of reference contained a clause that the arbitrator should publish his award "ready to be delivered to the parties in difference, or such of them as require the same (or their respective personal representatives, if either of the said parties die before the making of the award)." After the hearing of the reference had been concluded, but before the award was made, the Plaintiff died. The arbitrator afterwards published the award, and the executors of the Plaintiff having proved his will, took up the award :—*Held*, that the cause of action being in tort died with the Plaintiff and did not pass to his personal representatives by force of the clause above mentioned, which in an action of tort was inoperative, and that the executors were not entitled to be substituted as Plaintiffs in place of their testator. BOWKER *v.* EVANS 15 Q. B. D. 565

5. —— Death of Party—*Revivor—Appeal—Rules of Court, 1875, Order L.*] A Defendant, P., gave notice of appeal from a judgment, and set it down. After this he died, and his executrix obtained an order of course at the Rolls that the appeal might be carried on and prosecuted by her in like manner as it might have been carried on and prosecuted by P. if he had not died.—*Held*, that the order was sufficient, and that the executrix was entitled to proceed with the appeal. RANSON *v.* PATTON　-　-　17 Ch. D. 767

6. —— Death of Party—*Revivor—Discretion of Court — Suit abated for more than Twenty*

VII. PRACTICE—SUPREME COURT—CHANGE OF PARTIES—*continued.*

Years—Rules of Court, 1875, *Order L.*] It is in the discretion of the Court whether it will allow an action which has become defective by the death of a party or otherwise, to be revived.—An administration suit in which a decree was made by the Court of Chancery in the year 1833, having become defective by the deaths of some parties and the bankruptcy of another, and no step having been taken in it for thirty-nine years, an order of revivor was allowed for the purpose of enabling a party to appeal from an order made in the year 1836 (in case the Court of Appeal should give leave to appeal), the Court being of opinion that no person had altered his position, or incurred any liability, or suffered any loss on the faith of the order from which it was desired to appeal. CURTIS *v.* SHEFFIELD　　　**20 Ch. D. 398**

7. —— Death of Party—*Revivor—Order of Course—Person attending Proceedings—Rules of Court,* 1875, *Order L.*] A person served with notice of an administration judgment, and having obtained liberty to attend the proceedings under it, is in the same position as a party to the action, and is entitled to obtain an order of course to revive the action on the death of the sole Plaintiff.—*Delaney* v. *Delaney* (27 Sol. J. 418) distinguished.—*Dobson* v. *Faithwaite* (30 Beav. 228) followed. BURSTALL *v.* FEARON　　**24 Ch. D. 126**

—— Death of Defendant who has delivered counter-claim—Revivor　　　**21 Ch. D. 175**
See PRACTICE—SUPREME COURT—COUNTER-CLAIM. 6.

VIII. PRACTICE — SUPREME COURT — CONDUCT OF CAUSE.

1. —— Concurrent Suits—*Bankrupt Administrator—Receiver.*] An action was commenced in the Court of one of the Vice-Chancellors for the administration of the estate of a testator, against the administrator with the will annexed. The administrator, being interested in that capacity in the estate of another testator, commenced an action for the administration of his estate in the Court of a different Vice-Chancellor, and then became bankrupt. The Plaintiff in the first suit moved in that suit that a receiver of the estate might be appointed, and that the Plaintiff might be permitted to prosecute the second action in the name of the administrator:—*Held,* that the Plaintiff was entitled to the order asked for, and that it was properly made in that Court to which the first action was attached.—In such a case it is not the modern practice to permit the receiver to carry on an action in the name of a bankrupt executor or administrator. *In re* HOPKINS. DOWD *v.* HAWTIN　　-　　-　　**19 Ch. D. 61**

2. —— Concurrent Suits — *Conduct of Proceedings—Stay of Proceedings—Lancaster Palatine Court.*] A judgment creditor of the Defendant brought an action in the Court of the County Palatine of Lancaster to obtain a declaration that he had a charge upon certain lands of the Defendant comprised in a certain deed of settlement, and to carry into effect the trusts of the settlement. He obtained judgment for a declaration of his charge, and for administration, inquiries,

VIII. PRACTICE — SUPREME COURT — CONDUCT OF CAUSE—*continued.*

and a receiver. Afterwards one of the beneficiaries under the settlement brought an action in the High Court to carry into effect the trusts of the settlement, and charging the trustees with a breach of trust. Judgment was obtained and inquiries directed, including one as to the breach of trust:—*Held,* that the Plaintiff in the Palatine action was not a stranger to the action in the High Court, and was entitled to the conduct of that action; and he undertaking to add the inquiry as to the breach of trust to the inquiry in the Palatine action, the Court stayed all proceedings in the action in the High Court. TOWNSEND *v.* TOWNSEND -　　**23 Ch. D. 100**

3. —— Concurrent Suits—*Lancaster Palatine Court.*] The general rule that where two actions have been commenced for the administration of the same estate the conduct of the proceedings will be given to the Plaintiff in the first action, although the decree in the second has been obtained first, applies to actions commenced in the Palatine Court of Lancaster, as well as to those commenced in the High Court of Justice. In considering whether the rule ought to be applied the Court will have regard to the special circumstances, and will take into account the amount of the interest of the Plaintiff in the first action, and his object in bringing his action. The fact of a plaintiff, being a stranger to the family, who had bought up the reversionary interests of some of the residuary legatees, *held,* not a sufficient reason for not giving him the conduct of the proceedings, although his purchase of some of the shares was disputed on the ground of inadequacy of consideration and undue influence.—The decision of Bacon, V.C., reversed. *In re* SWIRE. MELLOR *v.* SWIRE　　**21 Ch. D. 647**

4. —— First Action defective — *Action by Joint Creditors for Administration of Separate Estate of deceased Partner.*] A creditor of a partnership firm brought an administration action against the executor of a deceased partner. Afterwards a separate creditor of the same partner brought an administration action against the executor and obtained judgment: — *Held,* on an application by the Plaintiff in the first action for the conduct of the proceedings in the second action, that a joint creditor of a firm could not maintain a simple action for the administration of the estate of a deceased partner, and therefore that the first action was not properly constituted. The application of the Plaintiff was consequently refused.—Decision of Kay, J., affirmed. *In re* McRAE. FORSTER *v.* DAVIS. NORDEN *v.* McRAE　　　**[25 Ch. D. 16**

IX. PRACTICE—SUPREME COURT—DEFENCE.

—— Action for Recovery of Land—*Defence that Defendant is in possession of Land—Omission to deny Plaintiff's Title—Rules of Court,* 1875, *Order XLV., rr.* 15, 17.] In an action for the recovery of land a defence simply alleging that the Defendant is in possession thereof, operates as a denial of the Plaintiff s title and requires him to prove the truth of the allegations in the claim. DANFORD *v.* McANULTY　　　**6 Q. B. D. 645 ;**
[8 App. Cas. 456

X. PRACTICE—SUPREME COURT—COUNTER-CLAIM.

1. —— **Connection with the original Cause—** *Third Party—Judicature Act, 1873, s. 24, sub-s. 3, Rules of Court, 1875, Order XVI., r. 17.*] An action asking relief as in detinue was brought against a sole Defendant who had seized goods which B. had assigned to the Plaintiff under a bill of sale.—The sole Defendant filed a statement of defence and a counter-claim impeaching the bona fides of the Plaintiff's bill of sale, and alleging a bill of sale by B. to himself, and by such counter-claim claimed, (1) relief against the Plaintiff, and (2) as against B. the money due under the bill of sale from B to himself, and damages for the alleged fraud. The counter-claim against the Plaintiff was abandoned at the hearing:—*Held*, that the relief asked by the Defendant against B. was not a matter sufficiently " relating to or connected with the original cause or matter " to be the subject of a claim under sect. 24 of the Judicature Act, 1873. BARBER *v.* BLAIBERG
[19 Ch. D. 473

2. —— **Connection with the Original Cause—** *Rules of Court, 1875, Order XIX., r. 3; Order XXVII., r. 9; Order XXVII., r. 1.*] Order XIX., rule 3, is sufficiently general to allow a counter-claim by way of defence whether or not it is connected with or of the same character as the Plaintiff's claim, and whether it sounds in damages or not. —But the Court has a discretion to exclude a counter-claim which may unduly delay the action. GRAY *v.* WEBB　-　21 Ch. D. 802

3. —— **Counter-claim against Non-party—** *Service necessary before Defendant to Counter-claim can appear—Rules of Court, 1875, Order XXII., rr. 5, 6, 7.*] A person not a party to an action, when made a defendant to a counter-claim, is not entitled to enter an appearance gratis. FRASER *v.* COOPER HALL & Co. WADDELL *v.* FRASER
[23 Ch. D. 685

4. —— **Extent of Relief—** *Judicature Act, 1873 (36 & 37 Vict. c. 66), s. 24, sub-s. 3—Rules of Court, 1875, Order XIX., r. 3; Order XX., r. 1.*] Relief can be given on a counter-claim in respect of a cause of action accrued to the Defendant subsequently to the issue of the writ in the original action.—*Original Hartlepool Collieries Company* v. *Gibb* (5 Ch. D. 713) not followed.— *Semble*, that a counter-claim is an independent action and not part of the original action, though for convenience the two are tried together.— *Vavasseur* v. *Krupp.* (15 Ch. D. 474) questioned. BEDDALL *v.* MAITLAND　-　17 Ch. D. 174

5. —— **Recovery of Land—** *Joinder of other Cause of Action—Rules of Court, 1875, Order XVII., r. 2; Order XIX., r. 3; Order XXII., r. 9—Judicature Act, 1873 (36 & 37 Vict. c. 66), s. 24, sub-s. 3.*] The provision of rule 2 of Order XVII., that no cause of action, except those specified in that rule, shall, unless by leave of the Court, be joined with an action for the recovery of land, applies to a counter-claim. as well as to an original action. —Order made to exclude a counter-claim, on the ground that in it such a joinder of causes of action had been made without the leave of the Court, and that the fair trial of the action would be embarrassed. COMPTON *v.* PRESTON　21 Ch. D. 138

X. PRACTICE—SUPREME COURT—COUNTER-CLAIM—continued.

6. —— **Revivor—** *Rules of Court, 1875, Order XIV., r. 3; Order L.*] On the death of a Defendant who has delivered a counter-claim, it is necessary that his representatives, if they wish to prosecute the counter-claim against the Plaintiff in the original action, should obtain an order of revivor against him.—An order of revivor of the original action obtained by the Plaintiff against them does not authorize them to prosecute the counter-claim against him. ANDREW *v.* AITKEN　-　-　-　-　21 Ch. D. 175

7. —— **Set-off—** *Incumbents Resignation Act, 1871 (34 & 35 Vict. c. 44), s. 10.*] To a claim in an action brought to recover the arrears of a pension due by virtue of the Incumbents Resignation Act, 1871, the Defendant by way of set-off and counter-claim, pleaded that a larger sum than the amount of pension was due to him from the Plaintiff upon a judgment, and he claimed to recover the balance:—*Held*, by Baggallay, and Lush, L.JJ., that as there can be no set-off to a pension created under the Incumbents Resignation Act, 1871, the set-off and counter-claim must be dismissed.—By Bramwell, L.J., that the Plaintiff must have a judgment for the arrears of the pension owing to him, but that the Defendant was entitled to a separate and independent judgment for the amount due under the set-off and counter-claim. GATHERCOLE *v.* SMITH
[7 Q. B. D. 626

8. —— **Set-off—** *Rules of Court, 1875, Order XIX., r. 3.*] Rule 3 of Order XIX., Rules of Court, 1875, was not intended to give rights against third parties which did not exist before; but it is a rule of procedure designed to prevent the necessity of bringing a cross-action in all cases where the counter-claim may conveniently be tried in the original action. *In re* MILAN TRAMWAYS COMPANY. *Ex parte* THEYS 22 Ch. D. 122

9. —— **Third-party—** *Counter-claim by Third Party against Plaintiff — Rules of Court, 1883, Order XVI., rr. 48, 52, 53; Order XIX., r. 3.*] The Court has no power to give a third party who has been served with notice by a defendant under Order XVI., r. 48, leave to file a counter-claim against the original plaintiff. EDEN *v.* WEARDALE IRON AND COAL COMPANY　28 Ch. D. 333

—— Costs—Claim and counter-claim.
See Cases under PRACTICE — SUPREME COURT—COSTS. 10—13.

—— Counter-claim in reply　-　8 Q. B. D. 428
See PRACTICE—SUPREME COURT—REPLY. 1.

—— Discontinuance of action　11 Q. B. D. 464
See PRACTICE—SUPREME COURT — DISCONTINUANCE.

XI. PRACTICE—SUPREME COURT—REPLY.

1. —— **Counter-claim and Set-off in Reply—** *Judicature Act, 1873, s. 24, sub-ss. 3, 7—Rules of Court, 1875, Order XIX., rr. 3, 19; Order XX., r. 1.*] A Plaintiff may, in his reply to a counter-claim of the Defendant, counter-claim in respect of a cause of action accrued after the issue of the writ, but arising at the same time and out of the same transaction as the counter-claim of the Defendant. TOKE *v.* ANDREWS　8 Q. B. D. 428

XI. PRACTICE—SUPREME COURT—REPLY— *continued.*

2. —— Time—*Delivery of Reply after Time —Judgment on Admissions in Pleadings—Rules of Court*, 1875, *Order XXIX.*, r. 12—*Order XL.*, r. 11.] The Plaintiff delivered his reply after three weeks had elapsed from delivery of the statement of defence, and subsequently the Defendant, treating the facts stated in the defence as admitted, under Order XXIX., rule 12, by reason of the Plaintiff's failure to reply in time, gave notice of motion for judgment under Order XL., rule 11 :—*Held*, that, the reply having been actually delivered before the notice of motion was given, the Defendant was not entitled to judgment. GRAVES *v.* TERRY　　9 Q. B. D. 170

3. —— Time — *Leave to deliver Reply after Time—Rules of Court*, 1875, *Order XXIV.*, r. 1; *Order LVII.*, r. 6.] The time for delivering a reply which would have expired on the 25th of July was extended to the 22nd of August, and then to the 19th of September. On the 26th of September no reply having been delivered the Defendant served notice of motion for judgment. On the same day the Plaintiff, by leave of the Judge, served notice of motion for the following day for leave to deliver a reply, and on the 27th the Judge refused the Plaintiff's motion on the ground of unexplained delay :—*Held*, on appeal, that the application ought to have been granted, on the terms of the Plaintiff's paying the costs of it. EATON *v.* STORER　　-　　- 22 Ch. D. 91

XII. PRACTICE — SUPREME COURT — PAYMENT INTO COURT.

1. —— Acceptance by Defendant—*Discretion of Court—Rules of Court*, 1875, *Order XXX.*. rr. 1, 4 —*Order LV.*, r. 1.] Order XXX. applies only to an action which is strictly brought to recover a debt or damages.—If an account is claimed the order does not apply, and even if the Plaintiff accepts in satisfaction of his whole cause of action a sum paid into Court by the Defendant, the Court has a discretion as to the costs. NICHOLS *v.* EVENS　　22 Ch. D. 611

2. —— Admission—*Evidence.*] Trust funds may be ordered to be brought into Court by the trustee, an accounting party, upon admissions contained in letters written before action brought that he has received the money, and a recital to that effect contained in the settlement, his execution of which as trustee has been proved, although there is no formal admission in his pleadings or affidavits that he has received and holds the money. HAMPDEN *v.* WALLIS
[27 Ch. D. 251

3. —— Denial of Liability—*Action for several Breaches of Contract—Payment into Court in respect of One Breach—Acceptance in Satisfaction of all Demands — Rules of Court*, 1883, *Order XXII.*, rr. 6, 7.] In an action for breach of contract assigning two distinct breaches, the Defendants pleaded denying the breaches, and alternatively paid money into Court with regard to one of the breaches. The Plaintiffs gave notice under Order XXII., r. 7, that they accepted the money paid into Court in full satisfaction of the causes of action in the statement of claim :—*Held*, that the Plaintiffs were entitled,

XII. PRACTICE — SUPREME COURT — PAYMENT INTO COURT—*continued.*

without proceeding to judgment, to their costs of the action; for by accepting the money paid into Court in satisfaction of all their alleged causes of action they had in effect discontinued or withdrawn the action as to the breach, in respect of which the money was not paid in.—Decision of the Queen's Bench Division affirmed. M'ILWRAITH *v.* GREEN　　13 Q. B. D. 997 ; 14 Q. B. D. 766

4. —— Denial of Liability—*Rules of Supreme Court*, 1875, *Order XXX.*, r. 1 — *Payment into Court without admitting Liability.*] Where the Defendant succeeds at the trial on an issue on money paid into Court under Order XXX., rule 1, of the Rules of 1875, with a defence stating such payment as an alternative defence to the action, he is entitled to have judgment entered for him in the action.—In an action for trespass in breaking and entering the Plaintiff's land, the Defendants paid money into Court under Order XXX., rule 1, of the Rules of 1875. and in their defence denied the Plaintiff's possession of the land, and also stated that without admitting any kind of liability the sum paid into Court was sufficient to satisfy any damage which the Plaintiff might have sustained in consequence of any acts of theirs. The Plaintiff joined issue upon these defences, but failed at the trial to establish any damages exceeding the sum paid into Court, though he succeeded on the other issue. The Court of Appeal treated such defence of payment into Court as an alternative payment, and as it went to the whole cause of action :—*Held*, reversing the decision of Williams, J., that the Defendants were entitled to judgment. WHEELER *v.* UNITED TELEPHONE COMPANY 13 Q. B. D. 597
[*See also* GOTTARD *v.* CARR, 13 Q. B. D. 598, n.]

5. —— Investment of Money in Court—*Cash under Control of the Court—Money paid under Lands Clauses Act*, 1845 (8 & 9 Vict. c. 18)—*Law of Property Act*, 1860 (25 & 24 Vict. c. 38), s. 10—*General Order, Feb.* 1, 1861.] Money paid into Court under the Lands Clauses Act is "cash under the control of the Court" within the meaning of the Act 23 & 24 Vict. c. 38, s. 10, and the General Order of the 1st of February, 1861, and may be invested in any of the securities sanctioned by the Court. The expression "cash under the control of the Court" means cash standing in Court in any cause or matter.—*In re Boyd's Settled Estates* (21 W. R. 667) overruled.—Cash under the control of the Court may be invested in East India 3½ per cent. Stock created since the date of the General Order. *Ex parte* ST. JOHN BAPTIST COLLEGE, OXFORD. *In re* METROPOLITAN AND DISTRICT RAILWAYS ACT
[22 Ch. D. 93

6. —— Order to pay Plaintiff *instead of paying into Court—Appeal—Service on Solicitor—Continuance of Authority of Solicitor.*] By order on further consideration the Defendant was ordered to pay money into Court, which was then to be carried to the credit of an action for administering the estate of a testator whose executrix was the Plaintiff in the present action. The Defendant went abroad without complying with the order. On appeal the order was varied by ordering the Defendant to pay the money to

XII. PRACTICE — SUPREME COURT — PAYMENT INTO COURT—*continued.*

the Plaintiff, who was then to pay it into Court in the administration action, such an order being capable of being better enforced against the Defendant's property than the order as originally framed.—The notice of appeal was served on the Defendant's solicitors, who stated that they had ceased to act for him, but they were still his solicitors on the record :—*Held*, that as the order on further consideration had not been worked out, they still represented him, and that service of the notice on them was good service.—Whether the solicitors on the record do not continue to represent their client until the expiration of the time allowed for appealing, *quære.* LADY DE LA POLE *v.* DICK　-　　-　　- 29 Ch. D. 351

XIII. PRACTICE — SUPREME COURT — PAYMENT OUT OF COURT.

—— **Probate**—*Petitioner entitled under Will —New Zealand—English Probate necessary.*] A Petitioner asked for payment out of Court of money to which he was entitled under an appointment by will :—*Held*, that probate of the will in the Supreme Court of New Zealand was not sufficient for this Court to act upon, but the will must be proved in England. *Ex parte* LIMEHOUSE BOARD OF WORKS. *In re* VALLANCE
[24 Ch. D. 177

—— Lands Clauses Act.
　　See Cases under PRACTICE—SUPREME COURT—CHAMBERS. 11—16.

XIV. PRACTICE—SUPREME COURT—DEMURRER (and POINT OF LAW).

　1. —— **Demurrer for want of Parties**—*Rules of Court, 1875, Order XXVIII., r. 1.*] Under the practice established by the Judicature Acts a demurrer for want of parties will not lie. WERDERMAN *v.* SOCIÉTÉ GÉNÉRALE D'ÉLECTRICITÉ
[19 Ch. D. 246

　2. —— **Form of General Demurrer**—*Rules of Court, 1875, Order XXVIII., r. 2.*] The equity in a statement of claim was not apparent, but had to be collected from a long and complicated series of facts. A Defendant put in a general demurrer on the ground "that the facts alleged do not shew any cause of action to which effect can be given as against this Defendant" :—*Held* (affirming the decision of Kay, J.), that notwithstanding Order XXVIII., rule 2, a demurrer in this form was in such a case sufficient. BIDDER *v.* MCLEAN -　　　-　　　20 Ch. D. 512

　3. —— **Point of Law**—*Proceedings in lieu of Demurrer* — *Disposal of Action* — *Rules of Court, 1883, Order XXV., rr. 1, 2, 3.*] An action having been by the consent of the parties set down for hearing under Rules of Supreme Court, 1883, Order XXV., rule 2, upon a "point of law" raised by the defence, and the point having been decided in favour of the Defendant, the Judge, as the decision substantially disposed of the whole action, dismissed the action under rule 3, and with costs, by analogy to the former practice on demurrer. O'BRIEN *v.* TYSSEN
[28 Ch. D. 372

　4. —— **Point of Law**—*Disposal of Action— Rules of Court, 1883, Order XXV., rr. 2, 3.*]

XIV. PRACTICE—SUPREME COURT—DEMURRER (and POINT OF LAW)—*continued.*
The decision of the Judge on a "point of law" raised in an action under Rules of Supreme Court, 1883, Order XXV., rule 2, having substantially disposed of the whole action, the action was, under rule 2, dismissed with costs. PERCIVAL *v.* DUNN　　　-　　　-　　- 29 Ch. D. 128

—— Cross-demurrers—Right to begin
[7 Q. B. D. 38
　　See PRACTICE — SUPREME COURT—APPEAL. 10.

—— Notice in lieu of claim　　　10 Q. B. D. 516
　　See PRACTICE—SUPREME COURT—WRIT SPECIALLY INDORSED. 1.

XV. PRACTICE — SUPREME COURT — PARTICULARS.

　1. —— **Claim for definite Sum.**] Where a Plaintiff claims to recover a definite sum made up of a number of items he will be ordered to give particulars of demand, though he will not be ordered to do so if he only claims an account.— The Plaintiffs by their statement of claim alleged that they and their testator had paid sums of money under a contract of suretyship under which the Defendant was also liable, and that, after deducting contributions received from other quarters, the balance paid by them was £16,233 ; that the Defendant had paid nothing, and was liable to pay to the Plaintiffs one half of this balance, and the Plaintiffs claimed payment of £8116. The Defendant, before putting in his defence, applied for an order that the Plaintiffs might give particulars of the sums making up the £16,233. The application was refused by Mr. Justice Pearson :—*Held*, on appeal, that, as the Plaintiffs did not ask merely for an account, but claimed payment of a definite sum, they must give particulars of demand. BLACKIE *v.* OSMASTON
[28 Ch. D. 119

　2. —— **Defamation**—*Slander*—*Particulars of Persons to whom Slander was uttered.*] A statement of claim alleged that T., "at the request and by the direction of the Defendant, falsely and maliciously spoke and published of and concerning the Plaintiff" certain slanderous words, which were set out :—*Held*, that the Defendant was entitled to particulars of the persons to whom the words were uttered. BRADBURY *v.* COOPER
[12 Q. B. D. 94

　3. —— **Equitable Claim.**] The administratrix of A.. by statement of claim in an action against the administratrix of G., alleged that an arrangement had been made between A. and G. that sums contributed by them for the purpose of being lent to or applied for the benefit of C., to enable him to carry on a litigation, should be treated as a joint transaction, and that as soon as C. had established his title to the property for which he was suing, and could repay the advances made him, the advances made by A. and G. should be repaid out of the moneys recovered from him ; that during the litigation A. advanced, in pursuance of this arrangement, sums amounting to about £27,000 ; that the advances made to C. were made through G. and in his name ; that the Defendant had recovered a judgment against C. for the advances to him, and that a sum had been

XV. PRACTICE—SUPREME COURT—PARTI-CULARS—continued.

set apart in a suit in Chancery in satisfaction of this judgment. The Plaintiff claimed that it might be declared that the loans by G., in respect of which the judgment was recovered, were trans-actions for the joint benefit of A. and G. as part-ners, and to have the sums contributed by them respectively ascertained; and asked that the Plaintiff might be declared entitled to a share in the benefit of the judgment, and in the fund set aside to satisfy it. The Defendant, before putting in a defence, applied for an account with dates and items of the particulars of the £27,000 mentioned in the statement of claim, and Pol-lock, B., made an order accordingly :—*Held*, on appeal, that the action not being a mere legal demand for an ascertained sum, but an equitable claim for an amount to be ascertained by an ac-count, the particulars asked for were not required to enable the Defendant to frame her defence, and that the Plaintiff ought not to be ordered to furnish them. AUGUSTINUS *v.* NERINCKX

[16 Ch. D. 13

XVI. PRACTICE — SUPREME COURT—STRIK-ING OUT PLEADINGS.

1. —— Breach of Promise of Marriage—*Spe-cial Damage—Matter of Aggravation—Averment of—Rules of Court,* 1875, *Order XIX.,* r. 4 ; *Order XXVII.,* r. 1.] A statement of claim, after alleging a promise by the Defendant to marry the Plain-tiff, went on to allege in paragraph 4, that, " the Plaintiff relying upon the said promise permitted the Defendant to debauch and carnally know her, whereby the Defendant infected her with a venereal disease." It then alleged a breach of the said promise. An order having been made at chambers to strike out paragraph 4 of the claim : —*Held*, reversing the decision of the Common Pleas Division, that the order was wrongly made, and upon two grounds; first, that the facts alleged in the paragraph complained of, were " material facts" within the meaning of Order XIX., rule 4, and as such were properly plead-able ; and secondly, that, even if they were not, the Court had no power to strike the paragraph out, the statements therein neither being scan-dalous nor tending to prejudice or embarrass the fair trial of the action within the meaning of Order XXVII., rule 1. MILLINGTON *v.* LORING

[6 Q. B. D. 190

2. —— Covenants in a Lease—*Statement of Claim—Title to Reversion—Pleading tending to embarrass — Rules of Court,* 1883, *Order XIX.,* rr. 4, 27.] In an action upon covenants in an expired lease, the Plaintiff stated the lease, that the term had expired, that at its expiration the Defendants were the assigns of the lease, and liable to perform the lessee's covenants, that the Plaintiff became, and at the expiration of the term was entitled to the immediate reversion in the demised property, subject only to the term that he was and is entitled to enforce all the lessee's covenants, and that the Defendants had for eight years paid him rent :—*Held*, such plead-ing was insufficient, and that the Plaintiff ought also to have shewn what the reversion was which the lessor had, and how the Plaintiff derived his title to that particular reversion.—Accordingly a

XVI. PRACTICE—SUPREME COURT—STRIK-ING OUT PLEADINGS—continued.

statement of claim containing the statements so held to be insufficient was ordered to be struck out under Order XIX., rule 27, as a pleading tend-ing to embarrass the fair trial of the action.— *Philipps* v. *Philipps* (4 Q. B. D. 127) followed. DAVIS *v.* JAMES - 26 Ch. D. 778

3. —— Prolixity—*Affidavit—Rules of Court,* 1883, *Order XXXVIII.,* r. 11 ; *Order LXV.,* r. 27, *sub-s.* 20.] Although there is no rule of Court specially giving power to the Court to take plead-ings or affidavits off the file for prolixity, yet the Court has an inherent power to do so in order to prevent its records from being made the instru-ments of oppression. Where however an affidavit of documents was of oppressive length, but it appeared to the Court that delay and expense would be caused by filing a fresh one, the Court permitted it to remain on the file but ordered the party filing it to pay the costs of it. HILL *v.* HART-DAVIS 26 Ch. D. 470

—— Affidavit of documents—Prolixity

[21 Ch. D. 835

See PRACTICE—SUPREME COURT—PRO-DUCTION OF DOCUMENTS. 1.

XVII. PRACTICE—SUPREME COURT—DISCON-TINUANCE.

—— Counter-claim — *Rules of Court,* 1875, *Order XIX.,* r. 3 ; *Order XXIII.,* r. 1.] By dis-continuing an action after a counter-claim has been delivered, a Plaintiff cannot put an end to it so as to prevent the Defendant from enforcing against him the causes of action contained in the counter-claim.—*Vavasseur* v. *Krupp* (15 Ch. D. 474) overruled. McGOWAN *v.* MIDDLETON

[11 Q. B. D. 464

XVIII. PRACTICE—SUPREME COURT—STAY-ING PROCEEDINGS.

(a.) GENERAL.

1. —— Bankruptcy of Plaintiff—*Refusal of Trustee to proceed with Action.*] Where the Plain-tiff is adjudicated bankrupt after action brought and his trustee declines to proceed with the action, it may be stayed by an order in Chambers, and the Defendant need not plead the bankruptcy in bar. WARDER *v.* SAUNDERS 10 Q. B. D. 114

2. —— Payment of Costs—*Interlocutory Pro-ceeding—Order for Payment—Default of Payment.*] The Plaintiff obtained a verdict in an action, and the Queen's Bench Division having refused to grant a rule nisi for a new trial, the Defendant obtained a rule absolute in the Court of Appeal. By the rule the Plaintiff was ordered to pay the costs of the applications, which he failed to do :— *Held* by Mathew and Cave, JJ., that the Defen-dant was not entitled to an order to stay the pro-ceedings until the costs were paid. MORTON *v.* PALMER - 9 Q. B. D. 89

3. —— Probate of Will—*Action by Execu-tors.*] A testatrix having indorsed and delivered a bill of exchange to her bankers for collection at maturity, died before the bill became due, and her executors, before probate of the will was granted, sued the bankers for a return of the bill or its value. The Defendants were always will-ing to pay over the proceeds of the bill to the

XVIII. PRACTICE—SUPREME COURT—STAY-
ING PROCEEDINGS—*continued.*

(a.) GENERAL—*continued.*

Plaintiffs upon production of probate :—*Held*, that
all proceedings in the action ought to be stayed
until the Plaintiffs obtained probate.—*Webb* v.
Adkins (14 C. B. 401; 23 L. J. (C. P.) 96) followed. TARN v. COMMERCIAL BANKING COMPANY
OF SYDNEY　　-　　-　　12 Q. B. D. 294

4. —— Reference to Arbitration—*Railways
Passengers Assurance Company's Act*, 1864 (27 &
28 *Vict. c. cxxv.*] By the Act regulating an insurance company it was provided that any question arising under any policy should, if either the
company or the assured or the representatives of
the assured required it, be referred to arbitration
under the Act, and it was provided that if a
policy-holder or his representatives commenced
any action a Judge might, on the application of the
company " upon being satisfied that no sufficient
reason exists why the matter cannot be or ought
not to be referred to arbitration " stay proceedings in the action. An action having been commenced by the representatives of the policy-holder
to recover the sum assured, the company disputing their liability, the company obtained an order
to stay proceedings in the action in order that
the dispute might be referred to arbitration :—
Held, that the burden lay on the Plaintiffs to shew
that some sufficient reason existed why the dispute should not be referred to arbitration, and
not on the company to shew that no such reason
existed, and that as no such reason had been shewn
the order to stay proceedings was right. HODGSON
v. RAILWAY PASSENGERS ASSURANCE COMPANY
[9 Q. B. D. 188

(b.) CONCURRENT ACTIONS.

5. —— Burden of Proof — *Order directing
that One of Two Cross Actions be stayed, and
that a Counter-claim be delivered in the other
—Supreme Court of Judicature Act*, 1873 (36 & 37
Vict. c. 66), s. 24, *sub-s.* 7.] When an order is
made under the Supreme Court of Judicature
Act, 1873, sect. 24, sub-sect. 7, to stay one of
two cross actions between the same parties arising out of the same matter, the action brought
against the party on whom the burden of proof
lies ought to be stayed, and the action brought
by him ought to be allowed to proceed, the other
party to the litigation being at liberty to raise by
defence, set-off, and counter-claim, all questions
intended to be raised by him in the action which
is stayed.—In an action, commenced on the 28th
of November, 1881, the Plaintiffs, Messrs. T.,
claimed £7000, the balance of the price of a
steamship built by them for the Defendants, a
railway company, and certain other sums as
extras; in a cross-action, commenced on the
30th of November, 1881, the railway company
as Plaintiffs claimed a return of all the moneys
paid by them to Messrs. T. on account of the
steamship and £15,000 damages, and in the alternative £50,000 damages. Upon the facts the
burden of proof lay upon the railway company.
The Queen's Bench Division ordered that the
action brought by the railway company should
be stayed, with liberty to raise their claim by
way of counter-claim in the action brought by
Messrs. T., on the ground that Messrs. T. had

XVIII. PRACTICE—SUPREME COURT—STAY-
ING PROCEEDINGS—*continued.*

(b.) CONCURRENT ACTIONS—*continued.*

been the first to commence legal proceedings :—
Held, reversing the decision of the Queen's Bench
Division, that as the burden of proof lay upon
the railway company, the action brought by the
railway company should be allowed to proceed,
Messrs. T. being at liberty to raise all questions
by counter-claim, and that the action brought by
Messrs. T. should be stayed. THOMSON v. SOUTH
EASTERN RAILWAY COMPANY. SOUTH EASTERN
RAILWAY COMPANY v. THOMSON　　9 Q. B. D. 320

6. —— English and Foreign Actions—*Two
Actions in this Country—Action in Foreign Country—Lis alibi pendens.*] When a Plaintiff sues a
Defendant for the same matter in two Courts in
this country, such a proceeding is primâ facie
vexatious, and the Court will generally, as of
course, put the Plaintiff to his election and stay
one of the suits. And the same principle applies
where one of the actions is in the Queen's Courts
in Scotland or Ireland, or any other part of the
Queen's dominions. Under the present practice
Lord Dillon v. *Alvares* (4 Ves. 357) cannot be
relied on as an authority. But if one of the
actions is in a foreign country where there are
different forms of procedure and different remedies, there is no presumption that the multiplicity
of actions is vexatious, and a special case must
be made out to induce the Court to interfere.
The Court has, however, power to interfere in
such a case under its general jurisdiction to restrain vexatious and oppressive litigation, and
will interfere in a proper case even before decree.
—And *semble.* after a decree has been made in
one of the actions, the Court will be more willing
to exercise its jurisdiction.—*Cox* v. *Mitchell* (7
C. B. (N.S.) 55) considered. MCHENRY v. LEWIS
[21 Ch. D. 202; 22 Ch. D. 397

7. —— English and Foreign Actions—*Election.*] An action was brought in this Court by
an English company against a firm of French
merchants for the delivery of the cargoes of certain
ships, or in the alternative for damages, and for
an injunction and receiver.—At the commencement of the action the ships were in British
waters, but they had since been removed by the
direction of the Defendants to ports in France, and
the cargoes had been taken possession of by the
Defendants. Proceedings had been instituted by
the Plaintiffs in a French Court for recovery of
the cargoes. The English action comprised a
claim for the cargo of one ship which was not
claimed in the French action.—A motion on
behalf of the Defendants, that the Plaintiffs
might be ordered to elect whether they would
proceed with the English action or with the
French proceedings was refused. PERUVIAN
GUANO COMPANY v. BOCKWOLDT　　23 Ch. D. 225

8. —— English and Foreign Actions.] B., resident in San Francisco, brought an action against
C. in England alleging that C. had been B.'s
agent to purchase for him goods in England, that
B. had recently discovered that C. had in the
accounts rendered charged more for the goods than
he had paid for them, and asking for an account
against C. as agent. C., by his statement of defence
denied agency, alleged that he had as principal

XVIII. PRACTICE—SUPREME COURT—STAY-
ING PROCEEDINGS—*continued.*

(b.) CONCURRENT ACTIONS—*continued.*

sold the goods to B., insisted on the accounts rendered as settled accounts, and alleged that a large balance was due. C. then commenced an action in San Francisco against B. to recover the amount which he so alleged to be due. B. moved to restrain this action :—*Held*, by Chitty, J., and by the Court of Appeal, that the action ought not to be restrained, for that there was no primâ facie inference that the bringing the action abroad, during the pendency of an action in England in which the matters in dispute could be determined, was vexatious, since the course of procedure in San Francisco might be such as to give advantages to C. of which he was entitled to avail himself, and that the burden lay on B. to prove that C.'s action was vexatious, which he had failed to do. HYMAN *v.* HELM   -   -   - **24 Ch. D. 531**

9. —— **Payment of Costs**—*Second Suit for same Matter—Costs of former Suit.*] A bill for an account of the personal estate of W. J., an intestate, was filed by the legal personal representative of E. B. against the personal representatives of the deceased administrators of W. J., alleging that the administrators of W. J. had got in the greater part of the estate, and that E. B. was the sole next of kin. The suit was revived in 1877 by M., a subsequent personal representative of E. B., against X. and Y., as representatives of one of the administrators, and Z., as representative of the others, and was ultimately dismissed in 1880 with costs as against all three Defendants on the ground that the title of E. B. as next of kin was not proved. After this M. took out administration de bonis non to W. J., and brought his action as such administrator against Z. for an account of the personal estate of W. J. received by the administrators whom Z. represented :—*Held* (affirming the decision of Pearson, J.), that although M. formerly sued as personal representative of E. B., and now sued as personal representative of W. J., the action was in substance a second proceeding for the same matter under the same alleged title, and that proceedings must be stayed until the costs of the old suit had been paid.   MARTIN *v.* EARL BEAUCHAMP   -   - **25 Ch. D. 12**

10. —— **Two Actions by Married Woman—** *Next Friend—Costs in Former Action by a different Next Friend not paid.*] An action was brought by a married woman by her next friend, and an order was made that the next friend should give security for costs on the ground of poverty. That order not having been complied with the action was dismissed with costs. Afterwards the Plaintiff by a different next friend brought another action for the same purpose :—*Held* (reversing the decision of Bacon, V.C.), that the second action ought to be stayed till the costs of the first action were paid.—*Hind* v. *Whitmore* (2 K. & J. 458) not followed. *In re* PAYNE. RANDLE *v.* PAYNE   **23 Ch. D. 288**

(c.) PENDING APPEAL.

11. —— **Action dismissed**—*Rules of Court,* 1875, *Order* LVIII., rr. 16, 17.] Where an action has been dismissed with costs, an application to

XVIII. PRACTICE—SUPREME COURT—STAY-
ING PROCEEDINGS—*continued.*

(c.) PENDING APPEAL—*continued.*

stay proceedings for costs pending an appeal must be made in the first instance to the Court below and not to the Court of Appeal.—*Wilson* v. *Church* (11 Ch. D. 576) explained.   OTTO *v.* LINDFORD
[18 Ch. D. 394

12. —— **Appeal to House of Lords**—*Stay of Execution—No Special Grounds alleged.*] Execution for costs pending an appeal from the Court of Appeal to the House of Lords will not be stayed, unless evidence be adduced to shew that the Respondent to the appeal will be unable to repay the amount levied by execution, if the Appellant be successful before the House of Lords   BARKER *v.* LAVERY   **14 Q. B. D. 769**

13. —— **Costs of Sale and Reinvestment**—*Interest.*] An order was made by the Court of Appeal directing a sum of Consols in Court to be sold and the proceeds paid to B. Y. appealed to the House of Lords and after sale but before payment out applied to stay proceedings pending the appeal, asking to have the proceeds of the sale of the fund reinvested and retained in Court :—*Held*, that, as a condition of obtaining the order, Y. must undertake that in case his appeal was unsuccessful, he would make good the difference between the income actually produced by the fund and interest at £4 per cent. per annum, and would also pay the costs of the sale and reinvestment.   BREWER *v.* YORKE.   YORKE *v.* BREWER
[20 Ch. D. 669

14. —— **Payment of Fund out of Court—** *Rules of Court,* 1883, *Order* LVIII., r. 16.] In the absence of special circumstances it is not the practice of the Court to retain in Court pending an appeal a fund which has been ordered to be paid out, because there is an appeal from the order.—An order directing the payment of a fund out of Court to the Plaintiff having been made just before the commencement of the Long Vacation, and an appeal having been presented, a suspension of the payment out was granted over the Long Vacation, in order to enable the Appellant to apply to the Court of Appeal.—*Wilson* v. *Church* (12 Ch. D. 454) and *Walburn* v. *Ingilby* (1 My. & K. 79) considered.—On appeal, it being shewn that the Plaintiff had been abroad for two years, and that the applicant could not discover his address, it was held that payment out ought to be stayed if the applicant would give security to pay to the Plaintiff interest at £4 per cent. on the present value of the funds in Court, and to make good to the Plaintiff, if the appeal was unsuccessful, the difference between the highest market price of the investments at any time before the hearing of the appeal and their market price on the day of the hearing of the appeal.   BRADFORD *v.* YOUNG.   *In re* FALCONAR'S TRUSTS
[28 Ch. D. 18

15. —— **Refusal by Court below to stay—** *Time within which Application may be made to Court of Appeal—Rules of Court,* 1875, *Order* LVIII., rr. 16, 17.] In an action by patentees judgment was given referring it to the official referee to assess the damages occasioned to the Plaintiffs by the Defendants' infringement, and ordering

XVIII. PRACTICE—SUPREME COURT—STAYING PROCEEDINGS—continued.

(c.). PENDING APPEAL—continued.

payment within twenty-one days after service of the report. The Defendants appealed, and set down their appeal on the 18th of April, and then moved to stay proceedings under the judgment pending the appeal. This was refused by Chitty, J. On the 25th of June, the official referee made his report, and on the 14th of July, more than twenty-one days after the above refusal, the Defendants gave notice of motion before the Court of Appeal that the time for payment of the damages might be extended till after the hearing of the appeal. The Plaintiffs took the objection that the application could not be made as an original motion, and as an appeal motion was out of time :—Held, that Order LVIII., r. 16, gives concurrent jurisdiction to the Court below and to the Court of Appeal as to staying proceedings pending an appeal; that rule 17 does not take away any of the jurisdiction thus given to the Court of Appeal, but only requires that it shall not be exercised till an application has first been made to the Court below, and that the application to the Court of Appeal to stay proceedings when an order for that purpose has been refused by the Court below, is not properly an appeal motion, and need not be brought within twenty-one days from the refusal. — *Attorney-General v. Swansea Improvements and Tramways Company* (9. Ch. D. 46) considered. CROPPER *v.* SMITH　　-　　24 Ch. D. 305

16. —— Trial of Issue of Fact—*Appeal on Question of Law—Rules of Court, 1875, Order LVIII., r. 18.*] Where a question of law has been decided on demurrer, or on a preliminary objection, and an appeal has been brought, the Court will not in general stay the trial of the issues of fact pending the appeal. *In re* J. B. PALMER's APPLICATION. *In re* TRADE-MARKS REGISTRATION ACT, 1875　　-　　22 Ch. D. 88

XIX. PRACTICE — SUPREME COURT — DEFAULT.

1. —— Appeal—*Rules of Court, 1883, Order XXXVI., r. 33.*] Although the Court of Appeal has jurisdiction to hear a direct appeal from a judgment by default, such appeals will not be encouraged. The proper course for a party against whom judgment has been given by default is to apply to the Judge who heard the cause to set aside the judgment and to re-hear the cause. VINT *v.* HUDSPITH　　-　　29 Ch. D. 322

2. —— Counter-claim—*Motion for Judgment —Rules of Court, 1883, Order XXIII., r. 4; Order XXVII., rr. 11, 12.*] Order XXIII., rule 4, and Order XXVII., rules 11, 12, of the Rules of 1883, apply when a motion for judgment in default of pleading is made after, although the default itself was made before, they came into operation.—And these rules apply to a case where a Defendant to a counter-claim has made default in pleading to it, and entitle the Plaintiff in the counter-claim to move for judgment against the defaulting Defendant. STREET *v.* CRUMP　　-　　25 Ch. D. 68

3. —— Defence delivered after Time—*Rules of Court, 1875, Order XXIX., rr. 10, 14—Rules of Court, 1883, Order XXVII., 11, 15.*] S. gave to G. a charge upon costs due from B. to S. G.

XIX. PRACTICE — SUPREME COURT — DEFAULT—continued.

brought his action against S. and B., asking for an account and foreclosure against S., and that B. might be ordered to pay the amount of the bill of costs, £359, into Court. The time for delivering defence was enlarged from the 1st of August to the 16th of August, 1882. No defence having been delivered, notice of motion for judgment was served on the 18th of November. On the second of December B. took out a summons for leave to deliver defence, which was dismissed on the 6th. The defence which he proposed to put in alleged that there were other dealings between B. and S., and that no substantial part of the bill of costs was due, and moreover that B. was going to have the bill taxed. On the 19th of February, 1883, the motion for judgment came on for hearing. The Court refused to look at the defence, and gave a judgment directing an account against S., and ordering B. to bring the £359 into Court. B. appealed.—Held, that on motion for judgment for want of defence, if a defence has been put in, though irregularly, the Court will not disregard it, but will see whether it sets up grounds of defence which, if proved, will be material, and if so, will deal with the case in such manner that justice can be done; and that in the present case the order for bringing the £359 into Court must be discharged, and an account directed of what was due from B. to S. in respect of the bill of costs. GIBBINGS *v.* STRONG [26 Ch. D. 66

4. —— Defence delivered after Time—*Rules of Court, 1875, Order XXIX., r. 10—Amendment of Notice of Motion by Court of Appeal—Rules of Court, 1883, Order LVIII., r. 4.*], A Defendant made default in putting in a statement of defence under Order XXIX., r. 10 (1875), and the Plaintiff gave notice of motion for judgment in default of defence. But before the motion was heard the Defendant put in a statement of defence :—Held, that the statement of defence, though put in after time, could not be treated as a nullity, and that the Plaintiff was not entitled to judgment in default of defence.—But as the statement of defence disclosed no real defence to the action, the Court of Appeal ordered the notice of motion to be amended and judgment to be given for the Plaintiff on the admissions in the statement of defence. GILL *v.* WOODFIN [25 Ch. D. 707

5. —— Dismissal for want of Prosecution—*Appeal from Order—Power to enlarge Time—Rules of Court, 1875, Order LVII., r. 6.*] A Judge has jurisdiction under Order LVII., rule 6, to enlarge the time for appealing against an order dismissing the action for want of prosecution, even after the order has taken effect and the action has therefore become dismissed; and he has also jurisdiction when he has so enlarged the time for appealing to vary or amend the order dismissing the action, and in the exercise of such jurisdiction his discretion is not limited by any fixed or arbitrary rules. CARTER *v.* STUBBS　6 Q. B. D. 116

6. —— Dismissal for want of Prosecution—*Motion—Affidavit of Service.*] An order dismissing an action for want of prosecution was made subject to production of an affidavit of service, no

XIX. PRACTICE — SUPREME COURT — DEFAULT—*continued.*

one appearing for the Plaintiff. Shortly afterwards counsel appeared for the Plaintiff, but the Judge refused to have the case argued. No affidavit of service was sworn or filed until after the day on which the motion was made. The Registrar drew up the order on production of an office copy of an affidavit of service sworn and filed after that day, omitting in the order the date of the affidavit. It appears that since the passing of the Judicature Acts the rule in *Lord Milltown* v. *Stuart* (8 Sim. 34) had not been uniformly observed by the Registrars :—*Held*, that, assuming the drawing up of the order on an affidavit sworn and filed after the day on which the motion was made to be irregular, the irregularity was not such that the Court ought on that ground to discharge the order. SEEAR *v.* WEBB - - **25 Ch. D. 84**

7. —— **Dismissal for want of Prosecution—** *Notice of Trial given, but Trial not entered—Rules of Court*, 1883, *Order XXXVI.*, *rr.* 12, 16.] A Plaintiff gave notice of trial (in Middlesex) within the six weeks limited by rule 12 of Order XXXVI.; but did not, as required by rule 16, enter the trial within six days after the notice of trial was given. The trial not having been entered :—*Held*, that the Defendant was entitled to move to dismiss for want of prosecution, and an order dismissing the action was accordingly made. CRICK *v.* HEWLETT
[**27 Ch. D. 354**]

8. —— **Reply—***Effect of non-delivery of Judgment on Admissions in Pleadings—Counter-claim —Rules of Court*, 1875, *Order XXIX.*, r. 12 ; *Order XL.*, r. 11.] The Plaintiff having made default in delivery of reply to Defendant's statement of defence and counter-claim :—The Court ordered final judgment to be entered for the Defendant in respect of both the claim and counter-claim under Order XL., rule 11. LUMSDEN *v.* WINTER
[**8 Q. B. D. 650**]

XX. PRACTICE—SUPREME COURT—AMENDMENT.

1. —— **Embarrassing Statement of Claim—** *Right of Way—Rules of Court*, 1875, *Order XXVII.*, r. 1.] In an action to restrain the obstruction of an alleged private right of way, the Plaintiff ought to shew in his statement of claim whether he claims the right by prescription or by grant.—He ought also to allege with reasonable certainty the termini of the way and its course.—If the Plaintiff omits to do this his statement of claim is embarrassing, and the Court will order it to be amended. HARRIS *v.* JENKINS - **22 Ch. D. 481**

2. —— **Foreclosure —** *Judgment not drawn up and entered — Discovery of Puisne Mortgagees—Rules of Court*, 1883, *Order XVI.*, *r.* 11— *Leave to amend by adding Defendants.*] Where judgment in a foreclosure action had been pronounced, but had not been drawn up and entered, and it was discovered that there were puisne mortgagees, leave was given under Rules of Supreme Court, 1883, Order XVI., rule 11, to amend the writ and statement of claim by making the puisne mortgagees Defendants. KEITH *v.* BUTCHER - - - **25 Ch. D. 750**

3. —— **New Defence—***Fraud of Solicitor— Rehearing.*] Where a solicitor has put in a

XX. PRACTICE—SUPREME COURT—AMENDMENT—*continued.*

fraudulent defence for his client without the knowledge of the client, making admissions on which judgment was obtained against the client : —*Held*, that the Court had jurisdiction to set aside the judgment and permit the client to withdraw the defence, and put in a fresh defence. WILLIAMS *v.* PRESTON - **20 Ch. D. 672**

4. —— **Qualifying Words.**] In an action to restrain the removal of shingle from, and the placing of bathing-machines upon, a part of the foreshore of the sea at M., the Plaintiff claimed to be tenant in possession of the locus in quo under a building agreement granted him by the lord of the manor of M., who was tenant for life of the property under a settlement. By his statement of defence the Defendant set up a forty years' uninterrupted user and enjoyment of the locus in quo by himself and his predecessors in title for the purposes complained of, and denied that the Plaintiff was or ever had been in possession of the locus in quo " save subject to the right of the Defendant." At the trial, Fry, J., refused the Defendant leave to amend his statement of defence by striking out the qualifying words, so as to make his denial of the Plaintiff's possession an unqualified one :—*Held*, on appeal, that the amendment ought to have been allowed.—*Golding* v. *Wharton Saltworks Company* (1 Q. B. D. 374) explained. LAIRD *v.* BRIGGS **16 Ch. D. 440**;
[**19 Ch. D. 22**]

5. —— **Record of Trial—***Power of Court of Appeal to amend—Rules of Court*, 1875, *Order LVIII.*, r. 5 ; *LIX.* r. 2.] At the trial of an action the jury found certain issues in favour of the Plaintiff, and the Judge reserved judgment. The verdict was entered as a general verdict for the Plaintiff, but the Judge notwithstanding the verdict gave judgment for the Defendant.—On an appeal by the Plaintiff from the judgment, the Court of Appeal amended the record by entering the verdict for the Plaintiff on the issues only, and affirmed the judgment. CLACK *v.* WOOD - **9 Q. B. D. 276**

—— Alteration in judgment—Accidental slip
[**29 Ch. D. 827**]
See PRACTICE—SUPREME COURT—JUDGMENT. 8.

—— Special case - - **22 Ch. D. 495**
See PRACTICE — SUPREME COURT — SPECIAL CASE. 1.

XXI. PRACTICE—SUPREME COURT—INTERROGATORIES.

(a.) GENERAL.

1. —— **Action for Penalties—***Rules of Court*, 1875, *Order XXXI.*, *rr.* 1, 12.] In an action for penalties the Plaintiff is not entitled to administer interrogatories or to discovery of documents under Order XXXI., that order not being intended to give the right to discovery in cases where prior to the Judicature Acts discovery was not obtainable. HUNNINGS *v.* WILLIAMSON **10 Q. B. D. 459**

2. —— **Conversations—***Right of Way—Rules of Court*, 1875, *Order XXXI.*, *rr.* 1, 10.] An action was brought by the Attorney-General and a local board to restrain the Defendant from building across a public footpath. The amended statement

XXI. PRACTICE—SUPREME COURT—INTER-
ROGATORIES—continued.

(a.) GENERAL—continued.

of claim alleged that at a meeting of the board held after the commencement of the action the Defendant had attended and signed an agreement for settling the action on certain terms, and the Plaintiffs sought to enforce this agreement, or, in the alternative, to restrain interference with the footpath by virtue of their original title. The Defendant, by his defence, denied the existence of any public right of way over the ground. He admitted the signature of the agreement, but alleged that it was obtained by threats and pressure after a long conversation and argument, and without his having it read and explained to him. The Plaintiffs delivered interrogatories as to the existence of a public right of way over the land, and as to what passed in the conversation at the board meeting and at a conversation between the Defendant and the Plaintiffs' solicitor before that meeting. The Defendant declined to answer those interrogatories, alleging that as to the right of way he was not bound to answer as to a right which he had denied by his pleadings; and that as to the conversations he ought not to be called upon to answer till the Plaintiffs' solicitor had been examined and cross-examined as to the conversation:—*Held*, by Bacon, V.C., that the Defendant having by the statement of defence denied the existence of the right of way was not bound to answer as to it; and that he was not bound to answer as to the conversations, no discovery being requisite as to facts which the Plaintiffs had the means of establishing :—*Held*, by the Court of Appeal, that the Defendant was bound to answer as to the existence of the right of way, for that one object of interrogatories is to enable a party to obtain admissions from the other party, and so to relieve him from the necessity of adducing evidence :—*Held*, also, that as the conversations were material on the issue whether the agreement had been unduly obtained, the Defendant must answer as to them; and that it would not be right to allow him to delay answering until he saw what account another person would give of what had taken place.—The right of discovery as existing in the Court of Chancery still exists, except so far as it is modified by the Judicature Acts and the General Orders ; and a party still has a right to exhibit interrogatories, not only for the purpose of obtaining from the opposite party information as to material facts which are not within his own knowledge and are within the knowledge of the opposite party, but also for the purpose of obtaining from the opposite party admissions which will make it unnecessary for him to enter into evidence as to the facts admitted. ATTORNEY-GENERAL v. GASKILL

[20 Ch. D. 519

3. —— Denial of Plaintiff's Title—*Rules of Court*, 1875, *Order* XXXI., rr. 5, 19.] Where a Defendant's answering an interrogatory cannot help the Plaintiff to obtain a decree, but will only be of use to him if he obtains a decree, the Court has a discretion whether to oblige the Defendant to answer it before trial, and will not do so where compelling such discovery would be oppressive.—The Plaintiff alleged that G. had

XXI. PRACTICE—SUPREME COURT—INTER-
ROGATORIES—continued.

(a.) GENERAL—continued.

deposited money with the Defendant E. in trust for S. and A. (both since deceased) successively for their lives, and then for the Plaintiff and another person absolutely. That E. had employed it in trade and made large profits, and had paid the interest to S. and A. for their lives, but now refused to pay over the principal. E., by his defence, admitted the deposit, but denied the trust, and stated that he had only held the money for G. to draw upon, and had many years ago paid it away by G.'s directions; he denied payment of interest to S. and A. The Plaintiff delivered, amongst others, interrogatories requiring E. to set out (1) the dates and particulars of the payments made by him out of the deposit sum ; (2) an account of the profits made by the employment of the money in trade ; (3) whether E. had not paid to S. and A. quarterly sums by way of interest on the moneys, and if not, then he was asked whether he had not during some and what years paid to S. and A. certain and what moneys, and whether or not quarterly, or at some and what dates and under what agreement, or for what reason or in respect of what matters ; and was required to set out an account of all moneys paid by him since 1854 to S. and A., or either of them.—E. filed an affidavit verifying his defence and denying the trust, denying the payment of any interest to S. or A. on the deposited sum, denying the Plaintiff's title, and declining to make any further answer. Fry, J., ordered E. to make a further answer as to (1) and (3). E. appealed.—*Held*, on appeal, that E. was not bound to answer interrogatory 1, as an answer to it could not furnish evidence to establish the alleged trust, and could not be of any use to the Plaintiff except by discrediting E.'s evidence if he made erroneous statements as to the particulars of his payments, and that it would be oppressive to require him to go through his books for a number of years for that purpose :—*Held*, further, that E. ought not to be compelled to answer as to the profits, for that it would be oppressive to call upon him to enter into a difficult account, which could not help the Plaintiff to obtain a decree and would be useless if a decree was not obtained : —*Held*, that the third interrogatory was too wide, as it extended to payments not connected with the sums to which the action related, and that the Plaintiff was not entitled to a full answer ;— *Held*, further, by Jessel, M.R., and Brett, L.J., that as the Plaintiff had not in the Court below asked for a qualified order but had insisted on a full answer, the order for a further answer ought simply to be discharged.—Dissentiente, Cotton, L.J., who was of opinion that an order ought to be made for a further answer to a limited extent. PARKER v. WELLS -　- 18 Ch. D. 477

4. —— Guardian ad litem :— "*Party*" to *Action—Judicature Act*, 1873 (36 & 37 Vict. c. 66), s. 100—*Rules of Court*, 1875, *Order* XVIII.— *Order* XXXI., r. 1.] A guardian ad litem is not a party to the action within the meaning of Order XXXI., rule 1, and therefore cannot be compelled to answer interrogatories. INGRAM v. LITTLE

[11 Q. B. D. 251

XXI. PRACTICE—SUPREME COURT—INTER-
ROGATORIES—*continued*.

(a.) GENERAL—*continued*.

5. —— Knowledge of Agent—*Servant of a Person interrogated.*] A party to a cause is not excused from answering interrogatories relevant to the question in issue on the ground that they are as to matters which are not within such party's own knowledge, but are only within the knowledge of his agents or servants, if derived in the ordinary course of their employment; and he is bound to obtain the information from such agents or servants, unless he shew that it would be unreasonable to require him to do so, as that either such agents or servants have left his employment, or it would occasion unreasonable expense or an unreasonable amount of detail or the like. Therefore in an action by cargo owners against the owners of a ship, for a loss alleged to have arisen from negligence in the navigation of such ship by which she ran ashore and was stranded, an answer by the Defendants to interrogatories as to what was done by those on board with regard to such navigation at the time of the accident, which stated in substance that the Defendants were not on board at the time and had no knowledge or information respecting the matters inquired into, except as appeared by the protest of which the Plaintiffs had had inspection, was held insufficient, as it did not appear that there was any difficulty in the Defendants' obtaining the required information from those who were in charge of the ship at the time of the accident. BOLCKOW *v.* FISHER

[10 Q. B. D. 161

6. —— Knowledge of Agent.] In an action by owners of water mills to restrain a canal company, who had statutory power to take water from the river on which the Plaintiffs' mills were situate, from wrongfully diminishing the quantity of water in the river to the injury of the Plaintiffs, the Defendants interrogated the Plaintiffs and asked them to give a list of the days between specified dates on which they alleged that the working of their mills was interfered with by the negligence of the Defendants. The Plaintiffs answered that they were unable to specify the particular days:—*Held,* that this answer was sufficient, and that the Plaintiffs were not bound to state whether they had made inquiries of their agents, servants, and workmen.—*Bolckow v. Fisher* (10 Q. B. D. 161) distinguished. RASBOTHAM *v.* SHROPSHIRE UNION RAILWAYS AND CANAL COMPANY　-　24 Ch. D. 110

7. —— Libel — *Matters in Issue — Rules of Court, 1883, Order XXXI., r. 1 — Comparison of Handwriting.*] In order to prove that the Defendant was the writer of a libellous letter, he may be interrogated as to whether or not he was the writer of another letter addressed to a third person,—as leading up to a matter in issue in the cause, and therefore relevant. JONES *v.* RICHARDS

[15 Q. B. D. 439

8. —— Plaintiff's Evidence.] B. and N., two landowners in the parish of M., brought an action for a declaration that a piece of land formed part of M. Common, and to establish commonable rights thereover. N. sued as owner in fee of a beerhouse and three cottages, and the Plaintiffs pleaded the

XXI. PRACTICE—SUPREME COURT—INTER-
ROGATORIES—*continued*.

(a.) GENERAL—*continued*.

exercise of the rights claimed from time immemorial. The Defendant was the lord of an adjacent manor, and his defence was that the piece of land never formed part of M. Common, but was common land forming part of his own manor; that if the Plaintiffs ever had any rights of common thereon such rights had been extinguished; that some of the rights claimed could only be used in respect of ancient tenements, and that the beerhouse and three cottages in respect of which N. sued had no land held therewith. After the defence had been delivered the Defendant administered interrogatories to the Plaintiffs, asking in effect:—1. How long the Plaintiffs had been owners or occupiers of their properties, and for what estates, what was the tenure thereof, and whether those lands were within the limits of any and what actual or reputed manors, and whether any such premises were ancient messuages, and whether the beerhouse and three cottages had any and what lands appurtenant thereto or held therewith. 2ndly. Whether the Plaintiffs or their predecessors in title, as proprietors or occupiers of any lands in M., or under any other alleged title, had exercised the rights claimed upon any and what parts of M. Common, or upon any and what part of the piece of land in question. 3rdly. The Plaintiffs were asked to set forth particulars of their exercise of such rights, and whether they did so by any license or in consideration of any and what payment. The Plaintiffs objected to answer these interrogatories on the ground that they related exclusively to their own title and to the evidence they should adduce at the hearing.—Upon a summons that the Plaintiffs might be ordered to make a sufficient answer:— *Held,* by Kay, J., that the Plaintiff N. must answer so much of the first interrogatory as asked, whether the beerhouse and cottages had any lands appurtenant thereto or held therewith because he had not pleaded that they had, and the Defendant had pleaded that they had not; but that the rest of the interrogatories need not be answered, because they were in effect directed to the discovery of the evidence by which the Plaintiffs intended to prove their case at the hearing.—*Eade v. Jacobs* (3 Ex. D. 335) and *Hoffmann v. Postill* (Law Rep. 4 Ch. 673) explained.—*Lowndes* v. *Davies* (6 Sim. 468) dissented from.—On appeal by the Defendant the question was left to the Judges of the Court of Appeal as arbitrators to settle what parts of the interrogatories should be answered, and the Plaintiffs were directed to answer further parts of them. BIDDER *v.* BRIDGES　-　29 Ch. D. 29

9. —— Plaintiff's Evidence—*Infringement of Trade-Name—Accounts of Goods sold—Rules of Court, 1875, Order XXXI.*] In an action to restrain the Defendants from using a trade-name and from selling their goods as the goods of the Plaintiffs, the Defendants by counter-claim claimed the like relief, and also an account of the goods sold by the Plaintiffs as and for the goods of the Defendants, and of the profits of such sale. Both Plaintiffs and Defendants claimed to derive their title under a partnership that had been dissolved in

XXI. PRACTICE—SUPREME COURT—INTER-ROGATORIES—*continued.*

(a.) GENERAL—*continued.*

1861, and both had since that time carried on the same business. An interrogatory exhibited by the Defendants required the Plaintiffs to set forth the quantities of goods sold by them since 1861, distinguishing the quantities sold in each year :—*Held* (affirming the decision of Bacon, V.C.), that the interrogatory was not for the ordinary purposes of discovery, but was directed to the details of the Plaintiff's evidence, and was rightly disallowed.—*Saunders* v. *Jones* (7 Ch. D. 435) explained and discussed. BENBOW *v.* Low

[16 Ch. D. 93

10. —— **Recollection of Written Document.**] In an action for libel, one of the Plaintiff's interrogatories required the Defendant to state whether she had not written and sent letters to a third person making certain defamatory statements of the Plaintiff set out in the interrogatory, or statements to the same purport and effect, and to set out as fully as she could what her statements were. The Defendant answered that to the best of her recollection and belief she never wrote any letters making the statements set out in the interrogatory, " or any of those exact statements set out in the interrogatory," " or any of those exact statements:" that she did write a letter to the third person, but that she had no copy of it, and was unable to recollect " with exactness " what the statements contained in it were :—*Held*, that the answer was sufficient. DALRYMPLE *v.* LESLIE   8 Q. B. D. 5

11. —— **Recovery of Land**—*Legal Title*—*Rules of Court, 1875, Order XXXI., r. 1.*] In an action for the recovery of land the Plaintiff is entitled to discovery as to all matters relevant to his own and not to the Defendant's case.—In an action for the recovery of land the Plaintiff claimed as assignee of co-heiresses of a deceased intestate owner of the land, and the Defendant relied on his possession and also set up the Statute of Limitations : —*Held*, reversing the decision of the Court of Appeal, that the Plaintiff was entitled to interrogate the Defendant as to matters relevant to the pedigree and heirship of his assignors and as to alleged admissions by the Defendant that his possession of the land was as trustee for the intestate and her heirs, even though the Plaintiff might have other means of proving the facts inquired after; and that the Defendant must answer the interrogatories in substance subject to any privilege against particular discovery which he might be entitled to claim.—*Held*, also, that the Defendant must file a proper affidavit of documents. LYELL *v.* KENNEDY   20 Ch. D. 484; 8 App. Cas.

[217

(b.) PRIVILEGE.

12. —— **Attempt to falsify Claim for Privilege**—*Rules of Court, 1875, Order XXXI., rr. 9, 10, 23*—*Rules of Court, 1883, Order XXXI., rr. 10, 11, 24.*] Where in an answer to interrogatories the party interrogated declines to give certain information on the ground of professional privilege, and the privilege is properly claimed in law, the Court will not require a further answer to be put in, unless it is clearly satisfied, either from the nature of the subject-matter for which privilege is

XXI. PRACTICE—SUPREME COURT—INTER-ROGATORIES—*continued.*

(b.) PRIVILEGE—*continued.*

claimed, or from statements in the answer itself, or in documents so referred to as to become part of the answer, that the claim for privilege cannot possibly be substantiated.—The mere existence of a reasonable suspicion which is sufficient to justify the Court in requiring a further affidavit of documents is not enough when a claim for privilege in an answer to interrogatories is sought to be falsified.—The duty of the Court with reference to answers to interrogatories is now regulated by Order XXXI., rules 10, 11, and limited to considering the sufficiency or insufficiency of the answer, *i.e.*, whether the party interrogated has answered that which he has no excuse for not answering;—and only in the case of insufficiency can it require a further answer :—*Semble* (per Bowen, L.J.), that an embarrassing answer to interrogatories may be dealt with as insufficient.—A party interrogated may, on a question of sufficiency, refer to his whole affidavit in answer to interrogatories, and is not restricted to the passages dealing with any particular interrogatory, and all embarrassment to the interrogating party is now obviated by the provisions of Order XXXI., rule 24 ; but he must not endeavour to import into an. admission matter which has no connection with the matter admitted.—The Defendant K. in his answer to interrogatories objected to disclose certain information asked for by the Plaintiff. L. on the ground of professional privilege, which the Court held properly claimed in law. L. sought by reference to certain admissions in the answer itself, and from documents referred to in the interrogatories and answer, as well as from documents scheduled to K.'s affidavit of documents, to shew that the information sought was obtained under circumstances which negatived the claim of privilege, and sought a further answer :—*Held* (affirming Bacon, V.C.), that no further answer should be required, as the admissions in the answer and in the documents referred to therein only raised a case of suspicion at the most, which might be capable of explanation if K. were at liberty to make an affidavit.—The Court declined to decide how far, under the present practice, reference could be made, as against the interrogated party, to any document in possession not referred to in his answer, but only scheduled to his affidavit of documents. LYELL *v.* KENNEDY - 27 Ch. D. 1

13. —— **Belief founded on Privileged Communications.**] A party to an action cannot be compelled to answer interrogatories asking as to his knowledge, information, or belief with regard to matters of fact, if he swears that he has no knowledge or information with regard to those matters except such as he has derived from privileged communications made to him by his solicitors or their agents; for since under those circumstances his knowledge and information are protected, so also is his belief when derived solely from such communications.—The Plaintiff having been interrogated as to his knowledge, information and belief upon matters relevant to the Defendant's case answered that he had no personal knowledge of any of the matters inquired into; that such information as he had

XXI. PRACTICE—SUPREME COURT—INTER-
ROGATORIES—*continued.*

(*b.*) PRIVILEGE—*continued.*

received in respect of those matters had been derived from information procured by his solicitors
or their agents in and for the purpose of his own
case :—*Held,* affirming the decision of the Court
of Appeal, that the answer was sufficient. LYELL
v. KENNEDY (No. 2) 23 Ch. D. 387 ; 9 App. Cas. 81

14. —— Professional Confidence—*Solicitor and
Client.*] The privilege from discovery resulting
from professional confidence does not extend to
facts communicated by the solicitor to the client
which cannot be the subject of a confidential communication between them, even though such facts
have a relation to the case of the client in the
action.—A Plaintiff interrogated a Defendant as
to whether interviews and correspondence had not,
between certain dates, taken place between their
respective solicitors, and also between the Defendant's solicitor and a third person, in reference to
an agreement the specific performance of which
it was the object of the action to enforce.—The
Defendant declined to answer the interrogatory,
so far as it related to communications between
his solicitor and other persons, on the ground that
he had no personal knowledge, and the only information he had was derived from confidential
communications between him and his solicitor in
reference to his defence in the action :—*Held,* that
he must make a further answer. FOAKES *v.*
WEBB　　　-　　　26 Ch. D. 287

15. —— Publication of Libel—*Refusal to
answer—Incrimination.*] An objection to answer
interrogatories which is made by affidavit on the
ground of the tendency of the answer to criminate
the person interrogated may be valid, although
not expressed in any precise form of words, if,
from the nature of the question and the circumstances, such a tendency seems likely or probable.
In an action for libel the Defendant pleaded a
denial of the publication, and to interrogatories
asking him, in effect, whether he published the
libel he stated by his affidavit in answer : " I
decline to answer all the interrogatories upon
the ground that my answer to them ' might '
tend to criminate me." :—*Held,* that his answer
was sufficient. LAMB *v.* MUNSTER　　10 Q. B. D.
[110

—— Deposit—Discretion of Judge 13 Q. B. D. 326
See PRACTICE—SUPREME COURT—SECU-
RITY FOR COSTS. 13.

XXII. PRACTICE — SUPREME COURT — PRO-
DUCTION OF DOCUMENTS.

(*a.*) GENERAL.

1. —— Affidavit—*Prolixity.*] An affidavit as
to documents setting out a very large number of
letters instead of referring to them in bundles
properly identified, was ordered to be taken off
the file, the costs to be paid by the Defendants.
WALKER *v.* POOLE　　-　　-　　21 Ch. D. 835

2. —— Arbitrator—*Order of Reference—Jurisdiction—Rules of Court, 1875, Ord. XXXI., r. 12—
" Matter in question in the action"— Liberty to
apply, Omission of.*] An order was taken by consent in an action referring the action and all
matters in difference to the award of an arbitrator

XXII. PRACTICE — SUPREME COURT — PRO-
DUCTION OF DOCUMENTS—*continued.*

(*a.*) GENERAL—*continued.*

named in the order. The order provided that the
parties should produce before the arbitrator all
documents in their or either of their custody or
power relating to the matter in difference ; also
that the party in whose favour the award should
be made should be at liberty, after the service of
a copy of the award on the other party, to apply
for final judgment in accordance with the award.
The Plaintiff having during the pendency of the
arbitration applied by summons in the action
under Rules of Court, 1875, Order XXXI., r. 12, for
an affidavit of documents, the application was dismissed on the ground, (1) That in consequence of
the order of reference the Court has no jurisdiction to grant the application, not having before it
" any matter in question in the action" within
the meaning of the rule ; and (2) that under the
order the whole jurisdiction as to discovery was
in the hands of the arbitrator.—The rule that an
order of the Court carries with it "liberty to
apply," though not expressly reserved, only
applies where the order is one not of a final
character. PENRICE *v.* WILLIAMS　　23 Ch. D. 353

3. —— Documents held in Right of another—
*Company — Voluntary Winding-up — Liquidator
— Companies Act, 1862 (25 & 26 Vict. c. 89),
s. 155.*] In an action on a promissory note, made
by the Defendant as security for the repayment
of moneys due to the Plaintiffs from a limited
company, the Defendant objected to produce documents relating to the matters in question in the
action, being the banker's pass-book and directors'
minute-book of the company, on the ground
that they were in his custody only as liquidator
in the voluntary winding-up of the company.
The company had been dissolved before the
application for the discovery of documents was
made, but no resolution had been passed under
the Companies Act, 1862, s. 155, for the disposal
of the documents belonging to it :—*Held,* that
the Plaintiffs were entitled to the inspection of
the documents, inasmuch as the Defendant had
them in his absolute control. — Decision of the
Queen's Bench Division affirmed. LONDON AND
YORKSHIRE BANK *v.* COOPER　　15 Q. B. D. 7, 473

4. —— Husband and Wife—*Joint Possession
—Affidavit as to Documents.*] A husband and wife
sued as co-Plaintiffs in respect of an alleged
breach of trust by the trustees of their marriage
settlement. The wife had a life estate for her
separate use, and sued without a next friend.
An order was made that the Plaintiffs should
file an affidavit stating " whether they or either
of them " had in the possession or power " of
them or either of them," any documents relating
to the matters in question. They filed an affidavit admitting the possession of various documents, which they scheduled, and going on to
say, " We have not now, and never had, in our
possession, custody, or power, or in the possession,
custody, or power of any other person or persons
on our behalf, any deed, &c., other than and
except the documents set forth in the said schedule" :—*Held* (reversing the decision of Bacon,
V.C.), that the Plaintiffs must be ordered to file
a further and better affidavit, for that an affidavit

**XXII. PRACTICE — SUPREME COURT — PRO-
DUCTION OF DOCUMENTS—**continued.

(a.) GENERAL—continued.

relating only to documents in the joint custody
of the husband and wife did not comply with the
order, and that the order was right in requiring
them to answer as to documents in the possession
of either of them. FENDALL v. O'CONNELL
[29 Ch. D. 899

5. —— Infant—Next Friend—Affidavit as to
Documents—Rules of Court, 1883, Order XXXI.,
r. 12.] The Court refused either to order the
next friend of an infant Plaintiff to make an
affidavit as to documents, or stay the action till
he made such affidavit.—Higginson v. Hall (10
Ch. D. 235) dissented from. DYKE v. STEPHENS
[30 Ch. D. 189

6. —— Interrogatory— Discovery of Documents—Sufficient Affidavit.] After a Defendant
has made a sufficient affidavit of documents the
Plaintiff will not be allowed to administer to him
a general roving interrogatory as to documents in
his possession, the effect of which would be to
compel the Defendant to make a further affidavit
as to documents.—There may possibly be cases in
which, after a sufficient affidavit as to documents
has been made, the Court will allow the plaintiff to
deliver an interrogatory as to some specific document or documents, but whether this shall be allowed is a matter within the discretion of the Judge
in each particular case, and, though his decision
can be appealed from, the Court of Appeal will
not readily reverse it.—Jones v. Monte Video Gas
Company (5 Q. B. D. 556) explained. HALL v.
TRUMAN, HANBURY, & CO. - 29 Ch. D. 307

7. —— Joint Possession—Documents of Title.]
In an action for the seizure of the goods of the
Plaintiff, which was justified by the Defendant
under an alleged power of distress in a mortgage
deed, the Defendant stated in his affidavit of
documents that he and one B., who was not
a party to the action, jointly had in their possession or power certain documents specified in a
schedule to such affidavit and that they were the
muniments of title of himself and the said B. as
mortgagees, and that he the Defendant objected
to their production :—Held, affirming the decision
of the Queen's Bench Division, that such affidavit
shewed sufficient reason for not making an order
for inspection of the documents. — Murray v.
Walter (Cr. & Ph. 114) followed. KEARSLEY v.
PHILIPS   10 Q. B. D. 36, 465

8. —— "Material to any Matter in Question"
— Rules of Court, 1875, Order XXXI., r. 12.]
Documents are material to the matters in question in the action within the meaning of Order
XXXI., rule 12, if it is not unreasonable to suppose that they may contain information directly
or indirectly enabling the party seeking discovery
either to advance his own case, or to damage
the case of his adversary. — The Plaintiff company sued the Defendant company for breach
of contract ; the defence to the action was that
no contract had been concluded, and that only
negotiations had taken place between the parties.
The Defendants having obtained an order for an
affidavit of documents, the Plaintiffs set out,
amongst others, their minute-book, which referred

**XXII. PRACTICE — SUPREME COURT — PRO-
DUCTION OF DOCUMENTS—**continued.

(a.) GENERAL—continued.

to certain documents and letters ; the entries as
to these documents and letters were of a date
subsequent to the date of the alleged breach of
contract ; the documents and letters were not set
out by the Plaintiffs in their affidavit. The
Defendants claimed a further and better affidavit
from the Plaintiffs, setting out the documents and
letters above-mentioned, on the ground that they
might shew that after the alleged breach the
parties were still negotiating, and might tend to
disprove the Plaintiffs' allegation that a contract
had been concluded :—Held, that the Plaintiffs
were bound to make a further affidavit of documents. COMPAGNIE FINANCIÈRE ET COMMERCIALE
DU PACIFIQUE v. PERUVIAN GUANO CO.
[11 Q. B. D. 55

9. —— Official Referee—Jurisdiction—Rules
of Court, 1875, Order XXXI., rr. 11, 18, 20 ; Order
XXXVI., r. 32.] The official referees have no
jurisdiction to make an order for the production
of documents, the proper course being to take out
a summons for the purpose in the Chambers of
the Judge to whom the action is attached. DAU-
VILLIER v. MYERS   17 Ch. D. 346

10. —— Opening Settled Account—Allegations
of Fraud — Rules of Court, 1883, Order XIX.,
r. 6; Order XXXI., rr. 12, 20.] The Plaintiffs
employed the Defendants to purchase goods, as
their agents, at the lowest possible prices. The
Plaintiffs sued for an account, and in their statement of claim alleged that the Defendants had
purchased goods at prices higher than the current
prices, and had secretly received from the vendors
allowances or commissions. The charges against
the Defendants were stated in general terms, no
particulars being mentioned. The Defendants
denied the charges, and pleaded a settled account.
The Plaintiffs applied for production of documents :— Held, by Cotton, L.J., affirming the
decision of Bacon, V.C. (dissentiente, Fry, L.J.)
that the Plaintiffs were not bound to give particulars of fraud under Order XIX., rule 6, before
obtaining discovery of documents :— Held, by
Fry, L.J., that the allegations of fraud in the
pleadings not being sufficient to enable the Plaintiffs to open a settled account, discovery ought to
be refused until the allegations had been made
sufficient. WHYTE v. AHRENS - 26 Ch. D. 717

11. —— Place of Production—Alteration of
Order.] Where an order has been made for production of documents at a particular place the
Judge, or his successor, may at any time make a
fresh order appointing a different place if the circumstances render it advisable. And although
such an order may be appealed from, the Court
will not interfere with the Judge's discretion except on some special ground. The common order
having been made for production of documents by
the Defendants at the solicitor's office in London,
the Judge, six months afterwards, made another
order that the documents should be produced at
Colchester. The documents consisted principally
of ancient charters and books of account belonging
to the corporation :—Held, by the Court of Appeal,
that the order was right : but a direction was
added that the Plaintiffs should be at liberty to

XXII. PRACTICE—SUPREME COURT — PRO-DUCTION OF DOCUMENTS—continued.

(a.) GENERAL—continued.

apply for the production of any documents which might be more conveniently examined in London; and that the Defendants should undertake to pay any additional costs caused by the alteration in the place of production. PRESTNEY v. CORPORA-TION OF COLCHESTER　　24 Ch. D. 376

12. —— Plaintiff's Documents—Action brought in the Name of Third Parties.] Goods shipped by R. & Co. having been lost at sea, the under-writers, who had insured the cargo, paid R. & Co. for a total loss, and then commenced an action against the shipowners in the name of R. & Co. to recover the value of the goods. An order having been made by consent that the Plaintiffs should make an affidavit stating what documents were in their possession relating to the matters in question in the action, and a further order having been made by the Master in Chambers that both members of the firm of R. & Co. should put in a further and better affidavit, the solicitor of the underwriters deposed that the members of the firm of R. & Co. were abroad, and would not give any further discovery, and that the real Plaintiffs had done all they could do to comply with the order:—Held, reversing the decision of the Queen's Bench Division, that the case must be treated as if the nominal Plaintiffs on the record were suing for their own benefit, and that the making a further affidavit could not be dispensed with. WILSON v. RAFFALOVICH
[7 Q. B. D. 553

13. —— Plaintiff's Documents—Documents referred to in Pleadings—Rules of Court, 1875, Order XXXI., rr. 14–17.] The Plaintiff by his statement of claim referred to certain entries in his own books, to two letters written to himself, and to two letters written by himself. The Defendant as soon as the statement of claim was delivered applied for production of the books, of the letters written to the Plaintiff, and of copies of the letters written by the Plaintiff. The Plaintiff's solicitors refused to produce any of them as the Defendant had not delivered statement of defence. The De-fendant then applied to the Court for production:—Held, by Chitty, J., that production ought not to be ordered till a statement of defence had been delivered.—Held, on appeal, that production must be ordered at once of documents referred to in the pleadings unless some special reason against it can be shewn, and that the Plaintiff must pro-duce his books, with the usual liberty to seal up the parts other than the entries, and must also produce the letters written to himself, but that he could not be ordered to produce copies of letters written by himself, there being no reference to such copies in the statement of claim.—Webster v. Whewall (15 Ch. D. 120) observed upon. QUILTER v. HEATLY　　-　　- 23 Ch. D. 42

14. —— Policy, Action on—Insurance—Marine—Discovery of Ship's Papers—Form of Order—Whether rightly made on all Persons interested—Continuance of Practice in Force before Judica-ture Acts—Rules of Court, 1875, Order XXXI., r. 11, and Order LX., A., r. 12.] In an action on a policy of marine insurance, underwriters are entitled to discovery of ship's papers, in accordance with the practice in force before the Judicature Acts, with-out an affidavit, and from all persons interested in the proceedings. CHINA TRANSPACIFIC STEAM-SHIP COMPANY v. COMMERCIAL UNION ASSURANCE COMPANY　　-　　-　8 Q. B. D. 142

15. —— Sealing up Entries — Partnership Books — Surviving Partner.] The Defendant and W. P. were partners. W. P. died and ap-pointed the Defendant his executor. In an action by a person interested under W. P.'s will against the Defendant a decree was made for adminis-tration of W. P.'s estate, and for taking accounts of the partnership as between the Defendant as surviving partner and W. P.'s estate. An order having been made for the production of the part-nership books by the Defendant, he claimed to seal up such entries as related to his own private affairs:—Held (affirming the decision of Chitty, J.), that inasmuch as the Plaintiff and Defendant were both interested in the partnership property, the Defendant was not entitled to the ordinary power to seal up such entries as he might swear to be ir-relevant to the matters at issue in the action, but only to seal up entries which related to certain specified private matters mentioned in the order. In re PICKERING.　PICKERING v. PICKERING
[25 Ch. D. 247

16. —— Service—Attachment—Rules of Court, 1875, Order XXXI., r. 21.] In an action for the specific performance of an agreement by the De-fendant to sell two leasehold houses to the Plaintiff, judgment for specific performance was given, and an order was afterwards made that the Defendant should within four days after service of the order, produce to the Plaintiff "the ab-stract, and at the same time produce upon oath for inspection all deeds and writings in his pos-session or power" relating to the property:—Held, that under rule 21 of Order XXXI., service of this order on the Defendant's solicitors was sufficient service to found an application to attach the Defendant for disobedience of the order. JOY v. HADLEY　　-　　-　22 Ch. D. 571

17. —— Title Deeds in Custody of Court.] In an action of trespass to land brought against the committee of a lunatic whose title-deeds are in the custody of the Court having jurisdiction in Lunacy, an order on the Defendant for inspection of the documents ought not to be made, as they are not in his possession or control. VIVIAN v. LITTLE　　-　　-　　-　11 Q. D. 370

(b.) PRIVILEGE.

18. —— Affidavit—Sufficiency—Rules of Court, 1875, Order XXXI., rr. 11, 12.] The Defendants in an affidavit of documents made pursuant to Order XXXI., rule 12, stated as follows:—"We have in our possession or power certain documents numbered 101 to 110 inclusive, which are tied up in a bundle marked with the letter A., and initialed by the deponent" C. G.; "the said documents relate solely to the case of the Defendants and not to the case of the Plaintiff, nor do they tend to support it, and they do not, to the best of our knowledge, information, and belief, contain any-thing impeaching the case of the said Defendants,

XXII. PRACTICE—SUPREME COURT — PRODUCTION OF DOCUMENTS—continued.

(b.) Privilege—continued.

wherefore we object to produce the same, and say they are privileged from production." A Judge at Chambers and the Divisional Court (W. Williams, J., dissenting), refused to order, under Order XXXI., rule 11, the production of the documents which the Defendants so objected to produce :—*Held,* by the Court of Appeal, that the affidavit sufficiently described such documents for the purpose of identification, and that as the affidavit was conclusive against the Plaintiff seeking inspection, the Judge and the Divisional Court rightly refused to order their production. Bewicke v. Graham - - 7 Q. B. D. 400

19. —— **Affidavit** — *Sufficiency—Power of the Court to disregard the Affidavit as to the Nature and Effect of the Documents.*] Although a Defendant to an action swears that certain documents which are in his possession and are material to the matter in issue, form and support his own title, and do not contain anything which could form or support the Plaintiff's case, or impeach the defence, the Court will not act on such oath (at least in proceedings excepted by Order LXII. from the rules under the Judicature Act, 1875), but will order such documents to be produced, if from the whole of the Defendant's answer or from the description of the documents given by the Defendant, the Court is reasonably certain that the Defendant has erroneously represented or misconceived the nature of such documents. Attorney-General v. Emerson - - 10 Q. B. D. 191

20. —— **Affidavit** — *Sufficiency — Documents referred to in Pleadings—Rules of Court, 1883, Order XXXI. r. 15.*] Where a party claims privilege against the production of documents on the ground that they supported his own title and do not relate to that of his opponent, his affidavit must be taken as conclusive, unless the Court can see from the nature of the case or of the documents that the party has misunderstood the effect of the documents.—*Attorney-General* v. *Emerson* (10 Q. B. D. 191) distinguished.—The privilege claimed for documents is not lost merely by their being referred to in the pleadings. The penalty for non-production is that they cannot afterwards be used in evidence, the decision of Kay, J., affirmed. Roberts v. Oppenheim 26 Ch. D. 724

21. —— **Attempt to falsify Claim for Privilege** — *Affidavit of Documents — Rules of Court, 1875, Order XXXI., r. 11—Rules of Court, 1883, Order XXXI., r. 14.*] A waiver of privilege in respect of some out of a larger number of documents for all of which privilege was originally claimed does not preclude the party from still asserting his claim of privilege for the rest. — Although primâ facie privilege cannot be claimed for copies of or extracts from public records or documents which are publici juris, a collection of such copies or extracts will be privileged when it has been made or obtained by the professional advisers of a party for his defence to the action, and is the result of the professional knowledge, research, and skill of those advisers.—The Defendant K.'s solicitors had for the purposes of K.'s defence in the action procured copies of and extracts from certain entries in public registers,

XXII. PRACTICE—SUPREME COURT—PRODUCTION OF DOCUMENTS—continued.

(b.) Privilege—continued.

and also photographs of certain tombstones and houses to be taken, for which K. in his affidavit of documents claimed protection :—*Held* (affirming Bacon, V.C.), that although mere copies of unprivileged documents were themselves unprivileged, the whole collection being the result of the professional knowledge, skill, and research of his solicitors, must be privileged—any disclosure of the copies and photographs might afford a clue to the view entertained by the solicitors of their client's case. Lyell v. Kennedy 27 Ch. D. 1

22. —— **Plaintiff's Documents** — *Documents privileged in Previous Action by Plaintiff against Third Party—Rules of Court, 1883, Order XXXI., rr. 12–14.*] An order having been made for discovery of documents by the Plaintiff in an action, the Plaintiff stated on affidavit that, among other documents relating to the matters in question in the action, he had in his possession certain documents partially prepared by his solicitors in an action previously brought by him against one D. (a person other than the Defendant) for future use in carrying on the said action, but which were, in fact, never completed or used owing to such action not proceeding in consequence of D.'s death, and that the whole of the said documents were of a private and confidential nature between counsel, solicitor, and client :—*Held,* that the documents were privileged from discovery in the action.—*Bullock* v. *Corry* (3 Q. B. D. 356) followed. Pearce v. Foster - - - 15 Q. B. D. 114

23. —— **Notes of Proceedings in Arbitration** —*Transcript.*] The corporation of P. took compulsorily some of R.'s land, and at an arbitration to ascertain the sum to be paid, R. claimed a right of way over other land to a river, and such alleged right had to be considered in regard to the sum to be assessed.—R. employed a shorthand writer to take notes of the evidence and arguments, and afterwards had them transcribed for his own purposes. Subsequently he brought an action for a mandatory injunction to compel the corporation to remove materials which they had put on the land over which he claimed the right of way. The relevancy of the notes was admitted. On motion by the corporation for the production of the transcript, R. objected on the ground that it was privileged, as the notes were taken at his expense and in anticipation of other proceedings against the corporation : — *Held,* that the transcript of the notes was not privileged, and that it must be produced. Rawstone v. Preston Corporation

[30 Ch. D. 116

24. —— **Notes of Proceedings in previous Action.**] An action having been commenced to determine whether the Defendant had or had not executed a certain agreement, the Defendant, while the action was pending, commenced an action against other persons whom he charged with a conspiracy to defraud him, and to utter the agreement as binding upon him, knowing it to be a forgery. After the commencement of the second action, the Defendant caused shorthand notes to be taken of the evidence, speeches, and summing-up at the trial of the first action, as he deposed for the purpose [" amongst others "], of

**XXII. PRACTICE — SUPREME COURT — PRO-
DUCTION OF DOCUMENTS—**continued.

(b.) PRIVILEGE—continued.

his case in the second action:—*Held*, upon the above facts, that the shorthand notes were privileged from inspection in the second action, and that the affidavit need not shew that the notes came into existence exclusively for the purposes of such action. NORDON *v.* DEFRIES
[8 Q. B. D. 508

25. —— Opinions of Counsel—*Reports of Sub-Committees.*] Upon a summons by the Defendant that the Plaintiffs—the corporation—might be ordered to produce the documents comprised in their affidavit or documents :—*Held*, that opinions of counsel with reference to these proceedings, whether taken before or after the commencement of the action, were privileged; and the fact that the Defendant was a ratepayer and the opinions might have been paid for out of the parish rates gave the Defendant no special claim to inspection; and also the minutes of the corporation and sub-committees appointed by them to report concerning matters connected with the litigation were also privileged. MAYOR AND CORPORATION OF BRISTOL *v.* COX
26 Ch. D. 678

26. —— Solicitors and Surveyors—*Correspondence.*] In an action for specific performance of a building contract to take on lease building land from the Defendants, the Defendants sought to protect from production letters which had passed between their solicitors and their surveyors:—*Held*, by Bacon, V.C., that their letters were privileged.—*Held*, on appeal, that the Defendants must produce the letters except such of them (if any) as the Defendants should state by affidavit to have been prepared confidentially after dispute had arisen between the Plaintiff and the Defendants, and for the purpose of obtaining information, evidence, or legal advice with reference to litigation existing or contemplated between the parties to the action. WHEELER *v.* LE MARCHANT
[17 Ch. D. 675

27. —— Trustee and Cestui que Trust—*Correspondence with Solicitors ante litem motam.*] In an action by cestuis que trust against their trustees to compel them to make good a breach of trust :—*Held*, that the trustees must produce letters and copies of letters from and to their solicitors in relation to matters in question in the action ante litem motam.—*Talbot v. Marshfield* (2 Dr. & Sm. 549) followed. *In re* MASON. MASON *v.* CATTLEY
22 Ch. D. 609

—— Recovery of land by legal title 20 Ch. D. 484;
[8 App. Cas. 217

See PRACTICE—SUPREME COURT—INTERROGATORIES. 11.

XXIII. PRACTICE—SUPREME COURT—SECURITY FOR COSTS.

(a.) GENERAL.

1. —— Company Plaintiffs—*Time for making Application—Rules of Court, 1875, Order LV., r. 2—Companies Act, 1862 (25 & 26 Vict. c. 89), s. 69.*] The old rule of the Court of Chancery, that an application for security for the costs of an action must be made promptly is inconsistent with the provision of rule 2 of Order LV., that

XXIII. PRACTICE—SUPREME COURT—SECURITY FOR COSTS—continued.

(a.) GENERAL—continued.

security for costs may be given "at such time or times as the Court may direct," and must be taken to have been abrogated.—*Held*, therefore, that an application by a Defendant for security for the costs of an action brought against him by a limited company might be made after reply and notice of trial. LYDNEY AND WIGPOOL IRON ORE COMPANY *v.* BIRD -
23 Ch. D. 358

2. —— Counter-claim — *Defendant out of Jurisdiction.*] Where a claim and counter-claim arise out of different matters, so that the counter-claim is really in the nature of a cross action, the Defendant, if he is residing out of the jurisdiction, may be required to give security for the Plaintiff's costs of the counter-claim, and, if the only dispute remaining arises on the counter-claim, it is beyond doubt right that he should be so required. SYKES *v.* SACERDOTI -   -   - 15 Q. B. D. 423

3. —— Interpleader by Sheriff—*Defendant in Issue liable to give Security for Costs.*] In an interpleader issue directed upon an application by a sheriff, who has received a notice of a claim to goods seized by him under a writ of fieri facias in execution of a judgment, both the Plaintiff and the Defendant in the issue are really in the position of the Plaintiffs in an ordinary action, and, therefore, the Defendant in the interpleader issue may be ordered to give security for costs in any case in which a Plaintiff may be so ordered, and the rule, that a Defendant cannot be compelled to give security for costs, does not apply.—*Williams* v. *Crosling* (3 C. B. 957) followed.—*Belmonte* v. *Aynard* (4 C. P. D. 221, 352) distinguished. TOMLINSON *v.* LAND AND FINANCE CORPORATION
[14 Q. B. D. 539

4. —— Married Woman *suing separately — Rules of Court, 1875, Order XVI., r. 8.*] The rule as to giving security for costs before a married woman can be allowed to sue separately under Order XVI., rule 8, is the same as in the ordinary case of giving security for costs by an Appellant, and therefore she is to give such security if she has no available means to pay the costs if she loses, but not where she has such means. BROWN *v.* NORTH
9 Q. B. D. 52

5. —— Married Woman *suing without Husband or Next Friend—No Separate Estate—Security for Costs of Action—Married Women's Property Act, 1882, s. 1, sub-s. 2—Rules of Court, 1883, Order XVI., r. 16.*] A married woman being empowered by sect. 1, sub-sect. 2, of the Married Women's Property Act, 1882, to sue as a feme sole, may sue without her husband or a next friend, and cannot be ordered to give security for the costs of the action, even although she have at the time of action no separate estate, and there be nothing upon which, if she fails, the Defendant can issue available execution. *In re* ISAAC. JACOB *v.* ISAAC
30 Ch. D. 418

6. —— Residence Abroad—*Joint Plaintiffs, one residing Abroad—Joint and Separate Claims—Rules of Court, 1875, Order XVI., r. 1.*] An action was brought against the Defendant as a common carrier by two Plaintiffs, one residing abroad. The statement of claim alleged a cou-

XXIII. PRACTICE—SUPREME COURT—SECURITY FOR COSTS—continued.

(a.) GENERAL—continued.

tract by the Defendant with the Plaintiffs jointly, and in the alternative with each of the Plaintiffs separately : — Held, that the Plaintiff residing abroad could not be ordered to give security for costs. D'HORMUSGEE v. GREY   10 Q. B. D. 13

7. —— Residence Abroad— One of Several Plaintiffs coming within Jurisdiction before Appeal.] An action was brought by a mercantile firm, all the members of which were in America, against a firm at Manchester. The Defendants put in a defence and counter-claim, and then applied to the Judge for an order for the Plaintiffs to give security for costs. The Plaintiffs filed an affidavit stating that they with other persons carried on business at Manchester, and that the firm there had assets amounting to £2000. The Judge refused the application. On the appeal the Plaintiffs produced an affidavit stating that since the order one of the Plaintiffs had come to Manchester for the purpose of carrying on the action :—Held, by the Court of Appeal, that the affidavit as to the property of the Plaintiffs in England was ambiguous and was not sufficient to support the order in the Court below.—But held, that as one of the Plaintiffs had come to England since the order was made, although for a temporary purpose, the Defendants were not entitled to security for costs, and therefore the order must be affirmed.—Redondo v. Chaytor (4 Q. B. D. 453) followed. EBBARD v. GASSIER   -   28 Ch. D. 232

8. —— Trustee of Bankrupt's Estate suing in his Official Name — Insolvency — Bankruptcy Act, 1883 (46 & 47 Vict. c. 52), s. 83—Rules of Court, 1883, Order XVII., rr. 4, 5.] A trustee of the property of a bankrupt brought an action in his official name, his own name not being mentioned. The Defendants moved for security for costs on the ground of his insolvency, and of his suing solely in his official name. Evidence was given that he had been bankrupt ten years previously, and had also compounded with his creditors four years before the action was brought :—Held (affirming the decision of Pearson, J.), that the evidence of the insolvency of the Plaintiff was insufficient; and that the fact of his suing solely in his official name was not a ground for ordering him to give security for costs.—When a trustee in bankruptcy suing in his official name is removed, and a new trustee appointed, the new trustee must obtain an order to continue the action, and give notice thereof to the other parties, under Order XVII., rr. 4, 5.—Whether a trustee in bankruptcy suing in his official name would, if insolvent, be ordered to give security for costs, quære.—Denston v. Ashton (Law Rep. 4 Q. B. 590) questioned. POOLEY'S TRUSTEE IN BANKRUPTCY v. WHETHAM   -   28 Ch. D. 38

(b.) APPEAL.

9. —— Delay in making Application—Appellant out of Jurisdiction.] An application for security for costs of an appeal must be made promptly. As a general rule it is too late if it is made when the appeal is in the paper for hearing. But the Court will take into account special circumstances. Where a motion for security for

XXIII. PRACTICE—SUPREME COURT—SECURITY FOR COSTS—continued.

(b.) APPEAL—continued.

costs and the appeal came into the paper on the same day, and it appeared that notice of appeal had been given in the Long Vacation, and that the motion for security had been delayed by reason of the Court not having sat to hear such applications on the usual day, the application was granted.—Semble, the Court will be more strict in enforcing promptness where the application is on the ground of poverty than where it is on the ground of the Appellant being out of the jurisdiction. In re INDIAN, KINGSTON, AND SANDHURST MINING COMPANY   22 Ch. D. 83

10. —— Dismissal of Appeal — For want of Security.] Where an order has been made for the Appellant to give security for the costs of an appeal, if he does not give it within a reasonable time, the Court will dismiss the appeal without giving further time, unless there are extenuating circumstances.—As a general rule a period of three months is more than a reasonable time. WASHBURN AND MOEN MANUFACTURING COMPANY v. PATTERSON   -   -   29 Ch. D. 48

11. —— Poverty of Appellant—Rules of Court, 1875, Order LVIII., r. 15.] The fact that an Appellant would be unable through poverty to pay the costs of the Respondent if the appeal should be unsuccessful is in itself sufficient ground for requiring security for costs. HARLOCK v. ASHBERRY   -   -   19 Ch. D. 84

12. —— Question of Law—Security.] There is no general rule that an insolvent appellant will be exempted from giving security for the costs of the appeal because the case involves a question of law which has not been previously considered by a Court of Error.—Rourke v. White Moss Colliery Company (1 C. P. D. 556) explained. FARBER v. LACY, HARTLAND, & Co. -   28 Ch. D. 482

(c.) DISCOVERY.

13. —— Discretion of Judge—Rules of Court, 1883, Order XXXI., rr. 25, 26.] A party to a cause is not entitled to obtain as a matter of right an order to administer interrogatories without making a deposit under Rules of the Supreme Court, Order XXXI., rules 25, 26, merely because the other party consents to it. The Judge at Chambers has upon an application of that kind a discretion, and in the exercise of that discretion may order the deposit to be made, notwithstanding that the party to be interrogated is ready to dispense with a deposit. ASTE v. STUMORE -   13 Q. B. D. 326

—— Next friend of married women 19 Ch. D. 94

See PRACTICE—SUPREME COURT—NEXT FRIEND. 2.

XXIV. PRACTICE — SUPREME COURT — INQUIRIES AND ACCOUNTS.

1. —— Administration Action—Preliminary Accounts and Inquiries—Rules of Court, 1883, Order XV., r. 1; Order LV., r. 10.] A mortgagee of shares of the proceeds of the residuary real and personal estate of a testator who died in 1872, brought an action in 1884 for the administration of the estate, alleging misapplication by one of the trustees of moneys raised by mortgage of parts of the real estate, and advances to the same trustee

XXIV. PRACTICE — SUPREME COURT — INQUIRIES AND ACCOUNTS—*continued.*

of parts of the testator's estate on equitable mortgage. The Plaintiff applied under Order xv., rule 1, for the common accounts and inquiries in an administration suit, and also for inquiries as to mortgages of the real estate and as to advances to the trustees. Bacon, V.C., refused to make any order:—*Held*, on appeal, that only common accounts and inquiries could be directed on an application under the rule, and not accounts and inquiries the right to which depended on the Plaintiff establishing a case for them at the hearing, and that the special inquiries therefore could not be directed.—*Held* further, that Order xv., rule 1, must be read in connection with Order LV., rule 10, which makes it not obligatory on the Court to order a general administration, and that the Vice-Chancellor was right in refusing the common accounts and inquiries in a case where, having regard to the period elapsed since the testator's death, it was uncertain whether a general administration order would be found at the hearing to be desirable, and where, if the Plaintiff at the hearing established a case of breach of trust, accounts and inquiries would have to be directed, going over in part the same ground as the common accounts and inquiries. *In re* GYHON. ALLEN *v.* TAYLOR　　　-　　　29 Ch. D. 834

2. —— *Foreclosure* — *Rules of Court*, 1883, *Order* XXXIII., *r.* 2.] The Plaintiff, an equitable mortgagee, brought an action for foreclosure or sale against several other mortgagees, insisting that under the circumstances she was entitled to priority over the Defendants. The alleged priority of the Plaintiff to the Defendants depended on questions of notice and fraud. On the application of the Plaintiff, Kay, J., on summons under Order XXXIII., rule 2, made an order directing an inquiry what were the respective priorities of the incumbrances of the Plaintiff and the respective Defendants, and an account of what was due to the incumbrancers respectively. One of the Defendants appealed:—*Held*, on appeal, that this order must be discharged, for that Order XXXIII., rule 2, was not intended to authorize the sending the whole of the questions in a cause to be tried in Chambers, but only to authorize the Court to direct, before trial, accounts and inquiries which would otherwise have been directed at the trial. GARNHAM *v.* SKIPPER　　　-　　　29 Ch. D. 566

3. —— *Foreclosure*—*Rules of Supreme Court*, 1883, *Order* XV., *rr.* 1, 2.] In foreclosure actions where there is no preliminary question to be tried, the Plaintiff may obtain, under Rules of Supreme Court, 1883, Order xv., an order for an account with all necessary inquiries, and the usual directions as in a common foreclosure judgment nisi. Such order should be applied for by summons in Chambers and not by motion in Court, and only the costs of a summons in Chambers attended by counsel will be allowed. SMITH *v.* DAVIES　　-　　28 Ch. D. 650
[*But see* BLAKE *v.* HARVEY, 29 Ch. D. 827] .

XXV. PRACTICE — SUPREME COURT — SPECIAL CASE.

1. —— *Amendment.*] In an action for the administration of the testator's estate it was ordered that a special case should be stated to obtain the opinion of the Court on the effect of the codicil. The case made it appear that the £3000 had been paid by the testator before the date of the codicil, and the declaration made by the Court of Appeal and the consequent inquiry went on this footing, and referred only to sums paid by him before the date of the codicil. A certificate was made accordingly, and the balance due from J. T. was found to be £453. The £3000 had in fact been paid by the testator after the date of the codicil, though he had been called upon for payment before. No subsequent order had been made giving effect to the certificate. The executors on discovering the error applied for leave to amend the special case, which was refused by Kay, J., on the ground of want of jurisdiction:—*Held*, by the Court of Appeal, that the special case could not be amended. But that where a special case is stated in an action, and a decision given upon it under a mistake of fact, the Court is not bound by that decision unless it has been adopted by subsequent orders, but may disregard it, direct the action to go on to trial, and direct inquiries to ascertain the real facts.— On the present occasion, the parties waiving all technical objections, and the payment of the £3000 after the date of the codicil being admitted, the Court decided that the legacy must be reduced by £3453, it not being material whether the £3000 was paid before or after the date of the codicil. *In re* TAYLOR'S ESTATE. TOMLIN *v.* UNDERHAY　　　-　　　22 Ch. D. 495

2. —— *Form of Answers* — *Rules of Court*, 1875, *Order* XXXIV., *r.* 1.] Where a special case for the opinion of the Court is stated in an action pursuant to the Rules of Court, 1875, Order XXXIV., rule 1, and the answers to the special case in fact dispose of the action, the proper course is to take the answers in the shape of a judgment, making declarations to the effect of the answers, the action being, if necessary, set down pro formâ for trial on motion for judgment. HARRISON *v.* CORNWALL MINERALS RAILWAY COMPANY　　　-　　　16 Ch. D. 66

—— Appeal from judgment　　9 Q. B. D. 632
See PRACTICE—SUPREME COURT—APPEAL. 19.

XXVI. PRACTICE — SUPREME COURT — DISTRICT REGISTRY.

—— *Administration Action*—*Taxation*—*Taxing Officer*—*District Registrar* — *Rules of Court*, 1883, *Order* XXXV., *r.* 4 ; *Order* LXV., *r.* 27, *sub-s.* 43 —*Supreme Court Funds Rules*, 1884, *rr.* 3, 11, 12, 98, 111.] The Court can, in its discretion, order the taxation of costs in an administration action commenced and prosecuted in a District Registry to be made by the District Registrar.—The term "Taxing Officer" in rules 3, 11, and 12 of Supreme Court Funds Rules, 1884, these rules being read in conjunction with Order LXV., rule 27, sub-s. 43 of Rules of Supreme Court, 1883, includes "District Registrar," where the Court has directed taxation to be made by that officer, and the Paymaster is bound to act on the certificate of taxation of a District Registrar, when the

XXVI. PRACTICE — SUPREME COURT — DISTRICT REGISTRY—continued.

Court, in the exercise of its discretion, has directed taxation in the District Registry.—The Court, however, following Day v. Whittaker (6 Ch. D. 734), will not, except under very special circumstances, direct the costs of an action commenced in a District Registry to be taxed otherwise than by a Taxing Master of the Chancery Division. In re Wilson. Wilson v. Alltree

[27 Ch. D. 242

XXVII. PRACTICE — SUPREME COURT — NOTICE OF TRIAL.

—— Right of Defendant to give—Abridgment of Time—Rules of Court, 1883, Order XXXVI., r. 12; Order LXIV., r. 7.] Order XXXVI. r. 12, provides that, if the Plaintiff does not within six weeks after the close of the pleadings, or within such extended time as the Court or a Judge may allow, give notice of trial, the Defendant may, before notice of trial given by the Plaintiff, give notice of trial, or may apply to the Court or Judge to dismiss the action for want of prosecution.—Order LXIV., rule 7, provides that the Court or a Judge shall have power to enlarge or abridge the time appointed by the rules, or fixed by any order enlarging time, for doing any act or taking any proceeding, upon such terms (if any) as the justice of the case may require:—Held, that the period of six weeks mentioned in Order XXXVI., rule 12, is not a time appointed for doing any act or taking any proceeding within Order LXIV., rule 7, and consequently that the Court could not make an order giving the Defendant leave to give notice of trial, if the Plaintiff did not give such notice within a shorter period than six weeks from the close of the pleadings. Saunders v. Pawley

[14 Q. B. D. 234

XXVIII. PRACTICE — SUPREME COURT — TRIAL.

1. —— Administration Action—Allegations of Fraud—Wilful Default—Reference to Chambers.] In an action for ordinary administration it is competent for the Court to allow a case of wilful default, though not stated in the pleadings, to be raised at any time during the action, but allegations of fraud and wilful default ought not generally to be adjourned, but should be disposed of at the hearing. Smith v. Armitage 24 Ch. D. 727

2. —— Trial by Jury—Action assigned to Chancery Division—Official Referee—Judicature Act, 1873 (36 & 37 Vict. c. 66), s. 57—Rules of Court, 1883, Order XXXVI., r. 3.] An action, which falls within one of the classes of actions which, by sect. 34 of the Judicature Act, 1873, are specially assigned to the Chancery Division, will not be sent for trial by a jury unless it involves a simple issue of fact, the determination of which will decide the action.—If such an action depends on the determination of mixed questions of law and fact, it ought to be tried by a Judge without a jury, and an order will be made for its trial by the Judge of the Chancery Division to whom it has been assigned, without a jury, even though the Plaintiff has by his statement of claim proposed a different venue.—The mere fact that the action will be tried more quickly, is not a sufficient reason for sending it to be tried at the

XXVIII. PRACTICE — SUPREME COURT — TRIAL—continued.

Assizes.—It was not intended by the Judicature Act that an official referee should decide the issue in an action; he is only to ascertain the facts so as to enable the Court to decide the issue. Cardinall v. Cardinall.   25 Ch. D. 772

3. —— Trial by Jury—Action assigned to Chancery Division—Joinder of Cause of Action not so assigned—Rules of Court, 1883, Order XXXVI., rr. 3, 6.] The Plaintiff commenced an action in the Chancery Division alleging that the Defendant was trustee of a sum of £700 for her, and claiming payment of that sum with interest, and, if necessary, an account of profits made by the Defendant by using it in his business, and also claiming the return of certain chattels, or their value, and damages for their detention. The Defendant denied the trust, stated that the money had been lent to him by the Plaintiff, and long ago repaid, and denied that he ever had any chattels of the Plaintiff in his possession. The Plaintiff, after the defence had been put in, applied to have the issues of fact tried by a jury:— Held, by Pearson, J., and by the Court of Appeal, that the action came within Order XXXVI., rule 3, and not within rule 6 of the same Order. That the action therefore was to be tried by a Judge without a jury, unless it could be made out that it was better to have it tried by jury, and that in the present case this was not shewn. Gardner v. Jay   -   -   -   - 29 Ch. D. 50

4. —— Trial by Jury—Discretion of Court to direct Trial without a Jury—Rules of Court, 1875, Order XXXVI., rr. 3, 26—Appeal from Discretion of Judge.] Either party to an action has an absolute right under Order XXXVI., rule 3, to have the action or the issues tried before a jury, without assigning any reasons, unless it shall appear to the Judge that there are special grounds rendering it desirable to try the action before a Judge without a jury; the onus in such cases being on the party who desires it not to be tried before a jury—Bacon, V.C., having made an order under Order XXXVI., rule 26, that the issues in an action should be tried before himself without a jury, on the ground that no sufficient reason had been shewn for its being tried by a jury:—Held, on appeal, that the Judge having placed the onus of proof on the wrong party, had not exercised his discretion in accordance with the rule, and the Court overruled his decision.—Semble, even if the Judge exercises his discretion in accordance with the rule his decision is subject to appeal, though the Court will not interfere with his discretion except in a very strong case.—Where the whole case is a proper one to be tried by a jury, it is the more convenient practice to transfer the action altogether to the Queen's Bench Division.—Buston v. Tobin (10 Ch. D. 558) commented on. In re Martin. Hunt v. Chambers   -   20 Ch. D. 365

5. —— Trial by Jury—Waiver of Option—Rules of Court, 1875, Order XXXVI., rr. 3, 26.] The hearing of a motion for an injunction was (with the consent of the Defendants), ordered to stand to the hearing, with liberty to either party to apply to expedite the trial:—Held, that the Defendants by consenting to such order were not

2 Q

XXVIII. PRACTICE — SUPREME COURT — TRIAL—*continued.*

deprived of their option to have the issues of fact tried by a jury, although the effect might be to prevent the Plaintiffs from having the trial expedited. CLARKE *v.* SKIPPER - 21 Ch. D. 134

6. —— *Venue—Change of Venue—Action assigned to Chancery Division—Rules of Court*, 1883, *Order XXXVI., r.* 1.] Under Order XXXVI., rule 1, a Plaintiff is entitled to lay the venue of an action in any place that he pleases, although it is specially assigned to the Chancery Division, and has been commenced in that Division. PHILIPS *v.* BEALE - - 26 Ch. D. 621

7. —— *Venue—Mode of Trial—Rules of Court*, 1883, *Order XXXVI., r.* 1.] The Plaintiff in an action to set aside deeds on the ground of fraud, named Cardigan as the place of trial in his statement of claim. On motion by a Defendant before issue joined, the Court ordered the action to be tried in the Chancery Division without a jury, and this decision was affirmed by the Court of Appeal. POWELL *v.* COBB - 29 Ch. D. 486

XXIX. PRACTICE — SUPREME COURT — REFEREE.

1. —— *Compulsory Reference—Official Referee—Judicature Act*, 1873, *ss.* 56, 57—*Appeal from Judicial Discretion in directing Trial before an Official Referee.*] The Court of Appeal has power to review the order made by a Judge under sect. 57 of the Judicature Act, 1873, who, having jurisdiction to make such order, has in the exercise of his discretion ordered the issues of fact in an action to be tried by an official referee, on the ground that they required prolonged examination of documents and also scientific and local investigation ; but the Court of Appeal, whose discretion in such case is to be substituted for that of the Judge, will not exercise such discretion except in a strong case where it clearly thinks the Judge has wrongly exercised his discretion, and that an injustice has been done by the order he has so made.—So *held* by Brett and Holker, L.JJ. (Lord Coleridge, C.J., doubting if the Court had jurisdiction to review the discretion of the Judge).— *Semble*, per Brett, L.J., that the "prolonged examination of documents," intended by sect. 57 of the Judicature Act, 1873, is an examination required to enable the Judge to leave questions of fact to the jury ; and not an examination to enable him to determine a question of legal right. ORMEROD *v.* TODMORDEN MILL COMPANY

[8 Q. B. D. 664

2. —— *Report—Form of—Official Referee—Supreme Court of Judicature Act*, 1873 (36 & 37 *Vict. c.* 66), *ss.* 56, 57.] A referee under the Supreme Court of Judicature Act, 1873, s. 57, is not bound to give his reasons for his findings ; he may simply find the affirmative or the negative of the issues, and the issues in an action cannot be sent back to him for re-trial or further consideration merely on the ground that his report does not set out the reasons for his findings. MILLER *v.* PILLING

[9 Q. B. D. 736

3. —— *Report—Motion for Judgment—Official Referee—Judicature Act*, 1873, *ss.* 56, 57, 58— *Rules of Court*, 1875, *Order XXXVI., r.* 34.] In an

XXIX. PRACTICE — SUPREME COURT — REFEREE—*continued.*

action for an account an order was made under Order XXXIII. to take an account, without prejudice to the proceedings in the action generally being carried on. By a subsequent order it was directed that the accounts should be taken by the official referee. The referee made a report finding a sum due from the Plaintiff. The Plaintiff moved that the report might be set aside and the accounts remitted to the referee, and that he might be directed to state his reasons. The Defendant at the same time moved that the report might be confirmed and the Plaintiff ordered to pay the sum found due. Kay, J., refused both motions, holding that a motion to confirm the report was unnecessary, that the action ought to be set down for trial, and that the Plaintiff could object to the report at the hearing. The Defendant appealed :—*Held*, by the Court of Appeal, that the proper course was not to set down the action for trial, but for the Defendant to move for judgment on the report, and for the Plaintiff to move to set the report aside. Both the orders of Kay, J., were discharged, and the two motions remitted to him to be disposed of on the merits :—*Held*, also, that the proviso as to the order to take the accounts being without prejudice to the proceedings in the action generally being carried on ought not to have been inserted. WALKER *v.* BUNKEEL - - 22 Ch. D. 722

4. —— *Report—Setting aside—Application where and within what Time made—Judicature Act*, 1873, *ss.* 56-58.] Application to set aside the findings of a referee appointed under sect. 57 of the Judicature Act, 1873, to try the issues of fact in an action and report to the Judge making the order of reference, must be made to a Divisional Court and not to the Judge, as such findings are by sect. 58 equivalent to the verdict of a jury and can only be set aside by the Court.—*Quære*, whether the time for making the application runs from the time when the report is made to the Judge. COOKE *v.* NEWCASTLE AND GATESHEAD WATER COMPANY 10 Q. B. D. 332

5. —— *Report — Setting aside — Application within what Time and how made—Judicature Act*, 1873, *ss.* 56-58—*Rules of Court*, 1875, *Order XXXVI., r.* 34—*Order XXXIX., r.* 1 a—*Order LIII., rr.* 2, 3.] Where on a reference under sect. 57 of the Judicature Act the unsuccessful party desires to question the findings of the referee, the proper course is to move the Court on notice under Order LIII. to the other party, and such a motion need not be made within the time limited by Order XXXIX., rule 1A for moving for a new trial in an action tried by a jury. DYKE *v.* CANNELL - - - - 11 Q. B. D. 180

6. —— *Report—Varying Report—Official Referee—Further Consideration.*] Where, in an action which has by the judgment been referred to the official referee and in which further consideration has been adjourned, either party desires to vary the referee's report, he should serve the opposite party with a notice of motion to vary, such notice to be given for the usual motion day. The motion will then be adjourned, as a matter of course, to come on with the further consideration. Where further consideration has not been adjourned, the

XXIX. PRACTICE — SUPREME COURT — RE-FEREE—*continued.*

proceeding to vary may be either a motion or a summons. BURRARD *v.* CALISHER - 19 Ch. D. 644

—— Order for production of documents

[17 Ch. D. 346

See PRACTICE—SUPREME COURT—PRO-DUCTION OF DOCUMENTS. 9.

XXX. PRACTICE — SUPREME COURT — EVI-DENCE.

(a.) GENERAL.

1. —— Affidavit—*Agreement to take Evidence by Affidavit—Examination of Witnesses de bene esse—Rules of Court, 1875, Order XXXVII., r. 4; Order XXXVIII.*] Where the parties to an action agree under Order XXXVIII. to take the evidence in the action by affidavit, and either party subsequently finds himself unable to procure affidavit evidence, either by reason of the reluctance of some of his witnesses to make affidavits or other good cause, his proper course is to take out a summons for leave to be relieved from the agreement, and the Court will, in a proper case, make an order that the reluctant witnesses be examined vivâ voce at the trial, or, at the option of the other party, discharge the agreement and direct all the evidence to be taken vivâ voce at the trial.—Whenever a necessary witness is going abroad, or is from illness, age, or other infirmity likely to be unable to attend the trial, an order will be made under Order XXXVII., rule 4, for his examination before an officer of the Court in the presence of both parties.—A like order will be made whenever it shall appear to the Court necessary for the purposes of justice. WARNER *v.* MOSSES - - - 16 Ch. D. 100

2. —— Affidavit — *Cross-examination — Production of Deponent—Expenses—Rules of Court, 1883, Order XXXVII., r. 21 ; Order XXXVIII., r. 28 —15 & 16 Vict. c. 86, ss. 38, 41.*] The direction in Order XXXVIII., rule 28, of Rules of the Supreme Court, 1883, that the party producing a deponent for cross-examination shall not be entitled to demand the expenses thereof in the first instance from the party requiring such production, must be taken in conjunction with Order XXXVII., rule 21, of the same rules, which provides that evidence taken subsequently to the hearing or trial of any cause or matter shall be taken as nearly as may be in the same manner as evidence taken at or with a view to a trial, is not confined to the cross-examination of the deponent before the Court at the trial of the action, but applies also to a cross-examination before the Chief Clerk in Chambers or before an Examiner. BACKHOUSE *v.* ALCOCK

[28 Ch. D. 669

3. —— Affidavit — *Cross-Examination — Expenses of producing Affidavit Witness for Cross-examination—Rules of Court, 1875, Order XXXVIII., r. 4.*] The provision in Rules of Court, 1875, Order XXXVIII., rule 4, that the party producing deponents for cross-examination upon their affidavits shall not be entitled to demand the expenses thereof in the first instance from the party requiring such production, is confined to a cross-examination of the deponents before the Court at the trial of the action, and does not apply to a cross-examination on an affidavit filed after decree

XXX. PRACTICE — SUPREME COURT — EVI-DENCE—*continued.*

(a.) GENERAL—*continued.*

for the purpose of proceedings in Chambers.—Decision of Bacon, V.C., reversed. *In re* KNIGHT. KNIGHT *v.* GARDNER 24 Ch. D. 606 ; 25 Ch. D. 297

4. —— Affidavit — *Cross-Examination — Expenses of Deponent—Rules of Court, 1883, Order XXXVII., rr. 9, 13, 20, 21 ; Order XXXVIII., r. 28.*] Plaintiff after judgment in an administration action having obtained an order for cross-examination of Defendant (the executor) upon his affidavit, in answer to inquiries directed by the judgment, denying possession of any part of the testator's estate, Defendant declined to attend before the examiner until Plaintiff had paid his expenses. Plaintiff having subsequently served Defendant with a subpoena moved that he be ordered to attend at his own expense :—*Held,* that it was open to the Plaintiff to combine the two methods of procedure, and that the Defendant was bound to produce himself at his own expense for cross-examination ; and further, that regarding the Defendant as a deponent whose attendance was required for cross-examination, the penalty imposed by Order XXXVIII., rule 28 of having his affidavit rejected did not relieve him from the obligation to attend at his own expense. *In re* BAKER. CONNELL *v.* BAKER 29 Ch. D. 711

5. —— Affidavit—*Cross-Examination—Withdrawal of Affidavit—15 & 16 Vict. c. 86, s. 40.*] Where a person has made and filed an affidavit for the purpose of being used in a matter pending before the Court, he cannot be exempted from cross-examination by the withdrawal of the affidavit.—*Clarke* v. *Law* (2 K. & J. 28) approved and held to be applicable where the person making the affidavit is not a party to the proceedings. *In re* QUARTZ HILL, &C., COMPANY. *Ex parte* YOUNG

[21 Ch. D. 642

6. —— Affidavit in Reply—*Rules of Court, 1875, Order XXXVIII., r. 3—Cons. Ord. XXXIII., r. 7.*] Affidavits filed by a Plaintiff in reply will not upon interlocutory motion be ordered to be taken off the file upon an allegation by the Defendant that they are not confined to matters strictly in reply ; though at the hearing, if it should turn out to be so, the Court will not regard them, or may give leave to the Defendant to answer them. GILBERT *v.* COMEDY OPERA COMPANY - 16 Ch. D. 594

7. —— Witness—*Action in Chancery Division—Arbitrator—Compelling Attendance of Witness—Subpoena—3 & 4 Will. 4, c. 42, s. 40—Judicature Act, 1873, ss. 3, 16.*] An order may now be made on summons in the Chancery Division under 3 & 4 Will. c. 42, s. 40, requiring the attendance of a witness before an arbitrator appointed in an action in that Division, and the order will be directed to be served as an ordinary subpoena. CLARBROUGH *v.* TOOTHILL

[17 Ch. D. 787

8. —— Witness—*Right to subpoena Witness—Evidence after Decree — Leave of the Court—Proceedings in Chambers—15 & 16 Vict. c. 86, ss. 40, 41—Rules of Court, 1875, Order XXXVII., r. 4.*] Any party may without leave of the Court issue a subpoena for the examination of a witness

XXX. PRACTICE — SUPREME COURT — EVI-
DENCE—*continued.*

(a.) GENERAL—*continued.*

at any stage of an action; but the Court will exercise a control over this privilege to prevent its being oppressively used. In an action for the redemption of a mortgage the usual judgment was obtained and the Defendant, the mortgagee, proceeded to vouch his accounts in Chambers. The Plaintiffs subpœnaed a solicitor who had acted for both parties in the mortgage transactions, in order to examine him with respect to the moneys received by him on account of both parties:—*Held*, that the Plaintiff was entitled to issue the subpœna and to examine the witness. RAYMOND *v.* TAPSON　　-　　22 Ch. D. 430

(b.) ABROAD.

9. —— Affidavit—*Foreign Country—Notary Public—Consul*—15 & 16 *Vict. c.* 86, *s.* 22—*Court of Probate Act,* 1858 (21 & 22 *Vict. c.* 95), *s.* 31 —*Rules of Court,* 1883, *Order XXXVIII., r.* 6; *Order LXXII., r.* 2.] Before and after the Act 15 & 16 Vict. c. 86, affidavits sworn in foreign parts out of Her Majesty dominions before a notary public might be filed, and that practice continued in force down to the time when the Rules of the Supreme Court, 1883, came into operation.—*Held*, that this practice is not abrogated by Order XXXVIII., rule 6, and Order LXXII.. rule 2, of the Rules of 1883, and may be followed at any rate in cases where the practice under the Rules of 1883 would be very inconsistent. COOKE *v.* WILBY　-　　~　　25 Ch. D. 769

10. —— Commission to Foreign Court—*Witness resident Abroad—Rules of Court,* 1875, *Order XXXVII., r.* 4.] Upon an application for a commission to take the evidence of a witness who is abroad, the Court ought to be satisfied that the application is made bonâ fide, and that the claim in support of which the evidence is desired is one which the Court ought to try, but it ought not to go any further into the merits of the claim. —In a case in which a claim was made under very suspicious circumstances, and the Court was of opinion that a person resident abroad, whose evidence was desired in support of it, ought to be subjected to a drastic cross-examination:— *Held*, that a commission ought not to be issued to a foreign Court for the examination of the witness abroad, because it appeared that under the procedure of that Court he would not be cross-examined in the ordinary way. *In re* BOYES. CROFTON *v.* CROFTON　　20 Ch. D. 760

11. —— Commission to examine Plaintiff— *Rules of Court,* 1875, *Order XXXVII., r.* 4.] A commission to examine the Plaintiff abroad was applied for by the Plaintiff on the ground that the state of his health was such that a voyage to England would be dangerous to his life. The Court refused the commission, holding that his cross-examination before the English Court was required in the interests of justice, and that he had not proved the truth of his allegation that the voyage would be dangerous to his life. BERDAN *v.* GREENWOOD　　-　　20 Ch. D. 764, n.

12. —— Commission to examine Witness— *Single Commissioner—Administration of Oath— Rules of Court, April,* 1880, *Schedule, Form G.*

XXX. PRACTICE — SUPREME COURT — EVI-
DENCE—*continued.*

(b.) ABROAD—*continued.*

11.] When a single Commissioner is appointed to take evidence abroad the commission should authorize him to administer the oath to himself. WILSON *v.* DE COULON　　-　　22 Ch. D. 841

13. —— Commission to examine Witness — *Rules of Court,* 1875, *Order XXXVII., r.* 4.] L. granted to T. an exclusive licence to use in England a certain patented invention for making sugar. This invention was also patented in America, and M., an American sugar manufacturer, had a licence for its use in the United States. L. brought his action against T., to have the licence rectified, alleging that the real agreement between the parties was that the licence was not to interfere with the importation into England of sugar made abroad under the patent. The statement of claim alleged that M. had introduced L. to T., and that the negotiations between L. and T. had proceeded on the understanding that sugar made abroad under the patent might be imported; but there was no allegation, nor did it appear in evidence, that M. had taken part in the negotiations. L. applied to have a commission to examine M. in America:—*Held*, by Chitty, J., that the application must be refused as in *Berdan* v. *Greenwood* (20 Ch. D. 764, n.) for that it was essential that M., an interested witness, should be examined and cross-examined orally before the Judge who tried the case.—*Held*, by the Court of Appeal, that if it appeared that the evidence of M. would be material, the commission ought to be granted, there being nothing to shew that M. was keeping out of the way to avoid cross-examination; and that *Berdan* v. *Greenwood* turned on the fact that the Court was convinced that the plaintiff there was so keeping out of the way.—But, *held*, that on the materials before the Court the commission was rightly refused, there being nothing to shew that M. had taken such part in the negotiations as to make his evidence material. The Court, however, as an indulgence, gave the Plaintiff an opportunity of adducing evidence to shew that M. could give material evidence. LANGEN *v.* TATE

[24 Ch. D. 522

14. —— Commission to examine Witness — *Rules of Court,* 1883, *Order XXXVII., r.* 5.] If it is shewn that there are material witnesses resident abroad whom a party wishes to examine, a commission to examine them abroad will be granted if there is any reasonable ground for their not coming here, unless a case is made shewing that it is necessary for the purposes of justice that they should be examined in England. ARMOUR *v.* WALKER　　-　　25 Ch. D. 673

15. —— Commission to examine Witness— *Rules of Court,* 1883, *Order XXXVII., r.* 5.] Where it is sought to have a material witness examined abroad, and the nature of the case is such that it is important that he should be examined here, the party asking to have him examined abroad must shew clearly that he cannot bring him to this country to be examined at the trial. LAWSON *v.* VACUUM BRAKE COMPANY　　27 Ch. D. 137

16. —— Commission to examine Witness—

**XXX. PRACTICE — SUPREME COURT — EVI-
DENCE**—*continued*.

(b.) ABROAD—*continued*.

*Examination of Parties to the Suit—Rules of Court,
1875, Order XXXVII., r. 4—Rules of Court, 1883,
Order XXXVII., r. 5.*] A Plaintiff residing in
New Zealand brought an action for redemption
alleging himself to be the heir-at-law of a person
who had died intestate entitled to a remainder in
fee in the equity of redemption which had fallen
into possession since his death. The Plaintiff's
case was that he had been long resident in New
Zealand and had had no communication with his
family since 1860, and had only been recently
informed of his title. The Defendant was a
person to whom the property had been sold by a
person whose elder brother the Plaintiff alleged
himself to be. The Defendant did not dispute
the Plaintiff's right to redeem if he was the person
he represented himself to be, but required proof
of his identity. The Plaintiff applied for a commission to examine himself, two persons named
and others residing in New Zealand. Mr. Justice
Kay made the order, and directed that the depositions might be given in evidence at the trial
" without prejudice to the right of the Defendant
to cross-examine the Plaintiff at the trial in the
presence of witnesses in England who can speak
to his identity." The Defendant appealed from
the order :—*Held*, that there was jurisdiction to
appoint examiners for the examination of a party
to the cause as well as of a mere witness :—But,
held, that the deposition of the Plaintiff ought
not to be admitted at the trial if the Defendant
required him to appear at the trial to be examined and cross-examined, it not being shewn
that there was any practical impossibility of his
attending :—*Held*, further, that the order need
not be confined to witnesses mentioned in it by
name, but that the Plaintiff must give notice to
the other side in New Zealand of the witnesses
he proposed to call. NADIN v. BASSETT

[25 Ch. D. 21

(c) DE BENE ESSE.

17. —— **Old Suit.**] In 1815 some customary
tenants of a manor filed their bill on behalf of
themselves and all other the customary tenants
to establish their right to work minerals under
their tenements without the consent of the lord.
A commission was taken out in the same year to
examine certain old persons de bene esse, and
they were examined. After this the suit abated,
was revived, and answers were put in 1819,
after which nothing further was done. In 1871
a bill of the same nature was filed by customary
tenants, who did not interfere under any of the
persons named as Plaintiffs in the suit of 1815.—
Held, by Hall, V.C., and by the Court of Appeal,
that the evidence taken de bene esse in the
former suit was admissible on behalf of the Plaintiffs in the latter suit, the issue in the two suits
being the same, and there being privity of estate
between the parties to the two suits respectively.
LLANOVER v. HOMFRAY.　PHILLIPS v. LLANOVER

[19 Ch. D. 224

18. —— **Witness above seventy years of age**
—*Affidavit — Sufficiency of — Rules of Court,
1883, Order XXXVII., rr. 1-5 ; Order XXXVIII.,
r. 3.*] The Court has jurisdiction on a proper

**XXX. PRACTICE —SUPREME COURT — EVI-
DENCE**—*continued*.

(c.) DE BENE ESSE—*continued*.

occasion when it is "necessary for the purpose of justice," to make an order for an examination de bene esse of witnesses upon an ex parte
application, the order being taken by the applicant at his peril, and subject to the risk of being
discharged on sufficient grounds. An order was
made in Chambers on an ex parte application by
the Plaintiffs to examine de bene esse thirty
witnesses upon an affidavit of the Plaintiffs' solicitor merely stating that he was advised that they
were material witnesses—that they were all above
seventy years of age, and that he was advised and
believed that by reason of their age it was desirable that their examination should be taken
without delay. This order was discharged by
Kay, J., on motion in Court, mainly on the ground
that the affidavit was insufficient :—*Held*, by the
Court of Appeal (affirming Kay, J.), that the affidavit did not satisfy the requirements of Order
XXXVIII., rule 3, but leave was given to put in a
further affidavit stating what information had
been obtained, and what steps had been taken to
obtain such information as to the age of the different witnesses, and also stating generally the
facts which the particular witnesses were going
to depose to. Although the fact that a witness is
seventy years old is generally a good primâ facie
ground for an order for his examination de bene
esse, such a practice will not necessarily be applied
to an extraordinary case, e.g., where an order has
been made to examine thirty witnesses. On a
subsequent application made on a further affidavit
of the solicitor, in which he divided the witnesses
into four classes who were to depose to four
different heads of evidence.—The Court declined
to allow the examination de bene esse of ten of
the proposed witnesses who were between seventy
and seventy-five years old, without prejudice to a
subsequent application for leave to examine them
on grounds other than age, but allowed the other
twenty witnesses above seventy-five to be examined de bene esse upon the undertaking of the
Plaintiff's counsel to produce at the trial, if so
requested by the Defendant, any of such witnesses
who might be then alive. BIDDER v. BRIDGES

[26 Ch. D. 1

**XXXI. PRACTICE—SUPREME COURT — NEW
TRIAL.**

1. —— **County Court** — *Action remitted for
Trial to County Court under 19 & 20 Vict. c. 108, s.
26—Rules of Court, 1883, Order XXXIX., r. 1—
Trial before Judge without Jury.*] In an action
remitted for trial to a County Court and tried by
the County Court Judge without a jury, an application for a new trial must, under the Rules of
the Supreme Court, 1883, be made to the Divisional Court. SWANSEA CO-OPERATIVE BUILDING
SOCIETY v. DAVIES - - 12 Q. B. D. 21

2. —— **County Court**—*Action remitted to the
County Court for Trial of Issues under 19 & 20 Vict.
c. 108, s. 26—Order XXXIX. of the Rules of 1883
—Order LII., r. 1—County Courts Act, 1875 (38
& 39 Vict. c. 50), s. 6.*] Rules 3 and 4 of Order
XXXIX., and Rule 1 of Order LII. (of 1883),
have no application to cases sent for trial to a

XXXI. PRACTICE—SUPREME COURT—NEW TRIAL—continued.

County Court under 19 & 20 Vict. c. 108, s. 26; applications for new trials, therefore, are still regulated by the old practice. PRITCHARD v. PRITCHARD - 14 Q. B. D. 55

[*But see* Rules of Court, December, 1885, Order LIX., rr. 9–17.]

3. —— County Court—*Improper Rejection of Evidence—Rules of Court, 1883, Order xxxix., r. 6 —County Courts Act, 1875 (38 & 39 Vict. c. 50), s. 6.*] Order xxxix., rule 6, provides that a new trial shall not be granted on the ground (inter alia) of the improper rejection of evidence, unless in the opinion of the Court some substantial wrong or miscarriage has been thereby occasioned in the trial:—*Held*, that the above rule applies to a motion in the High Court for a new trial in a County Court action. SHAPCOTT v. CHAPPELL
[12 Q. B. D. 58

4. —— Damages excessive—*Power of Court to reduce Damages.*] In a case where the Plaintiff is entitled to substantial damages, and a verdict for the Plaintiff cannot be impeached except on the ground that the damages are excessive, the Court has power to refuse a new trial, on the Plaintiff alone, and without the Defendant, consenting to the damages being reduced to such an amount as the Court would consider not excessive had they been given by the jury. BELT v. LAWES
[12 Q. B. D. 356

5. —— Verdict against Evidence—*Principle on which New Trial allowed.*] The question whether a new trial should be granted on the ground that the verdict was against the weight of evidence, must depend upon whether the verdict was such as reasonable men ought to have given, and not upon whether the learned Judge who tried the action was dissatisfied or not with the verdict. SOLOMON v. BITTON 8 Q. B. D. 176

XXXII. PRACTICE—SUPREME COURT — MOTION FOR JUDGMENT.

1. —— Admissions in Pleadings—*Admission of Claim—Counter-claim—Rules of Court, 1875, Order xix., r. 3, Order xl., r. 11.*] In an action for a liquidated demand the Defendants pleaded admitting the claim, but setting up a counter-claim for unliquidated damages to a greater amount.—The Court refused an application under Order xl., r. 11, for an order to sign judgment for the Plaintiffs upon the claim, and for payment of the amount thereof by the Defendants into Court to abide the result of the action. MERSEY STEAMSHIP CO. v. SHUTTLEWORTH - 10 Q. B. D. 468;
[11 Q. B. D. 531

2. —— Admissions in Pleadings — *Indorsement on Writ—" Pleading"—Rules of Court, 1875, Order ii., r. 1; Order xl., r. 11—Judicature Act, 1873, s. 100.*] The indorsement on a writ is not a "pleading" so as to entitle a Plaintiff, without the consent of the Defendant, to move thereon for an order on admissions in the pleadings under Rules of Court, 1875, Order xl., r. 11, in a case where the Defendant, admitting the Plaintiff's claim, has given notice that he does not require the delivery of a statement of claim. WALLIS v. JACKSON - 23 Ch. D. 204

3. —— Admissions in Pleadings — *Specific*

XXXII. PRACTICE—SUPREME COURT—MOTION FOR JUDGMENT—continued.

Performance—Rules of Court, 1875, Order xl., r. 11.] A plaintiff may move for judgment upon admissions in the pleadings at any stage in the action and notwithstanding that he has joined issue on the defence and given notice of trial. BROWN v. PEARSON - 21 Ch. D, 716

XXXIII. PRACTICE — SUPREME COURT — JUDGMENT.

1. —— Action against Firm—*Rules of Court, 1875, Order ix., r. 6, and Order xlii., r. 8.*] Where the writ in an action is issued against a partnership firm in the name of the firm the judgment must be against the firm, and it cannot be separately entered against an individual member of the firm who has made default in appearing to the action. JACKSON v. LITCHFIELD 8 Q. B. D. 474

2. —— Action against Firm—*Service of Writ on one Member of a Trading Partnership—Appearance by him only "as a partner of the firm"—Rules of Court, 1883, Order xii., r. 15.*] A writ was issued against a trading partnership (unincorporated), and served upon a member of the firm, who entered an appearance, "W. N., a partner of the firm of W. T. & Co." There was no service upon or appearance by the other members of the firm:—*Held*, that leave to sign judgment against the firm for default of appearance could not be granted.—*Jackson* v. *Litchfield* (8 Q. B. D. 474) followed. ADAM v. TOWNEND 14 Q. B. D. 103

3. —— Judgment against Firm — *Action on Judgment—Execution—Rules of Court, 1875, Order xlii., r. 8.*] Where judgment has been recovered against a partnership firm in the name of the firm, the Plaintiff may bring an action on the judgment against the individual members of the firm, and is not confined to the remedy given by Order xlii., rule 8, with respect to the issue of execution. CLARK v. CULLEN 9 Q. B. D. 355

4. —— No Proceeding for a Year—*Notice—Rules of Court, 1883, Order xiii., r. 3; Order lxiv., r. 13.*] Where on default of appearance by the Defendant the Plaintiff takes no step in the cause for a year, Order lxiv., r. 13, applies, and notice is necessary before judgment can be signed. WEBSTER v. MYER - 14 Q. B. D. 231

5. —— Setting aside Judgment—*Application by a Person not party to the Record—Judicature Act, 1873, s. 24, sub-s. 5—Rules of Court, 1883, Order xxvii., r. 15.*] If a person, who is not a party to the record, seeks to set aside a judgment by which he is injuriously affected, which the Defendant in the action has allowed to go by default, he ought by summons, taken out in the name of the Defendant, or if not entitled to use the Defendant's name, then taken out in his own name, but in that case served on both the Plaintiff and the Defendant, to apply for leave to have the judgment set aside, and to be allowed either to defend the action on such terms of indemnifying the Defendant as the Judge may consider right, or to intervene in the action in the manner pointed out by the Judicature Act, 1873, s. 24, sub-s. 5. Order xxvii., rule 15, is designed to enable judgments by default to be set aside by those who have or who can acquire a locus standi,

XXXIII. PRACTICE — SUPREME COURT — JUDGMENT—*continued:*

and does not give a locus standi to those who have none. JACQUES v. HARRISON

[12 Q. B. D. 136, 165

6. —— Varying Minutes—*Order of Appeal Court—Notice of Motion to vary.*] Where any party is dissatisfied with an order as settled by the Registrar, and desires to bring the matter before the Court, he must, whether the order be an order of the Court of Appeal or of a Court of first instance, give notice of motion to vary the minutes. GENERAL SHARE AND TRUST COMPANY v. WETLEY BRICK AND POTTERY COMPANY

[20 Ch. D. 130

7. —— Varying Minutes—*Production of Registrar's Note.*] On the hearing of a motion to vary the minutes of an order the solicitor of the moving party ought to produce a copy of the Registrar's note of what took place when the order was made. ROBINSON v. LOCAL BOARD OF BARTON

[21 Ch. D. 621

8. —— Varying Order—*Foreclosure Order—Rules of Court, 1883, Order* XV., r. 1—*Order* XXVIII., r. 11.] The Plaintiffs in a foreclosure action applied by summons under Order XV., rule 1, for an account. The Chief Clerk pronounced the usual order for an account and foreclosure. The Defendants objected to the direction for foreclosure, and the Plaintiffs assenting, the order was drawn up for an account only, and was passed and entered in that form. When the parties came before the Chief Clerk to proceed with the account he objected to the order as not being the one he had pronounced, and refused to proceed with the account. Subsequently the Registrar, at the instance of the Chief Clerk, without any motion or summons, altered the order by adding the usual directions for foreclosure. The Defendants moved to strike out the additions. Kay, J., declined to do so, as he considered that the parties were not at liberty to have an order drawn up, different from the order pronounced, without applying to the Court for the purpose; but, being of opinion that the addition had been irregularly made, he stayed proceedings under the existing order, giving the Plaintiffs liberty to apply for a fresh order for accounts and foreclosure. The Defendants appealed :—*Held*, that assuming the order as passed and entered to contain an error arising from an accidental slip or omission, an alteration made in it without any motion or summons for the purpose was irregular, and must be discharged, and that the Plaintiffs must pay the costs, as they ought to have applied to the Judge when the Chief Clerk refused to proceed with the accounts.—Whether a foreclosure Order can be made under Order XV., rule 1, as in *Smith* v. *Davies* (28 Ch. D. 650), *quære.*—Whether there was jurisdiction to stay proceedings under the order against the wish of the Defendants, *quære.* BLAKE v. HARVEY

[29 Ch. D. 827

9. —— Varying Order—*Correcting Error—Order passed and entered—Order not conformable to what the Court intended.*] An order of the Court of Appeal was drawn up, passed and entered, in such a form that it might be contended to decide questions which had not been before the Court, and which it had not intended to de-

XXXIII. PRACTICE — SUPREME COURT — JUDGMENT—*continued.*

cide :—*Held*, that the Court had jurisdiction to alter the record of its order, so as to make it conformable to the order which the Court had pronounced, and the record was altered accordingly, but as the applicant had not adopted the usual and proper course of applying to vary the minutes, he was ordered to pay the costs of the application. *In re* SWIRE. MELLOR v. SWIRE

[30 Ch. D. 239

—— Judgment against partnership — Action against partners in name of firm

See Cases under PRACTICE — SUPREME COURT—PARTIES. 10—15.

XXXIV. PRACTICE — SUPREME COURT—SEQUESTRATION.

1. —— Chose in Action—*Bankers.*] Where a sequestration had been issued against A. :—*Held*, that A.'s balance at his bankers might be attached under it, and that the Court had jurisdiction to order the bankers to verify and pay the balance to the sequestration account. MILLER v. HUDDLESTONE　　　- 　- 22 Ch. D. 233

2. —— Enforcing Sequestration—*Divorce Action.*] A co-Respondent in a divorce action was ordered to pay damages and costs, and a writ of sequestration was issued by the Probate and Divorce Division to enforce such order. He was entitled to certain trust moneys which were being administered in the Chancery action :—*Held*, that the Court of Chancery had jurisdiction on motion of the sequestrators in the Chancery action to order the trust moneys to be paid to the sequestrators. *In re* SLADE. SLADE v. HULME

[18 Ch. D. 653

3. —— Non-Payment of Costs—*Rules of Court of April, 1880 [Order* XLVII., r. 2]—*Subpœna for Costs—Chambers.*] On a motion the Court gave leave in its discretion, under the Rules of Court of April, 1880, to issue a sequestration for the payment of costs.—Where such application is made in an action which is transferred for hearing only to a Judge who does not sit in Chambers, it is properly made to such Judge in Court, otherwise in Chambers. SNOW v. BOLTON

[17 Ch. D. 433

XXXV. PRACTICE — SUPREME COURT—ATTACHMENT.

1. —— Defaulting Trustee—*Debtors Act, 1869 (32 & 33 Vict. c. 62), s. 4—Debtors Act, 1878 (41 & 42 Vict. c. 54), s. 1.*] On application for an attachment against a defaulting trustee, the Court has jurisdiction to inquire into the circumstances of the case, and where there has been no actual fraud or embezzlement, but merely an erroneous application of the trust fund, may refuse the application for an attachment.—*Barrett* v. *Hammond* (10 Ch. D. 285) followed.—*Marris* v. *Ingram* (13 Ch. D. 338) distinguished. HOLROYDE v. GARNETT　　　- 　20 Ch. D. 532

2. —— Discharge of Prisoner—*Custody for Contempt — Sheriff—Debtors Act, 1869 (32 & 33 Vict. c. 62), s. 4.*] No order is necessary for the discharge of a prisoner in custody for contempt under any of the exceptions contained in sect. 4 of the Debtor's Act, 1869, where the writ of

XXXV. PRACTICE—SUPREME COURT—AT-TACHMENT—continued.

attachment has appended to it a note in the following terms: "NOTE.—This writ does not authorize an imprisonment for any longer period than one year." It is now the usual practice to append the above note to all writs of attachment issued under the above section. *In re* EDWARDS. BROOKE *v.* EDWARDS　　　21 Ch. D. 230

3. —— Indorsement on Order—*Cons. Ord.xxIII. r.* 10.] On the 20th of May, 1881, an order was made for the Defendants within seven days after service, to file an affidavit as to documents. The copy served had no such indorsement as is required by Cons. Ord. XXIII. r. 10. The Defendants filed successively three affidavits, which were successively held insufficient, and on the 10th of February, 1882, filed a fourth. A summons was taken out to consider its sufficiency, and on its being attended on the 24th of February, the Defendant's solicitor stated that the draft of a further affidavit had been sent into the country, and that the affidavit would be filed as soon as possible, and requested an adjournment. The Chief Clerk refused to adjourn; held the affidavit of the 10th of February 'to be insufficient, and ordered the Defendants to pay the costs. On the 25th the Plaintiffs served notice of motion for attachment for the 3rd of March. On the 28th of February the Defendants filed a further affidavit, and on the first of March asked the Plaintiffs' solicitors whether they proposed to withdraw their notice of motion. The Plaintiffs' solicitors replied that they did not, as their briefs had been delivered before the affidavit was filed, but that they would consider any proposal the Defendants had to make. The Defendant's solicitors wrote in answer, making no offer to pay any costs, but saying that they should deliver their briefs. North, J., refused the motion with costs:—*Held*, on appeal, that the Plaintiffs were right in giving their notice of motion, and that as the Defendants had made no offer to pay any costs, the Plaintiffs were entitled to bring on their motion, and must have the costs of it. Under the practice established by the Judicature Acts, it is not necessary that the copy of an order which is served should have the indorsement required by Cons. Ord. XXIII., r. 10, stating the consequences of failing to obey the order. THOMAS *v.* PALIN　　-　　21 Ch. D. 360

4. —— Indorsement on Order — *Rules of Court*, 1883, *Order XLI., r.* 5 — *Form of Notice of Motion for Attachment — Order LII., r.* 4.] By order of the 13th of February, 1884, the Defendant was directed to pay a sum into Court by the 13th of March. This order not having been served before the 13th of March, an order was made on the 3rd of April enlarging the time until four days after service of the two orders. The Plaintiff served the two orders, indorsing on the former the notice given in Order I. of the 7th of January, 1870, but putting no indorsement on the latter. The money not having been paid in, the Plaintiff moved for an attachment "for your default in obeying the orders made herein on the 28th of February last and the 3rd of April last," supporting it by an affidavit that the Defendant had not borrowed the order for the purpose of paying in the money, nor given

XXXV. PRACTICE—SUPREME COURT — AT-TACHMENT—continued.

notice of having paid in the money :—*Held*, that as the second order did not require the Defendant to do any act, but only extended the time for doing the act mentioned in the first order, it was sufficient to indorse the first order only:—*Held*, also, that the indorsement was sufficient in form, for that although not in the words of the indorsement given in the rules of 1883, Order XLI., rule 5, it was to the same effect:—*Held*, also, that, having regard to the nature of the orders, a notice of motion to attach "for default in obeying" them sufficiently stated the grounds of the application within the meaning of Order LII., rule 4: —*Held*, also, that though the affidavit in support of the application would probably have been held insufficient to support an attachment, if the motion had been heard on affidavit of service, the defect was cured by the Defendant's appearing and resisting the application on other grounds. TREHERNE *v.* DALE　　-　　27 Ch. D. 66

5. —— Leave to issue—*Judge at Chambers, Jurisdiction of—Judicature Act*, 1873, *s.* 39—*Rules of Court*, 1883, *Order XLIV., r.* 2.] A Judge at chambers has power to give leave to issue a writ of attachment.—So held by Grove, J., and Huddleston, B., Day, J., dissenting. SALM KYRBURG *v.* POSNANSKI　　-　　[13 Q. B. D. 218

6. —— Order for Delivery up of Deeds—*Execution of Writ—Breaking open outer Door.*] Where a writ of attachment has issued against a party to an action for contempt of Court in non-compliance with an order for the delivery over of deeds and documents, the officer charged with the execution of the writ may break open the outer door of the house in order to execute it. —*Burdett* v. *Abbot* (14 East, 1) and *In re Freston* (11 Q. B. D. 545) discussed. HALVEY *v.* HARVEY　　-　　-　　26 Ch. D. 644

7. —— Order for Discovery — *Service — Omission to serve Copy of Affidavit with Notice of Motion—Rules of Court*, 1883, *Order XXXI., r.* 21 ; *Order LII., r.* 4.] On giving a notice of motion to commit a Defendant for contempt in disobeying an order for discovery, the Plaintiffs omitted to serve with the notice of motion a copy of an affidavit which they stated in the notice that they should read in support of the motion :—*Held*, that rule 4 of Order LII. applied to such a notice of motion, and not only to a case in which a writ of attachment would have issued under the old Common Law practice, and that the notice of motion was, therefore, irregular.—But *held*, that the motion should not be at once dismissed, but should be ordered to stand over until after the hearing of a summons by the Defendant for further time to make the discovery. LITCHFIELD *v.* JONES [25 Ch. D. 64

8. —— Order for Production of Documents—*Service on Solicitor—Indorsement on Order—Rules of Court*, 1883, *Order XXXI., rr.* 21, 22, 23 ; *Order XLI., r.* 5 ; *Order LII., r.* 4.] Order XLI., rule 5, which requires every order to bear an indorsement warning the party bound by it of the consequences of disobedience, applies to an order for discovery of documents of which service on the solicitor is permitted. And a writ of attachment cannot be issued against a person who

XXXV. PRACTICE — SUPREME COURT — AT-TACHMENT—*continued*.

disobeys such an order unless the copy served on his solicitor bore the required indorsement.—A party whose solicitor was served with such an order without the required indorsement took out a summons for further time :—*Held* (dissentiente Lindley, L.J.), that he did not thereby waive the irregularity of the service. — The decision of Chitty, J., reversed.—The affidavit in support of a motion for attachment was not served with the notice of motion as it ought to have been under Order LII., rule 4, but was served two clear days before the day named in the notice of motion for moving the Court :—*Held*, by Chitty, J., that this was not such an irregularity as made the notice invalid. HAMPDEN *v.* WALLIS 26 Ch. D. 746

9. —— Service — *Non-service of Order — Notice to Defendant*.] In order to justify the committal of a defendant for breach of an injunction it is not necessary that the order granting the injunction should have been served upon him if it is proved that he had notice of the order aliunde, and knew that the plaintiff intended to enforce it.—This rule is not limited to cases in which a breach is committed before there has been time for the plaintiff to get the order drawn up and entered—*James v. Downes* (18 Ves. 522) and *Vansandau v. Rose* (2 Jac. & W. 264) discussed and explained. UNITED TELEPHONE COMPANY *v.* DALE - - 25 Ch. D. 778

—— Appeal from refusal to commit
[20 Ch. D. 493
See PRACTICE — SUPREME COURT—AP-PEAL. 1.

—— Removing goods from custody of sheriff—Notice of motion necessary
[9 Q. B. D. 335
See PRACTICE—SUPREME COURT—NOTICE OF MOTION. 1.

XXXVI. PRACTICE—SUPREME COURT—GAR-NISHEE ORDERS.

1. —— Debt — *Default of Appearance — Unliquidated Claim—Rules of Court*, 1883, *Order XLV., r. 1—Assignment—Interpleader*.] A claim on a fire policy having been made against an insurance company for unliquidated damages, the Plaintiff, a judgment creditor of the assured for £127, duly served an ex parte garnishee order, under Order XLV., rule 1, on the company, attaching all debts owing or accruing from them to the assured. The company did not appear to shew cause against it, and the order was made absolute. An award on the claim was afterwards made of £248 due to the assured, who assigned it to trustees for his creditors. The Plaintiff demanded payment under his garnishee order of £127 out of the sum payable by the company, and threatened them with execution, and the trustees ,claiming the £248, the company took out an interpleader summons on which an order was made directing the sum of £127 to be paid into Court, and an issue to be tried as to whether that sum was the property of the Plaintiff or the trustees.—On appeal ;—*Held*, that although no attachable debt was in existence at the date of the garnishee order, yet it, not having been set aside, entitled the Plaintiff to issue execution for

XXXVI. PRACTICE—SUPREME COURT—GAR-NISHEE ORDERS—*continued*.

£127, and that the interpleader order was wrong. RANDALL *v.* LITHGOW - 12 Q. B. D. 525

2. —— Debt — *Conditional Debt — Railway Company—Verdict by Jury—Statutory Contract—Specific Performance — Purchase-money—"Debt due or accruing in hands of Garnishee"—Lands Clauses Consolidation Act*, 1845, *ss.* 49, 50—*Rules of Court*, 1875, *Order XLV., rr.* 3, 8.] A "debt due or accruing" to a judgment debtor and therefore capable of being attached by a garnishee order under Rules of Court, 1875, Order XLV., rule 3, must be an absolute and not merely a conditional debt.—Thus, where, after notice to treat by a railway company to a landowner, the purchase-money has been fixed by the verdict of a jury and judgment of the sheriff under sects. 49 and 50 of the Lands Clauses Act, the purchase-money cannot be attached by a garnishee order nisi served upon the company by a judgment creditor of the landowner after the verdict but before the execution or tender of a conveyance ; for the proceedings under the above sections do not of themselves create an absolute debt due from the company to the landowner, his right to the purchase-money being conditional upon the execution or tender of a conveyance.—Accordingly in a case where the landowner has brought an action and obtained judgment against the company for specific performance of the statutory contract :—*Held*, that the purchase-money could not be attached by garnishee orders nisi served upon the company, some before and others after the commencement of the action, notwithstanding that a good title had been shewn ; nor even by a garnishee order served after the execution of the conveyance when the money had been paid into Court by the company under the judgment, the money not being "a debt in the hands" of the garnishee within. rule 3 of Order XLV.—The provisions of rule 8 of Order XLV., as to payment or execution being. a valid discharge to the garnishee, are inapplicable to a debt due to the judgment debtor that is conditional only. HOWELL *v.* METROPOLITAN DISTRICT RAILWAY COMPANY 19 Ch. D. 508

3. —— Debt—Joint Debt.] The debt, legal or equitable, owing by a garnishee to a judgment debtor, which can be attached to answer the judgment debt, must be a debt due to such judgment debtor alone, and where it is only due to him jointly with another person it cannot be so attached. MACDONALD *v.* TACQUAH GOLD MINES COMPANY - - - - 13 Q. B. D. 535

4. —— "Debt, legal or equitable"—*Common Law Procedure Act*, 1854 (17 & 18 *Vict. c.* 125), *s.* 61—*Rules of Court*, 1883, *Order XLV.*] In July, 1882, the Plaintiff obtained a judgment against W., for £574 in an action for breach of promise of marriage commenced in August, 1881. In May, 1881, W. became entitled to a. legacy of £500 under a will of which the Defendant was executor. This legacy was in hand and ready to be paid over in October, 1881. On the 31st of May, 1881, and before the legacy became actually payable to W., he married ; and on the 17th of October, 1881, he by deed between himself of the one part and the Defendant of the other part assigned the £500 to the Defendant upon trust to

XXXVI. PRACTICE—SUPREME COURT—GAR-NISHEE ORDERS—*continued.*

invest the money and pay the annual income to his wife for her separate use for life, and afterwards upon other trusts. On the 4th of January, 1883, the Plaintiff obtained an order under sect. 61 of the Common Law Procedure Act, 1854, attaching any sum or sums of money then in or which might come to the hands of the Defendant, to answer the judgment recovered by her against W.—Upon an issue directed to try whether on the 4th of January, 1883, there was a sum of money which the Plaintiff was entitled, under Order XLV. (1883), and under the Common Law Procedure Act, 1854, to attach in the hands of the Defendant, to satisfy the Plaintiff's judgment debt against W.:—*Held* —by Williams, J., upon further consideration— that, even assuming the settlement of October, 1881, to be impeachable, there was nothing in the nature of a debt, either legal or equitable, due or accruing due from the Defendant to W. (the judg-ment debtor) which could be attached to satisfy the judgment-debt. VYSE *v.* BROWN

[13 Q. B. D. 199

5. —— "Debt owing"—*Income from Trust Fund—Rules of Court, 1875, Order XLV., r. 2.*] A judgment debtor was entitled for his life to the income arising from a fund vested in trustees, payable half-yearly in February and August. Upon application by the judgment creditor in Novem-ber for a garnishee order attaching the debtor's share of the income in the hands of the trustees, it appeared that the last half-yearly payment had been made, and that there was no money the proceeds of the trust property in the hands of the trustees:—*Held,* affirming the decision of the Queen's Bench Division, that there was no debt "owing or accruing" at the time when the order was applied for which could be attached under Order XLV., rule 2.—*Semble,* that the proper course for the judgment creditor to pursue was to apply for the appointment of a receiver, under the practice of the Chancery Division. WEBB *v.* STENTON

[11 Q. B. D. 518

6. —— Examination of Judgment Debtor— *Rules of Court, 1875, Order XLV., r. 1.*] The ex-amination of a judgment debtor under Rules of Court, 1875, Order XLV., rule 1, touching the debts due to him is intended to be a cross-ex-amination of the strictest character, and the debtor when under such an examination is bound to answer all questions relevant to the subject-matter, and cannot insist on the examination being confined to the simple question "whether any and what debts are due to him." REPUBLIC OF COSTA RICA *v.* STROUSBERG -   16 Ch. D. 8

7. —— Lapse of Six Years—*Garnishee Order to pay—Rules of Court, 1883, Order XLII., rr. 6, 8, 22, 23—Order XLV., r. 1.*] A garnishee against whom proceedings under Order XLV. have been duly taken, may be ordered to pay to a judgment creditor a debt due from such garnishee to the judgment debtor, although more than six years have elapsed since the judgment. FELLOWS *v.* THORNTON -   -   14 Q. B. D. 335

8. —— Mortgagor—*Right of Holder of Gar-nishee Order against Mortgaged Estate—Rules of Court, 1875, Order XLV., rr. 2, 3—27 & 28 Vict. c. 112, s. 1.*] M. mortgaged a leasehold to W.,

XXXVI. PRACTICE—SUPREME COURT—GAR-NISHEE ORDERS—*continued.*

and then to B. A judgment creditor of B. ob-tained a garnishee order against M. After this W. sold the property under a power of sale, and an action was brought to distribute the surplus proceeds :—*Held,* by the Court of Appeal (affirm-a decision of Bacon, V.-C.), that the judgment creditor had no claim against the surplus proceeds of sale, for that a garnishee order has not the effect of transferring the debt due from the gar-nishee with the benefit of the securities for it, and that to treat the garnishee order as affecting the land before execution would conflict with the provisions of 27 & 28 Vict. c. 112. CHATTERTON *v.* WATNEY -   16 Ch. D. 378; 17 Ch. D. 259

9. —— Partnership Firm—*Rules of Court,* 1875, *Order XLV., r. 2.*] A garnishee order cannot be made under Order XLV., rule 2, attaching a debt due from a partnership firm described by its part-nership name. WALKER *v.* BOOKE **6 Q. B. D. 631**

10. —— Superannuation Allowance—*Police Constable—Rules of Court,* 1883, *Order XLV., r. 1* —"*Debt owing or accruing"—Wages Attachment Abolition Act,* 1870 (33 & 34 *Vict. c.* 30).] A sum already accrued due to a retired police constable in respect of his superannuation allowance under 11 & 12 Vict. c. 14, may be attached in execution. —*Semble,* the Wages Attachment Abolition Act, 1870, only applies to inferior Courts of record and not to the High Court of Justice. BOOTH *v.* TRAIL

[12 Q. B. D. 8

11. —— Trust Money—*Attaching Debt under Garnishee Order—Rules of Court,* 1875, *Order XLV., rr.* 6, 7.] A garnishee order nisi, obtained by a judgment creditor to attach money owing to the judgment debtor, ought not to be made abso-lute if it be suggested, and there is reasonable ground for so suggesting, that the money sought to be attached is trust money, and not really the money of the judgment debtor, even though such suggestion be not made by the garnishee, and the case, therefore, is not within Order XLV., rules 6 and 7. If the fact suggested be disputed, the proper order to make would be that the money should be paid into Court to abide the event of any inquiry, whether it be trust money or not. ROBERTS *v.* DEATH -   -   8 Q. B. D. 319

XXXVII. PRACTICE — SUPREME COURT— CHARGING ORDERS (and STOP ORDERS).

1. —— Charging Order—"*In trust for him"— Stock vested in Trustees for Judgment Debtor and others — Interest determinable on Alienation— Chargeable Interest—1 & 2 Vict. c.* 110, *s.* 14.] An order was made under 1 & 2 Vict. c. 110, s. 14, and 3 & 4 Vict. c. 82, charging a judgment debtor's interest in the dividends on certain bank stock. It appeared that by the terms of a will certain property, including this stock, was be-queathed to trustees on trust as to one moiety thereof for the testatrix's niece, and as to the other moiety in trust to pay the income thereof to her nephew, the judgment debtor, for life, or until he should attempt to alien or charge the same. And upon his interest determining, there were limitations over in favour of his wife for life, and after her death in favour of his children, with an ultimate remainder in the event of the

XXXVII. PRACTICE — SUPREME COURT — CHARGING ORDERS (and STOP ORDERS)— *continued.*

failure of the preceding trusts to the judgment debtor absolutely. At the time when the charging order was made, there was a dividend on the stock accrued due, but which the trustees had not yet received from the bank :—*Held*, that the fact that the stock stood in the name of the trustees in trust for another, besides the judgment debtor, did not prevent its being stock " standing in the name of any person in trust for him,' within the words of 1 & 2 Vict. c. 110, s. 14.—*Held*, also that the accrued dividend and the ultimate remainder to the judgment debtor after failure of the preceding trusts constituted a sufficient chargeable interest, whatever might have been the case with regard to the interest determinable on alienation, if that had stood alone ; and that the order was therefore rightly made, the trustees being responsible upon its being made for the due application of the fund according to the legal effect of the order, whatever it might be. SOUTH WESTERN LOAN AND DISCOUNT COMPANY v. ROBERTSON **3 Q. B. D. 17**

2. —— Charging Order — *Judicature Act, 1873 (36 & 37 Vict. c. 66), s. 24—Rules of Court, 1883, Order. XLVI. r. 1 — Jurisdiction — Debtor and Creditor — Company — Shares — Order for Sale of Shares subject to Charging Order.*] The Plaintiff having recovered judgment in an action, obtained an order absolute under Order XLVI., charging shares of the Defendant in a company with the payment of the judgment debt and interest, and then applied to the Court for an order for sale of the shares :—*Held*, that sect. 24 of the Judicature Act, 1873, did not give the Court jurisdiction to order the sale. LEGGOTT v. WESTERN - - .. **12 Q. B. D. 287**

3. —— Stop Order — *Mortgagor — Fund in Court — Priority — Notice.*] As against a stop order obtained by an incumbrancer upon a fund in Court in an administration suit, and in respect of which orders have been made directing payment of interest to the parties entitled, notice to the trustees, though given by another incumbrancer before the stop order was obtained, does not give priority. PINNOCK v. BAILEY **23 Ch. D. 497**

XXXVIII. PRACTICE — SUPREME COURT— WRIT OF POSSESSION.

—— *Mortgagee—Order for Foreclosure absolute—Action for Recovery of Land—Action for the Recovery of the Possession of Land—Rules of Court, 1875, Order XVII., r. 2; Order XLII., r. 3.*] A order for foreclosure absolute is not a judgment for the recovery of the possession of land within the meaning of Order XLII., rule 3, of Rules of Court, 1875.—Hence after foreclosure absolute the Plaintiff is not entitled to a writ of possession. WOOD v. WHEATER **22 Ch. D. 281**

XXXIX. PRACTICE — SUPREME COURT — TRANSFER.

1. —— Pending Action—*Winding up of Company—Jurisdiction—Rules of Court, 1875, Order LI., rr. 1, 2a.*] When an order has been made by a Judge of the Chancery Division for the winding-up of a company under the Companies Acts, 1862 and 1867, the Judge in whose Court such wind-

XXXIX. PRACTICE — SUPREME COURT — TRANSFER—*continued.*

ing-up shall be pending has no jurisdiction under Order LI., rule 2a, to order the transfer to him of an action pending against the company in another Court of the same Division : such a transfer can only be made by the Lord Chancellor under Order LI., rule 1.—*In re Landore Siemens Steel Company* (10 Ch. D. 489) not followed. *In re* MADRAS IRRIGATION AND CANAL COMPANY **[16 Ch. D. 702**

2. —— Transfer to Chancery Division — *Vendor and Purchaser - Action for Return of Deposit—Counterclaim for Specific Performance —Rules of Court, 1883, Order XLIX., rr. 1, 3.*] In an action by purchaser of land against vendor for return of deposit the Defendant counterclaimed specific performance :—*Held*, that the action ought to be transferred to the Chancery Division. LONDON LAND CO. v. HARRIS **[13 Q. B. D. 540**

—— Transfer to County Court—Interim jurisdiction - - **27 Ch. D. 533**
See PRACTICE—SUPREME COURT—JURISDICTION. 3.

XL. PRACTICE—SUPREME COURT —INSPECTION OF PROPERTY.

—— Authority to dig up Soil — *Rules of Court, 1883, Order L., r. 3.*] Under rule 3 of Order L. the Court has power to make an interlocutory order before trial, giving liberty to a plaintiff to enter upon land belonging to the defendant, and to excavate the soil thereof for the purposes of inspection:—The decision in *Ennor* v. *Barwell* (1 D. F. & J. 529) has no application to this rule. LUMB v. BEAUMONT - **27 Ch. D. 356**

—— Costs—Appeal for—Discretion of Court
[10 Q. B. D. 457
See PRACTICE — SUPREME COURT — APPEAL. 29.

XLI. PRACTICE — SUPREME COURT — INJUNCTION.

1.—— Illegal Act—*Injury to Public—Right of Attorney-General to sue—Evidence of Injury — Company — Excess of Statutory Powers— Costs.*] When an illegal act is being committed, which in its nature tends to the injury of the public (such as an interference with a public highway or a navigable stream), the Attorney-General can maintain an action on behalf of the public to restrain the commission of the act, without adducing any evidence of actual injury to the public, and in such a case an injunction will be granted with costs, although no evidence of actual injury is given.—*Attorney-General* v. *Great Eastern Railway Company* (11 Ch. D. 449), *Attorney-General* v. *Cockermouth Local Board* (Law Rep. 18 Eq. 172), and *Attorney-General* v. *Ely, Haddenham, and Sutton Railway Company* (Law Rep. 4 Ch. 194) considered. ATTORNEY-GENERAL v. SHREWSBURY (KINGSLAND) BRIDGE COMPANY
[21 Ch. D. 752

2. —— In lieu of Distringas—*Injunction to restrain Transfer of Stock—5 & 6 Vict. c. 5, ss. 4, 5 —Rules of Court, 1875, Order XLVI, rr. 2a, 4, 7, 10.*] A notice having been served on the Bank of England under rules 4 and 7 of Order XLVI,

XLI. PRACTICE—SUPREME COURT—INJUNC-
TION—*continued.*

to prevent the transfer of stock or the payment of
dividends thereon without notice to the persons
serving the notice, the bank gave notice to them
that an application had been made to the bank to
allow the transfer of stock and to pay the dividends thereon, and that they should comply with
the application, unless an order of the Court
should be served on them within eight days.—A
motion was then made ex parte for an order to
restrain the bank from permitting the transfer or
paying the dividends.—*Held*, that the proper
course was to grant an interim injunction over the
next regular motion day, and that notice of the
order must be served on the legal owners of the
stock. *In re* BLAKSLEY'S TRUSTS. **23 Ch. D. 549**

3. —— Libel—*Company—Interlocutory Application—Privileged Communication—Common Law
Procedure Act*, 1854 (17 & 18 *Vict. c.* 125), *ss.* 79,
82—*Judicature Act*, 1873 (36 & 37 *Vict. c.* 66),
s. 25, *sub-s.* 8.] A solicitor, acting for some shareholders in a company, printed and circulated, but
only among the shareholders, a circular containing very strong reflections on the mode in which
the company had been brought out, and on the
conduct of the promoters and directors, and proposing a meeting of shareholders to take steps to
protect their interests. The company commenced
an action to restrain the further publication, and
applied for an interlocutory injunction, which was
granted by Bacon, V.-C.:—*Held*, on appeal that
the Court has jurisdiction to interfere on interlocutory application to restrain the publication of
a libel.—But *held*, that this jurisdiction is to be
exercised with great caution, and will not in
general be exercised unless the applicant satisfies
the Court that the statements in the document
complained of are untrue.—*Held*, further, that
still more caution is requisite where the document
in question is primâ facie a privileged communication, so as not to be actionable unless express
malice is proved, the question of malice being one
which cannot conveniently be tried on interlocutory application.—In the present case the Court
not being satisfied on the evidence that the statements in the document were false or malicious,
the order for an injunction was discharged.
QUARTZ HILL CONSOLIDATED GOLD MINING COM-
PANY *v.* BEALL　　-　　**20 Ch. D. 501**

4. —— Libel—*Friendly Society—38 & 39 Vict.
c.* 60, *s.* 23.] A injunction can be granted to
restrain a libel likely to injure a friendly society
or joint stock company.—A member of a friendly
society issued to persons not members of the
society circulars containing inaccurate statements
as to the financial condition of the society:—*Held*,
that such circulars ought to be restrained by injunction. HILL *v.* HART DAVIES　　**21 Ch. D. 798**

5. —— Married Woman—*Separate Estate—
General Engagements — Action by Creditor —
Injunction to restrain Dealing with Separate Estate—Judicature Act*, 1873 (36 & 37 *Vict. c.* 66),
s. 25, *sub-s.* 8.] In an action by a creditor to
enforce against the separate estate of a married
woman a general engagement entered into with
her on the credit of that estate, the Court will not,
before the creditor has established his right by
obtaining a judgment, restrain the married woman

XLI. PRACTICE—SUPREME COURT—INJUNC-
TION—*continued.*

from dealing with her separate estate.—Decision
of Malins, V.-C., reversed. ROBINSON *v.* PICKERING
[16 Ch. D, 371, 660

6. —— Protection of Property —*Equitable
Mortgage—Ex parte Injunction to restrain parting with Legal Estate.*] In an action by an equitable mortgagee for sale or foreclosure the Court
granted an interim injunction to restrain dealing
with the legal estate till the next motion day, on
an ex parte application by the Plaintiff; there
being ground for believing that the Defendants
intended to part with the legal estate pendente
lite. LONDON AND COUNTY BANKING COMPANY *v.*
LEWIS　　　　-　　　　**21 Ch. D. 490**

7. —— Trespass—*Jurisdiction—Proceedings
before Justices.*] Where the Legislature has
pointed out a special tribunal for determining a
question, as a general rule no other Court ought
to restrain the proceedings before it; but where
the question has come before another Court in
independent proceedings in which it is necessary
to decide the whole matter between the parties,
the Court may in such case restrain the proceedings elsewhere by injunction in order to save
expenses.—A dispute having arisen between the
Defendants, who were a local authority, and the
Plaintiff about a drain which the Plaintiff had
interfered with, the Defendants gave notice to
the Plaintiff that they would enter on his land
and reinstate the drain ; but they afterwards
abandoned their intention, and instead took proceedings against him before the magistrate. The
Plaintiff then brought an action against the Defendants, claiming an injunction to restrain them
from trespassing on his land, and from proceeding
against him before the magistrate. In the statement of claim the Plaintiff did not in terms allege
that the Defendants threatened and intended to
trespass on the land :—*Held* (affirming the decision of Bacon, V.C.), that as no intention to
commit a trespass was proved or alleged, the
Plaintiff had not made out his case for an injunction against the trespass ; and that being so, the
Court had no jurisdiction to restrain the proceedings before the magistrate.—*Hedley* v. *Bates*
(13 Ch. D. 498) and *Great Western Railway
Company* v. *Waterford and Limerick Railway
Company* (17 Ch. D. 493) explained. STANNARD
v. VESTRY OF SAINT GILES, CAMBERWELL
[20 Ch. D. 190

8. —— Undertaking as to Damages—*Inquiry
as to Damages.*] An injunction to restrain the
Defendant from building so as to prevent access
of light and air to the Plaintiff's windows was
granted ex parte on the 4th of November, 1879,
and on the 27th of November was continued until
the trial or further order, the Plaintiff giving the
usual undertaking as to damages. On the 18th
of February, 1880, the Court of Appeal discharged
the order. On the 11th of November, 1880, a
perpetual injunction as to access of air was
granted ; but on the 21st of June, 1881, the Court
of Appeal dismissed the action with costs. On
the 16th of February, 1882, the Defendant gave
notice of motion for an inquiry as to damages
which was refused by Bacon, V.C. The only
damage alleged was that the Defendant had

XLI. PRACTICE—SUPREME COURT—INJUNC-TION—continued.

agreed to let part of the property with the new buildings to a tenant, and was prevented from carrying this out by the injunction preventing his building. It was not proved, however, that there was any binding agreement to take a lease, nor did it appear that the injunction interfered with the erection of the buildings to such an extent as would have entitled the intended tenant to throw up the agreement if binding :—*Held*, by the Court of Appeal, that an inquiry as to damages ought not to be granted.—Whether where an interlocutory injunction has been wrongly granted, owing to a mistake of law by the Judge, without any misrepresentation, suppression, or other default on the part of the Plaintiff, an inquiry as to damages can be directed under the undertaking, *quære*. Jessel, M.R., and Cotton, L.J., differed, and Brett, L.J., gave no opinion.—The Court is not bound to grant an inquiry as to damages whenever the Defendant has sustained some damage by the granting the injunction ; but it has a discretion, and may refuse any inquiry if the damage restrained is trivial or remote, or if there has been great delay in making the application.—The question considered at what time the application for an inquiry as to damages ought to be made :—*Held*, that, even if there had been a binding agreement by the proposed tenant to take a lease, and the injunction had so interfered with the building as to entitle the tenant to be off the bargain, damages ought not to be granted in respect of it, for that damages must be confined to the immediate natural consequences of the injunction, under the circumstances which were within the knowledge of the party obtaining the injunction. SMITH *v*. DAY　　　- 21 Ch. D. 421

9. —— **Undertaking as to Damages**—*Interlocutory Injunction.*] *Per* Baggallay, Cotton, and Lindley, L.JJ., where an interlocutory injunction has been granted on the usual undertaking as to damages, if it afterwards is established at the trial that the plaintiff is not entitled to an injunction, an inquiry as to damages may be directed, though the plaintiff was not guilty of misrepresentation, suppression, or other default in obtaining the injunction.—*Dictum* of Jessel, M.R., in *Smith v. Day* (21 Ch. D. 421) dissented from. GRIFFITH *v*. BLAKE　　　-　-　- 27 Ch. D. 474

—— Costs—Appeal for　-　　- 29 Ch. D. 60
See PRACTICE — SUPREME COURT — APPEAL. 28.

XLII. PRACTICE — SUPREME COURT — RECEIVER.

1. —— ·**After Final Judgment**—*Whether New Action necessary—"Cause or Matter pending"—Judicature Act, 1873, s. 24—Rules of Court, 1875, Order XLII.—Bankruptcy—Execution Creditor—Equitable Execution—Bankruptcy Act, 1869 (32 & 33 Vict. c. 71), s. 95, sub-s. 2; s. 125, sub-s. 5.*] *Held*, by the Master of the Rolls, that so long as the final judgment in an action remains unsatisfied, the action is a "cause or matter pending" within the meaning of sect. 24, sub-sect. 7, of the Judicature Act, 1873, and that consequently, in an action by a creditor against a debtor in which the Plaintiff has obtained final judgment, the

XLII. PRACTICE — SUPREME COURT — RECEIVER—continued.

Court has power, under that sub-section in order to satisfy the judgment, to grant equitable execution against the Defendant by appointing a receiver upon motion in that action, although the writ may not have been indorsed with a claim for a receiver ; it being unnecessary in such a case to bring another action for the purpose.— S. recovered judgment for a debt against C. and issued an elegit. The sheriff returned that the debtor had no lands which he could seize. C. had leasehold property which was subject to mortgages. S. thereupon obtained the appointment of a receiver of the rents of the leasehold property without prejudice to the rights of the prior incumbrancers. On the same day a petition for adjudication in bankruptcy was filed against C., and a receiver was appointed in bankruptcy a few minutes before the appointment of the receiver in the action. C. afterwards filed a petition for liquidation ; the same receiver was appointed in the liquidation as had been appointed in the bankruptcy, and resolutions were passed for liquidation of his affairs by arrangement. S. had not, until some days after the appointment of his receiver, any notice that C. had committed an act of bankruptcy, or that any proceedings in bankruptcy were pending against him :—*Held*, by the Master of the Rolls and by the Court of Appeal, that as, at the time when S. obtained equitable execution by the appointment of a receiver, the property was legally though not actually in the possession of the receiver appointed by the Court of Bankruptcy, the equitable execution was ineffectual, and was not protected by sect. 95, sub-sect. 2, of the Bankruptcy Act, 1869. SALT *v*. COOPER　　16 Ch. D. 544

2. —— **Judgment Creditor**—*Application for Receiver—Elegit—Equity of Redemption—Interlocutory Order — Judicature Act, 1873, s. 25, sub-s. 8.*] The words "interlocutory order" in s. 25, sub-s. 8 of the Judicature Act, 1873, are not confined in their meaning to an order made between writ and final judgment, but mean an order other than final judgment in an action, whether such order be made before judgment or after.—A creditor who had recovered judgment in an action sued out a writ of elegit, to which writ the sheriff returned that there were no goods or lands of the debtor which he could deliver. It appearing, however, that the debtor was entitled to an equity of redemption of certain land, the creditor, without commencing any fresh action for the purpose, made an application to a Judge at Chambers for the appointment of a receiver :—*Held*, that such application was rightly made in the original action, and that it was unnecessary to commence a new action for the purpose. SMITH *v*. COWELL　　　-　　-　　- 6 Q. B. D. 75

3. —— **Judgment Creditor**—*Defaulting Trustee—Equitable Execution—Rules of Court, 1883, Order XLII, rr. 4, 28—Judicature Act, 1873, s. 25, sub-s. 8.*] Under the general power to appoint receivers given by the Judicature Act, 1873, s. 25, sub-s. 8, and. having regard to Rules of Supreme Court, 1883, Order XLII., rules 4 and 28, the Court has jurisdiction to enforce a judgment for payment of money into Court by a defaulting trustee, by

XLII. PRACTICE — SUPREME COURT — RE-CEIVER—*continued.*

the appointment of a receiver of his equitable interest in property in this country; and order accordingly where, from the debtor being out of the jurisdiction, service of a writ of attachment could not be effected. *In re* CONEY. CONEY *v.* BENNETT
[29 Ch. D. 399

4. —— Judgment Creditor—*Equitable Execution—Debts and Sums of Money—Judgment Creditor—Judicature Act*, 1873 (36 & 37 *Vict.* c. 66), s. 25, *sub-s.* 8—*Rules of Court*, 1883, *Order L.*, *r.* 6.] Since the Judicature Acts the Court can grant equitable execution by the appointment of a receiver at the instance of a judgment creditor against debts and sums of money payable to the judgment debtor to which garnishee proceedings are not applicable. WESTHEAD *v.* RILEY
[25 Ch. D. 413

5. —— Mortgage—*Receiver and Manager—Legal Mortgagee—Business—Hotel—Injunction—Form of Order.*] A legal mortgagee of business premises, such as an hotel, who is prevented by the mortgagor from taking possession under the mortgage, may obtain, upon an interlocutory application, an order for the appointment of a receiver and manager, and an injunction restraining the mortgagor from interfering with the management of the business and the possession of the premises.—Form of order appointing a receiver and manager, with an injunction. TRUMAN & CO. *v.* REDGRAVE - - - 18 Ch. D. 547

6. —— Question of Title—*Reference to Master—Appeal—Supreme.Court of Judicature Act*, 1873 (36 & 37 *Vict.* c. 66), s. 24, *sub-s.* 7; s. 25, *sub-s.* 8.] The Plaintiff, having obtained judgment, was by an order made at Chambers appointed receiver of the rents of some houses belonging to the Defendant; the order was made without prejudice to prior incumbrances. G. having applied to discharge the order appointing the receiver on the ground that he was a second mortgagee under a deed executed by the Defendant before the judgment in the action, the Queen's Bench Division referred the question as to the validity of G.'s mortgage to a Master, who after hearing evidence reported that the mortgage was a sham and had been executed in order to defeat the Defendant's creditors. The Queen's Bench Division declined to review the evidence upon which the Master had acted, accepted his report as conclusive, and refused G.'s application :—*Held*, that inasmuch as the receiver was appointed under an equitable jurisdiction now vested in the Queen's Bench Division, the evidence before the Master might have been reviewed; and the Court of Appeal being of opinion on the evidence that the mortgage had been executed in good faith, discharged the order made at Chambers, whereby the Plaintiff was appointed receiver. WALMSLEY *v.* MUNDY
[13 Q. B. D. 807

7. —— Restraining Receiver appointed in another Action — *Judicature Act*, 1873, s. 24, *sub-ss.* 5, 7.] A person who is prejudiced by the conduct of a receiver appointed in an action by way of equitable execution, ought not without leave of the Court to commence a fresh action to restrain the proceedings of the receiver, even

XLII. PRACTICE — SUPREME COURT — RE-CEIVER—*continued.*

though the act complained of was beyond the scope of the receiver's authority; but ought to make an application for such relief as he is entitled to in the action in which the receiver was appointed. SEARLE *v.* CHOAT - 25 Ch. D. 723

8. —— Reversionary Interest—*Judicature Act*, 1873, s. 25, *sub-s.* 8.] The Plaintiff, who had obtained judgment against the Defendants, husband and wife, was upon his application ex parte appointed receiver of the income of the wife's reversionary interest under a will. FUGGLE *v.* BLAND
[11 Q. B. D. 711

XLIII. PRACTICE—SUPREME COURT — SALE BY COURT.

—— Opening Biddings—30 & 31 *Vict.* c. 48, s. 7—*Principle applicable to Private Contract.*] In an administration suit an estate was ordered to be sold by auction, but the reserved price not having been reached, the sale by auction became inoperative. A subsequent offer to purchase subject to the approval of the Court within ten days was carried in before the Chief Clerk, who approved of the offer, and ordered the contract to be carried out, whereupon the deposit was paid and the abstract delivered. Before the order had been passed and entered a much higher price was offered.— Upon summons to vary the Chief Clerk's certificate by setting aside the sale and directing the order for a larger amount to be accepted :—*Held*, that the certificate of the Chief Clerk, although not passed and entered, was tantamount to a confirmation of the contract; and that the principle of the Act 30 & 31 *Vict.* c. 48, s. 7, by which the old practice of opening biddings on a sale by auction was discontinued, except upon the ground of fraud or improper conduct, applied equally to a sale by private contract entered into under the sanction of the Court, and that such a contract could not be discharged where no unfairness existed. The Chief Clerk's certificate was therefore confirmed. *In re* BARTLETT. NEWMAN *v.* HOOK - - - - 16 Ch. D. 56

XLIV. PRACTICE—SUPREME COURT—NOTICE OF MOTION.

1. —— Attachment—*Rules of Court*, 1875, *Order XLIV.*, *r.* 2.] Under Order XLIV., rule 2, a motion for an attachment for removing goods out of the custody of the sheriff can only be made on notice.—*Jupp* v. *Cooper* (5 C. P. D. 26) considered. EYNDE *v.* GOULD - 9 Q. B. D. 335

2. —— Short Notice of Motion—*Power of Court to disregard Irregularities—Rules of Court*, 1875, *Order LIII.*, *r.* 4; *Order LIX.*, *r.* 1.] Where a party applies for special leave to serve short notice of motion he must distinctly state to the Court that the notice applied for is short; and the same fact must distinctly appear on the face or the notice served on the other party.—But in a case where short notice of a motion had been irregularly applied for and served, but the party served had not been injured by the irregularity, the Court exercised its discretion under Order LIX., rule 1, and disregarded the irregularity and heard the motion on the merits. DAWSON *v.* BEESON
[22 Ch. D. 504

XLV. PRACTICE—SUPREME COURT—CHAMBERS.

(a.) GENERAL.

1. —— Accounts —*Adjournment of disputed Items before the Judge—Costs.*] Where accounts are being taken in Chambers before the Chief Clerk, either party has a right to have an item which has been found against him adjourned before the Judge without taking out a summons for that purpose. And where a question of principle is involved in a particular item it may be necessary to do this. But the ordinary practice is to wait till the account is completed, and then take the adjournment once for all before the Judge.—If a solicitor so insist upon his right to take particular items before the Judge in an unreasonable manner, the Court might make him pay the costs personally. UPTON *v.* BROWN
[20 Ch. D. 731

2. —— Accounts—*Settled Account—Order for Account not directing that Settled Account shall not be disturbed.*] By the rules of a benefit society it was provided that the accounts should be audited, and that after they had been audited and signed by the auditors, the secretary and treasurer should not be answerable for any mistakes, omissions, or errors that might afterwards be proved in them. An action for an account was commenced by two shareholders, on behalf of themselves and all other the shareholders, against the secretary. No pleadings were delivered, and on a motion for a receiver being made the Defendant submitted to an order for an account of all moneys and property of the society come to his hands, without any direction as to settled accounts. The Defendant carried in a complete account, and the Plaintiffs carried in a surcharge. The Defendant then set up certain accounts which had been audited under the rules, as vouching his account for the period over which they extended. The point was brought before the Judge, who was stated to have expressed his opinion that the audited accounts must be treated as conclusive. The Plaintiffs then applied for a direction that in taking the accounts the audited accounts might be disregarded, on the ground that as the order did not save the settled accounts, they could not be attended to. The application was refused, and the Plaintiffs appealed:—*Held*, that the audited accounts ought not to be disregarded, and that the appeal must be dismissed; but the dismissal was prefaced by a statement of the opinion of the Court, that the Plaintiffs, in taking the accounts under the order, were at liberty to impeach the audited accounts for fraud. HOLGATE *v.* SHUTT
[27 Ch. D. 111

3. —— Chief Clerk's Certificate—*Application to vary—Rules of Court, 1883, Order* LV., *rr.* 70, 71.] On an application upon the further consideration of an action for an extension of the time, under rule 71 of Order LV., for applying to vary a finding in a Chief Clerk's certificate :— *Held*, that the applicant should take out a summons for the purpose. *In re* DOVE. BOUSFIELD *v.* DOVE　　-　　27 Ch. D. 687

4. —— Judge at Chambers—*Jurisdiction.*] A Judge at Westminster sitting, not in open Court, but as a Judge at Chambers, has jurisdiction to

hear a summons referred to him by the Judge at Chambers. HARTMONT *v.* FOSTER　8 Q. B. D. 82

5. —— Motion to discharge Order — *Time within which such Motion may be brought—Judicature Act, 1873, s.* 50—*Rules of Court, 1875, Order* LVIII., *r.* 15.] A motion to a Judge in Court under the Judicature Act, 1873, s. 50, to discharge an order made by him in Chambers may be made at any time within twenty-one days from the drawing up of the order unless the order is simply a refusal of an application, in which case the twenty-one days must be reckoned from the refusal. HEATLEY *v.* NEWTON　19 Ch. D. 326

6. —— Summons—*Substituted Service—Party to Action evading Service—Solicitor—Charging Order—23 & 24 Vict.* c. 127, *s.* 28.] A sum of money having been paid into Court for the benefit of the Defendant, M., his solicitor, obtained a charging order for costs upon it under 23 & 24 Vict. c. 127, s. 28. The costs had been taxed ex parte. M. then took out a summons to shew cause why the sum of money paid into Court should not be paid out to him in part satisfaction of his taxed costs. This summons could not be served upon the Defendant, who appeared to be wilfully evading service of it. L. had acted for the Defendant after M. had ceased to do so, and H. had introduced the Defendant to M. :—*Held*, that substituted service of the summons should be allowed, that a notice calling upon the Defendant to appear in one month should be put up at the master's office, and served upon L. and H., and advertised in the *Times* newspaper, and thereupon, if the Defendant did not appear, an order might be made on the summons. HUNT *v.* AUSTIN. *Ex parte* MASON　-　-　9 Q. B. D. 598

(b.) ADMINISTRATION SUMMONS.

7. —— Action commenced before the 24th of October, 1883—*Rules of Court, 1883, Order* LV., *r.* 10.] Rule 10 of Order LV. of the Rules of the Supreme Court, 1883, applies to an administration action commenced before, but tried after, those rules came into operation.—An order was therefore made referring such an action to Chambers to determine whether it was necessary that a general administration of the estate should be directed. *In re* LLEWELLYN. LANE *v.* LANE
[25 Ch. D. 66

8. —— Determination of Questions at issue— *Rules of Court, 1883, Order* LV., *r.* 10.] Except to the extent to which special provisions are made by the rules, as, for instance, by Order XV., the plaintiff in an action is not entitled to take out a summons for the determination of the questions which are at issue in the action, and which will properly be decided at the trial. BORTHWICK *v.* RANSFORD　-　28 Ch. D. 79

9. —— Infants—*Rules of Court, 1883, Order* LV., *rr.* 3, 10.] Discussion of the principles on which the Court will act in the exercise of its discretion under Order LV., r. 10, whether or not to make a general order for administration. *In re* WILSON. ALEXANDER *v.* CALDER 28 Ch. D. 457

10. —— Infants—*Cestui que trust—Residuary Legatee—Limited Accounts and Inquiries—Costs*

XLV. PRACTICE—SUPREME COURT—CHAM-
BERS—*continued.*

(b.) ADMINISTRATION SUMMONS—*continued.*

—*Rules of Court,* 1883, Order LV., rr. 3, 4, 10 :
Order LXV., r. 1.] A party interested in the
estate of a deceased person, even though that
party be an infant, is not entitled, as a matter of
course, to an administration judgment at the
expense of the estate. Having regard to Rules
of Supreme Court, 1883, Order LV., rule 10, a
party interested is only entitled to an administration judgment where there are questions which
cannot be properly determined except by an administration action ; but the Court has power
under that rule to order a limited administration
only, that is, to direct particular accounts and inquiries, if it sees that the questions can thus be
properly determined, the object of the rule being
to prevent general administration except in case
of necessity ; and the Court, in the exercise of its
discretion as to costs under Order LXV., rule 1,
will order the Plaintiff—if an infant, then the
next friend—to pay the costs of any unnecessary
or improper administration proceedings.—Order
of Kay, J., varied.—*In re Wilson* (28 Ch. D. 457)
considered. *In re* BLAKE. JONES *v.* BLAKE
[29 Ch. D. 913

(c.) LANDS CLAUSES ACT.

11. —— Payment out of Court—*Deposit in
Court—Fund not exceeding £1000—Petition or
Summons—Rules of Court,* 1883, Order LV., r. 2,
sub-ss. 2–7—*Railway Company—Payment out to
Third Person—Company's Seal.*] The general
expressions of sub-sect. 2 of Order LV., rule 2
(Rules of Court, 1883), are not to be construed
as in any way qualified or modified by the
subsequent sub-sections. Therefore, an application by a landowner and a railway company for
payment out of a sum not exceeding £1000 deposited in Court under sect. 85 of the Lands
Clauses Consolidation Act, 1845, should be made
by summons in Chambers and not by petition.—
Any such summons asking for payment out to a
person on behalf of the company, should be sealed
with the company's seal, by analogy to the practice on petition. *Ex parte* MAIDSTONE AND ASH-
FORD RAILWAY COMPANY. *Ex parte* BALA AND
FESTINIOG RAILWAY COMPANY -   25 Ch. D. 168

12. —— Payment out of Court—*Money paid
in under Lands Clauses Consolidation Act,* 1845
—*Sum under £1000 — Rules of Court,* 1883,
Order LV., r. 2, *sub-ss.* 2, 6, 7.] An application
for the payment or transfer out of Court to a person absolutely entitled of a fund of less amount
than £1000 paid into Court under the Lands
Clauses Act is governed by sub-sect. 2 of rule 2
of Order LV., and ought now to be made by summons in Chambers. *In re* CALTON'S WILL
[25 Ch. D. 240

13. —— Payment out of Court—*Petition or
Summons — Fund exceeding £1000 — Rules of
Court,* 1883, Order LV., r. 2, *sub-s.* 1.] Freehold hereditaments in the city of London, to a
moiety of which A. B. was entitled after the
death of a tenant for life, subject to four life annuities of £50 payable from the death of the
tenant for life, were taken by the Metropolitan
Board of Works, and the money paid into Court

XLV. PRACTICE—SUPREME COURT—CHAM-
BERS—*continued.*

(c.) LANDS CLAUSES ACT—*continued.*.

under the Lands Clauses Act, 1845. In 1866 an
order was made on petition, whereby a sum of
£7000 was ordered to be invested to provide for
the annuities when they should become payable,
and the balance of a moiety of the fund, after
providing for the tenant for life's interest, was
directed to be paid to A. B. In 1868 one of the
expectant annuitants died ; in 1869 the tenant for
life died and in 1870 another order was made on
petition, whereby a sum of stock which would
have been sufficient to pay an annuity of £50,
was ordered to be transferred to A. B.—A second
annuitant having died in May, 1883, A. B. claimed
a sum of £1666 13s. 4d. Consols, being so much of
the residue of the investment of £7000 as had
sufficed to provide for the second annuity of £50.
—*Held,* that the orders of the Court in 1866 and
1870, amounted "to an order declaring the rights
of" A. B. within the meaning of sub-sect. 1 of
rule 2 of Order LV. of 1883 ; and that the application ought to be by summons.—The generality
of sub-sect. 1 of rule 2 of Order LV. is not cut
down or qualified by sub-sect. 7 or any of the sub-
sections of rule 2 following sub-sect. 1. *In re*
BRANDRAM -   25 Ch. D. 366

14. —— Payment out of Court—*Petition or
Summons — Sum not exceeding £1000 — Lands
Clauses Consolidation Act,* 1845—*Rules of Court,*
1883, Order LV., r. 2, *sub-s.* 2.] An application
for payment out of Court to a person absolutely
entitled of a sum of cash not exceeding £1000
paid in under the Lands Clauses Consolidation
Act, 1845, is rightly made by summons, not by
petition. *In re* MADGWICK   25 Ch. D. 371

15. —— Payment out of Court—*Re-investment of Moneys — Summons — Judicature Acts,*
1873, *ss.* 16, 24, 73 ; 1875, s. 17 ; *Appellate Jurisdiction Act,* 1876, s. 17 ; *Judicature Act,* 1881,
s. 19 — 18 & 19 Vict. c. 134, s. 16—*Rules of
Court,* 1883, Order LV., r. 2, *sub-s.* 7, *not ultrà
vires.*] The 16th section of the Despatch of
Business, Court of Chancery, Act (18 & 19 Vict.
c. 134), giving power to the Lord Chancellor, with
the advice and assistance of the Master of the
Rolls and the Vice-Chancellors, or any two of
them, to make general orders as to the business
to be disposed of in Chambers, has not been repealed either expressly or by implication ; and
the effect of the 76th section of the Judicature
Act of 1873 was to substitute three Judges of the
High Court of Justice for the three Vice-Chancellors mentioned in such 16th section. Accordingly such power may now be properly exercised
by the Lord Chancellor, with the advice and
assistance of the Master of the Rolls, and any two
Judges of the High Court of Justice, and the fact
that the Rule Committee who framed the Rules of
the Supreme Court, 1883, comprised other Judges
as well as these, does not invalidate the exercise
of the power. Therefore it appearing from the
reference in Order LV., rule 2, sub-sect. 7, to the
14th of August, 1855, the date on which the Despatch of Business, Court of Chancery Act, received the royal assent, that the Rule Committee
intended to act under the powers conferred by
that Act, the order contained in such sub-section

XLV. PRACTICE—SUPREME COURT—CHAMBERS—*continued.*

(c.) LANDS CLAUSES ACT—*continued.*

is not ultrà vires, and in accordance therewith all applications for interim and permanent investments and for payment of dividends under the Lands Clauses Consolidation Act, 1845, and any other Act passed before the 14th of August, 1855, whereby the purchase-money of any property sold is directed to be paid into Court, must be made upon summons at Chambers. *Ex parte* MAYOR OF LONDON - - - - 25 Ch. D. 384

16. —— **Payment out of Court**—*Permanent Investment—Settled Land Act, 1882, s. 25* (iv.)—*Rules of Court, 1883, Order LV., r. 2, sub-r. 7.*] In applications for payment out of Court and investment under the Settled Land Act, 1882, of funds in Court representing the purchase-money of lands taken under the provisions of the Lands Clauses Act, 1845, the Court has a discretion under the Rules of Supreme Court, 1883, Order LXX., rule 1, and, where an application by petition is cheaper and more expeditious than by summons, will not disallow the costs of a petition, although the proceeding falls within the Rules of Supreme Court, 1883, Order LV., r. 2, sub-r. 7, as business to be transacted in Chambers.—In such cases, however, the option of proceeding by petition or summons is at the applicant's risk. *In re* BETHLEHEM AND BRIDEWELL HOSPITALS

[30 Ch. D. 541

—— Counsel—Solicitor and client—Taxation

[10 Q. B. D. 54

See PRACTICE—SUPREME COURT—COSTS. 18.

XLVI. PRACTICE—SUPREME COURT—COSTS.

1. —— **Abandoned Appeal.**] On the 20th of December, 1880, C. gave notice of appeal, but did not set it down. On the 11th of January he sent a letter withdrawing his notice of appeal. On the next day the solicitor for the Respondents wrote to C. saying that he had delivered briefs, and that unless C. would undertake to pay the Respondents' costs of the appeal the usual proceeding would be taken to enforce payment of them. C. did not answer this letter. The Respondents then moved that the appeal might be dismissed, and that C. might be ordered to pay the costs of the appeal and of this application, and an order was made accordingly. CHARLTON *v.* CHARLTON

[16 Ch. D. 273

2. —— **Abandoned Motion**—*Discontinuance of Action — Taxation — Incomplete — Affidavits or Pleadings.*] Statement of practice as to taxation of costs of an abandoned motion, or on discontinuance of action. HARRISON *v.* LEUTNER

[16 Ch. D. 559

3. —— **Admissions** *between co-Defendants—Rules of Court, 1883, Order XXXII., r. 2.*] Admissions between co-Defendants under Rules of Supreme Court, 1883, Order XXXII., r. 2, to which the Plaintiff is not a party, cannot be entered as evidence against the Plaintiff, and therefore cannot be included in an order for taxation and payment of the general costs of the action. DODDS *v.* TUKE - - - 25 Ch. D. 617

4. —— **Affidavit of Increase.**] Upon summons to review the taxation of costs, the Court

XLVI. PRACTICE—SUPREME COURT—COSTS—*continued.*

refused to direct the Taxing Master to adopt the practice in the Queen's Bench Division of requiring the solicitor to make an "affidavit of increase," since evidence could be obtained without such affidavit of all matters necessary for the information of the Taxing Master. But the Court declined to lay down any rule that such affidavit of increase should in no case be required. SMITH *v.* DAY - - - - - 16 Ch. D. 726

5. —— **Amendment of Pleadings.**] An amendment to the pleadings made at the trial by the Court, *mero motu,* in order to raise the real point at issue, is no ground for departing from the usual rule as to the costs of the action. NOTTAGE *v.* JACKSON - - - 11 Q. B. D. 627

6. —— **Appeal**—*Note of Judgment of Court below.*] A decision on the construction of a will was reversed on appeal, but the Court, on the ground that it was not furnished with any information as to the reasons given by the Judge for his decision, refused to make any order as to the costs of the appeal. *In re* MCCONNELL. SAUNDERS *v.* MCCONNELL - - 29 Ch. D. 76

7. —— **Apportionment**—*Cross-Notice of Appeal—Rules of Court, 1875, Order LVIII., r. 6.*] A Respondent who has given cross-notice of appeal under Order LVIII., rule 6, is in the same position as to costs as if he had presented a cross-appeal.—Where there were two Respondents to an appeal, one of whom gave cross-notice of appeal affecting his co-Respondent, the Court made an apportionment of the costs of the appeal. HARRISON *v.* CORNWALL MINERALS RAILWAY COMPANY

[18 Ch. D. 334

8. —— **Apportionment**—*Notice by Respondent to vary Order—Rules of Court, 1875, Order LVIII., r. 6.*] In an action for redemption of a mortgage vested in the Defendant R. as a trustee for the Defendant C., who was in possession, D. set up the case that he was not in possession by virtue of the mortgage, but under a lease. The Court decided that he was in possession as mortgagee, and made a decree on that footing, but without rests. The Defendants appealed. The Plaintiff gave notice that at the hearing of the appeal he should ask to have the decree varied by directing the account to be taken with rests. The Court of Appeal held that the decree was right in treating D. as mortgagee in possession, but refused to direct rests:—*Held,* that as the case was one where the costs could not have been materially increased by the notice, the costs ought not to be apportioned as in *Harrison v. Cornwall Minerals Railway Company* (18 Ch. D. 334), but that the Defendants should have £5 for their costs incidental to the notice. ROBINSON *v.* DRAKES

[23 Ch. D. 98

9. —— **Apportionment**—*Plaintiff succeeding upon one Item out of three of his Claim—Apportionment of Costs under Special Order.*] The Plaintiff sued for three items of a claim for work done, and recovered a sum in respect of one of such items only. By an order of the Court it was ordered "that the Plaintiff recover against the Defendants" that sum, "and such costs as one of

XLVI. PRACTICE—SUPREME COURT—COSTS
—continued.

the Masters may find that he has rightly incurred in recovering the above amount, and that the Defendants recover against the Plaintiff such costs as they have rightly incurred in defending themselves on those points on which they have succeeded, to be also taxed."—On taxation the Master allowed the Plaintiff the general costs of the cause, disallowing only those which applied exclusively to the parts of his claim on which he failed; and he allowed the Defendants such costs only as were incurred by them by reason of the two items of claim which they successfully resisted :— *Held*, reversing the decision of the Queen's Bench Division, that the Master had construed the order rightly, and had taxed the costs on the right principle. SPARROW *v.* HILL
[7 Q. B. D. 362; 8 Q. B. D. 479

10. —— **Claim and Counter-claim—*Costs where both succeed—Apportionment of Costs.*] When the Plaintiff's claim and the Defendant's counter-claim have both been successful, the Plaintiff, in the absence of any special directions to the contrary, is entitled to the general costs of the action, notwithstanding that the result of the litigation is in favour of the Defendant. There will be no apportionment of such costs as would have been duplicated had the counter-claim been the subject of an independent action, but the Plaintiff is not to recover as costs of the action any costs fairly attributable to the counter-claim. The decision of Chitty, J., affirmed. *In re* BROWN. WARD *v.* MORSE - 23 Ch. D. 377

11. —— **Claim and Counter-claim—*Costs of the Cause—Judgment—Certificate of Associate.*] The Plaintiff claimed to recover commission due to him from the Defendants on an agreement. The Defendants denied the claim, and claimed by way of counter-claim £230 0s. 9d. for goods sold: The jury found a verdict for the Plaintiff on the claim for £114 17s. 6d., and a verdict for the Defendants on the counter-claim for £280 0s. 9d. The judgment entered was "that the Plaintiff recover against the Defendants £ · · for his costs of suit," and "that the Defendants recover against the Plaintiff £115 3s. 3d. on the counter-claim and £ for their costs of the counter-claim " :—*Held*, reversing the decision of Pollock, B., that on taxing the costs according to the judgment the Plaintiff and not the Defendants was entitled to the costs of the cause.—*Semble*, per Brett, L.J., that where there is a claim with issues on it and a counter-claim (which is not a set-off but is in the nature of a cross-action) with issues on it, and the Plaintiff succeeds on the claim, and the Defendant succeeds on such counter-claim, the taxation, if not otherwise ordered, should be by taxing the claim as if it and its issues were an action, and by taxing the counter-claim as if it and its issues were also an action, and the allocatur for costs should be given for the balance in favour of the party in whose favour is such balance ; the Master on such taxation dividing items which are common to both actions. BAINES *v.* BROMLEY
[6 Q. B. D. 197, 691

12. —— **Claim and Counter-claim —*Judgment, Form of—Rules of Court, 1875, Order LV., r. 1.*] The Plaintiff's claim being for the balance

of the contract price of work done, after giving credit for money paid on account, the Defendants by way of set-off and counter-claim claimed in respect of the inferiority and defective character of the work. The action being referred for trial to an official referee, he found by his report that a balance of £32 18s. 6d. remained due to the Plaintiff on his claim in respect of the contract price of the work, and that £34 10s. 6d. was due to the Defendants on their counter-claim :—*Held*, that the proper judgment on these findings was that the Defendants do recover the balance of £1 12s., and the costs of the action, on the ground, either that the inferiority of the work, though pleaded by way of counter-claim in form, in reality amounted to a defence, or that, even if the Plaintiff were technically entitled by the findings to the costs of the action, the Court ought to interfere under Order LV., rule 1, and give the costs to the Defendants who had substantially succeeded in the action. LOWE *v.* HOLME -   10 Q. B. D. 286

13. —— **Claim and Counter-claim — *Debt — Arbitration—Order of Reference—" Costs of cause, reference, and award, shall abide the event"—Award — Entry of Judgment — Costs where the Plaintiff succeeds on Claim, and the Defendant on Counter-claim—Costs of Issues found in favour of Party, against whom Judgment in Action is entered.*] A Plaintiff having claimed for goods sold and delivered, and for commission, and the Defendants having counter-claimed for moneys collected by the Plaintiff on the Defendants' account and for work and labour, the action was referred to an arbitrator under an order of reference whereby "the costs of the cause, and the costs of the reference and award shall abide the event." The arbitrator found the issues on the claim in favour of the Plaintiff, and awarded him a sum of money in respect thereof, and found the issues on the counter-claim in favour of the Defendants, and awarded to them a sum of money in respect thereof. After deducting the sum found for the Plaintiff from the sum found for the Defendants, a balance of £97 was due to the Defendants :—*Held*, that the word "event" in the order of reference must be construed distributively, and that judgment must be entered for the Defendants, who were entitled to the costs of the action, reference, and award, but that the Plaintiff was entitled to the costs of the issues found in his favour.—*Baines v. Bromley* (6 Q. B. D. 691) explained. LUND *v.* CAMPBELL -   14 Q. B. D. 821

14. —— **Co-Defendants—*Contribution.*] Where co-Defendants are decreed to pay the costs of an action, one co-Defendant cannot, by an independent proceeding, obtain contribution in respect of such costs against the other. DEABSLEY *v.* MIDDLEWEEK -   -   - 18 Ch. D. 236

15. —— **Co-Defendants—*Payment to one Another.*] In cases where under the old practice in Chancery the Court would have ordered the Plaintiff to pay the costs of one Defendant and have them over against another Defendant, an order will now be made at once for the one Defendant to pay them to the other. RUDOW *v.* GREAT BRITAIN MUTUAL LIFE ASSURANCE SOCIETY
[17 Ch. D. 600

XLVI. PRACTICE—SUPREME COURT—COSTS
—continued.

16. —— Copies of Pleadings on Interlocutory
Application— Rules of Supreme Court (Costs),
August, 1875, r. 26.] An order had been made
by the Court of Appeal on the application of the
Defendants directing part of an affidavit to be
struck out as scandalous and giving the Defendants the costs of the application. Among the
items in the bill of costs of the Defendants were
charges for four copies of the pleadings, one for
the use of counsel and three for the use of the
Judges of the Court of Appeal. The Taxing
Master, without entering into the consideration of
the question whether the copies were necessary
for the purpose of the application, disallowed them
on the ground that it was the general rule not to
allow the costs of copies of pleadings on an interlocutory application :— Held, by the Court, of
Appeal, that no such general rule as was alleged
to exist in the Taxing Masters' office could be
sustained : that it was the duty of the Taxing
Master, under the Rules of the Supreme Court
(Costs), rule 26, to consider in each case whether
the copies were "necessary or proper for the
attainment of justice," and that as the copies in
the present case were necessary for the hearing of
the application, the costs of them must be allowed.
WARNER v. MOSSES - 　 - 　 - 　 19 Ch. D. 72

17. —— Costs by way of Penalty—Appeal for
Costs.] The Judge, at the trial of an action in
which there was a claim and counter-claim, thinking both parties in the wrong, dismissed the
action without costs, and also dismissed the
counter-claim with costs, but ordered that if the
costs of the counter-claim should not amount to
half the whole costs of the action the Defendant
should pay the difference to the Plaintiff :— Held,
that the order as to costs was irregular, inasmuch
as, after dismissing the action without costs, it
imposed part of the costs of the action upon the
Defendant by way of penalty ; but that in substance the order was within the discretion of the
Judge, as it amounted to dismissing the claim
and counter-claim and directing the Defendant
to pay half the whole costs of the action. WILL-
MOTT v. BARBER 　 - 　 - 　 17 Ch. D. 772

18. —— Counsel at Chambers—Solicitor and
Client— Taxation— Special Allowances— Rules
of Court (Costs), 1875, Special Allowances, Rule 14.]
The Supreme Court Rules, Special Allowances,
rule 14, that "as to counsel attending at Judge's
Chambers no costs thereof shall in any case be
allowed unless the Judge certifies it to be a
proper case for counsel to attend", applies to
taxation of costs between solicitor and client as
well as between party and party. In re CHAPMAN
　　　　 [9 Q. B. D. 254; 10 Q. B. D. 54

19. —— County Court— Action of Contract
which could not have been brought in County Court
—Judgment for Sum not exceeding £50—Rules of
Court, 1883, Order LXV., r. 12.] By Order LXV.,
rule 12, in actions founded on contract in which
the Plaintiff recovers by judgment or otherwise a
sum (exclusive of costs) not exceeding £50, he
shall be entitled to no more costs than he would
have been entitled to had he brought his action
in a County Court, unless the Court or a Judge
otherwise orders :— Held, that this rule does not

XLVI. PRACTICE—SUPREME COURT—COSTS
—continued.

apply to actions which could not have been
brought in a County Court. SAYWOOD v. CROSS
　　　　　　　　　　　 [14 Q. B. D. 53

20. —— County Court—Action remitted for
Trial to County Court—Rules of Court, 1883,
Order LXV., rr. 1, 4.] By Order LXV., rule 1
(Rules of the Supreme Court, 1883) the costs of
and incident to proceedings in the Supreme Court
are to be in the discretion of the Court or Judge,
subject to a proviso where an action is tried with
a jury. By rule 4 of the same Order, where an
action is ordered to be tried in a County Court
under 19 & 20 Vict. c. 108, s. 26, the costs of the
action are subject to these rules to follow the
event, unless by the Registrar's certificate of the
result of the trial, it appears that the County
Court Judge was of opinion that the question
ought to be referred to a Judge of the High
Court, in which case no costs are to be recovered
unless ordered by the Court or a Judge.—Where
an action has been ordered to be tried in a County
Court under 19 & 20 Vict. c. 108, s. 26, and has
been so tried there, the High Court retains its
power under Order LXV., rule 1, of dealing with
the costs of the action, notwithstanding rule 4
of that order, and the absence in the Registrar's
certificate of any expression of opinion by the
County Court Judge as provided for by that
rule. EMENY v. SANDES - 　 - 　 14 Q. B. D. 6

21. —— County Court—Admiralty Jurisdiction Act, 1868 (31 & 32 Vict. c. 71)—Rules of
Court, 1875, Order LV., rule 1.] Sect. 9 of the
County Courts Admiralty Jurisdiction Act, 1868,
which enacts that persons taking proceedings in a
superior Court, which they might under sect. 3 of
that Act have taken in a County Court, shall not
be entitled to costs, unless the Judge before whom
the cause was tried shall certify that it was a
proper cause to be tried in a superior Court, is inconsistent with and repealed by Order LV., rule 1,
of the Rules of the Supreme Court, 1875. TENANT
v. ELLIS 　 - 　 - 　 6 Q. B. D. 46

22. —— Cross-examination — Affidavit — Expenses of producing Affidavit Witness for Cross-
examination — Rules of Court, 1875, Order
XXXVIII., r. 4.] The provision in Rules of Court,
1875, Order XXXVIII., rule 4, that the party producing deponents for cross-examination upon their
affidavits shall not be entitled to demand the expenses thereof in the first instance from the party
requiring such production, is confined to a cross-
examination of the deponents before the Court at
the trial of the action, and does not apply to a
cross-examination on an affidavit filed after decree
for the purpose of proceedings in Chambers.—
Decision of Bacon, V.C., reversed. In re KNIGHT.
KNIGHT v. GARDNER 24 Ch. D. 606 ; 25 Ch. D. 297

23. —— Defendant—Withdrawal of Defence
—Common Law Procedure Act, 1852, s. 205—
Rules of Court, 1875, Order XXIII., r. 1.] Leave
was given to one of two Defendants in an action
of ejectment to withdraw his defence on the
terms of his paying to the Plaintiffs their costs of
the action, "so far as they were occasioned by
the said defence of the said Defendant" :— Held,
that the only costs which such Defendant was
liable to pay under this order were the increased

XLVI. PRACTICE—SUPREME COURT—COSTS
—*continued.*

costs occasioned by such Defendant having defended the action; and that he was not liable to pay an apportioned part of the Plaintiffs' general costs. REAL AND PERSONAL ADVANCE COMPANY *v.* MCCARTHY - - - **18 Ch. D. 362**

24. —— **Discretion of Court**—*Payment out of Court—Company—Compulsory Purchase of Land —Owner under Disability—Rules of Court, 1875, Order LV.*] When the purchase-money of land, taken by a company under compulsory powers conferred on them by a special Act passed before the Judicature Act, has been paid into Court by reason of the disability of the person entitled to the land, the Court has, under the general discretion as to costs given to it by Order LV., power to order the company to pay the costs of a petition for payment of the money out to a person absolutely entitled, even though the special Act contains no provision to that effect.—*Ex parte Mercers' Company* (10 Ch. D. 481) followed. *In re* LEE AND HEMINGWAY - - **24 Ch. D. 669**

25. —— **Dismissal for want of Prosecution**— *Rules of Court, 1883, Order LXV., r. 1.*] The costs of the Defendant where an action is dismissed for want of prosecution are now in the discretion of the Judge. SNELLING *v.* PULLING
[29 Ch. D. 85

26. —— **Entering Cause for Trial**—*Order as to Supreme Court Fees, 1884, Schedule 52—Fee for "entering cause or matter for trial or hearing"— Rule ordering Justice to hear Application for Summons.*] Under the Order as to Supreme Court Fees, 1884, Schedule 52—which directs that a fee of £2 shall be paid " on entering or setting down, or re-entering or re-setting down an appeal to the Court of Appeal, or a cause or matter for trial or hearing in any Court in London or Middlesex, or at any assizes "—such fee is payable though the matter for hearing does not arise in an action, as in the case of a rule nisi against a justice under 11 & 12 Vict. c. 44, s. 5. *Ex parte* HASKER **14 Q. B. D. 82**

27. —— **Executor of defaulting Executor**— *Defendant appearing in two Capacities—Apportionment of Costs.*] Where an action was brought for the administration of a testator's estate against the executor of a defaulting executor; whose estate was insolvent :—*Held,* that the Defendant being before the Court in a double capacity should have his costs of taking the accounts of the original testator's estate and half the rest of the costs of the action out of the estate.—*Palmer* v. *Jones* (43 L. J. (Ch.) 349) and *Kitto* v. *Luke* (28 W. R. 411) followed. *In re* GRIFFITHS. GRIFFITHS *v.* LEWIS - - **26 Ch. D. 465**

28. —— **Formâ pauperis**—*Taxation of Plaintiff's Costs—Remuneration for Solicitor and Fees for Counsel—Rules of Court, 1883, Order XVI., rr. 24, 25, 26, 27, 31.*] Under the Rules of the Supreme Court, 1883, Order XVI., rr. 24, 25, 26, 27, 31, a successful Plaintiff in an action in formâ pauperis tried before a Judge and jury is entitled upon taxation as against the Defendant to costs out of pocket only, and cannot be allowed anything for remuneration to his solicitor or fees to counsel. CARSON *v.* PICKERSGILL
[14 Q. B. D. 859

XLVI. PRACTICE—SUPREME COURT—COSTS
—*continued.*

29. —— **Higher or Lower Scale**—*Injunction— "Injury to Property"—Trespass.*] In Order VI., rule 2, of the Rules of the Supreme Court (Costs) which allows costs on the higher scale in actions— for special injunctions to restrain the commission or continuance of waste, nuisances, breaches of covenant, injuries to property, &c.—the "injury to property" must be a substantial physical injury, and does not include a trespass upon land without injury to the soil, though of a permanent character and committed in the assertion of title.—*Chapman* v. *Midland Railway Company* (5 Q. B. D. 167, 431) discussed. GOODHAND *v.* AYSCOUGH - - **10 Q. B. D. 71**

30. —— **Higher or Lower Scale**—*Rules of the Supreme Court (Costs), August, 1875, Order VI., rr. 1, 3.*] An appeal will lie from a decision by a Judge under Rules of the Supreme Court (Costs), August, 1875, Order VI., rule 3, as to the taxation of costs on the higher or lower scale; but where he has exercised his discretion the Court of Appeal will not interfere unless he has proceeded on a wrong principle or made a manifest slip.—An action for the recovery of large estates, the statement of claim in which set up a case of concealed fraud to avoid the operation of the Statutes of Limitation, was dismissed without costs. The Taxing Master in taxing the costs of the Plaintiff as between the solicitor and a person who had guaranteed their payment taxed them on the lower scale as coming within Order VI., rule 1, and Bacon, V.C., affirmed his decision :—*Held,* that the fact of the issue of fraud being raised was not a sufficient reason for directing the costs to be taxed on the higher scale, but that, to take the case out of the general rule that the costs of an action for the recovery of land are to be taxed on the lower scale, the solicitor must shew that the case was one requiring extra skill or labour. *In re* TERRELL **22 Ch. D. 473**

31. —— **Higher or Lower Scale**—*Rules of Supreme Court (Costs), Order VI., rr. 2, 3.*] The Plaintiff brought an action for damages for an alleged trespass under a claim of right, and prayed an injunction to restrain the Defendant from a repetition of it. The issue was one of considerable importance as between the parties, and involved a lengthened and expensive inquiry into the title of property which had been in the possession of the Plaintiff's family for more than three centuries. Upon the trial (without a jury) the Plaintiff obtained judgment for nominal damages :—*Held,* not a case in which the Court, in the exercise of its discretion under Order VI., rule 3, Rules of the Supreme Court (Costs) would order the costs to be taxed upon the higher scale.—*Semble,* that Order VI., rule 3, of the Rules of the Supreme Court (Costs) allowing costs upon the "higher scale " is not limited to costs in actions brought in the Chancery Division of the High Court, but gives the Common Law Divisions a discretionary power to order costs to be taxed upon the higher scale, even though the cause of action involves no equitable element. DUKE OF NORFOLK *v.* ARBUTHNOT
[6 Q. B. D. 279

32. —— **Higher or Lower Scale**—*Rules of Supreme Court (Costs), August, 1875, Order VI.*] In

XLVI. PRACTICE—SUPREME COURT—COSTS
—continued.

an action, which was dismissed with costs, to cancel an allotment of shares on the ground of fraudulent misrepresentation and suppression of material facts by the directors; to recover the amount paid upon the shares, and to be indemnified against the remaining balance—the fact that the pecuniary amount at issue was £110 only, and that the Plaintiff in issuing the writ had certified for the lower scale of costs, does not affect the discretion given to the Court by Rules of Supreme Court (Costs), August, 1875, Order VI., rule 3, to direct the costs payable by Plaintiff to be taxed on the higher and not on the lower scale.
HARRISON *v.* LEUTNER - 24 Ch. D. 594

33. —— **Inquiry as to Damages.**] When an injunction is granted to restrain the committing of a nuisance, and an inquiry as to damages is directed in Chambers, though the Plaintiff is entitled to the general costs of the action, the costs of the inquiry will be reserved in order that the Judge may have complete control over them, and be able to see that they are not unreasonably exaggerated. SLACK *v.* MIDLAND RAILWAY COMPANY - 16 Ch. D. 81

34. —— *Interrogatories—Insufficient Answers —Vivâ voce Examination—Costs—Order for Payment " in any Event"—Jurisdiction of Master— Rules of Court, 1875, Order XXXI., r. 10—Order LIV., r. 2—Order LV., r. 1.*] Where, in consequence of the party interrogated answering insufficiently, an order was made by the Master for his examination vivâ voce before a special examiner :—*Held,* that there was power under Order XXXI., rule 10, and Order LV., rule 1, or the general practice of the Court, to make it a term of the order that the costs of, and occasioned by, the application should be paid by the party interrogated " in any event."
VICARY *v.* GREAT NORTHERN RAILWAY COMPANY
[9 Q. B. D. 168

35. —— **Married Woman—***Action by Executrix and her Husband—Bankruptcy of Husband—Dismissal of Action with Costs—Liability of Husband for the Costs—Bankruptcy Act,* 1869 (32 & 33 Vict. c. 71), s. 31.] A feme coverte sued as executrix, and (the action being brought before the Married Women's Property Act, 1882, came into operation) her husband was joined as co-Plaintiff. After the action was set down, but before trial, the husband filed a liquidation petition, and obtained his discharge thereunder. When the action came on for trial the Plaintiffs did not appear, and the action was dismissed with costs :—*Held* (affirming the judgment of Pollock, B., for Pearson, J.), that the husband, who had no beneficial interest which could pass to the trustee under his liquidation, having allowed the action (which was a continuing action after his liquidation) to come on for trial, was liable for the costs.—*Semble,* per Lindley, L.J.:—A possibility of having to pay costs is not a debt provable in bankruptcy, though it may in some cases be a " contingent liability." VINT *v.* HUDSFITH - 30 Ch. D. 24

36. —— **Parties having Liberty to attend.**] Mere liberty to attend the proceedings under an administration judgment does not entitle the parties having the liberty to the costs of their attendance in Chambers as a matter of course.

XLVI. PRACTICE—SUPREME COURT—COSTS
—continued.

In order to entitle such parties to such costs the order giving the liberty to attend should expressly provide that they are to be entitled thereto.
DAY *v.* BATTY - - 21 Ch. D. 830

37. —— **Perusal of Exhibits** — *Affidavits — Special Order—Rules of Court (Costs), August,* 1875, *Order VI., Schedule. "Perusals."*] Order made that the Taxing Master should be at liberty to allow a special charge for the perusal of exhibits to affidavits, the amount thereof (if any) to be in his discretion. *In re* DE ROSAZ. RYMER *v.* DE ROSAZ 24 Ch. D. 684

38. —— **Production and Inspection—***Counsel's Fees and Refreshers.*] When an order is made in an action in the Chancery Division for the production of documents at the office of the producing party's solicitor, that party, if ultimately successful in the action, is not entitled, as between party and party, to his solicitor's costs of the production, nor to his own costs of inspecting the documents of the other party.—When the trial of an action commences on one day and is concluded on the next next day, refreshers to counsel will not be allowed unless the trial occupied in the whole more than one day's sittings, i.e., six hours.—The Taxing Master's decision as to the amount of counsel's fees will not be interfered with unless a gross mistake is made. BROWN *v.* SEWELL
[16 Ch. D. 517

39. —— **Purchase of Land—***Reinvestment of Money—Redemption of Land Tax—Private Act —Rules of Court,* 1875, *Order LV.—Discretion of Court.*] A company purchased lands under a private Act of Parliament, which provided that the company should pay the costs of reinvestment of purchase-money in " lands, tenements, and hereditaments " :—*Held,* that the costs of reinvestment in the redemption of land tax must be paid by the company. The purchase-money having amounted to £125,000, the Court did not consider six applications for reinvestment, still leaving £38,440 uninvested, to be unreasonable.— The Court has now, under the Judicature Act, 1875, and Order LV. of Rules of Court, 1875, a discretion as to directing payment of costs where a provision as to costs is omitted in any public or private Act. *Ex parte* HOSPITAL OF ST. KATHARINE - - 17 Ch. D. 378

40. —— **Reference—***Consent—Costs to abide the Event—County Courts Act,* 1867 (30 & 31 Vict. c. 142), s. 5.] By an order made by consent of the parties, an action on a building contract was referred to an arbitrator to ascertain the amount, if any, due from the Defendant to the Plaintiff, " the costs of the action, reference, and award, to abide the event." The arbitrator found the sum due to the Plaintiff was £19 2s. 7d. upon which an order was made for judgment for the Plaintiff for that sum, without costs :—*Held,* that the Plaintiff had recovered in the action by judgment a sum not exceeding £20, and that he was therefore deprived of his costs of the action by the County Courts Act, 1867 (30 & 31 Vict. c. 142), s. 5, unless he got a certificate or order for costs under that section.—*Jones* v. *Jones* (7 C. B. (N.S.) 832) overruled. FERGUSSON *v.* DAVISON
[8 Q. B. D. 470

XLVI. PRACTICE—SUPREME COURT—COSTS
—continued.

41. —— **Reference**—*Costs to abide "Event"*
—General Award in favour of Defendant on Coun-
ter-claim—Reference back to find Specific Issues.]
The Plaintiff, who had built two houses for the
Defendant at a contract price of £1135, sued for
£169 16s., the balance of the price, and for other
small items.—The Defendant raised various defences, and also counter-claimed £1200 for penalties for delay and for damages arising from bad
work. The pleadings went as far as surrejoinder,
after which the cause, with all matters in difference, was referred to an architect as arbitrator,
upon the terms, inter alia, that the costs of action,
reference, and award, should follow the event,
unless the arbitrator should otherwise order. The
arbitrator by an award, silent as to costs, awarded
£3 2s. 6d. to the Defendant in respect of the
action and matters in difference :—*Held*, affirming the judgment of the Queen's Bench Division,
that the word "event" ought to be construed
distributively, and the award remitted to the
arbitrator to find specific issues. ELLIS v. DESILVA
[6 Q. B. D. 521]

42. —— **Reference**—*Costs to abide Event—*
"Event" construed distributively.] An action and
all matters in difference were referred, the costs
of the cause, reference, and award to abide the
event :—*Held*, on the authority of *Ellis* v. *Desilva*
(6 Q. B. D. 521), that the word "event" must be
construed distributively; and that consequently,
upon an award by which the arbitrator decided
in the Plaintiff's favour upon the claim in the
action, but in the Defendant's favour upon a matter
in difference not raised in the action, the Plaintiff
was entitled to the costs of the action and the
Defendant to the costs of the matter on which he
had succeeded.—*Gribble* v. *Buchanan* (18 C. B.
691; 26 L. J. (C.P.) 24) not followed. HAWKE v.
BREAR　-　-　-　14 Q. B. 841

43. —— **Set-off**—*Rules of Court,* 1883, *Order*
LXV., r. 27, *sub-s.* 21.] Under sub-sect. 21 of
rule 27 of Order LXV. of the Rules of the Supreme
Court, 1883, costs which a party is ordered to pay
personally may be set off against costs which he
is entitled to receive out of a fund in Court. BAT-
TEN v. WEDGWOOD COAL AND IRON COMPANY
[28 Ch. D. 317]

44. —— **Set-off for Damages or Costs**—*Soli-*
citor's Lien—Cross Judgments in Separate Actions
—Rules of Court, 1883, *Order* LXV., *r.* 14.] The
Court upon an application to set off cross judgments in distinct actions are entitled, notwithstanding Order LXV., r. 14, to order that the set-
off shall be subject to the lien for costs of the
solicitor of the opposite party—for assuming that
rule 14 applies to a set-off in distinct actions, it
leaves the Court a discretion to allow the set-
off, either subject to or notwithstanding the solicitor's lien, and if it has no application the Court
have the same discretion by the practice previous
to Reg. Hil. Term, 1853, r. 63, which, since the
repeal of that rule by the new rules, is revived.
EDWARDS v. HOPE　-　-　14 Q. B. D. 922

45. —— **Short-hand Notes**—*Evidence.*] The
rule is now well settled that the costs of shorthand writer's notes of evidence will not be allowed
on taxation unless a direction to that effect has
been inserted in the order; for which special application must be made at the hearing. And
such a direction will only be inserted in exceptional cases, the Judge's notes, supplemented by
those of counsel, being in general a sufficient
record of the evidence. EARL DE' LA WARR v.
MILES　-　-　-　19 Ch. D. 80

46. —— **Short-hand Notes**—*Evidence at Trial*
—Special Direction.] It is competent to the
Court to make an order for the allowance, on
taxation between party and party, of the expense
of the short-hand notes of the evidence given at
the trial, as part of the costs of a rule for a new
trial on the ground that the verdict was against
the weight of evidence, in a case where from the
nature and extent of the evidence it is manifest
that the matter could not have been properly
disposed of without their aid. WATSON v. GREAT
WESTERN RAILWAY COMPANY　6 Q. B. D. 163

47. —— **Solicitor**—*Defendant in Person—Costs*
as Solicitor — Taxation.] Where an action is
brought against a solicitor who defends it in
person and obtains judgment, he is entitled upon
taxation to the same costs as if he had employed
a solicitor, except in respect of items which the
fact of his acting directly renders unnecessary.—
Judgment of the Queen's Bench Division affirmed.
LONDON SCOTTISH BENEFIT SOCIETY v. CHORLEY.
[12 Q. B. D. 452; 13 Q. B. D. 872]

48. —— **Third Party**—*Jurisdiction of Court*
to order to pay Plaintiff's Costs—Appeal as to
Costs—Judicature Act, 1873, *s.* 24, *sub-s.* 3, *and*
s. 49—*Rules of Court,* 1875, *Order* LV.—*Contract*
of sub-Tenant to perform Covenants of head-Lease,
whether Contract of Indemnity.] The High Court
has jurisdiction to order a third party to pay to
an unsuccessful Defendant the costs payable by
such Defendant to the Plaintiff.—*Per* Brett and
Cotton, L.JJ.: The contract of a sub-tenant to
perform the covenants of the head-lease is a contract of indemnity.—The Plaintiff let to the Defendant a house, for twenty-one years with option
to determine the lease at the end of seven or
fourteen, by deed containing covenants by the
Defendant to repair and paint and leave in repair.
The Defendant, after having occupied for five
years, sublet the house to H. for the remainder of
the first seven years by a writing with a clause,
that "the letting should be subject in all respects
to the terms of the existing lease and the covenants and stipulations contained therein." At
the end of the seven years, the Defendant having
determined the lease in the exercise of his option,
the Plaintiff claimed from the Defendant, and
the Defendant claimed from H., the amount at
which dilapidations had been assessed by the
Plaintiff's surveyor. H. declined to pay or to give
the Defendant an indemnity, or to take any responsibility in the matter. The Plaintiff sued
the Defendant, who brought in H. as third party.
The issues, as between the Plaintiff and the Defendant, and the Defendant and H., were referred
separately to an official referee, who reported that
the sum claimed by the Plaintiff was due from
the Defendant to the Plaintiff, and that a similar
sum was due from H. to the Defendant.—A Divisional Court (Lord Coleridge, C.J., and Field, J.),

XLVI. PRACTICE—SUPREME COURT—COSTS
—*continued.*

on adopting the second report, ordered H. to pay all costs as between the Plaintiff and the Defendant:—*Held*, by the Court of Appeal (Jessel, M.R., Brett and Cotton, L.JJ.), that these were costs within the discretion of the High Court, and therefore that this order was not appealable; and by Brett and Cotton, L.JJ., that H.'s contract was a contract of indemnity, under which the Defendant was entitled to recover from H. all the costs of an action by the Plaintiff against the Defendant reasonably defended. HORNBY *v.* CARDWELL　-　- 8 Q. B. D. 329

· **49. —— Trial by Jury**—*Nonsuit—Costs of Issues upon which Plaintiff has been nonsuited—Rules of Court, 1875, Order* LV., r. 1—*Procedure where Ambiguity in Judgment as to Costs.*] In an action tried by a jury where the Plaintiff succeeds upon some issues but is nonsuited upon others, and no order is made as to costs, the Defendant is entitled under Order LV., rule 1, to the costs of the issues upon which the Plaintiff was nonsuited. —Where there is an ambiguity in the terms of a judgment with respect to costs, and the Master in consequence refuses to tax the costs of one of the parties, the proper course is to apply for a direction to the Judge who tried the cause, and not to appeal against the Master's decision. ABBOTT *v.* ANDREWS　-　-　- - 8 Q. B. D. 648

50. —— Trial by Jury—*Rules of Court, 1883, Order* LXV., r. 1—*Jurisdiction of Judge to make Order as to Costs—" Good Cause "—Appeal—Action for Recovery of Land—Separate Issues—Taxation of Costs in such Action.*] Where an action is tried with a jury the Judge before whom it is tried has no jurisdiction under Order LXV., rule 1, to make an order by which the costs will not follow the event unless there exist " good cause " within the meaning of that rule, and consequently there is an appeal with respect to the existence of the facts necessary to give the Judge jurisdiction to make such order.—To be " good cause " within that rule there must be facts shewing that it would be more just not to allow the costs to follow the event, as, for example, oppression or misconduct of either of the parties by which costs have been unnecessarily increased.—The fact that the action is for the recovery of several closes of land, that the only defence is that the defendant is in possession, and that the verdict is for the plaintiff for some only of the closes claimed, does not by itself constitute " good cause " within Order LXV., rule 1, since the verdict in such a case is distributive, and the costs, if properly taxed, would be as on a finding by the jury on separate issues. JONES *v.* CURLING
· [13 Q. B. D. 262

—— Appeal for.
　　See Cases under PRACTICE—SUPREME COURT—APPEAL. 24—33.

—— Appeal for—Interpleader　8 Q. B. D. 82
　　See PRACTICE—SUPREME COURT—INTERPLEADER. 1.

—— Successful party deprived of costs 7 Q. B. D.
[641
·.·.　*See* PRACTICE—SUPREME COURT—APPEAL. 39.

XLVII. PRACTICE — SUPREME COURT — INTERPLEADER.
(*a.*) RULES OF COURT, 1875.

1. —— Appeal—*Costs—Judicature Act, 1873, s. 49—Order* I., r. 2.] Order I., rule 2, which preserves the procedure and practice under the Interpleader Acts in actions in the High Court, does not contradict sect. 49 of the Judicature Act, 1873, which enacts that no order of a Judge of the High Court as to costs only, shall be subject to appeal without leave of such Judge; and such enactment applies to a Judge's order in interpleader as well as in other proceedings. HARTMONT *v.* FOSTER　·　8 Q. B. D. 82

2. —— Jurisdiction of Judge—*Trial without Jury—1 & 2 Will. 4, c. 58—Order* I., r. 2—*Order* XXXVI., rr. 2 and 3.] An interpleader issue cannot be tried by a Judge without a jury in pursuance of a notice of that mode of trial, under Order XXXVI., rules 2 and 3. HAMLYN *v.* BETTELEY
[6 Q. B. D. 63

3. —— Summary Decision—*Reference by Judge at Chambers to the Court—Appeal—Common Law Procedure Act, 1860 (23 & 24 Vict. c. 126), ss. 14, 17.*] A Judge at Chambers referred an interpleader summons to a Divisional Court. The Court barred the claimant and decided the case without ordering an interpleader issue:—*Held*, that such a decision was given in exercise of the summary jurisdiction of a Court or Judge under the Common Law Procedure Act, 1860 (23 & 24 Vict. c. 126), s. 14, and was therefore final and without appeal. TURNER *v.* BRIDGETT 9 Q. B. D. 55

(*b.*) RULES OF COURT, 1883.

4. —— Appeal—*Application for New Trial—Court of Appeal.*] Under the Rules of 1883, Order LVII., rule 11, where an interpleader issue has been tried by a jury, and judgment given according to their finding by the presiding Judge, application for a new trial must be made to the Court of Appeal and not to the Divisional Court. BURSTALL *v.* BRYANT　-　12 Q. B. D. 103

5. —— Appeal—*Judge finally disposing of whole Matter—Supreme Court of Judicature Act, 1873 (36 & 37 Vict. c. 66), s. 19—Order* XL., r. 5; *Order* LVII., r. 13.] When an interpleader issue has been tried by a Judge and a jury, and upon the finding of the jury the Judge has, under Order LVII., r. 13, pronounced judgment disposing of the whole matter of the interpleader proceedings, but has given leave to appeal, a party to the issue who is dissatisfied with both the finding of the jury and the judgment of the Judge, may appeal under Order XL., r. 5, to a Divisional Court of the Queen's Bench Division, and under the Supreme Court of Judicature Act, 1873, s. 19, from that Court to the Court of Appeal.—*Semble*, that *Burstall* v. *Bryant* (12 Q. B. D. 103) was wrongly decided. ROBINSON *v.* TUCKER
[14 Q. B. D. 371

6. —— Appeal—*Summary Decision at Chambers—Appeal from Queen's Bench Division to Court of Appeal—Common Law Procedure Act, 1860 (23 & 24 Vict. c. 126), s. 17—Appellate Jurisdiction Act, 1876 (39 & 40 Vict. c. 59), s. 20—Order* LVII., rr. 8, 11.] By the combined operation of the Common Law Procedure Act, 1860, sect. 17, and of the Appellate Jurisdiction

XLVII. PRACTICE — SUPREME COURT — IN-
TERPLEADER—*continued.*

(b.) RULES OF COURT, 1883—*continued.*

Act, 1876, sect. 20, no appeal lies to the Court
of Appeal from a decision of the Queen's Bench
Division upon an appeal from the summary decision at Chambers of an interpleader summons, and
r. 11 of the Rules of the Supreme Court, 1883,
Order LVII., does not confer any power to give
leave to appeal. WATERHOUSE *v.* GILBERT
[15 Q. B. D. 569

7. —— **Appeal** — *Trial of Issue — Judgment
of Judge on Trial.*] Where it is sought to impeach the judgment of a Judge on the trial of
an interpleader issue with respect only to the finding of the facts, or the ruling of the law, and not
with respect to the final disposal of the whole
matter of the interpleader proceedings, an appeal
will lie from such judgment under sect. 19 of the
Judicature Act, 1873, as it will from any other
judgment or order of a Judge. DAWSON *v.* FOX
[14 Q. B. D. 377

8. —— **Indemnity to Stakeholder**—*Objection
by Claimant indemnifying to Interpleader Issue—
Order LVII., r. 2 (b).*] The objection that a stakeholder has, by merely taking an indemnity from
one of two rival claimants to property in his
hands, disentitled himself to relief under the
Interpleader Acts because he has identified himself with and must be taken to "collude" with
the claimant who gave the indemnity, cannot be
raised by that claimant himself, and the decisions
in *Tucker* v. *Morris* (1 Cr. & M. 73) and *Belcher*
v. *Smith* (9 Bing. 82) do not apply. THOMPSON
v. WRIGHT　　-　　13 Q. B. D. 632

9. —— **Power of Master to award Costs**—
*Order LIV., r. 12 (i.)—Order LVII., rr, 5, 9, 10, 15
—Order barring Claimant—Costs of Defendant
in Action as distinct from those in Interpleader
Proceedings—Judicature Act, 1873, s. 49.*] Under
the Rules of 1883, Order LIV., rule 12 (i), limiting
the power of the Master to award costs other than
those of any proceeding before him or those specially authorized—the Master in making an order
barring the claimant upon an interpleader summons under Order LVII., when the applicant is
a defendant, has no power under rule 15 to make
it a term of the order that the plaintiff shall pay
the costs of the defendant in the original action,
apart from those in the interpleader proceedings,
and an order to this effect is, notwithstanding
36 & 37 Vict. c. 66, *s.* 49, subject to appeal.
HANSEN *v.* MADDOX　　-　　12 Q. B. D. 100

10. —— **Sale**—*Receiver and Manager—Judicature Act, 1873, s. 25, sub-s. 8—Order LVII., r. 15.*]
An interpleader issue being ordered to try the
right to goods seized in execution, the Court or a
Judge may, under the Judicature Act, 1873, s. 25,
sub-s. 8, and Order LVII., rule 15, order that,
instead of a sale by the sheriff, a receiver and
manager of the property be appointed. HOWELL
v. DAWSON　　-　　-　　13 Q. B. D. 67

11. —— **Sheriff**—*Possession Money—Sheriff's
Fees—1 & 2 Will. 4, c. 58, s. 6; 23 & 24 Vict.
c. 126, ss. 13, 14, 17.*] On the 17th of February, 1881, the sheriff seized goods under an
elegit against D. for £72, and interest, and costs.
W. claimed the goods as his. On the 19th of

XLVII. PRACTICE — SUPREME COURT — IN-
TERPLEADER—*continued.*

(b.) RULES OF COURT, 1883—*continued.*

February the sheriff took out an interpleader
summons. On the 15th of July an order was
made for the sheriff to withdraw on W. giving
security, in default of security the sheriff was
ordered to sell the goods and pay the net proceeds into Court. Security was not given, and
on the 12th of August the sheriff paid £52, the
net proceeds of the goods, into Court. On the
21st of June, 1882, Chitty, J., made an order that
W. should be barred, that the fund in Court
should be paid to the execution creditor, and that
W. should pay to the execution creditor and the
sheriff their costs of the interpleader summons,
including in the costs of the sheriff his possession money caused by W.'s claim. The sheriff,
not being satisfied that W. could pay him, appealed, asking that his possession money might
be paid out of the fund in Court in priority to the
claim of the execution creditor. In the meantime
the money had been paid to the Plaintiff :—*Held,*
by Cotton and Bowen, L.JJ. (dissentiente, Fry,
L.J.), that 23 & 24 Vict. c. 126, s. 17, making a
summary decision under the Act final and conclusive against "the parties," did not make it
final against the sheriff, and that he could appeal :—*Held,* by the whole Court, that where an
interpleader has been directed on the application
of the sheriff, and the claim of the third party
fails, the strict form of order upon which the execution creditor is entitled to insist, is to direct the execution creditor to pay the sheriff's charges of the
interpleader, with a remedy over to the execution
creditor against the third party, though it is a
common form of order simply to order the third
party to pay them to the sheriff. SMITH *v.*
DARLOW　　-　　-　　26 Ch. D. 605

12. —— **Sheriff**—*Proceeds or Value of Goods
taken in Execution—Money paid to Sheriff under
Protest—Order LVII., r. 1 (b)—Trespass on Land
of Person other than Execution Debtor — Protection to Sheriff against Action for Trespass.*]
Where the sheriff seized goods under a fi. fa.
and a person other than the person against
whom the process issued claimed the goods and
paid out the sheriff under protest :—*Held,* that
the money so paid to the sheriff under protest
was the proceeds of goods taken in execution
within the meaning of Order LVII., rule 1 (b),
and that therefore the sheriff was entitled to interplead in respect thereof.—By the Court,—Where
the sheriff in the execution of a fi. fa. enters the
premises of a person other than the execution
debtor and there seizes goods believing erroneously that such goods belong to the execution
debtor, the sheriff may, upon interpleader proceedings, be protected against an action for trespass to the land as well as against an action for
seizure of the goods, if no substantial grievance
has been done to the person whose premises are
wrongfully entered.—*Hollier* v. *Laurie* (3 C. B.
334) discussed, and *Winter* v. *Bartholomew* (11 Ex.
704; 25 L. J. (Ex.) 62) approved. SMITH *v.*
CRITCHFIELD　　-　　-　　14 Q. B. D. 873
—— Service out of the jurisdiction 12 Q. B. D. 171
　　See PRACTICE—SUPREME COURT—SER-
　　VICE. 7.

XLVIII. PRACTICE—SUPREME COURT—CONSENT.

—— **Facts not mentioned to Court—** *Withdrawal of Consent.*] An action was brought against a local board to restrain them from pulling down certain houses of the Plaintiff's and for damages. On a motion for an injunction coming on, the Defendants' counsel by the authority of his clients, consented to an order for a perpetual injunction with costs, and an inquiry as to damages, and such order was taken by consent without opening the case to the Court. Before the order had been passed, the Defendants formally withdrew their consent, and the Registrar thereupon declined to pass the order without the direction of the Court. The Plaintiff moved that he might be directed to proceed to perfect the order. The Defendants alleged that their instructions to consent had been given under a misapprehension, but did not enter into any evidence in support of that allegation:— *Held*, by Pearson, J., that up to the time of a consent order being passed, any party can withdraw his consent, except where he consents to a decree of the Court after the case has been before the Judge, and that the application must be refused:— *Held*, on appeal, that where counsel by the authority of their clients consent to an order, the clients cannot arbitrarily withdraw such consent, and that the Registrar must be directed to proceed to perfect the order, without prejudice to any application which the Defendants might make to the Court below to be relieved from their consent, on the ground of mistake or surprise or for other sufficient reason. HARVEY *v.* CROYDON UNION RURAL SANITARY AUTHORITY

[26 Ch. D. 249

XLIX. PRACTICE—SUPREME COURT—APPEAL.

(a.) GENERAL.

1. —— **Attachment—***Refusal to commit for Contempt—Discretion of Judge—Right to appeal.*] Where a Judge has refused to commit for contempt, an appeal lies from such refusal, although where that refusal has been simply an exercise of judicial discretion, the Court of Appeal, while entertaining an appeal, will be slow to alter the decision of the Court below.—*Ashworth v. Outram* (5 Ch. D. 943) must not be treated as laying down a general rule that no appeal lies from a refusal to commit. JARMAIN *v.* CHATTERTON

[20 Ch. D. 493

2. —— **Case stated by Arbitrator—***Interlocutory or Final Order.*] An arbitrator, under an order of reference, stated a case for the opinion of the Court, which provided that, if the opinion of the Court should be one way the case was to be referred back to the arbitrator ; if the other way judgment was to be entered for the Defendant with costs. A Divisional Court decided in favour of the Plaintiffs, and referred the case back to the arbitrator. The Defendant appealed :—*Held*, first, that an appeal could be brought from the order; secondly, that it was a final order, and that the appeal must be entered in the general and not in the interlocutory list.—*Collins v. Vestry of Paddington* (5 Q. B. D. 368) distinguished. SHUBROOK *v.* TUFNELL　　9 Q. B. D. 621

XLIX. PRACTICE — SUPREME COURT — APPEAL—*continued.*

(a.) GENERAL—*continued.*

3. —— **Case stated by Judge's Order—***Poorrate—12 & 13 Vict. c. 45, s. 11—Supreme Court of Judicature Act,* 1873 (36 & 37 Vict. c. 66), *s.* 19.] An appeal will lie to the Court of Appeal from the decision of the Queen's Bench Division upon a case stated under 12 & 13 Vict. c. 45, s. 11, in an appeal against a poor-rate ; for the decision of the Queen's Bench Division is an " order " within the meaning of the Supreme Court of Judicature Act, 1873, s. 19. CORPORATION OF PETERBOROUGH *v.* OVERSEERS OF WILSTHORPE　　12 Q. B. D. 1

4. —— **Case stated by Judge's Order—***Poor Law —* 12 & 13 *Vict. c.* 45, *s.* 11 — *Supreme Court of Judicature Act,* 1873, *ss.* 19, 45.] An appeal lies to the Court of Appeal from the decision of the Divisional Court upon a case stated under 12 & 13 Vict. c. 45, s. 11, on an appeal from an order of the justices to the quarter sessions, it not being a decision of the Divisional Court on an appeal from petty or quarter sessions within the meaning of sect. 45 of the Judicature Act, 1873, and it being an " order " within sect. 19 of that Act. GUARDIANS OF HOLBORN *v.* GUARDIANS OF CHERTSEY　－　　15 Q. B. D. 76

5. —— **Case stated by Quarter Sessions** *for Opinion of Queen's Bench Division—Appeal to the Court of Appeal— Leave to appeal when necessary —Judicature Act,* 1873 (36 & 37 *Vict. c.* 66), *s.* 45.] Where the Queen's Bench Division in the exercise of its original common law jurisdiction affirms or quashes an order of sessions, an appeal lies to the Court of Appeal although no leave to appeal be given. THE QUEEN *v.* SAVIN　　6 Q. B. D. 309

6. —— **County Court—***Action remitted to County Court—County Courts Act,* 1867 (30 & 31 *Vict. c.* 142), *s.* 10—*Judicature Act,* 1873 (36 & 37 *Vict. c.* 66), *s.* 45.] Where a cause has been remitted for trial before a County Court under sect. 10 of the County Courts Act, 1867 (30 & 31 Vict. c. 142), it becomes a County Court cause, and the determination of a Divisional Court, on appeal from the decision of the County Court Judge, is within sect. 45 of the Judicature Act, 1873, and therefore final, unless special leave to appeal be given. BOWLES *v.* DRAKE

[8 Q. B. D. 325

7. —— **County Court—***County Courts Act,* 1875 (38 & 39 *Vict. c.* 50), *s.* 6—*Rules of Supreme Court,* 1883, *Orders XXXIX. and LII.*] An appeal from the decision of a County Court Judge should be by motion ex parte in the first instance under the County Courts Act, 1875, s. 6, and not by giving notice of motion under Order XXXIX., rule 3. *Shapcott v. Chappell* (12 Q. B. D. 58) questioned. MATHEWS *v.* OVEY　　13 Q. B. D. 403 [*But see* Rules of Supreme Court, December, 1885, rr. 9–17.]

8. —— **Criminal Matter** — *Jurisdiction — Supreme Court of Judicature Act,* 1873 (36 & 37 *Vict. c.* 66), *s.* 47—*Public Health Act,* 1875 (38 & 39 *Vict. c.* 55), *ss.* 92, 94.] An order was made by justices directing the Defendant to fill up an ash-pit, so as to be no longer a nuisance. The Queen's Bench Division made absolute an order for a certiorari to quash this order, on the ground

XLIX. PRACTICE — SUPREME COURT — AP-
PEAL—continued.

(a.) GENERAL—continued.

that it was not warranted by the Public Health
Act, 1875, ss. 94, 96:—Held, that the order of
the justices was made in a "criminal cause or
matter" within the meaning of the Supreme
Court of Judicature Act, 1873, s. 47, and that an
appeal from the judgment of the Queen's Bench
Division could not be entertained.—Mellor v.
Denham (5 Q. B. D. 467) followed. THE QUEEN
v. WHITCHURCH　-　　-　　7 Q. B. D. 534

9. —— Criminal Matter—Jurisdiction—Bail
—36 & 37 Vict. c. 66, ss. 19, 47.] A prisoner
applied for bail to a Divisional Court of the
Queen's Bench Division but was refused; he
then appealed to the Court of Appeal :—Held,
that the decision of the Divisional Court was a
judgment of the High Court in a criminal matter,
and therefore that the Court of Appeal had no
jurisdiction to entertain the appeal. THE QUEEN
v. FOOTE　-　　-　　-　　10 Q. B. D. 378

10. —— Cross-demurrers— Right to begin.]
Where there are cross appeals on cross demurrers
before the Court of Appeal, and the burden of
proof lies on the Defendant, so that if he fails in
his appeal the cross appeal becomes immaterial,
the Defendant will be entitled to begin. CLARKE
v. BRADLAUGH　-　　-　　7 Q. B. D. 38

11. —— Cross Notice—Notice by Respondent
to ask for Variation—Rules of Court, 1875, Order
LVIII., r. 6.] A Respondent who seeks to have
an order varied on a point in which the Appellant has no interest, cannot proceed by notice
under Rules of Court, 1875, Order LVIII., rule 6,
but must give notice of appeal. In re CAVAN-
DER'S TRUSTS　-　　-　　16 Ch. D. 270

12. —— Death of Appellant—Revivor by Executor.] A Defendant, P., gave notice of appeal
from a judgment, and set it down. After this he
died, and his executrix obtained an order of
course at the Rolls that the appeal might be
carried on and prosecuted by her in like manner
as it might have been carried on and prosecuted
by P. if he had not died.—Held, that the order
was sufficient, and that the executrix was entitled
to proceed with the appeal. RANSON v. PATTON
[17 Ch. D. 767

13. —— Election Petition—Corrupt Practices
Prevention Act (26 & 27 Vict. c. 29), s. 7 —
Certificate to Witness—Mandamus—Jurisdiction
to hear Appeal— Supreme Court of Judicature
Act, 1873, s. 47—Criminal Matter.] Where the
Commissioners appointed to inquire into corrupt
practices at a parliamentary election have, with
reference to a witness before them on such inquiry, exercised their judgment as to the right of
such witness to receive their certificate under
sect. 7 of Corrupt Practices Prevention Act (26 &
27 Vict. c. 29), their decision refusing such certificate is conclusive, and cannot be reviewed by
mandamus.—Reg. v. Price (Law Rep. 6 Q. B.
411) dissented from.—The decision of a Divisional Court discharging a rule for a mandamus
to such Commissioners to grant such certificate,
which certificate if given would be a protection
to the witness against criminal proceedings for
bribery, does not relate to a criminal cause or

XLIX. PRACTICE — SUPREME COURT — AP-
PEAL—continued.

(a.) GENERAL—continued.

matter, within the meaning of the Supreme Court
of Judicature Act, 1873, s. 47, and the Court of
Appeal is not therefore deprived of jurisdiction
to hear an appeal against such decision. THE
QUEEN v. HOLL　-　　-　　7 Q. B. D. 575

14. —— Fresh Evidence—Claim in Administration Action — Order, whether interlocutory
or final—Rules of Court, 1883—Order LVIII.,
rr. 4, 15.] Although an order made on a summons by a creditor in an administration action is
considered as if interlocutory for the purpose of
determining the time within which an appeal must
be brought, for other purposes it is a final order,
and therefore fresh evidence cannot be given on
the appeal without the special leave of the Court.
In re COMPTON. NORTON v. COMPTON 27 Ch. D. 392

15. —— One of several Plaintiffs.] Two of
the three trustees of a settlement brought an
action to have the trusts administered under the
direction of the Court. Malins, V.C., dismissed
the action with costs. One of the Plaintiffs
having declined to concur in an appeal, the other
appealed alone.—The Court of Appeal held that
such an appeal was regular, and must be allowed
to proceed; and, being of opinion that a sufficient
ground has been shewn for asking the direction
of the Court, a decree for administration of the
trusts was made. BECKETT v. ATTWOOD
[18 Ch. D. 54

16. —— Person not a Party—Leave to appeal.]
Leave to a person interested in, but not a party to
an action, to appeal from an order, may be obtained by ex parte application to the Court of
Appeal. In re MARKHAM. MARKHAM v. MARKHAM
[16 Ch. D. 1

17. —— Person not a Party—Representative
Suit—Person represented by the Plaintiff.] In an
action commenced by a bondholder on behalf of
himself and all other bondholders, the Plaintiff
obtained an order for a receiver. One of the
bondholders represented by the Plaintiff, being
dissatisfied with the order, applied for leave to
appeal:—Held, that the order having been made
in favour of the class to which the applicant belonged, and having been obtained by the Plaintiff, who represented him in the action, he could
not appeal against it.—Semble, the proper course
for the dissentient shareholder to pursue was to
apply to the Court below to be made a Defendant
to the action. WATSON v. CAVE (No. 1)
[17 Ch, D. 19

18. —— Person not a Party—Setting aside
Judgment obtained by Collusion—Rules of Court,
1883, Order XVI., r. 40.] D., the residuary legatee
of Mrs. Y., brought her action for administration
of Mrs. Y.'s estate against R., the surviving executor. Mrs. Y. had been the surviving executrix
of her husband. V., one of the residuary legatees
of the husband, shortly afterwards, brought her
action against R. as sole Defendant, for administration of the husband's estate, alleging breaches
of trust by Mrs. Y., and asking administration of
her estate if R., as her representative, did not
admit assets to pay what should be found due
from her estate to the husband's estate. On the

XLIX. PRACTICE — SUPREME COURT — APPEAL—*continued.*

(a.) GENERAL—*continued.*

28th of February, 1885, V. moved for judgment. There was no evidence before the Court that Mrs. Y. was indebted to her husband's estate, or that she had been guilty of wilful neglect and default. R., by his counsel, admitted that she was so indebted, and he submitted to a judgment directing an account of personal estate of the husband which she had received, or but for her wilful neglect or default might have received, with an inquiry as to balances in her hands, and directing administration of her estate. It appeared that, from information R. had received, he felt sure that Mrs. Y. would be found a debtor to her husband's estate, and that wilful default would be established against her, and that it was not advisable to incur the expense of contesting these points at the hearing. D., on the 26th of June, 1885, moved before Pearson, J., under Order XVI., r. 40, to discharge or vary the judgment of February, 1885. This motion was refused on the ground that D. had not been served with the judgment. D. appealed from this refusal and also applied for leave to appeal from the judgment:—*Held*, that leave cannot be given to a residuary legatee to appeal from a decree made against the executor at the suit of a creditor, as the executor completely represents the estate for the purposes of such a suit, and the residuary legatee could not be made a party to the suit, and the case is quite different from one where leave to appeal is applied for by a person who, though not according to the present practice a necessary party to the suit, would have been a proper party to it:—*Held*, further, that the application of June, 1885, to vary the judgment was not supported by Order XVI., r. 40, the case not falling within that rule, which only applies to cases where service of an order is necessary in order to make it binding, whereas here the order was binding without service, and D. was not a proper person to be served:—*Held*, further, that although R. might have acted injudiciously in submitting in February, 1885, to an order which went further than any order that could have been made adversely on the materials before the Court, the order could not be discharged unless the Court was satisfied that R. had submitted to it fraudulently in collusion with V., and in this case the Court was satisfied that R. had acted bonâ fide. *In re* YOUNGS. DOGGETT *v.* REVETT. *In re* YOUNGS. VOLLUM *v.* REVETT   -   -   -   **30 Ch. D. 421**

19. —— **Special Case—**Appeal by Party not appearing at Hearing.] Whether a party to a special case who does not appear at the hearing before the Divisional Court can appeal from the judgment, quære. ALLUM *v.* DICKENSON   -   -   -   **[9 Q. B. D. 632**

20. —— **Summons heard in Chambers.**] A party desiring to appeal from an order made by the Judge in Chambers on a summons which has not been adjourned into Court for argument or judgment, should move in Court, on notice, to discharge the order, so as to afford the Judge an opportunity of stating, for the information of the Court of Appeal, his reasons for his decision. HOLLOWAY *v.* CHESTON   -   -   **19 Ch. D. 516**

XLIX. PRACTICE — SUPREME COURT — APPEAL—*continued.*

(a.) GENERAL—*continued.*

21. —— **Summons heard in Chambers.—**Desire to appeal — Motion for Certificate of Judge.] Where, on a summons heard in Chambers, an order has been made by the Judge and not adjourned into Court, and there is a desire to appeal against it, the proper course is not to move in Court, on notice, to discharge the order, or for a certificate that the Judge does not desire it to be reheard, but to make an application in Chambers. —*Holloway v. Cheston* (19 Ch. D. 516) not followed. *In re* BUTLER'S WHARF COMPANY. ANDERSON *v.* BUTLER'S WHARF COMPANY
[21 Ch. D. 131

22. —— **Summons, Originating—**Dismissal of —Time for appealing — Rules of Court, 1883, Order I., r. 1 ; Order II., r. 1 ; Order LV., r. 3 ; Order LVIII., r. 15; Order LXXI., r. 1—Judicature Act, 1873, s. 100.] An originating summons taken out under Order LV., r. 3, is a civil proceeding commenced otherwise than by writ in manner prescribed by a Rule of Court, and is consequently an action within the definition of that word in sect. 100 of the Judicature Act, 1873. Therefore an order made upon such a summons is appealable at any time within one year from its date. *In re* FAWSITT. GALLAND *v.* BURTON   -   -   -   **30 Ch. D. 231**

23. —— **Withdrawal of Appeal—**Revocation of Withdrawal.] The Defendant in an action having given notice of appeal against an order, wrote to the Plaintiff saying that he proposed to withdraw his appeal, and asking for his consent to his doing so. The Plaintiff at once consented to the withdrawal. Two days afterwards the Defendant wrote to say that he was under misapprehension as to a material fact, and intended to go on with the appeal. No step was taken by either side to remove the appeal from the list of appeals, and both parties filed affidavits in support of their case :—*Held*, that the Defendant had no power to revoke his withdrawal of the appeal, and that the appeal could not be heard. WATSON *v.* CAVE (No. 2)   -   -   -   -   **17 Ch. D. 23**

(b) APPEAL FOR COSTS.

24. —— **Administration Action—**Executor— Residuary Legatee—Rules of Court, 1875, Order LV., r. 1 — Supreme Court of Judicature Act, 1873 (36 & 37 Vict. c. 66), s. 49.] A married woman, who was one of the executors of a testator and also tenant for life of the residue, filed a bill for administration of the estate. Upon the accounts being taken it turned out the residuary estate was insufficient for payment of debts and costs, and that it would be necessary to resort to specifically bequeathed property. Malins, V.C., on further consideration, refused to give the Plaintiff any costs of the suit, and ordered the next friend to pay the costs of taking an account of what, if anything, was due from another of the executors on an account current between him and the testator. The Plaintiff appealed :— *Held*, that as a residuary legatee or executor filing a bill for administration is entitled to costs out of the estate unless some special grounds are shewn for depriving him of them, the costs in question

XLIX. PRACTICE — SUPREME COURT — AP-
PEAL—*continued.*

(b.) APPEAL FOR COSTS—*continued.*

were not costs in the discretion of the Court
within the meaning of the Supreme Court of Judicature Act, 1873 (36 & 37 Vict. c. 66), s. 49, and
that an appeal would lie. FARROW v. AUSTIN
[18 Ch. D. 58

25. —— Administration Action — *Trustee —
Judicature Act, 1873, s. 49—Rules of Court, 1875,
Order LV.*] The right of a trustee to his costs,
like that of a mortgagee, is a matter of contract,
and is not in the discretion of the Judge; although
he may be deprived of them for misconduct.—
Therefore the costs of a trustee are not within
sect. 49 of the Judicature Act, 1873, and an
appeal may be brought from a decision in respect
of them.—*Cotterell v. Stratton* (Law Rep. 8 Ch. 295)
and *Farrow* v. *Austin* (18 Ch. D. 58) followed.
In re Hoskins (6 Ch. D. 281) disapproved.—The
mere fact that a trustee denies that he is indebted
to the estate, and on taking the accounts turns
out to be indebted, is no reason for depriving
him of his costs. TURNER v. HANCOCK
[20 Ch. D. 303

26. —— Administration Action — *Residuary
Legatee—Rules of Court,* 1883, *Order LXV., r.* 1
—*Pending Cause — Rules of Court,* 1875, *Order
LV., r.* 1.] Order LXV., r. 1, of the Rules of
the Supreme Court, 1883, directing that the costs
of all proceedings in the Supreme Court, including the administration of estates and trusts shall
be in the discretion of the Court or a Judge, applies in the case of causes and matters pending on
the 24th of October, 1883, when those rules came
into operation, only to the costs of proceedings
taken on and after that day; and the costs incurred in proceedings taken in such causes and
matters before that day, although not adjudicated
upon until afterwards, are not within that rule.—
In an action for administration by one of several
residuary legatees, all the proceedings except
those on subsequent further consideration were
taken before Order LXV., r. 1, came into operation,
though the costs were not adjudicated upon until
the order on further consideration which was made
afterwards:—*Held,* that an appeal would lie as to
the costs of such prior, though not as to the costs of
such subsequent proceedings.—*Farrow v. Austin*
(18 Ch. D. 58) followed. *In re* McCLELLAN.
McCLELLAN v. McCLELLAN　　29 Ch. D. 495

27. —— Dismissal for want of Prosecution—
4 & 5 *Anne, c.* 3, *s.* 23—42 & 43 *Vict. c.* 59,
ss. 2, 4 — *Repeal with Qualification — Rules of
Court,* 1883, *Order LXV., r.* 1—*Discretion of Judge
as to Costs.*] The statutable right of a defendant
to the costs of an action in the Chancery Division
which had been dismissed for want of prosecution was repealed by 42 & 43 Vict. c. 59, which
repeals so much of 4 & 5 Anne, c. 3, as gives
such costs, and though the practice in accordance
with such statutable right, and as regulated by
Order XXXIII, rule 10, of the Chancery Consolidation Orders of 1860, was preserved by sect. 4 of
42 & 43 Vict. c. 59, yet Order LXV., rule 1, of
the Rules of 1883 has changed such practice, so
that the costs of a defendant where such action
has been dismissed for want of prosecution are
now in the discretion of the Judge, and there-

XLIX. PRACTICE — SUPREME COURT — AP-
PEAL—*continued.*

(b.) APPEAL FOR COSTS—*continued.*

fore his order as to such costs is by sect. 49 of
the Judicature Act, 1873, not subject to appeal.
SNELLING v. PULLING　　-　　29 Ch. D. 85

28. —— Injunction—*Order for Costs alone—
Rules of Court,* 1883, *Order LXV., r.* 1.] Where
the jurisdiction of a Judge to inflict costs on a
party arises from his being guilty of breach of an
injunction or other misconduct, an appeal lies as
to costs, although the Judge makes no order
except that the party shall pay costs.—*Witt v.
Corcoran* (2 Ch. D. 69) followed.　STEVENS v.
METROPOLITAN DISTRICT RAILWAY COMPANY
[29 Ch. D. 60

29. —— Inspection of Property—*Discretion of
Court—Judicature Act,* 1873 (36 & 37 *Vict. c.* 66),
s. 49—*Rules of Court,* 1875, *Order LII., r.* 3.] An
order was made in Chambers for the inspection
of the Defendant's property, the costs of the
inspection to be paid by the Plaintiff:—*Held,*
that under Order LII, rule 3, the Judge had a
discretion to order the Plaintiff to pay the costs,
and the order being made in his discretion the
Plaintiff had no right without leave to appeal from
it. MITCHELL v. DARLEY MAIN COLLIERY COM-
PANY　　　　　　　　　　10 Q. B. D. 457

30. —— Mortgage Suit—*Costs of Appeal on
Cross Notice—Priority of Charge—Gazetting Retirement of Officer.*] After receipt by the army
agents of the money payable to an officer on his
retirement continual notices of charges on the
money were given to the army agents by each of
the three assignees. One of the assignees brought
an action against the two others, claiming priority
over them:— *Held,* by Bacon, V.C., that the
notices given before the retirement was gazetted
were of no avail, and that of the two assignees
who gave notice on the day after the retirement
was gazetted the Defendant whose security was
prior in date had priority over the Plaintiff and
over the other Defendant, and that the costs of the
action were to be paid out of the fund.—The Defendant who had obtained priority appealed as to
the costs, and the other Defendant gave notice of
cross-appeal on the merits :—*Held,* that an appeal
would lie from the order as to costs. Order as to
priority affirmed, but the costs of action ordered
to be added to the securities. Appellant's costs
of appeal to be paid in moieties by the Respondents. JOHNSTONE v. COX　　-　　19 Ch. D. 17

31. —— Partnership Suit — *Costs of Unsuccessful Claim—Rules of Court,* 1875, *Order LV.,
r.* 1.] By articles of partnership between three
partners, on the death of any partner the survivors were entitled to take his share at a valuation.　One of the partners having died, his
executrix brought her action to have it declared
that the goodwill was to be included in the
valuation, and to have the value of the deceased
partner's share in the assets ascertained.　A
decree was made declaring that the goodwill
must be valued as part of the assets, and directing
accounts.　The Chief Clerk made his general
certificate, finding (inter alia) that two specified
leaseholds belonging to the partnership were of
no value.　The Plaintiff took out a summons to

XLIX. PRACTICE — SUPREME COURT — APPEAL—continued.

(b.) APPEAL FOR COSTS—continued.

vary the certificate by estimating these leaseholds as worth a considerable sum. The summons was adjourned into Court, and Bacon, V.C., refused to vary the certificate, but ordered the costs of both parties to be paid out of the estate. The Defendants appealed :—*Held*, that the case did not come within the rule in *Foster* v. *Great Western Railway Company* (8 Q. B. D. 25, 515) that the Court cannot make a successful defendant pay the costs of a plaintiff who has wholly failed; but that it was within the discretion of the Court to order all costs reasonably incurred in ascertaining the fund to be paid out of the fund, and that an appeal would not lie. BUTCHER *v.* POOLER - - - 24 Ch. D. 273

32. —— Solicitor—*Order on Solicitor personally to pay Costs—Judicature Act, 1873, s. 49.*] An order that the costs of an application at Chambers on behalf of a client shall be paid by his solicitor personally cannot be costs left to the discretion of the Court within s. 49 of the Judicature Act, 1873, unless the solicitor has been guilty of misconduct or negligence, and, therefore, an appeal lies from such order without leave as to whether there has been such misconduct or negligence.—Decision of the Queen's Bench Division reversed. *In re* BRADFORD
[11 Q. B. D. 373 ; 15 Q. B. D. 635

33. —— Special Leave—*Discretion of Judge—Judicature Act, 1873, s. 49.*] Where an appeal from an order as to costs which are left by law to the discretion of the Judge is brought by leave of the Judge under the 49th section of the Judicature Act, 1873, the Court of Appeal will still have regard to the discretion of the Judge, and will not overrule his order unless there has been a disregard of principle or misapprehension of facts. *In re* GILBERT. GILBERT *v.* HUDLESTONE
[28 Ch. D. 549

(c.) TIME FOR APPEALING.

34. —— Decree declaring Future Rights.] A testator gave after the death of his wife, a legacy to his son E. S. for life and after his death to his children, and if he died without issue it was to be divided among the testator's " surviving children." Six other legacies were given in a similar way. All the seven children survived the testator. A suit for administration was instituted to which all were parties. In 1836 an order on further consideration was made, at which time six of the children were living, and it was declared, that on the death of the widow, E. S. would become entitled to the interest on the legacy for life, that on his death it would be divisible among his children then living, but if he died without leaving issue, then among the children of the testator who were living at the testator's decease. The testator's widow died in 1838, and E. S. died in 1881 without ever having had a child. At this time one only child of the testator was living, and he applied for leave to appeal against the order of 1836, on the ground that it was irregular in making a prospective declaration as to future rights :—*Held*, that leave to appeal ought not to be granted, the fact that a declara-

XLIX. PRACTICE — SUPREME COURT — APPEAL—continued.

(c.) TIME FOR APPEALING—continued.

tion was made as to future rights being no sufficient reason for giving such leave in a case where all parties who could in any event be interested were before the Court and adult when the declaration was made.— *Brandon* v. *Brandon* (7 D. M. & G. 365) and *Walmsley* v. *Foxhall* (1 D. J. & S. 451) considered and distinguished.—Observations on the change of opinion in the Legislature and the Judges as to the period during which orders should be appealable. CURTIS *v.* SHEFFIELD
[21 Ch. D. 1

35. —— Extension of Time—*Final Order—Rules of Court, 1875, Order LVIII., rr. 9, 15.*] A petition having been presented for payment out of Court of a fund paid in under the Lands Clauses Act as the purchase-money of a devised estate, the Court, on the 18th of June, made an order declaring the construction of the will and directing inquiries as to the persons interested. An application was made on behalf of some of the parties who were resident in America to extend the time for appealing to four weeks from the 8th of July, in order to allow time for the persons acting for them under a power of attorney to consult them as to appealing :—*Held*, that, as the order was a final one, the case, though within the letter was not within the spirit of rule 9, the Rules of Court, 1875, Order LVIII., requiring an appeal to be brought within twenty-one days, and that the extension of time ought to be granted. *In re* LEONARD JACQUES - - 18 Ch. D. 392

36. —— Extension of Time—*Informal Notice of Appeal—Letters to Solicitors of Respondent—Accident or Mistake — Rules of Court, 1875, Order LVIII., rr. 3, 15—Costs of Respondent not served with Notice of Appeal.*] A petition for winding up a company having been dismissed, the Petitioner's solicitors wrote a letter to the company's solicitor urging him to get the order drawn up, adding, " as we are advised and intend to give notice of appeal." No formal notice of appeal was given till more than twenty-one days had elapsed from the dismissal of the petition, when the Petitioner gave a supplemental notice of appeal :—*Held*, that the letter could not be treated as an informal notice of appeal, and therefore the appeal was too late.—*Little's Case* (8 Ch. D. 806) considered and distinguished.—*Held*, also, that there was no such mistake or accident as would justify the Court in extending the time for appeal.—Mistake by Appellant may be a ground for extending the time for appeal without misconduct by Respondent.—Observations of James and Baggallay, L.JJ., in *In re Blyth and Young* (13 Ch. D. 416) upon *McAndrew* v. *Barker* (7 Ch. D. 701) respecting the grounds for extension of time for appeal, approved.—An Appellant ought to serve notice of appeal on all parties who will be affected by the order of the Court of Appeal, and if a party who would be so affected is not served, he may appear without service and obtain his costs. And this rule applies although the appeal fails through irregularity and never comes on to be heard. *In re* NEW CALLAO - - - - 22 Ch. D. 484

37. —— Extension of Time—*Special Grounds*

XLIX. PRACTICE — SUPREME COURT — APPEAL—*continued.*

(c.) TIME FOR APPEALING—*continued.*

—*Company* — *Order on Winding-up Petition* — *Rules of Court, 1875, Order LVIII., r. 15* — *Lancaster Court* — *Power of Rehearing* — *Transfer of Shares to escape Liability.*] The shareholders in a company passed an extraordinary resolution to wind up the company voluntarily, but the resolution was void, the majority of members who voted not being entitled to vote. A creditor filed a petition in the Chancery Court of the Duchy of Lancaster for a supervision order or for a compulsory winding-up order, and as the Court and the Petitioner were ignorant of the fact that the resolution was invalid, a supervision order was made. Five months afterwards the Petitioner discovered the invalidity of the resolution, and then moved before the Vice-Chancellor that the supervision order might be discharged, and a compulsory winding-up order made. This motion having been refused by the Vice-Chancellor on the ground of want of jurisdiction to rehear the petition, the Petitioner appealed from the refusal of the motion, and also applied to the Court of Appeal for leave to appeal against the original order notwithstanding the lapse of time. —The application for leave to appeal was opposed by the executors of a previous member who had transferred their testator's shares to escape liability less than twelve months before the presenting of the original petition, but more than twelve months before the case came before the Court of Appeal on the ground that if an order was now made on the original petition they would be made liable under the 38th section of the Companies Act, 1862 :—*Held,* that leave to appeal, notwithstanding the lapse of time, ought to be given, the mistake as to the validity of the resolution forming a special ground for the application, and the Respondents having no equity to resist it.—Observations on the principle on which the Court grants extension of time for appeal.—*In re New Callao* (22 Ch. D. 484) approved.—*Semble,* the Vice-Chancellor had no power to rehear the petition himself. *In re* MANCHESTER ECONOMIC BUILDING SOCIETY　-　-　- **24 Ch. D. 488**

38. —— *Extension of Time*—*Special Grounds* — *Revivor* — *Discretion of the Court* — *Rules of Court, 1883, Order XVII., r. 4.*] By a marriage settlement the property of the wife was vested in trustees upon trust for the wife, for her separate use, and in case there should be no issue (which event happened) for the wife, her executors, administrators, and assigns, if she survived her husband, but if she died in his lifetime then for the husband for his life; and subject thereto for such persons as should be of the wife's own kindred as she should by will appoint, and in default of appointment for such persons as would be entitled under the Statutes of Distribution, in case she had died intestate and unmarried.—The marriage was dissolved in 1871, and in 1872 the wife, in a suit instituted by her against her late husband and the trustees of the settlement, obtained a decree that she was absolutely entitled to the property comprised in the settlement.—By her will dated in 1877, the wife disposed of the property as if it was her own absolutely, and died in 1881,

in the lifetime of her late husband :—*Held,* in the absence of special circumstances, that the next of kin of the wife were not now entitled to an order to revive the suit or to carry on proceedings therein for the mere purpose of appealing against the decree of 1872. FUSSELL *v.* DOWDING
[27 Ch. D. 237

39. —— *Interlocutory Order*—*Appeal from Order of Judge at Trial depriving successful Party of Costs*—*Jurisdiction of Divisional Court.*] At the trial of an action the jury found for the Plaintiffs for a sum exceeding the amount which the Defendants had paid into Court; the Judge thereupon gave judgment for the Plaintiffs without costs. The High Court of Justice afterwards made an order that the Plaintiffs should have their costs. The Defendants applied to the Court of Appeal to annul the order of the High Court after the time had elapsed for appealing against an interlocutory order :—*Held,* that the order of the High Court was made on an appeal from a final judgment, and that the application to the Court of Appeal was not too late; but—*Held,* that the High Court had no jurisdiction to entertain an appeal from a final judgment, and that the order giving the Plaintiffs their costs must be annulled. MARSDEN *v.* LANCASHIRE AND YORKSHIRE RAILWAY COMPANY　　**7 Q. B. D. 641**

40. —— *Order in Winding-up and in an Action* —*Rules of Court, 1875, Order LVIII., r. 9.*] An action was brought by a debenture holder of a company on behalf of himself and the other debenture holders to enforce their securities. After this an order was made for winding up the company. An arrangement was proposed for the making over the undertaking to the Secretary of State for India on certain terms, and an order was made in the winding-up and in the action sanctioning the arrangement and declaring that no moneys payable by the Secretary of State to the stockholders and debenture holders of the company under the arrangement should be treated as assets of the company. An unsecured creditor of the company who did not know of this order at the time when it was made, applied after a lapse of more than twenty-one days from his receiving a copy of the order, but within the time for appealing from a final order in an action, for leave to appeal against it :—*Held,* that as the applicant had no such interest that he could have been a party to the action the order must, as regarded him, be treated as an order made only in the winding-up, that Order LVIII., r. 9, applied, and that he was out of time. *In re* MADRAS IRRIGATION AND CANAL COMPANY. WOOD *v.* MADRAS IRRIGATION AND CANAL COMPANY　　-　　**23 Ch. D. 248**

41. —— *Refusal of Application forming part of Judgment*—*Application at Trial for Leave to amend Pleadings*—*Rules of Court, 1875, Order LVIII., r. 15.*] When at the trial of an action an application for leave to amend the pleadings is refused, the refusal forms part of the judgment, and it is unnecessary to appeal separately from it; but on an appeal from the judgment the Court of Appeal has power, if it thinks fit, to give leave to amend. It is contrary to the practice to insert

**XLIX. PRACTICE — SUPREME COURT — AP-
PEAL—**continued.

(c.) TIME FOR APPEALING—continued.

in the judgment as drawn up any mention of the
refusal of leave to amend. LAIRD v. BRIGGS
[16 Ch. D. 663

42. —— Refusal of Application—Declaration
as to Rights—Rules of Court, 1875, Order LVII.,
r. 8 (April, 1880), LVIII., r. 15.] When an order
refusing an application contains a declaration or
expression of opinion of the Judge as to the rights
of the parties, it is not a mere refusal of the application so as to oblige an appeal to be brought
within twenty-one days from the date of the refusal
under Order LVIII., rule 15. In re CLAY AND
TETLEY　-　　-　　-　16 Ch. D. 3

43. —— Refusal of Application—Claim of
Creditor under Administration Judgment—Rules
of Court, 1875, Order LVIII., r. 15.] Where a creditor has brought in a claim in answer to advertisements for creditors issued under a judgment
for administration, and that claim is disallowed,
such disallowance is a refusal within the meaning
of Order LVIII., rule 15, and an appeal can be
brought from it without any order being drawn
up. In re CLAGETT. FORDHAM v. CLAGETT
[20 Ch. D. 134

44. —— Refusal of Application—Special Direction as to Costs—Rules of Court, 1883, Order LVIII.,
r. 15.] Where an application to a Judge is refused,
and the Judge adds special directions as to the
payment of the costs, that is a refusal of the application within the meaning of Order LVIII., rule 15,
and the time for appeal runs from the date of the
refusal not from the drawing up of the order.
In re SMITH. HOOPER v. SMITH　26 Ch. D. 614

—— Appeal from judgment by default
[29 Ch. D. 322; 6 Q. B. D. 116
See PRACTICE — SUPREME COURT—DE-
FAULT. 1, 5.

—— Interpleader.
See Cases under PRACTICE — SUPREME
COURT—INTERPLEADER. 1, 3—7.

**L. PRACTICE—SUPREME COURT—JURISDIC-
TION.**

1. —— Chancery Division—Recalling Probate
—Judicature Act, 1873, ss. 16, 34, 36—Judicature
Act, 1875, s. 11.] Though the Chancery Division may have jurisdiction to recall the probate of
a will, it ought not as a general rule to exercise
that jurisdiction, even if the estate of the testator
is in Court in a proceeding in that Division.—
Pinney v. Hunt (6 Ch. D. 98) followed. BRAD-
FORD v. YOUNG　-　　-　26 Ch. D. 656

2. —— Subject-matter below £10—Chancery
Action—Judicature Act, 1873 (36 & 37 Vict. c. 66),
ss. 16, 25, 34.] An action in the High Court,
claiming relief which, before the Judicature Act,
could have been given only by the Court of
Chancery, cannot now be maintained if the subject-matter is below £10 in value.—The old rule
of the Court of Chancery in this respect still
remains in force. WESTBURY-ON-SEVERN RURAL
SANITARY AUTHORITY v. MEREDITH 30 Ch. D. 387

3. —— Transfer to County Court—Plaintiff
failing to proceed—Jurisdiction of Superior Court
—County Courts Act, 1867, ss. 7, 8, 10—County

**L. PRACTICE — SUPREME COURT — JURIS-
DICTION—**continued.

Court Rules, 1875, Order XX. r. 1—Judicature
Act, 1873, s. 67.] Where an order has been made
for the transfer of a Chancery action to a County
Court under sect. 8 of the County Courts Act,
1867, the Superior Court retains its jurisdiction
in the action until the transfer has been completed by all necessary steps being taken for that
purpose. DAVID v. HOWE　　27 Ch. D. 533

—— Transfer—Winding-up of company
[16 Ch. D. 702
See PRACTICE—SUPREME COURT—TRANS-
FER. 1.

PRACTICE—SUPREME COURT—Abortive execution—Possession money 6 Q. B. D. 171
See SHERIFF. 2.

—— Action sent for trial to County Court—Unliquidated damages　-　10 Q. B. D. 11
See COUNTY COURT—JURISDICTION. 8.

—— Action to prove will and discharge protection order　-　　-　6 P. D. 54
See PROBATE—MARRIED WOMAN. 3.

—— Adding Plaintiff—Trustee in bankruptcy
[17 Ch. D. 768
See BANKRUPTCY—UNDISCHARGED BANK-
RUPT. 4.

—— Administration action.
See Cases under EXECUTOR—ACTIONS.

—— Administration order—Disputed debt
[30 Ch. D. 291
See LIMITATIONS, STATUTE OF — PER-
SONAL ACTIONS. 10.

—— Admissions between co-Defendants
[25 Ch. D. 617
See TRUSTEE—COSTS AND CHARGES. 6.

—— Amendment　-　　-　19 Ch. D. 22
See EASEMENT. 2.

—— Amendment—Adding Plaintiffs
[30 Ch. D. 57
See HUSBAND AND WIFE — SEPARATION
DEED. 2.

—— Appeal for costs　-　　-　18 Ch. D. 76
See COPYRIGHT—BOOKS. 5.

—— Appeal for costs　-　　-　20 Ch. D. 611
See VENDOR AND PURCHASER—PURCHASE
WITHOUT NOTICE. 1.

—— Appeal for costs　-　　-　23 Ch. D. 278
See VOLUNTARY CONVEYANCE. 5.

—— Appeal for costs—Appeal by liquidator
See COMPANY—COSTS. 1. [21 Ch. D. 381

—— Appeal—Election petition　6 Q. B. D. 323
See MUNICIPAL CORPORATION—ELECTION.
3.

—— Appeal—Right to raise new point
[19 Ch. D. 419
See BILL OF SALE—FORMALITIES. 18.

—— Appointment of guardian　-　19 Ch. D. 451
See INFANT—WARD OF COURT. 1.

—— Arbitration—Motion to set aside award
[19 Ch. D. 58
See ARBITRATION—AWARD. 3.

—— Arbitration—Submission　-　19 Ch. D. 56
See ARBITRATION—SUBMISSION. 3.

PRACTICE—SUPREME COURT—*continued.*

—— Landlord and tenant—Agreement to appoint valuers—Rule of Court **15 Q. B. D. 426**
See ARBITRATION—SUBMISSION. 4.

—— Lands Clauses Act.
See Cases under LANDS CLAUSES ACT—COSTS.

—— Legal demand—Pending litigation
See WILL—CONDITION. 1. [21 Ch. D. 278

—— Lunacy.
See Cases under LUNATIC—JURISDICTION.

—— Mandamus—Central Criminal Court
[11 Q. B. D. 479
See COURT—CENTRAL CRIMINAL COURT.

—— Mandamus—Return of unconditional compliance - - - **14 Q. B. D. 13**
See MANDAMUS. 1.

—— Married Women's Property Act.
See Cases under HUSBAND AND WIFE—MARRIED WOMEN'S PROPERTY ACTS.

—— Mayor's Court.
See Cases under COURT—MAYOR'S COURT.

—— Nautical assessors — Duty of — County Court - - - **6 P. D. 84**
See COUNTY COURT—PRACTICE. 2.

—— Parties—Claim against glebe land
[20 Ch. D. 208
See ECCLESIASTICAL COMMISSIONERS.

—— Partition suit.
See Cases under PARTITION SUIT.

—— Partnership—Judgment against firm
[19 Ch. D. 124
See BANKRUPTCY—ACT OF BANKRUPTCY. 16.

—— Patent action.
See Cases under PATENT—PRACTICE.

—— Patent—Notice not to sell patented article
[19 Ch. D. 386
See PATENT—INFRINGEMENT. 4.

—— Patent—Particulars of objection—Amendment - - **26 Ch. D. 700**
See PATENT—VALIDITY. 1.

—— Patent—Prolongation.
See Cases under PATENT—PROLONGATION.

—— Production of documents—Deceased lunatic
[16 Ch. D. 673
See LUNATIC—DECEASED LUNATIC.

—— Production of documents—Winding-up
[22 Ch. D. 714
See COMPANY—LIQUIDATOR. 1.

—— Railway Commissioners — Power to state case - - **15 Q. B. D. 505**
See RAILWAY COMPANY — RAILWAYS REGULATION ACTS. 4.

—— Res judicata — Order on petition—"Till further order" - - **22 Ch. D. 182**
See ESTOPPEL—JUDGMENT. 5.

—— Security for costs—Appeal from winding-up
See COMPANY—APPEAL. [23 Ch. D. 370

—— Security for costs—Winding-up petition
[19 Ch. D. 457
See COMPANY—WINDING-UP ORDER. 14.

PRACTICE—SUPREME COURT—*continued.*

—— Settled Estates Act.
See Cases under SETTLED ESTATES ACTS.

—— Settled Land Act.
See Cases under SETTLED LAND ACT.

—— Solicitor—Unqualified practitioner—Attachment—Contempt **8 Q. B. D. 187;**
[15 Q. B. D. 348
See SOLICITOR—UNQUALIFIED. 1, 2.

—— Solicitors' Remuneration Act
See Cases under SOLICITOR — BILL OF COSTS. 18—25.

—— Stop order—Mortgage—Priority
[29 Ch. D. 786
See MORTGAGE—PRIORITY. 10.

—— Trustee Acts.
See Cases under TRUSTEE ACTS.

—— Trustee Relief Act.
See Cases under TRUSTEE RELIEF ACT.

—— Variance between rules of Common Law and Admiralty Courts—Collision
[10 Q. B. D. 521
See SHIP—BILL OF LADING. 1.

—— Witness not within jurisdiction of Court—Subpœna [12 Q. B. D. 39
See EVIDENCE—WITNESS. 1.

—— Wreck Commissioner—Shipping casualty—Appeal—Evidence—Costs **6 P. D. 182**
See SHIP—MERCHANT SHIPPING ACTS. 8.

—— Writ specially indorsed—Action for arrears of alimony - - **13 Q. B. D. 855**
See ACTION. 1.

PRECATORY TRUST - - **27 Ch. D. 394;**
[7 App. Cas. 321
See WILL—PRECATORY TRUST. 1, 2.

PRECOGNITIONS—Admissibility of
[6 App. Cas. 489
See SCOTCH LAW—HUSBAND AND WIFE. 3.

PRE-EMPTION — Crown lands — Dedication to public purposes - **6 App. Cas. 636**
See COLONIAL LAW — NEW SOUTH WALES. 1.

—— Right of - **28 Ch. D. 486**
See LONDON—COMMISSIONERS OF SEWERS.

—— Right of—Superfluous lands **20 Ch. D. 418**
See LANDS CLAUSES ACT—SUPERFLUOUS LANDS. 1.

PREFERENCE SHARES—Alteration in rights—Ultra vires act - **30 Ch. D. 376**
See COMPANY — MEMORANDUM AND ARTICLES. 1.

—— Building society - - **23 Ch. D. 440;**
[9 App. Cas. 519
See BUILDING SOCIETY. 9.

—— Dividend out of profits—Reserved fund
[16 Ch. D. 344
See COMPANY—DIVIDEND. 4.

PREFERENTIAL DEBT—Bankruptcy
[26 Ch. D. 693
See BANKRUPTCY—PREFERENTIAL DEBTS.

—— Winding-up of company.
See COMPANY—PREFERENTIAL DEBTS—*Statutes.*

2 S

PREFERENTIAL DEBT—*continued.*

—— Winding-up of company - 16 Ch. D. 373
 See COMPANY—PREFERENTIAL DEBTS.

PRELIMINARY ACCOUNTS—Order for
      [29 Ch. D. 566, 834
 See PRACTICE — SUPREME COURT — IN-
 QUIRIES AND ACCOUNTS. 1, 2.

PREMIUM—Articled clerk—Death of solicitor
      [28 Ch. D. 409
 See SOLICITOR—ARTICLED CLERK.

—— Fire insurance — Payment out of rents —
 Right to money - - 23 Ch. D. 188
 See INSURANCE, FIRE. 2.

—— Life insurance—Payment by stranger
      [23 Ch. D. 552
 See INSURANCE, LIFE—ASSIGNMENT.

—— Partnership—Return of - 29 Ch. D. 170
 See PARTNERSHIP—DISSOLUTION. 2.

PREROGATIVE OF CROWN - 28 Ch. D. 643
 See CROWN.

—— - - 7 Q. B. D. 38 ; 8 App. Cas. 354
 See PENAL ACTION. 2.

PRESCRIPTION.

1. —— Right of Way—*Prescription Act* (2 & 3
Wm. 4, *c.* 71), ss. 2, 4, 5, 6—*Right to use Way for
the removal of Timber—User at long Intervals—
"Enjoyment for full period of Twenty Years."*]
In an action where a right of way was claimed
under the Prescription Act (2 & 3 Wm. 4, c. 71),
in respect of twenty years' user as of right it appeared that the way had only been used by the
party claiming it — the Defendant—for the removal of wood upon an adjoining close. The
wood was cut upon this close at intervals of
several years ; the last cutting having been in the
year before the action was commenced, the one
next previous twelve years before, and the next at
another interval of twelve years. Between these
intervals the road was occasionally stopped up,
but the Defendant used it as often as he wished
while the wood was being cut :—*Held,* that there
had not been an uninterrupted enjoyment of the
way for twenty years within the meaning of the
Prescription Act, which did not apply to so
discontinuous an easement as that claimed.—
Judgment of the Queen's Bench Division affirmed.
HOLLINS *v.* VERNEY 11 Q. B. D. 715 ;
      [13 Q. B. D. 304

2. —— Right of Way—*Prescription Act, 2 &
3 Wm.* 4, *c.* 71, *s.* 8—*Forty Years' Enjoyment—
Remainderman—"Reversion expectant" on Term
of Life or Years.*] Where a right of way is
claimed by virtue of forty years' enjoyment under
the Prescription Act, 2 & 3 Wm. 4, c. 71; the
period during which the servient tenement has
been vested in a tenant for life, with remainder in
fee, cannot be deducted from the period of forty
years' enjoyment—for the remainderman is not
"a person entitled to the reversion expectant on
a term" within s. 8. SYMONS *v.* LEAKER
      [15 Q. B. D. 629

—— Common—Estovers - - 17 Ch. D. 535
 See COMMON.

—— Easement - - 19 Ch. D. 22
 See EASEMENT. 2.

—— Fishery 7 Q. B. D. 106 ; 7 App. Cas. 633 ;
 See FISHERY. 1, 3. [8 App. Cas. 135

PRESCRIPTION—*continued.*

—— Liability by frontager to repair sea wall—
 Extraordinary violence of sea
 See SEA WALL [14 Q. B. D. 561

—— Light - 19 Ch. D. 462 ; 24 Ch. D. 1
 See LIGHT—TITLE. 3, 4.

—— Market - - 14 Q. B. D. 245
 See MARKET. 3.

—— Scotch law—Highway 10 App. Cas. 378
 See SCOTCH LAW—HIGHWAY. 2.

—— Support of house
 See Cases under SUPPORT.

—— Use of water—Roman-Dutch law
      [10 App. Cas. 336
 See COLONIAL LAW—CAPE OF GOOD
 HOPE. 4.

—— Watercourse—Unity of possession 17 Ch. D.
 See WATERCOURSE. 5. [391

PRESENTATION OF CHEQUE—Laches
 See BANKER—CHEQUE. 1. [3 Q. B. D. 288

PRESENTATION TO CHURCH — Consolidated
 benefice—Quare impedit 15 Q. B. D. 432
 See ADVOWSON. 2.

PRESSURE—Fraudulent preference
      [19 Ch. D. 580
 See BANKRUPTCY—FRAUDULENT PREFER-
 ENCE. 4.

PRESUMPTION—Ademption of legacy
 See WILL—ADEMPTION. [26 Ch. D. 552

—— Continuance of cohabitation between husband and wife - 11 Q. B. D. 118
 See CRIMINAL LAW—BIGAMY. 2.

—— Duration of life - - 6 Q. B. D. 366
 See CRIMINAL LAW—BIGAMY. 1.

—— Lost grant - - - 14 Q. B. D. 245
 See MARKET. 3.

—— Marriage—Law of Ceylon 6 App. Cas. 364
 See COLONIAL LAW—CEYLON. 3.

—— Purchase by conservators of river
 See RIVER. [6 App. Cas. 685

—— Woman past childbearing 18 Ch. D. 213
 See EVIDENCE—PRESUMPTION.

PRETENDED TITLE—Purchase of
     [9 Q. B. D. 126 ; 15 Q. B. D. 491
 See RIGHT OF ENTRY. 1, 2.

PREVENTION OF CRIME.
 See CRIMINAL LAW—PRACTICE—*Statutes.*

PRIMOGENITURE — Law of Malta—Construction of deed - 7 App. Cas. 156 ;
      [8 App. Cas. 106
 See COLONIAL LAW—MALTA. 1, 2.

PRINCIPAL AND AGENT :— Col.
 I. AGENT'S AUTHORITY - - 1252
 II. AGENT'S LIABILITY - - 1253
 III. PRINCIPAL'S LIABILITY - - 1257

**I. PRINCIPAL AND AGENT—AGENT'S AUTHO-
RITY.**

1. —— Vendor and Purchaser—*Misrepresentation by Vendor's Agent — Specific Performance
refused.*] An agent, commissioned by a vendor to
find a purchaser, has authority to describe the
property, and to state any fact or circumstance
which may affect the value, so as to bind the

I. PRINCIPAL AND AGENT—AGENT'S AUTHORITY—*continued.*

vendor; and if an agent so commissioned, makes a false statement as to the description or value (though not instructed so to do), which the purchaser is led to believe, and upon which he relies, the vendor cannot recover in an action for specific performance.—A surveyor was employed by the owner of a leasehold house to find a purchaser. He represented to the Defendant that another person, H., was ready to buy the property for £700, and that if the Defendant were to give £50 more, he would make a clear profit of 7 per cent.; that H. had further offered to rent the property at £300, or the ground floor only at £200. The Defendant, relying on the above representations and others, which were unauthorized by the vendor, and untrue, contracted to purchase for £750; but afterwards, finding out the falsehood, refused to complete.—The vendor himself also made a misleading statement to the purchaser:—*Held* (independently of the statement made by the vendor himself), that the false statements made by the agent, being within his authority, were sufficient to vitiate the contract; and specific performance refused. MULLENS *v.* MILLER
[22 Ch. D. 194

2. —— **Warranty of Authority**—*Liability of Agent—Measure of Damages—Contract to take Shares—Winding-up—Summons by Liquidator.*] L. instructed his brokers to apply for fifty shares at £1 each in a company which he named. They by mistake applied for and obtained an allotment to L. in another company. L. repudiated the shares, but his name was placed on the register. The company had at that time a very large number of shares unallotted, and in the opinion of the Court the shares were unsaleable in the market. The company was soon afterwards wound up; and the name of L. was removed on his application from the list of contributories. The official liquidator then claimed £50 from the brokers by way of damages for their misrepresentation of authority:—*Held,* that the general rule as to measure of damages for breach of warranty of authority was applicable; that the liquidator was entitled to recover from the brokers the amount which the company had lost by losing the contract with L.; and that as L. was solvent and the shares unsaleable in the market, that loss was represented by the whole sum of £50 payable for the shares. *In re* NATIONAL COFFEE PALACE COMPANY. *Ex parte* PANMURE   24 Ch. D. 367

II. PRINCIPAL AND AGENT—AGENT'S LIABILITY.

1. —— **Agent for Purchase**—*Sale of Agent's own Property to Principal — Non-disclosure — Rescission of Contract—Account of Profit made by Agent—Company—Winding-up—Director — Misfeasance—Companies Act,* 1862 (25 & 26 *Vict. c.* 89), *s.* 165.] In 1871 certain coal areas were purchased for £5500 by six persons, of whom F. was one, and were vested in G. as a trustee for them without disclosing the trust. In 1873 a company was formed for the purpose of purchasing these areas and other property. F. was one of the directors, and as such he concurred in effecting a purchase by the company from G. for £12,000

II. PRINCIPAL AND AGENT — AGENT'S LIABILITY—*continued.*

cash, and £30,000 in fully paid-up shares, without disclosing the fact that F. was a part owner. In 1875 the company was ordered to be wound up. In 1878 a meeting of contributories was called, at which two rival schemes were brought forward, one for repudiating the purchase of the coal areas, the other for adopting the purchase and selling the property. The latter scheme was adopted, and was confirmed by the Court. The liquidator accordingly sold the property, but at a heavy loss. A contributory then took out a summons under sect. 165 of the Companies Act, 1862, to make F. liable for misfeasance as a director in allowing the company's seal to be affixed to the agreement for purchase by the company. Mr. Justice Pearson dismissed the summons, holding that though the company would have been entitled to rescind the contract, yet as rescission had become impossible no relief could be given against F.; that as F. when he acquired his interest in the property was not a trustee for the company, he could not be treated as having purchased on behalf of the company at the price he gave, and therefore was not chargeable with the difference between the price at which he bought and the price paid by the company, and that he could not be charged with the difference between the price paid by the company and the value of the property when the company bought it, as this would be making a new contract between the parties:—*Held,* by Cotton and Fry, L.JJ., dissentiente Bowen, L.J., that this decision was right. *In re* CAPE BRETON COMPANY -   - 26 Ch. D. 221; 29 Ch. D. 795

2. —— **Broker signing as Principal**—*"Broker" —Sale of Goods—Arbitration—Award—Jurisdiction of Arbitrator—"Dispute arising on this Contract."*] By a contract in writing, the Defendants "sold to" the Plaintiffs a cargo of cotton seed cake of a specified quality. The contract contained a clause that "should any of the above goods turn out not equal to quality specified, they are to be taken at an allowance, which allowance together with any dispute arising on this contract is to be settled by arbitration." The Defendants signed the contract with the addition of the word "brokers," and were acting as agents. Some time after the contract was signed, the Defendants named their principals. The cargo proved to be of inferior quality, and an arbitration (which the Plaintiffs did not attend) to determine the liability of the Defendants was held; the arbitrators decided by their award that the Defendants were not liable, inasmuch as a custom existed that a broker upon naming his principals ceased to be liable on the contract. At the trial of the action, the jury found that the alleged custom did not exist:—*Held,* first, that the Defendants were personally liable on the contract: secondly, by Brett, M.R., and Bowen, L.J., Fry, L.J., dissenting, that the Defendants were not relieved from liability by the award, inasmuch as the arbitrators had exceeded their jurisdiction. HUTCHESON & CO. *v.* EATON & SON 13 Q. B. D. 861

3. —— **Foreign Commission Agent**—*Goods consigned not of Description ordered—Measure of Damages.*] The Plaintiff, a merchant in London, gave orders to the Defendants, commission agents

2 S 2

II. PRINCIPAL AND AGENT—AGENT'S LIA-
BILITY—*continued.*

in Hong Kong, to purchase for him a quantity of
a certain kind of opium. No such opium could
then be obtained at Hong Kong, but instead of
informing the Plaintiff of this fact, the Defendants by mistake informed him that they could
procure it, and they purchased and shipped to
the Plaintiff opium which they erroneously supposed to be such as was ordered, but which was
really of an inferior description :—*Held*, that the
relation between the Plaintiff and Defendants
was not that of vendor and purchaser but of principal and agent, and that therefore the true
measure of damages which the Plaintiff was
entitled to recover was not the difference between
the value of the opium ordered and that shipped,
but the loss actually sustained by the Plaintiff
in consequence of the opium not being of the
description ordered. CASSABOGLOU *v.* GIBB

[9 Q. B. D. 220; 11 Q. B. D. 797

4. —— Solicitor — *Money received by petitioning Creditor's Solicitor from Debtor during
pendency of Bankrupt Petition, and paid over to
petitioning Creditor.*] Pending the hearing of a
bankruptcy petition, and with notice of the act of
bankruptcy on which it was founded, the solicitor
of the petitioning creditor, as his agent, received
from the debtor various sums of money as consideration for successive adjournments of the
hearing of the petition, and these sums he paid
over, or accounted for, to his client (the petitioning creditor). Afterwards an adjudication was
made on the petition :—*Held*, that the solicitor
having received the money with notice of the act
of bankruptcy to which the title of the trustee
related back, the payment by him was a wrongful
act, and he was liable to repay the money to the
trustee, and was not discharged by the payment
to his own principal. *Ex parte* EDWARDS. *In re*
CHAPMAN - - - 13 Q. B. D. 747

5. —— Undisclosed Principal—*Consignor and
Consignee—Sub-Contract—Privity of Contract—
Right to follow Goods or Proceeds—Trustees.*] The
Plaintiffs, who were landowners in New Zealand,
were in the habit of shipping wheat from New
Zealand to England for sale on the London
market, taking bills of lading which made the
wheat deliverable to themselves in London, and
indorsing these bills to M. & T., merchants and
factors at Glasgow, with instructions to sell the
wheat in London. M. & T. having no house or
agency in London were themselves in the habit
of indorsing these bills of lading to the Defendants, who were cornfactors and brokers in London, for the purpose of their selling there the
wheat. When any sales were effected, M. & T.
delivered account sales to the Plaintiffs in the
usual form, deducting a del credere commission
of £3 per cent., while the terms upon which the
Defendants were employed by M. & T. were
different, being a factorage of £2 per cent. and
not a del credere commission. The indorsement
of the bills of lading by the Plaintiffs to M. & T.
and by M. & T. to the Defendants, was in each
case only for the purpose of selling the wheat
and without the intention of passing any property in it. The Plaintiffs knew that the sales
effected for them by M. & T. in London were

II. PRINCIPAL AND AGENT—AGENT'S LIA-
BILITY—*continued.*

made by brokers employed by M. & T., but the
Plaintiffs were in no way parties to the particular
contracts of sale, nor were their names disclosed
upon them. The Defendants effected sales of
certain cargoes of wheat which had been so consigned for sale by the Plaintiffs in the above
mode, and paid the proceeds into their own account with their bankers, and from time to time
made remittances to M. & T. on account of them ;
but upon reference to the Defendants' books of
account the proceeds of the particular cargoes
could be separated and identified.—M. & T. carried on a business at Leith as well as at Glasgow,
and they employed the Defendants in respect of
both, and when they stopped payment, which
they did, they were indebted to the Defendants
upon the Leith account but not on the Glasgow
account.—The Plaintiffs having brought an action
against the Defendants for the net balance of the
proceeds of the said cargoes of wheat after deducting the remittances made to M. & T in respect
thereof, but without giving credit due to them
from M. & T. on other transactions, the jury found
at the trial, first, that the Plaintiffs did not,
through their agents, employ the Defendants to
sell and account for the proceeds of the wheat ;
secondly, that the Defendants knew, or had reason
to believe, that M. & T. were acting in the sales as
agents for a third person :—*Held*, reversing the
judgment of Field, J., that the Plaintiffs were not
entitled to recover, as there was no privity of contract between them and the Defendants, and the
Defendants did not stand in any fiduciary character towards the Plaintiffs so as to entitle the
latter to follow the proceeds of their property in
the Defendants' hands, and as whatever right the
Plaintiffs might have had as owners to claim the
wheat before it had been sold, they had no right,
after such sale, to the proceeds, without giving
credit for the sum due to the Defendants from
M. & T. on their general account. NEW ZEALAND
AND AUSTRALIAN LAND COMPANY *v.* WATSON

[7 Q. B. D. 374

6. —— Undisclosed Principal — *Provision in
bought and sold Notes for Settlement of Disputes
by Brokers — Custom of Trade making Brokers
personally liable—Evidence of—Admissibility.*] A
written contract made by brokers on behalf of undisclosed principals for the sale of hides provided
that " if any difference or dispute shall arise under
this contract it is hereby mutually agreed 'between
the sellers and buyers that the same shall be
settled by the selling brokers, whose decision in
writing shall be final and binding on both sellers
and buyers."—In an action against the brokers
in respect of inferior hides delivered under the
contract, the buyers made a claim for the breach
against the brokers as principals by custom of the
trade :—*Held*, that evidence of a custom of the
trade that a broker who does not disclose his
principal is personally responsible for the performance of the contract and liable for the breach was
rightly rejected, as such custom was inconsistent
with the arbitration clause, which would, if the
custom were incorporated, make the brokers judges
in their own cause. BARROW *v.* DYSTER

[13 Q. B. D. 635

III. PRINCIPAL AND AGENT — PRINCIPAL'S LIABILITY.

1. —— Contractor—*Party Wall—Liability of adjoining Landowners.*] The Appellant and Respondent were owners of adjoining houses between which was a party-wall, the property of both. The Appellant's house also adjoined B.'s house and between them was a party-wall. The Appellant employed a builder to pull down his house and rebuild it on a plan which involved the tying together of the new house and the party-wall between it and the Respondent's house, so that if one fell the other would be damaged. In the course of the rebuilding the builder's workmen in fixing a staircase, negligently and without the knowledge of the Appellant, cut into the party-wall between the Appellant's house and B.'s house, in consequence of which the Appellant's house fell, and the fall dragged over the party-wall between it and the Respondent's house and injured the Respondent's house. The cutting into the party-wall was not authorized by the contract between the Appellant and his builder: — *Held*, affirming the decision of the Court of Appeal, that the law cast a duty upon the Appellant to see that reasonable care and skill were exercised in those operations which involved a use of the party-wall belonging to himself and the Respondent, exposing it to the risk above-mentioned; and that the Appellant could not get rid of responsibility by delegating the performance to a third person; and was liable to the Respondent for the injury to his house.—*Bower v. Peate* (1 Q. B. D. 321) commented on. PERCIVAL *v.* HUGHES　　　9 Q. B. D. 441; 8 App. Cas. 443

2. —— Discharge of Principal — *Mode of dealing with Agent—Delay—Ship's Husband.*] In order to discharge a principal from his liability for a debt contracted by his agent the principal must shew that the creditor has himself misled him into supposing that he has elected to give exclusive credit to the agent, and that the principal has been prejudiced by that supposition. Mere delay in enforcing payment from the agent will not be sufficient for the purpose.—The Plaintiff sold stores for a ship to T., who was ship's husband and managing owner. The Defendant was part owner of the ship, and was also interested jointly with T. in the adventure for which the ship was being fitted out. The Plaintiff applied to T. for payment, but did not obtain it. Three months after the goods were supplied, and again two years after that, the Defendant settled accounts with T. and gave him credit for the price of the goods, supposing that they had been paid for. More than three years after the goods had been supplied, T. having become bankrupt, the Plaintiff for the first time applied for payment to the Defendant and brought his action for the debt :—*Held*, that there had been no such conduct on the part of the Plaintiff as would discharge the Defendant from his liability.—*Irvine v. Watson* (5 Q. B. D. 102), *Heald v. Kenworthy* (10 Ex. 745), and *Smethurst v. Mitchell* (28 L. J. (Q. B.) 241) considered. DAVISON *v.* DONALDSON [9 Q. B. D. 623

3. —— Employment of Agent to bet—*Implied Authority to pay Bet—When Authority is irrevocable—8 & 9 Vict. c. 109, s. 18.*] The em-

III. PRINCIPAL AND AGENT — PRINCIPAL'S LIABILITY—*continued.*

ployment of an agent to make a bet in his own name on behalf of his principal may imply an authority to pay the bet if lost, and on the making of the bet that authority may become irrevocable.—So *held*, by Bowen and Fry, L.JJ., Brett, M.R., dissenting.—Judgment of Hawkins, J., affirmed. READ *v.* ANDERSON [10 Q. B. D. 100; 13 Q. B. D. 779

4. —— Stock Exchange—*Usage of—30 & 31 Vict. c. 29, s. 1—Omission to specify Numbers—Brokers' Right to Indemnity.*] The Defendant employed the Plaintiffs, who were stockbrokers on the Stock Exchange, to buy shares in a joint stock banking company. He had on many previous occasions employed the Plaintiffs to buy similar shares, and on none of those occasions did the contract or advice note forwarded to him specify the distinguishing numbers of the shares purchased. The Plaintiffs purchased the shares from a jobber on the Stock Exchange in the usual way, and forwarded to the Defendant a contract note in the usual form, stating that the contract was made subject to the rules and regulations of the Stock Exchange. The contract was not made with reference to any distinguishing numbers of the shares, nor did the contract note specify any numbers. It is not the practice on the Stock Exchange to specify the numbers of the shares in dealing in bank shares. The Defendant before the settling-day wrote to the Plaintiffs repudiating the contract, on the ground that the numbers of the shares were not specified pursuant to 30 & 31 Vict. c. 29, s. 1. Notwithstanding such repudiation, the Plaintiffs completed the contract and paid for the shares. By the rules of the Stock Exchange the committee only recognise the members of the Stock Exchange as the parties to contracts, and if a member does not carry out a contract he may be declared a defaulter and expelled from the Stock Exchange, and "no application, which has for its object to annul any bargain on the Stock Exchange, shall be entertained by the committee unless upon an allegation of fraud or wilful misrepresentation."—The plaintiffs sued the Defendant to recover the price of the shares paid by them :—*Held*, by Mathew, J., on the authority of *Read v. Anderson* (13 Q. B. D. 779), that the Plaintiffs were entitled to recover. SEYMOUR *v.* BRIDGE　　　-　　　14 Q. B. D. 460

5. —— Stock Exchange—*Usage of — Bank Shares, Contract for Sale of—Failure to specify Numbers of Shares—30 & 31 Vict. c. 29, s. 1—Brokers' Right to Indemnity.*] The Defendant instructed the Plaintiffs, who were stockbrokers at Bristol, to purchase for him shares in a joint stock banking company on the Stock Exchange. The Plaintiffs gave directions accordingly to their London agents, brokers on the Stock Exchange, who purchased the shares from jobbers on the Stock Exchange in the usual way, without having in the contract distinguishing numbers of the shares, it not being the practice on the London Stock Exchange to specify the numbers or otherwise to comply with 30 & 31 Vict. c. 29 (Leeman's Act), s. 1. By the Rules of such Stock Exchange it is provided that the Stock Exchange shall not recognise in its dealings any other persons than

III. PRINCIPAL AND AGENT—PRINCIPAL'S LIABILITY—*continued.*

its own members, such members, if they do not carry out contracts, being liable to be expelled from the Stock Exchange, and that no application to annul a contract shall be entertained by the committee of the Stock Exchange unless upon a specific allegation of fraud, or wilful misrepresentation. Before the settling day the Defendant repudiated the contract, but the committee of the Stock Exchange refused to annul the contract, and therefore the Plaintiffs completed it, and paid the price of the shares. The Defendant was ignorant of the usage of the London Stock Exchange with regard to dealings in shares of banking companies, and did not know that the purchasing broker was by such usage bound to perform a contract for the purchase of banking shares, though void at law under Leeman's Act:—*Held*, affirming the decision of Grove, J., that the Plaintiffs were not entitled to recover from the Defendant the money paid by them as the price of the shares, since the usage of the Stock Exchange to disregard Leeman's Act, and to recognise as valid a contract which was made contrary to that Act, was unreasonable as against strangers who did not know it, and therefore was not binding on the Defendant. PERRY *v.* BARNETT

[14 Q. B. D. 467 ; 15 Q. B. D. 388

6. —— Undisclosed Principal—*Privity of Contract between Principal and Consignee—Money had and received—Notice or Knowledge—Set-off—Factors Act (6 Geo. 4, c. 94), s. 1.*] Merchants in London, upon the instruction of shipping agents at Havannah with respect to a cargo of tobacco to be consigned to the London merchants and after receiving the shipping documents, effected policies of marine insurance in the ordinary form on behalf and for the benefit of all parties whom it might concern. The Havannah agents shipped and consigned the tobacco in their own names, but were in fact acting as commission agents for Havannah merchants to whom the tobacco belonged; and the London merchants before effecting the policies had notice that the Havannah agents had an unnamed principal. A total loss having occurred the London merchants received the policy moneys, but before receipt had notice that the moneys were claimed by the Havannah principals :—*Held*, affirming the decision of the Court of Appeal, that an action lay by the Havannah principals against the London merchants for the policy moneys; that the London merchants were not entitled to a lien upon the moneys for the balance of their general account with the Havannah agents, and could not in that action set off their claim to that balance, or set off anything except the premium, stamps and commission in respect of the insurance.—*Held* also by Lord Blackburn, that the case fell within the Factors Act (6 Geo. 4, c. 94), s. 1.—*Sed quære* by Lord FitzGerald. MASPONS *v.* MILDRED - 9 Q. B. D. 530 ; 8 App. Cas. 874

7. —— Wagering— *Agent betting for Principal—Action for the Money received—8 & 9 Vict. c. 109, s. 18.*] The Plaintiff employed the Defendant for a commission to make bets for him on horses. The Defendant accordingly made such bets, and he received the winnings from the persons with whom he had so betted. In an

III. PRINCIPAL AND AGENT—PRINCIPAL'S LIABILITY—*continued.*

action by the Plaintiff for the amount which the Defendant had so received:—*Held*, that 8 & 9 Vict. c. 109, s. 18, which makes null and void all contracts by way of wagering, did not apply to the contract between the Plaintiff and Defendant, and that, therefore, notwithstanding that statute. the Plaintiff was entitled to recover in respect of the bets which had been so paid to the Defendant.—*Beyer* v. *Adams* (26 L. J. (Ch.) 841) overruled. BRIDGER *v.* SAVAGE - 15 Q. B. D. 363

PRINCIPAL AND AGENT—Agent for sale—Duty on purchase-money - 8 App. Cas. 309
　　See COLONIAL LAW — CAPE OF GOOD HOPE. 3.

—— Authority to receive mortgage debts
　　　　　　　　　　　　[30 Ch. D. 249
　　See SOLICITOR—AUTHORITY.

—— Commission agent—Goods bought for foreign principal—Stoppage in transitu
　　　　　　　　　　　　[15 Q. B. D. 39
　　See SALE OF GOODS—LIEN. 4.

—— Commission on sale, subject to title being approved by solicitor - 9 Q. B. D. 276
　　See CONDITION. 2.

—— Committee of voluntary fund 28 Ch. D. 426
　　See CHARITY—MANAGEMENT. 4.

—— Company—Share certificate issued by secretary 13 Q. B. D. 103
　　See ESTOPPEL—CONDUCT. 2.

—— Contractor—Support of adjacent soil
　　　　　[19 Ch. D. 281 ; 6 App. Cas. 740
　　See SUPPORT. 2, 3.

—— Factor—Lien 24 Ch. D. 54 ; 25 Ch. D. 31 ; [9 Q. B. D. 530 ; 8 App. Cas. 874 ; *See* FACTOR. 1, 2, 3. [10 App. Cas. 617

—— Liability of agent 24 Ch. D. 339
　　See BANKRUPTCY—ASSETS. 9.

—— Power of attorney 9 App. Cas. 561
　　See POWER OF ATTORNEY. 1.

—— Privity of contract—Shipowners—Charterer
　　　　　　　　　　　　[8 App. Cas. 120
　　See COLONIAL LAW—QUEENSLAND.

—— Right to follow trust funds—Bankruptcy
　　　　　　　　　　　　[9 Q. B. D. 264
　　See BANKRUPTCY—ORDER AND DISPOSITION. 7.

—— Securities for bills of exchange 29 Ch. D. 813
　　See BILL OF EXCHANGE—SECURITIES FOR. 4.

—— Ship's necessaries — Managing owner — Authority 6 Q. B. D. 93
　　See SHIP—OWNERS. 2.

—— Statement by agent—Evidence
　　　　　　　　　　　　[22 Ch. D. 593
　　See EVIDENCE—GENERAL. 4.

—— Warranty of authority—Building society
　　　　　　　　　　　　[6 Q. B. D. 696
　　See BUILDING SOCIETY. 10.

—— Wife—Liability of husband 6 App. Cas. 24
　　See HUSBAND AND WIFE — LIABILITY OF HUSBAND.

PRINCIPAL AND SURETY:—

I. PRINCIPAL AND SURETY—CONTRACT.

—— Guarantee — *Construction* — *Determination*—*Death of Guarantor*—*Contract for Benefit of Third Party*—*Right to sue*—*Measure of Damages*—*Trustee.*] In May, 1863, a father on the occasion of the admission of his son as an underwriting member of Lloyd's, addressed to the managing committee of that body a letter, by which he held himself responsible for all his son's engagements in that capacity. Lloyd's was then a voluntary association, governed by certain by-laws, under which a person once admitted a member could not be excluded from membership except in the event of his bankruptcy or insolvency. The association consisted of underwriting members, non-underwriting members, and subscribers. The practice of the underwriting members was to underwrite policies of marine insurance for the benefit of various owners of property, both members of the association and outsiders, but the policies with outsiders could only be effected through the agency of insurance brokers who were either members of or subscribers to the association. The association as such incurred no liability on the policies underwritten by its members. In 1871 the Society was incorporated by Act of Parliament, all the rights of the committee on behalf of the members being vested by the Act in the corporation. In 1876 the father died, and notice of his death was shortly afterwards given to Lloyd's. In 1878 the son became bankrupt, and thereupon ceased to be a member of Lloyd's:—*Held*, by the Court of Appeal, affirming the decision of Fry, J.:—(1.) That the guarantee was not determined by the death of the father or by the notice of it, but that his estate was liable in respect of engagements contracted by the son after his death:—(2.) That the guarantee extended to all engagements contracted by the son as an underwriting member of Lloyd's, whether with members or with outsiders:—(3.) That the committee of Lloyd's and the corporation of Lloyd's as their successors, were trustees of the benefit of the guarantee for all the persons, whether members or outsiders, with whom the son had contracted engagements as an underwriting member, and that the corporation could maintain an action to enforce the guarantee against the father's estate for the benefit of all those persons; on the ground, as to the outsiders, that the brokers, through whom the son's engagements with them were contracted, were trustees for their principals of the right which they themselves had to call on their own agents, Lloyd's, to enforce the guarantee for their benefit.—A guarantee the consideration for which is given once for all, cannot be determined by the guarantor, and does not cease on his death. —Whether a guarantee for future advances, which the party guaranteed is not bound to make, is not determinable by the guarantor, and whether it does not cease on notice of his death, *quære.* LLOYD'S v. HARPER - 16 Ch. D. 290

II. PRINCIPAL AND SURETY—CONTRIBUTION.

1. —— *Co-Sureties—Bankruptcy Petition— Petitioning Creditor's Debt.*] A surety is not entitled to call upon his co-surety for contribution until he has paid more than his proportion of the debt due to the principal creditor, even though the co-surety has not been required by the creditor to pay anything, provided that the co-surety has not been released by the creditor.—*Davies* v. *Humphreys* (6 M. & W. 153) followed.—*Craythorne* v. *Swinburne* (14 Ves. 160) discussed. *Ex parte* SNOWDON. *In re* SNOWDON　　17 Ch. D. 44

2. —— *Co-Sureties — Promissory Notes for Mon-ys borrowed—Action against one Surety— Payment of Debt—Policies effected on Life of Principal Debtor—Assignment of Policies after Assured's Death to Surety's Father who had paid the Premiums—Right to Policy Moneys.*] C. being indebted to D., four of his friends joined him in signing and giving four promissory notes to secure the payment to D., of the sum of £13,000 and interest. D. effected three policies on the life of C. for, in the aggregate, £10,000.—In 1867, Lord H. of E., one of the co-sureties, having been sued by D. on the notes, paid, with the assistance of his father, the Earl of E., the £13,000 and interest by a mortgage of estates which were settled upon the Earl for life with remainder to Lord H. of E.; and the Earl having paid the premiums and kept the policies on foot, in September, 1871, shortly after the death of C. obtained an assignment from D. of the policies and received the £10,000 from the insurance office.—A. another of the four sureties died. His estate, which was stated to be insolvent, was being administered by the Court, and Lord H. of E. brought in a claim against it for contribution in respect of the sum paid to D. on the notes:—*Held*, that, under all the circumstances of the case, Lord H. of E. and his father, the Earl, must be treated as one person, and that the claim for contribution would be allowed, but only after Lord H. of E. had brought into account, as a set-off, the moneys which were received on the three policies assigned to the Earl, credit being first given for the premiums and other moneys which had been paid in reference to the transaction. *In re* ARCEDECKNE. ATKINS v. ARCEDECKNE - - - 24 Ch. D. 709

3. —— *Co-Sureties—Security given by principal Debtor to one co-Surety.*] A surety, who has obtained from the principal debtor a countersecurity for the liability which he has undertaken, is bound to bring into hotchpot, for the benefit of his co-sureties, whatever he receives from that source, even though he consented to be a surety only upon the terms of having the security, and the co-sureties were, when they entered into the contract of suretyship, ignorant of his agreement for security.—The American cases *Miller* v. *Sawyer* (30 Vermont, 412) and *Hall* v. *Robinson* (8 Iredell, 56) followed. STEEL v. DIXON - - - 17 Ch. D. 825

III. PRINCIPAL AND SURETY—DISCHARGE.

1. —— *Co-Sureties in Severalty—Release— Pleading.*] Where two or more sureties contract severally the creditor does not break the contract with one of them by releasing the other. The contract remaining entire, the surety in order to

III. PRINCIPAL AND SURETY—DISCHARGE
—*continued.*

escape liability must shew an existing right to contribution from his co-surety which has been taken away or injuriously affected by his release. —*Held*, in an action upon a guarantee, that a plea to the effect that M. was the Defendant's co-surety, and had been released in consideration of a new guarantee given to the Plaintiff, constituted no defence : the plea nowhere averring or implying that the liability was joint, or that the Defendant became surety on the faith of M.'s co-suretyship, or that any right of contribution had arisen against M. which had been taken away or injuriously affected, or that the Defendant had suffered any damage or injury by the substitution described. WARD *v.* NATIONAL BANK OF NEW ZEALAND　　**8 App. Cas. 755**

2. —— Death of Co-Surety—*Joint and Several continuing Guarantee—Liability of surviving Co-surety.*] The death of one of the co-sureties under a joint and several continuing guarantee does not by itself determine the future liability of the surviving co-surety.—Claim, that by a bond G. and H., as principals, and the Defendant and W., since deceased, as sureties, became jointly and severally bound to the Plaintiffs, subject to a condition that if the obligors should repay to the obligees all sums of money to be by them advanced to G. and H., so that the Defendant and W. should not be responsible for more than £250, the bond should become void : that W. died before action : that after his death the Plaintiffs made advances to G. and H. : that G. and H. liquidated their affairs by arrangement pursuant to the Bankruptcy Act, 1869 : that more than £250 was owing from them to the Plaintiffs.— Defence, that shortly after the decease of W. the Plaintiffs had notice of the existence of his will, and that executors thereunder had proved it :— *Held*, upon demurrer, that the defence was bad. BECKETT *v.* ADDYMAN　　**9 Q. B. D. 783**

3. —— Laches—*Acceptance of Bill of Exchange in Blank—Omission to fill up Drawer's Name after Death of Acceptor.*] A debtor gave his creditor a bill of exchange accepted by himself, but with the drawer's name left blank. The Plaintiff at the same time, as a surety, deposited with the creditor certificates of stock in a joint stock company as collateral security for the debt.—The debtor died without the creditor having filled in the name of the drawer, and his estate was insolvent.—The bill was never presented for payment, nor was notice given to the Plaintiff of its non-payment :—*Held*, that the creditor had not discharged the Plaintiff from his suretyship by his omission to fill up the drawer's name and to give notice of the non-payment of the bill to the Plaintiff. CARTER *v.* WHITE　　**25 Ch. D. 666**

IV. PRINCIPAL AND SURETY—INDEMNITY.

1. —— Indorser of Bill of Exchange—*Surety — Securities.*] The acceptor of a bill of exchange knows that, by his acceptance, he does an act which will make him liable to indemnify any indorser of it who may afterwards pay it. The indorser is a surety for the payment to the holder, and having paid it, is entitled to the benefit of any securities to cover it deposited

IV. PRINCIPAL AND SURETY—INDEMNITY
—*continued.*

with the holder by the acceptor.—He is so entitled whether at the time of his indorsement he knew, or did not know, of the deposit of those securities.—The surety's right in this respect in no way depends on contract, but is the result of the equity of indemnification attendant on the suretyship.—S. C. R., one of the partners of S. R. & Sons, in December, 1874, deposited with the N. & S. W. Bank the title deeds of two of his own freehold properties, and signed a memorandum acknowledging them to be deposited as securities for what the N. & S. W. Bank might advance to the firm in the way of discounts.—In November, 1875, D. & Co. sold to R. & Sons a cargo of corn to be paid for in cash. Cash was paid only for part. R. & Sons offered a bill of exchange for the rest, which was declined. D. & Co. were customers of the N. & S. W. Bank. R. & Sons said if D. & Co. would inquire of those bankers they would find it would be all right with the R. bills. The bank manager refused to discount the bill without the indorsement of D. & Co., but said that he believed D. & Co. would incur no more than a nominal liability by putting their names on the bill. D. & Co. thereupon consented to take the bill, indorsed it in the ordinary way, and it was discounted by the bank and carried to their credit. In January, 1876, R. & Sons stopped payment. The bill became due in February, and was dishonoured. D. & Co., who then became acquainted with the fact that securities had been deposited with the bankers to cover advances on R. & Son's bills, brought an action against the N. & S. W. Bank to have the benefit, so far as they would go, of the securities deposited in December, 1874, claiming to be sureties to the bankers for what was due upon the bill.—*Held*, that D. & Co. were sureties on the bill, and that as such they were entitled to the benefit of these securities. DUNCAN, FOX & CO. *v.* NORTH AND SOUTH WALES BANK **[6 App. Cas. 1**

2. —— Mortgage of Premises and Policy—*Proviso for Redemption—Surety, Covenant by, to pay Interest and Premiums—Subsequent Advances by Mortgagee—Payment of Interest and Premiums by Surety—Right of Surety to a Transfer of the Securities.*] In December, 1854, S. assigned certain premises and a policy of assurance to secure the repayment of a sum of £200 advanced to him by W., and interest. The proviso for redemption was that on payment of the money W. would re-assign the premises and policy unto S., his executors, administrators, or assigns, or as he or they should direct. F. by the same indenture, as surety, covenanted, for himself only, with W. that while the £200 or any part should remain owing he would pay the interest and premiums, and he also assigned a policy on his own life, and covenanted to pay the premiums. W. at four different periods between May, 1856, and May, 1866, advanced moneys amounting to £530 to S. on the security of the same premises. S. made default in the payment of interest. W. died in 1878, and his executors made a demand upon F. for all arrears, which he paid, and he also paid the premiums on the policy of S. :—*Held*, that F.

IV. PRINCIPAL AND SURETY—INDEMNITY— *continued.*

was entitled to have a transfer of all the securities on payment of what was due upon the mortgage of December, 1854.—*Williams* v. *Owen* (13 Sim. 597) not followed. *Newton* v. *Chorlton* (10 Hare, 646) followed. FORBES *v.* JACKSON - 19 **Ch. D.** 615

V. PRINCIPAL AND SURETY—LIABILITY.

1. —— Bond to Guardians—*Collection of Rates —Overseers.*] The Defendant as surety gave a bond to the guardians of the poor for the M. Union conditioned for the due discharge by C. of his duties as collector of poor-rates for the parish of N. C. absconded, having embezzled part of the rates and allowed others to be lost by not applying for them. The guardians sued the Defendant for the loss. The Defendant admitted his liability as to the sums embezzled, but disputed his liability as to the sums lost by C.'s negligence, on the ground that the loss would not have occurred if C. had been called upon to account as he ought to have been. It appeared that no negligence could be imputed to the guardians, but there appeared some ground to believe that if the overseers of the parish of N. had discharged their statutory duties with reasonable care the loss would not have occurred :—*Held,* affirming the decision of Watkin Williams, J., that the Plaintiffs were entitled to recover from the Defendants the moneys lost through failure of C. to collect them, for that there had been no negligence on the part of the Plaintiffs, and they were not answerable for the negligence of the overseers. GUARDIANS OF MANS-FIELD UNION *v.* WRIGHT -   9 **Q. B. D.** 683

2. —— Guarantee of Account at Bank—*Debtor and Creditor—Death of Surety—Appropriation of Payments.*] S. guaranteed the account of T. at a bank by two guarantees, one for £150, the other for £400. By the terms of the guarantees the surety guaranteed to the bank "the repayment of all moneys which shall at any time be due from" the customer "to you on the general balance of his account with you;" the guarantee was moreover to be "a continuing guarantee to the extent at any one time of" the sums respectively named, and was not to be considered as wholly or partially satisfied by the payment at any time of any sums due on such general balance; and any indulgence granted by the bank was not to prejudice the guarantee.—S. having died, leaving T. and another executors, the bank on receiving notice of his death, without any communication with the executors beyond what would appear in T.'s pass-book, closed T.'s account, which was overdrawn, and opened a new account with him, in which they did not debit him with the amount of the overdraft, but debited him with interest on the same; and continued the account until he went into liquidation, when it also was overdrawn :—*Held,* by Bacon, V.C., that payments in after the death of the surety went in discharge of the overdraft, alike on the terms of guarantee, and on the principle of *Clayton's Case* (1 Mer. 572, 605), and that, as the amount of such payments exceeded the overdraft, the bank were not entitled to prove against the estate of the father-in-law.—*Held,* on appeal, that there was no contract express 'or implied which obliged the debtor and creditor to appropriate to the old over-

V. PRINCIPAL AND SURETY—LIABILITY— *continued.*

draft the payments made by the debtor after the determination of the guarantee, and that the bank were entitled to prove against the estate of S. for the amount of the old overdraft less the amount of the dividend which they had received on it in the liquidation. *In re* SHERRY. LONDON AND COUNTY BANKING COMPANY *v.* TERRY   [25 **Ch. D.** 692

3. —— Judgment against Principal—*Evidence Liability of Surety.*] In the absence of special agreement a judgment or an award against a principal debtor is not binding on the surety, and is not evidence against him in an action against him by the creditor, but the surety is entitled to have the liability proved as against him in the same way as against the principal debtor.—The American case *Douglass* v. *Howland* (24 Wendell, 35) followed. *Ex parte* YOUNG. *In re* KITCHEN   [17 **Ch. D.** 668

PRINCIPAL AND SURETY—Liability of surety —Proof in bankruptcy   17 Ch. D. 98
See BANKRUPTCY—PROOF. 11.

—— Liability of surety—Debt due to principal
See SET-OFF. 2.   [6 **Q. B. D.** 540

PRINTING—Evidence in previous action—Costs   [9 **P. D.** 126
See PRACTICE—ADMIRALTY—COSTS. 6.

PRIORITY—Administration action—Secured creditors -   20 **Ch. D.** 545
See EXECUTOR—ACTIONS. 20.

—— Administration action—Unregistered judgment -   21 **Ch. D.** 189
See EXECUTOR—ACTIONS. 6.

—— Assignment of chose in action—Notice   [18 **Ch. D.** 381
See BANKRUPTCY—ASSETS. 15.

—— Contemporaneous deeds -   21 **Ch. D.** 762
See DEED. 1.

—— Contribution—Indorsers of promissory note   [8 **App. Cas.** 733
See BILL OF EXCHANGE—LIABILITY OF PARTIES.

—— Costs in winding-up—Liquidator—Litigation   · 23 **Ch. D.** 511 ; 27 **Ch. D.** 33
See COMPANY—COSTS. 2, 3.

—— Debentures   16 **Ch. D.** 411 ; 18 **Ch. D.** 334 ; [28 **Ch. D.** 317 ; 8 **App. Cas.** 780
See COMPANY—DEBENTURES. 1, 6, 7.

—— Judgment   29 **Ch. D.** 527
See JUDGMENT. 4.

—— Legacies -   17 **Ch. D.** 798
See WILL—PRIORITY OF LEGACIES.

—— Lunatic—Maintenance—Claims of creditors   [23 **Ch. D.** 577
See LUNATIC—MAINTENANCE. 2.

—— Material men—Wages   9 **P. D.** 37
See SHIP—MARITIME LIEN. 5.

—— Mortgages.
See Cases under MORTGAGE—PRIORITY.

—— Mortgage—Creditors' deed -   29 **Ch. D.** 745
See CREDITORS' DEED.

—— Mortgage—Middlesex registry
See REGISTRY ACTS.   [29 **Ch. D.** 702

PRIORITY—*continued.*.

—— Mortgage—Money entrusted to solicitor
　　　　　　　　　　　　 .. [19 Ch. D. 207
　, *See* SOLICITOR—LIABILITIES. 3.

—— Mortgage to building society
　　　　　　　　　 [28 Ch. D. 298, 398
　See BUILDING SOCIETY. . 12, 13.

—— Mortgage—Renewable lease　29 Ch. D. 231
　See LEASEHOLD—RENEWABLE LEASE. 4.

—— Mortgage of shares—Lien of company
　　　　　　　　　　　　 [29 Ch. D. 149
　See COMPANY—SHARES—TRANSFER. 3.

—— Patent—Publication　　　　21 Ch. D. 720
　See PATENT—VALIDITY. 2.

—— Patent—User　　-　　. 19 Ch. D. 268
　See PATENT—VALIDITY. 4.

—— Shares held in trust—Lien of company on
　shares　　-　　-　　-　21 Ch. D. 302
　See COMPANY—MEMBER'S LIABILITY. 3.

—— Stop order　　　-　　　23 Ch. D. 497
　See PRACTICE—SUPREME COURT—CHARG-
　ING ORDERS. 3.

—— Winding-up of company—Directors' fees
　See COMPANY—PROOF. 1. [30 Ch. D. 629

PRISON.

*The Act 44 & 45 Vict. c. 64 (the Central
Criminal Court Prisons Act, 1881) applies the
rules made under sect. 24 of the Prisons Act, 1877
(40 & 41 Vict. c. 21) to the Central Criminal Court
District.*

*The Act 47 & 48 Vict. c. 51, removes doubts as
to the powers of the Secretary of State in relation
to the altering, enlarging, rebuilding, and building
of prisons and appropriating any building for a
prison under the Prison Act, 1877 (40 & 41 Vict.
c. 21).*

Repeal.] *Sect. 2 (5) repeals sects. 23 to 29
inclusive of the Prison Act, 1865 (28 & 29 Vict.
c. 126).*

Prison Charity.] *By 45 & 46 Vict. c. 65 (the
Prisons Charity Act, 1882), s. 2, the Charity Commissioners may, on the application of the Secretary
of State, make an order for the establishment of a
scheme for the administration of a prison charity.*

*The expression "prison charity" means a charity
the endowment of which or part of the endowment
of which is applicable for the benefit of any prisoners, or for any purpose connected with any
prisoners or prison, whether the prisoners be confined in or the prison be a common gaol, house of
correction, or other place of confinement.*

1. —— Governor— *Superannuation—Compensation Allowance--Special Minute--Superannuation
Act 1859 (22 Vict. c. 26) ss. 2, 4, 7—Prison Act
1877 (40 & 41 Vict. c. 21) s. 36.*—At the time when
the Prison Act 1877 (40 & 41 Vict. c. 21) came
into force C. was the governor of a prison which
by that Act was transferred to the Home Secretary. Up to that time the county justices had
been the . prison authority. Soon after the Act
came into force C. retired, and the Lords Commissioners of the Treasury awarded him an
annuity calculated upon ³⁄₆₀ths of his salary and
emoluments, or ₄₀th per annum for thirty-eight
years ; viz. ³³⁄₆₀ths for his twenty-three years of
actual service under the county justices ; with
¹⁵⁄₆₀ths added for ten years because he had retired

PRISON—*continued.*

for the purpose of facilitating improvements in
the organisation of the prison department; and
₅⁄₆₀ths added for five years under sect. 4 of the
Superannuation Act 1859 (22 Vict. c. 26). The
Commissioners apportioned ³⁸⁄₆₀ths of the annuity
to be paid by- the county justices out of the
county rates, leaving the ¹⁵⁄₆₀ths to be paid out of
grants provided by Parliament. C. was under
sixty years of age, and was not incapacitated by
illness or otherwise. The Commissioners did not
make or lay before Parliament a special minute
within the meaning of sect. 7 of the Superannuation Act 1859 :—*Held,* affirming the decision of
the Court of Appeal, that the provision in sect. 7
of the Superannuation Act, 1859 as to a special
minute was directory only ; that the Commissioners had power to make the award under the
Prison Act 1877, s. 36, and the Superannuation
Act 1859, ss. 2. 4, and 7; and that the county
justices were liable for the proportion charged
upon them. JUSTICES OF MIDDLESEX *v.* THE
QUEEN　-　11 Q. B. D. 656 ; 9 App. Cas. 757

2. —— Maintenance of Prisoners—*Committal
to Prison—Expenses of conveying to Prison—
Prison Act, 1877 (40 & 41 Vict. c. 21), ss. 4, 57.*]
The expenses of conveying to prison persons
who are committed to prison either for punishment or to take their trial and are unable to
pay those expenses are "expenses incurred in
respect of the maintenance of prisoners," within
sects. 4 and 57 of the Prison Act, 1877 (40 & 41
Vict. c. 21), and those sections transfer the liability for such expenses from county rates to
moneys provided by Parliament. MULLINS *v.*
TREASURER OF THE COUNTY OF SURREY
　　　　　 [6 Q. B. D. 156; 7 App. Cas. 1

3. —— Purchase of Land—*Land bought for
the purpose of rendering Prison more commodious
or safe—Prison Commissioners—Prison Act, 1865
(28 & 29 Vict. c. 126), ss. 4, 5, 8, 23, 44—Prison
Act, 1877 (40 & 41 Vict. c. 21), ss. 5, 48, 60—Evidence—Sale of Land—Intention of Parties to Conveyance.*] In 1867 the justices of the county of
M. bought land covered with houses subject to
leases for long terms, several years of which remained unexpired. The land and the houses
were conveyed to the clerk of the peace for the
county, "upon trust for Justices of the county of
M., for the purposes of the Prison Act, 1865, and
upon or for no other trust, intent, or purpose
whatsoever." The land and houses were never
used as part of the prison. An action having
been brought to try whether the reversion in the
land and houses was in the Prison Commissioners
or the justices, the Defendant proposed to adduce
as evidence the minutes of the proceedings of the
justices in order to shew that the land had been
bought for the purpose of rendering the prison
more commodious or safe :—*Held,* that the reversion in the land and the houses standing thereon
had passed to the Prison Commissioners by virtue
of the Prison Act, 1877.—*Per* Jessel, M.R., that
the conveyance having been executed, the minutes
of the proceedings of the justices were inadmissible as evidence shewing the purpose for which
the land and the houses had been bought. PRISON
COMMISSIONERS *v.* CLERK OF THE PEACE FOR MID-
DLESEX　　-　　-　　9 Q. B. D. 506

PRISONER—Expense of conveying to prison·
[6 Q. B. D. 156; 7 App. Cas. 1
See PRISON. 2.
—— Habeas corpus -   -   - 15 Q. B. D. 471
See HABEAS CORPUS.

PRIVATE IMPROVEMENT EXPENSES
[17 Ch. D. 782
See LOCAL GOVERNMENT—STREETS. 8.

PRIVILEGE—Annexed to heritable property
[6 App. Cas. 295
See SCOTCH LAW — HERITABLE PRO-
PERTY. 3.

—— Criminating interrogatories—Divorce
[10 P. D. 122
See PRACTICE — DIVORCE—NULLITY OF
MARRIAGE. 8.

—— Interrogatories.
See Cases under PRACTICE—SUPREME
COURT—INTERROGATORIES. 12—15.

—— Libel.
See Cases under DEFAMATION—PRIVI-
LEGE.

—— Libel—Injunction -   - 20 Ch. D. 501;
[21 Ch. D. 798
See PRACTICE — SUPREME COURT — IN-
JUNCTION. 3, 4.

—— Production of documents.
See Cases under PRACTICE—SUPREME
COURT—PRODUCTION OF DOCUMENTS.
18—27.

—— Solicitor—Evidence -   18 Ch. D. 30
See EVIDENCE—WITNESS. 3.

—— Witness—Answer tending to criminate
[20 Ch. D. 294
See EVIDENCE—WITNESS. 2.

PRIVITY OF CONTRACT   - 19 Ch. D. 246
See PATENT—ASSIGNMENT. 2.

——   -   - 24 Ch. D. 54; 10 App. Cas. 617
See FACTOR. 1.

PRIVY COUNCIL.
Judicial Committee.] The Act 44 & 45 Vict.
c. 3 (the Judicial Committee Act, 1881) provides
that Lords Justices of Appeal, if members of Her
Majesty's Privy Council in England, shall be
members of the Judicial Committee of the Privy
Council.

—— Practice.
See Cases under PRACTICE — PRIVY
COUNCIL.

PRIZE FIGHT—Aiding and abetting
[8 Q. B. D. 534
See CRIMINAL LAW—OFFENCES AGAINST
PERSON. 7.

PROBATE:—   Col.
I. EXECUTION   -   -   -   1269
II. GRANT   -   -   -   1270
III. KNOWLEDGE OF CONTENTS   1272
IV. MARRIED WOMAN   -   -   1273

I. PROBATE—EXECUTION.

1. —— Acknowledgment of Signature—Testator's Signature not seen by Attesting Witnesses—
Wills Act, 1837 (1 Vict. c. 26), s. 9.] To constitute
a sufficient acknowledgment, within sect 9 of the
Wills Act, the witnesses must at the time of the
acknowledgment see, or have the opportunity of

I. PROBATE—EXECUTION—continued.
seeing, the signature of the testator, and if such
be not the case it is immaterial whether the signature be, in fact, there at the time of attestation,
or whether the testator say that the paper to be
attested is his will, or that his signature is inside
the paper.—Hudson v. Parker (1 Robert. 14) followed.—Gwillim v. Gwillim (3 Sw. & Tr. 200)
and Becket v. Howe (Law Rep. 2 P. & M. 1) disapproved. IN THE GOODS OF GUNSTAN. BLAKE v.
BLAKE -   -   -   7 P. D. 102

2. —— Alterations.] The clause appointing
executors was written partly on the second and
partly on the third side of a will. Subsequently
the testator altered the clause, but his signature
and those of the attesting witnesses appeared
opposite only to the alterations which were made
on the second side. The Court granted probate
of all the alterations. IN THE GOODS OF WILKIN-
SON   .   - 6 P. D. 100

3. —— Duplicate — Mistake.] An intended
will was written in duplicate, one copy of which
was signed only by the deceased and the other
only by the attesting witnesses:—Held, that
neither paper was entitled to probate. IN THE
GOODS OF HATTON -   -   6 P. D. 204

4. —— Evidence of attesting Witnesses.] In
1878 the testator, who was a good man of
business but not a lawyer, wrote a holograph
codicil upon the same paper as a will which he
had made in 1868, and wrote at the end of it an
attestation clause adapting that at the end of the
will to the case of a codicil. He called the nurse
into the schoolroom, and asked her and the
nursery-governess to "sign this paper." There
was evidence that he took his own pen into the
room. Both witnesses signed. At the trial, which
took place between four and five years afterwards,
the codicil was produced bearing the testator's
signature, and both the attesting witnesses were
examined. The governess deposed that she had
designedly abstained from looking at any of the
writing on the paper, and the nurse it appeared
had been very nervous. Neither of them could
say anything as to what writing was on the paper,
nor as-to whether the testator's signature was
there when they signed, and both said that they
did not see him sign. The President pronounced
for the validity of the codicil:—Held, by Earl of
Selborne, L.C., that the reasonable conclusion was,
that the codicil was signed by the testator in the
presence of the witnesses:—Held, by Cotton, L.J.,
that on the evidence he should have come to the
contrary conclusion, but that the finding of the President, who had seen and heard the witnesses, ought
not to be reversed:—Held, by Fry, L.J., that as the
codicil ex facie appeared to be properly executed,
and the presumption omnia rite esse acta was
strengthened by the conduct of the testator, which
shewed an anxious and intelligent desire to do
everything regularly, that presumption was not
rebutted by the evidence of the witnesses, who
appeared to have been nervous and confused on
the occasion of the attestation, and whose recollection of what took place was evidently imperfect.
WRIGHT v. SANDERSON   -   - 9 P. D. 149

II. PROBATE—GRANT.

1. —— Alien—English Form—Execution—

II. PROBATE—GRANT—*continued.*

24 & 25 *Vict. c.* 114—*Naturalization Act,* 1870.]
A will of a foreigner executed abroad according
to the formalities required by the English law is
invalid, notwithstanding the provisions of 24 &
25 Vict. c. 114, and the Naturalization Act, 1870.
IN THE GOODS OF VON BUSECK　　6 P. D. 211

2. —— **Alien**—*Execution*—24 & 25 *Vict. c.* 114
—*Naturalization Act,* 1870 (33 & 34 *Vict. c.* 14).] A
will made by an alien who was domiciled abroad at
the time of making her will and of her death, and
executed according to the forms required by English law, but not in manner required by the law
of the country of her domicil, is not entitled to
probate, though her domicil of origin was English—Decision of Sir J. Hannen affirmed. BLOXAM
v. FAVRE　　8 P. D. 101 ; 9 P. D. 130

3. —— **Conditional.**] A testator, being about to
travel, made his will, which contained the following words :—" On leaving this station for *T.* and
M., in case of my death on the way, know all men
this is a memorandum of my last will and testament :"—*Held,* that the will was not contingent
upon his death before arriving at *T.* or *M.* Will
admitted to probate. IN THE GOODS OF MAYD
[6 P. D. 17

4. —— **Domicil**—*Will*—*Construction of Will
expressed in Terms of Foreign Law.*] The fact
that probate of a will has been granted by an
English Court is not conclusive that the testator
was domiciled in England.—If a domiciled Englishman makes a will expressed in the technical
terms of the law of a foreign country, so as to
manifest an intention that it should operate
according to that law, the meaning of the will
must be ascertained by the foreign law, and then
an equivalent effect must be given to the will in
England.—*Studd* v. *Cook* (8 App. Cas. 577) discussed. BRADFORD *v.* YOUNG　　-　　26 Ch. D. 656

5. —— **Equitable Conversion**—*Right to Probate — Property — Probate and Legacy Duty.*]
Where freehold property is, by the doctrine of
equitable conversion, to be considered as personalty, it is liable to probate and legacy duty, and
a will disposing of it is entitled to probate. IN
THE GOODS OF GUNN -　　9 P. D. 242

6. —— **Executor according to the Tenor.**] A
testator by his will said, " I appoint R. H. P.
and J. E. W.," but did not state in what capacity
he appointed them. He also bequeathed legacies
to " each of my executors," and gave to his " said
executors" the residue of his property, with certain directions as to it. The Court *held,* upon
motion, that by the words of the will R. H. P.
and J. E. W. were appointed executors, and granted
probate to them accordingly. IN THE GOODS OF
BRADLEY　　-　　-　　8 P. D. 215

7. —— **Foreign Law**—*Royal Family of Russia
—Will and Codicils superseded—Probate of Acte
Definitif — Certificate of Ambassador.*] By the
law of Russia no will or codicil of a deceased
member of the Royal Family has any effect as
such, but the deceased's property is distributed
according to an acte definitif decreed by the other
members of the family and confirmed by the
Emperor. Probate of the acte definitif granted
notwithstanding the execution of a will and codicils.—The law of a foreign country is sufficiently

II. PROBATE—GRANT—*continued.*

proved by the certificate of the ambassador for
that country. IN THE GOODS OF PRINCE OLDEN-
BURG　　9 P. D. 234

8. —— **Foreign Probate**—*Probate of Codicil.*]
If a will has been proved abroad, probate of the
codicils, if any, must be granted by the Court
which granted probate of the will. IN THE GOODS
OF MILLER　　·　　8 P. D. 167

9. —— **Foreign Will**—*English and Spanish
Wills—Probate of English Will only.*] A testator
made a will in England which disposed only of
English property. Subsequently he made abroad
another will which disposed of property abroad
and cancelled all previous dispositions. The Court,
with the consent of all the parties interested,
ordered probate of the English will only, and
allowed the foreign will to be delivered out of
the registry for probate abroad. IN THE GOODS
OF SMART　　9 P. D. 64

10. —— **Mistake** — *Inconsistent Attestation
Clause.*] In an attestation clause of a third codicil
it was stated by mistake that the first codicil was
cancelled :—*Held,* that an attestation clause forms
no part of a codicil, and that therefore the first
codicil must be admitted to probate. IN THE
GOODS OF ATKINSON -　　8 P. D. 165

11. —— **Omission of Paragraph**—*Words introduced without Instructions — Amendment of
Probate.*] There is no difference between the
words which a testator himself uses in drawing
up his will, and the words which are bonâ fide
used by one whom he trusts to draw it up for him.
The Court in either case must take the words as
it finds them, and therefore *held* that the Plaintiff,
the natural daughter, was not entitled to have
probate amended by omitting the words " from
and after the decease of my said wife without
leaving issue of our said marriage," on the ground
that the draughtsman introduced them without
reason or special directions, and that the effect of
the same had not been intelligently appreciated
by the testator.—Where a portion of a will has
been introduced through fraud or perhaps inadvertence, it may be rejected and probate granted
of the remainder, if the two are severable. But
where the rejection of part alters the sense of the
remainder, *quære,* whether there is a valid will
within the meaning of 7 Will. 4 & 1 Vict. c. 26,
s. 9. RHODES *v.* RHODES　　7 App. Cas. 192

III. PROBATE—KNOWLEDGE OF CONTENTS.

—— **Capacity**—*Memory.*] If a testatrix has
given instructions for her will, and it is prepared
in accordance with them, the Will will be valid
though at the time of execution the testatrix merely
recollects that she has given those instructions but
believes that the will which she is executing is in
accordance with them. PARKER *v.* FELGATE AND
TILLY　　-　　-　　8 P. D. 171

IV. PROBATE—MARRIED WOMAN.

1. —— **Husband's Assent.**] A will was made
by a married woman who appointed her husband
one of the executors. He assented to the making
of the will, and after her death expressed his intention to take probate, but died before doing so :
—*Held,* that he had assented to the probate. IN
THE GOODS OF COOPER　　6 P. D. 34

2. —— **Husband's Assent**—20 & 21 *Vict.* c. 77,

IV. PROBATE—MARRIED WOMAN—*contd.*
s. 73.] A married woman having been appointed sole executrix and universal legatee, her husband objected to her taking probate. The Court, under sect. 73 of 20 & 21 Vict. c. 77, made the grant to her attorney :—*Quære*, whether a husband has an absolute right to object to his wife's taking probate of a will of which she is executrix. CLERKE *v.* CLERKE　　　6 P. D. 103

· 3. —— **Protection Order**—*Wife's Lifetime—Action to prove Will and to discharge Order.*] An application to discharge a protection order is not limited to the lifetime of the married woman. —A claim to pronounce against the validity of the will of a married woman who had obtained a protection order, and a counter-claim to discharge the protection order, may be included in the same action. MUDGE *v.* ADAMS　　　6 P. D. 54

4. —— **Realty**—*Appointment of Executors—Probate—Jurisdiction—Judicature Acts.*] A will of a married woman made during coverture, under a power and disposing of real property only, is not entitled to probate, though there is an appointment of executors.—The Judicature Acts do not alter the jurisdiction of the Court of Probate in non-contentious matters. IN THE GOODS OF TOMLINSON -　　-　　-　　6 P. D. 209

5. —— **Realty**—*Appointment of Executor—Arrears of Rent personalty—Right to Probate.*] A married woman having a power of appointment over real property executed the power in favour of herself. She afterwards made her will, by which she directed (amongst other things) that a portion of the property should be sold to pay legacies and to erect a memorial window. She also appointed an executor. There were arrears of rent due at the time of her death and subsequently :—*Held*, that as she possessed the property as separate estate, and had appointed an executor and directed him to pay the legacies, &c., and as the arrears of rent were part of her personal estate, the will was entitled to probate. BROWNRIGG *v.* PIKE　　　7 P. D. 61

PROBATE—Action by executor before probate—
　　Stay of proceedings　-　12 Q. B. D. 294
　　See PRACTICE—SUPREME COURT—STAYING PROCEEDINGS. 3.

—— Domicil—Abandonment　29 Ch. D. 617
　　See DOMICIL. 1.

—— Domicil—Estoppel　-　29 Ch. D. 268
　　See ESTOPPEL—JUDGMENT. 4.

—— New Zealand—Payment out of Court
　　　　　　　　　　[24 Ch. D. 177
　　See PRACTICE—SUPREME COURT—PAYMENT OUT OF COURT.

—— Obtaining by unqualified person
　　　　[9 Q. B. D. 1; 8 App. Cas. 407
　　See SOLICITOR—UNQUALIFIED. 4.

—— Revocation of　-　21 Ch. D. 581
　　See EXECUTOR—ACTIONS. 7.

—— Revocation—Jurisdiction of Chancery Division　-　-　9 P. D. 210
　　See ESTOPPEL—JUDGMENT. 1.

—— Revocation—Jurisdiction of Chancery Division　-　-　26 Ch. D. 656
　　See PRACTICE—SUPREME COURT—JURISDICTION. 1.

PROBATE—*continued.*
—— Unattested will made abroad· 25 Ch. D. 373
　　See POWER—EXECUTION. 4.

—— Where necessary.
　　See REVENUE—PROBATE DUTY—*Statutes.*

—— Will of real estate in Victoria　21 Ch. D. 674
　　See PARTITION SUIT—SALE. 2.

PROBATE DUTY.
　　See Cases and Statutes under REVENUE —PROBATE DUTY.

—— Application for return—Mandamus—Commissioners of Inland Revenue
　　See MANDAMUS. 2.　　[12 Q. B. D. 461

—— Law of Victoria　-　8 App. Cas. 82
　　See COLONIAL LAW—VICTORIA. 3.

PROCTOR—Unqualified person—Penalty
　　　　[9 Q. B. D. 1; 8 App. Cas. 407
　　See SOLICITOR—UNQUALIFIED. 4.

PROCURATION.
　　See CRIMINAL LAW—OFFENCES AGAINST WOMEN—*Statutes.*

PRODUCTION OF DOCUMENTS.
　　See Cases under PRACTICE — SUPREME COURT—PRODUCTION OF DOCUMENTS.

—— Acknowledgment of right　25 Ch. D. 600
　　See VENDOR AND PURCHASER — TITLE DEEDS.

—— Costs of　　-　16 Ch. D. 517
　　See PRACTICE—SUPREME COURT—COSTS. 38.

—— Depositions before receiver of wreck 9 P. D. 6
　　See PRACTICE — ADMIRALTY — PRODUCTION OF DOCUMENTS.

—— Solicitor's lien　-　23 Ch. D. 169
　　See SOLICITOR—LIEN. 8.

—— Title deeds.
　　See TITLE DEEDS—*Statutes.*

—— Winding-up—Official liquidator　22 Ch. D.
　　See COMPANY—LIQUIDATOR. 1.　　[714

PROFESSIONAL WITNESS—Expenses
　　　　　　　　　　[21 Ch. D. 831
　　See EVIDENCE—WITNESS. 4.

PROFIT À PRENDRE—Fishery.
　　See Cases under FISHERY.

PROFITS—Account of　-　17 Ch. D. 423
　　See PATENT—ASSIGNMENT. 1.

—— Business—Assignment of—Bankruptcy
　　　　　　　　　　[22 Ch. D. 782
　　See BANKRUPTCY—ASSETS. 6.

—— Business settled on successive tenants for life　-　-　26 Ch. D. 588
　　See TENANT FOR LIFE.

—— Foreign patent—Prolongation—Accounts
　　　　[6 App. Cas. 176; 9 App. Cas. 592
　　See PATENT—PROLONGATION. 1, 2.

—— Income tax.
　　See Cases under REVENUE—INCOME TAX.

—— Made by agent　-　29 Ch. D. 795
　　See PRINCIPAL AND AGENT—AGENT'S LIABILITY. 1.

—— Mine—Income tax　-　6 App. Cas. 315
　　See SCOTCH LAW—REVENUE.

—— Participation in　-　-　18 Ch. D. 698
　　See PARTNERSHIP—CONTRACT. 3.

PROFITS—*continued.*

—— Participation in—Policy-holder.
See Cases under COMPANY—LIFE INSURANCE COMPANY.

—— Payment of dividend out of　16 Ch. D. 344
See COMPANY—DIVIDEND. 4.

—— Proof in bankruptcy — Infringement of patent　-　-　20 Ch. D. 780
See BANKRUPTCY—PROOF. 7.

—— Trade carried on by executors　26 Ch. D. 42
See EXECUTOR—ADMINISTRATION. 4.

—— Trespasser—Action surviving against executors　-　24 Ch. D. 439
See TRESPASS. 1.

PROHIBITION.

—— Jurisdiction— *Inferior Court* — *Salford Hundred Court of Record Act,* 1868 (31 & 32 Vict. c. cxxx.), s. 7.] Sect. 7 of the Salford Hundred Court of Record Act, 1868, enacts that "no defendant shall be permitted to object to the jurisdiction of the Court otherwise than by special plea, and, if the want of jurisdiction be not so pleaded, the Court shall have jurisdiction for all purposes":—*Held,* that the Defendant, against whom judgment had been recovered in the Salford Hundred Court, he not having pleaded to the jurisdiction, could not have a writ of prohibition on the ground of want of jurisdiction, inasmuch as the above-mentioned section under the circumstances conferred jurisdiction on the Salford Hundred Court.—*Oram v. Brearey* (2 Ex. D. 346) overruled. CHADWICK v. BALL　-　14 Q. B. D. 855

—— Appeal　-　8 Q. B. D. 9
See COUNTY COURT—PRACTICE. 5.

—— Demurrer　-　6 Q. B. D. 586
See RAILWAY COMPANY — RAILWAYS REGULATION ACTS. 5.

—— Ecclesiastical Court　-　6 App. Cas. 424
See PRACTICE—ECCLESIASTICAL—MONITION.

—— Ecclesiastical Court　-　7 App. Cas. 240
See PRACTICE—ECCLESIASTICAL—PUBLIC WORSHIP ACT. 1.

—— Ecclesiastical Court　-　22 Ch. D. 316
See PRACTICE—ECCLESIASTICAL—JURISDICTION. 2.

—— Local Government Board　10 Q. B. D. 309
See LOCAL GOVERNMENT—STREETS. 9.

—— Mayor's Court — Jurisdiction — Cause of action arising wholly or in part within city of London　-　14 Q. B. D. 1
See COURT—MAYOR'S COURT. 4.

—— Railway company—Arbitration
[17 Ch. D. 493
See RAILWAY COMPANY — RAILWAYS REGULATION ACTS. 1.

PROLIXITY—Affidavit of documents
[21 Ch. D. 835
See PRACTICE—SUPREME COURT—PRODUCTION OF DOCUMENTS. 1.

—— Affidavit—Taking off the file　26 Ch. D. 470
See PRACTICE—SUPREME COURT—STRIKING OUT PLEADINGS. 3.

PROLONGATION OF PATENT.
See Cases under PATENT—PROLONGATION.

PROMISSORY NOTE — Banker—Bank Charter Act, 1834—Penalties　12 Q. B. D. 605
See BANKER—NOTES.

—— Conditional payment,—Bankruptcy notice
[12 Q. B. D. 506
See BANKRUPTCY—ACT OF BANKRUPTCY. 6.

—— Joint note—Sureties—Contribution
[24 Ch. D. 709
See PRINCIPAL AND SURETY—CONTRIBUTION. 2.

—— Liability of parties　-　8 App. Cas. 733
See BILL OF EXCHANGE—LIABILITY OF PARTIES.

—— Statutory enactments respecting.
See BILL OF EXCHANGE—*Statutes.*

PROMOTER OF COMPANY—Contract by
[16 Ch. D. 125
See COMPANY—CONTRACT. 2.

—— Contract by—Costs of formation of company　-　-　25 Ch. D. 103
See COMPANY—FORMATION.

—— Fiduciary relation—Secret profit　17 Ch. D.
See BANKRUPTCY—PROOF. 22.　[122

—— Misrepresentation by　-　20 Ch. D. 27 ;
[9 App. Cas. 187
See COMPANY—PROSPECTUS. 1.

—— Qualification of director　-　27 Ch. D. 322
See COMPANY — DIRECTOR'S QUALIFICATION. 2.

—— Railway company—Deposit　28 Ch. D. 652
See RAILWAY COMPANY—ABANDONMENT. 3.

PROOF OF DEBTS—Administration of estate
[17 Ch. D. 342; 18 Ch. D. 370 ;
[20 Ch. D. 545
See EXECUTOR—ACTIONS. 19, 20, 21.

—— Bankruptcy.
See Cases under BANKRUPTCY—PROOF.

—— Bankruptcy Act, 1883.
See BANKRUPTCY — BANKRUPTCY ACT. 1883—*Statutes.*

—— Bankruptcy—Amendment of　14 Q. B. D. 121
See BANKRUPTCY—SECURED CREDITOR. 12.

—— Bankruptcy—Breach of covenant　22 Ch. D.
See BANKRUPTCY—DISTRESS. 5.　[410

—— Bankruptcy — Rejection of — Appeal — Notice of motion　-　14 Q. B. D. 385
See BANKRUPTCY—APPEAL. 14.

—— Bankruptcy—Secured creditor
[19 Ch. D. 105 ; 8 App. Cas. 606
See BANKRUPTCY—SECURED CREDITOR. 7, 8.

—— Winding-up of company　17 Ch. D. 337 ;
[28 Ch. D. 634; 30 Ch. D. 629
See COMPANY—PROOF. 1, 2, 3.

—— Winding-up of company　18 Ch. D. 587
See COMPANY—DEBENTURES. 2.

—— Winding-up—Secured creditor　16 Ch. D. 590
See COMPANY—SECURED CREDITOR. 2.

PROPERTY—Bankrupt.
See Cases under BANKRUPTCY—ASSETS.

—— Dead body　-　-　20 Ch. D. 659
See EXECUTOR—POWERS. 3.

PROPERTY—*continued*.

—— Infant
　　See Cases under INFANT—PROPERTY.

—— Lunatic.
　　See Cases under LUNATIC—PROPERTY.

—— Passing of—Indorsement of bill of lading
　　　　[13 Q. B. D. 159; 10 App. Cas. 74
　　See SHIP—BILL OF LADING. 4.

—— Railway company -　　- 6 Q. B. D. 36;
　　　　[9 Q. B. D. 424; 13 Q. B. D. 320
　　See RAILWAY COMPANY—PROPERTY. 1,
　　2, 3.

—— Recovered—Solicitor's lien
　　See Cases under SOLICITOR—LIEN. 1—7.

PROSECUTION—Expenses before magistrate.
　　See JUSTICES—PRACTICE—*Statutes.*

PROSPECTUS.
　　See Cases under COMPANY—PROSPECTUS.

PROTECTED TRANSACTION—Bankruptcy.
　　See Cases under BANKRUPTCY — PRO-
　　TECTED TRANSACTION.

—— Equitable execution　　-　16 Ch. D. 544
　　See PRACTICE—SUPREME COURT—RE-
　　CEIVER. 1.

—— Winding-up -　　-　-　28 Ch. D. 634
　　See COMPANY—PROOF. 3.

PROTECTION OF ESTATE—Costs incurred by
　　tenant for life -　16 Ch. D. 587, 588, n.
　　See TRUSTEE RELIEF ACT. 4, 5.

—— Settled estates.
　　See SETTLED LAND ACT—*Statutes.*

PROTECTION OF POST-OFFICES AND LETTERS.
　　See POST-OFFICE—*Statutes.*

PROTECTION OF PROPERTY — Practice — In-
　　junction　　-　　21 Ch. D. 490
　　See PRACTICE—SUPREME COURT—IN-
　　JUNCTION. 6.

PROTECTOR OF SETTLEMENT—Estate tail—
　　Appointment by settlor　16 Ch. D. 176
　　See TENANT IN TAIL. 2.

—— Lunacy　　-　　-　　20 Ch. D. 320
　　See LUNATIC—PROPERTY. 3.

**PROVIDENT NOMINATIONS AND SMALL IN-
TESTACIES ACT, 1883.**
　　See FRIENDLY SOCIETY—*Statutes.*

PROVISIONAL SPECIFICATION—Patent
　　See PATENT—VALIDITY. 2. [21 Ch. D. 720

PROXIMATE CAUSE—Negligence 11 Q. B. D. 776
　　See ESTOPPEL—CONDUCT. 3.

PROXY—General meeting of shareholders
　　　　　　　　[23 Ch. D. 14
　　See COMPANY—MANAGEMENT. 4.

PUBLIC BODY—Nuisance by -　20 Ch. D. 595;
　　　　　[22 Ch. D. 221; 23 Ch. D. 767
　　See NUISANCE—REMEDIES. 4, 5, 6.

—— Nuisance by -　　-　　29 Ch. D. 39
　　See NUISANCE—DEFINITION.

PUBLIC HEALTH ACTS.
　　See Cases and Statutes under LOCAL
　　GOVERNMENT.

PUBLIC-HOUSE.
　　See Cases and Statutes under INN.

—— Covenant not to keep -　16 Ch. D. 645, 718
　　See LANDLORD AND TENANT—LEASE. 6, 7.

PUBLIC-HOUSE—*continued.*

—— Covenant not to sell land for　19 Ch. D. 258
　　See COVENANT—RUNNING WITH LAND. 1.

—— Covenant to buy beer of landlord
　　　　　　　　[13 Ch. D. 199
　　See LANDLORD AND TENANT—LEASE. 8.

—— Goodwill　　-　　-　-　16 Ch. D. 226
　　See BANKRUPTCY—DISTRESS. 2.

PUBLIC LIBRARY.
　　*The Act 47 & 48 Vict. c. 37 (the Public Libra-
ries Act, 1884), amends the Public Libraries Act,
1855, and gives power to establish a library,
museum, or school of art in connection with any
other of such institutions.*

—— **Meeting of Ratepayers** — *Poll — Public
Libraries Act, 1855 (18 & 19 Vict. c. 70), s. 6—
Public Libraries Amendment Act (England and
Scotland), 1866 (29 & 30 Vict. c. 114), ss. 5, 7—
Public Libraries Amendment Act, 1877 (40 & 41
Vict. c. 54), s. 1.]* A meeting of ratepayers was
summoned for the purpose of determining whether
the provisions of the Public Libraries Act should
be adopted in the Defendants' district.. A chairman having been chosen, the resolution to adopt
the Acts was carried upon a show of hands; a
poll was demanded, but the chairman refused to
grant it. The Defendants declined to put in
force the Acts :—*Held,* that the right to demand
a poll existed by the Common Law, and had not
been taken away by any of the provisions contained in the Public Libraries Acts, and that the
Defendants could not be compelled by mandamus
to carry out the Acts. THE QUEEN *v.* WIM-
BLEDON LOCAL BOARD　　8 Q. B. D. 459

PUBLIC OFFICER—Suit against 6 App. Cas. 619
　　See COLONIAL LAW—NATAL. 1.

PUBLIC POLICY 7 Q. B. D. 548; 15 Q. B. D. 561
　　See CONTRACT—VALIDITY. 1, 2.

PUBLIC PROSECUTOR.
　　See CRIMINAL LAW—PRACTICE—*Statutes.*

PUBLIC RECREATION—Land for—Power to
　　make road over　　-　6 App. Cas. 833
　　See SCOTCH LAW—HIGHWAY. 1.

PUBLIC REGISTER—Jersey -　8 App. Cas. 542
　　See COLONIAL LAW—JERSEY. 2.

PUBLIC WORSHIP ACT.
　　See Cases under PRACTICE—ECCLESIASTI-
　　CAL—PUBLIC WORSHIP ACT.

PUBLICATION—Drama—Copyright　21 Ch. D.
　　See COPYRIGHT—DRAMATIC. 3.　[232

—— Lecture—Copyright　　-　26 Ch. D. 374
　　See COPYRIGHT—BOOKS. 2.

—— Libel -　　　-　　11 Q. B. D. 43
　　See DEFAMATION—PRIVILEGE. 3.

—— Patent　　-　　　21 Ch. D. 720
　　See PATENT—VALIDITY. 2.

PUBLICI JURIS—Trade-mark—Registration
　　　　　　　　[26 Ch. D. 409
　　See TRADE-MARK—REGISTRATION. 16.

PUBLISHER—Registration of copyright
　　See COPYRIGHT—BOOKS 3. [23 Ch. D. 727

PURCHASE-MONEY—Advanced by trustee
　　　　　　　　[22 Ch. D. 255
　　See TRUSTEE—INDEMNITY. 2.

PURCHASE-MONEY—*continued*.

—— Application of—Settled Land Act.
　　See Cases under SETTLED LAND ACT—
　　PURCHASE-MONEY.

—— Authority to receive　-　24 Ch. D. 387 ;
　　　　　　　　　　　　　　[27 Ch. D. 592
　　See VENDOR AND PURCHASER—CONVEY-
　　ANCE. 5, 6.

—— Devise of estate—Ademption　30 Ch. D. 92
　　See WILL—WORDS.

—— Duty on　-　　8 App. Cas. 309
　　See COLONIAL LAW—CAPE OF GOOD
　　HOPE. 3.

—— Interest on　-　-　27 Ch. D. 555
　　See VENDOR AND PURCHASER—CONDI-
　　TIONS OF SALE. 10.

—— Interest on—Lands Clauses Act
　　　　　　　　　　　[18 Ch. D. 146
　　See LANDS CLAUSES ACTS—COMPULSORY
　　POWERS. 5.

—— Interest on—Payment by mistake
　　　　　　　　　　　[29 Ch. D. 691
　　See VENDOR AND PURCHASER—CONDI-
　　TIONS OF SALE. 2.

—— Land in foreign country—Parties in Eng-
　　land　-　-　　23 Ch. D. 743
　　See JURISDICTION. 1.

PURCHASE-MONEY—*continued*.

—— Lands Clauses Act—Investment.
　　See Cases under LANDS CLAUSES ACT—
　　PURCHASE-MONEY.

—— Leasehold for lives—Settled Estates Act
　　　　　　　　　　　[18 Ch. D. 624
　　See LEASEHOLD—RENEWABLE LEASE. 3.

—— Mortgaged estate—Second mortgagee
　　　　　　　　　　　[29 Ch. D. 954
　　See MORTGAGE—REDEMPTION. 5.

—— Reinvestment—Private Act—Costs
　　　　　　　　　　　[17 Ch. D. 378
　　See PRACTICE—SUPREME COURT—COSTS.
　　39.

—— Vendor's lien for　-　-　21 Ch. D. 243 ;
　　　　　　　　　　　　　[26 Ch. D. 501
　　See VENDOR AND PURCHASER—LIEN. 1, 2.

PURCHASE WITHOUT NOTICE　20 Ch. D. 611
　　See VENDOR AND PURCHASER — PUR-
　　CHASE WITHOUT NOTICE. 1.

—— Conveyance obtained by undue influence
　　See UNDUE INFLUENCE.　[18 Ch. D. 188

—— Debentures—Estoppel　-　24 Ch. D. 85
　　See COMPANY—DEBENTURES. 3.

—— Negligence—Priority　　29 Ch. D. 725
　　See MORTGAGE—PRIORITY. 9.

Q.

QUALIFICATION—Director　25 Ch. D. 283 ;
　　　　　　　　　　　　[27 Ch. D. 322
　　See COMPANY — DIRECTOR'S QUALIFCA-
　　TIONS. 1, 2.

QUANTUM MERUIT—Barrister—Law of Que-
　　bec　-　-　-　9 App. Cas. 745
　　See COLONIAL LAW—CANADA—QUEBEC.
　　7.

QUARE IMPEDIT—Consolidated benefice—Right
　　of presentation　15 Q. B. D. 432
　　See ADVOWSON. 2.

—— Refusal of bishop to institute clerk—Offences
　　against ecclesiastical law
　　　　　　　　　　　[12 Q. B. D. 404
　　See ECCLESIASTICAL LAW—BISHOP.

QUARTER SESSIONS　-　-　8 Q. B. D. 586
　　See SESSIONS.

QUEBEC—Law of.
　　See Cases under COLONIAL LAW —
　　CANADA—QUEBEC.

QUEEN'S BENCH—Canada　-　6 App. Cas. 644
　　See COLONIAL LAW—CANADA—ONTARIO.
　　1.

QUESTION OF TITLE.
　　See HUSBAND AND WIFE — MARRIED
　　WOMEN'S PROPERTY ACTS—*Statutes*.

QUIA TIMET ACTION—Pollution of stream
　　　　　　　　　　　[28 Ch. D. 688
　　See NUISANCE—REMEDIES. 1.

—— Trustee—Indemnity　　22 Ch. D. 561
　　See TRUSTEE—INDEMNITY. 3.

"QUICQUID PLANTATUR SOLO SOLO CEDIT."
　　　　　[7 Q. B. D. 295 ; 8 App. Cas. 195
　　See MINE—WORKING. 1.

QUIT RENT—Redemption of.
　　See RENT-CHARGE—*Statutes*.

QUORUM—Directors of company　23 Ch. D. 413
　　See COMPANY—SHARES—ALLOTMENT. 3.

—— Local board　-　-　30 Ch. D. 350
　　See LOCAL GOVERNMENT—LOCAL AU-
　　THORITY. 15.

R.

RAILWAY—Bookstands on platform—Poor-rate
　　　　　　　　　[10 Q. B. D. 327
　See POOR-RATE—OCCUPATION. 1.
—— Bridge over—Paving expenses
　　　　　[9 Q. B. D. 412 ; 8 App. Cas. 687
　See METROPOLIS—MANAGEMENT ACTS.
　12.
—— Construction.
　See RAILWAY COMPANY—CONSTITUTION
　—*Gazette.*
—— Penalty for travelling with intent to avoid
　payment of fare—Justices—Procedure
　　　　　　　　　[8 Q. B. D. 151
　See JUSTICES—PRACTICE. 4.
—— Transfer of—Canada　　7 App. Cas. 178
　See COLONIAL LAW — CANADA—DOMI-
　NION. 1.

RAILWAY COMMISSIONERS.
　See Cases and Statutes under RAILWAY
　COMPANY — RAILWAYS REGULATION
　ACTS.

RAILWAY COMPANY :—

—— Lands Clauses Act.
　See LANDS CLAUSES ACT.

I. RAILWAY COMPANY—ABANDONMENT.

1. —— **Parliamentary Deposit** — *Judgment Creditor—Undertaking—Receiver—Unpaid Calls—Railway Companies Act, 1867 (30 & 31 Vict. c. 127), ss. 4, 31, 35—Abandonment of Railways Act, 1869 (32 & 33 Vict. c. 114).]* A railway company which has never commenced to acquire the lands or construct the railways authorized by their Act is not an "undertaking," within the meaning of sect. 4 of the Railways Companies Act, 1867, of which a receiver can be appointed under that section.—*Semble,* the powers of a receiver appointed under the above section do not extend to getting in unpaid calls. *In re* BIRMINGHAM AND LICHFIELD JUNCTION RAILWAY COMPANY
　　　　　　　　　[18 Ch. D. 155

2. —— **Parliamentary Deposit**—*Landowner—Diminution of Value of Land — Measure of Damages.]* A railway company being about to apply for an Act of Parliament for making an extension line, assented to F., an owner of land over which the line was intended to pass, commencing the line over his own land. F. accordingly made an embankment over his land, and

I. RAILWAY COMPANY — ABANDONMENT—
continued.

was paid for the work by the company. After a considerable part of the work on F.'s land had been done the company obtained their Act giving power to construct the railway in the proposed line. The Act contained a proviso that if the new line were not opened for traffic within five years the parliamentary deposit should be applied towards compensating landowners or other persons whose land had been interfered with or rendered less valuable "by the commencement, construction or abandonment of the railway." The extension railway was not completed within five years, but no warrant of abandonment was obtained under the Railways Abandonment Act. A fresh Act was passed authorizing a petition for winding up the company and the sale of the undertaking by the official liquidator.—A petition having been presented by F.'s mortgagees and the trustee in his liquidation for the application of the parliamentary deposit in compensation for the injury done to his estate by the commencement, construction, or abandonment of the works :—*Held,* that the undertaking was abandoned within the meaning of the Act ;—That the words "commencement, construction, or abandonment," must be read disjunctively :—That F., having commenced the works on his own land before the company had obtained their Act, on the speculation that they would obtain power to construct the railway, the Petitioners had no claim for compensation for injury to the estate by the commencement or construction of the railway ; but they had a claim for compensation for injury done by the abandonment of the railway :—That the measure of injury must be determined by comparing the value of the estate immediately before with its value immediately after the abandonment.—Whether the words "commencement of the railway" must be confined to its commencement by the company under its parliamentary powers, or would include its commencement in anticipation of such powers, *quære.*—*Held,* also that mortgagees of the landowner might be persons entitled to claim compensation under the Act. *In re* POTTERIES, SHREWSBURY, AND NORTH WALES RAILWAY COMPANY　25 Ch. D. 251

3. —— **Parliamentary Deposit** — *Promoters and Parliamentary Agents.]* Under the usual provision, in an Act incorporating a railway company, that in the event of the undertaking being abortive the parliamentary deposit shall either be forfeited to the Crown, or, in the discretion of the Court, be wholly or in part applied, as part of the assets of the company, for the benefit of the creditors thereof, the Court will not apply the deposit for the benefit of all the creditors without distinction as to the nature and merit of their claims ; and, accordingly the promoters and the parliamentary agents claiming in respect of costs incurred in obtaining the Act, or in relation to the promotion of the company, not being

2 T

I. RAILWAY COMPANY — ABANDONMENT —
continued.

"meritorious creditors" (*In re Lowestoft, Yarmouth, and Southwold Tramways Company* (6 Ch. D. 484)), will not be admitted to share in the distribution of the fund. *In re* BIRMINGHAM AND LICHFIELD JUNCTION RAILWAY COMPANY
[28 Ch. D. 652

II. RAILWAY COMPANY — BY-LAWS.

—— Validity and Construction—8 & 9 *Vict. c.* 20, *ss.* 108, 109.] By a by-law of a railway company "any person travelling without special permission of the company duly authorized servant of the company, in a' carriage or by a train of a class superior to that for which his ticket was issued, is hereby subject to a penalty not exceeding 40*s.*, and shall, in addition, be liable to pay his fare according to the class of carriage in which he is travelling from the station where the train originally started, unless he shews that he had no intention to defraud." The Defendant, with the intention of defrauding the company, travelled in a carriage of a superior class to that for which his ticket was issued, and having been charged under the by-law was convicted in a penalty of 10*s.* and costs :—*Held*, that the by-law was illegal and void, for assuming that it could be divided after the words "penalty of 40*s.*" and that each part was capable of being enforced apart from the other, the first part was repugnant to 8 & 9 Vict. c. 20, s. 103, which makes a fraudulent intention the gist of the offence of travelling without having paid the fare, and that, if taken as a whole and indivisible, it was unreasonable according to *Watson* v. *London and Brighton Railway Company* (4 C. P. D. 118), and *Saunders* v. *South Eastern Railway Company* (5 Q. B. D. 456) :— *Held*, further, that the conviction must be quashed, for it was founded upon the by-law, and could not be upheld as disclosing an offence under 8 & 9 Vict. c. 20, s. 103. DYSON v. LONDON AND NORTH WESTERN RAILWAY COMPANY   7 Q. B. D. 32

III. RAILWAY COMPANY — CONSTITUTION.

Railways Construction Facilities Act, 1864.] *Rule made by Board of Trade under sect.* 64 *of this Act with respect to application for a certificate for promoters.* Sept. 4*th*, 1883 L. G., 1883, p. 4361

1. —— Borrowing Powers—*Sale and Hiring of Rolling Stock—Ultra vires act—30 & 31 Vict.* c. 127, s. 4—*Rights of Debenture Holders.*] A Railway Company being in want of money, and being advised that they had no power to borrow, sold part of their rolling-stock to a Wagon Company for £30,000, at the same time making a contract with the Wagon Company for the hire of the same rolling-stock at a rent which would repay the £30,000 with interest in five years, and then for its re-purchase at a nominal price. At the same time three of the directors guaranteed to the Wagon Company the payment of the rent.—The Wagon Company brought an action against the Railway Company and the sureties for non-payment of rent due.—Kay, J., having held that the transaction was void as against the Railway Company, but could be enforced against the sureties: —*Held*, by the Court of Appeal, that the transaction was not a borrowing of money, but a bonâ fide sale and hiring of the rolling-stock, and was

III. RAILWAY COMPANY — CONSTITUTION —
continued.

valid both against the Railway Company and the sureties.—Observations on the rights of debenture holders over the rolling stock of a railway company. YORKSHIRE RAILWAY WAGON COMPANY v. MACLURE   19 Ch. D. 478 ; 21 Ch. D. 309

IV. RAILWAY COMPANY — LIABILITIES.

1. —— Cattle Station—*Nuisance—Additional Lands.*] A railway company were by their Act authorized, among other things, to carry cattle, and were also authorized to purchase by agreement (in addition to the lands which they were empowered to purchase compulsorily) any lands not exceeding in the whole fifty acres, in such places as should be deemed eligible, for the purpose of providing additional station yards, &c., for receiving, loading, or keeping any cattle or any goods, &c., conveyed or intended to be conveyed by the railway, and for making convenient ways thereto, or for any other purposes connected with the undertaking which the company should judge requisite; and they were empowered to sell the additional lands, and to purchase in lieu thereof other lands which they should deem more eligible for their additional purposes, and afterwards to sell the same as aforesaid, and so from time to time. The company bought under this power a piece of land adjoining one of their stations and used it as a cattle dock. The noise of the cattle and drovers was a nuisance to the occupiers of certain houses near the station, and they brought an action to restrain the company from continuing the nuisance :—*Held* (affirming the decision of North, J.), that the Plaintiffs were entitled to an injunction, for that there was nothing in the Act which by necessary implication authorized the creation of a nuisance on the additional lands. TRUMAN v. LONDON, BRIGHTON, AND SOUTH COAST RAILWAY COMPANY   25 Ch. D. 423 ; 29 Ch. D. 89 [Reversed by the House of Lords, 11 App. Cas. 45.]

2. —— "Detention"—*Reduced Rate—Conditions — Wrongful Refusal to deliver at end of Transit—Mistake as to whether Carriage was paid.*] The Plaintiff delivered cattle, carriage prepaid, to the Defendant railway company for carriage on the terms of signed conditions whereby, in consideration of an alternative reduced rate, it was agreed that the company were "not to be liable in respect of any loss or detention of or injury to the said animals, or any of them, in the receiving, forwarding, or delivery thereof, except upon proof that such loss, detention, or injury, arose from the wilful misconduct of the company or its servants." —The cattle were carried; but, on application made for them by the Plaintiff, the Defendants, in consequence of their clerk having negligently omitted to enter the cattle on the consignment note as "carriage paid," refused to deliver them, and alleged that the carriage was not paid. The cattle were kept exposed to the weather until the next day, when the mistake having been ascertained, they were delivered. They were damaged by the exposure. In an action for damages by reason of wrongful detention and negligence :— *Held*, that the withholding of the cattle, under a groundless claim to retain them, at the end of the transit, was not "detention" within the condi-

IV. RAILWAY COMPANY — LIABILITIES — *continued.*

tions, and the company were therefore liable.
GORDON *v.* GREAT WESTERN RAILWAY COMPANY
[8 **Q. B. D. 44**

3. —— Power to underpin Buildings—*Adjoining Lands—Retaining Wall of Railway—Wall built with double Object.*] A railway company had power to underpin or strengthen buildings on lands adjoining their line. They carried their line in a deep cutting close beside a building belonging to the Plaintiffs, and having given the required notice that they intended to underpin this building, they made a wall of concrete to support the Plaintiffs' building, part of the thickness of which was under the Plaintiffs' building, and part on the company's land, the whole wall forming the retaining wall of the railway cutting : —*Held* (reversing the decision of Chitty, J.), that the fact that the concrete wall was also the retaining wall of the railway did not make it the less an "underpinning" within the meaning of the Act; and therefore that the company had not acted beyond their powers in making the wall on the Plaintiffs' land. STEVENS *v.* METROPOLITAN DISTRICT RAILWAY COMPANY　　29 **Ch. D. 60**

V. RAILWAY COMPANY—PASSENGER DUTY.

The Act 46 & 47 Vict. c. 34, amends the law relating to Railway Passenger Duty, and amends and consolidates the law relating to the Conveyance of the Queen's Forces by Railway.

Sect. 1. Act to be cited as the Cheap Trains Act, 1883.

By sect. 2 fares not exceeding the rate of a penny are exempt from duty ; but fares for return or periodical tickets are exempt from duty only where the ordinary fare for the single journey does not exceed that rate.

Duty is payable at the rate of two per cent. on fares exceeding the rate of one penny a mile, or conveyance between railway stations within one urban district certified so to be in manner provided in the section.

Where the Board of Trade are satisfied that any two or more railway stations are within an area which has a continuous urban as distinguished from a rural or suburban character, and contains a population of not less than 100,000 inhabitants, the Board of Trade may certify that those stations are within one urban district for the purposes of the Act.

Power to Board of Trade at any time to rescind or vary any certificate given under the section.

Sect. 3 provides for proper third-class accommodation and workmen's trains.

Sect. 4. Provision as to special mileage and exceptional charges.

Sect. 5. Proviso as to fractions of miles.

Sect. 6 provides for the conveyance at reduced rates of the Queen's Forces on any occasion of public service.

Sect. 7 amends sections 4 and 7 of the Act 5 & 6 Vict. c. 79.

Sect. 8. Definitions.

Sect. 9. Commencement of Act—1st Oct. 1883.

Sect. 10 repeals—

5 & 6 Vict. c. 55, s. 20.
7 & 8 Vict c. 85, ss. 6—10, and s. 12.
16 & 17 Vict. c. 69, s. 18.
21 & 22 Vict. c. 75, ss. 1 and 2.
26 & 27 Vict. c. 33, s. 14.

V. RAILWAY COMPANY—PASSENGER DUTY
—continued.

—— Duty upon Sums charged to cover Duty
—*Conveyance of Passengers — Duty upon Sum charged for Sleeping Accommodation—5 & 6 Vict. c. 79, s. 2.*] By the 2nd section of 5 & 6 Vict. c. 79, and the schedule to that Act, a duty at the rate of 5 per cent. is made payable upon all sums received or charged for the hire, fare, or conveyance of passengers conveyed for hire upon any railway. The Defendants, by a local Act, were prohibited from charging to their passengers more than certain specified sums per mile, which sums were to include all expenses incidental to their conveyance, except government duty. The Defendants, in addition to the sum charged by them to their passengers for conveyance, charged to and received from such passengers a further sum at the rate of 5 per cent. on the former, to cover the government duty. The Crown claimed duty on the latter sum as well as on the former :—*Held,* affirming the decision of the Exchequer Division, that the Crown was entitled to duty on the whole amount received from the passengers, even though such amount should exceed the maximum charge for conveyance fixed by the local Act.—The Defendants attached to certain of their night trains sleeping carriages for the accommodation of such of their first-class passengers as might choose to avail themselves of it. For the use of these carriages such passengers were charged an extra sum in addition to the ordinary first-class fare. In addition to couches with pillows, sheets, and blankets, each carriage contained a lavatory, water-closet, and other conveniences. Passengers using such carriages were not disturbed during the night by demands for their tickets; and if they arrived at their destination in the middle of the night the carriage was put into a siding, and the passengers allowed to remain in their beds until the morning. A special servant was employed to wait upon them, call them in the morning, and bring them hot water. The Crown claimed duty upon the sums charged to passengers for the accommodation provided in the sleeping carriages :—*Held,* affirming the decision of the Exchequer Division, that such accommodation was incidental to the conveyance of the passengers, and that the Crown was entitled to the duty claimed. ATTORNEY-GENERAL *v.* LONDON AND NORTH WESTERN RAILWAY COMPANY　　6 **Q. B. D. 216**

VI. RAILWAY COMPANY—PASSENGER'S LUGGAGE.

1. —— Delivery to Passenger—*Termination of Company's Risk.*] The Plaintiff arrived at a station on the Defendants' railway with her luggage contained in two boxes which were taken from the luggage-van by a porter in the employ of the company. The porter asked the Plaintiff if he should engage a cab for her. In reply she said she would walk to her destination, and would leave her luggage at the station for a short time, and send for it. The porter said : "All right; I'll put them on one side and take care of them ;" Thereupon the Plaintiff quitted the station leaving her boxes in the custody of the porter. One of them was lost :—*Held,* that the transaction amounted to a delivery of the luggage by the

2 T 2

VI. RAILWAY COMPANY—PASSENGER'S LUGGAGE—*continued.*

company to the Plaintiff, and a re-delivery of it by her to the porter as her agent to take care of, and that consequently the company were not responsible for the loss.—*Patscheider* v. *Great Western Ry. Co.* (3 Ex. D. 153) distinguished. HODKINSON *v.* LONDON AND NORTH WESTERN RAILWAY COMPANY - **14 Q. B. D. 228**

VII. RAILWAY COMPANY—PROPERTY.

1. —— **Dock Company**—*Railway ancillary to Docks—" Company " — Railway Companies Act, 1867* (30 & 31 *Vict. c.* 127), *ss.* 3, 4.] The protection against seizure in execution afforded by the Railway Companies Act, 1867, ss. 3, 4, applies to the railway plant of every company constituted by a statute for the purpose of constructing or working a railway, even although the railway is merely a subordinate and ancillary part of the undertaking authorized by the statute.—By two local statutes a company was authorized to construct a wet dock, a lock forming an entrance to the dock, and two short railways, each about half a mile long, to connect the dock with other railways. The Plaintiffs had lent money to the company upon mortgage-debentures. The Defendants were creditors of the company, and having obtained judgment seized in execution certain railway plant belonging to it. The Plaintiffs having brought an action for an injunction to prevent the Defendants from realizing their execution :—*Held,* that the dock company was a " company " within the Railway Companies Act, 1867, sect. 3, and that the railway plant belonging to it was protected from seizure by sect. 4. GREAT NORTHERN RAILWAY COMPANY *v.* TAHOURDIN **13 Q. B. D. 320**

2. —— **Execution**—*Judgment Creditor—Protection of Rolling Stock and Plant—Railway Companies Act, 1867* (30 & 31 *Vict. c.* 127), *ss.* 4, 23.] The protection from seizure in execution by a judgment creditor, given by the Railway Companies Act, 1867, s. 4, to the rolling stock and plant of a railway, after such railway is open for public traffic, continues although the railway is afterwards closed for traffic. MIDLAND WAGGON COMPANY *v.* POTTERIES, SHREWSBURY, AND NORTH WALES RAILWAY COMPANY **6 Q. B. D. 36**

3. —— **Land required for Undertaking** — *Lands Clauses Act, 1845* (8 & 9 *Vict. c.* 18), *s.* 127)— *Adverse Possession—Statutes of Limitation,* 3 & 4 *Will.* 4, *c.* 27, *s.* 7 ; 37 & 38 *Vict. c.* 57, *s.* 1—*Evidence.*] The mere fact that land of a railway company is required for the purposes of their undertaking, and is not superfluous land, does not prevent an occupier who has exclusive adverse possession for twelve years becoming thereby entitled to the land under the Statutes of Limitations. BOBBETT *v.* SOUTH EASTERN RAILWAY COMPANY **9 Q. B. D. 424**

VIII. RAILWAY COMPANY — RAILWAYS CLAUSES ACT.

1. —— **Accommodation Works**—*Compulsory Powers—Railways Clauses Consolidation Act, 1845* (8 & 9 *Vict. c.* 20), *ss.* 15, 16, 68—*Discretion of Company as to the most convenient Mode of doing the Works.*] Lands required by a railway company for accommodation works are lands required for the purposes of " the undertaking " or " of the

railway."—Every work which a railway company is empowered to do, not merely what it is compelled to do, is a purpose of the undertaking.— The word " necessary " in the 68th section of the Railways Clauses Consolidation Act, 1845, refers to the obligation to make good the interruption, and does not confine the company to any particular mode of doing the works. Where there are several modes of doing the works, the company, acting under the advice of their engineer, are the sole judges which mode should be adopted : but if they do not act bonâ fide the Court will interfere.—A railway company having intersected the lands of two adjoining landowners, A. and B., by an embankment, proposed to connect the severed portions of A.'s land by an arch through the embankment, and to give B. a right of way through the same arch, which they proposed to connect with his land by an occupation road carried through A.'s land. The strip of A.'s land proposed to be taken for this road was included in the lands delineated. A. objected to this arrangement as being beyond the powers of the company :—*Held* (reversing the decision of Kay, J.), that the company had power to take the strip of land compulsorily for the proposed purpose. WILKINSON *v.* HULL, &c., RAILWAY AND DOCK COMPANY - **20 Ch. D. 323**

2. —— **Carrier**—8 & 9 *Vict. c.* 20, *s.* 90—" *Passing only over the same Portion of the Line*"— " *Under the like circumstances*"—" *In favour of or against any particular Person*"—*Unequal Tolls— Group Rates—Undue Preference — Railway and Canal Traffic Act,* 1854 (17 & 18 *Vict. c.* 31), *ss.* 2, 3, 6—*Action for Breach of Railway and Canal Traffic Act,* 1854, *whether maintainable.*] No action will lie in respect of any breach of the provisions of the Railway and Canal Traffic Act, 1854, s. 2.— Judgment of the Queen's Bench Division as to this point affirmed.—A railway company carried coals eastwards to various towns from a group of collieries situate at different points along their line, and charged one uniform set of rates in respect of the carriage to all the collieries comprised in the group. In an action for overcharges by the owners of the colliery lying furthest eastwards :— *Held,* that inasmuch as the terminus of the transit over the company's line differed with respect to each colliery comprised in the group, the company had not contravened the provisions of the Railways Clauses Consolidation Act, 1845, s. 90, and therefore were not liable in the action. —Judgment of the Queen's Bench Division as to this point reversed. — A railway company carried coal from certain collieries, including the D. colliery, situate in the Y. coalfield, to the port of G., where a line of steamers called which traded to the West Indies; in order to introduce the coal carried by them to the West Indian market, the railway company agreed to allow B. 8*d.* per ton in respect of all coal shipped on board the steamers in order to be carried to the West Indies. The railway company agreed also to allow B. 6*d.* per ton upon all coal shipped for certain ports, in view of the anticipated advantage to themselves by the increased tonnage

VIII. RAILWAY COMPANY, — RAILWAYS CLAUSES ACT—*continued.*

· to be carried over their line. The owners of the D. colliery also sent coals over the line of the railway company to the same port of G., but not for shipment to the West Indies or to the ports above-mentioned, and claimed to recover from the railway company overcharges in respect of the coal thus sent by them, on the ground of the allowances of 8*d.* per ton and 6*d.* per ton made to B. :—*Held,* as to the coals carried by the railway company for B. from the Y. coalfield other than those coming from the D. colliery, that the termini of the transit from the collieries being different, the owners of the D. colliery could not recover for overcharges :—*Held,* as to the coals carried by the railway company for B. coming from the D. colliery, on the authority of *Great Western Ry. Co.* v. *Sutton* (Law Rep. 4 H. L. 226), and *London and North Western Ry. Co.* v. *Evershed* (3 App. Cas. 1029), that the railway company, by making the allowances of 8*d.* per ton and 6*d.* per ton, had contravened the Railways Clauses Consolidation Act, 1845, s. 90, but that the owners of the D. colliery had not proved any damage by reason of the allowances to B., and therefore could not recover from the railway company for overcharges.—A railway company were carriers of coal for B. and J., who were coal merchants, to G. The trucks with the coals intended for them upon the arrival at G. were taken direct to their yards, and it cost the railway company less to deliver the trucks straight into the yards of B. and J., than to keep the trucks in the goods-yard of the company until the trucks should be unloaded. The railway company thereupon allowed B. sometimes 2*d.* and sometimes 6*d,* per ton, and J. 4*d.* per ton. B. and J. obtained coals from many collieries situate upon the line of the railway company, and the railway company, as might be convenient to them, returned the trucks of B. and J. to any colliery with which they had dealings. It was cheaper for the railway company to be at liberty to send the trucks at their pleasure to any colliery with which B. and J. had dealings than to be compelled to return them to a particular colliery, and therefore they allowed B. and J. a rebate of 2 per cent. upon their respective nett debits. The saving to the railway company did not adequately represent the allowances of 6*d.* or 4*d.* per ton, or the rebate of 2 per cent. The owners of a colliery also sent their coals along the line of the railway company to G., but their trucks were kept in the goods-yards of the railway company until they were unloaded, and after being unloaded were returned straight to the colliery. The owners of the colliery having claimed to recover from the railway company overcharges in respect of the allowance of 6*d.,* 2*d.,* and 4*d.* per ton, and of the rebate of 2 per cent. :—*Held,* that the railway company carried for B. and J. under circumstances different from those under which they carried for the owners of the colliery, and that the latter were not entitled to recover in respect of the alleged overcharges. MANCHESTER, SHEFFIELD, AND LINCOLNSHIRE RAILWAY COMPANY *v.* DENABY MAIN COLLIERY COMPANY   13 Q. B. D. 674; 14 Q. B. D. 209 [Affirmed in part, reversed in part, by the House of Lords.]

VIII. RAILWAY COMPANY — RAILWAYS CLAUSES ACT—*continued.*

3. —— Liability to fence—*Adjoining Lands —Railways Clauses Consolidation Act, 1845 (8 & 9 Vict. c. 20), s. 68—Injury to Cattle—Owner releasing Right to Accommodation Works—Rights of Occupier.*] The Plaintiff in 1846 became tenant from year to year of land belonging to one G. In 1847 the Defendants, a railway company, acquired part of the land in the exercise of their statutory powers, and by arrangement with G. paid him compensation in lieu of all accommodation works, including the right to have his land fenced from the railway, G. releasing the Defendants from their statutory obligation in that respect. The Defendants, however, made a fence of posts and rails between the land so occupied by the Plaintiff and a ditch in the Defendants' land adjoining the railway, and they planted a hedge on the side of the ditch nearest the railway itself, sufficient to prevent animals from straying thereon. They, however, neglected to keep up the posts and rails, and in consequence of their neglect to do so a cow belonging to the Plaintiff, in 1879, whilst the Plaintiff so continued in the occupation of the land under the original tenancy which had never been determined, fell into the ditch and was killed :—*Held,* affirming the decision of the Common Pleas Division, that the Defendants were liable for the loss of the cow, for that their arrangement with the owner did not exonerate them from their liability under the Railways Clauses Act, 1845 (8 & 9 Vict. c. 20), s. 68, to maintain the fence for the benefit of the occupier, and so as to prevent his cattle from straying from his land. CORRY *v.* GREAT WESTERN RAILWAY COMPANY -   6 Q. B. D. 237 ; [7 Q. B. D. 322

4. —— Mines—*Compulsory Purchase—Subsequent Purchase of Minerals under Lands previously acquired — " Expressly purchased " — Lands Clauses Consolidation Act, 1845 (8 & 9 Vict. c. 18), ss. 6, 16, et seq.—Railways Clauses Consolidation Act, 1845 (8 & 9 Vict. c. 20), ss. 6, 77, 78, 79.*] A railway company having the usual power to purchase lands under its special Act, has, by virtue of the 6th section of the Lands Clauses Act, 1845, power also to purchase the minerals under those lands compulsorily at any time before the expiration of the time limited for the exercise of its compulsory powers, if it should deem it advisable.— That power is not taken away by the 77th and following sections of the Railways Clauses Act, 1845, which are for the benefit not of the mine owner but of the company, and only exempt the company from the obligation of buying the minerals at once together with the surface lands.— The words " expressly purchased " in the 77th section are not to be confined to " purchased by agreement." There is no distinction between the severance of ownership vertically, that is, of the surface lands from the mines beneath, and the severance of ownership laterally by the taking by successive purchases of surface lands from the same landowner. So a railway company having already acquired surface lands may subsequently purchase compulsorily the minerals under those lands.—The opinion of the company's engineer, if

VIII. RAILWAY COMPANY — RAILWAYS CLAUSES ACT—*continued.*

bonâ fide, is the only evidence required by the Court as to the necessity or propriety of any purchase, and the onus of proving want of bona fides rests upon the party opposing the purchase:—Injunction granted against the company by Hall V.C., discharged. ERRINGTON *v.* METROPOLITAN DISTRICT RAILWAY COMPANY　　**19 Ch. D. 559**

5. —— Mines—*Minerals—Clay—Conveyance —Railways Clauses Consolidation Act,* 1845 *(8 & 9 Vict. c.* 20), *s.* 77.] The word "mines" in the 77th section of the Railways Clauses Act, 1845, includes minerals whether got by underground or by open workings; and therefore a bed of clay, on which the railway had been made, was as a mine excepted out of the conveyance of the land to the railway company, and might, unless the company were willing to make compensation to the landowner, be dug and worked by him. MIDLAND RAILWAY COMPANY *v.* HAUNCHWOOD BRICK AND TILE COMPANY　-　　**20 Ch. D. 552**

6. —— Mines—*Right of Owner to work Mines — Minerals under or near Railway — Mineral Estate intersected by Railway—Railways Clauses Consolidation Act,* 1845 *(8 & 9 Vict. c.* 20), *ss.* 77–82.] Sect. 80 of the Railways Clauses Consolidation Act, 1845, applies to minerals lying more than forty yards from a line of railway, and enables the owner of minerals, whose access to them is cut off, by reason of a railway company having purchased from him the minerals lying under their line of railway, or within forty yards from it, to tunnel under the railway for the purpose of working his minerals which are on the other side of it. And this power extends, not only to minerals in the ordinary sense of the word, but also to such a substance as clay, which is usually worked from the surface. — And by sect. 81 the mineral owner is entitled to be compensated by the company for any additional expense caused by his having to work the minerals in this way.—The Defendant was the owner of the minerals lying in and under a triangular piece of land, which was completely surrounded by three lines of railway belonging to the Plaintiffs, and also of the minerals lying under certain portions of those three lines. The company had purchased the surface of the triangular piece of land, and also the surface of the land on which those parts of the three lines were constructed. The minerals in and under the lands so purchased were not in the first instance purchased by the company. The Defendant, in April, 1885, gave the company notice, under sect. 78 of the Railways Clauses Consolidation Act, 1845, of his intention to work the minerals belonging to him in and under the triangular piece of land, and also under the lines of railway. The company gave the Defendant notice that they were willing to make compensation for the minerals under the lines of railway, and arbitrators were appointed to assess the compensation. The Defendant then gave the company notice that he intended to work the minerals in and under the triangular piece of land, and for that purpose to enter upon and across the line of railway:—*Held,* that such a mode of working would be a trespass, and that the Defendant must be restrained from working

VIII. RAILWAY COMPANY — RAILWAYS CLAUSES ACT—*continued.*

in that way, but that he would be entitled to tunnel under the railway in order to work the minerals in and under the triangular piece of land, and that the company must compensate him for the extra expense of so working. MIDLAND RAILWAY COMPANY *v.* MILES　-　**30 Ch. D. 634**

7. —— Mines—*Right of Support to Surface Land—Railways Clauses Consolidation Act,* 1845 *(8 & 9 Vict. c.* 20), *ss.* 77, 78, 79.] In 1865 the owner of land demised the minerals under it to the Defendant for a term of years, and in 1867 such owner conveyed the surface of the land to a railway company under the compulsory powers of the Lands Clauses Consolidation Act, 1845, which was incorporated with the company's special Act, and some years afterwards the company sold part of such land as superfluous land to persons who ultimately sold it to the Plaintiff. The railway company never purchased the minerals or made compensation to the Defendant as such lessee under the powers conferred on them by the Railways Clauses Consolidation Act, 1845, and the Defendant worked the mines in the usual manner of working in the district, and by so doing caused a subsidence which damaged some houses erected by the Plaintiff upon the land.—In an action against the Defendant for working the mines without leaving a sufficient support for the Plaintiff's land:—*Held,* that the Defendant had not interfered with any right of the Plaintiff, who could have no greater right than the railway company from whom he derived his title, and that upon the construction of sects. 77, 78, and 79 of the Railways Clauses Consolidation Act, 1845, if a railway company has exercised the option it has under that Act of purchasing land under their compulsory powers without the mines and minerals thereunder, the owner, lessee, or occupier of such mines and minerals has a right to work the same without regard to whether such working will let down the surface, provided the working is according to the usual way in the district. POUNTNEY *v.* CLAYTON　-　-　**11 Q. B. D. 820**

8. —— Siding—*Right to use—Landowner—Branch Railway—Renewing Junction—Board of Trade Order—Interlocking and Signalling Apparatus—Liability of Landowner—Removing Junction—Injunction—Regulation of Railways*—3 & 4 Vict. c. 97, s. 5—5 & 6 Vict. c. 55, ss. 4, 6, 12—*Railways Clauses Consolidation Act,* 1845, s. 76.] The Plaintiff, and his predecessors in title, as owners of land adjoining a single line of railway, had ever since the year 1861 used a junction siding connecting the railway with a foundry on their land, the siding being the only access to the foundry. The Defendants, the railway company, having doubled their line, the Board of Trade, acting on the report of their inspector and as a condition for certifying the line to be fit for traffic, required the company either to provide the junction of the siding with the modern and improved system of interlocking and signalling apparatus, or to remove the junction, which was of an old-fashioned description. The company then called upon the Plaintiff to execute the work or pay the costs of it, but this the Plaintiff declined to do, whereupon the company took up the junction

VIII. RAILWAY COMPANY — RAILWAYS CLAUSES ACT—*continued.*

points:—*Held*, by Bacon, V.C., that the Plaintiff had, under sect. 76 of the Railways Clauses Consolidation Act, 1845, a statutory right to the use of his siding in connection with the company's railway, the company's parliamentary powers being subject to that right; and an injunction was therefore granted restraining the company from continuing to prevent communication between his siding and the railway, and compelling the company to restore the junction.—*Powell Duffryn Steam Coal Company* v. *Taff Vale Railway Company* (Law Rep. 9 Ch. 331) distinguished. —*Held*, on appeal, that as the Plaintiff's predecessors in title had acquired a perpetual right to use the siding under a clause as to sidings in an old local Act for making a tramway, which had since been converted into the railway of the Defendants, and the subsequent Acts contained saving clauses sufficient to protect all rights acquired by the Plaintiff under the old Act, the case did not depend on the Railways Clauses Act, and that the Plaintiff retained the right acquired under the old Act to use the siding without contributing to the expense of the new apparatus, such Act containing nothing to oblige the Plaintiff to make or pay for the interlocking apparatus.—*Held*, also, that if the case had turned on the 76th section of the Railways Clauses Act, the Court would not have decided the question whether the Plaintiff was bound to pay for the interlocking apparatus, without first ascertaining what, in the year 1845, was included in the terms "offset plates" and " switches" used in that section. WOODRUFF *v.* BRECON AND MERTHYR TYDFIL JUNCTION RAILWAY COMPANY   **28 Ch. D. 190**

IX. RAILWAY COMPANY—RAILWAYS REGULATION ACTS.

Railway Commissioners.] *The Act 48 & 49 Vict. c. 59, continues the Regulation of Railways Acts, 1873 (37 & 38 Vict. c. 48), until the 31st of December, 1886.*

1. —— Arbitration— *Reference to Railway Commissioners—Jurisdiction of Railway Commissioners—Regulation of Railways Act, 1873 (36 & 37 Vict. c. 48), s. 8—Injunction—Prohibition.*] Two railway companies were empowered by a special Act to enter into a working agreement, but no provision was made respecting arbitration. The agreement made under this Act contained a clause providing that any difference between the companies should be determined by arbitration in accordance with the provisions of the Railway Arbitration Act, 1859. Differences having arisen, one of the companies called upon the Railway Commissioners to decide the differences under the 8th section of the Regulation of Railways Act, 1873.—The other company accordingly issued a writ for an injunction against the first company, which was amended by making the Railway Commissioners parties, and asking for a prohibition:—*Held* (reversing the decision of Jessel, M.R.), that the! Railway Commissioners had no jurisdiction to undertake the arbitration, and a prohibition was issued accordingly.—The clause in the 88th section of the Regulation of Railways Act, 1873, which enables one party to apply for the arbitration of the Railway Commissioners,

IX. RAILWAY COMPANY—RAILWAYS REGULATION ACTS—*continued.*

" where any difference between railway companies is, under the provisions of any general or special Act, required or authorized to be referred to arbitration," does not apply to all cases in which the agreement under which the difference has arisen has been made under the provisions of a general or special Act, but only to cases in which the specific difference has been required or authorized by a general or special Act to be referred to arbitration.—*Stokes Bay Railway and Pier Company* v. *London and South Western Railway Company* (2 Nev. & Mac. 143) and *Portpatrick Railway Company* v. *Caledonian Railway Company* (3 Nev. & Mac. 189) disapproved. GREAT WESTERN RAILWAY COMPANY *v.* WATERFORD AND LIMERICK RAILWAY COMPANY -   - **17 Ch. D. 493**

2. —— Costs—*Railway Commissioners—Successful Defendant not liable to be ordered to pay unsuccessful Applicant's Costs—Regulation of Railways Act, 1873 (36 & 37 Vict. c. 48), s. 28—Rules of Supreme Court, 1875, Order LV.*] The Railway Commissioners have no jurisdiction under the Regulation of Railways Act, 1873, s. 28, to order a railway company, in whose favour they have decided upon an application to them against such company, to pay costs to the unsuccessful applicant. — Judgment of the Queen's Bench Division reversed. FOSTER *v.* GREAT WESTERN RAILWAY COMPANY -   **8 Q. B. D. 25, 515**

3. —— Excessive Charges — *Conveyance of Passengers by Railway—Neglect to afford "Reasonable Facilities"—Jurisdiction of Railway Commissioners—Regulation of Railways Act, 1873 (36 & 37 Vict. c. 48)—Railway and Canal Traffic Act, 1854 (17 & 18 Vict. c. 31), s. 2.*] The mere fact that railway companies make charges for the conveyance of passengers in excess of those authorized by their special Acts, but without any undue preference, is not a breach of their obligation under 17 & 18 Vict. c. 31, s. 2, to " afford according to their respective powers all reasonable facilities for the receiving and forwarding and delivering of traffic upon and from the several railways and canals belonging to or worked by such companies respectively and for the return of carriages, trucks, boats, and other vehicles." And the Railway Commissioners have no jurisdiction to grant an injunction to restrain the making of such excessive charges.—*Semble*, per Brett, L.J., and Cotton, L.J., that if the overcharges were of such an amount and of such a nature that they had the effect, or it could be presumed that they were made with the intention, of preventing the use by passengers of particular trains and stations, the Commissioners might have jurisdiction to entertain a complaint in respect of them as being a refusal of "facilities" within the meaning of 17 & 18 Vict. c. 31, s..2. GREAT WESTERN RAILWAY COMPANY *v.* RAILWAY COMMISSIONERS   **[7 Q. B. D. 182**

4. —— Excessive Charges — Railway Commissioners—*Terminal Charges—Stations, Sidings, &c. — Services incidental to the Business of a Carrier—Special Case—Power to state—36 & 37 Vict. c. 48, ss. 15, 26—26 & 27 Vict. c. ccxviii., s. 51.*] On the hearing of an application made under the Regulation of Railways Act, 1873

IX. RAILWAY COMPANY—RAILWAYS REGU-LATION ACTS—continued.

(36 & 37 Vict. c. 48), s. 15, the Railway Commissioners have power to state a special case for the opinion of the High Court.—By the London, Brighton, and South Coast Railway Act, 1863 (26 & 27 Vict. c. ccxviii.), s. 51: "The maximum rates of charges to be made by the company for the conveyance of animals and goods, including the tolls for the use of their railways and waggons or trucks and for locomotive power, and every other expense incidental to such conveyance (except a reasonable sum for loading, covering, and unloading the goods at any terminal station of such goods, and for delivery and collection, and any other services incidental to the duty or business of a carrier, where such services or any of them are or is performed by the company), shall not exceed" certain sums prescribed:—Held, that station accommodation, the use of sidings, weighing, checking, clerkage, watching, and labelling, provided and performed by the company in respect of goods traffic carried by them as carriers, may be, and primâ facie are "services incidental to the duty or business of a carrier" within s. 51; whether they are so in any particular case is a question of fact for the Railway Commissioners to decide, and, if found by them to be so, such services may be the subject of a separate reasonable charge in addition to the rates prescribed. HALL & CO. v. LONDON, BRIGHTON, AND SOUTH COAST RAILWAY COMPANY   15 Q. B. D. 505

5. —— Jurisdiction of Railway Commissioners —Demurrer—Regulation of Railways Act, 1873 (36 & 37 Vict. c. 48)—Railway and Canal Traffic Act, 1854 (17 & 18 Vict. c. 31).] The Railway Commissioners, to whom has been transferred the jurisdiction of the Court of Common Pleas under the Railway and Canal Traffic Act, 1854 (17 & 18 Vict. c. 31), have under that Act jurisdiction to hear and determine a complaint against a railway company of not, according to its powers, affording all reasonable facilities for receiving, forwarding, and delivering passengers and other traffic at and from any of its stations which are used by the company for such passengers or other traffic ; and although the commissioners have no jurisdiction to order the company to make a new railway station, or to order any particular works, or otherwise to interfere with the discretion of the company in the mode of performing its obligation to afford such facilities, according to its powers, for the receiving, forwarding, and delivering of the traffic, yet they have jurisdiction to order such facilities, even if their doing so would necessitate the making by the company of some structural alteration of such station.—If the Railway Commissioners act beyond their powers, prohibition will lie, notwithstanding the power of the Court of Common Pleas over railways under 17 & 18 Vict. c. 31, was transferred to such commissioners by 36 & 37 Vict. c. 48.—In a declaration in prohibition by a railway company against the Railway Commissioners it appeared that a complaint, under the Railway and Canal Traffic Act, 1854, had been made to the commissioners against the company, and that the commissioners proposed to order certain things to be done by the company

IX. RAILWAY COMPANY—RAILWAYS REGU-LATION ACTS—continued.

in respect of such complaint, and that the company denied the jurisdiction of the commissioners to hear and determine the complaint or any part of it, and prayed for a writ to prohibit the commissioners "from further proceeding in any way touching the premises before them."—The Court, being of opinion that the commissioners had jurisdiction over the general matter of the complaint, and that they had jurisdiction to order some of the things they proposed ordering, though not to order the others:—Held (Brett, L.J., dissenting), that a general demurrer by the commissioners to the whole declaration should be allowed. SOUTH EASTERN RAILWAY COMPANY v. RAILWAY COMMISSIONERS AND MAYOR OF HASTINGS
[6 Q. B. D. 586

6. —— Through Traffic—Facilities for forwarding—Through Rate—Intermediate Railway Company, whether entitled to require through Rate for Traffic to and from Termini off their own Line —Regulation of Railways Act, 1873 (36 & 37 Vict. c. 48), s. 11.] By sect. 2 of the Railway and Canal Traffic Act, 1854, every railway company shall afford all reasonable facilities for the receiving, forwarding, and delivering of traffic upon its railway whether belonging to or worked by such company, and by sect. 14 of the Regulation of Railways Act, 1876, the facilities to be so afforded are declared to be and shall include "the due and reasonable receiving, forwarding, and delivering by every railway company, at the request of any other such company, of through traffic to and from the railway of any other such company at through rates." The Central Wales Railway Company applied to the Railway Commissioners for an order under sect. 11 allowing through rates in respect of the traffic in certain goods between Chester and Haverfordwest, the route claimed being from Chester, over lines owned or worked by the London and North Western Railway Company, and over the applicants' own line, which was worked by the same company under an agreement with the applicants, and thence to Haverfordwest over the Great Western Company's line. which was worked and owned exclusively by that company, and vice versâ from Haverfordwest to Chester. The applicants had no rolling stock, and did not work their railway, but maintained and managed their line, and collected, forwarded, and delivered their own traffic, the whole of the staff at their stations being employed and paid by them, and subject to their orders:—Held, that the traffic was "through traffic to and from" the applicants' railway, and that the applicants were a railway company entitled to request a through rate in respect of such traffic, within the meaning of sect. 11, and therefore that the Railway Commissioners had jurisdiction to make the order. GREAT WESTERN RAILWAY COMPANY v. CENTRAL WALES RAILWAY COMPANY   10 Q. B. D. 231

X. RAILWAY COMPANY—TRAFFIC MANAGEMENT.

1. —— Carrier—Railway and Canal Traffic Act, 1854 (17 & 18 Vict. c. 31), s. 7—Alternative Rates—Special Condition.] A fish merchant delivered fish to a railway company to carry upon a signed contract relieving the company as to all

**X. RAILWAY COMPANY—TRAFFIC MANAGE-
MENT**—*continued.*

fish delivered by him "from all liability for loss
or damage by delay in transit or from whatever
other cause arising," in consideration of the rates
being one-fifth lower than where no such undertaking was granted; the contract to endure for
five years. The servants of the company accepted
the fish, although from pressure of business they
could not carry it in time for the intended
market, and the fish lost the market :—*Held*,
·reversing the decision of the Court of Appeal,
that upon the facts the merchant had a bonâ fide
·option to send fish at a reasonable rate with liability on the company as common carriers, or at
the lower rate upon the terms of the contract;
that the contract was in point of fact just and
reasonable within the Railway and Canal Traffic
Act, 1854 (17 & 18 Vict. 31), s. 7, and covered
the delay; and that the company were not liable
for the loss. BROWN *v.* MANCHESTER, SHEFFIELD,
AND LINCOLNSHIRE RAILWAY COMPANY
[9 Q. B. D. 230; 10 Q. B. D. 250; 8 App. Cas. 703

2. —— Contract — *Ultrà Vires—Charge for
Weighing Goods carried by Railway Company.*]
A railway company carried coals on their line for
the Defendants, who were coal merchants, and
delivered them at the Defendants' wharf which
adjoined a siding at one of the company's stations,
and they allowed the Defendants, in consideration
of paying a specified reasonable charge, to weigh
out the coals to customers by a machine belonging to the company placed in the station yard.
The company had no express statutory power to
make charges for the use of their weighing
machines :—*Held*, that the charges were not ultrà
vires, and the company could maintain an action
to recover them from the Defendants. LONDON
AND NORTH WESTERN RAILWAY COMPANY *v.* PRICE
[11 Q. B. D. 485

3. —— Mileage Charges—*Lump Charges—
Statute — Repeal by Implication — Government
Duty—" Tolls " — Omission to put Milestones —
Railways Clauses Consolidation Act,* 1845, *s.* 95.]
The W. Company by their original Act were
·authorized to charge reasonable rates for the conveyance of passengers. By a subsequent Act the
company were empowered to extend their line,
and to charge a lump sum for carrying passengers
over that extension. A third and later Act
allowed the W. Company to amalgamate with
another company, provided that they reduced
their charges to the same scale as that of the
other company. That scale was one penny a
mile for each third-class passenger. The Plaintiff
travelled over the line of the W. Company with a
third-class ticket, and was charged as his fare at
more than the rate of one penny a mile. In the
course of his journey he travelled over the extension. The W. Company also charged the Plaintiff
with the Government duty :—*Held*, that the W.
Company were not entitled to charge the Plaintiff
more than one penny per mile, but that they were
entitled to charge him with the Government duty.
—By one of the clauses in an Act relating to the
W. Company they were forbidden to take tolls,
unless milestones were maintained along the line;
and another Act relating to the W. Company in-
·corporated the Railways Clauses Consolidation

**X. RAILWAY COMPANY—TRAFFIC MANAGE-
MENT**—*continued.*

Act, 1845, which, in sect. 95, contains a similar
provision :—*Held*, that the word "tolls" related
to tolls properly so called, and did not extend to
charges for carrying passengers in the company's
own carriages. BROWN *v.* GREAT WESTERN RAIL-
WAY COMPANY　　　9 Q. B. D. 744

RAILWAY COMPANY—Abandonment—Costs
[26 Ch. D. 237
　　See LANDS CLAUSES ACT—COSTS　6.

——Canada—Power to levy tolls 8 App. Cas. 723
　　See COLONIAL LAW — CANADA—DOMI-
　　NION.　4.

—— Contagious Diseases (Animals) Act—Movement into proscribed district
[12 Q. B. D. 629
　　See CONTAGIOUS DISEASES (ANIMALS)
　　ACT.

—— Negligence—Charge or control of points
[12 Q. B. D. 208
　　See MASTER AND SERVANT—MASTER'S
　　LIABILITY.　17.

—— Negligence—Delivery order—Estoppel
[11 Q. B. D. 776
　　See ESTOPPEL—CONDUCT.　3.

—— Negligence—Level crossing　12 Q. B. D. 70
　　See NEGLIGENCE—EVIDENCE.　3.

—— Power of general meeting　23 Ch. D. 654 ;
[25 Ch. D. 320
　　See COMPANY—MANAGEMENT.　2, 5.

—— Purchase of lands.
　　See Cases under LANDS CLAUSES ACT—
　　COMPULSORY POWERS.

—— Purchase of land—Right of way—Purposes
of railway　　　26 Ch. D. 434
　　See WAY.　2.

—— Running powers—Fixed rent—Rateability
[15 Q. B. D. 597
　　See POOR-RATE—RATEABLE VALUE.　5.

—— Scotch law.
　　See Cases under SCOTCH LAW—RAILWAY
　　COMPANY.

—— Superfluous lands.
　　See Cases under LANDS CLAUSES ACT—
　　SUPERFLUOUS LANDS.

—— West Australia—Compensation
[9 App. Cas. 142
　　See COLONIAL LAW—WEST AUSTRALIA.
　　2.

**RAILWAY CONSTRUCTION FACILITIES ACT,
1864.**
　　See RAILWAY COMPANY—CONSTITUTION
　　—*Gazette.*

RAPE.
　　See CRIMINAL LAW—OFFENCES AGAINST
　　WOMEN—*Statutes.*

—— Girl between twelve and thirteen
[10 Q. B. D. 74
　　See CRIMINAL LAW—OFFENCES AGAINST
　　WOMEN.

RATEABLE VALUE.
　　See Cases under POOR-RATE—RATEABLE
　　VALUE.

RATES — Borough — Municipal election — Expenses of Court   9 Q. B. D. 494
  See MUNICIPAL CORPORATION—ELECTION. 1.

—— Company in liquidation — Occupation by liquidator - 23 Ch. D. 500; 28 Ch. D.
  See COMPANY—RATES. 1, 2, 3. [470, 474

—— Highway   13 Q. B. D. 946
  See LOCAL GOVERNMENT—RATES. 1.

—— Mortgage of—Mortmain   22 Ch. D. 202
  See CHARITY—MORTMAIN. 4.

—— Order to levy—Sealing—Issue of order
                [14 Q. B. D. 328
  See METROPOLIS—MANAGEMENT ACTS. 8.

—— Owner rated instead of occupier—Tenements whether occupied or unoccupied
              [8 Q. B. D. 486
  See LOCAL GOVERNMENT—RATES. 2.

—— Parish—Winding-up of company—Apportionment - 19 Ch. D. 640
  See APPORTIONMENT. 2.

—— Procedure for recovery of.
  See JUSTICES—PRACTICE—RATES—*Statutes.*

—— Poor-rates.
  See Cases under POOR-RATE.

—— Waterworks company—"Rateable value"
    [10 Q. B. D. 337; 9 App. Cas. 49
  See WATERWORKS COMPANY — WATER-RATE. 3.

RATIFICATION—Contract by promoter 16 Ch. D.
  See COMPANY—CONTRACTS. 2.   [125

—— Ultra vires act - 26 Ch. D. 107
  See COMPANY—MEMORANDUM AND ARTICLES. 3.

REAL AND PERSONAL ESTATE—Administration action—Apportionment of costs
              [19 Ch. D. 552
  See EXECUTOR—ACTIONS. 11.

——Fire insurance—Right to money
  See INSURANCE, FIRE. 2. [23 Ch. D. 188

—— Larch trees   28 Ch. D. 220; 30 Ch. D. 485
  See TIMBER. 1, 2.

REAL AND PERSONAL REPRESENTATIVES—Partition suit—Proceeds of sale
              [19 Ch. D. 302
  See PARTITION SUIT—SALE. 6.

—— Option of purchasing freehold 27 Ch. D. 394
  See LEASE—LANDLORD AND TENANT. 16.

REAL ESTATE.
  The statute 47 & 48 *Vict. c.* 71, *s.* 4, *extends the law of escheat to any estate or interest, whether legal or equitable in any incorporeal hereditament, and to any equitable estate or interest in any corporeal hereditaments.*
  By sect. 5 (1) *the High Court of Justice or the Court of Chancery of Lancaster may with consent of Attorney-General, notwithstanding that no office has been found and no commission issued, order a sale of any land or legal or equitable interest of the Crown, the same to be disposed of under* 39 & 40 *Vict. c.* 18.
  (2.) 15 & 16 *Vict. c.* 55, *s.* 1, *to apply to such sale as if to the property of a subject.*
  By sect. 6 *a Treasury warrant may waive rights*

REAL ESTATE—*continued.*
of Crown in certain cases where a person dies without an heir, and intestate in respect of real estate.
  By sect. 7 *the offices of the Duchy of Lancaster are substituted for the ordinary offices of the Crown in matters appertaining to that Duchy.*
  See also ADMINISTRATOR.

—— Assets—Right of retainer—Heir-at-law
  See RETAINER.   [27 Ch. D. 478

—— Contract by wife to assign to husband—Heir-at-law - 9 Q. B. D. 576
  See HUSBAND AND WIFE—WIFE'S REAL ESTATE. 6.

—— Cultivation of - 27 Ch. D. 553
  See SETTLEMENT—MANAGEMENT. 6.

—— Debt payable out of   19 Ch. D. 156
  See CHARITY—MORTMAIN 2.

—— Descended—Costs of administration action
              [28 Ch. D. 159
  See EXECUTOR—ACTIONS. 12.

—— Devise by will—Leaseholds   28 Ch. D. 66
  See WILL—WORDS. 16.

—— Equitable assets—Retainer   18 Ch. D. 182
  See EXECUTOR—RETAINER. 7.

—— Infant—Power of Court to mortgage
              [21 Ch. D. 786
  See INFANT—PROPERTY. 1.

—— Power of appointment—Failure by death of appointee   16 Ch. D. 18
  See POWER—EXECUTION. 6.

—— Will—Married woman—Probate Division—Jurisdiction—Appointment of executors
              [6 P. D. 209
  See PROBATE—MARRIED WOMAN. 4.

—— Will—Probate - 9 P. D. 242
  See PROBATE—GRANT. 5.

REAL SECURITY—Turnpike road bonds
  See WILL—WORDS. 17. [30 Ch. D. 227

REASONABLE AND PROBABLE CAUSE—Malicious prosecution.
  See Cases under MALICIOUS PROSECUTION.

REASONABLENESS OF CHARGES — Railway tolls—Canada   8 App. Cas. 723
  See COLONIAL LAW — CANADA—DOMINION. 4.

RECEIPT IN DEED—Effect of.
  See DEED—*Statutes.*

—— Mortgage debt—Building society
              [28 Ch. D. 298
  See BUILDING SOCIETY. 12.

RECEIVER—Abandoned railway 18 Ch. D. 155
  See RAILWAY COMPANY—ABANDONMENT. 1.

—— Appointment—Effect on right of retainer
              [22 Ch. D. 604
  See EXECUTOR—RETAINER. 2.

—— Balance due from—Debt of record
              [18 Ch. D. 296
  See LIMITATIONS, STATUTE OF—PERSONAL ACTIONS. 11.

—— Bankruptcy.
  See Cases under BANKRUPTCY—RECEIVER.

RECEIVER—*continued.*

—— Bankruptcy—Contract in his own name
[22 Ch. D. 470
See BANKRUPTCY—JURISDICTION. 5.

—— Bankruptcy—Right to complain of trustee
[16 Ch. D. 501
See BANKRUPTCY—APPEAL. 9.

—— Bankruptcy—Ship—Engineer's lien
[16 Ch. D. 604
See SHIP—MARITIME LIEN. 6.

—— Conduct of action—Bankrupt executor
[19 Ch. D. 61
See PRACTICE—SUPREME COURT—CON-
DUCT OF CAUSE. 1.

——Interpleader—Practice - 13 Q. B. D. 67
See PRACTICE—SUPREME COURT—INTER-
PLEADER. 10.

—— Leaseholds—Repairs—Indemnity to trustees - 16 Ch. D. 723
See TRUSTEE—LIABILITIES. 9.

—— Manager of company—Action by debenture
holder - 23 Ch. D. 317
See COMPANY—DEBENTURES. 6.

—— Mortgage—Conveyancing Act, 1881
[25 Ch. D. 236
See MORTGAGE—FORECLOSURE. 20.

—— Mortgagee—Appointment by.
See MORTGAGE—POWERS—*Statutes.*

—— Official—Power to sell bankrupt's property
[15 Q. B. D. 196
See BANKRUPTCY—RECEIVER. 11.

—— Official—Report as to composition or scheme
of arrangement—How far primâ facie
evidence 15 Q. B. D. 213
See BANKRUPTCY—SCHEME OF ARRANGE-
MENT. 2.

—— Settled Estates Act - - 24 Ch. D. 238
See SETTLED ESTATES ACT. 4.

—— Supreme Court—Practice.
See Cases under PRACTICE—SUPREME
COURT—RECEIVER.

RECEIVING ORDER—Bankruptcy.
See BANKRUPTCY—STATUTES.

—— Bankruptcy.
See Cases under BANKRUPTCY—RE-
CEIVER. 4—10.

RECEIVING STOLEN GOODS—Evidence—Guilty
knowledge - 12 Q. B. D. 522
See CRIMINAL LAW—EVIDENCE. 6.

RECITAL—Construction of general words
See ADVOWSON. 1. [30 Ch. D. 298

—— Deed more than twenty years old
[24 Ch. D. 11
See VENDOR AND PURCHASER—CONDI-
TIONS OF SALE. 4.

—— Implied covenant - - 18 Ch. D. 354
See SETTLEMENT—FUTURE PROPERTY. 7.

—— Mistake in—Will . - 22 Ch. D. 495
See WILL—MISTAKE. 2.

—— Notice of trust - - 24 Ch. D. 720
See VENDOR AND PURCHASER—TITLE. 4.

—— Power of attorney 29 Ch. D. 500
See POWER OF ATTORNEY. 2.

RECONSTRUCTION OF COMPANY—Arbitration
[28 Ch. D. 620
See COMPANY—RECONSTRUCTION.

RECONVEYANCE — Mortgage—Right of mortgagor to call for assignment 20 Ch. D.
See MORTGAGE—REDEMPTION. 2. [724

—— Mortgage to building society—Priority
[28 Ch. D. 398
See BUILDING SOCIETY. 13.

—— Unstamped deed—Compulsory purchase
[24 Ch. D. 119
See REVENUE—STAMPS. 5.

RECORD—Transcript of—Irish inquisition
[20 Ch. D. 269
See LUNATIC—JURISDICTION. 1.

RECORD OFFICE.
Rules under 40 & 41 *Vict. c.* 55 (*the Public
Record Office Act,* 1877), *for the disposal of valueless documents of public offices. Dated August* 11*th,*
1883 - - - L. G., 1883, p. 2921

RECOVERY OF LAND—Action for—Interroga-
tories 20 Ch. D. 484; 8 App. Cas. 217
See PRACTICE—SUPREME COURT—INTER-
ROGATORIES. 11.

—— Action for—Pleading 6 Q. B. D. 645;
[8 App. Cas. 456
See PRACTICE — SUPREME COURT — DE-
FENCE.

—— Action for—Writ of possession 22 Ch. D. 281
See PRACTICE—SUPREME COURT—WRIT
OF POSSESSION.

—— Joinder of causes of action—Counter-claim
[21 Ch. D. 138
See PRACTICE — SUPREME COURT —
COUNTER-CLAIM. 5.

RECTIFICATION—Disentailing deed 29 Ch. D.
See TENANT IN TAIL. 1. [133

—— Lease - 28 Ch. D. 255
See MISTAKE. 4.

—— Register of shares - 24 Ch. D. 149
See COMPANY—PROSPECTUS. 6.

—— Register of trade-marks - 27 Ch. D. 646
[29 Ch. D. 551
See TRADE-MARK—REGISTRATION. 2, 3.

—— Voluntary settlement - 29 Ch. D. 212
See VOLUNTARY SETTLEMENT. 4.

REDEMPTION.
See Cases under
MORTGAGE—CONSOLIDATION.
MORTGAGE—REDEMPTION.

—— Mortgage payable by instalments: 22 Ch. D.
See MORTGAGE—CONTRACT. 10. [549

—— Mortgage—Period of—Foreclosure action.
See Cases under MORTGAGE — FORE-
CLOSURE.

—— Mortgage—Statute of Limitations
[17 Ch. D. 104, 132
See LIMITATIONS, STATUTE OF—REALTY.
6, 7.

—— Rent-charges and quit-rents.
See RENT-CHARGE—*Statutes.*

—— Second mortgage—Extinguishment of first
mortgage - - 24 Ch. D. 618
See MORTGAGE—PRIORITY. 1.

REGISTER—REGISTRATION—_continued._

—— Yorkshire registry · **26 Ch. D. 501**
　See VENDOR AND PURCHASER—LIEN. 2.

REGISTRAR—Bankruptcy—Approval of composition or scheme of arrangement—Discretion　-　- **15 Q. B. D. 213**
　See BANKRUPTCY—SCHEME OF ARRANGEMENT. 2.

—— Bankruptcy—Discretion **16 Ch. D. 283**
　See BANKRUPTCY—ADJUDICATION. 1.

—— County Court—Notice of appeal **19 Ch. D.**
　See BANKRUPTCY—APPEAL. 6.　[169

—— Note of—Varying minutes **21 Ch. D. 621**
　See PRACTICE—SUPREME COURT—JUDGMENT. 7.

—— Ship—Bottomry—Registrar and merchants
　　　　　　　　　　　　　[9 P. D. 177
　See SHIP—MARITIME LIEN. 2.

REGISTRATION ACT, 1885.
　See PARLIAMENT—REGISTRATION—Statutes.

REGISTRATION OF BIRTHS AND DEATHS.
　The *Burial and Registration Acts (Doubts Removal) Act,* 1881—44 & 45 Vict. c. 2—sect. 1, enacts: Nothing in the 11th section of the Burial Laws Amendment Act, 1880, shall have, or be deemed in law to have had, the effect of repealing, or in any manner altering, any of the provisions contained in the 17th section of the Births and Deaths Registration Act, 1874, in any case whatever, save and except only the case of a burial under the Burial Laws Amendment Act, 1880.

REGISTRY ACTS.
　The Act 47 & 48 Vict. c. 54 (*Yorkshire Registries Act,* 1884) consolidates and amends the law relating to the Registration of Deeds and other matters affecting lands and hereditaments within the North, East, and West Ridings of Yorkshire, and town of Kingston-upon-Hull.
　Sect. 3. Interpretation clause.
　Sect. 4. All assurances made after commencement of this Act (1st January, 1885), and all wills of any testators dying after that date, affecting lands within above limits may be registered.
　Sect. 5. The registration of any assurance, will, or other instrument under this Act, shall be effected in the following manner:
　(1.) There shall be presented for enrolment in the register—
　　(a.) In the case of deeds, wills or other assurances which may be registered under this Act, except private Acts of Parliament or memoranda of charge, or affidavits of vesting under any Act of Parliament, a memorial thereof prepared in accordance with the provisions of this Act, and any rules made thereunder, or such deed, will or other assurance as aforesaid, at full length at the option of the person registering the same;
　　(b.) In the case of a private Act of Parliament, a Queen's Printer's copy of such Act, or a memorial thereof prepared in accordance with the provisions of this Act, and any rules made thereunder;
　　(c.) In the case of any memorandum of charge,

REGISTRY ACTS—_continued._
　caveat, notice, or affidavit which may be registered under this Act, such memorandum, caveat, notice or affidavit at full length;
　(2.) Immediately on receipt of any instrument or memorial thereof presented for enrolment in the register, an entry shall be made in a book of reference to be kept for that purpose setting forth—
　(a.) The date of the instrument.
　(b.) (1.) In the case of a deed, the names of the parties.
　　(2.) In the case of a will, the name of the testator.
　　(3.) In the case of an order of Court or certificate of appointment of trustee in bankruptcy, the title of the cause or matter wherein the same purports to be made, and the names of the parties thereto, if any.
　　(4.) In the case of a private Act of Parliament the title of the Act.
　　(5.) In the case of an order of the Land Commissioners, the name of the landowner whose lands are charged.
　　(6.) In the case of an award of the Land Commissioners, the names of the persons in whose favour the award is made.
　　(7.) In the case of a memorandum of charge, the name of the landowner whose lands are charged.
　　(8.) In the case of a caveat, the names of the persons by and in whose favour the same is given.
　　(9.) In the case of a notice of a will, the names of the testator, and of the person by whom such notice is given.
　　(10.) In the case of an affidavit of intestacy, the names of the deceased and of the deponent.
　　(11.) In the case of an affidavit of vesting, the title of the Act of Parliament under which such vesting has been effected, and the name of the deponent.
　(c.) The names of all the parishes in which the lands affected by such instrument are situate.
　(d.) The volume, page, and number of the register where such instrument or memorial thereof is, or is intended to be enrolled.
　(e.) The date, hour, and minute when such instrument or memorial thereof was received at the office for the purpose of registration.
　And upon such entry being duly made, such instrument shall be deemed to have been registered under this Act, and the date, hour, and minute so entered as aforesaid shall be deemed for all purposes to be the date of registration, provided that if such entry be duly made in respect of part only of the lands affected by any such instrument, such instrument shall as to the lands with respect to which such entry has been duly made, but not as to the residue of the lands affected thereby, be deemed to have been registered under this Act: Provided that if such instrument shall afterwards be registered as to the omitted lands, a note of such registration

REGISTRY ACTS—*continued.*

and of the date thereof shall be made in the book of reference, and such registration shall thenceforth be valid and effectual as to such omitted lands.

(3.) As soon as conveniently may be after the presentation of any instrument or memorial thereof for enrolment in the register, such instrument or memorial thereof shall be duly enrolled in the register and the volume, page, and number of the register where the same is so enrolled, shall correspond with the entry made or to be made in the book of reference relating to such instrument, and an entry shall be made in the margin of the register opposite any instrument or memorial thereof so enrolled of the date of registration.

Sect. 6 prescribes the regulation to which memorials of (1) deeds, (2) wills, (3) orders or certificates, (4) private Acts, (5) awards, (6) orders of Land Commissioners shall be subject.

Sect. 7 prescribes regulations for a memorandum of lien or charge.

Sect. 8. Originals of deeds, &c., to be produced.

Sect. 9. Indorsement of registrar to be made on every deed, &c., produced.

Sect. 10 repealed by 48 & 49 Vict. c. 26, which enacts in lieu of the repealed provisions, new rules for registering a caveat with respect to lands in above limits.

Sect. 11 enables a person claiming an interest under a will, if unable to register the will within six months after death of testator, to register a notice of the will.

Sect. 12. A person claiming as heir or through intestacy may register an affidavit of intestacy.

Sect. 13. Where lands are vested by payment, &c., under an Act, an affidavit of such vesting may be registered.

Sect. 14. Assurances are entitled to priority according to dates of registration and not according to their respective dates. Every will [entitled to be (48 & 49 Vict. c. 26)] registered under this Act to have priority according to the date of the death of the testator if the date of registration thereof be within, or under this Act to be deemed to be within, a period of six months after the death of the testator, or according to the date of registration thereof, if such date of registration be not within, or under this Act to be deemed to be within, such period of six months. Where dates of registration of assurances or wills are identical, the Act does not interfere with the priorities. Priorities given by this Act have no effect in cases of actual fraud.

Sect. 15. Repealed by 48 & 49 Vict. c. 26.

Sect. 16. No priority or protection shall be given by reason of any interest within the limits of this Act being tacked to any legal or other estate, except where any interest has existed prior to this Act.

Sect. 17. The rights of purchasers to relief shall be the same as those of the persons through whom they may claim.

Sect. 18. The registrar shall register all assurances, &c. The rules of priority of instruments delivered through the post.

Sect. 19. Searches may be made and copies taken by any person.

Sect. 20. Any person may require an official search to be made.

Sect. 21. Certificate of such search receivable in evidence.

Sect. 22. Certified copies to be given.

REGISTRY ACTS—*continued.*

Sect. 23. Solicitor, trustee, or person in fiduciary position not to be answerable for error in certificate or copy from the register.

Sect. 24. Pages of register to be numbered and signed.

Sect. 25. Any person claiming interest may apply to the Chancery Division of the High Court for an order that the register, or rules under this Act, be rectified, or that any certificate or deed be cancelled, &c.

This jurisdiction of Chancery Division may be exercised at Chambers. The Lord Chancellor may make rules for carrying out this section. Right of appeal from any such order is given.

Sect. 26. Statutory receipts, where required.

Sect. 27. Stamp duty.

Sect. 28. The Act does not extend to copyhold hereditaments, nor to lease not exceeding twenty-one years, nor to assignment thereof accompanied by actual possession from the making of lease or assignment.

Sect. 29. Shares in companies, &c., not affected by the Act.

Sect. 30. Crown land not affected by the Act.

Register Offices.] Sect. 31. Offices where to be situated.

Sect. 32. Judicial notice to be taken of seal, and of registrar's signature.

Sect. 33. Offices and property of registry vested in clerk of the peace.

Sect. 34. County authority may purchase land, &c., for the registry and may build and repair same.

Sect. 35. Subject to the provisions of this Act, the county authority may from time to time make, and when made may rescind, amend, or add to, rules in respect to all or any of the following matters :

(1.) The form of the register and the mode in which the same is to be made and kept :

(2.) The preparation and keeping at the register office of any books and indexes, and the entries to be made therein for the purpose of effecting any registration :

(3.) The mode in which registration is to be conducted :

(4.) The making of entries in the register where any mortgage, lien, or charge with reference to which any instrument has been registered under this Act has been satisfied or discharged :

(5.) The forms of memorials, certificates, and other instruments to be prepared for the purposes of this Act :

(6.) The making of searches and the giving of certified copies :

(7.) The fees to be taken by the registrar where such fees are not paid to and retained by an existing registrar for his own use :

(8.) The custody of the register and other documents connected with the business of registration :

(9.) The transmission by post of applications for registration and for search, and of registered documents and certificates of registration and search ;

(10.) Generally in relation to any matters, whether similar or not to those above mentioned, as to which it may be expedient

REGISTRY ACTS—*continued.*

to make rules for carrying into effect the objects of this Act :

Provided that no such rules shall have any force or effect unless and until they have been confirmed by the Lord Chancellor and published in such manner as he may direct, and that a copy thereof shall be laid before both Houses of Parliament within fourteen days after the confirmation thereof if Parliament be then sitting, or if Parliament be not then sitting, within fourteen days after the next meeting thereof.

Any rules made, confirmed, and published in pursuance of this Act shall be deemed to be within the powers conferred by this Act, and shall be of the same force as if enacted in this Act, and shall be judicially noticed.

Sect. 36. Existing registrars to be the first registrars under this Act.

Sect. 37. Appointment of officers.

Sects. 38 and 39. Fees to be taken in registry.

Sects. 40 and 41. Application of fees and accounts.

Sect. 42. Expenses to be defrayed out of county rate and be considered to be within meaning of 45 & 46 Vict. c. 50.

Sect. 43. Registering of memorials, &c., where assurances made, or testators died, before [the passing (amended by 48 & 49 Vict. c. 4)] of this Act.

Sect. 44. Books, &c., connected with the old registries.

Sect. 45. Copies of old registers.

Sect. 46. Frauds by registrar punished as misdemeanor, by imprisonment, with or without hard labour, not exceeding two years.

Sect. 47. Making a false affidavit punishable as perjury.

Sect. 48. An affidavit under this Act may be sworn before Commissioners to Administer Oaths, and out of Great Britain and Ireland may be sworn before a magistrate of the country, certified to be such by a British consul or by a notary public.

Sect. 49. When and so soon as the right of appointment of the registrar under this Act is vested in and has been exercised by the county authority, the following provisions shall have effect :

(a.) *Every action which may be brought by any person to recover damages for or by reason of any loss or damage occasioned by any neglect, omission, mistake, or misfeasance of the registrar or any person employed in the register office in connection with the business of such office shall be brought against the registrar as the nominal defendant by his name of office, and no such action shall abate by reason of the death or removal from office of any such registrar :*

(b.) *A writ or process shall not be sued out against or served on the registrar for anything done or intended to be done or omitted to be done under the provisions of this Act until the expiration of one month after notice in writing has been served on such registrar, clearly stating the cause of action and the names and place of abode of the intended plaintiff and of his solicitor or agent in the cause :*

(c.) *The registrar, with the consent of the county authority, may enter into and conclude a*

REGISTRY ACTS—*continued.*

compromise with any body or person claiming a right of action against him under this section, or may agree with such body or person that any question relating to such right of action should be referred to arbitration :

(d.) *All damages, costs, and expenses payable by the registrar in respect of any such action, compromise, or arbitration as in this section above mentioned shall be paid by him out of moneys to be provided by the county authority, and the county authority shall provide all moneys which may be necessary in that behalf.*

Sect. 50. No matter or thing done and no contract entered into by any county authority, and no matter or thing done by any member of any such authority, or by any officer of such authority, or other person whomsoever appointed by and acting under the direction of such authority, shall, if the matter or thing were done or the contract were entered into bonâ fide for the purpose of executing this Act, subject them or any of them personally to any action, liability, claim, or demand whatsoever, and any expense incurred by any such county authority, member, officer, or other person acting as last aforesaid shall be paid by the county authority :

Provided that nothing in this section shall exempt any member of any county authority from liability to be surcharged with the amount of any payment which may be disallowed by the auditor in the accounts of such authority, and which such member authorized or joined in authorizing.

Repeal.] *Sect. 51. Repeal of Acts 2 & 3 Anne, c. 4, 6 Anne, cc. 20 and 62, 8 Geo. 2, c. 6.*

Amendment.] *This Act is amended by 48 & 49 Vict. cc. 4 and 26 respectively.*

—— **Middlesex Registry Act** — *Mortgage— Share in Proceeds of Sale of—Priority—7 Anne, c. 20), s. 1—Notice to Trustees—Equitable Execution.*] The local Registry Acts are intended to apply only to dealings at law or in equity with the land itself. Accordingly an incumbrancer upon a share in the proceeds of real estate in Middlesex devised in trust for sale obtains no priority over other incumbrancers on such share by registering his mortgage deed, and the priorities of such incumbrancers rank according to the dates of their respective notices to the trustees.— *Malcolm v. Charlesworth* (1 Keen, 36) approved. —Although formal notice to the trustee of the proceeds of real estate devised in trust for sale or of a chose in action, of an incumbrance thereupon does not give priority over an earlier incumbrance of which the trustee may have obtained accidental notice, the converse proposition that incumbrances are to rank not in the order of notices given by the incumbrancers but of accidental knowledge obtained by the trustees, does not hold good.—A judgment creditor cannot, by giving notice to the trustee, put himself in a better position than the judgment debtor ; and a judgment creditor who has obtained equitable execution by the appointment of a receiver subject to existing incumbrances was held to have obtained no priority by giving notice of the appointment to the trustee of the judgment debtor. ARDEN *v.* ARDEN

[29 Ch. D. 702

REGISTRY ACTS—*continued*.
—— Middlesex - - - 20 Ch. D. 611
　　See VENDOR AND PURCHASER—PURCHASE
　　WITHOUT NOTICE. 1.
—— Yorkshire - 26 Ch. D. 501
　　See VENDOR AND PURCHASER—LIEN. 2.

REGULATION OF THE FORCES ACT, 1881.
　　See ARMY—*Statutes*.

REGULATIONS FOR PREVENTING COLLISIONS
AT SEA.
　　See Cases under SHIP — NAVIGATION.
　　8—26.
　　And SHIP—NAVIGATION—*Gazette*.

RE-HEARING—Bankruptcy - 22 Ch. D. 529
　　See BANKRUPTCY—APPEAL. 5.

—— Fraud of solicitor - 20 Ch. D. 672
　　See PRACTICE — SUPREME COURT —
　　AMENDMENT. 3.

—— Lancaster Court—Jurisdiction
　　　　　　　[24 Ch. D. 488
　　See PRACTICE—SUPREME COURT — AP-
　　PEAL. 37.

RE-INDORSEMENT—Circuity of action
　　　　　　　[7 Q. B. D. 636
　　See BILL OF EXCHANGE—TRANSFER.

RE-INSURANCE — Constructive total loss —
　　Notice of abandonment 15 Q. B. D. 11
　　See INSURANCE, MARINE—LOSS, TOTAL.

RE-INVESTMENT—Money in Court—Petition or
　　summons - - 25 Ch. D. 384
　　See PRACTICE—SUPREME COURT—CHAM-
　　BERS. 15.

RELATION OF TITLE—Trustee in bankruptcy.
　　See Cases under BANKRUPTCY—ASSETS.
　　6—11.

RELATIONS OF LUNATIC—Allowance to
　　　　　　　[21 Ch. D. 297
　　See LUNATIC—PROPERTY. 2.

RELEASE OF SURETY - - 9 Q. B. D. 783;
　　　　[25 Ch. D. 666; 8 App. Cas. 755
　　See PRINCIPAL AND SURETY — DIS-
　　CHARGE. 1, 2, 3.

RELIGIOUS EDUCATION—Infant 21 Ch. D. 817;
　　　　　　　[28 Ch. D. 82
　　See INFANT—EDUCATION. 2, 3.

RELIGIOUS WORSHIP—Registration of building
　　　　　　　[21 Ch. D. 513
　　See CHARITY—COMMISSIONERS. 3.

RELINQUISHMENT OF DEBT—Condition
　　See WILL—CONDITION. 8. [21 Ch. D. 431

REMAINDERMAN — Easement—Prescription—
　　Forty years' enjoyment—Reversion ex-
　　pectant on term of life or years
　　See PRESCRIPTION. 2. [15 Q. B. D. 629

REMOTENESS—Appointment - 29 Ch. D. 521;
　　　　　　　[30 Ch. D. 172
　　See POWER—EXECUTION. 12, 18.

—— Covenant to re-convey 20 Ch. D. 562
　　See LANDS CLAUSES ACT—SUPERFLUOUS
　　LANDS. 2.

—— Damage.
　　See Cases under DAMAGES—REMOTENESS.

—— Power of sale—Settlement 19 Ch. D. 624
　　See SETTLEMENT—POWERS. 15.

REMOTENESS—*continued*.
—— Will—Construction.
　　See Cases under WILL—PERPETUITY.

REMOVAL OF PAUPER.
　　See Cases under POOR LAW—SETTLE-
　　MENT.

REMUNERATION—Agent—Commission on sale
　　of land - 9 Q. B. D. 276
　　See CONDITION. 2.

—— Barrister—Law of Quebec 9 App. Cas. 745
　　See COLONIAL LAW—CANADA—QUEBEC.
　　7.

—— Directors—Power of general meeting
　　　　　　　[28 Ch. D. 654
　　See COMPANY—MANAGEMENT. 4.

—— Solicitors' Remuneration Act.
　　See Cases under SOLICITOR — BILL OF
　　COSTS. 18—25.

RENEWABLE LEASE.
　　See Cases under LEASEHOLD—RENEW-
　　ABLE LEASE.

—— Charity scheme - 20 Ch. D. 516
　　See CHARITY—MANAGEMENT 1.

RENEWAL OF LEASE—Covenant
　　　[18 Ch. D. 238; 22 Ch. D. 640;
　　　　　　　[9 App. Cas. 844
　　See LANDLORD AND TENANT — LEASE.
　　12, 13, 14.

—— Executor—Mortgage for his own debts
　　　　　　　[18 Ch. D. 93
　　See EXECUTOR—ADMINISTRATION. 3.

RENEWAL OF PATENT.
　　See Cases under PATENT — PROLONGA-
　　TION.

RENEWAL OF REGISTRATION—Bill of sale
　　　　　　　[22 Ch. D. 136
　　See BILL OF SALE—FORMALITIES. 6.

RENT—Apportionment — Assignment of rever-
　　sion - - 10 Q. B. D. 48
　　See LANDLORD AND TENANT—ASSIGN-
　　MENT. 2.

—— Distress after bankruptcy.
　　See Cases under BANKRUPTCY — DIS-
　　TRESS.

—— Distress—Winding-up of company.
　　See Cases under COMPANY—DISTRESS.

—— Gas company—Money due from consumer
　　—How far preferential debt — Bank-
　　ruptcy - 13 Q. B. D. 753
　　See BANKRUPTCY—DISTRESS. 1.

—— Mortgagee in possession 18 Ch. D. 449
　　See MORTGAGE—POWERS. 6.

—— Payable in advance—Distress 21 Ch. D. 9
　　See LANDLORD AND TENANT — AGREE-
　　MENT. 4.

—— Peppercorn rent 30 Ch. D. 344
　　See VENDOR AND PURCHASER—TITLE. 2.

RENT-CHARGE.
　　By 44 & 45 *Vict. c.* 41 (*Conveyancing Act,* 1881),
　　Sect. 44.—(1.) *Where a person is entitled to re-
　　ceive out of any land, or out of the income of any
　　land, any annual sum, payable half-yearly or
　　otherwise, whether charged on the land or on the
　　income of the land, and whether by way of rent-
　　charge or otherwise, not being rent incident to a*

RENT-CHARGE—*continued.*

reversion, then, subject and without prejudice to all estates, interests, and rights having priority to the annual sum, the person entitled to receive the same shall have such remedies for recovering and compelling payment of the same as are described in this section as far as those remedies might have been conferred by the instrument under which the annual sum arises, but not further.

(2.) If at any time the annual sum or any part thereof is unpaid for twenty-one days next after the time appointed for any payment in respect thereof, the person entitled to receive the annual sum may enter into and distrain on the land charged or any part thereof, and dispose according to law of any distress found, to the intent that thereby or otherwise the annual sum and all arrears thereof, and all costs and expenses occasioned by non-payment thereof, may be fully paid.

(3.) If at any time the annual sum or any part thereof is unpaid for forty days next after the time appointed for any payment in respect thereof, then, although no legal demand has been made for payment thereof, the person entitled to receive the annual sum may enter into possession of and hold the land charged or any part thereof, and take the income thereof, until thereby or otherwise the annual sum and all arrears thereof due at the time of his entry, or afterwards becoming due during his continuance in possession, and all costs and expenses occasioned by non-payment of the annual sum, are fully paid; and such possession when taken shall be without impeachment of waste.

(4.) In the like case the person entitled to the annual charge, whether taking possession or not, may also by deed demise the land charged, or any part thereof, to a trustee for a term of years, with or without impeachment of waste, on trust, by mortgage, or sale, or demise, for all or any part of the term, of the land charged, or of any part thereof, or by receipt of the income thereof, or by all or any of those means, or by any other reasonable means, to raise and pay the annual sum and all arrears thereof due or to become due, and all costs and expenses occasioned by non-payment of the annual sum, or incurred in compelling or obtaining payment thereof, or otherwise relating thereto, including the costs of the preparation and execution of the deed of demise, and the costs of the execution of the trusts of that deed; and the surplus, if any, of the money raised, or of the income received under the trusts of that deed, shall be paid to the person for the time being entitled to the land therein comprised in reversion immediately expectant on the term thereby created.

(5.) This section applies only if and as far as a contrary intention is not expressed in the instrument under which the annual sum arises, and shall have effect subject to the terms of that instrument and to the provisions therein contained.

(6.) This section applies only where that instrument comes into operation after the commencement of the Act—31st December, 1881.

Sect. 45.—(1.) Where there is a quit-rent, chief rent, rent-charge, or other annual sum issuing out of land (in this section referred to as the rent), the Copyhold Commissioners shall at any time, on the requisition of the owner of the land, or of any person interested therein, certify the amount of money in consideration whereof the rent may be redeemed.

RENT-CHARGE—*continued.*

(2.) Where the person entitled to the rent is absolutely entitled thereto in fee simple in possession, or is empowered to dispose thereof absolutely, or to give an absolute discharge for the capital value thereof, the owner of the land, or any person interested therein, may, after serving one month's notice on the person entitled to the rent, pay or tender to that person the amount certified by the Commissioners.

(3.) On proof to the Commissioners that payment or tender has been so made, they shall certify that the rent is redeemed under this Act; and that certificate shall be final and conclusive and the land shall be thereby absolutely freed and discharged from the rent.

(4.) Every requisition under this section shall be in writing; and every certificate under this section shall be in writing, sealed with the seal of of the Commissioners.

(5.) This section does not apply to tithe rent-charge, or to a rent reserved on a sale or lease, or to a rent made payable under a grant or license for building purposes, or to any sum or payment issuing out of land not being perpetual.

(6.) This section applies to rents payable at, or created after, the commencement of this Act.

(7.) This section does not extend to Ireland.

—— **Apportionment** — *Release of Part of the Hereditaments*—22 & 23 Vict. c. 35, s. 10.] The effect of 22 & 23 Vict. c. 35, s. 10, is that where the owner of land, which is subject to a rent-charge, sells and conveys such land in separate portions to different persons, and the person entitled to the rent-charge joins in the conveyance of one only of such portions and releases it from the rent-charge, without the concurrence of the person to whom the other portion has been conveyed, the whole of such rent-charge is not extinguished, but only a proportionate part of it can be recovered from the person to whom the unreleased portion was conveyed. BOOTH *v.* SMITH
[14 Q. B. D. 318

—— Assignee of land—Liability on covenant
[8 Q. B. D. 403 ; 22 Ch. D. 218
See COVENANT—RUNNING WITH LAND. 2, 3.

—— Land drainage company—Glebe lands
[20 Ch. D. 208
See ECCLESIASTICAL COMMISSIONERS.

—— Land drainage company—Glebe lands
[20 Ch. D. 203
See LANDS CLAUSES ACT—PURCHASE-MONEY. 6.

—— Tithes -   -   -.   - 30 Ch. D. 84
See TITHES.

—— Tithes—Redemption of.
See TITHE RENT-CHARGE—*Statutes.*

—— Vote for Parliament   12 Q. B. D. 365, 369
See PARLIAMENT—FRANCHISE. 11, 12.

RENTS AND PROFITS—Application of, during minority—Settled Land Act 24 Ch. D.129
See SETTLED LAND ACT—TRUSTEES. 6.

—— Portions payable out of   -   23 Ch. D. 472
See SETTLEMENT—POWERS. 14.

RENUNCIATION—Executor   - 16 Ch. D. 3
See ADMINISTRATOR—WITH WILL ANNEXED. 1.

2 U

RE-OPENING BANKRUPTCY 20 Ch. D. 306
   See BANKRUPTCY—UNDISCHARGED BANK-
     RUPT. 1.

REPAIRS—Highway.
   See Cases under HIGHWAY—REPAIR.
—— House—Tenancy in common 15 Q. B. D. 60
   See TENANT IN COMMON.
—— Infant's estate - 21 Ch. D. 786
   See INFANT—PROPERTY. 1.
—— Investment of purchase-money — Lands
   Clauses Act - 21 Ch. D. 228
   See LANDS CLAUSES ACT—PURCHASE-
   MONEY. 7.
—— Leaseholds—Duty of trustees 16 Ch. D. 723
   See TRUSTEE—LIABILITIES. 9.
—— Pipes—Easement 25 Ch. D. 182
   See WATERCOURSE. 3.
—— Power to lease—Repairing lease
       [20 Ch. D. 251
   See SETTLEMENT—POWERS. 3.
—— Power to mortgage for—Administrator
       [20 Ch. D. 745
   See ADMINISTRATOR—POWERS. 3.

REPEALED STATUTE—Bills of Sale Act
       [23 Ch. D. 409
   See BANKRUPTCY—ORDER AND DISPO-
   SITION. 3.
—— Interval before repeal 23 Ch. D. 440 ;
       [9 App. Cas. 519
   See BUILDING SOCIETY. 9.

REPLY.
   See Cases under PRACTICE—SUPREME
   COURT—REPLY.

REPLY POST-CARDS.
   See POST-OFFICE—*Statutes.*

REPORT—Official referee.
   See Cases under PRACTICE—SUPREME
   COURT—REFEREE.
—— Sub-committee—Privilege - 26 Ch. D. 678
   See PRACTICE—SUPREME COURT—PRO-
   DUCTION OF DOCUMENTS. 25.

REPRESENTATION—Dramatic entertainment
       [11 Q. B. D. 102 ; 13 Q. B. D. 843
   See COPYRIGHT—DRAMATIC. 1, 2.

REPRESENTATION OF THE PEOPLE ACTS.
   See PARLIAMENT—FRANCHISE—*Statutes.*

REPRESENTATIVE SUIT—Appeal by person re-
   presented by Plaintiff 17 Ch. D. 19
   See PRACTICE — SUPREME COURT—AP-
   PEAL. 17.
—— Costs - - 18 Ch. D. 530
   See COMPANY—COSTS. 4.

REPUDIATION—Contract for shares
       [23 Ch. D. 413
   See COMPANY—SHARES—ALLOTMENT. 3.

REPUGNANCY—Will 18 Ch. D. 17
   See WILL—REPUGNANCY.
—— Conditional limitation - 21 Ch. D. 638 ;
       [26 Ch. D. 792, 801
   See WILL—CONDITION. 2, 3, 5.

REPUTED OWNERSHIP—Bankruptcy.
   See Cases under BANKRUPTCY—ORDER
   AND DISPOSITION.

REPUTED OWNERSHIP—*continued.*
—— Chattels comprised in lease—Disclaimer
       [20 Ch. D. 341
   See BANKRUPTCY—DISCLAIMER. 4.

REQUISITIONS—Time for sending in
       [20 Ch. D. 465
   See VENDOR AND PURCHASER—TITLE. 8.

RES JUDICATA.
   See Cases under ESTOPPEL—JUDGMENT.
—— Discovery of fresh evidence 28 Ch. D. 516
   See NATIONAL DEBT COMMISSIONERS.
—— Summary proceeding before justices
       [6 Q. B. D. 300
   See LOCAL GOVERNMENT—STREETS. 1.

RESCISSION OF CONTRACT 29 Ch. D. 795
   See PRINCIPAL AND AGENT—AGENT'S
   LIABILITY. 1.
—— Misrepresentation 20 Ch. D. 1
   See FALSE REPRESENTATION. 1.
—— Sale of goods 7 Q. B. D. 92 ; 9 Q. B. D. 648 ;
       [9 App. Cas. 434
   See SALE OF GOODS—RESCISSION. 1, 2.
—— Sale of land 22 Ch. D. 105 ; 29 Ch. D. 661
   See VENDOR AND PURCHASER — RE-
   SCISSION. 1, 2.
—— Sale of land—Conditions of sale.
   See Cases under VENDOR AND PURCHASER
   —CONDITIONS OF SALE. 6—11.
—— To take shares - - 29 Ch. D. 421
   See COMPANY—SHARES—ALLOTMENT. 1.
—— Vendor's lien - 24 Ch. D. 94
   See WILL—EXONERATION. 3.

RESERVATION OF MINERALS 21 Ch. D. 18 ;
       [8 App. Cas. 508
   See LANDLORD AND TENANT—CUSTOM OF
   COUNTRY.
—— Scotch law - - 10 App. Cas. 813
   See SCOTCH LAW—MINE. 1.

RESERVATION OF RIGHT OF WAY—Absolute
   conveyance 24 Ch. D. 572
   See VENDOR AND PURCHASER—AGREE-
   MENT. 1.
—— Settled Land Act—Power of trustees
       [24 Ch. D. 129
   See SETTLED LAND ACT—TRUSTEES. 6.

RESERVE FORCES ACT, 1882.
   See ARMY—*Statutes.*

RESERVE FUND—Profits of company
       [16 Ch. D. 344
   See COMPANY—DIVIDENDS. 4.

RESERVOIR—Escape of water 7 App. Cas. 694
   See SCOTCH LAW—STATUTORY DUTY.

RESIDENCE — Debtor — Debtor's summons —
   Jurisdiction - 16 Ch. D. 484
   See BANKRUPTCY—ACT OF BANKRUPTCY.
   14.
—— Debtor—Out of jurisdiction 25 Ch. D. 500
   See BANKRUPTCY—ACT OF BANKRUPTCY.
   26.
—— Devise of house—Forfeiture for non-resi-
   dence - - 25 Ch. D. 605
   See WILL—CONDITION. 6.

RESIDENCE—*continued.*

—— Domicil.
　　See Cases under DOMICIL.

—— Pauper.
　　See Cases under POOR LAW — SETTLE-
　　MENT.

—— Statement of—Bill of sale　　21 Ch. D. 871 ;
　　　　　　　　[22 Ch. D. 136 ; 10 Q. B. D. 90
　　See BILL OF SALE—FORMALITIES. 5, 6, 7.

RESIDUARY GIFT.
　　See Cases under WILL — RESIDUARY
　　GIFT.

—— Exception from residue—Void bequest
　　See WILL—LAPSE. 7.　　[23 Ch. D. 218

—— Separate use　-　　-　　19 Ch. D. 277
　　See HUSBAND AND WIFE — SEPARATE
　　ESTATE. 13.

—— Specific legacy　-　　-　20 Ch. D. 676 ;
　　　　　　　　　　　　[8 App. Cas. 812
　　See WILL—SPECIFIC LEGACY.

—— Void appointment　　-　　18 Ch. D. 499
　　See POWER—EXECUTION. 8.

RESIDUARY LEGATEE—Costs as between soli-
　　citor and client -　　　　26 Ch. D. 179
　　See EXECUTOR—ACTIONS. 14.

RESIDUE—Legacy payable out of—Interim in-
　　come　　-　　　　　　　25 Ch. D. 743
　　See WILL—INTERIM INCOME. 3.

RESIGNATION — Corporate office — Power to
　　withdraw resignation　　14 Q. B. D. 908
　　See MUNICIPAL CORPORATION—RESIGNA-
　　TION.

RESOLUTION—Altering memorandum of asso-
　　ciation　　-　　　　-　　30 Ch. D. 376
　　See COMPANY—MEMORANDUM AND AR-
　　TICLES. 1.

—— Creditors—Bankruptcy—Direction as to ad-
　　ministration　　-　　　　21 Ch. D. 397
　　See BANKRUPTCY—TRUSTEE. 1.

—— Creditors—For composition.
　　See Cases under BANKRUPTCY—COMPO-
　　SITION. 1—8.

—— Creditors—For liquidation.
　　See Cases under BANKRUPTCY—LIQUIDA-
　　TION. 6—9.

—— Voluntary winding-up — Appointment of
　　liquidator　　-　　　　26 Ch. D. 70
　　See COMPANY—VOLUNTARY WINDING-UP.
　　2.

RESTITUTIO IN INTEGRUM—Scotch law
　　　　　　　　　　　　[7 App. Cas. 547
　　See SCOTCH LAW—PUBLIC RIGHTS.

RESTITUTION OF CONJUGAL RIGHTS
　　　　　　　　　　[9 P. D. 52 ; 10 P. D. 72
　　See PRACTICE — DIVORCE—RESTITUTION
　　OF CONJUGAL RIGHTS. 1, 2.

——

　　See PRACTICE—DIVORCE — RESTITUTION
　　OF CONJUGAL RIGHTS—*Statutes.*

—— Agreement by wife not to sue　10 P. D. 188
　　See PRACTICE — DIVORCE— SEPARATION
　　DEED. 1.

—— Service of petition—Jurisdiction
　　　　　　　　　　　　　[10 P. D. 186
　　See PRACTICE—DIVORCE—SERVICE.

RESTITUTION OF GOODS—Sale of stolen beasts
　　in market overt—Claim by purchaser
　　against owner for cost of keeping
　　　　　　　　　　　　[8 Q. B. D. 109
　　See SALE OF GOODS—CONTRACT. 2.

RESTRAINT OF MARRIAGE—Covenant not to
　　revoke will　　-　　-　23 Ch. D. 285
　　See COVENANT—VALIDITY.

—— Restriction of marriage with domestic ser-
　　vant　　　　　　　　16 Ch. D. 188
　　See WILL—CONDITION. 10.

RESTRAINT OF SHIP— Bail bond—Form —
　　Value of Plaintiff's shares　10 P. D. 15
　　See PRACTICE—ADMIRALTY—ARREST OF
　　SHIP. 1.

RESTRAINT OF TRADE—Covenant in lease.
　　See Cases under LANDLORD AND TENANT
　　—LEASE. 4—8.

—— Scotch law　　-　　-　7 App. Cas. 427
　　See SCOTCH LAW — HERITABLE PRO-
　　PERTY. 1.

RESTRAINT ON ALIENATION　26 Ch. D. 801
　　See WILL—REPUGNANCY.

RESTRAINT ON ANTICIPATION　18 Ch. D. 531
　　See SETTLEMENT—FUTURE PROPERTY. 2.

——

　　See Cases under HUSBAND AND WIFE—
　　SEPARATE ESTATE. 8—15.

—— Election　　-　27 Ch. D. 606 ; 28 Ch. D. 124
　　See ELECTION. 5, 6.

—— Perpetuity　-　　-　-　17 Ch. D. 368
　　See WILL—PERPETUITY. 6.

—— When removeable.
　　See HUSBAND AND WIFE — SEPARATE
　　ESTATE—*Statutes.*

RESTRICTIONS IN FEU CHARTER
　　　　　　　　　　　　[7 App. Cas. 427
　　See SCOTCH LAW — HERITABLE PRO-
　　PERTY. 1.

RESTRICTIVE COVENANT

—— Conveyance settled by Judge 21 Ch. D. 466
　　See VENDOR AND PURCHASER—CONVEY-
　　ANCE. 1.

—— In lease.
　　See Cases under LANDLORD AND TENANT
　　—LEASE. 2—8.

—— Objection to title 17 Ch. D. 353 ; 21 Ch. D. 95
　　See VENDOR AND PURCHASER—TITLE.
　　3, 6.

RETAINER.

—— Heir-at-Law—*Real Estate*—3 & 4 *Will.* 4,
　c. 104—*Hinde Palmer's Act* (32 & 33 *Vict. c.* 46).]
　　An heir-at-law or devisee has no right of retainer,
　　either out of the proceeds of sale of real estate,
　　or out of rents received by him, for a debt due
　　to him on simple contract from the testator or
　　intestate.　Such right of retainer arises only
　　where the creditor is a person liable to be sued
　　at law for debts of the same nature owing by
　　the testator or intestate, so that other creditors
　　might gain priority over him if he had not a right
　　to retain, and therefore an heir or devisee, as he
　　cannot be sued at law for simple contract debts,
　　has no right of retainer for them.—*Semble,* that
　　notwithstanding Hinde Palmer's Act (32 & 33 Vict.
　　c. 46), an heir-at-law or devisee where the estates
　　are not charged with debts, may retain a debt to

RETAINER—*continued.*

which he is entitled by specialty in which the heirs are bound.—*Ferguson v. Gibson* (Law Rep. 14 Eq. 379) considered. *In re* ILLIDGE. DAVIDSON *v.* ILLIDGE　-　24 Ch. D. 654; 27 Ch. D. 478

—— Executor.

　　See Cases under EXECUTOR—RETAINER.

RETAINER OF SOLICITOR　　26 Ch. D. 169

　　See SOLICITOR—RETAINER.

RETAINING WALL—Railway cutting

[29 Ch. D. 60

　　See RAILWAY COMPANY—LIABILITIES. 1.

RETIREMENT—Directors　　17 Ch. D. 373

　　See COMPANY—PROSPECTUS. 2.

—— Incumbent—Incumbents' Resignation Act

[17 Ch. D. 1

　　See ECCLESIASTICAL LAW—CLERGY. 3.

—— Shareholder—Cost-book company

[23 Ch. D. 52

　　See COMPANY—COST-BOOK COMPANY. 4.

—— Trustee　-　-　27 Ch. D. 333

　　See SETTLEMENT—POWERS. 9.

RETURN TO MANDAMUS—Pleading

　　See MANDAMUS. 1.　　[14 Q. B. D. 13

RETURNING OFFICER—Municipal corporation —Election　　-　6 Q. B. D. 323

　　See MUNICIPAL CORPORATION — ELECTION. 3.

—— Parliament—Election.

　　See PARLIAMENT—ELECTION—*Statutes.*

REVENUE :　　　　　　　　　　　　　Col.

I. REVENUE — COLLECTION (and MANAGEMENT.)

Buildings.] *The Act 44 & 45 Vict. c. 10, provides for the transfer of property held for the use and service of the Inland Revenue to the Commissioners of Her Majesty's Works and Public Buildings.*

Taxes.] *By 45 & 46 Vict. c. 72, s. 7, the words " and all such orders shall be final and conclusive on all parties " in sub-sect. (b), the words " of the High Court" after the word "orders" in sub-sect. (d), and sub-sect. (e), in sect. 59 of the Taxes Management Act, 1880, are repealed.*

Act of 1883.] *The Act 46 & 47 Vict. c. 55 (Revenue Act, 1883), amends the law relating to Inland Revenue.*

Sect. 12 *extends sect. 26 of the Taxes Management Act, 1880, as to places of meeting of Land Tax Commissioners.*

Sect. 13 *extends sect. 38 of the Taxes Management Act, 1883, as to cases in which the jurisdiction vested in Board of Inland Revenue by that section may be exercised.*

Sect. 14 *removes doubts as to construction and*

I. REVENUE — COLLECTION (and MANAGEMENT)—*continued.*

application of ss. 90 and 97 of the Taxes Management Act, 1880.

Act of 1884.] *The Act 47 & 48 Vict. c. 62 (Revenue Act, 1884), s. 7, amends the Taxes Management Act, 1880, and explains s. 90 of the same.*

Post Office.] *The Act 47 & 48 Vict. c. 62, s. 13, amends 16 & 17 Vict. c. 45, 27 & 28 Vict. c. 43, and 35 & 36 Vict. c. 67, with respect to claims on the Post Office for granting Government annuities.*

Vouchers.] *The Act 47 & 48 Vict. c. 62, s. 14, amends 29 & 30 Vict. c. 39, with respect to what constitutes a voucher in the case of certain payments out of money granted for army and navy services.*

II. REVENUE—CUSTOMS.

The Act 44 & 45 Vict. c. 12 (the Customs and Inland Revenue Act, 1881).

Sect. 3 *alters the Customs duties on beer.*

Sect. 4 *provides for drawbacks on the exportation of imported beer.*

Sect. 5. *Provisions as to importation of beer.*

Sect. 6. *Beer imported may be exported.*

Sect. 7. *Alteration of duties on spirits imported.*

Sect. 8. *Mode of testing in cases of obscuration.*

Sect. 9. *Time and place for landing goods inwards.*

Sect. 10. *Time and places for landing and shipping coastwise.*

Sect. 11. *As to delivery of specifications for free goods six days after clearance, except salmon.*

Sect. 12. *Persons may be searched if officers have reason to suspect smuggled goods are concealed upon them. Rescuing goods. Rescuing persons. Assaulting or obstructing officers. Attempting the foregoing offences. Penalty.*

Sect. 13 *incorporates sects. 5–12, both inclusive, with the Customs Consolidation Act, 1876.*

Sect. 48 *repeals 30 & 31 Vict. c. 23, ss. 5, 6. and Schedule E ; 32 & 33 Vict. c. 103, ss. 3, 4, 5, 9, 10, and 11 ; 39 & 40 Vict. c. 35, part of Schedule ; and 39 & 40 Vict. c. 36 (Customs Consolidation Act, 1876), ss. 48, 110, 143, 144, and 147.*

Act of 1882.] *The Act 45 & 46 Vict. c. 72, amends the laws relating to Customs and Inland Revenue.*

Sect. 2. *Upon revocation of approval of Customs warehouse goods to be cleared or removed.*

Sect. 3. *Salaries and superannuation allowances of officers not to be subject to execution or attachment under any process.*

Sect. 4. *Repealed by 48 & 49 Vict. c. 51.*

Sect. 5 *amends sect. 9 of 43 & 44 Vict. c. 24.*

Sect. 6. *Person charged with an offence against sect. 4 of 23 & 24 Vict. c. 90, may be convicted of an offence against sect. 7 of 33 & 34 Vict. c. 57.*

Sect. 7 *re-enacts sect. 60 of 43 Geo. 3, c. 161.*

Act of 1883.] *The Act 46 & 47 Vict. c. 55 (the Revenue Act, 1883), amends the Customs Consolidation Act (39 & 40 Vict. c. 36), 1876.*

Sect. 2 *amends sect. 42 of 39 & 40 Vict. c. 36.*

Sect. 3. *Foreign spirits racked into casks, not less than nine gallons, may be exported.*

Sect. 4 *provides for recovery of penalties under Customs Acts where judgment has been obtained in a superior Court.*

Execution may be issued both against the person and the real and personal property of the party in default.

Sect. 5. *Vessel arriving at port to come quickly*

II. REVENUE—CUSTOMS—continued.

to place of unloading and bring to at the stations for boarding officers. Penalty for neglect £20.

Sect. 6. Accommodation for custom officers to be provided on board. Penalty £20.

Sect. 7. If seals upon stores inwards be broken or the stores secretly conveyed away, master to forfeit £20.

Sect. 8 amends sect. 230 of 39 & 40 Vict. c. 36.

Sect. 9 extends the word "ship" in 39 & 40 Vict. c. 38, to sea-fishing boats.

Sect. 11. Act to be construed as one with 39 & 40 Vict. c. 36.

Sect. 19. Repeals in part 39 & 40 Vict. c. 36.

Act of 1884.] The Act 47 & 48 Vict. c. 62 (the Revenue Act, 1884), enacts sect. 2—(1.) That vessels with inward cargo for more than one port may convey certain goods coastwise. (2.) Repeals part of sect. 142 of 39 & 40 Vict. c. 36 (Customs Consolidation Act, 1876).

Sect. 3. The master or owner is to deliver a manifest of goods shipped, and in the case of steamships a certificate of the coal to be used on board.

The sect. 111 of 39 & 40 Vict. c. 36 (the Customs Consolidation Act, 1876), is repealed.

Sect. 5. Construction of this Act.

Sect. 8 amends ss. 4 and 11, and Schedule B. of 30 & 31 Vict. c. 23.

Plate.] By 46 & 47 Vict. c. 55 (the Revenue Act, 1883), s. 10, provision is made for securing with more certainty the marking of all gold and silver plate of standard quality imported into Great Britain or Ireland to be sold, exchanged, or exposed for sale; and also for allowing the exportation of imported plate of coarser alloy than the said respective standards.

The Act 47 & 48 Vict. c. 62, s. 4, exempts certain oriental plate from assay in the United Kingdom, but subject to the payment of customs duties.

Act of 1885.] The Act of 48 & 49 Vict. c. 51, s. 2, continues duties on tea.

III. REVENUE—EXCISE. [1]

The Act 44 & 45 Vict. c. 12 (the Customs and Inland Revenue Act, 1881).

Sect. 14 grants a duty on brewer's licence where annual value of the house exceeds £10 and does not exceed £15.

Sect. 15 allows deductions and exemptions from duty with regard to brewers other than brewers for sale.

Sect. 16 repealed by 48 & 49 Vict. c. 51.

Sect. 17. Provisions as to warehousing foreign wine in an excise warehouse.

Sect. 18. Goods liable to duty of custom or excise may be warehoused in a custom or excise warehouse.

Sect. 48 repeals 23 & 24 Vict. c. 129, ss. 2 and 3; 32 & 33 Vict. c. 103, ss. 3, 4, 5, 9, 10, and 11.

Chicory and Coffee.] The Act 45 & 46 Vict. c. 41, repeals the customs and excise duties on vegetable matters (other than chicory) applicable to the uses of chicory and coffee and imposes a duty on substances intended to serve as imitations or substitutes for chicory or coffee.

Act of 1883.] The Act 46 & 47 Vict. c. 10, grants certain duties of Customs and Inland Revenue, alters other duties, and amends the law relating to Customs and Inland Revenue.

III. REVENUE—EXCISE—continued.

Sect. 1. Act to be cited as the Customs and Inland Revenue Act, 1883.

Sect. 2 continues duties on tea.

Sect. 3. All explosives as defined by the Explosives Act, 1875, and the Explosive Substances Act, 1883, to be deemed restricted goods within 39 & 40 Vict. c. 36.

Sect. 4 alters date of expiration of game licences.

Sect. 5. Game licences may be taken out for 14 days.

Sect. 6 alters date of expiration of gun licences.

Sect. 7 extends the expression "carriage" in subsection 6 of sect. 19 of 32 & 33 Vict. c. 14. to any vehicle drawn or propelled upon a road or tramway, or elsewhere than upon a railway, by steam or electricity, or any other mechanical power.

Act of 1884.] The Act 47 & 48 Vict. c. 25 (Customs and Inland Revenue Act, 1884).

Sect. 2 continues duties on tea.

Sect. 3 fixes duty on licence for hackney carriage at fifteen shillings.

Sect. 4 reduces duties on carriages commenced to be used on or after 1st October in any year.

Tobacco on Railways.] The Act 47 & 48 Vict. c. 62 (the Revenue Act, 1884), s. 12, declares it to be lawful for any railway company to obtain licences from the Inland Revenue to sell tobacco and snuff in railway carriages. Any railway company dealing in tobacco or snuff without a licence is liable to a fine of £50.

Act of 1885.] The Act 48 & 49 Vict. c. 51 (Customs and Inland Revenue Act, 1885), amends the laws relating to Inland Revenue.

Sect. 3 regulates allowances on British spirits exported or used in warehouse.

Sect. 4 extends term "beer" in 43 & 44 Vict. c. 20, and in Excise Licence Acts.

Sect. 5. Duty for private brewers' licence.

Sect. 6 amends 43 & 44 Vict. c. 20, s. 20, as to worts.

Sect. 7. Sugar store to be entered by brewer for sale, and accounts of sugar to be kept.

Sect. 8. Prohibition against adulteration of beer by brewers for sale, and dealers and retailers of beer.

Sect. 9. Provision as to penalties.

Repeal.] Sect. 10 repeals 56 Geo. 3, c. 58: sect. 4 of 23 & 24 Vict. c. 129; sect. 20 of 25 & 26 Vict. c. 22; sect. 12 of 27 & 28 Vict. c. 12; sect. 12 of 28 & 29 Vict. c. 98; sect. 16 of 44 & 45 Vict. c. 12; sect. 4 of 45 & 46 Vict. c. 72.

———— Beer—Brewer other than a Brewer for Sale — Exemption from Duty—Annual Value of House occupied not exceeding £10—Inland Revenue Act, 1880 (43 & 44 Vict. c. 20) s. 33, sub-s. 3.] By the Inland Revenue Act, 1880, s. 33, sub-s. 3, if the annual value of the house occupied by a brewer other than a brewer for sale does not exceed £10, the beer brewed by him shall not be charged with duty. The Respondent brewed beer (not for sale) in a house occupied by him of an annual value not exceeding £10, and he occupied, as a residence, another house which was of greater annual value than £10:—Held, that the exemption from duty did not apply to the beer so brewed. TIPPETT v. HART　-　-　- 10 Q. B. D. 483

IV. REVENUE—HOUSE DUTY :—

The Statute 44 & 45 Vict. c. 12 (Customs and Inland Revenue Act, 1881) *— Sect.* 24 *interprets the meaning of "servant" and "other person" in exemption from inhabited house duty under the Customs and Inland Revenue Act,* 1878, *s.* 13, *sub-s.* 2.

1. —— **Dwelling-house let in Tenements—** *House, Definition of—*41 *&* 42 *Vict. c.* 15, *s.* 13*— Necessity of structural Severance—Occupation of Part by Landlord—*57 *Geo.* 3, *c.* 25.] The statute 41 & 42 Vict. c. 15, s. 13, sub-s. 1, provides that, when any house being one property shall be divided into and let in different tenements, and any of such tenements are occupied solely for the purposes of any trade or business, or of any profession or calling by which the occupier seeks a livelihood or profit, or are unoccupied, the person chargeable as occupier of the house shall be at liberty to give notice in writing at any time during the year of assessment to the surveyor of taxes stating therein the facts, and after the receipt of such notice by the surveyor the Commissioners acting in the execution of the Acts relating to the inhabited house duties shall, upon proof of the facts to their satisfaction, grant relief from the amount of duty charged in the assessment, so as to confine the same to the duty on the value according to which the house should, in their opinion, have been assessed if it had been a house comprising only the tenements other than such as are occupied as aforesaid or are unoccupied :—*Held,* that the provisions of the sub-section only apply in cases where the house is divided into different tenements structurally severed from each other, as for instance in the case of flats and sets of chambers.—Where a part on the ground floor and basement of a building was severed from the rest of the building by a party-wall, and, had its own separate entrance, there being no communication between it and the rest of the building, and the part so separated was used wholly for the purposes of a bank :— *Held,* that such part of the premises constituted a separate house, and being used solely for business purposes was exempt from inhabited house duty. —*Semble, per* Hawkins, J., that, when a house is substantially within the words of the sub-section above referred to as being a house structurally divided into and let in different tenements, the mere fact that the landlord occupied one of such tenements forming a small portion of the whole, would not disentitle him to the relief given by the sub-section. CHAPMAN *v.* ROYAL BANK OF SCOTLAND　-　-　7 Q. B. D. 136

2. —— **Dwelling-house let in Tenements—** 41 *& 42 Vict. c.* 15, *s.* 13.] By 41 & 42 Vict. c. 15, s. 13,where any house being one property is divided into and let in different tenements, and any of such tenements are occupied solely for the purpose of any trade or business or of any profession or calling, by which the occupier seeks a livelihood or profit, or are unoccupied, inhabited house duty is to be assessed as if the house comprised only the tenements other than those so occupied as aforesaid, or unoccupied ; and a house or tenement occupied solely as aforesaid is exempt, although a servant or other person may dwell in such house or tenement for the protection thereof.

IV. REVENUE—HOUSE DUTY—*continued.*

—A house had one entrance into the street, and the rooms in it opened on a hall, passages, and staircase, common to all the tenants. Some of the rooms on the ground floor were occupied by the landlords, the Appellants, as offices, and the remainder, and the rooms on the first floor, were let to tenants who occupied them as offices. The rooms on the second floor were occupied partly by tenants who resided, and the remainder by a caretaker and his wife, who acted as servants to the residents and cleaned the several portions occupied by the Appellants as offices or let off. The Appellants claimed relief from being assessed on the portions used as offices :—*Held,* affirming the decision of the Queen's Bench Division, that the portions so used were not exempt, as the exemption applies to houses let in separate and distinct tenements each complete in itself, and not to rooms in a house. YORKSHIRE FIRE AND LIFE INSURANCE COMPANY *v.* CLAYTON
[6 Q. B. D. 557 ; 8 Q. B. D. 421

3. —— **Exemption—***" Servant or other Person "* —32 *&* 33 *Vict. c.* 14, *s.* 11.] The Respondent was a hop-merchant, and was possessed of certain houses having an internal communication throughout, and used for the purposes of his trade. K. lived in the houses in order to take care of them, but he was a clerk in the Respondent's employ at a salary of £150 a year, and he resided in the houses together with his wife, children, and servant :—*Held,* that K. was not "a servant or other person" within the meaning of 32 & 33 Vict. c. 14, s. 11, and that the Respondent was not exempt from inhabited house duty in respect of the houses. YEWENS *v.* NOAKES 6 Q. B. D. 530

4. —— **Exemption—***" Servant or other Person "* —41 *&* 42 *Vict. c.*15, *s.* 13, *part* 2.] The Respondents, wholesale clothiers, were possessed of premises the whole of which were used as warehouses and counting-houses, except a sitting-room and bedroom on the top storey occupied by their cashier, who had a salary of £200 a year, and who slept on the premises solely as caretaker and for their protection, this being considered as part of his duty :—*Held,* that the Income Tax Commissioners were warranted in finding that the cashier was "a servant or other person" within 41 & 42 Vict. c. 15, s. 13, part 2, and that the premises were accordingly exempt from house duty.— *Yewens* v. *Noakes* (6 Q. B. D. 530) explained. ROLFE *v.* HYDE　-　　6 Q. B. D. 673

5. —— **Exemption—***" Servant or other Person " —Caretaker—Customs and Inland Revenue Act,* 1878 (41 *&* 42 *Vict. c.* 15), *s.* 13, *sub-s.* 2*—Customs and Inland Revenue Act,* 1881 (44 *& 45 Vict. c.* 12), *s.* 24.] A female caretaker resided on premises, and it was a condition of her employment that her son, who was a clerk employed elsewhere, should sleep on the premises for their better protection :—*Held,* that the premises were not exempt from inhabited house duty under 41 & 42 Vict. c. 15, s. 13, sub-s. 2. WEGUELLIN *v.* WAYALL　　　-　　14 Q. B. D. 838

V. REVENUE—INCOME-TAX.

Act of 1881.] *By* 44 *&* 45 *Vict. c.* 12 (*the Customs and Inland Revenue Act,* 1881), *s.* 23, *the particulars of the property assessed, &c., are to be*

V. REVENUE—INCOME TAX—*continued.*

inserted in the collector's receipt when they have not been stated in the demand note.

Customs Act of 1884.] *By the 47 & 48 Vict. c. 25 (Customs and Inland Revenue Act, 1884), s. 7 (1) if any dividends, &c., payable half-yearly or quarterly shall have become due in the course of the year commencing 6th of April, 1884, and shall have been paid to any person prior to the passing of this Act, without deduction of income tax, such tax may be added to the assessment on the next half-yearly or quarterly payment. (2.) A similar enactment for rent or other annual payment.*

Revenue Act of 1884.] *By the Act 47 & 48 Vict. c. 62 (the Revenue Act, 1884), s. 6, the poor law parishes in England, under 32 & 33 Vict. c. 67, elsewhere than in the city of London, shall be parishes for purposes of income tax and inhabited house duties. The union or grouping of parishes under 43 & 44 Vict. c. 19, shall be subject to this section.*

Income Tax Act of 1885.] *The Act 48 & 49 Vict. c. 1, grants to her Majesty additional rates of income tax.*

Customs Act, 1885.] *The Act 48 & 49 Vict. c. 51 (the Customs and Inland Revenue Act, 1885).*

Sect. 22 grants duties of income tax.

Sect. 23. Application of provisions of Income Tax Acts.

Sect. 24. Provisions as to duty on dividends, &c., paid prior to the passing of this Act.

Sect. 25. Allowances to assessors and collectors.

Foreign and Colonial Dividends.] *Sect. 26. The following enactments, viz., sect. 96 of 5 & 6 Vict. c. 35, sect. 2 of 5 & 6 Vict. c. 80, sect. 10 of 16 & 17 Vict. c. 34, and sect. 36 of 24 & 25 Vict. c. 91, being enactments to secure payment of income tax upon dividends of foreign and colonial securities, are to be read as if among the persons entrusted with payment of dividends, were* (a.) *any banker;* (b.) *any person who obtains payment of dividends for another elsewhere than in the United Kingdom;* (c.) *any dealer in coupons payable out of the United Kingdom.*

A person entrusted with payment of dividends and causing income tax to be paid, is entitled to a remuneration of not less than 3d. in the pound of the amount paid, as may be fixed by the Treasury.

1886.] *Sect. 27. Income Tax Acts to apply to duties granted for 1886.*

1. —— Assize Courts—*Police Stations*—5 & 6 Vict. c. 35—16 & 17 Vict. c. 34, *Schedules A and B.*] The justices of a county in the due exercise of statutory powers erected assize courts with the usual rooms and offices, and a county police station with the usual offices and accommodation for constables living there and for prisoners. The land on which they were built was conveyed under 21 & 22 Vict. c. 92, to the clerk of the peace to hold to him and his successors for ever upon trust for the construction of a police station and otherwise for such uses as the county justices should from time to time order. The buildings formed one block and were used for the administration of justice and for police purposes. Parts of the buildings were also used for holding county and committee meetings and various other occasional purposes, but no rent or profit was received or made in respect of the buildings or any part of them:—*Held,* affirming

V. REVENUE—INCOME TAX—*continued.*

the judgment of the Court of Appeal, that income tax was not payable in respect of the buildings under Scheds. A or B of 5 & 6 Vict. c. 35, and 16 & 17 Vict. c. 34.—*Clerk* v. *Dumfries Commissioners of Supply* (7 Court Sess. Cas. 4th Series, 1157) disapproved. COOMBER v. JUSTICES OF THE COUNTY OF BERKS　　9 Q. B. D. 17; 10 Q. B. D.
[267; 9 App. Cas. 61

2. —— Burial Board—*Application of Surplus Income in aid of Poor-rate*—"*Profit*"—5 & 6 Vict. c. 35, s. 60; 15 & 16 Vict. c. 85, s. 22.] A burial board was constituted under 15 & 16 Vict. c. 85, and in pursuance of the Act a burial ground was provided with money charged upon the poor-rate of the parish, and the surplus over expenditure of the income derived from the fees charged by the board was regularly applied in aid of the poor-rate :—*Held,* that the board were liable to be assessed to the income tax in respect of such surplus, inasmuch as the provision requiring it to be applied in aid of the poor-rate did not prevent it from being a "profit" within 5 & 6 Vict. c. 35, s. 60. PADDINGTON BURIAL BOARD v. COMMISSIONERS OF INLAND REVENUE　　-　　13 Q. B. D. 9

3. —— Coal Mines—*Partnership—Incorporation of—Succession—Diminution of Profits from Extraordinary Depression of Trade — "Specific Cause"*—5 & 6 Vict. c. 35, s. 60, Scheds. A and D—Rules—29 & 30 Vict. c. 36, s. 8.] A partnership, after working certain coal mines for more than five years, was on the 21st of December, 1875, incorporated as a limited company, and sold to the company the assets, subject to the liabilities, of the partnership. The partners became holders of all the shares in the limited company according to their interests. After the 3rd of August, 1876, changes took place in the shareholders. The company, being assessed by the Income Tax Commissioners to the income tax under 5 & 6 Vict. c. 35, Sched. D, for the year ending the 5th of April, 1877, on an average of the five preceding years, appealed, and contended that they were only to pay on a computation for one year on the average of the profits from the 21st of December, 1875, the date of the incorporation.—The Commissioners stated a case in which they found that "the profits and gains of the Appellants' business had fallen short since the 21st of December, 1875," from the following specific causes, viz., "the extraordinary depression in the iron and coal trades whereby the Appellants were unable to sell either so large a quantity of their coals as they had formerly been enabled to do, or to obtain anything like so good a price for such coals." Figures shewing that the annual profits had fallen short by one-half were set out :—*Held,* that Sched. A, rule 4, clause 6, which prescribes that if it shall appear that the account required by the rules "cannot be made out by reason of the possession or interest of the party to be charged thereon having commenced within the time for which the account is directed to be made out, the profits of one year shall be estimated in proportion to the profits received within the time elapsed since the commencement of such possession or interest," did not apply.—That the business was a "trade . . . adventure or concern," within Sched. D, rule 1, of

V. REVENUE—INCOME TAX—*continued.*

the rules for ascertaining the duties to be charged thereon, and was not within the terms of the proviso "set up and commenced" within the period of three years.—That the company was a new association carrying on an old concern; and had "succeeded" to it within clause 4 of the third set of Rules in Sched. D, but that, since such succession, the profits had fallen short from a "specific cause" within the exception in that clause.—And that the sixth case of the said rules applied, and under it the computation should be made "on the amount of the full value of the profits and gains received annually," i.e., for the current year. RY-HOPE COAL COMPANY *v.* FOYER　　**7 Q. B. D. 485**

4. —— **Coal Mines**—*Royalties—Dead Rent—Deductions from Gross Profits—Provision for recouping Dead Rents out of Royalties, Effect of—5 & 6 Vict. c. 35, s. 60 (Sched. A), r. 3; Sect. 100 (Sched. D)—29 & 30 Vict. c. 36, s. 8.*] By an agreement for lease of coal mines for a term of years from March, 1874, the lessees agreed to pay a dead rent for the mines, and royalties at specified rates per ton on all coal worked; the dead rent to be recoupable out of royalties during the first sixteen years of the term—the effect being, that the lessor received on account of his share of the profits of the concern not less than a fixed annual sum; so that when his share of the royalties did not amount to the fixed sum he received that sum; but when his share of the royalties exceeded the fixed sum he received that sum only until the lessees had been reimbursed the excess paid to the lessor when his share of the royalties did not amount to the fixed sum. The lessees worked the mines for the first time in October, 1880, having paid the dead rent, less income-tax, to the lessor up to that year. Upon an assessment to the income tax, made upon the lessees under Schedule D, for the year 1881–2, it appeared that the lessor's share of the royalties for that year had exceeded the dead rent by the sum of £1477:—*Held,* that, in estimating the profits of the concern for the particular year for the purpose of being assessed under the Income Tax Acts, the lessees were not entitled to deduct the £1477 from their gross profits. BROUGHTON COAL COMPANY *v.* KIRKPATRICK　　**14 Q. B. D. 491**

5. —— **Company**—*Debenture Coupons payable Abroad—Deduction from Tax of Sums payable Abroad—5 & 6 Vict. c. 35, ss. 100, 102, 159, & Sched. D.*] An English company carrying on their business in Alexandria where their gains and profits were earned were held to be properly assessed to the income tax in respect of the whole of the profits of the concern, without any deduction on account of the interest on the debenture bonds of the company paid to the holders of such bonds in Alexandria ; there being nothing in sects. 102 and 159 of the Income Tax Act (5 & 6 Vict. c. 35) to limit rule 4 in sect. 100, which states that "no deduction shall be made on account of any annual interest or any annuity or other annual payment payable out of such profits or gains." ALEXANDRIA WATER COMPANY *v.* MUSGRAVE　　-　　**11 Q. B. D. 174**

6. —— **Corporation** *appropriated by Statute to certain Purposes—5 & 6 Vict. c. 35, s. 60, Sched. A. No. III.*] A corporation was constituted for the management of the Mersey Dock estate

V. REVENUE—INCOME TAX—*continued.*

by an Act which provided that the moneys to be received by them from their dock dues and other sources of revenue should be applied in payment of expenses, interest upon debts, construction of works and management of the estate ; and that the surplus should be applied to a sinking fund for the extinguishment of the principal of the debts ; and that after such extinguishment the rates should be reduced ; and that except as aforesaid the moneys should not be applied for any other purpose whatsoever ; and that nothing should affect their liability to parochial or local rates :—*Held,* affirming the decision of the Court of Appeal, that under the Income Tax Acts the corporation was liable to income tax in respect of the surplus though applicable to the above-named purposes only. MERSEY DOCKS AND HARBOUR BOARD *v.* LUCAS -　　**8 App. Cas. 891**

7. —— **Foreign Corporation** — *Dividends to Shareholders in the United Kingdom—Dividends intrusted to Agents for Payment—16 & 17 Vict. c. 34, s. 10.*] A foreign company carrying on business and earning profits abroad, had an agency in London which conducted a branch and earned profits. The dividends of the company were payable, at the option of the shareholders, abroad or by the London agency. In a particular year the London agency earned an amount of profits which enabled them to pay all the dividends demanded of them in that year without requiring or obtaining any remittance from the company abroad. The London agency were assessed to income tax under Sched. D on the profits earned in the United Kingdom on an average of the three preceding years, the amount on which they were so assessed being less than the amount actually earned by them in that year. They further made a return under 16 & 17 Vict. c. 34, s. 10, that no interest, dividends, or other annual payments payable out of or in respect of the stock, funds, or shares of the company had been intrusted to them for payment in the United Kingdom, and appealed against an assessment of the Commissioners whereby they were assessed in respect of the dividends paid by them :—*Held,* affirming the judgment of the Exchequer Division, that the London agency were intrusted with the payment of dividends in the United Kingdom, within the meaning of 16 & 17 Vict. c. 34, s. 10, and that they were liable to be assessed on the full amount of the dividends they so paid in the year, but that since the dividends were payable out of the general earnings of the company, consisting of profits made partly in the United Kingdom and partly elsewhere, and the London agency had already been assessed to income tax on the former under Sched. D, they ought not to be further assessed under 16 & 17 Vict. c. 34, s. 10, and pay income tax in respect of that portion of the dividends which represented profits arising out of the United Kingdom. GILBERTSON *v.* FERGUSSON　　-　　**7 Q. B. D. 562**

8. —— **Foreign Telegraph Company**—*Marine Cables—Exercising Trade in England—Messages forwarded from England to remote Parts of the World—16 & 17 Vict. c. 34; 5 & 6 Vict. c. 35.*] The Appellants, a foreign company domiciled in Copenhagen, had three marine cables in connection with Aberdeen and Newcastle, commu-

V. REVENUE—INCOME TAX—*continued.*

nicating with the telegraph lines of the Post Office in the United Kingdom. They had also work-rooms with clerks in London, Newcastle, and Aberdeen. Messages from this country were forwarded over the lines of the Post Office and the cables of the Appellants to Denmark, and thence by their wires and the wires of foreign governments to Russia, China, Japan, and India. The total charges paid for transmitting such messages were collected by the Post Office, and, after deducting their dues, handed to the Appellants, who retained the amount due to them for the transmission of messages over their cables and lines, and paid the residue to the various governments and companies respectively entitled to it. No profits were made by the Appellants from the transmission of messages over the land lines in the United Kingdom :—*Held*, affirming the decision of the Queen's Bench Division, that the Appellants must be taken to exercise a trade in the United Kingdom under 16 & 17 Vict. c. 34, s. 2, Sched. D, and that they were chargeable to income tax on the balance of profits or gains from their receipts in this country from the transmission of messages. ERICHSEN *v.* LAST

[7 Q. B. D. 12 ; 8 Q. B. D. 414

9. —— Insurance Company—*"Annual Profits or Gains"* — *Sums paid as Bonuses to participating Policy-holders—Dividend—5 & 6 Vict. c. 35, s. 54.*] A life insurance company issued " participating policies " at an increased premium, according to the terms of which at the end of each quinquennial period " the gross profits " of such policies were thus dealt with : two-thirds were returned by way of bonus or abatement of premiums to the holders of such policies then in force : the remaining third went to the company, who bore the whole expenses of the business, the portion remaining after payment of expenses constituting the only profit available for division among the shareholders :—*Held*, reversing the decision of the Court of Appeal, by Lords Blackburn and FitzGerald, Lord Bramwell dissenting, that the two-thirds returned to the policy-holders were "annual profits or gains" and assessable to income tax. LAST *v.* LONDON ASSURANCE CORPORATION - 12 Q. B. D. 389 ; 14 Q. B. D. 239 ;

[10 App. Cas. 438

VI. REVENUE—LEGACY DUTY.

By the Customs and Inland Revenue Act, 1881 (44 & 45 Vict. c. 12), s. 41, where the ad valorem duty has been paid on the affidavit or account, in conformity with the Act, in respect of any legacy, residue, or share of residue payable out of or consisting of any estate, the duty at the rate of £1 per cent. imposed by the Act 55 Geo. 3, c. 184, is not payable.

[*See also, infra*, REVENUE—STAMPS—*Statutes.*]

Sect. 42. Subject to the relief from legacy duty given by sect. 13 of the Customs and Inland Revenue Act, 1880, every pecuniary legacy or residue, or share of residue under the will or intestacy of a person dying on or after the 1st day of June, 1881, although not of an amount or value of £20, shall be chargeable to the duties imposed by the said Act 55 Geo. 3, c. 184, as modified by this Act.

Sect. 43 confers a discretionary power upon the Commissioners of Inland Revenue, upon the appli-

VI. REVENUE—LEGACY DUTY—*continued.*

cation of the person acting in the execution of the will of any deceased person, and upon the delivery to them of an account shewing the amount of the estate and effects in respect whereof legacy duty is payable, together with the names or description of the class of persons entitled thereto and every part thereof, in possession or expectancy, and their degrees of consanguinity to the testator, to compound the amount of the duty shewn by such account.

If the Commissioners are of opinion that an application should receive the assent of any person, they shall refuse to entertain the application until such assent shall have been given.

1. —— Valuation of Property — *Executor — " Property which shall not be reduced into Money" —36 Geo. 3, c. 52, ss. 6, 22.*] By 36 Geo. 3, c. 52, s. 6, legacy duty shall be paid by the person taking the burden of the execution of the will upon delivery or payment of the residue of any personal estate to the person entitled, and by sect. 22, where the residue shall consist of "property which shall not be reduced into money," the executor may set a value thereon, and the Commissioners of the Inland Revenue may accept duty upon that value. Shortly after the death of a testatrix her executor brought into the Inland Revenue Office the residuary account of her property, in which a value was set upon certain pictures and other personal property not reduced into money, and the Commissioners accepted duty upon that value. Subsequently—the residuary legatee and the executor having always intended that the pictures should be sold in the course of the administration—the executor sold them for a sum greatly in excess of the value upon which duty had been paid, and accounted to the residuary legatee for the proceeds :—*Held*, that the provisions of sect. 22 apply to property which shall not be reduced into money during the course of the administration by the executor, and not merely to property which shall not have been reduced into money when the residuary account is brought in ; that the pictures, &c., therefore did not satisfy the description in sect. 22, and that the Crown were entitled to duty under sect. 6 upon the amount paid to the legatee. ATTORNEY-GENERAL *v.* DARDIER - - 11 Q. B. D. 16

VII. REVENUE—PROBATE DUTY.

By 44 & 45 Vict. c. 12 (the Customs and Inland Revenue Act, 1881), s. 27, the following duties are charged and made payable on and after the 1st day of June, 1881, on the affidavit to be required and received from the person applying for the probate or letters of administration in England; that is to say

| Where the estate and effects for or in respect of which the probate or letters of administration is or are to be granted, exclusive of what the deceased shall have been possessed of or entitled to as trustee, and not beneficially, shall be above the value of £100 and not above the value of £500. | Duty, At the rate of £1 for every full sum of £50 and for any fractional part of £50 over any multiple of £50. |

VII. REVENUE—PROBATE DUTY—_continued._

	Duty.
Where such estate and effects shall be above the value of £500, and not above the value of £1000.	At the rate of 25s. for every full sum of £50 and for any fractional part of £50 over any multiple of £50.
Where such estate and effects shall be above the value of £1000.	At the rate of £3 for every full sum of £100, and for any fractional part of £100 over any multiple of £100.

Sect. 28. _In the case of a person dying domiciled in any part of the United Kingdom, it shall be lawful for the person applying for the probate or letters of administration to state in his affidavit the fact of such domicil, and to deliver therewith or annex thereto a schedule of the debts due from the deceased to persons resident in the United Kingdom, and the funeral expenses, and in that case for the purpose of the charge of duty on the affidavit the aggregate amount of the debts and funeral expenses appearing in the schedule shall be deducted from the value of the estate and effects as specified in the account delivered with or annexed to the affidavit._

Debts to be deducted under this power are to be debts due and owing from the deceased and payable by law out of any part of the estate and effects comprised in the affidavit, and are not to include voluntary debts expressed to be payable on the death of the deceased, or payable under any instrument which shall not have been bonâ fide delivered to the donee thereof three months before the death of deceased, or debts in respect whereof any real estate may be primarily liable, or a re-imbursement may be capable of being claimed from any real estate of the deceased or from any other estate or person. Funeral expenses to be deducted under this power are to include only such expenses as are allowable as reasonable funeral expenses according to law.

Sect. 29. _The affidavit must extend to the verification of the account of the estate and effects, or to the verification of such account and the schedule of debts and funeral expenses, as the case may be, and must be in the prescribed form._

Sect. 30. _Every grant of probate or letters of administration must bear a certificate in writing under the hand of the proper officer of the Court, shewing that the affidavit has been delivered, and that such affidavit, if liable to stamp duty, was duly stamped, and stating the amount of the gross value of the estate and effects as shewn by the account._

Sect. 31. _If at any time after the grant of probate or letters of administration, and during the administration of the estate, the value mentioned in the certificate of the officer of the Court shall be found to exceed the true value of the personal estate and effects of the deceased, or if at any time within three years after the grant, or within such further period as the Commissioners of Inland Revenue may allow, it shall appear that no amount or an insufficient amount was deducted on account of debts and funeral expenses, it shall be lawful for the said Commissioners, upon proof of the facts to their satisfaction, to return the amount of stamp duty which shall have been overpaid._

Certificate of authorized officer of Inland Revenue in such case substituted for certificate of the officer of the Court.

Sect. 32. _If at any time it shall be discovered that the personal estate and effects of the deceased were at the time of the grant of probate or letters of administration of greater value than the value mentioned in the certificate, or that any deduction for debts or funeral expenses was made erroneously, the person acting in the administration of such estate and effects shall, within six months after the discovery, deliver a further affidavit with an account to the Commissioners of Inland Revenue, duly stamped for the amount which with the duty (if any) previously paid on an affidavit in respect of such estate and effects, shall be sufficient to cover the duty chargeable according to the true value thereof, and shall at the same time pay to the said Commissioners interest upon such amount at the rate of £5 per cent. per annum from the date of the grant, or from such subsequent date as the said Commissioners may in the circumstances think proper._

Certificate of authorized officer of Inland Revenue substituted in such cases for certificate of the officer of the Court.

Sect. 33. (1.) _Where the whole personal estate and effects of any person dying on or after the 1st day of June, 1881 (inclusive of property by law made such personal estate and effects for the purpose of the charge of duty, and any personal estate and effects situate out of the United Kingdom), without any deduction for debts or funeral expenses, shall not exceed the value of £300, it shall be lawful for the person intending to apply for probate or letters of administration to deliver to the proper officer of the Court or to any officer of Inland Revenue duly appointed for the purpose a notice in writing in the prescribed form setting forth the particulars of such estate and effects, and such further particulars as may require to, be stated therein, and to deposit with him the sum of 15s. for fees of Court and expenses, and also in case the estate and effects shall exceed the value of £100, the further sum of 30s. for stamp duty._

(2.) _If the officer has good reason to believe that the whole personal estate and effects of the deceased exceeds the value of £300, he shall refuse to accept the notice and deposit until he is satisfied of the true value thereof._

(3.) _As to the form of notice._

(4.) _Empowers officers of Inland Revenue to administer all necessary oaths or affirmations, and to attest administration bonds._

(5.) _Where the estate and effects shall exceed the value of £100 the stamp duty payable on the affidavit shall be the fixed duty of 30s. and no more._

Sect. 34 _applies to Scotland._

[_As to compensation to officers for loss of fees under the two preceding sections, see_ 45 & 46 Vict. c. 72, s. 12.

Sect. 35. _Where representation has been obtained in conformity with either of the two preceding sections, and it shall be at any time afterwards discovered that the whole personal estate and effects of the deceased were of a value exceeding £300, then a sum equal to the stamp duty payable on an affidavit in respect of the true value of such estate and effects shall be a debt due to Her Majesty from_

VII. REVENUE—PROBATE DUTY—*continued.*

the person acting in the administration of such estate and effects, and no allowance shall be made in respect of the sums deposited or paid by him, nor shall the relief afforded by the next succeeding section be claimed or allowed by reason of the deposit or payment of any sum.

Sect. 36. The payment of the sum of 30s. for the fixed duty on the affidavit in conformity with the Act shall be deemed to be in full satisfaction of any claim to legacy or succession duty in respect of the estate and effects to which such affidavit relates.

Sect. 37 empowers the Commissioners at any time and from time to time within three years after the grant of probate or letters of administration, as they may think necessary, to require the person acting in the administration of the estate and effects of any deceased person to furnish such explanations, and to produce such documentary or other evidence respecting the contents of or particulars verified by the affidavit as the case may seem to them to require.

Sect. 40. If any person who ought to obtain probate or letters of administration or deliver a further affidavit shall neglect to do so within the period prescribed by law for the purpose, he shall be liable to pay to Her Majesty double the amount of duty chargeable, and the same shall be a debt due from him to the Crown, and be recoverable by any of the ways and means now in force for the recovery of probate duty.

Act of 1884.] By the Act 47 & 48 Vict. c. 62 (the Revenue Act, 1884), s. 11, notwithstanding any local or private Act, probate, or letters of administration, or confirmation, from a Court of the United Kingdom is necessary to constitute title to assets situated therein. Saving as to certain insurances with grant of representation from India or the colonies, and under some other circumstances.

1. —— Lunatic—*Accumulations of Personal Estate—Investment in Realty—Conversion.*] The committees of a lunatic acting under the orders of the Lords Justices of Appeal sitting in Lunacy invested the accumulations of the personal estate of the lunatic in the purchase of land. The conveyances to the committees contained, in conformity with such orders, declarations that the land purchased should to all intents and purposes be considered as part of the personal estate of the lunatic, but contained no trust for sale:—*Held,* that on the death of the lunatic the value of the investment was personal estate liable to probate duty. ATTORNEY-GENERAL *v.* MARQUESS OF AILESBURY -   . 14 Q. B. D. 895 [Reversed by the Court of Appeal, 16 Q. B. D. 408.]

2. —— Realty—*Partnership Assets—Conversion.*] The shares of partners in realty forming part of the partnership property must be regarded as personal estate in the absence of any binding agreement between the partners to the contrary ; and probate duty is payable on a deceased partner's share in such realty irrespective of the question whether or not there is in the event any actual conversion into personalty.—*Custance v. Bradshaw* (4 Hare, 315) discussed.—Judgment of Queen's Bench Division affirmed. ATTORNEY-GENERAL *v.* HUBBUCK   - 10 Q. B. D. 488 ; [13 Q. B. D. 275

VIII. REVENUE—STAMPS.

The Customs and Inland Revenue Act, 1881 (44 & 45 Vict. c. 12) *repeals* (sect. 48) *the Act 3 & 4 Vict. c. 96 ; amends* (sect. 44) *sects.* 16, 117 (sub-sect. 2), *and* 119 *of the Stamp Act,* 1870 ; *and provides* (sect. 47) *that on and after the 1st day of June,* 1881, *any stamp duties of one penny which may legally be denoted by adhesive stamps not appropriated by any word or words on the face of them to any particular description of instrument may be denoted by adhesive penny postage stamps ; and on and after that date postage duties may be paid by the use of penny adhesive stamps not appropriated by any word or words on the face of them to postage duty or to any particular description of instrument.*

By 45 & 46 Vict. c. 72, s. 13, *any stamp duties of an amount not exceeding* 2s. 6d. *which may legally be denoted by adhesive stamps not appropriated by any word or words on the face of them to any particular description of instrument, and any postage duties to the · like amount, may be denoted by the same adhesive stamps.*

With a view to exhaust any adhesive postage stamps denoting an amount not exceeding 2s. 6d. *which may have been unissued or unused, such stamps to a proper amount may be used to denote any stamp duties of an amount not exceeding* 2s. 6d., *which may legally be denoted by adhesive stamps not appropriated by any word or words on the face of them to any particular description of instrument.*

Sect. 14. Where two or more adhesive stamps are used to denote a stamp duty upon an instrument, such instrument is not to be deemed duly stamped unless the person upon whom the duty of cancellation is by law imposed cancels each and every stamp by writing on or across the same his name or initials, or the name or initials of his firm, together with the true date of his so writing, so that both or all and every of the stamps may be effectually cancelled and rendered incapable of being used for any other instrument, or for any postal purpose, or unless it is otherwise proved that the stamps appearing on the instrument were affixed thereto at the proper time.

Penalty for contravening the section.

Sect. 15 extends interpretation of sect. 25 of the Stamp Act, 1870, *to any letter or cover within sect. 23 of the Post Office Duties Act,* 1840, *and any postal packet and the cover thereof which is a letter or cover within the Post Office Act,* 1875.

Sect. 16. The stamp duties granted in respect of letters patent for inventions, and on the certificate of registration of a design, to be deemed public office fees and not stamp duties.

Sect. 17. Provision for composition for stamp duty on certain Canadian Government stock.

Accounts, Duties on.] *By* 44 & 45 Vict. c. 12 (the Customs and Inland Revenue Act, 1881) *sect. 38* (1) *stamp duties at the like rates as are by the Act charged on affidavits are charged and made payable on accounts.*

(2.) *The personal or moveable property to be included in an account shall be property of the following descriptions, viz :—*

(a.) *Any property taken as a donatio mortis causâ made by any person dying on or after the 1st day of June,* 1881, *or taken*

VIII. REVENUE—STAMPS—*continued.*

under a voluntary disposition made by any person so dying purporting to operate as an immediate gift inter vivos whether by way of transfer, delivery, declaration of trust, or otherwise, which shall not have been bona fide made three months before the death of the deceased.

(b.) *Any property which a person dying on or after such day having been absolutely entitled thereto has voluntarily caused or may voluntarily cause to be transferred to or vested in himself, and any other person jointly, whether by disposition or otherwise, so that the beneficial interest therein or in some part thereof passes or accrues by survivorship on his death to such other person.*

(c.) *Any property passing under any past or future voluntary settlement made by any person dying on or after such day by deed or any other instrument not taking effect as a will whereby an interest in such property for life or any other period determinable by reference to death is reserved either expressly or by implication to the settlor or whereby the settlor may have reserved to himself the right by the exercise of any power to restore to himself or to reclaim the absolute interest in such property.*

(3.) *Where an account delivered duly stamped comprises property passing under a voluntary settlement, and upon the production of the settlement it shall appear that the stamp duty of 5s. per centum has been paid thereon according to the amount or value of the property so passing or any part thereof, the amount of such stamp duty shall be returned to the person delivering the account.*

Sect. 39. *Every person who as beneficiary, trustee, or otherwise, acquires possession, or assumes the management of any personal or moveable property of a description to be included in an account according to the preceding section, shall upon retaining the same for his own use or distributing or disposing thereof, and in any case within six calendar months after the death of the deceased, deliver to the Commissioners of Inland Revenue a full and true account verified by oath of such property duly stamped as required by this Act. Any officer authorized by the Commissioners for the purpose may administer the oath.*

Sect. 40. *If any person who is required to deliver such an account as aforesaid shall neglect to do so within the period prescribed by law for the purpose, he shall be liable to pay Her Majesty double the amount of duty chargeable, and the same shall be a debt due from him to the Crown, and be recoverable by any of the ways or means now in force for the recovery of legacy or succession duty.*

County Stock.] *By sect. 45 where the justices of any county, liberty, riding, parts, or divisions of a county, shall be empowered by any Act of Parliament to create " county stock," the transfers of such stock shall be chargeable with stamp duty as if they were transfers of the debenture stock of a company or corporation.*

Patent,] *The Act 47 & 48 Vict. c. 62, s. 9, exempts from stamp duty of Stamp Act, 1870, any*

VIII. REVENUE—STAMPS—*continued.*

statutory declaration forming part of an application for a patent.

Mortgage.] *The Revenue Act (46 & 47 Vict. c. 55), 1883, s. 15, enacts—*

In lieu of the stamp duty now payable under the Stamp Act, 1870, there shall be charged upon mortgage, bond, debenture, covenant and foreign security of any kind—

Being a security for the payment or repayment of money not exceeding £10 .   8d.

The Act 48 & 49 Vict. c. 51 (the Customs and Inland Revenue Act, 1885), provides:—

Securities to Bearer.] *Sect. 21. In lieu of the stamp duties payable upon any security for money bearing date or signed or offered for subscription after the passing of this Act, and given to a subscriber in respect of a loan raised by any company or corporation, and transferable by delivery, and upon a foreign security bearing date or signed, or offered for subscription, after the passing of this Act, and transferable by delivery, there shall be charged a duty at the rate of one shilling for every ten pounds, and also for any fractional part of ten pounds of the money thereby secured.*

And in lieu of any other stamp duties there shall be charged upon any such security given in substitution for a like security, duly stamped in conformity with the law in force at the time when such last mentioned security became subject to duty, a duty at the rate of sixpence for every twenty pounds, and also for any fractional part of twenty pounds of the money thereby secured.

The term "foreign security" shall not include a security by or on behalf of any Colonial Government, but shall otherwise have the meaning assigned to it by 34 & 35 Vict. c. 4, and shall also include a security which, though originally issued to the holder out of the United Kingdom, is offered by him for subscription, and given or delivered to a subscriber in the United Kingdom.

And see sect. 26 of this Act under head REVENUE. —INCOME TAX—*Statutes.*

Solicitor.] *The Act 47 & 48 Vict. c. 62, s. 10, amends the Stamp Act, 1870, s. 59, and renders it unnecessary for a person by law authorized to act as solicitor of a public department without admission, or officer under him, to take out a stamped certificate.*

Stock Certificate to Bearer.] *By the Act 44 & 45 Vict. c. 12, s. 46* (1) *Every " stock certificate to bearer " which shall after the passing of the Act (3rd of June, 1881) be issued under the provisions of the Local Authorities Loans Act, 1875, or of any other Act authorizing the creation of debenture stock, county stock, corporation stock, municipal stock, or funded debt, by whatever name known, shall be charged with the stamp duty of 7s. 6d. for every full sum of £100, and also for any fraction less than £100, or over and above £100, or a multiple of £100, of the nominal amount of the stock described in the certificate.*

(2.) *Where the holder of any stock certificate to bearer so issued shall have been entered on the register of the local authority as the owner of the share of stock described in the certificate, such certificate shall be forthwith cancelled so as to be incapable of being re-issued to any person.*

(3.) *The foregoing charge of stamp duty shall not be applicable where a composition has been*

VIII. REVENUE—STAMPS—*continued.*

paid under the provisions of the 53rd section of the Inland Revenue Act, 1880, for the stamp duty on transfers of the stock described in the certificate.

Superannuation Annuity.] *By 45 & 46 Vict. c. 72, s. 8, the stamp duty on any grants or contract for the payment of a superannuation annuity is—*

6d. *for every full sum of £5, and also for any fraction less than £5, or over and above £5, or a multiple of £5 of the annuity.*

Sect. 9. *No stamp duty is chargeable upon—*

Draft *or order drawn upon any banker in the United Kingdom by an officer of a public department of the State for the payment of money out of a public account.*

Receipt *given by an officer of a public department of the State for money paid by way of imprest or advance, or in adjustment of an account, where he derives no personal benefit therefrom.*

The Act 48 & 49 Vict. c. 51 (*the Customs and Inland Revenue Act*), 1885, *provides :—*

Duty on Property of Bodies corporate and unincorporate.] *Sect.* 1. *Certain property by reason of being vested in bodies corporate or unincorporate, escapes liability to probate, legacy, or succession duties, it is therefore enacted that there shall be levied and paid to Her Majesty in respect of all real and personal property which shall have belonged to or being vested in any body corporate or unincorporate during the yearly period ending on the 5th day of April, 1885, or during any subsequent yearly period ending on the same day in any year, a duty at the rate of £5 per centum upon the annual value, income or profits of such property accrued to such body corporate or unincorporate in the same yearly period, after deducting therefrom all necessary outgoings, including the receiver's remuneration, and costs, charges and expenses properly incurred in the management of such property. Subject to exemption from such duty in favour of property of the descriptions following (that is to say) :—*

(1.) *Property vested in or under the control or management of " The Commissioners of Works and Public Buildings " or " The Commissioners of Woods and Forests," or any department of Government.*

(2.) *Property which, or the income or profits whereof, shall be legally appropriated and applied for the benefit of the public at large or of any county, shire, borough, or place, or the ratepayers or inhabitants thereof, or in any manner expressly prescribed by Act of Parliament.*

(3.) *Property which, or the income or profits whereof, shall be legally appropriated and applied for any purpose connected with any religious persuasion, or for any charitable purpose, or for the promotion of education, literature, science, or the fine arts.*

(4.) *Property of any friendly society or savings bank established according to Act of Parliament.*

(5.) *Property belonging to or constituting the capital of a body corporate or unincorporate established for any trade or business, or being the property of a body whose capital stock is so divided and held as to be liable to be charged to legacy duty or succession duty.*

(6.) *Property acquired by or with funds volun-*

VIII. REVENUE—STAMPS—*continued.*

tarily contributed to any body corporate or unincorporate within a period of thirty years immediately preceding.*

(7.) *Property acquired by any body corporate or unincorporate within a period of thirty years immediately preceding where legacy duty or succession duty shall have been paid upon the acquisition thereof.*

Sect. 12. *In the construction and for the purposes of this part of this Act,—*

The term " body unincorporate " *includes every unincorporated company, fellowship, society, association, and trustee, or number of trustees, to or in whom respectively any real or personal property shall belong in such manner, or be vested upon such permanent trusts, that the same shall not be liable to legacy duty or succession duty,*

The term " accountable officer " *means every chamberlain, treasurer, bursar, receiver, secretary, or other officer, trustee, or member of a body corporate or unincorporate by whom the annual income or profits of property in respect whereof duty is chargeable under this Act shall be received, or in whose possession or under whose control the same shall be.*

Sect. 13. *The duty hereby imposed shall be considered as a stamp duty, and shall be under the care and management of the Commissioners of Inland Revenue hereinafter called the Commissioners, who by themselves and their officers shall have the same powers and authorities for the collection, recovery, and management thereof as are vested in them for the collection, recovery, and management of the succession duty, and shall have all other powers and authorities requisite for carrying this part of this Act into execution.*

Sect. 14. *The duty hereby imposed shall be a first charge on all the property in respect whereof the same shall be payable while such property shall remain in the possession or under the control of the body corporate or unincorporate chargeable with such duty, or of any party or parties acquiring the same, with notice of any such duty being in arrear, and every such body corporate or unincorporate, and every accountable officer, shall, to the full extent thereof, be answerable to Her Majesty for the payment of the duty charged thereon.*

Sect. 15. *Return of property to be made to the Commissioners.*

Sect. 16. *Power for persons answerable to retain moneys for payment of duty.*

Sect. 17. *Power to Commissioners to assess duty according to accounts rendered or to obtain other accounts.*

Sect. 18. *Penalty for not making returns and for non-payment of duty.*

Sect. 19. *Application of enactments as to succession duty to this part of the Act.*

Sect. 20. *In administration of property chargeable under this Act, the Court shall provide for payment of duty.*

1. —— **Charterparty**—*Stamp Act, 1870.*] A charterparty executed entirely abroad and stamped within two months after it has been received in this country can be received in evidence, since it falls within the provisions of 33 & 34 Vict. c. 97, s. 15, and not of sects. 67 and 68 of that Act. THE " BELFORT " - - - - **9 P. D. 215**

VIII. REVENUE—STAMPS—continued.

2. —— Debenture—*Promissory-note*—33 & 34 *Vict. c.* 97, *s.* 18, *and Sched.*—"*Debenture*"—*Joint' Stock Company.*] An instrument issued by a company incorporated under the Joint Stock Companies Acts, 1856 and 1862, purporting upon the face of it to be a "debenture," with coupons for the payment of interest half-yearly attached to it, and containing an engagement on the part of the company to pay "the amount of this indenture" to A. B. or order on a given day, with interest at 5 per cent., is under the Stamp Act, 1870, chargeable with a debenture-stamp at 2s. 6d., and not with a promissory-note stamp. BRITISH INDIA STEAM NAVIGATION COMPANY *v.* COMMISSIONERS OF INLAND REVENUE 　7 Q. B. D. 165

3. —— Mortgage Deed—*Vendor and Purchaser—Ad valorem Stamp—Stamp Act*, 1870.] A ten shilling deed stamp on a mortgage deed is insufficient; therefore a purchaser is entitled, on a contract for sale with a mortgagor, to require the mortgage deed, where so stamped, to be stamped before completion to the full ad valorem duty at the vendor's expense, notwithstanding that the mortgagee may have consented to join in conveyance. WHITING TO LOOMES 17 Ch. D. 10

4. —— Settlement by Court.] An order of the Court making a settlement should bear the usual settlement stamp. *In re* GOWAN. GOWAN *v.* GOWAN 　·—　　17 Ch. D. 778

5. —— Unstamped Deed—*Vendor and Purchaser— Title— Compulsory Purchase — Payment into Court—Costs of Petition—Lands Clauses Consolidation Act*, 1845 (8 & 9 Vict. c. 18), *ss.* 75, 80, 82.] A freehold land society in 1871 purchased some land in Epping Forest, which was conveyed to them in fee. They conveyed it in allotments to various members of the society who respectively paid for their allotments. Afterwards the Epping Forest Act, 1878, was passed, and it provided that the land (together with other lands) should be thrown open to the public, certain compensation, the amount of which was to be ascertained by an arbitrator, being paid by the Conservators appointed by the Act to the owner of the soil of any land thrown open. With the Act were incorporated the provisions of the Lands Clauses Act, 1845, with respect to the purchase-money or compensation coming to parties having limited interests, or prevented from treating, or not making title, and with respect to the conveyances of lands. After the passing of the Act the land society repurchased the allotments from the allottees, repaying them their purchase-moneys. The allottees· reconveyed the plots to the trustees of the society, the reconveyances being indorsed on the original conveyances, but the reconveyances were not stamped within the proper time after execution. The arbitrator determined the amount of compensation to be paid by the Conservators to the·society, and the society furnished an abstract of title to the Conservators. The Conservators made no objection to the title, except that the reconveyances ought to be stamped, and they required the society to have them stamped at their own expense. The society declined to do this, but offered that the allottees should join with the trustees of the society in a conveyance to the Conservators. The Conservators would not accept

VIII. REVENUE—STAMPS—continued.

this offer, but paid the compensation money into Court, and, under sect. 75 of the Lands Clauses Act, executed a deed-poll vesting the land in themselves in fee. The society petitioned for payment of the money to them :—*Held*, that it was not necessary that the reconveyances should be stamped; that the Conservators ought to have been satisfied with the conveyance offered them by the society; and that the Conservators must pay the costs of the petition.—*Whiting to Loomes* (14 Ch. D. 822 ; 17 Ch. D. 10) distinguished. *Ex parte* BIRKBECK FREEHOLD LAND SOCIETY
　　　　　　　　　　　　　　[24 Ch. D. 119

IX. REVENUE—SUCCESSION DUTY.

By the Customs and Inland Revenue Act, 1881 (44 & 45 *Vict.* c. 12), *s.* 41, *where the ad valorem duty has been paid on the affidavit or account, in conformity with the Act, in respect of any succession to property, the duty at the rate of £1 per cent. imposed by the Act* 55 *Geo.* 3, *c.* 184, *is not payable.*

1. —— Appointment under General Power—*Predecessor—Legacy Duty—Succession Duty Act,* 1853 (16 & 17 *Vict. v.* 51), *ss.* 2, 18—36 *Geo.* 3, *c.* 52, *s.* 18.] In cases of appointments by donees of general powers which fall within sect. 2 and do not fall within sect. 4 of the Succession Duty Act, 1853 (16 & 17 Vict. c. 51), the canon of construction adopted in *In re Barker* (7 H. & N. 109 ; 30 L. J. (Ex.) 404) and *Charlton v. Attorney -General* (4 App. Cas. 427) is to be applied whether the power be joint or sole, and the appointees must be held to derive their interest from the donor of the power as "predecessor," and not from the donee.—Testator, in 1826, bequeathed personalty in trust for his daughter for life, and afterwards (in the event which happened) for such persons as she should by deed appoint, and in default of appointment for her next of kin. Testator died before the coming into operation of the Succession Duty Act, 1853, and legacy duty at 1 per cent. was paid upon the whole absolute interest of the trust fund. After that Act came into operation the daughter, by deed, appointed the trust fund to her sister's daughters:—*Held*, by Grove and Lindley, JJ., that, as owing to the date of the testator's death sect. 4 did not apply, the appointees derived their interest from their grandfather, the testator, as predecessor, within sect. 2, and not from their aunt, the appointor, and that succession duty was therefore payable on their succession at the death of the appointor at 1 and not at 3 per cent. :—*Held*, also, that the payment of legacy duty under 36 Geo. 3, c. 52, s. 18, did not exempt the appointees from succession duty, since their succession did not come within the exemption granted by sect. 18 of the Succession Duty Act, 1853, to persons already charged with legacy duty "in respect of the same acquisition of the same property." ATTORNEY-GENERAL *v.* MITCHELL - - - - 6 Q. B. D. 548

2. —— Illegitimate Children —*Proceeds of Real Estate in Court—Petition by Natural Children of an Englishman domiciled in Rome — Status—Succession Duty Act,* 1853 (16 & 17 *Vict.* c. 51), *s.* 10.] J. A., a native of Cumberland,

IX. REVENUE—SUCCESSION DUTY—contd.

went about forty years before his death in 1877 to reside in Rome, and there acquired a Roman or Italian domicil. He cohabited with an Italian woman, by whom he had four children, sons, all born in Rome prior to 1862. The parents were never married. J. A. inherited real estate in England. By his will, made in English form, he gave all his real estate whether in Italy or England to his four children, nominatim. The will was not valid in regard to his personal estate in Rome, but as he had acknowledged his natural children in his lifetime they were allowed to succeed to that estate as heredes ab intestato. The real estate in England was sold and the proceeds paid into Court:—On petition by the children for distribution of the fund, held, that their status was that of strangers in blood to the testator, and that the Crown was entitled to be paid 10 per cent. duty under the Succession Duty Act, 1853. ATKINSON v. ANDERSON

[21 Ch. D. 100

3. —— Letters of Administration—*Reversion* — *Cesser of Succession Duty* — *Succession Duty Act, 1853* (16 & 17 Vict. c. 51), s. 10—*Customs and Inland Revenue Act, 1881* (44 & 45 Vict. c. 12), *ss.* 27, 41.] A. died intestate and without having been married. He was entitled to an interest in reversion expectant on his father's death, in a settled fund. The father, to whom letters of administration of A.'s estate were granted, paid 3 per cent. administration duty under sect. 27 of the Customs and Inland Revenue Act, 1881, upon the estimated value of A.'s estate, including the above reversionary interest :—*Held*, that the father was exempted by sect. 41 of the same Act from paying duty at £1 per cent. in respect of A.'s succession to his father, under sect. 10 of the Succession Duty Act, 1853. *In re* HAYGARTH'S TRUSTS   22 Ch. D. 545

4. —— Predecessor—*Settlement—Resettlement* —*Succession Duty Act, 1853* (16 & 17 Vict. c. 51), s. 2.] A lunatic was tenant in tail in possession of land with remainder to his younger brother R. and his sister D. successively in tail. R. converted his estate tail into a base fee in remainder, and mortgaged his interest to secure a debt of £124,000 which was more than the fee simple value of the land, so that he had no beneficial interest in the equity of redemption. His sister D. married, and by her marriage settlement made before such marriage her estate in remainder was settled to the use of herself for life, with remainder to the use of the first and other sons of such marriage. The Defendant was the only son of that marriage. For the benefit of all parties a family arrangement was made with the consent of the Lord Chancellor (as protector and in lieu of the lunatic under 3 & 4 Will. 4, c. 74, s. 83), in pursuance of which R. and his sister D. and the mortgagees all joined in deeds of settlement, whereby the land was conveyed to trustees in fee simple, subject to the estate tail of the lunatic, but discharged from the mortgage and from the equity of redemption of R. upon trust after the determination of the lunatic's estate to raise £37,000 by sale or mortgage, and to pay that sum to the mortgagees, and subject thereto to hold the land to the use of D. for life

IX. REVENUE—SUCCESSION DUTY—*contd.*

with remainder to her sons successively in tail. This arrangement was carried out, and upon the death of the lunatic D. became tenant for life in possession and upon her death the Defendant, as her son, became tenant in tail in possession :— *Held*, that the Defendant derived his interest as successor from his mother D. and not from his uncle R. as predecessor, under the Succession Duty Act, 1853 (16 & 17 Vict. c. 51), s. 2, and was therefore liable to duty at £1 per cent., and not at £3 per cent. ' ATTORNEY-GENERAL *v.* DOWLING   - - 6 Q. B. D. 177

5. —— Sale under Settled Estates Act, 1877 (40 & 41 Vict. c. 18), s. 22 — *Succession Duty Act, 1853* (16 & 17 Vict. c. 51), *ss.* 39, 41, 42— *Vendor and Purchaser Act, 1874* (37 & 38 Vict. c. 78.] The effect of a sale by the Court under the powers conferred by the Settled Estates Act, 1877, of any settled estates, is, by the operation of the 22nd section of that Act, to revoke the uses of the settlement; and by the operation of the 42nd section of the Succession Duty Act, 1853, the duty is shifted from the land sold to the purchase-money or its investments, and the land in the hands of the purchaser is freed from the succession duty. *In re* WARNER'S SETTLED ESTATES. WARNER TO STEEL - 17 Ch. D. 711

6. —— Settlement—*Reservation of Interest to Settlor — Alternative Conditions of Succession — Succession at a fixed Time or on Death of Settlor — Succession Duty Act, 1853* (16 & 17 Vict. c. 51), *ss.* 2, 5, 10, 32.] A settlor, by deed containing no power of revocation, settled personal property upon trust for himself for a term of four years, if he should so long live, and at the end of the term, or at his death, whichever should first happen, upon trust for other persons. Before the end of the term the settlor died, and the persons entitled in remainder came into possession of the settled property :—*Held*, by the Court of Appeal (Jessel, M.R., Brett and Cotton, L.JJ.), that as the succession actually took effect on the death of the settlor, succession duty was payable on the whole of the fund, and not merely on the income of it for the period between the death of the settlor and the end of the term. ATTORNEY-GENERAL *v.* NOYES - 8 Q. B. D. 125

REVENUE—Canadian law—Duty on exhibits

[10 App. Cas. 141
See COLONIAL LAW—CANADA, QUEBEC. 4.

—— Cape of Good Hope—Duty on purchase-money - - - 8 App. Cas. 309
See COLONIAL LAW — CAPE OF GOOD HOPE. 3.

—— Commissioners of Inland Revenue — Mandamus - - - 12 Q. B. D. 461
See MANDAMUS. 2.

—— Scotch law - - - 6 App. Cas. 315
See SCOTCH LAW—REVENUE.

REVERSION—Action by assignee of reversion
[9 Q. B. D. 366
See LANDLORD AND TENANT—ASSIGNMENT. 1.

—— Appointment of receiver   11 Q. B. D. 711
See PRACTICE — SUPREME COURT—RECEIVER. 8.

REVERSION—continued.

—— Injury to—Trespass   - 20 Ch. D. 589
    See NUISANCE—REMEDIES. 2.

—— Owner of—Prescription—Tenant at will
    See EASEMENT. 2.   [19 Ch. D. 22

—— Married woman 18 Ch. D. 106; 25 Ch. D. 620
    See HUSBAND AND WIFE—WIFE'S RE-
    VERSION. 1, 2.

—— Married Women's Property Act
    [27 Ch. D. 604; 29 Ch. D. 127
    See HUSBAND AND WIFE — MARRIED
    WOMEN'S PROPERTY ACTS. 7, 8.

—— Succession duty   -   - 22 Ch. D. 545
    See REVENUE—SUCCESSION DUTY. 3.

—— Temporary nuisance to—Injunction
    [20 Ch. D. 589
    See NUISANCE—REMEDIES. 2.

REVISION OF VOTES.
    See PARLIAMENT—REGISTRATION — Sta-
    tutes.

REVIVOR—Appeal   -   - 17 Ch. D. 767
    See PRACTICE — SUPREME COURT —
    CHANGE OF PARTIES. 5.

—— Appeal   -   - 27 Ch. D. 237
    See PRACTICE—SUPREME COURT—AP-
    PEAL. 38.

—— Counter-claim   -   21 Ch. D. 175
    See PRACTICE — SUPREME COURT —
    COUNTER-CLAIM. 6.

—— Death of sole Plaintiff—Person attending
    proceedings   -   24 Ch. D. 126
    See PRACTICE — SUPREME COURT —
    CHANGE OF PARTIES. 7.

—— Discretion of Court   20 Ch. D. 398
    See PRACTICE — SUPREME COURT —
    CHANGE OF PARTIES. 6.

REVOCATION — Marriage settlement—Children
    of prior marriage   9 App. Cas. 303
    See SCOTCH LAW—HUSBAND AND WIFE. 5.

—— Marriage settlement   - 20 Ch. D. 742;
    [26 Ch. D. 191
    See SETTLEMENT—REVOCATION. 1, 2.

—— Power of—Voluntary settlement
    [18 Ch. D. 668 ; 29 Ch. D. 212
    See VOLUNTARY CONVEYANCE. 4, 6.

—— Probate—Jurisdiction of Chancery Divi-
    sion   -   - 26 Ch. D. 656
    See PRACTICE—SUPREME COURT—JURIS-
    DICTION. 1.

—— Probate—Jurisdiction of Chancery Division
    See ESTOPPEL—JUDGMENT. 1.[9 P. D. 210

—— Will 23 Ch. D. 337; 8 P. D. 169; 9 P. D. 237
    See WILL—REVOCATION. 1, 2, 3.

—— Will — Appointment — General clause of
    revocation   20 Ch. D. 99
    See POWER—EXECUTION. 13.

—— Withdrawal of appeal   17 Ch. D. 23
    See PRACTICE — SUPREME COURT — AP-
    PEAL. 23.

RIGHT OF ACTION—Covenant—Stranger
    [30 Ch. D. 57
    See HUSBAND AND WIFE—SEPARATION
    DEED. 2.

RIGHT OF COMMON   - 20 Ch. D. 753
    See COPYHOLD—CUSTOM. 1.

RIGHT OF ENTRY.

1. —— Title to Land—"*Pretenced* | *Title*"—
Buying of — *Forfeiture* — 32 Hen. 8, c. 9, s. 2 ;
8 & 9 Vict. c. 106, s. 6—*Knowledge of Buyer.*] In
an action for a forfeiture under 32 Hen. 8, c. 9,
s. 2, against the buyer of a right of entry, since
8 & 9 Vict. c. 106, s. 6, the onus is upon the Plaintiff to prove not only that the title purchased was
bad, but also that the buyer knew that it was
"pretenced," i.e. fictitious, or bad in fact. The
mere fact that the right purchased was barred by
the Statute of Limitations at the time of the purchase does not necessarily render the title "pretenced" within the meaning of the 32 Hen. 8,
c. 9. KENNEDY *v.* LYELL   - 15 Q. B. D. 491

2. —— Validity of Grant—32 Hen. 8, c. 9,
s. 2—8 & 9 Vict. c. 106, s. 6 — *Measure of
Damages—Sale of Land—Covenants for Title
and quiet Enjoyment.*] Although 32 Hen. 8,
c. 9, s. 2, cannot be said to have been repealed
by 8 & 9 Vict. c. 106, s. 6, nevertheless since
the passing of the latter statute a grant of lands
to which the grantor has a title existing in fact,
but of which he has never been in possession,
and on which he is entitled only to a right of
entry, will be valid, even although at the time of
the grant a litigation is pending as to the title to
the lands.—A. sought to recover by ejectment
certain lands ; the person in possession, amongst
other defences, alleged that one-fourth share
thereof belonged to B., who had never been in
possession. Thereupon A., for the sum of £10,
took from B. a conveyance dated the 4th of July,
1877, of his share, containing covenants for title
and quiet enjoyment. The actual value of B.'s
share was £500. A. then recovered possession of
the lands. Before the date of the conveyance B.
had been bankrupt, and after A. had recovered
possession of the lands, B.'s trustees in bankruptcy recovered possession from A. of the one-
fourth share which had been conveyed by B. to
A. In an action by A. against B. for damages
for breach of the covenants for title and quiet
enjoyment :—*Held*, that the conveyance to A.
from B. was not rendered void by 32 Hen. 8, c. 9,
s. 2.—*Held*, also, that A. was entitled to recover
from B. the sum of £500 as damages. JENKINS *v.*
JONES   -   -   - 9 Q. B. D. 128

RIGHT OF WAY 18 Ch. D. 616; 26 Ch. D. 434
    See WAY. 1, 2.

RIOT.

—— Action against Hundred — *Damage to
Houses—Larceny therefrom by Rioters—Felonious
Demolition — Intention to destroy — Evidence —
Compensation from Hundred—7 & 8 Geo. 4, c. 31,
s. 2 ; 24 & 25 Vict. c. 97, ss. 11, 12.*] A house
damaged by rioters is not "feloniously demo-
lished wholly or in part" so as to entitle the
person damnified to compensation from the Hundred under 7, & 8 Geo. 4, c. 31, s. 2, unless the
rioters when attacking the house had an intention wholly to destroy it.—During an election
riot, and before the Riot Act was read, the
rioters attacked many houses, broke the windows
and damaged the walls by throwing stones, and
stole tobacco from a house so damaged :—*Held*,
that there was no evidence of felonious demolition for which the Hundred was liable to

RIOT—*continued.*
compensate the persons damnified. DRAKE *v.*
FOOTITT. DRAKE *v.* HANKIN - 7 Q. B. D. 201
RIPARIAN OWNER—Canadian law
[9 App. Cas. 170
See COLONIAL LAW—CANADA—QUEBEC. 8.
—— Right to use water - 27 Ch. D. 122;
See WATERCOURSE. 1, 2. [11 Q. B. D. 155
—— River—Towing path 6 App. Cas. 685
See RIVER.
—— Roman-Dutch law—Prescription
[10 App. Cas. 336
See COLONIAL LAW — CAPE OF GOOD
HOPE. 4.
—— Scotch law—Clyde navigation 6 App. Cas.
See SCOTCH LAW—RIVER. [273
RISK—Marine insurance - 7 Q. B. D. 456
See INSURANCE, MARINE—RISK.
RIVER.
Thames.] *The Act 48 & 49 Vict. c. 76 (the
Thames Preservation Act, 1885), preserves the
River Thames above Teddington Lock for purposes
of public recreation, regulates the pleasure traffic
thereon, and enables Conservators to make by-laws
for the purposes mentioned in this Act, in addition
to the powers of making by-laws already possessed
by them under earlier statutes.*
Locks on the Thames.] *Order in Council of
3rd May, 1882, under 41 & 42 Vict. c. ccxvi., s. 35,
amends by-law No. 2 in the Rules and By-laws
for the Regulation of the Navigation of the River
Thames, allowed by Her Majesty in Council, on
the 17th day of May, 1879* L. G., 1882, p. 2129
Boat-races on the Thames.] *Order in Council
of 19th March, 1883, revokes certain by-laws of
11th Nov., 1869, and 17th March, 1875, and provides that any vessel being on the River Thames
between Cricklade in the county of Wilts and
Yantlet Creek in the county of Kent on the occasion
of any boat-race, regatta, public procession or
launch of any vessel, or on any other occasion when
large crowds assemble thereon, shall not pass thereon
so as to obstruct, impede or interfere with the boat-
race, regatta, procession or launch, or endanger the
safety of persons assembling on the river or prevent
the maintenance of order thereon, and the master of
every such vessel on any such occasion as aforesaid
shall observe the directions of the officer of the
Conservators engaged in superintending the execution of this by-law, and if any such master fails in
any respect to comply with the requirements of this
by-law or does anything in contravention thereof,
he shall be deemed guilty of an offence against this
by-law, and shall for every such offence be liable to
a penalty of not exceeding £5* L. G., 1883, p. 1626
And see FISHERY ACTS—THAMES BY-LAWS.

—— *Lee Navigation — Towing Path — Evidence of Ownership — Presumption — Onus Probandi.]* Provisions in different Acts of Parliament appointed Conservators of a river navigation,
and gave them full powers to do what was necessary for carrying the object of the Acts into
effect, including powers to purchase land and
levy tolls. The Conservators executed the powers
of the Acts so far as related to the improvement
of the river navigation, and the making of towing-
paths—and they levied tolls. There was no evi-

dence that they had actually purchased any of
the land that lay along the course of the navigation, and had been used to form the towing-paths :
—*Held,* that, as the Acts might be carried into
effect without purchasing, the burden of proof lay
on the Conservators to shew that they had purchased ; and since they had failed to shew it,
though they were entitled to an injunction to
prevent any owner of adjoining land from so
using the towing-paths as to obstruct in any way
their free use for the purposes of the navigation,
they were not entitled to be treated as owners of
the soil of the towing-paths. CONSERVATORS OF
THE RIVER LEE NAVIGATION *v.* BUTTON
[6 App. Cas. 685
—— Right of fishery.
See Cases under FISHERY.
—— "Tributary"—Salmon fishery 10 Q. B. D.
See FISHERY ACTS. 1. [131
ROAD—Power of magistrates to make
[6 App. Cas. 833
See SCOTCH LAW—HIGHWAY. 1.
—— Repair of.
See Cases under HIGHWAY—REPAIR.
ROADS AND BRIDGES ACT—Scotland
[6 App. Cas. 881
See SCOTCH LAW—HIGHWAY. 3.
ROLLER—Steam roller—Repair of highway—
Injury to gas pipes 15 Q. B. D. 1
See GAS COMPANY.
ROLLING STOCK—Railway—Execution
[6 Q. B. D. 36
See RAILWAY COMPANY—PROPERTY. 2.
—— Sale and hire of—Fictitious sale—Ultra
vires - 21 Ch. D. 309
See RAILWAY COMPANY — CONSTITU-
TION. .
ROMAN-DUTCH LAW - 6 App. Cas. 364;
[9 App. Cas. 571
See COLONIAL LAW—CEYLON. 3, 4.
—— - - - - 10 App. Cas. 336
See COLONIAL LAW — CAPE OF GOOD
HOPE. 4.
ROYAL PECULIAR—Ecclesiastical jurisdiction
[22 Ch. D. 316
See PRACTICE—ECCLESIASTICAL—JURIS-
DICTION. 2.
ROYAL RESIDENCE—Ecclesiastical jurisdiction
[22 Ch. D. 316
See PRACTICE—ECCLESIASTICAL—JURIS-
DICTION. 2.
ROYAL SOCIETY—Purchase of land—Consent of
Charity Commissioners 17 Ch. D. 407
See CHARITY—COMMISSIONERS. 6.
ROYAL WARRANT—Booty of war 7 App. Cas.
See BOOTY OF WAR. [619
ROYALTY—Assignment of part of 17 Ch. D. 423
See PATENT—ASSIGNMENT. 1.
RULE OF COURT—Award - 19 Ch. D. 56
See ARBITRATION—SUBMISSION. 3.
**RULES FOR PREVENTING COLLISIONS AT
SEA**
See Cases and Gazette under SHIP—
NAVIGATION.

2 X

RULES OF THE SUPREME COURT, 1875—*contd.*

—— **Order XIX.,** r. 4 - - 6 Q. B. D. 190
See PRACTICE—SUPREME COURT—STRIK-
ING OUT PLEADINGS. 1.

—— —— - 8 Q. B. D. 491
See DEFAMATION—LIBEL. 2.

—— —— rr. 5, 7 - 8 P. D. 227
See PRACTICE — ADMIRALTY — PLEAD-
ING. 2.

—— —— rr. 15, 17 6 Q. B. D. 645 ; 8 App. Cas. 456
See PRACTICE—SUPREME COURT—DE-
FENCE.

—— **Order XX.,** r. 1 - 17 Ch. D. 174
See PRACTICE—SUPREME COURT—COUN-
TER-CLAIM. 4.

—— —— - 8 Q. B. D. 428
See PRACTICE — SUPREME COURT —
REPLY. 1.

—— **Order XXI.,** r. 4 - 10 Q. B. D. 516
See PRACTICE—SUPREME COURT—WRIT
SPECIALLY INDORSED. 1.

—— —— rr. 11, 12 - 7 Q. B. D. 400
See PRACTICE—SUPREME COURT—PRO-
DUCTION OF DOCUMENTS. 18.

—— **Order XXII.,** r. 9 - 21 Ch. D. 138, 802
See PRACTICE—SUPREME COURT—COUN-
TER-CLAIM. 2, 5.

—— **Order XXIII.,** r. 1 - 18 Ch. D. 362
See PRACTICE — SUPREME COURT —
COSTS. 23.

—— —— - 11 Q. B. D. 464
See PRACTICE — SUPREME COURT—DIS-
CONTINUANCE.

—— **Order XXIV.,** r. 1 - 22 Ch. D. 91
See PRACTICE — SUPREME COURT —
REPLY. 3.

—— **Order XXVII.,** r. 1 - 6 Q. B. D. 190
See PRACTICE—SUPREME COURT—STRIK-
ING OUT PLEADINGS. 1.

—— —— - 21 Ch. D. 802
See PRACTICE—SUPREME COURT—COUN-
TER-CLAIM. 2.

—— —— - 22 Ch. D. 481
See PRACTICE — SUPREME COURT —
AMENDMENT. 1.

—— —— r. 2 17 Ch. D. 721 ; 8 App. Cas. 5
See PATENT—INFRINGEMENT. 6.

—— **Order XXVIII.,** r. 1 19 Ch. D. 246
See PRACTICE — SUPREME COURT—DE-
MURRER. 1.

—— —— r. 2 - - 20 Ch. D. 512
See PRACTICE—SUPREME COURT—DE-
MURRER. 2.

—— **Order XXIX.,** rr. 10, 14 25 Ch. D. 707 ;
[26 Ch. D. 66
See PRACTICE — SUPREME COURT—DE-
FAULT. 3, 4.

—— —— r. 12 - 8 Q. B. D. 650
See PRACTICE—SUPREME COURT—DE-
FAULT. 8.

—— —— - 9 Q. B. D. 170
See PRACTICE — SUPREME COURT —
REPLY. 2.

RULES OF THE SUPREME COURT, 1875—*contd.*

—— **Order XXX.,** rr. 1, 4 - 22 Ch. D. 611 ;
[13 Q. B. D. 597
See PRACTICE—SUPREME COURT — PAY-
MENT INTO COURT. 1, 4.

—— **Order XXXI.,** rr. 1–10.
See Cases under PRACTICE — SUPREME
COURT—INTERROGATORIES.

—— —— rr. 1, 4 - 16 Ch. D. 58
See COMPANY—EVIDENCE. 1.

—— —— rr. 9, 10, 11, 23 27 Ch. D. 1
See PRACTICE—SUPREME COURT—INTER-
ROGATORIES. 12.

—— —— r. 10 - 9 Q. B. D. 168
See PRACTICE — SUPREME COURT —
COSTS. 34.

—— —— rr. 11–18.
See Cases under PRACTICE—SUPREME
COURT—PRODUCTION OF DOCUMENTS.

—— —— r. 12 10 Q. B. D. 459
See PRACTICE — SUPREME COURT — IN-
TERROGATORIES. 1.

—— —— r. 19 - 18 Ch. D. 477
See PRACTICE—SUPREME COURT — IN-
TERROGATORIES. 2.

—— —— r. 21 - 22 Ch. D. 571
See PRACTICE—SUPREME COURT—PRO-
DUCTION OF DOCUMENTS. 16.

—— **Order XXXII.,** r. 1 9 P. D. 32
See PRACTICE—ADMIRALTY—SALVAGE.
1.

—— **Order XXXIII.** 21 Ch. D. 757
See EXECUTOR—ACTIONS. 9.

—— **Order XXXIV.,** r. 1 - 16 Ch. D. 66
See PRACTICE—SUPREME COURT—SPE-
CIAL CASE. 2.

—— **Order XXXV.,** rr. 1a, 4 - 20 Ch. D. 538
See EXECUTOR—ACTIONS. 8.

—— —— rr. 3, 26 20 Ch. D. 365
See PRACTICE—SUPREME COURT—TRIAL.
1.

—— **Order XXXVI.,** rr. 2, 3 - 6 Q. B. D. 63
See PRACTICE—SUPREME COURT—INTER-
PLEADER. 2.

—— —— rr. 3, 26 - 21 Ch. D. 134
See PRACTICE—SUPREME COURT—TRIAL.
5.

—— —— rr. 3, 26 - - 8 P. D. 205
See PRACTICE—PROBATE—TRIAL.

—— —— r. 32 - 17 Ch. D. 346
See PRACTICE—SUPREME COURT—PRO-
DUCTION OF DOCUMENTS. 9.

—— —— r. 34 22 Ch. D. 722 ; 11 Q. B. D. 180
See PRACTICE — SUPREME COURT—RE-
FEREE. 3, 5.

—— **Order XXXVII.,** r. 4.
See Cases under PRACTICE—SUPREME
COURT—EVIDENCE.

—— **Order XXXVIII.,** r. 1 - 16 Ch. D. 100
See PRACTICE—SUPREME COURT—EVI-
DENCE. 1.

—— —— r. 3 - 16 Ch. D. 594
See PRACTICE—SUPREME] COURT—EVI-
DENCE. 6.

RULES OF THE SUPREME COURT, 1875—*contd.*
—— Order LVIII., r. 9   16 Ch. D. 501
 See BANKRUPTCY—APPEAL. 9.
—— —— —— - 18 Ch. D. 392; 23 Ch. D. 248
 See PRACTICE — SUPREME COURT—AP-
 PEAL. 35, 40.
—— —— r. 15.
 See Cases under PRACTICE—SUPREME
 COURT—APPEAL.
—— —— —— -   22 Ch. D. 529
 See BANKRUPTCY—APPEAL. 5.
—— —— —— - -   19 Ch. D. 326
 See PRACTICE—SUPREME COURT—CHAM-
 BERS. 5.
—— —— rr. 16, 17 18 Ch. D. 394; 22 Ch. D. 88;
        [24 Ch. D. 305
 See PRACTICE—SUPREME COURT—STAY-
 ING PROCEEDINGS. 11, 15, 16.
—— Order LIX., r. 1   22 Ch. D. 504
 See PRACTICE—SUPREME COURT—NOTICE
 OF MOTION. 2.
—— —— r. 2 - -   9 Q. B. D. 276
 See PRACTICE — SUPREME COURT —
 AMENDMENT. 5.
—— Order LXa., r. 12 ·   8 Q. B. D. 142
 See PRACTICE—SUPREME COURT—PRO-
 DUCTION OF DOCUMENTS. 14.
—— Order LXII., r. 2 -   6 Q. B. D. 139
 See POOR-RATE— PROCEDURE. 4.
—— —— Sched. App, G. 11   22 Ch. D. 841
 See PRACTICE—SUPREME COURT—EVI-
 DENCE. 12.
RULES OF THE SUPREME COURT (Costs),
 August, 1875, Order VI., rr. 1, 3
   [22 Ch. D. 473; 24 Ch. D. 594
 See PRACTICE—SUPREME COURT—COSTS.
 30, 32.
—— —— rr. 2, 3 6 Q. B. D. 279; 10 Q. B. D. 71
 See PRACTICE—SUPREME COURT—COSTS.
 29, 31.
—— —— r. 26 - -   19 Ch. D. 72
 See PRACTICE—SUPREME COURT—COSTS.
 16.
—— —— rr. 30, 32 -   8 Q. B. D. 479
 See PRACTICE—SUPREME COURT—COSTS.
 9.
—— —— Sched. r. 17 - -   21 Ch. D. 855
 See TRUSTEE RELIEF ACT. 2.
—— —— Sched. r. 27 -   24 Ch. D. 684
 See PRACTICE—SUPREME COURT—COSTS.
 37.
RULES OF THE SUPREME COURT, 1883, Order I.,
 r. 1   30 Ch. D. 231
 See PRACTICE—SUPREME COURT—AP-
 PEAL. 22.
—— Order II., r. 1 -   30 Ch. D. 231
 See PRACTICE—SUPREME COURT — AP-
 PEAL. 22.
—— Order III., r. 6 (f) - 13 Q. B. D. 302, 347
 See PRACTICE—SUPREME COURT—WRIT
 SPECIALLY INDORSED. 2, 5.
—— Order IX., rr. 11, 12   10 P. D. 62
 See PRACTICE—ADMIRALTY—SERVICE. 3.
—— Order XI., r. 1 (b) (e)   14 Q. B. D. 78
 See PRACTICE—SUPREME COURT—SER-
 VICE. 2.

RULES OF THE SUPREME COURT, 1883—*contd.*
—— Order XI., rr. 1 (e), and 2 -   12 Q. B. D. 50
 See PRACTICE—SUPREME COURT—SER-
 VICE. 10.
—— —— r. 1 (f)   15 Q. B. D. 680
 See PRACTICE—SUPREME COURT— SER-
 VICE. 6.
—— —— r. 1 (g) - -   13 Q. B. D. 96
 See PRACTICE—SUPREME COURT—THIRD
 PARTY. 10.
—— Order XII., r. 15 - -   14 Q. B. D. 103
 See PRACTICE—SUPREME COURT—JUDG-
 MENT. 2.
—— Order XIII., r. 3 -   14 Q. B. D. 231
 See PRACTICE—SUPREME COURT—JUDG-
 MENT. 4.
—— —— rr. 12, 13 - -   9 P. D. 84
 See PRACTICE—ADMIRALTY—DEFAULT.
—— —— rr. 12, 13   10 P. D. 62
 See PRACTICE—ADMIRALTY—SERVICE. 3
—— Order XIV.   13 Q. B. D. 302, 347, 691
 See PRACTICE—SUPREME COURT—WRIT
 SPECIALLY INDORSED. 2, 4, 5.
—— —— - - -   13 Q. B. D. 855
 See ACTION. 1.
—— Order XV., r. 1 28 Ch. D. 650; 29 Ch. D. 834
 See PRACTICE—SUPREME COURT—INQUI-
 RIES AND ACCOUNTS. 1, 3.
—— Order XVI., r. 2   30 Ch. D. 57
 See HUSBAND AND WIFE— SEPARATION
 DEED. 2.
—— —— r. 11   28 Ch. D. 414; 29 Ch. D.
        [190, 584
 See PRACTICE — SUPREME COURT —
 PARTIES. 2, 3, 5.
—— —— —— —   25 Ch. D. 750
 See PRACTICE — SUPREME COURT —
 AMENDMENT. 2.
—— —— r. 16 -   30 Ch. D. 418
 See PRACTICE— SUPREME COURT— SE-
 CURITY FOR COSTS. 5.
—— —— rr. 24, 25, 26, 31 - 14 Q. B. D. 859
 See PRACTICE—SUPREME COURT—COSTS.
 28.
—— —— r. 40 · -   30 Ch. D. 421
 See PRACTICE — SUPREME COURT—AP-
 PEAL. 18.
—— —— rr. 48, 55.
 See Cases under PRACTICE—SUPREME
 COURT—THIRD PARTY.
—— Order XVII., r. 4 -   27 Ch. D. 237
 See PRACTICE—SUPREME COURT—AP-
 PEAL. 28.
—— —— rr. 4, 5   28 Ch. D. 38
 See PRACTICE—SUPREME COURT—SECU-
 RITY FOR COSTS. 8.
—— —— —— -   26 Ch. D. 181
 See PRACTICE — SUPREME COURT —
 CHANGE OF PARTIES. 3.
—— Order XVIII., r. 1 -   26 Ch. D. 35
 See PRACTICE—SUPREME COURT—PAR-
 TIES. 16.
—— Order XIX., r. 3 -   28 Ch. D. 333
 See PRACTICE—SUPREME COURT—COUN-
 TER-CLAIM. 9.

RULES OF THE SUPREME COURT, 1883—*contd.*

—— Order XIX., r. 3　　　9 Q. B. D. 648 ;
　　　　　　　　　　　　　[9 App. Cas. 434
　　See SALE OF GOODS—RESCISSION. 2.

—— —— rr. 4, 27　-　　　26 Ch. D. 778
　　See PRACTICE — SUPREME COURT —
　　STRIKING OUT PLEADINGS. 2.

—— —— r. 27　-　-　-　9 P. D. 68
　　See PRACTICE—PROBATE—PLEADING.

—— —— r. 6　-　　　26 Ch D. 717
　　See PRACTICE—SUPREME COURT—PRO-
　　DUCTION OF DOCUMENTS. 10.

—— Order XXII., rr. 6, 7　14 Q. B. D. 766
　　See PRACTICE—SUPREME COURT—PAY-
　　MENT INTO COURT. 3.

—— Order XXIII., r. 4　　　25 Ch. D. 68
　　See PRACTICE—SUPREME COURT — DE-
　　FAULT. 2.

—— Order XXV., rr. 1, 2, 3　28 Ch. D. 372
　　See PRACTICE—SUPREME COURT — DE-
　　MURRER. 3.

—— —— rr. 1, 3, 4　-　26 Ch. D. 35
　　See PRACTICE — SUPREME COURT —
　　PARTIES. 16.

—— —— rr. 2, 3 -　-　29 Ch. D. 128
　　See PRACTICE — SUPREME COURT — DE-
　　MURRER. 4.

—— —— r. 4　-　　10 App. Cas. 210
　　See CHAMPERTY. 2.

—— Order XXVII., rr. 11, 12　-　25 Ch. D. 68 ;
　　　　　　　　　　　　　　　[26 Ch. D. 66
　　See PRACTICE—SUPREME COURT — DE-
　　FAULT. 2, 3.

—— —— r. 15　-　　12 Q. B. D. 165
　　See PRACTICE—SUPREME COURT—JUDG-
　　MENT. 5.

—— Order XXXI., r. 1 -　　15 Q. B. D. 439
　　See PRACTICE—SUPREME COURT—INTER-
　　ROGATORIES. 7.

—— —— rr. 10, 11, 14, 24　-　27 Ch. D. 1
　　See PRACTICE—SUPREME COURT—INTER-
　　ROGATORIES. 12.

—— —— rr. 12–14　　　15 Q. B. D. 114 ;
　　　　　　　　　　　　　[30 Ch. D. 189
　　See PRACTICE—SUPREME COURT—PRO-
　　DUCTION OF DOCUMENTS. 5, 22.

—— —— rr. 12, 20　-　　26 Ch. D. 717
　　See PRACTICE—SUPREME COURT—PRO-
　　DUCTION OF DOCUMENTS. 10.

—— —— r. 15　-　-　26 Ch. D. 724
　　See PRACTICE—SUPREME COURT — PRO-
　　DUCTION OF DOCUMENTS. 20.

—— —— rr. 21, 22, 23　　　25 Ch. D. 64 ;
　　　　　　　　　　　　　[26 Ch. D. 746
　　See PRACTICE — SUPREME COURT—AT-
　　TACHMENT. 7, 8.

—— —— rr. 25, 26　-　　13 Q. B. D. 326
　　See PRACTICE — SUPREME COURT—SE-
　　CURITY FOR COSTS. 13.

—— Order XXXII., r. 2　-　25 Ch. D. 617
　　See PRACTICE—SUPREME COURT—COSTS.
　　3.

—— Order XXXIII., r. 2　-　29 Ch. D. 566
　　See PRACTICE — SUPREME COURT —IN-
　　QUIRIES AND ACCOUNTS. 2.

RULES OF THE SUPREME COURT, 1883—*contd.*

—— Order XXXV., r. 4 -　　27 Ch. D. 242
　　See PRACTICE — SUPREME COURT—DIS-
　　TRICT REGISTRY.

—— Order XXXVI., r. 1　-　26 Ch. D. 621 ;
　　　　　　　　　　　　　　[29 Ch. D. 486
　　See PRACTICE—SUPREME COURT—TRIAL.
　　6, 7.

—— —— r. 3　　25 Ch. D. 772 ; 29 Ch. D. 50
　　See PRACTICE—SUPREME COURT—TRIAL.
　　2, 3.

—— —— r. 6　-　-　29 Ch. D. 50
　　See PRACTICE—SUPREME COURT—TRIAL.
　　3.

—— —— r. 12 -　-　-　14 Q. B. D. 234
　　See PRACTICE—SUPREME COURT—NOTICE
　　OF TRIAL.

—— —— rr. 12, 16　-　27 Ch. D. 354
　　See PRACTICE — SUPREME COURT—DE-
　　FAULT. 7.

—— —— r. 33　-　-　29 Ch. D. 322
　　See PRACTICE—SUPREME COURT—DE-
　　FAULT. 1.

—— Order XXXVII., r. 1–5　25 Ch. D. 21, 673 ;
　　　　　　　　　　　　[26 Ch. D. 1 ; 27 Ch. D. 137
　　See PRACTICE—SUPREME COURT—EVI-
　　DENCE. 14, 15, 16, 18.

—— —— r. 21　-　28 Ch. D. 669
　　See PRACTICE—SUPREME COURT—EVI-
　　DENCE. 2.

—— —— r. 35　-　9 P. D. 120
　　See PRACTICE—DIVORCE—EVIDENCE. 2.

—— Order XXXVIII., r. 3　-　26 Ch. D. 1
　　See PRACTICE—SUPREME COURT—EVI-
　　DENCE. 18.

—— —— r. 6　-　-　25 Ch. D. 769
　　See PRACTICE—SUPREME COURT—EVI-
　　DENCE. 9.

—— —— rr. 9, 13, 20, 21　　29 Ch. D. 711
　　See PRACTICE—SUPREME COURT—EVI-
　　DENCE. 4.

—— —— r. 11　-　-　26 Ch. D. 470
　　See PRACTICE—SUPREME COURT—STRIK-
　　ING OUT PLEADINGS. 3.

—— —— r. 28　28 Ch. D. 669 ; 29 Ch. D. 711
　　See PRACTICE—SUPREME COURT—EVI-
　　DENCE. 2, 4.

—— Order XXXIX.　-　13 Q. B. D. 403
　　See PRACTICE—SUPREME COURT—AP-
　　PEAL. 7.

—— —— r. 1　-　12 Q. B. D. 21 ; 14 Q. B. D. 55
　　See PRACTICE—SUPREME COURT—NEW
　　TRIAL. 1, 2.

—— —— r. 6　-　-　12 Q. B. D. 58
　　See PRACTICE — SUPREME COURT—NEW
　　TRIAL. 3.

—— Order XL., r. 5　　　14 Q. B. D. 371
　　See PRACTICE—SUPREME COURT—INTER-
　　PLEADER. 5.

—— Order XLI., r. 5　26 Ch. D. 746 ; 27 Ch. D. 66
　　See PRACTICE — SUPREME COURT—AT-
　　TACHMENT. 4, 8.

—— Order XLII., rr. 6, 8, 22, 23　14 Q. B. D. 335
　　See PRACTICE — SUPREME COURT—GAR-
　　NISHEE ORDERS. 7.

S.

SAILING RULES.
　See Cases under
　　SHIP—NAVIGATION. 8—26.
　　SHIP—NAVIGATION—*Gazette.*
—— Action in rem—Contributory negligence
　　　　　[9 P. D. 96; 10 App. Cas. 59
　　See PRACTICE—ADMIRALTY — JURISDIC-
　　TION. 1.
ST. LAWRENCE—Navigation—Policy of insur-
　　ance　　　　9 App. Cas. 345
　　See INSURANCE, MARINE—POLICY. 9.
SALARY—Bankruptcy—Voluntary allowance
　　　　　[17 Ch. D. 70
　　See BANKRUPTCY—ASSETS. 14.
—— Bankruptcy—Judge of colony 21 Ch. D. 85
　　See BANKRUPTCY—ASSETS. 13.
SALE—Assets of partnership　-　18 Ch. D. 698
　　See PARTNERSHIP—CONTRACT. 3.
—— By agent to principal　　-　29 Ch. D. 795
　　See PRINCIPAL AND AGENT — AGENT'S
　　LIABILITY. 1.
—— By auction　　　-　　　29 Ch. D. 790
　　See SOLICITOR—BILL OF COSTS. 25.
—— By auctioneer—Right to proceeds 19 Ch. D.
　　See BAILMENT.　　　　　　[86
—— By Court　　-　　　16 Ch. D. 561
　　See PRACTICE—SUPREME COURT—SALE
　　BY COURT.
—— By Court　　-　　　21 Ch. D. 466
　　See VENDOR AND PURCHASER—CONVEY-
　　ANCE. 1.
—— By Court—Leave to Defendant's solicitor to
　　bid　-　-　27 Ch. D. 302
　　See SOLICITOR—LIABILITIES, 6.
—— By Court—Misrepresentation 27 Ch. D. 424
　　See FALSE REPRESENTATION. 2.
—— By mortgagee.
　　See Cases under MORTGAGE—POWERS.
—— By solicitor—Fiduciary relation　16 Ch. D.
　　See SOLICITOR—LIABILITIES. 7.　　[393
—— Glebe land—Land drainage company
　　　　　[20 Ch. D. 208
　　See ECCLESIASTICAL COMMISSIONERS.
—— Goods.
　　See Cases under SALE OF GOODS.
—— Goodwill　　19 Ch. D. 355; 27 Ch. D. 145
　　See GOODWILL. 2, 3.
—— Infant's property　-　-　16 Ch. D. 161
　　See INFANT—PROPERTY. 2.
—— Infant's property—Settled Land Act
　　　　　[27 Ch. D. 552
　　See SETTLED LAND ACT—DISABILITIES.
　　1.
—— Land.
　　See Cases under VENDOR AND PUR-
　　CHASER.
—— Land—Charity—Royal Society 17 Ch. D. 407
　　See CHARITY—COMMISSIONERS. 6.

SALE—*continued.*
—— Leaseholds—Administrator　27 Ch. D. 220
　　See ADMINISTRATOR—GRANT. 8.
—— Medical practice　　　20 Ch. D. 705
　　See SPECIFIC PERFORMANCE. 4.
—— Mortgaged estate—Second mortgagee
　　　　　[29 Ch. D. 954
　　See MORTGAGE—REDEMPTION. 5.
—— Order for—Conversion　　25 Ch. D. 735
　　See EXECUTOR—ACTIONS. 4.
—— Order for—Mortgage—Foreclosure
　　　　　[20 Ch. D. 463; 22 Ch. D. 235
　　See MORTGAGE—FORECLOSURE: 21, 22.
—— Order for—Mortgage—Redemption action
　　　　　[21 Ch. D. 169
　　See MORTGAGE—REDEMPTION. 4.
—— Partition suit.
　　See Cases under PARTITION SUIT—SALE.
—— Partition suit—Trust for sale 22 Ch. D. 284
　　See PARTITION SUIT—JURISDICTION. 2.
—— Partition suit—Vesting order 19 Ch. D. 646
　　See TRUSTEE ACTS—VESTING ORDERS. 10.
—— Rolling stock—Railway company
　　　　　[19 Ch. D. 478
　　See RAILWAY COMPANY—CONSTITUTION.
—— Salvage—Costs—Tender after action
　　　　　[10 P. D. 1
　　See PRACTICE—ADMIRALTY—COSTS. 8.
—— Salvage money—Winding-up of company—
　　Running contract　-　30 Ch. D. 216
　　See COMPANY—CONTRACTS. 4.
—— Settled Estates Act　-　21 Ch. D. 41, 123
　　See SETTLED ESTATES ACTS. 1, 5.
—— Settled Estates Act—Succession duty
　　　　　[17 Ch. D. 711
　　See REVENUE—SUCCESSION DUTY. 5.
—— Settled Land Act.
　　See Cases and Statutes under SETTLED
　　LAND ACT.
—— Settled Land Act—Remuneration of solici-
　　tor　-　-　24 Ch. D. 608
　　See SOLICITOR—BILL OF COSTS. 18.
—— Ship—Disagreement between co-owners
　　See SHIP—OWNERS. 1.　　[10 P. D. 4
—— Ship—Wreck—Authority of master
　　See SHIP—MASTER. 1.　[16 Ch. D. 574

SALE OF GOODS :—　　　　　　Col.
　I. CONTRACT　-　　　-　　1362
　II. LIEN　　-　　　　-　1364
　III. RESCISSION　-　　-　　-　1366

I. SALE OF GOODS—CONTRACT.

　　1. —— **Manufacturer**—*Implied Contract that
Goods are of Manufacturer's make—Evidence—
Custom.*] On the sale of goods by a manufacturer of such goods, who is not otherwise a dealer
in them, there is, in the absence of any usage in
the particular trade or as regards·the particular

I. SALE OF GOODS—CONTRACT—*continued.*

goods to supply goods of other makers, an implied contract that the goods shall be those of the manufacturer's own make.—The Plaintiffs, who were manufacturers but not dealers in iron, by a written contract, on the margin of which was their trade-mark (a crown with their initials), contracted to sell to the Defendants, who thereby contracted to buy of the Plaintiffs, 2000 tons of ship-plates of the quality known as "Crown," to pass Lloyd's survey to be delivered monthly, at the Defendants' shipyard. The contract contained a strike clause by which the supply of the iron contracted for might be suspended during the continuance of any strike of workmen; but it had no express stipulation that the plates should be of the Plaintiffs' manufacture. Before the contract was completed the Plaintiffs closed their works, and proposed to complete the contract by delivery of ship-plates of the quality mentioned in the contract made by another firm. The Defendants having refused to accept these, the Plaintiffs sued them for breach of contract.—At the trial the Defendants tendered evidence to shew that in the iron trade there is a custom that, under a contract between a manufacturer of iron plates and a customer for the supply of them, the seller must, in the absence of stipulation to the contrary, supply plates of his own make, and that the purchaser is entitled to reject other plates if tendered though of the quality contracted for. The learned Judge at the trial rejected this evidence, and gave judgment for the Plaintiffs :—*Held,* that such evidence was improperly rejected.—*Held,* also, by Brett and Cotton, L.JJ. (Bramwell, L.J., dissenting), that without such evidence the Defendants were entitled to succeed, as the contract implied that the plates to be supplied should be of the manufacture of the Plaintiffs, and that therefore the Plaintiffs could not require the Defendants to accept plates not of their own manufacture even though of the quality contracted for and as good as those made by the Plaintiffs themselves. JOHNSON *v.* RAYLTON   7 Q. B. D. 438

2. —— **Market overt—***Felony—Sale of stolen Beasts—Conviction of Thief—Restitution—Claim by Purchaser against Owner for Cost of keeping the Beasts.*] The bonâ fide purchaser of stolen beasts sold in market overt, cannot, in answer to a claim for them by the original owner after the conviction of the thief, counter-claim for the cost of their keep while the beasts were in the possession of the purchaser, for they were his own property until, on the conviction, the property revested in the original owner. WALKER *v.* MATTHEWS -   -   -   8 Q. B. D. 109

3. —— **Statute of Frauds** (29 *Car.* 2, *c.* 3), *s.* 17 —*Acceptance—Act recognising the Contract.*] It is not necessary in order to satisfy the requirements of the 17th section of the Statute of Frauds that there should be an absolute acceptance of goods: there is sufficient evidence of an acceptance of goods within the section where upon delivery of the goods the purchaser has received them and done any act in relation thereto recognising the existence of a contract for the purchase of them by him, though he subsequently refuses the goods. So, where there was a sale of wheat by sample, and the purchaser, having received a number of

I. SALE OF GOODS—CONTRACT—*continued.*

sacks of wheat delivered under the contract into his premises, opened the sacks and examined their contents to see if they were equal to sample, but immediately after so doing gave notice to the seller that he refused the wheat as not being equal to sample :—*Held,* that there was evidence of an acceptance.—*Kibble* v. *Gough* (38 L. T. (N.S.) 204) followed.—*Rickard* v. *Moore* (38 L. T. (N.S.) 841) discussed. PAGE *v.* MORGAN [15 Q. B. D. 228

4. —— **Tender of Bill of Lading —** *Bill of Lading drawn in Sets of Three—Tender of Two only—Time when Tender to be made—Right of Vendee to reject.*] Where by the terms of the contract of sale of goods to be shipped payment is to be made in exchange for bills of lading of each shipment the purchaser is bound to pay when a duly indorsed bill of lading, effectual to pass the property in the goods, is tendered to him, although the bill of lading be drawn in triplicate, and all the three are not then tendered or accounted for; and, if he refuses to accept and pay, he does so at his own risk as to whether it may turn out to be the fact or not that the bill of lading tendered was an effectual one, or whether there was another of the set which had been so dealt with as to defeat the title of the purchaser as indorsee of the one tendered.—*Per* Brett, M.R., the seller of such goods should make every reasonable exertion to forward the bills of lading to the purchaser as soon as possible after the shipment, but there is no implied condition in such a contract that the bills of lading shall be delivered to the purchaser in time for him to send them forward so as to be at the port of delivery, either before the arrival of the vessel with the goods or before charges are incurred there in respect of them. SANDERS *v.* MACLEAN [11 Q. B. D. 327

II. SALE OF GOODS—LIEN.

1. —— **Stoppage in transitu—***Bill of Lading, Indorsement of—Sub-sale.*] The purchaser of goods (shipped by the vendor) consigned them abroad, and indorsed the bill of lading to a bank as security for an advance. Afterwards and before the arrival of the ship the consignees sold the goods "to arrive" to sub-purchasers, to whom they were delivered. The purchaser having become bankrupt, the unpaid vendor gave notice to the master, after the sub-sales but before delivery and before payment of the freight, to stop the goods in transitu. The consignees remitted the proceeds of the sub-sales to the bank, who after repaying themselves their advance handed to the trustee of the bankrupt the balance, which was less than the original purchase-money :— *Held,* affirming the decision of the Court of Appeal, that the principles established by *In re Westzinthus* (5 B. & Ad. 817) and *Spalding* v. *Ruding* (6 Beav. 376; 12 L. J. (Ch.) 503) were applicable; that the right of stoppage in transitu was not at an end when the notice was given; and that the vendor was entitled to the balance after satisfaction of the bank's claim. KEMP *v.* FALK -   -   -   7 App. Cas. 573

2. —— **Stoppage in transitu—***Notice to Consignees to hold Proceeds of Goods.*] The Plaintiffs

II. SALE OF GOODS—LIEN—continued.

were the holders for value of bills drawn on a Liverpool firm, the goods having been shipped by B. at New York to a firm at Pernambuco, and the bills of lading being also sent to that firm.—On the 10th of June, 1879, the Liverpool firm stopped payment, and on the same day B. telegraphed to the Pernambuco firm as follows : " Having pledged documents and shipments (naming the vessel) hold proceeds for P. & Co. (the Plaintiffs)." The ship arrived on the 11th of June, but the bills of lading had been previously delivered to the purchasers of the goods.—The bills having been dishonoured by the Liverpool firm, the Plaintiffs brought an action against the Pernambuco firm claiming to have the bills paid out of the proceeds of the goods as having been specifically appropriated to meet the bills, and also relying on the telegram as having stopped the goods in transitu : *Held*, that the telegram to the Pernambuco firm was not effectual to stop the goods in transitu.— *Quære*, whether under any circumstances a notice to stop goods in transitu can be effectual, if addressed to the consignees only, and not to the owner or master of the ship which carries them. PHELPS, STOKES & Co. *v.* COMBER	29 Ch. D. 813

3. —— Stoppage in transitu—*Termination of Transit—Ulterior and Subsequent Transit—Goods stopped in Possession of Forwarding Agent of Vendee.*] When goods have been sent by an unpaid vendor through a carrier to a forwarding agent, who has been appointed by the vendee, and who receives the necessary orders from the vendee and not from the vendor, the transit of the goods upon reaching the hands of the forwarding agent is at an end and the right to stop in transitu is lost. even although the goods may have been intended to be sent to an ulterior and subsequent destination.—L. bought certain goods of W. at Bolton, saying nothing as to the place of delivery. L. afterwards arranged with M. that the goods should be sent by steamer from Garston to Rouen. L. then instructed W. to send the goods to M. at Garston. W. accordingly despatched the goods by railway. The railway company gave notice to M. of the arrival of the goods, and further gave notice that they would hold the goods as warehousemen. L. then filed a petition for the liquidation of his affairs by arrangement; he had not paid W. for the goods. W. thereupon stopped the delivery of the goods, and M. returned them to him. The trustee in liquidation of L. having brought an action against M. & W. to recover the value of the goods:—*Held*, that the transit of the goods had ceased when the goods reached Garston and came into the possession of M., as forwarding agent for L., that the right to stop in transitu was then at an end, and that the trustee was entitled to recover the value of the goods. KENDAL *v.* MARSHALL, STEVENS & Co.

[11 Q. B. D. 356

4. —— Stoppage in transitu—*Termination of Transit—Destination—Goods bought by Commission Agent in England for Foreign Principal— Bankruptcy of Agent.*] A commission agent in London was employed by merchants at Kingston, Jamaica, to buy goods for them in England. He ordered the goods of the manufacturers " for this mark," there being in the margin of the letter

II. SALE OF GOODS—LIEN—continued.

which gave the order a mark consisting of two letters, with " Kingston, Jamaica," added. The manufacturers knew from previous dealings that this mark had been used by the Jamaica firm. The goods were to be paid for by six months' bills drawn by the manufacturers on the commission agent and accepted by him. On the 11th of September the commission agent wrote to the manufacturers, telling them to pack the goods and mark them with the mark previously mentioned, and to forward them to specified shipping agents at Southampton, for shipment by a particular ship, " advising them with particulars for clearance." On the 13th of September the manufacturers sent the invoice of the goods to the commission agent, telling him that they had that day forwarded the goods by railway to the shipping agents " with the usual particulars for clearance." The same day the manufacturers wrote to the shipping agents, sending them the particulars of the goods, and adding, "which please forward as directed." The particulars described the goods as marked with the letters originally given by the commission agent, and the words " Kingston, Jamaica," and numbered with specified numbers, but the columns for " consignee" and " destination" were left in blank. The cost of the carriage to Southampton was paid by the manufacturers. On the 14th of September the commission agent sent to the shipping agents particulars of the goods, giving the name of the Jamaica firm as consignees, and stating the destination of the goods to be Kingston, Jamaica. The goods were shipped on board the vessel, the bills of lading describing the commission agent as consignor, and the Jamaica firm as consignees. After the ship had sailed, but before her arrival at Jamaica, the commission agent stopped payment, and the manufacturers, who had not been paid for the goods, gave notice to the shipowners to stop them in transitu :—*Held*, that, as between the commission agent and the manufacturers, the transit was at an end when the goods arrived at Southampton, and that the notice to stop was given too late.— *Ex parte Watson* (5 Ch. D. 35), distinguished *Ex parte* MILKS.	*In re* ISAACS -	15 Q. B. D. 39

III. SALE OF GOODS—RESCISSION.

1. —— Instalments—*Failure as to one Instalment—Right to cancel Contract.*] The Defendant in October, 1879, sold to the Plaintiff, and the Plaintiff bought of the Defendant, 2000 tons of pig iron at 42s. a ton, to be delivered to the Plaintiff free on board at maker's wharf, at Middlesborough, " in November, 1879, or equally over November, December, and January next, at 6d. per ton extra."—The Plaintiff failed to take delivery of any of the iron in November, but claimed to have delivery of one-third of the iron in December and one-third in January. The Defendant refused to deliver these two-thirds, and gave notice that he considered that the contract was cancelled by the Plaintiff's breach to take any iron in November:—*Held*, in an action by the Plaintiff for damages, in respect of the Defendant's refusal (Brett, L.J., dissenting), that by the Plaintiff's failure to take one-third of the iron in November, the Defendant was justified in refusing to deliver the other two-thirds afterwards.—The decision in

III. SALE OF GOODS—RESCISSION—*continued.*
Hoare v. Rennie (5 H. & N. 19) held to be right by Bramwell and Baggallay, L.JJ., and wrong by Brett, L.J. HONCK *v.* MULLER - 7 Q. B. D. 92

2. —— Instalments—*Winding-up of Company —Set-off of unliquidated Damages against Claim of Company in Winding-up—Counterclaim—Judicature Act, 1875 (38 & 39 Vict. c. 77), s. 10—Order XIX. r. 3.*] The Respondents bought from the Appellant company 5000 tons of steel of the company's make. to be delivered 1000 tons monthly, commencing January, 1881, payment within three days after receipt of shipping documents. In January the company delivered part only of that month's instalment, and in the beginning of February made a further delivery. On the 2nd of February, shortly before payment for these deliveries became due, a petition was presented to wind up the company. The Respondents bonâ fide, under the erroneous advice of their solicitor that they could not without leave of the Court safely pay pending the petition, objected to make the payments then due unless the company obtained the sanction of the Court, which they asked the company to obtain. On the 10th of February the company informed the Respondents that they should consider the refusal to pay as a breach of contract, releasing the company from any further obligations. On the 15th of February an order was made to wind up the company by the Court. A correspondence ensued between the Respondents and the liquidator, in which the Respondents claimed damages for failure to deliver the January instalment, and a right to deduct those damages from any payments then due ; and said that they always had been and still were ready to accept such deliveries and make such payments as ought to be accepted and made under the contract, subject to the right of set-off. The liquidator made no further deliveries, and brought an action in the name of the company for the price of the steel delivered. The Respondents counter-claimed for damages for non-delivery :—*Held*, affirming the decision of the Court of Appeal, that, upon the true construction of the contract, payment for a previous delivery was not a condition precedent to the right to claim the next delivery ; that the Respondents had not, by postponing payment under erroneous advice, acted so as to shew an intention to repudiate the contract, or so as to release the company from further performance.— That sect. 10 of the Judicature Act, 1875, imported into the winding-up of companies the rules as to set-off in bankruptcy; that the Respondents were entitled, after the winding-up order was made, to set off damages for non-delivery against the payments due from them, and to counter-claim for damages in this action. MERSEY STEEL AND IRON COMPANY *v.* NAYLOR, BENZON & Co.　　9 Q. B. D. 648 ; 9 App. Cas. 434

SALE OF GOODS—Bill of lading—Title of first indorsee 6 Q. B. D. 475 ; 7 App. Cas. 591
　See TROVER.

—— Breach of contract—Measure of damages
　　　　　　　　　　　　　[15 Q. B. D. 85
　See DAMAGES—CONTRACT. 2.

—— Contract not to sell—Injunction 22 Ch. D.
　See SPECIFIC PERFORMANCE. 3.　[835

SALE OF GOODS—*continued.*
—— Passing of property—Goods free on board— Insurable interest　　12 Q. B. D. 564 ;
　　　　　　　　　　　　　[10 App. Cas. 263
　See INSURANCE, MARINE—INSURABLE INTEREST.

—— Prevention of performance of condition
　　　　　　　　　　　　　[6 App. Cas. 251
　See SCOTCH LAW—SALE OF GOODS. 1.

—— Sale note—Signature by broker—Liability
　　　　　　　　　　　　　[13 Q. B. D. 635, 861
　See PRINCIPAL AND AGENT — AGENT'S LIABILITY. 2, 6.

—— Unfinished article—Bankruptcy
　　　　　　　　　　　　　[6 App. Cas. 588
　See SCOTCH LAW—SALE OF GOODS. 2.

SALMON FISHERY ACTS—Inspectors under.
　See FISHERY ACTS—*Statutes.*

SALVAGE.
　See Cases under
　　SHIP—SALVAGE.
　　PRACTICE — ADMIRALTY — SALVAGE.

—— Assistance rendered by pilot—Remuneration　　　-　　-　7 Q. B. D. 129
　See SHIP—PILOT. 8.

—— Damages—Commission for bail—Salvage action　　　　-　9 P. D. 128
　See DAMAGES—REMOTENESS. 2.

—— Marine insurance -　　-　9 Q. B. D. 633 ;
　　　　　　　　　　　　　[7 App. Cas. 333
　See INSURANCE, MARINE—SALVAGE.

—— Payment of premiums of life policy
　　　　　　　　　　　　　[23 Ch. D. 552
　See INSURANCE, LIFE—ASSIGNMENT. 1.

—— Pleading—Statement of claim 8 P. D. 227
　See PRACTICE—ADMIRALTY—PLEADING. 2.

—— Practice—Costs on the higher scale
　　　　　　　　　　　　　[9 P. D. 86
　See PRACTICE—ADMIRALTY—COSTS. 5.

—— Wrongdoer—Cargo　　　6 P. D. 127
　See PRACTICE—ADMIRALTY—LIMITATION OF LIABILITY. 5.

SALVAGE MONEY—Contract with company
　　　　　　　　　　　　　[30 Ch. D. 216
　See COMPANY—CONTRACTS. 4.

SAMPLE—Adulteration -　　6 Q. B. D. 17 ;
　See ADULTERATION. 4, 5. [9 Q. B. D. 172

SANCTION OF COURT—Petition for—Company —Reduction of capital　23 Ch. D. 542
　See COMPANY—REDUCTION OF CAPITAL. 3.

SATISFACTION.—Accord and satisfaction
　　　　　[9 Q. B. D. 37; 11 Q. B. D. 221 ;
　　　　　　　　　　　　　[9 App. Cas. 605
　See ACCORD AND SATISFACTION. 1, 2.

—— Mortgage　　-　　22 Ch. D. 614
　See LIMITATIONS, STATUTE OF—TRUSTS. 3.

—— Payment into Court -　22 Ch. D. 611
　See PRACTICE—SUPREME COURT—PAYMENT INTO COURT. 1.

SAVINGS BANK ACTS.
See FRIENDLY SOCIETY— *Statutes.*

SCHEME FOR CHARITY.
See Cases under CHARITY — MANAGE-
MENT.

—— Church Building Acts - 24 Ch. D. 213
See CHURCH BUILDING ACTS.

SCHEME FOR ENDOWED SCHOOL
[7 App. Cas. 91, 463 ; 10 App. Cas. 304
See ENDOWED SCHOOLS ACT. 1, 2, 3.

SCHEME OF ARRANGEMENT — Bankruptcy
Act, 1869.
See Cases under BANKRUPTCY—ANNUL-
MENT. 2—6.

—— Bankruptcy Act, 1883.
See BANKRUPTCY — BANKRUPTCY ACT,
1883—*Statutes.*

—— Bankruptcy Act, 1883 13 Q. B. D. 426, 438 ;
[15 Q. B. D. 213
See BANKRUPTCY—SCHEME OF ARRANGE-
MENT. 1, 2, 3.

SCHOOL—Endowed - 7 App. Cas. 91, 463 ;
[10 App. Cas. 304
See ENDOWED SCHOOLS ACT. 1, 2, 3.

SCHOOL BOARD—Action to recover fees—Implied
contract - - 12 Q. B. D. 578
See ELEMENTARY EDUCATION ACTS—
FEES. 2.

—— Attendance order.
See Cases under ELEMENTARY EDUCA-
TION ACTS—ATTENDANCE.

—— Clerk — Disqualification as guardian of
parish or union 15 Q. B. D. 382
See POOR-RATE—GUARDIANS.

—— Contract not under seal—Appointment of
architect—Minutes of board 14 Q. B. D.
See CORPORATION. 3. [500

—— Home lessons—Unlawful detention of scholar
[13 Q. B. D. 225
See ELEMENTARY EDUCATION ACTS—
HOME LESSONS.

—— Non-payment of fees for tuition—Penalty
[15 Q. B. D. 415
See ELEMENTARY EDUCATION ACTS—AT-
TENDANCE. 7.

—— Poor-rate—Rateability - 13 Q. B. D. 929
See POOR-RATE—RATEABLE VALUE. 3.

SCHOOL OF ART.
See PUBLIC LIBRARY—*Statutes.*

SCOPE OF BUSINESS—Solicitor—Partnership
[28 Ch. D. 340
See PARTNERSHIP—LIABILITIES.

SCOTCH ASSETS—Administration action in England 22 Ch. D. 456 ; 9 App. Cas. 34
See EXECUTOR—ACTIONS. 16.

SCOTCH CHARITY— Application for scheme
[22 Ch. D. 827
See CHARITY—MANAGEMENT. 2.

SCOTCH DIVORCE—Validity—English wife
[6 P. D. 35 ; 8 App. Cas. 43
See HUSBAND AND WIFE—DIVORCE.

SCOTCH LAW :—

	Col.
I. BANKRUPTCY - -	1370
II. BILL OF EXCHANGE	1371
III. BUILDING SOCIETY -	1374
IV. CONVEYANCE -	1374
V. ENTAIL - -	1376
VI. HARBOUR - -	1377
VII. HERITABLE PROPERTY	1379
VIII. HIGHWAY - -	1384
IX. HUSBAND AND WIFE	1388
X. JURISDICTION -	1392
XI. LANDLORD AND TENANT	1393
XII. MINE - - -	1394
XIII. NUISANCE - -	1395
XIV. PARTNERSHIP -	1395
XV. PATENT - -	1396
XVI. PEERAGE - -	1396
XVII. PUBLIC RIGHTS -	1396
XVIII. RAILWAY COMPANY -	1397
XIX. REVENUE - -	1401
XX. RIVER - -	1402
XXI. SALE OF GOODS -	1402
XXII. STATUTORY DUTY -	1403
XXIII. TRUSTEE - -	1404
XXIV. WILL - - -	1405
XXV. PRACTICE - -	1405

I. SCOTCH LAW—BANKRUPTCY.

—— *Notour Bankruptcy — Statutes* 19 & 20
Vict. c. 79; 43 & 44 Vict. c. 34—*Sequestration
—Contingent Debt—Bankruptcy (Scotland) Act,*
1856, ss. 14, 31.] The Debtors (Scotland) Act,
1880 (43 & 44 Vict. c. 34), s. 6, enacts that in
any case in which, under the provisions of this
Act, imprisonment is rendered incompetent, notour
bankruptcy shall be constituted by insolvency,
concurring with a duly executed charge for payment followed by the expiry of the days of
charge without payment, or where a charge is
not necessary or not competent, by insolvency
concurring with an extracted decree for payment, followed by the lapse of the days intervening prior to execution without payment having
been made.—The Court of Session decerned A.
to pay to B., with an execution of charge thereon
indorsed, dated the 8th of June, 1883. The days
of charge on the said decree expired on the 14th
of June, 1883, and payment had not been then
made ; but on the 13th of June A. intimated to
B. that he had appealed to this House against
the decree, and on the 20th of June the usual
order of service in the said appeal granted on the
18th of June was duly served on B. :—*Held*,
affirming the decision of the Court below, that
there was no notour bankruptcy under the statute,
which could not be affected by the appeal.—By
letters C. agreed that any advances he made to
A. on I. O. U.s should not be an obligation
against A. upon which he could sue A., or use
diligence against him, but that they should until
final adjustment of a joint adventure be retained
as vouchers of the current account, "upon which
I cannot use you or use diligence for them against
you." A. became notour bankrupt, and C., the
petitioning creditor, in a petition for sequestra-

I. SCOTCH LAW—BANKRUPTCY—*continued.*

tion founded on the debt forming the balance of the accounts current, which he vouched by the I. O. U.s.:—*Held*, affirming the decision of the Court below, that the debtor having become notour bankrupt, C. was not barred by the agreement from applying for sequestration.—*Per* Lord Watson :—A contingent debt within the meaning of sect. 14 of the statute of 1856 is a debt which has no existence now, but will only emerge and become due upon the occurrence of some future event. FLEMING *v.* YEAMAN　　9 App. Cas. 966

II. SCOTCH LAW—BILL OF EXCHANGE.

1. —— Cheque—*Negotiability—Countermand of Drawer—Onerous Indorsee—Findings of the Court of Session on Appeal from Sheriff's Court—Judicature Act of Scotland*, 1825 (6 Geo. 4, c. 120), s. 40—*Bills of Exchange Act*, 1882 (45 & 46 Vict. c. 61, ss. 3, 73.] A banker's draft or cheque is substantially a bill of exchange, attended with many, though not all of the privileges of such ; and both in England and Scotland it is as much a negotiable instrument ; consequently, the holder, to whom the property in it 'has been transferred for value, either by delivery, or by indorsation, is entitled to sue upon it if upon due presentation it is not paid.—*Per* Lord Blackburn : The definition given in sect. 3 of the Bills of Exchange Act, 1882, embraces in it a cheque : and that Act is declaratory of the prior law.—On a Saturday A. granted a cheque on his account with the Bank of S. for, inter alia, £250, crossed blank in favour of B. On the same day B. indorsed the cheque, and paid it into the Bank of C., of which he was a customer. The Bank of C. immediately on receipt of the cheque carried the amount to B.'s credit, and thus reduced a debit balance standing against him. On the Monday following A. stopped payment of the cheque at the Bank of S., consequently when the Bank of C. presented it, payment was refused. The Bank of C. sued A. in the Sheriff's Court for the amount. On appeal, the Court of Session found that the cheque was granted to B. to reduce the balance at his debit with the Bank of C. ; that A. agreed the cheque should be so used ; and that in pursuance of that agreement the cheque was indorsed to the Bank of C. and given to them as cash, and the contents being put to B.'s credit the balance at his debit was thereby reduced :—*Held*, that in accordance with *Mackay* v. *Dick* (6 App. Cas. 251) : statute 1825, s. 40, this House was limited to the findings of the Court of Session and the record ; that the findings in fact were distinct, intelligible, and within the record ; that it followed from them as a matter of law that the Bank of C. were onerous holders of the cheque, and therefore the Bank of S. not having paid the cheque on 'demand, the Court below was right in holding that A. was liable.—*Currie* v. *Misa* (1876, Law Rep. 10 Ex. 153 ; 1 App. Cas. 554) commented on.—*De la Chaumette* v. *Bank of England* (1829, 9 B. & C. 208) explained. Dicta of the Judges in *Macdonald* v. *Union Bank* (1864, 2 Court Sess. Cas. 3rd Series, 963) approved. M'LEAN *v.* CLYDESDALE BANKING COMPANY　　9 App. Cas. 95

2. —— Forgery—*Estoppel—Conduct—Silence—Adoption of Signature.*] A person who knows that a bank is relying upon his forged signature

II. SCOTCH LAW — BILL OF EXCHANGE — *continued.*

to a bill, cannot lie by and not divulge the fact until he sees that the position of the bank is altered for the worse. But there is no principle on which his mere silence for a fortnight from the time when he first knew of the forgery, during which the position of the bank was in no way altered or prejudiced. can be held to be an admission or adoption of liability, or an estoppel. The names of A. and B. appeared on a bill as drawers and indorsers to the B. L. Co. The B. L. Co.'s Inverness bank discounted it for C., who signed it as acceptor. They had had no previous dealings with A. or B. Being dishonoured when due, notice to that effect was sent to A. and B., and received late on a Saturday, but they did not communicate with the bank. On the following Monday, being the 14th of April, C. brought to the B. L. Co. a blank bill with A. and B.'s names as drawers and indorsers, apparently in the same handwriting as the previous bill. It was agreed to accept it as a renewal of the previous bill but for a less amount, the difference being paid in cash by C. Three days before it was due, notice was sent to A. and B., and again when it was dishonoured, and then through the B. L. Co.'s law agent. A fortnight after the first notice the B. L. Co. were informed for the first time that A. and B.'s signatures were forgeries, and that they declined to pay the amount in the bill. A. alleged that he called on C. on the 14th of April about the first bill, that C. admitted that he had forged his name, handed him the bill, and solemnly assured him that it had been taken up by cash ; and so assured he did not think it necessary to communicate with the bank. He admitted that on that day he drank with C. and borrowed £4 of him. He denied positively any knowledge of the second bill until he received the bank notices. C. was convicted of the forgery. The B. L. Co. charged A. with payment of the bill on the ground that he had either authorized the use of his name, or had subsequently adopted, and accredited the bill, and therefore was estopped from denying his liability : *Held*, reversing the decision of the Court below, that on the facts proved A. had neither authorized nor assented to the use of his name : nor did the circumstances of the case raise any estoppel against him.—Dictum of Parke, B., as to estoppel in *Freeman* v. *Cooke* (2 Ex. 654), approved of. M'KENZIE *v.* BRITISH LINEN COMPANY

[6 App. Cas. 82

3. —— Securities for —*Bankruptcy—Lien—Bills accepted against Goods—Bankruptcy of both Drawer and Acceptor during Currency of Bills—English Rule of Ex parte Waring* (19 Ves. 345 ; 2 Rose, 182) *inconsistent with Scotch Bankruptcy System.*] Rule of the English bankruptcy system fixed by *Ex parte Waring* (19 Ves. 345 ; 2 Rose, 182), and as extended in subsequent cases, has not been adopted in Scotland and is inconsistent with Scotch bankruptcy law.—In Scotch practice where B. accepts bills drawn by A. against goods left in B.'s hands as security, if both become bankrupt, the bill-holder can rank on the estate of each for the amount of the bills to the effect of recovering full payment, but B.'s estate is entitled to be indemnified for any dividends which his estate may be required to pay in respect of the bills, A.'s

II. SCOTCH LAW — BILL OF EXCHANGE — *continued.*

estate having a right to the balance of the proceeds of the goods, after such indemnity has been given. —By agreement between A. and B., the latter undertook to employ his works in heckling and spinning yarns at a specific rate. By the 8th article of the agreement it was provided that all material and yarn at B.'s works should continue to be the sole property of A., subject only to the lien of B. for the cost of manufacture and for advances made by him, or other debts due to him by A. By the 9th article B. became bound to give his acceptances for a sum not exceeding three-fourths of the value of the raw material and yarn held by him on A.'s account, and should be entitled to " a right of lien or retention of goods to a value sufficient to cover such acceptances."— Both A. and B. became bankrupt. At the date of the bankruptcy B. was liable as acceptor on bills drawn by A. to the amount of £16,000, and he held goods belonging to A. (since sold for £4025 14s. 2d.), on which he had a right of lien or retention to indemnify him from that liability. The holders of the bills claimed to have the whole proceeds applied, in the first place in payment of the bills, as far as they would extend, so as to reduce their amount of proof against the two estates to about £12,000 instead of £16,000, relying upon the English case of *Ex parte Waring* (19 Ves. 345 ; 2 Rose, 182)—B.'s trustees maintained that the bill-holders must continue to rank on both bankrupt estates for the full amount of the bills, and claimed that all dividends paid by them to the bill-holders out of B.'s estate should be repaid to them from the fund in medio :—*Held*, affirming the decision of the Court below, that in view of the agreement, and in accordance with the principles on which the bankruptcy laws have hitherto been administered by the Courts of Scotland, B.'s trustees were entitled to the fund in medio, in order that they might apply it towards their relief from the payments which they were liable to make in the shape of dividends to the holders of the bills ; (2.) That the balance of the fund, if any, was payable to A.'s trustee :—*Held*, also, if the security were sufficient to cover the whole amount of the acceptances, the rule of *Ex parte Waring* might be the most convenient practicable way of giving effect to the contract between the drawers and acceptors, but where the securities are insufficient, the rule confers a benefit on the bill-holders to which they are not entitled, at the expense of the acceptors, which was inequitable, nor could it be reconciled with the reasons of Lord Eldon's judgment in *Ex parte Waring.*—*Per* Lord Selborne, L.C.: Assuming that the positive rule of administration which has been accepted as the law in England since the rule of *Ex parte Waring* was made, must be understood in accordance with the determination in *Powles* v. *Hargreaves* (3 D. M. & G. 453), still so far as it is a positive rule, and not the necessary result of equitable principles, it cannot be held to be of force in Scotland, merely because it is so in England.—And : The reasons assigned by Lord Cranworth in *Powles* v. *Hargreaves* (3 D. M. & G. 453) to justify the extension of *Ex parte Waring* to the case of a deficient security are unsatisfactory if applied to such a contract as this, and appear to overlook the fact that, when the

II. SCOTCH LAW — BILL OF EXCHANGE — *continued.*

whole benefit of a deficient security is given to the bill-holder, the estate of the bankrupt acceptor may lose some part of the indemnity, to which by the contract he is entitled. ROYAL BANK OF SCOTLAND v. COMMERCIAL BANK OF SCOTLAND. 7 App. Cas. 366

III. SCOTCH LAW—BUILDING SOCIETY.

1. —— Bond of Corroboration—Ultrà vires.] A building society advanced in 1876 to A., a member, £1000. A. disponed in security an ex facie absolute disposition of certain subjects. which were already heavily burdened by prior mortgages. In 1879 A.'s estates were sequestrated, and the directors of the society, in order to prevent a sale of the subjects at an alleged loss, granted B. a bond of corroboration guaranteeing the payment of his prior mortgage.—In 1882 an order for the voluntary winding-up of the society was made, and the liquidators instituted this action concluding for reduction of the bond of corroboration granted to B. as being ultrà vires of the directors and in violation of the rules and constitution of the society :—*Held*, affirming the decision of the Court below, that the bond was ultrà vires, being a transaction not authorized by the rules, and not incidental to the conduct of the society's business. SMALL v. SMITH

[10 App. Cas. 119

IV. SCOTCH LAW—CONVEYANCE.

1. —— Construction — *Heritage* — *Mid-superiority* — *Meaning of Clause " All other lands and others," following and concluding a Specific Enumeration and Description of Separate Subjects* — *When Reference to prior Letters to control Language of Dispositive Clause not allowed* — *Ambiguity.*] According to the Law of Scotland the execution of a formal conveyance, even when it expressly bears to be an implement of a previous contract, supersedes that contract in toto, and the conveyance thenceforth becomes the sole measure of the rights and liabilities of the contracting parties; and a reference to an antecedent agreement is not warranted either by the fact that the subjects conveyed are described in general terms in the dispositive clause of the deed, or by the fact that, in the narrative of the deed, the parties are represented as having agreed upon certain points, which were presumably matters of stipulation, in any written agreement which preceded its execution. Although subsidiary clauses of a deed may be legitimately referred to for the purpose of solving any ambiguity which is raised by the terms of the dispositive clause, yet if the terms of the dispositive clause are per se sufficient to give a right, they cannot be controlled by a reference to the other clauses of the disposition. Where one of a set of heads in the dispositive clause of a disposition is expressed in general terms and concludes a specific enumeration and description of separate subjects, primâ facie, and unless the contrary appear, it must be presumed that it was merely intended to carry rights ejusdem generis with those previously described and disponed. A completed disposition, dated 1879, and made inter alia by A. in favour of B. of certain superiorities, proceeded on the narrative that it was granted in

IV. SCOTCH LAW—CONVEYANCE—*continued.*

consideration of an agreement between the parties. It conveyed to B. the dominium directum of separate parcels of land by five clauses. Of the land described in four the dominium utile had been conveyed by A. and his predecessors at various dates before 1873 out and out to the G. and S. W. Railway Company. None of these conveyances was of the nature of a feu right, and no mid-superiority was thereby created, and consequently the railway company held the lands thereby disponed (sect. 126 Lands Clauses Consolidation (Scotland) Act, 1845), under those who were the immediate superiors at the dates of the several conveyances in their favour. The 5th clause was, inter alia, in these terms : " And all other lands and others in the county of Ayr, parts of the said estates of Ballochmyle, ... and have been disponed by me," &c., to the said G. and S. W. Railway Company. In 1878 A. had disponed an acre of land to the same railway for a reservoir, together with the servitude right of conveying water from it by means of pipes through his intervening lands to the railway station. That deed declares that the said acre of land and servitude are to be holden of the disponer in feu farm fee and heritage for ever; and the lands thus feued are described as parts of " all and whole the lands and tenandry of Ballochmyle and others, being the lands and others particularly described in a writ of clare constat granted by A. in favour of himself in 1864." In 1863 A. had completed his title as superior under the Crown of "all and whole the lands and tenandry of Ballochmyle." In 1864 he made up a feudal title to the dominium utile of these lands by obtaining from himself, as his own immediate superior, the writ of clare referred to. These several estates of superiority and fee remain vested in A. under separate titles. The effect, therefore, of the feu disposition of 1878 was to split the dominium utile of the acre of ground and its accompanying servitude rights, as vested in A. by the writ of 1864, into two estates; one an estate of fee belonging to the railway company, and the other a subordinate (yet independent) estate of superiority, belonging to A., interposed between his vassal's estate of fee and his own estate of superiority under the Crown. B., under the above 5th clause, claimed the mid-superiority of the acre of ground feued in 1878 to the railway company. A. adduced proof to shew that the land in question was misdescribed in the deed of 1878, that it did not "belong to the lands and tenandry of Ballochmyle," but was part and parcel of other lands ; he also sought to refer to previous letters to shew what the contract was :—*Held*, affirming the judgment of the Court below, but not on the same reasoning, that the evidence was not sufficient to discredit the description of the lands, the onus probandi being on A.; that there was not in the dispositive clause any ambiguity of expression such as to necessitate or justify a reference to the other clauses of the deed or to the previous letters for aid in its interpretation ; but the terms of that clause did not sustain the claim made by B. LEE *v.* ALEXANDER - - 8 App. Cas. 853

2. —— *Construction—Similar restrictive Conditions appearing in Feu Charters from Common Superior—What necessary to give each Feuar a*

IV. SCOTCH LAW—CONVEYANCE—*continued.*

*Title to enforce them —Suing with another Person's Consent and Concurrence—Strangers to the Action—Practice—Amendment of the Record—*31 & 32 Vict. c. 100, *s.* 29.] It is settled by a series of decisions in the law of Scotland that where it appears that the restrictions in a feu contract are entered into for the benefit of other feus, either already existing, or to be created by the superior thereafter, the restrictions may be enforced by each co-feuar as far as his interest is concerned. But the fact of several feuars of neighbouring plots of building land in the same street, holding from a common superior, does not, by itself, entitle one of those feuars to claim the benefit of restrictions contained in the feu contract of another, unless some mutuality and community of rights and obligations is otherwise established between them, which can only be done by express stipulations in their respective contracts with the superior, or by reasonable implication from reference in both contracts to a common plan or scheme of building, or by mutual agreement between the feuars themselves. —A.'s author was a party to a feu contract of a piece of land upon which a house was already built, and he was taken bound not to build any other buildings on the said piece of land except offices. The adjoining pieces of land were feued off, some being taken not to build and others having that right. It was not indicated in A.'s feu that the restrictions were imposed for the benefit of the co-feuars, beyond the facts that the feus were all given out nearly at the same time ; that some of the conditions inserted in the feus are similar to each other ; and that the houses being built in a square, produce a considerable degree of uniformity.—B. and C., proprietors of a neighbouring feu, sought to prevent A. building a carriage show room on the ground intervening between his house and the street of the square, and raised an interdict with the " consent and concurrence " of the superior ; there was no condescendence or pleas in law for the superior :—*Held*, reversing the decision of the Court below (1), that the restrictive conditions as to building in A.'s feu contract was not in any sense jus quæsitum tertio ; and (2), that the superior was not a party complainant in the action for his own separate interest ; and therefore B. and C. being strangers to A.'s contract, A. ought to have been assoilzied from the action.—Persons who have no title in their own persons to raise and insist in an action, cannot have the right to sue, where nil, validated by the consent and concurrence of the party to whom alone such right or title of action belong.— B. and C., owners of an adjoining feu, raised an action with "consent and concurrence" of the common superior to enforce building restrictions contained in A.'s feu contract :—*Held*, that B. and C. were strangers to the action, and therefore had no title to sue.—See remarks of Lord Watson as to the question of the importation of new parties into the suit under the Court of Sessions Act, 1865 (31 & 32 Vict. c. 100). HISLOP *v.* LECKIE

[6 App. Cas. 560

V. SCOTCH LAW—ENTAIL.

—— *Trust to make strict Entail—Destination to Heirs whatsoever—Construction of.*] A. in his final general settlement dated 1853, revoking all

V. SCOTCH LAW—ENTAIL—*continued.*

prior deeds so far as inconsistent therewith, conveyed his whole estates to trustees with directions to execute a deed of strict entail of his lands "to and in favour of B. and his heirs whatsoever, whom failing to and in favour of C. and his heirs whatsoever," whom failing to persons thereafter to be nominated by him (the truster), always excluding heirs portioners, and failing such nomination, then to "my own heirs whatsoever and their assignees;" but declaring that any member of a family in possession of the entailed estate of M. should be excluded; and also the descendants of the body of his sister Charlotte. B. and C. were A.'s natural sons. C. predeceased A., unmarried. A. died without executing any deed of nomination of fresh heirs. His trustees executed, in 1859, a deed in the form of an entail conveying the estates to B., exactly in terms of the destination in A.'s deed, leaving out C. B. treated the estates as fee-simple, and left them in certain directions on his death without issue.—Thereupon the heir-at-law of A. (his brother's son) raised an action against A.'s trustees and others concluding for reduction of the deed of 1859, and all subsequent writs, on the ground, inter alia, that the directions as to entailing the estates contained in his uncle's settlements had not been carried out by the trustees in respect that the said deed was not a valid entail under the Act of 1685; and for a declaration that the trustees are bound to execute a new deed of entail in favour of himself as institute and of several other descendants of A.'s brother and sisters as substitute heirs of entail: or alternatively, assuming the deed of 1859 was executed in terms of the truster's intentions, to have it found that it was an effectual entail, and that he was entitled to succeed as heir of entail next in succession to B. He relied on the various prior deeds and settlements, which he contended should be read along with the deed of 1853, which if done, made it clear that A.'s intention was to limit the class of heirs whatsoever of B. to heirs of the body, and also by the term "my own heirs whatsoever," he intended to designate his nearest heir of line and the heirs of the body of such heir, whom failing his own heirs whatsoever:—*Held,* affirming the decision of the Court below, that the deed of entail of 1859 had been executed in conformity with the terms of A.'s final trust, the terms of which were clear and unambiguous. That the Pursuer had failed to establish that he either possessed or was entitled to claim the character of an heir of provision and tailzie under the entail directed by the trust deed of 1853: that the only ulterior destination being to the truster's own "heirs whatsoever and assignees" the entail came to an end in the person of B., and he could dispose of the estates as he pleased. That it was competent to read all the prior deeds to see how far any of them were to receive effect, along with his final trust settlement—but not competent to use them to put a construction on words bearing a clear and well understood technical meaning and which they do not bear if the deed be construed by itself. GORDON *v.* GORDON
　　　　　　　　　　　　　　　　[7 App. Cas. 713

VI. SCOTCH LAW—HARBOUR.

　1. —— Compulsory Purchase of Land—*Har-*

VI. SCOTCH LAW—HARBOUR—*continued.*

bour Trustees—Powers under Special Act—Compensation—Invalidity of Agreement purporting to restrain Powers over Land taken—Lands Clauses Consolidation (Scotland) Act, 1845, ss. 48 and 61.] Where the Legislature confers powers on any body, whether one which is seeking to make a profit for shareholders, or one acting solely for the public good, to take lands compulsorily for a particular purpose, it is on the ground that the using of that land for that purpose will be for the public good; and a contract purporting to bind such a body and their successors not to use those powers is void. Harbour trustees, constituted for the management and improvement of a public harbour by a special Act, which incorporated the Lands Clauses Consolidation (Scotland) Act, 1845, were empowered to take lands scheduled (which included that part of O.'s land having an unrestricted frontage to the harbour) for the undertaking. While the question of compensation to O. for his land was before the arbiter the trustees lodged a minute agreeing that the conveyance should restrict their use of the ground taken so as not to interfere with the access from the remaining property of O. to the harbour. To this minute O. did not assent. The arbiter found £4900 payable by the trustees as compensation for an unrestricted use, or £2786 if it were competent for the trustees to bind themselves and their successors by the above-mentioned minute. O. raised an action for declarator of an absolute purchase and unrestricted right in the subject, and for payment of the larger sum :—*Held,* affirming the decision of the Court below, that the trustees had power under their special Act, now or at any future time, to make erections on the piece of ground taken, which would effectually destroy the frontage of O.'s remaining property to the harbour; secondly, that it was not competent to the trustees to dispense with future exercise of their powers by themselves and their successors.— *Per* Lord Blackburn : If the trustees could bind themselves and their successors by the agreement, and that agreement would prevent O.'s land from being injuriously affected, O., by refusing his assent, could not get compensation for the injury he might have prevented. AYR HARBOUR TRUSTEES *v.* OSWALD　　　- 8 App. Cas. 623

　2. —— Dues leviable — *Timber floated in Chains — Usage and contemporanea expositio — Clyde Navigation Consolidation Act,* 1858 (21 & 22 *Vict. c. cxlix.*), *ss.* 98, 99, *Sched. H.*] Where a statute gave trustees appointed for the improvement of a navigable river and harbour power to charge dues on all timber "shipped or unshipped within the harbour or river" :—*Held,* that, to attach a tow-rope to a log of timber or a number of logs loosely connected at one of the ends for the purpose of towing them, is not to "ship" those logs, and that to cast off the tow-rope is not to "unship" them.—*Query,* whether a raft of logs so constructed as to be capable of being navigated can be said to be "unshipped" when on reaching its destination it is taken to pieces and landed.—By an Act dated 1770, the Clyde trustees had power to charge rates on "all timber or wood either carried in boats or other vessels, or floated in and upon the said River

2 Y

VI. SCOTCH LAW—HARBOUR—continued.

Clyde within those points aforesaid" (that is above Dumbuck). By a statute in 1840 the Clyde trustees' jurisdiction was extended down the river to Newark Castle, and the duties were imposed by that Act on "all goods carried or conveyed on the river." By the statute in force at present, dated 1858, all the prior Acts are totally repealed. By sect. 75 the limits of the river are to include the whole channel or waterway forming the harbour, and the whole works within certain given limits, and the whole lands acquired for the purposes of such works, or occupied by the trustees in connection with the navigation of the said river. By sect. 98 it is enacted that the trustees are to have power to levy on goods "shipped or unshipped" in the river or harbour the rates specified in the first and second columns of part 1 of Schedule H. Schedule H. is headed "Rates on goods conveyed upon or shipped or unshipped in the river or harbour." In 1876 the trustees under their Act of 1858 sought to levy rates on timber in logs, which were taken out of the vessels importing them from abroad outside the jurisdiction of the trustees, and then floated or towed chained together over the old, shallow channel of the river, to storing ponds situate within the trustees' jurisdiction. In a note for suspension and interdict at the instance of the owners :—*Held*, affirming the decision of the Court below, that the word "river" as it occurs in sect. 98 comprehended the whole waters of the Clyde, within the limits defined in sect. 75, and cannot be restricted to those portions of the channel which have been artificially deepened ; but that the statute of 1858 confers no authority on the trustees to levy rates on timber towed in the manner mentioned.—See Lords Blackburn (p. 670) and Watson (p. 673) as to the value of contemporanea expositio of an Act so late as 1858.
TRUSTEES OF CLYDE NAVIGATION *v.* LAIRD
[8 App. Cas. 658

VII. SCOTCH LAW—HERITABLE PROPERTY.

—— Feu Duties—*Superior and Vassal—Restrictions in Feu Charter not to sell or retail any kind of Malt Liquor in Houses erected on the Feu—Relevancy—Interest.*] A restriction in a feu charter, purporting to bind not only the original contracting feuar and his heirs, but also his assignee or any tenant or possessor of the houses to be erected on the feu, and power to enforce or dispense with it, is given not to the disponer or his heirs, but to the superior for the time being ; the restriction, unless repugnant to the nature of the estate taken by the feuar or to public policy, is a condition of the feu, and runs with the land against singular successors.—In all cases of restrictive conditions in a feu charter, the superior must have power to enforce them, or to dispense with them according to his own will or not, whether the charter is so expressed or not, unless the benefit of them and the right to enforce them are communicated to other feuars.—A restraint against carrying on the trade of a publican is as good in law, and as capable of running with the land, as a restraint against carrying on any other business ; and the fact that restrictions are placed by statute upon the freedom of that particular trade constitutes no reason why a private

VII. SCOTCH LAW—HERITABLE PROPERTY
continued.

contract to prevent it from being carried on, without the consent of the superior, should be held invalid or contrary to law.—Feu rights of land in Grangemouth, a town of 5000 inhabitants, contained restrictions against retailing malt or spirituous liquors, or allowing the same to be sold or retailed within the buildings erected on the feus without the superior's permission. The superior sought an interdict to prohibit the Defenders, the feuars, from continuing to sell any kind of malt or spirituous liquors, &c., alleging that the whole of the town was built on ground held of him as superior ; that he was proprietor of certain houses in the heart of the town at a rental of £750 ; that he had still a large extent of ground in and adjacent to the town available for feuing, and that his mansion-house was within half a mile of the town ; and that these properties were damaged by the existence of so many public-houses. The Defenders pleaded no interest to sue the action, acquiescence, and prescriptive use. On the question of relevancy :—*Held*, reversing the decision of the Court below, first, that the restrictions sought to be imposed were not personal, or inconsistent with public policy, nor repugnant to the Pursuer's estate, they relating to the use and employment of buildings erected on the land ; secondly, that the interest to sue the action was connected with patrimonial rights, and that the superior's case, as shewn on the record, was sufficient to entitle him to the relief which he prayed :—*Held*, also, that it was the plain intention of the contracting parties that the superior should determine, whether there are to be public-houses upon any of the feus, and if so, their number and position, and accordingly the superior in granting his license to certain feuars to sell liquor was in no sense departing from or waiving the prohibition. But it was a different question in all or some of the cases, whether the Pursuer might not be seeking to enforce the restrictions under circumstances, or in a manner, which ought to deprive him of the assistance of the Court, there being facts averred, from which, if proved or admitted, it might be legally inferred that successive superiors had so acquiesced in the feuars' use of their premises for the sale of liquor that the prohibition must be held to have been unconditionally discharged. But the record leaving it open to the superior to adduce evidence which might give a different colour to these facts, the parties must proceed to proof before the questions of acquiescence and waiver, and prescriptive use, could be decided.—*Per* Lord Watson : Though *Tailors of Aberdeen v. Coutts* (1 Rob. App. Cas. 296) does determine, that the superior cannot enforce a restriction on property, unless he has some legitimate interest ; that case does not lay down the doctrine, that an action at the superior's instance, which merely sets forth the condition of his feu right and its violation by the vassal must be dismissed as irrelevant, because the Pursuer has failed to allege interest. The vassal in consenting to be bound by the restriction concedes the interest of the superior, and therefore the onus is upon the vassal, who is pleading a release from his contract, to prove that any legitimate interest which

VII. SCOTCH LAW—HERITABLE PROPERTY
—continued.

the Pursuer may originally have had in maintaining the restriction has ceased to exist.—*Tailors of Aberdeen v. Coutts* (1 Rob. App. Cas. 296) followed. EARL OF ZETLAND *v.* HISLOP　　7 App. Cas. 427

2. —— Liferent and Fiar—*Unworked Coal Mines—Liferentrix not entitled to Profits though opened during her Life—Testator's Intention—Trusts (Scotland) Act, 1867 (30 & 31 Vict. c. 97), s. 2, sub-s. 3.*] A testator directed his trustees to pay to his wife " the whole annual produce and rents of the residue of his estates both heritable and moveable." Coal and iron mines were leased by the testator before his death. His trustees afterwards leased others. In a question whether the wife was entitled to the rents of those opened after the testator's death :—*Held*, affirming the decision of the Court below, that in law she was not entitled ; and that there was nothing in the trust deed which shewed that she was to have such a benefit :—Also, the Trusts (Scotland) Act of 1867 was merely an Act to facilitate administration without disturbing the interests of the beneficiaries under the trust, i.e., it enables trustees who also have the testator's authority to let minerals, to let them for the customary period instead of a lease for an uncertain period, namely, a tenancy for life.—Whether the power to let minerals on long leases under sub-sect. 3, sect. 2, of the Act includes a power to open up and let new mineral fields not decided. CAMPBELL *v.* WARDLAW　　8 App. Cas. 641

3. —— Personal and Real Property—*Privileges stipulated for in Conveyance of Heritable Subjects —Jus quæsitum tertio—Theatre.*] Trustees acting for the shareholders or rentallers of a theatre called the Queen's Theatre and Opera House, who had obtained a feu right to the site, granted in 1858 a disposition of the ground and buildings to one J. B., subject, inter alia, to the real burden of a perpetual annuity of £2 per share to each rentaller of the said Queen's Theatre and Opera House, and to the successors or assignees of them ; and it was further declared that each of the said rentallers, or the assignee or successors of such, should at all time be entitled, inter alia, to free admission to the auditorium of the said Queen's Theatre and Opera House ; also declaring that J. B. should not convert the said theatre to any other use ; and that he should keep it open for performance six months in each year. There was no stipulation as to insurance of the theatre or as to the rebuilding of it in case of destruction by fire or otherwise.—In 1865 the theatre was entirely destroyed by fire, and was rebuilt by J. B.'s trustee and called by another name.—In 1875 it was again entirely burnt down and again rebuilt.—From 1865 to 1879 the theatre, under the new name, was twice sold, but in each case the conveyance was granted subject to the " real burdens, conditions, provisions, declarations, and others," specified in the original disposition of 1858, and especially under the burden of payment of the annuities to the rentallers, and of allowing " these parties the privileges to which they are entitled." The privilege of free admission was enjoyed by the rentallers for fourteen years after the destruction of the first theatre.

VII. SCOTCH LAW—HERITABLE PROPERTY
—continued.

But in 1879 disputes arose as to the validity of the rentallers' right to, inter alia, the privilege of free admission. The trustees maintained that the rentallers were entitled under the disposition of 1858 and the succeeding conveyances to the same privileges in the new theatre which they had in the first :—*Held*, affirming the decision of the Court below, that the privileges conferred on the rentallers by the original dispositions—other than the payment of the annuities, which was constituted a real burden—rested only on the personal obligation of the original disponee, and were confined to the theatre then in existence ; and that the subsequent deeds to which the rentallers were not parties, were not intended to, and did not, confer on them any new right. SCOTT *v.* HOWARD　　6 App. Cas. 295

4. —— Succession — *English Will devising English and Scotch Lands in tail male, Effect as to Scotch Heritage—Construction—Intention of Testator—Titles to Land Consolidation (Scotland) Act, 1868 (31 & 32 Vict. c. 101), ss. 19, 20.*] Where a testator, in a foreign will, expresses himself in technical language of the place where made and where he is domiciled, to obtain the intention the technical terms must be interpreted by the meaning put on them in the system of law from which they are borrowed.—By the common law of Scotland the actual intention of the maker of any validly executed settlement of moveables received effect when duly ascertained ; and now by the Titles to Land Consolidation (Scotland) Act, 1868, the Scotch law—which would previously have rejected as inoperative a foreign will dealing with Scotch lands not executed with all the required formalities ; and not expressed in appropriate terms of de presenti conveyance—must, so far as may be practicable with the principles of that law, give effect to the intention as expressed in the will, just the same as if it dealt with moveables and not heritage. The technical rule of Scotch law applicable to moveable and immoveable property, that a gift or devise to a parent in liferent, and after his death to his unborn or unnamed children in fee, confers a fee on the parent and a spes successionis only on the children—(*Frog's Creditors*, Mor. 4262)—is excluded by anything in the gift itself, shewing beyond doubt that the intention was to give nothing more than a life interest to the parent. A testator, domiciled in England, who died possessed of lands in England and Scotland, left a will executed according to the forms of English law, by which he devised all his lands as consisted of " freehold of inheritance " to the use of his eldest son, E. F. S., and his assigns for his life " without impeachment of waste," and after the death of E. F. S. to the use of the first and every other son of E. F. S. successively, according to their respective seniorities in tail male, with remainders over. Under a subsequent clause, E. F. S. took as residuary legatee all property not otherwise disposed of. Subsequent to the date of the will children were born to E. F. S. He claimed the Scotch estate as vested in him absolutely, or alternatively that the estate belonged to him as residuary legatee or as heir-at-

VII. SCOTCH LAW—HERITABLE PROPERTY
—continued.

law. This claim was opposed on behalf of his infant children :—*Held,* affirming the decision of the Court below, that under the statute of 1868 the law of Scotland must, so far as practicable, give effect to the intention of the testator, as gathered from the whole context interpreted by English law; and (2) that undoubtedly the intention of the testator was that E. F. S. should take a life interest only; and that of the fee the Scotch estates should go to the eldest son of E. F. S., and the others nominated. (3) That the intention, so far as the separate destination of the liferent and fee of the estate, could be carried out substantially without inconsistency with the practice or policy of the law of Scotland,—the rule being valeat quantum valere potest. (4) That a registrable title fell to be made up in accordance with such intention; but that the technical way in which effect might be given to the intention by the Scotch law was immaterial. —See Lord Watson as to the non-vesting of the beneficial fee until the death of the liferenter, p. 602. STUDD *v.* COOK   **8 App. Cas. 577**

5. —— Superior and Vassal — *Irritancy ob non solutum canonem—Statute 1597, c. 250 — Extinction of Sub-feu held under defaulting Vassal —Right of Sub-feuar to purge the Irritancy.*] An action of declarator of tinsel of a feu ob non solutum canonem is an irredeemable adjudication of the feu in favour of the superior; but the sub-feuar can protect himself from eviction by paying the superior's full preferable debt, and when he does so he has a claim of relief pro ratâ against all the owners of the land on which the debt is charged.—It is provided by the Scotch Statute 1597, c. 250, that the vassal shall lose the feu of his lands by his failure to pay the feu duty for two years together, in like manner as if an irritant clause to that effect had existed in his feu contract.—By feu contract A. disponed in feu farm to B. and C. five acres of building land, with an annual reddendo of £480. The contract of feu contained the express declaration "that in case at any time two years' feu duty shall be fully resting, owing and unpaid together, then this present feu right, and all that may follow hereon, shall, in the option of the superior, become void and null. B. and C. divided the lands between them, and each granted, inter alia, sub-feus (narrating in the deeds conveying the land the above-mentioned feu contract) of portions of the five acres to D. and E. respectively.—Upwards of four years' feu duties became due. A. raised an action of declarator of irritancy ob non solutum canonem. D. and E. contended that the irritancy must be confined to the mid-superiorities created by B. and C. and had no effect on the portions of land sub-fued on their tendering the sub-feu duty reserved on each :—*Held,* reversing the decision appealed from, but affirming *Cassels* v. *Lamb* (12 Court Sess. Cas. 4th Series, 722), that the superior's right was not merely a charge upon the mid-superiorities, but a right to annul the charter of his feuars and all sub-feus made by them, to the effect of resuming the full beneficial possession of the lands feued.—*Held,* also, that the circumstances did not warrant the conclusion that the

VII. SCOTCH LAW—HERITABLE PROPERTY
—continued.

superior had consented to the sub-infeudation. SANDEMAN *v.* SCOTTISH PROPERTY SOCIETY
    [10 App. Cas. 553

VIII. SCOTCH LAW—HIGHWAY.

1. —— Power of *Magistrates in the exercise of Administration to make Road over Land held for Public Recreation—Constitution of new Rights and Burdens—Alienation of Solum—Costs—Alteration of Interlocutor.*] Magistrates for a burgh held the links from time immemorial for behoof of the inhabitants, and, inter alia, subject to the obligation of preserving the same for the purposes of the game of golf and for the recreation and amusement of the inhabitants. They had from time to time exercised powers of administration and management over the links, such as the letting of the pasturage, the regulation of bleaching clothes on the links, the construction of a sloping walk, and the levelling and filling up other portions of the ground. The magistrates proposed to make a macadamised road along the outside boundary of the links, where that boundary adjoins certain feus let off by them in 1820, which feus are no longer, in point of law, part of the links.—P., an inhabitant of the burgh and member of the principal golfing club there, and others, the Appellants, sought by note of suspension and interdict to restrain the magistrates either from making the road or from permitting any road to be used in that place for wheel traffic :—*Held,* substantially affirming the decision of the Judges of the Court below, but altering their interlocutor, that the evidence proved that the proposed road would have no substantial interference with the obligation of golfing, &c., and that the road might be reconciled with its due observance; but that it was inconsistent with that obligation for the magistrates to alienate any part of the solum of the ground in question, or to abdicate their existing powers of administration either by granting private easements to particular individuals, or, having made the road, to create a public easement by dedicating it to the public.—*Held,* also that the Respondents were not entitled to their costs in the appeal on the grounds that the alteration made in the interlocutor of the Court below was wanted to give complete security to the interests represented by the Appellants; and because the attitude of both sets of Respondents before action brought was such as to justify the institution of some action for the purpose of obtaining the declarations now obtained. PATERSON *v.* PROVOST, &c., OF ST. ANDREWS
    [6 App. Cas. 833

2. —— Prescription—*Non-user for a long Period—Presumption—Scotch Law.*] According to the law of Scotland, the constitution of a public right of way does not depend on any legal fiction, but upon the fact of user by the public as matter of right, continuously and without interruption for forty years.—And the amount of user must be such as might have been reasonably expected, if the road in dispute had been an undoubted public highway.—Also, the user must be a user of the whole road as a means of passage from one terminus to the other, and must not be such a user

VIII. SCOTCH LAW—HIGHWAY—*continued.*

as can be reasonably ascribed either to private servitude rights or to the license of the proprietor. —The continued exclusion of the public from the use of an alleged public road for thirty-seven years will not, per se, destroy a pre-existent right of public way. unless it is maintained for the prescriptive period of forty years, but it is strong evidence that no such public right ever existed. —Observations on the difference of English law. MANN *v.* BRODIE - **10 App. Cas. 378**

3. —— Roads and Bridges (Scotland) Act, 1878 (41 & 42 *Vict. v.* 51), *ss.* 4, 5, 6, 7, *and* 37— *Construction of.*] The trustees of the W. S. bridge, which spans the River Dee and connects the counties of Kincardine and Aberdeen, sought to have it found that the local Acts 10 Geo. 4, c. 43, and 23 Vict. c. 26, being the W. S. Bridge and Road Acts—had ceased to be of force and effect within the county of Kincardine (that county having adopted the Roads and Bridges Act, 1878): That the trustees have ceased to be under any obligation as regards the management or maintenance of the bridge or road, and that the Defenders, the county road trustees of Kincardine, and the commissioners of supply of the county of Aberdeen, are bound to maintain and keep in proper repair the bridge and road : and further, that the trustees have ceased to be liable for the debts incurred by them as trustees. By the local Act, of 1865 tolls were abolished in the county of Aberdeen; but from its provisions the burgh was excluded. The Aberdeenshire portion of the road and part of the bridge are within the burgh boundary.—The county of Aberdeen has not adopted the Act of 1878, and the commissioners of supply of that county deny any liability in respect to the maintenance, &c., of the bridge and road.—*Held*, reversing the interlocutors of the Court below, that that the true effect of the Roads and Bridges Act, 1878, in the circumstances, was to continue in force the local Acts so far as the powers and duties thereby imposed on the trustees for the management, &c., of that part of the bridge and road which is within the county and parliamentary burgh of Aberdeen, together with the powers of demanding and taking tolls within the county and burgh conferred by such Acts so long as the Roads and Bridges Act, 1878, shall not be in force therein : that the liability of the trustees to the debts incurred under the local Acts had now ceased and fallen severally upon the Defenders : that the commissioners of supply are entitled to receive from the W. S. bridge and road trustees all surplus of income accruing to them from tolls exacted on the bridge and road within the county and parliamentary burgh of Aberdeen, after providing for the expenses of management, &c., and on doing so, are entitled to be relieved by them from the proportion of the debts belonging under the Roads and Bridges Act, 1878, to the county and parliamentary burgh of Aberdeen ; and that as regards that part of the bridge and roads within the county of Kincardine, the local Acts had ceased to be in force : and the road trustees of that county are bound to maintain and keep in repair that part of the bridge and road. COMMISSIONERS OF SUPPLY OF COUNTY OF ABERDEEN *v.* MORICE

[**6 App. Cas. 881**

IX. SCOTCH LAW—HUSBAND AND WIFE.

1. —— Divorce—*Wife's Adultery—Condonation — Subsequent acts of Misconduct — Doctrine of Canon Law—Non-revival of condoned Adultery in Scotch · Law — Weight of English Divorce Cases.*] By the law of Scotland full condonation of adultery (remission expressly or by implication in full knowledge of the acts forgiven), followed by cohabitation as man and wife, is a remissio injuriæ absolute and unconditional, and affords an absolute bar to any action of divorce founded on the condoned acts of adultery. Nor can condonation of adultery—cohabitation following—be made conditional by any arrangement between the spouses.—Although the condoned adultery cannot be founded on, condonation does not extinguish the guilty acts entirely, and they may be proved so far as they tend to throw light upon charges of adultery posterior to the condonation.—A wife confessed to several acts of adultery with E. Her husband forgave her and resumed cohabitation on the alleged condition that she should not speak or hold any communication with E. again. Subsequently she met E. by appointment several times under suspicious circumstances; but, admittedly, no act of adultery could be proved. The husband sued for a dissolution of the marriage on the ground that the condoned adultery was revived by the wife's subsequent conduct :—*Held* (affirming the decision of the Court below), that to obtain a divorce he must prove adultery subsequent to the condonation, and no less.—The doctrine laid down in *Durant* v. *Durant* (1 Hagg. Ecc. Rep. at p. 761) not approved without qualification.— *Dent* v. *Dent* (34 L. J. (P. M. & Ad.) 118 ; 4 Sw. & Tr. at p. 106). Direction of Lord Penzance to the jury questioned on principle; and that case distinguished from *Blandford* v. *Blandford* (8 P. D. 19), adultery reviving desertion.—*Per* Lord Blackburn : The doctrine of revival of adultery as a ground on which a divorce has been granted is to be strongly objected to as varying the status of married persons. On principle, a reconciliation being entered into with full knowledge of the guilt and with free and deliberate intention to forgive it, where that reconciliation is followed by living together as man and wife, the status of the couple ought to be the same and not more precarious than if there was a new marriage.—*Per* Lord Blackburn : Assuming it to be now established English law that any matrimonial offence, though forgiven, may be revived by any other matrimonial offence of which the Courts take cognizance, it is very modern law, and not so obviously just and expedient that this House ought to infer that it either was or ought to have been introduced into the law of Scotland. —See Lord Watson's opinion (p. 257), for the terms of a remission of adultery which would not constitute plena condonatio in the law of Scotland. COLLINS *v.* COLLINS   **9 App. Cas. 205**

2. —— Marriage—*Evidence—Certificate and Relative Affidavit— Admissible Evidence—Legitimation of Children by subsequent Marriage—Marriage on Death-bed—Succession to Real Estate.*] Where a marriage is proved to have been solemnized de facto 113 years ago by people who intended that it should be a good marriage, and it is done bonâ

IX. SCOTCH LAW — HUSBAND AND WIFE —
continued.

fide and openly, the maxim omnia rite acta præsumuntur applies.—The marriage of a domiciled Scotchman legitimates his children born previous to the marriage, and the children's right to succeed to his heritable estate is not prejudiced by the marriage taking place on death-bed.—By the law of Scotland statements of a deceased person in relation to facts, which must presumably have been within his personal knowledge, and to which, if alive, he could have been examined as a witness, may after his death be received as secondary evidence through the medium of writing, or through the medium of a living person who heard the statement. Where, therefore, a member of the family writes a note in a manuscript book to the effect that he has sent original letters to a certain person, and they cannot be found, the copies of such letters, the handwriting, and that the copies were from original letters being proved, the note, and the copies of the letters, are evidence of the truth of the statements within the writer's personal knowledge, and appearing to be so by the letters themselves.—So also a statement, whether oral or written, is not vitiated if made with a purpose, where the object was an obvious and legitimate one and one supporting and not discrediting the presumption of truth. But the statement of a deceased person is not admissible as evidence when its terms, or the circumstances in which it was made, are such as to beget a reasonable suspicion either that the statement was not in accordance with the truth, or that it was a coloured or one-sided version of the truth ; and this rule should be applied with greater strictness in criminal cases : *Magistrates of Aberdeen* v. *More* (1813. Hume's Dec. 502); *Geils* v. *Geils* (1855. 17 Court Sess. Cas. 2nd Series, 397) ; *Gordon* v. *Grant* (13 Ibid. 1); *Madeline Smith* (1857. 2 Irving's Justiciary Rep. 653) ; *Macdonald* v. *Union Bank* (1864. 2 Court Sess. Cas. 3rd Series, 963), examined.—A minute of date 1749, from an original unsigned minute book, produced from the proper custody and kept in accordance with a charter of a society, is admissible evidence.—A memorandum in a register of a church by its deceased rector made about 108 years ago, though not a contemporaneous entry made in the regular course of the register, is admissible as evidence, and goes to prove that the rector did the things stated in the memorandum.—A change of domicil must be a residence sine animo revertendi. A temporary residence for the purposes of health, travel, or business does not change the domicil. Also, (1) every presumption is to be made in favour of the original domicil ; (2) no change can occur without an actual residence in a new place ; and (3) no new domicil can be obtained without a clear intention of abandoning the old.—A., then ill of the malady of which he died, and two days before his death, was married in 1772 in New York to B. by C., an ordained clergyman of the Church of England, then assistant minister of Trinity Church, New York. There was produced, inter alia, in support of the marriage from the custody of the family a certificate signed by C., that he had married A. and B. according to the rites of the Church of England as by law established, and an affidavit, signed by the mayor of

IX. SCOTCH LAW — HUSBAND AND WIFE—
continued.

New York, to the effect that C. had made an oath of the truth of the statements in the certificate ; a will of date anterior to the marriage, by which A. left all his property to B. and the children then born ; copies of letters shewing that one of the executors wrote to his co-executor in England, a brother of A., stating that he was a witness to the ceremony of marriage ; that B. signed herself in A.'s surname ; that the children were recognised and taken care of by members of the family as A.'s children ; and also War Office records shewing that B. received a pension as A.'s widow : —Held, that there was ample proof of a legal marriage.—*Per* Lord Blackburn : When English settlers go out to a colony and settle there they carry with them, so far as may be applicable to their purpose, all the immunities and privileges of the law of England as the law of England was at that time. LAUDERDALE PEERAGE CASE

[10 App. Cas. 692

3. —— Marriage—*Habit and repute—Mutual Consent de præsenti before Witnesses—Evidence— Admissibility of Statement not on Oath of deceased Person—Statements post litem motam—Statutes 15 & 16 Vict. c. 27; 16 & 17 Vict. c. 20; and 37 & 38 Vict. c. 64—Precognitions—Admissibility of.*] The law of Scotland accepts the continued cohabitation of a man and woman as spouses, coupled with the general repute of their being married persons, as complete evidence of their having deliberately consented to marry ; but in order to sustain that inference their cohabitation must be within the realm of Scotland.—Cohabitation outside Scotland will not constitute marriage, although it may be competently founded on, either as corroborative evidence of a ceremony in Scotland, or as evidence that a ceremony proved to have taken place in Scotland was truly intended by the parties as a present interchange of matrimonial consent.—A. alleged that she was lawfully married to B. by interchange of mutual consent de præsenti before witnesses in 1844 in Scotland, and that having remained in Scotland for about a month, B. and she cohabited at divers places in England as husband and wife, and that a son now living was born of the marriage in 1863. —Between 1844 and 1849, when B. deserted A., three daughters were born, one of whom B. registered as legitimate. In 1851 B. married C. at a parish church in England and had children. A. was informed of this marriage shortly after its celebration, but took no steps to have the validity of the averred irregular Scotch marriage of 1844, or the nullity of the marriage of 1851, judicially declared, until 1880. The alleged witnesses to A.'s marriage were admitted now to be dead, but they were alive in 1853, when they might have been judicially examined in an action brought against B. for the board and lodging of A. :— Held, that the evidence completely disproved the allegation of a marriage between A. and B.—B. married C. in facie ecclesiæ in 1851, had issue, and died in 1872. In an attempt by A. to set up a previous irregular Scotch marriage, a witness gave evidence that B. told him repeatedly after 1851 that A. was his wife and not C. :—Held, that such evidence was not admissible.—Effect of the

IX. SCOTCH LAW—HUSBAND AND WIFE—
continued.

statute 37 & 38 Vict. c. 64 (1874) *held* not necessary to decide.—In an attempt on the part of A. to set up an irregular marriage according to the law of Scotland between herself and B., statements prepared by D., the Plaintiff, in an action against B. as the alleged husband of A. for A.'s board and lodging; which statement was signed—and in one case corrected by interlineations—by deceased persons who, if alive, would have been competent witnesses, were sought to be used as evidence :—*Held*, that they were not admissible. DYSART PEERAGE CASE   -   6 App. Cas. 489

4. —— Marriage—*Habit and Repute—Declaration of Deceased Person—Statements Post litem Motam.*] The general rule of the law of Scotland is that hearsay of a deceased person who, if alive, would have been a competent witness, is admissible evidence; but if the fact, to which the deceased testified, was such as he could not have had any special means of knowledge it is not receivable; and this applies to written as well as oral statements.—Deliberate statements made by deceased members of a family, who, if alive, could have been competent witnesses, are generally admissible—but a statement by one member of a family that B., another member, did a certain act, which act, if done at all, was done before the deceased narrator's birth, and there being nothing to shew what were his grounds of knowledge, and the fact not otherwise being proved, is not evidence that the particular act was done by any one; and though the statement cannot be altogether rejected, yet it can only be received as mere family tradition :— When a person leaves his native place and goes to another place to pursue a claim to an estate or title of nobility, and on his return tells certain persons what was said to him by persons connected with the family while so pursuing his inquiries; these statements are not admissible evidence.— Rule laid down in *Dysart Case* (6 App. Cas. p. 507) followed. LOVAT PEERAGE CASE 10 App. Cas. 763

5. —— Marriage Contract—*Provision to Children of prior Marriage—Rule of Law—Intention of Truster—Trust—Irrevocability.*] The general rule of law is that the Courts will not enforce a marriage settlement in favour of stranger volunteers who are not parties to the contract, on the ground that they are not within the consideration of the marriage. But when the persons who are within the consideration of the marriage take only on terms which admit to a participation with them others who would not otherwise be within the consideration, then, not the matrimonial consideration, but the consideration of the mutual contract extend to and comprehend them.—Where in an ante-nuptial contract of marriage, the intention of the owner of the property, a widow with children, was to make the children of the prior marriage and those procreated of the second marriage *a single class*, the members of which class were to take equally among them, subject to a power of apportionment, it is inconsistent with this intention to hold that some of the children take vested interests, as they come into existence, and that others take nothing except subject to a testamentary power: and in such a case the vested interest of

the children of the earlier marriage is not contingent on there being children of the second marriage, for the effect and operation of the deed must be determined at the time it was executed. —A widow possessed of certain heritable and movable property, who had children alive by her first husband, by deed before her second marriage, to which her husband was a party, conveyed her property to trustees for behoof of herself "in liferent for her liferent alimentary use of the annual proceeds thereof allenarly and seclusive of the jus mariti of" her husband, "and not affectable by his or her debts or deeds or by the diligence of their creditors, and for behoof of the children procreated or to be procreated of" her body, "in such proportions and on such terms and conditions as she might appoint by a writing under her hand, which failing, equally among them share and share alike," &c., "in fee." The trustees entered into possession, and applied the income for the behoof of the wife. She died without issue by the second marriage, leaving testamentary deeds by which she cut down one of the children's interest to a sum much less than he would have taken under an equal division of her estate. He raised this action for declarator of his right to an equal share of her estate; and the sole question *now* for decision was whether the marriage contract was revocable :—*Held*, reversing the decision of the Court below, that the provision of the marriage contract in favour of the children of the prior marriage was irrevocable. MACKIE v. HERBERTSON   9 App. Cas. 303

6. —— Married Women's Property (Scotland) Act—*Succession to Personalty*—44 & 45 Vict. c. 21 —*Applicability of Sect. 6 to Marriages entered into before the Act.*] The 6th section of the Married Women's Property (Scotland) Act, 1881, enacts, " After the passing of this Act the husband of any woman who may die domiciled in Scotland shall take by operation of law the same share and interest in her moveable estate which is taken by a widow in her deceased husband's moveable estate, according to the law and practice of Scotland, and subject always to the same rules of law in relation to the nature and amount of such share and interest, and the exclusion, discharge, or satisfaction thereof, as the case may be."—A woman, married before the passing of the above cited Act, succeeded to moveable property, some before and some after the date of the Act, which was settled upon her for her personal use, and free from the jus mariti of her husband. She died, without issue, intestate, and domiciled in Scotland. In a claim by A., her husband, against her executrix :—*Held*, affirming the decision of the Court below, that sect. 6 of the Married Women's Property (Scotland) Act, 1881, applies to marriages entered into before the passing of that Act as well as to those contracted after that date; and that, therefore, A. was entitled in accordance with that section to half his wife's personal estate.—Also, that sub-sect. 2 of sect. 3 applies only to the preceding sections. PATERSON v. POE   -   8 App. Cas. 678

7. —— Nullity of Marriage—*Impotence of the Man—Want of Sincerity as a Bar to the Action—*

IX. SCOTCH LAW—HUSBAND AND WIFE—
continued.

Canon Law—Triennial Cohabitation.] In a suit for nullity of marriage on the ground of impotency, there may be facts and circumstances proved, which so plainly imply on the part of the complaining spouse a recognition of the existence and validity of the marriage, as to render it most inequitable, and contrary to public policy, that he or she should be permitted to go on to challenge it with effect: but the doctrine, designated as the "doctrine of want of sincerity" in an action of this kind, has been too much extended in recent English decisions, and that doctrine, apart from "approbate" and "reprobate," has never been recognised by the law of Scotland.—Delay in raising a suit of nullity on the ground of impotency is a material element in the investigation of a case which upon the facts is doubtful; but there is no definite or absolute bar arising from it. The Canon Law rule of triennial cohabitation has not been recognised in England beyond this point, that where a husband or a wife seeks a decree of nullity on the ground of propter impotentiam, if there is no more evidence than that they have for a period of three years lived together in the same house and with ordinary opportunities of intercourse, and it is clearly proved there has been no consummation, then if that is the whole state of the evidence, inability on the part of the one or of the other will be presumed. On the other hand, the presumption to be drawn from non-consummation during a period of three years or more cohabitation, is capable, by evidence sufficient for the purpose, of being rebutted. But every case need not be fortified with the presumption; for although no presumption can be raised from the absence of consummation within a less period than three years, yet positive evidence may be given, from which the same inference of inability may be drawn. See Lord Watson's opinion (p. 198), that to this extent the Court of Session would not hesitate to adopt the rule.—G. and M. were married in 1877. They slept in the same bed for about nineteen months, but during only two months and a half of that time did G., the husband, make any attempt to consummate the marriage. He desisted on account, he alleged, of his wife's increasing coldness and repugnance to him. It was admitted that the marriage had never been consummated. In 1879 the parties finally separated, the wife living on her own income with her relations, the husband not giving anything towards her support. In 1882 the wife gave birth to a child of which G. was not the father. G. instituted an action for divorce which M. defended, and she then raised this action of declarator of nullity of marriage on the ground of G.'s impotence. G. denied his impotence. He was personally examined, and the medical evidence was that no malformation was apparent from his appearance:—*Held*, affirming the decision of the Court below, that M. was not barred personali exceptione from insisting in this action; and that G.'s impotence had been proved. G. v. M.

[10 App. Cas. 171

—— *Divorce—English marriage* - 6 P. D. 35 ;
[8 App. Cas. 43

See HUSBAND AND WIFE—DIVORCE.

X. SCOTCH LAW—JURISDICTION.

—— Administration — *Estate of domiciled Scotch Testator—Jurisdiction, Conflict of—Trust Funds partly in Scotland partly in England—Power of Scotch Courts to sequestrate Estate and appoint Judicial Factor — Forum conveniens—Confirmation and Probate Act (21 & 22 Vict. c. 56), s. 12—Treaty of Union, 1706 (6 Anne, c. 11), art. 19.*] A resident and domiciled Scotchman died leaving a trust disposition and settlement appointing six trustees; three were resident in Scotland, one being a Scotch member of parliament resided in Scotland when parliament was not sitting, and the other two were resident in England. The truster had a very large amount of personalty in Scotland as well as heritable estate; and a trifling amount of personal estate only in England. The trustees proved the trust deed in Scotland, and were confirmed as executors. They then had the Scotch probate sealed in accordance with 21 & 22 Vict. c. 56, s. 12, and thus became the personal representatives in England. They removed all but a small portion of the personalty in England into Scotland. A person resident in England, who was entitled to a share of a large legacy, and also to a share of the residue, brought an action in England to administer the estate. The trustees were served and entered an appearance. The Plaintiff, an infant, in the English action moved for judgment for administration of the whole estate, and on the 29th of November, 1882, the Court of Appeal granted the order. The trustees lodged an appeal to this House. In June, 1883, the trustees carried certain accounts into Chambers in the English action. On the 5th of July, 1883, four of the residuary legatees commenced this action in Scotland against the trustees for, inter alia, declarator that the trustees were bound to administer the estate in Scotland, subject to the Scotch law and under the authority and jurisdiction of the Scottish Courts *alone*: and that they were not entitled to place the estate under the control of the English Court or any other foreign tribunal furth of Scotland, and for interdict; or, alternatively, to the conclusion for interdict for the removal of the trustees, for sequestration of the estate, the appointment of a judicial factor and for interdict until the estate should be vested in the judicial factor. On the 30th of November, 1883, this House affirmed the order of the Court of Appeal. On the 29th of February, 1884, the Court of Session granted an interlocutor finding in terms of the declaratory conclusions of the summons: sequestrating the estate, appointing a judicial factor and interdicting the trustees from removing any title deeds, &c. from Scotland, or accounting to any one otherwise than the judicial factor.—On appeal taken by order of the Court of Chancery in England:—*Held*, that the decerniture in terms of the declaratory conclusions of the summons, which in effect affirms the exclusive competency of the Scottish jurisdiction, was not supported by statute nor authority; and, therefore, that part of the principal interlocutor and that part of the interdict relating to accounting must be reversed; but the remaining portion of the principal interlocutor and the others appealed from must be affirmed, because the Scotch Courts had (1) full jurisdiction to sequestrate the estate in Scotland—the

X. SCOTCH LAW—JURISDICTION—*continued.*

persons of the trustees and the trust property being there—and to appoint a judicial factor; and (2), because in-the circumstances and on the undertaking given as to the infant Plaintiff becoming a party to the Scotch administration, a primâ facie case of convenience in favour of a judicial administration in Scotland had been made out.—Lord Cottenham in *Preston* v. *Melville* (2 Rob. App. 107) explained, and Lord Westbury in *Enohin* v. *Wylie* (10 H. L. C. 13) dissented from. EWING v. ORR EWING 10 App. Cas. 453

XI. SCOTCH LAW—LANDLORD AND TENANT.

—— Construction of Agreement—*Holograph Writing—Agreement between Tenant and Landlord, written from the latter's Dictation.*] Tenants of quarries situated about three miles from their works, who were accustomed to convey the stones from the quarries to the works by carts, entered into an agreement with their landlord to construct a tramway from the quarry to the works, to run, inter alia, "by the end of the policy" of the landlord: and they further agreed to compensate the farm tenants along the line for any damage done to their farms during the currency of their leases. The landlord agreed, inter alia, to give gratuitously the land required for the tramway. Outside the policy ground there was a private road the property of the landlord, which, before it reached the tenant's works, ran through another tenant's stone pavement yard. This was the only practical route outside the policy for the tramway: and it was alleged that the only obstacle to laying it along that road was that the other tenant might refuse to allow it being laid on that part passing through his yard, but for this there were no termini habiles.—The tenants claimed that the landlord was bound to give them the use and possession of land for the purpose of the tramway, and that either (1) "within and by the end of the policy," or (2) "in any other place as suitable or convenient for them in every respect":—*Held*, reversing the decision of the Court below, that under the agreement the stipulation was that the tramway should pass outside the walls which enclose the policy of the landlord; and that by agreeing to give gratuitously the lands required, the landlord merely undertook to give the tenants such rights as were vested in him, leaving them (with the power to use his name) to settle with any persons who might have a right or interest entitling them to object to the formation of the tramway.—A landlord entered into an agreement with a tenant the terms of which were dictated by the landlord to a person who acted as his factor. The agreement was then handed unsigned to the tenant, who was present. The factor's name did not appear in the agreement, nor had he any authority to make the agreement for the landlord. Subsequently the tenant resiled from the agreement:—*Held*, affirming the decision of the Court below, that the writing was not a valid holograph writ, and therefore the tenant could resile from it.—Lord Watson doubted whether the document would be valid even if the factor had been the sole negotiator acting in the landlord's absence and by his instructions. SINCLAIR v. CAITHNESS FLAGSTONE QUARRYING COMPANY - - 6 App. Cas. 340

XII. SCOTCH LAW—MINE.

1. —— Reservation—"*Disposition of Lands with a Reservation of the "Liberty of working the Coal"—Right of Property retained.*] Where the owner conveys lands to a singular successor or other person, reserving the "liberty of working the coal" in those lands, he must be taken to have reserved the estate of coal (unless there are clear words in the deed qualifying that right of property) with which he stands vested by infeftment at the date of the conveyance. DUKE OF HAMILTON v. DUNLOP - - 10 App. Cas. 813

2. —— Support—*Inherent Right of the Surface Owner to necessary Support—Express Obligation to pay Compensation for Damage done by "the foresaid Operations" Meaning of—Construction of Titles.*] If the owner of a piece of land sells the surface and reserves the minerals below it, with power to get them, he must, if he intends to have the power of destroying or letting down the surface by subsidence in getting them, frame his power in such language that the Court may be able to say from the titles that such was clearly the intention of the parties.—A. was the owner of 500 acres of land. He, in 1800, feued the whole coal, &c., therein to B with full power to work and win the same, and for that purpose to set down pits, &c., but expressly providing that B. should not be at liberty to sink pits, or break the surface of the land lying on the north of a certain line: with full power, however, to work the coal there, provided it was done from pits situate on the south of the line, without breaking the surface of the land on the north; but for the "whole damage and injury occasioned by the foresaid operations," A. and his successors "shall be completely paid and indemnified by" by B. In 1801 A., by disposition and sale, conveyed to C.'s predecessor all his right and title in a parcel of land situate on the north of the line, reserving to himself and his feuars the liberty to take the coal, substantially in the terms given above, and providing that the persons carrying on these operations were to be liable to C.'s predecessor "for the whole damage thereby occasioned:" declaring that the rules contained in the above feu right should be the rule of settlement between C.'s predecessor and B. In 1799 A. had feued to another predecessor of C. a parcel of land contiguous to the above and also to the north of the line, under reservation of the minerals, and with liberty to work the same "so as not to break the surface of the said lands or injure the springs therein upon payment to" C.'s predecessors "any damage that may be occasioned to the said lands by the working of the minerals." B. claimed an absolute right to work out the whole of the coal, under the obligation to pay C. a money compensation for any damage done to the surface:—*Held*, affirming the decision of the Court below, that there was nothing in the titles of the parties which had the effect of taking away or derogating from the common law right of the owner of the surface to insist that the owner of the minerals shall leave sufficient supports to sustain the surface uninjured; and that the provision as to payment of compensation clearly meant payment of compensation for damage done by accident or negligence.—The rule established in *Rowbotham* v. *Wilson* (8 H. L. Cas.

XII. SCOTCH LAW—MINE—*continued.*

348) and *Andrew* v. *Buchanan* (Law Rep. 2 H. L., Sc. 286) cited.—*Aspden* v. *Seddon* (Law Rep. 10 Ch. App. 394) approved but distinguished. DIXON v. WHITE   -   **8 App. Cas. 833**

XIII. SCOTCH LAW—NUISANCE.

—— Calcining—*Damage to Plantation—Interdict—Distance fixed.*] The Shotts Iron Company possessed valuable mining leases of the iron ore under the estate of, inter alia, Penicuik, under the condition not to calcine within a certain area. They calcined beyond this area, but near to the boundary of the lands of Glencorse. The calcining was carried on in open bings eight feet high.—The proprietor of Glencorse on the ground, inter alia, that his ornamental plantations were being destroyed by the fumes from the bings, raised an action concluding for interdict against the company calcining within two miles of his estate:—*Held*, affirming the decision of the Court below—but altering the terms of the interlocutor pronounced—that, the Glencorse plantations had been injured by the calcining, and that the Pursuer was entitled to interdict to prevent the company from carrying on their calcining within one mile of his lands, in the same manner hitherto pursued by them, or in any other manner whereby noxious vapours may be caused to pass over the Pursuer's lands, or any part thereof, to the damage or injury of his plantations or estate. SHOTT'S IRON COMPANY v. INGLIS -   **7 App. Cas. 518**

XIV. SCOTCH LAW—PARTNERSHIP.

—— Retirement—*Assignment by one Partner of his whole Interest to another.*] A prosperous partnership came to consist of three partners, A., B., and C., having equal shares. The contract of co-partnership contained, inter alia, a clause that it should not be in the power of any of the partners to assign all or any part of their shares or interest in the capital, stock, or profits of the concern to any person or persons, or give them a right to inspect the company's books, or to interfere in any way with the business; and should any such assignation be granted the same was declared of no effect as far as regards the company. There was also a clause that on the retirement of a partner the remaining partners should have power to buy his interest at the amount standing to his credit at the last balance. A. entered into an agreement by which he sold to B. his whole interest. A.'s name remained on the books, and he signed all deeds relating to the business till his death seven years after. C. was not till then informed of the agreement. He then claimed to participate on the grounds of (1) an alleged mandate to B. to purchase for the company A.'s interest; (2) that the agreement could only be legally made under the contract of co-partnership with his consent; and (3) that B. had secretly acquired a benefit for himself within the scope of the partnership business:—*Held*, affirming the decision of the Court below, that in point of fact no agreement had been made between B. and C. to the effect that B. was to buy A.'s interest for the partnership. And in respect to the articles of co-partnership they did not prevent the agreement being made, and otherwise

XIV. SCOTCH LAW—PARTNERSHIP—*contd.*

it was perfectly legal. Therefore C. was not entitled to any benefit under it. CASSELS v. STEWART   **6 App. Cas. 64**

XV. SCOTCH LAW—PATENT.

—— Infringement.] Decision of the Court of Session, Scotland, granting an interdict to restrain infringement of patent affirmed. CLIPPENS OIL COMPANY v. HENDERSON -   **8 App. Cas. 873**

XVI. SCOTCH LAW—PEERAGE.

1. —— Dysart Peerage—*Held*, that William John Manners had made out, and established, his right to the dignities of Earl of Dysart and Lord Huntingtower in the peerage of Scotland. DYSART PEERAGE CASE   -   **6 App. Cas. 489**

2. —— Lauderdale Peerage—*Held*, that Major Frederick Henry Maitland had made out his claim to the Earldom of Lauderdale and the other honours connected therewith in the Peerage of Scotland. LAUDERDALE PEERAGE CASE
[10 App. Cas. 692

3. —— Lovat Peerage — *Evidence—Family Repute—Statements Post litem Motam.*] *Held*, that John Fraser of Carnarvonshire, mining engineer, had no right to the title, dignity and honour of the Barony of Lovat in the Peerage of Scotland. LOVAT PEERAGE CASE **10 App. Cas. 763**

XVII. SCOTCH LAW—PUBLIC RIGHTS.

—— Burgh—*Common Good of Burgh—Encroachment by Magistrates on Burgh Property—Equitable Jurisdiction of Court of Session where restitutio in integrum impossible or attended with unreasonable Loss—Actio Popularis—Res Noviter —Interdict — Necessary Proceedings—Costs.*] A superior Court, having equitable jurisdiction, has a discretion in exceptional cases to withhold from parties applying for it that remedy to which, in ordinary circumstances, they would be entitled as a matter of course. But to justify the exercise of such a discretionary power, there must be some very cogent reason.—A. suing, not as owner of the soil, nor as the proprietor of a dominant tenement, but as one of the community, applied for suspension and interdict on the 4th of May, 1878, against magistrates of a burgh, who were also police commissioners, building municipal stables on a piece of ground vested in them for the common use and enjoyment of the community. No interim interdict was granted, and the magistrates, who had accepted contracts for the work, went on building, and before the interdict sought was granted, on the 19th of June, 1879, the stables were completed at a cost to the community of about £1900. Thereupon in March, 1880, A. raised this action, concluding for, inter alia, a declaration that the ground in question was vested in the magistrates in perpetuity for the use and enjoyment of the inhabitants, and that they had no right as police commissioners to build thereon; and that they ought to be ordered to remove the stables. The magistrates offered to dedicate to the use of the inhabitants in lieu of the site of the stables another piece of ground which they had acquired by feu charter dated December, 1880:—*Held*, agreeing with the judgment of the Court below, that in the peculiar circumstances of this case and on the considera-

XVII. SCOTCH LAW—PUBLIC RIGHTS—*contd.*

tions (1) that the community of the burgh had an interest on both sides of the present litigation; and (2) that the tender of a substituted piece of ground was res noviter, affecting the relations of the parties which had emerged since the date of the final judgment of interdict, it was not too late for the Court to exercise its discretionary power, and to refuse the remedy which A. asked so far as the removal of the stables was demanded.—*Held,* reversing interlocutor of the Court below, that A. was entitled to a declaratory decree affirming the right of the community in the ground in question; and to the action being kept in Court until the substituted ground had been dedicated in perpetuity to the uses of the inhabitants; and his action being necessary for the vindication of the community's rights, he was entitled to his whole expenses in the Court below and in this House.— Per Lord Watson : Were A. seeking to enforce the decree which he holds in his own private right and interest, the considerations of inconvenience and pecuniary loss, arising from the position in which the magistrates have placed themselves, by their own acts, would not afford a relevant answer to his demand in the present action.—*Macnair* v. *Cathcart* (Morr. Dic. 12,832); *Sanderson* v. *Geddes* (1 Court Sess. Cas. 4th Series, 1198); *Begg* v. *Jack* (3 Court Sess. Cas. 4th Series, 35), approved, as authorities in favour of the equitable jurisdiction of the Court; but see Lord Watson as to his disapproval of the result at which the Court arrived in *Begg* v. *Jack.* GRAHAME *v.* SWAN   -   -   -   7 App. Cas. 547

XVIII. SCOTCH LAW—RAILWAY COMPANY.

1. —— Construction of Act—*Broken Bridge in navigable River—Removal of Débris to Satisfaction of Board of Trade, Meaning of—Construction of Statute.*] The North British Railway (New Tay Bridge) Act,1881, gave the North British Railway authority to erect a new bridge over the Tay a little higher up the river than one blown down on the 28th of December, 1879. Sect. 21 of this Act provided, "The company shall abandon and cause to be disused as a railway so much of the North British Railway as lies between the respective points of junction therewith of railway No. 1 and railway No. 2; and shall remove the ruins and débris of the old bridge, and all obstructions interfering with the navigation caused by the old bridge, to the satisfaction of the Board of Trade." The magistrates of Perth, whose jurisdiction extends down the river to within about three miles of the old bridge, raised an action for declarator and implement:—*Held,* (1) that the special Act imposed an absolute obligation to remove the whole ruins and débris of the old bridge; and sect. 21 did not give the Board of Trade a discretionary power to dispense with the performance of any part of this obligation; and it followed that the Respondents had an interest to obtain a declarator as to the extent of the obligation; but (2), dissenting from the judgment of the Court below, the obligation did not become immediately prestable; and (3) the import of the expression "to the satisfaction of the Board of Trade" was, that though not bound to submit their plans of removal, including the time and manner, yet, as a matter of

XVIII. SCOTCH LAW—RAILWAY COMPANY— *continued.*

prudence, the company ought to do so; (4) that in the circumstances it would be inexpedient, though hardly incompetent, to do more now than simply ordain the company to remove the whole ruins and débris in terms of sect. 21, for to order the removal "forthwith" might unduly hamper the discretion of the Board of Trade ; and if the company were guilty of undue delay in applying to the Board of Trade ; or if they should proceed at their own hand so as to cause obstruction to navigation ; or if after obtaining the sanction of the Board of Trade to some scheme of removal, they failed to properly execute it, or any conditions attached, the Respondents, on application to the Court, had an effective remedy. NORTH BRITISH RAILWAY COMPANY *v.* LORD PROVOST OF PERTH   -   -   -   10 App. Cas. 579

2. —— Construction of Act—*Statute* 42 & 43 *Vict. c. clv., ss.* 3, 6 (*Local*)—*Commencement of Payment.*] The Caledonian Railway Company for thirteen years up to July, 1879. had been proprietors of the D. and A. Railway, and had incurred certain liabilities in respect to payment of dividends to preference and ordinary shareholders of the D. & A. line. The preamble of the North British Railway (D, and A. Joint Line) passed July, 1879 (42 & 43 Vict. c. clv.), set forth that it was expedient that the Caledonian and North British Companies should have equal rights and powers, and be subject to equal liabilities over and with respect to the D. & A. line. Sect. 3 provided that on and after the 1st of February, 1880, called the "vesting period," all interest which the Caledonian possessed should be transferred to the Caledonian and North British jointly and in equal proportions in manner hereinafter provided by the Act. Sect. 6 provided that the consideration for the transfer of the joint line shall be as follows : "(1.) From and after the vesting period the company (the North British) shall pay to the Caledonian Railway Company half-yearly on the 1st of March and 1st of September in each year a sum equal to one-half of the aggregate of the following half-yearly payments for which the Caledonian Railway Company are now liable in respect of their acquisition of the D. and A. Railway." The Caledonian Railway Company claimed that under this section there was a half-yearly payment amounting to £5903.15s. due on the 1st of March, 1880 :—*Held,* affirming the decision of the Court below, that the liability to make payment in 1880 did not arise till September, the time of payment applicable to the first six months following the 1st of February, 1880. —Per Lord Selborne, L.C. : The more literal construction of a section of a statute ought not to prevail if it is opposed to the intentions of the Legislature as apparent by the statute; and if the words are sufficiently flexible to admit of some other construction by which that intention will be better effectuated. CALEDONIAN RAILWAY COMPANY *v.* NORTH BRITISH RAILWAY COMPANY

[6 App. Cas. 114

3. —— Contract to stop all Passenger Trains— *Construction of Feu. Contract.*] By feu contract, dated 1863, between A., the proprietor of land

XVIII. SCOTCH LAW—RAILWAY COMPANY
—*continued.*

through which a railway was authorized to run, and the railway company, it was provided that the company should be bound to erect on a piece of ground conveyed to them by A. at a nominal feu rent, "a station for passengers and goods travelling by the said" railway, "at which all passenger trains shall regularly stop," to be called Crathes Station.—The station was erected. Subsequently certain trains were run, namely (1) excursion trains at low fares to certain places on the line, but not to Crathes Station. They were advertised by special handbills, and were not included in the time-tables except in error; (2) trains called the Queen's messenger trains, run by arrangement with the Home Office, who paid the railway company a subsidy; (3) trains called the Post Office trains, run by arrangement with the Post Office, who also paid a subsidy. The Queen's messenger trains and the Post Office trains only ran during Her Majesty's stay at Balmoral; but they were advertised in the railway company's time-table, and through passengers were allowed to travel by them. They stopped at Crathes by signal, but did not stop regularly for setting down or taking up passengers. There was no contract with the Home Office or Post Office that they should not do so.—A. sought declarator that all trains, including the above, except only such as might be hired for an individual or individuals for his or their exclusive use, should regularly stop:—*Held*, reversing the decision of the Court below, that the trains called the Queen's messenger trains, and the Post Office trains, fell within the terms of the contract; but, agreeing with the decision of the Court below, that the excursion trains in the circumstances materially differed from ordinary passenger trains and did not come within the obligation. BURNETT *v.* GREAT NORTH OF SCOTLAND RAILWAY COMPANY　　10 App. Cas. 147

4. —— Land injuriously affected—*Compensation—Railways Clauses Consolidation (Scotland) Act,* 1845 (8 & 9 Vict. c. 33), s. 6, *and Lands Clauses Consolidation (Scotland) Act,* 1845 (8 & 9 Vict. c. 19)—*Agreement that Claim should not be barred by reason of no Land being taken—Conflicting Decisions of House of Lords.*] The 6th section of the Scotch Railways Clauses Act of 1845 (similar in the English Act), provides, inter alia, that the railway company " shall make to the owners and occupiers of, and all other parties interested in, any lands taken . . . . or injuriously affected by the construction thereof, full compensation for the value of the lands so taken, and for all damage sustained by such owners," &c. And it then cites the Lands Clauses Consolidation (Scotland) Act, 1845, as the machinery by which compensation is to be adjudged.—In order to found a claim for compensation under this section, some special or peculiar damage must be done to the lands by reason of the construction of the works, which diminishes the value of the lands, which damage would have been the subject of an action at law before the statute.—Where, therefore, an access to private property by a public highway or private way is interfered with by the construction of the works,

XVIII. SCOTCH LAW—RAILWAY COMPANY
—*continued.*

and the value of the property, irrespective of any particular use which may be made of it, is so dependent upon the existence of that access as to be substantially diminished by its obstruction, then the owner is entitled to compensation for such interference.—But no compensation is given for damages if the thing done was one for which, if done without any statutory power, no action could have been maintained; nor when a right of action, which would have existed if the works had not been authorized by statute, would have been merely personal. Nor when damage arises, not out of the execution, but only out of the subsequent use of the works. Nor for the loss of trade or custom by reason of a work not otherwise affecting the house in or upon which the trade has been carried on.—Trustees were possessed of a spinning mill ninety yards from an important main thoroughfare in Glasgow, having parallel accesses on the level from two sides of the mill to the thoroughfare.—A railway company under their special Act cut off entirely one access, substituting therefor a deviated road over a bridge with steep gradients. And the other access they diverted and made less convenient. But none of the operations were carried on ex adverso the premises. When the Bill was before Parliament the trustees were induced to withdraw their opposition in consideration of an agreement, by which the company undertook, that in the event of the land of the trustees and of others being injuriously affected by the construction of any of the works proposed by the Bill, their claim to compensation should not be barred by reason of the company not taking part of their land. The trustees claimed compensation for the diminished value of their premises by reason of the detour and gradients:—*Held*, affirming the decision of the Court below, that though the agreement gave no right to compensation, the trustees were entitled to it under the Railways and Lands Clauses Consolidation (Scotland) Acts, 1845.—Per Lord Selborne, L.C.: The obstruction of access to a private property by a public road need not be ex adverso, but it must be proximate and not remote or indefinite to entitle the owner of that property to compensation for the loss of it.—And—It is a question whether a mere change of gradient alone would be a proper subject for compensation.—*Metropolitan Board of Works* v. *McCarthy* (Law Rep. 7 H. L. 243) held undistinguishable.—*The Caledonian Railway Company* v. *Ogilvy* (2 Macq. 229) explained; and distinguished.—*Chamberlain* v. *West End of London Railway Company* (2 B. & S. 605), and *Beckett* v. *Midland Railway Company* (Law Rep. 3 C. P. 82) approved.—*Ricket* v. *Metropolitan Railway Company* (Law Rep. 2 H. L. 175) examined.—Per Lord Selborne, L.C.: It is the duty of this House to maintain as far as possible the authority of all former decisions of this House; and although later decisions may have interpreted and limited the application of earlier, they ought not (without some unavoidable necessity) to be treated as conflicting.—And—All the above decisions of this House appear to be capable of being explained and justified upon consistent principles.—See remarks of Lord Blackburn, as to the

XVIII. SCOTCH LAW—RAILWAY COMPANY—
continued.

cases of *Ogilvy* and *McCarthy* not being reconcilable, pp. 294, 302. CALEDONIAN RAILWAY COMPANY *v.* WALKER'S TRUSTEES **7 App. Cas. 259**

5. —— Land injuriously affected—*Superior and Vassal—Construction of Feu Contract—Interdict to restrain Action for Compensation—Railways Clauses Consolidation (Scotland) Act, 1845, s. 6—Exercise of reserved Powers ; what not equivalent to.*] In January, 1872, A.'s predecessor in title obtained by feu contract from a superior a building lot situated at the south side of an estate. With the contract was incorporated a plan which shewed the whole estate divided into feuing lots with several streets running east and west ; and one street twenty-four feet wide connecting the turnpike road on the north to another road on the south, and forming one side of A.'s feu. The lot was disponed "together with free ish and entry thereto by the streets laid down on the said plan, but in so far only as tho same may be opened and not altered in virtue of the reserved power after mentioned." The reserved power was, that "the superior should have full power and liberty to vary and alter the said plan or streets or roads thereon in so far as regards the ground not already feued." In July, 1872, a railway company gave the superior statutory notice that they intended to take a strip of ground running from east to west through the estate. In 1877 they executed the works and, inter alia, cut off all access for carriages by the street-marked on the plan running from south to north, twenty-four feet wide. None of A.'s land was taken. In an action by the railway company for interdict against A. taking further proceedings in a claim for compensation in respect that his lands were injuriously affected, under sect. 6 of the Railway Clauses (Scotland) Act, 1845 :—*Held*, affirming the decision of the Court below (Earl of Selborne, L.C., doubting), that A. was not entitled to compensation, because, 1, the access in question had not been "opened" in the sense meant in his feu contract before the statutory notice, and 2, there was no obligation in the feu contract cast upon the superior to pursue his feuing scheme, and give the feuars at some future time access along any of the roads or streets marked on the plan Also—when there is an implied obligation by the superior to prosecute his feuing scheme for the benefit of the feuars, the feuars have a vested interest de futuro in the roads and streets shewn on the feuing plan, sufficient to sustain a claim for compensation under the Railways Clauses Consolidation (Scotland) Act, 1845. The compulsory taking by a railway company, under their statutory powers, of part of a superior's estate, cannot be regarded as equivalent, either in fact or law, to an exercise of a power reserved by the superior himself.—*Solway Railway Company v. Jackson* (1 Ct. Sess. Cas. 4th Series, 831) affirmed.—*Henderson v. Nimmo and Colquhoun* (2 Ibid. 2nd Series, 8C9) and *Crawford v. Field* (2 Ibid. 4th Series, 20) distinguished. FLEMING *v.* NEWPORT RAILWAY COMPANY **8 App. Cas. 265**

XIX. SCOTCH LAW—REVENUE.

—— *Income Tax—Coal Mines—Exhaustion of Pits—Deductions from Gross Profits—Statutes 5 & 6*

XIX. SCOTCH LAW—REVENUE—*continued.*

Vict. c. 35, ss. 100 (Rule 3) and 159 ; 29 & 30 Vict. c. 36, s. 8.] A tenant of minerals, though he may be under a constant vanishing expense in sinking new pits as the old ones become exhausted, is not entitled, in computing the profits for assessment of income tax, to deduct from the gross profits a sum estimated as representing the amount of capital expended in making bores and sinking pits, which have been exhausted by the year's working.—See Lord Penzance's opinion as to the method of taxation intended by the Legislature to be applicable to mines.—*Knowles* v. *McAdam* (3 Ex. D. 23) held wrongly decided. COLTNESS IRON COMPANY *v.* BLACK - **6 App. Cas. 315**

XX. SCOTCH LAW—RIVER.

—— The Clyde—*Right of the Clyde Trustees to dredge Foreshore, the Property of the Riparian Proprietor—Clyde Navigation Consolidation Act* (21 & 22 Vict. c. cxlix.), ss. 76, 84.] The Clyde Navigation Trustees, being empowered by sects. 76 and 84 of 21 & 22 Vict. c. cxlix.), to dredge the bed of the River Clyde to a depth of seventeen feet, cannot be interdicted from dredging ground which has been declared the property of the riparian owner, subject to any right which the public may have over it, and subject also to any rights conferred on the trustees by their Acts of Parliament. —*Held*, so, affirming the decision of the Court below, but without prejudice to the question of their liability to subsequent compensation for damage. LORD BLANTYRE *v.* CLYDE NAVIGATION TRUSTEES **6 App. Cas. 273**

XXI. SCOTCH LAW—SALE OF GOODS.

1. —— Condition Precedent—*Implement of Condition prevented—Remedy.*] If, in the case of a contract of sale and delivery, which makes acceptance of the thing sold and payment of the price conditional on a certain thing being done by the seller, the buyer prevents the possibility of the seller fulfilling the condition, the contract is to be taken as satisfied.—By a written contract A. agreed to buy of B. a digging machine, if it fulfilled certain conditions, one of which was that it should be capable of excavating a given quantity of clay in a fixed time on a "properly opened-up face" at the C. railway cutting. The machine failed at another cutting to excavate the required quantity, and on its being removed to the "C." cutting and tried at a face not a "properly opened-up" one, and breaking down, after a few days work, A. refused to give it any further trial or to pay the price of the machine :—*Held*, affirming the decision of the Court below, that B. was entitled to a decree against A. for payment of the price of the machine. MACKAY *v.* DICK **[6 App. Cas. 251**

2. —— Non-Delivery before Sequestration—*Article in Course of Completion—Unfinished Ship — Bankruptcy — Security — Mercantile Law Amendment (Scotland) Act, 1856 (19 & 20 Vict. c. 60), s. 1.*] By the law of Scotland there must be delivery to give effect to a contract of sale, but the Mercantile Law Amendment (Scotland) Act for the express purpose of assimilating the law of Scotland to that of England on such points, enacts : "Where goods have been sold but the same have not been delivered to the pur-

XXI. SCOTCH LAW—SALE OF GOODS—contd.

chaser, and have been allowed to remain in the custody of the seller, it shall not be competent for any creditor of such seller after the date of such sale to attach such goods as belong to the seller by any diligence or process of law, including sequestration, to the effect of preventing the purchaser or others in his right from enforcing the delivery of the same."—B. & C., by verbal communing, agreed to make advances to A. on the security of a ship he had nearly completed building on his own account, provided A. entered into an absolute contract of sale of the vessel. An unqualified contract of sale was completed by which A. agreed to complete and deliver to B. & C. the vessel, for a price to be paid in two instalments, with power to B. & C., in the event of A. failing to complete the contract, to enter into possession of the vessel and complete it, or sell it.—In a correspondence between A. and B. & C. and a shipbroker and others subsequent to the contract, and for the purpose of getting a purchaser for the vessel, the ship was called A.'s ship; but no letters were written to any persons who were induced by their means to deal with the ship upon the footing of its being the property of A.—From the date of the contract B. & C. gave, by cheques at various dates, advances to A., taking a receipt on account of the purchase of the ship; at the same time bills for like amounts were accepted by A. The advances equalled the full price of the ship. Before it was completed or delivered A.'s estate was sequestrated. The bills accepted by A. were paid by B. & C. In a question between A.'s trustee and B. & C.:—Held, (1) affirming the decision of the Court below, that there was here a bonâ fide sale in fact and intent unaccompanied by delivery, and —whether security was the object or not—every condition of the statute was fulfilled; (2) that no reputation of ownership had been created in the seller A. Therefore B. & C. had a right to the ship—Held, that where there is an absolute bonâ fide contract of sale of an article, which is not delivered before the bankruptcy of the seller, the right of the buyer under the contract to have delivery cannot be defeated by proof that the character of buyer had been conferred on him merely for the purpose of his having a security for money intended to be advanced by him. M'BAIN v. WALLACE & CO.　-　**6 App. 588**

XXII. SCOTCH LAW—STATUTORY DUTY.

—— **Waterworks Act**—Damage to Lands by extraordinary Flood—Escape of Water from Reservoir—Liability of Water Commissioners—Damnum fatale—Kirkcaldy and Dysart Waterworks Act, 1867 (30 & 31 Vict. c. cxxxix.), ss. 43, 49.] By the 43rd section of the Kirkcaldy and Dysart Waterworks Act, 1867, it was provided that the commissioners under the Act " should be bound to make good to the Countess of Rothes and her heirs, &c., all damages which may be occasioned to her or them, by reason of, or in consequence of any bursting, or flow, or escape of water from any reservoir, or acqueduct, or pipe, or other work connected therewith " which may be constructed by the commissioners. The Countess is proprietrix of lands situated below the site of one of the reservoirs, and during an extraordinary rainfall a great quantity of water was continuously dis-

XXII. SCOTCH LAW — STATUTORY DUTY — continued.

charged from the reservoir, through a waste weir into the watercourse of a burn, and did much damage to the Countess's lands. She claimed compensation. There was no failure or insufficiency of the works and no negligence :—Held, reversing the decision of the Court below (Lord Blackburn dissenting), that on the construction of the above clause the Countess was entitled to compensation for damage by flood waters from the reservoir, no matter how caused. — Per Lord Watson : Statutory provisions, such as here, in a local and personal Act must be regarded as a contract between the parties, whether made by their mutual agreement, or forced on them by the legislature. COUNTESS OF ROTHES v. KIRKCALDY AND DYSART WATERWORKS COMMISSIONERS
[7 App. Cas. 694

XXIII. SCOTCH LAW—TRUSTEE.

—— **Severance of Funds** — Investment for Behoof of Distinct Parties—Indemnity of Trustees for Liability incurred.] A testatrix directed her trustees to pay the interest or annual rent of £2000 to Mrs. A. during her life and after her death to divide that sum among her children ; and to pay the interest or annual rent of a similar amount to Mrs. B. in life-rent, with the fee to her children.—The trustees were empowered by the deed to realize, or to continue to "hold any or all of such shares or stocks" as might belong to the testatrix at her decease, should they consider it advisable or expedient to do so, without any personal responsibility to them, if any, thereby sustained;" with power also " to lend or place out on such securities, heritable or moveable, as they shall consider advantageous, the foresaid legacies of £2000 and £2000 respectively, the securities to be conceived in favour of my trustees, and that for the purposes of this trust and no otherwise."—The testatrix at her death held £850 stock of a unlimited bank. The trustee, at the desire of Mrs. A. and without consulting Mrs. B., set £200 of this stock aside as part of the fund appropriated to Mrs. A., and realized the remainder. They afterwards on the narrative of the purposes of the trust deed, and of the sums invested for the two specific legacies of £2000, and that they had paid the residue, received their discharge from Mrs. A. and Mrs. B. Statements and separate accounts of interest on the investments allocated to each were sent half-yearly to Mrs. A. and Mrs. B. All the investments stood in the names of the testatrix's trustees.—The bank became insolvent, and calls were made upon the trustees in respect of the £200 stock. They sought to indemnify themselves for payment of the calls out of the whole trust estate. Mrs. B. objected to any portion of her legacy being taken :—Held, reversing the decision of the Court below, that the trustees had the power to sever and had severed the two legacies, and had placed them in separate investments for behoof of the respective beneficiaries, and therefore the trustees had no right to relief from the investments allotted to Mrs. B. and her family for liabilities incurred on those allotted to Mrs. A. and her family.—Ex parte Garland (10 Ves. 110) followed. FRASER v. MURDOCK　-　**6 App. Cas 855**

XXIV. SCOTCH LAW—WILL.

—— Ambiguity—*Holograph Document, signed and headed "Notes of intended Settlement."*] In the repositories of the deceased who left no other testamentary instrument was found a holograph writing, signed and dated and complete in its testamentary provisions; but headed "Notes of intended settlement by" the deceased. The proof allowed threw no light on the intentions of the deceased:—*Held,* affirming the decision of the Court below that the document was the last will and settlement of the deceased.— *Per* Lord Watson: A mere ambiguity occuring in the descriptive title written by the testator cannot qualify the terms or destroy the validity of the document which it professes to describe, when the legal character and effect of the document taken by itself are not doubtful. Such an ambiguity will justify inquiry; but should the parties lead no proof, or should the proof adduced by them be inconclusive, the document must receive effect according to its tenor and substance. WHYTE *v.* POLLOK - - - - 7 App. Cas. 400

XXV. SCOTCH LAW—PRACTICE.

1. —— Appeal—*Bankruptcy.*] Where an appeal involves a question of the Appellant's status, the House will allow it to be proceeded with notwithstanding the bankruptcy of the Appellant. G. *v.* M, - 10 App. Cas. 171

2. —— Appeal—*Findings of Fact—Judicature Act of Scotland, 1825 (6 Geo. 4, c. 120), s. 40—Cases commenced in Sheriff's Court—Remit to Court below—Proof.*] The 40th section of the Judicature Act of Scotland, 1825, enacts, inter alia, that the judgment in cases commenced in the Sheriff's Court shall be subject to appeal to the House of Lords only so far as the same depends on, or is affected by, matters of law; but shall, in so far as relates to the facts, be held to have the force and effect of a special verdict of the jury, finally and conclusively fixing the several facts specified in the interlocutor.—In appeals falling within the scope of this section, the House of Lords has no concern with the facts which has been led in the Sheriff's Court. When it can be shewn that the Court of Session has not exhausted the issue before it, and that there are material questions of fact left undetermined, a remit will be made to the Court below to pronounce findings upon these questions, but that can only be shewn by a reference to the record, and not to the proof. And if the questions are not raised by the record, no remit will be made. MACKAY *v.* DICK - - 6 App. Cas. 251

3. —— Appeal—*Findings of Fact—Sheriff's Court — Competency of Appeal under sect. 40, 6 Geo. 4, c. 120—Issue raised in the Pleadings—Ship—Acceptance of Abandonment — Matter of Law or Fact.*] The 40th section of 6 Geo. 4, c. 120, provides: "When in causes commenced in any of the courts of the sheriffs, or of the magistrates of burghs, or other inferior courts, matter of fact shall be disputed, and a proof shall be allowed and taken according to the present practice, the Court of Session shall, in reviewing the judgment proceeding on such proof, distinctly specify in their interlocutor the several facts material to the case which they find to be established by the proof, and express how far their judgment proceeds

XXV. SCOTCH LAW—PRACTICE—*continued.*

on the matters of fact so found, or on matter of law, and the several points of law which they mean to decide; and the judgment on the cause thus pronounced shall be subject to appeal to the House of Lords, in so far only as the same depends on or is affected by matter of law."—A. raised an action in the Sheriff's Court against B. for £50, the sum payable by him as underwriter on a policy of insurance on A.'s vessel the *Krishna.* On the 23rd of May the vessel was driven on a sandy beach on the West Court of India, during a violent storm. Soon afterwards the usual monsoon commenced and lasted till October. On the 7th of June A., on hearing from the master that it was impossible to save the ship, gave notice of abandonment to the underwriters; which they refused to accept. On the 1st of October A. raised this action averring that the vessel had become a wreck, and in his amended pleadings he set out that the underwriters had taken possession of the vessel on the 15th of October and had floated her on the 16th of November, and taken her to Bombay and had docked her and executed certain repairs and that thus the underwriters had accepted the abandonment. — The underwriters alleged that they only took possession of the vessel as salvors, that no repairs were done except for the safety of the ship, and that A. was informed of all they were doing, and to the last it was intimated to A. that the vessel was lying at Bombay at his risk.—The Court of Session found, inter alia, "that the underwriters did not accept the abandonment: that there was on the 7th of June and continued thereafter to be a reasonable prospect of the ship being got off the sandy shore on which she lay without greater expense than a prudent uninsured owner would reasonably incur," therefore that there was not at that date a constructive total loss of the ship.—A. contended on the question of the competency of his appeal (1) that the finding that the underwriters did not accept the abandonment, was a matter of mixed law and fact; (2), that the findings of fact were incomplete and ought to be rectified on remit:—Held, applying the rule of *Mackay v. Dick* (6 App. Cas. 251) that the Court had decided the issue submitted to them, an issue of fact and not of law; namely, that the underwriters did not accept the abandonment, and accordingly their finding was not open to impeachment under sect. 40 of 6 Geo. 4, c. 120; and (2), that looking at the controversy raised by the record, the findings in fact were reasonably complete.—*Per* Lord Penzance: The question whether the underwriters accept the abandonment or not is a question of fact; but the circumstances of the case may be such, that a jury may be told as a matter of law, that if they think the underwriters have done certain acts which are consistent only with their having accepted the abandonment, then they ought to find that the abandonment has been accepted.—Remarks, whether in Scotland constructive total loss is to be taken from the date of notice of abandonment, or from the date of commencement of action. SHEPHERD *v.* HENDERSON [7 App. Cas. 49

—— Amendment of record   6 App. Cas. 560
See SCOTCH LAW—CONVEYANCE. 2.

XXV. SCOTCH LAW—PRACTICE—*continued.*

——— Evidence　　　　　　- 6 App. Cas. 489;
[10 App. Cas. 692, 763
See SCOTCH LAW—HUSBAND AND WIFE.
2, 3, 4.

SCOTCH SEQUESTRATION—Subsequent bankruptcy in England　　22 Ch. D. 816
See BANKRUPTCY—ADJUDICATION. 4.

SCOTCH WILL—Scotch assets—Administration action in England　　22 Ch. D. 456;
[9 App. Cas. 34
See EXECUTOR—ACTIONS. 16.

SCOTLAND—Service of bastardy summons in
[12 Q. B. D. 261; 10 App. Cas. 45
See BASTARDY. 6.

——— Service of writ 12 Q. B. D. 50; 14 Q. B. D. 78;
[20 Ch. D. 240
See PRACTICE—SUPREME COURT—SERVICE. 2, 3, 10.

——— Will proved in—Assets in Scotland and England　　　　　　6 P. D. 19
See ADMINISTRATOR—GRANT. 4.

SEA FISHERIES.
See FISHERY ACTS—*Statutes.*
SHIP—MERCHANT SHIPPING ACTS—*Statutes.*

SEA WALL.

——— Liability to repair — *Frontager—Prescription—Extraordinary Violence of the Sea—Act of God—Sewers, Commissioners of, Order by, to repair Sea Wall, Effect of—Land Drainage Act, 1861 (24 & 25 Vict. c. 133), s. 33 —Disqualification of Commissioners by reason of Interest—23 Hen. 8, c. 5; 13 Eliz. c. 9.*] The extent of the liability of a frontager to repair a sea wall, whether arising by tenure, prescription, or custom, can only be ascertained by usage.—J. A. was a frontager in a level on the Essex shore of the Thames under the jurisdiction of Commissioners of Sewers. An ancient sea wall protected the level against incursions of the sea. There was evidence proving a prescriptive liability on the part of the frontagers in the level to maintain and repair this sea wall. A portion of the sea wall in front of J. A.'s land was destroyed by an extraordinary storm and high tide. The wall was previously in good repair, and in a proper condition to resist the ordinary action of the sea:—*Held*, on the authority of *Keighley's Case* (10 Rep. 139) and *R. v. Commissioners of Sewers for Somerset* (8 T. R. 312), that, in the absence of evidence sufficient to shew that the prescriptive liability of the frontagers extended to the repair of damage occasioned by extraordinary violence of the sea J. A. was not liable to repair the damage thus occasioned to the wall at his own expense, but the expense of so doing must fall on the whole of the level.—By sect. 33 of the Land Drainage Act, 1861 (24 & 25 Vict. c. 133), it is provided that commissioners of sewers acting within their jurisdiction may, without the presentment of a jury, make any order in respect of the execution of any work, the levying of any rate, or doing any act which they might but for this section have made with such presentment, subject to a proviso that any person aggrieved by any such order may appeal therefrom to the quarter sessions.—Orders were

SEA WALL—*continued.*

made by the Commissioners of Sewers upon J. A. to execute repairs to the sea wall rendered necessary by the aforesaid extraordinary storm and high tide. Among the commissioners making the orders were two persons who were interested in lands in the level, liable to be rated to a general rate :— *Held*, by the Queen's Bench Division, that these orders had, by virtue of the above-mentioned section, the same effect as if made on the presentment of a jury, and that therefore so long as they stood they had the effect of adjudications against J. A. rendering him liable to do such repairs to the wall :—But *held*, also, by the Queen's Bench Division and the Court of Appeal, that such orders must be quashed on certiorari on the ground that two of the commissioners making them were interested parties. THE QUEEN *v.* COMMISSIONERS OF SEWERS FOR FOBBING
[14 Q. B. D. 561

SEAL—Company — Lands Clauses Act — Summons in Chambers　　25 Ch. D. 168
See PRACTICE—SUPREME COURT—CHAMBERS. 11.

——— Contract not under—Local board.
See Cases under LOCAL GOVERNMENT—LOCAL AUTHORITY. 1—4.

——— Contract not under—School Board
See CORPORATION. 3.　[14 Q. B. D. 500

SEALING UP ENTRIES　　25 Ch. D. 247
See PRACTICE — SUPREME COURT — PRODUCTION OF DOCUMENTS. 15.

SEAMAN—Neglect to join ship　11 Q. B. D. 225
See SHIP—SEAMEN.

——— Wages and rating.
See SHIP—MERCHANT SHIPPING ACTS—*Gazette.*

——— Wages—Priority of lien 8 P. D. 129; 9 P. D.
See SHIP—MARITIME LIEN. 3, 5.　[37

SEARCH—For incumbrances.
See VENDOR AND PURCHASER—TITLE—*Statutes.*

——— Women detained for immoral purposes.
See CRIMINAL LAW—OFFENCES AGAINST WOMEN—*Statutes.*

SEAWORTHINESS—Warranty　　10 P. D. 103
See SHIP—SALVAGE. 13.

SECOND COUSINS—Will—Construction
[17 Ch. D. 262; 19 Ch. D. 201
See WILL—WORDS. 5, 6.

SECOND MORTGAGEE—Right of redemption
[24 Ch. D. 618
See MORTGAGE—PRIORITY. 1.

——— Sale—Right to balance of purchase-money
[29 Ch. D. 954
See MORTGAGE—REDEMPTION. 5.

SECRET TRUST—Mortmain　　28 Ch. D. 372
See CHARITY—MORTMAIN. 6.

SECURED CREDITOR—Bankruptcy.
See Cases under BANKRUPTCY—SECURED CREDITOR.

——— Bankruptcy　　　　- 25 Ch. D. 716
See BANKRUPTCY—MUTUAL DEALINGS. 4.

——— Composition -　　- 16 Ch. D. 534
See BANKRUPTCY—COMPOSITION. 1.

SECURED CREDITOR—*continued.*

—— Proof in administration suit   **18 Ch. D. 370**
    See EXECUTOR—ACTIONS. 21.

—— Winding-up—Proof - **16 Ch. D. 337, 590**
    See COMPANY—SECURED CREDITOR. 1, 2.

SECURITY—Bill of sale—Order and disposition
                        [**24 Ch. D. 210**
    See BANKRUPTCY—ORDER AND DISPOSI-
    TION. 2.

—— Debtor's summons - - **22 Ch. D. 312**
    See BANKRUPTCY—ACT OF BANKRUPTCY.
    18.

—— For bills of exchange.
    See Cases under BILL OF EXCHANGE—
    SECURITIES FOR.

—— For bills of exchange—Indorser
                        [**6 App. Cas. 1**
    See PRINCIPAL AND SURETY—INDEM-
    NITY. 1.

—— For bills of exchange—Scotch law
                        [**7 App. Cas. 366**
    See SCOTCH LAW—BILL OF EXCHANGE. 3.

—— For costs.
    See Cases under PRACTICE—SUPREME
    COURT—SECURITY FOR COSTS.

—— For costs—Divorce—Attachment   **10 P. D.**
    See ARREST—DEBTORS ACT. 2.   [**183**

—— For costs—Next friend of married woman
                        [**19 Ch. D. 94**
    See PRACTICE—SUPREME COURT—NEXT
    FRIEND. 2.

—— For costs—Remission of action to County
    Court - - **13 Q. B. D. 835**
    See COUNTY COURT—PRACTICE. 4.

—— For costs—Winding-up petition
                        [**19 Ch. D. 457**
    See COMPANY—WINDING-UP ORDER. 14.

—— For costs—Winding-up—Appeal
    See COMPANY—APPEAL.   [**23 Ch. D. 370**

—— For damages—Collision—Counter-claim
                        [**10 P. D. 33**
    See PRACTICE—ADMIRALTY—COUNTER-
    CLAIM.

—— Innkeeper—Lien - **23 Ch. D. 380**
    See INN—INNKEEPER. 2.

—— Insufficient—Liability of trustees
                [**23 Ch. D. 483; 29 Ch. D. 889;**
                [**30 Ch. D. 490**
    See TRUSTEE—LIABILITIES. 3, 4, 5.

—— One of two co-sureties - **17 Ch. D. 825**
    See PRINCIPAL AND SURETY—CONTRIBU-
    TION. 3.

—— Right of surety to - **19 Ch. D. 615**
    See PRINCIPAL AND SURETY—INDEMNITY.
    2.

—— Valuation of—Proof in bankruptcy .
                [**19 Ch. D. 105; 13 Q. B. D. 128;**
                [**14 Q. B. D. 121; 8 App. Cas. 606**
    See BANKRUPTCY — SECURED CREDITOR.
    7, 8, 11, 12.

SEIZURE WITHOUT SALE   **17 Ch. D. 839**
    See BANKRUPTCY—PROTECTED TRANSAC-
    TION. 3.

SENTENCE—Ecclesiastical law—Process to en-
    force - - **6 App. Cas. 424**
    See PRACTICE—ECCLESIASTICAL—MONI-
    TION.

SEPARATE ESTATE OF WIFE.
    See Cases under HUSBAND AND WIFE—.
    SEPARATE ESTATE.

—— Bequest to husband and wife — Married
    Women's Property Act   **27 Ch. D. 166**
    See WILL—JOINT TENANCY.

—— Charge on—Interim injunction
                        [**16 Ch. D. 660**
    See PRACTICE — SUPREME COURT — IN-.
    JUNCTION. 5.

—— Covenant to settle after-acquired property
                [**18 Ch. D. 354, 531; 22 Ch. D. 275;**
                [**24 Ch. D. 195**
    See SETTLEMENT — FUTURE PROPERTY..
    2, 7, 9, 10.

—— Deed of separation—Married woman
                        [**8 P. D. 16**
    See ADMINISTRATOR—MARRIED WOMAN.
    2.

—— Election -   **27 Ch. D. 606; 28 Ch. D. 124**
    See ELECTION. 5, 6.

—— Married Women's Property Act.
    See Cases and Statutes under HUSBAND
    AND WIFE—MARRIED WOMEN'S PRO-
    PERTY ACTS.

—— Partnership—Marshalling of securities
                        [**25 Ch. D. 148**
    See BANKRUPTCY—SECURED CREDITOR. 6.

—— Policy effected under Married Women's Pro-
    perty Act - **23 Ch. D. 525**
    See HUSBAND AND WIFE—MARRIED WO-
    MEN'S PROPERTY ACT. 5.

—— Post-nuptial settlement - **24 Ch. D. 597**
    See VOLUNTARY CONVEYANCE. 8.

—— Power of testamentary disposition
                        [**27 Ch. D. 264**
    See POWER—EXECUTION. 16.

—— Sale of, under Lands Clauses Act—Dis-
    ability - **18 Ch. D. 429**
    See LANDS CLAUSES ACT—COMPULSORY
    POWERS. 8.

—— Taxation of costs - **24 Ch. D. 405**
    See SOLICITOR—BILL OF COSTS. 9.

SEPARATE EXAMINATION—Married woman
                        [**16 Ch. D. 362**
    See PARTITION SUIT—SALE. 3.

SEPARATE USE—Will—Construction
                [**17 Ch. D. 794; 24 Ch. D. 703**
    See WILL—SEPARATE USE. 1, 2.

—— Will—Restraint on anticipation
    See WILL—PERPETUITY. 6. [**17 Ch. D. 368**

SEPARATION DEED.
    See Cases under HUSBAND AND WIFE—
    SEPARATION DEED.

—— Variation—Dissolution of marriage **9 P. D. 76**
    See PRACTICE—DIVORCE—SETTLEMENTS.
    8.

SEQUESTRATION—Evasion of service
                        [**10 P. D. 187**
    See PRACTICE — DIVORCE —SEQUESTRA-
    TION. 2.

—— Injunction to restrain—Bankruptcy
                        [**16 Ch. D. 665**
    See BANKRUPTCY—STAYING PROCEEDINGS
    1.

                                    2 Z

SEQUESTRATION—*continued.*

—— Pension of Indian officer　-　**8 P. D. 163**
　　See PRACTICE — DIVORCE — SEQUESTRA-
　　TION. 1.

—— Practice—Supreme Court　**17 Ch. D. 433;**
　　　　[**18 Ch. D. 653; 22 Ch. D. 233**
　　See PRACTICE — SUPREME COURT — SE-
　　QUESTRATION. 1, 2, 3.

—— Repairs done by sequestrator—Objection to
　　accounts—Dilapidations to glebe build-
　　ings　-　-　**15 Q. B. D. 222**
　　See ECCLESIASTICAL LAW — DILAPIDA-
　　TIONS.

—— Scotch bankruptcy　　**9 App. Cas. 966**
　　See SCOTCH LAW—BANKRUPTCY.

—— Scotch bankruptcy　-　**6 App. Cas. 588**
　　See SCOTCH LAW-- SALE OF GOODS. 2.

—— Scotch bankruptcy—Subsequent bankruptcy
　　in England　-　**22 Ch. D. 816**
　　See BANKRUPTCY—ADJUDICATION. 4.

SERVANT.

　　See Cases under
　　　　APPRENTICE.
　　　　MASTER AND SERVANT.

—— Knowledge of—Interrogatories
　　　　[**10 Q. B. D. 161; 24 Ch. D. 110**
　　See PRACTICE—SUPREME COURT—INTER-
　　ROGATORIES. 5, 6.

—— Marriage with—Condition forbidding
　　See WILL—CONDITION. 10. [**16 Ch. D. 188**

SERVICE—Affidavit of　-　**25 Ch. D. 84**
　　See PRACTICE — SUPREME COURT — DE-
　　FAULT. 6.

—— Appeal in bankruptcy　-　**20 Ch. D. 703**
　　See BANKRUPTCY—LIQUIDATION. 7.

—— Attachment—Solicitor　-　**22 Ch. D. 571**
　　See PRACTICE—SUPREME COURT—PRO-
　　DUCTION OF DOCUMENTS. 16.

—— Bastardy summons—Scotland
　　　　[**12 Q. B. D. 261; 10 App. Cas. 45**
　　See BASTARDY. 6.

—— Debtor's summons　-　**25 Ch. D. 112, 336**
　　See BANKRUPTCY—ACT OF BANKRUPTCY.
　　19, 20.

—— Evasion of—Writ of sequestration
　　　　[**10 P. D. 187**
　　See PRACTICE — DIVORCE — SEQUESTRA-
　　TION. 2.

—— Injunction—Committal for breach
　　　　[**25 Ch. D. 778**
　　See PRACTICE—SUPREME COURT—AT-
　　TACHMENT. 9.

—— Judgment—Partition suit　-　**16 Ch. D. 360**
　　See PARTITION SUIT—SALE. 1.

—— Lunatic—Business carried on in name of
　　firm　　**10 Q. B. D. 471**
　　See PRACTICE—SUPREME COURT—SER-
　　VICE. 1.

—— Motion for attachment—Copy of affidavit
　　　　[**25 Ch. D. 64**
　　See PRACTICE — SUPREME COURT — AT-
　　TACHMENT. 7.

—— Notice of appeal—Solicitor who has ceased
　　to act　-　-　**29 Ch. D. 351**
　　See PRACTICE—SUPREME COURT—PAY-
　　MENT INTO COURT. 6.

SERVICE—*continued.*

—— Notice—Shareholder　　**24 Ch. D. 149**
　　See COMPANY—PROSPECTUS. 6.

—— Notice to determine lease　**15 Q. B. D. 256**
　　See LANDLORD AND TENANT—RE-ENTRY.
　　9.

—— Notice to treat　-　**30 Ch. D. 553**
　　See LANDS CLAUSES ACT—COMPULSORY
　　POWERS. 6.

—— Order of magistrate　-　**27 Ch. D. 362**
　　See METROPOLIS—MANAGEMENT ACTS. 3.

—— Out of jurisdiction.
　　See Cases under PRACTICE—SUPREME
　　COURT—SERVICE. 2—11.

—— Out of jurisdiction—Interpleader
　　　　[**12 Q. B. D. 171**
　　See PRACTICE — SUPREME COURT — SER-
　　VICE. 7.

—— Out of jurisdiction—Lancaster Court
　　　　[**24 Ch. D. 280**
　　See COURT—LANCASTER COURT.

—— Out of jurisdiction—Restitution of conjugal
　　rights—Petition　　**10 P. D. 186**
　　See PRACTICE—DIVORCE—SERVICE.

—— Out of jurisdiction—Third-party notice
　　　　[**13 Q. B. D. 96**
　　See PRACTICE—SUPREME COURT—THIRD
　　PARTY. 10.

—— Partner, in action against firm **19 Ch. D. 124**
　　See PRACTICE—SUPREME COURT—PAR-
　　TIES. 11.

—— Process.
　　See JUSTICE OF THE PEACE—PRACTICE
　　—*Statutes.*

—— Substituted—Notice of appeal **24 Ch. D. 364**
　　See BANKRUPTCY—APPEAL. 3.

—— Substituted, on solicitor—Attachment
　　　　[**26 Ch. D. 746**
　　See PRACTICE — SUPREME COURT — AT-
　　TACHMENT. 8.

—— Summons—Settled Land Act **27 Ch. D. 179**
　　See SETTLED LAND ACT—RESTRICTIONS.
　　1.

—— Warrant of arrest—City of London Court
　　　　[**10 P. D. 36**
　　See PRACTICE—ADMIRALTY—SERVICE. 1.

—— Writ—Admiralty　-　**10 P. D. 62**
　　See PRACTICE—ADMIRALTY—SERVICE. 3.

SESSIONS.

—— Case stated—*Quarter Sessions*—12 & 13
Vict. c. 45, *s.* 11—*Agreement for Entry of Judgment according to the Opinion of the Court.*] A
case stated for the opinion of the Queen's Bench
Division, under sect. 11 of 12 & 13 Vict. c. 45,
should contain a statement of the agreement of
the parties that judgment in conformity with the
decision of the Court may be entered at Quarter
Sessions in the manner provided by the section.
CORPORATION OF PETERBOROUGH *v.* OVERSEERS OF
THURLBY　-　-　-　**8 Q. B. D. 586**

—— Appeal — Metropolis Local Management
　　Acts—Order for demolition **9 Q. B. D. 41**
　　See METROPOLIS—MANAGEMENT ACTS. 1.

—— Appeal against order of removal—Corrobora-
　　tive evidence　-　**6 Q. B. D. 31**
　　See POOR LAW—SETTLEMENT. 15.

SESSIONS—continued.

—— Appeal against rate—Time for giving notice
of appeal　-　-　6 Q. B. D. 100
See POOR-RATE—PROCEDURE. 5.

—— Case stated—Practice—Civil proceeding
[6 Q. B. D. 139
See POOR-RATE—PROCEDURE. 4.

—— Case stated — Queen's Bench Division—
Leave to appeal　6 Q. B. D. 309
See PRACTICE — SUPREME COURT — AP-
PEAL. 5.

SET-OFF.

1. —— Army Agents—Banker's Lien—Value
of Commission.] K., an officer in the army, mortgaged to R., to secure £5000, all moneys which
should be realized by sale of his commission. In
December, 1877, K. obtained leave to retire from
the army, and his commission was valued at
£3000, which on the 6th of December, 1877, was
paid by the Paymaster-General to C. & Co., the
army agents of the regiment, and was carried to
the deposit account kept by C. & Co. with the
Army Purchase Commissioners, there to remain
till K.'s retirement was gazetted. K. kept an
account current with C. & Co. as his bankers,
which was overdrawn to the amount of £647. K.'s
retirement was gazetted on the evening of the
18th of December, and as soon as C. & Co.'s office
opened on the 19th, R. gave them notice of his
security. R. having claimed payment of the
£3000, C. & Co. claimed to retain out of it the
£647 :—Held, by Bacon, V.C., that C. & Co. received the £3000 as K.'s bankers, and had a
banker's lien upon it for the balance due to them,
and were therefore entitled to retain the £647.—
Held, on appeal, that as soon as K.'s retirement
was gazetted the £3000 became money had and
received by C. & Co. for his use, and for which he
could have brought an action at law; that they
had a right to set off the balance due to them
against this demand; that this set-off was equally
available against R., of whose security C. & Co.
had no notice until after their right to set off had
arisen; and that, therefore, independently of any
question of banker's lien, C. & Co. were entitled
to retain the £647. ROXBURGHE v. COX
[17 Ch. D. 520

2. —— Surety—Debt due to Principal.] Action on a covenant to pay all liabilities which
the Plaintiff might incur under a deed of assignment made between the Plaintiff and other
parties. The Defendant pleaded that the covenant was the joint and several covenant of himself and one Wilson, and that, before action the
Plaintiff was indebted to Wilson in an amount
exceeding the Plaintiff's claim against the Defendant; and that Wilson had assigned the Plaintiff's
debt to himself and the Defendant in equal shares
as tenants in common. As to one half of the
Plaintiff's claim the Defendant claimed to set off
one-half of the debt so assigned, and as to the
other half, the Defendant said that he was entitled to be exonerated by his co-surety Wilson,
and to call upon him to contribute in equal shares
to the payment of the Plaintiff's claim, and was
entitled to set off the share remaining vested in
Wilson against this part of the Plaintiff's claim :—
Held, by Watkin Williams and Mathew, JJ., that

SET-OFF—continued.
the defence was no answer to the Plaintiff's claim.
BOWYEAR v. PAWSON　-　6 Q. B. D. 540

3. —— Trustees, Debtors to Estate—Bankruptcy of Trustee—Costs—Bankruptcy Act, 1869.]
Crombie and Storer were two trustees of an estate
administered by the Court. Crombie became
bankrupt after 1869. A balance of £896 was
found due from Crombie to the estate, and a
balance of £745 was found due from the estate to
the two trustees jointly :—Held, that the debt due
from the estate to the two trustees could not be
set off against the debt due from one; that the
Plaintiffs were entitled to an inquiry what part
of the £745 found due to the two trustees was,
as between the two, due to Crombie the bankrupt, but as that inquiry was not asked for, and
as there was evidence shewing that all the
money was in fact due to Storer, the debt so due
must be paid to him. The insolvent trustee
being indebted to the estate and the solvent
trustee not being responsible for that debt; and
the Bankruptcy Act, 1869, having made a debt
arising from a breach of trust to continue notwithstanding the bankruptcy :—Held, that a
reference be directed to the Taxing-Master to
apportion the costs of the trustees appearing by
the same solicitor, and that the costs of the
solvent trustee be paid out of the estate, and the
costs apportioned as the costs of the insolvent
trustee be set off against the amount found due
from him to the estate.—Whether under this
direction the whole of the common costs of the
two trustees would be allowed to the solvent
trustee or divided, must depend on the settled
practice of the Taxing-Master's office. MCEWAN
v. CROMBIE -　-　-　-　25 Ch. D. 175

—— Bankruptcy—Mutual dealings.
See Cases under BANKRUPTCY—MUTUAL
DEALINGS.

—— Bankruptcy -　-　-　22 Ch. D. 586
See EXECUTOR—ACTIONS. 18.

—— Between Crown and subject 9 App. Cas. 571
See COLONIAL LAW—CEYLON. 4.

—— Company—Contract—Winding-up. [30 Ch.
See COMPANY—CONTRACTS. 4. [D. 216

—— Company—Winding-up -　25 Ch. D. 587;
[8 Q. B. D. 179
See COMPANY—SET-OFF. 1, 2.

—— Company—Winding-up　-　27 Ch. D. 322
See COMPANY—DIRECTOR'S QUALIFICA-
TION. 2.

—— Company—Winding-up -　9 Q. B. D. 648;
[9 App. Cas. 434
See SALE OF GOODS—RESCISSION. 2.

—— Damages and costs—Solicitors lien
[14 Q. B. D. 922
See PRACTICE—SUPREME COURT—COSTS.
44.

—— Executor—Costs in probate suit—Legacies
[18 Ch. D. 300
See EXECUTOR—RETAINER. 5.

—— Landlord and tenant—Breaches of covenant
[22 Ch. D. 410
See BANKRUPTCY—DISTRESS. 5.

—— Law of Jersey -　-　9 App. Cas. 726
See COLONIAL LAW—JERSEY. 3.

2 Z 2

SET-OFF—*continued.*

—— Misappropriation of money by directors
[21 Ch. D. 519

See COMPANY—DIRECTOR'S LIABILITY. 5.

—— Pension of retired clerk　　17 Ch. D. 1
See ECCLESIASTICAL LAW—CLERGY. 3.

—— Pleading—Counter-claim　22 Ch. D. 122 ;
[7 Q. B. D. 626

See PRACTICE — SUPREME COURT —
COUNTER-CLAIM. 7, 8.

—— Pleading—Counter-claim—Reply
[8 Q. B. D. 428
See PRACTICE—SUPREME COURT—REPLY.
1.

—— Undisclosed principal　　9 Q. B. D. 530 ;
[8 App. Cas. 874
See PRINCIPAL AND AGENT—PRINCIPAL'S
LIABILITY. 6.

SETTING ASIDE AWARD　19 Ch. D. 58 ; 6 Q. B. D.
See ARBITRATION—AWARD. 2, 3.　　[67

SETTING ASIDE JUDGMENT—Collusion
[30 Ch. D. 421
See PRACTICE — SUPREME COURT—AP-
PEAL. 18.

SETTING ASIDE SETTLEMENT　18 Ch. D. 668 ;
[23 Ch. D. 278
See VOLUNTARY CONVEYANCE. 5, 6.

SETTLED ACCOUNT -　　　6 App. Cas. 181
See MORTGAGE—CONTRACT. 11.

—— Audit—Building society -　28 Ch. D. 111
See BUILDING SOCIETY. 3.

—— Impeaching accounts　　27 Ch. D. 111
See PRACTICE — SUPREME COURT —
CHAMBERS. 2.

—— Opening of　-　　　26 Ch. D. 717
See PRACTICE—SUPREME COURT—PRO-
DUCTION OF DOCUMENTS. 10.

SETTLED ESTATE—Fire insurance 23 Ch. D. 188
See INSURANCE, FIRE. 2.

SETTLED ESTATES ACTS.

1. —— **Irregular Order**—*40 & 41 Vict. c. 18*
—*Conveyancing and Law of Property Act, 1881
(44 & 45 Vict. c. 41), s. 70—Protection of Purchaser under Order.*] An order for sale under
the Settled Estates Act, 1877, contained a direction dispensing with the concurrence or consent
of the persons entitled, whether beneficially or
otherwise, to any estate or interest subsequent
to a certain estate tail, without naming them.
The purchaser objected to the title on the ground
that the order on the face of it was irregular :—
Held, by Hall, V.C., that under the special circumstances of the case it was unnecessary for the
parties whose concurrence was dispensed with
to be named in the order :—*Held*, by the Court of
Appeal, that under the 70th section of the Conveyancing and Law of Property Act, 1881, the
purchaser would in any event have a good title—
that section being applicable whether the objection to the order appears on the face of it or not,
and that the purchaser must complete. *In re* HALL-
DARE'S CONTRACT　　-　　21 Ch. D. 41

2. —— **Married Woman**—*Petition for Confirmation of Contract for Sale—Settled Estates Act,
1877 (40 & 41 Vict. c. 18), s. 50—Consent of Married*

SETTLED ESTATES ACTS—*continued.*
*Woman — Examination—Married Women's Pro-
perty Act, 1882 (45 & 46 Vict. c. 75), ss. 1, 2.*]
Notwithstanding the provisions of sect. 50 of the
Settled Estates Act, 1877, that when a married
woman consents to an application to the Court
under the Act, she is to be examined apart from
her husband as to her consent, such an examination is not now necessary in the case of a woman
who has married since the commencement of the
Married Women's Property Act, 1882. RIDDELL
v. ERRINGTON　　-　　-　　26 Ch. D. 220

3. ——**Married Woman**—*Separate Examination—Settled Estates Act, 1877 (40 & 41 Vict. c.
18), s. 50—Married Women's Property Act, 1882
(45 & 46 Vict. c. 75), s. 1.*] In the case of a
woman married before the commencement of the
Married Women's Property Act, 1882, sect. 1 of
the Act applies only as to property acquired by
her after the commencement of the Act.—Therefore, if such a woman is a petitioner, or a Respondent to a petition, under the Settled Estates Act,
1877, relating to property her interest in which
was acquired before the commencement of the
Act of 1882, she must be examined separately, as
provided by sect. 50 of the Act of 1877. *In re*
HARRIS' SETTLED ESTATES　-　28 Ch. D. 171

4. —— **No Beneficial Owner**—*40 & 41 Vict. c.
18, ss. 4, 13, 23, 46—Legal Estate—Trustees—
Persons to present Petition—Receiver.*] Where
an estate is vested in trustees and there is not for
the time being any beneficial owner of the rents
and profits, the trustees are persons who may,
under the 23rd section of the Settled Estates Act,
1877, apply to the Court by petition in a summary
way to exercise the powers conferred by the Act.
—*Wolley* v. *Jenkins* (23 Beav. 53) discussed.
VINE *v.* RALEIGH　　-　　-　24 Ch. D. 238

5. —— **Sale out of Court**—*40 & 41 Vict. c. 18,
s. 16.*] The Court has no jurisdiction to direct a
sale under the Settled Estates Act, 1877, to be
conducted out of Court.—*In re Adams' Settled
Estates* (9 Ch. D. 116) not followed. *In re* HAR-
VEY'S SETTLED ESTATE　-　-　21 Ch. D. 123

—— Conversion　　-　　-　19 Ch. D. 302
See PARTITION SUIT—SALE. 6.

—— Leaseholds for lives　-　18 Ch. D. 624
See LEASEHOLD—RENEWABLE LEASE. 3.

—— Sale under—Succession duty 17 Ch. D. 711
See REVENUE—SUCCESSION DUTY. 5.

SETTLED LAND ACT :—　　　　　　Col.

I. SETTLED LAND ACT—STATUTES.

*The Act 45 & 46 Vict. c. 38 (the Settled Land
Act, 1882), which came into operation on the 31st
of December, 1882, repeals (sect. 64)—*
23 & 24 Vict. c. 145, Parts 1 and 4,
27 & 28 Vict. c. 114, ss. 17, 18, and part of 21,
40 & 41 Vict. c. 18, s. 17,

I. SETTLED LAND ACT—STATUTES—*contd.*

and facilitates sales, leases, and other dispositions of settled land, and promotes the execution of improvements thereon.

1. Definitions.
2. Powers of tenant for life.
3. Investment of capital moneys.
4. Improvement of settled estates.
5. Protection of settled estates.
6. Trustees.
7. Limited owners.
8. Settlements by way of trust for sale.
9. Procedure—Land Commissioners.

1. DEFINITIONS.

Sect. 2 defines (amongst other things), " a settlement for the purposes of the Act," to be any deed, will, agreement or a settlement, or other agreement, covenant to surrender, copy of Court roll, Act of Parliament, or other instrument, or any number of instruments, whether made or passed before or after, or partly before and partly after the commencement of the Act, under or by virtue of which instrument or instruments any land, or any estate or interest in land, stands for the time being limited to or in trust for any persons by way of succession.

An estate or interest in remainder or reversion not disposed of by a settlement, and reverting to the settlor or descending to the testator's heir, is for the purposes of the Act an estate or interest coming to the settlor or heir under or by virtue of the settlement and comprised in the subject of the settlement.

" Settled land " for the purposes of the Act, to be land, and any estate or interest therein, which is the subject of a settlement.

The determination of the question whether land is settled land, for the purposes of the Act, or not, is governed by the state of facts, and the limitations of the settlement, at the time of the settlement taking effect.

" The tenant for life " of settled land for the purposes of the Act, to be the person who is for the time being, under a settlement, beneficially entitled to possession of settled land, for his life.

If, in any case, there are two or more persons so entitled as tenants in common, or as joint tenants, or for other concurrent estates or interests, they together constitute the tenant for life for purposes of the Act.

A person being tenant for life within the foregoing definitions shall be deemed to be such notwithstanding that, under the settlement or otherwise, the settled land, or his estate or interest therein, is incumbered or charged in any manner or to any extent.

" Trustees " of a settlement for the purposes of the Act to be the persons, if any, who are for the time being, under a settlement, trustees with power of sale of settled land, or with power of consent to or approval of the exercise of such a power of sale, or if under a settlement there are no such trustees, then the persons, if any, for the time being, who are by the settlement declared to be trustees thereof for purposes of the Act.

" Capital money " arising under the Act to be capital money arising under the Act, and receivable for the trusts and purposes of the settlement.

" Person " includes corporation.

The Act 47 & 48 Vict. c. 18, s. 8, for the purposes

I. SETTLED LAND ACT—STATUTES—*contd.*

of the Act of 1882, defines the estate of a tenant by the curtesy to be an estate arising under a settlement made by his wife.

Infants—Married Women—Lunatics.] By the Act 45 & 46 Vict. c. 38, s. 59, where a person who is in his own right seised of or entitled in possession to land is an infant, then for the purposes of this Act the land is settled land, and the infant shall be deemed tenant for life thereof.

Sect. 60. Where a tenant for life, or a person having the powers of a tenant for life under this Act, is an infant, or an infant would, if he were of full age, be a tenant for life, or have the powers of a tenant for life under this Act, the powers of a tenant for life under this Act may be exercised on his behalf by the trustees of the settlement, and if there are none, then by such person and in such manner as the Court, on the application of a testamentary or other guardian, or next friend of the infant, either generally or in a particular instance, order.

Sect. 61.—(1.) The foregoing provisions of this Act do not apply in the case of a married woman.

(2.) Where a married woman who, if she had not been a married woman, would have been a tenant for life or would have had the powers of a tenant for life under the foregoing provisions of this Act, is entitled for her separate use, or is entitled under any statute, passed or, to be passed, for her separate property, or as a feme sole, then she, without her husband, shall have the powers of a tenant for life under this Act.

(3.) Where she is entitled otherwise than as aforesaid, then she and her husband together shall have the power of a tenant for life under this Act.

(4.) The provisions of this Act referring to a tenant for life and a settlement and settled land shall extend to the married woman without her husband, or to her and her husband together, as the case may require, and to the instrument under which her estate or interest arises, and to the land therein comprised.

(5.) The married woman may execute, make, and do all deeds, instruments, and things necessary or proper for giving effect to the provisions of this section.

(6.) A restraint on anticipation in the settlement shall not prevent the exercise by her of any power under this Act.

Sect. 62. Where a tenant for life, or a person having the powers of a tenant for life under this Act, is a lunatic, so found by inquisition, the committee of his estate may, in his name and on his behalf, under an order of the Lord Chancellor, or other person intrusted by virtue of the Queen's Sign Manual with the care and commitment of the custody of the persons and estates of lunatics, exercise the powers of a tenant for life under this Act; and the order may be made on the petition of any person interested in the settled land, or of the committee of the estate.

2. POWERS OF TENANT FOR LIFE.

Contracts.] Sect. 31.—(1.) A tenant for life—
(i.) May contract to make any sale, exchange, partition, mortgage, or charge; and
(ii.) May vary or rescind, with or without consideration, the contract, in the like cases and manner in which, if he were absolute

I. SETTLED LAND ACT—STATUTES—*contd.*

owner of the settled land, he might lawfully vary or rescind the same, but so that the contract as varied be in conformity with this Act; and any such consideration, if paid in money, shall be capital money arising under this Act; and

(iii.) *May contract to make any lease; and in making the lease may vary the terms, with or without consideration, but so that the lease be in conformity with this Act; and*

(iv.) *May accept a surrender of a contract for a lease, in like manner and on the like terms in and on which he might accept a surrender of a lease; and thereupon may make a new or other contract, or new or other contracts, for or relative to a lease or leases, in like manner and on the like terms in and on which he might make a new or other lease, or new or other leases, where a lease had been granted; and*

(v.) *May enter into a contract for or relating to the execution of any improvement authorized by this Act, and may vary or rescind the same; and*

(vi.) *May, in any other case, enter into a contract to do any act for carrying into effect any of the purposes of this Act, and may vary or rescind the same.*

(2.) Every contract shall be binding on and shall enure for the benefit of the settled land, and shall be enforceable against and by every successor in title for the time being of the tenant for life, and may be carried into effect by any such successor; but so that it may be varied or rescinded by any such successor, in the like case and manner, if any, as if it had been made by himself.

(3.) The Court may, on the application of the tenant for life, or of any such successor, or of any person interested in any contract, give directions respecting the enforcing, carrying into effect, varying, or rescinding thereof.

(4.) Any preliminary contract under this Act for or relating to a lease shall not form part of the title or evidence of the title of any person to the lease, or to the benefit thereof.

Heirlooms.] *Sect.* 37.—(1.) *Where personal chattels are settled on trust so as to devolve with land until a tenant in tail by purchase is born or attains the age of twenty-one years, or so as otherwise to vest in some person becoming entitled to an estate of freehold of inheritance in the land, a tenant for life of the land may sell the chattels or any of them.*

(2.) *The money arising by the sale shall be capital money arising under this Act, and shall be paid, invested, or applied, and otherwise dealt with in like manner in all respects as by this Act directed with respect to other capital money arising under this Act, or may be invested in the purchase of other chattels, of the same or any other nature, which, when purchased, shall be settled and held on the same trusts, and shall devolve in the same manner as the chattels sold.*

(3.) *A sale or purchase of chattels under this section shall not be made without an order of the Court.*

Leases and Sales, &c.] *Sect.* 6. *A tenant for life may lease the settled land, or any part thereof, or any easement, right, or privilege of any kind,*

over or in relation to the same, for any purpose whatever, whether involving waste or not, for any term not exceeding—

(i.) *In case of a building lease, ninety-nine years:*

(ii.) *In case of a mining lease, sixty years:*

(iii.) *In case of any other lease, twenty-one years.*

Sect. 7.—(1.) *Every lease shall be by deed, and be made to take effect in possession not later than twelve months after its date.*

(2.) *Every lease shall reserve the best rent that can reasonably be obtained, regard being had to any fine taken, and to any money laid out or to be laid out for the benefit of the settled land, and generally to the circumstances of the case.*

(3.) *Every lease shall contain a covenant by the lessee for payment of the rent, and a condition of re-entry on the rent not being paid within a time therein specified not exceeding thirty days.*

(4.) *A counterpart of every lease shall be executed by the lessee and delivered to the tenant for life; of which execution and delivery the execution of the lease by the tenant for life shall be sufficient evidence.*

(5.) *A statement, contained in a lease or in an indorsement thereon, signed by the tenant for life, respecting any matter of fact or of calculation under this Act in relation to the lease, shall, in favour of the lessee and of those claiming under him, be sufficient evidence of the matter stated.*

Sect. 8.—(1.) *Every building lease shall be made partly in consideration of the lessee, or some person by whose direction the lease is granted, or some other person, having erected, or agreeing to erect, buildings, new or additional, or having improved or repaired, or agreeing to improve or repair, buildings, or having executed, or agreeing to execute, on the land leased, an improvement authorized by this Act, for or in connection with building purposes.*

(2.) *A peppercorn rent or a nominal or other rent less than the rent ultimately payable, may be made payable for the first five years or any less part of the term.*

(3.) *Where the land is contracted to be leased in lots, the entire amount of rent to be ultimately payable may be apportioned among the lots in any manner; save that—*

(i.) *The annual rent reserved by any lease shall not be less than ten shillings; and*

(ii.) *The total amounts of the rents reserved on all leases for the time being granted shall not be less than the total amount of the rents which, in order that the leases may be in conformity with this Act, ought to be reserved in respect of the whole land for the time being leased; and*

(iii.) *The rent reserved by any lease shall not exceed one fifth part of the full annual value of the land comprised in that lease with the buildings thereon when completed.*

Sect. 9.—(1.) *In a mining lease—*

(i.) *The rent may be made to be ascertainable by or to vary according to the acreage worked, or by or according to the quantities of any mineral or substance gotten, made merchantable, converted, carried*

I. SETTLED LAND ACT—STATUTES—*contd.*

away, or disposed of, in or 'from the settled land, or any other land, or by or according to any 'facilities given in that behalf; and

(ii.) *A fixed or minimum rent may be made payable with or without power for the lessee in case the rent, according to acreage or quantity, in any specified period does not produce an amount equal to the fixed or minimum rent, to make up the deficiency in any subsequent specified period 'free of rent other than the fixed or minimum rent.*

(2.) *A lease may be made partly in consideration of the lessee having executed, or his agreeing to execute, on the land leased, an improvement authorized by this Act, for or in connection with mining purposes.*

Sect. 10.—(1.) *Where it is shewn to the Court with respect to the district in which any settled land is situate, either—*

(i.) *That it is the custom for land therein to be leased or granted for building or mining purposes for a longer term or on other conditions than the term or conditions specified in that behalf in this Act, or in perpetuity; or*

(ii.) *That it is difficult to make leases or grants for building or mining purposes of land therein, except for a longer term or on other conditions than the term and conditions specified in that behalf in this Act, or except in perpetuity;*

the Court may, if it thinks fit, authorize generally the tenant for life to make 'from time to time leases or grants of or affecting the settled land in that district, or parts thereof, for any term or in perpetuity, at fee 'farm or other rents, secured by condition of re-entry, or otherwise, as in the order of the Court expressed, or may, if it thinks fit, authorize the tenant for life to make any such lease or grant in any particular case.

(2.) *Thereupon the tenant for life, and subject to any direction in the order of the Court to the contrary, each of his successors in title being a tenant for life, or having the powers of a tenant for life under this Act, may make in any case, or in the particular case, a lease or grant of or affecting the settled land, or part thereof, in conformity with the order.*

Sect. 11. *Under a mining lease, whether the mines or minerals leased are already opened or in work or not, unless a contrary intention is expressed in the settlement, there shall be 'from time to time set aside, as capital money arising under this Act, part of the rent as 'follows, namely,—where the tenant for life is impeachable for waste in respect of minerals, three 'fourth parts of the rent, and otherwise one 'fourth part thereof, and in every such case the residue of the rent shall go as rents and profits.*

Sect. 12. *The leasing power of a tenant for life extends to the making of—*

(i.) *A lease for giving effect to a contract entered into by any of his predecessors in title for making a lease, which, if made by the predecessor, would have been binding on the successors in title; and*

(ii.) *A lease for giving effect to a covenant of*

I. SETTLED LAND ACT—STATUTES—*contd.*

renewal, performance whereof could be enforced against the owner for the time being of the settled land; and

(iii.) *A lease for confirming, as far as may be, a previous lease, being void or voidable; but so that every lease, as and when confirmed, shall be such a lease as might at the date of the original lease have been lawfully granted, under this Act, or otherwise, as the case may require.*

Sect. 13.—(1.) *A tenant for life may accept, with or without consideration, a surrender of any lease of settled land, whether made under this Act or not, in respect of the whole land leased, or any part thereof with or without an exception of all or any of the mines and minerals therein, or in respect of mines and minerals, or any of them.*

(2.) *On a surrender of a lease in respect of part only of the land or mines and minerals leased, the rent may be apportioned.*

(3.) *On a surrender, tenant for life may make of the land or mines and minerals surrendered, or of any part thereof, a new or other lease, or new or other leases in lots.*

(4.) *A new or other lease may comprise additional land or mines and minerals, and may reserve any apportioned or other rent.*

(5.) *On a surrender, and the making of a new or other lease, whether for the same or for any extended or other term, and whether or not subject to the same or to any covenants, provisions, or conditions, the value of the lessee's interest in the lease surrendered may be taken into account in the determination of the amount of the rent to be reserved, and of any fine to be taken, and of the nature of the covenants, provisions, and conditions to be inserted in the new or other lease.*

(6.) *Every new or other lease shall be in conformity with this Act.*

Sect. 3. *A tenant for life—*

(i.) *May sell the settled land, or any part thereof, or any easement, right, or privilege of any kind, over or in relation to the same; and*

(ii.) *Where the settlement comprises a manor—may sell the seigniory of any 'freehold land within the manor, or the 'freehold and inheritance of any copyhold or customary land, parcel of the manor, with or without any exception or reservation of all or any mines or minerals, or of any rights or powers relative to mining purposes, so as in every case to effect an enfranchisement; and*

(iii.) *May make an exchange of the settled land, or any part thereof, for other land, including an exchange in consideration of money paid for equality of exchange; and*

(iv.) *Where the settlement comprises an undivided share in land, or, under the settlement, the settled land has come to be held in undivided shares,—may concur in making partition of the entirety, including a partition in consideration of money paid for equality of partition.*

Sect. 4.—(1.) *Every sale shall be made at the best price that can reasonably be obtained.*

(2.) *Every exchange and every partition shall be made for the best consideration in land or in land and money that can reasonably be obtained.*

I. SETTLED LAND ACT—STATUTES—*contd.*

(3.) *A sale may be made in one lot or in several lots, and either by auction or by private contract.*

(4.) *On a sale the tenant for life may fix reserve biddings and buy in at an auction.*

(5.) *A sale, exchange, or partition may be made subject to any stipulations respecting title, or evidence of title, or other things.*

(6.) *On a sale, exchange, or partition, any restriction or reservation with respect to building on or other user of land, or with respect to mines and minerals, or with respect to or for the purpose of the more beneficial working thereof, or with respect to any other thing, may be imposed or reserved and made binding, as far as the law permits, by covenant, condition, or otherwise, on the tenant for life and the settled land, or any part thereof, or on the other party and any land sold or given in exchange or on partition to him.*

(7.) *An enfranchisement may be made with or without a re-grant of any right of common or other right, easement, or privilege theretofore appendant or appurtenant to or held or enjoyed with the land enfranchised, or reputed so to be.*

(8.) *Settled land in England shall not be given in exchange for land out of England.*

Sect. 5. Where on a sale, exchange, or partition there is an incumbrance affecting land sold or given in exchange or on partition, the tenant for life, with the consent of the incumbrancer, may charge that incumbrance on any other part of the settled land, whether already charged therewith or not, in exoneration of the part sold or so given, and, by conveyance of the fee simple, or other estate or interest the subject of the settlement, or by creation of a term of years in the settled land, or otherwise, make provision accordingly.

Completion of Sale, Lease, &c.] *Sect. 20—*(1.) *On a sale, exchange, partition, lease, mortgage, or charge, the tenant for life may, as regards land sold, given in exchange or on partition, leased, mortgaged, or charged or intended so to be, including copyhold or customary or leasehold land vested in trustees, or as regards easements or other rights or privileges sold or leased, or intended so to be, convey or create the same by deed, for the estate or interest the subject of the settlement, or for any less estate or interest, to the uses and in the manner requisite for giving effect to the sale, exchange, partition, lease, mortgage, or charge.*

(2.) *Such a deed, to the extent, and in the manner to and in which it is expressed or intended to operate and can operate under this Act, is effectual to pass the land conveyed, or the easements, rights, or privileges created, discharged from all the limitations, powers, and provisions of the settlement, and from all estates, interests, and charges subsisting or to arise thereunder, but subject to and with the exception of—*

(i.) *All estates, interests, and charges having priority to the settlement ; and*

(ii.) *All such other, if any, estates, interests, and charges as have been conveyed or created for securing money actually raised at the date of the deed ; and*

(iii.) *All leases and grants at feefarm rents or otherwise, and all grants of easements, rights of common, or other rights or privileges granted or made for value in money or money's worth, or agreed so to be, before*

I. SETTLED LAND ACT—STATUTES—*contd.*

the date of the deed, by the tenant for life, or by any of his predecessors in title, or by any trustees for him or them, under the settlement, or under any statutory power, or being otherwise binding on the successors in title of the tenant for life.

(3.) *In case of a deed relating to copyhold or customary land it is sufficient that the deed be entered on the Court rolls of the manor, and the steward is hereby required on production to him of the deed to make the proper entry ; and on that production, and on payment of customary fines, fees, and other dues or payments, any person whose title under the deed requires to be perfected by admittance shall be admitted accordingly ; but if the steward so requires there shall also be produced to him so much of the settlement as may be necessary to shew the title of the person executing the deed ; and the same may, if the steward thinks fit, be also entered on the Court rolls.*

Copyholds.] *Sect. 14.—*(1.) *A tenant for life may grant to a tenant of copyhold or customary land, parcel of a manor comprised in the settlement, a licence to make any such lease of that land, or of a specified part thereof, as the tenant for life is by this Act empowered to make of freehold land.*

(2.) *The licence may fix the annual value whereon fines, fees, or other customary payments are to be assessed, or the amount of those fines, fees, or payments.*

(3.) *The licence shall be entered on the Court rolls of the manor, of which entry a certificate in writing of the steward shall be sufficient evidence.*

Mansion and Park.] *Sect. 15. Notwithstanding anything in this Act the principal mansion-house on any settled land, and the demesnes thereof, and other lands usually occupied therewith, shall not be sold or leased by the tenant for life, without the consent of the trustee of the settlement, or an order of the Court.*

Mortgage for Equality Money, &c.] *Sect. 18. Where money is required for enfranchisement, or for equality of exchange or partition, the tenant for life may raise the same on mortgage of the settled land, or of any part thereof, by conveyance of the fee simple, or other estate or interest the subject of the settlement, or by creation of a term of years in the settled land, or otherwise, and the money raised shall be capital money arising under this Act.*

Streets and Open Spaces.] *Sect. 16. On or in connection with a sale or grant for building purposes, or a building lease, the tenant for life, for the general benefit of the residents on the settled land or on any part thereof,—*

(i.) *May cause or require any parts of the settled land to be appropriated and laid out for streets, roads, paths, squares, gardens, or other open spaces, for the use, gratuitously or on payment, of the public or of individuals, with sewers, drains, watercourses, fencing, paving, or other works necessary or proper in connexion therewith ; and*

(ii.) *May provide that the parts so appropriated shall be conveyed to or vested in the trustees of the settlement, or other trustees, or any company or public body, on trusts or subject to provisions for securing the continued appropriation thereof to the*

I. SETTLED LAND ACT—STATUTES—*contd.*

purposes *aforesaid, and the continued repair or maintenance of streets and other places and works aforesaid, with or without provision for appointment of new trustees when required; and*

(iii.) *May execute any general or other deed necessary or proper for giving effect to the provisions of this section (which deed may be inrolled in the Central Office of the Supreme Court of Judicature), and thereby declare the mode, terms, and conditions of the appropriation, and the manner in which and the persons by whom the benefit thereof is to be enjoyed, and the nature and extent of the privileges and conveniences granted.*

Surface and Minerals Apart.] *Sect.* 17.—(1.) *A sale, exchange, partition, or mining lease, may be made either of land, with or without an exception or reservation of all or any of the mines and minerals therein, or of any mines and minerals, and in any such case with or without a grant or reservation of powers of working, wayleaves or rights of way, rights of water and drainage, and other powers, easements, rights, and privileges for or incident to or connected with mining purposes, in relation to the settled land, or any part thereof, or any other land.*

(2.) *An exchange or partition may be made subject to and in consideration of the reservation of an undivided share in mines or minerals.*

Undivided Shares.] *Sect.* 19. *Where the settled land comprises an undivided share in land, or, under the settlement, the settled land has come to be held in undivided shares, the tenant for life of an undivided share may join or concur, in any manner and to any extent necessary or proper for any purpose of this Act, with any person entitled to or having power or right of disposition of or over another undivided share.*

Waste.] *Sect.* 35—(1.) *Where a tenant for life is impeachable for waste in respect of timber, and there is on the settled land timber ripe and fit for cutting, the tenant for life, on obtaining the consent of the trustee of the settlement or an order of the Court, may cut and sell that timber, or any part thereof.*

(2.) *Three fourth parts of the net proceeds of the sale shall be set aside as and be capital money arising under this Act, and the other fourth part shall go as rents and profits.*

Restrictions, Savings, and General Provisions.] *Sect.* 50.—(1.) *The powers under this Act of a tenant for life are not capable of assignment or release, and do not pass to a person as being, by operation of law or otherwise, an assignee of a tenant for life, and remain exercisable by the tenant for life after and notwithstanding any assignment, by operation of law or otherwise, of his estate or interest under the settlement.*

(2.) *A contract by a tenant for life not to exercise any of his powers under this Act is void.*

(3.) *But this section shall operate without prejudice to the rights of any person being an assignee for value of the estate or interest of the tenant for life; and in that case the assignee's rights shall not be affected without his consent, except that, unless the assignee is actually in possession of the settled land or part thereof, his consent shall*

I. SETTLED LAND ACT—STATUTES—*contd.*

not be requisite for the making of leases thereof to the tenant for life, provided the leases are made at the best rent that can reasonably be obtained, without fine, and in other respects are in conformity with this Act.

(4.) *This section extends to assignments made or coming into operation before or after and to acts done before or after the commencement of this Act; and in this section assignment includes assignment by way of mortgage, and any partial or qualified assignment, and any charge or incumbrance; and assignee has a meaning corresponding with that of assignment*

Sect. 51—(1.) *If in a settlement, will, assurance, or other instrument executed or made before or after, or partly before and partly after, the commencement of this Act a provision is inserted purporting or attempting, by way of direction, declaration, or otherwise, to forbid a tenant for life to exercise any power under this Act, or attempting, or tending, or intended, by a limitation, gift, or disposition over of settled land, or by a limitation, gift, or disposition of other real or any personal property, or by the imposition of any condition, or by forfeiture, or in any other manner whatever, to prohibit or prevent him from exercising, or to induce him to abstain from exercising, or to put him into a position inconsistent with his exercising, any power under this Act, that provision, as far as it purports, or attempts, or tends, or is intended to have, or would or might have, the operation aforesaid, shall be deemed to be void.*

(2.) *For the purposes of this section an estate or interest limited to continue so long only as a person abstains from exercising any power shall be and take effect as an estate or interest to continue for the period for which it would continue if that person were to abstain from exercising the power, discharged from liability to determination or cesser by or on his exercising the same.*

Sect. 52. *Notwithstanding anything in a settlement, the exercise by the tenant for life of any power under this Act shall not occasion a forfeiture.*

Sect. 53. *A tenant for life shall, in exercising any power under this Act, have regard to the interest of all parties entitled under the settlement, and shall, in relation to the exercise thereof by him, be deemed to be in the position and to have the duties and liabilities of a trustee for those parties.*

Sect 54. *On a sale, exchange, partition, lease, mortgage, or charge, a purchaser, lessee, mortgagee, or other person dealing in good faith with a tenant for life shall, as against all parties entitled under the settlement, be conclusively taken to have given the best price, consideration, or rent, as the case may require, that could reasonably be obtained by the tenant for life, and to have complied with all the requisitions of this Act.*

Sect. 55—(1.) *Powers and authorities conferred by this Act on a tenant for life or trustees or the Court or the Land Commissioners are exercisable from time to time.*

(2.) *Where a power of sale, enfranchisement, exchange, partition, leasing, mortgaging, charging, or other power is exercised by a tenant for life, or by the trustees of a settlement, he and they may respectively execute, make, and do all deeds,*

I. SETTLED LAND ACT—STATUTES—*contd.*

instruments, and things necessary or proper in their behalf.

(3.) *Where any provision in this Act refers to sale, purchase, exchange, partition, leasing or other dealing, or to any power, consent, payment, receipt, deed, assurance, contract, expenses, act or transaction, the same shall be construed to extend only (unless it is otherwise expressed) to sales, purchases. exchanges, partitions, leasings, dealings, powers, consents, payments, receipts, deeds, assurances, contracts, expenses, acts, and transactions under this Act.*

Sect. 56.—(1.) *Nothing in this Act shall take away, abridge, or prejudicially affect any power for the time being subsisting under a settlement, or by statute or otherwise, exerciseable by a tenant for life, or by trustees with his consent, or on his request, or by his direction or otherwise; and the powers given by this Act are cumulative.*

(2.) *But in cases of conflict between the provisions of a settlement and the provisions of this Act, relative to any matter in respect whereof the tenant for life exercises or contracts or intends to exercise any power under this Act, the provisions of this Act shall prevail; and, accordingly, notwithstanding anything in the settlement, the consent of the tenant for life shall, by virtue of this Act, be necessary to the exercise by the trustees of the settlement or other person of any power conferred by the settlement exerciseable for any purpose provided for in this Act.*

(3.) *If a question arises, or a doubt is entertained, respecting any matter within this section, the Court may, on the application of the trustees of the settlement, or of the tenant for life, or of any other person interested, give its decision, opinion, advice or direction thereon.*

Sect. 57.—(1.) *Nothing in this Act shall preclude a settlor from conferring on the tenant for life, or the trustees of the settlement, any powers additional to or larger than those conferred by this Act.*

(2.) *Any additional or larger powers so conferred shall, as far as may be, notwithstanding anything in this Act, operate and be exercisable in the like manner, and with all the like incidents, effects, and consequences, as if they were conferred by this Act, unless a contrary intention is expressed in the settlement.*

3. INVESTMENT OF CAPITAL MONEY.

Sect. 21. *Capital money arising under this Act, subject to payment of claims properly payable thereout, and to application thereof for any special authorized object for which the same was raised, shall, when received, be invested or otherwise applied wholly in one, or partly in one and partly in another or others, of the following modes (namely):—*

(i.) *In investment on government securities, or on other securities on which the trustees of the settlement are by the settlement or by law authorized to invest trust money of the settlement, or on the security of the bonds, mortgages, or debentures, or in the purchase of the debenture stock of any railway company in Great Britain or Ireland incorporated by special Act of Parliament, and having for ten years next*

I. SETTLED LAND ACT—STATUTES—*contd.*

before the date of the investment paid a dividend on its ordinary stock or shares, with power to vary the investment into or for any other such securities:

(ii.) *In discharge, purchase, or redemption of incumbrances affecting the inheritance of the settled land, or other the whole estate the subject of the settlement, or of land tax, rentcharge in lieu of tithe, Crown rent, chief rent, or quit rent, charged on or payable out of the settled land:*

(iii.) *In payment for any improvement authorized by this Act:*

(iv.) *In payment for equality of exchange or partition of settled land:*

(v.) *In purchase of the seigniory of any part of the settled land, being freehold land, or in purchase of the fee simple of any part of the settled land, being copyhold or customary land:*

(vi.) *In purchase of the reversion or freehold in fee of any part of the settled land, being leasehold land held for years, or life, or years determinable on life:*

(vii.) *In purchase of land in fee simple, or of copyhold or customary land, or of leasehold land held for sixty years or more unexpired at the time of purchase, subject or not to any exception or reservation of or in respect of mines or minerals therein, or of or in respect of rights or powers relative to the working of mines or minerals therein, or in other land:*

(viii.) *In purchase, either in fee simple, or for a term of sixty years or more, of mines and minerals convenient to be held or worked with the settled land, or of any easement, right, or privilege convenient to be held with the settled land for mining or other purposes:*

(ix.) *In payment to any person becoming absolutely entitled or empowered to give an absolute discharge:*

(x.) *In payment of costs, charges, and expenses of or incidental to the exercise of any of the powers, or the execution of any of the provisions, of this Act:*

(xi.) *In any other mode in which money produced by the exercise of a power of sale in the settlement is applicable thereunder.*

Sect. 22.—(1.) *Capital money arising under this Act shall, in order to its being invested or applied as aforesaid, be paid either to the trustees of the settlement or into Court, at the option of the tenant for life, and shall be invested or applied by the trustees, or under the direction of the Court, as the case may be, accordingly.*

(2.) *The investment or other application by the trustees shall be made according to the direction of the tenant for life, and in default thereof, according to the discretion of the trustees, but in the last-mentioned case subject to any consent required or direction given by the settlement with respect to the investment or other application by the trustees of trust money of the settlement; and any investment shall be in the names or under the control of the trustees.*

(3.) *The investment or other application under the direction of the Court shall be made on the*

I. SETTLED LAND ACT—STATUTES—contd.

application of the tenant for life, or of the trustees.

(4.) Any investment or other application shall not during the life of the tenant for life be altered without his consent.

(5.) Capital money arising under this Act while remaining uninvested or unapplied, and securities on which an investment of any such capital money is made, shall, for all purposes of disposition, transmission, and devolution, be considered as land, and the same shall be held for and go to the same persons successively, in the same manner and for and on the same estates, interests, and trusts, as the land whered'rom the money arises would, if not disposed of, have been held and have gone under the settlement.

(6.) The income of those securities shall be paid or applied as the income of that land, if not disposed of, would have been payable or applicable under the settlement.

(7.) Those securities may be converted into money, which shall be capital money arising under this Act.

Sect. 23. Capital money arising under this Act from settled land in England shall not be applied in the purchase of land out of England, unless the settlement expressly authorizes the same.

Sect. 24.—(1.) Land acquired by purchase or in exchange, or on partition, shall be made subject to the settlement in manner directed in this section.

(2.) Freehold land shall be conveyed to the uses, on the trusts, and subject to the powers and provisions which, under the settlement, or by reason of the exercise of any power of charging therein contained, are subsisting with respect to the settled land, or as near thereto as circumstances permit, but not so as to increase or multiply charges or powers of charging.

(3.) Copyhold, customary, or leasehold land shall be conveyed to and vested in the trustees of the settlement on trusts and subject to powers and provisions corresponding, as nearly as the law and circumstances permit, with the uses, trusts, powers, and provisions to on and subject to which freehold land is to be conveyed as aforesaid; so nevertheless that the beneficial interest in land held by lease for years shall not vest absolutely in a person who is by the settlement made by purchase tenant in tail, or in tail male, or in tail female, and who dies under the age of twenty-one years, but shall, on the death of that person under that age, go as freehold land conveyed as aforesaid would go.

(4.) Land acquired as aforesaid may be made a substituted security for any charge in respect of money actually raised, and remaining unpaid, from which the settled land, or any part thereof, or any undivided share therein, has heretofore been released on the occasion and in order to the completion of a sale, exchange, or partition.

(5.) Where a charge does not affect the whole of the settled land, then the land acquired shall not be subjected thereto, unless the land is acquired either by purchase with money arising from sale of land which was before the sale subject to the charge, or by an exchange or partition of land which, or an undivided share wherein, was before the exchange or partition subject to the charge.

(6.) On land being so acquired, any person who, by the direction of the tenant for life, so conveys the

land as to subject it to any charge, is not concerned to inquire whether or not it is proper that the land should be subjected to the charge.

(7.) The provisions of this section referring to land extend and apply, as far as may be, to mines and minerals, and to easements, rights, and privileges over and in relation to land.

Sect. 32. Where, under an Act incorporating or applying, wholly or in part, the Lands Clauses Consolidation Acts, 1845, 1860, and 1869, or under the Settled Estates Act, 1877, or under any other Act, public, local, personal, or private, money is at the commencement of this Act in Court, or is afterwards paid into Court, and is liable to be laid out in the purchase of land to be made subject to a settlement, then, in addition to any mode of dealing therewith authorized by the Act under which the money is in Court, that money may be invested or applied as capital money arising under this Act, on the like terms, if any, respecting costs and other things, as nearly as circumstances admit, and (notwithstanding anything in this Act) according to the same procedure, as if the modes of investment or application authorized by this Act were authorized by the Act under which the money is in Court.

Sect. 33. Where, under a settlement, money is in the hands of trustees, and is liable to be laid out in the purchase of land to be made subject to the settlement, then in addition to such powers of dealing therewith as the trustees have independently of this Act, they may, at the option of the tenant for life, invest or apply the same as capital money arising under this Act.

Sect. 34. Where capital money arising under this Act is purchase-money paid in respect of a lease for years, or life, or years determinable on life, or in respect of any other estate or interest in land less than the fee simple, or in respect of a reversion dependent on any such lease, estate, or interest, the trustees of the settlement or the Court, as the case may be, and in the case of the Court on the application of any party interested in that money, may, notwithstanding anything in this Act, require and cause the same to be laid out, invested, accumulated, and paid in such manner as, in the judgment of the trustees or of the Court, as the case may be, will give to the parties interested in that money the like benefit thered'rom as they might lawfully have had from the lease, estate, interest, or reversion in respect whered' the money was paid, or as near thereto as may be.

4. IMPROVEMENTS OF SETTLED ESTATES.

Sect. 25. Improvements authorized by this Act are the making or the execution on, or in connexion with, and for the benefit of settled land, of any of the following works, or of any works for any of the following purposes, and any operation incident to or necessary or proper in the execution of any of those works, or necessary or proper for carrying into effect any of those purposes, or for securing the full benefit of any of those works or purposes (namely):

(i.) Drainage, including the straightening, widening, or deepening of drains, streams, and watercourses:

(ii.) Irrigation; warping:

(iii.) Drains, pipes, and machinery for supply and distribution of sewage as manure:

I. SETTLED LAND ACT—STATUTES—contd.

(iv.) Embanking or weiring from a river or lake, or from the sea, or a tidal water .

(v.) Groynes; sea walls; defences against water:

(vi.) Inclosing; straightening of fences; redivision of fields :

(vii.) Reclamation; dry warping:

(viii.) Farm roads; private roads; roads or streets in villages or towns:

(ix.) Clearing; trenching; planting:

(x.) Cottages for labourers, farm servants, and artisans, employed on the settled land or not :

(xi.) Farmhouses, offices, and outbuildings, and other buildings for farm purposes:

(xii.) Saw-mills, scutch-mills, and other mills, water-wheels, engine-houses, and kilns, which will increase the value of the settled land for agricultural purposes or as woodland or otherwise:

(xiii.) Reservoirs, tanks, conduits, watercourses, pipes, wells, ponds, shafts, dams, weirs, sluices, and other works and machinery for supply and distribution of water for agricultural, manufacturing, or other purposes, or for domestic or other consumption;

(xiv.) Tramways; railways; canals; docks:

(xv.) Jetties, piers, and landing places on rivers, lakes, the sea, or tidal waters, for facilitating transport of persons and of agricultural stock and produce, and of manure and other things required for agricultural purposes, and of minerals, and of things required for mining purposes:

(xvi.) Markets and market-places:

(xvii.) Streets, roads, paths, squares, gardens, or other open spaces for the use, gratuitously or on payment, of the public or of individuals, or for dedication to the public, the same being necessary or proper in connection with the conversion of land into building land :

(xviii.) Sewers, drains, watercourses, pipe-making, fencing, paving, brick-making, tile-making, and other works necessary or proper in connection with any of the objects aforesaid :

(xix.) Trial pits for mines, and other preliminary works necessary or proper in connection with development of mines:

(xx.) Reconstruction, enlargement, or improvement of any of those works.

Sect. 26.—(1.) Where the tenant for life is desirous that capital money arising under this Act shall be applied in or towards payment for an improvement authorized by this Act, he may submit for approval to the trustees of the settlement, or to the Court, as the case may require, a scheme for the execution of the improvement, shewing the proposed expenditure thereon.

(2.) Where the capital money to be expended is in the hands of trustees, then, after a scheme is approved by them, the trustees may apply that money in or towards payment for the whole or part of any work or operation comprised in the improvement, on—

(i.) A certificate of the Land Commissioners

I. SETTLED LAND ACT—STATUTES—contd.

certifying that the work or operation, or some specified part thereof, has been properly executed, and what amount is properly payable by the trustees in respect thereof, which certificate shall be conclusive in favour of the trustees as an authority and discharge for any payment made by them in pursuance thereof ; or on

(ii.) A like certificate of a competent engineer or able practical surveyor nominated by the trustees and approved by the Commissioners or by the Court, which certificate shall be conclusive as aforesaid; or on

(iii.) An order of the Court directing or authorizing the trustees to so apply a specified portion of the capital money.

(3) Where the capital money to be expended is in Court, then, after a scheme is approved by the Court, the Court may, if it thinks fit, on a report or certificate of the Commissioner or of a competent engineer or able practical surveyor approved by the Court, or on such other evidence as the Court thinks sufficient, make such order and give such directions as it thinks fit for the application of that money, or any part thereof, in or towards payment for the whole or part of any work or operation comprised in the improvement.

Sect. 27. The tenant for life may join or concur with any other person interested in executing any improvement authorized by this Act, or in contributing to the cost thereof.

Sect. 28.—(1.) The tenant for life and each of his successors in title having, under the settlement, a limited estate or interest only in the settled land, shall during such period, if any, as the Land Commissioners by certificate in any case prescribe, maintain and repair, at his own expense, every improvement executed under the foregoing provisions of this Act, and where a building or work in its nature insurable against damage by fire is comprised in the improvement, shall insure and keep insured the same, at his own expense, in such amount, if any, as the Commissioners by certificate in any case prescribe.

(2.) The tenant for life or any of his successors as aforesaid, shall not cut down or knowingly permit to be cut down, except in proper thinning, any trees planted as an improvement under the foregoing provisions of this Act.

(3.) The tenant for life and each of his successors as aforesaid, shall from time to time if required by the Commissioners, on or without the suggestion of any person having, under the settlement, any estate or interest in the settled land in possession, remainder, or otherwise, report to the Commissioners the state of every improvement executed under this Act, and the fact and particulars of fire insurance, if any.

(4.) The Commissioners may vary any certificate made by them under this section, in such manner or to such extent as circumstances appear to them to require, but not so as to increase the liabilities of the tenant for life, or any of his successors as aforesaid.

(5.) If the tenant for life, or any of his successors as aforesaid fail in any respect to comply with the requisitions of this section, or does any act in contravention thereof, any person having under the settlement, any estate or interest in the settled land

I. SETTLED LAND ACT—STATUTES—*contd.*

in possession, remainder, or reversion, shall have a right of action, in respect of that default or act, against the tenant for life; and the estate of the tenant for life, after his death, shall be liable to make good to the persons entitled under the settlement any damages occasioned by that default or act.

Execution and Repair of Improvements.] *Sect.* 29. *The tenant for life, and each of his successors in title having, under the settlement, a limited estate or interest only in the settled land, and all persons employed by or under contract with the tenant for life, or any such successor, may from time to time enter on the settled land, and without impeachment of waste by any remainderman or reversioner, thereon execute any improvement authorized by this Act, or inspect, maintain, and repair the same, and, for the purposes thereof, on the settled land, do, make, and use all acts, works, and conveniences proper for the execution, maintenance, repair, and use thereof, and get and work freestone, limestone, clay, sand, and other substances, and make tramways and other ways, and burn and make bricks, tiles, and other things, and cut down and use timber and other trees not planted or left standing for shelter or ornament.*

Improvement of Land Act, 1864.] *Sect.* 30. *The enumeration of improvements contained in sect. 9 of the Improvement of Land Act, 1864, is hereby extended so as to comprise, subject and according to the provisions of that Act, but only as regards applications made to the Land Commissioners after the commencement of this Act, all improvements authorized by this Act.*

5. PROTECTION OF SETTLED ESTATES.

Sect. 36. *The Court may, if it thinks fit, approve of any action, defence, petition to Parliament, parliamentary opposition, or other proceeding taken or proposed to be taken for protection of settled land, or of any action or proceeding taken or proposed to be taken for recovery of land, being, or alleged to be, subject to a settlement, and may direct that any costs, charges, or expenses incurred or to be incurred in relation thereto, or any part thereof, be paid out of property subject to the settlement.*

6. TRUSTEES.

Sect. 38.—(1). *If at any time there are no trustees of a settlement within the definition in this Act, or where in any other case it is expedient, for purposes of this Act, that new trustees of a settlement be appointed, the Court may, if it thinks fit, on the application of the tenant for life or of any other person having under the settlement an estate or interest in the settled land, in possession, remainder, or otherwise, or, in the case of an infant, if his testamentary or other guardian, or next friend, appoint fit persons to be trustees under the settlement for purposes of this Act.*

(2.) *The person so appointed, and the survivors and survivor of them, while continuing to be trustees or trustee, and, until the appointment of new trustees, the personal representatives or representative for the time being of the last surviving or continuing trustee, shall, for the purposes of this Act, become and be the trustees or trustee of the settlement.*

Sect. 39.—(1.) *Notwithstanding anything in this*

I. SETTLED LAND ACT—STATUTES—*contd.*

Act capital money arising under this Act shall not be paid to fewer than two persons as trustees of a settlement, unless the settlement authorizes the receipt of capital trust money of the settlement by one trustee.

(2.) *Subject thereto, the provisions of this Act referring to the trustees of a settlement apply to the surviving or continuing trustees or trustee of the settlement for the time being.*

Sect. 40. *The receipt in writing of the trustees of a settlement, or where one trustee is empowered to act, of one trustee, or of the personal representatives or representative of the last surviving or continuing trustee, for any money or securities, paid or transferred to the trustees, trustee, representatives, or representative, as the case may be, effectually discharges the payer or transferor therefrom, and from being bound to see to the application or being answerable for any loss or misapplication thereof, and, in case of a mortgages or other person advancing money, from being concerned to see that any money advanced by him is wanted for any purpose of this Act, or that no more than is wanted is raised.*

Sect. 41. *Each person who is for the time being trustee of a settlement is answerable for what he actually receives only, notwithstanding his signing any receipt for conformity, and in respect of his own acts, receipts, and defaults only, and is not answerable in respect of those of any other trustee, or of any banker, broker, or other person, or for the insufficiency or deficiency of any securities, or for any loss not happening through his own wilful default.*

Sect. 42. *The trustees of a settlement, or any of them, are not liable for giving any consent, or for not making, bringing, taking, or doing any such application, action, proceeding, or thing, as they might make, bring, take, or do; and in case of purchase of land with capital money arising under this Act, or of an exchange, partition, or lease, are not liable for adopting any contract made by the tenant for life, or bound to inquire as to the propriety of the purchase, exchange, partition, or lease, or answerable as regards any price, consideration, or fine, and are not liable to see to or answerable for the investigation of the title, or answerable for a conveyance of land, if the conveyance purports to convey the land in the proper mode, or liable in respect of purchase-money paid by them by direction of the tenant for life to any person joining in the conveyance as a conveying party, or as giving a receipt for the purchase-money, or in any other character, or in respect of any other money paid by them by direction of the tenant for life on the purchase, exchange, partition, or lease.*

Sect. 43. *The trustees of a settlement may reimburse themselves or pay and discharge out of the trust property all expenses properly incurred by them.*

Sect. 44. *If at any time a difference arises between a tenant for life and the trustees of the settlement, respecting the exercise of any of the powers of this Act, or respecting any matter relating thereto, the Court may, on the application of either party, give such directions respecting the matter in difference, and respecting the costs of the application, as the Court thinks fit.*

Sect. 45.—(1.) *A tenant for life when intending*

I. SETTLED LAND ACT—STATUTES—*contd.*

to make a sale, exchange, partition, lease, mortgage, or charge, shall give notice *of* his intention in that behalf to each *of* the trustees *of* the settlement, by posting registered letters, containing the notice, addressed to the trustees, severally, each at his usual or last known place *of* abode in the United Kingdom, and shall give like notice to the solicitor *for* the trustees, *if* any such solicitor is known to the tenant *for* life, by posting a registered letter, containing the notice, addressed to the solicitor at his place *of* business in the United Kingdom, every letter under this section being posted not less than one month before the making by the tenant *for* life *of* the sale, exchange, partition, lease, mortgage, or charge, or *of* a contract *for* the same.

(2.) Provided that at the date *of* notice given the number *of* trustees shall ·not· be less than two, unless a contrary intention is expressed in the settlement.

(3.) · A person dealing in good *faith* with the tenant *for* life is not concerned to inquire respecting the giving *of* any such notice as is required by this section.

Notice.] The Act 47 & 48 *Vict.* c. 18, ss. 5 and 6, modifies the above requirements as to notice. .

7. LIMITED OWNERS.

Sect. 58 *of* the Act 45 & 46 *Vict.* c. 38.—(1.) Each person as *follows* shall, when the estate or interest *of* each *of* them is in possession, have the powers *of* a tenant *for* life under this Act, as *if* each *of* them were a tenant *for* life as defined in this Act (namely):

(i.) A tenant in tail, including a tenant in tail *who* is by Act *of* Parliament restrained *from* barring or defeating his estate tail, ·and although the reversion is in the Crown, and so that the exercise by him of his powers under this Act shall bind the Crown, but not including such a tenant in tail where the land whereof he is so restrained was purchased with money provided by Parliament in consideration *of* public services :

(ii.) A tenant in fee simple, with an executory limitation, gift, or disposition over, on *failure of* his issue, or in any other event :

(iii.) A person entitled to a base fee, although the reversion is in the Crown, and so that the exercise by him *of* his powers under this Act shall bind the Crown :

(iv.) A tenant *for* years determinable on life, not holding merely under a lease at a rent :

(v.) A tenant *for* the life *of* another, not holding merely under a lease at a rent :

(vi.) A tenant *for* his own or any other life. or *for* years determinable on life, whose estate is liable to cease in any event during that life, whether by expiration *of* the estate, or by conditional limitation, or otherwise, or ·to· be defeated by an executory limitation, gift, or disposition over, or is subject to a trust *for* accumulation *of* income *for* payment *of* debts or other purpose :

(vii.) A tenant in tail after possibility *of* issue extinct :

(viii.) A tenant by the curtesy :

(ix.) A person entitled to the income *of* land under a trust or direction *for* payment

---

I. SETTLED LAND ACT—STATUTES—*contd.*

thereof to him during his own or any other life, whether subject to expenses *of* management or not, or until sale *of* the land, or until *forfeiture* of his interest therein on bankruptcy or other event.

(2.) In every such case, the provisions *of* this Act referring to a tenant for life, either as conferring powers on him or otherwise, and to a settlement, and to settled land shall extend to each *of* the persons aforesaid, and to the instrument under which his estate or interest arises, and to the land therein comprised.

(3.) In any such case any reference in this Act to death as regards a tenant for life, shall, where necessary, be deemed to refer to the determination by death or otherwise *of* such estate or interest as last aforesaid.

8. SETTLEMENT BY WAY OF TRUSTS FOR SALE.

Sect. 63.—(1.) Any land, or any estate or interest in land, which under or by virtue *of* any deed. will, or agreement, covenant to surrender, copy *of* Court roll, Act *of* Parliament, or other instrument or any number *of* instruments, whether made or passed before or after, or partly before and partly after, the commencement *of* this Act, is subject to a trust or direction for sale *of* that land, estate, or interest, and *for* the application or disposal of the money to arise *from* the sale, or the income *of* that money, or the income *of* the land until sale, or any part *of* that money or income, for the benefit *of* any person for his life, or any other limited period, or *for* the benefit of two or more persons concurrently *for* any limited period, and whether absolutely, or subject to a trust *for* accumulation *of* income for payment *of* debts or other purpose, or to any other restriction, shall be deemed to be settled land, and the instrument or instruments under which the trust arises shall be deemed to be a settlement ; and the person *for* the time being beneficially entitled to the income *of* the land, estate, or interest aforesaid until sale, whether absolutely or subject as aforesaid, shall be deemed to be tenant *for* life thereof ; or if two or more persons are so entitled concurrently, then those persons shall be deemed to constitute together the tenant *for* life thereof ; and the persons, if any, who are *for* the time being under the settlement trustees *for* sale *of* the settled land, or having power *of* consent to, or approval *of*, or control over the sale, or if under the settlement there are no such trustees, then the persons, if any, for the time being, who are by the settlement declared to be trustees thereof *for* purposes *of* this Act are *for* purposes *of* this Act trustees *of* the settlement.

(2.) In every such case the provisions *of* this Act referring to a tenant *for* life, and to a settlement, and to settled land, shall extend to the person or persons aforesaid, and to the instrument or instruments under which his or their estate or interest arises, and to the land therein comprised, subject and except as in this section provided (that is to say):

(i.) Any reference in this Act to the predecessors or successors in title *of* the tenant *for* life, or to the remaindermen, or reversioners or other persons interested in the settled land, shall be deemed to refer to the persons interested in succession or otherwise in the

I. SETTLED LAND ACT—STATUTES—cotnd.

money to arise from sale of the land, or the income of that money, or the income of the land, until sale (as the case may require).

(ii.) Capital money arising under this Act from the settled land shall not be applied in the purchase of land unless such application is authorized by the settlement in the case of capital money arising thereunder from sales or other dispositions of the settled land, but may, in addition to any other mode of application authorized by this Act, be applied in any mode in which capital money arising under the settlement from any such sale or other disposition is applicable thereunder, subject to any consent required or direction given by the settlement with respect to the application of trust money of the settlement.

(iii.) Capital money arising under this Act from the settled land and the securities in which the same is invested, shall not for any purpose of disposition, transmission, or devolution, be considered as land unless the same would, if arising under the settlement from a sale or disposition of the settled land, have been so considered, and the same shall be held in trust for and shall go to the same persons successively in the same manner, and for and on the same estates, interests, and trusts as the same would have gone and been held if arising under the settlement from a sale or disposition of the settled land, and the income of such capital money and securities shall be paid or applied accordingly.

Restrictions.] The Act 47 & 48 Vict. c. 18, s. 7, enacts that these powers shall only be exercised by leave of the Court, and makes other provisions with regard to them.

9. PROCEDURE.—LAND COMMISSIONERS.

Sect. 46 of the Act 45 & 46 Vict. c. 38.—(1.) All matters within the jurisdiction of the Court under this Act shall, subject to the Act regulating the Court, be assigned to the Chancery Division of the Court.

(2.) Payment of money into Court effectually exonerates therefrom the person making the payment.

(3.) Every application to the Court shall be by petition, or by summons at Chambers.

(4.) On an application by the trustees of a settlement notice shall be served in the first instance on the tenant for life.

(5.) On an application notice shall be served on such persons, if any, as the Court thinks fit.

(6.) The Court shall have full power and discretion to make such order as it thinks fit respecting the costs, charges, or expenses of all or any of the parties to any application, and may, if it thinks fit, order that all or any of those costs, charges, or expenses be paid out of property subject to the settlement.

(7.) General Rules for purposes of this Act shall be deemed Rules of Court within sect. 17 of the Appellate Jurisdiction Act, 1876, as altered by sect. 19 of the Supreme Court of Judicature Act, 1881, and may be made accordingly.

(8.) The powers of the Court may, as regards land in the County Palatine of Lancaster, be exercised also by the Court of Chancery of the County Palatine; and Rules for regulating proceedings in that Court shall be from time to time made by the Chancellor of the Duchy of Lancaster, with the advice and consent of a Judge of the High Court acting in the Chancery Division, and of the Vice-Chancellor of the County Palatine.

(9.) General Rules, and Rules for the Court of Chancery of the County Palatine, may be made at any time after the passing of this Act, to take effect on or after the commencement of this Act.

(10.) The powers of the Court may, as regards land not exceeding in capital value £500, or in annual rateable value £30, and, as regards capital money arising under this Act, and securities in which the same is invested, not exceeding in amount or value £500, and as regards personal chattels settled or to be settled, as in this Act mentioned, not exceeding in value £500, be exercised by any County Court within the district whereof is situate any part of the land which is to be dealt with in the Court, or from which the capital money to be dealt with in the Court arises under this Act, or in connexion with which the personal chattels to be dealt with in the Court are settled.

(47.) Where the Court directs that any costs, charges, or expenses be paid out of property subject to a settlement, the same shall, subject and according to the directions of the Court, be raised and paid out of capital money arising under this Act, or other money liable to be laid out in the purchase of land to be made subject to the settlement, or out of investments representing such money, or out of income of any such money or investments, or out of any accumulations of income of land, money, or investments, or by means of a sale of part of the settled land in respect whereof the costs, charges, or expenses are incurred, or of other settled land comprised in the same settlement and subject to the same limitations, or by means of a mortgage of the settled land or any part thereof, to be made by such person as the Court directs, and either by conveyance of the fee simple or other estate or interest the subject of the settlement, or by creation of a term, or otherwise, or by means of a charge on the settled land or any part thereof, or partly in one of those modes and partly in another or others, or in any such other mode as the Court thinks fit.

Land Commissioners.] Sect. 48.—(1.) The Commissioners now bearing the three several styles of the Inclosure Commissioners for England and Wales, and the Copyhold Commissioners, and the Tithe Commissioners for England and Wales, shall, by virtue of this Act, become and shall be styled the Land Commissioners for England.

(2.) The Land Commissioners shall cause one seal to be made with their style as given by this Act, and in the execution and discharge of any power or duty under any Act relating to the three several bodies of Commissioners aforesaid, they shall adopt and use the seal and style of the Land Commissioners for England and no other.

(3.) Nothing in the foregoing provisions of this section shall be construed as altering in any respect the powers, authorities, or duties of the Land Commissioners, or as affecting in respect of appointment, salary, pension, or otherwise any of those Commissioners, in office at the passing of this Act,

I. SETTLED LAND ACT—STATUTES—contd.

or any assistant Commissioner, secretary, or other officer or person then in office or employed under them.

(4.) *All Acts of Parliament, judgments, decrees, or orders of any Court, awards, deeds, and other documents, passed or made before the commencement of this Act, shall be read and have effect as if the Land Commissioners were therein mentioned instead of one or more of the three several bodies of Commissioners aforesaid.*

(5.) *All acts, matters, and things commenced by or under the authority of any one or more of the three several bodies of Commissioners aforesaid before the commencement of this Act, and not then completed, shall and may be carried on and completed by or under the authority of the Land Commissioners; and the Land Commissioners for the purpose of prosecuting, or defending, and carrying on any action, suit or proceeding pending at the commencement of this Act, shall come into the place of any one or more, as the case may require, of the three several bodies of Commissioners aforesaid.*

(6.) *The Land Commissioners shall, by virtue of this Act, have, for the purposes of any Act, public, local, personal, or private, passed or to be passed, making provisions for the execution of improvements on settled land, all such powers and authorities as they have for the purposes of the Improvement of Land Act, 1864, and the provisions of the last mentioned Act relating to their proceedings and inquiries, and to authentication of instruments, and to declarations, statements, notices, applications, forms, security for expenses, inspections, and examinations, shall extend and apply, as far as the nature and circumstances of the case admit, to acts and proceedings done or taken by or in relation to the Land Commissioners under any Act making provision as last aforesaid; and the provisions of any Act relating to fees or to security for costs to be taken in respect of the business transacted under the Acts administered by the three several bodies of Commissioners aforesaid shall extend and apply to the business transacted by or under the direction of the Land Commissioners under any Act, public, local, personal, or private, passed or to be passed, by which any power or duty is conferred or imposed on them.*

Sect. 49.—(1.) *Every certificate and report approved and made by the Land Commissioners under this Act shall be filed in their office.*

(2.) *An office copy of any certificate or report as filed shall be delivered out of their office to any person requiring the same, on payment of the proper fee, and shall be sufficient evidence of the certificate or report whereof it purports to be a copy.*

(4.) *Land of whatever tenure acquired under this Act by purchase or in exchange, or on partition, shall be conveyed to and vested in the trustees of the settlement, on the trusts and subject to the powers and provisions which, under the settlement or by reason of the exercise of any power of appointment or charging therein contained, are subsisting with respect to the settled land, or would be so subsisting if the same had not been sold, or as near thereto as circumstance permit, but so as not to increase or multiply charges or powers of charging.*

Buildings for Working Classes.] *The Act*

I. SETTLED LAND ACT—STATUTES—contd.

48 & 49 *Vict. c.* 72, *s.* 11, *amends the Settled Land Act, 1882, with regard to any sale, exchange, or lease of land for buildings for the working classes.*

II. SETTLED LAND ACT—DEFINITIONS.

1. —— **Limited Owner** — *Contingency of attaining Twenty-one—Executory Limitations—Infant—Appointment of Trustee*—45 & 46 *Vict.* c. 38, *s.* 58, *sub-s* 1, *cl.* (*ii.*).] Certain estates were devised to the use of the testator's wife and G. T., upon trust to pay the net rents and income of the estates to the wife for the maintenance, education, and benefit of the testator's son until he should attain twenty-one, and without being liable to account to the trustees or to the son for the same; and upon the son's attaining twenty-one, then upon trust for him absolutely: but if he should die under twenty-one without leaving issue, then upon trust to permit the wife to receive such rents and income for her life, and after her death upon the trusts therein mentioned:—*Held*, under the Settled Land Act, 1882, s. 58, sub-s. 2, that the infant son had the powers of a tenant for life, being tenant in fee simple with an executory limitation over in case of dying under twenty-one without issue. The trustees of the will appointed trustees for the purposes of the Act. *In re* MORGAN
[24 Ch. D. 114

2. —— **Limited Owner** — *Conditional Life Estate*—45 & 46 *Vict.* c. 38, *ss.* 51, 58, *sub-s.* 1, *cl.* vi. —*Person having Powers of Tenant or Life—Invalidity of Condition—Application of Proceeds of Sale of Estate.*] A testator devised his B. estate to the use of his son, " so long as he shall reside in my present dwelling-house, or upon some part of my B. estate, for not less than three months in each year after he shall become entitled to the actual possession thereof;" and, after the death of the son, provided that he should have complied with the condition, to such uses for the benefit of his children as he should by will appoint; and, in default of such appointment, or, if he should fail in compliance with the above condition, on the determination of his estate therein, to the use of trustees, on trust for sale and distribution of the proceeds of sale among the son's children:—*Held*, that the son had the powers of a tenant for life under the Settled Land Act, and could sell the estate, and that, notwithstanding the condition as to residence, he would, by virtue of sect. 51 of the Act, be entitled to the income of the proceeds of sale during his life. *In re* PAGET'S SETTLED ESTATES   -   **30 Ch. D. 161**

3. —— **Limited Owner**—*Settled Land Act,* 1882 (45 & 46 *Vict.* c. 38), *s.* 58, *sub-ss.* 1, *cl.* (*iv.*), (*vi.*).— *Leasehold Interest — Estate determinable with Lease.*] A testator who had granted a lease of a house for a term of thirty-one years from the 25th of March, 1859, at a rent of £50 a year, by his will, dated the 20th of June, 1866, devised his freehold interest in such house to trustees upon trust to permit his wife to receive the rent for her own benefit " during the remainder of the term granted by the said lease if she should so long live " and in case she should die " before the expiration of the term created by such lease " then he gave and devised the house to the children of his brother in fee, and he directed that if his wife should " happen to live after the expiration of the term

I. SETTLED LAND ACT — DEFINITIONS — continued.

created by such lease" then the trustees should sell the house, and out of the income from the interest of the proceeds pay £50 a year to his wife during her life, and subject thereto he gave the residue of the proceeds for his brother's children. The testator died in 1866, and the question being raised whether his widow could, under the Settled Land Act, 1882, accept a surrender of such lease and grant a new lease of the house for a term of twenty-one years from the 25th of December, 1883, at an increased rent :—*Held* (affirming the decision of Pearson, J.), that the widow was not a person under sect. 58 of that Act entitled to the powers of a tenant for life and was therefore not able to accept a surrender and make a new lease of the house *In re* HAZLE'S SETTLED ESTATES　　　　-　26 Ch. D. 428 ; 29 Ch. D. 78

4. —— **Limited Owner** — *Settled Land Act, 1882 (45 & 46 Vict. c. 38), s. 2, sub-ss. 5, 7, 10, cl. (i.) ; s. 58, sub-s. 1, cl. (ix.)—Power of Sale— ' Person entitled to the income of land."*] Subject to a term for raising certain sums, freehold estates were devised to the use of trustees during the life of A.'s children and issue. The trustees of the life estate were directed to enter into possession of and manage the property, pay outgoings, keep down the interest on incumbrances, and during A.'s life pay out of the residue an annuity of £400 to the person next entitled in remainder, and pay the ultimate residue to A. The estates were so heavily encumbered that after payment of outgoings and interest there was not enough to pay the annuity of £400. A. therefore had received nothing, and there was no prospect of his receiving anything for many years : —*Held*, (affirming the decision of Bacon, V.C.), that A. was a person entitled to the income of land under a trust or direction for payment thereof to him during his life, subject to expenses of management within the meaning of the Settled Land Act, 1882, sect. 58, sub-sect. 1, clause (ix.), and therefore possessed the power of selling given by the Act to tenants for life. *In re* JONES　-　24 Ch. D. 583 ; [26 Ch. D. 736

5. —— **Limited Owner**—*45 & 46 Vict. c. 38, s. 2, sub-s. 5 ; s. 56, sub-s. 2, s. 58, sub-s. 1, cl. (ix.)—Tenant for Life.*] Testator by will, dated the 8th of August, 1883, limited an estate to the use of trustees for a term of 1300 years, and subject thereto to his second son H. S. for life, with remainders over in strict settlement. The trusts of the term were to raise portions, to pay annuities, H. S. himself being one of the annuitants, and to apply the residue as a sinking fund to pay off mortgage debts and other charges. The income of the estate was about £26,000 a year, and the amount of the charges about £175,000. It was estimated that the trusts of the term would require from fifteen to twenty years for their fulfilment. The testator directed that the trustees should "during the continuance of the last mentioned trusts" enter into and hold possession of the rents and profits of the estate, and not deliver the same to any *person* beneficially interested in any part thereof," and manage the estate as therein mentioned. Very full powers of management were given to the trustees, and

II. SETTLED LAND ACT —DEFINITIONS — continued.

the testator provided that when all the trusts of the term should have been fully paid and satisfied the term should then cease. He moreover gave to the trustees such other powers over the estate as were given to a tenant for life in possession by the Settled Land Act, 1882:—*Held*, that H. S. was not a mere annuitant, but was tenant for life, or a person having the powers of a tenant for life, of the estate within the meaning of sect. 58, sub-sect. 1, cl. (ix.) of the Settled Land Act, 1882, and that his consent was necessary under sect. 56, sub-sect. 2, to the effectual exercise by the trustees of the powers of sale and enfranchisement contained in the will. *In re* CLITHEROE ESTATE [28 Ch. D. 378 [Affirmed by the Court of Appeal, 31 Ch. D. 135.]

6. —— **Limited Owner**—*Tenant for Life— Persons having Powers of Tenant for Life—Discretionary Trust for Application of Income during Life —Forfeiture in Event of Bankruptcy—Settled Land Act, 1882 (45 & 46 Vict. c. 38), s. 2, sub-ss. 5, 6, 10, cl. i. 51, 58, sub-s. 1, cls. vi. ix.*] The words "entitled to possession of settled land for his life," as used in sub-sect. 5 of sect. 2 of the Settled Land Act, 1882, mean entitled " in possession" as distinguished from entitled "in reversion," and the words in sub-sect. 6, "two or more persons so entitled as tenants in common, or as joint tenants," mean entitled " for life." — A testator devised real estate to the use of trustees in fee during the life of his son, on trust to receive the rents, and after payment of costs and outgoings, to hold the residue of the rents upon the trusts thereinafter mentioned. And after the death of the son, to the use of his first and other sons successively in tail male, with remainders over. And the testator directed that his trustees should during the life of the son pay and apply the residue of the rents which should during his life become payable to them in such manner in all respects as they should think best for the maintenance, or otherwise for the benefit of the son and of his wife and his child and children, or for the benefit of any one or more of them, and so that, in case the son should at any time assign, charge, or attempt to anticipate his interest under the will, or should do any act whereby, either directly or by operation of law, he would, if absolutely entitled to such interest, be deprived, or liable to be deprived, of the benefit or enjoyment thereof, then the trust thereinbefore declared in his favour should absolutely cease, and the rents should thenceforth during his life be applied by the trustees, either for the maintenance, support, or benefit of the son, or for such other purposes and in such manner in all respects as the trustees should in their absolute discretion think fit. There being no children of the son and he not having forfeited his interest under the will :—*Held*, that he and his wife did not together constitute a tenant for life of the estate by virtue of sub-sect. 6 of sect. 2 of the Settled Land Act, 1882, and that they had not, by virtue of sect. 58, the powers of a tenant for life under the Act. *In re* ATKINSON. ATKINSON *v.* BRUCE　-　-　-　30 Ch. D. 605 [Affirmed by the Court of Appeal.]

7. —— **Settlement**—*45 & 46 Vict. c. 38, s. 2,*

3 A

II. SETTLED LAND ACT—DEFINITIONS— *continued.*

sub-s. 1 — *Original and derivative Settlements.*] When a complete settlement of land has been made, and derivative settlements have been afterwards made by persons who take interests (not yet in possession) under the original settlement, the original settlement alone is the settlement for the purposes of the Settled Land Act. *In re* KNOWLES' SETTLED ESTATES　　27 Ch. D. 707

III. SETTLED LAND ACT—DISABILITIES.

1. —— Infant — *Trustees — Sale out of Court —Settled Land Act, 1882 (45 & 46 Vict. c. 38), ss.* 3, 59, 60.] In appointing trustees under the Settled Land Act, 1882, to sell an infant's estate (ss. 3, 59, 60), the Court has jurisdiction to authorize the sale to be made out of Court. *In re* PRICE. LEIGHTON *v.* PRICE　　27 Ch. D. 552

2. —— Lunatic—*Notice to Trustees—Sale by Tenant for Life—45 & 46 Vict. c. 38, s. 45—Sanction of Court of Lunacy.*] The committee of a lunatic tenant for life cannot give a valid notice under sect. 45 unless he has previously obtained authority from the Court of Lunacy to do so. *In re* RAY'S SETTLED ESTATES　　25 Ch. D. 464

IV. SETTLED LAND ACT—PURCHASE-MONEY.

1. —— Improvements—*Heirlooms—Power of Tenant for Life to sell—Leave of the Court— Settled Land Act, 1882 (45 & 46 Vict. c. 38), s.* 21, *sub-s.* vii.; *s.* 25, *sub-ss.* 1., iii., x., xi., xiii.; *s.* 37—*Settled Land Act, 1884 (47 & 48 Vict. c.* 18), *s.* 7.] A tenant for life under a settlement containing a discretionary trust for sale of the settled estates, and also a power to sell certain settled heirlooms, asked leave of the Court under sect. 37 of the Settled Land Act, 1882, that he might be authorized to sell part of the settled estates, and also a specified portion of the heirlooms; that the money might be paid to the trustees, and that such part as might be necessary might be applied by them in paying for certain improvements, consisting of (1) a larger and better supply of water to a mansion-house; (2) a new and improved system of drainage of the mansion-house; (3) rebuilding of the stables, which were out of repair; (4) the building of an agent's house; and (5) the building of two cottages.—The trustees submitted that the proposed improvements (except the cottages) were not within the 25th section of the Act of 1882; and, that even if they were the Court would not supersede the power of the trustees by giving leave to the tenant for life to sell either the estate or the heirlooms:—*Held,* that the proposed outlay was all within sect. 25 of the Settled Land Act, 1882; and would have been authorized without the statute; and leave given to the tenant for life to sell both the settled estates and the heirlooms, and for the application of the proceeds as prayed. *In re* HOUGHTON ESTATE　　30 Ch. D. 102

2. —— Income—45 & 46 Vict. c. 38, s. 34— *Lands Clauses Consolidation Act, 1845 (8 & 9 Vict. c.* 18), *s.* 74—*Purchase-money of Lands subsequent to beneficial Lease—Tenant for Life and Remainderman—Application of Income.*] Sect. 34 of the Settled Land Act, 1882, and 74 of the Lands Clauses Consolidation Act, 1845, are similar enactments, so that where the facts are similar decisions on

IV. SETTLED LAND ACT—PURCHASE-MONEY —*continued.*

sect. 74 are authorities on sect. 34.—As between tenant for life and remainderman, where lands subject to a beneficial lease are sold under the Settled Land Act, 1882, the tenant for life will, during the unexpired period of the term, be entitled to so much only of the income of the invested purchase-moneys as equals the rents under the lease, and the rest of that income must be accumulated and invested for the benefit of the inheritance until the date when the lease would have expired.—*In re Mette's Estate* (Law Rep. 7 Eq. 72), *In re Wootton's Estate* (Law Rep. 1 Eq. 589), and *In re Wilkes' Estate* (16 Ch. D. 597) approved. COTTRELL *v.* COTTRELL　28 Ch. D. 628

3. —— Incumbrances — *Discharge of Incumbrances affecting part of Estate—Settled Land Act, 1882 (45 & 46 Vict. c.* 38), *ss.* 21, 51, 53, 56.] A settlement of land was made in 1853 by a private Act of Parliament. By this Act the estates were vested in the trustees thereby appointed, upon trust by sale or mortgage thereof to raise money for the purpose of discharging certain incumbrances and liabilities. The Act provided that the trustees might from time to time absolutely sell and dispose of all or any part of the estates mentioned in a schedule, provided that the trustees should not sell any of the lands situate in the parishes of C. and H., unless it should be absolutely necessary for the purposes of the Act to do so, and in case of such necessity should not sell any of those lands until all the rest of the estates were sold. —After the Settled Land Act, 1882, had come into operation the tenant for life entered into a contract to sell some of the lands situate in the parishes of C. and H. The whole of the rest of the estates had not then been sold :—*Held,* that under sub-sect. 2 of sect. 21 of the Settled Land Act, the purchase-money could be applied in discharging a mortgage which affected part of the land sold and another mortgage which affected another part of the settled estate, and that it was not necessary that the other mortgage should be one affecting the whole of the settled estates. *In re* CHAYTOR'S SETTLED ESTATE ACT　25 Ch. D. 651

4. —— Incumbrances—45 & 46 Vict. c. 38, ss. 21, sub-s. ii., 37, 53—*Heirlooms—Sale—Application of Proceeds—Discharge of Incumbrances.*] The money arising by the sale, on the application of the tenant for life with the sanction of the Court, of chattels treated in a settlement as heirlooms, and so far as the rules of law and equity would permit annexed to the settled freehold land, may be applied in the discharge of incumbrances affecting the inheritance of settled land, without keeping such incumbrances on foot for the benefit of the infant remainderman in whom the heirlooms would, if unsold, have vested absolutely on his attaining twenty-one. *In re* DUKE OF MARLBOROUGH'S SETTLEMENT. DUKE OF MARLBOROUGH *v.* MARJORIBANKS -　　30 Ch. D. 127
[Affirmed by the Court of Appeal.]

5. —— Incumbrances—45 & 46 Vict. c. 38, ss. 21, 25, 26, 53—*Land Drainage Charges—Improvement of Land Act, 1864 (27 & 28 Vict. c.* 114), ss. 49, 51, 66.] Where a tenant for life of settled land has prior to the Settled Land Act, 1882, created charges for land drainage and improve-

IV. SETTLED LAND ACT—PURCHASE-MONEY
—*continued.*

ments under the Improvement of Land Act, 1864, and other Acts, which were repayable by instalments, he will not be entitled under the Settled Land Act, s. 21, sub-s. 2. to have these charges paid out of the capital of the settled estates so as to relieve him from the payment of the instalments. Trustees who purchase such charges will hold them upon trust to receive the instalments payable by the tenant for life, and to treat them as capital. The decision of Pearson, J., affirmed. *In re* KNATCHBULL'S SETTLED ESTATE   27 Ch. D. 349; 29 Ch. D. 588

6. —— Investment—*Charity—Settled Land Act,* 1882 (45 & 46 *Vict. c.* 38), *ss.* 21,'32.] Lands belonging absolutely to a charity were taken by a public body, and the purchase-money paid into Court under the Lands Clauses Act :—*Held,* that the purchase-money could be dealt with under the provisions of the 62nd section of the Settled Land Act, 1882, as " money liable to be laid out in the purchase of land to be made subject to a settlement." *In re* BYRON'S CHARITY
[23 Ch. D. 171

7. —— Investment — *Debenture Stock—Petition for Advice—Will—Money to be laid out in the purchase of Land to be settled in Strict Settlement —Settled Land Act,* 1882 (45 & 46 *Vict. c.* 38), *ss.* 2 (1), 21, 22 (2), (4), 33, 44, 51, 56 (2).] Where under a will money is bequeathed to trustees in trust to lay it out in the purchase of land, to be settled in strict settlement, the trustees may invest it in debenture stock in accordance with the provisions of sect. 21 of the Settled Land Act, 1882. *In re* MACKENZIE'S TRUSTS
[23 Ch. D. 750

V. SETTLED LAND ACT—RESTRICTIONS.

1. —— Mansion-house — Heirlooms — *Tenant for Life—Sale—Settled Land Act,* 1883 (45 & 46 *Vict. c.* 38), *ss.* 3, 15, 37—*Practice—Service.*] A testator bequeathed to his trustees certain articles as heirlooms to be annexed to his mansion-house and held in trust for the person for the time being entitled to the mansion-house under the equitable limitations thereinafter contained ; and he devised his mansion-house and estate, comprising about 360 acres, to the trustees upon trust for his son for life, with equitable remainders over in strict settlement for the benefit of the son's issue : and the testator directed that his mansion-house and certain lands thereto belonging, comprising about thirty acres, and described on a plan indorsed on the will, should be kept up as a place of residence for the person for the time being entitled to the possession thereof under his will, and that the heirlooms should at all times be kept in the mansion-house. Powers were given to the trustees to let, sell, or exchange any part of the settled estate except the mansion-house and lands described on the plan.—The testator's son, the tenant for life, being desirous of selling the whole estate under the powers of the Settled Land Act, 1882, applied to the Court under sect. 15 for leave to sell the excepted mansion-house and lands, on the ground that, owing to ill-health and permanent residence elsewhere, he was unable to reside in the man-

V. SETTLED LAND ACT — RESTRICTIONS —
continued.

sion-house, and also that inasmuch as the estate was in proximity to a large town, the bulk of the estate could not be sold advantageously without the mansion-house and adjoining lands. The summons did not ask for the sale of or contain any reference to the heirlooms :—*Held,* that, on the evidence, the case was a proper one for a sale of the mansion-house and adjoining lands, but that leave for sale would not be granted without some direction as to the disposal of the heirlooms. —The summons was then amended, with the consent of the trustees, by asking for leave to sell the heirlooms also, under sect. 37 of the Settled Land Act, 1882, by reference to an inventory verified by affidavit, whereupon an order was made for the sale of the heirlooms with liberty for the tenant for life to bid at such sale.—Service of the summons on the children of the tenant for life was dispensed with, their interests being sufficiently represented by the trustees, who had been served. *In re* BROWN'S WILL 27 Ch. D. 179

2. —— Title of Dignity—*Heirlooms—Incorporeal Hereditament — Land—Heirlooms devolving with Dignity—Sale of Heirlooms—Settled Land Act,* 1882 (45 & 46 *Vict. c.* 38), *s.* 2, *sub-s.* 10, *ss.* 37, 58—*Statute De Donis* (13 *Ed.* 1)—*Statute Westminster Second.*] A dignity or title of honour, as an incorporeal hereditament, is " land " within the meaning of the 37th section of the Settled Land Act, 1882.—When a dignity is limited to the heirs of the body, then although no place be named in the creation of the title, the dignity is within the statute *De Donis,* and descendible as an estate tail. and the patent does not create a fee simple conditional. — There is no difference in these respects between a baronetcy and other descendible dignities. The resolution reported 12 Rep. 81, *held* to be overruled.—The Settled Land Act, 1883, does not enable a limited owner to sell any property which, when vested in a tenant in fee simple, is by law inalienable. *In re* SIR J. RIVETT-CARNAC'S WILL   30 Ch. D. 136

VI. SETTLED LAND ACT—TENANT FOR LIFE (and LIMITED OWNER).

1. —— Sale——*Pendency of Administration Action*—45 & 46 *Vict. c.* 38, *s.* 3.] The pendency of an action by tenant for life in which a decree has been made for execution of the trusts of a settlement, does not prevent him from exercising his power of sale under the Settled Land Act, 1882, without the sanction of the Court. CARDIGAN *v.* CURZON-HOWE -   -   30 Ch. D. 531

2. —— Sale—*Private Act authorizing Trustees to sell—Restriction on Exercise—Power of Tenant for Life to sell—Settled Land Act,* 1882 (45 & 46 *Vict. v.* 38), *ss.* 21, 51, 53, 56.] A settlement of land was made in 1853 by a private Act of Parliament. By this Act the estates were vested in the trustees thereby appointed, upon trust by sale or mortgage thereof to raise money for the purpose of discharging certain incumbrances and liabilities. The Act provided that the trustees might from time to time absolutely sell and dispose of all or any part of the estates mentioned in a schedule, provided that the trustees should not sell any of the lands situate

VI. SETTLED LAND ACT—TENANT FOR LIFE (and LIMITED OWNER)—*continued.*

in the parishes of C. and H., unless it should be absolutely necessary for the purpose of the Act to do so, and in case of such necessity should not sell any of those lands until all the rest of the estates were sold.—After the Settled Land Act, 1882, had come into operation the tenant for life entered into a contract to sell some of the lands situate in the parishes of C. and H. The whole of the rest of the estates had not then been sold :—*Held,* that the power of sale conferred on the tenant for life by the Settled Land Act was an absolute power over and above that given to the trustees by the private Act, and that he was therefore entitled to sell free from the restriction imposed by the private Act on the trustees. *In re* CHAYTOR'S SETTLED ESTATE ACT **25 Ch. D. 651**

3. —— *Sale—Trust for Sale by Trustees after Death of Tenant for Life—Power of Tenant for Life to sell the Fee Simple—45 & 46 Vict. c. 38, s. 45—Will made in 1834—Sale of Property by the Reversioner in 1880—Notice under sect. 45 by Tenant for Life to Trustees of Settlement.*] J. W., by his will, devised an estate to trustees upon trust to receive and pay the rents to his grandson for life, and after his decease to sell and to stand possessed of the moneys for all the grandson's children. The tenant for life was upwards of seventy years of age, and a widower. He had one child only, a daughter, and she and her husband in July, 1880, contracted to sell her reversion in the estate of the Plaintiff. The Settled Land Act (45 & 46 Vict. c 38) came into operation in January, 1883, and the tenant for life at the end of that month advertised the estate for sale under the powers of the Act. The Plaintiff brought an action for an injunction to restrain the tenant for life from selling ; and to restrain the other Defendants, devisees of the legal estate under the will of the survivor of trustees of J. W.'s will appointed by the Court, from executing any assurance of the estate, and on motion for that purpose :—*Held,* that the tenant for life had power under the Act to sell the fee simple and inheritance of the property if he should comply with the provisions of the Act ; but held also that there were no trustees to whom he could under sect. 45, give notice ; and an injunction was granted to restrain him from selling until trustees had been properly appointed for the purposes of the Act.—*Held,* also, that the Plaintiff was entitled to be served with any summons for the appointment of new trustees, and (the Plaintiff objecting) that the Defendant's solicitor ought not to be appointed. WHEELWRIGHT *v.* WALKER **[23 Ch. D. 752**

VII. SETTLED LAND ACT—TRUSTEES.

1. —— *Appointment—Payment of Money out of Court.*] Where a testator's daughter was beneficial tenant for life of a fund paid into Court upon the compulsory purchase of the testator's property, the daughter being one of the two trustees of the will, and both trustees being desirous of resigning their trusts ; and there being no power of sale in the will.—The Court appointed two new trustees of the settlement effected by the will for the purposes of the Settled Land Act, 1882, and ordered the fund to be paid out to such

VII. SETTLED LAND ACT—TRUSTEES—*contd.*

trustees, to be held by them upon the trusts of the will. *In re* WRIGHT'S TRUSTS -　**24 Ch. D 662**

2. —— *Appointment—Payment of Money out of Court.*] A testator devised freehold property to trustees in trust for his grandson for life, and then for his issue in tail. There were four trustees of the will, and the testator's grandson was one of such trustees. The will contained no power of sale. Shortly after the testator's death a portion of the property comprised in the will was purchased by a railway company under their powers, and the money was paid into Court.— Upon petition for payment of the money out of Court, an order was made appointing three of the trustees of the will, omitting the testator's grandson (the tenant for life), to be trustees of the settlement effected by the will for the purposes of the Settled Land Act, 1882 : and the fund was ordered to be paid out to such three trustees to be held by them upon the trusts of the will.—And it appearing that the trustees of the will had advanced a large sum of money on mortgage including, by anticipation, a sum of money equivalent to the fund in Court—It was ordered that the three trustees appointed by the Court be at liberty to pay the fund to the four trustees of the will upon the execution by them of a declaration of trust in favour of the three trustees of so much of the principal sum secured by the mortgage as should be equivalent to the proceeds of the fund ordered to be paid out of Court. *In re* HARBOP'S TRUSTS. **24 Ch. D. 717**

3. —— *Appointment—Relatives.*] The Court will not in general appoint as trustees of a settlement for the purposes of the Act two persons who are near relatives to each other. There ought to be two independent trustees. *In re* KNOWLES' SETTLED ESTATES -　　-　**27 Ch. D. 707**

4. —— *Appointment—Solicitor for the Tenant for Life—45 & 46 Vict. c. 38, s. 38.*] A testator devised his real estate to the use of G. & W. in fee upon trusts in strict settlement, and bequeathed to them his residuary personal estate upon trust to invest it in the purchase of land to be conveyed to them upon the same trusts. The will contained no power of sale. W. was the family solicitor, a person of good position and high character, and after the death of the testator he acted as solicitor to the trustees and also to the tenant for life. The tenant for life being desirous of selling part of the estates under the powers of the Settled Land Act, applied to the Court to appoint G. and W. trustees for the purposes of the Act :—*Held* (affirming the decision of Kay, J.), that W. ought not to be appointed, for that although he was in all other respects a most proper person, his being solicitor to the tenant for life, made him unsuitable for an office the duties of which required him to check the proceedings of the tenant for life. *In re* KEMP'S SETTLED ESTATES **24 Ch. D. 485**

5. —— *Notice to Trustees—Sale or Lease by Tenant for Life—Settled Land Act, 1882 (45 & 46 Vict. c. 38), s. 45.*] The notice, to be given, under sect. 45 of the Settled Land Act, 1882, by the tenant for life of settled land to the trustees of the settlement for the purposes of the Act, when he is intending to make a sale or lease, must be—

VII. SETTLED LAND ACT—TRUSTEES—contd.

not a merely general notice of an intention to sell or lease all or any part of the estate at any time after the expiration of one month from the date of the notice as and when a proper opportunity shall from time to time occur—but a notice of a specific sale or lease which is contemplated at the time when the notice is given. In re RAY'S SETTLED ESTATES -   -   25 Ch. D. 464

6. ——Powers of leasing, sale and exchange —45 & 46 Vict. c. 38, ss. 2, 3, 6, 11, 17, 25, 33, 56, 60—Infant Tenant in Tail—Mining Leases—Surface Land apart from Mines — Application of Rents—Proceeds of Sale—Conflict between Settlement and Act.] Upon a summons under 'the Settled Land Act to obtain the opinion and direction of the Court as to the effect of the Act upon certain clauses in a settlement where an infant tenant in tail was entitled to possession, the following questions were decided:—1. The settlement gave the trustees power during the minority of any person entitled to possession to receive and apply rents and profits in management of estate and maintenance of infant, and to accumulate and apply the surplus in paying off charges or in purchase of real estate to be settled to the same uses : —Held, that the rents and profits received by the trustees during the minority were to be treated in manner directed by the settlement and without regard to the Act.—2. Power in the settlement to the trustees with the consent of the tenant for life, if of age, and if not, of his guardians, to sell or exchange :—Held, that this power was exercisable by the trustees during the minority at the request and by the direction of the guardians of the infant tenant in tail.—3. Power in the settlement for the guardians during minority to grant leases for twenty-one years, building leases for ninety-nine years, and mining leases for sixty years:—Held, that this power was exercisable during minority by the guardians with the consent of the trustees; —4. Held, that the rents derived from mining leases were to be applied by the trustees in manner directed by the settlement as coming within the term "contrary intention" expressed in the 11th section of the Act.—5. Held, that there being no power in the settlement to sell surface land apart from minerals the trustees could exercise that power under sect. 17 of the Act; and this being an execution of a statutory power, the consent of the guardians would not be necessary. In re DUKE OF NEWCASTLE'S ESTATES
[24 Ch. D. 129

7. —— Power of Sale—Settled Land Act, 1882 (45 & 46 Vict. c. 38), ss. 2 (8), 38, 39, 45 (2).] By settlement (a), executed upon the marriage of A. and B., it was declared that the trustees C. and M. should stand possessed of money, upon trust that they and the survivor of them, his executors, administrators, and assigns, should continue the money on the present investments, or with the consent in writing of A. and B. or the survivor, and after the death of the survivor then of the proper authority of such trustees or trustee to sell and transfer the securities and lay out and invest the proceeds, with power from time to time with such consent as aforesaid to vary the securities. All after-acquired property, both real and personal, to be assured and settled upon the same

VII. SETTLED LAND ACT—TRUSTEES—contd.

trusts, &c., as the principal sum. Power to appoint new trustees, and to maintain, enlarge, or diminish the original number : every new trustee to have the power, &c., of the trustee in whose place he was appointed.—By settlement (b), executed upon the marriage of C. and D. (the sister of B.), it was declared that the trustees M. & N. should stand possessed of money upon trust to continue the same upon its then present security, or with the consent in writing of C. and D. or the survivor, and after the death of the survivor, of the proper authority of such trustees or trustee to call in the said principal money and again lay out the same in their or his names or name upon the securities therein mentioned, with power for the trustees or trustee for the time being with such consent or at such discretion as aforesaid to alter, vary, and transpose the stocks, funds, or investments to be from time to time made under the authority of the aforesaid power in any other stocks, &c., of the nature or description contemplated by the trust for investment. Covenant to settle after-acquired property similar in terms to that in settlement (a).—M. had died and three new trustees of settlement (a) had been appointed by A. and B. N. was the sole present trustee of settlement (b). — Real estate had descended during their coverture upon B. and D. as co-heiresses in undivided moieties. A contract for the sale of this real estate having been entered into by A. and B. and C. and D. as vendors :— Held, upon summons under the Vendor and Purchaser Act, 1874, that under the express power contained in settlement (a), and the implied power in settlement (b), the existing trustees of both settlements had full power within the meaning of the Settled Land Act, 1882, s. 2 (8), to act as trustees under the Act, and that it was not necessary to apply to the Court under the Settled Land Act, 1882, s. 38, for the appointment of new trustees for the purposes of the Act. In re GARNETT ORME AND HARGREAVES' CONTRACT
[25 Ch. D. 595

8. —— Trust for Sale—Consent of Beneficiaries—45 & 46 Vict. s. 38, s. 63.] In determining whether land vested in trustees on an absolute trust for sale is subject to the provisions of sect. 63 of the Settled Land Act, 1882, the Court must look simply at the instrument which created the trust, and if at the time when a contract for sale is entered into by the trustees, there is no person who, by virtue of the provisions of that instrument, is entitled to the income of the money arising from the sale, or of the land until sale, for his life, or any other limited period, sect. 63 does not apply, but the trustees can exercise the trust for sale just as they could have done prior to the passing of the Act. In re EARLE AND WEBSTER'S CONTRACT   -   24 Ch. D. 144

9. —— Trust for Sale—Order of the Court for Sale—Concurrence of Tenant for Life not required—45 & 46 Vict. c. 38, ss. 56, 63.] A testator devised all his real and personal estate to trustees upon trust after the death of his wife absolutely to sell the whole of his property in such manner as they should think fit, and to pay one fourteenth part of the proceeds to each of his fourteen children at twenty-one or marriage, with

VII. SETTLED LAND ACT—TRUSTEES—*contd.*
further provisions under which his daughters'
shares were settled on them for life with remainders over.—A suit having been instituted for
the administration of the estate, and the wife
being dead, an order was made in the suit for sale
of part of the estate by the trustees :—*Held*, that
the concurrence of the children constituting the
tenant for life under the Settled Land Act, 1882,
was not necessary upon the sale by the trustees ;
but even if such concurrence would be necessary
the order of the Court was sufficient to enable
the trustees to sell without joining the fourteen
children or any of them in the conveyance to the
purchaser. TAYLOR *v.* PONCIA -   **25 Ch. D. 646**

SETTLED LAND ACT—Appointment of trustees
—Pending action   **24 Ch. D. 558**
See SETTLEMENT—POWERS. 17.

—— Payment out of Court   **30 Ch. D. 541**
See PRACTICE—SUPREME COURT—PAY-
MENT OUT OF COURT.

—— Sale under—Remuneration of solicitor
[**24 Ch. D. 608**
See SOLICITOR—BILL OF COSTS. 18.

—— By DIVORCE COURT.
See PRACTICE—DIVORCE—SETTLEMENTS.

—— By WILL.
See WILL.

—— FRAUDULENT.
See FRAUDULENT CONVEYANCE.

—— SETTLED ESTATES ACT.
See SETTLED ESTATES ACTS.

—— SETTLED LAND ACT.
See SETTLED LAND ACT.

—— VOLUNTARY.
See VOLUNTARY CONVEYANCE.

I. SETTLEMENT—ARTICLES.

1. —— **Marriage** — *Promise to settle—Subse-*
quent Settlement—Lapse of Time.] The father of
a lady wrote to her intended husband that he and
his wife had determined to settle on their daughter
£2000, and that in addition she would have
£2000 on her mother's death, and at least as
much on her father's death. Eleven months
afterwards the marriage took place ; and on that
occasion a formal agreement for a settlement of
£2000 was executed, the letter not being in any
way referred to. The mother died sixteen years
and the father died twenty-five years after the
marriage. The husband then claimed from the
father's estate £4000 under the promises contained in the letter :—*Held*, that the letter had,
under the circumstances, been superseded by the
agreement for a settlement, and claim disallowed.
In re BADCOCK. KINGDON *v.* TAGERT **17 Ch. D. 361**

2. —— **Marriage**—*Promise by Letter to make*
a Settlement.] Shortly before a marriage the in-

I. SETTLEMENT—ARTICLES—*continued.*
tended husband, at the request of a friend of the
lady, wrote a letter to the lady promising to
settle her property, which was reversionary. At
the same time negotiations as to a settlement
were going on between the respective solicitors :
but the marriage took place without any settlement being executed :—*Held*, that this was a
valid agreement for a settlement ; and a settlement in the usual form was ordered to be executed.
VIRET *v.* VIRET   -   -   **17 Ch. D. 365, n**

II. SETTLEMENT—CONSTRUCTION.

1. —— Covenant for Payment of Money "Free
from all Deductions"—*Whether Succession Duty*
or Legacy Duty payable—Succession Duty Act
(16 & 17 *Vict.* c. 51), *ss.* 1, 42, 44—*Legacy Duty*
Act (36 *Geo.* 3, c. 52), s. 6.] By a post-nuptial
settlement the settlor, the wife's father, covenanted with the trustees for payment to them
during his life, or within twelve calendar months
after his death, of the sum of £10,000, "free from
all deductions whatsoever," and an annuity of
£200 in the meantime. On the death of the
settlor his executor paid the full £10,000 to the
trustees :—*Held*, that succession duty on the
£10,000 was payable by the trustees and not by
executor. *In re* HIGGINS. DAY *v.* TURNELL
[**29 Ch. D. 697**
[Affirmed by the Court of Appeal, **31 Ch. D. 142.**]

2. —— "Eldest Son"—*Portions for Younger*
Children—Younger becoming the elder Son—Estates
sold under paramount Title, and also under Incum-
bered Estates Act to pay off Incumbrances.] By a
marriage settlement an estate was settled on the
wife and the husband successively for life, with
remainder to trustees for a term of 600 years, and
subject thereto to the first and other sons in tail.
Other estates were settled free from the portions
term, but subject to prior charges which entirely
absorbed them. The trusts of the term were if
there should be any child or children of the husband and wife other than or besides an eldest or
only son, who by virtue of the limitations should
for the time being be entitled to the hereditaments
and premises, to raise for the portions of such
child or children other than or besides such eldest
or only son, £5000, to be vested in such of them
as the husband and wife, or the survivor, should
appoint, and in default of appointment equally.
There were three children of the marriage, two
sons and a daughter. In 1841 the estate was sold,
under a paramount title, and produced a sum of
about £2400. In 1841 the eldest son died an
infant. In 1882 the surviving tenant for life died
and the portions became payable. There had
been no appointment. The younger son who
had become the elder and had attained twenty-
one claimed to take a share with his sister of the
£2400 :—*Held*, that the effect of the settlement
was to give £5000 to the sister as a first charge
on the estate, and the rest of the estate to the
brother, and whether the value of the residue
were more or less than the portion, or as in this
case, nothing at all, the brother had no right to
claim any share in the prior charge. REID *v.*
HOARE   -   -   -   **26 Ch. D. 363**

3. —— "Eldest or only Son."] Sir C. D.
(who died in 1857), by deed in 1852, appointed a

II. SETTLEMENT—CONSTRUCTION—_contd._

fund to trustees in trust for his daughter Lady W. for life, and after her death in trust for the child or all the children, "except an eldest or only son," if more than one, of Lady W., who should attain twenty-one or marry; and failing such trusts then over. Lady W. died in 1883, having had four children only, viz., Thomas, her eldest born son, who attained twenty-one in January, 1869, and died in April following, Sir F. W., who attained twenty-one in 1880, Helena, who attained twenty-one in 1865, and Edith, who died in infancy, in 1864; so that the fund vested in Helena (subject to let in other children) in the lifetime of the eldest born son, and before he attained twenty-one. At the date of the deed certain estates stood limited under a settlement, to which Sir C. D. was a party, to the use of Sir T. W. (the husband of Lady W.) for life with remainder to the use of the first and other sons of Sir T. and Lady W., in tail male. In March, 1869, Sir T. W. and his son Thomas, disentailed the estates, and limited them to the appointees of both, or of the survivor. The joint power was not exercised; but after the death of Thomas, Sir T. W. by will appointed the estates to Sir F. W. for life, with remainder to his sons in tail male. Upon Lady W.'s death Sir F. W. claimed half the fund, and Helena, the whole of it :— _Held_, that, if the expression "eldest or only son," was to be read as referring to a son entitled under a settlement to settled estates, the time for ascertaining the excluded son would be the time for distributing the younger children's portions ; but that if that expression was to be read according to its natural meaning, the time of vesting would be the time for exclusion :—_Held_, also, that the words an "eldest or only son" primâ facie mean an individual, and that as there was an eldest son in existence when the provision vested in Helena, the clause of exclusion applied to him, and its operation was exhausted, so that any other son who attained twenty-one was entitled to take. And _held_, accordingly, that Sir F. W. was entitled to one half of the fund.—_Mathews_ v. _Paul_ (3 Sw. 328) observed upon. DOMVILE v. WINNINGTON

[26 Ch. D. 382]

4. —— Forfeiture—_Bankruptcy—Bankruptcy Act, 1869, s. 126—Composition._] Presentation by a firm of a petition for liquidation under the Bankruptcy Act, 1869, followed by acceptance by the creditors of a composition, operates as a forfeiture of an interest limited in 1862 to the use of A., who was a member of the firm, during his life, " or until he should be outlawed or declared bankrupt, or become an insolvent within the meaning of some Act of Parliament for the relief of insolvent debtors." NIXON v. VEERY 29 Ch. D. 196

5. —— Forfeiture—_Bankruptcy—Tenant for Life and in Remainder — Insolvency in New South Wales—Bankruptcy Act, 1869 (32 & 33 Vict. c. 71), s. 74._] In 1838 a settlement of real estate in England was made, and thereby the trustees were to pay the rents and profits to S. L. for life or until he should commit an act of bankruptcy, or commit any act, or any event should occur, whereby the rents, if settled absolutely upon or in trust for him, should be forfeited to or become vested in any other person whomsoever, and

II. SETTLEMENT—CONSTRUCTION—_contd._

there was a gift over upon the happening of any such event. S. L. in 1875 was residing in New South Wales, and was adjudged insolvent by the Court of the colony, the Act of the colony vesting all property of the insolvent "wheresoever the same might be known or found" in the Commissioner therein mentioned. On summons taken out by S. L. under the Settled Land Act of 1882, to have trustees appointed :—_Held_, that in consequence of the insolvency in New South Wales, the property had become forfeited and had gone over to those in remainder. _In re_ LEVY'S TRUSTS

[30 Ch. D. 119]

6. —— Forfeiture—_Bankruptcy— Discharge of Bankrupt—Life Estate — Reassignment of Estate._] Under the trusts of a marriage settlement a life interest in property brought into settlement by the wife was given, after her death, to the husband, but the trust in his favour was to cease in the event of his bankruptcy or liquidation and there was a gift over on that event. In August, 1881, he filed a liquidation petition under which, in October, 1881, a trustee of his property was appointed. In January, 1883, he obtained a discharge. In April, 1884, the wife died. In March, 1885, the trustees assigned for value to the debtor all the property belonging to him at the commencement of the liquidation and devolving on him subsequently, up to the date of the discharge, other than that which had been already received by the trustee. The liquidation was never formally closed, but the trustee had never made any claim to the income of the settled fund :—_Held_, that, inasmuch as, before the reassignment by the trustee to the debtor, income had become due to him, which, but for the forfeiture clause, the trustee might have received, the forfeiture had taken effect.—_White_ v. _Chitty_ (Law Rep. 1 Eq. 372), _Lloyd_ v. _Lloyd_ (Law Rep. 2 Eq. 722), and _Ancona_ v. _Waddell_ (10 Ch. D. 157) distinguished. ROBERTSON v. RICHARDSON

[30 Ch. D. 623]

7. —— Power of Appointment—_"Issue"— Invalid Appointment by Will—Election._] There is no inflexible rule that if the word "issue" is evidently used in one clause of a settlement as meaning "children" only, it must be construed in the same sense in every other clause. A marriage settlement contained a power for the wife to appoint by will among the issue of the marriage, and, in default of appointment, the trust fund was to be in trust for the issue of the marriage, if more than one in equal shares, the son or sons at twenty-one, and the daughter or daughters at twenty-one or marriage; and, in case there should be but one child issue of the marriage, or, if more than one, all but one should die without having become entitled, then in trust for such only or surviving child; and in case there should not be any issue of the marriage, or all such issue should die without having become entitled, then upon other trusts :—_Held_, that the word "issue" in the power of appointment must be construed in the strict technical sense, and that an appointment by the wife to the children of a deceased son was valid. The wife appointed another part of the fund on trust for another living son for his life, with remainder to his child

II. SETTLEMENT—CONSTRUCTION—*contd.*

or children who should attain twenty-one, if more than one in equal shares. The testatrix also bequeathed property of her own to the persons who were entitled in default of appointment. It was admitted that the appointment to the children of the living son was void for remoteness:—*Held*, that, the appointment being ex facie void, the will must be read as if the appointment had not been contained in it, and that the persons entitled in default of appointment were not bound to elect between the interest which they took in that way, and the benefits given to them by the testatrix out of her own property. *In re* WARREN'S TRUSTS 　　　　　　　　26 Ch. D. 208

8. ——— **Power of Appointment**—*Trust for Children—Default of Appointment—Class when to be ascertained.*] By a settlement dated in May, 1833, a leasehold house was assigned to trustees upon trust for A. for life, and after her decease for B., her husband, for life, and after the decease of the survivor of A. and B. upon trust to assign the premises unto and amongst such of the children of A. and B. then living in such manner, shares, times, and proportions as A. and B. jointly, or the survivor of them separately, should by any writing appoint, and in case there should be no such child or children, then upon trust for C. for life, and after his decease upon trust to assign the premises unto and amongst such of his children, and in such manner, shares, times, and proportions, as he should by any writing appoint.—A. died in 1876 without leaving issue. B. died in 1880. C. died in 1863 without having exercised the power of appointment, having had ten children, of whom three died before him, two after and before the death of A., and one after the death of A. and before that of B.:—*Held*, that all the children of C. took as tenants in common in equal shares. WILSON *v.* DUGUID 　　　　　　　　　　　　　　　[24 Ch. D. 244

9. ——— **Vested Interest**—*Marriage Settlement —"Payable" meaning "vested"—Shares "to be paid" at twenty-one—Gift over on Death before Share "payable."*] By a marriage settlement lands were conveyed upon trust for husband and wife successively for life, and after the death of the survivor, "to levy out of the said lands and premises . . . . the sum of £3000 . . . . to be divided to and among all the children of the said intended marriage, save and except such child and children as under the limitations aforesaid shall succeed to the enjoyment of the lands and premises hereby conveyed . . . . in equal shares and proportions as tenants in common and not as joint tenants, the share of such child or children as shall be a son or sons to be paid to him or them upon his or their respectively arriving at the full age of twenty-one years, and the share or shares of such of them as shall be daughters to be paid upon their respectively arriving at their full age of twenty-one years, or day or days of marriage, whichever shall first happen: Provided always that such marriage during minority shall be had by and with the consent and approbation of" the parents "or the survivor of them: with interest for the same by way of maintenance at the rate of £6 by the hundred to be computed from the day of the death of the survivor of" the parents:

II. SETTLEMENT—CONSTRUCTION—*contd.*

"with benefit of survivorship to the survivors or survivor of such children if any of such children shall die before his, her, or their share or shares shall become payable unmarried and without leaving issue as aforesaid, it being the true intent and meaning of these presents that none of the children of the said intended marriage, who under the limitations herein contained shall become entitled to an estate in possession in any part of the lands and premises hereby conveyed . . . . shall be entitled to any part of" the said sum.—A son attained twenty-one and died in the lifetime of his father:—*Held*, affirming the decision of the Court of Appeal in Ireland, that there being no words indicating a clear intention to postpone the vesting of children's portions till the death of the survivor of the parents, the rule laid down in *Emperor v. Rolfe* (1 Ves. Sen. 208) applied, and the son took a vested interest in his portion on attaining twenty-one. WAKEFIELD *v.* MAFFET 　　　　　　　　　　　　　　　[10 App. Cas. 422

III. SETTLEMENT—EQUITY TO SETTLEMENT.

1. ——— **Form of Settlement**—*Joint Power of Appointment among Children — Stamp.*] In settling a fund in pursuance of a will by which the fund was bequeathed to a man until marriage and then to be settled on his wife and children, the Court inserted a power for the husband and wife jointly by deed, and for the survivor by deed or will, to appoint among the children.—Observations on *Oliver v. Oliver* (10 Ch. D. 765). —Form of judgment settling a fund.—An order of the Court making a settlement should bear the usual settlement stamp. *In re* GOWAN. GOWAN *v.* GOWAN - 　　　　　17 Ch. D. 778

2. ——— **Infant**—*Consent—Waiver of Equity.*] A fund in Court belonging to an infant married woman will not be paid out to her husband, as she cannot waive her equity to a settlement.—*In re* D'Angibau (15 Ch. D. 228) noticed. SHIPWAY *v.* BALL - 　　　　　　　- 16 Ch. D. 376

3. ——— **Whole Fund**—*Desertion by Husband.*] A husband entitled to leaseholds in right of his wife, deserted her and their children, and for eight years contributed nothing towards her or their support, except the rents of the leaseholds. During the desertion the leaseholds were sold by the wife for £250 to a purchaser, who expended the greater part of the proceeds upon the maintenance of the wife and children. In an action by the husband against the wife and the purchaser to set aside the sale and recover the leaseholds or the proceeds:—*Held*, that, under her equity to a settlement, the wife was entitled to have the entire proceeds of the sale secured to herself, and such proceeds having practically been expended for her benefit, the action must be dismissed with costs. BOXALL *v.* BOXALL 　　　　　27 Ch. D. 220

IV. SETTLEMENT—FUTURE PROPERTY.

1. ——— **Estate Tail**—*Real and Personal Property of which Wife "should become seised or possessed of or entitled to."*] A marriage settlement contained an agreement and declaration by the parties that, if the wife then was, or if, during the coverture, she, or the husband in her right, should become seised or possessed of or entitled to any real or personal property (of a specified

IV. SETTLEMENT — FUTURE PROPERTY — *continued.*

value) for any estate or interest whatsoever, in possession, reversion, remainder, or expectancy, then and in every such case, the husband and wife, and all necessary parties, should, as soon as circumstances would admit, convey, assign, and assure the said real and personal property to, or otherwise cause the same to be vested in, the trustees of the settlement, upon the trusts thereof. —*Held,* that an estate tail in possession to which the wife became entitled during the coverture was not bound by this agreement, and that she could not be compelled either to execute a disentailing deed, and to convey the estate in fee thus acquired by her to the trustees, or to execute a conveyance of the property to the trustees, so that they could by enrolling the deed acquire an estate in fee simple.—*Held,* that the agreement extended only to the wife's estate or interest in the property acquired by her, and that it was impossible that she could convey an estate tail to the trustees. HILBERS *v.* PARKINSON

[25 Ch. D. 200

2. —— Infant—*Restraint on Application—Existing Property — Voidable Covenant — Election.*] An agreement by husband and wife, in an ante-nuptial settlement for the settlement by the husband and wife of the wife's after-acquired property, is a covenant by the wife as well by the husband, whether the wife is a minor or of full age. If the wife is a minor, and the covenant is for her benefit, it is voidable only and not void, and is binding upon all property coming to her during the coverture for her separate use, without a restraint on anticipation, until she avoids or disaffirms the covenant as to such property; for she may, after attaining twenty-one, and during the coverture, elect whether the covenant shall be binding on her separate estate or not, such right of election being a necessary consequence of a married woman's power to dispose of, without her husband's consent, property settled to her separate use : but—inasmuch as a contract by a married woman, while under coverture, affecting her separate property binds only her then existing separate property, and not separate property which she may thereafter acquire (*Pike* v. *Fitzgibbon,* 17 Ch. D. 454)—the wife, in electing to confirm the covenant, thereby binds only that separate property to which she is entitled at the date of the confirmation, and not that to which she may subsequently become entitled during the coverture.—*Semble,* the doctrine of election or compensation does not apply in the case of a married woman entitled for her separate use with a restraint on anticipation.—*Willoughby* v. *Middleton* (2 J. & H. 344) questioned on this point.—By an ante-nuptial settlement, dated in 1856, the lady being then a minor, after reciting that she would be entitled on attaining twenty-one to a share of her deceased father's estate, and the intention to settle the same, it was agreed and declared between the parties thereto, and the husband covenanted with the trustees, that the husband and wife and all other necessary parties would, as soon as the wife attained twenty-one, convey the share to the trustees upon trust for the wife during her life for her separate use without

IV. SETTLEMENT — FUTURE PROPERTY — *continued.*

power of anticipation, and after her death for the husband till bankruptcy or alienation, with remainder for the issue of the marriage. And it was further agreed and declared that if the wife then was, or if at any time or times during the coverture she or her husband in her right should become seised or possessed of or entitled to any real or personal property for any estate or interest whatsoever, then and in every such case the husband and wife and all other necessary parties should assure the same to the trustees upon the trusts thereinbefore declared. The settlement contained a power for the trustees, at the request of the wife, to lend any of the trust funds to the husband on his personal security.—The wife attained twenty-one in 1857, and in 1858 she and her husband, in pursuance of the covenant in that behalf in the settlement, conveyed her share of her father's estate to the trustees of the settlement.—In 1863, upon the death of a brother, the wife became entitled under his will to certain funds thereby bequeathed to her for her separate use. These funds, and also funds arising from her share of her father's estate, were, with the assent of the wife, paid to the trustees of the settlement, and by them lent, at her request, to the husband on his personal security. In 1880 the wife became entitled under the will of her mother to a sum of £4000, and a share of her residuary estate thereby bequeathed respectively to her for her separate use :—*Held,* that the wife could elect to retain the £4000 and share of residue for her separate use unbound by the covenant for the settlement of her after-acquired property. SMITH v. LUCAS　　・　18 Ch. D. 531

3. —— Infant—*Deed acknowledged by Wife after full age — Confirmation of Settlement—Election by Married Woman—Wife of Unsound Mind—Jurisdiction of Court to elect for.*] By a marriage settlement made in January, 1874, the wife being an infant, personal property derived under her father's marriage settlement was assigned by the husband and wife to trustees upon the usual trusts. There was a covenant by the husband that he and his wife would so soon as she should attain the age of twenty-one years convey and assign real and personal property to which she was entitled under the will of her father ; and it was provided that if the wife should refuse or neglect to do so it should be lawful for the trustees to accumulate any part of the income payable to her for the other persons interested under the settlement. There was an agreement to settle the wife's after-acquired personal property. The wife, on the 13th of April, 1874, a week after she attained the age of twenty-one, and her husband executed a deed, which she acknowledged, by which she assigned all the personal property expressed to be assigned by the settlement which had not become vested in possession, and conveyed property purported to be conveyed by the settlement upon the trusts thereof.—At the date of the settlement she was contingently entitled to a reversionary interest in personal estate, but it was not actually assigned by the deed of confirmation because it did not come within the provisions of Sir R. Malin's Act,

IV. SETTLEMENT — FUTURE PROPERTY — *continued.*

20 & 21 Vict. c. 57. It fell into possession, and it was by the direction of the wife and her husband invested in the names of the trustees. The husband had died, and the wife had become of unsound mind, but not so found by inquisition. On summons by the infant children, by their next friend :—*Held*, following the cases of *Barrow v. Barrow* (4 K. & J. 409) and *Smith v. Lucas* (18 Ch. D. 531), that the wife could during her coverture elect to confirm the settlement, and that she had by her acts elected.—The wife having become of unsound mind, if she had not elected the Court would have made an election on her behalf, it having jurisdiction to bind the equitable interests of lunatics, not so found by inquisition, when it appears to be for their benefit.—*Jones* v. *Lloyd* (Law Rep. 18 Eq. 265) followed. WILDER *v.* PIGOTT - - **22 Ch. D. 263**

4. —— Judicial Separation—*"Feme Sole"*— 20 & 21 *Vict. c.* 85, *ss.* 7, 21, 25, 26.] A married woman, subsequently to obtaining a decree of judicial separation from her husband, became absolutely entitled to certain sums of stock :—*Held*, that under 20 & 21 Vict. c. 85, s. 25, the stock belonged to her as if she were a feme sole, and was not included in a covenant in her marriage settlement to settle all property which she or her husband in her right might acquire "during the coverture." DAWES *v.* CREYKE - - - **30 Ch. D. 500**

5. —— Life Annuities.] By an ante-nuptial settlement made in 1870 the intended husband and wife respectively covenanted with the trustees that all the estate, property, and effects, real or personal, of or to which the wife, or the husband in her right, should at any time during the coverture become seised, possessed, or entitled, should be assured and settled, as regarded personal estate, upon trust, to such part thereof as should not consist of money or authorized investments, or of interest determinable on the death of the wife, upon trust to convert it, and to invest the proceeds, and such part of the estate as should consist of money, upon such investments as therein mentioned, and during the joint lives of husband and wife pay "the interest, dividends, and annual proceeds thereof" to them in equal shares, the share of the wife to be for her separate use without power of anticipation. By a deed of the same date the wife's father covenanted with the trustees to pay to them an annuity of £500 to be applied by them upon trusts corresponding with those of the income of the personal property mentioned in the covenant. In 1874 the wife's father bought up the husband's interest in this annuity, and assigned it to trustees for the wife's separate use with no restraint on anticipation :—*Held* (affirming the decision of Pollock, B.), that the covenant to settle included life annuities given to the wife, that the share assigned by the wife's father in the annuity of £500 was bound by the covenant, and that during the joint lives of the husband and wife, three-fourths of the annuity belonged to the wife for her separate use with a restraint on anticipation and the remaining fourth to the trustee of the husband, who had become bankrupt, and that persons to whom the wife had

IV. SETTLEMENT — FUTURE PROPERTY — *continued.*

mortgaged the interest assigned in 1874 took nothing. Where a covenant has been entered into for settlement of the future property of a married woman, and a gift is afterwards made to her of such a nature as to come within the terms of the covenant, no expression of the intention of the donor that it shall not be settled will exclude it from the operation of the covenant.—*In re Mainwaring's Settlement* (Law Rep. 2 Eq. 487) observed upon. SCHOLFIELD *v.* SPOONER - **26 Ch. D. 94**

6. —— Property before Marriage—*Covenant to settle Property to which Wife or Husband in her right " shall become entitled."*] In a settlement made before marriage there was a covenant to settle upon certain trusts all real and personal property to which the wife or the husband " in her right at any time during her now intended coverture shall become entitled (except jewels and ' certain other articles " which it is hereby declared shall belong to" the wife "for her separate use). The trusts included a power of sale, the moneys arising from the sale to be held upon the trusts declared concerning such part of the personal estate of or to which the wife "now is or she or" the husband "in her right shall become possessed or entitled as aforesaid " :— *Held*, affirming the decision of the Court of Appeal, that on the true construction of the covenant, read in conjunction with the context, it included property to which the wife was entitled before marriage; and therefore that jewels given to the wife before marriage were within the exception and belonged to the wife for her separate use. WILLIAMS *v.* MERCIER   **9 Q. B. D. 337;** [10 App. Cas. 1

7. —— Separate Estate.] By a marriage settlement, after a recital that on the treaty for the marriage it was agreed that all real and personal property which during the coverture should devolve upon or vest in the wife or the husband in her right to the value of £200 at any one time should be settled upon the trusts thereinafter declared, it was witnessed that it was thereby agreed and declared between and by the parties thereto, and the husband thereby covenanted with the trustees that if at any time during the coverture any real or personal estate should devolve on or vest in the wife or the husband in her right to the amount in value of £200 at any one time, the husband would make, do, and execute, or cause and procure to be made, done, and executed, and join and concur in making, doing, and executing all such conveyances, &c., as would effectually vest such real and personal estate in the trustees upon the trusts therein declared. After the marriage the deed was executed by the wife's mother, under which, during the coverture, a sum exceeding £200 became payable to the wife for her separate use :—*Held*, by Fry, J., that this sum was within the covenant, and must be settled.— *Held*, by the Court of Appeal, that as the operative part of the deed was clear, the recital could not control it—that as the operative part of the deed only related to acts to be done by the husband, the agreement and declaration between and by the parties that those acts should be done did not import a covenant by any other party that

IV. SETTLEMENT — FUTURE PROPERTY — continued.

they should be done, and that there was, therefore, no covenant by any one but the husband—that the covenant by him could not be held to relate to property over which he had no power and in which he had no interest—and that the wife therefore was not bound to bring into settlement property given to her separate use. DAWES v. TREDWELL - 18 Ch. D. 354

8. —— Separate Estate—*Covenant to settle future Property except such as should be otherwise settled—Will—Legacy to Wife for Separate Use.*] A marriage settlement, in which the wife's property was vested in trustees for her separate use without power of anticipation, contained a covenant by the husband and wife that if at any time during the joint lives of them any further portion, fortune, or estate should come to or devolve upon either of them by or under any will, or otherwise, they would effectually settle the same (except such future portion, fortune, or estate as should be otherwise settled previously to the same devolving as aforesaid) upon the trusts of the settlement :—*Held*, that a gift of a legacy to the wife for her own sole and separate use, free from the debts, control, and engagements of her husband, was excluded from the operation of the covenant. KANE v. KANE - 16 Ch. D. 207

9. —— Separate Estate—*Property to separate use excepted—Married Women's Property Act, 1882 (45 & 46 Vict. c. 75), ss. 5, 19—Settlement not affected by Act.*] A marriage settlement made in 1862 contained an agreement for the settlement of any future acquired property of the wife to a specified amount (except interests settled and limited to her separate use). The wife after the commencement of the Married Women's Property Act, 1882, became entitled absolutely to a bequest above the specified amount, without any limitation as to separate use :—*Held*, that by the 19th section of the above Act the marriage settlement was exempted from the 5th and other sections; and that the bequest to the wife came within the covenant to settle future acquired property and must be dealt with as if the Act had never been passed. *In re* STONOR'S TRUSTS
[24 Ch. D. 195

10. —— Separate Estate—*Will — Legacy to Wife for Separate Use.*] By an ante-nuptial settlement the husband and wife covenanted with the trustees to settle all property to which the wife then was or during the coverture she or her husband in her right should become entitled by devise, bequest, or otherwise "for any estate or interest whatsoever."—During the coverture the wife's father died, having by his will devised and bequeathed a moiety of his residuary real and personal estate to her "for her separate use, independently of any husband."—*Held*, that the moiety was bound by the covenant.—*In re* Mainwaring's Settlement (Law Rep. 2 Eq. 487) not followed. *In re* ALLNUTT. POTT v. BRASSEY
[22 Ch. D. 275

V. SETTLEMENT—POWERS.

1. —— Leasing — *Charge on Inheritance — Tenant for Life—Mortgagor and Mortgagee—Consolidation—Coal Workings—Removal of Pillars —Injunction.*] A testator devised his real estates

V. SETTLEMENT—POWERS—*continued.*

in strict settlement, making M. first tenant for life, without impeachment of waste, and, after giving to male tenants for life powers to jointure their wives and provide portions for younger children, proceeded to authorize the tenants for life when in possession and the guardians of infant tenants for life in possession to demise any parts of the estates, except the mansion-house, for any term not exceeding twenty-one years at the best rent without fine or premium. He then empowered such tenants for life and guardians to grant any lease or leases of any mines or collieries or of any parcels of land for the purpose of digging for, winning, or gaining minerals or coal in any part of his estates "for such term or number of years, and under and subject to such rents or reservations and agreements, as to such tenant for life or guardian or guardians shall seem reasonable and proper," and also to grant building or repairing leases for any term not exceeding ninety-nine years without any fine or premium. In 1843, M., the tenant for life, by a deed reciting the leasing power, in consideration of £6000 paid to him by C., demised the mines included in a mining lease made by the testator to E. in 1829, which would expire in 1848, to C. for ninety-nine years at a peppercorn rent, subject to redemption on payment of £6000 and interest. The deed contained an appointment of a receiver of the rents and royalties payable by the present and future tenants, and did not oblige C. to work the mines; but the tenant for life covenanted to grant, or concur in granting, such further leases as C. should require :—*Held*, by Bacon, V.-C., and by the Court of Appeal, that this deed was a valid exercise of the power of leasing mines, and created a good legal mortgage for an absolute term of ninety-nine years.—By a deed of April, 1850, reciting the will and the power of leasing mines, and that M. was indebted to S. P. & B. in £60,000 and that it had been agreed that S. P. & B. should pay what was due on the mortgage of 1843, and take a transfer of that security, and that for securing to S. P. & B. the payment of the debt due to them from M. and any other moneys they might advance to him, it had been agreed that such further mortgage as thereinafter contained should be made; the mortgage debt of £60,000 was assigned to S. P. & B., and the term was also assigned to them subject to the existing equity of redemption, and M. granted his life estate to J. C. as a trustee for S. P. & B. It was declared that the collieries and property assigned to S. P. & B. should be subject to the proviso for redemption thereinafter contained. There followed a proviso for redemption of all the mortgaged property on payment of £67,000, being the aggregate of the £60,000 and the moneys secured by the mortgage of 1843 :—*Held*, by Bacon, V.-C., and by the Court of Appeal, that the £60,000 was effectually charged on the ninety-nine years term as well as on the life interest, for that this deed was a good exercise of the leasing power by varying the proviso for redemption in the deed of 1843, and that even if it were a defective exercise of that power the defect was one which a Court of Equity would make good.—The lease of 1829 contained covenants by the lessee to leave sufficient pillars of coal to support the roof, and these

V. SETTLEMENT—POWERS—continued.

covenants were embodied by reference in the mortgage of 1843. In May, 1850, M. granted to J. C. as a trustee for S. P. & B. an ordinary mining lease for forty years, subject to a dead rent and royalties, which contained a covenant by the lessee not to remove pillars without the consent of M. or his assigns, or other the persons entitled to the colliery. M. after this conveyed absolutely all his interest in the property to the trustees of his eldest son, who had become entitled in fee in remainder. Afterwards J. C., with the concurrence of the parties claiming under S. P. & B., granted an underlease to L. & S. authorizing them to remove some of the pillars, which they proceeded to do, alleging that J. C. and the persons claiming under S. P. & B. were the persons entitled to consent : — Held, that during the continuance of the lease of May, 1850, the pillars could not be worked without the consent of the assigns of M., who became such after the execution of that deed, and that such working must be restrained at the suit of the son's trustees. —But, held, that if M. should survive the expiration of the lease of May, 1850, the parties claiming under the deed of April, 1850, as assigns of M.'s life estate, could during the remainder of M.'s life effectually consent to the removal of the pillars by persons interested under the deed of 1843. MOSTYN v. LANCASTER. TAYLOR v. MOSTYN

[23 Ch. D. 583

2. —— **Leasing**—Infant Remainderman — Tenant for Life —Trustees — Effectuating Predecessor's Contract for Lease.] By a will devising real estate in strict settlement powers of granting building leases were given to any tenant for life and to trustees during the minority of any tenant in tail. The tenant for life, in pursuance of his power entered into a contract to grant a building lease, but died without having executed a lease, and was succeeded by an infant tenant in tail :— Held, that the trustees had power to effectuate the contract of the tenant for life by executing a lease. DAVIS v. HARFORD 22 Ch. D. 128

3. —— **Leasing**—Repairing Lease — Tenant to do necessary Repairs.] A settlement of house property gave power to the trustees to demise or agree to demise all or any of the messuages "to any person or persons who shall improve or repair the same, or covenant or agree to improve or repair the same, or shall expend or agree to expend such sum or sums of money in improvements thereof respectively as shall be thought adequate for the interests therein respectively." The trustees agreed to let a house on the terms of a letter by which the tenant undertook "to do necessary repairs" :—Held, by Chitty, J., that the agreement did not satisfy the terms of the power, and that specific performance of it could not be decreed at the suit of the trustees.— Held, by the Court of Appeal, that the agreement imposed upon the tenant the burden of doing all repairs which were requisite during the term, and that it satisfied the requisitions of the power.— Doe v. Withers (2 B. & Ad. 896) doubted. TRUSCOTT v. DIAMOND ROCK BORING COMPANY

[20 Ch. D. 251

4. —— **Leasing** — Will — Building Leases — Ordinary Leases—Invalid Lease—Deviation from

V. SETTLEMENT—POWERS—continued.

Terms of Power—Contract for Grant of valid Lease under 12 & 13 Vict. c. 26—Option to purchase.] A testator by his will devised and bequeathed freehold and leasehold lands upon trusts, and empowered the trustees to contract for leases thereof with or without optional powers of purchase in the lessees, and to grant leases thereof either for building or other purposes, so that no lease of the site of a building should be made for more than ninety-nine years, and no lease for any other purpose for more than twenty-one years, and so that while leases for twenty-one years were to be at the best rents which could be obtained, building leases might be at a rent to increase progressively. After the testator's death the trustees granted to A. B. a lease of part of the freehold and leasehold lands of the testator for thirty-five years, with an option to purchase during the first twenty-one years of the term, and at an increasing rent as to the freehold part, by an indenture which recited that they had power to grant building leases, but contained no covenant to build, though it contained covenants to repair, amend, and keep, and to insure all messuages erected or to be erected on the land demised.—A. B. exercised his option to purchase as to a leasehold portion of the demised property, which was duly assigned to him, and he afterwards sold and assigned part of those leaseholds to C. D. C. D. contracted to sell to a purchaser, and in order to avoid any question as to the validity of the lease by the trustees, a memorandum was indorsed upon it signed by A. B. and the trustees declaring that pursuant to the Act 12 & 13 Vict. c. 26, the lease should be considered in equity as a contract for the grant of a valid lease for twenty-one years. The purchaser, however, took the objection that the lease was invalid.—Upon a summons taken out under the Vendor and Purchaser Act of 1874 :—Held, that the lease though intended to be a building lease was invalid as such, owing to the absence of any covenant to build, and that being bad as a building lease under the power it could not by the operation of 12 & 13 Vict. c. 26, be turned into a contract for the grant of a valid lease of a kind different from that which it was originally intended to be ; moreover, that even if it could by this means be turned into an ordinary lease, it would be bad as such, inasmuch as the rent reserved on the freehold part was an increasing rent, which was not authorized by the power to grant ordinary leases :—Held, also, that as there was no power to grant an option to purchase otherwise than in a valid lease under the power, and the lease granted was invalid, the option to purchase must fall with the lease. HALLETT to MARTIN　　-　　　-　24 Ch. D. 624

5. —— **Maintenance** — Power or Trust — Direction to apply the whole or part of Income "for or towards maintenance"—Right of Father to claim Application of Income to Maintenance.] By a marriage settlement certain personal property was settled upon trust for the wife for life, and after her death for the children ; and it was declared that the trustees should after the death of the wife apply the whole or such part as the trustees should think fit of the annual income of

V. SETTLEMENT—POWERS—*continued.*

the expectant share of any child for or towards the maintenance of such child. The trustees after the death of the wife paid the whole income of the trust fund to the husband during the infancy of the child of the marriage without exercising any discretion as to its application to his maintenance :—*Held* (affirming the decision of Bacon, V.C.), that there was no absolute trust to apply the income to the maintenance of the children, but a discretionary trust equivalent to a power ; and that as the trustees had not exercised any discretion, the estate of the husband must be held liable to repay the whole amount of the income received.—*Ransome* v. *Burgess* (Law Rep. 3 Eq. 773) disapproved.—*Mundy* v. *Earl Howe* (4 Bro. C. C. 224) commented on.　WILSON *v.* TURNER

[22 Ch. D. 521

6. —— **Management**—*Cultivation of Farm—Investment of Personal Estate to cultivate Real Estate.*] The trustees of real and residuary personal estate devised and bequeathed in trust for A. for life, with remainder to his children, who were infants (there being no investment clause in the will) were authorized to advance to the tenant for life part of the residuary personal estate for the purpose of stocking and cultivating a farm forming part of the real estate, on evidence that the outlay would be to the advantage of the infant remaindermen. *In re* HOUSEHOLD.　HOUSEHOLD *v.* HOUSEHOLD　-　27 Ch. D. 553

7. —— **Management**—*Permanent Improvements—Tenant for Life—Trusts of Minority Term—Option to Trustees to pay Charges out of Income or Capital—Incidence of Charges paid for out of Income during Minority.*] By a deed, executed two years before his will, a testator devised estates in Glamorganshire, which comprised a canal, harbour and docks at Cardiff, and also estates in the counties of Bedford, Herts, and Durham, to A., B., and C., upon trust out of rents and profits and sums to be raised by sale or mortgage, to pay expenses, salaries, mortgage debts, and the residue to the settlor. He empowered the trustees to enlarge, improve and make additional works at Cardiff, and to manage the estates, with powers of leasing, sale and mortgage.—By his will, dated two months before the birth of his first son, the testator devised the Glamorganshire estates (except Cardiff Castle, park, and lands adjoining) to B. and C. and their heirs for a term of 1500 years, and subject thereto to the use of his first son for life, remainder to his first and other sons in tail male. The trusts of the 1500 years term were declared to be, after payment out of income of certain annuities, of a specified sum for certain repairs, "by mortgaging or otherwise disposing of the term . . . or by, with and out of the rents, issues and profits of the same hereditaments . . . or by one . . . or all of the aforesaid ways and means, or by any other reasonable ways and means" to raise moneys sufficient for the above purposes, and with the moneys to arise from the sale of the estates in Bedford, Herts, and Durham, to satisfy the trusts of such sale. The trustees of the term were empowered to manage and improve the hereditaments comprised in the term in the same manner as the trustees of the deed.—Testator then directed that, during the minority of a tenant

V. SETTLEMENT—POWERS—*continued.*

for life of the Glamorganshire estates, D. and A. should enter into possession and receipt of the rents and profits of the same hereditaments, and thereout keep down the interest on mortgages, and maintain mansion-houses and grounds, and pay the surplus to the trustees of the 1500 years term for the purposes thereof, and "subject thereto, and after the trusts of the said term of 1500 years shall be fully performed or satisfied" apply any annual sum they might think proper for the maintenance of the minor, and invest the surplus and accumulate the income for his benefit on attaining majority.—The trusts of the proceeds of the sale of the Bedford, Herts, and Durham estates were declared to be : 1. to pay debts, including mortgage debts on the Glamorganshire estates ; and 2. to purchase lands to be settled as before.—Six months after the birth of his first son, testator died, and during the minority the trustees of the 1500 years term laid out upwards of £1,000,000 in enlarging and improving the canal, docks, and harbour, and in other works. This sum was largely paid out of income :—*Held*, that the expenditure was a charge on the corpus of the estates comprised in the term. *In re* MARQUESS OF BUTE.　MARQUESS OF BUTE *v.* RYDER

[27 Ch. D. 196

8. —— **New Trustees**—"*Continuing*" *Trustees*—23 & 24 *Vict. c.* 145, *s.* 27.] A trustee who has made up his mind to retire, may be a "continuing" trustee, until he has executed the deed appointing new trustees.—Decision in *Travis* v. *Illingworth* (2 Dr. & Sm. 344, 346) to the contrary, not followed.—By a settlement in 1867 (Lord Cranworth's Act having been passed in 1860), it was declared that it should be lawful for "the surviving or continuing trustees, in the event of any trustees declining to act, to discharge such trustees, and to appoint any new trustees ; and it was provided that nothing should authorize the discharge of the only continuing trustees without the substitution of others. Of three original trustees, one having died, the other two, by deed in 1874, after reciting that they themselves "declined to act" and "desired to be discharged," and had "determined to appoint" three other persons to be trustees, "in exercise of the power for this purpose vested in them" by the settlement, appointed the three persons "to be trustees in the place of" themselves and the deceased trustee respectively :—*Held*, that the appointment was good. *In re* GLENNY AND HARTLEY　　　　　　　　　25 Ch. D. 611

9. —— **New Trustees**—*Continuing Trustee—Retirement of Trustee—Validity of Appointment by continuing Trustee—Exercise of Power after Judgment for Administration of Trusts—Approval of Court—Solicitor of continuing Trustee.*] When a power of appointing new trustees authorizes the continuing trustee or trustees to appoint a new trustee or trustees in the place of a trustee or trustees becoming unwilling to act, an appointment by a sole continuing trustee, in the place of a trustee who desires to retire, is valid ; it is not necessary that the retiring trustee should join in making the appointment.—*In re Glenny and Hartley* (25 Ch. D. 611) commented on, and dicta of Bacon, V.C., dissented from.—*Travis*

V. SETTLEMENT—POWERS—*continued.*

v. *Illingworth* (2 Dr. & Sm. 344) approved and followed.—On the retirement of one of two trustees of a will, the continuing trustee, who was the solicitor to the trustees, appointed his son, who was his partner in his business, to be a new trustee. The trusts of the will were being administered by the Court :—*Held*, that, without any reference to the personal fitness of the son, by reason of his position the appointment was one which the Court ought not to approve, though it would not have been invalid if the Court had not been administering the trusts. *In re* NORRIS. ALLEN *v.* NORRIS   **27 Ch. D. 333**

10. —— **New Trustees**—*Continuing Trustee—Trustees appointed by Court—Conveyancing and Law of Property Act, 1881 (44 & 45 Vict. c. 41), ss. 31, 33.*] A settlement of real estate of which there were four trustees, provided that if the trustees thereby appointed "or any future trustee or trustees to be appointed in the place of them or any of them as hereinafter mentioned " should die or be desirous of being discharged, &c., it should be lawful for "the surviving or continuing trustee or trustees for the time being," with the consent of the tenant for life or in tail for the time being entitled in possession, to appoint a new trustee or new trustees in the place of the trustee or trustees so dying, &c. In 1872, four new trustees were appointed under the Trustee Act, 1850, in the place of two deceased and two retiring trustees. After this a decree was made for carrying the trusts of the settlement into execution. Two of the trustees of 1872 being dead, and another desiring to retire, the Plaintiff, who was an infant tenant in tail in possession, took out a summons to appoint new trustees, W. the continuing trustee took out a summons asking that he might be at liberty to appoint new trustees. A reference to chambers being directed, W. proposed new trustees whom the Court considered to be proper persons, but to whom all the persons beneficially interested objected :—*Held* (affirming the decision of Pearson, J.), that the persons nominated by W. must be appointed, though the tenant in tail in possession did not consent, for that as the power in the settlement only applied to filling up vacancies in the number of original trustees, or trustees appointed under the power, it had come to an end when new trustees were appointed by the Court in 1872, and that the fetter imposed by the settlement on the exercise of that power did not apply to the new power given to the continuing trustee by the Conveyancing and Law of Property Act, 1881, which enabled him to fill up vacancies in a body of trustees not coming within the scope of the power in the settlement. CECIL *v.* LANGDON - **28 Ch. D. 1**

11. —— **New Trustees** — *Executor of sole Trustee—Conveyancing and Law of Property Act, 1881 (44 & 45 Vict. c. 41), s. 31.*] The power of appointing new trustees given by sect. 31 of the Conveyancing Act, 1881, to "the personal representatives of the last surviving or continuing trustee" includes the case of an executor of a sole trustee. *In re* SHAFTO'S TRUSTS   **29 Ch. D. 247**

12. —— **New Trustees**—*One in place of two—23 & 24 Vict. c. 145.*] The power of appointing new trustees given by sect. 27 of the Act 23 & 24

V. SETTLEMENT—POWERS—*continued.*

Vict. c. 145, authorizes a retiring trustee, one of two originally appointed, to appoint a single trustee in place of himself, the other original trustee having previously disclaimed without acting. WEST OF ENGLAND AND SOUTH WALES DISTRICT BANK *v.* MURCH   **23 Ch. D. 138**

13. —— **New Trustees** — *Trustee remaining Abroad for more than Twelve Months—Person to exercise Power—Conveyancing and Law of Property Act, 1881 (44 & 45 Vict. c. 41), s. 31—Settlement executed before Act.*] A settlement executed in 1878 contained no express power to appoint new trustees, but there was a declaration that the husband and wife during their joint lives, and the survivor of them during his or her life, "shall have power to appoint new trustees or a new trustee for this settlement." There was no express reference to the power of appointing new trustees conferred by sect. 27 of Lord Cranworth's Act, which was then in force :—*Held*, that after the commencement of the Conveyancing Act, 1881, the husband and wife were the proper persons to exercise the power conferred by sect. 31 of that Act of appointing a new trustee in place of one of the trustees who had remained out of the United Kingdom for more than twelve months, though sect. 27 of Lord Cranworth's Act did not provide for, and the parties when they executed the settlement probably did not contemplate, the occurrence of a vacancy in that event. *In re* WALKER AND HUGHES' CONTRACT   **24 Ch. D. 698**

14. —— **Portions** — *Interest on Portions charged on Land in Ireland—Right of Donee of Power to fix Rate of Interest—Portions payable out of "rents and profits."*] By a settlement made in England on the marriage of D. certain real estates in Ireland were limited to trustees for 1000 years, upon trust by mortgaging the said estates, or out of the rents and profits thereof, to raise £15,000, to be divided among the younger children of the marriage as D. should appoint. D. appointed the whole of the portions among his children, appointing £4000 to his daughter, to be raised at certain specified times, with interest in the meantime at 5 per cent. The trustees being unable to raise the portions by mortgage, an action was brought to carry the trusts into effect :—*Held* (reversing the decision of Pearson, J.), that D. having only a power of distributing the portions and not of charging them, had no power to fix the rate of interest ; but that the land being in Ireland 5 per cent. was the proper rate to be fixed by the Court.—*Lewis* v. *Freke* (2 Ves. 507) and *Young* v. *Lord Waterpark* (13 Sim. 199) distinguished.—*Held*, also, that under the terms of the settlement the trustees of the term had right to apply the rents and profits first in payment of the interest, and secondly in reduction of the capital. BALFOUR *v.* COOPER - **23 Ch. D. 472**

15. —— **Sale** — *Duration — Determination — Intention of Settlor — Remoteness.*] A power given to the trustees of a settlement or will to sell land comprised in it can be exercised by them after the property has, under the trusts, become absolutely vested in persons who are sui juris, if on the construction of the instrument it appears to be the intention of the settlor or testator that it should be then exercised, provided that the

V. SETTLEMENT—POWERS—continued.

power in its creation was not obnoxious to the rule against perpetuities, and that the cestui que trustent have not put an end to the trusts by electing to take the property as it stands. *In re* COTTON'S TRUSTEES AND THE SCHOOL BOARD FOR LONDON　　　　-　　19 Ch. D. 624

16. —— Sale—*Extinction—Disentailing Deed.*] An estate was devised to uses to secure certain annuities, and subject thereto in strict settlement, with power for trustees to sell at the request of the tenant for life under the will. The estate was disentailed and resettled (the existing life estate being postponed to certain charges and the powers of the will being expressed to be kept alive):—*Held*, that the trustees for sale and the tenant for life could make a good title. *In re* WRIGHT'S TRUSTEES AND MARSHALL　28 Ch. D. 93

17. —— Sale—*Tenant for Life—Settled Land Act, 1882 (45 & 46 Vict. c. 38), ss. 3, 53—Appointment of New Trustee — Pending Action.*] Independently of the cumulative powers of sale given to tenants for life by the Settled Land Act, 1882, the tenant for life, and the trustees under a will which gives them power to sell the estate at the request and by the direction of the person or persons for the time being entitled to the actual freehold of the devised property, will not be restrained from selling the estate at the request and for the benefit of the tenant for life on merely speculative evidence adduced by the remainderman objecting to an immediate sale, of an expected future increase in the value of the property from the development of coal mines, and the construction of a railway through the estate. THOMAS *v.* WILLIAMS　　-　　-　24 Ch. D. 558

18. —— Sale—*Trust exercisable without Consent of Cestuis que Trust.*] Real property was vested in trustees upon trust at the request of A. and B. and the survivor, and after their death at discretion, to sell and hold the proceeds upon trust for A. and B. successively for life, and then for the children equally. After the deaths of A. and B. there were three adult children:—*Held*, that the trust for sale was not spent, but was exercisable by the trustees without the concurrence of the beneficiaries. *In re* TWEEDIE AND MILES　　　-　　　27 Ch. D. 315

VI. SETTLEMENT—REVOCATION.

1. —— Non-*solemnization of Marriage.*] By a settlement executed in 1877, in consideration of a then intended marriage, it was declared that a sum of stock, the property of the intended wife, which had been transferred by her two trustees, should be held by them on trust for the benefit of the intended wife, the intended husband, and the issue of the intended marriage. The marriage was not solemnized, but the parties cohabited without marriage, and three children were born. In 1883 an action was brought by the father and mother against the trustees of the settlement, to obtain a transfer of the fund to the mother:—*Held*, that the contract to marry had been absolutely put an end to, and that the Court could order the stock to be tranferred to the lady. ESSERY *v.* COWLARD　　-　　26 Ch. D. 191

2. —— Volunteers—*Wife's Property—Gift to Next of Kin of Wife in Default of Wife's Assign-*

VI. SETTLEMENT—REVOCATION—continued.

ment by Will—Power of Revocation.] By a marriage settlement the wife's property was settled, after life estates in the husband and wife and in default of children, in the event of the wife surviving, on her, and in the event of the husband surviving, as the wife should by will appoint, and in default, on her next of kin, excluding the husband:—*Held* (affirming the decision of Fry, J.), that the trust in favour of the next of kin could not be revoked, and that although there was no possibility of issue, the husband and wife together were not entitled to the corpus of the settled fund.—*Paul* v. *Paul* (15 Ch. D. 580) overruled. PAUL *v.* PAUL
[19 Ch. D. 47; 20 Ch. D. 742

VII. SETTLEMENT—SATISFACTION.

—— Double Portions — Bond — *Articles of Partnership.*] L. bound himself by bond to pay to his reputed son £10,000 on a certain day four years later. A few weeks before the day of payment he took his son into partnership, and it was provided in the articles that the capital should consist of £37,500 to be brought in by L., of which £19,000 should be considered as belonging to his son. He also assigned to his son the lease of the premises on which the business was carried on. L. died without having paid any part of the £10,000 secured by the bond:—*Held*, in a suit for the administration of L.'s estate (affirming the decision of Fry, J.), that the rule against double portions applied; and that the benefit given to the son under the partnership articles must be taken in satisfaction of the sum due under the bond.—*Holmes* v. *Holmes* (1 Bro. C. C. 555) and *Bengough* v. *Walker* (15 Ves. 507) considered. *In re* LAWES. LAWES v. LAWES　20 Ch. D. 81

SETTLEMENT—Accumulations　25 Ch. D. 729 ;
　　See ACCUMULATIONS. 1, 2. [30 Ch. D. 649

—— Covenant to settle—Severance of joint tenancy　-　　　　28 Ch. D. 416
　　See JOINT TENANT. 1.

—— Derivative—Settled Land Act 27 Ch. D. 707
　　See SETTLED LAND ACT—DEFINITIONS. 7.

—— Discretion of trustees — Interference of Court　-　　21 Ch. D. 571, 576, n. ;
　　　　　　　　　　　[29 Ch. D. 913
　　See TRUSTEE—POWERS. 4, 5, 6.

—— Female infant—Covenant to settle
　　See ELECTION. 6.　　[28 Ch. D. 124

—— Fraudulent—13 Eliz. c. 5　20 Ch. D. 389 ;
　　　　　　　　　[22 Ch. D. 74; 27 Ch. D. 523
　　See FRAUDULENT CONVEYANCE. 1, 2, 3.

—— Notice of—Negligence of solicitor 17 Ch. D.
　　See SOLICITOR—LIABILITIES. 2.　[437

—— Power of appointment.
　　See Cases under POWER—EXECUTION.

—— Power to appoint new trustees 26 Ch. D. 417
　　See POWER—EXTINCTION. 1.

—— Scotch law—Children of prior marriage
　　　　　　　　　　[9 App. Cas. 303
　　See SCOTCH LAW—HUSBAND AND WIFE. 5.

—— Share of residue　-　　-　30 Ch. D. 234
　　See WILL—LAPSE. 9.

SETTLEMENT—*continued.*
—— Timber—Larch trees—Windfalls
　　　　　　　[28 Ch. D. 220; 30 Ch. 485
　　See TIMBER. 1, 2.
—— Variation of.
　　See Cases under PRACTICE—DIVORCE—
　　SETTLEMENTS.
—— Variation of—Nullity of marriage　10 P. D.
　　　　　　　　　　　　[178
　　See PRACTICE—DIVORCE—NULLITY OF
　　MARRIAGE. 9.
—— Void under Bankruptcy Act　19 Ch. D. 588;
　　　　　　　　[15 Q. B. D. 682
　　See BANKRUPTCY—VOID SETTLEMENT.
　　1, 2.
—— Ward of Court　　　　25 Ch. D. 482
　　See INFANT—SETTLEMENT.

SETTLEMENT OF POOR.
　　See Cases under POOR LAW—SETTLE-
　　MENT.

SETTLING DAY—Appointment of　20 Ch. D. 356
　　See STOCK EXCHANGE. 2.

SEVERANCE—Compulsory powers of vestry—
　　Part of building　　　30 Ch. D. 642
　　See METROPOLIS—MANAGEMENT ACTS.
　　10.
—— From soil　-　　-　　-　30 Ch. D. 485
　　See TIMBER. 2.
—— Joint tenancy　17 Ch. D. 388; 28 Ch. D. 416
　　See JOINT TENANT. 1, 2.

SEWAGE—Nuisance by local board 22 Ch. D. 221
　　See NUISANCE—REMEDIES. 4.

SEWER—Accumulation of water—Negligence—
　　Liability of Metropolitan Board of
　　Works　-　　　　　7 Q. B. D. 418
　　See METROPOLIS—MANAGEMENT ACTS. 4.
—— Obligation to support—Local Government
　　Acts　　·　　　　8 Q. B. D. 86
　　See LOCAL GOVERNMENT—SEWERS. 1.
—— Power to make branch drains—Metropolis
　　Management Acts　-　15 Q. B. D. 652
　　See METROPOLIS—MANAGEMENT ACTS.
　　14.
—— Right of access to—Obstruction—Compen-
　　sation　　　　-　9 Q. B. D. 572
　　See LANDS CLAUSES ACT — COMPENSA-
　　TION. 4.
—— Support of.
　　See　LOCAL　GOVERNMENT — PUBLIC
　　HEALTH ACTS—*Statutes.*
—— Vesting in local authority　28 Ch. D. 283
　　See LOCAL GOVERNMENT—SEWERS. 2.

SEWERING AND PAVING—Expenses—Justices
　　—Jurisdiction—Appeal to Local Govern-
　　ment Board　　-　12 Q. B. D. 142
　　See LOCAL GOVERNMENT—PRACTICE. 2.
—— New street.
　　See Cases under
　　　　LOCAL GOVERNMENT—STREETS.
　　　　METROPOLIS—MANAGEMENT ACTS.

SEWERS BOARD—Arbitration—Judge of County
　　Court　　　-　9 Q. B. D. 723
　　See COUNTY COURT—JURISDICTION. 6.

SHADE—Lopping trees, &c., to avert.
　　See HIGHWAY—REPAIR—*Statutes.*

SHANGHAI—A port of registry.
　　See SHIP—MERCHANT SHIPPING ACTS—
　　Gazette.
—— Registrar for.
　　See SHIP—MERCHANT SHIPPING ACTS—
　　Gazette.

SHARE OF PARTNERSHIP—Assignment of
　　　　　　　　　[6 App. Cas. 64
　　See SCOTCH LAW—PARTNERSHIP.
—— Deceased partner—Proof　16 Ch. D. 620
　　See BANKRUPTCY—PROOF. 18.

SHAREHOLDER—Cost-book company
　　　　　[18 Ch. D. 660; 23 Ch. D. 52
　　See COMPANY—COST-BOOK COMPANY. 2, 4.
—— Majority of shareholders　20 Ch. D. 151
　　See COMPANY—WINDING-UP ORDER. 5.
—— Married woman　　　18 Ch. D. 581
　　See COMPANY—CONTRIBUTORY. 1.
—— Meeting of shareholders　23 Ch. D. 1
　　See COMPANY — DIRECTOR'S APPOINT-
　　MENT. 2.
—— Meeting of shareholders　-　23 Ch. D. 14;
　　　　　　　　　[25 Ch. D. 320
　　See COMPANY—MANAGEMENT. 4, 5.
—— Preference　-　　-　16 Ch. D. 344
　　See COMPANY—DIVIDENDS. 4.
—— Removal of name　-　-　17 Ch. D. 373
　　See COMPANY—PROSPECTUS. 2.
—— Service of notice on -　-　24 Ch. D. 149
　　See COMPANY—PROSPECTUS. 6.

SHARES—Allotment of.
　　See Cases under COMPANY — SHARES—
　　ALLOTMENT.
—— Bankruptcy—Order and disposition
　　　　　　　　　[30 Ch. D. 261
　　See BANKRUPTCY—ORDER AND DISPOSI-
　　TION. 11.
—— Contract to take—Agent's authority
　　　　　　　　　[24 Ch. D. 367
　　See PRINCIPAL AND AGENT — AGENT'S
　　AUTHORITY. 2.
—— Indemnity against calls—Trustee
　　　　　　　　　[22 Ch. D. 561
　　See TRUSTEE—INDEMNITY. 3.
—— Issue of, -　23 Q. B. D. 545, n.; 30 Ch. D. 153
　　See COMPANY—SHARES—ISSUE. 1, 2.
—— Not issued　-　　-　17 Ch. D. 715
　　See COMPANY—DIRECTOR'S AUTHORITY.
　　2.
—— Pledge of—Blank transfer -　26 Ch. D. 257
　　See COMPANY—SHARES—TRANSFER. 1.
—— Power to company to purchase　17 Ch. D. 76
　　See COMPANY—REDUCTION OF CAPITAL.
　　1.
—— Preference—Building society 23 Ch. D. 440;
　　　　　　　　　[9 App. Cas. 519
　　See BUILDING SOCIETY. 9.
—— Preference—Rights of shareholders
　　　　　　　　　[30 Ch. D. 376
　　See COMPANY—MEMORANDUM AND ARTI-
　　CLES. 1.
—— Purchase by company of its own shares
　　　　　　　　　[27 Ch. D. 268
　　See COMPANY—REDUCTION OF CAPITAL.
　　2.

SHARES—*continued.*

—— Transfer.

   See Cases under COMPANY—SHARES— TRANSFER.

SHELLEY'S CASE—Rule in - 9 Q. B. D. 643;
                      [9 App. Cas. 890
   See WILL—ESTATE IN REALTY. 2, 3.

SHERIFF.

   1. —— **Duty of Sheriff**—*Seizure in Execution—Equity of Redemption—Common Law Procedure Act*, 1860 (23 & 24 Vict. c. 126), s. 13.] Where goods seized in execution by a sheriff under a fi. fa. have been previously assigned by the execution debtor to a third person as security for a debt, the sheriff is not bound to interplead and thereby enable proceedings to be taken for an order to sell being made by a Judge under sect. 13 of the Common Law Procedure Act, 1860, but is at liberty to withdraw, though the value of the goods seized exceed the sum secured by the bill of sale, and the execution debtor therefore has an equity of redemption which is valuable. SCARLETT *v.* HANSON - - - 12 Q. B. D. 213

   2. —— **Possession Money**—*Sheriff's Officer—Abortive Execution—Who liable to pay.*] The solicitors of a judgment creditor, in the course of their duty as such solicitors, lodged a writ of fi. fa. at the office of the sheriff, with a request for execution, giving however no instructions as to the selection of any particular bailiff. The sheriff employed one of his officers to execute the writ, which the officer thereupon proceeded to do. On an action being brought by such sheriff's officer against the solicitors of the judgment creditor to recover his fees for executing the writ:—*Held* (affirming the judgment of Bowen, J.), that the solicitors were not liable to pay the fees; that the law, apart from a contract to pay them (express or implied), cast no such liability upon them; and that, from the mere fact that they in the ordinary course of their duty lodged the writ at the sheriff's office for execution, no such contract could be implied.—*Maybery* v. *Mansfield* (9 Q. B. 754) followed.—*Brewer* v. *Jones* (10 Ex. 655) dissented from ROYLE *v.* BUSBY - 6 Q. B. D. 171

   3. —— **Wrongful Seizure**—*Execution Creditor—Liability for wrongful Seizure under Fi. fa.—Implied Authority of Solicitor—Direction to levy on particular Goods.*] Whether a seizure of particular goods under a fi. fa. was directed by the execution creditor, so as to make him liable for the act of the sheriff, is a question of fact.—It is not within the scope of the implied authority of the solicitor of a judgment creditor issuing a fi. fa. to direct the sheriff to seize particular goods.—*Jarmain* v. *Hooper* (6 Man. & G. 827) distinguished. SMITH *v.* KEAL 9 Q. B. D. 340

   4. —— **Wrongful Seizure**—*Fi. fa.—Injunction—Costs.*] Under a writ of fi. fa. against a son, the sheriff seized goods of his father, in whose house the son lived. The son had in fact no goods there, except some wearing apparel. The writ was indorsed with a statement that the son lived at a certain address, which was in fact the father's house, though the indorsement did not state this. The father gave verbal notice to the bailiff that he claimed the goods, and the next day the sheriff issued an interpleader summons.

SHERIFF—*continued.*

Meanwhile the father had commenced an action against the sheriff alone, claiming an injunction to restrain him from remaining in possession, and Hall, V.C., without requiring notice to be given to the execution creditor, granted the injunction. The sheriff appealed, and meanwhile the execution creditor, on the hearing of the interpleader summons, had admitted that the goods seized were the father's. No misconduct on the part of the sheriff was proved.:—*Held*, that the action was premature; that the father ought to have waited to see the result of the interpleader proceedings; and that he must bear his own costs of the motion for the injunction in both Courts:—*Held*, also, that the Vice-Chancellor ought not to have granted the injunction without hearing the execution creditor, who should have been made a party to the action, or at any rate served with notice of it. HILLIARD *v.* HANSON 21 Ch. D. 69

  —— Forcible entry—Attachment 26 Ch. D. 644
     See PRACTICE—SUPREME COURT—ATTACHMENT. 6.

  —— Interpleader—Action of trespass—Protection - - - 14 Q. B. D. 873
     See PRACTICE—SUPREME COURT—INTERPLEADER. 12.

  —— Interpleader—Costs 22 Ch. D. 136
     See BILL OF SALE—FORMALITIES. 6.

  —— Interpleader—Sheriff's fees 26 Ch. D. 605
     See PRACTICE—SUPREME COURT—INTERPLEADER. 11.

  —— Notice of bankruptcy petition—Sale.
        [11 Q. B. D. 430; 14 Q. B. D. 966
     See BANKRUPTCY—ASSETS. 1, 2.

  —— Notice of bankruptcy petition—Sale under execution 15 Q. B. D. 48
     See BANKRUPTCY—PROTECTED TRANSACTION. 6.

  —— Notice of winding-up order 16 Ch. D. 337
     See COMPANY—SECURED CREDITOR. 1.

  —— Possession of—Apparent possession
                   [16 Ch. D. 668
     See BILL OF SALE—APPARENT POSSESSION. 2.

  —— Poundage—Costs of execution
                   [13 Q. B. D. 415
     See BANKRUPTCY—COSTS. 6.

  —— Removing goods from sheriff's custody—Attachment - 9 Q. B. D. 335
     See PRACTICE—SUPREME COURT—NOTICE OF MOTION. 1.

  —— Sale under execution—Application ex parte to sell by private contract
                   [12 Q. B. D. 162
     See BANKRUPTCY—SECURED CREDITOR. 9.

  —— Sale under execution—Fixed machinery—Law of Lower Canada 10 App. Cas. 843
     See COLONIAL LAW—CANADA—QUEBEC. 1.

SHERIFF'S COURT—Scotland 6 App. Cas. 251
     See SCOTCH LAW—SALE OF GOODS. 1.

  —— Scotland—Practice—Appeal 7 App. Cas. 49
     See SCOTCH LAW—PRACTICE. 3.

SHIP :—

I. SHIP—BILL OF LADING.

1. —— Exceptions — *Collision between Two Ships belonging to the same Owner—Negligence of Master and Crew—Action of Tort—Variance between Rules of Admiralty Court and Courts of Common Law—Supreme Court of Judicature Act, 1873 (36 & 37 Vict. c. 66), s. 25, sub-s. 9.*] The Plaintiffs shipped goods on board the Defendant's vessel, the *Crown Prince,* under a bill of lading, which contained exceptions of, among other things, " collision," and " accidents, loss, or damage, from any act, neglect, or default whatsoever of the pilots, master, or mariners, or other servants of the company, in navigating the ship." In the course of the voyage the *Crown Prince* came into collision with another vessel of the Defendants, the *Atjeh.* The Plaintiffs' goods were in consequence lost. The collision was due to negligence, for which the *Atjeh* was mainly in fault; but the *Crown Prince* also was in some degree to blame :—*Held,* that the Defendants had not committed a breach of the contract created by the bill of lading, and that no action could be maintained against them on the ground of failure to perform the undertaking therein contained to carry the goods safely upon the voyage.—*Per* Brett, L.J.: No stipulation on the part of the Defendants could be implied as to the conduct of those on board the *Atjeh,* and although the negligence of the *Atjeh* was not within the exceptions, nevertheless it was not within the contract created by the bill of lading :—*Per* Baggallay and Lindley, L.JJ. :—The exception " collision," although it did not cover the negligence of the *Crown Prince,* covered the negligence of the *Atjeh,* and the Defendants were expressly relieved from liability for the negligence of the *Crown Prince* by the other exceptions in the bill of lading :—*Held,* further, that the Defendants were liable in tort for the negligence of those engaged in navigating the *Atjeh,* but that the amount payable by the Defendants must be limited to one half of the loss sustained by the Plaintiffs, pursuant to the Supreme Court of Judicature Act, 1873, s. 25, sub-s. 9. CHARTERED MERCANTILE BANK OF INDIA v. NETHERLANDS INDIA STEAM NAVIGATION CO.
[9 Q. B. D. 118; 10 Q. B. D. 521

2. —— Exceptions—*Matters occurring during the Voyage—Breach of Obligation to provide reasonably fit Ship—Clause limiting Liability of Shipowners, Scope of.*] The Plaintiff shipped certain cattle on board the Defendants' ship for carriage from London to New York under a bill of lading

I. SHIP—BILL OF LADING—continued.

which provided as follows :— " These animals being in sole charge of shipper's servants, it is hereby expressly agreed that the shipowners, or their agents or servants, are, as respects these animals, in no way responsible either for their escape from the steamer or for accidents, disease, or mortality, and that under no circumstances shall they be held liable for more than £5 for each of the animals." The ship had on her previous voyage carried cattle suffering from foot and mouth disease. Some of the cattle shipped under the bill of lading were during the voyage infected with that disease, owing to the negligence of the Defendants' servants in not cleansing and disinfecting the ship before receiving the Plaintiff's cattle on board, and signing the bill of lading, and the Plaintiff in consequence suffered damage amounting to more than £5 for each of the said cattle :—*Held,* that the provision in the bill of lading limiting liability to £5 for each of the cattle did not apply to damage occasioned by the Defendants not providing a ship reasonably fit for the purposes of the carriage of the cattle which they had contracted to carry. TATTERSALL v. NATIONAL STEAMSHIP COMPANY　　12 Q. B. D. 297

3. —— Exceptions—*Perils of the Sea—Collision—Negligence.*] A collision between two vessels brought about by the negligence of either of them, without the waves or wind or difficulty of navigation contributing to the accident, is not " a peril of the sea " within the terms of that exception in a bill of lading. WOODLEY v. MICHELL
[11 Q. B. D. 47

4. —— Indorsement—" *Passing of Property* " *in Goods shipped—Indorsement by way of Pledge —Bills of Lading Act (18 & 19 Vict. c. 111), s. 1.*] The mere indorsement and delivery of a bill of lading by way of pledge for a loan does not pass " the property in the goods " to the indorsee, so as to transfer to him all liabilities in respect of the goods within the meaning of the Bills of Lading Act (18 & 19 Vict. c. 111), s. 1.—Goods were shipped to a foreign port under bills of lading making the goods deliverable to the shipper or assigns. After the goods had arrived and been warehoused the shipper indorsed the bills of lading in blank and deposited them with the indorsees as security for a loan. The indorsees never took possession of or dealt with the goods :—*Held,* reversing the judgment of the Court of Appeal, and restoring the judgment of Field, J., that " the property " in the goods did not " pass " to the indorsees within the meaning of the Bills of Lading Act so as to make them liable in an action by the shipowner for the freight. SEWELL v. BURDICK　　- 10 Q. B. D. 363; 13 Q. B. D. 159;
[10 App. Cas. 74

II. SHIP—CHARTERPARTY.

1. —— Bill of Lading—*Freight—Incorporation of Conditions of Charterparty in Bill of Lading—Lien.*] A charterparty contained a stipulation in the usual form for payment of freight at the rate of £1 11s. per ton ; it also contained a clause that the shipowner should have " an absolute lien on the cargo for freight, dead freight, demurrage, lighterage at port of discharge, and average ; " and a further clause that the captain was to sign bills of lading at any rate of freight ;

II. SHIP—CHARTERPARTY—*continued.*

"but should the total freight as per bills of lading be under the amount estimated to be earned by this charter, the captain to demand payment of any difference in advance." Certain goods were put on board the chartered ship, and were made deliverable to the Plaintiffs (who were not the charterers) by a bill of lading, whereby freight was made payable at 22*s.* 6*d.* per ton; the bill of lading contained also a clause, whereby it was provided that extra expenses should be borne by the receivers and "other conditions as per charterparty." Upon the arrival of the ship at the port of discharge the Defendant, who was the ship-owner, claimed and compelled payment of freight at the rate mentioned in the charterparty. The Plaintiffs having sued to recover back the difference between the freight as specified in the charterparty and the freight as specified in the bill of lading:—*Held,* that the bill of lading did not incorporate the stipulation in the charterparty as to the payment of freight, that no right of lien existed for the freight mentioned in the charterparty, and that the Plaintiffs were entitled to delivery of the goods upon payment of the freight specified in the bill of lading. GARDNER *v.* TRECHMANN 　-　**15 Q. B. D. 154**

2. —— Construction — *Demurrage — Ready Quay Berth as ordered by Charterer.*] By a charterparty it was agreed that the Plaintiff's vessel after loading a certain cargo should proceed "to London or Tyne dock to such ready quay berth as ordered by the charterers," "demurrage to be at the rate of £30 per running day," in no case unless in berth before noon were the lay days to count before the day following that on which the vessel was in berth, and the captain or owners were to have an absolute lien on the cargo for all freight and demurrage in respect thereof.— The vessel was ordered by the charterers to a certain London dock, but when the vessel arrived at such dock there was no quay berth ready for her, and she was consequently detained one day beyond the time required for discharging her had she been able to have got alongside a quay berth on her arrival in the dock:—*Held,* on the construction of this charterparty, that the charterers were bound to name such a quay berth as was ready, and that for the detention caused by the charterers neglecting to do so the Plaintiffs were entitled to a lien on the cargo for demurrage, the damage for the detention being sufficiently in the nature of demurrage to come within the demurrage clause. HARRIS AND DIXON *v.* MARCUS JACOBS & CO. 　-　**15 Q. B. D. 247**

3. —— Construction—*Final sailing from last Port—" Port"—Freight.*] By terms of a charterparty the owners were entitled to an advance of one-third of the freight within eight days "from final sailing of the vessel from her last port in United Kingdom." The vessel was loaded at Penarth Dock, and was towed by a steam-tug seven or eight miles, bringing her out about three miles into the Bristol Channel. She there cast anchor, as the weather was threatening. While she was lying at anchor a storm broke her cable, and she ultimately ran ashore on Penarth beach, and the cargo was spoiled. The vessel had never been beyond the limits of the port of Cardiff as

II. SHIP—CHARTERPARTY—*continued.*

defined for fiscal purposes, but she had left what, for commercial purposes, is considered the port, and had been out at sea. She went ashore within the limits of the port in its commercial sense. The owners sued for one-third of the freight, and the charterers resisted the claim on the ground that the vessel had never sailed from her last port in the United Kingdom:—*Held,* affirming the decision of Lopes, J., that the word "port" must be taken in its ordinary commercial sense, and that as the vessel had got out to sea without any intention of returning, she must be taken to have finally sailed from her last port, that her being driven back into it by the weather made no difference, and that the one-third of the freight was payable. PRICE *v.* LIVINGSTONE 　9 Q. B. D. 679

4. —— Construction—*Final sailing of Ship from last Port—Freight—" Port."*] The word "port" in a charterparty is to be understood in its popular, or business, or commercial sense; it does not in such a document necessarily mean the port as defined for revenue or pilotage purposes.— Tests for determining the business meaning of the word "port" considered.—A charterparty provided that a ship should load a cargo of coals at Cardiff, and then proceed to Bombay, the freight to be paid two-thirds in cash "ten days after the final sailing of the vessel from her last port in Great Britain," and the remainder in cash on delivery of the cargo. The ship loaded the coals in the Bute Docks, at Cardiff, and, having cleared at the Custom House, started on her voyage to Bombay. She proceeded down the artificial channel leading from the docks to the River Taff, and, when about 300 yards beyond the junction of the channel with the river, she came into collision with a steamer, and was so much injured that she was compelled to return the next day to the docks for repairs:—*Held,* that at the time of the collision the ship was not outside the limits of the port, in the popular, business, or commercial sense of the word; that, consequently, she had not finally sailed from her last port; and that no freight was payable. SAILING-SHIP "GARSTON" CO. *v.* HICKIE 　　**15 Q. B. D. 580**

5. —— Delay in discharging — *Discharge in Dock as ordered "if sufficient water."*] A charterparty provided that the ship should load with a cargo and proceed therewith to a port "to discharge in a dock as ordered on arriving, if sufficient water, or so near thereto as she may safely get always afloat":—*Held,* that the ship was only bound to discharge in the dock named if there was sufficient water there at the time the order was given. ALLEN *v.* COLTART 　　**11 Q. B. D. 782**

6. —— Delay in discharging — *Docks — Demurrage — Charterer's Duties.*] A charterparty for a ship to sail to "London Surrey Commercial Docks" is not satisfied by the ship arriving at the gate of the docks but not entering into the docks. There is no established custom in the port of London by which the charterer of a timber-loaded ship is bound to secure for the vessel, on its arrival in the river, and in close contiguity to the docks named, the authority to enter into the docks. The charterparty was to "London Surrey Commercial Docks, or as near thereto as she may safely get, and lie always afloat." As the docks were full

3 B 2

II. SHIP—CHARTERPARTY—*continued.*

the ship could not be given a discharging berth, and the dock manager therefore refused it entrance into the docks. Both parties having named these docks in the charterparty, this refusal of the dock authorities was held not to be the fault of either party. The cause of the delay as to being admitted into the docks was immaterial; the length of the delay was material. The charterer would not name any other docks to which the ship might be taken. The ship's master therefore took it to the Deptford Buoys (the nearest place to the Surrey Commercial Docks where it could lie in safety afloat) and there discharged the cargo by lighters carrying the timber into the Surrey Commercial Docks, where it was afterwards sorted and put in order on the wharf :—*Held*, that under the circumstances existing in this case, the delay in discharging the cargo was to be attributed to the charterer, who therefore became liable to demurrage, and to the charges for unloading. The contract in the charterparty as to demurrage was this : The cargo was to be supplied as fast as it could be taken on board, "and to be received at port of discharge as fast as steamer can deliver as above . . . and ten days demurrage over and above the said laying days" [there were no laying days mentioned in the charterparty] "at £30 per day payable day by day, it being agreed that for the payment of all freight, dead freight, and demurrage, the owner shall have absolute charge and lien on the said cargo . . ." "The cargo to be brought to and taken from alongside the ship at merchants' risk and expense." The ship did not fulfil the engagement in the charterparty to proceed to the Surrey Commercial Docks by merely going to the gates of the docks, but when it had fulfilled the alternative to go as near thereto as it could safely get, the charterer was bound to take the cargo from alongside at his risk and expense. The shipowner was not bound to wait for an unreasonable period, until the dock authorities should be able to assign the ship a discharging berth in the docks. When that difficulty arose about the ship being admitted into the Surrey Commercial Docks, and the charterer would not name any other docks or place where the vessel might be unloaded, the shipowner gave notice to the charterer of the discharge of the cargo by lighters, and on taking the timber into the docks, gave notice to the dock authorities that it was delivered there subject to the claim for freight, demurrage, and delivery charges :—*Held*, that he was warranted in so doing.　DAHL *v.* NELSON

[6 App. Cas. 38

7. —— Demurrage— *Cesser Clause* — *Bill of Lading—Incorporation of Conditions of Charterparty in Bill of Lading.*] A charterparty contained stipulations in the usual form for payment of freight and demurrage, and also a stipulation that " as this charterparty is entered into by the charterers on account of another party, their liability ceases as soon as the cargo is on board, the vessel holding a lien upon the cargo for freight and demurrage." The charterers having placed the cargo on board at the port of loading, a bill of lading was signed whereby the goods were made deliverable to themselves at the port of discharge, " they paying freight, and all other conditions as

II. SHIP—CHARTERPARTY—*continued.*

per charterparty." In an action by the shipowner against them, as consignees of the cargo, for demurrage in respect of delay at the port of discharge :—*Held*, that the cesser clause in the charterparty must be rejected as inapplicable in reading the bill of lading which incorporated all the conditions of the charterparty applicable to the reception of the goods at the port of discharge, and therefore that the Plaintiff was entitled to maintain the action.—Judgment of the Queen's Bench Division affirmed. GULLISCHEN *v.* STEWART BROTHERS　-　11 Q. B. D. 186; 13 Q. B. D. 317

8. —— Demurrage — *Customary Manner of Loading—Detention by Frost.*] By the terms of a charterparty the ship was to proceed to Cardiff, East Bute Dock, and there load in the customary manner from the agents of the freighters a cargo of rail iron, the cargo to be loaded as fast as ship could take on board and stow within the customary working hours of the port, commencing when ship was in berth and ready to load, " detention by frost, floods, &c., not to be reckoned as lay days." At Cardiff there are two docks, the East Bute Dock and the West Bute Dock, connected by a canal, and the West Bute Dock is connected by a junction canal with the Glamorganshire Canal. The shipowner, when the charterparty was made, did not know who were the freighters' agents at Cardiff. There were about six manufacturers of rail iron there, and all of them (with the exception of the freighters' agents) had wharves in the East or West Bute Dock. The agents' wharf was on the Glamorganshire Canal, nearly opposite the junction canal, and their rail iron was loaded on ships berthed in the East Bute Dock by means of lighters passing down the junction canal, through the West Bute Dock, and from thence through the connecting canal to the East Bute Dock. The other manufacturers loaded ships in the East Bute Dock, either from the quay or by lighters coming from their wharves.—The ship on arrival was berthed in the East Bute Dock, and the loading was commenced, but it was delayed afterwards for sixteen days by frost, which covered with ice the junction canal, from the agents' wharf to the West Bute Dock, and prevented there the passage of the lighters, though the water in the docks was not frozen :— *Held*, reversing the decision of Pollock, B., that the exception in the charterparty with respect to detention by frost did not apply to relieve the freighters from liability for demurrage, as the lighters with the cargo for the ship had not got within the limits of the East Bute Dock where the ship was to be loaded, before the detention by frost had happened. KAY *v.* FIELD

[8 Q. B. D. 594; 10 Q. B. D. 241

9. —— Demurrage—*" Frost preventing loading."*] By a charterparty a ship was to proceed to Cardiff, East Bute Dock, and there load in the customary manner from the agents of the freighters a cargo of iron, " Cargo to be supplied as fast as steamer can receive. . . . . Time to commence from the vessel being ready to load and unload and ten days on demurrage, over and above the said lay days, at £40 per day. (Except in case of hands striking work, or frosts or floods, or any other unavoidable accidents preventing

II. SHIP—CHARTERPARTY—_continued._

the loading . . . . ; in which case owners to have the option of employing the steamer in some short voyage trade until receipt of written notice from charterers that they are ready to resume employment without delay to the ship.)"—The ship arrived at the East Bute Dock and loaded part of her cargo. A frost then set in and made a canal which communicated with the dock impassable, so that the remainder of the cargo which was ready at a wharf on the canal could not for several days be brought in lighters to the dock. The cargo could not have been brought into the dock by carting or otherwise at any reasonable expense. The dock itself was not frozen over and if the cargo had been in the dock the loading might have proceeded :—_Held_, affirming the decision of the Court of Appeal, that the frost did not " prevent the loading" within the meaning of the exception. GRANT & Co. _v._ COVERDALE, TODD & Co.　　8 Q. B. D. 600; 11 Q. B. D. 543;
[9 App. Cas. 470

10. —— Demurrage— _Lay Days — Usual Place of Discharge — Custom to lighten Vessel at Entrance to Port before proceeding to Place of Discharge._] By charterparty it was agreed that the Plaintiffs' steamship should proceed to Cronstadt and load a cargo of wheat and therewith proceed to a port in the English or Bristol channel as ordered, " or so near thereto as she may safely get at all times of tide and always afloat, and deliver the same. Eight running days, Sundays excepted, to be allowed the merchants, if the ship be not sooner dispatched, for loading and discharging the steamer, and ten days on demurrage if required over and above the laying days at £25 per day." The steamer arrived at Cronstadt, occupied six running days in loading a cargo of 4325 quarters of wheat, and was ordered to Gloucester, Bristol Channel, for discharge. She arrived at Sharpness Dock in the Bristol Channel on the 13th of November. Sharpness Dock is within the port of Gloucester, and about seventeen miles from the basin within the city of Gloucester where grain cargoes are usually discharged if the burthen of the ship will admit. The steamer was ready to commence the discharge of her cargo on the 13th, but could not get nearer to Gloucester than Sharpness until part of her cargo was first discharged at Sharpness. On the 14th and 15th of November the consignees discharged into lighters 1585 quarters of the cargo, and then required the master to take the steamer through the canal to a place of discharge within the basin at Gloucester. The master proceeded, and arrived in the basin on the 17th. On the 18th the residue of the cargo was discharged and the vessel returned to Sharpness, where she arrived on the 19th. In an action for demurrage evidence was given of a custom of the port of Gloucester, according to which the usual place of discharging grain cargoes was at the basin within the city, and when vessels with grain cargoes destined for Gloucester were of too heavy a burthen to come up the canal they were lightened at Sharpness, and during the discharge at Sharpness of so much of the cargo as it was necessary to discharge in order to enable the vessel to proceed by the canal to Gloucester Basin the lay

II. SHIP—CHARTERPARTY—_continued._

days counted, but the time occupied by coming up the canal to discharge at Gloucester Basin and by returning to Sharpness was not counted :—_Held_, first, that the custom was reasonable, as the effect of it was not to detain the ship longer than if she had been wholly discharged at Sharpness; secondly, that it was not inconsistent with the express provision in the charterparty as to running days, for the proper inference from the facts was that the discharge of the vessel except for the purpose of lightening her did not commence until she arrived within Gloucester Basin. That, therefore the time occupied by the vessel in going from Sharpness to the basin and in returning to Sharpness ought to be excluded from the lay days, and the Plaintiffs were entitled to one day's demurrage only.—_Caffarini v. Walker_ (Ir. Rep. 9 C. L. 431; Ir. Rep. 10 C. L. 250) and _McIntosh v. Sinclair_ (Ir. Rep. 11 C. L. 456) considered. NIELSEN _v._ WAIT　　14 Q. B. D. 516
[Affirmed by the Court of Appeal, 16 Q. B. D. 67.]

11. —— Demurrage—_Completion of Voyage— Charterer's Option to order Ship to one of several Places in Dock — Discharge of Cargo._] By the terms of a charterparty the ship was to load from the charterers' agents at Cardiff a cargo of coals, " and therewith proceed to Dieppe and deliver the same alongside consignee's or railway wharf, or into lighters, or any vessel or wharf where she may safely deliver, as ordered, cargo to be loaded and discharged in forty-eight running hours, &c. Demurrage over and above the said lying time at 10s. per hour." The ship arrived in the dock at Dieppe, and was ordered to discharge at the railway wharf, but in consequence of all the discharging berths being occupied, she was not berthed at the railway wharf until twenty-four hours after her arrival in the dock. In an action by shipowner against charterers for demurrage :—_Held_, that the voyage was not completed, and the lying time did not commence under the charterparty until the ship was berthed at the railway wharf, and therefore that the Defendants were not liable to pay demurrage for delay in respect of the period which elapsed between the ship's arrival in the dock at Dieppe and her being berthed at the railway wharf.—_Davies v. McVeagh_ (4 Ex. D. 265) considered. MURPHY _v._ COFFIN
[12 Q. B. D. 87

12. —— Demurrage—_Loading and unloading at fixed daily Rate—Right to include whole Time occupied in Loading and Unloading._] By charterparty between the Plaintiff and the Defendants it was agreed that the Plaintiff's ship should proceed to Bilbao and there load a full and complete, or part, cargo of iron ore, and deliver the same at Middlesborough. " 400/500 tons per working day (Sundays and holidays excepted) to be allowed the charterers for loading, and 300 discharging, all demurrage over and above the said days at the rate of 2s. per hour for every 100 tons cargo. The lay days to commence day after arrival, and being ready to load or discharge respectively. The captain to have a lien on the cargo for freight or demurrage." " If the ship is loaded at other than Portugalette or Lucana shipping staithes, the loading and discharging to be at the rate of 300 tons per working day."—The

II. SHIP—CHARTERPARTY—*continued.*

vessel having loaded at a place other than those last mentioned at a rate less than 300 tons per working day, proceeded to Middlesborough, where she discharged her cargo at a higher rate per day :—*Held*, that, in calculating the demurrage, the days for loading and unloading must be kept separate, and that the charterers had no right to add together the whole number of days occupied in loading and unloading for the purpose of ascertaining the average amount of work done on each day. MARSHALL *v.* BOLCKOW, VAUGHAN, & CO.

[6 Q. B. D. 231

13. —— **Demurrage**—*Port of unloading—"At all times of tide and always afloat."*] A ship was chartered to unload at S. or "so near thereto as she may safely get at all times of tide and always afloat," and for delay in unloading the charterers were to pay demurrage.—The state of the tide prevented the ship from reaching S. for four days after she arrived at the nearest point where she was able to float :—*Held*, that, according to the terms of the charterparty this was a sufficient arrival of the ship at S. to found a claim for demurrage. HORSLEY *v.* PRICE 　　11 Q. B. D. 244

14. —— **"Excepted Dangers"**—*Option to cancel for non-arrival at Loading Port.*] By a charterparty of a steamship it was agreed that she should go to "three safe loading places" between two named ports and there load from the charterers a cargo of oranges and being so loaded proceed to London . . . and deliver the same pursuant to bills of lading . . . . (the act of God . . . . and all dangers of the seas, rivers, and steam navigation of what nature and kind soever during the said voyage always excepted), and the charterers thereby promised to load the cargo, and stipulated, after a provision for working and lay days, that "should the steamer not be arrived at first loading port free of pratique and ready to load on or before the 15th of December next, charterers have the option of cancelling or confirming this charterparty."—By dangers of the seas, the steamer, although arrived at the first loading port, was not free of pratique and ready to load on the 15th of December, and the charterers therefore cancelled the charterparty. At the trial of an action against them for not loading the cargo, the judge left to the jury the disputed question whether the port was a "safe loading place," but being asked by them for his opinion thereon, gave it, and they found in the affirmative :—*Held*, (1) that this expression of opinion was under the circumstances no misdirection ; (2) that the excepted dangers clause applied only to the voyage, and not to the clause giving the option to cancel the charterparty if the ship was not ready to load on the day fixed, and therefore the cancellation was justified. SMITH *v.* DART & SON 　—　14 Q. B. D. 105

15. —— **Managing Owner**—*Co-ownership—Commission.*] A vessel was chartered for twelve months, and during the currency of the charter the charterers made default in certain payments and the charter lapsed. The vessel was rechartered by a voyage charter from K. to England During the performance of this voyage the Defendant purchased a share in this vessel :—*Held*, on objection to the registrar's report in a co-

II. SHIP—CHARTERPARTY—*continued.*

ownership action, that the Defendant was not liable to bear any of the losses occasioned by the time charter :—*Held*, also, that a part owner being the manager of a ship, is entitled to remuneration for his services, but that there is no fixed rate applicable. THE "MEREDITH"　　-　　10 P. D. 69

16. —— **"Safe Port, or as near thereunto as she can safely get, and always lay and discharge afloat"**—*Rights of Parties when Ship is unable to lie afloat in Port of Discharge without being lightened—Evidence of Custom of Port.*] Where a vessel is chartered to proceed with cargo to a "safe port . . . . as ordered, or as near thereunto as she can safely get, and always lay and discharge afloat," the master is not bound to discharge at a port where she cannot, by reason of her draught of water, "always lie and discharge afloat" without being lightened, even if she can be lightened with reasonable dispatch and safety in the immediate vicinity of the port or in the port itself. A vessel was chartered to proceed with a cargo of grain from Baltimore to Falmouth for orders, "thence to a safe port in the United Kingdom as ordered, or as near thereunto as she could safely get, and always lay and discharge afloat." The vessel was ordered to Lowestoft. Her draught of water when loaded was such that she could not lie afloat in Lowestoft Harbour without discharging a portion of her cargo, but the discharge of cargo might have been carried on with reasonable safety in Lowestoft Roads. The consignee offered at his own expense to lighten the vessel in the roads, but the master refused to proceed to Lowestoft to discharge, and went to Harwich as the nearest safe port, and there discharged the cargo : —*Held*, reversing the decision of Sir R. Phillimore, that the consignee could not recover damages against the shipowner for the refusal of the master to discharge at Lowestoft. *Held*, also, that evidence that it was the custom of the port of Lowestoft for vessels to be lightened in the roads before proceeding into the harbour was not admissible. THE "ALHAMBRA"　　-　　6 P. D. 68

III. SHIP—FREIGHT.

1. —— **Collision**—*Sum in the Nature of Freight—Bill of Lading—Right of Action.*] A ship *A.* and her cargo belonged to the same owners, and the Plaintiffs advanced £1000 as a loan to such owners, and received as security, in conformity with the agreement made between them and the borrowers, the bill of lading, on which the master indorsed a receipt for £1000 as advanced freight, and also a policy of insurance on advanced freight. Ship *A.* was lost through a collision with the Defendants' vessel, whose negligence was admitted. It was proved that the difference between the value of the cargo at the port of destination and at the port of loading would have considerably exceeded £1000. In an action by the holders of the bill of lading for £1000 against the Defendants' ship :—*Held*, that the Plaintiffs were entitled to recover the sum, though it was not, strictly speaking, advanced freight, but a prospective increase in the value of the cargo, but that the insurers were subrogated to the rights of the Plaintiffs.—A sum in respect of disbursements for ship *A.* on her voyage and wages paid in advance had been awarded to the

III. SHIP—FREIGHT—continued.

owners of the A. by the registrar and merchants: Held, further, that this was no bar to the Plaintiffs' right to recover in this action. THE " THYATIRA "　　-　　8 P. D. 155

2. —— Derelict—Right to Freight after Abandonment of Ship.] By the abandonment of a ship by its crew during a voyage, without any intention to retake possession, a right is given to the owner of cargo on board to treat the contract of affreightment as at an end.—A ship with a cargo of resin in barrels, on a voyage from America to Rotterdam, was, owing to the perils of the sea, abandoned by her crew off the American coast. She was afterwards saved by another vessel, and brought with her cargo by the salvors into a port in England, and there arrested in an action for salvage by her salvors. Before the shipowner had released the ship or cargo, the owners of the cargo applied for and obtained from the Admiralty Court an order for the release of the cargo to them without payment of any freight, upon their giving bail to the salvors:—Held, that the cargo owners were entitled to treat the contract of affreightment as at an end, and that therefore the order of the Admiralty was rightly made. THE " CITO "　　-　　7 P. D. 5

—— Final sailing from last port — Right to freight　9 Q. B. D. 679; 15 Q. B. D. 580 See SHIP—CHARTERPARTY. 3, 4.

IV. SHIP—GENERAL AVERAGE.

1. —— Deck Cargo.] The Plaintiffs shipped certain cattle as a deck cargo on board the Defendants' vessel : during the voyage a storm arose, and owing to stress of weather the master jettisoned the deck cargo by throwing the cattle overboard. The act of jettison was proper and necessary on the part of the master for the safety of the Defendants' vessel :—Held, that the Plaintiffs could not recover from the Defendants a general average contribution for the loss of the cattle.—Johnson v. Chapman (19 C. B. (N.S.) 563 ; 35 L. J. (C.P.) 23) commented on. WRIGHT v. MARWOOD. GORDON v. MARWOOD　7 Q. B. D. 62

2. —— Deck Cargo—Charterparty—' At Merchant's risk."] It was stipulated in a charterparty that the "ship should be provided with a deck cargo if required at full freight, but at merchant's risk" :—Held, reversing the decision of the Queen's Bench Division, that the words "at merchant's risk" did not exclude the right of the charterers to general average contribution from the shipowners in respect of deck cargo, shipped by the charterers, and necessarily jettisoned to save the ship and the rest of the cargo. BURTON v. ENGLISH [10 Q. B. D. 426 ; 12 Q. B. D. 218

3. —— Liability of Cargo—General Average Contribution.] When ship and cargo are in peril, the fact that the shipowners have by the act of the master become bound to pay and have paid a sum of money for preservation of ship and cargo, and that the master in so binding them pursued a reasonable course under the circumstances, is not conclusive that the whole sum was chargeable to general average so as to bind the cargo owners to pay their proportion.—The decision of the Court of Appeal reversed and a new trial ordered on the

IV. SHIP—GENERAL AVERAGE—continued.

ground that the question of the amount chargeable to general average ought to have been submitted to the jury. ANDERSON v. OCEAN STEAMSHIP COMPANY 13 Q. B. D. 651 ; 10 App. Cas. 107

4. —— Reshipping Cargo—Expenses of Ship leaving Port of Refuge.] A ship on a voyage having sprung a dangerous leak, the captain, acting justifiably for the safety of the whole adventure, put into a port of refuge to repair. In port the cargo was reasonably, and with a view to the common safety of ship, cargo and freight, landed in order to repair the ship. The ship was repaired, the cargo reloaded and the voyage completed :—Held, affirming the decision of the Court of Appeal, that the cargo owners were not chargeable with a general average contribution in respect of the expenses of reshipping the cargo.—Atwood v. Sellar (4 Q. B. D. 342 ; 5 Q. B. D. 286) discussed. SVENDSEN v. WALLACE 11 Q. B. D. 616 ; [13 Q. B. D. 69 ; 10 App. Cas. 404

5. —— Ship on Fire—Water poured upon Cargo — Termination of Maritime Adventure — Arrival of Ship at Port of Destination — Cargo remaining on Board.] To pour water upon the cargo pursuant to the master's orders for the purpose of extinguishing a fire which has broken out in a ship's hold, is a general average act, and if the cargo is thereby injured, the owner is entitled to a contribution.—Whilst the cargo remains on board a ship after her arrival at the port of destination, the maritime adventure is not terminated so as to absolve the owners of the cargo and the ship from mutual rights and liabilities.—The Defendants were the owners of the H., which having arrived at her port of destination at the end of a voyage, unloaded about 1300 tons of her cargo ; about 100 tons remained on board. Whilst she was lying at a wharf, a fire broke out in her hold, and in order to extinguish it her master caused water to be poured into her, whereby some goods, forming part of the cargo and belonging to the Plaintiffs, were damaged. The H. might have been scuttled and raised again ; but if the fire had not been extinguished, she would have been in peril of partial destruction :—Held, that the Defendants were liable to contribute by way of general average for the damage done to the Plaintiffs' goods. WHITECROSS WIRE AND IRON COMPANY v. SAVILL　-　8 Q. B. D. 653

V. SHIP—MARITIME LIEN.

1. —— Bottomry—Necessaries—Foreign Vessel — 3 & 4 Vict. c. 65, s. 6—24 & 25 Vict. c. 10, s. 5— Bottomry Bond.] A foreign vessel was in an English port, and the owner, being temporarily in England and in want of funds for the purchase of necessaries, made an agreement with the Plaintiffs by which, in consideration of their advancing him by cash or acceptance £600 for necessaries supplied to and for the use of the vessel, he thereby undertook to return them the amount so advanced with interest and all charges on the return of the vessel from her voyage. And the Plaintiffs were thereby authorized "to cover the amount advanced the owner by insurance on ship, &c., out and home at owner's cost."—In an action in rem for necessaries in respect of the amount so

V. SHIP—MARITIME LIEN—continued.

advanced :—Held, by the Court of Appeal (Bowen and Fry, L.JJ., Brett, M.R., doubting), first, that this agreement was not equivalent to a bottomry bond ; secondly (by the whole Court) that there was no lien for necessaries ; for that before 3 & 4 Vict. c. 65, s. 6, there was no maritime lien on a foreign ship for necessaries supplied to her, that that section did not give any maritime lien but only a right to seize the ship on the institution of an action, and therefore that the Plaintiffs were not entitled to recover against the vessel.—Judgment of Sir J. Hannen reversed.— The Ella A. Clark (Br. & L. 32) overruled.—The Two Ellens (Law Rep. 4 P. C. 161) explained. THE "HEINRICH BJÖRN" -   3 P. D. 151 ; 10 P. D. 44

[Affirmed by the House of Lords.]

2. —— Bottomry—Necessaries — Reference to Registrar and Merchants.] To constitute a valid bottomry bond the money must be required for the necessities of the ship, and the authority of the master to borrow money on bottomry is based on such necessity. Reasonable inquiries by a lender may be evidence of his bona fides, but will not make a bond valid in respect of the several items for which it is given to the full extent of such items unless they are actually and entirely necessary :—Held, therefore, by the Court of Appeal, that the decision of Butt, J., was right, whereby he upheld the finding of the registrar and merchants who reduced the amount payable under a bond given by the master to a banker at St. Michaels, in respect of the charges for goods supplied, commissions, and premium.—The Prince of Saxe Coburg (3 Moo. P. C. 1) explained. THE "PONTIDA"   -   9 P. D. 102, 177

3. —— Damages—Wages—Priority of Liens.] The maritime lien for damages, arising out of damage done by a foreign vessel in a collision for which she is to blame, takes precedence of the maritime lien of the seamen for wages earned by them since the collision on board such vessel. THE "ELIN"   -   8 P. D. 39, 129

4. —— Disbursements—Admiralty Court Act, 1861 (24 & 25 Vict. c. 10), s. 10—Liability in respect of Judgment recovered in Action on Bill of Exchange drawn by Master and dishonoured.] In April and May, 1880, the master of a steamship obtained at a British colonial port coals for the ship, and paid for them by bills of exchange drawn on the charterers of the ship. The bills were dishonoured by the charterers, and in August, 1880, the master was served with a writ in an action brought to recover the amount of the bills. Judgment in this action was recovered against the master in July, 1881. In October, 1881, the steamship was sold, and the master in November, 1882, instituted an action of disbursements against her and her freight. The purchasers appeared and put in bail. At the hearing of the action the judgment recovered against the Plaintiff in August, 1881, remained still in force and unsatisfied, and the Plaintiff claimed to recover as a disbursement the amount for which he was liable under it :—Held, that the liability of the Plaintiff to satisfy the judgment against him must be considered as a disbursement in respect of which a maritime lien existed under the 10th section of the Admiralty Court Act, 1861 :—Held, also, that the right to enforce such

V. SHIP—MARITIME LIEN—continued.

lien had not been lost by any want of reasonable diligence on the part of the Plaintiff, and that his claim must be pronounced for. THE "FAIRPORT" [8 P. D. 48

5. —— Material Men — Wages — Priority— Lien—Costs.] When a fund, by a sale of a ship, is placed in Court by one set of claimants, so as to be available for other claimants, the former are entitled to their costs up to and inclusive of the sale, though they do not rank first in respect of their actual claim.—Mariners have priority of wages over persons with a possessory common law lien up to the time of the beginning of such lien, and they are entitled to subsistence money from the time they leave the ship to the time they return home: this and the expenses of the journey home, and the costs of the action, rank with their prior wages. THE " IMMACOLATA CONCEZIONE " [9 P. D. 37

6. —— Necessaries—Artificer's Lien on Ship —Contract to take Bills in Payment—Possession —Negotiation of Acceptance.] Engineers contracted with the debtor, the owner of a barge, to supply steam machinery to the vessel, at the docks of a dock company, for the price of £1050, to be paid by approved bills ; one at three months for £260 when the boiler and engine should be placed in the vessel, one at three months for £260, and one at six months for £530, when the vessel should have made a trial trip. The vessel having been taken to the docks, was there entered in the name of one of the engineers ; and whilst shipwrights and other agents of the debtor were occasionally or constantly on board, the vessel remained in the possession of the engineers till the boat was ready to make a trial trip. In the interim the engineers had been paid £360, partly in cash, and partly by the debtor's acceptance, which they discounted. On the day appointed for the trial trip the debtor filed a liquidation petition, and a receiver took possession of the vessel. A few days afterwards the debtor's acceptance was dishonoured :—Held, that the lien of the engineers for the unpaid price for the machinery and their labour was not affected by their having agreed to take bills in payment, nor by the nature of the possession, nor by their having discounted the debtor's acceptance. Ex parte WILLOUGHBY. In re WESTLAKE [16 Ch. D. 604

7. —— Necessaries — Vice-Admiralty Jurisdiction—26 & 27 Vict. c. 24, s. 10, sub-s. 10.] No maritime lien attaches to a ship in respect of coals or other necessaries supplied to it.—Vice-Admiralty Courts have not (apart from statute) more than the ordinary Admiralty jurisdiction, i.e., as it existed before 3 & 4 Vict. c. 65, enlarged it. The Vice-Admiralty Act, 1863 (26 & 27 Vict. c. 24), s. 10, sub-s. 10, does not create a maritime lien with respect to necessaries supplied within the possession. LAWS v. SMITH. THE "RIO TINTO" [9 App. Cas. 356

VI. SHIP—MASTER.

1. —— Sale — Wreck — Necessity.] On the 19th of April an Austrian ship with a valuable cargo on board ran upon a rock on the eastern side of Algoa Bay, distant fifty miles by sea and about eighty by land from Port Elizabeth.

VI. SHIP—MASTER—*continued.*

The Austrian consul at Port Elizabeth came to the spot, and there being no hope of getting the vessel off, he advised the master to sell her with the cargo. The master accordingly advertised the ship and cargo for sale, and they were sold in one lot by auction on the 30th of April for £9500, after a brisk competition. The purchaser got some part of the cargo out of the wreck, but on the 19th of June the ship went to pieces with the rest of the cargo on board. The owners of the cargo having abandoned it to the underwriters as a total loss, the underwriters filed their bill to have the goods which had been brought to land delivered to them as not having been effectually sold. The master had not gone to Port Elizabeth, nor endeavoured to procure funds to enable him to save the cargo; nor had he made any effort to induce any persons to undertake the salvage of the cargo. Several witnesses at Port Elizabeth deposed that in their opinion no person could have been induced to undertake the salvage; others gave their opinion that offers to save the cargo could have been obtained if a large percentage of the net proceeds had been offered. There was a good deal of evidence to shew that, in the opinion of persons on the spot, the course which had been adopted of selling the wreck and cargo was the most advisable one in the interest of all parties concerned :—*Held,* by the Court of Appeal (affirming the decision of the Master of the Rolls), that no such necessity was proved to have existed as would make the master the agent of the owners of the cargo to effect a sale; that the sale was void; and that the Plaintiffs were entitled to the cargo saved, subject to a proper allowance for salvage and other expenses. ATLANTIC MUTUAL INSURANCE COMPANY *v.* HUTH

[16 Ch. D. 474

2. —— Wages—*Misconduct—Mortgage.*] A mortgagee took possession of a ship by putting a man on board and giving notice to the master. The latter, by order of the mortgagor, took the vessel to sea with the man in possession on board. In an action by the master for wages, and for compensation for wrongful dismissal, the registrar awarded him a sum as compensation, being the amount of wages payable for two months after the mortgagee took possession :—*Held,* on appeal, that the master had been guilty of misconduct in taking the vessel to sea, and could not as against the mortgagee be properly awarded any sum as compensation for wrongful dismissal. THE "FAIRPORT"

10 P. D. 13

VII. SHIP—MERCHANT SHIPPING ACTS.

The Act 45 & 46 Vict. c. 55 (the Merchant Shipping Expenses Act, 1882), repeals 40 & 41 Vict. c. 44, amends the Merchant Shipping Acts, 1854 and 1876 and certain other enactments, provides for the adjustment of the receipts and expenditure under the Merchant Shipping Acts between the Mercantile Marine Fund and moneys provided by Parliament, and also amends the law with respect to Expenses of Prosecutions for Offences committed at Sea.

Colonial Courts of Inquiry.] *The Act 45 & 46 Vict. c. 76, amends the Merchant Shipping Acts, 1854 to 1880, with respect to inquiries held in British possessions abroad into charges of incom-*

VII. SHIP — MERCHANT SHIPPING ACTS — *continued.*

petency or misconduct on the part of masters, mates, or engineers of ships, or into shipwrecks or other casualties affecting ships.

Act of 1883.] *The Act 46 & 47 Vict. c. 41, (Merchant Shipping Fishing Boats Act, 1883) amends the Merchant Shipping Acts, 1854 to 1880, with respect to fishing vessels and apprenticeship to the sea fishing service and otherwise.*

PART I. FISHING BOATS AND THE SEA FISHING SERVICE.

Sect. 3. *Application of first part of this Act, and definitions.*

Apprenticeship to the Sea Fishing Service, and agreements with boys under 16 with respect to such service.

Sect. 4. *Apprenticeship indentures and agreements with boys under 16 how to be entered into.*

Sect. 5. *Indentures of apprenticeship and agreements to contain provisions set forth in 2nd Schedule, otherwise to be void.*

Sect. 6. *Limits of age for lads employed in sea fishing.*

Sect. 7. *Penalty on persons receiving money for binding apprentice.*

Sect. 8. *Indentures and agreements with boys to be void if not entered into before a superintendent of mercantile marine.*

Sect. 9. *Penalty for taking boy to sea under void indenture or agreement, and powers of superintendent in such case.*

Sect. 10. *Power of mercantile marine superintendents to enforce indentures or agreements.*

Sect. 11. *Shipping masters to assist in binding apprentices and making agreements, and to be under the control of the Board of Trade.*

Sect. 12. *Guardian and overseers of the poor to apprentice in conformity with this Act.*

AGREEMENTS WITH SEAMEN.

Sect. 13. *Agreements to be made with seamen containing certain particulars,*

Sect. 14. *Manner of entering into agreements.*

Sect. 15. *Special engagements may be made for several fishing boats belonging to the same owners, and owners may enter into agreements instead of skippers.*

Sect. 16. *Fishing boats making short voyages may have running agreements.*

Sect. 17. *Engagement and discharge of seamen pending a running agreement.*

Sect. 18. *Definition of "voyage" of a fishing boat.*

Sect. 19. *Reports of a fishing boat's crew on a voyage to be made.*

Sect. 20. *Penalty for shipping seamen without agreement duly executed.*

Sect. 21. *Changes in crew to be reported.*

Sect. 22. *Alterations, &c., in agreements to be void unless attested.*

Sect. 23. *Penalty for falsifying or delivering false copy of an agreement.*

WAGES AND DISCHARGES OF SEAMEN.

Sect. 24. *Skipper to deliver account of wages.*

Sect. 25. *Seamen to have inspection of owner's accounts and books relating to catch.*

Sect. 26. *Skipper to give seamen certificate of discharge.*

VII. SHIP—MERCHANT SHIPPING ACTS— *continued.*

Sect. 27. Seamen discharged without fault to recover compensation in same manner as wages.

DISCIPLINE.

Sect. 28. Offences of seamen and apprentices, and their punishments. Desertion. Neglect or refusal to join or proceed to sea, and absence without leave. Quitting boat before it is in security. Disobedience and neglect of duty. Continuous disobedience or neglect of duty. Assaults. Combinations to disobey or neglect duty. Damage to boat, or stores, or cargo, and embezzlement. Smuggling.

Sect. 29. Questions of forfeiture may be decided in suits for wages

Sect. 30. How things forfeited are to be disposed of.

Sect. 31. Deserters and others may be sent back to their boats.

Sect. 32. How seamen and apprentices deserting, or neglecting or refusing to join or proceed to sea, or absent without leave, or guilty of disobedience or neglect of duty, may be dealt with.

Sect. 33. Notice by seaman that he intends to absent himself from his ship and effect thereof.

Sect. 34. How wages are to accrue and to be calculated. Forfeiture of whole if voyage or trip shorter than the period of forfeiture.

Sect. 35. Facilities for proving desertion so far as concerns forfeiture of wages.

CERTIFICATES TO SKIPPERS AND SECOND HANDS.

Sect. 36. Certificates for fishing boats heretofore granted to be deemed to have been granted under 17 & 18 Vict. c. 104 (Part III).

Sect. 37. Power of Board of Trade to issue certificates for fishing boats.

Sect. 38. Availability of certificates referred to in this Act.

Sect. 39. Provisions in the Merchant Shipping Acts to apply to certificates referred to in this Act.

Sect. 40. Certificates of service to be given to certain skippers of fishing boats.

Sect. 41. Board of Trade may establish a register of certificates. Copy or extract from register or register of shipping at any port to be evidence.

Sect. 42. No fishing boat to proceed to sea without duly certified skipper and penalty for so doing.

ENACTMENTS RELATING TO DEATHS, INJURIES, PUNISHMENTS, ILL-TREATMENT AND CASUALTIES.

Sect. 43. Skipper of fishing boat to record cases of death, injury, or ill-treatment.

Sect. 44. Skippers to make special reports of death, injuries, ill-treatment, punishment, and casualties.

Sect. 45. Inquiry into cause of death, injury, ill-treatment, punishment, or casualty.

DISPUTES BETWEEN SKIPPERS OR OWNERS AND SEAMEN.

Sect. 46. Superintendent of Mercantile Marine Office to decide disputes between seamen and owners and masters.

Sect. 47. Masters and others to produce documents to superintendent of Mercantile Marine Office, and to give evidence.

VII. SHIP—MERCHANT SHIPPING ACTS— *continued.*

PART II. MISCELLANEOUS.

Sect. 48. Seamen's lodging-houses.

Sect. 49. Declaration of the meaning of 17 & 18 Vict. c. 104, s. 109.

Sect. 50. Incorporation of Part I. of 17 & 18 Vict. c. 104.

Sect. 51. Legal proceedings in cases of offences.

Sect. 52. Fishing tenders to be trawlers.

Sect. 53. Vessels engaged in certain fisheries to be deemed to be foreign going ships.

Sect. 54. 17 & 18 Vict. c. 104, s. 243, and s. 35 of this Act not to take away remedy for breach of contract.

Sect. 55. Repeal of enactments and saving.

Passenger Ships.] *Notice by Board of Trade of 9th June, 1882, under the Passengers Act, 1855, and the Passengers Act Amendment Act, 1863, varying the declared length of voyage to certain places for certain passenger ships*
[L. G., 1882, p. 2739

Passengers Act, 1885, s. 71, new form of passenger's contract ticket prescribed by Board of Trade. Order of 13th July, 1883
[L. G., 1883, p. 3588

Shanghai.] *Order in Council of 22nd May, 1883, providing for the appointment of a Registrar for Shanghai, a port of registry under the Merchant Shipping Act, 1873 (36 & 37 Vict.) c. 85, s. 29*
[L. G., 1883, p. 2790

Unlawfully entering Foreign Ship within British Jurisdiction.] *The following Orders in Council apply sect. 5 of the Act 43 & 44 Vict. c. 16 (Merchant Seamen Payment of Wages and Rating Act, 1880), to the foreign ships hereinafter mentioned. This section provides that where a ship is about to arrive, is arriving, or has arrived at the end of her voyage every person not being in Her Majesty's service, or not being duly authorized who —*

(a.) *Goes on board the ship without the permission of the master before the seamen lawfully leave the ship at the end of their engagement or are discharged (whichever last happens) or,*

(b.) *Being on board the ship remains there after being warned to leave by the master, or by a police officer, or by any officer of the Board of Trade or of the Customs, shall for every such offence be liable on summary conviction to a fine not exceeding twenty pounds, or at the discretion of the Court to imprisonment for any term not exceeding six months, and the master of the ship or any officer of the Board of Trade may take him into custody, and deliver him up forthwith to a constable to be taken before a Court or magistrate capable of taking cognizance of the offence and dealt with according to law;*

And is further provided, sect. 6, that whenever it is made to appear that any foreign country has provided that unauthorized persons going on board of British ships under similar circumstances shall be subject to similar provisions as above; and that such foreign country is desirous that the said section shall apply to ships of such foreign country within British jurisdiction, an Order in Council may declare that the provisions of sect. 5 shall

VII. SHIP — MERCHANT SHIPPING ACTS —
continued.

·apply to the ships of such foreign country as if they
·were British ships.

The Order in Council of October 17th, 1884,
·applies sect. 5 of this Act to the ships of Austro-
·Hungary　-　-　L. G., 1884, p. 4580

The Order in Council of May 22nd, 1883, applies
the same section to American ships　L. G., 1883,
[p. 2789

The Order in Council of Nov. 30th, 1882, applies
·the same section to German ships　L. G., 1882,
[p. 6139

. The Order in Council of March 2nd, 1881,
·applies the same section to ships of Italy
[L. G., 1881, p. 990

The Order in Council of Oct. 25th, 1881, applies
·the same section to Sweden and Norway
[L. G., 1881, p. 5294

Measurement of Tonnage.] The following
Orders in Council apply the rules made under
·25 & 26 Vict. c. 63 (the Merchant Shipping Act
Amendment Act, 1862), s. 60, to the merchant ships
·of the foreign countries hereinafter mentioned.

Order in Council of 19th March, 1883, relative
to the measurement of the tonnage of merchant
ships of the United States of America L. G., 1883,
[p. 168]

Order in Council of 17th Oct., 1884, relative to
the measurement of the tonnage of Belgian mer-
·chant ships　-　-　L. G., 1884, p. 4580

Order in Council of 20th April, 1883, relative
·to the measurement of the tonnage of merchant
·ships of Denmark　-　-　L. G., 1883, p. 2154

Order in Council of 14th Feb., 1883, relative to
the measurement of the tonnage of steam ships of
·Italy　-　-　-　L. G., 1883, p. 910

Order in Council of 27th January, 1885, relative
·to the measurement of the tonnage of Japanese
·ships -　-　-　L. G., 1885, p. 473

Order in Council of 2nd Feb., 1884, relative to
the measurement of the tonnage of merchant sailing
·ships of the United Kingdom of Norway
[L. G., 1884, p. 527

Order in Council of 18th Aug., 1882, relative to
the measurement of the tonnage of Swedish mer-
·chant ships　-　-　L. G., 1882, p. 3906

Certificate of Competency—Colonial.] Orders
in Council made in pursuance of 32 & 33 Vict. c. 11
·(the Merchant Shipping (Colonial) Act, 1869), s. 8,
which enacts, that where the Legislature of any
·British possession provides for the examination of
and grant of certificates of competency to persons
intending to act as masters, mates, or engineers on
board British ships, and the Board of Trade
reports to Her Majesty that they are satisfied that
·the examinations are so conducted as to be equally
efficient as the examinations for the same purpose
in the United Kingdom under the Acts relating to
merchant shipping, and that the certificates are
: granted on such principles as to shew the like qualifications and competency as those granted under the
said Acts, and are liable to be forfeited for the like
reasons, and in the like manner, it shall be lawful
·for Her Majesty by Order in Council,—

1. To declare that the said certificates shall be of
the same force as if they had been granted under
the said Acts.

2. To declare that all or any of the provisions of
·the said Acts which relate to certificates of compe-

VII. SHIP — MERCHANT SHIPPING ACTS —
continued.

tency granted under those Acts shall apply to the
certificates referred to in the said Order.

3. To impose such conditions and to make such
regulations with respect to the said certificates and
to the use, issue, delivery, cancellation, and suspension thereof as to Her Majesty may seem fit, and to
impose penalties not exceeding fifty pounds for the
breach of such conditions and regulations.

The Order in Council of June 29th, 1882, declares the efficiency, in the different degrees therein
stated, of certificates of competency of the following
British possessions:—

Canada.
Malta and its Dependencies.
Victoria.
New Zealand.
New South Wales.
South Australia.
Tasmania.
Bengal.
Newfoundland.
Bombay.
Queensland.　　L. G., 1882, p. 3065

The Order in Council of Dec. 31st, 1883, declares with regard to the efficiency of certificates of
competency granted by Hong Kong
[L. G., 1884, p. 186

Certificate of Survey—Colonial.] Orders in
Council made in pursuance of 39 & 40 Vict. c. 80,
(the Merchant Shipping Act, 1876), s. 17, which enacts that, when the legislature of any British possession provides for the survey of and grant of
certificates for passenger steamers, and the Board
of Trade report to Her Majesty that they are satisfied that the certificates are to the like effect, and
are granted after a like survey, and in such manner
as to be equally efficient with the certificates granted
for the same purpose in the United Kingdom under
the Acts relating to merchant shipping, it shall be
lawful for Her Majesty by Order in Council to declare the efficiency of such certificates, or impose
conditions on the same.

Order in Council of 26th June, 1884, referring
to certificates of survey granted by Bombay
[L. G., 1884, p. 2994

Ditto of 17th October, 1884, as to same granted
by Bengal -　-　[L. G., 1884, p. 4579

Lighthouses.] Order in Council of 12th Dec.,
1885, under 17 & 18 Vict. c. 104, s. 410, that every
ship, British or foreign, deriving benefit from the
light vessel at Skulmartin Reef, County Down, shall
pay certain tolls to the officers authorized in that
behalf　-　-　L. G., 1885, p. 6039

Order in Council of 12th Dec., 1885, under
17 & 18 Vict. c. 104, s. 410, that every ship, British
or foreign, deriving benefit from the light vessel off
the Middle Cross Sand, near Yarmouth, shall pay
certain tolls to Corporation of Trinity House
[L. G., 1885, p. 6039

Order in Council of 12th, Dec. 1885, under
18 & 19 Vict. c. 91, s. 2, that tolls shall cease to be
levied on ships for the lighthouse on Cape Race,
Colony of Newfoundland　L. G., 1885, p. 6129

1. —— Detention of British Ship—"Unfit to
proceed to Sea without serious Danger to Human
Life"—"Reasonable and Probable Cause for Provisional Detention of Ship"—Merchant Shipping

VII. SHIP — MERCHANT SHIPPING ACTS —
continued.

Act, 1876 (39 & 40 *Vict.* c. 80), *ss.* 6, 10.] The
Plaintiff was the owner of a British ship named
the *L.*, which was at the British port of S., and
was intended to be employed in the foreign cattle
trade. Certain surveyors of the Board of Trade
reported in doubtful terms that owing to her unusual proportions the *L.* was an unsafe ship. The
Board of Trade thereupon ordered the *L.* to be
provisionally detained. A court of survey was
held as to the condition of the *L.*, and the members thereof reported that the *L.* was not unsafe,
and that she ought not to have been detained.
The *L.* was accordingly released. The Plaintiff
then brought an action against the secretary of
the Board of Trade to recover compensation for
the loss to him by reason of the provisional detention. At the trial it was admitted that the *L.*
was a safe ship. The Judge in substance directed
the jury to consider whether it was reasonable in
the Board of Trade to detain the *L.* for survey
without a direct affirmation by their surveyors that
in their opinion she was unsafe :— *Held*, a misdirection, for the proper question to be left to the
jury was whether the facts with regard to the *L.*
as she lay at S., which would have been apparent
to a person of ordinary skill on examining her and
inquiring about her, would have given him reasonable and probable cause to suspect her safety and
to detain her for survey and inquiry. THOMPSON
v. FARRER -   -   -   **9 Q. B. D. 372**

2. —— Duty of Master—*Investigation—Shipping Casualty—Appeal—Merchant Shipping Act,*
1854 (17 & 18 *Vict.* c. 104), *ss.* 242, 432—" *Wrongful act or default*"—*Fresh Evidence on Appeal—
Costs.*] On a shipping casualty appeal where it
is desired to adduced fresh evidence at the hearing of the appeal, application for leave to do so
should be made to the Court of Appeal by motion
prior to the hearing of the appeal.—An error of
judgment on the part of the master of a vessel at
a moment of great difficulty and danger does not
amount to a wrongful act *or* default, within the
meaning of the 242nd section of the Merchant
Shipping Act, 1854, so as to justify the suspension
or cancellation of the master's certificate.—On a
successful appeal the Board of Trade having appeared in support of the decision appealed from
were directed to pay the costs of the appeal. THE
" FAMENOTH "   **7 P. D. 207**

3. —— Duty of Owner—*Engaging or supplying Seamen or Apprentices—Merchant Shipping
Act,* 1854 (17 & 18 *Vict.* c. 104), *s.* 147, *sub-s.* 1.]
By sect. 147, sub-sect. 1, of the Merchant Shipping Act, 1854 (17 & 18 *Vict.* c. 104), if any person not licensed by the Board of Trade other than
" the owner *or* master *or* mate of a ship, *or* some
person who is bonâ fide the servant and in the
constant employ of the owner, *or* a shipping
master duly appointed as aforesaid, engages or
supplies any seaman *or* apprentice to be entered
on board any ship in the United Kingdom," he
incurs a penalty.—The Respondent having bonâ
fide contracted to purchase one sixty-fourth share
in a British ship from P., who, though not registered as the owner, had the full possession and
control of the ship under a contract to purchase
the sixty-four shares, supplied an apprentice to P.,

VII. SHIP — MERCHANT SHIPPING ACTS —
continued.

who engaged the apprentice for the ship :—*Held*,
that the Respondent was an " owner " within the
meaning of the exemption, since though not a
registered owner he had a contract enforceable in
Equity for the purchase of a share in the ship.
HUGHES *v.* SUTHERLAND -   **7 Q. B. D. 160**

4. —— Duty of Owner —*Failure of Cargo
Owner to take Goods—Bill of Lading—Merchant
Shipping Amendment Act,* 1862 (25 & 26 *Vict.*
c. 63), *s.* 67—*Notice.*] When goods are landed
under sub-sect. 6, 25 & 26 Vict. c. 63, s. 67, sub-
sect. 7, does not apply, for the latter refers only to
the discharging of cargo overside, and not to the
landing of it for the purposes of assortment on
the wharf, and the written notice referred to in
sub-sect. 7 applies, therefore, to cases arising
under that sub-section only.—It is the duty of the
owner of the goods who receives either a written
or verbal notice that he can have them to take them
away within a reasonable time, and that whether
sub-sect. 6 or 7 applies to the case.—Notice to the
lightermen employed by the owner of the goods
is notice to the owner himself.—A ship arrived
in dock with a general cargo on the 12th of December, and began to unload on the quay on the
13th. The Plaintiffs (owners of some of the
goods) sent a lighterman and barge to receive
their portion of the cargo on the 13th. It was
not then ready. On the 14th the lighterman
again attended but could obtain no information.
On the 14th the firm of lightermen wrote to the
Defendants (the shipowners), stating they had
made application for the goods and enclosing a
notice requiring twenty-four hours' notice of the
Defendants' readiness to deliver the goods, and
stating that they would not be responsible for
any landing charges. On the 15th the landing of
the cargo was completed, and the lighterman was
that day verbally informed he could have the
goods on the morning of the 16th. He did not
attend, and the goods were not taken away till
the 29th. The Plaintiffs paid the dock charges
under protest, and brought an action to recover
them back :—*Held*, that they could not recover
them. THE " CLAN MACDONALD " -   **8 P. D. 178**

5. —— Duty of Owner—*Investigation—Appeal
—Shipping Casualties Investigations Act,* 1879
(42 & 43 *Vict.* c. 72), *s.* 2.] A shipowner, who
has appeared as a party at the hearing of an investigation under the Merchant Shipping Acts
into the circumstances attending the loss of a
ship owned by him, has no right of appeal, notwithstanding that the tribunal investigating the
case has given a decision suspending the certificate of the master of the ship, and condemning
the shipowner in costs.—The Wreck Commissioner, having been requested to hold an investigation into the loss and abandonment of a British
ship, found that the loss of the ship was due to
certain improper ballast taken on board her at an
English port having been converted into mud by
mixture with the water made by her during the
voyage, and so choking the pumps that they
could not be used, whereby the ship foundered,
and for these wrongful acts and defaults suspended the certificate of the master of the ship
for three months. The master appealed. The

VII. SHIP — MERCHANT SHIPPING ACTS — *continued.*

Probate, Divorce, and Admiralty Division being of opinion that the evidence before the Wreck Commissioner established that the master had authority from his owner to provide ballast for the vessel without restriction as to the price, and had been aware of the character of the ballast which she had taken on board, and that the carrying of such ballast contributed to her loss, dismissed the appeal with costs. THE "GOLDEN SEA"

[7 P. D. 194

6. —— Duty of Owner—*Penalty—Action for Breach of Statutory Duty — Merchant Shipping Act,* 1854 (17 & 18 Vict. c. 104), s. 172—*Refusal to give Certificate of discharge to Seaman.*] An action will not lie for the refusal to give to a seaman the certificate of discharge directed to be given by the 172nd section of the Merchant Shipping Act, 1854, the only remedy for such refusal being the penalty provided by that section. VALLANCE v. FALLE - - 13 Q. B. D. 109

7. —— Registration of British Ship—*Sale by Licitation—Transfer — Merchant Shipping Act,* 1854 (17 & 18 Vict. c. 104), ss. 55, 58.] The transfer of a British ship is governed by the express provisions of the Merchant Shipping Acts, which make a clear distinction between the legal estate and mere beneficial interests therein :—*Held,* that a sale by licitation of a British ship (or of a share therein) without a conveyance by bill of sale did not create such an interest in the purchasers as rendered it compulsory on the Registrar, under the Merchant Shipping Act, 1854, to register them as owners, and that the Registrar was right in refusing so to do, and to erase from his books the inscriptions contained in the register against the ship in the names of the mortgagees. —*Held,* also, that a purchaser under a judicial sale, of a beneficial interest in a British ship is not entitled to be registered as owner of it. There is no provision in the Merchant Shipping Acts which authorizes the Registrar to erase entries of mortgages. In case of their having been duly discharged, an entry to that effect may be made under sect. 68 of the Act of 1854. CHASTEAUNEUF v. CAPEYRON 7 App. Cas. 127

8. —— Wreck Commissioner—*Shipping Casualty—Appeal—Shipping Casualties Investigations Act,* 1879 (42 & 43 Vict. c. 72), s. 2—*Materials on which Appeal heard—Practice—Evidence of Experts not admissible on Questions of Nautical Skill and Knowledge — Costs.*] Although the Wreck Commissioner, or other authority, holding a formal investigation into a shipping casualty under the Merchant Shipping Acts, must, if he deals with the certificate of a master or certified officer, give his decision in open Court, yet he may, subsequently in his report to the Board of Trade, state reasons for his decision not mentioned by him at the time when the judgment was delivered.—In appeals under the Shipping Casualties Investigations Act, 1879, the Court of Appeal will not permit witnesses to be called to give evidence on questions of nautical knowledge and skill.— Where, on an appeal under the Shipping Casualties Investigations Act, 1879, the decision of the Wreck Commissioner, suspending the certificate of a master, was affirmed, but the Court of Appeal

VII. SHIP — MERCHANT SHIPPING ACTS — *continued.*

recommended that the Board of Trade should shorten the time for which the certificate had been suspended, the parties to the appeal were left to bear their own costs of the appeal. THE "KESTREL" - - - 6 P. D. 182

—— Neglect of seaman to join ship 11 Q. B. D. *See* SHIP—SEAMEN. [225

VIII. SHIP—NAVIGATION.

REGULATIONS FOR PREVENTING COLLISIONS AT SEA, UNDER THE MERCHANT SHIPPING ACT AMENDMENT ACT, 1862, 25 & 26 VICT. c. 63, ss. 57, 58.

Order in Council of 26th August, 1881, *suspends until 1st September,* 1882, *article* 10 *of the Regulations of* 1879, *for preventing collisions at sea (for ships of countries mentioned in the 2nd Schedule of the Regulations, whether within British jurisdiction or not), and continues in force in lieu thereof article* 9 *of the Regulations of* 1863 - L. G., 1881, p. 4531 *Order in Council of* 18th *August,* 1882, *extends the above until 1st September,* 1883

[L. G., 1882, p. 3907 *Order in Council of 23rd August,* 1883, *further extends the above until 1st March,* 1884

[L. G., 1883, p. 4211 *Ditto 2nd February,* 1884, *further extends to* 1st *September,* 1884 - L. G., 1884, p. 582 *Order in Council of 11th August,* 1884, *substitutes the following regulations in lieu of the Regulations of* 1879, *so far as regards British ships and boats, and to take effect from 1st September,* 1884

Art. 1. *In the following rules every steamship which is under sail and not under steam is to be considered a sailing ship; and every steamship which is under steam, whether under sail or not, is to be considered a ship under steam.*

Rules concerning Lights.

Art. 2. *The lights mentioned in the following Articles, numbered* 3, 4, 5, 6, 7, 8, 9, 10, 11, *and no others, shall be carried in all weathers, from sunset to sunrise.*

Art. 3. *A seagoing steamship when under way shall carry—*

(a.) *On or in front of the foremast, at a height above the hull of not less than* 20 *feet, and if the breadth of the ship exceeds* 20 *feet then at a height above the hull not less than such breadth, a bright white light, so constructed as to show an uniform and unbroken light over an arc of the horizon of* 20 *points of the compass, so fixed as to throw the light* 10 *points on each side of the ship, viz., from right ahead to two points abaft the beam on either side, and of such a character as to be visible on a dark night, with a clear atmosphere, at a distance of at least five miles.*

(b.) *On the starboard side a green light so constructed as to shew an uniform and unbroken light over an arc of the horizon of* 10 *points of the compass, so fixed as to throw the light from right ahead to two points abaft the beam on the starboard side, and of such a character as to be visible on a*

VIII. SHIP—NAVIGATION—continued.

dark night, with a clear atmosphere, at a distance of at least two miles.

(c.) *On the port side a red light, so constructed as to shew an uniform and unbroken light over an arc of the horizon of 10 points of the compass, so fixed as to throw the light from right ahead to two points abaft the beam on the port side, and of such a character as to be visible on a dark night, with a clear atmosphere, at a distance of at least two miles.*

(d.) *The said green and red side lights shall be fitted with inboard screens projecting at least 3 feet forward from the light, so as to prevent these lights from being seen across the bow.*

Art. 4. *A steamship, when towing another ship, shall, in addition to her side lights, carry two bright white lights in a vertical line one over the other, not less than 3 feet apart, so as to distinguish her from other steamships. Each of these lights shall be of the same construction and character, and shall be carried in the same position, as the white light which other steamships are required to carry.*

Art. 5 (a.) *A ship, whether a steamship or a sailing ship, which from any accident is not under command, shall at night carry, in the same position as the white light which steamships are required to carry, and, if a steamship, in place of that light, three red lights in globular lanterns, each not less than 10 inches in diameter, in a vertical line one over the other, not less than three feet apart, and of such a character as to be visible on a dark night with a clear atmosphere at a distance of at least two miles ; and shall by day carry in a vertical line one over the other, not less than 3 feet apart, in front of but not lower than her foremast head, three black balls or shapes, each 2 feet in diameter.*

(b.) *A ship, whether a steamship or a sailing ship, employed in laying or in picking up a telegraph cable, shall at night carry in the same position as the white light which steamships are required to carry, and, if a steamship, in place of that light, three lights in globular lanterns each not less than 10 inches in diameter, in a vertical line over one another, not less than 6 feet apart ; the highest and lowest of these lights shall be red, and the middle light shall be white, and they shall be of such a character that the red lights shall be visible at the same distance as the white light. By day she shall carry in a vertical line one over the other not less than six feet apart, in front of but not lower than her foremast head, three shapes not less than 2 feet in diameter, of which the top and bottom shall be globular in shape and red in colour, and the middle one diamond in shape and white.*

(c.) *The ships referred to in this Article, when not making any way through the water, shall not carry the side lights, but when making way shall carry them.*

(d.) *The lights and shapes required to be shewn by this Article are to be taken by other ships as signals that the ship shewing them is not under command, and cannot therefore get out of the way. The signals to be made by ships in distress and requiring assistance are contained in Article 27.*

Art. 6. *A sailing ship under way, or being towed, shall carry the same lights as are provided by*

VIII. SHIP—NAVIGATION—continued.

Article 3 for a steamship under way, with the exception of the white light, which she shall never carry.

Art. 7. *Whenever, as in the case of small vessels during bad weather, the green and red side lights cannot be fixed, these lights shall be kept on deck, on their respective sides of the vessel, ready for use ; and shall, on the approach of or to other vessels, be exhibited on their respective sides in sufficient time to prevent collision. in such manner as to make them most visible, and so that the green light shall not be seen on the port side nor the red light on the starboard side.*

To make the use of these portable lights more certain and easy, the lanterns containing them shall each be painted outside with the colour of the light they respectively contain, and shall be provided with proper screens.

Art. 8. *A ship, whether a steamship or a sailing ship, when at anchor, shall carry, where it can best be seen, but at a height not exceeding 20 feet above the hull, a white light, in a globular lantern of not less than 8 inches in diameter, and so constructed as to shew a clear uniform and unbroken light visible all round the horizon, at a distance of at least one mile.*

Art. 9. *A pilot vessel, when engaged on her station on pilotage duty, shall not carry the lights required for other vessels, but shall carry a white light at the masthead, visible all round the horizon, and shall also exhibit a flare-up light or flare-up lights at short intervals, which shall never exceed fifteen minutes.*

A pilot vessel, when not engaged on her station on pilotage duty, shall carry lights similar to those of other ships.

Art. 10. *Open boats and fishing vessels of less than 20 tons net registered tonnage, when under way and when not having their nets, trawls, dredges, or lines in the water, shall not be obliged to carry the coloured side lights ; but every such boat and vessel shall in lieu thereof have ready at hand a lantern with a green glass on the one side and a red glass on the other side, and on approaching to or being approached by another vessel such lantern shall be exhibited in sufficient time to prevent collision, so that the green light shall not be seen on the port side nor the red light on the starboard side.*

The following portion of this article applies only to fishing vessels and boats when in the sea off the coast of Europe lying north of Cape Finisterre :—

(a.) *All fishing vessels and fishing boats of 20 tons net registered tonnage, or upwards, when under way and when not required by the following regulations in this article to carry and shew the lights therein named, shall carry and shew the same lights as other vessels under way.*

(b.) *All vessels when engaged in fishing with drift nets shall exhibit two white lights from any part of the vessel where they can be best seen. Such lights shall be placed so that the vertical distance between them shall be not less than 6 feet and not more than 10 feet ; and so that the horizontal distance between them measured in a line with the keel of the vessel shall be not less than 5 feet and not more than 10 feet. The lower of these two lights shall be the more*

VIII. SHIP—NAVIGATION—continued.

forward, and both of them shall be of such a character, and contained in lanterns of such construction as to shew all round the horizon, on a dark night with a clear atmosphere, for a distance of not less than three miles.

(c.) A vessel employed in line fishing with her lines out shall carry the same lights as a vessel when engaged in fishing with drift nets.

(d.) If a vessel when fishing becomes stationary in consequence of her gear getting fast to a rock or other obstruction, she shall shew the light and make the fog signal for a vessel at anchor.

(e.) Fishing vessels and open boats may at any time use a flare-up in addition to the lights which they are by this article required to carry and shew. All flare-up lights exhibited by a vessel when trawling, dredging, or fishing with any kind of drag net shall be shewn at the after part of the vessel, excepting that, if the vessel is hanging by the stern to her trawl, dredge, or drag net, they shall be exhibited from the bow.

(f.) Every fishing vessel and every open boat when at anchor between sunset and sunrise shall exhibit a white light visible all round the horizon at a distance of at least one mile.

(g.) In fog, mist, or falling snow, a drift net vessel attached to her nets and a vessel when trawling, dredging, or fishing with any kind of drag net, and a vessel employed in line fishing with her lines out, shall at intervals of not more than two minutes make a blast with her fog horn and ring her bell alternately.

Art. 11. A ship which is being overtaken by another shall shew from her stern to such last-mentioned ship a white light or a flare-up light.

Sound Signals for Fog, &c.

Art. 12. A steamship shall be provided with a steam whistle or other efficient steam sound signal, so placed that the sound may not be intercepted by any obstructions, and with an efficient fog horn to be sounded by a bellows or other mechanical means, and also with an efficient bell.* A sailing ship shall be provided with a similar fog horn and bell.

In fog, mist, or falling snow, whether by day or night, the signals described in this article shall be used as follows; that is to say,—

(a.) A steamship under way shall make with her steam whistle, or other steam sound signal, at intervals of not more than two minutes, a prolonged blast.

(b.) A sailing ship under way shall make with her fog horn, at intervals of not more than two minutes, when on the starboard tack one blast, when on the port tack two blasts in succession, and when with the wind abaft the beam three blasts in succession.

(c.) A steamship and a sailing ship, when not under way, shall, at intervals of not more than two minutes ring the bell.

* In all cases where the regulations require a bell to be used, a drum will be substituted on board Turkish vessels.

VIII. SHIP—NAVIGATION—continued.

Speed of Ships to be moderate in Fog, &c.

Art. 13. Every ship, whether a sailing ship or steam ship, shall in a fog, mist, or falling snow, go at a moderate speed.

Steering and Sailing Rules.

Art. 14. When two sailing ships are approaching one another, so as to involve risk of collision, one of them shall keep out of the way of the other as follows, viz.:

(a.) A ship which is running free shall keep out of the way of a ship which is close-hauled.

(b.) A ship which is close-hauled on the port tack shall keep out of the way of a ship which is close-hauled on the starboard tack.

(c.) When both are running free with the wind on different sides, the ship which has the wind on the port side shall keep out of the way of the other.

(d.) When both are running free with the wind on the same side, the ship which is to windward shall keep out of the way of the ship which is to leeward.

(e.) A ship which has the wind aft shall keep out of the way of the other ship.

Art. 15. If two ships under steam are meeting end on, or nearly end on, so as to involve risk of collision, each shall alter her course to starboard, so that each may pass on the port side of the other.

This Article only applies to cases where ships are meeting end on, or nearly end on, in such a manner as to involve risk of collision, and does not apply to two ships which must, if both keep on their respective courses, pass clear of each other.

The only cases to which it does apply are, when each of the two ships is end on, or nearly end on, to the other; in other words, to cases in which, by day, each ship sees the masts of the other in a line, or nearly in a line, with her own; and by night, to cases in which each ship is in such a position as to see both the side lights of the other.

It does not apply by day, to cases in which a ship sees another ahead crossing her own course; or by night to cases where the red light of one ship is opposed to the red light of the other, or where the green light of one ship is opposed to the green light of the other, or where a red light without a green light, or a green light without a red light, is seen ahead, or where both green and red lights are seen anywhere but ahead.

Art. 16. If two ships under steam are crossing, so as to involve risk of collision, the ship which has the other on her own starboard side shall keep out of the way of the other.

Art. 17. If two ships, one of which is a sailing ship and the other a steamship, are proceeding in such directions as to involve risk of collision, the steamship shall keep out of the way of the sailing ship.

Art. 18. Every steamship, when approaching another ship, so as to involve risk of collision, shall slacken her speed or stop and reverse, if necessary.

Art. 19. In taking any course authorized or required by these regulations, a steamship under way may indicate that course to any other ship

VIII. SHIP—NAVIGATION—*continued.*

which she has in sight by the following signals on her steam whistle, viz. :—

One short blast to mean "I am directing my course to starboard."

Two short blasts to mean "I am directing my course to port."

Three short blasts to mean "I am going full speed astern."

The use of these signals is optional, but if they are used the course of the ship must be in accordance with the signal made.

Art. 20. *Notwithstanding anything contained in any preceding Article, every ship, whether a sailing ship or a steamship, overtaking any other shall keep out of the way of the overtaken ship.*

Art. 21. *In narrow channels every steamship shall, when it is safe and practicable, keep to that side of the fairway or mid-channel which lies on the starboard side of such ship.*

Art. 22. *Where by the above rules one of two ships is to keep out of the way, the other shall keep her course.*

Art. 23. *In obeying and construing these rules due regard shall be had to all dangers of navigation, and to any special circumstances which may render a departure from the above rules necessary in order to avoid immediate danger.*

No Ship, under any circumstances, to neglect proper Precautions.

Art. 24. *Nothing in these rules shall exonerate any ship, or the owner, or master, or crew thereof, from the consequences of any neglect to carry lights or signals, or of any neglect to keep a proper lookout, or of the neglect of any precaution which may be required by the ordinary practice of seamen, or by the special circumstances of the case.*

Reservation of Rules for Harbours and Inland Navigation.

Art. 25. *Nothing in these rules shall interfere with the operation of a special rule duly made by local authority, relative to the navigation of any harbour, river, or inland navigation.*

Special Lights for Squadrons and Convoys.

Art. 26. *Nothing in these rules shall interfere with the operation of any special rules made by the Government of any nation with respect to additional station and signal lights for two or more ships of war or for ships sailing under convoy.*

Art. 27. *When a ship is in distress and requires assistance from other ships or from the shore, the following shall be the signals to be used or displayed by her, either together or separately, that is to say:—*

In the daytime—
1. *A gun fired at intervals of about a minute;*
2. *The International Code signal of distress indicated by N C;*
3. *The distant signal, consisting of a square flag, having either above or below it a ball, or anything resembling a ball.*

At night—
1. *A gun fired at intervals of about a minute;*
2. *Flames on the ship (as from a burning tar barrel, oil barrel, &c.);*
3. *Rockets or shells, throwing stars of any*

VIII. SHIP—NAVIGATION—*continued.*

colour or description, fired one at a time, at short intervals.

[L. G., 1884, p. 3818

Modification of above Regulations as regards British fishing vessels—steam or sailing—trawling off the coast of Europe lying north of Cape Finisterre. Order in Council, 30th Dec., 1884
[L. G., 1885, p. 4

Further modifications of above Regulations as regards British sailing fishing vessels trawling and situate as above. Order in Council, 24th June, 1885 -　-　-　-　L. G., 1885, p. 2988

Order in Council of 30th Dec., 1884, applying the Regulations of 11th August, 1884, to the ships of Greece, Portugal, and Italy, whether within British jurisdiction or not -　-　L. G., 1885, p. 1

Order in Council of 19th May, 1885, applying the regulations of 11th August, 1884, to the ships of Norway and Sweden, and Brazil, whether within British jurisdiction or not　L. G., 1885, p. 2334

Order in Council of 9th Sept., 1884, applying the Regulations to the ships of France, whether within British jurisdiction or not　L. G., 1884, p. 4116

Order in Council of 9th July, 1885, applying the Regulations to the ships of Turkey, whether within British jurisdiction or not　L. G., 1885, p. 3233

Order in Council of 17th Sept., 1885, applying the Regulations to the ships of Chili, whether within British jurisdiction or not　L. G., 1885, p. 4430

1. —— Consequential Loss—*Collision—Damage—Registrar and Merchants—Loss of Fishing—Evidence.*] A French fishing brig of 142 tons, employed in the cod fishery off the banks of Newfoundland, came into collision on the 6th of July, 1881, with an Italian barque, and in consequence of the collision was compelled to put into port for repairs, but, her repairs having been completed, returned to the fishing ground before the close of the fishing season. In an action of damage instituted on behalf of the owners of the brig against the barque, the Court pronounced the barque solely to blame for the collision, and referred the question of damages to the registrar and merchants. At the reference the Plaintiffs claimed £1200 for demurrage of their vessel from the date of the collision to the 26th of August, 1881, the date of her return to the fishing ground, and of the amount so claimed, the registrar, by his report, allowed the Plaintiffs £880 as the loss sustained by the interruption of their fishing. The Defendants moved the Court in objection to the report :—*Held*, that the motion must be dismissed. THE "RISOLUTO"　　　　8 P. D. 109

2. —— Contributory Negligence—*Collision—Negligence by Complaining Vessel.*] Where there has been a departure from an important rule of navigation, if the absence of due observance of the rule can by any possibility have contributed to the accident, then the party in default cannot be excused.—Where the lights of the complaining vessel were not properly burning, and were not visible on board the other vessel, *held*, that in the absence of proof that this latter was also to blame, the suit must be dismissed. EMERY *v.* CICHERO. THE "ARKLOW"　　　　9 App. Cas. 136

3. —— Damages—*Collision—Cargo—Re-shipment—Use of Damaged Cargo.*] Plaintiffs' cargo of coals on board the K. was damaged by a collision

VIII. SHIP—NAVIGATION—*continued.*

at C., the port of loading, and had to be unloaded. It was ultimately reshipped and carried on to B., and used by the Plaintiffs in smithies, though it was not purchased for this purpose. The shipowner was not willing to ship a fresh cargo except on fresh terms, and the Plaintiffs did not ascertain what those terms were. On a reference as to damages, in an action between the owners of the coal and the owners of the vessel with which the K. came into collision, the assistant registrar decided that the Plaintiffs were only entitled to recover the difference between the value of sound and damaged coal at the port of loading, and that if the value was that at the port of destination it must be taken to be the value of smithy coal. On objection to this report :—*Held,* that the shipowner had a right to insist on carrying on the same cargo; that it appearing that he had been willing to take a fresh cargo on fresh terms, it was the duty of the Plaintiffs to have ascertained what those terms were, so as to diminish the loss as much as possible, before comparing the loss on the damaged cargo at B., and that from the sale of it at C., and shipping a fresh one :—*Held,* also, that the coal having been used for a particular purpose, was not a reason for estimating its value at that of coal ordinarily used for such purpose. The "BLENHEIM" - **10 P. D. 167**

4. —— **Danube Commission Rules, Rule 34, Chapter II.** — *Collision — Negligence.*] Under Rule 34, Chapter II. of the Danube Commission Rules, vessels going down the Danube should keep to the right bank.—Where a vessel going down the the Danube, when there was a fog and approaching night, went to the left bank, *held,* that, according to the true construction of the rule, that was neglect of duty; and that such negligence was the cause of a collision which occurred with a vessel coming up, although the absence of lights on the latter vessel might have partly contributed to the accident. RUSSIAN S.S. "YOURRI" *v* BRITISH S.S. "SPEARMAN" - **10 App. Cas. 276**

5. —— **Evidence of Negligence**—*Steam-steering Gear.*] A steamship fitted with a patent steam-steering gear ran into a vessel at anchor in the Thames, owing to the steering gear suddenly not acting; every effort was unavailingly made to avoid the collision. A few days before, on the previous voyage of the same steamship, the same apparatus had similarly refused to act, but no cause for it so doing could be seen on examination. Large numbers of the gears were in use on steamers. In an action of damage :— *Held,* first, that the Defendants were not liable for damage caused by the use of this apparatus without negligence. Secondly, that the use of this apparatus on the Thames after it had acted wrongly on a previous occasion, was evidence of negligence, and that the Defendants were liable for the damage caused thereby. The "EUROPEAN" **10 P. D. 99**

6. —— **Launch**—*Duty of Vessels anchored in Track of Launch—Compulsory Pilotage— Mersey Docks Consolidation Act,* 1858 (21 & 22 Vict. c. xcii.), s. 139—Meaning of "Proceed to Sea."] A barque was at anchor in the Mersey in the way of the C., a vessel about to be launched. The launch was delayed as long as was prudent, but the barque not having been got out of the way

VIII. SHIP—NAVIGATION—*continued.*

in time was struck by the C. in coming off the ways and both vessels were damaged. Reasonable notice had been given of the launch, and a steam-tug had been sent by those superintending the launch to tow the barque out of danger, and would have done so in time to have prevented the collision but for the obstinacy of those on board the barque :—*Held,* that the barque was alone to blame for the collision.—The barque had been towed out of dock into the river the previous day in order that she might proceed to sea before daybreak on the morning on which the collision happened. But an accident having happened to the mainyard of the barque she was unable to proceed to sea as intended, and at the time of the collision was waiting in the river to have repairs executed. She had on board of her a duly licensed Mersey pilot :—*Held,* that she was not at the time of the collision proceeding to sea within the meaning of the Mersey Docks Consolidation Act, 1858, s. 139, and that the pilot on board her was not at the time employed by compulsion of law.—*Rodrigues* v. *Melhuish* (10 Ex. 110) followed. THE "CACHAPOOL" **7 P. D. 217**

7. —— **Launch**—*Duty of Tugs in the Mersey.*] Persons in charge of a launch are bound to take the utmost precautions to avoid injury to passing vessels, such precautions being in the circumstances no more than reasonable. It is their duty to have a tug in attendance on a launch in the Mersey, decorated so as to indicate that a launch is imminent, and, if necessary, to warn approaching vessels. The "GEORGE ROPER" - **8 P. D. 119**

8. —— **Sailing Rules,** *Art. 2—Humber Rules—Stern Light—Compulsory Pilotage—*25 & 26 Vict. c. 63, s. 32—36 & 37 Vict. c. 85, s. 17.] The R. in charge of a tug was dropping stern foremost up the Humber with the tide, and was eventually brought athwart the tide to go into dock. The R. was exhibiting, in addition to the mast head and side lights, a white light from the main peak shewing astern, which had been placed there by order of the pilot who was by compulsion of law in charge of the R. The Rules for the Navigation of the River Humber, made by Order in Council in pursuance of 25 & 26 Vict. c. 63, s. 32, incorporate the Regulations for Preventing Collisions at Sea. The E. coming down the Humber and the R. came into collision. At the hearing it was admitted that the E. was to blame :—*Held,* that the R. was also to blame, for that as the Humber Rules were within the purview of 36 & 37 Vict. c. 85, s. 17, there had been, by the exhibition of a stern light, a breach of a statutory regulation, namely, of art. 2, which it was impossible to say might not have contributed to the collision, and there was no circumstance to make a departure from the regulation necessary :—*Held,* also, that the light having been exhibited by order of the pilot, did not exempt the owner of the R. from liability, as the master should not have permitted an infringement of the regulations. THE "RIPON"

[10 P. D. 65

9. —— **Sailing Rules,** *Arts.* 2 *and* 11.] A ship shewed a flare-up light to a steamer approaching on her starboard side :—*Held,* not an infringement of arts. 2 and 11, as such light was not calculated

3 C

VIII. SHIP—NAVIGATION—*continued.*

in the circumstances to mislead the approaching vessel. THE "MERCHANT PRINCE" 10 P. D. 139

10. —— Sailing Rules. *Arts.* 3, 10, *and* 1863, *Art.* 9—*Collision—Order in Council, March* 24, 1880—36 & 37 *Vict.* c. 85, *s.* 17.] A steam trawler, whilst engaged in trawling at the rate of 2½ knots an hour through the water and 4½ knots an hour over the ground, carrying a single white light, was run down by the *D.*; it being admitted that the *D.* was to blame, the question arose whether the trawler was not also to blame for not carrying side lights:—*Held*, by Butt, J., that the trawler was also to blame, since she was a vessel under way, and therefore subject to art. 3 of the Regulations for Preventing Collisions at Sea, 1880, and not to art. 9 of the Regulations for Preventing Collisions at Sea, 1863, substituted by Order in Council, 1880, for Art. 10 of the Regulations of 1880.—*Held*, by the Court of Appeal, that the decision of Butt, J., was right, but on the ground that though the trawler was one of a class of vessels within art. 9 of the Regulations of 1863, she, in order to be " stationary " within the meaning of that article, was bound not to go faster than was necessary to keep herself under command whilst fishing, and that as her speed was greater than was necessary for so doing, she was, at the time of the collision, within art. 3 of the Regulations of 1880. THE "DUNELM" 9 P. D. 164

11. —— Sailing Rules, *Arts.* 5, 6—*Inevitable Accident—Costs—Infringement of Regulations for Preventing Collisions at Sea—Merchant Shipping Act,* 1873 (36 & 37 *Vict.* c. 85,) *s.* 17.] A sailing ship in a gale drove from her anchors across a sand, and her rudder was so damaged as to render the ship unmanageable; in this condition she came into collision after sunset with a brig at anchor. At the time of the collision the ship had her anchor light exhibited and no other light. In an action of damage by the owners of the brig against the ship it was held that the collision was occasioned by inevitable accident, and that the ship in the circumstances of the case was not to be deemed in fault for not carrying side lights or the three red lights prescribed by Article 5 of the Regulations for Preventing Collisions at Sea, and that the suit ought to be dismissed without costs. THE " BUCKHURST " - 6 P. D. 152

12. —— Sailing Rules, *Art.* 11.] A ship does not, by carrying a fixed white binnacle light in such a position as to be reflected astern, comply with the provisions of the eleventh article of the Regulations for Preventing Collisions at Sea, which provides that a ship which is being overtaken by another, shall shew from her stern to such last-mentioned ship a white light or a flareup light. THE " BREADALBANE " - 7 P. D. 186

13. —— Sailing Rules, *Art.* 11—*Speed.*] A smack with her trawl down had a globular white light exhibited from her weather crosstree partially hidden from overtaking vessels by her sails, and did not exhibit any other white light or flareup to an overtaking steamer :—*Held*, that this was an infringement of art. 11.—The steamer being in the North Sea, and the weather fine and clear, though the night was dark, was proceeding at the rate of eight to nine knots an hour :—*Held*,

VIII. SHIP—NAVIGATION—*continued.*

that she was not, under the circumstances, going at too high a rate of speed. THE "PACIFIC " [9 P. D. 124

14. —— Sailing Rules, *Arts.* 12, 13, 18 — *Merchant Shipping Act,* 1873 (36 & 37 *Vict.* c. 85), *s.* 17—*Fog.*] A barque, provided only with a fog-horn, sounded by means of the breath, came into collision, during a fog, with a steamship. The fog-horn was duly sounded before the collision, and was heard by those on board the steamship, and those on board the steamship neglected, for some time after they heard the fog-horn, to stop or reverse the engines. The steamship was held to blame. The barque was held to be deemed in fault for not using a fog-horn, to be sounded by mechanical means, as required by Article 12 of the Regulations for Preventing Collisions at Sea, 1879. — The circumstance that the barque left port a few days before the regulations came into force was held not to afford any valid excuse for the neglect of those in charge of her to furnish her with a fog-horn, to be sounded by mechanical means, they well knowing, before she left port, that the regulations would come into force in a few days, and there being no evidence to shew that they could not obtain a fog-horn, according to the regulations, before she left port. THE " LOVE BIRD " 6 P. D. 80

15. —— Sailing Rules, *Arts.* 12 (*b*), 13—*Fog.*] A collision happened between the steamship *I.* and the barque *Z.* in a fog. It was proved that the *I.* had reduced her speed so far as was possible without stopping her way altogether:—*Held*, that she had not infringed article 13 of the Regulations for Preventing Collisions at Sea.—It was further proved that the *Z.* was proceeding at more than four knots an hour:—*Held*, an infringement of article 13, for the term "moderate speed " means that a vessel is to reduce her speed so far as she can consistently with keeping steerage way.—It was further proved that a fog-horn was blown on the *Z.* but not heard on the *I.* :—*Held*, that this was not primâ facie evidence of negligence of those on the *I.* THE " ZADOK " 9 P. D. 114

16. —— Sailing Rules, *Art.* 13—*Fog.*] The term "moderate speed " used in Art. 13 of the Regulations for Preventing Collisions at Sea is a relative term, depending upon the circumstances. —When a sailing ship was going in a dense fog at a speed greater than was enough to keep her under control:—*Held*, that she had infringed Art. 13. THE " BETA " - 9 P. D. 134

17. —— Sailing Rules, *Arts.* 13, 18, 20 — *Fog—Duty of Steamship.*] It is the duty of those who have charge of a steamship in motion during a dense fog, on first hearing the whistle of a steamship in such close proximity to them that risk of collision between the two vessels is involved, to bring their vessel immediately to a standstill on the water, and not execute any manœuvre with their helm until they have definitely ascertained the position and course of the other ship. THE " KIRBY HALL " - 8 P. D. 71

18. —— Sailing Rules, *Arts.* 13, 18—*Fog.*] A steamship the *D.* in a dense fog off Ushant proceeding at slow speed heard a whistle about three points on her starboard bow; the whistle was

VIII. SHIP—NAVIGATION—continued.

repeated several times and answered by the D. In about a quarter of an hour from the first sound of the whistle the steamship E. appeared about a length from the D. crossing from starboard to port. The engines of the D. were reversed full speed but a collision occurred. Butt, J., having held both ships to blame, the owners of the D. appealed :—Held, by the Court of Appeal (affirming the decision of Butt, J.), that the D. was also to blame, for she should have been brought to as complete a standstill as possible, without getting out of command, at an early period after the first sound of the whistle, and should have also stopped and reversed sooner.—Per Brett, M.R. : Under art. 13 (1) "a moderate speed"—in a river or narrow channel—means that a vessel shall be brought nearly to a standstill, whether the whistle or fog-horn of another vessel is heard or not, but in the open sea the article need not be so strictly construed, unless a whistle or fog-horn is heard.— Under art. 18 (2) as soon as it is perceived by those on a steamer in a dense fog that a vessel is coming substantially nearer, the steamer should stop and reverse.—Semble, though art. 18 does not apply to a sailing ship, yet she ought in similar circumstances to take off sail so as to come to as complete a standstill as possible, without getting out of command. THE "DORDOGNE" 10 P. D. 6

19. —— Sailing Rules, 1880, Arts. 16, 20— Crossing Ships.] When a vessel is at the same time overtaking and crossing the course of another vessel, she is to be deemed an overtaking, and not a crossing ship under Art. 16, and is bound therefore to obey the directions of Art. 20, and keep out of the way of the other vessel. THE "SEATON" [9 P. D. 1

20. —— Sailing Rules, Arts. 16, 18, 22—Crossing Ships.] The A. and B. were crossing within the meaning of Art. 16, and it was the duty of the A. to keep out of the way of the B., but she did not do so. The B. when from a quarter to half a mile distant slackened her speed and continued with slackened speed to within 300 yards of the A., and then stopped and reversed, but not in time to prevent a collision :—Held, on appeal, that the B. must be held, for not stopping and reversing sooner, to blame as well as the A. Arts. 16 and 18 are intended to be applicable according to the circumstances as they would present themselves to the mind of a prudent sailor, and come into force before the risk of collision is fixed and determined.—Held, also, that the word "course" in Art. 22, refers to the direction of the vessel's head and not to her speed.—Per Brett, M.R. : If the Judge of the Court below differs from his assessors, he is bound to decide in accordance with his own opinion. THE "BERYL" - 9 P. D. 4, 137

21. —— Sailing Rules, Art. 18—Damage—Equal Negligence.] In accordance with the 18th sailing rule, under Order in Council, 14th of August, 1879, it is the duty of those in charge of a steamship in motion, when they perceive that a risk of collision is involved, to reverse their engines and bring their ship to a standstill on the water.— A collision occurred between the steamship A. and the steamship B. The evidence was most contradictory. It was, however, satisfactorily proved that although the crew of the ship B. had been

VIII. SHIP—NAVIGATION—continued.

until a few minutes before the collision engaged in getting the anchors on board in shipshape order, and that the captain had left the deck when he ought to have been there, yet that when it was perceived the two vessels were approaching in such a manner as to involve risk of collision the engines were reversed, and the ship stopped. On board the ship A. everything was proved to have been in good order at the time of the collision. But her captain did not stop his engines until almost the moment of collision, and consequently the ship A. cut into the ship B. to the water's edge :—Held, reversing the decision of the Court below, that there was fault on both sides, contributing to the damage and loss which had been suffered, and therefore neither were entitled to costs. MACLAREN v. COMPAGNIE FRANÇAISE DE NAVIGATION À VAPEUR 9 App. Cas. 640

22. —— Sailing Rules, Art. 18—Probability of Risk.] The S. and the C. were approaching each other at night on opposite courses, so as to pass starboard to starboard. The master of the C. saw the green and white lights of the S., somewhat more than a quarter of a mile distant, coming into line. This indicated a probability that the S. was porting, which would cause a risk of collision ; soon after the red light of the S. was seen. The engines of the C. had been previously stopped, but the master did not reverse her engines till the red light of the S. was seen ; the vessels soon after came into collision :—Held, that the C. was to blame for infringing art. 18 of the Regulations for Preventing Collisions at Sea, because as there was a probability of risk of collision when the master of the C. saw the green and white lights of the S. coming into line, he should, being aware of such probability, have then reversed the engines of the C. THE "STANMORE" - 10 P. D. 134

23. —— Sailing Rules, Art. 18—Fog.] A steamer heard a whistle on her port bow in a dense fog, and it was repeated, shewing that the vessel from which it was sounded was approaching and was in her vicinity :—Held, that under such circumstances it is a general rule of conduct that there is a necessity to stop and reverse, and that she had disobeyed Art. 18 by not so doing. THE "JOHN McINTYRE" - 9 P. D. 135

24. —— Sailing Rules, Art. 18—Standing by.] The E. H., after a collision with the M., burnt rockets and blue lights as signals of distress, but the M. did not, as she might have done, reply to these signals :—Held, a breach of the statutory duty of rendering assistance under 36 & 37 Vict. c. 85, s. 16, and that the M. was therefore to be deemed to blame. The E. H. did not stop and reverse under Article 18 as soon as she might have done :—Held, that she was also to blame, but that instantaneous compliance with Art. 18 is not necessary. THE "EMMY HAASE" [9 P. D. 81

25. —— Sailing Rules, Arts. 18, 23.] A steamer, the G., saw a green light at some distance and starboarded her helm ; soon after the port side of the B., without a red light, came into view, so close that the only chance of avoiding a collision was for the G. to continue at full speed ahead and starboard her helm, which she did. The B. struck the G. on her starboard

3 C 2

VIII. SHIP—NAVIGATION—*continued.*

side :—*Held*, that the *B.* was alone to blame for the collision, and that Art. 18 of the Regulations did not apply under the circumstances to the *G.*, and that Art. 23 was applicable.—*The Khedive* (5 App. Cas. 876) explained.　THE " BENABES "

[9 P. D. 16]

26. —— **Sailing Rules,** *Art.* 21 — *Narrow Channel—Collision.*] The Strait of Messina is a narrow channel within the meaning of Art. 21 of the Admiralty Regulations for Preventing Collisions at Sea ; as to what particular width or length will constitute a narrow channel, *quære —Held*, that the *A. L.* by infringing the said article occasioned the collision which afterwards happened, and failed to establish that the *R.* by anything which she did contributed to it or could in any way have avoided it.—*Held*, that the *R.'s* helm having been put hard aport in a way which if successful would have put her on such a course as would have determined the risk of collision, the duty of reversing her engines did not arise till it was discovered that the vessel, owing to the action of a current, was not obeying her helm. SCICLUNA *v.* STEVENSON. THE " RHONDDA " 8 App. Cas. 549

27. —— **Tees Conservancy Regulations** — " *Maximum Speed of Six Miles per Hour.*"] The 22nd clause of the by-laws of the river Tees, which provides that no steamship shall be navigated on any part of the river Tees at a higher rate of speed than six miles per hour, is to be construed as prohibiting a steamship proceeding against the tide being navigated at a greater speed than six miles per hour over the ground. THE " R. L. ALSTON "　7 P. D. 49 ; 8 P. D. 5

28. —— **Thames Rules**—*Negligence—Contributory Negligence — Damages — Infringement of Thames By-laws—Cause of Action.*] A dumb barge, by the negligent navigation of those in charge of her, was suffered to come into contact with a schooner moored to a mooring buoy in the river Thames. The schooner had her anchor hanging over her bow with the stock above water, contrary to the Thames by-laws. The anchor made a hole in the barge and caused damage to her cargo. But for the improper position of the anchor neither the barge nor her cargo would have received any damage. In an action of damage by the owners of the barge against the schooner :—*Held*, reversing the decision of the Admiralty Court, that both vessels were to blame, and that therefore the owners of the barge were entitled to half the damage sustained. THE " MARGARET "　6 P. D. 76

29. —— **Thames Rules,** *r.* 14 — *Collision—Merchant Shipping Act,* 1873 (36 & 37 *Vict.* c. 85), *s.* 17.] A steamer having stopped but not having, as she should have done, reversed immediately before a collision, though the Court found as a fact that her not having done so did not affect the collision, and having thus infringed rule 14 of the Thames Rules :—*Held*, that she was nevertheless not to blame, for the Thames Rules do not fall within the operation of sect. 17 of the Merchant Shipping Act, 1873 (36 & 37 Vict. c. 85). THE " HARTON "　9 P. D. 44

30. —— **Thames Rules.** *r.* 22, 23 — *Coming to Points—Porting.*] The 22nd and 23rd rules for the navigation of the Thames are not inconsistent,

VIII. SHIP—NAVIGATION—*continued.*

and the intention is that when the 23rd rule (as to passing a point) applies, the case for the 22nd (as to porting) shall not arise, but if the case does arise the rule will apply. A steam vessel coming down the Thames against tide to a point on the north shore, and being nearer to mid-channel than to the north shore, eased, and then seeing danger of collision with a vessel coming up with tide, starboarded and reversed. The other vessel was coming up with the tide also near the north shore and rounded the point under a port helm ; seeing the other vessel, she ported hard, and stopped, but a collision occurred :—*Held*, that under the circumstances the 22nd rule applied, and that the vessel which had starboarded was to blame. By Jessel, M.R., and Brett, L J. (Cotton, L.J., doubting), that under the 23rd rule the vessel navigating against tide is to wait until she has been passed by the other vessel, and not merely until the other vessel has passed the point. THE " LIBRA "　6 P. D. 139

31. —— **Thames Rules,** *r.* 23 — *Collision — Negligence—Contributory Negligence.*] Rule 23 of the Thames Rules is not confined to the seaward side of " a line drawn from Blackwall Point to Bow Creek."—The order of the Court of Appeal reversed and the order of Butt, J., restored, on the ground that even assuming (but without deciding) that the construction put by the Court of Appeal upon rule 23 was correct and that the *Clan Sinclair* had transgressed that rule, yet such transgression was not the cause of the collision ; that ordinary care on the part of the *Margaret* would have enabled her to avoid the collision, and that she alone was to blame. CAYZER *v.* CARRON COMPANY (THE " MARGARET ") 8 P. D. 126 ;

[9 P. D. 47 ; 9 App. Cas. 873]

32. —— **Towage**—*Condition of Contract exempting Tug Owners from Liability—Negligence of Tug Master.*] The master of a steam tug who had contracted to tow a fishing smack out of the harbour of Great Yarmouth to sea on the terms that his owners should not be liable for damage arising from any negligence or default of themselves or their servants after the towage had been in part performed, took in tow in addition to the smack six other vessels, and in consequence was unable to keep the fishing smack in her course, so that she went aground and was lost. By having more than six vessels in tow at once the master of the tug disobeyed a regulation made by the harbour-master of Great Yarmouth under statutory authority :—*Held*, that the loss of the smack was occasioned by the negligence of the master of the tug, but that the owners were protected from liability by the terms of the towage contract. THE " UNITED SERVICE "

[8 P. D. 56 ; 9 P. D. 3]

IX. SHIP—OWNERS.

1. —— **Co-ownership**—*Sale* — 24 & 25 *Vict.* c. 10, s. 8.] The Court will not exercise the power of sale conferred on it by 24 & 25 Vict. c. 10, s. 8 (2), by ordering the sale of a ship, unless a part owner —whether he be the owner of a minority or majority of shares—makes out a very strong case. Continued and embittered disagreements between two part owners were held not to constitute suffi-

IX. SHIP—OWNERS—*continued.*

cient reason for the interference of the Court.
THE "MARION"   10 P. D. 4

2. —— **Managing Owner**—*Entry on Register as—Authority to bind other Owners—Ship's Necessaries.*] W. was the registered owner of certain shares in a ship, and had been entered on the register as managing owner. The Defendant subsequently became the registered owner of other shares in the ship. The Defendant was not aware in fact that W. was so registered as managing owner. W. sent the ship on a voyage without the Defendant's knowledge, and contrary to the terms of an agreement made between them. The Defendant did not participate in the adventure, and had previously informed W. that he did not intend to navigate the ship or take any part in her management. The Plaintiffs supplied necessaries for the ship previous to such voyage, upon the order of W. without the knowledge or consent of the Defendant. The Plaintiffs, before supplying the goods, consulted the register, and found the Defendant's name entered therein as part owner of the ship:—*Held*, by Bowen, J., that the fact that the Defendant had allowed the entry on the register describing W. as managing owner to remain unaltered did not per se amount to a holding out of W. as his agent, so as to render the Defendant liable for the necessaries supplied by the Plaintiffs, and that inasmuch as W. had not in fact authority to bind the Defendant, the Plaintiffs could not recover against the Defendant for such necessaries. FRAZER & Co v CUTHBERTSON   6 Q. B. D. 93

X. SHIP—PILOT.

1. —— **Compulsory Pilotage**—*Collision with Pier—Non-liability of Shipowners for Negligence of Pilot in charge by Compulsion of Law—Harbours, Docks, and Piers Clauses Act, 1847* (10 & 11 *Vict.* c. 27), *s.* 74—*New Brighton Pier Act,* 1864 (27 & 28 *Vict.* c. cclxvii.), *ss.* 2, 39—*Merchant Shipping Act,* 1854 (17 & 18 *Vict.* c. 104), *s.* 388.] The 74th section of the Harbours, Docks, and Piers Clauses Act, 1847, which Act is incorporated with the New Brighton Pier Act, 1864, save and so far as any of the clauses and provisions of the two Acts are inconsistent, declares that the owner of every vessel shall be answerable to the undertakers of every pier to which the Harbours Docks and Piers Clauses Act, 1847, is applied, for any damage done to such pier, but provides that nothing therein contained shall extend to impose any liability for such damage upon the owner of any vessel where such vessel shall at the time when such damage is caused be in charge of a duly licensed pilot whom such owner or master is bound by law to employ. By the 39th section of the New Brighton Pier Act, 1864, it is enacted that if any person having the care of any ship shall wilfully or carelessly cause, permit, or suffer any damage or injury to be done to the New Brighton Pier then and in every such case the owners of every such ship shall be answerable and liable to make satisfaction to the New Brighton Pier Company for all such damage or injury. A steamship came into collision with and did damage to the New Brighton Pier, and to recover for the damage so done the New Brighton Pier Company brought an action against the steamship. The owners of

X. SHIP—PILOT—*continued.*

the steamship alleged in their statement of defence that at the time the damage was done the steamship was in charge of a pilot employed by compulsion of law; that the collision was not caused or contributed to by the negligence of the Defendants or any other persons than the pilot of the steamship, and that the damage was not permitted or suffered by any persons having the care of the steamship within the meaning of the New Brighton Pier Act, 1864. The Plaintiffs demurred to these allegations in the statement of defence:—*Held*, that the provisions of the New Brighton Pier Act, 1864, did not preclude the Defendants from setting up the defence of compulsory pilotage and that the demurrer must be overruled. THE "CLAN GORDON"   7 P. D. 190

2. —— **Compulsory Pilotage**—*Damage*—25 & 26 *Vict.* c. 63, *s.* 41.] The word "loading" in 25 & 26 *Vict.* c. 63, *s.* 41, does not refer to the taking on board of cargo only. Therefore when a steamer anchored in Dartmouth Harbour and took on board twenty tons of coal for the purposes of the voyage, and was bound from a place out of the outport district to a destination also out of it:—*Held*, that she was not exempt from the obligation to employ a pilot. THE "WINSTON"
                           [8 P. D. 176; 9 P. D. 85

3. —— **Compulsory Pilotage**—*Damage—Hull Pilot Act* (2 & 3 *Wm.* 4, c. cv.)—*Default of Pilot.*] A collision occurred in the Humber Dock, Hull, between a fly-boat and a foreign schooner bound to the Prince's Dock. The schooner was in charge of a duly licensed Humber pilot who had taken over the charge of the schooner while she was moored at a pier in the Humber from the pilot who had brought her in from sea. One sum was paid for the services of the two pilots:—*Held*, that the schooner was in charge of a pilot whose employment was compulsory by law. The damage was done by the fluke of the schooner's anchor piercing the side of the fly-boat. The Court found that there was no want of care in the crew in lowering the anchor. The other allegations against the schooner were that the anchor was improperly slung; that she came too fast up the dock and without a check rope:—*Held*, that the damage was caused by the fault of the pilot in the course of his duty. THE "RIGBORGS MINDE"
                                        [8 P. D. 132

4. —— **Compulsory Pilotage**—*Damage—Measure of Damages.*] Where a collision has occurred between two vessels through the bad navigation of each of them, and where one of the vessels, by compulsion of law, has had on board a pilot whose default has contributed to the accident, the owner of that vessel is entitled to recover a moiety of the damage sustained by her without any deduction on account of the damage sustained by the other. THE "HECTOR"   8 P. D. 218

5. —— **Compulsory Pilotage**—*London Trinity House District—Foreign Vessels carrying Passengers from London to Hamburg—Pilotage Act,* 1825 (6 *Geo.* 4, c. 125), *s.* 59—*Pilotage Amendment Act,* 1853 (16 & 17 *Vict.* c. 129), *s.* 21—*Order in Council, February 18th,* 1854—*Merchant Shipping Act,* 1854 (17 & 18 *Vict.* c. 104), *ss.* 353, 370, 376, 388—*Harbours and Passing Tolls Act,* 1861 (24 & 25 *Vict.* c. 47), *s.* 10.] Sections 353 and

X. SHIP—PILOT—*continued.*

376 of the Merchant Shipping Act, 1854, render foreign vessels trading with cargo and passengers from the port of London to ports between Boulogne and the Baltic subject to compulsory pilotage on their outward passages between London and Gravesend, unless their masters or mates have pilotage certificates from the London Trinity House; and the operation of these sections, so far as such vessels are concerned, is not affected either by the Order in Council of February 18th, 1854, or by the provisions contained in the Harbours and Passing Tolls Act, 1861.—*The Hanna* (Law Rep. 1 A. & E. 283) followed. THE "VESTA"
[7 P. D. 240

6. —— Compulsory Pilotage — *Pilot compulsorily taken on Board but not compulsorily in Charge— Liability of Shipowner for Collision in Suez Canal solely caused by Negligence of Suez Canal Company's Pilot.*] Where a collision in the Suez Canal has been caused by the negligence of a Suez Canal Company's pilot compulsorily taken on board the wrongdoing ship, the owner of such ship is not exempt from liability for the damage arising out of the collision.—The effect of the Regulations for the Navigation of the Suez Canal is to constitute a pilot taken on board a ship traversing the canal the adviser of the master, and to leave the control of the navigation of the ship solely with the master. THE "GUY MANNERING" - 7 P. D. 52, 132

7. —— Compulsory Pilotage—*Sea Damage— Steam-tug.*] Where a vessel is under the charge of a licensed pilot, the employment of whom is compulsory, and is, at the same time, in tow of a steam-tug, the latter is bound to obey the orders of the pilot. In case of a mischief occurring to the vessel, occasioned directly by the conduct of the steam-tug, the tug (which had not noticed the pilot's signal), cannot in an action brought by the owners of the vessel for damage, set up, as a legal defence, contributory negligence, upon the ground that if the pilot, when the mischief was about to happen, had himself done a certain thing, the mischief might possibly have been avoided.—*Bland* v. *Ross* (*The Julia*) (Lush. 231; 14 Moo. P. C. 210) commented on, and approved. SPAIGHT v. TEDCASTLE 6 App. Cas. 217

8. —— Salvage—*Remuneration.*] When a pilot has assisted in navigating a vessel from a dangerous situation to a safe anchorage, the test whether he is entitled to be remunerated for salvage services, is not, on the one hand, whether the vessel was at the time of succour in distress, or, on the other hand, whether she was then damaged; but the test is whether the risk attending the services to the vessel was such that the pilot could not be reasonably expected to perform them for the ordinary pilot's fees, or even for extraordinary pilotage reward. — A vessel was, during a heavy storm, being driven to leeward towards dangerous sands : her captain was ignorant of the locality, and her loss appeared almost inevitable : some pilots, seeing her danger, put off to sea at the peril of their lives in order to assist her ; they were unable to board her by reason of the height of the sea ; but by preceding her and signalling to her, they guided her to a safe anchorage. The vessel had sustained no damage :

X. SHIP—PILOT—*continued.*

—*Held,* that the pilots were entitled to be remunerated for salvage services. AKERBLOM v. PRICE.
[7 Q. B. D. 129

XI. SHIP—SALVAGE.

1. —— Agreement—*Cargo—Liability of Shipowner—Average Bond.*] The *G.* fell in with the *R.* which was in distress. The following agreement was signed by the two captains: "At my request the captain of the *G.* will tow my ship the *R.* to St. Nazaire, that being the nearest port, for repairs. The matter of compensation to be left to arbitrators at home." The *G.* towed the *R.* safely to St. Nazaire. The *R.* discharged her cargo at Dunkirk, and an average bond in the usual form was taken from the consignees of the cargo. The owners of the *G.* brought an action for salvage of the ship and freight against the *R.,* and were awarded salvage. They also brought an action in France for the salvage of the cargo against the cargo owners, but failed in it. They then brought this action in personam against the owners of the *R.* to recover salvage in respect of the services to the cargo or, in the alternative, damages from the Defendants, for not taking a proper bond to secure salvage from the cargo owners :—*Held,* that the Defendants were not primarily liable to pay salvage in respect of the cargo, that they had not bound themselves by the above agreement to do so, and that it was not their duty to obtain a bond from the cargo owners for the proportion of any salvage which might be due. THE "RAISBY" - 10 P. D. 114

2. —— Agreement — *Life Salvage — No Res saved—Right of Salvors to bring Action—Validity of Salvage Agreement.*] A steamship was requested by another steamship in distress to stand by her. An agreement was accordingly made between the two masters for a fixed sum that the sound vessel would remain by the damaged one till she was in a safe position to get to port. The sound vessel remained by the damaged one until the latter was about to sink, when she took her crew on board, and the damaged steamer immediately afterwards sank. The owners, master, and crew of the salving ship brought an action for life salvage:—*Held,* that as no res was saved the action would not lie either as a salvage action simply or on the agreement.—Observations of Brett, M.R., as to the implied authority of shipmasters to enter into salvage agreements. THE "RENPOR" - - - 8 P. D. 115

3. —— Amount — *Apportionment — Derelict.*] The master of a Norwegian brig bound to Cardiff, with a crew of nine men, fell in, in the North Sea, between Heligoland and the Dogger Bank, with a derelict vessel in a very crippled condition, and put his mate and two of his crew on board her. The mate and the two men on board the derelict, shortly after they had boarded her, fearing that she was about to founder, endeavoured to leave her, but their boat was swamped, and one of the men drifted astern, and was picked up by a fishing smack. The mate and the other hand succeeded in bringing the derelict safely into the English Channel, and within three miles of Dungeness; she was then taken in tow by a steamship and towed to the entrance of Dover Harbour, within which she was subsequently placed in

XI. SHIP—SALVAGE—*continued.*

safety.—Actions of salvage were instituted by the owners, master, and crew of the brig, and by the owners, master, and crew of the steamship against the derelict vessel and her cargo, and the Court awarded a moiety of the value of the property proceeded against, and apportioned three-fifths of the amount to the owners, master, and crew of the brig. THE "LIVIETTA" - 8 P. D. 24

4. —— Amount—*Damage to Salvor.*] Where the property saved is ample, losses voluntarily incurred by the salvor should be transferred to the owner of the property saved, and in addition the salvor should receive a compensation for his exertions and for the risk he runs of not receiving any compensation in the event of his services proving ineffectual.—The losses should be ascertained with precision where practicable, but in that case the salvage remuneration added thereto should be fixed on a more moderate scale than where the losses cannot be fixed with precision.— Where a Judge had awarded £3500 for losses and £5000 for remuneration (the property saved being £67,000) :—*Held*, that a total of £6000 was sufficient. BIRD *v.* GIBB, THE "DE BAY"
[8 App. Cas. 559

5. —— Amount—*Damage to Salvor — Evidence.*] In an action of salvage in which the value of the salving steamer was £85,000 and of her cargo and freight £104,047, and of the salved steamer £90,000 and of her cargo and freight £89,535, the Court awarded £4500 to the owners, £500 to the master, and £1500 to the crew. During the hearing the owners tendered evidence of the particular injuries to their steamer caused by the performance of the services, of the costs of the repairs and of the pecuniary loss caused by the detention of their steamer whilst such repairs were being executed. Butt, J., refused to receive this evidence or to refer it to the registrar and merchants to assess the amount of such costs and losses.—On appeal from this decision :—*Held*,— Per Brett, M.R. : That the Judge of the Admiralty Court is not bound *ex debito justitiæ* to admit such evidence or to decree in terms that a specific and ascertained amount shall be paid to salvors in respect of damages or costs caused by rendering salvage services, for he is not bound always to award a sum sufficient to indemnify a salvor. But the Judge may in his discretion receive such evidence, and may, if it be proper under the circumstances, include an amount in respect of damages in his award. Having regard to the large value in the present case, the decree should be varied by awarding £1000 to the ship-owners for the actual services rendered, and by referring the costs of repairs to, and of the detention of, the salvor's steamer to be ascertained by the registrar and merchants, unless the Appellants were willing that the decree of the Court below should stand.—Per Baggallay and Lindley, L.JJ. : Where salvage services have occasioned salvors serious pecuniary loss, and where the value of the ship and cargo saved is ample not only to defray loss sustained by a salvor, in addition to a proper sum for the master and crew, but also to leave a substantial surplus for the owner of the property saved, the salvor should be remunerated where possible with a sum sufficient

XI. SHIP—SALVAGE—*continued.*

to reward him for the risk and labour and to cover damages and expenses incurred through rendering the service, and evidence of the damages and expenses ought to be received by the Judge, so that they may be ascertained with precision. The present case should be determined as stated by Brett, M.R.—*The De Bay* (8 App. Cas. 559) considered. THE "CITY OF CHESTER"
[9 P. D. 182

6. —— Amount—*Evidence—Loss of Earnings by and Damage to Salving Ship.*] In an action for salvage, evidence of the loss of earnings by and of the costs of repairing damage done to the salving vessel in consequence of rendering salvage services is admissible. But these sums are to be regarded as elements for consideration in estimating the amount of the salvage reward, but are not to be considered as fixed amounts to be awarded to the salvors in respect of these matters. THE "SUNNISIDE" - - - 8 P. D. 137

7. —— Amount—*Rule of Court of Appeal in Salvage Appeals.*] Where a salvage award is appealed against the Court of Appeal adheres to the rule laid down in the Privy Council, and will not alter the sum unless it has been given on wrong principles, or with a misapprehension of the facts, or it is exorbitant and out of reason. —£6000 was awarded for services rendered to a steamer which had run aground on a reef in the Red Sea, nearly five miles from Suez, and which, owing to the heavy sea and the nature of her position, was in imminent peril. The services were rendered at much peril to the salving ship.— The Court of Appeal refused to alter this award. THE "LANCASTER" 8 P. D. 65 ; 9 P. D. 14

8. —— Appeal *from Justices—Jurisdiction— Merchant Shipping Act*, 1854 (17 & 18 Vict. c. 104), *ss.* 2, 458, 460—*Meaning of "Ship or Boat stranded or otherwise in distress on the Shore of any Sea or Tidal Water."*] Justices awarded salvage in respect of services rendered to a hopper barge, which had been found adrift without any person on board of her in the Wash about three miles from Boston. The barge was not furnished with any means by which she could be propelled, and was used for dredging purposes : —*Held*, that the barge was a "ship in distress on the shore of a sea or tidal water" within the meaning of the Merchant Shipping Act, 1854, s. 458, and that the justices had jurisdiction to award salvage.—*The Leda* (Sw. 40) followed. THE "MAC" - - - 7 P. D. 38, 126

9. —— Costs—*Success—Abandonment.*] The *V.* fell in with the *C.*, shewing signals of distress, with her propeller shaft broken, about thirty miles out of her usual course from America to England, and took her in tow. After the *V.* had towed the *C.* from 8.10 P.M. to 7.45 A.M. the hawser broke, and owing to the danger to the cattle on board the *V.* would not take the *C.* again in tow. By the services of the *V.* the *C.* was brought ten to fourteen miles nearer her proper track, and towed eighty-five miles on her course, and thus brought into greater comparative safety. The *C.* subsequently arrived safely at Queenstown :—*Held*, that the *V.* was entitled to some salvage reward, and she was accordingly awarded

XI. SHIP—SALVAGE—*continued.*

£200—*Held*, also, that the Plaintiffs were entitled to the general costs of the action, but not to those of a special issue as to damage to machinery on which they had failed. THE " CAMELLIA "
[9 P. D. 27

10. —— **Misconduct of Salvors — Counter-claim.**] The master and crew of the Y., a vessel in distress, got on board the K., a steamer standing by her. The mate and two of the crew of the K. afterwards went on board the Y. but refused to take her master back with them. The mate subsequently also refused the services of a steam-tug, and finally having from want of local knowledge anchored the Y. in an insecure place, she began to drift, was forsaken by the salvors, and sank. She was subsequently raised by her owners at considerable expense. In an action for salvage the owners of the Y. denied that a reward was due, and counter-claimed for damages :—*Held*, that the mate was guilty of misconduct in refusing to take the master of the Y. on board of her, and to engage the services of the tug; but that if the Y. had been ultimately saved such misconduct would have worked a partial forfeiture of the reward only :—*Held*, further, that as the loss arising from the misconduct of the salvors was probably equal to that from which the Y. was first rescued, no salvage reward was due.—Counter-claim for damages dismissed. THE " YAN-YEAN "　-　8 P. D. 147

11. —— **Priority of Claims—Foreign Consul—Payments of Viaticum—Solicitor—23 & 24 Vict. c. 127, s. 28.**] Salvage actions were brought against an Italian vessel, and she was sold by order of the Court. After the salvors had been remunerated, the balance of the fund in Court was insufficient to satisfy the costs of the solicitors who had appeared in the above actions for the parties interested in the ship, and who sought to enforce their claim for such costs by virtue of 23 & 24 Vict. c. 127, s. 28, as well as the claim of the Italian consul in respect of the expenses of sending the crew back to Italy. It was proved that by the law of Italy such expenses and the keep of the master and crew ranked next to the salvage payments :—*Held*, that the claim of the Italian consul had priority to that of the solicitors. THE " LIVIETTA "　　　8 P. D. 209

12. —— **Service to two Vessels—Constructive Acceptance of Salvage Service.**] Where two vessels are in collision and are entangled together in a position dangerous to both, salvors who, by towing one of the vessels clear, free both vessels from danger, are entitled to recover salvage reward from the owners of both vessels.—A screw steam-ship drifted, during a gale of wind, across the bows of a ship at anchor in the Mersey, and with her propeller caught the anchor chains of the ship, and the two vessels were held together in a position dangerous to both. A steam-tug went to the assistance of the ship, and held her whilst her chains were slipped and towed her clear of the steamship :—*Held*, that the owners, master, and crew of the tug were entitled to recover salvage reward from the owners of the steamship. THE " VANDYCK "　　　7 P. D. 42

13. —— **Ships belonging to same Owners—**

XI. SHIP—SALVAGE—*continued.*

Warranty of Seaworthiness—Bill of Lading—Exceptions—" Dangers and accidents of the seas."] A steamship laden with cargo became disabled at sea in consequence of the breaking of her crank shaft. Such breakage was caused by a latent defect in the shaft, arising from a flaw in the welding, which it was impossible to discover. Her cargo was shipped under bills of lading which contained among the excepted perils " all and every the dangers and accidents of the seas and of navigation of whatsoever nature or kind." Another vessel belonging to the same owners towed the disabled vessel to a place of safety. In an action of salvage brought by the owners, master, and crew of the salving vessel against the owners of cargo on the salved ship :—*Held*, that the master and crew were entitled to salvage, but that the owners were not, for that there was an implied warranty by them that the vessel was seaworthy at the beginning of the voyage :—*Held*, also, that the exceptions in the bill of lading had no application to a vessel not seaworthy at the time of sailing, and that the Defendants were entitled to judgment on their counter-claim for the salvage awarded to the master and crew. THE " GLENFRUIN "
[10 P. D. 103

—— Assistance rendered by pilot　7 Q. B. D. 129
See SHIP—PILOT.　8.

XII. SHIP—SEAMEN.

—— **Neglect to join Ship—Merchant Shipping Act (17 & 18 Vict. c. 104), s. 243—Summary Proceeding before Justices—Exclusion of Civil Remedy—Employers and Workmen Act (38 & 39 Vict. c. 90), s. 4.**] The Merchant Shipping Act, 1854 (17 & 18 Vict. c. 104), s. 243—which enables a seaman who neglects without reasonable cause to join his ship to be punished upon proceedings before a court of summary jurisdiction with imprisonment and forfeiture of part of his wages—by implication takes away any other remedy against the seaman for the breach of contract, and the shipowner cannot, where the amount which he claims does not exceed £10, take proceedings for the recovery of damages under the Employers and Workmen Act, 1875 (38 & 39 Vict. c. 90), s. 4. GREAT NORTHERN STEAMSHIP FISHING COMPANY v. EDGEHILL　　　11 Q. B. D. 225

SHIP—Arrest—Bail for exorbitant sum—Costs
[9 P. D. 46
See PRACTICE—ADMIRALTY—COSTS. 1.

—— Arrest—Notice—Removal—Contempt
[10 P. D. 120
See PRACTICE—ADMIRALTY—ARREST OF SHIP. 2.

—— Carriage of goods—Liability of shipowner —Admission by master—Evidence
[10 P. D. 137
See PRACTICE—ADMIRALTY—EVIDENCE. 1.

—— County Court — Admiralty jurisdiction — Goods carried on ship
[7 P. D. 247; 12 Q. B. D. 115
See COUNTY COURT—JURISDICTION. 2, 3.

—— Discovery of ship's papers　8 Q. B. D. 142
See PRACTICE—SUPREME COURT—PRODUCTION OF DOCUMENTS. 14.

SHIP—*continued.*

—— Insurance.
　See Cases under INSURANCE, MARINE.

—— Jurisdiction of Admiralty Division.
　See Cases under PRACTICE—ADMIRALTY
　—JURISDICTION.

—— Larceny from British ship in foreign port
　See JURISDICTION. 2. [10 Q. B. D. 76

—— Malicious arrest—Commission on bail bond
　—Damages　　-　-　10 P. D. 158
　See PRACTICE—ADMIRALTY—SALVAGE.
　6.

—— Maritime lien—Jurisdiction -　6 P. D. 106
　See FOREIGN JUDGMENT. 2.

—— Mortgage of -　　-　18 Ch. D. 254
　See LIMITATIONS, STATUTE OF—TRUSTS.
　2.

—— Order given by harbour master—Liability
　of harbour commissioners　10 P. D. 131
　See NEGLIGENCE—LIABILITY. 10.

—— Owner domiciled in Great Britain—Neces-
　saries—County Court　　6 Q. B. D. 165
　See COUNTY COURT—JURISDICTION. 1.

—— Owner—Limitation of liability.
　See Cases under PRACTICE—ADMIRALTY
　—LIMITATION OF LIABILITY.

—— Owner—Privity of contract—Charterer
　　　　　　[8 App. Cas. 120
　See COLONIAL LAW—QUEENSLAND.

—— Re-insurance — Voyage over when policy
　effected　　-　　7 Q. B. D. 456
　See INSURANCE, MARINE—RISK.

—— Unfinished—Sale of　-　6 App. Cas. 588
　See SCOTCH LAW—SALE OF GOODS. 2.

SHIPBUILDING CONTRACT—Validity
　　　　　　[26 Ch. D. 510
　See CONTRACT—VALIDITY. 3.

SHIP'S HUSBAND—Discharge of principal by
　mode of dealing with agent—Delay
　　　　　　[9 Q. B. D. 623
　See PRINCIPAL AND AGENT—PRINCIPAL'S
　LIABILITY. 2.

SHOOTING, RIGHT OF—Overstocking land with
　game—Injury to crops　15 Q. B. D. 258
　See GAME. 1.

—— Statute of Frauds -　　9 Q. B. D. 315
　See FRAUDS, STATUTE OF. 3.

—— Woodlands—Poor-rate　-　6 Q. B. D. 13
　See POOR-RATE—RATEABLE VALUE. 4.

SHORT NOTICE OF MOTION　22 Ch. D. 504
　See PRACTICE—SUPREME COURT—NOTICE
　OF MOTION. 2.

SHORTHAND NOTES—Costs of　19 Ch. D. 80;
　　　　　　[6 Q. B. D. 163
　See PRACTICE—SUPREME COURT—COSTS.
　45, 46.

—— Costs of—Taxation—Solicitor and client
　　　　　　[10 Q. B. D. 207
　See SOLICITOR—BILLS OF COSTS. 13.

—— Meeting of creditors　-　20 Ch. D. 281
　See BANKRUPTCY—COMPOSITION. 3.

SHORTHAND NOTES—*continued.*

—— Evidence　-　-　-　29 Ch. D. 448
　See ESTOPPEL—JUDGMENT. 2.

—— Production of—Privilege　30 Ch. D. 116
　See PRACTICE—SUPREME COURT—PRO-
　DUCTION OF DOCUMENTS. 23.

—— Publication of lecture　-　26 Ch. D. 374
　See COPYRIGHT—BOOKS. 2.

SIAM—Order in Council
　See JURISDICTION—*Gazette.*

SIDING—Railway—Rights of landowner
　　　　　　[26 Ch. D. 190
　See RAILWAY COMPANY — RAILWAYS
　CLAUSES ACT. 8.

SIGNATURE—Acknowledgment of—Will
　　　　　　[7 P. D. 103
　See PROBATE—EXECUTION. 1.

—— Forged documents—Estoppel
　　　[13 Q. B. D. 103; 6 App. Cas. 82
　See ESTOPPEL—CONDUCT. 1, 2.

SIGNIFICAVIT—Writ of　-　6 Q. B. D. 376
　See PRACTICE — ECCLESIASTICAL —
　CHURCH DISCIPLINE ACT. 2.

SIMILARITY—Trade-mark—Registration
　　　　　　[30 Ch. D. 505
　See TRADE-MARK—REGISTRATION. 13.

SIMPLE CONTRACT DEBT—Retainer by heir-at-
　law　　-　　-　27 Ch. D. 478
　See RETAINER.

SITE FOR PLACES OF WORSHIP.
　See CHURCH BUILDING ACT;—*Statutes.*

SLANDER.
　See Cases under DEFAMATION—SLANDER.

—— Judicial proceedings—Advocate
　　　　　　[11 Q. B. D. 588
　See DEFAMATION—PRIVILEGE. 2.

—— Law of New South Wales—Costs
　　　　　　[10 App. Cas. 279
　See COLONIAL LAW—NEW SOUTH WALES.
　3.

—— Witness—House of Commons—Privilege
　　　　　　[6 Q. B. D. 307
　See DEFAMATION—PRIVILEGE. 4.

SLANDER OF TITLE—Notice against purchas-
　ing patented articles　-　19 Ch. D. 386
　See PATENT—INFRINGEMENT. 4.

SLATE MINES (GUNPOWDER) ACT, 1882.
　See MINE—MINES REGULATION ACTS—
　Statutes.

SMALL BANKRUPTCIES.
　See BANKRUPTCY — BANKRUPTCY ACT,
　1883—*Statutes.*

SOIL—Alienation of—Land for public recreation
　　　　　　[6 App. Cas. 833
　See SCOTCH LAW—HIGHWAY. 1.

" SOLE USE AND DISPOSAL "—Will—Construc-
　tion　　-　　-　17 Ch. D. 794
　See WILL—SEPARATE USE. 2.

SOLICITING CUSTOMERS—Partners
　　　　　　[22 Ch. D. 504
　See PARTNERSHIP—DISSOLUTION. 3.

—— Sale of goodwill -　　-　19 Ch. D. 355;
　See GOODWILL. 2, 3. [27 Ch. D. 145

SOLICITOR:—   Col.
    I. ARTICLED CLERK   -   1523
    II. AUTHORITY   -   - 1523
    III. BILL OF COSTS -   -   - 1524
        (a.) GENERAL.
        (b.) REMUNERATION ACT.
    IV. CERTIFICATE   -   1534
    V. LIABILITIES   1534
    VI. LIEN   1538
    VII. MISCONDUCT   1542
    VIII. RETAINER   1542
    IX. UNQUALIFIED   1543

I. SOLICITOR—ARTICLED CLERK.

1. —— Return of Premium.] A solicitor who had received a premium on taking an articled clerk died during the term of the articles:—*Held*, that his estate was not liable for the return of any part of the premium. FERNS *v.* CARR
[**28 Ch. D. 409**

II. SOLICITOR—AUTHORITY.

—— Agency—*Authority of Solicitor to receive Mortgage Money—Possession by Solicitor of Transfer Deed executed by Client.*] G. and H. were mortgagees for £1000 on property of S. Their solicitors, D. & P., who had the deeds in their custody, applied to the Defendant, who was also a client of theirs, saying that they believed he had £1000 to invest on mortgage, and that G. and H. wanted £1000 on a transfer of S.'s mortgage. The Defendant inspected the property, and being satisfied, he, on the 19th of June, 1878, sent the £1000 to D. & P., who gave him a receipt for it. In July, D. & P. fraudulently induced G. and H. to execute a deed of transfer to the Defendant with a receipt indorsed, which deed they stated to be a deed of reconveyance to S. on his paying off the mortgage. D. & P. shortly afterwards handed this deed with the title deeds to the Defendant, and went on paying him interest as if they had received it from S. who was in fact paying his interest to the agents of G. and H. G. and H. made no inquiry as to the mortgage, and this went on till 1883, when D. & P. became bankrupts, and the £1000 received from the Defendant, which had never been handed over to G. and H., was lost. G. and H. then brought their action against the Defendant, asserting a right against the property in the nature of an unpaid vendor's lien :—*Held*, by the Vice-Chancellor of the county palatine that on the evidence in the case D. & P. had authority to receive mortgage money on behalf of the Plaintiffs, and must be taken to have received the £1000 on their behalf, and that the action must be dismissed.—On appeal, Cotton, L.J., expressed great doubt (the other Judges giving no opinion on the point) whether D. & P., assuming them to have authority to receive mortgage money on behalf of the Plaintiffs, could be taken ever to have, in fact, received this £1000 on their behalf.—But *held*, by the Court of Appeal, that the decision must be affirmed on the ground that as the Plaintiffs by the deed of transfer and receipt which they handed to D. & P. enabled them to represent to the Defendant that the £1000 which he had previously handed to D. & P. had come to the

hands of the Plaintiffs, they had raised a counter equity which prevented their claiming a vendor's lien, though this would not have been the case if (D. & P. having no authority to receive money for the Plaintiffs) the Defendant had paid the £1000 to D. & P. at the time when the deeds were delivered to him, since he would then have known that the Plaintiffs had not received the money.—*Ex parte Swinbanks* (11 Ch. D. 525) distinguished. GORDON *v.* JAMES -   - **30 Ch. D. 249**

III. SOLICITOR—BILL OF COSTS.

Solicitors' Remuneration.] *The Act* 44 & 45 *Vict. c.* 44 *(the Solicitors Remuneration Act,* 1881) *provides for the making of General Orders to prescribe and regulate the remuneration of solicitors in respect of conveyancing and other non-contentious business.*

Sect. 5. *Any General Order under the Act may authorize and regulate the taking by a solicitor from his client of security for future remuneration, to be ascertained by taxation or otherwise, and the allowance of interest.*

Sect. 7. *As long as any General Order under the Act is in operation the taxation of bill of costs is to be regulated thereby.*

By sect. 8 (1) *it is competent for a solicitor, with respect to any business to which the provisions of the Act relates, whether any General Order under the Act is in operation or not, to make an agreement with his client, and, for a client to make an agreement with his solicitor, before or after or in the course of the transaction of any such business, for the remuneration of the solicitor in such amount and in such manner as the solicitor and client think fit, either by a gross sum, or by commission or percentage, or by salary, or otherwise ; and it is competent for the solicitor to accept from the client, and for the client to give to the solicitor, remuneration accordingly.*

(2.) *The agreement must be in writing, signed by the person to be bound thereby or by his agent in that behalf.*

(3.) *The agreement may, if the solicitor and the client think fit, be made on the terms that the amount of the remuneration therein stipulated for either shall include or shall not include all or any disbursements made by the solicitor in respect of searches, plans, travelling, stamps, fees, or other matters.*

(4.) *The agreement may be sued and recovered on or impeached or set aside in the like manner and on the like grounds as an agreement not relating to the remuneration of a solicitor ; and if, under any order for taxation of costs, such agreement being relied on by the solicitor shall be objected to by the client as unfair or unreasonable, the taxing master or officer of the Court may inquire into the facts, and certify the same to the Court ; and if, upon such certificate, it shall appear to the Court or Judge that just cause has been shewn either for cancelling the agreement, or for reducing the amount payable under the same, the Court or Judge has power to order such cancellation or reduction, and to give all such directions necessary or proper for the purpose of carrying such order into effect, or otherwise consequential thereon, as to the Court or Judge may seem fit.*

Sect. 9. *The Attorneys and Solicitors Act,* 1870,

III. SOLICITOR—BILL OF COSTS—*continued.*
does not apply to any business to which this Act relates.

(a.) GENERAL.

1. —— After Payment—*Order for Delivery of Bill after Payment*—6 & 7 *Vict.* c. 73, s. 41.] Where twelve calendar months have elapsed since payment of a solicitor's bill of costs by his client, such bill, although not signed by the solicitor, is prohibited by 6 & 7 Vict. c. 73, s. 41, from being referred to taxation. *In re* SUTTON & ELLIOTT
[11 Q. B. D. 377

2. —— After Payment — "*Special Circumstances*"—*Solicitors Act*, 1843 (6 & 7 *Vict.* c. 73), s. 41.] Mortgagees for £2000 were proceeding to sell the mortgaged estates. On the 1st of September, S., the mortgagor's solicitor, wrote to B., the mortgagee's solicitor, informing him that he had found a transferee, and proposing to complete the transfer on the 3rd. B. wrote back proposing the 10th for completion, and afterwards postponed the appointment to the 13th. His bill of costs, which amounted with surveyor's charges to more than £450, was received by S. on the 9th. On that day S. wrote to B., saying that the bill of costs appeared excessive, and would require to be carefully gone into, but did not propose to postpone the completion. On the 12th S. took with him a written protest against the bill, and had two interviews with B., at which arrangements were made for completion. S. did not mention the subject of costs at either interview, but deposed that he had intended to do so at a third appointment on the same day, which B. did not keep. On the 13th the parties met, the transfer was completed, and the bill of costs paid, B. refusing to part with the deeds unless it was paid. S. delivered his written protest, and it appeared that B. expressed willingness to reconsider his bill if any item were shewn to be erroneous, but said nothing to the effect that it was to be treated as open to taxation. The mortgagor applied for taxation, alleging pressure and overcharge, but not referring to any specific items of overcharge. Bacon, V.C., made an order for taxation, and B. appealed :—*Held*, by Cotton and Fry, L.JJ. (dissentiente Bowen, L.J.), that the order for taxation must be discharged, for that as the shortness of the interval between the delivery of the bill and the time fixed for completion did not arise from any act of the mortgagee's solicitor, but was owing only to the desire of the mortgagor for speedy completion, there was no pressure such as to justify taxation, though the case would have been otherwise if the mortgagee had been pressing for an early settlement :—*Held*, by Bowen, L.J., that the Solicitors Act, 1843, sect. 41, authorizes taxation after payment where there are special circumstances which, in the opinion of the Judge, require the same ; that there is no inflexible rule that the special circumstances must be pressure with overcharge, or overcharge so gross as to amount to fraud ; and that in the present case, as the parties did not at completion treat the bill as finally settled, and B. had taken advantage of the inconvenience which a postponement of the settlement would have occasioned to the mortgagor, there were special circumstances justifying taxation :—*Held*, by Bowen, L.J., that where a bill is

III. SOLICITOR—BILL OF COSTS—*continued.*

(a.) GENERAL—*continued.*

so large as to be redolent of overcharge it is not necessary that specific items of overcharge should be pointed out :—*Held*, by Fry, L.J., that though the bill appeared excessive, the Court could not treat overcharge as shewn, unless specific items were pointed out on which it could exercise its judgment. *In re* BOYCOTT - 29 Ch. D. 571

3. —— Agency Charges—*Country Solicitor and London Agent — Charge for Counsel's Fee not yet paid.*] London solicitors acted as agents in London for a country solicitor during the years 1877 to 1884 inclusive. The agency was terminated in 1884. During the period of the agency the London agents delivered to the country solicitor, generally once a year but sometimes oftener, detailed bills of the charges which they claimed against him in each of the actions or other matters in which they had acted for him. They also delivered to him a cash account for each year, in which he was credited with all payments made by him to them, and all moneys received by them on his behalf, and was debited with all payments made by them to him or on his behalf, and with the gross amounts of the several bills of charges which had been delivered. The balance appearing to be due from him on each account but the last, was carried on to the next account. Some of the actions continued during several years, and one of them (*Rhodes v. Jenkins*) continued during the whole period of the agency, and was not then concluded. After the close of the agency the country solicitor claimed a taxation of the whole of the bills :—*Held*, by Pearson, J., that only those bills which had been delivered within twelve months could be taxed, and that the earlier bills must be treated as having been settled in account and thus paid.—*Held*, by the Court of Appeal, that the bills of costs in *Rhodes* v. *Jenkins* (to which the appeal was limited), notwithstanding the fact that all the costs in it had not yet been taxed, being in fact separate bills, could not be treated as one continuous bill, at the option of the country solicitor. — The London agents had charged the country solicitor with fees to counsel which had not yet been paid, but the country solicitor had not supplied them with sufficient funds to pay the fees :—*Held*, by Pearson, J., that this charge was not a circumstance sufficient to justify a taxation. *In re* NELSON, SON, & HASTINGS
[30 Ch. D. 1

4. —— Assignee — *Costs — Taxation*—6 & 7 *Vict.* c. 73, s. 37.] Whether an assignee of costs due to a solicitor is such an "assignee" of the solicitor as is, under sect. 37 of the Act 6 & 7 Vict. c. 73, entitled to obtain a taxation of the costs, *quære.*—But if an assignee of costs can obtain a taxation, he cannot obtain an order of course to tax one bill of costs out of several, even if that bill only has been assigned to him. An order to tax one bill out of several alone can only be obtained by means of a special application. *In re* WARD - - 28 Ch. D. 719

5. —— Assignee—*Solicitors Act*, 1843 (6 & 7 *Vict.* c. 73), s. 37—*Signature—Judicature Act*, 1873 (36 & 37 *Vict.* c. 66), s. 25, sub-s. 6.] A solicitor assigned his bill of costs and the right

III. SOLICITOR—BILL OF COSTS—continued.

(a.) GENERAL—continued.

to recover on it, and the assignee gave notice of the assignment and delivered the bill to the party to be charged inclosed in a letter signed by himself. After the expiration of a month he brought an action in his own name on the bill of costs :— Held, that the Plaintiff was an assignee within sect. 37 of the Solicitors' Act, 1843, and was entitled to maintain the action. INGLE v. M'CUTCHAN　-　-　12 Q. B. D. 518

6. —— Costs of Taxation—Offer by Solicitor to reduce the Amount—Certifying special Circumstances—6 & 7 Vict. c. 73, s. 37.] O., a solicitor, sent in to executors a bill of costs for £83, writing at the foot, "say £78," and the £78 was paid. The residuary legatee obtained an order to tax the bill, which was taxed at £66, being more than five-sixths of £78, but less than five-sixths of £83. The residuary legatee objected to certain items as excessive, and the Taxing Master considered that they were excessive ; but held, that, as the executors had authorized them and admitted their liability to pay them, the residuary legatee could not have them reduced :— Held, by Chitty, J., that the Taxing Master was right in allowing these items ; that the bill must be treated as a bill for £78, from which less than one-sixth had been taxed off, and that the solicitor was entitled to the costs of the reference.—P., a solicitor, delivered a bill for £362, but stated that he would only claim £320, and the £320 only was entered in the cash account which he delivered to his clients. The clients obtained an order for taxation. The Taxing Master taxed the bill at £280, being more than five-sixths of £320, but less than five-sixths of £362, and certified that he had allowed the solicitor the costs of the reference, as he considered that since he had never claimed more than £320, the difference of £42 between this sum and the amount of the whole bill, ought to be deducted from the sums taxed off, thus reducing them to £40, which was less than a sixth of the sum he had claimed :—Held, by Pearson, J., that the solicitor must pay the costs of the reference.—Held, on appeal, that in C.'s Case, the bill delivered, within the meaning of 6 & 7 Vict. c. 73, s. 37, was a bill for £83, and that, as more than one-sixth had been taxed off, the solicitor must, according to that section, pay the costs of the reference ; the case not coming within the proviso giving the Court a discretion where special circumstances are certified.—Held, in P.'s Case, that special circumstances were certified, so as to give the Court a discretion as to the costs of the reference, but that the special circumstances were not such as to induce the Court to depart from the general rule that the costs of the reference should follow the event of the taxation, and that in this case also, more than one-sixth having been taxed off the £362, the solicitor must pay the costs of the reference. In re CARTHEW. In re PAULL　-　27 Ch. D. 485

7. —— Delivery of Bill — Condition— Withdrawal — Delivery of Second Bill — Taxation, Common Order for—Practice—Solicitors Act (6 & 7 Vict. c. 73), s. 37.] A solicitor may, when sending in his bill of costs to his client, reserve to himself the right to withdraw or alter it on

III. SOLICITOR—BILL OF COSTS—continued.

(a.) GENERAL—continued.

condition, provided the condition is fully and clearly stated to the client : but if the solicitor has sent in his bill without any condition, or with a condition which he could not fairly impose, he cannot afterwards withdraw it or send in an amended bill.—A firm of solicitors, on being pressed by their clients to send in their bill of costs, delivered a bill accompanied by a letter saying that there were certain charges which, owing to haste, had not been included in the bill, but that they were willing to accept a stated sum in full discharge, though if such sum was not paid within eight days, they reserved to themselves the right to withdraw the bill and deliver another. The clients, however, insisting on being furnished with the particulars of further charges, the solicitors wrote withdrawing the bill. The clients then obtained a common order for taxation of that bill, and for delivery and taxation of a further bill.—On motion by the solicitors, Bacon, V.C., discharged the common order on the ground that no bill had been "delivered" within the meaning of sect. 37 of the Solicitors Act, 6 & 7 Vict. c. 73 ; but ordered the solicitors to deliver a bill within fourteen days, such bill to be taxed.—The solicitors, in pursuance of that order, delivered a second bill, but of a considerably less amount than the first, whereupon the clients appealed to reverse that order and to have it declared that the bill to be taxed was that first delivered :—Held, by Cotton and Lindley, L.JJ., discharging the last-mentioned order, that the first bill was conditional, but that the condition was one which a solicitor could not impose on his client, and that therefore the original common order for taxation must stand.—Held, also, that the clients should under the circumstances, instead of obtaining the common order to tax, have obtained a special order on petition raising the question as to the right of the solicitors to withdraw their bill : they were therefore allowed no costs of the proceedings in the Court below, but only the costs of the appeal. In re THOMPSON　　30 Ch. D. 441

8. —— Journeys—Practice—Taxation of Costs —Country Solicitor—Journeys to London.] Upon a summons by a solicitor for an order directing the Taxing Master to review his taxation of a bill of costs :—Held, that the journeys of a country solicitor to town to attend counsel and otherwise to conduct the proceedings in an action ought to be allowed, where the solicitor had authority from his client to make these charges ; but that such journeys to town ought not to be allowed simply on the principle that the country solicitor would probably be better acquainted with the subject-matter than his London agent.—In re Foster (8 Ch. D. 598) dissented from. In re STORER [26 Ch. D. 189

9. —— Married Woman—Receiver—Taxation of Solicitor's Bill—Solicitors Act (6 & 7 Vict. c. 73), s. 43—Judicature Act, 1873, s. 25, sub-s. 8.] M., a married woman, by her next friend, applied to tax the bill of costs of her solicitor incurred in a suit relating to her separate estate. After the Taxing Master's certificate had been filed, an order was made on the application of the solicitor directing an inquiry of what M.'s separate estate

III. SOLICITOR—BILL OF COSTS—*continued.*

(a.) GENERAL—continued.

consisted at the date of the filing of the certificate capable of being reached by the judgment and execution of the Court, and appointing a person to receive it until the amount found due on taxation was paid:—*Held*, that this order was proper, and that it was not necessary to take separate proceedings by action to enforce the demand against the separate estate. *In re* PEACE & WALLER　　-　　24 Ch. D. 405

10. —— **Mortgage**—*Taxation—Mortgagor and Mortgagee—Trustee—Profit Costs.*] Where one of a body of mortgagees is a solicitor and acts as such in enforcing the mortgage security, he is entitled to charge profit costs against the mortgagor, whether the mortgagees are trustees or not.—If in such a case the mortgagor, in applying for an order to tax the bill of the solicitor-mortgagee, desires to raise the objection to profit costs, he should state his objection in his petition for taxation. *In re* DONALDSON　　27 Ch. D. 544

11. —— **Negligence** — *Taxation — Power of Taxing Master to disallow Items caused by Negligence.*] The Taxing Master in taxing a bill of costs between a solicitor and his client has power to disallow the costs of proceedings in an action conducted by the solicitor which were occasioned by the negligence or ignorance of the solicitor. But if the negligence goes to the loss of the whole action, he ought not to disallow them, but to leave the client to bring an action for negligence against the solicitor. *In re* MASSEY & CAREY　　26 Ch. D. 459

12. —— **Past Costs**—*Ex parte Order for Taxation—Motion to discharge — Parol Agreement to pay a Lump Sum—Attorneys and Solicitors Act,* 1870 (33 & 34 Vict. c. 28), s. 4.] Since the Attorneys and Solicitors Act, 1870, a verbal agreement by a client to pay his solicitor a lump sum in discharge of past costs is not binding on the client. *In re* RUSSELL, SON, & SCOTT　　[30 Ch. D. 114

13. —— **Shorthand Notes**—*Solicitor and Client—Taxation.*] Where a solicitor proposes to incur unusual expense in the course of an action, such as taking shorthand notes of the evidence or procuring the attendance of experts and scientific witnesses, it is his duty to point out to his client that such expense might not be allowed on taxation as between party and party, and might therefore have to be borne by the client whatever might be the result of the trial. Therefore, where the solicitor had omitted such duty, he was not allowed on taxation as between solicitor and client the cost of shorthand notes of the evidence, although the client authorized him to employ a shorthand writer to take such notes and used and otherwise availed himself of them after they had been so taken. *In re* BLYTH & FANSHAWE　　[10 Q. B. D. 207

14. —— **Third Counsel**—*Costs of Third Counsel on Appeal.*] The rule laid down in *In re Blyth and Fanshawe* (10 Q. B. D. 207) applies to the costs of employing a third counsel on the hearing of an appeal, the expense being an unusual one.— Therefore, even if a solicitor has obtained his client's sanction to the employment of a third

III. SOLICITOR—BILL OF COSTS—*continued.*

(a.) GENERAL—continued.

counsel on an appeal, the costs will not be allowed on taxation between solicitor and client, unless the solicitor has also explained to the client that the costs will probably not be allowed as between party and party, and that, even if he succeeds on his appeal, he may have to pay the costs of the third counsel himself. — Decision of Divisional Court affirmed. *In re* BROAD AND BROAD　　[15 Q. B. D. 252, 420

15. —— **Trustee of Will**—*Authority by Testator to charge for non-professional Business.*] A testator by his will authorized any trustee thereof who might be a solicitor to make the usual professional or other proper and reasonable charges, for all business done and time expended in relation to the trusts of the will, whether such business was usually within the business of a solicitor or not. On the further consideration of an action for the administration of the testator's estate an order was made for the taxation of the costs, charges, and expenses of the trustees, and it was directed that the Taxing Master should have regard to the terms of the will as to the costs of the trustees:— *Held*, that the Taxing Master had power to allow to a trustee who was a solicitor the proper charges for business not strictly of a professional nature transacted by him in relation to the trust estate. *In re* AMES. AMES *v.* TAYLOR　　25 Ch. D. 72

16. —— **Trustee of Will**—*Executor—Direction Professional Charges—Construction.*] A testatrix by her will appointed her solicitor (who prepared her will) one of her two executors and trustees, and, stating that it was her desire that he should continue to act as solicitor in relation to her property and affairs, and should "make the usual professional charges," expressly directed that notwithstanding his acceptance of the office of trustee and executor he should be entitled to make the same professional charges and to receive the same pecuniary emoluments and remuneration for all business done by him, and all attendances, time, and trouble given and bestowed by him in or about the execution of the trusts and powers of the will, and the management and administration of the trust estate, real or personal, as if he, not being himself a trustee or executor, were employed by the trustee or executor. Under this direction the solicitor-executor delivered bills of costs which included charges for all business done by him, whether such business was strictly professional or could have been transacted by a lay executor without the assistance of a solicitor :— *Held*, that all items which were not of a strictly professional character ought to be disallowed.— *In re Ames* (25 Ch. D. 72) distinguished. *In re* CHAPPLE. NEWTON *v.* CHAPMAN　　27 Ch. D. 584

17. —— **Undertaking to pay Costs**—*Party and Party—Taxation—Attorneys and Solicitors Act* (6 & 7 Vict. c. 73), *s.* 38.] A creditor's petition to wind up a company having been withdrawn on payment of the debt, the solicitors for the company undertook by letter with the petitioning creditor's solicitors "to pay all proper costs and charges incidental to and recoverable under such petition, such costs, in case of difference, to be taxed."—The amount of the costs not being agreed upon, the company obtained,

IIL. SOLICITOR—BILL OF COSTS—*continued.*

(a.) GENERAL—*continued.*

ex parte, an order to tax under the third party clause (sect. 38) of the Attorneys and Solicitors Act, and served it on the solicitors of the petitioning creditors :—*Held*, on motion to discharge the order, that the undertaking was a personal undertaking to pay the costs, such costs being costs as between party and party; that the 38th section of the Act had reference only to the taxation of costs as between solicitor and client; that the order, therefore, was irregular, and must be discharged with costs to be paid by the company.—*Re Hartley* (30 Beav. 620) considered and explained. *In re* GRUNDY, KERSHAW, & Co.

[**17 Ch. D. 108**

(b.) REMUNERATION ACT.

18. —— Conducting Sale—*Settled Land Act, 1882—Sale by Tenant for Life—General Order of August, 1882—Solicitor's Remuneration in respect of Business connected with Sales — Auctioneer's Charges.*] Settled property which had been put up for sale by auction by the tenant for life under the Settled Land Act, 1882, but withdrawn for want of any sufficient offer, having been sold by private contract on the same day :—*Held*, on summons by the trustees for the decision of the Court, that one charge, according to the scale set out in Part I. of Schedule 1 of the General Order under the Solicitors' Remuneration Act, 1881, was payable out of the purchase-money to the tenant for life's solicitor for conducting the sale, including the conditions of sale, and one charge for deducing the title and completing the conveyance, including the preparation of the contract; and that the costs of the concurrence in the sale by the mortgagees of the tenant for life, and a proper sum for the auctioneer's charges, were also payable out of the purchase-money. *In re* BECK. *In re* CARTINGTON ESTATE **24 Ch. D. 608**

19. —— Conveyancing—*Charges for Pressure —Taxation—General Order, August, 1882 (44 & 45 Vict. c. 44)—Percentage.*] A tenant having an option of purchase of the fee at a given price on the terms of his paying all the vendor's costs, gave notice in December, 1882, of his exercise of the option, and stated that he should not require an abstract of title. The time for completion was the 25th of March, 1883, but it was arranged for the tenant's convenience that the completion should be six weeks earlier, and that the property should be conveyed in two lots. He sent his draft conveyances for perusal before the end of December. On the 2nd of February, 1883, the vendor's solicitors sent in their bill of costs, in which they charged 30s. per cent. on the purchase-money of each lot, considering that this was the proper charge under Schedule I. to the general rules under the Solicitors' Remuneration Act, 1881, which provides that amount of remuneration to a vendor's solicitor " for deducing title to freehold, copyhold, or leasehold property, and perusing and completing conveyance (including preparation of contract or conditions of sale, if any)." The purchaser's solicitors objected to these charges, but the vendor's solicitors refused to allow completion unless they were paid, and on the 14th of February the purchaser paid them under protest, and completed the purchase. After

III. SOLICITOR—BILL OF COSTS—*continued.*

(b.) REMUNERATION ACT—*continued.*

this he applied for taxation of the bill :—*Held*, by Bacon, V.C., that an order must be made for taxation of the bill with a direction that the taxation should be on the old system prevailing before the Solicitors' Remuneration Act, 1881 :— *Held*, on appeal, that the case was governed by the new Rules, but that the bill was framed on an erroneous footing, for that the ad valorem remuneration authorized by Schedule I. was chargeable only where the whole of the business in respect of which it was imposed, viz., the deducing title and perusing and completing conveyance, was done; that here, as there was no deducing of title, but only perusal and completion of the conveyances, Schedule I. did not apply, but that under the General Order, rule 2 (c), the solicitor's remuneration was to be regulated by the old system as modified by Schedule II.—But *held*, that, having regard to the dates, there was no pressure, and that there was no overcharge amounting to fraud, and that there were therefore no special circumstances to authorize taxation after payment. *In re* LACY & SON

[**25 Ch. D. 301**

20. —— Conveyancing—*Perusing Abstracts— Taxation — Solicitors' Remuneration Act, 1881 (44 & 45 Vict. c. 44) — General Order, August, 1882, Sched. II.*] Upon the construction of Sched. II. of the General Order (containing scales of charges) made in pursuance of the Solicitors' Remuneration Act, 1881, abstracts of title are not included in the words " deeds, wills, and other documents," the charge for perusing which is therein fixed at 1s. per folio; but the old scale of 6s. 8d. for perusal of every three brief sheets of eight folios each remains unaltered. *In re* PARKER

[**29 Ch. D. 199**

21. —— Conveyancing—*Suit for Administration—Taxation of Costs—Solicitors' Remuneration Act, 1881 (44 & 45 Vict. c. 44)—General Order, August, 1882, r. 2—Costs for Conveyancing Business in an Action.*] Solicitors who transact conveyancing business in an action will, under the Solicitors' Remuneration Act, 1881 (44 & 45 Vict. c. 44), and the General Order of August, 1882 (W. N. (1882) pt. II. p. 358), be allowed taxed costs and charges for such business, according to the scales set forth in the schedules to the General Order.—The proper construction of the language of sect. 2 of the Solicitors' Remuneration Act, 1881, is that it refers to conveyancing matters which take place in an action as well as to those out of Court, and that the exception is only from "other business " not being conveyancing business; and accordingly where the Taxing Master had disallowed certain charges made for conveyancing business in an action, and under the scales of charges contained in the schedules to the General Order of August, 1882, he was directed to review his taxation. STANFORD *v.* ROBERTS

[**26 Ch. D. 155**

22. —— Lands Clauses Act (8 & 9 *Vict* c. 18), *Sale under—Reinvestment' of Proceeds— Costs — Solicitors' Remuneration Act, 1881 (44 & 45 Vict. c. 44) — General Order, August, 1882, r. 2, Sched. I., pt. 1. r. 11 — Scale Charges.*] Money arising from the sale of land belonging

III. SOLICITOR—BILL OF COSTS—*continued.*

(b.) REMUNERATION ACT—*continued.*

to a corporation, and taken by a railway company under their statutory powers, was reinvested in land under the direction of the Court. The solicitor of the corporation charged the ad valorem scale fee prescribed by the rules under the Solicitors' Remuneration Act, 1881, Schedule I. Part I., " for investigating title and preparing and completing conveyance " :—*Held* (affirming the decision of Chitty, J.), that the exception in Schedule I., Part I., rule 11, which provides that the scale shall not apply in case of sales under the Lands Clauses Act, or any other private or public Act under which the vendor's charges are paid by the purchaser, was not applicable to the case.—*Held*, also (approving the decision of Kay, J., in *Stanford* v. *Roberts* (26 Ch. D. 155), that the words of rule 2 " not being business in any action or transacted in any Court or in the chambers of any Judge or Master," apply only to the " other business " mentioned immediately before, i.e., to business not being conveyancing business, and do not exclude from the scale conveyancing business done under the direction of the Court.—*Held*, also, that as the purchaser's solicitor had had to do all the things which he would have had to do in a purchase not under the direction of the Court, the case was not taken out of the scale by the fact that, in a purchase under the direction of the Court, he did not incur as much responsibility as in a private purchase :—*Held*, therefore, that the scale fee was properly chargeable. *In re* MERCHANT TAYLORS' COMPANY - - 29 Ch. D. 209 ; 30 Ch. D. 28

23. —— Non-professional Work—*Taxation of Bill—Ex parte Order—Special Agreement—Solicitors' Remuneration Act, 1881 (44 & 45 Vict. c. 44), s. 8.*] Where an agreement has been made for the remuneration of a solicitor, and the solicitor alleges that the remuneration was for non-professional work, the person chargeable cannot obtain the common ex parte order for the delivery and taxation of the bill of costs. The Solicitors' Remuneration Act, 1881, s. 8, has made no difference in the practice in this respect. *In re* INDERWICK - - 25 Ch. D. 279

24. —— Pending Business—*Negotiations for Lease—Solicitors' Remuneration Act, 1881 (44 & 45 Vict. c. 44), s. 7 — General Order, August, 1882, r. 2 (a), (b), (c) ; Sched. I., Part II.*] Negotiations for a lease were carried on through the lessor's solicitor for two years before the rules under the Solicitors' Remuneration Act, 1881, came into operation. After they came into operation terms were come to, and a lease executed. The solicitor in his bill charged for the negotiations, and also charged the amount fixed by Sched. I., Part II., to the rules, as remuneration " for preparing, settling, and completing lease and counterpart." The Taxing Master disallowed all the items for negotiations, and Mr. Justice Chitty affirmed his decision. The solicitor appealed :—*Held*, by the Court of Appeal, that though the business had been commenced before the rules came into operation, the taxation must be conducted according to the rules, the solicitor not having declared his election to the contrary.—Whether he might on the

III. SOLICITOR—BILL OF COSTS—*continued.*

(b.) REMUNERATION ACT—*continued.*

rules coming into operation have effectually declared such election, *quære.*—*Held*, further, that having regard to rule 2, the amount fixed by Sched. I., Part II., included the charges for negotiations, and that the appeal must be dismissed. *In re* FIELD - - 29 Ch. D. 608

25. —— Sale by Auction — *General Order under Solicitors' Remuneration Act, 1881, r. 4 ; Sched. I., Part I., r. 11—Commission to Auctioneer.*] Property of a lunatic in Lancashire was put up for sale by auction under an order in lunacy, but was not sold. The solicitor charged £16 12s. 6d. remuneration according to the scale in the order under the Solicitors' Remuneration Act, 1881, on £8300, the amount of the reserved prices. He also paid the auctioneer £5 5s., which was allowed against the estate, and the surveyor's bill of £40 3s. was allowed at £31 10s. against the estate, but the Taxing Master disallowed the £16 12s. 6d., and only allowed £2 2s. for instructing the auctioneer and surveyor, and £3 3s. for particulars, &c. His reasons were, first, that the solicitor had not in fact conducted the sale, the auctioneer and surveyor having done most of the work, and been paid by the client ; and, secondly, that the scale did not apply, for that a commission had been paid to the auctioneer by the client within the meaning of rule 11 to Part I. of Sched. I. to the General Order.—*Held*, by the Court of Appeal, that as the bill of the surveyor contained charges for various things which it was the duty of the person conducting the sale to do, the solicitor had not done the whole of the work for which the ad valorem remuneration was provided, and the scale did not apply.—*Semble*, also, that the case was taken out of rule 4 by the specific provision of rule 11 to Part I. of Sched. I. to the Order, which provides that the scale for conducting a sale by auction shall apply only in cases where no commission is paid by the client to an auctioneer. *In re* WILSON - - 29 Ch. D. 790

IV. SOLICITOR—CERTIFICATE.

—— Certificate — *40 & 41 Vict. c. 25, s. 23, and Sched. II.*] Where a solicitor has neglected for a whole year to renew his certificate, the Master of the Rolls alone has power to order the registrar of certificates (the Incorporated Law Society) to grant him a certificate for the current year.—The right of a solicitor who has neglected to renew his certificate to apply for a fresh one is not a " right acquired or accrued " within 40 & 41 Vict. c. 25, s. 23, Proviso (B.) *In re* CHAFFERS [15 Q. B. D. 467

V. SOLICITOR—LIABILITIES.

1. —— Acting against Former Client—*Injunction.*] *Held*, by Hall, V.C., that the jurisdiction to restrain a solicitor from acting for the antagonist of his former client is founded upon the principle that a man ought to be restrained from doing any act contrary to the duty he owes to another ; and that it will be exercised at the instance of the former client irrespective of the question whether the solicitor was discharged by him. or had discharged himself, whenever the transaction in reference to which the injunction is sought so flows out of or is connected with

V. SOLICITOR—LIABILITIES—_continued._

that in which the solicitor was formerly retained that the same matter of dispute may probably arise.—_Hutchins_ v. _Hutchins_ (1 Hogan, 315) and _Biggs_ v. _Head_ (Sausse & Scully, 335) approved and adopted.—On appeal, the injunction granted by the Vice-Chancellor was disapproved and dissolved by consent, the solicitor undertaking not to disclose his client's secrets.　LITTLE _v._ KINGSWOOD COLLIERIES COMPANY　　　**20 Ch. D. 733**

2. —— Constructive Trust—_Notice of Settlement—Sales._] A settlement of land in Wales, the property of the husband, was executed shortly after a marriage, which took place in India. The husband and wife went to reside in Wales, and the husband employed a solicitor to make his will and to sell part of the land, the solicitor concluding from the statement of the husband that there had not been any marriage settlement. The husband died leaving his widow trustee and executrix, and directing his debts to be paid out of his estate. The widow employed the same solicitor to sell other part of the land, and the solicitor received the purchase moneys and applied them in payment of the debts of the husband. The deed of settlement had been in the possession of the wife, but had been by her given to the husband. There was no evidence as to what had become of it, but after the sales had been made a copy was found. The solicitor had concluded from what he was told by the husband that there had been no settlement, and though, before all the sales were completed, his clerk had been told by the wife that there had been a settlement, the solicitor continued to believe that there had been none.— An action was brought by the children of the marriage, entitled under the settlement, claiming to recover from the solicitor the money which had so passed through his hands :—_Held_, that under the circumstances, although the solicitor might have been negligent in that character, he could not be held to have had such notice of the settlement as to be treated as constructively a trustee, and therefore liable for the money which had passed through his hands.—Notice to raise a constructive trust is different from notice to an actual trustee.—_Cothay_ v. _Sydenham_ (2 Bro. C. C. 391) discussed.　WILLIAMS _v._ WILLIAMS **17 Ch. D. 437**

3. —— Constructive Trust—_Solicitor receiving money to invest on a Specified Security—Legal Estate—Tacking—Priority._] The owner of a copyhold, which was subject to a mortgage by conditional surrender for £350, made by a former owner, instructed S., his solicitor, to procure him, on the security of the property, a loan of £550, out of which the old mortgage was to be paid off. S., in July, 1876, obtained the money from the Plaintiff, who was also his client. In July, 1877, S. took a security for £700 on the property in his own name, the mortgagee assigning the old mortgage debt, and the mortgagor covenanting to surrender. The old mortgagee was paid by a cheque drawn by S. on B. & Co., his bankers. S.'s account was already overdrawn, but on the same day he applied to them for leave further to overdraw, which was granted on his depositing with them the security for £700, and the cheque when presented was honoured. B. & Co. had no notice of the Plaintiff's claim. Some time after this S. put

V. SOLICITOR—LIABILITIES—_continued._

his account in credit, but it shortly afterwards became again overdrawn. S. handed over some of the other muniments of title to the Plaintiff. The Plaintiff commenced his action to establish his right to rank as incumbrancer for £550 in priority to B. & Co. After this, B. & Co. procured the old mortgage to be admitted under the old conditional surrender, and to surrender to them :—_Held_, by Malins, V.C., that after the account of S. with B. & Co. had once been put in credit, their security must, as against other incumbrances on the property, be taken to have been discharged, and that the Plaintiff was entitled to priority over B. & Co.—B. & Co. appealed, asking for priority over the Plaintiff to the extent of the old mortgage which had been paid off with their money :—_Held_, by the Court of Appeal, that S., having received money from the Plaintiff for the purpose of being invested on a mortgage of specified property, and having taken a security on that property in his own name, was a trustee of that security for the Plaintiff to the extent of the money received from him, and that this equitable title must prevail against the deposit with B. & Co., and that the £350 mortgage could not be set up against the Plaintiff :—_Held_, also, that B. & Co. did not acquire priority by having got the legal estate, for that an equitable incumbrancer cannot, after receiving notice of a prior incumbrance, obtain priority over it by getting in a legal estate from a bare trustee.　HARPHAM _v._ SHACKLOCK
　　　　　　　　　　　　　　　　　[19 Ch. D. 207

4. —— Contempt of Court—_Attachment—Privilege—Police Court—Debtors Act_, 1869 (32 & 33 _Vict._ c. 62), _s._ 4, _sub-s._ 4—_Debtors Act_, 1878 (41 & 42 _Vict._ c. 54), s. 1.] Disobedience by a solicitor to an order of Court made against him as an officer of the Court is a contempt of a criminal nature, and an attachment granted to enforce compliance with the order of Court is process of a punitive and disciplinary character; and therefore no privilege from arrest exists or can be claimed against the execution of the attachment. —Privilege from arrest for contempt of Court, where it otherwise exists, can be claimed in respect of attendance as an advocate at a police court as well as at any other Court, although the proceedings at the police court consist merely of a preliminary inquiry on a charge of felony.—F. was a solicitor, and an order was made at chambers that he should deliver up certain documents and should pay the sum of £10 and certain costs. This order was made against F. as an officer of the Court. F. delivered up the documents, but he did not pay the sum of £10 or the costs. An order for the attachment of F. for contempt of Court was thereupon made at Chambers. F. then paid the sum of £10, but he did not pay the costs. He was arrested under the attachment, whilst he was on his return to his offices from a metropolitan police court, where he had been as advocate attending to defend certain persons at a preliminary inquiry on a charge of treason-felony :— _Held_, that he was not entitled to be discharged from custody on the ground of privilege from arrest, the attachment having been granted for a contempt of a criminal nature.　_In re_ FRESTON
　　　　　　　　　　　　　　　　　[11 Q. B. D. 545

V. SOLICITOR—LIABILITIES—*continued.*

5. —— Contempt of Court—*Attachment—Order for Payment of Money — Punitive and Disciplinary Process.*] A solicitor received on behalf of a client a sum of £339, which he paid into his account with his own bankers and dealt with as his own money. He afterwards forwarded to his client a sum of £100, and refused to pay the balance, on the ground that he had a claim against an agent whom his client had employed to communicate with him. Application having been made to the Queen's Bench Division to compel the solicitor to pay the money, the matter was referred to a Master, who reported that the balance was due from the solicitor to his client. An order was made by the Queen's Bench Division, and also a subsequent order was made at Chambers, that the solicitor should pay the balance claimed to his client. These orders not having been complied with, an order for the attachment of the solicitor was made by a Judge at Chambers :—*Held*, that the orders for the payment of the balance claimed were not merely in the nature of civil process, but were orders made against the solicitor as an officer of the Court, and that the attachment was properly granted.—*In re Ball* (Law Rep. 8 C. P. 104) explained.—*In re Freston* (11 Q. B. D. 545) followed. *In re* DUDLEY - · 12 Q. B. D. 44

6. —— Fiduciary Relation—*Duty to disclose Facts—Solicitor in Administration Action—Leave to bid at Sale.*] In an administration action part of the property of the testator was ordered to be put up for sale by auction, and leave was given to the solicitor for the Defendant (the executor) to bid at the sale, which was to be conducted by the Plaintiffs' solicitors independently of him. At the auction the property was not sold, and the Court afterwards sanctioned a contract for its sale to the Defendant's solicitor and another person :—*Held*, that the effect of the order giving leave to the solicitor to bid and of the subsequent approval of the contract was entirely to put an end to the fiduciary relation in which he formerly stood, and to place him in the position of a mere stranger, and that consequently he was under no obligation to disclose to the Court any facts within his knowledge affecting the value of the property. BOSWELL *v.* COAKS - 23 Ch. D. 302
[**Reversed** on other grounds by Court of Appeal, 27 Ch. D. 424.]

7. —— Improper Sale—*Measure of Damage—Costs as between Solicitor and Client.*] The Defendant (who was the Plaintiff's solicitor) improperly sold the Plaintiff's property without giving him notice of the sale, and a decree was made against the solicitor directing him to pay damages and costs :—*Held*, that the damages ought to include the difference between the Plaintiff's solicitor and client costs and the party and party costs which he could get under the order for costs. COCKBURN *v.* EDWARDS - 16 Ch. D. 393

8. —— Summary Jurisdiction—*Liability of Town Agent of Country Solicitor to pay to Client amount of Debt received in an Action.*] The town agent of the solicitor of the Plaintiff, in an action in which judgment had been recovered for a debt, refused to pay over to the Plaintiff the amount of the debt which had been received by

V. SOLICITOR—LIABILITIES—*continued.* ·

him from the sheriff under a writ of fi. fa., on the ground that he was entitled to retain such amount for a debt due to him from the country solicitor of equal amount.—The country solicitor had no lien on such amount against his client, the Plaintiff :—*Held*, affirming the decision of the Queen's Bench Division, that the Court in the exercise of its summary jurisdiction over its own officers would order the town agent to pay over the amount of the debt to the Plaintiff.—In such a case the Court will exercise its summary jurisdiction, although there be no fraud imputed to the town agent. *Ex parte* EDWARDS
[7 Q. B. D. 155; 8 Q. B. D. 262

VI. SOLICITOR—LIEN.

1. —— Charging Order—*"Property recovered or preserved"—23 & 24 Vict. c. 127, s. 28.*] An undischarged bankrupt, without the knowledge of the trustee in his bankruptcy, brought an action, claiming (inter alia) remuneration for services rendered by him as an architect to the Defendant, and damages for wrongful dismissal. The Defendant, without admitting any legal liability to the Plaintiff, paid £360 into Court. The Plaintiff took out a summons to have the money paid out to him, but before the summons was heard the action came to the knowledge of the trustee, and he obtained an order joining him as co-Plaintiff in the action, on the ground that the remuneration and damages claimed were his property. The bankrupt's solicitor then applied for a charging order on the £360 in respect of his costs, charges, and expenses of or in reference to the action :—*Held* (reversing the decision of Fry, J.), that the bankrupt's solicitor was entitled to a charging order for his costs up to the time of the intervention of the trustee.—When the Court makes an order under the Solicitors' Act (23 & 24 Vict. c. 127), s. 28, declaring a solicitor entitled to a charge upon the property recovered or preserved in an action, it is the duty of the Judge to limit the order to costs properly incurred in recovering or preserving the property.—Money paid into Court by a Defendant, although accompanied by a defence denying legal liability, may be taken out of Court by the Plaintiff; and is, therefore, property "recovered or preserved" within the 28th section of the Solicitors' Act.—*Berdan* v. *Greenwood* (3 Ex. D. 251) followed. EMDEN *v.* CARTE - - 19 Ch. D. 311

2. —— Charging Order—*23 & 24 Vict. c. 127, s. 28—Property recovered or preserved—Property of Person not employing the Solicitor—Property of Infant.*] The charge declared in pursuance of the 28th section of the Solicitors Act, 1860, on the property recovered or preserved in favour of the solicitor employed is in the nature of salvage, and may be made on the interest of persons who did not employ the solicitor and who were not parties to the suit, if they adopt the benefit obtained in the suit.—It makes no difference that the persons whose interests are charged are infants, but the Court will not make the order until the infants have an opportunity of being heard on it.—P. and Y. were trustees under the will of G. P. misapplied some of the trust funds and died. The suit of *M.* v. *P.* was brought for the administration of P.'s estate, and a proof was carried in by Y. on

3 D

VI. SOLICITOR—LIEN—continued.

behalf of the trust in respect of the breaches of trust by P. Afterwards the action of *G.* v. *Y.* was brought by some of the cestuis que trust under *G.*'s will to establish the liability of **Y.** and to appoint new trustees, in which a small dividend was recovered from Y.'s estate. The solicitor who acted for the Plaintiffs in *G.* v. *Y.* applied for a charging order for his costs on the dividend recovered from P.'s and Y.'s estates, which was opposed by the new trustees on behalf of the infant cestuis que trust :—*Held,* that the solicitor was entitled to a charge upon the dividend recovered in the action from Y.'s estate as against the infant cestui que trust, but not on the dividend recovered from P.'s estate, as it was not recovered in the action. GREER *v.* YOUNG

[**24 Ch. D. 545**

3. —— Charging Order—"*Property recovered or preserved*"—*Jurisdiction of Judge at Chambers —23 & 24 Vict. c. 127, s. 28—Judicature Act,* 1873 (36 & 37 Vict. c. 66), *s.* 39.] The Defendant having paid money into Court in the action, the Plaintiff's solicitor declined to proceed with the action, except on terms to which the Plaintiff would not assent. Thereupon the Plaintiff retained fresh solicitors and obtained an order for a change of solicitors. After the order was made the solicitor obtained a Judge's order at Chambers charging the money in Court with his costs in the action :—*Held,* by Grove and Lindley, JJ., 1, that when an action is pending a Judge at Chambers has jurisdiction to make such an order; 2, that the money in Court was "property recovered or preserved" within 23 & 24 Vict. c 127, s. 28; 3, that the order was valid though the Plaintiff's solicitor had ceased to be such when it was made; 4, that though he had discharged himself from the position of Plaintiff's solicitor, yet as he had not done so wrongfully or improperly the order was right. CLOVER *v.* ADAMS - 6 Q. B. D. 622

4. —— Charging Order—*Property recovered— Garnishee Summons — Priority — 23 & 24 Vict.* c. 127, s. 28.] The proceeds of a fi. fa., issued on behalf of the successful Plaintiff in an action, were attached in the hands of the sheriff by a garnishee summons from a County Court to answer a judgment obtained against the Plaintiff in that Court. The Plaintiff's solicitor in the action, who had received notice of the service of the garnishee summons, subsequently obtained an order under 23 & 24 Vict. c. 127, s. 28, charging the fund recovered with costs of the action remaining due to him :— *Held,* that such order was rightly made, and the solicitor's claim was entitled to priority over the claim of the judgment creditor of the Plaintiff under the garnishee summons.—Decision of the Queen's Bench Division affirmed. DALLOW *v.* GARROLD. *Ex parte* ADAMS 13 Q. B. D. 543;

[**14 Q. B. D. 543**

5. —— Charging Order — *Property recovered —Money paid into Court of Bankruptcy by Plaintiff—Application by Plaintiff's Solicitor—23 & 24 Vict.* c. 127, s. 28.] An action having been brought to recover a sum of £727. C., one of the Defendants, counter-claimed against the Plaintiff for the sum of £700, C. presented also a petition in bankruptcy against the Plaintiff, who was ordered to bring into Court a sum of £300. The action

VI. SOLICITOR—LIEN—continued.

and the proceedings in bankruptcy ultimately were referred to an arbitrator, who, by his award, found that the Plaintiff was entitled to judgment in the action for £157, that no debt was due from the Plaintiff to C., and that the sum of £300 must be paid to the Plaintiff out of the Court of Bankruptcy. The Plaintiff's solicitors having applied to the Queen's Bench Division for a charging order on the sum of £300 for their costs in the action :—*Held,* that they were not entitled to an order. PIERSON *v.* KNUTSFORD ESTATES COMPANY

[**13 Q. B. D. 666**

6. —— Charging Order—*Property* "*recovered or preserved*"—*Solicitor discharged before Trial —23 & 24 Vict.* c. 127, s. 28.] A solicitor, through whose instrumentality property has been recovered or preserved in an action, is entitled under the 28th section of the Attorneys and Solicitors Act, 1860, to a declaration of charge upon such property, although his client may have discharged him before the trial of the action.— In such a case his charge will be subject to the lien for costs of the client's solicitor for the time being.—Money paid into Court as a security for the costs of a party to an action is not in case by the success of the party it becomes repayable to him, property "preserved" in the action within the meaning of the Act. *In re* WADSWORTH. RHODES *v.* SUGDEN 29 Ch. D. 517

7. —— Charging Order—*23 & 24 Vict.* c. 127, s. 28—*Time for raising Costs.*] A decree for administration of a testator's estate was made at the suit of an infant who was entitled to a contingent reversionary share in the estate. R. was solicitor for the Plaintiff and for J. and A., two of the persons entitled to the other shares. After decree he ceased to be solicitor for these parties, and obtained an order directing taxation of his costs as their solicitor in the action, including the costs of the application, and charging their shares in the estate with the payment of such costs, with liberty to apply to have them raised. He now, the cause not yet having been heard for further consideration, applied to have the costs raised by a sale of the shares charged :—*Held,* affirming the decision of Bacon, V.C., that the application was premature, and that no order ought to be made for raising the costs until the cause was heard for further consideration. *In re* GREEN. GREEN *v.* GREEN - 26 Ch. D. 16

8. —— Lien on Deeds—*Change of Solicitor— Administration Action.*] The solicitor for the parties to an administration action will not, on a change of solicitor, be allowed to assert his lien for costs on papers in his possession in such a way as to embarrass the proceedings in the action.—On the contrary, he must produce the papers when they are required for the carrying on of the proceedings. *In re* BOUGHTON. BOUGHTON *v.* BOUGHTON - - - - 23 Ch. D. 169

9. —— Lien on Deeds—*Change of Solicitor in Action.*] In a suit instituted by a debenture-holder of a company, on behalf of himself and the other debenture-holders, against the company the original Plaintiff became bankrupt in the course of the proceedings, and another debenture-holder was substituted for him as Plaintiff.—An order was made that the solicitors of the first Plaintiff

VI. SOLICITOR—LIEN—continued.

should, without prejudice to their lien (if any) deliver up to the solicitor of the second Plaintiff all documents in their possession relating to the conduct and prosecution of the suit :—Held, that the solicitors of the first Plaintiff had no lien on the documents which could entitle them to priority in respect of their costs. BATTEN v. WEDGWOOD COAL AND IRON CO.   -   - 28 Ch. D. 317

10. —— Lien on Deeds—Deeds deposited by Mortgagee with Solicitor—Subsequent Employment of Solicitor by Mortgagor.] A mortgage deed and the title deeds to the mortgaged property were deposited by the mortgagees with their solicitors for safe custody. Afterwards the mortgagor instructed the same solicitors to sell the property, and they employed an auctioneer for the purpose, and made use of the deeds in preparing particulars and conditions of sale. The property was put up for sale, but was not sold. The mortgagor then filed a liquidation petition, and the trustee contracted to sell the mortgaged property :—Held, that the solicitors had no lien on the deeds as against the trustee in respect of their costs of the abortive sale. Ex parte FULLER. In re LONG
[16 Ch. D. 617

11. —— Lien on Deeds—Summary Jurisdiction—Delivery of Documents.] The Court will not summarily order a solicitor to deliver up a deed to his client unless it be clearly shewn not only that the solicitor has no lien upon it, but that he is holding it for the applicant alone, and as his solicitor. Ex parte COBELDICK
[12 Q. B. D. 149

12. —— Lien on Deeds—Winding-up.] An order having been made for winding up a company, applications were made by the official liquidator against B., a solicitor employed by the company before the winding-up, that B. might be ordered to deliver up the following documents : 1. The share register and minute book, which were in B.'s hands before the commencement of the winding-up ; 2 Other documents which came to B.'s hands after the presentation of the winding-up petition, but before the winding-up order ; 3. Documents relating to allotments of shares which had come to B.'s hands before the presentation of the petition. B. resisted the applications on the ground that he claimed a lien. Mr. Justice Chitty ordered that all the documents should be delivered to the liquidator subject to the lien, if any, of B. :—Held, on appeal, that the order was right as regarded the share register and minute book, for that the directors had no power to create any lien on them which could interfere with their being used for the purposes of the company :—Held, also, that the order was right as to class 2 ; for that a solicitor could not assert against documents which came to his hands pending the winding-up any such lien as would interfere with the prosecution of the winding-up.—But held, that the order for delivery of class 3 must be discharged, for that the winding-up order could not defeat any valid lien existing at the time when the winding-up petition was presented.—Belaney v. Ffrench (Law Rep. 8 Ch. 918) and Boughton v. Boughton (23 Ch. D. 169) distinguished. In re CAPITAL FIRE INSURANCE ASSOCIATION
[24 Ch. D. 408

VII. SOLICITOR—MISCONDUCT.

1. —— Appeal—Order striking off the Rolls—Summary Jurisdiction—Judicature Act, 1873, s. 47.] When the High Court makes an order ordering a solicitor to be struck off the rolls for misconduct, it does so in exercise of a disciplinary jurisdiction over its own officers, and not of a jurisdiction in any criminal cause or matter within the meaning of sect. 47 of the Judicature Act, 1873, and therefore an appeal lies from such order to the Court of Appeal. In re HARDWICK
[12 Q. B. D. 148

2. —— Court of Appeal—Striking off the Roll—Jurisdiction.] From the evidence given by a solicitor in an action in the Court of the County Palatine of Lancaster he appeared to have been guilty of gross misconduct in his character of solicitor as to one of the mortgages to which the action related. The Plaintiffs in the action having appealed, the conduct of the solicitor came under the consideration of the Court of Appeal, who directed the official solicitor to take proceedings. The official solicitor accordingly moved in the Court of Appeal for an order calling on the solicitor to explain his conduct, or that he might be struck off the roll :—Held, that the Court of Appeal had jurisdiction to entertain the application, although not brought before them by way of appeal. The solicitor had not taken out his certificate for several years, and did not take any notice of the application. The Court, under the special circumstances of the case, did not think fit to strike him off the roll or suspend him, but made an order restraining him from applying to renew his certificate without the leave of the Court. In re WHITEHEAD   - 28 Ch. D. 614

VIII. SOLICITOR—RETAINER.

—— Authority to issue Writ.] A retainer to a country solicitor does not justify an action in which his London agents are the solicitors on the record.—A., an illiterate woman, being desirous of knowing whether there was any balance coming to her, as administratrix of C., her deceased husband, out of the proceeds of a sale by the mortgagee of property mortgaged by C., gave to B., a country solicitor (who had recovered judgment in an action against her, as administratrix, for a debt due to him from her deceased husband) this written retainer : " I hereby authorize you to act as my solicitor in the administration of my late husband's estate, and authorize you to investigate the accounts of the mortgagee, and take such steps as you may think proper in the matter on my behalf."—A writ was subsequently issued by a London firm of solicitors in the names of A. and B., as Plaintiffs, claiming an account of the proceeds of sale of the mortgaged property and payment of the balance, the claim by A. being "as legal representative of C." by B. "as a creditor of C. who had obtained judgment against A., and had obtained execution by the appointment of a receiver of the balance due from C."—Upon motion by A. that her name might be struck out of the writ, as having been issued without her knowledge and without any authority on her part :—Held, that the retainer was not sufficient to justify the issue of the writ ; but whether sufficient or not, it was a retainer to B.,

VIII. SOLICITOR—RETAINER—continued.

and did not authorize the London firm to issue th writ in the name of A. as her solicitors. WHAY v. KEMP　-　-　-　**26 Ch. D. 169**

IX. SOLICITOR—UNQUALIFIED.

1. —— **Attachment**—*Acting as a Solicitor in the Name of a qualified Solicitor—6 & 7 Vict. c. 73, s. 2; 23 & 24 Vict. c. 127, s. 26.*] An unqualified person who acts as a solicitor commits an offence against 6 & 7 Vict. c. 73, s. 2, though he acts in the name and with the consent of a duly qualified solicitor.—H. who had carried on the business of an accountant, arranged with C., who had been admitted as a solicitor, that he should use H.'s offices, and any business H. had he was to allow C. to attend to, H. to share in the profits, but in what proportion was not settled,—or, according to H.'s version of the arrangement, H. was to be paid, as a commission, one half-share of profits after deducting all expenses, including rent of offices, and was to find money and clerk to carry on the business. Pursuant to this arrangement, H., sometimes with C. and sometimes alone, transacted various matters which it was alone competent to a solicitor to transact, generally using the name of C. & Co., but sometimes not, and not always with the knowledge or express sanction of C.:—*Held*, by the Court of Appeal, affirming the Queen's Bench Division, that H. had been guilty of a contempt of Court, and that an attachment must issue against him. ABERCROMBIE v. JORDAN

[**8 Q. B. D. 187**

2. —— **Attachment**—*Acting as a Solicitor— 6 & 7 Vict. c. 73, s. 2—23 & 24 Vict. c. 127, s. 26.*] Every person who acts as a solicitor contrary to sect. 2 of 6 & 7 Vict. c. 73, is liable to attachment for contempt of Court under 23 & 24 Vict. c. 127, s. 26, whether he so acts in the name of any other person or in his own name, unless such person be duly qualified. — Although the Court will generally adopt the findings of the master as to such conduct, his report is not conclusive. *In re* SIMMONS　　　　　　**15 Q. B. D. 348**

3. —— **Practising** — *Certificate — Stamp — Attendance of Country Solicitor at a Taxation in London—33 & 34 Vict. c. 97, s. 59—Schedule.*] By 33 & 34 Vict. c. 97, s. 59, every person who "acts or practises" in any Court as a solicitor without having in force at the time a duly stamped certificate shall forfeit £50, and shall be incapable of maintaining any action or suit for the recovery of any fee on account of any act or proceeding done or taken by him in any such capacity. By the schedule the certificate if such person "practises or carries on his business" within ten miles from the General Post Office of the City of London is of a certain amount, and if he practises or carries on his business beyond the above-mentioned limits, is of a less amount. A solicitor, with a country certificate, and whose offices were at Birmingham, came up on a retainer and attended the taxation of a bill of costs within the ten miles radius:—*Held*, that he did not, by this one transaction, act or practise in London within the meaning of the statute. *In re* HORTON

[**8 Q. B. D. 434**

4. —— **Proctor**—*6 & 7 Vict. c. 73, s. 2—23 & 24*

IX. SOLICITOR—UNQUALIFIED—continued.

Vict. c. 127, s. 26—Legal Practitioners Act, 1877 (40 & 41 Vict. c. 62), ss. 2, 3—Rules of Probate Division.] Law stationers, not qualified as solicitors or proctors, were accustomed upon the instruction and in the names of London or country solicitors, to take to the Registry of the Probate Division original wills and the engrossments thereof, with the proper affidavits, and if these were in order, to fetch away the probate; if any question arose as to the sufficiency of the documents the stationers communicated it to the solicitors. All the charges between solicitor and client were made by the solicitors, and the stationers charged the solicitors for their clerk's time only :—*Held*, affirming the decision of the Court of Appeal, that the stationers had not acted as solicitors or proctors, and were not liable to the penalties imposed by 23 & 24 Vict. c. 127, s. 26. LAW SOCIETY v. WATERLOW. LAW SOCIETY v. SKINNER　　**9 Q. B. D. 1 ; 8 App. Cas. 407**

SOLICITOR—Adopting Conveyancing Act—Protection of.
　　See CONVEYANCING ACT, 1881.—*Statutes.*

—— Appointment as trustee　　**24 Ch. D. 485**
　　See SETTLED LAND ACT—TRUSTEES. 4.

—— Appointment by testator—Duty of trustees to continue　-　**19 Ch. D. 518**
　　See WILL—TRUSTEES. 3.

—— Authority—Payment of costs personally
　　　　　　　　　　　　[**19 Ch. D. 94**
　　See PRACTICE—SUPREME COURT—NEXT FRIEND. 2.

—— Authority to direct sheriff to seize particular goods—Liability of execution creditor
　　See SHERIFF. 3.　　[**9 Q. B. D. 340**

—— Authority to receive purchase-money—Conveyancing Act, 1881　　**24 Ch. D. 387**
　　See VENDOR AND PURCHASER—CONVEYANCE. 5.

—— Clerk—Scope of authority　**6 Q. B. D. 318**
　　See NEGLIGENCE—LIABILITY. 11.

—— Client—Counsel at Chambers—Taxation
　　　　　　　　　　　　[**10 Q. B. D. 54**
　　See PRACTICE—SUPREME COURT—COSTS. 18.

—— Client — Substituted service on solicitor— Practice　-　**9 Q. B. D. 598**
　　See PRACTICE—SUPREME COURT—CHAMBERS. 6.

—— Conflict of interest and duty　**22 Ch. D. 604**
　　See EXECUTOR—RETAINER. 2.

—— Constructive notice—Equitable mortgage
　　　　　　　　　　　　[**16 Ch. D. 178**
　　See MORTGAGE—CONTRACT. 9.

—— Costs—Defending action in person
　　　　　　　　　　　　[**13 Q. B. D. 872**
　　See PRACTICE—SUPREME COURT—COSTS. 47.

—— Costs in County Court　-　**18 Ch. D. 521 ;**
　　　　　　　　[**6 Q. B. D. 607 ; 9 Q. B. D. 406**
　　See COUNTY COURT—COSTS. 1, 2. 3,

—— Costs in County Court.
　　See COUNTY COURT—COSTS—*Statutes.*

—— Explanation by—Bill of sale　**21 Ch. D. 543**
　　See BILL OF SALE—FORMALITIES. 23.

SOLICITOR—*continued.*

—— Fraud in conduct of action—New defence
[20 Ch. D. 672
See PRACTICE — SUPREME COURT —
AMENDMENT. 3.

—— Joint retainer by two defendants
[18 Ch. D. 516
See EXECUTOR—ACTIONS. 10.

—— Law of Victoria—Order to deliver bill
[10 App. Cas. 300
See COLONIAL LAW—VICTORIA. 5.

—— Liability—Scope of business — Deposit of
bonds　-　-　- 28 Ch. D. 340
See PARTNERSHIP—LIABILITIES.

—— Lien—Setting off damages and costs
[14 Q. B. D. 922
See PRACTICE—SUPREME COURT—COSTS.
44.

—— Money paid by debtor to his solicitor to
oppose petition—Adjudication—Title of
trustee -　-　- 15 Q. B. D. 616
See BANKRUPTCY—ASSETS. 8.

—— Mortgage by client to solicitor—Breach of
duty　-　18 Ch. D. 449; 24 Ch. D. 289
See MORTGAGE—POWERS. 4, 6.

—— Order on solicitor to pay costs personally—
Appeal -　-　- 15 Q. B. D. 635
See PRACTICE — SUPREME COURT —AP-
PEAL. 32.

—— Petitioning creditor—Payment to client with
notice of act of bankruptcy
[13 Q. B. D. 747
See BANKRUPTCY—ASSETS. 7.

—— Privilege　-　-　- 18 Ch. D. 30
See EVIDENCE—WITNESS. 3.

—— Privilege—Professional confidence
[28 Ch. D. 287
See PRACTICE—SUPREME COURT—INTER-
ROGATORIES. 14.

—— Privileged communication—Criminal law
[14 Q. B. D. 153
See CRIMINAL LAW—EVIDENCE. 5.

—— Promoters of company—Claim against company　-　-　- 25 Ch. D. 103
See COMPANY—FORMATION.

—— Right of audience — Bankruptcy—Appeal
from County Court　- 15 Q. B. D. 169
See BANKRUPTCY— STAYING PROCEED-
INGS. 3.

—— Right of audience—Bankruptcy—Examination of debtor　　15 Q. B. D. 54
See BANKRUPTCY—EXAMINATION. 1.

—— Salvage—Payment of viaticum—Priority of
claim　-　-　8 P. D. 209
See SHIP—SALVAGE. 11.

—— Service on, after he has ceased to act
[29 Ch. D. 351
See PRACTICE—SUPREME COURT—PAY-
MENT INTO COURT. 6.

—— Service on—Attachment　- 22 Ch. D. 571
See PRACTICE—SUPREME COURT—PRO-
DUCTION OF DOCUMENTS. 16.

—— Solicitor of trustee in bankruptcy—Costs
[20 Ch. D. 685; 15 Q. B. D. 340
See BANKRUPTCY—COSTS. 1, 3.

SOLICITOR—*continued.*

—— To public department—Certificate.
See REVENUE—STAMPS—*Statutes.*

—— Trustee—Appointment of new trustee
[27 Ch. D. 333
See SETTLEMENT—POWERS. 9.

—— Victoria, Law of—Order to deliver bill
[10 App. Cas. 300
See COLONIAL LAW—VICTORIA. 5.

SOLICITORS REMUNERATION ACT, 1881.
See Cases and Statutes under SOLICITOR
—BILL OF COSTS.

SOUTH AFRICA—Church of　7 App. Cas. 484
See COLONIAL LAW—CAPE OF GOOD
HOPE. 1.

SPANISH LAW—Trinidad.　10 App. Cas. 312
See COLONIAL LAW—TRINIDAD.

SPECIAL ACT—Compulsory purchase—Costs
[24 Ch. D. 669
See PRACTICE—SUPREME COURT—COSTS.
24.

—— Power under—Harbour trustees　8 App. Cas.
See SCOTCH LAW—HARBOUR　1.　[623

SPECIAL CASE—Amendment　22 Ch. D. 495
See PRACTICE — SUPREME COURT—SPE-
CIAL CASE. 1.

—— Disposing of action—Form of answers—
Judgment　-　16 Ch. D. 66
See PRACTICE—SUPREME COURT—SPE-
CIAL CASE. 2.

SPECIAL CIRCUMSTANCES — Taxation after
payment -　-　29 Ch. D. 571
See SOLICITOR—BILL OF COSTS. 2.

SPECIAL REFEREE　-　- 20 Ch. D. 351
See COMPANY — LIFE INSURANCE COM-
PANY. 6.

SPECIALTY DEBT.

—— Breach of Trust—*Devastavit—Covenant—
Waiver—Laches.*] There is no rule in equity any
more than at law, that the mere non-suing by a
specialty creditor for any period within the statutory limit of twenty years is such negligence as
deprives him of the right of requiring payment
of the specialty debt. — S. covenanted with B.
for immediate payment of a sum of money in exoneration of B., and in substitution for a similar
sum which B. was liable to pay within six months
of his death.—S. died without having paid, or
been called on to pay that sum, leaving property
amply sufficient to meet it, but her executor, instead of providing out of her estate funds to meet
the liability on her covenant, left her estate, consisting entirely of shares in a bank, which afterwards failed, unconverted. The investment in
bank shares was authorized by the will of S. :—
Held (reversing the decision of Kay, J.), that the
executors of B. were entitled, after a lapse of 18½
years, to enforce that covenant against the estate
of S., and that the executor of S., having committed a devastavit in not converting the shares
to provide for payment of the debt, was liable to
make good the amount for which his testatrix
was so liable under her covenant. *In re* BAKER.
COLLINS *v.* RHODES. *In re* SEAMAN. RHODES *v.*
WISH　-　- 20 Ch. D. 230

SPECIALTY DEBT—*continued*.

—— Retainer—Heir-at-law or devisee
　　See RETAINER.　　　　　[27 Ch. D. 478

SPECIFIC DEVISE—After-acquired property
　　　　　　　　　　　　　[30 Ch. D. 50
　　See WILL—SPEAKING FROM DEATH.　3.

SPECIFIC LEGACY　　-　　-　20 Ch. D. 676;
　　　　　　　　　　　　　[8 App. Cas. 812
　　See WILL—SPECIFIC LEGACY.

—— Ademption of　　-　　-　22 Ch. D. 622
　　See WILL—ADEMPTION.

—— Disclaimer of　　-　　22 Ch. D. 573
　　See WILL—DISCLAIMER.　1.

SPECIFIC PERFORMANCE.

1. —— **Agreement in several Documents**—
*Failure to prove one of the Documents—Literary
Work—Misstatement as to Authorship—Fraud on
Public.*] The Plaintiffs claimed the specific performance of an agreement for the composition of
a literary work by the Defendant, alleging that
the agreement was contained in three written
documents. At the trial the first and third of
the documents were proved; the second was not
produced, nor was any evidence given of its
contents. The Defendant, by his statement of
defence, denied that he had agreed with the
Plaintiffs, as alleged by them, with reference to
the second document:—*Held*, that the Plaintiffs
were not entitled to specific performance of the
agreement contained in the first and third documents, or to damages for the breach of it. The
Plaintiffs alleged that the Defendant had agreed
that his name should not appear on the title-page
of the work as the author of it; the Defendant
alleged that it was part of the agreement that his
name should so appear. The Plaintiffs proposed
to publish the book with a title-page, stating that
it was "Edited by K. (assisted by M. (the Defendant)") K. was known as having published
other books of a similar description, and had
allowed the Plaintiffs to make use of his name,
but he had taken no part whatever in the compilation:—*Held*, that the proposed title-page
would be a fraud on the public, and that on this
ground also the Plaintiffs were disentitled to
relief. POST *v.* MARSH　-　　- 16 Ch. D. 395

2. —— **Alternative Claim** — *Amendment of
Pleadings.*] The Plaintiff by his statement of
claim claimed specific performance of a contract
by which he agreed to sell and the Defendant
agreed to purchase the lease, goodwill, fixtures
and stock-in-trade of a business; the Plaintiff
alleging that he was and always had been able
and willing to perform the contract, but that the
Defendant refused to perform the same. The
statement of claim in the alternative claimed
£100 as liquidated damages fixed by the contract
for the refusal to perform the contract. The
statement of defence alleged false representations
by the Plaintiff as to the character of the business,
and denied that the Plaintiff was able and willing
to perform the contract. The Plaintiff, after the
close of the pleadings, gave notice to the Defendant that, unless the Defendant completed the
purchase within a week, he should re-sell the
business, which he accordingly did. No amendment of the pleadings was then asked for by the
Plaintiff, and the action went on to trial. At the

SPECIFIC PERFORMANCE—*continued*.

trial before Bacon, V.C., the Plaintiff's counsel,
admitting that the claim for specific performance
must be abandoned, sought to recover the £100
as liquidated damages. He did not apply for any
amendment of the pleadings. The Vice-Chancellor dismissed the action on the ground that the
claim for specific performance failing through the
Plaintiff's own act the alternative claim for
damages must fall also:—*Held*, on appeal, affirming the decision of Bacon, V.C., that, in the
absence of any amendment of the pleadings (which
ought not at that stage of the action to be allowed),
the action must be treated as one for specific performance with a claim for damages in the alternative as a substitute for specific performance,
according to the practice existing before the Judicature Act in the Court of Chancery, and that the
Plaintiff, having by his own act rendered specific
performance impossible, was not in such action
entitled to damages. HIPGRAVE *v.* CASE
　　　　　　　　　　　　　　　　[28 Ch. D. 356

3. —— **Chattels**—*Injunction.*] A contract for
the sale of chattels to the Plaintiff contained an
express negative stipulation not to sell to any
other manufacturer. The Court granted an injunction to restrain the breach of the negative
stipulation although the contract was one of
which specific performance would not have been
granted.—*Wolverhampton and Walsall Railway
Company v. London and North Western Railway
Company* (Law Rep. 16 Eq. 433) considered.
DONNELL *v.* BENNETT　　　　22 Ch. D. 835

4. —— **Sale of Medical Practice**—*Stipulation
for Personal Introduction—Agreement by Letter—
Reference to formal Contract—Statute of Frauds.*]
The Plaintiff wishing to sell a medical practice
with the lease of the house where it was carried
on, placed it on the books of a medical agent.
This led to negotiations with the Defendant. The
premiums asked for the practice and for the lease
were stated in a letter from the agent to the Defendant, but no time for completing the purchase
was mentioned. The Defendant replied in a
letter to the agent accepting the terms offered,
and adding that he should be ready to pay the
deposit money "on receipt of corrected agreement," and at the same time he wrote to the
Plaintiff personally, also accepting the terms
offered, and adding, "I shall trust to you to give
me the best introduction you can during three
months and afterwards, if necessary." The
Plaintiff replied, thanking the Defendant for
acceding to his terms and saying that "it would
be his aim as well as his duty to give him an
effectual introduction to his patients." A formal
agreement was drawn up but never signed, and
after some further correspondence the Defendant refused to complete the purchase:—*Held*
(affirming the decision of Bacon, V.C.), that inasmuch as the time for the commencement of the
purchase was left uncertain, and the stipulation
as to the three months' introduction was not
agreed to, and as the parties contemplated a
formal agreement, there was no binding contract
between the parties, and the action was dismissed.—Whether the Court can enforce specific
performance of a contract to sell a medical practice—*Quære.* MAY *v.* THOMSON　20 Ch. D. 705

SPECIFIC PERFORMANCE—*continued.*

—— Agreement for lease　-　19 Ch. D. 175, 233
　　See LANDLORD AND TENANT—AGREE-
　　MENT. 1, 3.

—— Agreement for sale of land.
　　See Cases under VENDOR AND PUR-
　　CHASER.

—— Counter-claim—Action to recover deposit—
　　Transfer to Chancery Division
　　　　　　　　　　　[13 Q. B. D. 540
　　See PRACTICE—SUPREME COURT—TRANS-
　　FER. 2.

—— Covenant—Alteration of property
　　See COVENANT—BREACH. [28 Ch. D. 103

—— Covenant to renew lease　-　22 Ch. D. 640
　　See LANDLORD AND TENANT—LEASE. 13.

—— Doubtful title　-　-　18 Ch. D. 381
　　See BANKRUPTCY—ASSETS. 15.

—— Misrepresentation　-　-　20 Ch. D. 1
　　See FALSE REPRESENTATION. 1.

—— Misrepresentation by vendor's agent
　　　　　　　　　　　[22 Ch. D. 194
　　See PRINCIPAL AND AGENT — AGENT'S
　　AUTHORITY. 1.

—— Separation deed　-　18 Ch. D. 670
　　See HUSBAND AND WIFE—SEPARATION
　　DEED. 1.

SPECIFICATION—Amendment
　　　　　　[26 Ch. D. 105 ; 28 Ch. D. 149
　　See PATENT—AMENDMENT. 1, 2.

—— Sufficiency -　21 Ch. D. 720 ; 29 Ch. D. 366
　　See PATENT—VALIDITY. 2, 5.

SPIRITS—Duty on.
　　See REVENUE—EXCISE—*Statutes.*

SPORTING—Overstocking land with game—In-
　　jury to crops -　　15 Q. B. D. 258
　　See GAME. 1.

—— Poor-rate—Woodlands　-　6 Q. B. D. 13
　　See POOR-RATE—RATEABLE VALUE. 4.

—— Statute of Frauds　　9 Q. B. D. 315
　　See FRAUDS, STATUTE OF. 3.

STAMP.
　　See Cases and Statutes under REVENUE
　　—STAMPS.

—— Acting or practising as solicitor　8 Q. B. D.
　　See SOLICITOR—UNQUALIFIED. 3. [434

—— Fictitious.
　　See POST OFFICE—*Statutes.*

—— Law of Penang　-　7 App. Cas. 172
　　See COLONIAL LAW—STRAITS SETTLE-
　　MENTS. 1.

—— Registration of resolutions for liquidation—
　　Return of duty　-　20 Ch. D. 703
　　See BANKRUPTCY—LIQUIDATION. 7.

—— Settlement by Court　-　17 Ch. D. 778
　　See SETTLEMENT—EQUITY TO SETTLE-
　　MENT. 1.

STANNARIES COURT.
　　See Cases under COMPANY—COST-BOOK
　　COMPANY.

STATEMENT OF CLAIM—Embarrassing plead-
　　ing　-　-　26 Ch. D. 778
　　See PRACTICE — SUPREME COURT —
　　STRIKING OUT PLEADINGS. 2.

STATEMENT OF CLAIM—*continued.*

—— Embarrassing pleading　.　22 Ch. D. 481
　　See PRACTICE—SUPREME COURT—AMEND-
　　MENT. 1.

STATEMENT OF CONSIDERATION—Bill of sale.
　　See Cases under BILL OF SALE—FOR-
　　MALITIES. 15—26.

—— Judgment debt—Debtor's summons
　　　　　　　　　　　[22 Ch. D. 529
　　See BANKRUPTCY—APPEAL. 5.

STATEMENT OF DEBTS AND ASSETS — Com-
　　pounding debtor　-　16 Ch. D. 131 ;
　　　　　　[20 Ch. D. 281 ; 23 Ch. D. 706
　　See BANKRUPTCY—COMPOSITION. 3, 9, 10.

—— Liquidation　16 Ch. D. 513 ; 21 Ch. D. 594 ;
　　　　　　　　　　　[25 Ch. D. 338
　　See BANKRUPTCY—LIQUIDATION. 10, 11,
　　12.

STATEMENT OF DEFENCE—Action for recovery
　　of land　6 Q. B. D. 645 ; 8 App. Cas. 456
　　See PRACTICE—SUPREME COURT—DE-
　　FENCE.

STATUS OF MARRIED WOMAN.
　　See HUSBAND AND WIFE—MARRIED WO-
　　MEN'S PROPERTY ACTS—*Statutes.*

STATUTE.

—— Marginal Notes.] The marginal notes to
the sections of an Act of Parliament are not to be
taken as part of the Act.—Dictum in *In re Venour's
Settled Estates* (2 Ch. D. 522, 525) corrected.
SUTTON *v.* SUTTON -　-　-　22 Ch. D. 511

—— Commencement of　-　8 Q. B. D. 119
　　See INN—OFFENCES. 5.

—— Construction -　-　-　17 Ch. D. 746
　　See BANKRUPTCY—DISCLAIMER. 15.

—— Construction — Public and private Act of
　　Parliament　　15 Q. B. D. 597
　　See POOR-RATE—RATEABLE VALUE. 5.

—— Divided into headings　-　9 App. Cas. 365
　　See COLONIAL LAW—VICTORIA. 4.

—— Repeal by implication　-　11 Q. B. D. 120
　　See COURT—MAYOR'S COURT. 2.

—— Summary proceeding before justices—Ex-
　　clusive of civil remedy　11 Q. B. D. 225
　　See SHIP—SEAMEN.

STATUTE OF FRAUDS.
　　See FRAUDS, STATUTE OF.

STATUTE OF LIMITATIONS.
　　See LIMITATIONS, STATUTE OF.

**STATUTES SPECIALLY REFERRED TO IN THIS
DIGEST.**
　　See TABLE OF STATUTES (*ante*, p. cxliii).

STATUTORY CHARGE—Execution of works by
　　company　-　-　16 Ch. D. 411
　　See COMPANY—DEBENTURES. 7.

STATUTORY CONTRACT—Attachment of pur-
　　chase-money　-　-　19 Ch. D. 506
　　See PRACTICE—SUPREME COURT—GAR-
　　NISHEE ORDERS. 2.

STATUTORY DUTY—Local and personal Act
　　　　　　　　　　　[7 App. Cas. 694
　　See SCOTCH LAW—STATUTORY DUTY.

—— Penalty—Refusal to give certificate of dis-
　　charge to seaman　.　13 Q. B. D. 109
　　See SHIP—MERCHANT SHIPPING ACTS. 6.

STATUTORY FORM—Mortgage.
  See MORTGAGE — STATUTORY FORM —
    Statutes.

STATUTORY POWERS—Excess of 21 Ch. D. 752
  See PRACTICE — SUPREME COURT — IN-
    JUNCTION.

STATUTORY RECEIPT—Mortgage to building
  society - 26 Ch. D. 273; 28 Ch. D. 298
  See BUILDING SOCIETY. 34.

STATUTORY RIGHTS—Waiver of—Charter
      [22 Ch. D. 287; 25 Ch. D. 511;
  See MARKET. 1, 2.   [9 App. Cas. 927

STAYING PROCEEDINGS—Action pending for
  same cause of action   10 P. D. 141
  See PRACTICE—ADMIRALTY—LIS ALIBI
    PENDENS. 2.

—— Bankruptcy 16 Ch. D. 665; 13 Q. B. D. 235;
      [15 Q. B. D. 169
  See BANKRUPTCY — STAYING PROCEED-
    INGS. 1, 2, 3.

—— Bankruptcy   16 Ch. D. 283
  See BANKRUPTCY—ADJUDICATION. 1.

—— Bankruptcy—Debtor's summons
      [16 Ch. D. 675
  See BANKRUPTCY—ACT OF BANKRUPTCY.
    22.

—— County Court—Trial in Superior Court
      [14 Q. B. D. 905
  See MASTER AND SERVANT—MASTER'S
    LIABILITY. 11.

—— Supreme Court.
  See Cases under PRACTICE—SUPREME
    COURT—STAYING PROCEEDINGS.

—— Supreme Court -   - 19 Ch. D. 326
  See PRACTICE—SUPREME COURT—CHAM-
    BERS. 5.

—— Supreme Court—Concurrent actions
      [21 Ch. D. 647; 23 Ch. D. 100
  See PRACTICE—SUPREME COURT—CON-
    DUCT OF CAUSE. 2, 3.

—— Supreme Court—Winding-up petition
      [23 Ch. D. 210
  See COMPANY—WINDING-UP ORDER. 10.

STEAM-TUG—Duty to obey pilot 6 App. Cas. 217
  See SHIP—PILOT. 7.

STOCK—Certificate to bearer.
  See REVENUE—STAMPS—*Statutes.*

—— Conversion of.
  See NATIONAL DEBT COMMISSIONERS—
    Statutes.

—— Petition to transfer -   - 28 Ch. D. 516
  See NATIONAL DEBT COMMISSIONERS.

—— Transfer of—Notice to retain 23 Ch. D. 549
  See PRACTICE — SUPREME COURT — IN-
    JUNCTION. 2.

—— Vesting order—Standing in name of testator
      [22 Ch. D. 535
  See TRUSTEE ACTS—VESTING ORDER. 11.

STOCK-IN-TRADE—Exempt from poor-rate.
  See POOR-RATE—EXEMPTIONS—*Statutes.*

STOCKBROKER—Bankruptcy 22 Ch. D. 132
  See BANKRUPTCY—ADJUDICATION. 2.

—— Employment of, by trustee—Loss of fund
      [22 Ch. D. 727; 9 App. Cas. 1
  See TRUSTEE—LIABILITIES. 2.

STOCKBROKER—*continued.*
—— Member of committee — Appointment of
  settling day.   -   - 20 Ch. D. 356
  See STOCK EXCHANGE. 2.

—— Sale of bank shares—Negligence
  See STOCK EXCHANGE. 1. [9 Q. B. D. 546

STOCK EXCHANGE.
  1. —— Sale of Shares—*Name of Shareholder—
  30 & 31 Vict. c. 29, s. 1—Custom of Stock Exchange.*]
  The Defendant, a stockbroker, who had undertaken to sell shares of a joint stock bank for the
  Plaintiff, a shareholder, sold them to a jobber on
  the Stock Exchange and sent an advice note of
  such sale to the Plaintiff, but in accordance with
  the custom of the Stock Exchange, the bought
  and sold notes between the Defendant and the
  jobber omitted to state the name of the registered
  proprietor of the shares as required by 30 & 31 Vict.
  c. 29, s. 1, by reason of which the contract for sale
  was void, and the bank having stopped, and an
  order for its winding-up having been made before
  the day on which the jobber was entitled to name
  the person willing to be the purchaser, the contract for sale was repudiated, and the Plaintiff
  remained the holder of the shares :—*Held,* that
  the Defendant had committed a breach of duty in
  not making a valid contract for sale, notwithstanding the custom of the Stock Exchange to
  disregard the said statute, as such custom was
  both unreasonable and illegal, and that for such
  breach of duty the Plaintiff was entitled to recover from the Defendant by way of damages the
  price at which the shares had been sold. NEILSON
  v. JAMES   -   - 9 Q. B. D. 546

  2. —— Settling Day—*Rules of London Stock
  Exchange—Appointment of Settling Day obtained
  by Fraud—Defaulter—Private Administration of
  Assets by Official Assignee—Member of Committee
  —Disqualification by reason of Interest.*] By one
  of the rules of the London Stock Exchange bar-
  gains in the shares of a new company are contingent on the appointment of a special settling day
  by the committee :—*Held,* that, if the appointment
  of a settling day has been obtained by fraud, the
  validity of contracts in relation to the shares of
  the company, entered into by persons who were
  not actors in or parties to the fraud, is unaffected.
  —A member of the committee of the Stock Exchange who takes part in the appointment of a
  settling day is not in so doing acting in a judicial
  capacity, and is not, therefore, disqualified from
  acting by reason of his having a personal interest
  in the matter.—A creditor of a defaulter on the
  Stock Exchange who has taken the benefit of the
  private distribution of Stock Exchange assets,
  made by the official assignee of the Stock Exchange under its rules, is not precluded from
  afterwards taking ordinary legal proceedings for
  the recovery of his debt, though he must give
  credit for what he has received from the official
  assignee. *Ex parte* WARD. *In re* WARD
      [20 Ch. D. 356.

—— Usage — Principal and agent— Shares in
  banking company - 14 Q. B. D. 460;
      [15 Q. B. D. 388
  See PRINCIPAL AND AGENT—PRINCIPAL'S
    LIABILITY. 4, 5.

STOLE - - - - **7 App. Cas. 240**
  See PRACTICE—ECCLESIASTICAL—PUBLIC
  WORSHIP ACT. 1.

STOLEN GOODS—Receiving—Guilty knowledge
  —Evidence - - **12 Q. B. D. 522**
  See CRIMINAL LAW—EVIDENCE. 6.

STOP ORDER—Mortgage—Priority
  [26 Ch. D. 686; 29 Ch. D. 786
  See MORTGAGE—PRIORITY. 10, 11.

—— Priority - **23 Ch. D. 497**
  See PRACTICE—SUPREME COURT—CHARG-
  ING ORDERS. 3.

—— Priority—Notice - - **18 Ch. D. 381**
  See BANKRUPTCY—ASSETS. 15.

STOPPAGE IN TRANSITU.
  See Cases under SALE OF GOODS—LIEN.

STRAITS SETTLEMENTS - **7 App. Cas. 172;**
  [8 App. Cas. 751
  See COLONIAL LAW—STRAITS SETTLE-
  MENTS. 1, 2.

STRATIFIED IRONSTONE MINES (GUN-
  POWDER) ACT, 1881.
  See MINE—MINES REGULATION ACTS—
  Statutes.

STREET—Dedication to public - **29 Ch. D. 750**
  See HIGHWAY—DEDICATION.

—— Definition **10 Q. B. D. 394 ; 13 Q. B. D. 184;**
  [10 App. Cas. 364
  See LOCAL GOVERNMENT—STREETS. 2, 10.

—— Expense of sewering and paving—Formation
  and width.
  See Cases under
    LOCAL GOVERNMENT—STREETS.
    METROPOLIS—MANAGEMENT ACTS.

—— Limits of metropolitan.
  See METROPOLIS — POLICE ACTS — *Sta-*
  tutes.

—— Repair—Use of steam roller **15 Q. B. D. 1**
  See GAS COMPANY.

STRIKE—Begging for assistance—Vagrancy
  See VAGRANT ACTS. 3. [12 Q. B. D. 306

STRIKING OFF ROLLS - **12 Q. B. D. 148;**
  [28 Ch. D. 614
  See SOLICITOR—MISCONDUCT. 1, 2.

STRIKING OUT PLEADINGS 26 Ch. D. 470, 778 ;
  [6 Q. B. D. 190
  See PRACTICE—SUPREME COURT—STRIK-
  ING OUT PLEADINGS. 1, 2, 3.

SUB-FEU—Held under defaulting vassal
  [10 App. Cas. 553
  See SCOTCH LAW — HERITABLE PRO-
  PERTY. 5.

SUBMARINE TELEGRAPH.
  See TELEGRAPH—*Statutes.*

SUBMISSION — Revocation—No agreement to
  make submission a rule of Court
  [12 Q. B. D. 310
  See ARBITRATION—SUBMISSION. 2.

SUB-MORTGAGE—Improper investment
  [30 Ch. D. 490
  See TRUSTEE—LIABILITIES. 5.

SUBPŒNA—Arbitration—Witness out of jurisdiction of Court - **12 Q. B. D. 39**
  See EVIDENCE—WITNESS. 1.

—— Witness before arbitrator **17 Ch. D. 787**
  See PRACTICE—SUPREME COURT—EVI-
  DENCE. 7.

SUBROGATION—Insurance, Fire — Sale — Fire
  before completion—Right to insurance
  money - - - **11 Q. B. D. 380**
  See INSURANCE—FIRE. 4.

—— Insurance, Marine—Constructive total loss
  Collision—Recovery of damages
  [13 Q. B. D. 706
  See INSURANCE, MARINE—POLICY. 7.

SUB-SALE—Stoppage in transitu **7 App. Cas. 573**
  See SALE OF GOODS—LIEN. 1.

—— Vendor's lien for unpaid purchase-money
  [26 Ch. D. 501
  See VENDOR AND PURCHASER—LIEN. 2.

SUBSCRIBER OF MEMORANDUM 25 Ch. D. 283
  See COMPANY—DIRECTOR'S QUALIFICA-
  TION. 1.

SUBSIDENCE—Action for, after compensation
  for previous subsidence **14 Q. B. D. 125**
  See LIMITATIONS, STATUTE OF—PERSONAL
  ACTIONS. 2.

SUBSTITUTED SERVICE—Debtor's summons
  [25 Ch. D. 336
  See BANKRUPTCY—ACT OF BANKRUPTCY.
  20.

—— Solicitor—Summons **9 Q. B. D. 598**
  See PRACTICE—SUPREME COURT—CHAM-
  BERS. 6.

—— Notice of appeal - - **24 Ch. D. 364**
  See BANKRUPTCY—APPEAL. 3.

SUBSTITUTIONAL GIFT - **17 Ch. D. 788;**
  [23 Ch. D. 737
  See WILL—SUBSTITUTIONAL GIFT. 1, 2.

—— - - - **18 Ch. D. 441**
  See WILL—PERPETUITY. 4.

—— - - - **19 Ch. D. 470**
  See WILL—DEATH COUPLED WITH CON-
  TINGENCY. 3.

—— - - - **25 Ch. D. 212**
  See WILL—WORDS. 10.

SUCCESSION — Personalty — Married Women's
  Property Act (Scotland) **8 App. Cas. 678**
  See SCOTCH LAW—HUSBAND AND WIFE.
  6.

—— Real estate—Scotch law - **8 App. Cas. 577**
  See SCOTCH LAW—HERITABLE PROPERTY.
  4.

SUCCESSION DUTY.
  See Cases under REVENUE—SUCCESSION
  DUTY.

—— Covenant to pay money free from all deductions - - **29 Ch. D. 697**
  See SETTLEMENT—CONSTRUCTION. 1.

—— Customs Inland Revenue Act, 1881.
  See REVENUE—SUCCESSION DUTY—*Sta-*
  tutes.

SUEZ CANAL—Negligence of pilot   **7 P. D. 132**
　　See SHIP—PILOT. 6.

SUING AND LABOURING CLAUSE—Re-insurance—Constructive total loss—Notice of abandonment   -   -   **15 Q. B. D. 11**
　　See INSURANCE, MARINE—LOSS, TOTAL.

SULPHATE OF AMMONIA WORKS.
　　See LOCAL GOVERNMENT — PUBLIC HEALTH ACTS—*Statutes.*

SULPHURIC ACID WORKS.
　　See LOCAL GOVERNMENT — PUBLIC HEALTH ACTS—*Statutes.*

SUMMARY JURISDICTION ACTS.
　　See JUSTICES—PRACTICE—*Statutes.*

SUMMONS — Amendment — Foreclosure — Accounts   -   -   -   **25 Ch. D. 48**
　　See MORTGAGE—FORECLOSURE. 1.

——— Bastardy—Service in Scotland
　　　　　[12 Q. B. D. 261; 10 App. Cas. 45
　　See BASTARDY. 6.

——— Jurisdiction on—Infant   -   **19 Ch. D. 305**
　　See INFANT—MAINTENANCE. 3.

——— Order on—Whether final or interlocutory
　　　　　　　　　[27 Ch. D. 392
　　See PRACTICE — SUPREME COURT—APPEAL. 14.

——— Originating—Appeal   -   **30 Ch. D. 231**
　　See PRACTICE—SUPREME COURT—APPEAL. 22.

——— Practice in Chambers.
　　See Cases under PRACTICE — SUPREME COURT—CHAMBERS.

——— Substituted service on solicitor **9 Q. B. D. 598**
　　See PRACTICE—SUPREME COURT—CHAMBERS. 6.

SUNDAY—Closing public-house   **8 Q. B. D. 119;**
　　See INN—OFFENCES. 5, 6.   **[11 Q. B. D. 71**

SUNDAY OBSERVANCE.
　　The Act 48 & 49 *Vict.* c. 59, *continues the Sunday Observance Prosecution Act,* 1871 (34 & 35 *Vict.* c. 87) *until the* 31*st of December,* 1886.

SUPERANNUATION—Governor of prison
　　　　　[11 Q. B. D. 656 ; 9 App. Cas. 757
　　See PRISON. 1.

SUPERANNUATION ACT, 1881.
　　See PENSION—*Statutes.*

SUPERFLUOUS LANDS—Lands Clauses Act.
　　　　　　　　　[21 Ch. D. 95
　　See VENDOR AND PURCHASER—TITLE. 6.

———
　　See Cases under LANDS CLAUSES ACT—SUPERFLUOUS LANDS.

SUPERIOR AND VASSAL   -   **7 App. Cas. 427 ;**
　　　　　　　　　[10 App. Cas. 553
　　See SCOTCH LAW—HERITABLE PROPERTY. 1, 5.

——— Compensation   -   -   **8 App. Cas. 265**
　　See SCOTCH LAW—RAILWAY COMPANY. 5.

SUPPLEMENTAL ACTION   -   **26 Ch. D. 181**
　　See PRACTICE — SUPREME COURT — CHANGE OF PARTIES. 3.

SUPPLEMENTAL ACTION—*continued.*
——— Nuisance—District Board   **17 Ch. D. 685**
　　See LOCAL GOVERNMENT—LOCAL AUTHORITY. 13.

SUPPLEMENTAL DEED.
　　See DEED—*Statutes.*

SUPPORT.

　1. ——— **Implied Grant.**] The corporation of L. put up a piece of land for sale in lots, the interest acquired by each purchaser being a right to a lease of the lot purchased by him, and he being bound to build upon the lot according to plans to be approved by the corporation. None of the lots were sold, and in July, 1868, the Plaintiff agreed for the purchase of one of the lots by private contract, subject to the original conditions. He furnished plans shewing a foundation 10 feet 9 inches deep ; but finding the subsoil unsafe he laid his foundation at a depth of 8 feet 3 inches, to the knowledge of the corporation, whose officer inspected the operations and made no objections. In June, 1869, the Plaintiff's house was carried to the joists of the ground floor. In August, 1869, the Defendant purchased from the corporation the adjoining lot. In October, 1869, when the Plaintiff's house was nearly finished the corporation granted him his lease. After this the Defendant got his lease, and in 1881, wishing to carry his foundations lower than those of the Plaintiff, excavated to a considerably greater depth and endangered the foundations of the Plaintiff's house :—*Held* (affirming the decision of the Vice-Chancellor of Lancaster), that the Plaintiff was entitled to restrain the Defendant from excavating so as to let down the Plaintiff's house, for that there was not enough in the special circumstances of the case to take away the right of support from the adjoining lands of the grantor which is implied in a grant of land for the purpose of building.—How the case would have stood if the grants to the Plaintiff and the Defendant had been contemporaneous, or if the right of support claimed would have prevented the corporation from building in a reasonable way on the adjoining lot, *quære.*   RIGBY *v.* BENNETT
　　　　　　　　　[21 Ch. D. 559

　2. ——— **Prescription** — *Ancient Buildings* — *Rebuilding Tenement* — *Damage to Neighbour's Vault*—*Estate of Ecclesiastical Corporation*—*Prescription Act*—*Owner and Contractor jointly responsible.*] Where ancient buildings belonging to different owners adjoin each other there is a right of support from the building as well as from the land ; and this right of support can be claimed under the provisions of the Prescription Act (2 & 3 Will. 4, c. 71). The mere fact that the support is derived from property which belongs to an ecclesiastical corporation does not prevent the right of support being acquired under the Act. But the enjoyment of right must have been open and not surreptitious to come within the provisions of the Act. Damage having been done by the wrongful acts of a contractor or his workmen, employed under a contract and specification, to a neighbour's vault, it was held, under the circumstances, that both the employer and contractor were liable

SUPPORT—*continued.*

for it, and judgment was given for the Plaintiff, with costs against both Defendants. LEMAITRE *v.* DAVIS　-　-　-　- 19 Ch. D. 281

3. —— Prescription—*House*—*Adjoining Soil* —*Prescription Act (2 & 3 Will. 4, c. 71), s. 2* —*Principal and Agent* or *Contractor*—*Liability of Principal for Acts of Contractor.*] A right to lateral support from adjoining land may be acquired by twenty years' uninterrupted enjoyment for a building proved to have been newly built, or altered so as to increase the lateral pressure, at the beginning of that time ; and it is so acquired if the enjoyment is peaceable and without deception or concealment and so open that it must be known that some support is being enjoyed by the building.—*Semble,* per Lord Selborne, L.C.: Such a right of support is an easement within the meaning of the Prescription Act, 2 & 3 Will. 4, c. 71, s. 2. Two dwelling-houses adjoined, built independently, but each on the extremity of its owner's soil and having lateral support from the soil on which the other rested. This having continued for much more than twenty years, one of the houses (the Plaintiffs') was, in 1849, converted into a coach factory, the internal walls being removed and girders inserted into a stack of brickwork in such a way as to throw much more lateral pressure than before upon the soil under the adjoining house. The conversion was made openly, and without deception or concealment. More than twenty years after the conversion the owners of the adjoining house employed a contractor to pull down their house and excavate, the contractor being bound to shore up adjoining buildings and make good all damage. The contractor employed a sub-contractor upon similar terms. The house was pulled down, and the soil under it excavated to a depth of several feet, and the Plaintiffs' stack being deprived of the lateral support of the adjacent soil sank and fell, bringing down with it most of the factory :— *Held,* that the Plaintiffs ha acquired a right of support for their factory by dhe twenty years' enjoyment, and could sue the owners of the adjoining house and the contractor for the injury.—*Bower* v. *Peate* (1 Q. B. D. 321) approved. DALTON *v.* ANGUS　-　-　-　- 6 App. Cas. 740

4. —— Prescription—*Enjoyment as of Right.*] In 1856 A. built on a wall belonging to B., the rest of the building being on land laid out by B. for a street. By a deed made in 1864, A. covenanted with B. that A. would on three months' notice macadamise the street and keep it in repair. This deed was recited in another deed made between A. and B. in 1877, in which the proposed street was referred to. The street was never made, and the design had been abandoned : —*Held,* that A.'s enjoyment of support from the wall was not as of right, and that no easement was acquired.—*Dalton* v. *Angus* (6 App. Cas. 740) discussed. TONE *v.* PRESTON 24 Ch. D. 739

—— Action for subsidence—Compensation for previous subsidence—Limitation
[14 Q. B. D. 125
See LIMITATIONS, STATUTE OF—PERSONAL ACTIONS. 2.

SUPPORT—*continued.*

—— Houses abutting on highway—Subsidence
[6 Q. B. D. 264
See LOCAL GOVERNMENT — COMPENSATION. 8.

—— Mine—Clause in lease　- 23 Ch. D. 81 ;
See MINE—LEASE. 1, 2. [6 App. Cas. 460

—— Mine—Inclosure Act—Manorial rights
[10 Q. B. D. 547 ; 9 App. Cas. 286
See INCLOSURE. 1.

—— Mine—Scotch law　-　- 8 App. Cas. 833
See SCOTCH LAW—MINE. 2.

—— Party-wall—Contractor's work
[9 Q. B. D. 441 ; 8 App. Cas. 443
See PRINCIPAL AND AGENT—PRINCIPAL'S LIABILITY. 1.

—— Surface—Mine—Railway company
[11 Q. B. D. 820
See RAILWAY COMPANY — RAILWAYS CLAUSES ACT. 7.

SUPREME COURT OF CANADA—Jurisdiction
[6 App. Cas. 644
See COLONIAL LAW—CANADA—ONTARIO. 1.

SUPREME COURT OF JUDICATURE ACT, 1881.
See COURT—*Statutes.*
　　MUNICIPAL CORPORATION—*Statutes.*
　　PARLIAMENT—*Statutes.*
　　PRACTICE—DIVORCE—APPEAL—*Statutes.*

SUPREME COURT OF JUDICATURE ACT, 1884.
See COURT—*Statutes.*

SUPREME COURT OF JUDICATURE (FUNDS, &c.) ACT, 1883.
See COURT—*Statutes.*

SURCHARGE—Mortgagee in possession
[30 Ch. D 336
See MORTGAGE—MORTGAGEE IN POSSESSION. 4.

SURETY.
See Cases under PRINCIPAL AND SURETY.

—— Administration bond -　- 10 P. D. 196
See ADMINISTRATOR—GRANT. 2.

—— Bail in criminal case—Indemnity—Act on to recover deposit—Illegality 15 Q. B.D.
See CONTRACT—VALIDITY. 2.　　[561

—— Bond by—Mortgage　　 30 Ch. D. 291
See LIMITATIONS, STATUTE OF — PERSONAL ACTIONS. 10.

—— Composition -　　-　 16 Ch. D. 505
See BANKRUPTCY—ANNULMENT. 4.

—— Guarantee society—Probate action
[7 P. D. 235
See ADMINISTRATOR—LIMITED. 7.

SURFACE—Mine—Clause in lease 23 Ch. D. 81 ;
See MINE—LEASE. 1, 2. [6 App. Cas. 460

—— Support of
See Cases under SUPPORT.

—— Support of—Scotch law　- 8 App. Cas. 833
See SCOTCH LAW—MINE. 2.

—— Support—Mine—Railway company
[11 Q. B. D. 820
See RAILWAY COMPANY — RAILWAYS CLAUSES ACT. 7.

SURPLUS INCOME—Ecclesiastical Commissioners
[18 Ch. D. 596
See CHARITY—COMMISSIONERS. 1.

SURRENDER OF LEASE—Infant   29 Ch. D. 248
See INFANT—PROPERTY. 3.

SURVEY—Colonial certificate of.
See SHIP—MERCHANT SHIPPING ACTS—
Gazette.

SURVEYOR—Certificate of—Evidence of title
[30 Ch. D. 344
See VENDOR AND PURCHASER—TITLE. 2.

SURVIVOR — Death of child before testator,
leaving issue   -   -   22 Ch. D. 663
See WILL—LAPSE. 5.

—— Will—Construction   -   19 Ch. D. 186;
See WILL—SURVIVOR. 1, 2. [29 Ch. D. 839

—— Will—Death without issue — Woman past
childbearing   -   18 Ch. D. 213
See EVIDENCE—PRESUMPTION.

SURVIVORSHIP—Husband and wife—Joint in-
vestments   -   -   28 Ch. D. 705
See HUSBAND AND WIFE—SEPARATE ES-
TATE. 4.

—— Husband—Wife's reversionary interest in
term   -   -   -   25 Ch. D. 620
See HUSBAND AND WIFE—WIFE'S REVER-
SION. 1.

SUSPENDING ORDER—Certificate of conformity
[27 Ch. D. 687
See BANKRUPTCY—DISCHARGE. 2.

SWINE—Nuisance—Dwelling-house—By-law
[12 Q. B. D. 617
See LOCAL GOVERNMENT—BY-LAWS.

—— Nuisance—Keeping near dwelling-house
[8 Q. B. D. 97
See LOCAL GOVERNMENT—OFFENCES. 3.

SYNOD—Lower Canada   -   7 App. Cas. 136
See COLONIAL LAW — CANADA—QUEBEC.
3.

T.

TACKING—Mortgage — Priorities — Receipt by
trustees of building society
[**12 Q. B. D. 423**
    See MORTGAGE—PRIORITY. 2.

—— Mortgage—Priority   -   **19 Ch. D. 207**
    See SOLICITOR—LIABILITIES. 3.

TATENHILL RECTORY.
    See ECCLESIASTICAL COMMISSIONERS—Statutes.

TAXATION OF COSTS—County Court.
    See Cases under COUNTY COURT—COSTS.

—— District registry   -   **27 Ch. D. 242**
    See PRACTICE — SUPREME COURT—DIS-
    TRICT REGISTRY.

—— Solicitor and client—Bill of costs.
    See Cases under SOLICITOR—BILL OF
    COSTS.

—— Solicitor and client—Bill of costs—After
payment—Lands Clauses Act
[**23 Ch. D. 167**
    See LANDS CLAUSES ACT—COSTS. 2.

—— Supreme Court.
    See Cases under PRACTICE — SUPREME
    COURT—COSTS.

TEES—Conservancy regulations—Damage
    See SHIP—NAVIGATION. 27. [**8 P. D. 5**

TELEGRAPH.
Post Office.]   *The Act 48 & 49 Vict. c. 58, re-
peals sect. 15 of 31 & 32 Vict. c. 100 (the Telegraph
Act, 1868), and provides for sixpenny telegrams.
Sect. 23 of the latter Act to apply to regulations
made under this Act.*

    *Sect. 4. This Act to extend to the Isle of Man and
Channel Islands.*

    *Sect. 1. This Act to be read with the Telegraphs
Acts, 1863 to 1878, and to be a Post Office Act,
within the Post Office (Offences) Act, 1837 (1 Vict.
c. 36).*

Telegrams.]   *Regulations of 10th August, 1885,
for Inland Telegrams*   -   **L. G. 1885, p. 4450**
Submarine Cable.]   *The Act 48 & 49 Vict. c. 49,
carries into effect the International Convention of
March 14th, 1884, between Great Britain, Germany,
the Argentine Confederation, Austria, Belgium,
Brazil, Costa Rica, Denmark, Dominican Re-
public, Spain, United States of America, Columbia,
France, Guatemala, Greece, Italy, Turkey, Holland,
Duchy of Luxemburg, Persia, Portugal, Roumania,
Russia, Salvador, Servia, Sweden and Norway,
Uruguay. The Convention applies (outside ter-
ritorial waters) to submarine cables landed on the
territories, colonies, or possessions of the Powers,
but does not apply to the following British colonies,
viz.: Canada, Newfoundland, Cape, Natal, New
South Wales, Victoria, Queensland, Tasmania,
South Australia, Western Australia, New Zealand.
They are at liberty however to accede to the Con-
vention hereafter.*

    *Sect. 2. The above-named Convention is part of
this Act.*

    *Sect. 3. Punishment for any person who within
or (being a subject of Her Majesty) without Her*

TELEGRAPH—*continued.*
*Majesty's dominions unlawfully or by culpable
negligence breaks or injures a submarine cable.*

    Sect. 4. Repairing breakage or injury.

    *Sect. 5. Application of certain enactments of
25 & 26 Vict. c. 63 (the Merchant Shipping Act,
1862), and of sect. 6 of 46 & 47 Vict. c. 22 (Sea
Fisheries Act, 1883) to this Act for purposes of
lights, signals and fishing vessels.*

    *Sect. 6. (1.) A commander of a British or foreign
ship of war may exercise the powers conferred by
the Convention.*

    (2.) Punishment for obstructing such officers.

    *(3.) (4.) and (5.) Actions and proceedings against
such officers.*

    Legal Procedure.]   *Sect. 7. Incorporation of
Part X. of 17 & 18 Vict. c. 104 (Merchant Shipping
Act, 1854) with this Act.*

    *Sect. 8. (1.), (2.), (3.). Admissibility of docu-
ments drawn up under the Convention in civil or
criminal proceedings.*

    (4.) Forgery of signature of officer.

    *Sect. 9. The master of a vessel by which an offence
has been committed is primâ facie liable.*

    *Sect. 10. Provisions of this Act to be in addition
to, and not in derogation of, other British laws.*

    *Sect. 11. This Act applies to the whole of Her
Majesty's dominions and to the Admiralty.*

    Sect. 12. Definitions.

    *Sect. 13. This Act comes into force on date pub-
lished in " London Gazette " and ends when the
Convention ceases to be binding on Great Britain.
It had not come into force on the 1st January,
1886.*

—— Address—Trade-name   -   **30 Ch. D. 156**
    See TRADE-NAME. 1.

—— Fictitious telegrams.
    See POST OFFICE—Statutes.

—— Rateability of wires   -   **12 Q. B. D. 552**
    See POOR-RATE—OCCUPATION. 5.

TELEGRAPH COMPANY.

—— **Postmaster General** — *Telephone—Telegraph Acts, 1863 (26 & 27 Vict. c. 112), s. 3 ; 1868
(31 & 32 Vict. c. 110); and 1869 (32 & 33 Vict.
c. 73), ss. 3, 4, 5, 6.]*   Edison's telephone, for which
patents were granted in 1877 and 1878, consists
of a transmitter, a wire, and a receiver. When
sounds are spoken into the transmitter, electric
currents of varying intensity pass along the wire,
so that corresponding or equivalent sounds are
heard at the receiver, and two persons at a distance can thus converse with one another. A
company leased these telephones to subscribers at
yearly rents which produced a profit to the company, and arranged the wires so that subscribers
could converse with one another when put into
communication by a servant of the company :—
Held, that Edison's telephone was a " telegraph "
within the meaning of the Telegraph Acts, 1863
and 1869, although the telephone was not invented or contemplated in 1869.—*Held,* also, that
a conversation through the telephone was a

TELEGRAPH COMPANY—*continued.*

" message," or at all events " a communication transmitted by a telegraph," and therefore a " telegram " within the meaning of those Acts; and that since the company made a profit out of the rents, conversations held by subscribers through their telephones were infringements of the exclusive privilege of transmitting telegrams granted to the Postmaster-General by the Act of 1869, and were not within the exceptions mentioned in sect. 5. ATTORNEY-GENERAL *v.* EDISON TELEPHONE COMPANY OF LONDON   -   6 Q. B. D. 244

TELEGRAPHY—Book of words—Copyright
[26 Ch. D. 637
See COPYRIGHT—BOOKS. 4.

TELEPHONE—Company—Rateable occupation—
Wayleaves   14 Q. B. D. 267
See POOR-RATE—OCCUPATION. 6.

—— Rights of Postmaster-General 6 Q. B. D. 244
See TELEGRAPH COMPANY.

—— Wire extending across street—Trespass—
Rights of vestry or district board
[13 Q. B. D. 904
See METROPOLIS—MANAGEMENT ACTS. 7.

TEMPORARY NUISANCE—Reversioner
[20 Ch. D. 589
See NUISANCE—REMEDIES. 2.

TENANT AT WILL—Attornment clause in mortgage   -   21 Ch. D. 442
See BANKRUPTCY—DISTRESS. 4.

—— Mortgagor—Satisfied mortgagee
[22 Ch. D. 614
See LIMITATIONS, STATUTE OF—TRUSTS. 3.

TENANT FOR LIFE.

—— Settlement of Business — *Successive Tenants for Life—Loss during First Tenancy for Life—Profit during Second Tenancy for Life— Apportionment of Loss between Persons interested.*]
In an action to execute the trusts of a settlement, by which (inter alia) a business was assigned to trustees on trust for successive tenants for life and remainderman, a receiver and manager was appointed to carry on the business. During the life of the first tenant for life the business was carried on by the receiver at a loss; during the life of the second tenant for life profits were earned:—*Held,* that the loss must be made good out of the subsequent profits, and not out of capital. UPTON *v.* BROWN   -   26 Ch. D. 588

—— Apportionment—Income of legacy
See APPORTIONMENT. 1. [18 Ch. D. 160

—— Building contract by   -   19 Ch. D. 22
See EASEMENT. 2.

—— Consent by—Assignment of life estate
[23 Ch. D. 583
See SETTLEMENT—POWERS. 1.

—— Contract for lease   -   22 Ch. D. 128
See SETTLEMENT—POWERS. 2.

—— Costs incurred for protection of estate
[16 Ch. D. 587
See TRUSTEE RELIEF ACT. 4.

—— Custody of deeds   -   -   26 Ch. D. 31
See TITLE DEEDS.

—— Leaseholds—Duty of trustee — Repairs — Covenant   -   -   16 Ch. D. 723
See TRUSTEE—LIABILITIES. 9.

TENANT FOR LIFE—*continued.*

—— Lunacy—Allowance to tenant in remainder
[20 Ch. D. 320
See LUNATIC—PROPERTY. 3.

—— Mortgage to be paid off out of accumulations—Rights of tenant for life
See ACCUMULATIONS. 1. [30 Ch. D. 649

—— Mortgaged estate—Keeping down interest
[30 Ch. D. 614
See WILL—DISCLAIMER. 2.

—— Order to redeem — Assignment to third party   -   -   -   26 Ch. D. 567
See MORTGAGE—REDEMPTION. 3.

—— Ordinary outgoings -   -   28 Ch. D. 431
See WILL—WORDS. 14.

—— Permanent improvements   27 Ch. D. 196
See SETTLEMENT—POWERS. 7.

—— Power of leasing mines—Mortgage
[23 Ch. D. 583
See SETTLEMENT—POWERS. 1.

—— Power of sale—Settlement—Injunction
[24 Ch. D. 558
See SETTLEMENT—POWERS. 17.

—— Powers of sale and leasing under Settled Land Act.
See Cases and Statutes under SETTLED LAND ACT.

—— Power to consent to advancement—Bankruptcy   27 Ch. D. 565
See POWER—EXTINCTION. 2.

—— Protector of settlement—Death of protector appointed by settlor   16 Ch. D. 176
See TENANT IN TAIL. 2.

—— Purchase-money under Lands Clauses Act
[16 Ch. D. 597
See LANDS CLAUSES ACT—PURCHASE-MONEY. 2.

—— Remaindermen—Apportionment
[26 Ch. D. 672
See EXECUTOR—ADMINISTRATION. 1.

—— Remainderman—Bonus   29 Ch. D. 635
See COMPANY—DIVIDENDS. 1.

—— Renewable leaseholds—Purchase of reversion   -   26 Ch. D. 590; 29 Ch. D. 673
See LEASEHOLD — RENEWABLE LEASE. 1, 2.

—— Sale under Lands Clauses Act 18 Ch. D. 146
See LANDS CLAUSES ACT—COMPULSORY POWERS. 5.

TENANT FROM YEAR TO YEAR 16 Ch. D. 274
See BANKRUPTCY—DISTRESS. 2.

—— Assignment   -   9 Q. B. D. 366
See LANDLORD AND TENANT—ASSIGNMENT. 1.

—— Notice to quit.
See LANDLORD AND TENANT—YEARLY TENANT—*Statutes.*

TENANT IN COMMON.

—— Use and Occupation — *Contribution — Tenants in Common of a House—Landlord and Tenant—Tenant by Sufferance—Ordinary Repairs.*]
Where one tenant in common has by lease demised his interest to his co-tenant in common, if the tenant in common who was lessee continues in occupation as tenant at sufferance after the

TENANT IN COMMON—*continued.*

expiration of the lease, he will be liable in an action for use and occupation at the suit of his co-tenant in common who was lessor.—One tenant in common of a house who expends money on ordinary repairs has no right of action against his co-tenant for contribution.—Judgment of Pollock, B., affirmed. LEIGH *v.* DICKESON　　12 Q. B. D. 194;
[15 Q. B. D. 60

—— Joint tenant -　　-　　21 Ch. D. 352
See POWER—EXECUTION. 3.

—— Partition suit　　-　　- 21 Ch. D. 674
See PARTITION SUIT—SALE. 2.

—— "Share and share alike"　-　21 Ch. D. 811
See WILL—CLASS. 2.

TENANT IN TAIL.

1. —— **Disentailing Deed**—*Enrolment—Settlement — Mistake — Rectification — Jurisdiction—.Fines and Recoveries Act (3 & 4 Will. 4, c. 74), ss. 40, 47.]* Having regard to sects. 40 and 47 of the Fines and Recoveries Act (3 & 4 Will. 4, c. 74), the Court has no jurisdiction to rectify, on the ground of mistake, a deed which has been enrolled as a disentailing assurance under the Act, although the rectification asked is not in the disentailing part of the deed, but in a re-settlement added to it, which might have been effected by a separate unenrolled deed.—A testator, who died in 1836, devised his estates, subject to a prior limitation to A. for life, to the use of B. for life, with remainder to the use of "the first and other sons of B. in tail," with remainders over. In 1878, by a deed enrolled as a disentailing assurance under the Fines and Recoveries Act (3 & 4 Will. 4, c. 74), B., and C. his then only son, with the consent of A. as protector of the settlement, conveyed the estates subject to A.'s life estate, but discharged from B.'s life estate and C.'s estate tail in remainder under the will, to the use of B. for life, with remainder to the use of C. in tail, with remainder to uses in favour of the Defendant and his issue.—It appeared to have been the intention of the parties to this re-settlement to preserve therein the limitation in the will to "the first and other sons of B. in tail," but shortly after the death, in 1880, of C., a bachelor, B. being still living, it was discovered that this limitation had been omitted, and that consequently the limitations over in favour of the Defendant and his issue took effect to the exclusion or B.'s future issue, if any.—In an action by A. and B. against the Defendant, who was an infant, to have the deed of 1878 rectified by the insertion, next after C.'s estate tail, of a limitation to B.'s "second and other sons in tail :"—*Held*, that by sect. 47 of the above Act the Court was prohibited, in such a case, from exercising its ordinary jurisdiction as to the rectification of mistakes in deeds
HALL-DARE *v.* HALL-DARE　-　29 Ch. D. 133
[Reversed by the Court of Appeal, 31 Ch. D. 251.]

2. —— **Disentailing Deed**—*Protector of Settlement—Trustees—Death—Tenant for Life—3 & 4 Will. 4, c. 74, s. 22.]* The trustees of the real estate under a will were appointed also protectors of the estates tail created by the will. They all died, and new trustees of the real estate were appointed by the Court :—*Held*, that the tenant for

TENANT IN TAIL—*continued.*

life had become protector of the settlement, and that he and the first tenant in tail could convey.
CLARKE *v.* CHAMBERLIN　-　16 Ch. D. 176

—— Fire insurance—Right to policy-money
See INSURANCE, FIRE. 2. [23 Ch. D. 188

—— Heirlooms—Vesting　-　24 Ch. D. 102
See WILL—HEIRLOOM. 1.

—— Infant—Powers of trustees—Settled Land Act　-　-　-　24 Ch. D. 129
See SETTLED LAND ACT—TRUSTEES. 6.

—— Lunacy—Allowance -　-　20 Ch. D. 320
See LUNATIC—PROPERTY. 3.

TENANT OF MANOR—Rights of common
See INCLOSURE.: 3.　　[20 Ch. D. 380

TENANT PUR AUTRE VIE　　18 Ch. D. 624
See LEASEHOLD—RENEWABLE LEASE. 3.

TENDENCY TO DECEIVE 18 Ch. D. 395; 8 App.
See TRADE NAME. 3.　　[Cas. 315

TENDER—After action — Costs — Salvage suit
[10 P. D. 1
See PRACTICE—ADMIRALTY—COSTS. 8.

—— Bill of lading in exchange for payment—Bills of lading drawn in sets
[11 Q. B. D. 327
See SALE OF GOODS—CONTRACT 4.

—— Costs—Trustee　-　21 Ch. D. 855
See TRUSTEE RELIEF ACT. 2.

—— Salvage—Plea—Payment into Court
[10 P. D. 41
See PRACTICE—ADMIRALTY—SALVAGE. 2.

TERMINAL CHARGES — Railway — Stations, sidings, &c.　-　- 15 Q. B. D. 505
See RAILWAY COMPANY—RAILWAYS REGULATION ACTS. 4.

TERRITORIAL SOVEREIGNTY 6 App. Cas. 143
See COLONIAL LAW—HONDURAS.

TESTAMENTARY POWER.
See Cases under POWER — EXECUTION. 8—19.

THAMES—Fishery bye-laws.
See FISHERY ACTS—*Gazette.*

—— Preservation of.
See RIVER—*Statutes.*

—— Rules for navigation—Infringement.
See Cases under SHIP — NAVIGATION. 28—31.

THEATRE.

—— **Licence**—*Having or keeping a House for the Public Performance of Stage Plays—6 & 7 Vict. c. 68, s. 2.]* The Appellant was the owner and occupier of a building which he gratuitously allowed to be used on a few occasions for the performance of stage plays, to which the public were admitted on payment, for the benefit of a charity. The Appellant had no licence for the performance of stage plays in such building :—*Held*, that he was rightly convicted, of having or keeping a house for the public performance of stage plays without a licence, under 6 & 7 Vict. c. 68, s. 2. SHELLEY
v. BETHELL　-　-　-　12 Q. B. D. 11

—— Free admission—Real burden
[6 App. Cas. 295
See SCOTCH LAW — HERITABLE PROPERTY. 3.

THEATRE—continued.

—— Right of representing dramatic piece—Place
of entertainment   11 Q. B. D. 102;
                              [13 Q. B. D. 843
   See COPYRIGHT—DRAMATIC. 1, 2.

THIRD COUNSEL—Appeal—Costs 15 Q. B. D. 420
   See SOLICITOR—BILL OF COSTS. 14.

THIRD PARTY—Claim against.
   See Cases under PRACTICE — SUPREME
   COURT—THIRD PARTY.

—— Contract to perform covenants in head lease
—Indemnity -   8 Q. B. D. 329
   See PRACTICE—SUPREME COURT—COSTS.
   48.

—— Damage by collision   -   -   8 P. D. 91
   See PRACTICE — ADMIRALTY — THIRD
   PARTY.

—— Entry of appearance   23 Ch. D. 685
   See PRACTICE—SUPREME COURT—COUN-
   TER-CLAIM. 3.

—— Right to compel action against—Nuisance
                              [23 Ch. D. 767
   See NUISANCE—REMEDIES. 6.

TIDAL RIVER—Fishery   -   8 App. Cas. 135
   See FISHERY. 1. .

TIERCE OPPOSITION — Law of Mauritius —
Award   -   -   -   8 App. Cas. 296
   See COLONIAL LAW—MAURITUS. 1.

TIMBER.

   1. —— Windfalls—Larch Trees.] An estate
which comprised larch plantations was settled
as personalty by the medium of trustees for sale.
The trustees had power to pay all outgoings, and
to determine what part of the property was corpus
and what income. A large number of trees were
blown down by extraordinary gales, and the plantations were so much injured that it became
necessary to clear and replant the ground.—The
income from the plantations was derived from
thinnings, and varied considerably according to
the age of the trees. The trees blown down were
about thirty-five years old, and in ordinary course
would have come to full maturity in fifteen or
twenty years, and they would then have been cut
down and the ground cleared and replanted :—
Held, the proceeds of the sale of the larch trees
blown down and felled by reason of the gales did
not belong to the equitable tenant for life, but
must be invested by the trustees. But the Court,
having regard to the average income which would
have been derived from the plantations if no gales
had occurred, fixed an annual sum to be paid to
the tenant for life out of the income, and, if necessary, the capital of the invested fund; subject to
the right of the trustees to have recourse to the
fund in order to replant the plantations. In re
HARRISON'S TRUSTS. HARRISON v. HARRISON
                              [28 Ch. D. 220

   2. —— Windfalls — Larch Trees — Real and
Personal Estate—Tenant for Life.] A testator
devised estates upon which there were plantations of larch trees. At the time of his death a
great number of the larch trees had been more or
less blown down by extraordinary gales.—It was
held by Pearson, J., that as between the devisees
and the executors of the testator the trees which
had been blown down to such an extent that they

TIMBER—continued.

could not grow as trees usually grow were severed
and belonged to the executors, and that the trees
which were merely lifted but would have to be
cut for the proper cultivation of the plantations
belonged to the devisees :—But, held, by the Court
of Appeal, in allowing an appeal, that, having
regard to the maxim "quicquid plantatur solo,
solo cedit," the principle applicable was that if a
tree was attached to the soil it was real estate, and
if severed, personalty; that the life and manner
of growth of any particular tree was no test of its
attachment to the soil, and that the degree of
attachment or severance was a question of fact in
the case of each particular tree. In re AINSLIE.
SWINBURN v. AINSLIE 28 Ch. D. 89; 30 Ch. D. 485

—— Floats—Harbour dues   -   8 App. Cas. 658
   See SCOTCH LAW—HARBOUR. 2.

—— Right to float down stream 9 App. Cas. 392
   See COLONIAL LAW — CANADA — ON-
   TARIO. 5.

—— Timber limits   -   -   9 App. Cas. 150
   See COLONIAL LAW—CANADA—QUEBEC.
   9.

TIME—Appeal—Application to stay proceedings
                              [24 Ch. D. 305
   See PRACTICE—SUPREME COURT—STAY-
   ING PROCEEDINGS. 15.

—— Appeal in bankruptcy.
   See Cases under BANKRUPTCY—APPEAL.
   6—9.

—— Appeal—Practice—Supreme Court.
   See Cases under PRACTICE—SUPREME
   COURT—APPEAL. 34—44.

—— Appeal—Probate and Divorce Division
                [10 P. D. 110; 9 App. Cas. 631
   See PRACTICE—DIVORCE—APPEAL. 1, 2.

—— Application for security for costs
                              [23 Ch. D. 358
   See PRACTICE—SUPREME COURT—SECU-
   RITY FOR COSTS. 1.

—— Appointment of trustee in liquidation
                              [24 Ch. D. 353
   See BANKRUPTCY—LIQUIDATION. 4.

—— Computation of — Notice of meeting of
shareholders   -   29 Ch. D. 204
   See COMPANY—REDUCTION OF CAPITAL.
   5.

—— Delivery of reply   -   -   22 Ch. D. 91
   See PRACTICE — SUPREME COURT —
   REPLY. 3.

—— Extension of—Appeal.
   See Cases under PRACTICE—SUPREME
   COURT—APPEAL. 35—38.

—— Extension of—Appeal from order in Cham-
bers   -   -   -   6 Q. B. D. 116
   See PRACTICE — SUPREME COURT—DE-
   FAULT. 5.

—— Extension of—Indorsement of writ
                              [16 Ch. D. 734
   See PRACTICE—SUPREME COURT—WRIT.
   1.

—— Motion to discharge order in Chambers
                              [19 Ch. D. 326
   See PRACTICE—SUPREME COURT—CHAM-
   BERS. 5.

TIME—*continued.*

—— Rehearing in bankruptcy - **22 Ch. D. 529**
　See BANKRUPTCY—APPEAL. 5.

—— Sending in requisitions **20 Ch. D. 465**
　See VENDOR AND PURCHASER—TITLE. 8.

—— Writ taking effect—Fraction of day
　　　　　　　　[8 Q. B. D. 63
　See PRACTICE—SUPREME COURT—WRIT.
　　2.

TIME POLICY—Average under 3 per cent.—
　Adding losses - **14 Q. B. D. 555**
　See INSURANCE, MARINE—POLICY. 8.

—— Negative words **9 App. Cas. 345**
　See INSURANCE, MARINE—POLICY. 9.

TITHES.

Redemption.] *By the Act* 48 & 49 Vict. c. 32, *the provisions of certain Acts respecting the re-demption of rent-charge (except as otherwise pro-vided by this Act) are extended to all corn-rents, rent-charges, and money payments payable out of lands by virtue of any Act of Parliament in lieu of tithes.*

—— Arrears—*Not recoverable by Sale*—*Tithes Commutation Act* (6 & 7 Will. 4, c. 71), s. 67.] By the 67th section of the Tithes Commutation Act (6 & 7 Will. 4, c. 71) the sum thenceforth pay-able in lieu of tithes is declared to be "in the nature of a rent-charge issuing out of the lands charged therewith."—Lands in respect of which a tithe rent-charge was payable having become unproductive, and the remedy by distress and entry having become ineffectual :—*Held*, that the sum payable in lieu of tithes is not by the statute rendered a charge on the inheritance ; and that the owner of the rent-charge was not entitled to claim a sale of the lands in order to recover the arrears of his rent-charge. BAILEY *v.* BADHAM - **30 Ch. D. 84**

—— Payment under mistake—Delay in reclaim-ing - - **6 Q. B. D. 234**
　See MISTAKE. 3.

—— Statute of Limitations - **10 App. Cas. 14**
　See LIMITATIONS, STATUTE OF—REALTY.
　　8.

TITLE—Sale of land.
　See Cases and Statutes under
　　VENDOR AND PURCHASER—TITLE.
　　VENDOR AND PURCHASER—CONDITIONS
　　OF SALE.

—— Sale of land—Defects in—Notice
　　　　　　　[29 Ch. D. 661
　See VENDOR AND PURCHASER—RESCIS-
　　SION. 1.

TITLE DEEDS.

By 44 & 45 Vict. c. 41 (*Conveyancing Act*, 1881). Sect. 9.—(1.) *Where a person retains possession of documents, and gives to another an acknowledg-ment in writing of the right of that other to pro-duction of those documents, and to delivery of copies thereof (in this section called an acknowledgment), that acknowledgment shall have effect as in this section provided.*

(2.) *An acknowledgment shall bind the documents to which it relates in the possession or under the control of the person who retains them, and in the possession or under the control of every other person having possession or control thereof from time to time, but shall bind each individual possessor or*

TITLE DEEDS—*continued.*

person as long only as he has possession or control thereof ; and every person so having possession or control from time to time shall be bound specifically to perform the obligations imposed under this section by an acknowledgment, unless prevented from so doing by fire or other inevitable accident.

(3.) *The obligations imposed under this section by an acknowledgment are to be performed from time to time at the request in writing of the person to whom an acknowledgment is given, or of any person, not being a lessee at a rent, having or claiming any estate, interest, or right through or under that person, or otherwise becoming through or under that person interested in or affected by the terms of any document to which the acknowledgment relates.*

(4.) *The obligations imposed under this section by an acknowledgment are—*

(i.) *An obligation to produce the documents or any of them at all reasonable times for the purpose of inspection, and of comparison with abstracts or copies thereof, by the person entitled to request production or by any one by him authorized in writing ; and*

(ii.) *An obligation to produce the documents or any of them at any trial, hearing, or ex-amination in any Court, or in the execution of any commission, or elsewhere in the United Kingdom, on any occasion on which production may properly be required, for proving or supporting the title or claim of the person entitled to request production, or for any other purpose relative to that title or claim ; and*

(iii.) *An obligation to deliver to the person en-titled to request the same true copies or extracts attested or unattested, of or from the documents or any of them.*

(5.) *All costs and expenses of or incidental to the specific performance of any obligation imposed under this section by an acknowledgment shall be paid by the person requesting performance.*

(6.) *An acknowledgment shall not confer any right to damages for loss or destruction of, or injury to, the documents to which it relates, from whatever cause arising.*

(7.) *Any person claiming to be entitled to the benefit of an acknowledgment may apply to the Court for an order directing the production of the documents to which it relates, or any of them, or the delivery of copies of or extracts from those documents or any of them to him ; or some person on his be-half ; and the Court may, if it thinks fit, order production, or production and delivery accordingly, and may give directions respecting the time, place, terms, and mode of production and delivery, and may make such order as it thinks fit respecting the costs of the application or any other matter connected with the application.*

(8.) *An acknowledgment shall by virtue of this Act satisfy any liability to give a covenant for production and delivery of copies of or extracts from documents.*

(9.) *Where a person retains possession of docu-ments and gives to another an undertaking in writing for safe custody thereof, that undertaking shall impose on the person giving it, and on every person having possession or control of the documents*

3 E

TITLE DEEDS—*continued.*

from time to time, but on each individual possessor or person as long only as he has possession or control thereof, an obligation to keep the documents safe, whole, uncancelled, and undefaced, unless prevented from so doing by fire or other inevitable accident.

(10.) *Any person claiming to be entitled to the benefit of such an undertaking may apply to the Court to assess damages for any loss, destruction of, or injury to the documents or any of them, and the Court may, if it thinks fit, direct an inquiry respecting the amount of damages and order the payment thereof by the person liable, and may make such order as it thinks fit respecting the costs of the application, or any other matter connected with the application.*

(11.) *An undertaking for safe custody of documents shall by virtue of this Act satisfy any liability to give a covenant for safe custody of documents.*

(12.) *The rights conferred by an acknowledgment or an undertaking under this section shall be in addition to all such other rights relative to the production, or inspection, or the obtaining of copies of documents as are not, by virtue of this Act, satisfied by the giving of the acknowledgment or undertaking, and shall have effect subject to the terms of the acknowledgment and undertaking, and to any provisions therein contained.*

(13.) *This section applies only if and as far as a contrary intention is not expressed in the acknowledgment or undertaking.*

(14.) *This section applies only to an acknowledgment or undertaking given, or a liability respecting documents incurred, after the commencement of this Act*—31st December 1881.

—— Custody of—*Trustee in Bankruptcy—Life Estate of Bankrupt's Wife.*] The trustee in bankruptcy of a husband, whose wife is legal tenant for life of land (not to her separate use) has no absolute right to the custody of the title deeds of the land during the coverture, but the Court has a discretion as to the custody.—In a case in which there was evidence that a bankrupt's wife was about to apply to the Divorce Court for the dissolution of the marriage :—*Held*, that the title deeds of land, of which she was legal tenant for life, ought not to be delivered to the trustee in the bankruptcy, but ought to be retained in Court, where the County Court Judge had, upon the trustee's application for delivery to him, ordered them to be deposited.—Per Cotton, L.J.: Whether, under ordinary circumstances, an assignee from a husband of his right to receive during the coverture the rents of land of which his wife is legal tenant for life, is entitled as a matter of course to the custody of the title deeds. *Quære. Ex parte* ROGERS. *In re* PYATT - - **26 Ch. D. 31**

—— Inspection by mortgagee.
  See MORTGAGE—REDEMPTION—*Statutes.*

—— Not in vendor's possession—Costs
                        [30 Ch. D. 42
  See VENDOR AND PURCHASER—TITLE. 1.

—— Order to deliver up—Purchaser without notice - **20 Ch. D. 611**
  See VENDOR AND PURCHASER—PURCHASE WITHOUT NOTICE. 1.

TITLE DEEDS—*continued.*

—— Order to give up—Equitable mortgagee
                        [18 Ch. D. 93
  See EXECUTOR—ADMINISTRATION. 3.

—— Possession of—Priority.
  See Cases under MORTGAGE—PRIORITY. 5—9.

—— Right to retain - - **30 Ch. D. 396**
  See MORTGAGE—CONTRACT. 8.

—— Solicitor's lien on.
  See Cases under SOLICITOR—LIEN. 8—12.

TITLE OF ACTION—Amendment—Assignment pendente lite - - **16 Ch. D. 121**
  See PRACTICE — SUPREME COURT — PARTIES. 6.

TITLE OF BOOK—Copyright   **18 Ch. D. 76**
  See COPYRIGHT—BOOKS. 5.

TITLE OF DIGNITY—Heirlooms **30 Ch. D. 136**
  See SETTLED LAND ACT—RESTRICTIONS. 2.

TOBACCO.
  See REVENUE—EXCISE—*Statutes.*

TOLLS—Power to levy—Canadian railway
                        [8 App. Cas. 723
  See COLONIAL LAW — CANADA — DOMINION. 4.

—— Railway company — Inequality — Undue preference -   **14 Q. B. D. 209**
  See RAILWAY COMPANY — RAILWAYS CLAUSES ACT. 2.

TOLZEY COURT OF BRISTOL.
  See COURT—GAZETTE.

TONNAGE—Measurement of.
  See SHIP—MERCHANT SHIPPING ACTS—Gazette.

TORT—Abatement of action by death of Plaintiff—Order of reference **15 Q. B. D. 565**
  See PRACTICE — SUPREME COURT — CHANGE OF PARTIES. 4.

TOWAGE—Condition of contract exempting owner of tug from liability - **9 P. D. 3**
  See SHIP—NAVIGATION. 32.

—— Damage to ship - **6 App. Cas. 217**
  See SHIP—PILOT. 7.

TOWING-PATH - **6 App. Cas. 685**
  See RIVER.

TRADE — Bankruptcy — Farming and market-gardening for pleasure **14 Q. B. D. 950**
  See BANKRUPTCY—ORDER AND DISPOSITION. 9.

—— Carried on by executors - **18 Ch. D. 93;**
                        [26 Ch. D. 19, 42
  See EXECUTOR—ADMINISTRATION. 2, 3, 4.

—— Carried on by trustee - **26 Ch. D. 245**
  See TRUSTEE—POWERS. 3.

—— Carried on by trustee in bankruptcy
                        [17 Ch. D. 35
  See BANKRUPTCY—TRUSTEE. 2.

TRADE OR BUSINESS—Covenant not to exercise
                  [27 Ch. D. 71, 81, n.
  See LANDLORD AND TENANT — LEASE. 4. 5.

TRADE-MARK :—   Col.
  I. INFRINGEMENT -   - **1573**
  II. REGISTRATION - - - **1573**

I. TRADE-MARK—INFRINGEMENT.

1. —— Injunction—*Tendency to mislead.*] No trader has a right to use a trade-mark so nearly resembling that of another trader as to be calculated to mislead incautious purchasers.—The use of such a trade-mark may be restrained by injunction, although no purchaser has actually been misled; for the very life of a trade-mark depends upon the promptitude with which it is vindicated.—So *held*, affirming the decision of the Court of Appeal. JOHNSTON *v.* ORR EWING

[**7 App. Cas. 219**

2. —— Innocent Consignee — *User* — *Costs.*] The Defendant, who was a china manufacturer, purchased abroad for his own private use a large number of cigars which were consigned to him at the docks here in cases bearing a spurious brand, purporting to be that of the Plaintiffs, who were cigar manufacturers. The Defendant was not aware that the brand was spurious, nor, except from seeing it on the invoice, that any such brand was in use. Immediately upon the Plaintiffs issuing their writ and serving the Defendant with notice of motion for an injunction to restrain him from selling the cigars, the Defendant stated that he had no intention of selling the cigars, and offered all the relief asked for by the writ, and afterwards at the motion agreed to an undertaking in the terms of the writ, the question of costs being reserved :—*Held*, that the Defendant must pay all the costs of the action. UPMANN *v.* FORESTER - - **24 Ch. D. 231**

II. TRADE-MARK—REGISTRATION.

The Act *of* 1883, 46 & 47 *Vict. c.* 57, s. 113, *repeals* (inter alia) *the Trade-marks Registration Acts, 1875, 1876 and 1877, and consolidates and amends the law relating to the registration of Trade-marks.*

Registration.] *Sect.* 62.—(1.) *The Comptroller may on application by or on behalf of any person claiming to be the proprietor of a trade-mark register the trade-mark.*

(2.) *The application must be made in the form set forth in the first schedule to this Act, or in such other form as may be from time to time prescribed, and must be left at, or sent by post to, the Patent Office in the prescribed manner.*

(3.) *The application must be accompanied by the prescribed number of representations of the trade-mark, and must state the particular goods or classes of goods in connexion with which the applicant desires the trade-mark to be registered.*

(4.) *The Comptroller may, if he thinks fit, refuse to register a trade-mark, but any such refusal shall be subject to appeal to the Board of Trade, who shall, if required, hear the applicant and the Comptroller, and may make an order determining whether and subject to what conditions, if any, registration is to be permitted.*

(5.) *The Board of Trade may, however, if it appears expedient, refer the appeal to the Court; and in that event the Court shall have jurisdiction to hear and determine the appeal and may make such order as aforesaid.*

Sect. 63. *Where registration of a trade-mark has not been or shall not be completed within twelve months from the date of the application, by reason of default on the part of the applicant, the application shall be deemed to be abandoned.*

II. TRADE-MARK—REGISTRATION—*contd.*

Sect. 64.—(1.) *For the purposes of this Act, a trade-mark must consist of or contain at least one of the following essential particulars:*

(a.) *A name of an individual or firm printed, impressed, or woven in some particular and distinctive manner; or*

(b.) *A written signature or copy of a written signature of the individual or firm applying for registration thereof as a trade-mark; or*

(c.) *A distinctive device, mark, brand, heading, label, ticket, or fancy word or words not in common use.*

(2.) *There may be added to any one or more of these particulars any letters words or figures, or combination of letters words or figures, or any of them.*

(3.) *Provided that any special and distinctive word or words, letter, figure, or combination of letters or figures or of letters and figures used as a trade mark before the 13th day of August, 1875, may be registered as a trade-mark under this part of this Act.*

Sect. 65. *A trade-mark must be registered for particular goods or classes of goods.*

Sect. 66. *When a person claiming to be the proprietor of several trade-marks which, while resembling each other in the material particulars thereof, yet differ in respect of (a) the statement of the goods for which they are respectively used or proposed to be used, or (b) statements of numbers, or (c) statements of price, or (d) statements of quality, or (e) statements of names of places, seeks to register such trade-marks they may be registered as a series in one registration. A series of trade-marks shall be assignable and transmissible only as a whole, but for all other purposes each of the trade-marks composing a series shall be deemed and treated as registered separately.*

Sect. 67. *A trade-mark may be registered in any colour, and such registration shall (subject to the provisions of this Act) confer on the registered owner the exclusive right to use the same in that or any other colour.*

Sect. 68. *Every application for registration of a trade-mark under this part of this Act shall as soon as may be after its receipt be advertised by the Comptroller.*

Sect. 69.—(1.) *Any person may within two months of the first advertisement of the application, give notice in duplicate at the Patent Office of opposition to registration of the trade-mark, and the Comptroller shall send one copy of such notice to the applicant.*

(2.) *Within two months after receipt of such notice or such further time as the Comptroller may allow, the applicant may send to the Comptroller a counter-statement in duplicate of the grounds on which he relies for his application, and if he does not do so, shall be deemed to have abandoned his application.*

(3.) *If the applicant sends such counter-statement the Comptroller shall furnish a copy thereof to the person who gave notice of opposition and shall require him to give security in such manner and to such amount as the Comptroller may require for such costs as may be awarded in respect of such opposition; and if such security is not given within fourteen days after such requirement was*

3 E 2

II. TRADE-MARK—REGISTRATION—contd.

made or such further time as the Comptroller may allow, the opposition be deemed to be withdrawn.

(4.) If the person who gave notice of opposition duly gave such security as aforesaid the Comptroller shall inform the applicant thereof in writing, and thereupon the case shall be deemed to stand for the determination of the Court.

Sect. 70. A trade-mark when registered shall be assigned and transmitted only in connexion with the goodwill of the business concerned in the particular goods or classes of goods for which it has been registered and shall be determinable with that goodwill.

Sect. 71. Where each of several persons claims to be registered as proprietor of the same trade mark, the Comptroller may refuse to register any of them until their rights have been determined according to law, and the Comptroller may himself submit or require the claimants to submit their rights to the Court.

Sect. 72.—(1.) Except where the Court has decided that two or more persons are entitled to be registered as proprietors of the same trade-mark, the Comptroller shall not register in respect of the same goods or description of goods a trade-mark identical with one already on the register with respect to such goods or description of goods.

(2.) The Comptroller shall not register with respect to the same goods or description of goods a trade-mark so nearly resembling a trade-mark already on the register with respect to such goods or description of goods as to be calculated to deceive.

Sect. 73. It shall not be lawful to register as part of or in combination with a trade-mark any words the exclusive use of which would by reason of their being calculated to deceive or otherwise, be deemed disentitled to protection in a Court of justice, or any scandalous design.

Sect. 74. (1.) Nothing in this Act shall be construed to prevent the Comptroller entering on the the register, in the prescribed manner, and subject to the prescribed conditions, as an addition to any trade-mark—

    (a.) In the case of an application for registration of a trade-mark used before the 13th day of August, 1875,

        Any distinctive device, mark, brand, heading, label, ticket, letter, word, or figure, or combination of letters, words, or figures, though the same is common to the trade in the goods with respect to which the application is made;

    (b.) In the case of an application for registration of a trade-mark not used before the 13th day of August, 1875,

        Any distinctive word or combination of words, though the same is common to the trade in the goods with respect to which the application is made;

    (2.) The applicant for entry of any such common particular or particulars must, however, disclaim in his application any right to the exclusive use of the same, and a copy of the disclaimer shall be entered on the register.

    (3.) Any device, mark, brand, heading, label, ticket, letter, word, figure, or combination of letters, words, or figures, which was or were, before the 13th day of August, 1875, publicly used by more than

II. TRADE-MARK—REGISTRATION—contd.

three persons on the same or a similar description of goods shall, for the purposes of this section, be deemed common to the trade in such goods.

Effects of Registration.] Sect. 75. Registration of a trade-mark shall be deemed to be equivalent to public use of the trade-mark.

Sect. 76. The registration of a person as proprietor of a trade-mark shall be primâ facie evidence of his right to the exclusive use of the trade-mark, and shall, after the expiration of five years from the date of the registration, be conclusive evidence of his right to the exclusive use of the trade-mark, subject to the provisions of this Act.

Sect. 77. A person shall not be entitled to institute any proceeding to prevent or to recover damages for the infringement of a trade-mark, unless in the case of a trade-mark capable of being registered under this Act, it has been registered in pursuance of this Act, or of an enactment repealed by this Act, or in the case of any other trade-mark in use before the 13th of August, 1875, registration thereof under this part of this Act, or of an enactment repealed by this Act, has been refused. The Comptroller may on request, and on payment of the prescribed fee, grant a certificate that such registration has been refused.

Register of Trade-marks.] Sect. 78. There shall be kept at the Patent Office a book called the Register of Trade Marks, wherein shall be entered the names and addresses of proprietors of registered trade-marks, notifications of assignments and of transmissions of trade-marks, and such other matters as may be from time to time prescribed.

Sect. 79.—(1.) At a time not being less than two months nor more than three months before the expiration of fourteen years from the date of the registration of a trade-mark, the Comptroller shall send notice to the registered proprietor that the trade-mark will be removed from the register unless the proprietor pays to the Comptroller before the expiration of such fourteen years (naming the date at which the same will expire) the prescribed fee; and if such fee be not previously paid, he shall at the expiration of one month from the date of the giving of the first notice send a second notice to the same effect.

(2.) If such fee be not paid before the expiration of such fourteen years the Comptroller may after the end of three months from the expiration of such fourteen years remove the mark from the register, and so from time to time at the expiration of every period of fourteen years.

(3.) If before the expiration of the said three months the registered proprietor pays the said fee, together with the additional prescribed fee, the Comptroller may without removing such trade-mark from the register accept the said fee as if it had been paid before the expiration of the said fourteen years.

(4.) Where after the said three months a trade-mark has been removed from the register for non-payment of the prescribed fee, the Comptroller may, if satisfied that it is just so to do, restore such trade-mark to the register on payment of the prescribed additional fee.

(5.) Where a trade-mark has been removed from the register for non-payment of the fee or otherwise, such trade-mark shall nevertheless for the purposes of any application for registration during the five

II. TRADE-MARK—REGISTRATION—*contd.*

years next after the date of such removal be deemed to be a trade-mark which is already registered.

Fees.] *Sect. 80. There shall be paid in respect of applications and registration and other matters under this part of this Act, such fees as may be from time to time, with the sanction of the Treasury, prescribed by the Board of Trade; and such fees shall be levied and paid to the account of Her Majesty's Exchequer in such manner as the Treasury may from time to time direct.*

Sect. 81. Provisions as to registration by Cutlers' Company of Sheffield marks.

Sects. 82—102 provide for the constitution of the Patent Office and the proceedings therein, including the rectification and alteration of the register.

Sect. 103 relates to International and Colonial arrangements.

Sect. 105 as to offences against the Act.

[*See also* PATENT—STATUTES.]

1. —— Cancelling of Registration—*Lapse of Five Years—" Distinctive Words "—Registration of Mark not authorized to be registered — Trade-marks Registration Act,* 1875 (38 & 39 *Vict.* c. 91), *ss.* 3, 5, 10.] P. registered " braided fixed stars " as a trade-mark for matches, alleging that he had used it as a trade-mark before the passing of the Act. He also at the same time registered a label enveloping the boxes in which his matches were sold, which contained the words " braided fixed stars " in two places so as to be conspicuous on each side of the boxes, but also contained a number of other words. It was shewn that at the time when P. introduced the term " braided fixed stars " the term " fixed stars " was known in the trade as denoting a particular class of fusees, and that he had just bought a patent for enveloping the stems of fusees with wire by means of a braiding machine. This patent expired in August, 1881. It appeared from the evidence that P. had not before the Act used " braided fixed stars " separately as a trade-mark, or otherwise than as a part of the above-mentioned label. In October, 1881, an application was made by a rival trader to expunge the registration :—*Held,* that the registration must be expunged, for that to entitle P. to register these words as a trade-mark he must before the Act have used them as such alone, and not merely in conjunction with other words.— *Held,* further, that if they had been so used alone they ought not to have been registered, for that they were only words properly descriptive of the patented article, and that P. had no exclusive right to their use after the patent had expired. *In re* J. B. PALMER'S TRADE-MARK 21 Ch. D. 47; [24 Ch. D. 504

2. —— Cancelling of Registration—*Lapse of Five Years—Patents, Designs, and Trade-Marks Act,* 1883 (46 & 47 *Vict.* c. 57), *ss.* 76, 90, 113.] The right to the exclusive use of a trade-mark, after the expiration of five years from the date of registration, given by the Trade-marks Act, 1883, s. 76, is subject to and controlled by sect. 90, and therefore any person who considers himself aggrieved by any entry made in the register without sufficient cause is not precluded by the expiration of five years from the date of such registration from shewing that the mark ought

II. TRADE-MARK—REGISTRATION—*contd.*

not to have been registered. *In re* LLOYD AND SONS' TRADE-MARK. LLOYD v. BOTTOMLEY

[27 Ch. D. **646**

3. —— Cancelling of Registration—*Lapse of Five Years—Label—Indefeasible Title—" Common to the Trade "—" Three Marks Rule "—Patents, Designs, and Trade-marks Act,* 1883 (46 & 47 *Vict.* c. 57), *ss.* 74, 76, 90.] The registration of a mark as a trade-mark and the lapse of five years do not, under sect. 76 of the Trade-marks Act, 1883 confer on the person who has made the registration an indefeasible title to the use of the mark as a trade-mark if, by reason of its being at the time of registration in common use in the trade, it ought not to have been registered.—The lapse of five years cannot make good a registration which was in its inception invalid.—A trade-mark which was originally improperly registered ought, even after the lapse of five years, to be removed from the register, because the registration might enable the person who has made it to commit a fraud.—*Held,* that a mark which had been registered as a trade-mark, was, at the time of registration, " common to the trade " because similar (though not in each case identical) marks were then in use by more than three persons engaged in the same trade, although in some of the cases the mark was not actually placed on the goods, but was only used on bill-heads, trade circulars, advertisements, or show-cards. *In re* WRAGG'S TRADE-MARK - 29 Ch. D. 551

4. —— Cancelling of Registration—*New Name for New Article—Improper Registration—Injunction—" Heading "—" Distinctive Word "—Trade-marks Registration Act,* 1875 (38 & 39 *Vict.* c. 91), *ss.* 3, 5, 10.] L. & E. invented in 1873 a process for making a certain description of lubricating oil which they called " Valvoline," and in that year registered in America as their trade-mark, the word accompanied by a device. In August, 1877, they registered the same trade-mark in England, and in February, 1878, registered the word " Valvoline " alone as their trade-mark. After this mark had been five years on the register they commenced an action against W. to restrain him from selling under the name of Valvoline any oil not made by the Plaintiffs. W. moved to rectify the register by striking out the trade-mark " Valvoline." The Court came to the conclusion on the evidence that L. & E. had not used " Valvoline " alone as a trade-mark, either in America or England before the passing of the Trade-marks Registration Act, 1875, but only in conjunction with a device, and that " Valvoline " was a word invented to describe the particular class of oil at the same time as the process was invented, and was used as a descriptive term for that particular kind of oil. The process was not the subject of a patent :—*Held,* that where a person seeks to remove a trade-mark from the register the onus is upon him to shew that it ought to be removed, but though his own evidence may be insufficient for the purpose, the onus is discharged if it appears from the evidence of the owner of the mark that it ought not to be on the register.—Whether a word used alone as a trade-mark in a foreign country before the passing of the Trade-marks Act, 1875, can be registered under the Act if it has not been so used in

II. TRADE-MARK—REGISTRATION—*contd.*

this country, *quære* :—*Held*, further, that a single word cannot be registered under the Act, on the ground that it was used as a "heading," unless it was so used before the passing of the Act :—*Held*, therefore, affirming the decision of Pearson, J., that the trade-mark "Valvoline" must be removed from the register.—If a person who invents a new process for making a new article invents at the same time a new name for describing such article, and the article comes to be known by that name only, he cannot afterwards, when everybody is at liberty to make that article, claim a monopoly in the name :—*Held*, therefore, affirming the decision of Pearson, J., that the Defendants were not by using the name "Valvoline," which was the only name by which the substance in question was known, infringing any rights of the Plaintiffs, or representing their goods as made by the Plaintiffs, and that the fact that the Plaintiffs had in consequence of the registration enjoyed a practical monopoly of the name for five years did not, as the name had been improperly put in the register, give them any better right than they would otherwise have had.—Per Fry, L.J., *semble*, a "special and distinctive" word within the meaning of the Act, must be a word intended to distinguish articles manufactured by one person from similar articles manufactured by other persons, and not a word merely descriptive of the articles themselves. *In re* LEONARD & ELLIS'S TRADE-MARK. LEONARD & ELLIS *v.* WELLS -   **26 Ch. D. 288**

5. —— Distinctive Letters—*Name of Firm— Fancy Words not in Common Use—Identical Label —Power of Comptroller—Sanction of Court—Refusal to register.*] An application was made for an order upon the Comptroller of Trade-marks to register a mark having the words " Price's Patent Candle Company " in common letters round the upper border and "National Sperm" in the centre, with the address of the company round the lower border. The Comptroller refused to register the mark, on the ground that there was a mark so nearly resembling this, already on the register, as to be calculated to deceive, and also because it was not a distinctive label within the terms of the Patents Act, 1883 :—*Held*, that the name of the firm printed in common letters not being distinctive, and the words "National Sperm" not being fancy words "not in common use," the label did not fulfil the requirements of the Patents, Designs, and Trade-marks Act, 1883, s. 64 :—*Held*, also, that the Comptroller would be justified in refusing to register a label so nearly resembling another label already on the register as to be calculated to deceive, until the opinion of the Court should have been obtained authorizing him to do so. *In re* PRICE'S PATENT CANDLE COMPANY
                                [**27 Ch. D. 681**

6. —— Fancy Word—*Patents, Designs and Trade-marks Act, 1883 (46 & 47 Vict. c. 57), s. 64, snb-s. (1) (c).*] The word "Alpine," and words of such class, although words in common use and not strictly fancy words, may, when applied to articles such as woollen and cotton goods, be registered as a trade-mark, as they are, if not "fancy words," at least fanciful words when applied to such goods, and so fall within sect. 64, sub-sect. (1) (c), of the Patents, Designs and Trade-marks

II. TRADE-MARK—REGISTRATION—*contd.*

Act, 1883 (46 & 47 Vict. c. 57). *In re* TRADE-MARK "ALPINE" -   -   - **29 Ch. D. 877**

7. —— Length of adverse User—*Fraudulent Commencement — Continuing Misrepresentation— Foreign Proprietor.*] Mere length of adverse user will not of itself make a mark which was originally a trade-mark publici juris, where such user was originally fraudulent and is still calculated to deceive, but it throws upon the trader claiming an exclusive right to the mark the onus of proving such original fraud and continuing misrepresentation, and the longer the user the stronger must be the evidence.—Upon this principle an application to register under the Trade-marks Acts in combination with the name of the applicants, a foreign trade-mark which had been used by the applicants and by thirty other firms in this country in combination with their own respective names or with some device for fifty years, was refused upon the opposition of the foreign proprietor of the mark who had only recently discovered such user. The owners of ironworks at Leufsta, in Sweden, had, in 1718, registered in Sweden, as a trade-mark, the letter L within a circle (called in the trade the Hoop L), and their iron so marked had acquired a high reputation, particularly for manufacture into blister steel. By Swedish law all bar iron must be stamped with a duly registered mark before it is exported, and, from the year 1835 the Leufsta iron was exported to England marked with the hoop L in combination either with the name of the English consignee, or with the word "Leufsta," or with both. In 1878 the Hoop L was registered in England by the Leufsta owners as a trade-mark both alone and in combination with the word "Leufsta."—In 1882 the B. Company, a firm of English steel manufacturers, applied to register under the Trade-marks Acts the Hoop L in combination with the words "B. Company, Warranted," and produced evidence to shew that for fifty years they and thirty other firms had used the Hoop L in combination with a name or with a device upon all blister steel manufactured from Swedish iron, whether Leufsta iron or not, cutting off from inferior iron its distinctive stamp and substituting the Hoop L.— The Leufsta owners opposed the application, and proved that this adverse user was not discovered by them until 1881 :—*Held*, that the Hoop L mark had not become publici juris, and that the application to register it must be dismissed with costs. *In re* HEATON'S TRADE-MARK **27 Ch. D. 570**

8. —— Limitation of User—*Application Ex parte—Trade-marks Rules, 1883, r. 32.*] Objections having been raised by the owner of a registered trade-mark to the proposed registration of another trade-mark for use in connection with goods included in classes for which the first mark was used, but no formal opposition having been lodged to the application for registration, an agreement was entered into between the registered owner and the applicant that no formal opposition should be lodged; that the applicant should use his mark in connection only with goods actually exported to certain specified countries; and that he would, in connection with the registration, cause a note of this restriction on the

II. TRADE-MARK—REGISTRATION—contd.

use of his trade-mark to be entered on the register. Upon an ex parte application by the applicant, in pursuance of this agreement, the Court directed the Comptroller of Trade-marks to enter such a note on the register. *In re* KEEP'S TRADE-MARK   **26 Ch. D. 187**

· 9. —— Limitation of User—*Entry of Undertaking on Register—Patents, Designs and Trade-marks Act, 1883 (46 & 47 Vict. c. 57), s. 85.*] The entry, on the register of two similar trade-marks in the same class, of a note that the use of the marks registered is restricted by an agreement between the respective owners (the effect of which is not stated) is irregular, and contrary to the provisions of the Patents, Designs and Trade-marks Act, 1888; but, following *In re Rabone & Co.* (Seb. Dig. 395), a note of the mutual undertakings not to use the marks except in a certain manner and within specified districts may be entered on the register. *In re* MITCHELL & CO.'s TRADE-MARK. *In re* HOUGHTON & HALL-MARK'S TRADE-MARK   **28 Ch. D. 666**

10. —— Limitation of User—*Registration for part of a Class—Registration of New Mark for other Goods in same Class—Limited Registration—Trade-marks Registration Act, 1875 (38 & 39 Vict. c. 91), t. 6—Trade-mark Rules, 1876, rr. 17, 19.*] A new mark may be registered for some one of the goods in a class, even though an old mark of a similar kind has been already registered for other goods in the same class, provided that the goods and the trades of the proprietors are sufficiently distinct for no confusion to take place. *In re* F. BRABY & CO.'s APPLICATION. *In re* SHROPSHIRE IRON COMPANY'S TRADE-MARKS -   **21 Ch. D. 223**

11. —— Limitation of User—*Registration for entire Class of Goods—Five Years' Registration—User for part of Class only—Exclusive Title for Entire Class—Assignment—Goodwill—Infringement—Rectification of Register—Limitation to Part of Class—Trade-marks Registration Act, 1875, ss. 2, 3, 4, 5, 10—Trade-marks Registration Amendment Act, 1876, s. 1.*] An assignee of the goodwill of a business with the right to a trade-mark which has been registered by the assignor under the Trade-marks Registration Act, 1875, in respect of an entire class, but of which the articles dealt with in such business form part only, is not entitled to the exclusive user of the trade-mark for the entire class, but only for the particular articles in connection with which it is actually used, even though the trade-mark may have been on the register for five years.—Sects. 3 and 4 of the Trade-marks Registration Act, 1875, do not confer on the first or subsequent registered proprietor of a trade-mark who has been on the register for five years the absolute right to the exclusive use of his trade-mark as against all the world: the intention of the sections is merely to afford him assistance in bringing an action for infringement by dispensing with the necessity of his adducing evidence in that action of exclusive user; and the sections are no bar to an application under sect. 5 to rectify the register on the ground that the trade-mark is improperly on the register or should be restricted to certain goods.—*Semble*, it is not the intention of the Act that a man registering a trade-mark for an entire class, and yet only using

II. TRADE-MARK—REGISTRATION—contd.

it for one description of goods in that class, shall be able to claim for himself the exclusive right to use it for every description of goods in that class. If he desires to extend his business and apply his trade-mark to a new description of goods in the class, he should have his trade-mark registered in respect of those goods.—*Quære*, whether a man can claim the exclusive use of a registered trade-mark not in actual use in connection with particular goods at the time of registration.—In 1883 E. purchased and took an assignment of the goodwill of the business of an iron merchant and manufacturer, and also of the right to a trade-mark, consisting of a device of Neptune holding a trident with the word "Neptune" added, which had been registered by the assignor in 1878, under the Trade-marks Registration Acts, 1875 and 1876, for the whole of Class 5, described in the *Trade-marks Journal* as "unwrought and partly wrought metals used in manufacture," E. duly getting himself registered as proprietor of the trade-mark. The only business actually carried on by E. and his assignor was and had been that of a manufacturer of iron sheets. In 1880 D. registered a trade-mark bearing the word "Neptune" for "steel wire and iron wire" in Class 5, his business consisting solely of the manufacture and sale of wire. In 1884 E. brought an action against D. for infringement on the ground of the alleged similarity of D.'s trade-mark. D. then applied by summons under sect. 5 of the Act of 1875 to have the register rectified by limiting E.'s trade-mark to the articles in Class 5 other than steel and iron wire :—*Held*, in the action, reversing A. L. Smith, J., that inasmuch as the goods sold by E. and D. were entirely distinct, E. was not entitled to an injunction :—*Held*, also, upon the summons (affirming Bacon, V.C., with a variation), that, notwithstanding the five years' registration of E.'s trade-mark for the whole of Class 5, his trade-mark must be limited to those articles in the class in connection with which it was being actually used, namely, iron sheets. EDWARDS *v.* DENNIS. *In re* EDWARDS' TRADE-MARK

[**30 Ch. D. 454**

12. —— Non-user—*Abandonment.*] In order to deprive a manufacturer of his right to a trade-mark, the use of which has been practically given up for a period of five years, mere discontinuance of user for lack of demand, though coupled with non-registration, and non-assertion of any right, is not enough, there must be evidence of distinct intention to abandon.—In 1874, A., a German soap manufacturer, adopted a trade-mark for a particular kind of soap, which for about two years was manufactured and sent to this country in large quantities for exportation to Australia, but from 1876 until 1882 the manufacture and sale of soap thus marked fell off, until it practically ceased, and the existence of the particular mark was in May, 1882, forgotten by A.—In 1880, B., a manufacturer of soap in the same part of Germany, adopted, in complete ignorance of A.'s mark, a precisely similar mark for soap sent to this country for exportation to Australia, and in August, 1880, he registered his mark under the Trade-marks Acts in this country.—In July, 1882, after the commencement of proceedings by B. to

II. TRADE-MARK—REGISTRATION—contd.

restrain an infringement of his registered trade-mark by A., A. applied for registration of his mark of 1874.—Upon application (1) by B. to restrain the infringement of his trade-mark; (2) by A. to have his trade-mark registered; (3) by A. to have B.'s trade-mark removed from the register:—Held (1), that mere non-user by A. of his mark between 1876 and 1882, although coupled with non-registration, did not, having regard to the fact that he had not ceased to carry on his business, and had not broken up the mould, and that a number indicating soap thus marked was retained on his price lists, did not amount to an abandonment by A. of the mark, so as to give B. any exclusive right to his registered mark.—(2) That the existence upon the register of B.'s mark did not prevent the Court from granting leave for the registration of A.'s mark.—(3) That previous bonâ fide registration of B.'s mark in ignorance of any claim by A., followed by large dealings under that mark, prevented A., after the lapse of two years, from getting B.'s mark expunged from the register. MOUSON & Co. v. BOEHM　-　-　26 Ch. D. 398

13. —— Old Mark—Similarity—Patents, Designs, and Trade-marks Act, 1883 (46 & 47 Vict. c. 57), s. 62.] An application made in November, 1884, by an American firm of oil manufacturers for the registration under the Act of 1883 of a trade-mark for illuminating oils, which mark had been used by them in America since 1872, and had been known in England as the "White Rose" mark prior to 1875, was refused by the Comptroller upon the ground that there had been on the register since 1878 a similar mark for illuminating oils called the "Rosaline" mark, of which an English firm were the proprietors:—Held, that although there was enough similarity between the two marks to render it possible for the public to mistake the one for the other, yet as the "White Rose" was to all intents and purposes an old mark, it ought to be admitted to registration. In re "WHITE ROSE" TRADE-MARK　30 Ch. D. 505

14. —— Person aggrieved — Person not carrying on Business in England—Trade-marks Registration Act, 1875 (38 & 39 Vict. c. 91), s. 5.] R. & Co. registered a trade-mark for brandy in England. M. & Co., who carried on business at Madras, but neither carried it on nor intended to carry it on in England, applied to rectify the register by striking out the name of R. & Co. and substituting that of M. & Co. as owners of the trade-mark, alleging that they, M. & Co., were the owners of the trade-mark, and had instructed R. & Co. to register it in the name of M. & Co., instead of which R. & Co. had registered it in their own name.—Held, by Pearson, J., that as M. & Co. neither used nor intended to use the trade-mark in England they were not entitled to registration of it in England, and could not be persons aggrieved within the meaning of the Trade-marks Act, 1875, sect. 5, and that on this ground the application must be refused without entering on the merits.—Held, on appeal, that assuming M. & Co. to have no right to register the trade-mark in England, it did not follow as a necessary consequence that they could not be aggrieved by its being registered here in the name

II. TRADE-MARK—REGISTRATION—contd.

of another person, and that the case must be dealt with on the merits.—Whether in order to entitle a person to have a trade-mark registered, he must be carrying on or intending to carry on business in England, quære. In re RIVIÈRE'S TRADE-MARK
　　　　　　[26 Ch. D. 48

15. —— Person aggrieved — Trade-marks Act, 1875 (38 & 39 Vict. c. 91), r. 33—Proprietor of Trade-mark not carrying on Business.] The owner of a patent for a washing machine called the "Home-washer," which had been exclusively manufactured by a licensee upon payment of a royalty, registered "The Home-washer" as his trade-mark, a year before the expiration of the patent, and claimed the exclusive use of that name. The patentee had not carried on any trade connected with the manufacture of these machines for a year and nine months after the patent had expired. The licensee moved under the 23rd of the rules framed under the Trade-marks Act to have the trade-mark expunged from the register:—Held, that the licensee, who had been the sole manufacturer of the machines, was a person aggrieved within the terms of the 33rd rule, and that the patentee not having been engaged in any business concerning the goods within the same class for more than one year, was not entitled to retain his trade-mark. Semble, that the name of a patented article which has become known in the trade is not a fitting trade-mark after the expiration of the patent, since it would have the effect of extending the patent beyond its legal limit. In re RALPH'S TRADE-MARK. RALPH v. TAYLOR　-　　25 Ch. D. 194

16. —— Words Publici Juris—Trade-marks Act, 1875 (38 & 39 Vict. c. 91), ss. 6, 10.] A term which by judicial decision has become open to the trade as the proper description of an article made in accordance with the recipe of the original inventor, and is therefore publici juris, cannot be registered as a trade-mark either alone or in combination with a portrait of the original inventor; and such portrait is not a sufficiently "distinctive device" within the Trade-marks Act, 1875, s. 10, to be capable of registration as a trade-mark per se. In re ANDERSON'S TRADE-MARK
　　　　　　[26 Ch. D. 409

TRADE-MARK RULES, 1876, rr. 17, 19
　　　　　　[21 Ch. D. 223
See TRADE-MARK—REGISTRATION. 10.
—— —— 1883, r. 32　-　26 Ch. D. 187
See TRADE-MARK—REGISTRATION. 8.

TRADE NAME.

1. —— Jurisdiction—Injunction— Telegraphic Address.] The short address "Street, London," was used for many years in sending telegrams from abroad to Street & Co. of Cornhill. A bank adopted by arrangement with the Post Office the phrase "Street, London," as a cypher address for telegrams from abroad to themselves:—Held, that the Court had no jurisdiction to restrain the bank from using such cypher address. STREET v. UNION BANK OF SPAIN AND ENGLAND　30 Ch. D. 156

2. —— Mortgagee — User of Name.] The mortgagee of stock-in-trade and goodwill, and of the right to use a name, never having used the

TRADE NAME—*continued.*

name and not intending to use the name, cannot obtain an injunction to restrain persons claiming under the mortgagor from using the name. BEAZLEY *v.* SOARES   22 Ch. D. 660

3. —— **Reference to Rival's Name**—*User of Name*—*Tendency to deceive.*] A trader has a right to make and sell machines similar in form and construction to those made and sold by a rival trader, and in describing and advertising his own machines to refer to his rival's machines and his rival's name, provided he does this in such a way as to obviate any reasonable possibility of misunderstanding or deception. SINGER MANUFACTURING COMPANY *v.* LOOG - 18 Ch. D. 395;
[8 App. Cas. 15

TRADE UNION.

—— Contract — *Direct Enforcement* — *Trade Unions Act, 1871* (34 & 35 *Vict.* c. 31), *ss.* 2, 3, 4.] By the Trade Unions Act, 1871, sect. 4, it is provided that nothing in the Act shall enable the Court to entertain any legal proceeding instituted with the object of directly enforcing an agreement for the application of the funds of a trade union to provide benefits to its members.—The Plaintiffs, members of a trade union within the Act, sought for an injunction to restrain other members from applying the funds in a manner contrary to an agreement to provide benefits to members:—*Held,* that such an injunction would not be a direct enforcement of the alleged agreement and that the Court might entertain the proceeding. WOLFE *v.* MATTHEWS 21 Ch. D. 194

—— Sums not exceeding £100.
See FRIENDLY SOCIETY—*Statutes.*

TRADER—Bankruptcy.
See Cases under BANKRUPTCY—TRADER.

—— Bankruptcy — Business carried on by receiver   11 Q. B. D. 241
See BANKRUPTCY—ASSETS. 5.

—— Defeating and delaying creditors
[25 Ch. D. 500
See BANKRUPTCY—ACT OF BANKRUPTCY. 26.

—— Voluntary settlement by 19 Ch. D. 588
See BANKRUPTCY—VOID SETTLEMENT. 1.

TRAFFIC—Highway — Extraordinary expenses —Excessive weight - 6 Q. B. D. 206;
[8 Q. B. D. 59, 466
See HIGHWAY—REPAIR. 8, 9, 10.

—— Railway company.
See Cases under RAILWAY COMPANY—TRAFFIC MANAGEMENT.

—— Railway company — Tolls — Undue preference - - 14 Q. B. D. 209
See RAILWAY COMPANY — RAILWAYS CLAUSES ACT. 2.

TRAMWAY—Law of New South Wales
[9 App. Cas. 720
See COLONIAL LAW—NEW SOUTH WALES. 5.

TRAMWAY COMPANY.

1. —— **Flange Wheels**—*Tramways Act, 1870* (33 & 34 *Vict.* c. 78), s. 54—*User of Wheels substantially flanged.*] Sect. 54 of the Tramways Act, 1870 (33 & 34 Vict. c. 78), prohibits the

TRAMWAY COMPANY—*continued.*

user of the tramway by unlicensed persons with carriages " having flange-wheels or other wheels suitable only to run on the rail of such tramway." The Appellant, an omnibus proprietor, attached to his vehicle a lever with arms having a small revolving disc or roller which the driver might drop into the groove of the rail at the lower side of each fore-wheel when on the tramway, such discs operating when down as a flange at the point of contact with the rails, but when withdrawn by means of the lever leaving the vehicle free to travel over any part of the road: —*Held,* that this contrivance (though no obstruction to the tramway) was within the prohibition of the statute. COTTAM *v.* GUEST 6 Q. B. D. 70

2. —— **Repair of Road**—*Tramways Act, 1870* (33 & 34 *Vict.* c. 78), *ss.* 28, 29, 55—*Contract with Road Authority*—*Transfer of Liability.*] Where a tramway company enters into a contract with the road authority under 33 & 34 Vict. c. 78, s. 29, whereby the road authority undertakes the repair of the portion of the road upon which the tramway is laid, the liability for damage occasioned by the non-repair of that part of the road, which would but for such contract be cast by sect. 28 upon the tramway company, is transferred to the road authority. HOWITT *v.* NOTTINGHAM AND DISTRICT TRAMWAYS COMPANY 12 Q. B. D. 16

TRANSCRIPT OF RECORD—Irish inquisition
[20 Ch. D. 269
See LUNATIC—JURISDICTION.

TRANSFER—Action - 16 Ch. D. 702;
[13 Q. B. D. 540
See PRACTICE — SUPREME COURT — TRANSFER. 1, 2.

—— Action—County Court - 27 Ch. D. 533.
See PRACTICE—SUPREME COURT—JURISDICTION. 3.

—— Action—Inferior Court—Action pending in High Court - - 8 P. D. 34
See PRACTICE—ADMIRALTY — JURISDICTION. 4.

—— Action—Inferior Court — Cross action in High Court   9 P. D. 34
See PRACTICE — ADMIRALTY — CONCURRENT ACTIONS.

—— Administration of estate of deceased debtor —Transfer to Bankruptcy Court
[13 Q. B. D. 552; 15 Q. B. D. 159;
[29 Ch. D. 236
See BANKRUPTCY—DECEASED DEBTOR. 1, 2, 3.

—— Bankruptcy proceedings—County Court
[13 Q. B. D. 484; 15 Q. B. D. 335
See BANKRUPTCY—TRANSFER. 1, 2.

—— Debentures_ - - 24 Ch. D. 85
See COMPANY—DEBENTURES. 3.

—— Liquidation proceedings - 19 Ch. D. 367
See BANKRUPTCY—LIQUIDATION. 13.

—— Mortgage.
See MORTGAGE—REDEMPTION—*Statutes.*

—— Mortgage—Equitable—Deposit
[30 Ch. D. 396
See MORTGAGE—CONTRACT. 8.

—— Mortgage—Notice - 16 Ch. D. 178.
See MORTGAGE—CONTRACT. 9.

TRANSFER—*continued.*

—— Railway—Canada   **7 App. Cas. 178**
  See COLONIAL LAW — CANADA — DO-
  MINION. 1.

—— Shares.
  See Cases under COMPANY—SHARES—
  TRANSFER.

—— Ship   -   **7 App. Cas. 127**
  See SHIP—MERCHANT SHIPPING ACTS. 7.

—— Stock—National Debt Commissioners
  [**25 Ch. D. 231**
  See NATIONAL DEBT COMMISSIONERS.

—— Stock—Injunction to restrain **23 Ch. D. 549**
  See PRACTICE—SUPREME COURT—IN-
  JUNCTION. 2.

—— Stock—Into joint names   -   **27 Ch. D. 341**
  See ADVANCEMENT. 2.

TRANSSHIPMENT—Foreign manufacture
  [**17 Ch. D. 721 ; 8 App. Cas. 5**
  See PATENT—INFRINGEMENT. 6.

TRESPASS.

1. —— *Actio personalis moritur cum persona
—Benefit received by Trespasser.*] By the decree
in 1870 it was declared that H. and F. and the
estate of their deceased partner were liable to the
Plaintiffs for minerals taken by them under the
Plaintiffs' farm, and that H. & F. were liable to
compensate the Plaintiffs for user of all roads and
passages under the farm, and inquiries were
directed—1. As to the quantity of minerals taken
and the value. 2. What quantities of minerals
had been carried by the Defendants through the
roads or passages under the farm. 3. What upon
the result of the second inquiry ought to be paid
by the Defendants as wayleave for the user of the
roads and passages. 4. Whether the farm, and
the mineral property of the Plaintiffs under it,
had sustained any and what damage by reason of
the way in which the Defendants had worked
under the farm. Pending these inquiries F. died,
and his executrix moved to stay proceedings under
the second, third, and fourth inquiries:—*Held,* by
Pearson, J., that the fourth inquiry must be
stayed, but that as the estate of F. had derived
profit from the trespasses to which the second and
third inquiries related, it was liable after his death,
and that these inquiries must be prosecuted:—
Held, on appeal by Cotton and Bowen, L.JJ., dissentiente Baggallay. L.J., that proceedings under
the second and third inquiries must also be stayed,
for that, apart from cases of breach of contract, a
remedy for a wrongful act done by a deceased
person cannot be pursued against his estate, unless property or the proceeds or value of property
belonging to another person have been appropriated by the deceased person and added to his
estate. PHILIPS *v.* HOMFRAY   -   **24 Ch. D. 439**

2. —— *Injury by Cattle—Entry of Ox into
Shop adjoining Street—Absence of Negligence—
Liability.*] An ox belonging to the Defendant
and while being driven by his servants through
the streets of a country town entered the Plaintiff's shop, which adjoined the street, through the
open doorway and damaged his goods. No negligence on the part of the persons in charge of the
ox was proved:—*Held,* that the Defendant was
not liable. TILLETT *v.* WARD   **10 Q. B. D. 17**

TRESPASS—*continued.*

—— Injunction to restrain   -   **20 Ch. D. 190**
  See PRACTICE—SUPREME COURT—IN-
  JUNCTION. 7.

—— Injury to reversion -   **20 Ch. D. 589**
  See NUISANCE—REMEDIES. 2.

TRIAL.
  See Cases under PRACTICE — SUPREME
  COURT—TRIAL.

—— Notice of—Abridgment of time **14 Q. B. D. 234**
  See PRACTICE—SUPREME COURT—NOTICE
  OF TRIAL.

TRIAL OF LUNATICS ACT, 1883.
  See LUNATIC—CRIMINAL—*Statutes.*

TRICYCLE—Steam power—Locomotive—Highway   -   -   **7 Q. B. D. 313**
  See HIGHWAY—LOCOMOTIVE.

TRINITY MASTER—Inspection of lights—Col-
  lision   -   -   **10 P. D. 40**
  See PRACTICE—ADMIRALTY—INSPECTION
  OF PROPERTY.

TROVER.

—— Bill of Lading—*Sale of Goods—Merchant Shipping Act,* 1862 (25 & 26 Vict. c. 63),
ss. 66–78—*Warehouseman, Liability of—Conversion.*] When goods are shipped under a bill of
lading drawn in parts, to be delivered to the consignee "or his assigns, the one of which bills
being accomplished, the others to stand void," the
master, or the warehouseman who has the custody
of the goods under the Merchant Shipping Act,
1862, ss. 66–78, is justified in delivering to the
consignee on production of one part, although
there has been a prior indorsement for value to
the holder of another part ; provided the delivery
be bonâ fide and without notice or knowledge of
such prior indorsement. — Goods having been
shipped for London consigned to C. & Co. the
shipmaster signed a set of three bills of lading
marked "First," "Second," and "Third," respectively, making the goods deliverable to C. &
Co., or their assigns, freight payable in London,
the one of the bills being accomplished, the
others to stand void. During the voyage C. &
Co. indorsed the bill of lading marked "First" to
a bank in consideration of a loan. Upon the
arrival of the ship at London the goods were
landed and placed in the custody of a dock company in their warehouses : the master lodging with
them notice under the Merchant Shipping Act,
1862, sect. 68, &c., to detain the cargo until the
freight should be paid. C. & Co. then produced
to the dock company the bill of lading marked
"Second" unindorsed, and the dock company
entered C. & Co. in their books as proprietors of
the goods. The stop for freight being afterwards
removed, the dock company bonâ fide and without notice or knowledge of the bank's claim
delivered the goods to other persons upon delivery
orders signed by C. & Co.:—*Held,* affirming the
decision of the Court of Appeal, that the dock
company had not been guilty of a conversion, and
that the bank could not maintain any action
against them.—*Fearon* v. *Bowers* (1 H. Bl. 364)
reflected on. GLYN MILLS, CURRIE & Co. *v.* EAST
AND WEST INDIA DOCK COMPANY **6 Q. B. D. 475** ;
  [**7 App. Cas. 591**

TRUST—Bequest on indefinite trust
　　See WILL—TRUSTEES. 2. [26 Ch. D. 531

—— Breach of—Making good by trustee
　　　　　　　　　　　　　　[17 Ch. D. 58
　　See BANKRUPTCY — FRAUDULENT PRE-
　　　FERENCE. 1.

—— Breach of—Trustee's liability.
　　See Cases under TRUSTEE—LIABILITIES.

—— Declaration of　-　-　17 Ch. D. 416
　　See VOLUNTARY CONVEYANCE. 1.

—— Discretionary　　　　21 Ch. D. 332
　　See POWER—EXECUTION. 3.

—— For maintenance—Settlement 22 Ch. D. 521
　　See SETTLEMENT—POWERS. 5.

—— For payment of debts—Exoneration of per-
　　sonalty　-　-　-　28 Ch. D. 446
　　See EXECUTOR—ADMINISTRATION. 9.

—— For sale—Charge of debts　20 Ch. D. 465 ;
　　　　　　　　　　　　　[23 Ch. D. 138
　　See VENDOR AND PURCHASER—TITLE. 7,
　　8.

—— For sale—Consent of cestui que trust
　　　　　　　　　　　　　[27 Ch. D. 315
　　See SETTLEMENT—POWERS. 18.

—— For sale—Discretion—Interference of Court.
　　　　　　　　　　　　　[29 Ch. D. 913
　　See PRACTICE—SUPREME COURT—CHAM-
　　BERS. 10.

—— For sale—Partition suit　-　22 Ch. D. 284
　　See PARTITION SUIT—JURISDICTION. 2.

—— For sale—Settled Land Act　24 Ch. D. 144 ;
　　　　　　　　　　　　　[25 Ch. D. 646
　　See SETTLED LAND ACT—TRUSTEES. 8, 9.

—— For sale—Will—Power to postpone
　　　　　　　　　　　　　[26 Ch. D. 42
　　See EXECUTOR—ADMINISTRATION. 4.

—— Notice of　　-　　24 Ch. D. 720
　　See VENDOR AND PURCHASER—TITLE. 4.

—— Solicitor　17 Ch. D. 437 ; 19 Ch. D. 207
　　See SOLICITOR—LIABILITIES. 2, 3.

—— To make strict entail　-　7 App. Cas. 713
　　See SCOTCH LAW—ENTAIL.

—— Transfer into joint names　-　27 Ch. D. 341
　　See ADVANCEMENT. 2.

TRUST ESTATE—Charge on—Creditor
　　See TRUSTEE—POWERS. 3. [26 Ch. D. 245

—— Devolution of.
　　See WILL—TRUST ESTATES—Statutes.

—— Indemnity of trustees　-　22 Ch. D. 255, 561
　　See TRUSTEE—INDEMNITY. 2, 3.

—— Retainer of income—Expenses of action
　　　　　　　　　　　　　[25 Ch. D. 710
　　See TRUSTEE—COSTS AND CHARGES. 5.

I. TRUSTEE—APPOINTMENT.

The Act 44 & 45 Vict. c. 41 (Conveyancing Act, 1881) enacts—

Sect. 31.—(1.) Where a trustee, either original or substituted, and whether appointed by a Court or otherwise, is dead, or remains out of the United Kingdom for more than twelve months, or desires to be discharged from the trusts or powers reposed in or conferred on him, or refuses or is unfit to act therein, or is incapable of acting therein, then the person or persons nominated for this purpose by the instrument, if any, creating the trust, or if there is no such person, or no such person able and willing to act, then the surviving or continuing trustees or trustee for the time being, or the personal represen- tatives of the last surviving or continuing trustee, may. by writing, appoint another person or other persons to be a trustee or trustees in the place of the trustee dead, remaining out of the United Kingdom, desiring to be discharged, refusing or being unfit, or being incapable, as aforesaid.

(2.) On an appointment of a new trustee, the number of trustees may be increased.

(3.) On an appointment of a new trustee, it shall not be obligatory to appoint more than one new trustee, where only one trustee was originally ap- pointed, or to fill up the original number of trustees, where more than two trustees were originally ap- pointed ; but, except where only one trustee was originally appointed, a trustee shall not be dis- charged under this section from his trust unless there will be at least two trustees to perform the trust.

(4.) On an appointment of a new trustee any assurance or thing requisite for vesting the trust property, or any part thereof, jointly in the persons who are the trustees, shall be executed or done.

(5.) Every new trustee so appointed, as well before as after all the trust property becomes by law, or by assurance, or otherwise, vested in him, shall have the same powers, authorities, and discretions, and may in all respects act, as if he had been originally appointed a trustee by the instrument, if any, creating the trust.

(6.) The provisions of this section relative to a trustee who is dead include the case of a person nominated trustee in a will but dying before the testator ; and those relative to a continuing trustee include a refusing or retiring trustee, if willing to act in the execution of the provisions of this section.

(7.) This section applies only if and as far as a contrary intention is not expressed in the instrument, if. any, creating the trust, and shall have effect subject to the terms of that instrument and to any provisions therein contained.

(8.) This section applies to trusts created either before or after the commencement of this Act.

Sect. 33.—(1.) Every trustee appointed by the Court of Chancery, or by the Chancery Division of the Court, or by any other Court of competent jurisdiction, shall, as well before as after the trust property becomes by law, or by assurance, or other- wise, vested in him, have the same powers, autho- rities, and discretions, and may in all respects act, as if he had been originally appointed a trustee by the instrument, if any, creating the trust.

(2.) This section applies to appointments made either before or after the commencement of this Act.

Vesting of Trust Property :] Sect. 34.—(1.) Where a deed by which a new trustee is appointed

I. TRUSTEE—APPOINTMENT—*continued.*

to perform any trust contains a declaration by the appointer to the effect that any estate or interest in any land subject to the trust, or in any chattel so subject, or the right to recover and receive any debt or other thing in action so subject shall vest in the persons who by virtue of the deed become and are the trustees for performing the trust, the declaration shall, without any conveyance or assignment, operate to vest in those persons, as joint tenants, and for the purposes of the trust, that estate, interest, or right.

(2.) *Applies to retiring trustees.*

(3.) *This section does not extend to any legal estate or interest in copyhold or customary land, or to land conveyed by way of mortgage for securing money subject to the trust, or to any such share, stock, annuity or property as is only transferable in books kept by a company or other body, or in manner prescribed by or under Act of Parliament.*

(4.) *For purposes of registration of the deed in any registry, the person or persons making the declaration shall be deemed the conveying party or parties, and the conveyance shall be deemed to be made by him or them under a power conferred by this Act.*

(5.) *This section applies only to deeds executed after the commencement of the Act*—31st Dec. 1881.

Separate Trustees.] *By* 45 & 46 *Vict. c.* 39 (*Conveyancing Act,* 1882)—*Sect.* 5.—(1.) *On an appointment of new trustees, a separate set of trustees may be appointed for any part of the trust property held on trusts distinct from those relating to any other part or parts of the trust property; or, if only one trustee was originally appointed, then one separate trustee may be so appointed for the first-mentioned part.*

(2.) *This section applies to trusts created either before or after the commencement of the Act.*—31st Dec. 1882.

II. TRUSTEE—COSTS AND CHARGES.

1. —— Defaulting Trustee—*Bankruptcy*—*Costs.*] Where the trustee of a settlement became bankrupt shortly after the commencement of an action for the execution of the trusts, and an order was made for payment by him into Court of a sum of money certified to be due from him to the estate, he was held entitled to his costs of the action, though he was not to receive them until he had made good his default.—*Bowyer v. Griffin* (Law Rep. 9 Eq. 340) considered. LEWIS *v.* TRASK　　-　　21 Ch. D. 862

2. —— Defaulting Trustee—*Bankruptcy of*—*Executor*—*Costs of Trustee subsequent to Bankruptcy*—*Bankruptcy Act,* 1869 (32 & 33 *Vict. c.* 71), *s.* 49.] In an administration action one Defendant was an executor. He was a defaulting trustee under a settlement. After the action was commenced he was adjudicated bankrupt, and a trustee in bankruptcy was appointed and made a Defendant:—*Held,* that the defaulting trustee was entitled to be paid his costs incurred after his bankruptcy.—*Bowyer v. Griffin* (Law Rep. 9 Eq. 340) followed. CLARE *v.* CLARE　　21 Ch. D. 865

3. —— Defaulting Trustee — *Bankruptcy* — *Executor*—*Bankruptcy Act,* 1869, *s.* 49.] Where, after the commencement of an administration action against a defaulting executor or trustee, he

II. TRUSTEE—COSTS AND CHARGES—*contd.*

becomes bankrupt, and, under sect. 49 of the Bankruptcy Act, 1869, his debt remains undischarged by the bankruptcy, he is not entitled to be paid any of his costs of the action, whether incurred before or after the bankruptcy, until he has made good his default.—But where the debt of the defaulting executor or trustee has been discharged by his bankruptcy—as where the bankruptcy has taken place prior to the Bankruptcy Act, 1869; or where, after the bankruptcy, his debt remaining undischarged, he renders services in the action in his character of executor or trustee, he is entitled to be paid his costs incurred subsequently to his bankruptcy, though his prior costs must be set off against his debt.—*Lewis* v. *Trask* (21 Ch. D. 862) followed.—*Clare* v. *Clare* (21 Ch. D. 865) not followed. *In re* BASHAM. HANNAY *v.* BASHAM　　-　　23 Ch. D. 195

4. ——　Defaulting Trustee—*Co-Trustee not indebted*—*Bankruptcy of Trustee.*] There were two trustees of an estate administered by the Court. One trustee was indebted to the estate and became bankrupt. The other trustee, who was solvent, was not indebted to the estate:—*Held,* that a reference be directed to the Taxing Master to apportion the costs of the trustees appearing by the same solicitor, and that the costs of the solvent trustee be paid out of the estate, and the costs apportioned as the costs of the insolvent trustee be set off against the amount found due from him to the estate.—Whether under this direction the whole of the common costs of the two trustees would be allowed to the solvent trustee or divided, must depend on the settled practice of the Taxing Master's office. McEWAN *v.* CROMBIE -　　25 Ch. D. 175

5. ——　Expenses of Actions—*Retainer of Income.*] The trustees of a freehold estate of which the Plaintiff was equitable tenant for life under a will, brought actions under the advice of counsel against two persons for interfering with the property, and compromised them before trial. The Plaintiff had no notice of the proceedings, but had some time previously warned the trustees on the occasion of an injury done by persons other than the Defendants to these actions, that he should hold them liable if they did not take all necessary steps to protect the property. In December, 1881, the Plaintiff applied to the trustees for the rents accrued since May, 1880. The trustees' solicitor answered stating the amount of the rents received, and saying that it was less than the costs incurred by the trustees in the action, and that they were out of pocket. A correspondence ensued, in the course of which the trustees expressed their willingness to concur in any arrangement for raising the costs out of the estate, but the Plaintiff insisted on having the rents paid to him irrespective of any arrangement for raising the costs, and brought his action to enforce payment. The Vice-Chancellor of the Lancaster Court made an order declaring that as the actions were brought without the knowledge or consent of the Plaintiff, the costs were not chargeable against the income. And the Court "being of opinion that the actions were commenced under the advice of counsel," ordered the trustees' costs of them to be raised and paid out

II. TRUSTEE—COSTS AND CHARGES—contd.

of the estate, but ordered the trustees to pay the Plaintiff his costs of the present action up to the hearing. The Plaintiff appealed against the direction to raise the costs of the former actions out of the estate, and the trustees from the order as to the costs of the present action.—Held, on appeal that the direction to raise the costs of the trustees of the old actions out of the estate ought to be affirmed, for that the actions appeared to have been brought bonâ fide and to have been beneficial to the estate, but that the reason given in the decree for allowing them ought to be varied, as that result did not necessarily follow from their having been commenced under the advice of counsel. But held, that the order on the trustees to pay costs must be reversed, and directions given for raising their costs of this action out of the estate, for that the costs of trustees properly incurred in the administration of the trust are a first charge on both the capital and income of the trust estate, and that the trustees were not bound to part with the income till their costs had been otherwise provided for, and they therefore had been guilty of no misconduct. STOTT v. MILNE - **25 Ch. D. 710**

6. —— Insufficient Estate—Priority.] If, in action by cestuis que trust under a creditors' trust deed against their trustees for accounts, and to have the rights of the parties ascertained, the costs of all parties are ordered to be paid out of the trust fund, and it appears probable that the fund will not be sufficient for payment of all the costs in full, the trustees are entitled to a direction for payment of their costs, charges, and expenses in priority to the costs of all other parties. DODDS v. TUKE - - **25 Ch. D. 617**

7. —— Litigation between Trustees—Costs between Solicitor and Client.] One of two executors and trustees commenced an action against the other for the administration of the estate, and a decree was made. There was no allegation of any misconduct on the part of the Defendant. On the action coming on for further consideration, Mr. Justice Kay gave the Plaintiff his costs as between solicitor and client, but gave the Defendant costs only as between party and party, holding that two sets of costs as between solicitor and client ought not to be allowed to the trustees :—Held, on appeal, that a trustee is entitled to costs as between solicitor and client in an administration action, unless a case of misconduct is made out against him, and that the Defendant must have costs as between solicitor and client. In re LOVE. HILL v. SPURGEON **29 Ch. D. 348**

8. —— Obstruction to Cestui que Trust—Refusal of Representative of deceased Trustee to appoint new Trustees—Conveyancing and Law of Property Act, 1881 (44 & 45 Vict. c. 41), s. 31—Rules of Supreme Court, 1883, Order LXV., r. 1—Jurisdiction to order Respondent to pay costs on Petition under Trustee Act, 1850.] The executors of the sole executor of a deceased sole trustee whose sole executor had never acted in the trust, were applied to in April, 1883, to take steps to enable the tenant for life of a small sum of stock standing in the name of the deceased trustee to receive the dividends. In May, 1883, the executors handed to the solicitor of the tenant for

II. TRUSTEE—COSTS AND CHARGES—contd.

life the probate of their testator's will, that he might produce it at the Bank of England, which he did. After some correspondence, in the course of which the executors asked for evidence of the title of the cestuis que trust, which did not appear to have been produced, the solicitor of the tenant for life about the end of May sent a power of attorney to be executed by the executors to enable her to receive the dividends. The executors did not execute or return the power. In July the solicitor of the tenant for life applied to the executors to appoint new trustees under the Conveyancing and Law of Property Act, 1881, to which the executors replied, stating their ignorance of the title of the cestuis que trust. Ultimately, in November, 1883, the cestuis que trust presented a petition for the appointment of new trustees and a vesting order:—Held, by Pearson, J., that the representative of a deceased trustee is not bound at the request of the cestuis que trust to exercise the power of appointing new trustees given by the Conveyancing and Law of Property Act, 1881 ; and that the refusal to do so was not a sufficient reason for ordering the executors to pay the costs of a petition for the appointment of new trustees :—But held by Pearson. J., that the conduct of the executors, who on the materials before him appeared to have accepted the trust by taking a transfer of the stock into their own names, had been vexatious, and that they must pay the costs which would have been occasioned by a petition simply asking for payment of dividends to the tenant for life, and that they could not be allowed any costs out of the fund.—The executors appealed :—Held, that an objection that this was an appeal for costs only was not sustainable :—Held, also, that as the cestuis que trust had not taken proper steps to satisfy the executors as to their title, the executors had not been guilty of any such misconduct as is necessary to deprive a trustee of his right to costs out of the trust fund, and that they must have their costs below, but that as the Court of Appeal was not satisfied with their conduct they ought to have no costs of their appeal.—Whether under the Judicature Acts and the Orders of 1883, Order LXV., rule 1, the Court has jurisdiction to order a respondent to a petition under the Trustee Act, 1850, to pay costs, quære. In re SARAH KNIGHT'S WILL
[26 Ch. D. 82

III. TRUSTEE—INDEMNITY.

1. —— Concurrence of Cestui que Trust—Married Woman.] Where a cestui que trust, who is party to a breach of trust, is a married woman, and the trustees claim a right of retainer against her life interest in the settled funds to indemnify them against their breach of trust, they are bound to shew that she acted for herself in the breach of trust, and was fully informed of the state of the case. SAWYER v. SAWYER - **28 Ch. D. 595**

2. —— Purchase of Land—Advance by Trustee of Part of Purchase-money—Lien.] Under a marriage settlement the trustees were empowered at the request of the husband and wife to invest the trust fund in the purchase of real estate, and to re-sell the same. In exercise of this power the trustees, at the request of the husband and wife, bought certain real estate at a price which

III. TRUSTEE—INDEMNITY—continued.

·exceeded the whole of the trust fund, the husband promising to provide the balance out of his own moneys. The husband could not fulfil his promise, and C. P., one of the trustees, at the request of the husband and wife, borrowed the sum necessary to complete the purchase from a bank, and deposited with them the title deeds of tho estate.—C. P. died, and the husband was unable to repay the loan.—In an action brought by the bank for an account and the realization of their security, and for administration of C. P.'s estate:—Held, that the trust estate was entitled to a first charge upon the real estate purchased for the full amount of the trust fund; that subject to such charge the estate of C. P. was entitled to be indemnified out of such real estate for the amount borrowed by him, and actually invested in or about the purchase, and to enforce such indemnity by sale of ·such real estate without the consent of the ·husband and wife : the bank being entitled to stand in the place of C. P. as against the trust estate for the amount due to them. In re PUMFREY. WORCESTER CITY AND COUNTY BANKING COMPANY v. BLICK

[22 Ch. D. 255

3. —— Shares in Company—Indemnity against Future Liability—Quia Timet Action.] A trustee held shares in a company on trust for an adult cestui que trust. He had applied for them at the request of the cestui que trust, who paid the money due to the company on the application and allotment. The trustee executed a transfer of the shares to the cestui que trust, and the latter sent it to the company for registration, but the directors refused to register it, and when an order was made to wind up the company the name of the trustee remained on the company's register as the holder of the shares. No further call had been made on them. The trustee brought an action against the cestui que trust, claiming an indemnity against liability on the shares. There was no evidence to shew whether calls were likely to be made in the winding-up:—Held, that the action was a mere quia timet one, and that it was premature and could not be maintained.—Lord Ranelaugh v. Hayes (1 Vern. 189) not followed. HUGHES-HALLETT v. INDIAN MAMMOTH GOLD MINES COMPANY   22 Ch. D. 561

IV. TRUSTEE—LIABILITIES.

1. —— Employment of Agent—Loss by Insolvency of Agent—Onus probandi.] A common order having been made for the administration of a testator's estate, the district registrar by his certificate found the outstanding personal estate to consist in part of book debts amounting nominally to £291, as to £113 part of which he certified that it represented a portion of book debts which the executors had employed H. to collect, and for which H. had not accounted, and had claimed to deduct £55 for remuneration, but that £25 was enough. The certificate went on to say that H. had gone into liquidation, and that no part of the £113 was likely to be recovered. No application was made to vary this certificate. It appeared that H. had collected in all £168, had paid to the executors in April, May, and June, 1880, sums amounting in all to £55, and had gone on collecting without making any

IV. TRUSTEE—LIABILITIES—continued.

further payment to the executors till July, 1881, when a receiver was appointed in the action, but it did not appear when he became insolvent nor at what times the moneys received came to his hands. The action having come on for further consideration :—Held, by Chitty, J., that the executors having received the £113 by their agent must be charged with it, less the £25 which the Registrar had held to be the proper amount of remuneration to the agent for collecting :—Held, on appeal, that this decision must be reversed, for that where an executor or trustee employs an agent to collect money under circumstances which make such employment proper, and the money collected is lost by the agent's insolvency, the burden of proof is not on the executor to shew that the loss was not attributable to his own default, but on the persons seeking to charge him to prove that it was. In re BRIER. BRIER v. EVISON   -   -   - 26 Ch. D. 238

2. —— Employment of Broker—Cestui que Trust—Liability of Trustee for Trust Moneys lost through Broker.]. A trustee investing trust funds is justified in employing a broker to procure securities authorized by the trust and in paying the purchase-money to the broker, if he follows the usual and regular course of business adopted by ordinary prudent men in making such investments.—A broker employed by a trustee to buy securities of municipal corporations authorized by the trust, gave the trustee a bought-note which purported to be subject to the rules of the London Stock Exchange and obtained the purchase-money from the trustee upon the representation that it was payable the next day, which was the next account day on the London Exchange. The broker never procured the securities but appropriated the money to his own use and finally became insolvent. Some of the securities were procurable only from the corporations direct and were not bought and sold in the market, and there was evidence that the form of the bought-note would have suggested to some experts that the loans were to be direct to the corporations; but (as the House held on the facts) there was nothing calculated to excite suspicion in the mind of the trustee or of an ordinary prudent man of business; and such payment to a broker was in accordance with the usual course of business in purchases on the London Exchange :—Held, affirming the decision of the Court of Appeal (Lord FitzGerald doubting), that the trustee was not liable to the cestuis que trust for the loss of the trust funds.—Semble, by the Earl of Selborne, L.C., that if the broker had represented to the trustee that the contracts were with the corporations for loans direct to them from the trustee he would not have been justified in paying the money to the broker, for which in such a case there would have been no moral necessity or sufficient practical reason. SPEIGHT v. GAUNT   22 Ch. D. 727; 9 App. Cas. 1

3. —— Improvident Investment—Mortgage— Advance on Valuation made on behalf of Vendor of Mortgagor—Failure of Security—Advance to more than Two-thirds of Estimated Value—Liability of Trustees.] In May, 1870, F. and G., the trustees of a will, one of whom, F., was an experienced farmer, and the other, G., a solicitor, advanced a

IV. TRUSTEE—LIABILITIES—*continued.*

sum of £2400, part of the trust estate, along with another sum of £2600, not part of the estate, making together £5000, at £4 per cent., on the security of a freehold farm, which in 1868 had been sold to the mortgagor, who was farming that and neighbouring land on a peculiar system of husbandry. The trustees had power to advance on contributory mortgages. In 1868 the farm had been valued on behalf of the vendors, of whom G. was one, and also the solicitor, at £6895. This valuation was communicated to F. at the time of the mortgage; and no other valuation was made. Interest was paid in full, but irregularly, down to November, 1877, since which time the farm, which was situated on clay soil, in a wet situation, had become unsaleable and unlettable, owing to unfavourable seasons, and had yielded no income. The mortgagor became insolvent.—Upon claim by the cestui que trust against F. and the executors of G. to be declared entitled to payment of the £2400 and interest since November, 1877:—*Held*, notwithstanding that no valuation was used at the date of the mortgage other than the valuation made on behalf of the vendors at the time of the sale to the mortgagor: that G., the trustee, was himself one, and solicitor of the others, of the vendors to the mortgagor; and that the sum advanced was more than two-thirds of the estimated value of the farm—that the trustees were not liable to make good the deficient security.—The test of liability always is, whether or not the trustees have acted as prudent men would have acted in dealing with their own property.—The "two-thirds" rule is not enforceable with exact strictness. *In re* GODFREY. GODFREY *v.* FAULKNER

[23 Ch. D. 483

4. —— Improvident Investment — *Mortgage on House Property — Employment of Agents — Valuation by Mortgagor's Surveyor—Selection of Valuer—Negligence—Liability of Trustees.*] The rule that trustees, acting according to the ordinary course of business, and employing agents as prudent men of business would do on their own behalf, are not liable for the default of the agent so employed, is subject to the limitation that the agent must not be employed out of the ordinary scope of his business.—Trustees empowered to invest on mortgage lent under the advice of their solicitors a sum of £5000 upon mortgage of a freehold house and grounds at Liverpool, valued to them at from £7000 to £8000. The trustees did not exercise their own judgment as to the choice of a valuer, but accepted the suggestion of their solicitors that a London surveyor who had introduced the security to them, and was in fact the agent of the mortgagor with a pecuniary interest in the completion of the mortgage, should value the property for the trustees, and they acted upon the report of this valuer, which was of an inflated character.—The mortgagor afterwards became bankrupt, and the property would not realize the sum advanced:—*Held*, that the trustees were jointly and severally liable to replace the sum advanced, with interest at 4 per cent. from the date of the loan. FRY *v.* TAPSON

28 Ch. D. 268

5. —— Improvident Investment — *Sub-mortgage—Building Estate — Speculative Security —*

IV. TRUSTEE—LIABILITIES—*continued.*

Separate Mortgages—Breach of Trust—Transfer of Securities—Executors—Waiver—Adoption and Acquiescence.] Under a settlement S. was tenant for life with an ultimate trust, in default of children (which happened), for her testamentary appointees. The trustees, having power to invest on leasehold securities, invested the trust funds, with S.'s consent, on separate sub-mortgages of leasehold houses, unfinished and unlet, on a building estate of which the roads and drainage were in a defective condition. The investment was made without an independent or reliable valuation, and more than half the value of the house was lent on each sub-mortgage. S. died, having by will disposed of the trust funds and appointed executors. The executors, with the sanction of the Chief Clerk in an action establishing S.'s testamentary appointment, had the sub-mortgages transferred to them by the trustees, and subsequently, finding them an insufficient security, brought an action against the trustees to make them personally liable for the deficiency :—*Held*, that, although the sub-mortgages were not improper investments in point of form, the trustees, having invested the trust funds on insufficient security of a speculative character, and without proper precautions, must make good the loss; and that the executors, having taken the transfers in ignorance of the circumstances attending the investment, were not bound by adoption or acquiescence. SMETHURST *v.* HASTINGS - - - - 30 Ch. D. 490

6. —— Improvident Investment—*Uncontrolled Discretion.*] A testator directed that his trustees should invest the moneys coming to their hands in respect of his estate in their names or under their control in such mode or modes of investment as they in their uncontrolled discretion should think fit. Before the commencement of an action to administer the testator's estate, the trustees (who were also executors) invested moneys forming part of it in the purchase of bonds of a foreign Government, bonds of a colonial railway company, and shares of a bank on which there was a further liability. The Chief Clerk, in taking the accounts of the testator's estate, disallowed the trustees the sums which they had expended in the purchase of these bonds and shares. The shares in the bank had been previously sold at a profit:—*Held*, that, though the investments in question ought not to be retained by the trustees, yet, as they had acted bonâ fide, and no loss had resulted to the trust estate, they ought not to be disallowed the sums which they had laid out in making the investments. *In re* BROWN. BROWN *v.* BROWN

[29 Ch. D. 889

7. —— Interest, Rate of—*Breach of Trust—Accumulation Clause—Compound Interest.*] The trustee of a will held a fund upon trust (after the determination of a previous life interest) to transfer and pay the same to a child when and as he should attain twenty-one, with a proviso that in case the child should be under age at the determination of the life interest the income of the fund or any part thereof should or might be applied for or towards his maintenance, education and advancement, and the surplus, if any, should accumulate to and become part of the fund.—After the child attained twenty-one (the life interest having

IV. TRUSTEE—LIABILITIES—*continued.*

previously determined), the trustee retained the fund without making any arrangement with the child or explaining to him his rights:—*Held,* that the trustee must be taken to have continued to hold the fund after the child attained twenty-one upon the same trusts and with the same obligations to accumulate as before, and that he was liable to account for the fund with compound interest.—*Wilson v. Peake* (3 Jur. (N.S.) 155) distinguished.—*Amiss v. Hall* (3 Jur. (N.S.) 584) observed upon.—Part of the fund had been invested at 5 per cent. or other rates of interest upon authorized securities, and the rest of it had been either improperly invested or had not been kept separate from the trustee's own moneys:—*Held,* that as to so much of the fund as had been invested at 5 per cent. or any other rate upon authorized securities interest must be calculated at the rate actually yielded; that the rest of the fund must be treated as having been in the trustee's hands uninvested, and that under the circumstances he must be charged with interest thereon calculated at 4 per cent. only. *In re* EMMET'S ESTATE. EMMET *v.* EMMET

[17 Ch. D. 142

8. —— **Lapse of Time**—*Waiver*—*Stale Demand.*] A cestui que trust who with knowledge that his trustee has committed a breach of trust obtains from him a part only of that to which he is entitled, does not thereby waive his right to such further relief as he may be able to obtain unless an intention so to do can be clearly inferred from the surrounding circumstances.—In November, 1860, an order was made in a suit for administering the trusts of the will of J. C., to which H. C., a former trustee, was Defendant, directing her to pay into Court a sum of money in respect of breaches of trust committed in 1843 and 1845, the amount of which had been ascertained by the Chief Clerk in the suit. H. C. went abroad, and substituted service of the order was made upon her. By the order on further consideration in 1863, H. C. appearing by counsel, certain sums of money to which she was entitled, and her life interest under the testator's will, were ordered to be impounded and paid over to "the account of H. C. funds applicable for the repayment of trust funds misappropriated," and an inquiry was directed as to what steps should be taken to obtain restitution of the funds. Certain other orders were made in the suit, but no personal order was made on H. C. for payment of the amount of her defalcations, nor any steps taken against her, although she returned to England in 1870, where she remained till her death in 1880, and her residence was known to the then trustees of the will and some of the cestuis que trust. On her death the surviving trustee of the will of J. C. brought this action against her executors, claiming the administration of her real and personal estate on behalf of himself and all other the creditors, alleging himself a creditor in respect of the unpaid balance of the sum representing the breach of trust.—At the date of the institution of the action several beneficiaries under J. C.'s will were infants:—*Held* (reversing the decision of Fry, J.), that the action was not an attempt to enforce a stale demand, and that the cestuis que trust must

IV. TRUSTEE—LIABILITIES—*continued.*

not be taken to have elected to abandon their claim against her and to rest content with impounding her life interest:—That, there being a debt due from H. C. at her death to the estate of J. C. and the trusts of his will not being completed, the surviving trustee was the proper person to bring the action, and that the cestuis que trust need not be parties:—Although as between the cestui que trust and a stranger the claim of the cestui que trust is barred by lapse of time operating against his trustee, lapse of time is no bar as between cestui que trust and trustee. *In re* CROSS. HARSTON *v.* TENISON　-　**20 Ch. D. 109**

9. —— **Leaseholds**—*Tenant for Life and Remainderman*—*Repairs*—*Receiver.*] When leasehold houses are vested in trustees on behalf of a tenant for life and remaindermen, it is the duty of the trustees to keep the property free from the risk of forfeiture by a breach of the covenants of the lease, and they are entitled to have the rents applied in keeping the houses in a proper state of repair.—The trustees are not bound to be content with the setting apart of a sum of money in the joint names of themselves and the tenant for life as an indemnity against the consequences of a breach of the covenants of the lease, but are entitled to require the covenants to be specifically performed.—When a tenant for life of leasehold houses is allowed by the trustees to receive the rents, and the houses are not kept in a proper state of repair according to the covenants of the lease, the Court will, at the instance of one of the trustees, appoint a receiver of the rents, for the purpose of enforcing the proper repair of the houses. *In re* FOWLER. FOWLER *v.* ODELL

[16 Ch. D. 723

10. —— **Second Set of Trustees**—*Persons entitled to possession of the Fund.*] Property was assigned to trustees on trust for S. for life, and after her death to such of her issue as she should by will appoint; the settlor and S. during their joint lives, and the survivor, had a power of appointment of new trustees and discretion as to the investments, and the settlor had a power of revocation, which however he did not exercise. S. by her will appointed to B. and N. the property as trustees for her son. After her death the settlor appointed L. and N. trustees of the settlement, and the property was transferred to them. The son of S. died, and B. died. L. had allowed the property to remain in the hands of N., who had made away with it.—The persons beneficially entitled under the will of the son recovered judgment for the property made away with against the executor of the son on the ground of wilful default. The executor brought an action against L. for the property as having been lost by his wilful default in allowing it to remain in the hands of N.:—*Held,* that S. had power to appoint the property to trustees for her son; that as he took the whole beneficial interest the trustees of the settlement had no duties to perform except to hand the property over to the surviving trustee of the will; that therefore N. was rightfully in possession of the property, and L. was not liable for having allowed it to remain in the hands of N.—*In re* Pocock's *Policy* (Law Rep. 6 Ch. 445), *Ferrier v. Jay* (Law Rep. 10 Eq. 550), and *Busk*

IV. TRUSTEE—LIABILITIES—*continued.*

v. *Aldam* (Law Rep. 19 Eq. 16), observed upon.— *Held*, that as the persons entitled under the will of the son of S. had chosen to proceed and recover against his executor, the executor could recover again from the trustee of the settlement if he had been guilty of wilful default.　Scotney *v.* Lomer
[29 Ch. D. 535
[Affirmed on different grounds by the Court of Appeal, 31 Ch. D. 380.]

V. TRUSTEE—POWERS.

The *Act* 44 & 45 *Vict.* c. 41 (*Conveyancing Act,* 1881) *enacts—*

Sect. 35.—(1.) *Where a trust for sale or a power of sale of property is vested in trustees, they may sell or concur with any other person in selling all or any part of the property, either subject to prior charges or not and either together or in lots, by public auction or by private contract, subject to any such conditions respecting title or evidence of title, or other matter as the trustees think fit, with power to vary any contract for sale, and to buy in at any auction, or to rescind any contract for sale, and to re-sell, without being answerable for any loss.*

(2.) *This section applies only if and as far as a contrary intention is not expressed in the instrument creating the trust or power, and shall have effect subject to the terms of that instrument and to the provisions therein contained.*

(3.) *This section applies to trusts created either before or after the commencement of this Act.*

Sect. 37.—(1.) *An executor may pay or allow any debt or claim on any evidence that he thinks sufficient.*

(2.) *An executor or two or more trustees acting together, or a sole acting trustee where, by the instrument, if any, creating the trust, a sole trustee is authorized to execute the trusts and powers thereof, may, if and as he or they think fit, accept any composition, or any security real or personal for any debt, or for any property, real or personal, claimed, and may allow any time for payment of any debt, and may compromise, compound, abandon, submit to arbitration, or otherwise settle any debt, account, claim, or thing whatever relating to the testator's estate, or to the trust, and for any of those purposes may enter into, give, execute, and do such agreements, instruments of composition or arrangement, releases, and other things, as to him or them seem expedient, without being responsible for any loss occasioned by any act or thing so done by him or them in good faith.*

(3.) *As regards trustees, this section applies only if and as far as a contrary intention is not expressed in the instrument, if any, creating the trust, and shall have effect subject to the terms of that instrument and to the provisions therein contained.*

· (4.) *This section applies to executorships and trusts constituted or created either before or after the commencement of this Act.*

Sect. 38.—(1.) *Where a power or trust is given to or vested in two or more executors or trustees jointly, then, unless the contrary is expressed in the instrument, if any, creating the power or trust, the same may be exercised or performed by the survivor or survivors of them for the time being.*

(2.) *This section applies only to executorships and trusts constituted after or created by instru-*

V. TRUSTEE—POWERS—*continued.*

ments coming into operation after the commencement of the Act—31st Dec. 1881.

1. —— To appoint new Trustees—*Exercise of Power after Decree for Administration of Trusts.*] A decree for the administration of the trusts of a will directed "that some proper person be appointed" a trustee of the will in the place of a deceased trustee.　The power of appointing new trustees was given by the will to the surviving trustee, who was the Defendant.　The Plaintiff took out a summons to have A. B. appointed trustee, and the Defendant a summons to have C. D. appointed.　The summonses were adjourned into Court, and Bacon, V.C., appointed the nominee of the Plaintiff:—*Held*, on appeal, that the decree did not take away from the Defendant the power of appointing new trustees, though after decree he could only exercise it subject to the supervision of the Court; that if he nominated a fit and proper person such person must be appointed, and the Court would not appoint some one else on the ground that such other person was in the opinion of the Court more eligible, and that if he nominated a person whom the Court did not approve the Court would not itself make the choice, but would call on him to make a fresh nomination:—*Held*, therefore, that the appointment of A. B. must be discharged.—*Middleton* v. *Reay* (7 Hare, 106) distinguished.　*In re* Gadd.　Eastwood *v.* Clark
[23 Ch. D. 134

2. —— To appoint new Trustees—*Power to appoint one in place of two*—23 & 24 *Vict.* c. 145, s. 27.] The power of appointing new trustees given by sect. 27 of the Act 23 & 24 Vict. c. 145, authorizes a retiring trustee, one of two originally appointed, to appoint a single trustee in place of himself, the other original trustee having previously disclaimed without acting.　West of England and South Wales District Bank *v.* Murch　　　-　　　23 Ch. D. 138

3. —— To carry on Business — *Advances—Charge of Trustee—Right of Creditor against Trust Funds.*] By a marriage settlement a lunatic asylum was assigned to trustees on trust at the request of the husband and wife to sell and stand possessed of the proceeds of the sale for the benefit of the wife and children; but the trustees were to allow the husband to carry on the business of the asylum without paying any rent, but paying certain premiums and other moneys.　The husband became bankrupt, and thereupon the surviving trustee of the settlement entered into possession of the asylum and carried on the business until the asylum was sold for a large sum of money.　A tradesman had supplied the trustee with goods for the use of the asylum, and brought an action claiming payment out of the trust funds of the settlement :—*Held*, that, whether the trustee would or not have been entitled to be indemnified for moneys advanced by him for the purposes of the asylum, the tradesman had no right to recover his debt out of the trust funds, no special part of the estate having been appropriated for carrying on the asylum.　*Ex parte Garland* (10 Ves. 110) considered.　Strickland *v.* Symons　　　22 Ch. D. 666;
[26 Ch. D. 245
3 F

V. TRUSTEE--POWERS—*continued.*

4. —— **To manage Estate**—*Special Power of leasing Mansion-house—Discretion of Trustees.*] A testator gave to his trustees a special power of leasing at their absolute discretion ; which formed part of a special scheme of management of his mansion-house and estate for a limited period :— *Held,* in a suit for the execution of the trusts of the will that the Court would compel the trustees to exercise the power of leasing. TEMPEST *v.* LORD CAMOYS   - 21 Ch. D. 576, n.

5. —— **To purchase Real Estate**—*Power of mortgaging—Jurisdiction of Court to interfere with Discretion of Trustees.*] Where absolute discretion has been given to trustees as to the exercise of a power the Court will not compel them to exercise it, but if they propose to exercise it, the Court will see that they do not exercise it improperly or unreasonably.—Where the power is coupled with a trust or duty the Court will enforce the proper and timely exercise of the power, but will not interfere with the discretion of the trustees as to the particular time or manner of their bonâ fide exercise of it.—A testator gave his trustees a power to be exercised at their absolute discretion of selling real estates, with a declaration that the proceeds should be applied, at the like discretion, in the purchase of other real estates. He also gave them power at their absolute discretion to raise money by mortgage for the purchase of real estates. A suit having been instituted for the execution of the trusts of the will, and a sum of money, the proceeds of the sale of real estate, having been paid into Court, one of the trustees proposed to purchase a large estate and to apply the fund in Court in part payment of the purchase-money, and to raise the remainder of the purchase-money by mortgage of the purchased estate. The other trustee refused to concur in the purchase :—*Held* (affirming the decree of Chitty, J.), that the Court could not control the dissentient trustee in the exercise of his discretion in refusing to make the purchase, or in refusing to exercise his power of raising money by mortgage for the proposed purpose. TEMPEST *v.* LORD CAMOYS   21 Ch. D. 571

6. —— **To sell Real Estate**—*Power to postpone Sale—Discretion of Trustees.*] Where real estate is devised to trustees in trust for sale, with a discretionary power to postpone the sale, the Court will not interfere with a bonâ fide exercise of their discretion as to the time and mode of sale. *In re* BLAKE.   JONES *v.* BLAKE   29 Ch. D. 913

VI. TRUSTEE—RETIREMENT.

The Act 44 & 45 *Vict. c.* 41 (*Conveyancing Act,* 1881) *enacts*—

Sect. 32.—(1.) *Where there are more than two trustees, if one of them declares that he is desirous of being discharged from the trust, and if his co-trustees and such other person, if any, as is empowered to appoint trustees, by deed consent to the discharge of the trustee, and to the vesting in the co-trustees alone of the trust property, then the trustee desirous of being discharged shall be deemed to have retired from the trust, and shall, by the deed, be discharged therefrom under this Act, without any new trustee being appointed in his place.*

(2.) *Any assurance or thing requisite for vesting*

VI. TRUSTEE—RETIREMENT—*continued.*

the trust property in the continuing trustees alone shall be executed or done.

(3.) *This section applies only if and as far as a contrary intention is not expressed in the instrument, if any, creating the trust, and shall have effect subject to the terms of that instrument and to any provisions therein contained.*

(4.) *This section applies to trusts created either before or after the commencement of this Act.*

Vesting of Trust Property.] *Sect.* 34.—(2.) *Where a deed by which a retiring trustee is discharged under this Act contains such a declaration as is in this section mentioned (see sect. 34. (1)) by the retiring and continuing trustees, and by the other person, if any, empowered to appoint trustees, that declaration shall, without any conveyance or assignment operate, to vest in the continuing trustees alone as joint tenants, and for the purposes of the trust, the estate, interest, or right to which the declaration relates.*

Sub-sects. 3, 4 *and* 5 *apply to the retirement of a trustee as well as to the appointment of a new trustee.*

[*See* TRUSTEE—APPOINTMENT—*Statutes.*]

TRUSTEE—Admission to copyholds—Escheat
[27 Ch. D. 298
See COPYHOLD — SURRENDER — ADMITTANCE. 3.

—— Adopting Conveyancing Act, 1881—Protection of.
See CONVEYANCING ACT, 1881—*Statutes.*

—— Appointment of—Settled Land Act.
See SETTLED LAND ACT—STATUTES.
And Cases under SETTLED LAND ACT—TRUSTEES. 1—4.

—— Appointment of—Trustee Act.
See Cases under TRUSTEE ACTS—NEW TRUSTEES.

—— Bankruptcy—Petitioning creditor—Joining equitable owner of debt 14 Q. B. D. 184
See BANKRUPTCY — BANKRUPTCY PETITION. 6.

—— Bare trustee—Vendor and Purchaser Act
[29 Ch. D. 693
See VENDOR AND PURCHASER—CONVEYANCE. 3.

—— Costs of—Appeal   - 20 Ch. D. 303 ;
[29 Ch. D. 495
See PRACTICE—SUPREME COURT—APPEAL. 25, 26.

—— Costs of—Appeal   -   - 19 Ch. D. 588
See BANKRUPTCY—VOID SETTLEMENT. 1.

—— Costs of—Appeal—Setting aside settlement
[23 Ch. D. 278
See VOLUNTARY CONVEYANCE. 5.

—— Costs of—Solicitor trustee of will
[25 Ch. D. 72 ; 27 Ch. D. 584
See SOLICITOR—BILL OF COSTS. 15, 16.

—— Costs of—Trustee Relief Act 21 Ch. D. 855
See TRUSTEE RELIEF ACT. 2.

—— Creditor's deed — Liability to account — Bankruptcy   14 Q. B. D. 25
See BANKRUPTCY—TRUSTEE. 3.

—— Defaulting—Debtors' Act - 20 Ch. D. 532
See PRACTICE — SUPREME COURT — ATTACHMENT. 1.

TRUSTEE IN BANKRUPTCY—*continued*.
—— Security for costs—Official name
[28 Ch. D. 38
See PRACTICE—SUPREME COURT—SECURITY FOR COSTS. 8.

—— Vesting of property — Pension of retired
Judge　　　　　　　21 Ch. D. 85
See BANKRUPTCY—ASSETS. 13.

TRUSTEE IN LIQUIDATION—Appointment
[24 Ch. D. 353
See BANKRUPTCY—LIQUIDATION. 4.

—— Exercise of power of appointment
[29 Ch. D. 1005
See BANKRUPTCY—TRUSTEE. 11.

—— Removal of　　-　　-　14 Q. B. D. 177
See BANKRUPTCY—TRUSTEE. 8.

—— Shareholder in company　　28 Ch. D. 363
See COMPANY—SHARES—TRANSFER. 5.

TRUSTEE ACTS :—　　　　　　　Col.
　I. NEW TRUSTEES　-　　-　　1607
　II. VESTING ORDERS　-　　-　　1608

I. TRUSTEE ACTS—NEW TRUSTEES.

1. —— Deceased Lunatic—*Appointment of New Trustee after Death of Lunatic—Trustee Extension Act, 1852 (15 & 16 Vict. c. 55), s. 9—Affidavit—Description of Deponent as a " Gentleman."*] The Court sitting in lunacy, has power under the 9th section of the Trustee Extension Act, 1852, to appoint new trustees of the will of a deceased lunatic, where the trustees appointed by the lunatic have died in his lifetime, for the purpose of getting rid of the funds standing in Court to the credit of the lunacy.—It is not sufficient to describe a person making an affidavit of the fitness of a new trustee merely as a "gentleman." *In re* ORDE　　　　　24 Ch. D. 271

2. —— " Incapable to act "—*Personal Incapacity — Appointment of new Trustee — " Expedient "—Trustee Act, 1850, s. 32.*] The Court has jurisdiction, under sect. 32 of the Trustee Act, 1850, to appoint a new trustee in the place of a trustee who has become incapable—as, for instance, through age and infirmity—of acting in the trusts.—A will contained a power for the trustees or the survivors of them to appoint a new trustee in the place of any trustee who should be "incapable to act." One of the surviving trustees, the testator's widow, having become, through age and infirmity, incapable of acting in the trusts, or of concurring in the appointment of a new trustee, or in a transfer of the trust estate :—The Court appointed a new trustee in her place and made a vesting order. *In re* LEMANN'S TRUSTS　　　　22 Ch. D. 633

3. —— No Trustee appointed by Will—*Interpretation Clause—Appointment of Trustee to perform Duties incident to Office of Executor.*] Where a testator had, by his will, left all his property to his wife for life, and appointed her his sole executrix, and had also left legacies of considerable amount to be paid after her death, but had not constituted any persons trustees thereof :—*Held*, upon petition intituled in an administration action commenced for the purpose and in the Trustee Act, 1850, that upon the retirement of the widow the Court had jurisdiction under the Trustee Act,

I. TRUSTEE ACTS—NEW TRUSTEES—*contd*.
1850, to appoint in her place a trustee or trustees to perform the duties incident to the office of an executor. *In re* MOORE. MCALPINE *v.* MOORE
[21 Ch. D. 778

4. —— Reappointment of existing Trustees *in the place of existing Trustees and a Lunatic Trustee—Trustee Act, 1850, s. 32.*] Where one of several trustees is of unsound mind, the Court will not reappoint the other trustees as trustees in the place of themselves and the lunatic trustee, for the purpose of excluding the lunatic trustee from the trust; but a new trustee must be appointed in his place.—*In re Harford's Trusts* (13 Ch. D. 135) not followed. *In re* ASTON
[23 Ch. D. 217

5. —— Re-appointment of existing Trustees *as sole Trustees in place of themselves and a bankrupt and absconding Trustee—Trustee Act, 1850(13 & 14 Vict. c. 60, ss. 32, 34.*] It is the settled practice of the Court under the Trustee Acts, when there is a continuing trust, not simply to remove or discharge a trustee, without appointing a new trustee in his place, by appointing the remaining trustees to be sole trustees in place of themselves and him. And, though the Court will deviate from this rule and make such an appointment if the trustees have no duty to perform but to distribute a fund which is immediately divisible, it will adhere to the ordinary rule if there is a continuing trust as regards even a relatively small part of the trust fund. *In re* LAMB'S TRUSTS　　-　　28 Ch. D. 77

6. —— Separate Trustees of distinct Part of Trust Property—*Conveyancing Act, 1882 (45 & 46 Vict. c. 39), s. 5.*] Appointment made of new trustees to act in conjunction with a sole continuing trustee of a will in relation to a distinct part of the trust property. *In re* PAINE'S TRUSTS
[28 Ch. D. 725

II. TRUSTEE ACTS—VESTING ORDERS.

1. —— Amending Order — Death of Sole Trustee intestate—*Vesting Order—Conveyancing and Law of Property Act, 1881, s. 30.*] Upon the death of a sole surviving trustee intestate, the Court made an order for the appointment of new trustees, and ordered certain lands forming part of the estate to vest in the new trustees " for the estate therein now vested in the heir-at-law of the deceased trustee." After the order had been passed and entered administration was taken out to the estate of the deceased trustee. Upon motion that the order of the Court might be altered by substituting the legal personal representative for the heir-at-law of the intestate trustee in accordance with sect. 30 of the Conveyancing and Law of Property Act, 1881, the Court made a new order, that notwithstanding the previous order, the land should vest in the new trustees " for all the estate therein now vested in the legal personal representative" of the deceased trustee. *In re* PILLING'S TRUSTS
[26 Ch. D. 432

2. —— Chambers, Business in—*Appointment of new Trustees—Petition—Vesting Order in Chambers—Transfer of Stock — Jurisdiction — Trustee Act, 1850, ss. 2, 32, 35, 40—Trustee Extension Act, 1852, s. 6—Master in Chancery Abolition Act, 1852 (15 & 16 Vict. c. 80), ss. 11, 26, 27—Despatch*

II. TRUSTEE ACTS—VESTING ORDERS—*contd.*
of Business Act, 1855 (18 & 19 *Vict.* o. 134), s. 16—
Cons. Ord. XXXV., r. 1—*Judicature Act*, 1873, s. 16
—*Rules of Supreme Court*, 1883, *Order LV.*, r. 2
(8), (18)—*Statute Law Revision and Civil Procedure Act*, 1883, s. 5.] On a petition for the
appointment of new trustees and a vesting order,
an order was made in Court on the 28th of June,
1884, that two or more proper persons should be
appointed trustees, and that an inquiry should be
made of what the trust funds consisted : and the
parties were to be at liberty to apply in Chambers
for an order to vest the trust property in the new
trustees when appointed. On the 22nd of July,
before any certificate as to the trust funds had
been made, an order was made in Chambers
appointing new trustees, and directing that the
right to call for a transfer of, and to transfer into
their own names, certain sums of stock specified
in the order "may" vest in the new trustees.
This order mentioned, but did not recite, the order
of the 28th of June. The Bank of England refused to act on it, and Bacon, V.C., on the 28th
of November, made an order directing them to do
so. The bank appealed :—*Held*, that, the matter
having been properly brought before the Court on
petition, the Judge had power under the provisions of the Masters Abolition Act, 1852 (15 & 16
Vict. c. 80), to dispose in Chambers of such parts
of the matters brought before him on the petition
as he thought could be more conveniently disposed
of in Chambers than in Court, and that there was
therefore jurisdiction to make the order of the
22nd of July.—*Frodsham v. Frodsham* (15 Ch. D.
317) distinguished.—But *held*, that the order was
so irregular in form that the bank were justified
in declining to act upon it, they being entitled to
require a vesting order to be in such a form as to
shew that the statutory requirements have been
satisfied.—Statement of the recitals which ought
to be contained in a vesting order made in
Chambers under the Trustee Act. *In re* TWEEDY
[28 Ch. D. 529

3. —— Coparceners—"*Seised jointly*"—*Trustee Act*, 1850 (13 & 14 *Vict.* c. 60), s. 10.]
The words "seised jointly" in sect. 10 of the
Trustee Act, 1850, are not limited strictly to a
legal joint tenancy, but are used in the widest
sense, and they include the case of land vested
in coparceners, one of whom is out of the jurisdiction of the Court.—*In re Templer's Trusts* (4
N. R. 494) and *McMurray* v. *Spicer* (Law Rep.
5 Eq. 527) considered. *In re* GREENWOOD's
TRUSTS   -   27 Ch. D. 359

4. —— Copyholds—*Dying without an Heir—
Petition by Person absolutely entitled — Trustee
Act*, 1850 (13 & 14 *Vict.* c. 60), ss. 15, 28.] The
sole trustee of copyholds held in trust for A. B.
absolutely having died intestate and without an
heir, A. B. presented a petition under the Trustee
Act, 1850, asking that the property might be
vested in himself :—*Held*, that the Court had
jurisdiction to make the order under the combined operation of sects. 15 and 28 of the Act.
In re GODFREY'S TRUSTS   23 Ch. D. 205

5. —— Infant—*Stock in Name of Infant and
another to which Infant was entitled—Trustee Extension Act*, 1852 (15 & 16 *Vict.* c. 55), s. 3.]
Where stock to which an infant was beneficially

II. TRUSTEE ACTS—VESTING ORDERS—*contd.*
entitled had been invested in the joint names of
himself and another person : — *Held*, that the
Court had jurisdiction under the 3rd section of
the Trustee Extension Act, 1852, to make an
order vesting in such other person the right to
transfer such stock. *In re* HARWOOD
[20 Ch. D. 536

6. —— Lunatic Trustee—13 & 14 *Vict.* c. 60,
s. 3.] A trustee of property held in trust for
A. B. absolutely having become lunatic, A. B.
presented a petition asking that the property
might be vested in himself :—*Held*, that such
an order ought not to be made, but that a new
trustee ought to be appointed and the property
vested in him. *In re* HOLLAND. *In re* HOWARTH's
TRUSTS   16 Ch. D. 672

7. —— Lunatic Trustee—13 & 14 *Vict.* c. 60,
s. 5.] When one of several trustees of stock
becomes lunatic or of unsound mind, the Court,
although it may have jurisdiction under sect. 5 of
the Trustee Act, 1850, to make an order vesting
the right to transfer the stock solely in the co-trustees, will not do so, but a new trustee in the
place of the lunatic must be appointed before a
vesting order will be made. *In re* NASH
[16 Ch. D. 503

8. —— Lunatic Trustee—*Trustee Act*, 1850,
s. 5—*Order vesting Right to Stock in the other
Trustees.*] One of three trustees of a sum of
stock had been found lunatic. The fund having
become divisible, a petition intituled both in
Lunacy and in Chancery was presented for the
appointment of a new trustee and a vesting
order : — *Held*, that the appointment of a new
trustee was unnecessary, and that the petition
ought to be intituled in Lunacy only. Order
made vesting the right to call for a transfer of
and to transfer the stock in the two trustees who
were not under disability.—*In re Nash* (16 Ch. D.
503) not followed. *In re* WATSON   19 Ch. D. 384

9. —— Lunatic Trustee—*Order vesting Right
to deal with the Trust Fund in the Trustees of
Sound Mind.*] Although, where one of the
trustees of a trust fund becomes lunatic, the Court
will not in general vest the right to deal with
the trust funds in the trustees of sound mind,
but will require a new trustee to be appointed in
the place of the lunatic, an order vesting the
right to the fund in the trustees of sound mind
will be made where the fund is immediately
divisible. *In re* MARTYN, A LUNATIC. *In re*
TOUTT'S WILL   -   26 Ch. D. 745

10. —— Partition Action—*Sale—Parties not
under Disability—Appointing Person to convey—
Partition Acts*, 1868 and 1876—*Trustee Extension
Act*, 1852 (15 & 16 *Vict.* c. 55), s. 1.] Sect. 1 of
the Trustee Extension Act, 1852 (15 & 16 Vict.
c. 55), applies to sales under the Partition Acts,
1868 and 1876, and is not limited to cases of
persons under disability. BECKETT v. SUTTON
[19 Ch. D. 648

11. —— Stock standing in the Name of Testator — *One of several Executors a Lunatic—
Trustee Act*, 1850, s. 5.] Where one of three executors of the surviving executor of a testator was
of unsound mind an order was made under the
5th section of the Trustee Act, 1850, giving the

II. TRUSTEE ACTS—VESTING ORDERS—*contd.*

right to transfer a sum of stock belonging to the estate of the original testator, although the stock still remained standing in the name of the original testator. *In re* WACHER   22 Ch. D. 535

12. —— Trustees of Stock refusing to transfer —"*Sole*" *Trustee—Trustee Act*, 1850, *ss.* 2, 23.] Having regard to the interpretation clause (sect. 2) of the Trustee Act, 1850, the expression "sole trustee" in the Act includes all trustees who are jointly entitled. Consequently, where two trustees of stock refused to transfer it to two new trustees duly appointed under a power:—*Held*, that the Court had jurisdiction under the 23rd section to make an order vesting the stock in the new trustees. *In re* HYATT'S TRUSTS   21 Ch. D. 846

TRUSTEE ACTS—Costs   26 Ch. D. 82
See TRUSTEE—COSTS AND CHARGES. 8.

TRUSTEE RELIEF ACT.

1. —— Adjournment into Chambers—*Payment out of Court—Jurisdiction—Trustee Relief Act,* 1847 (10 & 11 *Vict. c.* 96), *s.* 2—*Masters Abolition Act,* 1852 (15 & 16 *Vict. c.* 80), *ss.* 26, 27—*Despatch of Business Act,* 1855 (18 & 19 *Vict. c.* 134), *s.* 16—*Cons. Ord. XXXV., r.* 1.] A trust fund having been paid into Court under the Trustee Relief Act by the trustee of a will, a petition was presented by parties interested for an inquiry as to the persons entitled and for payment out to the persons found entitled under that inquiry. Upon the petition coming on for hearing an order was made directing the inquiry, and adjourning the further hearing of the petition into Chambers:—*Held*, that the proceeding having been properly commenced by petition under sect. 2 of the Trustee Relief Act, the Court had jurisdiction, under sect. 27 of the Masters Abolition Act, 1852 (15 & 16 Vict. c. 80), to adjourn the petition into Chambers.—*Frodsham* v. *Frodsham* (15 Ch. D. 317) distinguished. *In re* MOATE'S TRUST   - 22 Ch. D. 635

2. —— Costs of Trustee — *Payment out of Court*—10 & 11 *Vict. c.* 96—*Tender of 42s.*—*Costs of Appearance—Rules of Court,* 1875 (*Costs*), *Sched. r.* 17.] Trustees who are Respondents to a petition under the Trustee Relief Act for payment of a fund out of Court, and have been tendered and have accepted 42s. for their costs under Rules of Court, 1875 (Costs) Sched. rule 17, are not, as a general rule, entitled to their costs of appearance on the petition. *In re* SUTTON   [21 Ch. D. 855

3. —— Lunacy — *Payment out of Court —Jurisdiction.*] Where a person who has been found lunatic is entitled to a fund which has been paid into Court under the Trustee Relief Act, a

TRUSTEE RELIEF ACT—*continued.*

petition may be presented in Chancery under the Trustee Relief Act and in Lunacy, and the Court has jurisdiction to make an immediate order for the transfer of the fund to the account of the lunatic. *In re* TATE   - 20 Ch. D. 135

4. —— Petition for advice of Court—*Costs of Protecting Estate—Costs of Tenant for Life permitted to be paid out of Proceeds of Sale of Part of the Estate—Trustee Relief Act* (22 & 23 *Vict. c.* 35), *s.* 30.] Where proceedings have been instituted (though without the preliminary sanction of the Court), whether by claim in an action, or by defence to an action, for the protection of a settled estate, the Court will, if it sees fit, give permission to the trustees to apply the proceeds of the sale of a portion of the estate in defraying the costs already incurred, and which must necessarily be incurred, by the tenant for life, in instituting such proceedings. *Ex parte* EARL DE LA WARR'S ESTATE   - 18 Ch. D. 587

5. —— Petition for advice of Court—*Costs of protecting Estate—Trustees*—22 & 23 *Vict. c.* 35, *s.* 30.] On a petition presented by trustees of settled estate for the advice of the Court, the Court permitted them to apply certain funds not exceeding £3000 in payment of the costs of litigation for the protection of the estate. *In re* LORD RIVERS' ESTATE   - 16 Ch. D. 588, n.

TUNIS—Order in Council
See JURISDICTION—*Gazette.*

TURNPIKE ACTS.

The Act 45 & 46 *Vict. c.* 52, *s.* 8, *continues the liability of any individual or corporation to repair, &c., a turnpike road, notwithstanding the expiration of the trust, where such liability was created by any contract or obligation not expressly made determinable on the happening of that event.*

The Act 4 & 5 *Vict. c.* 59, *which makes highway rates applicable in certain cases to the repair of turnpike roads, is continued by the Act 48 & 49 Vict. c. 59, until the 31st of December,* 1886.

The 48 & 49 *Vict. c.* 37 (*the Annual Turnpike Acts Continuance Act,* 1885), *continues certain Turnpike Acts, and repeals others.*

TURNPIKE BONDS—Real security 30 Ch. D. 227
See WILL—WORDS. 17.

TURNPIKE DEBENTURES — Law of Upper Canada   - 7 App. Cas. 473
See COLONIAL LAW—CANADA—QUEBEC. 10.

TURNPIKE ROAD — Repair of—Disturnpiked road.
See Cases under HIGHWAY—REPAIR. 1—7.

U.

ULTRA VIRES ACT—Acquiescence 26 Ch. D. 107
　　See COMPANY—MEMORANDUM AND ARTI-
　　CLES. 3.

—— Alteration of memorandum of association
　　　　　　　　　　[30 Ch. D. 376
　　See COMPANY—MEMORANDUM AND ARTI-
　　CLES. 1.

—— Application of funds of company
　　　　　　　　　　[24 Ch. D. 611
　　See COMPANY—DIRECTOR'S AUTHORITY.
　　1.

—— Building society—Bond of corroboration
　　　　　　　　　　[10 App. Cas. 119
　　See SCOTCH LAW—BUILDING SOCIETY.

—— Building society—Borrowing powers.
　　See Cases under BUILDING SOCIETY. 5—
　　10.

—— Call—Forfeiture　-　　-　16 Ch. D. 681
　　See COMPANY—DIRECTOR'S AUTHORITY.
　　3.

—— Canadian law—Powers of provincial Legis-
　　lature -　　　　　10 App. Cas. 141
　　See COLONIAL LAW—CANADA—QUEBEC.
　　4.

—— Conveyance of superfluous lands
　　　　　　　　　[20 Ch. D. 418, 562
　　See LANDS CLAUSES ACT—SUPERFLUOUS
　　LANDS. 1, 2.

—— Corporation　　　-　10 App. Cas. 354
　　See CORPORATION. 2.

—— Issue of shares at a discount—Reduction of
　　capital　-　.　　　23 Ch. D. 545, n.
　　See COMPANY—SHARES—ISSUE. 1.

—— Local board -　　-　-　27 Ch. D. 665
　　See LOCAL GOVERNMENT — LOCAL AU-
　　THORITY. 14.

—— Mortgage by directors　　17 Ch. D. 715
　　See COMPANY—DIRECTOR'S AUTHORITY.
　　2.

—— Public injury　-　　-　21 Ch. D. 752
　　See PRACTICE — SUPREME COURT — IN-
　　JUNCTION. 1.

—— Purchase of shares by company 17 Ch. D. 76
　　See COMPANY—REDUCTION OF CAPITAL. 1.

—— Sale and hire of rolling stock 21 Ch. D. 309
　　See RAILWAY COMPANY—CONSTITUTION.

UMPIRE—Appointment of.
　　See LANDS CLAUSES ACT—*Statutes.*

UNCERTAINTY—Limitation of heirlooms
　　See WILL—HEIRLOOM 4. [23 Ch. D. 158

—— Will—Gift over of such part of legacy as had
　　not been paid　　　　16 Ch. D. 218
　　See WILL—DEATH COUPLED WITH CON-
　　TINGENCY. 2.

UNCLAIMED DIVIDENDS.
　　See BANKRUPTCY—STATUTES.

UNDERGROUND WATER—Pollution
　　See WATER. 3.·　　　[29 Ch. D. 115

UNDERLEASE—Administrator—Power to grant
　　　　　　　　　　[16 Ch. D. 236
　　See ADMINISTRATOR—POWERS. 1.

—— Covenants of lease　　30 Ch. D. 404
　　See LANDLORD AND TENANT—LEASE. 3.

UNDERTAKING—As to damages 21 Ch. D. 421;
　　　　　　　　　　[27 Ch. D. 474
　　See PRACTICE — SUPREME COURT — IN-
　　JUNCTION. 8, 9.

—— As to damages—Receiver in bankruptcy
　　　　　　　　　　[23 Ch. D. 644
　　See BANKRUPTCY—RECEIVER. 1.

—— As to user of trade-mark　28 Ch. D. 666
　　See TRADE-MARK—REGISTRATION. 9.

UNDERTAKING OF COMPANY—Railway com-
　　pany—Receiver -　　-　18 Ch. D. 155
　　See RAILWAY COMPANY—ABANDONMENT.
　　1.

UNDERPINNING BUILDINGS　·　29 Ch. D. 60
　　See RAILWAY COMPANY—LIABILITIES. 3.

UNDERVALUE—Sale by mortgagee
　　　　　　　　　　[20 Ch. D. 220
　　See MORTGAGE—POWERS. 5.

UNDERWOOD—Waste of manor—Right of tenants
　　See INCLOSURE. 3.　　[20 Ch. D. 380

UNDERWRITER—Total loss—Sale of wreck
　　See SHIP—MASTER. 1. [16 Ch. D. 474

UNDISCHARGED BANKRUPT.
　　See Cases under BANKRUPTCY—UNDIS-
　　CHARGED BANKRUPT.

UNDISCLOSED PRINCIPAL　29 Ch. D. 795;
　　　　　　　　　　[13 Q. B. D. 635
　　See PRINCIPAL AND AGENT — AGENT'S
　　LIABILITY. 1, 6.

————　-　9 Q. B. D. 530; 3 App. Cas. 874
　　See PRINCIPAL AND AGENT—PRINCIPAL'S
　　LIABILITY. 6.

UNDUE INFLUENCE.

———— Father and Child—*Deed executed by
Child in favour of Father—Onus Probandi—Purchaser for Value without Notice.*] When a deed·
conferring a benefit on a father is executed by a
child who is not emancipated from the father's
control, if the deed is subsequently impeached by
the child, the onus is on the father to shew that
the child had independent advice, and that he
executed the deed with full knowledge of its contents, and with a free intention of giving the
father the benefit conferred by it. If this onus be
not discharged the deed will be set aside.—This
onus extends to a volunteer claiming through the
father, and to any person taking with notice of
the circumstances which raise the equity, but not
further.—If a solicitor purports to act in the
transaction on behalf of the child, a purchaser for
value is entitled to assume that he has given the
child proper advice even though he be also acting
as the father's solicitor.—There is no absolute
rule that in such a transaction the father and the

UNDUE INFLUENCE—*continued.*
child must be advised by different solicitors.
BAINBRIGGE *v.* BROWNE　　　-　　18 Ch. D. 188
—— Gift by infant　　　-　　19 Ch. D. 603
　　See INFANT—ACTS.

UNFINISHED ARTICLE—Sale of—Scotch law
　　　　　　　　　　[6 App. Cas. 588
　　See SCOTCH LAW—SALE OF GOODS. 2.

UNITY OF PERSON—Gift to husband and wife
　　　　　　　　　　[27 Ch. D. 166
　　See WILL—JOINT TENANCY.

UNITY OF POSSESSION—Prescription
　　See WATERCOURSE. 5.　　[17 Ch. D. 391
—— Right of way—" Occupied and enjoyed "
　　See WAY. 2.　　　　　[26 Ch. D. 434

UNLIQUIDATED DAMAGES — Proof in bankruptcy　　　　　　　17 Ch. D. 122
　　See BANKRUPTCY—PROOF. 22.

"UNMARRIED"—Construction of will 16 Ch. D.
　　　　　　　　　[715; 26 Ch. D. 575
　　See WILL—WORDS. 18, 19.
—— " Sole and unmarried "　　-　　24 Ch. D. 703
　　See WILL—SEPARATE USE. 1

UNQUALIFIED PERSON—Acting as solicitor—
Penalty.
　　See Cases under SOLICITOR—UNQUALI-
FIED.
—— Medical practitioner　　29 Ch. D. 596
　　See MEDICAL PRACTITIONER.

UNREGISTERED BILL OF SALE　16 Ch. D. 668
　　See BILL OF SALE—APPARENT POSSES-
SION. 2.

—————
　　See Cases under BILL OF SALE—REGIS-
TRATION.
—— Administration of estate of deceased person
　　　　　　　　　　[20 Ch. D. 217
　　See EXECUTOR—ACTIONS. 17.

UNREGISTERED COMPANY.
　　See Cases under COMPANY — UNREGIS-
TERED COMPANY.

UNREGISTERED DEED—South Australia
　　　　　　　　　　[8 App. Cas. 314
　　See COLONIAL LAW—SOUTH AUSTRALIA.

UNREGISTERED WILL—Middlesex registry
　　　　　　　　　　[20 Ch. D. 611
　　See VENDOR AND PURCHASER—PURCHASE
WITHOUT NOTICE. 1.

UNSOUND MIND.
　　See Cases under LUNATIC.
—— Person of—Power of Court to elect for
　　　　　　　　　　[22 Ch. D. 263
　　See SETTLEMENT—FUTURE PROPERTY. 3.
—— Person of—Trustee Act—Appointment of
new trustee 23 Ch. D. 217; 24 Ch. D. 271
　　See TRUSTEE ACTS — NEW TRUSTEES.
1, 4.
—— Person of—Trustee—Vesting order.
　　See Cases under TRUSTEE ACTS—VEST-
ING ORDERS. 6—9, 11.

UNSTAMPED DEED—Re-conveyance — Compulsory purchase　　-　　-　24 Ch. D. 119
　　See REVENUE—STAMPS. 5.

URBAN AUTHORITY—By-law　21 Ch. D. 621;
　　　　　　　　　　[8 App. Cas. 798
　　See LOCAL GOVERNMENT—STREETS. 4.
—— Contract with.
　　See Cases under LOCAL GOVERNMENT—
LOCAL AUTHORITY. 1—8.

URINAL—Nuisance　　　16 Ch. D. 449
　　See METROPOLIS — MANAGEMENT ACTS.
6.

USAGE—Bought and sold notes — Liability of
brokers—Admissibility of evidence
　　　　　　　　　　[13 Q. B. D. 635
　　See PRINCIPAL AND AGENT — AGENT'S
LIABILITY. 6.
—— Harbour dues　　　-　　8 App. Cas. 658
　　See SCOTCH LAW—HARBOUR. 2.
—— Presumption of lost grant　14 Q. B. D. 245
　　See MARKET. 2.
—— Stock Exchange — Principal and agent —
Shares in banking company
　　[14 Q. B. D. 460; 15 Q. B. D. 388
　　See PRINCIPAL AND AGENT—PRINCIPAL'S
LIABILITY. 4, 5.
—— Trade—Hiring furniture　　18 Ch. D. 30;
　　　　　　　　　　[23 Ch. D. 261
　　See BANKRUPTCY—ORDER AND DISPOSI-
TION. 4, 5.
—— Trade—Implied contract between manufac-
turer and customer　-　7 Q. B. D. 438
　　See SALE OF GOODS—CONTRACT. 1.

USE AND OCCUPATION—Lease by tenant in
common to co-tenant—Holding over
　　　　　　　　　　[15 Q. B. D. 60
　　See TENANT IN COMMON.
—— Mortgagee in possession　　21 Ch. D. 469
　　See MORTGAGE—MORTGAGEE IN POSSES-
SION. 5.

USER—Fishery 7 Q. B. D. 106; 7 App. Cas. 633;
　　See FISHERY. 1, 3.　　[8 App. Cas. 135
—— Patent　-　17 Ch. D. 721; 26 Ch. D. 766;
　　　　　　[29 Ch. D. 164; 8 App. Cas. 5
　　See PATENT—INFRINGEMENT. 6, 7, 8.
—— Trade-mark　　　　24 Ch. D. 231
　　See TRADE-MARK—INFRINGEMENT. 2.
—— Trade-mark—Length of time 27 Ch. D. 570
　　See TRADE-MARK—REGISTRATION. 7.
—— Trade-mark—Limitation of—Registration of
trade-mark 21 Ch. D. 223; 26 Ch. D. 187;
　　　　　　[28 Ch. D. 666; 30 Ch. D. 454
　　See TRADE-MARK—REGISTRATION. 8—11.
—— Trade name　　　　22 Ch. D. 660
　　See TRADE NAME. 2.

UTILITY—Patent -　　-　-　29 Ch. D. 366
　　See PATENT—VALIDITY. 5.

V.

VACANT LAND—General line of buildings
[27 Ch. D. 362
 See METROPOLIS—MANAGEMENT ACTS. 3.

VACATING REGISTRATION—Composition
[20 Ch. D. 438
 See BANKRUPTCY—COMPOSITION. 8.

—— Trade-mark.
 See Cases under TRADE-MARK—REGISTRATION. 1—4.

VAGRANT ACTS.

1. —— **Frequenting a Public Thoroughfare**—*Intent to commit a Felony*—*Vagrant Act* (5 Geo. 4, c. 83), s. 4.] A man who *frequents* a public street, having in his mind the intent to commit a felony when and wheresoever opportunity arises, is liable to the penalties of the Vagrant Act, 5 Geo. 4, c. 83, s. 4, even though no opportunity should arise, and may be committed as a rogue and vagabond, if the justices are satisfied on sufficient evidence, first, that he frequented the street, and secondly, that he did so with intent to commit a felony. The overt act, or the attempt to carry out the intent, is not an essential part of the offence against the Act.—The Appellant was found and apprehended by two constables at about two o'clock in the morning in a public thoroughfare called Victoria Road, having in his possession a portion of a brass pump which appeared to have been wrenched off from the continuation-pipe. Being stopped and questioned as to how he became possessed of it and whither he was taking it, he gave an account which proved to be false, and also a false name and address. Being charged before two justices on suspicion of having stolen the pump, and the proof failing, he was then charged under 5 Geo. 4, c. 83, s. 4, with frequenting the street in question with intent to commit a felony ; and on proof that he was an associate of thieves, and had four years before been convicted and sentenced to imprisonment for felony, —although there was no proof that he had ever before been seen in the street in question, or that the pump had been stolen, he was convicted as a rogue and vagabond under the 4th section of the Vagrant Act, for "frequenting the public thoroughfare with intent to commit a felony," and sentenced to be imprisoned :—*Held*, that the evidence did not warrant the conviction, inasmuch as it did not shew a frequenting of Victoria Road with intent to commit a felony. CLARK *v.* THE QUEEN
[14 Q. B. D. 92

2. —— **Gaming** — *Vagrant Act Amendment Act, 1873 (36 & 37 Vict. c. 38), s. 3*—" *Open and public Place to which the Public have or are permitted to have Access*"—*Railway Carriage.*] The Vagrant Act Amendment Act, 1873 (36 & 37 Vict. c. 38), s. 3, imposes a penalty upon "every person playing or betting by way of wagering or gaming in any street, road, highway, or other open and public place, or in any open place to which the public have or are permitted to have access at or with any coin, card, &c., used as an instrument or

VAGRANT ACTS—*continued.*
means of such wagering or gaming, at any game or pretended game of chance ":—*Held*, that a railway carriage while travelling on its journey is within the definition of "an open and public place to which the public have or are permitted to have access" in the section. LANGRISH *v.* ARCHER - 10 Q. B. D. 44

3. —— **Wandering abroad to beg**—*Vagrant Act (5 Geo. 4, c. 83), s. 3*—*Idle and disorderly Persons — Colliers "on strike."*] Colliers "on strike" who were householders in a colliery district, and had wives and families, went from house to house in a street of a town four miles distant with a waggon inscribed "Children's Bread Waggon," and begged for assistance in money or kind. They were not disorderly. Having been convicted under the Vagrant Act (5 Geo. 4, c. 83), s. 3, which enacts that every person wandering abroad in any public highway to beg or gather alms shall be deemed an idle and disorderly person :—*Held*, that, as it was not their habit and mode of life to wander abroad and beg, they were not within the meaning of the Act, and the conviction was wrong. POINTON *v.* HILL
[12 Q. B. D. 306

VALIDITY—Contract.
 See Cases under CONTRACT—VALIDITY.

—— Covenant—Restraint of marriage
[23 Ch. D. 285
 See COVENANT—VALIDITY.

—— Patent.
 See Cases under PATENT—VALIDITY.

—— Trade-mark.
 See Cases under TRADE-MARK · REGISTRATION.

VALUATION—Crops—Incoming tenant
[22 Ch. D. 769
 See LANDLORD AND TENANT—LEASE. 15.

—— Landlord and tenant—Agreement to appoint valuers—Rule of Court 15 Q. B. D. 426
 See ARBITRATION—SUBMISSION. 4.

—— Lands Clauses Act—Appointment of trustee as valuer - - 18 Ch. D. 429
 See LANDS CLAUSES ACT—COMPULSORY POWERS. 8.

—— Security—Bankruptcy 25 Ch. D. 716
 See BANKRUPTCY—MUTUAL DEALINGS. 4.

—— Security—Bankruptcy 19 Ch. D. 394;
[20 Ch. D. 289 ; 14 Q. B. D. 121
 See BANKRUPTCY — SECURED CREDITOR. 3, 5, 12.

—— Security—Liability of trustees
[23 Ch. D. 483 ; 28 Ch. D. 268
 See TRUSTEE—LIABILITIES. 3, 4.

VALUATION LIST.
 See METROPOLIS — VALUATION ACTS — *Statutes.*

—— Alterations - - 18 Q. B. D. 364
 See METROPOLIS—VALUATION ACTS.

VALUATION LIST—*continued.*

—— Assessment committee—Failure to obtain relief　-　**15 Q. B. D. 451**
See POOR-RATE—PROCEDURE. 2.

—— Metropolis—Discretion of overseers
[14 Q. B. D. 351
See POOR-RATE—PROCEDURE. 1.

—— Power to amend omission to give notice of meeting of assessment committee
[14 Q. B. D. 83
See POOR-RATE—PROCEDURE. 3.

VALUED POLICY 6 Q. B. D. 633 ; 7 App. Cas. 333
See INSURANCE, MARINE—SALVAGE.

VARIANCE—Articles and memorandum
[22 Ch. D. 349
See COMPANY—MEMORANDUM AND AR-TICLES. 2.

—— Complete and provisional specifications
[21 Ch. D. 720
See PATENT—VALIDITY. 2.

VARYING MINUTES—Motion for　**20 Ch. D. 130 ;
[21 Ch. D. 621**
See PRACTICE—SUPREME COURT—JUDG-MENT. 6,.7.

VASSAL—Defaulting　-　**10 App. Cas. 553**
See SCOTCH LAW — HERITABLE PRO-PERTY. 5.

VENDOR AND PURCHASER :—　　Col.

I. VENDOR AND PURCHASER—AGREEMENT.

1. —— Reservation—*Absolute Conveyance.*] In June, 1870, an·agreement was entered into by a railway company for the purchase, at a price named, of land for the purpose of carrying a road over the line at an incline, and the agreement contained a proviso that the vendor, &c., should have a right of access to other lands belonging to him by and over any of the slopes which the company might arrange on their intended works, and through, over and upon any occupation roads which they might from adjacent to the said lands. This agreement was executed by the secretary of the company, but was not under seal.—Possession was taken by the company, and a bridge was constructed over the line which was reached by a road carried over the land purchased at a steep incline. In April, 1871, the land, with all ways, rights of pre-emption, and other rights, members, easements, and appurtenances, was, in considera-tion of the price named in the agreement, which was stated to include the value of the mines and also all right of pre-emption and compensation for damage sustained by vendor in the execution of the works, conveyed to the company, without

I. VENDOR AND PURCHASER—AGREEMENT
—*continued.*
reserving any right of access to the vendor or in any way referring to the proviso contained in the agreement of June, 1870 :—*Held*, in an action by the vendor to restrain the company from obstruc-ting, by fences and retaining walls rendered ne-cessary by a widening of the road, the right of access stipulated for by the proviso in the pre-liminary agreement, but not claiming a rectifica-tion of the subsequent conveyance, that as the vendor by the terms of the conveyance had abso-lutely conveyed to the company every interest which he possessed in the land, any right of access previously stipulated for was thereby absolutely extinguished. TREBAY *v.* MANCHESTER, SHEF-FIELD, AND LINCOLNSHIRE RAILWAY COMPANY
[24 Ch. D. 572

2. —— Statute of Frauds—*Description of Pro-perty.*] A house and premises were put up for sale by auction under conditions of sale which did not contain any description of what was sold, but were so expressed that it could be inferred from them that the subject of sale was real estate. A. Shardlow became the purchaser. After the sale, the auctioneer signed and gave to him the following memorandum at the foot of the con-ditions : "The property duly sold to A. Shardlow, Butcher, Pinxton, and deposit paid at close of sale," and at the same time signed and gave to him the following receipt : "Pinxton, March 29, 1880. Received of Mr. A Shardlow the sum of £21 as deposit on property purchased at £420 at Sun Inn, Pinxton, on the above date. Mr. G. Cotterell, owner :"—*Held*, reversing the decision of Kay, J., that the receipt, memorandum, and conditions contained a sufficiently definite de-scription of the property sold to enable the Court to receive parol evidence of what the property consisted, and that the Statute of Frauds was no defence to an action by the purchaser for specific performance.—*Held*, by Jessel, M.R., and Bag-gallay, L.J., that the receipt alone without the memorandum and conditions was a memorandum sufficient to satisfy the requirement of the statute. SHARDLOW *v.* COTTERELL　　**18 Ch. D. 280 ;
[20 Ch. D. 90**

3. —— Statute of Frauds—*Two Documents referring to same parol Contract of Sale—Suffi-cient Memorandum—Specific Performance.*] Two or more documents which do not refer to each other, but do refer to the same parol contract, and which, when taken together, contain all the terms of the parol contract, may together constitute a sufficient memorandum within the Statute of Frauds.—On the 22nd of September, 1882, the Defendant verbally agreed with the Plaintiff to sell her share in certain property for £200, and signed and gave to him the following receipt : "Sept. 22nd, 1882. Received of J. Studds one pound of my share in the Barrett's Grove property the sum of two hundred pounds." No time was fixed for completion, and no abstract was delivered, and on the 19th of March, 1883, the Defendant wrote to Plaintiff : "Mr. Studds,—Sir,—If the balance of £199 on account of the purchase of my share of the property be not paid on or before the 22nd instant I shall consider the agreement (made 22nd of September, 1882) not

I. VENDOR AND PURCHASER—AGREEMENT
—continued.

any longer binding" : — *Held,* that the word "balance" in the letter sufficiently referred to the receipt to enable the two documents to be read together, and that they constituted a sufficient memorandum within the Statute of Frauds, sect. 4:—*Held,* also, that even if the word "balance" was not sufficient to connect the two documents, yet that as they both referred to the same parol contract, all the terms of which were contained in one or other of them, they could be read together, and together constituted a good memorandum within the statute. STUDDS *v.* WATSON - - - 28 Ch. D. 305

II. VENDOR AND PURCHASER — COMPENSATION.

1. —— Claim after Completion—*False Representation, Action for, Moral Fraud essential to—Sale of Land—Compensation for Misdescription.*] In an action for damages for a misrepresentation with reference to the subject-matter of a contract, in the absence of any breach of contract or warranty, fraud is an essential element of the cause of action.—There is no such thing as "legal" fraud in the absence of moral fraud.—A vendor of real property, during the negotiations for the sale, made a representation to the purchaser, bonâ fide, and believing it to be true, that the pieces of land sold contained three acres, whereas in truth they contained a less quantity. After completion of the contract and execution of the conveyance, the purchaser sought to recover compensation from the vendor for the false representation :—*Held,* that, after completion, such compensation could not be recovered unless there had been fraud or the breach of some contract or warranty contained in the conveyance, and, therefore, the action would not lie. JOLIFFE *v.* BAKER
[11 Q. B. D. 255

2. —— Discovery after Completion— *Misdescription in Particulars of Sale.*] The Plaintiff purchased at a sale by auction certain property belonging to the Defendant described in the particulars of sale as producing a net annual rental of £39, and one of the conditions of sale was, " if any error, misstatement, or omission in the particulars be discovered, the same shall not annul the sale but compensation shall be allowed by the vendor or purchaser as the case may require." After the conveyance (without any covenants) had been executed by the Defendant to the Plaintiff, it was discovered by the Plaintiff that the rental of £39 was a gross rental, the net rental being considerably less :—*Held,* that, notwithstanding the error was not discovered until after the conveyance, the Plaintiff was entitled to compensation under the conditions of sale.—*Cann* v. *Cann* (3 Sim. 447) and *Bos* v. *Helsham* (Law Rep. 2 Ex. 72) followed.— *Manson* v. *Thacker* (7 Ch. D. ·620), *Besley* v. *Besley* (9 Ch. D. 103), and *Allen* v. *Richardson* (13 Ch. D. 524) dissented from. PALMER *v.* JOHNSON 12 Q. B. D. 32;
[13 Q. B. D. 351

III. VENDOR AND PURCHASER—CONDITIONS OF SALE.

By 44 & 45 *Vict. c.* 41 (*Conveyancing Act,* 1881), s. 2, the word "*property,*" *unless a contrary inten-*

III. VENDOR AND PURCHASER—CONDITIONS OF SALE—*continued.*

tion appears in the Act, includes real and personal property, and any estate or interest in any property, real or personal, and any debt, and any thing in action, and any other right or interest.

"*Land,*" *unless a contrary intention appears, includes land of any tenure, and tenements and hereditaments, corporeal or incorporeal, and houses and other buildings, also an undivided share in land.*

"*Purchaser,*" *unless a contrary intention appears, includes a lessee or mortgagee, and an intending purchaser, lessee, or mortgagee, or other person, who, for valuable consideration, takes or deals for any property ; and purchase, unless a contrary intention appears, has a meaning corresponding with that of purchaser ; but sale means only a sale properly so called.*

Sect. 3.—(1.) *Under a contract to sell and assign a term of years derived out of a leasehold interest in land, the intended assign shall not have the right to call for the title to the leasehold reversion.*

(2.) *Where land of copyhold or customary tenure has been converted into freehold by enfranchisement, then, under a contract to sell and convey the freehold, the purchaser shall not have the right to call for the title to make the enfranchisement.*

(3.) *A purchaser of any property shall not require the production, or any abstract or copy, of any deed, will, or other document, dated or made before the time prescribed by law, or stipulated for commencement of the title, even though the same creates a power subsequently exercised by an instrument abstracted in the abstract furnished to the purchaser ; nor shall he require any information, or make any requisition, objection, or inquiry with respect to any such deed, will, or document, or the title prior to that time, notwithstanding that any such deed, will, or other document, or that prior title, is recited, covenanted to be produced, or noticed, and he shall assume, unless the contrary appears, that the recitals, contained in the abstracted instruments, of any deed, will, or other document forming part of that prior title, are correct, and give all the material contents of the deed, will, or other document so recited, and that every document so recited was duly executed by all necessary parties, and perfected, if and as required, by fine, recovery, acknowledgment, inrolment, or otherwise.*

(4.) *Where land sold is held by lease (not including under-lease), the purchaser shall assume, unless the contrary appears, that the lease was duly granted : and, on production of the receipt for the last payment due for rent under the lease before the date of actual completion of the purchase, he shall assume, unless the contrary appears, that all the covenants and provisions of the lease have been duly performed and observed up to the date of actual completion of the purchase.*

(5.) *Where land sold is held by under-lease, the purchaser shall assume, unless the contrary appears, that the under-lease and every superior lease were duly granted ; and, on production of the receipt for the last payment due for rent under the under-lease before the date of actual completion of the purchase, he shall assume, unless the contrary appears, that all the covenants and provisions of the under-lease have been duly performed and observed up to the date of actual completion of the purchase, and*

III. VENDOR AND PURCHASER—CONDITIONS OF SALE—continued.

further that all rent due under every superior lease, and all the covenants and provisions of every superior lease, have been paid and duly performed and observed up to that date.

(6.) *On a sale of any property, the expenses of the production and inspection of all Acts of Parliament, inclosure awards, records, proceedings of courts, court rolls, deeds, wills, probates, letters of administration, and other documents, not in the vendor's possession, and the expenses of all journeys incidental to such production or inspection, and the expenses of searching for, procuring, making, verifying, and producing all certificates, declarations, evidences, and information not in the vendor's possession, and all attested, stamped, office, or other copies or abstracts of, or extracts from, any Acts of Parliament or other documents aforesaid, not in the vendor's possession, if any such production, inspection, journey, search, procuring, making, or verifying is required by a purchaser, either for verification of the abstract, or for any other purpose, shall be borne by the purchaser who requires the same ; and where the vendor retains possession of any document, the expenses of making any copy thereof, attested or unattested, which a purchaser requires to be delivered to him, shall be borne by that purchaser.*

(7.) *On a sale of any property in lots, a purchaser of two or more lots, held wholly or partly under the same title, shall not have a right to more than one abstract of the common title, except at his own expense.*

(8.) *This section applies only to titles and purchasers on sales properly so called, notwithstanding any interpretation in this Act.*

(9.) *This section applies only if and as far as a contrary intention is not expressed in the contract of sale, and shall have effect subject to the terms of the contract and to the provisions therein contained.*

(10.) *This section applies only to sales made after the commencement of this Act.*

(11.) *Nothing in this section shall be construed as binding a purchaser to complete his purchase in any case where, on a contract made independently of this section, and containing stipulations similar to the provisions of this section, or any of them, specific performance of the contract would not be enforced against him by the Court.*

Sect. 13.—(1.) On a contract to grant a lease for a term of years to be derived out of a leasehold interest, with a leasehold reversion, the intended lessee shall not have the right to call for the title to that reversion.

(2.) *This section applies only if and as far as a contrary intention is not expressed in the contract, and shall have effect subject to the terms of the contract and to the provisions therein contained.*

By 45 & 46 Vict. c. 39 (Conveyancing Act, 1882) —Sect. 4.—(1.) Where a lease is made under a power contained in a settlement, will, Act of Parliament, or other instrument, any preliminary contract for or relating to the lease shall not, for the purpose of the deduction of title to an intended assign, form part of the title, or evidence of the title, to the lease.

(2.) *This section applies to leases made either before or after the commencement of the Act.*

1. —— **Depreciatory Conditions**—*Sale by Trus-*

tees.] Trustees for sale under a will put up for sale by auction certain lands in numerous small lots, with conditions providing (inter alia) that the title should commence with the conveyance to the testator ten years before ; that every recital in any abstracted document should be conclusive evidence of the fact stated ; and that the lots were sold "subject to the existing tenancies, restrictive covenants, and all easements and quit-rents (if any) affecting the same ;" and that the purchasers were to indemnify the vendors against the breach of any restrictive covenants contained in the abstracted muniments of title. The sale was made also subject to certain general conditions restricting the occupation of the land. The abstracted documents contained no other restrictive covenants than those comprised in the general conditions ; and the vendors stated that they knew of no other restrictive covenants, and of no existing tenancies, easements or quit-rents affecting the property :—*Held*, that the condition as to existing tenancies and restrictive covenants was depreciatory, and that the objection was a good defence to an action for specific performance by the trustees against a purchaser.—But, *semble*, the condition limiting the title to ten years, having regard to the number and smallness of the lots, was not unreasonable. DUNN *v.* FLOOD

[**25 Ch. D. 629 ; 28 Ch. D. 586**]

2. —— Interest—*Mistake—Repayment—Summons—Jurisdiction—Vendor and Purchaser Act, 1874 (37 & 38 Vict. c. 78), s. 9.*] A purchaser who has, under his contract, erroneously paid the vendor interest on the purchase-money cannot recover it by summons under sect. 9 of the Vendor and Purchaser Act, 1874, but must proceed by action in the ordinary way. *In re* YOUNG & HARSTON'S CONTRACT   -   29 Ch. D. 691

[Question left undecided by the Court of Appeal, 31 Ch. D. 681.]

3. —— Leaseholds—*Performance of Covenants —Specific Performance.*] A leasehold public-house was sold subject to a condition that the production of the last receipt for rent paid should be taken as conclusive evidence of the due performance of the lessee's covenants or the waiver of any breaches up to the time of completion, whether the lessor should be cognizant of such breaches or not. The lease contained a covenant to use the premises for the business of a public-house only, and not to permit any other trade to be carried on on any part of the premises without the lessor's written consent. The particulars on which the contract of purchase was indorsed shewed that parts of the premises were underlet to persons who carried on other trades there. From the answers to objections to title it appeared that the lessors had received rent with knowledge of the underlettings, and the last receipt for rent was produced. Specific performance of the contract having been decreed and a reference as to title directed by an order which was not appealed from :—*Held* (affirming the decision of the Court of Appeal) that whether the breach of covenant was or was not a continuing breach such as to render the purchaser liable to be ejected after the completion of the purchase,

III. VENDOR AND PURCHASER—CONDITIONS OF SALE—*continued.*

and whether this would or would not have furnished a valid reason for not decreeing specific performance, the vendor had made a good title in accordance with the contract, which the purchaser was bound to accept, the decree for specific performance having been made and not appealed from.　LAWRIE *v.* LEES -　　　**7 App. Cas. 19**

4. —— **Misleading** Condition—*Limited Title —Voluntary Deed—Evidence — Recital in Deed more than Twenty Years Old—Vendor and Purchaser Act,* 1874 (37 & 38 *Vict.* c. 78), s. 2.] A contract entered into in 1882 for the sale of freehold estate provided that the title should commence " with an indenture dated the 18th of October, 1845," and made between persons whose names were mentioned, and that the earlier title should not be investigated or objected to. From the abstract of title delivered by the vendors to the purchaser it appeared that the deed of 1845 was a conveyance by a person, who purported to be the absolute owner, of freehold and leasehold property to trustees, on trust for himself for life, and after his death on trust to sell the property, and to hold the proceeds of sale on the trusts declared by a deed of even date. An express power was reserved to the grantor to revoke the trusts. The deed was a voluntary one, except for the consideration which resulted from the liability assumed by the trustees in respect of the leaseholds :—*Held*, by Fry, J., and by the Court of Appeal, that, inasmuch as the fact that the deed of 1845 was a voluntary one, would influence the purchaser in determining whether he would agree to accept a title commencing within forty years, the vendors ought to have stated in the condition of sale the nature of the deed: that the omission to state this rendered the condition a misleading one; and that the purchaser was not bound by the contract to accept a title commencing with that deed.—By a deed executed in 1858 (after the death of the settlor) the trustees conveyed the property to a purchaser for value. This deed contained a recital of the deed of 1845, and a recital that the trustees " in pursuance of the trust for sale conferred on them " by that deed had caused the property to be put up for sale :—*Held*, by Fry, J., that by virtue of sect. 2 of the Vendor and Purchaser Act, 1874, this recital, not being shewn to be inaccurate, was conclusive evidence that the deed of 1845 had not been revoked either by an exercise by the settlor of the power of revocation, or by a sale of the property by him for value during his lifetime, *In re* MARSH AND EARL GRANVILLE　-　　**24 Ch. D. 11**

5. —— **Misleading** Condition—*Statement in Auction Room—Specific Performance refused.*] A dwelling-house and offices were put up for sale by public auction, under a printed condition in a common form, that the lot was sold subject to any existing rights and easements of whatever nature—and the printed particulars made no mention of any easement, or of any claim to an easement. As the result of evidence, it appeared that the house was subject to an easement belonging to the owner of a neighbouring tenement to use the kitchen for particular purposes, and that

III. VENDOR AND PURCHASER—CONDITIONS OF SALE—*continued.*

the vendor's solicitor knew of the rumoured existence of some such easement, but forbore to make inquiries. No grant of an easement appeared from the abstract, and its existence was, in fact, disputed on the pleadings. In the auction room the Plaintiff's solicitor said he had heard of some such claim, but had no definite information about it, and the auctioneer, in hearing of the Plaintiff's solicitor, on being questioned, told the audience that they might dismiss the subject of the rumoured claims from their minds, as nobody would probably ever hear of them again :—*Held*, that the conditions were misleading, and the statements in the auction room insufficient, and specific performance of the contract refused. HEYWOOD *v.* MALLALIEU　-　**25 Ch. D. 357**

6. —— **Right** to rescind—*Discharge of Incumbrances on Sale—Conveyancing and Law of Property Act,* 1881 (44 & 45 *Vict.* c. 41), s. 5.] The Court will not, under the power given to it by sect. 5 of the Conveyancing Act, 1881, compel a vendor of land to pay money into Court for the purpose of discharging an incumbrance upon the land, when the result of so doing would be to inflict a great hardship on him, as, for instance, if the incumbrance is a perpetual rent-charge, and the sum necessary to procure its discharge would far exceed the amount of the purchase-money payable to the vendor.—A railway company contracted to sell some superfluous land " free from incumbrances," for £868. The contract provided that, if the purchaser should decline to waive any valid objection to the title, the company might at any time rescind the contract, without paying the purchaser any costs or compensation. The abstract of title shewed that the land was subject to a perpetual rent-charge of £63 issuing out of it, this being the consideration for which the company had purchased it under their statutory powers, for the making of a railway, which, by a subsequent Act, they were authorized to abandon.—The purchaser required the company to procure the release of the land from the rent-charge. This they declined to do, but offered to indemnify him against it. He declined to waive his requisition :—*Held*, that the company were entitled to rescind the contract under the condition, and that they were not bound to apply to the Court, under sect. 5 of the Conveyancing Act, 1881, to declare the land freed from the rent-charge, or to take any other steps to procure the release of the rent-charge. *In re* GREAT NORTHERN RAILWAY COMPANY AND SANDERSON -　**25 Ch. D. 788**

7. —— **Right** to rescind—*Misrepresentation.*] The particulars of sale of a freehold property described the garden as " inclosed by a rustic wall with tradesmen's side entrance." The wall did not form part of the property, and the tradesmen's side entrance was used on sufferance. This was known to the vendor, but not disclosed to the purchaser. The conditions of sale provided that mistakes or errors in the description of particulars should not annul the sale, but that compensation should be given :—*Held*, that it was not a case for compensation, and that the purchaser was entitled to have the contract rescinded. BREWER *v.* BROWN. **[28 Ch. D. 309.**

III. VENDOR AND PURCHASER—CONDITIONS OF SALE—continued.

8. —— Right to rescind—Non-disclosure of Restrictive Covenants—Conditions of Sale precluding Objections as to Omissions in Contract, Effect of—Conveyancing Act, 1881 (44 & 45 Vict. c. 41), s. 3, sub-ss. 3, 11.] The owner in fee of land sold and conveyed it, during the years 1865, 1866, and 1867, in thirteen lots to different purchasers, each lot being subject to covenants entered into by the purchasers restricting the use of the land as a brickyard and in other respects. The Defendant subsequently became the purchaser of Lot 11, but the deed of conveyance to him did not contain the restrictive covenants. In 1882, the Plaintiffs, a company for manufacturing bricks, contracted to purchase Lot 11 from the Defendant under conditions of sale which stated that the property was sold subject to any matter or thing affecting the same, whether disclosed at the time of sale or not ; and provided that any error or omission in the particulars should not annul the sale, nor entitle the purchaser to compensation. The existence of the restrictive covenants was not mentioned in the contract, but during the negotiations the Defendant stated that there were covenants restricting the use of the land as a brickyard, but his solicitor, who was present, and to whom the Plaintiffs' solicitor applied for information, stated that he was not aware of any such covenants. The Plaintiffs paid a deposit upon the purchase-money, and having subsequently discovered that there were restrictive covenants, claimed to rescind their contract and sued the Defendant to recover the amount of the deposit :—Held, that the Plaintiffs, if their contract with the Defendant were carried out, would be bound by the restrictive covenants, and that the owners of the other twelve lots purchased from the original vendor would be entitled to enforce those covenants against the Plaintiffs : that the Plaintiffs were not precluded by the terms of the conditions of sale, nor by s. 3, sub-s. 3, of the Conveyancing Act, 1881, from refusing to complete the purchase, and that they were therefore entitled to recover the amount of the deposit. NOTTINGHAM PATENT BRICK AND TILE COMPANY v. BUTLER - - 15 Q. B. D. 261

[Affirmed by the Court of Appeal.]

9. —— Right to rescind—Objection to Conveyance—Specific Performance.] Trustees of a will put up land for sale, subject to a condition that, if any objection or requisition as to (inter alia) title, or abstract, or conveyance should be insisted on, and the vendors should be unable or unwilling to remove or comply therewith, they should be at liberty to annul the sale. The abstract delivered to the purchaser shewed that the conveyance to the vendor's testator was of the land, together with a wall on the east side of it, "which wall is to be ever hereafter repaired and kept in repair" by the testator, his heirs, and assigns. This obligation was not mentioned in the particulars and conditions of sale, and the purchaser did not know of it until the delivery of the abstract. He accepted the title, and tendered to the vendors the draft of a conveyance to himself of the land with the wall, omitting all reference to the obligation to repair the wall. The vendor's solicitors

III. VENDOR AND PURCHASER—CONDITIONS OF SALE—continued.

added the words "subject to and with the liability for ever to repair the wall" by the purchaser, his heirs and assigns. The purchaser would not agree to the addition, and the vendors thereupon gave notice to rescind the contract. The purchaser then brought an action for specific performance of the contract, claiming the right to a conveyance without the additional words :—Held, that, if the obligation to repair the wall ran with the land, it was immaterial whether it was mentioned in the conveyance or not, because the purchaser would be bound by it in either case ; but that, if it did not run with the land, the vendors, not having mentioned it in the particulars of sale, could not impose it on the purchaser. Consequently, the vendors were not entitled to rescind the contract.—Semble, that a condition of sale giving the vendor a right to rescind the contract, in the event of his being unable or unwilling to comply with a purchaser's requisition as to conveyance, is not in general a proper condition. HARDMAN v. CHILD - 28 Ch. D. 712

10. —— Right to rescind—Purchase-money—Deposit — Separate Account — Interest.] On a sale of a freehold house by auction one of the conditions of sale provided that "all objections and requisitions in respect of the title, or the abstract, or particulars, or anything appearing therein respectively shall be sent to the vendors' solicitors within fourteen days from the delivery of the abstract, and all objections and requisitions not sent in within that time shall be considered to be waived. If any objection or requisition shall be made and insisted on, which the vendors shall be unable or unwilling to remove or comply with, the vendors shall be at liberty by notice in writing to rescind the sale." The purchaser accepted the vendors' title as shewn by the abstract and sent them a draft conveyance for approval. The vendors then required that the conveyance should be taken subject to certain "covenants, conditions, and restrictions," the nature of which they did not explain, but which, they alleged, were contained in a deed recited in an abstracted deed forming the commencement of title. As the abstract did not shew the existence of any such covenants, conditions, or restrictions, and as the conveyance to the vendors' immediate predecessor in title did not in any way refer to them, the purchaser declined to take a conveyance subject to them without, at all events, being first informed of their nature, whereupon the vendors wrote purporting to rescind the contract :—Held, upon a summons by the purchaser under the Vendor and Purchaser Act, 1874, that the vendors had no power to rescind, and that the purchaser was entitled to a conveyance without the insertion of the words required by the vendors.—Another condition of sale provided for payment of a deposit and for the completion of the purchase on a certain day ; and that "if from any cause whatever," the purchase should not be completed on that day the purchaser should pay interest at 5 per cent. per annum on the remainder of his purchase-money until completion. After receiving the vendors' notice of rescission the purchaser," on the day fixed for

III. VENDOR AND PURCHASER—CONDITIONS OF SALE—continued.

completion, placed the balance of her purchase-money to a separate account on deposit with a bank at 2½ per cent. interest, and gave notice of the deposit to the vendors :—*Held,* that the purchaser could not, under the circumstances, be required to pay, on actual completion, higher interest than that allowed by the bank. *In re* MONCKTON AND GILZEAN - 　27 Ch. D. 555

11. —— Right to rescind—*Withdrawal of Objections.*] Land was contracted to be sold under a condition that "if the purchaser shall take any objection or make any requisition" as to the title which the vendor " is unable or unwilling to remove or comply with,' the vendor, might rescind the contract. The purchasers made requisitions with several of which the vendor, for reasons stated, "declined to comply." The purchasers insisted on their requisitions, and the vendor served the purchasers with notice to rescind.—The purchasers, in reply, denied the vendor's right to rescind, withdrew their requisitions, and stated that they were willing to complete :—*Held* (affirming the decision of Bacon, V.C.), that the contract had been duly rescinded *In re* DAMES AND WOOD 　-　27 Ch. D. 172 ; 29 Ch. D. 626

IV. VENDOR AND PURCHASER — CONVEYANCE.

Death of Vendor.] *The Act* 44 & 45 *Vict.* c. 41 (*Conveyancing Act,* 1881) *enacts,* s. 4—(1.) *Where at the death of any person there is subsisting a contract, enforceable against his heir, or devisee, for the sale of the fee simple or other freehold interest, descendible to his heirs general, in any land, his personal representatives shall, by virtue of this Act, have power to convey the land for all the estate and interest vested in him at his death, in any manner proper for giving effect to the contract.*

(2.) *A conveyance made under this section shall not affect the beneficial rights of any person claiming under any testamentary disposition or as heir or next of kin of a testator or intestate.*

(3.) *This section applies only in cases of death after the commencement of this Act—31st December,* 1881.

Discharge of Incumbrances.] *Sect.* 2. " *Incumbrance*" *includes a mortgage in fee or for a less estate, and a trust for securing money, and a lien, and a charge of a portion, annuity, or other capital or annual sum; and "incumbrancer" has a meaning corresponding with that of incumbrance, and includes every person entitled to the benefit of an incumbrance, or to require payment or discharge thereof.*

Sect. 5.—(1.) *Where land subject to any incumbrance, whether immediately payable or not, is sold by the Court, or out of Court, the Court may, if it thinks fit, on the application of any party to the sale, direct or allow payment in Court, in case of an annual sum charged on the land, or of a capital sum charged on a determinable interest in the land, of such amount as, when invested in Government securities, the Court considers will be sufficient, by means of the dividends thereof, to keep down or otherwise provide for that charge, and in any other case of capital money charged on the land, of the amount sufficient to meet the incumbrance and any interest due thereon; but in either case there shall*

IV. VENDOR AND PURCHASER—CONVEYANCE—continued.

also be paid into Court such additional amount as the Court considers will be sufficient to meet the contingency of further costs, expenses, and interest, and any other contingency, except depreciation of investments, not exceeding one tenth part of the original amount to be paid in, unless the Court for special reason thinks fit to require a larger additional amount.

(2.) *Thereupon the Court may, if it thinks fit, and either after or without any notice to the incumbrancer, as the Court thinks fit, declare the land to be freed from the incumbrance, and make any order for conveyance, or vesting order, proper for giving effect to the sale, and give directions for the retention and investment of the money in Court.*

(3.) *After notice served upon the person interested in or entitled to the money or fund in Court, the Court may direct payment or transfer thereof, to the person entitled to receive or give a discharge for the same, and generally may give directions respecting the application or distribution of the capital or income thereof.*

(4.) *This section applies to sales not completed at the commencement of the Act, and to sales thereafter made.*

Execution of Purchase Deed.] *Sect.* 8.—(1.) *On sale, the purchaser shall not be entitled to require that the conveyance to him be executed in his presence, or in that of his solicitor, as such; but shall be entitled to have, at his own cost, the execution of the conveyance attested by some person appointed by him, who may if he thinks fit be his solicitor.*

1. —— Covenant—*Sale by Court—Restricted Covenant — Qualifying Proviso — Appeal from Form settled by Judge.*] In a sale by the Court the particulars of sale contained certain reservations and stipulations as to the property, and one of the conditions of sale provided that the conveyances should contain covenants by the purchasers for securing the liabilities and rights under such reservations and stipulations, the form of such covenants, in case of dispute, to be settled by the Judge.—A dispute having arisen between a purchaser and a vendor concerning the form of the covenant, the Judge settled the covenant, adding a proviso that if the purchaser assigned his purchase, and the assignee entered into a similar covenant, the purchaser should be freed from further liability :—*Held,* that the vendor was entitled to an unqualified covenant, and that the proviso must be struck out.—The order of a Judge settling the form of a conveyance is subject to appeal. POLLOCK *v.* RABBITS 　21 Ch. D. 466

2. —— Covenant for quiet Enjoyment—*Decree in Equity a Disturbance in Possession.*] In a conveyance of land by the Defendant to the Plaintiff the Defendant covenanted for title and quiet enjoyment notwithstanding any act or thing done or suffered by him or by any of his ancestors or predecessors in title. After the conveyance a decree was made in a suit in Chancery in which the Plaintiff, though not a party, was represented as being one of a class of persons against whom the suit was brought, and by the decree the land so conveyed by the Defendant was declared to be subject to a general right of common over it :—*Held,* that the decree alone, without any entry or

IV. VENDOR AND PURCHASER—CONVEY-ANCE—*continued.*

actual disturbance of the Plaintiff in his possession, was no breach of the Defendant's covenant for quiet enjoyment:—*Held*, also, that the Court, in the absence of evidence of a grant of such right of common by some predecessor in title of the Defendant, would not infer that there must have been such grant so as to be a breach of his covenant for title within the meaning of the covenant. HOWARD *v.* MAITLAND -   11 Q. B. D. 695

3. —— **Married Woman**—*Trust for Sale—"Bare Trustee"—Administration Action—Order for Sale—Conveyance—Acknowledgment — Fines and Recoveries Act (3 & 4 Will. 4, c. 74), ss. 77, 79—Vendor and Purchaser Act, 1874 (37 & 38 Vict. c. 78), s. 6.*] A testator devised his real estate to trustees for sale, who were married women, one of them having married before and the other after the Married Women's Property Act, 1882. Both of them also took beneficial interests in the proceeds of sale. Under the judgment in an action for the administration of the testator's estate, part of the real estate was sold by the trustees, the purchaser paying his purchase-money into Court:—*Held*, that the married women were "bare trustees" within sect. 6 of the Vendor and Purchaser Act, 1874, and that the conveyance to the purchaser did not require the concurrence of the husbands, or acknowledgment under the Fines and Recoveries Act. *In re* DOCWRA. DOCWRA *v.* FAITH -   29 Ch. D. 693

4. —— **Payment of Purchase-money**—*Payment into Court—Conveyancing and Law of Property Act, 1881 (44 & 45 Vict. c. 41), s. 5.*] A mortgage deed gave the mortgagee an option to purchase in case the debt was not paid on a day named. The trustees in bankruptcy of the mortgagors sold the mortgaged property. A part of the purchase-money was deposited to provide against the mortgage. Pending proceedings on the part of the trustees to set aside the mortgage on the ground of fraudulent preference, an order was made that the money deposited should be paid into Court, and on such further sum being paid in as would cover the principal and interest due, and 10 per cent. extra, the property should vest in the purchaser. MILFORD HAVEN RAILWAY AND ESTATE COMPANY *v.* MOWATT. *In re* LAKE & TAYLOR'S MORTGAGE. SPAIN *v.* MOWATT
[28 Ch. D. 402

5. —— **Payment of Purchase-money**—*Sale by Trustees—Authority to Solicitor to receive Purchase-money—Breach of Trust—Conveyancing and Law of Property Act, 1881 (44 & 45 Vict. c. 41), s. 56.*] The 56th section of the Conveyancing Act, 1881, does not authorize vendors who are trustees with a power of sale to require the purchaser to pay the purchase-money to their solicitor on production of the deed of conveyance duly executed in cases where before the Act they could not have required the purchaser to pay the purchase-money to their solicitor under a special authority.—Trustees of real estate with a power to sell and give receipts, sold the estate. The purchasers required that the vendors should attend in person to receive the purchase-money, or should authorize the purchaser to pay it into a bank to the joint account of the vendors. The

IV. VENDOR AND PURCHASER — CONVEY-VANCE—*continued.*

vendors insisted that the money should be paid to their solicitor on his producing the conveyance duly executed. They gave no special reason why the money should be paid to the solicitor, but relied on the 56th section of the Conveyancing Act, 1881. A summons having been taken out under the Vendor and Purchaser Act:—*Held* (dissentiente Baggallay, L.J.), that the 56th section had no application, and that the purchasers had a right to insist on their requisition.—The decision of Kay, J., reversed. *In re* BELLAMY AND METROPOLITAN BOARD OF WORKS
[24 Ch. D. 387

6. —— **Payment of Purchase-money**—*Sale of Real Estate by Trustees—Requisition by Purchasers that all the Trustees should attend to receive Purchase-moneys, or direct payment into a Bank.*] Trustees of real estate sold parts of it to the Metropolitan Board of Works, and they sent in a requisition that the vendors should attend personally to receive the purchase-moneys, or direct the moneys to be paid to their joint account at a bank. One or more of the trustees resided in the country. On summonses taken out under the Vendor and Purchaser Act, 1874, by the board:—*Held*, that the requisition must be complied with by the trustees, and that they must pay the costs of the application.—*In re Bellamy and Metropolitan Board of Works* (24 Ch. D. 387) followed. *In re* FLOWER AND METROPOLITAN BOARD OF WORKS
[27 Ch. D. 592

V. VENDOR AND PURCHASER—DEPOSIT.

1. —— **Possessory Title**—*Land over Railway Arch—Ultrà vires Sale by Railway Company to Vendor—Sale of Possessory Title only—Forfeiture of Deposit on refusal to complete.*] The Defendant purchased from a railway company land over a tunnel, which, not being "superfluous," the company had no power to sell, and the Plaintiff contracted to purchase the land from the Defendant as freehold building land. One of the conditions of sale was that the title should commence with the conveyance from the company; another, that the purchaser should not require the production of, or investigate or make any objection or requisition in respect of, such conveyance; and another, that the purchaser should send his objections, if any, to the title within seven days from the delivery of the abstract. The Plaintiff declined to complete after the expiration of the seven days, and sued for the deposit:—*Held*, by the Court of Appeal (Jessel, M.R., and Brett and Cotton, L.JJ.) reversing the decision of Lindley, J., that the deposit could not be recovered. ROSENBERG *v.* COOK
[8 Q. B. D. 162

2. —— **Purchaser's Failure to complete.**] On a sale of real estate the purchaser paid £500, which was stated in the contract to be paid "as a deposit, and in part payment of the purchase-money." The contract provided that the purchase should be completed on a day named, and that if the purchaser should fail to comply with the agreement the vendor should be at liberty to re-sell and to recover any deficiency in price as liquidated damages. The purchaser was not ready with his purchase-money, and,

V. VENDOR AND PURCHASER — DEPOSIT — *continued.*

after repeated delays, the vendor re-sold the property for the same price.—The original purchaser having brought an action for specific performance, it was held by the Court of Appeal, affirming the decision of Kay, J., that the purchaser had lost by his delay his right to enforce specific performance :—*Held*, also, that the deposit, although to be taken as part payment if the contract was completed, was also a guarantee for the performance of the contract, and that the Plaintiff, having failed to perform his contract within a reasonable time, had no right to a return of the deposit.—*Palmer* v. *Temple* (9 Ad. & E. 508) distinguished. Howe v. Smith 27 Ch. D. 89

3. —— **Purchaser's Knowledge of Defect of Title**—*Right to rescind.*] T. agreed to sell to C. certain freehold houses, and to make a good marketable title. On investigation of the title it appeared that the houses were part of a property which had been sold by a building society in lots, subject to stringent restrictive covenants which were admitted to make the title not a marketable one. T. having declined to procure a release of the covenants, C. brought an action to recover back his deposit. T. adduced evidence that C. knew of the restriction at the time of the contract, and the jury found that he did :—*Held*, affirming the decision of Lopes, J., that this evidence could not be admitted to modify the terms of the express contract, and that the Plaintiff was entitled to recover.—*Farebrother* v. *Gibson* (1 De G. & J. 602) and *Leyland* v. *Illingworth* (2 De G. F. & J. 248) distinguished. Cato v. Thompson
[9 Q. B. D. 616

4. —— **Vendor's right to follow the Money**—*Forfeiture for Non-completion—Payment by Bankrupt in Fraud of Creditors.*] A bankrupt having disposed of his goods in fraud of his creditors, opened an account in a bank with the proceeds, and having entered into a contract for the purchase of land in an assumed name, paid a deposit to the Defendant, the auctioneer, by a cheque drawn upon the bank. The vendor and the Defendant acted bonâ fide and without notice of the bankruptcy or of the fraudulent conduct of the bankrupt :—*Held*, that the bankrupt's trustee was not entitled to recover the deposit from the Defendant so as to prevent it from being forfeited to the vendor upon the non-completion of the contract. Collins v. Stimson　　　　　　- 11 Q. B. D. 142

VI. VENDOR AND PURCHASER—FRAUD.

1. —— **Fiduciary Relation**—*Executor—Purchase of Testator's Estate by an Executor who has not proved—Suit to set aside Sale.*] Held, that a sale is not to be avoided merely because when entered upon the purchaser has the power to become trustee of the property purchased, as for instance by proving the will which relates thereto, though in point of fact he never does become such. Such a purchaser is under no disability, and in order to avoid such sale it must be shewn that he in fact used his power in such a way as to render it inequitable that the sale should be upheld. Clark v. Clark　　　　-　　- 9 App. Cas. 733

2. —— **Misrepresentation.**] The Plaintiffs put up an hotel for sale on the 4th of August, 1882,

VI. VENDOR AND PURCHASER — FRAUD — *continued.*

stating in the particulars that it was let to "F. (a most desirable tenant), at a rental of £400 for an unexpired term of 27½ years." The L. Co. sent M., their secretary, to inspect the property. M. reported that F., from the business he was doing, could hardly pay the rent, and that the town in which it was situate seemed to be in the last stage of decay. The directors on receiving this report, directed M. to bid up to £5000. M. went and bought for £4700. Before completion, F. went into liquidation, and the L. Co. refused to complete. The Plaintiffs sued for specific performance. It was proved that on the 1st of May, 1882, the Lady Day quarter's rent was wholly unpaid ; that a distress was then threatened, and that F. paid £30 on the 6th of May, £40 on the 13th of June, and the remaining £30 shortly before the auction, and that no part of the quarter's rent due at Midsummer had been paid. The chairman of the company was orally examined, and deposed most positively, that the company would not have bought but for the representation in the particulars that F. was a most desirable tenant. Mr. Justice Denman held that there was a material misrepresentation, and that the contract had been entered into in reliance upon it. His Lordship accordingly dismissed the action, and on a counter-claim by the Defendants, rescinded the contract.—*Held*, on appeal, that the description of F. as a most desirable tenant was not a mere expression of opinion, but contained an implied assertion that the vendors knew of no facts leading to the conclusion that he was not ; that the circumstances relating to the Lady Day rent shewed that he was not a desirable tenant ; and that there was a misrepresentation :—*Held*, also, that, as the positive testimony of the chairman, that but for this representation the company would not have bought, was not shaken on cross-examination, and was believed by the Judge who saw and heard the witness, the Court of Appeal would not disturb the finding that the representation had induced the company to enter into the contract, and that the appeal must be dismissed. Smith v. Land and House Property Corporation　　　　-　　　28 Ch. D. 7

VII. VENDOR AND PURCHASER—LIEN.

1. —— **Money expended on Land**—*Refusal to perform Contract.*] A man who enters into a contract to expend a certain sum of money on land, and after spending part of it declines to perform the contract, has no lien on the land for the money which he has expended. Wallis v. Smith
[21 Ch. D. 243

2. —— **Waiver of Lien**—*Vendor's Lien for unpaid Purchase-money—Land in Register County.—West Riding Registry Act (2 & 3 Anne, c. 4)—Sub-Purchaser—Notice.*] A vendor of land in a register county, part of whose purchase-money remains unpaid, is under no obligation to register a memorial of the vendor's lien, but is entitled to rely on his equitable lien against sub-purchasers who have notice of it actual or constructive.—A purchaser of land in a register county is bound to inquire for and examine the deeds and documents memorials of which are registered.—Land belonging to the trustees of a charity, situated in

3 G

VII. VENDOR AND PURCHASER — LIEN —
continued.

the West Riding of Yorkshire, was sold by the
trustees to R. & W., who were estate agents, and
bought the land with the intention of selling it
in lots for building purposes. Part of the purchase-money remained unpaid, and the vendors
retained the deed of conveyance in their possession, but at the request of the purchasers, the
vendors' solicitor registered a memorial of it in
the West Riding registry. The vendors took no
written security for their unpaid purchase-money,
but relied on their equitable lien. R. & W. sold
the land again in lots.—P., one of the sub-purchasers, who took a mortgage on a small lot,
made no inquiries himself, but left it, as he said,
to R. & W. to "manage the whole business"
for him, and they prepared the conveyance to
him.—The original vendors having brought an
action to enforce their lien for the unpaid purchase-money against some of the sub-purchasers:
—*Held,* that there was no obligation on the
original vendors to register a memorial of the
vendor's lien. Whether the neglect of the sub-
purchasers to search the register and inquire for
the deed affected them with constructive notice
of the Plaintiffs' lien, *quære.*—But the Court
being convinced on the evidence that the vendors
knew that R. & W. wanted the deed of conveyance registered for the purpose of selling, and
that they did sell, the land in lots, and that by
their conduct in registering the deed they had
led the sub-purchasers to believe that R. & W. had
power to dispose of the land as absolute owners:
—*Held,* that the vendors had waived their lien and
could not enforce it against the sub-purchasers.
—*Semble,* the fact of P. having left R. & W. to
manage the business for him was not in itself
sufficient to affect him with their knowledge of
the lien. KETTLEWELL *v.* WATSON

[21 Ch. D. 685 ; 26 Ch. D. 501

**VIII. VENDOR AND PURCHASER — PURCHASE
WITHOUT NOTICE.**

By 45 & 46 Vict. c. 39 (*Conveyancing Act,*1882),
s. 3.—(1.) *A purchaser shall not be prejudicially
affected by notice of any instrument, fact, or thing,
unless—*

(i.) *It is within his own knowledge, or would
have come to his knowledge if such inquiries and inspections had been made as
ought reasonably to have been made by
him ; or*

(ii.) *In the same transactions with respect to
which a question of notice to the purchaser
arises, it has come to the knowledge of his
counsel, as such, or of his solicitor, or other
agent, as such, or would have come to the
knowledge of his solicitor, or other agent,
as such, if such inquiries and inspections
had been made as ought reasonably to have
been made by the solicitor or other agent.*

(2.) *This section shall not exempt a purchaser
from any liability under, or any obligation to
perform or observe, any covenant, condition, provision, or restriction contained in any instrument
under which his title is derived mediately or immediately ; and such liability or obligation may be
enforced in the same manner and to the same
extent as if this section had not been enacted.*

**VIII. VENDOR AND PURCHASER — PURCHASE
WITHOUT NOTICE—**—*continued.*

(3.) *A purchaser shall not by reason of anything
in this section be affected by notice in any case
where he would not have been so affected if this
section had not been enacted.*

(4.) *This section applies to purchases made either
before or after the commencement of the Act, 31st
December, 1882 ; save that, where an action is
pending at the commencement of the Act, the rights
of the parties shall not be affected by this section.*

1. —— Forged Deed—*Fraud—Personation—
Purchaser for Value without Notice—Middlesex
Registry Act (7 Anne, c. 20)—Unregistered Will
—Conveyance by Heir-at-law—Order for delivery
up of Title Deeds—Execution of Deed—Presumption of Knowledge of Contents—Costs. Appeal for
—Parties—Trustee and Cestui que Trust—Judicature Act, 1873, s. 49—Rules of Court, 1875,
Order* XVI., *r.* 7—*Order* LV.] A son who was
heir-at-law to his father, who was one of the
executors and trustees of his father's will, though
he had not proved the will, and whose Christian
names and description were identical with those
of his father, after his father's death, executed
mortgages of freehold and leasehold property of
the father and applied the mortgage money to
his own purposes. He handed over the title
deeds to the mortgagees. The transaction took
place without the knowledge of his mother and
sister, who were co-trustees and co-executrixes
with him, and who had proved the will. The
will had not been registered in the Middlesex
Registry, though the property was situate in that
county. The mortgage deeds were registered.
They purported to be executed by the absolute
owner of the property, and the solicitor who
acted for both parties believed the son to be the
absolute owner. The son told him nothing about
the father's will. The solicitor searched the
Middlesex Registry. The son took a beneficial
interest under the trusts of the father's will.
After the son's death the fraud was discovered,
and the mother and sister, as trustees of the
father's will, brought an action against the mortgagees, claiming a declaration that the mortgages
were void against them, and delivery up of the
title deeds. The other beneficiaries under the
will were made Defendants:—*Held* (by Kay, J.,
and the Court of Appeal), that the son in executing the mortgage deeds was personating his
father; that the deeds were forgeries and passed
nothing to the mortgagees, except the son's beneficial interest under the father's will; and that
the mortgagees could obtain no title by virtue
of the Middlesex Registry Act:—*Held,* also, that
the mortgagees must deliver up the title deeds to
the Plaintiffs:—*Held,* by Kay, J., that the mortgagees must pay the Plaintiff's costs of the action,
and also the costs of the co-Defendants :—*Held,*
by the Court of Appeal, that, inasmuch as, by
virtue of rule 7 of Order XVI., trustees may sue on
behalf of their cestuis que trust, the beneficiaries
ought not to have been made parties to the action.
Consequently, the order that the mortgagees
should pay their costs, could be appealed from,
and that order was discharged.—Since the Judicature Act the Chancery Division has jurisdiction
on the application of the legal owner of title

VIII. VENDOR AND PURCHASER—PURCHASE WITHOUT NOTICE—*continued.*

deeds to order them to be delivered up by a purchaser for value without notice. — *McLeod* v. *Drummond* (14 Ves. 353 ; 17 Ves. 152) distinguished.—*Per* Lindley, L.J.: The son could have been convicted of forgery by reason of his executing the mortgage deeds.—*Per* Jessel, M.R. : In the absence of evidence to the contrary there is a legal presumption that a man knows the contents of a deed which he executes. *In re* COOPER. COOPER *v.* VESEY - 20 Ch. D. 611

2. —— **Married Woman**—*Notice of Settlement.*] When a married woman executes a mortgage there is no obligation on the mortgagee to inquire whether a settlement was made on her marriage. LLOYD'S BANKING CO. *v.* JONES - 29 Ch. D. 221

IX. VENDOR AND PURCHASER—RESCISSION

1. —— **Notice of Defects of Title**—*Repudiation by Purchaser—Licence to assign.*] A railway company agreed to demise to E. for building purposes certain lands which they had acquired under their compulsory powers. E. was restrained from assigning without licence. The property had formerly belonged to a building society, which had sold it in lots, each purchaser entering into restrictive covenants for the benefit of the owners of the other lots, and the conveyance to the company was expressly made subject to these covenants. E. agreed to sell his interest under the contract to R. R. at the time of the contract knew of the restrictive covenants, but believed that the compulsory purchase by the railway company had extinguished them. E. did not know of their existence. R.'s solicitors having discovered the existence of the covenants objected to the title. E.'s solicitors replied that the compulsory purchase had extinguished them. R. then refused to proceed with the purchase. E. brought a bill for specific performance, but having afterwards resumed possession, and built, in order to avoid a forfeiture, the action came on as an action for damages. E. had never obtained a licence to assign :—*Held*, by Kay, J., that as E. had not either at the time of the repudiation of the contract by the Defendant, or subsequently, obtained a licence to assign, he never was in a position to perform his part of the contract, and therefore could not recover damages. *Semble*, also, that R. had not such knowledge that the property was still subject to the covenants as to debar him from requiring a title free from them. —*Held*, on appeal, that R. was entitled to object to the title on the ground of the restrictive covenants, for that in order to take a case out of the general rule that a purchaser is entitled to require a good title, it must be shewn that at the time of the contract he knew that a good title could not be made, and that here such knowledge was not shewn, as R. believed that the covenants had been extinguished.—*Semble*, that R.'s objection on the ground that a licence to assign had not been obtained was not valid, inasmuch as he had repudiated the contract before the time had arrived at which it was necessary for the vendor to produce a licence. ELLIS *v.* ROGERS

[29 Ch. D. 661

2. —— **Voidable Lease.**] A vendor contracted

IX. VENDOR AND PURCHASER—RESCISSION —*continued.*

to sell and a purchaser to purchase an agreement for a lease. The purchaser afterwards repudiated the contract.—At the date of the agreement, and of the repudiation, the agreement to lease was voidable at the will of a third party, but the third party took no steps to avoid the agreement, but was willing to confirm it on certain conditions :— *Held*, that the purchaser was entitled to repudiate the contract. BREWER *v.* BROADWOOD

[22 Ch. D. 105

—— Right to rescind under conditions of sale. *See* Cases under VENDOR AND PURCHASER—CONDITIONS OF SALE. 6—11.

X. VENDOR AND PURCHASER—TITLE.

Orders of Court.] *By* 44 & 45 *Vict.* c. 41 (*Conveyancing Act*, 1881), s. 70.—(1.) *An order of the Court under any statutory or other jurisdiction shall not as against a purchaser be invalidated on the ground of want of jurisdiction, or want of any concurrence, consent, notice, or service, whether the purchaser has notice of any such want or not.*

(2.) *This section applies to leases and sales made under the Settled Estates Act*, 1877.

(3.) *This section applies to all orders made before commencement of the Act, except any order which had been set aside, or questioned in a pending suit.*

Searches.] *By* 45 & 46 *Vict.* c. 39 (*Conveyancing Act*, 1882)—

Sect. 2.—(1.) *Where any person requires, for purposes of this section, search to be made in the Central Office of the Supreme Court of Judicature for entries of judgments, deeds, or other matters or documents, whered entries are required or allowed to be made in that office by any Act described in Part I. of the First Schedule to the Conveyancing Act of* 1881, *or by any other Act, he may deliver in the office a requisition in that behalf, referring to this section.*

(2.) *Thereupon the proper officer shall diligently make the search required, and shall make and file in the office a certificate setting forth the result thereof ; and office copies of that certificate shall be issued on requisition, and an office copy shall be evidence of the certificate.*

(3.) *In favour of a purchaser, as against persons interested under or in respect of judgments, deeds or other matters or documents, whered entries are required or allowed as aforesaid, the certificate, according to the tenor thereof, shall be conclusive, affirmatively or negatively, as the case may be.*

(4.) *Every requisition under this section shall be in writing, signed by the person making the same, specifying the name against which he desires search to be made, or in relation to which he requires an office copy certificate of result of search, and other sufficient particulars ; and the person making any such requisition shall not be entitled to a search, or an office copy certificate, until he has satisfied the proper officer that the same is required for the purposes of this section.*

(5.) *General Rules shall be made for purposes of this section, prescribing forms and contents of requisitions and certificates, and regulating the practice of the office, and prescribing, with the concurrence of the Commissioners of Her Majesty's Treasury, the fees to be taken therein ; which Rules*

3 G 2

X. VENDOR AND PURCHASER—TITLE—contd.

shall be deemed Rules of Court within section seventeen of the Appellate Jurisdiction Act, 1876, as altered by section nineteen of the Supreme Court of Judicature Act, 1881, and may be made, at any time after the passing of this Act, to take effect on or after the commencement of this Act.

(6.) If any officer, clerk, or person employed in the office commits, or is party or privy to, any act of fraud or collusion, or is wilfully negligent in the making of or otherwise in relation to any certificate or office copy under this section, he shall be guilty of a misdemeanor.

(7.) Nothing in this section or in any rule made thereunder shall take away, abridge, or prejudicially affect any right which any person may have independently of this section to make any search in the office ; and every such search may be made as if this section or any such rule had not been enacted or made.

(8.) Where a solicitor obtains an office copy certificate of result or search under this section, he shall not be answerable in respect of any loss that may arise from error in the certificate.

(9.) Where the solicitor is acting for trustees, executors, agents, or other persons in a fiduciary position, those persons also shall not be so answerable.

(10.) Where such persons obtain such an office copy without a solicitor, they shall also be protected in like manner.

(11.) Nothing in this section applies to deeds enrolled under the Fines and Recoveries Act, or under any other Act, or under any statutory rule.

(12.) This section does not extend to Ireland.

1. —— Expense of Abstract—Deed not in Vendor's Possession—Expense of making—Conveyancing and Law of Property Act, 1881 (44 & 45 Vict. c. 41), s. 3, sub-s. 6.] A vendor is bound at his own expense to produce to the purchaser a proper abstract of title, either for the statutory period of forty years, or for such other period as may be agreed upon, and sect. 3, subsect. 6, of the Conveyancing Act, 1881, is not intended to interfere with the performance by the vendor of that duty, but proceeds on the assumption that the vendor has produced such an abstract.—Therefore on an open contract the vendor must bear the expense of procuring and making an abstract of any deed forming part of the forty years' title, although such deed be not in his possession.—The word "abstract" in that sub-section is to be distinguished from the "abstract" of title to which the purchaser is entitled ; and a purchaser cannot be said to "require an abstract of a particular deed," merely because he requires an abstract of title for the prescribed length of time, which involves the abstracting of that deed.—Decision of Pearson, J., reversed. In re JOHNSON AND TUSTIN　28 Ch. D. [84; 30 Ch. D. 42

2. —— Leasehold—Evidence of performance of Covenant—Conveyancing and Law of Property Act, 1881 (44 & 45 Vict. c. 41), s. 3, sub-ss. 4, 6 —Peppercorn Rent.] The Conveyancing and Law of Property Act, 1881, s. 3, sub-s. 4, does not apply to a peppercorn rent so as by production of a receipt for a peppercorn to relieve the vendors of a building lease from the obligation of shewing

X. VENDOR AND PURCHASER—TITLE—contd..

that the covenants with their lessor (to finish the house within —— months to the satisfaction of the lessor's surveyor) have been duly performed and observed.—The certificate of the lessor's surveyor that the house has been finished to his satisfaction is not a "certificate" or "evidence" within sect. 3, sub-sect. 6, the expense of obtaining which must be borne by the purchaser, but a part of the title itself. Decision of Chitty, J., affirmed. In re MOODY AND YATES' CONTRACT [28 Ch. D. 661 ; 30 Ch. D. 344

3. —— Leasehold — Restrictive Covenant — Constructive Notice—Lessor's Title—Vendor and Purchaser Act, 1874 (37 & 38 Vict. c. 78), s. 2, sub-s. 1.] A purchaser or lessees having notice of a deed forming part of the chain of title of his vendor or lessor, has constructive notice of the contents of such deed, and is not protected from the consequences of not looking at the deed, even by the most express representation on the part of the vendor or lessor that it contains no restrictive covenants, nor anything in any way affecting the title.—The rule that a lessee has constructive notice of his lessor's title has not been altered by sect. 2, sub-sect 1, of the Vendor and Purchaser Act, 1874, but a lessee is now in the same position with regard to notice as if he had, before the Act, stipulated not to inquire into his lessor's title.—Wilson v. Hart (Law Rep. 1 Ch. [463) observed upon. PATMAN v. HARLAND [17 Ch. D. 353

4. —— Notice of Trust—Objections to Title—Recitals in Deed.] In 1840 property was mortgaged to W. in fee, there being nothing in the mortgage deed to shew that he was not the beneficial owner of the mortgage money. He died in 1842, having by his will devised and bequeathed his real and personal estate to three trustees (of whom his wife was one), on trusts for the benefit of his wife and children, and having appointed the same three persons executors. He also devised and bequeathed his trust and mortgage estates to the same three persons, subject to the trusts and equities affecting the same respectively. The widow alone proved the will, and alone acted as trustee. The other two trustees disclaimed the trusts. In 1854 the widow obtained a decree absolute foreclosing the mortgages. In 1865 she, by a deed indorsed on the mortgage deed, conveyed the property, without receiving any pecuniary consideration for it, to K., C., and B., in fee, as joint tenants at law and in equity. The conveyance contained a recital that the testator held the mortgage money on an account under which K., C., and B. were then solely entitled thereto, as was thereby acknowledged, whereby the widow, as trustee under the testator's will, was trustee only of the property for K., C., and B., and they had requested her to convey it to them. On a subsequent sale of the property by persons who had purchased it from K., C., and B., the purchasers required evidence of the truth of the recital in the deed of 1865 that K., C., and B. were entitled to the mortgage money. And, assuming that the testator was a trustee of the mortgage money, the purchasers required the vendors to shew that the property sold was comprised in the trust ; that K., C., and B. were duly

X. VENDOR AND PURCHASER—TITLE—*contd.*

appointed to succeed the testator in the trust: and that they had an effectual power of sale and of giving a receipt for the purchase-money:—*Held*, that it would be contrary to the practice of the Court to go behind a recital evidently framed for the purpose of keeping notice of trusts off the conveyance; that the requisitions need not be answered; and that a good title had been shewn by the vendors. *In re* HARMAN AND UXBRIDGE AND RICKMANSWORTH RAILWAY COMPANY

[24 Ch. D. 720

5. —— Order of Court—*Irregularity—Protection of Purchaser—Conveyancing and Law of Property Act*, 1881 (44 & 45 *Vict.* c. 41), s. 70—*Settled Estates Act*, 1877 (40 & 41 *Vict.* c. 18).] An order for sale under the Settled Estates Act, 1877, contained a direction dispensing with the concurrence or consent of the persons entitled, whether beneficially or otherwise, to any estate or interest subsequent to a certain estate tail, without naming them. The purchaser objected to the title on the ground that the order on the face of it was irregular:—*Held*, by Hall, V.C., that under the special circumstances of the case it was unnecessary for the parties whose concurrence was dispensed with to be named in the order:—*Held*, by the Court of Appeal, that under the 70th section of the Conveyancing and Law of Property Act, 1881, the purchaser would in any event have a good title—that section being applicable whether the objection to the order appears on face of it or not, and that the purchaser must complete. *In re* HALL DARE'S CONTRACT - 21 Ch. D. 41

6. —— Restrictive Covenant—*Railway Company—Superfluous Lands—Lands Clauses Consolidation Act*, 1845 (8 & 9 *Vict.* c. 18), *ss.* 127, 128.] Upon delivery of the abstract by a vendor who had contracted to deduce a good title in fee simple, it appeared that one of his predecessors had covenanted in his purchase deed not to use the property (which was a semi-detached villa standing on an eighth of an acre in a residential neighbourhood) or any part of it for the purpose of gasworks or a public-house:—*Held*, that this was such a restriction upon the user and enjoyment of the property as to constitute a fatal objection to the title.—A railway company selling its superfluous land is at liberty to impose such restrictive conditions upon the use and enjoyment of the land as may most conduce to their advantage as vendors, and there is nothing in the Lands Clauses Consolidation Act, 1845, to deprive them in this respect of the rights of ordinary vendors. *In re* HIGGINS AND HITCHMAN'S CONTRACT - - 21 Ch. D. 95

7. —— Trust for Sale — *Will — Charge of Debts—Partnership Property—Power of Executor to sell.*] A testator, who carried on business in partnership with his brother, by his will, dated the 23rd of November, 1861, directed payment of his debts, and, after bequeathing specific and pecuniary legacies, he devised and bequeathed all his real and leasehold and personal estate to trustees, upon trust for sale and conversion into money, and to hold the proceeds of sale on certain trusts. In 1872 the brother and the testator's widow, who was then the sole trustee and

X. VENDOR AND PURCHASER—TITLE—*contd.*

executrix of the will, joined in selling and conveying real estate, of which the brother and the testator had been tenants in common, and which was in fact partnership property, to a limited company who purchased the business. The purchase-money was to be paid partly in cash and partly in fully paid-up shares and debentures of the company. At the same time an arrangement was made for the handing over of the whole purchase-money to the bankers of the partnership, to whom the partnership was largely indebted, and whose debt was secured by mortgages of the partnership property, in satisfaction of the debt due to the bankers, the bankers undertaking to pay the other creditors of the partnership, and handing back to the executrix a sum of cash and some of the debentures, and providing certain other benefits for the brother. The conveyance of the real estate to the company contained a recital that the brother and the widow were entitled to the property in equal undivided moieties, and the widow purported to convey as trustee of her husband's will, but it was not stated in the deed that she was his executrix or that the property was partnership property.—On a subsequent sale of the property by the company, the purchaser objected that the sale by the widow was not authorized by the trust for sale, the consideration not being entirely paid in money:—*Held*, that the arrangement as to the disposition of the purchase-money received from the company amounted to a compromise by the widow with the creditors and with the surviving partner into which it was competent to her as executrix to enter under sect. 30 of the Act 23 & 24 Vict. c. 145:—And *held*, on the authority of *Corser* v. *Cartwright* (Law Rep. 7 H. L. 731), that this being so, and the real estate being partnership property which the widow, as executrix, was entitled to sell, and, inasmuch as she, as trustee, had the legal estate, and as executrix was the proper person to receive the purchase-money, the sale to the company was a valid one and their title good. WEST OF ENGLAND AND SOUTH WALES DISTRICT BANK *v.* MURCH 23 Ch. D. 138

8. —— Trust to pay or permit to receive—*Charge of Debts—Devise to Executors—Inquiry as to Existence of Debts—Requisitions—Objection to Root of Title not too late though stipulated Time expired.*] A testator directed that his debts should be paid by his executrix and executor thereinafter named. He then devised all his freehold and copyhold estates to his wife and son, and bequeathed to them his leaseholds and other personal estate and declared that his real and personal estates were devised and bequeathed to them "upon trust to pay the rents, issues, and profits, and the interest, dividends, and income of my said real and personal estates unto or permit the same to be received by my said wife during her life," and after her decease to raise and pay certain legacies to other persons which were to be treated as vested from his decease, and as to all the rest, residue and remainder of his real and personal estates after the death of his wife he devised and bequeathed the same to his said son, his heirs, executors, administrators, and assigns, according to the natures and qualities thereof,

X. VENDOR AND PURCHASER—TITLE—contd.

and empowered him to postpone payment of the legacies for two years from the widow's death, the legacies to carry interest from her death. The widow and son were appointed executors. The testator died in May, 1871, and the will was proved by the executors. In June, 1881, the widow and son put up for sale part of the freehold estate, under conditions of sale providing that requisitions must be delivered within ten days from the delivery of the abstract; time to be of the essence of the contract. The purchaser made a requisition that the legatees must release the estate from their legacies. The vendors refused to procure their concurrence, on the ground that the real estates were charged with debts, and that the vendors could sell discharged from the legacies. The purchaser then asked whether any debts remained unpaid. The vendors declined to answer the question, and the point was then raised, after the time for sending in requisitions had expired, whether any charge of debts was created. The vendors persisting in their refusal to answer the question whether any debts remained unpaid, the purchaser took out a summons to have it declared that no charge of debts was created by the will, and if it was, then that the vendors were bound to answer the inquiry as to debts.—*Held*, by Kay, J., that as the purchaser's objection went to the question whether the vendors had any power to sell he was not precluded by the conditions from raising it.—*Held*, further that as the real estate was not devised to the executors in trust for other persons, nor devised to them beneficially in such a way as to give them equal beneficial interests, the question whether the direction to them to pay debts charged the real estate with debts was too doubtful for the title to be forced on the purchaser.—*Held*, on appeal, that the legal estate in the widow for life with remainder to the son, but was vested in the two as joint tenants in fee.—*Doe v. Biggs* (2 Taunt. 109) distinguished.—*Held*, further that as the executors took the whole legal fee as joint tenants, the direction to them to pay debts charged the real estate with debts, though they took unequal beneficial interests in it.— *Held*, further that where executors in whom the legal fee is vested are selling real estate charged with debts, a purchaser is not bound or entitled to inquire whether debts remain unpaid unless twenty years have elapsed from the testator's decease. *In re* TANQUERAY-WILLAUME AND LANDAU　-　-　-　20 Ch. D. 465

9. —— Waiver of Objections—*Possession taken by Purchaser before Completion—Notice of Defects of Title—Distinction between removeable and irremoveable Defects.*] If a contract for the sale of land is silent as to the title which is to be shewn by the vendor, the legal implication that the purchaser is entitled to a good title may be rebutted by evidence that, before the execution of the contract, the purchaser had notice of defects in the vendor's title.—But, if the contract expressly provides that a good title shall be shewn the purchaser is entitled to insist on a good title, notwithstanding that before the execution of the contract he had notice of defects in the vendor's title.—If the contract contains no stipulation as

X. VENDOR AND PURCHASER—TITLE—contd.

to possession being taken by the purchaser before completion, and he takes possession with knowledge that there are defects in the title which the vendor cannot remove, the taking possession amounts to a waiver of the purchaser's right to require the removal of those defects, or to repudiate his contract. If, on the other hand, the defects are removable by the vendor, the taking of possession does not amount to such a waiver. *In re* GLOAG AND MILLER'S CONTRACT
[23 Ch. D. 320

XI. VENDOR AND PURCHASER — TITLE DEEDS.

—— Copyholds — *Enfranchisement — Acknowledgment of Right to produce Documents—Lands Clauses Consolidation Act*, 1845 (8 & 9 Vict. c. 18), s. 96—*Conveyancing and Law of Property Act*, 1881 (44 & 45 Vict. c. 41), s. 3, sub-s. 2, s. 9.] Copyhold land having been taken by a corporation under the powers of the Lands Clauses Act, and a draft conveyance from the copyholder being in the course of settlement, the corporation applied to the lord of the manor under sect. 96, for enfranchisement upon certain terms, which were agreed to. In settling the draft enfranchisement deed, the corporation claimed to have from the lord and his trustee to uses an acknowledgment of the right of the corporation to production of the documents of title to the manor, and of the Court rolls, relating to the hereditaments enfranchised, and to delivery of copies thereof, and, also from both, an undertaking for the safe custody of the same:—*Held*, that the corporation were entitled to no more than an acknowledgment by the lord and his trustee of the right of the corporation to the production of the documents of title to the manor, and of the Court rolls, so far as they related to the hereditaments enfranchised, and to delivery of copies thereof; and an undertaking by the lord alone for safe custody.—Whether the corporation were entitled to so much as the above, *quære. In re* AGG-GARDNER　-　-　-　25 Ch. D. 600

VENDOR AND PURCHASER—Action to recover deposit—Counter-claim for specific performance—Transfer to Chancery Division　-　13 Q. B. D. 540
See PRACTICE—SUPREME COURT—TRANSFER. 2.

—— Attachment of purchase-money
[19 Ch. D. 508
See PRACTICE—SUPREME COURT—GARNISHEE ORDERS. 2.

—— Conditions of sale—Approval of title
See CONDITION. 2.　　[9 Q. B. D. 276

—— Conveyance—Execution by attorney
See POWER OF ATTORNEY—*Statutes.*

—— Doubtful title　　　18 Ch. D. 381
See BANKRUPTCY—ASSETS. 15.

—— Evidence—Intention of parties to conveyance　-　-　-　9 Q. B. D. 506
See PRISON. 3.

—— Fire insurance—Fire after contract
[18 Ch. D. 1; 11 Q. B. D. 380
See INSURANCE, FIRE. 3, 4.

VETERINARY SURGEON.

The Act 44 & 45 Vict. c. 62, amends the law relating to Veterinary Surgeons.

Sect. 1. Act to be cited as the Veterinary Surgeons Act, 1881.

Sect. 2. Definitions and interpretations.

Sect. 3. Provisions as to register of veterinary surgeons.

Sect. 4. Provision for examination of students in Scotland.

Sect. 5. Power to registrar to correct the register.

Sect. 6. Empowers council of the Royal College of Veterinary Surgeons to remove names from the register.

Sect. 7. Empowers the council to restore names to the register.

Sect. 8. Proceedings for removal or restoration of names.

Sect. 9. Copy of register to be evidence of registration.

Sect. 10. Notice of death of practitioners to be sent by registrar of deaths.

Sect. 11. Penalty on obtaining registration by false representation.

Sect. 12. Penalty for wilful falsification of register.

Sect. 13. Provisions for registration of colonial or foreign practitioners with recognised diploma.

Sect. 14. Confirmation of charter of Royal College of Veterinary Surgeons.

VETERINARY SURGEON—continued.

Sect. 15. *Title of existing veterinary surgeons to be registered in college.*

Sect. 16. *Penalty on false representation as to membership of college.*

Sect. 17. *Penalty on misrepresentation after 1883 as to qualification to practise, and incapacity to recover fee, &c.*

Sect. 18. *Exercise of powers of Privy Council.*

Sect. 19. *Fines and imprisonment to be recovered and imposed summarily.*

Sect. 20. *Saving rights of the Royal College of Veterinary Surgeons.*

VICE-ADMIRALTY COURT—Jurisdiction
[9 App. Cas. 356
See SHIP—MARITIME LIEN. 7.

—— - 8 App. Cas. 329
See PRACTICE—ADMIRALTY—JURISDICTION. 5.

VICTORIA—Bankruptcy in—Will proved in
[21 Ch. D. 674
See PARTITION SUIT—SALE. 2.

—— Law of - - 9 App. Cas. 365
See COLONIAL LAW—VICTORIA. 4.

VIS MAJOR—Contract governed by lex loci—
War - 12 Q. B. D. 589
See CONFLICT OF LAWS. 1.

VISITOR—Lunatic—Order for access
[18 Ch. D. 26
See LUNATIC—INQUISITION. 1.

VOLUNTARY ALLOWANCE—Bankrupt
[17 Ch. D. 70
See BANKRUPTCY—ASSETS. 14.

VOLUNTARY CONVEYANCE.

1. —— **Gift of Furniture by Letters—***No Declaration of Trust—Subsequent Will of Husband—Wife not entitled to the Gift.*] A husband, by three letters written and signed by him and handed to his wife, gave her furniture and other articles for her sole and absolute use. He afterwards made his will, bequeathing certain legacies and making other dispositions of his property, and giving the residue of it to trustees in trust for his wife for life with remainder to six nieces absolutely. The furniture and other articles were at the time of the husband's death in the house which had been occupied by him and his wife, and the whole had been used by them in the ordinary way :—*Held*, that the furniture, &c., formed part of the husband's estate.—*Baddeley* v. *Baddeley* (9 Ch. D. 113) and *Fox* v. *Hawks* (13 Ch. D. 822) observed upon, and *Milroy* v. *Lord* (4 D. F. & J. 264) followed. *In re* BRETON'S ESTATE. BRETON *v.* WOOLLVEN - - - 17 Ch. D. 416

2. —— **Mortgagor—***Sale by Mortgagees under Power—Title to Surplus.*] A. B. having mortgaged estates in fee simple, subsequently made a voluntary settlement of the same estates and all his interest therein to grantees to uses to hold, subject to the mortgage and to a power of raising a sum of money for himself, to the use of himself for life with remainder to his first and other sons in tail, with remainders over.—The mortgagee afterwards sold the estates under the power of sale

VOLUNTARY CONVEYANCE—continued.

in the mortgage, and after retainer of his debt and costs paid the balance of the sale moneys into Court under the Trustee Relief Act. Upon a petition for payment out A. B. contended that the sale had destroyed the voluntary settlement, and that the persons claiming thereunder had no equity against the sale moneys, which must be treated as if the sale had been made by A. B. himself :—*Held*, that the voluntary settlement was a complete disposition by the settlor of the proceeds of the sale of the estate in case the prior mortgagee should exercise his power, and that the volunteers under the settlement were entitled as against the settlor to the fund in Court. *In re* WALHAMPTON ESTATE 26 Ch. D. 391

3. —— **Post-nuptial Settlement—***Conveyance by Husband and Wife of Wife's Separate Freeholds, and Demise by Husband of Wife's Separate Leaseholds — Subsequent Mortgage by Husband and Wife—Settlement held voluntary and void as against Mortgagee—27 Eliz. c. 4, s. 1.*] A married woman, having become entitled under a will to freehold and leasehold property for her sole and separate use, joined her husband in making a settlement, whereby the husband and wife conveyed the freeholds, and the husband alone demised the leaseholds, subject to the annual payment of a shilling, if demanded, to trustees, upon trust for the wife for her separate use for life, remainder to the husband for life, remainder for the children (if any), with ultimate remainder to the wife absolutely. Two years afterwards the husband and wife (there being no children of the marriage) made a mortgage of the property :—*Held*, that the conveyance by the husband, though binding on the estate by the curtesy which he would have had in his wife's freeholds if there had been issue, in the absence of any conveyance by her was not sufficient to raise a consideration moving from the husband; and that the settlement was voluntary and void under the statute as against the mortgagee. SHURMUR *v.* SEDGWICK. CROSSFIELD *v.* SHURMUR
[24 Ch. D. 597

4. —— **Rectification—***Power of Revocation.*] By a voluntary settlement property was assigned to trustees in trust for the settlor for life, remainder for any wife he might marry for life, with remainders to his issue, and in default or failure of issue in trust for his paternal next of kin :—*Held*, that though a settlement was proper to be made, and though the settlor understood the terms of this settlement, yet as his attention was not drawn to the fact that he might have had a power of disposition over the property in default or failure of issue, such a power ought to be given, and the settlement must be rectified accordingly. JAMES *v.* COUCHMAN 29 Ch. D. 212

5. —— **Setting aside—***Grounds for setting aside—Improper Clauses—Trustee—Appeal for Costs.*] Where an action is brought by the settlor against the trustees to set aside a voluntary settlement, the Court will not consider the propriety or impropriety of the clauses, except as evidence that the settlor did not understand what he was doing; the only question being whether the settlor understood what he was doing and its effect on his position with regard to the property.

VOLUNTARY CONVEYANCE—*contiuued.*

—Per Cotton, L.J.: But *quære* whether this applies to cases in which there are persons claiming adversely to the settlor.—Where a settlement is set aside the trustee has no claim to his costs as a matter of right, there being no contract in existence ; and, therefore, if costs are given against him he has no right of appeal. DUTTON *v.* THOMPSON   -   -   -   **23 Ch. D. 278**

6. —— **Setting aside**—*Onus*—*Power of Revocation.*] When a voluntary deed is impeached the onus of supporting it does not necessarily rest upon those who set it up. Nor is a voluntary deed of settlement voidable by the settlor merely because it does not contain a power of revocation HENRY *v.* ARMSTRONG   -   -   **18 Ch. D. 668**

—— Bankruptcy   19 Ch. D. 588 ; 15 Q. B. D. 682
    See BANKRUPTCY—VOID SETTLEMENT.
    1, 2.

—— Commencement of—Title   -   **24 Ch. D. 11**
    See VENDOR AND PURCHASER—CONDI-
    TIONS OF SALE. 4.

—— Duties on—Accounts under.
    See REVENUE—STAMPS—*Statutes.*

VOLUNTARY SUBSCRIPTIONS — Committee —
Action by some against others
    [28 Ch. D. 426
    See CHARITY—MANAGEMENT. 4.

VOLUNTARY WINDING-UP—Distress
    [17 Ch. D. 250
    See COMPANY—DISTRESS. 3.

—— Poor-rates   -   -   **23 Ch. D. 500**   .
    See COMPANY—RATES. 1.

—— Resolution for   26 Ch. D. 70 ; 29 Ch. D. 159
    See COMPANY—VOLUNTARY WINDING-UP.
    1, 2.

VOLUNTEER—Military.
    See ARMY AND NAVY—*Gazette.*

—— Next of kin—Marriage settlement—Default
    of appointment   .   -   **20 Ch. D. 742**
    See SETTLEMENT—REVOCATION. 2.

—— Settlement—Children of prior marriage
    [9 App. Cas. 303
    See SCOTCH LAW—HUSBAND AND WIFE.
    5.

VOTE—Municipal.
    See MUNICIPAL CORPORATION—ELECTION
    —*Statutes.*

—— Parliament—Employé—Time to record.
    See PARLIAMENT—ELECTION—*Statutes.*

—— Parliament—Multiplication of votes.
    See PARLIAMENT—FRANCHISE—*Statutes.*

VOTING PAPER   ..   -   **13 Q. B. D. 388**
    See MUNICIPAL CORPORATION — ELEC-
    TION. 9.

VOUCHERS—Army and navy service.
    See REVENUE—COLLECTION—*Statutes.*

W.

WAGER—Agent betting for principal **13 Q. B. D.**
[**779 ; 15 Q. B. D. 363**
See PRINCIPAL AND AGENT—PRINCIPAL'S
LIABILITY. 3, 7.

WAGES—Action for—Master of ship—Mortgage
of ship—Misconduct **10 P. D. 13**
See SHIP—MASTER. 2.

—— Foreign ship—Jurisdiction　-　**8 P. D. 121**
See JURISDICTION. 3.

—— Material men—Priority—Lien—Costs.
[**9 P. D. 37**
See SHIP—MARITIME LIEN. 5.

—— Payment in public-houses prohibited.
See MASTER AND SERVANT—WAGES—
Statutes.

—— Preferential debt—Bankruptcy **26 Ch. D. 393**
See BANKRUPTCY—PREFERENTIAL DEBTS.

—— Preferential debt—Winding-up
[**16 Ch. D. 373**
See COMPANY—PREFERENTIAL DEBTS.

—— Preferential debt — Winding-up — Statute
respecting.
See COMPANY—PREFERENTIAL DEBTS—
Statutes.

—— Seamen **8 App. Cas. 329**
See PRACTICE—ADMIRALTY — JURISDIC-
TION. 5.

—— Seamen—Priority of lien **8 P. D. 129**
See SHIP—MARITIME LIEN. 3.

WAIVER—Breach of trust　-　**20 Ch. D. 109**
See TRUSTEE—LIABILITIES. 8.

—— Devastavit—Lapse of time　- **20 Ch. D. 230**
See SPECIALTY DEBT.

—— Infant—Equity to settlement **16 Ch. D. 376**
See SETTLEMENT—EQUITY TO SETTLE-
MENT. 2.

—— Objection to title　-　**23 Ch. D. 320**
See VENDOR AND PURCHASER—TITLE. 8.

—— Penalty **16 Ch. D. 675**
See BANKRUPTCY—ACT OF BANKRUPTCY.
22.

—— Statutory rights—Charter - **25 Ch. D. 511 ;**
See MARKET. 2. [**9 App. Cas. 927**

—— Vendor's lien　-　-　**26 Ch. D. 501**
See VENDOR AND PURCHASER—LIEN. 2.

WARD OF COURT 19 Ch. D. 451 ; 25 Ch. D. 56 ;
[**28 Ch. D. 186**
See INFANT—WARD OF COURT. 1, 2, 3.

—— Access to mother—Years of discretion
[**24 Ch. D. 317**
See INFANT—EDUCATION. 1.

—— Custody—Covenant in separation deed
[**28 Ch. D. 606**
See HUSBAND AND WIFE—SEPARATION
DEED. 5.

—— Settlement　-　**25 Ch. D. 482**
See INFANT—SETTLEMENT.

WAREHOUSEMAN—Breach of contract—Damages　-　**7 Q. B. D. 510**
See DAMAGES—REMOTENESS. 5.

—— Liability of **6 Q. B. D. 475 ; 7 App. Cas. 591**
See TROVER.

WARRANT OF ARREST—Admiralty—Notice—
Telegram **10 P. D. 120**
See PRACTICE—ADMIRALTY—ARREST OF
SHIP. 2.

WARRANT OF DISTRESS, Service of.
See JUSTICE OF THE PEACE—PRACTICE—
Statutes.

WARRANTY—Answers to queries of life insurance company **9 App. Cas. 671**
See INSURANCE, LIFE—POLICY. 3.

—— Written warranty— Adulteration — Sale of
Food and Drugs Act, 1875 **12 Q. B. D. 97**
See ADULTERATION. 1.

WASTE—Tenant **21 Ch. D. 18 ; 8 App. Cas. 508**
See LANDLORD AND TENANT—CUSTOM
OF COUNTRY.

WATER.

1. —— **Nuisance** — *Flood* — *Adjoining Landowners—Liability for sending Water on adjoining
Lands.*] By reason of an unprecedented rainfall a
quantity of water was accumulated against one of
the sides of the Defendants' railway embankment,
to such an extent as to endanger the embankment,
when in order to protect their embankment, the
Defendants cut trenches in it by which the water
flowed through, and went ultimately on to the land
of the Plaintiff, which was on the opposite side of
the embankment and at a lower level, and flooded
and injured it to a greater extent than it would
have done had the trenches not been cut. In an
action for damages for such injury the jury found
that the cutting of the trenches was reasonably
necessary for the protection of the Defendants'
property, and that it was not done negligently :—
Held, that though the Defendants had not brought
the water on their land, they had no right to protect
their property by transferring the mischief from
their own land to that of the Plaintiff, and that
they were therefore liable. WHALLEY *v.* LANCA-
SHIRE AND YORKSHIRE RAILWAY COMPANY
[**13 Q. B. D. 131**

2. —— *Nuisance—Percolation of Water.*] Defendant allowed water to collect in his cellar and
to percolate into the Plaintiff's cellar.—*Held*, that
this was a wrong within the decision of *Fletcher
v. Rylands* (Law Rep. 3 H. L. 330), and that the
Plaintiff was entitled to damages. SNOW *v.* WHITE-
HEAD　-　-　**27 Ch. D. 588**

3. —— *Nuisance—Underground Water—Pollution of Well—Injunction.*] No one has a right
to use his own land in such a way as to be a nuisance
to his neighbour, and therefore if a man puts filth
or poisonous matter on his land, he must take care
that it does not escape so as to poison water which
his neighbour has a right to use, although his
neighbour may have no property in such water at

WATER—*continued.*

the time it is fouled. The Plaintiff and Defendant were adjoining landowners, and had each a deep well on his own land, the Plaintiff's land being at a lower level than the Defendant's. The Defendant turned sewage from his house into his well, and thus polluted the water that percolated underground from the Defendant's to the Plaintiff's land, and consequently the water which came into the Plaintiff's well from such percolating water when he used his well by pumping, came adulterated with the sewage from the Defendant's well :—*Held* (reversing the decision of Mr. Justice Pearson), that the Plaintiff had a right of action against the Defendant for so polluting the source of supply, although until the Plaintiff had appropriated it, he had no property in the percolating water under his land, and although he appropriated such water by the artificial means of pumping. BALLARD *v.* TOM-LINSON　　　**26 Ch. D. 194; 29 Ch. D. 115**

—— Damage from—Extraordinary flood—Liability of Water Commissioners
[7 App. Cas. 694
See SCOTCH LAW—STATUTORY DUTY.

—— Larceny　-　-　-　**11 Q. B. D. 21**
See CRIMINAL LAW—LARCENY. 5.

—— Right to accumulation　-　**9 App. Cas. 170**
See COLONIAL LAW—CANADA—QUEBEC. 8.

—— Right to use of.
See Cases under WATERCOURSE.

—— Supply of.
See Cases under WATERWORKS COMPANY.

—— Supply to house—Notice to owner to obtain supply—Power to charge rates.
[13 Q. B. D. 215
See LOCAL GOVERNMENT—RATES. 3.

WATERCOURSE.

1. —— **Abstraction of Water by non-riparian Owner**—*Riparian Owner—Absence of Damage—Right of Action—Injunction—Rights of riparian Owner in artificial Stream.*] The owner of land not abutting on a river with the license of a riparian owner took water from the river, and after using it for cooling certain apparatus returned it to the river unpolluted and undiminished:—*Held* (affirming the decision of Pollock, B.), that a lower riparian owner could not obtain an injunction against the landowner so taking the water, or against the riparian owner through whose land it was taken.—Observations on the rights which can be acquired by a riparian owner in an artificial stream. KENSIT *v.* GREAT EASTERN RAILWAY COMPANY　-　**23 Ch. D. 566; 27 Ch. D. 122**

2. —— **Diversion of Stream**—*Alteration of Natural Flow—Action by Riparian Owner—Grant to non-Riparian Landowner.*] A riparian owner cannot, except as against himself, confer on one who is not a riparian owner any right to use the water of the stream, and any user by a non-riparian proprietor, even under a grant from a riparian owner, is wrongful, if it sensibly affects the flow of the water by the lands of other riparian proprietors.—*Stockport Waterworks Company* v. *Potter* (3 H. & C. 300) approved. ORMEROD *v.* TODMORDEN JOINT STOCK MILL COMPANY　-　**11 Q. B. D. 155**

3. —— **Obstruction of Access** — *Conduit — Building — Previous Application — Costs.*] The

WATERCOURSE—*continued.*

owners of a house had had for many years a supply of water by pipes passing through the adjoining land under circumstances which in the view of the Court created an easement. The owner of part of the adjoining land proceeded to build a house over part of the line of pipes :—*Held*, that the owners of the house had a right to go on the adjoining land and repair the pipes when necessary, and that by building the house their means of access to the pipes would be materially interfered with and rendered more expensive; and an injunction was granted to restrain the building of the house.—The fact that an action has been brought without a previous application to the Defendant does not prevent the Plaintiff from getting his costs of the action. GOODHART *v.* HYETT　　**25 Ch. D. 182**

4. —— **Obstruction of Access** —*Sewer — Injunction.*] The owner of land through which a sewer ran, made an agreement that he would not set up any buildings so as to prevent reasonable access to the sewer. A subsequent owner of the land built a stable over the sewer :—*Held*, in an action by a local board, that there was no ground for a mandatory injunction to remove the building. SANDGATE LOCAL BOARD *v.* LENEY
[25 Ch. D. 183, n.

5. —— **Prescription**—*Unity of Possession.*] By deed in 1791 A. obtained a demise from B. of an underground goit or drain to be then constructed in B.'s land for the purpose of conducting water from A.'s mill so long as an annual rent of £2 2s. should be paid by A. to B.—In 1836 the demise of 1791 was put an end to, and liberty was given to A., who was at that time yearly tenant from B. of the land through which the goit ran, to change the goit or drain of 1791, and to substitute a new cut for conducting pure and clean water at the like rent of £2 2s.—The new cut was made and used for pure water, and the old goit (as the Plaintiff alleged) continued to be used for foul water.—In 1866 the land through which the goits ran was sold to C., and in 1867 A.'s yearly tenancy of the land was determined.—In an action by A. in 1879 to restrain C. from interfering with his use of the old goit, to which he claimed title by prescription from alleged open and uninterrupted use and enjoyment thereof from 1836 :—*Held*, that until 1867 A. could not acquire an easement in the land of which he was yearly tenant, distinct from the use and enjoyment of such land, as against B. his landlord, and accordingly that, assuming the open and uninterrupted user from 1836 to have been proved, he had failed to establish any title by prescription as against C. OUTRAM *v.* MAUDE
[17 Ch. D. 391

—— Prescription—Roman-Dutch Law
[10 App. Cas. 336
See COLONIAL LAW — CAPE OF GOOD HOPE. 4.

WATER-RATE.
See Cases under WATERWORKS COMPANY —WATER-RATE.

—— Covenant to pay rates　-　**13 Q. B. D. 202**
See LANDLORD AND TENANT—LEASE. 11.

WATERWORKS CLAUSES ACT.
See Statutes and Cases under WATERWORKS COMPANY.

WATERWORKS COMPANY:—　　　Col.
　I. Supply of Water　　-　1655
　II. Water-rate　-　　　　1657

I. WATERWORKS COMPANY — SUPPLY OF WATER.

1. —— Cutting off Supply — Injunction — Waterworks Clauses Act, 1847 (10 & 11 Vict. c. 17), s. 68—Jurisdiction.] Although the statutory remedy provided by sect. 68 of the Waterworks Clauses Act, 1847, for the settlement by two justices of disputes as to the annual value of a tenement supplied with water, and the special remedy by penalties given by sect. 43 against a company for withholding water, have not ousted the general jurisdiction to restrain the company by injunction from cutting off the supply of water pending proceedings for settling a dispute as to value, such injunction will not be granted on the application of an owner or occupier who will not undertake to commence proceedings with due speed before the justices under sect. 68. HAYWARD v. EAST LONDON WATERWORKS COMPANY 28 Ch. D.
[138

2. —— Measurement — Meter, Obligation to provide—Cutting off Supply—Waterworks Clauses Act, 1863 (26 & 27 Vict. c. 93), ss. 14, 16— Waterworks Clauses Act, 1847 (10 & 11 Vict. c. 17), ss. 43, 74 — Failure to pay or tender Rate in Advance.] The special Act of a water company provided for the supply of water to the inhabitants of the district for "family use" at certain rates calculated on the rental of the house supplied. The Act contained further provisions for the supply of water for schools, manufactories, &c., &c., and for other purposes than family consumption, and for baths, &c., and for the purposes of any trade or business whatsoever at certain rates per thousand gallons. The supply of water under these latter provisions having been held obligatory upon the company unless prevented by causes beyond their control :—Held, that, there being no provision in the special Act throwing upon the consumer the obligation of providing a meter to measure the water supplied for the purposes of a bath, no such obligation could be implied from the 14th section of the Waterworks Clauses Act, 1863, incorporated with the special Act, which section provides that where the undertakers are authorized by the special Act to supply water by measure they may let for hire to any consumer of water so supplied any meter or instrument for measuring the quantity of water supplied. The occupier of a house within the district of the above-mentioned company had a bath connected by means of a pipe with the house cistern, to which water was conveyed from the company's mains for "family use." The company required him to put up a meter for the purpose of measuring the water used for the bath, but he refused to do so. He had paid to the company in advance the proper amount in respect of the water supply "for family use" for the quarter ending the 29th of September, but had not paid or tendered any sum in respect of the water supply to the bath during such period. The company in consequence of his refusal to put up a meter or disconnect the bath, cut off the communication pipe from their main to his house upon the 20th of September. On the 29th of September, having cut off the pipe connecting the cistern with

I. WATERWORKS COMPANY — SUPPLY OF WATER—continued.

the bath, but not the waste or outlet pipe from the bath, he gave notice to the company of what he had done, and paid to the company in advance the proper amount for the supply of water for "family use" during the ensuing quarter, but did not restore the communication pipe between the company's mains and his cistern. The company refused to restore the supply on the ground that he had not cut off the waste-pipe from the bath, which he refused to do. The supply of water was not renewed till the 4th of November, when the company restored the communication pipe under protest :—Held, that the company were not entitled to insist on the consumer's providing a meter, but that they were not liable to a penalty under the Waterworks Clauses Act, 1847, s. 43, for not supplying water during the period between the 20th and the 29th of September, inasmuch as no payment or tender in respect of the water supply to the bath for such period had been made. But held that the company were liable to a penalty in respect of the period subsequent to the 29th of September; that they had no right to refuse the supply of water after that date, and that they were not justified in cutting off the supply, and were, therefore, not entitled to require the consumer to renew the communication. SHEFFIELD WATERWORKS COMPANY v. CARTER 8 Q. B. D. 632

3. —— Measurement—Private Baths—Meters supplied by Consumer.] The Sheffield Waterworks Company claimed a declaration that they were not bound under their Acts of Parliament to supply water for private baths except upon the terms of the consumer providing at his own expense a meter or other automatic self-registering instrument for the accurate measurement of the water used. The Defendant alleged that it was for the company who supplied the water to measure the quantity to be paid for :—Held, upon the construction of the various Acts under which the proceedings of the company were regulated, that it was not correct to treat the company as supplying the water to the consumer, but it was the consumer who was entitled to draw off from the main what water he required, and to fix pipes and apparatus at his own expense for the purpose of measuring the water so taken by him ; and such measurement could only be effected by some sufficient automatic self-registering meter or other instrument, or in some other equally accurate mode. SHEFFIELD WATERWORKS COMPANY v. BINGHAM　　　-　　25 Ch. D. 443

4. —— Private Baths.] Held, on the construction of the Sheffield Waterworks Company's Act that they have a right to make an extra charge for private baths. SHEFFIELD WATERWORKS COMPANY v. J. E. BINGHAM　25 Ch. D. 446, n.

5. —— Public Purposes—Workhouse—Waterworks Clauses Act, 1847 (10 & 11 Vict. c. 17), ss. 37-43.] By a special Act, incorporating the Waterworks Clauses Act, 1847, a waterworks company were bound at the request of the owner or occupier of any house to supply such person with water for domestic purposes at a minimum rate, to be increased if such house should be occupied by more than one family, and the Act further provided that a supply of water for domestic pur-

I. WATERWORKS COMPANY — SUPPLY OF WATER—*continued.*

poses should not include a supply of water for baths, washhouses, or public purposes. The Waterworks Clauses Act, 1847, deals with the supply of water for cleansing sewers and drains, cleansing and watering the streets, supplying any public pumps, baths, or washhouses, and imposes a penalty for neglect to supply water "for the public purposes aforesaid":—*Held* (by Lord Coleridge, C.J., Pollock, B., and Manisty, J.), that a workhouse was a house of which the guardians were owners, and the company were bound to supply them with water for domestic purposes, such supply not being a supply "for public purposes" within the meaning of the special Act or of the Waterworks Clauses Act, 1847, and that for the purposes of the special Act the inmates of the workhouse were to be treated as one family and the rate assessed accordingly. LISKEARD UNION *v.* LISKEARD WATERWORKS COMPANY - 　　**7 Q. B. D. 505**

6. —— " **Pure and Wholesome** " Water — *Contamination from Leaden Pipes—Deleterious Effect on Consumer — Waterworks Clauses Act, 1847 (10 & 11 Vict. c. 17), s. 35—Special Act (32 & 33 Vict. c. cx.).*] The Defendants were empowered by a special Act (32 & 33 Vict. c. cx.) incorporating the Waterworks Clauses Act of 1847 (10 & 11 Vict. c. 17), with the exception of certain provisions, to supply water for domestic use within the limits and from the sources described in their Act.—By sect. 66 of the special Act the Defendants were entitled to prescribe the material to be used for service-pipes by persons supplied with water, and by by-laws the Defendants prescribed that the material might be either lead or cast-iron. Leaden service-pipes were, upon the application of the landlord of the Plaintiff's house and of the Plaintiff, laid down by the Defendants from their mains to the house at the expense of the landlord and the Plaintiff. The service-pipes when laid belonged to the consumer of the water supplied through them.—By the Waterworks Clauses Act, 1847, s. 35, " the undertakers shall provide and keep in the pipes to be laid down by them a supply of pure and wholesome water sufficient for the domestic use of all the inhabitants of the town or district within the limits of the special Act, who shall be entitled to demand a supply, and shall be willing to pay water-rate for the same." Water which was pure and wholesome in the mains of the Defendants, was supplied by them to the Plaintiff, but in its passage from the mains through the service-pipes it was contaminated by the lead, and he, using the water, suffered from lead-poisoning. He sued the Defendants for injuries sustained from impure and unwholesome water:—*Held*, that he had no cause of action.—Judgment of Mathew, J., affirmed. ' MILNES *v.* MAYOR, &C., OF HUDDERSFIELD　**10 Q. B. D. 124;**
　　　　　　　　　　　　　[12 Q. B. D. 443

II. WATERWORKS COMPANY—WATER-RATE.
Waterworks Clauses Act.]　The Act 48 & 49 Vict. c. 34, declares the meaning of the words " the annual value of the tenement supplied with water " in sect. 68 of 10 & 11 Vict. c. 17 (Waterworks Clauses Act, 1847).

1. —— Annual Value—*Water Rate to be calculated on " Rateable Value "—Waterworks Clauses*

II. WATERWORKS COMPANY—WATER-RATE —*continued.*

Act, 1847 (10 & 11 *Vict.* c. 17), s. 68.] By the special Act of a water company, which incorporated the Waterworks Clauses Act, 1847, save so far as the clauses or provisions thereof were expressly varied or excepted, the company were obliged to supply water to the occupiers of dwelling houses for domestic purposes at a rate not exceeding £6 per cent. per annum upon the annual "rack rent or value" of the premises supplied. It was further provided in a subsequent section of the Act that the rate should be "payable according to the annual value at which the premises were from time to time assessed to the poor-rate if the same were so assessed, or if not according to the net annual value of the premises."—By the 68th section of the Waterworks Clauses Act, 1847, "the water-rates, except as hereinafter and in the special Act mentioned, shall be payable according to the annual value of the tenements supplied with water ":—*Held*, that the water rate charged by the company must be calculated on the " rateable value " not on the " gross estimated rental " of the premises supplied with water. WARRINGTON WATERWORKS COMPANY *v.* LONGSHAW　　　　　　**9 Q. B. D. 145**

2. —— Annual Value—*Annual Rent, how to be estimated—" Voids."—Owner compounding for Rates—Repairs and Insurance.*] It was provided by a Water Act that the charge to be made for the supply of water for domestic use should be at a rate varying according to the " annual rent " of the premises supplied.—The Appellant was the owner of certain houses supplied with water by the Respondents under the Act. The houses were let at weekly rents, the Appellant paying all rates charged thereon, and also for all repairs and insurances in respect thereof. He was allowed, as an owner, under 32 & 33 Vict. c. 41, s. 4 (the Poor-rate Assessment and Collection Act, 1869), a deduction of 30 per cent. from the full amount of the poor-rate which an occupier if rated would have paid.—The Respondents charged the Appellant with water-rates calculated on the following basis: they multiplied the weekly rents by fifty-two and deducted from the amount so arrived at the actual sums paid by the Appellant for rates, and then charged the water-rates upon the balance:—*Held*, that, in order to arrive at the " annual rent " upon which the water-rate was to be computed, an allowance should be made in respect of " voids," i.e., houses lying vacant from time to time; and that the actual amount of the poor-rates and other rates paid by the Appellant was rightly deducted, but that the Appellant was not entitled to deduct the full amount of the rates which an occupier if rated would have paid; nor the amount which he paid for repairs and insurances.—Meaning of the terms " annual rent " and " annual value " discussed.—*Dobbs* v. *Grand Junction Waterworks Co.* (10 Q. B. D. 337) followed. SMITH *v.* MAYOR, &C., OF BIRMINGHAM
　　　　　　　　　　　[11 Q. B. D. 195
　　　　　[But see next case.]

3. —— Annual Value—*Net annual or rateable Value.*] A water company by a special Act of 1826 were compellable to supply water to certain dwelling-houses in the metropolis for domestic purposes at certain rates per cent. per annum, payable "according to the actual amount of the

II. WATERWORKS COMPANY—WATER-RATE
—continued.

rent where the same can be ascertained, and where
the same cannot be ascertained according to the
actual amount or annual value upon which the
assessment to the poor's-rate is computed in the
parish or district where the house is situated."—
By a special Act of 1852 the company were compellable to furnish the water "where the annual
value of the dwelling-house or other place supplied
shall not exceed £200 at a rate per cent. per annum
on such value not exceeding £4; and where such
annual value shall exceed £200, at a rate per cent.
per annum on such value not exceeding £3."—The
occupier of one of the houses was lessee for a long
term at a ground rent, and paid no rent except the
ground rent :—*Held*, reversing the decision of the
Court of Appeal, that whether the later Act repealed the provisions of the former or not the case
must be dealt with under the later Act; and that
the words "annual value" in the later Act meant
"net annual value" as defined in the Parochial
Assessments Act, 1836 (6 & 7 Will. 4., c. 96), s. 1.
—*Held*, also, that "annual value" had the same
meaning in the earlier as in the later Act.—*Colvill
v. Wood* (2 C. B. 210) commented on. DOBBS *v.*
GRAND JUNCTION WATERWORKS COMPANY 9 Q. B. D.
[151; 10 Q. B. D. 337; 9 App. Cas. 49

4. —— Annual Value—*Supply for Domestic
Purposes — Premises used as a Public-house—
Licence—Premium.*] By the special Act of a
water company it was provided that water should
be supplied for domestic purposes by the company
at a rate per cent. upon the annual value of the
dwelling-house or other place supplied, that a supply of water for domestic purposes should not
include a supply of water for, among other things,
any trade or manufacture or business requiring an
extra supply of water, and that the company might
furnish water for other than domestic purposes on
such terms as might be agreed on between the
company and the consumer.—The company supplied water for domestic purposes to a house occupied as a licensed public-house. The company
contended that the annual value of the premises
as a licensed public-house should be taken as the
basis of the water-rate payable in respect of such
supply, and that therefore the fact of the premises
being licensed, and a premium which had been
paid for the lease of the premises as a public-house,
ought to be taken into consideration in fixing the
value. The occupier contended that such water-
rate should be based upon the value of the premises
for domestic purposes only :—*Held*, that the contention of the company was correct. WEST MIDDLE-
SEX WATERWORKS *v.* COLEMAN. COLEMAN *v.* WEST
MIDDLESEX WATERWORKS -   14 Q. B. D. 529

5. —— Annual Value — "*Water - rate*" —
"*Annual Rack-rent or Value*"—"*Gross sum assessed to the Poor-rate*"—*Bristol Waterworks Acts,
1862 and 1865—Pleasure Garden attached to and
occupied with a Dwelling-house—Extra Charge
for* "*a pipe and tap or other apparatus*" *used in
the garden.*] Sect. 68 of the Bristol Waterworks
Act, 1862, enacts that the company shall furnish to
every occupier of a private dwelling-house within
their limits a sufficient supply of water for the
domestic use of such occupier, at certain annual
rents or rates according to the "annual rack-rent

II. WATERWORKS COMPANY—WATER-RATE
—continued.

or value of the premises so supplied "—such supply
(by sect. 71) not to include, among other things, a
supply of water "for watering gardens by means
of a tap, tube, pipe, or other such like apparatus;"
and sect. 32 of the Bristol Waterworks Amendment
Act, 1865, enacts that "if any dispute shall arise
as to the amount of the annual rent or value of any
dwelling-house or premises supplied with water by
the company, such dispute shall be decided by two
justices : provided that the amount of the annual
rack-rent or value to be fixed by such justices shall
not be less than the gross sum assessed to the poor-
rate, or less than the rent actually paid for such
dwelling-house or premises." A dwelling-house
and garden in the occupation of the owner were
assessed to the poor-rate as follows :—"Gross estimated rental, £240 ; rateable value, £204." It was
proved that the value of the house without the
garden would be 10 per cent. less, and that the
owner contracted to pay and did pay £1 1s. annually
for the watering by means of a pipe and tap in the
garden which surrounded the dwelling-house and
was occupied and assessed therewith.—*Held*, upon
a case stated by the justices, that the words "gross
sum assessed to the poor-rate" meant the "gross
estimated rental," and not "rateable or net value;"
and that the water-rent was chargeable upon the
gross estimated rental of "the premises," including
the pleasure-garden occupied with the house, and
not merely upon the dwelling-house itself, the
extra charge for the garden supply being for using
a pipe and tap. BRISTOL WATERWORKS COMPANY
v. UREN -   15 Q. B. D. 637

6. —— Recovery of Arrears—*Distress—West
Middlesex Waterworks Acts* (46 *Geo.* 3, *c. cxix.;*
50 *Geo.* 3, *c. cxxxii.;* 15 & 16 *Vict. c cliz.*).—*Waterworks Clauses Consolidation Act*, 1847 (10 & 11
Vict. c. 17)—*Effect of, upon the Company's special
Acts.*] By an Act of 46 Geo. 3, c. cxix. s. 57, the
West Middlesex Waterworks Company were to
supply water to the occupiers of premises in certain
parishes, they paying to the company such rates
or sums of money for such water as should be
mutually agreed upon between them, and, in default
of payment, power was given to the company to
issue their warrants for the recovery of arrears by
distress and sale of the consumer's goods. By a
subsequent Act of 50 Geo. 3, c. cxxxii. s. 13, it
was provided that the company should not alienate
their powers, but only take and demand "such
sums *as should be reasonable*" for the water supplied under the provisions of that Act; and by 15
& 16 Vict. c. clix. (passed in 1852), which recited
the earlier Acts of the company, it was provided
that, "except as by this Act expressly provided, this
Act or anything therein contained shall not repeal,
alter, interpret, or in any manner affect any of the
provisions in force at the commencement of this
Act of the recited Acts or any of them; and,
except only so far as is requisite for the execution
of this Act, all those provisions, and all powers
thereby respectively created, conferred, or saved.
shall be and continue as valid and effectual as if
this Act had not passed ":—*Held*, that the effect
of s. 13 of 50 Geo. 3, c. cxxxii. was merely to
alter the mode of ascertaining the amount of the
rate, but not the mode of enforcing payment of

II. WATERWORKS COMPANY—WATER-RATE
—continued.

arrears; and that the power of distress given to the
company by s. 57 of the Act of 46 Geo. 3 was not
(either expressly or by implication) taken away by
the Act of 50 Geo. 3, or by any of the provisions
of the Waterworks Clauses Consolidation Act,
1847; but that such power of distress was expressly preserved to the company by sect. 48 of 15 &
16 Vict. c. clix.—Held, also, that the company
were not responsible for an assault committed by
the broker or his assistant when executing the
warrant. RICHARDS v. WEST MIDDLESEX WATER-
WORKS COMPANY   -   15 Q. B. D. 660

WATERWORKS COMPANY—Supply of water—
Larceny -   -   -   11 Q. B. D. 21
See CRIMINAL LAW—LARCENY. 5.

—— Water-rate—Covenant by lessor to pay rates
[13 Q. B. D. 202
See LANDLORD AND TENANT—LEASE. 11.

WAY.

1. —— Unity of possession—Owner of two
Tenements—Grant of one Tenement "together with
all Ways now used and enjoyed therewith."] A
grant by the owner of two tenements of one of
them, "together with all ways now used or enjoyed
therewith," will pass to the grantee a right of way
over a clearly defined path constructed over the
other tenement, and at the date of the grant actually used for the purposes of the tenement which
is granted, even though the path did not exist
prior to the unity of possession.—Thomson v. Waterlow (Law Rep. 6 Eq. 36) and Langley v. Hammond
(Law Rep. 3 Ex. 161), so far as they are contrary
to this view, must be taken to have been overruled
by Watts v. Kelson (Law Rep. 6 Ch. 166) and
Kay v. Oxley (Law Rep. 10 Q. B. 360). BARK-
SHIRE v. GRUBB   -   18 Ch. D. 616

2. —— Unity of possession—Right occupied
or enjoyed as "parcel or member" of the Tenement
granted—Purchase by Railway Company—User
for Purposes of Railway.] A railway company
purchased, under the powers of their Act, a piece
of land on which was a stable. By the conveyance
to the company the premises were granted together
with all "rights, members, and appurtenances to
the hereditaments belonging or occupied or enjoyed
as part, parcel, or member thereof." The vendor
had many years previously made a private road from
the highway to the stable over his own land for
his own convenience and had used it ever since.
The soil of this road was not conveyed to the
company and no express mention of it was made
in the conveyance. The Plaintiff refused to allow
the company to use the road:—Held (affirming the
judgment of Chitty, J.), first, that notwithstanding
the unity of possession of the stables and the private
road at the date of the conveyance to the company,
a right of way passed to the company under the
general words in the conveyance.—Kay v. Oxley
(Law Rep. 10 Q. B. 360) and Watts v. Kelson (Law
Rep. 6 Ch. 166) followed.—Secondly, that the fact
of the stable having been purchased by a railway
company for the purposes of their undertaking did
not preclude them from claiming the right of way
so long as they used the premises as a stable; which
they might lawfully do till such time as they were
required for the special purposes of the railway, or
were sold as superfluous land.—Whether the rail-

WAY—continued.

way company would be entitled to claim the right
of way after they had ceased to use the premises
as a stable, and had converted them to some purpose connected with the railway—Quære. BAYLEY
v. GREAT WESTERN RAILWAY COMPANY
[26 Ch. D. 434

—— Pleading—Statement of course and termini
[22 Ch. D. 481
See PRACTICE — SUPREME COURT —
AMENDMENT. 1.

—— Right of—Prescription—Forty years' enjoyment — Remainderman — "Reversion expectant on term of life or years"
See PRESCRIPTION. 2. [15 Q. B. D. 629

—— Reservation of, in agreement, not in convey-
ance   -   -   -   24 Ch. D. 572
See VENDOR AND PURCHASER—AGREE-
MENT. 1.

—— User at intervals—Twenty years' enjoyment
as of right   -   13 Q. B. D. 304
See PRESCRIPTION. 1.

WAYWARDEN—Meeting for election—Demand
of poll -   -   -   11 Q. B. D. 282
See HIGHWAY—WAYWARDEN.

WEIGHTS AND MEASURES.

Weights and Measures Act, 1878.] Orders in
council regulating the fees to be paid to inspectors.
May 18th, 1881   -   -   L. G., 1881, p. 2618
Altering the fees hitherto taken by inspectors.
Nov. 29th, 1881   -   L. G., 1881, p. 6533
Relative to fees. Aug. 18th, 1882   L. G., 1882,
[p. 3905
Increasing the fees payable to inspectors. June
26th, 1884 -   -   L. G., 1884, p. 2993
Defining the amount of errors to be tolerated in
local standards when verified by the Board of
Trade. June 29th, 1882 -   L. G., 1882, p. 3055
Denominations of Standards. Aug 23rd, 1883
[L. G., 1883, p. 4211

WELL—Pollution of   -   29 Ch. D. 115
See WATER. 3.

WEST AUSTRALIA—Law of   9 App. Cas. 142
See COLONIAL LAW—WEST AUSTRALIA. 2.

WEST RIDING REGISTRY   -   26 Ch. D. 501
See VENDOR AND PURCHASER—LIEN. 2.

WESTMINSTER, PALACE OF — Ecclesiastical
jurisdiction   -   -   22 Ch. D. 316
See PRACTICE—ECCLESIASTICAL—JURIS-
DICTION. 2.

WHARFINGER—Warrant—Indorsement
[28 Ch. D. 682
See BILL OF SALE—REGISTRATION. 5.

WHITE LEAD FACTORY.
See FACTORY ACTS—Statutes.

WIDOW—Annuity to—Voidable marriage
[25 Ch. D. 685
See WILL—CONDITION. 11.

WIFE.

See Cases under HUSBAND AND WIFE;
and PRACTICE—DIVORCE.

—— Invalid marriage—Legacy to widow
See WILL—MISTAKE. 2. [22 Ch. D. 597

WILD BIRDS PROTECTION ACT, 1881.
See BIRDS PROTECTION ACT—Statutes.

WILFUL DEFAULT—Executor—Administration
action　-　-　　24 Ch. D. 727
See PRACTICE—SUPREME COURT—TRIAL.
1.

—— Executor—Order for account　20 Ch. D. 538
See EXECUTOR—ACTIONS. 8.

WILL:—　　　　　　　　　　　Col.
　I. ABSOLUTE GIFT　-　-　1663
　II. ADEMPTION　　-　-　1664
　III. AMBIGUITY　　-　-　1664
　IV. ANNUITY　-　-　-　1664
　V. ATTESTING WITNESS -　-　1664
　VI. CHARGE OF DEBTS　-　-　1665
　VII. CHILDREN　　-　-　1666
　VIII. CLASS -　　-　-　1666
　IX. CONDITION.　-　-　1668
　X. CONTINGENT REMAINDER　-　1673
　XI. CONVERSION　　-　-　1673
　XII. CROSS REMAINDERS.　-　1673
　XIII. DEATH COUPLED WITH CONTIN-
　　GENCY　　　　　　　1674
　XIV. DISCLAIMER　-　　　1675
　XV. ESTATE IN REALTY　-　-　1676
　XVI. EXECUTORS　　-　-　1677
　XVII. EXONERATION -　　-　1678
　XVIII. HEIRLOOM　-　　-　1679
　XIX. INCORPORATED DOCUMENTS　-　1682
　XX. INTERIM INCOME　-　-　1682
　XXI. JOINT TENANCY　　-　1683
　XXII. LAPSE -　　　　-　1683
　XXIII. MISTAKE　-　　-　1685
　XXIV. PERPETUITY　　-　-　1687
　XXV. PRECATORY TRUST　-　1690
　XXVI. PRIORITY OF LEGACIES　-　1691
　XXVII. REPUGNANCY　　-　-　1691
　XXVIII. RESIDUARY GIFT　　-　1692
　XXIX. REVOCATION　-　　-　1693
　XXX. SATISFACTION　-　-　1694
　XXXI. SEPARATE USE　　-　1695
　XXXII. SPEAKING FROM DEATH　-　1696
　XXXIII. SPECIFIC LEGACY　　-　1697
　XXXIV. SUBSTITUTIONAL GIFT　-　1698
　XXXV. SURVIVOR　-　　-　1698
　XXXVI. TRUST ESTATES　-　-　1699
　XXXVII. TRUSTEES　-　　-　1699
　XXXVIII. VESTING　-　　-　1700
　XXXIX. WORDS　-　　-　1703

I. WILL—ABSOLUTE GIFT.

1.——Interest.] Under a gift by A. to his wife of £10,000 "afterwards to go to the understated residuary legatee E.":—*Held*, that the legacy of £10,000 was given to the wife absolutely, but that interest upon such legacy did not begin to run until after one year from the testator's death. *In re* PERCY. PERCY *v.* PERCY.　24 Ch. D. 616

2.—— Survivor—Life Estate—Intestacy.] The will of S. C. after bequeathing her property to A. C. and J. C., continued thus, "in case of the demise of either the said A. C. or J. C., I do hereby bequeath the same . . . to the survivor for her sole use and benefit during her or their natural

I. WILL—ABSOLUTE GIFT—*continued.*

lifetime":—*Held*, that the residue was not disposed of, and that A. C. and J. C. took only as tenants for life. WATSON *v.* WATSON　7 P. D. 10

II. WILL—ADEMPTION.

—— **Lunatic Testator**—*Lunacy Jurisdiction.*—*Specific Bequest — Order for Sale — Separate Account—Lunacy Regulation Act*, 1853 (16 & 17 *Vict. c.* 70), *ss.* 118, 119.] A testator made a specific bequest of stock in the G. railway company. After the date of his will he was found a lunatic. Under an order in the lunacy, the stock was sold and the proceeds were invested in a sum of consols, which was carried to the credit of the lunatic to an account intituled "Proceeds of the sale of stock in the G. railway company."—In an action for the administration of the testator's estate:—*Held*, that the specific legacy was adeemed by the sale in the lunacy, and that the consols therefore fell into the residue.—Observations on *Jones v. Green* (Law Rep. 5 Eq. 555) and *In re Leeming* (3 D. F. & J. 43). *In re* FREER. FREER *v.* FREER　　　　　　　[22 Ch. D. 622

—— Purchase-money of estate sold　30 Ch. D. 92
　See WILL—WORDS. 9.

—— Satisfaction by advance in lifetime of testator
　　[17 Ch. D. 701; 28 Ch. D. 552; 15 Q. B. D.
　See WILL—SATISFACTION. 1, 2, 3. [300

III. WILL—AMBIGUITY.

—— **Extrinsic Evidence**—*Misdescription.*] A testator appointed William McC. of Canonbury, an executor. The only persons at all answering the description were Thomas McC. and William Abraham McC.:—*Held*, that parol evidence was admissible to prove which person was intended by the testator. Probate granted to Thomas McC. IN THE GOODS OF BRAKE　　　6 P. D. 217

IV. WILL—ANNUITY.

1. —— **Charge on Income or Corpus**—*Continuing Charge.*] A testator directed his trustees to pay an annuity out of the rents and profits of a trust estate by half-yearly payments, and he bequeathed the remainder of such rents and income in trust for his sister for life, with remainder to her children:—*Held*, that the annuity was a continuing charge on the rents and profits.—*Stelfox v. Sugden* (Joh. 234) considered. WORMALD *v.* MUZEEN -　　　　　　17 Ch. D. 167

2. —— **For Life or Perpetual.**] A testatrix bequeathed an annuity payable out of the rental of certain hereditaments to her sister C. for life, with remainder for life to certain persons, and on their deaths the testatrix directed her executors to pay the annuity out of the said rental to the surviving children of B. :—*Held*, that the children of B. took the annuity for their lives only.—*Evans v. Walker* (3 Ch. D. 211) not followed. BLIGHT *v.* HARTNOLL -　　　　　19 Ch. D. 294

V. WILL—ATTESTING WITNESS.

—— **Marriage of Devisee**, *after Attestation, to attesting Witness*—1 *Vict. c.* 26, *s* 15.] Under the Wills Act (1 Vict. c. 26), s. 15, the marriage, after attestation of a will, of a devisee to the attesting witness, does not affect the validity of the devise. THORPE *v.* BESTWICK　6 Q. B. D. 311

VI. WILL—CHARGE OF DEBTS.

—— Legal Estate—*Direction to Executors to pay Debts—Devise to Executors—Inquiry as to Existence of Debts—Trust to pay or permit to receive—Requisitions—Objection to Root of Title not too late though stipulated Time expired.*] A testator directed that his debts should be paid by his executrix and executor thereinafter named. He then devised all his freehold and copyhold estates to his wife and son, and bequeathed to them his leaseholds and other personal estate and declared that his real and personal estates were devised and bequeathed to them "upon trust to pay the rents, issues, and profits, and the interest, dividends, and income of my said real and personal estates unto or permit the same to be received by my said wife during her life," and after her decease to raise and pay certain legacies to other persons which were to be treated as vested from his decease, and as to all the rest, residue and remainder of his real and personal estates after the death of his wife he devised and bequeathed the same to his said son, his heirs, executors, administrators, and assigns, according to the natures and qualities thereof, and empowered him to postpone payment of the legacies for two years from the widow's death, the legacies to carry interest from her death. The widow and son were appointed executors. The testator died in May, 1871, and the will was proved by the executors. In June, 1881, the widow and son put up for sale part of the freehold estate, under conditions of sale providing that requisitions must be delivered within ten days from the delivery of the abstract; time to be of the essence of the contract. The purchaser made a requisition that the legatees must release the estate from their legacies. The vendors refused to procure their concurrence, on the ground that the real estates were charged with debts, and that the vendors could sell discharged from the legacies. The purchaser then asked whether any debts remained unpaid. The vendors declined to answer the question, and the point was then raised, after the time for sending in requisitions had expired, whether any charge of debts was created. The vendors persisting in their refusal to answer the question whether any debts remained unpaid, the purchaser took out a summons to have it declared that no charge of debts was created by the will, and if it was, then that the vendors were bound to answer the inquiry as to debts.—*Held*, by Kay, J., that as the purchaser's objection went to the question whether the vendors had any power to sell he was not precluded by the conditions from raising it.—*Held*, further, that as the real estate was not devised to the executors in trust for other persons, nor devised to them beneficially in such a way as to give them equal beneficial interests, the question whether the direction to them to pay debts charged the real estate with debts was too doubtful for the title to be forced on the purchaser. —*Held*, on appeal, that the legal estate in the real property was not limited to the widow for life with remainder to the son, but was vested in the two as joint tenants in fee.—*Doe v. Biggs* (2 Taunt. 109) distinguished. — *Held*, further that as the executors took the whole legal fee as joint tenants, the direction to them to pay debts charged the real estate with debts, though they took unequal beneficial interests in it.—*Held*, further that where

VI. WILL—CHARGE OF DEBTS—*continued.*

executors in whom the legal fee is vested are selling real estate charged with debts, a purchaser is not bound or entitled to inquire whether debts remain unpaid unless twenty years have elapsed from the testator's decease. *In re* TANQUERAY-WILLAUME AND LANDAU   -   20 Ch. D. 465

VII. WILL—CHILDREN.

1. —— *Illegitimate Child—Gift to Children of deceased Person.*] A testatrix bequeathed to A., "the eldest daughter of my deceased daughter S., my gold watch." And she bequeathed other property to trustees "in trust for such of the children of my said deceased daughter S. who shall attain twenty-one, absolutely, equally share and share alike, the shares of such of them as shall be daughters to be for their sole and separate use." S. had two legitimate children, a son and a daughter, and she had also an illegitimate daughter, who was the person spoken of in the will as "A., the eldest daughter of S.":—*Held*, that there was a sufficient indication of an intention that A. should be included in the description of "the children of S." *In re* HUMPHRIES. SMITH *v.* MILLIDGE   24 Ch. D. 691

2. —— *Illegitimate Child—Class of Children.*] Testator by his will bequeathed to M. B. B., "daughter of my nephew J. B.," £200; and to T. B., "son of the said J. B.," £100. He directed his trustees to stand possessed of his residue upon trust for "all and every the children and child" of R. C. and J. B. respectively. By a codicil testator revoked the bequest of £200 "to my great-niece," M. B. B., and the bequest of £100 "to my great-nephew," T. B., and instead thereof bequeathed to M. B. B., £100; to T. B., £100; and to A. B., "another daughter of my nephew J. B.," £100.— M. B. B. was illegitimate; T. B. and A. B. were legitimate;—*Held*, that M. B. B. was sufficiently indicated as one of the persons who was to participate in the residue.—*Megson v. Hindle* (15 Ch. D. 198) distinguished. *In re* BRYON. DRUMMOND *v.* LEIGH   -   -   -   -   30 Ch. D. 110

VIII. WILL—CLASS.

1. —— " *According to the Stocks.*"] A testator gave the income of a trust fund to his wife for her life, and subject thereto the fund was to be held in trust for such of his cousins (the children of four deceased aunts and two deceased uncles of the testator named in the will) living at the determination of the wife's life interest, and such issue then living (if any) of his said cousins then dead as, either before or after the determination of such life interest, should attain twenty-one, or should die under twenty-one leaving issue living at his, her, or their death, to take (if more than one) in a course of distribution according to the stocks, and not according to the number of individuals. At the time of the death of the tenant for life there were living one cousin of the testator (a child of one of the uncles named in the will), and children and other issue of fifteen deceased cousins (children of the other uncle and of the four aunts named in the will):—*Held*, that the words "according to the stocks" applied to the descendants of cousins, and not to the cousins themselves, and that the fund was divisible into sixteen shares. —*Robinson v. Shepherd* (4 D. J. & S. 129) preferred to *Gibson v. Fisher* (Law Rep. 5 Eq. 51). *In re* WILSON. PARKER *v.* WINDER 24 Ch. D. 664

VIII. WILL—CLASS—continued.

2. —— Gift to **F. H. S. and R. S. share and share alike,** "and after the decease of the said F. H. S. and R. S. to their Children share and share alike, and to their Heirs for ever."] A testatrix bequeathed personalty in trust for A. B. for life, and after his decease for his issue, and on failure of his issue to F. H. S. and R. S. share and share alike, "and after the decease of the said F. S. H. and R. S. to their children share and share alike, and to their heirs for ever." F. H. S. died without having had issue, R. S. survived him and died leaving children, and A. B., who survived them both, died without issue.—Upon a petition by the children of R. S. for payment out of a portion of the trust fund which was in Court :—Held, that, upon the authorities, the bequest must be construed as a gift after the respective deaths of F. H. S. and R. S. to their respective children, and that there having been an absolute gift to each of them in the first instance only cut down in favour of his children, in the event which happened the fund was divisible in moieties between the representatives of F. H. S. and the children of R. S. In re HUT-CHINSON'S TRUSTS　　21 Ch. D. 811

3. —— **Gift to the Children of J. D. and R. A.** to be vested Legacies at Testator's Death—Death of R. A. before Testator—Children of R. A. not entitled—Residuary Legatee living at Death entitled.] Testator gave to trustees all his estates upon trust to sell, and directed that the proceeds of sale should be part of his personal estate and be subject to the dispositions concerning his residuary estate. and after giving legacies—one to R. A., and another to the children of J. D.—he gave the residue unto and equally amongst all the children of his brother-in-law, J. D., and the said R. A., and directed that the same should be vested legacies at the time of his decease. R. A. died before the testator, leaving children living at the testator's death. Three children of J. D. were living at the testator's death :—Held, that R. A. would, if living, have taken a share of the residue and not his children, and that, as he died before the testator, the share which he would have taken belonged to the three surviving residuary legatees, not as a class with R. A., but under the special terms of this will. In re FEATHERSTONE'S TRUSTS　　22 Ch. D. 111

4. —— **Next of Kin " by virtue of the Statutes "** of Distribution—Time of ascertaining Class—Artificial Class—Tenants for Life.] Where a testator gives property in trust for the benefit of the persons who at a time subsequent to his own death shall by virtue of the Statutes of Distribution be his next of kin, the class is an artificial class to be ascertained on the hypothesis that the testator lives up to and dies at the subsequent period of time. STURGE AND THE GREAT WESTERN RAILWAY COMPANY　　19 Ch. D. 444

5. —— **Personæ designatæ**—Gift to Individuals or to a Class.] Bequest of residue " In trust for my son George, my daughters Lydia, Mary Ann, Alice, and Frances, and such of my child or children, if any, hereafter to be born as shall attain the age of twenty-one years or marry, in equal shares as tenants in common, but subject, as to the share of any daughter, whether now living or a child hereafter to be born, to the trusts following—" the share of " such daughter " being settled. The

VIII. WILL—CLASS—continued.

testator had six children only, the five named and one other, all of whom had attained twenty-one at the date of the will. Of the named children two died in the testator's lifetime without issue, and three survived him:—Held, that the five named children took as a class and not as individuals, and that the whole residue was divisible among the three who survived the testator.—Re Stanhope's Trusts (27 Beav. 201) followed. In re JACKSON. SHIERS v. ASHWORTH　　25 Ch. D. 162

6. —— **Portions**—Period of Vesting—Variation between Words of Gift and Words of Gift over.] The rule that the Court will lean to a construction which will give portions to all of a class of children who may live to require them is not confined to settlements, but extends also to wills. —Jackson v. Dover (2 H. & M. 209) followed. In re KNOWLES. NOTTAGE v. BUXTON　　21 Ch. D. 806

IX. WILL—CONDITION.

1. —— **Forfeiture on Alienation**—Acceleration of subsequent Limitations—Want of Parties—Suit in Equity for Legal Demand pending at Commencement of Judicature Act—Judicature Act, 1873, s. 22—Rules of Court, 1875, Order XVI. r. 13.] Specified freeholds and leaseholds were given by will to trustees upon trust to permit the rents to be received by H. for life, and after his death to convey to his children on their attaining twenty-one, with a proviso that if H. charged or incumbered the property, the gift to him should be absolutely forfeited, and that in such case the gift in favour of his children should at once take effect, and be acted upon by the trustees as thereinbefore directed. H. by a memorandum in writing, in 1869, charged his life estate in favour of W. W. shortly afterwards, on hearing of the clause of forfeiture, and before he had taken any benefit under the charge, repudiated the security and obtained another security from H. In 1874 the trustee of the will, by leave of the Court in an administration suit, filed a bill against persons who were in possession of the property under a title derived from a lessee of H., to make them account for the rents. H. had no children.—Held, by Fry, J., and by the Court of Appeal, that the memorandum of charge produced a forfeiture of the life interest of H., although W. had never claimed any benefit thereunder, and had afterwards disclaimed it, and although H. had no children, so that there were no persons to take under the gift over.—Held, by the Court of Appeal, that though the claim of the Plaintiff was a purely legal demand in respect of which a bill in equity could not formerly have been maintained, a decree could be made after the Judicature Acts came into operation, inasmuch as sect. 22 of the Act of 1873 provides that the Court shall have the same jurisdiction in pending suits as if they had been commenced in the High Court of Justice. HURST v. HURST　　-　　21 Ch. D. 278

2. —— **Forfeiture on Alienation**—Repugnancy—Devise in Fee.] A condition in absolute restraint of alienation annexed to a devise in fee, even though its operation is limited to a particular time, e.g., to the life of another living person, is void in law as being repugnant to the nature of an estate in fee.—In re Macleay (Law Rep. 20 Eq. 186) commented on.—Large's Case (2 Leon. 82 ;

IX. WILL—CONDITION—continued.

3. Leon. 182) explained.—A testator devised an estate to his son in fee, provided always that if the son, his heirs or devisees, or any person claiming through or under him or them, should desire to sell the estate, or any part or parts thereof, in the lifetime of the testator's wife, she should have the option to purchase the same at the price of £3000 for the whole, and at a proportionate price for any part or parts thereof, and the same should accordingly be first offered to her at such price or proportionate price or prices. The real selling value of the estate was, at the date of the will and at the time of the testator's death, £15,000:—*Held*, that the proviso amounted to an absolute restraint on alienation during the life of the testator's widow; that it was void in law; and that the son was entitled to sell the estate as he pleased, without first offering it to the widow at the price named in the will. *In re* ROSHER. ROSHER *v.* ROSHER

                        [26 Ch. D. 801]

3. —— Forfeiture on Bankruptcy—*Fee-simple Estate—Condition—Conditional Limitation—Repugnancy.*] A testator devised a freehold estate to the use of his daughter, " her heirs and assigns," for her separate use, " subject, nevertheless, to the proviso hereinafter contained for determining her estate and interest in the event therein mentioned." In a subsequent part of the will was a proviso that in case his said daughter should at any time be declared a bankrupt, then and thenceforth the devise thereinbefore made to her should be void, and the premises should thenceforth go, remain and be to the use of her children:—*Held*, that the devise did not operate as a conditional limitation, and that the condition in the proviso was void for repugnancy; and accordingly that the daughter was entitled to the property for an absolute estate in fee simple. *In re* MACHU   21 Ch. D. 838

4. —— Forfeiture on Bankruptcy—*Life Estate determinable on Bankruptcy—Gift over to Children—Time for ascertaining Class—Canons of Construction.*] A testator gave a fund to trustees upon trust to pay the income to his son during his life, and after his death to pay and divide the fund equally among all the children which the son might have, as and when they should respectively attain twenty-one; and if the son should have no child who should attain twenty-one, the fund was to sink into the residue of the testator's estate. There was a proviso that if the son should be adjudicated bankrupt the fund and the income thereof should thenceforth immediately go and be payable or applicable to or for the benefit of the child or children of the son " in the same manner as if he was naturally dead " or in default of such child or children should sink into the residue. After the death of the testator the son was adjudicated a bankrupt. At the date of the adjudication he had two children : other children were born to him afterwards :—*Held* (affirming the decision of Pearson, J.), that the children born after the adjudication were entitled to share in the fund subject to the contingency of their attaining twenty-one.—Observations upon the force of canons of construction. *In re* BEDSON'S TRUSTS -   25 Ch. D. 458; 28 Ch. D. 523

5. —— Forfeiture—Name Clause—*Fee Simple Estate—Repugnancy.*] A testatrix, who died in 1832, settled her freehold estate upon her grand-

children, a share becoming vested in one of them, Lucy, in fee simple in possession; and the will contained a proviso that any person becoming entitled in possession to the estate should, within one year thereafter, take and use the name of Jones, and that in case any such person should refuse or neglect to use the name of Jones within one year, then the estate limited to him or her should be void, and should first go to her niece, Catherine Jones, since deceased, for her life, and after her decease to the person or persons next in remainder under the trusts of the will, in the same manner as if the person so refusing were dead. Lucy was twice married, and neither she nor either of her husbands ever took the name of Jones :—*Held*, that the gift being in fee simple, and there being necessarily no person entitled to remainder, the name clause was void, and that there had consequently been no forfeiture by Lucy. MUSGRAVE *v.* BROOKE

                        [26 Ch. D. 792]

6. —— Forfeiture for non-Residence—*Devise of House and Grounds—What will amount to Residence.*] Testator devised a messuage and hereditaments in the country to the use of his son G. for life, " provided as a sine quâ non " that he " within six calendar months after my decease shall enter upon and take actual possession of" the messuages and hereditaments " as and for his residence and place of abode ;" and " shall as such tenant for life thereinafter during his life continue to reside in or upon the same capital messuage for at least six calendar months (but not necessarily consecutively) in every year." After G.'s death " or his failing to take such possession as aforesaid and to reside in" the house, testator devised the same to G.'s first and other sons in tail male. G. entered and took possession within six months after the testator's decease; but as to residence, during the year following the expiration of six months, he was in the house for eighteen days only ; and from the 1st of January to the 28th of December in the year following the date of such expiration, for no more than twenty-four days. He had, however, placed the house in charge of a staff of servants, he had paid the rates, he had kept horses and poultry in the stables and on the grounds, and his son, who was at college near, had stayed at the house on an average on every alternate Saturday till Monday : —*Held*, that no forfeiture of G.'s life estate had taken place. *In re* MOIR. WARNER *v.* MOIR

                        [25 Ch. D. 605]

7. —— Option to purchase—*Interest not transmissible to Executors of Person to whom Option is given.*] A testator devised and bequeathed certain real and personal property, including an hotel, to trustees upon trust to pay out of the rents, issues, and income thereof, annuities to his widow and sister, and during their lives and the life of the survivor to divide the residue of the rents, issues, and income equally between his four children; and after the decease of the survivor of his wife and sister he declared that his son should have the option of purchasing the hotel at the price of £10,000, such sum to fall into testator's residuary personal estate; but if the son should decline to purchase the hotel at that price within six months after the decease of the survivor of the testator's wife and sister, he directed that his trustees should

                          3 H 2

IX. WILL—CONDITION—*continued.*

sell the hotel, and that the moneys arising from the sale thereof should fall into his residuary personal estate. The son died very soon after his father, the testator, also leaving a will whereby he appointed executors. The testator's wife and sister being also dead:—*Held*, that the option to purchase the hotel was a right personal to the son, and could not be exercised after his death by his executors. *In re* COUSINS. ALEXANDER *v.* CROSS
[30 Ch. D. 203

8. —— Relinquishment of Debt—*Death of Devisee before Testator.*] A testator devised land at M. to his son R. in fee, on the express condition that R., his executors or administrators, should, within three months after the testator's death, relinquish all claim to a sum of £3400 due to him by the testator. And he devised other land to trustees, on trust for sale, and to stand possessed of the proceeds of sale, after payment of the deficiency (if any) of his residuary personal estate to pay his debts as thereinafter mentioned, on trust for his wife for her life, with remainder in trust for some grandchildren. And he devised all other his real estate not thereinbefore disposed of to his sons J. and R. in fee, in equal shares. And, after making some specific bequests of personal estate, he bequeathed the residue of his personal estate to trustees upon trust for conversion, and to stand possessed of the proceeds upon trust to pay his debts (except the debt of £3400 due to R. and two other specified debts), and on trust to retain the surplus for the benefit of his sons J. and R. in equal shares. But, in case his residuary personal estate should be insufficient to pay his debts (except as aforesaid), he directed that the deficiency should be paid out of the proceeds of the sale of the real estate which he had directed to be sold. R. died before the testator without issue:—*Held* (affirming the decision of Fry, J.), that the condition bound the land at M. notwithstanding the lapse of the devise, and that the debt of £3400 must be discharged out of it. *In re* KIRK. KIRK *v.* KIRK
[21 Ch. D. 431

9. —— Restraint of Marriage—*Marriage with Consent—Guardians.*] A testator appointed his wife sole guardian of his infant children, and bequeathed a legacy to each of his daughters on her attaining twenty-one or marrying with the consent of her "guardian or guardians," which should first happen. He gave the residue to his wife for life, and, after her death, gave a further legacy to each daughter who should attain twenty-one or marry with the consent "of her guardian or guardians." He empowered the trustees during the minority of the daughters, to pay the income of their contingent legacies to his wife for their maintenance and education, and, in case of her decease, empowered them to apply so much of the income of the contingent legacies as they might think fit for the maintenance of the infant daughters presumptively entitled thereto, with power to pay it to the guardian or guardians of the daughters for that purpose. After the death of the wife, a daughter married under twenty-one without the consent of any guardian or guardians, there being none, and died shortly afterwards, under the age of twenty-one years:—*Held*, by Fry J., and by the Court of Appeal, that the condition was not complied with,

IX. WILL—CONDITION—*continued.*

and that the daughter took no vested interest in the legacies—the condition not being made inoperative by there being no guardians, since guardians could have been appointed by the Court, and the testator, on the language of his will, must be taken to have contemplated such an appointment.—By the testator's marriage settlement the trust funds, after the death of the husband and wife, were to be held in trust for such children as, being a son or sons, attained twenty-one, or, being a daughter or daughters, attained that age or married with the consent of their parents or guardians:—*Held*, by Fry, J., and by the Court of Appeal, that the same rule applied to this gift, and that the daughter took no vested interest :—*Held*, by the Court of Appeal, that the consent of a guardian appointed by the infant herself would not have satisfied the condition. *In re* BROWN'S WILL. *In re* BROWN'S SETTLEMENT　-　-　-　. 18 Ch. D. 61

10. —— Restraint of Marriage — *Restriction confined to the case of Marriage with a Domestic Servant—Condition valid.*] Testatrix devised real estate to her father for life, remainder to her brother for life, remainder to his first and other sons in tail, with remainders over. She then bequeathed the proceeds of her residuary personalty in trust for her brother absolutely. But, she declared, if her brother should thereafter, whether he should at the time be in possession as tenant for life or not, marry a domestic servant, or a person who had been a domestic servant, then the devises and bequests in favour of her brother and issue should be null and void, and in lieu thereof, she devised her real estate to the use of the Plaintiffs, and declared that the personalty was to be held and enjoyed with a specific part of the realty.— The father survived the testatrix and died. Thereupon the brother became entitled to the realty as tenant for life in possession. Afterwards, the brother married a person who at the time of her marriage was, and had previously been, a domestic servant:—*Held*, that the condition was valid, and that the real estate passed to the Plaintiff. JENNER *v.* TURNER　　　　16 Ch. D. 188

11. —— Widowhood—*Restraint of Marriage—Annuity to Wife "so long as she shall continue my Widow and unmarried"—Voidable Marriage—Substitutionary Gift.*] A testator, after giving a legacy of £200 to his wife, directed his trustees "in addition thereto to pay to my said wife, so long as she shall continue my widow and unmarried, an annuity of £300, or otherwise in lieu and in substitution of the said annuity, at the option of my said wife if she shall prefer it, a legacy of £2000." After the date of the will the marriage was declared null by the Divorce Court in a suit brought by the wife against the testator. After this the testator died leaving the lady surviving. Fry, J., held that she was entitled to the legacy of £200, but was not entitled either to the annuity or the £2000. She appealed from this decision so far as it was unfavourable to her :— *Held*, that although if the lady had been the testator's wife at his decease, the words "shall continue my widow and unmarried," might have been in substance the same as "shall continue unmarried," the reference to widowhood could not on that ground be treated as surplusage, but was the principal part of the

IX. WILL—CONDITION—continued.

condition, and that as the lady did not at the testator's death fill the position of the testator's widow, she could not take the annuity.—Held, further that she could not take the £2000, for that an option to take a legacy instead of an annuity could not exist if there was no right to take the annuity ; and, moreover, that a gift by way of substitution for another is subject to the same conditions as the original gift.—Rishton v. Cobb (5 My. & Cr. 145 doubted). In re BODDINGTON. BODDINGTON v. CLAIRAT   - 22 Ch. D. 597; 25 Ch. D. 685

X. WILL—CONTINGENT REMAINDER.

1. —— **Executory Devise**—Life Estate—Devise to such Children of Tenant for Life " as either before or after her decease " should attain twenty-one or marry.] A testatrix devised a freehold estate to her granddaughter E. during her life, and from and after her death to such of her children living at her death " as either before or after her decease " should, being males, attain twenty-one, or, being females, attain that age or marry, in fee simple as tenants in common : and if there should be no such child, then over. E. survived the testatrix, and died leaving seven children, of whom five had attained twenty-one at the time of her death, and two, a son and a daughter, were infants, the daughter being also a spinster :—Held, that the five children took vested interests liable to open to let in the two other children on their fulfilling the conditions of the will.—Brackenbury v. Gibbons (2 Ch. D. 417) not followed. In re LECHMERE & LLOYD
[18 Ch. D. 524

2. —— **Executory Devise**—Gift for Life—Gift to Children living at the time of the Decease of Tenant for Life or thereafter to be born.] Testator gave an estate to his wife Elizabeth and her assigns for her life, and after her decease unto all and every the lawful children of his son William living at the time of the decease of his wife Elizabeth or thereafter to be born, in equal shares as tenants in common :—Held, that this was an executory devise, and that the children born after the death of the tenant for life were entitled to share equally with those born before her death.—Brackenbury v. Gibbons (2 Ch. D. 417) and In re Lechmere and Lloyd (18 Ch. D. 524) observed upon. MILES v. JARVIS
[24 Ch. D. 633

XI. WILL—CONVERSION.

—— **Conversion imperative**—Power of Sale discretionary.] A testator gave an annuity to his wife, and he gave and bequeathed to his seven children all his real and personal estate after deducting the said annuity ; and after his wife's decease the annuity, together with all rents, interests, dividends and profits arising from his estate, to be divided between his seven children equally; and he directed his executors to sell and convert into money his furniture, lands, houses, tenements, and other property whenever it should appear to their satisfaction that such sale would be for the benefit of his children, and all the money arising from the sale to be invested for the benefit of his children :— Held, that the direction to convert was imperative, and operated from the death of the testator. In re RAW. MORRIS v. GRIFFITHS   26 Ch. D. 601

XII. WILL—CROSS REMAINDERS.

—— **Construction**—Cross Executory Limitations — Implication — Original and accruing

XII. WILL—CROSS REMAINDERS—continued.
Shares.] A will contained a trust of real and personal property during the lives of five children and the survivor to divide the income into five parts, and pay one-fifth to each, if living, or if dead to their respective children or issue, the latter taking equally between themselves in classes the one-fifth share which their parent if living would have taken. And if any one of the five children died without leaving children or issue, or if such issue failed during the period, the share of such children or issue to belong to the others of the testator's children and their issue in the same way as original shares. This clause to apply to accruing as well as original shares, and upon the death of the last surviving child the capital to testator's grandchildren in classes, per stirpes.—One child died leaving children. One of the grandchildren died, leaving one child, Lucia, who died unmarried before the period had expired : —Held, upon a special case to determine what became of Lucia's share of income—that she' took only a life interest, and that on her death her share went equally among her uncles and aunts and their issue per stirpes, cross limitations being implied to effect this.—Rules deducible from the authorities : —1. Cross executory limitations in the case of personal estate, like cross-remainders of real estate, are only implied to fill up a hiatus in the limitations which seems from the context to have been unintentional.—2. They cannot be implied—as cross-remainders could not—to divest an interest given by the will.—3. The existence of other cross-limitations between different persons does not prevent implication.—4. But where such ·express cross-limitations are in favour of the persons to whom the implied cross-remainders would convey the property, that circumstance is of weight in determining the intention. In re HUDSON. HUDSON v. HUDSON   -   -   -   20 Ch. D. 406

XIII. WILL—DEATH COUPLED WITH CONTINGENCY.

1. —— **Before final Division**—Gift over in case Legatee should die before "final division" of Estate.] A testator gave the residue of his estate equally between four persons, and gave the shares over to the children of the legatees in case the legatees respectively should die before the " final division " of his estate. Two of the legatees died more than a year after the death of the testator. The estate had not then been fully realized and distributed :—Held, that the " final division " of the estate meant the period of a year from the death of the testator, and that the shares of the deceased legatees had not gone over.—Johnson v. Crook (12 Ch. D. 639) approved. In re WILKINS. SPENCER v. DUCKWORTH 18 Ch. D. 634

2. —— **Before Payment**—Uncertainty—Gift over of Legacy or so much thereof as shall not have been paid to or received by Legatee— Words—Paid to or received by.] A gift over of a legacy or so much thereof as should not have been paid to or received by the legatee :—Held, not to be void for uncertainty, on the ground that the words referred, not to the time of actual payment or receipt, but to the time when it was the duty of the executors to pay the legacy.—In re Arrowsmith's Trusts (29 L. J. (Ch.) 774 ; 2 D. F. & J 474) approved and followed.—Hutchin v. Mannington (1 Ves. 366) and Martin v. Martin (Law

XIII. WILL—DEATH COUPLED WITH CONTINGENCY—continued.

Rep. 2 Eq. 404) distinguished.—*Bubb v. Padwick* (13 Ch. D. 517) disapproved.—*Johnson v. Crook* (12 Ch. D. 639) approved. *In re* CHASTON. CHASTON *v.* SEAGO　-　　18 Ch. D. 218

3. —— **Leaving a Family—**Death between Date of Will and Death of Testator—Substitutional Gift.] A testator bequeathed his residuary personalty to trustees in trust for the children of L., to be divided equally between them, and directed that " in case of the decease of either of them leaving a family, then such share as the parents ,would have taken shall be equally divided amongst the children of such deceased parents ":—*Held,* that " decease" meant decease during the testator's life —that the children of L. who survived the testator took absolutely—and that the children of one child of L., who died between the date of the will and the death of the testator, took the share which this parent would have taken. *In re* HAYWARD. CREERY *v.* LINGWOOD　　19 Ch. D. 470

4. —— **Leaving Children—**Gift of Property to Trustees to pay Debts and Annuities, and to convey, &c., Residue to Son absolutely—Death of Son leaving Children, Trustees to convey to them absolutely—Death of Son in Testatrix's Lifetime, without leaving Children, Gift over—Son survived Testatrix, and entitled absolutely.] Testatrix gave all her real and personal estate to trustees in trust to pay all her debts, &c., and certain annuities, and then as to the residue of her estate directed them to convey, assign, or otherwise assure the same unto and to the use of her son, his heirs, executors, &c., absolutely. And if her son should marry, and should die leaving children who should live to attain the age of twenty-one years, the trustees were to convey, &c., the residue to such children equally, as tenants in common absolutely, but if her son should die in her lifetime without leaving children or a child surviving, then the trustees were to convey, &c., the residue to the persons named for their absolute use and benefit. The son married after the date of the will in the lifetime of the testatrix, survived the testatrix, and had children living.—*Held,* that death leaving children meant death in the lifetime of the testatrix, and that that not having happened, the son became, subject to the payment of debts and annuities, entitled absolutely to the residue. *In re* LUDDY. PEARD *v.* MORTON　-　25 Ch. D. 394

XIV. WILL—DISCLAIMER.

1. —— **Onerous Legacies.**] When by a will two distinct legacies are bequeathed to the same person, one of them being onerous and the other beneficial, primâ facie the legatee is entitled to disclaim the onerous legacy and to take the other.— If, however, onerous property and beneficial property are included in the same gift, primâ facie the legatee cannot disclaim the onerous and accept the beneficial ; he must take the whole gift or none of it.—But this primâ facie rule may be rebutted if the will manifests a sufficient intention of the testator to the contrary.—*Green* v. *Britten* (42 L. J. (Ch.) 187) followed. GUTHRIE *v.* WALROND
[22 Ch. D. 573

2. —— **Onerous Property—**Mortgaged House.] A testator devised and bequeathed a freehold house

XIV. WILL—DISCLAIMER—continued. and the furniture and effects therein on trust for A. and B. for life. The house was subject to a mortgage for more than its value :—*Held,* that A. and B. were entitled to the use of the furniture without keeping down the interest on the mortgage. SYER *v.* GLADSTONE　　30 Ch. D. 614

XV. WILL—ESTATE IN REALTY.

1. —— **Legal Estate in Executors—**Vendor and Purchaser Act, 1874—Interest commensurate with Objects of Will.] A testator, after directing his debts to be paid, and setting apart certain sums to provide annuities for his two sons, devised and bequeathed all his real and personal estate to his wife and his four daughters, to be equally divided between them :—Provided as follows—that the share of his wife should be divided after her death between his four daughters or the survivors and their children : and the testator appointed his wife and T. Davies, his executors, to act jointly in carrying out all the intentions of his will, and to invest his daughters' shares for their benefit and the benefit of their children.—*Held,* upon an application under the Vendor and Purchaser Act, that the legal estate in the freeholds was vested in the executors who could make a good title to a purchaser. DAVIES to JONES AND EVANS　-　　24 Ch. D. 190

2. —— **Rule in Shelley's Case—**" Estate "— " Child or Children "—" Dying without Issue."} By a will made in 1820 the testatrix said " I give and devise unto my eldest son Thomas all my real and freehold estate and all leases and leasehold premises now in my possession (subject to the payment of the rents and the performance of the covenants mentioned in the said indentures of leases) during the term of his natural life, and after his decease to his legitimate child or children (if there be any); but if he dies without issue my will is it may go unto my other son William during the term of his natural life, and afterwards to his legitimate child or children (if any): but if he should likewise die without issue my will is it may go to my daughter Mary and to her heirs and assigns for ever."—The will then gave legacies to the second son and the daughters, with provisions for the daughters, to be paid in the first instance by Thomas, but to be repaid in part or in whole to him in certain events by his successor in the estate. Thomas died without issue.—*Held,* by Earl Cairns and Lords Blackburn and Fitz-Gerald, affirming the decision of the Court of Appeal, that reading the whole will together Thomas took an estate tail in the realty.—*Contrà,* by the Earl of Selborne, L.C., and Lord Bramwell, that Thomas took an estate for life, with remainder to his children (if any) in fee as purchasers. BOWEN *v.* LEWIS　　9 App. Cas. 890

3. —— **Rule in Shelley's Case—**" Issue and their Heirs "—Gift over on Death without leaving Children—Estate for Life or Estate Tail.] The owner of land devised it to his eldest son L. " for life, and after his decease to his lawful issue and their heirs for ever, if any," and " if he should die without leaving any children born in wedlock " then to the testator's son E. and his heirs :—*Held,* affirming the decision of Cave, J., that the devise gave a life estate only to L., and not an estate tail. MORGAN *v.* THOMAS　8 Q. B. D. 575; 9 Q. B. D. 643

XV. WILL—ESTATE IN REALTY—*continued.*

4. —— Words of Futurity—*Proviso*—"*Shall be born in my lifetime*" *construed as Words of Futurity.*] The testator devised an estate to his six grandsons (of whom the Appellant was one) "during their respective lives, in equal shares as tenants in common, and as to the respective shares therein of each of them, my said grandsons, after his decease, to the use of his first and every other son successively, according to seniority of birth in tail male, and on failure of the issue male of any one or more of my said grandsons, then and so often as the same shall happen, I give and devise as well the share or respective shares originally limited to the grandson whose issue shall so fail, as the share or respective shares which by virtue of this present clause shall have become vested in him or them, or his or their issue male, to the use of the other or others of my said grandsons during his or their life, or respective lives, as tenants in common. And after the decease of such last-mentioned grandsons, then I give and devise the share or shares lastly hereinbefore limited to him, to his first and every other son successively according to seniority of birth in tail male; and if there shall be a failure of such issue of all my said grandsons but one of them, I give and devise the entirety of all the said estates to the use of such only grandson for his life, and after his decease to the use of his and every other son successively according to their seniorities in tail male." By a proviso at the end of the will the testator directed—" Provided always, that if any person whom I have made tenant in tail male of my said estate shall be born in my lifetime, then and in such case I revoke the devise so made to him. In lieu thereof I give and devise the hereditaments comprised in such devise and appointment to the use of the same person respectively for the term of his or her natural life, and after his or her decease, to the use of his or her first and every other son successively according to their respective seniorities in tail male." Two out of the six grandsons died without issue. The eldest son of the Appellant was born before the date of the will, and by a disentailing deed executed after the testator's death conveyed to the Appellant his share and interest in the said estate in fee. In a suit for declaration of title and consequent relief :—*Held,* that the Appellant was entitled to an estate in fee simple in one fourth part of the hereditaments and premises, the subject of the suit. The words of the proviso must be construed in their grammatical sense, and be taken to mean a tenant in tail male born after the date of the will, and therefore not to include the eldest son of the Appellant. The words "shall be born in my lifetime," in the absence of any context to explain them, are to be taken as words of futurity. Consequently the gift of an estate tail to the Appellant's eldest son, who was born before the date of the will, was not revoked. GIBBONS *v.* GIBBONS

[6 App. Cas. 471

XVI. WILL—EXECUTORS.

· —— **Gift annexed to Office**—*Rebuttal of Presumption—Parol Evidence.*] The mere fact that the gift of the legacy precedes the appointment of the legatee as executor—or that the legacies to several persons appointed executors differ either in their amount or subject-matter—is not enough by itself to rebut the presumption, that a legacy

XVI. WILL—EXECUTORS—*continued.*

given to a person who is appointed executor is annexed to the office.—*Jewis v. Lawrence* (Law Rep. 8 Eq. 345) questioned.—*Wildes* v. *Davies* (1 Sm. & Giff. 475 ; 22 L. J. (Ch.) 497) explained. —Per Cotton, L.J. (dubitante, Fry, L.J.):—Parol evidence is admissible to rebut this, as well as any other presumption. *In re* APPLETON. BARBER *v.* TEBBIT   · -   **29 Ch. D. 893**

XVII. WILL—EXONERATION.

1. —— Lapsed Bequest— *Charge of Debts and Legacies — Mortmain Act.*] Where a testator, having bequeathed his personal estate, exonerates it from debts and legacies, which he charges on real estate, and part of the bequest lapses or fails under the Mortmain Act, the exemption does not extend to the lapsed portion. A testatrix devised her real estate to trustees in trust for sale, and directed them, out of the proceeds, to pay her funeral and testamentary expenses, debts, legacies, and duties ; and she directed her trustees to sell her leaseholds, and to apply the proceeds in payment of so much of her debts, &c., as the proceeds of her real estate should be insufficient to pay ; and she bequeathed all her personal estate to a charity. Part of the personal estate consisted of a mortgage debt, as to which the bequest failed and lapsed to the Crown, there being no next of kin :—*Held,* that the debts, expenses, legacies, and duties were chargeable, first, on the impure personalty ; secondly, on the real estate ; and thirdly, on the leaseholds. KILFORD *v.* BLANEY   -   -   **29 Ch. D. 145**
[Varied by Court of Appeal, 31 Ch. D. 56.]

2. —— Mixed Fund — Mortgaged Estates— *Payment pro ratâ—Locke King's Act* (17 & 18 *Vict. c.* 113).] A testator, by will made in 1866, after specifically disposing of certain parts of his property and giving certain real estate to his wife during widowhood, gave the rest and residue of his real and personal estate to trustees upon trust to convert the same into money and thereout pay his debts, including debts due on mortgage of the property given to his wife during widowhood, and his funeral and testamentary expenses, and the costs of proving and executing his will. He directed his trustees to pay the income of the fund to his wife during widowhood, and after her death or second marriage he gave so much of the fund as consisted of pure personalty to charitable purposes, and bequeathed the rest of it to his wife. In a subsequent part of his will he appointed executors, and gave a legacy to each of them who accepted the trusts. At his death part of the residuary real estate was subject to mortgages :—*Held,* by Fry, J., that the executor's legacies were charged on the real estate, and that as there was a mixed fund they must be paid pro ratâ out of the different parts of it.—*Held,* by the Court of Appeal, that the legacies were charged on the real estate, but only in aid of the personalty, the principle of pro ratâ payment only applying to payments which the testator had expressly directed to be made out of the mixed fund.—*Held,* by the Court of Appeal (affirming the decision of Fry, J.), that the will did not indicate any such "contrary intention" as to exclude the mortgages on the residuary real estate from the operation of Locke King's Act, and that they must be paid out of the proceeds of the mortgaged estate. ELLIOTT *v.* DEARSLEY   **16 Ch. D. 322**

XVII. WILL—EXONERATION—*continued.*

3. —— **Realty contracted to be purchased—** *Unpaid Purchase-money—Vendor's Lien—Rights of Devisees — Compromise — Rescission of Contract—Locke King's Acts Amendment Act (40 & 41 Vict. c. 34).*] A testator who had contracted to purchase real estate, and paid the deposit money, by will made in 1881, specifically devised such real estate to his daughter for life, with remainder to her children, without shewing any intention that the purchase-money should be paid out of his personal estate; and he died without having disposed of his personal estate; which was rather less in amount than the unpaid purchase-money, and without having completed the purchase or paid any further part of the purchase-money.—After his death an action by the vendor against the executor and trustee of the will for specific performance of the contract was compromised by the Defendant thereto, and the contract was put an end to upon the terms that the vendor should retain the deposit money and have his costs; and this compromise was confirmed by the Court by an order made by consent in an administration action in the presence of the tenant for life of the real estate and the trustee, all the remaindermen being infants.—Upon the further consideration of the administration action, the devisees contended that they were entitled to so much of the personal estate as was equivalent to the unpaid purchase-money, upon the ground that the purchase was a conversion by the testator of his personal estate to that extent, and that Locke King's Acts had not altered the law in that respect:—*Held*, that there was a vendor's lien, and that Locke King's Acts Amendment Act applied; that accordingly all the devisees were entitled to was the real estate charged with the unpaid purchase-money, and therefore on the facts to nothing; but *held*, moreover, that the order of compromise would be fatal to their claim, if otherwise good. *In re* COCKCROFT. BROADBENT *v.* GROVES **24 Ch. D. 94**

—— **House mortgaged for more than its value** **[30 Ch. D. 614**

See WILL—DISCLAIMER. **2.**

XVIII. WILL—HEIRLOOM.

1. —— **Contingent future Interest—***Transmissibility—Tenant in Tail—Personal Estate—Vesting.*] A testator by his will directed that his books and plate should be considered as heirlooms and should pass with his real estate in the same manner as if they were an estate of inheritance at Common Law, and should so continue annexed to his said real estate as long as the law would permit, to be inherited by the several persons who should succeed thereto; and he devised and bequeathed all his real and residuary personal estates to trustees upon trust for R. C. for life, and after the decease of R. C. for his first and other sons successively in tail male, and in default of such issue upon trust for Henry C., the eldest son of J. C., for life, and after his decease for his first and other sons successively in tail male, and in default of such issue upon trust for "the next eldest son of the said J. C. who shall survive the said Henry C." for life, and after his decease upon trust for "the first and other sons of the body of the said next eldest son of the said J. C. who shall survive the said

XVIII. WILL—HEIRLOOM—*continued.*

Henry C." successively in tail male, and in default of such issue upon trust for his, the testator's, own right heirs. R. C. and Henry C. died without having married. J. C. died in testator's lifetime. George was the next eldest son of J. C., who survived Henry. F. J. C. was the eldest son of George, and the first tenant in tail under the settlement, and he died an infant in the lifetime of R. C. and of Henry C.:—*Held*, that notwithstanding the death of F. J. C. before it could be known whether his father would survive Henry C., or whether there would be any issue male either of R. C. or Henry C., the heirlooms and residuary personalty vested absolutely in the legal personal representative of F. J. C.—*Hogg v. Jones* (32 Beav. 45) distinguished. *In re* CRESSWELL. PARKIN *v.* CRESSWELL - - - - **24 Ch. D. 102**

2. —— **Reference to Deed of Entail—***Non-existence of Deed—Non-failure of Gift.*] Testator bequeathed a collection of books, manuscripts, and pictures to his executors to hold as heirlooms, and suffer the same to be used and enjoyed by the person who for the time being under the limitations of "a certain deed of entail bearing date the day of shall be entitled to the possession of" M. House.—At the testator's death there was no such deed of entail as described in the will in existence, and the testator was entitled to the house absolutely in fee simple:—*Held*, that the collection belonged to the heir-at-law of the testator, as the person entitled in possession to M. House. *In re* MARQUESS OF BUTE. MARQUESS OF BUTE *v.* RYDER - **27 Ch. D. 196**

3. —— **"Successors"** — *Codicil — Plate — Leasehold House — "To A. and his successors to be enjoyed with and to go with the title"—Painting—Statuary and China—"To A. and his successors, to be held and settled as heirlooms and to go with the title"—Absolute Interest—Executory Trust—Settlement—Contents of House—Jewellery at Bankers — Legacies — Pecuniary—Specific—"All Legacies to be paid free of legacy duty"—Legacy Duty.*] A testatrix by a codicil to her will bequeathed to A. C., sixth Earl of E. and to his successors, all her plate, and also gave, devised, and bequeathed a leasehold house to him and "to his successors and to be enjoyed with and to go with the title," and as to all her household furniture, paintings, books, china, and the whole contents of her house, she bequeathed the same to her trustees and executors upon trust that they should in the first place "select and set aside a collection of the best paintings, statuary, and china for the said Earl of E., and his successors, to be held and settled as heirlooms, and to go with the title," and she authorized them to give to the said Earl or his successors any articles of furniture which they should think fit, and as to all the rest and residue of the contents of her house upon trust for her trustees to select presents for her friends, and directed them to present any portion of the residue of the contents of her house to her cousins if they should think fit, or to sell the same, and the moneys so received to form part of her residuary personal estate, and she directed all the legacies left by her will and codicil to be paid free of legacy duty. The testatrix died possessed of considerable personal estate, which comprised

XVIII. WILL—HEIRLOOM—continued.

amongst other things a number of articles of jewellery which were at her death in a box at her banker's, which jewellery had been bequeathed to her. It was proved that it had been the practice of the testatrix and also of the former owner to send such box for safe custody to the bankers when they respectively were away from London :—Held, first, that the plate and leasehold house passed to the sixth Earl absolutely ; the words " to be enjoyed with and go with the title" not being sufficient in themselves to create an executory trust or to cut down the interest to a life estate.—Montagu v. Lord Inchiquin (23 W. R. 592) discussed.— Secondly, that the gift to the trustees of the whole contents of the house upon trust to "select and set aside a collection of the best paintings, statuary, and china, for the said Earl of E. and his successors, to be held and settled as heirlooms and to go with the title" was a clear direction to settle and created an executory trust, and a settlement was directed (to be settled in Chambers) giving a life interest to the sixth Earl with remainder to the next heir to the Earldom for his life. Thirdly, that the box of jewellery passed to the trustees as part of the contents of the house, that being the locality to which the property ought to be ascribed, although jewellery is merely for personal use and is not appropriated to a house. Lastly, that under the words "all the legacies left by my will and codicil to be paid free of legacy duty," the legacy duty was to be paid out of the estate on all legacies as well pecuniary as specific, the word "paid" not being sufficient under the circumstances to cut down the direction to pecuniary legacies only.—Ansley v. Cotton (16 L. J. (Ch.) 35) discussed and followed. In re JOHNSTON. COCKERELL v. EARL OF ESSEX - 26 Ch. D. 538

4. —— Uncertainty—Trust—Validity—Condition subsequent.] When a trust is created to secure the devolution of chattels as heirlooms, any limitations which are to take effect by way of postponement or defeazance of an absolute interest are subject to all the rules which govern the validity of conditions subsequent. — Such limitations, therefore, must be certain, not only in expression, but also in operation, and it is essential to their validity that it should be capable of ascertainment at any given moment of time, whether the limitation has or has not taken effect. —A testator, who was a peer, bequeathed chattels to trustees, upon trust to permit and suffer the same to go and be held and enjoyed with the title, so far as the rules of law and equity would admit, by the person who for the time being should be actually possessed of the title, in the nature of heirlooms, and so that no person in existence at the time of the testator's decease, or born in due time afterwards, and afterwards coming to the title, should have any other than a life interest in the same, and so that no person should acquire an absolute interest in the same till the expiration of twenty-one years after the decease of all such persons as should be in existence at the time of the testator's decease and afterwards attaining the title :—Held, that the latter clause of the limitations was void for uncertainty in operation, and that the first person born after the death of the testator who attained the title acquired an absolute

XVIII. WILL—HEIRLOOM—continued.

interest in the chattels, notwithstanding that there was still living a person who was alive at the time of the testator's death, and who was capable of inheriting the title. In re VISCOUNT EXMOUTH. VISCOUNT EXMOUTH v. PRAED　　23 Ch. D. 158

XIX. WILL—INCORPORATED DOCUMENTS.

1. —— Codicil. Semble, a document containing the words, " This is the third codicil to my will," is not incorporated in a codicil of subsequent date by the words, " This is a fourth codicil to my will." STOCKIL v. PUNSHON - 6 P. D. 9

2. —— Codicil — Will of Married Woman.] S. M. H. while a married woman made a will which was invalid. Afterwards, when a widow, she executed a document beginning with the words, "this is a codicil to the last will and testament of me." The codicil was written on the same paper as the will and immediately after it, and it was proved that she had made no other will :—Held, that the will was incorporated in the codicil. Probate granted of both documents. IN THE GOODS OF HEATHCOTE　　6 P. D. 30

3. —— Codicil. A testator in a codicil referred to one gift as being contained in a list of gifts which he had previously deposited with his brother :—Held, under the circumstances, that the whole list was incorporated by the reference in the codicil. IN THE GOODS OF DANIELL 8 P. D. 14

XX. WILL—INTERIM INCOME.

1. —— Contingent Gift.] The interim income subject to the interim burden of a contingent specific legacy until the happening of the contingency falls into the residue of the testator's estate, or goes to his next of kin, as the case may be. GUTHRIE v. WALROND - 22 Ch. D. 573

2. —— Contingent Gift — Real and Personal Estate — Right to interim Income till happening of Contingency.] A testator devised his residuary real estate to trustees, on trust to pay the rents to his wife for her life, and upon her death to apply the rents for the maintenance of his daughter and to accumulate the surplus, and on the daughter attaining twenty-one to pay to her the accumulations and the future income for her life, and upon her death on trust to convey the residuary real estate unto and equally between all and every her child and children who should live to attain twenty-one, as tenants in common in fee. But in case his daughter should die without leaving any child or children who should attain twenty-one, then on trust to convey the residuary real estate to such person or persons as the daughter should by deed or will appoint. And by another clause the testator bequeathed his residuary personal estate to the same persons as trustees, on the same trusts as those declared of the real estate except the clause as to maintenance and accumulation.—The will contained no disposition of the income of the realty or the personalty during the suspense of vesting.—The daughter survived the testator and his wife, and died leaving an only daughter, who was an infant. The testator's daughter had, by her will, exercised the power of appointment in favour of other persons, in the event of her leaving no child who should live to attain a vested interest under the trusts of her father's will :—Held, that the testator had in

XX. WILL—INTERIM INCOME—continued.

effect mixed up the whole of his property in one mass, and that the rule in *Crenery* v. *Fitzgerald* (Jac. 468) applied, and that consequently the interim rents of the real estate, until the happening of the contingency, as well as the interim income of the personalty, must be accumulated, and follow the destination of the corpus. *In re* DUMBLE. WILLIAMS *v.* MURRELL **23 Ch. D. 360**

3. —— Contingent Legacy *payable out of Residue—Rest of Residue payable first—Gift of "rest" of Residuary Estate—Severance for Convenience of Estate.*] A testator by will, after giving his real and personal estate upon trust for sale and conversion and payment of debts and legacies, directed the trustees to stand possessed of the residue of the trust moneys upon trust, in the first place. to pay thereout £1500 to be equally divided between such of six legatees whom he named as should be alive at the death of A. B.; such shares to be paid to them respectively on attaining twenty-one or marriage. "And as to the rest of his residuary estate" upon trust for X. Y. A. B. and the six legatees all survived the testator and were still living. The trustees having set apart and invested £1500 to meet the legacy, X. Y., the six legatees, and the next of kin of the testator, all claimed to be entitled to the income thereof during the life of A. B. :—*Held*, that such income passed under the gift of the rest of the testator's residuary estate, and that X. Y. was entitled thereto during the life of A. B. Where a contingent deferred legacy has been severed from the general estate of a testator, such severance will not entitle the legatee to interim interest thereon unless the severance has been necessitated by something connected. with the legacy itself. *In re* JUDKIN'S TRUSTS · **25 Ch. D. 743**

XXI. WILL—JOINT TENANCY.

—— Gift to Husband and Wife and Third Person—*Unity of Person of Husband and Wife—Separate Use — Married Women's Property Act,* 1882 (45 & 46 Vict. c. 75), *ss.* 1, 5.] A testatrix, by her will, dated in 1880, gave her residuary personal estate "to C. J. M., and J. H. and E. his wife," to and for their own use and benefit absolutely, and appointed C. J. M., and J. H. and E. H. his wife, her executors.—The testatrix died in 1883, after the commencement of the Married Women's Property Act, 1882. J. H. and E. H. were married in 1864. — *Held* (reversing the decision of Chitty, J.), that as the will was made before the Married Women's Property Act came into operation, it must be construed in accordance with the law at that time, and that the three residuary legatees were entitled to the personal estate as joint tenants, C. J. M. taking one moiety, and J. H. and E. H., his wife, taking the other moiety between them, J. H. in his own right, and his wife for her separate use. How the Court would have construed the gift if the will had been made after the Married Women's Property Act, 1882, came into operation, *quære*. *In re* MARCH. MANDER *v.* HARRIS **24 Ch. D. 222; 27 Ch. D. 166**

XXII. WILL—LAPSE.

1. —— Appointment—*Failure of Appointment,* 1 *Vict.* c. 26, *s.* 25.] The word "devise" in the Wills Act includes in general a devise by way of ap-

XXII. WILL—LAPSE—continued.

pointment under a special or general power: consequently where a testator makes a will operating as an exercise of a special or general power, a devise of real estate by way of appointment which fails and is void, falls under sect. 25 into the residuary devise, if any, by way of appointment, unless a contrary intention appears by the will. FREME *v.* CLEMENT **18 Ch. D. 499**

2. —— Child of Testator — *Special Power of Appointment—Death of Appointee in Lifetime of Testator—Wills Act* (1 Vict. c. 26), s. 33.] The 33rd section of the Wills Act, which enacts that a devise or bequest to a child of the testator who dies in the lifetime of the testator leaving issue shall not lapse does not apply to an appointment under a special power.—*Freme* v. *Clement* (18 Ch. D. 499) disapproved. HOLYLAND *v.* LEWIN **26 Ch. D. 266**

3. —— Child of Testator—*Death of Child in Lifetime of Father—Devise by Child to Father—Lapse—Wills Act* (1 Vict. c. 26), s. 33.] A father by his will devised a freehold house to a son, and his residuary real estate to trustees in trust for other persons. The son died in his father's lifetime leaving issue living at his father's death, and having by his will devised all his real estate to his father :—*Held*, that as under the 33rd section of the Wills Act, the son must be deemed to have survived the father, the property passed to the son absolutely under his father's will, and became subject to testamentary disposition by the son :—~~~~~~~~ But that as by the will of the son the property was devised to his father, the devise by the son failed, and his heir-at-law was entitled to the property. *In re* HENSLER. JONES *v.* HENSLER **[19 Ch. D. 612**

4. —— Contingent Legacy.] A testatrix gave the residue of her estate equally between a number of persons whom she named, and such of the children of J. G, as were living at the date of her will. J. G. had died before the date of the will and had left no children :—*Held*, that there was no lapse of the share given to the children of J. G., but that the whole residue was divisible among the other persons named.—*Re Hornby* (7 W. R. 729) followed: *In re* SPILLER. SPILLER *v.* MADGE **[18 Ch. D. 614**

5. —— "Death"—Gift over.] A testator left legacies to three persons, and if any of them died their share was to go to the others. One of the legatees and the testator died at the same instant : —*Held*, that "death" must, according to the ordinary rule, mean death in the testator's lifetime, and that the legacy of the legatee so dying became part of the residue. ELLIOTT *v.* SMITH **[22 Ch. D. 236**

6. —— Direction to block up a House for Twenty Years—*Intestacy—Wills Act* (1 Vict. c. 26), *s.* 3.] Testatrix devised a freehold house, yard, garden, and out-buildings, to trustees and their heirs, upon trust to block up all the rooms of the house (except four rooms in which she directed that a housekeeper and his wife should be placed in occupation), and the coach-house, for twenty years; and subject thereto upon trust for a devisee in fee. She directed her trustees to visit the house. and premises once in every three months to see that the trusts were effectually carried out, and declared

XXII. WILL—LAPSE—continued.

that if any trustee should neglect or refuse to carry out the trusts aforesaid, any real or personal estate given or intended to be given to him by the will should go to the persons therein named, absolutely. Held, that there was an intestacy as to the twenty years' term in the house, yard, garden, and out-buildings. BROWN v. BURDETT - 21 Ch. D. 667

7. —— Exception from Residue—*Void Bequest of excepted Property—Excepted Property held to pass by Residuary Gift.*] A testatrix gave to C. H. all her personal property except a certain wharf which she bequeathed to other persons charged with certain debts and annuities. The bequest of the wharf failed for remoteness :—*Held* (affirming the decision of Fry, J.), that the wharf fell into the residue, and belonged to C. H.—*Wainman v. Field* (Kay, 507) distinguished. BLIGHT v. HARTNOLL - 23 Ch. D. 218

8. —— Settlement of Share — *Bequest to Daughter to be subject if she survived Testator to the Trusts of her Settlement—Death of Daughter in Testator's Lifetime leaving Issue living at his Death—Wills Act (1 Vict. c. 26), s. 33.*] A testator gave his residuary personal estate to his children in equal shares, and directed that the share of his daughter Mrs. B., if she survived him, should be subject to the trusts of her marriage settlement and paid to the trustees thereof. Mrs. B. died in the testator's lifetime, but left children surviving him: Her husband having taken out administration to her he claimed her share :—*Held*, that under section 33 of the Wills Act (1 Vict. c. 26), Mrs. B. must for all the purposes of the will be taken to have survived the testator, and that the share must be paid to the trustees of the marriage settlement and not the administrator. *In re* HONE's TRUSTS - 22 Ch. D. 663

9. —— Settlement of Share—*Bequest of Share of Residue to a Woman—Death of Legatee in Testator's Lifetime.*] A testator bequeathed the residue of his estate to trustees upon trust for a nephew and three nieces equally between them, and in case any or either of them should die under twenty-one then he directed that the share or shares of him, her, or them so dying, whether original or accruing, should go to the others or other of them, and if more than one in equal shares: "Provided and I declare that my trustees or trustee shall retain the share of each of my nieces of and in the said trust moneys upon the trusts following." Then followed trusts for the niece for life for her separate use, and after her decease as to the capital upon trust as she should by will appoint, and in default of appointment upon trust for her children who being sons should attain twenty-one, or being daughters attain that age or marry, and in default of such issue upon trust for such persons as should be next of kin to her at her decease. One of the nieces married and died before the testator, leaving a child who survived him :—*Held* (affirming the decision of Pearson, J.), that the share of the deceased niece had lapsed, and that there was an intestacy as to it. *In re* ROBERTS. TARLETON v. BRUTON
[27 Ch. D. 346; 30 Ch. D. 234

XXIII. WILL—MISTAKE.

1. —— Blank in Will—*Right of Court to look at Original Will.*] A testatrix in making her will

XXIII. WILL—MISTAKE—continued.

used a law stationer's form, which was partly in print, blanks being left in it which were to be filled up by the person who made use of it. After directing that her debts and funeral and testamentary expenses should be paid by her executrix thereinafter named, the testatrix gave all her property both real and personal "unto to and for her own use and benefit absolutely, and I nominate, constitute, and appoint my niece Catherine Hellard to be executrix of this my last will and testament":—*Held*, by Kay, J., and by the Court of Appeal, that there was an effectual gift of the residue to Catherine Hellard.—Per Lord Esher, M.R., and Baggallay, L.J. :—For the purpose of construing a will the Court is entitled to look at the original will as well as at the probate copy. *In re* HARRISON. TURNER v. HELLARD
[30 Ch. D. 390

2. —— Erroneous Statement of Fact.] A testator gave a legacy of £7000 in trust for his daughter, the wife of J. T., and her children, and after reciting that he had given a bond for £3000 for J. T. he directed that what should remain due on the bond at his death should be paid out of the legacy. By a codicil made about a year afterwards he recited that he had paid the £3000 and other sums for which he was bound for J. T. to an amount exceeding £5000 in the whole, and directed that if J. T. should not before his death have repaid to him £5000 at least, the sum of £5000 should be taken in part payment of the £7000, and to that extent he revoked the legacy: It was admitted that J. T. had not repaid the £5000, but the legatees disputed the fact that the testator had paid so much as £5000 for J. T. :—*Held*, by Hall, V.C., that the legacy must be reduced by £5000, for that the legatees could not dispute the statements made by the testator as to the payments made by him.—*Held*, by the Court of Appeal, that the legacy must be reduced only by the amount remaining unrepaid of sums advanced by the testator for J. T., and that an account must be directed.—*In re* AIRD's ESTATE (12 Ch. D. 291) not followed. *In re* TAYLOR's ESTATE. TOMLIN v. UNDERHAY - - - 22 Ch. D. 495

3. —— Manifest Incongruity—*Clerical Error in Description—Correction by Reference to Context.*] A clerical error may be corrected where, if uncorrected, it makes the will absurd, and the proper correction can be gathered from the context. —A testator devised an estate called Lea Knowl to trustees upon trusts for the benefit of his daughter W., her husband and children, and empowered his trustees, at the request of his daughter W., to sell the estate and stand possessed of the sale moneys upon the trusts thereinbefore declared "concerning the said Lea Knowl estate hereby devised, as to such and so many of them as shall at the time of sale have been existing undetermined and capable of taking effect." He then devised an estate called Croxton to trustees upon similar trusts for the benefit of his daughter C., her husband and children, and empowered his trustees, at the request of his daughter C., to sell the last-mentioned devised hereditaments and stand possessed of the sale moneys, "in trust for such person and persons, and for such estates, ends, intents and purposes, powers, provisoes, and conditions as are hereinbefore

XXIII. WILL—MISTAKE—*continued.*

limited, expressed, and declared, of and concerning the said Lea Knowl estate hereby devised, as to such and so many of them as shall at the time of sale have been existing undetermined and capable of taking effect":—*Held*, that the words, "the said Lea Knowl estate," in the trust of the moneys to arise from the sale of the Croxton estate had been inserted in the will through an obvious error: that to read the words, "the said Lea Knowl estate," literally and grammatically, would be making the will lead to a manifest absurdity or incongruity, and that the will must be read as if the words, "the said Croxton estate," were inserted in the place of the words, "the said Lea Knowl estate," in the trusts of the moneys to arise from the sale of the Croxton estate. *In re* NORTHEN'S ESTATE. SALT *v.* PYM - **28 Ch. D. 153**

4. —— **Reference to Codicil**—*Revival—Revocation.*] A testator made a will, and afterwards another, which by implication revoked the former will. Subsequently, by the terms of a duly executed codicil, he, by mistake, referred to the former instead of the later will:—*Held*, that the codicil by its language, revived the former will, and that as the later will was not revoked by the codicil all three documents must be admitted to probate. IN THE GOODS OF STEDHAM. IN THE GOODS OF DYKE **[6 P. D. 205, 207**

5. —— **Words introduced without the Knowledge of the Testator.**] A testator, in the instructions for his will, directed that all his B shares should be given to his nephews, but the word "forty," was inserted several times in the will before the word "shares,"and the will was executed with that word repeated several times before the word "shares." The jury found that the word "forty" was introduced by mistake, that the clauses including the word were never read over to the testator, and that he only approved of the will upon the supposition that all his B shares were given to his nephews, and thereupon the Court ordered the word "forty," wherever it occurred in the will, to be struck out. MORRELL *v.* MORRELL **[7 P. D. 68**

—— Erroneous reference to previous gift *See* WILL—VESTING. 7. [**16 Ch. D. 112**

—— Gift to wife during widowhood—Void marriage - **25 Ch. D. 685** *See* WILL—CONDITION. 11.

XXIV. WILL—PERPETUITY.

1. —— **Ascertainment of Class** — *Divisible Gift—Gift to Children of A. who should attain Twenty-one—Period for ascertaining Class—Prior Trust for Accumulation of Income.*] Devise of real estate to trustees in fee, upon trust for J. for life, and after his death upon trust for his children who should attain twenty-one, and the issue of any child who should die under twenty-one leaving issue who should attain that age; but, in case there should be no child, nor the issue of any child of J. who should attain twenty-one, the property was to be held on trust for the child or children of R. who should respectively attain twenty-one, if more than one in equal shares. Provided always, that the rents of the trust premises should, during the term of twenty years from the day next before the day of the testator's death, be

XXIV. WILL—PERPETUITY—*continued.*

accumulated by way of compound interest, and the accumulated fund should be held in trust for the child, if only one, or all the children equally, if more than one, of R. who should attain twenty-one. J. died without ever having a child. R. had six children who attained twenty-one. The youngest of them was born after the eldest had attained twenty-one, but before the end of the period of accumulation:—*Held*, that the gift over to the children of R. was divisible into two distinct alternative gifts, viz., (1) a gift over in the event of there never being any child of J.; (2) a gift over in the event of no child or issue of any child of J. attaining twenty-one; and that consequently the first alternative was not too remote, and the gift over was in the events which had happened good. —*Evers v. Challis* (7 H. L. C. 531) explained.— *Stuart* v. *Cockerell* (Law Rep. 5 Ch. 713) distinguished.—*Held*, also, that all the children of R. who were born during the period of accumulation, and who attained twenty-one, were entitled under the gift over. WATSON *v.* YOUNG **28 Ch. D. 436**

2. —— **Ascertainment of Class** *within prescribed Period.*] The rule against perpetuities requires that not only the extreme limit of the class of persons who may take, but the actual persons who are to take, should be ascertained within the prescribed period.—A testatrix directed property to be sold at a period beyond the limit prescribed by the rule against perpetuities and the proceeds to be divided between such of her grandchildren living at the time of the sale in such proportions as testatrix's sister should by will appoint:—*Held*, that an appointment made by a will of the sister before the sale was a bad exercise of the power:—*Held*, also, that as the class of grandchildren living at the time of the sale could not be ascertained within the prescribed limit, the gift was void for remoteness notwithstanding that the entire class of grandchildren must be ascertained within the prescribed limit. BLIGHT *v.* HARTNOLL **19 Ch. D. 294**

3. —— **Contingent Remainder** — *Executory Devise—Life Estate—Equitable Estate—Attaining Twenty-five—Name and Arms—Possession.*] A testator devised and bequeathed real and personal estate to trustees upon trust to pay the income to his wife during her life, and after her decease, if H. was then living, to retain the rents of the realty to their own use during his life, and to pay him the income of the personalty during his life, and after his death upon trust to convey and transfer the real and personal estate to such son of M. as should first attain the age of twenty-five years, upon condition that such son of M. as should become entitled to any property under the will should, within two years after he should so become entitled, take the name and arms of the testator. At the testator's decease M. was living and had no son who had attained twenty-five, but his eldest son attained that age during the lives of the widow and H. This son died in the lifetime of H. without having taken the name and arms of the testator:—*Held*, by Malins, V.C., that although the limitation of the personal estate to the first son of M. who should attain the age of twenty-five was void for remoteness, the direction to convey the real estate to him gave him a contingent remainder which was not void for remote-

XXIV. WILL—PERPETUITY—continued.

ness, although his estate was only equitable, the doctrine of contingent remainders being applicable to equitable as well as to legal estates ; that he was not bound to take the name and arms of the testator until his estate came into possession, and that the real estate devolved upon his heir.—*Held*, on appeal, that the limitation to such son of M. as should first attain the age of twenty-five years could not, as in *Riley* v. *Garnett* (3 De G. & Sm. 629), be treated as intended to give an immediately vested interest liable to be divested on death under twenty-five, but was a limitation contingent on the son's attaining the age of twenty-five years :—*Held*, also, that when the legal estate in fee is vested in trustees under the instrument which creates the beneficial limitations, the feudal rule by which a contingent remainder fails, if it does not vest before the determination of the particular estate, does not apply, and that the limitation to such son of M. as should attain twenty-five years, assuming it to have been an equitable remainder, would still have been void for remoteness :—*Held*, also, that the direction to the trustees to convey on the death of H. did not create a contingent equitable remainder, but was an executory devise. ABBISS *v.* BURNEY. *In re* FINCH

[17 Ch. D. 211

4. —— Gift to Class—*Substitution*.] A testator directed his trustees, after the death of the longest liver of his son, his daughter, and any widow whom the son might leave, to sell his real estate and to stand possessed of the proceeds and of the rents and profits until sale, upon trust to pay and apply them " unto and equally amongst all and every the child and children of my son W. and daughter M. share and share alike, and the lawful issue of such of them as may be then dead leaving issue, such issue to be entitled to no more than their parent or respective parents would have been if living." He directed that if his daughter's son then living should die without leaving issue, or leaving issue, all of them should die under age and unmarried, the trustees should pay the share which would have been payable to him under the above trusts to the children of J. ; and, that if the testator's son died without leaving issue, or all of them died under age and unmarried, the trustees should pay the share which would have been payable to them under the trusts aforesaid to the children of J. and M. The heir-at-law claimed the corpus as undisposed of, on the ground that the disposition of the proceeds of sale was void for remoteness as being a gift to a class not ascertainable till at or after the death of the son's widow, who might be a person unborn at the testator's death :—*Held*, that the gift was not a gift to such children of the son and daughter as should be living at the period of distribution and the issue of such of them as should be then dead, but a gift to all the children of the son and daughter, with a gift over by way of substitution of the shares of such of them as might die before the period of distribution leaving issue—that when the gift over of any share was void for remoteness the original gift remained unaffected—and that the. heir-at-law had no title. GOODIER *v.* JOHNSON　　　-　　-　18 Ch. D. 441

5. —— Gift to Descendants bearing a particular Name—*Life Estate to Unborn Persons*.]

XXIV. WILL—PERPETUITY—continued.

The testatrix, Miss R., had a brother, a widower advanced in life, who had assumed the name of R. G., and had two children, one a bachelor of unsound mind, the other a daughter. By her will she bequeathed a fund to trustees in trust to pay the income to her brother for life, then to his son for life, and from and after the decease of both of them, upon trust to pay the income " for life unto any immediate or direct descendants of my said brother or nephew who shall bear the name of R. G. only, and from and after his or her decease, or in case of failure of any such immediate or direct descendant of my said brother or nephew who shall bear the name of R. G. only," upon trust for certain specified charitable societies. There was a clause for determining the interests of any descendants who after becoming entitled to the receipt of the income should abandon the name of R. G. Before the death of the nephew, a son born after the death of the testatrix, of the daughter of the testatrix's brother, assumed by royal license the name of R. G., and at the decease of the survivor of the brother and nephew there was no other descendant of either of them who bore that name :—*Held*, by Hall, V.C., that the trusts subsequent to the life interests of the brother and nephew were void for remoteness, and that on the determination of those interests the fund fell into the residue.—*Held*, on appeal, that the limitations after the life interests were not void for remoteness :— *Held*, that the limitation to descendants was a gift for life to descendants living at the determination of the life interests and bearing the name of R. G. as joint tenants :—*Held*, that the gift was not, as in *Leigh* v. *Leigh* (15 Ves. 92), confined to persons entitled to the name of R. G. by birth, and that the brother's grandson, as he bore the name of R. G. at the determination of the life interests, was entitled for life, and that on his decease the gift to the charities would take effect. *In re* ROBERTS. REPINGTON *v.* ROBERTS-GAWEN

[19 Ch. D. 520

6. —— Restraint on Anticipation—*Daughters' Share—Rule against Perpetuities*.] A testator gave his property to trustees to pay the income to two persons for life, and after the death of the survivor to divide the capital between the children of A. B. and C. D., two females, the shares of sons to be paid on their attaining twenty-one, and the shares of daughters to be invested and the interest paid to such daughters for life for their separate use without power of anticipation, and on their deaths the capital to go as the daughters should by will appoint. A. B. was dead at the date of the will, and C. D. was sixty years of age, and therefore past child-bearing :—*Held*, that if the children of A. B. and C. D. had not necessarily been lives in esse at the date of the will, the restraint on anticipation in respect of the daughters' shares would have been bad, as infringing the rule against perpetuities ; but as A. B. was dead and C. D. past child-bearing, all the children were lives in esse, and the restraint on alienation was valid. COOPER *v.* LAROCHE　　-　　-　　-　17 Ch. D. 368

XXV. WILL—PRECATORY TRUST.

1. —— " Feeling confident."] A testator gave to his widow the whole of his real and personal property " feeling confident that she will act justly to our children in dividing the same when.

XXV. WILL—PRECATORY TRUST—*continued.*

no longer required by her ":—*Held*, that the widow took an absolute interest, and that the doctrine of precatory trusts did not apply. MUSSOORIE BANK *v.* RAYNOR - 7 App. Cas. 321

2. —— "In full confidence."] A testator gave all his real and personal estate unto and to the absolute use of his wife, her heirs, executors, administrators, and assigns, "in full confidence that she would do what was right as to the disposal thereof between his children, either in her lifetime or by will after her decease ":—*Held* (affirming the decision of Pearson, J.), that under these words the widow took an absolute interest in the property, unfettered by any trust in favour of the children. *In re* ADAMS AND THE KENSINGTON VESTRY　　　24 Ch. D. 199 ; 27 Ch. D. 394

XXVI. WILL—PRIORITY OF LEGACIES.

—— Legacy to Wife.] A testator gave to his wife all his furniture and effects together with the sum of £500 to be paid to her immediately after his decease.—He also directed his trustees to raise out of his estate the sums of £12,000 and £5000, and invest the same and pay the interest of the £12,000 to his wife during her life, and the interest of the £5000 to his brother and sisters during their lives, and after the death of his wife, brother, and sisters, those sums were to fall into the residue of his estate. He then gave his brother and sisters legacies of £6000 and £2000, and gave other smaller legacies.—His estate proved insufficient for the payment in full of all the legacies :—*Held*, that the legacy of £500 to the wife had priority over all the other pecuniary legacies :—*Held*, that the legacies of £12,000 and £5000 had priority over the other legacies.—*Blower v. Morrett* (2 Ves. Sen. 420) dissented from. *In re* HARDY. WELLS *v.* BORWICK - - 17 Ch. D. 798

XXVII. WILL—REPUGNANCY.

—— Direction as to Time of Payment—*Inconsistent Clause.*] A testator gave to his wife so long as she should continue his widow and until all his four daughters by his former wife should attain twenty-one or die under twenty-one, an annuity of £800, and a further annuity of £100 in respect of each of such daughters who should for the time being be under twenty-one, such annuities to be employed by her in maintaining herself and his said daughters, and in educating the daughters. After all his four daughters had attained twenty-one or died he bequeathed to his wife during widowhood £600 a year, and after her future marriage £200 a year. And if he should have any children by his then wife, he bequeathed to his wife in respect of each of such children who should for the time being be under twenty-one a further annuity of £150, to commence after all his said four daughters should have attained twenty-one or died, to be applied by his wife in maintaining and educating such children, and to be paid by equal half-yearly payments, the first of such payments to be made at the expiration of six calendar months from his decease. He gave his residuary estate among such of his children by both wives as being sons should attain twenty-one, or being daughters attain that age or marry, in equal shares, subject to a provision for making the share of each child by the second wife exceed the share of a child by

XXVII. WILL—REPUGNANCY—*continued.*

the former wife by £3000. There was the usual clause of maintenance, subject to a proviso that the power of giving maintenance should not be exercised as to any child while the annuity bequeathed to his wife in respect of such child was payable, unless the trustees thought the annuity insufficient. At the testator's death several of the daughters by the first wife were under twenty-one. —*Held*, by Jessel, M.R., that the annuities of £150 became payable from the testator's death, and were not postponed till all the daughters by the first wife had attained twenty-one or died, on the ground that, having regard to the scope of the will, the former of the two inconsistent clauses was to be rejected rather than the latter, independently of the rule that of two inconsistent clauses in a will the latter is to be preferred.—*Held*, on appeal, that this was not a case of two inconsistent gifts, but of a gift of something to arise at a future time with a subsequent direction as to the time of payment which was inconsistent with the terms of the original gift, and that such subsequent direction could not enlarge the gift, but must be rejected as inconsistent with it :—*Held*, that evidence that the latter of the two clauses was left in the will by mistake, and contrary to the testator's express instructions, was not admissible. *In re* BYWATER. BYWATER *v.* CLARKE - - 18 Ch. D. 17

—— Condition in restraint of alienation 26 Ch. D. *See* WILL—CONDITION. 2. [901

XXVIII. WILL—RESIDUARY GIFT.

1. —— "Everything I am possessed of."—"*I give and devise*" — "*Residuary Legatee*" — *No Real Estate at Date of Will or Codicil—After-acquired Real Estate—Residuary Devisee—Intestacy as to Real Estate—Vendor and Purchaser Act, 1874.*] A testatrix, by her will, dated in 1854, gave as follows : "I commit to paper my wishes respecting the disposal of my property. . . . Everything I am possessed of I leave to my sister for her life; after her decease I give and devise as here annexed." Then followed a number of legacies, and the will proceeded : "My two nephews, H. H. M. and F. P. M., I leave my executors, and the latter residuary legatee after the demise of my sister."—She also executed a codicil, but she had no real estate either at the date of the will or codicil. She afterwards purchased some freehold property, which she held at her death.—F. P. M. contracted for the sale of part of the real estate as absolute owner, and an objection having been taken by the purchaser that he had no title :—*Held*, that there was not sufficient context in the will to enable the Court to read the words "residuary legatee" as "residuary devisee," and that consequently, the real estate did not pass to F. P. M. —*Hughes* v. *Pritchard* (6 Ch. D. 24) distinguished. *In re* METHUEN AND BLORE'S CONTRACT 16 Ch. D. [696

2. —— "Fall into residue" — *Direction that Share "shall fall into residue."*] A testator bequeathed the residue of his personal estate to his wife for life, and after her death to his sister and three brothers in equal shares; but directed that in the event of his sister dying unmarried in his wife's lifetime (which happened) "her one-fourth should fall into the residue ":—*Held*, that there was no intestacy as to the sister's one-fourth, but

XXVIII. WILL—RESIDUARY GIFT—*continued.*

that the whole residue was, on the widow's death, divisible in thirds between three other legatees.—*Humble v. Shore* (7 Hare, 247; 1 H. & M. 550, n.), *Lightfoot v. Burstall* (1 H. & M. 546), and *Crawshaw v. Crawshaw* (14 Ch. D 817) considered. *In re* RHOADES. LANE *v.* RHOADES **29 Ch. D. 142**

3. —— "*Money*"—"*All the rest of my money however invested.*"] A testatrix, by her will, after giving a pecuniary legacy and bequeathing furniture, leaseholds, and dock shares, gave "all the rest of her money however invested" to her nephew R. J. F. "under deduction of £50 to be paid to each of her executors." She then gave a number of specified articles, such as ornaments, plate, pictures, and house linen, to various other nephews and nieces, and appointed executors:—*Held,* that the gift to R. J. F. was a general residuary gift, and included the furniture, leaseholds, and dock shares, the bequest of which had lapsed. *In re* PRINGLE. WALKER *v.* STEWART　-　-　**17 Ch. D. 819**

4. —— "*Money of which I am possessed.*"] In construing a will no absolute technical meaning should be given of such a word as "money," the meaning of which must depend upon the context, if any, and such surrounding circumstances as the Court can take into consideration. A testatrix who was possessed of cash, securities, leaseholds, furniture, and effects, by her will, made in expectation of her death, which occurred two days after its date, gave "one half of the money of which I am possessed to H., and the remainder equally between O. and S., and after them to their children":—*Held,* that the word "money" passed all the personal estate. *In re* CADOGAN. CADOGAN *v.* PALAGI　　-　　**25 Ch. D. 154**

5. —— "*Money, Residue of.*"] A testator bequeathed "the whole residue of money" to A. H. W., "excepting such things as the undermentioned," &c.:—*Held,* that the words were sufficient to pass the residue. IN THE GOODS OF WHITE **[7 P. D. 65**

6. —— "*Money, Stocks, Funds, or other Securities.*"] A gift of "such money, stocks, funds, or other securities, not hereafter specifically devised, as I may die possessed of," does not constitute a gift of residue. IN THE GOODS OF ASTON **[6 P. D. 203**

XXIX. WILL—REVOCATION.

1. —— Codicil.] T. M. B. having executed a codicil at the foot of his will cut off his signature to the will. Upon proof that he thereby intended to revoke the codicil the Court held that the codicil was also revoked. IN THE GOODS OF BLECKLEY **[8 P. D. 169**

2. —— *Codicil—Confirmation of Will by Codicil referring to Will by Date—Implied Revocation of Intermediate Codicil.*] A testator by will gave legacies to three of his daughters, and devised and bequeathed his residuary real and personal estate upon trusts for his wife and children.—By a first codicil in 1878 he revoked one of the legacies in his will and increased another, and concluded "in all other respects I confirm my said will."—By a second codicil after reciting that he was desirous of altering the residuary devise contained in his will, he made a specific devise, and in all other respects confirmed his will. He afterwards made

XXIX. WILL—REVOCATION—*continued.*

a third codicil, by which, after referring to his will by date and reciting a promise to that effect, he directed his trustees to grant an underlease of a house to his daughter-in-law, and gave his wife a pecuniary legacy in addition to the benefit she derived under his said will, and concluded "in all other respects I confirm my said will except as altered by a certain codicil made thereto in 1878, whereby I revoked a legacy to my daughter Mary":—*Held,* that the words of confirmation in the first and third codicils were to be read as meaning that the testator did not intend to alter his general testamentary dispositions further than in the specific way mentioned in those codicils; and that the devise in the second codicil being clear, no intention to revoke it had been shewn with sufficient clearness to enable the Court to reject that devise. FOLLETT *v.* PETTMAN　　-　**23 Ch. D. 337**

3. —— *Evidence—Revocation by subsequent Will—Admissibility of Memorandum.*] A testator made a will in 1864 appointing his wife sole executrix, and duly executed another document in 1877. There was no evidence of the contents of the second document except that after its execution the testator said, "I have made a will altering my affairs, and I have taken care of Ellen, and there will be something for Roby," and except a memorandum at the foot of the will as follows: "This will is now useless, a new will having been made in October 1877, upon my wife telling me she was sorry she had ever seen me," &c.:—*Held,* that in the absence of proof of an alteration of executrix or a revocatory clause or disposition wholly inconsistent with the first will, that will was not revoked, and was therefore entitled to probate.—*Quære,* whether the memorandum was admissible in evidence to shew an intention to revoke the first will. HELLIER *v.* HELLIER

[9 P. D. 237

XXX. WILL—SATISFACTION.

1. —— *Advance by Parent to Child—Debt due to Testator, whether released by Will—Bequest of Residue on Trust to pay Income to Widow, and subject thereto for equal Distribution among Children — Clause providing that Advances made to Children shall be brought into Hotchpot.*] A testator had advanced by way of loan to the defendant, one of his children, a sum of £2000, upon which sum interest was paid during the testator's lifetime. The testator, by his will, devised and bequeathed all his property, both real and personal, to trustees on trust to permit his widow to receive the income actually produced by such property, howsoever constituted or invested, during widowhood, and subject thereto on trust for his child, if only one, or all his children equally if more than one, who being a son or sons should attain the age of twenty-one years, or being a daughter or daughters should attain that age or marry. The will contained a proviso that any advances made by the testator to any child or to the husband of any child in his lifetime together with interest on such advances, as charged against such child or her husband in his private memorandum book in his own handwriting, should, according to the amount thereof, be taken in full or in part satisfaction of his or her share in the testator's property, unless the testator should

XXX. WILL—SATISFACTION—continued.

otherwise declare by writing under his hand. The sum advanced to the Defendant was charged against him in the testator's memorandum book, and such book contained an entry as follows: "This is the memorandum book named in my will as containing the advances made by me to my children or their husbands to be taken in satisfaction of their respective shares in my estate":—Held, by Brett, M.R., and Lindley, L.J., Cotton, L.J., dissenting, that the testator's widow was entitled to receive from the Defendant during her life, as part of the annual income given to her by the will, interest on the said sum of £2000.—Judgment of the Queen's Bench Division affirmed. LIMPUS v. ARNOLD **13 Q. B. D. 246; 15 Q. B. D. 300**

2. —— Hotchpot—*Gift of Residue to Widow for Life, with Remainder to Children—Advances—Interest.*] A testator gave his residuary estate to his widow for life, with remainder to his children equally, with a proviso, in the common form, for bringing into hotchpot all sums advanced to any of them by him during his lifetime. The testator made advances to some of his children. In distributing the residuary estate among the children after the death of the widow:—Held, that the advanced children must bring their advances into hotchpot, with interest at 4 per cent. per annum up to the distribution of the estate; such interest to be computed from the death of the widow, and not from the date of the respective advances or from the death of the testator. *In re* REES. REES v. GEORGE - **17 Ch. D. 701**

3. —— Moral Obligation *other than Parental.*] The doctrine of ademption of legacies founded on parental or *quasi*-parental relation applies also to cases where a moral obligation other than parental or *quasi*-parental is recognised in the will, though without reference to any special application of the money.—A testatrix by her will bequeathed to a niece of her deceased husband £500 with these words, "according to the wish of my late beloved husband," and she afterwards in her lifetime paid £300 to such legatee, with a contemporaneous entry in her diary that such payment was a "legacy from" the legatee's "uncle John":—Held, that the presumption was that such legacy was adeemed to the extent of £300, and that such presumption of ademption *pro tanto* only was not displaced by evidence that more than a year before the £300 was given the testatrix had said, that the legatee when then asked by the testatrix whether she would rather receive £300 down than a larger sum after the testatrix's death, had replied that she would prefer the £300 down. *In re* POLLOCK. POLLOCK v. WORRALL. **28 Ch. D. 552**

XXXI. WILL—SEPARATE USE.

1. —— "Sole and Unmarried."] A testatrix by her will made in 1860, bequeathed a fund to trustees, on trust to pay the income to her husband for his life, and on his death to divide the fund into four equal parts, and, as to one of the parts, "upon trust to pay the same to J. H., spinster, if she be then sole and unmarried, but, if she be then married," the testatrix directed her trustees to pay the income of the fourth part to J. H. for her life, for her separate use, and after her death to hold it on trust for her children. In June, 1878, the testatrix died, and her husband died in April, 1883.

XXXI. WILL—SEPARATE USE—continued.

In April, 1861, J. H. married, and in November, 1878, a decree absolute was made for the dissolution of her marriage. There were three children of the marriage. J. H. did not marry again:—Held, that the words "then sole and unmarried" meant "not having a husband" at the time of the death of the tenant for life, and that, in the events which had happened, J. H. was absolutely entitled to the one-fourth share. *In re* LESINGHAM'S TRUSTS **24 Ch. D. 703**

2. —— "Sole use and disposal."] A legacy given to a married woman for her "sole use and disposal" vests in her as separate estate. BLAND v. DAWES - - - - **17 Ch. D. 794**

—— Restraint on anticipation—Perpetuity [17 Ch. D. 368

See WILL—PERPETUITY. 6.

XXXII. WILL—SPEAKING FROM DEATH.

1. —— Curtesy—*Devise to Married Daughter—Death of Devisee in Lifetime of Testator—Wills Act (7 Will. 4 & 1 Vict. c. 26), ss. 3, 33—Seisin—Husband.*] A testator died in 1875, having by his will, dated in 1872, devised a freehold estate to his daughter (the Plaintiff's wife), her heirs and assigns, for her separate use.—The daughter died in 1874, in the lifetime of the testator, leaving an only child, who was her heiress at law.—The Plaintiff claimed to be entitled for his life as tenant by the curtesy.—Held, upon demurrer, that the Plaintiff was entitled for his life to the property devised by the testator as tenant by the curtesy. EAGER v. FURNIVALL - **17 Ch. D. 115**

2. —— Income of Share of Partnership Business—*Subsequent Acquisition of the entire Business—Wills Act, ss. 23, 24.*] The testator, William Russell, by a will, dated in 1857, after reciting that he was carrying on business as an iron manufacturer in partnership with his two brothers, bequeathed all his share and interest of and in the partnership business, and of and in the real and personal estate employed or invested therein, and of and in the partnership debts, securities, and moneys to which he might be entitled at his decease, to trustees, upon trust to continue the business during his wife's life, and to pay to her a sum equal to half the amount drawn out by the two other partners. The wife had a discretion to discontinue the business, and in case the business should be discontinued testator directed the trustees to get in the share then appertaining to his estate in "the said co-partnership trade or business," and, after making good to the wife "one half third share of the profits," invest the same, and pay the income to his wife for life. After the death of the wife, he directed the trustees out of the profits of his said share and interest in the business, if continued, and out of the trust fund, if the business should have been discontinued, to pay certain pecuniary legacies, and subject thereto to hold the fund in trust for A. B.—Testator died in 1881. After the date of the will, he acquired the shares of his two brothers in the partnership and carried on the business still under the firm of "Russell Brothers," as sole owner, until his death. A. B. died in the testator's lifetime. The widow had not discontinued the business:—Held, that the will operated upon the whole of the testator's

XXXII. WILL—SPEAKING FROM DEATH—
continued.

interest in the business at his death, and that the widow took the whole of the income for her life. *In re* RUSSELL. RUSSELL *v.* CHELL **19 Ch. D. 432**

3 —— "*In their present state*"—*Specific Devise of "my cottage and all my land at S." "in their present state"—Residuary Devise — Subsequent Contract to purchase a House and Land at S.—Wills Act,* 1837 (1 *Vict. c.* 26), *s.* 24.] A. devised to G. for life, "my cottage and all my land at S.," subject to the stipulation (among others) that the plantations, heather, and furze be all preserved "in their present state," and devised "all other, my freehold manor, messuages, lands, and real estate whatsoever and wheresoever" to trustees upon trust for sale. At the date of his will A. had a small cottage with twenty-two acres of rough land held with it, and he subsequently contracted to purchase from G. a house of considerable size with gardens and land comprising ten acres closely adjoining the cottage and land. The contract was not completed at his death:—*Held*, that a contrary intention within the meaning of the 24th section of the Wills Act was not shewn with sufficient clearness, but that, construing the will as if it had been made on the day of the testator's death, having regard to the circumstances at that date and to the residuary devise, the specific devise more aptly referred to the cottage and rough land, and did not carry the after-acquired property.— The words "all my land at S." would, if used alone, have been sufficient to carry the after-acquired land with the house standing upon it; but upon the authority of *Emer v. Hayden* (Cro. Eliz. 476, 658), by force of the context the word "land" must be taken as confined to lands in contradistinction from buildings.—Decision of Kay, J., reversed.—*Semble*, per Lindley, L.J.: Sect. 24 of the Wills Act, which provides that a will shall speak as to the real and personal estate comprised in it (*i.e.*, the will) from the day of the testator's death, leaves open the question whether a particular property passes by the specific or the residuary devise. *In re* PORTAL AND LAMB **27 Ch. D. 600;**
[30 Ch. D, 50

XXXIII. WILL—SPECIFIC LEGACY.

—— "*All personal estate*"—*Residuary Bequest.*] A testator by his will, after directing his executors to pay all his just debts and funeral and testamentary expenses, and giving pecuniary legacies to individuals and to charities, gave all his personal estate and effects of which he should die possessed, and which should not consist of money or securities for money, to E. A. Robertson absolutely. And he gave and devised all the rest, residue and remainder of his estate, both real and personal, to his executors upon certain trusts; all the legacies to be free of legacy duty; the legacies for charitable purposes to be paid exclusively out of such part of his personal estate as might lawfully be appropriated to such purposes and preferably to any other payment thereout:—*Held*, affirming the decision of the Court of Appeal, that the legacy to E. A. Robertson was not specific, and not exempt from the payment of the pecuniary legacies. *In re* OVEY. BROADBENT *v.* BARROW. ROBERTSON *v.* BROADBENT - **20 Ch. D. 676;**
[8 App. Cas. 812

XXXIV. WILL—SUBSTITUTIONAL GIFT.

1. —— Gift to Children of deceased Child, "*or in event of decease to their descendants*"— *Child of one of the Class who predeceased M. not entitled to share.*] Testator by will bequeathed all his share in an estate in Barbadoes "to all the children of "his dear departed wife's sister M: H. M., "or in event of decease to their descendants share and share alike." M. H. M. had six children, of whom five were living at the date of the will and at the death of the testator, and one had died prior to the date of the will leaving issue an only daughter:—*Held*, following the decision in *Christopherson v. Naylor* (1 Mer. 320), that the issue of the child of M. H. M. who was dead at the date of the will, was not entitled to a share of the property, but that it went to the five children of M. H. M. who survived the testator. *In re* WEBSTER'S ESTATE. WIDGEN *v.* MELLO
[23 Ch. D. 737

2. —— Issue of Child dead when the Will was made.] A testatrix by her will gave a sum of money to trustees on trust, after the death of the widow of a cousin, for the children of the cousin, share and share alike; provided that in case of any of the children dying in the lifetime of the testatrix leaving issue, such issue should take the share to which their parent would have been entitled if living.—One of the children was dead when the will was made, and a codicil shewed that the testatrix was aware of this:—*Held*, that the issue of that child took a share in the money.— *In re Potter's Trust* (Law Rep. 8 Eq. 52) followed. *In re* LUCAS'S WILL **17 Ch. D. 788**

—— Remoteness **18 Ch. D. 441**
See WILL—PERPETUITY. 4.

XXXV. WILL—SURVIVOR.

1. —— "*Other or others*"—*Gift to Children for Life with Remainder to their Children—Dying without Children—"Survivor or Survivors" not construed "other or others."*] Testator gave by will, made in 1834, the residue of his estate to trustees to pay the income, after the death of his wife, unto such of his four named children as should be living at the decease of his wife, during their lives; and after the decease of any one or more of such children who should leave children he gave the share, whether original or accruing, of the one so dying in trust for his or her children : and, in the event of any one of his children dying without leaving children who should attain the age of twenty-one years, then he gave the share, whether original or accruing, of such of them so dying in trust for the survivor or survivors of his said children during their lives, and after their deaths for their respective children, and their heirs, executors, and administrators. There was no gift over. The four children of the testator survived the widow. One child died leaving two children who attained the age of twenty-one years, and the other three children died without issue:—*Held*, that the words "survivor or survivors" must be so read, and not as "other or others." *In re* HORNER'S ESTATE. POMFRET *v.* GRAHAM
[19 Ch. D. 186

2. —— "Other or others"—"*Surviving.*"] A testator devised to each of his children an estate for the life of that child, with remainder to the children

8 I

XXXV. WILL—SURVIVOR—*continued.*

of that child, and in case any or either of the testator's children should die without leaving any child or children him, her or them surviving, then the testator devised the estates to which their child or children respectively would have been entitled under his will, if living, to his, the testator's, surviving children for their respective natural lives, and after their deceases respectively he gave their respective shares to their respective children, their heirs, executors, administrators, and assigns. There was no gift over on the death of all the testator's children without leaving children. C., one of the testator's children, died without leaving issue. Some of the other children were then living; others had died leaving children of theirs then living:—*Held*, that the word " surviving " was to be read in its proper sense, and that the children of those children of the testator who had predeceased C., took no interest in the estate of which C. was tenant for life.—The fact that the original shares are all settled by the will, and that the shares which the " survivors " take in the share of a child who dies without issue, are settled in the same way as their original shares, is not by itself sufficient to shew that " survivors " is used otherwise than in its proper sense. *In re* BENN. BENN *v.* BENN

[**29 Ch. D. 839**

XXXVI. WILL—TRUST ESTATES.

The Act 44 & 45 *Vict. c.* 41 (*Conveyancing Act*, 1881) *enacts*—

Sect. 30.—(1.) *Where an estate or interest of inheritance, or limited to the heir as special occupant, in any tenements or hereditaments, corporeal or incorporeal, is vested on any trust, or by way of mortgage in any person solely, the same shall, on his death, notwithstanding any testamentary disposition, devolve to and become vested in his personal representatives or representative from time to time, in like manner as if the same were a chattel real vesting in them or him; and accordingly all the like powers, for one only of several joint personal representatives, as well as for a single personal representative, and for all the personal representatives together to dispose of and otherwise deal with the same, shall belong to the deceased's personal representatives or representative from time to time, with all the like incidents, but subject to all the like rights, equities, and obligations, as if the same were a chattel real vesting in them or him; and, for the purposes of this section, the personal representatives for the time being, of the deceased, shall be deemed in law his heirs and assigns, within the meaning of all trusts and powers.*

(2.) *Section 4 of the Vendor and Purchaser Act, 1874, and section 48 of the Land Transfer Act, 1875, are hereby repealed.*

(3.) *This section, including the repeals therein, applies only in cases of death after the commencement of the Act—31st Dec. 1881.*

XXXVII. WILL—TRUSTEES.

1. —— Extent of Estate—*Direction to pay Debts—Contingent Remainder—Failure of particular Estate.*] A testator, by his will made in 1838, directed his debts to be paid. And he devised specific real estate to four persons (whom he afterwards named as his executors), their heirs and assigns, upon trust and for the intents and purposes thereinafter mentioned, viz., upon trust during the

XXXVII. WILL—TRUSTEES—*continued.*

minority of his daughter D. to receive the rents and apply the same for her benefit till she should attain twenty-one, and, on her attaining twenty-one, to pay to or permit and suffer her to receive the rents during her life for her separate use, without power of anticipation. And, from and after her death, upon trust for, and the testator thereby gave and devised the property to the issue children or child of the daughter who should live to attain twenty-one, in equal shares, if more than one, and to their respective heirs and assigns, with remainders over. And, after making other specific devises and bequests, the testator devised and bequeathed the residue of his estate and effects (subject to and charged with the payment of his debts) to one of his trustees absolutely, for his own use and benefit. The daughter D survived the testator, and she afterwards married and had three children, but she died before any of them had attained twenty-one:—*Held*, that, by reason of the direction that the testator's debts should be paid, the trustees took the whole legal estate in fee simple in the specifically devised estate, and consequently that the contingent remainder to the children of the daughter had not failed by reason of the determination of her life estate before the happening of the contingency.—*Festing* v. *Allen* (12 M. & W. 279) distinguished.— *Creaton* v. *Creaton* (3 Sm. & Giff. 386) followed. MARSHALL *v.* GINGELL -   **21 Ch. D. 790**

2. —— Indefinite Trust—*Communication of Object of Trust to Trustee after Testator's Death.*] A. B. instructed his solicitor to prepare for him a will leaving all his property to the solicitor himself absolutely, but to be held and disposed of by him according to written directions to be subsequently given, and a will was prepared and executed accordingly under which the solicitor was universal legatee and sole executor.—No such directions were however given to the solicitor by the testator in his lifetime, but after his death an unattested paper was found by which the testator stated his wish that X. Y. should have all his property except a small sum of money which he gave to the solicitor. The solicitor claimed no beneficial interest in the testator's property, except to the extent of his legacy, and claimed to hold the rest of the property as trustee for X. Y.:—*Held*, that as the testator had not in his own lifetime communicated to the solicitor the object of the trust no valid trust in favour of X. Y. had been constituted, and accordingly that the solicitor held the property as trustee for the next of kin of the testator. *In re* BOYES. BOYES *v.* CARRITT

[**26 Ch. D. 531**

3. —— Solicitor to Trust Estate.] A direction in a will appointing a particular person solicitor to the trust estate imposes no trust or duty on the trustees of the will to continue such person their solicitor in the management and affairs of the estate. FOSTER *v.* ELSLEY -   **19 Ch. D. 518**

XXXVIII. WILL—VESTING.

1. —— " From and after the Decease of my Wife."] Words are to be construed according to their plain ordinary meaning, unless the context shews them to have been used in a different sense, or unless the rule, if acted on, would lead to some

XXXVIII. WILL—VESTING—continued.

manifest absurdity or incongruity. A testator must not be presumed to intend an absurdity, nevertheless if shewn by the context, or by the whole will to have so intended, the intention, if not illegal, must be carried out.—A testator after making certain dispositions in favour of his wife, and others, directed that from and after the decease of his wife without leaving issue of his marriage, his trustees should stand possessed of all the undisposed of residue of his real and personal estate in trust for his natural daughter for the term of her natural life, with further provision in case of her death or marriage.—It appeared that there was no issue of the marriage, that the testator's widow was still living, and that the natural daughter was still unmarried.—Held, from an examination of the whole will, that, according to the intention therein appearing, the vesting in the natural daughter's estate was not postponed till after the death of the widow.—"From and after the decease of my said wife" must be construed as referring only to property in which the widow took an interest terminable at her death.—Quære, if the case arose whether they might be construed as referring also to property in which the widow's interest failed during her life. RHODES v. RHODES

[7 App. Cas. 192

2. —— Income until Marriage—Capital at the Time of Marriage.] A testatrix by her will, after specific bequests of bonds, gave all the rest of her stocks and shares upon trust to pay the income to G. until his marriage, and at the time of his marriage to hand over the stocks and shares to him:—Held, that G. took a vested interest under the gift, and, being of age, was entitled to have the stocks and shares comprised therein transferred to him, although he had not married.—Batsford v. Kebbel (3 Ves. 363) distinguished.—In re Bunn (16 Ch. D. 247) and Vize v. Stoney (2 D. & Wal. 659 ; S. C. 1 D & War. 337) observed upon. In re WREY. STUART v. WREY - - - 30 Ch. D. 507

3. —— Interim Trust for Maintenance—Gift at Twenty-one—Residuary Gift to Class—Interest whether vested or contingent.] A testatrix gave her residuary real and personal estate to trustees in trust for sale and conversion and investment of the proceeds, and to hold the investments upon trust to pay the income thereof, " or such part thereof as her said trustees" should " from time to time deem expedient," in or towards the maintenance and education of her children until they should attain their respective ages of twenty-one years ; and from and immediately after their attaining their respective ages of twenty-one years, then upon trust to pay and transfer the capital to her said children in equal shares, and to settle each daughter's " share whether original or accruing "; and the testatrix empowered her trustees to dispose of any competent part, not exceeding one-half, of " the presumptive share of any of her children," for their advancement in life.—The testatrix left three children, of whom two attained twenty-one, and the third died an infant :—Held, that the infant did not take a vested interest in his one-third share of the residuary estate of the testatrix.—Fox v. Fox (Law Rep. 19 Eq. 286) distinguished. In re PARKER. BARKER v. BARKER

[16 Ch. D. 44

XXXVIII. WILL—VESTING—continued.

4. —— Interim Trust for Maintenance—Gift over on Assignment—Life Interest—Remainder—Absolute Interest.] A testatrix by her will appointed two-fifths of certain property to trustees upon trust to pay the income to her son until he should attain the age of forty years, and then to hold the same in trust for her son his executors and administrators ; provided that in case her son should assign his share in the property, then the aforesaid bequests should be void, and the two-fifths should be held upon the trusts declared as to the other three-fifths. The son died before he attained the age of forty without having assigned : —Held, that the two-fifths vested in trust for the son absolutely so as to pass by his will. SCOTNEY v. LOMER - - - - 29 Ch. D. 534 [Affirmed by the Court of Appeal, 31 Ch. D. 380.]

5. —— Interim Trust for Maintenance—Residuary Gift to Individual—Gift at Thirty—Interest whether vested or contingent.] A testator bequeathed his residuary personal estate to trustees in trust for conversion and investment ; and to pay the income to B. for his maintenance and until he should attain the age of thirty ; and upon his attaining that age to pay or transfer the capital to him absolutely. B. survived the testator and died under thirty :—Held, that B. took a vested interest. In re BUNN. ISAACSON v. WEBSTER 16 Ch. D. 47

6. —— " Payable."] A testator by his will, bequeathed an annuity to his daughter, and directed that after her death the trustees should hold £2000, part of the fund set apart to secure the annuity, upon trust to pay and divide the same unto and equally between the child and children of the daughter as and when they should respectively attain twenty-one, and, in case any of the children should die before their shares should become " payable as aforesaid " without leaving issue, the share or shares of him, her, or them so dying should be paid to the survivor or survivors of them, equally if more than one, and, if but one, the whole to that one, with power for the trustees, during the respective minorities of the children, to apply the income of his, her, or their expectant share or shares towards his, her, or their maintenance and education. And if all such children should die under twenty-one, without leaving issue, the fund income was given over :—Held, that the children's absolutely vested at twenty-one, and were not divested by subsequent death without issue in the lifetime of their mother. PARTRIDGE v. BAYLIS

[17 Ch. D. 835

7. —— " Period of Distribution."—Erroneous Reference.] A testator gave the interest arising from a sum of stock to V. D., which interest he was to enjoy along with his wife, M. D., during their respective lives, but in the event of either dying and the survivor marrying again, then the capital to be divided, share and share alike, between their children ; an arrangement ultimately to take place at the death of their parents, should neither marry again. The testator then directed that the money should not be removed from the English funds during the lifetime of V. D. and M.D., not until the period arrived " for its distribution (after their death) among their children surviving, share and share alike ":—Held (affirming the decision of Jessel, M.R.), that the interests of the children

3 I 2

XXXVIII. WILL—VESTING—*continued.*

were not contingent on their surviving their parents, the concluding words not being sufficient to render the previously vested gift contingent. *In re* DUKE. HANNAH *v.* DUKE - **16 Ch. D. 112**

XXXIX. WILL—WORDS.

1. —— *Clear annual Income without " Deduction for the legacy tax, or any other matter, cause, or thing whatever "—Annuity held free of Income Tax.*] Testator directed trustees to stand possessed of residuary real and personal estate upon trust to pay thereout to his wife, during her life, such an annual sum as, together with the income of a settled fund of £10,000, should produce to her " a clear annual income of £1500." He gave several legacies and annuities, and towards the end of his will declared that " no deduction shall be made from any of the legacies given by this my will, or to be given by any codicil thereto, for legacy tax or any other matter, cause, or thing whatever."— An administration suit having been brought, an order was made in 1861 that the trustees of the will should repay to the widow certain sums which had been deducted from her annuity by mistake for succession duty, and that they should pay her until further order an annuity of £1500 free of all deductions except income tax; but no express declaration of her rights was made. This order was acted upon until 1882, when a petition was presented by the widow asking that the income tax which had been deducted might be paid to her, and that in future her annuity might be paid free of income tax:—*Held*, by Bacon, V.C., that the widow was entitled to receive from the trustees a clear annuity of £1500, without any deduction therefrom on account of income tax:—But *held*, by the Court of Appeal, discharging the order of Bacon, V.C,. that the order of 1861 amounted to a declaration of the right of the widow to receive the annuity free of all deductions except income tax, notwithstanding the words " until further order," and that the matter was res judicata and could not now be reconsidered.—*Quære*, whether, if the matter had not been res judicata, the decision of the Vice-Chancellor was correct. PEARETH *v.* MARRIOTT - **22 Ch. D. 182**

2. —— *" Clear yearly sums," " free from all deductions"—Income Tax deducted by Trustees—Annuitant entitled to Payment of all Sums deducted.*] A. B., in 1846, gave to his wife annuities or clear yearly sums for her life " free from all deductions in respect of any present or future taxes, charges, assessments, or impositions, or other matter, cause, or thing, whatsoever," and directed the trustees to appropriate and invest a sufficient part of his personal estate as a fund for the purpose of paying them. The trustees, acting upon the advice of counsel, deducted from all the payments to the widow the income tax:—*Held*, that the widow was entitled to be paid the annuities in full, free from any deduction; and also entitled to be paid all the sums which had been deducted.— *Lord Lovat v. Duchess of Leeds* (2 Dr. & Sm. 62) followed. *In re* BANNERMAN'S ESTATE. BANNERMAN *v.* YOUNG **21 Ch. D. 105**

3. —— *" Clear yearly sum "—" Free from all deductions and abatements whatsoever "—Annuitant to pay Income Tax.*] Testator declared that his trustees should stand possessed of his resi-

XXXIX. WILL—WORDS—*continued.*

duary estate and directed them out of the income to pay to his wife " the clear yearly sum of £600 " for life if she should remain his widow, but if she should marry again an annuity of £100 in lieu of the annuity of £600, " the said annuities of £600 and £100, as the case may be, to be paid free from all deductions and abatements whatsoever." By a codicil an annuity of £1000 was given in lieu of £600:—*Held*, that the annuity was not given free from income tax. GLEADOW *v.* LEETHAM **[22 Ch. D. 269**

4. —— *Cousins—First and Second Cousins—Gift over—Death before Payment of any Legacy.*] Testator bequeathed the residue of the proceeds of sale of his real and personal estates upon trust, after the deaths of his wife and sister, to be equally divided amongst all such of his first and second cousins, including his reputed cousin A. B. and his children, or reputed children, and the children of his reputed cousin S. G. deceased as should be then living, and if A. B. should be then dead, the share to which he would have been entitled, if then living, should be divided amongst his then surviving children. And by a codicil, the testator gave a legacy out of the same proceeds of sale " to each of my cousins J. B. and G. C.," in addition to any sum to which they might be entitled under his will, and directed that if any or either of his first or second cousins should die before the payment of any sum or share thereby or by his will directed to be paid to him or her, such sum or share should be equally divided among his or her wife or husband and children or child, if any, and if none should be paid to his or her next of kin. The testator had not, either at the date of his will, or at his death, any second cousin, but at the time of his death he had both first cousins and first cousins once removed, and also first cousins twice removed. A. B. and S. G., if they had been legitimate, would have been the testator's first cousins, and J. B. and G. C. were his first cousins once removed:—*Held*, that the first cousins once removed and their children were included in the gift:— *Held*, also, that the gift over on death before payment was to be construed as before becoming entitled to payment. WILKS *v.* BANNISTER **[30 Ch. D. 512**

5. —— *" Cousins "—" Second Cousins."*] A testator gave one-third of his property to his first cousins and two-thirds to his second cousins. At his death he left first cousins, second cousins, and children and grandchildren of first cousins:— *Held* (affirming the decision of the Master of the Rolls), that the term " second cousins " did not include children or grandchildren of first cousins. *In re* PARKER. BENTHAM *v.* WILSON **17 Ch. D. 262**

6. —— *' Cousins "—" Second Cousins "—First Cousins once removed.*] A testator, after giving to h's sister a life interest in the whole of his property, devised and bequeathed the same after her death upon trust for sale, and to divide the proceeds amongst " my second cousins."—The testator had no " second cousins " either at the date of his will or at his death, or any born afterwards:— *Held*, that first cousins once removed were entitled. —*Slade v Fooks* (9 Sim. 386) followed. *In re* BONNER. TUCKER *v.* GOOD - **19 Ch. D. 201**

XXXIX. WILL—WORDS—continued.

7. —— "Debt"—Locality—Domicil.] A testator resident in England at the time of his death bequeathed to his son "all his estate and effects in Mauritius." At the time of his death the purchase-money of real estate in Mauritius sold by him to persons residing in that island was due to him. He was not domiciled in Mauritius:—Held, that this debt was included in the bequest of his property in Mauritius. GUTHRIE v. WALROND
[22 Ch. D. 573

8. —— "Farming Stock"—Growing Crops.] A testatrix, after devising all her real estate to A., gave all the "farming stock, goods, chattels and effects in and about" one of her farms forming part of her real estate, to B.: and she gave the residue of her personal estate to other persons:—Held, that all crops growing on the farm at the testatrix's death passed to B.—Vaisey v. Reynolds (5 Russ. 12) disapproved of. In re ROORE. EVANS v. WILLIAMSON　　-　　17 Ch. D. 696

9. —— "Furniture, Goods, and Chattels"—Ejusdem Generis—Gift of "all my interest in C. Estate"—Purchase-money—Mixing with Money at Bankers — Deposit — Ademption.] A testator, after bequeathing pecuniary legacies, directed them "to be paid from such part of my personal estate as shall consist of money at my bankers or in the 3 per cent. consols." And after directing that the whole of his income should be devoted to the comfort and maintenance of his wife, and that she should have the use of his residence, he desired "that the furniture, goods, and chattels be not sold during my wife's lifetime, but at her decease be divided among the executors." And after the death of his wife he bequeathed to M. "all my interest in the C. estate." Prior to the date of the will, the C. estate, which had been appointed by will by the testator's wife to him absolutely, was taken by the M. Board of Works, the purchase-money being paid into Court. Subsequently the wife died, and administration with her will annexed was taken out by the testator, who then conveyed the C. estate to the Board, and obtained payment out to himself of the purchase-money, which he placed with his bankers partly on deposit and partly to his general account with his other moneys, from time to time drawing on that general account. At his death there stood to his credit at his bankers the sum on deposit and a balance on his general account:—Held, (1), applying the rule ejusdem generis, that the gift of "furniture, goods, and chattels," passed only such furniture, &c., as, on the house being let furnished, would go with the occupation of the house, and not such articles as jewellery, guns, pistols, tricycles, and scientific instruments; (2), that the gift of "all my interest in the C. estate," had been adeemed and did not pass the money on deposit or any part of the balance at the bankers.—Clark v. Brown (2 Sm. & Giff.,524) not followed.—Moore v. Moore (29 Beav. 496) distinguished. MANTON v. TABOIS
[30 Ch. D. 92

10. —— "Heirs"—Gift of real and personal Estate together—Substitution.] A testator gave, devised, and bequeathed to his wife all his property, real or personal, on trust for herself for her life, and after her death the whole of his property was to be equally divided among all his children,

XXXIX. WILL—WORDS—continued.

"or such of them as may be then surviving, or their heirs." The testator had five children, all of whom survived him. Of these children two daughters died before the wife, leaving children:—Held, that the word "heirs" had a twofold meaning, viz., heir-at-law as regarded the real estate and next of kin as regarded the personalty:—Held, also, that the property was divisible in fifths,—each surviving child of the testator taking one-fifth, and the heir-at-law and next of kin of each deceased daughter taking between them (according to the nature of the estate) one-fifth share.—Wingfield v. Wingfield (9 Ch. D. 658) followed.—Smith v. Butcher (10 Ch. D. 113) distinguished. KEAY v. BOULTON
[25 Ch. D. 212

11. —— "Husband"—Divorce.] A testator devised property to his daughter for life, and after her death in trust for "any husband with whom she might intermarry, if he should survive her, for his life."—The daughter married the Defendant, and was divorced from him on his petition, and he married again and survived her:—Held, that the Defendant was entitled to the property devised for his life. BULLMORE v. WYNTER　　22 Ch. D. 619

12. —— "Nephews and Nieces"—Consanguinity or affinity.] A testator devised freehold property to be divided between the children of his sister-in-law and A. and B., and "my niece M." (the last-named three devisees being nieces of his deceased wife). He gave other real property to trustees upon trust for sale, and to pay the income of the proceeds of sale amongst "all my nephews and nieces," for their lives and the life of the survivors of them, and bequeathed the capital to the survivor, and he gave other real property unto "all my said nephews and nieces" as tenants in common, and he gave his residuary realty upon trust to pay the income to "all my said nephews and nieces" for their lives and the life of the survivor, and then devised such residue to the survivor, and bequeathed his residuary personal estate equally amongst "all my nephews and nieces":—Held, that the circumstances of the testator having given property to his wife's nieces, and even having called one of them his niece, was not sufficient to include any of his wife's nephews and nieces in the subsequent gifts to all his nephews and nieces: and those only who were related by consanguinity were entitled to take.—Grant v. Grant (Law Rep. 5 C. P. 380, 727) dissented from. MERRILL v. MORTON　17 Ch. D. 382

13. —— "Nephews"— Construction—"Great Nephews, the Sons of his deceased Nephew T. G. A.'—Legitimacy—Domicil.] A bequest of personalty in an English will to the children of a foreigner must be construed to mean to his legitimate children, and by international law as recognised in this country those children are legitimate whose legitimacy is established by the law of their father's domicil. Accordingly where a testator bequeathed personalty to his "great nephews the sons of his deceased nephew T. G. A." and T. G. A. was domiciled in Guernsey:—Held, that a son of T. G. A. born before wedlock, but legitimated according to the law of Guernsey by the subsequent marriage of T. G. A. with that son's mother, was entitled to share with the sons of T. G. A born after the marriage in the testator's bequest.

XXXIX. WILL—WORDS—continued.

—Observations on *In re Goodman's Trusts* (17 Ch. D. 266) and *Boyes v. Bedale* (1 H. & M. 798). *In re* ANDROS. ANDROS *v.* ANDROS
[24 Ch. D. 637

14. —— "Ordinary Outgoings"—*Tenant for Life —Apportionment—Metropolis Local Management Act,* 1855 (18 & 19 Vict. c. 120), *s.* 73—*Metropolis Local Management Act,* 1862 (25 & 26 Vict. c. 102), ss. 96, 97.] A testator gave freehold and leasehold houses, bonds, and consols on trust to pay the income after deducting ordinary outgoings to his widow for life :—*Held,* that the tenant for life must bear the cost of drainage work required to be done to one of the leasehold houses by the vestry under the Metropolis Local Management Act, 1855, s. 73. *In re* CRAWLEY. ACTON *v.* CRAWLEY　　　　　　　　28 Ch. D. 431

15. —— "Paid free of legacy duty."] A testatrix gave several specific and pecuniary legacies, and directed that all her legacies should be "paid free of legacy duty."—*Held,* that under the words "all the legacies left by my will and codicil to be paid free of legacy duty," the legacy duty was to be paid out of the estate on all legacies as well pecuniary as specific, the word "paid" not being sufficient under the circumstances to cut down the direction to pecuniary legacies only.— *Ansley v. Cotton* (16 L. J. (Ch.) 55) discussed and followed. *In re* JOHNSTON. COCKERELL *v.* EARL OF ESSEX　-　　　　　　26 Ch. D. 538

16. —— "Real estates wheresoever situate" *Personal Estate—Leasehold for Years—Wills Act* (1 Vict. c. 26), *s.* 26.] A testator by his will, dated in 1870, declared that his trustees should stand possessed of and interested in the annual income and proceeds of his real and personal estate in trust to pay an annuity to his wife, and after her decease he declared and directed that his trustees should stand possessed of and interested in his real and personal estate upon the trusts and for the intents and purpose following, that is to say, "as to my real estates wheresoever situate (the Victoria Park Cemetery in the parish of St. Matthew, Bethnal Green, excepted)" in trust to pay the annual rents and proceeds thereof to two children as therein mentioned, "and as to my freehold estate called the Victoria Park Cemetery, and my personal estate wheresoever situated, upon trust to pay the dividends, interest and annual proceeds thereof," to his five daughters in equal proportions. —The personal estate comprised certain leaseholds for years.—*Held,* that according to the true construction of the 26th section of the Wills Act (1 Vict. c. 26) the leaseholds for years did not pass under the gift of the real estates.—*Wilson* v. *Eden* (11 Beav. 237; 5 Ex. 752; 14 Beav. 317; 18 Q. B. 474; 16 Beav. 153) discussed; *Turner* v. *Turner* (21 L. J. (Ch.) 843) and *Gully* v. *Davis* (Law Rep. 10 Eq. 562) discussed and distinguished. BUTLER *v.* BUTLER　-　　　28 Ch. D. 66

17. —— Real Security—*Construction—Turnpike Road Bonds.*] Specific bequest of all moneys, stocks, funds, shares, and other securities, "except mortgages on real and leasehold security" :—*Held,* that mortgages of turnpike road tolls, and mortgages of turnpike road tolls and toll-houses, were not mortgages on real security, and did not come

within the exception in the bequest. CAVENDISH *v.* CAVENDISH　-　24 Ch. D. 685 ; 30 Ch. D. 227

18. —— "Unmarried."] Property was given by will to trustees in trust for A. for life, "but if he should die unmarried," to be equally divided between the children of B. At the date of the will A. was a bachelor, and at the time of his death he was a widower :—*Held,* that in the absence of context shewing a contrary intention the word "unmarried" must be construed according to its ordinary or primary meaning as "never having been married," and therefore that the gift to the children of B. did not take effect. DALRYMPLE *v.* HALL　　　　-　　　16 Ch. D. 715

19. —— "Unmarried."] Although the word "unmarried" is one of flexible meaning, and may mean either "never having been married," or "not having a husband" at the time when a gift is to take effect, the former is the primary or natural meaning, and, in the absence of any context shewing a different intention, the word will be so construed. *In re* SERGEANT. MERTENS *v.* WALLEY
[26 Ch. D. 575

—— "Money."
See Cases under WILL—RESIDUE. 3—6.

WILL—Action before probate—Stay of proceedings　　-　　　12 Q. B. B. 294
See PRACTICE—SUPREME COURT—STAYING PROCEEDINGS. 3.

—— Appointment.
See Cases under POWER — EXECUTION. 8—19.

—— Apportionment of dividends　　26 Ch. D. 795
See APPORTIONMENT. 3.

—— Charge of debts—Administration with will annexed　　　　-　　16 Ch. D. 3
See ADMINISTRATOR—WITH WILL ANNEXED. 1.

—— Charitable legacy.
See Cases under CHARITY—MORTMAIN.

—— Contingent gift to infant—Maintenance
[26 Ch. D. 426 ; 29 Ch. D. 331
See INFANT—MAINTENANCE. 4, 6.

—— Covenant not to revoke　-　23 Ch. D. 285
See COVENANT—VALIDITY.

—— Direction as to disposition of dead body
See EXECUTOR—POWERS. 3 [20 Ch. D. 659

—— Election　　-　　-　22 Ch. D. 555
See ELECTION. 1.

—— Execution—Alien　6 P. D. 211 ; 9 P. D. 130
See PROBATE—GRANT. 1, 2.

—— Execution—Attesting witnesses—Evidence
[9 P. D. 149
See PROBATE—EXECUTION. 4.

—— Foreign law and foreigner—Will executed abroad according to English law　6 P. D. 6
See ADMINISTRATOR—LIMITED. 6

—— Foreign law—Construction　26 Ch. D. 656
See PROBATE—GRANT. 4.

—— Forgery—Actions in Probate and Chancery Divisions　　　　　　9 P. D. 210
See ESTOPPEL—JUDGMENT. 1.

WILL—*continued.*

—— Gift to separate use—Covenant to settle after-acquired property
See Cases under SETTLEMENT—FUTURE PROPERTY. 7—10.

—— Married woman — Testamentary appointment - - 22 Ch. D. 238
See POWER—EXECUTION. 11.

—— Power of leasing 24 Ch. D. 624
See SETTLEMENT—POWERS. 4.

—— Promise to devise interest in land by will
[10 Q. B. D. 148
See FRAUDS, STATUTE OF. 2.

—— Proved in Scotland 6 P. D. 19
See ADMINISTRATOR—GRANT. 4.

—— Proved in Victoria - - 21 Ch. D. 674
See PARTITION SUIT—SALE. 2.

—— Power to consent to advancement 27 Ch. D.
See POWER—EXTINCTION. 2. [565

—— Realty—Appointment of executors
[6 P. D. 209; 7 P. D. 61
See PROBATE—MARRIED WOMAN. 4, 5.

—— Revocation—Testamentary appointment
[20 Ch. D. 99
See POWER—EXECUTION. 13.

—— Scotch will - 7 App. Cas. 400
See SCOTCH LAW—WILL.

—— Scotch will - 8 App. Cas. 577
See SCOTCH LAW — HERITABLE PROPERTY. 4.

—— Survivor - - 18 Ch. D. 213
See EVIDENCE—PRESUMPTION.

—— Trustees—Appointment of new after decree
See TRUSTEE—POWERS. 1. [23 Ch. D. 134

—— Unregistered—Middlesex Registry Acts
[20 Ch. D. 611
See VENDOR AND PURCHASER — PURCHASE WITHOUT NOTICE. 1.

WINDFALLS—Larch trees - 28 Ch. D. 220;
See TIMBER. 1, 2. [30 Ch. D. 485

WINDING-UP.
See Cases under COMPANY.

—— Building society.
See Cases under BUILDING SOCIETY.

—— Company — Balance order — "Final judgment" 13 Q. B. D. 476
See BANKRUPTCY—ACT OF BANKRUPTCY. 7.

—— Lease to company—Clause of re-entry
[20 Ch. D. 260
See LANDLORD AND TENANT—RE-ENTRY. 8.

—— Lien of solicitor of company on documents
See SOLICITOR—LIEN. 12. [24 Ch. D. 408

—— Life insurance company.
See Cases under COMPANY—LIFE INSURANCE COMPANY.

—— Pending action—Transfer 16 Ch. D. 663
See PRACTICE—SUPREME COURT—TRANSFER. 1.

—— Petition—Order on—Appeal 16 Ch. D. 663;
[23 Ch. D. 248; 24 Ch. D. 488
See PRACTICE — SUPREME COURT — APPEAL. 37, 40, 41.

WINDOW—Entry by, to distrain 15 Q. B. D. 312
See LANDLORD AND TENANT—DISTRESS. 2.

WITHDRAWAL—Affidavit—Bankruptcy
[20 Ch. D. 126
See BANKRUPTCY—EVIDENCE. 1.

—— Affidavit—Cross-examination 21 Ch. D. 642
See PRACTICE—SUPREME COURT—EVIDENCE. 5.

—— Appeal - - 17 Ch. D. 23
See PRACTICE—SUPREME COURT—APPEAL. 23.

—— Bill of costs 30 Ch. D. 441
See SOLICITOR—BILL OF COSTS. 7.

—— Consent 26 Ch. D. 249
See PRACTICE—SUPREME COURT—CONSENT.

—— Defence—Costs - 18 Ch. D. 362
See PRACTICE—SUPREME COURT—COSTS. 23.

—— Members of company 24 Ch. D. 421, 425, n.;
[28 Ch. D. 559; 10 App. Cas. 33
See COMPANY—DISTRIBUTION OF ASSETS. 1, 2, 3.

—— Members of company—Building society.
[24 Ch. D. 421; 8 App. Cas. 235; 10 App.
See BUILDING SOCIETY. 14, 15. [Cas. 33

WITNESS.
See Cases under EVIDENCE—WITNESS.

—— Aged—Evidence de bene esse 26 Ch. D. 1
See PRACTICE—SUPREME COURT—EVIDENCE. 18.

—— Attendance before arbitrator 17 Ch. D. 787
See PRACTICE—SUPREME COURT—EVIDENCE. 7.

—— Bankruptcy.
See Cases under BANKRUPTCY — EVIDENCE.

—— Costs—Cross-examination 25 Ch. D. 297
See PRACTICE—SUPREME COURT—COSTS.

—— Cross-examination—Expenses 25 Ch. D. 297
See PRACTICE—SUPREME COURT—EVIDENCE. 3.

—— Examination abroad.
See Cases under PRACTICE — SUPREME COURT—EVIDENCE. 9—16.

—— Examination de bene esse - 16 Ch. D. 100
See PRACTICE—SUPREME COURT—EVIDENCE. 1.

—— Expenses—Certificate of Registrar—Taxation by Master - 7 Q. B. D. 477
See PARLIAMENT—ELECTION PETITION. 2.

—— Husband for wife, and *vice versâ.*
See HUSBAND AND WIFE — MARRIED WOMEN'S PROPERTY ACTS—*Statutes.*

—— Husband or wife of accused—Offences against women.
See CRIMINAL LAW—OFFENCES AGAINST WOMEN—*Statutes.*

—— Lunacy—Medical witnesses 18 Ch. D. 26
See LUNATIC—INQUISITION. 1.

—— Right to subpœna—Leave of Court
[22 Ch. D. 430
See PRACTICE—SUPREME COURT—EVIDENCE. 8.

WITNESS—*continued.*
—— Voluntary attendance—Refusal to give evidence—Power of justices to commit
 See BASTARDY. 7. [**14 Q. B. D. 364**
—— Winding-up.
 See Cases under COMPANY—EVIDENCE.

WOMAN PAST CHILDBEARING 18 Ch. D. 213
 See EVIDENCE—PRESUMPTION.

WOODS AND FORESTS.
 See CROWN LANDS—*Statutes.*

WORD—Registration of, as trade-mark
   [24 Ch. D. 504 ; 26 Ch. D. 288
 See TRADE-MARK—REGISTRATION. 1, 4.

WORDS—" According to the stocks "
 See WILL—CLASS. 1. [24 Ch. D. 664
—— " Act or practice " - 8 Q. B. D. 434
 See SOLICITOR—UNQUALIFIED. 3.
—— " Adjoining or abutting on " 9 Q. B. D. 183 ;
        [14 Q. B. D. 849
 See LOCAL GOVERNMENT—STREETS. 6, 7.
—— " All my land at S." 30 Ch. D. 50
 See WILL—SPEAKING FROM DEATH. 3.
—— " All other lands and others " 8 App. Cap. 853
 See SCOTCH LAW—CONVEYANCE. 1.
—— " All the rest of my money " 17 Ch. D. 819
 See WILL—RESIDUARY GIFT. 3.
—— " All ways now used and enjoyed"
 See WAY. 1. [18 Ch. D. 616
—— " Allowance " - 14 Q. B. D. 735
 See LOCAL GOVERNMENT—LOCAL AUTHORITY. 5.
—— " Annual profits or gains " 14 Q. B. D. 239 ;
        [10 App. Cas. 438
 See REVENUE—INCOME TAX. 9.
—— " Annual value."
 See Cases under WATERWORKS COMPANY
   —WATER-RATE. ·
—— " Assignee " - 28 Ch. D. 719
 See SOLICITOR—BILL OF COSTS. 4.
—— " At all times of tide and always afloat "
        [11 Q. B. D. 244
 See SHIP—CHARTERPARTY. 13.
—— " At merchant's risk " - 12 Q. B. D. 218
 See SHIP—GENERAL AVERAGE. 2.
—— " Author " 11 Q. B. D. 627
 See COPYRIGHT—PICTURES.
—— " Available for adjudication " 21 Ch. D. 605
 See BANKRUPTCY—PROTECTED TRANSACTION. 2.
—— " Beer-house " 16 Ch. D. 718
 See LANDLORD AND TENANT—LEASE. 7.
—— " Bonâ fide charitable gift " 7 Q. B. D. 539
 See POOR LAW—SETTLEMENT. 14.
—— " By virtue of Statute of Distributions "
 See WILL—CLASS. 4. [19 Ch. D. 444
—— " Capital not called up " 17 Ch. D. 715
 See COMPANY—DIRECTOR'S AUTHORITY. 2.
—— " Capture and seizure " 9 Q. B. D. 463 ;
 [10 Q. B. D. 432 ; 8 App. Cas. 393
 See INSURANCE, MARINE—POLICY. 3, 4.
—— " Carry out bread for sale in and from any cart "—" Carry out or deliver any bread "
 See BAKER. 1. [14 Q. B. D. 110

WORDS—*continued.*
—— " Cause or matter pending " 16 Ch. D. 544.
 See PRACTICE – SUPREME COURT – RECEIVER. 1.
—— " Cause shewn " 14 Q. B. D. 177
 See BANKRUPTCY—TRUSTEE. 8.
—— " Causing, directing, or permitting "
        [12 Q. B. D. 629
 See CONTAGIOUS DISEASES (ANIMALS) ACT.
—— " Charge or control " 12 Q. B. D. 208
 See MASTER AND SERVANT—MASTER'S LIABILITY. 17.
—— " Child or children " - 9 App. Cas. 890
 See WILL—ESTATE IN REALTY. 2.
—— " Clear annual income without deduction"
 See WILL—WORDS. 1. [22 Ch. D. 182
—— " Clear yearly sum " - 21 Ch. D. 105 ;
 See WILL—WORDS. 2, 3. [22 Ch. D. 226
—— " Common to the trade " 29 Ch. D. 551
 See TRADE-MARK—REGISTRATION. 3.
—— " Commonly understood. "– 15 Q. B. D. 273
 See MUNICIPAL CORPORATION—ELECTION. 6.
—— " Concerned or interested in any bargain or contract " 14 Q. B. D. 735, 739
 See LOCAL GOVERNMENT—LOCAL AUTHORITY. 5, 6.
—— " Continuing trustees " - 25 Ch. D. 611
 See SETTLEMENT—POWERS. 8.
—— " Contract " 17 Ch. D. 122
 See BANKRUPTCY—PROOF. 22.
—— " Contrary intention " 26 Ch. D. 426.
 See INFANT—MAINTENANCE. 4.
—— " Costs of reference " 9 Q. B. D. 434
 See ARBITRATION—COSTS.
—— " Cottage and land " 30 Ch. D. 50
 See WILL—SPEAKING FROM DEATH. 3.
—— " Course ' - · 9 P. D. 137
 See SHIP—NAVIGATION. 20.
—— " Cousins" 17 Ch. D. 262 ; 19 Ch. D. 201 ; 30
 See WILL—WORDS. 4, 5, 6. [Ch. D. 512.
—— " Criminal cause or matter " 7 Q. B. D. 534 ;
        [10 Q. B. D. 378
 See PRACTICE – SUPREME COURT—APPEAL. 8, 9.
—— " Criminal cause or matter ' 14 Q. B. D. 667
 See PARLIAMENT—ELECTION. 3.
—— " Dangers and accidents of the seas '
 See SHIP—SALVAGE. 13. [10 P. D. 103.
—— " Death " 22 Ch. D. 236
 See WILL—LAPSE. 3.
—— " Debt."
 See Cases under PRACTICE — SUPREME. COURT—GARNISHEE ORDERS.
—— " Debt incurred by fraud " 17 Ch. D. 122
 See BANKRUPTCY—PROOF. 22.
—— " Debt or liability " - 15 Q. B. D. 239
 See BANKRUPTCY—PROOF. 3.
—— " Decision " - 10 Q. B. D. 309
 See LOCAL GOVERNMENT—STREETS. 9.
—— " Desertion " 9 Q. B. D. 522
 See POOR LAW—SETTLEMENT. 8.
—— " Devise" 18 Ch. D. 499
 See POWER—EXECUTION. 8.

WORDS—continued.

—— " Heading " - - 26 Ch. D. 288
  See TRADE-MARK—REGISTRATION. 4.

—— " Heirs " - 25 Ch. D. 212
  See WILL—WORDS. 10.

—— " Heirs and successors " - 8 App. Cas. 751
  See COLONIAL LAW—STRAITS SETTLE-
  MENTS. 2.

—— " Held shares " - 21 Ch. D. 849
  See COMPANY—WINDING-UP ORDER. 13.

—— " House " - 27 Ch. D. 536
  See LANDS CLAUSES ACT—COMPULSORY
  POWERS. 7.

—— " Husband " - 22 Ch. D. 619
  See WILL—WORDS. 11.

—— " In their present state " 30 Ch. D. 50
  See WILL—SPEAKING FROM DEATH. 3.

—— " Incapable to act " 22 Ch. D. 633
  See TRUSTEE ACTS—NEW TRUSTEES. 2.

—— " Income " - 6 App. Cas. 373
  See COLONIAL LAW — CANADA — NEW
  BRUNSWICK.

—— " Income " 17 Ch. D. 70; 21 Ch. D. 85;
  [14 Q. B. D. 301
  See BANKRUPTCY—ASSETS. 12, 13, 14.

—— " Injury to property " - 10 Q. B. D. 71
  See PRACTICE—SUPREME COURT—COSTS.
  29.

—— " Injuriously affected " 14 Q. B. D. 747, 753
  See LANDS CLAUSES ACT — COMPENSA-
  TION. 2, 3.

—— " Interlocutory order 6 Q. B. D. 75
  See PRACTICE — SUPREME COURT — RE-
  CEIVER. 2.

—— " Issue " - 12 Q. B. D. 605
  See BANKER—NOTES.

—— " Issue and their heirs " - 9 Q. B. D. 643
  See WILL—ESTATE IN REALTY. 3.

—— " Just and equitable " 20 Ch. D. 151, 169
  See COMPANY—WINDING-UP ORDER. 4, 5.

—— " Land " 22 Ch. D. 677; 9 App. Cas. 787
  See LANDS CLAUSES ACT—COMPULSORY
  POWERS. 3.

—— " Land burdened with onerous covenants "
  [14 Q. B. D. 956
  See BANKRUPTCY—DISCLAIMER. 19.

—— " Loading " - - 9 P. D. 85
  See SHIP—PILOT. 2.

—— " Lodger " - 9 Q. B. D. 245; 12 Q. B. D. 4;
  [13 Q. B. D. 179
  See LANDLORD AND TENANT—LODGER.
  1, 2, 3.

—— " Material facts not brought before the Court "
  [9 P. D. 218
  See PRACTICE—DIVORCE—INTERVENTION.

—— " Matter in question in the action "
  [23 Ch. D. 353
  See PRACTICE—SUPREME COURT—PRO-
  DUCTION OF DOCUMENTS. 2.

—— " Means to pay " - 9 Q. B. D. 178;
  [14 Q. B. D. 597
  See ARREST—DEBTORS ACT. 4, 5.

—— " Milk " - - - 14 Q. B. D. 193
  See ADULTERATION. 2.

WORDS—continued.

—— " Mistake " - - 15 Q. B. D. 461
  See PARLIAMENT—FRANCHISE. 5.

—— " Moderate speed " 9 P. D. 114, 134
  See SHIP—NAVIGATION. 15, 16.

—— " Molestation " - - 14 Q. B. D. 792
  See HUSBAND AND WIFE—SEPARATION
  DEED. 3.

—— " Money " - - - 28 Ch. D. 464
  See CHARITY—GIFT TO. 1.

—— " Money " - - 6 P. D. 203; 7 P. D. 65
  See WILL—RESIDUARY GIFT. 5, 6.

—— " Money of which I am possessed "
  [25 Ch. D. 154
  See WILL—RESIDUARY GIFT. 4.

—— " Money value " 29 Ch. D. 1007, 1009, n.
  See LEASEHOLD—LONG TERMS. 1, 2.

—— " Mutual credits and dealings."
  See Cases under BANKRUPTCY—MUTUAL
  DEALINGS.

—— " My own heirs whatsoever " 7 App. Cas. 713
  See SCOTCH LAW—ENTAIL.

—— " Nature, substance, and quality "
  [14 Q. B. D. 193, 845
  See ADULTERATION. 2, 3.

—— " New street " 21 Ch. D. 621; 8 App. Cas. 798
  See LOCAL GOVERNMENT—STREETS. 4.

—— " Now paid " - - 14 Q. B. D. 43
  See BILL OF SALE—FORMALITIES. 13.

—— " Nuisance or injurious to health "
  [8 Q. B. D. 97; 10 Q. B. D. 138
  See LOCAL GOVERNMENT—OFFENCES. 1, 3.

—— " Objection made " 14 Q. B. D. 584
  See INN—LICENCE. 9.

—— " Open and public place " 10 Q. B. D. 44
  See VAGRANT ACTS. 2.

—— " Order " - - 15 Q. B. D. 76
  See PRACTICE — SUPREME COURT —
  APPEAL. 4.

—— " Ordinary outgoings " - 28 Ch. D. 431
  See WILL—WORDS. 14.

—— " Owner " - - 13 Q. B. D. 211
  See METROPOLIS—MANAGEMENT ACTS. 13.

—— " Owner " - - 7 Q. B. D. 160
  See SHIP—MERCHANT SHIPPING ACTS. 3.

—— " Parish " - - 6 Q. B. D. 576
  See POOR LAW—SETTLEMENT. 13.

—— " Party " - 15 Q. B. D. 54
  See BANKRUPTCY—EXAMINATION. 1.

—— " Party " - - 11 Q. B. D. 251
  See PRACTICE—SUPREME COURT—INTER-
  ROGATORIES. 4.

—— " Party grieved " - 7 Q. B. D. 465
  See PENAL ACTION. 1.

—— " Pave " - - 15 Q. B. D. 652
  See METROPOLIS—MANAGEMENT ACTS. 14.

—— " Payable " 17 Ch. D. 835
  See WILL—VESTING. 6.

—— " Payable " 10 App. Cas. 422
  See SETTLEMENT—CONSTRUCTION. 9.

—— " Pending action " - 28 Ch. D. 148
  See PATENT—AMENDMENT. 2.

WORDS—*continued.*

—— "Pending matter"　　–　　**20 Ch. D. 637**
　　See INSOLVENCY.

—— "Person aggrieved"　　–　　**16 Ch. D. 497**
　　See BANKRUPTCY—RECEIVER. 2.

—— "Person aggrieved"　　　**17 Ch. D. 518**
　　See BANKRUPTCY—TRUSTEE. 7.

—— "Person aggrieved"　　　**25 Ch. D. 194;**
　　　　　　　　　　　　　　　　[26 Ch. D. 48
　　See TRADE-MARK—REGISTRATION. 14, 15.

—— "Person entitled to the income of land"
　　　　　　　　　　　　　　　[26 Ch. D. 736
　　See SETTLED LAND ACT—DEFINITIONS. 4.

—— "Place used for betting"　　**8 Q. B. D. 275 ;**
　　　　　　[**13 Q. B. D. 377 ; 14 Q. B. D. 588**
　　See GAMING. 4, 6, 7.

—— "Pleading"　　　–　　　**23 Ch. D. 204**
　　See PRACTICE—SUPREME COURT—MOTION
　　FOR JUDGMENT. 2.

—— "Port"　–　**9 Q. B. D. 679 ; 15 Q. B. D. 580**
　　See SHIP—CHARTERPARTY. 3, 4.

—— "Practising"　　–　　　**8 Q. B. D. 434**
　　See SOLICITOR—UNQUALIFIED. 3.

—— "Present right to receive"　　**29 Ch. D. 964**
　　See LIMITATIONS, STATUTE OF—LEGACY.

—— "Pretenced rights or titles"　**15 Q. B. D. 491**
　　See RIGHT OF ENTRY. 1.

—— "Proceed to sea"　　　　**7 P. D. 217**
　　See SHIP—NAVIGATION. 6.

—— "Professional charges"　　**27 Ch. D. 584**
　　See SOLICITOR—BILL OF COSTS. 16.

—— "Profits or gains"　**14 Q. B. D. 239 ; 10 App.**
　　See REVENUE—INCOME TAX. 9. [Cas. 438

—— "Property"　　–　　　**21 Ch. D. 85**
　　See BANKRUPTCY—ASSETS. 13.

—— "Property"　　　–　**14 Q. B. D. 956**
　　See BANKRUPTCY—DISCLAIMER. 19.

—— "Property recovered or preserved."
　　See Cases under SOLICITOR—LIEN. 1—7.

—— "Provided the funds permit"　**24 Ch. D. 421 ;**
　　　　　　　　　　　　　　　[10 App. Cas. 33
　　See BUILDING SOCIETY. 15.

—— "Public purposes"　–　　**7 Q. B. D. 505**
　　See WATERWORKS COMPANY—SUPPLY OF
　　WATER. 5.

—— "Publisher"　　–　　　**23 Ch. D. 727**
　　See COPYRIGHT—BOOKS. 3.

—— "Pure and wholesome water"　**12 Q. B. D. 443**
　　See WATERWORKS COMPANY—SUPPLY OF
　　WATER. 6.

—— "Railway"　　　–　　**10 Q. B. D. 358**
　　See MASTER AND SERVANT—MASTER'S
　　LIABILITY. 19.

—— "Railway company"　　–　**26 Ch. D. 527**
　　See COMPANY—UNREGISTERED COMPANY.
　　9.

—— "Rash and hazardous speculations"
　　　　　　　　　　　　　[14 Q. B. D. 936
　　See BANKRUPTCY—DISCHARGE. 4.

—— "Real estate wheresoever situate"
　　See WILL—WORDS. 16.　[**28 Ch. D. 66**

—— "Real or personal property"　**8 Q. B. D. 283**
　　See CRIMINAL LAW—MALICIOUS INJURY
　　PROPE RTY.

WORDS—*continued.*

—— "Real security"　　–　　**30 Ch. D. 227**
　　See WILL—WORDS. 17.

—— "Residuary legatee"　　–　**16 Ch. D. 696**
　　See WILL—RESIDUARY GIFT. 1.

—— "Reversion expectant"　　**15 Q. B. D. 629**
　　See PRESCRIPTION. 2.

—— "Right acquired or accrued"　**15 Q. B. D. 467**
　　See SOLICITOR—CERTIFICATE.

—— "Right occupied and enjoyed"　**26 Ch. D. 434**
　　See WAY. 2.

—— "Safe port or as near thereunto as she can
　　safely get"　–　　–　–　**6 P. D. 68**
　　See SHIP—CHARTERPARTY. 16.

—— "Salary or income"　　–　**17 Ch. D. 70 ;**
　　　　　　[**21 Ch. D. 85 ; 14 Q. B. D. 301**
　　See BANKRUPTCY—ASSETS. 12, 13, 14.

—— "Sale by retail"　　–　　**8 Q. B. D. 373**
　　See INN—OFFENCES. 2.

—— "Second cousins"　　–　**17 Ch. D. 262 ;**
　　See WILL—WORDS. 5, 6.　[**19 Ch. D. 201**

—— "Seised jointly"　　　**27 Ch. D. 359**
　　See TRUSTEE ACTS—VESTING ORDERS 3.

—— "Seised or possessed or entitled to"
　　　　　　　　　　　　　[25 Ch. D. 200
　　See SETTLEMENT—FUTURE PROPERTY. 1.

—— "Seller"　　–　–　　**8 Q. B. D. 397**
　　See PHARMACY ACTS.

—— "Servant or other person"　　**6 Q. B. D. 530,**
　　　　　　　　　　[673 ; 14 Q. B. D. 838
　　See REVENUE—HOUSE DUTY. 3, 4, 5.

—— "Services incidental to the duty or business
　　of a carrier"　　–　　**15 Q. B. D. 505**
　　See RAILWAY COMPANY—RAILWAYS RE-
　　GULATION ACTS. 4.

—— "Settlement of property"　**15 Q. B. D. 682**
　　See BANKRUPTCY—VOID SETTLEMENT. 2.

—— "Sewer"　　　–　　　**28 Ch. D. 283**
　　See LOCAL GOVERNMENT—SEWERS. 2.

—— "Shall be born in my lifetime"　**6 App. Cas.**
　　See WILL—ESTATE IN REALTY. 4.　[471

—— "Shall become entitled"　–　**9 Q. B. D. 337 ;**
　　　　　　　　　　　　　　　[10 App. Cas. 1
　　See SETTLEMENT—FUTURE PROPERTY. 6.

—— "Sheriff"　　–　　–　**15 Q. B. D. 48**
　　See BANKRUPTCY—PROTECTED TRANSAC-
　　TION. 6.

—— "Ship or boat in distress on shore of sea or
　　tidal water"　　–　　**7 P. D. 126**
　　See SHIP—SALVAGE. 8.

—— "Site"　　–　　–　**14 Q. B. D. 479**
　　See METROPOLIS—BUILDING ACTS. 3.

—— "Situate in parish of D."　–　**30 Ch. D. 298**
　　See ADVOWSON. 1.

—— "Six months' notice"　　**15 Q. B. D. 501**
　　See LANDLORD AND TENANT—YEARLY
　　TENANT.

—— "Sole and unmarried"　–　**24 Ch. D. 703**
　　See WILL—SEPARATE USE. 1.

—— "Sole trustee"　　–　　**21 Ch. D. 846**
　　See TRUSTEE ACTS—VESTING ORDERS. 12.

WORDS—*continued.*

—— "Sole use and disposal" - 17 Ch. D. 794
See WILL—SEPARATE USE. 2.

—— "Solemnly and publicly made and subscribed"
[14 Q. B. D. 667
See PARLIAMENT—ELECTION. 3.

—— "Stationary" - - - 9 P. D. 164
See SHIP—NAVIGATION. 10.

—— "Street" - - - 10 Q. B. D. 394;
[13 Q. B. D. 184; 10 App. Cas. 364
See LOCAL GOVERNMENT—STREETS. 2, 10.

—— "Street" 13 Q. B. D. 904
See METROPOLIS—MANAGEMENT ACTS. 7.

—— "Subject as aforesaid" - 15 Q. B. D. 70
See HIGHWAY—REPAIR. 7.

—— "Subsequent action" 8 Q. B. D. 380
See HUSBAND AND WIFE—MARRIED WOMEN'S PROPERTY ACTS. 3.

—— "Successors" - 26 Ch. D. 538
See WILL—HEIRLOOM. 3.

—— "Suffering judicial proceedings"
[25 Ch. D. 311
See BANKRUPTCY — FRAUDULENT PREFERENCE. 6.

—— "Sufficient cause" - 15 Q. B. D. 399
See BANKRUPTCY—RECEIVER. 8.

—— "Sum previously offered." 12 Q. B. D. 481
See LANDS CLAUSES ACT—COSTS. 7.

—— "Sunday" - 11 Q. B. D. 71
See INN—OFFENCES. 6.

—— "Surviving"— "Survivor" 19 Ch. D. 186;
See WILL—SURVIVOR. 1, 2. [29 Ch. D. 839

—— "Survivor" - - 18 Ch. D. 213
See EVIDENCE—PRESUMPTION.

—— "Take" 22 Ch. D. 142
See LANDS CLAUSES ACT—COMPULSORY POWERS. 1.

—— "Taking land" - 28 Ch. D. 237
See LANDS CLAUSES ACT—COSTS. 6.

—— "Temperate" · - 9 App. Cas. 671
See INSURANCE, LIFE—POLICY. 3.

—— "Title to be approved by my solicitor"
See CONDITION. 2. [9 Q. B. D. 276

—— "Tolls" - - 9 Q. B. D. 744
See RAILWAY COMPANY—TRAFFIC MANAGEMENT. 3.

—— "Trade or business" - 14 Q B. D. 950
See BANKRUPTCY—ORDER AND DISPOSITION. 9.

—— "Trade or business" — Covenant not to exercise 27 Ch. D. 71, 81, n.
See LANDLORD AND TENANT — LEASE. 4, 5.

—— "Trader" - 11 Q. B. D. 241
See BANKRUPTCY—ASSETS. 5.

—— "Tributary" - 10 Q. B. D. 131
See FISHERY ACTS. 1.

—— "True copy" - - 21 Ch. D. 871
See BANKRUPTCY—ORDER AND DISPOSITION. 1.

WORDS—*continued.*

—— "Uncertain rent" 21 Ch. D. 442
See BANKRUPTCY—DISTRESS. 4.

—— "Union" - - 6 Q. B. D. 576
See POOR LAW—SETTLEMENT. 13.

—— "Unliquidated damages" 17 Ch. D. 122
See BANKRUPTCY—PROOF. 22.

—— "Unmarried" 16 Ch. D. 715; 26 Ch. D. 575
See WILL—WORDS. 18, 19.

—— "Until further order" 22 Ch. D. 182
See ESTOPPEL—JUDGMENT. 5.

—— "Visible means" - 13 Q. B. D. 835
See COUNTY COURT—PRACTICE. 4.

—— "Voids" - 11 Q. B. D. 195
See WATERWORKS COMPANY — WATERRATE. 2.

—— "Widow and unmarried" 25 Ch. D. 685
See WILL—CONDITION. 11.

—— "Workman" 6 Q. B. D. 182; 13 Q. B. D. 616
See MASTER AND SERVANT—REMEDIES. 2, 3.

—— "Wrongful act or default" - 7 P. D. 207
See SHIP—MERCHANT SHIPPING ACTS. 2.

WORDS OF LIMITATION.
See DEED—*Statutes.*

WORKMAN—Wages—Preferential debt
[26 Ch. D. 693
See BANKRUPTCY—PREFERENTIAL DEBT.

WORKING OF MINE - 7 App. Cas. 43
See MINE—WORKING. 2.

—— Consent to remove pillars 23 Ch. D. 583
See SETTLEMENT—POWERS. 1.

WRECK—Sale by master 16 Ch. D. 474
See SHIP—MASTER. 1.

WRECK COMMISSIONERS—Appeal
[6 P. D. 182; 7 P. D. 194, 207
See SHIP—MERCHANT SHIPPING ACTS. 2, 5, 8.

WRIT—Authority to issue 26 Ch. D. 169
See SOLICITOR—RETAINER.

—— De contumace capiendo—Significavit
[7 Q. B. D. 273; 6 App. Cas. 657
See PRACTICE — ECCLESIASTICAL—CONTEMPT. 2.

—— Fieri facias—Wrongful seizure 21 Ch. D. 69;
See SHERIFF. 3, 4. [9 Q. B. D. 340

—— In personam — Incorrect address of Defendant 7 P. D. 57
See PRACTICE—ADMIRALTY—SERVICE. 2.

—— Indorsement on—Motions on admissions
[23 Ch. D. 204
See PRACTICE—SUPREME COURT—MOTION FOR JUDGMENT. 2.

—— Indorsement—Time of making 16 Ch. D. 734
See PRACTICE—SUPREME COURT—WRIT. 1.

—— Inquiry as to lunacy—Trial by judge of High Court - 27 Ch. D. 116
See LUNATIC—INQUISITION. 2.

—— Of possession - 22 Ch. D. 281
See PRACTICE—SUPREME COURT—WRIT OF POSSESSION.

WRIT—*continued.*

—— Service.

    See Cases under PRACTICE—SUPREME COURT—SERVICE.

—— Service—Admiralty—Marshal   **10 P. D. 62**
    See PRACTICE—ADMIRALTY—SERVICE. 3.

—— Service on partnership—Appearance of one member only   -   **14 Q. B. D. 103**
    See PRACTICE—SUPREME COURT—JUDGMENT. 2.

—— Special indorsement—Power to sign final judgment under Order XIV.—Foreign judgment   -   **13 Q. B. D. 302**
    See PRACTICE—SUPREME COURT—WRIT SPECIALLY INDORSED. 2.

WRIT—*continued.*

—— Time of taking effect—Fraction of day
    [8 Q. B. D. 63
    See PRACTICE—SUPREME COURT—WRIT. 2.

WRITTEN AGREEMENT—Agency—Scotch law
    [6 App. Cas. 340
    See SCOTCH LAW — LANDLORD AND TENANT.

WRITTEN ORDER—Police Magistrate
    [27 Ch. D. 362
    See METROPOLIS—MANAGEMENT ACTS. 3.

WRONGFUL SEIZURE—Fieri facias
    [21 Ch. D. 69 ; 9 Q. B. D. 340
    See SHERIFF. 3, 4.

Y.

YEARLY RESTS—Administration of estate—Conversion   -   **24 Ch. D. 643**
    See EXECUTOR—ADMINISTRATION. 6.

YEARLY TENANT—Assignment **9 Q. B. D. 366**
    See LANDLORD AND TENANT—ASSIGNMENT. 1.

—— Distress—Bankruptcy   -   **16 Ch. D. 274**
    See BANKRUPTCY—DISTRESS 3.

—— Notice to quit.
    See LANDLORD AND TENANT—YEARLY TENANT—*Statutes.*

YEARS OF DISCRETION — Infant — Access to mother   -   **24 Ch. D. 317**
    See INFANT—EDUCATION. 1.

YORK—Province of—Jurisdiction
    [7 Q. B. D. 273 ; 6 App. Cas. 657
    See PRACTICE — ECCLESIASTICAL — CONTEMPT. 2.

YORKSHIRE REGISTRY   -   **26 Ch. D. 501**
    See VENDOR AND PURCHASER—LIEN. 2.

—— Act of 1884.
    See REGISTRY ACTS—*Statutes.*

YOUNGER SON—Becoming eldest **26 Ch. D. 363**
    See SETTLEMENT—CONSTRUCTION. 2.

YOUNGEST SON—Customary heir—Copyholds
    See COPYHOLD—CUSTOM. 2. **[18 Ch. D. 165**

Z.

ZANZIBAR—Order in Council. *See* JURISDICTION—*Gazette.*

Lightning Source UK Ltd.
Milton Keynes UK
UKHW011325220119
335966UK00006B/37/P